Victorian Literature

PROSE

VICTORIAN LITERATURE

PROSE

G. B. Tennyson
UNIVERSITY OF CALIFORNIA, LOS ANGELES

Donald J. Gray
INDIANA UNIVERSITY

MACMILLAN PUBLISHING CO., INC.
New York

Macmillan Publishing Co., Inc.
866 Third Avenue, New York, New York 10022

Collier Macmillan Canada, Ltd.

Library of Congress Cataloging in Publication Data
Main entry under title:

Victorian literature—prose.

  Includes bibliographies and indexes.
  1. English prose literature—19th century.
I. Tennyson, G. B. II. Gray, Donald J.
PR1304.V5   828'.8'08   74-25599
ISBN 0-02-419900-1

Printing: 1 2 3 4 5 6 7 8   Year: 6 7 8 9 0 1 2

ACKNOWLEDGMENTS

Jonathan Cape Ltd. "How to Make the Best of Life," from *Selected Essays by Samuel Butler;* "The 'Enfant Terrible' of Literature," from *The Note-Books of Samuel Butler,* edited by Henry Festing Jones. Reprinted by permission of the publisher and the Executors of the Samuel Butler Estate.

Houghton Mifflin Company. "Bentham," "Coleridge," "Thoughts on Poetry," "On Liberty," from John Stuart Mill, *Autobiography and Other Writings,* edited by Jack Stillinger (Riverside Editions). Copyright © 1969 by Jack Stillinger. Reprinted by permission of Houghton Mifflin Company.

PREFACE

UNTIL recent years it was widely, if tacitly, assumed that the Victorian age was distinguished chiefly for its great accomplishments in poetry and the novel. Students of the period, however, have come to realize that the achievements of Victorian writers in the area of nonfiction prose equal those of their contemporaries in the novel or in poetry and probably surpass the work in nonfiction prose of any other English literary era. Victorian prose constitutes the third great genre of literary activity in its age.

To be sure, it has long been acknowledged that Victorian prose contains within its broad compass many works of exceptional importance to the history of the nineteenth century. Several impressive anthologies have been built on the awareness of the social, intellectual, and historical significance of Victorian prose, but it is primarily within the past generation that attention has been devoted to the artistic dimensions of that prose. Various studies of Victorian prose writers and of individual works have illuminated the literary merits and complexities of writings once considered important solely to our understanding of the social temper of their time. These studies have enriched our grasp of the literary dimensions of nonfiction prose and our understanding of why certain works and authors commanded an attention in their age rivaling that accorded poets and novelists.

It is now becoming both possible and necessary to view the treasures of Victorian prose in their literary and their historical aspects simultaneously. Although much remains to be done in the study of the aesthetics and stylistics of Victorian prose, preliminary investigations have made it clear that the effort of further study will be amply rewarded. That this body of writing can tell us more than almost any other kind of literature about the character and concerns of the age that produced it is one of the long-acknowledged strengths of Victorian prose. Even the panoramic Victorian novel cannot rival the expository prose in direct and intellectually challenging treatment of the issues that made the Victorian age Victorian and that did so much to make our own age what it is. It remains to acquaint more students with the literary delights of this rich body of writing.

The present collection of works of Victorian prose is designed to illustrate the dual importance, aesthetic and historical, that we now ascribe to the nonfiction prose of the reign of Queen Victoria. The volume contains almost three times as many authors as the largest previous collection, with a corresponding increase in the number of selections. It presents works of virtually every sub-type under the umbrella of nonfiction prose—essays, sermons, history, speeches, art criticism, reviews, biography, autobiography, polemics, and humor—to name the most obvious. It contains works of the undisputed prose masters, like Carlyle, Newman, and Ruskin, and works of that great host of writers of the second rank who graced the profession of Man of Letters in the Victorian age. Many of these last have never before been represented in an anthology, and their merits have accordingly not been fully recognized in our time. For the first time, too, several of the women writers of the period are included.

In lieu of a historical introduction, the anthology provides introductions for each author designed to place the author in the intellectual and artistic context of the age as well as to condense standard biographical information. Since the authors included appear in chronological sequence, it is possible to trace the changing intellectual concerns of the period from 1832 to the end of the century by a sequential reading of the introductions. The large number of selections by which each major author is represented is sufficient to show the development of his mind and art throughout his literary career. Readers should, of course, also consult some of the many available literary and historical studies of the age as companion works to the study of the prose.

While the sum of authors and selections was perceived as providing a selective but thorough intellectual history of the period, individual works and selections were considered as independent pieces readable in their own right and for their own sake. By this second criterion of choice, the anthology makes possible a response to the *art* of Victorian prose—to the grace, the eloquence, the excitement, and the power that this literary genre possesses in abundance. In the case of major authors, whole works, or the greater part of whole works, have been given, as well as many full essays and chapters. For minor authors whole essays or self-contained portions of works have been selected. The result is a comprehensive survey of significant Victorian prose. I hope it will prove both a monument to the achievement of Victorian prose writers and a stimulus to our reading of their works.

A NOTE ON THE TEXTS

The textual authority for Victorian prose at the present time is not en-couraging. Very few of even the major figures have appeared in reliable modern editions of their works; exceptions are Ruskin and most of Arnold and Mill. Minor figures have in many cases not been reprinted at all in this century. The general procedure in this volume has been to use as text, unless otherwise noted, the last edition of the work in the author's lifetime or the last edition of the work to have authorial approval. In some cases this last edition is also the first or is even the original periodical publication. Generally the edition cited in the headnote is the edition followed. Although the original spelling and punctuation have been retained, some modernization in numbers and dates and forms of words has been made silently.

A NOTE ON REFERENCE MATERIALS

Every author has been provided with an introduction, a chronology, and a list of editions of his works and of works about him. Space allotted has been based on the author's prominence as a writer of nonfiction prose. Major authors receive long introductions, chronologies, and bibliographies. Titles in the bibliographies are listed alphabetically by title for works by the author, and alphabetically by author for works about the author. Minor writers have briefer introductions, chronologies, and lists of primary and secondary works chronologically by date of publication. Except for references to bibliographical resources, all titles listed are full-length works, not articles. Readers are referred to the annual bibliographies in *Victorian Studies*, *PMLA*, and the *Year's Work in English Studies* for other titles of secondary materials, including the numerous articles available on each author and work. For discussions of the research materials on major figures and many minor ones, students should consult *Victorian Prose: A Guide to Research*, edited by D. J. DeLaura (New York: Modern Language Association, 1973), and the annual supplement to that volume published in the autumn number of *Victorian Poetry*.

A NOTE ON ANNOTATION

The procedure on annotations has been to gloss more extensively the major works of major authors and, for reasons of space, to confine annotation of minor works and lesser authors to foreign words and phrases and to names of historical figures necessary to an understanding of the argument. Words, phrases, and historical and literary personages generally known or readily accessible in desk dictionaries and reference books have usually not been annotated in the minor pieces. Wherever available, an author's own notes identified as such have been retained.

A NOTE ON ILLUSTRATIONS

The illustrations are all taken from contemporary Victorian portraits, books, and periodicals. The source of each is identified in the illustration section. I am grateful to the Trustees of the National Portrait Gallery, London, for permission to reproduce the nineteen portraits of Victorian prose writers that appear among the illustrations.

In the preparation of this volume the editor was greatly aided by Mary Bisgay, Janet D. Keyes, Ellen Cole and staff, and Elliot Engel, all at University of California, Los Angeles. Elizabeth Tennyson made indispensable contributions in readying the mass of material for publication. The aid, encouragement, and patience of D. Anthony English at Macmillan are also gratefully acknowledged.

A NOTE ON EDITORIAL RESPONSIBILITY

Although *Victorian Literature: Prose* and its companion work, *Victorian Literature: Poetry*, were conceived and undertaken together, Donald Gray and I divided our editorial task between the volumes, Professor Gray assuming greater responsibility for the poetry; I bear the responsibility for most of the work on the prose.

G. B. T.

CONTENTS

Thomas Babington Macaulay

229

Jane Welsh Carlyle

269

John Henry Newman

276

Harriet Martineau

447

Richard Hurrell Froude

454

Benjamin Disraeli

460

Frederick Denison Maurice

467

Victorian Literature

PROSE

John Keble

1792-1866

JOHN KEBLE was credited by Newman and others with having begun the Oxford Movement with his sermon "National Apostasy" in 1833. Well before that time, however, Keble had established himself as a leading spiritual force in Oxford and in the Church of England at large. Born to a High Church family in Gloucestershire, Keble deeply absorbed his father's sacramental theology and his intense devotion to the Church of England. It was inevitable that Keble would attend Oxford and take holy orders and succeed his father as vicar of St. Mary's, Fairford, a post later also filled by Keble's brother Thomas. At Oxford Keble took double first-class honors and was quickly made a fellow of Oriel College. He gathered about him a group of like-minded churchmen, including Richard Hurrell Froude and John Henry Newman, who became the nucleus of the Oxford Movement. The great influence Keble exerted on his students and colleagues was extended to a wider public after 1827 by the publication of his volume of poems, *The Christian Year*, which became perhaps the most popular volume of verse in the nineteenth century. Keble held the post of Professor of Poetry at Oxford from 1831 to 1841, but from 1835 he was vicar at Hursley in Hampshire, which removed him from the main arena of contention in the growing agitation at Oxford over the pamphlet series of the Oxford Movement, the *Tracts for the Times*, and over what seemed to many the Romeward tendency of the Movement itself. With E. B. Pusey, the other major leader of the Movement, Keble stood firm for Tractarianism and the Church of England through the upheaval of Newman's defection to Rome in 1845. Although others before and after Newman went over to Rome, Keble's steadfastness kept many within the Church of England, and in the years after 1845 Keble was revered as the saintly father figure of the High Church movement. He was also a devoted and pious pastoral priest whose personal influence shaped the values reflected in the many novels of Charlotte Mary Yonge, one of Keble's parishioners.

Keble's own literary gifts found their chief expression in poetry like *The Christian Year* and the *Lyra Innocentium*, but he was also responsible for various prose works of a pastoral and theological character, most notably his *Sermons, Academical and Occasional* and his *On Eucharistical Adoration*. Keble's prose, like his own character, is usually serene and unostentatious. Much of its impact is

1

conveyed by the intensity of conviction and purity of motive that marked Keble's entire life.

CHRONOLOGY

1792   Born at Fairford, Gloucestershire.
1807   Attends Corpus Christi College, Oxford.
1810   Graduates with double first-class honors.
1811   Elected Fellow of Oriel College.
1815   Ordained Deacon in the Church of England.
1818–23   Serves as tutor at Oxford.
1827   *The Christian Year.*
1831–41   Serves as Oxford Professor of Poetry.
1833   Delivers "National Apostasy" Sermon.
1835   Marries and removes to Hursley, Hampshire.
1846   *Lyra Innocentium.*
1866   Dies at Hursley.

EDITIONS

The Christian Year (1827).
National Apostasy (1833).
Praelectiones Academicae (1844; trans. E. K. Francis as *Lectures on Poetry, 1832–1841*; 2 vols., 1912).
Lyra Innocentium (1846).
Sermons, Academical and Occasional (1848).
On Eucharistical Adoration (1857).
Miscellaneous Poems (1869).
Sermons for the Christian Year (11 vols., 1875–80).
Occasional Papers and Reviews, ed. E. B. Pusey (1877).

BIOGRAPHY AND CRITICISM

J. T. Colerige, *A Memoir of the Rev. John Keble* (2 vols., 1869).
Charlotte Mary Yonge, *John Keble's, Parishes* (1879).
R. W. Church, *The Oxford Movement, Twelve Years, 1833–1845* (1891).
Walter Locke, *John Keble* (1893).
E. F. L. Wood, *John Keble* (1909, 1932).
W. J. A. M. Beek, *John Keble's Literary and Religious Contribution to the Oxford Movement* (1959).
Georgina Battiscombe, *John Keble: A Study in Limitations* (1963).

National Apostasy

Keble preached the following sermon at the Oxford University church of St. Mary the Virgin before the session of the Court of the Assizes on July 14, 1833, and it is therefore sometimes called Keble's Assize Sermon. It proved to be the spark that set off the activity of spiritual renewal in the Church of England known as the Oxford Movement. The immediate provocation for Keble's sermon was the motion in Parliament to reduce in number and consolidate some of the sees of the Anglican Church of Ireland. Keble opposed the suppression of these sees but, even more, he opposed the imposition of such a judgment by Parliament, a body no longer composed exclusively of loyal sons of the Church of England. In Keble's view the action was a usurpation of the rights of bishops by a purely secular authority. Earlier parliamentary actions that involved Church affairs such as Catholic emancipation in 1829 were indications that church and state no longer spoke with one voice and that many considered the Church simply a department of the state. This is the position known as erastianism, and it was the antierastianism of Keble's stand, along with his devotion to the apostolicity and divinely constituted authority of the Church of England, that marked his position as new and forceful and that caused John Henry Newman to say of the event: "I have ever considered and kept the day, as the start of the religious movement of 1833."

The "Advertisement," or preface, that precedes the text was appended by Keble to the published sermon, as were the footnote references to Bible passages.

ADVERTISEMENT

SINCE the following pages were prepared for the press, the calamity, in anticipation of which they were written, has actually overtaken this portion of the Church of God. The Legislature of England and Ireland (*the members of which are not even bound to profess belief in the Atonement*), this body has virtually usurped the commission of those whom our Saviour entrusted with *at least one voice* in making ecclesiastical laws, on matters wholly or partly spiritual.[1] The same Legislature has also ratified, to its full extent, this principle—that the Apostolical Church in this realm is henceforth only to stand, in the eye of the state, as *one sect among many,* depending, for any preeminence she may still appear to retain, merely upon the accident of her having a strong party in the country.

It is a moment, surely, full of deep solicitude to all those members of the Church who still believe her authority divine, and the oaths and obligations, by which they are bound to her, undissolved and indissoluble by calculations of human expediency. Their anxiety turns not so much on the consequences to the State of what has been done (*they* are but too evident) as on the line of conduct which they are bound themselves to pursue. How may they continue their communion with the Church *established* (hitherto the pride and comfort of their lives) without any taint of those Erastian principles on which she is now avowedly to be governed? What answer can we make henceforth to the partisans of the Bishop of Rome when they taunt us with being a mere Parliamentarian Church? And how, consistently with our present relations to the State, can even the doctrinal purity and integrity of the MOST SACRED ORDER be preserved?

The attention of all who love the Church is most earnestly solicited to these questions. They are such, it will be observed, as cannot be answered by appealing to precedents in English History, because, at most, such could only show that the difficulty might have been raised before. It is believed that there are hundreds, nay thousands, of Christians, and that soon there will be tens of thousands, unaffectedly anxious to be rightly guided with regard to these and similar points. And they are mooted thus publicly for the chance of eliciting, from competent judges, a correct and early opinion.

If, under such trying and delicate circumstances, one could venture to be positive about any thing, it would seem safe to say that in such measure as it may be thought incumbent on the Church, or on Churchmen, to submit to any profane intrusion, it must at least be their sacred duty to declare, promulgate, and record, their full conviction, that it *is* intrusion, that they yield to it as they might to any other tyranny, but do from their hearts deprecate and abjure it. This seems the least that can be done, unless we would have our children's children say, "There was once here a glorious Church, but it was betrayed into the hands of Libertines for the real or affected love of a little temporary peace and good order."

July 22, 1833.

1 SAMUEL XII. 23

As for me, God forbid that I should sin against the Lord in ceasing to pray for you: but I will teach you the good and the right way.

[1] In the suppression of certain Irish Sees, *contrary to the suffrage of the Bishops of England and Ireland.*

On public occasions, such as the present, the minds of Christians naturally revert to that portion of Holy Scripture, which exhibits to us the will of the Sovereign of the world in more immediate relation to the civil and national conduct of mankind. We naturally turn to the Old Testament when public duties, public errors, and public dangers are in question. And what in such cases is natural and obvious is sure to be more or less right and reasonable. Unquestionably it is a mistaken theology which would debar Christian nations and statesmen from the instruction afforded by the Jewish Scriptures, under a notion, that the circumstances of that people were altogether peculiar and unique, and therefore irrelevant to every other case. True, there is hazard of misapplication, as there is whenever men teach by example. There is peculiar hazard, from the sacredness and delicacy of the subject; since dealing with things supernatural and miraculous as if they were ordinary human precedents, would be not only unwise, but profane. But these hazards are more than counterbalanced by the absolute certainty, peculiar to this history, that what is there commended was right, and what is there blamed, wrong. And they would be effectually obviated if men would be careful to keep in view this caution—suggested everywhere, if I mistake not, by the manner in which the Old Testament is quoted in the New—that, as regards reward and punishment, God dealt formerly with the Jewish people in a manner analogous to that in which He deals now, not so much with Christian nations as with the souls of individual Christians.

Let us only make due allowances for this cardinal point of difference and we need not surely hesitate to avail ourselves, as the time may require, of those national warnings which fill the records of the elder Church: the less so, as the discrepancy lies rather in what is revealed of God's providence than in what is required in the way of human duty. Rewards and punishments may be dispensed, visibly at least, with a less even hand; but what tempers and what conduct God will ultimately reward and punish, this is a point which cannot be changed, for it depends not on our circumstances, but on His essential unvarying Attributes.

I have ventured on these few general observations because the impatience with which the world endures any remonstrance on religious grounds is apt to show itself most daringly when the Law and the Prophets are appealed to. Without any scruple or ceremony, men give us to understand that they regard the whole as obsolete, thus taking the very opposite ground to that which was preferred by the same class of persons two hundred years ago, but, it may be feared, with much the same purpose and result. Then, the Old Testament was quoted at random for every excess of fanatical pride and cruelty: now, its authority goes for nothing, however clear and striking the analogies may be which appear to warrant us in referring to it. The two extremes, as usual, meet, and in this very remarkable point, that they both avail themselves of the supernatural parts of the Jewish revelation to turn away attention from that which they, of course, most dread and dislike in it—its authoritative confirmation of the plain dictates of conscience in matters of civil wisdom and duty.

That portion in particular of the history of the chosen people, which drew from Samuel, the truest of patriots, the wise and noble sentiment in the text, must ever be an unpleasing and perplexing page of Scripture to those who would fain persuade themselves that a nation, even a Christian nation, may do well enough, as such, without God and without His Church. For what if the Jews were bound to the Almighty by ties common to no other people? What if He had condescended to know them in a way in which He was as yet unrevealed to all families of the earth besides? What if, as their relation to Him was nearer, and their ingratitude more surpassing, so they might expect more exemplary punishment? Still, after all has been said, to exaggerate their guilt in degree beyond what is supposed possible in any nation whatever now, what can it come to, in kind and in substance, but only this: that they rejected God? that they wished themselves rid of the moral restraint implied in His peculiar presence and covenant? They said, what the prophet Ezekiel long after represents their worthy posterity as saying, "We will be as the heathen, the families of the countries,"[1] "Once for all we will get rid of these disagreeable unfashionable scruples which throw us behind, as we think, in the race of worldly honour and profit." Is this indeed a tone of thought which Christian nations cannot fall into? Or, if they should, has it ceased to be displeasing to God? In other words, has He forgotten to be angry with impiety and practical atheism? Either this must be affirmed, or men must own (what is clear at once to plain

[1] Ezekiel 20:32.

unsophisticated readers) that this first overt act, which began the downfall of the Jewish nation, stands on record, with its fatal consequences, for a perpetual warning to all nations, as well as to all individual Christians, who, having accepted God for their King, allow themselves to be weary of subjection to Him, and think they should be happier if they were freer, and more like the rest of the world.

I do not enter into the question, whether visible temporal judgements are to be looked for by Christian nations, transgressing as those Jews did. Surely common sense and piety unite in representing this inquiry as, practically, one of no great importance. When it is once known for certain that such and such conduct is displeasing to the King of kings, surely common sense and piety concur in setting their mark of reprobation on such conduct, whether the punishment, sure to overtake it, come to-morrow, or a year hence, or wait till we are in another world.

Waiving this question, therefore, I proceed to others which appear to me, I own, at the present moment especially, of the very gravest practical import.

What are the symptoms by which one may judge most fairly whether or no a nation, as such, is becoming alienated from God and Christ?

And what are the particular duties of sincere Christians whose lot is cast by Divine Providence in a time of such dire calamity?

The conduct of the Jews, in asking for a king, may furnish an ample illustration of the first point: the behaviour of Samuel, then and afterwards, supplies as perfect a pattern of the second as can well be expected from human nature.

I. The case is at least possible of a nation, having for centuries acknowledged, as an essential part of its theory of government, that, as a Christian nation, she is also a part of Christ's Church, and bound, in all her legislation and policy, by the fundamental rules of that Church— the case is, I say, conceivable, of a government and people so constituted deliberately throwing off the restraint which in many respects such a principle would impose on them, nay, disavowing the principle itself; and that on the plea that other states, as flourishing or more so in regard of wealth and dominion, do well enough without it. Is not this desiring, like the Jews, to have an earthly king over them, when the Lord their God is their King? Is it not saying in other words, "We will be as the heathen, the families

of the countries," the aliens to the Church of our Redeemer?

To such a change, whenever it takes place, the immediate impulse will probably be given by some pretence of danger from without, such as, at the time now spoken of, was furnished to the Israelites by an incursion of the children of Ammon; or by some wrong or grievance in the executive government, such as the malversation of Samuel's sons, to whom he had deputed his judicial functions. Pretences will never be hard to find; but, in reality, the movement will always be traceable to the same decay or want of faith, the same deficiency in Christian resignation and thankfulness, which leads so many, as individuals, to disdain and forfeit the blessings of the Gospel. Men not impressed with religious principle attribute their ill success in life—the hard times they have to struggle with—to anything rather than their own ill-desert: and the institutions of the country, ecclesiastical and civil, are always at hand to bear the blame of whatever seems to be going amiss. Thus, the discontent in Samuel's time, which led the Israelites to demand a change of constitution, was discerned by the Unerring Eye, though perhaps little suspected by themselves, to be no better than a fresh development of the same restless, godless spirit which had led them so often into idolatry. "They have not rejected thee, but they have rejected Me, that I should not reign over them. According to all the works, which they have done since the day that I brought them up out of Egypt even unto this day, wherewith they have forsaken Me, and served other gods, so do they also unto thee."[2]

The charge might perhaps surprise many of them, just as, in other times and countries, the impatient patrons of innovation are surprised at finding themselves rebuked on religious grounds. Perhaps the Jews pleaded the express countenance which the words of their Law in one place[3] seemed, by anticipation, to lend to the measure they were urging. And so, in modern times, when liberties are to be taken, and the intrusive passions of men to be indulged, precedent and permission, or what sound like them, may be easily found and quoted for everything. But Samuel, in God's name, silenced all this, giving them to understand that in His sight the whole was a question of motive and purpose, not of ostensible and colourable argument;—in His sight, I say, to Whom we, as well as they, are nationally responsible for much more than the

---

[2] 1 Samuel 8:7, 8.   [3] Deuteronomy 17:14–20.

soundness of our deductions as matter of disputation, or of law; we are responsible for the meaning and temper in which we deal with His Holy Church, established among us for the salvation of our souls.

These, which have been hitherto mentioned as omens and tokens of an Apostate Mind in a nation, have been suggested by the portion itself of sacred history to which I have ventured to direct your attention. There are one or two more, which the nature of the subject, and the palpable tendency of things around us, will not allow to be passed over.

One of the most alarming, as a symptom, is the growing indifference in which men indulge themselves, to other men's religious sentiments. Under the guise of charity and toleration we are come almost to this pass, that no difference, in matters of faith, is to disqualify for our approbation and confidence, whether in public or domestic life. Can we conceal it from ourselves that every year the practice is becoming more common of trusting men unreservedly in the most delicate and important matters, without one serious inquiry whether they do not hold principles which make it impossible for them to be loyal to their Creator, Redeemer, and Sanctifier? Are not offices conferred, partnerships formed, intimacies courted— nay (what is almost too painful to think of), do not parents commit their children to be educated, do they not encourage them to intermarry, in houses on which Apostolical Authority would rather teach them to set a mark, as unfit to be entered by a faithful servant of Christ?

I do not now speak of public measures only or chiefly; many things of that kind may be thought, whether wisely or no, to become from time to time necessary, which are in reality as little desired by those who lend them a seeming concurrence as they are in themselve undesirable. But I speak of the spirit which leads men to exult in every step of that kind, to congratulate one another on the supposed decay of what they call an exclusive system.

Very different are the feelings with which it seems natural for a true Churchman to regard such a state of things, from those which would arise in his mind on witnessing the mere triumph of any given set of adverse opinions, exaggerated or even heretical as he might deem them. He might feel as melancholy,—he could hardly feel so indignant.

But this is not a becoming place, nor are these safe topics, for the indulgence of mere feeling. The point really to be considered is, whether, according to the coolest estimate, the fashionable liberality of this generation be not ascribable, in a great measure, to the same temper which led the Jews voluntarily to set about degrading themselves to a level with the idolatrous Gentiles? And if it be true anywhere that such enactments are forced on the Legislature by public opinion, is APOSTASY too hard a word to describe the temper of that nation?

The same tendency is still more apparent, because the fair gloss of candour and forbearance is wanting, in the surly or scornful impatience often exhibited, by persons who would regret passing for unbelievers, when Christian motives are suggested, and checks from Christian principles attempted to be enforced on their public conduct. I say "their public conduct" more especially, because in that, I know not how, persons are apt to be more shameless and readier to avow the irreligion that is in them; amongst other reasons, probably, from each feeling that he is one of a multitude, and fancying, therefore, that his responsibility is divided.

For example:—whatever be the cause, in this country of late years (though we are lavish in professions of piety) there has been observable a growing disinclination, on the part of those bound by VOLUNTARY OATHS, to whatever reminds them of their obligation, a growing disposition to explain it all away. We know what, some years ago, would have been thought of such uneasiness, if betrayed by persons officially sworn, in private, legal, or commercial life. If there be any subjects or occasions now on which men are inclined to judge of it more lightly, it concerns them deeply to be quite sure that they are not indulging or encouraging a profane dislike of God's awful Presence, a general tendency, as a people, to leave Him out of all their thoughts.

They will have the more reason to suspect themselves, in proportion as they see and feel more of that impatience under pastoral authority, which our Saviour Himself has taught us to consider as a never-failing symptom of an unchristian temper. "He that heareth you, heareth Me; and he that despiseth you, despiseth Me."[4] Those words of divine truth put beyond all sophistical exception what common sense would lead us to infer, and what daily experience teaches—that disrespect to the Successors of the Apostles, as such, is an

[4] Luke 10:16.

unquestionable symptom of enmity to Him, Who gave them their commission at first, and has pledged Himself to be with them for ever. Suppose such disrespect general and national, suppose it also avowedly grounded not on any fancied tenet of religion, but on mere human reasons of popularity and expediency, either there is no meaning at all in these emphatic declarations of our Lord, or that nation, how highly soever she may think of her own religion and morality, stands convicted in His sight of a direct disavowal of His Sovereignty.

To this purpose it may be worth noticing that the ill-fated chief, whom God gave to the Jews, as the prophet tells us, in His anger,[5] and whose disobedience and misery were referred by himself to his "fearing the people, and obeying their voice,"[6] whose conduct, therefore, may be fairly taken as a sample of what public opinion was at that time supposed to require,—his first step in apostasy was, perhaps, an intrusion on the sacrificial office,[7] certainly an impatient breach of his engagement with Samuel, as the last and greatest of his crimes was persecuting David, whom he well knew to bear God's special commission. God forbid that any Christian land should ever, by her prevailing temper and policy, revive the memory and likeness of Saul, or incur a sentence of reprobation like this. But if such a thing should be, the crimes of that nation will probably begin in infringement on Apostolical Rights; she will end in persecuting the true Church; and in the several stages of her melancholy career she will continually be led on from bad to worse by vain endeavours at accommodation and compromise with evil. Sometimes toleration may be the word, as with Saul when he spared the Amalekites; sometimes state security, as when he sought the life of David; sometimes sympathy with popular feeling, as appears to have been the case when, violating solemn treaties, he attempted to exterminate the remnant of the Gibeonites in his zeal for the children of Israel and Judah.[8] Such are the sad but obvious results of separating religious resignation altogether from men's notions of civil duty.

II. But here arises the other question, on which it was proposed to say a few words, and with a view to which, indeed, the whole subject must be considered, if it is to lead to any practical improvement. What should be the tenor of their conduct who find themselves cast on such times of decay and danger? How may a man best reconcile his allegiance to God and his Church with his duty to his country, that country which now, by the supposition, is fast becoming hostile to the Church, and cannot therefore long be the friend of God?

Now in proportion as any one sees reason to fear that such is, or soon may be, the case in his own land, just so far may he see reason to be thankful, especially if he be called to any national trust, for such a complete pattern of his duty as he may find in the conduct of Samuel. That combination of sweetness with firmness, of consideration with energy, which constitutes the temper of a perfect public man, was never perhaps so beautifully exemplified. He makes no secret of the bitter grief and dismay with which the resolution of his countrymen has filled him. He was prepared to resist it at all hazards had he not received from God Himself directions to give them their own way, protesting, however, in the most distinct and solemn tone, so as to throw the whole blame of what might ensue on their wilfulness. Having so protested, and found them obstinate, he does not therefore at once forsake their service, he continues discharging all the functions they had left him with a true and loyal, though most heavy, heart. "God forbid that I should sin against the Lord in ceasing to pray for you: but I will teach you the good and the right way."

Should it ever happen (which God avert, but we cannot shut our eyes to the danger) that the Apostolical Church should be forsaken, degraded, nay trampled on and despoiled by the State and people of England, I cannot conceive a kinder wish for her, on the part of her most affectionate and dutiful children, than that she may consistently act in the spirit of this most noble sentence, nor a course of conduct more likely to be blessed by a restoration to more than her former efficiency. In speaking of the Church, I mean, of course, the laity as well as the clergy in their three orders,—the whole body of Christians united, according to the will of Jesus Christ, under the Successors of the Apostles. It may, by God's blessing, be of some use to show how, in the case supposed, the example of Samuel might guide her collectively, and each of her children individually, down even to minute details of duty.

The Church would, first of all, have to be constant, as before, in INTERCESSION. No despiteful usage, no persecution, could warrant her in

---

[5] I Samuel 15:24. [6] Hosea 13:11. [7] I Samuel 13:8–14. [8] 2 Samuel 21:2.

ceasing to pray, as did her first fathers and patterns, for the State and all who are in authority. That duty once well and cordially performed, all other duties, so to speak, are secured. Candour, respectfulness, guarded language, all that the Apostle meant in warning men not to "speak evil of dignities" may then, and then only, be practised, without compromise of truth and fortitude, when the habit is attained of praying as we ought for the very enemies of our precious and holy cause.

The constant sense of God's presence and consequent certainty of final success, which can be kept up no other way, would also prove an effectual bar against the more silent but hardly less malevolent feeling of disgust, almost amounting to misanthropy, which is apt to lay hold on sensitive minds when they see oppression and wrong triumphant on a large scale. The custom of interceding, even for the wicked, will keep the Psalmist's reasoning habitually present to their thoughts: "Fret not thyself because of the ungodly, neither be thou envious against the evildoers: for they shall soon be cut down like the grass, and be withered even as the green herb. . . . Leave off from wrath, and let go displeasure; fret not thyself, else shalt thou be moved to do evil."[9]

Thus not only by supernatural aid, which we have warrant of God's word for expecting, but even in the way of natural consequence, the first duty of the Church and of Churchmen, INTERCESSION, sincerely practised, would prepare them for the second;—which, following the words of Samuel as our clue, we may confidently pronounce to be REMONSTRANCE. "I will teach you the good and the right way." REMONSTRANCE, calm, distinct, and persevering, in public and in private, direct and indirect, by word, look, and demeanour is the unequivocal duty of every Christian, according to his opportunities, when the Church landmarks are being broken down.

Among laymen a deep responsibility would appear to rest on those particularly, whose profession leads them most directly to consider the boundaries of the various rights and duties which fill the space of civilized Society. The immediate machinery of change must always pass through their hands; and they have also very great power in forming and modifying public opinion. The very solemnity of this day may remind them, even more than others, of the close amity which must ever subsist between equal

justice and pure religion, Apostolical religion more especially, in proportion to her superior truth and exactness. It is an amity, made still more sacred, if possible, in the case of the Church and Law of England by historical recollections, associations, and precedents of the most engaging and ennobling cast.

But I return to the practical admonition afforded her, in critical periods, by Samuel's example.

After the accomplishment of the change which he deprecated, his whole behaviour, to Saul especially, is a sort of expansion of the sentiment in the text. It is all earnest INTERCESSION with God, grave, respectful, affectionate REMONSTRANCE with the misguided man himself. Saul is boldly rebuked, and that publicly, for his impious liberality in sparing the Amalekites, yet so as not to dishonour him in the presence of the people. Even when it became necessary for God's prophet to show that he was in earnest, and give the most effectual of warnings, by separating himself from so unworthy a person,—when "Samuel came no more to see Saul,"[10]—even then, we are told, he still "mourned for him."

On the same principle, come what may, we have ill learned the lessons of our Church if we permit out patriotism to decay together with the protecting care of the State. "The powers that be are ordained of God," whether they foster the true Church or no. Submission and order are still duties. They were so in the days of pagan persecution; and the more of loyal and affectionate feeling we endeavour to mingle with our obedience the better.

After all, the surest way to uphold or restore our endangered Church will be for each of her anxious children, in his own place and station, to resign himself more thoroughly to his God and Saviour in those duties, public and private, which are not immediately affected by the emergencies of the moment: the daily and hourly duties, I mean, of piety, purity, charity, justice. It will be a consolation understood by every thoughtful Churchman, that, let his occupation be, apparently, never so remote from such great interests, it is in his power, by doing all as a Christian, to credit and advance the cause he has most at heart; and what is more to draw down God's blessing upon it. This ought to be felt, for example, as one motive more to exact punctuality in those duties, personal and official, which the return of an Assize week offers to our practice; one reason

---

[9] Psalm 37:1, 2, 8.   [10] 1 Samuel 15:35.

more for veracity in witnesses, fairness in pleaders, strict impartiality, self-command, and patience, in those on whom decisions depend; and for an awful sense of God's presence in all. An Apostle once did not disdain to urge good conduct upon his proselytes of lowest condition, upon the ground that, so doing, they would adorn and recommend the doctrine of God our Saviour.[11] Surely, then, it will be no unworthy principle, if any man be more circumspect in his behaviour, more watchful and fearful of himself, more earnest in his petitions for spiritual aid, from a dread of disparaging the holy name of the English Church in her hour of peril by his own personal fault or negligence.

As to those who, either by station or temper, feel themselves most deeply interested, they cannot be too careful in reminding themselves that one chief danger, in times of change and excitement, arises from their tendency to engross the whole mind. Public concerns, ecclesiastical or civil, will prove indeed ruinous to those who permit them to occupy all their care and thoughts, neglecting or undervaluing ordinary duties, more especially those of a devotional kind.

These cautions being duly observed, I do not see how any person can devote himself too entirely to the cause of the Apostolical Church in these realms. There may be, as far as he knows, but a very few to sympathise with him. He may have to wait long, and very likely pass out of this world, before he see any abatement in the triumph of disorder and irreligion. But, if he be consistent, he possesses, to the utmost, the personal consolations of a good Christian: and as a true Churchman he has that encouragement which no other cause in the world can impart in the same degree:—he is calmly, soberly, demonstrably SURE, that, sooner or later, HIS WILL BE THE WINNING SIDE, and that the victory will be complete, universal, eternal.

He need not fear to look upon the efforts of Anti-christian powers, as did the Holy Apostles themselves, who welcomed the first persecution in the words of the Psalmist:

"Why do the heathen rage, and the people imagine a vain thing?

"The kings of the earth stand up, and the rulers take counsel together, against the Lord, and against His Anointed.

"For of a truth against Thy Holy Child Jesus, Whom Thou hast anointed, both Herod and Pontius Pilate, with the Gentiles, and the people of Israel, were gathered together,—

"FOR TO DO WHATSOEVER THY HAND AND THY COUNSEL DETERMINED BEFORE TO BE DONE."[12]

[11] Titus 2:10. [12] Acts 4:25–28.

Thomas Arnold

1795-1842

PERHAPS best known today as the father of Matthew Arnold, Thomas Arnold was, in his own day, one of the most distinguished educators and clergymen in Britain. He was cherished in his lifetime and long after his death as "Arnold of Rugby," and many Victorians formed their picture of him through Thomas Hughes's novel *Tom Brown's Schooldays* (1850), which glorified Headmaster Arnold and his educational ideals that combined discipline and moral earnestness. Born on the Isle of Wight, Arnold attended Winchester School and Corpus Christi College, Oxford. After graduation he became a fellow of Oriel where he became identified with the liberal wing of the Church of England and with the liberal-minded group known as the "Oriel Noëtics." This affiliation and the latitudinarian views expressed in his *Principles of Church Reform* (1833) were to bring him into conflict with the Oxford Movement, for in that work Arnold advocated a national church free of most formal theology and open to any who accepted Christ's divinity. Before the Movement was under way, however, he had left Oxford and in 1828 had accepted the headmastership of Rugby School. His tenure at Rugby transformed English public school education by raising both the intellectual and moral level of such schooling in a pattern widely imitated throughout the nation. Arnold was made Regius Professor of Modern History at Oxford in 1841, but he died suddenly in the following year. A decade and a half later Matthew Arnold wrote his celebrated tribute to his father in the poem "Rugby Chapel."

Thomas Arnold's prose writings fall chiefly in two categories, religious and historical. His religious works include the previously mentioned *Principles of Church Reform* and also a six-volume collection of his sermons. His historical works include the three-volume *History of Rome*, which carries the story only to the end of the Second Punic War, and his Oxford *Lectures on Modern History*.

CHRONOLOGY

1795	Born at Cowes, Isle of Wight.
1807	Attends Winchester School.
1811	Attends Corpus Christi College, Oxford.
1814	Graduates with first-class honors in classics.

1815   Elected Fellow of Oriel College.
1818   Ordained Deacon in the Church of England.
1820   Marries Mary Penrose.
1828   Assumes headmastership of Rugby School.
1833   *Principles of Church Reform.*
1838–43 *History of Rome.*
1841   Appointed Regius Professor of Modern History at Oxford.
1842   Dies June 12; buried in Rugby Chapel.

EDITIONS

Principles of Church Reform (1833; rpt. 1962).
History of Rome (3 vols., 1838–42).
Lectures on Modern History (1842).
Miscellaneous Works, ed. A. P. Stanley (1845).
Sermons (6 vols., 1878).

BIOGRAPHY AND CRITICISM

Arthur Penrhyn Stanley, *The Life and Correspondence of Thomas Arnold* (2 vols., 1844).
Joseph John Findlay, ed., *Arnold of Rugby: His School Life and Contributions to Education* (1897).
Lytton Strachey, *Eminent Victorians* (1918).
Reginald John Campbell, *Thomas Arnold* (1927).
Arnold Whitridge, *Dr. Arnold of Rugby* (1928).
Charles Richard Sanders, *Coleridge and the Broad Church Movement* (1942).
Basil Willey, *Nineteenth Century Studies* (1949).
Norman Wymer, *Dr. Arnold of Rugby* (1953).
Thomas W. Bamford, *Thomas Arnold* (1960).
Eugene L. Williamson, *The Liberalism of Thomas Arnold: A Study of His Religious and Political Writings* (1964).

The Oxford Malignants
and Dr. Hampden

Arnold took up the challenge laid down by the High Church party in what was called the Hampden Affair, one of many controversies at Oxford in the eighteen-thirties that involved the Oxford Movement. Briefly, the affair involved attacks by conservative churchmen, joined by members of the Oxford Movement, on the appointment of Renn Dickson Hampden to the Regius Professorship of Divinity at Oxford in 1836. Conservatives opposed Hampden because of his heterodox theology and his support for the abolition of religious tests for admission to Oxford. The affair resulted in a kind of pamphlet war touched off by Newman's Elucidations of

Hampden's Bampton lectures of 1832 as tending toward unitarianism and finally unbelief. Hampden and the liberals were incensed, and one of the resulting polemic essays in the campaign was Arnold's piece in the Edinburgh Review *of April 1836. Although opposition to Hampden came from the entire High Church party and some Evangelicals, Arnold, in his attack, had chiefly in mind the Oxford Movement, which he sought to link with the Nonjurors, who opposed the revolution of 1688, as opponents of progress. Arnold was not present at the scenes he describes in the essay, but his report reflects the views of Hampden's supporters at Oxford. Hampden survived the struggle, retained his multiple appointments, and in 1847 was made Bishop of Hereford.*

D<small>R.</small> H<small>AMPDEN</small>, the present Regius Professor of Divinity in the University of Oxford, after having obtained as a young man the highest academical distinctions, was appointed, in the year 1832, to preach what are called the "Bampton Lectures." These consist of a course of eight sermons, preached before the University every year on some point of Christian theology; and when the preacher is a man of any ability or reputation, the sermons, from their elaborate character, and from being delivered during a period of several weeks, always attract considerable attention. In the following year, Dr. Hampden was appointed by Lord Grenville, Principal of St. Mary's Hall; and, in 1834, he was elected Professor of Moral Philosophy, the electors being the Vice-chancellor and Proctors for the time, the Dean of Christ Church, and the Presidents of Magdalen and St. John's Colleges; and one of the qualifications required in the Professor by the statutes being, that he should be *sinceritate fidei commendatus.* The Dean of Christ Church, Dr. Gaisford, and the Presidents of Magdalen and St. John's, Drs. Routh and Dynter, held their present situations in the year 1834, and elected Dr. Hampden to the professorship. The "Purity of his Faith" received also, on the same occasion, the sanction of Dr. Rowley's approbation, the Master of University College, who was, in 1834, as he still is, the Vice-chancellor of the University.

A career so marked at every period by academical honours, pointed out Dr. Hampden as one of the most distinguished members of his University; and when the King's Government selected him to fill the important office of Regius Professor of Divinity, upon no other recommendation than that of his high public and academical character, it might have been supposed that their choice would have been received by the University, not with satisfaction merely,

but with gratitude.[1] The Government had, in a manner, believed the University's testimonial; and had attached so much weight to it as to be thereby influenced in the disposal of a piece of preferment not more lucrative than honourable.

But instead of peace there came a whirlwind. A numerous party in the University first took upon themselves, with characteristic modesty, to petition his Majesty to rescind his own appointment; and when this application was treated with due contempt, the baffled petitioners, or rather conspirators, commenced one of the most extraordinary courses of agitation ever yet witnessed even in the annals of party malignity.

As a first step, they met in the common room of Corpus Christi College, and named a committee to conduct their business. The committee drew up a declaration, which was submitted to the whole body of the conspirators, and then published, with a long list of names subscribed to it. The declaration contained a protest against Dr. Hampden's appointment: it charged him with having "contradicted the doctrinal truths which he was pledged to maintain;" and with having "asserted principles which necessarily tend to subvert, not only the authority of the Church, but the whole fabric and reality of Christian truth." By way of scholium on this declaration, the committee annexed to it an extract from their own report, in which they explained the mischievous principles ascribed to Dr. Hampden as no other than what they call the "Philosophy of Rationalism." "It is the theory of rationalism," they say, "[as set forth systematically in the Bampton Lectures of 1832, and still more recently asserted in lectures addressed to students,] which is to be considered the root of all the errors of Dr. Hampden's system."

We feel, that in this last quotation, we are drawing somewhat largely upon the confidence of our readers. We can indeed, to speak plainly,

---

[1] The appointment was made by the Whig ministry of Lord Melbourne in spite of the fact that Hampden's name had not been submitted by the Archbishop of Canterbury.

forgive them if they mistrust us. It is monstrous, it is almost incredible, that a charge of "mischievous principle" should be founded upon Dr. Hampden's Bampton Lectures of 1832; and not only this, but that these mischievous principles should be described as "SET FORTH SYSTEMATICALLY!" Mischievous principles, SET FORTH SYSTEMATICALLY, in a course of eight sermons preached successively in the University pulpit, before the Vice-chancellor and all the Dignitaries and Tutors of the University,—and no proceedings instituted, no censure passed, no accusation made,—but, on the contrary, the preacher subsequently receiving from the University the highest degree in Divinity—that degree which is virtually a professorship of theology—the University's commission to give lectures to its students in every branch of that faculty—receiving again the office of Head of a Hall—and lastly, the Professorship of Moral Philosophy? Such was the University of Oxford's censure upon eight sermons full of "SYSTEMATIC MISCHIEF," preached in her own church,—and in the presence of her highest authorities? And this statement comes not from an enemy, not from a rival; it is no dissenting slander; no *Edinburgh Review* calumny; but it is given out to the world from the very heart of Oxford herself; and subscribed with the names of five of her most devoted sons, who have known her long and well, who cannot misrepresent her in ignorance, who would not slander her in malice!

But the marvel is greater still. This charge against Dr. Hampden's Bampton Lectures, made by five individuals, has been adopted and sanctioned by seventy-six others—all of them masters of arts at the least—all describing themselves as persons "engaged or interested in the religious instruction of the University." All the five accusers, and an immense majority of the seventy-six sanctioners of the accusation, were exactly as much engaged and interested in the religious instruction of the University, in 1832, as they are now, in 1836. A reference to the Oxford calendar of 1832 will prove this at once to those to whom it is not notorious. Was there ever an accusation involving its unhappy promoters in such a dilemma of infamy? Compromisers of mischievous principles in 1832, 1833, 1834, and 1835,—or slanderers of a good and most Christian man in 1836—disqualified for the office of religious instructors, upon their own showing, by four years of either dullness or indifference, during which they could not understand, or did not notice, what was "mis-

chievous"—or else by one month of audacious and unprincipled calumny! We leave it to the nation to decide for which of these merits it will continue to respect and confide in the greater part of the eighty-one graduates, fellows, and tutors who have signed the declaration against Dr. Hampden.

Still, here is a phenomenon which requires explanation. What new circumstances have either enlightened the ignorance of these persons, or awakened their slanders? Whence this hurricane after so profound but, it seems, so treacherous a calm? Dr. Hampden, in 1834, published a pamphlet, entitled "Observations on Religious Dissent, with particular reference to the use of Religious tests in the University;" and, in 1835, he was a strenuous advocate for the measure, which had received, it is said, the sanction of the Duke of Wellington, the Chancellor of the University; namely, the substituting of a Declaration of Agreement with the doctrines of the Church, so far as the declarant's knowledge went, in the place of the unqualified subscription to the Thirty-nine Articles, now required of every young man who enters at Oxford. It was natural that these acts should throw a new light on all that Dr. Hampden had formerly written; nor can we be surprised that the eighty-one graduates, &c., should have partaken in this sudden illumination.

We return, however, to our narrative. The Corpus new Political Union petitioned the Board of Heads of Colleges and Halls, to propose to Convocation, two measures;—one, an address from the University to the Bishops, requesting them not to require from candidates for orders the usual certificate of having attended the lectures of the Regius Professor of Divinity, but to be satisfied with attendance on the lectures of the Margaret Professor of Divinity, Dr. Fawcett; —the other, a statute to be passed by the University itself, depriving the actual Regius Professor of his voice in the nomination of the select preachers, and also in the cognizance of any alleged heretical preaching. But the Heads of Houses refused to bring forward either of these measures before the Convocation.

Undismayed by this check, the unionists, by dint of sheer importunity and agitation, prevailed upon the Board to depart from their former resolution, and to propose the second of the two measures to Convocation,—the address of the Bishops being tacitly relinquished. Accordingly, notice was officially given, that on the 22d day of March a Convocation would be held for the consideration of the proposed statute. This precious bill of attainder states, in its preamble, that the University has no confidence in its Regius Professor of Divinity, in consequence of the manner in which he has treated theological subjects, in his published writings; and then, an enactment follows, divesting the said Professor of the powers which we have mentioned a little above, and which are attached to his office.

It were waste of time to comment on this proceeding; it were idle to dwell on the utter confusion which it exhibits of the simplest principles of good government—on the attempt to substitute the vote of a factious majority for the sober judgment of a court of justice—to put a vague charge of "having forfeited the confidence of the University" in the place of the definite, intelligible, and tangible accusation of "having preached doctrine contrary to the Articles of the Church." For the Church of England, like every other society, is not without a legal check upon the conduct of his ministers. If a clergyman's preaching be at variance with the tenets of the Church, the Bishop of his diocese may take cognizance of it; or if the alleged offence be committed in Oxford, the University statutes have provided that the Vice-chancellor, with the assistance of six doctors of divinity, shall inquire into the truth of the charge, and pass sentence accordingly. If Dr. Hampden had really published anything in opposition to the Articles of the Church of England, there was a ready way of substantiating the charge, and obtaining a censure upon him, from a competent authority. But the course of truth and honesty was not suited to the eighty-one conspirators. They thought that they had a secure majority in Convocation, which would vote for anything that they proposed to it. A *vote*, they knew, might give them what they could never dare to hope from a *verdict*. If Justice were to decide upon the case, they were sure to be disgracefully defeated; if Faction could be made the judge, they had a reasonable prospect of success.

Meantime, a charge that dared not abide the decision of a legal tribunal, was to be supported by evidence worthy of itself. A pamphlet was published, entitled "Elucidations of Dr. Hampden's Theological statements,"[2] consisting of a number of quotations from his work, classed in such an order, and separated in such a manner from the context, as might best serve the compiler's purposes. This was followed by another and more elaborate production, in which a number of propositions on different points of theology are professedly selected from Dr. Hampden's works, and contrasted with the Articles of the Church of England—a selection made precisely in the same spirit, and conducted with the same honesty, as the famous selection of articles from Wycliffe's works, which had the honour of being condemned by the Council of Constance.[3]

We have before us a copy of the "Elucidations," in which the *omissions* in the pretended quotations there given from Dr. Hampden's works have been carefully noted down; and these omissions happen so unluckily to fall upon passages which would have altered the whole tone and character of the quotation, that there is no possibility of acquitting the compiler of deliberate dishonesty. For instance, that person, in order to "elucidate," which, in his language, means "misrepresent," Dr. Hampden's Doctrine on the Trinity, begins a quotation with this sentence: "No one can be more convinced than I am, that there is a real mystery of God revealed in the Christian dispensation; and that no scheme of Unitarianism can solve the whole of the phenomena which Scripture records. But I am also as fully sensible, that there is a mystery attached to the subject, which is not a mystery of God;" and then follows the explanation of this last clause, for which the passage has been selected. The appearance, therefore, to the reader of the "Elucidations" is necessarily this, that Dr. Hampden, after one prefatory sentence expressing, for decency's sake, his belief that there was a *mystery* connected with the divine nature, goes on with great satisfaction to dispute, or undervalue the peculiar view of this mystery entertained by the Church of England. Accordingly, the pretended elucidator observes, in his introduction to this chapter of his work, that "Dr. Hampden holds that there is *some* mystery in the divine nature; but what that mystery is, or that it is the very mystery which the Catholic doctrine of the Trinity expresses, is, he considers, not revealed?" A grave charge undoubtedly against a member and minister of the Church of England, which professes its belief in the especial doctrine of the Trinity! But what shall we say to this elucidator, when we find that this serious charge rests only on his own direct falsification of what Dr. Hampden has written? For the quotation which we have copied is preceded by about a page and a half, in which Dr. Hampden has been

---

[2] By John Henry Newman.
[3] John Wycliffe (c. 1320–84), English precursor of the Reformation.

at great pains to distinguish between the doctrine of the Trinity itself, and the technical language in which it has been expressed in the writings of theologians; and to urge that it is only this language which has thrown a difficulty in the way of receiving the doctrine;—"causing," he says, "the wisdom of God to be received as the foolishness of man." And then the paragraph with which the elucidator's quotation begins, begins in reality with the following sentence, which alone is sufficient to refute the whole charge founded upon its deliberate suppression. "The truth itself, of the Trinitarian doctrine, emerges from these mists of human speculation, like the bold naked land on which an atmosphere of fog has for a while rested, and then been dispersed." It is apparent enough that the atmosphere of fog, of which Dr. Hampden speaks, has rested without being dispersed, upon the understanding or conscience of the "elucidator."

This same falsehood, for it deserves no lighter name, runs through all the second pamphlet, the preface to which is actually signed with the name of Dr. Pusey.[4] The technical language in which scriptural truths have been expressed is carefully confounded with the truths themselves. Dr. Hampden as carefully distinguishes them; repeating over and over again his firm belief that the scriptural truths are such in substance as the Church of England represents them,—but agreeing with many other good and sound divines, in regarding the language in which they are conveyed in theological writings, as perplexing; and as not setting forth the truth in the same practical manner as it is to be found in the Scripture. Now, if a minister of the Church of England did not believe that her articles expressed substantially the truth, as it is in the Scripture, he would undoubtedly be guilty of great inconsistency in subscribing them; but to account *historically* for the origin of the technical language of those articles,—and to separate it from the divine truth intended to be expressed by it, is neither inconsistent with the faith of an orthodox Christian, nor with the subscriptions signed by a clergyman of the Church of England.

With a natural and pardonable earnestness, yet paying, we think, far too great deference to charges so worthless in themselves, and known to proceed from authors whose censure was to be coveted by every good Christian minister, Dr. Hampden's friends were at the pains of publishing "statements of Christian doctrine," extracted also from his works; and containing a series of passages on every important point in theology, so full, so clear, so entirely in unison with the doctrines of the Church, and expressed with such intense earnestness of sincerity, that it might seem beyond the power of the very spirit of calumny itself to affix a charge of heresy on their author. It is very important also to observe, that these passages are extracted in great proportion from a published volume of Dr. Hampden's parochial sermons; a work which his calumniators took good care not to notice. Now, it is manifest, that the real nature of a man's religious views and feelings is to be collected most perfectly from his general pastoral preaching to his own congregation; and not from a set of sermons preached on a particular subject, and when that subject is in itself of an abstract and unimpassioned character. The subject of Dr. Hampden's Bampton Lectures was the influence of the Scholastic Philosophy on Christianity; his business therefore was less to enforce the original truths of the Gospel, than to condemn the corruptions of them; his statements were of necessity negative rather than positive; confuting error rather than inculcating truth. To quote, therefore, exclusively from such a work, even had the quotations been fairly made, was to give an utterly inadequate and unjust view of Dr. Hampden's character as an instructor in positive Christianity.

In the midst of all this ferment, the day arrived on which Dr. Hampden was to deliver his inaugural Lecture. As might have been expected, an immense crowd of hearers attended it. It was a trying moment; for as the Professor looked round upon his audience, he saw the well-known faces of his persecutors, who had already shown abundantly that they were of those who make a man an offender for a word, and who were come to his lecture not to be convinced, not to be softened, not to listen and to judge with fairness and truth; but to lay hold upon every expression, to misunderstand or misrepresent his matter, and to pervert his tone and manner;—ready to call conciliation cowardice, and firmness pride. Yet from this fiery ordeal Dr. Hampden came forth nobly triumphant. It was touching to observe the subdued emotions of his countenance, and the unequalled and unexcited dignity of his voice:— it was beautiful to mark how he had triumphed over opposite temptations,—how meekly and patiently he laboured to remove misunderstand-

---

[4] Edward Bouverie Pusey (1800–82), fellow of Oriel, one of the leaders of the Oxford Movement.

ing,—how honestly he abstained from one word of unworthy compromise,—yet how heroically he forebore from every expression of resentment or contempt towards the faction of his unworthy calumniators. We cannot resist the pleasure of copying the concluding passage of this most Christian address:—

"I appeal from an excited spirit to a spirit of soberness and candor; I demand not to be tried by the conclusions of an adverse school, but by the calm and gentle reason of men disposed to give me credit for no less love of the truth and the faith than themselves, and who will openly contend with me by argument, not by censure and intimidation, and the array of hostile numbers: 'Non tam bene cum rebus humanus agitur,' says an ancient philosopher, 'ut meliora pluribus placeant; argumentum pessimi, turba est.' And a far greater than the philosopher has said:— 'Woe unto you when all men shall speak well of you.'—'Blessed are ye when men shall revile you and persecute you, and shall say all manner of evil against you falsely for my sake.'—'If any man will come after me, let him deny himself, and take up his cross and follow me.' These words are my comfort; I trust he who spoke them will enable me to proceed on my way without repining at the suffering through which he has required that I should pass; and without relaxation of spirit in his work under the painfulness of the counteraction against which it must be done. I am at all times ready to meet fair and free discussion, but to misrepresentation, and clamour, and violence, with God's help I will never yield. I pray God to forgive those who may have employed such weapons against me, and to turn their hearts, and to grant them more of that mind which was in Christ Jesus.

"It is a great grief to me, I acknowledge, to know that there are any whose honest though mistaken zeal I may have offended. Such are, I trust, open to conviction and kinder feelings; I should, however, unless experience had furnished ample instances of it, wonder that Christian zeal should in any individual have carried him to proceedings destructive of Christian purity and peace. A sense of Christian duty and the kind feelings of the heart will never, I believe, be found apart from each other, and least of all, in doing 'the work of the Lord.'

"After all, however, I appear not here as a functionary of the University or of the Church alone, but as the servant of a Master in Heaven by whose judgment I must stand or fall. For let me say it with that humility which becomes me in applying to myself such sacred words: 'With me it is a very small thing that I should be judged of you or of man's judgment; yea, I judge not mine own self. For I know nothing by myself; yet am I not hereby justified: but he that judgeth me is the Lord. Therefore judge nothing before the time, until the Lord come, who both will bring to light the hidden things of darkness, and will make manifest the counsels of the hearts; and then shall every man have praise of God.'"

This might have been thought irresistible; but faction and fanaticism combined are proof against any impression of truth or goodness. The conspirators actually adjourned their meetings from Corpus common room to Mr. Baxter's Printing office; there, with the press before them, they issued with unabated zeal their placards, and circulars, and elucidations, and statements,—all designed to fanaticise their partizans amongst the country clergy, whom they had summoned up to Oxford to secure their expected triumph in the Convocation on the 22d of March.

There is no reason to doubt that their arts would have been successful; but the exemplary firmness of the Proctors saved the University, for a time at least, from the deep disgrace in which the party would have involved it. By the Constitution of Oxford, if two Proctors are agreed, they can interpose a *veto* upon any measure brought forward by the Heads of Houses; and thus prevent it from being submitted at all to the votes of the Convocation. On the 19th of March the Proctors gave official notice of their intention to negative the statute. The factious and fanatical party, deceived by the unscrupulous falsehoods of the Tory newspapers, still expected that there would be a division, and crowded up to Oxford. When the 22d of March arrived, they found out their error;—the Convocation was held, and the Proctors, as they had declared they would do, put their negative on the statute in the usual form. The conspirators and their country disciples consoled themselves by fresh placards, and by a meeting in Brazenose Hall, where they had the pleasure of listening to speeches from Lord Kenyon, Lord Encombe, Mr. A. Trevor, and Dr. Pusey.[5]

Thus the persecution rests for the present. But it will be renewed, in all probability, early in the

[5] Leaders of the High Church party.

next term, when new Proctors will have come into office. Meanwhile, we may be thought to have given undue importance to these Oxford squabbles; and to have unwisely gratified the vanity of a few obscure fanatics by noticing them in this Journal. The *individuals,* indeed, are sufficiently insignificant;—nor shall we, by naming them, confer on them that notoriety for which nature has not designed them. But the *party,* unworthy as it is, is yet strong enough to be mischievous. Always defeated in the end, it has yet always impeded the progress of good, and in some degree marred its triumph; so it did at the Revolution of 1688,—so it did at the Reformation.

The common language, which describes history to be philosophy teaching by examples, is an ambiguous expression of a great but ill-understood truth. No man would go to history for lessons of private morality: we have other far better and readier means of learning these. But what history does furnish, when read aright, is a mirror to reflect the true character of existing parties, and so, to determine our judgment, in taking part with one or another. It gives us this true mirror when we have learned, in the parties and revolutions of past times, to separate what is accidental and particular from what is essential and universal—to fix first the true standard of all political enterprise, and then to judge of parties, whatever may be their subordinate resemblances or differences, by their attachment or opposition to this one great end. Thus we find, that the zealous worshipper of the saints and apostles, in the sixteenth century, was the real moral successor of their persecutors in the first; and thus the fanatic who now spreads the no-popery war-cry, is the genuine representative of those very Papists of the sixteenth century, whose names he is overwhelming with obloquy.

This is consoling, because it shows that the world has on the whole advanced;—that the heresy of one period becomes the orthodox faith of another;—and that that which great and good men taught at the price of their blood, obtains in the end so sure a triumph, that even the low and the wicked are obliged to do it homage, and make use of its name to exclude that further

development of truth which is indeed its own genuine child. Thus, even the Tories of our day profess to admire the Revolution of 1688; but whilst exalting the individual of the race, as it were, who has done his appointed work, and has nearly lived out his generation, they would fain see his lineage become extinct for ever, and no heir born in due season to continue and improve what he had begun. For it is false to say that the reform, or the truth, of a later age undoes or despises the reforms and the truths which have preceded them. They do not destroy, but complete;—holding in honour, loving, and using the reforms and the truths achieved and discovered by their fathers,—but deeming it the worthiest tribute to their fathers' memory to imitate their example, by farther reforming and developing some farther truth, as they did.

But on the character of no party does history throw so full and clear a light as on the High Church party of the Church of England—the party of the Oxford conspirators. Unlike the political Tories, who are only analogously like the Tories of the Revolution, by being as much in the rear of the existing generation as the old Tories were in the rear of theirs, these Church Tories have stirred neither actually nor relatively; they are the very Nonjurors and High Church clergy of King William's, and Anne's, and George the First's reign, reproduced, with scarcely a shade of difference.[6] Now, as then, this party is made up of two elements; of the Hophni and Phinehas school, on the one hand—the mere low worldly clergy, careless and grossly ignorant,—ministers not of the Gospel but of the aristocracy, who belong to Christianity only from the accident of its being established by law; and of the formalist Judaizing fanatics, on the other hand, who have ever been the peculiar disgrace of the Church of England; for these High Church fanatics have imbibed, even of fanaticism itself, nothing but the folly and the virulence.[7] Other fanatics have persecuted, like the Romanists, in order to uphold a magnificent system, which, striking its roots deep, and stretching its branches wide, exercises a vast influence over the moral condition of man, and may almost excuse some

---

[6] The Nonjurors were Anglican bishops who refused to take the oath of allegiance to William and Mary in 1688 because they felt themselves bound to the deposed James II. They represented the continuation into the eighteenth century of the Caroline Anglo-Catholic spirit that was to be cultivated by the Oxford Movement. Throughout the essay Arnold cites instances of Nonjuror opposition to broad churchmen.

[7] Hophni and Phinehas (Phineas) were Old Testament brothers who abused their priestly office, using it for personal pleasure and gain. Here they represent the "High and Dry" Tory churchmen. The Judaizers represent the Oxford Movement.

extravagance of zeal in its behalf. Others again have been fanatics for freedom, and for what they deemed the due authority of God's own word. They were violent against human ceremonies— they despised learning—they cast away the delicacies, and almost the humanities of society, for the sake of asserting two great principles, noble even in their exaggeration,—entire freedom towards man, and entire devotion towards God. But the fanaticism of the English High Church-man has been the fanaticism of mere foolery. A dress, a ritual, a name, a ceremony;—a technical phraseology;—the superstition of a priesthood, without its power;—the form of Episcopal government, without the substance; a system imperfect and paralyzed, not independent, not sovereign,—afraid to cast off the subjection against which it is perpetually murmuring. Such are the objects of High Church fanaticism; objects so pitiful, that, if gained ever so completely, they would make no man the wiser or the better; they would lead to no good, intellectual, moral, or spiritual; to no effect, social or religious, except to the changing of sense into silliness, and holiness of heart and life into formality and hypocrisy.

Once, however, and once only, in the history of Christianity, do we find a heresy—for never was that term more justly applied—so degraded and low-principled as this. We must pass over the times of Romanists—we must go back to the very beginning of the Christian Church, and there, in the Jews and Judaizers of the New Testament, we find the only exact resemblance to the High Churchman of Oxford. In the zealots of circumcision and the ceremonies of the law,—in the slanderers and persecutors of St. Paul—the doters upon old wives' fables and endless genealogies—the men of "soft words and fair speeches,"—of a "voluntary humility," all the time that they were calumniating and opposing the Gospel and its great apostle;—in the malignant fanatics who, to the number of more than forty, formed a conspiracy to assassinate Paul, because he had denied the necessity of ceremonies to salvation—"the men of mint, and anise, and cummin," who cared not for judgment, mercy, and truth—the enemies and revilers of the holiest names which earth reverences, and who are condemned, in the most emphatic language, by

that authority which all Christians acknowledge as divine;—in these, and in these alone, can the party which has headed the late Oxford conspiracy find their perfect prototype.

But we may not press this farther *now*. Most true and complete as is the parallel, and most instructive as it is, towards setting a mark upon these revived Judaizers, to warn all Christians against their spirit and their practice, yet it would lead us into matter, and thoughts, and feelings too deep to find a place here. We turn to a comparison less solemn—to a period and a country less remote—to the events of scarcely more than a century ago—to the spirit and the proceedings of the High Church party under the Liberal Government that followed the Revolution. The tricks that have been now attempted to be played in the Convocation of the University were then played in the Convocation of the Clergy. There, we find the bigot Dr. Jane, who defeated the attempt of King William's government to effect a union between the Church and the Dissenters, by the parrot-like repetition of *Nolumus leges Angliæ mutari*.[8] There we find Burnet's[9] *Exposition of the Articles* condemned by the lower House of Convocation, on grounds similar to those now urged by the Oxford conspirators against the writings of Dr. Hampden; namely, "that it allowed a diversity of opinions, which the Articles were framed to avoid; that it contained many passages contrary to the true meaning of the Articles, and to other received doctrines of our Church; and that some things in it were of dangerous consequence to the Church, and derogated from the honour of the Reformation." Such was the sentence passed by the High Churchmen of the last century, upon a book which is now universally received as a correct statement of the doctrines of the Church, and which is commonly recommended by the Bishop as a companion to theological studies of candidates for orders! Again, the rancorous slanders of the High Churchmen against names amongst the most revered in the annals of the Church, may sufficiently console Dr. Hampden for the same slanders now vented against himself. The Irish nonjuror Lesley, in an anonymous pamphlet, professing to be written by "A true son of the Church," and published in 1695, writes thus of Archbishop Tillotson:[10]—"His politics are Levi-

---

[8] "We do not wish to change English laws"; said by William Jane (1645–1707), professor of divinity at Oxford.

[9] Gilbert Burnet (1643–1715), Bishop of Salisbury.

[10] Robert Lesley or Leslie, Bishop successively of Dromore, Raphoe, and Clogher in Ireland in the seventeenth century; John Tillotson (1630–94), Archbishop of Canterbury.

athan, and his religion is latitudinarian, which is none; that is, nothing that is positive, but against everything that is positive in other religions. . . . He is owned by the atheistical wits of all England as their true primate and apostle. They glory and rejoice in him, and make their public boasts of him. He leads them not only the length of Socinianism (they are but slender beaux who have got no further than that,) but to call in question all revelation, to turn Genesis, &c., into a mere romance—to ridicule the whole, as Blount, Gildon, and others of the doctor's disciples have done in print." Lesley goes on to call Tillotson's principles "diabolical," and says that he had by them "deeply poisoned" the nation.[11] And another nonjuror, Hickes, a man, like one or two of the Oxford conspirators, much vaunted by his party for the pretended holiness of his life, because he used a sentimental style of excessive religious feeling in his prayers and other compositions, found his religion perfectly compatible with falsehood and malignity; for he was privy to the writing of this wicked libel, and recommended it, hoping that it might see the light before the publication of his own discourses upon Dr. Burnet and Dr. Tillotson. These men, whose intellectual powers were so low, that Dr. Johnson himself, in spite of all his prejudices in their favour, declared, "that with one exception, he never knew a nonjuror who could reason," appear to have exactly reversed the precepts of St. Paul, which bids us "in malice to be children, but in understanding to be men."

But the Government held on its way in spite of the clamours, the constant libels, and the occasional treasons of the High Church clergy. It continued to advance real Christians, like Burnet and Tillotson, to such important stations in the Church as fell vacant. The higher clergy were thus gradually purified; and of the lower, the Hophni and Phinehas party, seeing which way promotion came, composed their outward bearing accordingly, while the more fanatical party died out in their own folly. Then came a period in which the spirit of the Heads of the Clergy was indeed an honour to the Church of England— the period marked by the names of Wake, of Butler, of the apostolical Bishop Wilson, and of Secker[12]—men firm and earnest in the faith of the Church of England; but in whom faith ministered to holiness and to charity, because

it was the faith of Christians, and not of Judaizers.

Yet the experience of the last century affords, in one respect, a warning by which we hope that the Liberal Government of the present day will not fail to profit. The poisonous plant of Judaism was cut down or withered away; but the root was left in the ground; and thus, when its season returned, it sprung up again, and is now again growing rankly. In other words, Oxford was allowed to retain its exclusive character—opinions and prejudices of one sort only found admission to it—it stood aloof from the great mass of the intelligence of the nation, neither influencing it, nor influenced by it. The consequences were doubly injurious: Oxford, on the one hand, lived wholly in the past, and that past continually viewed amiss; whilst the active part of the nation, finding one of its great seats of education thus incompetent to discharge its duties, could but supply its place imperfectly by other means. Men's views became too exclusively practical and utilitarian—they lived too entirely in the present; and thus learning decayed, and a narrow-mindedness of another sort began to prevail, equally injurious to that lofty wisdom, which, by ever looking at the present through the past, learns thus, and thus only, to provide aright for it and for the future. We are satisfied that there is a spirit, in an ancient and magnificent University like Oxford, far too valuable to be quietly suffered to taint and spoil itself by refusing the wholesome combinations of elements of a different species. If Oxford be left alone, and a substitute for it be sought in a new University, both will suffer, for both will remain more or less sectarian;—the High Church fanaticism will become more and more inveterate, while it will be met by extremes of another sort, not more respectable or profitable.

One word more in conclusion. We have used the language of severe condemnation in speaking of the late proceedings at Oxford, and of the party which originated them. We should be most unwilling to speak harshly of any mere differences of opinion, utterly false and mischievous as we hold the views of the High Church party to be; yet, if it were merely an *intellectual error*, it should be confuted, indeed, firmly and plainly, but still, with all tenderness to the persons of those who held it. But the attack on

---

[11] Birch, *Life of Tillotson*, p. 297, 2d edn 1753. [Arnold's note.]

[12] William Wake (1657–1737), Archbishop of Canterbury; Thomas Wilson (1663–1755), Bishop of Sodor and Man; Thomas Secker (1693–1768), Archbishop of Canterbury.

Dr. Hampden bears upon it the character, not of error, but of *moral wickedness*. When men break through the charities and decencies of life, to run down a good and pious individual—when they raise a cry against him which they know will arouse the worst passions, and be re-echoed by their baser followers with a violence to shame even themselves—when they appeal not to any legal and competent tribunal, but to the votes of an assembly where party spirit is notoriously virulent—when they garble the writings of their intended victim, wholly neglecting such as would palpably refute their charge, and so detaching the passages which they quote from the context, and keeping out of sight the writer's general object, as to produce an impression unfair and false—above all, when refusing to give credit to a good man's solemn declarations, they labour as far as in them lies to ruin his character,—to say nothing of the acute pain occasioned to a noble mind by being insulted with such suspicions,—in such a proceeding we see nothing of Christian zeal, but much of the mingled fraud, and baseness, and cruelty, of fanatical persecution. And, for such persecution, the plea of conscience is not admissible; it can only be a conscience so blinded by wilful neglect of the highest truth, or so corrupted by the habitual indulgence of evil passions, that it rather aggravates than excuses the guilt of those whom it misleads.

Thomas Carlyle

1795-1881

IT IS PERHAPS fitting that Thomas Carlyle should have had to endure what is probably the longest literary apprenticeship in English literature before attaining recognition, for the role he fashioned and won for himself was a role suited to a man of years and dignity. It was the role of the prophet and the sage. It is fitting too that he should have conceived such a role during the uncertain years of the Regency and have come upon the public at large at the very beginning of Victoria's reign, for by this timing he impressed his character on the age and contributed to shaping the character of that age.

Carlyle had none of the advantages of most of the other literary figures of his time. He was born to a poor, intensely Calvinistic stonemason's family in the Scottish hamlet of Ecclefechan. His extraordinary intelligence was early recognized and he was therefore destined for the ministry. His financial circumstances were such that he had to walk the almost one hundred miles to Edinburgh to begin his college education there. His college years were spent in a degree of frugality impressive even for a Scot, and his early years of schoolmastering, first at Annan Academy where he had studied as a boy and later in Kirkcaldy near Edinburgh, did not much improve his financial position. They did, however, bring him again into contact with Edward Irving, a man from Carlyle's native region and a brilliant preacher who was to go on to notorious success and finally notorious failure in London. Irving introduced Carlyle to his first love, Margaret Gordon, but there was no possibility of marriage because of the difference in her and Carlyle's stations. Irving also introduced Carlyle to his own former pupil, Jane Welsh of Haddington, who had once expected to marry Irving himself, but he was previously committed. Carlyle courted Jane for many years and finally married her in 1826, though still not yet financially well established, a matter of some concern to Jane's mother.

Carlyle had left off teaching at the end of 1818 and had settled in Edinburgh doing various literary odd jobs and hackwork. He wrote encyclopaedia articles, translated a French geometry text, wrote several reviews, but, above all, in 1819 he undertook on his own the study of German. This proved to be a momentous experience for the young Carlyle and the foundation of his first literary success. It preceded by about two years Carlyle's "mystical experience" in Leith Walk in Edinburgh, a perception of a transcendent reality that overcame his entire being and initiated a period of self-reconstitution after the near despair that attended upon his losing his traditional Calvinist Christian faith while a student at the university and after the onset of what was to prove a lifelong condition of chronic indigestion that Carlyle called dyspepsia. The combination of the Leith Walk experience and the growing awareness that in German literature he was finding answers to some of the spiritual problems that had been plaguing him gave Carlyle a new lease on life, not unlike that he attributes to Diogenes Teufelsdröckh in the latter part of Book Second of *Sartor Resartus*. Its practical results were increased literary activity, issuing in the translation of Goethe's *Wilhelm Meisters Lehrjahre* (Wilhelm Meister's Apprenticeship) and in a biography of Friedrich Schiller. He even engaged in a correspondence with Goethe, the German author whom he regarded most highly. Between 1822 and 1824 he was also tutoring the sons of Mr. and Mrs. Charles Buller with whom he traveled to London, where he was enabled to meet such literary figures as Coleridge.

After his marriage to Jane Welsh in 1826 the Carlyles settled in Edinburgh, and he began writing review articles on German literature for the *Edinburgh Review* and other journals. In 1828 the Carlyles removed to the isolated farm of Craigenputtock, a property owned by the Welsh family. There Carlyle wrote the critical and social essays like "Signs of the Times" and "Characteristics" that were to set forth the basis of his social ideas and to attract the enthusiastic response of such as Emerson, who sought Carlyle out in the moorlands and began a friendship that was to last for a half-century. There too Carlyle wrote the original and unconventional *Sartor Resartus*, but he was unable to find a publisher for it until *Fraser's Magazine* agreed to run it serially in 1833–34. It was not issued in book form until Emerson saw it through the press in Boston in 1836.

The Craigenputtock years were the years of Carlyle's consolidating his spiritual and social insights. By the time he and Jane moved to London in 1834 his views on life and society were fully formed and he was ready to make an assault on the citadel of English intellectual life. But even this effort was not immediately successful. Carlyle undertook to write a history of the French Revolution, but when the first volume was completed in manuscript he lent it to John Stuart Mill, and Mill's housemaid unknowingly burned the manuscript in the fireplace. Carlyle had to begin again, and with characteristic indomitability he did. Little wonder that he described the new version as having come "flamingly from the heart."

Sartor Resartus, which was to come to be an essential book in Victorian life, had had to make its way slowly, first in *Fraser's* where it aroused mainly hostility, then in Emerson's American edition, then with an English book edition in 1838. *The French Revolution*, however, was an immediate success. Carlyle had made history live, and the Victorian public read the work as avidly as they read popular novels by Carlyle's friend Dickens. From the moment of its favorable reception on, Carlyle's place as a leading man of letters was secure. His and Jane's home in Chelsea became a literary salon where such figures as Dickens, Tennyson, and Browning enjoyed the society of the Sage and his witty and captivating wive.

With the success of *The French Revolution* Carlyle was invited to give a series of public lectures. The first was delivered in 1837, and there were four courses in all, ranging from German literature to heroes and hero-worship, only this last series being published. In 1839 Carlyle published *Chartism* and he collected his earlier essays under the title of *Critical and Miscellaneous Essays*. Almost over-night it seemed—though for Carlyle himself it had been anything but over-night—Carlyle was a major literary figure in English life. And almost overnight he had become recognized as a sage and a prophet. He continued to discharge his responsibilities in this role for forty more years.

Carlyle's industry continued unabated through the eighteen-forties and fifties with such works as *Past and Present, Cromwell,* the *Latter-Day Pamphlets,* and *The Life of John Sterling,* In 1852 he commenced his "thirteen-years war" with *Frederick the Great,* the eighth and final volume not appearing until 1865, one year before the death of Jane Carlyle. During the forties and fifties Carlyle was at the peak of his influence. Matthew Arnold recalled later the force of Carlyle's "puissant voice" as it reached Oxford undergraduates in the forties through his works. Others heard that puissant voice in person, especially the English literary and intellectual world that clustered round the house in Chelsea, as well as numerous American literary visitors following in Emerson's wake.

After Jane's death Carlyle withdrew a good deal from society, first to work on his *Reminiscences,* including the reminiscence of Jane herself, then to assemble Jane's writings and correspondence for subsequent publication after his death. He opposed the Second Reform Bill in 1867 with *Shooting Niagara* and as late as 1875 he was still publishing such works as *The Early Kings of Norway.* In 1874 he received the Prussian Order of Merit but declined a pension and the Grand Cross of Bath from the British government. He died in 1881 and was buried in the town of his birth.

Carlyle has been called a "spiritual volcano," and it was as such that he struck his contemporaries. Although he propounded no systematic philosophy, he did affirm a series of propositions of a philosophic and religious character that his audience received eagerly and that forms the basis of his appeal. Carlyle asserts above all the existence of an all-powerful and all-just deity who created and governs the universe for a purpose. From this conviction come Carlyle's positive and negative insights and judgments—that modern man has forgotten God, that acquisitiveness has replaced brotherhood, that the ballot box has become a new altar, that only a spiritual rebirth can bring coherence out of the chaos of modern life, and much more. Man and society are always seen by Carlyle in the light of their relation to divine purpose and divine justice. Thus Carlyle's writings have a depth and perspective ordinarily absent from social commentary and history, and they carry the reader from the mundane to the transcendent in the manner of the sage and the prophet.

The style Carlyle developed to express his views reinforces those views by its very character. The combination of pulpit eloquence and biblical echoes, exhortation and the imperative mode, portentous language and wide-rever-berating allusion—all these reinforce the impact of the sage's utterances and seem to give them a divine imprimatur. Carlyle's style is today as interesting in its own right as his ideas, and it has come to be recognized as one of the most inventive and exuberant in all English literature and a source of Carlyle's abiding fascination for the modern reader.

To be sure, contemporary readers can hardly be expected to come to Carlyle with the same sense of reverence that the Victorians brought or even with the same intellectual background that disposed such readers to receive Carlyle favorably. Yet much in Carlyle continues to exert power over modern readers. Carlyle reminds us of the moral dimensions of all actions, and he calls upon the reader to ponder such concepts as justice, evil, blessedness, purpose, and the destiny of man.

CHRONOLOGY

1795	Born December 4 at Ecclefechan, Annandale, Scotland.
1806–9	Attends Annan Academy.
1809–14	Attends Edinburgh University.
1814	Returns to Annan Academy as mathematics instructor.
1816–18	Teaches in Burgh School, Kirkcaldy. Meets Margaret Gordon. Friendship with Edward Irving.
1819	Moves to Edinburgh. Begins study of German.
1821	Meets Jane Baillie Welsh in Haddington.
1822	Tutors Charles and Arthur Buller.
1824	Translates *Wilhelm Meister's Apprenticeship*.
1826	Marries Jane Welsh, October 17
1828–31	Contributes essays to *Edinburgh Review, Foreign Review, Fraser's Magazine*, etc.
1832	Death of James Carlyle, Carlyle's father.
1833–34	*Sartor Resartus* appears in *Fraser's*.
1834	Carlyles move to London, No. 5 Great Cheyne Row, Chelsea. Death of Edward Irving.
1837	*The French Revolution*.
1839	*Critical and Miscellaneous Essays*, 4 vols.
1841	*On Heroes, Hero-Worship*.
1843	*Past and Present*.
1844	Death of John Sterling.
1845	*Oliver Cromwell's Letters and Speeches*.
1846	Visits Ireland.
1850	*Latter-Day Pamphlets*.
1851	*Life of John Sterling*.
1852	Begins work on *Frederick the Great*. Tours Germany.
1853	Death of Margaret Aitken Carlyle, Carlyle's mother.
1858–65	*Frederick the Great*, 8 vols.
1866	Elected Rector of Edinburgh University. Death of Jane Welsh Carlyle. Begins *Reminiscences*.
1867	*Shooting Niagara: and After?*
1869	Audience with Queen Victoria.
1874	Receives Prussian Order of Merit.
1875	*The Early Kings of Norway* and *Portraits of John Knox*.
1881	Dies February 4; is buried in Ecclefechan churchyard.

EDITIONS

Works ed. H. D. Traill (30 vols., 1896–1901). [The standard edition.]
Correspondence between Goethe and Carlyle, ed. Charles Eliot Norton (1887).
Correspondence of Emerson and Carlyle, ed. Joseph Slater (1963).
The Letters of Thomas and Jane Welsh Carlyle, ed. C. R. Sanders et al. (4 vols., 1970—in progress). [Will be the standard edition.]
Letters of Thomas Carlyle 1826–1836, ed. Charles Eliot Norton (2 vols., 1888).

Letters of Thomas Carlyle to John Stuart Mill, John Sterling, and Robert Browning,
     ed. Alexander Carlyle (1923).
On Heroes, Hero-Worship, and the Heroic in History, ed. A. MacMechan (1902).
Past and Present, ed. A. M. D. Hughes (1918).
Reminiscences, ed. Charles Eliot Norton (2 vols., 1887).
Sartor Resartus, ed. Charles Frederick Harrold (1937).

BIOGRAPHY AND CRITICISM

Grace J. Calder, *The Writing of Past and Present* (1949).
Ian Campbell, *Thomas Carlyle* (1974).
Louis Cazamian, *Carlyle,* trans. E. K. Brown (1932).
Isaac Watson Dyer, *A Bibliography of Thomas Carlyle's Writing and Ana* (1928).
James Anthony Froude, *Thomas Carlyle: A History of the First Forty Years of His
     Life, 1795–1835* and *A History of His Life in London, 1834–1881* (4 vols.,
     1882–84).
Michael Goldberg, *Carlyle and Dickens* (1972).
Charles Frederick Harrold, *Carlyle and German Thought, 1819–1834* (1934).
John Holloway, *The Victorian Sage: Studies in Argument* (1953).
A. Abbott Ikeler, *Puritan Temper and Transcendental Faith: Carlyle's Literary
     Vision* (1972).
W. S. Johnson, *Thomas Carlyle: A Study of His Literary Apprenticeship, 1814–1831*
     (1911).
Albert J. LaValley, *Carlyle and the Idea of the Modern* (1968).
B. H. Lehman, *Carlyle's Theory of the Hero* (1928).
George Levine, *The Boundaries of Fiction: Carlyle, Macaulay, Newman* (1968).
Arthur Mämpel, *Thomas Carlyle als Künstler* (1935).
Emery Neff, *Carlyle* (1932).
———, *Carlyle and Mill: Mystic and Utilitarian* (1924).
Philip Rosenberg, *The Seventh Hero* (1974).
Hill Shine, *Carlyle's Early Reading to 1834* (1953).
Julian Symons, *Thomas Carlyle: The Life and Ideas of a Prophet* (1952).
G. B. Tennyson, *Sartor Called Resartus* (1965).
———, "Thomas Carlyle," in *Victorian Prose: A Guide to Research* (1973).
Rene Wellek, *Confrontations* (1965).
David Alec Wilson, *Life of Thomas Carlyle* (6 vols., 1923–34).

Signs of the Times

*Carlyle took the title of this essay from Christ's words reported in Matthew 16:3: "O ye
hypocrites, ye can discern the face of the sky; but can ye not discern the signs of the times?"
The essay, ostensibly a review of three recently published works—one of them by Edward
Irving—is Carlyle's first excursion into the realm of social and cultural criticism after almost a
decade of concern with German literature. In it he seeks to read the very signs of the times that*

others have ignored or misread. The characterization of the present age as mechanical was to become a frequently reiterated Carlyle idea, and many of the thoughts expressed in this essay are developed in subsequent works, especially the essay "Characteristics." "Signs of the Times" first appeared in the Edinburgh Review *of June 1829.*

I T IS NO very good symptom either of nations or individuals, that they deal much in vaticination. Happy men are full of the present, for its bounty suffices them; and wise men also, for its duties engage them. Our grand business undoubtedly is, not to *see* what lies dimly at a distance, but to *do* what lies clearly at hand.

> Know'st thou *Yesterday*, its aim and reason;
> Work'st thou well *Today*, for worthy things?
> Calmly wait the *Morrow's* hidden season,
> Need'st not fear what hap soe'er it brings.[1]

But man's 'large discourse of reason' *will* look 'before and after'; and, impatient of the 'ignorant present time,' will indulge in anticipation far more than profits him. Seldom can the unhappy be persuaded that the evil of the day is sufficient for it; and the ambitious will not be content with present splendour, but paints yet more glorious triumphs, on the cloud-curtain of the future.

The case, however, is still worse with nations. For here the prophets are not one, but many; and each incites and confirms the other; so that the fatidical fury spreads wider and wider, till at last even Saul must join in it. For there is still a real magic in the action and reaction of minds on one another. The casual deliration of a few becomes, by this mysterious reverberation, the frenzy of many; men lose the use, not only of their understandings, but of their bodily senses; while the most obdurate unbelieving hearts melt, like the rest, in the furnace where all are cast as victims and as fuel. It is grievous to think, that this noble omnipotence of Sympathy has been so rarely the Aaron's-rod[2] of Truth and Virtue, and so often the Enchanter's-rod of Wickedness and Folly! No solitary miscreant, scarcely any solitary maniac, would venture on such actions and imaginations, as large communities of sane men have, in such circumstances, entertained as sound wisdom. Witness long scenes of the French Revolution, in these late times! Levity is no protection against such visitations, nor the utmost earnestness of character. The New-England Puritan burns witches, wrestles for months with the horrors of Satan's invisible world, and all ghastly phantasms, the daily and hourly precursors of the Last Day; then suddenly bethinks him that he is frantic, weeps bitterly, prays contritely, and the history of that gloomy season lies behind him like a frightful dream.

Old England too has had her share of such frenzies and panics; though happily, like other old maladies, they have grown milder of late: and since the days of Titus Oates[3] have mostly passed without loss of men's lives; or indeed without much other loss than that of reason, for the time, in the sufferers. In this mitigated form, however, the distemper is of pretty regular recurrence; and may be reckoned on at intervals, like other natural visitations; so that reasonable men deal with it, as the Londoners do with their fogs,—go cautiously out into the groping crowd, and patiently carry lanterns at noon; knowing, by a well-grounded faith, that the sun is still in existence, and will one day reappear. How often have we heard, for the last fifty years, that the country was wrecked, and fast sinking; whereas up to this date, the country is entire and afloat! The 'State in Danger' is a condition of things, which we have witnessed a hundred times; and as for the Church, it has seldom been out of 'danger' since we can remember it.

All men are aware that the present is a crisis of this sort; and why it has become so. The repeal of the Test Acts, and then of the Catholic disabilities,[4] has struck many of their admirers with an indescribable astonishment. Those things seemed fixed and immovable; deep as the foundations of the world; and lo, in a moment they have vanished, and their place knows them no more! Our worthy friends mistook the slumbering Leviathan for an island; often as they had been assured, that Intolerance was, and could be nothing but a Monster; and so, mooring under the lee, they had anchored comfortably in his scaly

---

[1] Free translation by Carlyle of a Goethe poem published in *Zahme Xenien*, group 4.

[2] Miraculous Old Testament rod; see Exodus 7:9–12 and Numbers 17.

[3] Originator of false reports in 1678 that Charles II was to be murdered and Roman Catholicism to be established in England.

[4] The Test Acts imposed civil disabilities on Roman Catholics and dissenters and were repealed in 1828; Catholic Emancipation in 1829 permitted Catholics to serve in Parliament.

rind, thinking to take good cheer; as for some space they did. But now their Leviathan has suddenly dived under; and they can no longer be fastened in the stream of time; but must drift forward on it, even like the rest of the world: no very appalling fate, we think, could they but understand it; which, however, they will not yet, for a season. Their little island is gone; sunk deep amid confused eddies; and what is left worth caring for in the universe? What is it to them that the great continents of the earth are still standing; and the polestar and all our loadstars, in the heavens, still shining and eternal? Their cherished little haven is gone, and they will not be comforted! And therefore, day after day, in all manner of periodical or perennial publications, the most lugubrious predictions are sent forth. The King has virtually abdicated; the Church is a widow, without jointure; public principle is gone; private honesty is going; society, in short, is fast falling in pieces; and a time of unmixed evil is come on us.

At such a period, it was to be expected that the rage of prophecy should be more than usually excited. Accordingly, the Millennarians have come forth on the right hand, and the Millites on the left. The Fifth-monarchy men prophesy from the Bible, and the Utilitarians from Bentham.[5] The one announces that the last of the seals is to be opened, positively, in the year 1860; and the other assures us that 'the greatest-happiness principle' is to make a heaven of earth, in a still shorter time. We know these symptoms too well, to think it necessary or safe to interfere with them. Time and the hours will bring relief to all parties. The grand encourager of Delphic or other noises is—the Echo. Left to themselves, they will the sooner dissipate, and die away in space.

Meanwhile, we too admit that the present is an important time; as all present time necessarily is. The poorest Day that passes over us is the conflux of two Eternities; it is made up of currents that issue from the remotest Past, and flow onwards into the remotest Future. We were wise indeed, could we discern truly the signs of our own time; and by knowledge of its wants and advantages, wisely adjust our own position in it. Let us, instead of gazing idly into the obscure distance, look calmly around us, for a little on the perplexed

scene where we stand. Perhaps, on a more serious inspection, something of its perplexity will disappear, some of its distinctive characters and deeper tendencies more clearly reveal themselves; whereby our own relations to it, our own true aims and endeavours in it, may also become clearer.

Were we required to characterise this age of ours by any single epithet, we should be tempted to call it, not an Heroical, Devotional, Philosophical, or Moral Age, but, above all others, the Mechanical Age. It is the Age of Machinery, in every outward and inward sense of that word; the age which, with its whole undivided might, forwards, teaches and practices the great art of adapting means to ends. Nothing is now done directly, or by hand; all is by rule and calculated contrivance. For the simplest operation, some helps and accompaniments, some cunning abbreviating process is in readiness. Our old modes of exertion are all discredited, and thrown aside. On every hand, the living artisan is driven from his workshop, to make room for a speedier, inanimate one. The shuttle drops from the fingers of the weaver, and falls into iron fingers that ply it faster. The sailor furls his sail, and lays down his oar; and bids a strong, unwearied servant, on vaporous wings, bear him through the waters. Men have crossed oceans by steam; the Birmingham Fire-king has visited the fabulous East; and the genius of the Cape, were there any Camoens now to sing it, has again been alarmed, and with far stranger thunders than Gamas.[6] There is no end to machinery. Even the horse is stripped of his harness, and finds a fleet fire-hose yoked in his stead. Nay, we have an artist that hatches chickens by steam; the very brood-hen is to be superseded! For all earthly, and for some unearthly purposes, we have machines and mechanic furtherances; for mincing our cabbages; for casting us into magnetic sleep. We remove mountains, and make seas our smooth highway; nothing can resist us. We war with rude Nature; and, by our resistless engines, come off always victorious, and loaded with spoils.

What wonderful accessions have thus been made, and are still making, to the physical power of mankind; how much better fed, clothed, lodged

---

[5] Millenarians believed in a coming millennium of 1,000 years of holiness; Millites, followers of James Mill's utilitarian philosophy; Fifth-monarchy men in the seventeenth century believed that a 1,000-year reign of Christ, or the fifth monarchy, was imminent; Utilitarians were followers of Jeremy Bentham (1748–1832), who advocated the principle of utility as the measure of good.

[6] Luis de Camöens (1524–80), Portuguese poet, author of the *Lusiads* (1572), epic poem on Portuguese voyagers.

and, in all outward respects, accommodated men now are, or might be, by a given quantity of labour, is a grateful reflection which forces itself on every one. What changes, too, this addition of power is introducing into the Social System; how wealth has more and more increased, and at the same time gathered itself more and more into masses, strangely altering the old relations, and increasing the distance between the rich and the poor, will be a question for Political Economists, and a much more complex and important one than any they have yet engaged with.

But leaving these matters for the present, let us observe how the mechanical genius of our time has diffused itself into quite other provinces. Not the external and physical alone is now managed by machinery, but the internal and spiritual also. Here too nothing follows its spontaneous course, nothing is left to be accomplished by old natural methods. Everything has its cunningly devised implements, its prĕestablished apparatus; it is not done by hand, but by machinery. Thus we have machines for Education: Lancastrian machines; Hamiltonian machines;[7] monitors, maps and emblems. Instruction, that mysterious communing of Wisdom with Ignorance, is no longer an indefinable tentative process, requiring a study of individual aptitudes, and a perpetual variation of means and methods, to attain the same end; but a secure, universal, straightforward business, to be conducted in the gross, by proper mechanism, with such intellect as comes to hand. Then, we have Religious machines, of all imaginable varieties; the Bible-Society, professing a far higher and heavenly structure, is found, on inquiry, to be altogether an earthly contrivance: supported by collection of moneys, by fomenting of vanities, by puffing, intrigue and chicane; a machine for converting the Heathen. It is the same in all other departments. Has any man, or any society of men, a truth to speak, a piece of spiritual work to do; they can nowise proceed at once and with the mere natural organs, but must first call a public meeting, appoint committees, issue prospectuses, eat a public dinner; in a word, construct or borrow machinery, wherewith to speak it and do it. Without machinery they were hopeless, helpless; a colony of Hindoo weavers squatting in the heart of Lancashire. Mark, too, how every machine must have its moving power, in some of the great currents of society; every little sect among us, Unitarians, Utilitarians, Anabaptists, Phrenologists, must have its Periodical, its monthly or quarterly Magazine;—hanging out, like its windmill, into the *popularis aura,* to grind meal for the society.

With individuals, in like manner, natural strength avails little. No individual now hopes to accomplish the poorest enterprise single-handed and without mechanical aids; he must make interest with some existing corporation, and till his field with their oxen. In these days, more emphatically than ever, 'to live, signifies to unite with a party, or to make one.' Philosophy, Science, Art, Literature, all depend on machinery. No Newton, by silent meditation, now discovers the system of the world from the falling of an apple; but some quite other than Newton stands in his Museum, his Scientific Institution and behind whole batteries of retorts digesters and galvanic piles imperatively 'interrogates Nature,' —who, however, shows no haste to answer. In defect of Raphaels, and Angelos, and Mozarts, we have Royal Academies of Painting, Sculpture, Music; whereby the languishing spirit of Art may be strengthened, as by the more generous diet of a Public Kitchen. Literature, too, has its Paternoster-row[8] mechanism, its Trade-dinners, its Editorial conclaves, and huge subterranean, puffing bellows; so that books are not only printed, but, in a great measure, written and sold, by machinery.

National culture, spiritual benefit of all sorts, is under the same management. No Queen Christina, in these times, needs to send for her Descartes; no King Frederick for his Voltaire,[9] and painfully nourish him with pensions and flattery: any sovereign of taste, who wishes to enlighten his people, has only to impose a new tax, and with the proceeds establish Philosophic Institutes. Hence the Royal and Imperial Societies, the Bibliothèques, Glypothèques, Technothèques, which front us in all capital cities; like so many well-finished hives, to which it is expected the stray agencies of Wisdom will swarm of their own accord, and hive and make honey. In like manner, among ourselves, when it is thought that religion is declining, we have

---

[7] Systems of education of Joseph Lancaster (1778–1838), by which advanced students taught beginners, and of James Hamilton (1769–1829), who devised a method of foreign language instruction.

[8] Center of book publishing in London.

[9] Queen Christina of Sweden (1626–89) attracted the French philosopher René Descartes to her court; Frederick the Great (1712–86) of Prussia called Voltaire to his court.

only to vote half-a-million's worth of bricks and mortar, and build new churches. In Ireland it seems they have gone still farther, having actually established a 'Penny-a-week Purgatory-Society'! Thus does the Genius of Mechanism stand by to help us in all difficulties and emergencies, and with his iron back bears all our burdens.

These things, which we state lightly enough here, are yet of deep import, and indicate a mighty change in our whole manner of existence. For the same habit regulates not our modes of action alone, but our modes of thought and feeling. Men are grown mechanical in head and in heart, as well as in hand. They have lost faith in individual endeavour, and in natural force, of any kind. Not for internal perfection, but for external combinations and arrangements, for institutions, constitutions,—for Mechanism of one sort or other, do they hope and struggle. Their whole efforts, attachments, opinions, turn on mechanism, and are of a mechanical character.

We may trace this tendency in all the great manifestations of our time; in its intellectual aspect, the studies it most favours and its manner of conducting them; in its practical aspects, its politics, arts, religion, morals; in the whole sources, and throughout the whole currents, of its spiritual, no less than its material activity.

Consider, for example, the state of Science generally, in Europe, at this period. It is admitted, on all sides, that the Metaphysical and Moral Sciences are falling into decay, while the Physical are engrossing, every day, more respect and attention. In most of the European nations there is now no such things as a Science of Mind; only more or less advancement in the general science, or the special sciences, of matter. The French were the first to desert Metaphysics; and though they have lately affected to revive their school, it has yet no signs of vitality. The land of Malebranche, Pascal, Descartes and Fénelon, has now only its Cousins and Villemains;[10] while, in the department of Physics, it reckons far other names. Among ourselves, the Philosophy of Mind, after a rickety infancy, which never reached the vigour of manhood, fell suddenly into decay, languished and finally died out, with its last amiable cultivator, Professor Stewart.[11] In no nation but

Germany has any decisive effort been made in psychological science; not to speak of any decisive result. The science of the age, in short, is physical, chemical, physiological; in all shapes mechanical. Our favourite Mathematics, the highly prized exponent of all these other sciences, has also become more and more mechanical. Excellence in what is called its higher departments depends less on natural genius than on acquired expertness in wielding its machinery. Without undervaluing the wonderful results which a Lagrange or Laplace[12] educes by means of it, we may remark, that their calculus, differential and integral, is little else than a more cunningly-constructed arithmetical mill; where the factors being put in, are, as it were, ground into the true product, under cover, and without other effort on our part than steady turning of the handle. We have more Mathematics than ever; but less Mathesis. Archimedes and Plato could not have read the *Mécanique Céleste;* but neither would the whole French Institute see aught in that saying, 'God geometrises!' but a sentimental rodomontade.

Nay, our whole Metaphysics itself, from Locke's time downwards, has been physical; not a spiritual philosophy, but a material one. The singular estimation in which his Essay was so long held as a scientific work (an estimation grounded, indeed, on the estimable character of the man) will one day be thought a curious indication of the spirit of these times. His whole doctrine is mechanical, in its aim and origin, in its method and its results. It is not a philosophy of the mind: it is a mere discussion concerning the origin of our consciousness, or ideas, or whatever else they are called; a genetic history of what we see *in* the mind. The grand secrets of Necessity and Freewill, of the Mind's vital or non-vital dependence on Matter, of our mysterious relations to Time and Space, to God, to the Universe, are not, in the faintest degree touched on in these inquiries; and seem not to have the smallest connexion with them.

The last class of our Scotch Metaphysicians had a dim notion that much of this was wrong; but they knew not how to right it. The school of Reid[13] had also from the first taken a mechanical

---

[10] Malebranche, Pascal, and Fenelon were distinguished French philosophers of the seventeenth century; Cousin and Villemains were contemporary men of letters of the second rank.

[11] Dugald Stewart (1753–1828), professor at Edinburgh, last of the Common Sense school of philosophy.

[12] Joseph Louis LaGrange (1726–1813), French mathematician; Pierre Laplace (1749–1827), French astronomer, author of the *Mecanique Céleste* referred to subsequently.

[13] Thomas Reid (1710–96), chief of the Scottish Common Sense school of philosophy.

course, not seeing any other. The singular conclusions at which Hume, setting out from their admitted premises, was arriving, brought this school into being; they let loose Instinct, as an undiscriminating ban-dog, to guard them against these conclusions;—they tugged lustily at the logical chain by which Hume was so coldly towing them and the world into bottomless abysses of Atheism and Fatalism. But the chain somehow snapped between them; and the issue has been that nobody now cares about either,—any more than about Hartley's, Darwin's, or Priestley's[14] contemporaneous doings in England. Hartley's vibrations and vibratiuncles, one would think, were material and mechanical enough; but our Continental neighbours have gone still farther. One of their philosophers has lately discovered, that 'as the liver secretes bile, so does the brain secrete thought'; which astonishing discovery Dr. Cabanis,[15] more lately still, in his *Rapports du Physique et du Morale de l'Homme,* has pushed into its minutest developments.

The metaphysical philosophy of this last inquirer is certainly no shadowy or unsubstantial one. He fairly lays open our moral structure with his dissecting-knives and real metal probes; and exhibits it to the inspection of mankind, by Leuwenhoek microscopes, and inflation with the anatomical blowpipe. Thought, he is inclined to hold, is still secreted by the brain; but then Poetry and Religion (and it is really worth knowing) are 'a product of the smaller intestines'! We have the greatest admiration for this learned doctor: with what scientific stoicism he walks through the land of wonders, unwondering; like a wise man through some huge, gaudy, imposing Vauxhall,[16] whose fire-works, cascades and symphonies, the vulgar may enjoy and believe in,—but where he finds nothing but the saltpetre, pasteboard and catgut. His book may be regarded as the ultimatum of mechanical metaphysics in our time; a remarkable realisation of what in Martinus Scriblerus[17] was still only an idea, that 'as the jack had a meat-roasting quality, so had the body a thinking quality,'—upon the strength of which the Nurembergers were to build a wood-and-leather man, 'who

should reason as well as most country parsons.' Vaucanson[18] did indeed make a wooden duck, that seemed to eat and digest; but that bold scheme of the Nurembergers remained for a more modern virtuoso.

This condition of the two great departments of knowledge,—the outward, cultivated exclusively on mechanical principles; the inward, finally abandoned, because, cultivated on such principles, it is found to yield no result,—sufficiently indicates the intellectual bias of our time, its all-pervading disposition towards that line of inquiry. In fact, an inward persuasion has long been diffusing itself, and now and then even comes to utterance, That, except the external, there are no true sciences; that to the inward world (if there be any) our only conceivable road is through the outward; that, in short, what cannot be investigated and understood mechanically, cannot be investigated and understood at all. We advert the more particularly to these intellectual propensities, as to prominent symptoms of our age, because Opinion is at all times doubly related to Action, first as cause, then as effect; and the speculative tendency of any age will therefore give us, on the whole, the best indications of its practical tendency.

Nowhere, for example, is the deep, almost exclusive faith we have in Mechanism more visible than in the Politics of this time. Civil government does by its nature include much that is mechanical, and must be treated accordingly. We term it indeed, in ordinary language, the Machine of Society, and talk of it as the grand working wheel from which all private machines must derive, or to which they must adapt, their movements. Considered merely as a metaphor, all this is well enough; but here, in as so many other cases, the 'foam hardens itself into a shell,' and the shadow we have wantonly evoked stands terrible before us and will not depart at our bidding. Government includes much also that is not mechanical, and cannot be treated mechanically; of which latter truth, as appears to us, the political speculations and exertions of our time are taking less and less cognisance.

Nay, in the very outset, we might note the mighty interest taken in *mere political arrange-*

---

[14] David Hartley (1705–57), associationist psychologist; Erasmus Darwin (1733–1804), physiologist and poet, grandfather of Charles Darwin; Joseph Priestly (1733–1804), chemist, discoverer of oxygen.
[15] Pierre Cabanis (1757–1808), French physician and psychologist.
[16] London pleasure gardens on the south side of the Thames.
[17] Imaginary author of *Memoirs of Martinus Scriblerus* (1741).
[18] Jacques de Vaucanson (1709–82), French inventor.

ments, as itself the sign of a mechanical age. The whole discontent of Europe takes this direction. The deep, strong cry of all civilised nations,—a cry which, every one now sees, must and will be answered, is: Give us a reform of Government! A good structure of legislation, a proper check upon the executive, a wise arrangement of the judiciary, is *all* that is wanting for human happiness. The Philosopher of this age is not a Socrates, a Plato, a Hooker, or Taylor,[19] who inculcates on men the necessity and infinite worth of moral goodness, the great truth that our happiness depends on the mind which is within us, and not on the circumstances which are without us; but a Smith, a De Lolme,[20] a Bentham, who chiefly inculcates the reverse of this,—that our happiness depends entirely on external circumstances; nay, that the strength and dignity of the mind within us is itself the creature and consequence of these. Were the laws, the government, in good order, all were well with us; the rest would care for itself! Dissentients from this opinion, expressed or implied, are now rarely to be met with; widely and angrily as men differ in its application, the principle is admitted by all.

Equally mechanical, and of equal simplicity, are the methods proposed by both parties for completing or securing this all-sufficient perfection of arrangement. It is no longer the moral, religious, spiritual condition of the people that is our concern, but their physical, practical, economical condition, as regulated by public laws. Thus is the Body-politic more than ever worshipped and tendered; but the Soul-politic less than ever. Love of country, in any high or generous sense, in any other than an almost animal sense, or mere habit, has little importance attached to it in such reforms, or in the opposition shown them. Men are to be guided only by their self-interests. Good government is a good balancing of these; and, except a keen eye and appetite for self-interest, requires no virtue in any quarter. To both parties it is emphatically a machine: to the discontented, a 'taxing-machine'; to the contented, a 'machine for securing property.' Its duties and its faults are not those of a father, but of an active parish-constable.

Thus it is by the mere condition of the machine, by preserving it untouched, or else by reconstructing it, and oiling it anew, that man's salvation as a social being is to be ensured and indefinitely promoted. Contrive the fabric of law aright, and without farther effort on your part, that divine spirit of Freedom, which all hearts venerate and long for, will of herself come to inhabit it; and under her healing wings every noxious influence will wither, every good and salutary one more and more expand. Nay, so devoted are we to this principle, and at the same time so curiously mechanical, that a new trade, specially grounded on it, has arisen among us, under the name of 'Codification,' or codemaking in the abstract; whereby any people, for a reasonable consideration, may be accommodated with a patent code;—more easily than curious individuals with patent breeches, for the people does *not* need to be measured first.

To us who live in the midst of all this, and see continually the faith, hope and practice of every one founded on Mechanism of one kind or other, it is apt to seem quite natural, and as if it could never have been otherwise. Nevertheless, if we recollect or reflect a little, we shall find both that it has been, and might again be otherwise. The domain of Mechanism,—meaning thereby political, ecclesiastical or other outward establishments,—was once considered as embracing, and we are persuaded can at any time embrace, but a limited portion of man's interests, and by no means the highest portion.

To speak a little pedantically, there is a science of *Dynamics* in man's fortunes and nature, as well as of *Mechanics*. There is a science which treats of, and practically addresses, the primary, unmodified forces and energies of man, the mysterious springs of Love, and Fear, and Wonder, of Enthusiasm, Poetry, Religion, all which have a truly vital and *infinite* character; as well as a science which practically addresses the finite, modified developments of these, when they take the shape of immediate 'motives,' as hope of reward, or as fear of punishment.

Now it is certain, that in former times the wise men, the enlightened lovers of their kind, who appeared generally as Moralists, Poets or Priests, did, without neglecting the Mechanical province, deal chiefly with the Dynamical; applying themselves chiefly to regulate, increase and purify the inward primary powers of man;

---

[19] Richard Hooker (1554–1600), English divine, author of the *Laws of Ecclesiastical Polity;* Jeremy Taylor (1613–67), author of *Holy Living* and *Holy Dying.*

[20] Adam Smith (1723–90), author of *Wealth of Nations;* Jean Louis DeLolme (1740–1806), Swiss jurist.

and fancying that herein lay the main difficulty, and the best service they could undertake. But a wide difference is manifest in our age. For the wise men, who now appear as Political Philosophers, deal exclusively with the Mechanical province; and occupying themselves in counting-up and estimating men's motives, strive by curious checking and balancing, and other adjustments of Profit and Loss, to guide them to their true advantage: while, unfortunately, those same 'motives' are so innumerable, and so variable in every individual, that no really useful conclusion can ever be drawn from their enumeration. But though Mechanism, wisely contrived, has done much for man in a social and moral point of view, we cannot be persuaded that it has ever been the chief source of his worth or happiness. Consider the great elements of human enjoyment, the attainments and possessions that exalt man's life to its present height, and see what part of these he owes to institutions, to Mechanism of any kind; and what to the instinctive, unbounded force, which Nature herself lent him, and still continues to him. Shall we say, for example, that Science and Art are indebted principally to the founders of Schools and Universities? Did not Science originate rather, and gain advancement, in the obscure closets of the Roger Bacons, Keplers, Newtons; in the workshops of the Fausts and the Watts; wherever, and in what guise soever Nature, from the first times downwards, had sent a gifted spirit upon the earth? Again, were Homer and Shakspeare members of any beneficed guild, or made Poets by means of it? Were Painting and Sculpture created by forethought, brought into the world by institutions for that end? No; Science and Art have, from first to last, been the free gift of Nature; an unsolicited, unexpected gift; often even a fatal one. These things rose up, as it were, by spontaneous growth, in the free soil and sunshine of Nature. They were not planted or grafted, nor even greatly multiplied or improved by the culture or manuring of institutions. Generally speaking, they have derived only partial help from these; often enough have suffered damage. They made constitutions for themselves. They originated in the Dynamical nature of man, not in his Mechanical nature.

Or, to take an infinitely higher instance, that of the Christian Religion, which, under every theory of it, in the believing or unbelieving mind, must ever be regarded as the crowning glory, or rather the life and soul, of our whole modern culture: How did Christianity arise and spread abroad among men? Was it by institutions, and establishments and well-arranged systems of mechanism? Not so; on the contrary, in all past and existing institutions for those ends, its divine spirit has invariably been found to languish and decay. It arose in the mystic deeps of man's soul; and was spread abroad by the 'preaching of the word,' by simple, altogether natural and individual efforts; and flew, like hallowed fire, from heart to heart, till all were purified and illuminated by it; and its heavenly light shone, as it still shines, and (as sun or star) will ever shine, through the whole dark destinies of man. Here again was no Mechanism; man's highest attainment was accomplished Dynamically, not Mechanically.

Nay, we will venture to say, that no high attainment, not even any far-extending movement among men, was ever accomplished otherwise. Strange as it may seem, if we read History with any degree of thoughtfulness, we shall find that the checks and balances of Profit and Loss have never been the grand agents with men; that they have never been roused into deep, thorough, all-pervading efforts by any computable prospect of Profit and Loss, for any visible, finite object; but always for some invisible and infinite one. The Crusades took their rise in Religion; their visible object was, commercially speaking, worth nothing. It was the boundless Invisible world that was laid bare in the imaginations of those men; and in its burning light, the visible shrunk as a scroll. Not mechanical nor produced by mechanical means, was this vast movement. No dining at Freemasons' Tavern, with the other long train of modern machinery; no cunning reconciliation of 'vested interests,' was required here: only the passionate voice of one man,[21] the rapt soul looking through the eyes of one man; and rugged, steel-clad Europe trembled beneath his words, and followed him whither he listed. In later ages it was still the same. The Reformation had an invisible, mystic and ideal aim; the result was indeed to be embodied in external things; but its spirit, its worth, was internal, invisible, infinite. Our English Revolution too originated in Religion. Men did battle, in those old days, not for Purse-sake, but for Conscience-sake. Nay, in our own

---

[21] Peter the Hermit (c. 1050–c. 1115), French monk, by his preaching called into being the First Crusade (1096–99).

days, it is no way different. The French Revolution itself had something higher in it than cheap
bread and a Habeas-corpus act. Here too was an
Idea; a Dynamic, not a Mechanic force. It was
a struggle, though a blind and at last an insane
one, for the infinite, divine nature of Right, of
Freedom, of Country.

Thus does man, in every age, vindicate,
consciously or unconsciously, his celestial birthright. Thus does Nature hold on her wondrous,
unquestionable course; and all our systems and
theories are but so many froth-eddies or sandbanks, which from time to time she casts up, and
washes away. When we can drain the Ocean into
mill-ponds, and bottle-up the Force of Gravity, to
be sold by retail, in gas jars; then may we hope to
comprehend the infinitudes of man's soul under
formulas of Profit and Loss; and rule over this
too, as over a patent engine, by checks, and
valves, and balances.

Nay, even with regard to Government itself,
can it be necessary to remind any one that
Freedom, without which indeed all spiritual life
is impossible, depends on infinitely more complex
influences than either the extension or the
curtailment of the 'democratic interest'? Who is
there that, 'taking the high *priori* road,' shall
point out what these influences are; what deep,
subtle, inextricably entangled influences they
have been and may be? For man is not the
creature and product of Mechanism; but, in a
far truer sense, its creator and producer: it is the
noble People that makes the noble Government;
rather than conversely. On the whole, Institutions are much; but they are not all. The freest
and highest spirits of the world have often been
found under strange outward circumstances:
Saint Paul and his brother Apostles were
politically slaves; Epictetus was personally one.
Again, forget the influences of Chivalry and
Religion, and ask: What countries produced
Columbus and Las Casas?[22] Or, descending from
virtue and heroism to mere energy and spiritual
talent: Cortes, Pizarro, Alba, Ximenes?[23] The
Spaniards of the sixteenth century were indisputably the noblest nation of Europe: yet they
had the Inquisition and Philip II. They have the
same government at this day; and are the lowest

nation. The Dutch too have retained their old
constitution; but no Siege of Leyden, no William
the Silent, not even an Egmont or De Witt[24] any
longer appears among them. With ourselves also,
where much has changed, effect has nowise
followed cause as it should have done: two
centuries ago, the Commons Speaker addressed
Queen Elizabeth on bended knees, happy that
the virago's foot did not even smite him; yet the
people were then governed, not by a Castlereagh,
but by a Burghley; they had their Shakspeare
and Philip Sidney, where we have our Sheridan
Knowles and Beau Brummel.

These and the like facts are so familiar, the
truths which they preach so obvious, and have in
all past times been so universally believed and
acted on, that we should almost feel ashamed for
repeating them; were it not that, on every hand,
the memory of them seems to have passed away,
or at best died into a faint tradition, of no value as
a practical principle. To judge by the loud
clamour of our Constitution-builders, Statists,
Economists, directors, creators, reformers of
Public Societies; in a word, all manner of
Mechanists, from the Cartwright up to the
Code-maker; and by the nearly total silence of all
Preachers and Teachers who should give a voice
to Poetry, Religion and Morality, we might
fancy either that man's Dynamical nature was,
to all spiritual intents, extinct, or else so perfected
that nothing more was to be made of it by the
old means; and henceforth only in his Mechanical
contrivances did any hope exist for him.

To define the limits of these two departments of
man's activity, which work into one another, and
by means of one another, so intricately and
inseparably, were by its nature an impossible
attempt. Their relative importance, even to the
wisest mind, will vary in different times, according to the special wants and dispositions of those
times. Meanwhile, it seems clear enough that
only in the right coördination of the two, and the
vigorous forwarding of *both*, does our true line of
action lie. Undue cultivation of the inward or
Dynamical province leads to idle, visionary,
impracticable courses, and, especially in rude
eras, to Superstition and Fanaticism, with their
long train of baleful and well-known evils.

---

[22] Bartolomé de las Casas (1474–1566), Spanish missionary, the first priest ordained in the New
World.
[23] Fernando Alvarez de Toledo, Duke of Alba (1508–83), suppressed revolt in the Netherlands;
Francisco Ximenes, or Jimenes (1437–1517), Spanish prelate and cardinal.
[24] The city of Leyden was relieved from Spanish siege in 1547; William the Silent (1533–84), founder
of the Dutch Republic; Count Egmont (1522–68) opposed Alba in the Spanish-Dutch war; Jan De
Witt (1625–72), Dutch statesman.

Undue cultivation of the outward, again, though less immediately prejudicial, and even for the time productive of many palpable benefits, must, in the long-run, by destroying Moral Force, which is the parent of all other Force, prove not less certainly, and perhaps still more hopelessly, pernicious. This, we take it, is the grand characteristic of our age. By our skill in Mechanism, it has come to pass, that in the management of external things we excel all other ages: while in whatever respects the pure moral nature, in true dignity of soul and character, we are perhaps inferior to most civilised ages.

In fact, if we look deeper, we shall find that this faith in Mechanism has now struck its roots down into man's most intimate, primary sources of conviction; and is thence sending up, over his whole life and activity, innumerable stems,— fruit-bearing and poison-bearing. The truth is, men have lost their belief in the Invisible, and believe, and hope, and work only in the Visible; or, to speak it in other words: This is not a Religious age. Only the material, the immediately practical, not the divine and spiritual, is important to us. The infinite, absolute character of Virtue has passed into a finite, conditional one; it is no longer a worship of the Beautiful and Good; but a calculation of the Profitable. Worship, indeed, in any sense, is not recognised among us, or is mechanically explained into Fear of pain, or Hope of pleasure. Our true Deity is Mechanism. It has subdued external Nature for us, and we think it will do all other things. We are Giants in physical power: in a deeper than metaphorical sense, we are Titans, that strive, by heaping mountain on mountain, to conquer Heaven also.

The strong Mechanical character, so visible in the spiritual pursuits and methods of this age, may be traced much farther into the condition and prevailing disposition of our spiritual nature itself. Consider, for example, the general fashion of Intellect in this era. Intellect, the power man has of knowing and believing, is now nearly synonymous with Logic, or the mere power of arranging and communicating. Its implement is not Meditation, but Argument. 'Cause and effect' is almost the only category under which we look at, and work with, all Nature. Our first question with regard to any object is not, What is it? but, How is it? We are no longer instinctively driven

to apprehend, and lay to heart, what is Good and Lovely, but rather to inquire, as onlookers, how it is produced, whence it comes, whither it goes. Our favourite Philosophers have no love and no hatred; they stand among us not to do, nor to create anything, but as a sort of Logic-mills, to grind out the true causes and effects of all that is done and created. To the eye of a Smith, a Hume or a Constant,[25] all is well that works quietly. An Order of Ignatius Loyola, a Presbyterianism of John Knox, a Wickliffe or a Henry the Eighth, are simply so many mechanical phenomena, caused or causing.

The *Euphuist*[26] of our day differs much from his pleasant predecessors. An intellectual dapperling of these times boasts chiefly of his irresistible perspicacity, his 'dwelling in the daylight of truth,' and so forth; which, on examination, turns out to be a dwelling in the *rush*-light of 'closet-logic,' and a deep unconsciousness that there is any other light to dwell in or any other objects to survey with it. Wonder, indeed, is, on all hands, dying out: it is the sign of un-cultivation to wonder. Speak to any small man of a high, majestic Reformation, of a high majestic Luther; and forthwith he sets about 'accounting' for it; how the 'circumstances of the time' called for such a character, and found him, we suppose, standing girt and road-ready, to do its errand; how the 'circumstances of the time' created, fashioned, floated him quietly along into the result; how, in short, this small man, had he been there, could have performed the like himself! For it is the 'force of circumstances' that does everything; the force of one man can do nothing. Now all this is grounded on little more than a metaphor. We figure Society as a 'Machine,' and that mind is opposed to mind, as body is to body; whereby two, or at most ten, little minds must be stronger than one great mind. Notable absurdity! For the plain truth, very plain, we think is, that minds are opposed to minds in quite a different way; and *one* man that has a higher Wisdom, a hitherto unknown spiritual Truth in him, is stronger, not than ten men that have it not, or than ten thousand, but than *all* men that have it not; and stands among them with a quite ethereal, angelic power, as with a sword out of Heaven's own armory, sky-tempered, which no buckler, and no tower of brass, will finally withstand.

But to us, in these times, such considerations

---

[25] Benjamin Constant (1767–1830), French writer and politician.
[26] From John Lyly's *Euphues* (1579), denoting affectation.

rarely occur. We enjoy, we see nothing by direct vision; but only by reflection, and in anatomical dismemberment. Like Sir Hudibras,[27] for every Why we must have a Wherefore. We have our little *theory* on all human and divine things. Poetry, the workings of genius itself, which in all times, with one or another meaning, has been called Inspiration, and held to be mysterious and inscrutable, is no longer without its scientific exposition. The building of the lofty rhyme is like any other masonry or bricklaying: we have theories of its rise, height, decline and fall,—which latter, it would seem, is now near, among all people. Of our 'Theories of Taste,' as they are called, wherein the deep, infinite, unspeakable Love of Wisdom and Beauty, which dwells in all men, is 'explained,' made mechanically visible, from 'Association' and the like, why should we say anything? Hume has written us a 'Natural History of Religion'; in which one Natural History all the rest are included. Strangely too does the general feeling coincide with Hume's in this wonderful problem; for whether his 'Natural History' be the right one or not, that Religion must have a Natural History, all of us, cleric and laic, seem to be agreed. He indeed regards it as a Disease, we again as Health; so far there is a difference; but in our first principle we are at one.

To what extent theological Unbelief, we mean intellectual dissent from the Church, in its view of Holy Writ, prevails at this day, would be a highly important, were it not, under any circumstances, an almost impossible inquiry. But the Unbelief, which is of a still more fundamental character, every man may see prevailing, with scarcely any but the faintest contradiction, all around him; even in the Pulpit itself. Religion in most countries, more or less in every country, is no longer what it was, and should be,—a thousand-voiced psalm from the heart of Man to his invisible Father, the fountain of all Goodness, Beauty, Truth, and revealed in every revelation of these; but for the most part, a wise prudential feeling grounded on mere calculation; a matter, as all others now are, of Expediency and Utility; whereby some smaller quantum of earthly enjoyment may be exchanged for a far larger quantum of celestial enjoyment. Thus Religion too is Profit, a working for wages; not Reverence, but vulgar Hope or Fear. Many, we know, very many we hope, are still religious in a far different sense; were it not so, our case were too desperate: but to witness that such is the temper of the times, we take any calm observant man, who agrees or disagrees in our feeling on the matter, and ask him whether our *view* of it is not in general well-founded.

Literature too, if we consider it, gives similar testimony. At no former era has Literature, the printed communication of Thought, been of such importance as it is now. We often hear that the Church is in danger; and truly so it is,—in a danger it seems not to know of: for, with its tithes in the most perfect safety, its functions are becoming more and more superseded. The true Church of England, at this moment, lies in the Editors of its Newspapers. These preach to the people daily, weekly; admonishing kings themselves; advising peace or war, with an authority which only the first Reformers, and a long-past class of Popes, were possessed of; inflicting moral censure; imparting moral encouragement, consolation, edification; in all ways diligently 'administering the Discipline of the Church.' It may be said too, that in private disposition the new Preachers somewhat resemble the Mendicant Friars of old times: outwardly full of holy zeal; inwardly not without stratagem, and hunger for terrestrial things. But omitting this class, and the boundless host of watery personages who pipe, as they are able, on so many scrannel straws, let us look at the higher regions of Literature, where, if anywhere, the pure melodies of Poesy and Wisdom should be heard. Of natural talent there is no deficiency: one or two richly-endowed individuals even give us a superiority in this respect. But what is the song they sing? Is it a tone of the Memnon Statue,[28] breathing music as the *light* first touches it? A 'liquid wisdom,' disclosing to our sense the deep, infinite harmonies of Nature and man's soul? Alas, no! It is not a matin or vesper hymn to the Spirit of Beauty, but a fierce clashing of cymbals, and shouting of multitudes, as children pass through the fire to Moloch! Poetry itself has no eye for the Invisible. Beauty is no longer the god it worships, but some brute image of Strength; which we may call an idol, for true Strength is one and the same with Beauty, and its worship also is a hymn. The meek, silent Light can mould, create and purify all Nature; but the loud Whirlwind, the sign and product of Disunion, of Weakness, passes on, and is forgotten. How widely this veneration for the physically Strongest has

---

[27] From Samuel Butler's poem *Hudibras* (1663–78).
[28] A statue in ancient Thebes said to emit sounds when touched by the rays of the rising sun.

spread itself through Literature, any one may judge who reads either criticism or poem. We praise a work, not as 'true,' but as 'strong'; our highest praise is that it has 'affected' us, has 'terrified' us. All this, it has been well observed, is the 'maximum of the Barbarous,' the symptom, not of vigorous refinement, but of luxurious corruption. It speaks much, too, for men's indestructible love of truth, that nothing of this kind will abide with them; that even the talent of a Byron cannot permanently seduce us into idol-worship; that he too, with all his wild siren charming, already begins to be disregarded and forgotten.

Again, with respect to our Moral condition: here also he who runs may read that the same physical, mechanical influences are everywhere busy. For the 'superior morality,' of which we hear so much, we too would desire to be thankful: at the same time, it were but blindness to deny that this 'superior morality' is properly rather an 'inferior criminality,' produced not by greater love of Virtue, but by greater perfection of Police; and of that far subtler and stronger Police, called Public Opinion. This last watches over us with its Argus eyes more keenly than ever; but the 'inward eye' seems heavy with sleep. Of any belief in invisible, divine things, we find as few traces in our Morality as elsewhere. It is by tangible, material considerations that we are guided, not by inward and spiritual. Self-denial, the parent of all virtue, in any true sense of that word, has perhaps seldom been rarer: so rare is it, that the most, even in their abstract speculations, regard its existence as a chimera. Virtue is Pleasure, is Profit; no celestial, but an earthly thing. Virtuous men, Philanthropists, Martyrs are happy accidents; their 'taste' lies the right way! In all senses, we worship and follow after Power; which may be called a physical pursuit. No man now loves Truth, as Truth must be loved, with an infinite love; but only with a finite love, and as it were *par amours*. Nay, properly speaking, he does not *believe* and know it, but only '*thinks*' it, and that 'there is every probability!' He preaches it aloud, and rushes courageously forth with it,—if there is a multitude huzzaing at his back; yet ever keeps looking over his shoulder, and the instant the huzzaing languishes, he too stops short.

In fact, what morality we have takes the shape of Ambition, of 'Honour': beyond money and money's worth, our only rational blessedness is Popularity. It were but a fool's trick to die for conscience. Only for 'character,' by duel, or in case of extremity, by suicide, is the wise man bound to die. By arguing on the 'force of circumstances,' we have argued away all force from ourselves; and stand leashed together, uniform in dress and movement, like the rowers of some boundless galley. This and that may be right and true; *but* we must not do it. Wonderful 'Force of Public Opinion'! We must act and walk in all points as it prescribes; follow the traffic it bids us, realise the sum of money, the degree of 'influence' it expects of us, *or* we shall be lightly esteemed; certain mouthfuls of articulate wind will be blown at us, and this what mortal courage can front? Thus, while civil liberty is more and more secured to us, our moral liberty is all but lost. Practically considered, our creed is Fatalism; and, free in hand and foot, we are shackled in heart and soul with far straiter than feudal chains. Truly may we say, with the Philosopher, 'the deep meaning of the Laws of Mechanism lies heavy on us'; and in the closet, in the market-place, in the temple, by the social hearth, encumbers the whole movements of our mind, and over our noblest faculties is spreading a nightmare sleep.

These dark features, we are aware, belong more or less to other ages, as well as to ours. This faith in Mechanism, in the all-importance of physical things, is in every age the common refuge of Weakness and blind Discontent; of all who believe, as many will ever do, that man's true good lies without him, not within. We are aware also, that, as applied to ourselves in all their aggravation, they form but half a picture; that in the whole picture there are bright lights as well as gloomy shadows. If we here dwell chiefly on the latter, let us not be blamed: it is in general more profitable to reckon up our defects than to boast of our attainments.

Neither, with all these evils more or less clearly before us, have we at any time despaired of the fortunes of society. Despair, or even despondency, in that respect, appears to us, in all cases, a groundless feeling. We have a faith in the imperishable dignity of man; in the high vocation to which, throughout this his earthly history, he has been appointed. However it may be with individual nations, whatever melancholic speculators may assert, it seems a well-ascertained fact, that in all times, reckoning even from those of the Heraclides and Pelasgi,[29] the happiness and

29 Heraclides were legendary descendants of Hercules; Pelasgi were early inhabitants of Greece.

greatness of mankind at large have been continually progressive. Doubtless this age also is
advancing. Its very unrest, its ceaseless activity,
its discontent contains matter of promise.
Knowledge, education are opening the eyes of
the humblest; are increasing the number of
thinking minds without limit. This is as it should
be; for not in turning back, not in resisting, but
only in resolutely struggling forward, does our
life consist.

Nay, after all, our spiritual maladies are but of
Opinion; we are but fettered by chains of our
own forging, and which ourselves also can rend
asunder. This deep, paralysed subjection to
physical objects comes not from Nature, but from
our own unwise mode of *viewing* Nature. Neither
can we understand that man wants, at this hour,
any faculty of heart, soul or body, that ever
belonged to him. 'He, who has been born, has
been a First Man'; has had lying before his
young eyes, and as yet unhardened into scientific
shapes, a world as plastic, infinite, divine, as lay
before the eyes of Adam himself. If Mechanism,
like some glass bell, encircles and imprisons us;
if the soul looks forth on a fair heavenly country
which it cannot reach, and pines, and in its
scanty atmosphere is ready to perish,—yet the
bell is but of glass; 'one bold stroke to break the
bell in pieces, and thou art delivered!' Not the
invisible world is wanting, for it dwells in man's
soul, and this last is still here. Are the solemn
temples, in which the Divinity was once visibly
revealed among us, crumbling away? We can
repair them, we can rebuild them. The wisdom,
the heroic worth of our fore-fathers, which we
have lost, we can recover. That admiration of old
nobleness, which now so often shows itself as a
faint *dilettantism*, will one day become a generous
emulation, and man may again be all that he has
been, and more than he has been. Nor are these
the mere daydreams of fancy; they are clear
possibilities; nay, in this time they are even
assuming the character of hopes. Indications we
do see in other countries and in our own, signs
infinitely cheering to us, that Mechanism is not
always to be our hard taskmaster, but one day
to be our pliant, all-ministering servant; that a
new and brighter spiritual era is slowly evolving

itself for all men. But on these things our present
course forbids us to enter.

Meanwhile, that great outward changes are in
progress can be doubtful to no one. The time is
sick and out of joint. Many things have reached
their height; and it is a wise adage that tells us,
'the darkest hour is nearest the dawn.' Wherever
we can gather indication of the public thought,
whether from printed books, as in France or
Germany, or from Carbonari[30] rebellions and
other political tumults, as in Spain, Portugal,
Italy and Greece, the voice it utters is the same.
The thinking minds of all nations call for change.
There is a deep-lying struggle in the whole fabric
of society; a boundless grinding collision of the
New with the Old. The French Revolution, as
is now visible enough, was not the parent of this
mighty movement, but its offspring. Those two
hostile influences, which always exist in human
things, and on the constant intercommunion
of which depends their health and safety, had
lain in separate masses, accumulating through
generations, and France was the scene of their
fiercest explosion; but the final issue was not
unfolded in that country: nay, it is not yet
anywhere unfolded. Political freedom is hitherto
the object of these efforts; but they will not and
cannot stop there. It is towards a higher freedom
than mere freedom from oppression by his
fellow-mortal, that man dimly aims. Of this
higher, heavenly freedom, which is 'man's reasonable service,' all his noble institutions, his faithful
endeavours and loftiest attainments, are but the
body, and more and more approximated emblem.

On the whole, as this wondrous planet, Earth,
is journeying with its fellows through infinite
Space, so are the wondrous destinies embarked
on it journeying through infinite Time, under a
higher guidance than ours. For the present, as our
astronomy informs us, its path lies towards
Hercules, the constellation of *Physical Power*: but
that is not our most pressing concern. Go where it
will, the deep HEAVEN will be around it. Therein
let us have hope and sure faith. To reform a
world, to reform a nation, no wise man will
undertake; and all but foolish men know, that
the only solid, though a far slower reformation, is
what each begins and perfects on *himself*.

---

[30] Secret Italian political association that first met among charcoal burners (carbonari) in the
mountains.

On History

"On History" is Carlyle's earliest statement about the philosophy that was to guide him to such historical triumphs as The French Revolution. *Here he sets forth his views of the deficiencies of contemporary histories and of the need for history to capture the inward spirit of events as well as the outward appearances. Only in this way can history convey, says Carlyle, "some oversight of the Whole." This essay first appeared in* Fraser's Magazine *in November 1830.*

CLIO was figured by the ancients as the eldest daughter of Memory, and chief of the Muses;[1] which dignity, whether we regard the essential qualities of her art, or its practice and acceptance among men, we shall still find to have been fitly bestowed. History, as it lies at the root of all science, is also the first distinct product of man's spiritual nature; his earliest expression of what can be called Thought. It is a looking both before and after; as, indeed, the coming Time already waits, unseen, yet definitely shaped, predetermined and inevitable, in the Time come; and only by the combination of both is the meaning of either completed. The Sibylline Books, though old, are not the oldest. Some nations have prophecy, some have not: but of all mankind, there is no tribe so rude that it has not attempted History, though several have not arithmetic enough to count Five. History has been written with quipo-threads, with feather-pictures, with wampum-belts; still oftener with earth-mounds and monumental stone-heaps, whether as pyramid or cairn; for the Celt and the Copt, the Red man as well as the White, lives between two eternities, and warring against Oblivion, he would fain unite himself in clear conscious relation, as in dim unconscious relation he is already united, with the whole Future, and the whole Past.

A talent for History may be said to be born with us, as our chief inheritance. In a certain sense all men are historians. Is not every memory written quite full with Annals, wherein joy and mourning, conquest and loss manifoldly alternate; and, with or without philosophy, the whole fortunes of one little inward Kingdom, and all its politics, foreign and domestic, stand ineffaceably recorded? Our very speech is curiously historical. Most men, you may observe, speak only to narrate; not in imparting what they have thought, which indeed were often a very small matter, but in exhibiting what they have undergone or seen, which is a quite unlimited one, do talkers dilate. Cut us off from Narrative, how would the stream of conversation, even among the wisest, languish into detached handfuls, and among the foolish utterly evaporate! Thus, as we do nothing but enact History, we say little but recite it. Nay, rather, in that widest sense, our whole spiritual life is built thereon. For, strictly considered, what is all Knowledge too but recorded Experience, and a product of History; of which, therefore, Reasoning and Belief, no less than Action and Passion, are essential materials?

Under a limited, and the only practicable shape, History proper, that part of History which treats of remarkable action, has, in all modern as well as ancient times, ranked among the highest arts, and perhaps never stood higher than in these times of ours. For whereas, of old, the charm of History lay chiefly in gratifying our common appetite for the wonderful, for the unknown; and her office was but as that of a Minstrel and Story-teller, she has now farther become a School-mistress, and professes to instruct in gratifying. Whether, with the stateliness of that venerable character, she may not have taken up something of its austerity and frigidity; whether in the logical terseness of a Hume or Robertson, the graceful ease and gay pictorial heartiness of a Herodotus or Froissart may not be wanting, is not the question for us here. Enough that all learners, all inquiring minds of every order, are gathered round her footstool; and reverently pondering her lessons, as the true basis of Wisdom. Poetry, Divinity, Politics, Physics, have each their adherents and adversaries; each little guild supporting a defensive and offensive war for its own special domain; while the domain of History is as a Free Emporium, where all these belligerents peaceably meet and furnish themselves; and Sentimentalist and Utilitarian, Sceptic

---

[1] Clio was the muse of history.

and Theologian, with one voice advise us: Examine History, for it is 'Philosophy teaching by Experience.'

Far be it from us to disparage such teaching, the very attempt at which must be precious. Neither shall we too rigidly inquire: How much it has hitherto profited? Whether most of what little practical wisdom men have, has come from study of professed History, or from other less boasted sources, whereby, as matters now stand, a Marlborough may become great in the world's business, with no History save what he derives from Shakespeare's Plays? Nay, whether in that same teaching by Experience, historical Philosophy has yet properly deciphered the first element of all science in this kind: What the aim and significance of that wondrous changeful Life it investigates and paints may be? Whence the course of man's destinies in this Earth originated, and whither they are tending? Or, indeed, if they have any course and tendency, are really guided forward by an unseen mysterious Wisdom, or only circle in blind mazes without recognisable guidance? Which questions, altogether fundamental, one might think, in any Philosophy of History, have, since the era when Monkish Annalists were wont to answer them by the long-ago extinguished light of their Missal and Breviary, been by most philosophical Historians only glanced at dubiously and from afar; by many, not so much as glanced at.

The truth is, two difficulties, never wholly surmountable, lie in the way. Before Philosophy can teach by Experience, the Philosophy has to be in readiness, the Experience must be gathered and intelligibly recorded. Now, overlooking the former consideration, and with regard only to the latter, let any one who has examined the current of human affairs, and how intricate, perplexed, unfathomable, even when seen into with our own eyes, are their thousandfold blending movements, say whether the true representing of it is easy or impossible. Social Life is the aggregate of all the individual men's Lives who constitute society; History is the essence of innumerable Biographies. But if one Biography, nay, our own Biography, study and recapitulate it as we may, remains in so many points unintelligible to us; how much more must these mil-

lion, the very facts of which, to say nothing of the purport of them, we know not, and cannot know!

Neither will it adequately avail us to assert that the general inward condition of Life is the same in all ages; and that only the remarkable deviations from the common endowment and common lot, and the more important variations which the outward figure of Life has from time to time undergone, deserve memory and record. The inward condition of Life, it may rather be affirmed, the conscious or half-conscious aim of mankind, so far as men are not mere digesting-machines, is the same in no two ages; neither are the more important outward variations easy to fix on, or always well capable of representation. Which was the greatest innovator, which was the more important personage in man's history, he who first led armies over the Alps, and gained the victories of Cannæ and Thrasymene;[2] or the nameless boor who first hammered out for himself an iron spade? When the oak-tree is felled, the whole forest echoes with it; but a hundred acorns are planted silently by some unnoticed breeze. Battles and war-tumults, which for the time din every ear, and with joy or terror intoxicate every heart, pass away like tavern-brawls; and except some few Marathons and Morgartens,[3] are remembered by accident, not by desert. Laws themselves, political Constitutions, are not our Life, but only the house wherein our Life is led: nay, they are but the bare walls of the house: all whose essential furniture, the inventions and traditions, and daily habits that regulate and support our existence, are the work not of Dracos and Hampdens,[4] but of Phœnician mariners, of Italian masons and Saxon metallurgists, of philosophers, alchymists, prophets, and all the long-forgotten train of artists and artisans; who from the first have been jointly teaching us how to think and how to act, how to rule over spiritual and over physical Nature. Well may we say that of our History the more important part is lost without recovery; and,—as thanksgivings were once wont to be offered 'for unrecognized mercies,'—look with reverence into the dark untenanted places of the Past, where, in formless oblivion, our chief benefactors, with all their sedulous endeavours, but not with the fruit of these, lie entombed.

[2] Cannae and Thrasymene (Trasimene) were scenes of two of Hannibal's victories over Rome in 216 and 217 B.C. in the Second Punic War.

[3] Marathon, scene of an Athenian victory in 490 B.C. over the Persians; Morgarten, site of Swiss victory over Austria in 1315.

[4] Draco, Athenian jurist, seventh century B.C., famed for his severe code of laws; John Hampden (1594–1643), British parliamentarian, a leader of the Long Parliament.

So imperfect is that same Experience, by which Philosophy is to teach. Nay, even with regard to those occurrences which do stand recorded, which, at their origin have seemed worthy of record, and the summary of which constitutes what we now call History, is not our understanding of them altogether incomplete; is it even possible to represent them as they were? The old story of Sir Walter Raleigh's looking from his prison-window, on some street tumult, which afterwards three witnesses reported in three different ways, himself differing from them all, is still a true lesson for us. Consider how it is that historical documents and records originate; even honest records, where the reporters were unbiased by personal regard; a case which, were nothing more wanted, must ever be among the rarest. The real leading features of a historical Trans-action, those movements that essentially characterise it, and alone deserve to be recorded, are nowise the foremost to be noted. At first, among the various witnesses, who are also parties interested, there is only vague wonder, and fear or hope, and the noise of Rumour's thousand tongues; till, after a season, the conflict of testimonies has subsided into some general issue; and then it is settled, by majority of votes, that such and such a 'Crossing of the Rubicon,' an 'Impeachment of Strafford,' a 'Convocation of the Notables,' are epochs in the world's history, cardinal points on which grand world-revolutions have hinged. Suppose, however, that the majority of votes was all wrong; that the real cardinal points lay far deeper: and had been passed over unnoticed, because no Seer, but only mere Onlookers, chanced to be there! Our clock strikes when there is a change from hour to hour; but no hammer in the Horologe of Time peals through the universe when there is a change from Era to Era. Men understand not what is among their hands: as calmness is the characteristic of strength, so the weightiest causes may be most silent. It is, in no case, the real historical Trans-action, but only some more or less plausible scheme and theory of the Transaction, or the harmonised result of many such schemes, each varying from the other and all varying from truth, that we can ever hope to behold.

Nay, were our faculty of insight into passing things never so complete, there is still a fatal discrepancy between our manner of observing these, and their manner of occurring. The most gifted man can observe, still more can record, only the *series* of his own impressions: his observation, therefore, to say nothing of its other imperfections, must be *successive*, while the things done were often *simultaneous*; the things done were not a series, but a group. It is not in acted, as it is in written History: actual events are nowise so simply related to each other as parent and offspring are; every single event is the off-spring not of one, but of all other events, prior or contemporaneous, and will in its turn combine with all others to give birth to new: it is an ever-living, ever-working Chaos of Being, wherein shape after shape bodies itself forth from in-numerable elements. And this Chaos, boundless as the habitation and duration of man, un-fathomable as the soul and destiny of man, is what the historian will depict, and scientifically gauge, we may say, by threading it with single lines of a few ells in length! For as all Action is, by its nature, to be figured as extended in breadth and in depth, as well as in length; that is to say, is based on Passion and Mystery, if we investigate its origin; and spreads abroad on all hands, modifying and modified; as well as advances towards completion,—so all Narrative is, by its nature, of only one dimension; only travels forward towards one, or towards successive points: Narrative is *linear*, Action is *solid*. Alas for our 'chains,' or chainlets, of 'causes and effects,' which we so assiduously track through certain hand-breadths of years and square miles, when the whole is a broad, deep Immensity, and each atom is 'chained' and completed with all! Truly, if History is Philosophy teaching by Experience, the writer fitted to compose History is hitherto an unknown man. The Experience itself would require All-knowledge to record it,— were the All-wisdom needful for such Philosophy as would interpret it, to be had for asking. Better were it that mere earthly Historians should lower such pretensions, more suitable for Omniscience than for human science; and aiming only at some picture of the things acted, which picture itself will at best be a poor approximation, leave the inscrutable purport of them an acknowledged secret; or at most, in reverent Faith, far different from that teaching of Philosophy, pause over the mysterious vestiges of Him, whose path is in the great deep of Time, whom History indeed reveals, but only all History, and in Eternity, will clearly reveal.

Such considerations truly were of small profit, did they, instead of teaching us vigilance and reverent humility in our inquiries into History, abate our esteem for them, or discourage us from unweariedly prosecuting them. Let us search more and more into the Past; let all men explore it, as the true fountain of knowledge; by whose light alone, consciously or unconsciously employed, can the Present and the Future be interpreted or guessed at. For though the whole meaning lies far beyond our ken; yet in that complex Manuscript, covered over with formless inextricably-entangled unknown characters,—nay, which is a *Palimpsest*, and had once prophetic writing, still dimly legible there,—some letters, some words, may be deciphered; and if no complete Philosophy, here and there an intelligible precept, available in practice, be gathered: well understanding, in the mean while, that it is only a little portion we have deciphered; that much still remains to be interpreted; that History is a real Prophetic Manuscript, and can be fully interpreted by no man.

But the Artist in History may be distinguished from the Artisan in History; for here, as in all other provinces, there are Artists and Artisans; men who labour mechanically in a department, without eye for the Whole, not feeling that there is a Whole; and men who inform and ennoble the humblest department with an Idea of the Whole, and habitually know that only in the Whole is the Partial to be truly discerned. The proceedings and the duties of these two, in regard to History, must be altogether different. Not, indeed, that each has not a real worth, in his several degree. The simple husbandman can till his field, and by knowledge he has gained of its soil, sow it with the fit grain, though the deep rocks and central fires are unknown to him: his little crop hangs under and over the firmament of stars, and sails through whole untracked celestial spaces, between Aries and Libra: nevertheless it ripens for him in due season, and he gathers it safe into his barn. As a husbandman he is blameless in disregarding those higher wonders; but as a thinker, and faithful inquirer into Nature, he were wrong. So likewise is it with the Historian, who examines some special aspect of History; and from this or that combination of circumstances, political, moral, economical, and the issues it has led to, infers that such and such properties belong to human society, and that the like circumstances will produce the like issue; which inference, if other trials confirm it, must be held true and practically valuable. He is wrong only, and an artisan, when he fancies that these properties, discovered or discoverable, exhaust the matter; and sees not, at every step, that it is inexhaustible.

However, that class of cause-and-effect speculators, with whom no wonder would remain wonderful, but all things in Heaven and Earth must be computed and 'accounted for'; and even the Unknown, the Infinite in man's Life, had under the words *enthusiasm, superstition, spirit of the age* and so forth, obtained, as it were, an algebraical symbol and given value,—have now wellnigh played their part in European culture; and may be considered, as in most countries, even in England itself where they linger the latest, verging towards extinction. He who reads the inscrutable Book of Nature as if it were a Merchant's Ledger, is justly suspected of having never seen that Book, but only some school Synopsis thereof; from which, if taken for the real Book, more error than insight is to be derived.

Doubtless also, it is with a growing feeling of the infinite nature of History, that in these times, the old principle, division of labour, has been so widely applied to it. The Political Historian, once almost the sole cultivator of History, has now found various associates, who strive to elucidate other phases of human Life; of which, as hinted above, the political conditions it is passed under are but one, and though the primary, perhaps not the most important, of the many outward arrangements. Of this Historian himself, moreover, in his own special department, new and higher things are beginning to be expected. From of old, it was too often to be reproachfully observed of him, that he dwelt with disproportionate fondness in Senate-houses, in Battle-fields, nay, even in Kings' Antechambers; forgetting, that far away from such scenes, the mighty tide of Thought and Action was still rolling on its wondrous course, in gloom and brightness; and in its thousand remote valleys, a whole world of Existence, with or without an earthly sun of Happiness to warm it, with or without a heavenly sun of Holiness to purify and sanctify it, was blossoming and fading, whether the 'famous victory' were won or lost. The time seems coming when much of this must be amended; and he who sees no world but that of courts and camps; and writes only how soldiers were drilled and shot, and how this ministerial conjuror out-conjured that other, and then guided, or at least held, something which he called the rudder of Government, but which was rather the spigot of Taxation, wherewith, in place of steering, he could tap, and the more cunningly the nearer the lees,—will pass for a more or less instructive Gazetteer, but will no longer be called a Historian.

However, the Political Historian, were his work performed with all conceivable perfection, can accomplish but a part, and still leaves room for numerous fellow-labourers. Foremost among these comes the Ecclesiastical Historian; endeavouring, with catholic or sectarian view, to trace the progress of the Church; of that portion of the social establishments, which respects our religious condition; as the other portion does our civil, or rather, in the long-run, our economical condition. Rightly conducted, this department were undoubtedly the more important of the two; inasmuch as it concerns us more to understand how man's moral well-being had been and might be promoted, than to understand in the like sort his physical well-being; which latter is ultimately the aim of all Political arrangements. For the physically happiest is simply the safest, the strongest; and, in all conditions of Government, Power (whether of wealth as in these days, or of arms and adherents as in old days) is the only outward emblem and purchase-money of Good. True Good, however, unless we reckon Pleasure synonymous with it, is said to be rarely, or rather never, offered for sale in the market where that coin passes current. So that, for man's true advantage, not the outward condition of his life, but the inward and spiritual, is of prime influence; not the form of Government he lives under, and the power he can accumulate there, but the Church he is a member of, and the degree of moral elevation he can acquire by means of its instruction. Church History, then, did it speak wisely, would have momentous secrets to teach us: nay, in its highest degree, it were a sort of continued Holy Writ; our Sacred Books being, indeed, only a History of the primeval Church, as it first arose in man's soul, and symbolically embodied itself in his external life. How far our actual Church Historians fall below such unattainable standards, nay, below quite attainable approximations thereto, we need not point out. Of the Ecclesiastical Historian we have to complain, as we did of his Political fellow-craftsman, that his inquiries turn rather on the outward mechanism, the mere hulls and superficial accidents of the object, than on the object itself: as if the Church lay in Bishops' Chapterhouses, and Ecumenic Council-halls, and Cardinals' Conclaves, and not far more in the hearts of Believing Men; in whose walk and conversation, as influenced thereby, its chief manifestations were to be looked for, and its progress or decline ascertained. The History of the Church

is a History of the Invisible as well as of the Visible Church; which latter, if disjoined from the former, is but a vacant edifice; gilded, it may be, and overhung with old votive gifts, yet useless, nay, pestilentially unclean; to write whose history is less important than to forward its downfall.

Of a less ambitious character are the Histories that relate to special separate provinces of human Action; to Sciences, Practical Arts, Institutions and the like; matters which do not imply an epitome of man's whole interest and form of life; but wherein, though each is still connected with all, the spirit of each, at least its material results, may be in some degree evolved without so strict a reference to that of the others. Highest in dignity and difficulty, under this head, would be our histories of Philosophy, of man's opinions and theories respecting the nature of his Being, and relations to the Universe Visible and Invisible: which History, indeed, were it fitly treated, or fit for right treatment, would be a province of Church History; the logical or dogmatical province thereof; for Philosophy, in its true sense, is or should be the soul, of which Religion, Worship is the body; in the healthy state of things the Philosopher and Priest were one and the same. But Philosophy itself is far enough from wearing this character; neither have its Historians been men, generally speaking, that could in the smallest degree approximate it thereto. Scarcely since the rude era of the Magi and Druids has that same healthy identification of Priest and Philosopher had place in any country: but rather the worship of divine things, and the scientific investigation of divine things, have been in quite different hands, their relations not friendly but hostile. Neither have the Brückers and Bühles, to say nothing of the many unhappy Enfields[5] who have treated of that latter department, been more than barren reporters, often unintelligent and unintelligible reporters, of the doctrine uttered; without force to discover how the doctrine originated, or what reference it bore to its time and country, to the spiritual position of mankind there and then. Nay, such a task did not perhaps lie before them, as a thing to be attempted.

Art also and Literature are intimately blended with Religion; as it were, outworks and abutments, by which that highest pinnacle in our

---

[5] Probably Johann Jakob Brücker (1696–1770), German philosopher; probably Johann Gottlieb Bühle (1763–1821), German philosopher and philologist; William Enfield (1741–97), English dissenting divine and author.

inward world gradually connects itself with the general level, and becomes accessible therefrom. He who should write a proper History of Poetry, would depict for us the successive Revelations which man has obtained of the Spirit of Nature; under what aspects he had caught and endeavoured to body forth some glimpse of that unspeakable Beauty, which in its highest clearness is Religion, is the inspiration of a Prophet, yet in one or the other degree must inspire every true Singer, were his theme never so humble. We should see by what steps men had ascended to the Temple; how near they had approached; by what ill hap they had, for long periods, turned away from it, and grovelled on the plain with no music in the air, or blindly struggled towards other heights. That among all our Eichhorns and Wartons[6] there is no such Historian, must be too clear to every one. Nevertheless let us not despair of far nearer approaches to that excellence. Above all, let us keep the Ideal of it ever in our eye; for thereby alone have we even a chance to reach it.

Our histories of Laws and Constitutions, wherein many a Montesquieu and Hallam[7] has laboured with acceptance, are of a much simpler nature; yet deep enough if thoroughly investigated; and useful, when authentic, even with little depth. Then we have Histories of Medicine, of Mathematics, of Astronomy, Commerce, Chivalry, Monkery; and Goguets and Beckmanns[8] have come forward with what might be the most bountiful contribution of all, a History of Inventions. Of all which sorts, and many more not here enumerated, not yet devised and put in practice, the merit and the proper scheme may, in our present limits, require no exposition.

In this manner, though, as above remarked, all Action is extended three ways, and the general sum of human Action is a whole Universe, with all limits of it unknown, does History strive by running path after path, through the Impassable, in manifold directions and intersections, to secure for us some oversight of the Whole; in which endeavour, if each Historian look well around him from his path, tracking it out with the *eye*, not, as is more common, with the *nose*, she may at last prove not altogether unsuccessful. Praying only that increased division of labour do not here, as elsewhere, aggravate our already strong Mechanical tendencies, so that in the manual dexterity for parts we lose all command over the whole, and the hope of any Philosophy of History be farther off than ever,—let us all wish her great and greater success.

Characteristics

Probably the single most influential of Carlyle's many essays, "Characteristics" was an attempt to see into the character and indeed the soul of the age. Carlyle adapted the term from the use of the Charakteristik, *a character sketch or characterization, by German Romantic authors like the Schlegels. This essay, like "Signs of the Times," was technically a review—in this case of Thomas Hope's* The Origin and Prospects of Man *(1830) and Friedrich Schlegel's* Philosophische Vorlesungen *(1831)—but Carlyle ranges far beyond the limits of a review to consider the mechanical utilitarianism of the age in contrast to what he sees as needful, a spiritual rebirth. The essay was first published in the* Edinburgh Review *in December 1831.*

THE HEALTHY know not of their health, but only the sick: this is the Physician's Aphorism; and applicable in a far wider sense than he gives it. We may say, it holds no less in moral, intellectual, political, poetical, than in merely corporeal therapeutics; that wherever, or in what shape soever, powers of the sort which can be named *vital* are at work, herein lies the test of their working right or working wrong.

In the Body, for example, as all doctors are

---

[6] Johann Gottfried Eichhorn (1752–1827), German biblical scholar; Thomas Warton (1728–90), English scholar, author of *History of English Poetry*.

[7] Charles de Secondat, Baron Montesquieu (1689–1755), French jurist, author of *L'esprit des lois;* Henry Hallam (1777–1859), English historian, author of *The Constitutional History of England.*

[8] Antoine Yves Goguet (1716–58), French jurist and scholar; Johnan Beckmann (1739–1811), German scholar, author of *History of Inventions.*

agreed, the first condition of complete health is, that each organ perform its function unconsciously, unheeded; let but any organ announce its separate existence, were it even boastfully, and for pleasure, not for pain, then already has one of those unfortunate 'false centres of sensibility' established itself, already is derangement there. The perfection of bodily well-being is, that the collective bodily activities seem one; and be manifested, moreover, not in themselves, but in the action they accomplish. If a Dr. Kitchiner[1] boast that his system is in high order, Dietetic Philosophy may indeed take credit; but the true Peptician was that Countryman who answered that, "for his part, he had no system." In fact, unity, agreement is always silent, or soft-voiced; it is only discord that loudly proclaims itself. So long as the several elements of Life, all fitly adjusted, can pour forth their movement like harmonious tuned strings, it is a melody and unison; Life, from its mysterious fountains, flows out as in celestial music and diapason,—which also, like that other music of the spheres, even because it is perennial and complete, without interruption and without imperfection, might be fabled to escape the ear. Thus too, in some languages, is the state of health well denoted by a term expressing unity; when we feel ourselves as we wish to be, we say that we are *whole*.

Few mortals, it is to be feared, are permanently blessed with that felicity of 'having no system'; nevertheless, most of us, looking back on young years, may remember seasons of a light, aërial translucency and elasticity and perfect freedom; the body had not yet become the prison-house of the soul, but was its vehicle and implement, like a creature of the thought, and altogether pliant to its bidding. We knew not that we had limbs, we only lifted, hurled and leapt; through eye and ear, and all avenues of sense, came clear unimpeded tidings from without, and from within issued clear victorious force; we stood as in the centre of Nature, giving and receiving, in harmony with it all; unlike Virgil's Husbandmen, 'too happy *because* we did not know our blessedness.'[2] In those days, health and sickness were foreign traditions that did not concern us; our whole being was as yet One, the whole man like an incorporated Will. Such, were Rest or ever-successful Labour the human lot, might our life continue to be: a pure, perpetual, unregarded music; a beam of perfect white light,

rendering all things visible, but itself unseen, even because it was of that perfect whiteness, and no irregular obstruction had yet broken it into colours. The beginning of Inquiry is Disease: all Science, if we consider well, as it must have originated in the feeling of something being wrong, so it is and continues to be but Division, Dismemberment, and partial healing of the wrong. Thus, as was of old written, the Tree of Knowledge springs from a root of evil, and bears fruits of good and evil. Had Adam remained in Paradise, there had been no Anatomy and no Metaphysics.

But, alas, as the Philosopher declares, 'Life itself is a disease; a working incited by suffering'; action from passion! The memory of that first state of Freedom and paradisaic Unconsciousness has faded away into an ideal poetic dream. We stand here too conscious of many things: with Knowledge, the sympton of Derangement, we must even do our best to restore a little Order. Life is, in few instances, and at rare intervals, the diapason of a heavenly melody; oftenest the fierce jar of disruptions and convulsions, which, do what we will, there is no disregarding. Nevertheless, such is still the wish of Nature on our behalf; in all vital action, her manifest purpose and effort is, that we should be unconscious of it, and, like the peptic Countryman, never know that we 'have a system.' For, indeed, vital action everywhere is emphatically a means, not an end; Life is not given us for the mere sake of Living, but always with an ulterior external Aim: neither is it on the process, on the means, but rather on the result, that Nature, in any of her doings, is wont to intrust us with insight and volition. Boundless as is the domain of man, it is but a small fractional proportion of it that he rules with Consciousness and by Forethought: what he can contrive, nay, what he can altogether know and comprehend, is essentially the mechanical, small; the great is ever, in one sense or other, the vital; it is essentially the mysterious, and only the surface of it can be understood. But nature, it might seem, strives, like a kind mother, to hide from us even this, that she is a mystery: she will have us rest on her beautiful and awful bosom as if it were our secure home; on the bottomless boundless Deep, whereon all human things fearfully and wonderfully swim, she will have us walk and build, as if the film which supported us there (which any scratch of a bare bodkin will rend asunder, any

---

[1] William Kitchiner (1775?–1827), author of *Apicius Redivivus, or the Cook's Oracle.*
[2] Virgil, *Georgics*, ii, 458–59.

sputter of a pistol-shot instantaneously burn up) were no film, but a solid rock-foundation. Forever in the neighbourhood of an inevitable Death, man can forget that he is born to die; of his Life, which, strictly meditated, contains in it an Immensity and an Eternity, he can conceive lightly, as of a simple implement wherewith to do day-labour and earn wages. So cunningly does Nature, the mother of all highest Art, which only apes her from afar, 'body forth the Finite from the Infinite'; and guide man safe on his wondrous path, not more by endowing him with vision, than, at the right place, with blindness! Under all her works, chiefly under her noblest work, Life, lies a basis of Darkness, which she benignantly conceals; in Life too, the roots and inward circulations which stretch down fearfully to the regions of Death and Night, shall not hint of their existence, and only the fair stem with its leaves and flowers, shone on by the fair sun, shall disclose itself, and joyfully grow.

However, without venturing into the abstruse, or too eagerly asking Why and How, in things where our answer must needs prove, in great part, an echo of the question, let us be content to remark farther, in the merely historical way, how that Aphorism of the bodily Physician holds good in quite other departments. Of the Soul, with her activities, we shall find it no less true than of the Body: nay, cry the Spiritualists, is not that very division of the unity, Man, into a dualism of Soul and Body, itself the symptom of disease; as, perhaps, your frightful theory of Materialism, of his being but a Body, and therefore, at least, once more a unity, may be the paroxysm which was critical, and the beginning of cure! But omitting this, we observe, with confidence enough, that the truly strong mind, view it as Intellect, as Morality, or under any other aspect, is nowise the mind acquainted with its strength; that here as before the sign of health is Unconsciousness. In our inward, as in our outward world, what is mechanical lies open to us: not what is dynamical and has vitality. Of our Thinking, we might say, it is but the mere upper surface that we shape into articulate Thoughts;— underneath the region of argument and conscious discourse, lies the region of meditation; here, in its quiet mysterious depths, dwells what vital force is in us; here, if aught is to be created, and not merely manufactured and communicated, must the work go on. Manufacture is intelligible, but trivial; Creation is great, and cannot be under-

stood. Thus if the Debater and Demonstrator, whom we may rank as the lowest of true thinkers, knows what he has done, and how he did it, the Artist, whom we rank as the highest, knows not; must speak of Inspiration, and in one or the other dialect, call his work the gift of a divinity.

But on the whole, 'genius is ever a secret to itself'; of this old truth we have, on all sides, daily evidence. The Shakspeare takes no airs for writing *Hamlet* and the *Tempest*, understands not that it is anything surprising: Milton, again, is more conscious of his faculty, which accordingly is an inferior one. On the other hand, what cackling and strutting must we not often hear and see, when, in some shape of academical prolusion, maiden speech, review article, this or the other well-fledged goose has produced its goose-egg, of quite measurable value, were it the pink of its whole kind; and wonders why all mortals do not wonder!

Foolish enough, too, was the College Tutor's surprise at Walter Shandy: how, though unread in Aristotle, he could nevertheless argue; and not knowing the name of any dialectic tool, handled them all to perfection.[3] Is it the skilfulest anatomist that cuts the best figure at Sadler's Wells? or does the boxer hit better for knowing that he has a *flexor longus* and a *flexor brevis*? But indeed, as in the higher case of the Poet, so here in that of the Speaker and Inquirer, the true force is an unconscious one. The healthy Understanding, we should say, is not the Logical, argumentative, but the Intuitive; for the end of Understanding is not to prove and find reasons, but to know and believe. Of logic, and its limits, and uses and abuses, there were much to be said and examined; one fact, however, which chiefly concerns us here, has long been familiar: that the man of logic and the man of insight; the Reasoner and the Discoverer, or even Knower, are quite separable,—indeed, for most part, quite separate characters. In practical matters, for example, has it not become almost proverbial that the man of logic cannot prosper? This is he whom business-people call Systematic and Theoriser and Word-monger; his *vital* intellectual force lies dormant or extinct, his whole force is mechanical, conscious: of such a one it is foreseen that, when once confronted with the infinite complexities of the real world, his little compact theorem of the world will be found wanting; that unless he can throw it overboard and become a new creature, he will necessarily founder. Nay,

---

[3] Lawrence Sterne, *Tristram Shandy*, I, xix.

in mere Speculation itself, the most ineffectual of all characters, generally speaking, is your dialectic man-at-arms; were he armed cap-a-pie in syllogistic mail of proof, and perfect master of logic-fence, how little does it avail him! Consider the old Schoolmen, and their pilgrimage towards Truth: the faithfulest endeavour, incessant unwearied motion, often great natural vigour; only no progress: nothing but antic feats of one limb poised against the other; there they balanced, somersetted, and made postures; at best gyrated swiftly, with some pleasure, like Spinning Dervishes, and ended where they began. So it is, so will it always be, with all System-makers and builders of logical card-castles; of which class a certain remnant must, in every age, as they do in our own, survive and build. Logic is good, but it is not the best. The Irrefragable Doctor,[4] with his chains of induction, his corollaries, dilemmas and other cunning logical diagrams and apparatus, will cast you a beautiful horoscope, and speak reasonable things; nevertheless your stolen jewel, which you wanted him to find you, is not forthcoming. Often by some winged word, winged as the thunderbolt is, of a Luther, a Napoleon, a Goethe, shall we see the difficulty split asunder, and its secret laid bare; while the Irrefragable, with all his logical tools, hews at it, and hovers round it, and finds it on all hands too hard for him.

Again, in the difference between Oratory and Rhetoric, as indeed everywhere in that superiority of what is called the Natural over the Artificial, we find a similar illustration. The Orator persuades and carries all with him, he knows not how; the Rhetorician can prove that he ought to have persuaded and carried all with him: the one is in a state of healthy unconsciousness, as if he 'had no system'; the other, in virtue of regimen and dietetic punctuality, feels at best that 'his system is in high order.' So stands it, in short, with all the forms of Intellect, whether as directed to the finding of truth, or to the fit imparting thereof; to Poetry to Eloquence, to depth of Insight, which is the basis of both these; always the characteristic of right performance is a certain spontaneity, an unconsciousness; 'the healthy know not of their health, but only the sick.' So that the old precept of the critic, as crabbed as it looked to his ambitious disciple, might contain in it a most fundamental truth, applicable to us all, and in much else than

Literature: "Whenever you have written any sentence that looks particularly excellent, be sure to blot it out." In like manner, under milder phraseology, and with a meaning purposely much wider, a living Thinker has taught us: 'Of the Wrong we are always conscious, of the Right never,'[5]

But if such is the law with regard to Speculation and the Intellectual power of man, much more is it with regard to Conduct, and the power, manifested chiefly therein, which we name Moral. 'Let not thy left hand know what thy right hand doeth': whisper not to thy own heart, How worthy is this action!—for then it is already becoming worthless. The good man is he who *works* continually in welldoing; to whom welldoing is as his natural existence, awakening no astonishment, requiring no commentary; but there, like a thing of course, and as if it could not but be so. Self-contemplation, on the other hand, is infallibly the symptom of disease, be it or be it not the sign of cure. An unhealthy Virtue is one that consumes itself to leanness in repenting and anxiety; or, still worse, that inflates itself into dropsical boastfulness and vain-glory: either way, there is a self-seeking; an unprofitable looking behind us to measure the way we have made: whereas the sole concern is to walk continually forward, and make more way. If in any sphere of man's life, then in the Moral sphere, as the inmost and most vital of all, it is good that there be wholeness; that there be unconsciousness, which is the evidence of this. Let the free, reasonable Will, which dwells in us, as in our Holy of Holies, be indeed free, and obeyed like a Divinity, as is its right and its effort: the perfect obedience will be the silent one. Such perhaps were the sense of that maxim, enunciating, as is usual, but the half of a truth: To say that we have a clear conscience, is to utter a solecism; had we never sinned, we should have had no conscience. Were defeat unknown, neither would victory be celebrated by songs of triumph.

This, true enough, is an ideal, impossible state of being; yet ever the goal towards which our actual state of being strives; which it is the more perfect the nearer it can approach. Nor, in our actual world, where Labour must often prove *in*effectual, and thus in all senses Light alternate with Darkness, and the nature of an ideal Morality be much modified, is the case, thus far, materially different. It is a fact which escapes

---

[4] Alexander of Hales (d. 1245), English schoolman, author of *Summa Universae Theologiae.*
[5] Goethe, *Wilhelm Meister,* II.

no one, that, generally speaking, whoso is acquainted with his worth has but a little stock to cultivate acquaintance with. Above all, the public acknowledgment of such acquaintance, indicating that it has reached quite an intimate footing, bodes ill. Already, to the popular judgment, he who talks much about Virtue in the abstract, begins to be suspect; it is shrewdly guessed that where there is great preaching, there will be little almsgiving. Or again, on a wider scale, we can remark that ages of Heroism are not ages of Moral Philosophy; Virtue, when it can be philosophised of, has become aware of itself, is sickly and beginning to decline. A spontaneous habitual all-pervading spirit of Chivalrous Valour shrinks together, and perks itself up into shrivelled Points of Honour; humane Courtesy and Nobleness of mind dwindle into punctilious Politeness, 'avoiding meats'; 'paying tithe of mint and anise, neglecting the weightier matters of the law.'[6] Goodness, which was a rule to itself, must now appeal to Precept, and seek strength from Sanctions; the Freewill no longer reigns unquestioned and by divine right, but like a mere earthly sovereign, by expediency, by Rewards and Punishments: or rather, let us say, the Freewill, so far as may be, has abdicated and withdrawn into the dark, and a spectral nightmare of a Necessity usurps its throne; for now that mysterious Self-impulse of the whole man, heaven-inspired, and in all senses partaking of the Infinite, being captiously questioned in a finite dialect, and answering, as it needs must, by silence,—is conceived as non-extant, and only the outward Mechanism of it remains acknowledged: of Volition, except as the synonym of Desire, we hear nothing; of 'Motives,' without any Mover, more than enough.

So too, when the generous Affections have become wellnigh paralytic, we have the reign of Sentimentality. The greatness, the profitableness, at any rate the extremely ornamental nature of high feeling, and the luxury of doing good; charity, love, self-forgetfulness, devotedness and all manner of godlike magnanimity,—are everywhere insisted on, and pressingly inculcated in speech and writing, in prose and verse; Socinian[7] Preachers proclaim 'Benevolence' to all the four winds, and have TRUTH engraved on their watchseals: unhappily with little or no effect. Were the limbs in right walking order, why so much

demonstrating of motion? The barrenest of all mortals is the Sentimentalist. Granting even that he were sincere, and did not wilfully deceive us, or without first deceiving himself, what good is in him? Does he not lie there as a perpetual lesson of despair, and type of bedrid valetudinarian impotence? He is emphatically a Virtue that has become, through every fibre, conscious of itself; it is all sick, and feels as if it were made of glass, and durst not touch or be touched; in the shape of work, it can do nothing; at the utmost, by incessant nursing and caudling, keep itself alive. As the last stage of all, when Virtue, properly so called, has ceased to be practised, and become extinct, and a mere remembrance, we have the era of Sophists, descanting of its existence, proving it, denying it, mechanically 'accounting' for it;—as dissectors and demonstrators cannot operate till once the body be dead.

Thus is true Moral genius, like true Intellectual, which indeed is but a lower phasis thereof, 'ever a secret to itself.' The healthy moral nature loves Goodness, and without wonder wholly lives in it: the unhealthy makes love to it, and would fain get to live in it; or, finding such courtship fruitless, turns round, and not without contempt abandons it. These curious relations of the Voluntary and Conscious to the Involuntary and Unconscious, and the small proportion which, in all departments of our life, the former bears to the latter,—might lead us into deep questions of Psychology and Physiology: such, however, belong not to our present object. Enough, if the fact itself become apparent, that Nature so meant it with us; that in this wise we are made. We may now say, that view man's individual Existence under what aspect we will, under the highest spiritual, as under the merely animal aspect, everywhere the grand vital energy, while in its sound state, is an unseen unconscious one; or, in the words of our old Aphorism, 'the healthy know not of their health, but only the sick.'

To understand man, however, we must look beyond the individual man and his actions or interests, and view him in combination with his fellows. It is in Society that man first feels what he is; first becomes what he can be. In Society an altogether new set of spiritual activities are evolved in him, and the old immeasurably quickened and strengthened. Society is the genial

---

[6] See Matthew 23:23.
[7] Laelio and Faustus Socinus, sixteenth-century Italian theologians who denied the major doctrines of Christianity; their followers are called Socinians.

element wherein his nature first lives and grows; the solitary man were but a small portion of himself, and must continue forever folded in, stunted and only half alive. 'Already,' says a deep Thinker, with more meaning than will disclose itself at once, 'my opinion, my conviction, gains *infinitely* in strength and sureness, the moment a second mind has adopted it.'[8] Such, even in its simplest form, is association; so wondrous the communion of soul with soul as directed to the mere act of Knowing! In other higher acts, the wonder is still more manifest; as in that portion of our being which we name the Moral: for properly, indeed, all communion is of a moral sort, whereof such intellectual communion (in the act of knowing) is itself an example. But with regard to Morals strictly so called, it is in Society, we might almost say, that Morality begins; here at least it takes an altogether new form, and on every side, as in living growth, expands itself. The Duties of Man to himself, to what is Highest in himself, make but the First Table of the Law: to the First Table is now superadded a Second, with the Duties of Man to his Neighbour; whereby also the significance of the First now assumes its true importance. Man has joined himself with man; soul acts and reacts on soul; a mystic miraculous unfathomable Union establishes itself; Life, in all its elements, has become intensated, consecrated. The lightning-spark of Thought, generated, or say rather heaven-kindled, in the solitary mind, awakens its express likeness in another mind, in a thousand other minds, and all blaze-up together in combined fire; reverberated from mind to mind, fed also with fresh fuel in each, it acquires incalculable new light as Thought, incalculable new heat as converted into Action. By and by, a common store of Thought can accumulate, and be transmitted as an ever-lasting possession: Literature, whether as preserved in the memory of Bards, in Runes and Hieroglyphs engraved on stone, or in Books of written or printed paper, comes into existence, and begins to play its wondrous part. Polities are formed; the weak submitting to the strong; with a willing loyalty, giving obedience that he may receive guidance: or say rather, in honour of our nature, the ignorant submitting to the wise; for so it is in all even the rudest communities, man never yields himself wholly to brute Force, but always to moral Greatness; thus the universal title of respect, from the Oriental *Sheik*, from the *Sachem* of the Red Indians, down to our English *Sir*, implies only that he whom we mean to honour is our *senior*. Last, as the crown and all-supporting keystone of the fabric, Religion arises. The devout meditation of the isolated man, which flitted through his soul, like a transient tome of Love and Awe from unknown lands, acquires certainty, continuance, when it is shared-in by his brother men. 'Where two or three are gathered together' in the name of the Highest, then first does the Highest, as it is written, 'appear among them to bless them';[9] then first does an Altar and act of united Worship open a way from Earth to Heaven; whereon, were it but a simple Jacob's-ladder, the heavenly Messengers will travel, with glad tidings and unspeakable gifts for men. Such is SOCIETY, the vital articulation of many individuals into a new collective individual: greatly the most important of man's attainments on this earth; that in which, and by virtue of which, all his other attainments and attempts find their arena, and have their value. Considered well, Society is the standing wonder of our existence; a true region of the Supernatural; as it were, a second all-embracing Life, wherein our first individual Life becomes doubly and trebly alive, and whatever of Infinitude was in us bodies itself forth, and becomes visible and active.

To figure Society as endowed with life is scarcely a metaphor; but rather the statement of a fact by such imperfect methods as language affords. Look at it closely, that mystic Union, Nature's highest work with man, wherein man's volition plays an indispensable yet so subordinate a part, and the small Mechanical grows so mysteriously and indissolubly out of the infinite Dynamical, like Body out of Spirit,—is truly enough vital, what we can call vital, and bears the distinguishing character of life. In the same style also, we can say that Society has its periods of sickness and vigour, of youth, manhood, decrepitude, dissolution and new birth; in one or other of which stages we may, in all times, and all places where men inhabit, discern it; and do ourselves, in this time and place, whether as coöperating or as contending, as healthy members or as diseased ones, to our joy and sorrow, form part of it. The question, What is the actual condition of Society? has in these days unhappily become important enough. No one of us is unconcerned in that question; but for the majority of thinking men a true answer to it, such is the state of matters, appears almost as the one thing

---

[8] Novalis, *Fragmente*.   [9] Adapted from Matthew 28:20.

needful. Meanwhile, as the true answer, that is to say, the complete and fundamental answer and settlement, often as it has been demanded, is nowhere forthcoming, and indeed by its nature is impossible, any honest approximation towards such is not without value. The feeblest light, or even so much as a more precise recognition of the darkness, which is the first step to attainment of light, will be welcome.

This once understood, let it not seem idle if we remark that here too our old Aphorism holds; that again in the Body Politic, as in the animal body, the sign of right performance is Un-consciousness. Such indeed is virtually the mean-ing of that phrase, 'artifical state of society,' as contrasted with the natural state, and indicating something so inferior to it. For, in all vital things, men distinguish an Artificial and a Natural; founding on some dim perception or sentiment of the very truth we here insist on: the artificial is the conscious, mechanical; the natural is the unconscious, dynamical. Thus, as we have an artificial Poetry, and prize only the natural; so likewise we have an artificial Morality, an artificial Wisdom, an artificial Society. The artificial Society is precisely one that knows its own structure, its own internal functions; not in watching, not in knowing which, but in working outwardly to the fulfilment of its aim, does the wellbeing of a Society consist. Every Society, every Polity, has a spiritual principle; is the embodiment, tentative and more or less complete, of an Idea: all its tendencies of endeavour, specialities of custom, its laws, politics and whole procedure (as the glance of some Montesquieu,[10] across innumerable superficial entanglements, can partly decipher), are prescribed by an Idea, and flow naturally from it, as movements from the living source of motion. This Idea, be it of devotion to a man or class of men, to a creed, to an institution, or even, as in more ancient times, to a piece of land, is ever a true Loyalty; has in it something of a religious, paramount, quite infinite character; it is properly the Soul of the State, its Life; mysterious as other forms of Life, and like these working secretly, and in a depth beyond that of consciousness.

Accordingly, it is not in the vigorous ages of a Roman Republic that Treatises of the Common-wealth are written: while the Decii[11] are rushing with devoted bodies on the enemies of Rome, what need of preaching Patriotism? The virtue of Patriotism has already sunk from its pristine all-transcendent condition, before it has received a name. So long as the Commonwealth continues rightly athletic, it cares not to dabble in anatomy. Why teach obedience to the Sovereign; why so much as admire it, or separately recognise it, while a divine idea of Obedience perennially inspires all men? Loyalty, like Patriotism, of which it is a form, was not praised till it had begun to decline; the *Preux Chevaliers* first became rightly admirable, when 'dying for their king' had ceased to be a habit with chevaliers. For if the mystic significance of the State, let this be what it may, dwells vitally in every heart, encircles every life as with a second higher life, how should it stand self-questioning? It must rush outward, and express itself by works. Besides, if perfect, it is there as by necessity, and does not excite inquiry: it is also by nature infinite, has no limits; therefore can be circum-scribed by no conditions and definitions; cannot be reasoned of; except *musically*, or in the language of Poetry, cannot yet so much as be spoken of.

In those days, Society was what we name healthy, sound at heart. Not indeed without suffering enough; not without perplexities, diffi-culty on every side: for such is the appointment of man; his highest and sole blessedness is, that he toil, and know what to toil at: not in ease, but in united victorious labour, which is at once evil and the victory over evil, does his Freedom lie. Nay, often, looking no deeper than such super-ficial perplexities of the early Time, historians have taught us that it was all one mass of contra-diction and disease; and in the antique Republic or feudal Monarchy have seen only the confused chaotic quarry, not the robust labourer, or the stately edifice he was building of it.

If Society, in such ages, had its difficulty, it had also its strength; if sorrowful masses of rubbish so encumbered it, the tough sinews to hurl them aside, with indomitable heart, were not wanting. Society went along without complaint; did not stop to scrutinise itself, to say, How well I perform! or, Alas, how ill! Men did not yet feel themselves to be 'the envy of surrounding nations'; and were enviable on that very account. Society was what we can call *whole*, in both senses of the word. The individual man was in himself a whole, or complete union; and could combine with his

---

[10] Charles de Secondat, Baron Montesquieu (1689–1755), author of *L'esprit des lois*.
[11] Valorous Roman consuls of the third and fourth centuries B.C., who pledged themselves to defend Rome to the death.

fellows as the living member of a greater whole. For all men, through their life, were animated by one great Idea; thus all efforts pointed one way, everywhere there was *wholeness*. Opinion and Action had not yet become disunited; but the former could still produce the latter, or attempt to produce it; as the stamp does its impression while the wax is not hardened. Thought and the voice of thought were also a unison; thus, instead of Speculation, we had Poetry; Literature, in its rude utterance, was as yet a heroic Song, perhaps too a devotional Anthem.

Religion was everywhere; Philosophy lay hid under it, peaceably included in it. Herein, as in the life-centre of all, lay the true health and oneness. Only at a later era must Religion split itself into Philosophies; and thereby, the vital union of Thought being lost, disunion and mutual collision in all provinces of Speech and Action more and more prevail. For if the Poet, or Priest, or by whatever title the inspired thinker may be named, is the sign of vigour, and well-being; so likewise is the Logician, or uninspired thinker, the sign of disease, probably of decrepitude and decay. Thus, not to mention other instances, one of them much nearer hand,—so soon as Prophecy among the Hebrews had ceased, then did the reign of Argumentation begin; and the ancient Theocracy, in its Sadduceeisms and Phariseeisms,[12] and vain jangling of sects and doctors, give token that the *soul* of it had fled, and that the *body* itself, by natural dissolution, 'with the old forces still at work, but working in reverse order,' was on the road to final disappearance.

We might pursue this question into innumerable other ramifications; and everywhere, under new shapes, find the same truth, which we here so imperfectly enunciate, disclosed; that throughout the whole world of man, in all manifestations and performances of his nature, outward and inward, personal and social, the Perfect, the Great is a mystery to itself, knows not itself; whatsoever does know itself is already little, and more or less imperfect. Or otherwise, we may say, Unconsciousness belongs to pure unmixed life; Consciousness to a diseased mixture and conflict of life and death: Unconsciousness is the sign of creation; Consciousness, at best, that of manufacture. So deep, in this existence of ours,

is the significance of Mystery. Well might the Ancients make Silence a god; for it is the element of all godhood, infinitude, or transcendental greatness; at once the source and the ocean wherein all such begins and ends. In the same sense, too, have Poets sung 'Hymns to the Night';[13] as if Night were nobler than Day; as if Day were but a small motley-coloured veil spread transiently over the infinite bosom of Night, and did but deform and hide from us its purely transparent eternal deeps. So likewise have they spoken and sung as if Silence were the grand epitome and complete sum-total of all Harmony; and Death, what mortals call Death, properly the beginning of Life. Under such figures, since except in figures there is no speaking of the Invisible, have men endeavoured to express a great Truth;—a Truth, in our Times, as nearly as is perhaps possible, forgotten by the most; which nevertheless continues forever true, forever all-important, and will one day, under new figures, be again brought home to the bosoms of all.

But indeed, in a far lower sense, the rudest mind has still some intimation of the greatness there is in Mystery. If Silence was made a god of by the Ancients, he still continues a government-clerk among us Moderns. To all quacks, moreover, of what sort soever, the effect of Mystery is well known: here and there some Cagliostro,[14] even in latter days, turns it to notable account: the blockhead also, who is ambitious, and has no talent, finds sometimes in 'the talent of silence,' a kind of succedaneum. Or again, looking on the opposite side of the matter, do we not see, in the common understanding of mankind, a certain distrust, a certain contempt of what is altogether self-conscious and mechanical? As nothing that is wholly seen through has other than a trivial character; so anything professing to be great, and yet wholly to see through itself, is already known to be false, and a failure. The evil repute your 'theoretical men' stand in, the acknowledged inefficiency of 'paper constitutions,' and all that class of objects, are instances of this. Experience often repeated, and perhaps a certain instinct of something far deeper that lies under such experiences, has taught men so much. They know beforehand, that the loud is generally the insignificant, the

---

[12] Ancient Jewish sects known for their theological rigor and hair-splitting and strict observance of the law.

[13] Novalis, *Hymnen an die Nacht*.

[14] Count Alessandro Cagliostro (1743–95), notorious Italian charlatan.

empty. Whatsoever can proclaim itself from the house-tops may be fit for the hawker, and for those multitudes that must needs buy of him; but for any deeper use, might as well continue unproclaimed. Observe too, how the converse of the proposition holds; how the insignificant, the empty, is usually the loud; and, after the manner of a drum, is loud even because of its emptiness. The uses of some Patent Dinner Calefactor can be bruited abroad over the whole world in the course of the first winter; those of the Printing Press are not so well seen into for the first three centuries: the passing of the Select-Vestries Bill[15] raises more noise and hopeful expectancy among mankind than did the promulgation of the Christian Religion. Again, and again, we say, the great, the creative and enduring is ever a secret to itself; only the small, the barren and transient is otherwise.

If we now, with a practical medical view, examine, by this same test of Unconsciousness, the Condition of our own Era, and of man's Life therein, the diagnosis we arrive at is nowise of a flattering sort. The state of Society in our days is, of all possible states, the least an unconscious one: this is specially the Era when all manner of Inquiries into what was once the unfelt, involuntary sphere of man's existence, find their place, and, as it were, occupy the whole domain of thought. What, for example, is all this that we hear, for the last generation or two, about the Improvement of the Age, the Spirit of the Age, Destruction of Prejudice, Progress of the Species, and the March of Intellect, but an unhealthy state of self-sentience, self-survey; the precursor and prognostic of still worse health? That Intellect do march, if possible at double-quick time, is very desirable; nevertheless, why should she turn round at every stride, and cry: See you what a stride I have taken! Such a marching of Intellect is distinctly of the spavined kind; what the Jockeys call 'all action and no go.' Or at best, if we examine well, it is the marching of that gouty Patient, whom his Doctors had clapt on a metal floor artificially heated to the searing point, so that he was obliged to march, and did march with a vengeance—nowhither. Intellect did not awaken for the first time yesterday; but has been under way from Noah's Flood downwards: greatly her best progress, moreover, was in the

old times, when she said nothing about it. In those same 'dark ages,' Intellect (metaphorically as well as literally) could invent *glass*, which now she has enough ado to grind into *spectacles*. Intellect built not only Churches, but a Church, *the* Church, based on this firm Earth, yet reaching up, and leading up, as high as Heaven; and now it is all she can do to keep its doors bolted that there be no tearing of the Surplices, no robbery of the Alms-box. She built a Senate-house likewise, glorious in its kind; and now it costs her a well-nigh mortal effort to sweep it clear of vermin, and get the roof made rain-tight.

But the truth is, with Intellect, as with most other things, we are now passing from that first or boastful stage of Self-sentience into the second or painful one: out of these often-asseverated declarations that 'our system is in high order,' we come now, by natural sequence, to the melancholy conviction that it is altogether the reverse. Thus, for instance, in the matter of Government, the period of the 'Invaluable Constitution' has to be followed by a Reform Bill;[16] to laudatory De Lolmes succeed objurgatory Benthams. At any rate, what Treatises on the Social Contract, on the Elective Franchise, the Rights of Man, the Rights of Property, Codifications, Institutions, Constitutions, have we not, for long years, groaned under! Or again, with a wider survey, consider those Essays on Man, Thoughts on Man, Inquiries concerning Man; not to mention Evidences of the Christian Faith, Theories of Poetry, Considerations on the Origin of Evil, which during the last century have accumulated on us to a frightful extent. Never since the beginning of Time was there, that we hear or read of, so intensely self-conscious a Society. Our whole relations to the Universe and to our fellow-man have become an Inquiry, a Doubt; nothing will go on of its own accord, and do its function quietly; but all things must be probed into, the whole working of man's world be anatomically studied. Alas, anatomically studied, that it may be medically aided! Till at length indeed, we have come to such a pass, that except in this same *medicine*, with its artifices and appliances, few can so much as imagine any strength or hope to remain for us. The whole Life of Society must now be carried on by drugs: doctor after doctor appears with his nostrum, of Coöperative Societies, Universal Suffrage,

<hr>

[15] A measure to provide for an elected committee to manage parish affairs.
[16] First Reform Bill, passed in 1832; Louis DeLolme (1740–1806), Swiss jurist; Jeremy Bentham (1748–1832), Utilitarian philosopher.

Cottage-and-Cow systems, Repression of Population, Vote by Ballot. To such height has the dyspepsia of Society reached; as indeed the constant grinding internal pain, or from time to time the mad spasmodic throes, of all Society do otherwise too mournfully indicate.

Far be it from us to attribute, as some unwise persons do, the disease itself to this unhappy sensation that there is a disease! The Encyclopedists did not produce the troubles of France; but the troubles of France produced the Encyclopedists, and much else. The Self-consciousness is the symptom merely; nay, it is also the attempt towards cure. We record the fact, without special censure; not wondering that Society should feel itself, and in all ways complain of aches and twinges, for it has suffered enough. Napoleon was but a Job's-comforter, when he told his wounded staff-officer, twice unhorsed by cannon-balls, and with half his limbs blown to pieces: "*Vous vous écoutez trop!*"[17]

On the outward, as it were Physical diseases of Society, it were beside our purpose to insist here. There are diseases which he who runs may read; and sorrow over, with or without hope. Wealth has accumulated itself into masses; and Poverty, also in accumulation enough, lies impassably separated from it; opposed, uncommunicating, like forces in positive and negative poles. The gods of this lower world sit aloft on glittering thrones, less happy than Epicurus's gods, but as indolent, as impotent; while the boundless living chaos of Ignorance and Hunger welters terrific, in its dark fury, under their feet. How much among us might be likened to a whited sepulchre; outwardly all pomp and strength; but inwardly full of horror and despair and dead-men's bones! Iron highways, with their wains fire-winged, are uniting all ends of the firm Land; quays and moles, with their innumerable stately fleets, tame the Ocean into our pliant bearer of burdens; Labour's thousand arms, of sinew and of metal, all-conquering everywhere, from the tops of the mountain down to the depths of the mine and the caverns of the sea, ply unweariedly for the service of man: yet man remains unserved. He has subdued this Planet, his habitation and inheritance; yet reaps no profit from the victory.

Sad to look upon: in the highest stage of civilisation, nine tenths of mankind have to struggle in the lowest battle of savage or even animal man, the battle against Famine. Countries are rich, prosperous in all manner of increase, beyond example: but the Men of those countries are poor, needier than ever of all sustenance outward and inward; of Belief, of Knowledge, of Money, of Food. The rule, *Sic vos non vobis*,[18] never altogether to be got rid of in men's Industry, now presses with such incubus weight, that Industry must shake it off, or utterly be strangled under it; and, alas, can as yet but gasp and rave, and aimlessly struggle, like one in the final deliration. Thus Change, or the inevitable approach of Change, is manifest everywhere. In one Country we have seen lavatorrents of fever-frenzy envelop all things; Government succeed Government, like the phantasms of a dying brain. In another Country, we can even now see, in maddest alternation, the Peasant governed by such guidance as this: To labour earnestly one month in raising wheat, and the next month labour earnestly in burning it. So that Society, were it not by nature immortal, and its death ever a new-birth, might appear, as it does in the eyes of some, to be sick to dissolution, and even now writhing in its last agony. Sick enough we must admit it to be, with disease enough, a whole nosology of diseases; wherein he perhaps is happiest that is not called to prescribe as physician;—wherein, however, one small piece of policy, that of summoning the Wisest in the Commonwealth, by the sole method yet known or thought of, to come together and with their whole soul consult for it, might, but for late tedious experiences, have seemed unquestionable enough.

But leaving this, let us rather look within, into the Spiritual condition of Society, and see what aspects and prospects offer themselves there. For after all, it is there properly that the secret and origin of the whole is to be sought: the Physical derangements of Society are but the image and impress of its Spiritual; while the heart continues sound, all other sickness is superficial, and temporary. False Action is the fruit of false Speculation; let the spirit of Society be free and strong, that is to say, let true Principles inspire the members of Society, then neither can disorders accumulate in its Practice; each disorder will be promptly, faithfully inquired into, and remedied as it arises. But alas, with us the Spiritual condition of Society is no less sickly than the Physical. Examine man's internal world, in any of its social relations and performances, here too all seems diseased self-consciousness,

---

[17] "You pay too much attention to yourself."

[18] "Thus you labor, but not for yourselves."

collision and mutually-destructive struggle. Nothing acts from within outwards in undivided healthy force; everything lies impotent, lamed, its force turned inwards, and painfully 'listens to itself.'

To begin with our highest Spiritual function, with Religion, we might ask, Whither has Religion now fled? Of Churches and their establishments we here say nothing; nor of the unhappy domains of Unbelief, and how innumerable men, blinded in their minds, have grown to 'live without God in the world';[19] but, taking the fairest side of the matter, we ask, What is the nature of that same Religion, which still lingers in the hearts of the few who are called, and call themselves, specially the Religious? Is it a healthy religion, vital, unconscious of itself; that shines forth spontaneously in doing of the Work, or even in preaching of the Word? Unhappily, no. Instead of heroic martyr Conduct, and inspired and soul-inspiring Eloquence, whereby Religion itself were brought home to our living bosoms, to live and reign there, we have 'Discourses on the Evidences,' endeavouring, with smallest result, to make it probable that such a thing as Religion exists. The most enthusiastic Evangelicals do not preach a Gospel, but keep describing how it should and might be preached: to awaken the sacred fire of faith, as by a sacred contagion, is not their endeavour; but, at most, to describe how Faith shows and acts, and scientifically distinguish true Faith from false. Religion, like all else, is conscious of itself, listens to itself; it becomes less and less creative, vital; more and more mechanical. Considered as a whole, the Christian Religion of late ages has been continually dissipating itself into Metaphysics; and threatens now to disappear, as some rivers do, in deserts of barren sand.

Of Literature, and its deep-seated, widespread maladies, why speak? Literature is but a branch of Religion, and always participates in its character: however, in our time, it is the only branch that still shows any greenness; and, as some think, must one day become the main stem. Now, apart from the subterranean and tartarean regions of Literature;—leaving out of view the frightful, scandalous statistics of Puffing, the mystery of Slander, Falsehood, Hatred and other convulsion-work of rabid Imbecility, and all that has rendered Literature on that side a perfect 'Babylon the mother of Abominations,' in very deed, making the world 'drunk' with the wine of her iniquity;—forgetting all this, let us look only to the regions of the upper air; to such Literature as can be said to have some attempt towards truth in it, some tone of music, and if it be not poetical, to hold of the poetical. Among other characteristics, is not this manifest enough: that it knows itself? Spontaneous devotedness to the object, being wholly possessed by the object, what we can call Inspiration, has well-nigh ceased to appear in Literature. Which melodious Singer forgets that he is singing melodiously? We have not the love of greatness, but the love of the love of greatness. Hence infinite Affectations, Distractions; in every case inevitable Error. Consider, for one example, this peculiarity of Modern Literature, the sin that has been named View-hunting. In our elder writers, there are no paintings of scenery for its own sake; no euphuistic gallantries with Nature, but a constant heartlove for her, a constant dwelling in communion with her. View-hunting, with so much else that is kin to it, first came decisively into action through the *Sorrows of Werter*;[20] which wonderful Performance, indeed, may in many senses be regarded as the progenitor of all that has since become popular in Literature; whereof, in so far as concerns spirit and tendency, it still offers the most instructive image; for nowhere, except in its own country, above all in the mind of its illustrious Author, has it yet fallen wholly obsolete. Scarcely ever, till that late epoch, did any worshipper of Nature become entirely aware that he was worshipping, much to his own credit; and think of saying to himself: Come, let us make a description! Intolerable enough: when every puny whipster plucks out his pencil, and insists on painting you a scene; so that the instant you discern such a thing as 'wavy outline,' 'mirror of the lake,' 'stern head-land,' or the like, in any Book, you tremulously hasten on; and scarcely the Author of Waverley himself can tempt you not to skip.

Nay, is not the diseased self-conscious state of Literature disclosed in this one fact, which lies so near us here, the prevalence of Reviewing! Sterne's wish for a reader 'that would give up the reins of his imagination into his author's hands, and be pleased he knew not why, and cared not wherefore,' might lead him a long journey now.[21] Indeed, for our best class of readers, the chief

---

[19] Ephesians 2:12.   [20] Goethe's sentimental novel, published 1774.
[21] See *Tristram Shandy*, III, xii.

pleasure, a very stinted one, is this same knowing of the Why; which many a Kames and Bossu[22] has been, ineffectually enough, endeavouring to teach us: till at last these also have laid down their trade; and now your Reviewer is a mere *taster*; who tastes, and says, by the evidence of such palate, such tongue, as he has got, It is good, It is bad. Was it thus that the French carried out certain inferior creatures on their Algerine Expedition, to taste the wells for them, and try whether they were poisoned? Far be it from us to disparage our own craft, whereby we have our living! Only we must note these things: that Reviewing spreads with strange vigour; that such a man as Byron reckons the Reviewer and the Poet equal; that at the last Leipzig Fair, there was advertised a Review of Reviews. By and by it will be found that all Literature has become one boundless self-devouring Review; and, as in London routs, we have to *do* nothing, but only to *see* others do nothing.—Thus does Literature also, like a sick thing, superabundantly 'listen to itself.'

No less is this unhealthy symptom manifest, if we cast a glance on our Philosophy, on the character of our speculative Thinking. Nay, already, as above hinted, the mere existence and necessity of a Philosophy is an evil. Man is sent hither not to question, but to work: 'the end of man,' it was long ago written, 'is an Action, not a Thought.'[23] In the perfect state, all Thought were but the picture and inspiring symbol of Action; Philosophy, except as Poetry and Religion, would have no being. And yet how, in this imperfect state, can it be avoided, can it be dispensed with? Man stands as in the centre of Nature; his fraction of Time encircled by Eternity, his handbreadth of Space encircled by Infinitude: how shall he forbear asking himself, What am I; and Whence; and Whither? How too, except in slight partial hints, in kind asseverations and assurances, such as a mother quiets her fretfully inquisitive child with, shall he get answer to such inquiries?

The disease of Metaphysics, accordingly, is a perennial one. In all ages, those questions of Death and Immortality, Origin of Evil, Freedom and Necessity, must, under new forms, anew make their appearance; ever, from time to time, must the attempt to shape for ourselves some Theorem of the Universe be repeated. And ever unsuccessfully: for what Theorem of the Infinite can the Finite render complete? We, the whole species of Mankind, and our whole existence and history, are but a floating speck in the illimitable ocean of the All; yet *in* that ocean; indissoluble portion thereof; partaking of its infinite tendencies: borne this way and that by its deep-swelling tides, and grand ocean currents;— of which what faintest chance is there that we should ever exhaust the significance, ascertain the goings and comings? A region of Doubt, therefore, hovers in the background; in Action alone can we have certainty. Nay, properly Doubt is the indispensable inexhaustible material whereon Action works, which Action has to fashion into Certainty and Reality; only on a canvas of Darkness, such is man's way of being, could the many-coloured picture of our Life paint itself and shine.

Thus if our eldest system of Metaphysics is as old as the *Book of Genesis*, our latest is that of Mr. Thomas Hope, published only within the current year.[24] It is a chronic malady that of Metaphysics, as we said, and perpetually recurs on us. At the utmost, there is a better and a worse in it; a stage of convalescence, and a stage of relapse with new sickness: these forever succeed each other, as is the nature of all Life-movement here below. The first, or convalescent stage, we might also name that of Dogmatical or Constructive Metaphysics; when the mind constructively endeavours to scheme out and assert itself an actual Theorem of the Universe, and therewith for a time rests satisfied. The second or sick stage might be called that of Sceptical or Inquisitory Metaphysics; when the mind having widened its sphere of vision, the existing Theorem of the Universe no longer answers the phenomena, no longer yields contentment: but must be torn in pieces, and certainty anew sought for in the endless realms of denial. All Theologies and sacred Cosmogonies belong, in some measure, to the first class; in all Pyrrhonism, from Pyrrho down to Hume and the innumerable disciples of Hume, we have instances enough of the second.[25] In the former, so far as it affords satisfaction, a temporary anodyne to doubt, an arena for wholesome action, there may be much good; indeed in this case, it holds rather of Poetry than of Metaphysics, might be called Inspiration

---

[22] Henry Home, Lord Kames (1696–1782), Scottish critic; René Le Bossu (1631–80), French neoclassical critic.

[23] Adapted from Aristotle, *Ethics*.   [24] This is one of the volumes under review in this essay.

[25] Pyrrho (c. 360–270 B.C.), founder of the skeptical school of Athenian philosophy; David Hume (1711–1776), Scottish philosopher and skeptic.

rather than Speculation. The latter is Metaphysics proper; a pure, unmixed, though from time to time a necessary evil.

For truly, if we look into it, there is no more fruitless endeavour than this same, which the Metaphysician proper toils in: to educe Conviction out of Negation. How, by merely testing and rejecting what is not, shall we ever attain knowledge of what is? Metaphysical Speculation, as it begins in No or Nothingness, so it must needs end in Nothingness; circulates and must circulate in endless vortices; creating, swallowing—itself. Our being is made up of Light and Darkness, the Light resting on the Darkness, and balancing it; everywhere there is Dualism, Equipoise; a perpetual Contradiction dwells in us: 'where shall I place myself to escape from my own shadow?' Consider it well, Metaphysics is the attempt of the mind to rise above the mind; to environ and shut in, or as we say, *comprehend* the mind. Hopeless struggle, for the wisest, as for the foolishest! What strength of sinew, or athletic skill, will enable the stoutest athlete to fold his own body in his arms, and, by lifting, lift up *himself*? The Irish Saint swam the Channel, 'carrying his head in his teeth'; but the feat has never been imitated.

That this is the age of Metaphysics, in the proper, or sceptical Inquisitory sense; that there was a necessity for its being such an age, we regard as our indubitable misfortune. From many causes, the arena of free Activity has long been narrowing, that of sceptical Inquiry becoming more and more universal, more and more perplexing. The Thought conducts not to the Deed; but in boundless chaos, self-devouring, engenders monstrosities, phantasms, fire-breathing chimeras. Profitable Speculation were this: What is to be done; and How is it to be done? But with us not so much as the What can be got sight of. For some generations, all Philosophy has been a painful, captious, hostile question towards everything in the Heaven above, and in the Earth beneath: Why art thou there? Till at length it has come to pass that the worth and authenticity of all things seems dubitable or deniable: our best effort must be unproductively spent not in working, but in ascertaining our mere Whereabout, and so much as whether we are to work at all. Doubt, which, as was said, ever hangs in the background of our world, has now become our middleground and foreground; whereon, for the time, no fair Life-picture can be painted, but only the dark air-canvas itself flow round us, bewildering and benighting.

Nevertheless, doubt as we will, man is actually Here; not to ask questions, but to do work: in this time, as in all times, it must be the heaviest evil for him, if his faculty of Action lie dormant, and only that of sceptical Inquiry exert itself. Accordingly, whoever looks abroad upon the world, comparing the Past with the Present, may find that the practical condition of man in these days is one of the saddest; burdened with miseries which are in a considerable degree peculiar. In no time was man's life what he calls a happy one; in no time can it be so. A perpetual dream there has been of Paradises, and some luxurious Lubberland, where the brooks should run wine, and the trees bend with ready-baked viands; but it was a dream merely; an impossible dream. Suffering, contradiction, error, have their quite perennial, and even indispensable abode in this Earth. Is not labour the inheritance of man? And what labour for the present is joyous, and not grievous? Labour, effort, is the very interruption of that ease, which man foolishly enough fancies to be his happiness; and yet without labour there were no ease, no rest, so much as conceivable. Thus Evil, what we call Evil, must ever exist while man exists: Evil, in the widest sense we can give it, is precisely the dark, disordered material out of which man's Freewill has to create an edifice of order and Good. Ever must Pain urge us to Labour; and only in free Effort can any blessedness be imagined for us.

But if man has, in all ages, had enough to encounter, there has, in most civilised ages, been an inward force vouchsafed him, whereby the pressure of things outward might be withstood. Obstruction abounded; but Faith also was not wanting. It is by Faith that man removes mountains: while he had Faith, his limbs might be wearied with toiling, his back galled with bearing; but the heart within him was peaceable and resolved. In the thickest gloom there burnt a lamp to guide him. If he struggled and suffered, he felt that it even should be so; knew for what he was suffering and struggling. Faith gave him an inward Willingness; a world of Strength wherewith to front a world of Difficulty. The true wretchedness lies here: that the Difficulty remain and the Strength be lost; that Pain cannot relieve itself in free Effort; that we have the Labour, and want the Willingness. Faith strengthens us, enlightens us, for all endeavours and endurances; with Faith we can do all, and dare all, and life itself has a thousand times been joyfully given away. But the sum of man's misery is even this, that he feel himself crushed under the Juggernaut wheels, and know that Juggernaut is no divinity, but a dead mechanical idol.

Now this is specially the misery which has fallen on man in our Era. Belief, Faith has well-nigh vanished from the world. The youth on awakening in this wondrous Universe no longer finds a competent theory of its wonders. Time was, when if he asked himself, What is man, What are the duties of man? the answer stood ready written for him. But now the ancient 'ground-plan of the All' belies itself when brought into contact with reality; Mother Church has, to the most, become a superannuated Step-mother, whose lessons go disregarded; or are spurned at, and scornfully gainsaid. For young Valour and thirst of Action no ideal Chivalry invites to heroism, prescribes what is heroic: the old ideal of Manhood has grown obsolete, and the new is still invisible to us, and we grope after it in darkness, one clutching this phantom, another that; Werterism, Byronism, even Brummelism,[26] each has its day. For Contemplation and love of Wisdom, no Cloister now opens its religious shades; the Thinker must, in all senses, wander homeless, too often aimless, looking up to a Heaven which is dead for him, round to an Earth which is deaf. Action, in those old days, was easy, was voluntary, for the divine worth of human things lay acknowledged; Speculation was wholesome, for it ranged itself as the handmaid of Action; what could not so range itself died out by its natural death, by neglect. Loyalty still hallowed obedience, and made rule noble; there was still something to be loyal to: the God-like stood embodied under many a symbol in men's interests and business; the Finite shadowed forth the Infinite; Eternity looked through Time. The Life of man was encompassed and over-canopied by a glory of Heaven, even as his dwelling-place by the azure vault.

How changed in these new days! Truly may it be said, the Divinity has withdrawn from the Earth; or veils himself in that wide-wasting Whirlwind of a departing Era, wherein the fewest can discern his goings. Not Godhead, but an iron, ignoble circle of Necessity embraces all things; binds the youth of these times into a sluggish thrall, or else exasperates him into a rebel. Heroic Action is paralysed; for what worth now remains unquestionable with him? At the fervid period when his whole nature cries aloud for Action, there is nothing sacred under whose

banner he can act; the course and kind and conditions of free Action are all but undiscoverable. Doubt storms-in on him through every avenue; inquiries of the deepest, painfulest sort must be engaged with; and the invincible energy of young years waste itself in sceptical, suicidal cavillings; in passionate 'questionings of Destiny,' whereto no answer will be returned.

For men, in whom the old perennial principle of Hunger (be it Hunger of the poor Day-drudge who stills it with eighteenpence-a-day, or of the ambitious Placehunter who can nowise still it with so little) suffices to fill-up existence, the case is bad; but not the worst. These men have an aim, such as it is; and can steer towards it, with chagrin enough truly; yet, as their hands are kept full, without desperation. Unhappier are they to whom a higher instinct has been given; who struggle to be persons, not machines; to whom the Universe is not a warehouse, or at best a fancy-bazaar, but a mystic temple and hall of doom. For such men there lie properly two courses open. The lower, yet still an estimable class, take up with worn-out Symbols of the Godlike; keep trimming and trucking between these and Hypocrisy, purblindly enough, miserably enough. A numerous intermediate class end in Denial; and form a theory that there is no theory; that nothing is certain in the world, except this fact of Pleasure being pleasant; so they try to realise what trifling modicum of Pleasure they can come at, and to live contented therewith, winking hard. Of those we speak not here; but only of the second nobler class, who also have dared to say No, and cannot yet say Yea; but feel that in the No they dwell as in a Gologtha, where life enters not, where peace is not appointed them.

Hard, for most part, is the fate of such men; the harder the nobler they are. In dim forecastings, wrestles within them the 'Divine Idea of the World,'[27] yet will nowhere visibly reveal itself. They have to realise a Worship for themselves, or live unworshipping. The Godlike has vanished from the world; and they, by the strong cry of their soul's agony, like true wonder-workers, must again evoke its presence. This miracle is their appointed task; which they must accomplish, or die wretchedly: this miracle has been accomplished by such; but not in our land; our land yet knows not of it. Behold a Byron, in melodious tones, 'cursing his day': he mistakes earthborn

---

[26] After Goethe's Werther, Lord Byron, and Beau Brummel respectively.
[27] From Johann Gottlieb Fichte (1762–1814).

passionate Desire for heaven-inspired Freewill; without heavenly loadstar, rushes madly into the dance of meteoric lights that hover on the mad Mahlstrom; and goes down among its eddies. Hear a Shelley filling the earth with inarticulate wail; like the infinite, inarticulate grief and weeping of forsaken infants. A noble Friedrich Schlegel,[28] stupefied in that fearful loneliness, as of a silenced battle-field, flies back to Catholicism; as a child might to its slaim mother's bosom, and cling there. In lower regions, how many a poor Hazlitt must wander on God's verdant earth, like the Unblest on burning deserts; passionately dig wells, and draw up only the dry quicksand; believe that he is seeking Truth, yet only wrestle among endless Sophisms, doing desperate battle as with spectre-hosts; and die and make no sign!

To the better order of such minds any mad joy of Denial has long since ceased: the problem is not now to deny, but to ascertain and perform. Once in destroying the False, there was a certain inspiration; but now the genius of Destruction has done its work, there is now nothing more to destroy. The doom of the Old has long been pronounced, and irrevocable; the Old has passed away: but, alas, the New appears not in its stead; the Time is still in pangs of travail with the New. Man has walked by the light of conflagrations, and amid the sound of falling cities; and now there is darkness, and long watching till it be morning. The voice even of the faithful can but exclaim: 'As yet struggles the twelfth hour of the Night: birds of darkness are on the wing, spectres uproar, the dead walk, the living dream.—Thou, Eternal Providence, wilt cause the day to dawn!'[29]

Such being the condition, temporal and spiritual, of the world at our Epoch, can we wonder that the world 'listens to itself,' and struggles and writhes, everywhere externally and internally, like a thing in pain? Nay, is not even this unhealthy action of the world's Organisation, if the symptom of universal disease, yet also the symptom and sole means of restoration and cure? The effort of Nature, exerting her medicative force to cast-out foreign impediments, and once more become One, become whole? In Practice, still more in Opinion, which is the precursor and prototype of Practice, there must needs be collision, convulsion; much has to be ground away. Thought must needs be Doubt and Inquiry, before it can again be Affirmation and Sacred Precept. Innumerable 'Philosophies of Man,' contending in boundless hubbub, must annihilate each other, before an inspired Poesy and Faith for Man can fashion itself together.

From this stunning hubbub, a true Babel-like confusion of tongues, we have here selected two Voices; less as objects of praise or condemnation, than as signs how far the confusion has reached, what prospect there is of its abating. Friedrich Schlegel's *Lectures* delivered at Dresden, and Mr. Hope's *Essay* published in London, are the latest utterances of European Speculation: far asunder in external place, they stand at a still wider distance in inward purport; are, indeed, so opposite and yet so cognate that they may, in many senses, represent the two Extremes of our whole modern system of Thought; and be said to include between them all the Metaphysical Philosophies, so often alluded to here, which, of late times, from France, Germany, England, have agitated and almost overwhelmed us. Both in regard to matter and to form, the relation of these two Works is significant enough.

Speaking first of their cognate qualities, let us remark, not without emotion, one quite extraneous point of agreement; the fact that the Writers of both have departed from this world; they have now finished their search, and had all doubts resolved: while we listen to the voice, the tongue that uttered it has gone silent forever. But the fundamental, all-pervading similarity lies in this circumstance, well worthy of being noted, that both these Philosophies are of the Dogmatic or Constructive sort: each in its way is a kind of Genesis; an endeavour to bring the Phenomena of man's Universe once more under some theoretic Scheme: in both there is a decided principle of unity; they strive after a result which shall be positive; their aim is not to question, but to establish. This, especially if we consider with what comprehensive concentrated force it is here exhibited, forms a new feature in such works.

Under all other aspects, there is the most irreconcilable opposition; a staring contrariety, such as might provoke contrasts, were there far fewer points of comparison. If Schlegel's Work is the apotheosis of Spiritualism; Hope's again is the apotheosis of Materialism: in the one, all Matter is evaporated into a Phenomenon, and terrestrial Life itself, with its whole doings and showings, held out as a Disturbance (*Zerrüttung*)

---

[28] Schlegel's *Philosophic Lectures* is one of the volumes under review in this essay.
[29] Jean Paul's Hesperus (Vorrede). [Carlyle's note]

produced by the *Zeitgeist* (Spirit of Time); in the other, Matter is distilled and sublimated into some semblance of Divinity: the one regards Space and Time as mere forms of man's mind, and without external existence or reality; the other supposes Space and Time to be 'incessantly created,' and rayed-in upon us like a sort of 'gravitation.' Such is their difference in respect of purport: no less striking is it in respect of manner, talent, success and all outward characteristics. Thus, if in Schlegel we have to admire the power of Words, in Hope we stand astonished, it might almost be said, at the want of an articulate Language. To Schlegel his Philosophic Speech is obedient, dextrous, exact, like a promptly ministering genius; his names are so clear, so precise and vivid, that they almost (sometimes altogether) become things for him: with Hope there is no Philosophical Speech; but a painful, confused stammering, and struggling after such; or the tongue, as in doatish forgetfulness, maunders, low, long-winded, and speaks not the word intended, but another; so that here the scarcely intelligible, in these endless convolutions, becomes the wholly unreadable; and often we could ask, as that mad pupil did of his tutor in Philosophy, "But whether is Virtue a fluid, then, or a gas?" If the fact, that Schlegel, in the city of Dresden, could find audience for such high discourse, may excite our envy; this other fact, that a person of strong powers, skilled in English Thought and master of its Dialect, could write the *Origin and Prospects of Man*, may painfully remind us of the reproach, that England has now no language for Meditation; that England, the most calculative, is the least meditative, of all civilised countries.

It is not our purpose to offer any criticism of Schlegel's Book; in such limits as were possible here, we should despair of communicating even the faintest image of its significance. To the mass of readers, indeed, both among the Germans themselves, and still more elsewhere, it nowise addresses itself, and may lie forever sealed. We point it out as a remarkable document of the Time and of the Man; can recommend it, moreover, to all earnest Thinkers, as a work deserving their best regard; a work full of deep meditation, wherein the infinite mystery of Life, if not represented, is decisively recognised. Of Schlegel himself, and his character, and spiritual history, we can profess no thorough or final understanding; yet enough to make us view him with admiration and pity, nowise with harsh contemptuous censure; and must say, with clearest

persuasion, that the outcry of his being 'a renegade,' and so forth, is but like other such outcries, a judgment where there was neither jury, nor evidence, nor judge. The candid reader, in this Book itself, to say nothing of all the rest, will find traces of a high, far-seeing, earnest spirit, to whom 'Austrian Pensions,' and the Kaiser's crown, and Austria altogether, were but a light matter to the finding and vitally appropriating of Truth. Let us respect the sacred mystery of a Person; rush not irreverently into man's Holy of Holies! Were the lost little one, as we said already, found 'sucking its dead mother, on the field of carnage,' could it be other than a spectacle for tears? A solemn mournful feeling comes over us when we see this last Work of Friedrich Schlegel, the unwearied seeker, end abruptly in the middle; and, as if he *had not* yet found, as if emblematically of much, end with an '*Aber*—,' with a 'But—'! This was the last word that came from the Pen of Friedrich Schlegel: about eleven at night he wrote it down, and there paused sick; at one in the morning, Time for him had merged itself in Eternity; he was, as we say, no more.

Still less can we attempt any criticism of Mr. Hope's new Book of Genesis. Indeed, under any circumstances, criticism of it were now impossible. Such an utterance could only be responded to in peals of laughter; and laughter sounds hollow and hideous through the vaults of the dead. Of this monstrous Anomaly, where all sciences are heaped and huddled together, and the principles of all are, with a childlike innocence, plied hither and thither, or wholly abolished in case of need; where the First Cause is figured as a huge Circle, with nothing to do but radiate 'gravitation' towards its centre; and so construct a Universe, wherein all, from the lowest cucumber with its coolness, up to the highest seraph with his love, were but 'gravitation,' direct or reflex, 'in more or less central globes,'—what can we say, except, with sorrow and shame, that it could have originated nowhere save in England? It is a general agglomerate of all facts, notions, whims and observations, as they lie in the brain of an English gentleman; as an English gentleman, of unusual thinking power, is led to fashion them, in his schools and in his world: all these thrown into the crucible, and if not fused, yet soldered or conglutinated with boundless patience; and now tumbled out here, heterogeneous, amorphous, unspeakable, a world's wonder. Most melancholy must we name the whole business; full of long-continued thought, earnestness, loftiness of mind; not without glances into the Deepest, a constant fearless endeavour after truth; and with all this nothing accomplished, but the perhaps absurdest Book written in our century by a thinking man. A shameful Abortion; which, however, need not now be smothered or mangled, for it is already dead; only, in our love and sorrowing reverence for the writer of *Anastasius*,[30] and the heroic seeker of Light, though not bringer thereof, let it be buried and forgotten.

For ourselves, the loud discord which jars in these two Works, in innumerable works of the like import, and generally in all the Thought and Action of this period, does not any longer utterly confuse us. Unhappy who, in such a time, felt not, at all conjunctures, ineradicably in his heart the knowledge that a God made this Universe, and a Demon not! And shall Evil always prosper, then? Out of all Evil comes Good? and no Good that is possible but shall one day be real. Deep and sad as is our feeling that we stand yet in the bodeful Night; equally deep, indestructible is our assurance that the Morning also will not fail. Nay, already, as we look round, streaks of a dayspring are in the east; it is dawning; when the time shall be fulfilled, it will be day. The progress of man towards higher and nobler developments of whatever is highest and noblest in him, lies not only prophesied to Faith, but now written to the eye of Observation, so that he who runs may read.

One great step of progress, for example, we should say, in actual circumstances, was this same; the clear ascertainment that we are in progress. About the grand Course of Providence, and his final Purposes with us, we can know nothing, or almost nothing: man begins in darkness, ends in darkness; mystery is everywhere around us and in us, under our feet, among our hands. Nevertheless so much has become evident to every one, that this wondrous Mankind is advancing somewhither; that at least all human things are, have been and forever will be, in Movement and Change;—as, indeed, for beings that exist in Time, by virtue of Time, and are made of Time, might have been long since understood. In some provinces, it is true, as in Experimental Science, this discovery is an old one; but in most others it belongs wholly to these latter days. How often, in former ages, by eternal Creeds, eternal Forms

of Government and the like, has it been attempted, fiercely enough, and with destructive violence, to chain the Future under the Past; and say to the Providence, whose ways with man are mysterious, and through the great deep: Hitherto shalt thou come, but no farther! A wholly insane attempt; and for man himself, could it prosper, the frightfulest of all enchantments, a very Life-in-Death. Man's task here below, the destiny of every individual man, is to be in turns Apprentice and Workman; or say rather, Scholar, Teacher, Discoverer: by nature he has a strength for learning, for imitating; but also a strength for acting, for knowing on his own account. Are we not in a world seen to be Infinite; the relations lying closest together modified by those latest discovered and lying farthest asunder? Could you ever spell-bind man into a Scholar merely, so that he had nothing to discover, to correct; could you ever establish a Theory of the Universe that were entire, unimprovable, and which needed only to be got by heart; man then were spiritually defunct, the Species we now name Man had ceased to exist. But the gods, kinder to us than we are to ourselves, have forbidden such suicidal acts. As Phlogiston is displaced by Oxygen, and the Epicycles of Ptolemy by the Ellipses of Kepler;[31] so does Paganism give place to Catholicism, Tyranny to Monarchy, and Feudalism to Representative Government,— where also the process does not stop. Perfection of Practice, like completeness of Opinion, is always approaching, never arrived: Truth, in the words of Schiller, *immer wird, nie ist*; never *is*, always *is a-being*.

Sad, truly, were our condition did we know but this, that Change is universal and inevitable. Launched into a dark shoreless sea of Pyrrhonism, what would remain for us but to sail aimless, hopeless; or make madly merry, while the devouring Death had not yet ingulfed us? As indeed, we have seen many, and still see many do. Nevertheless so stands it not. The venerator of the Past (and to what pure heart is the Past, in that 'moonlight of memory,' other than sad and holy?) sorrows not over its departure, as one utterly bereaved. The true Past departs not, nothing that was worthy in the Past departs; no Truth or Goodness realised by man ever dies, or can die; but is all still here, and, recognised or not, lives

---

[30] A popular novel by Thomas Hope.
[31] Phlogiston was regarded as the fire principle in earlier chemistry; epicycles in Ptolemaic astronomy accounted for the individual motion of planets; they were displaced by elliptical orbits described by Kepler's astronomy.

and works through endless changes. If all things, to speak in the German dialect, are discerned by us, and exist for us, in an element of Time, and therefore of Mortality and Mutability; yet Time itself reposes on Eternity: the truly Great and Transcendental has its basis and substance in Eternity; stand revealed to us as Eternity in a vesture of Time. Thus in all Poetry, Worship, Art, Society, as one form passes into another, nothing is lost: it is but the superficial, as it were the *body* only, that grows obsolete and dies; under the mortal body lies a *soul* which is immortal; which anew incarnates itself in fairer revelation; and the Present is the living sum-total of the whole Past.

In Change, therefore, there is nothing terrible, nothing supernatural: on the contrary, it lies in the very essence of our lot and life in this world. Today is not yesterday: we ourselves change; how can our Works and Thoughts, if they are always to be the fittest, continue always the same? Change, indeed, is painful; yet ever needful; and if Memory have its force and worth, so also has Hope. Nay, if we look well to it, what is all Derangement, and necessity of great Change, in itself such an evil, but the product simply of *increased resources* which the old *methods* can no longer administer; of new wealth which the old coffers will no longer contain? What is it, for example, that in our own day bursts asunder the bonds of ancient Political Systems, and perplexes all Europe with the fear of Change, but even this: the increase of social resources, which the old social methods will no longer sufficiently administer? The new omnipotence of the Steam-engine is hewing asunder quite other mountains than the physical. Have not our economical distresses, those barnyard Conflagrations themselves, the frightfulest madness of our mad epoch, their rise also in what is a real increase: increase of Men; of human Force; properly, in such a Planet as ours, the most precious of all increases? It is true again, the ancient methods of administration will no longer suffice. Must the indomitable millions, full of old Saxon energy and fire, lie cooped-up in this Western Nook, choking one another, as in a Blackhole of Calcutta, while a whole fertile untenanted Earth, desolate for want of the ploughshare, cries: Come and till me, come and reap me? If the ancient Captains can no longer yield guidance, new must be sought after: for the difficulty lies not in nature, but in artifice; the European Calcutta-Blackhole has no walls but air ones and paper ones.—So too,

Scepticism itself, with its innumerable mischiefs, what is it but the sour fruit of a most blessed increase, that of Knowledge; a fruit too that will not always continue *sour*?

In fact, much as we have said and mourned about the unproductive prevalence of Metaphysics, it was not without some insight into the use that lies in them. Metaphysical Speculation, if a necessary evil, is the forerunner of much good. The fever of Scepticism must needs burn itself out, and burn out thereby the Impurities that caused it; then again will there be clearness, health. The principle of life, which now struggles painfully, in the outer, thin and barren domain of the Conscious or Mechanical, may then withdraw into its inner sanctuaries, its abysses of mystery and miracle; withdraw deeper than ever into that domain of the Unconscious, by nature infinite and inexhaustible; and creatively work there. From that mystic region, and from that alone, all wonders, all Poesies, and Religions, and Social Systems have proceeded: the like wonders, and greater and higher, lie slumbering there; and, brooded on by the spirit of the waters, will evolve themselves, and rise like exhalations from the Deep.

Of our Modern Metaphysics, accordingly, may not this already be said, that if they have produced no Affirmation, they have destroyed much Negation? It is a disease expelling a disease: the fire of Doubt, as above hinted, consuming away the Doubtful; that so the Certain come to light, and again lie visible on the surface. English or French Metaphysics, in reference to this last stage of the speculative process, are not what we allude to here; but only the Metaphysics of the Germans. In France or England, since the days of Diderot and Hume, though all thought has been of a sceptico-metaphysical texture, so far as there was any Thought, we have seen no Metaphysics; but only more or less ineffectual questionings whether such could be. In the Pyrrhonism of Hume and the Materialism of Diderot, Logic had, as it were, overshot itself, overset itself. Now, though the athlete, to use our old figure, cannot, by much lifting, lift up his own body, he may shift it out of a laming posture, and get to stand in a free one. Such a service have German Metaphysics done for man's mind. The second sickness of Speculation has abolished both itself and the first. Friedrich Schlegel complains much of the fruitlessness, the tumult and transiency of German as of all Metaphysics; and with reason. Yet in that wide-spreading, deep-whirling vortex of Kantism, so soon metamorphosed into Fichte-ism, Schellingism, and then as Hegelism, and Cousinism,[32] perhaps finally evaporated, is not this issue visible enough, That Pyrrhonism and Materialism, themselves necessary phenomena in European culture, have disappeared; and a Faith in Religion has again become possible and inevitable for the scientific mind; and the word *Free*-thinker no longer means the Denier or Caviller, but the Believer, or the Ready to believe? Nay, in the higher Literature of Germany, there already lies, for him that can read it, the beginning of a new revelation of the Godlike; as yet unrecognised by the mass of the world; but waiting there for recognition, and sure to find it when the fit hour comes. This age also is not wholly without its Prophets.

Again, under another aspect, if Utilitarianism, or Radicalism, or the Mechanical Philosophy, or by whatever name it is called, has still its long task to do; nevertheless we can now see through it and beyond it: in the better heads, even among us English, it has become obsolete; as in other countries, it has been, in such heads, for some forty or even fifty years. What sound mind among the French, for example, now fancies that men can be governed by 'Constitutions'; by the never so cunning mechanising of Self-interests, and all conceivable adjustments of checking and balancing; in a word, by the best possible solution of this quite insoluble and impossible problem, *Given a world of Knaves, to produce an Honesty from their united action?* Were not experiments enough of this kind tried before all Europe, and found wanting, when, in that doomsday of France, the infinite gulf of human Passion shivered asunder the thin rinds of Habit; and burst forth all-devouring, as in seas of Nether Fire? Which cunningly-devised 'Constitution,' constitutional, republican, democratic, sansculottic, could bind that raging chasm together? Were they not all burnt up, like paper as they were, in its molten eddies; and still the fire-sea raged fiercer than before? It is not by Mechanism, but by Religion; not by Self-interest, but by Loyalty, that men are governed or governable.

Remarkable it is, truly, how everywhere the eternal fact begins again to be recognised, that there is a Godlike in human affairs; that God not only made us and beholds us, but is in us and around us; that the Age of Miracles, as it ever was, now is. Such recognition we discern on all hands and in all countries: in each country after its own fashion. In France, among the younger nobler minds, strangely enough; where, in their loud contention with the Actual and Conscious, the Ideal or Unconscious is, for the time, without exponent; where Religion means not the parent of Polity, as of all that is highest, but Polity itself; and this and the other earnest man has not been wanting, who could audibly whisper to himself: "Go to, I will make a religion." In England still more strangely; as in all things, worthy England will have its way: by the shrieking of hysterical women, casting out of devils, and other 'gifts of the Holy Ghost.' Well might Jean Paul say, in this his twelfth hour of the Night, 'the living dream'; well might he say, 'the dead walk.'[33] Meanwhile let us rejoice rather that so much has been seen into, were it through never so diffracting media, and never so madly distorted; that in all dialects, though but half-articulately, this high Gospel begins to be preached: Man is still Man. The genius of Mechanism, as was once before predicted, will not always sit like a choking incubus on our soul; but at length, when by a new magic Word the old spell is broken, become our slave, and as familiar-spirit do all our bidding. 'We are near awakening when we dream that we dream.'[34]

He that has an eye and a heart can even now say: Why should I falter? Light has come into the world; to such as love Light, so as Light must be loved, with a boundless all-doing, all-enduring love. For the rest, let that vain struggle to read the mystery of the Infinite cease to harass us. It is a mystery which, through all ages, we shall only read here a line of, there another line of. Do we not already know that the name of the Infinite is GOOD, is GOD? Here on Earth we are Soldiers, fighting in a foreign land; that understand not the plan of the campaign, and have no need to understand it; seeing well what is at our hand to be done. Let us do it like Soldiers; with submission, with courage, with a heroic joy. 'Whatsoever thy hand findeth to do, do it

---

[32] References to the idealistic philosophic systems of Immanuel Kant (1724–1804), Johann Gottlieb Fichte (1762–1814), Friedrich von Schelling (1775–1854), Georg Wilhelm Friedrich Hegel (1770–1831), and Victor Cousin (1792–1867).
[33] Jean Paul, *Hesperus.*
[34] Novalis, *Fragmente.*

with all thy might.'[35] Behind us, behind each one of us, lie Six Thousand Years of human effort, human conquest: before us is the boundless Time, with its as yet uncreated and unconquered Continents and Eldorados, which we, even we, have to conquer, to create; and from the bosom of Eternity there shine for us celestial guiding stars.

'My inheritance how wide and fair!
Time is my fair seed-field, of Time I'm heir.'[36]

Biography

As a writer of history Carlyle has been identified with his dictum that history is the biography of great men. He demonstrated this in practice by writing many and lengthy biographies as well as by giving prominence to the biographical in his histories. The beginnings of Carlyle's theories of the relationship between biography and history can be seen in this essay, which was the first of two he wrote in response to the appearance of a new edition, by John Wilson Croker, of Boswell's Life of Johnson in 1831. The essay first appeared in the April issue of Fraser's in 1832.

MAN'S SOCIALITY of nature evinces itself, in spite of all that can be said, with abundant evidence by this one fact, were there no other: the unspeakable delight he takes in Biography. It is written, 'The proper study of mankind is man';[1] to which study, let us candidly admit, he, by true or by false methods, applies himself, nothing loath. 'Man is perennially interesting to man; nay, if we look strictly to it, there is nothing else interesting.' How inexpressibly comfortable to know our fellow-creature; to see into him, understand his goings-forth, decipher the whole heart of his mystery: nay, not only to see into him, but even to see out of him, to view the world altogether as he views it; so that we can theoretically construe him, and could almost practically personate him; and do now thoroughly discern both what manner of man he is, and what manner of thing he has got to work on and live on!

A scientific interest and a poetic one alike inspire us in this matter. A scientific: because every mortal has a Problem of Existence set before him, which, were it only, what for the most it is, the Problem of keeping soul and body together, must be to a certain extent *original*, unlike every other; and yet, at the same time, so *like* every other; like our own, therefore; instructive, moreover, since we also are indentured to *live*. A poetic interest still more: for precisely this same struggle of human Freewill against material

Necessity, which every man's Life, by the mere circumstance that the man continues alive, will more or less victoriously exhibit,—is that which above all else, or rather inclusive of all else, calls the Sympathy of mortal hearts into action; and whether as acted, or as represented and written of, not only is Poetry, but is the sole Poetry possible. Borne onwards by which two all-embracing interests, may the earnest Lover of Biography expand himself on all sides, and indefinitely enrich himself. Looking with the eyes of every new neighbour, he can discern a new world different for each: feeling with the heart of every neighbour, he lives with every neighbour's life, even as with his own. Of these millions of living men, each individual is a mirror to us; a mirror both scientific and poetic; or, if you will, both natural and magical;—from which one would so gladly draw aside the gauze veil; and, peering therein, discern the image of his own natural face, and the supernatural secrets that pro-phetically lie under the same!

Observe, accordingly, to what extent, in the actual course of things, this business of Biography is practised and relished. Define to thyself, judicious Reader, the real significance of these phenomena, named Gossip, Egoism, Personal Narrative (miraculous or not), Scandal, Raillery, Slander, and suchlike; the sum-total of which (with some fractional addition of a better

[35] Ecclesiastes 9:10.   [36] Goethe, *Wilhelm Meisters Wanderjahre.*
[1] Pope, *Essay on Man*, II, 2.

ingredient, generally too small to be noticeable) constitutes that other grand phenomenon still called 'Conversation.' Do they not mean wholly: *Biography* and *Autobiography*? Not only in the common Speech of men; but in all Art too, which is or should be the concentrated and conserved essence of what men can speak and show, Biography is almost the one thing needful.

Even in the highest works of Art, our interest, as the critics complain, is too apt to be strongly or even mainly of a Biographic sort. In the Art we can nowise forget the Artist: while looking on the *Transfiguration*, while studying the *Iliad*, we ever strive to figure to ourselves what spirit dwelt in Raphael; what a head was that of Homer, wherein, woven of Elysian light and Tartarean gloom, that old world fashioned itself together, of which these written Greek characters are but a feeble though perennial copy. The Painter and the Singer are present to us; we partially and for the time become the very Painter and the very Singer, while we enjoy the Picture and the Song. Perhaps too, let the critic say what he will, this is the highest enjoyment, the clearest recognition, we can have of these. Art indeed is Art, yet Man also is Man. Had the *Transfiguration* been painted without human hand; had it grown merely on the canvas, say by atmospheric influences, as lichen-pictures do on rocks,—it were a grand Picture doubtless; yet nothing like so grand as *the* Picture, which, on opening our eyes, we everywhere in Heaven and on Earth see painted; and everywhere pass over with indifference,— because the Painter was not a Man. Think of this; much lies in it. The Vatican is great; yet poor to Chimborazo or the Peak of Teneriffe: its dome is but a foolish Big-endian or Little-endian chip of an egg-shell,[2] compared with that star-fretted Dome where Arcturus and Orion glance forever; which latter, notwithstanding, who looks at, save perhaps some necessitous star-gazer bent to make Almanacs; some thick-quilted watchman, to see what weather it will prove? The Biographic interest is wanting: no Michael Angelo was He who built that 'Temple of Immensity'; therefore do we, pitiful Littlenesses as we are, turn rather to wonder and to worship in the little toybox of a Temple built by our like.

Still more decisively, still more exclusively does the Biographic interest manifest itself, as we descend into lower regions of spiritual communication; through the whole range of what is called Literature. Of History, for example, the most honoured, if not honourable species of composition, is not the whole purport Biographic? 'History,' it has been said, 'is the essence of innumerable Biographies.'[3] Such, at least, it should be: whether it is, might admit of question. But, in any case, what hope have we in turning over those old interminable Chronicles, with their garrulities and insipidities; or still worse, in patiently examining those modern Narrations, of the Philosophic kind, where 'Philosophy, teaching by Experience,' has to sit like owl on house-top, *seeing* nothing, *understanding* nothing, uttering only, with such solemnity, her perpetual most wearisome *hoo-hoo*:—what hope have we, except the for most part fallacious one of gaining some acquaintance with our fellow-creatures, though dead and vanished, yet dear to us; how they got along in those old days, suffering and doing; to what extent, and under what circumstances, they resisted the Devil and triumphed over him, or struck their colours to him, and were trodden under foot by him; how, in short, the perennial Battle went, which men name Life, which we also in these new days, with indifferent fortune, have to fight, and must bequeath to our sons and grandsons to go on fighting,—till the Enemy one day be quite vanquished and abolished, or else the great Night sink and part the combatants; and thus, either by some Millennium or some new Noah's Deluge, the Volume of Universal History wind itself up! Other hope, in studying such Books, we have none: and that it is a deceitful hope, who that has tried knows not? A feast of widest Biographic insight is spread for us; we enter full of hungry anticipations: alas, like so many other feasts, which Life invites us to, a mere Ossian's[4] 'feast of *shells*,'—the food and liquor being all emptied out and clean gone, and only the vacant dishes and deceitful emblems thereof left! Your modern Historical Restaurateurs are indeed little better than high-priests of Famine; that keep choicest china dinner-sets, only no dinner to serve therein. Yet such is our Biographic appetite, we run trying from shop to shop, with ever new hope; and, unless we could eat the wind, with ever new disappointment.

Again, consider the whole class of Fictitious Narratives; from the highest category of epic or dramatic Poetry, in Shakspeare and Homer, down to the lowest of froth Prose in the Fashionable Novel. What are all these but so many

---

[2] See Swift, *Gulliver's Travels*.   [3] By Carlyle himself; see "On History" in this volume.
[4] James Macpherson, *Ossian* (1762).

mimic Biographies? Attempts, here by an inspired Speaker, there by an uninspired Babbler, to deliver himself, more or less ineffectually, of the grand secret wherewith all hearts labour oppressed: The significance of Man's Life;—which deliverance, even as traced in the unfurnished head, and printed at the Minerva Press,[5] finds readers. For, observe, though there is *a* greatest Fool, as a superlative in every kind; and *the* most Foolish man in the Earth is now indubitably living and breathing, and did this morning or lately eat breakfast, and is even now digesting the same; and looks out on the world with his dim horn-eyes, and inwardly forms some unspeakable theory thereof: yet where shall the authentically Existing be personally met with! Can one of us, otherwise than by guess, know that we have got sight of him, have orally communed with him? To take even the narrower sphere of this our English Metropolis, can any one confidently say to himself, that he has conversed with the identical, individual Stupidest man now extant in London? No one. Deep as we dive in the Profound, there is ever a new depth opens: where the ultimate bottom may lie, through what new scenes of being we must pass before reaching it (except that we know it does lie somewhere, and might by human faculty and opportunity be reached), is altogether a mystery to us. Strange, tantalising pursuit! We have the fullest assurance, not only that there is a Stupidest of London men actually resident, with bed and board of some kind, in London; but that several persons have been or perhaps are now speaking face to face with him: while for us, chase it as we may, such scientific blessedness will too probably be forever denied!—But the thing we meant to enforce was this comfortable fact, that no known Head was so wooden, but there might be other heads to which it were a genius and Friar Bacon's Oracle.[6] Of no given Book, not even of a Fashionable Novel, can you predicate with certainty that its vacuity is absolute; that there are not other vacuities which shall partially replenish themselves therefrom, and esteem it a *plenum*. How knowest thou, may the distressed Novelwright exclaim, that I, here where I sit, am the Foolishest of existing mortals; that this my Long-ear of a Fictious Biography shall not find one and the other, into whose still longer ears

it may be the means, under Providence, of instilling somewhat? We answer, None knows, none can certainly know: therefore, write on, worthy Brother, even as thou canst, even as it has been given thee.

Here, however, in regard to 'Fictitious Biographies,' and much other matter of like sort, which the greener mind in these days inditeth, we may as well insert some singular sentences on the importance and significance of *Reality*, as they stand written for us in Professor Gottfried Sauerteig's *Æsthetische Springwurzeln*;[7] a Work, perhaps, as yet new to most English readers. The Professor and Doctor is not a man whom we can praise without reservation; neither shall we say that his *Springwurzeln* (a sort of magical picklocks, as he affectedly names them) are adequate to '*start*' every *bolt* that locks-up an æsthetic mystery: nevertheless, in his crabbed, one-sided way, he sometimes hits masses of the truth. We endeavour to translate faithfully, and trust the reader will find it worth serious perusal:

'The significance, even for poetic purposes,' says Sauerteig, 'that lies in REALITY is too apt to escape us; is perhaps only now beginning to be discerned. When we named *Rousseau's Confessions*[8] an elegiaco-didactic Poem, we meant more than an empty figure of speech; we meant a historical scientific fact.

'Fiction, while the feigner of it knows that he is feigning, partakes, more than we suspect, of the nature of *lying*; and has ever an, in some degree, unsatisfactory character. All Mythologies were once Philosophies; were *believed*: the Epic Poems of old time, so long as they continued *epic*, and had any complete impressiveness, were Histories, and understood to be narratives of *facts*. In so far as Homer employed his gods as mere ornamental fringes, and had not himself, or at least did not expect this hearers to have, a belief that they were real agents in those antique doings; so far did he fail to be *genuine*; so far was he a partially *hollow* and false singer; and sang to please only a portion of man's mind, not the whole thereof.

'Imagination is, after all, but a poor matter when it has to part company with Understanding, and even front it hostilely in flat contradiction. Our mind is divided in twain: there is contest; wherein that which is weaker must needs come to

---

[5] London publishing house, noted for sentimental novels.
[6] See Robert Greene, *Friar Bacon and Friar Bungay* (1594).
[7] Gottfried Sauerteig (Sourdough) and his *Aesthetische Srpingwurzeln* (Aesthetic mandrakes) are Carlyle creations.
[8] The posthumously published *Confessions* of Jean Jacques Rousseau (1712–78).

the worse. Now of all feelings, states, principles, call it what you will, in man's mind, is not Belief the clearest, strongest; against which all others contend in vain? Belief is, indeed, the beginning and first condition of all spiritual Force whatsoever: only in so far as Imagination, were it but momentarily, is *believed*, can there be any use or meaning in it, any enjoyment of it? And what is momentary Belief? The enjoyment of a moment. Whereas a perennial Belief were enjoyment perennially, and with the whole united soul.

'It is thus that I judge of the Supernatural in an Epic Poem; and would say, the instant it has ceased to be authentically supernatural, and become what you call "Machinery": sweep it out of sight (*schaff' es mir vom Halse*)! Of a truth, that same "Machinery," about which the critics make such hubbub, was well named *Machinery*; for it is in very deed mechanical, nowise inspired or poetical. Neither for us is there the smallest æsthetic enjoyment in it; save only in this way; that we believe it *to have been believed*,—by the Singer or his Hearers; into whose case we now laboriously struggle to transport ourselves; and so, with stinted enough result, catch some reflex of the Reality, which for them was wholly real, and visible face to face. Whenever it has come so far that your "Machinery" is avowedly mechanical and unbelieved,—what is it else, if we dare tell ourselves the truth, but a miserable, meaningless Deception, kept-up by old use-and-wont alone? If the gods of an *Iliad* are to us no longer authentic Shapes of Terror, heart-stirring, heart appalling, but only vague-glittering Shadows,—what must the dead Pagan gods of an *Epigoniad* be, the dead-living Pagan-Christian gods of a *Lusiad*,[9] the concrete-abstract, evangelical-metaphysical gods of a *Paradise Lost*? Superannuated lumber! Cast raiment, at best; in which some poor mime, strutting and swaggering, may or may not set forth new noble Human Feelings (again a Reality), and so secure, or not secure, our pardon of such hoydenish masking; for which, in any case, he has a pardon to *ask*.

'True enough, none but the earliest Epic Poems can claim this distinction of entire credibility, of Reality: after an *Iliad*, a *Shaster*,[10] a *Koran*, and other the like primitive performances, the rest seem, by this rule of mine, to be altogether excluded from the list. Accordingly, what *are* all

the rest, from Virgil's *Æneid* downwards, in comparison? Frosty, artificial, heterogeneous things; more of gumflowers than of roses; at the best, of the two mixed incoherently together: to some of which, indeed, it were hard to deny the title of Poems; yet to no one of which can that title belong in any sense even resembling the old high one it, in those old days, conveyed,—when the epithet "divine" or "sacred" as applied to the uttered Word of man, was not a vain metaphor, a vain sound, but a real name with meaning. Thus, too, the farther we recede from those early days, when Poetry, as true Poetry is always, was still sacred or divine, and inspired (what ours, in great part, only pretends to be),—the more impossible becomes it to produce any, we say not true Poetry, but tolerable semblance of such; the hollower, in particular, grow all manner of Epics; till at length, as in this generation, the very name of Epic sets men a-yawning, the announcement of a new Epic is received as a public calamity.

'But what if the *impossible* being once for all quite discarded, the *probable* be well adhered to: how stands it with fiction *then*? Why, then, I would say, the evil is much mended, but nowise completely cured. We have then, in place of the wholly dead modern Epic, the partially living modern Novel; to which latter it is much easier to lend that above mentioned, so essential "momentary credence" than to the former: indeed, infinitely easier; for the former being flatly incredible, no mortal *can* for a moment credit it, for a moment enjoy it. Thus, here and there, a *Tom Jones*, a *Meister*, a *Crusoe*, will yield no little solacement to the minds of men; though still immeasurably less than a *Reality* would, were the significance thereof as impressively unfolded, were the genius that could so unfold it once given us by the kind Heavens. Neither say thou that proper Realities are wanting: for Man's Life, now, as of old, is the genuine work of God; wherever there is a Man, a God also is revealed, and all that is Godlike: a whole epitome of the Infinite, with its meanings, lies enfolded in the Life of every Man. Only, alas, that the Seer to discern this same Godlike, and with fit utterance *unfold* it for us, is wanting, and may long be wanting!

'Nay, a question arises on us here, wherein the whole German reading-world will eagerly join:

---

[9] *Epigoniad*, Carlyle's coinage for a work that would treat the Epigoni, i.e., the Seven against Thebes; *The Lusiads*, Portuguese epic poem by Camoëns (1524–80).
[10] Hindu religious book.

Whether man *can* any longer be so interested by the spoken Word, as he often was in those primeval days, when rapt away by its inscrutable power, he pronounced it, in such dialect as he had, to be *transcendental* (to *transcend* all measure), to be sacred, prophetic and the inspiration of a god? For myself, I (*ich meines Ortes*), by faith or by insight, do heartily understand that the answer to such question will be, Yea! For never that I could in searching find out, has Man been, by Time which devours so much, deprivated of any faculty whatsoever that he in any era was possessed of. To my seeming, the babe born yesterday has all the organs of Body, Soul and Spirit, and in exactly the same combination and entireness, that the oldest Pelasgic Greek, or Mesopotamian Patriarch, or Father Adam himself could boast of. Ten fingers, one heart with venous and arterial blood therein, still belong to man that is born of woman: when did he lose any of his spiritual Endowments either; above all, his highest spiritual Endowment, that of revealing Poetic Beauty, and of adequately receiving the same? Not the material, not the susceptibility is wanting; only the Poet, or long series of Poets, to work on these. True, alas too true, the Poet *is* still utterly wanting, or all but utterly: nevertheless have we not centuries enough before us to produce him in? Him and much else!—I, for the present, will but predict that chiefly by working more and more on REALITY, and evolving more and more wisely *its* inexhaustible meanings; and, in brief, speaking forth in fit utterance whatsoever our whole soul *believes*, and ceasing to speak forth what thing soever our whole soul does not believe, —will this high emprise be accomplished, or approximated to.'

These notable, and not unfounded, though partial and *deep*-seeing rather than *wide*-seeing observations on the great import of REALITY, considered even as a poetic material, we have inserted the more willingly, because a transient feeling to the same purpose may often have suggested itself to many readers; and, on the whole, it is good that every reader and every writer understand, with all intensity of conviction, what quite infinite worth lies in *Truth*; how all-pervading, omnipotent, in man's mind, is the thing we name *Belief*. For the rest, Herr Sauerteig, though one-sided, on this matter of Reality, seems heartily persuaded, and is not perhaps so ignorant as he looks. It cannot be unknown to him, for example, what noise is

made about 'Invention'; what a supreme rank this faculty is reckoned to hold in the poetic endowment. Great truly is Invention; nevertheless, that is but a poor exercise of it with which Belief is not concerned. 'An Irishman with whisky in his head,' as poor Byron said, will invent you, in this kind, till there is enough and to spare. Nay, perhaps, if we consider well, the highest exercise of Invention has, in very deed, nothing to do with Fiction; but is an invention of new Truth, what we can call a Revelation; which does undoubtedly transcend all other poetic efforts, nor can Herr Sauerteig be too loud in its praises. But, on the other hand, whether such effort is still possible for man, Herr Sauerteig and the bulk of the world are probably at issue;—and will probably continue so till that same 'Revelation,' or new 'Invention of Reality,' of the sort he desiderates, shall itself make its appearance.

Meanwhile, quitting these airy regions, let any one bethink him how impressive the smallest historical *fact* may become, as contrasted with the grandest *fictitious event*; what an incalculable force lies for us in this consideration: The Thing which I here hold imaged in my mind did actually occur; was, in very truth, an element in the system of the All, whereof I too form part; had therefore, and has, through all time, an authentic being; is not a dream, but a reality! We ourselves can remember reading, in *Lord Clarendon*,[11] with feelings perhaps somehow accidentally opened to it,—certainly with a depth of impression strange to us then and now,—that insignificant-looking passage, where Charles, after the battle of Worcester, glides down, with Squire Careless, from the Royal Oak, at nightfall, being hungry: how, 'making a shift to get over hedges and ditches, after walking at least eight or nine miles, which were the more grievous to the King by the weight of his boots (for he could not put *them* off when he cut off his hair, for want of shoes), before morning they came to *a poor cottage, the owner whereof, being a Roman Catholic, was known to Careless.*' How this poor drudge, being knocked-up from his snoring, 'carried them into a little barn full of hay, which was a better lodging than he had for himself'; and by and by, not without difficulty, brought his Majesty 'a piece of bread and a great pot of buttermilk,' saying candidly that "he himself lived by his daily labour, and that what he had brought him was the fare he and his

---

[11] *History of the Rebellion*, iii, 625. [Carlyle's note]

wife had": on which nourishing diet his Majesty, 'staying upon the haymow,' feeds thankfully for two days; and then departs, under new guidance, having first changed clothes, down to the very shirt and 'old pair of shoes,' with his landlord; and so, as worthy Bunyan has it, 'goes on his way, and sees him no more.' Singular enough, if we will think of it! This, then, was a genuine flesh-and-blood Rustic of the year 1651: he did actually swallow bread and buttermilk (not having ale and bacon), and do field-labour: with these hobnailed 'shoes' has sprawled through mud-roads in winter, and, jocund or not, driven his team a-field in summer: he made bargains; had chafferings and higglings, now a sore heart, now a glad one; was born; was a son, was a father; toiled in many ways, being forced to it, till the strength was all worn out of him; and then—lay down 'to rest his galled back,' and sleep there till the long-distant morning!—How comes it, that he alone of all the British rustics who tilled and lived along with him, on whom the blessed sun on that same 'fifth day of September' was shining, should have chanced to rise on us; that this poor pair of clouted Shoes, out of the million million hides that have been tanned, and cut, and worn, should still subsist, and hang visibly together? We see him but for a moment; for one moment, the blanket of the Night is rent asunder, so that we behold and see, and then closes over him—forever.

So too, in some *Boswell's Life of Johnson*, how indelible and magically bright does many a little *Reality* dwell in our remembrance! There is no need that the personages on the scene be a King and Clown; that the scene be the Forest of the Royal Oak, 'on the borders of Staffordshire'; need only that the scene lie on this old firm Earth of ours, where we also have so surprisingly arrived; that the personages be *men*, and *seen* with the eyes of a man. Foolish enough, how some slight, perhaps mean and even ugly incident, if *real* and well presented, will fix itself in a susceptive memory, and lie ennobled there; silvered over with the pale cast of thought, with the pathos which belongs only to the Dead. For the Past is all holy to us; the Dead are all holy, even they that were base and wicked while alive. Their baseness and wickedness was not *They*, was but the heavy and unmanageable Environment that lay round them, with which they fought un-prevailing: *they* (the ethereal god-given Force that dwelt in them, and was their *Self*) have now

shuffled-off that heavy Environment, and are free and pure: their life-long Battle, go how it might, is all ended, with many wounds or with fewer; they have been recalled from it, and the once harsh-jarring battle-field has become a silent awe-inspiring Golgotha, and *Gottesacker* (Field of God)!—Boswell related this in itself smallest and poorest of occurrences: 'As we walked along the Strand tonight, arm in arm, a woman of the town accosted us in the usual enticing manner. "No, no, my girl," said Johnson; "it won't do." He, however, did not treat her with harshness; and we talked of the wretched life of such women.' Strange power of *Reality*! Not even this poorest of occurrences, but now, after seventy years are come and gone, has a meaning for us. Do but consider that it is *true*; that it did in very deed occur! That unhappy Outcast, with all her sins and woes, her lawless desires, too complex mischances, her wailings and her riotings, has departed utterly; alas! her siren finery has got all besmutched, ground, generations since, into dust and smoke; of her degraded body, and whole miserable earthly esixtence, all is away: *she* is no longer here, but far from us, in the bosom of Eternity,—whence we too came, whither we too are bound! Johnson said, "No, no, my girl; it won't do"; and then 'we talked';—and herewith the wretched one, seen but for the twinkling of an eye, passes on into the utter Darkness. No high Calista,[12] that ever issued from Story-teller's brain, will impress us more deeply than this meanest of the mean; and for a good reason: That *she* issued from the Maker of Men.

It is well worth the Artist's while to examine for himself what it is that gives such pitiable incidents their memorableness; his aim likewise is, above all things, to be *memorable*. Half the effect, we already perceive, depends on the object; on its being *real*, on its being really *seen*. The other half will depend on the observer; and the question now is: How are real objects to be *so* seen; on what quality of observing, or of style in describing, does this so intense pictorial power depend? Often a slight circumstance contributes curiously to the result: some little, and perhaps to appearance accidental, feature is presented; a light-gleam, which instantaneously *excites* the mind, and urges it to complete the picture, and evolve the meaning thereof for itself. By critics, such light-gleams and their almost magical influence have frequently been noted: but the power to produce such, to select such features as will produce them,

---

[12] The heroine of Nicholas Rowe's *The Fair Penitent* (1703).

is generally treated as a knack, or trick of the trade, a secret for being 'graphic'; whereas these magical feats are, in truth, rather inspirations; and the gift of performing them, which acts unconsciously, without forethought, and as if by nature alone, is properly a *genius* for description.

One grand, invaluable secret there is, however, which includes all the rest, and, what is comfortable, lies clearly in every man's power: *To have an open loving heart, and what follows from the possession of such.* Truly, it has been said, emphatically in these days ought it to be repeated: A loving Heart is the beginning of all Knowledge. This it is that opens the whole mind, quickens every faculty of the intellect to do its fit work, that of *knowing*; and therefrom, by sure consequence, of *vividly uttering-forth*. Other secret for being 'graphic' is there none, worth having: but this is an all-sufficient one. See, for example, what a small Boswell can do! Hereby, indeed, is the whole man made a living mirror, wherein the wonders of this ever-wonderful Universe are, in their true light (which is ever a magical, miraculous one) represented, and reflected back on us. It has been said, 'the heart sees farther than the head'; but, indeed, without the seeing heart, there is no true seeing for the head so much as possible; all is mere *oversight,* hallucination and vain superficial phantasmagoria, which can permanently profit no one.

Here, too, may we not pause for an instant, and make a practical reflection? Considering the multitude of mortals that handle the Pen in these days, and can mostly spell, and write without glaring violations of grammar, the question naturally arises: How is it, then, that no Work proceeds from them, bearing any stamp of authenticity and permanence; of worth for more than one day? Ship-loads of Fashionable Novels, Sentimental Rhymes, Tragedies, Farces, Diaries of Travel, Tales by flood and field, are swallowed monthly into the bottomless Pool: still does the Press toil; innumerable Paper-makers, Compositors, Printers' Devils, Book-binders, and Hawkers grown hoarse with loud proclaiming, rest not from their labour; and still, in torrents, rushes on the great array of Publications, unpausing, to their final home; and still Oblivion, like the Grave, cries, Give! Give! How is it that of all these countless multitudes, no one can attain to the smallest mark of excellence, or produce aught that shall endure longer than

'snow-flake on the river,' or the foam of penny-beer? We answer: Because they *are* foam; because there is no *Reality* in them. These Three Thousand men, women and children, that make up the army of British Authors, do not, if we will well consider it, *see* anything whatever; consequently *have* nothing that they can record and utter, only more or fewer things that they can plausibly pretend to record. The Universe, of Man and Nature, is still quite shut-up from them; the 'open secret' still utterly a secret; because no sympathy with Man or Nature, no love and free simplicity of heart has yet unfolded the same. Nothing but a pitiful Image of their own pitiful Self, with its vanities, and grudgings, and ravenous hunger of all kinds, hangs forever painted in the retina of these unfortunate persons; so that the starry ALL, with whatsoever it embraces, does but appear as some expanded magic-lantern shadow of that same Image,—and naturally looks pitiful enough.

It is vain for these persons to allege that they are naturally without gift, naturally stupid and sightless, and so *can* attain to no knowledge of anything; therefore, in writing of anything, must needs write falsehoods of it, there being in it no truth for them. Not so, good Friends The stupidest of you has a certain faculty; were it but that of articulate speech (say, in the Scottish, the Irish, the Cockney dialect, or even in 'Governess-English'), and of physically discerning what lies under your nose. The stupidest of you would perhaps grudge to be compared in faculty with James Boswell; yet see what he has produced! You do not use your faculty honestly; your heart is shut up; full of greediness, malice, discontent; so your intellectual sense cannot be open. It is vain also to urge that James Boswell had opportunities; saw great men and great things, such as you can never hope to look on. What make ye of Parson White in Selborne?[13] He had not only no great men to look on, but not even men; merely sparrows and cockchafers: yet had he left us a *Biography* of these; which, under its title *Natural History of Selborne*, still remains valuable to us; which has copied a little sentence or two *faithfully* from the Inspired Volume of Nature, and so is itself not without inspiration. Go ye and do likewise. Sweep away utterly all frothiness and falsehood from your heart; struggle unweariedly to acquire, what is possible for every god-created Man, a free, open, humble soul: *speak not at all, in any wise, till you have somewhat to speak;*

---

[13] Gilbert White of Selbourne (1720–93), naturalist.

care not for the *reward* of your speaking, but simply and with undivided mind for the *truth* of your speaking: then be placed in what section of Space and of Time soever, do but open your eyes, and they shall actually *see*, and bring you real *knowledge*, wondrous, worthy of *belief*; and instead of one Boswell and one White, the world will rejoice in a thousand,—stationed on their thousand several watch-towers, to instruct us by indubitable documents, of whatsoever in our so stupendous World comes to light and *is*! O, had the Editor of this Magazine but a magic rod to turn all that not inconsiderable Intellect, which now deluges us with artificial fictitious soap-lather, and mere Lying, into the faithful study of Reality,—what knowledge of great, everlasting Nature, and of Man's ways and doings therein, would not every year bring us in! Can we but change one single soap-latherer and mountebank Juggler, into a true Thinker and Doer, who even *tries* honestly to think and do,—great will be our reward.

But to return; or rather from this point to begin our journey! If now, what with Herr Sauerteig's *Springwurzeln,* what with so much lucubration of our own, it have become apparent how deep, immeasurable is the 'worth that lies in *Reality,*' and farther, how exclusive the interest which man takes in Histories of Man,—may it not seem lamentable, that so few genuinely good *Biographies* have yet been accumulated in Literature; that in the whole world, one cannot find, going strictly to work, above some dozen, or baker's dozen, and those chiefly of very ancient date? Lamentable; yet, after what we have just seen, accountable. Another question might be asked: How comes it that in England we have simply one good Biography, this *Boswell's Johnson*; and of good, indifferent, or even bad attempts at Biography, fewer than any civilised people? Consider the French and Germans, with their Moreris, Bayles, Jördenses, Jöchers,[14] their innumerable *Mémoires,* and *Schilderungen,* and *Biographies Universelles*; not to speak of Rousseaus, Goethes, Schubarts, Jung-Stillings;[15] and then contrast with these our poor Birches and Kippises and Pecks;[16] the whole breed of whom, moreover, is now extinct!

With this question, as the answer might lead us far, and come out unflattering to patriotic sentiment, we shall not intermeddle; but turn rather, with great pleasure, to the fact, that one excellent Biography *is* actually English;—and even now lies, in Five new Volumes, at our hand, soliciting a new consideration from us; such as, age after age (the Perennial showing ever new phases as *our* position alters), it may long be profitable to bestow on it;— to which task we here, in this position, in this age, gladly address ourselves.

First, however, let the foolish April-fool Day pass by; and our Reader, during these twenty-nine days of uncertain weather that will follow, keep pondering, according to convenience, the purport of BIOGRAPHY in general: then, with the blessed dew of May-day, and in unlimited convenience of space, shall all that we have written on *Johnson* and *Boswell's Johnson* and *Croker's Boswell's Johnson* be faithfully laid before him.[17]

from Sartor Resartus
The Life and Opinions of Herr Teufelsdröckh

Despite its inauspicious beginning, Sartor Resartus *eventually became and has remained Carlyle's best-known work. It has also been his most challenging, packed as it is with allusion and reference and defying as it does conventional literary forms and types. It has been called a*

[14] Louis Moreri (1643–80), Pierre Bayle (1647–1706), Karl Heinrich Jördens (1757–1835), Christian Gottlieb Jöcher (1694–1758) were French and German lexicographers and biographers.

[15] Christian Friedrich Daniel Schubart (1739–91) and Johann Heinrich Jung-Stilling (1740–1817), German romantic autobiographers.

[16] Thomas Birch (1705–66), Andrew Kippis (1725–95), Francis Peck (1692–1743) were British biographers and antiquarians.

[17] Carlyle here refers to the April number of *Fraser's* in which this essay appeared and to his forthcoming essay in the May number also on Croker's edition of Boswell's *Johnson*.

novel, a satire, a romance, an extended essay, a rhetorical argument, a spiritual biography or autobiography, and, by Carlyle himself, "a Satirical Extravaganza on Things in General." It is something of all of these and something more.

The Latin title of the work expresses its leading idea—sartor resartus, meaning "the tailor retailored" or "the patcher repatched." In an earlier form the work was titled "Thoughts on Clothes," indicating again the importance of the clothes metaphor. By clothes in Sartor the reader comes to understand all the outward appearances of society and culture—clothing itself, institutions, language, symbols, customs, and beliefs. Man as a symbol-making creature is forever fashioning "clothes" to live with and by. Carlyle is here looking at those clothes, seeing which are outworn and no longer serviceable, and offering advice on how to retailor or refashion the personal and social clothes of the age.

To present his case Carlyle divides his book into three parts. In Book First an unnamed English editor endeavors to present to a British audience the character of a strange book on clothes, Die Kleider, that has come to him from Germany. In Book Second the editor offers the biography of the author of the work, one Diogenes Teufelsdröckh, as a means of better understanding the nature of Teufelsdröckh's thought in the clothes volume. Book Third presents further excerpts from Teufelsdröckh's writings as they pertain to life and society and to philosophical and social questions of permanent relevance. It includes Teufelsdröckh's wide-ranging thoughts on the profoundest questions of the meaning of life and the destiny of man. The entire work thus develops the theme expressed in its title and subtitle: it is a retailoring of the tailor through a presentation of the life and opinions of Herr Teufelsdröckh. As such it is one of the most thoughtful and provocative works of the nineteenth century.

Written at Craigenputtock in 1830–1831, Sartor Resartus was first published serially in Fraser's Magazine in 1833–34. It was published in book form in Boston in 1836, then in London in 1838. After that it went through countless editions in the age, becoming one of the all-time Victorian best-sellers.

Mein Vermächtniss, wie herrlich weit und breit!
Die Zeit ist mein Vermächtniss, mein Acker ist die Zeit.

                                                                                        GOETHE

Die Welt ist ein Universaltropus des Geistes, ein
symbolisches Bild desselben . . .   NOVALIS

Nicht blosses Wissen, sondern nach deinem Wissen
Thun ist deine Bestimmung.   FICHTE*

BOOK FIRST

CHAPTER I

Preliminary

No Philosphy of Clothes yet, notwithstanding all our Science. Strangely forgotten that Man is by nature a *naked* animal. The English mind all-too practically absorbed for any such inquiry. Not so, deep-thinking Germany. Advantage of Speculation having free course. Editor receives from Professor Teufelsdröckh his new Work on Clothes.

CONSIDERING our present advanced state of culture, and how the Torch of Science has now been brandished and borne about, with more or less effect, for five thousand years and upwards; how, in these times especially, not only the Torch still burns, and perhaps more fiercely than ever, but innumerable Rush-lights, and Sulphur-matches, kindled thereat, are also glancing in every direction, so that not the smallest cranny or doghole in Nature or Art can remain unilluminated,—it might strike the reflective mind with some surprise that hitherto little or nothing of a fundamental character, whether in the way of Philosophy or History, has been written on the subject of Clothes.

Our Theory of Gravitation is as good as perfect: Lagrange, it is well known, has proved that the Planetary System, on this scheme, will endure forever; Laplace, still more cunningly, even guesses that it could not have been made on any other scheme.[1] Whereby, at least, our nautical

---

* The three epigraphs to the work read as follows: "My inheritance how wide and fair! Time is my fair seed-field, of Time I'm heir!" [Carlyle's translation.]—Goethe. "The world is a universal trope of the spirit, a symbolic picture of it."—Novalis. "Not mere knowledge, but according to your knowledge, *Doing* is your commitment."—Fichte.

[1] Joseph Louis Lagrange (1736–1813) and Pierre Simon Laplace (1749–1827), French astronomers.

Logbooks can be better kept; and water-transport of all kinds has grown more commodious. Of Geology and Geognosy we know enough: what with the labours of our Werners and Huttons,[2] what with the ardent genius of their disciples, it has come about that now, to many a Royal Society, the Creation of a World is little more mysterious than the cooking of a dumpling; concerning which last, indeed, there have been minds to whom the question, *How the apples were got in*, presented difficulties.[3] Why mention our disquisitions on the Social Contract, on the Standard of Taste, on the Migrations of the Herring? Then, have we not a Doctrine of Rent, a Theory of Value; Philosophies of Language, of History, of Pottery, of Apparitions, of Intoxicating Liquors? Man's whole life and environment have been laid open and elucidated; scarcely a fragment or fibre of his Soul, Body, and Possessions, but has been probed, dissected, distilled, desiccated, and scientifically decomposed: our spiritual Faculties, of which it appears there are not a few, have their Stewarts, Cousins, Royer Collards:[4] every cellular, vascular, muscular Tissue glories in its Lawrences, Majendies, Bichâts.[5]

How, then, comes it, may the reflective mind repeat, that the grand Tissue of all Tissues, the only real Tissue, should have been quite overlooked by Science,—The vestural Tissue, namely, of woollen or other cloth; which Man's Soul wears as its outmost wrappage and overall; wherein his whole other Tissues are included and screened, his whole Faculties work, his whole Self lives, moves, and has its being? For if, now and then, some straggling broken-winged thinker has cast an owl's-glance into this obscure region, the most have soared over it altogether heedless; regarding Clothes as a property, not an accident, as quite natural and spontaneous, like the leaves of trees, like the plumage of birds. In all speculations they have tacitly figured man as a *Clothed Animal*; whereas he is by nature a *Naked Animal*; and only in certain circumstances, by

purpose and device, masks himself in Clothes. Shakespeare says ,we are creatures that look before and after:[6] the more surprising that we do not look round a little, and see what is passing under our very eyes.

But here, as in so many other cases, Germany, learned, indefatigable, deep-thinking Germany comes to our aid. It is, after all, a blessing that, in these revolutionary times, there should be one country where abstract Thought can still take shelter; that while the din and frenzy of Catholic Emancipations, and Rotten Boroughs, and Revolts of Paris,[7] deafen every French and every English ear, the German can stand peaceful on his scientific watch-tower; and, to the raging, struggling multitude here and elsewhere, solemnly, from hour to hour, with preparatory blast of cowhorn, emit his *Höret ihr Herren und lasset's Euch sagen;*[8] in other words, tell the Universe, which so often forgets that fact, what o'clock it really is. Not unfrequently the Germans have been blamed for an unprofitable diligence; as if they struck into devious courses, where nothing was to be had but the toil of a rough journey; as if, forsaking the gold-mines of finance and that political slaughter of fat oxen whereby a man himself grows fat, they were apt to run goose-hunting into regions of bilberries and crowberries, and be swallowed up at last in remote peat-bogs. Of that unwise science, which, as our Humorist expresses it,

'By geometric scale
Doth take the size of pots of ale;'[9]

still more, of that altogether misdirected industry, which is seen vigorously thrashing mere straw, there can nothing defensive be said. In so far as the Germans are chargeable with such, let them take the consequence. Nevertheless be it remarked, that even a Russian steppe has tumuli and gold ornaments; also many a scene that looks desert and rock-bound from the distance, will unfold itself, when visited, into rare valleys. Nay, in any

---

[2] Abraham Gottlieb Werner (1750–1817), German geologist; James Hutton (1726–97), Scottish geologist.

[3] From *The Apple Dumplings and a King* by Peter Pindar, pseudonym of John Wolcot.

[4] Dugald Stewart (1753–1828), Scottish philosopher; Victor Cousin (1792–1867) and Pierre Royer Collard (1763–1845), French antimaterialist philosophers.

[5] Sir William Laurence (1783–1807), François Magendie (1783–1855), Maria François Xavier Bichât (1771–1802), contemporary physicians and surgeons.

[6] *Hamlet*, IV, iv, 37.

[7] Catholic Emancipation in 1829 removed civil disabilities from Roman Catholics; Rotten Boroughs, electoral districts lacking population but retaining parliamentary representation; the Revolt of Paris in 1830 overthrew Charles X.

[8] "Listen ye gentlemen and let it be told you." The cry of the German night watchman.

[9] Samuel Butler, *Hudibras*, I, i, 121–122.

case, would Criticism erect not only finger-posts and turnpikes, but spiked gates and impassable barriers, for the mind of man? It is written, 'Many shall run to and fro, and knowledge shall be increased.'[10] Surely the plain rule is, Let each considerate person have his way, and see what it will lead to. For not this man and that man, but all men make up mankind, and their united tasks the task of mankind. How often have we seen some such adventurous, and perhaps much-censured wanderer light on some out-lying neglected, yet vitally momentous province; the hidden treasures of which he first discovered, and kept proclaiming till the general eye and effort were directed thither, and the conquest was completed;—thereby, in these his seemingly so aimless rambles, planting new standards, founding new habitable colonies, in the immeasurable circumambient realm of Nothingness and Night! Wise man was he who counselled that Speculation should have free course, and look fearlessly towards all the thirty-two points of the compass, whithersoever and howsoever it listed.

Perhaps it is proof of the stunted condition in which pure Science, especially pure moral Science, languishes among us English; and how our mercantile greatness, and invaluable Constitution, impressing a political or other immediately practical tendency on all English culture and endeavour, cramps the free flight of Thought,—that this, not Philosophy of Clothes, but recognition even that we have no such Philosophy, stands here for the first time published in our language. What English intellect could have chosen such a topic, or by chance stumbled on it? But for that same unshackled, and even sequestered condition of the German Learned, which permits and induces them to fish in all manner of waters, with all manner of nets, it seems probable enough, this abstruse Inquiry might, in spite of the results it leads to, have continued dormant for indefinite periods. The Editor of these sheets, though otherwise boasting himself a man of confirmed speculative habits, and perhaps discursive enough, is free to confess, that never, till these last months, did the above very plain considerations, on our total want of a Philosophy of Clothes, occur to him; and then, by quite foreign suggestion. By the arrival, namely, of a new Book from Professor Teufelsdröckh of

Weissnichtwo; treating expressly of this subject, and in a style which, whether understood or not, could not even by the blindest be overlooked. In the present Editor's way of thought, this remarkable Treatise, with its Doctrines, whether as judicially acceded to, or judicially denied, has not remained without effect.

'*Die Kleider, ihr Werden und Wirken* (Clothes, their Origin and Influence): *von Diog. Teufelsdröckh, J.U.D. etc. Stillschweigen und Cognie. Weissnichtwo,* 1831.[11]

'Here,' says the *Weissnichtwo'sche Anzeiger*,[12] 'comes a Volume of that extensive, close-printed, close-meditated sort, which, be it spoken with pride, is seen only in Germany, perhaps only in Weissnichtwo. Issuing from the hitherto irreproachable Firm of Stillschweigen and Company, with every external furtherance, it is of such internal quality as to set Neglect at defiance.' * * * * 'A work,' concludes the well-nigh enthusiastic Reviewer, 'interesting alike to the antiquary, the historian, and the philosophic thinker; a masterpiece of boldness, lynx-eyed acuteness, and rugged independent Germanism and Philanthropy (*derber Kerndeutschheit und Menschenliebe*); which will not, assuredly, pass current without opposition in high places; but must and will exalt the almost new name of Teufelsdröckh to the first ranks of Philosophy, in our German Temple of Honour.'

Mindful of old friendship, the distinguished Professor, in this the first blaze of his fame, which however does not dazzle him, sends hither a Presentation-copy of his Book; with compliments and encomiums which modesty forbids the present Editor to rehearse; yet without indicated wish or hope of any kind, except what may be implied in the concluding phrase: *Möchte es* (this remarkable Treatise) *auch im Brittischen Boden gedeihen!*[13]

CHAPTER II

Editorial Difficulties

How to make known Teufelsdröckh and his Book to English readers; especially *such* a book? Editor receives from the Hofrath Heuschrecke a letter promising Biographic Docu-

---

[10] Daniel 12:4.
[11] "By Diogenes (God-born) Teufelsdröckh (Devil's dung; also asafoetida), Doctor of Jurisprudence, etc.; Silence and Co., Know-not-where, 1831." Cf. Sir Walter Scott's Kennaquhair in *The Monastery*.
[12] "Weissnichtwo Advertiser."   [13] "May it also thrive on British soil."

ments. Negotiations with Oliver Yorke. *Sartor Resartus* conceived. Editor's assurances and advice to his British reader.

I
F FOR A speculative man, 'whose seedfield,' in the sublime words of the Poet, 'is Time,'[1] no conquest is important but that of new ideas, then might the arrival of Professor Teufelsdröckh's Book be marked with chalk in the Editor's calendar. It is indeed an 'extensive Volume,' of boundless, almost formless contents, a very Sea of Thought; neither calm nor clear, if you will; yet wherein the toughest pearl-diver may dive to his utmost depth, and return not only with sea-wreck but with true orients.

Directly on the first perusal, almost on the first deliberate inspection, it became apparent that here a quite new Branch of Philosophy, leading to as yet undescribed ulterior results, was disclosed; farther, what seemed scarcely less interesting, a quite new human Individuality, an almost unexampled personal character, that, namely, of Professor Teufelsdröckh the Discloser. Of both which novelties, as far as might be possible, we resolved to master the significance. But as man is emphatically a proselytising creature, no sooner was such mastery even fairly attempted, than the new question arose: How might this acquired good be imparted to others, perhaps in equal need thereof: how could the philosophy of Clothes, and the Author of such Philosophy, be brought home, in any measure, to the business and bosoms of our own English Nation? For if new-got gold is said to burn the pockets till it be cast forth into circulation, much more may new truth.

Here, however, difficulties occurred. The first thought naturally was to publish Article after Article on this remarkable Volume, in such widely-circulating Critical Journals as the Editor might stand connected with, or by money or love procure access to. But, on the other hand, was it not clear that such matter as must here be revealed, and treated of, might endanger the circulation of any Journal extant? If, indeed, all party-divisions in the State, could have been abolished, Whig, Tory, and Radical, embracing in discrepant union; and all the Journals of the Nation could have been jumbled into one Journal, and the Philosophy of Clothes poured forth in incessant torrent therefrom, the attempt had seemed possible. But, alas, what vehicle of that sort have we, except *Fraser's Magazine*? A vehicle all strewed (figuratively speaking) with the maddest Waterloo-Crackers, exploding distractively and destructively, wheresoever the mystified passenger stands or sits; nay, in any case, understood to be, of late years, a vehicle full to overflowing, and inexorably shut! Besides, to state the Philosophy of Clothes without the Philosopher, the ideas of Teufelsdröckh without something of his personality, was it not to insure both of entire misapprehension? Now for Biography, had it been otherwise admissible, there were no adequate documents, no hope of obtaining such, but rather owing to circumstances, a special despair. Thus did the Editor see himself, for the while, shut out from all public utterance of these extraordinary Doctrines, and constrained to revolve them, not without disquietude, in the dark depths of his own mind.

So had it lasted for some months; and now the Volume on Clothes, read and again read, was in several points becoming lucid and lucent; the personality of its Author more and more surprising, but, in spite of all that memory and conjecture could do, more and more enigmatic; whereby the old disquietude seemed fast settling into fixed discontent,—when altogether unexpectedly arrives a Letter from Herr Hofrath[2] Heuschrecke, our Professor's chief friend and associate in Weissnichtwo, with whom we had not previously corresponded. The Hofrath, after much quite extraneous matter, began dilating largely on the 'agitation and attention' which the Philosophy of Clothes was exciting in its own German Republic of Letters; on the deep significance and tendency of his Friend's Volume; and then, at length, with great circumlocution, hinted at the practicability of conveying 'some knowledge of it, and of him, to England, and through England to the distant West': a work on Professor Teufelsdröckh 'were undoubtedly welcome to the *Family*, the *National*, or any other of those patriotic *Libraries*, at present the glory of British Literature'; might work revolutions in Thought; and so forth;—in conclusion, intimating not obscurely, that should the present Editor feel disposed to undertake a Biography of Teufelsdröckh, he, Hofrath Heuschrecke, had it in his power to furnish the requisite Documents.

As in some chemical mixture, that has stood long evaporating, but would not crystallise, instantly when the wire or other fixed substance is introduced, crystallisation commences, and

---

[1] From the Goethe motto prefixed to *Sartor Resartus*.   [2] "Councillor Grasshopper."

rapidly proceeds till the whole is finished, so was it with the Editor's mind and this offer of Heuschrecke's. Form rose out of void solution and discontinuity; like united itself with like in definite arrangement: and soon either in actual vision and possession, or in fixed reasonable hope, the image of the whole Enterprise had shaped itself, so to speak, into a solid mass. Cautiously yet courageously, through the twopenny post, application to the famed redoubtable OLIVER YORKE[3] was now made: an interview, interviews with that singular man have taken place; with more of assurance on our side, with less of satire (at least of open satire) on his, than we anticipated;—for the rest, with such issue as is now visible. As to those same 'patriotic *Libraries*,' the Hofrath's counsel could only be viewed with silent amazement; but with his offer of Documents we joyfully and almost instantaneously closed. Thus, too, in the sure expectation of these, we already see our task begun; and this our *Sartor Resartus*, which is properly a 'Life and Opinions of Herr Teufelsdröckh,' hourly advancing.

Of our fitness for the Enterprise, to which we have such title and vocation, it were perhaps uninteresting to say more. Let the British reader study and enjoy, in simplicity of heart, what is here presented him, and with whatever metaphysical acumen and talent for meditation he is possessed of. Let him strive to keep a free, open sense; cleared from the mists of prejudice, above all from the paralysis of cant; and directed rather to the Book itself than to the Editor of the Book. Who or what such Editor may be, must remain conjectural, and even insignificant:[4] it is a voice publishing tidings of the Philosophy of Clothes; undoubtedly a Spirit addressing Spirits: whoso hath ears, let him hear.

On one other point the Editor thinks it needful to give warning: namely, that he is animated with a true though perhaps a feeble attachment to the Institutions of our Ancestors; and minded to defend these, according to ability, at all hazards; nay, it was partly with a view to such defence that he engaged in this undertaking. To stem, or if that be impossible, profitably to divert the current of Innovation, such a Volume as Teufelsdröckh's if cunningly planted down, were no despicable pile, or floodgate, in the logical wear.

For the rest, be it nowise apprehended, that any personal connexion of ours with Teufelsdröckh, Heuschrecke, or this Philosophy of Clothes, can pervert our judgment, or sway us to extenuate or exaggerate. Powerless, we venture to promise, are those private Compliments themselves. Grateful they may well be; as generous illusions of friendship; as fair mementos of bygone unions, of those nights and suppers of the gods,[5] when, lapped in the symphonies and harmonies of Philosophic Eloquence, though with baser accompaniments, the present Editor revelled in that feast of reason, never since vouchsafed him in so full measure! But what then? *Amicus Plato, magis amica veritas*;[6] Teufelsdröckh is our friend, Truth is our divinity. In our historical and critical capacity, we hope we are strangers to all the world; have feud or favour with no one,—save indeed the Devil, with whom, as with the Prince of Lies and Darkness, we do at all times wage internecine war. This assurance, at an epoch when puffery and quackery have reached a height unexampled in the annals of mankind, and even English Editors, like Chinese Shopkeepers, must write on their door-lintels *No cheating here,*—we thought it good to premise.

CHAPTER III

Reminiscences

Teufelsdröckh at Weissnichtwo. Professor of Things in General at the University there: Outward aspect and character; memorable coffee-house utterances; domicile and watch-tower: Sights thence of City-Life by day and by night; with reflections thereon. Old 'Liza and her ways. Character of Hofrath Heuschrecke, and his relation to Teufelsdröckh.

To THE Author's private circle the appearance of this singular Work on Clothes must have occasioned little less surprise than it has to the rest of the world. For ourselves, at least, few things have been more unexpected. Professor Teufelsdröckh, at the period of our acquaintance

---

[3] Persona used by William Maginn (1794–1842), editor of *Fraser's*.
[4] With us even he still communicates in some sort of mask, or muffler; and, we have reason to think, under a feigned name!—O.Y. [Carlyle's note]
[5] Horace, *Satires*, II, vi, 65.   [6] "Plato is my friend, but truth is a greater friend."

with him, seemed to lead a quite still and self-contained life: a man devoted to the higher Philosophies, indeed; yet more likely, if he published at all, to publish a refutation of Hegel and Bardili,[1] both of whom, strangely enough, he included under a common ban; than to descend, as he has here done, into the angry noisy Forum, with an Argument that cannot but exasperate and divide. Not, that we can remember, was the Philosophy of Clothes once touched upon between us. If through the high, silent, meditative Transcendentalism of our Friend we detected any practical tendency whatever, it was at most Political, and towards a certain prospective, and for the present quite speculative, Radicalism; as indeed some correspondence, on his part, with Herr Oken[2] of Jena was now and then suspected; though his special contributions to the *Isis* could never be more than surmised at. But, at all events, nothing Moral, still less anything Didactico-Religious, was looked for from him.

Well do we recollect the last words he spoke in our hearing; which indeed, with the Night they were uttered in, are to be forever remembered. Lifting his huge tumbler of *Gukguk*,[3] and for a moment lowering his tobacco-pipe, he stood up in full coffeehouse (it was *Zur Grünen Gans*,[4] the largest in Weissnichtwo, where all the Virtuosity, and nearly all the Intellect of the place asembled of an evening); and there, with low, soul-stirring tone, and the look truly of an angel, though whether of a white or of a black one might be dubious, proposed this toast: *Die Sache der Armen in Gottes und Teufels Namen* (The Cause of the Poor, in Heavens' name and ———'s)! One full shout, breaking the leaden silence; then a gurgle of innumerable emptying bumpers, again followed by universal cheering, returned him loud acclaim. It was the finale of the night: resuming their pipes; in the highest enthusiasm, amid volumes of tobacco-smoke; triumphant, cloud-capt without and within, the assembly broke up, each to his thoughtful pillow. *Bleibt doch ein echter Spass- und Galgen-vogel*,[5] said several; meaning thereby that, one day, he would probably be hanged for his democratic sentiments. *Wo steckt doch der Schalk?*[6] added they, looking round: but Teufelsdröckh had retired by private alleys, and the Compiler of these pages beheld him no more.

In such scenes has it been our lot to live with this Philosopher, such estimate to form of his purposes and powers. And yet, thou brave Teufelsdröckh, who could tell what lurked in thee? Under those thick locks of thine, so long and lank, overlapping roof-wise the gravest face we ever in this world saw, there dwelt a most busy brain. In thy eyes too, deep under their shaggy brows, and looking out so still and dreamy, have we not noticed gleams of an ethereal or else a diabolic fire, and half-fancied that their stillness was but the rest of infinite motion, the *sleep* of a spinning-top? Thy little figure, there as, in loose ill-brushed threadbare habiliments, thou sattest, amid litter and lumber, whole days, to 'think and smoke tobacco,' held in it a mighty heart. The secrets of man's Life were laid open to thee; thou sawest into the mystery of the Universe, farther than another; thou hadst *in petto*[7] thy remarkable Volume on Clothes. Nay, was there not in that clear logically-founded Transcendentalism of thine; still more, in thy meek, silent, deep-seated Sansculottism,[8] combined with a true princely Courtesy of inward nature, the visible rudiments of such speculation? But great men are too often unknown, or what is worse, misknown. Already, when we dreamed not of it, the warp of thy remarkable Volume lay on the loom; and silently, mysterious shuttles were putting-in the woof!

How the Hofrath Heuschrecke is to furnish biographical data, in this case, may be a curious question; the answer of which, however, is happily not our concern, but his. To us it appeared, after repeated trial, that in Weissnichtwo, from the archives or memories of the best-informed classes, no Biography of Teufelsdröckh was to be gathered; not so much as a false one. He was a stranger there, wafted thither by what is called the course of circumstances; concerning whose parentage, birthplace, prospects, or pursuits, curiosity had indeed made inquiries, but satisfied herself with the most indistinct replies. For himself, he was a man so still and altogether unparticipating, that to question him even afar off on such particulars was a thing of more than usual delicacy: besides, in his sly way, he had ever some quaint turn, not without its satirical

---

[1] Georg Wilhelm Friedrich Hegel (1770–1831), C. G. Bardili (1761–1808), German philosophers.
[2] Lorenz Oken (1779–1851), German philosopher and editor, founder of the periodical *Isis*.
[3] Gukguk is unhappily only an academical beer. [Carlyle's note]
[4] "At the Green Goose."   [5] "He's a regular wag and gallows-bird."
[6] "Where's the rascal hiding?"   [7] "In secret" (lit., "in his breast").
[8] Philosophical radicalism; from the Sansculottes (lit., without breeches) of the French Revolution.

edge, wherewith to divert such intrusions, and deter you from the like. Wits spoke of him secretly as if he were a kind of Melchizedek,[9] without father or mother of any kind; sometimes, with reference to his great historic and statistic knowledge, and the vivid way he had of expressing himself like an eye-witness of distant transactions and scenes, they called him the *Ewige Jude*, Everlasting, or as we say, Wandering Jew.[10]

To the most, indeed, he had become not so much a Man as a Thing; which Thing doubtless they were accustomed to see, and with satisfaction; but no more thought of accounting for than for the fabrication of their daily *Allgemeine Zeitung*,[11] or the domestic habits of the Sun. Both were there and welcome; the world enjoyed what good was in them and thought no more of the matter. The man Teufelsdröckh passed and repassed, in his little circle, as one of those originals and nondescripts, more frequent in German Universities than elsewhere; of whom, though you see them alive, and feel enough that they must have a History, no History seems to be discoverable; or only such as men give of mountain rocks and antediluvian ruins: That they have been created by unknown agencies, are in a state of gradual decay, and for the present reflect light and resist pressure; that is, are visible and tangible objects in this phantasm world, where so much other mystery is.

It was to be remarked that though, by title and diploma *Professor der Allerley-Wissenschaft*, or as we should say in English, 'Professor of Things in General,' he had never delivered any Course; perhaps never been incited thereto by any public furtherance or requisition. To all appearance, the enlightened Government of Weissnichtwo, in founding their New University, imagined they had done enough, if 'in times like ours,' as the half-official Program expressed it, 'when all things are, rapidly or slowly, resolving themselves into Chaos, a Professorship of this kind had been established; whereby, as occasion called, the task of bodying somewhat forth again from such Chaos might be, even slightly, facilitated.' That actual Lectures should be held, and Public Classes for the 'Science of Things in General,' they doubtless considered premature; on which ground too they had only established the Professorship, nowise endowed it; so that Teufelsdröckh,

'recommended by the highest Names,' had been promoted thereby to a Name merely.

Great, among the more enlightened classes, was the admiration of this new Professorship: how an enlightened Government had seen into the Want of the Age (*Zeitbedürfniss*); how at length, instead of Denial and Destruction, we were to have a science of Affirmation and Reconstruction; and Germany and Weissnichtwo were where they should be, in the vanguard of the world. Considerable also was the wonder at the new Professor, dropt opportunely enough into the nascent University; so able to lecture, should occasion call; so ready to hold his peace for indefinite periods, should an enlightened Government consider that occasion did not call. But such admiration and such wonder, being followed by no act to keep them living, could last only nine days; and, long before our visit to that scene, had quite died away. The more cunning heads thought it was all an expiring clutch at popularity, on the part of a Minister, whom domestic embarrassments, court intrigues, old age, and dropsy soon afterwards finally drove from the helm.

As for Teufelsdröckh, except by his nightly appearances at the *Grüne Gans*, Weissnichtwo saw little of him, felt little of him. Here, over his tumbler of Gukguk, he sat reading Journals; sometimes comtemplatively looking into the clouds of his tobacco-pipe, without other visible employment: always, from his mild ways, an agreeable phenomenon there; more especially when he opened his lips for speech; on which occasions the whole Coffee-house would hush itself into silence, as if sure to hear something noteworthy. Nay, perhaps to hear a whole series and river of the most memorable utterances; such as, when once thawed, he would for hours indulge in, with fit audience: and the more memorable, as issuing from a head apparently not more interested in them, not more conscious of them, than is the sculptured stone head of some public fountain, which through its brass mouth-tube emits water to the worthy and the unworthy; careless whether it be for cooking victuals or quenching conflagrations; indeed, maintains the same earnest assiduous look, whether any water be flowing or not.

To the Editor of these sheets, as to a young enthusiastic Englishman, however unworthy,

[9] The prototype of the priest and the king. See Hebrews 4 and 5:6–7, Psalms 110.
[10] From the legend of the shoemaker who refused Christ rest on the road to the Cross and who was therefore condemned to wander the earth forever.
[11] "General News."

Teufelsdröckh opened himself perhaps more than to the most. Pity only that we could not then half guess his importance, and scrutinise him with due power of vision! We enjoyed, what not three men in Weissnichtwo could boast of, a certain degree of access to the Professor's private domicile. It was the attic floor of the highest house in the Wahngasse;[12] and might truly be called the pinnacle of Weissnichtwo, for it rose sheer up above the contiguous roofs, themselves rising from elevated ground. Moreover, with its windows it looked towards all the four *Orte*, or as the Scotch say, and we ought to say, *Airts*: the sitting-room itself commanded three; another came to view in the *Schlafgemach* (bed-room) at the opposite end; to say nothing of the kitchen, which offered two, as it were, *duplicates*, and showing nothing new. So that it was in fact the speculum[13] or watch-tower of Teufelsdröckh: wherefrom, sitting at ease, he might see the whole life-circulation of that considerable City; the streets and lanes of which, with all their doing and driving (*Thun und Treiben*), were for the most part visible there.

'I look down into all that wasp-nest or bee-hive,' have we heard him say, 'and witness their wax-laying and honey-making, and poison-brewing, and choking by sulphur. From the Palace esplanade, where music plays while Serene Highness is pleased to eat his victuals, down to the low lane, where in her door-sill the aged widow, knitting for a thin livelihood, sits to feel the afternoon sun, I see it all; for, except the Schlosskirche[14] weathercock, no biped stands so high. Couriers arrive bestrapped and bebooted, bearing Joy and Sorrow bagged-up in pouches of leather; there, topladen, and with four swift horses, rolls-in the country Baron and his household; here, on timber-leg, the lamed Soldier hops painfully along, begging alms: a thousand carriages, and wains, and cars, come tumbling-in with Food, with young Rusticity, and other Raw Produce, inanimate or animate, and go tumbling out again with Produce manufactured. That living flood, pouring through these streets, of all qualities and ages, knowest thou whence it is coming, whither it is going? *Aus der Ewigkeit, zu der Ewigkeit hin*: From Eternity, onwards to Eternity! These are Apparitions: what else? Are they not Souls rendered visible: in Bodies, that

took shape and will lose it, melting into air? Their solid Pavement is a Picture of the Sense; they walk on the bosom of Nothing, blank Time is behind them and before them. Or fanciest thou, the red and yellow Clothes-screen yonder, with spurs on its heels and feather in its crown, is but of Today, without a Yesterday or a Tomorrow; and had not rather its Ancestor alive when Hengst and Horsa[15] overran thy Island? Friend, thou seest here a living link in that Tissue of History, which inweaves all Being: watch well, or it will be past thee, and seen no more.

'*Ach, mein Lieber!*'[16] said he once, at midnight, when we had returned from the Coffee-house in rather earnest talk, 'it is a true sublimity to dwell here. These fringes of lamplight, struggling up through smoke and thousandfold exhalation, some fathoms into the ancient reign of Night, what thinks Boötes[17] of them, as he leads his Hunting-dogs over the Zenith in their leash of sidereal fire? That stifled hum of Midnight, when Traffic has lain down to rest; and the chariot-wheels of Vanity, still rolling here and there through distant streets, are bearing her to Halls roofed-in, and lighted to the due pitch for her; and only Vice and Misery, to prowl or to moan like nightbirds, are abroad: that hum, I say, like the stertorous, unquiet slumber of sick Life, is heard in Heaven! Oh, under that hideous coverlet of vapours, and putrefactions, and un-imaginable gases, what a Fermenting-vat lies simmering and hid! The joyful and the sorrowful are there; men are dying there, men are being born; men are praying,—on the other side of a brick partition, men are cursing; and around them all is the vast, void Night. The proud Grandee still lingers in his perfumed saloons, or reposes within damask curtains; Wretchedness cowers into truckle-beds, or shivers hunger-stricken into its lair of straw: in obscure cellars, *Rouge-et-Noir*[18] languidly emits its voice-of-destiny to haggard hungry Villains; while Councillors of State sit plotting, and playing their high chess-game, whereof the pawns are Men. The Lover whispers his mistress that the coach is ready; and she, full of hope and fear, glides down, to fly with him over the borders: the Thief, still more silently, sets-to his picklocks and crowbars, or lurks in wait till the watchmen first snore in their boxes. Gay mansions, with supper-rooms,

---

[12] "Illusion Lane" or "Folly Street."   [13] Should read *specula* (watch-tower).   [14] "Castle chapel."
[15] Anglo-Saxon invaders of Britain in the fifth century.   [16] "Oh, my dear sir!"
[17] The constellation showing a man with a crook accompanied by his hunting dogs chasing the Great Bear.
[18] A card game with red and black diamond-shaped marks for placing bets.

and dancing-rooms, are full of light and music and high-swelling hearts; but, in the Condemned Cells, the pulse of life beats tremulous and faint, and bloodshot eyes look-out through the darkness, which is around and within, for the light of a stern last morning. Six men are to be hanged on the morrow: comes no hammering from the *Rabenstein?*[19]—their gallows must even now be o' building. Upwards of five-hundred-thousand two-legged animals without feathers lie round us, in horizontal positions; their heads all in night-caps, and full of the foolishest dreams. Riot cries aloud, and staggers and swaggers in his rank dens of shame; and the Mother, with streaming hair, kneels over her pallid dying infant, whose cracked lips only her tears now moisten.—All these heaped and huddled together, with nothing but a little carpentry and masonry between them;—crammed in, like salted fish in their barrel;—or weltering, shall I say, like an Egyptian pitcher of tamed vipers, each struggling to get its *head above* the others: *such* work goes on under that smoke-counterpane!—But I, *mein Werther*,[20] sit above it all; I am alone with the Stars.'

We looked in his face to see whether, in the utterance of such extraordinary Night-thoughts, no feeling might be traced there; but with the light we had, which indeed was only a single tallow-light, and far enough from the window, nothing save that old calmness and fixedness was visible.

These were the Professor's talking seasons: most commonly he spoke in mere monosyllables, or sat altogether silent and smoked; while the visitor had liberty either to say what he listed, receiving for answer an occasional grunt; or to look round for a space, and then take himself away. It was a strange apartment; full of books and tattered papers, and miscellaneous shreds of all conceivable substances, 'united in a common element of dust,' Books lay on tables, and below tables; here fluttered a sheet of manuscript, there a torn handkerchief, or nightcap hastily thrown aside; ink-bottles alternated with bread-crusts, coffee-pots, tobacco-boxes, Periodical Literature, and Blücher Boots.[21] Old Lieschen (Lisekin, 'Liza), who was his bed-maker and stove-lighter, his washer and wringer, cook, errand-maid, and general lion's-provider, and for the rest a very orderly creature, had no sovereign authority in this last citadel of Teufelsdröckh; only some once in the month she half-forcibly made her way thither, with broom and duster, and (Teufels-dröckh hastily saving his manuscripts) effected a partial clearance, a jail-delivery of such lumber as was not Literary. These were her *Erdbeben* (earthquakes), which Teufelsdröckh dreaded worse than the pestilence; nevertheless, to such length he had been forced to comply. Glad would he have been to sit here philosophising forever, or till the litter, by accumulation, drove him out of doors: but Lieschen was his right-arm, and spoon, and necessary of life, and would not be flatly gainsayed. We can still remember the ancient woman; so silent that some thought her dumb; deaf also you would often have supposed her; for Teufelsdröckh, and Teufelsdröckh only, would she serve or give heed to; and with him she seemed to communicate chiefly by signs; if it were not rather by some secret divination that she guessed all his wants, and supplied them. Assiduous old dame! she scoured, and sorted, and swept, in her kitchen, with the least possible violence to the ear; yet all was tight and right there: hot and black came the coffee ever at the due moment; and the speechless Lieschen herself looked out on you, from under her clean white coif with its lappets, through her clean withered face and wrinkles, with a look of helpful intelligence, almost of benevolence.

Few strangers, as above hinted, had admittance hither: the only one we ever saw there, ourselves excepted, was the Hofrath Heuschrecke, already known, by name and expectation, to the readers of these pages. To us, at that period, Herr Heuschrecke seemed one of those purse-mouthed, crane-necked, clean-brushed, pacific individuals, perhaps sufficiently distinguished in society by this fact, that, in dry weather or in wet, 'they never appear without their umbrella.' Had we not known with what 'little wisdom' the world is governed; and how, in Germany as elsewhere, the ninety-and-nine Public Men can for most part be but mute train-bearers to the hundredth, perhaps but stalking-horses and willing or unwilling dupes,—it might have seemed wonderful how Herr Heuschrecke should be named a *Rath*, or Councillor, and Counsellor, even in Weissnichtwo. What counsel to any man, or to any woman, could this particular Hofrath give; in whose loose, zigzag figure; in whose thin visage, as it went to and fro, in minute incessant fluctuation,—you traced rather confusion worse confounded; at most, Timidity and physical Cold?

---

[19] The gallows (lit., raven-stone).   [20] "My good man."
[21] Short boots named for the Prussian general C. L. Blücher (1742–1819).

Some indeed said withal, he was 'the very Spirit of Love embodied': blue earnest eyes, full of sadness and kindness; purse ever open, and so forth; the whole of which, we shall now hope, for many reasons, was not quite groundless. Nevertheless friend Teufelsdröckh's outline, who indeed handled the burin like few in these cases, was probably the best: *Er hat Gemüth und Geist, hat wenigstens gehabt, doch ohne Organ, ohne Schicksals-Gunst; ist gegenwärtig aber halb-zerrüttet, halb-erstarrt,* 'He has heart and talent, at least has had such, yet without fit mode of utterance, or favour of Fortune; and so is now half-cracked, half-congealed.'—What the Hofrath shall think of this when he sees it, readers may wonder: we, safe in the stronghold of Historical Fidelity, are careless.

The main point, doubtless, for us all, is his love of Teufelsdröckh, which indeed was also by far the most decisive feature of Heuschrecke himself. We are enabled to assert that he hung on the Professor with the fondness of a Boswell for his Johnson. And perhaps with the like return; for Teufelsdröckh treated his gaunt admirer with little outward regard, as some half-rational or altogether irrational friend, and at best loved him out of gratitude and by habit. On the other hand, it was curious to observe with what reverent kindness, and a sort of fatherly protection, our Hofrath, being the elder, richer, and as he fondly imagined far more practically influential of the two, looked and tended on his little Sage, whom he seemed to consider as a living oracle. Let but Teufelsdröckh open his mouth, Heuschrecke's also unpuckered itself into a free doorway, besides his being all eye and all ear, so that nothing might be lost: and then, at every pause in the harangue, he gurgled-out his pursy chuckle of a cough-laugh (for the machinery of laughter took some time to get in motion, and seemed crank and slack), or else his twanging nasal, *Bravo! Das glaub' ich;*[22] in either case, by way of heartiest approval. In short, if Teufelsdröckh was Dalai-Lama, of which, except perhaps in his self-seclusion, and godlike indifference, there was no symptom, then might Heuschrecke pass for his chief Talapoin,[23] to whom no dough-pill he could knead and publish was other than medicinal and sacred.

In such environment, social, domestic, physical, did Teufelsdröckh, at the time of our acquaintance, and most likely does he still, live and meditate. Here, perched-up in his high Wahngasse watchtower, and often, in solitude, outwatching the Bear, it was that the indomitable Inquirer fought all his battles with Dulness and Darkness; here in all probability, that he wrote this surprising Volume on *Clothes.* Additional particulars: of his age, which was of that standing middle sort you could only guess at; of his wide surtout; the colour of his trousers, fashion of his broad-brimmed steeple-hat, and so forth, we might report, but do not. The Wisest truly is, in these times, the Greatest; so that an enlightened curiosity, leaving Kings and suchlike to rest very much on their own basis, turns more and more to the Philosophic Class: nevertheless, what reader expects that, with all our writing and reporting, Teufelsdröckh could be brought home to him, till once the Documents arrive? His Life, Fortunes, and Bodily Presence, are as yet hidden from us, or matter only of faint conjecture. But, on the other hand, does not his Soul lie enclosed in this remarkable Volume, much more truly than Pedro Garcia's did in the buried Bag of Doubloons?[24] To the soul of Diogenes Teufelsdröckh, to his opinions, namely, on the 'Origin and Influence of Clothes,' we for the present gladly return.

CHAPTER IV

Characteristics

Teufelsdröckh and his Work on Clothes: Strange freedom of speech; transcendentalism; force of insight and expression; multifarious learning: Style poetic, uncouth: Comprehensiveness of his humour and moral feeling. How the Editor once saw him laugh. Different kinds of Laughter and their significance.

IT WERE A piece of vain flattery to pretend that this Work on Clothes entirely contents us; that it is not, like all works of genius, like the very Sun, which, though the highest published creation, or work of genius, has nevertheless black spots and troubled nebulosities amid its effulgence,—a mixture of insight, inspiration, with dulness, double-vision, and even utter blindness.

---

[22] "I believe that."   [23] Buddhist monk.   [24] *Gil Blas*, Preface.

Without committing ourselves to those enthusiastic praises and prophesyings of the *Weissnichtwo'sche Anzeiger*, we admitted that the Book had in a high degree excited us to self-activity, which is the best effect of any book; that it had even operated changes in our way of thought; nay, that it promised to prove, as it were, the opening of a new mineshaft, wherein the whole world of Speculation might henceforth dig to unknown depths. More especially it may now be declared that Professor Teufelsdröckh's acquirements, patience of research, philosophic and even poetic vigour, are here made indisputably manifest; and unhappily no less his prolixity and tortuosity and manifold ineptitude; that, on the whole, as in opening new mine-shafts is not unreasonable, there is much rubbish in his Book, though likewise specimens of almost invaluable ore. A paramount popularity in England we cannot promise him. Apart from the choice of such a topic as Clothes, too often the manner of treating it betokens in the Author a rusticity and academic seclusion, unblamable, indeed inevitable in a German, but fatal to his success with our public.

Of good society Teufelsdröckh appears to have seen little, or has mostly forgotten what he saw. He speaks-out with a strange plainness; calls many things by their mere dictionary names. To him the Upholsterer is no Pontiff, neither is any Drawing-room a Temple, were it never so begilt and overhung: 'a whole immensity of Brussels carpets, and pier-glasses, and or-molu,' as he himself expresses it, 'cannot hide from me that such Drawing-room is simply a section of Infinite Space, where so many God-created Souls do for the time meet together.' To Teufelsdröckh the highest Duchess is respectable, is venerable; but nowise for her pearl bracelets and Malines laces: in his eyes, the star of a Lord is little less and little more than the broad button of Birmingham spelter in a Clown's smock; 'each is an implement,' he says, 'in its kind; a tag for *hooking-together*; and, for the rest, was dug from the earth, and hammered on a stithy before smith's fingers.' Thus does the Professor look in men's faces with a strange impartiality, a strange scientific freedom; like a man unversed in the higher circles, like a man dropped thither from the Moon. Rightly considered, it is in this peculiarity, running through his whole system of thought, that all these short-comings,

over-shootings, and multiform perversities, take rise: if indeed they have not a second source, also natural enough, in his Transcendental Philosophies, and humour of looking at all Matter and Material things as Spirit; whereby truly his case were but the more hopeless, the more lamentable.

To the Thinkers of this nation, however, of which class it is firmly believed there are individuals yet extant, we can safely recommend the Work: nay, who knows but among the fashionable ranks too, if it be true, as Teufelsdröckh maintains, that 'within the most starched cravat there passes a windpipe and weasand, and under the thickliest embroidered waistcoat beats a heart,'—the force of that rapt earnestness may be felt, and here and there an arrow of the soul pierce through? In our wild Seer, shaggy, unkempt, like a Baptist[1] living on locusts and wild honey, there is an untutored energy, a silent, as it were unconscious, strength, which except in the higher walks of Literature, must be rare. Many a deep glance, and often with unspeakable precision, has he cast into mysterious Nature, and the still more mysterious Life of Man. Wonderful it is with what cutting words, now and then, he severs asunder the confusion; shears down, were it furlongs deep, into the true centre of the matter; and there not only hits the nail on the head, but with crushing force smites it home, and buries it.—On the other hand, let us be free to admit, he is the most unequal writer breathing. Often after some such feat, he will play truant for long pages, and go dawdling and dreaming, and mumbling and maundering the merest commonplaces, as if he were asleep with eyes open, which indeed he is.

Of his boundless Learning, and how all reading and literature in most known tongues, from *Sanchoniathon* to *Dr. Lingard*,[2] from your Oriental *Shasters*, and *Talmuds*, and *Korans*, with Cassini's *Siamese Tables*,[3] and Laplace's *Mécanique Céleste*, down to *Robinson Crusoe* and the *Belfast Town and Country Almanack*, are familiar to him,— we shall say nothing: for unexampled as it is with us, to the Germans such universality of study passes without wonder, as a thing commendable, indeed, but natural, indispensable, and there of course. A man that devotes his life to learning, shall he not be learned?

In respect of style our Author manifests the same genial capability, marred too often by the

---

[1] John the Baptist.

[2] Sanchoniathon, legendary Phoenician, author of sacred works; John Lingard (1771–1851), British historian, author of *History of England* (1819–30).

[3] G. D. Cassini (1625–1712), Italian astronomer, author of *Tables of Siamese Astronomy*.

same rudeness, inequality, and apparent want of intercourse with the higher classes. Occasionally, as above hinted, we find consummate vigour, a true inspiration; his burning thoughts step forth in fit burning words, like so many full-formed Minervas, issuing amid flame and splendour from Jove's head; a rich, idiomatic diction, picturesque allusions, fiery poetic emphasis, or quaint tricksy turns; all the graces and terrors of a wild Imagination, wedded to the clearest Intellect, alternate in beautiful vicissitude. Were it not that sheer sleeping and soporific passages; circumlocutions, repetitions, touches even of pure doting jargon, so often intervene! On the whole, Professor Teufelsdröckh is not a cultivated writer. Of his sentences perhaps not more than nine-tenths stand straight on their legs; the remainder are in quite angular attitudes, buttressed-up by props (of parentheses and dashes), and ever with this or the other tagrag hanging from them; a few even sprawl-out helplessly on all sides, quite broken-backed and dismembered. Nevertheless, in almost his very worst moods, there lies in him a singular attraction. A wild tone pervades the whole utterance of the man, like its keynote and regulator; now screwing itself aloft as into the Song of Spirits, or else the shrill mockery of Fiends; now sinking in cadences, not without melodious heartiness, though sometimes abrupt enough, into the common pitch, when we hear it only as a monotonous hum; of which hum the true character is extremely difficult to fix. Up to this hour we have never fully satisfied ourselves whether it is a tone and hum of real Humour, which we reckon among the very highest qualities of genius, or some echo of mere Insanity and Inanity, which doubtless ranks below the very lowest.

Under a like difficulty, in spite even of our personal intercourse, do we still lie with regard to the Professor's moral feeling. Gleams of an ethereal love burst forth from him, soft wailings of infinite pity; he could clasp the whole Universe into his bosom, and keep it warm; it seems as if under that rude exterior there dwelt a very seraph. Then again he is so sly and still, so imperturbably saturnine; shows such indifference, malign coolness towards all that men strive after; and ever with some half-visible wrinkle of a bitter sardonic humour, if indeed it be not mere stolid callousness,—that you look

on him almost with a shudder, as on some incarnate Mephistopheles, to whom this great terrestrial and celestial Round, after all, were but some huge foolish Whirligig, where kings and beggars, and angels and demons, and stars and street-sweepings, were chaotically whirled, in which only children could take interest. His look, as we mentioned, is probably the gravest ever seen: yet it is not of that cast-iron gravity frequent enough among our own Chancery suitors; but rather the gravity as of some silent, high-encircled mountain-pool, perhaps the crater of an extinct volcano; into whose black deeps you fear to gaze: those eyes, those lights that sparkle in it, may indeed be reflexes of the heavenly Stars, but perhaps also glances from the region of Nether Fire!

Certainly a most involved, self-secluded, altogether enigmatic nature, this of Teufelsdröckh! Here, however, we gladly recall to mind that once we saw him *laugh*; once only, perhaps it was the first and last time in his life; but then such a peal of laughter, enough to have awakened the Seven Sleepers![4]. It was of Jean Paul's[5] doing: some single billow in that vast World-Mahlstrom of Humour, with its heaven-kissing coruscations, which is now, alas, all congealed in the frost of death! The large-bodied Poet and the small, both large enough in soul, sat talking miscellaneously together, the present Editor being privileged to listen; and now Paul, in his serious way, was giving one of those inimitable 'Extra-harangues'; and, as it chanced, On the Proposal for a *Cast-metal King*: gradually a light kindled in our Professor's eyes and face, a beaming, mantling, loveliest light; through those murky features, a radiant, ever-young Apollo looked; and he burst forth like the neighing of all Tattersall's,[6] —tears streaming down his cheeks, pipe held aloft, foot clutched into the air,—loud, long-continuing, uncontrollable; a laugh not of the face and diaphragm only, but of the whole man from head to heel. The present Editor, who laughed indeed, yet with measure, began to fear all was not right: however, Teufelsdröckh composed himself, and sank into his old stillness; on his inscrutable countenance there was, if anything a slight look of shame; and Richter himself could not rouse him again. Readers who have any tincture of Psychology know how much is to be inferred from this; and that no man who

---

[4] Christians who hid in a cave from the Decian persecutions in A.D. 250 and slept for almost two hundred years.
[5] Jean Paul Friedrich Richter (1763–1825), German romantic author.   [6] A horse market in London.

has once heartily and wholly laughed can be altogether irreclaimably bad. How much lies in Laughter: the cipher-key, wherewith we decipher the whole man! Some men wear an everlasting barren simper; in the smile of others lies a cold glitter as of ice: the fewest are able to laugh, what can be called laughing, but only sniff and titter and snigger from the throat outwards; or at best, produce some whiffling husky cachinnation, as if they were laughing through wool: of none such comes good. The man who cannot laugh is not only fit for treasons, stratagems, and spoils; but his whole life is already a treason and a stratagem.

Considered as an Author, Herr Teufelsdröckh has one scarcely pardonable fault, doubtless his worst: an almost total want of arrangement. In this remarkable Volume, it is true, his adherence to the mere course of Time produces, through the Narrative portions, a certain show of outward method; but of true logical method and sequence there is too little. Apart from its multifarious sections and subdivisions, the Work naturally falls into two Parts; a Historical-Descriptive, and a Philosophical-Speculative: but falls, unhappily, by no firm line of demarcation; in that labyrinthic combination, each Part overlaps, and indents, and indeed runs quite through the other. Many sections are of a debatable rubric, or even quite nondescript and unnameable; whereby the Book not only loses in accessibility, but too often distresses us like some mad banquet, wherein all courses had been confounded, and fish and flesh, soup and solid, oyster-sauce, lettuces, Rhine-wine and French mustard, were hurled into one huge tureen or trough, and the hungry Public invited to help itself. To bring what order we can out of this Chaos shall be part of our endeavour.

CHAPTER V

The World in Clothes

Futile cause-and-effect Philosophies. Teufelsdröckh's Orbis Vestitus. Clothes first invented for the sake of ornament. Picture of our progenitor, the Aboriginal Savage. Wonders of growth and progress in mankind's history. Man defined as a Tool-using Animal.

As MONTESQUIEU wrote a *Spirit of Laws*,' observes our Professor, 'so could I write a *Spirit of Clothes*; thus, with an *Esprit des Lois*, properly an *Esprit de Coutumes*, we should have an *Esprit de Costumes*. For neither in tailoring nor in legislating does man proceed by mere Accident, but the hand is ever guided on by mysterious operations of the mind. In all his Modes, and habilatory endeavours, an Architectural Idea will be found lurking; his Body and the Cloth are the site and materials whereon and whereby his beautified edifice, of a Person, is to be built. Whether he flow gracefully out in folded mantles, based on light sandals; tower-up in high headgear, from amid peaks, spangles and bell-girdles; swell-out in starched ruffs, buckram stuffings, and monstrous tuberosities; or girth himself into separate sections, and front the world an Agglomeration of four limbs,—will depend on the nature of such Architectural Idea: whether Grecian, Gothic, Later-Gothic, or altogether Modern, and Parisian or Anglo-Dandical. Again, what meaning lies in Colour! From the soberest drab to the high-flaming scarlet, spiritual idiosyncrasies unfold themselves in choice of Colour: if the Cut betoken Intellect and Talent, so does the Colour betoken Temper and Heart. In all which, among nations as among individuals, there is an incessant, indubitable, though infinitely complex working of Cause and Effect: every snip of the Scissors has been regulated and prescribed by ever-active Influences, which doubtless to Intelligences of a superior order are neither invisible nor illegible.

'For such superior Intelligences a Cause-and-Effect Philosophy of Clothes, as of Laws, were probably a comfortable winter-evening entertainment: nevertheless, for inferior Intelligences, like men, such Philosophies have always seemed to me uninstructive enough. Nay, what is your Montesquieu himself but a clever infant spelling Letters from a hieroglyphical prophetic Book, the lexicon of which lies in Eternity, in Heaven?—Let any Cause-and-Effect Philosopher explain, not why I wear such and such a Garment, obey such and such a Law; but even why *I* am *here*, to wear and obey anything!—Much, therefore, if not the whole, of that same *Spirit of Clothes* I shall suppress, as hypothetical, ineffectual, and even impertinent: naked Facts, and Deductions drawn therefrom in quite another than that omniscient style, are my humbler and proper province.'

Acting on which prudent restriction, Teufelsdröckh has nevertheless contrived to take-in a well-nigh boundless extent of field; at least, the boundaries too often lie quite beyond our horizon. Selection being indispensable, we shall here glance-over his First Part only in the most cursory manner.

This First Part is, no doubt, distinguished by omnivorous learning, and utmost patience and fairness: at the same time in its results and delineations, it is much more likely to interest the Compilers of some *Library* of General, Entertaining, Useful, or even Useless Knowledge than the miscellaneous readers of these pages. Was it this Part of the Book which Heuschrecke had in view, when he recommended us to that joint-stock vehicle of publication, 'at present the glory of British Literature'? If so, the Library Editors are welcome to dig in it for their own behoof.

To the First Chapter, which turns on Paradise and Fig-leaves, and leads us into interminable disquisitions of a mythological, metaphorical, cabalistico-sartorial and quite antediluvian cast, we shall content ourselves with giving an unconcerned approval. Still less have we to do with 'Lilis,[1] Adam's first wife, whom, according to the Talmudists, he had before Eve, and who bore him, in that wedlock, the whole progeny of aerial, aquatic, and terrestrial Devils,'—very needlessly, we think. On this portion of the Work, with its profound glances into the *Adam-Kadmon*,[2] or Primeval Element, here strangely brought into relation with the *Nifl* and *Muspel* (Darkness and Light) of the antique North, it may be enough to say, that its correctness of deduction, and depth of Talmudic and Rabbinical lore have filled perhaps not the worst Hebraist in Britain with something like astonishment.

But, quitting this twilight region, Teufelsdröckh hastens from the Tower of Babel, to follow the dispersion of Mankind over the whole habitable and habilable globe. Walking by the light of Oriental, Pelasgic, Scandinavian, Egyptian, Otaheitean,[3] Ancient and Modern researches of every conceivable kind, he strives to give us in compressed shape (as the Nürnbergers give an *Orbis Pictus*) an *Orbis Vestitus*;[4] or view of the costumes of all mankind, in all countries, in all times. It is here that to the Antiquarian, to the Historian, we can triumphantly say: Fall to! Here is learning: an irregular Treasury, if you will; but inexhaustible as the Hoard of King Nibelung, which twelve wagons in twelve days, at the rate of three journeys a day, could not carry off. Sheepskin cloaks and wampum belts; phylacteries, stoles, albs; chlamydes, togas, Chinese silks, Afghaun shawls, trunk-hose, leather breeches,

Celtic philibegs (though breeches, as the name *Gallia Braccata*[5] indicates, are the more ancient), Hussar cloaks, Vandyke tippets, ruffs, fardingales, are brought vividly before us,—even the Kilmarnock nightcap is not forgotten. For most part, too, we must admit that the Learning, heterogeneous as it is, and tumbled-down quite pell-mell, is true concentrated and purified Learning, the drossy parts smelted out and thrown aside.

Philosophical reflections intervene, and sometimes touching pictures of human life. Of this sort the following has surprised us. The first purpose of Clothes, as our Professor imagines, was not warmth or decency, but ornament. 'Miserable indeed,' says he, 'was the condition of the Aboriginal Savage, glaring fiercely from under his fleece of hair, which with the beard reached down to his loins, and hung round him like a matted cloak; the rest of his body sheeted in its thick natural fell. He loitered in the sunny glades of the forest, living on wild-fruits; or, as the ancient Caledonian, squatted himself in morasses, lurking for his bestial or human prey; without implements, without arms, save the ball of heavy Flint, to which, that his sole possession and defence might not be lost, he had attached a long cord of plaited thongs; thereby recovering as well as hurling it with deadly unerring skill. Nevertheless, the pains of Hunger and Revenge once satisfied, his next care was not Comfort but Decoration (*Putz*). Warmth he found in the toils of the chase; or amid dried leaves, in his hollow tree, in his bark shed, or natural grotto: but for Decoration he must have Clothes. Nay, among wild people, we find tattooing and painting even prior to Clothes. The first spiritual want of a barbarous man is Decoration, as indeed we still see among the barbarous classes in civilised countries.

'Reader, the heaven-inspired melodious Singer; loftiest Serene Highness; nay thy own amber-locked, snow-and-rose-bloom Maiden, worthy to glide sylphlike almost on air, whom thou lovest, worshippest as a divine Presence, which, indeed, symbolically taken, she is,—has descended, like thyself, from that same hair-mantled, flint-hurling Aboriginal Anthropophagus! Out of the eater cometh forth meat; out of the strong cometh forth sweetness.[6] What changes are wrought, not by Time, yet in Time! For not Mankind only,

---

[1] Or Lilith, legendary first wife of Adam.   [2] Hebrew, meaning "the first man."   [3] Tahitian.
[4] *Orbis Pictus*, "The World in Pictures," a seventeenth-century German school book; *Orbis Vestitus*, "The World in Clothes."
[5] "A Gaul in breeches."   [6] Cf. Judges 14:14.

but all that Mankind does or beholds, is in continual growth, regenesis and self perfecting vitality. Cast forth thy Act, thy Word, into the ever-living, ever-working Universe: it is a seed-grain that cannot die; unnoticed today (says one), it will be found flourishing as a Banyan-grove (perhaps, alas, as a Hemlock-forest!) after a thousand years.

'He who first shortened the labour of Copyists by device of *Movable Types* was disbanding hired Armies, and cashiering most Kings and Senates, and creating a whole new Democratic world: he had invented the Art of Printing. The first ground handful of Nitre, Sulphur, and Charcoal drove Monk Schwartz's[7] pestle through the ceiling: what will the last do? Achieve the final undisputed prostration of Force under Thought of Animal courage under Spiritual. A simple invention it was in the old-world Grazier,—sick of lugging his slow Ox about the country till he got it bartered for corn or oil,—to take a piece of Leather, and thereon scratch or stamp the mere Figure of an Ox (or *Pecus*); put it in his pocket, and call it *Pecunia*, Money. Yet hereby did Barter grow Sale, the Leather Money is now Golden and Paper, and all miracles have been out-miracled: for there are Rothschilds and English National Debts; and whoso has sixpence is sovereign (to the length of sixpence) over all men; commands cooks to feed him, philosophers to teach him, kings to mount guard over him,—to the length of sixpence.—Clothes too, which began in foolishest love of Ornament, what have they not become! Increased Security and pleasurable Heat soon followed: but what of these? Shame, divine Shame, (*Schaam*, Modesty), as yet a stranger to the Anthropophagus bosom, arose there mysteriously under Clothes; a mystic grove-encircled shrine for the Holy in man. Clothes gave us individuality, distinctions, social polity; Clothes have made Men of us; they are threatening to make Clothes-screens of us.

'But, on the whole,' continues our eloquent Professor, 'Man is a Tool-using Animal (*Hand-thierendes Thier*). Weak in himself, and of small stature, he stands on a basis, at most for the flattest-soled, of some half-square foot, insecurely enough; has to straddle out his legs, lest the very wind supplant him. Feeblest of bipeds! Three quintals are a crushing load for him; the steer stranger to the Anthropophagous bosom, arose of the meadow tosses him aloft, like a waste rag. Nevertheless he can use Tools, can devise Tools: with these the granite mountain melts into light dust before him; he kneads glowing iron, as if if were soft paste; seas are his smooth highway, winds and fire his unwearying steeds. Nowhere do you find him without Tools: without Tools he is nothing, with Tools he is all.'

Here may we not, for a moment, interrupt the stream of Oratory with a remark, that this Definition of the Tool-using Animal appears to us, of all that Animal-sort, considerably the precisest and best? Man is called a Laughing Animal: but do not the apes also laugh, or attempt to do it; and is the manliest man the greatest and oftenest laugher? Teufelsdröckh himself, as we said, laughed only once. Still less do we make of that other French Definition of the Cooking Animal; which, indeed for rigorous scientific purposes, is as good as useless. Can a Tartar be said to cook, when he only readies his steak by riding on it? Again, what Cookery does the Greenlander use, beyond stowing-up his whale-blubber, as a marmot, in the like case, might do? Or how would Monsieur Ude[8] prosper among those Orinocco Indians who, according to Humboldt,[9] lodge in crow-nests, on the branches of trees; and, for half the year, have not victuals but pipe-clay, the whole country being under water? But, on the other hand, show us the human being, of any period or climate, without his Tools: those very Caledonians, as we saw, had their Flint-ball, and Thong to it, such as no brute has or can have.

'Man is a Tool-using Animal,' concludes Teufelsdröckh in his abrupt way; 'of which truth Clothes are but one example: and surely if we consider the interval between the first wooden Dibble fashioned by man, and those Liverpool Steam-carriages,[10] or the British House of Commons, we shall note what progress he has made. He digs up certain black stones from the bosom of the earth, and says to them, *Transport me and this luggage at the rate of five-and thirty miles an hour*; and they do it; he collects, apparently by lot, six-hundred and fifty-eight miscellaneous individuals, and says to them, *Make this nation*

---

[7] Berthold Schwartz, nickname for Konstantin Anklitzen (fl. 1320), German Franciscan monk, inventor of gunpowder.

[8] Louis Eustache Ude, celebrated French chef.

[9] Alexander von Humboldt (1769–1859), German naturalist who explored the Orinoco.

[10] Reference to the first railway in England, which began service between Liverpool and Manchester in 1830.

toil for us, bleed for us, hunger and sorrow and sin for us; and they do it.'

BOOK SECOND

CHAPTER I

Genesis

Old Andreas Futteral and Gretchen his wife: their quiet home. Advent of a mysterious stranger, who deposits with them a young infant, the future Herr Diogenes Teufels-dröckh. After-yearnings of the youth for his unknown Father. Sovereign power of Names and Naming. Diogenes a flourishing Infant.

IN A psychological point of view, it is perhaps questionable whether from birth and gene-alogy, how closely scrutinised soever, much insight is to be gained. Nevertheless, as in every phenom-enon the Beginning remains always the most notable moment; so, with regard to any great man, we rest not till, for our scientific profit or not, the whole circumstances of his first appear-ance in this Planet, and what manner of Public Entry he made, are with utmost completeness rendered manifest. To the Genesis of our Clothes-Philosopher, then be this First Chapter conse-crated. Unhappily, indeed, he seems to be of quite obscure extraction; uncertain, we might almost say, whether of any: so that this Genesis of his can properly be nothing but an Exodus (or transit out of Invisibility into Visibility); whereof the preliminary portion is nowhere forthcoming.

'In the village of Entepfuhl,' thus writes he, in the Bag *Libra,* on various Papers, which we arrange with difficulty, 'dwelt Andreas Futteral[1] and his wife; childless, in still seclusion, and cheerful though now verging towards old age. Andreas had been grenadier Sergeant, and even regimental Schoolmaster under Frederick the Great; but now, quitting the halbert and ferule for the spade and pruning hook, cultivated a little Orchard, on the produce of which he, Cincinna-tus-like,[2] lived not without dignity. Fruits, the peach, the apple, the grape, with other varieties came in their season; all which Andreas knew how to sell: on evenings he smoked largely, or read (as beseemed a regimental Schoolmaster), and talked to neighbours that would listen about the Victory of Rossbach; and how Fritz the Only (*der Einzige*)[3] had once with his own royal lips spoken to him, had been pleased to say, when Andreas as camp-sentinel demanded the pass-word, "*Schweig Hund* (Peace, hound)!" before any of his staff-adjutants could answer. "*Das nenn' ich mir einen König*, There is what I call a King," would Andreas exclaim: "but the smoke of Kunersdorf was still smarting his eyes."[4]

'Gretchen, the housewife, won like Desdemona by the deeds rather than the looks of her now veteran Othello, lived not in altogether military subordination; for, as Andreas said, "the woman-kind will not drill (*wer kann die Weiberchen dressiren*): nevertheless she at heart loved him both for valour and wisdom; to her a Prussian grenadier Sergeant and Regiment's Schoolmaster was little other than a Cicero and Cid: what you see, yet cannot see over, is as good as infinite. Nay, was not Andreas in very deed a man of order, courage, downrightness (*Geradheit*); that understood Büsching's *Geography*,[5] had been in the victory of Rossbach, and left for dead in the camisade of Hochkirch[6] The good Gretchen, for all her fretting, watched over him and hovered round him as only a true housemother can: assiduously she cooked and sewed and scoured for him; so that not only his old regimental sword and grenadier-cap, but the whole habitation and environment, where on pegs of honour they hung, looked ever trim and gay: a roomy painted Cottage, embowered in fruit-trees and forest-trees, evergreens and honey-suckles; rising many-coloured from amid shaven grass-plots, flowers struggling-in through the very windows; under its long projecting eaves nothing

---

[1] Entepfuhl, lit. duck pond; Libra, zodiacal sign of the balance or scales, September 22–October 22; Futteral, lit. feed-all, cover-all.

[2] Cincinnatus was called from his farm to the leadership of the Roman republic during a war in 458 B.C. and returned immediately to the plough when the danger was over.

[3] Rossbach, site of a victory in 1757 by Frederick the Great over the French; Fritz the Only is Frederick the Great.

[4] Kunersdorf, scene of the defeat of Frederick the Great in 1759 by the Austrians and Russians.

[5] A. F. Busching (1724–93), German geographer.

[6] Or Hochkirchen, scene of an Austrian defeat of Frederick the Great in 1758.

but garden-tools in methodic piles (to screen them from rain), and seats where, especially on summer nights, a King might have wished to sit and smoke, and call it his. Such a *Bauergut* (Copyhold) had Gretchen given her veteran; whose sinewy arms, and long-disused gardening talent, had made it what you saw.

'Into this umbrageous Man's-nest, one meek yellow evening or dusk, when the Sun, hidden indeed from terrestrial Entepfuhl, did nevertheless journey visible and radiant along the celestial Balance (*Libra*), it was that a Stranger of reverend aspect entered; and, with grave salutation, stood before the two rather astonished housemates. He was close-muffled in a wide mantle; which without farther parley unfolding, he deposited therefrom what seemed some Basket, overhung with green Persian silk; saying only: *Ihr lieben Leute, hier bringe ein unschätzbares Verleihen; nehmt es in aller Acht, sorgfältigst benützt es: mit hohem Lohn, oder wohl mit schweren Zinsen, wird's einst zurückgefordert.* "Good Christian people, here lies for you an invaluable Loan; take all heed thereof, in all carefulness employ it: with high recompense, or else with heavy penalty, will it one day be required back." Uttering which singular words, in a clear bell-like, forever memorable tone, the Stranger gracefully withdrew; and before Andreas or his wife, gazing in expectant wonder, had time to fashion either question or answer, was clean gone. Neither out of doors could aught of him be seen or heard; he had vanished in the thickets, in the dusk; the Orchard-gate stood quietly closed: the Stranger was gone once and always. So sudden had the whole transaction been, in the autumn stillness and twilight, so gentle, noiseless, that the Futterals could have fancied it all a trick of Imagination, or some visit from an authentic Spirit. Only that the green-silk Basket, such as neither Imagination nor authentic Spirits are wont to carry, still stood visible and tangible on their little parlour-table. Towards this the astonished couple, now with lit candle, hastily turned their attention. Lifting the green veil, to see what invaluable it hid, they described there, amid down and rich white wrappages, no Pitt Diamond[7] or Hapsburg Regalia, but, in the softest sleep, a little red-colored Infant! Beside it, lay a roll of gold Friedrichs,[8] the exact amount of which was never publicly known; also a *Taufschein* (baptismal certificate), wherein unfortunately

nothing but the Name was decipherable; other document or indication none whatever.

'To wonder and conjecture was unavailing, then and always thenceforth. Nowhere in Entepfuhl, on the morrow or next day, did tidings transpire of any such figure as the Stranger; nor could the Traveller, who had passed through the neighbouring Town in coach-and-four, be connected with this Apparition, except in the way of gratuitous surmise. Meanwhile, for Andreas and his wife, the grand practical problem was: What to do with this little sleeping red-coloured Infant? Amid amazements and curiosities, which had to die away without external satisfying, they resolved, as in such circumstances charitable prudent people needs must, on nursing it, though with spoon-meat, into whiteness, and if possible into manhood. The Heavens smiled on their endeavour: thus has that same mysterious Individual ever since had a status for himself in this visible Universe, some modicum of victual and lodging and parade-ground; and now expanded in bulk, faculty and knowledge of good and evil, he, as HERR DIOGENES TEUFELSDRÖCKH, professes or is ready to profess, perhaps not altogether without effect, in the New University of Weissnichtwo, the new Science of Things in General.'

Our Philosopher declares here, as indeed we should think he well might, that these facts, first communicated, by the good Gretchen Futteral, in his twelfth year, 'produced on the boyish heart and fancy a quite indelible impression. Who this reverend Personage,' he says, 'that glided into the Orchard Cottage when the Sun was in Libra, and then, as on spirit's wings, glided out again, might be? An inexpressible desire, full of love and of sadness, has often since struggled within me to shape an answer. Ever, in my distresses and my loneliness, has Fantasy turned, full of longing (*sehnsuchtsvoll*), to that unknown Father, who perhaps far from me, perhaps near, either way invisible, might have taken me to his paternal bosom, there to lie screened from many a woe. Thou beloved Father, dost thou still, shut out from me only by thin penetrable curtains of earthly Space, wend to and fro among the crowd of the living? Or art thou hidden by those far thicker curtains of the Everlasting Night, or rather of the Everlasting Day, though which my mortal eye and outstretched arms need not strive to reach? Alas, I know not, and in vain vex myself

---

[7] Brought from India in 1702 by Thomas Pitt, grandfather of William Pitt the Elder.
[8] Prussian gold coins.

to know. More than once, heart-deluded, have I taken for thee this and the other noble-looking Stranger; and approached him wistfully, with infinite regard; but he too had to repel me, he too was not thou.

'And yet, O Man born of Woman,' cries the Autobiographer, with one of his sudden whirls, 'wherein is my case peculiar? Hadst thou, any more than I, a Father whom thou knowest? The Andreas and Gretchen, or the Adam and Eve, who led thee into Life, and for a time suckled and pap-fed thee there, whom thou namest Father and Mother; these were, like mine, but thy nursing-father and nursing-mother: thy true Beginning and Father is in Heaven, whom with the bodily eye thou shalt never behold, but only with the spiritual.'

'The little green veil,' adds he, among much similar moralising, and embroiled discoursing, 'I yet keep; still more inseparably the Name, Diogenes Teufelsdröckh. From the veil can nothings be inferred: a piece of now quite faded Persian silk, like thousands of others. On the Name I have many times meditated and conjectured; but neither in this lay there any clue. That it was my unknown Father's name I must hesitate to believe. To no purpose have I searched through all the Herald's Books, in and without the German Empire, and through all manner of Subscriber-Lists (*Pränumeranten*), Militia-Rolls, and other Name-catalogues; extraordinary names as we have in Germany, the name Teufelsdröckh, except as appended to my own person, nowhere occurs. Again, what may the unchristian rather than Christian "Diogenes" mean? Did that reverend Basket-bearer intend, by such designation, to shadow forth my future destiny, or his own present malign humour? Perhaps the latter, perhaps both. Thou ill-starred Parent, who like an Ostrich hadst to leave thy ill-starred offspring to be hatched into self-support by the mere sky-influences of Chance, can thy pilgrimage have been a smooth one? Beset by Misfortune thou doubtless hast been: or indeed by the worst figure of Misfortune, by Misconduct. Often have I fancied how, in thy hard life-battle, thou wert shot at, and slung at, wounded, hand-fettered, hamstrung, browbeaten and bedevilled by the Time-Spirit (*Zeitgeist*) in thyself and others, till the good soul first given thee was seared into grim rage; and thou hadst nothing for it but to leave in me an indignant appeal to the Future,

and living speaking Protest against the Devil, as the same Spirit not of the Time only, but of Time itself, is well named! Which Appeal and Protest, may I now modestly add, was not perhaps quite lost in air.

'For indeed, as Walter Shandy[9] often insisted, there is much, nay almost all, in Names. The Name is the earliest Garment you wrap round the earth-visiting ME; to which it thenceforth cleaves, more tenaciously (for there are Names that have lasted nigh thirty centuries) than the very skin. And now from without, what mystic influences does it not send inwards, even to the centre; especially in those plastic first-times, when the whole soul is yet infantine, soft, and the invisible seedgrain will grow to be an all over-shadowing tree! Names? Could I unfold the influence of Names, which are the most important of all Clothings, I were a second greater Trismegistus.[10] Not only all common Speech, but Science, Poetry itself is no other, if thou consider it, than a right *Naming*. Adam's first task was giving names to natural Appearances: what is ours still but a continuation of the same; be the Appearances exotic-vegetable, organic, mechanic, stars, or starry movements (as in Science); or (as in Poetry) passions, virtues, calamities, God-attributes, Gods?—In a very plain sense the Proverb says, *Call one a thief, and he will steal*; in an almost similar sense may we not perhaps say, *Call one Diogenes Teufelsdröckh, and he will open the Philosophy of Clothes?*'

'Meanwhile the incipient Diogenes, like others, all ignorant of his Why, his How or Whereabout, was opening his eyes to the kind Light; sprawling-out his ten fingers and toes; listening, tasting, feeling; in a word, by all his Five Senses, still more by his Sixth Sense of Hunger, and a whole infinitude of inward spiritual, half-awakened Senses, endeavouring daily to acquire for himself some knowledge of this strange Universe where he had arrived, be his task therein what it might. Infinite was his progress; thus in fifteen months, he could perform the miracle of—Speech! To hreed a fresh Soul, is it not like brooding a fresh (celestial) Egg; wherein as yet all is formless; powerless; yet by degrees organic elements and fibres shoot through the watery albumen; and out of vague Sensation grows Thought, grows Fantasy and Force, and we have Philosophies, Dynasties, nay Poetries and Religions!

---

[9] Father of Tristram Shandy in Sterne's novel.
[10] Hermes Trismegistus, Greek name for Egyptian god Thoth, god of speech, science, and letters.

'Young Diogenes, or rather young Gneschen,[11] for by such diminutive had they in their fondness named him, travelled forward to those high consummations, by quick yet easy stages. The Futterals, to avoid vain talk, and moreover keep the roll of gold Friedrichs safe, gave-out that he was a grand-nephew; the orphan of some sister's daughter, suddenly deceased, in Andreas's distant Prussian birthland; of whom, as of her indigent sorrowing widower, little enough was known at Entepfuhl. Heedless of all which, the Nurseling took to his spoon-meat, and throve. I have heard him noted as a still infant, that kept his mind much to himself; above all, that seldom or never cried. He already felt that time was precious; that he had other work cut-out for him than whimpering.'

Such, after utmost painful search and collation among these miscellaneous Paper-masses, is all the notice we can gather of Herr Teufelsdröckh's genealogy. More imperfect, more enigmatic it can seem to few readers than to us. The Professor, in whom truly we more and more discern a certain satirical turn, and deep under-currents of roguish whim, for the present stands pledged in honour, so we will not doubt him: but seems it not conceivable that, by the 'good Gretchen Futteral,' or some other perhaps interested party, he has himself been deceived? Should these sheets, translated or not, ever reach the Entepfuhl Circulating Library, some cultivated native of that district might feel called to afford explanation. Nay, since Books, like invisible scouts, permeate the whole habitable globe, and Timbuctoo itself is not safe from British Literature, may not some Copy find out even the mysterious basket-bearing Stranger, who in a state of extreme senility perhaps still exists; and gently force even him to disclose himself; to claim openly a son, in whom any father may feel pride?

CHAPTER II

Idyllic

Happy Childhood! Entepfuhl: Sights, hearings and experiences of the boy Teufelsdröckh; their manifold teaching. Education; what it can do, what cannot. Obedience our

universal duty and destiny. Gneschen sees the good Gretchen pray.

HAPPY season of Childhood!' exclaims Teufelsdröckh: 'Kind Nature, that art to all a bountiful mother; that visitest the poor man's hut with aural radiance; and for thy Nurseling hast provided a soft swathing of Love and infinite Hope, wherein he waxes and slumbers, danced-round (*umgaukelt*) by sweetest Dreams! If the paternal Cottage still shuts us in, its roof still screens us; with a Father we have as yet a prophet, priest and king, and an Obedience that makes us free. The young spirit has awakened out of Eternity, and knows not what we mean by Time; as yet Time is no fast-hurrying stream, but a sportful sunlit ocean; years to the child are as ages: ah! the secret of Vicissitude, of that slower or quicker decay and ceaseless down-rushing of the universal World-fabric, from the granite mountain to the man or day-moth is yet unknown; and in a motionless Universe, we taste, what afterwards in this quick-whirling Universe, is forever denied us, the balm of Rest. Sleep on, thou fair Child, for thy long rough journey is at hand! A little while, and thou too shalt sleep no more, but thy very dreams shall be mimic battles; thou too, with old Arnauld, wilt have to say in stern patience: "Rest? Rest? Shall I not have all Eternity to rest in?"[1] Celestial Nepenthe! though a Pyrrhus conquer empires, and an Alexander[2] sack the world, he finds thee not; and thou hast once fallen gently, of thy own accord, on the eyelids, on the heart of every mother's child. For as yet, sleep and waking are one: the fair Life-garden rustles infinite around, and everywhere is dewy fragrance, and the budding of Hope; which budding, if in youth, too frostnipt, it grow to flowers, will in manhood yield no fruit, but a prickly, bitter-rinded stone-fruit, of which the fewest can find the kernel.'

In such rose-coloured light does our Professor, as Poets are wont, look back on his childhood; the historical details of which (to say nothing of much other vague oratorical matter) he accordingly dwells on with an almost wearisome minuteness. We hear of Entepfuhl standing 'in trustful derangement' among the woody slopes; the paternal Orchard flanking it as extreme outpost

---

[11] Gneschen, "little Gene," nickname from Diogenes.
[1] Antoine Arnauld (1612–94), French theologian who replied as Carlyle cites in response to a fellow theologian's statement that he was weary of theological controversy.
[2] Pyrrhus (318–272 B.C.), King of Epirus; Alexander the Great (356–303 B.C.), King of Macedonia.

from below; the little Kuhbach[3] gushing kindly by, among beech-rows, through river after river, into the Donau,[4] into the Black Sea, into the Atmosphere and Universe; and how 'the brave old Linden,' stretching like a parasol of twenty ells in radius, overtopping all other rows and clumps, towered-up from the central *Agora* and *Campus Martius*[5] of the Village, like its Sacred Tree; and how the old men sat talking under its shadow (Gneschen often greedily listening), and the wearied labours reclined, and the unwearied children sported, and the young men and maidens often danced to flute-music. 'Glorious summer twilights,' cries Teufelsdröckh, 'when the Sun, like a proud Conqueror and Imperial Taskmaster, turned his back, with his gold-purple emblazonry, and all his fireclad body-guard (of Prismatic Colours); and the tired brickmakers of this clay Earth might steal a little frolic, and those few meek Stars would not tell of them!'

Then we have long details of the *Weinlesen* (Vintage), the Harvest-Home, Christmas, and so forth; with a whole cycle of the Entepfuhl Children's-games, differing apparently by mere superficial shades from those of other countries. Concerning all which, we shall here, for obvious reasons, say nothing. What cares the world for our as yet miniature Philosopher's achievements under that 'brave old Linden'? Or even where is the use of such practical reflections as the following? 'In all the sports of Children, were it only in their wanton breakages and defacements, you shall discern a creative instinct (*scaffenden Trieb*): the Mankin feels that he is a born Man, that his vocation is to work. The choicest present you can make him is a Tool; be it knife or pen-gun, for construction or for destruction; either way it is for Work, for Change. In gregarious sports of skill or strength, the Boy trains himself to Coöperation, for war or peace, as governor or governed: the little Maid again, provident of her domestic destiny, takes with preference to Dolls.'

Perhaps, however, we may give this anecdote, considering who it is that relates it: 'My first short-clothes were of yellow serge; or rather, I should say, my first short-cloth, for the vesture was one and indivisible, reaching from neck to ankle, a mere body with four limbs: of which fashion how little could I then divine the architectural, how much less the moral significance?'

More graceful is the following little picture:

'On fine evenings I was wont to carry-forth my supper (bread-crumb boiled in milk), and eat it out-of-doors. On the coping of the Orchard-wall, which I could reach by climbing, or still more easily if Father Andreas would set-up the pruning-ladder, my porringer was placed: there, many a sunset, have I, looking at the distant western Mountains, consumed, not without relish, my evening meal. Those hues of gold and azure, that hush of World's expectation as Day died, were still a Hebrew Speech for me: nevertheless I was looking at the fair illuminated Letters, and had an eye for their gilding.'

With 'the little one's friendship for cattle and poultry' we shall not much intermeddle. It may be that hereby he acquired a 'certain deeper sympathy with animated Nature': but when, we would ask, saw any man, in a collection of Biographical Documents, such a piece as this: 'Impressive enough (*bedeutungsvoll*) was it to hear, in early morning, the Swineherd's horn; and know that so many hungry happy quadrupeds were, on all sides, starting in hot haste to join him, for breakfast on the Heath. Or to see them at eventide, all marching-in again, with short squeak, almost in military order; and each, topographically correct, trotting-off in succession to the right or left, through its own lane, to its own dwelling; till old Kunz, at the Village head, now left alone, blew his last blast, and retired for the night. We are wont to love the Hog chiefly in the form of Ham; yet did not these bristly thick-skinned beings here manifest intelligence, perhaps humour of character; at any rate, a touching, trustful submissiveness to Man, who, were he but a Swineherd, in darned gabardine, and leather breeches, more resembling slate or discoloured-tin breeches, is still the Hierarch of this lower world?'

It is maintained, by Helvetius[6] and his set, that an infant of genius is quite the same as any other infant, only that certain surprisingly favourable influences accompany him through life, especially through childhood, and expand him, while others lie closefolded and continue dunces. Herein, say they, consists the whole difference between an inspired Prophet and a double-barrelled Game-preserver: the inner man of the one has been fostered into generous development; that of the other, crushed-down perhaps by vigour of animal digestion and the like, has exuded and evaporated, or at best sleeps now irresuscitably stagnant at

---

[3] Cowbrook.   [4] Danube.
[5] Agora, Greek marketplace; Campus Martius, Field of Mars, Roman field of assembly.
[6] Claude Adrien Helvétius (1715–71), French Encyclopaedist.

the bottom of his stomach. 'With which opinion,' cries Teufelsdröckh, 'I should as soon agree as with this other, that an acorn might, by favourable or unfavourable influences of soil and climate, be nursed into a cabbage, or the cabbage-seed into an oak.

'Nevertheless,' continues he, 'I too acknowledge the all-but omnipotence of early culture and nurture: hereby we have either a doddered dwarf bush, or a high-towering, wide-shadowing-tree; either a sick yellow cabbage, or an edible luxuriant green one. Of a truth, it is the duty of all men, especially of all philosphers, to note-down with accuracy the characteristic circumstances of their Education, what furthered, what hindered, what in any way modified it: to which duty, nowadays so pressing for many a German Autobiographer, I also zealously address myself.'—Thou rogue! Is it by short-clothes of yellow serge, and swineherd horns, that an infant of genius is educated? And yet, as usual, it ever remains doubtful whether he is laughing in his sleeve at these Autobiographical times of ours, or writing from the abundance of his own fond ineptitude. For he continues: 'If among the ever-streaming currents of Sights, Hearings, Feelings for Pain or Pleasure, whereby, as in a Magic Hall, young Gneschen went about environed, I might venture to select and specify, perhaps these following were also of the number:

'Doubtless, as childish sports call forth Intellect, Activity, so the young creature's Imagination was stirred up, and a Historical tendency given him by the narrative habits of Father Andreas; who with his battle· reminiscences, and gray austere yet hearty patriarchal aspect, could not but appear another Ulysses and "much-enduring Man." Eagerly I hung upon his tales, when listening neighbours enlivened the hearth; from these perils and these travels, wild and far almost as Hades itself, a dim world of Adventure expanded itself within me. Incalculable also was the knowledge I acquired in standing by the Old Men under the Linden-tree: the whole of Immensity was yet new to me; and had not these reverend seniors, talkative enough, been employed in partial surveys thereof for nigh fourscore years? With amazement I began to discover that Entepfuhl stood in the middle of a Country, of a World; that there was such a thing as History, as Biography; to which I also, one day, by hand and tongue, might contribute.

'In a like sense worked the *Postwagen* (Stage-coach), which, slow-rolling under it mountains of men and luggage, wended through our Village: northwards, truly, in the dead of night; yet southwards visibly at eventide. Not till my eighth year did I reflect that this Postwagen could be other than some terrestrial Moon, rising and setting by mere Law of Nature, like the heavenly one; that it came on made highways, from far cities towards far cities; weaving them like a monstrous shuttle into closer and closer union. It was then that, independently of Schiller's *Wilhelm Tell*, I made this not quite insignificant reflection (so true also in spiritual things): *Any road, this simple Entepfuhl road, will lead you to the end of the World!*

'Why mention our Swallows, which, out of far Africa, as I learned, threading their way over seas and mountains, corporate cities and belligerent nations, yearly found themselves, with the month of May, snug-lodged in our Cottage Lobby? The hospitable Father (for cleanliness' sake) had fixed a little bracket plumb under their nest: there they built, and caught flies, and twittered, and bred; and all, I chiefly, from the heart loved them. Bright, nimble creatures, who taught *you* the mason-craft; nay, stranger still, gave you a masonic incorporation, almost social police? For if, by ill chance, and when time pressed, your House fell, have I not seen five neighbourly Helpers appear next day; and swashing to and fro with animated, loud, long-drawn chirpings, and activity almost super-hirundine, complete it again before nightfall?

'But undoubtedly the grand summary of Entepfuhl child's-culture, where as in a funnel its manifold influences were concentrated and simultaneously poured-down on us, was the annual Cattle-fair. Here, assembling from all the four winds, came the elements of an unspeakable hurlyburly. Nutbrown maids and nutbrown men, all clear-washed, loud-laughing, bedizened and beribanded; who came for dancing, for treating, and if possible, for happiness. Topbooted Graziers from the North; Swiss Brokers, Italian Drovers, also topbooted, from the South; these with their subalterns in leather jerkins, leather skull-caps, and long oxgoads; shouting in half-articulate speech, amid the inarticulate barking and bellowing. Apart stood Potters from far Saxony, with their crockery in fair rows; Nürnberg Pedlars, in booths that to me seemed richer than Ormuz bazaars;[7] Showmen from the Lago Maggiore; detachments of the *Wiener Schub* (Offscourings of Vienna) vociferously superintending games of

---

[7] Ormuz, an island off Persia, famous for its bazaar; Lago Maggiore, lake on Italian-Swiss border.

chance. Ballad-singers brayed, Auctioneers grew hoarse; cheap New Wine (*heuriger*) flowed like water, still worse confounding the confusion; and high over all, vaulted, in ground-and-lofty tumbling, a particoloured Merry-Andrew, like the genius of the place and of Life itself.

'Thus encircled by the mystery of Existence; under the deep heavenly Firmament; waited-on by the four golden Seasons, with their vicissitudes of contribution, for even grim Winter brought its skating-matches and shooting-matches, its snow-storms and Christmas-carols,—did the Child sit and learn. These things were the Alphabet, whereby in aftertime he was to syllable and partly read the grand Volume of the World: what matters it whether such Alphabet be in large gilt letters or in small ungilt ones, so you have an eye to read it? For Gneschen, eager to learn, the very act of looking thereon was a blessedness that gilded all: his existence was a bright, soft element of Joy; out of which, as in Prospero's Island,[8] wonder after wonder bodied itself forth, to teach by charming.

'Nevertheless, I were but a vain dreamer to say that even then my felicity was perfect. I had, once for all, come down from Heaven into the Earth. Among the rainbow colours that glowed on my horizon, lay even in childhood a dark ring of Care, as yet no thicker than a thread, and often quite over-shone; yet always it reappeared, nay ever waxing broader and broader; till in after-years it almost over-shadowed my whole canopy, and threatened to engulf me in final night. It was the ring of Necessity whereby we are all begirt; happy he for whom a kind heavenly Sun brightens it into a ring of Duty, and plays round it with beautiful prismatic diffractions; yet ever, as basis and as bourne for our whole being, it is there.

'For the first few years of our terrestrial Apprenticeship, we have not much work to do; but, boarded and lodged gratis, are set down mostly to look about us over the workshop, and see others work, till we have understood the tools a little, and can handle this and that. If good Passivity alone, and not good Passivity and good Activity together, were the thing wanted, then was my early position favourable beyond the most. In all that respects openness of Sense, affectionate Temper, ingenuous Curiosity, and the fostering of these, what more could I have wished? On the other side, however, things went not so well. My Active Power (*Thatkraft*) was unfavourably

hemmed-in; of which misfortune how many traces yet abide with me! In an orderly house, where the litter of children's sports is hateful enough, your training is too stoical; rather to bear and forbear than to make and do. I was forbid much: wishes in any measure bold I had to renounce; everywhere a strait bond of Obedience inflexibly held me down. Thus already Freewill often came in painful collision with Necessity; so that my tears flowed, and at seasons the Child itself might taste that root of bitterness, wherewith the whole fruitage of our life is mingled and tempered.

'In which habituation to Obedience, truly, it was beyond measure safer to err by excess than by defect. Obedience is our universal duty and destiny; wherein whoso will not bend must break: too early and too thoroughly we cannot be trained to know that Would, in this world of ours, is as mere zero to Should, and for most part as the smallest of fractions even to Shall. Hereby was laid for me the basis of worldy Discretion, nay of Morality itself. Let me not quarrel with my upbringing. It was rigorous, too frugal, compressively secluded, everyway unscientific: yet in that very strictness and domestic solitude might there not lie the root of deeper earnestness, of the stem from which all noble fruit must grow? Above all, how unskilful soever, it was loving, it was well-meant, honest; whereby every deficiency was helped. My kind Mother, for as such I must ever love the good Gretchen, did me one altogether invaluable service: she taught me, less indeed by word than by act and daily reverent look and habitude, her own simple version of the Christian Faith. Andreas too attended Church; yet more like a parade-duty, for which he in the other world expected pay with arrears,—as, I trust, he has received; but my Mother, with a true woman's heart, and fine though uncultivated sense, was in the strictest acceptation Religious. How indestructibly the Good grows, and propagates itself, even among the weedy entanglements of Evil! The highest whom I knew on Earth I here saw bowed down, with awe unspeakable, before a Higher in Heaven: such things, especially in infancy, reach inwards to the very core of your being; mysteriously does a Holy of Holies build itself into visibility in the mysterious deeps; and Reverence, the divinest in man, springs forth undying from its mean envelopment of Fear. Wouldst thou rather be a peasant's son that knew, were it never so rudely, there was a God in Heaven and in Man; or a duke's son that only

---

[8] See Shakespeare's *The Tempest*.

knew there were two-and-thirty quarters[9] on the family-coach?'

To which last question we must answer: Beware, O Teufelsdröckh, of spiritual pride!

CHAPTER III

Pedagogy

Teufelsdröckh's School. His Education. How the ever-flowing Kuhbach speaks of Time and Eternity. The Hinter-schlag Gymnasium: rude Boys; and pedant Professors. The need of true Teachers, and their due recognition. Father Andreas dies; and Teufelsdröckh learns the secret of his birth: His reflections thereon. The Nameless University. Statistics of Imposture much wanted. Bitter fruits of Rationalism: Teufelsdröckh's religious difficulties. The young Englishman Herr Towgood. Modern Friendship.

HITHERTO we see young Gneschen, in his indivisible case of yellow serge, borne forward mostly on the arms of kind Nature alone; seated, indeed, and much to his mind, in the terrestrial workshop, but (except his soft hazel eyes, which we doubt not already gleamed with a still intelligence) called upon for little voluntary movement there. Hitherto, accordingly, his aspect is rather generic, that of an incipient Philosopher and Poet in the abstract; perhaps it would puzzle Herr Heuschrecke himself to say wherein the special Doctrine of Clothes is as yet foreshadowed or betokened. For with Gneschen, as with others, the Man may indeed stand pictured in the Boy (at least all the pigments are there); yet only some half of the Man stands in the Child, or young Boy, namely, his Passive endowment, not his Active. The more impatient are we to discover what figure he cuts in this latter capacity; how, when to use his own words, 'he understands the tools a little, and can handle this or that,' he will proceed to handle it.

Here, however, may be the place to state that, in much of our Philosopher's history, there is something of an almost Hindoo character: nay perhaps in that so well-fostered and every-way excellent 'Passivity' of his, which, with no free development of the antagonist Activity, distinguished his childhood, we may detect the

rudiments of much that, in after days, and still in these present days, astonishes the world. For the shallow-sighted, Teufelsdröckh is oftenest a man without Activity of any kind, a No-man; for the deep-sighted, again, a man with Activity almost superabundant yet so spiritual, close-hidden, enigmatic, that no mortal can foresee its explosions, or even when it has exploded, so much as ascertain its significance. A dangerous, difficult temper for the modern European; above all, disadvantageous in the hero of a Biography! Now as heretofore it will behove the Editor of these pages, were it never so unsuccessfully, to do his endeavour.

Among the earliest tools of any complicacy which a man, especially a man of letters, gets to handle, are his Class-books. On this portion of his History, Teufelsdröckh looks down professedly as indifferent. Reading he 'cannot remember ever to have learned'; so perhaps had it by nature. He says generally: 'Of the insignificant portion of my Education, which depended on Schools, there need almost no notice be taken. I learned what others learn; and kept it stored-by in a corner of my head, seeing as yet no manner of use in it. My Schoolmaster, a downbent, brokenhearted, underfoot martyr, as others of that guild are, did little for me, except discover that he could do little: he, good soul, pronounced me a genius, fit for the learned professions; and that I must be sent to the Gymnasium, and one day to the University. Meanwhile, what printed thing soever I could meet with I read. My very copper pocket-money I laid-out on stall-literature; which, as it accumulated, I with my own hands sewed into volumes. By this means was the young head furnished with a considerable miscellany of things and shadows of things: History in authentic fragments lay mingled with Fabulous chimeras, wherein also was reality; and the whole not as dead stuff, but as living pabulum, tolerably nutritive for a mind as yet so peptic.'

That the Entepfuhl Schoolmaster judged well, we now know. Indeed, already in the youthful Gneschen, with all his outward stillness, there may have been manifest an inward vivacity that promised much; symptoms of a spirit singularly open, thoughtful, almost poetical. Thus, to say nothing of his Suppers on the Orchard-wall, and other phenomena of that earlier period, have many readers of these pages stumbled, in their twelfth year, on such reflections as the following? 'It struck me much, as I sat by the Kuhbach, one

---

[9] Reference to quarterings in heraldry.

silent noontide, and watched it flowing, gurgling, to think how this same streamlet had flowed and gurgled, through all changes of weather and of fortune, from beyond the earliest date of History. Yes, probably on the morning when Joshua forded Jordan; even as at the mid-day when Cæsar, doubtless with difficulty, swam the Nile, yet kept his *Commentaries* dry,—this little Kuhbach, assiduous as Tiber, Eurotas or Siloa,[1] was murmuring on across the wilderness, as yet unnamed, unseen: here, too, as in the Euphrates and the Ganges, is a vein or veinlet of the grand World-circulation of Waters, which, with its atmospheric arteries, has lasted and lasts simply with the World. Thou fool! Nature alone is antique, and the oldest art a mushroom; that idle crag thou sittest on is six-thousand years of age.' In which little thought, as in a little fountain, may there not lie the beginning of those well-nigh unutterable meditations on the grandeur and mystery of TIME, and its relation to ETERNITY, which play such a part in this Philosophy of Clothes?

Over his Gymnasic and Academic years the Professor by no means lingers so lyrical and joyful as over his childhood. Green sunny tracts there are still; but intersected by bitter rivulets of tears, here and there stagnating into sour marshes of discontent. 'With my first view of the Hinterschlag[2] Gymnasium,' writes he, 'my evil days began. Well do I still remember the red sunny Whitsuntide morning, when, trotting full of hope by the side of Father Andreas, I entered the main street of the place, and saw its steeple-clock (then striking Eight) and *Schuldthurm* (Jail), and the aproned or disaproned Burghers moving-in to breakfast: a little dog, in mad terror, was rushing past; for some human imps had tied a tin-kettle to its tail; thus did the agonised creature, loud-jingling, career through the whole length of the Borough, and become notable enough. Fit emblem of many a Conquering Hero, to whom Fate (wedding Fantasy to Sense, as it often elsewhere does) has malignantly appended a tin-kettle of Ambition, to chase him on; which the faster he runs, urges him the faster, the more loudly and more foolishly! Fit emblem also of much that awaited myself, in that mischievous Den; as in the World, whereof it was a portion and epitome! 'Alas, the kind beech-rows of Entepfuhl were

hidden in the distance: I was among strangers, harshly, at best indifferently, disposed towards me; the young heart felt, for the first time, quite orphaned and alone.' His schoolfellows, as is usual, persecuted him: 'They were Boys,' he says, 'mostly rude Boys, and obeyed the impulse of rude, Nature, which bids the deerherd fall upon any stricken hart, the duck-flock put to death any broken-winged brother or sister, and on all hands the strong tyrannise over the weak.' He admits that though 'perhaps in an unusual degree morally courageous,' he succeeded ill in battle, and would fain have avoided it; a result, as would appear, owing less to his small personal stature (for in passionate seasons he was 'incredibly nimble'), than to his 'virtuous principles': 'if it was disgraceful to be beaten,' says he, 'it was only a shade less disgraceful to have so much as fought; thus was I drawn two ways at once, and in this important element of school-history, the war-element, had little but sorrow.' On the whole, that same excellent 'Passivity,' so notable in Teufelsdröckh's childhood, is here visibly enough again getting nourishment. 'He wept often; indeed to such a degree that he was nicknamed *Der Weinende* (the Tearful), which epithet, till towards his thirteenth year, was indeed not quite unmerited. Only at rare intervals did the young soul burst-forth into fire-eyed rage, and, with a stormfulness (*Ungestüm*) under which the boldest quailed, assert that he too had Rights of Man, or at least of Mankin.' In all which, who does not discern a fine flower-tree and cinnamon-tree (of genius) nigh choked among pumpkins, reed-grass and ignoble shrubs; and forced if it would live, to struggle upwards only, and not outwards; into a *height* quite sickly, and disproportioned to its *breadth*?

We find, moreover, that his Greek and Latin were 'mechanically' taught; Hebrew scarce even mechanically; much else which they called History, Cosmography, Philosophy, and so forth, no better than not at all. So that, except inasmuch as Nature was still busy; and he himself 'went about, as was of old his wont, among the Craftsmen's workshops, there learning many things'; and farther lighted on some small store of curious reading, in Hans Wachtel the Cooper's house, where he lodged,—his time, it would appear, was utterly wasted. Which facts the Professor has not

---

[1] Joshua 3:14–17; Plutarch's *Lives* relates the story of Caesar's swimming the Nile; the Tiber runs through Rome; Eurotas, river in Laconia in Greece where Sparta was located; Siloa, or Siloam, pool near Jerusalem.
[2] "Strike behind."

yet learned to look upon with any contentment. Indeed, throughout the whole of this Bag *Scorpio*,[3] where we now are, and often in the following Bag, he shows himself unusually animated on the matter of Education, and not without some touch of what we might presume to be anger.

'My Teachers,' says he, 'were hide-bound Pedants, without knowledge of man's nature, or of boy's; or of aught save their lexicons and quarterly account-books. Innumerable dead Vocables (no dead Language, for they themselves knew no Language) they crammed into us, and called it fostering the growth of mind. How can an inanimate, mechanical Gerund grinder, the like of whom will, in a subsequent century, be manufactured at Nürnberg out of wood and leather, foster the growth of anything; much more of Mind, which grows, not like a vegetable (by having its roots littered with etymological compost), but like a spirit, by mysterious contact of Spirit; Thought kindling itself at the fire of living Thought? How shall *he* give kindling, in whose own inward man there is no live coal, but all is burnt-out to a dead grammatical cinder? The Hinterschlag Professors knew syntax enough; and of the human soul thus much: that it had a faculty called Memory, and could be acted-on through the muscular integument by appliance of birch-rods.

'Alas, so is it everywhere, so will it ever be; till the Hodman is discharged, or reduced to hod-bearing; and an Architect is hired, and on all hands fitly encouraged: till communities and individuals discover, not without surprise, that fashioning the souls of a generation by Knowledge can rank on a level with blowing their bodies to pieces by Gunpowder; that with Generals and Fieldmarshals for killing, there should be world-honoured Dignitaries, and were it possible, true God-ordained Priests, for teaching. But as yet, though the Soldier wears openly, and even parades, his butchering-tool, nowhere, far as I have travelled, did the Schoolmaster make show of his instructing-tool: nay, were he to walk abroad with birch girt on thigh, as if he therefrom expected honour, would there not, among the idler class, perhaps a certain levity be excited?'

In the third year of this Gymnasic period, Father Andreas seems to have died: the young Scholar, otherwise so maltreated, saw himself for the first time clad outwardly in sables, and inwardly in quite inexpressible melancholy. 'The dark bottomless Abyss, that lies under our feet, had yawned open; the pale kingdoms of Death, with all their innumerable silent nations and generations, stood before him; the inexorable word, NEVER! now first showed its meaning. My Mother wept, and her sorrow got vent; but in my heart there lay a whole lake of tears, pent-up in silent desolation. Nevertheless the unworn Spirit is strong; Life is so healthful that it even finds nourishment in Death: these stern experiences, planted down by Memory in my Imagination, rose there to a whole cypress-forest, sad but beautiful; waving, with not unmelodious sighs, in dark luxuriance, in the hottest sunshine, through long years of youth:—as in manhood also it does, and will do; for I have now pitched my tent under a Cypress-tree; the Tomb is now my inexpugnable Fortress, ever close by the gate of which I look upon the hostile armaments, and pains and penalties of tyrannous Life placidly enough, and listen to its loudest threatenings with a still smile. O ye loved ones, that already sleep in the noiseless Bed of Rest, whom in life I could only weep for and never help; and ye, who wide-scattered still toil lonely in the monster-bearing Desert, dyeing the flinty ground with your blood, —yet a little while, and we shall all meet THERE, and our Mother's bosom will screen us all; and Oppression's harness, and Sorrow's fire-whip, and all the Gehenna Bailiffs that patrol and inhabit ever-vexed Time, cannot thenceforth harm us any more!'

Close by which rather beautiful apostrophe, lies a laboured Character[4] of the deceased Andreas Futteral; of his natural ability, his deserts in life (as Prussian Sergeant); with long historical inquiries into the genealogy of the Futteral Family, here traced back as far as Henry the Fowler:[5] the whole of which we pass over, not without astonishment. It only concerns us to add, that now was the time when Mother Gretchen revealed to her foster-son that he was not at all of this kindred; or indeed of any kindred, having come into historical existence in the way already known to us. 'Thus was I doubly orphaned,' says he; 'bereft not only of Possession, but even of Remembrance. Sorrow and Wonder, here suddenly united, could not but produce abundant fruit. Such a disclosure, in such a season, struck its roots through my whole nature: ever till the years of mature manhood, it mingled with my whole thoughts, was as the stem whereon

---

[3] Zodiacal sign of the Scorpion, October 23–November 21.
[4] I.e., a character sketch.   [5] Heinrich der Vogeler (876?–936), German Emperor.

all my day-dreams and night-dreams grew. A certain poetic elevation, yet also a corresponding civic depression, it naturally imparted: *I was like no other*; in which fixed-idea, leading sometimes to highest, and oftener to frightfullest results, may there not lie the first spring of tendencies, which in my Life have become remarkable enough? As in birth, so in action, speculation, and social position, my fellows are perhaps not numerous.'

In the Bag *Sagittarius*,[6] as we at length discover, Teufelsdröckh has become a University man; though how, when, or of what quality, will nowhere disclose itself with the smallest certainty. Few things, in the way of confusion and capricious indistinctness, can now surprise our readers; not even the total want of dates, almost without parallel in a Biographical work. So enigmatic, so chaotic we have always found, and must always look to find, these scattered Leaves. In *Sagittarius*, however, Teufelsdröckh begins to show himself even more than usually Sibylline: fragments of all sorts; scraps of regular Memoir, College-Exercises, Programs, Professional Testimoniums, Milkscores, torn Billets, sometimes to appearance of an amatory cast; all blown together as if by merest chance, henceforth bewilder the sane Historian. To combine any picture of these University, and the subsequent, years; much more, to decipher therein any illustrative primordial elements of the Clothes-Philosophy, becomes such a problem as the reader may imagine.

So much we can see; darkly, as through the foliage of some wavering thicket: a youth of no common endowment, who has passed happily through Childhood, less happily yet still vigorously through Boyhood, now at length perfect in 'dead vocables,' and set down, as he hopes, by the living Fountain, there to superadd Ideas and Capabilities. From such Fountain he draws, diligently, thirstily, yet never or seldom with his whole heart, for the water nowise suits his palate; discouragements, entanglements, aberrations are discoverable or supposable. Nor perhaps are even pecuniary distresses wanting; for 'the good Gretchen, who in spite of advices from not disinterested relatives has sent him hither, must after a time withdraw her willing but too feeble hand.' Nevertheless in an atmosphere of Poverty and manifold Chagrin, the Humour of that young Soul, what character is in him, first decisively reveals itself; and, like strong sunshine in weeping skies, gives out variety of colours, some of which are prismatic. Thus, with the aid of Time and of what Time brings, has the stripling Diogenes Teufelsdröckh waxed into manly stature; and into so questionable an aspect, that we ask with new eagerness, How he specially came by it, and regret anew that there is no more explicit answer. Certain of the intelligible and partially significant fragments, which are few in number, shall be extracted from that Limbo of a Paper-bag, and presented with the usual preparation.

As if, in the Bag *Scorpio*, Teufelsdröckh had not already expectorated his antipedagogic spleen; as if, from the name *Sagittarius*, he had thought himself called upon to shoot arrows, we here again fall-in with such matter as this: 'The University where I was educated still stands vivid enough in my remembrance, and I know its name well; which name, however, I, from tenderness to existing interests and persons, shall in nowise divulge. It is my painful duty to say that, out of England and Spain, ours was the worst of all hitherto discovered Universities. This is indeed a time when right Education is, as nearly as may be, impossible: however, in degrees of wrongness there is no limit: nay, I can conceive a worse system than that of the Nameless itself; as poisoned victual may be worse than absolute hunger.

'It is written, When the blind lead the blind, both shall fall into the ditch:[7] wherefore, in such circumstances, may it not sometimes be safer, if both leader and led simply—sit still? Had you, anywhere in Crim Tartary, walled-in a square enclosure; furnished it with a small, ill-chosen Library; and then turned loose into it eleven-hundred Christian striplings, to tumble about as they listed, from three to seven years: certain persons, under the title of Professors, being stationed at the gates, to declare aloud that it was a University, and exact considerable admission-fees,—you had, not indeed in mechanical structure, yet in spirit and result, some imperfect resemblance of our High Seminary. I say, imperfect; for if our mechanical structure was quite other, so neither was our result altogether the same: unhappily, we were not in Crim Tartary,[8] but in a corrupt European city, full of smoke and sin; moreover, in the middle of a Public, which, without far costlier apparatus than that of the Square Enclosure, and De-

---

[6] Sign of the Archer, November 22–December 21.   [7] Matthew 15:14.
[8] Crimea, formerly occupied by the Tartars.

claration aloud, you could not be sure of gulling.

'Gullible, however, by fit apparatus, all Publics are; and gulled, with the most surprising profit. Towards anything like a *Statistics of Imposture*, indeed, little as yet has been done: with a strange indifference, our Economists, nigh buried under Tables for minor Branches of Industry, have altogether overlooked the grand all-overtopping Hypocrisy Branch; as if our whole arts of Puffery, of Quackery, Priestcraft, Kingcraft, and the innumerable other crafts and mysteries of that genus, had not ranked in Productive Industry at all! Can any one, for example, so much as say, What moneys, in Literature and Shoeblacking, are realised by actual instruction and actual jet Polish; what by fictitious-persuasive Proclamation of such; specifying, in distinct items, the distributions, circulations, disbursements, incomings of said moneys, with the smallest approach to accuracy? But to ask, How far, in all the several infinitely-complected departments of social business, in government, education, in manual, commercial, intellectual fabrication of every sort, man's Want is supplied by true Ware; how far by the mere Appearance of true Ware:—in other words, To what extent, by what methods, with what effects, in various times and countries, Deception takes the place of wages of Performance: here truly is an Inquiry big with results for the future time, but to which hitherto only the vaguest answer can be given. If for the present, in our Europe, we estimate the ratio of Ware to Appearance of Ware so high even as at One to a Hundred (which, considering the Wages of a Pope, Russian Autocrat, or English Game-Preserver, is probably not far from the mark),—what almost prodigious saving may there not be anticipated, as the *Statistics of Imposture* advances, and so the manufacturing of Shams (that of Realities rising into clearer and clearer distinction therefrom) gradually declines, and at length becomes all but wholly unnecessary!

'This for the coming golden ages. What I had to remark, for the present brazen one, is, that in several provinces, as in Education, Polity, Religion, where so much is wanted and indispensable, and so little can as yet be furnished, probably Imposture is of sanative, anodyne nature, and man's Gullibility not his worst blessing. Suppose your sinews of war quite broken; I mean your military chest insolvent, forage all but exhausted; and that the whole army is about to mutiny, disband, and cut your

and each other's throat,—then were it not well could you, as if by miracle, pay them in any sort of fairy-money, feed them on coagulated water, or mere imagination of meat; whereby, till the real supply came up, they might be kept together and quiet? Such perhaps was the aim of Nature, who does nothing without aim, in furnishing her favourite, Man, with this his so omnipotent or rather omnipatient Talent of being Gulled.

'How beautifully it works, with a little mechanism; nay, almost makes mechanism for itself! These Professors in the Nameless lived with ease, with safety, by a mere Reputation, constructed in past times, and then too with no great effort, by quite another class of persons. Which Reputation, like a strong, brisk-going undershot wheel, sunk into the general current, bade fair, with only a little annual repainting on their part, to hold long together, and of its own accord assiduously grind for them. Happy that it was so, for the Millers! They themselves needed not to work; their attempts at working, at what they called Educating, now when I look back on it, fill me with a certain mute admiration.

'Besides all this, we boasted ourselves a Rational University; in the highest degree hostile to Mysticism; thus was the young vacant mind furnished with much talk about Progress of the Species, Dark Ages, Prejudice, and the like; so that all were quickly enough blown out into a state of windy argumentativeness; whereby the better sort had soon to end in sick, impotent Scepticism; the worser sort explode (*crepiren*) in finished Self-conceit, and to all spiritual intents become dead.—But this too is portion of mankind's lot. If our era is the Era of Unbelief, why murmur under it; is there not a better coming, nay come? As in long-drawn systole and long-drawn diastole, must the period of Faith alternate with the period of Denial; must the vernal growth, the summer luxuriance of all Opinions, Spiritual Representations and Creations, be followed by, and again follow, the autumnal decay, the winter dissolution. For man lives in Time, has his whole earthly being, endeavour and destiny shaped for him by Time: only in the transitory Time-Symbol is the ever-motionless Eternity we stand on made manifest. And yet, in such winter-seasons of Denial, it is for the nobler-minded perhaps a comparative misery to have been born, and to be awake and work; and for the duller a felicity, if, like hibernating animals, safe-lodged in some Salamanca University, or Sybaris City, or other superstitious or voluptuous Castle of

Indolence,[9] they can slumber-through in stupid dreams, and only awaken when the loud-roaring hailstorms have all done their work, and to our prayers and martyrdoms the new Spring has been vouchsafed.'

That in the environment, here mysteriously enough shadowed forth Teufelsdröckh must have felt ill at ease, cannot be doubtful. 'The hungry young,' he says, 'looked up to their spiritual Nurses; and, for food, were bidden eat the east-wind. What vain jargon of controversial Metaphysic, Etymology, and mechanical Manipulation falsely named Science, was current there, I indeed learned, better perhaps than the most. Among eleven-hundred Christian youths, there will not be wanting some eleven eager to learn. By collision with such, a certain warmth, a certain polish was communicated; by instinct and happy accident, I took less to rioting (*renommiren*), than to thinking and reading, which latter also I was free to do. Nay from the chaos of that Library, I succeeded in fishing-up more books perhaps than had been known to the very keepers thereof. The foundation of a Literary Life was hereby laid: I learned, on my own strength, to read fluently in almost all cultivated languages, on almost all subjects and sciences; farther, as man is ever the prime object to man, already it was my favourite employment to read character in speculation, and from the Writing to construe the Writer. A certain groundplan of Human Nature and Life began to fashion itself in me; wondrous enough, now when I look back on it; for my whole Universe, physical and spiritual, was as yet a Machine! However, such a conscious, recognised groundplan, the truest I had, *was* beginning to be there, and by additional experiments might be corrected and indefinitely extended.'

Thus from poverty does the strong educe nobler wealth; thus in the destitution of the wild desert does our young Ishmael[10] acquire for himself the highest of all possessions, that of Self-help. Nevertheless a desert this was, waste, and howling with savage monsters. Teufelsdröckh gives us long details of his 'fever-paroxysms of Doubt'; his Inquiries concerning Miracles, and the Evidences of religious Faith; and how 'in the silent night-watches, still darker in his heart than over sky and earth, he has cast himself before the All-seeing, and with audible prayers cried vehemently for Light, for deliverance from Death and the Grave. Not till after long years, and unspeakable agonies, did the believing heart surrender; sink into spell-bound sleep, under the nightmare, Unbelief; and, in this hag-ridden dream, mistake God's fair living world for a pallid, vacant Hades and extinct Pandemonium. But through such Purgatory pain,' continues he, 'it is appointed us to pass; first must the dead Letter of Religion own itself dead, and drop piecemeal into dust, if the living Spirit of Religion, freed from this its charnel-house, is to arise on us, newborn of Heaven, and with new healing under its wings.'

To which Purgatory pains, seemingly severe enough, if we add a liberal measure of Earthly distresses, want of practical guidance, want of sympathy, want of money, want of hope; and all this in the fervid season of youth, so exaggerated in imagining, so boundless in desires, yet here so poor in means,—do we not see a strong incipient spirit oppressed and overloaded from without and from within; the fire of genius struggling-up among fuel-wood of the greenest, and as yet with more of bitter vapour than of clear flame?

From various fragments of Letters and other documentary scraps, it is to be inferred that Teufelsdröckh, isolated, shy, retiring as he was, had not altogether escaped notice: certain established men are aware of his existence; and, if stretching-out no helpful hand, have at least their eyes on him. He appears, though in dreary enough humour, to be addressing himself to the Profession of Law;—whereof, indeed, the world has since seen him a public graduate. But omitting these broken, unsatisfactory thrums of Economical relation, let us present rather the following small thread of Moral relation; and therewith, the reader for himself weaving it in at the right place, conclude our dim arras-picture of these University years.

'Here also it was that I formed acquaintance with Herr Towgood, or, as it is perhaps better written, Herr Toughgut; a young person of quality (*von Adel*), from the interior parts of England. He stood connected, by blood and hospitality, with the Counts von Zähdarm,[11] in this quarter of Germany; to which noble Family I likewise was, by his means, with all friendliness, brought near. Towgood had a fair talent,

---

[9] Salamanca, Spanish university founded 1230; Sybaris, Greek city in southern Italy, famed for its luxury; *Castle of Indolence*, poem by James Thomson (1700–1748).
[10] See Genesis 16:1–16, 21:12–21.   [11] German for "Tough-gut."

unspeakably ill-cultivated; with considerable humour of character: and, bating his total ignorance, for he knew nothing except Boxing and a little Grammar, showed less of that aristocratic impassivity, and silent fury, than for most part belongs to Travellers of his nation. To him I owe my first practical knowledge of the English and their ways; perhaps also something of the partiality with which I have ever since regarded that singular people. Towgood was not without an eye, could he have come at any light. Invited doubtless by the presence of the Zähdarm Family, he had travelled hither, in the almost frantic hope of perfecting his studies; he, whose studies had as yet been those of infancy, hither to a University where so much as the notion of perfection, not to say the effort after it, no longer existed! Often we would condole over the hard destiny of the Young in this era: how, after all our toil, we were to be turned-out into the world, with beards on our chins indeed, but with few other attributes of manhood; no existing thing that we were trained to Act on, nothing that we could so much as Believe. "How has our head on the outside a polished Hat," would Towgood exclaim, "and in the inside Vacancy, or a froth of Vocables and Attorney-Logic! At a small cost men are educated to make leather into shoes; but at a great cost, what am I educated to make? By Heaven, Brother! what I have already eaten and worn, as I came thus far, would endow a considerable Hospital of Incurables."—"Man, indeed," I would answer, "has a Digestive Faculty, which must be kept working, were it even partly by stealth. But as for our Mis-education, make not bad worse; waste not the time yet ours, in trampling on thistles because they have yielded us no figs. *Frisch zu, Bruder!*[12] Here are Books, and we have brains to read them; here is a whole Earth and a whole Heaven, and we have eyes to look on them: *Frisch zu!*"

'Often also our talk was gay; not without brilliancy, and even fire. We looked-out on Life, with its strange scaffolding, where all at once harlequins dance, and men are beheaded and quartered: motley, not unterrific was the aspect; but we looked on it like brave youths. For myself, these were perhaps my most genial hours. Towards this young warmhearted, strongheaded and wrongheaded Herr Towgood I was even near experiencing the now obsolete sentiment of Friendship. Yes, foolish Heathen that I was, I felt that, under certain conditions, I could have loved this man, and taken him to my bosom, and been his brother once and always. By degrees, however, I understood the new time, and its wants. If man's *Soul* is indeed, as in the Finnish Language, and Utilitarian Philosophy, a kind of *Stomach*, what else is the true meaning of Spiritual Union but an Eating together? Thus we, instead of Friends, are Dinner-guests; and here as elsewhere have cast away chimeras.'

So ends, abruptly as is usual, and enigmatically, this little incipient romance. What henceforth becomes of the brave Herr Towgood, or Tough-gut? He has dived-under, in the Autobiographical Chaos, and swims we see not where. Does any reader 'in the interior parts of England' know of such a man?

Getting Under Way

The grand thaumaturgic Art of Thought. Difficulty in fitting Capability to Opportunity, or of getting under way. The advantage of Hunger and Bread-Studies. Teufelsdröckh has to enact the stern monodrama of *No object and no rest.* Sufferings as Auscultator. Given up as a man of genius. Zähdarm House. Intolerable presumption of young men. Irony and its consequences. Teufelsdröckh's Epitaph on Count Zähdarm.

T HUS nevertheless,' writes our Autobiographer, apparently as quitting College, 'was there realised Somewhat; namely, I, Diogenes Teufels-dröckh: a visible Temporary Figure (*Zeitbild*), occupying some cubic feet of Space, and containing within it Forces both physical and spiritual; hopes, passions, thoughts; the whole wondrous furniture, in more or less perfection, belonging to that mystery, a Man. Capabilities there were in me to give battle, in some small degree, against the great Empire of Darkness: does not the very Ditcher and Delver, with his spade, extinguish many a thistle and puddle; and so leave a little Order, where he found the opposite? Nay your very Daymoth has capabilities in this kind; and ever organises something (into its own Body, if no otherwise), which was before Inorganic; and of mute dead air makes

---

[12] "Get to work, Brother!"

living music, though only of the faintest, by humming.

'How much more, one whose capabilities are spiritual; who has learned, or begun learning, the grand thaumaturgic art of Thought! Thaumaturgic I name it; for hitherto all Miracles have been wrought thereby, and henceforth innumerable will be wrought; whereof we, even in these days, witness some. Of the Poet's and Prophet's inspired Message, and how it makes and unmakes whole worlds, I shall forbear mention: but cannot the dullest hear Steam-Engines clanking around him? Has he not seen the Scottish Brassmith's IDEA (and this but a mechanical one) travelling on fire-wings round the Cape, and across two Oceans;[1] and stronger than any other Enchanter's Familiar, on all hands unweariedly fetching and carrying: at home, not only weaving Cloth; but rapidly enough overturning the whole old system of Society; and, for Feudalism and Preservation of the Game, preparing us, by indirect but sure methods, Industrialism and the Government of the Wisest? Truly a Thinking Man is the worst enemy the Prince of Darkness can have; every time such a one announces himself, I doubt not, there runs a shudder through the Nether Empire; and new Emissaries are trained, with new tactics, to, if possible, entrap him, and hoodwink and handcuff him.

'With such high vocation had I too, as denizen of the Universe, been called. Unhappy it is, however, that though born to the amplest Sovereignty, in this way, with no less than sovereign right of Peace and War against the Time-Prince (*Zeitfürst*), or Devil, and all his Dominions, your coronation-ceremony costs such trouble, your sceptre is so difficult to get at, or even to get eye on!'

By which last wiredrawn similitude does Teufelsdröckh mean no more than that young men find obstacles in what we call 'getting under way'? 'Not what I Have,' continues he, 'but what I Do is my Kingdom. To each is given a certain inward Talent, a certain outward Environment of Fortune; to each, by wisest combination of these two, a certain maximum of Capability. But the hardest problem were ever this first: To find by study of yourself, and of the ground you stand on, what your combined inward and outward Capability specially is. For, alas, our young soul is all budding with Capabilities, and we see not yet which is the main and true one.

Always too the new man is in a new time, under new conditions; his course can be the *fac-simile* of no prior one, but is by its nature original. And then how seldom will the outward Capability fit the inward: though talented wonderfully enough, we are poor, unfriended, dyspeptical, bashful; nay what is worse than all, we are foolish. Thus, in a whole imbroglio of Capabilities, we go stupidly groping about, to grope which is ours, and often clutch the wrong one: in this mad work must several years of our small term be spent, till the purblind Youth, by practice, acquire notions of distance, and become a seeing Man. Nay, many so spend their whole term, and in ever-new expectation, ever-new disappointment, shift from enterprise to enterprise, and from side to side: till at length, as exasperated striplings of three-score-and-ten, they shift into their last enterprise, that of getting buried.

'Such, since the most of us are too ophthalmic, would be the general fate; were it not that one thing saves us: our Hunger. For on this ground, as the prompt nature of Hunger is well known, must a prompt choice be made: hence have we, with wise foresight, Indentures and Apprenticeships for our irrational young; whereby, in due season, the vague universality of a Man shall find himself ready-moulded into a specific Craftsman; and so thenceforth work, with much or with little waste of Capability as it may be; yet not with the worst waste, that of time. Nay even in matters spiritual, since the spiritual artist too is born blind, and does not, like certain other creatures, receive sight in nine days, but far later, sometimes never,—is it not well that there should be what we call Professions, or Bread-studies (*Brodzwecke*), pre-appointed us? Here, circling like the gin-horse, for whom partial or total blindness is no evil, the Bread-artist can travel contentedly round and round, still fancying that it is forward and forward; and realise much: for himself victual; for the world an additional horse's power in the grand corn-mill or hemp-mill of Economic Society. For me too had such a leading-string been provided; only that it proved a neck-halter, and had nigh throttled me, till I broke it off. Then, in the words of Ancient Pistol, did the world generally become mine oyster, which I, by strength or cunning, was to open, as I would and could. Almost had I deceased (*fast wär ich umgekommen*), so obstinately did it continue shut.'

We see here, significantly foreshadowed, the spirit of much that was to befall our Auto-

---

[1] James Watt (1736–1819), Scottish inventor of the steam engine.

biographer; the historical embodiment of which, as it painfully takes shape in his Life, lies scattered, in dim disastrous details, through this Bag *Pisces*, and those that follow. A young man of high talent, and high though still temper, like a young mettled colt, 'breaks-off his neck-halter,' and bounds forth, from his peculiar manger, into the wide world; which, alas, he finds all rigorously fenced-in. Richest clover-fields tempt his eye; but to him they are forbidden pasture: either pining in progressive starvation, he must stand; or, in mad exasperation, must rush to and fro, leaping against sheer stone-walls, which he cannot leap over, which only lacerate and lame him; till at last, after thousand attempts and endurances, he, as if by miracle, clears his way; not indeed into luxuriant and luxurious clover, yet into a certain bosky wilderness where existence is still possible, and Freedom, though waited on by Scarcity, is not without sweetness. In a word, Teufelsdröckh having thrown-up his legal Profession, finds himself without landmark of outward guidance; whereby his previous want of decided Belief, or inward guidance, is frightfully aggravated. Necessity urges him on; Time will not stop, neither can he, a Son of Time; wild passions without solacement, wild faculties without employment, ever vex and agitate him. He too must enact that stern Monodrama, *No Object and no Rest*; must front its successive destinies, work through to its catastrophe, and deduce therefrom what moral he can.

Yet let us be just to him, let us admit that his 'neck-halter' sat nowise easy on him; that he was in some degree forced to break it off. If we look at the young man's civic position, in this Nameless capital, as he emerges from its Nameless University, we can discern well that it was far from enviable. His first Law-Examination he has come through triumphantly; and can even boast that the *Examen Rigorosum* need not have frightened him: but though he is hereby 'an *Auscultator* of respectability,' what avails it?[2] There is next to no employment to be had. Neither, for a youth without connexions, is the process of Expectation very hopeful in itself; nor for one of his disposition much cheered from without. 'My fellow Auscultators,' he says, 'were Auscultators: they dressed, and digested, and talked articulate words; other vitality showed they almost none. Small speculation in those eyes, that they did glare withal! Sense neither for the high nor for the deep, nor

for aught human or divine, save only for the faintest scent of coming Preferment.' In which words, indicating a total estrangement on the part of Teufelsdröckh, may there not also lurk traces of a bitterness as from wounded vanity? Doubtless these prosaic Auscultators may have sniffed at him, with his strange ways; and tried to hate, and what was much more impossible, to despise him. Friendly communion, in any case, there could not be: already has the young Teufelsdröckh left the other young geese; and swims apart, though as yet uncertain whether he himself is cygnet or gosling.

Perhaps, too, what little employment he had was performed ill, at best unpleasantly. 'Great practical method and expertness' he may brag of; but is there not also great practical pride, though deep-hidden, only the deeper-seated? So shy a man can never have been popular. We figure to ourselves, how in those days he may have played strange freaks with his independence, and so forth: do not his own words betoken as much? 'Like a very young person, I imagined it was with Work alone, and not also with Folly and Sin, in myself and others, that I had been appointed to struggle.' Be this as it may, his progress from the passive Auscultatorship, towards any active Assessorship, is evidently of the slowest. By degrees, those same established men, once partially inclined to patronise him, seem to withdraw their countenance, and give him up as 'a man of genius': against which procedure he, in these Papers, loudly protests. 'As if,' says he, 'the higher did not presuppose the lower; as if he who can fly into heaven, could not also walk post if he resolved on it! But the world is an old woman, and mistakes any gilt farthing for a gold coin; whereby being often cheated, she will thenceforth trust nothing but the common copper.'

How our winged sky-messenger, unaccepted as a terrestrial runner, contrived, in the mean while, to keep himself from flying skyward without return, is not too clear from these Documents. Good old Gretchen seems to have vanished from the scene, perhaps from the Earth; other Horn of Plenty, or even of Parsimony, nowhere flows for him; so that 'the prompt nature of Hunger being well known,' we are not without our anxiety. From private Tuition, in never so many languages and sciences, the aid derivable is small; neither, to use his own words, 'does the young Adventurer hitherto suspect in himself any literary gift; but

---

[2] *Examen Rigorosum,* rigorous examination, the final law examination in a German university; Auscultator, beginning lawyer or lawyer's assistant.

at best earns bread-and-water wages, by his wide faculty of Translation. Nevertheless," continues he, 'that I subsisted is clear, for you find me even now alive.' Which fact, however, except upon the principle of our true-hearted, kind old Proverb, that 'there is always life for a living one,' we must profess ourselves unable to explain.

Certain Landlords' Bills, and other economic Documents, bearing the mark of Settlement, indicate that he was not without money; but, like an independent Hearth-holder, if not House-holder, paid his way. Here also occur, among many others, two little mutilated Notes, which perhaps throw light on his condition. The first has now no date, or writer's name, but a huge Blot; and runs to this effect: 'The (*Inkblot*), tied-down by previous promise, cannot, except by best wishes, forward the Herr Teufelsdröckh's views on the Assessorship in question; and sees himself under the cruel necessity of forbearing, for the present, what were otherwise his duty and joy, to assist in opening the career for a man of genius, on whom far higher triumphs are yet waiting.' The other is on gilt paper; and interests us like a sort of epistolary mummy now dead, yet which once lived and beneficently worked. We give it in the original: '*Herr Teufelsdröckh wird von der Frau Gräfinn, auf Donnerstag, zum ÆSTHETISCHEN THEE schönstens eingeladen.*' [3]

Thus, in answer to a cry for solid pudding, whereof there is the most urgent need, comes, epigrammatically enough, the invitation to a wash of quite fluid *Æsthetic Tea*! How Teufelsdröckh, now at actual handgrips with Destiny herself, may have comported himself among these Musical and Literary Dilettanti of both sexes, like a hungry lion invited to a feast of chickenweed, we can only conjecture. Perhaps in expressive silence, and abstinence: otherwise if the lion, in such case, is to feast at all, it cannot be on the chickenweed, but only on the chickens. For the rest, as this Frau Gräfinn dates from the *Zähdarm House*, she can be no other than the Countess and mistress of the same; whose intellectual tendencies, and good-will to Teufelsdröckh, whether on the footing of Herr Towgood, or on his own footing, are hereby manifest. That some sort of relation, indeed, continued, for a time, to connect our Autobiographer, though perhaps feebly enough, with this noble House, we have elsewhere express evidence. Doubtless, if he expected patronage, it was in vain; enough for him if he here obtained occasional glimpses of the great world, from which we at one time fancied him to have been always excluded. 'The Zähdarms,' says he, 'lived in the soft, sumptuous garniture of Aristocracy; whereto Literature and Art, attracted and attached from without, were to serve as the handsomest fringing. It was to the *Gnädigen Frau* (her Ladyship) that this latter improvement was due: assiduously she gathered, dextrously she fitted-on, what fringing was to be had; lace or cobweb, as the place yielded.' Was Teufelsdröckh also a fringe, of lace or cobweb; or promising to be such? 'With his *Excellenz* (the Count),' continues he, 'I have more than once had the honour to converse; chiefly on general affairs, and the aspect of the world, which he, though now past middle life, viewed in no unfavourable light; finding indeed, except the Outrooting of Journalism (*die auszurottende Journalistik*), little to desiderate therein. On some points, as his *Excellenz* was not uncholeric, I found it more pleasant to keep silence. Besides, his occupation being that of Owning Land, there might be faculties enough, which, as superfluous for such use, were little developed in him.'

That to Teufelsdröckh the aspect of the world was nowise so faultless, and many things besides 'the Outrooting of Journalism' might have seemed improvements, we can readily conjecture. With nothing but a barren Auscultatorship from without, and so many mutinous thoughts and wishes from within, his position was no easy one. 'The Universe,' he says, 'was as a mighty Sphinx-riddle, which I knew so little of, yet must rede, or be devoured. In red streaks of unspeakable grandeur, yet also in the blackness of darkness, was Life, to my too-unfurnished Thought, unfolding itself. A strange contradiction lay in me; and I as yet knew not the solution of it; knew not that spiritual music can spring only from discords set in harmony; that but for Evil there were no Good, as victory is only possible by battle.'

'I have heard affirmed (surely in jest),' observes he elsewhere, 'by not unphilanthropic persons, that it were a real increase of human happiness, could all young men from the age of nineteen be covered under barrels, or rendered otherwise invisible; and there left to follow their lawful studies and callings, till they emerged, sadder and wiser, at the age of twenty-five. With which suggestion, at least as considered in the light of a practical scheme, I need scarcely say that I nowise coincide. Nevertheless it is plausibly urged

---

[3] "Herr Teufelsdröckh is cordially invited by the Countess to Aesthetic Tea on Thursday."

that, as young ladies (*Mädchen*) are, to mankind, precisely the most delightful in those years; so young gentlemen (*Bübchen*) do then attain their maximum of detestability. Such gawks (*Gecken*) are they, and foolish peacocks, and yet with such a vulturous hunger for self-indulgence; so obstinate, obstreperous, vain-glorious; in all senses, so froward and so forward. No mortal's endeavour or attainment will, in the smallest, content the as yet unendeavouring, unattaining young gentleman; but he could make it all infinitely better, were it worthy of him. Life everywhere is the most manageable matter, simple as a question in the Rule-of-Three: multiply your second and third term together, divide the product by the first, and your quotient will be the answer,—which you are but an ass if you cannot come at. The booby has not yet found-out, by any trial, that, do what one will, there is ever a cursed fraction, oftenest a decimal repeater, and no net integer quotient so much as to be thought of.'

In which passage does not there lie an implied confession that Teufelsdröckh himself, besides his outward obstructions, had an inward, still greater, to contend with; namely, a certain temporary, youthful, yet still afflictive derangement of head? Alas, on the former side alone, his case was hard enough. 'It continues ever true,' says he, 'that Saturn, or Chronos, or what we call TIME, devours all his Children:[4] only by incessant Running, by incessant Working, may you (for some threescore-and-ten years) escape him; and you too he devours at last. Can any Sovereign, or Holy Alliance[5] of Sovereigns, bid Time stand still; even in thought, shake themselves free of Time? Our whole terrestrial being is based on Time, and built of Time; it is wholly a Movement, a Time-impulse; Time is the author of it, the material of it. Hence also our Whole Duty, which is to move, to work,—in the right direction. Are not our Bodies and our Souls in continual movement, whether we will or not; in a continual Waste, requiring a continual Repair? Utmost satisfaction of our whole outward and inward Wants were but satisfaction for a space of Time; thus, whatso we have done, is done, and for us annihilated, and ever must we go and do anew. O Time-Spirit, how hast thou environed and imprisoned us, and sunk us so deep in thy troublous dim Time-Element, that only in lucid moments can so much as glimpses of our upper Azure Home be revealed to us! Me, however, as a Son of Time, unhappier than some others, was Time threatening to eat quite prematurely; for, strive as I might, there was no good Running, so obstructed was the path, so gyved were the feet.' That is to say, we presume, speaking in the dialect of this lower world, that Teufelsdröckh's whole duty and necessity was, like other men's, 'to work,—in the right direction,' and that no work was to be had; whereby he became wretched enough. As was natural: with haggard Scarcity threatening him in the distance; and so vehement a soul languishing in restless inaction, and forced thereby, like Sir Hudibras's sword by rust,

> To eat into itself, for lack
> Of something else to hew and hack![6]

But on the whole, that same 'excellent Passivity,' as it has all along done, is here again vigorously flourishing; in which circumstance may we not trace the beginnings of much that now characterises our Professor; and perhaps, in faint rudiments, the origin of the Clothes-Philosophy itself? Already the attitude he has assumed towards the World is too defensive; not, as would have been desirable, a bold attitude of attack. 'So far hitherto,' he says, 'as I had mingled with mankind, I was notable, if for anything, for a certain stillness of manner, which, as my friends often rebukingly declared, did but ill express the keen ardour of my feelings. I, in truth, regarded men with an excess both of love and of fear. The mystery of a Person, indeed, is ever divine to him that has a sense for the Godlike. Often, notwithstanding, was I blamed, and by half-strangers hated, for my so-called Hardness (*Härte*), my Indifferentism towards men; and the seemingly ironic tone I had adopted, as my favourite dialect in conversation. Alas, the panoply of Sarcasm was but as a buckram case, wherein I had striven to envelope myself; that so my own poor Person might live safe there, and in all friendliness, being no longer exasperated by wounds. Sarcasm I now see to be, in general, the language of the Devil; for which reason I have long since as good as renounced it. But how many individuals did I, in

---

[4] Chronos, god of time, by confusion of name of Greek god Kronos with the Latin word for "time." The Greek Kronos deposed his father Uranos, then devoured his own children to avoid a similar fate.
[5] Allusion to agreement originally between Russia, Austria, and Prussia, signed in 1815, but later including other Christian nations.
[6] *Hudibras*, I, i, 359-362.

those days, provoke into some degree of hostility thereby! An ironic man, with his sly stillness, and ambuscading ways, more especially an ironic young man, from whom it is least expected, may be viewed as a pest to society. Have we not seen persons of weight and name coming forward, with gentlest indifference, to tread such a one out of sight, as an insignificancy and worm, start ceiling-high (*balkenhoch*), and thence fall shattered and supine, to be borne home on shutters, not without indignation, when he proved electric and a torpedo!'

Alas, how can a man with this devilishness of temper make way for himself in Life; where the first problem, as Teufelsdröckh too admits, is 'to unite yourself with some one and with somewhat (*sich anzuschliessen*)'? Division, not union, is written on most part of his procedure. Let us add too that, in no great length of time, the only important connexion he had ever succeeded in forming, his connexion with the Zähdarm Family, seems to have been paralysed, for all practical uses, by the death of the 'not uncholeric' old Count. This fact stands recorded, quite incidentally, in a certain *Discourse on Epitaphs*, huddled into the present Bag, among so much else; of which Essay the learning and curious penetration are more to be approved of than the spirit. His grand principle is, that lapidary inscriptions, of what sort soever, should be Historical rather than Lyrical. 'By request of that worthy Nobleman's survivors,' says he, 'I undertook to compose his Epitaph; and not unmindful of my own rules, produced the following; which however, for an alleged defect of Latinity, a defect never yet fully visible to myself, still remains unengraven;'— wherein, we may predict, there is more than the Latinity that will surprise an English reader:

HIC JACET

PHILIPPUS ZAEHDARM, COGNOMINE MAGNUS,

ZAEHDARMI COMES,

EX IMPERII CONCILIO,

VELLERIS AUREI, PERISCELIDIS, NECNON VULTURIS NIGRI EQUES,

QUI DUM SUB LUNA AGEBAT,

QUINQUIES MILLE PERDICES

PLUMBO CONFECIT:

VARII CIBI

CENTUMPONDIA MILLES CENTENA MILLIA,

PER SE, PERQUE SERVOS QUADRUPEDES BIPEDESVE,

HAUD SINE TUMULTU DEVOLVENS,

IN STERCUS

PALAM CONVERTIT.

NUNC A LABORE REQUIESCENTEM

OPERA SEQUUNTUR.

SI MONUMENTUM QUÆRIS,

FIMETUM ADSPICE.

PRIMUM IN ORBE DEJECIT [*sub dato*]; POSTREMUM [*sub dato*] [7]

CHAPTER V

Romance

Teufelsdröckh gives up his Profession. The heavenly mystery of Love. Teufelsdröckh's feeling of worship towards women. First and only love. Blumine. Happy hearts and free tongues. The infinite nature of Fantasy. Love's joyful progress; sudden dissolution; and final catastrophe.

'FOR long years,' writes Teufelsdröckh, 'had the poor Hebrew, in this Egypt of an Auscultatorship, painfully toiled, baking bricks without stubble, before ever the question once struck him with entire force: For what?—*Beym Himmel*! For Food and Warmth! And are Food and Warmth nowhere else, in the whole wide Universe, discoverable?—Come of it what might, I resolved to try.'

Thus then are we to see him in a new independent capacity, though perhaps far from an improved one. Teufelsdröckh is now a man without Profession. Quitting the common Fleet of herring-busses and whalers, where indeed his leeward, laggard condition was painful enough, he desperately steers off, on a course of his own, by sextant and compass of his own. Unhappy Teufelsdröckh! Though neither Fleet, nor Traffic, nor Commodores pleased thee, still was it not *a Fleet*, sailing in prescribed track, for fixed objects; above all, in combination, wherein, by mutual

---

[7] "Here lies Philip Zaehdarm, named the Great, Count of Zaehdarm, of the Imperial Council, Knight of the Golden Fleece, of the Garter, and of the Black Vulture. Who, while he lived on earth, shot five-thousand partridges; A hundred-million hundred-weights of various kinds of food, he, by himself and his servants, quadruped or bipeds, not without considerable tumult, converted into manure. Now, resting from his labors, his works follow him. If you seek his monument, look at this pile. Begun on (*date given*); completed on (*date given*)."

guidance, by all manner of loans and borrowings, each could manifoldly aid the other? How wilt thou sail in unknown seas; and for thyself find that shorter North-west Passage to thy fair Spice-country of a Nowhere?—A solitary rover, on such a voyage, with such nautical tactics, will meet with adventures. Nay, as we forthwith discover, a certain Calypso-Island[1] detains him at the very outset; and as it were falsifies and oversets his whole reckoning.

'If in youth,' writes he once, 'the Universe is majestically unveiling, and everywhere Heaven revealing itself on Earth, nowhere to the Young Man does this Heaven on Earth so immediately reveal itself as in the Young Maiden. Strangely enough, in this strange life of ours, it has been so appointed. On the whole, as I have often said, a Person (*Persönlichkeit*) is ever holy to us; a certain orthodox Anthropomorphism connects my *Me* with all *Thees* in bonds of Love: but it is in this approximation of the Like and Unlike, that such heavenly attraction, as between Negative and Positive, first burns-out into a flame. Is the pitifullest mortal Person, think you, indifferent to us? Is it not rather our heartfelt wish to be made one with him; to unite him to us, by gratitude, by admiration, even by fear; or failing all these, unite ourselves to him? But how much more, in this case of the Like-Unlike! Here is conceded us the higher mystic possibility of such a union, the highest in our Earth; thus, in the conducting medium of Fantasy, flames-forth that *fire-development* of the universal Spiritual Electricity, which, as unfolded between man and woman, we first emphatically denominate LOVE.

'In every well-conditioned stripling, as I conjecture, there already blooms a certain prospective Paradise, cheered by some fairest Eve; nor, in the stately vistas, and flowerage and foliage of that Garden, is a Tree of Knowledge, beautiful and awful in the midst thereof, wanting. Perhaps too the whole is but the lovelier, if Cherubim and a Flaming Sword divide it from all footsteps of men; and grant him, the imaginative stripling, only the view, not the entrance. Happy season of virtuous youth, when shame is still an impassable celestial barrier; and the sacred air-cities of Hope have not shrunk into the mean clay-hamlets of Reality; and man, by his nature, is yet infinite and free!

'As for our young Forlorn,' continues Teufelsdröckh, evidently meaning himself, 'in his se-cluded way of life, and with his glowing Fantasy, the more fiery that it burnt under cover, as in a reverberating furnace, his feeling towards the Queens of this Earth was, and indeed is, altogether unspeakable. A visible Divinity dwelt in them; to our young Friend all women were holy, were heavenly. As yet he but saw them flitting past, in their many-coloured angel-plumage; or hovering mute and inaccessible on the outskirts of *Æsthetic Tea*: all of air they were, all Soul and Form; so lovely, like mysterious priestesses, in whose hand was the invisible Jacob's-ladder, whereby man might mount into very Heaven.[2] That he, our poor Friend, should ever win for himself one of these Gracefuls (*Holden*)—*Ach Gott!* how could he hope it; should he not have died under it? There was a certain delirious vertigo in the thought.

'Thus was the young man, if all-sceptical of Demons and Angels such as the vulgar had once believed in, nevertheless not unvisited by hosts of true Sky-born, who visibly and audibly hovered round him wheresoever he went; and they had that religious worship in his thought, though as yet it was by their mere earthly and trivial name that he named them. But now, if on a soul so circumstanced, some actual Air-maiden, incorporated into tangibility and reality, should cast any electric glance of kind eyes, saying thereby, "Thou too mayst love and be loved"; and so kindle him,—good Heaven, what a volcanic, earthquake-bringing, all-consuming fire were probably kindled!'

Such a fire, it afterwards appears, did actually burst-forth, with explosions more or less Vesuvian, in the inner man of Herr Diogenes; as indeed how could it fail? A nature, which, in his own figurative style, we might say, had now not a little carbonised tinder, of Irritability; with so much nitre of latent Passion, and sulphurous Humour enough; the whole lying in such hot neighbourhood, close by 'a reverberating furnace of Fantasy': have we not here the components of driest Gunpowder, ready, on occasion of the smallest spark, to blaze-up? Neither, in this our Life-element, are sparks anywhere wanting. Without doubt, some Angel, whereof so many hovered round, would one day, leaving 'the outskirts of *Æsthetic Tea*,' flit nigher; and, by electric Promethean glance, kindle no despicable firework. Happy, if it indeed proved a Firework, and flamed-off rocket-wise, in successive beautiful

---

[1] In Homer's *Odyssey,* where the nymph Calypso beguiled Ulysses for seven years.
[2] Genesis 28:10–15.

bursts of splendour, each growing naturally from the other, through the several stages of a happy Youthful Love; till the whole were safely burnt-out; and the young soul relieved with little damage! Happy, if it did not rather prove a Conflagration and mad Explosion; painfully lacerating the heart itself; nay perhaps bursting the heart in pieces (which were Death); or at best, bursting the thin walls of your 'reverberating furnace,' so that it rage thenceforth all unchecked among the contiguous combustibles (which were Madness): till of the so fair and manifold internal world of our Diogenes, there remained Nothing, or only the 'crater of an extinct volcano'!

From multifarious Documents in this Bag *Capricornus*,[3] and in the adjacent ones on both sides thereof, it becomes manifest that our philosopher, as stoical and cynical as he now looks, was heartily and even frantically in Love: here therefore may our old doubts whether his heart were of stone or of flesh give way. He loved once; not wisely but too well.[4] And once only: for as your Congreve[5] needs a new case or wrappage for every new rocket, so each human heart can properly exhibit but one Love, if even one; the 'First Love which is infinite' can be followed by no second like unto it. In more recent years, accordingly, the Editor of these Sheets was led to regard Teufelsdröckh as a man not only who would never wed, but who would never even flirt; whom the grand-climacteric itself, and *St Martin's Summer*[6] of incipient Dotage, would crown with no new myrtle-garland. To the Professor, women are henceforth Pieces of Art; of Celestial Art, indeed; which celestial pieces he glories to survey in galleries, but has lost thought of purchasing.

Psychological readers are not without curiosity to see how Teufelsdröckh, in this for him unexampled predicament, demeans himself; with what specialties of successive configuration, splendour and colour, his Firework blazes-off. Small, as usual, is the satisfaction that such can meet with here. From amid these confused masses of Eulogy and Elegy, with their mad Petrarchan and Werterean[7] ware lying madly scattered among all sorts of quite extraneous matter, not so much as the fair one's name can be deciphered.

For, without doubt, the title *Blumine*, whereby she is here designated, and which means simply Goddess of Flowers, must be fictitious. Was her real name Flora, then? But what was her surname, or had she none? Of what station in Life was she; of what parentage, fortune, aspect? Specially, by what Preëstablished Harmony[8] of occurrences did the Lover and the Loved meet one another in so wide a world; how did they behave in such a meeting? To all which questions, not unessential in a Biographic work, mere Conjecture must for most part return answer. 'It was appointed,' says our Philosopher, 'that the high celestial orbit of Blumine should intersect the low sublunary one of our Forlorn; that he, looking in her empyrean eyes, should fancy the upper Sphere of Light was come down into this nether sphere of Shadows; and finding himself mistaken, make noise enough.'

We seem to gather that she was young, hazel-eyed, beautiful, and some one's Cousin; highborn, and of high spirit; but unhappily dependent and insolvent; living, perhaps, on the not too gracious bounty of moneyed relatives. But how came 'the Wanderer' into her circle? Was it by the humid vehicle of *Æsthetic Tea*, or by the arid one of mere Business? Was it on the hand of Herr Towgood; or of the Gnädige Frau, who, as an ornamental Artist, might sometimes like to promote flirtation, especially for young cynical Nondescripts? To all appearance, it was chiefly by Accident, and the grace of Nature.

'Thou fair Waldschloss,' writes our Autobiographer, 'what stranger ever saw thee, were it even an absolved Auscultator, officially bearing in his pocket the last *Relatio ex Actis*[9] he would ever write, but must have paused to wonder! Noble Mansion! There stoodest thou, in deep Mountain Amphitheatre, on umbrageous lawns, in thy serene solitude; stately, massive, all of granite; glittering in the western sunbeams, like a palace of El Dorado, overlaid with precious metal. Beautiful rose up, in wavy curvature, the slope of thy guardian Hills; of the greenest was their sward, embossed with its dark-brown frets of crag, or spotted by some spreading solitary Tree and its shadow. To the unconscious Wayfarer thou wert also as an Ammon's Temple, in

---

[3] Zodiacal sign of the goat for the period December 22–January 20.   [4] *Othello*, V, ii, 343.

[5] A military rocket named after the inventor Sir William Congreve (1772–1828).

[6] Indian Summer, from St. Martin's Day, November 11.

[7] Petrarch (1304–74), Italian poet and soneteer; Werterean, after Goethe's *Werther* (1774).

[8] After the philosophy of Gottfried Wilhelm Leibniz (1646–1716).

[9] Waldschloss, forest castle; absolved auscultator, lawyer who has completed his studies; *Relatio ex Actis*, law reports.

the Libyan Waste;[10] where, for joy and woe, the tablet of his Destiny lay written. Well might he pause and gaze; in that glance of his were prophecy and nameless forebodings.'

But now let us conjecture that the so presentient Auscultator has handed-in his *Relatio ex Actis*; been invited to a glass of Rhine-wine; and so, instead of returning dispirited and athirst to his dusty Town-home, is ushered into the Garden-house, where sit the choicest party of dames and cavaliers: if not engaged in Æsthetic Tea, yet in trustful evening conversation, and perhaps Musical Coffee, for we hear of 'harps and pure voices making the stillness live.' Scarcely, it would seem, is the Gardenhouse inferior in respectability to the noble mansion itself. 'Embowered amid rich foliage, rose-clusters, and the hues and odours of thousand flowers, here sat that brave company; in front, from the wide-opened doors, fair outlook over blossom and bush, over grove and velvet green, stretching, undulating onwards to the remote Mountain peaks: so bright, so mild, and everywhere the melody of birds and happy creatures: it was all as if man had stolen a shelter from the Sun in the bosom-vesture of Summer herself. How came it that the Wanderer advanced thither with such forecasting heart (*ahndungs-voll*),[11] by the side of his gay host? Did he feel that to these soft influences his hard bosom ought to be shut; that here, once more, Fate had it in view to try him; to mock him, and see whether there were Humour in him?

'Next moment he finds himself presented to the party; and especially by name to—Blumine! Peculiar among all dames and damosels glanced Blumine, there in her modesty, like a star among earthly lights. Noblest maiden! whom he bent to, in body and in soul; yet scarcely dared look at, for the presence filled him with painful yet sweetest embarrassment.

'Blumine's was a name well known to him; far and wide was the fair one heard of, for her gifts, her graces, her caprices: from all which vague colourings of Rumour, from the censures no less than from the praises, had our friend painted for himself a certain imperious Queen of Hearts,[12] and blooming warm Earth-angel, much more enchanting than your mere white Heaven-angels of women, in whose placid veins circulates too little naphtha-fire. Herself also he had seen in

public places; that light yet so stately form; those dark tresses, shading a face where smiles and sunlight played over earnest deeps: but all this he had seen only as a magic vision, for him inaccessible, almost without reality. Her sphere was too far from his; how should she ever think of him; O Heaven! how should they so much as once meet together? And now that Rose-goddess sits in the same circle with him; the light of *her* eyes has smiled on him; if he speak, she will hear it! Nay, who knows, since the heavenly Sun looks into lowest valleys, but Blumine herself might have aforetime noted the so unnotable; perhaps, from his very gainsayers, as he had from hers, gathered wonder, gathered favour for him? Was the attraction, the agitation mutual, then; pole and pole trembling towards contact, when once brought into neighbourhood? Say rather, heart swelling in presence of the Queen of Hearts; like the Sea swelling when once near its Moon! With the Wanderer it was even so: as in heavenward gravitation, suddenly as at the touch of a Seraph's wand, his whole soul is roused from its deepest recesses; and all that was painful and that was blissful there, dim images, vague feelings of a whole Past and a whole Future, are heaving in unquiet eddies within him.

'Often, in far less agitating scenes, had our still Friend shrunk forcibly together; and shrouded-up his tremors and flutterings, of what sort soever, in a safe cover of Silence, and perhaps of seeming Stolidity. How was it, then, that here, when trembling to the core of his heart, he did not sink into swoons, but rose into strength, into fearlessness and clearness? It was his guiding Genius (*Dämon*) that inspired him; he must go forth and meet his Destiny. Show thyself now, whispered it, or be forever hid. Thus sometimes it is even when your anxiety becomes transcendental, that the soul first feels herself able to transcend it; that she rises above it, in fiery victory; and borne on new-found wings of victory, moves so calmly, even because so rapidly, so irresistibly. Always must the Wanderer remember, with a certain satisfaction and surprise, how in this case he sat not silent, but struck adroitly into the stream of conversation; which thenceforth, to speak with an apparent not a real vanity, he may say that he continued to lead. Surely, in those hours, a certain inspiration was imparted him, such inspiration as

---

[10] Temple in a desert oasis to the Egyptian divinity Ammon or Amun.

[11] Probably an error for *ahnungsvoll*, full of foreboding.

[12] Elizabeth (1596–1662), Queen of Bohemia, daughter of James I of England; she married Frederick V, the "Winter King," so called for the brevity of his reign before he was routed by the Catholic League.

is still possible in our late era. The self-secluded unfolds himself in noble thoughts, in free, glowing words; his soul is as one sea of light, the peculiar home of Truth and Intellect; wherein also Fantasy bodies-forth form after form, radiant with all prismatic hues.'

It appears, in this otherwise so happy meeting, there talked one 'Philistine'; who even now, to the general weariness, was dominantly pouring-forth Philistinism (*Philistriositäten*); little witting what hero was here entering to demolish him! We omit the series of Socratic, or rather Diogenic utterances, not unhappy in their way, whereby the monster, 'persuaded into silence,' seems soon after to have withdrawn for the night. 'Of which dialectic marauder,' writes our hero, 'the discomfiture was visibly felt as a benefit by most: but what were all applauses to the glad smile, threatening every moment to become a laugh, wherewith Blumine herself repaid the victor? He ventured to address her, she answered with attention: nay what if there were a slight tremor in that silver voice; what if the red glow of evening were hiding a transient blush!

'The conversation took a higher tone, one fine thought called forth another: it was one of those rare seasons, when the soul expands with full freedom, and man feels himself brought near to man. Gaily in light, graceful abandonment, the friendly talk played round that circle; for the burden was rolled from every heart; the barriers of Ceremony, which are indeed the laws of polite living, had melted as into vapour; and the poor claims of *Me* and *Thee*, no longer parted by rigid fences, now flowed softly into one another; and Life lay all harmonious, many-tinted, like some fair royal champaign, the sovereign and owner of which were Love only. Such music springs from kind hearts, in a kind environment of place and time. And yet as the light grew more aërial on the mountain-tops, and the shadows fell longer over the valley, some faint tone of sadness may have breathed through the heart; and, in whispers more or less audible, reminded every one that as this bright day was drawing towards its close, so likewise must the Day of Man's Existence decline into dust and darkness; and with all its sick toilings, and joyful and mournful noises, sink in the still Eternity.

'To our Friend the hours seemed moments; holy was he and happy; the words from those sweetest lips came over him like dew on thirsty grass; all better feelings in his soul seemed to whisper, It is good for us to be here. At parting, the Blumine's hand was in his: in the balmy twilight, with the kind stars above them, he spoke something of meeting again, which was not contradicted; he pressed gently those small soft fingers, and it seemed as if they were not hastily, not angrily withdrawn.'

Poor Teufelsdröckh! it is clear to demonstration thou art smit: the Queen of Hearts would see a 'man of genius' also sigh for her; and there, by art-magic, in that preternatural hour, has she bound and spell-bound thee. 'Love is not altogether a Delirium,' says he elsewhere; 'yet has it many points in common therewith. I call it rather a discerning of the Infinite in the Finite, of the Idea made Real; which discerning again may be either true or false, either seraphic or demoniac, Inspiration or Insanity. But in the former case too, as in common Madness, it is Fantasy that superadds itself to sight; on the so petty domain of the Actual plants its Archimedes-lever,[13] whereby to move at will the infinite Spiritual. Fantasy I might call the true Heaven-gate and Hell-gate of man: his sensuous life is but the small temporary stage (*Zeitbühne*), whereon thick-streaming influences from both these far yet near regions meet visibly, and act tragedy and melo-drama. Sense can support herself handsomely, in most countries, for some eighteen-pence a day; but for Fantasy planets and solar-systems will not suffice. Witness your Pyrrhus conquering the world, yet drinking no better red wine than he had before.'[14] Alas! witness also your Diogenes, flame-clad, scaling the upper Heaven, and verging towards Insanity, for prize of a 'high-souled Brunette,' as if the earth held but one and not several of these!

He says that, in Town, they met again: 'day after day, like his heart's sun, the blooming Blumine shone on him. Ah! a little while ago, and he was yet in all darkness: him what Graceful (*Holde*) would ever love? Disbelieving all things, the poor youth had never learned to believe in himself. Withdrawn, in proud timidity, within his own fastnesses; solitary from men, yet baited by night-spectres enough, he saw himself, with a sad indignation, constrained to renounce the fairest hopes of existence. And now, O now! "She looks on thee," cried he: "she the fairest, noblest; do not her dark eyes tell thee, thou art not despised? The Heaven's-Messenger! All Heaven's

---

[13] Archimedes (287–212 B.C.), discoverer of the principle of the lever.
[14] Recorded in Plutarch's *Lives*.

blessings be hers!" Thus did soft melodies flow through his heart; tones of an infinite gratitude; sweetest intimations that he also was a man, that for him also unutterable joys had been provided.

'In free speech, earnest or gay, amid lambent glances, laughter, tears, and often with the inarticulate mystic speech of Music: such was the element they now lived in; in such a many-tinted, radiant Aurora,[15] and by this fairest of Orient Light-bringers must our Friend be blandished, and the new Apocalypse of Nature unrolled to him. Fairest Blumine! And, even as a Star, all Fire and humid Softness, a very Light-ray incarnate! Was there so much as a fault, a "caprice," he could have dispensed with? Was she not to him in very deed a Morning-Star; did not her presence bring with it airs from Heaven? As from Æolian Harps in the breath of dawn, as from the Memnon's Statue struck by the rosy finger of Aurora,[16] unearthly music was around him, and lapped him into untried balmy Rest. Pale Doubt fled away to the distance; Life bloomed-up with happiness and hope. The past, then, was all a haggard dream; he had been in the Garden of Eden, then, and could not discern it! But lo now! the black walls of his prison melt away; the captive is alive, is free. If he loved his Disenchantress? *Ach Gott!* His whole heart and soul and life were hers, but never had he named it Love: existence was all a Feeling, not yet shaped into a Thought.'

Nevertheless, into a Thought, nay into an Action, it must be shaped; for neither Disenchanter nor Disenchantress, mere 'Children of Time,' can abide by Feeling alone. The Professor knows not, to this day, 'how in her soft, fervid bosom the Lovely found determination, even on hest of Necessity, to cut asunder these so blissful bonds.' He even appears surprised at the 'Duenna Cousin,' whoever she may have been, 'in whose meagre, hunger-bitten philosophy, the religion of young hearts was, from the first, faintly approved of.' We, even at such distance, can explain it without necromancy. Let the Philosopher answer this one question. What figure, at that period, was a Mrs Teufelsdröckh likely to make in polished society? Could she have driven so much as a brass-bound Gig, or even a simple iron-spring one? Thou foolish 'absolved Auscultator,' before

whom lies no prospect of capital, will any yet known 'religion of young hearts' keep the human kitchen warm? Pshaw! thy divine Blumine, when she 'resigned herself to wed some richer,' shows more philosophy, though but 'a woman of genius,' than thou, a pretended man.

Our readers have witnessed the origin of this Love-mania, and with what royal splendour it waxes, and rises. Let no one ask us to unfold the glories of its dominant state; much less the horrors of its almost instantaneous dissolution. How from such inorganic masses, henceforth madder than ever, as lie in these Bags, can even fragments of a living delineation be organised? Besides, of what profit were it? We view, with a lively pleasure, the gay silk Montgolfier[17] start from the ground, and shoot upwards, cleaving the liquid deeps, till it dwindle to a luminous star: but what is there to look longer on, when once, by natural elasticity, or accident of fire, it has exploded? A hapless air-navigator, plunging, amid torn parachutes, sand-bags, and confused wreck, fast enough into the jaws of the Devil! Suffice it to know that Teufelsdröckh rose into the highest regions of the Empyrean, by a natural parabolic track, and returned thence in a quick perpendicular one. For the rest, let any feeling reader, who has been unhappy enough to do the like, paint it out for himself: considering only that if he, for his perhaps comparatively insignificant mistress, underwent such agonies and frenzies, what must Teufelsdröckh's have been, with a fire-heart, and for a nonpareil Blumine! We glance merely at the final scene:

'One morning, he found his Morning-star all dimmed and dusky-red; the fair creature was silent, absent, she seemed to have been weeping. Alas, no longer a Morning-star, but a troublous skyey Portent, announcing that the Doomsday had dawned! She said, in a tremulous voice, They were to meet no more.' The thunderstruck Air-sailor is not wanting to himself in this dread hour: but what avails it? We omit the passionate expostulations, entreaties, indignations, since all was vain, and not even an explanation was conceded him; and hasten to the catastrophe. ' "Farewell, then, Madam!" said he, not without sternness, for his stung pride helped him. She put her hand in his, she looked in his face, tears started to her eyes; in wild audacity he clasped

---

[15] Goddess of the dawn.

[16] Aeolian harps, after Aeolus, god of winds; harps that produce music when blown upon by the wind; Memnon's statue, a statue to King Memnon erected in Thebes, which was said to emit sound when struck by the first rays of dawn.

[17] An air-filled balloon, named after its inventors, the brothers Montgolfier, Joseph Michel (1740–1810) and Jacques Étienne (1745–99).

her to his bosom; their lips were joined, their two souls, like two dew-drops, rushed into one,—for the first time, and for the last!' Thus was Teufelsdröckh made immortal by a kiss.[18] And then? Why, then—'thick curtains of Night rushed over his soul, as rose the immeasurable Crash of Doom; and through the ruins as of a shivered Universe was he falling, falling, towards the Abyss.'

CHAPTER VI

Sorrows of Teufelsdröckh

Teufelsdröckh's demeanour thereupon. Turns pilgrim. A last wistful look on native Entepfuhl: Sunset amongst primitive Mountains. Basilisk-glance of the Barouche-and-four. Thoughts on View-hunting. Wanderings and Sorrowings.

W E HAVE long felt that, with a man like our Professor, matters must often be expected to take a course of their own; that in so multiplex, intricate a nature, there might be channels, both for admitting and emitting, such as the Psychologist had seldom noted; in short, that on no grand occasion and convulsion, neither in the joy-storm nor in the woe-storm, could you predict his demeanour.

To our less philosophical readers, for example, it is now clear that the so passionate Teufelsdröckh, precipitated through 'a shivered Universe' in this extraordinary way has only one of three things which he can next do: Establish himself in Bedlam; begin writing Satanic Poetry;[1] or blow-out his brains. In the progress towards any of which consummations, do not such readers anticipate extravagance enough; breast-beating, brow-beating (against walls), lion-bellowings of blasphemy and the like, stampings, smitings, breakages of furniture, if not arson itself?

Nowise so does Teufelsdröckh deport him. He quietly lifts his *Pilgerstab* (Pilgrim-staff), 'old business being soon wound-up'; and begins a perambulation and circumambulation of the terraqueous Globe! Curious it is, indeed, how with such vivacity of conception, such intensity of feeling, above all, with these unconscionable habits of Exaggeration in speech, he combines that wonderful stillness of his, that stoicism in external procedure. Thus, if his sudden bereavement, in this matter of the Flower-goddess, is talked of as a real Doomsday and Dissolution of Nature, in which light doubltess it partly appeared to himself, his own nature is nowise dissolved thereby; but rather is compressed closer. For once, as we might say, a Blumine by magic appliances has unlocked that shut heart of his, and its hidden things rush-out tumultuous, boundless, like genii enfranchised from their glass phial: but no sooner are your magic appliances withdrawn, than the strange casket of a heart springs-to again; and perhaps there is now no key extant that will open it; for a Teufelsdröckh, as we remarked, will not love a second time. Singular Diogenes! No sooner has that heart-rending occurrence fairly taken place, than he affects to regard it as a thing natural, of which there is nothing more to be said. 'One highest hope, seemingly legible in the eyes of an Angel, had recalled him as out of Death-shadows into celestial Life: but a gleam of Tophet[2] passed over the face of his Angel; he was rapt away in whirlwinds, and heard the laughter of Demons. It was a Calenture,'[3] adds he, 'whereby the Youth saw green Paradise-groves in the waste Ocean-waters: a lying vision, yet not wholly a lie, for *he* saw it.' But what things soever passed in him, when he ceased to see it; what ragings and despairings soever Teufelsdröckh's soul was the scene of, he has the goodness to conceal under a quite opaque cover of Silence. We know it well; the first mad paroxysm past, our brave Gneschen collected his dismembered philosophies, and buttoned himself together; he was meek, silent, or spoke of the weather and the Journals: only by a transient knitting of those shaggy brows, by some deep flash of those eyes, glancing one knew not whether with tear-dew or with fierce fire,— might you have guessed what a Gehenna was within; that a whole Satanic School were spouting, though inaudibly, there. To consume your own choler, as some chimneys consume their own smoke; to keep a whole Satanic School spouting, if it must spout, inaudibly, is a negative yet no

---

[18] Marlowe, *Dr. Faustus.*
[1] Bedlam, a London asylum for the insane, corrupted from *Bethlehem*; Satanic poetry, poetry in the style of Byron, so named by Robert Southey in his "Vision of Judgment" (1821).
[2] Old Testament term, equivalent to Gehenna.   [3] Spanish for a fever delirium.

slight virtue, nor one of the commonest in these times.

Nevertheless, we will not take upon us to say, that in the strange measure he fell upon, there was not a touch of latent Insanity; whereof indeed the actual condition of these Documents in *Capricornus* and *Aquarius*[4] is no bad emblem. His so unlimited Wanderings, toilsome enough, are without assigned or perhaps assignable aim; internal Unrest seems his sole guidance; he wanders, wanders, as if that curse of the Prophet had fallen on him, and he were 'made like unto a wheel.' Doubtless, too, the chaotic nature of these Paper-bags aggravates our obscurity. Quite without note of preparation, for example, we come upon the following slip: 'A peculiar feeling it is that will rise in the Traveller, when turning some hill-range in his desert road, he descries lying far below, embosomed among its groves and green natural bulwarks, and all diminished to a toy-box, the fair Town, where so many souls, as it were seen and yet unseen, are driving their multifarious traffic. Its white steeple is then truly a starward-pointing finger; the canopy of blue smoke seems like a sort of Life-breath: for always, of its own unity, the soul gives unity to whatso-ever it looks on with love; thus does the little Dwellingplace of men, in itself a congeries of houses and huts, become for us an individual, almost a person. But what thousand other thoughts unite thereto, if the place has to ourselves been the arena of joyous or mournful experiences; if perhaps the cradle we were rocked in still stands there, if our Loving ones still dwell there, if our Buried ones there slumber!' Does Teufelsdröckh, as the wounded eagle is said to make for its own eyrie, and indeed military deserters, and all hunted outcast creatures, turn as if by instinct in the direction of their birthland,—fly first, in this extremity, towards his native Entepfuhl; but reflecting that there no help awaits him, take only one wistful look from the distance, and then wend elsewhither?

Little happier seems to be his next flight: into the wilds of Nature; as if in her mother-bosom he would seek healing. So at least we incline to interpret the following Notice, separated from the former by some considerable space, wherein, however, is nothing noteworthy:

'Mountains were not new to him; but rarely are Mountains seen in such combined majesty and grace as here. The rocks are of that sort called Primitive by the mineralogists, which always arrange themselves in masses of a rugged, gigantic character; which ruggedness, however, is here tempered by a singular airiness of form, and softness of environment: in a climate favour-able to vegetation, the gray cliff, itself covered with lichens, shoots-up through a garment of foliage or verdure; and white, bright cottages, tree-shaded, cluster round the everlasting granite. In fine vicissitude, Beauty alternates with Grandeur: you ride through stony hollows, along strait passes, traversed by torrents, overhung by high walls of rock; now winding amid broken shaggy chasms, and huge fragments; now sud-denly emerging into some emerald valley, where the streamlet collects itself into a Lake, and man has again found a fair dwelling, and its seems as if Peace had established herself in the bosom of Strength.

'To Peace, however, in this vortex of existence, can the Son of Time not pretend: still less if some Spectre haunt him from the Past; and the Future is wholly a Stygian Darkness, spectre-bearing. Reasonably might the Wanderer exclaim to himself: Are not the gates of this world's Happi-ness inexorably shut against thee; hast thou a hope that is not mad? Nevertheless, one may still murmur audibly, or in the original Greek if that suit thee better: "Whoso can look on Death will start at no shadows."

'From such meditations is the Wanderer's attention called outwards; for now the Valley closes-in abruptly, intersected by a huge moun-tain mass, the stony water-worn ascent of which is not to be accomplished on horseback. Arrived aloft, he finds himself again lifted into the evening sunset light; and cannot but pause, and gaze round him, some moments there. An upland irregular expanse of wold, where valleys in complex branchings are suddenly or slowly arranging their descent towards every quarter of the sky. The mountain-ranges are beneath your feet, and folded together: only the loftier summits look down here and there as on a second plain; lakes also lie clear and earnest in their solitude. No trace of man now visible; unless indeed it were he who fashioned that little visible link of Highway, here, as would seem, scaling the inaccessible, to unite Province with Province. But sun-wards, lo you! how it towers sheer up, a world of Mountains, the diadem and centre of

---

[4] Capricorn, sign of the goat, December 22–January 20; Aquarius, the water-bearer, January 21–February 19.

the mountain region! A hundred and a hundred savage peaks, in the last light of Day; all glowing, of gold and amethyst, like giant spirits of the wilderness; there in their silence, in their solitude, even as on the night when Noah's Deluge first dried! Beautiful, nay solemn, was the sudden aspect to our Wanderer. He gazed over those stupendous masses with wonder, almost with longing desire; never till this hour had he known Nature, that she was One, that she was his Mother and divine. And as the ruddy glow was fading into clearness in the sky, and the Sun had now departed, a murmur of Eternity and Immensity, of Death and of Life, stole through his soul; and he felt as if Death and Life were one, as if the Earth were not dead, as if the Spirit of the Earth had its throne in that splendour, and his own spirit were therewith holding communion.

'The spell was broken by a sound of carriage-wheels. Emerging from the hidden Northward, to sink soon into the hidden Southward, came a gay Barouche-and-four:[5] it was open; servants and postillions wore wedding-favours: that happy pair, then, had found each other, it was their marriage evening! Few moments brought them near: *Du Himmel!*[6] It was Herr Towgood and—— Blumine! With slight unrecognising salutation they passed me; plunged down amid the neighbouring thickets, onwards, to Heaven, and to England; and I, in my friend Richter's words, *I remained alone, behind them, with the Night.*'[7]

Were it not cruel in these circumstances, here might be the place to insert an observation, gleaned long ago from the great *Clothes-Volume*, where it stands with quite other intent: 'Some time before Small-pox was extirpated,' says the Professor, there came a new malady of the spiritual sort on Europe: I mean the epidemic, now endemical, of View-hunting. Poets of old date, being privileged with Senses, had also enjoyed external Nature; but chiefly as we enjoy the crystal cup which holds good or bad liquor for us; that is to say, in silence, or with slight incidental commentary: never, as I compute, till after the *Sorrows of Werter*,[8] was there man found who would say: Come let us make a Description! Having drunk the liquor, come let us eat the glass! Of which endemic the Jenner[9] is unhappily still to seek.' Too true!

We reckon it more important to remark that the Professor's Wanderings, so far as his stoical and cynical envelopment admits us to clear insight, here first take their permanent character, fatuous or not. That Basilisk-glance[10] of the Barouche-and-four seems to have withered-up what little remnant of a purpose may have still lurked in him: Life has become wholly a dark labyrinth; wherein, through long years, our Friend, flying from spectres, has to stumble about at random, and naturally with more haste than progress.

Foolish were it in us to attempt following him, even from afar, in this extraordinary world-pilgrimage of his; the simplest record of which, were clear record possible, would fill volumes. Hopeless is the obscurity, unspeakable the confusion. He glides from country to country, from condition to condition; vanishing and re-appearing, no man can calculate how or where. Through all quarters of the world he wanders, and apparently through all circles of society. If in any scene, perhaps difficult to fix geographically, he settles for a time, and forms connexions, be sure he will snap them abruptly asunder. Let him sink out of sight as Private Scholar (*Privatisirender*), living by the grace of God in some European capital, you may next find him as Hadjee in the neighbourhood of Mecca.[11] It is an inexplicable Phantasmagoria, capricious, quick-changing; as if our Traveller, instead of limbs and highways, had transported himself by some wishing-carpet, or Fortunatus' Hat.[12] The whole, too, imparted emblematically, in dim multifarious tokens (as that collection of Street-Advertisements); with only some touch of direct historical notice sparingly interspersed: little light-islets in the world of haze! So that, from this point, the Professor is more of an enigma than ever. In figurative language, we might say he becomes, not indeed a spirit, yet spiritualised, vaporized. Fact unparalleled in Biography: The river of his History, which we have traced from its tiniest fountains, and hoped to see flow onward, with increasing current, into the ocean,

---

[5] Horse-drawn four-wheeled carriage with retractable top over the back seat.
[6] "Heavens!"   [7] Jean Paul, *Quintus Fixlein*.
[8] Goethe's *Die Leiden des jungen Werthers*.
[9] Inoculation, after Edward Jenner (1749–1823), who developed the vaccination for smallpox.
[10] From the legendary serpent whose glance killed.
[11] A Moslem who has made his *hadj*, or pilgrimage, to Mecca.
[12] In popular legend a magical cap given to Fortunatus that enabled him to be transported to any place he wished to be.

here dashes itself over that terrific Lover's Leap;[13] and, as a mad-foaming cataract, flies wholly into tumultuous clouds of spray! Low down it indeed collects again into pools and plashes; yet only at a great distance, and with difficulty, if at all, into a general stream. To cast a glance into certain of those pools and plashes, and trace whither they run, must, for a chapter or two, form the limit of our endeavour.

For which end doubtless those direct historical Notices, where they can be met with, are the best. Nevertheless, of this sort too there occurs much, which, with our present light, it were questionable to emit. Teufelsdröckh, vibrating everywhere between the highest and the lowest levels, comes into contact with public History itself. For example, those conversations and relations with illustrious Persons, as Sultan Mahmoud,[14] the Emperor Napoleon, and others, are they not as yet rather of a diplomatic character than of a biographic? The Editor, appreciating the sacredness of crowned heads, nay perhaps suspecting the possible trickeries of a Clothes-Philosoper, will eschew this province for the present; a new time may bring new insight and a different duty.

If we ask now, not indeed with what ulterior Purpose, for there was none, yet with what immediate outlooks; at all events, in what mood of mind, the Professor undertook and prosecuted this world-pilgrimage,—the answer is more distinct than favourable. 'A nameless Unrest,' says he, 'urged me forward; to which the outward motion was some momentary lying solace. Whither should I go? My Loadstars were blotted out; in that canopy of grim fire shone no star. Yet forward must I; the ground burnt under me; there was no rest for the sole of my foot. I was alone, alone! Ever too the strong inward longing shaped Fantasms for itself: towards these, one after the other, must I fruitlessly wander. A feeling I had, that for my fever-thirst there was and must be somewhere a healing Fountain. To many fondly imagined Fountains, the Saints' Wells[15] of these days, did I pilgrim; to great Men, to great Cities, to great Events: but found there no healing. In strange countries, as in the well-known; in savage deserts, as in the press of corrupt civilisation, it was ever the same: how could your

Wanderer escape from—*his own Shadow*? Nevertheless still Forward! I felt as if in great haste; to do I saw not what. From the depths of my own heart, it called to me, Forwards! The winds and the streams, and all Nature sounded to me, Forwards! *Ach Gott,* I was even, once for all, a Son of Time.'

From which is it not clear that the internal Satanic School was still active enough? He says elsewhere: 'The *Enchiridion of Epictetus*[16] I had ever with me, often as my sole rational companion; and regret to mention that the nourishment it yielded was trifling.' Thou foolish Teufelsdröckh! How could it else? Hadst thou not Greek enough to understand thus much: *The end of Man is an Action, and not a Thought,*[17] though it were the noblest?

'How I lived?' writes he once: 'Friend, hast thou considered the "rugged all-nourishing Earth," as Sophocles well names her; how she feeds the sparrow on the house-top, much more her darling, man? While thou stirrest and livest, thou hast a probability of victual. My breakfast of tea has been cooked by a Tartar woman, with water of the Amur,[18] who wiped her earthen kettle with a horse-tail. I have roasted wild-eggs in the sand of Sahara; I have awakened in Paris *Estrapades* and Vienna *Malzleins,*[19] with no prospect of breakfast beyond elemental liquid. That I had my Living to seek saved me from Dying,—by suicide. In our busy Europe, is there not an everlasting demand for Intellect, in the chemical, mechanical, political, religious, educational, commercial departments? In Pagan countries, cannot one write Fetishes? Living! Little knowest thou what alchemy is in an inventive Soul; how, as with its little finger, it can create provision enough for the body (of a Philosopher); and then, as with both hands, create quite other than provision; namely, spectres to torment itself withal.'

Poor Teufelsdröckh! Flying with Hunger always parallel to him; and a whole Infernal Chase in his rear; so that the countenance of Hunger is comparatively a friend's! Thus must he, in the temper of ancient Cain, or of the modern Wandering Jew,—save only that he feels himself not guilty and but suffering the pains of

---

[13] A promontory in the Ionian Sea from which Sappho is said to have thrown herself for love of Phaon.

[14] Mahmud II (1785–1839), Sultan of Turkey.

[15] Shrines with curative powers, popular in the Middle Ages.

[16] *Enchiridion,* manual or handbook, by the Stoic philosopher Epictetus, first century A.D.

[17] Adapted from Aristotle's *Ethics.*   [18] River in east Asia.

[19] *Estrapades,* street in Paris near the Pantheon; *Malzlein,* suburb of Vienna.

guilt,—wend to and fro with aimless speed. Thus must he, over the whole surface of the Earth (by footprints), write his *Sorrows of Teufelsdröckh*; even as the great Goethe, in passionate words, had to write his *Sorrows of Werter*, before the spirit freed herself, and he could become a Man. Vain truly is the hope of your swiftest Runner to escape 'from his own Shadow'! Nevertheless, in these sick days, when the Born of Heaven first descries himself (about the age of twenty) in a world such as ours, richer than usual in two things, in Truths grown obsolete, and Trades grown obsolete,—what can the fool think but that it is all a Den of Lies, wherein whoso will not speak Lies and act Lies, must stand idle and despair? Whereby it happens that, for your nobler minds, the publishing of some such Work of Art, in one or the other dialect, becomes almost a necessity. For what is it properly but an Alter-cation with the Devil, before you begin honestly Fighting him? Your Byron publishes his *Sorrows of Lord George*, in verse and in prose, and copiously otherwise:[20] your Bonaparte represents his *Sorrows of Napoleon* Opera, in an all-too stupendous style; with music of cannon-volleys, and murder-shrieks of a world; his stage-lights are the fires of Conflagration; his rhyme and recitative are the tramp of embattled Hosts and the sound of falling Cities.—Happier is he who, like our Clothes-Philosopher, can write such matter, since it must be written, on the insensible Earth, with his shoe-soles only; and also survive the writing thereof!

CHAPTER VII

The Everlasting No

Loss of Hope, and of Belief. Profit-and-Loss Philosophy. Teufelsdröckh in his darkness and despair still clings to Truth and follows Duty. Inexpressible pains and fears of Unbelief. Fever-crisis: Protest against the Everlasting No: Baphometic Fire-Baptism.

UNDER the strange nebulous envelopment, wherein our Professor has now shrouded himself, no doubt but his spiritual nature is nevertheless progressive, and growing: for how can the 'Son of Time,' in any case, stand still?

We behold him, through those dim years, in a state of crisis, of transition: his mad Pilgrimings, and general solution into aimless Discontinuity, what is all this but a mad Fermentation; where-from, the fiercer it is, the clearer product will one day evolve itself?

Such transitions are ever full of pain: thus the Eagle when he moults is sickly; and, to attain his new beak, must harshly dash-off the old one upon rocks. What Stoicism soever our Wanderer, in his individual acts and motions, may affect, it is clear that there is a hot fever of anarchy and misery raging within; coruscations of which flash out: as, indeed, how could there be other? Have we not seen him disappointed, bemocked of Destiny, through long years? All that the young heart might desire and pray for has been denied; nay, as in the last worst instance, offered and then snatched away. Ever an 'Excellent Passivity'; but of useful, reasonable Activity, essential to the former as Food to Hunger, nothing granted: till at length, in this wild Pilgrimage, he must forcibly seize for himself an Activity, though useless, unreasonable. Alas, his cup of bitterness, which had been filling drop by drop, ever since that first 'ruddy morning' in the Hinterschlag Gymnasium, was at the very lip; and then with that poison-drop, of the Towgood-and-Blumine business, it runs over, and even hisses over in a deluge of foam.

He himself says once, with more justice than originality: 'Man is, properly speaking, based upon Hope, he has no other possession but Hope; this world of his is emphatically the 'Place of Hope.' What, then, was our Professor's possession? We see him, for the present, quite shut-out from Hope; looking not into the golden orient, but vaguely all round into a dim copper firmament, pregnant with earthquake and tornado.

Alas, shut-out from Hope, in a deeper sense than we yet dream of! For, as he wanders weari-somely through this world, he has now lost all tidings of another and higher. Full of religion, or at least of religiosity, as our Friend has since exhibited himself, he hides not that, in those days, he was wholly irreligious: 'Doubt had darkened into Unbelief,' says he; 'shade after shade goes grimly over your soul, till you have the fixed, starless, Tartarean black.' To such readers as have reflected, what can be called reflecting, on man's life, and happily discovered, in contradic-tion to much Profit-and-Loss Philosophy,[1] specu-lative and practical, that Soul is *not* synonymous

---

[20] Reference to the flamboyant life and work of Lord Byron.   [1] Utilitarianism and materialism.

with Stomach; who understand, therefore, in our Friend's words, 'that, for man's well-being, Faith is properly the one thing needful; how, with it, Martyrs, otherwise weak, can cheerfully endure the shame and the cross; and without it, World-lings puke-up their sick existence, by suicide, in the midst of luxury': to such it will be clear that, for a pure moral nature, the loss of his religious Belief was the loss of everything. Unhappy young man! All wounds, the crush of long-continued Destitution, the stab of false Friendship and of false Love, all wounds in thy so genial heart, would have healed again, had not its life-warmth been withdrawn. Well might he exclaim, in his wild way: 'Is there no God, then; but at best an absentee God, sitting idle, ever since the first Sabbath, at the outside of his Universe, and *see*ing it go? Has the word Duty no meaning; is what we call Duty no divine Messenger and Guide, but a false earthly Fantasm, made-up of Desire and Fear, of emanations from the Gallows and from Doctor Graham's Celestial-Bed?[2] Happiness of an approving Conscience! Did not Paul of Tarsus, whom admiring men have since named Saint, feel that *he* was "the chief of sinners";[3] and Nero of Rome, jocund in spirit (*wohlgemuth*), spend much of his time in fiddling? Foolish Wordmonger and Motive-grinder, who in thy Logic-mill hast an earthly mechanism for the Godlike itself, and wouldst fain grind me out Virtue from the husks of Pleasure,—I tell thee, Nay! To the unregenerate Prometheus Vinctus[4] of a man, it is ever the bitterest aggravation of his wretchedness that he is conscious of Virtue, that he feels himself the victim not of suffering only, but of injustice. What then? Is the heroic inspiration we name Virtue but some Passion; some bubble of the blood, bubbling in the direction others *profit* by? I know not: only this I know, If what thou namest Happiness be our true aim, then are we all astray. With Stupidity and sound Digestion man may front much. But what, in these dull unimaginative days, are the terrors of Conscience to the diseases of the Liver! Not on Morality, but on Cookery, let us build our stronghold: there brandishing our frying-pan, as censer, let us offer sweet incense to the Devil, and live at ease on the fat things *he* has provided for his Elect!'

Thus has the bewildered Wanderer to stand, as so many have done, shouting question after question into the Sibyl-cave of Destiny, and receive no Answer but an Echo. It is all a grim Desert, this once-fair world of his; wherein is heard only the howling of wild-beasts, or the shrieks of despairing, hate-filled men; and no Pillar of Cloud by day, and no Pillar of Fire by night,[5] any longer guides the Pilgrim. To such length has the spirit of Inquiry carried him. 'But what boots it (*was thut's*)?' cries he: 'it is but the common lot in this era. Not having come to spiritual majority prior to the *Siècle de Louis Quinze*,[6] and not being born purely a Loghead (*Dummkopf*), thou hadst no other outlook. The whole world is, like thee, sold to Unbelief;[7] their old Temples of the Godhead, which for long have not been rainproof, crumble down; and men ask now: Where is the Godhead; our eyes never saw him?'

Pitiful enough were it, for all these wild utterances, to call our Diogenes wicked. Un-profitable servants as we all are,[8] perhaps at no era of his life was he more decisively the Servant of Goodness, the Servant of God, than even now when doubting God's existence. 'One circum-stance I note,' says he: 'after all the nameless woe that Inquiry, which for me, what it is not always, was genuine Love of Truth, had wrought me, I nevertheless still loved Truth, and would bate no jot of my allegiance to her. "Truth!" I cried, "though the Heavens crush me for following her: no Falsehood! though a whole celestial Lubber-land were the price of Apostasy." In conduct it was the same. Had a divine Messenger from the clouds, or miraculous Handwriting on the wall, convincingly proclaimed to me *This thou shalt do*, with what passionate readiness, as I often thought, would I have done it, had it been leaping into the infernal Fire. Thus, in spite of all Motive-grinders, and Mechanical Profit-and-Loss Philos-ophies, with the sick ophthalmia and hallucina-tion they had brought on, was the Infinite nature of Duty still dimly present to me: living without God in the world, of God's light I was not utterly bereft; if my as yet sealed eyes, with their un-speakable longing, could nowhere see Him, nevertheless in my heart He was present, and His heaven-written Law still stood legible and sacred there.'

Meanwhile, under all these tribulations, and

---

[2] A notorious contraption supposed to cure sterility, invented by James Graham (1745–94).
[3] I Timothy 1:15.   [4] "Prometheus Bound," as in Aeschylus.   [5] Exodus 13:21.
[6] The century of Louis XV, i.e., the age of the Encyclopaedists and Deists; also title of a history by Voltaire.
[7] Luke 17:10.   [8] Ephesians 2:12.

temporal and spiritual destitutions, what must the Wanderer, in his silent soul, have endured! 'The painfullest feeling,' writes he, 'is that of your own Feebleness (*Unkraft*); ever, as the English Milton says, to be weak is the true misery.[9] And yet of your Strength there is and can be no clear feeling, save by what you have prospered in, by what you have done. Between vague wavering Capability and fixed indubitable Performance, what a difference! A certain inarticulate Self-consciousness dwells dimly in us; which only our Works can render articulate and decisively discernible. Our Works are the mirror wherein the spirit first sees its natural lineaments. Hence, too, the folly of that impossible Precept, *Know thyself*; till it be translated into this partially possible one, *Know what thou canst work at*.

'But for me, so strangely unprosperous had I been, the net-result of my Workings amounted as yet simply to—Nothing. How then could I believe in my Strength, when there was as yet no mirror to see it in? Ever did this agitating, yet, as I now perceive, quite frivolous question, remain to me insoluble: Hast thou a certain Faculty, a certain Worth, such even as the most have not; or art thou the completest Dullard of these modern times? Alas, the fearful Unbelief is unbelief in yourself; and how could I believe? Had not my first, last Faith in myself, when even to me the Heavens seemed laid open, and I dared to love, been all-too cruelly belied? The speculative Mystery of Life grew ever more mysterious to me: neither in the practical Mystery had I made the slightest progress, but been everywhere buffeted, foiled, and contemptuously cast out. A feeble unit in the middle of a threatening Infinitude, I seemed to have nothing given me but eyes, whereby to discern my own wretchedness. Invisible yet impenetrable walls, as of Enchantment, divided me from all living: was there, in the wide world, any true bosom I could press trustfully to mine? O Heaven, No, there was none! I kept a lock upon my lips: why should I speak much with that shifting variety of so-called Friends, in whose withered, vain and too-hungry souls Friendship was but an incredible tradition? In such cases, your resource is to talk little, and that little mostly from the Newspapers. Now when I look back, it was a strange isolation I then lived in. The men and women around me, even speaking with me, were but Figures; I had, practically, forgotten that they were alive that they were not merely automatic. In the midst of

their crowded streets and assemblages, I walked solitary; and (except as it was my own heart, not another's, that I kept devouring) savage also, as the tiger in his jungle. Some comfort it would have been, could I, like a Faust, have fancied myself tempted and tormented of the Devil; for a Hell, as I imagine, without Life, though only diabolic Life, were more frightful: but in our age of Down-pulling and Disbelief, the very Devil has been pulled down, you cannot so much as believe in a Devil. To me the Universe was all void of Life, of Purpose, of Volition, even of Hostility: it was one huge, dead, immeasurable Steam-engine, rolling on, in its dead indifference, to grind me limb from limb. O, the vast, gloomy, solitary Golgotha, and Mill of Death! Why was the Living banished thither companionless, conscious? Why, if there is no Devil; nay, unless the Devil is your God?'

A prey incessantly to such corrosions, might not, moreover, as the worst aggravation to them, the iron constitution even of a Teufelsdröckh threaten to fail? We conjecture that he has known sickness; and, in spite of his locomotive habits, perhaps sickness of the chronic sort. Hear this, for example: 'How beautiful to die of broken-heart, on Paper! Quite another thing in practice; every window of your Feeling, even of your Intellect, as it were, begrimed and mud-bespattered, so that no pure ray can enter; a whole Drugshop in your inwards; the fordone soul drowning slowly in quagmires of Disgust!'

Putting all which external and internal miseries together, may we not find in the following sentences, quite in our Professor's still vein, significance enough? 'From Suicide a certain aftershine (*Nachschein*) of Christianity withheld me: perhaps also a certain indolence of character; for, was not that a remedy I had at any time within reach? Often, however, was there a question present to me: Should someone now, at the turning of that corner, blow thee suddenly out of Space, into the other World, or other No-world, by pistol-shot,—how were it? On which ground, too, I often, in sea-storms and sieged cities and other death-scenes, exhibited an imperturbability, which passed, falsely enough, for courage.'

'So had it lasted,' concludes the Wanderer, 'so had it lasted, as in bitter protracted Death-agony, through long years. The heart within me, unvisited by any heavenly dew-drop was smouldering in sulphurous, slow-consuming fire. Al-

[9] *Paradise Lost*, I, 157.

most since earliest memory I had shed no tear; or once only when I, murmuring half-audibly, recited Faust's Death-song, that wild *Selig der den er im Siegesglanze findet* (Happy whom *he* finds in Battle's splendour),[10] and thought that of this last Friend even I was not forsaken, that Destiny itself could not doom me not to die. Having no hope, neither had I any definite fear, were it of Man or of Devil: nay, I often felt as if it might be solacing, could the Arch-Devil himself, though in Tartarean terrors, but rise to me, that I might tell him a little of my mind. And yet, strangely enough, I lived in a continual, indefinite, pining fear; tremulous, pusillanimous, apprehensive of I knew not what; it seemed as if all things in the Heavens above and the Earth beneath would hurt me; as if the Heavens and the Earth were but boundless jaws of a devouring monster, wherein I, palpitating, waited to be devoured.

'Full of such humour, and perhaps the miserablest man in the whole French Capital or Suburbs, was I, one sultry Dog-day, after much perambulation, toiling along the dirty little *Rue Saint-Thomas de l'Enfer*,[11] among civic rubbish enough, in a close atmosphere, and over pavements hot as Nebuchadnezzar's Furnace;[12] whereby doubtless my spirits were little cheered; when, all at once, there rose a Thought in me, and I asked myself: "What *art* thou afraid of? Wherefore, like a coward, dost thou forever pip and whimper, and go cowering and trembling? Despicable biped! what is the sum-total of the worst that lies before thee? Death? Well, Death; and say the pangs of Tophet too, and all that the Devil and Man may, will or can do against thee! Hast thou not a heart; canst thou not suffer whatsoever it be; and, as a Child of Freedom, though outcast, trample Tophet itself under thy feet, while it consumes thee? Let it come, then; I will meet it and defy it!" And as I so thought, there rushed like a stream of fire over my whole soul; and I shook base Fear away from me forever. I was strong, of unknown strength; a spirit, almost a god. Ever from that time, the temper of my misery was changed: not Fear or whining Sorrow was it, but Indignation and grim fire-eyed Defiance.

'Thus had the EVERLASTING NO (*das ewige Nein*) pealed authoritatively through all the recesses of my Being, of my ME; and then was it that my whole ME stood up, in native God-created

majesty, and with emphasis recorded its Protest. Such a Protest, the most important transaction in Life, may that same Indignation and Defiance, in a psychological point of view, be fitly called. The Everlasting No had said: "Behold, thou art fatherless, outcast, and the Universe is mine (the Devil's)"; to which my whole ME now made answer: "*I* am not thine, but Free, and forever hate thee!"

'It is from this hour that I incline to date my Spiritual New-birth, or Baphometic Fire-baptism;[13] perhaps I directly thereupon began to be a Man.'

CHAPTER VIII

Centre of Indifference

Teufelsdröckh turns now outwardly to the *Not-me*; and finds wholesomer food. Ancient Cities: Mystery of their origin and growth: Invisible inheritances and possessions. Power and virtue of a true Book. Wagram Battlefield: War. Great Scenes beheld by the Pilgrim: Great Events, and Great Men. Napoleon, a divine missionary, preaching *La carriere ouvertè aux talens*. Teufelsdröckh at the North Cape: Modern means of self-defence. Gunpowder and duelling. The Pilgrim, despising his miseries, reaches the Centre of Indifference.

THOUGH, after this 'Baphometic Fire-baptism' of his, our Wanderer signifiest hat his Unrest was but increased; as, indeed, 'Indignation and Defiance,' especially against things in general, are not the most peaceable inmates; yet can the Psychologist surmise that it was no longer a quite hopeless Unrest; that henceforth it had at least a fixed centre to revolve round. For the fire-baptised soul, long so scathed and thunder-riven, here feels its own Freedom, which feeling is its Baphometic Baptism: the citadel of its whole Kingdom it has thus gained by assault, and will keep inexpugnable; outwards from which the remaining dominions, not indeed without hard battling, will doubtless by degrees be conquered and pacificated. Under another figure, we might

---

[10] Goethe's *Faust*, I, 1573–76.   [11] "The Street of St. Thomas of Hell."   [12] Daniel 3:19.
[13] *Baphometic* is of uncertain origin but suggests flamelike and blinding, from Baphomet, an idol associated with the Knights Templar, and from Baffometus, an outcast in Zacharias Werner's *Die Söhne des Thals* (The Sons of the Valley).

say, if in that great moment, in the *Rue Saint-Thomas de l'Enfer*, the old inward Satanic School was not yet thrown out of doors, it received peremptory judicial notice to quit;—whereby, for the rest, its howl-chantings, Ernulphus-cursings,[1] and rebellious gnashings of teeth, might, in the meanwhile, become only the more tumultuous, and difficult to keep secret.

Accordingly, if we scrutinise these Pilgrimings well, there is perhaps discernible henceforth a certain incipient method in their madness. Not wholly as a Spectre does Teufelsdröckh now storm through the world; at worst as a spectre-fighting Man, nay who will one day be a Spectre-queller. If pilgriming restlessly to so many 'Saints' Wells,' and ever without quenching of his thirst, he nevertheless finds little secular wells, whereby from time to time some alleviation is ministered. In a word, he is now, if not ceasing, yet intermitting to 'eat his own heart'; and clutches round him outwardly on the Not-me for wholesomer food. Does not the following glimpse exhibit him in a much more natural state?

'Towns also and Cities, especially the ancient, I failed not to look upon with interest. How beautiful to see thereby, as through a long vista, into the remote Time; to have as it were, an actual section of almost the earliest Past brought safe into the Present, and set before your eyes! There, in that old City, was a live ember of Culinary Fire put down, say only two-thousand years ago; and there, burning more or less triumphantly, with such fuel as the region yielded, it has burnt, and still burns, and thou thyself seest the very smoke thereof. Ah! and the far more mysterious live ember of Vital Fire was then also put down there; and still miraculously burns and spreads; and the smoke and ashes thereof (in these Judgment-Halls and Church-yards), and its bellows-engines (in these Chur-ches), thou still seest; and its flame, looking out from every kind countenance, and every hateful one, still warms thee or scorches thee.

'Of Man's Activity and Attainment the chief results are aeriform, mystic, and preserved in Tradition only: such are his Forms of Government, with the Authority they rest on; his Customs, or Fashions both of Cloth-habits and of Soul-habits; much more his collective stock of Handicrafts, the whole Faculty he has acquired of manipulating Nature: all these things, as indispensable and priceless as they are, cannot in any way be fixed under lock and key, but must flit, spirit-like, on impalpable vehicles, from Father to Son; if you demand sight of them, they are nowhere to be met with. Visible Ploughmen and Hammermen there have been, ever from Cain and Tubalcain downwards: but where does your accumulated Agricultural, Metallurgic, and other Manufacturing Skill lie warehoused? It transmits itself on the atmospheric air, on the sun's rays (by Hearing and by Vision); it is a thing aeriform, impalpable, of quite spiritual sort. In like manner, ask me not, Where are the Laws; where is the Government? In vain wilt thou go to Schönbrunn, to Downing Street, to the Palais Bourbon:[2] thou findest nothing there but brick or stone houses, and some bundles of Papers tied with tape. Where, then, is that same cunningly-devised almighty Government of theirs to be laid hands on? Everywhere, yet nowhere: seen only in its works, this too is a thing aeriform, invisible; or if you will, mystic and miraculous. So spiritual (*geistig*) is our whole daily Life: all that we do springs out of Mystery, Spirit, invisible Force; only like a little Cloud-image, or Armida's Palace,[3] air-built, does the Actual body itself forth from the great mystic Deep.

'Visible and tangible products of the Past, again, I reckon-up to the extent of three: Cities, with their Cabinets and Arsenals; then tilled Fields, to either or to both of which divisions Roads with their Bridges, may belong; and thirdly——Books. In which third truly, the last invented, lies a worth far surpassing that of the two others. Wondrous indeed is the virtue of a true Book. Not like a dead city of stones, yearly crumbling, yearly needing repair; more like a tilled field, but then a spiritual field: like a spiritual tree, let me rather say, it stands from year to year, and from age to age (we have Books that already number some hundred-and-fifty human ages); and yearly comes its new produce of leaves (Commentaries, Deductions, Philosophical, Political Systems; or were it only Sermons, Pamphlets, Journalistic Essays), every one of which is talismanic and thaumaturgic, for it can persuade men. O thou who art able to write a Book, which once in the two centuries or oftener there is a man gifted to do, envy not him whom they name City-builder, and inexpressibly pity

---

[1] After Ernulf (1040–1124), Bishop of Rochester.
[2] Sites of governmental offices and activities in Vienna, London, and Paris respectively.
[3] Palace of the enchantress Armida in *Jerusalem Delivered*, by Torquato Tasso.

him whom they name Conqueror or City-burner! Thou too art a Conqueror and Victor; but of the true sort, namely over the Devil: thou too hast built what will outlast all marble and metal, and be a wonder-bringing City of the Mind, a Temple and Seminary and Prophetic Mount, wherto all kindreds of the Earth will pilgrim.—Fool! why journeyest thou wearisomely, in thy antiquarian fervour, to gaze on the stone pyramids of Geeza, or the clay ones of Sacchara?[4] These stand there, as I can tell thee, idle and inert, looking over the Desert, foolishly enough, for the last three-thousand years: but canst thou not open thy Hebrew Bible, then, or even Luther's Version thereof?'

No less satisfactory is his sudden appearance not in Battle, yet on some Battle-field; which, we soon gather, must be that of Wagram;[5] so that here, for once, is a certain approximation to distinctiveness of date. Omitting much, let us impart what follows:

'Horrible enough! A whole Marchfeld[6] strewed with shell-splinters, cannon-shot, ruined tumbrils, and dead men and horses; stragglers still remaining not so much as buried. And those red mould heaps: ay, there lie the Shells of Men, out of which all the Life and Virtue has been blown; and now are they swept together, and crammed-down out of sight, like blown Egg-shells!—Did Nature, when she bade the Donau bring down his mould-cargoes from the Carinthian and Carpathian Heights, and spread them out here into the softest, richest level,—intend thee, O Marchfeld, for a corn-bearing Nursery, whereon her children might be nursed; or for a Cockpit, wherein they might the more commodiously be throttled and tattered? Were thy three broad Highways, meeting here from the ends of Europe, made for Ammunition-wagons, then? Were thy Wagrams and Stillfrieds but so many ready-built Casemates, wherein the house of Hapsburg might batter with artillery, and with artillery be battered? König Ottokar, amid yonder hillocks, dies under Rodolf's truncheon; here Kaiser Franz falls a-swoon under Napoleon's: within which five centuries, to omit the others, how has thy breast, fair Plain, been defaced and defiled! The green-sward is torn-up and trampled-down; man's fond care of it, his fruit-trees, hedge-rows, and pleasant dwellings, blown away with gunpowder; and the

kind seedfield lies a desolate, hideous Place of Sculls.—Nevertheless, Nature is at work; neither shall these Powder-Devilkins with their utmost devilry gainsay her: but all that gore and carnage will be shrouded-in, absorbed into manure; and next year the Marchfeld will be green, nay greener. Thrifty unwearied Nature, ever out of our great waste educing some little profit of thy own,—how dost thou, from the very carcass of the Killer, bring Life for the Living!

'What, speaking in quite unofficial language, is the net-purport and upshot of war? To my own knowledge, for example, there dwell and toil, in the British village of Dumdrudge,[7] usually some five-hundred souls. From these, by certain "Natural Enemies" of the French, there are successively selected, during the French war, say thirty able-bodied men: Dumdrudge, at her own expense, has suckled and nursed them: she has, not without difficulty and sorrow, fed them up to manhood, and even trained them to crafts, so that one can weave, another build, another hammer, and the weakest can stand under thirty stone avoirdupois. Nevertheless, amid much weeping and swearing, they are selected; all dressed in red; and shipped away, at the public charges, some two-thousand miles, or say only to the south of Spain; and fed there till wanted. And now to that same spot, in the south of Spain, are thirty similar French artisans, from a French Dumdrudge, in like manner wending: till at length, after infinite effort, the two parties come into actual juxtaposition; and Thirty stands fronting Thirty, each with a gun in his hand. Straightway the word "Fire!" is given: and they blow the souls out of one another; and in place of sixty brisk useful craftsmen, the world has sixty dead carcasses, which it must bury, and anew shed tears for. Had these men any quarrel? Busy as the Devil is, not the smallest! They lived far enough apart; were the entirest strangers; nay, in so wide a Universe, there was even, unconsciously, by Commerce, some mutual helpfulness between them. How then? Simpleton! their Governors had fallen-out; and, instead of shooting one another, had the cunning to make these poor blockheads shoot.—Alas, so is it in Deutschland, and hitherto in all other lands; still as of old, 'what devilry soever Kings do, the Greeks must pay the piper!'—In that fiction of the English

---

[4] Geeza and Saccara, sites of large pyramids near Cairo.
[5] Scene of Napoleon's victòry over the Austrians, 1809.
[6] On the same plain as Wagram, scene of the triumph of Rudolf von Hapsburg over Ottokar of Bohemia in 1278, in the Battle of Stillfried.
[7] Carlyle's coinage for a typical British village.

Smollet,[8] it is true, the final Cessation of War is perhaps prophetically shadowed forth; where the two Natural Enemies, in person, take each a Tobacco-pipe, filled with Brimstone; light the same, and smoke in one another's faces, till the weaker gives in: but from such predicted Peace-Era, what blood-filled trenches, and contentious centuries, may still divide us!'

Thus can the Professor, at least in lucid intervals, look away from his own sorrows, over the many-coloured world, and pertinently enough note what is passing there. We may remark, indeed, that for the matter of spiritual culture, if for nothing else, perhaps few periods of his life were richer than this. Internally, there is the most momentous instructive Course of Practical Philosophy, with Experiments, going on; towards the right comprehension of which his Peripatetic habits, favourable to Meditation, might help him rather than hinder. Externally, again, as he wanders to and fro, there are, if for the longing heart little substance, yet for the seeing eye sights enough: in these so boundless Travels of his, granting that the Satanic School was even partially kept down, what an incredible knowledge of our Planet, and its Inhabitants and their Works, that is to say, of all knowable things, might not Teufelsdröckh acquire!

'I have read in most Public Libraries,' says he, 'including those of Constantinople and Samarcand: in most Colleges, except the Chinese Mandarin ones, I have studied, or seen that there was no studying. Unknown Languages have I oftenest gathered from their natural repertory, the Air, by my organ of Hearing; Statistics, Geographics, Topographics came, through the Eye, almost of their own accord. The ways of Man, how he seeks food, and warmth, and protection for himself, in most regions, are ocularly known to me. Like the great Hadrian,[9] I meted-out much of the terraqueous Globe with a pair of compasses that belonged to myself only.

'Of great Scenes why speak? Three summer days, I lingered reflecting, and even composing (*dichtete*), by the Pine-chasms of Vaucluse;[10] and in that clear Lakelet moistened my bread. I have sat under the Palm-trees of Tadmor;[11] smoked a pipe among the ruins of Babylon. The great Wall of China I have seen; and can testify that it is of gray brick, coped and covered with granite, and shows only second-rate masonry.—Great Events, also, have not I witnessed? Kings sweated-down (*ausgemergelt*) into Berlin-and-Milan Customhouse-Officers; the World well won, and the World well lost; oftener than once a hundred-thousand individuals shot (by each other) in one day. All kindreds and peoples and nations dashed together, and shifted and shovelled into heaps, that they might ferment there, and in time unite. The birth-pangs of Democracy,[12] wherewith convulsed Europe was groaning in cries that reached Heaven, could not escape me.

'For great Men I have ever had the warmest predilection; and can perhaps boast that few such in this era have wholly escaped me. Great Men are the inspired (speaking and acting) Texts of that divine BOOK OF REVELATIONS, whereof a Chapter is completed from epoch to epoch, and by some named HISTORY; to which inspired Texts your numerous talented men, and your innumerable untalented men, are the better or worse exegetic Commentaries, and wagonload of too-stupid, heretical or orthodox, weekly Sermons. For my study, the inspired Texts themselves! Thus did not I, in very early days, having disguised me as tavern-waiter, stand behind the field-chairs, under that shady Tree at Treisnitz by the Jena Highway;[13] waiting upon the great Schiller and greater Goethe; and hearing what I have not forgotten. For——'

——But at this point the Editor recalls his principle of caution, some time ago laid down, and must suppress much. Let not the sacredness of Laurelled, still more, of Crowned Heads, be tampered with. Should we, at a future day, find circumstances altered, and the time come for Publication, then may these glimpses into the privacy of the Illustrious be conceded; which for the present were little better than treacherous, perhaps traitorous Eavesdroppings. Of Lord Byron, therefore, of Pope Pius, Emperor Tarakwang, and the 'White Water-roses' (Chinese Carbonari)[14] with their mysteries, no notice here! Of Napoleon himself we shall only, glancing from

---

[8] Tobias Smollett (1721–71), *The Adventures of Ferdinand, Count Fathom.*
[9] Emperor Hadrian (76–138) spent much of his reign visiting the provinces of the Roman empire.
[10] Village in southern France associated with Petrarch.
[11] The "City of Palms," also known as Palmyra, in Syria; built by Solomon.
[12] The Paris Revolution of 1830 and the Reform Bill agitation in Britain in 1830 and 1831.
[13] Near Jena in Germany where Goethe and Schiller collaborated in 1796.
[14] Pope Pius VII, Pope from 1800 to 1823; Emperor Tao Kuang (1781–1850) of China; Carbonari, early nineteenth-century Italian revolutionary society.

afar, remark that Teufelsdröckh's relation to him seems to have been of very varied character. At first we find our poor Professor on the point of being shot as a spy; then taken into private conversation, even pinched on the ear, yet presented with no money; at last indignantly dismissed, almost thrown out of doors, as an 'Ideologist.' 'He himself,' says the Professor, 'was among the completest Ideologists, at least Ideopraxists: in the Idea (*in der Idee*) he lived, moved and fought. The man was a Divine Missionary, though unconscious of it; and preached, through the cannon's throat, that great doctrine, *La carrière ouverte aux talens* (The Tools to him that can handle them), which is our ultimate Political Evangel, wherein alone can liberty lie. Madly enough he preached, it is true, as Enthusiasts and first Missionaries are wont, with imperfect utterance, amid much frothy rant; yet as articulately perhaps as the case admitted. Or call him, if you will, an American Backwoodsman, who had to fell unpenetrated forests, and battle with innumerable wolves, and did not entirely forbear strong liquor, rioting, and even theft; whom, notwithstanding, the peaceful Sower will follow, and, as he cuts the boundless harvest, bless.'

More legitimate and decisively authentic is Teufelsdröckh's appearance and emergence (we know not well whence) in the solitude of the North Cape, on that June Midnight. He has a 'light-blue Spanish cloak' hanging round him, as his 'most commodious, principal, indeed sole upper-garment'; and stands there, on the World-promontory, looking over the infinite Brine, like a little blue Belfry (as we figure), now motionless indeed, yet ready, if stirred, to ring quaintest changes.

'Silence as of death,' writes he; 'for Midnight, even in the Arctic latitudes, has its character: nothing but the granite cliffs ruddy-tinged, the peaceable gurgle of that slow-heaving Polar Ocean, over which in the utmost North the great Sun hangs low and lazy, as if he too were slumbering. Yet is his cloud-couch wrought of crimson and cloth-of-gold; yet does his light stream over the mirror of waters, like a tremulous fire-pillar, shooting downwards to the abyss, and hide itself under my feet. In such moments, Solitude also is invaluable; for who would speak, or be looked on when behind him lies all Europe and Africa, fast asleep, except the watchmen; and before him the

silent Immensity, and Palace of the Eternal, whereof our Sun is but a porch-lamp?

'Nevertheless, in this solemn moment comes a man, or monster, scrambling from among the rock-hollows; and, shaggy, huge as the Hyperborean[15] Bear, hails me in Russian speech: most probably, therefore, a Russian Smuggler. With courteous brevity, I signify my indifference to contraband trade, my humane intentions, yet strong wish to be private. In vain: the monster, counting doubtless on his superior stature, and minded to make sport for himself, or perhaps profit, were it with murder, continues to advance; ever assailing me with his importunate train-oil breath; and now has advanced, till we stand both on the verge of the rock, the deep Sea rippling greedily down below. What argument will avail? On the thick Hyperborean, cherubic reasoning, seraphic eloquence were lost. Prepared for such extremity, I, deftly enough, whisk aside one step; draw out, from my interior reservoirs, a sufficient Birmingham Horse-pistol, and say, "Be so obliging as retire, Friend (*Er ziehe sich zurück, Freund*), and with promptitude!" This logic even the Hyperborean understands: fast enough, with apologetic, petitionary growl, he sidles off; and, except for suicidal as well as homicidal purposes, need not return.

'Such I hold to be the genuine use of Gunpowder: that it makes all men alike tall. Nay, if thou be cooler, cleverer than I, if thou have more *Mind*, though all but no *Body* whatever, then canst thou kill me first, and art the taller. Hereby, at last, is the Goliath powerless, and the David resistless; savage Animalism is nothing, inventive Spiritualism is all.

'With respect to Duels, indeed, I have my own ideas. Few things, in this so surprising world, strike me with more surprise. Two little visual Spectra of men, hovering with insecure enough cohesion in the midst of the UNFATHOMABLE, and to dissolve therein, at any rate, very soon,—make pause at the distance of twelve paces asunder; whirl round; and, simultaneously by the cunningest mechanism, explode one another into Dissolution; and off-hand become Air, and Non-extant! Deuce on it (*verdammt*), the little spit-fires!—Nay, I think with old Hugo von Trimberg: "God must needs laugh outright, could such a thing be, to see his wondrous Manikins here below." '[16]

But amid these specialties, let us not forget the

---

[15] From Boreas, the north wind, thus "most northern."
[16] Hugo von Trimberg (1260–1309), German philosopher and Meistersinger.

great generality, which is our chief quest here: How prospered the inner man of Teufelsdröckh under so much outward shifting? Does Legion still lurk in him, though repressed; or has he exorcised that Devil's Brood? We can answer that the symptoms continue promising. Experience is the grand spiritual Doctor; and with him Teufelsdröckh has been long a patient, swallowing many a bitter bolus. Unless our poor Friend belong to the numerous class of Incurables, which seems not likely, some cure will doubtless be effected. We should rather say that Legion, or the Satanic School, was now pretty well extirpated and cast out, but next to nothing introduced in its room; whereby the heart remains, for the while, in a quiet but no comfortable state.

'At length, after so much roasting,' thus writes our Autobiographer, 'I was what you might name calcined. Pray only that it be not rather, as is the more frequent issue, reduced to a *caput-mortuum*![17] But in any case, by mere dint of practice, I had grown familiar with many things. Wretchedness was still wretched; but I could now partly see through it, and despise it. Which highest mortal, in this inane Existence, had I not found a Shadow-hunter, or Shadow-hunted; and, when I looked through his brave garnitures, miserable enough? Thy wishes have all been sniffed aside, thought I: but what, had they even been all granted! Did not the Boy Alexander weep because he had not two Planets to conquer; or a whole Solar System; or after that, a whole Universe? *Ach Gott*, when I gazed into these Stars, have they not looked-down on me as if with pity, from their serene spaces; like Eyes glistening with heavenly tears over the little lot of man! Thousands of human generations, all as noisy as our own, have been swallowed-up of Time, and there remains no wreck of them any more; and Arcturus and Orion and Sirius and the Pleiades are still shining in their courses, clear and young, as when the Shepherd first noted them in the plain of Shinar.[18] Pshaw! what is this paltry little Dog-cage[19] of an Earth; what art thou that sittest whining there? Thou art still Nothing, Nobody: true; but who, then, is Something, Somebody? For thee the Family of Man has no use; it rejects thee; thou art wholly as a dissevered limb: so be it; perhaps it is better so!'

Too-heavy-laden Teufelsdröckh! Yet surely his

bands are loosening; one day he will hurl the burden far from him, and bound forth free and with a second youth.

'This,' says our Professor, 'was the CENTRE OF INDIFFERENCE[20] I had now reached; through which whoso travels from the Negative Pole to the Positive must necessarily pass.'

CHAPTER IX

The Everlasting Yea

Temptations in the Wilderness: Victory over the Tempter. Annihilation of Self. Belief in God, and love to Man. The Origin of Evil, a problem ever requiring to be solved anew: Teufelsdröckh's solution. Love of Happiness a vain whim: A Higher in man than Love of Happiness. The Everlasting Yea. Worship of Sorrow. Voltaire: his task now finished. Conviction worthless, impossible, without Conduct. The true Ideal, the Actual: Up and work!

Temptations in the Wilderness!'[1] exclaims Teufelsdröckh: 'Have we not all to be tried with such? Not so easily can the old Adam, lodged in us by birth, be dispossessed. Our Life is compassed round with Necessity; yet is the meaning of Life itself no other than Freedom, than Voluntary Force: thus have we a warfare; in the beginning, especially, a hard-fought battle. For the God-given mandate, *Work thou in Well-doing*,[2] lies mysteriously written, in Promethean Prophetic Characters, in our hearts; and leaves us no rest, night or day, till it be deciphered and obeyed; till it burn forth, in our conduct, a visible, acted Gospel of Freedom. And as the clay-given mandate, *Eat thou and be filled*, at the same time persuasively proclaims itself through every nerve,—must not there by a confusion, a contest, before the better Influence can become the upper?

'To me nothing seems more natural than that the Son of Man, when such God-given mandate first prophetically stirs within him, and the Clay must now be vanquished or vanquish,—should be carried of the spirit into grim Solitudes, and

---

[17] Death's head; also the residue after distillation, hence any worthless leftover.
[18] Location of the Tower of Babel; see Genesis 11:1–9.
[19] A cage device in which a dog walked to turn the spit on which meat was roasted.
[20] In physics the midpoint between the two extremes of a magnet.
[1] Matthew 4:1.   [2] II Thessalonians 3:13.

there fronting the Tempter do grimmest battle with him; defiantly setting him at naught, till he yield and fly. Name it as we choose: with or without visible Devil, whether in the natural Desert of rocks and sands, or in the populous moral Desert of selfishness and baseness,—to such Temptation are we all called. Unhappy if we are not! Unhappy if we are but Half-men, in whom that divine handwriting has never blazed forth, all-subduing, in true sun-splendour; but quivers dubiously amid meaner lights: or smoulders, in dull pain, in darkness, under earthly vapours!— Our Wilderness is the wide World in an Atheistic Century; our Forty Days are long years of suffering and fasting: nevertheless, to these also comes an end. Yes, to me also was given, if not Victory, yet the consciousness of Battle, and the resolve to persevere therein while life or faculty is left. To me also, entangled in the enchanted forests, demon-peopled, doleful of sight and of sound, it was given, after weariest wanderings, to work out my way into the higher sunlight slopes—of that Mountain which has no summit, or whose summit is in Heaven only!'

He says elsewhere, under a less ambitious figure; as figures are, once for all, natural to him: 'Has not thy Life been that of most sufficient men (*tüchtigen Männer*) thou hast known in this generation? An outflush of foolish young Enthusiasm, like the first fallow-crop, wherein are as many weeds as valuable herbs: this all parched away, under the Droughts of practical and spiritual Unbelief, as Disappointment, in thought and act, often-repeated gave rise to Doubt, and Doubt gradually settled into Denial! If I have had a second-crop, and now see the perennial greensward, and sit under umbrageous cedars, which defy all Drought (and Doubt); herein too, be the Heavens praised, I am not without examples, and even exemplars.'

So that, for Teufelsdröckh also, there has been a 'glorious revolution': these mad shadow-hunting and shadow-hunted Pilgrimings of his were but some purifying 'Temptation in the Wilderness,' before his apostolic work (such as it was) could begin; which Temptation is now happily over, and the Devil once more worsted! Was 'that high moment in the *Rue de l'Enfer*,' then, properly the turning-point of the battle; when the Fiend said, *Worship me, or be torn in shreds*; and was answered valiantly with an *Apage Satana*?[3]—Singular Teufelsdröckh, would thou hadst told thy singular

story in plain words! But it is fruitless to look there, in those Paper-bags, for such. Nothing but innuendoes, figurative crotchets: a typical Shadow, fitfully wavering, prophetico-satiric; no clear logical Picture. 'How paint to the sensual eye,' asks he once, 'what passes in the Holy-of-Holies of Man's Soul; in what words, known to these profane times, speak even afar-off of the unspeakable?' We ask in turn: Why perplex these times, profane as they are, with needless obscurity, by omission and by commission? Not mystical only is our Professor, but whimsical; and involves himself, now more than ever, in eye-bewildering *chiaroscuro*. Successive glimpses, here faithfully imparted, our more gifted readers must endeavour to combine for their own behoof.

He says: 'The hot Harmattan wind[4] had raged itself out; its howl went silent within me; and the long-deafened soul could now hear. I paused in my wild wanderings; and sat me down to wait, and consider; for it was as if the hour of change drew nigh. I seemed to surrender, to renounce utterly, and say: Fly, then, false shadows of Hope; I will chase you no more, I will believe you no more. And ye too, haggard spectres of Fear, I care not for you; ye too are all shadows and a lie. Let me rest here: for I am way-weary and life-weary; I will rest here, were it but to die: to die or to live is alike to me; alike insignificant.'— And again: 'Here, then, as I lay in that CENTRE OF INDIFFERENCE; cast, doubtless by benignant upper Influence, into a healing sleep, the heavy dreams rolled gradually away, and I awoke to a new Heaven and a new Earth. The first preliminary moral Act, Annihilation of Self (*Selbsttödtung*), had been happily accomplished; and my mind's eyes were now unsealed, and its hands ungyved.'

Might we not also conjecture that the following passage refers to his Locality, during this same 'healing sleep'; that his Pilgrim-staff lies cast aside here, on 'the high table-land'; and indeed that the repose is already taking wholesome effect on him? If it were not that the tone, in some parts, has more of riancy, even of levity, than we could have expected! However, in Teufelsdröckh, there is always the strangest Dualism: light dancing, with guitar-music, will be going on in the fore-court, while by fits from within comes the faint whimpering of woe and wail. We transcribe the piece entire.

'Beautiful it was to sit there, as in my skyey

---

[3] "Get thee hence, Satan!"; Matthew 4:8–10.
[4] A dry wind from the interior that blows on the Atlantic coast of Africa.

Tent, musing and meditating; on the high table-land, in front of the Mountains; over me, as roof, the azure Dome, and around me, for walls, four azure-flowing curtains,—namely, of the Four azure Winds, on whose bottom-fringes also I have seen gilding. And then to fancy the fair Castles that stood sheltered in these Mountain hollows; with their green flower-lawns, and white dames and damosels, lovely enough: or better still, the straw-roofed Cottages, wherein stood many a Mother baking bread, with her children round her:—all hidden and protectingly folded-up in the valley-folds; yet there and alive, as sure as if I beheld them. Or to see, as well as fancy, the nine Towns and Villages, that lay round my mountain-seat, which, in still weather, were wont to speak to me (by their steeple-bells) with metal tongue; and, in almost all weather, proclaimed their vitality by repeated Smoke-clouds; whereon, as on a culinary horologe, I might read the hour of the day. For it was the smoke of cookery, as kind housewives at morning, midday, eventide, were boiling their husbands' kettles; and ever a blue pillar rose up into the air, successively or simultaneously, from each of the nine, saying, as plainly as smoke could say: Such and such a meal is getting ready here. Not uninteresting! For you have the whole Borough, with all its love-makings and scandal-mongeries, contentions and contentments, as in miniature, and could cover it all with your hat.—If, in my wide Wayfarings, I had learned to look into the business of the World in its details, here perhaps was the place for combining it into general propositions, and deducing inferences therefrom.

'Often also could I see the black Tempest marching in anger through the Distance: round some Schreckhorn,[5] as yet grim-blue, would the eddying vapour gather, and there tumultously eddy, and flow down like a mad witch's hair; till, after a space, it vanished, and, in the clear sunbeam, your Schreckhorn stood smiling grim-white, for the vapour had held snow. How thou fermentest and elaboratest, in thy great fermenting-vat and laboratory of an Atmosphere, of a World, O Nature!—Or what is Nature? Ha! why do I not name thee GOD? Art not thou the "Living Garment of God"? O Heavens, is it, in very deed, HE, then, that ever speaks through thee; that lives and loves in thee, that lives and loves in me?

'Fore-shadows, call them rather fore-splendours, of that Truth, and Beginning of Truths, fell mysteriously over my soul. Sweeter than Dayspring to the Shipwrecked in Nova Zembla;[6] ah, like the mother's voice to her little child that strays bewildered, weeping, in unknown tumults; like soft streamings of celestial music to my too-exasperated heart, came that Evangel. The Universe is not dead and demoniacal, a charnel-house with spectres; but godlike, and my Father's!

'With other eyes, too, could I now look upon my fellow man: with an infinite Love, an infinite Pity. Poor, wandering, wayward man! Art thou not tried, and beaten with stripes, even as I am? Ever, whether thou bear the royal mantle or the beggar's gabardine, art thou not so weary, so heavy-laden; and thy Bed of Rest is but a Grave. O my Brother, my Brother, why cannot I shelter thee in my bosom, and wipe away all tears from thy eyes!—Truly, the din of many-voiced Life, which, in this solitude, with the mind's organ, I could hear, was no longer a maddening discord, but a melting one; like inarticulate cries, and sobbings of a dumb creature, which in the ear of Heaven are prayers. The poor Earth, with her poor joys, was now my needy Mother, not my cruel Stepdame; Man, with his so mad Wants and so mean Endeavours, had become the dearer to me; and even for his sufferings and his sins, I now first named him Brother. Thus was I standing in the porch of that *"Sanctuary of Sorrow"*;[7] by strange, steep ways had I too been guided thither; and ere long its sacred gates would open, and the *"Divine Depth of Sorrow"* lie disclosed to me.'

The Professor says, he here first got eye on the Knot that had been strangling him, and straightway could unfasten it, and was free. 'A vain interminable controversy,' writes he, 'touching what is at present called Origin of Evil, or some such thing, arises in every soul, since the beginning of the world; and in every soul, that would pass from idle Suffering into actual Endeavouring, must first be put an end to. The most, in our time, have to go content with a simple, incomplete enough Suppression of this controversy; to a few some Solution of it is indispensable. In every new era, too, such Solution comes-out in different terms; and ever the Solution of the last era has become obsolete, and is found unserviceable. For it is man's nature to change his Dialect from century to century; he cannot help it though he would. The authentic *Church-Catechism* of our present century has not yet fallen into my hands:

---

[5] Lit. "terror peak," a mountain in the Swiss Alps.
[6] Off the Arctic coast of Russia.
[7] From Goethe's *Wilhelm Meister*.

meanwhile, for my own private behoof, I attempt to elucidate the matter so. Man's Unhappiness as I construe, comes of his Greatness; it is because there is an Infinite in him, which with all his cunning he cannot quite bury under the Finite. Will the whole Finance Ministers and Upholsterers and Confectioners of modern Europe undertake, in joint-stock company, to make one Shoeblack HAPPY? They cannot accomplish it, above an hour or two: for the Shoeblack also has a Soul quite other than his Stomach; and would require, if you consider it, for his permanent satisfaction and saturation, simply this allotment, no more, and no less: *God's infinite Universe altogether to himself*, therein to enjoy infinitely, and fill every wish as fast as it rose. Oceans of Hochheimer,[8] a Throat like that of Ophiuchus: speak not of them; to the infinite Shoeblack they are as nothing. No sooner is your ocean filled, than he grumbles that it might have been of better vintage. Try him with half of a Universe, of an Omnipotence, he sets to quarrelling with the proprietor of the other half, and declares himself the most maltreated of men.—Always there is a black spot in our sunshine: it is even, as I said, the *Shadow of Ourselves*.

'But the whim we have of Happiness is somewhat thus. By certain valuations, and averages, of our own striking, we come upon some sort of average terrestrial lot; this we fancy belongs to us by nature, and of indefeasible right. It is simple payment of our wages, of our deserts; requires neither thanks nor complaint; only such *overplus* as there may be do we account Happiness; any *deficit* again is Misery. Now consider that we have the valuation of our own deserts ourselves, and what a fund of Self-conceit there is in each of us, —do you wonder that the balance should so often dip the wrong way, and many a Blockhead cry: See there, what a payment; was ever worthy gentleman so used!—I tell thee, Blockhead, it all comes of thy Vanity; of what thou *fanciest* those same deserts of thine to be. Fancy that thou deservest to be hanged (as is most likely), thou wilt feel it happiness to be only shot: fancy that thou deservest to be hanged in a hair-halter, it will be a luxury to die in hemp.

'So true is it, what I then said, that *the Fraction of Life can be increased in value not so much by increasing your Numerator as by lessening your Denom-*

inator. Nay, unless my Algebra deceive me, *Unity* itself divided by *Zero* will give *Infinity*. Make thy claim of wages a zero, then; thou hast the world under thy feet. Well did the Wisest of our time write: "It is only with Renunciation (*Entsagen*) that Life, properly speaking, can be said to begin."[9]

'I asked myself: What is this that, ever since earliest years, thou hast been fretting and fuming, and lamenting and self-tormenting, on account of? Say it in a word: is it not because thou art not HAPPY? Because the THOU (sweet gentleman) is not sufficiently honoured, nourished, soft-bedded, and lovingly cared-for? Foolish soul! What Act of Legislature was there that *thou* shouldst be Happy? A little while ago thou hadst no right to *be* at all. What if thou wert born and predestined not to be Happy, but to be Unhappy! Art thou nothing other than a Vulture, then, that fliest through the Universe seeking after somewhat to *eat*; and shrieking dolefully because carrion enough is not given thee? Close thy *Byron*; open thy *Goethe*.'

'*Es leuchtet mir ein*, I see a glimpse of it!' cries he elsewhere: 'there is in man a HIGHER than Love of Happiness: he can do without Happiness, and instead thereof find Blessedness! Was it not to preach-forth this same HIGHER that sages and martyrs, the Poet and the Priest, in all times, have spoken and suffered; bearing testimony, through life and through death, of the Godlike that is in Man, and how in the Godlike only has he Strength and Freedom? Which God-inspired Doctrine art thou also honoured to be taught; O Heavens! and broken with manifold merciful Afflictions, even till thou become contrite, and learn it! O, thank thy Destiny for these; thankfully bear what yet remain: thou hadst need of them; the Self in thee needed to be annihilated. By benignant fever-paroxysms is Life rooting out the deep-seated chronic Disease, and triumphs over Death. On the roaring billows of Time, thou art not engulfed, but borne aloft into the azure of Eternity. Love not Pleasure; love God.[10] This is the EVERLASTING YEA, wherein all contradictions it solved: wherein whoso walks and works, it is well with him.'

And again: 'Small is it that thou canst trample the Earth with its injuries under thy feet, as old Greek Zeno[11] trained thee: thou canst love the

---

[8] Hochheimer, a Rhine wine from the town of Hochheim near Mainz, hence English "hock"; Ophiuchus, the serpent in the constellation south of Hercules.
[9] See Goethe's *Wilhelm Meister*, which is quoted in the next several paragraphs.
[10] Cf. II Timothy 3:4.   [11] Stoic philosopher of the third century B.C.

Earth while it injures thee, and even because it injures thee; for this a Greater than Zeno was needed, and he too was sent. Knowest thou that "*Worship of Sorrow*"? The Temple thereof, founded some eighteen centuries ago, now lies in ruins, overgrown with jungle, the habitation of doleful creatures: nevertheless, venture forward; in a low crypt, arched out of falling fragments, thou findest the Altar still there, and its sacred Lamp perennially burning.'

Without pretending to comment on which strange utterances, the Editor will only remark, that there lies beside them much of a still more questionable character; unsuited to the general apprehension; nay wherein he himself does not see his way. Nebulous disquisitions on Religion, yet not without bursts of splendour; on the 'perennial continuance of Inspiration'; on Prophecy; that there are 'true Priests, as well as Baal-Priests,[12] in our own day': with more of the like sort. We select some fractions, by way of finish to this farrago.

'Cease, my much-respected Herr von Voltaire,'[13] thus apostrophises the Professor: 'shut thy sweet voice; for the task appointed thee seems finished. Sufficiently hast thou demonstrated this proposition, considerable or otherwise: That the Mythus of the Christian Religion looks not in the eighteenth century as it did in the eighth. Alas, were thy six-and-thirty quartos, and the six-and-thirty thousand other quartos and folios, and flying sheets or reams, printed before and since on the same subject, all needed to convince us of so little! But what next? Wilt thou help us to embody the divine Spirit of that Religion in a new Mythus, in a new vehicle and vesture, that our Souls, otherwise too like perishing, may live? What! thou hast no faculty in that kind? Only a torch for burning, no hammer for building? Take our thanks, then, and——thyself away.

'Meanwhile what are antiquated Mythuses to me? Or is the God present, felt in my own heart, a thing which Herr von Voltaire will dispute out of me; or dispute into me? To the "*Worship of Sorrow*" ascribe what origin and genesis thou pleasest, *has* not that Worship originated, and been generated; is it not *here*? Feel it in thy heart, and then say whether it is of God! This is Belief; all else is Opinion,—for which latter whoso will, let him worry and be worried.'

'Neither,' observes he elsewhere, 'shall ye tear out one another's eyes, struggling over "Plenary Inspiration," and such-like: try rather to get a little even Partial Inspiration, each of you for himself. One BIBLE I know, of whose Plenary Inspiration doubt is not so much as possible; nay with my own eyes I saw the God's-Hand writing it: thereof all other Bibles are but Leaves,—say, in Picture-Writing to assist the weaker faculty.'

Or, to give the wearied reader relief, and bring it to an end, let him take the following perhaps more intelligible passage:

'To me, in this our life,' says the Professor, 'which is an internecine warfare with the Time-spirit, other warfare seems questionable. Hast thou in any way a Contention with thy brother, I advise thee, think well what the meaning thereof is. If thou gauge it to the bottom, it is simply this: "Fellow, see! thou art taking more than thy share of Happiness in the world, something from *my* share: which, by the Heavens, thou shalt not; nay I will fight thee rather."— Alas, and the whole lot to be divided is such a beggarly matter, truly a "feast of shells," for the substance has been spilled out: not enough to quench one Appetite; and the collective human species clutching at them!—Can we not, in all such cases, rather say: "Take it, thou too-ravenous individual; take that pitiful additional fraction of a share, which I reckoned mine, but which thou so wantest; take it with a blessing: would to Heaven I had enough for thee!"—If Fichte's *Wissenschaftslehre* be, "to a certain extent, Applied Christianity,"[14] surely to a still greater extent, so is this. We have here not a Whole Duty of Man,[15] yet a Half Duty, namely the Passive half: could we but do it, as we can demonstrate it!

'But indeed Conviction, were it never so excellent, is worthless till it convert itself into Conduct. Nay properly Conviction is not possible till then; inasmuch as all Speculation is by nature endless, formless, a vortex amid vortices: only by a felt indubitable certainty of Experience does it find any centre to revolve round, and so fashion itself into a system. Most true is it, as a wise man teaches us, that "Doubt of any sort cannot be removed except by Action." On which ground, too, let him who gropes painfully in dark-

---

[12] False priests; see I Kings 28:17–40.
[13] Voltaire (1694–1778), for Carlyle the representative man of the godless eighteenth century.
[14] Said by Novalis in his *Fragmente*.
[15] *Whole Duty of Man* (1659), an anonymous devotional work.

ness or uncertain light, and prays vehemently that the dawn may ripen into day, lay this other precept well to heart, which to me was of invaluable service: "*Do the Duty which lies nearest thee,*" which thou knowest to be a Duty! Thy second Duty will already have become clearer.

'May we not say, however, that the hour of Spiritual Enfranchisement is even this: When your Ideal World, wherein the whole man has been dimly struggling and inexpressibly languishing to work, becomes revealed, and thrown open; and you discover, with amazement enough, like the Lothario in *Wilhelm Meister,* that your "America is here or nowhere"?[16] The Situation that has not its Duty, its Ideal, was never yet occupied by man. Yes here, in this poor, miserable, hampered, despicable Actual, wherein thou even now standest, here or nowhere is thy Ideal: work it out therefrom; and working, believe, live, be free. Fool! the Ideal is in thyself, the impediment too is in thyself: thy Condition is but the stuff thou art to shape that same Ideal out of: what matters whether such stuff be of this sort or that, so the Form thou give it be heroic, be poetic? O thou that pinest in the imprisonment of the Actual, and criest bitterly to the gods for a kingdom wherein to rule and create, know this of a truth: the thing thou seekest is already with thee, "here or nowhere," couldst thou only see!

'But it is with man's Soul as it was with Nature: the beginning of Creation is—Light.[17] Till the eye have vision, the whole members are in bonds. Divine moment, when over the tempest-tost Soul, as once over the wild-weltering Chaos, it is spoken: Let there be Light! Ever to the greatest that has felt such moment, is it not miraculous and God-announcing; even as, under simpler figures, to the simplest and least. The mad primeval Discord is hushed; the rudely-jumbled conflicting elements bind themselves into separate Firmaments: deep silent rock-foundations are built beneath; and the skyey vault with its everlasting Luminaries above: instead of a dark wasteful Chaos, we have a blooming, fertile, heaven-encompassed World.

'I too could now say to myself: Be no longer a Chaos, but a World, or even Worldkin. Produce! Produce! Were it but the pitifullest infinitesimal fraction of a Product, produce it, in God's name! 'Tis the utmost thou hast in thee:

out with it, then. Up, up! Whatsoever thy hand findeth to do, do it with thy whole might. Work while it is called Today; for the Night cometh, wherein no man can work.'[18]

CHAPTER X

Pause

Conversion; a spiritual attainment peculiar to the modern Era. Teufelsdröckh accepts Authorship as his divine calling. The scope of the command *Thou shalt not steal.*—Editor begins to suspect the authenticity of the Biographical documents; and abandons them for the great Clothes volume. Result of the preceding ten Chapters: Insight into the character of Teufelsdröckh: His fundamental beliefs, and how he was forced to seek and find them.

THUS have we, as closely and perhaps satisfactorily as, in such circumstances, might be, followed Teufelsdröckh the various successive states and stages of Growth, Entanglement, Unbelief, and almost Reprobation, into a certain clearer state of what he himself seems to consider as Conversion. 'Blame not the word,' says he; 'rejoice rather that such a word, signifying such a thing, has come to light in our modern Era, though hidden from the wisest Ancients. The Old World knew nothing of Conversion; instead of an *Ecce Homo,* they had only some *Choice of Hercules.* It was a new-attained progress in the Moral Development of man: hereby has the Highest come home to the bosoms of the most Limited; what to Plato was but a hallucination, and to Socrates a chimera, is now clear and certain to your Zinzendorfs, your Wesleys, and the poorest of their Pietists and Methodists.'[1]

It is here, then, that the spiritual majority of Teufelsdröckh commences: we are henceforth to see him 'work in well-doing,' with the spirit and clear aims of a Man. He has discovered that the Ideal Workshop he so panted for is even this same Actual ill-furnished Workshop he has so long been stumbling in. He can say to himself: 'Tools?

---

[16] In *Wilhelm Meister* the character Lothario learns to do the duty which lies nearest him.
[17] Cf. Matthew 6:22–23.   [18] Cf. Ecclesiastes 9:10; John 9:4.
[1] Nicholas Ludwig Zinzendorf (1700–1760), leader of the Moravian sect; John Wesley (1703–91), founder of Methodism.

Thou hast no Tools? Why, there is not a Man, or a Thing, now alive but has tools. The basest of created animalcules, the Spider itself, has a spinning-jenny, and warping-mill, and power-loom within its head: the stupidest of Oysters has a Papin's-Digester,[2] with stone-and-lime house to hold it in: every being that can live can do something: this let him *do*.—Tools? Hast thou not a Brain, furnished, furnishable with some glimmerings of Light; and three fingers to hold a Pen withal? Never since Aaron's rod went out of practice, or even before it, was there such a wonder-working Tool: greater than all recorded miracles have been performed by Pens. For strangely in this so solid-seeming World, which nevertheless is in continual restless flux, it is appointed that *Sound*, to appearance the most fleeting, should be the most continuing of all things. The WORD[3] is well said to be omnipotent in this world; man, thereby divine, can create as by a *Fiat*. Awake, arise! Speak forth what is in thee; what God has given thee, what the Devil shall not take away. Higher task than that of Priesthood was allotted to no man: wert thou but the meanest in that sacred Hierarchy, is it not honour enough therein to spend and be spent?

'By this Art, which whoso will may sacrilegiously degrade into a handicraft,' adds Teufelsdröckh, 'have I thenceforth abidden. Writings of mine, not indeed known as mine (for what am *I*?), have fallen, perhaps not altogether void, into the mighty seed-field of Opinion; fruits of my unseen sowing gratifyingly meet me here and there. I thank the Heavens that I have now found my Calling; wherein, with or without perceptible result, I am minded diligently to persevere.

'Nay how knowest thou,' cries he, 'but this and the other pregnant Device, now grown to be a world-renowned far-working Institution; like a grain of right mustard-seed once cast into the right soil,[4] and now stretching-out strong boughs to the four winds, for the birds of the air to lodge in,—may have been properly my doing? Some one's doing, it without doubt was; from some Idea, in some single Head, it did first of all take beginning: why not from some Idea in mine?' Does Teufelsdröckh here glance at that 'SOCIETY FOR THE CONSERVATION OF PROPERTY (*Eigen-thums-conservirende Gesellschaft*),' of which so many ambiguous notices glide spectre-like through these inexpressible Paper-bags? 'An Institution,' hints he, 'not unsuitable to the wants of the time; as indeed such sudden extension proves: for already can the Society number, among its office-bearers or corresponding members, the highest Names, if not the highest Persons, in Germany, England, France; and contributions, both of money and of meditation, pour in from all quarters; to, if possible, enlist the remaining Integrity of the world, and, defensively and with forethought, marshal it round this Palladium.' Does Teufelsdröckh mean, then, to give himself out as the originator of that so notable *Eigen-thums-conservirende* ('Owndom-conserving') *Gesell-schaft*; and if so, what, in the Devil's name, is it? He again hints: 'At a time when the divine Commandment, *Thou shalt not steal*, wherein truly, if well understood, is comprised the whole Hebrew Decalogue, with Solon's and Lycurgus's Constitutions, Justinian's Pandects, the Code Napoléon,[5] and all Codes, Catechisms, Divinities, Moralities whatsoever, that man has hitherto devised (and enforced with Altar-fire and Gallows-ropes) for his social guidance: at a time, I say, when this divine Commandment has all-but faded away from the general remembrance; and, with little disguise, a new opposite Commandment, *Thou shalt steal*, is everywhere promulgated,—it perhaps behoved, in this universal dotage and deliration, the sound portion of mankind to bestir themselves and rally. When the widest and wildest violations of that divine right of Property, the only divine right now extant or conceivable, are sanctioned and recommended by a vicious Press, and the world has lived to hear it asserted that *we have no Property in our very Bodies, but only an accidental Possession and Life-rent*, what is the issue to be looked for? Hangmen and Catchpoles may, by their noose-gins and baited fall-traps, keep down the smaller sort of vermin; but what, except perhaps some such Universal Association, can protect us against whole meat-devouring and man-devouring hosts of Boa-constrictors? If, therefore, the more sequestered Thinker have wondered, in his privacy, from what hand that perhaps not ill-written *Program* in the Public Journals, with its

---

[2] Invention by Denis Papin (1647–c. 1712) that raised the boiling point of water.

[3] John 1:1–3. [4] Cf. Matthew 13:31–32.

[5] Solon, Athenian jurist of the seventh century B.C.; Lycurgus, Spartan lawgiver of the ninth century B.C.; Justinian (483–565) had jurists compile the *Pandectae*, containing all that was valuable in the work of previous jurists; Napoleon caused a code of laws to be compiled in 1802–8, the basis of modern French law.

high *Prize-Questions* and so liberal *Prizes*, could have proceeded,—let him now cease such wonder; and, with undivided faculty, betake himself to the *Concurrenz* (Competition).'

We ask: Has this same 'perhaps not ill-written *Program*,' or any other authentic Transaction of that Property-conserving Society, fallen under the eye of the British Reader, in any Journal foreign or domestic? If so, what are those *Prize-Questions*; what are the terms of Competition, and when and where? No printed Newspaper-leaf, no farther light of any sort, to be met with in these Paper-bags! Or is the whole business one other of those whimsicalities and perverse inexplicabilities, whereby Herr Teufelsdröckh, meaning much or nothing, is pleased so often to play fast-and-loose with us?

Here, indeed, at length, must the Editor give utterance to a painful suspicion, which, through late Chapters, has begun to haunt him; paralysing any little enthusiasm that might still have rendered his thorny Biographical task a labour of love. It is a suspicion grounded perhaps on trifles, yet confirmed almost into certainty by the more and more discernible humoristico-satirical tendency of Teufelsdröckh, in whom underground humours and intricate sardonic rogueries, wheel within wheel, defy all reckoning: a suspicion, in one word, that these Autobiographical Documents are partly a mystification! What if many a so-called Fact were little better than a Fiction; if here we had not direct Camera-obscura Picture of the Professor's History; but only some more or less fantastic Adumbration, symbolically, perhaps significantly enough, shadowing-forth the same! Our theory begins to be that, in receiving as literally authentic what was but hieroglyphically so, Hofrath Heuschrecke, whom in that case we scruple not to name Hofrath Nose-of-Wax,[6] was made a fool of, and set adrift to make fools of others. Could it be expected, indeed, that a man so known for impenetrable reticence as Teufelsdröckh, would all at once frankly unlock his private citadel to an English Editor and a German Hofrath; and not rather deceptively *in*lock both Editor and Hofrath in the labyrinthic tortuosities and covered-ways of said citadel (having enticed them thither), to see, in his half-devilish way, how the fools would look?

Of one fool, however, the Herr Professor will perhaps find himself short. On a small slip, formerly thrown aside as blank, the ink being all-but invisible, we lately notice, and with effort decipher, the following: 'What are your historical Facts; still more your biographical? Wilt thou know a Man, above all a Mankind, by stringing-together beadrolls of what thou namest Facts? The Man is the spirit he worked in; not what he did, but what he became. Facts are engraved Hierograms, for which the fewest have the key. And then how your Block-head (*Dummkopf*) studies not their Meaning; but simply whether they are well or ill cut, what he calls Moral or Immoral! Still worse is it with your Bungler (*Pfuscher*): such I have seen reading some Rousseau, with pretences of interpretation; and mistaking the ill-cut Serpent-of-Eternity for a common poisonous reptile.' Was the Professor apprehensive lest an Editor, selected as the present boasts himself, might mistake the Teufelsdröckh Serpent-of-Eternity in like manner? For which reason it was to be altered, not without underhand satire, into a plainer Symbol? Or is this merely one of his half-sophisms, half-truisms, which if he can but set on the back of a Figure, he cares not whither it gallop? We say not with certainty; and indeed, so strange is the Professor, can never say. If our suspicion be wholly unfounded, let his own questionable ways, not our necessary circumspectness, bear the blame.

But be this as it will, the somewhat exasperated and indeed exhausted Editor determines here to shut these Paper-bags for the present. Let it suffice that we know of Teufelsdröckh, so far, if 'not what he did, yet what he became': the rather, as his character has now taken its ultimate bent, and no new revolution, of importance, is to be looked for. The imprisoned Chrysalis is now a winged Psyche:[7] and such, wheresoever be its flight, it will continue. To trace by what complex gyrations (flights or involuntary waftings) through the mere external Life-element, Teufelsdröckh reaches his University Professorship, and the Psyche clothes herself in civic Titles, without altering her now fixed nature,—would be comparatively an unproductive task, were we even unsuspicious of its being, for us at least, a false and impossible one. His outward Biography, therefore, which, at the Blumine Lover's-Leap, we saw churned utterly into spray-vapour, may hover in that condition, for aught that concerns us here. Enough that by survey of certain 'pools and plashes,' we have ascertained its general direction; do we not already know that, by one

---

[6] From Burton's *Anatomy of Melancholy*.
[7] Greek personification of the soul; her symbol was the butterfly.

way and other, it *has* long since rained-down again into a stream; and even now, at Weissnicht-two, flows deep and still, fraught with the *Philosophy of Clothes*, and visible to whoso will cast eye thereon? Over much invaluable matter, that lies scattered, like jewels among quarry-rubbish, in those Paper-catacombs, we may have occasion to glance back, and somewhat will demand insertion at the right place: meanwhile be our tiresome diggings therein suspended.

If now, before reopening the great *Clothes-Volume*, we ask what our degree of progress, during these Ten Chapters, has been, towards right understanding of the *Clothes-Philosophy*, let not our discouragement become total. To speak in that old figure of the Hell-gate Bridge over Chaos, a few flying pontoons have perhaps been added, though as yet they drift straggling on the Flood; how far they will reach, when once the chains are straightened and fastened, can, at present, only be matter of conjecture.

So much we already calculate: Though many a little loophole, we have had glimpses into the internal world of Teufelsdröckh; his strange mystic, almost magic Diagram of the Universe, and how it was gradually drawn, is not hence-forth altogether dark to us. Those mysterious ideas on TIME, which merit consideration, and are not wholly unintelligible with such, may by and by prove significant. Still more may his some-what peculiar view of Nature, the decisive One-ness he ascribes to Nature. How all Nature and Life are but one *Garment*, a 'Living Garment,' woven and ever aweaving in the 'Loom of Time'; is not here, indeed, the outline of a whole *Clothes-Philosophy*; at least the arena it is to work in? Remark, too, that the Character of the Man, nowise without meaning in such a matter, becomes less enigmatic: amid so much tumul-tuous obscurity, almost like diluted madness, do not a certain indomitable Defiance and yet a boundless Reverence seem to loom forth, as the two mountain-summits, on whose rock-strata all the rest were based and built?

Nay further, may we not say that Teufels-dröckh's Biography, allowing it even, as suspected, only a hieroglyphical truth, exhibits a man, as it were preappointed for Clothes-Philosophy? To look through the Shows of things into Things themselves he is led and compelled. The 'Passiv-ity' given him by birth is fostered by all turns of his fortune. Everywhere cast out, like oil out of water, from mingling in any Employment, in any

public Communion, he has no portion but Solitude, and a life of Meditation. The whole energy of his existence is directed, through long years, on one task: that of enduring pain, if he cannot cure it. Thus everywhere do the Shows of things oppress him, withstand him, threaten him with fearfullest destruction: only by vic-toriously penetrating into Things themselves can he find peace and a stronghold. But is not this same looking-through the Shows, or Vestures, into the Things, even the first preliminary to a *Philosophy of Clothes*? Do we not, in all this, discern some beckonings towards the true higher purport of such a Philosophy; and what shape it must assume with such a man, in such an era?

Perhaps in entering on Book Third, the cour-teous Reader is not utterly without guess whither he is bound: nor, let us hope, for all the fantastic Dream-Grottoes through which, as is our lot with Teufelsdröckh, he must wander, will there be wanting between whiles some twinkling of a steady Polar Star.

.   .   .

BOOK THIRD

CHAPTER III

Symbols

The benignant efficacies of Silence and Secrecy. Symbols; revelations of the Infinite in the Finite: Man everywhere encompassed by them; lives and works by them. Theory of Motive-millwrights, a false account of human nature. Symbols of an extrinsic value; as Banners, Standards: Of intrinsic value; as Works of Art, Lives and Deaths of Heroic men. Religious Symbols; Christianity. Symbols hallowed by Time; but finally defaced and desecrated. Many superannuated Symbols in our time, needing removal.

PROBABLY it will elucidate the drift of these foregoing obscure utterances, if we here insert somewhat of our Professor's speculations on *Symbols*. To state his whole doctrine, indeed, were beyond our compass: nowhere is he more mysterious, impalpable, than in this of 'Fantasy being the organ of the Godlike';[1] and how 'Man thereby, though based, to all seeming, on the

---

[1] Friedrich von Schlegel, *Ideen*.

small Visible, does nevertheless extend down into the infinite deeps of the Invisible, of which Invisible, indeed, his Life is properly the bodying forth.' Let us, omitting these high transcendental aspects of the matter, study to glean (whether from the Paper-bags or the Printed Volume) what little seems logical and practical, and cunningly arrange it into such degree of coherence as it will assume. By way of proem, take the following not injudicious remarks:

'The benignant efficacies of Concealment,' cries our Professor, 'who shall speak or sing? SILENCE and SECRECY! Altars might still be raised to them (were this an altar-building time) for universal worship. Silence is the element in which great things fashion themselves together; that at length they may emerge, full-formed and majestic, into the daylight of Life, which they are thenceforth to rule. Not William the Silent[2] only, but all the considerable men I have known, and the most undiplomatic and unstrategic of these, forbore to babble of what they were creating and projecting. Nay, in thy own mean perplexities, do thou thyself but *hold thy tongue for one day*: on the morrow, how much clearer are thy purposes and duties; what wreck and rubbish have those mute workmen within thee swept away, when intrusive noises were shut out! Speech is too often not, as the Frenchman defined it, the art of concealing Thought; but of quite stifling and suspending Thought, so that there is none to conceal. Speech too is great, but not the greatest. As the Swiss Inscription says: *Sprechen ist silbern, Schweigen ist golden* (Speech is silvern, Silence is golden); or as I might rather express it: Speech is of Time, Silence is of Eternity.

'Bees will not work except in darkness; Thought will not work except in Silence: neither will Virtue work except in Secrecy. Let not thy left hand know what thy right hand doeth![3] Neither shalt thou prate even to thy own heart of "those secrets known to all."[4] Is not Shame (*Schaam*) the soil of all Virtue, of all good manners and good morals? Like other plants, Virtue will not grow unless its root be hidden, buried from the eye of the sun. Let the sun shine on it, nay do but look at it privily thyself, the root withers, and no flowers will glad thee. O my Friends, when we view the fair clustering flowers that over-wreathe, for example, the Marriage-bower, and encircle man's life with the fragrance and hues of Heaven, what hand will not smite the foul plunderer that grubs them up by the roots, and with grinning, grunting satisfaction, shows us the dung they flourish in! Men speak much of the Printing-Press with its Newspapers: *du Himmel!* what are these to Clothes and the Tailor's Goose?'[5]

'Of kin to the so incalculable influences of Concealment, and connected with still greater things, is the wondrous agency of *Symbols*. In a Symbol there is concealment and yet revelation: here therefore, by Silence and by Speech acting together, comes a double significance. And if both the Speech be itself high, and the Silence fit and noble, how expressive will their union be! Thus in many a painted Device, or simple Seal-emblem, the commonest Truth stands out to us proclaimed with quite new emphasis.

'For it is here that Fantasy with her mystic wonderland plays into the small prose domain of Sense, and becomes incorporated therewith. In the Symbol proper, what we can call a Symbol, there is ever, more or less distinctly and directly, some embodiment and revelation of the Infinite; the Infinite is made to blend itself with the Finite, to stand visible, and as it were, attainable there. By Symbols, accordingly, is man guided and commanded, made happy, made wretched. He everywhere finds himself encompassed with Symbols, recognised as such or not recognised: the Universe is but one vast Symbol of God; nay if thou wilt have it, what is man himself but a Symbol of God; is not all that he does symbolical; a revelation to Sense of the mystic god-given force that is in him; a "Gospel of Freedom," which he, the "Messias[6] of Nature," preaches, as he can, by act and word? Not a Hut he builds but is the visible embodiment of a Thought; but bears visible record of invisible things; but is, in the transcendental sense, symbolical as well as real.'

'Man,' says the Professor elsewhere, in quite antipodal contrast with these high-soaring delin-eations, which we have here cut-short on the verge of the inane, 'Man is by birth somewhat of an owl. Perhaps, too, of all the owleries that ever possessed him, the most owlish, if we consider it, is that of your actually existing Motive-Millwrights. Fantastic tricks enough man has played, in his time; has fancied himself to be most things, down even to an animated heap of Glass: but to fancy himself a dead Iron-Balance for weighing Pains and Pleasures on, was reserved for

---

[2] William the Silent (1533–84), founder of the Dutch Republic.   [3] Matthew 6:3.
[4] *Wilhelm Meister*.   [5] Tailor's iron.   [6] *Messias*, Greek form of Messiah.

this his latter era. There stands he, his Universe one huge Manger, filled with hay and thistles to be weighed against each other; and looks long-eared enough. Alas, poor devil! spectres are appointed to haunt him: one age he is hagridden, bewitched; the next, priestridden, befooled; in all ages, bedevilled. And now the Genius of Mechanism smothers him worse than any Nightmare did; till the Soul is nigh choked out of him, and only a kind of Digestive, Mechanic life remains. In Earth and in Heaven he can see nothing but Mechanism; has fear for nothing else, hope in nothing else: the world would indeed grind him to pieces; but cannot he fathom the Doctrine of Motives, and cunningly compute these, and mechanise them to grind the other way?

'Were he not, as has been said, purblinded by enchantment, you had but to bid him open his eyes and look. In which country, in which time, was it hitherto that man's history, or the history of any man, went-on by calculated or calculable "Motives"? What make ye of your Christianities, and Chivalries, and Reformations, and Marseillese Hymns, and Reigns of Terror?[7] Nay, has not perhaps the Motive-grinder himself been *in Love*? Did he never stand so much as a contested Election? Leave him to Time, and the medicating virtue of Nature.'

'Yes, Friends,' elsewhere observes the Professor, 'not our Logical, Mensurative faculty, but our Imaginative one is King over us; I might say, Priest and Prophet to lead us heavenward; or Magician and Wizard to lead us hellward. Nay, even for the basest Sensualist, what is Sense but the implement of Fantasy; the vessel it drinks out of? Ever in the dullest existence there is a sheen either of Inspiration or of Madness (thou partly hast it in thy choice, which of the two), that gleams-in from the circumambient Eternity, and colours with its own hues our little islet of Time. The Understanding is indeed thy window, too clear thou canst not make it; but Fantasy is thy eye, with its colour-giving retina, healthy or diseased. Have not I myself known five-hundred living soldiers sabred into crows'-meat for a piece of glazed cotton, which they called their Flag; which, had you sold it at any market-cross, would not have brought above three groschen? Did not the whole Hungarian Nation rise, like some tumultuous moon-stirred Atlantic, when Kaiser Joseph pocketed their Iron Crown;[8] an implement, as was sagaciously observed, in size and commercial value little differing from a horse-shoe? It is in and through *Symbols* that man, consciously or unconsciously, lives, works, and has his being: those ages, moreover, are accounted the noblest which can the best recognise symbolical worth, and prize it the highest. For is not a Symbol ever, to him who has eyes for it, some dimmer or clearer revelation of the Godlike?

'Of Symbols, however, I remark farther, that they have both an extrinsic and intrinsic value; oftenest the former only. What, for instance, was in that clouted Shoe, which the Peasants bore aloft with them as ensign in their *Bauernkrieg* (Peasants' War)?[9] Or in the Wallet-and-staff round which the Netherland *Gueux*,[10] glorying in that nickname of Beggars, heroically rallied and prevailed, though against King Philip himself? Intrinsic significance these had none; only extrinsic; as the accidental Standards of multitudes more or less sacredly uniting together; in which union itself, as above noted, there is ever something mystical and borrowing of the Godlike. Under a like category, too, stand, or stood, the stupidest heraldic Coats-of-arms; military Banners everywhere; and generally all national or other sectarian Costumes and Customs: they have no intrinsic, necessary divineness, or even worth; but have acquired an extrinsic one. Nevertheless through all these there glimmers something of a Divine Idea; as through military Banners themselves, the Divine Idea of Duty, of heroic Daring; in some instances of Freedom, of Right. Nay the highest ensign that men ever met and embraced under, the Cross itself, had no meaning save an accidental extrinsic one.

'Another matter it is, however, when your Symbol has intrinsic meaning, and is of itself *fit* that men should unite round it. Let but the Godlike manifest itself to Sense; let but Eternity look, more or less visibly, through the Time-Figure (*Zeitbild*)! Then is it fit that men unite there; and worship together before such Symbol; and so from day to day, and from age to age, superadd to it new divineness.

'Of this latter sort are all true Works of Art: in them (if thou know a Work of Art from a Daub of Artifice) wilt thou discern Eternity looking

---

[7] References to the French Revolution.

[8] Joseph II (1741–90), German Emperor, refused the traditional iron crown worn by Hungarian monarchs; his refusal provoked an armed uprising.

[9] The Peasants' War in 1524–25 was an aspect of the Reformation in Germany.

[10] Gueux (Beggars) were Dutch opponents of Spanish rule of Philip II in 1566.

though Time; the Godlike rendered visible. Here too may an extrinsic value gradually superadd itself: thus certain *Iliads,* and the like, have, in three-thousand years, attained quite new significance. But nobler than all in this kind are the Lives of heroic god-inspired Men; for what other Work of Art is so divine? In Death too, in the Death of the Just, as the last perfection of a Work of Art, may we not discern symbolic meaning? In that divinely transfigured Sleep, as of Victory, resting over the beloved face which now knows thee no more, read (if thou canst for tears) the confluence of Time with Eternity, and some gleam of the latter peering through.

'Highest of all Symbols are those wherein the Artist or Poet has risen into Prophet, and all men can recognise a present God, and worship the same: I mean religious Symbols. Various enough have been such religious Symbols, what we call *Religions*; as men stood in this stage of culture or the other, and could worse or better body-forth the Godlike: some Symbols with a transient intrinsic worth; many with only an extrinsic. If thou ask to what height man has carried it in this manner, look on our divinest Symbol: on Jesus of Nazareth, and his Life, and his Biography, and what followed therefrom. Higher has the human Thought not yet reached: this is Christianity and Christendom; a Symbol of quite perennial, infinite character; whose significance will ever demand to be anew inquired into, and anew made manifest.

'But, on the whole, as Time adds much to the sacredness of Symbols, so likewise in his progress he at length defaces, or even desecrates them; and Symbols, like all terrestrial Garments, wax old. Homer's Epos has not ceased to be true; yet it is no longer *our* Epos, but shines in the distance, if clearer and clearer, yet also smaller and smaller, like a receding Star. It needs a scientific telescope, it needs to be reinterpreted and artificially brought near us, before we can so much as know that it *was* a Sun. So likewise a day comes when the Runic Thor, with his Eddas, must withdraw into dimness; and many an African Mumbo-Jumbo and Indian Pawaw be utterly abolished. For all things, even Celestial Luminaries, much more atmospheric meteors, have their rise, their culmination, their decline.'

'Small is this which thou tellest me, that the Royal Sceptre is but a piece of gilt-wood; that

the Pyx has become a most foolish box, and truly, as Ancient Pistol[11] thought, "of little price." A right Conjuror might I name thee, couldst thou conjure back into these wooden tools the divine virtue they once held.'

'Of this thing, however, be certain: wouldst thou plant for Eternity, then plant into the deep infinite faculties of man, his Fantasy and Heart; wouldst thou plant for Year and Day, then plant into his shallow superficial faculties, his Self-love and Arithmetical Understanding, what will grow there. A Hierarch, therefore, and Pontiff of the World will we call him, the Poet and inspired Maker; who, Prometheus-like, can shape new Symbols, and bring new Fire from Heaven to fix it there. Such too will not always be wanting; neither perhaps now are. Meanwhile, as the average of matters goes, we account him Legislator and wise who can so much as tell when a Symbol has grown old, and gently remove it.

'When, as the last English Coronation[12] was preparing,' concludes this wonderful Professor, 'I read in their Newspapers that the "Champion of England,"[13] he who has to offer battle to the Universe for his new King, had brought it so far that he could now "mount his horse with little assistance," I said to myself: Here also we have a Symbol well-nigh superannuated. Alas, move whithersoever you may, are not the tatters and rags of superannuated worn-out Symbols (in this Ragfair of a World) dropping off everywhere, to hoodwink, to halter, to tether you; nay, if you shake them not aside, threatening to accumulate, and perhaps produce suffocation?'

CHAPTER IV

Helotage

Heuschrecke's Malthusian Tract, and Teufelsdröckh's marginal notes thereon. The true workman, for daily bread, or spiritual bread, to be honoured; and no other. The real privation of the Poor not poverty or toil, but ignorance. Over-population: With a world like ours and wide as ours, can there be too many men? Emigration.

---

[11] *Henry V,* III, vi, 47.
[12] That of George IV.—Ed. [Carlyle's note]
[13] The official protector of the monarch should anyone challenge his right to succession.

AT THIS point we determine on adverting shortly, or rather reverting, to a certain Tract of Hofrath Heuschrecke's, entitled *Institute for the Repression of Population*; which lies, dishonourably enough (with torn leaves, and a preceptible smell of aloetic drugs), stuffed into the Bag *Pisces*.[1] Not indeed for the sake of the Tract itself, which we admire little; but of the marginal Notes, evidently in Teufelsdröckh's hand, which rather copiously fringe it. A few of these may be in their right place here.

Into the Hofrath's *Institute*, with its extraordinary schemes, and machinery of Corresponding Boards and the like, we shall not so much as glance. Enough for us to understand that Heuschrecke is a disciple of Malthus;[2] and so zealous for the doctrine, that his zeal almost literally eats him up. A deadly fear of Population possesses the Hofrath; something like a fixed-idea; undoubtedly akin to the more diluted forms of Madness. Nowhere, in that quarter of his intellectual world, is there light; nothing but a grim shadow of Hunger; open mouths opening wider and wider; a world to terminate by the frightfullest consummation: by its too dense inhabitants, famished into delirium, universally eating one another. To make air for himself in which strangulation, choking enough to a benevolent heart, the Hofrath founds, or proposes to found, this *Institute* of his, as the best he can do. It is only with our Professor's comments thereon that we concern ourselves.

First, then, remark that Teufelsdröckh, as a speculative Radical, has his own notions about human dignity; that the Zähdarm palaces and courtesies have not made him forgetful of the Futteral cottages. On the blank cover of Heuschrecke's Tract we find the following indistinctly engrossed:

'Two men I honour, and no third. First, the toilworn Craftsman that with earth-made Implement laboriously conquers the Earth, and makes her man's. Venerable to me is the hard Hand; crooked, coarse; wherein notwithstanding lies a cunning virtue, indefeasibly royal, as of the Sceptre of this Planet. Venerable too is the rugged face, all weather-tanned, besoiled, with its rude intelligence; for it is the face of a Man living manlike. O, but the more venerable for thy rudeness, and even because we must pity as well as love thee! Hardly-entreated Brother! For us was thy back so bent, for us were thy straight limbs and fingers so deformed: thou wert our Conscript, on whom the lot fell, and fighting our battles wert so marred. For in thee too lay a god-created Form, but it was not to be unfolded; encrusted must it stand with the thick adhesions and defacements of Labour: and thy body, like thy soul, was not to know freedom. Yet toil on, toil on: *thou* art in thy duty, be out of it who may; thou toilest for the altogether indispensable, for daily bread.

'A second man I honour, and still more highly: Him who is seen toiling for the spiritually indispensable; not daily bread, but the bread of Life. Is not he too in his duty; endeavouring towards inward Harmony; revealing this, by act or by word, through all his outward endeavours, be they high or low? Highest of all, when his outward and his inward endeavour are one: when we can name him Artist; not earthly Craftsman only, but inspired Thinker, who with heaven-made Implement conquers Heaven for us! If the poor and humble toil that we have Food, must not the high and glorious toil for him in return, that he have Light, have Guidance, Freedom, immortality?—These two, in all their degrees, I honour: all else is chaff and dust, which let the wind blow whither it listeth.

'Unspeakably touching is it, however, when I find both dignities united; and he that must toil outwardly for the lowest of man's wants, is also toiling inwardly for the highest. Sublimer in this world know I nothing than a Peasant Saint, could such now anywhere be met with. Such a one will take thee back to Nazareth itself; thou wilt see the splendour of Heaven spring forth from the humblest depths of Earth, like a light shining in great darkness.'

And again: 'It is not because of his toils that I lament for the poor: we must all toil, or steal (howsoever we name our stealing), which is worse; no faithful workman finds his task a pastime. The poor is hungry and athirst; but for him also there is food and drink: he is heavy-laden and weary; but for him also the Heavens send Sleep, and of the deepest; in his smoky cribs, a clear dewy heaven of Rest envelops him, and fitful glitterings of cloud-skirted Dreams. But what I do mourn over is, that the lamp of his soul should go out; that no ray of heavenly, or

---

[1] Sign of the fish for the period February 20–March 20.
[2] Thomas Malthus (1766–1834), English economist who projected the theory of geometrical population increase exceeding the possibility of subsistence.

even of earthly knowledge, should visit him; but only, in the haggard darkness, like two spectres, Fear and Indignation bear him company. Alas, while the body stands so broad and brawny, must the Soul lie blinded, dwarfed, stupefied, almost annihilated! Alas, was this too a Breath of God; bestowed in Heaven, but on earth never to be unfolded!—That there should one Man die ignorant who had capacity for Knowledge, this I call a tragedy, were it to happen more than twenty times in the minute, as by some computations it does. The miserable fraction of Science which our united Mankind, in a wide Universe of Nescience, has acquired, why is not this, with all diligence, imparted to all?'

Quite in an opposite strain is the following: 'The old Spartans had a wiser method; and went out and hunted-down their Helots, and speared and spitted them, when they grew too numerous. With our improved fashions of hunting, Herr Hofrath, now after the invention of fire-arms, and standing-armies, how much easier were such a hunt! Perhaps in the most thickly-peopled country, some three days annually might suffice to shoot all the able-bodied Paupers that had accumulated within the year. Let Governments think of this. The expense were trifling: nay the very carcasses would pay it. Have them salted and barrelled; could not you victual therewith, if not Army and Navy, yet richly such infirm Paupers, in workhouses and elsewhere, as enlightened Charity, dreading no evil of them, might see good to keep alive?'

'And yet,' writes he farther on, 'there must be something wrong. A full-formed Horse will, in any market, bring from twenty to as high as two-hundred Friedrichs d'or: such is his worth to the world. A full-formed Man is not only worth nothing to the world, but the world could afford him a round sum would he simply engage to go and hang himself. Nevertheless, which of the two was the more cunningly-devised article, even as an Engine? Good Heavens! A white European Man, standing on his two Legs, with his two five-fingered Hands at his shackle-bones, and miraculous Head on his shoulders, is worth, I should say, from fifty to a hundred Horses'!

'True, thou Gold-Hofrath,' cries the Professor elsewhere: 'too crowded indeed! Meanwhile, what portion of this inconsiderable terraqueous Globe have ye actually tilled and delved, till it will grow no more? How thick stands your Population in the Pampas and Savannas of America; round ancient Carthage, and in the interior of Africa; on both slopes of the Altaic chain, in the central Platform of Asia; in Spain, Greece, Turkey, Crim Tartary, the Curragh of Kildare?[3] One man, in one year, as I have understood it, if you lend him Earth, will feed himself and nine others. Alas, where now are the Hengsts and Alarics[4] of our still-glowing, still-expanding Europe; who, when their home is grown too narrow, will enlist, and, like Fire-pillars, guide onwards those superfluous masses of indomitable living Valour; equipped, not now with the battle-axe and war-chariot, but with the steam-engine and ploughshare? Where are they? —Preserving their Game!'

CHAPTER V

The Phœnix[1]

Teufelsdröckh considers Society as dead; its soul (Religion) gone, its body (existing Institutions) going. Utilitarianism, needing little farther preaching, is now in full activity of destruction.—Teufelsdröckh would yield to the Inevitable, accounting that the best: Assurance of a fairer Living Society, arising, Phœnix-like, out of the ruins of the old dead one. Before that Phœnix death-birth is accomplished, long time, struggle, and suffering must intervene.

PUTTING which four singular Chapters together, and alongside of them numerous hints, and even direct utterances, scattered over these Writings of his, we come upon the startling yet not quite unlooked-for conclusion, that Teufelsdröckh is one of those who consider Society, properly so called, to be as good as extinct; and that only the gregarious feelings, and old inherited habitudes, at this juncture, hold us from Dispersion, and universal national, civil, domestic and personal war! He says expressly: 'For the last three centuries, above all for the last 'three quarters of a century, that same

---

[3] Altaic chain, mountains in Mongolia; Curragh of Kildare, plains in County Kildare, Ireland.
[4] Hengest, fifth-century conqueror of England; Alaric (c. 370–410), Visigothic plunderer of Rome in 410.
[1] A legendary bird said to live five hundred years, be consumed by fire, and then rise from its own ashes.

Pericardial Nervous Tissue (as we named it) of Religion, where lies the Life-essence of Society, has been smote-at and perforated, needfully and needlessly; till now it is quite rent into shreds; and Society, long pining, diabetic, consumptive, can be regarded as defunct; for those spasmodic, galvanic sprawlings are not life; neither indeed will they endure, galvanise as you may, beyond two days.'

'Call ye that a Society,' cries he again, 'where there is no longer any Social Idea extant; not so much as the Idea of a common Home, but only of a common over-crowded Lodging-house? Where each, isolated, regardless of his neighbour, turned against his neighbour, clutches what he can get, and cries "Mine!" and calls it Peace, because, in the cut-purse and cut-throat Scramble, no steel knives, but only a far cunninger sort, can be employed? Where Friendship, Communion, has become an incredible tradition; and your holiest Sacramental Supper is a smoking Tavern Dinner, with Cook for Evangelist? Where your Priest has no tongue but for plate-licking: and your high Guides and Governors cannot guide; but on all hands hear it passionately proclaimed: *Laissez faire*;[2] Leave us alone of *your* guidance, such light is darker than darkness; eat you your wages, and sleep!

'Thus, too,' continues he, 'does an observant eye discern everywhere that saddest spectacle: The Poor perishing, like neglected, foundered Draught-Cattle, of Hunger and Over-work; the Rich, still more wretchedly, of Idleness, Satiety, and Over-growth. The Highest in rank, at length, without honour from the Lowest; scarcely, with a little mouth-honour, as from tavern-waiters who expect to put it in the bill. Once-sacred Symbols fluttering as empty Pageants, whereof men grudge even the expense; a World becoming dismantled: in one word, the CHURCH fallen speechless, from obesity and apoplexy; the STATE shrunken into a Police-Office, straitened to get its pay!'

We might ask, are there many 'observant eyes,' belonging to practical men in England or elsewhere, which have descried these phenomena; or is it only from the mystic elevation of a German *Wahngasse* that such wonders are visible? Teufelsdröckh contends that the aspect of a 'deceased or expiring Society' fronts us everywhere, so that whoso runs may read. 'What, for example,' says he, 'is the universally-arrogated Virtue, almost the sole remaining Catholic Virtue, of these days? For some half century, it has been the thing you name "Independence." Suspicion of "Servility," of reverence for Superiors, the very dogleech is anxious to disavow. Fools! Were your Superiors worthy to govern, and you worthy to obey, reverence for them were even your only possible freedom. Independence, in all kinds, is rebellion; if unjust rebellion, why parade it, and everywhere prescribe it?'

But what then? Are we returning, as Rousseau prayed, to the state of Nature? 'The Soul Politic having departed,' says Teufelsdröckh, 'what can follow but that the Body Politic be decently interred, to avoid putrescence? Liberals, Economists, Utilitarians enough I see marching with its bier, and chanting loud pæans, towards the funeral-pile, where, amid wailings from some, and saturnalian revelries from the most, the venerable Corpse is to be burnt. Or, in plain words, that these men, Liberals, Utilitarians, or whatsoever they are called, will ultimately carry their point, and dissever and destroy most existing Institutions of Society, seems a thing which has some time ago ceased to be doubtful.

'Do we not see a little subdivision of the grand Utilitarian Armament come to light even in insulated England? A living nucleus, that will attract and grow, does at length appear there also; and under curious phasis; properly as the inconsiderable fag-end, and so far in the rear of the others as to fancy itself the van. Our European Mechanisers are a sect of boundless diffusion, activity, and coöperative spirit: has not Utilitarianism flourished in high places of Thought, here among ourselves, and in every European country, at some time or other, within the last fifty years? If now in all countries, except perhaps England, it has ceased to flourish, or indeed to exist, among Thinkers, and sunk to Journalists and the popular mass,—who sees not that, as hereby it no longer preaches, so the reason is, it now needs no Preaching, but is in full universal Action, the doctrine everywhere known, and enthusiastically laid to heart? The fit pabulum, in these times, for a certain rugged workshop intellect and heart, nowise without their corresponding workshop strength and ferocity, it requires but to be stated in such scenes to make proselytes enough.—Admirably calculated for destroying, only not for rebuilding! It spreads like a sort of Dog-madness; till the

[2] "Let do or make (what one chooses)," the motto of free-market economists in opposition to government interference.

whole World-kennel will be rabid: then woe to the Huntsmen, with or without their whips! They should have given the quadrupeds water,' adds he; 'the water, namely, of Knowledge and of Life, while it was yet time.'[3]

Thus, if Professor Teufelsdröckh can be relied on, we are at this hour in a most critical condition; beleaguered by that boundless 'Armament of Mechanisers' and Unbelievers, threatening to strip us bare! 'The World,' says he, 'as it needs must, is under a process of devastation and waste, which, whether by silent assiduous corrosion, or open quicker combustion, as the case chances, will effectually enough annihilate the past Forms of Society; replace them with what it may. For the present, it is contemplated that when man's whole Spiritual Interests are once *divested*, these innumerable stript-off Garments shall mostly be burnt; but the sounder Rags among them be quilted together into one huge Irish watch-coat for the defence of the Body only!'—This, we think, is but Job's-news[4] to the humane reader.

'Nevertheless,' cries Teufelsdröckh, 'who can hinder it; who is there that can clutch into the wheelspokes of Destiny, and say to the Spirit of the Time: Turn back, I command thee?—Wiser were it that we yielded to the Inevitable and Inexorable, and accounted even this the best.'

Nay, might not an attentive Editor, drawing his own inferences from what stands written, conjecture that Teufelsdröckh individually had yielded to this same 'Inevitable and Inexorable' heartily enough; and now sat waiting the issue, with his natural diabolico-angelical Indifference, if not even Placidity? Did we not hear him complain that the World was a 'huge Ragfair,' and the 'rags and tatters of old Symbols' were raining-down everywhere, like to drift him in, and suffocate him? What with those 'unhunted Helots' of his; and the uneven *sic vos non vobis*[5] pressure and hard-crashing collision he is pleased to discern in existing things; what with the so hateful 'empty Masks,' full of beetles and spiders, yet glaring out on him, from their glass eyes, 'with a ghastly affectation of life,'—we feel entitled to conclude him even willing that much should be thrown to the Devil, so it were but done gently! Safe himself in that 'Pinnacle of Weissnichtwo,' he would consent, with a tragic solemnity, that the monster UTILITARIA, held back, indeed, and moderated by nose-rings, halters, foot-shackles, and every conceivable modification of rope, should go forth to do her work;—to tread down old ruinous Palaces and Temples with her broad hoof, till the whole were trodden down, that new and better might be built! Remarkable in this point of view are the following sentences.

'Society,' says he, 'is not dead: that Carcass, which you call dead Society, is but her mortal coil which she has shuffled-off, to assume a nobler; she herself, through perpetual metamorphoses, in fairer and fairer development, has to live till Time also merge in Eternity. Wheresoever two or three Living Men are gathered together, there is Society; or there it will be, with its cunning mechanisms and stupendous structures, overspreading this little Globe, and reaching upwards to Heaven and downwards to Gehenna: for always, under one or the other figure, it has two authentic Revelations, of a God and of a Devil; the Pulpit, namely, and the Gallows.'

Indeed, we already heard him speak of 'Religion, in unnoticed nooks, weaving for herself new Vestures';—Teufelsdröckh himself being one of the loom-treadles? Elsewhere he quotes without censure that strange aphorism of Saint-Simon's,[6] concerning which and whom so much were to be said: '*L'âge d'or, qu'une aveugle tradition a placé jusqu'ici dans passé, est devant nous*; The golden age, which a blind tradition has hitherto placed in the past, is Before us.'—But listen again:

'When the Phœnix is fanning her funeral pyre, will there not be sparks flying! Alas, some millions of men, and among them such as a Napoleon, have already been licked into that high-eddying Flame, and like moths consumed there. Still also have we to fear that incautious beards will get singed.

'For the rest, in what year of grace such Phœnix-cremation will be completed, you need not ask. The law of Perseverance is among the deepest in man: by nature he hates change; seldom will he quit his old house till it has actually fallen about his ears. Thus have I seen Solemnities linger as Ceremonies, sacred Symbols as idle Pageants, to the extent of three-hundred years and more after all life and sacredness had evaporated out of them. And then, finally, what time the Phœnix Death-Birth itself will require,

---

[3] Genesis 2:8–10; Revelation 22:17.   [4] Bad or unwelcome news.
[5] "Thus ye labor but not for yourselves."
[6] Claude Henri de Saint-Simon (1760–1825), founder of French socialism.

depends on unseen contingencies.—Meanwhile, would Destiny offer Mankind, that after, say two centuries of convulsion and conflagration, more or less vivid, the fire-creation should be accomplished, and we to find ourselves again in a Living Society, and no longer fighting but working,—were it not perhaps prudent in Mankind to strike the bargain?'

Thus is Teufelsdröckh content that old sick Society should be deliberately burnt (alas, with quite other fuel than spice-wood); in the faith that she is a Phœnix; and that a new heavenborn young one will rise out of her ashes! We ourselves, restricted to the duty of Indicator, shall forbear commentary. Meanwhile, will not the judicious reader shake his head, and reproachfully, yet more in sorrow than in anger, say or think: From a *Doctor utriusque Juris*, titular Professor in a University, and man to whom hitherto, for his services, Society, bad as she is, has given not only food and raiment (of a kind), but books, tobacco and gukguk, we expected more gratitude to his benefactress; and less of a blind trust in the future, which resembles that rather of a philosophical Fatalist and Enthusiast, than of a solid householder paying scot-and-lot[7] in a Christian country.

CHAPTER VI

Old Clothes

Courtesy due from all men to all men: The Body of Man a Revelation in the Flesh. Teufelsdröckh's respect for Old Clothes, as the 'Ghosts of life.' Walk in Monmouth Street, and meditations there.

As MENTIONED above, Teufelsdröckh, though a sansculottist, is in practice probably the politest man extant: his whole heart and life are penetrated and informed with the spirit of politeness; a noble natural Courtesy shines through him, beautifying his vagaries; like sunlight, making a rosy-fingered, rainbow-dyed Aurora out of mere aqueous clouds; nay brightening London-smoke itself into gold vapour, as from the crucible of an alchemist. Hear in what

earnest though fantastic wise he expresses himself on this head:

'Shall Courtesy be done only to the rich, and only by the rich? In Good-breeding, which differs, if at all, from High-breeding, only as it gracefully remembers the rights of others, rather than gracefully insists on its own rights, I discern no special connexion with wealth or birth: but rather that it lies in human nature itself, and is due from all men towards all men. Of a truth, were your Schoolmaster at his post, and worth anything when there, this, with so much else, would be reformed. Nay, each man were then also his neighbour's schoolmaster; till at length a rude-visaged, unmannered Peasant could no more be met with, than a Peasant unacquainted with botanical Physiology, or who felt not that the clod he broke was created in Heaven.

'For whether thou bear a sceptre or a sledge-hammer, art not thou ALIVE; is not this thy brother ALIVE? "There is but one temple in the world," says Novalis, "and that temple is the Body of Man. Nothing is holier than this high Form. Bending before men is a reverence done to this Revelation in the Flesh. We touch Heaven, when we lay our hands on a human Body."

'On which ground, I would fain carry it farther than most do; and whereas the English Johnson[1] only bowed to every Clergyman, or man with a shovel-hat, I would bow to every Man with any sort of hat, or with no hat whatever. Is not he a Temple, then; the visible Manifestation and Impersonation of the Divinity? And yet, alas, such indiscriminate bowing serves not. For there is a Devil dwells in man, as well as a Divinity; and too often the bow is but pocketed by the *former*. It would go to the pocket of Vanity (which is your clearest phasis of the Devil, in these times); therefore must we withhold it.

'The gladder am I, on the other hand, to do reverence to those Shells and outer Husks of the Body, wherein no devilish passion any longer lodges, but only the pure emblem and effigies of Man: I mean, to Empty, or even to Cast Clothes. Nay, is it not to Clothes that most men do reverence: to the fine frogged broadcloth, nowise to the "straddling animal with bandy legs" which it holds, and makes a Dignitary of? Who ever saw any Lord my-lorded in tattered blanket fastened with wooden skewer? Nevertheless, I say, there is in such worship a shade of

---

[7] A parish tax formerly levied in Great Britain.
[1] English Johnson, Samuel Johnson; shovel hat, a bishop's mitre.

hypocrisy, a practical deception: for how often does the Body appropriate what was meant for the Cloth only! Whoso would avoid falsehood, which is the essence of all Sin, will perhaps see good to take a different course. That reverence which cannot act without obstruction and perversion when the Clothes are full, may have free course when they are empty. Even as, for Hindoo Worshippers, the Pagoda is not less sacred than the God; so do I too worship the hollow cloth Garment with equal fervour, as when it contained the Man: nay, with more, for I now fear no deception, of myself or of others.

'Did not King *Toomtabard,* or, in other words, John Baliol,[2] reign long over Scotland; the man John Baliol being quite gone, and only the "Toom Tabard" (Empty Gown) remaining? What still dignity dwells in a suit of Cast Clothes! How meekly it bears its honours! No haughty looks, no scornful gesture: silent and serene, it fronts the world; neither demanding worship, nor afraid to miss it. The Hat still carries the physiognomy of its Head: but the vanity and the stupidity, and goose-speech which was the sign of these two, are gone. The Coat-arm is stretched out, but not to strike; the Breeches, in modest simplicity, depend at ease, and now at last have a graceful flow; the Waistcoat hides no evil passion, no riotous desire; hunger or thirst now dwells not in it. Thus all is purged from the grossness of sense, from the carking cares and foul vices of the World; and rides there, on its Clothes-horse; as, on a Pegasus, might some skyey Messenger, or purified Apparition, visiting our low Earth.

'Often, while I sojourned in that monstrous tuberosity of Civilised Life, the Capital of England; and meditated, and questioned Destiny, under that ink-sea of vapour, black, thick, and multifarious as Spartan broth; and was one lone soul amid those grinding millions;—often have I turned into their Old-Clothes Market to worship. With awe-struck heart I walk through that Monmouth Street,[3] with its empty Suits, as through a Sanhedrim of stainless Ghosts. Silent are they, but expressive in their silence: the past witnesses and instruments of Woe and Joy, of Passions, Virtues, Crimes, and all the fathomless tumult of Good and Evil in "the Prison men call

Life." Friends! trust not the heart of that man for whom Old Clothes are not venerable. Watch, too, with reverence, that bearded Jewish High-priest, who with hoarse voice, like some Angel of Doom, summons them from the four winds! On his head, like the Pope, he has three Hats,[4]—a real triple tiara; on either hand are the similitude of wings, whereon the summoned Garments come to alight; and ever, as he slowly cleaves the air, sounds forth his deep fateful note, as if through a trumpet he were proclaiming: "Ghosts of Life, come to Judgment!" Reck not, ye fluttering Ghosts: he will purify you in his Purgatory, with fire and with water; and, one day, new-created ye shall reappear. O, let him in whom the flame of Devotion is ready to go out, who has never worshipped, and knows not what to worship, pace and repace, with austerest thought, the pavement of Monmouth Street, and say whether his heart and his eyes still continue dry. If Field Lane,[5] with its long fluttering rows of yellow handkerchiefs, be a Dionysius' Ear, where, in stifled jarring hubbub, we hear the Indictment which Poverty and Vice bring against lazy Wealth, that it has left them there cast-out and trodden under foot of Want, Darkness and the Devil,—then is Monmouth Street a Mirza's Hill,[6] where, in motley vision, the whole Pageant of Existence passes awfully before us; with its wail and jubilee, mad loves and mad hatreds, church-bells and gallows-ropes, farce-tragedy, beast-godhood,—the Bedlam of Creation!'

To most men, as it does to ourselves, all this will seem overcharged. We too have walked through Monmouth Street; but with little feeling of 'Devotion': probably in part because the contemplative process is so fatally broken in upon by the brood of money-changers who nestle in that Church, and importune the worshipper with merely secular proposals. Whereas Teufelsdröckh might be in that happy middle state, which leaves to the Clothes-broker no hope either of sale or of purchase, and so be allowed to linger there without molestation.—Something we would have given to see the little philosophical figure, with its steeple-hat and loose flowing skirts, and eyes in a fine frenzy, 'pacing and repacing in austerest thought' that foolish

---

[2] John de Baliol (1249–1315), reigned but four years, 1292–96.
[3] Now part of Shaftesbury Avenue, formerly noted for its secondhand clothing shops.
[4] The Pope's triple crown has three crowns topped by a globe and cross. The crowns symbolize the Pope's temporal, spiritual, and purgatorial sovereignty.
[5] Near Holborn Hill, a haunt of dealers in stolen goods.
[6] See Addison's "Vision of Mirza," *Spectator,* No. 159.

Street; which to him was a true Delphic avenue, and supernatural Whispering-gallery,[7] where the 'Ghosts of Life' rounded strange secrets in his ear. O thou philosophic Teufelsdröckh, that listenest while others only gabble, and with thy quick tympanum hearest the grass grow!

At the same time, is it not strange that, in Paper-bag Documents destined for an English work, there exists nothing like an authentic diary of this his sojourn in London; and of his Meditations among the Clothes-shops only the obscurest emblematic shadows? Neither, in conversation (for, indeed, he was not a man to pester you with his Travels), have we heard him more than allude to the subject.

For the rest, however, it cannot be uninteresting that we here find how early the significance of Clothes had dawned on the now so distinguished Clothes-Professor. Might we but fancy it to have been even in Monmouth Street, at the bottom of our own English 'ink-sea,' that this remarkable Volume first took being, and shot forth its salient point in his soul,—as in Chaos did the Egg of Eros, one day to be hatched into a Universe!

CHAPTER VII

Organic Filaments

Destruction and Creation ever proceed together; and organic filaments of the Future are even now spinning. Wonderful connection of each man with all men; and of each generation with all generations, before and after: Mankind is One. Sequence and progress of all human work, whether of creation or destruction, from age to age.—Titles, hitherto derived from Fighting, must give way to others. Kings will remain and their title. Political Freedom, not to be attained by any mechanical contrivance. Hero-worship, perennial amongst men; the cornerstone of politics in the Future. Organic filaments of the New Religion: Newspapers and Literature. Let the faithful soul take courage!

FOR US, who happen to live while the World-Phœnix is burning herself, and burning so slowly that, as Teufelsdröckh calculates, it were a handsome bargain would she engage to have done 'within two centuries,' there seems to lie but

an ashy prospect. Not altogether so, however, does the Professor figure it. 'In the living subject,' says he, 'change is wont to be gradual: thus, while the serpent sheds its old skin, the new is already formed beneath. Little knowest thou of the burning of a World-Phœnix, who fanciest that she must first burn-out, and lie as a dead cinereous heap; and therefrom the young one start-up by miracle, and fly heavenward. Far otherwise! In that Fire-whirlwind, Creation and Destruction proceed together; ever as the ashes of the Old are blown about, do organic filaments of the New mysteriously spin themselves: and amid the rushing and the waving of the Whirlwind-element come tones of a melodious Deathsong, which end not but in tones of a more melodious Birthsong. Nay, look into the Fire-whirlwind with thy own eyes, and thou wilt see.' Let us actually look, then: to poor individuals, who cannot expect to live two centuries, those same organic filaments, mysteriously spinning themselves, will be the best part of the spectacle. First, therefore, this of Mankind in general:

'In vain thou deniest it,' says the Professor; 'thou *art* my Brother. Thy very Hatred, thy very Envy, those foolish Lies thou tellest of me in thy splenetic humour: what is all this but an inverted Sympathy? Were I a Steam-engine, wouldst thou take the trouble to tell lies of me? Not thou! I should grind all unheeded, whether badly or well.

'Wondrous truly are the bonds that unite us one and all; whether by the soft binding of Love, or the iron chaining of Necessity, as we like to choose it. More than once have I said to myself, of some perhaps whimsically strutting Figure, such as provokes whimsical thoughts: "Wert thou, my little Brotherkin, suddenly covered-up within the largest imaginable Glass-bell,—what a thing it were, not for thyself only, but for the world! Post Letters, more or fewer, from all the four winds, impinge against thy Glass walls, but have to drop unread: neither from within comes there question or response into any Postbag; thy Thoughts fall into no friendly ear or heart, thy Manufacture into no purchasing hand: thou art no longer a circulating venous-arterial Heart, that, taking and giving, circulatest through all Space and all Time: there has a Hole fallen-out in the immeasurable, universal World-tissue, which must be darned-up again!"

'Such venous-arterial circulation, of Letters, verbal Messages, paper and other Packages, going out from him and coming in, are a blood-circulation, visible to the eye: but the finer nervous circulation, by which all things, the minutest that he does, minutely influence all men, and the very look of his face blesses or curses whomso it lights on, and so generates ever new blessing or new cursing: all this you cannot see, but only imagine. I say, there is not a red Indian, hunting by Lake Winnipic,[1] can quarrel with his squaw, but the whole world must smart for it: will not the price of beaver rise? It is a mathematical fact that the casting of this pebble from my hand alters the centre of gravity of the Universe.

'If now an existing generation of men stand so woven together, not less indissolubly does generation with generation. Hast thou ever meditated on that word, Tradition: how we inherit not Life only, but all the garniture and form of Life; and work, and speak, and even think and feel, as our Fathers, and primeval grandfathers, from the beginning, have given it us?—Who printed thee, for example, this unpretending Volume on the Philosophy of Clothes? Not the Herren Stillschweigen and Company; but Cadmus of Thebes, Faust of Mentz,[2] and innumerable others whom thou knowest not. Had there been no Mœsogothic Ulfila,[3] there had been no English Shakspeare, or a different one. Simpleton! it was Tubalcain that made thy very Tailor's needle, and sewed that court-suit of thine.

'Yes, truly, if Nature is one, and a living indivisible whole, much more is Mankind, the Image that reflects and creates Nature, without which Nature were not. As palpable life-streams in that wondrous Individual Mankind, among so many life-streams that are not palpable, flow on those main-currents of what we call Opinion; as preserved in Institutions, Polities, Churches, above all in Books. Beautiful it is to understand and know that a Thought did never yet die; that as thou, the originator thereof, hast gathered it and created it from the whole Past, so thou wilt transmit it to the whole Future. It is thus that the heroic heart, the seeing eye of the first times,

still feels and sees in us of the latest; that the Wise Man stands ever encompassed, and spiritually embraced, by a cloud of witnesses and brothers; and there is a living, literal *Communion of Saints*,[4] wide as the World itself, and as the History of the World.

'Noteworthy also, and serviceable for the progress of this same Individual, wilt thou find his subdivision into Generations. Generations are as the Days of toilsome Mankind: Death and Birth are the vesper and the matin bells, that summon Mankind to sleep, and to rise refreshed for new advancement. What the Father has made, the Son can make and enjoy; but has also work of his own appointed him. Thus all things wax, and roll onwards; Arts, Establishments, Opinions, nothing is completed, but ever completing. Newton has learned to see what Kepler saw;[5] but there is also a fresh heaven-derived force in Newton; he must mount to still higher points of vision. So too the Hebrew Lawgiver is, in due time, followed by an Apostle of the Gentiles.[6] In the business of Destruction, as this also is from time to time a necessary work, thou findest a like sequence and perseverance: for Luther it was as yet hot enough to stand by that burning of the Pope's Bull; Voltaire could not warm himself at the glimmering ashes, but required quite other fuel. Thus likewise, I note, the English Whig has, in the second generation, become an English Radical; who, in the third again, it is to be hoped, will become an English Rebuilder. Find Mankind where thou wilt, thou findest it in living movement, in progress faster or slower: the Phœnix soars aloft, hovers with outstretched wings, filling Earth with her music; or, as now, she sinks, and with spheral swan-song immolates herself in flame, that she may soar the higher and sing the clearer.'

Let the friends of social order, in such a disastrous period, lay this to heart, and derive from it any little comfort they can. We subjoin another passage, concerning Titles:

'Remark, not without surprise,' says Teufelsdröckh, 'how all high Titles of Honour come hitherto from Fighting. Your *Herzog* (Duke,

---

[1] Lake Winnipeg, Canada.

[2] Herren Stillschweigen, Messrs. Silence and Co., Weissnichtwo booksellers; Cadmus, legendary founder of Thebes, who introduced a sixteen-letter alphabet to Greece; Faust of Mentz, Johann Faust or Fust of Mainz who originated movable types in the fifteenth century.

[3] Wulfilas (c. 311–83), Bishop of the Visigoths who translated the Scriptures into Gothic.

[4] From the Apostles Creed.

[5] Sir Isaac Newton (1642–1727), English mathematician; Johann Kepler (1571–1630), German astronomer.

[6] Moses and St. Paul.

Dux) is Leader of Armies; your Earl (*Jarl*) is Strong Man; your Marshal cavalry Horse-shoer. A Millennium, or reign of Peace and Wisdom, having from of old been prophesied, and becoming now daily more and more indubitable, may it not be apprehended that such Fighting-titles will cease to be palatable, and new and higher need to be devised?

'The only Title wherein I, with confidence, trace eternity, is that of King. *König* (King), anciently *Könning*, means Ken-ning (Cunning), or which is the same thing, Can-ning. Ever must the Sovereign of Mankind be fitly entitled King.'[7]

'Well, also,' says he elsewhere, 'was it written by Theologians: a King rules by divine right. He carries in him an authority from God, or man will never give it him. Can I choose my own King? I can choose my own King Popinjay, and play what farce or tragedy I may with him: but he who is to be my Ruler, whose will is to be higher than my will, was chosen for me in Heaven. Neither except in such Obedience to the Heaven-chosen is Freedom so much as conceivable.'

The Editor will here admit that, among all the wondrous provinces of Teufelsdröckh's spiritual world, there is none he walks in with such astonishment, hesitation, and even pain, as in the Political. How, with our English love of Ministry and Opposition, and that generous conflict of Parties, mind warming itself against mind in their mutual wrestle for the Public Good, by which wrestle, indeed, is our invaluable Constitution kept warm and alive; how shall we domesticate ourselves in this spectral Necropolis, or rather City both of the Dead and of the Unborn, where the Present seems little other than an inconsiderable Film dividing the Past and the Future? In those dim long-drawn expanses, all is so immeasurable; much so disastrous, ghastly; your very radiances and straggling light-beams have a supernatural character. And then with such an indifference, such a prophetic peacefulness (accounting the inevitably coming as already here, to him all one whether it be distant by centuries or only by days), does he sit;—and live, you would say, rather in any other age than in his own! It is our painful duty to announce, or repeat, that, looking into this man, we discern a deep, silent, slow-burning, inextinguishable Radicalism, such as fills us with shuddering admiration.

Thus, for example, he appears to make little even of the Elective Franchise; at least so we interpret the following: 'Satisfy yourselves,' he says, 'by universal, indubitable experiment, even as ye are now doing or will do, whether FREEDOM, heavenborn and leading heavenward, and so vitally essential for us all, cannot peradventure be mechanically hatched and brought to light in that same Ballot-Box of yours; or at worst, in some other discoverable or devisable Box, Edifice, or Steam-mechanism. It were a mighty convenience; and beyond all, feats of manufacture witnessed hitherto.' Is Teufelsdröckh acquainted with the British Constitution, even slightly?—He says, under another figure: 'But after all, were the problem, as indeed it now everywhere is, To rebuild your old House from the top downwards (since you must live in it the while), what better, what other, than the Representative Machine will serve your turn? Meanwhile, however, mock me not with the name of Free, "when you have but knit-up my chains into ornamental festoons." '—Or what will any member of the Peace Society[8] make of such an assertion as this: 'The lower people everywhere desire War. Not so unwisely; there is then a demand for lower people—to be shot!'

Gladly, therefore, do we emerge from those soul-confusing labyrinths of speculative Radicalism, into somewhat clearer regions. Here, looking round, as was our hest, for 'organic filaments,' we ask, May not this, touching 'Hero-worship,' be of the number? It seems of a cheerful character; yet so quaint, so mystical, one knows not what, or how little, may lie under it. Our readers shall look with their own eyes:

'True is it that, in these days, man can do almost all things, only not obey. True likewise that whoso cannot obey cannot be free, still less bear rule; he that is the inferior of nothing, can be the superior of nothing, the equal of nothing. Nevertheless, believe not that man has lost his faculty of Reverence; that if it slumber in him, it has gone dead. Painful for man is that same rebellious Independence, when it has become inevitable; only in loving companionship with his fellows does he feel safe; only in reverently bowing down before the Higher does he feel himself exalted.

'Or what if the character of our so troublous

---

[7] This etymology is no longer held.   [8] A Quaker society founded 1816.

Era lay even in this: that man had forever cast away Fear, which is the lower; but not yet risen into perennial Reverence, which is the higher and highest?

'Meanwhile, observe with joy, so cunningly has Nature ordered it, that whatsoever man ought to obey, he cannot but obey. Before no faintest revelation of the Godlike did he ever stand irreverent; least of all, when the Godlike showed itself revealed in his fellow-man. Thus is there a true religious Loyalty forever rooted in his heart; nay in all ages, even in ours, it manifests itself as a more or less orthodox *Hero-worship*. In which fact, that Hero-worship exists, has existed, and will forever exist, universally among Mankind, mayest thou discern the corner-stone of living-rock, whereon all Polities for the remotest time may stand secure.'

Do our readers discern any such corner-stone, or even so much as what Teufelsdröckh is looking at? He exclaims, 'Or hast thou forgotten Paris and Voltaire?[9] How the aged, withered man, though but a Sceptic, Mocker, and millinery Court-poet, yet because even he seemed the Wisest, Best, could drag mankind at his chariot-wheels, so that princes coveted a smile from him, and the loveliest of France would have laid their hair beneath his feet! All Paris was one vast Temple of Hero-worship; though their Divinity, moreover, was of feature too apish.

'But if such things,' continues he, 'were done in the dry tree, what will be done in the green?[10] If, in the most parched season of Man's History, in the most parched spot of Europe, when Parisian life was at best but a scientific *Hortus Siccus*, bedizened with some Italian Gumflowers,[11] such virtue could come out of it; what is to be looked for when Life again waves leafy and bloomy, and your Hero-Divinity shall have nothing apelike, but be wholly human? Know that there is in man a quite indestructible Reverence for whatsoever holds of Heaven, or even plausibly counterfeits such holding. Show the dullest clodpole, show the haughtiest featherhead, that a soul higher than himself is actually here; were his knees stiffened into brass, he must down and worship.'

Organic filaments, of a more authentic sort, mysteriously spinning themselves, some will perhaps discover in the following passage:

'There is no Church, sayest thou? The voice of Prophecy has gone dumb? This is even what I dispute: but in any case, hast thou not still Preaching enough? A Preaching Friar settles himself in every village; and builds a pulpit, which he calls Newspaper. Therefrom he preaches what most momentous doctrine is in him, for man's salvation; and dost not thou listen, and believe? Look well, thou seest everywhere a new Clergy of the Mendicant Orders, some bare-footed, some almost bare-backed, fashion itself into shape, and teach and preach, zealously enough, for copper alms and the love of God. These break in pieces the ancient idols; and, though themselves too often reprobate, as idol-breakers are wont to be, mark out the sites of new Churches, where the true God-ordained, that are to follow, may find audience, and minister. Said I not, Before the old skin was shed, the new had formed itself beneath it?'

Perhaps also in the following; wherewith we now hasten to knit-up this ravelled sleeve:[12]

'But there is no Religion?' reiterates the Professor. 'Fool! I tell thee, there is. Hast thou well considered all that lies in this immeasurable froth-ocean we name LITERATURE? Fragments of a genuine Church-*Homiletic* lie scattered there, which Time will assort: nay fractions even of a *Liturgy* could I point out. And knowest thou no Prophet, even in the vesture, environment, and dialect of this age? None to whom the Godlike had revealed itself, through all meanest and highest forms of the Common; and by him been again prophetically revealed: in whose inspired melody, even in these rag-gathering and rag-burning days, Man's Life again begins, were it but afar off, to be divine? Knowest thou none such? I know him, and name him—Goethe.

'But thou as yet standest in no Temple; joinest in no Psalm-worship; feelest well that, where there is no ministering Priest, the people perish? Be of comfort! Thou art not alone, if thou have Faith. Spake we not of a Communion of Saints, unseen, yet not unreal, accompanying and brother-like embracing thee, so thou be worthy? Their heroic Sufferings rise up melodiously together to Heaven, out of all lands, and out of all times, as a sacred *Miserere*; their heroic Actions also, as a boundless everlasting Psalm of Triumph. Neither say that thou hast now no Symbol of the Godlike. Is not God's Universe a Symbol of the Godlike; is not Immensity a Temple; is not Man's History, and Men's

---

[9] Voltaire's triumphal return to Paris in 1778.   [10] Luke 23:31.
[11] *Hortus siccus*, dry garden, a plant collection for study; Gumflowers, artificial flowers.
[12] *Macbeth*, II, ii, 38.

History, a perpetual Evangel? Listen, and for organ-music thou wilt ever, as of old, hear the Morning Stars sing together.'

CHAPTER VIII

Natural Supernaturalism

Deep significance of Miracles. Littleness of human Science: Divine incomprehensibility of Nature. Custom blinds us to the miraculousness of daily-recurring miracles; so do Names. Space and Time, appearances only; forms of human Thought: A glimpse of Immortality. How Space hides from us the wondrousness of our commonest powers; and Time, the divinley miraculous course of human history.

IT IS IN his stupendous Section, headed *Natural Supernaturalism,* that the Professor first becomes a Seer; and, after long effort, such as we have witnessed, finally subdues under his feet this refractory Clothes-Philosophy, and takes victorious possession thereof. Phantasms enough he has had to struggle with; 'Cloth-webs and Cob-webs,' of Imperial Mantles, Superannuated Symbols, and what not: yet still did he courageously pierce through. Nay, worst of all, two quite mysterious, world-embracing Phantasms, Time and Space, have ever hovered round him, perplexing and bewildering: but with these also he now resolutely grapples, these also he victoriously rends asunder. In a word, he has looked fixedly on Existence, till, one after the other, its earthly hulls and garnitures have all melted away; and now, to his rapt vision, the interior celestial Holy of Holies lies disclosed.

Here, therefore, properly it is that the Philosophy of Clothes attains to Transcendentalism; this last leap, can we but clear it, takes us safe into the promised land, where *Palingenesia,*[1] in all senses, may be considered as beginning. 'Courage, then!' may our Diogenes exclaim, with better right than Diogenes the First once did.[2] This stupendous Section we, after long painful meditation, have found not to be unintelligible; but, on the contrary, to grow clear, nay radiant, and all-illuminating. Let the reader, turning on it what utmost force of speculative intellect is in him, do his part; as we, by judicious selection and adjustment, shall study to do ours:

'Deep has been, and is, the significance of Miracles,' thus quietly begins the Professor; 'far deeper perhaps than we imagine. Meanwhile, the question of questions were: What specially is a Miracle? To that Dutch King of Siam, an icicle had been a miracle; whoso had carried with him an air-pump, and vial of vitriolic ether, might have worked a miracle. To my Horse, again, who unhappily is still more unscientific, do not I work a miracle, and magical "*Open sesame!*" every time I please to pay twopence, and open for him an impassable *Schlagbaum,* or shut Turnpike?

' "But is not a real Miracle simply a violation of the Laws of Nature?" ask several. Whom I answer by this new question: Where are the Laws of Nature? To me perhaps the rising of one from the dead were no violation of these Laws, but a confirmation; were some far deeper Law, now first penetrated into, and by Spiritual Force, even as the rest have all been, brought to bear on us with its Material Force.

'Here too may some inquire, not without astonishment: On what ground shall one, that can make Iron swim,[3] come and declare that therefore he can teach Religion? To us, truly, of the Nineteenth Century, such declaration were inept enough; which nevertheless to our fathers, of the First Century, was full of meaning.

' "But is it not the deepest Law of Nature that she be constant?" cries an illuminated class: "Is not the Machine of the Universe fixed to move by unalterable rules?" Probable enough, good friends: nay I, too, must believe that the God, whom ancient inspired men assert to be "without variableness or shadow of turning,"[4] does indeed never change; that Nature, that the Universe, which no one whom it so pleases can be prevented from calling a Machine, does move by the most unalterable rules. And now of you, too, I make the old inquiry: What those same unalterable rules, forming the complete Statute-Book of Nature, may possibly be?

'They stand written in our Works of Science, say you; in the accumulated records of Man's Experience?—Was Man with his Experience

---

[1] New birth; the title of Teufelsdröckh's proposed second volume was *On the Palingenesia, or Newbirth of Society.*

[2] The cynic philosopher Diogenes Laertius is said to have exclaimed near the end of a wearisome lecture, "Courage, friends! I see land!"

[3] Cf. II Kings 6:6.   [4] James 1:17.

present at the Creation, then, to see how it all went on? Have any deepest scientific individuals yet dived down to the foundations of the Universe, and gauged everything there? Did the Maker take them into His counsel; that they read His groundplan of the incomprehensible All; and can say, This stands marked therein, and no more than this? Alas, not in anywise! These scientific individuals have been nowhere but where we also are; have seen some handbreadths deeper than we see into the Deep that is infinite, without bottom as without shore.

'Laplace's Book on the Stars, wherein he exhibits that certain Planets, with their Satellites, gyrate round our worthy Sun, at a rate and in a course, which, by greatest good fortune, he and the like of him have succeeded in detecting,—is to me as precious as to another. But is this what thou namest "Mechanism of the Heavens," and "System of the World"; this, wherein Sirius and the Pleiades, and all Herschel's[5] Fifteen-thousand Suns per minute, being left out, some paltry handful of Moons, and inert Balls, had been—looked at, nicknamed, and marked in the Zodiacal Way-bill; so that we can now prate of their Whereabout; their How, their Why, their What, being hid from us, as in the signless Inane?

'System of Nature! To the wisest man, wide as is his vision, Nature remains of quite *infinite* depth, of quite infinite expansion; and all Experience thereof limits itself to some few computed centuries and measured square-miles. The course of Nature's phases, on this our little fraction of a Planet, is partially known to us: but who knows what deeper courses these depend on; what infinitely larger Cycle (of causes) our little Epicycle revolves on? To the Minnow every cranny and pebble, and quality and accident, of its little native Creek may have become familiar: but does the Minnow understand the Ocean Tides and periodic Currents, the Trade-winds, and Monsoons, and Moon's Eclipses; by all which the condition of its little Creek is regulated, and may, from time to time (*un*miraculously enough), be quite overset and reversed? Such a minnow is Man; his Creek this Planet Earth; his Ocean the immeasurable All; his Monsoons and periodic Currents the mysterious Course of Providence through Æons of Æons.

'We speak of the Volume of Nature: and truly a Volume it is,—whose Author and Writer is God. To read it! Dost thou, does man, so much as well know the Alphabet thereof? With its Words, Sentences, and grand descriptive Pages, poetical and philosophical, spread out through Solar Systems, and Thousands of Years, we shall not try thee. It is a Volume written in celestial hieroglyphs, in the true Sacred-writing; of which even Prophets are happy that they can read here a line and there a line.[6] As for your Institutes, and Academies of Science, they strive bravely; and, from amid the thick-crowded, inextricably intertwisted hieroglyphic writing, pick out, by dextrous combination, some Letters in the vulgar Character, and therefrom put together this and the other economic Recipe, of high avail in Practice. That Nature is more than some boundless Volume of such Recipes, or huge, well-nigh inexhaustible Domestic-Cookery Book, of which the whole secret will in this manner one day evolve itself, the fewest dream.

'Custom,' continues the Professor, 'doth make dotards of us all.[7] Consider well, thou wilt find that Custom is the greatest of Weavers; and weaves air-raiment for all the Spirits of the Universe; whereby indeed these dwell with us visibly, as ministering servants, in our houses and workshops; but their spiritual nature becomes, to the most, forever hidden. Philosophy complains that Custom has hoodwinked us, from the first; that we do everything by Custom, even Believe by it; that our very Axioms, let us boast of Free-thinking as we may, are oftenest simply such Beliefs as we have never heard questioned. Nay, what is Philosophy throughout but a continual battle against Custom; an ever-renewed effort to *transcend* the sphere of blind Custom, and so become Transcendental?

'Innumerable are the illusions and legerdemain-tricks of Custom: but of all these, perhaps the cleverest is her knack of persuading us that the Miraculous, by simple repetition, ceases to be Miraculous. True, it is by this means we live; for man must work as well as wonder: and herein is Custom so far a kind nurse, guiding him to his true benefit. But she is a fond foolish nurse, or rather we are false foolish nurselings, when, in our resting and reflecting hours, we prolong the same deception. Am I to view the Stupendous with stupid indifference, because I have seen it twice, or two-hundred, or two-million times? There is no reason in Nature or in Art why I

---

[5] Sir William Herschel (1738–1822), English astronomer.
[6] Cf. Isaiah 28:10.   [7] Cf. *Hamlet*, III, i, 83.

should: unless, indeed, I am a mere Work-Machine, for whom the divine gift of Thought were no other than the terrestrial gift of Steam is to the Steam-engine; a power whereby cotton might be spun, and money and money's worth realised.

'Notable enough too, here as elsewhere, wilt thou find the potency of Names; which indeed are but one kind of such custom-woven, wonder-hiding Garments. Witchcraft, and all manner of Spectre-work, and Demonology, we have now named Madness and Diseases of the Nerves. Seldom reflecting that still the new question comes upon us: What is Madness, what are Nerves? Ever, as before, does Madness remain a mysterious-terrific, altogether *infernal* boiling-up of the Nether Chaotic Deep, through this fair-painted Vision of Creation, which swims thereon, which we name the Real. Was Luther's Picture of the Devil less a Reality, whether it were formed within the bodily eye, or without it?[8] In every the wisest Soul lies a whole world of internal Madness, an authentic Demon-Empire; out of which, indeed, his world of Wisdom has been creatively built together, and now rests there, as on its dark foundations does a habitable flowery Earth-rind.

'But deepest of all illusory Appearances, for hiding Wonder, as for many other ends, are your two grand fundamental world-enveloping Appearances, SPACE and TIME. These, as spun and woven for us from before Birth itself, to clothe our celestial ME for dwelling here, and yet to blind it,—lie all-embracing, as the universal canvas, or warp and woof, whereby all minor Illusions, in this Phantasm Existence, weave and paint themselves. In vain, while here on Earth, shall you endeavour to strip them off; you can, at best, but rend them asunder for moments, and look through.

'Fortunatus had a wishing Hat, which when he put on, and wished himself Anywhere, behold he was There. By this means had Fortunatus triumphed over Space, he had annihilated Space; for him there was no Where, but all was Here. Were a Hatter to establish himself, in the Wahngasse of Weissnichtwo, and make felts of this sort for all mankind, what a world we should have of it! Still stranger, should, on the opposite side of the street, another Hatter establish himself; and, as his fellow-craftsman made Space-annihilating Hats, make Time-annihilating! Of both would I purchase, were it with my last groschen;[9] but chiefly of this latter. To clap-on your felt, and, simply by wishing that you were Any*where,* straightway to be *There*! Next to clap-on your other felt, and, simply by wishing that you were Any*when,* straightway to be *Then*! This were indeed the grander: shooting at will from the Fire-Creation of the World to its Fire-Consummation; here historically present in the First Century, conversing face to face with Paul and Seneca;[10] there prophetically in the Thirty-first, conversing also face to face with other Pauls and Senecas, who as yet stand hidden in the depth of that late Time!

'Or thinkest thou it were impossible, unimaginable? Is the Past annihilated, then, or only past; is the Future non-extant, or only future? Those mystic faculties of thine, Memory and Hope, already answer: already through those mystic avenues, thou the Earth-blinded summonest both Past and Future, and communest with them, though as yet darkly, and with mute beckonings. The curtains of Yesterday drop down, the curtains of Tomorrow roll up; but Yesterday and Tomorrow both *are*. Pierce through the Time-element, glance into the Eternal. Believe what thou findest written in the sanctuaries of Man's Soul, even as all Thinkers, in all ages, have devoutly read it there: that Time and Space are not God, but creations of God; that with God as it is a universal HERE, so is it an everlasting Now.

'And seest thou therein any glimpse of IMMORTALITY?—O Heaven! Is the white Tomb of our Loved One, who died from our arms, and had to be left behind us there, which rises in the distance, like a pale, mournfully receding Milestone, to tell how many toilsome uncheered miles we have journeyed on alone,—but a pale spectral Illusion! Is the lost Friend still mysteriously *Here,* even as we are Here mysteriously, with God!—Know of a truth that only the Time-shadows have perished, or are perishable; that the real Being of whatever was, and whatever is, and whatever will be, *is* even now and forever. This, should it unhappily seem new, thou mayest ponder at thy leisure; for the next twenty years,

---

[8] The Devil appeared to Luther while he was translating the Bible, and Luther threw an inkstand at him.

[9] A small German coin.

[10] St. Paul; Lucius Annaeus Seneca (c. 4 B.C. A.D. 65), Roman philosopher and dramatist.

or the next twenty centuries: believe it thou must; understand it thou canst not.

'That the Thought-forms, Space and Time, wherein, once for all, we are sent into this Earth to live, should condition and determine our whole Practical reasonings, conceptions, and imagings or imaginings, seems altogether fit, just, and unavoidable. But that they should, furthermore, usurp such sway over pure spiritual Meditation, and blind us to the wonder every-where lying close on us, seems nowise so. Admit Space and Time to their due rank as Forms of Thought; nay even, if thou wilt, to their quite undue rank of Realities: and consider, then, with thyself how their thin disguises hide from us the brightest God-effulgences! Thus, were it not miraculous, could I stretch forth my hand and clutch the Sun? Yet thou seest me daily stretch forth my hand and therewith clutch many a thing, and swing it hither and thither. Art thou a grown baby, then, to fancy that the Miracle lies in miles of distance, or in pounds avoirdupois of weight; and not to see that the true inexplicable God-revealing Miracle lies in this, that I can stretch forth my hand at all; that I have free Force to clutch aught therewith? Innumerable other of this sort are the deceptions, and wonder-hiding stupefactions, which Space practises on us.

'Still worse is it with regard to Time. Your grand anti-magician, and universal wonder-hider, is this same lying Time. Had we but the Time-annihilating Hat, to put on for once only, we should see ourselves in a World of Miracles, wherein all fabled or authentic Thaumaturgy, and feats of Magic, were outdone. But unhappily we have not such a Hat; and man, poor fool that he is, can seldom and scantily help himself without one.

'Were it not wonderful, for instance, had Orpheus, or Amphion, built the walls of Thebes by the mere sound of his Lyre?[11] Yet tell me, Who built these walls of Weissnichtwo; summoning out all the sandstone rocks, to dance along from the *Steinbruch*[12] (now a huge Troglodyte Chasm, with frightful green-mantled pools); and shape themselves into Doric and Ionic pillars, squared ashlar houses and noble streets? Was it not the still higher Orpheus, or Orpheuses, who, in past centuries, by the divine Music of Wisdom, succeeded in civilising Man? Our highest Orpheus walked in Judea, eighteen-hundred years ago; his sphere-melody, flowing in wild native tones, took captive the ravished souls of men; and, being of a true sphere-melody still flows and sounds, though now with thousandfold accompaniments, and rich symphonies, through all our hearts; and modulates, and divinely leads them. Is that a wonder, which happens in two hours; and does it cease to be wonderful if happening in two million? Not only was Thebes built by the music of an Orpheus; but without the music of some inspired Orpheus was no city ever built, no work that man glories in ever done.

'Sweep away the Illusion of Time; glance, if thou have eyes, from the near moving-cause to its far-distant Mover: The stroke that came transmitted through a whole galaxy of elastic balls, was it less a stroke than if the last ball only had been struck, and sent flying? O, could I (with the Time-annihilating Hat) transport thee direct from the Beginnings to the Endings, how were thy eyesight unsealed, and thy heart set flaming in the Light-sea of celestial wonder! Then sawest thou that this fair Universe, were it in the meanest province thereof, is in very deed the star-domed City of God;[13] that through every star, through every grass-blade, and most through every Living Soul, the glory of a present God still beams. But Nature, which is the Time-vesture of God, and reveals Him to the wise, hides Him from the foolish.

'Again, could anything be more miraculous than an actual authentic Ghost? The English Johnson longed, all his life, to see one; but could not, though he went to Cock Lane, and thence to the church-vaults, and tapped on coffins.[14] Foolish Doctor! Did he never, with the mind's eye as well as with the body's, look round him into that full tide of human Life he so loved; did he never so much as look into Himself? The good Doctor was a Ghost, as actual and authentic as heart could wish; well-nigh a million of Ghosts were travelling the streets by his side. Once more I say, sweep away the illusion of Time; compress the threescore years into three minutes: what else was he, what else are we? Are we not Spirits, that are shaped into a body, into an Appearance; and that fade away again into air and Invisibility? This is no metaphor, it is a simple scientific *fact*; we start out of Nothingness, take figure, and are

---

[11] Orpheus, son of Apollo, whose lyre tamed wild beasts; Amphion, son of Jupiter, by his lyre caused Thebes to build itself.
[12] Quarry.   [13] St. Augustine, *De Civitate Dei* (City of God).
[14] Dr. Johnson and the Cock Lane ghost is reported by Boswell for the year 1763.

Apparitions; round us, as round the veriest spectre, is Eternity; and to Eternity minutes are as years and æons. Come there not tones of Love and Faith, as from celestial harp-strings, like the Song of beatified Souls? And again, do not we squeak and jibber (in our discordant, screech-owlish debatings and recriminatings); and glide bodeful, and feeble, and fearful; or uproar (*poltern*), and revel in our mad Dance of the Dead,—till the scent of the morning air summons us to our still Home; and dreamy Night becomes awake and Day? Where now is Alexander of Macedon: does the steel Host, that yelled in fierce battle-shouts at Issus and Arbela,[15] remain behind him; or have they all vanished utterly, even as perturbed Goblins must? Napoleon too, and his Moscow Retreats and Austerlitz Campaigns! Was it all other than the veriest Spectre-hunt; which has now, with its howling tumult that made Night hideous, flitted away?—Ghosts! There are nigh a thousand-million walking the Earth openly at noontide; some half-hundred have vanished from it, some half-hundred have arisen in it, ere thy watch ticks once.

'O Heaven, it is mysterious, it is awful to consider that we not only carry each a future Ghost within Him; but are, in very deed, Ghosts! These Limbs, whence had we them; this stormy Force; this life-blood with its burning Passion? They are dust and shadow,[16] a Shadow-system gathered round our ME; wherein, through some moments or years, the Divine Essence is to be revealed in the Flesh. That warrior on his strong war-horse, fire flashes through his eyes; force dwells in his arm and heart: but warrior and war-horse are a vision; a revealed Force, nothing more. Stately they tread the Earth, as if it were a firm substance: fool! the Earth is but a film; it

cracks in twain, and warrior and war-horse sink beyond plummet's sounding.[17] Plummet's? Fantasy herself will not follow them. A little while ago, they were not; a little while, and they are not, their very ashes are not.

'So has it been from the beginning, so will it be to the end. Generation after generation takes to itself the Form of a Body; and forth-issuing from Cimmerian Night, on Heaven's mission APPEARS. What Force and Fire is in each he expends: one grinding in the mill of Industry; one hunter-like climbing the giddy Alpine heights of Science; one madly dashed in pieces on the rocks of Strife, in war with his fellow:—and then the Heaven-sent is recalled; his earthly Vesture falls away, and soon even to sense becomes a vanished Shadow. Thus, like some wild-flaming, wild-thundering train of Heaven's Artillery, does this mysterious MANKIND thunder and flame, in long-drawn, quick-succeeding grandeur, through the unknown Deep. Thus, like a God-created, fire-breathing Spirit-host, we emerge from the Inane; haste stormfully across the astonished Earth; then plunge again into the Inane. Earth's mountains are levelled, and her seas filled up, in our passage: can the Earth, which is but dead and a vision, resist Spirits which have reality and are alive? On the hardest adamant some footprint of us is stamped-in; the last Rear of the host will read traces of the earliest Van. But whence?—O Heaven, whither? Sense knows not; Faith knows not; only that it is through Mystery to Mystery, from God and to God.

> "We *are such stuff*
> As dreams are made of, and our little Life
> Is rounded with a sleep!"[18]

from The French Revolution

Carlyle's claim to greatness as a historian was first established by the publication of The French Revolution *in 1837. It was an immediate success and confirmed Carlyle as a literary figure of the first rank. His method was radically different from traditional historians', for Carlyle stressed the dynamic movement of events and did not confine himself to conventional military and political history. Using some of the methods of the novelist and the poet, as well as those of the historian, Carlyle conveyed both the sweep of events and the texture of individual actions.*

[15] Cities in Asia Minor where Alexander defeated the Persians.
[16] Horace, *Odes*, IV, vii, 16.   [17] *The Tempest*, V, i, 56.   [18] *The Tempest*, IV, i, 156–58.

Throughout he maintained a stance that put all the action in the perspective of world history and of an unfolding divine drama. He saw the heedlessness of the aristocracy but also the ghastly excesses of mob violence.

The work was published in three volumes, each containing six to seven books, subdivided into chapters. The total runs to more than 300,000 words. The work covers the period from the death of Louis XV in 1774 to Vendémaire (October) of 1795. The selections that follow illustrate Carlyle's command of such diverse matters as the role of popular journalism in the Revolution, the opportunity lost through the death of Mirabeau, the last days of Marie-Antoinette, and finally his concluding statement on the universal import of the Revolution.

FROM VOLUME I, BOOK VI: "CONSOLIDATION"

CHAPTER V

[August–September 1789]

The Fourth Estate

PAMPHLETEERING opens its abysmal throat wider and wider; never to close more. Our Philosophes, indeed, rather withdraw; after the manner of Marmontel, 'retiring in disgust the first day.' Abbé Raynal,[1] grown grey and quiet in his Marseilles domicile, is little content with this work: the last literary act of the man will again be an act of rebellion; an indignant *Letter to the Constituent Assembly*; answered by 'the order of the day.' Thus also Philosophe Morellet[2] puckers discontent brows; being indeed threatened in his benefices by that Fourth of August: it is clearly going too far. How astonishing that those 'haggard figures in woollen jupes' would not rest as satisfied with Speculation, and victorious Analysis, as we!

Alas, yes: Speculation, Philosophism, once the ornament and wealth of the saloon, will now coin itself into mere Practical Propositions, and circulate on street and highway, universally; with results! A Fourth Estate, of Able Editors, springs up; increases and multiplies; irrepressible, incalculable. New Printers, new Journals, and ever new (so prurient is the world), let our Three Hundred curb and consolidate as they can! Loustalot, under the wing of Prudhomme dull-blustering Printer, edits weekly his *Révolutions de Paris*; in an acrid, emphatic manner. Acrid, corrosive, as the spirit of sloes and copperas, is Marat,[3] *Friend of the People*; struck already with the fact that the National Assembly, so full of Aristocrats, 'can do nothing,' except dissolve itself and make way for a better; that the Town-hall Representatives are little other than babblers and imbeciles, if not even knaves. Poor is this man; squalid, and dwells in garrets; a man unlovely to the sense, outward and inward; a man forbid;—and is becoming fanatical, possessed with fixed-idea. Cruel *lusus* of Nature! Did Nature, O poor Marat, as in cruel sport, knead thee out of her *leavings* and miscellaneous waste clay; and fling thee forth, stepdame-like, a Distraction into this distracted Eighteenth Century? Work is appointed thee there; which thou shalt do. The Three Hundred have summoned and will again summon Marat: but always he croaks-forth answer sufficient; always he will defy them, or elude them; and endure no gag.

Carra, 'Ex-secretary of a decapitated Hospo-dar,' and then of a Necklace-Cardinal; likewise Pamphleteer, Adventurer in many scenes and lands,—draws nigh to Mercier, of the *Tableau de Paris*; and, with foam on his lips, proposes an *Annales Patriotiques*. The *Moniteur* goes its prosperous way; Barrère 'weeps,' on Paper as yet loyal; Rivarol, Royou are not idle. Deep calls to deep: your *Domine Salvum Fac Regem* shall awaken *Pange Lingua*; with an *Ami-du-Peuple* there is a King's-Friend Newspaper, *Ami-du-Roi*. Camille Desmoulins[4] has appointed himself *Procureur-*

---

[1] François Raynal (1726–1810), French Benedictine.
[2] André Morellet (1727–1819), French abbé, philosophe, and economist.
[3] Jean Paul Marat (1743–93), revolutionary, slain by Charlotte Corday.
[4] Camille Desmoulins (1760–94), revolutionary pamphleteer, supporter of Danton; guillotined by Robespierre.

Général de la Lanterne, Attorney-General of the Lamp-iron; and pleads, *not* with atrocity, under an atrocious title; editing weekly his brilliant *Revolutions of Paris and Brabant.* Brilliant, we say; for if, in that thick murk of Journalism, with its dull blustering, with its fixed or loose fury, any ray of genius greet thee, be sure it is Camille's. The thing that Camille touches, he with his light finger adorns; brightness plays, gentle, unexpected, amid horrible confusions; often is the word of Camille worth reading, when no other's is. Questionable Camille, how thou glitterest with a fallen, rebellious, yet still semi-celestial light; as is the starlight on the brow of Lucifer! Son of the Morning, into what times and what lands art thou fallen!

But in all things there is good;—though it be not good for 'consolidating Revolutions.' Thousand wagon-loads of this Pamphleteering and Newspaper matter lie rotting slowly in the Public Libraries of our Europe. Snatched from the great gulf, like oysters by bibliomaniac pearl-divers, there must they first *rot*, then what was pearl, in Camille or others, may be seen as such, and continue as such.

Nor has public speaking declined, though Lafayette and his Patrols look sour on it. Loud always is the Palais Royal, loudest the Café de Foy; such a miscellany of Citizens and Citizenesses circulating there. 'Now and then,' according to Camille, 'some Citizens employ the liberty of the *press* for a private purpose; so that this or the other Patriot finds himself short of his watch or pocket-handkerchief!' But for the rest, in Camille's opinion, nothing can be a livelier image of the Roman Forum. 'A Patriot proposes his motion; if it finds any supporters, they make him mount on a chair, and speak. If he is applauded, he prospers and redacts; if he is hissed, he goes his ways.' Thus they, circulating and perorating. Tall shaggy Marquis Saint-Huruge,[5] a man that has had losses, and has deserved them, is seen eminent, and also heard. 'Bellowing' is the character of his voice, like that of a Bull of Bashan; voice which drowns all voices, which causes frequently the hearts of men to leap. Cracked or half-cracked is this tall Marquis's head; uncracked are his lungs; the cracked and the uncracked shall alike avail him.

Consider further that each of the Forty-eight Districts has its own Committee; speaking and motioning continually; aiding in the search for grain, in the search for a Constitution; checking and spurring the poor Three Hundred of the Townhall. That Danton,[6] with a 'voice reverberating from the domes,' is President of the Cordeliers District; which has already become a Goshen of Patriotism. That apart from the 'seventeen thousand utterly necessitous, digging on Montmartre,' most of whom, indeed, have got passes, and been dismissed into Space 'with four shillings,'—there is a *strike*, or union, of Domestics out of place; who assemble for public speaking: next, a strike of Tailors, for even they will strike and speak; further, a strike of Journeymen Cordwainers; a strike of Apothecaries: so dear is bread.[7] All these, having struck, must speak; generally under the open canopy; and pass resolutions;—Lafayette and his Patrols watching them suspiciously from the distance.

Unhappy mortals: such tugging and lugging, and throttling of one another, to divide, in some not intolerable way, the joint Felicity of man in this Earth; when the whole lot to be divided is such a 'feast of *shells*'!—Diligent are the Three Hundred; none equals Scipio-Americanus in dealing with mobs. But surely all these things bode ill for the consolidating of a Revolution.

FROM VOLUME II,
BOOK III:
"THE TUILERIES"

CHAPTER VI

[March 1791]

Mirabeau

THE SPIRIT of France waxes ever more acrid, fever-sick: towards the final outburst of dissolution and delirium. Suspicion rules all minds: contending parties cannot now commingle; stand separated sheer asunder, eyeing one another, in most aguish mood, of cold terror

---

[5] Marquis Saint-Huruge (1750–1810), politician.
[6] Georges Jacques Danton (1759–94), revolutionary, leader of the Cordeliers' Club; guillotined.
[7] *Histoire Parlementaire,* II, 359, 417, 423. [Carlyle's note]

or hot rage. Counter-Revolution, Days of Poniards, Castries Duels; Flight of Mesdames, of Monsieur and Royalty! Journalism shrills ever louder its cry of alarm. The sleepless Dionysius-Ear[1] of the Forty-eight Sections, how feverishly quick has it grown; convulsing with strange pangs the whole sick Body, as in such sleeplessness and sickness the ear will do!

Since Royalists get Poniards made to order, and a Sieur Motier is no better than he should be, shall not Patriotism too, even of the indigent sort, have Pikes, secondhand Firelocks, in readiness for the worst? The anvils ring, during this March month, with hammering of Pikes. A Constitutional Municipality promulgated its Placard, that no citizen except the 'active' or cash-citizen was entitled to have arms; but there rose, instantly responsive, such a tempest of astonishment from Club and Section, that the Constitutional Placard, almost next morning, had to cover itself up, and die away into inanity, in a second improved edition.[2] So the hammering continues; as all that it betokens does.

Mark, again, how the extreme tip of the Left is mounting in favour, if not in its own National Hall, yet with the Nation, especially with Paris. For in such universal panic of doubt, the opinion that is sure of itself, as the meagrest opinion may the soonest be, is the one to which all men will rally. Great is Belief, were it never so meagre; and leads captive the doubting heart. Incorruptible Robespierre has been elected Public Accuser in our new Courts of Judicature; virtuous Pétion,[3] it is thought, may rise to be Mayor. Cordelier Danton, called also by triumphant majorities, sits at the Departmental Council-table; colleague there of Mirabeau.[4] Of incorruptible Robespierre it was long ago predicted that he might go far, mean meagre mortal though he was; for Doubt dwelt not in him.

Under which circumstances ought not Royalty likewise to cease doubting, and begin deciding and acting? Royalty has always that sure trump-card in its hand: Flight out of Paris. Which sure trump-card Royalty, as we see, keeps ever and anon clutching at, grasping; and swashes it forth tentatively; yet never tables it, still puts it back

again. Play it, O Royalty! If there be a chance left, this seems it, and verily the last chance; and now every hour is rendering this a doubtfuler. Alas, one would so fain both fly and not fly; play one's card and have it to play. Royalty, in all human likelihood, will not play its trump-card till the honours, one after one, be mainly lost; and such trumping of it prove to be the sudden finish of the game!

Here accordingly a question always arises; of the prophetic sort; which cannot now be answered. Suppose Mirabeau, with whom Royalty takes deep counsel, as with a Prime Minister that cannot yet legally avow himself as such, had got his arrangements *completed*? Arrangements he has; far-stretching plans that dawn fitfully on us, by fragments, in the confused darkness. Thirty Departments ready to sign loyal Addresses, of prescribed tenor: King carried out of Paris, but only to Compiègne and Rouen, hardly to Metz, since, once for all, no Emigrant rabble shall take the lead in it: National Assembly consenting, by dint of loyal Addresses, by management, by force of Bouillé, to hear reason, and follow thither![5] Was it so, on *these* terms, that Jacobinism and Mirabeau were then to grapple, in their Hercules-and-Typhon duel; Death inevitable for the one or the other? The duel itself is determined on, and sure: but on what terms; much more, with what issue, we in vain guess. It is vague darkness all: unknown what is to be; unknown even what has already been. The giant Mirabeau walks in darkness, as we said; companionless, on wild ways: what his thoughts during these months were, no record of Biographer, nor vague *Fils Adoptif*, will now ever disclose.

To us, endeavouring to cast his horoscope, it of course remains doubly vague. There is one Herculean Man; in internecine duel with him, there is Monster after Monster. Emigrant Noblesse return, sword on thigh, vaunting of their Loyalty never sullied; descending from the air, like Harpy-swarms with ferocity, with obscene greed. Earthward there is the Typhon of Anarchy, Political, Religious; sprawling hundred-headed, say with Twenty-five million heads;

---

[1] Dionysius of Syracuse (405–367 B.C.) constructed a cave from which he could hear the conversations of prisoners.

[2] Ordonnance du 17 Mars 1791 (*Hist. Parl.* ix. 257). [Carlyle's note]

[3] Maximilien Marie Robespierre (1758–94), leader of the Jacobin party; guillotined; Jerome Pétion de Villeneuve (c. 1756–94), ally for a time of Robespierre.

[4] Honoré Gabriel Mirabeau (1754–92), endeavoured to negotiate with the monarchy; died a natural death.

[5] See *Fils Adoptif*, vii, 1.6: Dumont, c. 11, 12, 14. [Carlyle's note]

wide as the area of France; fierce as Frenzy; strong in very Hunger. With these shall the Serpent-queller do battle continually, and expect no rest.

As for the King, he as usual will go wavering chameleon-like; changing colour and purpose with the colour of his environment;—good for no Kingly use. On one royal person, on the Queen[6] only, can Mirabeau perhaps place dependence. It is possible, the greatness of this man, not unskilled too in blandishments, courtiership, and graceful adroitness, might, with most legitimate sorcery, fascinate the volatile Queen, and fix her to him. She has courage for all noble daring; an eye and a heart: the soul of Theresa's Daughter. '*Faut-il donc,* Is it fated then,' she passionately writes to her Brother, 'that I with the blood I am come of, with the sentiments I have, must live and die among such mortals?[7] Alas, poor Princess, Yes. 'She is the only *man,*' as Mirabeau observes, 'whom his Majesty has about him.' Of one other man Mirabeau is still surer: of himself. There lie his resources; sufficient or insufficient.

Dim and great to the eye of Prophecy looks that future. A perpetual life-and-death battle; confusion from above and from below;—mere confused darkness for us; with here and there some streak of faint lurid light. We see a King perhaps laid aside; not tonsured,—tonsuring is out of fashion now,—but say, sent away any-whither, with handsome annual allowance, and stock of smith-tools. We see a Queen and Dauphin, Regent and Minor; a Queen 'mounted on horseback,' in the din of battles, with *Moriamur pro rege nostro!*[8] 'Such a day,' Mirabeau writes, 'may come.'

Din of battles, wars more than civil, confusion from above and from below: in such environment the eye of Prophecy sees Comte de Mirabeau, like some Cardinal de Retz,[9] stormfully maintain himself; with head all-devising, heart all-daring, if not victorious, yet unvanquished, while life is left him. The specialities and issues of it, no eye of Prophecy can guess at: it is clouds, we repeat, and tempestuous night; and in the middle of it, now visible, far-darting, now labouring in eclipse, is Mirabeau indomitably struggling to be Cloud-Compeller!—One can say that, had Mirabeau lived, the History of France and of the World had been different. Further, that the man

would have needed, as few men ever did, the whole compass of that same 'Art of Daring, *Art d'Oser,*' which he so prized; and likewise that he, above all men then living, would have practised and manifested it. Finally, that some substan-tiality, and no empty simulacrum of a formula, would have been the result realised by him: a result you could have loved, a result you could have hated; by no likelihood, a result you could only have rejected with closed lips, and swept into quick forgetfulness for ever. Had Mirabeau lived one other year!

FROM VOLUME II,
BOOK: III
"THE TUILERIES"

CHAPTER VII

[April 1791]

Death of Mirabeau

BUT Mirabeau could not live another year, any more than he could live another thousand years. Men's years are numbered, and the tale of Mirabeau's was now complete. Important or unimportant; to be mentioned in World-History for some centuries, or not to be mentioned there beyond a day or two,—it matters not to peremptory Fate. From amid the press of ruddy busy Life, the Pale Messenger beckons silently: wide-spreading interests, pro-jects, salvation of French Monarchies, what thing soever man has on hand, he must suddenly quit it all, and go. Wert thou saving French Monarchies; wert thou blacking shoes on the Pont Neuf! The most important of men cannot stay; did the World's History depend on an hour, that hour is not to be given. Whereby, indeed, it comes that these same *would-have-beens* are mostly a vanity; and the World's History could never in the least be what it would, or

---

[6] Marie Antoinette (1755–93), Queen of France, daughter of Maria Theresa of Austria. See Carlyle's portrait in the selection that follows.

[7] *Fils Adoptif,* ubi supra. [Carlyle's note]   [8] "Let us die for our king!"

[9] Jean Paul de Gondi, Cardinal de Retz (1614–79), prelate, political intriguer.

might, or should, by any manner of potentiality, but simply and altogether what it *is*.

The fierce wear and tear of such an existence has wasted out the giant oaken strength of Mirabeau. A fret and fever that keeps heart and brain on fire: excess of effort, of excitement; excess of all kinds: labour incessant, almost beyond credibility! 'If I had not lived with him,' says Dumont, 'I never should have known what a man can make of one day; what things may be placed within the interval of twelve hours. A day for this man was more than a week or a month is for others: the mass of things he guided on together was prodigious; from the scheming to the executing not a moment lost.'—'Monsieur le Comte,' said his Secretary to him once, 'what you require is impossible.'—'Impossible!'—answered he, starting from his chair, '*Ne me dites jamais ce bête de mot*, Never name to me that blockhead of a word.'[1] And then the social repasts; the dinner which he gives as Commandant of National Guards, which 'cost five hundred pounds'; alas, and 'the Syrens of the Opera'; and all the ginger that is hot in the mouth:—down what a course is this man hurled! Cannot Mirabeau stop; cannot he fly, and save himself alive? No! there is a Nessus-Shirt on this Hercules; he must storm and burn there, without rest, till he be consumed. Human strength, never so Herculean, has its measure. Herald shadows flit pale across the fire-brain of Mirabeau; heralds of the pale repose. While he tosses and storms, straining every nerve, in that sea of ambition and confusion, there comes, sombre and still, a monition that for him the issue of it will be swift death.

In January last, you might see him as President of the Assembly; 'his neck wrapt in linen cloths, at the evening session': there was sick heat of the blood, alternate darkening and flashing in the eyesight; he had to apply leeches, after the morning labour, and preside bandaged. 'At parting he embraced me,' says Dumont, 'with an emotion I had never seen in him: "I am dying, my friend; dying as by slow fire; we shall perhaps not meet again. When I am gone, they will know what the value of me was. The miseries I have held back will burst from all sides on France." '[2] Sickness gives louder warning; but cannot be listened to. On the 27th day of March, proceeding towards the Assembly, he had to seek rest and help in Friend de Lamarck's, by the road; and lay there, for an hour, half-fainted, stretched on a sofa. To the Assembly nevertheless he went, as if in spite of Destiny itself; spoke, loud and eager, five several times; then quitted the Tribune—for ever. He steps out, utterly exhausted, into the Tuileries Gardens; many people press round him, as usual, with applications, memorials; he says to the Friend who was with him: 'Take me out of this!'

And so, on the last day of March 1791, endless anxious multitudes beset the Rue de la Chaussée d'Antin; incessantly inquiring: within doors there, in that House numbered, in our time, 42, the overwearied giant has fallen down, to die.[3] Crowds of all parties and kinds; of all ranks from the King to the meanest man! The King sends publicly twice a-day to inquire; privately besides: from the world at large there is no end of inquiring. 'A written bulletin is handed out every three hours,' is copied and circulated; in the end, it is printed. The People spontaneously keep silence; no carriage shall enter with its noise: there is crowding pressure; but the Sister of Mirabeau is reverently recognised, and has free way made for her. The People stand mute, heart-stricken; to all it seems as if a great calamity were nigh: as if the last man of France, who could have swayed these coming troubles, lay there at hand-grips with the unearthly Power.

The silence of a whole People, the wakeful toil of Cabanis,[4] Friend and Physician, skills not: on Saturday the second day of April, Mirabeau feels that the last of the Days has risen for him; that on this day he has to depart and be no more. His death is Titanic, as his life has been! Lit up, for the last time, in the glare of coming dissolution, the mind of the man is all glowing and burning; utters itself in sayings, such as men long remember. He longs to live, yet acquiesces in death, argues not with the inexorable. His speech is wild and wondrous: unearthly Phantasms dancing now their torch-dance round his soul; the soul itself looking out, fire-radiant, motionless, girt together for that great hour! At times comes a beam of light from him on the world he is quitting. 'I carry in my heart the death-dirge of the French Monarchy; the dead remains of it will now be the spoil of the factious.' Or again, when he heard the cannon fire, what is characteristic too: 'Have we the Achilles' Funeral

---

[1] Dumont, p. 311. [Carlyle's note]   [2] *Ibid.*, p. 267. [Carlyle's note]
[3] *Fils Adoptif*, viii. 420–79. [Carlyle's note]
[4] Pierre Jean Georges Cabanis (1757–1808), Mirabeau's physician.

already?' So likewise, while some friend is supporting him: 'Yes, support that head; would I could bequeath it thee!' For the man dies as he has lived; self-conscious, conscious of a world looking on. He gazes forth on the young Spring, which for him will never be Summer. The Sun has risen; he says, '*Si ce n'est pas là Dieu, c'est du moins son cousin germain.*'[5]—Death has mastered the outworks; power of speech is gone; the citadel of the heart still holding out: the moribund giant, passionately, by sign, demands paper and pen; writes his passionate demand for opium, to end these agonies. The sorrowful Doctor shakes his head: *Dormir,* 'To sleep,' writes the other, passionately pointing at it! So dies a gigantic Heathen and Titan; stumbling blindly, undismayed, down to his rest. At half-past eight in the morning, Doctor Petit, standing at the foot of the bed, says, '*Il ne souffre plus.*'[6] His suffering and his working are now ended.

Even so, ye silent Patriot multitudes, all ye men of France; this man is rapt away from you. He has fallen suddenly, without bending till he broke; as a tower falls, smitten by sudden lightning. His word ye shall hear no more, his guidance follow no more.—The multitudes depart, heart-struck; spread the sad tidings. How touching is the loyalty of men to their Sovereign Man! All theatres, public amusements close; no joyful meeting can be held in these nights, joy is not for them: the People break in upon private dancing-parties, and sullenly command that they cease. Of such dancing-parties apparently but two came to light, and these also have gone out. The gloom is universal; never in this City was such sorrow for one death; never since that old night when Louis XII. departed, 'and the *Crieurs des Corps* went sounding their bells, and crying along the streets: *Le bon roi Louis, père du peuple, est mort,* The good King Louis, Father of the People, is dead!'[7] King Mirabeau is now the lost King; and one may say with little exaggeration, all the People mourns for him.

For three days there is low wide moan; weeping in the National Assembly itself. The streets are all mournful; orators mounted on the *bornes,* with large silent audience, preaching the funeral sermon of the dead. Let no coachman whip fast, distractively with his rolling wheels, or almost at all, through these groups! His traces may be cut; himself and his fare, as incurable Aristocrats, hurled sulkily into the kennels. The bourne-stone orators speak as it is given them; the Sansculottic People, with its rude soul, listens eager,—as men will to any Sermon, or *Sermo,* when it *is* a spoken Word meaning a Thing, and not a Babblement meaning No-thing. In the Restaurateur's of the Palais-Royal, the waiter remarks, 'Fine weather, Monsieur':— 'Yes, my friend,' answers the ancient Man of Letters, 'very fine; but Mirabeau is dead.' Hoarse rhythmic threnodics come also from the throats of ballad-singers; are sold on grey-white paper at a *sou* each.[8] But of Portraits, engraved, painted, hewn and written; of Eulogies, Reminiscences, Biographies, nay *Vaudevilles,* Dramas and Melodramas, in all Provinces of France, there will, through these coming months, be the due immeasurable crop; thick as the leaves of Spring. Nor, that a tincture of burlesque might be in it, is Gobel's[9] Episcopal *Mandement* wanting; goose Gobel, who has just been made Constitutional Bishop of Paris. A Mandement wherein *Ça ira* alternates very strangely with *Nomine Domini*;[10] and you are, with a grave countenance, invited to 'rejoice at possessing in the midst of you a body of Prelates created by Mirabeau, zealous followers of his doctrine, faithful imitators of his virtues.'[11] So speaks, and cackles manifold, the Sorrow of France; wailing articulately, inarticulately, as it can, that a Sovereign Man is snatched away. In the National Assembly, when difficult questions are astir, all eyes will 'turn mechanically to the place where Mirabeau sat,'—and Mirabeau is absent now.

On the third evening of the lamentation, the fourth of April, there is solemn Public Funeral; such as deceased mortal seldom had. Procession of a league in length; of mourners reckoned loosely at a hundred thousand. All roofs are thronged with on-lookers, all windows, lampirons, branches of trees. 'Sadness is painted on every countenance; many persons weep.' There is double hedge of National Guards; there is National Assembly in a body; Jacobin Society,

---

[5] *Fils Adoptif,* viii, 450; *Journal de la maladie et de la mort de Mirabeau,* par P. J. G. Cabanis (Paris, 1803). [Carlyle's note]. Mirabeau's dying words are: "If that is not God, it is at least his cousin german."
[6] "He is no longer suffering." [7] Henault, *Abrégé chronologique.* p. 429. [Carlyle's note]
[8] *Fils Adoptif,* viii. 1. 10; Newspapers and Excerpts (in *Hist. Parl.* ix. 366–402). [Carlyle's note]
[9] Jean Baptiste Joseph Gobel (1727–94), Archbishop of Paris and professed atheist.
[10] *Ça ira,* "that will be"; *Nomine Domini,* "Name of the Lord."
[11] *Hist. Parl.* ix. 405. [Carlyle's note]

and Societies; King's Ministers, Municipals, and all Notabilities, Patriot or Aristocrat. Bouillé is noticeable there, 'with his hat on'; say, hat drawn over his brow, hiding many thoughts! Slow-wending, in religious silence, the Procession of a league in length, under the level sun-rays, for it is five o'clock, moves and marches: with its sable plumes; itself in a religious silence; but, by fits with the muffled roll of drums, by fits with some long-drawn wail of music, and strange new clangour of trombones, and metallic dirge-voice; amid the infinite hum of men. In the Church of Saint-Eustache, there is funeral oration by Cerutti; and discharge of fire-arms, which 'brings down pieces of the plaster.' Thence, forward again to the Church of Sainte-Geneviève; which has been consecrated, by supreme decree, on the spur of this time, into a Pantheon for the Great Men of the Fatherland, *Aux Grands Hommes la Patrie réconnaissante.* Hardly at midnight is the business done; and Mirabeau left in his dark dwelling: first tenant of that Fatherland's Pantheon.

Tenants, alas, who inhabits but at will, and shall be cast out. For, in these days of convulsion and disjection, not even the dust of the dead is permitted to rest. Voltaire's bones are, by and by, to be carried from their stolen grave in the Abbey of Scellières, to an eager *stealing* grave, in Paris his birth-city: all mortals processioning and perorating there; cars drawn by eight white horses, goadsters in classical costume, with fillets and wheat-ears enough;—though the weather is of the wettest.[12] Evangelist Jean Jacques too, as is most proper, must be dug up from Ermenonville, and processioned, with pomp, with sensibility, to the Pantheon of the Fatherland.[13] He and others: while again Mirabeau, we say, is cast forth from it, happily incapable of being *re*placed; and rests now, irrecognisable, reburied hastily at dead of night 'in the central part of the Churchyard Sainte-Catherine, in the Suburb Saint-Marceau,' to be disturbed no further.

So blazes out, far-seen, a Man's Life, and becomes ashes and a *caput mortuum,* in this World-Pyre, which we name French Revolution: not the first that consumed itself there; nor, by thousands and many millions, the last! A man who 'had swallowed all formulas'; who, in these strange times and circumstances, felt called to live Titanically, and also to die so. As he, for his part, had swallowed all formulas, what Formula is there, never so comprehensive, that will express truly the *plus* and the *minus* of him, give us the accurate net-result of him? There is hitherto none such. Moralities not a few must shriek condemnatory over this Mirabeau; the Morality by which he could be judged has not yet got uttered in the speech of men. We will say this of him again: That he is a Reality and no Simulacrum; a living Son of Nature our general Mother; not a hollow Artifice, and mechanism of Conventionalities, son of nothing, *brother* to nothing. In which little word, let the earnest man, walking sorrowful in a world mostly of 'Stuffed Clothes-suits,' that chatter and grin meaningless on him, quite *ghastly* to the earnest soul,—think what significance there is!

Of men who, in such sense, are alive, and see with eyes, the number is now got great; it may be well, if in this huge French Revolution itself, with its all-developing fury, we find some Three. Mortals driven rabid we find; sputtering the acridest logic; baring their breast to the battle-hail, their neck to the guillotine:—of whom it is so painful to say that they too are still, in good part, manufactured Formalities, not Facts but Hearsays!

Honour to the strong man, in these ages, who has shaken himself loose of shams, and *is* something. For in the way of being *worthy,* the first condition surely is that one *be.* Let Cant cease, at all risks and at all costs: till Cant cease, nothing else can begin. Of human Criminals, in these centuries, write the Moralist, I find but one unforgivable: the Quack. 'Hateful to God,' as divine Dante sings, 'and to the Enemies of God,

'A Dio spiacente ed a' nemici sui!'

But whoever will, with sympathy, which is the first essential towards insight, look at this questionable Mirabeau, may find that there lay verily in him, as the basis of all, a Sincerity, a great free Earnestness; nay call it Honesty, for the man did before all things see, with that clear flashing vision, into what *was,* into what existed as fact; and did, with his wild heart, follow that and no other. Whereby on what ways soever he travels and struggles, often enough falling, he is still a brother man. Hate him not; thou canst not hate him! Shining through such soil and tarnish,

---

[12] *Moniteur,* du 13 Juillet 1791. [Carlyle's note]
[13] *Ibid.* du 18 Septembre 1794. See also du 30 Âout, etc. 1791 [Carlyle's note]. The "Evangelist Jean Jacques" is Rousseau.

and now victorious effulgent, and oftenest struggling eclipsed, the light of genius itself is in this man; which was never yet base and hateful; but at worst was lamentable, lovable with pity. They say that he was ambitious, that he wanted to be Minister. It is most true. And was he not simply the one man in France who could have done any good as Minister? Not vanity alone, not pride alone; far from that! Wild burstings of affection were in this great heart; of fierce lightning, and soft dew of pity. So sunk bemired in wretchedest defacements, it may be said of him, like the Magdalen of old, that he loved much: his Father, the harshest of old crabbed men, he loved with warmth, with veneration.

Be it that his falls and follies are manifold,—as himself often lamented even with tears.[14] Alas, is not the Life of every such man already a poetic Tragedy; made up 'of Fate and of one's own Deservings,' of *Schicksal und eigene Schuld*; full of the elements of Pity and Fear? This brother man, if not Epic for us, is Tragic; if not great, is large, large in his qualities, world-large in his destinies. Whom other men, recognising him as such, may, through long times, remember, and draw nigh to examine and consider: these, in their several dialects, will say of him and sing of him,—till the right thing be said; and so the Formula that *can* judge him be no longer an undiscovered one.

Here then the wild Gabriel Honoré drops from the tissue of our History; not without a tragic farewell. He is gone: the flower of the wild Riquetti or Arrighetti kindred;[15] which seems as if in him, with one last effort, it had done its best, and then expired, or sunk down to the undistinguished level. Crabbed old Marquis Mirabeau, the Friend of Men, sleeps sound. The Bailli Mirabeau, worthy Uncle, will soon die forlorn, alone. Barrel-Mirabeau, already gone across the Rhine, his Regiment of Emigrants will drive nigh desperate. 'Barrel-Mirabeau,' says a biographer of his, 'went indignantly across the Rhine, and drilled Emigrant Regiments. But as he sat one morning in his tent, sour of stomach doubtless and of heart, meditating in Tartarean humour on the turn things took, a certain Captain or Subaltern demanded admittance on business. Such Captain is refused; he again demands, with refusal; and then again;

till Colonel Viscount Barrel-Mirabeau, blazing up into a mere burning brandy-barrel, clutches his sword, and tumbles out on this *canaille* of an intruder,—alas, on the *canaille*[16] of an intruder's sword-point, who had drawn with swift dexterity; and dies, and the Newspapers name it *apoplexy* and *alarming accident*.' So die the Mirabeaus.

New Mirabeaus one hears not of: the wild kindred, as we said, is gone out with this its greatest. As families and kindreds sometimes do; producing, after long ages of unnoted notability, some living quintessence of all the qualities they had, to flame forth as a man world-noted; after whom they rest as if exhausted; the sceptre passing to others. The chosen Last of the Mirabeaus is gone; the chosen man of France is gone. It was he who shook old France from its basis; and, as if with his single hand, has held it toppling there, still unfallen. What things depended on that one man! He is as a ship suddenly shivered on sunk rocks: much swims on the waste waters, far from help.

FROM VOLUME III,
BOOK IV: "TERROR"

CHAPTER VII

[October 1793]

Marie-Antoinette

ON Monday the Fourteenth of October 1793, a Cause is pending in the Palais de Justice, in the new Revolutionary Court, such as those old stone-walls never witnessed: the Trial of Marie-Antoinette. The once brightest of Queens, now tarnished, defaced, forsaken, stands here at Fouquier-Tinville's Judgment-bar; answering for her life. The Indictment was delivered her last night.[1] To such changes of human fortune what words are adequate? Silence alone is adequate.

---

[14] Dumont, p. 287. [Carlyle's note]
   [15] The Mirabeaus were descended from Italian families of these names. The fates of Mirabeau's relatives are cited in the following passage.
   [16] Riffraff, scum.   [1] *Procès de la Reine* (*Deux Amis*, xi. 251–381.) [Carlyle's note]

There are few Printed things one meets with of such tragic, almost ghastly, significance as those bald Pages of the *Bulletin du Tribunal Révolutionnaire,* which bear title, *Trial of the Widow Capet.* Dim, dim, as if in disastrous eclipse; like the pale kingdoms of Dis! Plutonic Judges, Plutonic Tinville; encircled, nine times, with Styx and Lethe, with Fire-Phlegethon and Cocytus named of Lamentation! The very witnesses summoned are like Ghosts: exculpatory, inculpatory, they themselves are all hovering over death and doom; they are known, in our imagination, as the prey of the Guillotine. Tall *ci-devant* Count d'Estaing, anxious to show himself Patriot, cannot escape; nor Bailly,[2] who, when asked If he knows the Accused, answers with a reverent inclination towards her, 'Ah, yes, I know Madame.' Ex-Patriots are here, sharply dealt with, as Procureur Manuel; Ex-Ministers, shorn of their splendour. We have cold Aristocratic impassivity, faithful to itself even in Tartarus; rabid stupidity, of Patriot Corporals, Patriot Washerwomen, who have much to say of Plots, Treasons, August Tenth, old Insurrection of Women. For all now has become a crime in her who has *lost.*

Marie-Antoinette, in this her utter abandonment, and hour of extreme need, is not wanting to herself, the imperial woman. Her look, they say, as that hideous Indictment was reading, continued calm; 'she was sometimes observed moving her fingers, as when one plays on the piano.' You discern, not without interest, across that dim Revolutionary Bulletin itself, how she bears herself queenlike. Her answers are prompt, clear, often of Laconic brevity; resolution, which has grown contemptuous without ceasing to be dignified, veils itself in calm words. 'You persist, then, in denial?'—'My plan is not denial: it is the truth I have said, and I persist in that.' Scandalous Hébert has borne his testimony as to many things: as to one thing, concerning Marie-Antoinette and her little Son,—wherewith Human Speech had better not further be soiled. She has answered Hébert;[3] a Juryman begs to observe that she has not answered as to *this.* 'I have not answered,' she exclaims with noble emotion, 'because Nature refuses to answer such a charge brought against a Mother. I appeal to all the Mothers that are here.' Robespierre, when he heard of it, broke out into something almost like swearing at the brutish blockheadism of this Hébert;[4] on whose foul head his foul lie has recoiled. At four o'clock on Wednesday morning, after two days and two nights of interrogating, jury-charging, and other darkening of counsel, the result comes out: sentence of Death. 'Have you anything to say?' The Accused shook her head, without speech. Night's candles are burning out; and with her too Time is finishing, and it will be Eternity and Day. This Hall of Tinville's is dark, ill-lighted except where she stands. Silently she withdraws from it, to die.

Two Processions, or Royal Progresses, three-and-twenty years apart, have often struck us with a strange feeling of contrast. The first is of a beautiful Archduchess and Dauphiness, quitting her Mother's City, at the age of Fifteen; towards hopes such as no other Daughter of Eve then had: 'On the morrow,' says Weber an eye-witness, 'the Dauphiness left Vienna. The whole city crowded out; at first with a sorrow which was silent. She appeared: you saw her sunk back into her carriage; her face bathed in tears; hiding her eyes now with her handkerchief, now with her hands; several times putting out her head to see yet again this Palace of her Fathers, whither she was to return no more. She motioned her regret, her gratitude to the good Nation, which was crowding here to bid her farewell. Then arose not only tears; but piercing cries, on all sides. Men and women alike abandoned themselves to such expression of their sorrow. It was an audible sound of wail, in the streets and avenues of Vienna. The last Courier that followed her disappeared, and the crowd melted away.'[5]

The young imperial Maiden of Fifteen has now become a worn discrowned Widow of Thirty-eight; grey before her time: this is the last Procession: 'Few minutes after the Trial ended, the drums were beating to arms in all Sections; at sunrise the armed force was on foot, cannons getting placed at the extremities of the Bridges, in the Squares, Crossways, all along from the Palais de Justice to the Place de la Révolution. By ten o'clock, numerous patrols were circulating in the Streets; thirty thousand foot and horse drawn up under arms. At eleven, Marie-

---

[2] Charles Hector Théodat, Comte d'Estaing (1729–94), royalist supporter; Jean Sylvain Bailly (1736–93), mayor of Paris.

[3] Jacques René Hébert (1755–94), extreme Jacobin, charged the Queen with incestuous relations with the Dauphin.

[4] Villate, *Causes secrètes de la Révolution de Thermidor* (Paris, 1825), p. 179. [Carlyle's note]

[5] Weber, i. 6. [Carlyle's note]

Antoinette was brought out. She had on an undress of *piqué blanc*: she was led to the place of execution, in the same manner as an ordinary criminal; bound, on a Cart; accompanied by a Constitutional Priest in Lay dress; escorted by numerous detachments of infantry and cavalry. These, and the double row of troops all along her road, she appeared to regard with indifference. On her countenance there was visible neither abashment nor pride. To the cries of *Vive la République* and *Down with Tyranny,* which attended her all the way, she seemed to pay no need. She spoke little to her Confessor. The tricolor Streamers on the housetops occupied her attention, in the Streets du Roule and Saint-Honoré; she also noticed the Inscriptions on the housefronts. On reaching the Place de la Révolution, her looks turned towards the *Jardin National,* whilom Tuileries; her face at that moment gave signs of lively emotion. She mounted the Scaffold with courage enough; at a quarter past Twelve, her head fell; the Executioner showed it to the people, amid universal long-continued cries of *Vive la République.*'[6]

FROM VOLUME III,
BOOK VII: "VENDÉMAIRE"

CHAPTER VIII

[October 1795]

Finis

Homer's Epos, it is remarked, is like a Bas-Relief sculpture: it does not conclude, but merely ceases. Such, indeed, is the Epos of Universal History itself. Directorates, Consulates, Emperorships, Restorations, Citizen-Kingships succeed this Business in due series, in due genesis one out of the other. Nevertheless the First-parent of all these may be said to have gone to air in the way we see. A Babœuf Insurrection, next year, will die in the birth; stifled by the Soldiery. A

Senate, if tinged with Royalism, can be purged by the Soldiery; and an Eighteenth of Fructidor transacted by the mere show of bayonets.[1] Nay Soldiers' bayonets can be used *à posteriori* on a Senate, and make it leap out of window,—still bloodless; and produce an Eighteenth of Brumaire.[2] Such changes must happen: but they are managed by intriguings, caballings, and then by orderly word of command; almost like mere changes of Ministry. Not in general by sacred right of Insurrection, but by milder methods growing ever milder, shall the events of French History be henceforth brought to pass.

It is admitted that this Directorate, which owned, at its starting, these three things, an 'old table, a sheet of paper, and an inkbottle,' and no visible money or arrangement whatever,[3] did wonders: that France, since the Reign of Terror hushed itself, has been a new France, awakened like a giant out of torpor; and has gone on, in the Internal Life of it, with continual progress. As for the External form and forms of Life, what can we say, except that out of the Eater there comes Strength; out of the Unwise there comes *not* Wisdom!—Shams are burnt up; nay, what as yet is the peculiarity of France, the very Cant of them is burnt up. The new Realities are not yet come: ah no, only Phantasms, Paper models, tentative Prefigurements of such! In France there are now Four Million Landed Properties; that black portent of an Agrarian Law is, as it were, *realised.* What is still stranger, we understand all Frenchmen have 'the right of duel'; the Hackney-coachman with the Peer, if insult be given: such is the law of Public Opinion. Equality at least in death! The Form of Government is by Citizen King, frequently shot at, not yet shot.

On the whole, therefore, has it not been fulfilled what was prophesied, *ex postfacto* indeed, by the Arch-quack Cagliostro, or another? He, as he looked in rapt vision and amazement into these things, thus spake:[4] 'Ha! What is *this*? Angels, Uriel, Anachiel, and ye other Five; Pentagon of Rejuvenescence; Power that destroyedst Original Sin; Earth, Heaven, and thou Outer Limbo, which men name Hell! Does the EMPIRE OF IMPOSTURE waver? Burst there, in starry sheen, updarting, Light-rays from out of *its* dark foundations; as it rocks and heaves, not

---

[6] *Deux Amis,* xi, 301. [Carlyle's note]
[1] *Moniteur,* du 4 Septembre 1797. [Carlyle's note]
[2] 9th November 1799 (*Choix des Rapports,* xvii. 1–96). [Carlyle's note]
[3] Bailleul, *Examen critique des considerations Mad. de Staël,* ii. 275. [Carlyle's note]
[4] *Diamond Necklace* (Carlyle's *Miscellanies*). [Carlyle's note]

in travail-throes but in death-throes? Yea, Light-rays, piercing, clear, that salute the Heavens,—lo, they *kindle* it; their starry clearness becomes as red Hellfire!

'IMPOSTURE is in flames, Imposture is burnt up: one red sea of Fire, wild-billowing, enwraps the World; with its fire-tongue licks at the very Stars. Thrones are hurled into it, and Dubois Mitres, and Prebendal Stalls that drop fatness, and—ha! what see I?—all the *Gigs* of Creation: all, all! Wo is me! Never since Pharaoh's Chariots, in the Red Sea of water, was there wreck of Wheel-vehicles like this in the Sea of Fire. Desolate, as ashes, as gases, shall they wander in the wind.

'Higher, higher yet flames the Fire-Sea; crackling with new dislocated timber; hissing with leather and prunella. The metal Images are molten; the marble Images become mortar-lime; the stone Mountains sulkily explode. RESPECT-ABILITY, with all her collected Gigs inflamed for funeral pyre, wailing, leaves the Earth: not to return save under new Avatar. Imposture how it burns, through generations: how it is burnt up; for a time. The World is black ashes;—which, ah, when will they grow green? The images all run into amorphous Corinthian brass; all Dwellings of men destroyed; the very mountains peeled and riven, the valleys black and dead: it is an empty World! Wo to them that shall be born then!—— A King, a Queen (ah me!) were hurled in; did rustle once; flew aloft, crackling, like paper-scroll. Iscariot Egalité was hurled in; thou grim De Launay, with thy grim Bastille; whole kindreds and peoples; five millions of mutually destroying Men. For it is the End of the dominion of IMPOSTURE (which is Darkness and opaque Fire-damp); and the burning up, with un-quenchable fire, of all the Gigs that are in the Earth.' This Prophecy, we say, has it not been fulfilled, is it not fulfilling?

And so here, O Reader, has the time come for us two to part. Toilsome was our journeying together; not without offence; but it is done. To me thou wert as a beloved shade, the disembodied or not yet embodied spirit of a Brother. To thee I was but as a Voice. Yet was our relation a kind of sacred one; doubt not that! For whatsoever once sacred things become hollow jargons, yet while the Voice of Man speaks with Man, hast thou not there the living fountain out of which all sacrednesses sprang, and will yet spring? Man, by the nature of him, is definable as 'an incarnated Word.' Ill stands it with me if I have spoken falsely: thine also it was to hear truly. Farewell.

from On Heroes, Hero-Worship, and the Heroic in History

In May of 1840 Carlyle delivered the series of six lectures that was published as On Heroes, Hero-Worship, and the Heroic in History *in 1841. It was the fourth lecture series he delivered between 1837 and 1840 and the only one Carlyle published. In the lectures Carlyle endeavored to penetrate the heart of the idea of heroism to demonstrate that heroism could manifest itself in many guises, not merely the military, and to show thereby the need for a modern hero to give purpose to contemporary life. He begins his consideration of the subject by taking up the concept of the hero as divinity in the form of Odin and pagan hero-worship, the section printed here. In each of the succeeding lectures he examines another and later stage of heroism and its representative examples—the hero as prophet (Mohammed), as poet (Shakespeare and Dante), as priest (Luther and John Knox), as a man of letters (Dr. Johnson, Rousseau, Burns), and as king (Cromwell and Napoleon). The whole work sets forth characteristic Carlyle ideas on the Great Man and his role in society.*

The first lecture, on Odin, was delivered on May, 5 1840. In addition to setting the stage for Carlyle's concept of the hero as a leader who is in harmony with the divine moral law, the lecture constitutes one of the earliest evidences of Victorian interest in nonclassical mythology and anticipates the use of such material for artistic purposes. It also shows signs of interest in cultural anthropology, a study that was to come into its own later in the century.

LECTURE I

The Hero as Divinity.
Odin. Paganism:
Scandinavian Mythology

WE HAVE undertaken to discourse here for a little on Great Men, their manner of appearance in our world's business, how they have shaped themselves in the world's history, what ideas men formed of them, what work they did;—on Heroes, namely, and on their reception and performance; what I call Hero-worship and the Heroic in human affairs. Too evidently this is a large topic; deserving quite other treatment than we can expect to give it at present. A large topic; indeed, an illimitable one; wide as Universal History itself. For, as I take it, Universal History, the history of what man has accomplished in this world, is at bottom the History of the Great Men who have worked here. They were the leaders of men, these great ones; the modellers, patterns, and in a wide sense creators, of whatsoever the general mass of men contrived to do or to attain; all things that we see standing accomplished in the world are properly the outer material result, the practical realisation and embodiment, of Thoughts that dwelt in the Great Men sent into the world: the soul of the whole world's history, it may justly be considered, were the history of these. Too clearly it is a topic we shall do no justice to in this place!

One comfort is, that Great Men, taken up in any way, are profitable company. We cannot look, however imperfectly, upon a great man, without gaining something by him. He is the living light-fountain, which it is good and pleasant to be near. The light which enlightens, which has enlightened the darkness of the world: and this not as a kindled lamp only, but rather as a natural luminary shining by the gift of Heaven; a flowing light-fountain, as I say, of native original insight, of manhood and heroic nobleness;—in whose radiance all souls feel that it is well with them. On any terms whatsoever, you will not grudge to wander in such neighbourhood for a while. These Six classes of Heroes, chosen out of widely-distant countries and epochs, and in mere external figure differing altogether, ought, if we look faithfully at them, to illustrate several things for us. Could we see *them* well, we should get some glimpses into the very marrow of the world's history. How happy, could I but, in any measure, in such times as these, make manifest to you the meanings of Heroism; the divine relation (for I may well call it such) which in all times unites a Great Man to other men; and thus, as it were, not exhaust my subject, but so much as break ground on it! At all events, I must make the attempt.

It is well said, in every sense, that a man's religion is the chief fact with regard to him. A man's, or a nation of men's. By religion I do not mean here the church-creed which he professes, the articles of faith which he will sign and, in words or otherwise, assert; not this wholly, in many cases not this at all. We see men of all kinds of professed creeds attain to almost all degrees of worth or worthlessness under each or any of them. This is not what I call religion, this profession and assertion; which is often only a profession and assertion from the outworks of the man, from the mere argumentative region of him, if even so deep as that. But the thing a man does practically believe (and this is often enough *without* asserting it even to himself, much less to others); the thing a man does practically lay to heart, and know for certain, concerning his vital relations to this mysterious Universe, and his duty and destiny there, that is in all cases the primary thing for him, and creatively determines all the rest. That is his *religion*; or, it may be, his mere scepticism and *no-religion*: the manner it is in which he feels himself to be spiritually related to the Unseen World or No-World; and I say, if you tell me what that is, you tell me to a very great extent what the man is, what the kind of things he will do. Of a man or of a nation we inquire, therefore, first of all, What religion they had? Was it Heathenism,—plurality of gods, mere sensuous representation of this Mystery of Life, and for chief recognised element therein Physical Force? Was it Christianism; faith in an Invisible, not as real only, but as the only reality; Time, through every meanest moment of it, resting on Eternity; Pagan empire of Force displaced by a nobler supremacy, that of Holiness? Was it Scepticism, uncertainty and inquiry whether there was an Unseen World, any Mystery of Life except a mad one;—doubt as to all this, or perhaps unbelief and flat denial? Answering of this question is giving us the soul of the history of the man or nation. The thoughts they had were the parents of the actions they did; their feelings were parents of their thoughts: it was the unseen and spiritual in them that determined the outward and actual;—their religion, as I say, was the great fact about them. In these Discourses, limited as we are, it will be good to direct our survey chiefly to that religious phasis of the matter. That once known well, all is known. We have chosen as the first Hero in our series, Odin the central figure of Scandinavian Paganism; an emblem to us of a most extensive province of things. Let us look for a little at the Hero as Divinity, the oldest primary form of Heroism.

Surely it seems a very strange-looking thing this Paganism; almost inconceivable to us in these days. A bewildering, inextricable jungle of delusions, confusions, falsehoods, and absurdities, covering the whole field of Life! A thing that fills us with astonishment, almost, if it were possible, with incredulity,—for truly it is not easy to understand that sane men could ever calmly, with their eyes open, believe and live by such a set of doctrines. That men should have worshipped their poor fellow-man as a God, and not him only, but stocks and stones, and all manner of animate and inanimate objects; and fashioned for themselves such a distracted chaos of hallucinations by way of Theory of the Universe: all this looks like an incredible fable. Nevertheless it is a clear fact that they did it. Such hideous inextricable jungle of misworships, misbeliefs, men, made as we are, did actually hold by, and live at home in. This is strange. Yes, we may pause in sorrow and silence over the depths of darkness that are in man; if we rejoice in the heights of purer vision he has attained to. Such things were and are in man; in all men; in us too.

Some speculators have a short way of accounting for the Pagan religion: mere quackery, priestcraft, and dupery, say they; no sane man ever did believe it,—merely contrived to persuade other men, not worthy of the name of sane, to believe it! It will be often our duty to protest against this sort of hypothesis about men's doings and history; and I here, on the very threshold, protest against it in reference to Paganism, and to all other *isms* by which man has ever for a length of time striven to walk in this world. They have all had a truth in them, or men would not have taken them up. Quackery and dupery do abound; in religions, above all in the more advanced decaying stages of religions, they have fearfully abounded: but quackery was never the originating influence in such things; it was not

the health and life of such things, but their disease, the sure precursor of their being about to die! Let us never forget this. It seems to me a most mournful hypothesis, that of quackery giving birth to any faith even in savage men. Quackery gives birth to nothing; gives death to all things. We shall not see into the true heart of anything, if we look merely at the quackeries of it; if we do not reject the quackeries altogether; as mere diseases, corruptions, with which our and all men's sole duty is to have done with them, to sweep them out of our thoughts as out of our practice. Man everywhere is the born enemy of lies. I find Grand Lamaism itself to have a kind of truth in it. Read the candid, clear-sighted, rather sceptical Mr. Turner's *Account of his Embassy* to that country, and see. They have their belief, these poor Thibet people, that Providence sends down always an Incarnation of Himself into every generation. At bottom some belief in a kind of Pope! At bottom still better, belief that there is a *Greatest* Man; that *he* is discoverable; that, once discovered, we ought to treat him with an obedience which knows no bounds! This is the truth of Grand Lamaism; the 'discoverability' is the only error here. The Thibet priests have methods of their own of discovering what Man is Greatest, fit to be supreme over them. Bad methods: but are they so much worse than our methods,—of understanding him to be always the eldest-born of a certain genealogy? Alas, it is a difficult thing to find good methods for!——We shall begin to have a chance of understanding Paganism, when we first admit that to its followers it was, at one time, earnestly true. Let us consider it very certain that men did believe in Paganism; men with open eyes, sound senses, men made altogether like ourselves; that we, had we been there, should have believed in it. Ask now, What Paganism could have been?

Another theory, somewhat more respectable, attributes such things to Allegory. It was a play of poetic minds, say these theorists; a shadowing-forth, in allegorical fable, in personification and visual form, of what such poetic minds had known and felt of this Universe. Which agrees, add they, with a primary law of human nature, still everywhere observably at work, though in less important things, That what a man feels intensely, he struggles to speak-out of him, to see represented before him in visual shape, and as if with a kind of life and historical reality in it. Now doubtless there is such a law, and it is one of the deepest in human nature; neither need we doubt that it did operate fundamentally in this business. The hypothesis which ascribes Paganism wholly or mostly to this agency, I call a little more respectable; but I cannot yet call it the true hypothesis. Think, would *we* believe, and take with us as our life-guidance, an allegory, a poetic sport? Not sport but earnest is what we should require. It is a most earnest thing to be alive in this world; to die is not sport for a man. Man's life never was a sport to him; it was a stern reality, altogether a serious matter to be alive!

I find, therefore, that though these Allegory theorists are on the way toward truth in this matter, they have not reached it either. Pagan Religion is indeed an Allegory, a Symbol of what men felt and knew about the Universe; and all Religions are symbols of that, altering always as that alters: but it seems to me a radical perversion, and even *inversion*, of the business, to put that forward as the origin and moving cause, when it was rather the result and termination. To get beautiful allegories, a perfect poetic symbol, was not the want of men; but to know what they were to believe about this Universe, what course they were to steer in it; what, in this mysterious Life of theirs, they had to hope and to fear, to do and to forbear doing. The *Pilgrim's Progress*[1] is an Allegory, and a beautiful, just and serious one: but consider whether Bunyan's Allegory could have *preceded* the Faith it symbolises! The Faith had to be already there, standing believed by everybody;—of which the Allegory could *then* become a shadow; and, with all its seriousness, we may say a *sportful* shadow, a mere play of the Fancy, in comparison with that awful Fact and scientific certainty which it poetically strives to emblem. The Allegory is the product of the certainty, not the producer of it; not in Bunyan's nor in any other case. For Paganism, therefore, we have still to inquire, Whence came that scientific certainty, the parent of such a bewildered heap of allegories, errors, and confusions? How was it, what was it?

Surely it were a foolish attempt to pretend 'explaining,' in this place, or in any place, such a phenomenon as that far-distant distracted cloudy imbroglio of Paganism,—more like a cloudfield than a distant continent of firm land and facts! It is no longer a reality, yet it was one. We ought to understand that this seeming cloudfield was once a reality; that not poetic allegory, least of all that dupery and deception was the origin of it. Men, I say, never did believe idle songs, never

riskcd their soul's life on allegories: men in all times, especially in early earnest times, have had an instinct for detecting quacks, for detesting quacks. Let us try if, leaving out both the quack theory and the allegory one, and listening with affectionate attention to that far-off confused rumour of the Pagan ages, we cannot ascertain so much as this at least, That there was a kind of fact at the heart of them; that they too were not mendacious and distracted, but in their own poor way true and sane!

You remember that fancy of Plato's, of a man who had grown to maturity in some dark distance, and was brought on a sudden into the upper air to see the sun rise. What would his wonder be, his rapt astonishment at the sight we daily witness with indifference! With the free open sense of a child, yet with the ripe faculty of a man, his whole heart would be kindled by that sight, he would discern it well to be Godlike, his soul would fall down in worship before it. Now, just such a childlike greatness was in the primitive nations. The first Pagan Thinker among rude men, the first man that began to think, was precisely this child-man of Plato's. Simple, open as a child, yet with the depth and strength of a man. Nature had as yet no name to him; he had not yet united under a name the infinite variety of sights, sounds, shapes and motions, which we now collectively name Universe, Nature, or the like,—and so with a name dismiss it from us. To the wild deep-hearted man all was yet new, not veiled under names or formulas; it stood naked, flashing-in on him there, beautiful, awful, unspeakable. Nature was to this man, what to the Thinker and Prophet it for ever is, *preternatural*. This green flowery rock-built earth, the trees, the mountains, rivers, many-sounding seas;—that great deep sea of azure that swims overhead; the winds sweeping through it; the black cloud fashioning itself together, now pouring out fire, now hail and rain; what *is* it? Ay, what? At bottom we do not yet know; we can never know at all. It is not by our superior insight that we escape the difficulty; it is by our superior levity, our inattention, out *want* of insight. It is by *not* thinking that we cease to wonder at it. Hardened round us, encasing wholly every notion we form, is a wrappage of traditions, hearsays, mere *words*. We call that fire of the black thunder-cloud 'electricity,' and lecture learnedly about it, and grind the like of it

---

[1] 1678, by John Bunyan (1628–88).

out of glass and silk: but *what* is it? What made it? Whence comes it? Whither goes it? Science has done much for us; but it is a poor science that would hide from us the great deep sacred infinitude of Nescience, whither we can never penetrate, on which all science swims as a mere superficial film. This world, after all our science and sciences, is still a miracle; wonderful, inscrutable, *magical* and more, to whosoever will *think* of it.

That great mystery of TIME, were there no other; the illimitable, silent, never-resting thing called Time, rolling, rushing on, swift, silent, like an all-embracing ocean-tide, on which we and all the Universe swim like exhalations, like apparitions which *are,* and then *are not*: this is for ever very literally a miracle; a thing to strike us dumb,—for we have no word to speak about it. This Universe, ah me—what could the wild man know of it; what can we yet know? That it is a Force, and thousandfold Complexity of Forces; a Force which is *not we*. That is all; it is not we, it is altogether different from *us*. Force, Force, everywhere Force; we ourselves a mysterious Force in the centre of that. 'There is not a leaf rotting on the highway but has Force in it: how else could it rot?' Nay surely, to the Atheistic Thinker, if such a one were possible, it must be a miracle too, this huge illimitable whirlwind of Force, which envelops us here; never-resting whirlwind, high as Immensity, old as Eternity. What is it? God's creation, the religious people answer; it is the Almighty God's! Atheistic science babbles poorly of it, with scientific nomenclatures, experiments and what-not, as if it were a poor dead thing, to be bottled-up in Leyden jars[2] and sold over counters: but the natural sense of man, in all times, if he will honestly apply his sense, proclaims it to be a living thing,—ah, an unspeakable, godlike thing; towards which the best attitude for us, after never so much science, is awe, devout prostration and humility of soul; worship if not in words, then in silence.

But now I remark further: What in such a time as ours it requires a Prophet or Poet to teach us, namely, the stripping-off of those poor undevout wrappages, nomenclatures and scientific hearsays,—this, the ancient earnest soul, as yet unencumbered with these things, did for itself. The world, which is now divine only to the gifted, was then divine to whosoever would turn

his eye upon it. He stood bare before it face to face. 'All was Godlike or God:'—Jean Paul still finds it so; the giant Jean Paul, who has power to escape out of hearsays: but there then were no hearsays. Canopus shining-down over the desert, with its blue diamond brightness (that wild blue spirit-like brightness, far brighter than we ever witness here), would pierce into the heart of the wild Ishmaelitish man, whom it was guiding through the solitary waste there. To his wild heart, with all feelings in it, with no *speech* for any feeling, it might seem a little eye, that Canopus, glancing-out on him from the great deep Eternity; revealing the inner Splendour to him. Cannot we understand how these men *worshipped* Canopus; became what we call Sabeans, worshipping the stars? Such is to me the secret of all forms of Paganism. Worship is transcendent wonder; wonder for which there is now no limit or measure; that is worship. To these primeval men, all things and everything they saw exist beside them were an emblem of the Godlike, or some God.

And look what perennial fibre of truth was in that. To us also, through every star, through every blade of grass, is not a God made visible, if we will open our minds and eyes? We do not worship in that way now: but is it not reckoned still a merit, proof of what we call a 'poetic nature,' that we recognise how every object has a divine beauty in it; how every object still verily is 'a window through which we may look into Infinitude itself'? He that can discern the loveliness of things, we call him Poet, Painter, Man of Genius, gifted, lovable. These poor Sabeans[3] did even what he does,—in their own fashion. That they did it, in what fashion soever, was a merit: better than what the entirely stupid man did, what the horse and camel did,— namely, nothing!

But now if all things whatsoever that we look upon are emblems to us of the Highest God, I add that more so than any of them is man such an emblem. You have heard of St. Chrysostom's[4] celebrated saying in reference to the Shekinah, or Ark of Testimony, visible Revelation of God, among the Hebrews: 'The true Shekinah is Man!' Yes, it is even so: this is no vain phrase; it is veritably so. The essence of our being, the mystery in us that calls itself 'I,'—ah, what words have we for such things?—is a breath of Heaven; the Highest Being reveals himself in man. This

---

[2] An electrical condenser.   [3] Mesopotamian star worshippers.
[4] St. John Chrysostom (347?–407), the "golden mouthed," Greek Church father.

body, these faculties, this life of ours, is it not all as a vesture for that Unnamed? 'There is but one Temple in the Universe,' says the devout Novalis, 'and that is the Body of Man. Nothing is holier than that high form. Bending before men is a reverence done to this Revelation in the Flesh. We touch Heaven when we lay our hand on a human body!' This sounds much like a mere flourish of rhetoric; but it is not so. If well meditated, it will turn out to be a scientific fact; the expression, in such words as can be had, of the actual truth of the thing. *We* are the miracle of miracles,—the great inscrutable mystery of God. We cannot understand it, we know not how to speak of it; but we may feel and know, if we like, that it is verily so.

Well; these truths were once more readily felt than now. The young generations of the world, who had in them the freshness of young children, and yet the depth of earnest men, who did not think that they had finished-off all things in Heaven and Earth by merely giving them scientific names, but had to gaze direct at them there, with awe and wonder: they felt better what of divinity is in man and Nature;—they, without being mad, could *worship* Nature, and man more than anything else in Nature. Worship, that is, as I said above, admire without limit: this, in the full use of their faculties, with all sincerity of heart, they could do. I consider Hero-worship to be the grand modifying element in that ancient system of thought. What I called the perplexed jungle of Paganism sprang, we may say, out of many roots: every admiration, adoration of a star or natural object, was a root or fibre of a root; but Hero-worship is the deepest root of all; the tap-root, from which in a great degree all the rest were nourished and grown.

And now if worship even of a star had some meaning in it, how much more might that of a Hero! Worship of a Hero is transcendent admiration of a Great Man. I say great men are still admirable; I say there is, at bottom, nothing else admirable! No nobler feeling than this of admiration for one higher than himself dwells in the breast of man. It is to this hour, and at all hours, the vivifying influence in man's life. Religion I find stand upon it; not Paganism only, but far higher and truer religions,—all religion hitherto known. Hero-worship, heartfelt religion hitherto known. Hero-worship, heartfelt prostrate admiration, submission, burning, boundless, for a noblest godlike Form of Man,—

is not that the germ of Christianity itself? The greatest of all Heroes is One—whom we do not name here! Let sacred silence meditate that sacred matter; you will find it the ultimate perfection of a principle extant throughout man's whole history on earth.

Or coming into lower, less *un*speakable provinces, is not all Loyalty akin to religious Faith also? Faith is loyalty to some inspired Teacher, some spiritual Hero. And what therefore is loyalty proper, the life-breath of all society, but an effluence of Hero-worship, submissive admiration for the truly great? Society is founded on Hero-worship. All dignities of rank, on which human association rests, are what we may call a *Hero*archy (Government of Heroes),—or a Hierarchy, for it is 'sacred' enough withal! The Duke means *Dux,* Leader; King is *Kön-ning, Kan-ning,* Man that *knows* or *cans.*[5] Society everywhere is some representation, not *in*supportably inaccurate, of a graduated Worship of Heroes;—reverence and obedience done to men really great and wise. Not *in*supportably inaccurate, I say! They are all as bank-notes, these social dignitaries, all representing gold;—and several of them, alas, always are *forged* notes. We can do with some forged false notes; with a good many even; but not with all, or the most of them forged! No: there have to come revolutions then; cries of Democracy, Liberty and Equality, and I know not what:—the notes being all false, and no gold to be had for *them,* people take to crying in their despair that there is no gold, that there never was any!—'Gold,' Hero-worship, *is* nevertheless, as it was always and everywhere, and cannot cease till man himself ceases.

I am well aware that in these days Hero-worship, the thing I call Hero-worship, professes to have gone out, and finally ceased. This, for reasons which it will be worth while some time to inquire into, is an age that as it were denies the existence of great men; denies the desirableness of great men. Show our critics a great man, a Luther for example, they begin to what they call 'account' for him; not to worship him, but take the dimensions of him,—and bring him out to be a little kind of man! He was the 'creature of the Time,' they say; the Time called him forth, the Time did everything, he nothing—but what we the little critic could have done too! This seems to me but melancholy work. The Time call forth? Alas, we have known Times *call* loudly enough for their great man; but not find him when they

---

[5] A mistaken etymology; see *Sartor,* Book Third: "Organic Filaments."

called! He was not there; Providence had not sent him; the Time, *calling* its loudest, had to go down to confusion and wreck because he would not come when called.

For if we will think of it, no Time need have gone to ruin, could it have *found* a man great enough, a man wise and good enough: wisdom to discern truly what the Time wanted, valour to lead it on the right road thither; these are the salvation of any Time. But I liken common languid Times, with their unbelief, distress, perplexity, with their languid doubting characters and embarrassed circumstances, impotently crumbling-down into ever worse distress towards final ruin;—all this I liken to dry dead fuel, waiting for the lightning out of Heaven that shall kindle it. The great man, with his free force direct out of God's own hand, is the lightning. His word is the wise healing word which all can believe in. All blazes round him now, when he has once struck on it, into fire like his own. The dry mouldering sticks are thought to have called him forth. They did want him greatly; but as to calling him forth—!—Those are critics of small vision, I think, who cry: 'See, is it not the sticks that made the fire?' No sadder proof can be given by a man of his own littleness than disbelief in great men. There is no sadder symptom of a generation than such general blindness to the spiritual lightning, with faith only in the heap of barren dead fuel. It is the last consummation of unbelief. In all epochs of the world's history, we shall find the Great Man to have been the indispensable saviour of his epoch;—the lightning, without which the fuel never would have burnt. The History of the World, I said already, was the Biography of Great Men.

Such small critics do what they can to promote unbelief and universal spiritual paralysis: but happily they cannot always completely succeed. In all times it is possible for a man to arise great enough to feel that they and their doctrines are chimeras and cobwebs. And what is notable, in no time whatever can they entirely eradicate out of living men's hearts a certain altogether peculiar reverence for Great Men; genuine admiration, loyalty, adoration, however dim and perverted it may be. Hero-worship endures for ever while man endures. Boswell venerates his Johnson, right truly even in the Eighteenth century. The unbelieving French believe in their Voltaire; and burst-out round him into very curious Hero-worship, in that last act of his life when they 'stifle him under roses.' It has always seemed to me extremely curious this of

Voltaire. Truly, if Christianity be the highest instance of Hero-worship, then we may find here in Voltaireism one of the lowest! He whose life was that of a kind of Antichrist, does again on this side exhibit a curious contrast. No people ever were so little prone to admire at all as those French of Voltaire. *Persiflage* was the character of their whole mind; adoration had nowhere a place in it. Yet see! The old man of Ferney comes up to Paris; an old, tottering, infirm man of eighty-four years. They feel that he too is a kind of Hero; that he has spent his life in opposing error and injustice, delivering Calases, unmasking hypocrites in high places;—in short that *he* too, though in a strange way, has fought like a valiant man. They feel withal that, if *persiflage* be the great thing, there never was such a *persifleur*. He is the realised ideal of every one of them; the thing they are all wanting to be; of all Frenchmen the most French. *He* is properly their god,—such god as they are fit for. Accordingly all persons, from the Queen Antoinette to the Douanier at the Porte St. Denis, do they not worship him? People of quality disguise themselves as tavern-waiters. The Maître de Poste, with a broad oath, orders his Postillion, '*Va bon train*; thou art driving M. de Voltaire.' At Paris his carriage is 'the nucleus of a comet, whose train fills whole streets.' The ladies pluck a hair or two from his fur, to keep it as a sacred relic. There was nothing highest, beautifulest, noblest in all France, that did not feel this man to be higher, beautifuler, nobler.

Yes, from Norse Odin to English Samuel Johnson, from the divine Founder of Christianity to the withered Pontiff of Encyclopedism, in all times and places, the Hero has been worshipped. It will ever be so. We all love great men; love, venerate and bow down submissive before great men: nay can we honestly bow down to anything else? Ah, does not every true man feel that he is himself made higher by doing reverence to what is really above him? No nobler or more blessed feeling dwells in man's heart. And to me it is very cheering to consider that no sceptical logic, or general triviality, insincerity and aridity of any Time and its influences can destroy this noble inborn loyalty and worship that is in man. In times of unbelief, which soon have to become times of revolution, much down-rushing, sorrowful decay and ruin is visible to everybody. For myself, in these days, I seem to see in this indestructibility of Hero-worship the everlasting adamant lower than which the confused wreck of revolutionary things cannot fall. The confused wreck of things crumbling and even crashing and tumbling all round us in these revolutionary ages, will get down so far; *no* farther. It is an eternal corner-stone, from which they can begin to build themselves up again. That man, in some sense or other, worships Heroes; that we all of us reverence and must ever reverence Great Men: this is, to me, the living rock amid all rushings-down whatsoever;—the one fixed point in modern revolutionary history, otherwise as if bottomless and shoreless.

So much of truth, only under an ancient obsolete vesture, but the spirit of it still true, do I find in the Paganism of old nations. Nature is still divine, the revelation of the workings of God; the Hero is still worshipable: this, under poor cramped incipient forms, is what all Pagan religions have struggled, as they could, to set forth. I think Scandinavian Paganism, to us here, is more interesting than any other. It is, for one thing, the latest; it continued in these regions of Europe till the eleventh century: eight-hundred years ago the Norwegians were still worshippers of Odin. It is interesting also as the creed of our fathers; the men whose blood still runs in our veins, whom doubtless we still resemble in so many ways. Strange: they did believe that, while we believe so differently. Let us look a little at this poor Norse creed, for many reasons. We have tolerable means to do it; for there is another point of interest in these Scandinavian mythologies: that they have been preserved so well.

In that strange island Iceland,—burst-up, the geologists say, by fire from the bottom of the sea; a wild land of barrenness and lava; swallowed many months of every year in black tempests, yet with a wild gleaming beauty in summer-time; towering up there, stern and grim, in the North Ocean; with its snow jokuls, roaring geysers, sulphur-pools and horrid volcanic chasms, like the waste chaotic battle-field of Frost and Fire;—where of all places we least looked for Literature or written memorials, the record of these things was written down. On the seaboard of this wild land is a rim of grassy country, where cattle can subsist, and men by means of them and of what the sea yields; and it seems they were poetic men these, men who had deep thoughts in them, and uttered musically their thoughts. Much would be lost, had Iceland not been burst-up from the sea, not been discovered by the Northmen! The old Norse Poets were many of them natives of Iceland.

Sæmund, one of the early Christian Priests there, who perhaps had a lingering fondness for Paganism, collected certain of their old Pagan songs, just about becoming obsolete then,—Poems or Chants of a mythic, prophetic, mostly all of a religious character: that is what Norse critics call the *Elder* or Poetic *Edda*. *Edda*, a word of uncertain etymology, is thought to signify *Ancestress*.[6] Snorro Sturleson, an Iceland gentleman, an extremely notable personage, educated by this Sæmund's grandson, took in hand next, near a century afterwards, to put together, among several other books he wrote, a kind of Prose Synopsis of the whole Mythology; elucidated by new fragments of traditionary verse. A work constructed really with great ingenuity, native talent, what one might call unconscious art; altogether a perspicuous clear work, pleasant reading still: this is the *Younger* or Prose *Edda*. By these and the numerous other *Sagas*, mostly Icelandic, with the commentaries, Icelandic or not, which go on zealously in the North to this day, it is possible to gain some direct insight even yet; and see that old Norse system of Belief, as it were, face to face. Let us forget that it is erroneous Religion; let us look at it as old Thought, and try if we cannot sympathise with it somewhat.

The primary characteristic of this old Northland Mythology I find to be Impersonation of the visible workings of Nature. Earnest simple recognition of the workings of Physical Nature, as a thing wholly miraculous, stupendous, and divine. What we now lecture of as Science, they wondered at, and fell down in awe before, as Religion. The dark hostile Powers of Nature they figure to themselves as '*Jötuns*,' Giants, huge shaggy beings of a demonic character. Frost, Fire, Sea-tempest; these are Jötuns. The friendly Powers again, as Summer-heat, the Sun, are Gods. The empire of this Universe is divided between these two; they dwell apart, in perennial internecine feud. The Gods dwell above in Asgard, the Garden of the Asen, or Divinities; Jötunheim, a distant dark chaotic land, is the home of the Jötuns.

Curious all this; and not idle or inane, if we will look at the foundation of it! The power of *Fire*, or *Flame*, for instance, which we designate by some trivial chemical name, thereby hiding from ourselves the essential character of wonder that

---

[6] *Edda* may also be originally a place name. The Elder Edda was collected by Saemund the Wise, the Younger Edda by Snorri Sturlason (1179–1241).

dwells in it as in all things, is with these old Northmen, Loke, a most swift subtle *Demon*, of the brood of the Jötuns. The savages of the Ladrones Islands too (say some Spanish voyagers) thought Fire, which they never had seen before, was a devil or god, that bit you sharply when you touched it, and that lived upon dry wood. From us too no Chemistry, if it had not Stupidity to help it, would hide that Flame is a wonder. What *is* Flame?—*Frost* the old Norse Seer discerns to be a monstrous hoary Jötun, the Giant *Thrym, Hrym*; or *Rime*, the old word now nearly obsolete here, but still used in Scotland to signify hoar-frost. *Rime* was not then as now a dead chemical thing, but a living Jötun or Devil; the monstrous Jötun *Rime* drove home his Horses at night, sat 'combing their manes,'—which Horses were *Hail-Clouds*, or fleet *Frost-Winds*. His Cows—No, not his, but a kinsman's, the Giant Hymir's Cows are *Icebergs*: this Hymir 'looks at the rocks' with his devil-eye, and they *split* in the glance of it.

Thunder was not then mere Electricity, vitreous or resinous; it was the God Donner (Thunder) or Thor,—God also of beneficent Summer-heat. The thunder was his wrath; the gathering of the black clouds is the drawing-down of Thor's angry brows; the fire-bolt bursting out of Heaven is the all-rending Hammer flung from the hand of Thor: he urges his loud chariot over the mountain-tops,—that is the peal; wrathful he 'blows in his red beard,'—that is the rustling stormblast before the thunder begin. Balder again, the White God, the beautiful, the just and benignant (whom the early Christian Missionaries found to resemble Christ), is the Sun,—beautifulest of visible things; wondrous too, and divine still, after all our Astronomies and Almanacs! But perhaps the notablest god we hear-tell-of is one of whom Grimm the German Etymologist finds trace: the God *Wünsch*, or Wish. The God *Wish*;[7] who could give us all that we *wished*! Is not this the sincerest and yet rudest voice of the spirit of man? The *rudest* ideal that man ever formed; which still shows itself in the latest forms of our spiritual culture. Higher considerations have to teach us that the God *Wish* is not the true God.

Of the other Gods or Jötuns I will mention only for etymology's sake, that Sea-tempest is the Jötun *Aegir*, a very dangerous Jötun;—and now to this day, on our river Trent, as I learn, the Nottingham bargemen, when the River is in a certain flooded state (a kind of backwater, or eddying swirl it has, very dangerous to them), call it *Eager*; they cry out, 'Have a care, there is the *Eager* coming!' Curious; that word surviving, like the peak of a submerged world! The *oldest* Nottingham bargemen had believed in the God Aegir. Indeed our English blood too in good part is Danish, Norse; or rather, at bottom, Danish and Norse and Saxon have no distinction, except a superficial one,—as of Heathen and Christian, or the like. But all over our Island we are mingled largely with Danes proper,—from the incessant invasions there were: and this, of course, in a greater proportion along the east coast; and greatest of all, as I find, in the North Country. From the Humber upwards, all over Scotland, the Speech of the common people is still in a singular degree Icelandic; its Germanism has still a peculiar Norse tinge. They too are 'Normans,' Northmen,—if that be any great beauty!—

Of the chief god, Odin, we shall speak by and by. Mark at present so much; what the essence of Scandinavian and indeed of all Paganism is: a recognition of the forces of Nature as godlike, stupendous, personal Agencies,—as Gods and Demons. Not inconceivable to us. It is the infant Thought of man opening itself, with awe and wonder, on this ever-stupendous Universe. To me there is in the Norse System something very genuine, very great and manlike. A broad simplicity, rusticity, so very different from the light gracefulness of the old Greek Paganism, distinguishes this Scandinavian System. It is Thought; the genuine Thought of deep, rude, earnest minds, fairly opened to the things about them; a face-to-face and heart-to-heart inspection of the things,—the first characteristic of all good Thought in all times. Not graceful lightness, half-sport, as in the Greek Paganism; a certain homely truthfulness and rustic strength, a great rude sincerity, discloses itself here. It is strange, after our beautiful Apollo statues and clear smiling mythuses, to come down upon the Norse Gods 'brewing ale' to hold their feast with Aegir, the Sea-Jötun; sending out Thor to get the caldron for them in the Jötun country; Thör, after many adventures, clapping the Pot on his head, like a huge hat, and walking off with it,—quite lost in it, the ears of the Pot reaching down to his heels! A kind of vacant hugeness, large awkward gianthood, characterises that Norse System; enormous force, as yet altogether

---

[7] Grimm's notion of a god Wünsch is no longer held.

untutored, stalking helpless with large uncertain strides. Consider only their primary mythus of the Creation. The Gods, having got the Giant Ymer slain, a Giant made by 'warm wind,' and much confused work, out of the conflict of Frost and Fire,—determined on constructing a world with him. His blood made the Sea; his flesh was the Land, the Rocks his bones; of his eyebrows they formed Asgard their Gods'-dwelling; his skull was the great blue vault of Immensity, and the brains of it became the Clouds. What a Hyper-Brobdingnagian business! Untamed Thought, great, giantlike, enormous;—to be tamed in due time into the compact greatness, not giantlike, but godlike and stronger than gianthood, of the Shakspeares, the Goethes!— Spiritually as well as bodily these men are our progenitors.

I like, too, that representation they have of the Tree Igdrasil. All Life is figured by them as a Tree. Igdrasil, the Ash-tree of Existence, has its roots deep-down in the kingdoms of Hela or Death; its trunk reaches up heaven-high, spreads its boughs over the whole Universe: it is the Tree of Existence. At the foot of it, in the Death-kingdom, sit Three *Nornas*, Fates,—the Past, Present, Future; watering its roots from the Sacred Well. Its 'boughs,' with their buddings and disleafings,—events, things suffered, things done, catastrophes,—stretch through all lands and times. Is not every leaf of it a biography, every fibre there an act or word? Its boughs are Histories of Nations. The rustle of it is the noise of Human Existence, onwards from of old. It grows there, the breath of Human Passion rustling through it;—or stormtost, the stormwind howling through it like the voice of all the gods. It is Igdrasil, the Tree of Existence. It is the past, the present, and the future; what was done, what is doing, what will be done; 'the infinite conjugation of the verb *To do*.' Considering how human things circulate, each inextricably in communion with all,—how the word I speak to you today is borrowed, not from Ulfila[8] the Mœsogoth only, but from all men since the first man began to speak,—I find no similitude so true as this of a Tree. Beautiful; altogether beautiful and great. The '*Machine* of the Universe,'—alas, do but think of that on contrast!

Well, it is strange enough this old Norse view of Nature; different enough from what we believe of Nature. Whence it specially came, one would not like to be compelled to say very minutely! One thing we may say: It came from the thoughts of Norse men;—from the thought, above all, of the *first* Norse man who had an original power of thinking. The First Norse 'man of genius,' as we should call him! Innumerable men had passed by, across this Universe, with a dumb vague wonder, such as the very animals may feel; or with a painful, fruitlessly inquiring wonder, such as men only feel;—till the great Thinker came, the *original* man, the Seer; whose shaped spoken Thought awakes the slumbering capability of all into Thought. It is ever the way with the Thinker, the spiritual Hero. What he says, all men were not far from saying, were longing to say. The Thoughts of all start up, as from painful enchanted sleep, round his Thought; answering to it, Yes, even so! Joyful to men as the dawning of day from night;—*is* it not, indeed, the awakening for them from no-being into being, from death into life? We still honour such a man; call him Poet, Genius, and so forth: but to these wild men he was a very magician, a worker of miraculous unexpected blessing for them; a Prophet, a God!—Thought once awakened does not again slumber; unfolds itself into a System of Thought; grows, in man after man, generation after generation,—till its full stature is reached, and *such* System of Thought can grow no further, but must give place to another.

For the Norse people, the Man now named Odin, and Chief Norse God, we fancy, was such a man. A Teacher, and Captain of soul and of body; a Hero, of worth *im*measurable; admiration for whom, transcending the known bounds, became adoration. Has he not the power of articulate Thinking; and many other powers, as yet miraculous? So, with boundless gratitude, would the rude Norse heart feel. Has he not solved for them the sphinx-enigma of this Universe; given assurance to them of their own destiny there? By him they know now what they have to do here, what to look for hereafter. Existence has become articulate, melodious by him; he first has made Life alive!—We may call this Odin, the origin of Norse Mythology: Odin, or whatever name the First Norse Thinker bore while he was a man among men. His view of the Universe once promulgated, a like view starts into being in all minds; grows, keeps ever growing, while it continues credible there. In all minds it lay written, but invisibly, as in sympathetic ink; at his word it starts into visibility in

[8] Or Wulfilas (c. 311–83), Gothic bishop and translator of the Bible.

all. Nay, in every epoch of the world, the great event, parent of all others, is it not the arrival of a Thinker in the world?—

One other thing we must not forget; it will explain, a little, the confusion of these Norse Eddas. They are not one coherent System of Thought; but properly the *summation* of several successive systems. All this of the old Norse Belief which is flung-out for us, in one level of distance in the Edda, like a picture painted on the same canvas, does not at all stand so in the reality. It stands rather at all manner of distances and depths, of successive generations since the Belief first began. All Scandinavian thinkers, since the first of them, contributed to that Scandinavian System of Thought; in ever-new elaboration and addition, it is the combined work of them all. What history it had, how it changed from shape to shape, by one thinker's contribution after another, till it got to the full final shape we see it under in the *Edda,* no man will now ever know: *its* Councils of Trebisond, Councils of Trent, Athanasiuses,[9] Dantes, Luthers, are sunk without echo in the dark night! Only that it had such a history we can all know. Wheresoever a thinker appeared, there in the thing he thought-of was a contribution, accession, a change or revolution made. Alas, the grandest 'revolution' of all, the one made by the man Odin himself, is not this too sunk for us like the rest! Of Odin what history? Strange rather to reflect that he *had* a history! That this Odin, in his wild Norse vesture, with his wild beard and eyes, his rude Norse speech and ways, was a man like us; with our sorrows, joys, with our limbs, features;—intrinsically all one as we: and did such a work! But the work, much of it, has perished; the worker, all to the name. 'Wednesday,' men will say tomorrow; Odin's day! Of Odin there exists no history; no document of it; no guess about it worth repeating.

Snorro indeed, in the quietest manner, almost in a brief business style, writes down in his *Heimskringla,* how Odin was a heroic Prince, in the Black-Sea region, with Twelve Peers, and a great people straitened for room. How he led these *Asen* (Asiatics) of his out of Asia; settled them in the North parts of Europe, by warlike conquest; invented Letters, Poetry and so forth,—

and came by and by to be worshipped as Chief God by these Scandinavians, his Twelve Peers made into Twelve Sons of his own, Gods like himself: Snorro has no doubt of this. Saxo Grammaticus,[10] a very curious Northman of that same century, is still more unhesitating; scruples not to find out a historical fact in every individual mythus, and writes it down as a terrestrial event in Denmark or elsewhere. Torfæus, learned and cautious, some centuries later, assigns by calculation a *date* for it: Odin, he says, came into Europe about the Year 70 before Christ. Of all which, as grounded on mere uncertainties, found to be untenable now, I need say nothing. Far, very far beyond the Year 70! Odin's date, adventures, whole terrestrial history, figure and environment are sunk from us for ever into unknown thousands of years.

Nay Grimm,[11] the German Antiquary, goes so far as to deny that any man Odin ever existed. He proves it by etymology. The word *Wuotan,* which is the original form of *Odin,* a word spread, as name of their chief Divinity, over all the Teutonic Nations everywhere; this word, which connects itself, according to Grimm, with the Latin *vadere,* with the English *wade* and suchlike,—means primarily *Movement,* Source of Movement, Power; and is the fit name of the highest god, not of any man. The word signifies Divinity, he says, among the old Saxon, German and all Teutonic Nations; the adjectives formed from it all signify *divine, supreme,* or something pertaining to the chief god. Like enough! We must bow to Grimm in matters etymological. Let us consider it fixed that *Wuotan* means *Wading,* force of *Movement.* And now still, what hinders it from being the name of a Herioic Man and *Mover,* as well as of a god? As for the adjectives, and words formed from it,—did not the Spaniards in their universal admiration for Lope, get into the habit of saying 'a Lope flower,' 'a Lope *dama,*' if the flower or woman were of surpassing beauty? Had this lasted, *Lope* would have grown, in Spain, to be an adjective signifying *godlike* also. Indeed, Adam Smith,[12] in his *Essay on Language,* surmises that all adjectives whatsoever were formed precisely in that way: some very green thing, chiefly notable for its greenness, got the appellative name *Green,* and then the next thing remarkable for

[9] Council of Trebisond, possibly Council of Chalcedon (451): there was no Council of Trebizond; Council of Trent (1545–64), Roman Catholic council; St. Athanasius (c. 296–373), early Church leader, opponent of Arian heresy.

[10] Saxo Grammaticus (c. 1140–1206), "the scholar," Danish chronicler, author of *Gesta Danorum.*

[11] Jakob Grimm (1785–1863), German philologist and folklorist.

[12] Adam Smith (1723–90), Scottish economist and philosopher.

that quality, a tree for instance, was named the *green* tree,—as we still say 'the *steam* coach,' 'four-horse coach,' or the like. All primary adjectives, according to Smith, were formed in this way; were at first substantives and things. We cannot annihilate a man for etymologies like that! Surely there was a First Teacher and Captain; surely there must have been an Odin, palpable to the sense at one time: no adjective, but a real Hero of flesh and blood! The voice of all tradition, history or echo of history, agrees with all that thought will teach one about it, to assure us of this.

How the man Odin came to be considered a *god,* the chief god?—that surely is a question which nobody would wish to dogmatise upon. I have said, his people knew no *limits* to their admiration of him; they had as yet no scale to measure admiration by. Fancy your own generous heart's-love of some greatest man expanding till it *transcended* all bounds, till it filled and overflowed the whole field of your thought! Or what if this man Odin,—since a great deep soul, with the afflatus and mysterious tide of vision and impulse rushing on him he knows not whence, is ever an enigma, a kind of terror and wonder to himself,—should have felt that perhaps *he* was divine; that *he* was some effluence of the 'Wuotan,' '*Movement,*' Supreme Power and Divinity, of whom to his rapt vision all Nature was the awful Flame-image; that some effluence of *Wuotan* dwelt here in him! He was not necessarily false; he was but mistaken, speaking the truest he knew. A great soul, any sincere soul, knows not *what* he is,—alternates between the highest height and the lowest depth; can, of all things, the least measure—Himself! What others take him for, and what he guesses that he may be; these two items strangely act on one another, help to determine one another. With all men reverently admiring him; with his own wild soul full of noble ardours and affections, of whirlwind chaotic darkness and glorious new light; a divine Universe bursting all into godlike beauty round him, and no man to whom the like ever had befallen, what could he think himself to be? 'Wuotan?' All men answered, 'Wuotan!'—

And then consider what mere Time will do in such cases; how if a man was great while living, he becomes tenfold greater when dead. What an enormous *camera-obscura* magnifier is Tradition! How a thing grows in the human Memory, in the human Imagination, when love, worship, and all that lies in the human Heart, is there to encourage it. And in the darkness, in the entire ignorance; without date or document, no book, no Arundel-marble;[13] only here and there some dumb monumental cairn. Why, in thirty or forty years, were there no books, any great man would grow *mythic,* the contemporaries who had seen him, being once all dead. And in three-hundred years, and in three-thousand years—!— To attempt *theorising* on such matters would profit little: they are matters which refuse to be *theoremed* and diagramed; which Logic ought to know that she *cannot* speak of. Enough for us to discern, far in the uttermost distance, some gleam as of a small real light shining in the centre of that enormous camera-obscura image; to discern that the centre of it all was not a madness and nothing, but a sanity and something.

This light, kindled in the great dark vortex of the Norse mind, dark but living, waiting only for light; this is to me the centre of the whole. How such light will then shine out, and with wondrous thousandfold expansion spread itself, in forms and colours, depends not on *it,* so much as on the National Mind recipient of it. The colours and forms of your light will be those of the *cut-glass* it has to shine through.—Curious to think how, for every man, any the truest fact is modelled by the nature of the man! I said, The earnest man, speaking to his brother men, must always have stated what seemed to him a *fact,* a real Appearance of Nature. But the way in which such Appearance or fact shaped itself,—what sort of *fact* it became for him,—was and is modified by his own laws of thinking; deep, subtle, but universal, ever-operating laws. The world of Nature, for every man, is the Phantasy of Himself; this world is the multiplex 'Image of his own Dream.' Who knows to what unnameable subtleties of spiritual law all these Pagan Fables owe their shape! The number *Twelve,* divisiblest of all, which could be halved, quartered, parted into three, into six, the most remarkable number, —this was enough to determine the *Signs of the Zodiac,* the number of Odin's *Sons,* and innumerable other Twelves. Any vague rumour of number had a tendency to settle itself into Twelve. So with regard to every other matter. And quite unconsciously too,—with no notion of building-up "Allegories'! But the fresh clear glance of those First Ages would be prompt in

---

[13] Greek marble tablet containing historical data, acquired by the Earl of Arundel and presented by his descendants to Oxford.

discerning the secret relations of things, and wholly open to obey these. Schiller finds in the *Cestus of Venus*[14] an everlasting æsthetic truth as to the nature of all Beauty; curious:—but he is careful not to insinuate that the old Greek Mythists had any notion of lecturing about the 'Philosophy of Criticism'!——On the whole, we must leave those boundless regions. Cannot we conceive that Odin was a reality? Error indeed, error enough: but sheer falsehood, idle fables, allegory aforethought,—we will not believe that our Fathers believed in these.

Odin's *Runes* are a significant feature of him. Runes, and the miracles of 'magic' he worked by them, make a great feature in tradition. Runes are the Scandinavian Alphabet; suppose Odin to have been the inventor of Letters, as well as 'magic,' among that people! It is the greatest invention man has ever made, this of marking-down the unseen thought that is in him by written characters. It is a kind of second speech, almost as miraculous as the first. You remember the astonishment and incredulity of Atahualpa[15] the Peruvian King; how he made the Spanish Soldier who was guarding him scratch *Dios* on his thumb-nail, that he might try the next soldier with it, to ascertain whether such a miracle was possible. If Odin brought Letters among his people, he might work magic enough!

Writing by Runes has some air of being original among the Norsemen: not a Phœnician Alphabet, but a native Scandinavian one. Snorro tells us further that Odin invented Poetry; the music of human speech, as well as that miraculous runic marking of it. Transport yourselves into the early childhood of nations; the first beautiful morning-light of our Europe, when all yet lay in fresh young radiance as of a great sunrise, and our Europe was first beginning to think, to be! Wonder, hope; infinite radiance of hope and wonder, as of a young child's thoughts, in the hearts of these strong men! Strong sons of Nature; and here was not only a wild Captain and Fighter; discerning with his wild flashing eyes what to do, with his wild lion-heart daring and doing it; but a Poet too, all that we mean by a Poet, Prophet, great devout Thinker and Inventor,—as the truly Great Man ever is. A Hero is a Hero at all points; in the soul and thought of him first of all. This Odin, in his rude semi-articulate way, had a word to speak. A great heart laid open to take in this great

Universe, and man's Life here, and utter a great word about it. A Hero, as I say, in his own rude manner; a wise, gifted, noble-hearted man. And now, if we still admire such a man beyond all others, what must these wild Norse souls, first awakened into thinking, have made of him! To them, as yet without names for it, he was noble and noblest; Hero, Prophet, God; *Wuotan*, the greatest of all. Thought is Thought, however it speak or spell itself. Intrinsically, I conjecture, this Odin must have been of the same sort of stuff as the greatest kind of men. A great thought in the wild deep heart of him! The rough words he articulated, are they not the rudimental roots of those English words we still use? He worked so, in that obscure element. But he was as a *light* kindled in it; a light of Intellect, rude Nobleness of heart, the only kind of lights we have yet; a Hero, as I say: and he had to shine there, and make his obscure element a little lighter,—as is still the task of us all.

We will fancy him to be the Type Norseman; the finest Teuton whom that race had yet produced. The rude Norse heart burst-up into *boundless* admiration round him; into adoration. He is as a root of so many great things; the fruit of him is found growing, from deep thousands of years, over the whole field of Teutonic Life. Our own Wednesday, as I said, is it not still Odin's Day? Wednesbury, Wansborough, Wanstead, Wandsworth: Odin grew into England too, these are still leaves from that root! He was the Chief God to all the Teutonic Peoples; their Pattern Norseman;—in such way did *they* admire their Pattern Norseman; that was the fortune he had in the world.

Thus if the man Odin himself have vanished utterly, there is this huge Shadow of him which still projects itself over the whole History of his People. For this Odin once admitted to be God, we can understand well that the whole Scandinavian Scheme of Nature, or dim No-scheme, whatever it might before have been, would now begin to develop itself altogether differently, and grow thenceforth in a new manner. What this Odin saw into, and taught with his runes and his rhymes, the whole Teutonic People laid to heart and carried forward. His way of thought became their way of thought:—such, under new conditions, is the history of every great thinker still. In gigantic confused lineaments, like some enormous camera-obscura shadow thrown upwards from

[14] Venus's girdle, capable of giving the wearer amatory powers.
[15] Atahualpa (c. 1502–33), the last of the Inca rulers.

the dead deeps of the Past, and covering the whole Northern Heaven, is not that Scandinavian Mythology in some sort the Portraiture of this man Odin? The gigantic image of *his* natural face, legible or not legible there, expanded and confused in that manner! Ah, Thought, I say, is always Thought. No great man lives in vain. The History of the world is but the Biography of great men.

To me there is something very touching in this primeval figure of Heroism; in such artless, helpless, but hearty entire reception of a Hero by his fellow-men. Never so helpless in shape, it is the noblest of feelings, and a feeling in some shape or other perennial as man himself. If I could show in any measure, what I feel deeply for a long time now, That it is the vital element of manhood, the soul of man's history here in our world,—it would be the chief use of this discoursing at present. We do not now call our great men Gods, nor admire *without* limit; ah no, *with* limit enough! But if we have no great men, or do not admire at all,—that were a still worse case.

This poor Scandinavian Hero-worship, that whole Norse way of looking at the Universe, and adjusting oneself there, has an indestructible merit for us. A rude childlike way of recognising the divineness of Nature, the divineness of Man; most rude, yet heartfelt, robust, giantlike; betokening what a giant of a man this child would yet grow to!—It was a truth, and is none. Is it not as the half-dumb stifled voice of the long-buried generations of our own Fathers, calling out of the depths of ages to us, in whose veins their blood still runs: 'This then, this is what *we* made of the world: this is all the image and notion we could form to ourselves of this great mystery of a Life and Universe. Despise it not. You are raised high above it, to large free scope of vision; but you too are not yet at the top. No, your notion too, so much enlarged, is but a partial, imperfect one; that matter is a thing no man will ever, in time or out of time, comprehend; after thousands of years of ever-new expansion, man will find himself but struggling to comprehend again a part of it: the thing is larger than man, not to be comprehended by him; an Infinite thing!'

The essence of the Scandinavian, as indeed of all Pagan Mythologies, we found to be recognition of the divineness of Nature; sincere communion of man with the mysterious invisible Powers visibly seen at work in the world round him. This, I should say, is more sincerely done in the Scandinavian than in any Mythology I know. Sincerity is the great characteristic of it. Superior sincerity (far superior) consoles us for the total want of old Grecian grace. Sincerity, I think, is better than grace. I feel that these old Northmen were looking into Nature with open eye and soul: most earnest, honest; childlike, and yet manlike; with a great-hearted simplicity and depth and freshness, in a true, loving, admiring, unfearing way. A right valiant, true old race of men. Such recognition of Nature one finds to be the chief element of Paganism: recognition of Man, and his Moral Duty, though this too is not wanting, comes to be the chief element only in purer forms of religion. Here, indeed, is a great distinction and epoch in Human Beliefs; a great landmark in the religious development of Mankind. Man first puts himself in relation with Nature and her Powers, wonders and worships over those; not till a later epoch does he discern that all Power is Moral, that the grand point is the distinction for him of Good and Evil, of *Thou shalt* and *Thou shalt not*.

With regard to all these fabulous delineations in the *Edda,* I will remark, moreover, as indeed was already hinted, that most probably they must have been of much newer date; most probably, even from the first, were comparatively idle for the old Norsemen, and as it were a kind of Poetic sport. Allegory and Poetic Delineation, as I said above, cannot be religious Faith; the Faith itself must first be there, then Allegory enough will gather round it, as the fit body round its soul. The Norse Faith, I can well suppose, like other Faiths, was most active while it lay mainly in the silent state, and had not yet much to say about itself, still less to sing.

Among those shadowy *Edda* matters, amid all that fantastic congeries of assertions, and traditions, in their musical Mythologies, the main practical belief a man could have was probably not much more than this: of the *Valkyrs* and the *Hall of Odin*; of an inflexible *Destiny*; and that the one thing needful for a man was *to be brave*. The *Valkyrs* are Choosers of the Slain: a Destiny inexorable, which it is useless trying to bend or soften, has appointed who is to be slain; this was a fundamental point for the Norse believer;—as indeed it is for all earnest men everywhere, for a Mahomet, a Luther, for a Napoleon too. It lies at the basis this for every such man; it is the woof out of which his whole system of thought is woven. The *Valkyrs*; and then that these *Choosers* lead the brave to a heavenly *Hall of Odin*; only the base and slavish being thrust elsewhither, into the realms of Hela the Death-goddess: I take this to have been the soul of the whole Norse Belief. They understood in their heart that it was indispensable to be brave; that Odin would have no favour for them, but despise and thrust them out, if they were not brave. Consider too whether there is not something in this! It is an everlasting duty, valid in our day as in that, the duty of being brave. *Valour* is still *value*. The first duty for a man is still that of subduing *Fear*. We must get rid of Fear; we cannot act at all till then. A man's acts are slavish, not true but specious; his very thoughts are false, he thinks too as a slave and coward, till he have got Fear under his feet. Odin's creed, if we disentangle the real kernel of it, is true to this hour. A man shall and must be valiant; he must march forward, and quit himself like a man,—trusting imperturbably in the appointment and *choice* of the upper Powers; and, on the whole, not fear at all. Now and always, the completeness of his victory over Fear will determine how much of a man he is.

It is doubtless very savage that kind of valour of the old Northmen. Snorro tells us they thought it a shame and misery not to die in battle; and if natural death seemed to be coming on, they would cut wounds in their flesh, that Odin might receive them as warriors slain. Old kings, about to die, had their body laid into a ship; the ship sent forth, with sails set and slow fire burning it; that, once out at sea, it might blaze-up in flame, and in such manner bury worthily the old hero, at once in the sky and in the ocean! Wild bloody valour; yet valour of its kind; better, I say, than none. In the old Sea-kings too, what an indomitable rugged energy! Silent, with closed lips, as I fancy them, unconscious that they were specially brave; defying the wild ocean with its monsters, and all men and things;—progenitors of our own Blakes and Nelsons! No Homer sang these Norse Sea-kings; but Agamemnon's was a small audacity, and of small fruit in the world, to some of them;—to Hrolf's[16] of Normandy, for instance! Hrolf, or Rollo Duke of Normandy, the wild Sea-king, has a share in governing England at this hour.

Nor was it altogether nothing, even that wild sea-roving and battling, through so many generations. It needed to be ascertained which was the *strongest* kind of men; who were to be ruler over whom. Among the Northland Sovereigns, too, I find some who got the title *Wood-cutter*; Forest-felling Kings. Much lies in that. I suppose at bottom many of them were forest-fellers, as well as fighters, though the Skalds talk mainly of the latter,—misleading certain critics not a little; for no nation of men could ever live by fighting alone; there could not produce enough come out of that! I suppose the right good fighter was oftenest also the right good forest-feller,—the right good improver, discerner, doer and worker in every kind; for true valour, different enough from ferocity, is the basis of all. A more legitimate kind of valour that; showing itself against the untamed Forests and dark brute Powers of Nature, to conquer Nature for us. In the same direction have not we their descendants since carried it far? May such valour last for ever with us!

That the man Odin, speaking with a Hero's voice and heart, as with an impressiveness out of Heaven, told his People the infinite importance of Valour, how man thereby became a god; and that his People, feeling a response to it in their own hearts, believed this message of his, and thought it a message out of Heaven, and him a Divinity for telling it them: this seems to me the primary seed-grain of the Norse Religion, from which all manner of mythologies, symbolic practices, speculations, allegories, songs and sagas would naturally grow. Grow,—how strangely! I called it a small light shining and shaping in the huge vortex of Norse darkness. Yet the darkness itself was *alive*; consider that. It was the eager inarticulate uninstructed Mind of the whole Norse People, longing only to become articulate, to go on articulating ever further! The living doctrine grows, grows;—like a Banyan-tree; the first *seed* is the essential thing: any branch strikes itself down into the earth, becomes a new root; and so, in endless complexity, we have a whole wood, a whole jungle, one seed the parent of it all. Was not the whole Norse Religion, accordingly, in some sense, what we called 'the enormous shadow of this man's likeness'? Critics trace some affinity in some Norse mythuses, of the Creation and suchlike, with those of the Hindoos. The Cow Adumbla, 'licking the rime from the rocks,' has a kind of Hindoo look. A Hindoo Cow, transported into frosty countries. Probably enough; indeed we may say undoubtedly, these things will have a kindred with the remotest lands, with the earliest times. Thought does not die, but only is changed. The

---

[16] Rollo (c. 860–932), ancestor of William the Conqueror, possibly the same as Rolf the Ganger, a Norwegian chief banished by Harald Haarfager c. 872.

first man that began to think in this Planet of ours, he was the beginner of all. And then the second man, and the third man;—nay, every true Thinker to this hour is a kind of Odin, teaches men *his* way of thought, spreads a shadow of his own likeness over sections of the History of the World.

Of the distinctive poetic character or merit of this Norse Mythology I have not room to speak; nor does it concern us much. Some wild Prophecies we have, as the *Völuspa* in the *Elder Edda*; of a rapt, earnest, sibylline sort. But they were comparatively an idle adjunct of the matter, men who as it were but toyed with the matter, these later Skalds; and it is *their* songs chiefly that survive. In later centuries, I suppose, they would go on singing, poetically symbolising, as our modern Painters paint, when it was no longer from the inner-most heart, or not from the heart at all. This is everywhere to be well kept in mind.

Gray's fragment's[17] of Norse Lore, at any rate, will give one no notion of it;—any more than Pope will of Homer. It is no square-built gloomy palace of black ashlar marble, shrouded in awe and horror, as Gray gives it us: no; rough as the North rocks, as the Iceland deserts, it is; with a heartiness, homeliness, even a tint of good humour and robust mirth in the middle of these fearful things. The strong old Norse heart did not go upon theatrical sublimities; they had not time to tremble. I like much their robust simplicity; their veracity, directness of conception. Thor 'draws down his brows' in a veritable Norse rage; 'grasps his hammer till the *knuckles grow white.*' Beautiful traits of pity too, an honest pity. Balder 'the white God' dies; the beautiful, benignant; he is the Sungod. They try all Nature for a remedy; but he is dead. Frigga, his mother, sends Hermoder to seek or see him: nine days and nine nights he rides through gloomy deep valleys, a labyrinth of gloom; arrives at the Bridge with its gold roof: the Keeper says, 'Yes, Balder did pass here; but the Kingdom of the Dead is down yonder, far towards the North.' Hermoder rides on; leaps Hell-gate, Hela's gate; does see Balder, and speaks with him: Balder cannot be delivered. Inexorable! Hela will not, for Odin or any God, give him up. The beautiful and gentle has to remain there. His Wife had volunteered to go with him, to die with him. They shall for ever remain there. He sends his ring to Odin; Nanna

his wife sends her *thimble* to Frigga, as a remembrance Ah me!

For indeed Valour is the fountain of Pity too;—of Truth, and all that is great and good in man. The robust homely vigour of the Norse heart attaches one much, in these delineations. Is it not a trait of right honest strength, says Uhland, who has written a fine *Essay* on Thor, that the old Norse heart finds its friend in the Thunder-god? That it is not frightened away by his thunder; but finds that Summer-heat, the beautiful noble summer, must and will have thunder withal! The Norse heart *loves* this Thor and his hammer-bolt; sports with him. Thor is Summer-heat; the god of Peaceable Industry as well as Thunder. He is the Peasant's friend; his true henchman and attendant is Thialfi, *Manual Labour.* Thor himself engages in all manner of rough manual work, scorns no business for its plebeianism; is ever and anon travelling to the country of the Jötuns, harrying those chaotic Frost-monsters, subduing them, at least straitening and damaging them. There is a great broad humour in some of these things.

Thor, as we saw above, goes to Jötun-land, to seek Hymir's Caldron, that the Gods may brew beer. Hymir the huge Giant enters, his grey beard all full of hoar-frost; splits pillars with the very glance of his eye; Thor, after much rough tumult, snatches the Pot, claps it on his head; the 'handles of it reach down to his heels.' The Norse Skald has a kind of loving sport with Thor. This is the Hymir whose cattle, the critics have discovered, are Icebergs. Huge untutored Brobdingnag genius,—needing only to be tamed-down; into Shakspeares, Dantes, Goethes! It is all gone now, that old Norse work,—Thor the Thunder-god changed into Jack the Giant-killer: but the mind that made it is here yet. How strangely things grow, and die, and do not die! There are twigs of that great world-tree of Norse Belief still curiously traceable. This poor Jack of the Nursery, with his miraculous shoes of swiftness, coat of darkness, sword of sharpness, he is one. *Hynde Etin,* and still more decisively *Red Etin of Ireland,* in the Scottish Ballads, these are both derived from Norseland; *Etin* is evidently a *Jötun.* Nay, Shakspeare's *Hamlet* is a twig too of this same world-tree; there seems no doubt of that. Hamlet, *Amleth,* I find, is really a mythic personage; and his Tragedy, of the poisoned Father, poisoned asleep by drops in his ear, and the rest, is a Norse mythus! Old Saxo, as his wont

---

[17] Reference to fragments of Norse legend in the poems of Thomas Gray (1716–71).

was, made it a Danish history; Shakspeare, out of Saxo, made it what we see. That is a twig of the world-tree that has *grown*, I think;—by nature or accident that one has grown!

In fact, these old Norse songs have a *truth* in them, an inward perennial truth and greatness,—as, indeed, all must have that can very long preserve itself by tradition alone. It is a greatness not of mere body and gigantic bulk, but a rude greatness of soul. There is a sublime uncomplaining melancholy traceable in these old hearts. A great free glance into the very deeps of thought. They seem to have seen, these brave old Northmen, what Meditation has taught all men in all ages, That this world is after all but a show,—a phenomenon or appearance, no real thing. All deep souls see into that,—the Hindoo Mythologist, the German Philosopher,—the Shakspeare, the earnest Thinker, wherever he may be:

'We are such stuff as Dreams are made of!'[18]

One of Thor's expeditions, to Utgard (the *Outer* Garden, central seat of Jötun-land), is remarkable in this respect. Thialfi was with him, and Loke. After various adventures, they entered upon Giant-land; wandered over plains, wild uncultivated places, among stones and trees. At nightfull they noticed a house; and as the door, which indeed formed one whole side of the house, was open, they entered. It was a simple habitation; one large hall, altogether empty. They stayed there. Suddenly in the dead of the night loud noises alarmed them. Thor grasped his hammer; stood in the door, prepared for fight. His companions within ran hither and thither in their terror, seeking some outlet in that rude hall; they found a little closet at last, and took refuge there. Neither had Thor any battle: for, lo, in the morning it turned-out that the noise had been only the *snoring* of a certain enormous but peaceable Giant, the Giant Skrymir, who lay peaceably sleeping near by; and this that they took for a house was merely his *Glove*, thrown aside there; the door was the Glove-wrist; the little closet they had fled into was the Thumb! Such a glove;—I remark too that it had not fingers as ours have, but only a thumb, and the rest undivided: a most ancient, rustic glove!

Skrymir now carried their portmanteau all day; Thor, however, had his own suspicions, did not like the ways of Skrymir; determined at night to put an end to him as he slept. Raising his hammer, he struck down into the Giant's face a right thunderbolt blow, of force to rend rocks. The Giant merely awoke; rubbed his cheek, and said, Did a leaf fall? Again Thor struck, so soon as Skrymir again slept; a better blow than before; but the Giant only murmured, Was that a grain of sand? Thor's third stroke was with both his hands (the 'knuckles white,' I suppose), and seemed to dint deep into Skrymir's visage; but he merely checked his snore, and remarked, There must be sparrows roosting in this tree, I think; what is that they have dropt?—At the gate of Utgard, a place so high that you had to 'strain your neck bending back to see the top of it,' Skrymir went his ways. Thor and his companions were admitted; invited to share in the games going on. To Thor, for his part, they handed a Drinking-horn; it was a common feat; they told him, to drink this dry at one draught. Long and fiercely, three times over, Thor drank; but made hardly any impression. He was a weak child, they told him: could he lift that Cat he saw there? Small as the feat seemed, Thor with his whole godlike strength could not; he bent-up the creature's back, could not raise its feet off the ground, could at the utmost raise one foot. Why, you are no man, said the Utgard people; there is an Old Woman that will wrestle you! Thor, heartily ashamed, seized this haggard Old Woman; but could not throw her.

And now, on their quitting Utgard, the chief Jötun, escorting them politely a little way, said to Thor: 'You are beaten then:—yet be not so much ashamed; there was deception of appearance in it. That Horn you tried to drink was the *Sea*; you did make it ebb; but who could drink that, the bottomless! The Cat you would have lifted,—why, that is the *Midgard-snake*, the Great World-serpent, which, tail in mouth, girds and keeps-up the whole created world; had you torn that up, the world must have rushed to ruin! As for the Old Woman, she was *Time*, Old Age, Duration: with her what can wrestle? No man nor no god with her; gods or men, she prevails over all! And then those three strokes you struck,—look at these *three valleys*; your three strokes made these!' Thor looked at his attendant Jötun: it was Skrymir;—it was, say Norse critics, the old chaotic rocky *Earth* in person, and that glove-*house* was some Earth-cavern! But Skrymir had vanished; Utgard with its skyhigh gates, when Thor grasped his hammer to smite them, had gone to air; only the Giant's voice was heard

---

[18] *The Tempest*, IV, i, 156-57; correctly "on" not "of."

mocking: 'Better come no more to Jötunheim!'—

This is of the allegoric period, as we see, and half play, not of the prophetic and entirely devout: but as a mythus is there not real antique Norse gold in it? More true metal, rough from the Mimer-stithy, than in many a famed Greek Mythus *shaped* far better! A great broad Brobdingnag grin of true humour is in this Skrymir; mirth resting on earnestness and sadness, as the rainbow on black tempest: only a right valiant heart is capable of that. It is the grim humour of our own Ben Jonson, rare old Ben; runs in the blood of us, I fancy; for one catches tones of it, under a still other shape, out of the American Backwoods.

That is also a very striking conception that of the *Ragnarök*, Consummation, or *Twilight of the Gods*. It is in the *Völuspa* Song; seemingly a very old, prophetic idea. The Gods and Jötuns, the divine Powers and the chaotic brute ones, after long contest and partial victory by the former, meet at last in universal world-embracing wrestle and duel; World-serpent against Thor, strength against strength; mutually extinctive; and ruin, 'twilight,' sinking into darkness, swallows the created Universe. The old Universe with its Gods is sunk; but it is not final death: there is to be a new Heaven and a new Earth; a higher supreme God, and Justice to reign among men. Curious: this law of mutation, which also is a law written in man's inmost thought, had been deciphered by these old earnest Thinkers in their rude style; and how, though all dies, and even gods die, yet all death is but a phœnix fire-death, and new-birth into the Greater and the Better! It is the fundamental Law of Being for a creature made of Time, living in this Place of Hope. All earnest men have seen into it; may still see into it.

And now, connected with this, let us glance at the *last* mythus of the appearance of Thor; and end there. I fancy it to be the latest in date of all these fables; a sorrowing protest against the advance of Christianity,—set forth reproachfully by some Conservative Pagan. King Olaf[19] has been harshly blamed for his over-zeal in introducing Christianity; surely I should have blamed him far more for an under-zeal in that! He paid dear enough for it; he died by the revolt of his Pagan people, in battle, in the year 1033, at Stickelstad, near that Drontheim, where the chief Cathedral of the North has now stood for many centuries, dedicated gratefully to his memory as *Saint* Olaf. The mythus about Thor is

to this effect. King Olaf, the Christian Reform King, is sailing with fit escort along the shore of Norway, from haven to haven; dispensing justice, or doing other royal work: on leaving a certain haven, it is found that a stranger, of grave eyes and aspect, red beard, of stately robust figure, has stept in. The courtiers address him; his answers surprise by their pertinency and depth: at length he is brought to the King. The stranger's conversation here is not less remarkable, as they sail along the beautiful shore; but after some time, he addresses King Olaf thus: 'Yes, King Olaf, it is all beautiful, with the sun shining on it there; green, fruitful, a right fair home for you; and many a sore day had Thor, many a wild fight with the rock Jötuns, before he could make it so. And now you seem minded to put away Thor. King Olaf, have a care!' said the stranger, drawing-down his brows;—and when they looked again, he was nowhere to be found.— This is the last appearance of Thor on the stage of this world!

Do we not see well enough how the Fable might arise, without unveracity on the part of any one? It is the way most Gods have come to appear among men: thus, if in Pindar's time 'Neptune was seen once at the Nemean Games,' what was this Neptune too but a 'stranger of noble grave aspect,'—*fit* to be 'seen'! There is something pathetic, tragic for me in this last voice of Paganism. Thor is vanished, the whole Norse world has vanished; and will not return ever again. In like fashion to that pass away the highest things. All things that have been in this world, all things that are or will be in it, have to vanish: we have our sad farewell to give them.

That Norse Religion, a rude but earnest, sternly impressive *Consecration of Valour* (so we may define it), sufficed for these old valiant Northmen. Consecration of Valour is not a *bad* thing! We will take it for good, so far as it goes. Neither is there no use in *knowing* something about this old Paganism of our Fathers. Unconsciously, and combined with higher things, it is in *us* yet, that old Faith withal! To know it consciously, brings us into closer and clearer relation with the Past,—with our own possessions in the Past. For the whole Past, as I keep repeating, is the possession of the Present; the Past had always something *true*, and is a precious possession. In a different time, in a different place, it is always some other *side* of our common Human Nature that has been developing itself. The actual True

[19] Olaf II Haraldson (c. 995–1030), king and patron saint of Norway.

is the *sum* of all these; not any one of them by itself constitutes what of Human Nature is hitherto developed. Better to know them all than misknow them. 'To which of these Three Religions do you specially adhere?' inquires Meister of his Teacher. 'To all the Three!' answers the other: 'To all the Three; for they by their union first constitute the True Religion.'

from Past and Present

In 1842–43 Carlyle interrupted his work on the life of Oliver Cromwell to write Past and Present. *He was stimulated to do so by a visit to a workhouse in St. Ives, Huntingdonshire, where the Poor Laws condemned unemployed but able-bodied men to reside. Not too far away in Suffolk Carlyle visited the ruins of the Abbey of St. Edmundsbury (Bury St. Edmunds, St. Edmund's Burg or Fortress). The Cambridge Camden Society had just published the Latin Chronicle of Jocelin of Brakelond, a monk at Bury St. Edmunds in the twelfth century.* Past and Present *contrasts the state of affairs in nineteenth-century England, as illustrated by such misery and disorder as the workhouse, with the state of affairs in the twelfth-century monastery of Bury St. Edmunds, as illustrated by Jocelin's* Chronicle *with its story of the firm but beneficent rule of Abbot Samson. The work is at once a scathing indictment of the ills of contemporary England and a powerful evocation of medieval monastic life. It was first published in 1843.*

BOOK FIRST

PROEM

CHAPTER I

Midas

THE condition of England, on which many pamphlets are now in the course of publication, and many thoughts unpublished are going on in every reflective head, is justly regarded as one of the most ominous, and withal one of the strangest, ever seen in this world. England is full of wealth, of multifarious produce, supply for human want in every kind; yet England is dying of inanition. With unabated bounty the land of England blooms and grows; waving with yellow harvests; thick-studded with workshops, industrial implements, with fifteen millions of workers, understood to be the strongest, the cunningest and the willingest our Earth ever had; these men are here; the work they have done, the fruit they have realised is here, abundant, exuberant on every hand of us: and behold, some baleful fiat as of Enchantment has gone forth, saying, 'Touch it not, ye workers, ye master-workers, ye master-idlers; none of you can touch it, no man of you shall be the better for it; this is enchanted fruit!' On the poor workers such fiat falls first, in its rudest shape; but on the rich master-workers too it falls; neither can the rich master-idlers, nor any richest or highest man escape, but all are like to be brought low with it, and made 'poor' enough, in the money sense or a far fataler one.

Of these successful skilful workers some two millions, it is now counted, sit in Workhouses, Poor-law Prisons; or have 'out-door relief' flung over the wall to them,—the workhouse Bastille being filled to bursting, and the strong Poor-law broken asunder by a stronger.[1] They sit there, these many months now; their hope of deliverance as yet small. In workhouses, pleasantly so-named, because work cannot be done in them. Twelve-hundred-thousand workers in England alone; their cunning right-hand lamed, lying idle in their sorrowful bosom; their hopes, outlooks, share of this fair world, shut-in by narrow walls. They sit there, pent up, as in a kind of horrid

---

[1] The return of Paupers for England and Wales, at Ladyday [March 25] 1842 is, 'Indoor 221,687, Out-door 1,207,402, Total 1,429,089.' *Official Report.* [Carlyle's note]

enchantment; glad to be imprisoned and enchanted, that they may not perish starved. The picturesque Tourist,[2] in a sunny autumn day, through this bounteous realm of England, descries the Union Workhouse on his path. 'Passing by the Workhouse of St. Ives in Huntingdonshire, on a bright day last autumn,' says the picturesque Tourist, 'I saw sitting on wooden benches, in front of their Bastille and within their ring-wall and its railings, some half-hundred or more of these men. Tall robust figures, young mostly or of middle age; of honest countenance, many of them thoughtful and even intelligent-looking men. They sat there, near by one another; but in a kind of torpor, especially in a silence, which was very striking. In silence: for, alas, what word was to be said? An Earth all lying round, crying, Come and till me, come and reap me;—yet we here sit enchanted! In the eyes and brows of these men hung the gloomiest expression, not of anger, but of grief and shame and manifold inarticulate distress and weariness; they returned my glance with a glance that seemed to say, "Do not look at us. We sit enchanted here, we know not why. The Sun shines and the Earth calls; and, by the governing Powers and Impotences of this England, we are forbidden to obey. It is impossible, they tell us!" There was something that reminded me of Dante's Hell in the look of all this; and I rode swiftly away.'

So many hundred thousands sit in workhouses: and other hundred thousands have not yet got even workhouses; and in thrifty Scotland itself, in Glasgow or Edinburgh City, in their dark lanes, hidden from all but the eye of God, and of rare Benevolence the minister of God, there are scenes of woe and destitution and desolation, such as, one may hope, the Sun never saw before in the most barbarous regions where men dwelt. Competent witnesses, the brave and humane Dr. Alison,[3] who speaks what he knows, whose noble Healing Art in his charitable hands becomes once more a truly sacred one, report these things for us: these things are not of this year, or of last year, have no reference to our present state of commercial stagnation, but only to the common state. Not in sharp fever-fits, but in chronic gangrene of this kind is Scotland suffering. A Poor-law, any and every Poor-law, it may be observed, is but a temporary measure; an anodyne, not a remedy: Rich and Poor, when once the naked facts of their condition have come into collision, cannot long subsist together on a mere Poor-law. True enough:—and yet, human beings cannot be left to die! Scotland too, till something better come, must have a Poor-law, if Scotland is not to be a byword among the nations. O, what a waste is there; of noble and thrice-noble national virtues; peasant Stoicisms, Heroisms; valiant manful habits, soul of a Nation's worth,—which all the metal of Potosi[4] cannot purchase back; to which the metal of Potosi, and all you can buy with *it,* is dross and dust!

Why dwell on this aspect of the matter? It is too indisputable, not doubtful now to any one. Descend where you will into the lower class, in Town or Country, by what avenue you will, by Factory Inquiries, Agricultural Inquiries, by Revenue Returns, by Mining-Labourer Committees, by opening your own eyes and looking, the same sorrowful result discloses itself: you have to admit that the working body of this rich English Nation has sunk or is fast sinking into a state, to which all sides of it considered, there was literally never any parallel. At Stockport Assizes, —and this too has no reference to the present state of trade, being of date prior to that,—a Mother and a Father are arraigned and found guilty of poisoning three of their children, to defraud a 'burial-society' of some 3*l.* 8*s.* due on the death of each child: they are arraigned, found guilty; and the official authorities, it is whispered, hint that perhaps the case is not solitary, that perhaps you had better not prove farther into that department of things. This is in the autumn of 1841; the crime itself is of the previous year or season. 'Brutal savages, degraded Irish,' mutters the idle reader of Newspapers; hardly lingering on this incident. Yet it is an incident worth lingering on; the depravity, savagery and degraded Irishism being never so well admitted. In the British land, a human Mother and Father, of white skin and professing the Christian religion, had done this thing; they, with their Irishism and necessity and savagery, had been driven to do it. Such instances are like the highest mountain apex emerged into view; under which lies a whole mountain region and land, not yet emerged. A human Mother and Father had said to themselves, What shall we do

---

[2] I.e., Carlyle.

[3] William P. Alison (1790–1859), Scottish physician, author of *Observations on the Management of the Poor in Scotland* (1840).

[4] Site of silver mines in Bolivia.

to escape starvation? We are deep sunk here, in our dark cellar; and help is far.—Yes, in the Ugolino Hunger-tower[5] stern things happen; best-loved little Gaddo fallen dead on his Father's knees!—The Stockport Mother and Father think and hint: Our poor little starveling Tom, who cries all day for victuals, who will see only evil and not good in this world: if he were out of misery at once; he well dead, and the rest of us perhaps kept alive? It is thought, and hinted; at last it is done. And now Tom being killed, and all spent and eaten, Is it poor little starveling Jack that must go, or poor little starveling Will?—What a committee of ways and means!

In starved sieged cities, in the uttermost doomed ruin of old Jerusalem fallen under the wrath of God, it was prophesied and said, 'The hands of the pitiful women have sodden their own children.' The stern Hebrew imagination could conceive no blacker gulf of wretchedness; that was the ultimatum of degraded god-punished man. And we here, in modern England, exuberant with supply of all kinds, besieged by nothing if it be not by invisible Enchantments, are we reaching that?— —How come these things? Wherefore are they, wherefore should they be?

Nor are they of the St. Ives workhouses, of the Glasgow lanes, and Stockport cellars, the only unblessed among us. This successful industry of England, with its plethoric wealth, has as yet made nobody rich; it is an enchanted wealth, and belongs yet to nobody. We might ask, Which of us has it enriched? We can spend thousands where we once spent hundreds; but can purchase nothing good with them. In Poor and Rich, instead of noble thrift and plenty, there is idle luxury alternating with mean scarcity and inability. We have sumptuous garnitures for our Life, but have forgotten to *live* in the middle of them. It is an enchanted wealth; no man of us can yet touch it. The class of men who feel that they are truly better off by means of it, let them give us their name!

Many men eat finer cookery, drink dearer liquors,—with what advantage they can report, and their Doctors can: but in the heart of them, if we go out of the dyspeptic stomach, what increase of blessedness is there? Are they better, beautifuler, stronger, braver? Are they even what

they call 'happier'? Do they look with satisfaction on more things and human faces in this God's-Earth; do more things and human faces look with satisfaction on them? Not so. Human faces gloom discordantly, disloyally on one another. Things, if it be not mere cotton and iron things, are growing disobedient to man. The Master Worker is enchanted, for the present, like his Workhouse Workman; clamours, in vain hitherto, for a very simple sort of 'Liberty': the liberty 'to buy where he finds it cheapest, to sell where he finds it dearest.' With guineas jingling in every pocket, he was no whit richer; but now, the very guineas threatening to vanish, he feels that he is poor indeed. Poor Master Worker! And the Master Unworker, is not he in a still fataler situation? Pausing amid his game-preserves, with awful eye,—as he well may! Coercing fifty-pound tenants;[6] coercing, bribing, cajoling; 'doing what he likes with his own.' His mouth full of loud futilities, and arguments to prove the excellence of his Corn-law; and in his heart the blackest misgiving, a desperate half-consciousness that his excellent Corn-law is *in*defensible, that his loud arguments for it are of a kind to strike men too literally *dumb*.

To whom, then, is this wealth of England wealth? Who is it that it blesses; makes happier, wiser, beautifuler, in any way better? Who has got hold of it, to make it fetch and carry for him, like a true servant, not like a false mock-servant; to do him any real service whatsoever? As yet no one. We have more riches than any Nation ever had before; we have less good of them than any Nation ever had before. Our successful industry is hitherto unsuccessful; a strange success, if we stop here! In the midst of plethoric plenty, the people perish; with gold walls, and full barns, no man feels himself safe or satisfied. Workers, Master Workers, Unworkers, all men, come to a pause; stand fixed, and cannot farther. Fatal paralysis spreading inwards, from the extremities, in St. Ives workhouses, in Stockport cellars, through all limbs, as if towards the heart itself. Have we actually got enchanted, then; accursed by some god?—

Midas longed for gold, and insulted the Olympians. He got gold, so that whatsoever he touched became gold,—and he, with his long ears, was little the better for it. Midas had misjudged the celestial music-tones; Midas had

---

[5] Count Ugolino was imprisoned with his sons and let starve to death. See Dante, *Inferno*, 33.
[6] Tenants paying £50 or more annual rent were enfranchised by the Reform Bill of 1832.

insulted Apollo and the gods: the gods gave him his wish, and a pair of long ears, which also were a good appendage to it. What a truth in these old Fables!

CHAPTER II

The Sphinx

How true, for example, is that other old Fable of the Sphinx, who sat by the wayside, propounding her riddle to the passengers, which if they could not answer she destroyed them! Such a Sphinx is this Life of ours, to all men and societies of men. Nature, like the Sphinx, is of womanly celestial loveliness and tenderness; the face and bosom of a goddess, but ending in claws and the body of a lioness. There is in her a celestial beauty,—which means celestial order, pliancy to wisdom; but there is also a darkness, a ferocity, fatality, which are infernal. She is a goddess, but one not yet disimprisoned; one still half-imprisoned,—the articulate, lovely, still encased in the inarticulate, chaotic. How true! And does she not propound her riddles to us? Of each man she asks daily, in mild voice, yet with a terrible significance, 'Knowest thou the meaning of this Day? What thou canst do Today; wisely attempt to do?' Nature, Universe, Destiny, Existence, howsoever we name this grand unnamable Fact in the midst of which we live and struggle, is as a heavenly bride and conquest to the wise and brave, to them who can discern her behests and do them; a destroying fiend to them who cannot. Answer her riddle, it is well with thee. Answer it not, pass on regarding it not, it will answer itself; the solution for thee is a thing of teeth and claws; Nature is a dumb lioness, deaf to thy pleadings, fiercely devouring. Thou art not now her victorious bridegroom; thou art her mangled victim, scattered on the precipices, as a slave found treacherous, recreant, ought to be and must.

With Nations it is as with individuals: Can they rede the riddle of Destiny? This English Nation, will it get to know the meaning of *its* strange new Today? Is there sense enough extant, discoverable anywhere or anyhow, in our united twenty-seven million heads to discern the same; valour enough in our twenty-seven million hearts to dare and do the bidding thereof? It will be seen!—

The secret of gold Midas, which he with his long ears never could discover, was, That he had offended the Supreme Powers;—that he had parted company with the eternal inner Facts of this Universe, and followed the transient outer Appearances thereof; and so was arrived *here*. Properly it is the secret of all unhappy men and unhappy nations. Had they known Nature's right truth, Nature's right truth would have made them free. They have become enchanted; stagger spell-bound, reeling on the brink of huge peril, because they were not wise enough. They have forgotten the right Inner True, and taken up with the Outer Sham-true. They answer the Sphinx's question *wrong*. Foolish men cannot answer it aright! Foolish men mistake transitory semblance for eternal fact, and go astray more and more.

Foolish men imagine that because judgment for an evil thing is delayed, there is no justice, but an accidental one, here below. Judgment for an evil thing is many times delayed some day or two, some century or two, but it is sure as life, it is sure as death! In the centre of the world-whirlwind, verily now as in the oldest days, dwells and speaks a God. The great soul of the world is *just*. O brother, can it be needful now, at this late epoch of experience, after eighteen centuries of Christian preaching for one thing, to remind theee of such a fact; which all manner of Mahometans, old Pagan Romans, Jews, Scythians and heathen Greeks, and indeed more or less all men that God made, have managed at one time to see into; nay which thou thyself, till 'redtape' strangled the inner life of thee, hadst once some inkling of: That there *is* justice here below; and even, at bottom, that there is nothing else but justice! Forget that, thou hast forgotten all. Success will never more attend thee: how can it now? Thou hast the whole Universe against thee. No more success: mere sham-success, for a day and days; rising ever higher,—towards its Tarpeian Rock.[1] Alas, how, in thy soft-hung Longacre vehicle, of polished leather to the bodily eye, of redtape philosophy, of expediencies, clubroom moralities, Parliamentary majorities to the mind's eye thou beautifully rollest: but knowest thou whitherward? It is towards the *road's end*. Old use-and-wont; established

---

[1] Criminals were cast from this precipice in Roman times.

methods, habitudes, *once* true and wise; man's noblest tendency, his perseverance, and man's ignoblest, his inertia; whatsoever of noble and ignoble Conservatism there is in men and Nations, strongest always in the strongest men and Nations: all this is as a road to thee, paved smooth through the abyss,—till all this *end*. Till men's bitter necessities can endure thee no more. Till Nature's patience with thee is done; and there is no road or footing any farther, and the abyss yawns sheer!—

Parliament and the Courts of Westminster are venerable to me; how venerable; gray with a thousand years of honourable age! For a thousand years and more, Wisdom and faithful Valour, struggling amid much Folly and greedy Baseness, not without most sad distortions in the struggle, have built them up; and they are as we see. For a thousand years, this English Nation has found them useful or supportable: they have served this English Nation's want; *been* a road to it through the abyss of Time. They are venerable, they are great and strong. And yet it is good to remember always that they are not the venerablest, not the greatest, nor the strongest! Acts of Parliament are venerable; but if they correspond not with the writing on the 'Adamant Tablet,'[2] what are they? Properly their one element of venerableness, of strength or greatness, is, that they at all times correspond therewith as near as by human possibility they can. They are cherishing destruction in their bosom every hour that they continue otherwise.

Alas, how many causes that can plead well for themselves in the Courts of Westminster; and yet in the general Court of the Universe, and free Soul of Man, have no word to utter! Honourable Gentlemen may find this worth considering, in times like ours. And truly, the din of triumphant Law-logic, and all shaking of horse-hair wigs and learned-serjeant gowns having comfortably ended, we shall do well to ask ourselves withal, What says that high and highest Court to the verdict? For it is the Court of Courts, that same; where the universal soul of Fact and very Truth sits President;—and thitherward, more and more swiftly, with a really terrible increase of swiftness, all causes do in these days crowd for revisal,—for confirmation, for modification, for reversal with costs. Dost thou know that Court; hast thou had any Law-practice there? What, didst thou never enter; never file any petition of redress, reclaimer,

disclaimer or demurrer, written as in thy heart's blood, for thy own behoof or another's; and silently await the issue? Thou knowest not such a Court? Hast merely heard of it by faint tradition as a thing that was or had been? Of thee, I think, we shall get little benefit.

For the gowns of learned-serjeants are good: parchment records, fixed forms, and poor terrestrial Justice, with or without horse-hair, what sane man will not reverence these? And yet, behold, the man is not sane but insane, who considers these alone as venerable. Oceans of horse-hair, continents of parchment, and learned-serjeant eloquence, were it continued till the learned tongue wore itself small in the indefatigable learned mouth, cannot make unjust just. The grand question still remains, Was the judgment just? If unjust, it will not and cannot get harbour for itself, or continue to have footing in this Universe, which was made by other than One Unjust. Enforce it by never such statuting, three readings, royal assents; blow it to the four winds with all manner of quilted trumpeters and pursuivants, in the rear of them never so many gibbets and hangmen, it will not stand, it cannot stand. From all souls of men, from all ends of Nature, from the Throne of God above, there are voices bidding it: Away, away! Does it take no warning; does it stand, strong in its three readings, in its gibbets and artillery-parks? The more woe is to it, the frightfuler woe. It will continue standing for its day, for its year, for its century, doing evil all the while; but it has One enemy who is Almighty: dissolution, explosion, and the everlasting Laws of Nature incessantly advance towards it; and the deeper its rooting, more obstinate its continuing, the deeper also and huger will its ruin and overturn be.

In this God's-world, with its wild-whirling eddies and mad foam-oceans, where men and nations perish as if without law, and judgment for an unjust thing is sternly delayed, dost thou think that there is therefore no justice? It is what the fool hath said in his heart.[3] It is what the wise, in all times, were wise because they denied, and knew forever not to be. I tell thee again, there is nothing else but justice. One strong thing I find here below: the just thing, the true thing. My friend, if thou hadst all the artillery of Woolwich[4] trundling at thy back in support of an unjust thing; and infinite bonfires visibly waiting ahead of thee, to blaze centuries long for thy

---

[2] In the ancient world laws were engraved on bronze tablets.
[3] Cf. Psalms 14:1.   [4] Location of government arsenal near London.

victory on behalf of it,—I would advise thee to call halt, to fling down thy baton, and say, 'In God's name, No!' Thy 'success'? Poor devil, what will thy success amount to? If the thing is unjust, thou hast not succeeded; no, not though bonfires blazed from North to South, and bells rang, and editors wrote leading-articles, and the just thing lay trampled out of sight, to all mortal eyes an abolished and annihilated thing. Success? In few years thou wilt be dead and dark,—all cold, eyeless, deaf; no blaze of bonfires, ding-dong of bells or leading-articles visible or audible to thee again at all forever: What kind of success is that!—

It is true, all goes by approximation in this world; with any not insupportable approximation we must be patient. There is a noble Conservatism as well as an ignoble. Would to Heaven, for the sake of Conservatism itself, the noble alone were left, and the ignoble, by some kind severe hand, were ruthlessly lopped away, forbidden evermore to show itself! For it is the right and noble alone that will have victory in this struggle; the rest is wholly an obstruction, a postponement and fearful imperilment of the victory. Towards an eternal centre of right and nobleness, and of that only, is all this confusion tending. We already know whither it is all tending; what will have victory, what will have none! The Heaviest will reach the centre. The Heaviest, sinking through complex fluctuating media and vortices, has its deflexions, its obstructions, nay at time its resiliences, its reboundings; whereupon some blockhead shall be heard jubilating, 'See, your Heaviest ascends!'—but at all moments it is moving centreward, fast as is convenient for it; sinking, sinking; and, by laws older than the World, old as the Maker's first Plan of the World, it has to arrive there.

Await the issue. In all battles, if you await the issue, each fighter has prospered according to his right. His right and his might, at the close of the account, were one and the same. He has fought with all his might, and in exact proportion to all his right he has prevailed. His very death is no victory over him. He dies indeed; but his work lives, very truly lives. A heroic Wallace,[5] quartered on the scaffold, cannot hinder that his Scotland become, one day, a part of England: but he does hinder that it become, on tyrannous unfair terms, a part of it; commands still, as with

a god's voice, from his old Valhalla and Temple of the Brave, that there be a just real union as of brother and brother, not a false and merely semblant one as of slave and master. If the union with England be in fact one of Scotland's chief blessings, we thank Wallace withal that it was not the chief curse. Scotland is not Ireland; no, because brave men rose there, and said, 'Behold, ye must not tread us down like slaves; and ye shall not,—and cannot!' Fight on, thou brave true heart, and falter not, through dark fortune and through bright. The cause thou fightest for, so far as it is true, no farther, yet precisely so far, is very sure of victory. The falsehood alone of it will be conquered, will be abolished, as it ought to be: but the truth of it is part of Nature's own Laws, coöperates with the World's eternal Tendencies, and cannot be conquered.

The *dust* of controversy, what is it but the *falsehood* flying off from all manner of conflicting true forces, and making such a loud dust-whirlwind,—that so the truths alone may remain, and embrace brother-like in some true resulting-force! It is ever so. Savage fighting Heptarchies:[6] their fighting is an ascertainment, who has the right to rule over whom; that out of such waste-bickering Saxondom a peacefully coöperating England may arise. Seek through this Universe; if with other than owl's eyes, thou wilt find nothing nourished there, nothing kept in life, but what has right to nourishment and life. The rest, look at it with other than owl's eyes, is not living; is all dying, all as good as dead! Justice was ordained from the foundations of the world; and will last with the world and longer.

From which I infer that the inner sphere of Fact, in this present England as elsewhere, differs infinitely from the outer sphere and spheres of Semblance. That the Temporary, here as elsewhere, is too apt to carry it over the Eternal. That he who dwells in the temporary Semblances, and does not penetrate into the eternal Substance, will *not* answer the Sphinx-riddle of Today, or of any Day. For the substance alone is substantial; that *is* the law of Fact; if you discover not that, Fact, who already knows it, will let you also know it by and by.

What is Justice? that, on the whole, is the question of the Sphinx to us. The law of Fact is, that Justice must and will be done. The sooner

---

[5] William Wallace (c. 1274–1305), Scottish patriot, hanged in London, his remains were quartered and the quarters sent to Newcastle, Berwick, Stirling, and Perth as admonitions.
[6] The kingdoms of Anglo-Saxon England.

the better; for the Time grows stringent, frightfully pressing! 'What is Justice?[7] ask many, to whom cruel Fact alone will be able to prove responsive. It is like jesting Pilate asking, What is Truth? Jesting Pilate had not the smallest chance to ascertain what was Truth. He could not have known it, had a god shown it to him. Thick serene opacity, thicker than amaurosis, veiled those smiling eyes of his to Truth; the inner *retina* of them was gone paralytic, dead. He looked at Truth; and discerned her not, there where she stood. 'What is Justice?' The clothed embodied Justice that sits in Westminster Hall, with penalties, parchments, tipstaves, is very visible. But the *un*embodied Justice, whereof that other is either an emblem, or else is a fearful indescribability, is not so visible! For the unembodied Justice is of Heaven; a Spirit, and Divinity of Heaven,—*in*visible to all but the noble and pure of soul. The impure ignoble gaze with eyes, and she is not there. They will prove it to you by logic, by endless Hansard Debatings[8] by bursts of Parliamentary eloquence. It is not consolatory to behold! For properly, as many men as there are in a Nation who *can* withal see Heaven's invisible Justice, and know it to be on Earth also omnipotent, so many men are there who stand between a Nation and perdition. So many, and no more. Heavy-laden England, how many hast thou in this hour? The Supreme Power sends new and ever new, all *born* at least with hearts of flesh and not of stone;—and heavy Misery itself, once heavy enough, will prove didactic!—

BOOK SECOND

THE ANCIENT MONK

CHAPTER II

St. Edmundsbury

THE *Burg,* Bury, or 'Berry' as they call it, of St. Edmund is still a prosperous brisk Town; beautifully diversifying, with its clear brick houses, ancient clean streets, and twenty or fifteen thousand busy souls, the general grassy face of Suffolk; looking out right pleasantly, from its hill-slope, towards the rising Sun: and on the eastern edge of it, still runs, long, black and massive, a range of monastic ruins; into the wide internal spaces of which the stranger is admitted on payment of one shilling. Internal spaces laid out, at present, as a botanic garden. Here stranger or townsman, sauntering at his leisure amid these vast grim venerable ruins, may persuade himself that an Abbey of St. Edmundsbury did once exist; nay there is no doubt of it: see here the ancient massive Gateway, of architecture interesting to the eye of Dilettantism; and farther on, that other ancient Gateway, now about to tumble, unless Dilettantism, in these very months, can subscribe money to cramp it and prop it![1]

Here, sure enough, is an Abbey; beautiful in the eye of Dilettantism. Giant Pedantry also will step in, with its huge *Dugdale* and other enormous *Monasticons*[2] under its arm, and cheerfully apprise you, That this was a very great Abbey, owner and indeed creator of St. Edmund's Town itself, owner of wide lands and revenues; nay that its lands were once a county of themselves; that indeed King Canute or Knut was very kind to it, and gave St. Edmund his own gold crown off his head, on one occasion: for the rest, that the Monks were of such and such a genus, such and such a number; that they had so many carucates of land in this hundred, and so many in that; and then farther that the large Tower or Belfry was built by such a one, and the smaller Belfry was built by etc. etc.—Till human nature can stand no more of it; till human nature desperately take refuge in forgetfulness, almost in flat disbelief of the whole business, Monks, Monastery, Belfries, Carucates and all! Alas, what mountains of dead ashes, wreck and burnt bones, does assiduous Pedantry dig up from the Past Time, and name it History, and Philosophy of History; till, as we say, the human soul sinks wearied and bewildered; till the Past Time seems all one infinite incredible gray void, without sun, stars, hearth-fires, or candle-light; dim offensive dust-whirlwinds filling universal Nature; and over your Historical Library, it is as if all the Titans had written for themselves: DRY RUBBISH SHOT HERE!

---

[7] John 18:38.
[8] The proceedings of the House of Commons, named after the printer Hansard.
[1] At the time of writing a campaign was under way to collect money to preserve the abbey.
[2] Sir William Dugdale (1605–86) wrote the *Monasticon Anglicanum,* a source book on the history of English monasteries.

And yet these grim old walls are not a dilettantism and dubiety; they are an earnest fact. It was a most real and serious purpose they were built for! Yes, another world it was, when these black ruins, white in their new mortar and fresh chiselling, first saw the sun as walls, long ago. Gauge not, with thy dilettante compasses, with that placid dilettante simper, the Heaven's-Watchtower of our Fathers, the fallen God's-Houses, the Golgotha of true Souls departed!

Their architecture, belfries, land-carucates? Yes,—and that is but a small item of the matter. Does it never give thee pause, this other strange item of it, that men then had a *soul*,—not by hearsay alone, and as a figure of speech; but as a truth that they *knew*, and practically went upon! Verily it was another world then. Their Missals have become incredible, a sheer platitude, sayest thou? Yes, a most poor platitude; and even, if thou wilt, an idolatry and blasphemy, should any one persuade *thee* to believe them, to pretend praying by them. But yet it is pity we had lost tidings of our souls:—actually we shall have to go in quest of them again, or worse in all ways will befall! A certain degree of soul, as Ben Jonson reminds us, is indispensable to keep the very body from destruction of the frightfulest sort; to 'save us,' says he, 'the expense of *salt*.'[3] Ben has known men who had soul enough to keep their body and five senses from becoming carrion, and save salt:—men, and also Nations. You may look in Manchester Hunger-mobs and Corn-law Commons Houses, and various other quarters, and say whether either soul or else salt is not somewhat wanted at present!—

Another world, truly: and this present poor distressed world might get some profit by looking wisely into it, instead of foolishly. But at lowest, O dilettante friend, let us know always that it *was* a world, and not a void infinite of gray haze with fantasms swimming in it. These old St. Edmundsbury walls, I say, were not peopled with fantasms; but with men of flesh and blood, made altogether as we are. Had thou and I then been, who knows but we ourselves had taken refuge from an evil Time, and fled to dwell here, and meditate on an Eternity, in such fashion as we could? Alas, how like an old osseous fragment, a broken blackened shinbone of the old dead Ages, this black ruin looks out, not yet covered by the soil; still indicating what a once gigantic Life lies buried there! It is dead now, and dumb; but

was alive once, and spake. For twenty generations, here was the earthly arena where painful living men worked out their life-wrestle,—looked at by Earth, by Heaven and Hell. Bells tolled to prayers; and men, of many humours, various thoughts, chanted vespers, matins;—and round the little islet of their life rolled forever (as round ours still rolls, though we are blind and deaf) the illimitable Ocean, tinting all things with *its* eternal hues and reflexes; making strange prophetic music! How silent now; all departed, clean gone. The World-Dramaturgist has written: *Exeunt*. The devouring Time-Demons have made away with it all: and in its stead, there is either nothing; or what is worse, offensive universal dust-clouds, and gray eclipse of Earth and Heaven, from 'dry rubbish shot here'!—

Truly it is no easy matter to get across the chasm of Seven Centuries, filled with such material. But here, of all helps, is not a Boswell the welcomest; even a small Boswell? Veracity, true simplicity of heart, how valuable are these always! He that speaks what *is* really in him, will find men to listen, though under never such impediments. Even gossip, springing free and cheery from a human heart, this too is a kind of veracity and *speech*;—much preferable to pedantry and inane gray haze! Jocelin is weak and garrulous, but he is human. Through the thin watery gossip of our Jocelin, we do get some glimpses of that deep-buried Time; discern veritably, though in a fitful intermittent manner, these antique figures and their life-method, face to face! Beautifully, in our earnest loving glance, the old centuries melt from opaque to partially translucent, transparent here and there; and the void black Night, one finds, is but the summing-up of innumerable peopled luminous *Days*. Not parchment Chartularies, Doctrines of the Constitution, O Dryasdust;[4] not altogether, my erudite friend!—

Readers who please to go along with us into this poor *Jocelini Chronica* shall wander inconveniently enough, as in wintry twilight, through some poor stript hazel-grove, rustling with foolish noises, and perpetually hindering the eyesight; but across which, here and there, some real human figure is seen moving: very strange; whom we could hail if he would answer;—and we look into a pair of eyes deep as our own, *imaging* our own, but all unconscious of us; to

---

[3] Ben Jonson, *Bartholomew Fair*, IV, ii, and *The Devil Is an Ass*, I, vi.
[4] Byword for the pedantic scholar; cf. Scott's *Ivanhoe*.

whom we, for the time, are become as spirits and invisible!

CHAPTER III

Landlord Edmund

SOME three centuries or so had elapsed since *Beodric's-worth*[1] became St. Edmund's *Stow*, St. Edmund's *Town* and Monastery, before Jocelin entered himself a Novice there. 'It was,' says he, 'the year after the Flemings were defeated at Fornham St. Genevieve.'

Much passes away into oblivion: this glorious victory over the Flemings at Fornham has, at the present date, greatly dimmed itself out of the minds of men. A victory and battle nevertheless it was, in its time: some thrice-renowned Earl of Leicester, not of the De Montfort breed (as may be read in Philosophical and other Histories, could any human memory retain such things), had quarrelled with his sovereign, Henry Second of the name; had been worsted, it is like, and maltreated, and obliged to fly to foreign parts; but had rallied there into new vigour; and so, in the year 1173, returns across the German Sea with a vengeful army of Flemings. Returns, to the coast of Suffolk; to Framlingham Castle, where he is welcomed; westward towards St. Edmundsbury and Fornham Church, where he is met by the constituted authorities with *posse comitatus*; and swiftly cut in pieces, he and his, or laid by the heels; on the right bank of the obscure river Lark,—as traces still existing will verify.

For the river Lark, though not very discoverably, still runs or stagnates in that country; and the battle-ground is there; serving at present as a pleasure-ground to his Grace of Northumberland. Copper pennies of Henry II. are still found there;—rotted out from the pouches of poor slain soldiers, who had not had *time* to buy liquor with them. In the river Lark itself was fished up, within man's memory, an antique gold ring; which fond Dilettantism can almost believe may have been the very ring Countess Leicester threw away, in her flight, into that same Lark river or ditch.[2] Nay, few years ago, in tearing out an enormous superannuated ash-tree, now grown quite corpulent, bursten, superfluous, but long a fixture in the soil, and not to be dislodged without revolution,—there was laid bare, under its roots, 'a circular mound of skeletons wonderfully complete,' all radiating from a centre, faces upwards, feet inwards; a 'radiation' not of Light, but of the Nether Darkness rather; and evidently the fruit of battle; for 'many of the heads were cleft, or had arrow-holes in them.' The Battle of Fornham, therefore, is a fact, though a forgotten one; no less obscure than undeniable,—like so many other facts.

Like the St. Edmund's Monastery itself! Who can doubt, after what we have said, that there was a Monastery here at one time? No doubt at all there was a Monastery here; no doubt, some three centuries prior to this Fornham Battle, there dwelt a man in these parts of the name of Edmund, King, Landlord, Duke or whatever his title was, of the Eastern Counties;—and a very singular man and landlord he must have been.

For his tenants, it would appear, did not in the least complain of him; his labourers did not think of burning his wheat-stacks, breaking into his game-preserves; very far the reverse of all that. Clear evidence, satisfactory even to my friend Dryasdust, exists that, on the contrary, they honoured, loved, admired this ancient Landlord to a quite astonishing degree,—and indeed at last to an immeasurable and inexpressible degree; for, finding no limits or utterable words for their sense of his worth, they took to beatifying and adoring him! 'Infinite admiration,' we are taught, 'means worship.'

---

[1] Dryasdust puzzles and pokes for some biography of this Beodric; and repugns to consider him a mere East-Anglian Person of Condition, not in need of a biography,—whose beoꝥð, *weorth* or *worth*, that is to say, *Growth*, Increase, or as we should now name it, *Estate*, that same Hamlet and wood Mansion, now St. Edmund's Bury, originally was. For, adds our erudite Friend, the Saxon beoꝥðan, Equivalent to the German *werden*, means to *grow*, to *become;* traces of which old vocable are still found in the North-country dialects; as, 'What is *word* of him?' meaning, 'What is *become* of him?' and the like. Nay we in modern English still say, 'Woe *worth* the hour' (Woe *befall* the hour), and speak of the 'Weird Sisters'; not to mention the innumerable other names of places still ending in *weorth* or *worth*. and indeed, our common noun *worth,* in the sense of *value,* does not this mean simply, What a thing has *grown* to, What a man has *grown* to, How much he amounts to,—by the Threadneedle-street standard or another! [Carlyle's note]

[2] Lyttelton's *History of Henry II.* (2d edition), v. 169, etc. [Carlyle's note]

Very singular,—could we discover it! What Edmund's specific duties were; above all, what his method of discharging them with such results was, would surely be interesting to know; but are *not* very discoverable now. His Life has become a poetic, nay a religious *Mythus*; though, undeniably enough, it was once a prose Fact, as our poor lives are; and even a very rugged unmanageable one. This landlord Edmund did go about in leather shoes, with *femoralia*[3] and bodycoat of some sort on him; and daily had his breakfast to procure; and daily had contradictory speeches, and most contradictory facts not a few, to reconcile with himself. No man becomes a Saint in his sleep. Edmund, for instance, instead of *reconciling* those same contradictory facts and speeches to himself,—which means *subduing*, and in a manlike and godlike manner conquering them to himself,—might have merely thrown new contention into them, new unwisdom into them, and so been conquered *by* them; much the commoner case! In that way he had proved no 'Saint,' or Divine-looking Man, but a mere Sinner, and unfortunate, blameable, more or less Diabolic-looking man! No landlord Edmund becomes infinitely admirable in his sleep.

With what degree of wholesome rigour his rents were collected, we hear not. Still less by what methods he preserved his game, whether by 'bushing' or how,—and if the partridge-seasons were 'excellent,' or were indifferent. Neither do we ascertain what kind of Corn-bill he passed, or wisely-adjusted Sliding-scale:—but indeed there were few spinners in those days; and the nuisance of spinning, and other dusty labour, was not yet so glaring a one.

How then, it may be asked, did this Edmund rise into favour; become to such astonishing extent a recognised Farmer's Friend?[4] Really, except it were by doing justly and loving mercy to an unprecedented extent, one does not know. The man, it would seem, 'had walked,' as they say, 'humbly with God';[5] humbly and valiantly with God; struggling to make the Earth heavenly as he could: instead of walking sumptuously and pridefully with Mammon, leaving the Earth to grow hellish as it liked. Not sumptuously with Mammon? How then could he 'encourage trade,'—cause Howel and James,[6] and many

wine-merchants, to bless him, and the tailor's heart (though in a very short-sighted manner) to sing for joy? Much in this Edmund's Life is mysterious.

That he could, on occasion, do what he liked with his own, is meanwhile evident enough. Certain Heathen Physical-Force Ultra-Chartists,[7] 'Danes' as they were then called, coming into his territory with their 'five points,' or rather with their five-and-twenty thousand *points* and edges too, of pikes namely and battle-axes; and proposing mere Heathenism, confiscation, spoliation, and fire and sword,—Edmund answered that he would oppose to the utmost such savagery. They took him prisoner; again required his sanction to said proposals. Edmund again refused. Cannot we kill you? cried they.— Cannot I die? answered he. My life, I think, is my own to do what I like with! And he died, under barbarous tortures, refusing to the last breath; and the Ultra-Chartist Danes *lost* their propositions;—and went with their 'points' and other apparatus, as is supposed, to the Devil, the Father of them. Some say, indeed, these Danes were not Ultra-Chartists, but Ultra-Tories, demanding to reap where they had not sown, and live in this world without working, though all the world should starve for it; which likewise seems a possible hypothesis. Be what they might, they went, as we say, to the Devil; and Edmund doing what he liked with his own, the Earth was got cleared of them.

Another version is, that Edmund on this and the like occasion stood by his order; the oldest, and indeed only true order of Nobility known under the stars, that of Just Men and Sons of God, in opposition to Unjust and Sons of Belial,— which latter indeed are *second*-oldest, but yet a very unvenerable order. This, truly, seems the likeliest hypothesis of all. Names and appearances alter so strangely, in some half-score centuries; and all fluctuates chameleon-like, taking now this hue, now that. Thus much is very plain, and does not change hue: Landlord Edmund was seen and felt by all men to have done verily a man's part in this life-pilgrimage of his; and benedictions, and outflowing love and admiration from the universal heart, were his meed. Well-done! Well-done! cried the hearts of all men.

---

[3] Breeches.
[4] The popular name of Richard Grenville (1797–1861), Duke of Buckingham and Chandos, supporter of the Corn Laws.
[5] Micah 6:8.
[6] Furniture dealers and interior decorators of the time.
[7] The Chartists were nineteenth-century agitators for voting reform. See Carlyle's *Chartism*.

They raised his slain and martyred body; washed its wounds with fast-flowing universal tears; tears of endless pity, and yet of a sacred joy and triumph. The beautifulest kind of tears,—indeed perhaps the beautifulest kind of thing: like a sky all flashing diamonds and prismatic radiance; all weeping, yet shone on by the everlasting Sun:—and *this* is not a sky, it is a Soul and living Face! Nothing liker the *Temple of the Highest,* bright with some real effulgence of the Highest, is seen in this world.

Oh, if all Yankee-land follow a small good 'Schnüspel the distinguished Novelist'[8] with blazing torches, dinner-invitations, universal hep-hep-hurrah, feeling that he, though small, *is* something; how might all Angle-land once follow a hero-martyr and great true Son of Heaven! It is the very joy of man's heart to admire, where he can; nothing so lifts him from all his mean imprisonments, were it but for moments, as true admiration. Thus it has been said, 'all men, especially all women, are born worshippers'; and will worship, if it be but possible. Possible to worship a Something, even a small one; not so possible a mere loud-blaring Nothing! What sight is more pathetic than that of poor multitudes of persons met to gaze at King's Progresses, Lord Mayors' Shows, and other gilt-gingerbread phenomena of the worshipful sort, in these times; each so eager to worship; each, with a dim fatal sense of disappointment, finding that he cannot rightly here! These be thy gods, O Israel?[9] And thou art so *willing* to worship,—poor Israel!

In this manner, however, did the men of the Eastern Counties take up the slain body of their Edmund, where it lay cast forth in the village of Hoxne; seek out the severed head, and reverently reunite the same. They embalmed him with myrrh and sweet spices, with love, pity, and all high and awful thoughts; consecrating him with a very storm of melodious adoring admiration, and sun-dyed showers of tears;—joyfully, yet with awe (as all deep joy has something of the awful in it), commemorating his noble deeds and godlike walk and conversation while on Earth. Till, at length, the very Pope and Cardinals at Rome were forced to hear of it; and they, summing up as correctly as they well could, with *Advocatus-Diaboli*[10] pleadings and their other

forms of process, the general verdict of mankind, declared: That he had, in very fact, led a hero's life in this world; and being now *gone,* was gone, as they conceived, to God above, and reaping his reward *there.* Such, they said, was the best judgment they could form of the case;—and truly not a bad judgment. Acquiesced in, zealously adopted, with full assent of 'private judgment,' by all mortals.

The rest of St. Edmund's history, for the reader sees he has now become a *Saint,* is easily conceivable. Pious munificence provided him a *loculus,* a *feretrum* or shrine; built for him a wooden chapel, a stone temple, ever widening and growing by new pious gifts;—such the overflowing heart feels it is blessedness to solace itself by giving. St Edmund's Shrine glitters now with diamond flowerages, with a plating of wrought gold. The wooden chapel, as we say, has become a stone temple. Stately masonries, long-drawn arches, cloisters, sounding aisles buttress it, begirdle it far and wide. Regimented companies of men, of whom our Jocelin is one, devote themselves, in every generation, to meditate here on man's Nobleness and Awfulness, and celebrate and show forth the same, as they best can,—thinking they will do it better here, in presence of God the Maker, and of the so Awful and so Noble made by Him. In one word, St. Edmund's Body has raised a Monastery round it. To such length, in such manner, has the Spirit of the Time visibly taken body, and crystallised itself here. New gifts, houses, farms, *katalla*[11]—come ever in. King Knut, whom men call Canute, whom the Oceantide would not be forbidden to wet,—we heard already of this wise King, with his crown and gifts; but of many others, Kings, Queens, wise men and noble loyal women, let Dryasdust and divine Silence be the record! Beodric's-Worth has become St. Edmund's *Bury*;—and lasts visible to this hour. All this that thou now seest and namest Bury Town, is properly the Funeral Monument of Saint or Landlord Edmund. The present respectable Mayor of Bury may be said, like a Fakeer (little as he thinks of it), to have his dwelling in the extensive, many-sculptured Tombstone of St. Edmund; in one of the brick niches thereof dwells the present respectable Mayor of Bury.

---

[8] Probably a reference to Dickens' tour of America in 1842.
[9] Exodus 32:4.   [10] Devil's advocate.
[11] Goods, properties, what we now call *chattels,* and still more singularly *cattle,* says my erudite friend! [Carlyle's note]

Certain Times do crystallise themselves in a magnificent manner; and others, perhaps, are like to do it in rather a shabby one!—But Richard Arkwright too will have his Monument, a thousand years hence: all Lancashire and Yorkshire, and how many other shires and countries, with their machineries and industries, for his monument! A true *py*ramid or '*flame-mountain*,' flaming with steam fires and useful labour over wide continents, usefully towards the Stars, to a certain height;—how much grander than your foolish Cheops Pyramids or Sakhara clay ones![12] Let us withal be hopeful, be content or patient.

CHAPTER IV

Abbot Hugo

I T IS TRUE all thing have two faces, a light one and a dark. It is true, in three centuries much imperfection accumulates; many an Ideal, monastic or other, shooting forth into practice as it can, grows to a strange enough Reality; and we have to ask with amazement, Is this your Ideal? For, alas, the Ideal always has to grow in the Real, and to seek out its bed and board there, often in a very sorry way. No beautifulest Poet is a Bird-of-Paradise, living on perfumes; sleeping in the æther with outspread wings. The Heroic, *independent* of bed and board, is found in Drury-Lane Theatre only; to avoid disappointments, let us bear this in mind.

By the law of Nature, too, all manner of Ideals have their fatal limits and lot; their appointed periods, of youth, of maturity or perfection, of decline, degradation, and final death and disappearance. There is nothing born but has to die. Ideal monasteries, once grown real, do seek bed and board in this world; do find it more and more successfully; do get at length too intent on finding it, exclusively intent on that. They are then like diseased corpulent bodies fallen idiotic, which merely eat and sleep; *ready* for 'dissolution,' by a Henry the Eighth or some other. Jocelin's St. Edmundsbury is still far from this last dreadful state: but here too the reader will prepare

himself to see an Ideal not sleeping in the æther like a bird-of-paradise, but roosting as the common wood-fowl do, in an imperfect, uncomfortable, more or less contemptible manner!—

Abbot Hugo, as Jocelin, breaking at once into the heart of the business, apprises us, had in those days grown old, grown rather blind, and his eyes were somewhat darkened, *aliquantulum caligaverunt oculi ejus*. He dwelt apart very much, in his *Talamus* or peculiar Chamber; got into the hands of flatterers, a set of mealy-mouthed persons who strove to make the passing hour easy for him,—for him easy, and for themselves profitable; accumulating in the distance mere mountains of confusion. Old Dominus Hugo sat inaccessible in this way, far in the interior, wrapt in his warm flannels and delusions; inaccessible to all voice of Fact; and bad grew ever worse with us. Not that our worthy old *Dominus Abbas* was inattentive to the divine offices, or to the maintenance of a devout spirit in us or in himself; but the Account-Books of the Convent fell into the frightfulest state, and Hugo's annual Budget grew yearly emptier, or filled with futile expectations, fatal deficit, wind and debts!

His one worldly care was to raise ready money; sufficient for the day is the evil thereof.[1] And how he raised it: From usurious insatiable Jews; every fresh Jew sticking on him like a fresh horseleech, sucking his and our life out; crying continually, Give, give! Take one example instead of scores. Our *Camera*[2] having fallen into ruin, William the Sacristan received charge to repair it; strict charge, but no money; Abbot Hugo would, and indeed could, give him no fraction of money. The *Camera* in ruins, and Hugo penniless and inaccessible, Willelmus Sacrista borrowed Forty Marcs (some Seven-and-twenty Pounds) of Benedict the Jew, and patched-up our Camera again. But the means of repaying him? There were no means. Hardly could *Sacrista, Cellerarius,* or any public officer, get ends to meet, on the indispensablest scale, with their shrunk allowances: ready money had vanished.

Benedict's Twenty-seven pounds grew rapidly at compound-interest; and at length, when it had amounted to a Hundred pounds, he, on a day of settlement, presents the account to Hugo himself. Hugo already owed him another Hundred of his own; and so here it has become Two Hundred! Hugo, in a fine frenzy, threatens to depose the

---

[12] The Cheops, or Great Pyramid, is of stone; some of the Sakkhara pyramids are of brick.
[1] Matthew 6:34.   [2] Storehouse.

Sacristan, to do this and do that; but, in the mean while, How to quiet your insatiable Jew? Hugo, for this couple of hundreds, grants the Jew his bond for Four hundred payable at the end of four years. At the end of four years there is, of course, still no money; and the Jew now gets a bond for Eight hundred and eighty pounds, to be paid by instalments, Fourscore pounds every year. Here was a way of doing business!

Neither yet is this insatiable Jew satisfied or settled with: he had papers against us of 'small debts fourteen years old'; his modest claim amounts finally to 'Twelve hundred pounds besides interest';—and one hopes he never got satisfied in this world; one almost hopes he was one of those beleaguered Jews who hanged themselves in York Castle shortly afterwards, and had his usances and quittances and horseleech papers summarily set fire to! For approximate justice will strive to accomplish itself; if not in one way, then in another. Jews, and also Christians and Heathens, who accumulate in this manner, though furnished with never so many parchments, do, at times, 'get their grinder-teeth successfully pulled out of their head, each day a new grinder,' till they consent to disgorge again. A sad fact,—worth reflecting on.

Jocelin, we see, is not without secularity: Our *Dominus Abbas* was intent enough on the divine offices; but then his Account-Books—?—One of the things that strike us most, throughout, in Jocelin's *Chronicle,* and indeed in Eadmer's *Anselm,*[3] and other old monastic Books, written evidently by pious men, is this, That there is almost no mention whatever of 'personal religion' in them; that the whole gist of their thinking and speculation seems to be the 'privileges of our order,' 'strict exaction of our dues,' 'God's honour' (meaning the honour of our Saint), and so forth. Is not this singular? A body of men, set apart for perfecting and purifying their own souls, do not seem disturbed about that in any measure; the 'Ideal' says nothing about its idea; says much about finding bed and board for itself! How is this?

Why, for one thing, bed and board are a matter very apt to come to speech: it is much easier to *speak* of them than of ideas; and they are sometimes much more pressing with some! Nay, for another thing, may not this religious reticence, in these devout good souls, be perhaps a merit, and sign of health in them? Jocelin, Eadmer, and

such religious men, have as yet nothing of 'Methodism'; no Doubt or even root of Doubt. Religion is not a diseased self-introspection, an agonising inquiry: their duties are clear to them, the way of supreme good plain, indisputable, and they are travelling on it. Religion lies over them like an all-embracing heavenly canopy, like an atmosphere and life-element, which is not spoken of, which in all things is presupposed without speech. Is not serene or complete Religion the highest aspect of human nature; as serene Cant, or complete No-religion, is the lowest and miserablest? Between which two, all manner of earnest Methodisms, introspections, agonising inquiries, never so morbid, shall play their respective parts, not without approbation.

But let any ready fancy himself one of the Brethren in St. Edmundsbury Monastery under such circumstances! How can a Lord Abbot, all stuck-over with horseleeches of this nature, front the world? He is fast losing his life-blood, and the Convent will be as one of Pharaoh's lean kine.[4] Old monks of experience draw their hoods deeper down; careful what they say: the monk's first duty is obedience. Our Lord the King, hearing of such work, sends down his Almoner to make investigations: but what boots it? Abbot Hugo assembles us in Chapter; asks, 'If there is any complaint?' Not a soul of us dare answer, 'Yes, thousands!' but we all stand silent, and the Prior even says that things are in a very comfortable condition. Whereupon old Abbot Hugo, turning to the royal messenger, says, 'You see!'— and the business terminates in that way. I, as a brisk-eyed noticing youth and novice, could not help asking of the elders, asking of Magister Samson in particular: Why he, well-instructed and a knowing man, had not spoken out, and brought matters to a bearing? Magister Samson was Teacher of the Novices, appointed to breed us up to the rules, and I loved him well. '*Fili mi,*' answered Samson, 'the burnt child shuns the fire. Dost thou not know, our Lord the Abbot sent me once to Acre in Norfolk, to solitary confinement and bread-and-water, already? The Hinghams, Hugo and Robert, have just got home from banishment for speaking. This is the hour of darkness: the hour when flatterers rule and are believed. *Videat Dominus,* let the Lord see, and judge.'

In very truth, what could poor old Abbot Hugo do? A frail old man, and the Philistines

<hr>

[3] Eadmer (d. c. 1124), monk of Canterbury, author of *Vita Anselmi* (*Life of St. Anselm*).
[4] Genesis 41:14–36.

were upon him,—that is to say, the Hebrews. He had nothing for it but to shrink away from them: get back into his warm flannels, into his warm delusions again. Happily, before it was quite too late, he bethought him of pilgriming to St. Thomas of Canterbury. He set out, with a fit train, in the autumn days of the year 1180; near Rochester City, his mule threw him, dislocated his poor kneepan, raised incurable inflammatory fever; and the poor old man got his dismissal from the whole coil at once. St. Thomas à Becket, though in a circuitous way, had *brought* deliverance! Neither Jew usurers, nor grumbling monks, nor other importunate despicability of men or mud-elements afflicted Abbot Hugo any more; but he dropt his rosaries, closed his account-books, closed his old eyes, and lay down into the long sleep. Heavy-laden hoary old Dominus Hugo, fare thee well!

One thing we cannot mention without a due thrill of horror: namely, that, in the empty exchequer of Dominus Hugo, there was not found one penny to distribute to the Poor that they might pray for his soul! By a kind of god-send, Fifty shillings did, in the very nick of time, fall due, or seem to fall due, from one of his Farmers (the *Firmarius* de Palegrava), and he paid it, and the Poor had it; though, alas, this too only *seemed* to fall due, and we had it to pay again afterwards. Dominus Hugo's apartments were plundered by his servants, to the last portable stool, in a few minutes after the breath was out of his body. Forlorn old Hugo, fare thee well forever.

CHAPTER V

Twelfth Century

OUR Abbot being dead, the *Dominus Rex*, HENRY II., or Ranulf de Glanvill *Justiciarius*[1] of England for him, set Inspectors or Custodiars over us;—not in any breathless haste to appoint a new Abbot, our revenues coming into his own *Scaccarium*, or royal Exchequer, in the mean while. They proceeded with some rigour, these Custodiars; took written inventories, clapt-on seals, exacted everywhere strict tale and measure: but wherefore should a living monk complain? The living monk has to do his devotional drill-exercise; consume his allotted *pitantia*, what we call *pittance*, or ration of victual; and possess his soul in patience.

Dim, as through a long vista of Seven Centuries, dim and very strange looks that monk-life to us; the ever-surprising circumstance this, That it is a *fact* and no dream, that we see it there, and gaze into the very eyes of it! Smoke rises daily from those culinary chimney-throats; there are living human beings there, who chant, loud-braying, their matins, nones, vespers; awakening *echoes*, not to the bodily ear alone. St. Edmund's Shrine, perpetually illuminated, glows ruddy through the Night, and through the Night of Centuries withal; St. Edmundsbury Town paying yearly Forty pounds for that express end. Bells clang out: on great occasions, all the bells. We have Processions, Preachings, Festivals, Christmas Plays, *Mysteries* shown in the Churchyard, at which latter the Townsfolk sometimes quarrel. Time was, Time is, as Friar Bacon's Brass Head[2] remarked; and withal Time will be. There are three Tenses, *Tempora*, or Times; and there is one Eternity; and as for us,

'We are such stuff as Dreams are made of!'[3]

Indisputable, though very dim to modern vision, rests on its hill-slope that same *Bury*, *Stow*, or Town of St. Edmund; already a considerable place, not without traffic, nay manufactures, would Jocelin only tell us what. Jocelin is totally careless of telling: but, through dim fitful apertures, we can see *Fullones*, 'Fullers,' see cloth-making; looms dimly going, dye-vats, and old women spinning yarn. We have Fairs too, *Nundinæ*, in due course; and the Londoners give us much trouble, pretending that they, as a metropolitan people, are exempt from toll. Besides there is Field-husbandry, with perplexed settlement of Convent rents: corn-ricks pile themselves within burgh, in their season; and cattle depart and enter; and even the poor weaver has his cow,—'dungheaps' lying quiet at most doors (*ante foras*, says the incidental Jocelin), for the Town has yet no improved police. Watch and ward nevertheless we do keep, and have Gates,—as what Town must not; thieves so

---

[1] Ranulf de Glanvill was justiciarius, or administrator of Justice, for Henry II from 1180 to 1189.
[2] See Robert Greene, *Friar Bacon and Friar Bungay*.
[3] *The Tempest*, IV, i, 156-57: correctly "on," not "of."

abounding; war, *werra,* such a frequent thing! Our thieves, at the Abbot's judgment-bar, deny; claim wager of battle; fight, are beaten, and *then* hanged. 'Ketel, the thief,' took this course; and it did nothing for him,—merely brought us, and indeed himself, new trouble!

Everyway a most foreign Time. What difficulty, for example, has our *Cellerarius* to collect the *repselver,* 'reaping silver,' or penny, which each householder is by law bound to pay for cutting down the Convent grain! Richer people pretend that it is commuted, that it is this and the other; that, in short, they will not pay it. Our *Cellerarius* gives up calling on the rich. In the houses of the poor, our *Cellerarius* finding, in like manner, neither penny nor good promise, snatches, without ceremony, what *vadium* (pledge, *wad*) he can come at: a joint-stool, kettle, nay the very house-door, '*hostium*'; and old women, thus exposed to the unfeeling gaze of the public, rush out after him with their distaffs and the angriest shrieks: '*vetulæ exibant cum colis suis,*' says Jocelin, '*minantes et exprobrantes.*'

What a historical picture, glowing visible, as St. Edmund's Shrine by night, after Seven long Centuries or so! *Vetulæ cum colis*: My venerable ancient spinning grandmothers,—ah, and ye too have to shriek, and rush out with your distaffs; and become Female Chartists, and scold all evening with void doorway;—and in old Saxon, as we in modern, would fain demand some Five-point Charter, could it be fallen-in with, the Earth being too tyrannous!—Wise Lord Abbots, hearing of such phenomena, did in time abolish or commute the reap-penny, and one nuisance was abated. But the image of these justly offended old women, in their old wool costumes, with their angry features, and spindles brandished, lives forever in the historical memory. Thanks to thee, Jocelin Boswell. Jerusalem was taken by the Crusaders, and again lost by them; and Richard Cœur-de-Lion 'veiled his face' as he passed in sight of it: but how many other things went on, the while!

Thus, too, our trouble with the Lakenheath eels is very great. King Knut namely, or rather his Queen who also did herself honour by honouring St. Edmund, decreed by authentic deed yet extant on parchment, that the Holders of the Town Fields, once Beodric's, should, for one thing, go yearly and catch us four thousand eels in the marsh-pools of Lakenheath. Well, they went, they continued to go; but, in later times,

got into the way of returning with a most short account of eels. Not the due six-score apiece; no, Here are two-score, Here are twenty, ten,— sometimes, Here are none at all; Heaven help us, we *could* catch no more, they were not there! What is a distressed *Cellerarius* to do? We agree that each Holder of so many acres shall pay one penny yearly, and let-go the eels as too slippery. But, alas, neither is this quite effectual: the Fields, in my time, have got divided among so many hands, there is no catching of *them* either; I have known our Cellarer get seven-and-twenty pence formerly, and now it is much if he get ten pence farthing (*vix decem denarios et obolum*). And then their sheep, which they are bound to fold nightly in our pens, for the manure's sake; and, I fear, do not always fold: and their *aver-pennies,* and their *avragiums,* and their *foder-corns,* and mill-and-market dues! Thus, in its undeniable but dim manner, does old St. Edmundsbury spin and till, and laboriously keep its pot boiling, and St. Edmund's Shrine lighted, under such conditions and averages as it can.

How much is still alive in England; how much has not yet come into life! A Feudal Aristocracy is still alive, in the prime of life; superintending the cultivation of the land, and less consciously the distribution of the produce of the land, the adjustment of the quarrels of the land; judging, soldiering, adjusting; everywhere governing the people,—so that even a Gurth, born thrall of Cedric, lacks not his due parings of the pigs he tends. Governing;—and, alas, also game-preserving; so that a Robert Hood,[4] a William Scarlet and others have, in these days, put on Lincoln coats, and taken to living, in some universal-suffrage manner, under the greenwood-tree!

How silent, on the other hand, lie all Cotton-trades and such-like; not a steeple-chimney yet got on end from sea to sea! North of the Humber, a stern Willelmus Conquæstor burnt the Country, finding it unruly, into very stern repose. Wild-fowl scream in those ancient silences, wild cattle roam in those ancient solitudes; the scanty sulky Norse-bred population all coerced into silence,— feeling that, under these new Norman Governors, their history has probably as good as *ended.* Men and Northumbrian Norse populations know little what has ended, what is but beginning! The Ribble and the Aire roll down, as yet unpolluted by dyers' chemistry; tenanted by merry trouts and piscatory otters; the sunbeam and the vacant

---

[4] I.e., Robin Hood.

wind's-blast alone traversing those moors. Side by side sleep the coal-strata and the iron-strata for so many ages; no Steam-Demon has yet risen smoking into being. Saint Mungo rules in Glasgow; James Watt still slumbering in the deep of Time.[5] *Mancunium*, Manceaster, what we now call Manchester, spins no cotton,—if it be not *wool* 'cottons,' clipped from the backs of mountain sheep. The Creek of the Mersey gurgles, twice in the four-and-twenty hours, with eddying brine, clangorous with sea-fowl; and is a *Lither*-Pool, a *lazy* or sullen Pool, no monstrous pitchy City, and Seahaven of the world! The Centuries are big; and the birth-hour is coming, not yet come. *Tempus ferax, tempus edax rerum.*[6]

CHAPTER VI

Monk Samson

WITHIN doors, down at the hill-foot, in our Convent here, we are a peculiar people,—hardly conceivable in the Arkwright Corn-Law ages, of mere Spinning-Mills and Joe-Mantons![1] There is yet no Methodism among us, and we speak much of Secularities: no Methodism; our Religion is not yet a horrible restless Doubt, still less a far horribler composed Cant; but a great heaven-high Unquestionability, encompassing, inter-penetrating the whole of Life. Imperfect as we may be, we are here, with our litanies, shaven crowns, vows of poverty, to testify incessantly and indisputably to every heart, That this Earthly Life and *its* riches and possessions, and good and evil hap, are not intrinsically a reality at all, but *are* a shadow of realities eternal, infinite; that this Time-world, as an air-image, fearfully *emblematic*, plays and flickers in the grand still mirror of Eternity; and man's little Life has Duties that are great, that are alone great, and go up to Heaven and down to Hell. This, with our poor litanies, we testify, and struggle to testify.

Which, testified or not, remembered by all men or forgotten by all men, does verily remain the fact, even in Arkwright Joe-Manton ages! But it is incalculable, when litanies have grown obsolete; when *fodercorns, avragiums*, and all human dues and reciprocities have been fully changed into one great due of *cash payment*; and man's duty to man reduces itself to handing him certain metal coins, or covenanted money-wages, and then shoving him out of doors; and man's duty to God becomes a cant, a doubt, a dim inanity, a 'pleasure of virtue' or suchlike; and the thing a man does infinitely fear (the real *Hell* of a man) is, 'that he do not make money and advance himself,'—I say, it is incalculable what a change has introduced itself everywhere into human affairs! How human affairs shall now circulate everywhere not healthy life-blood in them, but, as it were, a detestable copperas banker's ink; and all is grown acrid, divisive, threatening dissolution; and the huge tumultuous Life of Society is galvanic, devil-ridden, too truly possessed by a devil! For, in short, Mammon *is* not a god at all; but a devil, and even a very despicable devil. Follow the Devil faithfully, you are sure enough to *go* to the Devil: whither else can you go?—In such situations, men look back with a kind of mournful recognition even on poor limited Monk-figures, with their poor litanies; and reflect, with Ben Jonson, that soul is indispensable, some degree of soul, even to save you the expense of salt!—

For the rest, it must be owned, we Monks of St. Edmundsbury are but a limited class of creatures, and seem to have a somewhat dull life of it. Much given to idle gossip; having indeed no other work, when our chanting is over. Listless gossip, for most part, and a mitigated slander; the fruit of idleness, not of spleen. We are dull, insipid men, many of us; easy-minded; whom prayer and digestion of food will avail for a life. We have to receive all strangers in our Convent, and lodge them gratis; such and such sorts go by rule to the Lord Abbot and his special revenues; such and such to us and our poor Cellarer, however straitened. Jews themselves send their wives and little ones hither in war-time, into our *Pitanceria*;[2] where they abide safe, with due *pittances*,—for a consideration. We have the fairest chances for collecting news. Some of us have a turn for reading Books; for meditation, silence; at times we even write Books. Some of us can preach, in English-Saxon, in Norman-

---

[5] Saint Mungo, sixth-century saint, also known as Saint Kentigern; James Watt (1736–1819), inventor of the steam engine.
[6] "Time the bearer, time the devourer of things."
[1] Guns named after their maker.
[2] Chamber where "pittances" of food were distributed.

French, and even in Monk-Latin; others cannot in any language or jargon, being stupid.

Failing all else, what gossip about one another! This is a perennial resource. How one hooded head applies itself to the ear of another, and whispers—*tacenda*.[3] Willelmus Sacrista, for instance, what does he nightly, over in that Sacristy of his? Frequent bibations, *'frequentes bibationes et quædam tacenda,'*—eheu! We have *'tempora minutionis,'* stated seasons of blood-letting, when we are all let blood together; and then there is a general free-conference, a sanhedrim of clatter. Notwithstanding our vow of poverty, we can by rule amass to the extent of 'two shillings'; but it is to be given to our necessitous kindred, or in charity. Poor Monks! Thus too a certain Canterbury Monk was in the habit of 'slipping, *clanculo,* from his sleeve,' five shillings into the hand of his mother, when she came to see him, at the divine offices, every two months. Once, slipping the money clandestinely, just in the act of taking leave, he slipt it not into her hand, but on the floor, and another had it; whereupon the poor Monk, coming to know it, looked mere despair for some days; till Lanfranc the noble Archbishop, questioning his secret from him, nobly made the sum *seven* shillings,[4] and said, Never mind!

One Monk, of a taciturn nature, distinguishes himself among these babbling ones: the name of him Samson; he that answered Jocelin, *'Fili mi,* a burnt child shuns the fire.' They call him 'Norfolk *Barrator,'* or litigious person; for indeed, being of grave taciturn ways, he is not universally a favourite; he has been in trouble more than once. The reader is desired to mark this Monk. A personable man of seven-and-forty; stout-made, stands erect as a pillar; with bushy eyebrows, the eyes of him beaming into you in a really strange way; the face massive, grave, with 'a very eminent nose'; his head almost bald, its auburn remnants of hair, and the copious ruddy beard, getting slightly streaked with gray. This is Brother Samson; a man worth looking at.

He is from Norfolk, as the nickname indicates; from Tottington in Norfolk, as we guess; the son of poor parents there. He has told me Jocelin, for I loved him much, That once in his ninth year he had an alarming dream;—as indeed we are all somewhat given to dreaming here. Little Samson, lying uneasily in his crib at Tottington, dreamed that he saw the Arch Enemy in person, just alighted in front of some grand building, with outspread bat-wings, and stretching forth detestable clawed hands to grip him, little Samson, and fly-off with him: whereupon the little dreamer shrieked desperate to St. Edmund for help, shrieked and again shrieked; and St. Edmund, a reverend heavenly figure, did come,—and indeed poor little Samson's mother, awakened by his shrieking, did come; and the Devil and the Dream both fled away fruitless. On the morrow, his mother, pondering such an awful dream, thought it were good to take him over to St. Edmund's own Shrine, and pray with him there. See, said little Samson at sight of the Abbey-Gate; see, mother, this is the building I dreamed of! His poor mother dedicated him to St. Edmund, —left him there with prayers and tears: what better could she do? The exposition of the dream, Brother Samson used to say, was this: *Diabolus* with outspread bat-wings shadowed forth the pleasures of this world, *voluptates hujus sæculi*, which were about to snatch and fly away with me, had not St. Edmund flung his arms round me, that is to say, made me a monk of his. A monk, accordingly, Brother Samson is; and here to this day where his mother left him. A learned man, of devout grave nature; has studied at Paris, has taught in the Town Schools here, and done much else; can preach in three languages, and, like Dr. Caius,[5] 'has had losses' in his time. A thoughtful, firm-standing man; much loved by some, not loved by all; his clear eyes flashing into you, in an almost inconvenient way!

Abbot Hugo, as we said, had his own difficulties with him; Abbot Hugo had him in prison once, to teach him what authority was, and how to dread the fire in future. For Brother Samson, in the time of the Antipopes, had been sent to Rome on business; and, returning successful, was too late,—the business had all misgone in the interim! As tours to Rome are still frequent with us English, perhaps the reader will not grudge to look at the method of travelling thither in those remote ages. We happily have, in small compass, a personal narrative of it. Through the clear eyes and memory of Brother Samson one peeps direct into the very bosom of that Twelfth Century, and finds it rather curious. The actual *Papa*, Father, or universal President of Christendom, as yet not

---

[3] Things one should not speak of.   [4] *Eadmeri Hist.*, p. 8. [Carlyle's note]
[5] Apparently a mistake for Dogberry in *Much Ado About Nothing;* Dr. Caius is the physician in *The Merry Wives of Windsor*.

grown chimerical, sat there; think of that only! Brother Samson went to Rome as to the real Light-fountain of this lower world; we now—!— But let us hear Brother Samson, as to his mode of travelling:

'You know what trouble I had for that Church of Woolpit; how I was despatched to Rome in the time of the Schism between Pope Alexander and Octavian; and passed through Italy at that season, when all clergy carrying letters for our Lord Pope Alexander were laid hold of, and some were clapt in prison, some hanged; and some, with nose and lips cut off, were sent forward to our Lord the Pope, for the disgrace and confusion of him (*in dedecus et confusionem ejus*). I, however, pretended to be Scotch, and putting on the garb of a Scotchman, and taking the gesture of one, walked along; and when anybody mocked at me, I would brandish my staff in the manner of that weapon they call *gaveloc*,[6] uttering comminatory words after the way of the Scotch. To those that met and questioned me who I was, I made no answer but: *Ride, ride Rome; turne Cantwereberei*.[7] Thus did I, to conceal myself and my errand, and get safer to Rome under the guise of a Scotchman.

'Having at last obtained a Letter from our Lord the Pope according to my wishes, I turned homewards again. I had to pass through a certain strong town on my road; and lo, the soldiers thereof surrounded me, seizing me, and saying: "This vagabond (*iste solivagus*), who pretends to be Scotch, is either a spy, or has Letters from the false Pope Alexander." And whilst they examined every stitch and rag of me, my leggings (*caligas*), breeches, and even the old shoes that I carried over my shoulder in the way of the Scotch,—I put my hand into the leather scrip I wore, wherein our Lord the Pope's Letter lay, close by a little jug (*ciffus*) I had for drinking out of; and the Lord God so pleasing, and St. Edmund, I got out both the Letter and the jug together; in such a way that, extending my arm aloft, I held the Letter hidden between jug and hand: they saw the jug, but the Letter they saw not. And thus I escaped out of their hands in the name of the Lord. Whatever money I had, they took from me; wherefore I had to beg from door to door, without any payment (*sine omni expensa*) till I came to England again. But hearing that the Woolpit Church was already given to Geoffry Ridell, my soul was struck with sorrow because I had laboured in vain. Coming home, therefore, I sat me down secretly under the Shrine of St. Edmund, fearing lest our Lord Abbot should seize and imprison me, though I had done no mischief; nor was there a monk who durst speak to me, nor a laic who durst bring me food except by stealth.'[8]

Such resting and welcoming found Brother Samson, with his worn soles, and strong heart! He sits silent, revolving many thoughts, at the foot of St. Edmund's Shrine. In the wide Earth, if it be not Saint Edmund, what friend or refuge has he? Our Lord Abbot, hearing of him, sent the proper officer to lead him down to prison, and clap 'foot-gyves on him' there. Another poor official furtively brought him a cup of wine; bade him 'be comforted in the Lord." Samson utters no complaint; obeys in silence. 'Our Lord Abbot, taking counsel of it, banished me to Acre, and there I had to stay long.'

Our Lord Abbot next tried Samson with promotions; made him Subsacristan, made him Librarian, which he liked best of all, being passionately fond of Books: Samson, with many thoughts in him, again obeyed in silence; discharged his offices to perfection, but never thanked our Lord Abbot,—seemed rather as if looking into him, with those clear eyes of his. Whereupon Abbot Hugo said, *Se nunquam vidisee*, He had never seen such a man; whom no severity would break to complain, and no kindness soften into smiles or thanks:—a questionable kind of man!

In this way, not without troubles, but still in an erect clear-standing manner, has Brother Samson reached his forty-seventh year; and his ruddy beard is getting slightly grizzled. He is endeavouring, in these days, to have various broken things thatched in; nay perhaps to have the Choir itself completed, for he can bear nothing ruinous. He has gathered 'heaps of lime and sand'; has masons, slaters working, he and *Warinus monachus noster*,[9] who are joint keepers of the Shrine; paying out the money duly,— furnished by charitable burghers of St. Edmundsbury, they say. Charitable burghers of St. Edmundsbury? To me Jocelin it seems rather, Samson, and Warinus whom he leads, have privily hoarded the oblations at the Shrine itself,

---

[6] Javelin, missile pike. *Gaveloc* is still the Scotch name for *crowbar*. [Carlyle's note]

[7] Does this mean, 'Rome forever; Canterbury *not*' (which claims an unjust Supremacy over us)! Mr. Rokewood is silent. Dryasdust would perhaps explain it,—the course of a week or two of talking; did one dare to question him! [Carlyle's note]

[8] *Jocelini Chronica*, p. 36. [Carlyle's note]   [9] "Warrinus, our monk."

in these late years of indolent dilapidation, while Abbot Hugo sat wrapt inaccessible; and are struggling, in this prudent way, to have the rain kept out![10]—Under what conditions, sometimes, has Wisdom to struggle with Folly; get Folly persuaded to so much as thatch out the rain from itself! For, indeed, if the Infant govern the Nurse, what dextrous practice on the Nurse's part will not be necessary!

It is a new regret to us that, in these circumstances, our Lord the King's Custodiars, interfering, prohibited all building or thatching from whatever source; and no Choir shall be completed, and Rain and Time, for the present, shall have their way. Willelmus Sacrista, he of 'the frequent bibations and some things not to be spoken of'; he, with his red nose, I am of opinion, had made complaint to the Custodiars; wishing to do Samson an ill turn:—Samson his *Subsacristan*, with those clear eyes, could not be a prime favourite of his. Samson again obeys in silence.

CHAPTER VII

The Canvassing

Now, however, come great news to St. Edmundsbury: That there is to be an Abbot elected; that our interlunar obscuration is to cease; St. Edmund's Convent no more to be a doleful widow, but joyous and once again a bride! Often in our widowed state had we prayed to the Lord and St. Edmund, singing weekly a matter of 'one-and-twenty penitential Psalms, on our knees in the Choir,' that a fit Pastor might be vouchsafed us. And, says Jocelin, had some known what Abbot we were to get, they had not been so devout, I believe!—Bozzy Jocelin opens to mankind the floodgates of authentic Convent gossip; we listen, as in a Dionysius' Ear,[1] to the inanest hubbub, like the voices at Virgil's Horn-Gate of Dreams.[2] Even gossip, seven centuries off, has significance. List, list, how like men are to one another in all centuries:

'*Dixit quidam de quodam,* A certain person said of a certain person, "He, that *Frater,* is a good monk, *probabilis persona*; knows much of the order and customs of the church; and, though not so perfect a philosopher as some others, would make a very good Abbot. Old Abbot Ording, still famed among us, knew little of letters. Besides, as we read in Fables, it is better to choose a log for king, than a serpent never so wise, that will venomously hiss and bite his subjects."—"Impossible!" answered the other: "How can such a man make a sermon in the Chapter, or to the people on festival-days, when he is without letters? How can he have the skill to bind and to loose, he who does not understand the Scriptures? How—"?'

And then 'another said of another, *alius de alio,* "That *Frater* is a *homo literatus,* eloquent, sagacious; vigorous in discipline; loves the Convent much, has suffered much for its sake." To which a third party answers, "From all your great clerks, good Lord deliver us! From Norfolk barrators and surly persons, That it would please thee to preserve us, We beseech thee to hear us, good Lord"! Then another *quidam* said of another *quodam,* "That *Frater* is a good manager (*husebondus*)"; but was swiftly answered, "God forbid that a man who can neither read nor chant, nor celebrate the divine offices, an unjust person withal, and grinder of the faces of the poor, should ever be Abbot"!' One man, it appears, is nice in his victuals. Another is indeed wise, but apt to slight inferiors; hardly at the pains to answer, if they argue with him too foolishly. And so each *aliquis* concerning his *aliquo,*—through whole pages of electioneering babble. 'For,' says Jocelin, 'So many men, as many minds.' Our Monks 'at time of blood-letting, *tempore minutionis,*' holding their sanhedrim of babble, would talk in this manner: Brother Samson, I remarked, never said anything; sat silent, sometimes smiling; but he took good note of what others said, and would bring it up, on occasion, twenty years after. As for me Jocelin, I was of opinion that 'some skill in Dialectics, to distinguish true from false,' would be good in an Abbot. I spake, as a rash Novice in those days, some conscientious words of a certain benefactor of mine; 'and behold, one of those sons of Belial' ran and reported them to him, so that he never

---

[10] *Jocelini Chronica,* p. 7. [Carlyle's note]

[1] A cave in Syracuse built by the tyrant Dionysius to enable him to hear the conversations of prisoners.

[2] Cf. *Aeneid,* VI, 893–896.

after looked at me with the same face again! Poor Bozzy!—

Such is the buzz and frothy simmering ferment of the general mind and no-mind; struggling to 'make itself up,' as the phrase is, or ascertain what *it* does really want: no easy matter, in most cases. St. Edmundsbury, in that Candlemas season of the year 1182, is a busily fermenting place. The very clothmakers sit meditative at their looms; asking, Who shall be Abbot? The *sochemanni*[3] speak of it, driving their ox-teams afield; the old women with their spindles: and none yet knows what the days will bring forth.

The Prior, however, as our interim chief, must proceed to work; get ready 'Twelve Monks,' and set off with them to his Majesty at Waltham, there shall the election be made. An election, whether managed directly by ballot-box on public hustings, or indirectly by force of public opinion, or were it even by open alehouses, landlords' coercion, popular club-law, or whatever electoral methods, is always an interesting phenomenon. A mountain tumbling in great travail, throwing up dustclouds and absurd noises, is visibly there; uncertain yet what mouse or monster it will give birth to.

Besides, it is a most important social act; nay, at bottom, the one important social act. Given the men a People choose, the People itself, in its exact worth and worthlessness, is given. A heroic people chooses heroes, and is happy; a valet or flunky people chooses sham-heroes, what are called quacks, thinking them heroes, and is not happy. The grand summary of a man's spiritual condition, what brings out all his herohood and insight, or all his flunkyhood and horn-eyed dimness, is this question put to him, What man dost thou honour? Which is thy ideal of a man; or nearest that? So too of a People: for a People too, every People, *speaks* its choice,—were it only by silently obeying, and not revolting,—in the course of a century or so. Nor are electoral methods, Reform Bills and suchlike, unimportant. A People's electoral methods are, in the long-run, the express image of its electoral *talent*; tending and gravitating perpetually, irresistibly, to a conformity with that: and are, at all stages, very significant of the People. Judicious readers, of these times, are not disinclined to see how Monks elect their Abbot in the Twelfth Century: how the St. Edmundsbury mountain manages its mid-wifery; and what mouse or man the outcome is.

CHAPTER VIII

The Election

ACCORDINGLY our Prior assembles us in Chapter; and, we adjuring him before God to do justly, nominates, not by our selection, yet with our assent, Twelve Monks, moderately satisfactory. Of whom are Hugo Third-Prior, Brother Dennis a venerable man, Walter the *Medicus*, Samson *Subsacrista*, and other esteemed characters,—though Willelmus *Sacrista*, of the red nose, too is one. These shall proceed straight-way to Waltham; and there elect the Abbot as they may and can. Monks are sworn to obedience; must not speak too loud, under penalty of foot-gyves, limbo, and bread-and-water: yet monks too would know what it is they are obeying. The St. Edmundsbury Community has no hustings, ballot-box, indeed no open voting: yet by various vague manipulations, pulse-feelings, we struggle to ascertain what its virtual aim is, and succeed better or worse.

This question, however, rises; alas, a quite preliminary question: Will the *Dominus Rex* allow us to choose freely? It is to be hoped! Well, if so, we agree to choose one of our own Convent. If not, if the *Dominus Rex* will force a stranger on us, we decide on demurring, the Prior and his Twelve shall demur: we can appeal, plead, remonstrate; appeal even to the Pope, but trust it will not be necessary. Then there is this other question, raised by Brother Samson: What if the Thirteen should not themselves be able to agree? Brother Samson *Subsacrista*, one remarks, is ready oftenest with some question, some suggestion, that has wisdom in it. Though a servant of servants, and saying little, his words all tell, having sense in them; it seems by his light mainly that we steer ourselves in this great dimness.

What if the Thirteen should not themselves be able to agree? Speak, Samson, and advise.— Could not, hints Samson, Six of our venerablest elders be chosen by us, a kind of electoral committee, here and now: of these, 'with their hand on the Gospels, with their eye on the *Sacrosancta*,'[1] we take oath that they will do faithfully; let these, in secret and as before God, agree on Three whom they reckon fittest; write their names in a Paper, and deliver the same

---

[3] A type of freehold tenant.   [1] Holy objects such as the bones of St. Edmund.

sealed, forthwith, to the Thirteen: one of those Three the Thirteen shall fix on, if permitted. If not permitted, that is to say, if the *Dominus Rex* force us to demur,—the paper shall be brought back unopened, and publicly burned, that no man's secret bring him into trouble.

So Samson advises, so we act; wisely in this and in other crises of the business. Our electoral committee, its eye on the Sacrosancta, is soon named, soon sworn; and we, striking-up the Fifth Psalm, '*Verba mea,*

> 'Give ear unto my words, O Lord,
> My meditation weigh,'

march out chanting, and leave the Six to their work in the Chapter here. Their work, before long, they announce as finished: they, with their eye on the Sacrosancta, imprecating the Lord to weigh and witness their meditation, have fixed on Three Names, and written them in this Sealed Paper. Let Samson Subsacrista, general servant of the party, take charge of it. On the morrow morning, our Prior and his Twelve will be ready to get under way.

This, then, is the ballot-box and electoral winnowing-machine they have at St. Edmundsbury: a mind fixed on the Thrice Holy, an appeal to God on high to witness their meditation: by far the best, and indeed the only good electoral winnowing-machine,—if men have souls in them. Totally worthless, it is true, and even hideous and poisonous, if men have no souls. But without soul, alas, what winnowing-machine in human elections can be of avail? We cannot get along without soul; we stick fast, the mournfulest spectacle; and salt itself will not save us!

On the morrow morning, accordingly, our Thirteen set forth; or rather our Prior and Eleven; for Samson, as general servant of the party, has to linger, settling many things. At length he too gets upon the road; and, 'carrying the sealed Paper in a leather pouch hung round his neck; and *froccum bajulans in ulnis*' (thanks to thee, Bozzy Jocelin), 'his frockskirts looped over his elbow,' showing substantial stern-works, tramps stoutly along. Away across the Heath, not yet of Newmarket and horse-jockeying; across your Fleam-dike and Devil's-dike, no longer useful as a Mercian East-Anglian boundary or bulwark: continually towards Waltham, and the Bishop of Winchester's House there, for his Majesty is in that. Brother Samson, as purse-bearer, has the reckoning always, when there is one, to pay; 'delays are numerous,'[2] progress none of the swiftest.

But, in the solitude of the Convent, Destiny thus big and in her birthtime, what gossiping, what babbling, what dreaming of dreams! The secret of the Three our electoral elders alone know: some Abbot we shall have to govern us; but which Abbot, oh, which! One Monk discerns in a vision of the night-watches, that we shall get an Abbot of our own body, without needing to demur: a prophet appeared to him clad all in white, and said 'Ye shall have one of yours, and he will rage among you like a wolf, *sæviet ut lupus.*' Verily!—then which of ours? Another Monk now dreams: he has seen clearly which; a certain Figure taller by head and shoulders than the other two, dressed in alb and *pallium,* and with the attitude of one about to fight;—which tall Figure a wise Editor would rather not name at this stage of the business! Enough that the vision is true: that Saint Edmund himself, pale and awful, seemed to rise from his Shrine, with naked feet, and say audibly, 'He *ille,* shall veil my feet'; which part of the vision also proves true. Such guessing, visioning, dim perscrutation of the momentous future: the very clothmakers, old women, all townsfolk speak of it, 'and more than once it is reported in St. Edmundsbury, This one is elected; and then, This one, and That other.' Who knows?

But now, sure enough, at Waltham, 'on the second Sunday of Quadragesima,' which Dryasdust declares to mean the 22d day of February, year 1182, Thirteen St. Edmundsbury Monks are, at last, seen processioning towards the Winchester Manor-house; and, in some high Presence-chamber and Hall of State, get access to Henry II. in all his glory. What a Hall,—not imaginary in the least, but entirely real and indisputable, though so extremely dim to us; sunk in the deep distances of Night! The Winchester Manorhouse has fled bodily, like a Dream of the old Night; not Dryasdust himself can show a wreck of it. House and people, royal and episcopal, lords and varlets, where are they? Why *there,* I say, Seven Centuries off; sunk *so* far in the Night, there they *are;* peep through the blankets of the old Night, and thou wilt see! King Henry himself is visibly there; a vivid, noble-looking man, with grizzled beard, in glittering uncertain costume; with earls round him, and

[2] *Macbeth,* I, v, 54.

bishops, and dignitaries, in the like. The Hall is large, and has for one thing an altar near it,—chapel and altar adjoining it; but what gilt seats, carved tables, carpeting of rush-cloth, what arras-hangings, and huge fire of logs:—alas, it has Human Life in it; and is not that the grand miracle, in what hangings or costume soever?—

The *Dominus Rex,* benignantly receiving our Thirteen with their obeisance, and graciously declaring that he will strive to act for God's honour and the Church's good, commands, 'by the Bishop of Winchester and Geoffrey the Chancellor,'[3]—*Galfridus Cancellarius,* Henry's and the Fair Rosamond's authentic Son present here!—commands, 'That they, the said Thirteen, do now withdraw, and fix upon Three from their own Monastery.' A work soon done; the Three hanging ready round Samson's neck, in that leather pouch of his. Breaking the seal, we find the names,—what think *ye* of it, ye higher dignitaries, thou indolent Prior, thou Willelmus *Sacrista* with the red bottle-nose?—the names, in this order: of Samson *Subsacrista,* of Roger the distressed Cellarer, of Hugo *Tertius-Prior.*

The higher dignitaries, all omitted here, 'flush suddenly red in the face'; but have nothing to say. One curious fact and question certainly is, How Hugo Third-Prior, who was of the electoral committee, came to nominate *himself* as one of the Three? A curious fact, which Hugo Third-Prior has never yet entirely explained, that I know of!—However, we return, and report to the King our Three names; merely altering the order; putting Samson last, as lowest of all. The King, at recitation of our Three, asks us: 'Who are they? Were they born in my domain? Totally unknown to me! You must nominate three others.' Whereupon Willelmus Sacrista says, 'Our Prior must be named, *quia caput nostrum est,* being already our head.' And the Prior responds, 'Willelmus Sacrista is a fit man, *bonus vir est,*'—for all his red nose. Tickle me, Toby, and I'll tickle thee! Venerable Dennis too is named; none in his conscience can say nay. There are now Six on our List. 'Well,' said the King, 'they have done it swiftly, they! *Deus est cum eis.*' The Monks withdraw again; and Majesty revolves, for a little, with his *Pares* and *Episcopi,*[4] Lords or 'Law-wards' and Soul-Overseers, the thoughts of the royal breast. The Monks wait silent in an outer room.

In short while, they are next ordered, To add yet another three; but not from their own Convent; from other Convents, 'for the honour of my kingdom.' Here,—what is to be done here? We will demur, if need be! We do name three, however, for the nonce: the Prior of St. Faith's, a good Monk of St. Neot's, a good Monk of St. Alban's; good men all; all made abbots and dignitaries since, at this hour. There are now Nine upon our List. What the thoughts of the Dominus Rex may be farther? The Dominus Rex, thanking graciously, sends out word that we shall now strike off three. The three strangers are instantly struck off. Willelmus Sacrista adds, that he will of his own accord decline,—a touch of grace and respect for the *Sacrosancta,* even in Willelmus! The King then orders us to strike off a couple more; then yet one more: Hugo Third-Prior goes, and Roger *Cellerarius,* and venerable Monk Dennis;—and now there remain on our List two only, Samson Subsacrista and the Prior.

Which of these two? It were hard to say,—by Monks who may get themselves foot-gyved and thrown into limbo for speaking! We humbly request that the Bishop of Winchester and Geoffrey the Chancellor may again enter, and help us to decide. 'Which do you want?' asks the Bishop. Venerable Dennis made a speech, 'commending the persons of the Prior and Samson; but always in the corner of his discourse, *in angulo sui sermonis,* brought Samson in.' 'I see!' said the Bishop: 'We are to understand that your Prior is somewhat remiss; that you want to have him you call Samson for Abbot.' 'Either of them is good,' said venerable Dennis, almost trembling; 'but we would have the better, if it pleased God.' 'Which of the two *do* you want?' inquires the Bishop pointedly. 'Samson!' answered Dennis; 'Samson!' echoed all of the rest that durst speak or echo anything: and Samson is reported to the King accordingly. His Majesty, advising of it for a moment, orders that Samson be brought in with the other Twelve.

The King's Majesty, looking at us somewhat sternly, then says: 'You present to me Samson; I do not know him: had it been your Prior, whom I do know, I should have accepted him: however, I will now do as you wish. But have a care of yourselves. By the true eyes of God, *per veros oculos Dei,* if you manage badly, I will be upon you!' Samson, therefore, steps forward, kisses the King's feet; but swiftly rises erect again, swiftly turns towards the altar, uplifting with the other

---

[3] The reputed son of Henry II and his mistress Rosamond de Clifford.
[4] Peers and bishops.

Twelve, in clear tenor-note, the Fifty-first Psalm, *Miserere mei Deus,*

> 'After thy loving-kindness, Lord,
>   Have mercy upon *me*';

with firm voice, firm step and head, no change in his countenance whatever. 'By God's eyes,' said the King, 'that one, I think, will govern the Abbey well.' By the same oath (charged to your Majesty's account), I too am precisely of that opinion! It is some while since I fell in with a likelier man anywhere than this new Abbot Samson. Long life to him, and may the Lord *have* mercy on him as Abbot!

Thus, then, have the St. Edmundsbury Monks, without express ballot-box or other good winnowing-machine, contrived to accomplish the most important social feat a body of men can do, to winnow-out the man that is to govern them: and truly one sees not that, by any winnowing-machine whatever, they could have done it better. O ye kind Heavens, there is in every Nation and Community a *fittest,* a wisest, bravest, best; whom could we find and make King over us, all were in very truth well;—the best that God and Nature had permitted *us* to make it! By what art discover him? Will the Heavens in their pity teach us no art; for our need of him is great!

Ballot-boxes, Reform Bills, winnowing-machines: all these are good, or are not so good;—alas, brethren, how *can* these, I say, be other than inadequate, be other than failures, melancholy to behold? Dim all souls of men to the divine, the high and awful meaning of Human Worth and Truth, we shall never, by all the machinery in Birmingham, discover the True and Worthy. It is written, 'if we are ourselves valets, there shall exist no hero for us; we shall not know the hero when we see him';—we shall take the quack for a hero; and cry, audibly through all ballot-boxes and machinery whatsoever, Thou art he; be thou King over us!

What boots it? Seek only deceitful Speciosity, money with gilt-carriages, 'fame' with newspaper-paragraphs, whatever name it bear, you will find only deceitful Speciosity; godlike Reality will be forever far from you. The Quack shall be legitimate inevitable King of you; no earthly machinery able to exclude the Quack. Ye shall be born thralls of the Quack, and suffer under him, till your hearts are near broken, and no French Revolution or Manchester Insurrection, or partial or universal volcanic combustions and explosions, never so many, can do more than

'change the *figure* of your Quack'; the essence of him remaining, for a time and times.—'How long, O Prophet?' say some, with a rather melancholy sneer. Alas, ye *un*prophetic, ever till this come about: Till deep misery, if nothing softer will, have driven you out of your Speciosities *into* your Sincerities; and you find that there either is a Godlike in the world, or else ye are an unintelligible madness; that there is a God, as well as a Mammon and a Devil, and a Genius of Luxuries and canting Dilettantisms and Vain Shows! How long that will be, compute for yourselves. My unhappy brothers!—

CHAPTER IX

Abbot Samson

So, then, the bells of St. Edmundsbury clang out one and all, and in church and chapel the organs go: Convent and Town, and all the west side of Suffolk, are in gala; knights, viscounts, weavers, spinners, the entire population, male and female, young and old, the very sockmen with their chubby infants,—out to have a holiday, and see the Lord Abbot arrive! And there is 'stripping barefoot' of the Lord Abbot at the Gate, and solemn leading of him in to the High Altar and Shrine; with sudden 'silence of all the bells and organs,' as we kneel in deep prayer there; and again with outburst of all the bells and organs, and loud *Te Deum* from the general human windpipe; and speeches by the leading viscount, and giving of the kiss of brotherhood; the whole wound-up with popular games, and dinner within doors of more than a thousand strong, *plus quam mille comedentibus in gaudio magno.*

In such manner is the selfsame Samson once again returning to us, welcomed on *this* occasion. He that went away with his frock-skirts looped over his arm, comes back riding high; suddenly made one of the dignitaries of this world. Reflective readers will admit that here was a trial for a man. Yesterday a poor mendicant, allowed to possess not above two shillings of money, and without authority to bid a dog run for him,—this man today finds himself a *Dominus Abbas,* mitred Peer of Parliament, Lord of manorhouses, farms, manors, and wide lands; a man with 'Fifty Knights under him,' and dependent, swiftly obedient multitudes of men. It is a change greater than Napoleon's; so sudden withal. As if one of the Chandos day-drudges had,[1] on awakening some morning, found that *he* overnight was become Duke! Let Samson with his clear-beaming eyes see into that, and discern it if he can. We shall now get the measure of him by a new scale of inches, considerably more rigorous than the former was. For if a noble soul is rendered tenfold beautifuler by victory and prosperity, springing now radiant as into his own due element and sun-throne; an ignoble one is rendered tenfold and hundredfold uglier, pitifuler. Whatsoever vices, whatsoever weaknesses were in the man, the parvenu will show us them enlarged, as in the solar microscope, into frightful distortion. Nay, how many mere seminal principles of vice, hitherto all wholesomely kept latent, may we now see unfolded, as in the solar hothouse, into growth, into huge universally-conspicuous luxuriance and development!

But is not this, at any rate, a singular aspect of what political and social capabilities, nay, let us say, what depth and opulence of true social vitality, lay in those old barbarous ages, That the fit Governor could be met with under such disguises, could be recognised and laid hold of under such? Here he is discovered with a maximum of two shillings in his pocket, and a leather scrip round his neck; trudging along the highway, his frock-skirts looped over his arm. They think this is he nevertheless, the true Governor; and he proves to be so. Brethren, have we no need of discovering true Governors, but will sham ones forever do for us? These were absurd superstitious blockheads of Monks; and we are enlightened Ten-pound Franchisers, without taxes on knowledge! Where, I say, are our superior, are our similar or at all comparable discoveries? We also have eyes, or ought to have; we have hustings, telescopes; we have lights, link-lights and rush-lights of an enlightened free Press, burning and dancing everywhere, as in a universal torch-dance; singeing your whiskers as you traverse the public thoroughfares in town and country. Great souls, true Governors, go about under all manner of disguises now as then. Such telescopes, such enlightenment,—and such discovery! How comes it, I say; how comes it? Is it not lamentable; is it not even, in some sense, amazing?

Alas, the defect, as we must often urge and again urge, is less a defect of telescopes than of some eyesight. Those superstitious blockheads of the Twelfth Century had no telescopes, but they had still an eye; not ballot-boxes; only reverence for Worth, abhorrence of Unworth. It is the way with all barbarians. Thus Mr. Sale[2] informs me, the old Arab Tribes would gather in liveliest *gaudeamus,* and sing, and kindle bonfires, and wreathe crowns of honour, and solemnly thank the gods that, in their Tribe too, a Poet had shown himself. As indeed they well might; for what usefuler, I say not nobler and heavenlier thing could the gods, doing their very kindest, send to any Tribe or Nation, in any time or circumstances? I declare to thee, my afflicted quack-ridden brother, in spite of thy astonishment, it is very lamentable! We English find a Poet, as brave a man as has been made for a hundred years or so anywhere under the Sun; and do we kindle bonfires, or thank the gods? Not at all. We, taking due counsel of it, set the man to gauge ale-barrels in the Burgh of Dumfries; and pique ourselves on our 'patronage of genius.'

Genius, Poet: do we know what these words mean? An inspired Soul once more vouchsafed us, direct from Nature's own great fire-heart, to see the Truth, and speak it, and do it; Nature's own sacred voice heard once more athwart the dreary boundless element of hearsaying and canting, of twaddle and poltroonery, in which the bewildered Earth, nigh perishing, has *lost its way.* Hear once more, ye bewildered benighted mortals; listen once again to a voice from the inner Light-sea and Flame-sea, Nature's and Truth's own heart; know the Fact of your Existence what it is, put away the Cant of it which it is *not*; and knowing, do, and let it be well with you!—

George the Third is Defender of something we call 'the Faith' in those years; George the Third is head charioteer of the Destinies of England, to guide them through the gulf of French Revolutions, American Independences; and Robert Burns is Gauger of ale in Dumfries. It is an Iliad in a nut-shell. The physiognomy of a world now verging towards dissolution, reduced now to

---

[1] Reference to the Duke of Buckingham and Chandos, Richard Grenville. See Book Second: The Ancient monks, Chapter III, note 4.

[2] George Sale (1690–1736), in the introduction to his translation of the *Koran ; gaudeamus,* enjoyment, revelry.

spasms and death-throes, lies pictured in that one fact,—which astonishes nobody, except at me for being astonished at it. The fruit of long ages of confirmed Valethood, entirely confirmed as into a Law of Nature; cloth-worship and quack-worship: entirely *confirmed* Valethood,—which will have to *un*confirm itself again; God knows, with difficulty enough!—

Abbot Samson had found a Convent all in dilapidation; rain beating through it, material rain and metaphorical, from all quarters of the compass. Willelmus Sacrista sits drinking nightly, and doing mere *tacenda*. Our larders are reduced to leanness, Jew harpies and unclean creatures our purveyors; in our basket is no bread. Old women with their distaffs rush out on a distressed Cellarer in shrill Chartism. 'You cannot stir abroad but Jews and Christians pounce upon you with unsettled bonds'; debts boundless seemingly as the National Debt of England. For four years our new Lord Abbot never went abroad but Jew creditors and Christian, and all manner of creditors, were about him; driving him to very despair. Our Prior is remiss; our Cellarers, officials are remiss; out monks are remiss: what man is not remiss? Front this, Samson, thou alone art there to front it; it is thy task to front and fight this, and to die or kill it. May the Lord have mercy on thee!

To our antiquarian interest in poor Jocelin and his Convent, where the whole aspect of existence, the whole dialect, of thought, of speech, of activity, is so obsolete, strange, long-vanished, there now superadds itself a mild glow of human interest for Abbot Samson; a real pleasure, as at sight of man's work, especially of governing, which is man's highest work, done *well*. Abbot Samson had no experience in governing; had served no apprenticeship to the trade of governing,—alas, only the hardest apprenticeship to that of obeying. He had never in any court given *vadium* or *plegium*,[3] says Jocelin; hardly ever seen a court, when he was set to preside in one. But it is astonishing, continues Jocelin, how soon he learned the ways of business; and, in all sorts of affairs, became expert beyond others. Of the many persons offering him their service, 'he retained one Knight skilled in taking *vadia* and *plegia*'; and within the year was himself well skilled. Nay, by and by, the Pope appoints him

Justiciary in certain causes; the King one of his new Circuit Judges: official Osbert is heard saying, 'That Abbot is one of your shrewd ones, *disputator est*; if he go on as he begins, he will cut out every lawyer of us!'[4]

Why not? What is to hinder this Samson from governing? There is in him what far transcends all apprenticeships; in the man himself there exists a model of governing, something to govern by! There exists in him a heart-abhorrence of whatever is incoherent, pusillanimous, unveracious, that is to say, chaotic, *un*governed; of the Devil, not of God. A man of this kind cannot help governing! He has the living ideal of a governor in him; and the incessant necessity of struggling to unfold the same out of him. Not the Devil or Chaos, for any wages, will he serve; no, this man is the born servant of Another than them. Alas, how little avail all apprenticeships, when there is in your governor himself what we may well call *nothing* to govern by: nothing;—a general gray twilight, looming with shapes of expediencies, parliamentary traditions, division-lists, election-funds, leading-articles; this, with what of vulpine alertness and adroitness soever, is not much!

But indeed what say we, apprenticeship? Had not this Samson served, in his way, a right good apprenticeship to governing; namely, the harshest slave-apprenticeship to obeying! Walk this world with no friend in it but God and St. Edmund, you will either fall into the ditch, or learn a good many things. To learn obeying is the fundamental art of governing. How much would many a Serene Highness have learned, had he travelled through the world with water-jug and empty wallet, *sine omni expensa*; and, at his victorious return, sat down not to newspaper-paragraphs and city-illuminations, but at the foot of St. Edmund's Shrine to shackles and bread-and-water! He that cannot be servant of many, will never be master, true guide and deliverer of many;—that is the meaning of true mastership. Had not the Monk-life extraordinary 'political capabilities' in it; if not imitable by us, yet enviable? Heavens, had a Duke of Logwood, now rolling sumptuously to his place in the Collective Wisdom, but himself happened to plough daily, at one time, on seven-and-sixpence a week, with no out-door relief,—what a light, unquenchable by logic and statistic and arithmetic, would it have thrown on several things for him!

---

[3] Pledges and guarantees for one's appearance in court.
[4] *Jocelini Chronica,* p. 25. [Carlyle's note]

In all cases, therefore, we will agree with the judicious Mrs. Glass.[5] 'First catch your hare!' First get your man; all is got: he can learn to do all things, from making boots, to decreeing judgments, governing communities; and will do them like a man. Catch your no-man,—alas, have you not caught the terriblest Tartar in the world! Perhaps all the terribler, the quieter and gentler he looks. For the mischief that one blockhead, that every blockhead does, in a world so feracious, teeming with endless results as ours, no ciphering will sum up. The quack bootmaker is considerable; as corn-cutters can testify, and desperate men reduced to buckskin and list-shoes. But the quack priest, quack high-priest, the quack king! Why do not all just citizens rush, half-frantic, to stop him, as they would a conflagration? Surely a just citizen *is* admonished by God and his own Soul, by all silent and articulate voices of this Universe, to do what in *him* lies towards relief of this poor blockhead-quack, and of a world that groans under him. Run swiftly; relieve him,—were it even by extinguishing him! For all things have grown so old, tinder-dry, combustible; and he is more ruinous than conflagration. Sweep him *down,* at least; keep him strictly within the hearth: he will then cease to be conflagration; he will then become useful, more or less, as culinary fire. Fire is the best of servants; but what a master! This poor blockhead too is born for uses; why, elevating him to mastership, will you make a conflagration, a parish-curse or world-curse of him?

BOOK THIRD

THE MODERN WORKER

CHAPTER II

Gospel of Mammonism

READER, even Christian Reader as thy title goes, hast thou any notion of Heaven and Hell? I rather apprehend, not. Often as the words are on our tongue, they have got a fabulous or semi-fabulous character for most of us, and pass on like a kind of transient similitude, like a sound signifying little.

Yet it is well worth while for us to know, once and always, that they are not a similitude, not a fable nor semi-fable; that they are an everlasting highest fact! 'No Lake of Sicilian or other sulphur burns now anywhere in these ages,' sayest thou? Well, and if there did not! Believe that there does not; believe it if thou wilt, nay hold by it as a real increase, a rise to higher stages, to wider horizons and empires. All this has vanished, or has not vanished; believe as thou wilt as to all this. But that an Infinite of Practical Importance, speaking with strict arithmetical exactness, an *Infinite,* has vanished or can vanish from the Life of any Man: this thou shalt not believe! O brother, the Infinite of Terror, of Hope, of Pity, did it not at any moment disclose itself to thee, indubitable, unnameable? Came it never, like the gleam of *preter*natural eternal Oceans, like the voice of old Eternities, far-sounding through thy heart of hearts? Never? Alas, it was not thy Liberalism, then; it was thy Animalism! The Infinite is more sure than any other fact. But only men can discern it; mere building beavers, spinning arachnes, much more the predatory vulturous and vulpine species, do not discern it well!—

'The word Hell,' says Sauerteig, 'is still frequently in use among the English people: but I could not without difficulty ascertain what they meant by it. Hell generally signifies the Infinite Terror, the thing a man *is* infinitely afraid of, and shudders and shrinks from, struggling with his whole soul to escape from it. There is a Hell therefore, if you will consider, which accompanies man, in all stages of his history, and religious or other development: but the Hells of men and Peoples differ notably. With Christians it is the infinite terror of being found guilty before the Just Judge. With old Romans, I conjecture, it was the terror not of Pluto, for whom probably they cared little, but of doing unworthily, doing unvirtuously, which was their word for un-*man*fully. And now what is it, if you pierce through his Cants, his oft-repeated Hearsays, what he calls his Worships and so forth,—what is it that the modern English soul does, in very truth, dread infinitely, and contemplate with entire despair? What *is* his Hell, after all these reputable, oft-repeated Hearsays, what is it? With hesitation, with astonishment, I pronounce it to be: The terror of "Not succeeding"; of not making money, fame, or some other figure in the world,—chiefly of not making money! Is not that a somewhat singular Hell?'

Yes, O Sauerteig, it is very singular. If we do not 'succeed,' where is the use of us? We had better never have been born. 'Tremble intensely,' as our friend the Emperor of China[1] says: *there* is the black Bottomless of Terror; what Sauerteig calls the 'Hell of the English'!—But indeed this Hell belongs naturally to the Gospel of Mammonism, which also has its corresponding Heaven. For there *is* one Reality among so many Phantasms; about one thing we are entirely in earnest: The making of money. Working Mammonism does divide the world with idle game-preserving Dilettantism:—thank Heaven that there is even a Mammonism, *any*thing we are in earnest about! Idleness is worst, Idleness alone is without hope: work earnestly at anything, you will by degrees learn to work at almost all things. There is endless hope in work, were it even work at making money.

True, it must be owned, we for the present, with our Mammon-Gospel, have come to strange conclusions. We call it a Society; and go about professing openly the totalest separation, isolation. Our life is not a mutual helpfulness; but rather, cloaked under due laws-of-war, named 'fair competition' and so forth, it is a mutual hostility. We have profoundly forgotten everywhere that *Cash-payment* is not the sole relation of human beings; we think, nothing doubting, that *it* absolves and liquidates all engagements of man. 'My starving workers?' answers the rich mill-owner: 'Did not I hire them fairly in the market? Did I not pay them, to the last sixpence, the sum covenanted for? What have I to do with them more?'—Verily Mammon-worship is a melancholy creed. When Cain, for his own behoof, had killed Abel, and was questioned, 'Where is thy brother?' he too made answer, 'Am I my brother's keeper?' Did I not pay my brother *his* wages, the thing he had merited from me?

O sumptuous Merchant-Prince, illustrious game-preserving Duke, is there no way of 'killing' thy brother but Cain's rude way! 'A good man by the very look of him, by his very presence with us as a fellow wayfarer in this Life-pilgrimage, *promises* so much': woe to him if he forget all such promises, if he never know that they were given! To a deadened soul, seared with the brute Idolatry of Sense, to whom going to Hell is equivalent to not making money, all 'promises,' and moral duties, that cannot be pleased for in Courts of Requests,[2] address themselves in vain. Money he can be ordered to pay, but nothing more. I have not heard in all Past History, and expect not to hear in all Future History, of any Society anywhere under God's Heaven supporting itself on such Philosophy. The Universe is not made so; it is made otherwise than so. The man or nation of men that thinks it is made so, marches forward nothing doubting, step after step; but marches—whither we know! In these last two centuries of Atheistic Government (near two centuries now, since the blessed restoration of his Sacred Majesty, and Defender of the Faith, Charles Second), I reckon that we have pretty well exhausted what of 'firm earth' there was for us to march on;—and are now, very ominously, shuddering, reeling, and let us hope trying to recoil, on the cliff's edge!—

For out of this that we call Atheism come so many other *isms* and falsities, each falsity with its misery at its heels!—a SOUL is not like wind (*spiritus*, or breath) contained within a capsule; the ALMIGHTY MAKER is not like a Clockmaker that once, in old immemorial ages, having *made* his Horologe of a Universe, sits ever since and sees it go! Not at all. Hence comes Atheism; come, as we say, many other *isms*; and as the sum of all, comes Valetism, the *reverse* of Heroism; sad root of all woes whatsoever. For indeed, as no man ever saw the above-said wind-element enclosed within its capsule, and finds it at bottom more deniable than conceivable; so too he finds, in spite of Bridgwater Bequests;[3] your Clockmaker Almighty an entirely questionable affair, a deniable affair;—and accordingly denies, it and along with it so much else. Alas, one knows not what and how much else! For the faith in an Invisible, Unnameable, Godlike, present everywhere in all that we see and work and suffer, is the essence of all faith whatsoever; and that once denied, or still worse, asserted with lips only, and out of bound prayerbooks only, what other thing remains believable? That Cant well-ordered is marketable Cant; that Heroism means gas-

---

[1] Reference to the controversy with China in 1840 known as the "Opium War."

[2] Small claims courts.

[3] Reference to the bequest of £8,000 by the 8th Earl of Bridgwater (1758–1829) to be paid to the author of the best treatise on the theme "Power, Wisdom, and Goodness of God, as manifested in the Creation."

lighted Histrionism; that seen with 'clear eyes' (as they call Valet-eyes), no man is a Hero, or ever was a Hero, but all men are Valets and Varlets. The accursed practical quintessence of all sorts of Unbelief! For if there be now no Hero, and the Histrio himself begin to be seen into, what hope is there for the seed of Adam here below? We are the doomed, everlasting prey of the Quack; who, now in this guise, now in that, is to filch us, to pluck and eat us, by such modes as are convenient for him. For the modes and guises I care little. The Quack once inevitable, let him come swiftly, let him pluck and eat me;— swiftly, that I may at least have done with him; for in his Quack-world I can have no wish to linger. Though he slay me, yet will I *not* trust in him. Though he conquer nations, and have all the Flunkies of the Universe shouting at his heels, yet will I know well that *he* is an Inanity; that for him and his there is no continuance appointed, save only in Gehenna and the Pool. Alas, the Atheist world, from its utmost summits of Heaven and Westminster-Hall, downwards through poor seven-feet Hats and 'Unveracities fallen hungry,' down to the lowest cellars and neglected hunger-dens of it, is very wretched.

One of Dr. Alison's Scotch facts struck us much.[4] A poor Irish Widow, her husband having died in one of the Lanes of Edinburgh, went forth with her three children, bare of all resource, to solicit help from the Charitable Establishments of that City. At this Charitable Establishment and then at that she was refused; referred from one to the other, helped by none;—till she had exhausted them all; till her strength and heart failed her: she sank down in typhus-fever; died, and infected her Lane with fever, so that 'seventeen other persons' died of fever there in consequence. The humane Physician asks there-upon, as with a heart too full for speaking, Would it not have been *economy* to help this poor Widow? She took typhus-fever, and killed seventeen of you!—Very curious. The forlorn Irish Widow applies to her fellow-creatures, as if saying, 'Behold I am sinking, bare of help: ye must help me! I am your sister, bone of your bone; one God made us: ye must help me!' They answer, 'No, impossible; thou are no sister of ours.' But she proves her sisterhood; her typhus-fever kills *them*: they actually were her brothers, though denying it! Had human creature ever to go lower for a proof?

For, as indeed was very natural in such case, all government of the Poor by the Rich has long ago been given over to Supply-and-demand, Laissez-faire and suchlike, and universally declared to be 'impossible.' 'You are no sister of ours; what shadow of proof is there? Here are our parch-ments, our padlocks, proving indisputably our money-safes to be *ours*, and you to have no business with them. Depart! It is impossible!'— Nay, what wouldst thou thyself have us do? cry indignant readers. Nothing, my friends,—till you have got a soul for yourselves again. Till then all things are 'impossible.' Till then I cannot even bid you buy, as the old Spartans would have done, two-pence worth of powder and lead, and compendiously shoot to death this poor Irish Widow: even that is 'impossible' for you. Nothing is left but that she prove her sisterhood by dying, and infecting you with typhus. Seventeen of you lying dead will not deny such proof that she *was* flesh of your flesh; and perhaps some of the living may lay it to heart.

'Impossible': of a certain two-legged animal with feathers it is said, if you draw a distinct chalk-circle round him, he sits imprisoned, as if girt with the iron ring of Fate; and will die there, though within sight of victuals,—or sit in sick misery there, and be fatted to death. The name of this poor two-legged animal is—Goose; and they make of him, when well fattened, *Pâté de foie gras*, much prized by some!

CHAPTER III

Gospel of Dilettantism

BUT after all, the Gospel of Dilettantism, producing a Governing Class who do not govern, nor understand in the least that they are bound or expected to govern, is still mournfuler than that of Mammonism. Mammonism, as we said, at least works; this goes idle. Mammonism has seized some portion of the message of Nature to man; and seizing that, and following it, will seize and appropriate more and more of Nature's

---

[4] *Observations on the Management of the Poor in Scotland:* by William Pulteney Alison, M.D. (Edinburgh, 1840). [Carlyle's note]

message: but Dilettantism has missed it wholly. 'Make money': that will mean withal, 'Do work in order to make money.' But, 'Go gracefully idle in Mayfair,' what does or can that mean? An idle, game-preserving and even corn-lawing Aristocracy, in such an England as ours: has the world, if we take thought of it, even seen such a phenomenon till very lately? Can it long continue to see such?

Accordingly the impotent, insolent Dono-thingism in Practice and Saynothingism in Speech, which we have to witness on that side of our affairs, is altogether amazing. A Corn-Law demonstrating itself openly, for ten years or more, with 'arguments' to make the angels, and some other classes of creatures, weep! For men are not ashamed to rise in Parliament and elsewhere, and speak the things they do *not* think. 'Expediency,' 'Necessities of Party,' etc. etc.! It is not known that the Tongue of Man is a sacred organ; that Man himself is definable in Philosophy as an 'Incarnate *Word*'; the Word not there, you have no Man there either, but a Phantasm instead! In this way it is that Absurdities may live long enough,—still walking, and talking for themselves, years and decades after the brains are quite out! How are the 'knaves and dastards' ever to be got 'arrested' at that rate?—

'No man in this fashionable London of yours,' friend Sauerteig would say, 'speaks a plain word to me. Every man feels bound to be something more than plain; to be pungent withal, witty, ornamental. His poor fraction of sense has to be perked into some epigrammatic shape, that it may prick into me;—perhaps (this is the common-est) to be topsyturvied, left standing on its head, that I may remember it the better! Such grinning inanity is very sad to the soul of man. Human faces should not grin on one like masks; they should look on one like faces! I love honest laughter, as I do sunlight; but not dishonest: most kinds of dancing too; but the St.-Vitus kind not at all! A fashionable wit, *ach Himmel!* if you ask, Which, he or a Death's head, will be the cheerier company for me? pray send *not* him!'

Insincere Speech, truly, is the prime material of insincere Action. Action hangs, as it were, *dissolved* in Speech, in Thought whereof Speech is the Shadow; and precipitates itself therefrom. The kind of Speech in a man betokens the kind of Action you will get from him. Our Speech, in these modern days, has become amazing.

Johnson complained, 'Nobody speaks in earnest, Sir; there is no serious conversation.'[1] To us all serious speech of men, as that of Seventeenth-Century Puritans, Twelfth-Century Catholics, German Poets of this Century, has become jargon, more or less insane. Cromwell was mad and a quack; Anselm, Becket, Goethe, *ditto, ditto*.

Perhaps few narratives in History or Myth-ology are more significant than that Moslem one, of Moses and the Dwellers by the Dead Sea. A tribe of men dwelt on the shores of that same Asphaltic Lake; and having forgotten, as we are all too prone to do, the inner facts of Nature, and taken up with the falsities and outer semblances of it, were fallen into sad conditions,—verging indeed towards a certain far deeper Lake. Whereupon it pleased kind Heaven to send them the Prophet Moses, with an instructive word of warning, out of which might have sprung 'remedial measures' not a few. But no: the men of the Dead Sea discovered, as the valet-species always does in heroes or prophets, no comeliness in Moses; listened with real tedium to Moses, with light grinning, or with splenetic sniffs and sneers, affecting even to yawn; and signified, in short, that they found him a humbug, and even a bore. Such was the candid theory these men of the Asphalt Lake formed to themselves of Moses, That probably he was a humbug, that certainly he was a bore.

Moses withdrew; but Nature and her rigorous veracities did not withdraw. The men of the Dead Sea, when we next went to visit them, were all 'changed into Apes';[2] sitting on the trees there, grinning now in the most *un*affected manner; gibbering and chattering very genuine nonsense; finding the whole Universe now a most indisputable Humbug! The Universe has *become* a Humbug to these Apes who thought it one. There they sit and chatter, to this hour: only, I believe, every Sabbath there returns to them a bewildered half-consciousness, half-reminiscence; and they sit, with their wizened smoke-dried visages, and such an air of supreme tragicality as Apes may; looking out through those blinking smoke-bleared eyes of theirs, into the wonderfulest universal smoky Twilight and undecipherable disordered Dusk of Things; wholly an Un-certainty, Unintelligibility, they and it; and for commentary thereon, here and there an un-musical chatter or mew:—truest, tragicalest Humbug conceivable by the mind or man or

---

[1] Perhaps a reference to remarks in Boswell's *Johnson* for the year 1776.
[2] Sales *Koran* (Introduction). [Carlyle's note]

ape! They made no use of their souls; and so have lost them. Their worship on the Sabbath now is to roost there, with unmusical screeches, and half-remember that they had souls.

Didst thou never, O Traveller, fall-in with parties of this tribe? Meseems they are grown somewhat numerous in our day.

CHAPTER IV

Happy

ALL WORK, even cotton-spinning, is noble; work is alone noble: be that here said and asserted once more. And in like manner too, all dignity is painful; a life of ease is not for any man, nor for any god. The life of all gods figures itself to us as a Sublime Sadness,—earnestness of Infinite Battle against Infinite Labour. Our highest religion is named the 'Worship of Sorrow.' For the son of man there is no noble crown, well worn or even ill worn, but is a crown of thorns!—These things, in spoken words, or still better, in felt instincts alive in every heart, were once well known.

Does not the whole wretchedness, the whole *Atheism* as I call it, of man's ways, in these generations, shadow itself for us in that unspeakable Life-philosophy of his: The pretension to be what he calls 'happy'? Every pitifulest whipster that walks within a skin has his head filled with the notion that he is, shall be, or by all human and divine laws ought to be 'happy.' His wishes, the pitifulest whipster's, are to be fulfilled for him; his days, the pitifulest whipster's, are to flow on in ever-gentle current of enjoyment, impossible even for the gods. The prophets preach to us, Thou shalt be happy; thou shalt love pleasant things, and find them. The people clamour, Why have we not found pleasant things?

We construct our theory of Human Duties, not on any Greatest-Nobleness Principle, never so mistaken; no, but on a Greatest-Happiness Principle. 'The word *Soul* with us, as in some Slavonic dialects, seems to be synonymous with *Stomach*.' We plead and speak, in our Parliaments and elsewhere, not as from the Soul, but from the Stomach;—wherefore indeed our pleadings are so slow to profit. We plead not for God's Justice; we are not ashamed to stand clamouring and pleading for our own 'interests,' our own rents and trade-profits; we say, They are the 'interests' of so many; there is such an intense desire in us for them! We demand Free-Trade, with much just vociferation and benevolence, That the poorer classes, who are terribly ill-off at present, may have cheaper New-Orleans bacon. Men ask on Free-trade platforms, How can the indomitable spirit of Englishmen be kept up without plenty of bacon? We shall become a ruined Nation!—Surely, my friends, plenty of bacon is good and indispensable: but, I doubt, you will never get even bacon by aiming only at that. You are men, not animals of prey, well-used or ill-used! Your Greatest-Happiness Principle seems to me fast becoming a rather unhappy one.—What if we should cease babbling about 'happiness,' and leave *it* resting on its own basis, as it used to do!

A gifted Byron rises in his wrath; and feeling too surely that he for his part is not 'happy', declares the same in very violent language, as a piece of news that may be interesting. It evidently has surprised him much. One dislikes to see a man and poet reduced to proclaim on the streets such tidings: but on the whole, as matters go, that is not the most dislikable. Byron speaks the *truth* in this matter. Byron's large audience indicates how true it is felt to be.

'Happy,' my brother? First of all, what difference is it whether thou art happy or not! Today becomes Yesterday so fast, all Tomorrows become Yesterdays; and then there is no question whatever of the 'happiness', but quite another question. Nay, thou hast such a sacred pity left at least for thyself, thy very pains, once gone over into Yesterday, become joys to thee. Besides, thou knowest not what heavenly blessedness and indispensable sanative virtue was in them; thou shalt only know it after many days, when thou art wiser!—A benevolent old Surgeon sat once in our company, with a Patient fallen sick by gourmandising, whom he had just, too briefly in the Patient's judgment, been examining. The foolish Patient still at intervals continued to break in on our discourse, which rather promised to take a philosophic turn: 'But I have lost my appetite,' said he, objurgatively, with a tone of irritated pathos; 'I have no appetite; I can't eat!'—'My dear fellow,' answered the Doctor in mildest tone, 'it isn't of the slightest consequence';—and continued his philosophical discoursings with us!

Or does the reader not know the history of that Scottish iron Misanthrope? The inmates of some town mansion, in those Northern parts, were thrown into the fearfulest alarm by indubitable symptoms of a ghost inhabiting the next house, or perhaps even the partition-wall! Even at a certain hour, with preternatural gnarring growling, and screeching, which attended as running bass, there began, in a horrid, semi-articulate, unearthly voice, this song: 'Once I was hap-hap-happy, but now I am *mees*erable! Clack-clack-clack, gnarr-r-r, whuz-z: Once I was hap-hap-happy, but now I'm *mees*erable!'—Rest, rest, perturbed spirit;—or indeed, as the good old Doctor said: My dear fellow, it isn't of the slightest consequence! But no; the perturbed spirit could not rest; and to the neighbours, fretted, affrighted, or at least insufferably bored by him, it *was* of such consequence that they had to go and examine in his haunted chamber. In his haunted chamber, they find that the perturbed spirit is an unfortunate—Imitator of Byron? No, is an unfortunate rusty Meat-jack, gnarring and creaking with rust and work; and this, in Scottish dialect is *its* Byronian musical Life-philosophy, sung according to ability.

Truly, I think the man who goes about pothering and up-roaring for his 'happiness,'—pothering, and were it ballot-boxing, poem-making, or in what way soever fussing and exerting himself,—he is not the man that will help us to 'get our knaves and dastards arrested'! No; he rather is on the way to increase the number,—by at least one unit and his tail! Observe, too, that this is all a modern affair; belongs not to the old heroic times, but to these dastard new times. 'Happiness our being's end and aim,'[1] all that very paltry speculation is at bottom, if we will count well, not yet two centuries old in the world.

The only happiness a brave man ever troubled himself with asking much about was, happiness enough to get his work done. Not 'I can't eat!' but 'I can't work!' that was the burden of all wise complaining among men. It is, after all, the one unhappiness of a man, That he cannot work; that he cannot get his destiny as a man fulfilled. Behold, the day is passing swiftly over, our life is passing swiftly over; and the night cometh, wherein no man can work.[2] The night once come, our happiness, our unhappiness,—it

is all abolished; vanished, clean gone; a thing that has been: 'not of the slightest consequence' whether we were happy as eupeptic Curtis, as the fattest pig of Epicurus, or unhappy as Job with potsherds, as musical Byron with Giaours[3] and sensibilities of the heart; as the unmusical Meat-jack with hard labour and rust! But our work,—behold that is not abolished, that has not vanished our work, behold, it remains, or the want of it remains;—for endless Times and Eternities, remains; and that is now the sole question with us for evermore! Brief brawling Day, with its noisy phantasms, its poor paper-crowns tinsel-gilt, is gone; and divine everlasting Night, with her star-diadems, with her silences and her veracities, is come! What hast thou done, and how? Happiness, unhappiness: all that was but the *wages* thou hadst; thou hast spent all that, in sustaining thyself hitherward; not a coin of it remains with thee, it is all spent, eaten: and now thy work, where is thy work? Swift, out with it; let us see thy work!

Of a truth, if man were not a poor hungry dastard, and even much of a blockhead withal, he would cease criticising his victuals to such extent; and criticise himself rather, what he does with his victuals!

CHAPTER V

The English

AND YET, with all thy theoretic platitudes, what a depth of practical sense in thee, great England! A depth of sense, of justice, and courage; in which, under all emergencies and world-bewilderments, and under this most complex of emergencies we now live in, there is still hope, there is still assurance!

The English are a dumb people. They can do great acts, but not describe them. Like the old Romans, and some few others, *their* Epic Poem is written on the Earth's surface: England her Mark; It is complained that they have no artists: one Shakspeare indeed; but for Raphael

---

[1] Pope, *Essay on Man,* IV, i.
[2] John 9:4.
[3] Sir William Curtis (d. 1829), London merchant and noted epicure; Job with potsherds, see Job 2:8; Byron's poem *The Giaour.*

only a Reynolds; for Mozart nothing but a Mr. Bishop:[1] not a picture, not a song. And yet they did produce one Shakspeare: consider how the element of Shakspearean melody does lie imprisoned in their nature; reduced to unfold itself in mere Cotton-mills, Constitutional Governments, and suchlike;—all the more interesting when it does become visible, as even in such unexpected shapes it succeeds in doing! Goethe spoke of the Horse, how impressive, almost affecting it was that an animal of such qualities should stand obstructed so; its speech nothing but an inarticulate neighing, its handiness mere *hoof* iness, the fingers all constricted, tied together, the finger-nails coagulated into a mere hoof, shod with iron. The more significant, thinks he, are those eye-flashings of the generous noble quadruped; those prancings, curvings of the neck clothed with thunder.

A Dog of Knowledge has free utterance; but the War-horse is almost mute, very far from free! It is even so. Truly, your freest utterances are not by any means always the best: they are the worst rather; the feeblest, trivialist; their meaning prompt, but small, ephemeral. Commend me to the silent English, to the silent Romans. Nay the silent Russians, too, I believe to be worth something: are they not even now drilling, under much obloquy, an immense semi-barbarous half-world from Finland to Kamtschatka, into rule, subordination, civilisation,—really in an old Roman fashion; speaking no word about it; quietly hearing all manner of vituperative Able Editors speak! While your ever-talking, ever-gesticulating French, for example, what are they at this moment drilling?—Nay of all animals, the freest of utterance, I should judge, is the genus *Simia*: go into the Indian woods, say all Travellers, and look what a brisk, adroit, unresting Ape-population it is!

The spoken Word, the written Poem, is said to be an epitome of the man; how much more the done work. Whatsoever of morality and of intelligence; what of patience, perseverance, faithfulness, of method, insight, ingenuity, energy; in a word, whatsoever of Strength the man had in him will lie written in the Work he does. To work: why, it is to try himself against Nature, and her everlasting unerring Laws; these will tell a true verdict as to the man. So much of virtue and of faculty did *we* find in him; so much and no more! He had such capacity of harmonising himself with *me* and my unalterable ever-veracious Laws; of coöperating and working as *I* bade him;—and has prospered, and has not prospered, as you see!—Working as great Nature bade him: does not that mean virtue of a kind; nay of all kinds? Cotton can be spun and sold, Lancashire operatives can be got to spin it, and at length one has the woven webs and sells them, by following Nature's regulations in that matter: by not following Nature's regulations, you have them not. You have them not;—there is no Cotton-web to sell: Nature finds a bill against you; your 'Strength' is not Strength, but Futility! Let faculty be honoured, so far as it is faculty. A man that can succeed in working is to me always a man.

How one loves to see the burly figure of him, this thick-skinned, seemingly opaque, perhaps sulky, almost stupid Man of Practice, pitted against some light adroit Man of Theory, all equipt with clear logic, and able anywhere to give you Why for Wherefore! The adroit Man of Theory, so light of movement, clear of utterance, with his bow full-bent and quiver full of arrow-arguments,—surely he will strike down the game, transfix everywhere the heart of the matter; triumph everywhere, as he proves that he shall and must do? To your astonishment, it turns out oftenest No. The cloudy-browed, thick-soled, opaque Practicality, with no logic utterance, in silence mainly, with here and there a low grunt or growl, has n him what transcends all logic-utterance: a Congruity with the Unuttered. The Speakable, which lies atop, as a superficial film, or outer skin, is his or is not his: but the Doable, which reaches down to the World's centre, you find him there!

The rugged Brindley[2] has little to say for himself; the rugged Brindley, when difficulties accumulate on him, retires silent, 'generally to his bed'; retires 'sometimes for three days together to his bed, that he may be in perfect privacy there,' and ascertain in his rough head how the difficulties can be overcome. The ineloquent Brindley, behold he *has* chained seas together; his ships do visibly float over valleys, invisibly through the hearts of mountains; the Mersey and the Thames, the Humber and the Severn have shaken hands: Nature most audibly answers, Yea! The man of Theory twangs his full-bent bow: Nature's Fact ought to fall

---

[1] Sir Henry Bishop (1785–1855), contemporary musician and composer.
[2] James Brindley (1716–72), noted canal builder who remained illiterate all his life.

stricken, but does not: his logic-arrow glances from it as from a scaly dragon, and the obstinate Fact keeps walking its way. How singular! At bottom, you will have to grapple closer with the dragon; take it home to you, by real faculty, not by seeming faculty; try whether you are stronger, or it is stronger. Close with it, wrestle it: sheer obstinate toughness of muscle; but much more, what we call toughness of heart, which will mean persistence hopeful and even desperate, unsubduable patience, composed candid openness, clearness of mind: all this shall be 'strength' in wrestling your dragon; the whole man's real strength is in this work, we shall get the measure of him here.

Of all the Nations in the world at present the English are the stupidest in speech, the wisest in action. As good as a 'dumb' Nation, I say, who cannot speak, and have never yet spoken,—spite of the Shakspeares and Miltons who show us what possibilities there are!—O Mr. Bull, I look in that surly face of thine with a mixture of pity and laughter, yet also with wonder and veneration. Thou complainest not, my illustrious friend; and yet I believe the heart of thee is full of sorrow, of unspoken sadness, seriousness,—profound melancholy (as some have said) the basis of thy being. Unconsciously, for thou speakest of nothing, this great Universe is great to thee. Not by levity of floating, but by stubborn force of swimming, shalt thou make thy way. The Fates sing of thee that thou shalt many times be thought an ass and a dull ox, and shalt with a godlike indifference believe it. My friend,—and it is all untrue, nothing ever falser in point of fact! Thou art of those great ones whose greatness the small passer-by does not discern. The very stupidity is wiser than their wisdom. A grand *vis inertiæ*[3] is in thee; how many grand qualities unknown to small men! Nature alone knows thee, acknowledges the bulk and strength of thee: thy Epic, unsung in words, is written in huge characters on the face of this Planet,—sea-moles, cotton-trades, railways, fleets and cities, Indian Empires, Americas, New Hollands; legible throughout the Solar System!

But the dumb Russians too, as I said, they, drilling all wild Asia and wild Europe into military rank and file, a terrible yet hitherto a prospering enterprise, are still dumber. The old Romans also could not *speak*, for many centuries: —not till the world was theirs; and so many speaking Greekdoms, their logic-arrows all spent,

had been absorbed and abolished. The logic-arrows, how they glanced futile from obdurate thick-skinned Facts; Facts to be wrestled down only by the real vigour of Roman thews!—As for me, I honour, in these loud-babbling days, all the Silent rather. A grand Silence that of Romans;—nay the grandest of all, is it not that of the gods! Even Triviality, Imbecility, that can sit silent, how respectable is it in comparison! The 'talent of silence' is our fundamental one. Great honour to him whose Epic is a melodious hexameter Iliad; not a jingling Sham-Iliad, nothing true in it but the hexameters and forms merely. But still greater honour, if his Epic be a mighty Empire, slowly built together, a mighty Series of Heroic Deeds,—a mighty Conquest over Chaos; *which* Epic the 'Eternal Melodies' have, and must have, informed and dwelt in, as *it* sung itself! There is no mistaking that latter Epic. Deeds are greater than Words. Deeds have such a life, mute but undeniable, and grow as living trees and fruit-trees do; they people the vacuity of Time, and make it green and worthy. Why should the oak prove logically that it ought to grow, and will grow? Plant it, try it; what gifts of diligent judicious assimilation and secretion it has, of progress and resistance, of *force* to grow, will then declare themselves. My much-honoured, illustrious, extremely inarticulate Mr. Bull!—

Ask Bull his spoken opinion of any matter,—oftentimes the force of dulness can no farther go. You stand silent, incredulous, as over a platitude that borders on the Infinite. The man's Church-isms, Dissenterisms, Puseyisms, Benthamisms, College Philosophies, Fashionable Literatures, are unexampled in this world. Fate's prophecy is fulfilled; you call the man an ox and an ass. But set him once to work,—respectable man! His spoken sense is next to nothing, nine-tenths of it palpable *non*sense: but his unspoken sense, his inner silent feeling of what is true, what does agree with fact, what is doable and what is not doable,—this seeks its fellow in the world. A terrible worker; irresistible against marshes, mountains, impediments, disorder, incivilisation; everywhere vanquishing disorder, leaving it behind him as method and order. He 'retires to his bed three days,' and considers!

Nay withal, stupid as he is, our dear John,—ever, after infinite tumblings, and spoken platitudes innumerable from barrel-heads and parliament-benches, he does settle down somewhere about the just conclusion; you are certain

---

[3] Inert strength.

that his jumblings and tumblings will end, after years or centuries, in the stable equilibrium. Stable equilibrum, I say; centre-of-gravity lowest;—not the unstable, with centre-of-gravity highest, as I have known it done by quicker people! For indeed, do but jumble and tumble sufficiently, you avoid that worst fault, of settling with your centre-of-gravity highest; your centre-of-gravity is certain to come lowest, and to stay there. If slowness, what we in our impatience call 'stupidity,' be the price of stable equilibrium over unstable, shall we grudge a little slowness? Not the least admirable quality of Bull is, after all, that of remaining insensible to logic; holding out for considerable periods, ten years or more, as in this of the Corn-Laws, after all arguments and shadow of arguments have faded away from him, till the very urchins on the street titter at the arguments he brings. Logic,—Λογική,, the 'Art of Speech,'—does indeed speak so and so; clear enough: nevertheless Bull still shakes his head; will see whether nothing else *illogical*, not yet 'spoken,' not yet able to be 'spoken,' do not lie in the business, as there so often does!—My firm belief is, that finding himself now enchanted, hand-shackled, foot-shackled, in Poor-Law Bastilles and elsewhere, he will retire three days to his bed, and *arrive* at a conclusion or two! His three-years 'total stagnation of trade,' alas, is not that a painful enough 'lying in bed to consider himself'? Poor Bull!

Bull is a born Conservative; for this too I inexpressibly honour him. All great Peoples are conservative; slow to believe in novelites; patient of much error in actualities; deeply and forever certain of the greatness that is in LAW, in Custom once solemnly established, and now long recognised as just and final.—True, O Radical Reformer, there is no Custom that can, properly speaking, be final; none. And yet thou seest *Customs* which, in all civilised countries, are accounted final; nay, under the Old-Roman name of *Mores*, are accounted *Morality*, Virtue, Laws of God Himself. Such, I assure thee, not a few of them are: such almost all of them once were. And greatly do I respect the solid character,—a blockhead, thou wilt say; yes, but a well-conditioned blockhead, and the best-conditioned,—who esteems all 'Customs once solemnly acknowledged' to be ultimate, divine, and the rule for a man to walk by, nothing doubting, not

inquiring farther. What a time of it had we, were all men's life and trade still, in all parts of it, a problem, a hypothetic seeking, to be settled by painful Logics and Baconian Inductions! The Clerk in Eastcheap cannot spend the day in verifying his Ready-Reckoner; he must take it as verified, true and indisputable; or his Book-keeping by Double Entry will stand still. 'Where is your Posted Ledger?' asks the Master at night. —'Sir,' answers the other, 'I was verifying my Ready-Reckoner, and find some errors. The Ledger is—!'—Fancy such a thing!

True, all turns on your Ready-Reckoner being moderately correct, being *not* insupportably incorrect! A Ready-Reckoner, which has led to distinct entries in your Ledger such as these: '*Creditor* an English People by fifteen hundred years of good Labour; and *Debtor* to lodging in enchanted Poor-Law Bastilles: *Creditor* by conquering the largest Empire the Sun ever saw; and *Debtor* to Donothingism and "Impossible" written on all departments of the government thereof: *Creditor* by mountains of gold ingots earned; and *Debtor* to No Bread purchasable by them:'—*such* Ready-Reckoner, methinks is beginning to be suspect; nay is ceasing, and has ceased, to be suspect! Such Ready-Reckoner is a Solecism in Eastcheap; and must, whatever be the press of business, and will and shall be rectified a little. Business can go on no longer with *it*. The most Conservative English People, thickest-skinned, most patient of Peoples, is driven alike by its Logic and its Unlogic, by things 'spoken,' and by things not yet spoken or very speakable, but only felt and very unendurable, to be wholly a Reforming People. Their Life, as it is, has ceased to be longer possible for them.

Urge not this noble silent People; rouse not the Berserkir rage that lies in them! Do you know their Cromwells, Hampdens, their Pyms and Bradshaws?[4] Men very peaceable, but men that can be made very terrible! Men who, like their old Teutsch Fathers in Agrippa's days,[5] 'have a soul that despises ¯death'; to whom 'death,' compared with falsehoods and injustices, is light;—'in whom there is a rage unconquerable by the immortal gods'! Before this, the English People have taken very preternatural-looking Spectres by the beard; saying virtually: 'And if thou *wert* "preternatural"? Thou with thy

---

[4] Leaders of the seventeenth-century English Revolution.
[5] Teutsch fathers, German fathers; Agrippa's day, i.e., first century B.C. when Agrippa fought the Germans.

"divine-rights" grown diabolic-wrongs? Thou,— not even "natural"; decapitable; totally extinguishable!'— —Yes, just so godlike as this People's patience was, even so godlike will and must its impatience be. Away, ye scandalous Practical Solecisms, children actually of the Prince of Darkness; ye have near broken our hearts; we can and will endure you no longer. Begone, we say; depart, while the play is good! By the Most High God, whose sons and born missionaries true men are, ye shall not continue here! You and we have become incompatible; can inhabit one house no longer. Either you must go, or we. Are ye ambitious to try *which* it shall be?

On my Conservative friends, who still specially name and struggle to approve yourselves 'Conservative,' would to Heaven I could persuade you of this world-old fact, than which Fate is not surer, That Truth and Justice alone are *capable* of being 'conserved' and preserved! The thing which is unjust, which is *not* according to God's Law, will you, in a God's Universe, try to conserve that? It is so old, say you? Yes, and the hotter haste ought *you,* of all others, to be in, to let it grow no older! If but the faintest whisper in your hearts intimate to you that it is not fair,—hasten, for the sake of Conservatism itself, to probe it rigorously, to cast it forth at once and forever if guilty. How will or can you preserve *it,* the thing that is not fair? 'Impossibility' a thousandfold is marked on that. And ye call yourselves Conservatives, Aristocracies:—ought not honour and nobleness of mind, if they had departed from all the Earth elsewhere, to find their last refuge with you? Ye unfortunate!

The bough that is dead shall be cut away, for the sake of the tree itself. Old? Yes, it is too old. Many a weary winter has it swung and creaked there, and gnawed and fretted, with its dead wood, the organic substance and still living fibre of this good tree; many a long summer has its ugly naked brown defaced the fair green umbrage; every day it has done mischief, and that only: off with it, for the tree's sake, if for nothing more; let the Conservatism that would preserve cut *it* away. Did no wood-forester apprise you that a dead bough with its dead root left sticking there is extraneous, poisonous; is as a dead iron spike, some horrid rusty plough-share driven into the living substance;—nay is far worse; for in every wind-storm ('commercial crisis' or the like), it frets and creaks, jolts itself

to and fro, and cannot lie quiet as your dead iron spike would.

If I were the Conservative Party of England (which is another bold figure of speech), I would not for a hundred thousand pounds an hour allow those Corn-Laws to continue! Potosi and Golconda[6] put together would not purchase my assent to them. Do you count what treasuries of bitter indignation they are laying up for you in every just English heart? Do you know what questions, not as to Corn-prices and Sliding-scales alone, they are *forcing* every reflective Englishman to ask himself? Questions insoluble, or hitherto unsolved; deeper than any of our Logic-plummets hitherto will sound: questions deep enough,—which it were better that we did not name even in thought! You are forcing us to think of them, to begin uttering them. The utterance of them is begun; and where will it be ended, think you? When two millions of one's brother-men sit in Workhouses, and five millions, as is insolently said, 'rejoice in potatoes,' there are various things that must be begun, let them end where they can.

CHAPTER X

Plugson of Undershot

ONE thing I do know: Never, on this Earth, was the relation of man to man long carried on by Cash-payment alone. If, at any time, a philosophy of Laissez-faire, Competition and Supply-and-demand, start up as the exponent of human relations, expect that it will soon end.

Such philosophies will arise: for man's philosophies are usually the 'supplement of his practice'; some ornamental Logic-varnish, some outer skin of Articulate Intelligence, with which he strives to render his dumb Instinctive Doings presentable when they are done. Such philosophies will arise; be preached as Mammon-Gospels, the ultimate Evangel of the World; be believed, with what is called belief, with much superficial bluster, and a kind of shallow satisfaction real in its way:—but they are ominous gospels! They are the sure, and even swift, forerunner of great changes. Expect that the old System of Society

---

[6] Indian city famous for its diamonds.

is done, is dying and fallen into dotage, when it begins to rave in that fashion. Most Systems that I have watched the death of, for the last three thousand years, have gone just so. The Ideal, the True and Noble that was in them having faded out, and nothing new remaining but naked Egoism, vulturous Greediness, they cannot live; they are bound and inexorably ordained by the oldest Destinies, Mothers of the Universe, to die. Curious enough: they thereupon, as I have pretty generally noticed, devise some light comfortable kind of 'wine-and-walnuts philosophy' for themselves, this of Supply-and-demand or another; and keep saying, during hours of mastication and rumination, which they call hours of meditation; 'Soul, take thy ease;[1] it is all *well* that thou art a vulture-soul;'—and pangs of dissolution come upon them, oftenest before they are aware!

Cash-payment never was, or could except for a few years be, the union-bond of man to man. Cash never yet paid one man fully his deserts to another; nor could it, nor can it, now or henceforth to the end of the world. I invite his Grace of Castle-Rackrent[2] to reflect on this;—does he think that a Land Aristocracy when it becomes a Land Auctioneership can have long to live? Or that Sliding-scales will increase the vital stamina of it? The indomitable Plugson too, of the respected Firm of Plugson, Hunks and Company, in St. Dolly Undershot,[3] is invited to reflect on this; for to him also it will be new, perhaps even newer. Book-keeping by double entry is admirable, and records several things in an exact manner. But the Mother-Destinies also keep their Tablets; in Heaven's Chancery also there goes on a recording; and things, as my Moslem friends say, are 'written on the iron leaf.'

Your Grace and Plugson, it is like, go to Church occasionally: did you never in vacant moments, with perhaps a dull parson droning to you, glance into your New Testament, and the cash-account stated four times over, by a kind of quadruple entry,—in the Four Gospels there? I consider that a cash-account, and balance-statement of work done and wages paid, worth attending to. Precisely *such*, though on a smaller scale, go on at all moments under this Sun; and the statement and balance of them in the Plugson Ledgers and on the Tablets of Heaven's Chancery are discrepant exceedingly;—which ought really

to teach, and to have long since taught, an indomitable common-sense Plugson of Undershot, much more an unattackable *un*common-sense Grace of Rackrent, a thing or two!—In brief, we shall have to dismiss the Cash-Gospel rigorously into its own place; we shall have to know, on the threshold, that either there is some infinitely deeper Gospel, subsidiary, explanatory and daily and hourly corrective, to the Cash one; or else that the Cash one itself and all others are fast travelling!

For all human things do require to have an Ideal in them; to have some Soul in them, as we said, were it only to keep the Body unputrefied. And wonderful it is to see how the Ideal or Soul, place it in what ugliest Body you may, will irradiate said Body with its own nobleness; will gradually, incessantly, mould, modify, new-form or reform said ugliest Body, and make it at last beautiful, and to a certain degree divine!—Oh, if you could dethrone that Brute-god Mammon, and put a Spirit-god in his place! One way or other, he must and will have to be dethroned.

Fighting, for example, as I often say to myself, Fighting with steel murder-tools is surely a much uglier operation than Working, take it how you will. Yet even of Fighting, in religious Abbot Samson's days, see what a Feudalism there has grown, a 'glorious Chivalry,' much besung down to the present day. Was not that one of the 'impossiblest' things? Under the sky is no uglier spectacle than two men with clenched teeth, and hell-fire eyes, hacking one another's flesh; converting precious living bodies, and priceless living souls, into nameless masses of putrescence, useful only for turnip-manure. How did a Chivalry ever come out of that; how anything that was not hideous, scandalous, infernal? It will be a question worth considering by and by.

I remark, for the present, only two things: first, that the Fighting itself was not, as we rashly suppose it, a Fighting without cause, but more or less with cause. Man is created to fight; he is perhaps best of all definable as a born soldier; his life 'a battle and a march,' under the right General. It is forever indispensable for a man to fight: now with Necessity, with Barrenness, Scarcity, with Puddles, Bogs, tangled Forests, unkempt Cotton;—now also with the hallucina-

---

[1] Luke 12:19.
[2] *Castle Rackrent* (1800), novel by Maria Edgeworth. Rackrent was the practice of renting tenant cottages to the highest bidder.
[3] Carlyle coinages but based on contemporary factory devices and practices.

tions of his poor fellow Men. Hallucinatory visions rise in the head of my poor fellow man: make him claim over me rights which are not his. All fighting, as we noticed long ago, is the dusty conflict of strengths, each thinking itself the strongest, or, in other words, the justest;—of Mights which do in the long-run, and forever will in this just Universe in the long-run, mean Rights. In conflict the perishable part of them, beaten sufficiently, flies off into dust: this process ended, appears the imperishable, the true and exact.

And now let us remark a second thing: how, in these baleful operations, a noble devout-hearted Chevalier will comport himself, and an ignoble godless Bucanier and Chactaw Indian. Victory is the aim of each. But deep in the heart of the noble man it lies forever legible, that as an Invisible Just God made him, so will and must God's Justice and this only, were it never so invisible, ultimately prosper in all controversies and enterprises and battles whatsoever. What an Influence; ever-present,—like a Soul in the rudest Caliban[4] of a body; like a ray of Heaven, and illuminative creative *Fiat-Lux*, in the wastest terrestrial Chaos! Blessed divine Influence, trace-able even in the horror of Battlefields and gar-ments rolled in blood: how it ennobles even the Battlefield; and, in place of a Chactaw Massacre, makes it a Field of Honour! A Battlefield too is great. Considered well, it is a kind of Quin-tessence of Labour; Labour distilled into its utmost concentration; the significance of years of it compressed into an hour. Here too thou shalt be strong, and not in muscle only, if thou wouldst prevail. Here too thou shalt be strong of heart, noble of soul; thou shalt dread no pain or death, thou shalt not love ease or life; in rage, thou shalt remember mercy, justice;—thou shalt be a Knight and not a Chactaw, if thou wouldst prevail! It is the rule of all battles, against hallucinating fellow Men, against unkempt Cotton, or whatsoever battles they may be, which a man in this world has to fight.

Howel Davies[5] dyes the West-Indian Seas with blood, piles his decks with plunder; approves himself the expertest Seaman, the daringest Sea fighter: but he gains no lasting victory, lasting victory is not possible for him. Not, had he fleets larger than the combined British Navy, all united with him in bucaniering. He, once for all, cannot prosper in his duel. He strikes down his

man, yes; but his man, or his man's representative, has no notion to lie struck down; neither, though slain ten times, will he keep so lying;—nor has the Universe any notion to keep him so lying! On the contrary, the Universe and he have, at all moments, all manner of motives to start up again, and desperately fight again. Your Napoleon is flung out, at last, to St. Helena; the latter end of him sternly compensating the beginning. The Bucanier strikes down a man, a hundred or a million men: but what profits it? He has one enemy never to be struck down; nay two enemies: Mankind and the Maker of Men. On the great scale or on the small, in fighting of men or fighting of difficulties, I will not embark my venture with Howel Davies: it is not the Bucanier, it is the Hero only that can gain victory, that can do more than *seem* to succeed. These things will deserve meditating; for they apply to all battle and soldiership, all struggle and effort whatsoever in this Fight of Life. It is a poor Gospel, Cash-Gospel or whatever name it have, that does not, with clear tone, uncontradictable, carrying conviction to all hearts, forever keep men in mind of these things.

Unhappily, my indomitable friend Plugson of Undershot has, in a great degree, forgotten them; —as, alas, all the world has; as, alas, our very Dukes and Soul-Overseers have, whose special trade it was to remember them! Hence these tears.—Plugson, who has indomitably spun Cotton merely to gain thousands of pounds, I have to call as yet a Bucanier and Chactaw; till there come something better, still more indomit-able from him. His hundred Thousand-pound Notes, if there be nothing other, are to me but as the hundred Scalps in a Chactaw wigwam. The blind Plugson: he was a Captain of Industry, born member of the Ultimate genuine Aris-tocracy of this Universe, could he have known it! These thousand men that span and toiled round him, they were a regiment whom he had enlisted, man by man; to make war on a very genuine enemy: Bareness of back, and disobedient Cotton-fibre, which will not, unless forced to it, consent to cover bare backs. Here is a most genuine enemy; over whom all creatures will wish him victory. He enlisted his thousand men; said to them, 'Come, brothers, let us have a dash at Cotton!' They follow with cheerful shout; they gain such a victory over Cotton as the Earth has to admire and clap hands at: but, alas, it is yet only of the

---

[4] The monster in Shakespeare's *Tempest*.
[5] Possibly Edward Davis, English buccaneer captain in the seventeenth century.

Bucanier or Chactaw sort,—as good as no victory! Foolish Plugson of St. Dolly Undershot: does he hope to become illustrious by hanging up the scalps in his wigwam, the hundred thousands at his banker's, and saying, Behold my scalps? Why, Plugson, even thy own host is all in mutiny: Cotton is conquered; but the 'bare backs'—are worse covered than ever! Indomitable Plugson, thou must cease to be a Chactaw; thou and others; thou, thyself, if no other!

Did William the Norman Bastard, or any of his Taillefers,[6] *Ironcutters*, manage so? Ironcutter, at the end of the campaign, did not turn-off his thousand fighters, but said to them: 'Noble fighters, this is the land we have gained; be I Lord in it,—what we will call *Law-ward*, maintainer and *keeper* of Heaven's *Laws*: be I *Law-ward*, or in brief orthoepy *Lord* in it, and be ye Loyal Men around me in it; and we will stand by one another, as soldiers round a captain, for again we shall have need of one another!' Plugson, bucanier-like, says to them: 'Noble spinners, this is the Hundred Thousand we have gained, wherein I mean to dwell and plant vineyards; the hundred thousand is mine, the three and sixpence daily was yours: adieu, noble spinners; drink my health with this groat each, which I give you over and above!' The entirely unjust Captain of Industry, say I; not Chevalier, but Bucanier! 'Commercial Law' does indeed acquit him; asks, with wide eyes, What else? So too Howel Davies asks, Was it not according to the strictest Bucanier Custom? Did I depart in any jot or tittle from the Laws of the Bucaniers?

After all, money, as they say, is miraculous. Plugson wanted victory; as Chevaliers and Bucaniers, and all men alike do. He found money recognised, by the whole world with one assent, as the true symbol, exact equivalent and synonym of victory;—and here we have him, a grim-browed, indomitable Bucanier, coming home to us with a 'victory,' which the whole world is *ceasing* to clap hands at! The whole world, taught somewhat impressively, is beginning to recognise that such victory is but half a victory; and that now, if it please the Powers, we must—have the other half!

Money is miraculous. What miraculous facilities has it yielded, will it yield us; but also what never-imagined confusions, obscurations has it brought in; down almost to total extinction of the moral sense in large masses of mankind! 'Protection of property,' of what is '*mine*,' means with most men protection of money,—the thing which, had I a thousand padlocks over it, is least of all *mine*; is, in a manner, scarcely worth calling mine! The symbol shall be held sacred, defended everywhere with tipstaves, ropes and gibbets; the thing signified shall be composedly cast to the dogs. A human being who has worked with human beings clears all scores with them, cuts himself with triumphant completeness forever loose from them, by paying down certain shillings and pounds. Was it not the wages I promised you? There they are, to the last sixpence,—according to the Laws of the Bucaniers!—Yes, indeed;—and, at such times, it becomes imperatively necessary to ask all persons, bucaniers and others, Whether these same respectable Laws of the Bucaniers are written on God's eternal Heavens at all, on the inner Heart of Man at all; or on the respectable Bucanier Logbook merely, for the convenience of bucaniering merely? What a question;—whereat Westminster Hall shudders to its driest parchment; and on the dead wigs each particular horsehair stands on end!

The Laws of Laissez-faire, O Westminster, the laws of industrial Captain and industrial Soldier, how much more of idle Captain and industrial Soldier, will need to be remodelled, and modified, and rectified in a hundred and a hundred ways,—and *not* in the Sliding-scale direction, but in the totally opposite one! With two million industrial Soldiers already sitting in Bastilles, and five million pining on potatoes, methinks Westminster cannot begin too soon!—A man has other obligations laid on him, in God's Universe, than the payment of cash: these also Westminster, if it will continue to exist and have board-wages, must contrive to take some charge of:—by Westminster or by another, they must and will be taken charge of; be, with whatever difficulty, got articulated, got enforced, and to a certain approximate extent put in practice. And, as I say, it cannot be too soon! For Mammonism, left to itself, has become Midas-eared; and with all its gold mountains, sits starving for want of bread; and Dilettantism with its partridge-nets, in this extremely earnest Universe of ours, is playing somewhat too high a game. 'A man by the very look of him promises so much': yes; and by the rent-roll of him does he promise nothing?—

Alas, what a business will this be, which our Continental friends, groping this long while

6 The name of William the Conqueror's Norman minstrel; Taillefer means "cleaver of iron."

somewhat absurdly about it and about it, call 'Organisation of Labour';—which must be taken out of the hands of absurd windy persons, and put into the hands of wise, laborious, modest and valiant men, to begin with it straightway; to proceed with it, and succeed in it more and more, if Europe, at any rate if England, is to continue habitable much longer. Looking at the kind of most noble Corn-Law Dukes or Practical *Duces* we have, and also of right reverend Soul-Over-seers, Christian Spiritual *Duces* 'on a minimum of four thousand five hundred,' one's hopes are a little chilled. Courage, nevertheless; there are many brave men in England! My indomitable Plugson,—nay is there not even in thee some hope? Thou art hitherto a Bucanier, as it was written and prescribed for thee by an evil world: but in that grim brow, in that indomitable heart which *can* conquer Cotton, do there not perhaps lie other ten-times nobler conquests?

CHAPTER XI

Labour

FOR THERE IS a perennial nobleness, and even sacredness, in Work. Were he never so benighted, forgetful of his high calling, there is always hope in a man that actually and earnestly works: in Idleness alone is there perpetual despair. Work, never so Mammonish, mean, *is* in communication with Nature; the real desire to get Work done will itself lead one more and more to truth, to Nature's appointments and regulations, which are truth.

The latest Gospel in this world is, Know thy work and do it. 'Know thyself': long enough has that poor 'self' of thine tormented thee; thou wilt never get to 'know' it, I believe! Think it not thy business, this of knowing thyself; thou art an unknowable individual: know what thou canst work at; and work at it, like a Hercules! That will be thy better plan.

It has been written, 'an endless significance lies in Work'; a man perfects himself by working. Foul jungles are cleared away, fair seedfields rise instead, and stately cities; and withal the man himself first ceases to be a jungle and foul

¹ Jeremiah 18:2–3.

unwholesome desert thereby. Consider how, even in the meanest sorts of Labour, the whole soul of a man is composed into a kind of real harmony, the instant he sets himself to work! Doubt, Desire, Sorrow, Remorse, Indignation, Despair itself, all these like helldogs lie beleaguering the soul of the poor dayworker, as of every man: but he bends himself with free valour against his task, and all these are stilled, all these shrink murmuring far off into their caves. The man is now a man. The blessed glow of Labour in him, is it not as purifying fire, wherein all poison is burnt up, and of sour smoke itself there is made bright blessed flame!

Destiny, on the whole, has no other way of cultivating us. A formless Chaos, once set it *revolving*, grows round and ever rounder; ranges itself, by mere force of gravity, into strata, spherical courses; is no longer a Chaos, but a round compacted World. What would become of the Earth, did she cease to revolve? In the poor old Earth, so long as she revolves, all inequalities, irregularities disperse themselves; all irregularities are incessantly becoming regular. Hast thou looked on the Potter's wheel,—one of the venerablest objects; old as the Prophet Ezechiel¹ and far older? Rude lumps of clay, how they spin themselves up, by mere quick whirling, into beautiful circular dishes. And fancy the most assiduous Potter, but without his wheel; reduced to make dishes, or rather amorphous botches, by mere kneading and baking! Even such a Potter were Destiny, with a human soul that would rest and lie at ease, that would not work and spin! Of an idle unrevolving man the kindest Destiny, like the most assiduous Potter without wheel, can bake and knead nothing other than a botch; let her spend on him what expensive colouring, what gilding and enamelling she will, he is but a botch. Not a dish; no, a bulging, kneaded, crooked, shambling, squint-cornered, amorphous botch,—a mere enamelled vessel of dishonour! Let the idle think of this.

Blessed is he who has found his work; let him ask no other blessedness. He has a work, a life-purpose; he has found it, and will follow it! How, as a free-flowing channel, dug and torn by noble force through the sour mud-swamp of one's existence, like an ever-deepening river there, it runs and flows;—draining-off the sour festering water, gradually from the root of the remotest grass-blade; making, instead of pestilential swamp, a green fruitful meadow with its clear-flowing stream. How blessed for the meadow itself, let the stream and *its* value be great or small! Labour is Life: from the inmost heart of the Worker rises his god-given Force, the sacred celestial Life-essence breathed into him by Almighty God; from his inmost heart awakens him to all nobleness,—to all knowledge, 'self-knowledge' and much else, so soon as Work fitly begins. Knowledge? The knowledge that will hold good in working, cleave thou to that; for Nature herself accredits that, says Yea to that. Properly thou hast no other knowledge but what thou hast got by working: the rest is yet all a hypothesis of knowledge; a things to be argued of in schools, a thing floating in the clouds, in endless logic-vortices, till we try it and fix it. 'Doubt, of whatever kind, can be ended by Action alone.'[2]

And again, hast thou valued Patience, Courage, Perseverance, Openness to light; readiness to own thyself mistaken, to do better next time? All these, all virtues, in wrestling with the dim brute Powers of Fact, in ordering of thy fellows in such wrestle, there and elsewhere not at all, thou wilt continually learn. Set down a brave Sir Christopher[3] in the middle of black ruined Stone-heaps, of foolish unarchitectural Bishops, redtape Officials, idle Nell-Gwyn Defenders of the Faith; and see whether he will ever raise a Paul's Cathedral out of all that, yea or no! Rough, rude, contradictory are all things and persons, from the mutinous masons and Irish hodmen, up to the idle Nell-Gwyn Defenders, to blustering redtape Officials, foolish unarchitectural Bishops. All these things and persons are there not for Christopher's sake and his Cathedral's; they are there for their own sake mainly! Christopher will have to conquer and constrain all these,—if be he able. All these are against him. Equitable Nature herself, who carries her mathematics and architectonics not on the face of her, but deep in the hidden heart of her,—Nature herself is but partially for him; will be wholly against him, if he constrain her not! His very money, where is it to come from? The pious munificence of England lies far-scattered, distant, unable to speak, and say, 'I am here';—must be spoken to before it can speak. Pious munificence, and all help, is so silent, invisible like the gods; impediment, contradictions manifold are so loud and near! O brave Sir Christopher, trust thou in those

notwithstanding, and front all these; understand all these; by valiant patience, noble effort, insight, by man's-strength, vanquish and compel all these,—and, on the whole, strike down victoriously the last topstone of that Paul's Edifice; thy monument for certain centuries, the stamp 'Great Man' impressed very legibly on Portlandstone there!—

Yes, all manner of help, and pious response from Men or Nature, is always what we call silent; cannot speak or come to light, till it be seen, till it be spoken to. Every noble work is at first 'impossible.' In very truth, for every noble work the possibilities will lie diffused through Immensity; inarticulate, undiscoverable except to faith. Like Gideon thou shalt spread out thy fleece at the door of thy tent;[4] see whether under the wide arch of Heaven there be any bounteous moisture, or none. Thy heart and life-purpose shall be as a miraculous Gideon's fleece, spread out in silent appeal to Heaven: and from the kind Immensities, what from the poor unkind Localities and town and country Parishes there never could, blessed dew-moisture to suffice thee shall have fallen!

Work is of a religious nature:—work is of a *brave* nature; which it is the aim of all religion to be. All work of man is as the swimmer's: a waste ocean threatens to devour him; if he front it not bravely, it will keep its word. By incessant wise defiance of it, lusty rebuke and buffet of it, behold how it loyally supports him, bears him as its conqueror along. 'It is so,' says Goethe, 'with all things that man undertakes in this world.'[5]

Brave Sea-captain, Norse Sea-King,—Columbus, my hero, royalest Sea-king of all! it is no friendly environment this of thine, in the waste deep waters; around thee mutinous discouraged souls, behind thee disgrace and ruin, before thee the unpenetrated veil of Night. Brother, these wild water-mountains, bounding from their deep bases (ten miles deep, I am told), are not entirely there on thy behalf! Meseems *they* have other work than floating thee forward:—and the huge Winds, that sweep from Ursa Major to the Tropics and Equators, dancing, their giant-waltz through the kingdoms of Chaos and Immensity, they care little about filling rightly or filling wrongly the small shoulder-of-mutton sails in this cockle-skiff of thine! Thou art not

[2] Goethe, *Wilhelm Meister's Apprenticeship*.
[3] Sir Christopher Wren (1632–1723), architect of St. Paul's Cathedral.
[4] Judges 6:36–38.   [5] *Wilhelm Meister's Travels*.

among articulate-speaking friends, my brother; thou art among immeasurable dumb monsters, tumbling, howling wide as the world here. Secret, far off, invisible to all hearts but thine, there lies a help in them: see how thou wilt get at that. Patiently thou wilt wait till the mad Southwester spend itself, saving thyself by dextrous science of defence, the while: valiantly, with swift decision, wilt thou strike in, when the favouring East, the Possible, springs up. Mutiny of men thou wilt sternly repress; weakness, despondency, thou wilt cheerily encourage: thou wilt swallow down complaint, unreason, weariness, weakness of others and thyself;—how much wilt thou swallow down! There shall be a depth of Silence in thee, deeper than this Sea, which is but ten miles deep: a Silence unsoundable; known to God only. Thou shalt be a Great man. Yes, my World-Soldier, thou of the World Marine-serivce,—thou wilt have to be *greater* than this tumultuous unmeasured World here round thee is: thou, in thy strong soul, as with wrestler's arms, shalt embrace it, harness it down; and make it bear thee on,—to new Americas, or whither God wills!

BOOK FOURTH

Horoscope

CHAPTER IV

Captains of Industry

IF I BELIEVED that Mammonism with its adjuncts was to continue henceforth the one serious principle of our existence, I should reckon it idle to solicit remedial measures from any Government, the disease being insusceptible of remedy. Government can do much, but it can in nowise do all. Government, as the most conspicuous object in Society, is called upon to give signal of what shall be done; and, in many ways, to preside over, further, and command the doing of it. But the Government cannot do, by all its signaling and commanding, what the Society is radically indisposed to do. In the long-run every Government is the exact symbol of its People, with their wisdom and unwisdom; we have to say, Like People like Government.—The main substance of this immense Problem of Organising Labour, and first of all of Managing the Working Classes, will, it is very clear, have to be solved by those who stand practically in the middle of it; by those who themselves work and preside over work. Of all that can be enacted by any Parliament in regard to it, the germs must already lie potentially extant in those two Classes, who are to obey such enactment. A Human Chaos *in* which there is no light, you vainly attempt to irradiate by light shed *on* it; order never can arise there.

But it is my firm conviction that the 'Hell of England' will *cease* to be that of 'not making money'; that we shall get a nobler Hell and a nobler Heaven! I anticipate light *in* the Human Chaos, glimmering, shining more and more; under manifold true signals from without That light shall shine. Our deity no longer being Mammon,—O Heavens, each man will then say to himself: 'Why such deadly haste to make money? I shall not go to Hell, even if I do not make money! There is another Hell, I am told!' Competition, at railway-speed, in all branches of commerce and work will then abate:—good felt-hats for the head, in every sense, instead of seven-feet lath-and-plaster hats on wheels, will then be discoverable! Bubble-periods, with their panics and commercial crises, will again become infrequent; steady modest industry will take the place of gambling specualtion. To be a noble Master, among noble Workers, will again be the first ambition with some few; to be a rich Master only the second. How the Inventive Genius of England, with the whirr of its bobbins and billy-rollers shoved somewhat into the backgrounds of the brain, will contrive and devise, not cheaper produce exclusively, but fairer distribution of the produce at its present cheapness! By degrees, we shall again have a Society with something of Heroism in it, something of Heaven's Blessing on it; we shall again have, as my German friend asserts, 'instead of Mammon-Feudalism with unsold cotton-shirts and Preservation of the Game, noble just Industrialism and Government by the Wisest!'

It is with the hope of awakening here and there a British man to know himself for a man and divine soul, that a few words of parting admonition, to all persons to whom the Heavenly Powers have lent power of any kind in this land, may now be addressed. And first to those same Master-Workers, Leaders of Industry; who stand nearest and in fact powerfulest, though not most prominent, being as yet in too many senses a Virtuality rather than an Actuality.

The Leaders of Industry, if Industry is ever to be led, are virtually the Captains of the World! if there be no nobleness in them, there will never be an Aristocracy more. But let the Captains of Industry consider: once again, are they born of other clay than the old Captains of Slaughter; doomed forever to be no Chivalry, but a mere gold-plated *Doggery*,—what the French well name *Canaille*, 'Doggery' with more or less gold carrion at its disposal? Captains of Industry are the true Fighters, henceforth recognisable as the only true ones: Fighters against Chaos, Necessity and the Devils and Jötuns; and lead on Mankind in that great, and alone true, and universal warfare; the stars in their courses fighting for them, and all Heaven and all Earth saying audibly, Well done![1] Let the Captains of Industry retire into their own hearts, and ask solemnly, If there is nothing but vulturous hunger, for fine wines, valet reputation and gilt carriages, discoverable there? Of hearts made by the Almighty God I will not believe such a thing. Deep-hidden under wretchedest god-forgetting Cants, Epicurisms, Dead-Sea Apisms; forgotten as under foulest fat Lethe mud and weeds, there is yet, in all hearts born into this God's-World, a spark of the Godlike slumbering. Awake, O nightmare sleepers; awake, arise, or be forever fallen! This is not playhouse poetry; it is sober fact. Our England, our world cannot live as it is. It will connect itself with a God again, or go down with nameless throes and fire-consummation to the Devils. Thou who feelest aught of such a Godlike stirring in thee, any faintest intimation of it as through heavy-laden dreams, follow *it*, I conjure thee. Arise, save thyself, be one of those that save thy country.

Bucaniers, Chactaw Indians, whose supreme aim in fighting is that they may get the scalps, the money, that they may amass scalps and money: out of such came no Chivalry, and never will! Out of such came only gore and wreck, infernal rage and misery; desperation quenched in annihilation. Behold it, I bid thee, behold there, and consider! What is it that thou have a hundred thousand-pound bills laid-up in thy strong-room, a hundred scalps hung-up in thy wigwam? I value not them or thee. Thy scalps and thy thousand-pound bills are as yet nothing, if no nobleness from within irradiate them; if no Chivalry, in action, or in embryo ever struggling towards birth and action, be there.

Love of men cannot be bought by cash-payment; and without love men cannot endure to be together. You cannot lead a Fighting World without having it regimented, chivalried: the thing, in a day, becomes impossible; all men in it, the highest at first, the very lowest at last, discern consciously, or by a noble instinct, this necessity. And can you any more continue to lead a Working World unregimented, anarchic? I answer, and the Heavens and Earth are now answering, No! The thing becomes not 'in a day' impossible; but in some two generations it does. Yes, when fathers and mothers, in Stockport hunger-cellars, begin to eat their children, and Irish widows have to prove their relationship by dying of typhus-fever; and amid Governing 'Corporations of the Best and Bravest,' busy to preserve their game by 'bushing,' dark millions of God's human creatures start up in mad Chartisms, impracticable Sacred-Months, and Manchester Insurrections;—and there is a virtual Industrial Aristocracy as yet only half-alive, spell-bound amid money-bags and ledgers; and an actual Idle Aristocracy seemingly near dead in somnolent delusions, in trespasses and double-barrels; 'sliding,' as on inclined-planes, which every new year they *soap* with new Hansard's-jargon under God's sky, and so are 'sliding,' ever faster, towards a 'scale' and balance-scale whereon is written *Thou art found Wanting:*[2]—in such days, after a generation or two, I say, it does become, even to the low and simple, very palpably impossible! No Working World, any more than a Fighting World, can be led on without a noble Chivalry of Work, and laws and fixed rules which follow out of that,—far nobler than any Chivalry of Fighting was. As an anarchic multitude on mere Supply-and-demand, it is becoming inevitable that we dwindle in horrid suicidal convulsion and self-abrasion, frightful to the imagination, into *Chactaw* Workers. With wigwams and scalps,—with palaces and thousand-pound bills; with savagery, depopulation, chaotic desolation! Good Heavens, will not one French Revolution and Reign of Terror suffice us, but must there be two? There will be two if needed; there will be twenty if needed; there will be precisely as many as are needed. The Laws of Nature will have themselves fulfilled. That is a thing certain to me.

Your gallant battle-hosts and work-hosts, as the others did, will need to be made loyally yours; they must and will be regulated, methodically secured in their just share of conquest under

---

[1] Judges 5:20.   [2] Daniel 5:27.

you;—joined with you in veritable brotherhood, sonhood, by quite other and deeper ties than those of temporary day's wages! How would mere red-coated regiments, to say nothing of chivalries, fight for you, if you could discharge them on the evening of the battle, on payment of the stipulated shillings,—and they discharge you on the morning of it! Chelsea Hospitals,[3] pensions, promotions, rigorous lasting covenant on the one side and on the other, are indispensable even for a hired fighter. The Feudal Baron, much more,—how could he subsist with mere temporary mercenaries round him, at sixpence a day; ready to go over to the other side, if sevenpence were offered? He could not have subsisted;—and his noble instinct saved him from the necessity of even trying! The Feudal Baron had a Man's Soul in him; to which anarchy, mutiny, and the other fruits of temporary mercenaries, were intolerable: he had never been a Baron otherwise, but had continued a Chactaw and Bucanier. He felt it precious, and at last it became habitual, and his fruitful enlarged existence included it as a necessity, to have men round him who in heart loved him; whose life he watched over with rigour yet with love; who were prepared to give their life for him, if need came. It was beautiful; it was human! Man lives not otherwise, nor can live contented, anywhere or anywhen. Isolation is the sum-total of wretchedness to man. To be cut off, to be left solitary: to have a world alien, not your world; all a hostile camp for you; not a home at all, of hearts and faces who are yours, whose you are! It is the frightfulest enchantment; too truly a work of the Evil One. To have neither superior, nor inferior, nor equal, united manlike to you. Without father, without child, without brother. Man knows no sadder destiny. 'How is each of us,' exclaims Jean Paul, 'so lonely in the wide bosom of the All!'[4] Encased each as in his transparent 'ice-palace'; our brother visible in his, making signals and gesticulations to us;— visible, but forever unattainable: on his bosom we shall never rest, nor he on ours. It was not a God that did this; no!

Awake, ye noble Workers, warriors in the one true war: all this must be remedied. It is you who are already half-alive, whom I will welcome into life; whom I will conjure, in God's name, to shake off your enchanted sleep, and live wholly! Cease to count scalps, gold-purses; not in these lies your or our salvation. Even these, if you count only these, will not long be left. Let bucaniering be

put far from you; alter, speedily abrogate all laws of the bucaniers, if you would gain any victory that shall endure. Let God's justice, let pity, nobleness and manly valour, with more gold-purses or with fewer, testify themselves in this your brief Life-transit to all the Eternities, the Gods and Silences. It is to you I call; for ye are not dead, ye are already half-alive: there is in you a sleepless dauntless energy, the prime-matter of all nobleness in man. Honour to you in your kind. It is to you I call: ye know at least this, That the mandate of God to His creature man is: Work! The future Epic of the World rests not with those that are near dead, but with those that are alive, and those that are coming into life.

Look around you. Your world-hosts are all in mutiny, in confusion, destitution; on the eve of fiery wreck and madness! They will not march farther for you, on the sixpence a day and supply-and-demand principle: they will not; nor ought they, nor can they. Ye shall reduce them to order, begin reducing them. To order, to just subordination; noble loyalty in return for noble guidance. Their souls are driven nigh mad; let yours be sane and ever saner. Not as a bewildered bewildering mob; but as a firm regimented mass, with real captains over them, will these men march any more. All human interests, combined human endeavours, and social growths in this world, have, at a certain stage of their development, required organising: and Work, the grandest of human interests, does now require it.

God knows, the task will be hard: but no noble task was ever easy. This task will wear away your lives, and the lives of your sons and grandsons: but for what purpose, if not for tasks like this, were lives given to men? Ye shall cease to count your thousand-pound scalps, the noble of you shall cease! Nay the very scalps, as I say, will not long be left it you count only these. Ye shall cease wholly to be barbarous vulturous Chactaws, and become noble European Nineteenth-Century Men. Ye shall know that Mammon, in never such gigs and flunky 'respectabilities,' is not the alone God; that of himself he is but a Devil, and even a Brute-god.

Difficult? Yes, it will be difficult. The short-fibre cotton; that too was difficult. The waste cotton-shrub, long useless, disobedient, as the thistle by the wayside,—have ye not conquered it; made it into beautiful bandana webs; white woven shirts for men; bright-tinted air-garments wherein flit goddesses? Ye have shivered moun-

---

[3] An old soldiers' home and hospital, founded by Charles II.   [4] Jean Paul, *Siebenkäs*.

tains asunder, made the hard iron pliant to you as soft putty: the Forest-giants, Marsh-jötuns bear sheaves of golden-grain; Ægir the Sea-demon himself stretches his back for a sleek highway to you, and on Firehorses and Windhorses ye career.[5] Ye are most strong. Thor red-bearded, with his blue sun-eyes, with his cheery heart and strong thunder-hammer, he and you have prevailed. Ye are most strong, ye Sons of the icy North, of the far East,—far marching from your rugged Eastern Wildernesses, hitherward from the gray Dawn of Time! Ye are Sons of the *Jötun*-land; the land of Difficulties Conquered. Difficult? You must try this thing. Once try it with the understanding that it will and shall have to be done. Try it as ye try the paltrier thing, making of money! I will bet on you once more, against all Jötuns, Tailor-gods, Doublebarrelled Law-wards, and Denizens of Chaos whatsoever!

from The Life of John Sterling

John Sterling (1806–44) was an Anglican clergyman, son of Edward Sterling, the editor of the Times *known as "The Thunderer." Sterling had religious and literary leanings and he came under the influence of Coleridge in the late eighteen-twenties. Somewhat later he came to know Carlyle and the two became fast friends. This eventually led Carlyle to write a biography of Sterling in 1851, seven years after Sterling's early death. Carlyle shaped the biography to reflect not only Sterling's character but also his representative quality as a man caught in the Victorian dilemma of doubt. As an aspect of Sterling's development Carlyle treated the impact of Coleridge on the circle that gathered round him in Highgate in his later years. It is that chapter of Carlyle's biography of Sterling that has become in itself a classic, a portrait of Coleridge by one who was in many respects his successor in the Victorian age.*

CHAPTER VIII

Coleridge

COLERIDGE sat on the brow of Highgate Hill, in those years, looking down on London and its smoke-tumult, like a sage escaped from the inanity of life's battle; attracting towards him the thoughts of innumerable brave souls still engaged there. His express contributions to poetry, philosophy, or any specific province of human literature or enlightenment, had been small and sadly intermittent; but he had, especially among young inquiring men, a higher than literary, a kind of prophetic or magician character. He was thought to hold, he alone in England, the key of German and other Transcendentalisms; knew the sublime secret of believing by 'the reason' what 'the understanding' had been obliged to fling out as incredible; and could still, after Hume and Voltaire had done their best and worst with him, profess himself an orthodox Christian, and say and print to the Church of England, with its singular old rubrics and surplices at Allhallowtide, *Esto perpetua.*[1] A sublime man; who, alone in those dark days, had saved his crown of spiritual manhood; escaping from the black materialisms, and revolutionary deluges, with 'God, Freedom, Immortality' still his: a king of men. The practical intellects of the world did not much heed him, or carelessly reckoned him a metaphysical dreamer: but to the rising spirits of the young generation he had this dusky sublime character; and sat there as a kind of *Magus*, girt in mystery and enigma; his Dodona oak-grove (Mr. Gilman's house at Highgate)[2] whispering strange things, uncertain whether oracles or jargon.

---

[5] II Kings 2:11.   [1] "Be thou everlasting."
[2] Dr. James Gillman (1782–1839) took Coleridge into his home in Highgate and cared for him from 1816 to 1834 when Coleridge died.

The Gilmans did not encourage much company, or excitation of any sort, round their sage; nevertheless access to him if a youth did reverently wish it, was not difficult. He would stroll about the pleasant garden with you, sit in the pleasant rooms of the place,—perhaps take you to his own peculiar room, high up, with a rearward view, which was the chief view of all. A really charming outlook, in fine weather. Close at hand, wide sweep of flowery leafy gardens, their few houses mostly hidden, the very chimney-pots veiled under blossomy umbrage, flowed gloriously down hill, gloriously issuing in wide-tufted undulating plain-country, rich in all charms of field and town. Waving blooming country of the brightest green; dotted all over with handsome villas, handsome groves; crossed by roads and human traffic, here inaudible or heard only as a musical hum: and behind all swam, under olive-tinted haze, the illimitable limitary ocean of London, with its domes and steeples definite in the sun, big Paul's[3] and the many memories attached to it hanging high over all. Nowhere, of its kind, could you see a grander prospect on a bright summer day, with the set of the air going southward,—southward, and so draping with the city-smoke not *you* but the city. Here for hours would Coleridge talk, concerning all conceivable or inconceivable things; and liked nothing better than to have an intelligent, or failing that, even a silent and patient human listener. He distinguished himself to all that ever heard him as at least the most surprising talker extant in this world,—and to some small minority, by no means to all, as the most excellent.

The good man, he was now getting old, towards sixty perhaps; and gave you the idea of a life that had been full of sufferings; a life heavy-laden, half-vanquished, still swimming painfully in seas of manifold physical and other bewilderment. Brow and head were round, and of massive weight, but the face was flabby and irresolute. The deep eyes, of a light hazel, were as full of sorrow as of inspiration; confused pain looked mildly from them, as in a kind of mild astonishment. The whole figure and air, good and amiable otherwise, might be called flabby and irresolute; expressive of weakness under possibility of strength. He hung loosely on his limbs, with knees bent, and stooping attitude; in walking, he rather shuffled than decisively stept;

and a lady once remarked, he never could fix which side of the garden walk would suit him best, but continually shifted, in corkscrew fashion, and kept trying both. A heavy-laden, high-aspiring and surely much-suffering man. His voice, naturally soft and good, had contracted itself into a plaintive snuffle and singsong; he spoke as if preaching,—you would have said, preaching earnestly and also hopelessly the weightiest things. I still recollect his 'object' and 'subject,' terms of continual recurrence in the Kantean province; and how he sang and snuffled them into 'om-m-mject' and 'sum-m-mject,' with a kind of solemn shake or quaver, as he rolled along. No talk, in his century or in any other, could be more surprising.

Sterling, who assiduously attended him, with profound reverence, and was often with him by himself, for a good many months, gives a record of their first colloquy.[4] Their colloquies were numerous, and he has taken note of many; but they are all gone to the fire, except this first, which Mr. Hare has printed,—unluckily without date. It contains a number of ingenious, true and half-true observations, and is of course a faithful epitome of the things said; but it gives small idea of Coleridge's way of talking;—this one feature is perhaps the most recognisable, 'Our interview lasted for three hours, during which he talked two hours and three quarters.' Nothing could be more copious than his talk; and furthermore it was always, virtually or literally, of the nature of a monologue; suffering no interruption, however reverent; hastily putting aside all foreign additions, annotations, or most ingenuous desires for elucidation, as well-meant superfluities which would never do. Besides, it was talk not flowing anywhither like a river, but spreading everywhither in inextricable currents and regurgitations like a lake or sea; terribly deficient in definite goal or aim, nay often in logical intelligibility; *what* you were to believe or do, on any earthly or heavenly thing, obstinately refusing to appear from it. So that, most times, you felt logically lost; swamped near to drowing in this tide of ingenious vocables, spreading out boundless as if to submerge the world.

To sit as a passive bucket and be pumped into, whether you consent or not, can in the long-run be exhilarating to no creature; how eloquent soever the flood of utterance that is descending.

---

[3] St. Paul's Cathedral.

[4] *Biography,* by Hare, pp. xvi–xxvi. [Carlyle's note in reference to the 1848 biography of John Sterling by Julius Charles Hare which partly prompted Carlyle's biography.]

But if it be withal a confused unintelligible flood of utterance, threatening to submerge all known landmarks of thought, and drown the world and you!—I have heard Coleridge talk, with eager musical energy, two stricken hours, his face radiant and moist, and communicate no meaning whatsoever to any individual of his hearers,—certain of whom, I for one, still kept eagerly listening in hope; the most had long before given up, and formed (if the room were large enough) secondary humming groups of their own. He began anywhere: you put some question to him, made some suggestive observation: instead of answering this, or decidedly setting out towards answer of it, he would accumulate formidable apparatus, logical swim-bladders, transcendental life-preservers and other precautionary and vehiculatory gear, for setting out; perhaps did at last get under way,—but was swiftly solicited, turned aside by the glance of some radiant new game on this hand or that, into new courses; and ever into new; and before long into all the Universe, where it was uncertain what game you would catch, or whether any.

His talk, alas, was distinguished, like himself, by irresolution: it disliked to be troubled with conditions, abstinences, definite fulfilments;—loved to wander at its own sweet will, and make its auditor and his claims and humble wishes a mere passive bucket for itself! He had knowledge about many things and topics, much curious reading; but generally all topics led him, after a pass or two, into the high seas of theosophic philosophy, the hazy infinitude of Kantean transcendentalism, with its 'sum-m-mjects' and 'om-m-mjects.' Sad enough; for with such indolent impatience of the claims and ignorances of others, he had not the least talent for explaining this or anything unknown to them; and you swam and fluttered in the mistiest wide unintelligible deluge of things, for most part in a rather profitless uncomfortable manner.

Glorious islets, too, I have seen rise out of the haze; but they were few, and soon swallowed in the general element again. Balmy sunny islets, islets of the blest and the intelligible:—on which occasions those secondary humming groups would all cease humming, and hang breathless upon the eloquent words; till once your islet got wrapt in the mist again, and they could recommence humming. Eloquent artistically expressive words you always had; piercing radiances of a most subtle insight came at intervals; tones of

noble pious sympathy, recognisable as pious though strangely coloured, were never wanting long: but in general you could not call this aimless, cloudcapt, cloud-based, lawlessly meandering human discourse of reason by the name of 'excellent talk,' but only of 'surprising'; and were reminded bitterly of Hazlitt's[5] account of it: 'Excellent talker, very,—if you let him start from no premises and come to no conclusion.' Coleridge was not without what talkers call wit, and there were touches of prickly sarcasm in him, contemptuous enough of the world and its idols and popular dignitaries; he had traits even of poetic humour: but in general he seemed deficient in laughter; or indeed in sympathy for concrete human things either on the sunny or on the stormy side. One right peal of concrete laughter at some convicted flesh-and-blood absurdity, one burst of noble indignation at some injustice or depravity, rubbing elbows with is on this solid Earth, how strange would it have been in that Kantean haze-world, and how infinitely cheering amid its vacant-air castles and dim-melting ghosts and shadows! None such ever came. His life had been an abstract thinking and dreaming, idealistic, passed amid the ghosts of defunct bodies and of unborn ones. The moaning singsong of that theosophico-metaphysical monotony left on you, at last, a very dreary feeling.

In close colloquy, flowing within narrower banks, I suppose he was more definite and apprehensible; Sterling in aftertimes did not complain of his unintelligibility, or imputed it only to the abstruse high nature of the topics handled. Let us hope, so let us try to believe so! There is no doubt but Coleridge could speak plain words on things plain: his observations and responses on the trivial matters that occurred were as simple as the commonest man's, or were even distinguished by superior simplicity as well as pertinency. 'Ah, your tea is too cold, Mr. Coleridge!' mourned the good Mrs. Gilman once, in her kind, reverential and yet protective manner, handing him a very tolerable though belated cup.—'It's better than I deserve!' snuffed he, in a low hoarse murmur, partly courteous, chiefly pious, the tone of which still abides with me: 'It's better than I deserve!'

But indeed, to the young ardent mind, instinct with pious nobleness, yet driven to the grim deserts of Radicalism for a faith, his speculations had a charm much more than literary, a charm

---

[5] William Hazlitt (1778–1830), English essayist.

almost religious and prophetic. The constant gist of his discourse was lamentation over the sunk condition of the world; which he recognised to be given-up to Atheism and Materialism, full of mere sordid misbeliefs, mispursuits and mis-results. All Science had become mechanical; the science not of men, but of a kind of human beavers. Churches themselves had died away into a godless mechanical condition; and stood there as mere Cases of Articles, mere Forms of Churches; like the dried carcasses of once-swift camels, which you find left withering in the thirst of the universal desert,—ghastly portents for the present, beneficent ships of the desert no more. Men's souls were blinded, hebetated; and sunk under the influence of Atheism and Materialism, and Hume and Voltaire: the world for the present was as an extinct world, deserted of God, and incapable of welldoing till it changed its heart and spirit. This, expressed I think with less of indignation and with more of long-drawn querulousness, was always recognisable as the ground-tone:—in which truly a pious young heart, driven into Radicalism and the opposition party, could not but recognise a too sorrowful truth; and ask of the Oracle, with all earnestness, What remedy, then?

The remedy, though Coleridge himself pro-fessed to see it as in sunbeams, could not, except by processes unspeakably difficult, be described to you at all. On the whole, those dead Churches, this dead English Church especially, must be brought to life again. Why not? It was not dead; the soul of it, in this parched-up body, was tragically asleep only. Atheistic Philosophy was true on its side, and Hume and Voltaire could on their own ground speak irrefragably for them-selves against any Church: but lift the Church and them into a higher sphere of argument, *they* died into inanition, the Church revivified itself into pristine florid vigour,—became once more a living ship of the desert, and invincibly bore you over stock and stone. But how, but how! By attending to the 'reason' of man, said Coleridge, and duly chaining-up the 'understanding' of man: the *Vernunft* (Reason) and *Verstand* (Under-standing) of the Germans, it all turned upon these, if you could well understand them,—which you couldn't. For the rest, Mr. Coleridge had on the anvil various Books, expecially was about to write one grand Book *On the Logos*, which would help to bridge the chasm for us. So much appeared, however: Churches, though proved false (as you had imagined), were still true (as you were to imagine): here was an Artist who

could burn you up an old Church, root and branch; and then as the Alchymists professed to do with organic substances in general, distil you as 'Astral Spirit' from the ashes, which was the very image of the old burnt article, its airdrawn counterpart,—this you still had, or might get, and draw uses from, if you could. Wait till the Book on the Logos were done;—alas, till your own terrene eyes, blind with conceit and the dust of logic, were purged, subtilised and spiritual-ised into the sharpness of vision requisite for discerning such an 'om-m-mject.'—The in-genuous young English head, of those days, stood strangely puzzled by such revelations; uncertain whether it were getting inspired, or getting infatuated into flat imbecility; and strange effulgence, of new day or else of deeper meteoric night, coloured the horizon of the future for it.

Let me not be unjust to this memorable man. Surely there was here, in his pious, ever-labour-ing, subtle mind, a precious truth, or prefigure-ment of truth; and yet a fatal delusion withal. Prefigurement that, in spite of beaver sciences and temporary spiritual hebetude and cecity, man and his Universe were eternally divine; and that no past nobleness, or revelation of the divine, could or would ever be lost to him. Most true, surely, and worthy of all acceptance. Good also to do what you can with old Churches and practical Symbols of the Noble: nay, quit not the burnt ruins of them while you find there is still gold to be dug there. But, on the whole, do not think you can, by logical alchymy, distil astral spirits from them; or if you could, that said astral spirits, or defunct logical phantasms, could serve you in anything. What the light of your mind, which is the direct inspiration of the Almighty, pronounces incredible,—that, in God's name, leave uncredited; at your peril do not try believing that. No subtlest hocus-pocus of 'reason' *versus* 'understanding' will avail for that feat;—and it is terribly perilous to try it in these provinces!

The truth is, I now see, Coleridge's talk and speculation was the emblem of himself: in it, as in him, a ray of heavenly inspiration struggled, in a tragically ineffectual degree, with the weak-ness of flesh and blood. He says once, he 'has skirted the howling deserts of Infidelity'; this was evident enough: but he had not had the courage, in defiance of pain and terror, to press resolutely across said deserts to the new firm lands of Faith beyond; he preferred to create logical fatamorganas for himself on this hither side, and laboriously solace himself with these.

To the man himself Nature had given, in high measure, the seeds of a noble endowment; and to unfold it had been forbidden him. A subtle lynx-eyed intellect, tremulous pious sensibility to all good and all beautiful; truly a ray of empyrean light;—but imbedded in such weak laxity of character, in such indolences and esuriences as had made strange work with it. Once more, the tragic story of a high endowment with an insufficient will. An eye to discern the divineness of the Heaven's splendours and lightnings, the insatiable wish to revel in their godlike radiances and brilliances; but no heart to front the scathing terrors of them, which is the first condition of your conquering an abiding place there. The courage necessary for him above all things, had been denied this man. His life, with such ray of the empyrean in it, was great and terrible to him; and he had not valiantly grappled with it, he had fled from it; sought refuge in vague day-dreams, hollow compromises, in opium, in theosophic metaphysics. Harsh pain, danger, necessity, slavish harnessed toil, were of all things abhorrent to him. And so the empyrean element, lying smothered under the terrene, and yet inextinguishable there, made sad writhings. For pain, danger, difficulty, steady slaving toil, and other highly disagreeable behests of destiny, shall in no wise be shirked by any brightest mortal that will approve himself loyal to his mission in this world; nay, precisely the higher he is, the deeper will be the disagreeableness, and the detestability to flesh and blood, of the tasks laid on him; and the heavier too, and more tragic, his penalties, if he neglect them.

For the old Eternal Powers do live forever; nor do their laws know any change, however we in our poor wigs and church-tippets may attempt to read their laws. To *steal* into Heaven,—by the modern method, of sticking ostrich-like your head into fallacies on Earth, equally as by the ancient and by all conceivable methods,—is forever forbidden. High-treason is the name of that attempt; and it continues to be punished as such. Strange enough: here once more was a kind of Heaven-scaling Ixion;[6] and to him, as to the old one, the just gods were very stern! The ever-revolving, never-advancing Wheel (of a kind) was his, through life; and from his Cloud-Juno did not he too procreate strange Centaurs, spectral Puseyisms,[7] monstrous illusory Hybrids, and ecclesiastical Chimeras,—which now roam the earth in a very lamentable manner!

from Reminiscences

Carlyle's Reminiscences *were begun in 1866 after the death of Jane Welsh Carlyle but not published until after his own death in 1881, when they were issued by James Anthony Froude. When they appeared they provoked controversy because they showed Carlyle's intense grief at the loss of Jane and because they contained much outspoken comment on revered figures of the nineteenth century whom Carlyle had known. One of the more sharply etched of the briefer portraits in the* Reminiscences *is that of Wordsworth in old age. Carlyle himself was seventy-two when he recalled his meetings with Wordsworth up to thirty years before.*

Wordsworth

OF WORDSWORTH I have little to write that could ever be of use to myself or others. I did not see him much, or till latish in my course see him at all; nor did we deeply admire one another at any time! Of me in my first times he had little knowledge; and any feeling he had towards me, I suspect, was largely blended with abhorrence and perhaps a kind of fear. His works I knew; but never considerably reverenced,—could not, on attempting it. A man recognisably of strong intellectual powers, strong character;

---

[6] Ixion in Greek mythology sought to seduce Hera but was given a cloud in her shape instead, then bound by Zeus to a fiery wheel. The "cloud" later gave birth to the ancestor of the Centaurs.

[7] After E. B. Pusey (1801–86), leader of the Oxford Movement.

given to meditation, and much contemptuous of the *un*meditative world and its noisy nothing-nesses; had a fine limpid style of writing and delineating, in his small way; a fine limpid vein of melody too in him (as of an honest rustic *fiddle*, good, and well handled, but *wanting* two or more of the *strings*, and not capable of much!)—in fact, a rather dull, hard-tempered, unproductive and almost wearisome kind of man; not adorable, by any means, as a great Poetic Genius, much less as the Trismegistus of such; whom only a select few could even read, instead of mis-reading, which was the opinion his worshippers confidently entertained of him! Privately I had a real respect for him, withal, founded on his early Biography, which Wilson of Edinburgh had painted to me as of antique greatness signifying: "Poverty and Peasanthood, then; be it so. But we consecrate ourselves to the Muses, all the same, and will proceed on those terms, Heaven aiding!" This, and what of faculty I did recognise in the man, gave me a clear esteem of him, as of one remarkable and fairly beyond common;—not to disturb which, I avoided speaking of him to his worshippers; or, if the topic turned up, would listen with an acquiescing air. But to my private self his divine reflections and unfathomabilities seemed stinted, scanty; palish and uncertain;—perhaps in part a feeble *reflex* (derived at second hand through Coleridge) of the immense German fund of such?—and I reckoned his Poetic Storehouse to be far from an opulent or well furnished apartment!

It was perhaps about 1840 that I first had any decisive meeting with Wordsworth, or made any really personal acquaintance with him. In parties at Taylor's[1] I may have seen him before; but we had no speech together, nor did we specially notice one another:—one such time I do remember (probably *before*, as it was in my earlier days of Sterling acquaintanceship, when Sterling[2] used to argue much with me), Words-worth sat silent, almost next to me, while Sterling took to asserting the claims of Kotzebue[3] as a Dramatist ("recommended even by Goethe," as he likewise urged); whom I with pleasure did my endeavour to explode from that mad notion,—and thought (as I still recollect), "This will perhaps please Wordsworth, too;" who, however, gave not the least sign of that or any other feeling.

I had various dialogues with him in that same room; but these, I judge, were all or mostly of after date.

On a summer morning (let us call it 1840, then) I was apprised by Taylor that Wordsworth had come to Town; and would meet a small party of us at a certain Tavern in St. James's Street, at breakfast,—to which I was invited for the given day and hour. We had a pretty little room; quiet, though looking street-ward (Tavern's *name* is quite lost to me); the morning sun was pleasantly tinting the opposite houses, a balmy, calm and bright morning; Wordsworth, I think, arrived just along with me; we had still five minutes of sauntering and miscellaneous talking before the whole were assembled. I do not positively remem-ber any of them, except that James Spedding[4] was there; and that the others, not above five or six in whole, were polite intelligent quiet persons, and, except Taylor and Wordsworth, not of any special distinction in the world. Breakfast was pleasant, fairly beyond the common of such things; Wordsworth seemed in good tone, and, much to Taylor's satisfaction, talked a great deal. About "poetic" Correspondents of his own (i.e. correspondents for the sake of *his* Poetry,—especially, one such who had sent him, from Canton, an excellent *Chest of Tea*, correspondent grinningly applauded by us all); then about ruralities and miscellanies, "Countess of Pem-broke" (antique She-Clifford, glory of those Northern parts, who was not new to any of us, but was set forth by Wordsworth with gusto and brief emphasis, "You lily-livered" etc.) now the only memorable item under that head: these were the first topics. Then finally about *Literature*, literary laws, practices, observances,—at con-siderable length, and turning wholly on the mechanical part, including even a good deal of shallow enough *etymology*, from me and others, which was well received: on all this Wordsworth enlarged with evident satisfaction, and was joyfully reverent of the "wells of English un-defiled,"—though stone *dumb* as to the deeper rules, and wells of Eternal Truth and Harmony you were to try and set forth by said undefiled wells of *English* or what other Speech you had! To me a little disappointing, but not much;—though it would have given me pleasure, had the robust veteran man emerged a little out of

---

[1] Sir Henry Taylor (1800–86), English poet.
[2] John Sterling; see *Life of John Sterling* in this volume.
[3] August Friedrich Ferdinand von Kotzebue (1761–1819), German playwright.
[4] James Spedding (1808–81), English scholar, friend of Carlyle's.

vocables into things, now and then, as he never once chanced to do. For the rest, he talked well in his way; with veracity, easy brevity and force; as a wise tradesman would of his tools and workshop, —and as no unwise one could. His voice was good, frank and sonorous, though practically clear, distinct and forcible, rather than melodious; the tone of him business-like, sedately confident, no discourtesy, yet no anxiety about being courteous; a fine wholesome rusticity, fresh as his mountain breezes, sat well on the stalwart veteran, and on all he said and did. You would have said he was a usually taciturn man; glad to unlock himself, to audience sympathetic and intelligent, when such offered itself. His face bore marks of much, not always peaceful, meditation; the look of it not bland or benevolent, so much as close, impregnable and hard: a man *multa tacere loquive paratus*,[5] in a world where he had experienced no lack of contradictions as he strode along! The eyes were not very brilliant, but they had a quiet clearness; there was enough of brow, and well shaped; rather too much of cheek ("horse-face," I have heard satirists say), face of squarish shape and decidedly longish, as I think the head itself was (*its* "length" going *horizontal*): he was large-boned, lean, but still firm-knit, tall and strong–looking when he stood: a right good old steel-gray figure, with a fine rustic simplicity and dignity about him, and a veracious *strength* looking through him which might have suited one of those old steel-gray *Markgrafs* (Graf = *Grau*, "Steel-gray") whom Henry the Fowler set up to ward the "marches," and do battle with the intrusive Heathen, in a stalwart and judicious manner.

On this and other occasional visits of his, I saw Wordsworth a number of times, at dinners, in evening parties; and we grew a little more familiar, but without much increase of real intimacy or affection springing up between us. He was willing to talk with me in a corner, in noisy extensive circles; having weak eyes, and little loving the general babble current in such places. One evening, probably about this time, I got him upon the subject of great poets, who I thought might be admirable equally to us both; but was rather mistaken, as I gradually found. Pope's partial failure I was prepared for; less for the narrowish limits visible in Milton and others. I tried him with Burns, of whom he had sung tender recognition; but Burns also turned

out to be a limited inferior creature, any genius he had a theme for one's pathos rather; even Shakspeare himself had his blind sides, his limitations:—gradually it became apparent to me that of transcendent and unlimited there was, to this Critic, probably but one specimen known, Wordsworth himself! He by no means said so, or hinted so, in words; but on the whole it was all I gathered from him in this considerable *tête-à-tête* of ours; and it was not an agreeable conquest. New notion as to Poetry or Poet I had not in the smallest degree got; but my insight into the depths of Wordsworth's pride in himself had considerably augmented;—and it did not increase my love of him; though I did [not] in the least hate it either, so quiet was it, so fixed, *un*appealing, like a dim old lichened crag on the wayside, the private meaning of which, in contrast with any public meaning it had, you recognised with a kind of not wholly melancholy *grin*.—

Another and better corner dialogue I afterwards had with him, possible also about this time; which raised him intellectually some real degrees higher in my estimation than any of his deliverances written or oral had ever done; and which I may reckon as the best of all his discoursings or dialogues with me. He had withdrawn to a corner, out of the light and of the general babble, as usual with him; I joined him there, and knowing how little fruitful was the Literary topic between us, set him on giving me account of the notable practicalities he had seen in life, especially of the notable men. He went into all this with a certain alacrity; and was willing to speak, wherever able on the terms. He had been in France in the earlier or secondary stage of the Revolution; had witnessed the struggle of *Girondins* and *Mountain*,[6] in particular the execution of Gorsas, "the first *Deputy* sent to the Scaffold;" and testified strongly to the ominous feeling which that event produced in everybody, and of which he himself still seemed to retain something: "Where will it *end*, when you have set an example in *this* kind?" I knew well about Gorsas; but had found, in my readings, no trace of the public emotion his death excited; and perceived now that Wordsworth might be taken as a true supplement to my Book, on this small point. He did not otherwise add to or alter my ideas on the Revolution: nor did we dwell long there; but hastened over to England and to the noteworthy, or at least noted men of that

---

[5] "Often silent but ready to speak."
[6] Girondins and the Mountain were opposing rebel factions in the French Revolution.

and the subsequent time. "Noted" and named, I ought perhaps to say, rather than "noteworthy"; for in general I forget what men they were; and now remember only the excellent sagacity, distinctness and credibility of Wordsworth's little Biographic Portraitures of them. Never, or never but once, had I seen a stronger intellect, a more luminous and veracious power of insight, directed upon such a survey of fellow-men and their contemporary journey through the world. A great deal of Wordsworth lay in the mode and tone of drawing; but you perceived it to be faithful, accurate, and altogether life-like, though Wordsworthian. One of the best remembered Sketches (almost the only one now remembered at all) was that of Wilberforce,[7] the famous Nigger-Philanthropist, Drawing-room Christian, and busy man and Politician. In all which capacities Wordsworth's esteem of him seemed to be privately as small as my own private one, and was amusing to gather. No hard word of him did he speak or hint; told, in brief firm business terms, How he was born at or near the place called *Wilberforce* in Yorkshire ("force" signifying torrent or angry brook, I suppose, as in Cumberland?), where, probably, his forefathers may have been possessors, though he was poorish; how he did this and that, of insignificant (to Wordsworth, insignificant) nature;—"and then," added Wordsworth, "he took into the *Oil* trade" (I suppose the Hull whaling); which lively phrase, and the incomaprable historical tone it was given in: "*the* Oil Trade," as a thing perfectly natural, and proper for such a man,—is almost the only point in the delineation which is now vividly present to me. I remember only the rustic Picture, sketched as with a burnt stick on the board of a pair of bellows, seemed to me completely good; and that the general effect was, one *saw* the great Wilberforce and his existence, visible in all their main lineaments,—but only as through the *reversed* telescope, and reduced to the size of a mouse and its nest, or little more! This was, in most or in all cases, the result brought out; oneself and telescope of natural (or perhaps preternatural) size; but the object, so great to vulgar eyes, *reduced* amazingly, with all its lineaments recognisable. I found a very superior talent in these Wordsworth delineations. They might have reminded me, though I know not whether they did at the time, of a larger series

like them, which I had from my Father during two wet days which confined us to the house, the last time we met at Scotsbrig! These were of select Annandale Figures whom I had seen in my Boyhood; and of whom, now that they were all vanished, I was glad to have, for the first time, some real knowledge as facts, the outer *simulacra* in all their equipments, being still so pathetically vivid to me. My Father's, in rugged simple force, picturesque ingenuity, veracity and brevity, were, I do judge, superior to even Wordsworth's, as bits of human Portraiture; *without* flavour of contempt, too, but given out with judicial indifference;—and intermixed here and there with flashes of the *Poetical* and soberly Pathetic (e.g. the death of Bell of Dunnaby, and *why* the two joiners were seen sawing wood in a pour of rain) which the Wordsworth Sketches, mainly of distant and indifferent persons, altogether wanted. Oh my brave, dear, and ever-honoured Peasant Father, where among the Grandees, Sages, and recognised Poets of the world, did I listen to such sterling speech as yours,—golden product of a heart and brain all sterling and royal! That is a literal *fact*;—and it has often filled me with strange reflections, in the whirlpools of this mad world!

During the last seven or ten years of his life, Wordsworth felt himself to be a recognised lion, in certain considerable London Circles; and was in the habit of coming up to Town with his Wife for a month or two every season, to enjoy his quiet triumph and collect his bits of tribute *tales quales*.[8] The places where I met him oftenest, were Marshall's (the great Leeds linen-manufacturer, and excellent and very opulent man), Spring-Rice's (i.e. Lord Monteagle's, who and whose house was strangely intermarried with this Marshall's), and the *first* Lord Stanley's of Alderley (who then perhaps, was still Sir Thomas Stanley). Wordsworth took his bit of lionism very quietly, with a smile sardonic rather than triumphant; and certainly got no harm by it, if he got or expected little good. His Wife, a small, withered, puckered, winking lady, who never spoke, seemed to be more in earnest about the affair;—and was visibly and sometimes ridiculously assiduous to secure her proper place of precedence at Table. One evening at Lord Monteagle's—Ah, *who* was it that then made me laugh as we went home together: ah

---

[7] William Wilberforce (1759–1833), noted for his efforts to stop the slave trade in Britain and her colonies.
[8] "Such as they were."

me!— —Wordsworth generally spoke a little with me on those occasions; sometimes, perhaps, we sat by one another; but there came from him nothing considerable, and happily at least nothing with an effort. "If you think me dull, be it just so!" this seemed to a most respectable extent to be his inspiring humour. Hardly above once (perhaps at the Stanleys') do I faintly recollect something of the contrary on his part for a little while; which was not pleasant or successful while it lasted. The light was always afflictive to his eyes; he carried in his pocket something like a skeleton brass candlestick; in which, setting it on the dinner-table, between him and the most afflictive or nearest of the chief lights, he touched a little spring, and there flirted out, at the top of his brass implement, a small vertical green circle, which prettily enough threw his eyes into shade, and screened him from that sorrow. In proof of his equanimity as lion I remember, in connection with this green shade, one little glimpse; which shall be given presently as finis. But first let me say that all these Wordsworth phenomena appear to have been indifferent to [me], and have melted to steamy oblivion, in a singular degree. Of his talk to others in my hearing I remember simply nothing, not even a word or gesture. To myself it seemed once or twice as if he bore suspicions, thinking I was *not* a real worshipper, which threw him into something of embarrassment, till I hastened to get them laid, by frank discourse on some suitable thing (in the Stanley Drawing-room, I remember, he hit a stool, and kicked it over in striding forward to shake hands);—nor, when we did talk, was there on his side or on mine the least utterance worth noting. The tone of his voice when I did get him afloat, on some Cumberland or other matter germane to him, had a braced rustic vivacity, willingness, and solid precision, which alone rings in my ear when all else is gone. Of some Druid Circle, for example, he prolonged his response to me with the addition, "And there is another, some miles off; which the country people call *Long* MEG *and her* DAUGHTERS;" as to the now ownership of which, "It" etc.; "*and then* it came into the hands of a Mr. Crackenthorpe;"—the *sound* of these two phrases is still lively and present with me; meaning or sound of absolutely nothing more. Still more memorable is an ocular glimpse I had in one of these Wordsworthian lion-dinners, very symbolic to me of

his general deportment there, and far clearer than the little feature of opposite sort, ambiguously given above (recollection of that viz. of unsuccessful *exertion* at a Stanley Dinner being dubious and all but extinct, while this is still vivid to me as of yesternight). Dinner was large, luminous, sumptuous; I sat a long way from Wordsworth; dessert I think had come in; and certainly there reigned in all quarters a cackle as of Babel (only politer perhaps),—which far up, in Wordsworth's quarter (who was leftward on my side of the table), seemed to have taken a sententious, rather louder, logical and quasi-scientific turn,—heartily unimportant to gods and men, so far as I could judge of it and of the other babble reigning. I looked upwards, leftwards, the coast luckily being for a moment clear: there, far off, beautifully screened in the shadow of his vertical green circle, which was on the farther side of him, sat Wordsworth, silent, in rock-like indifference, slowly but steadily gnawing some portion of what I judged to be raisins, with his eye and attention placidly fixed on these and these alone. The sight of whom, and of his rock-like indifference to the babble, quasi-scientific and other, with attention turned on the small practical alone, was comfortable and amusing to me, who felt like him but could not eat raisins. This little glimpse I could still paint, so clear and bright is it, and this shall be symbolical of all.

In a few years, I forget in how many or when, these Wordsworth Appearances in London ceased; we heard, not of ill-health perhaps, but of increasing love of rest; at length of the long Sleep's coming; and never saw Wordsworth more.[9] One felt his death as the extinction of a public light, but not otherwise. The public itself found not much to say of him; and staggered on to meaner but more pressing objects.— —Why should I continue these melancholy jottings in which I have no interest; in which the one Figure that could interest me is almost wanting! I will cease. [Finished, after many miserable interruptions, catarrhal and other, at Mentone, 8th March 1867.]

On the same day Carlyle writes in his *Journal*:[10]
"Finished the rag on Wordsworth to the last tatter; won't begin another: *Cui bono*, it is wearisome and naught even to myself. . . . I live mostly alone; with vanished Shadows of the

---

[9] Wordsworth died April 23, 1850.
[10] The following passage was added by Charles Eliot Norton in his edition of the *Reminiscences*.

Past,—many of them rise for a moment, inexpressibly tender; One is never long absent from me.[11] Gone, gone, but very dear, very beautiful and dear! ETERNITY, which cannot be far off, is my one strong city. I look into it fixedly now and then; all terrors about it seem to me superfluous; all knowledge about it, any the least glimmer of certain knowledge, impossible to living mortal. The universe is full of love, and also of inexorable sterness and severity; and it remains for ever true that 'GOD reigns.' Patience, silence, hope!"

[11] I.e., Jane Welsh Carlyle.

Thomas Babington Macaulay

1800-1859

Thomas Babington Macaulay was born in Leicestershire to a family prominent in what was called the "Clapham sect," a group of Evangelicals devoted to such social goals as the abolition of slavery as well as to the spread of evangelical Christianity. Macaulay was to make his mark both as a reforming spokesman for Whig ideas and as a man of letters. The two functions are never entirely separate in Macaulay, for he pursued simultaneously a political and a literary career and enjoyed considerable success in both. His prose writings (he was also a successful narrative poet) consistently bring his Whig principles to bear on history and literature alike. He also exploits his skill at debating, demonstrated early in his college career and continued through a distinguished career in Parliament, to color his emphatic and antithetical style, lending both vitality and contentiousness to almost every topic he touches.

Macaulay first attracted attention when he was not yet twenty-five years old, with his brilliant essay on Milton for the *Edinburgh Review*. The essay also marked the beginning of almost twenty years' association with the influential *Edinburgh*, whose editorship he declined in 1829. He preferred to move directly in political and literary circles in London as the chief representative of the ideas espoused by the *Edinburgh* and the Whigs. Whether serving as a member of Parliament or on the Supreme Council in India, Macaulay continued to write his essays and eventually took up the task of writing a history of England from the accession of James II in 1685. The work proved to be immensely successful, and Macaulay was hailed as the premier writer of history of the age. By the time he had begun work on his history he had amassed a large private fortune. He continued to serve in Parliament for some years, but in 1847 he retired to devote his energies entirely to literature. Accordingly he spent the last dozen years of his life writing and publishing the *History* and filling a full-time social and intellectual role as a man of letters.

As the spokesman for Victorian Whig ideas, Macaulay was a staunch opponent of Toryism and certain kinds of traditionalism. He was so enthusiastic a battler for the Fist Reform Bill, for instance, that he did not mind when its passage eliminated the very "pocket borough" he represented in Parliament, and he subsequently became a representative from Leeds for one of the new boroughs created by the bill. Later, after his return from India, he served as a representative from Edinburgh. As a Whig Macaulay supported such measures as the removal of Catholic and Jewish disabilities, and in India as advisor he encouraged freedom of the press, legal equality for Indians and Europeans, and a program of national education. At the same time, Macaulay was not a philosophical radical in the Mill and Bentham tradition, and he opposed rigid utilitariansim, preferring the increasing participation of the middle class and the business class in the existing parliamentary government. He was also not above accepting a peerage in 1857. It was thus as Lord Macaulay (Baron Macaulay of Rothley) that he died in 1859 and was buried in Westminster Abbey.

Macaulay was perhaps the most eloquent Victorian spokesman for the idea of progress, an idea especially congenial to his middle-class audience in the mid-Victorian years. His portrayal of English history from 1685 was designed in large measure to glorify both the Bloodless Revolution that established the principle of a cooperative government of monarch and parliament and the march of material progress through the eighteenth into the nineteenth century. Macaulay saw much of English history and indeed English letters in the light of this Whig position, but he was also capable of finding fault on his own side. Even though some of Macaulay's facts have been corrected by later scholarship there is every reason to believe that in writing history Macaulay strove for accuracy and not mere partisanship.

Macaulay's style has been much commented upon, especially in regard to its most evident features—antithesis, paradox, exaggeration, and repetition. It often shows the evidences of Macaulay's oratorical skill as well as of his prodigious memory (he was said to be able to recite *Paradise Lost* by heart). But the style is also remarkably clear and forthright, and it corresponds well with Macaulay's direct, practical, and optimistic spirit. Macaulay's historical writings also display something of a novelist's skill in narrative and description, and his inclusion of abundant details of setting and of social habit and everyday life continue to lend his historical writings a vigor that conventional political history lacks.

Macaulay's essays and histories have fallen from their high place in the esteem of modern readers, but they still have qualities that will commend them to many. The style continues to exhibit a force and vividness that many readers will find compelling, even when they find the air of dogmatic assurance that Macaulay often adopts somewhat unappealing. Since Macaulay's approach to literature and history is so often colored by his Whig principles, readers can consider his works not only in their own right as works of enduring prose but also as illustrations of the ideas and values that guided middle-class thought in the first half of the nineteenth century.

CHRONOLOGY

1800	Born at Rothley Temple. Leicestershire, 25 October.
1812	Attends private school at Little Shelford, later (1814) at Aspenden Park.
1818	Enters Trinity College, Cambridge.
1824	Becomes fellow of Trinity.
1825	Essay on Milton, *Edinburgh Review*.

1829	Becomes Commissioner of Bankruptcy; declines editorship of *Edinburgh Review*.
1830	Becomes M.P. for Calne.
1832	Loses seat in Parliament with passage of First Reform Bill.
1833	Becomes M.P. for borough of Leeds.
1834–37	Serves in India on Supreme Council.
1838	Returns to England.
1839	Becomes Liberal M.P. for Edinburgh; becomes Secretary-at-War in Lord Melbourne's cabinet.
1842	*Lays of Ancient Rome.*
1843	Collected edition of *Essays.*
1847	Retires to work on *History.*
1848	*History of England*, Volumes I and II.
1849	Elected Lord Rector of Glasgow University; declines chair of history at Cambridge.
1855	*History of England*, Volumes III and IV.
1857	Elevated to peerage as Baron Macaulay of Rothley.
1859	Dies 28 December; buried Westminster Abbey 9 January 1860.

EDITIONS

Works, ed. Lady Trevelyan (8 vols., 1866; rpt. 12 vols., 1898).

Critical and Historical Essays Contributed to the Edinburgh Review (3 vols., 1843).

History of England (4 vols., 1848–55); *History of England*, Vol. V, ed. Lady Trevelyan (1861).

History of England, ed. Charles Harding Firth (6 vols., 1913–15).

Lays of Ancient Rome and Other Historical Poems, ed. G. M. Trevelyan (1928).

Macaulay's Prose and Poetry, ed. G. M. Young (1953).

Miscellaneous Writings, ed. T. F. Ellis (2 vols., 1860).

Speeches by Lord Macaulay, ed. G. M. Young (1935).

BIOGRAPHY AND CRITICISM

Frederick Arnold, *The Public Life of Lord Macaulay* (1862).

Richmond Croom Beatty, *Lord Macaulay: Victorian Liberal* (1938).

Arthur Bryant, *Macaulay* (1932).

John Clive, *Macaulay: The Shaping of the Historian* (1973).

————, and Thomas Pinney, "Thomas Babington Macaulay" in *Victorian Prose: A Guide to Research* (1973), pp. 17–30.

Sir Charles Firth, *Commentary on Macaulay's "History of England,"* ed. Godfrey Davis (1938).

Pieter Geyl, *Debates with Historians* (1955).

George Levine, *The Boundaries of Fiction* (1968).

William Madden, "Macaulay's Style" in *The Art of Victorian Prose* (1968), pp. 127–153.

Henry Hart Milman, *A Memoir of Lord Macaulay* (1862).

George Richard Potter, *Macaulay* (1959).

S. C. Roberts, *Lord Macaulay, the Pre-eminent Victorian* (1927)

Mark A. Thomson, *Macaulay* (1959).

G. O. Trevelyan, *Life and Letters of Lord Macaulay* (2 vols., 1876).

G. M. Young, *Daylight and Champaign* (1937).

Milton

Macaulay's celebrated essay on Milton was a review of Milton's then recently discovered, and just published, Of Christian Doctrine. *As Macaulay makes clear, he takes the occasion of the publication of this long-lost theological work to treat Milton's life and works in their entirety. In so doing he exhibits the brilliance of style that was to characterize all of his writing. The essay was first published in the* Edinburgh Review *in August 1825 and formed the basis for Macaulay's first widespread public recognition. The essay is given below in full.*

Joannis Miltoni, Angli, de Doctrinâ Christianâ libri duo posthumi. A treatise on Christian Doctrine, compiled from the Holy Scriptures alone. By JOHN MILTON, translated from the Original by Charles R. Sumner, M.A., &c. &c. 1825.

TOWARDS the close of the year 1823, Mr. Lemon, deputy keeper of the state papers, in the course of his researches among the presses of his office, met with a large Latin manuscript. With it were found corrected copies of the foreign despatches written by Milton, while he filled the office of Secretary, and several papers relating to the Popish Trials and the Rye-house Plot.[1] The whole was wrapped up in an envelope, superscribed *To Mr. Skinner, Merchant.*[2] On examination, the large manuscript proved to be the long lost Essay on the Doctrines of Christianity, which, according to Wood and Toland,[3] Milton finished after the Restoration, and deposited with Cyriac Skinner. Skinner, it is well known, held the same political opinions with his illustrious friend. It is therefore probable, as Mr. Lemmon conjectures, that he may have fallen under the suspicions of the government during that persecution of the Whigs which followed the dissolution of the Oxford parliament, and that, in consequence of a general seizure of his papers, this work may have been brought to the office in which it has been found. But whatever the adventures of the manuscript may have been, no doubt can exist that it is a genuine relic of the great poet.

Mr. Sumner, who was commanded by His Majesty to edit and translate the treatise, has acquitted himself of his task in a manner honourable to his talents and to his character.

His version is not indeed very easy or elegant; but it is entitled to the praise of clearness and fidelity. His notes abound with interesting quotations, and have the rare merit of really elucidating the text. The preface is evidently the work of a sensible and candid man, firm in his own religious opinions, and tolerant towards those of others.

The book itself will not add much to the fame of Milton. It is, like all his Latin works, well written, though not exactly in the style of the prize essays of Oxford and Cambridge. There is no elaborate imitation of classical antiquity, no scrupulous purity, none of the ceremonial cleanness which characterises the diction of our academical Pharisees. The author does not attempt to polish and brighten his composition into the Ciceronian gloss and brilliancy. He does not in short sacrifice sense and spirit to pedantic refinements. The nature of his subject compelled him to use many words

"That would have made Quintilian stare and gasp."[4]

But he writes with as much ease and freedom as if Latin were his mother tongue; and, where he is least happy, his failure seems to arise from the carelessness of a native, not from the ignorance of a foreigner. We may apply to him what Denham with great felicity says of Cowley.[5] He wears the garb, but not the clothes of the ancients.

Throughout the volume are discernible the traces of a powerful and independent mind, emancipated from the influence of authority, and devoted to the search of truth. Milton professes to form his system from the Bible alone; and his digest of scriptural texts is certainly among the

---

[1] Milton served as Latin Secretary to the Cromwell government; the Popish Trials (1678) and Rye House Plot (1683) occurred after Milton's death.

[2] Daniel Skinner, nephew of Cyriak Skinner to whom Milton addressed one of his sonnets.

[3] Anthony A. Wood (1632–95), biographer and antiquarian; John Toland (1670–1722), editor in 1698 of Milton's prose works.

[4] From Milton's sonnet, "A Book was writ of late called *Tetrachordon.*"

[5] John Denham (1615–69), "On Mr. Abraham Cowley."

best that have appeared. But he is not always so happy in his inferences as in his citations.

Some of the heterodox doctrines which he avows seemed to have excited considerable amazement, particularly his Arianism, and his theory on the subject of polygamy.[6] Yet we can scarcely conceive that any person could have read the Paradise Lost without suspecting him of the former; nor do we think that any reader, acquainted with the history of his life, ought to be much startled at the latter. The opinions which he has expressed respecting the nature of the Deity, the eternity of matter, and the observation of the Sabbath, might, we think, have caused more just surprise.

But we will not go into the discussion of these points. The book, were it far more orthodox or far more heretical than it is, would not much edify or corrupt the present generation. The men of our time are not to be converted or perverted by quartos. A few more days, and this essay will follow the *Defensio Populi*[7] to the dust and silence of the upper shelf. The name of its author, and the remarkable circumstances attending its publication, will secure to it a certain degree of attention. For a month or two it will occupy a few minutes of chat in every drawing-room, and a few columns in every magazine; and it will then, to borrow the elegant language of the playbills, be withdrawn, to make room for the forthcoming novelties.

We wish however to avail ourselves of the interest, transient as it may be, which this work has excited. The dexterous Capuchins never choose to preach on the life and miracles of a saint, till they have awakened the devotional feelings of their auditors by exhibiting some relic of him, a thread of his garment, a lock of his hair, or a drop of his blood. On the same principle, we intend to take advantage of the late interesting discovery, and, while this memorial of a great and good man is still in the hands of all, to say something of his moral and intellectual qualities. Nor, we are convinced, will the severest of our readers blame us if, on an occasion like the present, we turn for a short time from the topics of the day, to commemorate, in all love and reverence, the genius and virtues of John Milton, the poet, the statesman, the philosopher, the glory of English literature, the champion and the martyr of English liberty.

It is by his poetry that Milton is best known; and it is of his poetry that we wish first to speak. By the general suffrage of the civilised world, his place has been assigned among the greatest masters of the art. His detractors, however, though outvoted, have not been silenced. There are many critics, and some of great name, who contrive in the same breath to extol the poems and to decry the poet. The works they acknowledge, considered in themselves, may be classed among the noblest productions of the human mind. But they will not allow the author to rank with those great men who, born in the infancy of civilisation, supplied, by their own powers, the want of instruction, and, though destitute of models themselves, bequeathed to posterity models which defy imitation. Milton, it is said, inherited what his predecessors created; he lived in an enlightened age; he received a finished education; and we must therefore, if we would form a just estimate of his powers, make large deductions in consideration of these advantages.

We venture to say, on the contrary, paradoxical as the remark may appear, that no poet has ever had to struggle with more unfavorable circumstances than Milton. He doubted, as he has himself owned, whether he had not been born "an age too late." For this notion Johnson has thought fit to make him the butt of much clumsy ridicule. The poet, we believe, understood the nature of his art better than the critic. He knew that his poetical genius derived no advantage from the civilisation which surrounded him, or from the learning which he had acquired; and he looked back with something like regret to the ruder age of simple words and vivid impressions.

We think that, as civilisation advances, poetry almost necessarily declines. Therefore, though we fervently admire those great works of imagination which have appeared in dark ages, we do not admire them the more because they have appeared in dark ages. On the contrary, we hold that the most wonderful and splendid proof of genius is a great poem produced in a civilised age. We cannot understand why those who believe in that most orthodox article of literary faith, that the earliest poets are generally the best, should wonder at the rule as if it were the exception. Surely the uniformity of the phænomenon indictes a corresponding uniformity in the cause.

The fact is, that common observers reason from the progress of the experimental sciences to that

---

[6] Arianism, the fourth-century heresy that denied Christ's divinity.
[7] Milton's defense of the English people for the beheading of Charles I.

of the imitative arts. The improvement of the former is gradual and slow. Ages are spent in collecting materials, ages more in separating and combining them. Even when a system has been formed, there is still something to add, to alter or to reject. Every generation enjoys the use of a vast hoard bequeathed to it by antiquity, and transmits that hoard, augmented by fresh acquisitions, to future ages. In these pursuits, therefore, the first speculators lie under great disadvantages, and even when they fail, are entitled to praise. Their pupils, with far inferior intellectual powers speedily surpass them in actual attainments. Every girl who has read Mrs. Marcet's little dialogues on Political Economy could teach Montague or Walpole many lessons in finance.[8] Any intelligent man may now, by resolutely applying himself for a few years to mathematics, learn more than the great Newton knew after half a century of study and meditation.

But it is not thus with music, with painting, or with sculpture. Still less is it thus with poetry. The progress of refinement rarely supplies these arts with better objects of imitation. It may indeed improve the instruments which are necessary to the mechanical operations of the musician, the sculptor, and the painter. But language, the machine of the poet, is best fitted for this purpose in its rudest state. Nations, like individuals, first perceive, and then abstract. They advance from particular images to general terms. Hence the vocabulary of an enlightened society is philosophical, that of a half-civilised people is poetical.

This change in the language of men is partly the cause and partly the effect of a corresponding change in the nature of their intellectual operations, of a change by which science gains and poetry loses. Generalisation is necessary to the advancement of knowledge; but particularity is indispensable to the creations of the imagination. In proportion as men know more and think more, they look less at individuals and more at classes. They therefore make better theories and worse poems. They give us vague phrases instead of images, and personified qualities instead of men. They may be better able to analyse human nature than their precedessors. But analysis is not the business of the poet. His office is to portray, not to dissect. He may believe in a moral sense, like Shaftesbury; he may refer all human actions to self-interest, like Helvetius; or he may never think about the matter at all.[9] His creed on such subjects will no more influence his poetry, properly so called, than the notions which a painter may have conceived respecting the lacrymal glands, or the circulation of the blood, will affect the tears of his Niobe, or the blushes of his Aurora.[10] If Shakespeare had written a book on the motives of human actions, it is by no means certain that it would have been a good one. It is extremely improbable that it would have contained half so much able reasoning on the subject as is to be found in the Fable of the Bees. But could Mandeville have created an Iago?[11] Well as he knew how to resolve characters into their elements, would he have been able to combine those elements is such a manner as to make up a man, a real, living, individual man?

Perhaps no person can be a poet, or can even enjoy poetry, without a certain unsoundness of mind, if any thing which gives so much pleasure ought to be called unsoundness. By poetry we mean not all writing in verse, nor even all good writing in verse. Our definition excludes many metrical compositions which, on other grounds, deserve the highest praise. By poetry we mean the art of employing words in such a manner as to produce an illusion on the imagination, the art of doing by means of words what the painter does by means of colours. Thus the greatest of poets has described it, in lines universally admired for the vigour and felicity of their diction, and still more valuable on account of the just notion which they convey of the art in which he excelled:

"As imagination bodies forth
The forms of things unknown, the poet's pen
Turns them to shapes, and gives to airy nothing
A local habitation and a name."[12]

These are the fruits of the "fine frenzy" which

[8] Jane Marcet (1769–1858), author of *Conversations on Political Economy* (1816); Charles Montagu (1661–1715) and Sir Robert Walpole (1676–1745), eminent statesmen.

[9] Anthony Ashley Cooper, 3rd Earl of Shaftesbury (1671–1713), philosopher, author of *Characteristics of Men, Manners, Opinions, Times* (1711); Claude Adrien Helvetius (1715–71), French philosopher.

[10] Niobe, daughter of the king of Thebes, who wept when her children were slain; Aurora, goddess of the dawn.

[11] Bernard de Mandeville (1670?–1733), author of the *Fable of the Bees,* which maintains that vice is beneficial to society.

[12] *A Midsummer Night's Dream,* v, i, 14–17.

he ascribes to the poet,—a fine frenzy doubtless, but still a frenzy. Truth, indeed, is essential to poetry; but it is the truth of madness. The reasonings are just; but the premises are false. After the first suppositions have been made, every thing ought to be consistent; but those first suppositions require a degree of credulity which almost amounts to a partial and temporary derangement of the intellect. Hence of all people children are the most imaginative. They abandon themselves without reserve to every illusion. Every image which is strongly presented to their mental eye produces on them the effect of reality. No man, whatever his sensibility may be, is ever affected by Hamlet or Lear, as a little girl is affected by the story of poor Red Riding-hood. She knows that it is all false, that wolves cannot speak, that there are no wolves in England. Yet in spite of her knowledge she believes; she weeps; she trembles; she dares not go into a dark room lest she should feel the teeth of the monster at her throat. Such is the despotism of the imagination over uncultivated minds.

In a rude state of society men are children with a greater variety of ideas. It is therefore in such a state of society that we may expect to find the poetical temperament in its highest perfection. In an enlightened age there will be much intelligence, much science, much philosophy, abundance of just classification and subtle analysis, abundance of wit and eloquence, abundance of verses, and even of good ones; but little poetry. Men will judge and compare; but they will not create. They will talk about the old poets, and comment on them, and to a certain degree enjoy them. But they will scarcely be able to conceive the effect which poetry produced on their ruder ancestors, the agony, the ecstasy, the plenitude of belief. The Greek Rhapsodists, according to Plato, could scarce recite Homer without falling into convulsions. The Mohawk hardly feels the scalping knife while he shouts his death song. The power which the ancient bards of Wales and Germany exercised over their auditors seems to modern readers almost miraculous. Such feelings are very rare in a civilised community, and most rare among those who participate most in its improvements. They linger longest among the peasantry.

Poetry produces an illusion on the eye of the mind, as a magic lantern produces an illusion on the eye of the body. And, as the magic lantern acts best in a dark room, poetry effects its purpose most completely in a dark age. As the light of knowledge breaks in upon its exhibitions, as the outlines of certainty become more and more definite and the shades of probability more and more distinct, the hues and lineaments of the phantoms which the poet calls up grow fainter and fainter. We cannot unite the incompatible advantages of reality and deception, the clear discernment of truth and the exquisite enjoyment of fiction.

He who, in an enlightened and literary society, aspires to be a great poet, must first become a little child. He must take to pieces the whole web of his mind. He must unlearn much of that knowledge which has perhaps constituted hitherto his chief title to superiority. His very talents will be a hindrance to him. His difficulties will be proportioned to his proficiency in the pursuits which are fashionable among his contemporaries; and that proficiency will in general be proportioned to the vigour and activity of his mind. And it is well if, after all his sacrifices and exertions, his works do not resemble a lisping man or a modern ruin. We have seen in our own time great talents, intense labour, and long meditation, employed in this struggle against the spirit of the age, and employed, we will not say absolutely in vain, but with dubious success and feeble applause.

If these reasonings be too just, no poet has ever triumphed over greater difficulties than Milton. He received a learned education: he was a profound and elegant classical scholar: he had studied all the mysteries of Rabbinical literature: he was intimately acquainted with every language of modern Europe, from which either pleasure or information was then to be derived. He was perhaps the only great poet of later times who has been distinguished by the excellence of his Latin verse. The genius of Petrarch[13] was scarcely of the first order; and his poems in the ancient language, though much praised by those who have never read them, are wretched compositions. Cowley,[14] with all his admirable wit and ingenuity, had little imagination; nor indeed do we think his classical diction comparable to that of Milton. The authority of Johnson is against us on this point. But Johnson had studied the bad writers of the middle ages till he had become utterly insensible to the Augustan elegance, and was as ill qualified to

[13] Francesco Petrarch (1304–74), Italian Renaissance poet.
[14] Abraham Cowley (1618–67), poet.

judge between two Latin styles as a habitual drunkard to set up for a wine-taster.

Versification in a dead language is an exotic, a far-fetched, costly, sickly, imitation of that which elsewhere may be found in healthful and spontaneous perfection. The soils on which this rarity flourishes are in general as ill suited to the production of vigorous native poetry as the flower-pots of a hothouse to the growth of oaks. That the author of the Paradise Lost should have written the Epistle to Manso was truly wonderful.[15] Never before were such marked originality and such exquisite mimicry found together. Indeed in all the Latin poems of Milton the artificial manner indispensable to such works is admirably preserved, while, at the same time, his genius gives to them a peculiar charm, an air of nobleness and freedom, which distinguishes them from all other writings of the same class. They remind us of the amusements of those angelic warriors who composed the cohort of Gabriel:

"About him exercised heroic games
  The unarmed youth of heaven. But o'er their heads
Celestial armoury, shield, helm, and spear,
Hung high, with diamond flaming and with gold."[16]

We cannot look upon the sportive exercises for which the genius of Milton ungirds itself, without catching a glimpse of the gorgeous and terrible panoply which it is accustomed to wear. The strength of his imagination triumphed over every obstacle. So intense and ardent was the fire of his mind, that it not only was not suffocated beneath the weight of fuel, but penetrated the whole superincumbent mass with its own heat and radiance.

It is not our intention to attempt any thing like a complete examination of the poetry of Milton. The public has long been agreed as to the merit of the most remarkable passages, the incomparable harmony of the numbers, and the excellence of that style, which no rival has been able to equal, and no parodist to degrade, which displays in their highest perfection the idiomatic powers of the English tongue, and to which every ancient and every modern language has contributed something of grace, of energy, or of music. In the vast field of criticism on which we are entering, innumerable reapers have already put their sickles. Yet the harvest is so abundant

that the negligent search of a straggling gleaner may be rewarded with a sheaf.

The most striking characteristic of the poetry of Milton is the extreme remoteness of the associations by means of which it acts on the reader. Its effect is produced, not so much by what it expresses, as by what it suggests: not so much by the ideas which it directly conveys, as by other ideas which are connected with them. He electrifies the mind through conductors. The most unimaginative man must understand the Iliad. Homer gives him no choice, and requires from him no exertion, but takes the whole upon himself, and sets the images in so clear a light, that it is impossible to be blind to them. The works of Milton cannot be comprehended or enjoyed, unless the mind of the reader co-operate with that of the writer. He does not paint a finished picture, or play for a mere passive listener. He sketches, and leaves others to fill up the outline. He strikes the key-note, and expects his hearer to make out the melody.

We often hear of the magical influence of poetry. The expression in general means nothing: but, applied to the writings of Milton, it is most appropriate. His poetry acts like an incantation. Its merit lies less in its obvious meaning than in its occult power. There would seem, at first sight, to be no more in his words than in other words. But they are words of enchantment. No sooner are they pronounced, than the past is present and the distant near. New forms of beauty start at once into existence, and all the burial-places of the memory give up their dead. Change the structure of the sentence: substitute one synonyme for another, and the whole effect is destroyed. The spell loses its power; and he who should then hope to conjure with it would find himself as much mistaken as Cassim in the Arabian tale, when he stood crying, "Open Wheat," "Open Barley," to the door which obeyed no sound but "Open Sesame." The miserable failure of Dryden in his attempt to translate into his own diction some parts of the Paradise Lost, is a remarkable instance of this.[17]

In support of these observations we may remark, that scarcely any passages in the poems of Milton are more generally known or more frequently repeated than those which are little more than muster-rolls of names. They are not always more appropriate or more melodious than

---

[15] A Latin epistle by Milton to a distinguished Italian friend.
[16] *Paradise Lost,* iv, 551–54; quoted slightly inaccurately.
[17] Reference to Dryden's *The State of Innocence and the Fall of Man* (1677).

other names. But they are charmed names. Every one of them is the first link in a long chain of associated ideas. Like the dwelling-place of our infancy revisited in manhood, like the song of our country heard in a strange land, they produce upon us an effect wholly independent of their intrinsic value. One transports us back to a remote period of history. Another places us among the novel scenes and manners of a distant region. A third evokes all the dear classical recollections of childhood, the school-room, the dog-eared Virgil, the holiday, and the prize. A fourth brings before us the splendid phantoms of chivalrous romance, the trophied lists, the embroidered housings, the quaint devices, the haunted forests, the enchanted gardens, the achievements of enamoured knights, and the smiles of rescued princesses.

In none of the works of Milton is his peculiar manner more happily displayed than in the Allegro and the Penseroso. It is impossible to conceive that the mechanism of language can be brought to a more exquisite degree of perfection. These poems differ from others, as atar of roses differs from ordinary rose water, the close packed essence from the thin diluted mixture. They are indeed not so much poems, as collections of hints, from each of which the reader is to make out a poem for himself. Every epithet is a text for a stanza.

The Comus and the Samson Agonistes are works which, though of very different merit, offer some marked points of resemblance. Both are lyric poems in the form of plays. There are perhaps no two kinds of composition so essentially dissimilar as the drama and the ode. The business of the dramatist is to keep himself out of sight, and to let nothing appear but his characters. As soon as he attracts notice to his personal feelings, the illusion is broken. The effect is as unpleasant as that which is produced on the stage by the voice of a prompter or the entrance of a scene-shifter. Hence it was, that the tragedies of Byron were his least successful performances. They resemble those pasteboard pictures invented by the friend of children, Mr. Newberry,[18] in which a single moveable head goes round twenty different bodies, so that the same face looks out upon us successively, from the uniform of a hussar, the furs of a judge, and the rags of a beggar. In all the characters, patriots and tyrants, haters and lovers, the frown and sneer of Harold were

discernible in an instant.[19] But this species of egotism, though fatal to the drama, is the inspiration of the ode. It is the part of the lyric poet to abandon himself, without reserve, to his own emotions.

Between these hostile elements many great men have endeavoured to effect an amalgamation, but never with complete success. The Greek Drama, on the model of which the Samson was written, sprang from the Ode. The dialogue was ingrafted on the chorus, and naturally partook of its character. The genius of the greatest of the Athenian dramatists co-operated with the circumstances under which tragedy made its first appearance. Æschylus was, head and heart, a lyric poet. In his time, the Greeks had far more intercourse with the East than in the days of Homer; and they had not yet acquired that immense superiority in war, in science, and in the arts, which, in the following generation, led them to treat the Asiatics with contempt. From the narrative of Herodotus it should seem that they still looked up, with the veneration of disciples, to Egypt and Assyria. At this period, accordingly, it was natural that the literature of Greece should be tinctured with the Oriental style. And that style, we think, is discernible in the works of Pindar and Æschylus. The latter often reminds us of the Hebrew writers. The book of Job, indeed, in conduct and diction, bears a considerable resemblance to some of his dramas. Considered as plays, his works are absurd; considered as choruses, they are above all praise. If, for instance, we examine the address of Clytæmnestra to Agamemnon on his return, or the description of the seven Argive chiefs, by the principles of dramatic writing, we shall instantly condemn them as monstrous. But if we forget the characters, and think only of the poetry, we shall admit that it has never been surpassed in energy and magnificence. Sophocles made the Greek drama as dramatic as was consistent with its original form. His portraits of men have a sort of similarity; but it is the similarity not of a painting, but of a bas-relief. It suggests a resemblance; but it does not produce an illusion. Euripides attempted to carry the reform further. But it was a task far beyond his powers, perhaps beyond any powers. Instead of correcting what was bad, he destroyed what was excellent. He substituted crutches for stilts, bad sermons for good ones.

Milton, it is well known, admired Euripides

---

[18] John Newberry (1713 67), publisher of children's books.
[19] Reference to Byron's *Childe Harold*.

highly, much more highly than, in our opinion, Euripides deserved. Indeed the caresses which this partiality leads our countryman to bestow on "sad Electra's poet,"[20] sometimes remind us of the beautiful Queen of Fairy-land kissing the long ears of Bottom. At all events, there can be no doubt that this veneration for the Athenian, whether just or not, was injurious to the Samson Agonistes. Had Milton taken Æschylus for his model, he would have given himself up to the lyric inspiration, and poured out profusely all the treasures of his mind, without bestowing a thought on those dramatic proprieties which the nature of the work rendered it impossible to preserve. In the attempt to reconcile things in their own nature inconsistent he has failed, as every one else must have failed. We cannot identify ourselves with the characters, as in a good play. We cannot identify ourselves with the poet, as in a good ode. The conflicting ingredients, like an acid and an alkali mixed, neutralise each other. We are by no means insensible to the merits of this celebrated piece, to the severe dignity of the style, the graceful and pathetic solemnity of the opening speech, or the wild and barbaric melody which gives so striking an effect to the choral passages. But we think it, we confess, the least successful effort of the genius of Milton.

The Comus is framed on the model of the Italian Masque, as the Samson is framed on the model of the Greek Tragedy. It is certainly the noblest performance of the kind which exists in any language. It is as far superior to the Faithful Shepherdess, as the Faithful Shepherdess is to the Aminta, or the Aminta to the Pastor Fido.[21] It was well for Milton that he had here no Euripides to mislead him. He understood and loved the literature of modern Italy. But he did not feel for it the same veneration which he entertained for the remains of Athenian and Roman poetry, consecrated by so many lofty and endearing recollections. The faults, moreover, of his Italian predecessors were of a kind to which his mind had a deadly antipathy. He could stoop to a plain style, sometimes even to a bald style; but false brilliancy was his utter aversion. His Muse had no objection to a russet attire; but she turned with disgust from the

finery of Guarini, as tawdry and as paltry as the rags of a chimney-sweeper on May-day. Whatever ornaments she wears are of massive gold not only dazzling to the sight, but capable of standing the severest test of the crucible.

Milton attended in the Comus to the distinction which he afterwards neglected in the Samson. He made his Masque what it ought to be, essentially lyrical, and dramatic only in semblance. He has not attempted a fruitless struggle against a defect inherent in the nature of that species of composition; and he has therefore succeeded, wherever success was not impossible. The speeches must be read as majestic soliloquies; and he who so reads them will be enraptured with their eloquence, their sublimity, and their music. The interruptions of the dialogue, however, impose a constraint upon the writer, and break the illusion of the reader. The finest passages are those which are lyric in form as well as in spirit. "I should much commend," says the excellent Sir Henry Wotton[22] in a letter to Milton, "the tragical part if the lyrical did not ravish me with a certain Dorique delicacy in your songs and odes, whereunto, I must plainly confess to you, I have seen yet nothing parallel in our language." The criticism was just. It is when Milton escapes from the shackles of the dialogue, when he is discharged from the labour of uniting two incongruous styles, when he is at liberty to indulge his choral raptures without reserve, that he rises even above himself. Then, like his own good Genius bursting from the earthly form and weeds of Thyrsis, he stand forth in celestial freedom and beauty; he seems to cry exultingly,

> "Now my task is smoothly done,
> I can fly or I can run,"[23]

to skim the earth, to soar above the clouds, to bathe in the Elysian dew of the rainbow, and to inhale the balmy smells of nard and cassia, which the musky wings of the zephyr scatter through the cedared alleys of the Hesperides.

There are several of the minor poems of Milton on which we would willingly make a few remarks. Still more willingly would we enter into a detailed examination of that admirable poem, the *Paradise Regained*, which, strangely enough, is scarcely ever mentioned except as an instance of

---

[20] Milton's phrase describing Euripides in the sonnet, "When the Assault Was Intended to the City."

[21] *The Faithful Shepherdess* (1609) by John Fletcher; *Aminta* by Torquato Tasso (1544–95); *Pastor Fido* by Guarini (1537–1612)—all works in the pastoral mode.

[22] Sir Henry Wotton (1568–1639), poet and diplomat.

[23] *Comus*, 11, 1011–12. Macaulay echoes other phrases from the poem in this paragraph.

the blindness of the parental affection which men of letters bear towards the offspring of their intellects. That Milton was mistaken in preferring this work, excellent as it is, to the *Paradise Lost*, we readily admit. But we are sure that the superiority of the *Paradise Lost* to the *Paradise Regained* is not more decided, than the superiority of the *Paradise Regained* to every poem which has since made its appearance. Our limits, however, prevent us from discussing the point at length. We hasten on to that extraordinary production which the general suffrage of critics has placed in the highest class of human compositions.

The only poem of modern times which can be compared with the *Paradise Lost* is the *Divine Comedy*. The subject of Milton, in some points, resembled that of Dante; but he has treated it in a widely different manner. We cannot, we think, better illustrate our opinion, respecting our own great poet, than by contrasting him with the father of Tuscan literature.

The poetry of Milton differs from that of Dante, as the hieroglyphics of Egypt differed from the picture-writing of Mexico. The images which Dante employs speak for themselves; they stand simply for what they are. Those of Milton have a signification which is often discernible only to the initiated. Their value depends less on what they directly represent than on what they remotely suggest. However strange, however grotesque, may be the appearance which Dante undertakes to describe, he never shrinks from describing it. He gives us the shape, the colour, the sound, the smell, the taste; he counts the numbers; he measures the size. His similes are the illustrations of a traveller. Unlike those of other poets, and especially of Milton, they are introduced in a plain, business-like manner; not for the sake of any beauty in the objects from which they are drawn; not for the sake of any ornament which they may impart to the poem; but simply in order to make the meaning of the writer as clear to the reader as it is to himself. The ruins of the precipice which led from the sixth to the seventh circle of hell were like those of the rock which fell into the Adige on the south of Trent. The cataract of Phlegethon was like that of Aqua Cheta at the monastery of St. Benedict. The place where the heretics were confined in burning tombs resembled the vast cemetery of Arles.[24]

Now let us compare with the exact details of Dante the dim intimations of Milton. We will cite a few examples. The English poet has never thought of taking the measure of Satan. He gives us merely a vague idea of vast bulk. In one passage the fiend lies stretched out huge in length, floating many a rood, equal in size to the earth-born enemies of Jove, or to the sea-monster which the mariner mistakes for an island. When he addresses himself to battle against the guardian angels, he stands like Teneriffe or Atlas: his stature reaches the sky. Contrast with these descriptions the lines in which Dante has described the gigantic spectre of Nimrod. "His face seemed to me as long and as broad as the ball of St. Peter's at Rome; and his other limbs were in proportion; so that the bank, which concealed him from the waist downwards, nevertheless showed so much of him, that three tall Germans would in vain have attempted to reach to his hair." We are sensible that we do no justice to the admirable style of the Florentine poet. But Mr. Cary's translation is not at hand; and our version, however rude, is sufficient to illustrate our meaning.[25]

Once more, compare the lazar-house in the eleventh book of the *Paradise Lost* with the last ward of Malebolge in Dante. Milton avoids the loathsome details, and takes refuge in indistinct but solemn and tremendous imagery, Despair hurrying from couch to couch to mock the wretches with his attendance, Death shaking his dart over them, but, in spite of supplications, delaying to strike. What says Dante? "There was such a moan there as there would be if all the sick who, between July and September, are in the hospitals of Valdichiana, and of the Tuscan swamps, and of Sardinia, were in one pit together; and such a stench was issuing forth as is wont to issue from decayed limbs."

We will not take upon ourselves the invidious office of settling precedency between two such writers. Each in his own department is incomparable; and each, we may remark, has wisely, or fortunately, taken a subject adapted to exhibit his peculiar talent to the greatest advantage The *Divine Comedy* is a personal narrative. Dante is the eye-witness and ear-witness of that which he relates. He is the very man who has heard the tormented spirits crying out for the second death, who has read the dusky characters on the portal within which there is

---

[24] All of the comparisons are with places known to Dante in his lifetime.
[25] Reference to the translation of the *Divine Comedy* by Henry Francis Cary in 1805 and 1812.

no hope, who has hidden his face from the terrors of the Gorgon, who has fled from the hooks and the seething pitch of Barbariccia and Draghignazzo. His own hands have grasped the shaggy sides of Lucifer. His own feet have climbed the mountain of expiation. His own brow has been marked by the purifying angel. The reader would throw aside such a tale in incredulous disgust, unless it were told with the strongest air of veracity, with a sobriety even in its horrors, with the greatest precision and multiplicity in its details. The narrative of Milton in this respect differs from that of Dante, as the adventures of Amadis differ from those of Gulliver.[26] The author of Amadis would have made his book ridiculous if he had introduced those minute particulars which give such a charm to the work of Swift, the nautical observations, the affected delicacy about names, the official documents transcribed at full length, and all the unmeaning gossip and scandal of the court, springing out of nothing, and tending to nothing. We are not shocked at being told that a man who lived, nobody knows when, saw many very strange sights, and we can easily abandon ourselves to the illusion of the romance. But when Lemuel Gulliver, surgeon, resident at Rotherhithe, tells us of pygmies and giants, flying islands, and philosophising horses, nothing but such circumstantial touches could produce for a single moment a deception on the imagination.

Of all the poets who have introduced into their works the agency of supernatural beings, Milton has succeeded best. Here Dante decidedly yields to him: and as this is a point on which many rash and ill-considered judgments have been pronounced, we feel inclined to dwell on it a little longer. The most fatal error which a poet can possibly commit in the management of his machinery, is that of attempting to philosophise too much. Milton has been often censured for ascribing to spirits many functions of which spirits must be incapable. But these objections, though sanctioned by eminent names, originate, we venture to say, in profound ignorance of the art of poetry.

What is spirit? What are our own minds, the portion of spirit with which we are best acquainted? We observe certain phænomena. We cannot explain them into material causes. We therefore infer that there exists something which is not material. But of this something we have no idea. We can define it only by negatives. We can reason about it only by symbols. We use the word; but we have no image of the thing; and the business of poetry is with images, and not with words. The poet uses words indeed; but they are merely the instruments of his art, not its objects. They are the materials which he is to dispose in such a manner as to present a picture to the mental eye. And if they are not so disposed, they are no more entitled to be called poetry than a bale of canvass and a box of colours to be called a painting.

Logicians may reason about abstractions. But the great mass of men must have images. The strong tendency of the multitude in all ages and nations to idolatry can be explained on no other principle. The first inhabitants of Greece, there is reason to believe, worshipped one invisible Deity. But the necessity of having something more definite to adore produced, in a few centuries, the innumerable crowd of Gods and Goddesses. In like manner the ancient Persians thought it impious to exhibit the Creator under a human form. Yet even these transferred to the Sun the worship which, in speculation, they considered due only to the Supreme Mind. The history of the Jews is the record of a continued struggle between pure Theism, supported by the most terrible sanctions, and the strangely fascinating desire of having some visible and tangible object of adoration. Perhaps none of the secondary causes which Gibbon has assigned for the rapidity with which Christianity spread over the world, while Judaism scarcely ever acquired a proselyte, operated more powerfully than this feeling. God, the uncreated, the incomprehensible, the invisible, attracted few worshippers. A philosopher might admire so noble a conception: but the crowd turned away in disgust from words which presented no image to their minds. It was before Deity embodied in a human form, walking among men, partaking of their infirmities, leaning on their bosoms, weeping over their graves, slumbering in the manger, bleeding on the cross, that the prejudices of the Synagogue, and the doubts of the Academy, and the pride of the Portico, and the fasces of the Lictor, and the swords of thirty legions, were humbled in the dust.[27] Soon after Christianity had achieved its triumph, the principle which had

---

[26] Amadis of Gaul, the hero of medieval romances; Gulliver, the protagonist of Swift's *Gulliver's Travels*.

[27] Academy, Portico, and Lictor represent the philosophies of Plato, Stoicism, and Rome respectively.

assisted it began to corrupt it. It became a new Paganism. Patron saints assumed the offices of household gods. St. George took the place of Mars. St. Elmo consoled the mariner for the loss of Castor and Pollux. The Virgin Mother and Cecilia succeeded to Venus and the Muses. The fascination of sex and loveliness was again joined to that of celestial dignity; and the homage of chivalry was blended with that of religion. Reformers have often made a stand against these feelings; but never with more than apparent and partial success. The men who demolished the images in Cathedrals have not always been able to demolish those which were enshrined in their minds. It would not be difficult to show that in politics the same rule holds good. Doctrines, we are afraid, must generally be embodied before they can excite a strong public feeling. The multitude is more easily interested .for the most unmeaning badge, or the most insignificant name, than for the most important principle.

From these considerations, we infer that no poet, who should affect that metaphysical accuracy for the want of which Milton has been blamed, would escape a disgraceful failure. Still, however, there was another extreme which, though far less dangerous, was also to be avoided. The imaginations of men are in a great measure under the control of their opinions. The most exquisite art of poetical colouring can produce no illusion, when it is employed to represent that which is at once perceived to be incongruous and absurd. Milton wrote in an age of philosophers and theologians. It was necessary, therefore, for him to abstain from giving such a shock to their understandings as might break the charm which it was his object to throw over their imaginations. This is the real explanation of the indistinctness and inconsistency with which he has often been reproached. Dr. Johnson acknowledges that it was absolutely necessary that the spirits should be clothed with material forms. "But," says he, "the poet should have secured the consistency of his system by keeping immateriality out of sight, and seducing the reader to drop it from his thoughts." This is easily said; but what if Milton could not seduce his readers to drop immateriality from their thoughts? What if the contrary opinion had taken so full a possession of the minds of men as to leave no room even for the half belief which poetry requires? Such we suspect to have been the case. It was impossible for the poet

to adopt altogether the material or the immaterial system. He therefore took his stand on the debatable ground. He left the whole in ambiguity. He has doubtless, by so doing, laid himself open to the charge of inconsistency. But, though philosophically in the wrong, we cannot but believe that he was poetically in the right. This task, which almost any other writer would have found impracticable, was easy to him. The peculiar art which he possessed of communicating his meaning circuitously through a long succession of associated ideas, and of intimating more than he expressed, enabled him to disguise those incongruities which he could not avoid.

Poetry which relates to the beings of another world ought to be at once mysterious and picturesque. That of Milton is so, That of Dante is picturesque indeed beyond any that ever was written. Its effect approaches to that produced by the pencil or the chisel. But it is picturesque to the exclusion of all mystery. This is a fault on the right side, a fault inseparable from the plan of Dante's poem, which, as we have already observed, rendered the utmost accuracy of description necessary. Still it is a fault. The supernatural agents excite an interest; but it is not the interest which is proper to supernatural agents. We feel that we could talk to the ghosts and dæmons, without any emotion of unearthly awe. We could, like Don Juan, ask them to supper, and eat heartily in their company. Dante's angels are good men with wings. His devils are spiteful ugly executioners. His dead men are merely living men in strange situations. The scene which passes between the poet and Farinata is justly celebrated. Still, Farinata in the burning tomb is exactly what Farinata would have been at an *auto da fe*.[28] Nothing can be more touching than the first interview of Dante and Beatrice. Yet what is it, but a lovely woman chiding, with sweet austere composure, the lover for whose affection she is grateful, but whose vices she reprobates? The feelings which give the passage its charm would suit the streets of Florence as well as the summit of the Mount of Purgatory.

The spirits of Milton are unlike those of almost all other writers. His fiends, in particular, are wonderful creations. They are not metaphysical abstractions. They are not wicked men. They are not ugly beasts. They have no horns, no tails, none of the fee-faw-fum of Tasso and

---

[28] Farinata, see *Inferno*, x; *auto da fé*, the ceremony preceding execution in the Inquisition.

Klopstock.[29] They have just enough in common with human nature to be intelligible to human beings. Their characters are, like their forms, marked by a certain dim resemblance to those of men, but exaggerated to gigantic dimensions, and veiled in mysterious gloom.

Perhaps the gods and dæmons of Æschylus may best bear a comparison with the angels and devils of Milton. The style of the Athenian had, as we have remarked, something of the Oriental character; and the same peculiarity may be traced in his mythology. It has nothing of the amenity and elegance which we generally find in the superstitions of Greece. All is rugged, barbaric, and colossal. The legends of Æschylus seem to harmonise less with the fragrant groves and graceful porticoes in which his countrymen paid their vows to the God of Light and Goddess of Desire than with those huge and grotesque labyrinths of eternal granite in which Egypt enshrined her mystic Osiris, or in which Hindostan still bows down to her seven-headed idols. His favourite gods are those of the elder generation, the sons of heaven and earth, compared with whom Jupiter himself was a stripling and an upstart, the gigantic Titans, and the inexorable Furies. Foremost among his creations of this class, stands Prometheus, half fiend, half redeemer, the friend of man, the sullen and implacable enemy of heaven. Prometheus bears undoubtedly a considerable resemblance to the Satan of Milton. In both we find the same impatience of control, the same ferocity, the same unconquerable pride. In both characters also are mingled, though in very different proportions, some kind and generous feelings. Prometheus, however, is hardly superhuman enough. He talks too much of his chains and his uneasy posture: he is rather too much depressed and agitated. His resolution seems to depend on the knowledge which he possesses that he holds the fate of his torturer in his hands, and that the hour of his release will surely come. But Satan is a creature of another sphere. The might of his intellectual nature is victorious over the extremity of pain. Amidst agonies which cannot be conceived without horror, he deliberates, resolves, and even exults. Against the sword of Michael, against the thunder of Jehovah, against the flaming lake, and the marl burning with solid fire, against the prospect of an eternity of unintermitted misery, his spirit bears up unbroken, resting on its own innate energies, requiring no support from any thing external, nor even from hope itself.

To return for a moment to the parallel which we have been attempting to draw between Milton and Dante, we would add that the poetry of these great men has in a considerable degree taken its character from their moral qualities. They are not egotists. They rarely obtrude their idiosyncracies on their readers. They have nothing in common with those modern beggars for fame who extort a pittance from the compassion of the inexperienced by exposing the nakedness and sores of their minds. Yet it would be difficult to name two writers whose works have been more completely, though undesignedly, coloured by their personal feelings.

The character of Milton was peculiarly distinguished by loftiness of spirit; that of Dante by intensity of feeling. In every line of the Divine Comedy we discern the asperity which is produced by pride struggling with misery. There is perhaps no work in the world so deeply and uniformly sorrowful. The melancholy of Dante was no fantastic caprice. It was not, as far as at this distance of time can be judged, the effect of external circumstances. It was from within. Neither love nor glory, neither the conflicts of earth not the hope of heaven could dispel it. It turned every consolation and every pleasure into its own nature. It resembled that noxious Sardinian soil of which the intense bitterness is said to have been perceptible even in its honey. His mind was, in the noble language of the Hebrew poet, "a land of darkness, as darkness itself, and where the light was as darkness." The gloom of his character discolours all the passions of men and all the face of nature, and tinges with its own livid hue the flowers of Paradise and the glories of the eternal throne. All the portraits of him are singularly characteristic. No person can look on the features, noble even to ruggedness, the dark furrows of the cheek, the haggard and woful stare of the eye, the sullen and contemptuous curve of the lip, and doubt that they belong to a man too proud and too sensitive to be happy.

Milton was, like Dante, a statesman and a lover; and, like Dante, he had been unfortunate in ambition and in love. He had survived his health and his sight, the comforts of his home, and the

---

[29] Torquato Tasso, author of *Jerusalem Delivered*; Friedrich Gottlob Klopstock (1724–1803), author of *Messias*.

prosperity of his party. Of the great men by whom he had been distinguished at his entrance into life, some had been taken away from the evil to come; some had carried into foreign climates their unconquerable hatred of oppression; some were pining in dungeons; and some had poured forth their blood on scaffolds. Venal and licentious scribblers, with just sufficient talent to clothe the thoughts of a pandar in the style of a bellman, were now the favourite writers of the Sovereign and of the public. It was a loathsome herd, which could be compared to nothing so fitly as to the rabble of Comus, grotesque monsters, half bestial, half human, dropping with wine, bloated with gluttony, and reeling in obscene dances. Amidst these that fair Muse was placed, like the chaste lady of the Masque, lofty, spotless, and serene, to be chattered at, and pointed at, and grinned at, by the whole rout of Satyrs and Goblins. If ever despondency and asperity could be excused in any man, they might have been excused in Milton. But the strength of his mind overcame every calamity. Neither blindness, nor gout, not age, nor penury, nor domestic afflictions, nor political disappointments, nor abuse, nor proscription, nor neglect, has power to disturb his sedate and majestic patience. His spirits do not seem to have been high, but they were singularly equable. His temper was serious, perhaps stern; but it was a temper which no sufferings could render sullen or fretful. Such as it was when, on the eve of great events, he returned from his travels, in the prime of health and manly beauty, loaded with literary distinctions, and glowing with patriotic hopes, such it continued to be when, after having experienced every calamity which is incident to our nature, old, poor, sightless, and disgraced, he retired to his hovel to die.

Hence it was that, though he wrote the Paradise Lost at a time of life when images of beauty and tenderness are in general beginning to fade, even from those minds in which they have not been effaced by anxiety and disappointment, he adorned it with all that is most lovely and delightful in the physical and in the moral world. Neither Theocritus nor Ariosto[30] had a finer or a more healthful sense of the pleasantness of external objects, or loved better to luxuriate amidst sunbeams and flowers, the songs of nightingales, the juice of summer fruits, and the coolness of shady fountains. His conception of love unites all the voluptuousness of the Oriental haram, and all the gallantry of the chivalric tournament, with all the pure and quiet affection of an English fire-side. His poetry reminds us of the miracles of Alpine scenery. Nooks and dells, beautiful as fairy-land, are embosomed in its most rugged and gigantic elevations. The roses and myrtles bloom unchilled on the verge of the avalanche.

Traces, indeed, of the peculiar character of Milton may be found in all his works; but it is most strongly displayed in the Sonnets. Those remarkable poems have been under-valued by critics who have not understood their nature. They have no epigrammatic point. There is none of the ingenuity of Filicaja[31] in the thought, none of the hard and brilliant enamel of Petrarch in the style. They are simple but majestic records of the feelings of the poet; as little tricked out for the public eye as his diary would have been. A victory, an expected attack upon the city, a momentary fit of depression or exultation, a jest thrown out against one of his books, a dream which for a short time restored to him that beautiful face over which the grave had closed for ever, led him to musings which, without effort, shaped themselves into verse. The unity of sentiment and severity of style which characterise these little pieces remind us of the Greek Anthology,[32] or perhaps still more of the Collects of the English Liturgy. The noble poem on the massacres of Piedmont is strictly a collect in verse.[33]

The Sonnets are more or less striking, according as the occasions which gave birth to them are more or less interesting. But they are, almost without exception, dignified by a sobriety and greatness of mind to which we know not where to look for a parallel. It would, indeed, be scarcely safe to draw any decided inferences as to the character of a writer from passages directly egotistical. But the qualities which we have ascribed to Milton, though perhaps most strongly marked in those parts of his works which treat of his personal feelings, are distinguishable in every page, and impart to all his writings, prose and poetry, English, Latin, and Italian, a strong family likeness.

His public conduct was such as was to be

---

[30] Theocritus, Greek pastoral poet of the third century; Ariosto, Italian poet, author of *Orlando Furioso* (1532).

[31] Vincenzo da Filicaia (1642–1707), Florentine poet.

[32] The collection of Greek poems of the fifth and sixth centuries B.C.

[33] Milton's sonnet, "Avenge, O Lord, Thy slaughter'd saints."

expected from a man of a spirit so high and of an intellect so powerful. He lived at one of the most memorable eras in the history of mankind, at the very crisis of the great conflict between Oromasdes and Arimanes,[34] liberty and despotism, reason and prejudice. That great battle was fought for no single generation, for no single land. The destinies of the human race were staked on the same cast with the freedom of the English people. Then were first proclaimed those mighty principles which have since worked their way into the depths of the American forests, which have roused Greece from the slavery and degradation of two thousand years, and which, from one end of Europe to the other, have kindled an unquenchable fire in the hearts of the oppressed, and loosed the knees of the oppressors with an unwonted fear.

Of those principles, then struggling for their infant existence, Milton was the most devoted and eloquent literary champion. We need not say how much we admire his public conduct. But we cannot disguise from ourselves that a large portion of his countrymen still think it unjustifiable. The civil war, indeed, has been more discussed, and is less understood, than any event in English history. The friends of liberty laboured under the disadvantage of which the lion in the fable complained so bitterly. Though they were the conquerors, their enemies were the painters. As a body, the Roundheads[35] had done their utmost to decry and ruin literature; and literature was even with them as, in the long run, it always is with its enemies. The best book on their side of the question is the charming narrative of Mrs. Hutchinson. May's History of the Parliament is good; but it breaks off at the most interesting crisis of the struggle. The performance of Ludlow is foolish and violent; and most of the later writers who have espoused the same cause, Oldmixon for instance, and Catherine Macaulay, have, to say the least, been more distinguished by zeal than either by candour or by skill.[36] On the other side are the most authoritative and the most popular historical works in our language, that of Clarendon and that

of Hume.[37] The former is not only ably written and full of valuable information, but has also an air of dignity and sincerity which makes even the prejudices and errors with which it abounds respectable. Hume, from whose fascinating narrative the great mass of the reading public are still contented to take their opinions, hated religion so much that he hated liberty for having been allied with religion, and has pleaded the cause of tyranny with the dexterity of an advocate while affecting the impartiality of a judge.

The public conduct of Milton must be approved or condemned according as the resistance of the people to Charles the First shall appear to be justifiable or criminal. We shall therefore make no apology for dedicating a few pages to the discussion of that interesting and most important question. We shall not argue it on general grounds. We shall not recur to those primary principles from which the claim of any government to the obedience of its subjects is to be deduced. We are entitled to that vantage ground; but we will relinquish it. We are, on this point, so confident of superiority, that we are not unwilling to imitate the ostentatious generosity of those ancient knights, who vowed to joust without helmet or shield against all enemies, and to give their antagonists the advantage of sun and wind. We will take the naked constitutional question. We confidently affirm, that every reason which can be urged in favour of the Revolution of 1688 may be urged with at least equal force in favour of what is called the Great Rebellion.

In one respect, only, we think, can the warmest admirers of Charles venture to say that he was a better sovereign than his son. He was not, in name and profession, a Papist; we say in name and profession, because both Charles himself and his creature Laud,[38] while they abjured the innocent badges of Popery, retained all its worst vices, a complete subjection of reason to authority, a weak preference of form to substance, a childish passion for mummeries, an idolatrous veneration for the priestly character, and, above all, a merciless intolerance. This, however, we waive.

[34] The Parsee spirits of good and evil.
[35] The Puritans in the English Civil War.
[36] Lucy Hutchinson (b. 1620) wrote the *Life of Colonel Hutchinson*; Thomas May (1595–1650), author of *History of the Long Parliament* (1647); Edmund Ludlow (1617?–92), author of *Memoirs* (1698–99); John Oldmixon (1673–1742), Whig critic of Clarendon's *History*; Catherine Macaulay (1731–91), historian, no relation to T. B. Macaulay.
[37] Edward Hyde, Earl of Clarendon (1609–74), author of *History of the Rebellion*; David Hume (1711–76), author of *History of England*.
[38] William Laud (1573–1645), Archbishop of Canterbury, beheaded by the Puritans in 1644.

We will concede that Charles was a good Protestant; but we say that his Protestantism does not make the slightest distinction between his case and that of James.

The principles of the Revolution have often been grossly misrepresented, and never more than in the course of the present year.[39] There is a certain class of men, who, while they profess to hold in reverence the great names and great actions of former times, never look at them for any other purpose than in order to find in them some excuse for existing abuses. In every venerable precedent they pass by what is essential, and take only what is accidental: they keep out of sight what is beneficial, and hold up to public imitation all that is defective. If, in any part of any great example, there be any thing unsound, these flesh-flies detect it with an unerring instinct, and dart upon it with a ravenous delight. If some good end has been attained in spite of them, they feel, with their prototype, that

> "Their labour must be to pervert that end,
> And out of good still to find means of evil."[40]

To the blessings which England has derived from the Revolution these people are utterly insensible. The expulsion of a tyrant, the solemn recognition of popular rights, liberty, security, toleration, all go for nothing with them. One sect[41] there was, which, from unfortunate temporary causes, it was thought necessary to keep under close restraint. One part of the empire[42] there was so unhappily circumstanced, that at that time its misery was necessary to our happiness, and its slavery to our freedom. These are the parts of the Revolution which the politicians of whom we speak, love to contemplate, and which seem to them not indeed to vindicate, but in some degree to palliate, the good which it has produced. Talk to them of Naples, of Spain, or of South America.[43] They stand forth zealots for the doctrine of Divine Right which has now come back to us, like a thief from transportation, under the *alias* of Legitimacy. But mention the miseries of Ireland. Then William is a hero. Then Somers and Shrewsbury are great men.[44] Then the Revolution is a glorious era. The very same persons who, in this country, never omit an opportunity of reviving every wretched Jacobite slander respecting the Whigs of that period, have no sooner crossed St. George's Channel, than they begin to fill their bumpers to the glorious and immortal memory. They may truly boast that they look not at men, but at measures. So that evil be done, they care not who does it; the arbitrary Charles, or the liberal William, Ferdinand the Catholic, or Frederic the Protestant. On such occasions their deadliest opponents may reckon upon their candid construction. The bold assertions of these people have of late impressed a large portion of the public with an opinion that James the Second was expelled simply because he was a Catholic, and that the Revolution was essentially a Protestant Revolution.

But this certainty was not the case; nor can any person who has acquired more knowledge of the history of those times than is to be found in Goldsmith's Abridgment[45] believe that, if James had held his own religious opinions without wishing to make proselytes, or if, wishing even to make proselytes, he had contented himself with exerting only his constitutional influence for that purpose, the Prince of Orange would ever have been invited over. Our ancestors, we suppose, knew their own meaning; and, if we may believe them, their hostility was primarily not to popery, but to tyranny. They did not drive out a tyrant because he was a Catholic; but they excluded Catholics from the crown, because they thought them likely to be tyrants. The ground on which they, in their famous resolution, declared the throne vacant, was this, "that James had broken the fundamental laws of the kingdom." Every man, therefore, who approves of the Revolution of 1688 must hold that the breach of fundamental laws on the part of the sovereign justifies resistance. The question, then, is this; Had Charles the First broken the fundamental laws of England?

No person can answer in the negative, unless he refuses credit, not merely to all the accusations brought against Charles by his opponents, but to the narratives of the warmest Royalists, and to the confessions of the King himself. If there be

---

[39] Reference to the debates in 1825 on Catholic Emancipation.

[40] *Paradise Lost*, I, 164–65.

[41] I.e., the Roman Catholics.

[42] I.e., Ireland.

[43] Places where revolutions had recently occurred.

[44] Baron Somers (1651–1716) and Alexander Montgomerie, Earl of Eglinton (1660?–1729), advisors to William III.

[45] An abridgment of a *History of England*, possibly by Goldsmith.

any truth in any historian of any party who has related the events of that reign, the conduct of Charles, from his accession to the meeting of the Long Parliament, had been a continued course of oppression and treachery. Let those who applaud the Revolution, and condemn the Rebellion, mention one act of James the Second to which a parallel is not to be found in the history of his father. Let them lay their fingers on a single article in the Declaration of Right, presented by the two Houses to William and Mary, which Charles is not acknowledged to have violated. He had, according to the testimony of his own friends, usurped the functions of the legislature, raised taxes without the consent of parliament, and quartered troops on the people in the most illegal and vexatious manner. Not a single session of parliament had passed without some unconstitutional attack on the freedom of debate; the right of petition was grossly violated; arbitrary judgments, exorbitant fines, and unwarranted imprisonments, were grievances of daily occurrence. If these things do not justify resistance, the Revolution was treason; if they do, the Great Rebellion was laudable.

But, it is said, why not adopt milder measures? Why, after the King had consented to so many reforms, and renounced so many oppressive prerogatives, did the parliament continue to rise in their demands at the risk of provoking a civil war? The ship money had been given up. The Star Chamber had been abolished.[46] Provision had been made for the frequent convocation and secure deliberation of parliaments. Why not pursue an end confessedly good by peaceable and regular means? We recur again to the analogy of the Revolution. Why was James driven from the throne? Why was he not retained upon conditions? He too had offered to call a free parliament and to submit to its decision all the matters in dispute. Yet we are in the habit of praising our forefathers, who preferred a revolution, a disputed succession, a dynasty of strangers, twenty years of foreign and intestine war, a standing army, and a national debt, to the rule, however restricted, of a tried and proved tyrant. The Long Parliament acted on the same principle, and is entitled to the same praise. They could not trust the King. He had no doubt passed salutary laws; but what assurance was there that he would not break

them? He had renounced oppressive prerogatives; but where was the security that he would not resume them? The nation had to deal with a man whom no tie could bind, a man who made and broke promises with equal facility, a man whose honour had been a hundred times pawned, and never redeemed.

Here, indeed, the Long Parliament stands on still stronger ground than the Convention of 1688. No action of James can be compared to the conduct of Charles with respect to the Petition of Right. The Lords and Commons present him with a bill in which the constitutional limits of his power are marked out. He hesitates; he evades; at last he bargains to give his assent for five subsidies. The bill receives his solemn assent; the subsidies are voted; but no sooner is the tyrant relieved, than he returns at once to all the arbitrary measures which he had bound himself to abandon, and violates all the clauses of the very Act which he had been paid to pass.

For more than ten years the people had seen the rights which were theirs by a double claim, by immemorial inheritance and by recent purchase, infringed by the perfidious King who had recognised them. At length circumstances compelled Charles to summon another parliament: another chance was given to our fathers: were they to throw it away as they had thrown away the former? Were they again to be cozened by *le Roi le veut?*[47] Were they again to advance their money on pledges which had been forfeited over and over again? Were they to lay a second Petition of Right at the foot of the throne, to grant another lavish aid in exchange for another unmeaning ceremony, and then to take their departure, till, after ten years more of fraud and oppression, their prince should again require a supply, and again repay it with a perjury? They were compelled to choose whether they would trust a tyrant or conquer him. We think that they chose wisely and nobly.

The advocates of Charles, like the advocates of other malefactors against whom overwhelming evidence is produced, generally decline all controversy about the facts, and content themselves with calling testimony to character. He had so many private virtues! And had James the Second no private virtues? Was Oliver Cromwell, his bitterest enemies themselves being judges, destitute of private virtues? And what, after all,

---

[46] Ship-money, a port tax levied in time of war, one of the causes of the English Civil War; Star Chamber, an arbitrary, secret tribunal operating at the monarch's pleasure.
[47] "The King wills it," words indicating the king's assent to Parliamentary acts.

are the virtues ascribed to Charles? A religious zeal, not more sincere than that of his son, and fully as weak and narrow-minded, and a few of the ordinary household decencies which half the tombstones in England claim for those who lie beneath them A good father! A good husband! Ample apologies indeed for fifteen years of persecution, tyranny, and falsehood!

We charge him with having broken his coronation oath; and we are told that he kept his marriage vow! We accuse him of having given up his people to the merciless inflictions of the most hot-headed and hard-hearted of prelates; and the defence is, that he took his little son on his knee and kissed him! We censure him for having violated the articles of the Petition of Right, after having, for good and valuable consideration, promised to observe them; and we are informed that he was accustomed to hear prayers at six o'clock in the morning! It is to such considerations as these, together with his Vandyke dress, his handsome face, and his peaked beard, that he owes, we verily believe, most of his popularity with the present generation.

For ourselves, we own that we do not understand the common phrase, a good man, but a bad king. We can as easily conceive a good man and an unnatural father, or a good man and a treacherous friend. We cannot, in estimating the character of an individual, leave out of our consideration his conduct in the most important of all human relations; and if in that relation we find him to have been selfish, cruel, and deceitful, we shall take the liberty to call him a bad man, in spite of all his temperance at table, and all his regularity at chapel.

We cannot refrain from adding a few words respecting a topic on which the defenders of Charles are fond of dwelling. If, they say, he governed his people ill, he at least governed them after the example of his predecessors. If he violated their privileges, it was because those privileges had not been accurately defined. No act of oppression has ever been imputed to him which has not a parallel in the annals of the Tudors. This point Hume has laboured, with an art which is as discreditable in a historical work as it would be admirable in a forensic address. The answer is short, clear, and decisive. Charles had assented to the Petition of Right. He had renounced the oppressive powers said to have been exercised by his predecessors, and he had renounced them for money. He was not entitled to set up his antiquated claims against his own recent release.

These arguments are so obvious, that it may seem superfluous to dwell upon them. But those who have observed how much the events of that time are misrepresented and misunderstood will not blame us for stating the case simply. It is a case of which the simplest statement is the strongest.

The enemies of the Parliament, indeed, rarely choose to take issue on the great points of the question. They content themselves with exposing some of the crimes and follies to which public commotions necessarily give birth. They bewail the unmerited fate of Strafford.[48] They execrate the lawless violence of the army. They laugh at the Scriptural names of the preachers. Major-generals fleecing their districts; soldiers revelling on the spoils of a ruined peasantry; upstarts, enriched by the public plunder, taking possession of the hospitable firesides and hereditary trees of the old gentry; boys smashing the beautiful windows of cathedrals; Quakers riding naked through the market-place; Fifth-monarchy-men shouting for King Jesus; agitators lecturing from the tops of tubs on the fate of Agag; all these, they tell us, were the offspring of the Great Rebellion.[49]

Be it so. We are not careful to answer in this matter. These charges, were they infinitely more important, would not alter our opinion of an event which alone has made us to differ from the slaves who crouch beneath despotic sceptres. Many evils, no doubt, were produced by the civil war. They were the price of our liberty. Has the acquisition been worth the sacrifice? It is the nature of the Devil of tyranny to tear and rend the body which he leaves. Are the miseries of continued possession less horrible than the struggles of the tremendous exorcism?

If it were possible that a people brought up under an intolerant and arbitrary system could subvert that system without acts of cruelty and folly, half the objections to despotic power would be removed. We should, in that case, be compelled to acknowledge that it at least produces no pernicious effects on the intellectual and moral character of a nation. We deplore the outrages which accompany revolutions. But the more violent the outrages, the more assured we feel that

---

[48] Thomas Wentworth, 1st Earl of Strafford (1593-1641), minister to Charles I, executed by the Puritans.

[49] Macaulay is cataloguing some of the excesses of the Puritans.

a revolution was necessary. The violence of those outrages will always be proportioned to the ferocity and ignorance of the people; and the ferocity and ignorance of the people will be proportioned to the oppression and degradation under which they have been accustomed to live. Thus it was in our civil war. The heads of the church and state reaped only that which they had sown. The government had prohibited free discussion: it had done its best to keep the people unacquainted with their duties and their rights. The retribution was just and natural. If our rulers suffered from popular ignorance, it was because they had themselves taken away the key of knowledge. If they were assailed with blind fury, it was because they had exacted an equally blind submission.

It is the character of such revolutions that we always see the worst of them at first. Till men have been some time free, they know not how to use their freedom. The natives of wine countries are generally sober. In climates where wine is a rarity intemperance abounds. A newly liberated people may be compared to a northern army encamped on the Rhine or the Xeres.[50] It is said that, when soldiers in such a situation first find themselves able to indulge without restraint in such a rare and expensive luxury, nothing is to be seen but intoxication. Soon, however, plenty teaches discretion; and, after wine has been for a few months their daily fare, they become more temperate than they had ever been in their own country. In the same manner, the final and permanent fruits of liberty are wisdom, moderation, and mercy. Its immediate effects are often atrocious crimes, conflicting errors, scepticism on points the most clear, dogmatism on points the most mysterious. It is just at this crisis that its enemies love to exhibit it. They pull down the scaffolding from the half-finished edifice; they point to the flying dust, the falling bricks, the comfortless rooms, the frightful irregularity of the whole appearance; and then ask in scorn where the promised splendour and comfort is to be found. If such miserable sophisms were to prevail there would never be a good house or a good government in the world.

Ariosto tells a pretty story of a fairy,[51] who, by some mysterious law of her nature, was condemned to appear at certain seasons in the form of a foul and poisonous snake. Those who

injured her during the period of her disguise were for ever excluded from participation in the blessings which she bestowed. But to those who, in spite of her loathsome aspect, pitied and protected her, she afterwards revealed herself in the beautiful and celestial form which was natural to her, accompanied their steps, granted all their wishes, filled their houses with wealth, made them happy in love and victorious in war. Such a spirit is Liberty. At times she takes the form of a hateful reptile. She grovels, she hisses, she stings. But woe to those who in disgust shall venture to crush her! And happy are those who, having dared to receive her in her degraded and frightful shape, shall at length be rewarded by her in the time of her beauty and her glory!

There is only one cure for the evils which newly acquired freedom produces; and that cure is freedom. When a prisoner first leaves his cell he cannot bear the light of day: he is unable to discriminate colours, or recognise faces. But the remedy is, not to remand him into his dungeon, but to accustom him to the rays of the sun. The blaze of truth and liberty may at first dazzle and bewilder nations which have become half blind in the house of bondage. But let them gaze on, and they will soon be able to bear it. In a few years men learn to reason. The extreme violence of opinions subsides. Hostile theories correct each other. The scattered elements of truth cease to contend, and begin to coalesce. And at length a system of justice and order is educed out of the chaos.

Many politicians of our time are in the habit of laying it down as a self-evident proposition, that no people ought to be free till they are fit to use their freedom. The maxim is worthy of the fool in the old story, who resolved not to go into the water till he had learnt to swim. If men are to wait for liberty till they become wise and good in slavery, they may indeed wait for ever.

Therefore it is that we decidely approve of the conduct of Milton and the other wise and good men who, in spite of much that was ridiculous and hateful in the conduct of their associates, stood firmly by the cause of Public Liberty. We are not aware that the poet has been charged with personal participation in any of the blameable excesses of that time. The favourite topic of his enemies is the line of conduct which he pursued with regard to the execution of the King. Of that

---

[50] Xeres is a town, not a river, in Spain, the original source for sherry wine, which is derived from the name of the town.

[51] In *Orlando Furioso*.

celebrated proceeding we by no means approve. Still we must say, in justice to the many eminent persons who concurred in it, and in justice more particularly to the eminent person who defended it, that nothing can be more absurd than the imputations which, for the last hundred and sixty years, it has been the fashion to cast upon the Regicides. We have, throughout, abstained from appealing to first principles. We will not appeal to them now. We recur again to the parallel case of the Revolution. What essential distinction can be drawn between the execution of the father and the deposition of the son? What constitutional maxim is there which applies to the former and not to the latter? The King can do no wrong. If so, James was as innocent as Charles could have been. The minister only ought to be responsible for the acts of the Sovereign. If so, why not impeach Jefferies and retain James?[52] The person of a King is sacred. Was the person of James considered sacred at the Boyne?[53] To discharge cannon against an army in which a King is known to be posted is to approach pretty near to regicide. Charles, too, it should always be remembered, was put to death by men who had been exasperated by the hostilities of several years, and who had never been bound to him by any other tie than that which was common to them with all their fellow citizens. Those who drove James from his throne, who seduced his army, who alienated his friends, who first imprisoned him in his palace, and then turned him out of it, who broke in upon his very slumbers by imperious messages, who pursued him with fire and sword from one part of the empire to another, who hanged, drew, and quartered his adherents, and attainted his innocent heir, were his nephew and his two daughters. When we reflect on all these things, we are at a loss to conceive how the same persons who, on the fifth of November, thank God for wonderfully conducting his servant William, and for making all opposition fall before him until he became our King and Governor, can, on the thirtieth of January, contrive to be afraid that the blood of the Royal Martyr may be visited on themselves and their children.[54]

We disapprove, we repeat, of the execution of Charles; not because the constitution exempts the King from responsibility, for we know that all such maxims, however excellent, have their exceptions; nor because we feel any peculiar interest in his character, for we think that his sentence describes him with perfect justice as "a tyrant, a traitor, a murderer, and a public enemy;" but because we are convinced that the measure was most injurious to the cause of freedom. He whom it removed was a captive and a hostage: his heir, to whom the allegiance of every Royalist was instantly transferred, was at large. The Presbyterians could never have been perfectly reconciled to the father: they had no such rooted enmity to the son. The great body of the people, also, contemplated that proceeding with feelings which, however unreasonable, no government could safely venture to outrage.

But though we think the conduct of the Regicides blameable, that of Milton appears to us in a very different light. The deed was done. It could not be undone. The evil was incurred; and the object was to render it as small as possible. We censure the chiefs of the army for not yielding to the popular opinion; but we cannot censure Milton for wishing to change that opinion. The very feeling which would have restrained us from committing the act would have led us, after it had been committed, to defend it against the ravings of servility and superstition. For the sake of public liberty, we wish that the thing had not been done, while the people disapproved of it. But, for the sake of public liberty, we should also have wished the people to approve of it when it was done. If any thing more were wanting to the justification of Milton, the book of Salmasius would furnish it.[55] That miserable performance is now with justice considered only as a beacon to word-catchers, who wish to become statesmen. The celebrity of the man who refuted it, the "Æneæ magni dextra,"[56] gives it all its fame with the present generation. In that age the state of things was different. It was not then fully understood how vast an interval separates the mere classical scholar from the political philosopher. Nor can it be doubted that a treatise which, bearing the name of so eminent a critic, attacked the fun-

---

[52] George, Baron Jeffries (1648–89), Lord High Chancellor under James II.

[53] Scene in 1690 of the defeat of James II in Ireland at the hands of William of Orange.

[54] Fifth of November, anniversary of the foiled Gunpowder Plot (1605) and of William's landing in England (1688); thirtieth of January, anniversary of the execution of Charles I (1649).

[55] Claudius Salmasius (1588–1653), French author of *Defensio regia pro Carlo I* (1649), a defense of King Charles I.

[56] "The right hand of the great Aeneas" (*Aeneid*).

damental principles of all free governments, must, if suffered to remain unanswered have produced a most pernicious effect on the public mind.

We wish to add a few words relative to another subject, on which the enemies of Milton delight to dwell, his conduct during the administration of the Protector. That an enthusiastic votary of liberty should accept office under a military usurper seems, no doubt, at first sight, extraordinary. But all the circumstances in which the country was then placed were extraordinary. The ambition of Oliver was of no vulgar kind. He never seems to have coveted despotic power. He at first fought sincerely and manfully for the Parliament, and never deserted it, till it had deserted its duty. If he dissolved it by force, it was not till he found that the few members who remained after so many deaths, secessions, and expulsions, were desirous to appropriate to themselves a power which they held only in trust, and to inflict upon England the curse of a Venetian oligarchy. But even when thus placed by violence at the head of affairs, he did not assume unlimited power. He gave the country a constitution far more perfect than any which had at that time been known in the world. He reformed the representative system in a manner which has extorted praise even from Lord Clarendon. For himself he demanded indeed the first place in the commonwealth; but with powers scarcely so great as those of a Dutch stadtholder, or an American president. He gave the Parliament a voice in the appointment of ministers, and left to it the whole legislative authority, not even reserving to himself a veto on its enactments; and he did not require that the chief magistracy should be hereditary in his family. Thus far, we think if the circumstances of the time and the opportunities which he had of aggrandising himself be fairly considered, he will not lose by comparison with Washington or Bolivar. Had his moderation been met by corresponding moderation, there is no reason to think that he would have overstepped the line which he had traced for himself. But when he found that his parliaments questioned the authority under which they met, and that he was in danger of being deprived of the restricted power which was absolutely necessary to his personal safety, then, it must be acknowledged, he adopted a more arbritrary policy.

Yet, though we believe that the intentions of Cromwell were at first honest, though we believe that he was driven from the noble course which he had marked out for himself by the almost irresistible force of circumstances, though we admire, in common with all men of all parties, the ability and energy of his splendid administration, we are not pleading for arbitrary and lawless power, even in his hands. We know that a good constitution is infinitely better than the best despot. But we suspect, that at the time of which we speak, the violence of religious and political enmities rendered a stable and happy settlement next to impossible. The choice lay, not between Cromwell and liberty, but between Cromwell and the Stuarts. That Milton chose well, no man can doubt who fairly compares the events of the protectorate with those of the thirty years which succeeded it, the darkest and most disgraceful in the English annals. Cromwell was evidently laying, though in an irregular manner, the foundations of an admirable system. Never before had religious liberty and the freedom of discussion been enjoyed in a greater degree. Never had the national honour been better upheld abroad, or the seat of justice better filled at home. And it was rarely that any opposition which stopped short of open rebellion provoked the resentment of the liberal and magnanimous usurper. The institutions which he had established, as set down in the Instrument of Government, and the Humble Petition and Advice, were excellent. His practice, it is true, too often departed from the theory of these institutions. But, had he lived a few years longer, it is probable that his institutions would have survived him, and that his arbitrary practice would have died with him. His power had not been consecrated by ancient prejudices. It was upheld only by his great personal qualities. Little, therefore was to be dreaded from a second protector, unless he were also a second Oliver Cromwell. The events which followed his decease are the most complete vindication of those who exerted themselves to uphold his authority. His death dissolved the whole frame of society. The army rose against the parliament, the different corps of the army against each other. Sect raved against sect. Party plotted against party. The Presbyterians, in their eagerness to be revenged on the Independents, sacrificed their own liberty, and deserted all their old principles. Without casting one glance on the past, or requiring one stipulation for the future, they threw down their freedom at the feet of the most frivolous and heartless of tyrants.

Then came those days, never to be recalled without a blush, the days of servitude without loyalty and sensuality without love, of dwarfish talents and gigantic vices, the paradise of cold hearts and narrow minds, the golden age of the coward, the bigot, and the slave. The King cringed to his rival that he might trample on his people, sank into a viceroy of France, and pocketed, with complacent infamy, her degrading insults, and her more degrading gold. The caresses of harlots, and the jests of buffoons, regulated the policy of the state. The government had just ability enough to deceive, and just religion enough to persecute. The principles of liberty were the scoff of every grinning courtier, and the Anathema Maranatha of every fawning dean.[57] In every high place, worship was paid to Charles and James, Belial and Moloch; and England propitiated those obscene and cruel idols with the blood of her best and bravest children. Crime succeeded to crime, and disgrace to disgrace, till the race accursed of God and man was a second time driven forth, to wander on the face of the earth, and to be a by-word and a shaking of the head to the nations.

Most of the remarks which we have hitherto made on the public character of Milton, apply to him only as one of a large body. We shall proceed to notice some of the peculiarities which distinguished him from his contemporaries. And, for that purpose, it is necessary to take a short survey of the parties into which the political world was at that time divided. We must premise, that our observations are intended to apply only to those who adhered, from a sincere preference, to one or to the other side. In days of public commotion, every faction, like an Oriental army, is attended by a crowd of camp-followers, an useless and heartless rabble, who prowl round its line of march in the hope of picking up something under its protection, but desert it in the day of battle, and often join to exterminate it after a defeat. England, at the time of which we are treating, abounded with fickle and selfish politicians, who transferred their support to every government as it rose, who kissed the hand of the King in 1640, and spat in his face in 1649, who shouted with equal glee when Cromwell was inaugurated in Westminster Hall, and when he was dug up to be hanged at Tyburn, who dined on calves' heads, or struck up oak branches, as circumstances altered, without the slightest shame or repugnance.[58] These we leave out of the account. We take our estimate of parties from those who really deserve to be called partisans.

We would speak first of the Puritans, the most remarkable body of men, perhaps, which the world has ever produced. The odious and ridiculous parts of their character lie on the surface. He that runs may read them; nor have there been wanting attentive and malicious observers to point them out. For many years after the Restoration, they were the theme of unmeasured invective and derision. They were exposed to the utmost licentiousness of the press and of the stage, at the time when the press and the stage were most licentious. They were not men of letters; they were, as a body, unpopular; they could not defend themselves; and the public would not take them under its protection. They were therefore abandoned, without reserve, to the tender mercies of the satirists and dramatists. The ostentatious simplicity of their dress, their sour aspect, their nasal twang, their stiff posture, their long graces, their Hebrew names, the Scriptural phrases which they introduced on every occasion, their contempt of human learning, their detestation of polite amusements, were indeed fair game for the laughers. But it is not from the laughers alone that the philosophy of history is to be learnt. And he who approaches this subject should carefully guard against the influence of that potent ridicule which has already misled so many excellent writers.

> "Ecco il fonte del riso, ed ecco il rio
> Che mortali perigli in se contiene:
> Hor qui tener a fren nostro desio,
> Ed esser cauti molto a noi conviene."[59]

Those who roused the people to resistance, who directed their measures through a long series of eventful years, who formed, out of the most unpromising materials, the finest army that Europe had ever seen, who trampled down King, Church, and Aristocracy, who, in the short intervals of domestic sedition and rebellion, made the name of England terrible to every nation on the face of the earth, were no vulgar fanatics.

---

[57] Macaulay mistakenly joins the two expressions to mean simply *anathema*; *marantha* means "the Lord will come."

[58] The calf's head was a symbol of the regicides, the oak leaf of the Royalists.

[59] "Behold the fatal spring where laughter dwells,
    Dire poison lurking in its secret cells;
    Here let us guard our thoughts, our passions rein,
    And every loose desire in bonds detain." (*Jerusalem Delivered*)

Most of their absurdities were mere external badges, like the signs of freemasonry, or the dresses of friars. We regret that these badges were not more attractive. We regret that a body to whose courage and talents mankind has owed inestimable obligations had not the lofty elegance which distinguished some of the adjerents of Charles the First, or the easy good-breeding for which the court of Charles the Second was celebrated. But, if we must make our choice, we shall, like Bassanio in the play,[60] turn from the specious caskets which contain only the Death's head and the Fool's head, and fix on the plain leaden chest which conceals the treasure.

The Puritans were men whose minds had derived a peculiar character from the daily contemplation of superior beings and eternal interests. Not content with acknowledging, in general terms, an overruling Providence, they habitually ascribed every event to the will of the Great Being, for whose power nothing was too vast, for whose inspection nothing was too minute. To know him, to serve him, to enjoy him, was with them the great end of existence. They rejected with contempt the ceremonious homage which other sects substituted for the pure worship of the soul. Instead of catching occasional glimpses of the Deity through an obscuring veil, they aspired to gaze full on his intolerable brightness, and to commune with him face to face. Hence originated their contempt for terrestrial distinctions. The difference between the greatest and the meanest of mankind seemed to vanish, when compared with the boundless interval which separated the whole race from him on whom their own eyes were constantly fixed. They recognised no title to superiority but his favour; and, confident of that favour, they despised all the accomplishments and all the dignities of the world. If they were unacquainted with the works of philosophers and poets, they were deeply read in the oracles of God. If their names were not found in the registers of heralds, they were recorded in the Book of Life. If their steps were not accompanied by a splendid train of menials, legions of ministering angels had charge over them. Their palaces were houses not made with hands; their diadems crowns of glory which should never fade away. On the rich and the eloquent, on nobles and priests, they looked down with contempt: for they esteemed themselves rich in a more precious treasure, and eloquent in a more sublime language, nobles by the right of an earlier creation, and priests by the imposition of a mightier hand. The very meanest of them was a being to whose fate a mysterious and terrible importance belonged, on whose slightest action the spirits of light and darkness looked with anxious interest, who had been destined, before heaven and earth were created, to enjoy a felicity which should continue when heaven and earth should have passed away. Events which short-sighted politicians ascribed to earthly causes, had been ordained on his account. For his sake empires had risen, and flourished, and decayed. For his sake the Almighty had proclaimed his will by the pen of the Evangelist, and the harp of the prophet. He had been wrested by no common deliverer from the grasp of no common foe. He had been ransomed by the sweat of no vulgar agony, by the blood of no earthly sacrifice. It was for him that the sun had been darkened, that the rocks had been rent, that the dead had risen, that all nature had shuddered at the sufferings of her expiring God.

Thus the Puritan was made up of two different men, the one all self-abasement, penitence, gratitude, passion, the other proud, calm, inflexible, sagacious. He prostrated himself in the dust before his Maker: but he set his foot on the neck of his king. In his devotional retirement, he prayed with convulsions, and groans, and tears. He was half-maddened by glorious or terrible illusions. He heard the lyres of angels or the tempting whispers of fiends. He caught a gleam of the Beatific Vision, or woke screaming from dreams of everlasting fire. Like Vane, he thought himself intrusted with the sceptre of the millennial year. Like Fleetwood, he cried in the bitterness of his soul that God had hid his face from him.[61] But when he took his seat in the council, or girt on his sword for war, these tempestuous workings of the soul had left no perceptible trace behind them. People who saw nothing of the godly but their uncouth visages, and heard nothing from them but their groans and their whining hymns, might laugh at them. But those had little reason to laugh who encountered them in the hall of debate or in the field of battle. These fanatics brought to civil and military affairs a coolness of judgment and an immutability of purpose which some writers

---

[60] *Merchant of Venice.*

[61] Sir Henry Vane, the younger (1613–62), a Fifth Monarchy man; Charles Fleetwood (d. 1692), Cromwell's son-in-law.

have thought inconsistent with their religious zeal, but which were in fact the necessary effects of it. The intensity of their feelings on one subject made them tranquil on every other. One overpowering sentiment had subjected to itself pity and hatred, ambition and fear. Death had lost its terrors and pleasure its charms. They had their smiles and their tears, their raptures and their sorrows, but not for the things of this world. Enthusiasm had made them Stoics, had cleared their minds from every vulgar passion and prejudice, and raised them above the influence of danger and of corruption. It sometimes might lead them to pursue unwise ends, but never to choose unwise means. They went through the world, like Sir Artegal's iron man Talus with his flail,[62] crushing and trampling down oppressors, mingling with human beings, but having neither part nor lot in human infirmities, insensible to fatigue, to pleasure, and to pain, not to be pierced by any weapon, not to be withstood by any barrier.

Such we believe to have been the character of the Puritans. We perceive the absurdity of their manners. We dislike the sullen gloom of their domestic habits. We acknowledge that the tone of their minds was often injured by straining after things too high for mortal reach: and we know that, in spite of their hatred of Popery, they too often fell into the worst vices of that bad system, intolerance and extravagant austerity, that they had their anchorites and their crusades, their Dunstans and their De Montforts, their Dominics and their Escobars.[63] Yet, when all circumstances are taken into consideration, we do not hesitate to pronounce them a brave, a wise, an honest, and an useful body.

The Puritans espoused the cause of civil liberty mainly because it was the cause of religion. There was another party, by no means numerous, but distinguished by learning and ability, which acted with them on very different principles. We speak of those whom Cromwell was accustomed to call the Heathens, men who were, in the phraseology of that time, doubting Thomases or careless Gallios with regard to religious subjects, but passionate worshippers of freedom. Heated by the study of ancient litera-

ture, they set up their country as their idol, and proposed to themselves the heroes of Plutarch as their examples. They seem to have borne some resemblance to the Brissotines[64] of the French Revolution. But it is not very easy to draw the line of distinction between them and their devout associates, whose tone and manner they sometimes found it convenient to affect, and sometimes, it is probable, imperceptibly adopted.

We now come to the Royalists. We shall attempt to speak of them, as we have spoken of their antagonists, with perfect candour. We shall not charge upon a whole party the profligacy and baseness of the horseboys, gamblers and bravoes, whom the hope of license and plunder attracted from all the dens of Whitefriars[65] to the standard of Charles, and who disgraced their associates by excesses which, under the stricter discipline of the Parliamentary armies, were never tolerated. We will select a more favourable specimen. Thinking as we do that the cause of the King was the cause of bigotry and tyranny, we yet cannot refrain from looking with complacency on the character of the honest old Cavaliers. We feel a national pride in comparing them with the instruments which the despots of other countries are compelled to employ, with the mutes who throng their antechambers, and the Janissaries who mount guard at their gates.[66] Our royalist countrymen were not heartless, dangling courtiers, bowing at every step, and simpering at every word. They were not mere machines for destruction dressed up in uniforms, caned into skill, intoxicated into valour, defending without love, destroying without hatred. There was a freedom in their subserviency, a nobleness in their very degradation. The sentiment of individual independence was strong within them. They were indeed misled, but by no base or selfish motive. Compassion and romantic honour, the prejudices of childhood, and the venerable names of history, threw over them a spell potent as that of Duessa; and, like the Red-Cross Knight, they thought that they were doing battle for an injured beauty, while they defended a false and loathsome sorceress.[67] In truth they scarcely entered at all into the merits of the political

---

[62] *Faerie Queene*, v, i, 14.

[63] St. Dunstan (924–88), Archbishop of Canterbury; De Montfort (c. 1150–1218), crusader against the Albigensians; St. Dominic (1170–1221), founder of the Dominican order; Excobar, Spanish Jesuit and casuist of the seventeenth century.

[64] Another name for the Girondists or the moderate party in the French Revolution.

[65] A section of London where debtors were exempt from arrest, hence a place of lawless persons.

[66] Guards to the Turkish sultans.   [67] *Faerie Queene*, I, ii.

question. It was not for a treacherous king or an intolerant church that they fought, but for the old banner which had waved in so many battles over the heads of their fathers, and for the altars at which they had received the hands of their brides. Though nothing could be more erroneous than their political opinions, they possessed, in a far greater degree than their adversaries, those qualities which are the grace of private life. With many of the vices of the Round Table, they had also many of its virtues, courtesy, generosity, veracity, tenderness and respect for women. They had far more both of profound and of polite learning than the Puritans. Their manners were more engaging, their tempers more amiable, their tastes more elegant, and their households more cheerful.

Milton did not strictly belong to any of the classes which we have described. He was not a Puritan. He was not a freethinker. He was not a Royalist. In his character the noblest qualities of every party were combined in harmonious union. From the Parliament and from the Court, from the conventicle and from the Gothic cloister, from the gloomy and sepulchral circles of the Roundheads, and from the Christmas revel of the hospitable Cavalier, his nature selected and drew to itself whatever was great and good, while it rejected all the base and pernicious ingredients by which those finer elements were defiled. Like the Puritans, he lived

> "As ever in his great task-master's eye." [68]

Like them, he kept his mind continually fixed on an Almighty Judge and an eternal reward. And hence he acquired their contempt of external circumstances, their fortitude, their tranquillity, their inflexible resolution. But not the coolest sceptic or the most profane scoffer was more perfectly free from the contagion of their frantic delusions, their savage manners, their ludicrous jargon, their scorn of science, and their aversion to pleasure. Hating tyranny with a perfect hatred, he had nevertheless all the estimable and ornamental qualities which were almost entirely monopolised by the party of the tyrant. There was none who had a stronger sense of the value of literature, a finer relish for every elegant amusement, or a more chivalrous delicacy of honour and love. Though his opinions were democratic, his tastes and his associations were such as harmonise best with monarchy and aristocracy. He was under the influence of all the

feelings by which the gallant Cavaliers were misled. But of those feelings he was the master and not the slave. Like the hero of Homer, he enjoyed all the pleasures of fascination; but he was not fascinated. He listened to the song of the Syrens; yet he glided by without being seduced to their fatal shore. He tasted the cup of Circe; but he bore about him a sure antidote against the effects of its bewitching sweetness. The illusions which captivated his imagination never impaired his reasoning powers. The statesman was proof against the splendour, the solemnity, and the romance which enchanted the poet. Any person who will contrast the sentiments expressed in his treatises on Prelacy with the exquisite lines on ecclesiastical architecture and music in the Penseroso, which was published about the same time, will understand our meaning. This is an inconsistency which, more than any thing else, raises his character in our estimation, because it shows how many private tastes and feelings he sacrificed, in order to do what he considered his duty to mankind. It is the very struggle of the noble Othello. His heart relents; but his hand is firm. He does nought in hate, but all in honour. He kisses the beautiful deceiver before he destroys her.

That from which the public character of Milton derives its great and peculiar splendour still remains to be mentioned. If he exerted himself to overthrow a forsworn king and a persecuting hierarchy, he exerted himself in conjunction with others. But the glory of the battle which he fought for the species of freedom which is the most valuable, and which was then the least understood, the freedom of the human mind, is all his own. Thousands and tens of thousands among his contemporaries raised their voices against Ship-money and the Star-chamber. But there were few indeed who discerned the more fearful evils of moral and intellectual slavery, and the benefits which would result from the liberty of the press and the unfettered exercise of private judgment. These were the objects which Milton justly conceived to be the most important. He was desirous that the people should think for themselves as well as tax themselves, and should be emancipated from the dominion of prejudice as well as from that of Charles. He knew that those who, with the best intentions, overlooked these schemes of reform, and contented themselves with pulling down the King and imprisoning the malignants, acted like the heedless brothers in

---

[68] Milton's sonnet, "On his having arrived at the age of twenty-three."

his own poem, who, in their eagerness to disperse the train of the sorcerer, neglected the means of liberating the captive. They thought only of conquering when they should have thought of disenchanting.

"Oh, ye mistook! Ye should have snatched his wand
And bound him fast. Without the rod reversed,
And backward mutters of dissevering power,
We cannot free the lady that sits here
Bound in strong fetters fixed and motionless."[69]

To reverse the rod, to spell the charm backward, to break the ties which bound a stupefied people to the seat of enchantment, was the noble aim of Milton. To this all his public conduct was directed. For this he joined the Presbyterians: for this he forsook them. He fought their perilous battle; but he turned away with disdain from their insolent triumph. He saw that they like those whom they had vanquished, were hostile to the liberty of thought. He therefore joined the Independents, and called upon Cromwell to break the secular chain, and to save free conscience from the paw of the Presbyterian wolf. With a view to the same great object, he attacked the licensing system, in that sublime treatise[70] which every statesman should wear as a sign upon his hand and as frontlets between his eyes. His attacks were, in general, directed less against particular abuses than against those deeply-seated errors on which almost all abuses are founded, the servile worship of eminent men and the irrational dread of innovation.

That he might shake the foundations of these debasing sentiments more effectually, he always selected for himself the boldest literary services. He never came up in the rear, when the outworks had been carried and the breach entered. He pressed into the forlorn hope. At the beginning of the changes, he wrote with incomparable energy and eloquence against the bishops. But, when his opinion seemed likely to prevail, he passed on to other subjects, and abandoned prelacy to the crowd of writers who now hastened to insult a falling party. There is no more hazardous enterprise than that of bearing the torch of truth into those dark and infected recesses in which no light has ever shone. But it was the choice and the pleasure of Milton to

penetrate the noisome vapours, and to brave the terrible explosion. Those who most disapprove of his opinions must respect the hardihood with which he maintained them. He, in general, left to others the credit of expounding and defending the popular parts of his religious and political creed. He took his own stand upon those which the great body of his countrymen reprobated as criminal, or derided as paradoxical. He stood up for divorce and regicide. He attacked the prevailing systems of education. His radiant and beneficent career resembled that of the god of light and fertility.

"Nitor in adversum; nec me, qui cætera, vincit
Impetus, et rapido contrarius evehor orbi."[71]

It is to be regretted that the prose writings of Milton should, in our time, be so little read. As compositions, they deserve the attention of every man who wishes to become acquainted with the full power of the English language. They abound with passages compared with which the finest declamations of Burke sink into insignificance. They are a perfect field of cloth of gold. The style is stiff with gorgeous embroidery. Not even in the earlier books of the *Paradise Lost* has the great poet ever risen higher than in those parts of his controversial works in which his feelings, excited by conflict, find a vent in bursts of devotional and lyric rapture. It is, to borrow his own majestic language, "a sevenfold chorus of hallelujahs and harping symphonies."[72]

We had intended to look more closely at these performances, to analyse the peculiarities of the diction, to dwell at some length on the sublime wisdom of the Areopagitica and the nervous rhetoric of the Iconoclast, and to point out some of those magnificent passages which occur in the Treatise of Reformation, and the Animadversions on the Remonstrant. But the length to which our remarks have already extended renders this impossible.

We must conclude. And yet we can scarcely tear ourselves away from the subject. The days immediately following the publication of this relic[73] of Milton appear to be peculiarly set apart, and consecrated to his memory. And we shall scarcely be censured if, on this his festival, we be found lingering near his shrine, how

---

[69] *Comus*, 11, 815–19.
[70] Milton's defense of freedom of the press in *Areopagitica* (1644).
[71] "I strive against opposition, nor does that force that overcame others conquer me, and I hasten in opposition to the swiftly turning sphere" (Ovid, *Metamorphoses*, ii, 72).
[72] From Milton's *Reason of Church Government*.
[73] I.e., the treatise *On Christian Doctrine* that occasioned this review.

worthless soever may be the offering which we bring to it. While this book lies on our table, we seem to be contemporaries of the writer. We are transported a hundred and fifty years back. We can almost fancy that we are visiting him in his small lodging; that we see him sitting at the old organ beneath the faded green hangings; that we can catch the quick twinkle of his eyes, rolling in vain to find the day; that we are reading in the lines of his noble countenance the proud and mournful history of his glory and his affliction. We image to ourselves the breathless silence in which we should listen to his slightest word, the passionate veneration with which we should kneel to kiss his hand and weep upon it, the earnestness with which we should endeavour to console him, if indeed such a spirit could need consolation, for the neglect of an age unworthy of his talents and his virtues, the eagerness with which we should contest with his daughters, or with his Quaker friend Elwood, the privilege of reading Homer to him, or of taking down the immortal accents which flowed from his lips.[74]

These are perhaps foolish feelings. Yet we cannot be ashamed of them; nor shall we be sorry if what we have written shall in any degree excite them in other minds. We are not much in the habit of idolizing either the living or the dead. And we think that there is no more certain indication of a weak and ill-regulated intellect than that propensity which, for want of a better name, we will venture to christen Boswellism. But there are a few characters which have stood the closest scrutiny and the severest tests, which have been tried in the furnace and have proved pure, which have been weighed in the balance and have not been found wanting, which have been declared sterling by the general consent of mankind, and which are visibly stamped with the image and superscription of the Most High. These great men we trust that we know how to prize; and of these was Milton. The sight of his books, the sound of his name, are pleasant to us. His thoughts resemble those celestial fruits and flowers which the Virgin Martyr of Massinger[75] sent down from the gardens of Paradise to the earth, and which were distinguished from the productions of other soils, not only by superior bloom and sweetness, but by miraculous efficacy to invigorate and to heal. They are powerful, not only to delight, but to elevate and purify. Nor do we envy the man who can study either the life or the writings of the great poet and patriot, without aspiring to emulate, not indeed the sublime works with which his genius has enriched our literature, but the zeal with which he laboured for the public good, the fortitude with which he endured every private calamity, the lofty disdain with which he looked down on temptations and dangers, the deadly hatred which he bore to bigots and tyrants, and the faith which he so sternly kept with his country and with his fame.

from History of England

Macaulay's History of England *began appearing in 1850 and was an instant success. In five volumes (the last published posthumously) Macaulay traced English history from 1685 to about the year 1700. He intended to carry the history up to his own time, but his death in 1859 prevented his carrying out the plan, which would in any case have resulted in an enormous work. The work Macaulay did nevertheless established him in the front rank of popular Victorian historians. Macaulay sees English history as the gradual but triumphant march of material progress. The view suited many Victorian readers, but many also many responded to the more pessimistic views of such historians as Carlyle.*

The selections that follow are taken, first from Chapter III, "State of England in 1685," and next from Chapter IV, "Charles the Second". In the "State of England" Macaulay sets forth his convictions about the study of history. In "Charles the Second" he provides one of the colorful and detailed portraits for which he was famous, here mingled with scarcely veiled contempt for the dying Stuart monarch. (Notes to these selections are Macaulay's own.)

[74] Thomas Ellwood (1693–1713), who read to Milton daily.
[75] *The Virgin Martyr* (1622) by Philip Massinger and Thomas Dekker.

FROM CHAPTER III

"State of England in 1685"

I INTEND, in this chapter, to give a description of the state in which England was at the time when the crown passed from Charles the Second to his brother. Such a description, composed from scanty and dispersed materials, must necessarily be very imperfect. Yet it may perhaps correct some false notions which would make the subsequent narrative unintelligible or uninstructive.

If we would study with profit the history of our ancestors, we must be constantly on our guard against that delusion which the well known names of families, places, and offices naturally produce, and must never forget that the country of which we read was a very different country from that in which we live. In every experimental science there is a tendency towards perfection. In every human being there is a wish to ameliorate his own condition. These two principles have often sufficed, even when counteracted by great public calamities and by bad institutions, to carry civilisation rapidly forward. No ordinary misfortune, no ordinary misgovernment, will do so much to make a nation wretched, as the constant progress of physical knowledge and the constant effort of every man to better himself will do to make a nation prosperous. It has often been found that profuse expenditure, heavy taxation, absurd commercial restrictions, corrupt tribunals, disastrous wars, seditions, persecutions, conflagrations, inundations, have not been able to destroy capital so fast as the exertions of private citizens have been able to create it. It can easily be proved that, in our own land, the national wealth has, during at least six centuries, been almost uninterruptedly increasing; that it was greater under the Tudors than under the Plantagenets; that it was greater under the Stuarts than under the Tudors; that, in spite of battles, sieges, and confiscations, it was greater on the day of the Restoration than on the day when the Long Parliament met; that, in spite of maladministration, of extravagance, of public bankruptcy, of two costly and unsuccessful wars, of the pestilence and of the fire, it was greater on the day of the death of Charles the Second than on the day of his Restoration. This progress, having continued during many ages, became at length, about the middle of the eighteenth century, portentously

rapid, and has proceeded, during the nineteenth, with accelerated velocity. In consequence partly of our geographical and partly of our moral position, we have, during several generations, been exempt from evils which have elsewhere impeded the efforts and destroyed the fruits of industry. While every part of the Continent, from Moscow to Lisbon, has been the theatre of bloody and devastating wars, no hostile standard has been seen here but as a trophy. While revolutions have taken place all around us, our government has never once been subverted by violence. During more than a hundred years there has been in our island no tumult of sufficient importance to be called an insurrection; nor has the law been once borne down either by popular fury or by regal tyranny: public credit has been held sacred: the administration of justice has been pure: even in times which might by Englishmen be justly called evil times, we have enjoyed what almost every other nation in the world would have considered as an ample measure of civil and religious freedom. Every man has felt entire confidence that the state would protect him in the possession of what had been earned by his diligence and hoarded by his selfdenial. Under the benignant influence of peace and liberty, science has flourished, and has been applied to practical purposes on a scale never before known. The consequence is that a change to which the history of the old world furnishes no parallel has taken place in our country. Could the England of 1685 be, by some magical process, set before our eyes, we should not know one landscape in a hundred or one building in ten thousand. The country gentleman would not recognize his own fields. The inhabitant of the town would not recognise his own street. Everything has been changed, but the great features of nature, and a few massive and durable works of human art. We might find out Snowdon and Windermere, the Cheddar Cliffs and Beachy Head. We might find out here and there a Norman minster, or a castle which witnessed the wars of the Roses. But, with such rare exceptions, everything would be strange to us. Many thousands of square miles which are now rich corn land and meadow, intersected by green hedgerows, and dotted with villages and pleasant country seats, would appear as moors overgrown with furze, or fens abandoned to wild ducks. We should see straggling huts built of wood and covered with thatch, where we now see manufacturing towns and seaports renowned to the farthest ends of the world. The capital itself would shrink to dimensions not much exceeding those of its present suburb on the south of the Thames. Not less strange to us would be the garb and manners of the people, the furniture and the equipages, the interior of the shops and dwellings. Such a change in the state of a nation seems to be at least as well entitled to the notice of a historian as any change of the dynasty or of the ministry.[1]

One of the first objects of an inquirer, who wishes to form a correct notion of the state of a community at a given time, must be to ascertain of how many persons that community then consisted. Unfortunately the population of England in 1685 cannot be ascertained with perfect accuracy. For no great state had then adopted the wise course of periodically numbering the people. All men were left to conjecture for themselves; and, as they generally conjectured without examining facts, and under the influence of strong passions and prejudices, their guesses were often ludicrously absurd. Even intelligent Londoners ordinarily talked of London as containing several millions of souls. It was confidently asserted by many that, during the thirty-five years which had elapsed between the accession of Charles the First and the Restoration, the population of the City had increased by two millions.[2] Even while the ravages of the plague and fire were recent, it was the fashion to say that the capital still had a million and a half of inhabitants.[3] Some persons, disgusted by these exaggerations, ran violently into the opposite extreme. Thus Isaac Vossius, a man of undoubted parts and learning, strenuously maintained that there were only two millions of human beings in England, Scotland, and Ireland taken together.[4]

We are not, however, left without the means of correcting the wild blunders into which some minds were hurried by national vanity and others by a morbid love of paradox. There are extant three computations which seem to be entitled to peculiar attention. They are entirely independent of each other: they proceed on different principles; and yet there is little difference in the results.

One of these computations was made in the year 1696 by Gregory King, Lancaster herald, a political arithmetician of great acuteness and judgment. The basis of his calculations was the number of houses returned in 1690 by the officers who made the last collection of the hearth money. The conclusion at which he arrived was that the population of England was nearly five millions and a half.[5]

About the same time King William the Third was desirous to ascertain the comparative strength of the religious sects into which the community was divided. An inquiry was instituted; and reports were laid before him from all the dioceses of the realm. According to these reports the number of his English subjects must have been about five million two hundred thousand.[6]

Lastly, in our own days, Mr. Finlaison, an actuary of eminent skill, subjected the ancient parochial registers of baptisms, marriages, and burials, to all the tests which the modern improvements in statistical science enabled him to apply. His opinion was, that, at the close of the seventeenth century, the population of England was a little under five million two hundred thousand souls.[7]

---

[1] During the interval which has elapsed since this chapter was written, England has continued to advance rapidly in material prosperity. I have left my text nearly as it originally stood; but I have added a few notes which may enable the reader to form some notion of the progress which has been made during the last nine years; and, in general, I would desire him to remember that there is scarcely a district which is not more populous, or a source of wealth which is not more productive, at present than in 1848. (1857.)

[2] Observations on the Bills of Mortality, by Captain John Graunt (Sir William Petty), chap. xi.

[3] "She doth comprehend
Full fifteen hundred thousand which do spend
Their days within."

Great Britain's Beauty, 1671.

[4] Isaac Vossius, De Magnitudine Urbium Sinarum, 1685. Vossius, as we learn from Saint Evremond, talked on this subject oftener and longer than fashionable circles cared to listen.

[5] King's Natural and Political Observations, 1696. This valuable treatise, which ought to be read as the author wrote it, and not as garbled by Davenant, will be found in some editions of Chalmers's Estimate.

[6] Dalrymple's Appendix to Part II, Book I. The practice of reckoning the population by sects was long fashionable. Gulliver says of the King of Brobdignag; "He laughed at my odd arithmetic, as he was pleased to call it, in reckoning the numbers of our people by a computation drawn from the several sects among us in religion and politics."

[7] Preface to the Population Returns of 1831.

Of these three estimates, framed without concert by different persons from different sets of materials, the highest, which is that of King, does not exceed the lowest, which is that of Finlaison, by one twelfth. We may, therefore, with confidence pronounce that, when James the Second reigned, England contained between five million and five million five hundred thousand inhabitants. On the very highest supposition she then had less than one third of her present population, and less than three times the population which is now collected in her gigantic capital.

The increase of the people has been great in every part of the kingdom, but generally much greater in the northern than in the southern shires. In truth a large part of the country beyond Trent was, down to the eighteenth century, in a state of barbarism. Physical and moral causes had concurred to prevent civilisation from spreading to that region. The air was inclement; the soil was generally such as required skilful and industrious cultivation; and there could be little skill or industry in a tract which was often the theatre of war, and which, even when there was nominal peace, was constantly desolated by bands of Scottish marauders. Before the union of the two British crowns, and long after that union, there was as great a difference between Middlesex and Northumberland as there now is between Massachusetts and the settlements of those squatters who, far to the west of the Mississippi, administer a rude justice with the rifle and the dagger. In the reign of Charles the Second, the traces left by ages of slaughter and pillage were distinctly perceptible, many miles south of the Tweed, in the face of the country and in the lawless manners of the people. There was still a large class of mosstroopers, whose calling was to plunder dwellings and to drive away whole herds of cattle. It was found necessary, soon after the Restoration, to enact laws of great severity for the prevention of these outrages. The magistrates of Northumberland and Cumberland were authorised to raise bands of armed men for the defence of property and order; and provision was made for meeting the expense of these levies by local taxation.[8] The parishes were required to keep bloodhounds for the purpose of hunting the freebooters. Many old men who were living in the middle of the eighteenth century could well remember the time when those ferocious dogs were common.[9] Yet, even with such auxiliaries, it was often found impossible to track the robbers to their retreats among the hills and morasses. For the geography of that wild country was very imperfectly known. Even after the accession of George the Third, the path over the fells from Borrowdale to Ravenglas was still a secret carefully kept by the dalesmen, some of whom had probably in their youth escaped from the pursuit of justice by that road.[10] The seats of the gentry and the larger farmhouses were fortified. Oxen were penned at night beneath the overhanging battlements of the residence, which was known by the name of the Peel. The inmates slept with arms at their sides. Huge stones and boiling water were in readiness to crush and scald the plunderer who might venture to assail the little garrison. No traveller ventured into that country without making his will. The Judges on circuit, with the whole body of barristers, attorneys, clerks, and serving men, rode on horseback from Newcastle to Carlisle, armed and escorted by a strong guard under the command of the Sheriffs. It was necessary to carry provisions; for the country was a wilderness which afforded no supplies. The spot where the cavalcade halted to dine, under an immense oak, is not yet forgotten. The irregular vigour with which criminal justice was administered shocked observers whose lives had been passed in more tranquil districts. Juries, animated by hatred and by a sense of common danger, convicted housebreakers and cattle stealers with the promptitude of a court martial in a mutiny; and the convicts were hurried by scores to the gallows.[11] Within the memory of some whom this generation has seen, the sportsman who wandered in pursuit of game to the sources of the Tyne found the heaths round Keeldar Castle peopled by a race scarcely less savage than the Indians of California, and heard with surprise the half naked women chaunting a wild measure, while the men with brandished dirks danced a war dance.[12]

Slowly and with difficulty peace was established on the border. In the train of peace came industry and all the arts of life. Meanwhile it was discovered that the regions north of the Trent possessed in their coal beds a source of wealth far more precious than the gold mines of Peru. It was found that, in the neighbourhood of these

---

[8] Statutes 14 Car. II. c. 22.; 18 & 19 Car. II. c. 3.; 29 & 30 Car. II. c. 2.
[9] Nicholson and Bourne, Discourse on the Ancient State of the Border, 1777.
[10] Gray's Journal of a Tour in the Lakes, Oct. 3. 1769.
[11] North's Life of Guildford; Hutchinson's History of Cumberland, Parish of Brampton.
[12] See Sir Walter Scott's Journal, Oct. 7. 1827, in his Life by Mr. Lockhart.

beds, almost every manufacture might be most profitably carried on. A constant stream of emigrants began to roll northward. It appeared by the returns of 1841 that the ancient archiepiscopal province of York contained twosevenths of the population of England. At the time of the Revolution that province was believed to contain only one seventh of the population.[13] In Lancashire the number of inhabitants appears to have increased ninefold, while in Norfolk, Suffolk, and Northamptonshire it has hardly doubled.[14]

Of the taxation we can speak with more confidence and precision than of the population. The revenue of England, when Charles the Second died, was small, when compared with the resources which she even then possessed, or with the sums which were raised by the governments of the neighbouring countries. It had, from the time of the Restoration, been almost constantly increasing: yet it was little more than three fourths of the revenue of the United Provinces, and was hardly one fifth of the revenue of France.

.   .   .

It seems clear, therefore, that the wages of labour, estimated in money, were, in 1685, not more than half of what they now are; and there were few articles important to the working man of which the price was not, in 1685, more than half of what it now is. Beer was undoubtedly much cheaper in that age than at present. Meat was also cheaper, but was still so dear that hundreds of thousands of families scarcely knew the taste of it.[15] In the cost of wheat there has been very little change. The average price of the quarter, during the last twelve years of Charles the Second, was fifty shillings. Bread, therefore, such as is now given to the inmates of a workhouse, was then seldom seen, even on the trencher of a yeoman or of a shopkeeper. The great majority of the nation lived almost entirely on rye, barley, and oats.

The produce of tropical countries, the produce of the mines, the produce of machinery, was positively dearer than at present. Among the commodities for which the labourer would have

had to pay higher in 1685 than his posterity now pay were sugar, salt, coals, candles, soap, shoes, stockings, and generally all articles of clothing and all articles of bedding. It may be added, that the old coats and blankets would have been, not only more costly, but less serviceable than the modern fabrics.

It must be remembered that those labourers who were able to maintain themselves and their families by means of wages were not the most necessitous members of the community. Beneath them lay a large class which could not subsist without some aid from the parish. There can hardly be a more important test of the condition of the common people than the ratio which this class bears to the whole society. At present the men, women, and children who receive relief appear from the official returns to be, in bad years, one tenth of the inhabitants of England, and, in good years, one thirteenth. Gregory King estimated them in his time at about a fourth; and this estimate, which all our respect for his authority will scarcely prevent us from calling extravagant, was pronounced by Davenant eminently judicious.

We are not quite without the means of forming an estimate for ourselves. The poor rate was undoubtedly the heaviest tax borne by our ancestors in those days. It was computed, in the reign of Charles the Second, at near seven hundred thousand pounds a year, much more than the produce either of the excise or of the customs, and little less than half the entire revenue of the crown. The poor rate went on increasing rapidly, and appears to have risen in a short time to between eight and nine hundred thousand a year, that is to say, to one sixth of what it now is. The population was then less than a third of what it now is. The minimum of wages, estimated in money, was half of what it now is; and we can therefore hardly suppose that the average allowance made to a pauper can have been more than half of what it now is. It seems to follow that the proportion of the English people which received parochial relief then must have been larger than the proportion which receives relief now. It is good to speak on such questions with diffidence: but it has certainly

---

[13] Dalrymple, Appendix to Part II. Book I. The returns of the hearth money lead to nearly the same conclusion. The hearths in the province of York were not a sixth of the hearths of England.

[14] I do not, of course, pretend to strict accuracy here; but I believe that whoever will take the trouble to compare the last returns of hearth money in the reign of William the Third with the census of 1841, will come to a conclusion not very different from mine.

[15] King in his Natural and Political Conclusions roughly estimated the common people of England at 880,000 families. Of these families 440,000, according to him, ate animal food twice a week. The remaining 440,000 ate it not at all, or at most not oftener than once a week.

never yet been proved that pauperism was a less heavy burden or a less serious social evil during the last quarter of the seventeenth century than it is in our own time.[16]

In one respect it must be admitted that the progress of civilisation has diminished the physical comforts of a portion of the poorest class. It has already been mentioned that, before the Revolution, many thousands of square miles, now enclosed and cultivated, were marsh, forest, and heath. Of this wild land much was, by law, common, and much of what was not common by law was worth so little that the proprietors suffered it to be common in fact. In such a tract, squatters and trespassers were tolerated to an extent now unknown. The peasant who dwelt there could, at little or no charge, procure occasionally some palatable addition to his hard fare, and provide himself with fuel for the winter. He kept a flock of geese on what is now an orchard rich with apple blossoms. He snared wild fowl on the fen which has long since been drained and divided into corn fields and turnip fields. He cut turf among the furze bushes on the moor which is now a meadow bright with clover and renowned for butter and cheese. The progress of agriculture and the increase of population necessarily deprived him of these privileges. But against this disadvantage a long list of advantages is to be set off. Of the blessings which civilisation and philosophy bring with them a large proportion is common to all ranks, and would, if withdrawn, be missed as painfully by the labourer as by the peer. The market-place which the rustic can now reach with his cart in an hour was, a hundred and sixty years ago, a day's journey from him. The street which now affords to the artisan, during the whole night, a secure, a convenient, and a brilliantly lighted walk was, a hundred and sixty years ago, so dark after sunset that he would not have been able to see his hand, so ill paved that he would have run constant risk of breaking his neck, and so ill watched that he would have been in imminent danger of being knocked down

and plundered of his small earnings. Every bricklayer who falls from a scaffold, every sweeper of a crossing who is run over by a carriage, may now have his wounds dressed and his limbs set with a skill such as, a hundred and sixty years ago, all the wealth of a great lord like Ormond, or of a merchant prince like Clayton, could not have purchased. Some frightful diseases have been extirpated by science; and some have been banished by police. The term of human life has been lengthened over the whole kingdom, and especially in the towns. The year 1685 was not accounted sickly; yet in the year 1685 more than one in twenty-three of the inhabitants of the capital died.[17] At present only one inhabitant of the capital in forty dies annually. The difference in salubrity between the London of the nineteenth century and the London of the seventeenth century is very far greater than the difference between London in an ordinary year and London in a year of cholera.

Still more important is the benefit which all orders of society, and especially the lower orders, have derived from the mollifying influence of civilisation on the national character. The groundwork of that character has indeed been the same through many generations, in the sense in which the groundwork of the character of an individual may be said to be the same when he is a rude and thoughtless schoolboy and when he is a refined and accomplished man. It is pleasing to reflect that the public mind of England has softened while it has ripened, and that we have, in the course of ages, become, not only a wiser, but also a kinder people. There is scarcely a page of the history or lighter literature of the seventeenth century which does not contain some proof that our ancestors were less humane than their posterity. The discipline of workshops, of schools, of private families, though not more efficient than at present, was infinitely harsher. Masters, well born and bred, were in the habit of beating their servants. Pedagogues knew no way of imparting knowledge but by beating their pupils. Husbands,

[16] Fourteenth Report of the Poor Law Commissioners, Appendix B. No. 2. Appendix C. No. 1. 1848. Of the two estimates of the poor rate mentioned in the text one was formed by Arthur Moore, the other, some years later, by Richard Dunning. Moore's estimate will be found in Davenant's Essay on Ways and Means; Dunning's in Sir Frederic Eden's valuable work on the poor. King and Davenant estimate the paupers and beggars in 1696, at the incredible number of 1,330,000 out of a population of 5,500,000. In 1846 the number of persons who received relief appears from the official returns to have been only 1,332,089 out of a population of about 17,000,000. It ought also to be observed that, in those returns, a pauper must very often be reckoned more than once.

I would advise the reader to consult De Foe's pamphlet entitled "Giving Alms no Charity," and the Greenwich tables which will be found in Mr. M'Culloch's Commercial Dictionary under the head Prices.

[17] The deaths were 23,222. Petty's Political Arithmetic.

of decent station, were not ashamed to beat their wives. The implacability of hostile factions was such as we can scarcely conceive. Whigs were disposed to murmur because Stafford was suffered to die without seeing his bowels burned before his face. Tories reviled and insulted Russell as his coach passed from the Tower to the scaffold in Lincoln's Inn Fields.[18] As little mercy was shown by the populace to sufferers of a humbler rank. If an offender was put into the pillory, it was well if he escaped with life from the shower of brick-bats and paving stones.[19] If he was tied to the cart's tail, the crowd pressed round him, imploring the hangman to give it the fellow well, and make him howl.[20] Gentlemen arranged parties of pleasure to Bridewell on court days for the purpose of seeing the wretched women who beat hemp there whipped.[21] A man pressed to death for refusing to plead, a woman burned for coining, excited less sympathy than is now felt for a galled horse or an overdriven ox. Fights compared with which a boxing match is a refined and humane spectacle were among the favourite diversions of a large part of the town. Multitudes assembled to see gladiators hack each other to pieces with deadly weapons, and shouted with delight when one of the combatants lost a finger or an eye. The prisons were hells on earth, seminaries of every crime and of every disease. At the assizes the lean and yellow culprits brought with them from their cells to the dock an atmosphere of stench and pestilence which sometimes avenged them signally on bench, bar, and jury. But on all this misery society looked with profound indifference. Nowhere could be found that sensitive and restless compassion which has, in our time, extended a powerful protection to the factory child, to the Hindoo widow, to the negro slave, which pries into the stores and watercasks of every emigrant ship, which winces at every lash laid on the back of a drunken soldier, which will not suffer the thief in the hulks to be ill fed or overworked, and which has repeatedly endeavoured to save the life even of the murderer. It is true that compassion ought, like all other feelings, to be under the government of reason, and has, for want of such government, produced some ridiculous and some deplorable effects. But the more we study the annals of the past, the more shall we rejoice that we live in a merciful age, in an age in which cruelty is abhorred, and in which pain, even when

deserved, is inflicted reluctantly and from a sense of duty. Every class doubtless has gained largely by this great moral change: but the class which has gained most is the poorest, the most dependent, and the most defenceless.

The general effect of the evidence which has been submitted to the reader seems hardly to admit of doubt. Yet, in spite of evidence, many will still image to themselves the England of the Stuarts as a more pleasant country than the England in which we live. It may at first sight seem strange that society, while constantly moving forward with eager speed, should be constantly looking backward with tender regret. But these two propensities, inconsistent as they may appear, can easily be resolved into the same principle. Both spring from our impatience of the state in which we actually are. That impatience, while it stimulates us to surpass preceding generations, disposes us to overrate their happiness. It is, in some sense, unreasonable and ungrateful in us to be constantly discontented with a condition which is constantly improving. But, in truth, there is constant improvement precisely because there is constant discontent. If we were perfectly satisfied with the present, we should cease to contrive, to labour, and to save with a view to the future. And it is natural that, being dissatisfied with the present, we should form a too favourable estimate of the past.

In truth we are under a deception similar to that which misleads the traveller in the Arabian desert. Beneath the caravan all is dry and bare but far in advance, and far in the rear, is the semblance of refreshing waters. The pilgrims hasten forward and find nothing but sand where an hour before they had seen a lake. They turn their eyes and see a lake where, an hour before, they were toiling through sand. A similar illusion seems to haunt nations through every stage of the long progress from poverty and barbarism to the highest degrees of opulence and civilisation. But, if we resolutely chase the mirage backward, we shall find it recede before us into the regions of fabulous antiquity. It is now the fashion to place the golden age of England in times when noblemen were destitute of comforts the want of which would be intolerable to a modern footman, when farmers and shopkeepers breakfasted on loaves the very sight of which would raise a riot in a modern workhouse, when to have a clean shirt

---

[18] Burnet, i. 560.   [19] Muggleton's Acts of the Witness of the Spirit.
[20] Tom Brown describes such a scene in lines which I do not venture to quote.
[21] Ward's London Spy.

once a week was a privilege reserved for the higher class of gentry, when men died faster in the purest country air than they now die in the most pestilential lanes of our towns, and when men died faster in the lanes of our towns than they now die on the coast of Guiana. We too shall, in our turn, be outstripped, and in our turn be envied. It may well be, in the twentieth century, that the peasant of Dorsetshire may think himself miserably paid with twenty shillings a week; that the carpenter at Greenwich may receive ten shillings a day; that labouring men may be as little used to dine without meat as they now are to eat rye bread; that sanitary police and medical discoveries may have added several more years to the average length of human life; that numerous comforts and luxuries which are now unknown, or confined to a few, may be within the reach of every diligent and thrifty working man. And yet it may then be the mode to assert that the increase of wealth and the progress of science have benefited the few at the expense of the many, and to talk of the reign of Queen Victoria as the time when England was truly merry England, when all classes were bound together by brotherly sympathy, when the rich did not grind the faces of the poor, and when the poor did not envy the splendour of the rich.

FROM CHAPTER IV

"Charles the Second"

THE DEATH of King Charles the Second took the nation by surprise. His frame was naturally strong, and did not appear to have suffered from excess. He had always been mindful of his health even in his pleasures; and his habits were such as promise a long life and a robust old age. Indolent as he was on all occasions which required tension of the mind, he was active and persevering in bodily exercise. He had, when young, been renowned as a tennis player,[1] and was, even in the decline of life, an indefatigable walker. His ordinary pace was such that those who were admitted to the honour of his society found it difficult to keep up with him. He rose early, and generally passed three or four hours a day in the open air. He might be seen, before the dew was off the grass in St. James's Park, striding among the trees, playing with his spaniels, and flinging corn to his ducks; and these exhibitions endeared him to the common people, who always love to see the great unbend.[2]

At length, towards the close of the year 1684, he was prevented, by a slight attack of what was supposed to be gout, from rambling as usual. He now spent his mornings in his laboratory, where he amused himself with experiments on the properties of mercury. His temper seemed to have suffered from confinement. He had no apparent cause for disquiet. His kingdom was tranquil: he was not in pressing want of money: his power was greater than it had ever been: the party which had long thwarted him had been beaten down; but the cheerfulness which had supported him against adverse fortune had vanished in this season of prosperity. A trifle now sufficed to depress those elastic spirits which had borne up against defeat, exile, and penury. His irritation frequently showed itself by looks and words such as could hardly have been expected from a man so eminently distinguished by good humour and good breeding. It was not supposed however that his constitution was seriously impaired.[3]

His palace had seldom presented a gayer or a more scandalous appearance than on the evening of Sunday the first of February 1685.[4] Some grave persons who had gone thither, after the fashion of that age, to pay their duty to their sovereign, and who had expected that, on such a day, his court would wear a decent aspect, were struck with astonishment and horror. The great gallery of Whitehall, an admirable relic of the magnificence of the Tudors, was crowded with revellers and gamblers. The king sate there chatting and toying with three women, whose charms were the boast, and whose vices were the disgrace, of three nations. Barbara Palmer, Duchess of Cleveland, was there, no longer young, but still retaining some traces of that superb and voluptuous loveliness which twenty years before overcame the

---

[1] Pepys's Diary, Dec. 28. 1663, Sept. 2. 1667.

[2] Burnet, i. 606.; Spectator, No. 462.; Lords' Journals, October 28. 1678.; Cibber's Apology.

[3] Burnet, i. 605, 606.; Welwood; North's Life of Guildford, 251.

[4] I may take this opportunity of mentioning that whenever I give only one date, I follow the old style, which was, in the seventeenth century, the style of England; but I reckon the year from the first of January.

hearts of all men. There too was the Duchess of Portsmouth, whose soft and infantine features were lighted up with the vivacity of France. Hortensia Mancini, Duchess of Mazarin, and niece of the great Cardinal, completed the group. She had been early removed from her native Italy to the court where her uncle was supreme. His power and her own attractions had drawn a crowd of illustrious suitors round her. Charles himself, during his exile, had sought her hand in vain. No gift of nature or of fortune seemed to be wanting to her. Her face was beautiful with the rich beauty of the South, her understanding quick, her manners graceful, her rank exalted, her possessions immense; but her ungovernable passions had turned all these blessings into curses. She had found the misery of an ill assorted marriage intolerable, had fled from her husband, had abandoned her vast wealth, and, after having astonished Rome and Piedmont by her adventures, had fixed her abode in England. Her house was the favourite resort of men of wit and pleasure, who, for the sake of her smiles and her table, endured her frequent fits of insolence and ill humour. Rochester and Godolphin sometimes forgot the cares of state in her company. Barillon and Saint Evremond found in her drawing room consolation for their long banishment from Paris. The learning of Vossius, the wit of Waller, were daily employed to flatter and amuse her. But her diseased mind required stronger stimulants, and sought them in gallantry, in basset, and in usquebaugh.[5] While Charles flirted with his three sultanas, Hortensia's French page, a handsome boy, whose vocal performances were the delight of Whitehall, and were rewarded by numerous presents of rich clothes, ponies, and guineas, warbled some amorous verses.[6] A party of twenty courtiers was seated at cards round a large table on which gold was heaped in mountains.[7] Even then the King had complained that he did not feel quite well. He had no appetite for his supper: his rest that night was broken; but on the following morning he rose, as usual, early.

To that morning the contending factions in his council had, during some days, looked forward with anxiety. The struggle between Halifax and Rochester seemed to be approaching a decisive crisis. Halifax, not content with having already driven his rival from the Board of Treasury, had undertaken to prove him guilty of such dishonesty or neglect in the conduct of the finances as ought to be punished by dismission from the public service. It was even whispered that the Lord President would probably be sent to the Tower. The King had promised to enquire into the matter. The second of February had been fixed for the investigation; and several officers of the revenue had been ordered to attend with their books on that day.[8] But a great turn of fortune was at hand.

Scarcely had Charles risen from his bed when his attendants perceived that his utterance was indistinct, and that his thoughts seemed to be wandering. Several men of rank had, as usual, assembled to see their sovereign shaved and dressed. He made an effort to converse with them in his usual gay style; but his ghastly look surprised and alarmed them. Soon his face grew black; his eyes turned in his head; he uttered a cry, staggered, and fell into the arms of one of his lords. A physician who had charge of the royal retorts and crucibles happened to be present. He had no lancet; but he opened a vein with a penknife. The blood flowed freely; but the King was still insensible.

He was laid on his bed, where, during a short time, the Duchess of Portsmouth hung over him with the familiarity of a wife. But the alarm had been given. The Queen and the Duchess of York were hastening to the room. The favourite concubine was forced to retire to her own apartments. Those apartments had been thrice pulled down and thrice rebuilt by her lover to gratify her caprice. The very furniture of the chimney was massy silver. Several fine paintings, which properly belonged to the Queen, had been transferred to the dwelling of the mistress. The sideboards were piled with richly wrought plate. In the niches stood cabinets, the masterpieces of Japanese art. On the hangings, fresh from the looms of Paris, were depicted, in tints which no English tapestry could rival, birds of gorgeous plumage, landscapes, hunting matches, the lordly terrace of Saint Germains, the statues and fountains of Versailles.[9] In the midst of this splendour,

---

[5] Saint Evremond, *passim;* Saint Réal, Mémoires de la Duchesse de Mazarin; Rochester's Farewell; Evelyn's Diary, Sept. 6. 1676, June 11. 1699.

[6] Evelyn's Diary, Jan. 28. 168$\frac{4}{5}$; Saint Evremond's Letter to Déry.

[7] Evelyn's Diary, February 4. 168$\frac{4}{5}$.

[8] Roger North's Life of Sir Dudley North, 170.; The true Patriot vindicated, or a Justification of his Excellency the E—— of R——; Burnet, i. 605. The Treasury Books prove that Burnet had good intelligence.

[9] Evelyn's Diary, Jan. 24. 168$\frac{1}{2}$, Oct. 4. 1683.

purchased by guilt and shame, the unhappy woman gave herself up to an agony of grief, which, to do her justice, was not wholly selfish.

And now the gates of Whitehall, which ordinarily stood open to all comers, were closed. But persons whose faces were known were still permitted to enter. The antechambers and galleries were soon filled to overflowing; and even the sick room was crowded with peers, privy councillors, and foreign ministers. All the medical men of note in London were summoned. So high did political animosities run that the presence of some Whig physicians was regarded as an extraordinary circumstance.[10] One Roman Catholic, whose skill was then widely renowned, Doctor Thomas Short, was in attendance. Several of the prescriptions have been preserved. One of them is signed by fourteen Doctors. The patient was bled largely. Hot iron was applied to his head. A loathsome volatile salt, extracted from human skulls, was forced into his mouth. He recovered his senses; but he was evidently in a situation of extreme danger.

The Queen was for a time assiduous in her attendance. The Duke of York scarcely left his brother's bedside. The Primate and four other bishops were then in London. They remained at Whitehall all day, and took it by turns to sit up at night in the King's room. The news of his illness filled the capital with sorrow and dismay. For his easy temper and affable manners had won the affection of a large part of the nation; and those who most disliked him preferred his unprincipled levity to the stern and earnest bigotry of his brother.

On the morning of Thursday the fifth of February, the London Gazette announced that His Majesty was going on well, and was thought by the physicians to be out of danger. The bells of all the churches rang merrily; and preparations for bonfires were made in the streets. But in the evening it was known that a relapse had taken place, and that the medical attendants had given up all hope. The public mind was greatly disturbed; but there was no disposition to tumult. The Duke of York, who had already taken on himself to give orders, ascertained that the City was perfectly quiet, and that he might without difficulty be proclaimed as soon as his brother should expire.

The King was in great pain, and complained that he felt as if a fire was burning within him. Yet he bore up against his sufferings with a fortitude which did not seem to belong to his soft and luxurious nature. The sight of his misery affected his wife so much that she fainted, and was carried senseless to her chamber. The prelates who were in waiting had from the first exhorted him to prepare for his end. They now thought it their duty to address him in a still more urgent manner. William Sancroft, Archbishop of Canterbury, an honest and pious, though narrowminded, man, used great freedom. "It is time," he said, "to speak out; for, Sir, you are about to appear before a Judge who is no respecter of persons." The King answered not a word.

Thomas Ken, Bishop of Bath and Wells, then tried his powers of persuasion. He was a man of parts and learning, of quick sensibility and stainless virtue. His elaborate works have long been forgotten; but his morning and evening hymns are still repeated daily in thousands of dwellings. Though, like most of his order, zealous for monarchy, he was no sycophant. Before he became a Bishop, he had maintained the honour of his gown by refusing, when the court was at Winchester, to let Eleanor Gwynn lodge in the house which he occupied there as a prebendary.[11] The King had sense enough to respect so manly a spirit. Of all the prelates he liked Ken the best. It was to no purpose, however, that the good Bishop now put forth all his eloquence. His solemn and pathetic exhortation awed and melted the bystanders to such a degree that some among them believed him to be filled with the same spirit which, in the old time, had, by the mouths of Nathan and Elias, called sinful princes to repentance. Charles however was unmoved. He made no objection indeed when the service for the visitation of the sick was read. In reply to the pressing questions of the divines, he said that he was sorry for what he had done amiss; and he suffered the absolution to be pronounced over him according to the forms of the Church of England: but, when he was urged to declare that he died in the communion of that Church, he seemed not to hear what was said; and nothing could induce him to take the Eucharist from the hands of the Bishops. A table with bread and wine was brought to his bedside, but in vain. Sometimes he said that there was no hurry, and sometimes that he was too weak.

Many attributed this apathy to contempt for divine things, and many to the stupor which often precedes death. But there were in the palace a few persons who knew better. Charles had never

---

[10] Dugdale's Correspondence. [11] Hawkin's Life of Ken, 1713.

been a sincere member of the Established Church. His mind had long oscillated between Hobbism and Popery. When his health was good and his spirits high he was a scoffer. In his few serious moments he was a Roman Catholic. The Duke of York was aware of this, but was entirely occupied with the care of his own interests. He had ordered the outports to be closed. He had posted detachments of the Guards in different parts of the City. He had also procured the feeble signature of the dying King to an instrument by which some duties, granted only till the demise of the Crown, were let to farm for a term of three years. These things occupied the attention of James to such a degree that, though, on ordinary occasions, he was indiscreetly and unseasonably eager to bring over proselytes to his Church, he never reflected that his brother was in danger of dying without the last sacraments. This neglect was the more extraordinary because the Duchess of York had, at the request of the Queen, suggested, on the morning on which the King was taken ill, the propriety of procuring spiritual assistance. For such assistance Charles was at last indebted to an agency very different from that of his pious wife and sister in law. A life of frivolity and vice had not extinguished in the Duchess of Portsmouth all sentiments of religion, or all that kindness which is the glory of her sex. The French ambassador Barillon, who had come to the palace to enquire after the King, paid her a visit. He found her in an agony of sorrow. She took him into a secret room, and poured out her whole heart to him. "I have," she said, "a thing of great moment to tell you. If it were known, my head would be in danger. The King is really and truly a Catholic; but he will die without being reconciled to the Church. His bedchamber is full of Protestant clergymen. I cannot enter it without giving scandal. The Duke is thinking only of himself. Speak to him. Remind him that there is a soul at stake. He is master now. He can clear the room. Go this instant, or it will be too late."

Barillon hastened to the bedchamber, took the Duke aside, and delivered the message of the mistress. The conscience of James smote him. He started as if roused from sleep, and declared that nothing should prevent him from discharging the sacred duty which had been too long delayed. Several schemes were discussed and rejected. At last the Duke commanded the crowd to stand aloof, went to the bed, stooped down, and whispered something which none of the spectators could hear, but which they supposed to be some question about affairs of state. Charles answered in an audible voice, "Yes, yes, with all my heart." None of the bystanders, except the French Ambassador, guessed that the King was declaring his wish to be admitted into the bosom of the Church of Rome.

"Shall I bring a priest?" said the Duke. "Do, brother," replied the sick man. "For God's sake do, and lose no time. But no; you will get into trouble." "If it costs me my life," said the Duke, "I will fetch a priest."

To find a priest, however, for such a purpose, at a moment's notice, was not easy. For, as the law then stood, the person who admitted a proselyte into the Roman Catholic Church was guilty of a capital crime. The Count of Castel Melhor, a Portuguese nobleman, who, driven by political troubles from his native land, had been hospitably received at the English court, undertook to procure a confessor. He had recourse to his countrymen who belonged to the Queen's household; but he found that none of her chaplains knew English or French enough to shrive the King. The Duke and Barillon were about to send to the Venetian Minister for a clergyman when they heard that a Benedictine monk, named John Huddleston, happened to be at Whitehall. This man had, with great risk to himself, saved the King's life after the battle of Worcester, and had, on that account, been, ever since the Restoration, a privileged person. In the sharpest proclamations which had been put forth against Popish priests, when false witnesses had inflamed the nation to fury, Huddleston had been excepted by name.[12] He readily consented to put his life a second time in peril for his prince; but there was still a difficulty. The honest monk was so illiterate that he did not know what he ought to say on an occasion of such importance. He however obtained some hints, through the intervention of Castel Melhor, from a Portuguese ecclesiastic, and, thus instructed, was brought up the back stairs by Chiffinch, a confidential servant, who, if the satires of that age are to be credited, had often introduced visitors of a very different description by the same entrance. The Duke then, in the King's name, commanded all who were present to quit the room, except Lewis Duras, Earl of Feversham, and John Granville, Earl of Bath.

---

[12] See the London Gazette of Nov. 21. 1678. Barillon and Burnet say that Huddleston was excepted out of all the Acts of Parliament made against priests; but this is a mistake.

Both these Lords professed the Protestant religion; but James conceived that he could count on their fidelity. Feversham, a Frenchman of noble birth, and nephew of the great Turenne, held high rank in the English army, and was Chamberlain to the Queen. Bath was Groom of the Stole.

The Duke's orders were obeyed; and even the physicians withdrew. The back door was then opened; and Father Huddleston entered. A cloak had been thrown over his sacred vestments; and his shaven crown was concealed by a flowing wig. "Sir," said the Duke, "this good man once saved your life. He now comes to save your soul." Charles faintly answered, "He is welcome." Huddleston went through his part better than had been expected. He knelt by the bed, listened to the confession, pronounced the absolution, and administered extreme unction. He asked if the King wished to receive the Lord's supper. "Surely," said Charles, "if I am not unworthy." The host was brought in. Charles feebly strove to rise and kneel before it. The priest bade him lie still, and assured him that God would accept the humiliation of the soul, and would not require the humiliation of the body. The King found so much difficulty in swallowing the bread that it was necessary to open the door and to procure a glass of water. This rite ended, the monk held up a crucifix before the penitent, charged him to fix his last thoughts on the sufferings of the Redeemer, and withdrew. The whole ceremony had occupied about three quarters of an hour; and, during that time, the courtiers who filled the outer room had communicated their suspicions to each other by whispers and significant glances. The door was at length thrown open, and the crowd again filled the chamber of death.

It was now late in the evening. The King seemed much relieved by what had passed. His natural children were brought to his bedside, the Dukes of Grafton, Southampton, and Northumberland, sons of the Duchess of Cleveland, the Duke of Saint Albans, son of Eleanor Gwynn, and the Duke of Richmond, son of the Duchess of Portsmouth. Charles blessed them all, but spoke with peculiar tenderness to Richmond. One face which should have been there was wanting. The eldest and best beloved child was an exile and a wanderer. His name was not once mentioned by his father.

During the night Charles earnestly recommended the Duchess of Portsmouth and her boy to the care of James; "And do not," he good-naturedly added, "let poor Nelly starve." The Queen sent excuses for her absence by Halifax. She said that she was too much disordered to resume her post by the couch, and implored pardon for any offence which she might unwittingly have given. "She ask my pardon, poor woman!" cried Charles; "I ask hers with all my heart."

The morning light began to peep through the windows of Whitehall; and Charles desired the attendants to pull aside the curtains, that he might have one more look at the day. He remarked that it was time to wind up a clock which stood near his bed. These little circumstances were long remembered, because they proved beyond dispute that, when he declared himself a Roman Catholic, he was in full possession of his faculties. He apologised to those who had stood round him all night for the trouble which he had caused. He had been, he said, a most unconscionable time dying; but he hoped that they would excuse it. This was the last glimpse of that exquisite urbanity, so often found potent to charm away the resentment of a justly incensed nation. Soon after dawn the speech of the dying man failed. Before ten his senses were gone. Great numbers had repaired to the churches at the hour of morning service. When the prayer for the King was read, loud groans and sobs showed how deeply his people felt for him. At noon on Friday, the sixth of February, he passed away without a struggle.[13]

[13] Clarke's Life of James the Second, i. 746. Orig. Mem.; Barillon's Despatch of Feb. $\frac{8}{18}$. 1685; Van Citters's Despatches of Feb. $\frac{3}{13}$ and Feb. $\frac{6}{16}$. Huddleston's Narrative; Letters of Philip, second Earl of Chesterfield, 277.; Sir H. Ellis's Original Letters, First Series, iii. 333.; Second Series, iv. 74.; Chaillot MS.; Burnet, i. 606.; Evelyn's Diary, Feb. 4. 168$\frac{4}{5}$; Welwood's Memoirs, 140.; North's Life of Guildford, 252.; Examen, 648.; Hawkins's Life of Ken; Dryden's Threnodia Augustalis; Sir H. Halford's Essay on Deaths of Eminent Persons. See also a fragment of a letter written by the Earl of Ailesbury, which is printed in the European Magazine for April 1795. Ailesbury calls Burnet an imposter. Yet his own narrative and Burnet's will not, to any candid and sensible reader, appear to contradict each other. I have seen in the British Museum, and also in the Library of the Royal Institution, a curious broadside containing an account of the death of Charles. It will be found in the Somers Collection. The author was evidently a zealous Roman Catholic, and must have had access to good sources of information. I strongly suspect that he had been in communication, directly or indirectly, with James himself. No name is given at length; but the initials are perfectly intelligible, except in one place. It is said that the D. of Y. was reminded of the duty which he owed to his brother by P. M. A. C. F. I must own

myself quite unable to decipher the last five letters. It is some consolation that Sir Walter Scott was equally unsuccessful. (1848). Since the first edition of this work was published, several very ingenious conjectures touching these mysterious letters have been communicated to me; but I am convinced that the true solution has not yet been suggested. (1850). I still greatly doubt whether the riddle has been solved. But the most plausible interpretation is one which, with some variations, occurred, almost at the same time, to myself and to several other persons; I am inclined to read "Pére Mansuete A Cordelier Friar." Mansuete, a Cordelier, was then James's confessor. To Mansuete therefore it peculiarly belonged to remind James of a sacred duty which had been culpably neglected. The writer of the broadside must have been unwilling to inform the world that a soul which many devout Roman Catholics had left to perish had been snatched from destruction by the courageous charity of a woman of loose character. It is therefore not unlikely that he would prefer a fiction, at once probable and edifying, to a truth which could not fail to give scandal. (1856.)

It should seem that no transactions in history ought to be more accurately known to us than those which took place round the deathbed of Charles the Second. We have several relations written by persons who were actually in his room. We have several relations written by persons who, though not themselves eyewitnesses, had the best opportunity of obtaining information from eyewitnesses. Yet whoever attempts to digest this vast mass of materials into a consistent narrative will find the task a difficult one. Indeed James and his wife, when they told the story to the nuns of Chaillot, could not agree as to some circumstances. The Queen said that, after Charles had received the last sacraments, the Protestant Bishops renewed their exhortations. The King said that nothing of the kind took place. "Surely," said the Queen, "you told me so yourself." "It is impossible that I could have told you so," said the King; "for nothing of the sort happened."

It is much to be regretted that Sir Henry Halford should have taken so little trouble to ascertain the facts on which he pronounced judgment. He does not seem to have been aware of the existence of the narratives of James, Barillon, and Huddleston.

As this is the first occasion on which I cite the correspondence of the Dutch ministers at the English court, I ought here to mention that a series of their despatches, from the accession of James the Second to his flight, forms one of the most valuable parts of the Mackintosh collection. The subsequent despatches, down to the settlement of the government in February 1689, I procured from the Hague. The Dutch archives have been far too little explored. They abound with information interesting in the highest degree to every Englishman. They are admirably arranged; and they are in the charge of a gentleman whose courtesy, liberality, and zeal for the interests of literature, cannot be too highly praised. I wish to acknowledge, in the strongest manner, my own obligations to Mr. De Jonge and to Mr. Van Zwanne.

Jane Welsh Carlyle

1801-1866

K N O W N in her lifetime as the charming and witty wife of the pre-eminent Victorian Man of Letters, Thomas Carlyle, Jane Welsh Carlyle has since her death and the subsequent publication of her correspondence come into her own as one of the greatest letter writers in an age of great letter writers. Born the daughter of a well-to-do physician in Haddington, Scotland, Jane Baillie Welsh married Thomas Carlyle after a long courtship and in spite of her mother's reservations. After early years of struggle in Edinburgh and in rural Scotland, the Carlyles moved to London in 1834. When literary success came to Carlyle, Jane provided in their Chelsea home the ideal social setting for his literary friends and associates. Her own literary gifts, which some have held were suppressed in her devotion to accommodating Carlyle's irascible temper, found expression in the vast number of letters she wrote to many correspondents, including Carlyle himself whenever he made a trip without her. After Jane's death in London in 1866 while Carlyle was in Edinburgh to be installed as Rector of the university, Carlyle devoted himself to gathering and editing her letters. These were published after his death as the *Letters and Memorials of Jane Welsh Carlyle,* and they form the basis of her literary reputation.

Jane Carlyle's letters are always lively, often acerbic, and always possessed of a directness and clearsightedness that bring her own presence forcefully to life on the page. In contrast to Carlyle's own frequently gloomy if always absorbing letters, Jane's correspondence is bright and quick, even when she is complaining, and it carries the reader forward with speed and vigor. Her punctuation is erratic, often mere dashes, and her style relies heavily on colloquial expressions and colorful Scotticisms. She is an acute observer of manners and at least as percipient an opponent of cant as her celebrated husband. Her letters bring a brightness and intimacy to our understanding of an age sometimes thought to be stuffy, and they remain probably the most readable written in the period.

CHRONOLOGY

1801   Born July 14 at Haddington, East Lothian, Scotland.
1816   Is tutored by Carlyle's friend Edward Irving.
1821   Meets Thomas Carlyle through Edward Irving.

1826   Marries Carlyle 17 October; they take up residence in Edinburgh.
1828   Carlyles move to Craigenputtock.
1834   Carlyles move to London, settle in Cheyne Row, Chelsea.
1842   Carlyles meet Mr. and Mrs. Baring (afterwards Lord and Lady Ashburton).
1866   Dies April 21 in carriage in Hyde Park; is buried beside her father in Haddington churchyard.
1883   *Letters and Memorials of Jane Welsh Carlyle.*

EDITIONS

Letters and Memorials of Jane Welsh Carlyle, ed. J. A. Froude (3 vols., 1883).
New Letters and Memorials of Jane Welsh Carlyle, ed. Alexander Carlyle (2 vols., 1903).
Early Letters of Jane Welsh Carlyle, ed. David G. Ritchie (1889).
The Love Letters of Thomas Carlyle and Jane Welsh, ed. Alexander Carlyle (1909).
Jane Welsh Carlyle: Letters to Her Family 1839–1863, ed. Leonard Huxley (1924).
The Letters of Thomas and Jane Welsh Carlyle, ed. C. R. Sanders et al. (4 vols., 1970—in progress) [will be the standard edition].

BIOGRAPHY AND CRITICISM

Mrs. Alexander Ireland, *The Life of Jane Welsh Carlyle* (1891).
Elizabeth Drew, *Jane Welsh and Jane Carlyle* (1928).
Osburt Burdett, *The Two Carlyles* (1930).
Townsend Scudder, *Jane Welsh Carlyle* (1939).
Lawrence and Elisabeth Hanson, *Necessary Evil: The Life of Jane Welsh Carlyle* (1952).
Iris Origo, *A Measure of Love* (1957).
Elizabeth Drew, *The Literature of Gossip* (1964).
Thea Holme, *The Carlyles at Home* (1965).
G. B. Tennyson, "Jane Welsh Carlyle" in *Victorian Prose: A Guide to Research* (1973).

[Letters]

(Dickens' Theatricals and Alfred Tennyson)

The following letter was written to Carlyle in Scotland telling him of Jane's experiences in attending a performance of "amateur" theatricals arranged by Charles Dickens and his friend and later biographer, John Forster. Jane attended in the company of Carlyle's brother John. Her encounter there and later with Tennyson, not yet the Poet Laureate but already a friend of the Carlyles, is also treated in Jane's entertaining fashion.

To Thomas Carlyle, Scotsbrig.

Chelsea, Tuesday, September 23rd, 1845.

'Nothink' for you today in the shape of inclosure, unless I inclose a letter from Mrs. Paulet to myself, which you will find as 'entertaining' to the full as any of mine. And *nothink* to be *told* either, except all about *the Play*; and upon my honour, I do not feel as if I had penny-a-liner genius enough, this cold morning, to make much entertainment out of that. Enough to clasp one's hand, and exclaim, like Helen[1] before the *Virgin and Child*, '*Oh, how expensive!*' But 'how did the creatures get through it?' Too well; and *not well enough*! The public theatre, scenes painted by Stansfield, costumes 'rather exquisite', together with the *certain* amount of proficiency in the amateurs, overlaid all idea of private theatricals; and, considering it as public theatricals, the acting was 'most insipid', not one performer among them that could be called good, and none that could be called absolutely *bad*. Douglas Jerrold[2] seemed to me the best, the oddity of his appearance greatly helping him; he played Stephen the Cull. Forster as Kitely and Dickens as Captain Bobadil were much on a par; but Forster preserved his identity, even through his loftiest flights of *Macreadyism*; while poor little Dickens, all painted in black and red, and affecting the voice of a man of six feet, would have been unrecognisable for the mother that bore him! On the whole, to get up the smallest interest in the thing, one needed to be always reminding oneself: 'all these actors were once men!' and will be men again tomorrow morning. The greatest wonder for me was how they had contrived to get together some six or seven hundred *ladies and gentlemen* (judging from the clothes) at this season of the year; and all utterly unknown to me, except some half-dozen.

So long as I kept my seat in the dress circle I recognized only Mrs. Macready (in one of the four private boxes), and in my nearer neighbourhood Sir Alexander and Lady Gordon. But in the interval betwixt the play and the farce I took a notion to make my way to Mrs. Macready. John, of course, declared the thing 'clearly impossible no use trying it'; but a servant of the theatre, overhearing our debate, politely offered to escort me where I wished; and then John, having no longer any difficulties to surmount, followed, to have his share in what advantages might accrue from the change. Passing through a long dim passage, I came on a tall man leant to the wall, with his head touching the ceiling like a caryatid, to all appearance asleep, or resolutely *trying* it under most unfavourable circumstances. '*Alfred* Tennyson!' I exclaimed in joyful surprise. '*Well!*' said he, taking the hand I held out to him, and *forgetting* to let it go again. 'I did not know you were in town,' said I. 'I should like to know who you are,' said he; 'I *know* that I *know* you, but I cannot tell your name.' And I had actually to name myself to him. Then he woke up in good earnest, and said he had been meaning to come to Chelsea. 'But Carlyle is in Scotland,' I told him with due humility. 'So I heard from Spedding[3] already, but I asked Spedding, would he go with me to see Mrs. Carlyle? and he said he would.' I told him if he really meant to come, he had better not wait for backing, under the present circumstances; and then pursued my way to the Macready's box; where I was received by *William* (whom I had not divined) with a 'Gracious heavens!' and spontaneous dramatic start, which made me all but answer, 'Gracious heavens!' and start dramatically in my turn. And then I was kissed all round by his women: and poor Nell Gwyn, Mrs. Milner Gibson, seemed almost pushed by the general enthusiasm on the distracted idea of kissing me also! They would not let me return to my stupid place, but put in a third chair for me in front of their box: 'and the latter end of that *woman* was better than the beginning'. Macready was in perfect ecstasies over the 'Life of Schiller', spoke of it *with tears in his eyes*. As 'a sign of the times', I may mention that in the box opposite sat the Duke of Devonshire, with Payne Collier! Next to us were D'Orsay and 'Milady'![4]

Between eleven and twelve it was all over—and the practical result? Eight-and-sixpence for a fly, and a headache for twenty-four hours! I went to bed as wearied as a little woman could be, and dreamt that I was plunging through a quagmire seeking some herbs which were to save

---

[1] The Carlyles' housemaid.

[2] Douglas William Jerrold (1803–57), playwright, author, and editor. The play being performed is Ben Jonson's *Every Man in His Humour*.

[3] James Spedding (1808–81), scholar, editor of the works of Francis Bacon.

[4] John Payne Collier (1789–1883), Shakespeare scholar; Count Alfred D'Orsay (1801–52), "the last of the dandies" and intimate friend of the novelist Lady Blessington, who is the "Milady" referred to.

the life of Mrs. Maurice; and that Maurice was waiting at home for them in an agony of impatience, while I could not get out of the mud-water!

Craik[5] arrived next evening (Sunday), to make his compliments of 'Kerrag', all he had to be thankful for as *his* ticket was for another part of the house than John's and mine. Decidedly a man who cannot get in a finger without thrusting in a hand! Helen had gone to visit *Numbers*. John was smoking in the kitchen. I was lying on the sofa, headachey, leaving Craik to put himself to the chief expenditure of wind, when a cab drove up. Mr. Strachey? No. Alfred Tennyson *alone*!!! Actually, by a superhuman effort of volition he had put himself into a cab, nay, *brought himself* away from a dinner party, and was there to smoke and talk with me!—by myself—me! But no such blessedness was in store for him. Craik prosed, and John babbled for his entertainment; and I, whom he had come to see, got scarcely any

speech with him. The exertion, however, of having to provide him with tea, through my own unassisted ingenuity (Helen being gone for the evening), drove away my headache; also perhaps a little feminine vanity at having inspired *such* a man with the *energy* to take a cab on his own responsibility, and to throw himself on Providence for getting away again! He stayed till eleven, Craik sitting him out, as he sat out Lady Harriet, and would sit out the Virgin Mary and Monsieur Son Fils should he find them here.

What with these unfortunate mattresses (a work of necessity) and other processes almost equally indispensable, I have my hands full, and feel '*worried*', which is worse. I fancy my earthquake begins to 'come it rather strong' for John's comfort and ease, but I cannot help that; if I do not get on with my work, such as it is, what am I here for? . . .

Yours,

J. C.

(Mrs. Macready and John Carlyle)

Two days after the previous letter Jane writes Carlyle again, referring first to some brochures recently received, then back to the Dickens theatricals. She tells him of a visit she paid to the home of the actor William Charles Macready and some amusements back at home in Chelsea involving brother John

To Thomas Carlyle, Scotsbrig.
Chelsea, Thursday evening,
September 25, 1845.

Here is an inclosure that will 'do thee neither ill n'r gude!' It lay along with two brochures, one blue, one pea-green—the thinnest brochures in every sense that ever issued from 'the womb of uncreated night!' 'the insipid offspring' of that 'crack brained enthusiastic' who calls herself *Henri Paris;* one entitled *Grossmütterlein*, in verse, the other—oh, Heavens!—*La femme libre, et*

l'émancipation de la femme: Rhapsodie à propos des Saint-Simoniens, in prose—dead prose.[1]

I have looked into it over my tea, and find that the only emancipation for *femme* lies in her having '*le saint courage de rester vierge!*'[2] Glad tidings of great joy for—Robertson! '*Guerroyez donc, si vous pouvez, contre les hommes!*' exclaims the great female mind in an enthusiasm of platitude. '*Mais pour qu'ils daignent accepter votre défi, prouvez-leur, avant tout, que vous avez appris . . . à vous passer d'eux!*'[3]

I rose yesterday morning with an immense

[5] George Lillie Craik (1798–1866), Scottish literary scholar.
[1] The first pamphlet is titled "Little Grandmother"; the second is "The Free Woman and the Emancipation of Women; Rhapsody on the Saint-Simonians."
[2] "The holy courage to remain a virgin."
[3] "Make war, if you can, against men!" "But should they deign to accept your challenge, show them above all that you have learned to do without them!"

desire for 'change of air'. I had made the house into the liveliest representation of '*Hell and Tommy*' (I, 'Tommy'),[4] and it struck me that I should do well to escape from it for some hours; so John and I left together. In the King's road he picked up a cab to take back for his luggage, and I went on to Clarence Terrace, where I dined, and by six I was at home again to tea. Mrs. Macready had returned to Eastbourne, having only come up for the day to attend the play. That I was prepared for, as she had invited me to go along with her, but I was not prepared to find poor Macready ill in bed, with two doctors attending him. He had caught a horrible cold that night, from seeing Mrs. Milner Gibson to her carriage through the rain 'in thin shoes'; had been obliged to break an engagement at Cambridge. Poor *Letitia* was very concerned about him, but would still not let me go without some dinner. Today she writes to me that he is better. There seemed a good deal of jealousy in Macreadydom on the subject of the amateur actors. A '*tremendous* puff of the thing' had appeared in the 'Times'!— 'more *kind* really than ever the "Times" showed itself towards William!' John, when he came at night to pay 'his compliments of digestion', suggested with his usual originality, 'it was probably *that* (the puff) which had made Macready so ill just now!' Forster, it seems, bears away the palm; but they have all had their share of praise, 'and are in such a state of *excitement*, poor things, as never was seen!' 'It will not stop here,' Miss Macready thinks.

Today I have not been out at all. I rose at seven, to receive—a sweep! And have been helping Helen to scrub in the library till now—seven in the evening. John came rushing in soon after nine this morning; he had left a breast-pin in the glass-drawer, and 'supposed it would not be lost yet'! Then, having found it, he brought it to me in the library, where I was mounted on the steps, covered with dust, to ask whether I thought 'the diamonds real?' and what I thought 'such a thing would cost?' It was the pin he got years ago in Italy. I told him I would not take upon me to value it, but I could learn its value for him. 'From whom?' 'From Collier the jeweller.' 'Where does he live?' (with immense eagerness). 'At the top

of Sloane Street.' 'But wouldn't he tell me—if I asked him? *me, myself?*' 'I dare say he would,' said I soothingly, for he seemed to be going rapidly out of his wits, with all-absorbing desire to know the value of that pin! If I had not seen him the night before playing with his purse and some sovereigns, I might have thought he was on the point of carrying it to a pawnshop to get himself a morsel of victuals! But when, giving up the diamonds as glass, he passed to the individual value of the *turquoise* in the middle, flesh and blood could stand it no longer, and I returned to my dusting in *silence*; whereupon he looked at his watch, and found he 'was obliged to go off to the British Museum'. What in all the world will become of him? He seems to be more than ever without 'fixed point', without will, without so much as a good wish! unless it be to enjoy a tolerable share of material comfort, without 'Amt', and as much as possible without 'Geld'. However, now that he has 'concluded with his landlady', it is no business of mine how he flounders on, 'bating no jot of heart and hope', as he says. My own life is rather of the floundering sort, only I have the grace to have 'abated heart and hope' in it to such an extent as to think sometimes that 'if I were dead, and a stone at my head', perhaps it would be be——ter!

Not a soul has been here since Alfred Tennyson —except the 'dark-fated' Krasinski,[5] who did not get in. I know his rap, and signified to Helen to say 'I was sick—or dead'—what she liked! So she told him, 'the mistress was bad with her head tonight', which, if not precisely the naked truth, was a Gambardella '*Aspiration*' towards it. But besides Miss Macready yesterday I saw Helps,[6] who seems to me 'dwindling away into an unintelligible whinner'. I met him in the King's Road, just as John called his cab, and he walked back part of the way with me, decidedly too solemn for his size!

I get no letters in these days except from you. Geraldine[7] has even fallen dumb; still out of sorts I fancy, or absorbed in her 'one-eyed Egyptian'; perhaps scheming a new 'work'! I care very little which. Kind regards wherever they are due.

J. C.

---

[4] A domestic reference of the Carlyles to an engraving at Macready's house showing a scene that in Carlyle's words was "mad as bedlam, all, and with one 'small figure' ('Tommy') notably prominent."

[5] Count Krasinski, Polish exile.

[6] Sir Arthur Helps (1813–75), essayist and historian.

[7] Geraldine Endsor Jewsbury (1812–80), novelist and friend of Jane's.

(Lady Harriet Baring and Edward Sterling)

Harriet Baring, Lady Ashburton, was to become something of a rival for Carlyle's attention, though not his affections, in the decade to come when he was engaged in the writing of Frederick the Great. *In the following letter Jane tells Carlyle of a visit to Lady Harriet's and adds further comments on the theatricals of the previous week. Jane's independence of spirit in regard to Lady Harriet is clearly evident. Jane also tells Carlyle of a visit with the father of John Sterling, Carlyle's friend and later to be the subject of a biography by Carlyle. John Sterling had died the previous year; the elder Sterling, one-time editor of the* Times, *was seventy-two at the time Jane is writing.*

To Thomas Carlyle, Scotsbrig.
Chelsea, Sunday, September 28th, 1845.

Well, if yesterday was rainy and dreary enough to set one on reading 'The Purgatory of Suicides' (had there been time for it), today I have had, as Gambardella[1] would say, 'some pleasant excitements'—as pleasant almost as his last feat—which appeared in 'The Times'—running a race with Green's balloon and being *in at the Descent* ! Today I have sat an hour with—Lady Harriet! and a quarter of an hour with old Sterling!

Last night I received a note from Lady Harriet stating that she was in Town for only a few days; not able to go out, but would send the brougham for me today at two, if 'perchance' I could come and see her. Of course, today at two, I was all in readiness. Guy ticht aboot the head; I *think* I had on *my new bonnet* ! I was rather surprised to be set down at a great Unknown House and conducted thro' large Halls and staircases by unknown servants. If it had not been for the indubitability of the brougham, I should have begun to fancy myself kidnapped, or in a Fairy Tale! *Eventually*, in a large dressing room at the top of the house, I found the Lady on a sofa; a gentleman was just coming out—*Irish* I should fancy from the fact of his leaving his *hat* behind him! On search being made for it by a servant some five minutes later, it was found, with difficulty, under the chair I had sat down upon! The Lady was ill only in a feminine sense: 'My dear, I am not up to going out and that sort of thing just at present'; but she 'would be able to return to The Grange on Tuesday'. She spoke of being to dine at Lansdowne House on Monday.—She was very graci-ous and agreeable; repeated pressingly the invitation to Alverstoke. I told her all about the Play which she had heard of with immense applause from—Lady Holland! who was there! It seems that a great many of the aristocracy assisted at the tomfoolery,—'*entertained* (by *me* at least) *unawares*', I thought it rather a 'rum-looking' gathering! The German Books had reached her safely;—if you wrote about them, that letter had not yet reached her; the one you wrote on your arrival, she bade me say, was duly received, and she would have answered it before now, 'if she had not been moving about more than she anticipated'. When she got back to The Grange, she expected to rest for a while, and would then write. It was to Richard Milnes[2] I owed the pleasure of seeing her; he had been there the same evening he called on me, and mentioned having just seen me in an unprecedented state of confusion.

I recommended her to read 'Cecil' (which I like immensely), and she recommended me to read Blanco White's 'Memoirs', about which she was all agog. She asked what I had heard said about it, and I told her Darwin's criticism; that 'it greatly took away from one's sympathy with a man's religious scruples, to find that they were merely symptoms of a diseased liver':[3] To which she replied, very justly, that 'until the dominion of the liver was precisely ascertained, it was safer to speak respectfully of it'! The Brougham was waiting to take me back again and she was *on a sofa*; so for both reasons I was careful not to make my visit too long, although she did ask me in a *sort of way* to stay and dine with them at five o'clock. On the whole our interview went off

---

[1] Spiridione Gambardella, Italian refugee and fashionable portrait painter.
[2] Richard Monkton Milnes, 1st Baron Houghton (1809–85), English statesman, traveler, and essayist.
[3] *Cecil, or the Adventures of a Coxcomb* (1845), novel by Mrs. Catherine Gore (1799–1861); Joseph Blanco White (1775–1841), former Roman Catholic priest, then an Anglican, then a Unitarian; the Darwin referred to is Charles Darwin's brother Erasmus.

quite successfully; and I dare say, in spite of Mrs. Buller's predictions, we shall get on very well together; although I can see that the Lady has a genius for *ruling*, whilst I have a genius for—not being ruled!

On my return Helen met me with the surprising intelligence that old Sterling had called!—a lady in the carriage with him. 'Not very lady-like', she fancied it must be his landlady. 'So thin she could not have known him; and so glad that he even shaked hands with her!' It was 'most waesome to see him'!—John also had been down and left a note on the table, *in French*—longer and more genial than he is in the habit of writing in English. Decidedly he should stick to French! So soon as I had swallowed-in a mouthful of dinner I went off again to see the poor old goose, whose visit under such circumstances quite melted my hard and stony heart. I called for John on the way, in case he chose to walk up with me, but suggested he should not go in, in case Sterling fancied we wanted to make a job of him. 'Better not stay above five minutes, you may bring on another fit if you do,' were John's rather alarming last words. But I seemed to do the old man nothing but good. Physically he is stronger than I expected; can walk alone, staggering a little. I do not know whether it be his thinness, or the consciousness of death being quite near him, but he has much more dignity in his appearance than ever he had in his best days. In the first minutes I thought he looked more *intelligent*, too, than I had ever seen him. He made me less of a *scene* than was to have been expected;—merely stretched his arms towards Heaven as if 'thanking God for having created *friendship*—the consolation of the unfortunate'. Ah, but he is not laughable any more.—'I am very glad to see you so well as this,' said I. 'And I am very, very glad to see you —*at all*,' said he. He offered me the easiest chair, offered me wine, with a courtesy that reminded me of the German Noble (what was his name?) who took off his hat, when dying, to his Bishop.[4] None of the old bluster, but a quiet painful eagerness to do all that was polite and kind by me. After a few minutes' talk about his illness, he said in a whisper, pointing to his head, 'It is *here*, that all is over with me! gone, gone, gone!' and then tears ran down his cheeks; almost down mine too; for he said *that*, not as he used to say such things, but with the simplicity of truth. The *thought* about his head seemed to *produce* confusion in it; for from the minute he spoke of his head, he talked quite incoherently; could not remember any name or any date; began mysterious sentences and left them unfinished.—John was waiting in the street to go home to tea with me; he got afraid that I would stay till I 'brought on another fit'; so had himself shown up. I promised to go to him again tomorrow evening; and kissed his brow; and he gave me his *blessing*, which really sounds *now* as if it were worth something.—And here I am (John long gone) writing at half after eleven, —which is not wise. But tomorrow will bring its own business—I will send you a letter I have had from Julia Paulet; read it pray, and judge if it be not promising for a girl of fifteen.—Kind regards to all.

Your own
J. Carlyle.

---

[4] Franz von Sickingen (1481–1523), who when dying doffed his hat to the Archbishop of Trier.

John Henry Newman

1801-1890

BY ANY account John Henry Newman exerted more influence on English religious life in the Victorian era than any other single person. Newman's impact on the Church of England has been profound; his subsequent impact on the Church of Rome has proven to be almost equally profound, though slower in being recognized. In addition to his role in the center of the Victorian concern with religion, Newman enjoys a secure place as one of the greatest prose writers of the age. Newman is thus a major figure in the ecclesiastical and intellectual history of his age as well as in the literary history of that age.

Newman was born in London to a moderately devout but not especially High Church family. As early as 1816 he experienced his first "conversion," a powerful conviction of the existence of God. The rest of his life can be seen as a development and elaboration of the consequences of that experience. His early theology was essentially Evangelical with its stress on the personal relation of the individual to God; but his lifelong consistent development was always toward a more Catholic, more ecclesiastical interpretation of Christianity. It was to lead him, of course, ultimately to the Roman Catholic Church. But the process was a very extended one, lasting some decades, as he himself describes in his spiritual autobiography, *Apologia pro vita sua*. During the period of this intellectual development, Newman occupied positions of prominence in English church life; thus, the effects of his intellectual development went far beyond his own personal actions.

As a student at Trinity College, Oxford, Newman was early recognized as a brilliant scholar. His disappointment at failing to gain first-class honors in 1820 was shared by many of his associates; but he redeemed himself two years later by winning election to a fellowship at Oriel College, which was then regarded as the most intellectual and high-minded of Oxford colleges. At Oriel Newman came under the influence of the "Oriel Noetics," a group of liberal scholars and clergymen, one of whose number was the logician and rhetorician Richard Whatley, later Archbishop of Dublin. From Whatley Newman learned the power of rational argument, but he did not find in the liberal or Broad Church movement the religious fulfillment and certainty that he craved. Hence he was drawn increasingly away from the Noetics and toward the High Church and Catholic views of Richard Hurrell Froude and John Keble. These three, subsequently joined by E. B. Pusey, were to form a few years later the nucleus of the Oxford Movement.

Newman had been appointed in 1828 Vicar of the Church of St. Mary the Virgin, the University church of Oxford, and with it a rural chapel in the nearby village of Littlemore. He was to hold this post until 1841 and from it to exercise immense influence on the religious life of Oxford. But the controversial aspects of his influence did not emerge until after 1833 and the beginning of the Oxford Movement. Newman himself spent most of the year preceding John Keble's 1833 sermon touring in the Mediterranean with Hurrell Froude, whose health was already failing, though he was still a young man. Newman himself suffered a serious illness in Sicily which served to deepen yet further his religious commitment. It was during the Mediterranean trip that Newman wrote most of his poetry; it was published along with contributions by others in the volume *Lyra Apostolica* (1836), the apostolic lyre. And it was less than a week after Newman's return from his trip that Keble delivered his Assize Sermon, "National Apostasy," and initiated the Oxford Movement.

Newman hailed Keble's sermon as the opening shot in a campaign to combat the Erastianism, of the C. of E., that is, its dependence on decisions of state. Newman and the other members of the Movement soon began to express their anti-Erastian ideas and to stress the independence of the Church from state authority, the apostolicity of the Church of England (its descent from the Apostles through the Apostolic Succession), its sacramental and Catholic character, and its distinctness as a spiritual body from the secularizing rationalism of Whatley and the Noetics. These ideas were promulgated chiefly through the publication of the *Tracts for the Times*, a series of anonymous pamphlets, edited and largely written by Newman, that ran from 1833 to 1841. Through these and similar means the Oxford Movement began to change the face of the Church of England.

Newmans's industry in publication was the chief factor in spreading the Movement beyond Oxford; his eloquence as a preacher was perhaps the chief factor in spreading the Movement in Oxford itself. Oxonians flocked to his sermons, professing as their faith *Credo in Newmannum* ("I believe in Newman"), and much of the appeal of the Movement certainly rested on Newman's quiet brilliance as a speaker. But there was powerful opposition to the Movement as well. The storm broke in 1841 with the publication of Tract XC in which Newman argued that the Thirty-nine Articles of the Church of England were susceptible of a fully Catholic interpretation. The tract was condemned and Newman ceased publication of any future tracts at the request of the Bishop.

Tract XC was Newman's last attempt to salvage his belief in the Church of England as the via media, or middle way, between Rome and Protestantism. After the condemnation of the tract, Newman retired to Littlemore in semi-monastic seclusion. For some years he delayed taking any step, even while some of his more eager followers went over to Rome, but at last in October of 1845 he was received into the Roman Catholic Church. The event marks the end of the first phase of the Oxford Movement and the beginning of a new phase in Newman's own life.

From 1845 on Newman's career as a public figure was in eclipse. He became a priest in the Roman Catholic Church, established an oratory, a chapter of the Oratory of St. Philip Neri near Birmingham, and continued to write and to project many undertakings. Anglicans largely ignored him; his new fellow communicants often treated him with a suspicion bordering on mistrust. Numerous projects were undertaken by Newman—a translation of the scriptures, the establishment of a Roman Catholic university in Dublin with Newman as Rector—but they were all allowed to lapse. Newman, however, persevered, and in 1864 when he took the occasion of a slur by Charles Kingsley to write a defense of his own position, he succedeed at once in his immediate aim of justifying his conduct and establishing his honesty of motive; but more than that, he also succeeded in writing one of the great accounts of spiritual development in any language. He became again an honored figure in English religious and intellectual life.

Newman continued to be an active force in English religious life for a quarter-century after the publication of the *Apologia*. He was made an Honorary Fellow of Trinity College, Oxford, in 1878, which occasioned his first visit to Oxford in more than thirty years. The following year he was made a Cardinal in the Roman Church. When he died in 1890 he was almost a legend, having lived close to a century and having made an impact on nineteenth-century religious life such as no one else in the century could claim.

Newman's literary fame is inextricably intertwined with his religious position, for he wrote virtually nothing that was not more or less explicitly on religious subjects. Yet so compelling was his literary power that his works reached beyone the confines of a narrowly religious audience (large though that audience was in his own day) to appeal to persons of various intellectual persuasions. Many have attributed this appeal to Newman's stylistic elegance, and no doubt his subtle and persuasive style accounts for much of his readership. But no doubt too Newman's readership has rarely been interested in style alone. It is rather that Newman puts his style in the service of enduring questions of faith and belief that has secured for him so large and so persistent an audience.

The questions that Newman continually addresses in his writing are in the first instance questions that concerned his contemporaries: What is the role of the Church of England in relation to the state? What are the merits of the claims of the various Christian bodies to be the true spokesman for the Church established by Christ? How does one arrive at personal conviction in a time of doubt and skepticism? What is the function of education in relation to society and in relation to faith? But these are also questions that, with very little modification, continue to speak to our own age. Newman is therefore confronting the perennial philosophic questions that have occupied the thoughts of the most vigorous minds of all ages: What is belief? How do we arrive at it? How do we relate it to our everyday life, to education and society? In short, what is man?

Because Newman arrived at his position of orthodoxy only after the most prolonged thought, and even struggle, his responses to these questions are anything but facile. His careful style is a reflection of this penetrating and at times even painful self-examination and self-criticism. Newman's style thus works both by its appeal to rational argument and by what has often been called insinuation, the slow, carefully pursued argument over which hovers almost mystically the power of some superintending design that seems to lead by a force more powerful than that of mere reason to a destined conclusion.

Newman's literary genius is evident in his beautifully phrased sermons, his carefully studied histories, his brilliantly argued philosophic treatises, and above all in his intensely personal yet still quietly reserved account of his own spiritual development. His own motto, *Cor ad cor loquitur*, heart speaking to heart, is an appropriate motto to characterize both his thought and his moving style.

CHRONOLOGY

1801 Born February 21 in London.
1808 Attends private school in Ealing.
1816 Experiences first "conversion" to Evangelical principles.
1817 Enters Trinity College, Oxford.
1821 Graduates without winning first-class honors.
1822 Elected fellow of Oriel College.
1825 Takes Holy Orders in Church of England.
1828 Appointed Vicar of St. Mary's, the University church.
1832 Resigns Oriel tutorship; takes Mediterranean tour with R. Hurrell Froude and suffers serious illness in Sicily.
1833 Returns from Italy; begins *Tracts for the Times.*
1837 Publishes *Prophetical Office of the Church.*
1841 Publishes "Tract XC"; resigns editorship of *British Critic.*
1842 Retires to Littlemore; writes *Development of Christian Doctrine* (published 1845).
1845 Received October 9 into Roman Catholic Church.
1846 Ordained priest in Rome; joins Order of the Oratory of St. Philip Neri.
1847 Returns to England as head of the Oratory at Birmingham.
1850 Delivers lecture series published as *Difficulties of Anglicans.*
1851 *The Present Position of Catholics.*
1852 Loses libel suit to ex-Dominican Dr. Achili; made rector-elect of proposed Catholic University of Dublin; presents lectures published as *The Idea of a University.*
1864 *Apologia pro vita sua.*
1865 *The Dream of Gerontius and Other Poems.*
1870 Opposes promulgation of doctrine of papal infallibility by Vatican Council; publishes *The Grammar of Assent.*
1877 Republishes Anglican writings.
1878 Made Honorary Fellow of Trinity College, Oxford.
1879 Created Cardinal at Rome.
1890 Dies August 11; buried at Rednal near Birmingham.

EDITIONS

Works (41 vols., 1878–1921). [The standard edition.]
Apologia pro vita sua, ed. Wilfred Ward (1913), A. Dwight Culler (1956), Martin J. Svaglic (1967), David J. DeLaura (1968).
Essays and Sketches, ed. C. F. Harrold (3 vols., 1948).
The Essential Newman, ed. V. F. Blehl (1963).
Idea of a University, ed. C. F. Harrold (1947), George N. Shuster (1959), Martin J. Svaglic (1959).
Letters and Correspondence of John Henry Newman, ed. Anne Mozley (2 vols., 1891).
Letters and Diaries of John Henry Newman, ed. C. F. Dessain (11 vols., 1961—in progress). [Will be the standard edition.]
Lyra Apostolica, ed. H. C. Beeching (1903).
A Newman Treasury, ed. C. F. Harrold (1943).
Newman: Prose and Poetry, ed. Geoffry Tillotson (1957).

BIOGRAPHY AND CRITICISM

Thomas Bokenkotter, *Cardinal Newman as an Historian* (1959).

Louis Bouyer, *Newman: His Life and Spirituality* (1960).

Yngve Brilioth, *The Anglican Revival* (1925).

Owen Chadwick, *From Bossuet to Newman* (1957).

R. W. Church, *The Oxford Movement: Twelve Years, 1833–1845* (1891, rpt. 1972).

A. Dwight Culler, *The Imperial Intellect* (1955).

Christopher Dawson, *The Spirit of the Oxford Movement* (1955).

David J. DeLaura, *Hebrew and Hellene in Victorian England* (1969).

C. F. Harrold, *John Henry Newman: An Exposition and Critical Study of His Mind, Thought, and Art* (1945).

Walter E. Houghton, *The Art of Newman's "Apologia"* (1945).

Terrence Kenny, *The Political Thought of John Henry Newman* (1957).

Fergal McGrath, *Newman's University: Idea and Reality* (1951).

Martin Svaglic and C. F. Dessain, "John Henry Newman" in *Victorian Prose: A Guide to Research* (1973).

Meriol Trevor, *Newman: The Pillar of the Cloud* and *Light in Winter* (1962).

H. Tristram, *Newman and His Friends* (1933).

Thomas Vargish, *Newman: The Contemplation of Mind* (1970).

Maisie Ward, *Young Mr. Newman* (1948).

Wilfred Ward, *The Life of John Henry Cardinal Newman* (2 vols., 1912).

Harold L. Weatherby, *Cardinal Newman in His Age* (1973).

Wisdom and Innocence

The following sermon from the collection Sermons on Subjects of the Day, *published in 1844, was the sermon that, when pressed by Newman, Charles Kingsley cited as the source for his assertion that "Truth, for its own sake, had never been a virtue with the Roman clergy. Father Newman informs us that it need not, and on the whole ought not to be." Newman took vigorous issue with Kingsley over this charge and eventually was impelled to write his* Apologia *in response to it. (The notes are Newman's.)*

"Behold, I send you forth as sheep in the midst of wolves; be ye therefore wise as serpents, and harmless as doves."—MATT. 10:16.

SHEEP are defenceless, wolves are strong and fierce. How prompt, how frightful, how resistless, how decisive, would be the attack of a troop of wolves on a few straggling sheep which fell in with them! and how lively, then, is the image which our Lord uses to express the treatment which His followers were to receive from the world! He Himself was the great Exemplar of all such sufferings. When He was in the hands of His enemies, surrounded by a mad multitude, gazed on by relentless enemies, jeered at, struck, hurried along, tormented by rude soldiers, and at length nailed to the cross, what was He emphatically but a sheep among wolves? "He is brought as a lamb to the slaughter, and as a sheep before her shearers is dumb, so He openeth not His mouth." And what He foretold of His followers, that the Psalmist had declared of them at an earlier time, and His Apostle applies it to them on its fulfilment. "As it is written," says St. Paul, "For Thy sake we are killed all the day long; we are accounted as sheep for the slaughter."[1] Such was the Church of Christ in its beginnings, and such has it been in every age in proportion to its purity. The purer it has been, the more defenceless; whever it has been pure, it has, in one way or another, been defenceless. The less worldly it has been, and the more it has cultivated its proper gifts, and the less it has relied upon sword and bow, chariots and horses, and arm of man, the more it has been exposed to ill-usage; the more it has invited oppression, the more it has irritated the proud and powerful. This, I say, is exemplified in every age. Seasons of peace, indeed, have been vouchsafed to it from the first, and in the most fearful times; but not an age of peace. A reign of temporal peace it can hardly enjoy, except under the reign of corruption, and in an age of faithlessness. Peace and rest are future.

Now, then, what is it natural to suppose will be the conduct of those who are helpless and persecuted, as the Holy Spouse of Christ? Pain and hardship and disrepute are pleasant to no man: and though they are to be gloried in when they are undergone, yet they will rather, if possible, be shunned or averted. Such avoidance is sanctioned, nay, commanded, by our Lord. When trials are inevitable, we must cheerfully bear them; but when they can be avoided without sin, we ought to prevent them. But how were Christians to prevent them when they might not fight? I answer, they were allowed the arms, that is, the arts, of the defenceless. Even the inferior animals will teach us how wonderfully the Creator has compensated to the weak their want of strength, by giving them other qualities which may avail in their struggle with the strong. They have the gift of fleetness; or they have a certain make and colour; or certain habits of living; or some natural cunning, which enables them either to elude or even to destroy their enemies. Brute force is countervailed by flight, brute passion by prudence and artifice. Instances of a similar kind occur in our own race. Those nations which are destitute of material force, have recourse to the arts of the unwarlike; they are fraudulent and crafty; they dissemble, negotiate, procrastinate, evading what they cannot resist, and wearing out what they cannot crush. Thus is it with a captive, effeminate race, under the rule of the strong and haughty. So is it with slaves; so is it with ill-used and oppressed children; who learn to be cowardly and deceitful towards their tyrants. So is it with the subjects of a despot, who encounter his axe or bowstring with the secret influence of intrigue and conspiracy, the dagger and the poisoned cup. They exercise the unalienable right of self-defence by such methods as they best may; only, since human nature is unscrupulous, guilt or innocence is all the same to them, if it works their purpose.

Now, our Lord and Saviour did not forbid us the exercise of that instinct of self-defence which is born with us. He did not forbid us to defend ourselves, but He forbad certain *modes* of defence. All sinful means, of course, He forbad, as is plain without mentioning. But, besides these, He forbad us what is not sinful, but allowable by nature, though not in that more excellent and perfect way which He taught—He forbad us to defend ourselves by force, to return blow for blow. "Ye have heard," He says, "that it hath been said, An eye for an eye, and a tooth for a tooth; but I say unto you, That ye resist not evil: but whosoever shall smite thee on thy right cheek, turn to him the other also. And if any man will sue thee at the law, and take away thy coat, let him have thy cloke also. And whosoever shall compel thee to go a mile, go with him in twain." Thus the servants of Christ are forbidden to defend themselves by violence; but they are not forbidden other means; direct means are not allowed them, but others are even commanded. For instance, *foresight*; "beware of men:"[2] *avoidance*, "when they persecute you in this city, flee ye into another:" *prudence and skill*, as in the text, "be ye wise as serpents."

Here we are reminded of the awful history with which the sacred volume opens. In the beginning, "the serpent was more subtle than any beast of the field which the Lord God had made." First, observe then, our Lord in the text sanctions that very reference which I have been making to the instincts and powers of the inferior animals, and puts them forth as our example. As we are to learn industry from the ant, and reliance on Him from the ravens, so the dove is our pattern of innocence, and the serpent our pattern of wisdom. But, moreover, considering that the serpent was chosen by the Enemy of mankind, as the instrument of his temptations in Paradise, it is very remarkable that Christ should choose it as the pattern of wisdom for His followers. It is as if He appealed to the whole world of sin, and to the

---

[1] Rom. 8:36.   [2] Matt. 10:17.

bad arts by which the feeble gain advantages here over the strong. It is as if He set before us the craft, the treachery, the perfidy of the captive and the slave, and bade us extract a lesson even from so great an evil. It is as if the more we are forbidden violence, the more we are exhorted to prudence; as if it were our bounden duty to rival the wicked in endowments of mind, and to excel them in their exercise. And He makes a reference of this very kind in one of His parables, where "the lord commended the unjust steward, because he had done wisely; for the children of this world are in their generation wiser than the children of light." "Be ye wise as serpents," He said; then, knowing how dangerous such wisdom is, especially in times of temptation, if a severe conscientiousness is not awake, He added, "and harmless as doves." "Behold, I send you forth as sheep in the midst of wolves; be ye therefore wise as serpents, and harmless as doves."

It needs very little knowledge of the history of the Church, to understand how remarkably this exhortation to wisdom has been fulfilled in it. If there be one reproach more than another which has been cast upon it, it is that of fraud and cunning—cast upon it, even from St. Paul's day, whose word was accused of being "yea and nay;"[3] and himself of "walking in craftiness, and handling the word of God deceitfully;"[4] of being a "deceiver," though he was "true;"[5] of "terrifying by letters;"[6] and of "being crafty," and "catching" his converts "with guile."[7] Nay, cast upon it in the person of our Lord, who was called "a deceiver," and said to "deceive the people." Priestcraft has ever been considered the badge, and its imputation is a kind of note of the Church; and in part, indeed, truly, because the presence of powerful enemies, and the sense of their own weakness, has sometimes tempted Christians to the abuse, instead of the use of Christian wisdom, to be wise without being harmless; but partly— nay, for the most part—not truly, but slanderously, and merely because the world called their wisdom craft, when it was found to be a match for its own numbers and power. Christians were called crafty, because "they were, in fact, so strong, though professing to be weak." And next, in mere consistency, they were called hypocritical, because "they were, forsooth, so crafty, professing to be innocent." And thus whereas they have ever, in accordance with our Lord's words, been wise and harmless, they have ever been called instead crafty and hypocritical. The words "craft"

and "hypocrisy" are but the version of "wisdom" and "harmlessness," in the language of the world.

It is remarkable, however, that not only is harmlessness the corrective of wisdom, securing it against the corruption of craft and deceit, as stated in the text; but innocence, simplicity, implicit obedience to God, tranquillity of mind, contentment, these and the like virtues are themselves a sort of wisdom;—I mean, they produce the same results as wisdom, because God works for those who do not work for themselves; and thus Christians especially incur the charge of craft at the hands of the world, because they pretend to so little, yet effect so much. This circumstance admits dwelling on.

By innocence, or harmlessness, is meant simplicity in act, purity in motive, honesty in aim; acting conscientiously and religiously, according to the matter in hand, without caring for consequences or appearances; doing what appears one's duty, and being obedient for obedience' sake, and leaving the event to God. This is to be innocent as the dove; yet this conduct is the truest wisdom; and this conduct accordingly has pre-eminently the appearance of craft.

It appears to be craft, and is wisdom, in many ways.

1. First: sobriety, self-restraint, control of word and feeling, which religious men exercise, have about them an appearance of being artificial, because they are not natural; and of being artful, because artificial. I do not deny there is something very engaging in a frank and unpremeditating manner; some persons have it more than others; in some persons it is a great grace. But it must be recollected that I am speaking of times of persecution and oppression to Christians, such as the text foretells; and then surely frankness will become nothing else than indignation at the oppressor, and vehemence of speech, if it is permitted. Accordingly, as persons have deep feelings, so they will find the necessity of self-control, lest they should say what they ought not. All this stands to reason, without enlarging upon it. And to this must be added, that those who would be holy and blameless, the sons of God, find so much in the world to unsettle and defile them, that they are necessarily forced upon a strict self-restraint, lest they should receive injury from such intercourse with it as is unavoidable; and this self-restraint is the first thing which makes holy persons seem wanting in openness and manliness.

[3] 3 Cor. 1:17.   [4] 2 Cor. 4:2.   [5] 2 Cor. 6:8.   [6] 2 Cor. 10:9.   [7] 2 Cor. 12:16.

2. Next let it be considered that the world, the gross, carnal, unbelieving world, is blind to the peculiar feelings, objects, hopes, fears, affections of religious people. It cannot understand them. Religious men are a mystery to it; and, being a mystery, they will be called by the world, in mere self-defence, mysterious, dark, subtle, designing; and that the more, because, as living to God, they are at no pains to justify themselves to the world, or to open their hearts, or account to it for their conduct. The world will impute motives, either because it cannot find any, or because it simply will not believe these motives to be the real ones which are such, and are avowed as such. It cannot believe that men will deliberately sacrifice this life to the next; and when they profess to do so, it thinks that of necessity there must be something behind which they do not divulge. And, again, all the reasons which religious men allege, seem to the world unreal, and all the feelings fantastical and strained; and this strengthens it in its idea that it has not fathomed them, and that there is some secret to be found out. And indeed it has not fathomed them, and there is a secret; but it is the power of Divine grace, their state of heart, which is the secret; not their motives or their ends, which the world is told to the full. Here is a second reason why the dove seems but a serpent. Christians give up worldly advantages; they sacrifice rank or wealth; they prefer obscurity to station; they do penance rather than live delicately; and the world says, "Here are effects without causes sufficient for them; here is craft."

3. Further, let this be considered. The precept given us is, that "we resist not evil;" that we yield to worldly authority, and "give place unto wrath." This the early Christians did in an especial way. But it is very difficult to make the world understand the difference between an outward obedience, and an interior assent. When the Christians obeyed the heathen magistrate in all things not sinful, it was not that they thought the heathen right; they knew them to be idolaters. There are a multitude of cases, and very various, where it is our duty to obey those who nevertheless have no power over our belief or conviction. When, however, religious men outwardly conform, on the score of duty, to "the powers that be," the world is easily led into the mistake that they have renounced their opinions as well as submitted their actions; and it feels or affects surprise, to learn that their opinions remain; and this it considers or calls an inconsistency, or a

duplicity. It argues that they are breaking promise, cherishing what they disown, or resuming what they professed to abandon. And thus the very fact that they are so harmless, so inoffensive, that they do so much in the way of compliance, becomes a ground of complaint against them, that they do not do more—that they do not do more than they have a right to do. They yield outwardly; to assent inwardly would be to betray the faith; yet they are called deceitful and double-dealing, because they do as much as they can, and not more than they may.

4. Again: the cheerfulness, contentment, and readiness with which religious men resign their cause into God's hands, and are well-pleased that the world should seem to triumph over them, have still further an appearance of craft and deceit. For why should they be so satisfied to give up their wishes, unless they knew something which others did not know, or were really gaining while they seemed to lose? Other men make a great clamour and lamentation over their idols; there is no mistaking that they have lost them, and that they have no hope. But Christians resign themselves. They are silent; silence itself is suspicious—even silence is mystery. Why do they not speak out? why do they not show a natural, an honest indignation? The submitting to calumny is a proof that it is too true. They would set themselves right, if they could. Still more strange and suspicious is the confidence which religious men show, in spite of apparent weakness, that their cause will triumph. The boldness, decisiveness, calmness of speech, which are necessarily the result of Christian faith and hope, lead the world to the surmise of some hidden reliance, some secret support, to account for them; as if God's word, when received and dwelt on, were not a greater encouragement to the lonely combatant than any word of man, however powerful, or any conspiracy, however far-spreading.

5. And still stronger is this delusion on the part of the world, when the event justifies the confidence of religious men. The truest wisdom is to stand still and trust in God, and to the world it is also the strongest evidence of craft. God fights for those who do not fight for themselves; such is the great truth, such is the gracious rule, which is declared and exemplified in the Gospel: "Dearly beloved, avenge not yourselves," says St. Paul, "but rather give place unto wrath, for it is written, Vengeance is Mine, I will repay, saith the Lord."[8] Do nothing, and you have done

[8] Rom. 12:19.

every thing. The less you do, the more God will do for you. The more you submit to the violence of the world, the more powerfully will He rise against the world, who is irresistible. The less you ward off the world's blows from you, the more heavy will be His blows upon the world, if not in your cause, at least in His own. When, then, the world at length becomes sensible that it is faring ill, and receiving more harm than it inflicts, yet is unwilling to humble itself under the mighty hand of God, what is left but to attribute its failure to the power of those who seem to be weak? that is, to their craft, who pretend to be weak when really they are strong.

6. To this must be added, that the truth has in itself the gift of spreading, without instruments; it makes its way in the world, under God's blessing, by its own persuasiveness and excellence; "So is the kingdom of God," says our Lord, "as if a man should cast seed into the ground, and should sleep, and rise night and day, and the seed should spring and grow up, he *knoweth not* how."[9] The Word, when once uttered, runs its course. He who speaks it has done his work in uttering it, and cannot recall it if he would. It runs its course; it prospers in the thing whereunto God sends it. It seizes many souls at once, and subdues them to the obedience of faith. Now when bystanders see these effects and see no cause, for they will not believe that the Word itself is the cause, which is to them a dead-letter—when it sees many minds moved in one way in many places, it imputes to secret management that uniformity which is nothing but the echo of the One Living and True Word.

7. And of course all this happens to the surprise of Christians as well as of the world; they can but marvel and praise God, but cannot account for it more than the world. "When the Lord turned again the captivity of Sion," says the Psalmist, "then were we like unto them that dream."[10] Or as the Prophet says of the Church, "Thine heart shall fear and be enlarged; because the abundance of the sea shall be converted unto thee, the forces of the Gentiles shall come unto thee."[11] and here again the Christian's true wisdom looks like craft. It is true wisdom to leave the event to God; but when they are prospered, it looks like deceit to show surprise, and to disclaim the work themselves. Moreover, meekness, gentleness, patience, and love, have in themselves a strong power to melt the heart of those who witness them. Cheerful suffering, too, leads spectators to sympathy, till, perhaps, a reaction takes place in the minds of men, and they are converted by the sight, and glorify their Father which is in heaven. But it is easy to insinuate, when men are malevolent, that those who triumph through meekness have affected the meekness to secure the triumph.

8. Here a very large subject opens upon us, to which I shall but allude. Those who surrender themselves to Christ in implicit faith are graciously taken into His service; and, "as men under authority," they do great things without knowing it, by the Wisdom of their Divine Master. They act on conscience, perhaps in despondency, and without foresight; but what is obedience in them, has a purpose with God, and they are successful, when they do but mean to be dutiful. But what duplicity does the world think it, to speak of conscience, or honour, or propriety, or delicacy, or to give other tokens of personal motives, when the event seems to show that a calculation of results has been the actuating principle at bottom! It is God who designs, but His servants seem designing; and that the more, should it so happen that they really do themselves catch glimpses of their own position in His providential course. For then what they do from the heart, approves itself to their reason, and they are able to recognize the expedience of obedience.

How frequently is this remark in point in the history—nay, in the very constitution of the Church! Jacob, for instance, is thought worldly-wise in his dealings with Laban, whereas he was a "plain man," simply obedient to the Angel who "spake unto him in a dream," who took care of his worldly interests for him, and protected him against his avaricious kinsman. Moses, again, is sometimes called sagacious and shrewd in his measures or his laws, as if wise acts might not come from the Source of wisdom, and provisions were proved to be human, when they could be shown to be advisable. And so, again, in the Christian Church, bishops have been called hypocritical in submitting and yet opposing themselves to the civil power, in a matter of plain duty, if a popular movement was the consequence; and then hypocritical again, if they did their best to repress it. And in like manner, theological doctrines or ecclesiastical usages are styled politic if they are but salutary; as if the Lord of the Church, who has willed her sovereignty, might

---

[9] Mark 4:26, 27.   [10] Ps. 126:1.   [11] Isa. 60:5.

not effect it by secondary causes. What, for instance, though we grant that sacramental confession and the celibacy of the clergy do tend to consolidate the body politic in the relation of rulers and subjects, or, in other words, to aggrandize the priesthood? for how can the Church be one body without such relation, and why should not He, who had decreed that there should be unity, take measures to secure it? Marks of design are not elsewhere assumed as disproofs of His interference. Why should not the Creator, who has given us the feeling of hunger that we may eat and not die, and sentiments of compassion and benevolence for the welfare of our brethren, when He would form a more integral power than mankind had yet seen, adopt adequate means, and use His old world to create a new one? and why must His human instruments set out with a purpose, because they accomplish one? Nothing is safe in Revelation on such an interpretation. As the expedience of its provisions is made an objection to their honesty, so the beauty of its facts becomes an argument against their truth. The narratives in the Gospels have lately been viewed as mythical representations from their very perfection; as if a Divine work could not be most beautiful on the one hand and most expedient on the other.

The reason is this: men do not like to hear of the interposition of Providence in the affairs of the world; and they invidiously ascribe ability and skill to His agents, to escape the thought of an Infinite Wisdom and an Almighty Power. They will be unjust to their brethren, that they may not be just to Him; they will be wanton in their imputations, rather than humble themselves to a confession.

But for us, let us glory in what they disown; let us beg of our Divine Lord to take to Him His great power, and manifest Himself more and more, and reign both in our hearts and in the world. Let us beg of Him to stand by us in trouble, and guide us on our dangerous way. May He, as of old, choose "the foolish things of the world to confound the wise, and the weak things of the world to confound the things which are mighty"! May He support us all the day long, till the shades lengthen, and the evening comes, and the busy world is hushed, and the fever of life is over, and our work is done! Then in His mercy may He give us a safe lodging, and a holy rest, and peace at the last!

from Tract XC

This, the last of the Tracts for the Times, *appeared in 1841 and provoked a storm of controversy for its argument that the Thirty-nine Articles of the Church of England were susceptible of a Catholic interpretation. The censure of the tract led to Newman's withdrawal from Oxford life, which in turn presaged his eventual shift of allegiance to Rome. The introduction and conclusion of the tract are given below; the body of the essay is a point-by-point consideration of each of the thirty-nine Articles of Religion commonly affixed to the Book of Common Prayer. The text below is that of the second edition with Newman's notes and with his additions to the first edition in brackets.*

Introduction

IT IS often urged, and sometimes felt and granted, that there are in the Articles propositions or terms inconsistent with the Catholic faith; or, at least, when persons do not go so far as to feel the objection as of force, they are perplexed how best to reply to it, or how most simply to explain the passages on which it is made to rest. The following Tract is drawn up with the view of showing how groundless the objection is, and further of approximating towards the argumentative answer to it, of which most men have an implicit apprehension, though they may have nothing more. That there are real difficulties to a Catholic Christian in the Ecclesiastical position of our Church at this day, no one can deny; but the statements of the Articles are not in the number; and it may be right at the present moment to insist upon this. If in any quarter it is supposed that persons who profess to be disciples of the early Church will silently concur with those of very opposite sentiments in furthering a relaxation of subscriptions, which, it is imagined, are galling to both parties, though for different reasons, and that they will do this against the wish of the great body of the Church, the writer of the following pages would raise one voice, at least, in protest against any such anticipation. Even in such points as he may think the English Church deficient, never can he, without a great alteration of sentiment, be party to forcing the opinion or project of one school upon another. Religious changes, to be beneficial, should be the act of the whole body; they are worth little if they are the mere act of a majority.[1] No good can come of any change which is not heartfelt, a development of feelings springing up freely and calmly within the bosom of the whole body itself. Moreover, a change in theological teaching involves either the commission or the confession of sin; it is either the profession or renunciation of erroneous doctrine, and if it does not succeed in proving the fact of past guilt, it, *ipso facto*, implies present. In other words, every change in religion carries with it its own condemnation, which is not attended by deep repentance. Even supposing then that any changes in contemplation, whatever they were, were good in themselves, they would cease to be good to a Church, in which they were the fruits not of the quiet conviction of all, but of the agitation, or tyranny, or intrigue of a few; nurtured not in mutual love, but in strife and envying; perfected not in humiliation and grief, but in pride, elation, and triumph. Moreover, it is a very serious truth, that persons and bodies who put themselves into a disadvantageous state, cannot at their pleasure extricate themselves from it. They are unworthy of it; they are in prison, and CHRIST is the keeper. There is but one way towards a real reformation,—a return to Him in heart and spirit, whose sacred truth they have betrayed; all other methods, however fair they may promise, will prove to be but shadows and failures.

On these grounds, were there no others, the present writer, for one, will be no party to the ordinary political methods by which professed reforms are carried or compassed in this day. We can do nothing well till we act "with one accord;" we can have no accord in action till we agree together in heart; we cannot agree without a supernatural influence; we cannot have a supernatural influence unless we pray for it; we cannot pray acceptably without repentance and confession. Our Church's strength would be irresistible, humanly speaking, were it but at unity with itself: if it remains divided, part against part, we shall see the energy which was meant to subdue the world preying upon itself, according to our SAVIOUR's express assurance, that such a house "cannot stand." Till we feel this, till we seek one another as brethren, not lightly throwing aside our private opinions, which we seem to feel we have received from above, from an ill-regulated, untrue desire of unity, but returning to each other in heart, and coming together to GOD to do for us what we cannot do for ourselves, no change can be for the better. Till [we] [her children] are stirred up to this religious course, let the Church,[2] [our Mother,] sit still; let [us] be content to be in bondage; let [us] work in chains; let [us] submit to [our] imperfections as a punishment; let [us] go on teaching [through the medium of indeterminate statements[3]] and inconsistent precedents, and principles but partially developed. We are not better than our fathers; let us bear to be what Hammond was, or Andrews, or Hooker; let us not faint under that body of death, which they bore about in patience; nor shrink from the penalty of sins, which they inherited from the age before them.[4]

But these remarks are beyond our present scope, which is merely to show that, while our Prayer Book is acknowledged on all hands to be

---

[1] This is not meant to hinder acts of Catholic consent, such as occurred anciently, when the Catholic body aids one portion of a particular Church against another portion.

[2] "Let the Church sit still; let her be content to be in bondage," &c.—1st edition. [The author has lately heard that these words have been taken as spoken in an insulting and reproachful tone; he meant them in the sense of the lines in the Lyra Apostolica,—

> "Bide thou thy time!
> Watch with meek eyes the race of pride and crime:
> Sit in the gate and be the heathen's jest,
> Smiling and self-possest," &c.—3rd edition.]

[3] "With the stammering lips."—1st edition.

[4] "We, Thy sinful creatures," says the Service for King Charles the Martyr, "here assembled before Thee, do, in behalf of all the people of this land, humbly confess, that they were the *crying sins* of this nation, which brought down this judgment upon us," i.e. King Charles's murder.

of Catholic origin, our Articles also, the offspring of an uncatholic age, are, through GOD's good providence, to say the least, not uncatholic, and may be subscribed by those who aim at being catholic in heart and doctrine. . . .

Conclusion

ONE remark may be made in conclusion. It may be objected that the tenor of the above explanations is anti-Protestant, whereas it is notorious that the Articles were drawn up by Protestants, and intended for the establishment of Protestantism; accordingly, that it is an evasion of their meaning to give them any other than a Protestant drift, possible as it may be to do so grammatically, or in each separate part.

But the answer is simple:

1. In the first place, it is a *duty* which we owe both to the Catholic Church and to our own, to take our reformed confessions in the most Catholic sense they will admit; we have no duties toward their framers. [Nor do we receive the Articles from their original framers, but from several successive convocations after their time; in the last instance, from that of 1662.]

2. In giving the Articles a Catholic interpretation, we bring them into harmony with the Book of Common Prayer, an object of the most serious moment in those who have given their assent to both formularies.

3. Whatever be the authority of the [Declaration] prefixed to the Articles, so far as it has any weight at all, it sanctions the mode of interpreting them above given. For its enjoining the "literal and grammatical sense," relieves us from the necessity of making the known opinions of their framers, a comment upon their text; and its forbidding any person to "affix any *new* sense to any Article," was promulgated at a time when the leading men of our Church were especially noted for those Catholic views which have been here advocated.

4. It may be remarked, moreover, that such an interpretation is in accordance with the well-known general leaning of Melanchthon, from whose writings our Articles are principally drawn, and whose Catholic tendencies gained for him that same reproach of popery, which has ever been so freely bestowed upon members of our own reformed Church.

"Melanchthon was of opinion," says Mosheim, "that, for the sake of peace and concord, many things might be given up and tolerated in the Church of Rome, which Luther considered could by no means be endured. . . . In the class of matters indifferent, this great man and his associates placed many things which had appeared of the highest importance to Luther, and could not of consequence be considered as indifferent by his true disciples. For he regarded as such, the doctrine of justification by faith alone; the necessity of good works to eternal salvation; the number of the sacraments; the jurisdiction claimed by the Pope and the Bishops; extreme unction; the observation of certain religious festivals, and several superstitious rites and ceremonies."—*Cent.* XVI. § 3, part 2. 27, 28.

5. Further: the Articles are evidently framed on the principle of leaving open large questions, on which the controversy hinges. They state broadly extreme truths, and are silent about their adjustment. For instance, they say that all necessary faith must be proved from Scripture, but do not say *who* is to prove it. They say that the Church has authority in controversies, they do not say *what* authority. They say that it may enforce nothing beyond Scripture, but do not say *where* the remedy lies when it does. They say that works *before* grace *and* justification are worthless and worse, and that works *after* grace *and* justification are acceptable, but they do not speak at all of works *with* GOD's aid, *before* justification. They say that men are lawfully called and sent to minister and preach, who are chosen and called by men who have public authority *given* them in the congregation to call and send; but they do not add *by whom* the authority is to be given. They say that councils called *by princes* may err; they do not determine whether councils called *in the name of* CHRIST will err.

[6. The variety of doctrinal views contained in the Homilies, as above shown, views which cannot be brought under Protestantism itself, in its widest comprehension of opinions, is an additional proof, considering the connexion of the Articles with the Homilies, that the Articles are not framed on the principle of excluding those who prefer the theology of the early ages to that of the Reformation; or rather since both Homilies and Articles appeal to the Fathers and Catholic antiquity, let it be considered whether, in interpreting them by these, we are not going to the very authority to which they profess to submit themselves.]

7. Lastly, their framers constructed them in such a way as best to comprehend those who did not go so far in Protestantism as themselves.

Anglo-Catholics then are but the successors and representatives of those moderate reformers; and their case has been directly anticipated in the wording of the Articles. It follows that they are not perverting, they are using them, for an express purpose for which among others their authors framed them. The interpretation they take was intended to be admissible; though not that which their authors took themselves. Had it not been provided for, possibly the Articles never would have been accepted by our Church at all. If, then, their framers have gained their side of the compact in effecting the reception of the Articles, the Catholics have theirs too in retaining their own Catholic interpretation of them.

An illustration of this occurs in the history of the 28th Article. In the beginning of Elizabeth's reign a paragraph formed part of it, much like that which is now appended to the Communion Service, but in which the Real Presence was *denied in words*. It was adopted by the clergy at the first convocation, but not published. Burnet observes on it thus:—

"When these Articles were first prepared by the convocation in Queen Elizabeth's reign, this paragraph was made a part of them; for the original subscription by both houses of convocation, yet extant, shows this. But the *design of the government* was at that time much turned *to the drawing over the body of the nation to the Reformation*, in whom the old leaven had gone deep; and no part of it deeper than the belief of the corporeal presence of CHRIST in the Sacrament; therefore it was *thought not expedient* to *offend* them by so particular a definition in this matter; in which the very word Real Presence was rejected. It might, perhaps, be also suggested, that here a definition was made that went too much upon the principles of natural philosophy; which, how true soever, they might not be the proper subject of an article of religion. Therefore it was thought fit to suppress this paragraph; though it was a part of the Article that was subscribed, yet it was not published, but the paragraph that follows, 'The Body of CHRIST,' &c., was put in its stead, and was received and pub-

lished by the next convocation; which upon the matter was a full explanation of the way of CHRIST'S presence in this Sacrament; that 'He is present in a heavenly and spiritual manner, and that faith is the mean by which He is received.' This seemed to be more theological; and it does indeed amount to the same thing. But howsoever we see what was the sense of the first convocation in Queen Elizabeth's reign, it differed in nothing from that in King Edward's time; and therefore though this paragraph is now no part of our Articles, yet we are certain that the clergy at that time did not at all doubt of the truth of it; we are sure it was their opinion; since they subscribed it, though *they did not think fit* to publish it at first; and though it was afterwards changed for another, that was the same in sense."—*Burnet on Article* XXVIII., p. 416.

What lately has taken place in the political world will afford an illustration in point. A French minister, desirous of war, nevertheless, as a matter of policy, draws up his state papers in such moderate language, that his successor, who is for peace, can act up to them, without compromising his own principles. The world, observing this, has considered it a circumstance for congratulation; as if the former minister, who acted a double part, had been caught in his own snare. It is neither decorous, nor necessary, nor altogether fair, to urge the parallel rigidly; but it will explain what it is here meant to convey. The Protestant Confession was drawn up with the purpose of including Catholics; and Catholics now will not be excluded. What was an economy in the reformers, is a protection to us. What would have been a perplexity to us then, is a perplexity to Protestants now. We could not then have found fault with their words; they cannot now repudiate our meaning.

[J. H. N.]

OXFORD,
The Feast of the Conversion of St. Paul,
1841.

The Parting of Friends

The following address was Newman's farewell sermon at Littlemore, delivered in 1843 as he resigned his living at St. Mary's, and with it Littlemore, to retire into semi-monastic contemplation and study at his retreat called "The College" in Littlemore. The specific occasion was the consecration of the redesigned chapel at Littlemore. In the congregation at the time were many of the other principals of the Oxford Movement who knew the sermon to be Newman's farewell to the Church of England. It was his last public sermon as an Anglican; it was published in Sermons on Subjects of the Day *in 1844. (The notes to biblical allusions and the ellipses in the text are Newman's.)*

"Man goeth forth to his work and to his labour until the evening."—
Ps. 104:23.

WHEN the Son of Man, the First-born of the creation of God, came to the evening of His mortal life, He parted with His disciples at a feast. He had borne "the burden and heat of the day;" yet, when "wearied with His journey," He had but stopped at the well's side, and asked a draught of water for His thirst; for He had "meat to eat which" others "knew not of." His meat was "to do the will of Him that sent Him, and to finish His work;" "I must work the works of Him that sent Me," said He, "while it is day; the night cometh, when no man can work."[1] Thus passed the season of His ministry; and if at any time He feasted with Pharisee or publican, it was in order that He might do the work of God more strenuously. But "when the even was come He sat down with the Twelve." "And He said unto them, With desire have I desired to eat this Passover with you, before I suffer."[2] He was about to suffer more than man had ever suffered or shall suffer. But there is nothing gloomy, churlish, violent, or selfish in His grief; it is tender, affectionate, social. He calls His friends around Him, though He was as Job among the ashes; He bids them stay by Him, and see Him suffer; He desires their sympathy; He takes refuge in their love. He first feasted them, and sung a hymn with them, and washed their feet; and when his long trial began, He beheld them and kept them in His presence, till they in terror shrank from it. Yet, on St. Mary and St. John, His Virgin Mother and His Virgin Disciple, who remained, His eyes still rested; and in St. Peter, who was denying Him in the distance, His sudden glance wrought a deep repentance. O wonderful pattern, the type of all trial and of all duty under it, while the Church endures.

We indeed to-day have no need of so high a lesson and so august a comfort. We have no pain, no grief which calls for it; yet, considering it has been brought before us in this morning's service,[3] we are naturally drawn to think of it, though it be infinitely above us, under certain circumstances of this season and the present time. For now are the shades of evening falling upon the earth, and the year's labour is coming to its end. In Septuagesima the labourers were sent into the vineyard; in Sexagesima the sower went forth to sow;— that time is over; "the harvest is passed, the summer is ended,"[4] the vintage is gathered. We have kept the Ember-days for the fruits of the earth, in self-abasement, as being unworthy even of the least of God's mercies; and now we are offering up of its corn and wine as a propitiation, and are eating and drinking of them with thanksgiving.

"All things come of Thee, and of Thine own have we given Thee."[5] If we have had the rain in its season, and the sun shining in its strength, and the fertile ground, it is of Thee. We give back to Thee what came from Thee. "When Thou givest it them, they gather it, and when Thou openest Thy hand, they are filled with good. When Thou hidest Thy face, they are troubled; when Thou takest away their breath, they die, and are turned again to their dust. When Thou lettest Thy breath go forth, they shall be made, and Thou shalt renew the face of the earth."[6] He gives, He takes away. "Shall we receive good at the hand of God, and shall we not receive evil?"[7] May He not "do what He will with His own?"[8] May not His sun set as it has risen? and must it not set, if it is to rise again? and must not darkness come first, if there is ever to be morning? and must not the sky be blacker, before it can be brighter? And cannot He, who can do all things cause a light to arise even in the darkness? "I have thought upon Thy Name, O Lord, in the night season, and have kept Thy Law;" "Thou also shalt light my candle, the Lord my God shall make my darkness to be light;" or as the Prophet speaks, "At the evening time it shall be light."[9]

"All things come of Thee," says holy David, "for we are strangers before Thee and sojourners, as were all our fathers; our days on the earth are as a shadow, and there is none abiding."[10] All is vanity, vanity of vanities, and vexation of spirit.

---

[1] John 4:6. 34; 9:4.   [2] Matt. 26:20. Luke 22:15.   [3] Sept. 25, 1843.   [4] Jer. 8:20.
[5] I Chron. 29:14.   [6] Ps. 104:28–30.   [7] Job 2:10.   [8] Matt. 20:15.
[9] Zech. 14:7.   [10] I Chron. 29:15.

"What profit hath a man of all his labour which he taketh under the sun? One generation passeth away, and another generation cometh; but the earth abideth for ever; the sun also ariseth, and the sun goeth down; . . . all things are full of labour, man cannot utter it; . . . that which is crooked cannot be made straight, and that which is wanting cannot be numbered."[11] "To every thing there is a season, and a time to every purpose under heaven; a time to be born and a time to die; a time to plant and a time to pluck up that which is planted; a time to kill and a time to heal; a time to break down and a time to build up; . . . a time to get and a time to lose; a time to keep and a time to cast away."[12] And time, and matter, and motion, and force, and the will of man, how vain are they all, except as instruments of the grace of God, blessing them and working with them! How vain are all our pains, our thought, our care, unless God uses them, unless God has inspired them! how worse than fruitless are they, unless directed to His glory, and given back to the Giver!

"Of Thine own have we given Thee," says the royal Psalmist, after he had collected materials for the Temple. Because "the work was great," and "the palace, not for man, but for the Lord God," therefore he "prepared with all his might for the house of his God," gold, and silver, and brass, and iron, and wood, "onyx stones, and stones to be set, glistering stones, and of divers colours, and all manner of precious stones, and marble stones in abundance."[13] And "the people rejoiced, for that they offered willingly; . . . and David the king also rejoiced with great joy." We too, at this season, year by year, have been allowed in our measure, according to our work and our faith, to rejoice in God's Presence, for this sacred building which He has given us to worship Him in. It was a glad time when we first met here,—many of us now present recollect it; nor did our rejoicing cease, but was renewed every autumn, as the day came round. It has been "a day of gladness and feasting, and a good day, and of sending portions one to another."[14] We have kept the feast heretofore with merry hearts; we have kept it seven full years unto "a perfect end;" now let us keep it, even though in haste, and with bitter herbs, and with loins girded, and with a staff in our hand, as they who have "no continuing city, but seek one to come."[15]

So was it with Jacob, when with his staff he passed over that Jordan. He too kept feast before he set out upon his dreary way. He received a father's blessing, and then was sent afar; he left his mother, never to see her face or hear her voice again. He parted with all that his heart loved, and turned his face towards a strange land. He went with the doubt, whether he should have bread to eat, or raiment to put on. He came to "the people of the East," and served a hard master twenty years. "In the day the drought consumed him, and the frost by night; and his sleep departed from his eyes."[16] O little did he think, when father and mother had forsaken him, and at Bethel he lay down to sleep on the desolate ground, because the sun was set and even had come, that there was the house of God and the gate of heaven, that the Lord was in that place, and would thence go forward with him whithersoever he went, till He brought him back to that river in "two bands," who was then crossing it forlorn and solitary!

So had it been with Ishmael; though the feast was not to him a blessing, yet he feasted in his father's tent, and then was sent away. That tender father, who, when a son was promised him of Sarah, cried out to his Almighty Protector, "O that Ishmael might live before Thee!"[17]—he it was, who, under a divine direction, the day after the feast, "rose up early in the morning, and took bread, and a bottle of water, and gave it unto Hagar, putting it on her shoulder, and the child, and sent her away. And she departed, and wandered in the wilderness of Beersheba."[18] And little thought that fierce child, when for feasting came thirst and weariness and wandering in the desert, that this was not the end of Ishmael, but the beginning. And little did Hagar read his coming fortunes, when "the water was spent in the bottle, and she cast the child under one of the shrubs, and she went and sat down over against him a good way off; . . . for she said, Let me not see the death of the child. And she sat over against him, and lift up her voice, and wept."

So had it been with Naomi, though she was not quitting, but returning to her home, and going, not to a land of famine, but of plenty. In a time of distress, she had left her country, and found friends and made relatives among the enemies of her people. And when her husband and her children died, Moabitish women, who had once been the stumbling-block of Israel, became the support and comfort of her widowhood. Time had been

---

[11] Eccles. 1:3–15.   [12] Eccles. 3:1–6.   [13] 1 Chron. 29:1, 2, 9.   [14] Esther 9:19.
[15] Heb. 13:14.   [16] Gen. 31:40.   [17] Gen. 17:18.   [18] Gen. 21:14.

when, at the call of the daughters of Moab, the chosen people had partaken their sacrifices, and "bowed down to their gods. And Israel joined himself unto Baal-peor, and the anger of the Lord was kindled against Israel." Centuries had since passed away, and now of Moabites was Naomi mother; and to their land had she given her heart, when the call of duty summoned her back to Bethlehem. "She had heard in the country of Moab, how that the Lord had visited His people in giving them bread. Wherefore she went forth out of the place where she was, and her two daughters-in-law with her, and they went on the way to return unto the land of Judah."[19]

Forlorn widow, great was the struggle in her bosom, whether shall she do?—leave behind her the two heathen women, in widowhood and weakness like herself, her sole stay, the shadows of departed blessings? or shall she selfishly take them as fellow-sufferers, who could not be protectors? Shall she seek sympathy where she cannot gain help? shall she deprive them of a home, when she has none to supply? So she said, "Go, return each to her mother's house: the Lord deal kindly with you, as ye have dealt with the dead and with me!" Perplexed Naomi, torn with contrary feelings; which tried her the more, —Orpah who left her, or Ruth who remained? Orpah who was a pain, or Ruth who was a charge? "They lifted up their voice and wept again; and Orpah kissed her mother-in-law, but Ruth clave unto her. And she said, Behold, thy sister-in-law is gone back unto her people and unto her gods; return thou after thy sister-in-law. And Ruth said, Entreat me not to leave thee, or to return from following after thee: for whither thou goest, I will go; and where thou lodgest, I will lodge: thy people shall be my people, and thy God my God. Where thou diest, will I die, and there will I be buried; the Lord do so to me, and more also, if aught but death part thee and me."[20]

Orpah kissed Naomi, and went back to the world. There was sorrow in the parting, but Naomi's sorrow was more for Orpah's sake than for her own. Pain there would be, but it was the pain of a wound, not the yearning regret of love. It was the pain we feel when friends disappoint us, and fall in our esteem. That kiss of Orpah was no loving token; it was but the hollow profession of those who use smooth words, that they may part company with us with least trouble and dis-

comfort to themselves. Orpah's tears were but the dregs of affection; she clasped her mother-in-law once for all, that she might not cleave to her. Far different were the tears, far different the embrace, which passed between those two religious friends recorded in the book which follows, who loved each other with a true love unfeigned, but whose lives ran in different courses. If Naomi's grief was great when Orpah kissed her, what was David's when he saw the last of him, whose "soul had from the first been knit with his soul," so that "he loved him as his own soul"?[21] "I am distressed for thee, my brother Jonathan," he says; "very pleasant hast thou been unto me; thy love to me was wonderful, passing the love of women."[22] What woe was upon that "young man," "of a beautiful countenance and goodly to look to," and "cunning in playing, and a mighty valiant man, and a man of war, and prudent in matters;"[23] when his devoted affectionate loyal friend, whom these good gifts have gained, looked upon him for the last time! O hard destiny, except that the All-merciful so willed it, that such companions might not walk in the house of God as friends! David must flee to the wilderness, Jonathan must pine in his father's hall; Jonathan must share that stern father's death in battle, and David must ascend the vacant throne. Yet they made a covenant on parting: "Thou shalt not only," said Jonathan, "while yet I live, show me the kindness of the Lord, that I die not; but also thou shalt not cut off thy kindness from my house for ever; no, not when the Lord hath cut off the enemies of David, every one from the face of the earth. . . . And Jonathan caused David to swear again, because he loved him, for he loved him as he loved his own soul." And then, while David hid himself, Jonathan made trial of Saul, how he felt disposed to David; and when he found that "it was determined of his father to slay David," he "arose from the table in fierce anger, and did eat no meat the second day of the month; for he was grieved for David, because his father had done him shame." Then in the morning he went out into the field, where David lay, and the last meeting took place between the two. "David arose out of a place toward the south, and fell on his face to the ground, and bowed himself three times; and they kissed one another, and wept one with another, till David exceeded. And Jonathan said to David, Go in peace, forasmuch as we have sworn both of us in the Name of the Lord, saying,

[19] Ruth 1:6–8, 14, 15.   [20] Ruth 1:14–17.   [21] 1 Sam. 18:1–3.
[22] 2 Sam. 1:26.   [23] 1 Sam. 16:12, 18.

The Lord be between me and thee, and between my seed and thy seed for ever. And he arose and departed; and Jonathan went into the city."[24]

David's affection was given to a single heart; but there is another spoken of in Scripture, who had a thousand friends and loved each as his own soul, and seemed to live a thousand lives in them, and died a thousand deaths when he must quit them: that great Apostle, whose very heart was broken when his brethren wept; who "lived if they stood fast in the Lord;" who "was glad when he was weak and they were strong;" and who was "willing to have imparted unto them his own soul, because they were dear unto him."[25] Yet we read of his bidding farewell to whole Churches, never to see them again. At one time, to the little ones of the flock; "When we had accomplished those days," says the Evangelist, "we departed, and went our way, . . . with wives and children, till we were out of the city; and we kneeled down on the shore and prayed. And when we had taken our leave one of another, we took ship, and they returned home again." At another time, to the rulers of the Church: "And now behold," he says to them, "I know that ye all, among whom I have gone preaching the kingdom of God, shall see my face no more. Wherefore, I take you to record this day, that I am pure from the blood of all men, for I have not shunned to declare unto you all the counsel of God. . . . I have coveted no man's silver, or gold, or apparel; . . . I have showed you all things, how that so labouring he ought to support the weak; and to remember the words of the Lord Jesus, how he said, It is more blessed to give than to receive." And then, when he had finished, "he kneeled down, and prayed with them all. And they all wept sore, and fell on Paul's neck, and kissed him; sorrowing most of all for the words which he spake, that they should see his face no more. And they accompanied him unto the ship."[26]

There was another time, when he took leave of his "own son in the faith," Timothy, in words more calm, and still more impressive, when his end was nigh: "I am now ready to be offered," he says, "and the time of my departure is at hand. I have fought a good fight, I have finished my course, I have kept the faith. Henceforth there is laid up for me a crown of righteousness, which the Lord, the Righteous Judge, shall give me at that day."[27]

And what are all these instances but memorials and tokens of the Son of Man, when His work and His labour were coming to an end? Like Jacob, like Ishmael, like Elisha, like the Evangelist whose day is just passed, He kept feast before His departure; and, like David, He was persecuted by the rulers in Israel; and, like Naomi, He was deserted by His friends; and, like Ishmael, He cried out, "I thirst" in a barren and dry land; and at length, like Jacob, He went to sleep with a stone for His pillow, in the evening. And, like St. Paul, He had "finished the work which God gave Him to do," and had "witnessed a good confession;" and, beyond St. Paul, "the Prince of this world had come, and had nothing in Him."[28] "He was in the world, and the world was made by Him, and the world knew Him not. He came unto His own, and His own received Him not."[29] Heavily did He leave, tenderly did He mourn over the country and city which rejected Him. "When He was come near, He beheld the city, and wept over it, saying, If thou hadst known, even thou, at least in this thy day, the things which belong unto thy peace! but now they are hid from thine eyes." And again: "O Jerusalem, Jerusalem, which killest the prophets, and stonest them that are sent unto thee, how often would I have gathered thy children together, as a hen doth gather her brood under her wings, and ye would not! Behold, your house is left unto you desolate."[30]

A lesson surely, and a warning to us all, in every place where He puts His Name, to the end of time; lest we be cold towards His gifts, or unbelieving towards His word, or jealous of His workings, or heartless towards His mercies. . . . O mother of saints! O school of the wise! O nurse of the heroic! of whom went forth, in whom have dwelt, memorable names of old, to spread the truth abroad, or to cherish and illustrate it at home! O thou, from whom surrounding nations lit their lamps! O virgin of Israel! wherefore dost thou now sit on the ground and keep silence, like one of the foolish women who were without oil on the coming of the Bridegroom? Where is now the ruler in Sion, and the doctor in the Temple, and the ascetic on Carmel, and the herald in the wilderness, and the preacher in the market-place? where are thy "effectual fervent prayers," offered in secret, and thy alms and good works coming up as a memorial before God?

---

[24] I Sam. 20:14–42.   [25] Acts 21:21, 22. I Thess. 2:8; 3:8. 2 Cor. 14:9.
[26] Acts 21:5, 6; 20:25–27. 33. 35, 36–38.   [27] 2 Tim. 4:6–8.   [28] I Tim. 6:13. John 14:30.
[29] John 1:10, 11.   [30] Luke 19:41, 42; 13:34, 35.

How is it, O once holy place, that "the land mourneth, for the corn is wasted, the new wine is dried up, the oil languisheth, . . . because joy is withered away from the sons of men?" "Alas for the day! . . . how do the beasts groan! the herds of cattle are perplexed, because they have no pasture, yea, the flocks of sheep are made desolate." "Lebanon is ashamed and hewn down; Sharon is like a wilderness, and Bashan and Carmel shake off their fruits."[31] O my mother, whence is this unto thee, that thou hast good things poured upon thee and canst not keep them, and bearest children, yet darest not own them? why hast thou not the skill to use their services, nor the heart to rejoice in their love? how is it that whatever is generous in purpose, and tender or deep in devotion, thy flower and thy promise, falls from thy bosom and finds no home within thine arms? Who hath put this note upon thee, to have "a miscarrying womb, and dry breasts," to be strange to thine own flesh, and thine eye cruel towards thy little ones? Thine own offspring, the fruit of thy womb, who love thee and would toil for thee, thou dost gaze upon with fear, as though a portent, or thou dost loathe as an offence;—at best thou dost but endure, as if they had no claim but on thy patience, self-possession, and vigilance, to be rid of them as easily as thou mayest. Thou makest them "stand all the day idle," as the very condition of thy bearing with them; or thou biddest them be gone, where they will be more welcome; or thou sellest them for nought to the stranger that passes by. And what wilt thou do in the end thereof? . . .

Scripture is a refuge in any trouble; only let us be on our guard against seeming to use it further than is fitting, or doing more than sheltering ourselves under its shadow. Let us use it according to our measure. It is far higher and wider than our need; and its language veils our feelings while it gives expression to them. It is sacred and heavenly; and it restrains and purifies, while it sanctions them.

And now, my brethren, "bless God, praise Him and magnify Him, and praise Him for the things which He hath done unto you in the sight of all that live. It is good to praise God, and exalt His Name, and honourably to show forth the works of God; therefore be not slack to praise Him." "All the works of the Lord are good; and He will give every needful thing in due season; so that a man cannot say, This is worse than that; for in time they shall all be well approved. And therefore praise ye the Lord with the whole heart and mouth, and bless the Name of the Lord."[32]

"Leave off from wrath, and let go displeasure; flee from evil, and do the thing that is good." "Do that which is good, and no evil shall touch you." "Go your way; eat your bread with joy, and drink your wine with a merry heart, for God now accepteth your works; let your garments be always white, and let your head lack no ointment."[33]

And, O my brethren, O kind and affectionate hearts, O loving friends, should you know any one whose lot it has been, by writing or by word of mouth, in some degree to help you thus to act; if he has ever told you what you knew about yourselves, or what you did not know; has read to you your wants or feelings, and comforted you by the very reading; has made you feel that there was a higher life than this daily one, and a brighter world than that you see; or encouraged you, or sobered you, or opened a way to the inquiring, or soothed the perplexed; if what he has said or done has ever made you take interest in him, and feel well inclined towards him; remember such a one in time to come, though you hear him not, and pray for him, that in all things he may know God's will, and at all times he may be ready to fulfil it.

from The Idea of a University

As Rector of the proposed Catholic University of Dublin from 1851 to 1858 Newman delivered a series of lectures on his views of what a university should be. The lectures failed to win the support of Irish Catholics for the proposed university but when published as The Idea of a

[31] Joel 1:10–18. Isa. 33:9.   [32] Tob. 12:6. Ecclus. 39:33–35.
[33] Ps. 37:8. 27. Tob. 12:7. Eccles. 9:7. 8.

University *in* 1852 *they established themselves as one of the most eloquent statements of the aims of education ever presented. The discourses that constitute the* Idea *were variously numbered and organized in subsequent editions, but the final organization of the work into nine discourses and ten occasional lectures (of which the later selections "Christianity and Letters" and "Literature" are examples) has been the established one since* 1873. *The nine discourses form a coherent whole that argues the case for the fullness of a university education in terms of the cultivation of the intellect. The most celebrated of the discourses, Discourse V, "Knowledge Its Own End," is given below, along with Discourse VII, "Knowledge Viewed in Relation to Professional Skill," as being the two selections from the* Idea *most applicable to the continuing twentieth century debate on the aims of education. (Notes supplied by Newman are marked* [N].*)*

DISCOURSE V

Knowledge Its Own End

A UNIVERSITY may be considered with reference either to its Students or to its Studies; and the principle, that all Knowledge is a whole and the separate Sciences parts of one, which I have hitherto been using in behalf of its studies, is equally important when we direct our attention to its students. Now then I turn to the students, and shall consider the education which, by virtue of this principle, a University will give them; and thus I shall be introduced, Gentlemen, to the second question, which I proposed to discuss, viz, whether and in what sense its teaching, viewed relatively to the taught, carries the attribute of Utility along with it.

1

I have said that all branches of knowledge are connected together, because the subject-matter of knowledge is intimately united in itself, as being the acts and the work of the Creator. Hence it is that the Sciences, into which our knowledge may be said to be cast, have multiplied bearings one on another, and an internal sympathy, and admit, or rather demand, comparison and adjustment. They complete, correct, balance each other. This consideration, if well-founded, must be taken into account, not only as regards the attainment of truth, which is their common end, but as regards the influence which they exercise upon those whose education consists in the study of them. I have said already, that to give undue prominence to one is to be unjust to another; to neglect or supersede these

is to divert those from their proper object. It is to unsettle the boundary lines between science and science, to disturb their action, to destroy the harmony which binds them together. Such a proceeding will have a corresponding effect when introduced into a place of education. There is no science but tells a different tale, when viewed as a portion of a whole, from what it is likely to suggest when taken by itself, without the safeguard, as I may call it, of others.

Let me make use of an illustration. In the combination of colours, very different effects are produced by a difference in their selection and juxta-position; red, green, and white, change their shades, according to the contrast to which they are submitted. And, in like manner, the drift and meaning of a branch of knowledge varies with the company in which it is introduced to the student. If his reading is confined simply to one subject, however such division of labour may favour the advancement of a particular pursuit, a point into which I do not here enter, certainly it has a tendency to contract his mind. If it is incorporated with others, it depends on those others as to the kind of influence which it exerts upon him. Thus the Classics, which in England are the means of refining the taste, have in France subserved the spread of revolutionary and deistical doctrines. In Metaphysics, again, Butler's Analogy of Religion,[1] which has had so much to do with the conversion to the Catholic faith of members of the University of Oxford, appeared to Pitt and others, who had received a different training, to operate only in the direction of infidelity. And so again, Watson, Bishop of Llandaff,[2] as I think he tells us in the narrative of his life, felt the science of Mathematics to indispose the mind to religious belief, while others see in its investigations the best parallel,

---

[1] Joseph Butler (1692–1752), Bishop of Durham, author of *The Analogy of Religion Natural and Revealed* (1736).
[2] Richard Watson (1737–1816), author of *Anecdotes of the Life of Richard Watson* (1817).

and thereby defence, of the Christian Mysteries. In like manner, I suppose, Arcesilas[3] would not have handled logic as Aristotle, nor Aristotle have criticized poets as Plato; yet reasoning and poetry are subject to scientific rules.

It is a great point then to enlarge the range of studies which a University professes, even for the sake of the students; and, though they cannot pursue every subject which is open to them, they will be the gainers by living among those and under those who represent the whole circle. This I conceive to be the advantage of a seat of universal learning, considered as a place of education. An assemblage of learned men, zealous for their own sciences, and rivals of each other, are brought, by familiar intercourse and for the sake of intellectual peace, to adjust together the claims and relations of their respective subjects of investigation. They learn to respect, to consult, to aid each other. Thus is created a pure and clear atmosphere of thought, which the student also breathes, though in his own case he only pursues a few sciences out of the multitude. He profits by an intellectual tradition, which is independent of particular teachers, which guides him in his choice of subjects, and duly interprets for him those which he chooses. He apprehends the great outlines of knowledge, the principles on which it rests, the scale of its parts, its lights and its shades, its great points and its little, as he otherwise cannot apprehend them. Hence it is that his education is called "Liberal." A habit of mind is formed which lasts through life, of which the attributes are, freedom, equitableness, calmness, moderation, and wisdom; or what in a former Discourse I have ventured to call a philosophical habit. This then I would assign as the special fruit of the education furnished at a University, as contrasted with other places of teaching or modes of teaching. This is the main purpose of a University in its treatment of its students.

And now the question is asked me, What is the *use* of it? and my answer will constitute the main subject of the Discourses which are to follow.

2

Cautious and practical thinkers, I say, will ask of me, what, after all, is the gain of this Philosophy, of which I make such account, and from which I promise so much. Even supposing it to enable us to exercise the degree of trust exactly due to every science respectively, and to estimate precisely the value of every truth which is anywhere to be found, how are we better for this master view of things, which I have been extolling? Does it not reverse the principle of the division of labour? will practical objects be obtained better or worse by its cultivation? to what then does it lead? where does it end? what does it do? how does it profit? what does it promise? Particular sciences are respectively the basis of definite arts, which carry on to results tangible and beneficial the truths which are the subjects of the knowledge attained; what is the Art of this science of sciences? what is the fruit of such a Philosophy? what are we proposing to effect, what inducements do we hold out to the Catholic community, when we set about the enterprise of founding a University?

I am asked what is the end of University Education, and of the Liberal or Philosophical Knowledge which I conceive it to impart: I answer, that what I have already said has been sufficient to show that it has a very tangible, real, and sufficient end, though the end cannot be divided from that knowledge itself. Knowledge is capable of being its own end. Such is the constitution of the human mind, that any kind of knowledge, if it be really such, is its own reward. And if this is true of all knowledge, it is true also of that special Philosophy, which I have made to consist in a comprehensive view of truth in all its branches, of the relations of science to science, of their mutual bearings, and their respective values. What the worth of such an acquirement is, compared with other objects which we seek,— wealth or power or honour or the conveniences and comforts of life, I do not profess here to discuss; but I would maintain, and mean to show, that it is an object, in its own nature so really and undeniably good, as to be the compensation of a great deal of thought in the compassing, and a great deal of trouble in the attaining.

Now, when I say that Knowledge is, not merely a means to something beyond it, or the preliminary of certain arts into which it naturally resolves, but an end sufficient to rest in and to pursue for its own sake, surely I am uttering no paradox, for I am stating what is both intelligible in itself, and has ever been the common judgment of philosophers and the ordinary feeling of mankind. I am saying what at least the public opinion of this day ought to be slow to deny, considering how much we have heard of late years, in opposition to Religion, of entertaining,

---

[3] Arcesilas (c. 315–240 B.C.), skeptical philosopher who denied the possibility of certain knowledge.

curious, and various knowledge. I am but saying what whole volume have been written to illustrate, viz., by a "selection from the records of Philosophy, Literature, and Art, in all ages and countries, of a body of examples, to show how the most unpropitious circumstances have been unable to conquer an ardent desire for the acquisition of knowledge."[4] That further advantages accrue to us and redound to others by its possession, over and above what it is in itself, I am very far indeed from denying; but, independent of these, we are satisfying a direct need of our nature in its very acquisition; and, whereas our nature, unlike that of the inferior creation, does not at once reach its perfection, but depends, in order to it, on a number of external aids and appliances, Knowledge, as one of the principal of these, is valuable for what its very presence in us does for us after the manner of a habit, even though it be turned to no further account, nor subserve any direct end.

3

Hence it is that Cicero, in enumerating the various heads of mental excellence, lays down the pursuit of Knowledge for its own sake, as the first of them. "This pertains most of all to human nature," he says, "for we are all of us drawn to the pursuit of Knowledge; in which to excel we consider excellent, whereas to mistake, to err, to be ignorant, to be deceived, is both an evil and a disgrace."[5] And he considers Knowledge the very first object to which we are attracted, after the supply of our physical wants. After the calls and duties of our animal existence, as they may be termed, as regards ourselves, our family, and our neighbours, follows, he tells us, "the search after truth. Accordingly, as soon as we escape from the pressure of necessary cares, forthwith we desire to see, to hear, and to learn; and consider the knowledge of what is hidden or is wonderful a condition of our happiness."

This passage, though it is but one of many similar passages in a multitude of authors, I take for the very reason that it is so familiarly known to us; and I wish you to observe, Gentlemen, how distinctly it separates the pursuit of Knowledge from those ulterior objects to which certainly it can be made to conduce, and which are, I suppose, solely contemplated by the persons who would ask of me the use of a University or Liberal Education. So far from dreaming of the cultivation of Knowledge directly and mainly in order to our physical comfort and enjoyment, for the sake of life and person, of health, of the conjugal and family union, of the social tie and civil security, the great Orator implies, that it is only after our physical and political needs are supplied, and when we are "free from necessary duties and cares," that we are in a condition for "desiring to see, to hear, and to learn." Nor does he contemplate in the least degree the reflex or subsequent action of Knowledge, when acquired, upon those material goods which we set out by securing before we seek it; on the contrary, he expressly denies its bearing upon social life altogether, strange as such a procedure is to those who live after the rise of the Baconian philosophy, and he cautions us against such a cultivation of it aş will interfere with our duties to our fellow-creatures. "All these methods," he says, "are engaged in the investigation of truth; by the pursuit of which to be carried off from public occupations is a transgression of duty. For the praise of virtue lies altogether in action; yet intermissions often occur, and then we recur to such pursuits; not to say that the incessant activity of the mind is vigorous enough to carry us on in the pursuit of knowledge; even without any exertion of our own." The idea of benefiting society by means of "the pursuit of science and knowledge" did not enter at all into the motives which he would assign for their cultivation.

This was the ground of the opposition which the elder Cato made to the introduction of Greek Philosophy among his countrymen, when Carneades[6] and his companions, on occasion of their embassy, were charming the Roman youth with their eloquent expositions of it. The fit representative of a practical people, Cato estimated every thing by what it produced; whereas the Pursuit of Knowledge promised nothing beyond Knowledge itself. He despised that refinement or enlargement of mind of which he had no experience.

4

Things, which can bear to be cut off from every thing else and yet persist in living, must have life in themselves; pursuits, which issue in nothing, and still maintain their ground for ages, which are regarded as admirable, though they

---

[4] Pursuit of Knowledge under Difficulties. Introd. [N]   [5] Cicer. Offic. init. [N]
[6] Cato (234–149 B.C.), Roman censor, opponent of culture; Carneades (214–129 B.C.), Greek philosopher who influenced Cicero.

have not as yet proved themselves to be useful, must have their sufficient end in themselves, whatever it turn out to be. And we are brought to the same conclusion by considering the force of the epithet, by which the knowledge under consideration is popularly designated. It is common to speak of "*liberal* knowledge," of the "*liberal* arts and studies," and of a "*liberal* education," as the especial characteristic or property of a University and of a gentleman; what is really meant by the word? Now, first, in its grammatical sense it is opposed to *servile*; and by "servile work" is understood, as our catechisms inform us, bodily labour, mechanical employment, and the like, in which the mind has little or no part. Parallel to such servile works are those arts, if they deserve the name, of which the poet speaks,[7] which owe their origin and their method to hazard, not to skill; as, for instance, the practice and operations of an empiric. As far as this contrast may be considered as a guide into the meaning of the word, liberal education and liberal pursuits are exercises of mind, of reason, of reflection.

But we want something more for its explanation, for there are bodily exercises which are liberal, and mental exercises which are not so. For instance, in ancient times the practitioners in medicine were commonly slaves; yet it was an art as intellectual in its nature, in spite of the pretence, fraud, and quackery with which it might then, as now, be debased, as it was heavenly in its aim. And so in like manner, we contrast a liberal education with a commercial education or a professional; yet no one can deny that commerce and the professions afford scope for the highest and most diversified powers of mind. There is then a great variety of intellectual exercises, which are not technically called "liberal;" on the other hand, I say, there are exercises of the body which do receive that appellation. Such, for instance, was the palæstra, in ancient times; such the Olympic games, in which strength and dexterity of body as well as of mind gained the prize. In Xenophon we read of the young Persian nobility being taught to ride on horseback and to speak the truth; both being among the accomplishments of a gentleman. War, too, however rough a profession, has ever been accounted liberal, unless in cases when it becomes heroic, which would introduce us to another subject.

Now comparing these instances together, we

shall have no difficulty in determining the principle of this apparent variation in the application of the term which I am examining. Manly games, or games of skill, or military prowess, though bodily, are, it seems, accounted liberal; on the other hand, what is merely professional, though highly intellectual, nay, though liberal in comparison of trade and manual labour, is not simply called liberal, and mercantile occupations are not liberal at all. Why this distinction? because that alone is liberal knowledge, which stands on its own pretensions, which is independent of sequel, expects no complement, refuses to be *informed* (as it is called) by any end, or absorbed into any art, in order duly to present itself to our contemplation. The most ordinary pursuits have this specific character, if they are self-sufficient and complete; the highest lose it, when they minister to something beyond them. It is absurd to balance, in point of worth and importance, a treatise on reducing fractures with a game of cricket or a fox-chase; yet of the two the bodily exercise has that quality which we call "liberal," and the intellectual has it not. And so of the learned professions altogether, considered merely as professions; although one of them be the most popularly beneficial, and another the most politically important, and the third the most intimately divine of all human pursuits, yet the very greatness of their end, the health of the body, or of the commonwealth, or of the soul, diminishes, not increases, their claim to the appellation "liberal," and that still more, if they are cut down to the strict exigencies of that end. If, for instance, Theology, instead of being cultivated as a contemplation, be limited to the purposes of the pulpit or be represented by the catechism, it loses,—not its usefulness, not its divine character, not its meritoriousness (rather it gains a claim upon these titles by such charitable condescension),—but it does lose the particular attribute which I am illustrating; just as a face worn by tears and fasting loses its beauty, or a labourer's hand loses its delicateness;—for Theology thus exercised is not simple knowledge, but rather is an art or a business making use of Theology. And thus it appears that even what is supernatural need not be liberal, nor need a hero be a gentleman, for the plain reason that one idea is not another idea. And in like manner the Baconian Philosophy, by using its physical sciences in the service of man, does thereby

[7] Vid. Arist. Nic. Ethic. vi. [N]

transfer them from the order of Liberal Pursuits to, I do not say the inferior, but the distinct class of the Useful. And, to take a different instance, hence again, as is evident, whenever personal gain is the motive, still more distinctive an effect has it upon the character of a given pursuit; thus racing, which was a liberal exercise in Greece, forfeits its rank in times like these, so far as it is made the occasion of gambling.

All that I have been now saying is summed up in a few characteristic words of the great Philosopher. "Of possessions," he says, "those rather are useful, which bear fruit; those *liberal, which tend to enjoyment*. By fruitful, I mean, which yield revenue; by enjoyable, where *nothing accrues of consequence beyond the using*."[8]

5

Do not suppose, that in thus appealing to the ancients, I am throwing back the world two thousand years, and fettering Philosophy with the reasonings of paganism. While the world lasts, will Aristotle's doctrine on these matters last, for he is the oracle of nature and of truth. While we are men, we cannot help, to a great extent, being Aristotelians, for the great Master does but analyze the thoughts, feelings, views, and opinions of human kind. He has told us the meaning of our own words and ideas, before we were born. In many subject-matters, to think correctly, is to think like Aristotle; and we are his disciples whether we will or no, though we may not know it. Now, as to the particular instance before us, the word "liberal" as applied to Knowledge and Education, expresses a specific idea, which ever has been, and ever will be, while the nature of man is the same, just as the idea of the Beautiful is specific, or of the Sublime, or of the Ridiculous, or of the Sordid. It is in the world now, it was in the world then; and, as in the case of the dogmas of faith, it is illustrated by a continuous historical tradition, and never was out of the world, from the time it came into it. There have indeed been differences of opinion from time to time, as to what pursuits and what arts came under that idea, but such differences are but an additional evidence of its reality. That idea must have a substance in it, which has maintained its ground amid these conflicts and changes, which has ever served as a standard to measure things withal, which has passed from mind to mind unchanged, when there was so much to colour, so much to influence any notion

or thought whatever, which was not founded in our very nature. Were it a mere generalization, it would have varied with the subjects from which it was generalized; but though its subjects vary with the age, it varies not itself. The palæstra may seem a liberal exercise to Lycurgus, and illiberal to Seneca; coach-driving and prize-fighting may be recognized in Elis, and be condemned in England; music may be despicable in the eyes of certain moderns, and be in the highest place with Aristotle and Plato,—(and the case is the same in the particular application of the idea of Beauty, or of Goodness, or of Moral Virtue, there is a difference of tastes, a difference of judgments)— still these variations imply, instead of discrediting, the archetypal idea, which is but a previous hypothesis or condition, by means of which issue is joined between contending opinions, and without which there would be nothing to dispute about.

I consider, then, that I am chargeable with no paradox, when I speak of a Knowledge which is its own end, when I call it liberal knowledge, or a gentleman's knowledge, when I educate for it, and make it the scope of a University. And still less am I incurring such a charge, when I make this acquisition consist, not in Knowledge in a vague and ordinary sense, but in that Knowledge which I have especially called Philosophy or, in an extended sense of the word, Science; for whatever claims Knowledge has to be considered as a good, these it has in a higher degree when it is viewed not vaguely, not popularly, but precisely and transcendently as Philosophy. Knowledge, I say, is then especially liberal, or sufficient for itself, apart from every external and ulterior object, when and so far as it is philosophical, and this I proceed to show.

6

Now bear with me, Gentlemen, if what I am about to say, has at first sight a fanciful appearance. Philosophy, then, or Science, is related to Knowledge in this way:—Knowledge is called by the name of Science or Philosophy, when it is acted upon, informed, or if I may use a strong figure, impregnated by Reason. Reason is the principle of that intrinsic fecundity of Knowledge, which, to those who possess it, is its especial value, and which dispenses with the necessity of their looking abroad for any end to rest upon external to itself. Knowledge, indeed, when thus exalted into a scientific form, is also power; not only is it excellent in itself, but whatever such

---

[8] Aristot. Rhet. i. 5. [N]

excellence may be, it is something more, it has a result beyond itself. Doubtless; but that is a further consideration, with which I am not concerned. I only say that, prior to its being a power, it is a good; that it is, not only an instrument, but an end. I know well it may resolve itself into an art, and terminate in a mechanical process, and in tangible fruit; but it also may fall back upon that Reason which informs it, and resolve itself into Philosophy. In one case it is called Useful Knowledge, in the other Liberal. The same person may cultivate it in both ways at once; but this again is a matter foreign to my subject; here I do but say that there are two ways of using Knowledge, and in matter of fact those who use it in one way are not likely to use it in the other, or at least in a very limited measure. You see, then, here are two methods of Education; the end of the one is to be philosophical, of the other to be mechanical; the one rises towards general ideas, the other is exhausted upon what is particular and external. Let me not be thought to deny the necessity, or to decry the benefit, of such attention to what is particular and practical, as belongs to the useful or mechanical arts; life could not go on without them; we owe our daily welfare to them; their exercise is the duty of the many, and we owe to the many a debt of gratitude for fulfilling that duty. I only say that Knowledge, in proportion as it tends more and more to be particular, ceases to be Knowledge. It is a question whether Knowledge can in any proper sense be predicated of the brute creation; without pretending to metaphysical exactness of phraseology, which would be unsuitable to an occasion like this, I say, it seems to me improper to call that passive sensation, or perception of things, which brutes seem to possess, by the name of Knowledge. When I speak of Knowledge, I mean something intellectual, something which grasps what it perceives through the senses; something which takes a view of things; which sees more than the senses convey; which reasons upon what it sees, and while it sees; which invests it with an idea. It expresses itself, not in a mere enunciation, but by an enthymeme: it is of the nature of science from the first, and in this consists its dignity. The principle of real dignity in Knowledge, its worth, its desirableness, considered irrespectively of its results, is this germ within it of a scientific or a philosophical process. This is how it comes to be an end in itself; this is why it admits of being called Liberal. Not to know the relative disposition of things is the state of slaves or children; to have mapped out the Universe is the boast, or at least the ambition, of Philosophy.

Moreover, such knowledge is not a mere extrinsic or accidental advantage, which is ours to-day and another's to-morrow, which may be got up from a book, and easily forgotten again, which we can command or communicate at our pleasure, which we can borrow for the occasion, carry about in our hand, and take into the market; it is an acquired illumination, it is a habit, a personal possession, and an inward endowment. And this is the reason, why it is more correct, as well as more usual, to speak of a University as a place of education, than of instruction, though, when knowledge is concerned, instruction would at first sight have seemed the more appropriate word. We are instructed, for instance, in manual exercises, in the fine and useful arts, in trades, and in ways of business; for these are methods, which have little or no effect upon the mind itself, are contained in rules committed to memory, to tradition, or to use, and bear upon an end external to themselves. But education is a higher word; it implies an action upon our mental nature, and the formation of a character; it is something individual and permanent, and is commonly spoken of in connexion with religion and virtue. When, then, we speak of the communication of Knowledge as being Education, we thereby really imply that that Knowledge is a state or condition of mind; and since cultivation of mind is surely worth seeking for its own sake, we are thus brought once more to the conclusion, which the word "Liberal" and the word "Philosophy" have already suggested, that there is a Knowledge, which is desirable, though nothing come of it, as being of itself a treasure, and a sufficient remuneration of years of labour.

7

This, then, is the answer which I am prepared to give to the question with which I opened this Discourse. Before going on to speak of the object of the Church in taking up Philosophy, and the uses to which she puts it, I am prepared to maintain that Philosophy is its own end, and, as I conceive, I have now begun the proof of it. I am prepared to maintain that there is a knowledge worth possessing for what it is, and not merely for what it does; and what minutes remain to me to-day I shall devote to the removal of some portion of the indistinctness and confusion with which the subject may in some minds be surrounded.

It may be objected then, that, when we profess to seek Knowledge for some end or other beyond itself, whatever it be, we speak intelligibly; but that, whatever men may have said, however obstinately the idea may have kept its ground from age to age, still it is simply unmeaning to say that we seek Knowledge for its own sake, and for nothing else; for that it ever leads to something beyond itself, which therefore is its end, and the cause why it is desirable;—moreover, that this end is twofold, either of this world or of the next; that all knowledge is cultivated either for secular objects or for eternal; that if it is directed to secular objects, it is called Useful Knowledge, if to eternal, Religious or Christian Knowledge;— in consequence, that if, as I have allowed, this Liberal Knowledge does not benefit the body or estate, it ought to benefit the soul; but if the fact be really so, that it is neither a physical or a secular good on the one hand, nor a moral good on the other, it cannot be a good at all, and is not worth the trouble which is necessary for its acquisition.

And then I may be reminded that the professors of this Liberal or Philosophical Knowledge have themselves, in every age, recognized this exposition of the matter, and have submitted to the issue in which it terminates; for they have ever been attempting to make men virtuous; or, if not, at least have assumed that refinement of mind was virtue, and that they themselves were the virtuous portion of mankind. This they have professed on the one hand; and on the other, they have utterly failed in their professions, so as ever to make themselves a proverb among men, and a laughing-stock both to the grave and the dissipated portion of mankind, in consequence of them. Thus they have furnished against themselves both the ground and the means of their own exposure, without any trouble at all to any one else. In a word, from the time that Athens was the University of the world, what has Philosophy taught men, but to promise without practising, and to aspire without attaining? What has the deep and lofty thought of its disciples ended in but eloquent words? Nay, what has its teaching ever meditated, when it was boldest in its remedies for human ill, beyond charming us to sleep by its lessons, that we might feel nothing at all? like some melodious air, or rather like those strong and transporting perfumes, which at first

spread their sweetness over every thing they touch, but in a little while do but offend in proportion as they once pleased us. Did Philosophy support Cicero under the disfavour of the fickle populace, or nerve Seneca to oppose an imperial tyrant? It abandoned Brutus, as he sorrowfully confessed, in his greatest need, and it forced Cato, as his panegyrist strangely boasts, into the false position of defying heaven. How few can be counted among its professors, who, like Polemo, were thereby converted from a profligate course, or like Anaxagoras,[9] thought the world well lost in exchange for its possession? The philosopher in *Rasselas* taught a super-human doctrine, and then succumbed without an effort to a trial of human affection.

"He discoursed," we are told, "with great energy on the government of the passions. His look was venerable, his action graceful, his pronunciation clear, and his diction elegant. He showed, with great strength of sentiment and variety of illustration, that human nature is degraded and debased, when the lower faculties predominate over the higher. He communicated the various precepts given, from time to time, for the conquest of passion, and displayed the happiness of those who had obtained the important victory, after which man is no longer the slave of fear, nor the fool of hope . . . He enumerated many examples of heroes immove-able by pain or pleasure, who looked with indifference on those modes or accidents to which the vulgar give the names of good and evil."

Rasselas in a few days found the philosopher in a room half darkened, with his eyes misty, and his face pale. "Sir," said he, "you have come at a time when all human friendship is useless; what I suffer cannot be remedied, what I have lost cannot be supplied. My daughter, my only daughter, from whose tenderness I expected all the comforts of my age, died last night of a fever." "Sir," said the prince, "mortality is an event by which a wise man can never be surprised; we know that death is always near, and it should therefore always be expected." "Young man," answered the philosopher, "you speak like one who has never felt the pangs of separa-tion." "Have you, then, forgot the precept," said Rasselas, "which you so powerfully enforced? . . . consider that external things are naturally variable, but truth and reason are always the

---

[9] Polemo of Athens (d. 273 B.C.), converted from a dissolute life upon hearing a university lecture; Anaxagoras (d. 42 B.C.), philosopher banished for his advocacy of monotheism.

same." "What comfort," said the mourner, "can truth and reason afford me? Of what effect are they now, but to tell me that my daughter will not be restored?"

8

Better, far better, to make no professions, you will say, than to cheat others with what we are not, and to scandalize them with what we are. The sensualist, or the man of the world, at any rate is not the victim of fine words, but pursues a reality and gains it. The Philosophy of Utility, you will say, Gentlemen, has at least done its work; and I grant it,—it aimed low, but it has fulfilled its aim. If that man of great intellect who has been its Prophet in the conduct of life played false to his own professions, he was not bound by his philosophy to be true to his friend or faithful in his trust. Moral virtue was not the line in which he undertook to instruct men; and though, as the poet calls him, he were the "meanest" of mankind, he was so in what may be called his private capacity and without any prejudice to the theory of induction. He had a right to be so, if he chose, for any thing that the Idols of the den or the theatre had to say to the contrary. His mission was the increase of physical enjoyment and social comfort;[10] and most wonderfully, most awfully has he fulfilled his conception and his design. Almost day by day have we fresh and fresh shoots, and buds, and blososms, which are to ripen into fruit, on that magical tree of Knowledge which he planted, and to which none of us perhaps, except the very poor, but owes, if not his present life, at least his daily food, his health, and general well-being. He was the divinely provided minister of temporal benefits to all of us so great, that whatever I am forced to think of him as a man, I have not the heart, from mere gratitude, to speak of him severely. And, in spite of the tendencies of his philosophy, which are, as we see at this day, to depreciate, or to trample on Theology, he has himself, in his writings, gone out of his way, as if with a prophetic misgiving of those tendencies, to insist on it as the instrument of that beneficent Father,[11] who, when He came on earth in visible form, took on Him first and most prominently the office of assuaging the bodily wounds of human nature. And truly, like the old mediciner

in the tale, "he sat diligently at his work, and hummed, with cheerful countenance, a pious song;" and then in turn "went out singing into the meadows so gaily, that those who had seen him from afar might well have thought it was a youth gathering flowers for his beloved, instead of an old physician gathering healing herbs in the morning dew."[12]

Alas, that men, in the action of life or in their heart of hearts, are not what they seem to be in their moments of excitement, or in their trances or intoxications of genius,—so good, so noble, so serene! Alas, that Bacon too in his own way should after all be but the fellow of those heathen philosophers who in their disadvantages had some excuse for their inconsistency, and who surprise us rather in what they did say than in what they did not do! Alas, that he too, like Socrates or Seneca, must be stripped of his holy-day coat, which looks so fair, and should be but a mockery amid his most majestic gravity of phrase; and, for all his vast abilities, should, in the littleness of his own moral being, but typify the intellectual narrowness of his school! However, granting all this, heroism after all was not his philosophy:—I cannot deny he has abundantly achieved what he proposed. His is simply a Method whereby bodily discomforts and temporal wants are to be most effectually removed from the greatest number; and already, before it has shown any signs of exhaustion, the gifts of nature, in their most artificial shapes and luxurious profusion and diversity, from all quarters of the earth, are, it is undeniable, by its means brought even to our doors, and we rejoice in them.

9

Useful Knowledge then, I grant, has done its work; and Liberal Knowledge as certainly has not done its work,—that is, supposing, as the objectors assume, its direct end, like Religious Knowledge, is to make men better; but this I will not for an instant allow, and, unless I allow it, those objectors have said nothing to the purpose. I admit, rather I maintain, what they have been urging, for I consider Knowledge to have its end in itself. For all its friends, or its enemies, may say, I insist upon it, that it is as real a mistake to burden it with virtue or religion as with the mechanical arts. Its direct business is

---

[10] It will be seen that on the whole I agree with Lord Macaulay in his Essay on Bacon's Philosophy. I do not know whether he would agree with me. [N]

[11] De Augment. iv. 2, vid. Macaulay's Essay; vid. also *Praef.* Instur. Magn. [N]

[12] Fouqué's Unknown Patient. [N]

not to steel the soul against temptation or to console it in affliction, any more than to set the loom in motion, or to direct the steam carriage; be it ever so much the means or the condition of both material and moral advancement, still, taken by and in itself, it as little mends our hearts as it improves our temporal circumstances. And if its eulogists claim for it such a power, they commit the very same kind of encroachment on a province not their own as the political economist who should maintain that his science educated him for casuistry or diplomacy. Knowledge is one thing, virtue is another; good sense is not conscience, refinement is not humility, nor is largeness and justness of view faith. Philosophy, however enlightened, however profound, gives no command over the passions, no influential motives, no vivifying principles. Liberal Education makes not the Christian, not the Catholic, but the gentleman. It is well to be a gentleman, it is well to have a cultivated intellect, a delicate taste, a candid, equitable, dispassionate mind, a noble and courteous bearing in the conduct of life;—these are the connatural qualities of a large knowledge; they are the objects of a University; I am advocating, I shall illustrate and insist upon them; but still, I repeat, they are no guarantee for sanctity or even for conscientiousness, they may attach to the man of the world, to the profligate, to the heartless,—pleasant, alas, and attractive as he shows when decked out in them. Taken by themselves, they do but seem to be what they are not; they look like virtue at a distance, but they are detected by close observers, and on the long run; and hence it is that they are popularly accused of pretence and hypocrisy, not, I repeat, from their own fault, but because their professors and their admirers persist in taking them for what they are not, and are officious in arrogating for them a praise to which they have no claim. Quarry the granite rock with razors, or moor the vessel with a thread of silk; then may you hope with such keen and delicate instruments as human knowledge and human reason to contend against those giants, the passion and the pride of man.

Surely we are not driven to theories of this kind, in order to vindicate the value and dignity of Liberal Knowledge. Surely the real grounds on which its pretensions rest are not so very subtle or abstruse, so very strange or improbable. Surely it is very intelligible to say, and that is what I say here, that Liberal Education, viewed in itself, is simply the cultivation of the intellect, as such, and its object is nothing more or less than intellectual

excellence. Every thing has its own perfection, be it higher or lower in the scale of things; and the perfection of one is not the perfection of another. Things animate, inanimate, visible, invisible, all are good in their kind, and have a *best* of themselves, which is an object of pursuit. Why do you take such pains with your garden or your park? You see to your walks and turf and shrubberies; to your trees and drives; not as if you meant to make an orchard of the one, or corn or pasture land of the other, but because there is a special beauty in all that is goodly in wood, water, plain, and slope, brought all together by art into one shape, and grouped into one whole. Your cities are beautiful, your palaces, your public buildings, your territorial mansions, your churches; and their beauty leads to nothing beyond itself. There is a physical beauty and a moral: there is a beauty of person, there is a beauty of our moral being, which is natural virtue; and in like manner there is a beauty, there is a perfection, of the intellect. There is an ideal perfection in these various subject-matters, towards which individual instances are seen to rise, and which are the standards for all instances whatever. The Greek divinities and demigods, as the statuary has moulded them, with their symmetry of figure, and their high forehead and their regular features, are the perfection of physical beauty. The heroes, of whom history tells, Alexander, or Cæsar, or Scipio, or Saladin, are the representatives of that magnanimity or self-mastery which is the greatness of human nature. Christianity too has its heroes, and in the supernatural order, and we call them Saints. The artist puts before him beauty of feature and form; the poet, beauty of mind; the preacher, the beauty of grace: then intellect too, I repeat, has its beauty, and it has those who aim at it. To open the mind, to correct it, to refine it, to enable it to know, and to digest, master, rule, and use its knowledge, to give it power over its own faculties, application, flexibility, method, critical exactness, sagacity, resource, address, eloquent expression, is an object as intelligible (for here we are inquiring, not what the object of a Liberal Education is worth, nor what use the Church makes of it, but what it is in itself), I say, an object as intelligible as the cultivation of virtue, while, at the same time, it is absolutely distinct from it.

10

This indeed is but a temporal object, and a transitory possession; but so are other things in themselves which we make much of and pursue.

The moralist will tell us that man, in all his functions, is but a flower which blossoms and fades, except so far as a higher principle breathes upon him, and makes him and what he is immortal. Body and mind are carried on into an eternal state of being by the gifts of Divine Munificence; but at first they do but fail in a failing world; and if the powers of intellect decay, the powers of the body have decayed before them, and, as an Hospital or an Alms-house, though its end be ephemeral, may be sanctified to the service of religion, so surely may a University, even were it nothing more than I have as yet described it. We attain to heaven by using this world well, though it is to pass away; we perfect our nature, not by undoing it, but by adding to it what is more than nature, and directing it towards aims higher than its own.

DISCOURSE VII

Knowledge Viewed in Relation to Professional Skill

1

I HAVE been insisting, in my two preceding Discourses, first, on the cultivation of the intellect, as an end which may reasonably be pursued for its own sake; and next, on the nature of that cultivation, or what that cultivation consists in. Truth of whatever kind is the proper object of the intellect; its cultivation then lies in fitting it to apprehend and contemplate truth. Now the intellect in its present state, with exceptions which need not here be specified, does not discern truth intuitively, or as a whole. We know, not by a direct and simple vision, not at a glance, but, as it were, by piecemeal and accumulation, by a mental process, by going round an object, by the comparison, the combination, the mutual correction, the continual adaptation, of many partial notions, by the employment, concentration, and joint action of many faculties and exercises of mind. Such a union and concert of the intellectual powers, such an enlargement and development, such a comprehensiveness, is necessarily a matter of training. And again, such a training is a matter of rule; it is not mere application, however

exemplary, which introduces the mind to truth, nor the reading many books, nor the getting up many subjects, nor the witnessing many experiments, nor the attending many lectures. All this is short of enough; a man may have done it all, yet be lingering in the vestibule of knowledge:— he may not realize what his mouth utters; he may not see with his mental eye what confronts him; he may have no grasp of things as they are; or at least he may have no power at all of advancing one step forward of himself, in consequence of what he has already acquired, no power of dis-criminating between truth and falsehood, of sifting out the grains of truth from the mass, of arranging things according to their real value, and, if I may use the phrase, of building up ideas. Such a power is the result of a scientific formation of mind; it is an acquired faculty of judgment, of clearsightedness, of sagacity, of wisdom, of philosophical reach of mind, and of intellectual self-possession and repose,—qualities which do not come of mere acquirement. The bodily eye, the organ for apprehending material objects, is provided by nature; the eye of the mind, of which the object is truth, is the work of discipline and habit.

This process of training, by which the intellect, instead of being formed or sacrificed to some particular or accidental purpose, some specific trade or profession, or study or science, is disciplined for its own sake, for the perception of its own proper object, and for its own highest culture, is called Liberal Education; and though there is no one in whom it is carried as far as is conceivable, or whose intellect would be a pattern of what intellects should be made, yet there is scarcely any one but may gain an idea of what real training is, and at least look towards it, and make its true scope and result, not something else, his standard of excellence; and numbers there are who may submit themselves to it, and secure it to themselves in good measure. And to set forth the right standard, and to train according to it, and to help forward all students towards it according to their various capacities, this I conceive to be the business of a University.

2

Now this is what some great men are very slow to allow; they insist that Education should be confined to some particular and narrow end, and should issue in some definite work, which can be weighed and measured. They argue as if every thing, as well as every person, had its price; and that where there has been a great outlay, they have a right to expect a return in kind. This they call making Education and Instruction "useful," and "Utility" becomes their watchword. With a fundamental principle of this nature, they very naturally go on to ask, what there is to show for the expense of a University; what is the real worth in the market of the article called "a Liberal Education," on the supposition that it does not teach us definitely how to advance our manufactures, or to improve our lands, or to better our civil economy; or again, if it does not at once make this man a lawyer, that an engineer, and that a surgeon; or at least if it does not lead to discoveries in chemistry, astronomy, geology, magnetism, and science of every kind.

This question, as might have been expected, has been keenly debated in the present age, and formed one main subject of the controversy, to which I referred in the Introduction to the present Discourses, as having been sustained in the first decade of this century by a celebrated Northern Review on the one hand, and defenders of the University of Oxford on the other. Hardly had the authorities of that ancient seat of learning, waking from their long neglect, set on foot a plan for the education of the youth committed to them, than the representatives of science and literature in the city, which has sometimes been called the Northern Athens, remonstrated, with their gravest arguments and their most brilliant satire, against the direction and shape which the reform was taking. Nothing would content them, but that the University should be set to rights on the basis of the philosophy of Utility; a philosophy, as they seem to have thought, which needed but to be proclaimed in order to be embraced. In truth, they were little aware of the depth and force of the principles on which the academical authorities were proceeding, and, this being so, it was not to be expected that they would be allowed to walk at leisure over the field of controversy which they had selected. Accordingly they were encountered in behalf of the University by two men of great name and influence in their day, of very different minds, but united, as by Collegiate ties, so in the clear-sighted and large view which they took of the whole subject of Liberal Education; and the

defence thus provided for the Oxford studies has kept its ground to this day.

3

Let me be allowed to devote a few words to the memory of distinguished persons, under the shadow of whose name I once lived, and by whose doctrine I am now profiting. In the heart of Oxford there is a small plot of ground, hemmed in by public thoroughfares, which has been the possession and the home of one Society for above five hundred years. In the old time of Boniface the Eighth and John the Twenty-second, in the age of Scotus and Occam and Dante, before Wiclif or Huss had kindled those miserable fires which are still raging to the ruin of the highest interests of man, an unfortunate king of England, Edward the Second, flying from the field of Bannockburn, is said to have made a vow to the Blessed Virgin to found a religious house in her honour, if he got back in safety.[1] Prompted and aided by his Almoner, he decided on placing this house in the city of Alfred; and the Image of our Lady, which is opposite its entrance-gate, is to this day the token of the vow and its fulfilment. King and Almoner have long been in the dust, and strangers have entered into their inheritance, and their creed has been forgotten, and their holy rites disowned; but day by day a memento is still made in the holy Sacrifice by at least one Catholic Priest, once a member of that College, for the souls of those Catholic benefactors who fed him there for so many years. The visitor, whose curiosity has been excited by its present fame, gazes perhaps with something of disappointment on a collection of buildings which have with them so few of the circumstances of dignity or wealth. Broad quadrangles, high halls and chambers, ornamented cloisters, stately walks, or umbrageous gardens, a throng of students, ample revenues, or a glorious history, none of these things were the portion of that old Catholic foundation; nothing in short which to the common eye sixty years ago would have given tokens of what it was to be. But it had at that time a spirit working within it, which enabled its inmates to do, amid its seeming insignificance, what no other body in the place could equal; not

---

[1] Boniface VIII (c. 1234–1303), Pope from 1294; John XXII (1249–1334), Pope from 1316; Johannes Duns Scotus (c. 1264–1308), Franciscan philosopher at Oxford, known as the "Subtle Doctor"; William of Occam (c. 1300–1349), Franciscan philosopher at Oxford, known for nominalist philosophy; John Wycliffe (c. 1329–84), Oxford scholar, called precursor of Reformation; John Hus (c. 1369–1415), Bohemian ecclesiastical reformer, follower of Wycliffe; Edward II (1284–1327), defeated at Bannockburn in 1314 by Robert Bruce, later founded what was to become Oriel College, Oxford.

a very abstruse gift or extraordinary boast, but a rare one, the honest purpose to administer the trust committed to them in such a way as their conscience pointed out as best. So, whereas the Colleges of Oxford are self-electing bodies, the fellows in each perpetually filling up for themselves the vacancies which occur in their number, the members of this foundation determined, at a time when, either from evil custom or from ancient statute, such a thing was not known elsewhere, to throw open their fellowships to the competition of all comers, and, in the choice of associates henceforth, to cast to the winds every personal motive and feeling, family connexion, and friendship, and patronage, and political interest, and local claim, and prejudice, and party jealousy, and to elect solely on public and patriotic grounds. Nay, with a remarkable independence of mind, they resolved that even the table of honours, awarded to literary merit by the University in its new system of examination for degrees, should not fetter their judgment as electors; but that at all risks, and whatever criticism it might cause, and whatever odium they might incur, they would select the men, whoever they were, to be children of their Founder, whom they thought in their consciences to be most likely from their intellectual and moral qualities to please him, if (as they expressed it) he were still upon earth, most likely to do honour to his College, most likely to promote the objects which they believed he had at heart. Such persons did not promise to be the disciples of a low Utilitarianism; and consequently, as their collegiate reform synchronized with that reform of the Academical body, in which they bore a principal part, it was not unnatural that, when the storm broke upon the University from the North, their Alma Mater, whom they loved, should have found her first defenders within the walls of that small College, which had first put itself into a condition to be her champion.

These defenders, I have said, were two, of whom the more distinguished was the late Dr. Copleston,[2] then a Fellow of the College, successively its Provost, and Protestant Bishop of Llandaff. In that Society, which owes so much to him, his name lives, and ever will live, for the distinction which his talents bestowed on it, for the academical importance to which he raised it, for the generosity of spirit, the liberality of sentiment, and the kindness of heart, with which he adorned it, and which even those who had least sympathy with some aspects of his mind and character could not but admire and love. Men come to their meridian at various periods of their lives; the last years of the eminent person I am speaking of were given to duties which, I am told, have been the means of endearing him to numbers, but which afforded no scope for that peculiar vigour and keenness of mind which enabled him, when a young man, single-handed, with easy gallantry, to encounter and overthrow the charge of three giants of the North combined against him. I believe I am right in saying that, in the progress of the controversy, the most scientific, the most critical, and the most witty, of that literary company, all of them now, as he himself, removed from this visible scene, Professor Playfair, Lord Jeffrey, and the Rev. Sydney Smith,[3] threw together their several efforts into one article of their Review, in order to crush and pound to dust the audacious controvertist who had come out against them in defence of his own Institutions. To have even contended with such men was a sufficient voucher for his ability, even before we open his pamphlets, and have actual evidence of the good sense, the spirit, the scholar-like taste, and the purity of style, by which they are distinguished.

He was supported in the controversy, on the same general principles, but with more of method and distinctness, and, I will add, with greater force and beauty and perfection, both of thought and of language, by the other distinguished writer, to whom I have already referred, Mr. Davison,[4] who, though not so well known to the world in his day, has left more behind him than the Provost of Oriel, to make his name remembered by posterity. This thoughtful man, who was the admired and intimate friend of a very remarkable person, whom,

---

[2] Edward Copleston (1776–1849), professor of poetry at Oxford and later Bishop of Llandaff and Dean of St. Paul's.

[3] John Playfair (1748–1819), Scottish mathematician and geologist; Francis Lord Jeffrey (1773–1850), Scottish jurist and cofounder of the *Edinburgh Review;* Sydney Smith (1771–1845), English journalist, cofounder of the *Edinburgh Review.* Playfair, Smith, and Richard Payne Knight (1750–1824) wrote the article attacking Copleston to which Newman refers.

[4] John Davison (1777–1834), Fellow of Oriel; his essay on education from the *Quarterly Review* of October 1811 is quoted later in this discourse.

whether he wish it or not, numbers revere and love as the first author of the subsequent movement in the Protestant Church towards Catholicism,[5] this grave and philosophical writer, whose works I can never look into without sighing that such a man was lost to the Catholic Church, as Dr. Butler before him, by some early bias or some fault of self-education—he, in a review of a work by Mr. Edgeworth on Professional Education, which attracted a good deal of attention in its day, goes leisurely over the same ground, which had already been rapidly traversed by Dr. Copleston, and, though professedly employed upon Mr. Edgeworth, is really replying to the northern critic who had brought that writer's work into notice, and to a far greater author than either of them, who in a past age had argued on the same side.

4

The author to whom I allude is no other than Locke. That celebrated philosopher has preceded the Edinburgh Reviewers in condemning the ordinary subjects in which boys are instructed at school, on the ground that they are not needed by them in after life; and before quoting what his disciples have said in the present century, I will refer to a few passages of the master. " 'Tis matter of astonishment," he says in his work on Education, "that men of quality and parts should suffer themselves to be so far misled by custom and implicit faith. Reason, if consulted with, would advise, that their children's time should be spent in acquiring what might be *useful* to them, when they come to be men, rather than that their heads should be stuffed with a deal of trash, a great part whereof they usually never do ('tis certain they never need to) think on again as long as they live; and so much of it as does stick by them they are only the worse for."

And so again, speaking of verse-making, he says, "I know not what reason a father can have to wish his son a poet, who does not desire him to *bid defiance to all other callings and business*; which is not yet the worst of the case; for, if he proves a successful rhymer, and gets once the reputation of a wit, I desire it to be considered, what company and places he is likely to spend his time in, nay, and estate too; for it is very seldom seen that any one discovers *mines of gold or silver in*

Parnassus. 'Tis a pleasant air, but a barren soil."

In another passage he distinctly limits utility in education to its bearing on the future profession or trade of the pupil, that is, he scorns the idea of any education of the intellect, simply as such. "Can there be any thing more ridiculous," he asks, "than that a father should waste his own money, and his son's time, in setting him to *learn the Roman language*, when at the same time he *designs him for a trade*, wherein he, having no use of Latin, fails not to forget that little which he brought from school, and which 'tis ten to one he abhors for the ill-usage it procured him? Could it be believed, unless we have every where amongst us examples of it, that a child should be forced to learn the rudiments of a language, which *he is never to use in the course of life that he is designed to*, and neglect all the while the writing a good hand, and casting accounts, which are of great advantage in all conditions of life, and to most trades indispensably necessary?" Nothing of course can be more absurd than to neglect in education those matters which are necessary for a boy's future calling; but the tone of Locke's remarks evidently implies more than this, and is condemnatory of any teaching which tends to the general cultivation of the mind.

Now to turn to his modern disciples. The study of the Classics had been made the basis of the Oxford education, in the reforms which I have spoken of, and the Edinburgh Reviewers protested, after the manner of Locke, that no good could come of a system which was not based upon the principle of Utility.

"Classical Literature," they said, "is the great object at Oxford. Many minds, so employed, have produced many works and much fame in that department; but if all liberal arts and sciences, *useful to human life*, had been taught there, if *some* had dedicated themselves to *chemistry*, some to *mathematics*, some to *experimental philosophy*, and if *every* attainment had been honoured in the mixt ratio of its difficulty and *utility*, the system of such a University would have been much more valuable, but the splendour of its name something less."[6]

Utility may be made the end of education, in two respects: either as regards the individual educated, or the community at large. In which light do these writers regard it? in the latter. So far they differ from Locke, for they consider the

---

[5] Mr. Keble, Vicar of Hursley, late Fellow of Oriel and Professor of Poetry in the University of Oxford. [N]

[6] Newman is quoting from an article by Sydney Smith in the *Edinburgh Review* of October 1809.

advancement of science as the supreme and real end of a University. This is brought into view in the sentences which follow.

"When a University has been doing *useless* things for a long time, it appears at first degrading to them to be *useful*. A set of Lectures on Political Economy would be discouraged in Oxford, probably despised, probably not permitted. To discuss the inclosure of commons, and to dwell upon imports and exports, to come so near to common life, would seem to be undignified and contemptible. In the same manner, the Parr or the Bentley[7] of the day would be scandalized, in a University, to be put on a level with the discoverer of a neutral salt; and yet, *what other measure is there of dignity in intellectual labour but usefulness?* And what ought the term University to mean, but a place where every science is taught which is liberal, and at the same time useful to mankind? Nothing would so much tend to bring classical literature within proper bounds as *a steady and invariable appeal to utility* in our appreciation of all human knowledge. . . . *Looking always to real utility as our guide*, we should see, with equal pleasure, a studious and inquisitive mind arranging the productions of nature, investigating the qualities of bodies, or mastering the difficulties of the learned languages. We should not care whether he was chemist, naturalist, or scholar, because we know it to be as *necessary* that matter should be studied and subdued *to the use of man*, as that taste should be gratified, and imagination inflamed."

Such then is the enunciation, as far as words go, of the theory of Utility in Education; and both on its own account, and for the sake of the able men who have advocated it, it has a claim on the attention of those whose principles I am here representing. Certainly it is specious to contend that nothing is worth pursuing but what is useful; and that life is not long enough to expend upon interesting, or curious, or brilliant trifles. Nay, in one sense, I will grant it is more than specious, it is true; but, if so, how do I propose directly to meet the objection? Why, Gentlemen, I have really met it already, viz., in laying down, that intellectual culture is its own end; for what has its *end* in itself, has its *use* in itself also. I say, if a Liberal Education consists in the culture of the intellect, and if that culture be in itself a good, here, without going further, is an answer to Locke's question; for if a healthy body

is a good in itself, why is not a healthy intellect? and if a College of Physicians is a useful institution, because it contemplates bodily health, why is not an Academical Body, though it were simply and solely engaged in imparting vigour and beauty and grasp to the intellectual portion of our nature? And the Reviewers I am quoting seem to allow this in their better moments, in a passage which, putting aside the question of its justice in fact, is sound and true in the principles to which it appeals:—

"The present state of classical education," they say, "cultivates the *imagination* a great deal too much, and other *habits of mind* a great deal too little, and trains up many young men in a style of elegant imbecility, utterly unworthy of the talents with which nature has endowed them. . . . The matter of fact is, that a classical scholar of twenty-three or twenty-four is a man principally conversant with works of imagination. His feelings are quick, his fancy lively, and his taste good. Talents for *speculation* and *original inquiry* he has none, nor has he formed the invaluable *habit of pushing things up to their first principles*, or of collecting dry and unamusing facts as the materials for reasoning. All the solid and masculine parts of his *understanding* are left wholly without *cultivation*; he hates the pain of thinking, and suspects every man whose boldness and originality call upon him to defend his opinions and prove his assertions."

5

Now, I am not at present concerned with the specific question of classical education; else, I might reasonably question the justice of calling an intellectual discipline, which embraces the study of Aristotle, Thucydides, and Tacitus, which involves Scholarship and Antiquities, *imaginative*; still so far I readily grant, that the cultivation of the "understanding," of a "talent for speculation and original inquiry," and of "the habit of pushing things up to their first principles," is a principal portion of a *good* or *liberal* education. If then the Reviewers consider such cultivation the characteristic of a *useful* education, as they seem to do in the foregoing passage, it follows, that what they mean by "useful" is just what I mean by "good" or "liberal:" and Locke's question becomes a verbal one. Whether youths are to be taught Latin or verse-making will depend on the *fact*,

---

[7] Samuel Parr (1747–1825), an associate of Copleston; Richard Bentley (1662–1742), celebrated classical scholar and editor.

whether these studies tend to mental culture; but, however this is determined, so far is clear, that in that mental culture consists what I have called a liberal or non-professional, and what the Reviewers call a useful education.

This is the obvious answer which may be made to those who urge upon us the claims of Utility in our plans of Education; but I am not going to leave the subject here: I mean to take a wider view of it. Let us take "useful," as Locke takes it, in its proper and popular sense, and then we enter upon a large field of thought, to which I cannot do justice in one Discourse, though to-day's is all the space that I can give to it. I say, let us take "useful" to mean, not what is simply good, but what *tends* to good, or is the *instrument* of good; and in this sense also, Gentlemen, I will show you how a liberal education is truly and fully a useful, though it be not a professional, education. "Good" indeed means one thing, and "useful" means another; but I lay it down as a principle, which will save us a great deal of anxiety, that, though the useful is not always good, the good is always useful. Good is not only good, but reproductive of good; this is one of its attributes; nothing is excellent, beautiful, perfect, desirable for its own sake, but it overflows, and spreads the likeness of itself all around it. Good is prolific; it is not only good to the eye, but to the taste; it not only attracts us, but it communicates itself; it excites first our admiration and love, then our desire and our gratitude, and that, in proportion to its intenseness and fulness in particular instances. A great good will impart great good. If then the intellect is so excellent a portion of us, and its cultivation so excellent, it is not only beautiful, perfect, admirable, and noble in itself, but in a true and high sense it must be useful to the possessor and to all around him; not useful in any low, mechanical, mercantile sense, but as diffusing good, or as a blessing, or a gift, or power, or a treasure, first to the owner, then through him to the world. I say then, if a liberal education be good, it must necessarily be useful too.

6

You will see what I mean by the parallel of bodily health. Health is a good in itself, though nothing came of it, and is especially worth seeking and cherishing; yet, after all, the blessings which attend its presence are so great, while they are so close to it and so redound back upon it and encircle it, that we never think of it except as useful as well as good, and praise and prize it for what it does, as well as for what it is, though at the same time we cannot point out any definite and distinct work or production which it can be said to effect. And so as regards intellectual culture, I am far from denying utility in this large sense as the end of Education, when I lay it down, that the culture of the intellect is a good in itself and its own end; I do not exclude from the idea of intellectual culture what it cannot but be, from the very nature of things; I only deny that we must be able to point out, before we have any right to call it useful, some art, or business, or profession, or trade, or work, as resulting from it, and as its real and complete end. The parallel is exact:—As the body may be sacrificed to some manual or other toil, whether moderate or oppressive, so may the intellect be devoted to some specific profession; and I do not call *this* the culture of the intellect. Again, as some member or organ of the body may be inordinately used and developed, so may memory, or imagination, or the reasoning faculty; and *this* again is not intellectual culture. On the other hand, as the body may be tended, cherished, and exercised with a simple view to its general health, so may the intellect also be generally exercised in order to its perfect state; and this *is* its cultivation.

Again, as health ought to precede labour of the body, and as a man in health can do what an unhealthy man cannot do, and as of this health the properties are strength, energy, agility, graceful carriage and action, manual dexterity, and endurance of fatigue, so in like manner general culture of mind is the best aid to professional and scientific study, and educated men can do what illiterate cannot; and the man who has learned to think and to reason and to compare and to discriminate and to analyze, who has refined his taste, and formed his judgment, and sharpened his mental vision, will not indeed at once be a lawyer, or a pleader, or an orator, or a statesman, or a physician, or a good landlord, or a man of business, or a soldier, or an engineer, or a chemist, or a geologist, or an antiquarian, but he will be placed in that state of intellect in which he can take up any one of the sciences or callings I have referred to, or any other for which he has a taste or special talent, with an ease, a grace, a versatility, and a success, to which another is a stranger. In this sense then, and as yet I have said but a very few words on a large subject, mental culture is emphatically *useful*.

If then I am arguing, and shall argue, against Professional or Scientific knowledge as the sufficient end of a University Education, let me not be supposed, Gentlemen, to be disrespectful towards particular studies, or arts, or vocations, and those who are engaged in them. In saying that Law or Medicine is not the end of a University course, I do not mean to imply that the University does not teach Law or Medicine. What indeed can it teach at all, if it does not teach something particular? It teaches *all* knowledge by teaching all *branches* of knowledge, and in no other way. I do but say that there will be this distinction as regards a Professor of Law, or of Medicine, or of Geology, or of Political Economy, in a University and out of it, that out of a University he is in danger of being absorbed and narrowed by his pursuit, and of giving Lectures which are the Lectures of nothing more than a lawyer, physician, geologist, or political economist; whereas in a University he will just know where he and his science stand, he has come to it, as it were, from a height, he has taken a survey of all knowledge, he is kept from extravagance by the very rivalry of other studies, he has gained from them a special illumination and largeness of mind and freedom and self-possession, and he treats his own in consequence with a philosophy and a resource, which belongs not to the study itself, but to his liberal education.

This then is how I should solve the fallacy, for so I must call it, by which Locke and his disciples would frighten us from cultivating the intellect, under the notion that no education is useful which does not teach us some temporal calling, or some mechanical art, or some physical secret. I say that a cultivated intellect, because it is a good in itself, brings with it a power and a grace to every work and occupation which it undertakes, and enables us to be more useful, and to a greater number. There is a duty we owe to human society as such, to the state to which we belong, to the sphere in which we move, to the individuals towards whom we are variously related, and whom we successively encounter in life; and that philosophical or liberal education, as I have called it, which is the proper function of a University, if it refuses the foremost place to professional interests, does but postpone them to the formation of the citizen, and, while it subserves the larger interests of philanthropy, prepares also for the successful prosecution of those merely personal objects, which at first sight it seems to disparage.

7

And now, Gentlemen, I wish to be allowed to enforce in detail what I have been saying, by some extracts from the writings to which I have already alluded, and to which I am so greatly indebted.

"It is an undisputed maxim in Political Economy," says Dr. Copleston, "that the separation of professions and the division of labour tend to the perfection of every art, to the wealth of nations, to the general comfort and well-being of the community. This principle of division is in some instances pursued so far as to excite the wonder of people to whose notice it is for the first time pointed out. There is no saying to what extent it may not be carried; and the more the powers of each individual are concentrated in one employment, the greater skill and quickness will he naturally display in performing it. But, while he thus contributes more effectually to the accumulation of national wealth, he becomes himself more and more degraded as a rational being. In proportion as his sphere of action is narrowed his mental powers and habits become contracted; and he resembles a subordinate part of some powerful machinery, useful in its place, but insignificant and worthless out of it. If it be necessary, as it is beyond all question necessary, that society should be split into divisions and subdivisions, in order that its several duties may be well performed, yet we must be careful not to yield up ourselves wholly and exclusively to the guidance of this system; we must observe what its evils are, and we should modify and restrain it, by bringing into action other principles, which may serve as a check and counterpoise to the main force.

"There can be no doubt that every art is improved by confining the professor of it to that single study. But, *although the art itself is advanced by this concentration of mind in its service, the individual who is confined to it goes back*. The advantage of the community is nearly in an inverse ratio with his own.

"Society itself requires some other contribution from each individual, besides the particular duties of his profession. And, if no such liberal intercourse be established, it is the common failing of human nature, to be engrossed with petty views and interests, to underrate the importance of all in which we are not concerned, and to carry our partial notions into cases where they are inapplicable, to act, in short, as so many unconnected units, displacing and repelling one another.

"In the cultivation of literature is found that common link, which, among the higher and middling departments of life, unites the jarring sects and subdivisions into one interest, which supplies common topics, and kindles common feelings, unmixed with those narrow prejudices with which all professions are more or less infected. The knowledge, too, which is thus acquired, expands and enlarges the mind, excites its faculties, and calls those limbs and muscles into freer exercise which, by too constant use in one direction, not only acquire an illiberal air, but are apt also to lose somewhat of their native play and energy. And thus, without directly qualifying a man for any of the employments of life, it enriches and ennobles all. Without teaching him the peculiar business of any one office or calling, it enables him to act his part in each of them with better grace and more elevated carriage; and, if happily planned and conducted, is a main ingredient in that complete and generous education which fits a man 'to perform justly, skilfully, and magnanimously, all the offices, both private and public, of peace and war.' "[8]

8

The view of Liberal Education, advocated in these extracts, is expanded by Mr. Davison in the Essay to which I have already referred.[9] He lays more stress on the "usefulness" of Liberal Education in the larger sense of the word than his predecessor in the controversy. Instead of arguing that the Utility of knowledge to the individual varies inversely with its Utility to the public, he chiefly employs himself on the suggestions contained in Dr. Copleston's last sentences. He shows, first, that a Liberal Education is something far higher, even in the scale of Utility, than what is commonly called a Useful Education, and next, that it is necessary or useful for the purposes even of that Professional Education which commonly engrosses the title of Useful. The former of these two theses he recommends to us in an argument from which the following passages are selected:—

"It is to take a very contracted view of life," he says, "to think with great anxiety how persons may be educated to superior skill in their department, comparatively neglecting or excluding the more liberal and enlarged cultivation. In his (Mr. Edgeworth's) system, the value of every attainment is to be measured by its subserviency to a calling. The specific duties of that calling are exalted at the cost of those free and independent tastes and virtues which come in to sustain the common relations of society, and raise the individual in them. In short, a man is to be usurped by his profession. He is to be clothed in its garb from head to foot. His virtues, his science, and his ideas are all to be put into a gown or uniform, and the whole man to be shaped, pressed, and stiffened, in the exact mould of his technical character. Any interloping accomplishments, or a faculty which cannot be taken into public pay, if they are to be indulged in him at all, must creep along under the cloak of his more serviceable privileged merits. Such is the state of perfection to which the spirit and general tendency of this system would lead us.

"But the professional character is not the only one which a person engaged in a profession has to support. He is not always upon duty. There are services he owes, which are neither parochial, nor forensic, nor military, not to be described by any such epithet of civil regulation, and yet are in no wise inferior to those that bear these authoritative titles; inferior neither in their intrinsic value, nor their moral import, nor their impression upon society. As a friend, as a companion, as a citizen at large; in the connections of domestic life; in the improvement and embellishment of his leisure, he has a sphere of action, revolving, if you please, within the sphere of his profession, but not clashing with it; in which if he can show none of the advantages of an improved understanding, whatever may be his skill or proficiency in the other, he is no more than an ill-educated man.

"There is a certain faculty in which all nations of any refinement are great practitioners. It is not taught at school or college as a distinct science; though it deserves that what is taught there should be made to have some reference to it; nor is it endowed at all by the public; everybody being obliged to exercise it for himself in person, which he does to the best of his skill. But in nothing is there a greater difference than in the manner of doing it. The advocates of professional learning will smile when we tell them that this same faculty which we would have encouraged, is simply that of speaking good sense in English, without fee or reward, in common conversation. They will smile when we lay some stress upon it; but in reality it is no such trifle as they imagine. Look into the huts of savages, and see,

---

[8] Vid. Milton on Education. [N]   [9] See note 4 above.

for there is nothing to listen to, the dismal blank of their stupid hours of silence; their professional avocations of war and hunting are over; and, having nothing to do, they have nothing to say. Turn to improved life, and you find conversation in all its forms the medium of something more than an idle pleasure; indeed, a very active agent in circulating and forming the opinions, tastes, and feelings of a whole people. It makes of itself a considerable affair. Its topics are the most promiscuous—all those which do not belong to any particular province. As for its power and influence, we may fairly say that it is of just the same consequence to a man's immediate society, how he talks, as how he acts. Now of all those who furnish their share to rational conversation, a mere adept in his own art is universally admitted to be the worst. The sterility and uninstructiveness of such a person's social hours are quite proverbial. Or if he escape being dull, it is only by launching into ill-timed, learned loquacity. We do not desire of him lectures or speeches; and he has nothing else to give. Among benches he may be powerful; but seated on a chair he is quite another person. On the other hand, we may affirm, that one of the best companions is a man who, to the accuracy and research of a profession, has joined a free excursive acquaintance with various learning, and caught from it the spirit of general observation."

9

Having thus shown that a liberal education is a real benefit to the subjects of it, as members of society, in the various duties and circumstances and accidents of life, he goes on, in the next place, to show that, over and above those direct services which might fairly be expected of it, it actually subserves the discharge of those particular functions, and the pursuit of those particular advantages, which are connected with professional exertion, and to which Professional Education is directed.

"We admit," he observes, "that when a person makes a business of one pursuit, he is in the right way to eminence in it; and that divided attention will rarely give excellence in many. But our assent will go no further. For, to think that the way to prepare a person for excelling in any one pursuit (and that is the only point in hand), is to fetter his early studies, and cramp the first development of his mind, by a reference to the exigencies of that pursuit barely, is a very different notion, and one which, we apprehend, deserves to be exploded rather than received.

Possibly a few of the abstract, insulated kinds of learning might be approached in that way. The exceptions to be made are very few, and need not be recited. But for the acquisition of professional and practical ability such maxims are death to it. The main ingredients of that ability are requisite knowledge and cultivated faculties; but, of the two, the latter is by far the chief. A man of well improved faculties has the command of another's knowledge. A man without them, has not the command of his own.

"Of the intellectual powers, the judgment is that which takes the foremost lead in life. How to form it to the two habits it ought to possess, of exactness and vigour, is the problem. It would be ignorant presumption so much as to hint at any routine of method by which these qualities may with certainty be imparted to every or any understanding. Still, however, we may safely lay it down that they are not to be got 'by a gatherer of simples,' but are the combined essence and extracts of many different things, drawn from much varied reading and discipline, first, and observation afterwards. For if there be a single intelligible point on this head, it is that a man who has been trained to think upon one subject or for one subject only, will never be a good judge even in that one: whereas the enlargement of his circle gives him increased knowledge and power in a rapidly increasing ratio. So much do ideas act, not as solitary units, but by grouping and combination; and so clearly do all the things that fall within the proper province of the same faculty of the mind, intertwine with and support each other. Judgment lives as it were by comparison and discrimination. Can it be doubted, then, whether the range and extent of that assemblage of things upon which it is practised in its first essays are of use to its power?

"To open our way a little further on this matter, we will define what we mean by the power of judgment; and then try to ascertain among what kind of studies the improvement of it may be expected at all.

"Judgment does not stand here for a certain homely, useful quality of intellect, that guards a person from committing mistakes to the injury of his fortunes or common reputation; but for that master-principle of business, literature, and talent, which gives him strength in any subject he chooses to grapple with, and enables him to *seize the strong point* in it. Whether this definition be metaphysically correct or not, it comes home to the substance of our inquiry. It describes the power that every one desires to possess when he comes to act in a profession, or elsewhere; and corresponds with our best idea of a cultivated mind.

"Next, it will not be denied, that in order to do any good to the judgment, the mind must be employed upon such subjects as come within the cognizance of that faculty, and give some real exercise to its perceptions. Here we have a rule of selection by which the different parts of learning may be classed for our purpose. Those which belong to the province of the judgment are religion (in its evidences and interpretation), ethics, history, eloquence, poetry, theories of general speculation, the fine arts, and works of wit. Great as the variety of these large divisions of learning may appear, they are all held in union by two capital principles of connexion. First, they are all quarried out of one and the same great subject of man's moral, social, and feeling nature. And secondly, they are all under the control (more or less strict) of the same power of moral reason."

"If these studies," he continues, "be such as give a direct play and exercise to the faculty of the judgment, then they are the true basis of education for the active and inventive powers, whether destined for a profession or any other use. Miscellaneous as the assemblage may appear, of history, eloquence, poetry, ethics, etc., blended together, they will all conspire in an union of effect. They are necessary mutually to explain and interpret each other. The knowledge derived from them all will amalgamate, and the habits of a mind versed and practised in them by turns will join to produce a richer vein of thought and of more general and practical application than could be obtained of any single one, as the fusion of the metals into Corinthian brass gave the artist his most ductile and perfect material. Might we venture to imitate an author (whom indeed it is much safer to take as an authority than to attempt to copy), Lord Bacon, in some of his concise illustrations of the comparative utility of the different studies, we should say that history would give fulness, moral philosophy strength, and poetry elevation to the understanding. Such in reality is the natural force and tendency of the studies; but there are few minds susceptible enough to derive from them any sort of virtue adequate to those high expressions. We must be contented therefore to lower our panegyric to this, that a person cannot avoid receiving some infusion and tincture, at least, of those several qualities, from that course of diversified reading. One thing is unquestionable,

that the elements of general reason are not to be found fully and truly expressed in any one kind of study; and that he who would wish to know her idiom, must read it in many books.

"If different studies are useful for aiding, they are still more useful for correcting each other; for as they have their particular merits severally, so they have their defects, and the most extensive acquaintance with one can produce only an intellect either too flashy or too jejune, or infected with some other fault of confined reading. History, for example, shows things as they are, that is, the morals and interests of men disfigured and perverted by all their imperfections of passion, folly, and ambition; philosophy strips the picture too much; poetry adorns it too much; the concentrated lights of the three correct the false peculiar colouring of each, and show us the truth. The right mode of thinking upon it is to be had from them taken all together, as every one must know who has seen their united contributions of thought and feeling expressed in the masculine sentiment of our immortal statesman, Mr. Burke, whose eloquence is inferior only to his more admirable wisdom. If any mind improved like his, is to be our instructor, we must go to the fountain head of things as he did, and study not his works but his method; by the one we may become feeble imitators, by the other arrive at some ability of our own. But, as all biography assures us, he, and every other able thinker, has been formed, not by a parsimonious admeasurement of studies to some definite future object (which is Mr. Edgeworth's maxim), but by taking a wide and liberal compass, and thinking a great deal on many subjects with no better end in view than because the exercise was one which made them more rational and intelligent beings."

10

But I must bring these extracts to an end. To-day I have confined myself to saying that that training of the intellect, which is best for the individual himself, best enables him to discharge his duties to society. The Philosopher, indeed, and the man of the world differ in their very notion, but the methods, by which they are respectively formed, are pretty much the same. The Philosopher has the same command of matters of thought, which the true citizen and gentleman has of matters of business and conduct. If then a practical end must be assigned to a University course, I say it is that of training good members of society. Its art is the art of social life, and its end is fitness for the world. It neither confines its views to particular professions on the one hand, nor creates heroes or inspires genius on the other. Works indeed of genius fall under no art; heroic minds come under no rule; a University is not a birthplace of poets or of immortal authors, of founders of schools, leaders of colonies, or conquerors of nations. It does not promise a generation of Aristotles or Newtons, of Napoleons or Washingtons, of Raphaels or Shakespeares, though such miracles of nature it has before now contained within its precincts. Nor is it content on the other hand with forming the critic or the experimentalist, the economist or the engineer, though such too it includes within its scope. But a University training is the great ordinary means to a great but ordinary end; it aims at raising the intellectual tone of society, at cultivating the public mind, at purifying the national taste, at supplying true principles to popular enthusiasm and fixed aims to popular aspiration, at giving enlargement and sobriety to the ideas of the age, at facilitating the exercise of political power, and refining the intercourse of private life. It is the education which gives a man a clear conscious view of his own opinions and judgments, a truth in developing them, an eloquence in expressing them, and a force in urging them. It teaches him to see things as they are, to go right to the point, to disentangle a skein of thought, to detect what is sophistical, and to discard what is irrelevant. It prepares him to fill any post with credit, and to master any subject with facility. It shows him how to accommodate himself to others, how to throw himself into their state of mind, how to bring before them his own, how to influence them, how to come to an understanding with them, how to bear with them. He is at home in any society, he has common ground with every class; he knows when to speak and when to be silent; he is able to converse, he is able to listen; he can ask a question pertinently, and gain a lesson seasonably, when he has nothing to impart himself; he is ever ready, yet never in the way; he is a pleasant companion, and a comrade you can depend upon; he knows when to be serious and when to trifle, and he has a sure tact which enables him to trifle with gracefulness and to be serious with effect. He has the repose of a mind which lives in itself, while it lives in the world, and which has resources for its happiness at home when it cannot go abroad. He has a gift which serves him in public, and supports him in retirement, without which good fortune is but vulgar, and with which failure and disappointment have a charm. The art which tends to make a man all this, is in the object which it pursues as useful as the art of wealth or the art of health, though it is less susceptible of method, and less tangible, less certain, less complete in its result.

Literature

Newman's lecture to Dublin Catholics on literature has been cited as anticipating Pater's more widely known essay "On Style." It is certainly a document in the nineteenth-century concern for the relation between thought and word, between the style and the man. Newman emphasizes the personal element in writing and virtually dispenses with scientific writing as literature. Much of Newman's thought on literature and style as expressed in this lecture can be profitably applied to an analysis of his own personal and supple style. The lecture was first published with other university lectures in 1858 and later included in editions of the Idea of a University. *(The ellipses are Newman's.)*

1

WISHING to address you, Gentlemen, at the commencement of a new Session, I tried to find a subject for discussion, which might be at once suitable to the occasion, yet neither too large for your time, nor too minute or abstruse for your attention. I think I see one for my purpose in the very title of your Faculty. It is the Faculty of Philosophy and Letters. Now the question may arise as to what is meant by "Philosophy," and what is meant by "Letters." As to the other Faculties, the subject-matter which they profess is intelligible, as soon as named, and beyond all dispute. We know what Science is, what Medicine, what Law, and what Theology; but we have not so much ease in determining what is meant by Philosophy and Letters. Each department of that twofold province needs explanation: it will be sufficient on an occasion like this, to investigate one of them. Accordingly I shall select for remark the latter of the two, and attempt to determine what we are to understand by Letters or Literature, in what Literature consists, and how it stands relatively to Science. We speak, for instance, of ancient and modern literature, the literature of the day, sacred literature, light literature; and our lectures in this place are devoted to classical literature and English literature. Are Letters, then, synonymous with books? This cannot be, or they would include in their range Philosophy, Law, and, in short, the teaching of all the other Faculties. Far from confusing these various studies, we view the works of Plato or Cicero sometimes as philosophy, sometimes as literature; on the other hand, no one would ever be tempted to speak of Euclid as literature, or of Matthiæ's Greek Grammar. Is, then, literature synonymous with composition? with books written with an attention to style? is literature fine writing? again, is it studied and artificial writing?

There are excellent persons who seem to adopt this last account of Literature as their own idea of it. They depreciate it, as if it were the result of a mere art or trick of words. Professedly indeed, they are aiming at the Greek and Roman classics, but their criticisms have quite as great force against all literature as against any. I think I shall be best able to bring out what I have to say on the subject by examining the statements which they make in defence of their own view of it. They contend then, 1. that fine writing, as exemplified in the Classics, is mainly a matter of conceits, fancies, and prettinesses, decked out in choice words; 2. that this is the proof of it, that the classics will not bear translating;—(and this is why I have said that the real attack is upon literature altogether, not the classical only; for, to speak generally, all literature, modern as well as ancient, lies under this disadvantage. This, however, they will not allow; for they maintain,) 3. that Holy Scripture presents a remarkable contrast to secular writings on this very point, viz, in that Scripture does easily admit of translation, though it is the most sublime and beautiful of all writings.

2

Now I will begin by stating these three positions in the words of a writer, who is cited by the estimable Catholics in question as a witness, or rather as an advocate, in their behalf, though he is far from being able in his own person to challenge the respect which is inspired by themselves.

"There are two sorts of eloquence," says this writer, "the one indeed scarce deserves the name of it, which consists chiefly in laboured and polished periods, an over-curious and artificial arrangement of figures, tinselled over with a gaudy embellishment of words, which glitter, but convey little or no light to the understanding. This kind of writing is for the most part much affected and admired by the people of weak judgment and vicious taste; but it is a piece of affectation and formality the sacred writers are utter strangers to. It is a vain and boyish eloquence; and, as it has always been esteemed below the great geniuses of all ages, so much more so with respect to those writers who were actuated by the spirit of Infinite Wisdom, and therefore wrote with that force and majesty with which never man writ. The other sort of eloquence is quite the reverse to this, and which may be said to be the true characteristic of the Holy Scriptures; where the excellence does not arise from a laboured and far-fetched elocution, but from a surprising mixture of simplicity and majesty, which is a double character, so difficult to be united that it is seldom to be met with in compositions merely human. We see nothing in Holy Writ of affectation and superfluous ornament . . . Now, it is observable that the most excellent profane authors, whether Greek or Latin, lose most of their graces whenever we find them literally translated. Homer's famed representation of Jupiter—his cried-up description of a tempest, his relation of Neptune's shaking the earth and opening it to its centre, his description of Pallas's horses, with numbers of other long-since admired passages, flag, and almost vanish away, in the vulgar Latin translation.

"Let any one but take the pains to read the common Latin interpretations of Virgil Theocritus, or even of Pindar, and one may venture to affirm he will be able to trace out but few remains of the graces which charmed him so much in the original. The natural conclusion from hence is, that in the classical authors, the expression, the sweetness of the numbers, occasioned by a musical placing of words, constitute a great part of their beauties; whereas, in the sacred writings, they consist more in the greatness of the things themselves than in the words and expressions. The ideas and conceptions are so great and lofty in their own nature that they necessarily appear magnificent in the most artless dress. Look but into the Bible, and we see them shine through the most simple and literal translations. That glorious description which Moses gives of the creation of the heavens and the earth, which Longinus . . . was so greatly taken with, has not lost the least whit of its intrinsic worth, and though it has undergone so many translations, yet triumphs over all, and breaks forth with as much force and vehemence as in the original. . . . In the history of Joseph, where Joseph makes himself known, and weeps aloud upon the neck of his dear brother Benjamin, that all the house of Pharaoh heard him, at that instant none of his brethren are introduced as uttering aught, either to express their present joy or palliate their former injuries to him. On all sides there immediately ensues a deep and solemn silence; a silence infinitely more eloquent and expressive than anything else that could have been substituted in its place. Had Thucydides, Herodotus, Livy, or any of the celebrated classical historians, been employed in writing this history, when they came to this point they would doubtless have exhausted all their fund of eloquence in furnishing Joseph's brethren with laboured and studied harangues, which, however fine they might have been in themselves, would nevertheless have been unnatural, and altogether improper on the occasion."[1]

This is eloquently written, but it contains, I consider, a mixture of truth and falsehood, which it will be my business to discriminate from each other. Far be it from me to deny the unapproachable grandeur and simplicity of Holy Scripture; but I shall maintain that the classics are, as human compositions, simple and majestic and natural too. I grant that Scripture is concerned with things, but I will not grant that classical literature is simply concerned with words. I grant that human literature is often elaborate, but I will maintain that elaborate composition is not unknown to the writers of Scripture. I grant that human literature cannot easily be translated out of the particular language to which it belongs; but it is not at all the rule that Scripture can easily be translated either;—and now I address myself to my task:—

---

[1] Sterne, Sermon xlii. [N]

3

Here, then, in the first place, I observe, Gentlemen, that Literature, from the derivation of the word, implies writing, not speaking; this, however, arises from the circumstance of the copiousness, variety, and public circulation of the matters of which it consists. What is spoken cannot outrun the range of the speaker's voice, and perishes in the uttering. When words are in demand to express a long course of thought, when they have to be conveyed to the ends of the earth, or perpetuated for the benefit of posterity, they must be written down, that is, reduced to the shape of literature; still, properly speaking, the terms, by which we denote this characteristic gift of man, belong to its exhibition by means of the voice, not of handwriting. It addresses itself, in its primary idea, to the ear, not to the eye. We call it the power of speech, we call it language, that is, the use of the tongue; and, even when we write, we still keep in mind what was its original instrument, for we use freely such terms in our books as "saying," "speaking," "telling," "talking," "calling;" we use the terms "phraseology" and "diction;" as if we were still addressing ourselves to the ear.

Now I insist on this, because it shows that speech, and therefore literature, which is its permanent record, is essentially a personal work. It is not some production or result, attained by the partnership of several persons, or by machinery, or by any natural process, but in its very idea it proceeds, and must proceed, from some one given individual. Two persons cannot be the authors of the sounds which strike our ear; and, as they cannot be speaking one and the same speech, neither can they be writing one and the same lecture or discourse,—which must certainly belong to some one person or other, and is the expression of that one person's ideas and feelings, —ideas and feelings personal to himself, though others may have parallel and similar ones,— proper to himself, in the same sense as his voice, his air, his countenance, his carriage, and his action, are personal. In other words, Literature expresses, not objective truth, as it is called, but subjective; not things, but thoughts.

Now this doctrine will become clearer by considering another use of words, which does relate to objective truth, or to things; which relates to matters, not personal, not subjective to the individual, but which, even were there no individual man in the whole world to know them or to talk about them, would exist still. Such objects become the matter of Science, and words indeed are used to express them, but such words are rather symbols than language, and however many we use, and however we may perpetuate them by writing, we never could make any kind of literature out of them, or call them by that name. Such, for instance, would be Euclid's Elements; they relate to truths universal and eternal; they are not mere thoughts, but things: they exist in themselves, not by virtue of our understanding them, not in dependence upon our will, but in what is called the *nature* of things, or at least on conditions external to us. The words, then, in which they are set forth are not language, speech, literature, but rather, as I have said, symbols. And, as a proof of it, you will recollect that it is possible, nay usual, to set forth the propositions of Euclid in algebraical notation, which, as all would admit, has nothing to do with literature. What is true of mathematics is true also of every study, so far forth as it is scientific; it makes use of words as the mere vehicle of things, and is thereby withdrawn from the province of literature. Thus metaphysics, ethics, law, political economy, chemistry, theology, cease to be literature in the same degree as they are capable of a severe scientific treatment. And hence it is that Aristotle's works on the one hand, though at first sight literature, approach in character, at least a great number of them, to mere science; for even though the things which he treats of and exhibits may not always be real and true, yet he treats them as if they were, not as if they were the thoughts of his own mind; that is, he treats them scientifically. On the other hand, Law or Natural History has before now been treated by an author with so much of colouring derived from his own mind as to become a sort of literature; this is especially seen in the instance of Theology, when it takes the shape of Pulpit Eloquence. It is seen too in historical composition, which becomes a mere specimen of chronology, or a chronicle, when divested of the philosophy, the skill, or the party and personal feelings of the particular writer. Science, then, has to do with things, literature with thoughts; science is universal, literature is personal; science uses words merely as symbols, but literature uses language in its full compass, as including phraseology, idiom, style, composition, rhythm, eloquence, and whatever other properties are included in it.

Let us then put aside the scientific use of words, when we are to speak of language and literature.

Literature is the personal use or exercise of language. That this is so is further proved from the fact that one author uses it so differently from another. Language itself in its very origination would seem to be traceable to individuals. Their peculiarities have given it its character. We are often able in fact to trace particular phrases or idioms to individuals; we know the history of their rise. Slang surely, as it is called, comes of, and breathes of the personal. The connection between the force of words in particular languages and the habits and sentiments of the nations speaking them has often been pointed out. And, while the many use language as they find it, the man of genius uses it indeed, but subjects it withal to his own purposes, and moulds it according to his own peculiarities. The throng and succession of ideas, thoughts, feelings, imaginations, aspirations, which pass within him, the abstractions, the juxtapositions, the comparisons, the discriminations, the conceptions, which are are so original in him, his views of external things, his judgments upon life, manners, and history, the exercises of his wit, of his humour, of his depth, of his sagacity, all these innumerable and incessant creations, the very pulsation and throbbing of his intellect, does he image forth, to all does he give utterance, in a corresponding language, which is as multiform as this inward mental action itself and analogous to it, the faithful expression of his intense personality, attending on his own inward world of thought as its very shadow: so that we might as well say that one man's shadow is another's as that the style of a really gifted mind can belong to any but himself. It follows him about *as* a shadow. His thought and feeling are personal, and so his language is personal.

4

Thought and speech are inseparable from each other. Matter and expression are parts of one: style is a thinking out into language. This is what I have been laying down, and this is literature; not *things*, not the verbal symbols of things; not on the other hand mere *words;* but thoughts expressed in language. Call to mind, Gentlemen, the meaning of the Greek word which expresses this special prerogative of man over the feeble intelligence of the inferior animals. It is called Logos: what does Logos mean? it stands both for *reason* and for *speech*, and it is difficult to say which it means more properly. It means both at once: why? because really they cannot be divided,— because they are in a true sense one. When we can separate light and illumination, life and motion, the convex and the concave of a curve, then will it be possible for thought to tread speech under foot, and to hope to do without it—then will it be conceivable that the vigorous and fertile intellect should renounce its own double, its instrument of expression, and the channel of its speculations and emotions.

Critics should consider this view of the subject before they lay down such canons of taste as the writer whose pages I have quoted. Such men as he is consider fine writing to be an *addition from without* to the matter treated of,—a sort of ornament superinduced, or a luxury indulged in, by those who have time and inclination for such vanities. They speak as if *one* man could do the thought, and *another* the style. We read in Persian travels of the way in which young gentlemen go to work in the East, when they would engage in correspondence with those who inspire them with hope or fear. They cannot write one sentence themselves; so they betake themselves to the professional letter-writer. They confide to him the object they have in view. They have a point to gain from a superior, a favour to ask, an evil to deprecate; they have to approach a man in power, or to make court to some beautiful lady. The professional man manufactures words for them, as they are wanted, as a stationer sells them paper, or a schoolmaster might cut their pens. Thought and word are, in their conception, two things, and thus there is a division of labour. The man of thought comes to the man of words; and the man of words, duly instructed in the thought, dips the pen of desire into the ink of devotedness, and proceeds to spread it over the page of desolation. Then the nightingale of affection is heard to warble to the rose of loveliness, while the breeze of anxiety plays around the brow of expectation. This is what the Easterns are said to consider fine writing; and it seems pretty much the idea of the school of critics to whom I have been referring.

We have an instance in literary history of this very proceeding nearer home, in a great University, in the latter years of the last century. I have referred to it before now in a public lecture elsewhere[2]; but it is too much in point here to be omitted. A learned Arabic scholar had to deliver a set of lectures before its doctors and professors on an historical subject in which his reading had

lain. A linguist is conversant with science rather than with literature; but this gentleman felt that his lectures must not be without a style. Being of the opinion of the Orientals, with whose writings he was familiar, he determined to buy a style. He took the step of engaging a person, at a price, to turn the matter which he had got together into ornamental English. Observe, he did not wish for mere grammatical English, but for an elaborate, pretentious style. An artist was found in the person of a country curate, and the job was carried out. His lectures remain to this day, in their own place in the protracted series of annual Discourses to which they belong, distinguished amid a number of heavyish compositions by the rhetorical and ambitious diction for which he went into the market. This learned divine, indeed, and the author I have quoted, differ from each other in the estimate they respectively form of literary composition; but they agree together in this,—in considering such composition a trick and a trade; they put it on a par with the gold plate and the flowers and the music of a banquet, which do not make the viands better, but the entertainment more pleasurable; as if language were the hired servant, the mere mistress of the reason, and not the lawful wife in her own house.

But can they really think that Homer, or Pindar, or Shakespeare, or Dryden, or Walter Scott, were accustomed to aim at diction for its own sake, instead of being inspired with their subject, and pouring forth beautiful words because they had beautiful thoughts? this is surely too great a paradox to be borne. Rather, it is the fire within the author's breast which overflows in the torrent of his burning, irresistible eloquence; it is the poetry of his inner soul, which relieves itself in the Ode or the Elegy; and his mental attitude and bearing, the beauty of his moral countenance, the force and keenness of his logic, are imaged in the tenderness, or energy, or richness of his language. Nay, according to the well-known line, "facit indignatio *versus;*"[3] not the words alone, but even the rhythm, the metre, the verse, will be the contemporaneous offspring of the emotion or imagination which possesses him. "Poeta nascitur, non fit,"[4] says the proverb; and this is in numerous instances true of his poems, as well as of himself. They are born, not framed; they are a strain rather than a composition; and their perfection is the monument, not so

---

[2] "Position of Catholics in England," pp. 101–2. [N]
[3] Literally, "indignation makes the verse" (Cicero).
[4] "The poet is born, not made."

much of his skill as of his power. And this is true of prose as well as of verse in its degree: who will not recognize in the vision of Mirza a delicacy and beauty of style which is very difficult to describe, but which is felt to be in exact correspondence to the ideas of which it is the expression?

5

And, since the thoughts and reasonings of an author have, as I have said, a personal character, no wonder that his style is not only the image of his subject, but of his mind. That pomp of language, that full and tuneful diction, that felicitousness in the choice and exquisiteness in the collocation of words, which to prosaic writers seems artificial, is nothing else but the mere habit and way of a lofty intellect. Aristotle, in his sketch of the magnanimous man, tells us that his voice is deep, his motions slow, and his stature commanding. In like manner, the elocution of a great intellect is great. His language expresses, not only his great thoughts, but his great self. Certainly he might use fewer words than he uses; but he fertilizes his simplest ideas, and germinates into a multitude of details, and prolongs the march of his sentences, and sweeps round to the full diapason of his harmony, as if κύδεϊ γαίων, rejoicing in his own vigour and richness of resource. I say, a narrow critic will call it verbiage, when really it is a sort of fulness of heart, parallel to that which makes the merry boy whistle as he walks, or the strong man, like the smith in the novel, flourish his club when there is no one to fight with.

Shakespeare furnishes us with frequent instances of this peculiarity, and all so beautiful, that it is difficult to select for quotation. For instance, in Macbeth:—

> "Canst thou not minister to a mind diseased,
>   Pluck from the memory a rooted sorrow,
>   Raze out the written troubles of the brain,
>   And with some sweet oblivious antidote,
>   Cleanse the foul bosom of that perilous stuff,
>   Which weighs upon the heart?"[5]

Here a simple idea, by a process which belongs to the orator rather than to the poet, but still comes from the native vigour of genius, is expanded into a many-membered period.

The following from Hamlet is of the same kind:—

> "'Tis not alone my inky cloak, good mother,
>   Nor customary suits of solemn black,
>   Nor windy suspiration of forced breath,
>   No, nor the fruitful river in the eye,
>   Nor the dejected haviour of the visage,
>   Together with all forms, modes, shows of grief,
>   That can denote me truly."[6]

Now, if such declamation, for declamation it is, however noble, be allowable in a poet, whose genius is so far removed from pompousness or pretence, much more is it allowable in an orator, whose very province it is to put forth words to the best advantage he can. Cicero has nothing more redundant in any part of his writings than these passages from Shakespeare. No lover then at least of Shakespeare may fairly accuse Cicero of gorgeousness of phraseology or diffuseness of style. Nor will any sound critic be tempted to do so. As a certain unaffected neatness and propriety and grace of diction may be required of any author who lays claim to be a classic, for the same reason that a certain attention to dress is expected of every gentleman, so to Cicero may be allowed the privilege of the "os magna sonaturum,"[7] of which the ancient critic speaks. His copious, majestic, musical flow of language, even if sometimes beyond what the subject-matter demands, is never out of keeping with the occasion or with the speaker. It is the expression of lofty sentiments in lofty sentences, the "mens magna in corpore magno."[8] It is the development of the inner man. Cicero vividly realised the *status* of a Roman senator and statesman, and the "pride of place" of Rome, in all the grace and grandeur which attached to her; and he imbibed, and became what he admired. As the exploits of Scipio or Pompey are the expression of this greatness in deed, so the language of Cicero is the expression of it in word. And, as the acts of the Roman ruler or soldier represent to us, in a manner special to themselves, the characteristic magnanimity of the lords of the earth, so do the speeches or treatises of her accomplished orator bring it home to our imaginations as no other writing could do. Neither Livy, nor Tacitus, nor Terence, nor Seneca, nor Pliny, nor Quintilian, is an adequate spokesman for the Imperial City. They write Latin; Cicero writes Roman.

---

[5] *Macbeth*, V, iii, 40–45.
[6] *Hamlet*, I, ii, 77–83.
[7] "The great mouth of sounds."
[8] "Great mind in a great body."

6

You will say that Cicero's language is undeniably studied, but that Shakespeare's is as
undeniably natural and spontaneous; and that
this is what is meant, when the Classics are accused of being mere artists of words. Here we
are introduced to a further large question,
which gives me the opportunity of anticipating
a misapprehension of my meaning. I observe,
then, that, not only is that lavish richness of
style, which I have noticed in Shakespeare,
justifiable on the principles which I have been
laying down, but, what is less easy to receive,
even elaborateness in composition is no mark of
trick or artifice in an author. Undoubtedly the
works of the Classics, particularly the Latin, *are*
elaborate; they have cost a great deal of time,
care, and trouble. They have had many rough
copics; I grant it. I grant also that there are
writers of name, ancient and modern, who really
are guilty of the absurdity of making sentences,
as the very end of their literary labour. Such was
Isocrates;[9] such were some of the sophists; they
were set on words, to the neglect of thoughts or
things; I cannot defend them. If I must give an
English instance of this fault, much as I love and
revere the personal character and intellectual
vigour of Dr. Johnson, I cannot deny that his
style often outruns the sense and the occasion,
and is wanting in that simplicity which is the
attribute of genius. Still, granting all this, I
cannot grant, notwithstanding, that genius never
need take pains,—that genius may not improve by
practice,—that it never incurs failures, and
succeeds the second time,—that it never finishes
off at leisure what it has thrown off in the
outline at a stroke.

Take the instance of the painter or the sculptor;
he has a conception in his mind which he wishes
to represent in the medium of his art;—the
Madonna and Child, or Innocence, or Fortitude,
or some historical character or event. Do you
mean to say he does not study his subject? does
he not make sketches? does he not even call them
"studies"? does he not call his workroom a
studio? is he not ever designing, rejecting, adopting, correcting, perfecting? Are not the first
attempts of Michael Angelo and Raffaelle[10]
extant, in the case of some of the most celebrated
compositions? Will any one say that the Apollo
Belvidere is not a conception patiently elaborated
into its proper perfection? These departments of

taste, are according to the received notions of the
world, the very province of genius, and yet we
call them *arts;* they are the "Fine Arts." Why
may not that be true of literary composition
which is true of painting, sculpture, architecture,
and music? Why may not language be wrought
as well as the clay of the modeller? why may not
words be worked up as well as colours? why
should not skill in diction be simply subservient
and instrumental to the great prototypal ideas
which are the comtemplation of a Plato or a
Virgil? Our greatest poet tells us,

"The poet's eye, in a fine frenzy rolling,
  Doth glance from heaven to earth, from earth to
      heaven;
  And, as imagination bodies forth
  The forms of things unknown, the poet's pen
  Turns them to shapes, and gives to airy nothing
  A local habitation and a name."[11]

Now, is it wonderful that that pen of his should
sometimes be at fault for a while,—that it should
pause, write, erase, re-write, amend, complete,
before he satisfies himself that his language has
done justice to the conceptions which his mind's
eye contemplated?

In this point of view, doubtless, many or most
writers are elaborate; and those certainly not
the least whose style is furthest removed from
ornament, being simple and natural, or vehement, or severely business-like and practical.
Who so energetic and manly as Demosthenes?
Yet he is said to have transcribed Thucydides
many times over in the formation of his style.
Who so gracefully natural as Herodotus? yet his
very dialect is not his own, but chosen for the
sake of the perfection of his narrative. Who
exhibits such happy negligence as our own
Addison? yet artistic fastidiousness was so
notorious in his instance that the report has got
abroad, truly or not, that he was too late in his
issue of an important state-paper, from his habit
of revision and recomposition. Such great authors
were working by a model which was before the
eyes of their intellect, and they were labouring
to say what they had to say, in such a way as
would most exactly and suitably express it.
It is not wonderful that other authors, whose
style is not simple, should be instances of a
similar literary diligence. Virgil wished his
Æneid to be burned, elaborate as is its composition, because he felt it needed more labour still,

---

[9] Isocrates (436–338 B.C.), Greek rhetorician.
[11] *Midsummer Night's Dream*, V, 12–17.

[10] I.e., Raphael (1483–1520).

in order to make it perfect. The historian Gibbon in the last century is another instance in point. You must not suppose I am going to recommend his style for imitation, any more than his principles; but I refer to him as the example of a writer feeling the task which lay before him, feeling that he had to bring out into words for the comprehension of his readers a great and complicated scene, and wishing that those words should be adequate to his undertaking. I think he wrote the first chapter of his History three times over; it was not that he corrected or improved the first copy; but he put his first essay, and then his second, aside—he recast his matter, till he had hit the precise exhibition of it which he thought demanded by his subject.

Now in all these instances, I wish you to observe, that what I have admitted about literary workmanship differs from the doctrine which I am opposing in this,—that the mere dealer in words cares little or nothing for the subject which he is embellishing, but can paint and gild anything whatever to order; whereas the artist, whom I am acknowledging, has his great or rich visions before him, and his only aim is to bring out what he thinks or what he feels in a way adequate to the thing spoken of, and appropriate to the speaker.

7

The illustration which I have been borrowing from the Fine Arts will enable me to go a step further. I have been showing the connection of the thought with the language in literary composition; and in doing so I have exposed the unphilosophical notion, that the language was an extra which could be dispensed with, and provided to order according to the demand. But I have not yet brought out, what immediately follows from this, and which was the second point which I had to show, viz., that to be capable of easy translation is no test of the excellence of a composition. If I must say what I think, I should lay down, with little hesitation, that the truth was almost the reverse of this doctrine. Nor are many words required to show it. Such a doctrine, as is contained in the passage of the author whom I quoted when I began, goes upon the assumption that one language is just like another language,— that every language has all the ideas, turns of thought, delicacies of expression, figures, associations, abstractions, points of view, which every other language has. Now, as far as regards Science, it is true that all languages are pretty much alike for the purposes of Science; but

even in this respect some are more suitable than others, which have to coin words, or to borrow them, in order to express scientific ideas. But if languages are not all equally adapted even to furnish symbols for those universal and eternal truths in which Science consists, how can they reasonably be expected to be all equally rich, equally forcible, equally musical, equally exact, equally happy in expressing the idiosyncratic peculiarities of thought of some original and fertile mind, who has availed himself of one of them? A great author takes his native language, masters it, partly throws himself into it, partly moulds and adapts it, and pours out his multitude of ideas through the variously ramified and delicately minute channels of expression which he has found or framed:—does it follow that this his personal presence (as it may be called) can forthwith be transferred to every other language under the sun? Then may we reasonably maintain that Beethoven's *piano* music is not really beautiful, because it cannot be played on the hurdy-gurdy. Were not this astonishing doctrine maintained by persons far superior to the writer whom I have selected for animadversion, I should find it difficult to be patient under a gratuitous extravagance. It seems that a really great author must admit of translation, and that we have a test of his excellence when he reads to advantage in a foreign language as well as in his own. Then Shakespeare *is* a genius because he can be translated into German, and *not* a genius because he cannot be translated into French. Then the multiplication-table is the most gifted of all conceivable compositions, because it loses nothing by translation, and can hardly be said to belong to any one language whatever. Whereas I should rather have conceived that, in proportion as ideas are novel and recondite, they would be difficult to put into words, and that the very fact of their having insinuated themselves into one language would diminish the chance of that happy accident being repeated in another. In the language of savages you can hardly express any idea or act of the intellect at all: is the tongue of the Hottentot or Esquimaux to be made the measure of the genius of Plato, Pindar, Tacitus, St. Jerome, Dante, or Cervantes?

Let us recur, I say, to the illustration of the Fine Arts. I suppose you can express ideas in painting which you cannot express in sculpture; and the more an artist is of a painter, the less he is likely to be of a sculptor. The more he commits his genius to the methods and conditions of his own art, the less he will be able to throw himself into the circumstances of another. Is the genius of Fra Angelico, of Francia, or of Raffaelle disparaged by the fact that he was able to do that in colours which no man that ever lived, which no Angel, could achieve in wood? Each of the Fine Arts has its own subject-matter; from the nature of the case you can do in one what you cannot do in another; you can do in painting what you cannot do in carving; you can do in oils what you cannot do in fresco; you can do in marble what you cannot do in ivory; you can do in wax what you cannot do in bronze. Then, I repeat, applying this to the case of languages, why should not genius be able to do in Greek what it cannot do in Latin? and why are its Greek and Latin works defective because they will not turn into English? That genius, of which we are speaking, did not make English; it did not make all languages, present, past, and future; it did not make the laws of *any* language: why is it to be judged of by that in which it had no part, over which it has no control?

8

And now we are naturally brought on to our third point, which is on the characteristics of Holy Scripture as compared with profane literature. Hitherto we have been concerned with the doctrine of these writers, viz., that style is an *extra*, that it is a mere artifice, and that hence it cannot be translated; now we come to their fact, viz., that Scripture has no such artificial style, and that Scripture can easily be translated. Surely their fact is as untenable as their doctrine.

Scripture easy of translation! then why have there been so few good translators? why is it that there has been such great difficulty in combining the two necessary qualities, fidelity to the original and purity in the adopted vernacular? why is it that the authorized versions of the Church are often so inferior to the original as compositions, except that the Church is bound above all things to see that the version is doctrinally correct, and in a difficult problem is obliged to put up with defects in what is of secondary importance, provided she secure what is of first? If it were so easy to transfer the beauty of the original to the copy, she would not have been content with her received version in various languages which could be named.

And then in the next place, Scripture not elaborate! Scripture not ornamented in diction, and musical in cadence! Why, consider the Epistle to the Hebrews—where is there in the classics any composition more carefully, more artificially written? Consider the book of Job—is it not a sacred drama, as artistic, as perfect, as any Greek tragedy of Sophocles of Euripides? Consider the Psalter—are there no ornaments, no rhythm, no studied cadences, no responsive members, in that divinely beautiful book? And is it not hard to understand? are not the Prophets hard to understand? is not St. Paul hard to understand? Who can say that these are popular compositions? who can say that they are level at first reading with the understandings of the multitude?

That there are portions indeed of the inspired volume more simple both in style and in meaning, and that these are the more sacred and sublime passages, as, for instance, parts of the Gospels, I grant at once; but this does not militate against the doctrine I have been laying down. Recollect, Gentlemen, my distinction when I began. I have said Literature is one thing, and that Science is another; that Literature has to do with ideas, and Science with realities; that Literature is of a personal character, that Science treats of what is universal and eternal. In proportion, then, as Scripture excludes the personal colouring of its writers, and rises into the region of pure and mere inspiration, when it ceases in any sense to be the writing of man, of St. Paul or St. John, of Moses or Isaias, then it comes to belong to Science, not Literature. Then it conveys the things of heaven, unseen verities, divine manifestations, and them alone—not the ideas, the feelings, the aspirations, of its human instruments, who, for all that they were inspired and infallible, did not cease to be men. St. Paul's epistles, then, I consider to be literature in a real and true sense, *as* personal, *as* rich in reflection and emotion, as Demosthenes or Euripides; and, without ceasing to be revelations of objective truth, they are expressions of the subjective notwithstanding. On the other hand, portions of the Gospels, of the book of Genesis, and other passages of the Sacred Volume, are of the nature of Science. Such is the beginning of St. John's Gospel, which we read at the end of Mass. Such is the Creed. I mean, passages such as these are the mere enunciation of eternal things, without (so to say) the medium of any human mind transmitting them to us. The words used have the grandeur, the majesty, the calm, unimpassioned beauty of Science; they are in no sense Literature, they are in no sense personal; and therefore they are easy to apprehend, and easy to translate.

Did time admit I could show you parallel instances of what I am speaking of in the Classics, inferior to the inspired word in proportion as the subject-matter of the classical authors is immensely inferior to the subjects treated of in Scripture—but parallel, inasmuch as the classical author or speaker ceases for the moment to have to do with Literature, as speaking of things objectively, and rises to the serene sublimity of Science. But I should be carried too far if I began.

9

I shall then merely sum up what I have said, and come to a conclusion. Reverting, then, to my original question, what is the meaning of Letters as contained, Gentlemen, in the designation of your Faculty, I have answered, that by Letters or Literature is meant the expression of thought in language, where by "thought" I mean the ideas, feelings, views, reasonings, and other operations of the human mind. And the Art of Letters is the method by which a speaker or writer brings out in words, worthy of his subject, and sufficient for his audience or readers, the thoughts which impress him. Literature, then, is of a personal character; it consists in the enunciations and teachings of those who have a right to speak as representatives of their kind, and in whose words their brethren find an interpretation of their own sentiments, a record of their own experience, and a suggestion for their own judgments. A great author, Gentlemen, is not one who merely has a *copia verborum*,[12] whether in prose or verse, and can, as it were, turn on at his will any number of splendid phrases and swelling sentences; but he is one who has something to say and knows how to say it. I do not claim for him, as such, any great depth of thought, or breadth of view, or philosophy, or sagacity, or knowledge of human nature, or experience of human life, though these additional gifts he may have, and the more he has of them the greater he is; but I ascribe to him, as his characteristic gift, in a large sense the faculty of Expression. He is master of the two-fold Logos, the thought and the word, distinct, but inseparable from each other. He may, if so be, elaborate his compositions, or he may pour out his improvisations, but in either case he has but one aim, which he keeps steadily before him, and is conscientious and single-minded in fulfilling. That aim is to give forth what he has within him; and from his very earnestness it comes to pass that, whatever be the splendour of his diction or the harmony of his periods, he has with him the

charm of an incommunicable simplicity. Whatever be his subject, high or low, he treats it suitably and for its own sake. If he is a poet, "nil molitur *ineptè*."[13] If he is an orator, then too he speaks, not only "distinctè" and "splendidè," but also "*aptè*." His page is the lucid mirror of his mind and life—

"Quo fit, ut omnis
Votivâ pateat veluti descripta tabellâ
Vita senis."[14]

He writes passionately, because he feels keenly; forcibly, because he conceives vividly, he sees too clearly to be vague; he is too serious to be otiose; he can analyze his subject, and therefore he is rich; he embraces it as a whole and in its parts, and therefore he is consistent; he has a firm hold of it, and therefore he is luminous. When his imagination wells up, it overflows in ornament; when his heart is touched, it thrills along his verse. He always has the right word for the right idea, and never a word too much. If he is brief, it is because few words suffice; when he is lavish of them, still each word has its mark, and aids, not embarrasses, the vigorous march of his elocution. He expresses what all feel, but all cannot say; and his sayings pass into proverbs among his people, and his phrases become household words and idioms of their daily speech, which is tesselated with the rich fragments of his language, as we see in foreign lands the marbles of Roman grandeur worked into the walls and pavements of modern palaces.

Such pre-eminently is Shakespeare among ourselves; such pre-eminently Virgil, among the Latins; such in their degree are all those writers who in every nation go by the name of Classics. To particular nations they are necessarily attached from the circumstance of the variety of tongues, and the peculiarities of each; but so far they have a catholic and ecumenical character, that what they express is common to the whole race of man, and they alone are able to express it.

10

If then the power of speech is a gift as great as any that can be named,—if the origin of language is by many philosophers even considered to be nothing short of divine,—if by means of words the secrets of the heart are brought to light, pain of soul is relieved, hidden grief is carried off, sympathy conveyed, counsel imparted, experience

---

[12] Abundance of words.   [13] "Nothing is softened foolishly."
[14] "Made so that the whole life of an old man is laid forth like a painted votive tablet."

recorded, and wisdom perpetuated,—if by great authors the many are drawn up into unity, national character is fixed, a people speaks, the past and the future, the East and the West are brought into communication with each other,—if such men are, in a word, the spokesmen and prophets of the human family,—it will not answer to make light of Literature or to neglect its study; rather we may be sure that, in proportion as we master it in whatever language, and imbibe its spirit, we shall ourselves become in our own measure the ministers of like benefits to others, be they many or few, be they in the obscurer or the more distinguished walks of life,—who are united to us by social ties, and are within the sphere of our personal influence.

The Second Spring

One of Newman's most moving sermons, "The Second Spring," was preached at St. Mary's Church, Oscott, site of a Roman Catholic college. The "Second Spring" of the title and the subject of Newman's constant references in the sermon is the reestablishment of the Roman Catholic hierarchy in Great Britain in 1850, an event that extreme Protestants referred to as the "Papal Aggression." Newman sees it as a rebirth, a second spring of the true faith in England. The sermon was preached in 1852 and first published in Sermons Preached on Various Occassions *(1857).*

(Preached in St. Mary's, Oscott.[1])

CANT., *c.* ii. *v.* 10-12.

Surge, propera, amica mea, columba mea, formosa mea, et veni. Jam enim hiems transiit, imber abiit et recessit. Flores apparuerunt in terrâ nostrâ.

Arise, make haste, my love, my dove, my beautiful one, and come. For the winter is now past, the rain is over and gone. The flowers have appeared in our land.

W E HAVE familiar experience of the order, the constancy, the perpetual renovation of the material world which surrounds us. Frail and transitory as is every part of it, restless and migratory as are its elements, never-ceasing as are its changes, still it abides. It is bound together by a law of permanence, it is set up in unity; and, though it is ever dying, it is ever coming to life again. Dissolution does but give birth to fresh modes of organization, and one death is the parent of a thousand lives. Each hour, as it comes, is but a testimony, how fleeting, yet how secure, how certain, is the great whole. It is like an image on the waters, which is ever the same, though the waters ever flow. Change upon change—yet one change cries out to another, like the alternate Seraphim, in praise and in glory of their Maker. The sun sinks to rise again; the day is swallowed up in the gloom of the night, to be born out of it, as fresh as if it had never been quenched. Spring passes into summer, and through summer and autumn into winter, only the more surely, by its own ultimate return, to triumph over that grave, towards which it resolutely hastened from its first hour. We mourn over the blossoms of May, because they are to wither; but we know, withal, that May is one day to have its revenge upon November, by the revolution of that solemn circle which never stops—which teaches us in our height of hope, ever to be sober, and in our depth of desolation, never to despair.

And forcibly as this comes home to every one of us, not less forcible is the contrast which exists between this material world, so vigorous, so reproductive, amid all its changes, and the moral world, so feeble, so downward, so resourceless, amid all its aspirations. That which ought to come to nought, endures; that which promises a future, disappoints and is no more. The same sun shines in heaven from first to last, and the

---

[1] Dedication in the first Edition:—To the Fathers of the Synod at Oscott, to the Clergy who assisted at it, who, in the strength of the Most High, have begun a work which is to live after them, the following Sermon, preached under the Illumination of their presence, is humbly and affectionately inscribed, by their devoted servant in Christ, the Author. [N]

blue firmament, the everlasting mountains, reflect his rays; but where is there upon earth the champion, the hero, the lawgiver, the body politic, the sovereign race, which was great three hundred years ago, and is great now? Moralists and poets, often do they descant upon this innate vitality of matter, this innate perishableness of mind. Man rises to fall: he tends to dissolution from the moment he begins to be; he lives on, indeed, in his children, he lives on in his name, he lives not on in his own person. He is, as regards the manifestations of his nature here below, as a bubble that breaks, and as water poured out upon the earth. He was young, he is old, he is never young again. This is the lament over him, poured forth in verse and in prose, by Christians and by heathen. The greatest work of God's hands under the sun, he, in all the manifestations of his complex being, is born only to die.

His bodily frame first begins to feel the power of this constraining law, though it is the last to succumb to it. We look at the bloom of youth with interest, yet with pity; and the more graceful and sweet it is, with pity so much the more; for, whatever be its excellence and its glory, soon it begins to be deformed and dishonoured by the very force of its living on. It grows into exhaustion and collapse, till at length it crumbles into that dust out of which it was originally taken.

So is it, too, with our moral being, a far higher and diviner portion of our natural constitution; it begins with life, it ends with what is worse than the mere loss of life, with a living death. How beautiful is the human heart, when it puts forth its first leaves, and opens and rejoices in its spring-tide. Fair as may be the bodily form, fairer far, in its green foliage and bright blossoms, is natural virtue. It blooms in the young, like some rich flower, so delicate, so fragrant, and so dazzling. Generosity and lightness of heart and amiableness, the confiding spirit, the gentle temper, the elastic cheerfulness, the open hand, the pure affection, the noble aspiration, the heroic resolve, the romantic pursuit, the love in which self has no part,—are not these beautiful? and are they not dressed up and set forth for admiration in their best shapes, in tales and in poems? and ah! what a prospect of good is there! who could believe that it is to fade! and yet, as night follows upon day, as decrepitude follows upon health, so surely are failure, and overthrow, and annihilation, the issue of this natural virtue, if time only be allowed to it to run its course. There are those who are cut off in the first opening of this excellence, and then, if we may

trust their epitaphs, they have lived like angels; but wait a while, let them live on, let the course of life proceed, let the bright soul go through the fire and water of the world's temptations and seductions and corruptions and transformations; and, alas for the insufficiency of nature! alas for its powerlessness to persevere, its waywardness in disappointing its own promise! Wait till youth has become age; and not more different is the miniature which we have of him when a boy, when every feature spoke of hope, put side by side of the large portrait painted to his honour, when he is old, when his limbs are shrunk, his eye dim, his brow furrowed, and his hair grey, than differs the moral grace of that boyhood from the forbidding and repulsive aspect of his soul, now that he has lived to the age of man. For moroseness, and misanthropy, and selfishness, is the ordinary winter of that spring.

Such is man in his own nature, and such, too, is he in his works. The noblest efforts of his genius, the conquests he has made, the doctrines he has originated, the nations he has civilized, the states he has created, they outlive himself, they outlive him by many centuries, but they tend to an end, and that end is dissolution. Powers of the world, sovereignties, dynasties, sooner or later come to nought; they have their fatal hour. The Roman conqueror shed tears over Carthage, for in the destruction of the rival city he discerned too truly an augury of the fall of Rome; and at length, with the weight and the responsibilities, the crimes and the glories, of centuries upon centuries, the Imperial City fell.

Thus man and all his works are mortal; they die, and they have no power of renovation.

But what is it, my Fathers, my Brothers, what is it that has happened in England just at this time? Something strange is passing over this land, by the very surprise, by the very commotion, which it excites. Were we not near enough the scene of action to be able to say what is going on, —were we the inhabitants of some sister planet possessed of a more perfect mechanism than this earth has discovered for surveying the transactions of another globe,—and did we turn our eyes thence towards England just at this season, we should be arrested by a political phenomenon as wonderful as any which the astronomer notes down from his physical field of view. It would be the occurrence of a national commotion, almost without parallel, more violent than has happened here for centuries,—at least in the judgments and intentions of men, if not in act and deed. We should note it down, that soon after St. Michael's day, 1850,[2] a storm arose in the moral world, so furious as to demand some great explanation, and to rouse in us an intense desire to gain it. We should observe it increasing from day to day, and spreading from place to place, without remission, almost without lull, up to this very hour, when perhaps it threatens worse still, or at least gives no sure prospect of alleviation. Every party in the body politic undergoes its influence,—from the Queen upon her throne, down to the little ones in the infant or day school. The ten thousands of the constituency, the sum-total of Protestant sects, the aggregate of religious societies and associations, the great body of established clergy in town and country, the bar, even the medical profession, nay, even literary and scientific circles, every class, every interest, every fireside, gives tokens of this ubiquitous storm. This would be our report of it, seeing it from the distance, and we should speculate on the cause. What is it all about? against what is it directed? what wonder has happened upon earth? what prodigious, what preternatural event is adequate to the burden of so vast an effect?

We should judge rightly in our curiosity about a phenomenon like this; it must be a portentous event, and it is. It is an innovation, a miracle, I may say, in the course of human events. The physical world revolves year by year, and begins again; but the political order of things does not renew itself, does not return; it continues, but it proceeds; there is no retrogression. This is so well understood by men of the day, that with them progress is idolized as another name for good. The past never returns—it is never good; —if we are to escape existing ills, it must be by going forward. The past is out of date; the past is dead. As well may the dead live to us, well may the dead profit us, as the past return. *This*, then, is the cause of this national transport, this national cry, which encompasses us. The past *has* returned, the dead lives. Thrones are overturned, and are never restored; States live and die, and then are matter only for history. Babylon was great, and Tyre, and Egypt, and Nineve, and shall never be great again. The English Church was, and the English Church was not, and the English Church is once again. This is the portent, worthy of a cry. It is the coming in of a Second Spring; it is a restoration in the moral world, such as that which yearly takes place in the physical.

Three centuries ago, and the Catholic Church, that great creation of God's power, stood in this land in pride of place. It had the honours of near a thousand years upon it; it was enthroned on some twenty sees up and down the broad country; it was based in the will of a faithful people; it energized through ten thousand instruments of power and influence; and it was ennobled by a host of Saints and Martyrs. The churches, one by one, recounted and rejoiced in the line of glorified intercessors, who were the respective objects of their grateful homage. Canterbury alone numbered perhaps some sixteen, from St. Augustine to St. Dunstan and St. Elphege, from St. Anselm and St. Thomas down to St. Edmund. York had its St. Paulinus, St. John, St. Wilfrid, and St. William; London, its St. Erconwald; Durham, its St. Cuthbert; Winton, its St. Swithun. Then there were St. Aidan of Lindisfarne, and St. Hugh of Lincoln, and St. Chad of Lichfield, and St. Thomas of Hereford, and St. Oswald and St. Wulstan of Worcester, and St. Osmund of Salibury, and St. Birinus of Dorchester, and St. Richard of Chichester.[3] And then, too, its religious orders, its monastic establishments, its universities, its wide relations all over Europe, its high prerogatives in the temporal state, its wealth, its dependencies, its popular honours,—where was there in the whole of Christendom a more glorious hierarchy? Mixed up with the civil institutions, with kings and nobles, with the people, found in every village and in every town,— it seemed destined to stand, so long as England stood, and to outlast, it might be, England's greatness.

But it was the high decree of heaven, that the majesty of that presence should be blotted out. It is a long story, my Fathers and Brothers—you know it well. I need not go through it. The vivifying principle of truth, the shadow of St. Peter, the grace of the Redeemer, left it. That old Church in its day became a corpse (a marvellous, an awful change!); and then it did but corrupt the air which once it refreshed, and cumber the ground which once it beautified. So all seemed to be lost; and there was a struggle for a time, and then its priests were cast out or martyred. There were sacrileges innumerable. Its temples were profaned or destroyed; its revenues seized by covetous nobles, or squandered upon the ministers of a new faith. The presence

---

[2] 29 September, day on which the Roman Catholic hierarchy was established in England.

[3] As an Anglican, Newman had made a special study of English saints and had sponsored a series of lives of English saints written by the Tractarians. See the *Apologia*.

of Catholicism was at length simply removed, —its grace disowned,—its power despised,—its name, except as a matter of history, at length almost unknown. It took a long time to do this thoroughly; much time, much thought, much labour, much expense; but at last it was done. Oh, that miserable day, centuries before we were born! What a martyrdom to live in it and see the fair form of Truth, moral and material, hacked piecemeal, and every limb and organ carried off, and burned in the fire, or cast into the deep! But at last the work was done. Truth was disposed of, and shovelled away, and there was a calm, a silence, a sort of peace;—and such was about the state of things when we were born into this weary world.

My Fathers and Brothers, *you* have seen it on one side, and some of us on another; but one and all of us can bear witness to the fact of the utter contempt into which Catholicism had fallen by the time that we were born. You, alas, know it far better than I can know it; but it may not be out of place, if by one or two tokens, as by the strokes of a pencil, I bear witness to you from without, of what you can witness so much more truly from within. No longer the Catholic Church in the country; nay, no longer, I may say, a Catholic community;—but a few adherents of the Old Religion, moving silently and sorrowfully about, as memorials of what had been. "The Roman Catholics;"—not a sect, not even an interest, as men conceived of it,—not a body, however small, representative of the Great Communion abroad,—but a mere handful of individuals, who might be counted, like the pebbles and *detritus* of the great deluge, and who, forsooth, merely happened to retain a creed which, in its day indeed, was the profession of a Church. Here a set of poor Irishmen, coming and going at harvest time, or a colony of them lodged in a miserable quarter of the vast metropolis. There, perhaps an elderly person, seen walking in the streets, grave and solitary, and strange, though noble in bearing, and said to be of good family, and a "Roman Catholic." An old-fashioned house of gloomy appearance, closed in with high walls, with an iron gate, and yews, and the report attaching to it that "Roman Catholics" lived there; but who they were, or what they did, or what was meant by calling them Roman Catholics, no one could tell;—though it had an unpleasant sound, and told of form and superstition. And then, perhaps, as we went to and fro, looking with a boy's curious eyes through the great city, we might come to-day upon some

Moravian chapel, or Quaker's meeting-house, and to-morrow on a chapel of the "Roman Catholics": but nothing was to be gathered from it, except that there were lights burning there, and some boys in white, swinging censers; and what it all meant could only be learned from books, from Protestant Histories and Sermons; and they did not report well of "the Roman Catholics," but, on the contrary, deposed that they had once had power and had abused it. And then, again, we might on one occasion hear it pointedly put out by some literary man, as the result of his careful investigation, and as a recondite point of information, which few knew, that there was this difference between the Roman Catholics of England and the Roman Catholics of Ireland, that the latter had bishops, and the former were governed by four officials, called Vicars-Apostolic.

Such was about the sort of knowledge possessed of Christianity by the heathen of old time, who persecuted its adherents from the face of the earth, and then called them a *gens lucifuga*, a people who shunned the light of day. Such were Catholics in England, found in corners, and alleys, and cellars, and the housetops, or in the recesses of the country; cut off from the populous world around them, and dimly seen, as if through a mist or in twilight, as ghosts flitting to and fro, by the high Protestants, the lords of the earth. At length so feeble did they become, so utterly contemptible, that contempt gave birth to pity; and the more generous of their tyrants actually began to wish to bestow on them some favour, under the notion that their opinions were simply too absurd ever to spread again, and that they themselves, were they but raised in civil importance, would soon unlearn and be ashamed of them. And thus, out of mere kindness to us, they began to vilify our doctrines to the Protestant world, that so our very idiotcy or our secret unbelief might be our plea for mercy.

A *great* change, an *awful* contrast, between the time-honoured Church of St. Augustine and St. Thomas, and the poor remnant of their children in the beginning of the nineteenth century! It was a miracle, I might say, to have pulled down that lordly power; but there was a greater and a truer one in store. No one could have prophesied its fall, but still less would any one have ventured to prophesy its rise again. The fall was wonderful; still after all it was in the order of nature;—all things come to nought: its rise again would be a different sort of wonder, for it is in the order of grace,—and who can hope for miracles, and such a miracle as this? Has the whole course of history a like to show? I must speak cautiously and according to my knowledge, but I recollect no parallel to it. Augustine, indeed, came to the same island to which the early missionaries had come already; but they came to Britons, and he to Saxons. The Arian Goths and Lombards, too, cast off their heresy in St. Augustine's age, and joined the Church; but they had never fallen away from her. The inspired word seems to imply the almost impossibility of such a grace as the renovation of those who have crucified to themselves again, and trodden under foot, the Son of God. Who then could have dared to hope that, out of so sacrilegious a nation as this is, a people would have been formed again unto their Saviour? What signs did it show that it was to be singled out from among the nations? Had it been prophesied some fifty years ago, would not the very notion have seemed preposterous and wild?

My Fathers, there was one of your own order, then in the maturity of his powers and his reputation. His name is the property of this diocese; yet is too great, too venerable, too dear to all Catholics, to be confined to any part of England, when it is rather a household word in the mouths of all of us. What would have been the feelings of that venerable man, the champion of God's ark in an evil time, could *he* have lived to see this day? It is almost presumptuous for one who knew him not, to draw pictures about him, and his thoughts, and his friends, some of whom are even here present; yet am I wrong in fancying that a day such as this, in which we stand, would have seemed to him a dream, or, if he prophesied of it, to his hearers nothing but a mockery? Say that one time, rapt in spirit, he had reached forward to the future, and that his mortal eye had wandered from that lowly chapel in the valley which had been for centuries in the possession of Catholics, to the neighbouring height, then waste and solitary. And let him say to those about him: "I see a bleak mount, looking upon an open country, over against that huge town, to whose inhabitants Catholicism is of so little account. I see the ground marked out, and an ample enclosure made; and plantations are rising there, clothing and circling in the space.

"And there on that high spot, far from the haunts of men, yet in the very centre of the island, a large edifice, or rather pile of edifices, appears with many fronts, and courts, and long cloisters and corridors, and story upon story. And there it rises, under the invocation of the same sweet and powerful name which has been our strength and consolation in the Valley. I look more attentively at that building, and I see it is fashioned upon that ancient style of art which brings back the past, which had seemed to be perishing from off the face of the earth, or to be preserved only as a curiosity, or to be imitated only as a fancy. I listen, and I hear the sound of voices, grave and musical, renewing the old chant, with which Augustine greeted Ethelbert in the free air upon the Kentish strand. It comes from a long procession, and it winds along the cloisters. Priests and Religious, theologians from the schools, and canons from the Cathedral, walk in due precedence. And then there comes a vision of well-nigh twelve mitred heads; and last I see a Prince of the Church, in the royal dye of empire and of martyrdom, a pledge to us from Rome of Rome's unwearied love, a token that that goodly company is firm in Apostolic faith and hope. And the shadow of the Saints is there;— St. Benedict is there, speaking to us by the voice of bishop and of priest, and counting over the long ages through which he has prayed, and studied, and laboured; there, too, is St. Dominic's white wool, which no blemish can impair, no stain can dim:—and if St. Bernard be not there, it is only that his absence may make him be remembered more. And the princely patriarch, St. Ignatius, too, the St. George of the modern world, with his chivalrous lance run through his writhing foe, he, too, sheds his blessing upon that train. And others, also, his equals or his juniors in history, whose pictures are above our altars, or soon shall be, the surest proof that the Lord's arm has not waxen short, nor His mercy failed,—they, too, are looking down from their thrones on high upon the throng. And so that high company moves on into the holy place; and there, with august rite and awful sacrifice, inaugurates the great act which brings it thither." What is that act? it is the first synod of a new Hierarchy; it is the resurrection of the Church.

O my Fathers, my Brothers, had that revered Bishop so spoken then, who that had heard him but would have said that he spoke what could not be? What! those few scattered worshippers, *the* Roman Catholics, to form a Church! Shall the past be rolled back? Shall the grave open? Shall the Saxons live again to God? Shall the shepherds, watching their poor flocks by night, be visited by a multitude of the heavenly army, and hear how their Lord has been new-born in their own city? Yes; for grace can, where nature cannot. The world grows old, but the Church is ever young. She can, in any time, at her Lord's will, "inherit the Gentiles, and inhabit the desolate cities." "Arise, Jerusalem, for thy light is come, and the glory of the Lord is risen upon thee. Behold, darkness shall cover the earth, and a mist the people; but the Lord shall arise upon thee, and His glory shall be seen upon thee. Lift up thine eyes round about, and see; all these are gathered together, they come to thee; thy sons shall come from afar, and thy daughters shall rise up at thy side." "Arise, make haste, my love, my dove, my beautiful one, and come. For the winter is now past, and the rain is over and gone. The flowers have appeared in our land . . . the fig-tree hath put forth her green figs; the vines in flower yield their sweet smell. Arise, my love, my beautiful one, and come." It is the time for thy Visitation. Arise, Mary, and go forth in thy strength into that north country, which once was thine own, and take possession of a land which knows thee not. Arise, Mother of God, and with thy thrilling voice, speak to those who labour with child, and are in pain, till the babe of grace leaps within them! Shine on us, dear Lady, with thy bright countenance, like the sun in his strength, *O stella matutina*,[4] O harbinger of peace, till our year is one perpetual May. From thy sweet eyes, from thy pure smile, from thy majestic brow, let ten thousand influences rain down, not to confound or overwhelm, but to persuade, to win over thine enemies. O Mary, my hope, O Mother undefiled, fulfil to us the promise of this Spring. A second temple rises on the ruins of the old. Canterbury has gone its way, and York is gone, and Durham is gone, and Winchester is gone. It was sore to part with them. We clung to the vision of past greatness, and would not believe it could come to nought; but the Church in England has died, and the Church lives again. Westminster and Nottingham, Beverley and Hexham, Northampton and Shrewsbury, if the world lasts, shall be names as musical to the ear, as stirring to the heart, as the glories we have lost; and Saints shall rise out of them, if God so will, and Doctors once again shall give the law to Israel, and Preachers call to penance and to justice, as at the beginning.

Yes, my Fathers and Brothers, and if it be God's blessed will, not Saints alone, not Doctors only, not Preachers only, shall be ours—but Martyrs, too, shall re-consecrate the soil to God. We know not what is before us, ere we win our own; we are engaged in a great, a joyful work, but in proportion to God's grace is the fury of His

enemies. They have welcomed us as the lion greets his prey. Perhaps they may be familiarized in time with our appearance, but perhaps they may be irritated the more. To set up the Church again in England is too great an act to be done in a corner. We have had reason to expect that such a boon would not be given to us without a cross. It is not God's way that great blessings should descend without the sacrifice first of great sufferings. If the truth is to be spread to any wide extent among this people, how can we dream, how can we hope, that trial and trouble shall not accompany its going forth? And we have already, if it may be said without presumption, to commence our work withal, a large store of merits. We have no slight outfit for our opening warfare. Can we religiously suppose that the blood of our martyrs, three centuries ago and since, shall never receive its recompense? Those priests, secular and regular, did they suffer for no end? or rather, for an end which is not yet accomplished? The long imprisonment, the fetid dungeon, the weary suspense, the tyrannous trial, the barbarous sentence, the savage execution, the rack, the gibbet, the knife, the cauldron, the numberless tortures of those holy victims, O my God, are they to have no reward? Are Thy martyrs to cry from under Thine altar for their loving vengeance on this guilty people, and to cry in vain? Shall they lose life, and not gain a better life for the children of those who persecuted them? Is this Thy way, O my God, righteous and true? Is it according to Thy promise, O King of saints, if I may dare talk to Thee of justice? Did not Thou Thyself pray for Thine enemies upon the cross, and convert them? Did not Thy first Martyr win Thy great Apostle, then a persecutor, by his loving prayer? And in that day of trial and desolation for England, when hearts were pierced through and through with Mary's woe, at the crucifixion of Thy body mystical, was not every tear that flowed, and every drop of blood that was shed, the seeds of a future harvest, when they who sowed in sorrow were to reap in joy?

And as that suffering of the Martyrs is not yet recompensed, so, perchance, it is not yet exhausted. Something, for what we know, remains to be undergone, to complete the necessary sacrifice. May God forbid it, for this poor nation's sake! But still could we be surprised, my Fathers and my Brothers, if the winter even now should not yet be quite over? Have we any right to take

---

[4] "O morning star."

it strange, if, in this English land, the spring-time of the Church should turn out to be an English spring, an uncertain, anxious time of hope and fear, of joy and suffering,—of bright promise and budding hopes, yet withal, of keen blasts, and cold showers, and sudden storms?

One thing alone I know,—that according to our need, so will be our strength. One thing I am sure of, that the more the enemy rages against us, so much the more will the Saints in Heaven plead for us; the more fearful are our trials from the world, the more present to us will be our Mother Mary, and our good Patrons and Angel Guardians; the more malicious are the devices of men against us, the louder cry of supplication will ascend from the bosom of the whole Church to God for us. We shall not be left orphans; we shall have within us the strength of the Paraclete, promised to the Church and to every member of it. My Fathers, my Brothers in the priesthood, I speak from my heart when I declare my conviction, that there is no one among you here present but, if God so willed, would readily become a martyr for His sake. I do not say you would wish it; I do not say that the natural will would not pray that that chalice might pass away; I do not speak of what you can do by any strength of yours;—but in the strength of God, in the grace of the Spirit, in the armour of justice, by the consolations and peace of the Church, by the blessing of the Apostles Peter and Paul, and in the name of Christ, you would do what nature cannot do. By the intercession of the Saints on high, by the penances and good works and the prayers of the people of God on earth, you would be forcibly borne up as upon the waves of the mighty deep, and carried on out of yourselves by the fulness of grace, whether nature wished it or no. I do not mean violently, or with unseemly struggle, but calmly, gracefully, sweetly, joyously, you would mount up and ride forth to the battle, as on the rush of Angels' wings, as your fathers did before you, and gained the prize. You, who day by day offer up the Immaculate Lamb of God, you who hold in your hands the Incarnate Word under the visible tokens which He has ordained, you who again and again drain the chalice of the Great Victim; who is to make you fear? what is to startle you? what to seduce you? who is to stop you, whether you are to suffer or to do, whether to lay the foundations of the Church in tears, or to put the crown upon the work in jubilation?

My Fathers, my Brothers, one word more. It may seem as if I were going out of my way in thus addressing you; but I have some sort of plea to urge in extenuation. When the English College at Rome was set up by the solicitude of a great Pontiff in the beginning of England's sorrows, and missionaries were trained there for confessorship and martyrdom here, who was it that saluted the fair Saxon youths as they passed by him in the streets of the great city, with the salutation, "Salvete flores martyrum"?[5] And when the time came for each in turn to leave that peaceful home, and to go forth to the conflict, to whom did they betake themselves before leaving Rome, to receive a blessing which might nerve them for their work? They went for a Saint's blessing; they went to a calm old man, who had never seen blood, except in penance; who had longed indeed to die for Christ, what time the great St. Francis opened the way to the far East, but who had been fixed as if a sentinel in the holy city, and walked up and down for fifty years on one beat, while his brethren were in the battle. Oh! the fire of that heart, too great for its frail tenement, which tormented him to be kept at home when the whole Church was at war! and therefore came those bright-haired strangers to him, ere they set out for the scene of their passion, that the full zeal and love pent up in that burning breast might find a vent, and flow over, from him who was kept at home, upon those who were to face the foe. Therefore one by one, each in his turn, those youthful soldiers came to the old man; and one by one they persevered and gained the crown and the palm,—all but one, who had not gone, and would not go, for the salutary blessing.

My Fathers, my Brothers, that old man was my own St. Philip.[6] Bear with me for his sake. If I have spoken too seriously, his sweet smile shall temper it. As he was with you three centuries ago in Rome, when our Temple fell, so now surely when it is rising, it is a pleasant token that he should have even set out on his travels to you; and that, as if remembering how he interceded for you at home, and recognizing the relations he then formed with you, he should now be wishing to have a name among you, and to be loved by you, and perchance to do you a service, here in your own land.

---

[5] "Hail, pride of martyrs."

[6] St. Philip Neri (1515–95), Italian founder of the Congregation of the Oratory, the first English chapter of which Newman founded after his conversion to Rome.

from Apologia pro vita sua

The relatively petty attack on Newman offered by Charles Kingsley in a review in 1864 in Macmillan's magazine *of James Anthony Froude's* History of England *provoked what has come to be Newman's most enduring work. Kingsley took what must have seemed easy aim at Newman only to find himself challenged by Newman to prove his assertion that Newman had claimed that the Roman clergy consciously eschewed truth as a virtue. An acrimonious pamphlet exchange ensued, and Newman then issued in pamphlet form his apology, or justification, for his life. Assembled and reorganized without the polemic exchanges with Kingsley, it became the intensely personal yet restrained account of how Newman reached his religious position.*

The Apologia *is not a conventional autobiography. Much is omitted of Newman's family life and personal relationships. But all that is included is directed toward the overriding purpose of setting forth how Newman arrived at his conviction of 1845 that the Roman Catholic Church was the true representative of Christianity. The quiet sincerity of Newman's presentation not only won over many of his contemporaries, it has continued to win adherents ever since.*

Newman's procedure is strictly chronological, and he concentrates on the high points in his religious development. Of these the accounts of his early development and conversion and of the course of the Oxford Movement are the most absorbing. They constitute the first four chapters of the Apologia *and are given below along with Newman's lengthy end notes on liberalism, Note A, and on ecclesiastical miracles, Note B. (The ellipses in the* Apologia *are Newman's.)*

CHAPTER I

History of My Religious Opinions to the Year 1833

IT MAY easily be conceived how great a trial it is to me to write the following history of myself; but I must not shrink from the task. The words, "Secretum meum mihi,"[1] keep ringing in my ears; but as men draw towards their end, they care less for disclosures. Nor is it the least part of my trial, to anticipate that, upon first reading what I have written, my friends may consider much in it irrelevant to my purpose; yet I cannot help thinking that, viewed as a whole, it will effect what I propose to myself in giving it to the public.

I was brought up from a child to take great delight in reading the Bible; but I had no formed religious convictions till I was fifteen. Of course I had a perfect knowledge of my Catechism.

After I was grown up, I put on paper my recollections of the thoughts and feelings on religious subjects, which I had at the time that I was a child and a boy,—such as had remained on my mind with sufficient prominence to make me then consider them worth recording. Out of these, written in the Long Vacation of 1820, and transcribed with additions in 1823, I select two, which are at once the most definite among them, and also have a bearing on my later convictions.

1. "I used to wish the Arabian Tales were true: my imagination ran on unknown influences, on magical powers, and talismans. . . . . I thought life might be a dream, or I an Angel, and all this world a deception, my fellow-angels by a playful device concealing themselves from me, and deceiving me with the semblance of a material world."

Again: "Reading in the Spring of 1816 a sentence from [Dr. Watts's] 'Remnants of Time,'[2] entitled 'the Saints unknown to the world,' to the effect, that 'there is nothing in their figure or countenance to distinguish them,' &c, &c, I supposed he spoke of Angels who lived in the world, as it were disguised."

2. The other remark is this: "I was very superstitious, and for some time previous to my conversion" [when I was fifteen] "used constantly to cross myself on going into the dark."

Of course I must have got this practice from some external source or other; but I can make no

[1] "My secret is my own" (Isaiah 23:16).
[2] Isaac Watts (1674–1748), clergyman and hymnodist.

sort of conjecture whence; and certainly no one had ever spoken to me on the subject of the Catholic religion, which I only knew by name. The French master was an *émigré* Priest, but he was simply made a butt, as French masters too commonly were in that day, and spoke English very imperfectly. There was a Catholic family in the village, old maiden ladies we used to think; but I knew nothing about them. I have of late years heard that there were one or two Catholic boys in the school; but either we were carefully kept from knowing this, or the knowledge of it made simply no impression on our minds. My brother[3] will bear witness how free the school was from Catholic ideas.

I had once been into Warwick Street Chapel, with my father, who, I believe, wanted to hear some piece of music; all that I bore away from it was the recollection of a pulpit and a preacher, and a boy swinging a censer.

When I was at Littlemore,[4] I was looking over old copybooks of my school days, and I found among them my first Latin verse-book; and in the first page of it there was a device which almost took my breath away with surprise. I have the book before me now, and have just been showing it to others. I have written in the first page, in my school-boy hand, "John H. Newman, February 11th, 1811, Verse Book;" then follow my first Verses. Between "Verse" and "Book" I have drawn the figure of a solid cross upright, and next to it is, what may indeed be meant for a necklace, but what I cannot make out to be anything else than a set of beads suspended, with a little cross attached. At this time I was not quite ten years old. I suppose I got these ideas from some romance, Mrs. Radcliffe's or Miss Porter's;[5] or from some religious picture; but the strange thing is, how, among the thousand objects which meet a boy's eyes, these in particular should so have fixed themselves in my mind, that I made them thus practically my own. I am certain there was nothing in the churches I attended, or the prayer books I read, to suggest them. It must be recollected that Anglican churches and prayer books were not decorated in those days as I believe they are now.

When I was fourteen, I read Paine's Tracts against the Old Testament, and found pleasure in thinking of the objections which were contained in them. Also, I read some of Hume's Essays; and perhaps that on Miracles.[6] So at least I gave my Father to understand; but perhaps it was a brag. Also, I recollect copying out some French verses, perhaps Voltaire's, in denial of the immortality of the soul, and saying to myself something like "How dreadful, but how plausible!"

When I was fifteen, (in the autumn of 1816), a great change of thought took place in me. I fell under the influences of a definite Creed, and received into my intellect impressions of dogma, which, through God's mercy, have never been effaced or obscured. Above and beyond the conversations and sermons of the excellent man, long dead, the Rev. Walter Mayers, of Pembroke College, Oxford, who was the human means of this beginning of divine faith in me, was the effect of the books, which he put into my hands, all of the school of Calvin. One of the first books I read was a work of Romaine's,[7] I neither recollect the title nor the contents, except one doctrine, which of course I do not include among those which I believe to have come from a divine source, viz. the doctrine of final perseverance. I received it at once, and believed that the inward conversion of which I was conscious, (and, of which I still am more certain than that I have hands and feet,) would last into the next life, and that I was elected to eternal glory. I have no consciousness that this belief had any tendency whatever to lead me to be careless about pleasing God. I retained it till the age of twenty-one, when it gradually faded away; but I believe that it had some influence on my opinions, in the direction of those childish imaginations which I have already mentioned, viz. in isolating me from the objects which surrounded me, in confirming me in my mistrust of the reality of material phenomena, and making me rest in the thought of two and two only absolute and luminously self-evident beings, myself and my Creator;—for while I considered myself predestined to salvation, my mind did not dwell upon others, as fancying them simply passed over, not predestined to eternal death. I only thought of the mercy to myself.

The detestable doctrine last mentioned is simply denied and abjured, unless my memory strangely deceives me, by the writer who made a

---

[3] Francis William Newman (1805–97), in religious matters John Henry's opposite; author of *Phases of Faith* (1853).

[4] Site of a chapel near Oxford under Newman's care as Vicar of St. Mary's.

[5] Authors of historical romances.

[6] Reference to the skeptical views of Thomas Paine (1737–1807) and David Hume (1711–76).

[7] William Romaine (1714–95), Anglican author of the Calvinist school.

deeper impression on my mind than any other, and to whom (humanly speaking) I almost owe my soul,—Thomas Scott[8] of Aston Sanford. I so admired and delighted in his writings, that, when I was an undergraduate, I thought of making a visit to his Parsonage, in order to see a man whom I so deeply revered. I hardly think I could have given up the idea of this expedition, even after I had taken my degree; for the news of his death in 1821 came upon me as a disappointment as well as a sorrow. I hung upon the lips of Daniel Wilson, afterwards Bishop of Calcutta, as in two sermons at St. John's Chapel he gave the history of Scott's life and death.[9] I had been possessed of his "Force of Truth" and Essays from a boy; his Commentary I bought when I was an undergraduate.

What, I suppose, will strike any reader of Scott's history and writings, is his bold unworldliness and vigorous independence of mind. He followed truth wherever it led him, beginning with Unitarianism, and ending in a zealous faith in the Holy Trinity. It was he who first planted deep in my mind that fundamental truth of religion. With the assistance of Scott's Essays, and the admirable work of Jones of Nayland,[10] I made a collection of Scripture texts in proof of the doctrine, with remarks (I think) of my own upon them, before I was sixteen; and a few months later I drew up a series of texts in support of each verse of the Athanasian Creed. These papers I have still.

Besides his unworldliness, what I also admired in Scott was his resolute opposition to Antinomianism, and the minutely practical character of his writings. They show him to be a true Englishman, and I deeply felt his influence; and for years I used almost as proverbs what I considered to be the scope and issue of his doctrine, "Holiness rather than peace," and "Growth the only evidence of life."

Calvinists make a sharp separation between the elect and the world; there is much in this that is cognate or parallel to the Catholic doctrine; but they go on to say, as I understand them, very differently from Catholicism,—that the converted and the unconverted can be discriminated by man, that the justified are conscious of their state

of justification, and that the regenerate cannot fall away. Catholics on the other hand shade and soften the awful antagonism between good and evil, which is one of their dogmas, by holding that there are different degrees of justification, that there is a great difference in point of gravity between sin and sin, that there is a possibility and the danger of falling away, and that there is no certain knowledge given to any one that he is simply in a state of grace, and much less that he is to persevere to the end:—of the Calvinistic tenets the only one which took root in my mind was the fact of heaven and hell, divine favour and divine wrath, of the justified and the unjustified. The notion that the regenerate and the justified were one and the same, and that the regenerate, as such, had the gift of perseverance, remained with me not many years, as I have said already.

This main Catholic doctrine of the warfare between the city of God and the powers of darkness was also deeply impressed upon my mind by a work of a character very opposite to Calvinism, Law's "Serious Call."[11]

From this time I have held with a full inward assent and belief the doctrine of eternal punishment, as delivered by our Lord Himself, in as true a sense as I hold that of eternal happiness; though I have tried in various ways to make the truth less terrible to the imagination.

Now I come to two other works, which produced a deep impression on me in the same Autumn of 1816, when I was fifteen years old, each contrary to each, and planting in me the seeds of an intellectual inconsistency which disabled me for a long course of years. I read Joseph Milner's Church History,[12] and was nothing short of enamoured of the long extracts from St. Augustine, St. Ambrose, and the other Fathers which I found there. I read them as being the religion of the primitive Christians: but simultaneously with Milner I read Newton on the Prophecies,[13] and in consequence became most firmly convinced that the Pope was the Antichrist predicted by Daniel, St. Paul, and St. John. My imagination was stained by the effects of this doctrine up to the year 1843; it had been obliterated from my reason and judgment at an earlier date; but the thought remained

---

[8] Thomas Scott (1747–1821), evangelical clergyman.

[9] Daniel Wilson (1778–1858), Anglican divine.

[10] William Jones (1726–1800), Anglican clergyman of Nayland, Suffolk.

[11] William Law (1686–1761), Anglican divine, author of *A Serious Call to the Devout and Holy Life* (1729).

[12] Joseph Milner (1744–97), coauthor with his brother of *A History of the Church of Christ* (1794–1809).

[13] Thomas Newton's *Dissertations on the Prophecies* (1754, 1758).

upon me as a sort of false conscience. Hence came that conflict of mind, which so many have felt besides myself;—leading some men to make a compromise between two ideas, so inconsistent with each other,—driving others to beat out the one idea or the other from their minds,—and ending in my own case, after many years of intellectual unrest, in the gradual decay and extinction of one of them,—I do not say in its violent death, for why should I not have murdered it sooner, if I murdered it at all?

I am obliged to mention, though I do it with great reluctance, another deep imagination, which at this time, the autumn of 1816, took possession of me,—there can be no mistake about the fact; viz. that it would be the will of God that I should lead a single life. This anticipation, which has held its ground almost continuously ever since,—with the break of a month now and a month then, up to 1829, and, after that date, without any break at all,—was more or less connected in my mind with the notion, that my calling in life would require such a sacrifice as celibacy involved; as, for instance, missionary work among the heathen, to which I had a great drawing for some years. It also strengthened my feeling of separation from the visible world, of which I have spoken above.

In 1822 I came under the very different influences from those to which I had hitherto been subjected. At that time, Mr. Whately,[14] as he was then, afterwards Archbishop of Dublin, for the few months he remained in Oxford, which he was leaving for good, showed great kindness to me. He renewed it in 1825, when he became Principal of Alban Hall, making me his Vice-Principal and Tutor. Of Dr. Whately I will speak presently: for from 1822 to 1825 I saw most of the present Provost of Oriel, Dr. Hawkins,[15] at the time Vicar of St. Mary's; and, when I took orders in 1824 and had a curacy in Oxford, then, during the Long Vacations, I was especially thrown into his company. I can say with a full heart that I love him, and have never ceased to love him; and I thus preface what otherwise might sound rude, that in the course of the many years in which we were together afterwards, he provoked me very much from time to time, though I am perfectly certain that I have

provoked him a great deal more. Moreover, in me such provocation was unbecoming, both because he was the Head of my College, and because, in the first years that I knew him, he had been in many ways of great service to my mind.

He was the first who taught me to weigh my words, and to be cautious in my statements. He led me to that mode of limiting and clearing my sense in discussion and in controversy, and of distinguishing between cognate ideas, and of obviating mistakes by anticipation, which to my surprise has been since considered, even in quarters friendly to me, to savour of the polemics of Rome. He is a man of most exact mind himself, and he used to snub me severely, on reading, as he was kind enough to do, the first Sermons that I wrote, and other compositions which I was engaged upon.

Then as to doctrine, he was the means of great additions to my belief. As I have noticed elsewhere, he gave me the "Treatise on Apostolical Preaching," by Sumner,[16] afterwards Archbishop of Canterbury, from which I was led to give up my remaining Calvinism, and to receive the doctrine of Baptismal Regeneration. In many other ways too he was of use to me, on subjects semi-religious and semi-scholastic.

It was Dr. Hawkins too who taught me to anticipate that, before many years were over, there would be an attack made upon the books and the canon of Scripture. I was brought to the same belief by the conversation of Mr. Blanco White,[17] who also led me to have freer views on the subject of inspiration than were usual in the Church of England at the time.

There is one other principle, which I gained from Dr. Hawkins, more directly bearing upon Catholicism, than any that I have mentioned; and that is the doctrine of Tradition. When I was an Under-graduate, I heard him preach in the University Pulpit his celebrated sermon on the subject, and recollect how long it appeared to me, though he was at that time a very striking preacher; but, when I read it and studied it as his gift, it made a most serious impression upon me. He does not go one step, I think, beyond the high Anglican doctrine, nay he does not reach it; but he does his work thoroughly, and his view

---

[14] Richard Whately (1787–1863), Fellow of Oriel, afterwards Archbishop of Dublin.

[15] Edward Hawkins (1789–1882), Fellow of Oriel, later Provost and an opponent of "Tract XC."

[16] John Bird Sumner (1780–1862), Archbishop of Canterbury from 1848, author of *Apostolical Preaching* (1815).

[17] Joseph Blanco White (1775–1841), former Roman Catholic priest, then an Anglican, then a Unitarian.

was in him original, and his subject was a novel one at the time. He lays down a proposition, self-evident as soon as stated, to those who have at all examined the structure of Scripture, viz. that the sacred text was never intended to teach doctrine, but only to prove it, and that, if we would learn doctrine, we must have recourse to the formularies of the Church; for instance to the Catechism, and to the Creeds. He considers, that, after learning from them the doctrines of Christianity, the inquirer must verify them by Scripture. This view, most true in its outline, most fruitful in its consequences, opened upon me a large field of thought. Dr. Whately held it too. One of its effects was to strike at the root of the principle on which the Bible Society was set up. I belonged to its Oxford Association; it became a matter of time when I should withdraw my name from its subscription-list, though I did not do so at once.

It is with pleasure that I pay here a tribute to the memory of the Rev. William James, then Fellow of Oriel; who, about the year 1823, taught me the doctrine of Apostolical Succession in the course of a walk, I think, round Christ Church meadow; I recollect being somewhat impatient of the subject at the time.

It was at about this date, I suppose, that I read Bishop Butler's Analogy;[18] the study of which has been to so many, as it was to me, an era in their religious opinions. Its inculcation of a visible Church, the oracle of truth and a pattern of sanctity, of the duties of external religion, and of the historical character of Revelation, are characteristics of this great work which strike the reader at once; for myself, if I may attempt to determine what I most gained from it, it lay in two points, which I shall have an opportunity of dwelling on in the sequel; they are the underlying principles of a great portion of my teaching. First, the very idea of an analogy between the separate works of God leads to the conclusion that the system which is of less importance is economically or sacramentally connected with the more momentous system,[19] and of this conclusion the theory, to which I was inclined as a boy, viz. the unreality of material phenomena, is an ultimate resolution. At this time I did not make the distinction between matter itself and its phenomena, which is so necessary and so obvious

in discussing the subject. Secondly, Butler's doctrine that Probability is the guide of life, led me, at least under the teaching to which a few years later I was introduced, to the question of the logical cogency of Faith, on which I have written so much. Thus to Butler I trace those two principles of my teaching, which have led to a charge against me both of fancifulness and of scepticism.

And now as to Dr. Whately. I owe him a great deal. He was a man of generous and warm heart. He was particularly loyal to his friends, and to use the common phrase, "all his geese were swans." While I was still awkward and timid in 1822, he took me by the hand, and acted towards me the part of a gentle and encouraging instructor. He, emphatically, opened my mind, and taught me to think and to use my reason. After being first noticed by him in 1822, I became very intimate with him in 1825, when I was his Vice-Principal at Alban Hall. I gave up that office in 1826, when I became Tutor of my College, and his hold upon me gradually relaxed. He had done his work towards me or nearly so, when he had taught me to see with my own eyes and to walk with my own feet. Not that I had not a good deal to learn from others still, but I influenced them as well as they me, and co-operated rather than merely concurred with them. As to Dr. Whately, his mind was too different from mine for us to remain long on one line. I recollect how dissatisfied he was with an Article of mine in the London Review,[20] which Blanco White, good-humouredly, only called Platonic. When I was diverging from him in opinion (which he did not like), I thought of dedicating my first book to him, in words to the effect that he had not only taught me to think, but to think for myself. He left Oxford in 1831; after that, as far as I can recollect, I never saw him but twice,—when he visited the University; once in the street in 1834, once in a room in 1838. From the time that he left, I have always felt a real affection for what I must call his memory; for, at least from the year 1834, he made himself dead to me. He had practically indeed given me up from the time that he became Archbishop in 1831; but in 1834 a correspondence took place between us, which, though conducted especially on his side in a friendly spirit, was the expression

---

[18] Joseph Butler (1692–1752), author of *The Analogy of Religion* (1736).
[19] It is significant that Butler begins his work with a quotation from Origen. [Newman's note]. Origen was a proponent of the sacramental system which Newman first encountered in Butler.
[20] "On Poetry, with Reference to Aristotle's Poetics" (1829).

of differences of opinion which acted as a final close to our intercourse.[21] My reason told me that it was impossible we could have got on together longer, had he stayed in Oxford; yet I loved him too much to bid him farewell without pain. After a few years had passed, I began to believe that his influence on me in a higher respect than intellectual advance, (I will not say through his fault,) had not been satisfactory. I believe that he has inserted sharp things in his later works about me. They have never come in my way, and I have not thought it necessary to seek out what would pain me so much in the reading.

What he did for me in point of religious opinion, was, first, to teach me the existence of the Church, as a substantive body or corporation; next to fix in me those anti-Erastian views of Church polity,[22] which were one of the most prominent features of the Tractarian movement. On this point, and, as far as I know, on this point alone, he and Hurrell Froude[23] intimately sympathized, though Froude's development of opinion here was of a later date. In the year 1826, in the course of a walk, he said much to me about a work then just published, called "Letters on the Church by an Episcopalian." He said that it would make my blood boil. It was certainly a most powerful composition. One of our common friends told me, that, after reading it, he could not keep still, but went on walking up and down his room. It was ascribed at once to Whately; I gave eager expression to the contrary opinion; but I found the belief of Oxford in the affirmative to be too strong for me; rightly or wrongly I yielded to the general voice; and I have never heard, then or since, of any disclaimer of authorship on the part of Dr. Whately.

The main positions of this able essay are these; first that Church and State should be independent of each other:—he speaks of the duty of protesting "against the profanation of Christ's kingdom, by that *double usurpation*, the interference of the Church in temporals, of the State in spirituals," p. 191; and, secondly, that the Church may justly and by right retain its property, though separated from the State, "The clergy," he says p. 133, "though they ought not to be the hired servants of the Civil Magistrate, may justly retain their revenues; and the State, though it has no right of interference in spiritual concerns, not only is justly entitled to support from the ministers of religion, and from all other Christians, but would, under the system I am recommending, obtain it much more effectually." The author of this work, whoever he may be, argues out both these points with great force and ingenuity, and with a thoroughgoing vehemence, which perhaps we may refer to the circumstance, that he wrote, not in *propriâ personâ*, and as thereby answerable for every sentiment that he advanced, but in the professed character of a Scotch Episcopalian. His work had a gradual, but a deep effect on my mind.

I am not aware of any other religious opinion which I owe to Dr. Whately. In his special theological tenets I had no sympathy. In the next year, 1827, he told me he considered that I was Arianizing.[24] The case was this: though at that time I had not read Bishop Bull's *Defensio*[25] nor the Fathers, I was just then very strong for that ante-Nicene view of the Trinitarian doctrine, which some writers, both Catholic and non-Catholic, have accused of wearing a sort of Arian exterior. This is the meaning of a passage in Froude's Remains, in which he seems to accuse me of speaking against the Athanasian Creed. I had contrasted the two aspects of the Trinitarian doctrine, which are respectively presented by the Athanasian Creed and the Nicene. My criticisms were to the effect that some of the verses of the former Creed were unnecessarily scientific. This is a specimen of a certain disdain for Antiquity which had been growing on me now for several years. It showed itself in some flippant language against the Fathers in the Encyclopædia Metropolitana, about whom I knew little at the time, except what I had learnt as a boy from Joseph Milner. In writing on the Scripture Miracles in 1825-6, I had read Middleton on the Miracles of the early Church,[26] and had imbibed a portion of his spirit.

The truth is, I was beginning to prefer intellectual excellence to moral; I was drifting in the direction of the Liberalism of the day.[27] I

---

[21] Newman appended the correspondence between himself and Whately to the *Apologia,* here omitted.

[22] I.e., opposition to state dominance of the Church.

[23] Richard Hurrell Froude (1803–36); see selection in this volume.

[24] Arianism, the third-century heresy that denied the divinity of Christ.

[25] George Bull (1634–1710), author of *Defensio Fidei Nicaenae* (1685).

[26] Conyers Middleton (1683–1750), author of *Free Inquiry* (1749).

[27] Vide Note A., *Liberalism,* at the end of the volume. [Newman's note]

was rudely awakened from my dream at the end of 1827 by two great blows—illness and bereavement.[28]

In the beginning of 1829, came the formal break between Dr. Whately and me; the affair of Mr. Peel's re-election was the occasion of it.[29] I think in 1828 or 1827 I had voted in the minority, when the Petition to Parliament against the Catholic Claims was brought into Convocation. I did so mainly on the views suggested to me in the Letters of an Episcopalian. Also I shrank from the bigoted "two-bottle-orthodox,"[30] as they were invidiously called. When then I took part against Mr. Peel, it was on an academical, not at all an ecclesiastical or a political ground; and this I professed at the time. I considered that Mr. Peel had taken the University by surprise; that his friends had no right to call upon us to turn round on a sudden, and to expose ourselves to the imputation of time-serving; and that a great University ought not to be bullied even by a great Duke of Wellington. Also by this time I was under the influence of Keble and Froude; who, in addition to the reasons I have given, disliked the Duke's change of policy as dictated by liberalism.

Whately was considerably annoyed at me, and he took a humorous revenge, of which he had given me due notice beforehand. As head of a house he had duties of hospitality to men of all parties; he asked a set of the least intellectual men in Oxford to dinner, and men most fond of port; he made me one of this party; placed me between Provost This and Principal That, and then asked me if I was proud of my friends. However, he had a serious meaning in his act; he saw, more clearly than I could do, that I was separating from his own friends for good and all.

Dr. Whately attributed my leaving his *clientela* to a wish on my part to be the head of a party myself. I do not think that this charge was deserved. My habitual feeling then and since has been, that it was not I who sought friends, but friends who sought me. Never man had kinder or more indulgent friends than I have had; but I expressed my own feeling as to the mode in which I gained them, in this very year 1829, in the course of a copy of verses. Speaking of my blessings, I said, "Blessings of friends, which to my door *unasked, unhoped*, have come." They have come, they have gone; they came to my great joy, they went to my great grief. He who gave took away. Dr. Whately's impression about me, however, admits of this explanation:—

During the first years of my residence at Oriel, though proud of my College, I was not quite at home there. I was very much alone, and I used often to take my daily walk by myself. I recollect once meeting Dr. Copleston,[31] then Provost, with one of the Fellows. He turned round, and with the kind courteousness which sat so well on him, made me a bow and said, "Nunquam minus solus, quàm cùm solus."[32] At that time indeed (from 1823) I had the intimacy of my dear and true friend Dr. Pusey[33] and could not fail to admire and revere a soul so devoted to the cause of religion, so full of good works, so faithful in his affections; but he left residence when I was getting to know him well. As to Dr. Whately himself, he was too much my superior to allow of my being at my ease with him; and to no one in Oxford at this time did I open my heart fully and familiarly. But things changed in 1826. At that time I became one of the Tutors of my College, and this gave me position; besides, I had written one or two Essays which had been well received. I began to be known. I preached my first University Sermon. Next year I was one of the Public Examiners for the B.A. degree. In 1828 I became Vicar of St. Mary's. It was to me like the feeling of spring weather after winter; and, if I may so speak, I came out of my shell; I remained out of it till 1841.

The two persons who knew me best at that time are still alive, beneficed clergymen, no longer my friends. They could tell better than any one else what I was in those years. From this time my tongue was, as it were, loosened, and I spoke spontaneously and without effort. One of the two, Mr. Rickards, said of me, I have been told, "Here is a fellow who, when he is silent, will never begin to speak; and when he once begins to speak, will never stop." It was at this time that I began to have influence, which

---

[28] Reference to the death of Newman's sister Mary in January 1828.

[29] Sir Robert Peel (1788–1850), reelected in 1829.

[30] Based on the saying that High Churchmen drank two bottles of wine a day as a protest against puritanism.

[31] Edward Copleston (1776–1849), Provost of Oriel from 1814 to 1828, then Dean of St. Paul's.

[32] "Never less lonely than when alone" (Cicero).

[33] Edward Bouverie Pusey (1800–1882), Fellow of Oriel and leading participant in the Oxford Movement.

steadily increased for a course of years. I gained upon my pupils, and was in particular intimate and affectionate with two of our probationer Fellows, Robert Isaac Wilberforce (afterwards Archdeacon) and Richard Hurrell Froude.[34] Whately then, an acute man, perhaps saw around me the signs of an incipient party, of which I was not conscious myself. And thus we discern the first elements of that movement afterwards called Tractarian.

The true and primary author of it, however, as is usual with great motive-powers, was out of sight. Having carried off as a mere boy the highest honours of the University, he had turned from the admiration which haunted his steps, and sought for a better and holier satisfaction in pastoral work in the country. Need I say that I am speaking of John Keble? The first time that I was in a room with him was on occasion of my election to a fellowship at Oriel, when I was sent for into the Tower, to shake hands with the Provost and Fellows. How is that hour fixed in my memory after the changes of forty-two years, forty-two this very day on which I write! I have lately had a letter in my hands, which I sent at the time to my great friend, John William Bowden,[35] with whom I passed almost exclusively my Under-graduate years. "I had to hasten to the Tower," I say to him, "to receive the congratulations of all the Fellows. I bore it till Keble took my hand, and then felt so abashed and unworthy of the honour done me, that I seemed desirous of quite sinking into the ground." His had been the first name which I had heard spoken of, with reverence rather than admiration, when I came up to Oxford. When one day I was walking in High Street with my dear earliest friend just mentioned, with what eagerness did he cry out, "There's Keble!" and with what awe did I look at him! Then at another time I heard a Master of Arts of my College give an account how he had just then had occasion to introduce himself on some business to Keble, and how gentle, courteous, and unaffected Keble had been, so as almost to put him out of countenance. Then too it was reported, truly or falsely, how a rising man of brilliant reputation, the present Dean of St. Paul's, Dr. Milman,[36] admired and loved him, adding, that somehow he was strangely unlike any one else. However, at the time when I

was elected Fellow of Oriel he was not in residence, and he was shy of me for years in consequence of the marks which I bore upon me of the evangelical and liberal schools. At least so I have ever thought. Hurrell Froude brought us together about 1828: it is one of the sayings preserved in his "Remains,"—"Do you know the story of the murderer who had done one good thing in his life? Well; if I was ever asked what good deed I had ever done, I should say that I had brought Keble and Newman to understand each other."

The Christian Year made its appearance in 1827. It is not necessary, and scarcely becoming, to praise a book which has already become one of the classics of the language. When the general tone of religious literature was so nerveless and impotent, as it was at that time, Keble struck an original note and woke up in the hearts of thousands a new music, the music of a school, long unknown in England. Nor can I pretend to analyze, in my own instance, the effect of religious teaching so deep, so pure, so beautiful. I have never till now tried to do so; yet I think I am not wrong in saying, that the two main intellectual truths which it brought home to me, were the same two, which I had learned from Butler, though recast in the creative mind of my new master. The first of these was what may be called, in a large sense of the word, the Sacramental system; that is, the doctrine that material phenomena are both the types and the instruments of real things unseen,—a doctrine, which embraces in its fulness, not only what Anglicans, as well as Catholics, believe about Sacraments properly so called; but also the article of "the Communion of Saints;" and likewise the Mysteries of the faith.[37] The connexion of this philosophy of religion with what is sometimes called "Berkeleyism" has been mentioned above; I knew little of Berkeley at this time except by name; nor have I ever studied him.

On the second intellectual principle which I gained from Mr. Keble, I could say a great deal; if this were the place for it. It runs through very much that I have written, and has gained for me many hard names. Butler teaches us that probability is the guide of life. The danger of this doctrine, in the case of many minds, is, its tendency to destroy in them absolute certainty,

[34] Robert Isaac Wilberforce (1800–1857), like Newman and Froude a Fellow of Oriel, later a convert to Rome.

[35] John William Bowden (1798–1844), Newman's closest undergraduate friend.

[36] Henry Hart Milman (1791–1868), author of *History of Christianity* (1840).

[37] Vide Note B, *Ecclesiastical Miracles*, at the end of the volume. [Newman's note]

leading them to consider every conclusion as doubtful, and resolving truth into an opinion, which it is safe indeed to obey or to profess, but not possible to embrace with full internal assent. If this were to be allowed, then the celebrated saying, "O God, if there be a God, save my soul, if I have a soul!" would be the highest measure of devotion:—but who can really pray to a Being, about whose existence he is seriously in doubt?

I considered that Mr. Keble met this difficulty by ascribing the firmness of assent which we give to religious doctrine, not to the probabilities which introduced it, but to the living power of faith and love which accepted it. In matters of religion, he seemed to say, it is not merely probability which makes us intellectually certain, but probability as it is put to account by faith and love. It is faith and love which give to probability a force which it has not in itself. Faith and love are directed towards an Object; in the vision of that Object they live; it is that Object, received in faith and love, which renders it reasonable to take probability as sufficient for internal conviction. Thus the argument from Probability, in the matter of religion, became an argument from Personality, which in fact is one form of the argument from Authority.

In illustration, Mr. Keble used to quote the words of the Psalm: "I will guide thee with mine *eye*. Be ye not like to horse and mule, which have no understanding; whose mouths must be held with a bit and bridle, lest they fall upon thee." This is the very difference, he used to say, between slaves, and friends or children. Friends do not ask for literal commands; but, from their knowledge of the speaker, they understand his half-words, and from love of him they anticipate his wishes. Hence it is, that in his Poem for St. Bartholomew's Day, he speaks of the "Eye of God's word;" and in the note quotes Mr. Miller, of Worcester College, who remarks in his Bampton Lectures, on the special power of Scripture, as having "this Eye, like that of a portrait, uniformly fixed upon us, turn where we will." The view thus suggested by Mr. Keble, is brought forward in one of the earliest of the "Tracts for the Times." In No. 8 I say, "The Gospel is a Law of Liberty. We are treated as sons, not as servants; not subjected to a code of formal commandments, but addressed as those who love God, and wish to please Him."

I did not at all dispute this view of the matter, for I made use of it myself; but I was dissatisfied, because it did not go to the root of the difficulty.

It was beautiful and religious, but it did not even profess to be logical; and accordingly I tried to complete it by considerations of my own, which are to be found in my University Sermons, Essay on Ecclesiastical Miracles, and Essay on Development of Doctrine. My argument is in outline as follows: that that absolute certitude which we were able to possess, whether as to the truths of natural theology, or as to the fact of a revelation, was the result of an *assemblage* of concurring and converging possibilities, and that, both according to the constitution of the human mind and the will of its maker; that certitude was a habit of mind, that certainty was a quality of propositions; that probabilities which did not reach to logical certainty, might suffice for a mental certitude; that the certitude thus brought about might equal in measure and strength the certitude which was created by the strictest scientific demonstration; and that to possess such certitude might in given cases and to given individuals be a plain duty, though not to others in other circumstances:—

Moreover, that as there were probabilities which sufficed for certitude, so there were other probabilities which were legitimately adapted to create opinion; that it might be quite as much a matter of duty in given cases and to given persons to have about a fact an opinion of a definite strength and consistency, as in the case of greater or of more numerous probabilities it was a duty to have a certitude; that accordingly we were bound to be more or less sure, on a sort of (as it were) graduated scale of assent, viz. according as the probabilities attaching to a professed fact were brought home to us, and as the case might be, to entertain about it a pious belief, or a pious opinion, or a religious conjecture, or at least, a tolerance of such belief, or opinion or conjecture in others; that on the other hand, as it was a duty to have a belief, of more or less strong texture, in given cases, so in other cases it was a duty not to believe, not to opine, not to conjecture, not even to tolerate the notion that a professed fact was true, inasmuch as it would be credulity or superstition, or some other moral fault, to do so. This was the region of Private Judgment in religion; that is, of a Private Judgment, not formed arbitrarily and according to one's fancy or liking, but conscientiously, and under a sense of duty.

Considerations such as these throw a new light on the subject of Miracles, and they seem to have led me to reconsider the view which I had taken of them in my Essay in 1825-6. I do not know what was the date of this change in me, nor of the train of ideas on which it was founded. That there had been already great miracles, as those of Scripture, as the Resurrection, was a fact establishing the principle that the laws of nature had sometimes been suspended by their Divine Author, and since what had happened once might happen again, a certain probability, at least no kind of improbability, was attached to the idea taken in itself; of miraculous intervention in later times, and miraculous accounts were to be regarded in connexion with the verisimilitude, scope, instrument, character, testimony, and circumstances, with which they presented themselves to us; and, according to the final result of those various considerations, it was our duty to be sure, or to believe, or to opine, or to surmise, or to tolerate, or to reject, or to denounce. The main difference between my Essay on Miracles in 1826 and my Essay in 1842 is this: that in 1826 I considered that miracles were sharply divided into two classes, those which were to be received, and those which were to be rejected; whereas in 1842 I saw that they were to be regarded according to their greater or less probability, which was in some cases sufficient to create certitude about them, in other cases only belief or opinion.

Moreover, the argument from Analogy, on which this view of the question was founded, suggested to me something besides, in recommendation of the Ecclesiastical Miracles. It fastened itself upon the theory of Church History which I had learned as a boy from Joseph Milner. It is Milner's doctrine, that upon the visible Church come down from above, at certain intervals, large and temporary *Effusions* of divine grace. This is the leading idea of his work. He begins by speaking of the Day of Pentecost, as marking "the first of those *Effusions* of the Spirit of God, which from age to age have visited the earth since the coming of Christ." Vol. i p. 3. In a note he adds that "in the term 'Effusion' there is *not* here included the idea of the miraculous or extraordinary operations of the Spirit of God;" but still it was natural for me, admitting Milner's general theory, and applying to it the principle of analogy, not to stop short at his abrupt *ipse dixit*, but boldly to pass forward to the conclusion, on other grounds plausible, that as miracles accompanied the first effusion of grace, so they might accompany the later. It is surely a natural and on the whole, a true anticipation (though of course there are exceptions in particular cases), that gifts and graces go together; now, according to

the ancient Catholic doctrine, the gift of miracles was viewed as the attendant and shadow of transcendent sanctity: and moreover, since such sanctity was not of every day's occurrence, nay further, since one period of Church history differed widely from another, and, as Joseph Milner would say, there have been generations or centuries of degeneracy or disorder, and times of revival, and since one region might be in the mid-day of religious fervour, and another in twilight or gloom, there was no force in the popular argument, that, because we did not see miracles with our own eyes, miracles had not happened in former times, or were not now at this very time taking place in distant places:—but I must not dwell longer on a subject, to which in a few words it is impossible to do justice.

Hurrell Froude was a pupil of Keble's, formed by him, and in turn reacting upon him. I knew him first in 1826, and was in the closest and most affectionate friendship with him from about 1829 till his death in 1836. He was a man of the highest gifts,—so truly many-sided, that it would be presumptuous in me to attempt to describe him, except under those aspects in which he came before me. Nor have I here to speak of the gentleness and tenderness of nature, the playfulness, the free elastic force and graceful versatility of mind, and the patient winning considerateness in discussion, which endeared him to those to whom he opened his heart; for I am all along engaged upon matters of belief and opinion, and am introducing others into my narrative, not for their own sake, or because I love and have loved them, so much as because, and so far as, they have influenced my theological views. In this respect then, I speak of Hurrell Froude,—in his intellectual aspect,—as a man of high genius, brimful and overflowing with ideas and views, in him original, which were too many and strong even for his bodily strength, and which crowded and jostled against each other in their effort after distinct shape and expression. And he had an intellect as critical and logical as it was speculative and bold. Dying prematurely, as he did, and in the conflict and transition-state of opinion, his religious views never reached their ultimate conclusion, by the very reason of their multitude and their depth. His opinions arrested and influenced me, even when they did not gain my assent. He professed openly his admiration of the Church of Rome, and his hatred of the Reformers. He delighted in the notion of an hierarchical system, of sacerdotal power, and of full ecclesiastical liberty. He felt scorn of the maxim, "The Bible and the Bible only is the religion of Protestants;" and he gloried in accepting Tradition as a main instrument of religious teaching. He had a high severe idea of the intrinsic excellence of Virginity; and he considered the Blessed Virgin its great Pattern. He delighted in thinking of the Saints; he had a vivid appreciation of the idea of sanctity, its possibility and its heights; and he was more than inclined to believe a large amount of miraculous interference as occurring in the early and middle ages. He embraced the principle of penance and mortification. He had a deep devotion to the Real Presence,[38] in which he had a firm faith. He was powerfully drawn to the Medieval Church, but not to the Primitive.

He had a keen insight into abstract truth; but he was an Englishman to the backbone in his severe adherence to the real and the concrete. He had a most classical taste, and a genius for philosophy and art; and he was fond of historical inquiry, and the politics of religion. He had no turn for theology as such. He set no sufficient value on the writings of the Fathers, on the detail or development of doctrine, on the definite traditions of the Church viewed in their matter, on the teaching of the Ecumenical Councils, or on the controversies out of which they arose. He took an eager courageous view of things on the whole. I should say that his power of entering into the minds of others did not equal his other gifts; he could not believe, for instance, that I really held the Roman Church to be Antichristian. On many points he would not believe but that I agreed with him, when I did not. He seemed not to understand my difficulties. His were of a different kind, the contrariety between theory and fact. He was a high Tory of the Cavalier stamp, and was disgusted with the Toryism of the opponents of the Reform Bill.[39] He was smitten with love of the Theocratic Church; he went abroad and was shocked by the degeneracy which he thought he saw in the Catholics of Italy.

It is difficult to enumerate the precise additions to my theological creed which I derived from a friend to whom I owe so much. He taught me to look with admiration towards the Church of Rome, and in the same degree to dislike the Reformation. He fixed deep in me the idea of devotion to the Blessed Virgin, and he led me gradually to believe in the Real Presence.

There is one remaining source of my opinions to be mentioned, and that far from the least important. In proportion as I moved out of the shadow of that liberalism which had hung over my course, my early devotion towards the Fathers returned; and in the Long Vacation of 1828 I set about to read them chronologically beginning with St. Ignatius and St. Justin.[40] About 1830 a proposal was made to me by Mr. Hugh Rose, who with Mr. Lyall (afterwards Dean of Canterbury) was providing writers for a Theological Library, to furnish them with a History of the Principal Councils. I accepted it, and at once set to work on the Council of Nicæa. It was to launch myself on an ocean with currents innumerable; and I was drifted back first to the ante-Nicene history, and then to the Church of Alexandria. The work at last appeared under the title of "The Arians of the Fourth Century;" and of its 422 pages, the first 117 consisted of introductory matter, and the Council of Nicæa did not appear till the 254th, and then occupied at most twenty pages.

I do not know when I first learnt to consider that Antiquity was the true exponent of the doctrines of Christianity and the basis of the Church of England; but I take it for granted that the works of Bishop Bull, which at this time I read, were my chief introduction to this principle. The course of reading, which I pursued in the composition of my volume, was directly adapted to develop it in my mind. What principally attracted me in the ante-Nicene period was the great Church of Alexandria, the historical centre of teaching in those times. Of Rome for some centuries comparatively little is known. The battle of Arianism was first fought in Alexandria; Athanasius, the champion of the truth, was Bishop of Alexandria; and in his writings he refers to the great religious names of an earlier date, to Origen, Dionysius, and others, who were the glory of its see, or of its school. The broad philosophy of Clement and Origen carried me away; the philosophy, not the theological doctrine; and I have drawn out some features of it in my volume, and with the zeal and freshness,

---

[38] The doctrine of Christ's actual presence in the consecrated blood and wine, a Catholic teaching held by the Tractarians.
[39] The Reform Bill of 1832, which extended voting rights to larger segments of the population.
[40] St. Ignatius of Antioch (c. 35–107) and St. Justin Martyr (c. 100–c. 165), early Church Fathers.

but with the partiality, of a neophyte. Some portions of their teaching, magnificent in themselves, came like music to my inward ear, as if the response to ideas, which, with little external to encourage them, I had cherished so long. These were based on the mystical or sacramental principle, and spoke of the various Economies or Dispensations of the Eternal. I understood these passages to mean that the exterior world, physical and historical, was but the manifestation to our senses of realities greater than itself. Nature was a parable: Scripture was an allegory: pagan literature, philosophy, and mythology, properly understood, were but a preparation for the Gospel. The Greek poets and sages were in a certain sense prophets; for "thoughts beyond their thought to those high bards were given."[41] There had been a directly divine dispensation granted to the Jews; but there had been in some sense a dispensation carried on in favour of the Gentiles. He who had taken the seed of Jacob for His elect people had not therefore cast the rest of mankind out of His sight. In the fulness of time both Judaism and Paganism had come to nought; the outward framework, which concealed yet suggested the Living Truth, had never been intended to last, and it was dissolving under the beams of the Son of Justice which shone behind it and through it. The process of change had been slow; it had been done not rashly, but by rule and measure, "at sundry times and in divers manners,"[42] first one disclosure and then another, till the whole evangelical doctrine was brought into full manifestation. And thus room was made for the anticipation of further and deeper disclosures, of truths still under the veil of the letter, and in their season to be revealed. The visible world still remains without its divine interpretation; Holy Church in her sacraments and her hierarchical appointments, will remain, even to the end of the world, after all but a symbol of those heavenly facts which fill eternity. Her mysteries are but the expressions in human language of truths to which the human mind is unequal. It is evident how much there was in all this in correspondence with the thoughts which had attracted me when I was young, and with the doctrine which I have already associated with the Analogy and the Christian Year.

It was, I suppose, to the Alexandrian school and to the early Church, that I owe in particular what I definitely held about the Angels. I viewed them, not only as the ministers employed by the Creator in the Jewish and Christian dispensations, as we find on the face of Scripture, but as carrying on, as Scripture also implies, the Economy of the Visible World. I considered them as the real causes of motion, light, and life, and of those elementary principles of the physical universe, which, when offered in their developments to our senses, suggest to us the notion of cause and effect, and of what are called the laws of nature. This doctrine I have drawn out in my Sermon for Michaelmas day, written in 1831. I say of the Angels, "Every breath of air and ray of light and heat, every beautiful prospect, is, as it were, the skirts of their garments, the waving of the robes of those whose faces see God." Again, I ask what would be the thoughts of a man who, "when examining a flower, or a herb, or a pebble, or a ray of light, which he treats as something so beneath him in the scale of existence, suddenly discovered that he was in the presence of some powerful being who was hidden behind the visible things he was inspecting,—who, though concealing his wise hand, was giving them their beauty, grace, and perfection, as being God's instrument for the purpose,—nay, whose robe and ornaments those objects were, which he was so eager to analyze?" and I therefore remark that "we may say with grateful and simple hearts with the Three Holy Children, 'O all ye works of the Lord, &c., &c., bless ye the Lord, praise Him, and magnify Him for ever.' "

Also, besides the hosts of evil spirits, I considered there was a middle race, δαιμόνια,[43] neither in heaven, nor in hell; partially fallen, capricious, wayward; noble or crafty, benevolent or malicious, as the case might be. These beings gave a sort of inspiration or intelligence to races, nations, and classes of men. Hence the action of bodies politic and associations, which is often so different from that of the individuals who compose them. Hence the character and the instinct of states and governments, of religious communities and cummunions. I thought these assemblages had their life in certain unseen Powers. My preference of the Personal to the Abstract would naturally lead me to this view. I thought it countenanced by the mention of "the Prince of Persia" in the Prophet Daniel; and I think I considered that it was of such intermediate beings that the Apocalypse spoke, in its notice of "The Angels of the Seven Churches."[44]

---

[41] From Keble's *Christian Year*, "Third Sunday after Lent."
[42] Hebrews 1:1.   [43] Daimonia, "demons."   [44] Revelations 1:20.

In 1837 I made a further development of this doctrine. I said to an intimate and dear friend, Samuel Francis Wood, in a letter which came into my hands on his death. "I have an idea. The mass of the Fathers (Justin, Athenagoras, Irenæus, Clement, Tertullian, Origen, Lactantius, Sulpicius, Ambrose, Nazianzen) hold that, though Satan fell from the beginning, the Angels fell before the deluge, falling in love with the daughters of men. This has lately come across me as a remarkable solution of a notion which I cannot help holding. Daniel speaks as if each nation had its guardian Angel. I cannot but think that there are beings with a great deal of good in them, yet with great defects, who are the animating principles of certain institutions, &c., &c. . . . . Take England with many high virtues, and yet a low Catholicism. It seems to me that John Bull is a spirit neither of heaven nor hell . . . . Has not the Christian Church, in its parts, surrendered itself to one or other of these simulations of the truth? . . . . How are we to avoid Scylla and Charybdis and go straight on to the very image of Christ?" &c., &c.

I am aware that what I have been saying will, with many men, be doing credit to my imagination at the expense of my judgment—"Hippoclides doesn't care;"[45] I am not setting myself up as a pattern of good sense or of any thing else: I am but giving a history of my opinions, and that, with the view of showing that I have come by them through intelligible processes of thought and honest external means. The doctrine indeed of the Economy has in some quarters been itself condemned as intrinsically pernicious,—as if leading to lying and equivocation, when applied, as I have applied it in my remarks upon it in my History of the Arians, to matters of conduct. My answer to this imputation I postpone to the concluding pages of my Volume.

While I was engaged in writing my work upon the Arians, great events were happening at home and abroad, which brought out into form and passionate expression the various beliefs which had so gradually been winning their way into my mind. Shortly before, there had been a Revolution in France; the Bourbons had been dismissed: and I held that it was unchristian for nations to cast off their governors, and, much more, sovereigns who had the divine right of inheritance. Again, the great Reform Agitation was going on around me as I wrote. The Whigs had come into power; Lord Grey had told the Bishops to set their house in order, and some of the Prelates had been insulted and threatened in the streets of London. The vital question was, how were we to keep the Church from being liberalized? there was such apathy on the subject in some quarters, such imbecile alarm in others; the true principles of Churchmanship seemed so radically decayed, and there was such distraction in the councils of the Clergy. Blomfield, the Bishop of London of the day, an active and open-hearted man, had been for years engaged in diluting the high orthodoxy of the Church by the introduction of members of the Evangelical body into places of influence and trust. He had deeply offended men who agreed in opinion with myself, by an off-hand saying (as it was reported) to the effect that belief in the Apostolical succession had gone out with the Non-jurors.[46] "We can count you," he said to some of the gravest and most venerated persons of the old school. And the Evangelical party itself, with their late successes, seemed to have lost that simplicity and unworldliness which I admired so much in Milner and Scott. It was not that I did not venerate such men as Ryder, the then Bishop of Lichfield, and others of similar sentiments, who were not yet promoted out of the ranks of the Clergy, but I thought little of the Evangelicals as a class. I thought they played into the hands of the Liberals. With the Establishment thus divided and threatened, thus ignorant of its true strength, I compared that fresh vigorous Power of which I was reading in the first centuries. In her triumphant zeal on behalf of that Primeval Mystery, to which I had had so great a devotion from my youth, I recognized the movement of my Spiritual Mother. "Incessu patuit Dea."[47] The self-conquest of her Ascetics, the patience of her Martyrs, the irresistible determination of her Bishops, the joyous swing of her advance, both exalted and abashed me. I said to myself, "Look on this picture and on that;"[48] I felt affection for my own Church, but not tenderness; I felt dismay at her prospects, anger and scorn at her do-nothing perplexity. I thought that if

---

[45] From Herodotus' story of the uncaring bridegroom.

[46] Anglican clergymen of 1688 who refused to take the oath of allegiance to William and Mary because of their prior oaths to the Stuarts. The nonjurors held theological and liturgical views similar to those held by the Tractarians.

[47] "By her step she revealed herself a goddess" (Vergil).

[48] *Hamlet,* III, iv, 53.

Liberalism once got a footing within her, it was sure of the victory in the event. I saw that Reformation principles were powerless to rescue her. As to leaving her, the thought never crossed my imagination; still I ever kept before me that there was something greater than the Established Church, and that that was the Church Catholic and Apostolic, set up from the beginning, of which she was but the local presence and the organ. She was nothing, unless she was this. She must be dealt with strongly, or she would be lost. There was need of a second reformation.

At this time I was disengaged from College duties, and my health had suffered from the labour involved in the composition of my Volume. It was ready for the Press in July, 1832, though not published till the end of 1833. I was easily persuaded to join Hurrell Froude and his Father, who were going to the south of Europe for the health of the former.

We set out in December, 1832. It was during this expedition that my Verses which are in the Lyra Apostolica were written;—a few indeed before it, but not more than one or two of them after it. Exchanging, as I was, definite Tutorial work, and the literary quiet and pleasant friendships of the last six years, for foreign countries and an unknown future, I naturally was led to think that some inward changes, as well as some larger course of action, were coming upon me. At Whitchurch, while waiting for the down mail to Falmouth, I wrote the verses about my Guardian Angel, which begin with these words: "Are these the tracks of some unearthly Friend?" and which go on to speak of "the vision" which haunted me:—that vision is more or less brought out in the whole series of these compositions.

I went to various coasts of the Mediterranean; parted with my friends at Rome; went down for the second time to Sicily without companion, at the end of April; and got back to England by Palermo in the early part of July. The strangeness of foreign life threw me back into myself; I found pleasure in historical sites and beautiful scenes, not in men and manners. We kept clear of Catholics throughout our tour. I had a conversation with the Dean of Malta, a most pleasant man, lately dead; but it was about the Fathers, and the Library of the great church. I knew the Abbate Santini, at Rome, who did no more than copy for me the Gregorian tones. Froude and I made two calls upon Monsignore (now Cardinal) Wiseman[49] at the Collegio Inglese, shortly before we left Rome. Once we heard him preach at a church in the Corso. I do not recollect being in a room with any other ecclesiastics, except a Priest at Castro-Giovanni in Sicily, who called on me when I was ill, and with whom I wished to hold a controversy. As to Church Services, we attended the Tenebræ, at the Sestine, for the sake of the Miserere; and that was all. My general feeling was, "All, save the spirit of man, is divine." I saw nothing but what was external; of the hidden life of Catholics I knew nothing. I was still more driven back into myself, and felt my isolation. England was in my thoughts solely, and the news from England came rarely and imperfectly. The Bill for the Suppression of the Irish Sees[50] was in progress, and filled my mind. I had fierce thoughts against the Liberals.

It was the success of the Liberal cause which fretted me inwardly. I became fierce against its instruments and its manifestations. A French vessel was at Algiers; I would not even look at the tricolour. On my return, though forced to stop twenty-four hours at Paris, I kept indoors the whole time, and all that I saw of that beautiful city was what I saw from the Diligence. The Bishop of London had already sounded me as to my filling one of the Whitehall preacherships, which he had just then put on a new footing; but I was indignant at the line which he was taking, and from my Steamer I had sent home a letter declining the appointment by anticipation, should it be offered to me. At this time I was specially annoyed with Dr. Arnold,[51] though it did not last into later years. Some one, I think, asked, in conversation at Rome, whether a certain interpretation of Scripture was Christian? it was answered that Dr. Arnold took it; I interposed, "But is *he* a Christian?" The subject went out of my head at once; when afterwards I was taxed with it, I could say no more in explanation, than (what I believe was the fact) that I must have had in mind some free views of Dr. Arnold about the Old Testament:—I thought I must have meant, "Arnold answers for the interpretation, but who is to answer for Arnold?"

---

[49] Nicholas Wiseman (1802–1865), Roman Catholic prelate, later Cardinal and Archbishop of Westminster.

[50] A bill to reduce the number of sees of the Church of Ireland from twenty-two to twelve; opposed by Tractarians.

[51] Thomas Arnold.

344

It was at Rome, too, that we began the Lyra Apostolica which appeared monthly in the British Magazine.[52] The motto shows the feeling of both Froude and myself at the time: we borrowed from M. Bunsen[53] a Homer, and Froude chose the words in which Achilles, on returning to the battle, says, "You shall know the difference, now that I am back again."[54]

Especially when I was left by myself, the thought came upon me that deliverance is wrought, not by the many but by the few, not by bodies but by persons. Now it was, I think, that I repeated to myself the words, which had ever been dear to me from my school days, "Exoriare aliquis!"[55]—now too, that Southey's beautiful poem of Thalaba,[56] for which I had an immense liking, came forcibly to my mind. I began to think that I had a mission. There are sentences of my letters to my friends to this effect, if they are not destroyed. When we took leave of Monsignore Wiseman, he had courteously expressed a wish that we might make a second visit to Rome; I said with great gravity, "We have a work to do in England." I went down at once to Sicily, and the presentiment grew stronger. I struck into the middle of the island, and fell ill of a fever at Leonforte. My servant thought that I was dying, and begged for my last directions. I gave them, as he wished; but I said, "I shall not die." I repeated, "I shall not die, for I have not sinned against light, I have not sinned against light." I never have been able quite to make out what I meant.

I got to Castro-Giovanni, and was laid up there for nearly three weeks. Towards the end of May I left Palermo, taking three days for the journey. Before starting from my inn in the morning of May 26th or 27th, I sat down on my bed, and began to sob violently. My servant, who had acted as my nurse, asked what ailed me. I could only answer him, "I have a work to do in England."

I was aching to get home; yet for want of a vessel I was kept at Palermo for three weeks. I began to visit the Churches, and they calmed my impatience, though I did not attend any services. I knew nothing of the Presence of the Blessed Sacrament there. At last I got off in an orange boat, bound for Marseilles. Then it was that I wrote the lines, "Lead, kindly light," which have since become well known. We were becalmed a whole week in the Straits of Bonifacio. I was writing verses the whole time of my passage. At length I got to Marseilles, and set off for England. The fatigue of travelling was too much for me, and I was laid up for several days at Lyons. At last I got off again, and did not stop night or day, (except a compulsory delay at Paris,) till I reached England, and my mother's house. My brother had arrived from Persia only a few hours before. This was on the Tuesday. The following Sunday, July 14th, Mr. Keble preached the Assize Sermon in the University Pulpit. It was published under the title of "National Apostasy." I have ever considered and kept the day, as the start of the religious movement of 1833.

CHAPTER II

History of My Religious Opinions from 1833 to 1839

IN SPITE of the foregoing pages, I have no romantic story to tell; but I have written them, because it is my duty to tell things as they took place. I have not exaggerated the feelings with which I returned to England, and I have no desire to dress up the events which followed, so as to make them in keeping with the narrative which has gone before. I soon relapsed into the every-day life which I had hitherto led; in all things the same, except that a new object was given me. I had employed myself in my own rooms in reading and writing, and in the care of a Church, before I left England, and I returned to the same occupations when I was back again. And yet perhaps those first vehement feelings which carried me on, were necessary for the beginning of the Movement; and afterwards, when it was once begun, the special need of me was over.

---

[52] *The British Magazine,* a High Church organ, ran from 1832 to 1836.
[53] C. K. J. Bunsen (1791–1860), Prussian minister to the Vatican.
[54] *Iliad,* xviii, 125.
[55] "Arise some (Avenger)!" (Aeneid, IV, 625).
[56] *Thalaba* (1801) by Robert Southey tells of an Arab boy who persevered and triumphed over many obstacles.

When I got home from abroad, I found that already a movement had commenced, in opposition to the specific danger which at that time was threatening the religion of the nation and its Church. Several zealous and able men had united their counsels, and were in correspondence with each other. The principal of these were Mr. Keble, Hurrell Froude, who had reached home long before me, Mr. William Palmer of Dublin and Worcester College (not Mr. William Palmer of Magdalen, who is now a Catholic), Mr. Arthur Perceval, and Mr. Hugh Rose.[1]

To mention Mr. Hugh Rose's name is to kindle in the minds of those who knew him a host of pleasant and affectionate remembrances. He was the man above all others fitted by his cast of mind and literary powers to make a stand, if a stand could be made, against the calamity of the times. He was gifted with a high and large mind, and a true sensibility of what was great and beautiful; he wrote with warmth and energy; and he had a cool head and cautious judgment. He spent his strength and shortened his life, Pro Ecclesia Dei, as he understood that sovereign idea. Some years earlier he had been the first to give warning, I think from the University Pulpit at Cambridge of the perils to England which lay in the biblical and theological speculations of Germany. The Reform agitation followed, and the Whig Government came into power; and he anticipated in their distribution of Church patronage the authoritative introduction of liberal opinions into the country. He feared that by the Whig party a door would be opened in England to the most grievous of heresies, which never could be closed again. In order under such grave circumstances to unite Churchmen together, and to make a front against the coming danger, he had in 1832 commenced the British Magazine, and in the same year he came to Oxford in the summer term, in order to beat up for writers for his publication; on that occasion I became known to him through Mr. Palmer. His reputation and position came in aid of his obvious fitness, in point of character and intellect, to become the centre of an ecclesiastical movement, if such a movement were to depend on the action of a party. His delicate health, his premature death, would have frustrated the expectation, even though the new school of opinion had been more exactly thrown into the shape of a party, than in fact was the case. But he zealously backed up the first efforts of those who were principals in it; and, when he went abroad to die, in 1838, he allowed me the solace of expressing my feelings of attachment and gratitude to him by addressing him, in the dedication of a volume of my Sermons, as the man "who, when hearts were failing, bade us stir up the gift that was in us, and betake ourselves to our true Mother."

But there were other reasons, besides Mr. Roses' state of health, which hindered those who so much admired him from availing themselves of his close co-operation in the coming fight. United as both he and they were in the general scope of the Movement, they were in discordance with each other from the first in their estimate of the means to be adopted for attaining it. Mr. Rose had a position in the Church, a name, and serious responsibilities; he had direct ecclesiastical superiors; he had intimate relations with his own University, and a large clerical connexion through the country. Froude and I were nobodies; with no characters to lose, and no antecedents to fetter us. Rose could not go a-head across country, as Froude had no scruples in doing. Froude was a bold rider, as on horseback, so also in his speculations. After a long conversation with him on the logical bearing of his principles, Mr. Rose said of him with quiet humour, that "he did not seem to be afraid of inferences." It was simply the truth; Froude had that strong hold of first principles, and that keen perception of their value, that he was comparatively indifferent to the revolutionary action which would attend on their application to a given state of things; whereas in the thoughts of Rose, as a practical man, existing facts had the precedence of every other idea, and the chief test of the soundness of a line of policy lay in the consideration whether it would work. This was one of the first questions, which, as it seemed to me, on every occasion occurred to his mind. With Froude, Erastianism,—that is, the union (so he viewed it) of Church and State,—was the parent, or if not the parent, the serviceable and sufficient tool, of liberalism. Till that union was snapped, Christian doctrine never could be safe; and, while he well knew how high and unselfish was the temper of Mr. Rose, yet he used to apply to him an epithet, reproachful in his own mouth;— Rose was a "conservative." By bad luck, I brought out this word to Mr. Rose in a letter of my own, which I wrote to him in criticism of

---

[1] Newman is referring to the meetings in late July 1833 at Hadleigh Rectory in Suffolk where Hugh James Rose (1795–1838) was Vicar.

something he had inserted in his Magazine; I got a vehement rebuke for my pains, for though Rose pursued a conservative line, he had as high a disdain, as Froude could have, of a worldly ambition, and an extreme sensitiveness of such an imputation.

But there was another reason still, and a more elementary one, which severed Mr. Rose from the Oxford Movement. Living movements do not come of committees, nor are great ideas worked out through the post, even though it had been the penny post. This principle deeply penetrated both Froude and myself from the first, and recommended to us the course which things soon took spontaneously, and without set purpose of our own. Universities are the natural centres of intellectual movements. How could men act together, whatever was their zeal, unless they were united in a sort of individuality? Now, first, we had no unity of place. Mr. Rose was in Suffolk, Mr. Perceval in Surrey, Mr. Keble in Gloucestershire; Hurrell Froude had to go for his health to Barbadoes. Mr. Palmer was indeed in Oxford; this was an important advantage, and told well in the first months of the Movement;—but another condition, besides that of place, was required.

A far more essential unity was that of antecedents,—a common history, common memories, an intercourse of mind with mind in the past, and a progress and increase in that intercourse in the present. Mr. Perceval, to be sure, was a pupil of Mr. Keble's; but Keble, Rose, and Palmer, represented distinct parties, or at least tempers, in the Establishment. Mr. Palmer had many conditions of authority and influence. He was the only really learned man among us. He understood theology as a science; he was practised in the scholastic mode of controversial writing; and, I believe, was as well acquainted, as he was dissatisfied, with the Catholic schools. He was as decided in his religious views, as he was cautious and even subtle in their expression, and gentle in their enforcement. But he was deficient in depth; and besides, coming from a distance, he never had really grown into an Oxford man, nor was he generally received as such; nor had he any insight into the force of personal influence and congeniality of thought in carrying out a religious theory,—a condition which Froude and I considered essential to any true success in the stand which had to be made against Liberalism.

Mr. Palmer had a certain connexion, as it may be called, in the Establishment, consisting of high Church dignitaries, Archdeacons, London Rectors, and the like, who belonged to what was commonly called the high-and-dry school. They were far more opposed than even he was to the irresponsible action of individuals. Of course their *beau idéal* in ecclesiastical action was a board of safe, sound, sensible men. Mr. Palmer was their organ and representative; and he wished for a Committee, an Association, with rules and meetings, to protect the interests of the Church in its existing peril. He was in some measure supported by Mr. Perceval.

I, on the other hand, had out of my own head begun the Tracts; and these, as representing the antagonist principle of personality, were looked upon by Mr. Palmer's friends with considerable alarm. The great point at the time with these good men in London,—some of them men of the highest principle, and far from influenced by what we used to call Erastianism,—was to put down the Tracts. I, as their editor, and mainly their author, was of course willing to give way. Keble and Froude advocated their continuance strongly, and were angry with me for consenting to stop them. Mr. Palmer shared the anxiety of his own friends; and, kind as were his thoughts of us, he still not unnaturally felt, for reasons of his own, some fidget and nervousness at the course which his Oriel friends were taking. Froude, for whom he had a real liking, took a high tone in his project of measures for dealing with bishops and clergy, which must have shocked and scandalized him considerably. As for me, there was matter enough in the early Tracts to give him equal disgust; and doubtless I much tasked his generosity, when he had to defend me, whether against the London dignitaries or the country clergy. Oriel, from the time of Dr. Copleston to Dr. Hampden,[2] had had a name far and wide for liberality of thought; it had received a formal recognition from the Edinburgh Review, if my memory serves me truly, as the school of speculative philosophy in England; and on one occasion, in 1833, when I presented myself, with some of the first papers of the Movement, to a country clergyman in Northamptonshire, he paused awhile, and then, eyeing me with significance, asked, "Whether Whately was at the bottom of them?"

Mr. Perceval wrote to me in support of the

---

[2] Renn Dickson Hampden (1793–1868), then Fellow of Oriel.

judgment of Mr. Palmer and the dignitaries. I replied in a letter, which he afterwards published. "As to the Tracts," I said to him (I quote my own words from his Pamphlet), "every one has his own taste. You object to some things, another to others. If we altered to please every one, the effect would be spoiled. They were not intended as symbols *è cathedrâ*, but as the expression of individual minds; and individuals, feeling strongly, while on the one hand, they are incidentally faulty in mode or language, are still peculiarly effective. No great work was done by a system; whereas systems rise out of individual exertions. Luther was an individual. The very faults of an individual excite attention; he loses, but his cause (if good and he powerful-minded) gains. This is the way of things; we promote truth by a self-sacrifice."

The visit which I made to the Northamptonshire Rector was only one of a series of similar expedients, which I adopted during the year 1833. I called upon clergy in various parts of the country, whether I was acquainted with them or not, and I attended at the houses of friends where several of them were from time to time assembled. I do not think that much came of such attempts, not were they quite in my way. Also I wrote various letters to clergymen, which fared not much better, except that they advertised the fact, that a rally in favour of the Church was commencing. I did not care whether my visits were made to high Church or low Church; I wished to make a strong pull in union with all who were opposed to the principles of liberalism, whoever they might be. Giving my name to the Editor, I commenced a series of letters in the Record Newspaper: they ran to a considerable length; and were borne by him with great courtesy and patience. The heading given to them was, "Church Reform." The first was on the revival of Church Discipline; the second, on its Scripture proof; the third, on the application of the doctrine; the fourth was an answer to objections; the fifth was on the benefits of discipline. And then the series was abruptly brought to a termination. I had said what I really felt, and what was also in keeping with the strong teaching of the Tracts, but I suppose the Editor discovered in me some divergence from his own line of thought; for at length he sent a very civil letter, apologizing for the non-appearance of my sixth communication, on the ground that it contained an attack upon "Temperance Societies," about which he did not wish a controversy in his columns. He added, however, his serious regret at the theological views of the Tracts. I had subscribed a small sum in 1828 towards the first start of the Record.

Acts of the officious character, which I have been describing, were uncongenial to my natural temper, to the genius of the Movement, and to the historical mode of its success:—they were the fruit of that exuberant and joyous energy with which I had returned from abroad, and which I never had before or since. I had the exultation of health restored, and home regained. While I was at Palermo and thought of the breadth of the Mediterranean, and the wearisome journey across France, I could not imagine how I was ever to get to England; but now I was amid familiar scenes and faces once more. And my health and strength came back to me with such a rebound, that some friends at Oxford, on seeing me, did not well know that it was I, and hesitated before they spoke to me. And I had the consciousness that I was employed in that work which I had been dreaming about, and which I felt to be so momentous and inspiring. I had a supreme confidence in our cause; we were upholding that primitive Christianity which was delivered for all time by the early teachers of the Church, and which was registered and attested in the Anglican formularies and by the Anglican divines. That ancient religion had well nigh faded away out of the land, through the political changes of the last 150 years, and it must be restored. It would be in fact a second Reformation:—a better reformation, for it would be a return not to the sixteenth century, but to the seventeenth. No time was to be lost, for the Whigs had come to do their worst, and the rescue might come too late. Bishoprics were already in course of suppression; Church property was in course of confiscation; Sees would soon be receiving unsuitable occupants. We knew enough to begin preaching upon, and there was no one else to preach. I felt as on board a vessel, which first gets under weigh, and then the deck is cleared out, and luggage and live stock stowed away into their proper receptacles.

Nor was it only that I had confidence in our cause, both in itself, and in its polemical force, but also, on the other hand, I despised every rival system of doctrine and its arguments too. As to the high Church and the low Church, I thought that the one had not much more of a logical basis than the other; while I had a thorough contempt for the controversial position of the latter. I had a real respect for the character of many of the advocates of each party, but that did not give cogency to their arguments; and I thought, on the contrary, that the Apostolical form of doctrine was essential and imperative, and its grounds of evidence impregnable. Owing to this supreme confidence, it came to pass at that time, that there was a double aspect in my bearing towards others, which it is necessary for me to enlarge upon. My behaviour had a mixture in it both of fierceness and of sport; and on this account, I dare say, it gave offence to many; nor am I here defending it.

I wished men to agree with me, and I walked with them step by step, as far as they would go; this I did sincerely; but if they would stop, I did not much care about it, but walked on, with some satisfaction that I had brought them so far. I liked to make them preach the truth without knowing it, and encouraged them to do so. It was a satisfaction to me that the Record had allowed me to say so much in its columns, without remonstrance. I was amused to hear of one of the Bishops, who, on reading an early Tract on the Apostolical Succession, could not make up his mind whether he held the doctrine or not. I was not distressed at the wonder or anger of dull and self-conceited men, at propositions which they did not understand. When a correspondent, in good faith, wrote to a newspaper, to say that the "Sacrifice of the Holy Eucharist," spoken of in the Tract, was a false print for "Sacrament," I thought the mistake too pleasant to be corrected before I was asked about it. I was not unwilling to draw an opponent on step by step, by virtue of his own opinions, to the brink of some intellectual absurdity, and to leave him to get back as he could. I was not unwilling to play with a man, who asked me impertinent questions. I think I had in my mouth the words of the Wise man, "Answer a fool according to his folly,"[3] especially if he was prying or spiteful. I was reckless of the gossip which was circulated about me; and, when I might easily have set it right, did not deign to do so. Also I used irony in conversation, when matter-of-fact-men would not see what I meant.

This kind of behaviour was a sort of habit with me. If I have ever trifled with my subject, it was a more serious fault. I never used arguments which I saw clearly to be unsound. The nearest approach which I remember to such conduct, but which I consider was clear of it nevertheless, was in the case of Tract 15. The matter of this Tract was

furnished to me by a friend, to whom I had applied for assistance, but who did not wish to be mixed up with the publication. He gave it me, that I might throw it into shape, and I took his arguments as they stood. In the chief portion of the Tract I fully agreed; for instance, as to what it says about the Council of Trent; but there were arguments, or some argument, in it which I did not follow; I do not recollect what it was. Froude, I think, was disgusted with the whole Tract, and accused me of *economy* in publishing it. It is principally through Mr. Froude's Remains that this word has got into our language. I think, I defended myself with arguments such as these:— that, as every one knew, the Tracts were written by various persons who agreed together in their doctrine, but not always in the arguments by which it was to be proved; that we must be tolerant of difference of opinion among ourselves; that the author of the Tract had a right to his own opinion, and that the argument in question was ordinarily received; that I did not give my own name or authority, nor was asked for my personal belief, but only acted instrumentally, as one might translate a friend's book into a foreign language. I account these to be good arguments; nevertheless I feel also that such practices admit of easy abuse and are consequently dangerous; but then, again, I feel also this,—that if all such mistakes were to be severely visited, not many men in public life would be left with a character for honour and honesty.

This absolute confidence in my cause, which led me to the negligence or wantonness which I have been instancing, also laid me open, not unfairly, to the opposite charge of fierceness in certain steps which I took, or words which I published. In the Lyra Apostolica, I have said that before learning to love, we must "learn to hate;" though I had explained my words by adding "hatred of sin." In one of my first Sermons I said, "I do not shrink from uttering my firm conviction that it would be a gain to the country were it vastly more superstitious, more bigoted, more gloomy, more fierce in its religion than at present it shows itself to be." I added, of course, that it would be an absurdity to suppose such tempers of mind desirable in themselves. The corrector of the press bore these strong epithets till he got to "more fierce," and then he put in the margin a *query*. In the very first page of the first Tract, I said of the Bishops, that, "black event though it would be for the country, yet we could

³ Proverbs 26:5.

not wish them a more blessed termination of their course, than the spoiling of their goods and martyrdom." In consequence of a passage in my work upon the Arian History, a Northern dignitary wrote to accuse me of wishing to re-establish the blood and torture of the Inquisition. Contrasting heretics and heresiarchs, I had said, "The latter should meet with no mercy: he assumes the office of the Tempter; and, so far forth as his error goes, must be dealt with by the competent authority, as if he were embodied evil. To spare him is a false and dangerous pity. It is to endanger the souls of thousands, and it is uncharitable towards himself." I cannot deny that this is a very fierce passage; but Arius was banished, not burned; and it is only fair to myself to say that neither at this, nor any other time of my life, not even when I was fiercest, could I have even cut off a Puritan's ears, and I think the sight of a Spanish *auto-da-fè* would have been the death of me. Again, when one of my friends, of liberal and evangelical opinions, wrote to expostulate with me on the course I was taking, I said that we would ride over him and his, as Othniel prevailed over Chushan-rishathaim, king of Mesopotamia. Again, I would have no dealings with my brother, and I put my conduct upon a syllogism. I said, "St. Paul bids us avoid those who cause divisions; you cause divisions: therefore I must avoid you." I dissuaded a lady from attending the marriage of a sister who had seceded from the Anglican Church. No wonder that Blanco White, who had known me under such different circumstances, now hearing the general course that I was taking, was amazed at the change which he recognized in me. He speaks bitterly and unfairly of me in his letters contemporaneously with the first years of the Movement; but in 1839, on looking back, he uses terms of me, which it would be hardly modest in me to quote, were it not that what he says of me in praise occurs in the midst of blame. He says: "In this party [the anti-Peel, in 1829] I found, to my great surprise, my dear friend, Mr. Newman of Oriel. As he had been one of the annual Petitioners to Parliament for Catholic Emancipation, his sudden union with the most violent bigots was inexplicable to me. That change was the first manifestation of the mental revolution, which has suddenly made him one of the leading persecutors of Dr. Hampden, and the most active and influential member of that association called the Puseyite party, from which we have those very strange productions, entitled, Tracts for the Times. While stating these public facts, my heart feels a pang at the recollection of the affectionate and mutual friendship between that excellent man and myself; a friendship, which his principles of orthodoxy could not allow him to continue in regard to one, whom he now regards as inevitably doomed to eternal perdition. Such is the venomous character of orthodoxy. What mischief must it create in a bad heart and narrow mind, when it can work so effectually for evil, in one of the most benevolent of bosoms, and one of the ablest of minds, in the amiable, the intellectual, the refined John Henry Newman!" (Vol. iii. p. 131.) He adds that I would have nothing to do with him, a circumstance which I do not recollect, and very much doubt.

I have spoken of my firm confidence in my position; and now let me state more definitely what the position was which I took up, and the propositions about which I was so confident. These were three:—

1. First was the principle of dogma: my battle was with liberalism; by liberalism I mean the anti-dogmatic principle and its developments. This was the first point on which I was certain. Here I make a remark: persistance in a given belief is no sufficient test of its truth: but departure from it is at least a slur upon the man who has felt so certain about it. In proportion, then, as I had in 1832 a strong persuasion of the truth of opinions which I have since given up, so far a sort of guilt attaches to me, not only for that vain confidence, but for all the various proceedings which were the consequence of it. But under this first head I have the satisfaction of feeling that I have nothing to retract, and nothing to repent of. The main principle of the movement is as dear to me now, as it ever was. I have changed in many things: in this I have not. From the age of fifteen, dogma has been the fundamental principle of my religion: I know no other religion; I cannot enter into the idea of any other sort of religion; religion, as a mere sentiment, is to me a dream and a mockery. As well can there be filial love without the fact of a father, as devotion without the fact of a Supreme Being. What I held in 1816, I held in 1833, and I hold in 1864. Please God, I shall hold it to the end. Even when I was under Dr. Whately's influence, I had no temptation to be less zealous for the great dogmas of the faith, and at various times I used to resist such trains of thought on his part as seemed to me (rightly or wrongly) to obscure them. Such was the fundamental principle of the Movement of 1833.

2. Secondly, I was confident in the truth of a certain definite religious teaching, based upon this foundation of dogma; viz. that there was a visible Church, with sacraments and rites which are the channels of invisible grace. I thought that this was the doctrine of Scripture, of the early Church, and of the Anglican Church. Here again, I have not changed in opinion; I am as certain now on this point as I was in 1833, and have never ceased to be certain. In 1834 and the following years I put this ecclesiastical doctrine on a broader basis, after reading Laud, Bramhall, and Stillingfleet[4] and other Anglican divines on the one hand, and after prosecuting the study of the Fathers on the other; but the doctrine of 1833 was strengthened in me, not changed. When I began the Tracts for the Times I rested the main doctrine, of which I am speaking, upon Scripture, on the Anglican Prayer Book, and on St. Ignatius's Epistles. (1) As to the existence of a visible Church, I especially argued out the point from Scripture, in Tract 11, viz. from the Acts of the Apostles and the Epistles. (2) As to the Sacraments and Sacramental rites, I stood on the Prayer Book. I appealed to the Ordination Service, in which the Bishop says, "Receive the Holy Ghost;" to the Visitation Service, which teaches confession and absolution; to the Baptismal Service, in which the Priest speaks of the child after baptism as regenerate; to the Catechism, in which Sacramental Communion is receiving "verily and indeed the Body and Blood of Christ;" to the Commination Service, in which we are told to do "works of penance;" to the Collects, Epistles, and Gospels, to the calendar and rubrics, portions of the Prayer Book, wherein we find the festivals of the Apostles, notice of certain other Saints, and days of fasting and abstinence.

(3) And further, as to the Episcopal system, I founded it upon the Epistles of St. Ignatius, which inculcated it in various ways. One passage especially impressed itself upon me: speaking of cases of disobedience to ecclesiastical authority, he says, "A man does not deceive that Bishop whom he sees, but he practises rather with the Bishop Invisible, and so the question is not with flesh, but with God, who knows the secret heart." I wished to act on this principle to the letter, and I may say with confidence that I never consciously transgressed it. I loved to act as feeling myself in my Bishop's sight, as if it were the sight of God. It was one of my special supports and safeguards against myself; I could not go very wrong while I had reason to believe that I was in no respect displeasing him. It was not a mere formal obedience to rule that I put before me, but I desired to please him personally, as I considered him set over me by the Divine Hand. I was strict in observing my clerical engagements, not only because they *were* engagements, but because I considered myself simply as the servant and instrument of my Bishop. I did not care much for the Bench of Bishops, except as they might be the voice of my Church: nor should I have cared much for a Provincial Council; nor for a Diocesan Synod presided over by my Bishop; all these matters seemed to me to be *jure ecclesiastico*, but what to me was *jure divino* was the voice of my Bishop in his own person. My own Bishop was my Pope; I knew no other; the successor of the Apostles, the Vicar of Christ. This was but a practical exhibition of the Anglican theory of Church Government, as I had already drawn it out myself, after various Anglican Divines. This continued all through my course; when at length, in 1845, I wrote to Bishop Wiseman, in whose Vicariate I found myself, to announce my conversion, I could find nothing better to say to him than that I would obey the Pope as I had obeyed my own Bishop in the Anglican Church. My duty to him was my point of honour; his disapprobation was the one thing which I could not bear. I believe it to have been a generous and honest feeling; and in consequence I was rewarded by having all my time for ecclesiastical superior a man, whom, had I had a choice, I should have preferred, out and out, to any other Bishop on the Bench, and for whose memory I have a special affection, Dr. Bagot[5]—a man of noble mind, and as kind-hearted and as considerate as he was noble. He ever sympathized with me in my trials which followed; it was my own fault, that I was not brought into more familiar personal relations with him, than it was my happiness to be. May his name be ever blessed!

And now in concluding my remarks on the second point on which my confidence rested, I repeat that here again I have no retractation to announce as to its main outline. While I am now as clear in my acceptance of the principle of

[4] William Laud (1573–1645), Edward Stillingfleet (1635–99), John Bramhall (1594–1663), seventeenth-century High Church Anglicans.
[5] Richard Bagot (1782–1854), Bishop of Oxford during the time of the Oxford Movement.

dogma, as I was in 1833 and 1816, so again I am now as firm in my belief of a visible Church, of the authority of Bishops, of the grace of the sacraments, of the religious worth of works of penance, as I was in 1833. I have added Articles to my Creed: but the old ones, which I then held with a divine faith, remain.

3. But now, as to the third point on which I stood in 1833, and which I have utterly renounced and trampled upon since,—my then view of the Church of Rome;—I will speak about it as exactly as I can. When I was young, as I have said already, and after I was grown up, I thought the Pope to be Antichrist. At Christmas 1824–5 I preached a sermon to that effect. But in 1827 I accepted eagerly the stanza in the Christian Year, which many people thought too charitable, "Speak *gently* of thy sister's fall." From the time that I knew Froude I got less and less bitter on the subject. I spoke (successively, but I cannot tell in what order or at what dates) of the Roman Church as being bound up with "the *cause* of Antichrist," as being *one* of the "*many* antichrists" foretold by St. John, as being influenced by "the *spirit* of Antichrist," and as having something "very Antichristian" or "unchristian" about her. From my boyhood and in 1824 I considered, after Protestant authorities, that St. Gregory I. about A.D. 600 was the first Pope that was Antichrist, though, in spite of this, he was also a great and holy man; but in 1832–3 I thought the Church of Rome was bound up with the cause of Antichrist by the Council of Trent.[6] When it was that in my deliberate judgment I gave up the notion altogether in any shape, that some special reproach was attached to her name, I cannot tell; but I had a shrinking from renouncing it, even when my reason so ordered me, from a sort of conscience or prejudice, I think up to 1843. Moreover, at least during the Tract Movement, I thought the essence of her offence to consist in the honours which she paid to the Blessed Virgin and the Saints; and the more I grew in devotion, both to the Saints and to our Lady, the more impatient was I at the Roman practices, as if those glorified creations of God must be gravely shocked, if pain could be theirs, at the undue veneration of which they were the objects.

On the other hand, Hurrell Froude in his familiar conversations was always tending to rub the idea out of my mind. In a passage of one of his letters from abroad, alluding, I suppose, to what I used to say in opposition to him, he observes: "I think people are injudicious who talk against the Roman Catholics for worshipping Saints, and honouring the Virgin and images, &c. These things may perhaps be idolatrous; I cannot make up my mind about it; but to my mind it is the Carnival that is real practical idolatry, as it is written, 'the people sat down to eat and drink, and rose up to play,'"[7] The Carnival, I observe in passing, is, in fact, one of those very excesses, to which, for at least three centuries, religious Catholics have ever opposed themselves, as we see in the life of St. Philip, to say nothing of the present day; but this we did not then know. Moreover, from Froude I learned to admire the great medieval Pontiffs; and, of course, when I had come to consider the Council of Trent to be the turning-point of the history of Christian Rome, I found myself as free, as I was rejoiced, to speak in their praise. Then, when I was abroad, the sight of so many great places, venerable shrines, and noble churches, much impressed my imagination. And my heart was touched also. Making an expedition on foot across some wild country in Sicily, at six in the morning, I came upon a small church; I heard voices, and I looked in. It was crowded, and the congregation was singing. Of course it was the mass, though I did not know it at the time. And, in my weary days at Palermo, I was not ungrateful for the comfort which I had received in frequenting the churches; nor did I ever forget it. Then, again, her zealous maintenance of the doctrine and the rule of celibacy, which I recognized as Apostolic, and her faithful agreement with Antiquity in so many other points which were dear to me, was an argument as well as a plea in favour of the great Church of Rome. Thus I learned to have tender feelings towards her; but still my reason was not affected at all. My judgment was against her, when viewed as an institution, as truly as it ever had been.

This conflict between reason and affection I expressed in one of the early Tracts, published July, 1834. "Considering the high gifts and the strong claims of the Church of Rome and its dependencies on our admiration, reverence, love, and gratitude, how could we withstand it, as we do, how could we refrain from being melted into tenderness, and rushing into communion with it, but for the words of Truth itself, which bid us

---

[6] Roman Catholic council (1545–63) called in response to the Reformation.
[7] Exodus 32:6; I Corinthians 10:7.

prefer It to the whole world? 'He that loveth father or mother more than Me, is not worthy of me.' How could 'we learn to be severe, and execute judgment,' but for the warning of Moses against even a divinely-gifted teacher, who should preach new gods; and the anathema of St. Paul even against Angels and Apostles, who should bring in a new doctrine?''—*Records,* No. 24. My feeling was something like that of a man, who is obliged in a court of justice to bear witness against a friend; or like my own now, when I have said, and shall say, so many things on which I had rather be silent.

As a matter, then, of simple conscience, though it went against my feelings, I felt it to be a duty to protest against the Church of Rome. But besides this, it was a duty, because the prescription of such a protest was a living principle of my own Church, as expressed not simply in a *catena,* but by a *consensus* of her divines, and by the voice of her people. Moreover, such a protest was necessary as an integral portion of her controversial basis; for I adopted the argument of Bernard Gilpin,[8] that Protestants "were *not able* to give any *firm and solid* reason of the separation besides this, to wit, that the Pope is Antichrist," But while I thus thought such a protest to be based upon truth, and to be a religious duty, and a rule of Anglicanism, and a necessity of the case, I did not at all like the work. Hurrell Froude attacked me for doing it; and, besides, I felt that my language had a vulgar and rhetorical look about it. I believed, and really measured, my words, when I used them; but I knew that I had a temptation, on the other hand, to say against Rome as much as ever I could, in order to protect myself against the charge of Popery.

And now I come to the very point, for which I have introduced the subject of my feelings about Rome. I felt such confidence in the substantial justice of the charges which I advanced against her, that I considered them to be a safeguard and an assurance that no harm could ever arise from the freest exposition of what I used to call Anglican principles. All the world was astounded at what Froude and I were saying: men said that it was sheer Popery. I answered, "True, we seem to be making straight for it; but go on awhile, and you will come to a deep chasm across the path, which makes real approximation impossible." And I urged in addition, that many

Anglican divines had been accused of Popery, yet had died in their Anglicanism;—now, the ecclesiastical principles which I professed, they had professed also; and the judgment against Rome which they had formed, I had formed also. Whatever deficiencies then had to be supplied in the existing Anglican system, and however boldly I might point them out, any how that system would not in the process be brought nearer to the special creed of Rome, and might be mended in spite of her. In that very agreement of two forms of faith, close as it might seem, would really be found, on examination, the elements and principles of an essential discordance.

It was with this absolute persuasion on my mind that I fancied that there could be no rashness in giving to the world in fullest measure the teaching and the writings of the Fathers. I thought that the Church of England was substantially founded upon them. I did not know all that the Fathers had said, but I felt that, even when their tenets happened to differ from the Anglican, no harm could come of reporting them. I said out what I was clear they had said; I spoke vaguely and imperfectly, of what I thought they said, or what some of them had said. Any how, no harm could come of bending the crooked stick the other way, in the process of straightening it; it was impossible to break it. If there was any thing in the Fathers of a startling character, this would be only for a time; it would admit of explanation, or it might suggest something profitable to Anglicans; it could not lead to Rome. I express this view of the matter in a passage of the Preface to the first volume, which I edited, of the Library of the Fathers.[9] Speaking of the strangeness at first sight, in the judgment of the present day, of some of their principles and opinions, I bid the reader go forward hopefully, and not indulge his criticism till he knows more about them, than he will learn at the outset. "Since the evil," I say, "is in the nature of the case itself, we can do no more than have patience, and recommend patience to others, and with the racer in the Tragedy, look forward steadily and hopefully to the *event,* τῷ τέλει πίστιν φέρων,[10] when, as we trust, all that is inharmonious and anomalous in the details, will at length be practically smoothed."

Such was the position, such the defences, such the tactics, by which I thought that it was both

---

[8] Bernard Gilpin (1517–83), English Protestant clergyman.
[9] A series of translations undertaken by the Tractarians under the title "The Library of Fathers of the Holy Catholic Church, anterior to the division of East and West."
[10] Sophocles, *Electra.*

incumbent on us, and possible for us, to meet that onset of Liberal principles, of which we were all in immediate anticipation, whether in the Church or in the University. And during the first year of the Tracts, the attack upon the University began. In November, 1834, was sent to me by Dr. Hampden the second edition of his Pamphlet, entitled, "Observations on Religious Dissent, with particular reference to the use of religious tests in the University." In this Pamphlet it was maintained, that "Religion is distinct from Theological Opinion," pp. 1. 28. 30, &c.; that it is but a common prejudice to identify theological propositions methodically deduced and stated, with the simple religion of Christ, p. 1; that under Theological Opinion were to be placed the Trinitarian doctrine, p. 27, and the Unitarian, p. 19; that a dogma was a theological opinion formally insisted on, pp. 20, 21; that speculation always left an opening for improvement, p. 22; that the Church of England was not dogmatic in its spirit, though the wording of its formularies might often carry the sound of dogmatism, p. 23.

I acknowledged the receipt of this work in the following letter:—

"The kindness which had led to your presenting me with your late Pamphlet, encourages me to hope that you will forgive me, if I take the opportunity it affords of expressing to you my very sincere and deep regret that it has been published. Such an opportunity I could not let slip without being unfaithful to my own serious thoughts on the subject.

"While I respect the tone of piety which the Pamphlet displays, I dare not trust myself to put on paper my feelings about the principles contained in it; tending as they do, in my opinion, altogether to make shipwreck of Christian faith. I also lament, that, by its appearance, the first step has been taken towards interrupting that peace and mutual good understanding which has prevailed so long in this place, and which, if once seriously disturbed, will be succeeded by dissensions the more intractable, because justified in the minds of those who resist innovation by a feeling of imperative duty."

Since that time Phaeton has got into the chariot of the sun; we, alas! can only look on, and watch him down the steep of heaven. Meanwhile, the lands, which he is passing over, suffer from his driving.

Such was the commencement of the assault of Liberalism upon the old orthodoxy of Oxford and England; and it could not have been broken, as it was, for so long a time, had not a great change taken place in the circumstances of that counter-movement which had already started with the view of resisting it. For myself, I was not the person to take the lead of a party; I never was, from first to last, more than a leading author of a school; nor did I ever wish to be anything else. This is my own account of the matter; and I say it, neither as intending to disown the responsibility of what was done, or as if ungrateful to those who at that time made more of me than I deserved, and did more for my sake and at my bidding than I realized myself. I am giving my history from my own point of sight, and it is as follows:—I had lived for ten years among my personal friends; the greater part of the time, I had been influenced, not influencing; and at no time have I acted on others, without their acting upon me. As is the custom of a University, I had lived with my private, nay, with some of my public, pupils, and with the junior fellows of my College, without form or distance, on a footing of equality. Thus it was through friends, younger, for the most part, than myself, that my principles were spreading. They heard what I said in conversation, and told it to others. Under-graduates in due time took their degree, and became private tutors themselves. In their new *status*, they in turn preached the opinions, with which they had already become acquainted. Others went down to the country, and became curates of parishes. Then they had down from London parcels of the Tracts, and other publications. They placed them in the shops of local booksellers, got them into newspapers, introduced them to clerical meetings, and converted more or less their Rectors and their brother curates. Thus the Movement, viewed with relation to myself, was but a floating opinion; it was not a power. It never would have been a power, if it had remained in my hands. Years after, a friend, writing to me in remonstrance at the excesses, as he thought them, of my disciples, applied to me my own verse about St. Gregory Nazianzen, "Thou couldst a people raise, but couldst not rule." At the time that he wrote to me, I had special impediments in the way of such an exercise of power; but at no time could I exercise over others that authority, which under the circumstances was imperatively required. My great principle ever was, Live and let live. I never had the staidness or dignity necessary for a leader. To the last I never recognized the hold I had over young men. Of late years I have read and heard that they even imitated me in various ways. I was quite unconscious of it, and I think my immediate friends knew too well how disgusted I should be at such proceedings, to have the heart to tell me. I felt great impatience at our being called a party, and would not allow that we were such. I had a lounging, free-and-easy way of carrying things on. I exercised no sufficient censorship upon the Tracts. I did not confine them to the writings of such persons as agreed in all things with myself; and, as to my own Tracts, I printed on them a notice to the effect, that any one who pleased, might make what use he would of them, and reprint them with alterations if he chose, under the conviction that their main scope could not be damaged by such a process. It was the same with me afterwards, as regards other publications. For two years I furnished a certain number of sheets for the British Critic from myself and my friends, while a gentleman was editor, a man of splendid talent, who, however, was scarcely an acquaintance of mine, and had no sympathy with the Tracts. When I was Editor myself, from 1838 to 1841, in my very first number I suffered to appear a critique unfavourable to my work on Justification, which had been published a few months before, from a feeling of propriety, because I had put the book into the hands of the writer who so handled it. Afterwards I suffered an article against the Jesuits to appear in it, of which I did not like the tone. When I had to provide a curate for my new church at Littlemore, I engaged a friend, by no fault of his, who, before he had entered into his charge, preached a sermon, either in depreciation of baptismal regeneration, or of Dr. Pusey's view of it. I showed a similar easiness as to the Editors who helped me in the separate volumes of Fleury's Church History; they were able, learned, and excellent men, but their after-history has shown, how little my choice of them was influenced by any notion I could have had of any intimate agreement of opinion between them and myself. I shall have to make the same remark in its place concerning the Lives of the English Saints, which subsequently appeared. All this may seem inconsistent with what I have said of my fierceness. I am not bound to account for it; but there have been men before me, fierce in act, yet tolerant and moderate in their reasonings; at least, so I read history. However, such was the case, and such its effect upon the Tracts. These at first starting were short, hasty, and some of them

ineffective; and at the end of the year, when collected into a volume, they had a slovenly appearance.

It was under these circumstances, that Dr. Pusey joined us. I had known him well since 1827–8, and had felt for him an enthusiastic admiration. I used to call him ὁ μέγας.[11] His great learning, his immense diligence, his scholarlike mind, his simple devotion to the cause of religion, overcame me; and great of course was my joy, when in the last days of 1833 he showed a disposition to make common cause with us. His Tract on Fasting appeared as one of the series with the date of December 21. He was not, however, I think, fully associated in the Movement till 1835 and 1836, when he published his Tract on Baptism, and started the Library of the Fathers. He at once gave to us a position and a name. Without him we should have had little chance, especially at the early date of 1834, of making any serious resistance to the Liberal aggression. But Dr. Pusey was a Professor and Canon of Christ Church; he had a vast influence in consequence of his deep religious seriousness, the munificence of his charities, his Professorship, his family connexions, and his easy relations with University authorities. He was to the Movement all that Mr. Rose might have been, with that indispensable addition, which was wanting to Mr. Rose, the intimate friendship and the familiar daily society of the persons who had commenced it. And he had that special claim on their attachment, which lies in the living presence of a faithful and loyal affectionateness. There was henceforth a man who could be the head and centre of the zealous people in every part of the country, who were adopting the new opinions; and not only so, but there was one who furnished the Movement with a front to the world, and gained for it a recognition from other parties in the University. In 1829, Mr. Froude, or Mr. Robert Wilberforce, or Mr. Newman were but individuals; and, when they ranged themselves in the contest of that year on the side of Sir Robert Inglis, men on either side only asked with surprise how they got there, and attached no significancy to the fact; but Dr. Pusey was, to use the common expression, a host in himself; he was able to give a name, a form, and a personality, to what was without him a sort of mob; and when various parties had to meet together in order to resist the liberal acts of the Government, we of the Movement took our place by right among them.

---

[11] "The Great One."

Such was the benefit which he conferred on the Movement externally; nor were the internal advantages at all inferior to it. He was a man of large designs; he had a hopeful, sanguine mind; he had no fear of others; he was haunted by no intellectual perplexities. People are apt to say that he was once nearer to the Catholic Church than he is now; I pray God that he may be one day far nearer to the Catholic Church than he was then; for I believe that, in his reason and judgment, all the time that I knew him, he never was near to it at all. When I became a Catholic, I was often asked, "What of Dr. Pusey?" when I said that I did not see symptoms of his doing as I had done, I was sometimes thought uncharitable. If confidence in his position is, (as it is,) a first essential in the leader of a party, this Dr. Pusey possessed pre-eminently. The most remarkable instance of this, was his statement, in one of his subsequent defences of the Movement, when moreover it had advanced a considerable way in the direction of Rome, that among its more hopeful peculiarities was its "stationariness." He made it in good faith; it was his subjective view of it.

Dr. Pusey's influence was felt at once. He saw that there ought to be more sobriety, more gravity, more careful pains, more sense of responsibility in the Tracts and in the whole Movement. It was through him that the character of the Tracts was changed. When he gave to us his Tract on Fasting, he put his initials to it. In 1835 he published his elaborate Treatise on Baptism, which was followed by other Tracts from different authors, if not of equal learning, yet of equal power and appositeness. The Catenas of Anglican divines, projected by me, which occur in the Series were executed with a like aim at greater accuracy and method. In 1836 he advertised his great project for a Translation of the Fathers: —but I must return to myself. I am not writing the history either of Dr. Pusey or of the Movement; but it is a pleasure to me to have been able to introduce here reminiscences of the place which he held in it, which have so direct a bearing on myself, that they are no digression from my narrative.

I suspect it was Dr. Pusey's influence and example which set me, and made me set others, on the larger and more careful works in defence of the principles of the Movement which followed in a course of years,—some of them demanding and receiving from their authors, such elaborate treatment that they did not make their appearance till both its temper and its fortunes had changed. I set about a work at once; one in which was brought out with precision the relation in which we stood to the Church of Rome. We could not move a step in comfort, till this was done. It was of absolute necessity and a plain duty from the first, to provide as soon as possible a large statement, which would encourage and reassure our friends, and repel the attacks of our opponents. A cry was heard on all sides of us, that the Tracts and the writings of the Fathers would lead us to become Catholics, before we were aware of it. This was loudly expressed by members of the Evangelical party, who in 1836 had joined us in making a protest in Convocation against a memorable appointment of the Prime Minister.[12] These clergymen even then avowed their desire, that the next time they were brought up to Oxford to give a vote, it might be in order to put down the Popery of the Movement. There was another reason still, and quite as important. Monsignore Wiseman, with the acuteness and zeal which might be expected from that great Prelate, had anticipated what was coming, had returned to England by 1836, had delivered Lectures in London on the doctrines of Catholicism, and created an impression through the country, shared in by ourselves, that we had for our opponents in controversy, not only our brethren, but our hereditary foes. These were the circumstances, which led to my publication of "The Prophetical office of the Church viewed relatively to Romanism and Popular Protestantism."

This work employed me for three years, from the beginning of 1834 to the end of 1836, and was published in 1837. It was composed, after a careful consideration and comparison of the principal Anglican divines of the 17th century. It was first written in the shape of controversial correspondence with a learned French Priest; then it was re-cast, and delivered in Lectures at St. Mary's; lastly, with considerable retrenchments and additions, it was rewritten for publication.

It attempts to trace out the rudimental lines on which Christian faith and teaching proceed, and to use them as means of determining the relation of the Roman and Anglican systems to each other. In this way it shows that to confuse the two together is impossible, and that the Anglican can be as little said to tend to the

---

[12] The appointment of Hampden as Regius Professor of Divinity.

Roman, as the Roman to the Anglican. The spirit of the Volume is not so gentle to the Church of Rome, as Tract 71 published the year before; on the contrary, it is very fierce; and this I attribute to the circumstance that the Volume is theological and didactic, whereas the Tract, being controversial, assumes as little and grants as much as possible on the points in dispute, and insists on points of agreement as well as of difference. A further and more direct reason is, that in my Volume I deal with "Romanism" (as I call it), not so much in its formal decrees and in the substance of its creed, as in its traditional action and its authorized teaching as represented by its prominent writers,—whereas the Tract is written as if discussing the differences of the Churches with a view to a reconciliation between them. There is a further reason too, which I will state presently.

But this Volume had a larger scope than that of opposing the Roman system. It was an attempt at commencing a system of theology on the Anglican idea, and based upon Anglican authorities. Mr. Palmer, about the same time, was projecting a work of a similar nature in his own way. It was published, I think, under the title, "A Treatise on the Christian Church." As was to be expected from the author, it was a most learned, most careful composition; and in its form, I should say, polemical. So happily at least did he follow the logical method of the Roman Schools, that Father Perrone[13] in his Treatise on dogmatic theology, recognized in him a combatant of the true cast, and saluted him as a foe worthy of being vanquished. Other soldiers in that field he seems to have thought little better than the *Lanzknechts* of the middle ages, and, I dare say, with very good reason. When I knew that excellent and kind-hearted man at Rome at a later time, he allowed me to put him to ample penance for those light thoughts of me, which he had once had, by encroaching on his valuable time with my theological questions. As to Mr. Palmer's book, it was one which no Anglican could write but himself,—in no sense, if I recollect aright, a tentative work. The ground of controversy was cut into squares, and then every objection had its answer. This is the proper method to adopt in teaching authoritatively young men; and the work in fact was intended for students in theology. My own book, on the other hand, was of a directly tentative and empirical character. I wished to build up an

Anglican theology out of the stores which already lay cut and hewn upon the ground, the past toil of great divines. To do this could not be the work of one man; much less, could it be at once received into Anglican theology, however well it was done. This I fully recognized; and, while I trusted that my statements of doctrine would turn out to be true and important, still I wrote, to use the common phrase, "under correction."

There was another motive for my publishing, of a personal nature, which I think I should mention. I felt then, and all along felt, that there was an intellectual cowardice in not finding a basis in reason for my belief, and a moral cowardice in not avowing that basis. I should have felt myself less than a man, if I did not bring it out, whatever it was. This is one principal reason why I wrote and published the "Prophetical Office." It was from the same feeling, that in the spring of 1836, at a meeting of residents on the subject of the struggle then proceeding against a Whig appointment, when some one wanted us all merely to act on college and conservative grounds (as I understood him), with as few published statements as possible, I answered, that the person whom we were resisting had committed himself in writing, and that we ought to commit ourselves too. This again was a main reason for the publication of Tract 90. Alas! it was my portion for whole years to remain without any satisfactory basis for my religious profession, in a state of moral sickness, neither able to acquiesce in Anglicanism, nor able to go to Rome. But I bore it, till in course of time my way was made clear to me. If here it be objected to me, that as time went on, I often in my writings hinted at things which I did not fully bring out, I submit for consideration whether this occurred except when I was in great difficulties, how to speak, or how to be silent, with due regard for the position of mind or the feelings of others. However, I may have an opportunity to say more on this subject. But to return to the "Prophetical Office."

I thus speak in the Introduction to my Volume:—

"It is proposed," I say, "to offer helps towards the formation of a recognized Anglican theology in one of its departments. The present state of our divinity is as follows: the most vigorous, the clearest, the most fertile minds, have through God's mercy been employed in the service of our Church: minds too as reverential and holy,

---

[13] Giovanni Perrone (1794–1876), Jesuit, author of *Praelectiones Theologicae*.

and as fully imbued with Ancient Truth, and as well versed in the writings of the Fathers, as they were intellectually gifted. This is God's great mercy indeed, for which we must ever be thankful. Primitive doctrine has been explored for us in every direction, and the original principles of the Gospel and the Church patiently brought to that. But one thing is still wanting: our champions and teachers have lived in stormy times: political and other influences have acted upon them variously in their day, and have since obstructed a careful consolidation of their judgments. We have a vast inheritance, but no inventory of our treasures. All is given us in profusion; it remains for us to catalogue, sort, distribute, select, harmonize, and complete. We have more than we know how to use; stores of learning, but little that is precise and serviceable; Catholic truth and individual opinion, first principles and the guesses of genius, all mingled in the same works, and requiring to be discriminated. We meet with truths overstated or misdirected, matters of detail variously taken, facts incompletely proved or applied, and rules inconsistently urged or discordantly interpreted. Such indeed is the state of every deep philosophy in its first stages, and therefore of theological knowledge. What we need at present for our Church's well-being, is not invention, nor originality, nor sagacity, nor even learning in our divines, at least in the first place, though all gifts of God are in a measure needed, and never can be unseasonable when used religiously, but we need peculiarly a sound judgment, patient thought, discrimination, a comprehensive mind, an abstinence from all private fancies and caprices and personal tastes,—in a word, Divine Wisdom."

The subject of the Volume is the doctrine of the *Via Media*, a name which had already been applied to the Anglican system by writers of repute. It is an expressive title, but not altogether satisfactory, because it is at first sight negative. This had been the reason of my dislike to the word "Protestant;" viz. it did not denote the profession of any particular religion at all, and was compatible with infidelity. A *Via Media* was but a receding from extremes,—therefore it needed to be drawn out into a definite shape and character: before it could have claims on our respect, it must first be shown to be one, intelligible, and consistent. This was the first condition of any reasonable treatise on the *Via Media*. The second condition, and necessary too, was not in my power. I could only hope that it would one day be fulfilled. Even if the *Via Media* were ever so positive a religious system, it was not as yet objective and real; it had no original any where of which it was the representative. It was at present a paper religion. This I confess in my Introduction; I say, "Protestantism and Popery are real religions . . . but the *Via Media*, viewed as an integral system, has scarcely had existence except on paper." I grant the objection, though I endeavour to lessen it:—"It still remains to be tried, whether what is called Anglo-Catholicism, the religion of Andrewes, Laud, Hammond, Butler, and Wilson,[14] is capable of being professed, acted on, and maintained on a large sphere of action, or whether it be a mere modification or transition-state of either Romanism or popular Protestantism." I trusted that some day it would prove to be a substantive religion.

Lest I should be misunderstood, let me observe that this hesitation about the validity of the theory of the *Via Media* implied no doubt of the three fundamental points on which it was based, as I have described them above, dogma, the sacramental system, and anti-Romanism.

Other investigations which had to be followed up were of a still more tentative character. The basis of the *Via Media*, consisting of the three elementary points, which I have just mentioned, was clear enough; but, not only had the house itself to be built upon them, but it had also to be furnished, and it is not wonderful if, after building it, both I and others erred in detail in determining what its furniture should be, what was consistent with the style of building, and what was in itself desirable. I will explain what I mean.

I had brought out in the "Prophetical Office" in what the Roman and the Anglican systems differed from each other, but less distinctly in what they agreed. I had indeed enumerated the Fundamentals, common to both, in the following passage:—"In both systems the same Creeds are acknowledged. Beside other points in common, we both hold, that certain doctrines are necessary to be believed for salvation; we both believe in the doctrines of the Trinity, Incarnation, and Atonement; in original sin; in the necessity of regeneration; in the supernatural grace of the Sacraments; in the Apostolical succession; in the obligation of faith and obedience, and in the eternity of future punishment,"—pp. 55, 56. So

---

[14] Earlier High Church divines.

much I had said, but I had not said enough. This enumeration implied a great many more points of agreement than were found in those very Articles which were fundamental. If the two Churches were thus the same in fundamentals, they were also one and the same in such plain consequences as were contained in those fundamentals and in such natural observances as outwardly represented them. It was an Anglican principle that "the abuse of a thing doth not take away the lawful use of it;" and an Anglican Canon in 1603 had declared that the English Church had no purpose to forsake all that was held in the Churches of Italy, France, and Spain, and reverenced those ceremonies and particular points which were Apostolic. Excepting then such exceptional matters, as are implied in this avowal, whether they were many or few, all these Churches were evidently to be considered as one with the Anglican. The Catholic Church in all lands had been one from the first for many centuries; then, various portions had followed their own way to the injury, but not to the destruction, whether of truth or of charity. These portions or branches were mainly three:—Greek, Latin, and Anglican. Each of these inherited the early undivided Church *in solido* as its own possession. Each branch was identical with that early undivided Church, and in the unity of that Church it had unity with the other branches. The three branches agreed together in *all but* their later accidental errors. Some branches had retained in detail portions of Apostolical truth and usage, which the others had not; and these portions might be and should be appropriated again by the others which had let them slip. Thus, the middle age belonged to the Anglican Church, and much more did the middle age of England. The Church of the 12th century was the Church of the 19th. Dr. Howley sat on the seat of St. Thomas the Martyr;[15] Oxford was a medieval University. Saving our engagements to Prayer Book and Articles, we might breathe and live and act and speak, as in the atmosphere and climate of Henry III.'s day, or the Confessor's, or of Alfred's. And we ought to be indulgent to all that Rome taught now, as to what Rome taught then, saving our protest. We might boldly welcome, even what we did not ourselves think right to adopt. And, when we were obliged on the contrary boldly to denounce, we should do so with pain, not with exultation. By very reason

of our protest, which we had made, and made *ex animo,* we could agree to differ. What the members of the Bible Society did on the basis of Scripture, we could do on the basis of the Church; Trinitarian and Unitarian were further apart than Roman and Anglican. Thus we had a real wish to co-operate with Rome in all lawful things, if she would let us, and if the rules of our own Church let us; and we thought there was no better way towards the restoration of doctrinal purity and unity. And we thought that Rome was not committed by her formal decrees to all that she actually taught: and again, if her disputants had been unfair to us, or her rulers tyrannical, we bore in mind that on our side too there had been rancour and slander in our controversial attacks upon her, and violence in our political measures. As to ourselves being direct instruments in improving her belief or practice, I used to say, "Look at home; let us first, (or at least let us the while,) supply our own shortcomings, before we attempt to be physicians to any one else." This is very much the spirit of Tract 71, to which I referred just now. I am well aware that there is a paragraph inconsistent with it in the Prospectus to the Library of the Fathers; but I do not consider myself responsible for it. Indeed, I have no intention whatever of implying that Dr. Pusey concurred in the ecclesiastical theory, which I have been now drawing out; nor that I took it up myself except by degrees in the course of ten years. It was necessarily the growth of time. In fact, hardly any two persons, who took part in the Movement, agreed in their view of the limit to which our general principles might religiously be carried.

And now I have said enough on what I consider to have been the general objects of the various works, which I wrote, edited, or prompted in the years which I am reviewing. I wanted to bring out in a substantive form a living Church of England, in a position proper to herself, and founded on distinct principles; as far as paper could do it, as far as earnestly preaching it and influencing others towards it, could tend to make it a fact;—a living Church, made of flesh and blood, with voice, complexion, and motion and action, and a will of its own. I believe I had no private motive, and no personal aim. Nor did I ask for more than "a fair stage and no favour," nor expect the work would be accomplished in

---

[15] Reference to the then Archbishop of Canterbury, William Howley (1766–1848), as occupant of the see once held by Thomas à Becket.

my days; but I thought that enough would be secured to continue it in the future, under, perhaps, more hopeful circumstances and prospects than the present.

I will mention in illustration some of the principal works, doctrinal and historical, which originated in the object which I have stated.

I wrote my Essay on Justification in 1837; it was aimed at the Lutheran dictum that justification by faith only was the cardinal doctrine of Christianity. I considered that this doctrine was either a paradox or a truism,—a paradox in Luther's mouth, a truism in Melanchthon's.[16] I thought that the Anglican Church followed Melanchthon, and that in consequence between Rome and Anglicanism, between high Church and low Church, there was no real intellectual difference on the point. I wished to fill up a ditch, the work of man. In this Volume again, I express my desire to build up a system of theology out of the Anglican divines, and imply that my dissertation was a tentative Inquiry. I speak in the Preface of "offering suggestions towards a work, which must be uppermost in the mind of every true son of the English Church at this day,—the consolidation of a theological system, which, built upon those formularies, to which all clergymen are bound, may tend to inform, persuade, and absorb into itself religious minds, which hitherto have fancied, that, on the peculiar Protestant questions, they were seriously opposed to each other."—P. vii.

In my University Sermons there is a series of discussions upon the subject of Faith and Reason; these again were the tentative commencement of a grave and necessary work, viz. an inquiry into the ultimate basis of religious faith, prior to the distinction into Creeds.

In like manner in a Pamphlet, which I published in the summer of 1838, is an attempt at placing the doctrine of the Real Presence on an intellectual basis. The fundamental idea is consonant to that to which I had been so long attached: it is the denial of the existence of space except as a subjective idea of our minds.

The Church of the Fathers is one of the earliest productions of the Movement, and appeared in numbers in the British Magazine, being written with the aim of introducing the religious sentiments, views, and customs of the first ages into the modern Church of England.

The Translation of Fleury's Church History was commenced[17] under these circumstances:—I was fond of Fleury for a reason which I express in the Advertisement; because it presented a sort of photograph of ecclesiastical history without any comment upon it. In the event, that simple representation of the early centuries had a good deal to do with unsettling me in my Anglicanism; but how little I could anticipate this, will be seen in the fact that the publication of Fleury was a favourite scheme with Mr. Rose. He proposed it to me twice, between the years 1834 and 1837; and I mention it as one out of many particulars curiously illustrating how truly my change of opinion arose, not from foreign influences, but from the working of my own mind, and the accidents around me. The date, from which the portion actually translated began, was determined by the Publisher on reasons with which we were not concerned.

Another historical work, but drawn from original sources, was given to the world by my old friend Mr. Bowden, being a Life of Pope Gregory VII. I need scarcely recall to those who have read it, the power and the liveliness of the narrative. This composition was the author's relaxation, on evenings and in his summer vacations, from his ordinary engagements in London. It had been suggested to him originally by me, at the instance of Hurrell Froude.

The Series of the Lives of the English Saints was projected at a later period, under circumstances which I shall have in the sequel to describe. Those beautiful compositions have nothing in them, as far as I recollect, simply inconsistent with the general objects which I have been assigning to my labours in these years, though the immediate occasion which led to them, and the tone in which they were written, had little that was congenial with Anglicanism.

At a comparatively early date I drew up the Tract on the Roman Breviary. It frightened my own friends on its first appearance; and several years afterwards, when younger men began to translate for publication the four volumes *in extenso*, they were dissuaded from doing so by advice to which from a sense of duty they listened. It was an apparent accident, which introduced me to the knowledge of that most wonderful and most attractive monument of the devotion of saints. On Hurrell Froude's death, in 1836, I was asked to select one of his books as a keepsake. I selected Butler's Analogy; finding that it had

---

[16] Philip Melancthon (1497–1560), modified Luther's doctrine of justification by faith.
[17] Claude Fleury's *Ecclesiastical History* was translated by Newman in 1842–44.

been already chosen, I looked with some perplexity along the shelves as they stood before me,
when an intimate friend at my elbow said, "Take
that." It was the Breviary which Hurrell had had
with him at Barbadoes. Accordingly I took it,
studied it, wrote my Tract from it, and have it
on my table in constant use till this day.

That dear and familiar companion, who thus
put the Breviary into my hands, is still in the
Anglican Church. So, too, is that early venerated
long-loved friend, together with whom I edited a
work which, more perhaps than any other,
caused disturbance and annoyance in the
Anglican world,—Froude's Remains; yet, however judgments might run as to the prudence of
publishing it, I never heard any one impute to
Mr. Keble the very shadow of dishonesty or
treachery towards his Church in so acting.

The annotated Translation of the Treatises of
St. Athanasius was of course in no sense of a
tentative character; it belongs to another order of
thought. This historico-dogmatic work employed
me for years. I had made preparations for
following it up with a doctrinal history of the
heresies which succeeded to the Arian.

I should make mention also of the British
Critic. I was Editor of it for three years, from
July 1838 to July 1841. My writers belonged to
various schools, some to none at all. The subjects
are various,—classical, academical, political,
critical, and artistic, as well as theological, and
upon the Movement none are to be found which
do not keep quite clear of advocating the cause
of Rome.

So I went on for years up to 1841. It was, in a
human point of view, the happiest time of my
life. I was truly at home. I had in one of my
volumes appropriated to myself the words of
Bramhall, "Bees, by the instinct of nature, do
love their hives, and birds their nests." I did not
suppose that such sunshine would last, though I
knew not what would be its termination. It was
the time of plenty, and, during its seven years, I
tried to lay up as much as I could for the dearth
which was to follow it. We prospered and spread.
I have spoken of the doings of these years, since I
was a Catholic, in a passage, part of which I will
here quote:

"From beginnings so small," I said, "from
elements of thought so fortuitous, with prospects
so unpromising, the Anglo-Catholic party suddenly became a power in the National Church,
and an object of alarm to her rulers and friends.
Its originators would have found it difficult to

say what they aimed at of a practical kind; rather,
they put forth views and principles for their
own sake, because they were true, as if they
were obliged to say them; and, as they might be
themselves surprised at their earnestness in
uttering them, they had as great cause to be
surprised at the success which attended their
propagation. And, in fact, they could only say
that those doctrines were in the air; that to assert
was to prove, and that to explain was to persuade;
and that the Movement in which they were taking
part was the birth of a crisis rather than of a place.
In a very few years a school of opinion was formed,
fixed in its principles, indefinite and progressive
in their range; and it extended itself into every
part of the country. If we inquire what the world
thought of it, we have still more to raise our
wonder; for, not to mention the excitement it
caused in England, the Movement and its
party-names were known to the police of Italy
and to the back-woodmen of America. And so
it proceeded, getting stronger and stronger
every year, till it came into collision with the
Nation, and that Church of the Nation, which it
began by professing especially to serve."

The greater its success, the nearer was that
collision at hand. The first threatenings of what
was coming were heard in 1838. At that time, my
Bishop in a Charge made some light animadversions, but they *were* animadversions, on the
Tracts for the Times. At once I offered to stop
them. What took place on the occasion I prefer to
state in the words, in which I related it in a
Pamphlet addressed to him in a later year, when
the blow actually came down upon me.

"In your Lordship's Charge for 1838," I
said, "an allusion was made to the Tracts for
the Times. Some opponents of the Tracts said
that you treated them with undue indulgence. . . .
I wrote to the Archdeacon on the subject, submitting the Tracts entirely to your Lordship's
disposal. What I thought about your Charge will
appear from the words I then used to him. I
said, 'A Bishop's lightest word *ex cathedrâ* is
heavy. His judgment on a book cannot be light.
It is a rare occurrence.' And I offered to withdraw any of the Tracts over which I had control,
if I were informed which were those to which your
Lordship had objections. I afterwards wrote to
your Lordship to this effect, that 'I trusted I
might say sincerely, that I should feel a more
lively pleasure in knowing that I was submitting
myself to your Lordship's expressed judgment in
a matter of that kind, than I could have even in
the widest circulation of the volumes in question.'

Your Lordship did not think it necessary to proceed to such a measure, but I felt, and always have felt, that, if ever you determined on it, I was bound to obey."

That day at length came, and I conclude this portion of my narrative, with relating the circumstances of it.

From the time that I had entered upon the duties of Public Tutor at my College, when my doctrinal views were very different from what they were in 1841, I had meditated a comment upon the Articles. Then, when the Movement was in its swing, friends had said to me, "What will you make of the Articles?" but I did not share the apprehension which their question implied. Whether, as time went on, I should have been forced, by the necessities of the original theory of the Movement, to put on paper the speculations which I had about them, I am not able to conjecture. The actual cause of my doing so, in the beginning of 1841, was the restlessness, actual and prospective, of those who neither liked the *Via Media,* nor my strong judgment against Rome. I had been enjoined, I think by my Bishop, to keep these men straight, and I wished so to do: but their tangible difficulty was subscription to the Articles; and thus the question of the Articles came before me. It was thrown in our teeth; "How can you manage to sign the Articles? they are directly against Rome." "Against Rome?" I made answer, "What do you mean by 'Rome?' " and then I proceeded to make distinctions, of which I shall now give an account.

By "Roman doctrine" might be meant one of three things: 1, the *Catholic teaching* of the early centuries; or 2, the *formal dogmas of Rome* as contained in the later Councils, especially the Council of Trent, and as condensed in the Creed of Pope Pius IV.; 3, the *actual popular beliefs and usages* sanctioned by Rome in the countries in communion with it, over and above the dogmas; and these I called "dominant errors." Now Protestants commonly thought that in all three senses, "Roman doctrine" was condemned in the Articles: I thought that the *Catholic teaching* was not condemned; that the *dominant errors* were; and as to the *formal dogmas,* that some were, some were not, and that the line had to be drawn between them. Thus, 1. The use of Prayers for the dead was a Catholic doctrine,—not condemned in the Articles; 2. The prison of Purgatory was a Roman dogma,—which was condemned in them; but the infallibility of Ecumenical Councils was a Roman dogma,—not condemned; and 3. The fire of Purgatory was an authorized and popular error, not a dogma,—which was condemned.

Further, I considered that the difficulties, felt by the persons whom I have mentioned, mainly lay in their mistaking, 1, Catholic teaching, which was not condemned in the Articles, for Roman dogma which was condemned; and 2, Roman dogma, which was not condemned in the Articles, for dominant error which was. If they went further than this, I had nothing more to say to them.

A further motive which I had for my attempt, was the desire to ascertain the ultimate points of contrariety between the Roman and Anglican creeds, and to make them as few as possible. I thought that each creed was obscured and misrepresented by a dominant circumambient "Popery" and "Protestantism."

The main thesis then of my Essay was this:— the Articles do not oppose Catholic teaching; but they partially oppose Roman dogma; they for the most part oppose the dominant errors of Rome. And the problem was, as I have said, to draw the line as to what they allowed and what they condemned.

Such being the object which I had in view, what were my prospects of widening and of defining their meaning? The prospect was encouraging; there was no doubt at all of the elasticity of the Articles: to take a palmary instance, the seventeenth was assumed by one party to be Lutheran, by another Calvinistic, though the two interpretations were contradictory of each other; why then should not other Articles be drawn up with a vagueness of an equally intense character? I wanted to ascertain what was the limit of that elasticity in the direction of Roman dogma. But next, I had a way of inquiry of my own, which I state without defending. I instanced it afterwards in my Essay on Doctrinal Development. That work, I believe, I have not read since I published it, and I do not doubt at all I have made many mistakes in it;—partly, from my ignorance of the details of doctrine, as the Church of Rome holds them, but partly from my impatience to clear as large a range for the *principle* of doctrinal Development (waiving the question of historical *fact*) as was consistent with the strict Apostolicity and identity of the Catholic Creed. In like manner, as regards the 39 Articles, my method of inquiry was to leap *in medias res.* I wished to institute an inquiry how far, in critical fairness, the text *could* be opened; I was aiming far more at ascertaining what a man who subscribed it might hold than what he must, so that my conclusions were negative rather than positive. It was but a first essay. And I made it with the full recognition and consciousness, which I had already expressed in my Prophetical Office, as regards the *Via Media,* that I was making only "a first approximation to the required solution;"—"a series of illustrations supplying hints for the removal" of a difficulty, and with full acknowledgment "that in minor points, whether in question of fact or of judgment, there was room for difference or error of opinion," and that I "should not be ashamed to own a mistake, if it were proved against me, nor reluctant to bear the just blame of it."—Proph. Off. p. 31.

I will add, I was embarrassed in consequence of my wish to go as far as was possible in interpreting the Articles in the direction of Roman dogma, without disclosing what I was doing to the parties whose doubts I was meeting; who, if they understood at once the full extent of the licence which the Articles admitted, might be thereby encouraged to proceed still further than at present they found in themselves any call to go.

1. But in the way of such an attempt comes the prompt objection that the Articles were actually drawn up against "Popery," and therefore it was transcendently absurd and dishonest to suppose that Popery, in any shape,—patristic belief, Tridentine dogma, or popular corruption authoritatively sanctioned,—would be able to take refuge under their text. This premiss I denied. Not any religious doctrine at all, but a political principle, was the primary English idea of "Popery" at the date of the Reformation. And what was that political principle, and how could it best be suppressed in England? What was the great question in the days of Henry and Elizabeth? The *Supremacy;*—now, was I saying one single word in favour of the Supremacy of the Holy See, in favour of the foreign jurisdiction? No, I did not believe in it myself. Did Henry VIII. religiously hold Justification by faith only? did he disbelieve Purgatory? Was Elizabeth zealous for the marriage of the Clergy? or had she a conscience against the Mass? The Supremacy of the Pope was the essence of the "Popery" to which, at the time of the composition of the Articles, the Supreme Head or Governor of the English Church was so violently hostile.

2. But again I said this:—let "Popery" mean what it would in the mouths of the compilers of the Articles, let it even, for argument's sake, include the doctrines of that Tridentine Council, which was not yet over when the Articles were drawn up, and against which they could not be simply directed, yet, consider, what was the object of the Government in their imposition? merely to get rid of "Popery?" No; it had the further object of gaining the "Papists." What then was the best way to induce reluctant or wavering minds, and these, I supposed, were the majority, to give in their adhesion to the new symbol? how had the Arians drawn up their Creeds? was it not on the principle of using vague ambiguous language, which to the subscribers would seem to bear a Catholic sense, but which, when worked out on the long run, would prove to be heterodox? Accordingly, there was great antecedent probability, that, fierce as the Articles might look at first sight, their bark would prove worse than their bite. I say antecedent probability, for to what extent that surmise might be true, could only be ascertained by investigation.

3. But a consideration came up at once, which threw light on the surmise:—what if it should turn out that the very men who drew up the Articles, in the very act of doing so, had avowed, or rather in one of those very Articles themselves had imposed on subscribers, a number of those very "Papistical" doctrines, which they were now thought to deny, as part and parcel of that very Protestantism, which they were now thought to consider divine? and this was the fact, and I showed it in my Essay.

Let the reader observe:—the 35th Article says: "The second Book of Homilies[18] doth contain *a godly and wholesome doctrine, and necessary for* these times, as doth the former Book of Homilies." Here the *doctrine* of the Homilies is recognized as godly and wholesome, and concurrence in that recognition is imposed on all subscribers of the Articles. Let us then turn to the Homilies, and see what this godly doctrine is: I quoted from them to the following effect:

1. They declare that the so-called "apocryphal" book of Tobit is the teaching of the Holy Ghost, and is Scripture.

2. That the so-called "apocryphal" book of Wisdom is Scripture, and the infallible and undeceivable word of God.

---

[18] The Homilies are two volumes of sermons prepared in the sixteenth century for the use of Anglican clergymen and generally considered as expansions of the Thirty-Nine Articles.

3. That the Primitive Church, next to the Apostles' time, and, as they imply, for almost 700 years, is no doubt most pure.

4. That the Primitive Church is specially to be followed.

5. That the Four first General Councils belong to the Primitive Church.

6. That there are Six Councils which are allowed and received by all men.

7. Again, they speak of a certain truth, and say that it is declared by God's word, the sentences of the ancient doctors, and judgment of the Primitive Church.

8. Of the learned and holy Bishops and doctors of the Church of the first eight centuries being of great authority and credit with the people.

9. Of the declaration of Christ and His Apostles and all the rest of the Holy Fathers.

10. Of the authority both of Scripture and also of Augustine.

11. Of Augustine, Chrysostom, Ambrose, Jerome, and about thirty other Fathers, to some of whom they give the title of "Saint," to others of "ancient Catholic Fathers and doctors, &c."

12. They declare that, not only the holy Apostles and disciples of Christ, but the godly Fathers also, before and since Christ, were endued without doubt with the Holy Ghost.

13. That the ancient Catholic Fathers say that the "Lord's Supper" is the salve of immortality, the sovereign preservative against death, the food of immortality, the healthful grace.

14. That the Lord's Blessed Body and Blood are received under the form of bread and wine.

15. That the meat in the Sacrament is an invisible meat and a ghostly substance.

16. That the holy Body and Blood of thy God ought to be touched with the mind.

17. That Ordination is a Sacrament.

18. That Matrimony is a Sacrament.

19. That there are other Sacraments besides "Baptism and the Lord's Supper," though not "such as" they.

20. That the souls of the Saints are reigning in joy and in heaven with God.

21. That alms-deeds purge the soul from the infection and filthy spots of sin, and are a precious medicine, an inestimable jewel.

22. That mercifulness wipes out and washes away sins, as salves and remedies to heal sores and grievous diseases.

23. That the duty of fasting is a truth more manifest than it should need to be proved.

24. That fasting, used with prayer, is of great efficacy and weigheth much with God; so the Angel Raphael told Tobias.

25. That the puissant and mighty Emperor Theodosius was, in the Primitive Church which was most holy and godly, excommunicated by St. Ambrose.

26. That Constantine, Bishop of Rome, did condemn Philippicus, then Emperor, not without a cause indeed, but very justly.

Putting altogether aside the question how far these separate theses came under the matter to which subscription was to be made, it was quite plain, that in the minds of the men who wrote the Homilies, and who thus incorporated them into the Anglican system of doctrine, there was no such nice discrimination between the Catholic and the Protestant faith, no such clear recognition of formal Protestant principles and tenets, no such accurate definition of "Roman doctrine," as is received at the present day:—hence great probability accrued to my presentiment, that the Articles were tolerant, not only of what I called "Catholic teaching," but of much that was "Roman."

4. And here was another reason against the notion that the Articles directly attacked the Roman dogmas as declared at Trent and as promulgated by Pius the Fourth:—the Council of Trent was nor over, nor its Canons promulgated at the date when the Articles were drawn up,[19] so that those Articles must be aiming at something else? What was that something else? The Homilies tell us: the Homilies are the best comment upon the Articles. Let us turn to the Homilies, and we shall find from first to last that, not only is not the Catholic teaching of the first centuries, but neither again are the dogmas of Rome, the objects of the protest of the compilers of the Articles, but the dominant errors, the popular corruptions, authorized or suffered by the high name of Rome. The eloquent declamation of the Homilies finds its matter almost exclusively in the dominant errors. As to Catholic teaching, nay as to Roman dogma, of such theology those Homilies, as I have shown, contained no small portion themselves.

5. So much for the writers of the Articles and Homilies;—they were witnesses, not authorities,

---

[19] The Pope's Confirmation of the Council by which its canons became *de fide*, and his Bull *super confirmatione*, by which they were promulgated to the world, are dated January 26, 1564. The Articles are dated 1562. [Newman's note]

and I used them as such; but in the next place, who were the actual authorities imposing them? I reasonably considered the authority *imponens* to be the Convocation of 1571; but here again, it would be found that the very Convocation, which received and confirmed the 39 Articles, also enjoined by Canon that "preachers should be *careful,* that they should *never* teach aught in a sermon, to be religiously held and believed by the people, except that which is agreeable to the doctrine of the Old and New Testament, and *which the Catholic Fathers and ancient Bishops have collected* from that very doctrine." Here, let it be observed, an appeal is made by the Convocation *imponens* to the very same ancient authorities, as had been mentioned with such profound veneration by the writers of the Homilies and the Articles, and thus, if the Homilies contained views of doctrine which now would be called Roman, there seemed to me to be an extreme probability that the Convocation of 1571 also countenanced and received, or at least did not reject, those doctrines.

6. And further, when at length I came actually to look into the text of the Articles, I saw in many cases a patent justification of all that I had surmised as to their vagueness and indecisiveness, and that, not only on questions which lay between Lutherans, Calvinists, and Zuinglians, but on Catholic questions also; and I have noticed them in my Tract. In the conclusion of my Tract I observe: The Articles are "evidently framed on the principle of leaving open large questions on which the controversy hinges. They state broadly extreme truths, and are silent about their adjustment. For instance, they say that all necessary faith must be proved from Scripture, but do not say *who* is to prove it. They say, that the Church has authority in controversies; they do not say *what* authority. They say that it may enforce nothing beyond Scripture, but do not say *where* the remedy lies when it does. They say that works *before* grace *and* justification are worthless and worse, and that works *after* grace *and* justification are acceptable, but they do not speak at all of works *with* God's aid *before* justification. They say that men are lawfully called and sent to minister and preach, who are chosen and called by men who have public authority *given* them in the Congregation; but they do not add *by whom* the authority is to be

given. They say that Councils called by *princes* may err; they do not determine whether Councils called in the name of Christ may err."

Such were the considerations which weighed with me in my inquiry how far the Articles were tolerant of a Catholic, or even a Roman interpretation; and such was the defence which I made in my Tract for having attempted it. From what I have already said, it will appear that I have no need or intention at this day to maintain every particular interpretation which I suggested in the course of my Tract, nor indeed had I then. Whether it was prudent or not, whether it was sensible or not, any how I attempted only a first essay of a necessary work, as essay which, as I was quite prepared to find, would require revision and modification by means of the lights which I should gain from the criticism of others. I should have gladly withdrawn any statement, which could be proved to me to be erroneous; I considered my work to be faulty and open to objection in the same sense in which I now consider my Anglican interpretations of Scripture to be erroneous; but in no other sense. I am surprised that men do not apply to the interpreters of Scripture generally the hard names which they apply to the author of Tract 90. He held a large system of theology, and applied it to the Articles: Episcopalians, or Lutherans, or Presbyterians, or Unitarians, hold a large system of theology and apply it to Scripture. Every theology has its difficulties; Protestants hold justification by faith only, though there is no text in St. Paul which enunciates it, and though St. James expressly denies it; do we therefore call Protestants dishonest? they deny that the Church has a divine mission, though St. Paul says that it is "the Pillar and ground of Truth;" they keep the Sabbath, though St. Paul says, "Let no man judge you in meat or drink or in respect of . . . the sabbath days."[20] Every creed has texts in its favour, and again texts which run counter to it: and this is generally confessed. And this is what I felt keenly:—how had I done worse in Tract 90 than Anglicans, Wesleyans, and Calvinists did daily in their Sermons and their publications? how had I done worse, than the Evangelical party in their *ex animo* reception of the Services for Baptism and Visitation of the Sick?[21] Why was I to be dishonest and they immaculate? There was an

---

[20] I Timothy 3:15; Colossians 2:16.

[21] For instance, let candid men consider the form of Absolution contained in that Prayer Book, of which all clergymen, Evangelical and Liberal as well as high Church, and (I think) all persons in University office declare that "it containeth nothing *contrary to the Word of God.*"

occasion on which our Lord gave an answer, which seemed to be appropriate to my own case, when the tumult broke out against my Tract:— "He that is without sin among you, let him first cast a stone at him."[22] I could have fancied that a sense of their own difficulties of interpretation would have persuaded the great party I have mentioned to some prudence, or at least moderation, in opposing a teacher of an opposite school. But I suppose their alarm and their anger overcame their sense of justice.

In the sudden storm of indignation with which the Tract was received throughout the country on its appearance, I recognize much of real religious feeling, much of honest and true principle, much of straightforward ignorant common sense. In Oxford there was genuine feeling too; but there had been a smouldering, stern, energetic animosity, not at all unnatural, partly rational, against its author. A false step had been made; now was the time for action. I am told that, even before the publication of the Tract, rumours of its contents had got into the hostile camp in an exaggerated form; and not a moment was lost in proceeding to action, when I was actually fallen into the hands of the Philistines. I was quite unprepared for the outbreak, and was startled at its violence. I do not think I had any fear. Nay, I will add, I am not sure that it was not in one point of view a relief to me.

I saw indeed clearly that my place in the Movement was lost; public confidence was at an end; my occupation was gone. It was simply an impossibility that I could say any thing henceforth to good effect, when I had been posted up by the marshal on the buttery-hatch of every College of my University, after the manner of discommoned pastry-cooks, and when in every part of the country and every class of society, through every organ and opportunity of opinion, in newspapers, in periodicals, at meetings, in pulpits, at dinner-tables, in coffee-rooms, in railway carriages, I was denounced as a traitor

who had laid his train and was detected in the very act of firing it against the time-honoured Establishment. There were indeed men, besides my own immediate friends, men of name and position, who gallantly took my part, as Dr. Hook,[23] Mr. Palmer, and Mr. Perceval; it must have been a grievous trial for themselves; yet what after all could they do for me? Confidence in me was lost;—but I had already lost full confidence in myself. Thoughts had passed over me a year and a half before in respect to the Anglican claims, which for the time had profoundly troubled me. They had gone: I had not less confidence in the power and the prospects of the Apostolical movement than before; not less confidence than before in the grievousness of what I called the "dominant errors" of Rome: but how was I any more to have absolute confidence in myself? how was I to have confidence in my present confidence? how was I to be sure that I should always think as I thought now? I felt that by this event a kind Providence had saved me from an impossible position in the future.

First, if I remember right, they wished me to withdraw the Tract. This I refused to do: I would not do so for the sake of those who were unsettled or in danger of unsettlement. I would not do so for my own sake; for how could I acquiesce in a mere Protestant interpretation of the Articles? how could I range myself among the professors of a theology, of which it put my teeth on edge even to hear the sound?

Next they said, "Keep silence; do not defend the Tract;" I answered, "Yes, if you will not condemn it,—if you will allow it to continue on sale." They pressed on me whenever I gave way; they fell back when they saw me obstinate. Their line of action was to get out of me as much as they could; but upon the point of their tolerating the Tract I *was* obstinate. So they let me continue it on sale; and they said they would not condemn it. But they said that this was on condition that I did not defend it, that I stopped the

---

I challenge, in the sight of all England, Evangelical clergymen generally to put on paper an interpretation of this form of words, consistent with their sentiments, which shall be less forced than the most objectionable of the interpretations which Tract 90 puts upon any passage in the Articles.

"Our Lord Jesus Christ who hath left *power* to His Church to absolve all sinners who truly repent and believe in Him, of His great mercy forgive thee thine offenses; and by *His authority committed to me, I absolve thee from all thy sins,* in the Name of the Father, and of the Son, and of the Holy Ghost. Amen."

I subjoin the Roman form as used in England and elsewhere: "Dominus noster Jesus Christus te absolvat; et ego auctoritate ipsius te absolve, ab omni vinculo excommunicationis et interdicti, in quantum possum et tu indiges. Deinde ego te absolve à peccatis tuis, in nomine Patris et Filii et Spiritûs Sancti. Amen." [Newman's note]

[22] John 8:7.

[23] Walter F. Hook (1798–1875), Vicar of Leeds.

series, and that I myself published my own condemnation in a letter to the Bishop of Oxford. I impute nothing whatever to him, he was ever most kind to me. Also, they said they could not answer for what some individual Bishops might perhaps say about the Tract in their own charges. I agreed to their conditions. My one point was to save the Tract.

Not a line in writing was given me, as a pledge of the observance of the main article on their side of the engagement. Parts of letters from them were read to me, without being put into my hands. It was an "understanding." A clever man had warned me against "understandings" some thirteen years before. I have hated them ever since.

In the last words of my letter to the Bishop of Oxford I thus resigned my place in the Movement:—

"I have nothing to be sorry for," I say to him, "except having made your Lordship anxious, and others whom I am bound to revere. I have nothing to be sorry for, but everything to rejoice in and be thankful for. I have never taken pleasure in seeming to be able to move a party, and whatever influence I have had, has been found, not sought after. I have acted because others did not act, and have sacrificed a quiet which I prized. May God be with me in time to come, as He has been hitherto! and He will be, if I can but keep my hand clean and my heart pure. I think I can bear, or at least will try to bear, any personal humiliation, so that I am preserved from betraying sacred interests, which the Lord of grace and power has given into my charge."[24]

CHAPTER III

History of My Religious Opinions from 1839 to 1841

AND NOW that I am about to trace, as far as I can, the course of that great revolution of mind, which led me to leave my own home, to which I was bound by so many strong and tender ties, I feel overcome with the difficulty of satisfying myself in my account of it, and have recoiled from the attempt, till the near approach of the day, on which these lines must be given to the world, forces me to set about the task. For who can know himself, and the multitude of subtle influences which act upon him? And who can recollect, at the distance of twenty-five years, all that he once knew about his thoughts and his deeds, and that, during a portion of his life, when, even at the time, his observation, whether of himself or of the external world, was less than before or after, by very reason of the perplexity and dismay which weighed upon him,—when, in spite of the light given to him according to his need amid his darkness, yet a darkness it emphatically was? And who can suddenly gird himself to a new and anxious undertaking, which he might be able indeed to perform well, were full and calm leisure allowed him to look through every thing that he had written, whether in published works or private letters, yet again, granting that calm contemplation of the past, in itself so desirable, who could afford to be leisurely and deliberate, while he practices on himself a cruel operation, the ripping up of old griefs, and the venturing again upon the "infandum dolorem"[1] of years, in which the stars of this lower heaven were one by one going out? I could not in cool blood, nor except upon the imperious call of duty, attempt what I have set myself to do. It is both to head and heart an extreme trial, thus to analyze what has so long gone by, and to bring out the results of that examination. I have done various bold things in my life: this is the boldest: and, were I not sure I should after all succeed in my object, it would be madness to set about it.

In the spring of 1839 my position in the Anglican Church was at its height. I had supreme confidence in my controversial status, and I had a great and still growing success, in recommending it to others. I had in the foregoing autumn been somewhat sore at the Bishop's Charge, but I have a letter which shows that all annoyance had passed from my mind. In January, if I recollect aright, in order to meet the popular clamour against myself and others, and to satisfy the Bishop, I had collected into one all the strong things which they, and especially I, had said against the Church of Rome, in order to their insertion among the advertisements appended to

[24] To the Pamphlets published in my behalf at this time I should add "One Tract more," an able and generous defence of Tractarianism and No. 90, by the present Lord Houghton. [Newman's note]
[1] "Unspeakable sorrow" (Aeneid).

our publications. Conscious as I was that my opinions in religion were not gained, as the world said, from Roman sources, but were, on the contrary, the birth of my own mind and of the circumstances in which I had been placed, I had a scorn of the imputations which were heaped upon me. It was true that I held a large bold system of religion, very unlike the Protestantism of the day, but it was the concentration and adjustment of the statements of great Anglican authorities, and I had as much right to hold it, as the Evangelical, and more right than the Liberal party could show, for asserting their own respective doctrines. As I declared on occasion of Tract 90, I claimed, in behalf of who would in the Anglican Church, the right of holding with Bramhall a comprecation with the Saints, and the Mass all but Transubstantiation with Andrewes, or with Hooker that Transubstantiation itself is not a point for Churches to part communion upon, or with Hammond that a General Council, truly such, never did, never shall err in a matter of faith, or with Bull that man had in paradise and lost on the fall, a supernatural habit of grace, or with Thorndike that penance is a propitiation for post-baptismal sin, or with Pearson[2] that the all-powerful name of Jesus is no otherwise given than in the Catholic Church. "Two can play at that," was often in my mouth, when men of Protestant sentiments appealed to the Articles, Homilies, or Reformers; in the sense that, if they had a right to speak loud, I had the liberty to speak out as well as they, and had the means, by the same or parallel appeals, of giving them tit for tat. I thought that the Anglican Church was tyrannized over by a mere party, and I aimed at bringing into effect the promise contained in the motto to the Lyra,[3] "They shall know the difference now." I only asked to be allowed to show them the difference.

What will best describe my state of mind at the early part of 1839, is an Article in the British Critic for that April. I have looked over it now, for the first time since it was published; and have been struck by it for this reason:—it contains the last words which I ever spoke as an Anglican to Anglicans. It may now be read as my parting address and valediction, made to my friends. I little knew it at the time. It reviews the actual state of things, and it ends by looking towards the future. It is not altogether mine; for my memory goes to this,—that I had asked a friend to do the work; that then, the thought came on me, that I would do it myself: and that he was good enough to put into my hands what he had with great appositeness written, and that I embodied it in my Article. Every one, I think, will recognize the greater part of it as mine. It was published two years before the affair of Tract 90, and was entitled "The State of Religious Parties."

In this Article, I begin by bringing together testimonies from our enemies to the remarkable success of our exertions. One writer said: "Opinions and views of a theology of a very marked and peculiar kind have been extensively adopted and strenuously upheld, and are daily gaining ground among a considerable and influential portion of the members, as well as ministers of the Established Church." Another: The Movement has manifested itself "with the most rapid growth of the hot-bed of these evil days." Another: "The *Via Media* is crowded with young enthusiasts, who never presume to argue, except against the propriety of arguing at all." Another: "Were I to give you a full list of the works, which they have produced within the short space of five years, I should surprise you. You would see what a task it would be to make yourself complete master of their system, even in its present probably immature state. The writers have adopted the motto, 'In quietness and confidence shall be your strength.' With regard to confidence, they have justified their adopting it; but as to quietness, it is not very quiet to pour forth such a succession of controversial publications." Another: "The spread of these doctrines is in fact now having the effect of rendering all other distinctions obsolete, and of severing the religious community into two portions, fundamentally and vehemently opposed one to the other. Soon there will be no middle ground left; and every man, and especially every clergyman, will be compelled to make his choice between the two." Another: "The time has gone by, when those unfortunate and deeply regretted publications can be passed over without notice, and the hope that their influence would fail is now dead." Another: "These doctrines had already made fearful progress. One of the largest churches in Brighton is crowded to hear them; so is the church at Leeds. There are few towns of note, to which they have not extended. They are preached in small towns in Scotland. They obtain in

---

[2] Those cited in the rest of the paragraph are Anglican divines of the sixteenth and seventeenth centuries.

  [3] I.e., the volume of verse, *Lyra Apostolica*.

Elginshire, 600 miles north of London. I found them myself in the heart of the highlands of Scotland. They are advocated in the newspaper and periodical press. They have even insinuated themselves into the House of Commons." And, lastly, a bishop in a charge:—It "is daily assuming a more serious and alarming aspect. Under the specious pretence of deference to Antiquity and respect for primitive models, the foundations of the Protestant Church are undermined by men, who dwell within her walls, and those who sit in the Reformers' seat are traducing the Reformation."

After thus stating the phenomenon of the time, as it presented itself to those who did not sympathize in it, the Article proceeds to account for it, and this it does by considering it as a re-action from the dry and superficial character of the religious teaching and the literature of the last generation, or century, and as a result of the need which was felt both by the hearts and the intellects of the nation for a deeper philosophy, and as the evidence and as the partial fulfilment of that need, to which even the chief authors of the then generation had borne witness. First, I mentioned the literary influence of Walter Scott, who turned men's minds in the direction of the middle ages. "The general need," I said, "of something deeper and more attractive, than what had offered itself elsewhere, may be considered to have led to his popularity; and by means of his popularity he re-acted on his readers, stimulating their mental thirst, feeding their hopes, setting before them visions, which, when once seen, are not easily forgotten, and silently indoctrinating them with nobler ideas, which might afterwards be appealed to as first principles."

Then I spoke of Coleridge, thus: "While history in prose and verse was thus made the instrument of Church feelings and opinions, a philosophical basis for the same was laid in England by a very original thinker, who, while he indulged a liberty of speculation, which no Christian can tolerate, and advocated conclusions which were often heathen rather than Christian, yet after all installed a higher philosophy into inquiring minds, than they had hitherto been accustomed to accept. In this way he made trial of his age, and succeeded in interesting its genius in the cause of Catholic truth."

Then come Southey and Wordsworth, "two living poets, one of whom in the department of

fantastic fiction, the other in that of philosophical meditation, have addressed themselves to the same high principles and feelings, and carried forward their readers in the same direction."

Then comes the prediction of this re-action hazarded by "a sagacious observer withdrawn from the world, and surveying its movements from a distance," Mr. Alexander Knox.[4] He had said twenty years before the date of my Article: "No Church on earth has more intrinsic excellence than the English Church, yet no Church probably has less practical influence. . . . The rich provision, made by the grace and providence of God, for habits of a noble kind, is evidence that men shall arise, fitted both by nature and ability, to discover for themselves, and to display to others, whatever yet remains undiscovered, whether in the words or works of God." Also I referred to "a much venerated clergyman of the last generation," who said shortly before his death, "Depend on it, the day will come, when those great doctrines, now buried, will be brought out to the light of day, and then the effect will be fearful." I remarked upon this, that they who "now blame the impetuosity of the current, should rather turn their aminadversions upon those who have dammed up a majestic river, till it has become a flood."

These being the circumstances under which the Movement began and progressed, it was absurd to refer it to the act of two or three individuals. It was not so much a movement as a "spirit afloat;" it was within us, "rising up in hearts where it was least suspected, and working itself, though not in secret, yet so subtly and impalpably, as hardly to admit of precaution or encounter on any ordinary human rules of opposition. It is," I continued, "an adversary in the air, a something one and entire, a whole wherever it is, unapproachable and incapable of being grasped, as being the result of causes far deeper than political or other visible agencies, the spiritual awakening of spiritual wants."

To make this clear, I proceed to refer to the chief preachers of the revived doctrines at that moment, and to draw attention to the variety of their respective antecedents. Dr. Hook and Mr. Churton represented the high Church dignitaries of the last century; Mr. Perceval, the Tory aristocracy; Mr. Keble came from a country parsonage; Mr. Palmer from Ireland; Dr. Pusey from the Universities of Germany, and the study of Arabic MSS.; Mr. Dodsworth from the study

---

[4] Alexander Knox (1757–1831), often cited as a forerunner of the Tractarians.

of Prophecy; Mr. Oakeley had gained his views, as he himself expressed it, "partly by study, partly by reflection, partly by conversation with one or two friends, inquirers like himself:" while I speak of myself as being "much indebted to the friendship of Archbishop Whately." And thus I am led on to ask, "What head of a sect is there? What march of opinions can be traced from mind to mind among preachers such as these? They are one and all in their degree the organs of one Sentiment, which has risen up simultaneously in many places very mysteriously."

My train of thought next led me to speak of the disciples of the Movement, and I freely acknowledged and lamented that they needed to be kept in order. It is very much to the purpose to draw attention to this point now, when such extravagances as then occurred, whatever they were, are simply laid to my door, or to the charge of the doctrines which I advocated. A man cannot do more than freely confess what is wrong, say that it need not be, that it ought not to be, and that he is very sorry that it should be. Now I said in the Article, which I am reviewing, that the great truths themselves, which we were preaching, must not be condemned on account of such abuse of them. "Aberrations there must ever be, whatever the doctrine is, while the human heart is sensitive, capricious, and wayward. A mixed multitude went out of Egypt with the Israelites." "There will ever be a number of persons," I continued, "professing the opinions of a movement party, who talk loudly and strangely, do odd or fierce things, display themselves unnecessarily, and disgust other people; persons, too young to be wise, too generous to be cautious, too warm to be sober, or too intellectual to be humble. Such persons will be very apt to attach themselves to particular persons, to use particular names, to say things merely because others do, and to act in a party-spirited way."

While I thus republish what I then said about such extravagances as occurred in these years, at the same time I have a very strong conviction that those extravagances furnished quite as much the welcome excuse for those who were jealous or shy of us, as the stumbling-blocks of those who were well inclined to our doctrines. This too we felt at the time; but it was our duty to see that our good should not be evil-spoken of; and accordingly, two or three of the writers of the Tracts for the Times had commenced a Series of what they called "Plain Sermons" with the avowed purpose of discouraging and correcting whatever was uppish or extreme in our followers: to this Series I contributed a volume myself.

Its conductors say in their Preface: "If therefore as time goes on, there shall be found persons, who admiring the innate beauty and majesty of the fuller system of Primitive Christianity, and seeing the transcendent strength of its principles, *shall become loud and voluble advocates* in their behalf, speaking the more freely, *because they do not feel them deeply as founded* in divine and eternal truth, of such persons *it is our duty to declare plainly*, that, as we should contemplate their condition with serious misgiving, *so would they be the last persons from whom we should* seek support.

"But if, on the other hand, there shall be any, who, in the silent humility of their lives, and in their unaffected reverence for holy things, show that they in truth accept these principles as real and substantial, and by habitual purity of heart and serenity of temper, give proof of their deep veneration for sacraments and sacramental ordinances, those persons, *whether our professed adherents or not,* best exemplify the kind of character which the writers of the Tracts for the Times have wished to form."

These clergymen had the best of claims to use these beautiful words, for they were themselves, all of them, important writers in the Tracts, the two Mr. Kebles, and Mr. Isaac Williams.[5] And this passage, with which they ushered their Series into the world, I quoted in the Article, of which I am giving an account, and I added, "What more can be required of the preachers of neglected truth, than that they should admit that some, who do not assent to their preaching, are holier and better men than some who do?" They were not answerable for the intemperance of those who dishonoured a true doctrine, provided they protested, as they did, against such intemperance. "They were not answerable for the dust and din which attends any great moral movement. The truer doctrines are, the more liable they are to be perverted."

The notice of these incidental faults of opinion or temper in adherents of the Movement, led on to a discussion of the secondary causes, by means of which a system of doctrine may be embraced, modified, or developed, of the variety of schools which may all be in the One Church, and of the succession of one phase of doctrine to another, while that doctrine is ever one and the same.

[5] John Keble and his brother Thomas; Isaac Williams (1802–65), Tractarian poet.

Thus I was brought on to the subject of Antiquity, which was the basis of the doctrine of the *Via Media,* and by which was not to be understood a servile imitation of the past, but such a re-production of it as is really new, while it is old. "We have good hope," I say, "that a system will be rising up, superior to the age, yet harmonizing with, and carrying out its higher points, which will attract to itself those who are willing to make a venture and to face difficulties, for the sake of something higher in prospect. On this, as on other subjects, the proverb will apply, 'Fortes fortuna adjuvat.' "[6]

Lastly, I proceeded to the question of that future of the Anglican Church, which was to be a new birth of the Ancient Religion. And I did not venture to pronounce upon it. "About the future, we have no prospect before our minds whatever, good or bad. Ever since that great luminary, Augustine, proved to be the last bishop of Hippo, Christians have had a lesson against attempting to foretell, *how* Providence will prosper and" [or?] "bring to an end, what it begins." Perhaps the lately-revived principles would prevail in the Anglican Church; perhaps they would be lost in "some miserable schism, or some more miserable compromise; but there was nothing rash in venturing to predict that "neither Puritanism nor Liberalism had any permanent inheritance within her."

Then I went on: "As to Liberalism, we think the formularies of the Church will ever, with the aid of a good Providence, keep it from making any serious inroads upon the clergy. Besides, it is too cold a principle to prevail with the multi-tude." But as regarded what was called Evan-gelical Religion or Puritanism, there was more to cause alarm. I observed upon its organization; but on the other hand it had no intellectual basis; no internal idea, no principle of unity, no theology. "Its adherents," I said, "are already separating from each other; they will melt away like a snow-drift. It has no straightforward view on any one point, on which it professes to teach, and to hide its poverty, it has dressed itself out in a maze of words. We have no dread of it at all; we only fear what it may lead to. It does not stand on intrenched ground, or make any pre-tence to a position; it does but occupy the space between contending powers, Catholic Truth and Rationalism. Then indeed will be the stern encounter, when two real and living principles,

simple, entire, and consistent, one in the Church, the other out of it, at length rush upon each other, contending not for names and words, or half-views, but for elementary notions and distinctive moral characters."

Whether the ideas of the coming age upon religion were true or false, at least they would be real. "In the present day," I said, "mistiness is the mother of wisdom. A man who can set down a half-a-dozen general propositions, which escape from destroying one another only by being diluted into truisms, who can hold the balance between opposites so skilfully as to do without fulcrum or beam, who never enunciates a truth without guarding himself against being supposed to exclude the contradictory,—who holds that Scripture is the only authority, yet that the Church is to be deferred to, that faith only justifies, yet that it does not justify without works, that grace does not depend on the sacraments, yet is not given without them, that bishops are a divine ordinance, yet those who have them not are in the same religious condition as those who have,—this is your safe man and the hope of the Church; this is what the Church is said to want, not party men, but sensible, temperate, sober, well-judging persons, to guide it through the channel of no-meaning, between the Scylla and Charybdis of Aye and No."

This state of things, however, I said, could not last, if men were to read and think. They "will not keep in that very attitude which you call sound Church-of-Englandism or orthodox Protestantism. They cannot go on for ever standing on one leg, or sitting without a chair, or walking with their feet tied, or like Tityrus's stags grazing in the air. They will take one view or another, but it will be a consistent view. It may be Liberalism, or Erastianism, or Popery, or Catholicity; but it will be real."

I concluded the Article by saying, that all who did not wish to be "democratic, or pantheistic, or popish," must "look out for *some* Via Media which will preserve us from what threatens, though it cannot restore the dead. The spirit of Luther is dead; but Hildebrand and Loyola are alive.[7] Is it sensible, sober, judicious, to be so very angry with those writers of the day, who point to the fact, that our divines of the seven-teenth century have occupied a ground which is the true and intelligible mean between extremes? Is it wise to quarrel with this ground, because it is

---

[6] "Fortune favors the brave."

[7] Hildebrand, Pope Gregory VII; Ignatius Loyola, the founder of the Jesuits.

not exactly what we should choose, had we the power of choice? Is it true moderation, instead of trying to fortify a middle doctrine, to fling stones at those who do? . . . Would you rather have your sons and daughters members of the Church of England or of the Church of Rome?"

And thus I left the matter. But, while I was thus speaking of the future of the Movement, I was in truth winding up my accounts with it, little dreaming that it was so to be;—while I was still, in some way or other, feeling about for an available *Via Media*, I was soon to receive a shock which was to cast out of my imagination all middle courses and compromises for ever. As I have said, this Article appeared in the April number of the British Critic; in the July number, I cannot tell why, there is no Article of mine; before the number for October, the event had happened to which I have alluded.

But before I proceed to describe what happened to me in the summer of 1839, I must detain the reader for a while, in order to describe the *issue* of the controversy between Rome and the Anglican Church, as I viewed it. This will involve some dry discussion; but it is as necessary for my narrative, as plans of buildings and homesteads are at times needed in the proceedings of our law courts.

I have said already that, though the object of the Movement was to withstand the Liberalism of the day, I found and felt this could not be done by mere negatives. It was necessary for us to have a positive Church theory erected on a definite basis. This took me to the great Anglican divines; and then of course I found at once that it was impossible to form any such theory, without cutting across the teaching of the Church of Rome. Thus came in the Roman controversy.

When I first turned myself to it, I had neither doubt on the subject, nor suspicion that doubt would ever come upon me. It was in this state of mind that I began to read up Bellarmine[8] on the one hand, and numberless Anglican writers on the other. But I soon found, as others had found before me, that it was a tangled and manifold controversy, difficult to master, more difficult to put out of hand with neatness and precision. It was easy to make points, not easy to sum up and settle. It was not easy to find a clear issue for the dispute, and still less by a logical process to decide it in favour of Anglicanism. This difficulty,

however, had no tendency whatever to harass or perplex me: it was a matter which bore not on convictions, but on proofs.

First I saw, as all see who study the subject, that a broad distinction had to be drawn between the actual state of belief and of usage in the countries which were in communion with the Roman church, and her formal dogmas; the latter did not cover the former. Sensible pain, for instance, is not implied in the Tridentine decree upon Purgatory; but it was the tradition of the Latin Church, and I had seen the pictures of souls in flames in the streets of Naples. Bishop Lloyd[9] had brought this distinction out strongly in an Article in the British Critic in 1825; indeed, it was one of the most common objections made to the Church of Rome, that she dared not commit herself by formal decree, to what nevertheless she sanctioned and allowed. Accordingly, in my Prophetical Office, I view as simply separate ideas, Rome quiescent, and Rome in action. I contrasted her creed on the one hand, with her ordinary teaching, her controversial tone, her political and social bearing, and her popular beliefs and practices, on the other.

While I made this distinction between the decrees and the traditions of Rome, I drew a parallel distinction between Anglicanism quiescent, and Anglicanism in action. In its formal creed Anglicanism was not at a great distance from Rome: far otherwise, when viewed in its insular spirit, the traditions of its establishment, its historical characteristics, its controversial rancour, and its private judgment. I disavowed and condemned those excesses, and called them "Protestantism" or "Ultra-Protestantism:" I wished to find a parallel disclaimer, on the part of Roman controversialists, of that popular system of beliefs and usages in their own Church, which I called "Popery." When that hope was a dream, I saw that the controversy lay between the book-theology of Anglicanism on the one side, and the living system of what I called Roman corruption on the other. I could not get further than this; with this result I was forced to content myself.

These then were the *parties* in the controversy:— the Anglican *Via Media* and the popular religion of Rome. And next, as to the *issue*, to which the controversy between them was to be brought, it was this:—the Anglican disputant took his stand upon Antiquity or Apostolicity, the Roman upon Catholicity. The Anglican said to the

---

[8] Robert Bellarmine (1542–1621), Cardinal and spokesman for the Counter-Reformation.
[9] Charles Lloyd (1784–1829), High Church Bishop of Oxford.

Roman: "There is but One Faith, the Ancient, and you have not kept to it;" the Roman retorted: "There is but One Church, the Catholic, and you are out of it." The Anglican urged "Your special beliefs, practices, modes of action, are nowhere in Antiquity;" the Roman objected: "You do not communicate with any one Church besides your own and its offshoots, and you have discarded principles, doctrines, sacraments, and usages, which are and ever have been received in the East and the West." The true Church, as defined in the Creeds, was both Catholic and Apostolic; now, as I viewed the controversy in which I was engaged, England and Rome had divided these notes or prerogatives between them: the cause lay thus, Apostolicity *versus* Catholicity.

However, in thus stating the matter, of course I do not wish it supposed that I allowed the note of Catholicity really to belong to Rome, to the disparagement of the Anglican Church; but I considered that the special point or plea of Rome in the controversy was Catholicity, as the Anglican plea was Antiquity. Of course I contended that the Roman idea of Catholicity was not ancient and apostolic. It was in my judgment at the utmost only natural, becoming, expedient, that the whole of Christendom should be united in one visible body; while such a unity might, on the other hand, be nothing more than a mere heartless and political combination. For myself, I held with the Anglican divines, that, in the Primitive Church, there was a very real mutual independence between its separate parts, though, from a dictate of charity, there was in fact a close union between them. I considered that each See and Diocese might be compared to a crystal, and that each was similar to the rest, and that the sum total of them all was only a collection of crystals. The unity of the Church lay, not in its being a polity, but in its being a family, a race, coming down by apostolical descent from its first founders and bishops. And I considered this truth brought out, beyond the possibility of dispute, in the Epistles of St. Ignatius, in which the Bishop is represented as the one supreme authority in the Church, that is, in his own place, with no one above him, except as, for the sake of ecclesiastical order and expedience, arrangements had been made by which one was put over or under another. So much for our own claim to Catholicity, which was so perversely appropriated by our opponents to themselves:—on the other hand, as

to our special strong point, Antiquity, while, of course, by means of it, we were able to condemn most emphatically the novel claim of Rome to domineer over other Churches, which were in truth her equals, further than that, we thereby especially convicted her of the intolerable offence of having added to the Faith. This was the critical head of accusation urged against her by the Anglican disputant; and as he referred to St. Ignatius in proof that he himself was a true Catholic, in spite of being separated from Rome, so he triumphantly referred to the Treatise of Vincentius of Lerins upon the "Quod semper, quod ubique, quod ab omnibus,"[10] in proof that the controversialists of Rome, in spite of their possession of the Catholic name, were separated in their creed from the Apostolical and primitive faith.

Of course those controversialists had their own mode of answering him, with which I am not concerned in this place; here I am only concerned with the issue itself, between the one party and the other—Antiquity *versus* Catholicity.

Now I will proceed to illustrate what I have been saying of the *status* of the controversy, as it presented itself to my mind, by extracts from my writings of the dates of 1836, 1840, and 1841. And I introduce them with a remark, which especially applies to the paper, from which I shall quote first, of the date of 1836. That paper appeared in the March and April numbers of the British Magazine of that year, and was entitled "Home Thoughts Abroad." Now it will be found, that, in the discussion which it contains, as in various other writings of mine, when I was in the Anglican Church, the argument in behalf of Rome is stated with considerable perspicuity and force. And at the time my friends and supporters cried out, "How imprudent!" and, both at the time, and especially at a later date, my enemies have cried out, "How insidious!" Friends and foes virtually agreed in their criticism; I had set out the cause which I was combating to the best advantage: this was an offence; it might be from imprudence, it might be with a traitorous design. It was from neither the one nor the other; but for the following reasons. First, I had a great impatience, whatever was the subject, of not bringing out the whole of it, as clearly as I could; next I wished to be as fair to my adversaries as possible; and thirdly I thought that there was a great deal of shallowness

---

[10] "That which has been believed always, everywhere, and by all," a formula for determining orthodoxy of belief.

among our own friends, and that they under-valued the strength of the argument in behalf of Rome, and that they ought to be roused to a more exact apprehension of the position of the controversy. At a later date, (1841,) when I really felt the force of the Roman side of the question myself, as a difficulty which had to be met, I had a fourth reason for such frankness in argument, and that was, because a number of persons were unsettled far more than I was, as to the Catholic-ity of the Anglican Church. It was quite plain that, unless I was perfectly candid in stating what could be said against it, there was no chance that any representations, which I felt to be in its favour, or at least to be adverse to Rome, would have had any success with the persons in question. At all times I had a deep conviction, to put the matter on the lowest ground, that "honesty was the best policy." Accordingly, in July 1841, I expressed myself thus on the Anglican difficulty: "This is an objection which we must honestly say is deeply felt by many people, and not inconsiderable ones; and the more it is openly avowed to be a difficulty, the better; for there is then the chance of its being acknowledged, and in the course of time obviated, as far as may be, by those who have the power. Flagrant evils cure themselves by being flagrant; and we are sanguine that the time is come when so great an evil as this is, cannot stand its ground against the good feeling and common sense of religious persons. It is the very strength of Romanism against us; and, unless the proper persons take it into their serious consideration, they may look for certain to undergo the loss, as time goes on, of some whom they would least like to be lost to our Church." The measure which I had especially in view in this passage, was the project of a Jerusalem Bishopric, which the then Archbishop of Canterbury was at that time concocting with M. Bunsen, and of which I shall speak more in the sequel. And now to return to the Home Thoughts Abroad of the spring of 1836:—

The discussion contained in this composition runs in the form of a dialogue. One of the dis-putants says: "You say to me that the Church of Rome is corrupt. What then? to cut off a limb is a strange way of saving it from the influence of some constitutional ailment. Indigestion may cause cramp in the extremities; yet we spare our poor feet notwithstanding. Surely there is such a

religious *fact* as the existence of a great Catholic body, union with which is a Christian privilege and duty. Now, we English are separate from it."

The other answers: "The present is an un-satisfactory, miserable state of things, yet I can grant no more. The Church is founded on a doctrine,—on the gospel of Truth; it is a means to an end. Perish the Church, (though, blessed be the promise! this cannot be,) yet let it perish *rather* than the Truth should fail. Purity of faith is more precious to the Christian than unity itself. If Rome has erred grievously in doctrine, then it is a duty to separate even from Rome."

His friend, who takes the Roman side of the argument, refers to the image of the Vine and its branches, which is found, I think, in St. Cyprian,[11] as if a branch cut from the Catholic Vine must necessarily die. Also he quotes a passage from St. Augustine in controversy with the Donatists[12] to the same effect; viz. that, as being separated from the body of the Church, they were *ipso facto* cut off from the heritage of Christ. And he quotes St. Cyril's[13] argument drawn from the very title Catholic, which no body or communion of men has ever dared or been able to appropriate, besides one. He adds, "Now I am only contending for the fact, that the communion of Rome constitutes the main body of the Church Catholic, and that we are split off from it, and in the condition of the Donatists."

The other replies by denying the fact that the present Roman communion is like St. Augustine's Catholic Church, inasmuch as there must be taken into account the large Anglican and Greek communions. Presently he takes the offensive, naming distinctly the points, in which Rome has departed from Primitive Christianity, viz. "the practical idolatry, the virtual worship of the Virgin and Saints, which are the offence of the Latin Church, and the degradation of moral truth and duty, which follows from these." And again: "We cannot join a Church, did we wish it ever so much, which does not acknowledge our orders, refuses us the Cup, demands our acquiescence in image-worship, and excommuni-cates us, if we do not receive it and all other decisions of the Tridentine Council."

His opponent answers these objections by referring to the doctrine of "developments of gospel truth." Besides, "The Anglican system itself is not found complete in those early cen-

---

[11] St. Cyprian (c. 200–258), early Church Father.
[12] Donatists were a schismatic North African sect of the fourth century that held sacraments invalid if the priest were unworthy.
[13] St. Cyril (c. 315–386), Eastern Church Father.

turies; so that the [Anglican] principle [of Antiquity] is self-destructive." "When a man takes up this *Via Media,* he is a mere *doctrinaire;"* he is like those, "who, in some matter of business, start up to suggest their own little crochet, and are ever measuring mountains with a pocket ruler, or improving the planetary courses." "The *Via Media* has slept in libraries; it is a substitute of infancy for manhood."

It is plain, then, that at the end of 1835 or beginning of 1836, I had the whole state of the question before me, on which, to my mind, the decision between the Churches depended. It is observable that the question of the position of the Pope, whether as the centre of unity, or as the source of jurisdiction, did not come into my thoughts at all; nor did it, I think I may say, to the end. I doubt whether I ever distinctly held any of his powers to be *de jure divino,*[14] while I was in the Anglican Church;—not that I saw any difficulty in the doctrine; not that in con-nexion with the history of St. Leo,[15] of which I shall speak by and by, the idea of his infallibility did not cross my mind, for it did,—but after all, in my view the controversy did not turn upon it; it turned upon the Faith and the Church. This was my issue of the controversy from the beginning to the end. There was a contrariety of claims between the Roman and Anglican religions, and the history of my conversion is simply the process of working it out to a solution. In 1838 I illus-trated it by the contrast presented to us between the Madonna and Child, and a Calvary. The peculiarity of the Anglican theology was this,— that it "supposed the Truth to be entirely objective and detached, not" (as in the theology of Rome) "lying hid in the bosom of the Church as if one with her, clinging to and (as it were) lost in her embrace, but as being sole and un-approachable, as on the Cross or at the Resur-rection, with the Church close by, but in the background."

As I viewed the controversy in 1836 and 1838, so I viewed it in 1840 and 1841. In the British Critic of January 1840, after gradually in-vestigating how the matter lies between the Churches by means of a dialogue, I end thus: "It would seem, that, in the above discussion, each disputant has a strong point: our strong point is the argument from Primitiveness, that of Roman-ists from Universality. It is a fact, however it is to be accounted for, that Rome has added to the Creed; and it is a fact, however we justify

ourselves, that we are estranged from the great body of Christians over the world. And each of these two facts is at first sight a grave difficulty in the respective systems to which they belong." Again, "While Rome, though not deferring to the Fathers, recognizes them, and England, not deferring to the large body of the Church, recognizes it, both Rome and England have a point to clear up."

And still more strongly, in July, 1841:

"If the Note of schism, on the one hand, lies against England, an antagonist disgrace lies upon Rome, the Note of idolatry. Let us not be mistaken here; we are neither accusing Rome of idolatry nor ourselves of schism; we think neither charge tenable; but still the Roman Church practises what is so like idolatry, and the English Church makes much of what is so very like schism, that without deciding what is the duty of a Roman Catholic towards the Church of England in her present state, we do seriously think that members of the English Church have a prov-idential direction given them, how to comport themselves towards the Church of Rome, while she is what she is."

One remark more about Antiquity and the *Via Media.* As time went on, without doubting the strength of the Anglican argument from Antiquity, I felt also that it was not merely our special plea, but our only one. Also I felt that the *Via Media,* which was to represent it, was to be a sort of remodelled and adapted Antiquity. This I advanced both in Home Thoughts Abroad and in the Article of the British Critic which I have analyzed above. But this circumstance, that after all we must use private judgment upon Antiquity, created a sort of distrust of my theory altogether, which in the conclusion of my Volume on the Prophetical office (1836–7) I express thus: "Now that our discussions draw to a close, the thought, with which we entered on the subject, is apt to recur, when the excitement of the inquiry has subsided, and weariness has succeeded, that what has been said is but a dream, the wanton exercise, rather than the practical conclusions of the intellect." And I conclude the paragraph by anticipating a line of thought into which I was, in the event, almost obliged to take refuge: "After all," I say, "the Church is ever invisible in its day, and faith only apprehends it." What was this, but to give up the Notes of a visible Church altogether, whether the Catholic Note or the Apostolic?

---

[14] "By divine right."   [15] Leo the Great, Pope from 440 to 461.

The Long Vacation of 1839 began early. There had been a great many visitors to Oxford from Easter to Commemoration; and Dr. Pusey's party had attracted attention, more, I think, than in any former year. I had put away from me the controversy with Rome for more than two years. In my Parochial Sermons the subject had at no time been introduced: there had been nothing for two years, either in my Tracts or in the British Critic, of a polemical character. I was returning, for the Vacation, to the course of reading which I had many years before chosen as especially my own. I have no reason to suppose that the thoughts of Rome came across my mind at all. About the middle of June I began to study and master the history of the Monophysites.[16] I was absorbed in the doctrinal question. This was from about June 13th to August 30th. It was during this course of reading that for the first time a doubt came upon me of the tenableness of Anglicanism. I recollect on the 30th of July mentioning to a friend, whom I had accidentally met, how remarkable the history was; but by the end of August I was seriously alarmed.

I have described in a former work, how the history affected me. My stronghold was Antiquity; now here, in the middle of the fifth century, I found, as it seemed to me, Christendom of the sixteenth and the nineteenth centuries reflected. I saw my face in that mirror, and I was a Monophysite. The Church of the *Via Media* was in the position of the Oriental communion, Rome was where she now is; and the Protestants were the Eutychians.[17] Of all passages of history, since history has been, who would have thought of going to the sayings and doings of old Eutyches, that *delirus senex*, as (I think) Petavius[18] calls him, and to the enormities of the unprincipled Dioscorus, in order to be converted to Rome!

Now let it be simply understood that I am not writing controversially, but with the one object of relating things as they happened to me in the course of my conversion. With this view I will quote a passage from the account, which I gave in 1850, of my reasonings and feelings in 1839:

"It was difficult to make out how the Eutychians or Monophysites were heretics, unless Protestants and Anglicans were heretics also; difficult to find arguments against the Tridentine Fathers, which did not tell against the Fathers of Chalcedon; difficult to condemn the Popes of the sixteenth century, without condemning the Popes of the fifth. The drama of religion, and the combat of truth and error, were ever one and the same. The principles and proceedings of the Church now, were those of the Church then; the principles and proceedings of heretics then, were those of Protestants now. I found it so,—almost fearfully; there was an awful similitude, more awful, because so silent and unimpassioned, between the dead records of the past and the feverish chronicle of the present. The shadow of the fifth century was on the sixteenth. It was like a spirit rising from the troubled waters of the old world, with the shape and lineaments of the new. The Church then, as now, might be called peremptory and stern, resolute, overbearing, and relentless; and heretics were shifting, changeable, reserved, and deceitful, ever courting civil power, and never agreeing together, except by its aid; and the civil power was ever aiming at comprehensions, trying to put the invisible out of view, and substituting expediency for faith. What was the use of continuing the controversy, or defending my position, if, after all, I was forging arguments for Arius or Eutyches, and turning devil's advocate against the much-enduring Athanasius and the majestic Leo? Be my soul with the Saints! and shall I lift up my hand against them? Sooner may my right hand forget her cunning, and wither outright, as his who once stretched it out against a prophet of God! anathema to a whole tribe of Cramners, Ridleys, Latimers, and Jewels! perish the names of Bramhall, Ussher, Taylor, Stillingfleet, and Barrow[19] from the face of the earth, ere I should do ought but fall at their feet in love and in worship, whose image was continually before my eyes, and whose musical words were ever in my ears and on my tongue!"

Hardly had I brought my course of reading to a close, when the Dublin Review of that same August was put into my hands, by friends who were more favourable to the cause of Rome than I was myself. There was an article in it on the

---

[16] The Monophysite heresy held that Christ had a single divine nature rather than a double nature, divine and human.

[17] Eutychianism, after Eutyches (c. 378–454), held that Christ had a single blended divine and human nature. The doctrine was condemned at the Council of Chalcedon (451).

[18] Dionysius Petavius (1583–1652), French theologian, called Eutyches a "*delirus senex*" (crazy old man); Dioscorus (d. 454), Patriarch of Alexandria, and a supporter of Eutyches.

[19] Anglican divines of the sixteenth and seventeenth centuries.

"Anglican Claim" by Dr. Wiseman. This was about the middle of September. It was on the Donatists, with an application to Anglicanism. I read it, and did not see much in it. The Donatist controversy was known to me for some years, as has appeared already. The case was not parallel to that of the Anglican Church. St. Augustine in Africa wrote against the Donatists in Africa. They were a furious party who made a schism within the African Church, and not beyond its limits, It was a case of Altar against Altar, of two occupants of the same See, as that between the Non-jurors in England, and the Established Church; not the case of one Church against another, as of Rome against the Oriental Monophysites. But my friend, an anxiously religious man, now, as then, very dear to me, a Protestant still, pointed out the palmary words of St. Augustine, which were contained in one of the extracts made in the Review, and which had escaped my observation. "Securus judicat orbis terrarum."[20] He repeated these words again and again, and, when he was gone, they kept ringing in my ears. "Securus judicat orbis terrarum;" they were words which went beyond the occasion of the Donatists: they applied to that of the Monophysites. They gave a cogency to the Article, which had escaped me at first. They decided ecclesiastical questions on a simpler rule than that of Antiquity; nay, St. Augustine was one of the prime oracles of Antiquity; here then Antiquity was deciding against itself. What a light was hereby thrown upon every controversy in the Church! not that, for the moment, the multitude may not falter in their judgment,— not that, in the Arian hurricane, Sees more than can be numbered did not bend before its fury, and fall off from St. Athanasius,—not that the crowd of Oriental Bishops did not need to be sustained during the contest by the voice and the eye of St. Leo; but that the deliberate judgment, in which the whole Church at length rests and acquiesces, is an infallible prescription and a final sentence against such portions of it as protest and secede. Who can account for the impressions which are made on him? For a mere sentence, the words of St. Augustine, struck me with a power which I never had felt from any words before. To take a familiar instance, they were like the "Turn again Whittington" of the chime;[21] or, to take a more serious one, they were like the "Tolle, lege,—Tolle, lege," of the child, which converted St. Augustine himself.[22] "Securus judicat orbis terrarum!" By those great words of the ancient Father, interpreting and summing up the long and varied course of ecclesiastical history, the theory of the *Via Media* was absolutely pulverized.

I became excited at the view thus opened upon me. I was just starting on a round of visits; and I mentioned my state of mind to two most intimate friends: I think to no others. After a while, I got calm, and at length the vivid impression upon my imagination faded away. What I thought about it on reflection, I will attempt to describe presently. I had to determine its logical value, and its bearing upon my duty. Meanwhile, so far as this was certain,— I had seen the shadow of a hand upon the wall. It was clear that I had a good deal to learn on the question of the Churches, and that perhaps some new light was coming upon me. He who has seen a ghost, cannot be as if he had never seen it. The heavens had opened and closed again. The thought for the moment had been, "The Church of Rome will be found right after all;" and then it had vanished. My old conviction remained as before.

At this time, I wrote my Sermon on Divine Calls, which I published in my volume of Plain Sermons. It ends thus:—

"O that we could take that simple view of things, as to feel that the one thing which lies before us is to please God! What gain is it to please the world, to please the great, nay even to please those whom we love, compared with this? What gain is it to be applauded, admired, courted, followed,—compared with this one aim, of 'not being disobedient to a heavenly vision?' What can this world offer comparable with that insight into spiritual things, that keen faith, that heavenly peace, that high sanctity, that everlasting righteousness, that hope of glory, which they have, who in sincerity love and follow our Lord Jesus Christ? Let us beg and pray Him day by day to reveal Himself to our souls more fully, to quicken our senses, to give us sight and hearing, taste and touch of the world to come; so

---

[20] "Securely the world judges," the beginning of Augustine's statement that goes on to say: "Securely the world judges that they are not good men who, wherever in the world, separate themselves from the rest of the world."

[21] Reference to the story of Dick Whittington who was turned back from running away by the sound of Bow Bells and eventually rose to become Lord Mayor of London.

[22] "Take up and read," the words which turned St. Augustine to scripture and led to his conversion.

to work within us, that we may sincerely say, 'Thou shalt guide me with Thy counsel, and after that receive me with glory. Whom have I in heaven but Thee? and there is none upon earth that I desire in comparison of Thee. My flesh and my heart faileth, but God is the strength of my heart, and my portion for ever.' "

Now to trace the succession of thoughts, and the conclusions, and the consequent innovations on my previous belief, and the general conduct, to which I was led, upon this sudden visitation. And first, I will say, whatever comes of saying it, for I leave inferences to others, that for years I must have had something of an habitual notion, though it was latent, and had never led me to distrust my own convictions, that my mind had not found its ultimate rest, and that in some sense or other I was on journey. During the same passage across the Mediterranean in which I wrote "Lead kindly light," I also wrote the verses, which are found in the Lyra under the head of "Providences," beginning, "When I look back." This was in 1833; and, since I have begun this narrative, I have found a memorandum under the date of September 7, 1829, in which I speak of myself, as "now in my rooms in Oriel College, slowly advancing &c. and led on by God's hand blindly, not knowing whither He is taking me." But, whatever this presentiment be worth, it was no protection against the dismay and disgust, which I felt, in consequence of the dreadful misgiving, of which I have been relating the history. The one question was, what was I to do? I had to make up my mind for myself, and others could not help me. I determined to be guided, not by my imagination, but by my reason. And this I said over and over again in the years which followed, both in conversation and in private letters. Had it not been for this severe resolve, I should have been a Catholic sooner than I was. Moreover, I felt on consideration a positive doubt, on the other hand, whether the suggestion did not come from below. Then I said to myself, Time alone can solve that question. It was my business to go on as usual, to obey those convictions to which I had so long surrendered myself, which still had possession of me, and on which my new thoughts had no direct bearing. That new conception of things should only so far influence me, as it had a logical claim to do so. If it came from above, it would come

again;—so I trusted,—and with more definite outlines and greater cogency and consistency of proof. I thought of Samuel, before "he knew the word of the Lord;" and therefore I went, and lay down to sleep again. This was my broad view of the matter, and my *primâ facie* conclusion.

However, my new historical fact had already to a certain point a logical force. Down had come the *Via Media* as a definite theory or scheme, under the blows of St. Leo. My "Prophetical Office" had come to pieces; not indeed as an argument against "Roman errors," nor as against Protestantism, but as in behalf of England. I had no longer a distinctive plea for Anglicanism, unless I would be a Monophysite. I had, most painfully, to fall back upon my three original points of belief, which I have spoken so much of in a former passage,—the principle of dogma, the sacramental system, and anti-Romanism. Of these three, the first two were better secured in Rome than in the Anglican Church. The Apostolical Succession, the two prominent sacraments, and the primitive Creeds, belonged, indeed, to the latter; but there had been and was far less strictness on matters of dogma and ritual in the Anglican system than in the Roman: in consequence, my main argument for the Anglican claims lay in the positive and special charges, which I could bring against Rome. I had no positive Anglican theory. I was very nearly a pure Protestant. Lutherans had a sort of theology, so had Calvinists. I had none.

However, this pure Protestantism, to which I was gradually left, was really a practical principle. It was a strong, though it was only a negative ground, and it still had great hold on me. As a boy of fifteen, I had so fully imbibed it, that I had actually erased in my *Gradus ad Parnassum*, such titles, under the word "Papa," as "Christi Vicarius," "sacer interpres," and "sceptra gerens," and substituted epithets so vile that I cannot bring myself to write them down here.[23] The effect of this early persuasion remained as, what I have already called it, a "stain upon my imagination." As regards my reason, I began in 1833 to form theories on the subject, which tended to obliterate it; yet by 1838 I had got no further than to consider Antichrist, as not the Church of Rome, but the spirit of the old pagan city, the fourth monster of Daniel, which was still alive, and which had corrupted the Church which was planted there. Soon after this indeed, and before

[23] In his metrical dictionary Newman had erased under the title "Pope" the phrases "Vicar of Christ," "sacred mediator," and "scepter-bearing."

my attention was directed to the Monophysite controversy, I underwent a great change of opinion. I saw that, from the nature of the case, the true Vicar of Christ must ever to the world seem like Antichrist, and be stigmatized as such, because a resemblance must ever exist between an original and a forgery; and thus the fact of such a calumny was almost one of the notes of the Church. But we cannot unmake ourselves or change our habits in a moment. Though my reason was convinced, I did not throw off, for some time after,—I could not have thrown off,—the unreasoning prejudice and suspicion, which I cherished about her at least by fits and starts, in spite of this conviction of my reason. I cannot prove this, but I believe it to have been the case from what I recollect of myself. Nor was there any thing in the history of St. Leo and the Monophysites to undo the firm belief I had in the existence of what I called the practical abuses and excesses of Rome.

To her inconsistencies then, to her ambition and intrigue, to her sophistries (as I considered them to be) I now had recourse in my opposition to her, both public and personal. I did so by way of a relief. I had a great and growing dislike, after the summer of 1839, to speak against the Roman Church herself or her formal doctrines. I was very averse to speaking against doctrines, which might possibly turn out to be true, though at the time I had no reason for thinking they were; or against the Church, which had preserved them. I began to have misgivings, that, strong as my own feelings had been against her, yet in some things which I had said, I had taken the statements of Anglican divines for granted without weighing them for myself. I said to a friend in 1840, in a letter, which I shall use presently, "I am troubled by doubts whether as it is, I have not, in what I have published, spoken too strongly against Rome, though I think I did it in a kind of faith, being determined to put myself into the English system, and say all that our divines said, whether I had fully weighed it or not." I was sore about the great Anglican divines, as if they had taken me in, and made me say strong things, which facts did not justify. Yet I *did* still hold in substance all that I had said against the Church of Rome in my Prophetical Office. I felt the force of the usual Protestant objections against her; I believed that we had the Apostolical succession in the Anglican Church, and the grace of the sacraments; I was not sure

that the difficulty of its isolation might not be overcome, though I was far from sure that it could. I did not see any clear proof that it had committed itself to any heresy, or had taken part against the truth; and I was not sure that it would not revive into full Apostolic purity and strength, and grow into union with Rome herself (Rome explaining her doctrines and guarding against their abuse), that is, if we were but patient and hopeful. I began to wish for union between the Anglican Church and Rome, if, and when, it was possible; and I did what I could to gain weekly prayers for that object. The ground which I felt to be good against her was the moral ground: I felt I could not be wrong in striking at her political and social line of action. The alliance of a dogmatic religion with liberals, high or low, seemed to me a providential direction against moving towards Rome, and a better "Preservative against Popery," than the three volumes in folio, in which, I think, that prophylactic is to be found. However, on occasions which demanded it, I felt it a duty to give out plainly all that I thought, though I did not like to do so. One such instance occurred, when I had to publish a Letter about Tract 90. In that Letter, I said, "Instead of setting before the soul the Holy Trinity, and heaven and hell, the Church of Rome does seem to me, as a popular system to preach the Blessed Virgin and the Saints, and purgatory." On this occasion I recollect expressing to a friend the distress it gave me thus to speak; but, I said, "How can I help saying it, if I think it? and I *do* think it; my Bishop calls on me to say out what I think; and that is the long and the short of it." But I recollected Hurrell Froude's words to me, almost his dying words, "I must enter another protest against your cursing and swearing. What good can it do? and I call it uncharitable to an excess. How mistaken we may ourselves be, on many points that are only gradually opening on us!"

Instead then of speaking of errors in doctrine, I was driven, by my state of mind, to insist upon the political conduct, the controversial bearing, and the social methods and manifestations of Rome. And here I found a matter ready to my hand, which affected me the more sensibly for the reason that it lay at our very doors. I can hardly describe too strongly my feeling upon it. I had an unspeakable aversion to the policy and acts of Mr. O'Connell,[24] because, as I thought, he associated himself with men of all religions

---

[24] Daniel O'Connell (1775–1847), Irish politican, called "The Liberator."

and no religion against the Anglican Church, and advanced Catholicism by violence and intrigue. When then I found him taken up by the English Catholics, and, as I supposed, at Rome, I considered I had a fulfilment before my eyes how the Court of Rome played fast and loose, and justified the serious charges which I had seen put down in books against it. Here we saw what Rome was in action, whatever she might be when quiescent. Her conduct was simply secular and political.

This feeling led me into the excess of being very rude to that zealous and most charitable man, Mr. Spencer,[25] when he came to Oxford in January, 1840, to get Anglicans to set about praying for Unity. I myself, at that time, or soon after, drew up such prayers; their desirableness was one of the first thoughts which came upon me after my shock; but I was too much annoyed with the political action of the Catholic body in these islands to wish to have anything to do with them personally. So glad in my heart was I to see him, when he came to my rooms with Mr. Palmer of Magdalen,[26] that I could have laughed for joy; I think I did laugh; but I was very rude to him, I would not meet him at dinner, and that, (though I did not say so,) because I considered him "in loco apostatæ"[27] from the Anglican Church, and I hereby beg his pardon for it. I wrote afterwards with a view to apologize, but I dare say he must have thought that I made the matter worse, for these were my words to him:—

"The news that you are praying for us is most touching, and raises a variety of indescribable emotions. . . . May their prayers return abundantly into their own bosoms. . . . Why then do I not meet you in a manner conformable with these first feelings? For this single reason, if I may say it, that your acts are contrary to your words. You invite us to a union of hearts, at the same time that you are doing all you can, not to restore, not to reform, not to re-unite, but to destroy our Church. You go further than your principles require. You are leagued with our enemies. 'The voice is Jacob's voice, but the hands are the hands of Esau.' This is what especially distresses us; this is what we cannot understand; how Christians, like yourselves, with the clear view you have that a warfare is ever waging in the world between good and evil, should, in the present state of England, ally yourselves with the side of evil against the side of good. . . . Of parties now in the country, you cannot but allow, that next to yourselves we are nearest to revealed truth. We maintain great and holy principles; we profess Catholic doctrines. . . . So near are we as a body to yourselves in modes of thinking, as even to have been taunted with the nicknames which belong to you; and, on the other hand, if there are professed infidels, scoffers, sceptics, unprincipled men, rebels, they are found among our opponents. And yet you take part with them against us. . . . You consent to act hand in hand [with these and others] for our overthrow. Alas! all this it is that impresses us irresistibly with the notion that you are a political, not a religious party; that in order to gain an end on which you set your hearts,— an open stage for yourselves in England,—you ally yourselves with those who hold nothing against those who hold something. This is what distresses my own mind so greatly, to speak of myself, that, with limitations which need not now be mentioned, I cannot meet familiarly any leading persons of the Roman Communion, and least of all when they come on a religious errand. Break off, I would say, with Mr. O'Connell in Ireland and the liberal party in England, or come not to us with overtures for mutual prayer and religious sympathy."

And here came in another feeling, of a personal nature, which had little to do with the argument against Rome, except that, in my prejudice, I viewed what happened to myself in the light of my own ideas of the traditionary conduct of her advocates and instruments. I was very stern in the case of any interference in our Oxford matters on the part of charitable Catholics, and of any attempt to do me good personally. There was nothing, indeed, at the time more likely to throw me back. "Why do you meddle? why cannot you let me alone? You can do me no good; you know nothing on earth about me; you may actually do me harm; I am in better hands than yours. I know my own sincerity of purpose; and I am determined upon taking my time." Since I have been a Catholic, people have sometimes accused me of backwardness in making converts; and Protestants have argued

---

[25] George Spencer (1799–1864), a convert to Rome who worked for the return of Anglicans to Rome.

[26] William Palmer (1811–79) of Magdalen, High Church theologian and later convert to Roman Catholicism.

[27] "In the state of an apostate."

from it that I have no great eagerness to do so. It would be against my nature to act otherwise than I do; but besides, it would be to forget the lessons which I gained in the experience of my own history in the past.

This is the account which I have to give of some savage and ungrateful words in the British Critic of 1840 against the controversialists of Rome: "By their fruits ye shall know them. . . . We see it attempting to gain converts among us by unreal representations of its doctrines, plausible statements, bold assertions, appeals to the weaknesses of human nature, to our fancies, our eccentricities, our fears, our frivolities, our false philosophies. We see its agents, smiling and nodding and ducking to attract attention, as gipsies make up to truant boys, holding out tales for the nursery, and pretty pictures, and gilt gingerbread, and physic concealed in jam, and sugar-plums for good children. Who can but feel shame when the religion of Ximenes, Borromeo, and Pascal,[28] is so overlaid? Who can but feel sorrow, when its devout and earnest defenders so mistake its genius and its capabilities? We Englishmen like manliness, openness, consistency, truth. Rome will never gain on us, till she learns these virtues, and uses them; and then she *may* gain us; but it will be by ceasing to be what we now mean by Rome, by having a right, not to 'have dominion over our faith,' but to gain and possess our affections in the bonds of the gospel. Till she ceases to be what she practically is, a union is impossible between her and England; but, if she does reform, (and who can presume to say that so large a part of Christendom never can?) then it will be our Church's duty at once to join in communion with the continental Churches, whatever politicians at home may say to it, and whatever steps the civil power may take in consequence. And though we may not live to see that day, at least we are bound to pray for it; we are bound to pray for our brethren that they and we may be led together into the pure light of the gospel, and be one as we once were one. It was most touching news to be told, as we were lately, that Christians on the Continent were praying together for the spiritual well-being of England. May they gain light, while they aim at unity, and grow in faith while they manifest their love! We too have our duties to them; not of reviling, not of slandering, not of hating, though political

interests require it; but the duty of loving brethren still more abundantly in spirit, whose faces, for our sins and their sins, we are not allowed to see in the flesh."

No one ought to indulge in insinuations; it certainly diminishes my right to complain of slanders uttered against myself, when, as in this passage, I had already spoken in disparagement of the controversialists of that religious body, to which I myself now belong.

I have thus put together, as well as I can, what has to be said about my general state of mind from the autumn of 1839 to the summer of 1841; and, having done so, I go on to narrate how my new misgivings affected my conduct, and my relations towards the Anglican Church.

When I got back to Oxford in October, 1839, after the visits which I had been paying, it so happened, there had been, in my absence, occurrences of an awkward character, compromising me both with my Bishop and also with the authorities of the University;[29] and this drew my attention at once to the state of the Movement party there, and made me very anxious for the future. In the spring of the year, as has been seen in the Article analyzed above, I had spoken of the excesses which were to be found among persons commonly included in it:— at that time I thought little of such an evil, but the new views, which had come on me during the Long Vacation, on the one hand made me comprehend it, and on the other took away my power of effectually meeting it. A firm and powerful control was necessary to keep men straight; I never had a strong wrist, but at the very time, when it was most needed, the reins had broken in my hands. With an anxious presentiment on my mind of the upshot of the whole inquiry, which it was almost impossible for me to conceal from men who saw me day by day, who heard my familiar conversation, who came perhaps for the express purpose of pumping me, and having a categorical *yes* or *no* to their questions,—how could I expect to say any thing about my actual, positive, present belief, which would be sustaining or consoling to such persons as were haunted already by doubts of their own? Nay, how could I, with satisfaction to myself, analyze my own mind, and say what I held and what I did not hold? or how could I say with

---

[28] Francisco Ximenes (1436–1517), Spanish Cardinal; St. Charles Borromeo (1538–84), Italian Cardinal; Blaise Pascal (1623–62), French theologian.
[29] Reference to Catholic excesses by Newman's followers.

what limitations, shades of difference, or degree of belief, I still held that body of Anglican opinions which I had openly professed and taught? how could I deny or assert this point or that, without injustice to the new light, in which the whole evidence for those old opinions presented itself to my mind?

However, I had to do what I could, and what was best, under the circumstances; I found a general talk on the subject of the Article in the Dublin Review; and, if it had affected me, it was not wonderful, that it affected others also. As to myself, I felt no kind of certainty that the argument in it was conclusive. Taking it at the worst, granting that the Anglican Church had not the Note of Catholicity; yet there were many Notes of the Church. Some belonged to one age or place, some to another. Bellarmine had reckoned Temporal Prosperity among the Notes of the Church; but the Roman Church had not any great popularity, wealth, glory, power, or prospects, in the nineteenth century. It was not at all certain as yet, even that we had not the Note of Catholicity; but, if not this, we had others. My first business then, was to examine this question carefully, and see, whether a great deal could not be said after all for the Anglican Church, in spite of its acknowledged short-comings. This I did in an Article "on the Catholicity of the English Church," which appeared in the British Critic of January, 1840. As to my personal distress on the point, I think it had gone by February 21st in that year, for I wrote then to Mr. Bowden about the important Article in the Dublin, thus: "It made a great impression here [Oxford]; and, I say what of course I would only say to such as yourself, it made me for a while very uncomfortable in my own mind. The great speciousness of his argument is one of the things which have made me despond so much," that is, as anticipating its effect upon others.

But, secondly, the great stumbling-block lay in the 39 Articles. It was urged that here was a positive Note *against* Anglicanism:—Anglicanism claimed to hold, that the Church of England was nothing else than a continuation in this country, (as the Church of Rome might be in France or Spain,) of that one Church of which in old times Athanasius and Augustine were members. But, if so, the doctrine must be the same; the doctrine of the Old Church must live and speak in Anglican formularies, in the 39 Articles. Did it?

Yes, it did; that is what I maintained; it did in substance, in a true sense. Man had done his worst to disfigure, to mutilate, the old Catholic Truth; but there it was, in spite of them, in the Articles still. It was there,—but this must be shown. It was a matter of life and death to us to show it. And I believed that it could be shown; I considered that those grounds of justification, which I gave above, when I was speaking of Tract 90, were sufficient for the purpose; and therefore I set about showing it at once. This was in March, 1840, when I went up to Little-more. And, as it was a matter of life and death with us, all risks must be run to show it. When the attempt was actually made, I had got reconciled to the prospect of it, and had no apprehensions as to the experiment; but in 1840, while my purpose was honest, and my grounds of reason satisfactory, I did nevertheless recognize that I was engaged in an *experimentum crucis*.[30] I have no doubt that then I acknowledged to myself that it would be a trial of the Anglican Church, which it had never undergone before,—not that the Catholic sense of the Articles had not been held or at least suffered by their framers and promulgators, not that it was not implied in the teaching of Andrewes or Beveridge, but that it had never been publicly recognized, while the interpretation of the day was Protestant and exclusive. I observe also, that, though my Tract was an experiment, it was, as I said at the time, "no *feeler*"; the event showed this; for, when my principle was not granted, I did not draw back, but gave up. I would not hold office in a Church which would not allow my sense of the Articles. My tone was, "This is necessary for us, and have it we must and will, and, if it tends to bring men to look less bitterly on the Church of Rome, so much the better."

This then was the second work to which I set myself; though when I got to Littlemore, other things interfered to prevent my accomplishing it at the moment. I had in mind to remove all such obstacles as lay in the way of holding the Apostolic and Catholic character of the Anglican teaching; to assert the right of all who chose, to say in the face of day, "Our Church teaches the Primitive Ancient faith." I did not conceal this: in Tract 90, it is put forward as the first principle of all, "It is a duty which we owe both to the Catholic Church, and to our own, to take our reformed confessions in the most Catholic sense they will admit: we have no duties towards their framers."

[30] "Crucial experiment."

And still more pointedly in my Letter, explanatory of the Tract, addressed to Dr. Jelf,[31] I say: "The only peculiarity of the view I advocate, if I must so call it, is this—that whereas it is usual at this day to make the *particular belief of their writers* their true interpretation, I would make the *belief of the Catholic Church such.* That is, as it is often said that infants are regenerated in Baptism, not on the faith of their parents, but of the Church, so in like manner I would say that the Articles are received, not in the sense of their framers, but (as far as the wording will admit or any ambiguity requires it) in the one Catholic sense."

A third measure which I distinctly contemplated, was the resignation of St. Mary's, whatever became of the question of the 39 Articles; and as a first step I meditated a retirement to Littlemore. Littlemore was an integral part of St. Mary's Parish, and between two and three miles distant from Oxford, I had built a Church there several years before; and I went there to pass the Lent of 1840, and gave myself up to teaching in the Parish School, and practising the choir. At the same time, I had in view a monastic house there. I bought ten acres of ground and began planting; but this great design was never carried out. I mention it, because it shows how little I had really the idea at that time of ever leaving the Anglican Church. That I contemplated as early as 1839 the further step of giving up St. Mary's, appears from a letter which I wrote in October, 1840, to Mr. Keble, the friend whom it was most natural for me to consult on such a point. It ran as follows:—

"For a year past a feeling has been growing on me that I ought to give up St. Mary's, but I am no fit judge in the matter. I cannot ascertain accurately my own impressions and convictions, which are the basis of the difficulty, and though you cannot of course do this for me, yet you may help me generally, and perhaps supersede the necessity of my going by them at all.

"First, it is certain that I do not know my Oxford parishioners;[32] I am not conscious of influencing them, and certainly I have no insight into their spiritual state. I have no personal, no pastoral acquaintance with them. To very few have I any opportunity of saying a religious word. Whatever influence I exert on them is precisely that which I may be exerting on persons out of my parish. In my excuse I am accustomed to say to myself that I am not adapted to get on with them while others are. On the other hand, I am conscious that by means of my position at St. Mary's, I do exert a considerable influence on the University, whether on Undergraduates or Graduates. It seems, then, on the whole that I am using St. Mary's, to the neglect of its direct duties, for objects not belonging to it; I am converting a parochial charge into a sort of University office.

"I think I may say truly that I have begun scarcely any plan but for the sake of my parish, but every one has turned, independently of me, into the direction of the University. I began Saints' days Services, daily Services, and Lectures in Adam de Brome's Chapel,[33] for my parishioners; but they have not come to them. In consequence I dropped the last mentioned, having, while it lasted, been naturally led to direct it to the instruction of those who did come, instead of those who did not. The Weekly Communion, I believe, I did begin for the sake of the University.

"Added to this the authorities of the University, the appointed guardians of those who form great part of the attendants of my Sermons, have shown a dislike of my preaching. One dissuades men from coming;—the late Vice-Chancellor threatens to take his own children away from the Church; and the present, having an opportunity last spring of preaching in my parish pulpit, gets up and preaches against doctrine with which I am in good measure identified. No plainer proof can be given of the feeling in these quarters, than the absurd myth, now a second time put forward, 'that Vice-Chancellors cannot be got to take the office on account of Puseyism.'

"But further than this, I cannot disguise from myself that my preaching is not calculated to defend that system of religion which has been received for 300 years, and of which the Heads of Houses are the legitimate maintainers in this place. They exclude me, as far as may be, from the University Pulpit; and, though I never have preached strong doctrine in it, they do so rightly, so far as this, that they understand that my sermons are calculated to undermine things established. I cannot disguise from myself that they are. No one will deny that most of my

---

[31] Richard William Jelf (1798–1871), canon of Christ Church, Oxford.
[32] Newman means the nonuniversity members of the parish.
[33] A chapel within St. Mary's Church.

sermons are on moral subjects, not doctrinal; still I am leading my hearers to the Primitive Church, if you will, but not to the Church of England. Now, ought one to be disgusting the minds of young men with the received religion, in the exercise of a sacred office, yet without a commission, and against the wish of their guides and governors?

"But this is not all. I fear I must allow that, whether I will or no, I am disposing them towards Rome. First, because Rome is the only representative of the Primitive Church besides ourselves; in proportion then as they are loosened from the one, they will go to the other. Next, because many doctrines which I have held have far greater, or their only scope, in the Roman system. And, moreover, if, as is not unlikely, we have in process of time heretical Bishops or teachers among us, an evil which *ipso facto* infects the whole community to which they belong, and if, again (what there are at this moment symptoms of), there be a movement in the English Roman Catholics to break the alliance of O'Connell and of Exeter Hall,[34] strong temptations will be placed in the way of individuals, already imbued with a tone of thought congenial to Rome, to join her Communion.

"People tell me, on the other hand, that I am, whether by sermons or otherwise, exerting at St. Mary's, a beneficial influence on our prospective clergy; but what if I take to myself the credit of seeing further than they, and of having in the course of the last year discovered that what they approve so much is very likely to end in Romanism?

"The *arguments* which I have published against Romanism seem to myself as cogent as ever, but men go by their sympathies, not by argument; and if I feel the force of this influence myself, who bow to the arguments, why may not others still more, who never have in the same degree admitted the arguments?

"Nor can I counteract the danger by preaching or writing against Rome. I seem to myself almost to have shot my last arrow in the Article on English Catholicity. It must be added, that the very circumstance that I have committed myself against Rome has the effect of setting to sleep people suspicious about me, which is painful now that I begin to have suspicions about myself. I mentioned my general difficulty to Rogers a year since, than whom I know no one of a more fine and accurate conscience, and it was his

spontaneous idea that I should give up St. Mary's, if my feelings continued. I mentioned it again to him lately, and he did not reverse his opinion, only expressed great reluctance to believe it must be so."

Mr. Keble's judgment was in favour of my retaining my living; at least for the present; what weighed with me most was his saying, "You must consider, whether your retiring either from the Pastoral Care only, or from writing and printing and editing in the cause, would not be a sort of scandalous thing, unless it were done very warily. It would be said, 'You see he can go on no longer with the Church of England, except in mere Lay Communion;' or people might say you repented of the cause altogether. Till you see your way to mitigate, if not remove this evil I certainly should advise you to stay." I answered as follows:—

"Since you think I *may* go on, it seems to follow that, under the circumstances, I *ought* to do so. There are plenty of reasons for it, directly it is allowed to be lawful. The following considerations have much reconciled my feelings to your conclusion.

"1. I do not think that we have yet made fair trial how much the English Church will bear. I know it is a hazardous experiment,—like proving cannon. Yet we must not take it for granted that the metal will burst in the operation. It has borne at various times, not to say at this time, a great infusion of Catholic truth without damage. As to the result, viz. whether this process will not approximate the whole English Church, as a body, to Rome, that is nothing to us. For what we know, it may be the providential means of uniting the whole Church in one, without fresh schismatizing or use of private judgment."

Here I observe, that, what was comtemplated was the bursting of the *Catholicity* of the Anglican Church, that is, my *subjective idea* of that Church. Its bursting would not hurt her with the world, but would be a discovery that she was purely and essentially Protestant, and would be really the "hoisting of the engineer with his own petard." And this was the result. I continue:—

"2. Say, that I move sympathies for Rome: in the same sense does Hooker, Taylor, Bull, &c. Their *arguments* may be against Rome, but the sympathies they raise must be towards Rome, *so far* as Rome maintains truths which our Church does not teach or enforce. Thus it is a question of *degree* between our divines and me. I may, if so

---

[34] Exeter Hall, London center of Evangelical activity.

be, go further; I may raise sympathies *more;* but I am but urging minds in the same direction as they do. I am doing just the very thing which all our doctors have ever been doing. In short, would not Hooker, if Vicar of St. Mary's, be in my difficulty?"—Here it may be objected, that Hooker could preach against Rome and I could not; but I doubt whether he could have preached effectively against Transubstantiation better than I, though neither he nor I held that doctrine.

"3. Rationalism is the great evil of the day. May not I consider my post at St. Mary's as a place of protest against it? I am more certain that the Protestant [spirit], which I oppose, leads to infidelity, than that which I recommend, leads to Rome. Who knows what the state of the University may be, as regards Divinity Professors in a few years hence? Anyhow, a great battle may be coming on, of which Milman's book is a sort of earnest. The whole of *our* day may be a battle with this spirit. May we not leave to another age *its own* evil,—to settle the question of Romanism?"

I may add that from this time I had a curate at St. Mary's,[35] who gradually took more and more of my work.

Also, this same year, 1840, I made arrangements for giving up the British Critic, in the following July, which were carried into effect at that date.

Such was about my state of mind, on the publication of Tract 90 in February 1841. I was indeed in prudence taking steps towards eventually withdrawing from St. Mary's, and I was not confident about my permanent adhesion to the Anglican creed; but I was in no actual perplexity or trouble of mind. Nor did the immense commotion consequent upon the publication of the Tract unsettle me again; for I fancied I had weathered the storm, as far as the Bishops were concerned: the Tract had not been condemned: that was the great point, and I made much of it.

To illustrate my feelings during this trial, I will make extracts from my letters addressed severally to Mr. Bowden and another friend, which have come into my possession.

1. March 15.—"The Heads, I believe, have just done a violent act: they have said that my interpretation of the Articles is an *evasion.* Do not think that this will pain me. You see, no *doctrine* is censured, and my shoulders shall manage to bear the charge. If you knew all, or were here, you would see that I have asserted a great principle, and I *ought* to suffer for it:—that the Articles are to be interpreted, not according to the meaning of the writers, but (as far as the wording will admit) according to the sense of the Catholic Church."

2. March 25.—"I do trust I shall make no false step, and hope my friends will pray for me to this effect. If, as you say, a destiny hangs over us, a single false step may ruin all. I am very well and comfortable; but we are not yet out of the wood."

3. April 1.—"The Bishop sent me word on Sunday to write a Letter to him '*instanter.*' So I wrote it on Monday: on Tuesday it passed through the press: on Wednesday it was out: and to-day [Thursday] it is in London.

"I trust that things are smoothing now; and that we have made a *great step* is certain. It is not right to boast, till I am clear out of the wood, i.e. till I know how the Letter is received in London. You know, I suppose, that I am to stop the Tracts; but you will see in the Letter, though I speak *quite* what I feel, yet I have managed to take out on *my* side my snubbing's worth. And this makes me anxious how it will be received in London.

"I have not had a misgiving for five minutes from the first: but I do not like to boast, lest some harm come."

4. April 4.—"Your letter of this morning was an exceedingly great gratification to me; and it is confirmed, I am thankful to say, by the opinion of others. The Bishop sent me a message that my Letter had his unqualified approbation; and since that, he has sent me a note to the same effect, only going more into detail. It is most pleasant too to my feelings, to have such a testimony to the substantial truth and importance of No. 90, as I have had from so many of my friends, from those who, from their cautious turn of mind, I was least sanguine about. I have not had one misgiving myself about it throughout; and I do trust that what has happened will be overruled to subserve the great cause we all have at heart."

5. May 9.—"The Bishops are very desirous of hushing the matter up: and I certainly have done my utmost to co-operate with them, on the understanding that the Tract is not to be withdrawn or condemned."

Upon this occasion several Catholics wrote to

---

[35] Frederic Rogers (1811–89), a friend of the Movement and former student under Newman.

me; I answered one of my correspondents in the same tone:—

"April 8.—You have no cause to be surprised at the discontinuance of the Tracts. We feel no misgivings about it whatever, as if the cause of what we hold to be Catholic truth would suffer thereby. My letter to my Bishop has, I trust, had the effect of bringing the preponderating *authority* of the Church on our side. No stopping of the Tracts can, humanly speaking, stop the spread of the opinions which they have inculcated.

"The Tracts are not *suppressed*. No doctrine or principle has been conceded by us, or condemned by authority. The Bishop has but said that a certain Tract is 'objectionable,' no reason being stated. I have no intention whatever of yielding any one point which I hold on conviction; and that the authorities of the Church know full well."

In the summer of 1841, I found myself at Littlemore without any harass or anxiety on my mind. I had determined to put aside all controversy, and I set myself down to my translation of St. Athanasius; but, between July and November, I received three blows which broke me.

1. I had got but a little way in my work, when my trouble returned on me. The ghost had come a second time. In the Arian History I found the very same phenomenon, in a far bolder shape, which I had found in the Monophysite. I had not observed it in 1832. Wonderful that this should come upon me! I had not sought it out; I was reading and writing in my own line of study, far from the controversies of the day, on what is called a "metaphysical" subject; but I saw clearly, that in the history of Arianism, the pure Arians were the Protestants, the semi-Arians were the Anglicans, and that Rome now was what it was then. The truth lay, not with the *Via Media,* but with what was called "the extreme party." As I am not writing a work of controversy, I need not enlarge upon the argument; I have said something on the subject in a Volume, from which I have already quoted.

2. I was in the misery of this new unsettlement, when a second blow came upon me. The Bishops one after another began to charge against me. It was a formal, determinate movement. This was the real "understanding;" that, on which I had acted on the first appearance of Tract 90, had come to nought. I think the words, which had then been used to me, were, that "perhaps two or three of them might think it necessary to say

something in their charges;" but by this time they had tided over the difficulty of the Tract, and there was no one to enforce the "understanding." They went on in this way, directing charges at me, for three whole years. I recognized it as a condemnation; it was the only one that was in their power. At first I intended to protest, but I gave up the thought in despair.

On October 17th, I wrote thus to a friend: "I suppose it will be necessary in some shape or other to re-assert Tract 90; else, it will seem, after these Bishops' Charges, as if it were silenced, which it has not been, nor do I intend it should be. I wish to keep quiet; but if Bishops speak, I will speak too. If the view were silenced, I could not remain in the Church, nor could many others; and therefore, since it is *not* silenced, I shall take care to show that it isn't."

A day or two after, Oct. 22, a stranger wrote to me to say, that the Tracts for the Times had made a young friend of his a Catholic, and to ask "would I be so good as to convert him back;" I made answer:

"If conversions to Rome take place in consequence of the Tracts for the Times, I do not impute blame to them, but to those who, instead of acknowledging such Anglican principles of theology and ecclesiastical polity as they contain, set themselves to oppose them. Whatever be the influence of the Tracts, great or small, they may become just as powerful for Rome, if our Church refuses them, as they would be for our Church if she accepted them. If our rulers speak either against the Tracts, or not at all, if any number of them, not only do not favour, but even do not suffer the principles contained in them, it is plain that our members may easily be persuaded either to give up those principles, or to give up the Church. If this state of things goes on, I mournfully prophesy, not one or two, but many secessions to the Church of Rome."

Two years afterwards, looking back on what had passed, I said, "There were no converts to Rome, till after the condemnation of No. 90."

3. As if all this were not enough, there came the affair of the Jerusalem Bishopric; and, with a brief mention of it, I shall conclude.

I think I am right in saying that it had been long a desire with the Prussian Court to introduce Episcopacy into the new Evangelical Religion, which was intended in that country to embrace both the Lutheran and Calvinistic bodies. I almost think I heard of the project, when I was at Rome in 1833, at the Hotel of the Prussian Minister, M. Bunsen, who was most hospitable and kind, as to other English visitors, so also to my friends and myself. The idea of Episcopacy, as the Prussian king understood it, was, I suppose, very different from that taught in the Tractarian School: but still, I suppose also, that the chief authors of that school would have gladly seen such a measure carried out in Prussia, had it been done without compromising those principles which were necessary to the being of a Church. About the time of the publication of Tract 90, M. Bunsen and the then Archbishop of Canterbury were taking steps for its execution, by appointing and consecrating a Bishop for Jerusalem. Jerusalem, it would seem, was considered a safe place for the experiment; it was too far from Prussia to awaken the susceptibilities of any part at home; if the project failed, it failed without harm to any one; and, if it succeeded, it gave Protestantism a *status* in the East, which, in association with the Monophysite or Jacobite and the Nestorian bodies, formed a political instrument for England, parallel to that which Russia had in the Greek Church, and France in the Latin.

Accordingly, in July 1841, full of the Anglican difficulty on the question of Catholicity, I thus spoke of the Jerusalem scheme in an Article in the British Critic: "When our thoughts turn to the East, instead of recollecting that there are Christian Churches there, we leave it to the Russians to take care of the Greeks, and the French to take care of the Romans, and we content ourselves with erecting a Protestant Church at Jerusalem, or with helping the Jews to rebuild their Temple there, or with becoming the august protectors of Nestorians, Monophysites, and all the heretics we can hear of, or with forming a league with the Mussulman against Greeks and Romans together."

I do not pretend, so long after the time, to give a full or exact account of this measure in detail. I will but say that in the Act of Parliament, under date of October 5, 1841, (if the copy, from which I quote, contains the measure as it passed the Houses,) provision is made for the consecration of "British subjects, or the subjects or citizens of any foreign state, to be Bishops in any foreign country, whether such foreign subjects or citizens be or be not subjects or citizens of the country in which they are to act, and . . . without requiring such of them as may be subjects or citizens of any foreign kingdom or state to take the oaths of allegiance and supremacy, and the

oath of due obedience to the Archbishop for the time being" . . . also "that such Bishop or Bishops, so consecrated, may exercise, within such limits, as may from time to time be assigned for that purpose in such foreign countries by her Majesty, spiritual jurisdiction over the ministers of British congregations of the United Church of England and Ireland, and over *such other Protestant* Congregations, as may be desirous of placing themselves under his or their authority."

Now here, at the very time that the Anglican Bishops were directing their censure upon me for avowing an approach to the Catholic Church not closer than I believed the Anglican formularies would allow, they were on the other hand, fraternizing, by their act or by their sufferance, with Protestant bodies, and allowing them to put themselves under an Anglican Bishop, without any renunciation of their errors or regard to their due reception of baptism and confirmation; while there was great reason to suppose that the said Bishop was intended to make converts from the orthodox Greeks, and the schismatical Oriental bodies, by means of the influence of England. This was the third blow, which finally shattered my faith in the Anglican Church. That Church was not only forbidding any sympathy or concurrence with the Church of Rome, but it actually was courting an inter-communion with Protestant Prussia and the heresy of the Orientals. The Anglican Church might have the Apostolical succession, as had the Monophysites; but such acts as were in progress led me to the gravest suspicion, not that it would soon cease to be a Church, but that, since the 16th century, it had never been a Church all along.

On October 12th, I wrote to Mr. Bowden:— "We have not a single Anglican in Jerusalem; so we are sending a Bishop to *make* a communion, not to govern our own people. Next, the excuse is, that there are converted Anglican Jews there who require a Bishop; I am told there are not half-a-dozen. But for *them* the Bishop is sent out, and for them he is a Bishop of the *circumcision*" (I think he was a converted Jew, who boasted of his Jewish descent), "against the Epistle to the Galatians pretty nearly. Thirdly, for the sake of Prussia, he is to take under him all the foreign Protestants who will come; and the political advantages will be so great, from the influence of England, that there is no doubt they *will* come. They are to sign the Confession of Augusburg[36]

---

[36] The Lutheran confession of belief (1530).

and there is nothing to show that they hold the doctrine of Baptismal Regeneration.

"As to myself, I shall do nothing whatever publicly, unless indeed it were to give my signature to a Protest; but I think it would be out of place in *me* to agitate, having been in a way silenced; but the Archbishop is really doing most grave work, of which we cannot see the end."

I did make a solemn Protest, and sent it to the Archbishop of Canterbury, and also sent it to my own Bishop with the following letter:—

"It seems as if I were never to write to your Lordship, without giving you pain, and I know that my present subject does not specially concern your Lordship; yet, after a great deal of anxious thought, I lay before you the enclosed Protest.

"Your Lordship will observe that I am not asking for any notice of it, unless you think that I ought to receive one. I do this very serious act in obedience to my sense of duty.

"If the English Church is to enter on a new course, and assume a new aspect, it will be more pleasant to me hereafter to think, that I did not suffer so grievous an event to happen, without bearing witness against it.

"May I be allowed to say, that I augur nothing but evil, if we in any respect prejudice our title to be a branch of the Apostolic Church? That Article of the Creed, I need hardly observe to your Lordship, is of such constraining power, that, if *we* will not claim it, and use it for ourselves, *others* will use it in their own behalf against us. Men who learn whether by means of documents or measures, whether from the statements of the acts of persons in authority, that our communion is not a branch of the One Church, I foresee with much grief, will be tempted to look out for that Church elsewhere.

"It is to me a subject of great dismay, that, as far as the Church has lately spoken out, on the subject of the opinions which I and others hold, those opinions are, not merely not *sanctioned* (for that I do not ask), but not even *suffered*.

"I earnestly hope that your Lordship will excuse my freedom in thus speaking to you of some members of your Most Rev. and Right Rev. Body. With every feeling of reverent attachment to your Lordship,

"I am, &c."

PROTEST

"Whereas the Church of England has a claim on the allegiance of Catholic believers only on the ground of her own claim to be considered a branch of the Catholic Church:

"And whereas the recognition of heresy, indirect as well as direct, goes far to destroy such claim in the case of any religious body:

"And whereas to admit maintainers of heresy to communion, without formal renunciation of their errors, goes far towards recognizing the same:

"And whereas Lutheranism and Calvinism are heresies, repugnant to Scripture, springing up three centuries since, and anathematized by East as well as West:

"And whereas it is reported that the Most Reverend Primate and other Right Reverend Rulers of our Church have consecrated a Bishop with a view to exercising spiritual jurisdiction over Protestant, that is, Lutheran and Calvinist congregations in the East (under the provisions of an Act made in the last session of Parliament to amend an Act made in the 26th year of the reign of his Majesty King George the Third, intituled, 'An Act to empower the Archbishop of Canterbury, or the Archbishop of York for the time being, to consecrate to the office of Bishop persons being subjects or citizens of countries out of his Majesty's dominions'), dispensing at the same time, not in particular cases and accidentally, but as if on principle and universally, with any abjuration of error on the part of such congregations, and with any reconciliation to the Church on the part of the presiding Bishop; thereby giving some sort of formal recognition to the doctrines which such congregations maintain:

"And whereas the dioceses in England are connected together by so close an intercommunion, that what is done by authority in one, immediately affects the rest:

"On these grounds, I in my place, being a priest of the English Church and Vicar of St. Mary the Virgin's, Oxford, by way of relieving my conscience, do hereby solemnly protest against the measure aforesaid, and disown it, as removing our Church from her present ground and tending to her disorganization.

"JOHN HENRY NEWMAN.
"November 11, 1841."

Looking back two years afterwards on the above-mentioned and other acts, on the part of Anglican Ecclesiastical authorities, I observed: "Many a man might have held an abstract theory about the Catholic Church, to which it was difficult to adjust the Anglican,—might have admitted a suspicion, or even painful doubts about the latter,—yet never have been impelled onwards, had our Rulers preserved the quiescence of former years; but it is the corroboration of a present, living, and energetic heterodoxy, that realizes and makes such doubts practical; it has been the recent speeches and acts of authorities, who had so long been tolerant of Protestant error, which has given to inquiry and to theory its force and its edge."

As to the project of a Jerusalem Bishopric, I never heard of any good or harm it has ever done, except what it has done for me; which many think a great misfortune, and I one of the greatest of mercies. It brought me on to the beginning of the end.

CHAPTER IV

History of My Religious Opinions from 1841 to 1845

1

FROM the end of 1841, I was on my death-bed, as regards my membership with the Anglican Church, though at the time I became aware of it only by degrees. I introduce what I have to say with this remark, by way of accounting for the character of this remaining portion of my narrative. A death-bed has scarcely a history; it is a tedious decline, with seasons of rallying and seasons of falling back; and since the end is foreseen, or what is called a matter of time, it has little interest for the reader, especially if he has a kind heart. Moreover, it is a season when doors are closed and curtains drawn, and when the sick man neither cares nor is able to record the stages of his malady. I was in these circumstances, except so far as I was not allowed to die in peace, —except so far as friends, who had still a full right to come in upon me, and the public world which had not, have given a sort of history to those last four years. But in consequence, my narrative must be in great measure documentary, as I cannot rely on my memory, except for definite particulars, positive or negative. Letters of mine to friends since dead have come into my hands; others have been kindly lent me for the occasion;

and I have some drafts of others, and some notes which I made, though I have no strictly personal or continuous memoranda to consult, and have unluckily mislaid some valuable papers.

And first as to my position in the view of duty; it was this:— 1. I had given up my place in the Movement in my letter to the Bishop of Oxford in the spring of 1841; but 2. I could not give up my duties towards the many and various minds who had more or less been brought into it by me; 3. I expected or intended gradually to fall back into Lay Communion; 4. I never contemplated leaving the Church of England; 5. I could not hold office in its service, if I were not allowed to hold the Catholic sense of the Articles; 6. I could not go to Rome, while she suffered honours to be paid to the Blessed Virgin and the Saints which I thought in my conscience to be incompatible with the Supreme, Incommunicable Glory of the One Infinite and Eternal; 7. I desired a union with Rome under conditions, Church with Church; 8. I called Littlemore my Torres Vedras,[1] and thought that some day we might advance again within the Anglican Church, as we had been forced to retire; 9. I kept back all persons who were disposed to go to Rome with all my might.

And I kept them back for three or four reasons; 1. because what I could not in conscience do myself, I could not suffer them to do; 2. because I thought that in various cases they were acting under excitement; 3. because I had duties to my Bishop and to the Anglican Church; and 4, in some cases, because I had received from their Anglican parents or superiors direct charge of them.

This was my view of my duty from the end of 1841, to my resignation of St. Mary's in the autumn of 1843. And now I shall relate my view, during that time, of the state of the controversy between the Churches.

As soon as I saw the hitch in the Anglican argument, during my course of reading in the summer of 1839, I began to look about, as I have said, for some ground which might supply a controversial basis for my need. The difficulty in question had affected my view both of Antiquity and Catholicity; for, while the history of St. Leo showed me that the deliberate and eventual consent of the great body of the Church ratified a doctrinal decision as a part of revealed truth, it also showed that the rule of Antiquity was not

---

[1] Town near Lisbon that Wellington held before advancing to win the Peninsular War in 1811.

infringed, though a doctrine had not been publicly recognized as so revealed, till centuries after the time of the Apostles. Thus, whereas the Creeds tell us that the Church is One, Holy, Catholic, and Apostolic, I could not prove that the Anglican communion was an integral part of the One Church, on the ground of its teaching being Apostolic or Catholic, without reasoning in favour of what are commonly called the Roman corruptions; and I could not defend our separation from Rome and her faith without using arguments prejudicial to those great doctrines concerning our Lord, which are the very foundation of the Christian religion. The Via Media was an impossible idea; it was what I had called "standing on one leg;" and it was necessary, if my old issue of the controversy was to be retained, to go further either one way or the other.

Accordingly, I abandoned that old ground and took another. I deliberately quitted the old Anglican ground as untenable; though I did not do so all at once, but as I became more and more convinced of the state of the case. The Jerusalem Bishopric was the ultimate condemnation of the old theory of the Via Media:—if its establishment did nothing else, at least it demolished the sacredness of diocesan rights. If England could be in Palestine, Rome might be in England. But its bearing upon the controversy, as I have shown in the foregoing chapter, was much more serious than this technical ground. From that time the Anglican Church was, in my mind, either not a normal portion of that One Church to which the promises were made, or at least in an abnormal state; and from that time I said boldly (as I did in my Protest, and as indeed I had even intimated in my Letter to the Bishop of Oxford), that the Church in which I found myself had no claim on me, except on condition of its being a portion of the One Catholic Communion, and that that condition must ever be borne in mind as a practical matter, and had to be distinctly proved. All this is not inconsistent with my saying above that, at this time, I had no thought of leaving the Church of England; because I felt some of my old objections against Rome as strongly as ever. I had no right, I had no leave, to act against my conscience. That was a higher rule than any argument about the Notes of the Church.

Under these circumstances I turned for protection to the Note of Sanctity, with a view of showing that we had at least one of the necessary Notes, as fully as the Church of Rome; or at least, without entering into comparisons, that we had it in such a sufficient sense as to reconcile us to our position, and to supply full evidence, and a clear direction, on the point of practical duty. We had the Note of Life,—not any sort of life, not such only as can come of nature, but a supernatural Christian life, which could only come directly from above. Thus, in my Article in the British Critic, to which I have so often referred, in January, 1840 (before the time of Tract 90), I said of the Anglican Church that "she has the note of possession, the note of freedom from party titles, the note of life,—a tough life and a vigorous; she has ancient descent, unbroken continuance, agreement in doctrine with the Ancient Church." Presently I go on to speak of sanctity: "Much as Roman Catholics may denounce us at present as schismatical, they could not resist us if the Anglican communion had but that one note of the Church upon it,—sanctity. The Church of the day [4th century] could not resist Meletius;[2] his enemies were fairly overcome by him, by his meekness and holiness, which melted the most jealous of them." And I continue, "We are almost content to say to Romanists, account us not yet as a branch of the Catholic Church, though we be a branch, till we are like a branch, provided that when we do become like a branch, then you consent to the acknowledge us," &c. And so I was led on in the Article to that sharp attack on English Catholics, for their shortcomings as regards this Note, a good portion of which I have already quoted in another place. It is there that I speak of the great scandal which I took at their political, social, and controversial bearing; and this was a second reason why I fell back upon the Note of Sanctity, because it took me away from the necessity of making any attack upon the doctrines of the Roman Church, nay, from the consideration of her popular beliefs, and brought me upon a ground on which I felt I could not make a mistake; for what is a higher guide for us in speculation and in practice, than that conscience of right and wrong, of truth and falsehood, those sentiments of what is decorous, consistent, and noble, which our Creator has made a part of our original nature? Therefore I felt I could not be wrong in attacking what I fancied was a fact,—the unscrupulousness, the deceit, and the intriguing spirit of the agents and representatives of Rome.

This reference to Holiness as the true test of a Church was steadily kept in view in what I wrote

---

[2] Meletius, fourth-century Bishop of Antioch.

in connexion with Tract 90. I say in its Introduction, "The writer can never be party to forcing the opinions or projects of one school upon another; religious changes should be the act of the whole body. No good can come of a change which is not a development of feelings springing up freely and calmly within the bosom of the whole body itself; every change in religion" must be "attended by deep repentance, changes" must be "nurtured in mutual love; we cannot agree without a supernatural influence;" we must come "together to God to do for us what we cannot do for ourselves." In my Letter to the Bishop I said, "I have set myself against suggestions for considering the differences between ourselves and the foreign Churches with a view to their adjustment." (I meant in the way of negotiation, conference, agitation, or the like.) "Our business is with ourselves,—to make ourselves more holy, more self-denying, more primitive, more worthy of our high calling. To be anxious for a composition of differences is to begin at the end. Political reconciliations are but outward and hollow, and fallacious. And till Roman Catholics renounce political efforts, and manifest in their public measures the light of holiness and truth, perpetual war is our only prospect."

According to this theory, a religious body is part of the One Catholic and Apostolic Church, if it has the succession and the creed of the Apostles, with the note of holiness of life; and there is much in such a view to approve itself to the direct common sense and practical habits of an Englishman. However, with the events consequent upon Tract 90, I sunk my theory to a lower level. For what could be said in apology, when the Bishops and the people of my Church, not only did not suffer, but actually rejected primitive Catholic doctrine, and tried to eject from their communion all who held it? after the Bishops' charges? after the Jerusalem "abomination?"[3] Well, this could be said; still we were not nothing: we could not be as if we never had been a Church; we were "Samaria." This then was that lower level on which I placed myself, and all who felt with me, at the end of 1841.

To bring out this view, was the purpose of Four Sermons preached at St. Mary's in December of that year. Hitherto I had not introduced the exciting topics of the day into the Pulpit;[4] on this occasion I did. I did so, for the moment was urgent; there was great unsettlement of mind among us, in consequence of those same events which had unsettled me. One special anxiety, very obvious, which was coming on me now, was, that what was "one man's meat was another man's poison." I had said even of Tract 90, "It was addressed to one set of persons, and has been used and commented on by another;" still more was it true now, that whatever I wrote for the service of those whom I knew to be in trouble of mind, would become on the one hand matter of suspicion and slander in the mouths of my opponents, and of distress and surprise to those on the other hand, who had no difficulties of faith at all. Accordingly, when I published these Four Sermons at the end of 1843, I introduced them with a recommendation that none should read them who did not need them. But in truth the virtual condemnation of Tract 90, after that the whole difficulty seemed to have been weathered, was an enormous disappointment and trial. My Protest also against the Jerusalem Bishopric was an unavoidable cause of excitement in the case of many; but it calmed them too, for the very fact of a Protest was a relief to their impatience. And so, in like manner, as regards the Four Sermons, of which I speak, though they acknowledge freely the great scandal which was involved in the recent episcopal doings, yet at the same time they might be said to bestow upon the multiplied disorders and shortcomings of the Anglican Church a sort of place in the Revealed Dispensation, and an intellectual position in the controversy, and the dignity of a great principle, for unsettled minds to take and use,—a principle which might teach them to recognize their own consistency, and to be reconciled to themselves, and which might absorb and dry up a multitude of their grudgings, discontents, misgivings, and questionings, and lead the way to humble, thankful, and tranquil thoughts;—and this was the effect, which certainly it produced on myself.

The point of these Sermons is, that, in spite of the rigid character of the Jewish law, the formal and literal force of its precepts, and the manifest schism, and worse than schism, of the Ten Tribes, yet in fact they were still recognized as a people by the Divine Mercy; that the great prophets Elias and Eliseus were sent to them; and not only so, but were sent to preach to them and reclaim them, without any intimation that they must be reconciled to the line of David and the Aaronic priesthood, or go up to Jerusalem to worship.

---

[3] Matthew 24:15. [Newman's note]. Newman is referring to the affair of the Jerusalem bishopric.
[4] Vide Note C. *Sermon on Wisdom and Innocence*. [Newman's note]

They were not in the Church, yet they had the means of grace and the hope of acceptance with their Maker. The application of all this to the Anglican Church was immediate;—whether, under the circumstances, a man could assume or exercise ministerial functions, or not, might not clearly appear (though it must be remembered that England had the Apostolic Priesthood, whereas Israel had no priesthood at all), but so far was clear, that there was no call at all for an Anglican to leave his Church for Rome, though he did not believe his own to be part of the One Church:—and for this reason, because it was a fact that the kingdom of Israel was cut off from the Temple; and yet its subjects, neither in a mass, nor as individuals, neither the multitudes on Mount Carmel, nor the Shunammite and her household, had any command given them, though miracles were displayed before them, to break off from their own people, and to submit themselves to Judah.[5]

It is plain that a theory such as this,—whether the marks of a divine presence and life in the Anglican Church were sufficient to prove that she was actually within the covenant, or only sufficient to prove that she was at least enjoying extraordinary and uncovenanted mercies,—not only lowered her level in a religious point of view, but weakened her controversial basis. Its very novelty made it suspicious; and there was no guarantee that the process of subsidence might not continue, and that it might not end in a submersion. Indeed, to many minds, to say that England was wrong was even to say that Rome was right; and no ethical or casuistic reasoning whatever could overcome in their case the argument from prescription and authority. To this objection, as made to my new teaching, I could only answer that I did not make my circumstances. I fully acknowledged the force and effectiveness of the genuine Anglican theory, and that it was all but proof against the disputants of Rome; but still like Achilles, it had a vulnerable point, and that St. Leo had found it out for me, and that I could not help it—that, were it not for matter of fact, the theory would be great indeed; it would be irresistible, if it were only true. When I became a Catholic, the Editor of the Christian Observer, Mr. Wilkes, who had in former days accused me, to my indignation, of tending towards Rome, wrote to me to ask, which of the

two was now right, he or I? I answered him in a letter, part of which I here insert, as it will serve as a sort of leave-taking of the great theory, which is so specious to look upon, so difficult to prove, and so hopeless to work.

"Nov. 8, 1845. I do not think, at all more than I did, that the Anglican principles which I advocated at the date you mention, lead men to the Church of Rome. If I must specify what I mean by 'Anglican principles,' I should say, e. g. taking *Antiquity*, not the *existing Church*, as the oracle of truth; and holding that the *Apostolical Succession* is a sufficient guarantee of Sacramental Grace, *without union with the Christian Church throughout the world*. I think these still the firmest, strongest ground against Rome—that is, *if they can be held*" [as truths or facts.] "They *have* been held by many, and are far more difficult to refute in the Roman controversy, than those of any other religious body.

"For myself, I found *I could not* hold them. I left them. From the time I began to suspect their unsoundness, I ceased to put them forward. When I was fairly sure of their unsoundness, I gave up my Living. When I was fully confident that the Church of Rome was the only true Church, I joined her.

"I have felt all along that Bp. Bull's theology was the only theology on which the English Church could stand. I have felt, that opposition to the Church of Rome was *part* of that theology; and that he who could not protest against the Church of Rome was no true divine in the English Church. I have never said, nor attempted to say, that any one in office in the English Church, whether Bishop or incumbent, could be otherwise than in hostility to the Church of Rome."

The *Via Media* then disappeared for ever, and a Theory, made expressly for the occasion, took its place. I was pleased with my new view. I wrote to an intimate friend, Samuel F. Wood, Dec. 13, 1841: "I think you will give me the credit, Carissime, of not undervaluing the strength of the feelings which draw one [to Rome], and yet I am (I trust) quite clear about my duty to remain where I am; indeed, much clearer than I was some time since. If it is not presumptuous to say, I have . . . a much more definite view of the promised inward Presence of Christ with us in

---

[5] As I am not writing controversially, I will only here remark upon this argument, that there is a great difference between a command which implies physical conditions, and one which is moral. To go to Jerusalem was a matter of the body, not of the soul. [Newman's note]

the Sacraments now that the outward notes of it are being removed. And I am content to be with Moses in the desert, or with Elijah excommunicated from the Temple. I say this, putting things at the strongest."

However, my friends of the moderate Apostolical party, who were my friends for the very reason of my having been so moderate and Anglican myself in general tone in times past, who had stood up for Tract 90 partly from faith in me, and certainly from generous and kind feeling, and had thereby shared an obloquy which was none of theirs, were naturally surprised and offended at a line of argument, novel, and, as it appeared to them, wanton, which threw the whole controversy into confusion, stultified my former principles, and substituted, as they would consider, a sort of methodistic self-contemplation, especially abhorrent both to my nature and to my past professions, for the plain and honest tokens, as they were commonly received, of a divine mission in the Anglican Church. They could not tell whither I was going; and were still further annoyed when I persisted in viewing the condemnation of Tract 90 by the public and the Bishops as so grave a matter, and when I threw about what they considered mysterious hints of "eventualities," and would not simply say, ' An Anglican I was born, and an Anglican I will die." One of my familiar friends, Mr. Church,[6] who was in the country at Christmas, 1841-2, reported to me the feeling that prevailed about me; and how I felt towards it will appear in the following letter of mine, written in answer:—

"Oriel, Dec. 24, 1841. Carissime, you cannot tell how sad your account of Moberly[7] has made me. His view of the sinfulness of the decrees of Trent is as much against union of Churches as against individual conversions. To tell the truth, I never have examined those decrees with this object, and have no view; but that is very different from having a deliberate view against them. Could not he say which they are? I suppose Transubstantiation is one. Charles Marriott, though of course he would not like to have it

repeated,[8] does not scruple at that. I have not my mind clear. Moberly must recollect that Palmer [of Worcester] thinks they all bear a Catholic interpretation. For myself, this only I see, that there is indefinitely more in the Fathers against our own state of alienation from Christendom than against the Tridentine Decrees.

"The only thing I can think of," [that I can have said of a startling character,] "is this, that there were persons who, if our Church committed herself to heresy, sooner than think that there was no Church any where, would believe the Roman to be the Church; and therefore would on faith accept what they could not otherwise acquiesce in. I suppose, it would be no relief to him to insist upon the circumstance that there is no immediate danger. Individuals can never be answered for of course; but I should think lightly of that man, who, for some act of the Bishops, should all at once leave the Church. Now, considering how the Clergy really are improving, considering that this row is even making them read the Tracts, is it not possible we may all be in a better state of mind seven years hence to consider these matters? and may we not leave them meanwhile to the will of Providence? I cannot believe this work has been of man; God has a right to His own work, to do what He will with it. May we not try to leave it in His hands, and be content?

"If you learn any thing about Barter, which leads you to think that I can relieve him by a letter, let me know. The truth is this,—our good friends do not read the Fathers; they assent to us from the common sense of the case: then, when the Fathers, and we, say more than their common sense, they are dreadfully shocked.

"The Bishop of London has rejected a man, 1. For holding any Sacrifice in the Eucharist. 2. The Real Presence. 3. That there is a grace in Ordination.[9]

"Are we quite sure that the Bishops will not be drawing up some stringent declarations of faith? Is this what Moberly fears? Would the Bishop of Oxford accept them? If so, I should be driven into the Refuge for the Destitute [Little-

---

[6] R. W. Church (1815–90), Fellow of Oriel and later Dean of St. Paul's and author of a history of the Oxford Movement.

[7] George Moberly (1803–85), later Bishop of Salisbury.

[8] As things stand now, I do not think he would have objected to his opinion being generally known. [Newman's note]

[9] I cannot prove at this distance of time; but I do not think it wrong to introduce here the passage containing it, as I am imputing to the Bishop nothing which the world would think disgraceful, but, on the contrary, what a large religious body would approve. [Newman's note]

more]. But I promise Moberly, I would do my utmost to catch all dangerous persons and clap them into confinement there."

Christmas Day, 1841. "I have been dreaming of Moberly all night. Should not he and the like see, that it is unwise, unfair, and impatient to ask others, What will you do under circumstances, which have not, which may never come? Why bring fear, suspicion, and disunion into the camp about things which are merely *in posse*?[10] Natural, and exceedingly kind as Barter's and another friend's letters were, I think they have done great harm. I speak most sincerely when I say, that there are things which I neither contemplate, nor wish to contemplate; but, when I am asked about them ten times, at length I begin to contemplate them.

"He surely does not mean to say, that *nothing* could separate a man from the English Church, e. g. its avowing Socinianism;[11] its holding the Holy Eucharist in a Socinian sense. Yet, he would say, it was not *right* to contemplate such things.

"Again, our case is [diverging] from that of Ken's. To say nothing of the last miserable century, which has given us to *start* from a much lower level and with much less to *spare* than a Churchman in the 17th century, questions of *doctrine* are now coming in; with him, it was a question of discipline.

"If such dreadful events were realized, I cannot help thinking we should all be vastly more agreed than we think now. Indeed, is it possible (humanly speaking) that those, who have so much the same heart, should widely differ? But let this be considered, as to alternatives. *What* communion could we join? Could the Scotch or American sanction the presence of its Bishops and congregations in England, without incurring the imputation of schism, unless indeed (and is that likely?) they denounced the English as heretical?

"Is not this a time of strange providences? is it not our safest course, without looking to consequences, to do simply *what we think right* day by day? shall we not be sure to go wrong, if we attempt to trace by anticipation the course of divine Providence?

"Has not all our misery, as a Church, arisen from people being afraid to look difficulties in the face? They have palliated acts, when they should have denounced them. There is that good fellow, Worcester Palmer, can whitewash the Ecclesiastical Commission and the Jerusalem Bishopric. And what is the consequence? that our Church has, through centuries, ever been sinking lower and lower, till good part of its pretensions and professions is a mere sham, though it be a duty to make the best of what we have received. Yet, though bound to make the best of other men's shams, let us not incur any of our own. The truest friends of our Church are they, who say boldly when her rulers are going wrong, and the consequences; and (to speak catachrestically) *they* are most likely to die in the Church, who are, under these black circumstances, most prepared to leave it.

"And I will add, that, considering the traces of God's grace which surround us, I am very sanguine, or rather confident, (if it is right so to speak,) that our prayers and our alms will come up as a memorial before God, and that all this miserable confusion tends to good.

"Let us not then be anxious, and anticipate differences in prospect, when we agree in the present.

"P.S. I think when friends" [i. e. the extreme party] "get over their first unsettlement of mind and consequent vague apprehensions, which the new attitude of the Bishops, and our feelings upon it, have brought about, they will get contented and satisfied. They will see that they exaggerated things. . . . Of course it would have been wrong to anticipate what one's feelings would be under such a painful contingency as the Bishops' charging as they have done,—so it seems to me nobody's fault. Nor is it wonderful that others" [moderate men] "are startled" [i. e. at my Protest, &c. &c.]; "yet they should recollect that the more implicit the reverence one pays to a Bishop, the more keen will be one's perception of heresy in him. The cord is binding and compelling, till it snaps.

"Men of reflection would have seen this, if they had looked that way. Last spring, a very high churchman talked to me of resisting my Bishop, of asking him for the Canons under which he acted, and so forth; but those, who have cultivated a loyal feeling towards their superiors, are the most loving servants, or the most zealous protestors. If others became so too, if the clergy of Chester denounced the heresy of their diocesan, they would be doing their duty, and relieving

---

[10] Possible, potential.
[11] Socinianism was a sixteenth-century Italian heresy that denied the Trinity.

themselves of the share which they otherwise have in any possible defection of their brethren.

"St. Stephen's [Day, December 26]. How I fidget! I now fear that the note I wrote yesterday only makes matters worse by *disclosing* too much. This is always my great difficulty.

"In the present state of excitement on both sides, I think of leaving out altogether my re-assertion of No. 90 in my Preface to Volume 6 [of Parochial Sermons], and merely saying, 'As many false reports are at this time in circulation about him, he hopes his well-wishers will take this Volume as an indication of his real thoughts and feelings: those who are not, he leaves in God's hand to bring them to a better mind in His own time.' What do you say to the logic, sentiment, and propriety of this?"

An old friend, at a distance from Oxford, Archdeacon Robert I. Wilberforce, must have said something to me at this time, I do not know what, which challenged a frank reply; for I disclosed to him, I do not know in what words, my frightful suspicion, hitherto only known to two persons, viz. his brother Henry[12] and Mr. Frederic Rogers,[13] that, as regards my Anglican-ism, perhaps I might break down in the event,— that perhaps we were both out of the Church. I think I recollect expressing my difficulty, as derived from the Arian and Monophysite history, in a form in which it would be most intelligible to him, as being in fact an admission of Bishop Bull's; viz. that in the controversies of the early centuries the Roman Church was ever on the right side, which was of course a *primâ facie* argument in favour of Rome and against An-glicanism now. He answered me thus, under date of Jan. 29, 1842: "I don't think that I ever was so shocked by any communication, which was ever made to me, as by your letter of this morning. It has quite unnerved me. . . . I cannot but write to you, though I am at a loss where to begin. . . . I know of no act by which we have dissevered ourselves from the communion of the Church Universal. . . . The more I study Scripture, the more I am impressed with the resemblance be-tween the Romish principle in the Church and the Babylon of St. John. . . . I am ready to grieve that I ever directed my thoughts to theology, if it is indeed so uncertain, as your doubts seem to indicate."

While my old and true friends were thus in trouble about me, I suppose they felt not only anxiety but pain, to see that I was gradually surrendering myself to the influence of others, who had not their own claims upon me, younger men, and of a cast of mind in no small degree uncongenial to my own. A new school of thought was rising, as is usual in doctrinal inquiries, and was sweeping the original party of the Movement aside, and was taking its place. The most prom-inent person in it, was a man of elegant genius, of classical mind, of rare talent in literary com-position:—Mr. Oakeley. He was not far from my own age; I had long known him, though of late years he had not been in residence at Oxford; and quite lately, he has been taking several signal occasions of renewing that kindness, which he ever showed towards me when we were both in the Anglican Church. His tone of mind was not unlike that which gave a character to the early Move-ment; he was almost a typical Oxford man, and, as far as I recollect, both in political and ec-clesiastical views, would have been of one spirit with the Oriel party of 1826–1833. But he had entered late into the Movement; he did not know its first years; and, beginning with a new start, he was naturally thrown together with that body of eager, acute, resolute minds who had begun their Catholic life about the same time as he, who knew nothing about the *Via Media*, but had heard much about Rome. This new party rapidly formed and increased, in and out of Oxford, and, as it so happened, contemporaneously with that very summer, when I received so serious a blow to my ecclesiastical views from the study of the Mono-physite controversy. These men cut into the original Movement at an angle, fell across its line of thought, and then set about turning that line in its own direction. They were most of them keenly religious men, with a true concern for their souls as the first matter of all, with a great zeal for me, but giving little certainty at the time as to which way they would ultimately turn. Some in the event have remained firm to Anglicanism, some have become Catholics, and some have found a refuge in Liberalism. Nothing was clearer concerning them, than that they needed to be kept in order; and on me who had had so much to do with the making of them, that duty was as clearly incumbent; and it is equally clear, from

[12] Robert and Henry Wilberforce were sons of William Wilberforce, famous evangelical reformer. Robert became a High Churchman; Henry converted to Rome in 1850.
[13] Now Lord Blachford. [Newman's note]

what I have already said, that I was just the person, above all others, who could not undertake it. There are no friends like old friends; but of those old friends, few could help me, few could understand me, many were annoyed with me, some were angry, because I was breaking up a compact party, and some, as a matter of conscience, could not listen to me. When I looked round for those whom I might consult in my difficulties, I found the very hypothesis of those difficulties acting as a bar to their giving me their advice. Then I said, bitterly, "You are throwing me on others, whether I will or no." Yet still I had good and true friends around me of the old sort, in and out of Oxford too, who were a great help to me. But on the other hand, though I neither was so fond (with few exceptions) of the persons, nor of the methods of thought, which belonged to this new school, as of the old set, though I could not trust in their firmness of purpose, for, like a swarm of flies, they might come and go, and at length be divided and dissipated, yet I had an intense sympathy in their object and in the direction in which their path lay, in spite of my old friends, in spite of my old life-long prejudices. In spite of my ingrained fears of Rome, and the decision of my reason and conscience against her usages, in spite of my affection for Oxford and Oriel, yet I had a secret longing love of Rome the Mother of English Christianity, and I had a true devotion to the Blessed Virgin, in whose College I lived, whose Altar I served, and whose Immaculate Purity I had in one of my earliest printed Sermons made much of. And it was the consciousness of this bias in myself, if it is so to be called, which made me preach so earnestly against the danger of being swayed in religious inquiry by our sympathy rather than by our reason. And moreover, the members of this new school looked up to me, as I have said, and did me true kindnesses, and really loved me, and stood by me in trouble, when others went away, and for all this I was grateful; nay, many of them were in trouble themselves, and in the same boat with me, and that was a further cause of sympathy between us; and hence it was, when the new school came on in force, and into collision with the old, I had not the heart, any more than the power, to repel them; I was in great perplexity, and hardly knew where I stood; I took their part; and, when I wanted to be in peace and silence, I had to speak out, and I incurred the charge of weakness from some men, and of mysteriousness, shuffling, and underhanded dealing from the majority.

Now I will say here frankly, that this sort of charge is a matter which I cannot properly meet, because I cannot duly realize it. I have never had any suspicion of my own honesty; and, when men say that I was dishonest, I cannot grasp the accusation as a distinct conception, such as it is possible to encounter. If a man said to me, "On such a day and before such persons you said a thing was white, when it was black," I understand what is meant well enough, and I can set myself to prove an *alibi* or to explain the mistake; or if a man said to me, "You tried to gain me over to your party, intending to take me with you to Rome, but you did not succeed," I can give him the lie, and lay down an assertion of my own as firm and as exact as his, that not from the time that I was first unsettled, did I ever attempt to gain any one over to myself or to my Romanizing opinions, and that it is only his own coxcombical fancy which has bred such a thought in him: but my imagination is at a loss in presence of those vague charges, which have commonly been brought against me, charges, which are made up of impressions, and understandings, and inferences, and hearsay, and surmises. Accordingly, I shall not make the attempt, for, in doing so, I should be dealing blows in the air; what I shall attempt is to state what I know of myself and what I recollect, and leave to others its application.

While I had confidence in the *Via Media*, and thought that nothing could overset it, I did not mind laying down large principles, which I saw would go further than was commonly perceived. I considered that to make the *Via Media* concrete and substantive, it must be much more than it was in outline; that the Anglican Church must have a ceremonial, a ritual, and a fulness of doctrine and devotion, which it had not at present, if it were to compete with the Roman Church with any prospect of success. Such Additions would not remove it from its proper basis, but would merely strengthen and beautify it: such, for instance, would be confraternities, particular devotions, reverence for the Blessed Virgin, prayers for the dead, beautiful churches, munificent offerings to them and in them, monastic houses, and many other observances and institutions, which I used to say belonged to us as much as to Rome, though Rome had appropriated them and boasted of them, by reason of our having let them slip from us. The principle, on which all this turned, is brought out in one of the Letters I published on occasion of Tract 90. "The age is moving," I said, "towards something;

and most unhappily the one religious communion among us, which has of late years been practically in possession of this something,—is the Church of Rome. She alone, amid all the errors and evils of her practical system, has given free scope to the feelings of awe, mystery, tenderness, reverence, devotedness, and other feelings which may be especially called Catholic. The question then is, whether we shall give them up to the Roman Church or claim them for ourselves. . . . But if we do give them up, we must give up the men who cherish them. We must consent either to give up the men, or to admit their principles." With these feelings I frankly admit, that, while I was working simply for the sake of the Anglican Church, I did not at all mind, though I found myself laying down principles in its defence, which went beyond that particular kind of defence which high-and-dry men thought perfection, and even though I ended in framing a kind of defence, which they might call a revolution, while I thought it a restoration. Thus, for illustration, I might discourse upon the "Communion of Saints" in such a manner, (though I do not recollect doing so,) as might lead the way towards devotion to the Blessed Virgin and the Saints on the one hand, and towards prayers for the dead on the other. In a memorandum of the year 1844 or 1845, I thus speak on this subject: "If the Church be not defended on establishment grounds, it must be upon principles, which go far beyond their immediate object. Sometimes I saw these further results, sometimes not. Though I saw them, I sometimes did not say that I saw them:—so long as I thought they were inconsistent, *not* with our Church, but only with the existing opinions, I was not unwilling to insinuate truths into our Church, which I thought had a right to be there."

To so much I confess; but I do not confess, I simply deny that I ever said any thing which secretly bore against the Church of England, knowing it myself, in order that others might unwarily accept it. It was indeed one of my great difficulties and causes of reserve, as time went on, that I at length recognized in principles which I had honestly preached as if Anglican, conclusions favourable to the cause of Rome. Of course I did not like to confess this; and, when interrogated, was in consequence in perplexity. The prime minister of this was the appeal to Antiquity; St. Leo had overset, in my own judgment, its force as the special argument for Anglicanism; yet I was committed to Antiquity, together with the whole Anglican school; what then was I to say, when acute minds urged this or that application of it against the *Via Media*? it was impossible that, in such circumstances, any answer could be given which was not unsatisfactory, or any behaviour adopted which was not mysterious. Again, sometimes in what I wrote I went just as far as I saw, and could as little say more, as I could see what is below the horizon; and therefore, when asked as to the consequences of what I had said, I had no answer to give. Again, sometimes when I was asked, whether certain conclusions did not follow from a certain principle, I might not be able to tell at the moment, especially if the matter were complicated; and for this reason, if for no other, because there is great difference between a conclusion in the abstract and a conclusion in the concrete, and because a conclusion may be modified in fact by a conclusion from some opposite principle. Or it might so happen that my head got simply confused, by the very strength of the logic which was administered to me, and thus I gave my sanction to conclusions which really were not mine; and when the report of those conclusions came round to me through others, I had to unsay them. And then again, perhaps I did not like to see men scared or scandalized by unfeeling logical inferences, which would not have troubled them to the day of their death, had they not been forced to recognize them. And then I felt altogether the force of the maxim of St. Ambrose, "Non in dialecticà complacuit Deo salvum facere populum suum;"[14]—I had a great dislike of paper logic. For myself, it was not logic that carried me on; as well might one say that the quicksilver in the barometer changes the weather. It is the concrete being that reasons; pass a number of years, and I find my mind in a new place; how? the whole man moves; paper logic is but the record of it. All the logic in the world would not have made me move faster towards Rome than I did; as well might you say that I have arrived at the end of my journey, because I see the village church before me, as venture to assert that the miles, over which my soul had to pass before it got to Rome, could be annihilated, even though I had been in possession of some far clearer view than I then had, that Rome was my ultimate destination. Great acts take time. At least this is what I felt in my own case; and therefore to come to me with methods

___

[14] "God was not pleased to save his people by means of logic." This was to become Newman's motto for *The Grammar of Assent*.

of logic had in it the nature of a provocation, and, though I do not think I ever showed it, made me somewhat indifferent how I met them, and perhaps led me, as a means of relieving my impatience, to be mysterious or irrelevant, or to give in because I could not meet them to my satisfaction. And a greater trouble still than these logical mazes, was the introduction of logic into every subject whatever, so far, that is, as this was done. Before I was at Oriel, I recollect an acquaintance saying to me that "the Oriel Common Room stank of Logic." One is not at all pleased when poetry, or eloquence, or devotion, is considered as if chiefly intended to feed syllogisms. Now, in saying all this, I am saying nothing against the deep piety and earnestness which were characteristics of this second phase of the Movement, in which I had taken so prominent a part. What I have been observing is, that this phase had a tendency to bewilder and to upset me; and, that, instead of saying so, as I ought to have done, perhaps from a sort of laziness I gave answers at random, which have led to my appearing close or inconsistent.

I have turned up two letters of this period, which in a measure illustrate what I have been saying. The first was written to the Bishop of Oxford on occasion of Tract 90:

"March 20, 1841. No one can enter into my situation but myself. I see a great many minds working in various directions and a variety of principles with multiplied bearings; I act for the best. I sincerely think that matters would not have gone better for the Church, had I never written. And if I write I have a choice of difficulties. It is easy for those who do not enter into those difficulties to say, 'He ought to say this and not say that,' but things are wonderfully linked together, and I cannot, or rather I would not be dishonest. When persons too interrogate me, I am obliged in many cases to give an opinion, or I seem to be underhand. Keeping silence looks like artifice. And I do not like people to consult or respect me, from thinking differently of my opinions from what I know them to be. And again (to use the proverb) what is one man's food is another man's poison. All these things make my situation very difficult. But that collision must at some time ensue between members of the Church of opposite sentiments, I have long been aware. The time and mode has been in the hand of Providence; I do not mean to exclude my own

great imperfections in bringing it about; yet I still feel obliged to think the Tract necessary."

The second is taken from the notes of a letter which I sent to Dr. Pusey in the next year:

"October 16, 1842. As to my being entirely with Ward,[15] I do not know the limits of my own opinions. If Ward says that this or that is a development from what I have said, I cannot say Yes or No. It is plausible, it *may* be true. Of course the fact that the Roman Church *has* so developed and maintained, adds great weight to the antecedent plausibility. I cannot assert that it is not true; but I cannot, with that keen perception which some people have, appropriate it. It is a nuisance to me to be *forced* beyond what I can fairly accept."

There was another source of the perplexity with which at this time I was encompassed, and of the reserve and mysteriousness, of which that perplexity gained for me the credit. After Tract 90 the Protestant world would not let me alone; they pursued me in the public journals to Littlemore. Reports of all kinds were circulated about me. "Imprimis, why did I go up to Littlemore at all? For no good purpose certainly; I dared not tell why." Why, to be sure, it was hard that I should be obliged to say to the Editors of newspapers that I went up there to say my prayers; it was hard to have to tell the world in confidence, that I had a certain doubt about the Anglican system, and could not at that moment resolve it, or say what would come of it; it was hard to have to confess that I had thought of giving up my Living a year or two before, and that this was a first step to it. It was hard to have to plead, that, for what I knew, my doubts would vanish, if the newspapers would be so good as to give me time and let me alone. Who would ever dream of making the world his confidant? yet I was considered insidious, sly, dishonest, if I would not open my heart to the tender mercies of the world. But they persisted: "What was I doing at Littlemore?" Doing there! have I not retreated from you? have I not given up my position and my place? am I alone, of Englishmen, not to have the privilege to go where I will, no questions asked? am I alone to be followed about by jealous prying eyes, which take note whether I go in at a back door or at the front, and who the men are who happen to call on me in the afternoon? Cowards! if I advanced one step, you would run away; it is not you that I fear: "Di me terrent, et Jupiter hostis."[16] It is because the Bishops still go on

[15] William George Ward (1812–82), a zealous Tractarian who converted in 1845.
[16] "The Gods terrify me and the enmity of Jove" (Aeneid).

charging against me, though I have quite given up: it is that secret misgiving of heart which tells me that they do well, for I have neither lot nor part with them: this it is which weighs me down. I cannot walk into or out of my house, but curious eyes are upon me. Why will you not let me die in peace? Wounded brutes creep into some hole to die in, and no one grudges it them. Let me alone, I shall not trouble you long. This was the keen feeling which pierced me, and, I think, these are the very words in which I expressed it to myself. I asked, in the words of a great motto, "Ubi lapsus? quid feci?"[17] One day when I entered my house, I found a flight of Under-graduates inside. Heads of Houses, as mounted patrols, walked their horses round those poor cottages. Doctors of Divinity dived into the hidden recesses of that private tenement un-invited, and drew domestic conclusions from what they saw there. I had thought that an Englishman's house was his castle; but the newspapers thought otherwise, and at last the matter came before my good Bishop. I insert his letter, and a portion of my reply to him:—

"April 12, 1842. So many of the charges against yourself and your friends which I have seen in the public journals have been, within my own knowledge, false and calumnious, that I am not apt to pay much attention to what is asserted with respect to you in the newspapers.

"In" [a newspaper] "however, of April 9, there appears a paragraph in which it is asserted, as a matter of notoriety, that a 'so-called Anglo-Catholic Monastery is in the process of erection at Littlemore, and that the cells of dormitories, the chapel, the refectory, the cloisters all may be seen advancing to perfection, under the eye of a Parish Priest of the Diocese of Oxford.'

"Now, as I have understood that you really are possessed of some tenements at Littlemore,—as it is generally believed that they are destined for the purposes of study and devotion,—and as much suspicion and jealousy are felt about the matter, I am anxious to afford you an opportunity of making me an explanation on the subject.

"I know you too well not to be aware that you are the last man living to attempt in my Diocese a revival of the Monastic orders (in any thing approaching to the Romanist sense of the term) without previous communication with me,—or indeed that you should take upon yourself to originate any measure of importance without authority from the heads of the Church,—and

therefore I at once exonerate you from the accusation brought against you by the newspaper I have quoted, but I feel it nevertheless a duty to my Diocese and myself, as well as to you, to ask you to put it in my power to contradict what, if uncontradicted, would appear to imply a glaring invasion of all ecclesiastical discipline on *your* part, or of inexcusable neglect and indifference to my duties on *mine*."

I wrote in answer as follows:—

"April 14, 1842. I am very much obliged by your Lordship's kindness in allowing me to write to you on the subject of my house at Littlemore; at the same time I feel it hard both on your Lordship and myself that the restlessness of the public mind should oblige you to require an explanation of me.

"It is now a whole year that I have been the subject of incessant misrepresentation. A year since I submitted entirely to your Lordship's authority; and, with the intention of following out the particular act enjoined upon me, I not only stopped the series of Tracts, on which I was engaged, but withdrew from all public discussion of Church matters of the day, or what may be called ecclesiastical politics. I turned myself at once to the preparation for the Press of the translations of St. Athanasius to which I had long wished to devote myself, and I intended and intend to employ myself in the like theological studies, and in the concerns of my own parish and in practical works.

"With the same view of personal improvement I was led more seriously to a design which had been long on my mind. For many years, at least thirteen, I have wished to give myself to a life of greater religious regularity than I have hitherto led; but it is very unpleasant to confess such a wish even to my Bishop, because it seems arrogant, and because it is committing me to a profession which may come to nothing. For what have I done that I am to be called to account by the world for my private actions, in a way in which no one else is called? Why may I not have that liberty which all others are allowed? I am often accused of being underhand and uncandid in respect to the intentions to which I have been alluding: but no one likes his own good resolutions noised about, both from mere common delicacy and from fear lest he should not be able to fulfil them. I feel it very cruel, though the parties in fault do not know what they are doing, that very sacred matters between me and my

_____

[17] "Where did I err? What have I done?"

conscience are made a matter of public talk. May I take a case parallel though different? suppose a person in prospect of marriage; would he like the subject discussed in newspapers, and parties, circumstances, &c., &c., publicly demanded of him, at the penalty of being accused of craft and duplicity?

"The resolution I speak of has been taken with reference to myself alone, and has been contemplated quite independent of the co-operation of any other human being, and without reference to success or failure other than personal, and without regard to the blame or approbation of man. And being a resolution of years, and one to which I feel God has called me, and in which I am violating no rule of the Church any more than if I married, I should have to answer for it, if I did not pursue it, as a good Providence made openings for it. In pursuing it then I am thinking of myself alone, not aiming at any ecclesiastical or external effects. At the same time of course it would be a great comfort to me to know that God had put it into the hearts of others to pursue their personal edification in the same way, and unnatural not to wish to have the benefit of their presence and encouragement, or not to think it a great infringement on the rights of conscience if such personal and private resolutions were interfered with. Your Lordship will allow me to add my firm conviction that such religious resolutions are most necessary for keeping a certain class of minds firm in their allegiance to our Church; but still I can as truly say that my own reason for any thing I have done has been a personal one, without which I should not have entered upon it, and which I hope to pursue whether with or without the sympathies of others pursuing a similar course. . . .

"As to my intentions, I purpose to live there myself a good deal, as I have a resident curate in Oxford. In doing this, I believe I am consulting for the good of my parish, as my population at Littlemore is at least equal to that of St. Mary's in Oxford, and the *whole* of Littlemore is double of it. It has been very much neglected; and in providing a parsonage-house at Littlemore, as this will be, and will be called, I conceive I am doing a very great benefit to my people. At the same time it has appeared to me that a partial or temporary retirement from St. Mary's Church might be expedient under the prevailing excitement.

"As to the quotation from the [newspaper], which I have not seen, your Lordship will perceive from what I have said, that no 'monastery is in process of erection;' there is no 'chapel;' no 'refectory,' hardly a dining-room or parlour. The 'cloisters' are my shed connecting the cottages. I do not understand what 'cells of dormitories' means. Of course I can repeat your Lordship's words that 'I am not attempting a revival of the Monastic Orders, in any thing approaching to the Romanist sense of the term,' or 'taking on myself to originate any measure of importance without authority from the Heads of the Church.' I am attempting nothing ecclesiastical, but something personal and private, and which can only be made public, not private, by newspapers and letter-writers, in which sense the most sacred and conscientious resolves and acts may certainly be made the objects of an unmannerly and unfeeling curiosity."

One calumny there was which the Bishop did not believe, and of which of course he had no idea of speaking. It was that I was actually in the service of the enemy. I had forsooth been already received into the Catholic Church, and was rearing at Littlemore a nest of Papists, who, like me, were to take the Anglican oaths which they disbelieved, by virtue of a dispensation from Rome, and thus in due time were to bring over to that unprincipled Church great numbers of the Anglican Clergy and Laity. Bishops gave their countenance to this imputation against me. The case was simply this:—as I made Littlemore a place of retirement for myself, so did I offer it to others. There were young men in Oxford, whose testimonials for Orders had been refused by their Colleges; there were young clergymen, who had found themselves unable from conscience to go on with their duties, and had thrown up their parochial engagements. Such men were already going straight to Rome, and I interposed; I interposed for the reasons I have given in the beginning of this portion of my narrative. I interposed from fidelity to my clerical engagements, and from duty to my Bishop; and from the interest which I was bound to take in them, and from belief that they were premature or excited. Their friends besought me to quiet them, if I could. Some of them came to live with me at Littlemore. They were laymen, or in the place of laymen. I kept some of them back for several years from being received into the Catholic Church. Even when I had given up my living, I was still bound by my duty to their parents or friends, and I did not forget still to do what I could for them. The immediate occasion of my resigning St. Mary's, was the unexpected conversion of one of them.[18] After that, I felt it was impossible to keep my post there, for I had been unable to keep my word with my Bishop.

The following letters refer, more or less, to these men, whether they were actually with me at Littlemore or not:—

1. "March 6, 1842. Church doctrines are a powerful weapon; they were not sent into the world for nothing. God's word does not return unto Him void: If I have said, as I have, that the doctrines of the Tracts for the Times would build up our Church and destroy parties, I meant, if they were used, not if they were denounced. Else, they will be as powerful against us, as they might be powerful for us.

"If people who have a liking for another, hear him called a Roman Catholic, they will say, 'Then after all Romanism is no such bad thing.' All these persons, who are making the cry, are fulfilling their own prophecy. If all the world agree in telling a man, he has no business in our Church, he will at length begin to think he has none. How easy is it to persuade a man of any thing, when numbers affirm it! so great is the force of imagination. Did every one who met you in the streets look hard at you, you would think you were somehow in fault. I do not know any thing so irritating, so unsettling, especially in the case of young persons, as, when they are going on calmly and unconsciously, obeying their Church and following its divines, (I am speaking from facts,) as suddenly to their surprise to be conjured not to make a leap, of which they have not a dream and from which they are far removed."

2. 1843 or 1844. "I did not explain to you sufficiently the state of mind of those who were in danger. I only spoke of those who were convinced that our Church was external to the Church Catholic, though they felt it unsafe to trust their own private convictions; but there are two other states of mind; 1. that of those who are unconsciously near Rome, and whose *despair* about our Church would at once develop into a state of conscious approximation, or a *quasi*-resolution to go over; 2. those who feel they can with a safe conscience remain with us *while* they are allowed to *testify* in behalf of Catholicism, i.e. as if by such acts they were putting our Church, or at least that portion of it in which they were included, in the position of catechumens."

3. "June 20, 1843. I return the very pleasing letter you have permitted me to read. What a sad

thing it is, that it should be a plain duty to restrain one's sympathies, and to keep them from boiling over; but I suppose it is a matter of common prudence.

"Things are very serious here; but I should not like you to say so, as it might do no good. The Authorities find, that, by the Statutes, they have more than military power; and the general impression seems to be, that they intend to exert it, and put down Catholicism at any risk. I believe that by the Statutes, they can pretty nearly suspend a Preacher, as *seditiosus* or causing dissension, without assigning their grounds in the particular case, nay, banish him, or imprison him. If so, all holders of preferment in the University should make as quiet an *exit* as they can. There is more exasperation on both sides at this moment, as I am told, than ever there was."

4. "July 16, 1843. I assure you that I feel, with only too much sympathy, what you say. You need not be told that the whole subject of our position is a subject of anxiety to others beside yourself. It is no good attempting to offer advice, when perhaps I might raise difficulties instead of removing them. It seems to me quite a case, in which you should, as far as may be, make up your mind for yourself. Come to Littlemore by all means. We shall all rejoice in your company; and, if quiet and retirement are able, as they very likely will be, to reconcile you to things as they are, you shall have your fill of them. How distressed poor Henry Wilberforce must be! Knowing how he values you, I feel for him; but, alas! he has his own position, and every one else has his own, and the misery is that no two of us have exactly the same.

"It is very kind of you to be so frank and open with me, as you are; but this is a time which throws together persons who feel alike. May I without taking a liberty sign myself, yours affectionately, &c."

5. "August 30, 1843. A. B.[19] has suddenly conformed to the Church of Rome. He was away for three weeks. I suppose I must say in my defence, that he promised me distinctly to remain in our Church three years, before I received him here."

6. "June 17, 1845. I am concerned to find you speak of me in a tone of distrust. If you knew me ever so little, instead of hearing of me from persons who do not know me at all, you would think differently of me, whatever you thought of my

---

[18] William Lockhart, the first Tractarian to submit to Rome.
[19] Lockhart.

opinions. Two years since, I got your son to tell you my intention of resigning St. Mary's, before I made it public, thinking you ought to know it. When you expressed some painful feeling upon it, I told him I could not consent to his remaining here, painful as it would be to me to part with him, without your written sanction. And this you did me the favour to give.

"I believe you will find that it has been merely a delicacy on your son's part, which has delayed his speaking to you about me for two months past; a delicacy, lest he should say either too much or too little about me. I have urged him several times to speak to you.

"Nothing can be done after your letter, but to recommend him to go to A. B. (his home) at once. I am very sorry to part with him."

7. The following letter is addressed to Cardinal Wiseman, then Vicar Apostolic, who accused me of coldness in my conduct towards him:—

"April 16, 1845. I was at that time in charge of a ministerial office in the English Church, with persons entrusted to me, and a Bishop to obey; how could I possibly write otherwise than I did without violating sacred obligations and betraying momentous interests which were upon me? I felt that my immediate, undeniable duty, clear if any thing was clear, was to fulfil that trust. It might be right indeed to give it up, that was another thing; but it never could be right to hold it, and to act as if I did not hold it. . . . If you knew me, you would acquit me, I think, of having ever felt towards your Lordship in an unfriendly spirit, or ever having had a shadow on my mind (as far as I dare witness about myself) of what might be called controversial rivalry or desire of getting the better, or fear lest the world should think I had got the worse, or irritation of any kind. You are too kind indeed to imply this, and yet your words lead me to say it. And now in like manner, pray believe, though I cannot explain it to you, that I am encompassed with responsibilities, so great and so various, as utterly to overcome me, unless I have mercy from Him, who all through my life has sustained and guided me, and to whom I can now submit myself, though men of all parties are thinking evil of me."

Such fidelity, however, was taken *in malam partem*[20] by the high Anglican authorities; they thought it insidious. I happen still to have a correspondence which took place in 1843, in which the chief place is filled by one of the most eminent Bishops of the day, a theologian and reader of the Fathers, a moderate man, who at one time was talked of as likely on a vacancy to succeed to the Primacy. A young clergyman in his diocese became a Catholic;[21] the papers at once reported on authority from "a very high quarter," that, after his reception, "the Oxford men had been recommending him to retain his living." I had reasons for thinking that the allusion was made to me, and I authorized the Editor of a Paper, who had inquired of me on the point, to "give it, as far as I was concerned, an unqualified contradiction;"—when from a motive of delicacy he hesitated, I added "my direct and indignant contradiction." "Whoever is the author of it," I continued to the Editor, "no correspondence or intercourse of any kind, direct or indirect, has passed between Mr. S. and myself, since his conforming to the Church of Rome, except my formally and merely acknowledging the receipt of his letter, in which he informed me of the fact, without, as far as I recollect, my expressing any opinion upon it. You may state this as broadly as I have set it down." My denial was told to the Bishop; what took place upon it is given in a letter from which I copy. "My father showed the letter to the Bishop, who, as he laid it down, said, 'Ah, those Oxford men are not ingenuous.' 'How do you mean?' asked my father. 'Why,' said the Bishop, 'they advised Mr. B. S. to retain his living after he turned Catholic. I know that to be a fact, because A. B. told me so.'" "The Bishop," continues the letter, "who is perhaps the most influential man in reality on the bench, evidently believes it to be the truth." Upon this Dr. Pusey wrote in my behalf to the Bishop; and the Bishop instantly beat a retreat. "I have the honour," he says in the autograph which I transcribe, "to acknowledge the receipt of your note, and to say in reply that it has not been stated by me, (though such a statement has, I believe, appeared in some of the Public Prints,) that Mr. Newman had advised Mr. B. S. to retain his living, after he had forsaken our Church. But it has been stated to me, that Mr. Newman was in close correspondence with Mr. B. S., and, being fully aware of his state of opinions and feelings, yet advised him to continue in our communion. Allow me to add," he says to Dr. Pusey, "that neither your name, nor that of Mr. Keble, was mentioned to me in connexion with that of Mr. B. S."

I was not going to let the Bishop off on this

[20] In bad part, unfavorably.   [21] Bernard Smith, who converted in 1842.

evasion, so I wrote to him myself. After quoting his Letter to Dr. Pusey, I continued, "I beg to trouble your Lordship with my own account of the two allegations" [*close correspondence* and *fully aware,* &c.] "which are contained in your statement, and which have led to your speaking of me in terms which I hope never to deserve. 1. Since Mr. B. S. has been in your Lordship's diocese, I have seen him in Common rooms or private parties in Oxford two or three times, when I never (as far as I can recollect) had any conversation with him. During the same time I have, to the best of my memory, written to him three letters. One was lately, in acknowledgment of his informing me of his change of religion. Another was last summer, when I asked him (to no purpose) to come and stay with me in this place. The earliest of the three letters was written just a year since, as far as I recollect, and it certainly was on the subject of his joining the Church of Rome. I wrote this letter at the earnest wish of a friend of his. I cannot be sure that, on his replying, I did not send him a brief note in explanation of points in my letter which he had misapprehended. I cannot recollect any other correspondence between us.

"2. As to my knowledge of his opinions and feelings, as far as I remember, the only point of perplexity which I knew, the only point which to this hour I know, as pressing upon him, was that of the Pope's supremacy. He professed to be searching Antiquity whether the see of Rome had formerly that relation to the whole Church which Roman Catholics now assign to it. My letter was directed to the point, that it was his duty not to perplex himself with arguments on [such] a question, . . . and to put it altogether aside. . . . It is hard that I am put upon my memory, without knowing the details of the statement made against me, considering the various correspondence in which I am from time to time unavoidably engaged. . . . Be assured, my Lord, that there are very definite limits, beyond which persons like me would never urge another to retain preferment in the English Church, nor would retain it themselves; and that the censure which has been directed against them by so many of its Rulers has a very grave bearing upon those limits." The Bishop replied in a civil letter, and sent my own letter to his original informant, who wrote to me the letter of a gentleman. It seems that an anxious lady had said something or other which had been misinterpreted, against her real meaning, into the calumny which was circulated, and so the report vanished into thin air. I closed the correspondence with the following Letter to the Bishop:—

"I hope your Lordship will believe me when I say, that statements about me, equally incorrect with that which has come to your Lordship's ears, are from time to time reported to me as credited and repeated by the highest authorities in our Church, though it is very seldom that I have the opportunity of denying them. I am obliged by your Lordship's letter to Dr. Pusey as giving me such an opportunity." Then I added, with a purpose, "Your Lordship will observe that in my Letter I had no occasion to proceed to the question, whether a person holding Roman Catholic opinions can in honesty remain in our Church. Lest then any misconception should arise from my silence, I here take the liberty of adding, that I see nothing wrong in such a person's continuing in communion with us, provided he holds no preferment or office, abstains from the management of ecclesiastical matters, and is bound by no subscription or oath to our doctrines."

This was written on March 8, 1843, and was in anticipation of my own retirement into lay communion. This again leads me to a remark:— for two years I was in lay communion, not indeed being a Catholic in my convictions, but in a state of serious doubt, and with the probable prospect of becoming some day, what as yet I was not. Under these circumstances I thought the best thing I could do was to give up duty and to throw myself into lay communion, remaining an Anglican. I could not go to Rome, while I thought what I did of the devotions she sanctioned to the Blessed Virgin and the Saints. I did not give up my fellowship, for I could not be sure that my doubts would not be reduced or overcome, however unlikely I might consider such an event. But I gave up my living; and, for two years before my conversion, I took no clerical duty. My last Sermon was in September, 1843; then I remained at Littlemore in quiet for two years. But it was made a subject of reproach to me at the time, and is at this day, that I did not leave the Anglican Church sooner. To me this seems a wonderful charge; why, even had I been quite sure that Rome was the true Church, the Anglican Bishops would have had no just subject of complaint against me, provided I took no Anglican oath, no clerical duty, no ecclesiastical administration. Do they force all men who go to their Churches to believe in the 39 Articles, or to join in the Athanasian Creed? However, I was to have other measure dealt to me; great authorities ruled it so; and a great controversialist, Mr. Stanley Faber,[22] thought it a shame that I did not leave the Church of England as much as ten years sooner than I did. He said this in print between the years 1847 and 1849. His nephew, an Anglican clergyman, kindly wished to undeceive him on this point. So, in the latter year, after some correspondence, I wrote the following letter, which will be of service to this narrative, from its chronological notes:—

"Dec. 6, 1849. Your uncle says, 'If he (Mr. N.) will declare, *sans phrase*,[23] as the French say, that I have laboured under an entire mistake, and that he was not a concealed Romanist during the ten years in question,' (I suppose, the last ten years of my membership with the Anglican Church,) 'or during any part of the time, my controversial antipathy will be at an end, and I will readily express to him that I am truly sorry that I have made such a mistake."

"So candid an avowal is what I should have expected from a mind like your uncle's. I am extremely glad he has brought it to this issue.

"By a 'concealed Romanist' I understand him to mean one, who, professing to belong to the Church of England, in his heart and will intends to benefit the Church of Rome, at the expense of the Church of England. He cannot mean by the expression merely a person who in fact is benefiting the Church of Rome, while he is intending to benefit the Church of England, for that is no discredit to him morally, and he (your uncle) evidently means to impute blame.

"In the sense in which I have explained the words, I can simply and honestly say that I was not a concealed Romanist during the whole, or any part of, the years in question.

"For the first four years of the ten, (up to Michaelmas, 1839,) I honestly wished to benefit the Church of England, at the expense of the Church of Rome:

"For the second four years I wished to benefit the Church of England without prejudice to the Church of Rome:

"At the beginning of the ninth year (Michaelmas, 1843) I began to despair of the Church of England, and gave up all clerical duty; and then, what I wrote and did was influenced by a mere wish not to injure it, and not by the wish to benefit it:

"At the beginning of the tenth year I distinctly contemplated leaving it, but I also distinctly told my friends that it was in my contemplation.

"Lastly, during the last half of that tenth year I was engaged in writing a book (Essay on Development) in favour of the Roman Church, and indirectly against the English; but even then, till it was finished, I had not absolutely intended to publish it, wishing to reserve to myself the chance of changing my mind when the argumentative views which were actuating me had been distinctly brought out before me in writing.

"I wish this statement, which I make from memory, and without consulting any document, severely tested by my writings and doings, as I am confident it will, on the whole, be borne out, whatever real or apparent exceptions (I suspect none) have to be allowed by me in detail.

"Your uncle is at liberty to make what use he pleases of this explanation."

I have now reached an important date in my narrative, the year 1843; but before proceeding to the matters which it contains, I will insert portions of my letters from 1841 to 1843, addressed to Catholic acquaintances.

1. "April 8, 1841. . . . The unity of the Church Catholic is very near my heart, only I do not see any prospect of it in our time; and I despair of its being effected without great sacrifices on all hands. As to resisting the Bishop's will, I observe that no point of doctrine or principle was in dispute, but a course of action, the publication of certain works. I do not think you sufficiently understood our position. I suppose you would obey the Holy See in such a case; now, when we were separated from the Pope, his authority reverted to our Diocesans. Our Bishop is our Pope. It is our theory, that each diocese is an integral Church, intercommunion being a duty, (and the breach of it a sin,) but not essential to Catholicity. To have resisted my Bishop, would have been to place myself in an utterly false position, which I never could have recovered. Depend upon it, the strength of any party lies in its being *true to its theory*. Consistency is the life of a movement.

"I have no misgivings whatever that the line I have taken can be other than a prosperous one: that is, in itself, for of course Providence may refuse to us its legitimate issues for our sins.

"I am afraid, that in one respect you may be disappointed. It is my trust, though I must not be

[22] George Stanley Faber (1773–1854), author of *Letters on Tractarian Secessions to Popery* (1846).
[23] Directly, straight out.

too sanguine, that we shall not have individual members of our communion going over to yours. What one's duty would be under other circumstances, what our duty ten or twenty years ago, I cannot say; but I do think that there is less of private judgment in going with one's Church, than in leaving it. I can earnestly desire a union between my Church and yours. I cannot listen to the thought of your being joined by individuals among us."

2. "April 26, 1841. My only anxiety is lest your branch of the Church should not meet us by those reforms which surely are *necessary*. It never could be, that so large a portion of Christendom should have split off from the communion of Rome, and kept up a protest for 300 years for nothing. I think I never shall believe that so much piety and earnestness would be found among Protestants, if there were not some very grave errors on the side of Rome. To suppose the contrary is most unreal, and violates all one's notions of moral probabilities. All aberrations are founded on, and have their life in, some truth or other—and Protestantism, so widely spread and so long enduring, must have in it, and must be witness for, a great truth or much truth. That I am an advocate for Protestantism, you cannot suppose;—but I am forced into a *Via Media,* short of Rome, as it is at present."

3. "May 5, 1841. While I most sincerely hold that there is in the Roman Church a traditionary system which is not necessarily connected with her essential formularies, yet, were I ever so much to change my mind on this point, this would not tend to bring me from my present position, providentially appointed in the English Church. That your communion was unassailable, would not prove that mine was indefensible. Nor would it at all affect the sense in which I receive our Articles; they would still speak against certain definite errors, though you had reformed them.

"I say this lest any lurking suspicion should be left in the mind of your friends that persons who think with me are likely, by the growth of their present views, to find it imperative on them to pass over to your communion. Allow me to state strongly, that if you have any such thoughts, and proceed to act upon them, your friends will be committing a fatal mistake. We have (I trust) the principle and temper of obedience too intimately wrought into us to allow of our separating ourselves from our ecclesiastical superiors because in many points we may sympathize with others. We have too great a horror of the principle of private judgment to trust it in so immense a

matter as that of changing from one communion to another. We may be cast out of our communion, or it may decree heresy to be truth,—you shall say whether such contingencies are likely; but I do not see other conceivable causes of our leaving the Church in which we were baptized.

"For myself, persons must be well acquainted with what I have written before they venture to say whether I have much changed my main opinions and cardinal views in the course of the last eight years. That my *sympathies* have grown towards the religion of Rome I do not deny; that my *reasons* for *shunning* her communion have lessened or altered it would be difficult perhaps to prove. And I wish to go by reason, not by feeling."

4. "June 18, 1841. You urge persons whose views agree with mine to commence a movement in behalf of a union between the Churches. Now in the letters I have written, I have uniformly said that I did not expect that union in our time, and have discouraged the notion of all sudden proceedings with a view to it. I must ask your leave to repeat on this occasion most distinctly, that I cannot be party to any agitation, but mean to remain quiet in my own place, and to do all I can to make others take the same course. This I conceive to be my simple duty; but, over and above this, I will not set my teeth on edge with sour grapes. I know it is quite within the range of possibilities that one or another of our people should go over to your communion; however, it would be a greater misfortune to you than grief to us. If your friends wish to put a gulf between themselves and us, let them make converts, but not else. Some months ago, I ventured to say that I felt it a painful duty to keep aloof from all Roman Catholics who came with the intention of opening negotiations for the union of the Churches: when you now urge us to petition our Bishops for a union, this, I conceive, is very like an act of negotiation."

5. I have the first sketch or draft of a letter, which I wrote to a zealous Catholic layman: it runs as follows, as far as I have preserved it, but I think there were various changes and additions:—"September 12, 1841. It would rejoice all Catholic minds among us, more than words can say, if you could persuade members of the Church of Rome to take the line in politics which you so earnestly advocate. Suspicion and distrust are the main causes at present of the separation between us, and the nearest approaches in doctrine will but increase the hostility, which,

alas, our people feel towards yours, while these causes continue. Depend upon it, you must not rely upon our Catholic tendencies till they are removed. I am not speaking of myself, or of any friends of mine; but of our Church generally. Whatever *our* personal feelings may be, we shall but tend to raise and spread a *rival* Church to yours in the four quarters of the world, unless *you* do what none but you *can* do. Sympathies, which would flow over to the Church of Rome, as a matter of course, did she admit them, will but be developed in the consolidation of our own system, if she continues to be the object of our suspicions and fears. I wish, of course I do, that our own Church may be built up and extended, but still, not at the cost of the Church of Rome, not in opposition to it. I am sure, that, while you suffer, we suffer too from the separation; *but we cannot remove the obstacles*; it is with you to do so. You do not fear us; we fear you. Till we cease to fear you, we cannot love you.

"While you are in your present position, the friends of Catholic unity in our Church are but fulfilling the prediction of those of your body who are averse to them, viz. that they will be merely strengthening a rival communion to yours. Many of you say that *we* are your greatest enemies; we have said so ourselves: so we are, so we shall be, as things stand at present. We are keeping people from you, by supplying their wants in our own Church. We *are* keeping persons from you: do you wish us to keep them from you for a time or for ever? It rests with you to determine. I do not fear that you will succeed among us; you will not supplant our Church in the affections of the English nation; only through the English Church can you act upon the English nation. I wish of course our Church should be consolidated, with and through and in your communion, for its sake, and your sake, and for the sake of unity.

"Are you aware that the more serious thinkers among us are used, as far as they dare form an opinion, to regard the spirit of Liberalism as the characteristic of the destined Antichrist? In vain does any one clear the Church of Rome from the badges of Antichrist, in which Protestants would invest her, if she deliberately takes up her position in the very quarter, whither we have cast them, when we took them off from her. Antichrist is described as the ανομος,[24] as exalting himself above the yoke of religion and law. The spirit of lawlessness came in with the Reformation, and Liberalism is its offspring.

[24] The lawless one.

"And now I fear I am going to pain you by telling you, that you consider the approaches in doctrine on our part towards you, closer than they really are. I cannot help repeating what I have many times said in print, that your services and devotions to St. Mary in matter of fact do most deeply pain me. I am only stating it as a fact.

"Again, I have nowhere said that I cannot accept the decrees of Trent throughout, nor implied it. The doctrine of Transubstantiation is a great difficulty with me, as being, as I think, not primitive. Nor have I said that our Articles in all respects admit of a Roman interpretation; the very word 'Transubstantiation' is disowned in them.

"Thus, you see, it is not merely on grounds of expedience that we do not join you. There are positive difficulties in the way of it. And, even if there were not, we shall have no divine warrant for doing so, while we think that the Church of England is a branch of the true Church, and that intercommunion with the rest of Christendom is necessary, not for the life of a particular Church, but for its health only. I have never disguised that there are actual circumstances in the Church of Rome, which pain me much; of the removal of these I see no chance, while we join you one by one; but if our Church were prepared for a union, she might make her terms; she might gain the cup; she might protest against the extreme honours paid to St. Mary; she might make some explanation of the doctrine of Transubstantiation. I am not prepared to say that a reform in other branches of the Roman Church would be necessary for our uniting with them, however desirable in itself, so that we were allowed to make a reform in our own country. We do not look towards Rome as believing that its communion is infallible, but that union is a duty."

6. The following letter was occasioned by the present made to me of a book by the friend to whom it is written; more will be said on the subject of it presently:—

"Nov. 22, 1842. I only wish that your Church were more known among us by such writings. You will not interest us in her, till we see her, not in politics, but in her true functions of exhorting, teaching, and guiding. I wish there were a chance of making the leading men among you understand, what I believe is no novel thought to yourself. It is not by learned discussions, or acute arguments, or reports of miracles, that the heart of England can be gained. It is by men 'approving themselves,' like the Apostle, 'ministers of Christ.'

"As to your question, whether the Volume you have sent is not calculated to remove my apprehensions that another gospel is substituted for the true one in your practical instructions, before I can answer it in any way, I ought to know how far the Sermons which it comprises are *selected* from a number, or whether they are the whole, or such as the whole, which have been published of the author's. I assure you, or at least I trust, that, if it is ever clearly brought home to me that I have been wrong in what I have said on this subject, my public avowal of that conviction will only be a question of time with me.

"If, however, you saw our Church as we see it, you would easily understand that such a change of feeling, did it take place, would have no necessary tendency, which you seem to expect, to draw a person from the Church of England to that of Rome. There is a divine life among us, clearly manifested, in spite of all our disorders, which is as great a note of the Church, as any can be. Why should we seek our Lord's presence elsewhere, when He vouchsafes it to us where we are? What *call* have we to change our communion?

"Roman Catholics will find this to be the state of things in time to come, whatever promise they may fancy there is of a large secession to their Church. This man or that may leave us, but there will be no general movement. There is, indeed, an incipient movement of our *Church* towards yours, and this your leading men are doing all they can to frustrate by their unwearied efforts at all risks to carry off individuals. When will they know their position, and embrace a larger and wiser policy?"

2

The letter which I have last inserted, is addressed to my dear friend, Dr. Russell, the present President of Maynooth.[25] He had, perhaps, more to do with my conversion than any one else. He called upon me, in passing through Oxford in the summer of 1841, and I think I took him over some of the buildings of the University. He called again another summer, on his way from Dublin to London. I do not recollect that he said a word on the subject of religion on either occasion. He sent me at different times several

letters; he was always gentle, mild, unobtrusive, uncontroversial. He let me alone. He also gave me one or two books. Veron's Rule of Faith and some Treatises of the Wallenburghs was one; a volume of St. Alfonso Liguori's Sermons was another; and it is to those Sermons that my letter to Dr. Russell relates.

Now it must be observed that the writings of St. Alfonso, as I knew them by the extracts commonly made from them, prejudiced me as much against the Roman Church as any thing else, on account of what was called their "Mariolatry;" but there was nothing of the kind in this book. I wrote to ask Dr. Russell whether any thing had been left out of the translation; he answered that there certainly were omissions in one Sermon about the Blessed Virgin. This omission, in the case of a book intended for Catholics, at least showed that such passages as are found in the works of Italian Authors were not acceptable to every part of the Catholic world. Such devotional manifestations in honour of our Lady had been my great *crux* as regards Catholicism; I say frankly, I do not fully enter into them now; I trust I do not love her the less, because I cannot enter into them. They may be fully explained and defended; but sentiment and taste do not run with logic: they are suitable for Italy, but they are not suitable for England. But, over and above England, my own case was special; from a boy I had been led to consider that my Maker and I, His creature, were the two beings, luminously such, *in rerum naturâ*.[26] I will not here speculate, however, about my own feelings. Only this I know full well now, and did not know then, that the Catholic Church allows no image of any sort, material or immaterial, no dogmatic symbol, no rite, no sacrament, no Saint, not even the Blessed Virgin herself, to come between the soul and its Creator. It is face to face, "solus cum solo," in all matters between man and his God. He alone creates; He alone has redeemed; before His awful eyes we go in death; in the vision of Him is our eternal beatitude.

1. Solus cum solo:—I recollect but indistinctly what I gained from the Volume of which I have been speaking; but it must have been something considerable. At least I had got a key to a difficulty; in these Sermons, (or rather heads of sermons, as they seem to be, taken down by a hearer,) there is much of what would be called legendary illustration; but the substance of them

---

[25] Charles William Russell (1812–80); Maynooth, a Catholic seminary in Ireland.
[26] In the nature of things.

is plain, practical, awful preaching upon the great truths of salvation. What I can speak of with greater confidence is the effect produced on me a little later by studying the Exercises of St. Ignatius.[27] For here again, in a matter consisting in the purest and most direct acts of religion,— in the intercourse between God and the soul, during a season of recollection, of repentance, of good resolution, of inquiry into vocation,—the soul was "sola cum solo;" there was no cloud interposed between the creature and the Object of his faith and love. The command practically enforced was, "My son, give Me thy heart." The devotions then to Angels and Saints as little interfered with the incommunicable glory of the Eternal, as the love which we bear our friends and relations, our tender human sympathies, are inconsistent with that supreme homage of the heart to the Unseen, which really does but sanctify and exalt, not jealously destroy, what is of earth. At a later date Dr. Russell sent me a large bundle of penny or half-penny books of devotion, of all sorts, as they are found in the booksellers' shops at Rome; and, on looking them over, I was quite astonished to find how different they were from what I had fancied, how little there was in them to which I could really object. I have given an account of them in my Essay on the Development of Doctrine. Dr. Russell sent me St. Alfonso's book at the end of 1842; however, it was still a long time before I got over my difficulty, on the score of the devotions paid to the Saints; perhaps, as I judge from a letter I have turned up, it was some way into 1844 before I could be said fully to have got over it.

2. I am not sure that I did not also at this time feel the force of another consideration. The idea of the Blessed Virgin was as it were *magnified* in the Church of Rome, as time went on,—but so were all the Christian ideas; as that of the Blessed Eucharist. The whole scene of pale, faint, distant Apostolic Christianity is seen in Rome, as through a telescope or magnifier. The harmony of the whole, however, is of course what it was. It is unfair then to take one Roman idea, that of the Blessed Virgin, out of what may be called its context.

3. Thus I am brought to the principle of development of doctrine in the Christian Church, to which I gave my mind at the end of 1842. I had made mention of it in the passage, which I quoted many pages back (vide p. 372), in "Home Thoughts Abroad," published in 1836; and even at an earlier date I had introduced it into my History of the Arians in 1832; nor had I ever lost sight of it in my speculations. And it is certainly recognized in the Treatise of Vincent of Lerins, which has so often been taken as the basis of Anglicanism. In 1843 I began to consider it attentively; I made it the subject of my last University Sermon on February 2; and the general view to which I came is stated thus in a letter to a friend of the date of July 14, 1844;— it will be observed that, now as before, my *issue* is still Creed *versus* Church:—

"The kind of considerations which weighs with me are such as the following:—1. I am far more certain (according to the Fathers) that we *are* in a state of culpable separation, *than* that developments do *not* exist under the Gospel, and that the Roman developments are not the true ones. 2. I am far more certain, that *our* (modern) doctrines are wrong, *than* that the *Roman* (modern) doctrines are wrong. 3. Granting that the Roman (special) doctrines are not found drawn out in the early Church, yet I think there is sufficient trace of them in it, to recommend and prove them, *on the hypothesis* of the Church having a divine guidance, though not sufficient to prove them by itself. So that the question simply turns on the nature of the promise of the Spirit, made to the Church. 4. The proof of the Roman (modern) doctrine is as strong (or stronger) in Antiquity, as that of certain doctrines which both we and Romans hold: e.g. there is more of evidence in Antiquity for the necessity of Unity, than for the Apostolical Succession; for the Supremacy of the See of Rome, than for the Presence in the Eucharist; for the practice of Invocation, than for certain books in the present Canon of Scripture, &c. &c. 5. The analogy of the Old Testament, and also of the New, leads to the acknowledgment of doctrinal developments."

4. And thus I was led on to a further consideration. I saw that the principle of development not only accounted for certain facts, but was in itself a remarkable philosophical phenomenon, giving a character to the whole course of Christian thought. It was discernible from the first years of the Catholic teaching up to the present day, and gave to that teaching a unity and individuality. It served as a sort of test, which the Anglican could not exhibit, that modern Rome was in truth ancient Antioch, Alexandria, and Constantinople, just as a mathematical curve has its own law and expression.

---

[27] St. Ignatius Loyola (1491–1556), author of the *Spiritual Exercises* and founder of the Jesuit order.

5. And thus again I was led on to examine more attentively what I doubt not was in my thoughts long before, viz. the concatenation of argument by which the mind ascends from its first to its final religious idea; and I came to the conclusion that there was no medium, in true philosophy, between Atheism and Catholicity, and that a perfectly consistent mind, under those circumstances in which it finds itself here below, must embrace either the one or the other. And I hold this still: I am a Catholic by virtue of my believing in God; and if I am asked why I believe in God, I answer that it is because I believe in myself, for I feel it impossible to believe in my own existence (and of that fact I am quite sure) without believing also in the existence of Him, who lives as a Personal, All-seeing, All-judging Being in my conscience. Now, I dare say, I have not expressed myself with philosophical correctness, because I have not given myself to the study of what metaphysicians have said on the subject, but I think I have a strong true meaning in what I say which will stand examination.

6. Moreover, I found a corroboration of the fact of the logical connexion of Theism with Catholicism in a consideration parallel to that which I had adopted on the subject of development of doctrine. The fact of the operation from first to last of that principle of development in the truths of Revelation, is an argument in favour of the identity of Roman and Primitive Christianity; but as there is a law which acts upon the subject-matter of dogmatic theology, so is there a law in the matter of religious faith. In the first chapter of this Narrative I spoke of certitude as the consequence, divinely intended and enjoined upon us, of the accumulative force of certain given reasons which, taken one by one, were only probabilities. Let it be recollected that I am historically relating my state of mind, at the period of my life which I am surveying. I am not speaking theologically, nor have I any intention of going into controversy, or of defending myself; but speaking historically of what I held in 1843-4, I say, that I believed in a God on a ground of probability, that I believed in Christianity on a probability, and that I believed in Catholicism on a probability, and that these three grounds of probability, distinct from each other of course in subject matter, were still all of them one and the same in nature of proof, as being probabilities—probabilities of a special kind, a cumulative, a transcendent probability but still probability; inasmuch as He who made us has so willed, that in mathematics indeed we should arrive at certitude by rigid demonstration, but in religious inquiry we should arrive at certitude by accumulated probabilities;—He has willed, I say, that we should so act, and, as willing it, He co-operates with us in our acting, and thereby enables us to do that which He wills us to do, and carries us on, if our will does but co-operate with His, to a certitude which rises higher than the logical force of our conclusions. And thus I came to see clearly, and to have a satisfaction in seeing, that, in being led on into the Church of Rome, I was not proceeding on any secondary or isolated grounds of reason, or by controversial points in detail, but was protected and justified, even in the use of those secondary or particular arguments, by a great and broad principle. But, let it be observed, that I am stating a matter of fact, not defending it; and if any Catholic says in consequence that I have been converted in a wrong way, I cannot help that now.

I have nothing more to say on the subject of the change in my religious opinions. On the one hand I came gradually to see that the Anglican Church was formally in the wrong, on the other that the Church of Rome was formally in the right; then, that no valid reasons could be assigned for continuing in the Anglican, and again that no valid objections could be taken to joining the Roman. Then, I had nothing more to learn; what still remained for my conversion, was, not further change of opinion, but to change opinion itself into the clearness and firmness of intellectual conviction.

Now I proceed to detail the acts, to which I committed myself during this last stage of my inquiry.

In 1843, I took two very significant steps:—1. In February, I made a formal Retractation of all the hard things which I had said against the Church of Rome. 2. In September, I resigned the Living of St. Mary's, Littlemore included:—I will speak of these two acts separately.

1. The words, in which I made my Retractation, have given rise to much criticism. After quoting a number of passages from my writings against the Church of Rome, which I withdrew, I ended thus:—"If you ask me how an individual could venture, not simply to hold, but to publish such views of a communion so ancient, so widespreading, so fruitful in Saints, I answer that I said to myself, 'I am not speaking my own words, I am but following almost a *consensus* of the divines of my own Church. They have ever used the strongest language against Rome, even

the most able and learned of them. I wish to throw myself into their system. While I say what they say, I am safe. Such views, too, are necessary for our position.' Yet I have reason to fear still, that such language is to be ascribed, in no small measure, to an impetuous temper, a hope of approving myself to persons I respect, and a wish to repel the charge of Romanism."

These words have been, and are, again and again cited against me, as if a confession that, when in the Anglican Church, I said things against Rome which I did not really believe.

For myself, I cannot understand how any impartial man can so take them; and I have explained them in print several times. I trust that by this time their plain meaning has been satisfactorily brought out by what I have said in former portions of this Narrative; still I have a word or two to say in addition to my former remarks upon them.

In the passage in question I apologize for *saying out* in controversy charges against the Church of Rome, which withal I affirm that I fully *believed* at the time when I made them. What is wonderful in such an apology? There are surely many things a man may hold, which at the same time he may feel that he has no right to say publicly, and which it may annoy him that he has said publicly. The law recognizes this principle. In our own time, men have been imprisoned and fined for saying true things of a bad king. The maxim has been held, that, "The greater the truth, the greater is the libel." And so as to the judgment of society, a just indignation would be felt against a writer who brought forward wantonly the weaknesses of a great man, though the whole world knew that they existed. No one is at liberty to speak ill of another without a justifiable reason, even though he knows he is speaking truth, and the public knows it too. Therefore, though I believed what I said against the Roman Church, nevertheless I could not religiously speak it out, unless I was really justified, not only in believing ill, but in speaking ill. I did believe what I said on what I thought to be good reasons; but had I also a just cause for saying out what I believed? I thought I had, and it was this, viz. that to say out what I believed was simply necessary in the controversy for self-defence. It was impossible to let it alone: the Anglican position could not be satisfactorily maintained, without assailing the Roman. In this, as in most cases of conflict, one party was right or the other, not both; and the best defence was to attack. Is not this almost a truism in the

Roman controversy? Is it not what every one says, who speaks on the subject at all? does any serious man abuse the Church of Rome, for the sake of abusing her, or because that abuse justifies his own religious position? What is the meaning of the very word "Protestantism," but that there is a call to speak out? This then is what I said; "I know I spoke strongly against the Church of Rome; but it was no mere abuse, for I had a serious reason for doing so."

But, not only did I think such language necessary for my Church's religious position, but I recollected that all the great Anglican divines had thought so before me. They had thought so, and they had acted accordingly. And therefore I observe in the passage in question, with much propriety, that I had not used strong language simply out of my own head, but that in doing so I was following the track, or rather reproducing the teaching, of those who had preceded me.

I was pleading guilty to using violent language, but I was pleading also that there were extenuating circumstances in the case. We all know the story of the convict, who on the scaffold bit off his mother's ear. By doing so he did not deny the fact of his own crime, for which he was to hang; but he said that his mother's indulgence when he was a boy, had a good deal to do with it. In like manner I had made a charge, and I had made it *ex animo*; but I accused others of having, by their own example, led me into believing it and publishing it.

I was in a humour, certainly, to bite off their ears. I will freely confess, indeed I said it some pages back, that I was angry with the Anglican divines. I thought they had taken me in; I had read the Fathers with their eyes; I had sometimes trusted their quotations or their reasonings; and from reliance on them, I had used words or statements, which by right I ought rigidly to have examined myself. I had thought myself safe, while I had their warrant for what I said. I had exercised more faith than criticism in the matter. This did not imply any broad misstatements on my part, arising from reliance on their authority, but it implied carelessness in matters of detail, and this of course was a fault.

But there was a far deeper reason for my saying what I said in this matter, on which I have not hitherto touched; and it was this:—The most oppressive thought, in the whole process of my change of opinion, was the clear anticipation, verified by the event, that it would issue in the triumph of Liberalism. Against the Anti-dogmatic principle I had thrown my whole mind; yet now

I was doing more than any one else could do, to promote it. I was one of those who had kept it at bay in Oxford for so many years; and thus my very retirement was its triumph. The men who had driven me from Oxford were distinctly the Liberals; it was they who had opened the attack upon Tract 90, and it was they who would gain a second benefit if I went on to abandon the Anglican Church. But this was not all. As I have already said, there are but two alternatives, the way to Rome, and the way to Atheism: Anglicanism is the halfway house on the one side, and Liberalism is the halfway house on the other. How many men were there, as I knew full well, who would not follow me now in my advance from Anglicanism to Rome, but would at once leave Anglicanism and me for the Liberal camp. It is not at all easy (humbly speaking) to wind up an Englishman to a dogmatic level. I had done so in good measure, in the case both of young men and of laymen, the Anglican *Via Media* being the representative of dogma. The dogmatic and the Anglican principle were one, as I had taught them; but I was breaking the *Via Media* to pieces, and would not dogmatic faith altogether be broken up, in the minds of a great number, by the demolition of the *Via Media?* Oh! how unhappy this made me! I heard once from an eye-witness the account of a poor sailor whose legs were shattered by a ball, in the action off Algiers in 1816, and who was taken below for an operation. The surgeon and the chaplain persuaded him to have a leg off; it was done and the tourniquet applied to the wound. Then, they broke it to him that he must have the other off too. The poor fellow said, "You should have told me that, gentlemen," and deliberately unscrewed the instrument and bled to death. Would not that be the case with many friends of my own? How could I ever hope to make them believe in a second theology, when I had cheated them in the first? with what face could I publish a new edition of a dogmatic creed, and ask them to receive it as gospel? Would it not be plain to them that no certainty was to be found any where? Well, in my defence I could but make a lame apology; however, it was the true one, viz. that I had not read the Fathers cautiously enough; that in such nice points, as those which determine the angle of divergence between the two Churches, I had made considerable miscalculations. But how came this about? why, the fact was, unpleasant

as it was to avow, that I had leaned too much upon the assertions of Ussher, Jeremy Taylor, or Barrow, and had been deceived by them. Valeat quantum,[28]—it was all that *could* be said. This then was a chief reason of that wording of the Retractation, which has given so much offence, because the bitterness, with which it was written, was not understood;—and the following letter will illustrate it:—

"April 3, 1844. I wish to remark on William's[29] chief distress, that my changing my opinion seemed to unsettle one's confidence in truth and falsehood as external things, and led one to be suspicious of the new opinion as one became distrustful of the old. Now in what I shall say, I am not going to speak in favour of my second thoughts in comparison of my first, but against such scepticism and unsettlement about truth and falsehood generally, the idea of which is very painful.

"The case with me, then, was this, and not surely an unnatural one:—as a matter of feeling and of duty I threw myself into the system which I found myself in. I saw that the English Church had a theological idea or theory as such, and I took it up. I read Laud on Tradition, and thought it (as I still think it) very masterly. The Anglican Theory was very distinctive. I admired it and took it on faith. It did not (I think) occur to me to doubt it; I saw that it was able, and supported by learning, and I felt it was a duty to maintain it. Further, on looking into Antiquity and reading the Fathers, I saw such portions of it as I examined, fully confirmed (e.g. the supremacy of Scripture). There was only one question about which I had a doubt, viz. whether it would *work,* for it has never been more than a paper system. . . .

"So far from my change of opinion having any fair tendency to unsettle persons as to truth and falsehood viewed as objective realities, it should be considered whether such change is not *necessary,* if truth be a real objective thing, and be made to confront a person who has been brought up in a system *short* of truth. Surely the *continuance* of a person, who wishes to go right, in a wrong system, and not his *giving it up,* would be that which militated against the objectiveness of Truth, leading, as it would, to the suspicion, that one thing and another were equally pleasing to our Maker, where men were sincere.

"Nor surely is it a thing I need be sorry for,

----

[28] Whatever it may be worth.
[29] William Froude (1810–79), brother of Richard Hurrell Froude.

that I defended the system in which I found myself, and thus have had to unsay my words. For is it not one's duty, instead of beginning with criticism, to throw oneself generously into that form of religion which is providentially put before one? Is it right, or is it wrong, to begin with private judgment? May we not, on the other hand, look for a blessing *through* obedience even to an erroneous system, and a guidance even by means of it out of it? Were those who were strict and conscientious in their Judaism, or those who were lukewarm and sceptical, more likely to be led into Christianity, when Christ came? Yet in proportion to their previous zeal, would be their appearance of inconsistency. Certainly, I have always contended that obedience even to an erring conscience was the way to gain light, and that it mattered not where a man began, so that he began on what came to hand, and in faith; and that any thing might become a divine method of Truth; that to the pure all things are pure, and have a self-correcting virtue and a power of germinating. And though I have no right at all to assume that this mercy is granted to me, yet the fact, that a person in my situation *may* have it granted to him, seems to me to remove the perplexity which my change of opinion may occasion.

"It may be said,—I have said it to myself,— 'Why, however, did you *publish?* had you waited quietly, you would have changed your opinion without any of the misery, which now is involved in the change, of disappointing and distressing people.' I answer, that things are so bound up together, as to form a whole, and one cannot tell what is or is not a condition of what. I do not see how possibly I could have published the Tracts, or other works professing to defend our Church, without accompanying them with a strong protest or argument against Rome. The one obvious objection against the whole Anglican line is, that it is Roman; so that I really think there was no alternative between silence altogether, and forming a theory and attacking the Roman system."

2. And now, in the next place, as to my Resignation of St. Mary's, which was the second of the steps which I took in 1843. The ostensible, direct, and sufficient reason for my doing so was the persevering attack of the Bishops on Tract 90. I alluded to it in the letter which I have inserted above, addressed to one of the most influential among them. A series of their *ex cathedrâ* judg-

ments, lasting through three years, and including a notice of no little severity in a Charge of my own Bishop, came as near to a condemnation of my Tract, and, so far, to a repudiation of the ancient Catholic doctrine, which was the scope of the Tract, as was possible in the Church of England. It was in order to shield the Tract from such a condemnation, that I had at the time of its publication in 1841 so simply put myself at the disposal of the higher powers in London. At that time, all that was distinctly contemplated in the way of censure, was contained in the message which my Bishop sent me, that the Tract was "objectionable." That I thought was the end of the matter. I had refused to suppress it, and they had yielded that point. Since I published the former portions of this Narrative, I have found what I wrote to Dr. Pusey on March 24, while the matter was in progress. "The more I think of it," I said, "the more reluctant I am to suppress Tract 90, though *of course* I will do it if the Bishop wishes it; I cannot, however, deny that I shall feel it a severe act." According to the notes which I took of the letters or messages which I sent to him on that and the following days, I wrote successively, "My first feeling was to obey without a word; I will obey still; but my judgment has steadily risen against it ever since." Then in the Postscript, "If I have done any good to the Church, I do ask the Bishop this favour, as my reward for it, that he would not insist on a measure, from which I think good will not come. However, I will submit to him." Afterwards, I got stronger still and wrote: "I have almost come to the resolution, if the Bishop publicly intimates that I must suppress the Tract, or speaks strongly in his charge against it, to suppress it indeed, but to resign my living also. I could not in conscience act otherwise. You may show this in any quarter you please."

All my then hopes, all my satisfaction at the apparent fulfilment of those hopes was at an end in 1843. It is not wonderful then, that in May of that year, when two out of the three years were gone, I wrote on the subject of my retiring from St. Mary's to the same friend,[30] whom I had consulted upon it in 1840. But I did more now; I told him my great unsettlement of mind on the question of the Churches. I will insert portions of two of my letters:—

"May 4, 1843. . . . At present I fear, as far as I can analyze my own convictions, I consider the Roman Catholic Communion to be the Church

---

[30] I.e., John Keble.

of the Apostles, and that what grace is among us (which, through God's mercy, is not little) is extraordinary, and from the overflowings of His dispensation. I am very far more sure that England is in schism, than that the Roman additions to the Primitive Creed may not be developments, arising out of a keen and vivid realizing of the Divine Depositum of Faith.

"You will now understand what gives edge to the Bishops' Charges, without any undue sensitiveness on my part. They distress me in two ways:—first, as being in some sense protests and witnesses to my conscience against my own unfaithfulness to the English Church, and next, as being samples of her teaching, and tokens how very far she is from even aspiring to Catholicity.

"Of course my being unfaithful to a trust is my great subject of dread,—as it has long been, as you know."

When he wrote to make natural objections to my purpose, such as the apprehension that the removal of clerical obligations might have the indirect effect of propelling me towards Rome, I answered:—

"May 18, 1843. . . . My office or charge at St. Mary's is not a mere *state,* but a continual *energy.* People assume and assert certain things of me in consequence. With what sort of sincerity can I obey the Bishop? how am I to act in the frequent cases, in which one way or another the Church of Rome comes into consideration? I have to the utmost of my power tried to keep persons from Rome, and with some success; but even a year and a half since, my arguments, though more efficacious with the persons I aimed at than any others could be, were of a nature to infuse great suspicion of me into the minds of lookers-on.

"By retaining St. Mary's, I am an offence and a stumbling-block. Persons are keen-sighted enough to make out what I think on certain points, and then they infer that such opinions are compatible with holding situations of trust in our Church. A number of younger men take the validity of their interpretation of the Articles, &c. from me on *faith.* Is not my present position a cruelty, as well as a treachery towards the Church?

"I do not see how I can either preach or publish again, while I hold St. Mary's;—but consider again the following difficulty in such a resolution, which I must state at some length.

"Last Long Vacation the idea suggested itself to me of publishing the Lives of the English Saints; and I had a conversation with [a publisher] upon it. I thought it would be useful, as employing the minds of men who were in danger of running wild, bringing them from doctrine to history, and from speculation to fact;—again, as giving them an interest in the English soil, and the English Church, and keeping them from seeking sympathy in Rome, as she is; and further, as tending to promote the spread of right views.

"But, within the last month, it has come upon me, that, if the scheme goes on, it will be a practical carrying out of No. 90, from the character of the usages and opinions of ante-reformation times.

"It is easy to say, 'Why *will* you do *any* thing? why won't you keep quiet? what business had you to think of any such plan at all?' But I cannot leave a number of poor fellows in the lurch. I am bound to do my best for a great number of people both in Oxford and elsewhere. If *I* did not act, others would find means to do so.

"Well, the plan has been taken up with great eagerness and interest. Many men are setting to work. I set down the names of men, most of them engaged, the rest half engaged and probable, some actually writing." About thirty names follow, some of them at that time of the school of Dr. Arnold, others of Dr. Pusey's, some my personal friends and of my own standing, others whom I hardly knew, while of course the majority were of the party of the new Movement. I continue:—

"The plan has gone so far, that it would create surprise and talk, were it now suddenly given over. Yet how is it compatible with my holding St. Mary's, being what I am?"

Such was the object and the origin of the projected Series of the English Saints; and, since the publication was connected, as has been seen, with my resignation of St. Mary's, I may be allowed to conclude what I have to say on the subject here, though it may read like a digression. As soon then as the first of the Series got into print, the whole project broke down. I had already anticipated that some portions of the Series would be written in a style inconsistent with the professions of a beneficed clergyman, and therefore I had given up my Living; but men of great weight went further in their misgivings than I, when they saw the Life of St. Stephen Harding, and decided that it was of a character inconsistent even with its proceeding from an Anglican publisher: and so the scheme was given up at once. After the two first numbers, I retired from the Editorship, and those Lives only were published in addition, which were then already finished, or in advanced preparation. The following passages from what I or others wrote at the time will illustrate what I have been saying:—

In November, 1844, I wrote thus to the author of one of them: "I am not Editor, I have no direct control over the Series. It is T.'s work; he may admit what he pleases; and exclude what he pleases. I was to have been Editor. I did edit the two first numbers. I was responsible for them, in the way in which an Editor is responsible. Had I continued Editor, I should have exercised a control over all. I laid down in the Preface that doctrinal subjects were, if possible, to be excluded. But, even then, I also set down that no writer was to be held answerable for any of the Lives but his own. When I gave up the Editorship, I had various engagements with friends for separate Lives remaining on my hands. I should have liked to have broken from them all, but there were some from which I could not break, and I let them take their course. Some have come to nothing; others like yours have gone on. I have seen such, either in MS. or Proof. As time goes on, I shall have less and less to do with the Series. I think the engagement between you and me should come to an end. I have any how abundant responsibility on me, and too much. I shall write to T. that if he wants the advantage of your assistance, he must write to you direct."

In accordance with this letter, I had already advertised in January 1844, ten months before it, that "other Lives," after St. Stephen Harding, would "be published by their respective authors on their own responsibility." This notice was repeated in February, in the advertisement to the second number entitled "The Family of St. Richard," though to this number, for some reason which I cannot now recollect, I also put my initials. In the Life of St. Augustine, the author,[31] a man of nearly my own age, says in like manner, "No one but himself is responsible for the way in which these materials have been used." I have in MS. another advertisement to the same effect, but I cannot tell whether it ever appeared in print.

I will add, since the authors have been considered "hot headed fanatic young men," whom I was in charge of, and whom I suffered to do intemperate things, that, while the writer

of St. Augustine was in 1844 past forty, the author of the proposed Life of St. Boniface, Mr. Bowden, was forty-six; Mr. Johnson,[32] who was to write St. Aldhelm, forty-three; and most of the others were on one side or other of thirty. Three, I think, were under twenty-five. Moreover, of these writers some became Catholics, some remained Anglicans, and others have professed what are called free or liberal opinions.[33]

The immediate cause of the resignation of my Living is stated in the following letter, which I wrote to my Bishop:—

"August 29, 1843. It is with much concern that I inform your Lordship, that Mr. A. B.,[34] who has been for the last year an inmate of my house here, has just conformed to the Church of Rome. As I have ever been desirous, not only of faithfully discharging the trust, which is involved in holding a living in your Lordship's diocese, but of approving myself to your Lordship, I will for your information state one or two circumstances connected with this unfortunate event. . . . I received him on condition of his promising me, which he distinctly did, that he would remain quietly in our Church for three years. A year has passed since that time, and, though I saw nothing in him which promised that he would eventually be contented with his present position, yet for the time his mind became as settled as one could wish, and he frequently expressed his satisfaction at being under the promise which I had exacted of him."

I felt it impossible to remain any longer in the service of the Anglican Church, when such a breach of trust, however little I had to do with it, would be laid at my door. I wrote in a few days to a friend:

"September 7, 1843. I this day ask the Bishop leave to resign St. Mary's. Men whom you little think, or at least whom I little thought, are in almost a hopeless way. Really we may expect any thing. I am going to publish a Volume of Sermons, including those Four against moving."

I resigned my living on September the 18th. I had not the means of doing it legally at Oxford. The late Mr. Goldsmid was kind enough to aid me in resigning it in London. I found no fault with the Liberals; they had beaten me in a fair field. As to the act of the Bishops, I thought, to borrow a Scriptural image from Walter Scott,

---

[31] Frederick Oakeley.
[32] Manuel Johnson (1805–59), keeper of the Radcliffe Observatory at Oxford.
[33] Vide Note D, *Lives of the English Saints*. [Newman's note]
[34] Lockhart (see note 18 above).

that they had "seethed the kid in his mother's milk."[35]

I said to a friend:—

"Victrix causa diis placuit, sed victa Catoni."[36]

And now I may be almost said to have brought to an end, as far as is necessary for a sketch such as this is, the history both of my changes of religious opinion and of the public acts which they involved.

I had one final advance of mind to accomplish, and one final step to take. That further advance of mind was to be able honestly to say that I was *certain* of the conclusions at which I had already arrived. That further step, imperative when such certitude was attained, was my *submission* to the Catholic Church.

This submission did not take place till two full years after the resignation of my living in September 1843; nor could I have made it at an earlier day, without doubt and apprehension, that is, with any true conviction of mind or certitude.

In the interval, of which it remains to speak, viz. between the autumns of 1843 and 1845, I was in lay communion with the Church of England, attending its services as usual, and abstaining altogether from intercourse with Catholics, from their places of worship, and from those religious rites and usages, such as the Invocation of Saints, which are characteristics of their creed. I did all this on principle; for I never could understand how a man could be of two religions at once.

What I have to say about myself between these two autumns I shall almost confine to this one point,—the difficulty I was in, as to the best mode of revealing the state of my mind to my friends and others, and how I managed to reveal it.

Up to January, 1842, I had not disclosed my state of unsettlement to more than three persons,[37] as has been mentioned above, and as is repeated in the course of the letters which I am now about to give to the reader. To two of them, intimate and familiar companions, in the Autumn of 1839: to the third, an old friend too, whom I have also named above, I suppose, when I was in great distress of mind upon the affair of the Jerusalem Bishopric. In May, 1843, I made it known, as has been seen, to the friend[38] by whose advice I wished, as far as possible, to be guided.

To mention it on set purpose to any one, unless indeed I was asking advice, I should have felt to be a crime. If there is any thing that was abhorrent to me, it was the scattering doubts, and unsettling consciences without necessity. A strong presentiment that my existing opinions would ultimately give way, and that the grounds of them were unsound, was not a sufficient warrant for disclosing the state of my mind. I had no guarantee yet, that that presentiment would be realized. Supposing I were crossing ice, which came right in my way, which I had good reasons for considering sound, and which I saw numbers before me crossing in safety, and supposing a stranger from the bank, in a voice of authority, and in an earnest tone, warned me that it was dangerous, and then was silent, I think I should be startled, and should look about me anxiously, but I think too that I should go on, till I had better grounds for doubt; and such was my state, I believe, till the end of 1842. Then again, when my dissatisfaction became greater, it was hard at first to determine the point of time, when it was too strong to suppress with propriety. Certitude of course is a point, but doubt is a progress; I was not near certitude yet. Certitude is a reflex action; it is to know that one knows. Of that I believe I was not possessed, till close upon my reception into the Catholic Church. Again, a practical, effective doubt is a point too, but who can easily ascertain it for himself? Who can determine when it is, that the scales in the balance of opinion begin to turn, and what was a greater probability in behalf of a belief becomes a positive doubt against it?

In considering this question in its bearing upon my conduct in 1843, my own simple answer to my great difficulty had been, *Do* what your present state of opinion requires in the light of duty, and let that *doing* tell: speak by *acts*. This I had done; my first *act* of the year had been in February. After three months' deliberation I had published my retractation of the violent charges which I had made against Rome: I could not be wrong in doing so much as this; but I did no more at the time: I did not retract my Anglican teaching. My second *act* had been in September in the same year; after much sorrowful lingering and hesitation, I had resigned my Living. I tried indeed, before I did so, to keep Littlemore for myself, even though it was still to remain an

---

[35] Exodus 23:19.
[36] "The victorious cause pleased the gods, but the vanquished one pleased Cato" (Lucan's *Civil War*).
[37] Frederick Rogers and the Wilberforce brothers.
[38] Keble.

integral part of St. Mary's. I had given to it a Church and a sort of Parsonage; I had made it a Parish, and I loved it. I thought in 1843 that perhaps I need not forfeit my existing relations towards it. I could indeed submit to become the curate at will of another, but I hoped an arrangement was possible, by which, while I had the curacy, I might have been my own master in serving it. I had hoped an exception might have been made in my favour, under the circumstances; but I did not gain my request. Perhaps I was asking what was impracticable, and it is well for me that it was so.

These had been my two acts of the year, and I said, "I cannot be wrong in making them; let that follow which must follow in the thoughts of the world about me, when they see what I do." And, as time went on, they fully answered my purpose. What I felt it a simple duty to do, did create a general suspicion about me, without such responsibility as would be involved in my initiating any direct act for the sake of creating it. Then, when friends wrote me on the subject, I either did not deny or I confessed my state of mind, according to the character and need of their letters. Sometimes in the case of intimate friends, whom I should otherwise have been leaving in ignorance of what others knew on every side of them, I invited the question.

And here comes in another point for explanation. While I was fighting in Oxford for the Anglican Church, then indeed I was very glad to make converts, and, though I never broke away from that rule of my mind, (as I may call it,) of which I have already spoken, of finding disciples rather than seeking them, yet, that I made advances to others in a special way, I have no doubt; this came to an end, however, as soon as I fell into misgivings as to the true ground to be taken in the controversy. For then, when I gave up my place in the Movement, I ceased from any such proceedings: and my utmost endeavour was to tranquillize such persons, especially those who belonged to the new school, as were unsettled in their religious views, and, as I judged, hasty in their conclusions. This went on till 1843; but, at that date, as soon as I turned my face Romeward, I gave up, as far as ever was possible, the thought of in any respect and in any shape acting upon others. Then I myself was simply my own concern. How could I in any sense direct others, who had to be guided in so momentous a matter myself? How could I be considered in a position, even to

say a word to them one way or the other? How could I presume to unsettle them, as I was unsettled, when I had no means of bringing them out of such unsettlement? And, if they were unsettled already, how could I point to them a place of refuge, when I was not sure that I should choose it for myself? My only line, my only duty, was to keep simply to my own case. I recollected Pascal's words, "Je mourrai seul."[39] I deliberately put out of my thoughts all other works and claims, and said nothing to any one, unless I was obliged.

But this brought upon me a great trouble. In the newspapers there were continual reports about my intentions; I did not answer them; presently strangers or friends wrote, begging to be allowed to answer them; and, if I still kept to my resolution and said nothing, then I was thought to be mysterious, and a prejudice was excited against me. But, what was far worse, there were a number of tender, eager hearts, of whom I knew nothing at all, who were watching me, wishing to think as I thought, and to do as I did, if they could but find it out; who in consequence were distressed, that, in so solemn a matter, they could not see what was coming, and who heard reports about me this way or that, on a first day and on a second; and felt the weariness of waiting, and the sickness of delayed hope, and did not understand that I was as perplexed as they were, and, being of more sensitive complexion of mind than myself, were made ill by the suspense. And they too of course for the time thought me mysterious and inexplicable. I ask their pardon as far as I was really unkind to them. There was a gifted and deeply earnest lady, who in a parabolical account of that time, has described both my conduct as she felt it, and her own feelings upon it. In a singularly graphic, amusing vision of pilgrims, who were making their way across a bleak common in great discomfort, and who were ever warned against, yet continually nearing, "the king's highway" on the right, she says, "All my fears and disquiets were speedily renewed by seeing the most daring of our leaders, (the same who had first forced his way through the palisade, and in whose courage and sagacity we all put implicit trust,) suddenly stop short, and declare that he would go on no further. He did not, however, take the leap at once, but quietly sat down on the top of the fence with his feet hanging towards the road, as if he meant to take his time about it, and let himself down easily." I do not

[39] I shall die alone.

wonder at all that I thus seemed so unkind to a lady, who at that time had never seen me. We were both in trial in our different ways. I am far from denying that I was acting selfishly both in her case and in that of others; but it was a religious selfishness. Certainly to myself my own duty seemed clear. They that are whole can heal others; but in my case it was, "Physician, heal thyself." My own soul was my first concern, and it seemed an absurdity to my reason to be converted in partnership. I wished to go to my Lord by myself, and in my own way, or rather His way. I had neither wish, nor, I may say, thought of taking a number with me. Moreover, it is but the truth to say, that it had ever been an annoyance to me to seem to be the head of a party; and that even from fastidiousness of mind, I could not bear to find a thing done elsewhere, simply or mainly because I did it myself, and that, from distrust of myself, I shrank from the thought, whenever it was brought home to me, that I was influencing others. But nothing of this could be known to the world.

The following three letters are written to a friend, who had every claim upon me to be frank with him, Archdeacon Manning:[40]—it will be seen that I disclose the real state of my mind in proportion as he presses me.

1. "October 14, 1843. I would tell you in a few words why I have resigned St. Mary's, as you seem to wish, were it possible to do so. But it is most difficult to bring out in brief, or even *in extenso,* any just view of my feelings and reasons.

"The nearest approach I can give to a general account of them is to say, that it has been caused by the general repudiation of the view, contained in No. 90, on the part of the Church. I could not stand against such an unanimous expression of opinion from the Bishops, supported, as it has been, by the concurrence, or at least silence, of all classes in the Church, lay and clerical. If there ever was a case, in which an individual teacher has been put aside and virtually put away by a community, mine is one. No decency has been observed in the attacks upon me from authority; no protests have been offered against them. It is felt,—I am far from denying, justly felt,—that I am a foreign material, and cannot assimilate with the Church of England.

"Even my own Bishop has said that my mode of interpreting the Articles makes them mean *any thing or nothing.* When I heard this delivered, I did not believe my ears. I denied to others that it was said. . . . Out came the charge, and the words could not be mistaken. This astonished me the more, because I published that Letter to him, (how unwillingly you know,) on the understanding that *I* was to deliver his judgment on No. 90 *instead* of him. A year elapses, and a second and heavier judgment came forth. I did not bargain for this,—nor did he, but the tide was too strong for him.

"I fear that I must confess, that, in proportion as I think the English Church is showing herself intrinsically and radically alien from Catholic principles, so do I feel the difficulties of defending her claims to be a branch of the Catholic Church. It seems a dream to call a communion Catholic, when one can neither appeal to any clear statement of Catholic doctrine in its formularies, nor interpret ambiguous formularies by the received and living Catholic sense, whether past or present. Men of Catholic views are too truly but a party in our Church. I cannot deny that many other independent circumstances, which it is not worth while entering into, have led me to the same conclusion.

"I do not say all this to every body, as you may suppose; but I do not like to make a secret of it to you."

2. "Oct. 25, 1843. You have engaged in a dangerous correspondence; I am deeply sorry for the pain I shall give you.

"I must tell you then frankly, (but I combat arguments which to me, alas, are shadows,) that it is not from disappointment, irritation, or impatience, that I have, whether rightly or wrongly, resigned St. Mary's; but because I think the Church of Rome the Catholic Church, and ours not part of the Catholic Church, because not in communion with Rome; and because I feel that I could not honestly be a teacher in it any longer.

"This thought came to me last summer four years. . . . I mentioned it to two friends in the autumn. . . . It arose in the first instance from the Monophysite and Donatist controversies, the former of which I was engaged with in the course of theological study to which I had given myself. This was at a time when no Bishop, I believe, had declared against us,[41] and when all was progress

---

[40] Henry Edward Manning (1808–92), at the time Archdeacon of Chichester, later a Roman Catholic and the Cardinal Archbishop of Westminster.
[41] I think Sumner, Bishop of Chester, must have done so already. [Newman's note]

and hope. I do not think I have ever felt disappointment or impatience, certainly not then; for I never looked forward to the future, nor do I realize it now.

"My first effort was to write that article on the Catholicity of the English Church; for two years it quieted me. Since the summer of 1839 I have written little or nothing on modern controversy. . . . You know how unwillingly I wrote my letter to the Bishop in which I committed myself again, as the safest course under circumstances. The article I speak of quieted me till the end of 1841, over the affair of No. 90, when that wretched Jerusalem Bishopric (no personal matter) revived all my alarms. They have increased up to this moment. At that time I told my secret to another person in addition.

"You see then that the various ecclesiastical and quasi-ecclesiastical acts, which have taken place in the course of the last two years and a half, are not the *cause* of my state of opinion, but are keen stimulants and weighty confirmations of a conviction forced upon me, while engaged in the *course of duty,* viz. that theological reading to which I had given myself. And this last-mentioned circumstance is a fact, which has never, I think, come before me till now that I write to you.

"It is three years since, on account of my state of opinion, I urged the Provost in vain to let St. Mary's be separated from Littlemore; thinking I might with a safe conscience serve the latter, though I could not comfortably continue in so public a place as a University. This was before No. 90.

"Finally, I have acted under advice, and that, not of my own choosing but what came to me in the way of duty, nor the advice of those only who agree with me, but of near friends who differ from me.

"I have nothing to reproach myself with, as far as I see, in the matter of impatience; i.e. practically or in conduct. And I trust that He, who has kept me in the slow course of change hitherto, will keep me still from hasty acts, or resolves with a doubtful conscience.

"This I am sure of, that such interposition as yours, kind as it is, only does what *you* would consider harm. It makes me realize my own views to myself; it makes me see their consistency; it assures me of my own deliberateness; it suggests to me the traces of a Providential Hand; it takes away the pain of disclosures; it relieves me of a heavy secret.

"You may make what use of my letters you think right."

3. My correspondent wrote to me once more, and I replied thus: "October 31, 1843. Your letter has made my heart ache more, and caused me more and deeper sighs than any I have had a long while, though I assure you there is much on all sides of me to cause sighing and heartache. On all sides:—I am quite haunted by the one dreadful whisper repeated from so many quarters, and causing the keenest distress to friends. You know but a part of my present trial, in knowing that I am unsettled myself.

"Since the beginning of this year I have been obliged to tell the state of my mind to some others; but never, I think, without being in a way obliged, as from friends writing to me as you did, or guessing how matters stood. No one in Oxford knows it or here" [Littlemore], "but one near friend whom I felt I could not help telling the other day. But, I suppose, many more suspect it."

On receiving these letters, my correspondent, if I recollect rightly, at once communicated the matter of them to Dr. Pusey, and this will enable me to describe, as nearly as I can, the way in which he first became aware of my changed state of opinion.

I had from the first a great difficulty in making Dr. Pusey understand such differences of opinion as existed between himself and me. When there was a proposal about the end of 1838 for a subscription for a Cranmer Memorial,[42] he wished us both to subscribe together to it. I could not, of course, and wished him to subscribe by himself. That he would not do; he could not bear the thought of our appearing to the world in separate positions, in a matter of importance. And, as time went on, he would not take any hints, which I gave him, on the subject of my growing inclination to Rome. When I found him so determined, I often had not the heart to go on. And then I knew, that, from affection to me, he so often took up and threw himself into what I said, that I felt the great responsibility I should incur, if I put things before him just as I might view them myself. And, not knowing him so well as I did afterwards, I feared lest I should unsettle him. And moreover, I recollected well, how prostrated he had been with illness in 1832, and I used always to think that the start of the Move-

---

[42] A memorial to the Reformation martyrs designed to embarrass the Tractarians. Most of them refused to support it.

ment had given him a fresh life. I fancied that his physical energies even depended on the presence of a vigorous hope and bright prospects for his imagination to feed upon; so much so, that when he was so unworthily treated by the authorities of the place in 1843,[43] I recollect writing to the late Mr. Dodsworth to state my anxiety, lest, if his mind became dejected in consequence, his health should suffer seriously also. These were difficulties in my way; and then again, another difficulty was, that, as we were not together under the same roof, we only saw each other at set times; others indeed, who were coming in or out of my rooms freely, and according to the need of that moment, knew all my thoughts easily; but for him to know them well, formal efforts were necessary. A common friend of ours broke it all to him in 1841, as far as matters had gone at that time, and showed him clearly the logical conclusions which must lie in propositions to which I had committed myself; but somehow or other in a little while, his mind fell back into its former happy state, and he could not bring himself to believe that he and I should not go on pleasantly together to the end. But that affectionate dream needs must have been broken at last; and two years afterwards, that friend to whom I wrote the letters which I have just now inserted, set himself, as I have said, to break it. Upon that, I too begged Dr. Pusey to tell in private to any one he would, that I thought in the event I should leave the Church of England. However, he would not do so; and at the end of 1844 had almost relapsed into his former thoughts about me, if I may judge from a letter of his which I have found. Nay, at the Commemoration of 1845, a few months before I left the Anglican Church, I think he said about me to a friend, "I trust after all we shall keep him."

In that autumn of 1843, at the time that I spoke to Dr. Pusey, I asked another friend also to communicate in confidence, to whom he would, the prospect which lay before me.

To another friend, Mr. James Hope, now Mr. Hope Scott, I gave the opportunity of knowing it, if he would, in the following Postscript to a letter:—

"While I write, I will add a word about myself. You may come near a person or two who, owing to circumstances, know more exactly my state of feeling than you do, though they would not tell you. Now I do not like that you should not be

aware of this, though I see no *reason* why you should know what they happen to know. Your wishing it would *be* a reason."

I had a dear and old friend,[44] near his death; I never told him my state of mind. Why should I unsettle that sweet calm tranquillity, when I had nothing to offer him instead? I could not say, "Go to Rome;" else I should have shown him the way. Yet I offered myself for his examination. One day he led the way to my speaking out; but, rightly or wrongly, I could not respond. My reason was, "I have no certainty on the matter myself. To say 'I think' is to tease and to distress, not to persuade."

I wrote to him on Michaelmas Day, 1843: "As you may suppose, I have nothing to write to you about, pleasant. I *could* tell you some very painful things; but it is best not to anticipate trouble, which after all can but happen, and, for what one knows, may be averted. You are always so kind, that sometimes, when I part with you, I am nearly moved to tears, and it would be a relief to be so, at your kindness and at my hardness. I think no one ever had such kind friends as I have."

The next year, January 22, I wrote to him: "Pusey has quite enough on him, and generously takes on himself more than enough, for me to add burdens when I am not obliged; particularly too, when I am very conscious, that there *are* burdens, which I am or shall be obliged to lay upon him some time or other, whether I will or no."

And on February 21: "Half-past ten. I am just up, having a bad cold; the like has not happened to me (except twice in January) in my memory. You may think you have been in my thoughts, long before my rising. Of course you are so continually, as you well know. I could not come to see you; I am not worthy of friends. With my opinions, to the full of which I dare not confess, I feel like a guilty person with others, though I trust I am not so. People kindly think that I have much to bear externally, disappointment, slander, &c. No, I have nothing to bear, but the anxiety which I feel for my friends' anxiety for me, and their perplexity. This is a better Ash-Wednesday than birthday present;" [his birthday was the same day as mine; it was Ash-Wednesday that year;] "but I cannot help writing about what is uppermost. And now, my dear B., all kindest and best wishes to you, my oldest friend, whom I must not speak more

[43] Reference to a censure placed on Pusey in 1843 for preaching on the doctrine of the Real Presence.
[44] John William Bowden, died 15 September 1844.

about, and with reference to myself, lest you should be angry." It was not in his nature to have doubts: he used to look at me with anxiety, and wonder what had come over me.

On Easter Monday: "All that is good and gracious descend upon you and yours from the influences of this Blessed Season; and it will be so, (so be it!) for what is the life of you all, as day passes after day, but a simple endeavour to serve Him, from whom all blessing comes? Though we are separated in place, yet this we have in common, that you are living a calm and cheerful time, and I am enjoying the thought of you. It is your blessing to have a clear heaven, and peace around, according to the blessing pronounced on Benjamin.[45] So it is, my dear B., and so may it ever be."

He was in simple good faith. He died in September of the same year. I had expected that his last illness would have brought light to my mind, as to what I ought to do. It brought none. I made a note, which runs thus: "I sobbed bitterly over his coffin, to think that he left me still dark as to what the way of truth was, and what I ought to do in order to please God and fulfil His will." I think I wrote to Charles Marriott to say, that at that moment, with the thought of my friend before me, my strong view in favour of Rome remained just what it was. On the other hand, my firm belief that grace was to be found within the Anglican Church remained too.[46] I wrote to another friend thus:—

"Sept. 16, 1844. I am full of wrong and miserable feelings, which it is useless to detail, so grudging and sullen, when I should be thankful. Of course, when one sees so blessed an end, and that, the termination of so blameless a life, of one who really fed on our ordinances and got strength from them, and sees the same continued in a whole family, the little children finding quite a solace of their pain in the Daily Prayer, it is impossible not to feel more at ease in our Church, as at least a sort of Zoar, a place of refuge and temporary rest, because of the steepness of the way. Only, may we be kept from unlawful security, lest we have Moab and Ammon for our progeny, the enemies of Israel."

I could not continue in this state, either in the light of duty or of reason. My difficulty was this: I had been deceived greatly once; how could I be sure that I was not deceived a second time? I thought myself right then; how was I to be certain that I was right now? How many years had I thought myself sure of what I now rejected? how could I ever again have confidence in myself? As in 1840 I listened to the rising doubt in favour of Rome, now I listened to the waning doubt in favour of the Anglican Church. To be certain is to know that one knows; what inward test had I, that I should not change again, after that I had become a Catholic? I had still apprehension of this, though I thought a time would come, when it would depart. However, some limit ought to be put to these vague misgivings; I must do my best and then leave it to a higher Power to prosper it. So, at the end of 1844, I came to the resolution of writing an Essay on Doctrinal Development; and then, if, at the end of it, my convictions in favour of the Roman Church were not weaker, of taking the necessary steps for admission into her fold.

By this time the state of my mind was generally known, and I made no great secret of it. I will illustrate it by letters of mine which have been put into my hands.

"November 16, 1844. I am going through what must be gone through; and my trust only is that every day of pain is so much taken from the necessary draught which must be exhausted. There is no fear (humanly speaking) of my moving for a long time yet. This has got out without my intending it; but it is all well. As far as I know myself, my one great distress is the perplexity, unsettlement, alarm, scepticism, which I am causing to so many; and the loss of kind feeling and good opinion on the part of so many, known and unknown, who have wished well to me. And of these two sources of pain it is the former that is the constant, urgent, unmitigated one. I had for days a literal ache all about my heart; and from time to time all the complaints of the Psalmist seemed to belong to me.

"And as far as I know myself, my one paramount reason for contemplating a change is my deep, unvarying conviction that our Church is in schism, and that my salvation depends on my joining the Church of Rome. I may use *argumenta ad hominem* to this person or that;[47] but I am not conscious of resentment, or disgust, at any thing that has happened to me. I have no visions whatever of hope, no schemes of action, in any other sphere more suited to me. I have no

---

[45] Deuteronomy 33:12. [Newman's note]

[46] On this subject, vide my Third Lecture on "Anglican Difficulties," also Note E, *Anglican Church.* [Newman's note]

[47] Vide supr. [p. 416] etc. Letter of Oct. 14, 1842, compared with that of Oct. 25. [Newman's note]

existing sympathies with Roman Catholics; I hardly ever, even abroad, was at one of their services; I know none of them, I do not like what I hear of them.

"And then, how much I am giving up in so many ways! and to me sacrifices irreparable, not only from my age, when people hate changing, but from my especial love of old associations and the pleasures of memory. Nor am I conscious of any feeling, enthusiastic or heroic, of pleasure in the sacrifice; I have nothing to support me here.

"What keeps me yet is what has kept me long; a fear that I am under a delusion; but the conviction remains firm under all circumstances, in all frames of mind. And this most serious feeling is growing on me; viz. that the reasons for which I believe as much as our system teaches, *must* lead me to believe more, and that not to believe more is to fall back into scepticism.

"A thousand thanks for your most kind and consoling letter; though I have not yet spoken of it, it was a great gift."

Shortly after I wrote to the same friend thus: "My intention is, if nothing comes upon me, which I cannot forsee, to remain quietly *in statu quo* for a considerable time, trusting that my friends will kindly remember me and my trial in their prayers. And I should give up my fellowship some time before any thing further took place."

There was a lady, now a nun of the Visitation, to whom at this time I wrote the following letters:—

1. "November 7, 1844. I am still where I was; I am not moving. Two things, however, seem plain, that every one is prepared for such an event, next, that every one expects it of me. Few, indeed, who do not think it suitable, fewer still, who do not think it likely. However, I do not think it either suitable or likely. I have very little reason to doubt about the issue of things, but the when and the how are known to Him, from whom, I trust, both the course of things and the issue come. The expression of opinion, and the latent and habitual feeling about me, which is on every side and among all parties, has great force. I insist upon it, because I have a great dread of going by my own feelings, lest they should mislead me. By one's sense of duty one must go; but external facts support one in doing so."

2. "January 8, 1845. What am I to say in answer to your letter? I know perfectly well, I ought to let you know more of my feelings and state of mind than you do know. But how is that possible in a few words? Any thing I say must be abrupt; nothing can I say which will not leave a bewildering feeling, as needing so much to explain it, and being isolated, and (as it were) unlocated, and not having any thing with it to show its bearings upon other parts of the subject.

"At present, my full belief is, in accordance with your letter, that, if there is a move in our Church, very few persons indeed will be partners to it. I doubt whether one or two at the most among residents at Oxford. And I don't know whether I can wish it. The state of the Roman Catholics is at present so unsatisfactory. This I am sure of, that nothing but a simple, direct call of duty is a warrant for any one leaving our Church; no preference of another Church, no delight in its services, no hope of greater religious advancement in it, no indignation, no disgust, at the persons and things, among which we may find ourselves in the Church of England. The simple question is, Can *I* (it is personal, not whether another, but can *I*) be saved in the English Church? am *I* in safety, were I to die to-night? Is it a mortal sin in *me*, not joining another communion?

"P.S. I hardly see my way to concur in attendance, though occasional, in the Roman Catholic chapel, unless a man has made up his mind pretty well to join it eventually. Invocations are not *required* in the Church of Rome; somehow, I do not like using them except under the sanction of the Church, and this makes me unwilling to admit them in members of our Church."

3. "March 30. Now I will tell you more than any one knows except two friends. My own convictions are as strong as I suppose they can become: only it is so difficult to know whether it is a call of *reason* or of conscience. I cannot make out, if I am impelled by what seems *clear,* or by a sense of *duty.* You can understand how painful this doubt is; so I have waited, hoping for light, and using the words of the Psalmist, 'Show some token upon me.' But I suppose I have no right to wait for ever for this. Then I am waiting, because friends are most considerately bearing me in mind, and asking guidance for me; and, I trust, I should attend to any new feelings which came upon me, should that be the effect of their kindness. And then this waiting subserves the purpose of preparing men's minds. I dread shocking, unsettling people. Any how, I can't avoid giving incalculable pain. So, if I had my will, I should like to wait till the summer of 1846, which would be a full seven years from the time

that my convictions first began to fall on me. But I don't think I shall last so long.

"My present intention is to give up my Fellowship in October, and to publish some work or treatise between that and Christmas. I wish people to know *why* I am acting, as well as *what* I am doing; it takes off that vague and distressing surprise, 'What *can* have made him?'

4. "June 1. What you tell me of yourself makes it plain that it is your duty to remain quietly and patiently, till you see more clearly where you are; else you are leaping in the dark."

In the early part of this year, if not before, there was an idea afloat that my retirement from the Anglican Church was owing to my distress that I had been so thrust aside, without any one's taking my part. Various measures were, I believe, talked of in consequence of this surmise. Coincidently with it appeared an exceedingly kind article about me in a Quarterly, in its April number. The writer praised me in kind and beautiful language far above my deserts. In the course of his remarks, he said, speaking of me as Vicar of St. Mary's: "He had the future race of clergy hearing him. Did he value and feel tender about, and cling to his position? . . . Not at all. . . . No sacrifice to him perhaps, he did not care about such things."

There was a censure implied, however covertly, in these words; and it is alluded to in the following letter, addressed to a very intimate friend:—

"April 3, 1845. . . . Accept this apology, my dear Church, and forgive me. As I say, tears come into my eyes;—that arises from the accident of this time, when I am giving up so much I love. Just now I have been overset by James Mozley's article in the Remembrancer;[48] yet really, my dear Church, I have never for an instant had even the temptation of repenting my leaving Oxford. The feeling of repentance has not even come into my mind. How could it? How could I remain at St. Mary's a hypocrite? how could I be answerable for souls, (and life so uncertain,) with the convictions, or at least persuasions, which I had upon me? It is indeed a responsibility to act as I am doing; and I feel His hand heavy on me without intermission, who is all Wisdom and Love, so that my heart and mind are tired out, just as the limbs might be from a load on one's back. That sort of dull aching pain is mine; but my responsibility really is nothing to what it would be, to be answerable for souls, for confiding loving souls, in the English Church, with my convictions. My love to Marriott, and save me the pain of sending him a line."

I am now close upon the date of my reception into the Catholic Church; at the beginning of the year a letter had been addressed to me by a very dear friend, now no more, Charles Marriott. I quote some sentences from it, for the love which I bear him and the value that I set on his good word.

"January 15, 1845. You know me well enough to be aware, that I never see through any thing at first. Your letter to Badeley[49] casts a gloom over the future, which you can understand, if you have understood me, as I believe you have. But I may speak out at once, of what I see and feel at once, and doubt not that I shall ever feel: that your whole conduct towards the Church of England and towards us, who have striven and are still striving to seek after God for ourselves, and to revive true religion among others, under her authority and guidance, has been generous and considerate, and, were that word appropriate, dutiful, to a degree that I could scarcely have conceived possible, more unsparing of self than I should have thought nature could sustain. I have felt with pain every link that you have severed, and I have asked no questions, because I felt that you ought to measure the disclosure of your thoughts according to the occasion, and the capacity of those to whom you spoke. I write in haste, in the midst of engagements engrossing in themselves, but partly made tasteless, partly embittered by what I have heard; but I am willing to trust even you, whom I love best on earth, in God's Hand, in the earnest prayer that you may be so employed as is best for the Holy Catholic Church."

In July, a Bishop thought it worth while to give out to the world that "the adherents of Mr. Newman are few in number. A short time will now probably suffice to prove this fact. It is well known that he is preparing for secession; and, when that event takes place, it will be seen how few will go with him."

I had begun my Essay on the Development of Doctrine in the beginning of 1845, and I was hard at it all through the year till October. As I advanced, my difficulties so cleared away that I

---

[48] James B. Mozley (1813–78), editor of the *Christian Remembrancer*. His two brothers married Newman's sisters.

[49] Edward L. Badeley (d. 1868), Newman's friend and ecclesiastical lawyer.

ceased to speak of "the Roman Catholics," and boldly called them Catholics. Before I got to the end, I resolved to be received, and the book remains in the state in which it was then, unfinished.

One of my friends at Littlemore[50] had been received into the Church on Michaelmas Day, at the Passionist House at Aston, near Stone, by Father Dominic, the Superior.[51] At the beginning of October the latter was passing through London to Belgium; and, as I was in some perplexity what steps to take for being received myself, I assented to the proposition made to me that the good priest should take Littlemore in his way, with a view to his doing for me the same charitable service as he had done to my friend.

On October the 8th I wrote to a number of friends the following letter:—

"Littlemore, October 8th, 1845. I am this night expecting Father Dominic, the Passionist, who, from his youth, has been led to have distinct and direct thoughts, first of the countries of the North, then of England. After thirty years' (almost) waiting, he was without his own act sent here. But he has had little to do with conversions. I saw him here for a few minutes on St. John Baptist's day last year.

"He is a simple, holy man; and withal gifted with remarkable powers. He does not know of my intention; but I mean to ask of him admission into the One Fold of Christ. . . .

"I have so many letters to write, that this must do for all who choose to ask about me. With my best love to dear Charles Marriott, who is over your head, &c., &c.

"P.S. This will not go till all is over. Of course it requires no answer."

For a while after my reception, I proposed to betake myself to some secular calling. I wrote thus in answer to a very gracious letter of congratulation sent me by Cardinal Acton:—

"Nov. 25, 1845. I hope you will have anticipated, before I express it, the great gratification which I received from your Eminence's letter. That gratification, however, was tempered by the apprehension, that kind and anxious well-wishers at a distance attach more importance to my step than really belongs to it. To me indeed personally it is of course an inestimable gain; but persons and things look great at a distance, which are not so when seen close; and, did your Eminence know me, you would see that I was one, about whom there has been far more talk for good and bad than he deserves, and about whose movements far more expectation has been raised than the event will justify.

"As I never, I do trust, aimed at any thing else than obedience to my own sense of right, and have been magnified into the leader of a party without my wishing it or acting as such, so now, much as I may wish to the contrary, and earnestly as I may labour (as is my duty) to minister in a humble way to the Catholic Church, yet my powers will, I fear, disappoint the expectations of both my own friends, and of those who pray for the peace of Jerusalem.

"If I might ask of your Eminence a favour, it is that you would kindly moderate those anticipations. Would it were in my power to do, what I do not aspire to do! At present certainly I cannot look forward to the future, and, though it would be a good work if I could persuade others to do as I have done, yet it seems as if I had quite enough to do in thinking of myself."

Soon, Dr. Wiseman, in whose Vicariate Oxford lay, called me to Oscott; and I went there with others; afterwards he sent me to Rome, and finally placed me in Birmingham.

I wrote to a friend:—

"January 20, 1846. You may think how lonely I am. 'Obliviscere populum tuum et domum patris tui,'[52] has been in my ears for the last twelve hours. I realize more that we are leaving Littlemore, and it is like going on the open sea."

I left Oxford for good on Monday, February 23, 1846. On the Saturday and Sunday before, I was in my house at Littlemore simply by myself, as I had been for the first day or two when I had originally taken possession of it. I slept on Sunday night at my dear friend's, Mr. Johnson's, at the Observatory. Various friends came to see the last of me; Mr. Copeland, Mr. Church, Mr. Buckle, Mr. Pattison, and Mr. Lewis.[53] Dr. Pusey too came up to take leave of me; and I called on Dr. Ogle, one of my very oldest friends, for he was my private Tutor, when I was an

[50] J. B. Dalgairns, who later joined the Oratory.

[51] Blessed Dominic Barberi, the Italian Passionist priest who received Newman into the Roman Catholic Church.

[52] "Forget thine own people and thy father's house." (Psalms).

[53] W. J. Copeland, Newman's curate at Littlemore; R. W. Church (see note 6 above); George Buckle, Fellow of Oriel; Mark Pattison, later Rector of Lincoln and a skeptic, but then a Tractarian; David Lewis, Fellow of Jesus College.

Undergraduate. In him I took leave of my first College, Trinity, which was so dear to me, and which held on its foundation so many who had been kind to me both when I was a boy and all through my Oxford life. Trinity had never been unkind to me. There used to be much snapdragon growing on the walls opposite my freshman's rooms there, and I had for years taken it as the emblem of my own perpetual residence even unto death in my University.

On the morning of the 23rd I left the Observatory. I have never seen Oxford since, excepting its spires, as they are seen from the railway.[54]

Note A: Liberalism
Note B: Ecclesiastical Miracles

The following Notes, A and B, are the first two of seven "Notes" Newman appended to the Apologia. *Note C, "Wisdom and Innocence," is omitted because the sermon itself is included in this volume; Note D concerns the series of saints' lives undertaken in 1843–44; Note E expands Newman's views on the Anglican Church; Notes F and G refer to passages in the final chapter of the* Apologia.

Note A

LIBERALISM

I HAVE been asked to explain more fully what it is I mean by "Liberalism," because merely to call it the Anti-dogmatic Principle is to tell very little about it. An explanation is the more necessary, because such good Catholics and distinguished writers as Count Montalembert and Father Lacordaire use the word in a favourable sense, and claim to be Liberals themselves. "The only singularity," says the former of the two in describing his friend, "was his Liberalism. By a phenomenon, at that time unheard of, this convert, this seminarist, this confessor of nuns, was just as stubborn a liberal, as in the days when he was a student and a barrister."—Life (transl.), p. 19.

I do not believe that it is possible for me to differ in any important matter from two men whom I so highly admire. In their general line of thought and conduct I enthusiastically concur, and consider them to be before their age. And it would be strange indeed if I did not read with a special interest, in M. de Montalembert's

beautiful volume, of the unselfish aims, the thwarted projects, the unrequited toils, the grand and tender resignation of Lacordaire. If I hesitate to adopt their language about Liberalism, I impute the necessity of such hesitation to some differences between us in the use of words or in the circumstances of country; and thus I reconcile myself to remaining faithful to my own conception of it, though I cannot have their voices to give force to mine. Speaking then in my own way, I proceed to explain what I meant as a Protestant by Liberalism, and to do so in connexion with the circumstances under which that system of opinion came before me at Oxford.

If I might presume to contrast Lacordaire and myself, I should say, that we had been both of us inconsistent;—he, a Catholic, in calling himself a Liberal; I, a Protestant, in being an Anti-liberal; and moreover, that the cause of this inconsistency had been in both cases one and the same. That is, we were both of us such good conservatives, as to take up with what we happened to find established in our respective countries, at the time when we came into active life. Toryism was the creed of Oxford; he inherited, and made the best of, the French Revolution.

---

[54] At length I revisited Oxford on February 26th, 1878, after an absence of just 32 years. Vide Additional Note at the end of the Volume. [Newman's note]

When, in the beginning of the present century, not very long before my own time, after many years of moral and intellectual declension, the University of Oxford woke up to a sense of its duties, and began to reform itself, the first instruments of this change, to whose zeal and courage we all owe so much, were naturally thrown together for mutual support, against the numerous obstacles which lay in their path, and soon stood out in relief from the body of residents, who, though many of them men of talent themselves, cared little for the object which the others had at heart. These Reformers, as they may be called, were for some years members of scarcely more than three or four Colleges; and their own Colleges, as being under their direct influence, of course had the benefit of those stricter views of discipline and teaching, which they themselves were urging on the University. They had, in no long time, enough of real progress in their several spheres of exertion, and enough of reputation out of doors, to warrant them in considering themselves the *élite* of the place; and it is not wonderful if they were in consequence led to look down upon the majority of Colleges, which had not kept pace with the reform, or which had been hostile to it. And, when those rivalries of one man with another arose, whether personal or collegiate, which befall literary and scientific societies, such disturbances did but tend to raise in their eyes the value which they had already set upon academical distinction, and increase their zeal in pursuing it. Thus was formed an intellectual circle or class in the University,—men, who felt they had a career before them, as soon as the pupils, whom they were forming, came into public life; men, whom non-residents, whether country parsons or preachers of the Low Church, on coming up from time to time to the old place, would look at, partly with admiration, partly with suspicion, as being an honour indeed to Oxford, but withal exposed to the temptation of ambitious views, and to the spiritual evils signified in what is called the "pride of reason."

Nor was this imputation altogether unjust; for, as they were following out the proper idea of a University, of course they suffered more or less from the moral malady incident to such a pursuit. The very object of such great institutions lies in the cultivation of the mind and the spread of knowledge: if this object, as all human objects, has its dangers at all times, much more would these exist in the case of men, who were engaged in a work of reformation, and had the oppor-

tunity of measuring themselves, not only with those who were their equals in intellect, but with the many, who were below them. In this select circle or class of men, in various Colleges, the direct instruments and the choice fruit of real University Reform, we see the rudiments of the Liberal party.

Whenever men are able to act at all, there is the chance of extreme and intemperate action; and therefore, when there is exercise of mind, there is the chance of wayward or mistaken exercise. Liberty of thought is in itself a good; but it gives an opening to false liberty. Now by Liberalism I mean false liberty of thought, or the exercise of thought upon matters, in which, from the constitution of the human mind, thought cannot be brought to any successful issue, and therefore is out of place. Among such matters are first principles of whatever kind; and of these the most sacred and momentous are especially to be reckoned the truths of Revelation. Liberalism then is the mistake of subjecting to human judgment those revealed doctrines which are in their nature beyond and independent of it, and of claiming to determine on intrinsic grounds the truth and value of propositions which rest for their reception simply on the external authority of the Divine Word.

Now certainly the party of whom I have been speaking, taken as a whole, were of a character of mind out of which Liberalism might easily grow up, as in fact it did; certainly they breathed around an influence which made men of religious seriousness shrink into themselves. But, while I say as much as this, I have no intention whatever of implying that the talent of the University, in the years before and after 1820, was liberal in its theology, in the sense in which the bulk of the educated classes through the country are liberal now. I would not for the world be supposed to detract from the Christian earnestness, and the activity in religious works, above the average of men, of many of the persons in question. They would have protested against their being supposed to place reason before faith, or knowledge before devotion; yet I do consider that they unconsciously encouraged and successfully introduced into Oxford a licence of opinion which went far beyond them. In their day they did little more than take credit to themselves for enlightened views, largeness of mind, liberality of sentiment, without drawing the line between what was just and what was inadmissible in speculation, and without seeing the tendency of their own principles; and engrossing, as they did, the mental energy of the University, they met for a time with no effectual hindrance to the spread of their influence, except (what indeed at the moment was most effectual, but not of an intellectual character) the thorough-going Toryism and traditionary Church-of-England-ism of the great body of the Colleges and Convocation.

Now and then a man of note appeared in the Pulpit or Lecture Rooms of the University, who was a worthy representative of the more religious and devout Anglicans. These belonged chiefly to the High-Church party; for the party called Evangelical never has been able to breathe freely in the atmosphere of Oxford, and at no time has been conspicuous, as a party, for talent or learning. But of the old High Churchmen several exerted some sort of Anti-liberal influence in the place, at least from time to time, and that influence of an intellectual nature. Among these especially may be mentioned Mr. John Miller, of Worcester College, who preached the Bampton Lecture in the year 1817. But, as far as I know, he who turned the tide, and brought the talent of the University round to the side of the old theology, and against what was familiarly called "march-of-mind," was Mr. Keble. In and from Keble the mental activity of Oxford took that contrary direction which issued in what was called Tractarianism.

Keble was young in years, when he became a University celebrity, and younger in mind. He had the purity and simplicity of a child. He had few sympathies with the intellectual party, who sincerely welcomed him as a brilliant specimen of young Oxford. He instinctively shut up before literary display, and pomp and donnishness of manner, faults which always will beset academical notabilities. He did not respond to their advances. His collision with them (if it may be so called) was thus described by Hurrell Froude in his own way. "Poor Keble!" he used gravely to say, "he was asked to join the aristocracy of talent, but he soon found his level." He went into the country, but his instance serves to prove that men need not, in the event, lose that influence which is rightly theirs, because they happen to be thwarted in the use of the channels natural and proper to its exercise. He did not lose his place in the minds of men because he was out of their sight.

Keble was a man who guided himself and formed his judgments, not by processes of reason, by inquiry or by argument, but, to use the word in a broad sense, by authority. Conscience is an authority; the Bible is an authority; such is the Church; such is Antiquity; such are the words of the wise; such are hereditary lessons; such are ethical truths; such are historical memories, such are legal saws and state maxims; such are proverbs; such are sentiments, presages, and prepossessions. It seemed to me as if he ever felt happier, when he could speak or act under some such primary or external sanction; and could use argument mainly as a means of recommending or explaining what had claims on his reception prior to proof. He even felt a tenderness, I think, in spite of Bacon, for the Idols of the Tribe and the Den, of the Market and the Theatre. What he hated instinctively was heresy, insubordination, resistance to things established, claims of independence, disloyalty, innovation, a critical, censorious spirit. And such was the main principle of the school which in the course of years was formed around him; nor is it easy to set limits to its influence in its day; for multitudes of men, who did not profess its teaching, or accept its peculiar doctrines, were willing nevertheless, or found it to their purpose, to act in company with it.

Indeed for their time it was particularly the champion and advocate of the political doctrines of the great clerical interest through the country, who found in Mr. Keble and his friends an intellectual, as well as moral support to their cause, which they looked for in vain elsewhere. His weak point, in their eyes, was his consistency; for he carried his love of authority and old times so far, as to be more than gentle towards the Catholic Religion, with which the Toryism of Oxford and of the Church of England had no sympathy. Accordingly, if my memory be correct, he could never get himself to throw his heart into the opposition made to Catholic Emancipation, strongly as he revolted from the politics and the instruments by means of which that Emancipation was won. I fancy he would have had no difficulty in accepting Dr. Johnson's saying about "the first Whig;" and it grieved and offended him that the "Via prima salutis" should be opened to the Catholic body from the Whig quarter. In spite of his reverence for the Old Religion, I conceive that on the whole he would rather have kept its professors beyond the pale of the Constitution with the Tories, than admit them on the principles of the Whigs. Moreover, if the Revolution of 1688 was too lax in principle for him and his friends, much less, as is very plain, could they endure to subscribe to the revolutionary doctrines of 1776 and 1789, which they felt to be absolutely and entirely out of keeping with theological truth.

The Old Tory or Conservative party in Oxford had in it no principle or power of development, and that from its very nature and constitution: it was otherwise with the Liberals. They represented a new idea, which was but gradually learning to recognize itself, to ascertain its characteristics and external relations, and to exert an influence upon the University. The party grew, all the time that I was in Oxford, even in numbers, certainly in breadth and definiteness of doctrine, and in power. And, what was a far higher consideration, by the accession of Dr. Arnold's pupils, it was invested with an elevation of character which claimed the respect even of its opponents. On the other hand, in proportion as it became more earnest and less self-applauding, it became more free-spoken; and members of it might be found who, from the mere circumstance of remaining firm to their original professions, would in the judgment of the world, as to their public acts, seem to have left it for the Conservative camp. Thus, neither in its component parts nor in its policy, was it the same in 1832, 1836, and 1841, as it was in 1845.

These last remarks will serve to throw light upon a matter personal to myself, which I have introduced into my Narrative, and to which my attention has been pointedly called, now that my Volume is coming to a second edition.

It has been strongly urged upon me to reconsider the following passages which occur in it: "The men who had driven me from Oxford were distinctly the Liberals, it was they who had opened the attack upon Tract 90," [p. 410], and "I found no fault with the Liberals; they had beaten me in a fair field," [p. 413].

I am very unwilling to seem ungracious, or to cause pain in any quarter; still I am sorry to say I cannot modify these statements. It is surely a matter of historical fact that I left Oxford upon the University proceedings of 1841; and in those proceedings, whether we look to the Heads of Houses or the resident Masters, the leaders, if intellect and influence make men such, were members of the Liberal party. Those who did not lead, concurred or acquiesced in them,—I may say, felt a satisfaction. I do not recollect any Liberal who was on my side on that occasion. Excepting the Liberal, no other party, as a party, acted against me. I am not complaining of them; I deserved nothing else at their hands. They could not undo in 1845, even had they wished it, (and there is no proof they did,) what they had done in 1841. In 1845, when I had already given up the contest for four years, and

my part in it had passed into the hands of others, then some of those who were prominent against me in 1841, feeling (what they had not felt in 1841) the danger of driving a number of my followers to Rome, and joined by younger friends who had come into University importance since 1841 and felt kindly towards me, adopted a course more consistent with their principles, and proceeded to shield from the zeal of the Hebdomadal Board, not me, but, professedly, all parties through the country,—Tractarians, Evangelicals, Liberals in general,—who had to subscribe to the Anglican formularies, on the ground that those formularies, rigidly taken, were, on some point or other, a difficulty to all parties alike.

However, besides the historical fact, I can bear witness to my own feelings at the time, and my feeling was this:—that those who in 1841 had considered it to be a duty to act against me, had then done their worst. What was it to me what they were now doing in opposition to the New Test proposed by the Hebdomadal Board? I owed them no thanks for their trouble. I took no interest at all, in February, 1845, in the proceedings of the Heads of Houses and of the Convocation. I felt myself *dead* as regarded my relations to the Anglican Church. My leaving it was all but a matter of time. I believe I did not even thank my real friends, the two Proctors, who in Convocation stopped by their Veto the condemnation of Tract 90; nor did I make any acknowledgement to Mr. Rogers, not to Mr. James Mozley, nor, as I think, to Mr. Hussey, for their pamphlets in my behalf. My frame of mind is best described by the sentiment of the passage in Horace, which at the time I was fond of quoting, as expressing my view of the relation that existed between the Vice-Chancellor and myself.

> "Pentheu,
> Rector Thebarum quid me perferre patique
> Indignum cogas?" "Adimam bona." "Nempe pecus, rem,
> Lectos, argentum; tollas licet." "In manicis et
> Compedibus, sævo te sub custode tenebo." (*viz. the* 39 *Articles.*)
> "*Ipse Deus, simul atque volam, me solvet.*" Opinor,
> Hoc sentit: *Moriar. Mors ultima linea rerum est.*

I conclude this notice of Liberalism in Oxford, and the party which was antagonistic to it, with some propositions in detail, which, as a member of the latter, and together with the High Church, I earnestly denounced and abjured.

1. No religious tenet is important, unless reason shows it to be so.

Therefore, e.g. the doctrine of the Athanasian Creed is not to be insisted on, unless it tends to convert the soul; and the doctrine of the Atonement is to be insisted on, if it does convert the soul.

2. No one can believe what he does not understand.

Therefore, e.g. there are no mysteries in true religion.

3. No theological doctrine is any thing more than an opinion which happens to be held by bodies of men.

Therefore, e.g. no creed, as such, is necessary for salvation.

4. It is dishonest in a man to make an act of faith in what he has not had brought home to him by actual proof.

Therefore, e.g. the mass of men ought not absolutely to believe in the divine authority of the Bible.

5. It is immoral in a man to believe more than he can spontaneously receive as being congenial to his moral and mental nature.

Therefore, e.g. a given individual is not bound to believe in eternal punishment.

6. No revealed doctrines or precepts may reasonably stand in the way of scientific conclusions.

Therefore, e.g. Political Economy may reverse our Lord's declarations about poverty and riches, or a system of Ethics may teach that the highest condition of body is ordinarily essential to the highest state of mind.

7. Christianity is necessarily modified by the growth of civilization, and the exigencies of times.

Therefore, e.g. the Catholic priesthood, though necessary in the Middle Ages, may be superseded now.

8. There is a system of religion more simply true than Christianity as it has ever been received.

Therefore, e.g. we may advance that Christianity is the "corn of wheat" which has been dead for 1800 years, but at length will bear fruit; and that Mahometanism is the manly religion, and existing Christianity the womanish.

9. There is a right of Private Judgment: that is, there is no existing authority on earth competent to interfere with the liberty of individuals in reasoning and judging for themselves about the Bible and its contents, as they severally please.

Therefore, e.g. religious establishments requiring subscription are Anti-christian.

10. There are rights of conscience such, that every one may lawfully advance a claim to profess and teach what is false and wrong in matters, religious, social, and moral, provided that to his private conscience it seems absolutely true and right.

Therefore, e.g. individuals have a right to preach and practise fornication and polygamy.

11. There is no such thing as a national or state conscience.

Therefore, e.g. no judgments can fall upon a sinful or infidel nation.

12. The civil power has no positive duty, in a normal state of things, to maintain religious truth.

Therefore, e.g. blasphemy and sabbath-breaking are not rightly punishable by law.

13. Utility and expedience are the measure of political duty.

Therefore, e.g. no punishment may be enacted, on the ground that God commands it: e.g. on the text, "Whoso sheddeth man's blood, by man shall his blood be shed."

14. The Civil Power may dispose of Church property without sacrilege.

Therefore, e.g. Henry VIII. committed no sin in his spoliations.

15. The Civil Power has the right of ecclesiastical jurisdiction and administration.

Therefore, e.g. Parliament may impose articles of faith on the Church or suppress Dioceses.

16. It is lawful to rise in arms against legitimate princes.

Therefore, e.g. the Puritans in the 17th century, and the French in the 18th, were justifiable in their Rebellion and Revolution respectively.

17. The people are the legitimate source of power.

Therefore, e.g. Universal Suffrage is among the natural rights of man.

18. Virtue is the child of knowledge, and vice of ignorance.

Therefore, e.g. education, periodical literature, railroad travelling, ventilation, drainage, and the arts of life, when fully carried out, serve to make a population moral and happy.

All of these propositions, and many others too, were familiar to me thirty years ago, as in the number of the tenets of Liberalism, and, while I gave into none of them except No. 12, and perhaps No. 11, and partly No. 1, before I began to publish, so afterwards I wrote against most of them in some part or other of my Anglican works.

If it is necessary to refer to a work, not simply my own, but of the Tractarian school, which contains a similar protest, I should name the *Lyra Apostolica*. This volume, which by accident has been left unnoticed, except incidentally, in my Narrative, was collected together from the pages of the "British Magazine," in which its contents originally appeared, and published in a separate form, immediately after Hurrell Froude's death in 1836. Its signatures, α, β, γ, δ, ε, ζ, denote respectively as authors, Mr. Bowden, Mr. Hurrell Froude, Mr. Keble, Mr. Newman, Mr. Robert Wilberforce, and Mr. Isaac Williams.

There is one poem on "Liberalism," beginning "Ye cannot halve the Gospel of God's grace;" which bears out the account of Liberalism as above given; and another upon "the Age to come," defining from its own point of view the position and prospects of Liberalism.

I need hardly to say that the above Note is mainly historical. How far the Liberal party of 1830-40 really held the above eighteen Theses, which I attributed to them, and how far and in what sense I should oppose those Theses now, could scarcely be explained without a separate Dissertation.

Note B

ECCLESIASTICAL MIRACLES

THE writer, who gave occasion for the foregoing Narrative, was very severe with me for what I had said about Miracles in the Preface to the Life of St. Walburga. I observe therefore as follows:—

Catholics believe that miracles happen in any age of the Church, though not for the same purposes, in the same number, or with the same evidences, as in Apostolic times. The Apostles wrought them in evidence of their divine mission; and with this object they have been sometimes wrought by Evangelists of countries since, as even Protestants allow. Hence we hear of them in the history of St. Gregory in Pontus, and St. Martin in Gaul; and in their case, as in that of the Apostles, they were both numerous and clear. As they are granted to Evangelists, so they are granted, though in less measure and evidence, to other holy men; and as holy men are not found equally at all times and in all places, therefore miracles are in some places and times more than in others. And since, generally, they are granted to faith and prayer, therefore in a country in which faith and prayer abound, they will be more likely to concur, than where and when faith and prayer are not; so that their occurrences is irregular. And further, as faith and prayer obtain miracles, so still more commonly do they gain from above the ordinary interventions of Providence; and, as it is often very difficult to distinguish between a providence and a miracle, and there will be more providences than miracles, hence it will happen that many occurrences will be called miraculous, which, strictly speaking, are not such, that is, not more than providential mercies, or what are sometimes called "*grazie*" or "favours."

Persons, who believe all this, in accordance with Catholic teaching, as I did and do, they, on the report of a miracle, will of necessity, the necessity of good logic, be led to say, first, "It *may* be," and secondly, "But I must have *good evidence* in order to believe it."

1. It *may* be, because miracles take place in all ages; it must be clearly *proved*, because perhaps after all it may be only a providential mercy, or an exaggeration, or a mistake, or an imposture. Well, this is precisely what I had said, which the writer, who has given occasion to this Volume, considered so irrational. I had said, as he quotes

me, "In this day, and under our present circumstances, we can only reply, that there is no reason why they should not be." Surely this is good logic, *provided* that miracles *do* occur in all ages; and so again I am logical in saying, "There is nothing, *primâ facie*, in the miraculous accounts in question, to repel a *properly taught* or religiously disposed mind." What is the matter with this statement? My assailant does not pretend to say *what* the matter is, and he cannot; but he expresses a rude, unmeaning astonishment. Accordingly, in the passage which he quotes, I observe, "Miracles are the kinds of facts proper to ecclesiastical history, just as instances of sagacity or daring, personal prowess, or crime, are the facts proper to secular history." What is the harm of this?

2. But, though a miracle be conceivable, it has to be *proved*. What has to be proved? (1.) That the event occurred as stated, and is not a false report or an exaggeration. (2.) That it is clearly miraculous, and not a mere providence or answer to prayer within the order of nature. What is the fault of saying this? The inquiry is parallel to that which is made about some extraordinary fact in secular history. Supposing I hear that King Charles II. died a Catholic, I am led to say: It *may* be, but what is your *proof?*

In my Essay on Miracles of the year 1826, I proposed three questions about a professed miraculous occurrence: 1. is it antecedently *probable?* 2. is it in its *nature* certainly miraculous? 3. has it sufficient *evidence?* To these three heads I had regard in my Essay of 1842; and under them I still wish to conduct the inquiry into the miracles of Ecclesiastical History.

So much for general principles; as to St. Walburga, though I have no intention at all of denying that numerous miracles have been wrought by her intercession, still, neither the Author of her Life, nor I, the Editor, felt that we had grounds for binding ourselves to the belief of certain alleged miracles in particular. I made, however, one exception; it was the medicinal oil, which flows from her relics. Now as to the *verisimilitude*, the *miraculousness*, and the *fact*, of this medicinal oil.

1. The *verisimilitude*. It is plain there is nothing extravagant in this report of her relics having a supernatural virtue; and for this reason, because there are such instances in Scripture, and Scripture cannot be extravagant. For instance, a man was restored to life by touching the relics of the Prophet Eliseus. The sacred text runs thus:— "And Elisha died, and they buried him. And the bands of the Moabites invaded the land at the coming in of the year. And it came to pass, as they were burying a man, that, behold, they spied a band of men; and they cast the man into the sepulchre of Elisha. And, when the man was let down, *and touched the bones of Elisha, he revived*, and stood upon his feet." Again, in the case of an inanimate substance, which had touched a living Saint: "And God wrought *special miracles* by the hands of Paul; so that *from his body* were brought unto the sick *handkerchiefs or aprons*, and the *diseases departed from them*." And again in the case of a pool: "An *Angel went down* at a certain season into the pool, and troubled the water, whosoever then first, after the troubling of the water, stepped in, *was made whole of whatsoever disease* he had." 2 Kings [4 Kings] xiii. 20, 21. Acts xix. 11, 12. John v. 4. Therefore there is nothing *extravagant* in the *character* of the miracle.

2. Next, the *matter of fact*:—is there an oil flowing from St. Walburga's tomb, which is medicinal? To this question I confined myself in my Preface. Of the accounts of medieval miracles, I said, that there was no *extravagance* in their *general character*, but I could not affirm that there was always *evidence* for them. I could not simply accept them as *facts*, but I could not reject them in their *nature*;—they *might* be true, for they were not impossible; but they were *not proved* to be true, because there was not trustworthy testimony. However, as to St. Walburga, I repeat, I made *one* exception, the fact of the medicinal oil, since for that miracle there was distinct and successive testimony. And then I went on to give a chain of witnesses. It was my duty to state what those witnesses said in their very words; so I gave the testimonies in full, tracing them from the Saint's death. I said, "She is one of the principal Saints of her age and country." Then I quoted Basnage, a Protestant, who says, "Six writers are extant, who have employed themselves in relating the deeds of miracles of Walburga." Then I said that her "renown was not the mere natural *growth* of ages, but begins with the very century of the Saint's death." Then I observed that only two miracles seem to have been "distinctly reported of her as occurring in her lifetime; and they were handed down apparently by tradition." Also, that such miracles are said to have commenced about A.D. 777. Then I spoke of the medicinal oil as having testimony to it in 893, in 1306, after 1450, in 1615, and 1620. Also, I said that Mabillon seems not to have believed some of her miracles; and that the earliest witness had got into trouble with his Bishop. And so I

left the matter, as a question to be decided by evidence, not deciding any thing myself.

What was the harm of all this? but my Critic muddled it together in a most extraordinary manner, and I am far from sure that he knew himself the definite categorical charge which he intended it to convey against me. One of his remarks is, "What has become of the holy oil for the last 240 years, Dr. Newman does not say," p. 324. Of course I did not, because I did not know; I gave the evidence as I found it; he assumes that I had a point to prove, and then asks why I did not make the evidence larger than it was.

I can tell him more about it now: the oil still flows; I have had some of it in my possession; it is medicinal still. This leads to the third head.

3. Its *miraculousness*. On this point, since I have been in the Catholic Church, I have found there is a difference of opinion. Some persons consider that the oil is the natural produce of the rock, and has ever flowed from it; others, that by a divine gift, it flows from the relics; and others, allowing that it now comes naturally from the rocks, are disposed to hold that it was in its origin miraculous, as was the virtue of the pool of Bethsaida.

The point must be settled of course before the virtue of the oil can be ascribed to the sanctity of St. Walburga; for myself, I neither have, nor ever have had, the means of going into the question; but I will take the opportunity of its having come before me, to make one or two remarks, supplemental of what I have said on other occasions.

1. I frankly confess that the present advance of science tends to make it probable that various facts take place, and have taken place, in the order of nature, which hitherto have been considered by Catholics as simply supernatural.

2. Though I readily make this admission, it must not be supposed in consequence that I am disposed to grant at once, that every event was natural in point of fact, which *might* have taken place by the laws of nature; for it is obvious, no Catholic can bind the Almighty to act only in one and the same way, or to the observance always of His own laws. An event which is possible in the way of nature, is certainly possible too to Divine Power without the sequence of natural cause and effect at all. A conflagration, to take a parallel, may be the work of an incendiary, or the result of a flash of lightning; nor would a jury think it safe to find a man guilty of arson, if a dangerous thunderstorm was raging at the very time when the fire broke out. In like manner, upon the

hypothesis that a miraculous dispensation is in operation, a recovery from diseases to which medical science is equal, may nevertheless in matter of fact have taken place, not by natural means, but by a supernatural interposition. That the Lawgiver always acts through His own laws, is an assumption, of which I never saw proof. In a given case, then, the possibility of assigning a human cause for an event does not *ipso facto* prove that it is not miraculous.

3. So far, however, is plain, that, till some *experimentum crucis* can be found, such as to be decisive against the natural cause or the super-natural, an occurrence of this kind will as little convince an unbeliever that there has been a divine interference in the case, as it will drive the Catholic to admit that there has been no interference at all.

4. Still there is this gain accruing to the Catholic cause from the larger views we now possess of the operation of natural causes, viz. that our opponents will not in future be so ready as hitherto, to impute fraud and falsehood to our priests and their witnesses, on the ground of their pretending or reporting things that are incredible. Our opponents have again and again accused us of false witness, on account of state-ments which they now allow are either true, or may have been true. They account indeed for the strange facts very differently from us; but still they allow the fact they were. It is a great thing to have our characters cleared; and we may reasonably hope that, the next time our word is vouched for occurrences which appear to be miraculous, our facts will be investigated, not our testimony impugned.

5. Even granting that certain occurrences, which we have hitherto accounted miraculous, have not absolutely a claim to be so considered, nevertheless they constitute an argument still in behalf of Revelation and the Church. Providences, or what are called *grazie*, though they do not rise to the order of miracles, yet, if they occur again and again in connexion with the same persons, institutions, or doctrines, may supply a cumula-tive evidence of the fact of a supernatural presence in the quarter in which they are found. I have already alluded to this point in my Essay on Ecclesiastical Miracles, and I have a particular reason, as will presently be seen, for referring here to what I said in the course of it.

In that Essay, after bringing its main argument to an end, I append to it a review of "the evidence for particular alleged miracles." "It does not strictly fall within the scope of the Essay," I observe, "to pronounce upon the truth or falsehood of this or that miraculous narrative, as it occurs in ecclesiastical history; but only to furnish such general considerations, as may be useful in forming a decision in particular cases." p. cv. However, I thought it right to go farther and "to set down the evidence for and against certain miracles as we meet with them," ibid. In discussing these miracles separately, I make the following remarks, to which I have just been referring.

After discussing the alleged miracle of the Thundering Legion, I observe: "Nor does it concern us much to answer the objection, that there is nothing strictly miraculous in such an occurrence, because sudden thunderclouds after drought are not unfrequent; for, I would answer, Grant me such miracles ordinarily in the early Church, and I will ask no other; grant that, upon prayer, benefits are vouchsafed, deliverances are effected, unhoped-for results obtained, sicknesses cured, tempests laid, pestilences put to flight, famines remedied, judgments inflicted, and there will be no need of analyzing the causes, whether supernatural or natural, to which they are to be referred. They may, or they may not, in this or that case, follow or surpass the laws of nature, and they may do so plainly or doubtfully, but the common sense of mankind will call them miraculous; for by a miracle is popularly meant, whatever be its formal definition, an event which impresses upon the mind the immediate presence of the Moral Governor of the world. He may sometimes act through nature, sometimes beyond or against it; but those who admit the fact of such interferences, will have little difficulty in admitting also their strictly miraculous character, if the circumstances of the case require it, and those who deny miracles to the early Church will be equally strenuous against allowing her the grace of such intimate influence (if we may so speak) upon the course of divine Providence, as is here in question, even though it be not miraculous."—p. cxxi.

And again, speaking of the death of Arius: "But after all, was it a miracle? for, if not, we are labouring at a proof of which nothing comes. The more immediate answer to this question has already been suggested several times. When a Bishop with his flock prays night and day against a heretic, and at length begs of God to take him away, and when he *is* suddenly taken away, almost at the moment of his triumph, and that by a death awfully significant, from its likeness to one recorded in Scripture, is it not trifling to ask whether such an occurrence comes up to the definition of a miracle? The question is not whether it is formally a miracle, but whether it is an event, the like of which persons, who deny that miracles continue, will consent that the Church should be considered still able to perform. If they are willing to allow to the Church such extraordinary protection, it is for them to draw the line to the satisfaction of people in general, between these and strictly miraculous events; if, on the other hand, they deny their occurrence in the times of the Church, then there is sufficient reason for our appealing here to the history of Arius in proof of the affirmative."—p. clxxii.

These remarks, thus made upon the Thundering Legion and the death of Arius, must be applied, in consequence of investigations made since the date of my Essay, to the apparent miracle wrought in favour of the African confessors in the Vandal persecution. Their tongues were cut out by the Arian tyrant, and yet they spoke as before. In my Essay I insisted on this fact as being strictly miraculous. Among other remarks (referring to the instances adduced by Middleton and others in disparagement of the miracle, viz. of "a girl born without a tongue, who yet talked as distinctly and easily, as if she had enjoyed the full benefit of that organ," and of the boy who lost his tongue at the age of eight, or nine, yet retained his speech, whether perfectly or not,) I said, "Does Middleton mean to say, that, if certain of men lost their tongues *at the command of a tyrant* for the *sake of their religion,* and then spoke *as plainly* as before, nay *if only one person was so mutilated* and so gifted, it would not be a miracle?"—p. ccx. And I enlarged upon the minute details of the fact as reported to us by eye-witnesses and contemporaries. "Out of the seven writers adduced, six are contemporaries; three, if not four, are eye-witnesses of the miracle. One reports from an eye-witness, and one testifies to a fervent record at the burial-place of the subjects of it. All seven were living, or had been staying, at one or other of the two places which are mentioned as their abode. One is a Pope, a second a Catholic Bishop, a third a Bishop of a schismatical party, a fourth an emperor, a fifth a soldier, a politician, and a suspected infidel, a sixth a statesman and courtier, a seventh a rhetorician and philosopher. 'He cut out the tongues by the roots,' says Victor, Bishop of Vito; 'I perceived the tongues entirely gone by the roots,' says Aeneas; 'as low down as the throat,' says Procopius; 'at the roots,' say Justinian and St. Gregory; 'he spoke like an educated man, without impediment, says Victor of Vito; 'with articulateness,' says Aeneas; 'better than before;' 'they talked without any impediment,' says Procopius; 'speaking with perfect voice,' says Marcellinus; 'they spoke perfectly, even to the end,' says the second Victor; 'the words were formed, full, and perfect,' says St. Gregory."—p. ccviii.

However, a few years ago an Article appeared in "Notes and Queries" (No. for May 22, 1858), in which various evidence was adduced to show that the tongue is not necessary for articulate speech.

1. Col. Churchill, in his "Lebanon," speaking of the cruelties of Djezzar Pacha, in extracting to the root the tongues of some Emirs, adds, "It is a curious fact, however, that the tongues grow again, sufficiently for the purposes of speech."

2. Sir John Malcolm, in his "Sketches of Persia," speaks of Zâb, Khan of Khisht, who was condemned to lose his tongue. "This mandate," he says, "was imperfectly executed, and the loss of half this member deprived him of speech. Being afterwards persuaded that its being cut close to the root would enable him to speak so as to be understood, he submitted to the operation; and the effect has been, that his voice, though indistinct and thick, is yet intelligible to persons accustomed to converse with him. . . . I am not an anatomist, and I cannot therefore give a reason, why a man, who could not articulate with half a tongue, should speak when he had none at all; but the facts are as stated."

3. And Sir John McNeill says, "In answer to your inquiries about the powers of speech retained by persons who have had their tongues cut out, I can state from personal observation, that several persons whom I knew in Persia, who had been subjected to that punishment, spoke so intelligibly as to be able to transact important business. . . . The conviction in Persia is universal, that the power of speech is destroyed by merely cutting off the tip of the tongue; and is to a useful extent restored by cutting off another portion as far back as a perpendicular section can be made of the portion that is free from attachment at the lower surface. . . . I never had to meet with a person who had suffered this punishment, who could not speak so as to be quite intelligible to his familiar associates."

I should not be honest, if I professed to be simply converted, by these testimonies, to the belief that there was nothing miraculous in the case of the African confessors. It is quite as fair to be sceptical on one side of the question as on the other; and if Gibbon is considered worthy of praise for his stubborn incredulity in receiving the evidence for this miracle, I do not see why I am to be blamed, if I wish to be quite sure of the full appositeness of the recent evidence which is brought to its disadvantage. Questions of fact cannot be disproved by analogies or presumptions; the inquiry must be made into the particular case in all its parts, as it comes before us. Meanwhile, I fully allow that the points of evidence brought in disparagement of the miracle are *primâ facie* of such cogency, that, till they are proved to be irrelevant, Catholics are prevented from appealing to it for controversial purposes.

from An Essay in Aid of a Grammar of Assent

Newman's Grammar of Assent *is at once his most philosophical and his most psychological work. It is the culmination of his lifelong preoccupation with the relation of faith and reason. Newman was concerned to explore what it means to give assent to intellectual propositions. He found that the mind gives assent on grounds other than purely logical ones, that certitude follows not from demonstration by syllogism but from a multitude of antecedent accumulated probabilities. In exploring thus the actions of the mind Newman was engaging in a psychological examination that went beyond traditional or modern logic. He found it necessary therefore to create his own term to describe the faculty of mind that enabled man to reach the certitude that contained but also surpassed rational argument. He called it the "Illative Sense," adapting a term from logic used to relate to inferences and deductions from propositions. The chapter on the Illative Sense is given below.* The Grammar of Assent *was written between 1866 and 1869 and published in 1870.*

The Illative Sense

MY OBJECT in the foregoing pages has been, not to form a theory which may account for those phenomena of the intellect of which they treat, viz. those which characterize inference and assent, but to ascertain what is the matter of fact as regards them, that is, when it is that assent is given to propositions which are inferred, and under what circumstances. I have never had the thought of an attempt which in me would be ambitious and which has failed in the hands of others,—if that attempt may fairly be called unsuccessful, which, though made by the acutest minds, has not succeeded in convincing opponents. Especially have I found myself unequal to antecedent reasonings in the instance of a matter of fact. There are those, who, arguing *à priori*, maintain, that, since experience leads by syllogism only to probabilities, certitude is ever a mistake. There are others, who, while they deny this conclusion, grant the *à priori* principle assumed in the argument, and in consequence are obliged, in order to vindicate the certainty of our knowledge, to have recourse to the hypothesis of intuitions, intellectual forms, and the like, which belong to us by nature, and may be considered to elevate our experience into something more than it is in itself. Earnestly maintaining, as I would, with this latter school of philosophers, the certainty of knowledge, I think it enough to appeal to the common voice of mankind in proof of it. That is to be accounted a normal operation of our nature, which men in general do actually instance. That is a law of our minds, which is exemplified in action on a large scale, whether *à priori* it ought to be a law or no. Our hoping is a proof that hope, as such, is not an extravagance; and our possession of certitude is a proof that it is not a weakness or an absurdity to be certain. How it comes about that we can be certain is not my business to determine; for me it is sufficient that certitude is felt. This is what the schoolmen, I believe, call treating a subject *in facto esse,* in contrast with *in fieri.*[1] Had I attemp-

ted the latter, I should have been falling into metaphysics; but my aim is of a practical character, such as that of Butler in his *Analogy,* with this difference, that he treats of probability, doubt, expedience, and duty, whereas in these pages, without excluding, far from it, the question of duty, I would confine myself to the truth of things, and to the mind's certitude of that truth.

Certitude is a mental state: certainty is a quality of propositions. Those propositions I call certain, which are such that I am certain of them. Certitude is not a passive impression made upon the mind from without, by argumentative compulsion, but in all concrete questions (nay, even in abstract, for though the reasoning is abstract, the mind which judges of it is concrete) it is an active recognition of propositions as true, such as it is the duty of each individual himself to exercise at the bidding of reason, and, when reason forbids, to withhold. And reason never bids us be certain except on an absolute proof; and such a proof can never be furnished to us by the logic of words, for as certitude is of the mind, so is the act of inference which leads to it. Every one who reasons, is his own centre; and no expedient for attaining a common measure of minds can reverse this truth;—but then the question follows, is there any *criterion* of the accuracy of an inference, such as may be our warrant that certitude is rightly elicited in favour of the proposition inferred, since our warrant cannot, as I have said, be scientific? I have already said that the sole and final judgment on the validity of an inference in concrete matter is committed to the personal action of the ratiocinative faculty, the perfection or virtue of which I have called the Illative Sense, a use of the word "sense" parallel to our use of it in "good sense," "common sense," a "sense of beauty," &c.;—and I own I do not see any way to go farther than this in answer to the question. However, I can at least explain my meaning more fully; and therefore I will now speak, first of the sanction of the Illative Sense, next of its nature, and then of its range.

---

[1] *In facto esse,* in a completed state; *in fieri,* in a state of development or process.

§ 1. THE SANCTION OF THE ILLATIVE SENSE

We are in a world of facts, and we use them; for there is nothing else to use. We do not quarrel with them, but we take them as they are, and avail ourselves of what they can do for us. It would be out of place to demand of fire, water, earth, and air their credentials, so to say, for acting upon us, or ministering to us. We call them elements, and turn them to account, and make the most of them. We speculate on them at our leisure. But what we are still less able to doubt about or annul, at our leisure or not, is that which is at once their counterpart and their witness, I mean, ourselves. We are conscious of the objects of external nature, and we reflect and act upon them, and this consciousness, reflection, and action we call our rationality. And as we use the (so called) elements without first criticizing what we have no command over, so is it much more unmeaning in us to criticize or find fault with our own nature, which is nothing else than we ourselves, instead of using it according to the use of which it ordinarily admits. Our being, with its faculties, mind and body, is a fact not admitting of question, all things being of necessity referred to it, not it to other things.

If I may not assume that I exist, and in a particular way, that is, with a particular mental constitution, I have nothing to speculate about, and had better let speculation alone. Such as I am, it is my all; this is my essential stand-point, and must be taken for granted; otherwise, thought is but an idle amusement, not worth the trouble. There is no medium between using my faculties, as I have them, and flinging myself upon the external world according to the random impulse of the moment, as spray upon the surface of the waves, and simply forgetting that I am.

I am what I am, or I am nothing. I cannot think, reflect, or judge about my being, without starting from the very point which I aim at concluding. My ideas are all assumptions, and I am ever moving in a circle. I cannot avoid being sufficient for myself, for I cannot make myself anything else, and to change me is to destroy me. If I do not use myself, I have no other self to use. My only business is to ascertain what I am, in order to put it to use. It is enough for the proof of the value and authority of any function which I possess, to be able to pronounce that it is natural. What I have to ascertain is the laws under which I live. My first elementary lesson of duty is that of resignation to the laws of my nature, whatever they are; my first disobedience is to be impatient at what I am, and to indulge an ambitious aspiration after what I cannot be, to cherish a distrust of my powers, and to desire to change laws which are identical with myself.

Truths such as these, which are too obvious to be called irresistible, are illustrated by what we see in universal nature. Every being is in a true sense sufficient for itself, so as to be able to fulfil its particular needs. It is a general law that, whatever is found as a function or an attribute of any class of beings, or is natural to it, is in its substance suitable to it, and subserves its existence, and cannot be rightly regarded as a fault or enormity. No being could endure, of which the constituent parts were at war with each other. And more than this; there is that principle of vitality in every being, which is of a sanative and restorative character, and which brings all its parts and functions together into one whole, and is ever repelling and correcting the mischiefs which befall it, whether from within or without, while showing no tendency to cast off its belongings as if foreign to its nature. The brute animals are found severally with limbs and organs, habits, instincts, appetites, surroundings, which play together for the safety and welfare of the whole; and, after all exceptions, may be said each of them to have, after its own kind, a perfection of nature. Man is the highest of the animals, and more indeed than an animal, as having a mind; that is, he has a complex nature different from theirs, with a higher aim and a specific perfection; but still the fact that other beings find their good in the use of their particular nature, is a reason for anticipating that to use duly our own is our interest as well as our necessity.

What is the peculiarity of our nature, in contrast with the inferior animals around us? It is that, though man cannot change what he is born with, he is a being of progress with relation to his perfection and characteristic good. Other beings are complete from their first existence, in that line of excellence which is allotted to them; but man begins with nothing realized (to use the word), and he has to make capital for himself by the exercise of those faculties which are his natural inheritance. Thus he gradually advances to the fulness of his original destiny. Nor is this progress mechanical, nor is it of necessity; it is committed to the personal efforts of each individual of the species; each of us has the prerogative of completing his inchoate and rudimental nature, and of developing his own perfection out of the living elements with which his mind began to be. It is his gift to be the creator of his own sufficiency; and to be emphatically self-made. This is the law of his being, which he cannot escape; and whatever is involved in that law he is bound, or rather he is carried on, to fulfil.

And here I am brought to the bearing of these remarks upon my subject. For this law of progress is carried out by means of the acquisition of knowledge, of which inference and assent are the immediate instruments. Supposing, then, the advancement of our nature, both in ourselves individually and as regards the human family, is, to every one of us in his place, a sacred duty, it follows that that duty is intimately bound up with the right use of these two main instruments of fulfilling it. And as we do not gain the knowledge of the law of progress by any *à priori* view of man, but by looking at it as the interpretation which is provided by himself on a large scale in the ordinary action of his intellectual nature, so too we must appeal to himself, as a fact, and not to any antecedent theory, in order to find what is the law of his mind as regards the two faculties in question. If then such an appeal does bear me out in deciding, as I have done, that the course of inference is ever more or less obscure, while assent is ever distinct and definite, and yet that what is in its nature thus absolute does, in fact follow upon what in outward manifestation is thus complex, indirect, and recondite, what is left to us but to take things as they are, and to resign ourselves to what we find? that is, instead of devising, what cannot be, some sufficient science of reasoning which may compel certitude in concrete conclusions, to confess that there is no ultimate test of truth besides the testimony born to truth by the mind itself, and that this phenomenon, perplexing as we may find it, is a normal and inevitable characteristic of the mental constitution of a being like man on a stage such as the world. His progress is a living growth, not a mechanism; and its instruments are mental acts, not the formulas and contrivances of language.

We are accustomed in this day to lay great stress upon the harmony of the universe; and we have well learned the maxim so powerfully inculcated by our own English philosopher, that in our inquiries into its laws, we must sternly destroy all idols of the intellect, and subdue nature by co-operating with her. Knowledge is power, for it enables us to use eternal principles which we cannot alter. So also is it in that microcosm, the human mind. Let us follow Bacon[2] more closely than to distort its faculties according to the demands of an ideal optimism, instead of looking out for modes of thought proper to our nature, and faithfully observing them in our intellectual exercises.

Of course I do not stop here. As the structure of the universe speaks to us of Him who made it, so the laws of the mind are the expression, not of mere constituted order, but of His will. I should be bound by them even were they not His laws; but since one of their very functions is to tell me of Him, they throw a reflex light upon themselves, and, for resignation to my destiny, I substitute a cheerful concurrence in an over-ruling Providence. We may gladly welcome such difficulties as are to be found in our mental constitution, and in the interaction of our faculties, if we are able to feel that He gave them to us, and He can over-rule them for us. We may securely take them as they are, and use them as we find them. It is He who teaches us all knowledge; and the way by which we acquire it is His way. He varies that way according to the subject-matter; but whether He has set before us in our particular pursuit the way of observation or of experiment, of speculation or of research, of demonstration or of probability, whether we are inquiring into the system of the universe, or into the elements of matter and of life, or into the history of human society and past times, if we take the way proper to our subject-matter, we have His blessing upon us, and shall find, besides abundant matter for mere opinion, the materials in due measure of proof and assent.

And especially, by this disposition of things, shall we learn, as regards religious and ethical inquiries, how little we can effect, however much we exert ourselves, without that Blessing; for, as if on set purpose, He has made this path of thought rugged and circuitous above other investigations, that the very discipline inflicted on our minds in finding Him, may mould them into due devotion to Him when He is found. "Verily Thou art a hidden God, the God of Israel, the Saviour,"[3] is the very law of His dealings with us. Certainly we need a clue into the labyrinth which

---

[2] Francis Bacon (1561–1626), English philosopher and author whose philosophy was based on empiricism—the doctrine that all knowledge is derived from experience and observation.
[3] Isaiah 45:15.

is to lead us to Him; and who among us can hope to seize upon the true starting-points of thought for that enterprise, and upon all of them, who is to understand their right direction, to follow them out of their just limits, and duly to estimate, adjust, and combine the various reasonings in which they issue, so as safely to arrive at what it is worth any labour to secure, without a special illumination from Himself? Such are the dealings of Wisdom with the elect soul. "She will bring upon him fear, and dread, and trial; and She will torture him with the tribulation of Her discipline, till She try him by Her laws, and trust his soul. Then She will strengthen him, and make Her way straight to him, and give him joy."[4]

§ 2. THE NATURE OF THE ILLATIVE SENSE.

It is the mind that reasons, and that controls its own reasonings, not any technical apparatus of words and propositions. This power of judging and concluding, when in its perfection, I call the Illative Sense, and I shall best illustrate it by referring to parallel faculties, which we commonly recognize without difficulty.

For instance, how does the mind fulfil its function of supreme direction and control, in matters of duty, social intercourse, and taste? In all of these separate actions of the intellect, the individual is supreme, and responsible to himself, nay, under circumstances, may be justified in opposing himself to the judgment of the whole world; though he uses rules to his great advantage, as far as they go, and is in consequence bound to use them. As regards moral duty, the subject is fully considered in the well-known ethical treatises of Aristotle.[5] He calls the faculty which guides the mind in matters of conduct, by the name of *phronesis*, or judgment. This is the directing, controlling, and determining principle in such matters, personal and social. What it is to be virtuous, how we are to gain the just idea and standard of virtue, how we are to approximate in practice to our own standard, what is right and wrong in a particular case, for the answers in fulness and accuracy to these and similar questions, the philosopher refers us to no

code of laws, to no moral treatise, because no science of life, applicable to the case of an individual, has been or can be written. Such is Aristotle's doctrine, and it is undoubtedly true. An ethical system may supply laws, general rules, guiding principles, a number of examples, suggestions, landmarks, limitations, cautions, distinctions, solutions of critical or anxious difficulties; but who is to apply them to a particular case? whither can we go, except to the living intellect, our own, or another's? What is written is too vague, too negative for our need. It bids us avoid extremes; but it cannot ascertain for us, according to our personal need, the golden mean. The authoritative oracle, which is to decide our path, is something more searching and manifold than such jejune generalizations as treatises can give, which are most distinct and clear when we least need them. It is seated in the mind of the individual, who is thus his own law, his own teacher, and his own judge in those special cases of duty which are personal to him. It comes of an acquired habit, though it has its first origin in nature itself, and it is formed and matured by practice and experience; and it manifests itself, not in any breadth of view, any philosophical comprehension of the mutual relations of duty towards duty, or any consistency in its teachings but it is a capacity sufficient for the occasion, deciding what ought to be done here and now, by this given person, under these given circumstances. It decides nothing hypothetical, it does not determine what a man should do ten years hence, or what another should do at this time. It may indeed happen to decide ten years hence as it does now, and to decide a second case now as it now decides a first; still its present act is for the present, not for the distant or the future.

State or public law is inflexible, but this mental rule is not only minute and particular, but has an elasticity, which, in its application to individual cases, is, as I have said, not studious to maintain the appearance of consistency. In old times the mason's rule which was in use at Lesbos was, according to Aristotle, not of wood or iron, but of lead, so as to allow of its adjustment to the uneven surface of the stones brought together for the work. By such the philosopher illustrates the nature of equity in contrast with law, and such is

---

[4] Ecclesiasticus 4: 19–20.

[5] Though Aristotle in his Nicomachean Ethics, speaks of φρόνησις as the virtue of the δοξαστικὸν generally, and as being concerned generally with contingent matter (vi.4), or what I have called the concrete, and of its function being, as regards that matter, ἀληθεύειν τῷ καταφάναι ἢ ἀποφάναι (ibid. 3), he does not treat of it in that work in its general relation to truth and the affirmation of truth, but only as it bears upon τὰ πρακγά. [Newman's note]

that *phronesis*, from which the science of morals forms its rules, and receives its complement.

In this respect of course the law of truth differs from the law of duty, that duties change, but truths never; but, though truth is ever one and the same, and the assent of certitude is immutable, still the reasonings which carry us on to truth and certitude are many and distinct, and vary with the inquirer; and it is not with assent, but with the controlling principle in inferences that I am comparing *phronesis*. It is with this drift that I observe that the rule of conduct for one man is not always the rule for another, though the rule is always one and the same in the abstract, and in its principle and scope. To learn his own duty in his own case, each individual must have recourse to his own rule; and if his rule is not sufficiently developed in his intellect for his need, then he goes to some other living, present authority, to supply it for him, not to the dead letter of a treatise or a code. A living, present authority, himself or another, is his immediate guide in matters of a personal, social, or political character. In buying and selling, in contracts, in his treatment of others, in giving and receiving, in thinking, speaking, doing, and working, in toil, in danger, in his recreations and pleasures, every one of his acts, to be praiseworthy, must be in accordance with this practical sense. Thus it is, and not by science, that he perfects the virtues of justice, self-command, magnanimity, generosity, gentleness, and all others. *Phronesis* is the regulating principle of every one of them.

These last words lead me to a further remark. I doubt whether it is correct, strictly speaking, to consider this *phronesis* as a general faculty, directing and perfecting all the virtues at once. So understood, it is little better than an abstract term, including under it a circle of analogous faculties, severally proper to the separate virtues. Properly speaking, there are as many kinds of *phronesis* as there are virtues: for the judgment, good sense, or tact which is conspicuous in a man's conduct in one subject-matter, is not necessarily traceable in another. As in the parallel cases of memory and reasoning, he may be great in one aspect of his character, and little-minded in another. He may be exemplary in his family, yet commit a fraud on the revenue; he may be just and cruel, brave and sensual, imprudent and patient. And if this be true of the moral virtues, it holds good still more fully when we compare what is called his private character

with his public. A good man may make a bad king; profligates have been great statesmen, or magnanimous political leaders.

So, too, I may go on to speak of the various callings and professions which give scope to the exercise of great talents, for these talents also are matured, not by mere rule, but by personal skill and sagacity. They are as diverse as pleading and cross-examining, conducting a debate in Parliament, swaying a public meeting, and commanding an army; and here, too, I observe that, though the directing principle in each case is called by the same name,—sagacity, skill, tact, or prudence,—still there is no one ruling faculty leading to eminence in all these various lines of action in common, but men will excel in one of them, without any talent for the rest.

The parallel may be continued in the case of the Fine Arts, in which, though true and scientific rules may be given, no one would therefore deny that Phidias or Rafael[6] had a far more subtle standard of taste and a more versatile power of embodying it in his works, than any which he could communicate to others in even a series of treatises. And here again genius is indissolubly united to one definite subject-matter; a poet is not therefore a painter, or an architect a musical composer.

And, so, again, as regards the useful arts and personal accomplishments, we use the same word "skill," but proficiency in engineering or in ship-building, or again in engraving, or again in singing, in playing instruments, in acting, or in gymnastic exercises, is as simply one with its particular subject-matter, as the human soul with its particular body, and is, in its own department, a sort of instinct or inspiration, not an obedience to external rules of criticism or of science.

It is natural, then, to ask the question, why ratiocination should be an exception to a general law which attaches to the intellectual exercises of the mind; why it is held to be commensurate with logical science; and why logic is made an instrumental art sufficient for determining every sort of truth, while no one would dream of making any one formula, however generalized, a working rule at once for poetry, the art of medicine, and political warfare?

This is what I have to remark concerning the Illative Sense, and in explanation of its nature and claims; and on the whole, I have spoken of it in four respects,—as viewed in itself, in its

---

[6] Phidias (8th Century B.C.), Greek sculptor; Rafael, or Raphael (1483–1520), Italian painter.

subject-matter, in the process it uses, and in its function and scope.

First, viewed in its exercise, it is one and the same in all concrete matters, though employed in them in different measures. We do not reason in one way in chemistry or law, in another in morals or religion; but in reasoning on any subject whatever, which is concrete, we proceed, as far indeed as we can, by the logic of language, but we are obliged to supplement it by the more subtle and elastic logic of thought; for forms by themselves prove nothing.

Secondly, it is in fact attached to definite subject-matters, so that a given individual may possess it in one department of thought, for instance, history, and not in another, for instance, philosophy.

Thirdly, in coming to its conclusion, it proceeds always in the same way, by a method of reasoning, which, as I have observed above, is the elementary principle of that mathematical calculus of modern times, which has so wonderfully extended the limits of abstract science.

Fourthly, in no class of concrete reasonings, whether in experimental science, historical research, or theology, is there any ultimate test of truth and error in our inferences besides the trustworthiness of the Illative Sense that gives them its sanction; just as there is no sufficient test of poetical excellence, heroic action, or gentleman-like conduct, other than the particular mental sense, be it genius, taste, sense of propriety, or the moral sense, to which those subject-matters are severally committed. Our duty in each of these is to strengthen and perfect the special faculty which is its living rule, and in every case as it comes to do our best. And such also is our duty and our necessity, as regards the Illative Sense.

§ 3. The Range of the Illative Sense.

Great as are the services of language in enabling us to extend the compass of our inferences, to test their validity, and to communicate them to others, still the mind itself is more versatile and vigorous than any of its works, of which language is one, and it is only under its penetrating and subtle action that the margin disappears, which I have described as intervening between verbal argumentation and conclusions in the concrete. It determines what science cannot determine, the limit of converging probabilities and the reasons sufficient for a proof. It is the ratiocinative mind itself, and no trick of art, however simple in its form and sure in operation, by which we are able to determine, and thereupon to be certain, that a moving body left to itself will never stop, and that no man can live without eating.

Nor, again, is it by any diagram that we are able to scrutinize, sort, and combine the many premises which must be first run together before we answer duly a given question. It is to the living mind that we must look for the means of using correctly principles of whatever kind, facts or doctrines, experiences or testimonies, true or probable, and of discerning what conclusion from these is necessary, suitable, or expedient, when they are taken for granted; and this, either by means of a natural gift, or from mental formation and practice and a long familiarity with those various starting-points. Thus, when Laud[7] said that he did not see his way to come to terms with the Holy See, "till Rome was other than she was," no Catholic would admit the sentiment: but any Catholic may understand that this is just the judgment consistent with Laud's actual condition of thought and cast of opinions, his ecclesiastical position, and the existing state of England.

Nor, lastly, is an action of the mind itself less necessary in relation to those first elements of thought which in all reasoning are assumptions, the principles, tastes, and opinions, very often of a personal character, which are half the battle in the inference with which the reasoning is to terminate. It is the mind itself that detects them in their obscure recesses, illustrates them, establishes them, eliminates them, resolves them into simpler ideas, as the case may be. The mind contemplates them without the use of words, by a process which cannot be analyzed. Thus it was that Bacon separated the physical system of the world from the theological; thus that Butler connected together the moral system with the religious. Logical formulas could never have sustained the reasonings involved in such investigations.

Thus the Illative Sense, that is, the reasoning faculty, as exercised by gifted, or by educated or otherwise well-prepared minds, has its function in the beginning, middle, and end of all verbal discussion and inquiry, and in every step of the process. It is a rule to itself, and appeals to no judgment beyond its own; and attends upon the whole course of thought from antecedents to

---

[7] William Laud (1573–1645), Archbishop of Canterbury.

consequents, with a minute diligence and unwearied presence, which is impossible to a cumbrous apparatus of verbal reasoning, though, in communicating with others, words are the only instrument we possess, and a serviceable, though imperfect instrument.

One function indeed there is of Logic, to which I have referred in the preceding sentence, which the Illative Sense does not and cannot perform. It supplies no common measure between mind and mind, as being nothing else than a personal gift or acquisition. Few there are, as I said above, who are good reasoners on all subject-matters. Two men, who reason well each in his own province of thought, may, one or both of them, fail and pronounce opposite judgments on a question belonging to some third province. Moreover, all reasoning being from premisses, and those premisses arising (if it so happen) in their first elements from personal characteristics, in which men are in fact in essential and irremediable variance one with another, the ratiocinative talent can do no more than point out where the difference between them lies, how far it is immaterial, when it is worth while continuing an argument between them, and when not.

Now of the three main occasions of the exercise of the Illative Sense, which I have been insisting on, and which are the measure of its range, the start, the course, and the issue of an inquiry, I have already, in treating of Informal Inference, shown the place it holds in the final resolution of concrete questions. Here then it is left to me to illustrate its presence and action in relation to the elementary premisses, and, again, to the conduct of an argument. And first of the latter.

1

There has been a great deal written of late years on the subject of the state of Greece and Rome during the pre-historic period; let us say before the Olympiads in Greece, and the war with Pyrrhus in the annals of Rome. Now, in a question like this, it is plain that the inquirer has first of all to decide on the point from which he is to start in the presence of the received accounts; on what side, from what quarter he is to approach them; on what principles his discussion is to be conducted; what he is to assume, what opinions or objections he is summarily to put aside as nugatory, what arguments, and when, he is to

consider as apposite, what false issues are to be avoided, when the state of his arguments is ripe for a conclusion. Is he to commence with absolutely discarding all that has hitherto been received; or to retain it in outline; or to make selections from it; or to consider and interpret it as mythical, or as allegorical; or to hold so much to be trustworthy, or at least of *primâ facie* authority, as he cannot actually disprove; or never to destroy except in proportion as he can construct? Then, as to the kind of arguments suitable or admissible, how far are tradition, analogy, isolated monuments and records, ruins, vague reports, legends, the facts or sayings of later times, language, popular proverbs, to tell in the inquiry? what are marks of truth, what of falsehood, what is probable, what suspicious, what promises well for discriminating facts from fictions? Then, arguments have to be balanced against each other, and then lastly the decision is to be made, whether any conclusion at all can be drawn, or whether any before certain issues are tried and settled, or whether a probable conclusion or a certain. It is plain how incessant will be the call here or there for the exercise of a definitive judgment, how little that judgment will be helped on by logic, and how intimately it will be dependent upon the intellectual complexion of the writer.

This might be illustrated at great length, were it necessary, from the writings of any of those able men, whose names are so well known in connexion with the subject I have instanced; such as Niebuhr, Mr. Clinton, Sir George Lewis, Mr. Grote, and Colonel Mure.[8] These authors have severally views of their own on the period of history which they have selected for investigation, and they are too learned and logical not to know and to use to the utmost the testimonies by which the facts which they investigate are to be ascertained. Why then do they differ so much from each other, whether in their estimate of those testimonies or of those facts? because that estimate is simply their own, coming of their own judgment; and that judgment coming of assumptions of their own, explicit or implicit; and those assumptions spontaneously issuing out of the state of thought respectively belonging to each of them; and all these successive processes of minute reasoning superintended and directed by an intellectual instrument far too subtle and spiritual to be scientific.

---

[8] Barthold Georg Niebuhr (1776–1831), German historian; Henry Fynes Clinton (1781–1852), English classicist; Sir George Cornewall Lewis (1806–63), English historian; George Grote (1794–1871), English historian and politician; Newman cites from these authors throughout this section; see his reference note 10, below.

What was Niebuhr's idea of the office he had undertaken? I suppose it was to accept what he found in the historians of Rome, to interrogate it, to take it to pieces, to put it together again, to re-arrange and interpret it. Prescription together with internal consistency was to him the evidence of fact, and if he pulled down he felt he was bound to build up. Very different is the spirit of another school of writers, with whom prescription is nothing, and who will admit no evidence which has not first proved its right to be admitted. "We are able," says Niebuhr, "to trace the history of the Roman constitution back to the beginning of the Commonwealth, as accurately as we wish, and even more perfectly than the history of many portions of the middle ages." But, "we may rejoice," says Sir George Lewis, "that the ingenuity or learning of Niebuhr should have enabled him to advance many noble hypotheses and conjectures respecting the form of the early constitution of Rome, but, unless he can support those hypotheses by sufficient evidence, they are not entitled to our belief." "Niebuhr," says a writer nearly related to myself, "often expresses much contempt for mere incredulous criticism and negative conclusions; . . yet wisely to disbelieve is our first grand requisite in dealing with materials of mixed worth." And Sir George Lewis again, "It may be said that there is scarcely any of the leading conclusions of Niebuhr's work which has not been impugned by some subsequent writer."

Again, "It is true," says Niebuhr, "that the Trojan war belongs to the region of fable, yet undeniably it has an historical foundation." But Mr. Grote writes, "If we are asked whether the Trojan war is not a legend . . raised upon a basis of truth, . . our answer must be, that, as the possibility of it cannot be denied, so neither can the reality of it be affirmed." On the other hand, Mr. Clinton lays down the general rule, "We may acknowledge as real persons, all those whom there is no reason for rejecting. The presumption is in favour of the early tradition, if no argument can be brought to overthrow it." Thus he lodges the *onus probandi*[9] with those who impugn the received accounts; but Mr. Grote and Sir George Lewis throw it upon those who defend them. "Historical evidence," says the latter, "is founded on the testimony of credible witnesses." And again, "It is perpetually assumed in practice, that historical evidence is different in its nature from

other sorts of evidence. This laxity seems to be justified by the doctrine of taking the best evidence which can be obtained. The object of [my] inquiry will be to apply to the early Roman history the same rules of evidence which are applied by common consent to modern history." Far less severe is the judgment of Colonel Mure: "Where no positive historical proof is affirmable, the balance of historical probability must reduce itself very much to a reasonable indulgence to the weight of national conviction, and a deference to the testimony of the earliest native authorities." "Reasonable indulgence" to popular belief, "deference" to ancient tradition, are principles of writing history abhorrent to the judicial temper of Sir George Lewis. He considers the words "reasonable indulgence" to be "ambiguous," and observes that "the very point which cannot be taken for granted, and in which writers differ, is, as to the extent to which contemporary attestation may be presumed without direct and positive proof, . . the extent to which the existence of a popular belief concerning a supposed matter of fact authorizes the inference that it grew out of authentic testimony." And Mr. Grote observes to the same effect: "The word *tradition* is an equivocal word, and begs the whole question. It is tacitly understood to imply a tale descriptive of some real matter of fact, taking rise at the time when the fact happened, originally accurate, but corrupted by oral transmission." And Lewis, who quotes the passage, adds, "This *tacit understanding* is the key-stone of the whole argument."

I am not contrasting these various opinions of able men, who have given themselves to historical research, as if it were any reflection on them that they differ from each other. It is the cause of their differing on which I wish to insist. Taking the facts by themselves, probably these authors would come to no conclusion at all; it is the "tacit understandings" which Mr. Grote speaks of, the vague and impalpable notions of "reasonableness" on his own side as well as on that of others, which both make conclusions possible, and are the pledge of their being contradictory. The conclusions vary with the particular writer, for each writes from his own point of view and with his own principles, and these admit of no common measure.

This in fact is their own account of the matter: "The results of speculative historical inquiry," says Colonel Mure, "can rarely amount to more than fair presumption of the reality of the events in question, as limited to their general substance, not as extending to their details. Nor can there consequently be expected in the minds of different inquirers any such unity regarding the precise degree of reality, as may frequently exist in respect to events attested by documentary evidence." Mr. Grote corroborates this decision by the striking instance of the diversity of existing opinions concerning the Homeric Poems. "Our means of knowledge," he says, "are so limited, that no one can produce arguments sufficiently cogent to contend against opposing preconceptions, and it creates a painful sensation of diffidence, when we read the expressions of equal and absolute persuasion with which the two opposite conclusions have both been advanced." And again, "There is a difference of opinion among the best critics, which is probably not destined to be adjusted, since so much depends partly upon critical feeling, partly upon the general reasonings in respect to ancient epical unity, with which a man sits down to the study." Exactly so; every one has his own "critical feeling," his antecedent "reasonings," and in consequence his own "absolute persuasion," coming in fresh and fresh at every turn of the discussion; and who, whether stranger or friend, is to reach and affect what is so intimately bound up with the mental constitution of each?

Hence the categorical contradictions between one writer and another, which abound. Colonel Mure appeals in defence of an historical thesis to the "fact of the Hellenic confederacy combining for the adoption of a common national system of chronology in 776 B.C." Mr. Grote replies: "Nothing is more at variance with my conception,"—he just now spoke of the preconceptions of others,—"of the state of the Hellenic world in 776 B.C., than the idea of a combination among all the members of the race for any purpose, much more for the purpose of adopting a common national system of chronology." Colonel Mure speaks of the "bigoted Athenian public;" Mr. Grote replies that "no public ever less deserved the epithet of 'bigoted' than the Athenian." Colonel Mure also speaks of Mr. Grote's "arbitrary hypothesis;" and again (in Mr. Grote's words), of his "unreasonable scepticism." He cannot disprove by mere argument the conclusions of Mr. Grote; he can but have recourse to a personal criticism. He virtually says, "We differ in our personal view of things." Men become personal when logic fails; it is their mode of appealing to their own primary elements of thought, and their own illative sense, against the principles and the judgment of another.

I have already touched upon Niebuhr's method of investigation, and Sir George Lewis's dislike of it: it supplies us with as apposite an instance of a difference in first principles as is afforded by Mr. Grote and Colonel Mure. "The main characteristic of his history," says Lewis, "is the extent to which he relies upon internal evidence, and upon the indications afforded by the narrative itself, independently of the testimony of its truth." And, "Ingenuity and labour can produce nothing but hypotheses and conjectures, which may be supported by analogies, but can never rest upon the solid foundation of proof." And it is undeniable, that, rightly or wrongly, disdaining the scepticism of the mere critic, Niebuhr does consciously proceed by the high path of divination. "For my own part," he says, "I *divine* that, since the censorship of Fabius and Decius falls in the same year, that Cn. Flavius became mediator between his own class and the higher orders." Lewis considers this to be a process of guessing; and says, "Instead of employing those tests of credibility which are consistently applied to modern history," Niebuhr, and his followers, and most of his opponents, "attempt to guide their judgment by the indication of internal evidence, and assume that the truth is discovered by an occult faculty of historical divination." Niebuhr defends himself thus: "The real geographer has a tact which determines his judgment and choice among different statements. He is able from isolated statements to draw inferences respecting things that are unknown, which are closely approximate to results obtained from observation of facts, and may supply their place. He is able with limited data to form an image of things which no eye-witness has described." He applies this to himself. The principle set forth in this passage is obviously the same as I should myself advocate; but Sir George Lewis, though not simply denying it as a principle, makes little account of it, when applied to historical research. "It is not enough," he says, "for an historian to claim the possession of a retrospective second-sight, which is denied to the rest of the world— of a mysterious doctrine, revealed only to the initiated." And he pronounces, that "the history of Niebuhr has opened more questions than it has closed, and it has set in motion a large body of combatants, whose mutual variances are not at present likely to be settled by deference to a common principle."[10]

We see from the above extracts how a controversy, such as that to which they belong, is carried on from starting-points, and with collateral aids, not formally proved, but more or less assumed, the process of assumption lying in the action of the Illative Sense, as applied to primary elements of thought respectively congenial to the disputants. Not that explicit argumentation on these minute or minor, though important, points is not sometimes possible to a certain extent; but, as I have said, it is too unwieldy an expedient for a constantly recurring need, even when it is tolerably exact.

2

And now secondly, as to the first principles themselves. In illustration, I will mention under separate heads some of those elementary contrarieties of opinion, on which the Illative Sense has to act, discovering them, following them out, defending or resisting them, as the case may be.

1. As to the statement of the case. This depends on the particular aspect under which we view a subject, that is, on the abstraction which forms our representative notion of what it is. Sciences are only so many distinct aspects of nature; sometimes suggested by nature itself, sometimes created by the mind. (1) One of the simplest and broadest aspects under which to view the physical world, is that of a system of final causes, or, on the other hand, of initial or effective causes. Bacon, having it in view to extend our power over nature, adopted the latter. He took firm hold of the idea of causation (in the common sense of the word) as contrasted with that of design, refusing to mix up the two ideas in one inquiry, and denouncing such traditional interpretations of facts, as did but obscure the simplicity of the aspect necessary for his purpose. He saw what others before him might have seen in what they saw, but who did not see as he saw it. In this achievement of intellect, which has been so fruitful in results, lie his genius and his fame.

(2) So again, to refer to a very different subject-matter, we often hear of the exploits of some great lawyer, judge or advocate, who is able in perplexed cases, when common minds see nothing

but a hopeless heap of facts, foreign or contrary to each other, to detect the principle which rightly interprets the riddle, and, to the admiration of all hearers, converts a chaos into an orderly and luminous whole. This is what is meant by originality in thinking: it is the discovery of an aspect of a subject-matter, simpler, it may be, and more intelligible than any hitherto taken.

(3) On the other hand, such aspects are often unreal, as being mere exhibitions of ingenuity, not of true originality of mind. This is especially the case in what are called philosophical views of history. Such seems to me the theory advocated in a work of great learning, vigour, and acuteness, Warburton's "Divine Legation of Moses." I do not call Gibbon[11] merely ingenious; still his account of the rise of Christianity is the mere subjective view of one who could not enter into its depth and power.

(4) The aspect under which we view things is often intensely personal; nay, even awfully so, considering that, from the nature of the case, it does not bring home its idiosyncrasy either to ourselves or to others. Each of us looks at the world in his own way, and does not know that perhaps it is characteristically his own. This is the case even as regards the senses. Some men have little perception of colours; some recognize one or two; to some men two contrary colours, as red and green, are one and the same. How poorly can we appreciate the beauties of nature, if our eyes discern, on the face of things, only an Indian-ink or a drab creation!

(5) So again, as regards form: each of us abstracts the relation of line to line in his own personal way,—as one man might apprehend a curve as convex, another as concave. Of course, as in the case of a curve, there may be a limit to possible aspects; but still, even when we agree together, it is not perhaps that we learn one from another, or fall under any law of agreement, but that our separate idiosyncrasies happen to concur. I fear I may seem trifling, if I allude to an illustration which has ever had a great force with me, and that for the very reason it is so trivial and minute. Children, learning to read, are sometimes presented with the letters of the alphabet turned into the figures of men in various attitudes. It is curious to observe from such representations, how

[10] Niebuhr, "Roman History," vol. i. p. 177; vol. iii. pp. 262. 318. 3221 "Lectures," vol. iii. App. p. xxii. Lewis, "Roman History," vol. i. pp. 11–17; vol. ii. pp. 489–492. F. W. Newman, "Regal Rome," p. v. Grote, "Greece," vol. ii. pp. 67, 68. 218. 630–639. Mure, "Greece," vol. iii. p. 503; vol. iv. p. 318. Clinton, ap. Grote, supra. [Newman's note]

[11] Edward Gibbon (1737–1794), English historian, author of *The History of the Decline and Fall of the Roman Empire* in which he attributes the collapse of the Roman Empire to Christian superstition.

differently the shape of the letters strikes different minds. In consequence I have continually asked the question in a chance company, which way certain of the great letters look, to the right or the left; and whereas nearly every one present had his own clear view, so clear that he could not endure the opposite view, still I have generally found that one half of the party considered the letters in question to look to the left, while the other half thought they looked to the right.

(6) This variety of interpretation in the very elements of outlines seems to throw light upon other cognate differences between one man and another. If they look at the mere letters of the alphabet so differently, we may understand how it is they form such distinct judgments upon handwriting; nay, how some men may have a talent for deciphering from it the intellectual and moral character of the writer, which others have not. Another thought that occurs is, that perhaps here lies the explanation why it is that family likenesses are so variously recognized, and how mistakes in identity may be dangerously frequent.

(7) If we so variously apprehend the familiar objects of sense, still more various, we may suppose, are the aspects and associations attached by us, one with another, to intellectual objects. I do not say we differ in the objects themselves, but that we may have interminable differences as to their relations and circumstances. I have heard say (again to take a trifling matter) that at the beginning of this century, it was a subject of serious, nay, of angry controversy, whether it began with January 1800, or January 1801. Argument, which ought, if in any case, to have easily brought the question to a decision, was but sprinkling water upon a flame. I am not clear that, if it could be fairly started now, it would not lead to similar results; certainly I know those who studiously withdraw from giving an opinion on the subject, when it is accidentally mooted, from their experience of the eager feeling which it is sure to excite in some one or other who is present. This eagerness can only arise from an overpowering sense that the truth of the matter lies in the one alternative, and not in the other.

These instances, because they are so casual, suggest how it comes to pass, that men differ so widely from each other in religious and moral perceptions. Here, I say again, it does not prove that there is no objective truth, because not all men are in possession of it; or that we are not responsible for the associations which we attach, and the relations which we assign, to the objects of the intellect. But this it does suggest, to us that there is something deeper in our differences than the accident of external circumstances; and that we need the interposition of a Power, greater than human teaching and human argument, to make our beliefs true and our minds one.

2. Next I come to the implicit assumption of definite propositions in the first start of a course of reasoning, and the arbitrary exclusion of others, of whatever kind. Unless we had the right, when we pleased, of ruling that propositions were irrelevant or absurd, I do not see how we could conduct an argument at all; our way would be simply blocked up by extravagant principles and theories, gratuitous hypotheses, false issues, unsupported statements, and incredible facts. There are those who have treated the history of Abraham as an astronomical record, and have spoken of our Adorable Saviour as the sun in *Aries*. Arabian Mythology has changed Solomon into a mighty wizard. Noah has been considered the patriarch of the Chinese people. The ten tribes have been pronounced still to live in their descendants, the Red Indians; or to be the ancestors of the Goths and Vandals, and thereby of the present European races. Some have conjectured that the Apollos of the Acts of the Apostles was Apollonius Tyaneus. Able men have reasoned out, almost against their will, that Adam was a negro. These propositions, and many others of various kinds, we should think ourselves justified in passing over, if we were engaged in a work on sacred history; and there are others, on the contrary, which we should assume as true by our own right and without notice, and without which we could not set about or carry on our work.

(1) However, the right of making assumptions has been disputed; but, when the objections are examined, I think they only go to show that we have no right in argument to make any assumption we please. Thus, in the historical researches which just now came before us, it seems fair to say that no testimony should be received, except such as comes from competent witnesses, while it is not unfair to urge, on the other side, that tradition, though unauthenticated, being (what is called) in possession, has a prescription in its favour, and may, *primâ facie*, or provisionally, be received. Here are the materials of a fair dispute; but there are writers who seem to have gone far beyond this reasonable scepticism, laying down as a general proposition that we have no right in philosophy to make any assumption whatever, and that we ought to begin with a universal

doubt. This, however, is of all assumptions the greatest and to forbid assumptions universally is to forbid this one in particular. Doubt itself is a positive state, and implies a definite habit of mind, and thereby necessarily involves a system of principles and doctrines all its own. Again, if nothing is to be assumed, what is our very method of reasoning but an assumption? and what our nature itself? The very sense of pleasure and pain, which is one of the most intimate portions of ourselves, inevitably translates itself into intellectual assumptions.

Of the two, I would rather have to maintain that we ought to begin with believing everything that is offered to our acceptance, than that it is our duty to doubt of everything. The former, indeed, seems the true way of learning. In that case, we soon discover and discard what is contradictory to itself; and error having always some portion of truth in it, and the truth having a reality which error has not, we may expect, that when there is an honest purpose and fair talents, we shall somehow make our way forward, the error falling off from the mind, and the truth developing and occupying it. Thus it is that the Catholic religion is reached, as we see, by inquirers from all points of the compass, as if it mattered not where a man began, so that he had an eye and a heart for the truth.

(2) An argument has been often put forward by unbelievers, I think by Paine,[12] to this effect, that "a revelation, which is to be received as true, ought to be written on the sun." This appeals to the commonsense of the many with great force, and implies the assumption of a principle which Butler, indeed, would not grant, and would consider unphilosophical, and yet I think something may be said in its favour. Whether abstractedly defensible or not, Catholic populations would not be averse, *mutatis mutandis*, to admitting it. Till these last centuries, the Visible Church was, at least to her children, the light of the world, as conspicuous as the sun in the heavens; and the Creed was written on her forehead, and proclaimed through her voice, by a teaching as precise as it was emphatical; in accordance with the text, "Who is she that looketh forth at the dawn, fair as the moon, bright as the sun, terrible as an army set in array?" It was not, strictly speaking, a miracle, doubtless; but in its effect, nay, in its circumstances, it was little less. Of course I would not allow that the Church fails in this manifestation of the truth now, any more than in former times,

though the clouds have come over the sun; for what she has lost in her appeal to the imagination, she has gained in philosophical cogency, by the evidence of her persistent vitality. So far is clear, that if Paine's aphorism has a *primâ facie* force against Christianity, it owes this advantage to the miserable deeds of the fifteenth and sixteenth centuries.

(3) Another conflict of first principles or assumptions, which have often been implicit on either side, has been carried through in our day, and relates to the end and scope of civil society, that is, whether government and legislation ought to be of a religious character, or not; whether the state has a conscience; whether Christianity is the law of the land; whether the magistrate, in punishing offenders, exercises a retributive office or a corrective; or whether the whole structure of society is raised upon the basis of secular expediency. The relation of philosophy and the sciences to theology comes into the question. The old time-honoured theory has, during the last forty years, been vigorously contending with the new; and the new is in the ascendant.

(4) There is another great conflict of first principles, and that among Christians, which has occupied a large space in our domestic history, during the last thirty or forty years, and that is the controversy about the Rule of Faith. I notice it as affording an instance of an assumption so deeply sunk into the popular mind, that it is a work of great difficulty to obtain from its maintainers an acknowledgment that it is an assumption. That Scripture is the Rule of Faith is in fact an assumption so congenial to the state of mind and course of thought usual among Protestants, that it seems to them rather a truism than a truth. If they are in controversy with Catholics on any point of faith, they at once ask, "Where do you find it in Scripture?" and if Catholics reply, as they must do, that it is not necessarily in Scripture in order to be true, nothing can persuade them that such an answer is not an evasion, and a triumph to themselves. Yet it is by no means self-evident that all religious truth is to be found in a number of works, however sacred, which were written at different times, and did not always form one book; and in fact it is a doctrine very hard to prove. So much so, that years ago, when I was considering it from a Protestant point of view, and wished to defend it to the best of my power, I was unable to give any better account of it than

---

[12] Thomas Paine (1737–1809), noted skeptic.

the following, which I here quote from its appositeness to my present subject.

"It matters not," I said, speaking of the first Protestants, "whether or not they only happened to come right on what, in a logical point of view, are faulty premisses. They had no time for theories of any kind; and to require theories at their hand argues an ignorance of human nature, and of the ways in which truth is struck out in the course of life. Common sense, chance, moral perception, genius, the great discoverers of principles do not reason. They have no arguments, no grounds, they see the truth, but they do not know how they see it; and if at any time they attempt to prove it, it is as much a matter of experiment with them, as if they had to find a road to a distant mountain, which they see with the eye; and they get entangled, embarrassed, and perchance overthrown in the superfluous endeavour. It is the second-rate men, though most useful in their place, who prove, reconcile, finish, and explain. Probably, the popular feeling of the sixteenth century saw the Bible to be the Word of God, so as nothing else is His Word, by the power of a strong sense, by a sort of moral instinct, or by a happy augury."[13]

That is, I considered the assumption an act of the Illative Sense;—I should now add, the Illative Sense, acting on mistaken elements of thought.

3. After the aspects in which a question is to be viewed, and the principles on which it is to be considered, come the arguments by which it is decided; among these are antecedent reasons, which are especially in point here, because they are in great measure made by ourselves and belong to our personal character, and to them I shall confine myself.

Antecedent reasoning, when negative, is safe. Thus no one would say that, because Alexander's rash heroism is one of the leading characteristics of his history, therefore we are justified, except in writing a romance, in asserting that at a particular time and place, he distinguished himself by a certain exploit about which history is altogether silent; but, on the other hand, his notorious bravery would be almost decisive against any charge against him of having on a particular occasion acted as a coward.

In like manner, good character goes far in destroying the force of even plausible charges There is indeed a degree of evidence in support, of an allegation, against which reputation is no defense; but it must be singularly strong to overcome an established antecedent probability which stands opposed to it. Thus historical personages or great authors, men of high and pure character, have had imputations cast upon them, easy to make, difficult or impossible to meet, which are indignantly trodden under foot by all just and sensible men, as being as anti-social as they are inhuman. I need not add what a cruel and despicable part a husband or a son would play, who readily listened to a charge against his wife or his father. Yet all this being admitted, a great number of cases remain which are perplexing, and on which we cannot adjust the claims of conflicting and heterogeneous arguments except by the keen and subtle operation of the Illative Sense.

Butler's argument in his *Analogy*[14] is such a presumption used negatively. Objection being brought against certain characteristics of Christianity, he meets it by the presumption in their favour derived from their parallels as discoverable in the order of nature, arguing that they do not tell against the Divine origin of Christianity, unless they tell against the Divine origin of the natural system also. But he could not adduce it as a positive and direct proof of the Divine origin of the Christian doctrines that they had their parallels in nature, or at the utmost as more than a recommendation of them to the religious inquirer.

Unbelievers use the antecedent argument from the order of nature against our belief in miracles. Here, if they only mean that the fact of that system of laws, by which physical nature is governed, makes it antecedently improbable that an exception should occur in it, there is no objection to the argument; but if, as is not uncommon, they mean that the fact of an established order is absolutely fatal to the very notion of an exception, they are using a presumption as if it were a proof. They are saying,—What has happened 999 times one way cannot possibly happen on the 1000th time another way, *because* what has happened 999 times one way is likely to happen in the same way on the 1000th. But unlikely things do happen sometimes. If, however, they mean that the existing order of nature constitutes a physical necessity, and that a law is an unalterable fact, this is to assume the very point

---

[13] "Prophetical Office of the Church," pp. 347, ed. 1837. [Newman's note]

[14] Bishop Joseph Butler (1692–1752), author of the *Analogy of Religion* (1736), a favorite work among the Tractarians.

in debate, and is much more than asserting its antecedent probability.

Facts cannot be proved by presumptions, yet it is remarkable that in cases where nothing stronger than presumption was even professed, scientific men have sometimes acted as if they thought this kind of argument, taken by itself, decisive of a fact which was in debate. Thus in the controversy about the Plurality of worlds, it has been considered, on purely antecedent grounds, as far as I see, to be so necessary that the Creator should have filled with living beings the luminaries which we see in the sky, and the other cosmical bodies which we imagine there, that it almost amounts to a blasphemy to doubt it.

Theological conclusions, it is true, have often been made on antecedent reasonings; but then it must be recollected that theological reasoning professes to be sustained by a more than human power, and to be guaranteed by a more than human authority. It may be true, also, that conversions to Christianity have often been made on antecedent reasons; yet, even admitting the fact, which is not quite clear, a number of antecedent probabilities, confirming each other, may make it a duty in the judgment of a prudent man, not only to act as if a statement were true, but actually to accept and believe it. This is not unfrequently instanced in our dealings with others, when we feel it right, in spite of our misgivings, to oblige ourselves to believe their honesty. And in all these delicate questions there is constant call for the exercise of the Illative Sense.

Harriet Martineau

1802-1876

ARRIET MARTINEAU was born into a Unitarian family at Norwich, and her early works were chiefly religious in nature, though later she came to be identified with Victorian free thought. She was the sister of James Martineau (1805–1900), who attained fame as a Unitarian minister and professor of philosophy. Harriet had begun writing for Unitarian publications as early as 1821, but she first gained widespread attention in 1832 as the author of *Illustrations of Political Economy,* a series of didactic tales. With the success of this work her literary focus became increasingly social and reformist.

In 1834–36 Harriet Martineau visited America and subsequently wrote *Society in America* (1837). She was also a novelist with *Deerbrook* and a writer of stories, especially for children. After several years of serious illness from 1839 to 1844, Miss Martineau regained her health through mesmerism. Her devotion to this therapy was held by many to be one of the marks of her eccentricity. She continued to write and travel, issuing *Eastern Life* in 1848 after a trip to Egypt and Turkey. After 1850 she became increasingly agnostic and radical. Her *Letters on Man's Social Nature,* written with H. G. Atkinson, and her translation of Auguste Comte's *Philosophie positive* are among the chief expressions of her later social and political views. She wrote also widely for newspapers and reviews.

Harriet Martineau's health was never strong; she had been deaf since 1820. But her industry was unflagging. Her association with many of the leading literary figures of the day gives a special interest to her posthumously published *Autobiography,* written in 1855. She died on 27 June 1876 and was buried in Birmingham.

Like many an unconventional Victorian authoress, Harriet Martineau could be seen as a forerunner of some aspects of the contemporary women's liberation movement. But her primary concern was not women's rights as such, but rather a drive to liberalize social and economic conditions in general. She belongs to the sober, freethinking, reformist side of Victorian life that welcomed material progress, encouraged the spread of education, and looked with suspicion on traditional beliefs, customs, and privileges. Her writings are less valuable for their own sake than as representative works of a powerful strain in Victorian thinking.

CHRONOLOGY

EDITIONS

There are no modern editions of Harriet Martineau's works. Following are
some representative titles.
Illustrations of Political Economy (1832–34).
Society in America (1837).
How to Observe: Morals and Manners (1838).
Eastern Life (1848).
Letters on the Laws of Man's Social Nature, with H. G. Atkinson (1851).
Philosophie positive, by Auguste Comte (trans.) (1853).
Autobiography (1877).

BIOGRAPHY AND CRITICISM

Janet Courtney, *Freethinkers of the Nineteenth Century* (1920).
Theodora Bosanquet, *Life of Harriet Martineau* (1927).
J. C. Nevill, *Life of Harriet Martineau* (1943).
Joseph B. Rivlin, *Harriet Martineau: A Bibliography of Her Separately Printed
Books* (1947).
Vera Wheatley, *The Life and Work of Harriet Martineau* (1957).
Robert K. Webb, *Harriet Martineau: A Radical Victorian* (1960).

---

from How to Observe:
Morals and Manners

Harriet Martineau's How to Observe: Morals and Manners *is at once a Victorian
primer in social observation and a statement of the author's concern for individual liberty and
harmonious relations between social classes. The passage given below is the "Idea of Liberty,"
which Miss Martineau claims arises from the social interaction of many minds. She illustrates
her views by reference to social classes in various countries of Western Europe and in the United States.*

Idea of Liberty

IT IS obvious enough that the Idea of Liberty, which can originate only in the intercourse of many minds, as the liberty itself can be wrought out only by the labours of many united hands, is not to be looked for where the people live apart, and are destitute of any knowledge of the interests and desires of the community at large.

Whether the society is divided into Two Classes, or whether there is a Gradation, is another important consideration. Where there are only two, proprietors and labourers, the Idea of Liberty is deficient or absent. The proprietory class can have no other desires on the subject than to repress the encroachments of the sovereign above them, or of the servile class below them: and in the servile class the conception of liberty is yet unformed. Only in barbarous countries, in countries where slavery subsists, and in some few strongholds of feudalism, is this decided division of society into two classes now to be found. Everywhere else there is more or less gradation; and in the most advanced countries the classes are least distinguishable. Below those members who, in European societies, are distinguished by birth, there is class beneath class of capitalists, though it is usual to comprehend them all, for convenience of speech, under the name of the middle class. Thus society in Great Britain, France, and Germany is commonly spoken of as consisting of three classes; while the divisions of the middle class are, in fact, very numerous. The small shopkeeper is not of the same class with the landowner, or wealthy banker, or professional man; while their views of life, their political principles, and their social aspirations, are as different as those of the peer and the mechanic.

There are two pledges of the advancement of the idea of liberty in a community:—the one is the mingling of the functions of proprietor and labourer throughout the whole of a society ruled by a representative government; the other is the graduation of ranks by some other principle than hereditary succession.

In ancient times most men were proprietors and labourers too; but under despotic rule. Societies which have once come under the representative principle are not likely to retrograde to this state; while there are influences ever at work to exalt the function of labour, and to extend that of proprietorship. Wherever this mixture of functions has gone the furthest,—wherever the mechanic classes are becoming capitalists, and proprietors are liable to sink down from their ancient honour, unless they can secure respect by personal qualifications, the idea of liberty is, to a considerable degree, confirmed and elevated. In such a case, it is clear that both the power and the desire of encroachment on the part of the upper class must be lessened, and that of resistance on the part of the lower increased.— The other improvement follows upon this. Proprietorship, with its feudal influences, having lost caste (though it has gained in true dignity), some other ground of distinction must succeed. If we may judge by what is before our eyes in the Western world, talent is likely to be the next successor. It is to be hoped that talent will, in its turn, give way to moral worth,—the higher degrees of which imply, however, superiority of mental power. The preference of personal qualifications to those of external endowment has already begun in the world, and is fast making its way. Such distinction of ranks as there is in America originates in mental qualifications. Statesmen, who rise by their own power, rank highest; and then authors. The wealthiest capitalist gives place, in the estimation of all, to a popular orator, a successful author, or an eminent clergyman.—In France, the honours of the peerage and the offices of the state are given to men of science, philosophy, and literature. The same is the case in some parts of Germany: and, even in aristocratic England, the younger members of her Upper House are unsatisfied with being merely peers, and are anxious to push their way in literature, as well as in politics.—The traveller must give earnest heed to symptoms like these, knowing that as the barriers of ranks are thrown down, and personal obtain the ascendant over hereditary qualifications, social coercion must be relaxed, and the sentiment of liberty exalted.

In close connexion with this, he must observe the condition of Servants. The treatment and conduct of domestics depend on causes which lie far deeper than the principles and tempers of particular servants and masters, as may be seen by a glance at domestic service in England, Scotland, and Ireland. In England, the old Saxon and Norman feud smoulders, (however unconscious the parties may be of the fact,) in the relation of master and servant. Domestics who never heard of either Norman or Saxon entertain a deep-rooted conviction of their masters' interests and their own being directly opposed, and are subject to a strong sense of injury. Masters who never bestow a thought on the transactions of the twelfth century, complain of a doggedness, selfishness, and case-hardened indifference in the class of domestics, which kindness cannot penetrate, or penetrates only to pervert. The relation is therefore a painful one in England. There is little satisfaction to be obtained between the extremes of servility and defiance, by which the conduct of servants is almost as distinctly marked now as when the nation was younger by seven centuries. The English housewives complain that confidence only makes their maid servants conceited, and that indulgence spoils them.—In Ireland, the case is of the same nature, but much aggravated. The injury of having an aristocracy of foreigners forced on the country, to whom the natives are to render service, is more recent, and the impression more consciously retained. The servants are ill-treated, and they yield bad service in return. It is mournful to see the arrangement of Dublin houses. The drawing-rooms are palace-like, while the servants' apartments are dark and damp dungeons. It is wearisome to hear the complaints of the dirt, falsehood, and faithlessness of Irish servants,—complaints which their mistresses have ever ready for the ear of the stranger; and it is disgusting to witness the effects in the household. It is equally sad and ludicrous to see the mistress of some families enter the breakfast room, with a loaf of bread under her arm, the butter-plate in one hand, and a bunch of keys in the other;—to see her cut from the loaf the number of slices required, and send them down to be toasted,—explaining that she is obliged to lock up the very bread from the thievery of her servants, and informing against them as if she expected them to be worthy of trust, while she daily insults them with the refusal of all trust,—even to the care of the bread-pan. In Scotland, the case is widely different. Servitude and clanship are there connected, instead of servitude and conquest. The service is willing in proportion; and the faults of domestics are not those common to the oppressed, but rather those proceeding from pride and self-will. The Scotch domestic has still the pride in the chief of the name which cherishes the self-respect of every member of a clan; and in the service of the chief there is scarcely any exertion which the humblest of his name would not make. The results are obvious. There is a better understanding between the two classes than in the other divisions of the kingdom: and Scotch masters and

mistresses obtain a satisfaction from their domestics which no degree of justice and kindness in English and Irish housekeepers can secure. The dregs of an oppression of centuries cannot be purged away by the action of individual tempers, be they of the best. The causes of misunderstandings, as we have said, lie deep.

The principles which regulate the condition of domestic servants in every country form thus a deep and wide subject for the traveller's inquiries. In America, he will hear frequent complaints from the ladies of the pride of their maid servants, and of the difficulty of settling them, while he sees that some are the most intimate friends of the families they serve; and that not a few collect books, and attend courses of scientific lectures. The fact is that, in America, a conflict is going on between opposite principles, and the consequences of the struggle show themselves chiefly in the relation between master and servant. The old European notions of the degradation of servitude survive in the minds of their American descendants, and are nourished by the presence of slavery on the same continent, and by the importation of labourers from Europe which is perpetually going on. In conflict with these notions are the democratic ideas of the honourableness of voluntary service by contract. It is found difficult, at first, to settle the bounds of the contract; and masters are liable to sin, from long habit, on the side of imperiousness, and the servants on that of captiousness and jealousy of their own rights. Such are the inconveniences of a transition state; —a state, however, upon which it should be remembered that other societies have yet to enter. In an Irish country-house, the guest sometimes finds himself desired to keep his wardrobe locked up.—In England, he perceives a restraint in the address of each class to the class above it.— In France, a washerwoman speaks with as much ease to a duchess as a duchess to a washerwoman. In Holland, the domestics have chambers as scrupulously neat as their masters'.—In Ireland, they sleep in underground closets.—In New York, they can command their own accommodation.— In Cuba they sleep, like dogs, in the passages of the family dwellings. These are some of the facts from which the observer is to draw his inferences, rather than from the manners of some individuals of the class whom he may meet. In his conclusions from such facts he can hardly be wrong, though he may chance to become acquainted with a footman of the true heroic order in Dublin, and a master in Cuba who respects his own servants, and a cringing lackey in New York.

A point of some importance is whether the provincial inhabitants depend upon the management and imitate the modes of life of the metropolis, or have principles and manners of their own. Where there is least freedom and the least desire of it, everything centres in the metropolis. Where there is most freedom, each "city, town, and vill," thinks and acts for itself. In despotic countries, the principle of centralization actuates everything. Orders are issued from the central authorities, and the minds of the provinces are saved all trouble of thinking for themselves. Where self-government is permitted to each assemblage of citizens, they are stimulated to improve their idea and practice of liberty, and are almost independent of metropolitan usages. The traveller will find that "Paris is France," as everybody has heard, and that the government of France is carried on in half-a-dozen apartments in the capital, with little reference to the unrepresented thousands who are living some hundreds of miles off: while, if he casts a glance over Norway, he may see the people on the shores of the fiords, or in the valleys between the pine-steeps, quietly making their arrangements for controlling the central authority, even abolishing the institution of hereditary nobility in opposition to the will of the king; but legally, peaceably, and in all the simplicity of determined independence,—the result of a matured idea of liberty. The observer will note whether the pursuits and amusements of the provincial inhabitants originate in the circumstances of the locality, or whether they are copies from those of the metropolis; whether the great city be spoken of with reverence, scorn, or indifference, or not spoken of at all: whether, as in a Pennsylvanian village, the society could go on if the capital were swallowed up by an earthquake; or whether, as in Prussia, the favour of the central power is as the breath of the nostrils of the people.

Newspapers are a strong evidence of the political ideas of a people;—not individual newspapers; for no two, perhaps, fully agree in principles and sentiment, and it is to be feared that none are positively honest. Not by individual newspapers must the traveller form his judgment, but by the freedom of discussion which he may find to be permitted, or the restraints upon discussion imposed. The idea of liberty must be low and feeble among a people who permit the government to maintain a severe censorship; and it must be powerful and effectual in a society which can make all its complaints through a newspaper,—be the reports of the newspapers upon the state of social affairs as dismal as they may. Whatever revilings of a tyrannical president, or of a servile congress, a traveller may meet with in any number of American journals, he may fairly conclude that both the one and the other must be nearly harmless if they are discussed in a newspaper. The very existence of the newspapers he sees testifies to the prevalence of a habit of reading, and consequently of education—to the wide diffusion of political power—and to the probable safety and permanence of a government which is founded on so broad a basis, and can afford to indulge so large a licence. Whatever he may be told of the patriotism of a sovereign, let him give it to the winds if he finds a space in a newspaper made blank by the pen of a censor. The tameness of the Austrian journals tells as plain a tale as if no censor had ever suppressed a syllable;—as much so as the small size of a New Orleans paper compared with one of New York, or as the fiercest bluster of a Cincinnati Daily or Weekly, on the eve of the election of a president.

In countries where there is any Free Education, the traveller must observe its nature; and especially whether the subjects of it are distinguished by any sort of badge. The practice of badging, otherwise than by mutual consent, is usually bad: it is always suspicious. The traveller will note whether free education is conferred by charitable bequest, (a practice originating in times when the doctrine of expiation was prevalent, and continued to this day by its union with charity,) or whether it is framed at the will of the sovereign, that his young subjects may be trained to his own purposes,—as in the case of the Emperor of Russia and his young Polish victims; or whether it arises from the union of such a desire with a more enlightened object,—as may be witnessed in Prussia; or whether it is provided by the sovereign people,—by universal consent, as the right of every individual born into the community, and as the necessary qualification for the enjoyment of social privileges,—as in the United States. The English Christ Hospital boys are badged: Napoleon's Polytechnic pupils were badged; so are the Czar's orphan charge. Wherever the meddling or ostentatious charity of antique times is in existence,—times when the idea of liberty was low and confined,—this badging is to be looked for; and also wherever it is necessary to the purposes of the potentate to keep a register of the young subjects who may become his instruments or his foes:—but where education is absolutely universal, where any citizen has a right to put every child, not otherwise educated, into the school-house of his township, and where the rising generation are destined to take care of themselves, and legislate after their own will, no badging will be found. This apparently trifling fact is worth the attention of the observer.

The extent of popular education is a fact of the deepest significance. Under despotisms there will be the smallest amount of it; and in proportion to the national idea of the dignity and importance of man,—idea of liberty, in short,—will be its extent, both in regard to the number it comprehends, and to the enlargement of their studies. The universality of education is inseparably connected with a lofty idea of liberty; and till the idea is realized in a constantly expanding system of national education, the observer may profitably note for reflection the facts whether he is surrounded on a frontier by a crowd of whining young beggars, or whether he sees a parade of charity scholars,—these all in blue caps and yellow stockings, and those all in white tippets and green aprons; or whether he falls in with an annual or quarterly assembly of teachers, met to confer on the best principles and methods of carrying on an education which is itself a matter of course.

In countries where there is any popular Idea of Liberty, the universities are considered its stronghold, from their being the places where the young, active, hopeful, and aspiring meet,—the youths who are soon to be citizens, and who have here the means of daily communication of their ideas, for many years together. It would be an interesting inquiry how many revolutions, warlike or bloodless, have issued from seats of learning; and yet more, how many have been planned for which the existing powers, or the habits of society, have been too strong. If the universities are not so constituted as to admit of this fostering of free principles, they are pretty sure to retain the antique notions in accordance with which they were instituted, and to fall into the rear of society in morals and manners. It is the traveller's business to observe the characteristics of these institutions, and to reflect whether they are likely to aid or to retard the progress of the nation in which they stand.

There are universities in almost every country; but they are as little like one another as the costumes that are found in Switzerland and India; and the one speak as plainly of morals and manners as the other of climate. It is needless to point out that countries which contain only aristocratic halls of learning, or schools otherwise devoid of an elastic principle, must be in a state of comparative barbarism; because, in such a case, learning (so called there) must be confined to a few, and probably to the few who can make the least practical use of it. Where the universities are on such a plan as that, preserving their primary form, they can admit increasing numbers, the state of intellect is likely to be a more advanced one. But a more favourable symptom is where seats of learning are multiplied as society enlarges, modified in their principles as new departments of knowledge open, and as new classes arise who wish to learn. That country is in a state of transition—of progression—where the ancient universities are honoured for as much as they can give, while new schools arise to supply their deficiencies, and Mechanics' Institutes, or some kindred establishments, flourish by the side of both. This state of things, this variety in the pursuit of knowledge, can exist only where there is a freedom of thought, and consequent diversity of opinion, which argues a vigorous idea of liberty.

The observer must not, however, rest satisfied with ascertaining the proportion of the means of education to the people who have to be educated. He must mark the objects for which learning is pursued. The two most strongly contrasted cases which can be found are probably those of Germany and (once more) the United States. In the United States, it is well known, a provision of university education is made as ample as that of schools for an earlier stage; yet no one pretends that a highly finished education is to be looked for in that country. The cause is obvious. In a young nation, the great common objects of life are entered upon earlier, and every preparatory process is gone through in a more superficial manner. Seats of learning are numerous and fully attended, both in Germany and America, and they testify in each to a pervading desire of knowledge. Here the agreement ends. The German student may, without being singular, remain within the walls of his college till time silvers his hairs; or he has even been known to pass eighteen years among his books, without once crossing the threshold of his study. The young American, meanwhile, satisfied at the end of three years that he knows as much as his neighbours, settles in a home, engages in farming or commerce, and plunges into what alone he considers the business of life. Each of these pursues his appropriate objects: each is right in his own way: but the difference of pursuit indicates a wider difference of sentiment between the two countries than the abundance of the means of learning in each indicates a resemblance. The observer must therefore mark, not only what and how many are the seats of learning, but who frequent them; whether there are many, past the season of youth, who make study the business of their lives; or whether all are of that class who regard study as a part of the preparation which they are ordained to make for the accomplishment of the commonest aims of life. He can scarcely take his evening walk in the precincts of a university without observing a difference so wide as this.

The great importance of the fact lies in this,—that increase of knowledge is necessary to the secure enlargement of freedom. Germany may not, it is true, require learning in her youth for political purposes, but because learning has become the taste, the characteristic honour of the nation; but this knowledge will infallibly work out, sooner or later, her political regeneration. America requires knowledge in her sons because her political existence itself depends upon their mental competency. The two countries will probably approximate gradually towards a sympathy which is at present out of the question. As America becomes more fully peopled, a literature will grow up within her, and study will assume its place among the chief objects of life. The great ideas which are the emplyoment of the best minds of Germany must work their way out into action; and new and immediately practical kinds of knowledge will mingle themselves, more and more largely, with those to which she has been, in times past, devoted. The two countries may thus fall into a sympathetic correspondence on the mighty subjects of human government and human learning, and the grand idea of liberty may be made more manifest in the one, and disciplined and enriched in the other.

Richard Hurrell Froude

1803-1836

ONE OF THE three begetters of the Oxford Movement, Richard Hurrell Froude has remained the least known, largely because he died only a few years after the Movement got under way. Yet it was the influence of Froude more than any single person that gave the Oxford Movement its intensely apostolic and Catholic cast.

Froude was the older brother of the historian and biographer James Anthony Froude (see selection by him in this volume) and the son of the High Churchman Archdeacon Robert Froude. He was from an old established family in Devonshire and was educated at Ottery, Eton, and Oriel College, Oxford, where he was subsequently a Fellow. A brilliant and intense thinker, Froude was closely associated with John Keble and John Henry Newman. With Newman he traveled to the Mediterranean in 1832–33 and with him he contributed poems to the *Lyra Apostolica*. His health obliged him to go abroad again, this time to the West Indies in 1834–35. He died of consumption in England the year following his return.

Froude's writings consist only of his poems, three of the *Tracts for the Times,* and his literary *Remains,* which Keble and Newman edited and presented to the public in four volumes in 1838–39. The *Remains* failed of their purpose in arousing sympathy for the memory of Froude and the aims of the Oxford Movement because they contained so many adverse judgments against the English reformation and so many instances of Froude's severe self-mortification. Popular sentiment was repelled rather than won over by what seemed to many a combination of virulently Catholic theology coupled with morbid self-torment over relatively slight sins. But to the Tractarians Froude remained always a symbol of the uncompromising commitment to holiness and purity of faith.

Both as a Tractarian document and as an example of Victorian soul searching, the *Remains* constitutes one of the fascinating and neglected prose documents of the early Victorian period.

CHRONOLOGY

1803   Born 25 March at Dartington, Devonshire.
1816   Attends Eton College.
1821–24   Attends Oriel College, Oxford.

EDITIONS, BIOGRAPHY, AND CRITICISM

Remains of the Late Reverend Richard Hurrell Froude, ed. J. Keble and J. H. Newman (4 vols., 1838–39).

R. W. Church, *The Oxford Movement* (1891).

Louise Imogen Guiney, *Hurrell Froude: Memoranda and Comments* (1904).

Yngve Brilioth, *The Anglican Revival* (1925).

Gordon Huntington Harper, *The Froude Family in the Oxford Movement* (1933).

Herbert Clegg, "Froude's *Remains,*" *Church Quarterly Review* (1966).

Marvin R. O'Connell, *The Oxford Conspirators* (1969).

William J. Baker, "Hurrell Froude and the Reformers," *Journal of Ecclesiastical History* (1970).

---

from Remains

As the only work of one of the prime movers of Tractarianism, Froude's Remains *has a special historical value in illuminating the spirituality and psychology of the Movement. But it is also of interest as a record of the scrupulous self-examination of an earnest Victorian. The selections below are taken from the private journal Froude kept during the period January 1826 to March 1827.*

Extracts from Journals, 1826-1827

Oxford, Oct. 22 [1826]. I turn back to this part of my book, in hopes that I shall, in another sense also, turn over a new leaf. I have not made much of a beginning. I have felt anxious that H. should think me steadier. Talked smartly to S. against Paley.[1] Ate little. Been at both sermons. I thought a great deal of H.'s, especially of the remark, that the records of God's miraculous providence in the Old Testament are meant to be witnesses of His faithfulness to us; and to give us, as it were, experience of His power and intention to make up to us, when we feel in this world borne down with misery.

Oct. 23. Up at six, and got the Psalms and Second Lesson read before chapel. . . . . .

Oct. 24. After chapel, found a letter from K. which gave me greater pleasure than I have had since my Mother's death. Read, and then had a walk with N. Our conversation did not leave a pleasing impression on my mind. We began about ghosts. I went on, by degrees, to argue

---

[1] William Paley (1743–1805), author of *Natural Theology* (1802). The initials of persons referred to were not identified by the original editors, but "N." and "K." presumably refer to Newman and Keble.

about our dwelling among spirits: I did not talk with any clearness, or talent, and perhaps this may account for a dissatisfied feeling. It seemed, too, that I had been intruding on hallowed precincts; and that a conversation, held in a manner not consistent with a serious belief, shook for a moment the steadiness of my faith.

I have been put out this evening, by hearing that I am not to receive any thing for my fellowship till this time next year, and that in the mean time I must continue a burden to my Father. I ought to acquiesce in it with complete indifference, but it will cut me off for a time from exercises of virtue, which I intended to have begun with directly. However, I can make it up by other additional austerity and self-denial, in order to compensate for not giving alms. It is also a trial to confess to my Father how much I owe, in order to clear my way preparatory to the first start. Felt provoked and silly, at hearing that —— had told —— that I was not in the least clever! How very weak! But all these things help to keep in my mind what I am. Above all things I must be careful not to talk σιγητὰ,[2] to which I am constantly tempted by habitual levity, and the example of those I live with.

Oct. 25.   Wrote to my Father for 6o*l.*; first of all in a very serious way, but afterward I made it a common sort of letter. Read steadily to-day; had no dinner, but a bit of bread. Somehow I feel, that I go to chapel more to pass away the time than from a love of God; and that the little good I do is attributable to the same motive. My annoyance, whenever I am worsted in an argument, shows me that theories of my own, rather than the word of God, are the rules on which I act. I talked sillily to-day, as I used to do last term; but took no pleasure in it: so am not ashamed. Although I don't recollect any harm of myself, yet I don't feel that I have made a clean breast of it.

Oct. 26.   Felt an impulse of pleasure, on finding W. was not at chapel this morning. I am always trying to persuade myself that I endeavour to be better than other people. Disgustingly self-complacent thoughts have kept continually obtruding themselves upon me, on the score of my little paltry abstinences. What I give up costs me no great effort; it is no sacrifice of pleasure for the sake of virtue. It is what I am glad to have, a motive to act, from a conviction that it is the means of getting the greatest quantity of happiness. I will persevere in the course I have pre-

scribed to myself, let my enemy do what he will to defile it; for, if I *do* nothing ostentatious, I cannot be forming the habit. Only I must prescribe to myself some exercises that I really dislike, that I may feel my weakness. I think it was ostentatious in me to hint to S. that I got up at six o'clock. To-morrow is a fasting-day. I am afraid I shall sleep a great deal. I can easily fast, but cannot shake off sloth. I feel as if I should not like to be laughed at for being serious when grace is saying.

Oct. 27.   I forgot to mention, that I had been looking round my rooms, and thinking they looked comfortable and nice, and that I said, in my heart, "Ah! ah! I am warm;" and felt less anxious to find an opportunity of giving them up to Mr. ——, which, however, I am resolved to do. It is disgusting for a fellow, like me, to be enjoying the fat of the land. Also, when I went to Lloyd's Lecture, just now, a thought crossed me that I should feel elevated by a visit from ——. I was not up till half past six; slept on the floor, and a nice uncomfortable time I had of it. I had on a mustard plaister nearly three hours after I returned from Lloyd's; could not bear it longer: I believe it has answered. Tasted nothing to-day till tea time, and then only one cup, and dry bread. Somehow it has not made me at all uneasy.

Oct. 28.   Was a good deal put out in my attention to the service this morning, by being sent to read the Lessons unexpectedly. I was provoked at knowing it was W.'s turn, and that H. would reckon me careless without reason: but I will say nothing about it. What I do, I do unto the Lord, and not unto men; at least that is the only motive I will allow. I am afraid it was a sort of breach of promise in me yesterday, not to give Lloyd ——'s excuse, and will tell him, as soon as I see him, that when it came to the point, I could not make up my mind to be responsible for his humbug. If I do not express myself as strongly as this, I shall be a coward. I was fool enough to be a little jealous at hearing Lloyd kept old —— an hour talking, and caught myself just now speculating whether he might not ask *me* to stay next lecture. I forgot to go to the sermon to-day.

.   .   .

Nov. 10.   Fell quite short of my wishes with respect to the rigour of to-day's fast, though I am quite willing to believe not unpardonably: I

[2] Foolishly.

tasted nothing till after half-past eight in the evening, and before that had undergone more uncomfortableness, both of body and mind, than any fast has as yet occasioned me, having, I hope, laid a sort of foundation, on which I may gradually build up the fit spending of a fast in calling my sins to remembrance. But I made rather a more hearty tea than usual [quite giving up the notion of a fast] in W.'s rooms, and by this weakness have occasioned another slip. For having been treated, as I think, without sufficient respect by the youngest ——, I allowed myself to be vexed, and to think of how I ought to have set him down all the rest of the evening, instead of receiving it with thankfulness from God as an instrument of humility. Also I will record another error, common indeed with me, and which for that reason I have hitherto overlooked, *i.e.* speaking severely of another without a cause. I said I thought —— an ass, when there was not the least occasion for me to express my sentiments about him. And yet I, so severe on the follies, and so bitter against the slightest injuries I get from others, am now presenting myself before my great Father to ask for mercy on my most foul sins, and forgiveness for the most incessant injuries. "How shall I be delivered from the body of this death!"

Nov. 11. I have become comfortable again, and cannot help thinking that it is owing, in a great measure, to my having seen that it was not from a deliberate intention to slight me, that young —— was pert, and from my interest in the argument with N. having died away. How feeble my mind has become, from my having left it so long uncontrolled. I am conscious that I have merited no respect from my past conduct, and always measure the slights offered me by what I know I deserve, and what I should be forced to put up with: and when external trifles make me uncomfortable, then I think it is repentance. Yet, I cannot but think that the consciousness of my great sinfulness had much to do with my wretchedness yesterday: and that our minds are so contrived, that this misery must have something external to fasten on, so that it may not be weighing us down continually. This is the first day I have not been to chapel in Oriel; but I was obliged to stay away, out of civility to ——. I went to Magdalen instead; and though I could not do all the forms, without obtruding myself on notice, yet it seems to me to have been a very impressive service, partly from the difficulty of reading; a subject connected with which I have been making a speculation, which I don't recollect having

dated. I have again been talking freely of people, partly out of habit, and partly to have something to say to ——. Laughed at ——, when uncalled for. Have not been the least abstemious in any of my meals.

Nov. 12. Felt great reluctance to sleep on the floor last night, and was nearly arguing myself out of it; was not up till half-past six. —— was sitting under me in chapel; and I was actually prevented from giving my mind to a great deal of the early part of the service, by the thought crossing me at each response, that he must be thinking I was become a Don, and was affecting religious out of compliance.

Felt ashamed that my trowsers were dirty whilst I was sitting next ——, but resolved not to hide them. This sort of shame [about what] we ourselves esteem matters of indifference, because they do not seem so to other people, brings home to our minds what depravity it proves in us to pay so little attention to what we know is serious. I cannot look on this Sunday with any pleasure. I have been inattentive again at evening chapel, and have made the day too much a holiday in the ordinary sense.

Nov. 13. This morning I found one of my old theme books, and the reading it presented to my recollection in a more lively way, the very wretched state into which my mind has fallen, than the mere reflection on that period of my life does usually suggest. The pain which, on this occasion, got hold of my mind was, I am willing to believe, more pure and genuine than any I had hitherto experienced; though, not having recorded my feelings at the time, they now present to me only an indistinct representation of wretchedness. Certainly, if I am now indeed in a better way, it is not by any effort of my own that I have been led into it; but the change has resulted from a combination of accidents, in the disposal of which I had no voice, and for which I ought to bow before God in affrighted gratitude. How I have become what I am, I cannot trace, yet I fear that the change, whatever it is, is much less than it appears; and that it, rather than [it is rather that] the circumstances in which I have been placed, have freed my will, than that my will is really more hearty. It is but little I do, and nothing that I sacrifice; and every return of old temptations raises thoughts and impulses, just like what I used to be overcome by.

To-day, when —— called on me, I was forced to watch myself at every turn, for fear of saying something irreligious, or uncharitable; and, perhaps as it was, I offended in both. I laughed at ——, when I had nothing else to say; and, as an apology for having altered my views of life, talked of the equality of dulness which attended all. I am not sure how far this was wrong; it is never right to intrude religion upon people: yet I feel that, in my case, I shrink from being connected with those people who are generally called religious, rather than avoid being thought well of. I felt quite annoyed, because of something said by ——, which gave me a notion that men thought I attended church regularly, because I wished to be a tutor. I must be on the watch, to purify my actions from the intrusion of any feeling, except a steady determination to act right, and shape all my conduct as if I was in solitude, where the likelihood of being approved tempts me to go farther; only allowing myself to meet the prejudices of others, when so doing is a greater instance of self-denial than the conduct I think exactly right. I have been quite overcome this evening by a tendency to sleep, and have not been able to command my attention since tea.

Nov. 14. It struck me to day, that forcing myself to take a walk for a certain time every day, would be a good sort of self-denial. I will try it. I was a little uneasy, just now, at not having been severe on ——, for a pert thing he said to me. I believe I gave him the right answer, but not in a sufficiently marked way; being taken by surprise. I think I should look on it as a duty to repress impertinence; but I must learn to be indifferent to it. I thought myself great, from some hints I wrote in my other book this morning.

Nov. 15. I should have felt much ashamed to have exposed how ignorant I was at Lloyd's Lecture, and ought to be as much ashamed at knowing it myself. Uncommon weakness of mind is the necessary consequence, and part of the natural punishment of my past habits; and these silly littlenesses and false shames are what I must be contented with, as with bodily diseases, till the Lord thinks fit gradually to remove them. All that I must be careful is, never to allow them to influence my voluntary actions.

I went to New College Chapel; in consequence of which, and being in the anti-chapel, could not go through the right forms of standing and kneeling, without attracting attention; as it was, I was much distracted by the thoughts that men were observing me. I was much delighted with the anthem, but caught myself giving way to the emotion it produced from the notion. . . . . How these things linger by me! I have been μαλακὸς [3]

---

[3] Morally weak.

this evening, and felt a wish that I had not resolved to live strictly; and indulged, for a moment, the intention of giving it up in some degree next term.

Nov. 16. I had a walk by myself, in which I was thinking over my condition, and trying to make out what I must guard against if I go home; and to plan the safest way of spending my time there; and yet here I am weary of finishing the course which I have prescribed to myself: the enthusiasm which set me off has gradually died away, and I am left to go on resolutions, the aim of which I often lose sight of, in spite of discouragements, for which I had hardly prepared myself. My friendlessness, and the consciousness that no one enters into my condition, and the consequent necessity of painful reserve, as well as the everlasting mortifications arising from the footing, on which my past life has placed me, and for rising above which, the habits I have contracted unfit me,—all tend to weigh me down, and repress my spirit. Yet it is my duty to acquiesce in them, as punishment richly deserved; and to be thankful for them as opportunities of practising more constantly the contrary habits to those which I have contracted. Perseverance, without regard to events; indifference to the praise, or censure of others; quietness in doing my own business. Strengthen me, O Lord, that I may perform effectually what I intend piously.

· · · ·

March 3 [1827]. O Lord God, who by the things which Thou sufferest us to do amiss, shewest us the weaknesses through which sin has access to us, work in me at the same time such hearty sorrow for my transgressions that its remembrance may, by Thy grace, protect me for the future.

March 4. I am getting into a bad way, am carelessly indulgent in my food; idle, arrogant, selfish, spiteful, detracting, irritable, inattentive in chapel. I feel to have lost all rule about expense, and am unstable in all my sentiments which regard my intercourse with others, conscious that I cannot set up for myself a consistent standard in the face of general though mistaken opinion, yet aware that my vanity so strongly inclines me to compliance, that it is the side on which I must be most on my guard. That I ought to comply in some degree is, I think, certain; but in what degree I am very doubtful. I must be energetic about abstinence, or I shall quickly drop back into lazy fatness. Besides, I am much in want of lowering, to tame my rising insolence of feeling.

O God, keep up in me now, while I am in the sunshine, that consciousness of my wretchedness which the day of darkness forced on me. Or if by no other means I can be preserved from arrogance, bow me down again, O Lord, and let Thy storms pass over me. O may it please Thee, of Thy goodness, to render its accomplishment unnecessary.

March 5.   O Lord, who, as a punishment for long neglect, permittest our souls to become so distorted and deformed, that we, when seeing the necessity of acting differently, and anxiously desiring to renew our lives, still through the imperfection of our misshapen faculties are unable to perform what we even earnestly attempt, yet Thou hast said, that seeking we shall find, and knocking we shall gain admittance, and that Thou wilt give Thy Spirit without measure to those that ask it; O work in me to will as well as to do Thy good pleasure, and make me to obey Thy godly motions in righteousness and true holiness. I will walk in the way of Thy commandments, when Thou hast set my heart at liberty. And, in the meantime, make me ever watchful for an opportunity of resisting evil, and working to obtain this rich inheritance. Let me find the narrow course between Pharisaical scrupulosity in things to which, I as yet annex no meaning, and using this as a pretext for real negligence.

March 15.   O Lord God, Thou art always with me, and spiest out all my ways; whatever I do, I do in Thy sight, and my inconsistencies are spread out at one view before Thee. O teach me to dread Thy contempt, as I do that of Thy servants; keep the thoughts of it before my own conscience, when I can no longer see its reflection in that of others, and bring me by degrees to such steady constancy in all my thoughts and actions, as suits Thy unchangeable pleasure and uninterrupted presence.

O God, who, by the image of Thy fearful wrath, presented in the thought of Thy trusty servants, teachest those who shrink from Thy displeasure, to flee the evil ways which Thou dost hate; make me, when unconscious of this reflected light, still to recollect its bright original, and preserve in me, through all the changes in society, such steadiness of thought and action as may suit Thy unvarying will and uninterrupted presence.

March 22.   I am in a very odd way just now, and should like to leave some monument of it. I am sure it is owing to some bodily derangement, but it has filled my head with all sorts of fancies. I got hold of a notion that K. slighted me and thought me a bore; and then I bothered myself with fancying the disgust which he must feel towards me, if he had seen any thing to suggest that my letters to him last Christmas were insincere.

Also, whether justly or not, I have been accusing myself of sneaking in mentioning ——'s work to ——, without alluding to my reason for being interested in it, &c.

When will the time come when I may be as sincere and open as the day, and my undisguised feelings will, on impulse, always come uppermost.

Grant it, O merciful Father. O leave me not a prey to them that will eat me up.

I have found out, within a few days, that I have very odd notions about other people, and that I cannot fancy them really endowed with capacities for any pain or pleasure, except as they come in contact with myself; and yet I quite forget all my scepticism directly I fancy myself the object of their perception. I wonder what I shall detect in myself next. But experience makes me conscious, these things will soon fade, and that they are only fancies for the moment.

Benjamin Disraeli

1804-1881

BENJAMIN DISRAELI, the first Earl of Beaconsfield, was born in London the son of the man of letters Isaac D'Israeli (1776–1848). Although the family was Jewish, Isaac D'Israeli had Benjamin christened in the Church of England in 1817, and Benjamin himself regularized the spelling of his surname. He was to surpass his father as a literary figure and to exceed that attainment by becoming Prime Minister of England and a special favorite of Queen Victoria.

Educated privately and by wide independent reading in his father's library, Disraeli entered Lincoln's Inn in 1824. Two years later, when he was but twenty-two years old, he published his first novel, *Vivian Grey*. It was a sensation, and Disraeli was launched on a career as a novelist of fashionable society. During the next ten years he published more than a half-dozen novels, including *The Young Duke* (1831) and *Contarini Fleming* (1832), and even after entering Parliament in 1837 he continued writing fiction, though his later and better known works like *Coningsby* (1844) and *Sybil* (1845) treat political rather than society themes.

As a member of Parliament Disraeli led a group of young Tories known as "Young England." He was first identified with Tory protectionism in his support of the Corn Laws, but later he changed his position and became Chancellor of the Exchequer under Lord Derby in 1852. Disraeli's great parliamentary opponent was Gladstone, and Disraeli spent many years in opposition to Gladstone and the Liberals as power seesawed between the two parties in the sixties and seventies. As Chancellor of the Exchequer in 1866 Disraeli introduced and carried the Second Reform Bill, and in 1868 he succeeded to the prime ministership in a short-lived administration. He returned to the post again in 1874 and began a series of international moves that endeared him to the Queen. It was under Disraeli's leadership that Britain took possession of the Suez Canal and that Victoria was proclaimed Empress of India. He was made Earl of Beaconsfield in 1876 and thenceforth operated from the House of Lords. In 1880 Disraeli retired from politics. He produced one final novel, *Endymion*. He died in 1881.

As a writer Disraeli is remembered chiefly for his novels, but he was also the author of nonfiction works on politics and political biography. His political speeches are also works of considerable literary skill. Disraeli served in Parliament for more than thirty years before his first administration as prime minister. During that time he perfected his rhetorical skills in wide debate and lecturing and thus became one of the most effective orators of his age.

CHRONOLOGY

1804	Born in London, 21 December.
1817	Baptized a Christian.
1824	Enters Lincoln's Inn.
1826–27	*Vivian Grey*.
1837	Enters Parliament.
1852	Chancellor of the Exchequer in Lord Derby's cabinet.
1858	Chancellor of the Exchequer in Lord Derby's second cabinet.
1866	Chancellor of the Exchequer in Lord Derby's third cabinet.
1867	Carries Reform Bill through Parliament.
1868	Prime Minister.
1874–80	Prime Minister in second administration.
1876	Elevated to peerage as First Earl of Beaconsfield.
1880	Retires from politics.
1881	Dies 19 April; buried at Hughenden.

EDITIONS

Works, ed. Edmund Gosse and Robert Arnot, Empire Edition (20 vols., 1904–5).
Novels, Hughenden Edition (11 vols., 1881).
Selected Speeches, ed. T. E. Kebbel (2 vols., 1882).
Lord Beaconsfield's Home Letters, ed. R. Disraeli (1885).
Correspondence with His Sister, 1832–52, ed. R. Disraeli (1886).
The Radical Tory, ed. H. W. J. Edwards (1937).

BIOGRAPHY AND CRITICISM

George H. Francis, *The Right Honourable Benjamin Disraeli* (1852).
Thomas Macknight, *The Right Honourable Benjamin Disraeli, M.P.* (1854).
W. F. Moneypenny and G. E. Buckle, *The Life of Benjamin Disraeli* (6 vols., 1910–20; rev. ed., 2 vols., 1929).
Hesketh Pearson, *Dizzy* (1951).
John Holloway, *The Victorian Sage* (1953).
Arthur H. Frietzsche, *The Monstrous Clever Young Man* (1959).
Harold J. Hanham, *Elections and Party Management* (1959).
B. R. Jerman, *The Young Disraeli* (1960).
Curtis Dahl, "Benjamin Disraeli," in *Victorian Fiction: A Guide to Research* (1964).
Robert Blake, *Disraeli* (1967).

Speeches on the Second Reform
Bill, 1867

*As the leading conservative politician of the age Disraeli surprised many Victorians when
he championed the Second Reform Bill of 1867, for in so doing he reversed himself and adopted
the program of the Liberals. But his eloquence and zeal carried the day for this proposal to extend the
franchise yet further than had been done by the First Reform Bill of 1832. The selections
below are taken from Disraeli's speeches on the first and third readings of the bill in Parliament.
They show Disraeli defending the bill and at the same time justifying his own change of position.*

THE Chancellor of the Exchequer; Sir, I rise to ask leave to introduce a Bill further to amend the laws for regulating the representation of the people in Parliament. Sir, the principles of political representation, and especially as applied to the circumstances of this country, have of late years been so profoundly and so extensively discussed and investigated that it is scarcely necessary on this occasion that I should advert to them. I propose, therefore, to confine my observations to two points. I will endeavour, in the first place, clearly to convey to the House the object of the Government in the Bill which I am asking leave to introduce; and, secondly, I will detail the means by which that purpose, in their opinion, can be accomplished. It will be for the House, first, to decide whether that object is desirable, and, secondly, if desirable, whether the means which we propose are adequate; and, in the first place, I would say that our object is, not only to maintain, but to strengthen the character and functions of this House. They are peculiar; not only rare, but perhaps unexampled in any other popular assembly which has existed. The House of Commons has combined national representation with the attributes of a senate. That peculiar union has, in our opinion, been owing to the variety of elements of which it is formed. Its variety of character has given to it its deliberative power, and it owes to its deliberative power its general authority. We wish, I repeat, not only to maintain, but to strengthen that character and those functions; and we believe that, in the present age, and under the existing circumstances of the country, the best way to do so is to establish them on a broad popular basis.

I know that there are some persons in whose minds the epithet which I have just used may create a feeling of distrust; but I attribute the sentiment of alarm which is associated with it to a misapprehension of its meaning, and to that perplexity of ideas which too often confounds popular privileges with democratic rights. They are not identical: they are not similar. More than that; they are contrary. Popular privileges are consistent with a state of society in which there is great inequality of conditions. Democratic rights, on the contrary, demand that there should be equality of conditions as the fundamental basis of the society which they regulate. Now, that is, I think, a distinction which ought to be borne in mind by the House in dealing with the provisions of the Bill which I am about to ask leave to introduce. If this Bill be a proposal that Her Majesty shall be enabled to concede to her subjects with the advice and concurrence of her Parliament a liberal measure of popular privileges, then there may be many of its provisions which will be regarded as prudent, wise, and essentially constitutional. If, on the other hand, it be looked upon as a measure having for its object to confer democratic rights, then I admit much that it may contain may be viewed in the light of being indefensible and unjust. We do not, however, live—and I trust it will never be the fate of this country to live—under a democracy. The propositions which I am going to make to-night certainly have no tendency in that direction. Generally speaking, I would say that, looking to what has occurred since the Reform Act of 1832 was passed—to the increase of population, the progress of industry, the spread of knowledge, and our ingenuity in the arts—we are of opinion that numbers, thoughts and feelings have since that time been created which it is desirable should be admitted within the circle of the Constitution. We wish that admission to take place in the spirit of our existing institutions, and with a due deference to the traditions of an ancient State.

In dealing with the question of the distribution of power in such a State—which is really the question before us—I would, in the first place, call the attention of the House to that part of it which is perhaps the most important, and which certainly to the greatest extent commands the interest of the public. I allude to the franchise and especially that which would prevail in towns. I would ask the House at the outset to consider the principles upon which the occupation franchise in boroughs ought to rest, and upon which it is expedient to base it. In 1832 the borough franchise was founded on the principle of value. Those who paid £10 for the house in which they lived, subject to certain regulations as regards rates and residence, had the borough franchise conferred upon them. I believe that franchise may be fairly considered as having been an efficient and satisfactory franchise, and as having in its generation operated with advantage to the country. My own opinion from the commencement has always been that seed was sown in that arrangement which would necessarily in the course of time lead to some disturbance. That is, however, a question of controversy, and I will not indulge in controversy at the present moment. It is, nevertheless, an historic fact that only twenty years after the passing of the great measure of 1832 the principal, or at least one of the principal authors of that measure announced in this House that the arrangement which had been entered into, especially with respect to the borough franchise, was no longer satisfactory, and invited us to consider a new arrangement which might command a more complete assent. That is a fact which cannot be denied.

·   ·   ·

I have placed before the House the principal features of the Bill which I am asked to introduce. The Bill itself will be in the hands of the members to-morrow, and then they will be perfectly well qualified to form an opinion upon the manner in which the principles I have laid down are acted on. I hope that the House will candidly consider this measure. As far as we are concerned, we have spared no pains, no thought, and have not shrunk from what was more important, perhaps, in endeavouring to bring it before the House. I will not advert unnecessarily to the circumstances attending the framing of this measure, which has now been brought before the House of Commons, under very great difficulties and at very great sacrifices. I do not wish to disguise that I have felt great chagrin and great mortification in connection with what has taken place; but I believe I have done my duty, and under the circumstances I do not think I could have done other than I have. In attempting to bring the question to this point we have lost those whose absence from our councils we more than regret; we have had to appeal to a high-spirited party to make what no doubt to some was to a certain extent a sacrifice of principle, much sacrifice of sentiment, and much sacrifice of interest. But we have not appealed in vain, because the members of that party were animated by the same feeling which influenced us—a sense of duty and conviction. They felt that the time had arrived when this question must be dealt with and settled extensively and completely. I hope, therefore, the House of Commons will give this measure a fair and candid consideration. We believe it is one which, if adopted in spirit, will settle its long differences; and that it is qualified to meet the requirements of the country. I am told for certain that there are objections against it; but I beg to remind the House of the distinction which we draw between popular privileges and democratic rights. I am told that in this measure there are checks and counterpoises in our scheme. We live under a Constitution of which we boast that it is a Constitution of checks and counterpoises. If the measure bears some reference to existing classes in this country, why should we conceal from ourselves, or omit from our discussions, the fact that this country is a country of classes, and a country of classes it will ever remain? What we desire to do is to give everyone who is worthy of it a fair share in the government of the country by means of the elective franchise; but, at the same time, we have been equally anxious to maintain the character of the House, to make propositions in harmony with the circumstances of the country, to prevent a preponderance of any class, and to give a representation to the nation.

·   ·   ·

Well, Sir, under these circumstances we acceded to power last year, and we found it was absolutely necessary to deal with this question; we came into power unpledged, and I have heard with some astonishment reproaches in regard to our change of opinion. I am not here to defend, to vindicate, or even to mitigate every expression I may have used on this subject during the course of many years, but I can appeal to the general tenor of the policy we have recom-

mended. I have always said that the question of
Parliamentary Reform was one which it was
quite open to the Conservative party to deal with.
I have said so in this House, and on the hustings,
in the presence of my countrymen, a hundred
times. I have always said, and I say so now, that
when you come to a settlement of this question,
you cannot be bound to any particular scheme, as
if you were settling the duties on sugar, but dealing with the question on great constitutional
principles, and which I hope to show have not
been deviated from, you must deal with it also
with a due regard to the spirit of the time and the
requirements of the country. I will not dwell upon
the excitement which then prevailed in the country, for I can say most sincerely that, without
treating that excitement with contempt, or in
any spirit analogous to contempt, we considered
this question only with reference to the fair
requirements of the country. But having to deal
with this question, and being in office with a large
majority against us, and finding that ministers of
all colours of party and politics, with great majorities, had failed to deal with it successfully, and
believing that another failure would be fatal not
merely to the Conservative party, but most
dangerous to the country, we resolved to settle
it if we could. Having accepted office unpledged,
what was the course we adopted? Believing that
it was a matter of the first State necessity that the
question should be settled; knowing the majority
was against us, and knowing the difficulties we
had to deal with, being in a minority—and even
with a majority our predecessors had not succeeded—after due deliberation we were of
opinion that the only mode of arriving at a
settlement was to take the House into council
with us, and by our united efforts, and the frank
communication of ideas, to attain a satisfactory
solution.

.   .   .

... I say that if we could not carry out our
policy of 1859, the logical conclusion was that in
settling the question we should make the proposition which you, after due consideration, have
accepted, and which I hope you will to-night pass.
Let us look at the other divisions of the subject.
I will not test by little points the question of
whether we have carried substantially the policy
which we recommended. I say look to the distribution of seats. I am perfectly satisfied on the part
of Her Majesty's Government with the distribution of seats which the House in its wisdom has

sanctioned. I think it is a wise and prudent
distribution of seats. I believe that upon reflection
it will satisfy the country. It has been modified in
one instance, to a certain degree, in favour of
views which in principle we do not oppose; but
we have succeeded in limiting the application of
that principle; and, on the whole, the policy
which is embodied in the distribution of seats,
which by reading this Bill a third time I hope you
are going to adopt, is the policy of redistribution
which on the part of the Conservative party I
have now for nearly twenty years impressed on
this House. And what is that policy? That you
should completely disfranchise no single place;
that it would be most unwise without necessity
to disfranchise any centre of representation; that
you should take the smaller boroughs with two
members each and find the degree of representation which you wanted to supply in their surplus
and superfluity of representation. You have
acted upon that principle. But, above all, year
after year I have endeavoured to impress on this
House the absolute necessity of your doing justice
to those vast, I may almost say, unrepresented
millions, but certainly most indaequately represented millions, who are congregated in your
counties. You may depreciate what you have
agreed to, but in my opinion you have agreed
to a very great measure. At any rate it is the first,
and it is a very considerable, attempt to do
justice in regard to the representation the of
counties.

Then although I am the last person in any
way to underrate the value of the assistance
which Her Majesty's Government have received
from the House in the management of this
measure; although I believe there is no other
example in the annals of Parliament when there
has been such a fair interchange of ideas between
the two sides of the House, and when, notwithstanding some bitter words and burning sentiments which we have occasionally listened to—
and especially to-night—there has been, on the
whole, a greater absence of party feeling and party
management than has ever been exhibited in the
conduct of a great measure; although personally
I am deeply grateful to many honourable gentlemen opposite for the advice and aid I have
received from them, yet I am bound to say that
in the carrying of this measure with all that assistance, and with an unaffected desire on our part
to defer to the wishes of the House wherever
possible, I do think the Bill embodies the chief
principles of the policy that we have professed,
and which we have always advocated.

Well, but there is a right honourable gentle-man[1] who has to-night told us that he is no prophet, but who for half an hour indulged in a series of the most doleful vaticinations that were ever listened to. He says that everything is ruined, and he begins with the House of Lords. Such a singular catalogue of political catastrophes, and such a programme of the injurious consequences of this legislation, were never heard of. The right honourable gentleman says, 'There is the House of Lords; it is not of the slightest use now, and what do you think will happen to it when this Bill passes?' That was his argument. Well, my opinion is, if the House of Lords is at present in the position which the right honourable gentle-man describes—and I am far from admitting it—then the passing of the Bill can do the House of Lords no harm, and it is very likely may do it a great deal of good. I think the increase of sym-pathy between the great body of the people and their natural leaders will be more likely to incite the House of Lords to action and to increased efforts to deserve and secure the gratitude and good feeling of the nation. 'But,' says the right honourable gentleman, 'what is most terrible about the business of carrying this Bill is the treachery by which it has been accomplished.' What I want to know from the right honourable gentleman is, when did the treachery begin? The right honourable gentleman thinks that a measure of Parliamentary Reform is an act of treachery, in consequence of what took place last year, when those who now bring it forward were in frequent council and co-operation with those who then and now oppose it. I can only say, for myself, that I hear of these mysterious councils for the first time. But if a compact was entered into last year, when we were in Opposition, that no measure of Parliamentary Reform should pass, or any pro-posal with that object be made by us—if such a proposal is an act of treason, then the noble lord the member for Stamford and his friends are as guilty of treachery as we who sit on these benches. Really I should have supposed that the right honourable gentleman would have weighed his words a little more; that when he talks of treach-ery he would have tried to define what he means, and that he would have drawn some hard and straight line to tell us where this treachery com-menced. The right honourable gentleman, how-ever, throws no light on the subject. He made a speech to-night which reminded me of the production of some inspired schoolboy, all about the battles of Chæronea and of Hastings.[2] I think he said that the people of England should be educated, but that the quality of the education was a matter of no consequence as compared with the quantity. Now, the right honourable gentle-man seems to be in doubt as to what may be his lot in the new Parliament, and what I should recommend him to be—if he will permit me to give him advice—is the schoolmaster abroad. I should think that with his great power of classical and historical illustration the right honourable gentleman might soon be able to clear the minds of the new constituency of all 'perilous stuff,' and thus render them as soundly Conservative as he himself could desire.

I must, however, remind the right honourable gentleman when he tells us of the victims at Chæronea, to whom he likens himself, that they died for their country, and died expressing their proud exultation that their blood should be shed in so sacred a cause. But this victim of Chæronea takes the earliest opportunity, not of expressing his glory in his achievements and his sacrifice, but of absolutely announcing the conditions on which he is ready to join with those who have brought upon him so disgraceful a discomfiture. He has laid before us a programme to-night of all the revolutionary measures which he detests, but which in consequence of the passing of this Bill he is now prepared to adopt. The right honour-able gentleman concluded his attack upon us by accusing us of treachery, and by informing us that he is going to support all those measures which he has hitherto opposed in this House—though I believe he advocated them elsewhere—and that he will recur, I suppose, to those Australian politics which rendered him first so famous.

The right honourable gentleman told us that in the course we are pursuing there is infamy. The expression is strong; but I never quarrel with that sort of thing, nor do I like on that account to disturb an honourable gentleman in his speech, particularly when he happens to be approaching his peroration. Our conduct, how-ever, according to him, is infamous—that is his statement—because in office we are supporting measures of Parliamentary Reform which we disapprove, and to which we have hitherto been opposed. Well, if we disapprove the Bill which

---

[1] Robert Lowe, Member of Parliament for Calne, opponent of the bill.

[2] Battle of Chærona, 338 B.C., a defeat of the Greek citizen armies by Philip II of Macedon; Battle of Hastings, 1066, defeat of the English by William the Conqueror.

we are recommending the House to accept and
sanction to-night, our conduct certainly would be
objectionable. If we, from the bottom of our
hearts do not believe that the measure which we
are now requesting you to pass is on the whole the
wisest and best that could be passed under the
circumstances, I would even admit that our conduct was infamous. But I want to know what the
right honourable gentleman thinks of his own
conduct when, having assisted in turning out the
Government of Lord Derby in 1859, because they
would not reduce the borough franchise, he—if
I am not much mistaken, having been one of the
most active managers in that intrigue—the right
honourable gentleman accepted office in 1860
under the Government of Lord Palmerston, who,
of course, brought forward a measure of Parliamentary Reform which, it would appear, the

right honourable gentleman also disapproved of,
and more than disapproved, inasmuch as,
although a member of the Government, he
privately and successfully· solicited his political
opponents to defeat it. And yet this is the right
honourable gentleman who talks of infamy!

Sir, the prognostications of evil uttered by the
noble lord I can respect, because I know that
they are sincere; the warnings and prophecies of
the right honourable gentleman I treat in another
spirit. For my part, I do not believe that the
country is in danger. I think England is safe in the
race of men who inhabit her; that she is safe in
something much more precious than her accumulated capital—her accumulated experience; she
is safe in her national character, in her fame, in
the traditions of a thousand years, and in that
glorious future which I believe awaits her.

John Frederick Denison Maurice

1805-1872

REDERICK DENISON MAURICE, as he is usually known, was born the son of a Unitarian minister near Lowestoft. His family of seven sisters and other relations was frequently in religious turmoil over which denomination to adhere to. He studied at Trinity College and Trinity Hall, Cambridge, but, being a dissenter, he was obliged to leave without taking a degree. He removed to London in 1827 and embarked on a literary career, which included for a time the editorship of the *Athenaeum*. But Maurice's interests were always theological, and under the influence of Coleridge and the Broad Church movement, he took holy orders in the Church of England and embarked on a distinguished theological career, the first fruits of which was *The Kingdom of Christ* (1838).

Maurice served as Chaplain at Guy's Hospital and at Lincoln's Inn, but eventually he turned to teaching and became Professor of Literature at King's College, London. Later, from 1846 to 1853, he served as Professor of Theology at King's, but he lost this post for his unorthodox theology as expressed in his *Theological Essays* (1853). From 1866 until his death he served as Professor of Moral Theology at Cambridge. It was on the occasion of Maurice's expulsion from King's as Professor of Theology that Tennyson wrote a poem praising Maurice and referring to him as "the man that is dear to God."

Through his writings and lectures Maurice established himself as the principle spokesman for the Broad Church point of view, which held a liberal but sacramental theology much indebted to Coleridge and romantic philosophy and touched also by such diverse strains as biblical criticism and modern science. Maurice advanced as his primary view God's infinite love for all His creation. The *Theological Essays* in which he advanced this idea expressed doubts about the traditional theory of eternal punishment. Maurice also declared himself a Christian socialist and as such was aligned with Charles Kingsley and those advocating a form of enlightened individual benevolence, though not necessarily social revolution. However, Maurice provoked much criticism by his association with more radical socialists. He established the Working Man's College and the Queen's College for Women.

F. D. Maurice's theology has come in for renewed attention in the twentieth century and his reputation is higher now that it has been for many decades. His theology is held to be more original and creative than that of most of his contemporaries, and his stress on the goodness of God and the need for a humane social order has found a warm reception from many contemporary thinkers.

CHRONOLOGY

1805	Born 29 August at Normanston near Lowestoft.
1823	Enters Trinity College, Cambridge.
1827	Leaves Cambridge without taking degree.
1828–30	Edits *Athenaeum*.
1834	Ordained priest in Church of England.
1838	*The Kingdom of Christ*.
1840	Becomes Professor of Literature, King's College, London.
1846–53	Professor of Theology, King's College.
1853	*Theological Essays*.
1866	Professor of Moral Philosophy, Cambridge.
1872	Dies 1 April; buried in Highgate Cemetery.

EDITIONS

The Kingdom of Christ, ed. A. R. Vidler (1958).
Moral and Metaphysical Philosophy (4 vols., 1850–62; rev. ed., 2 vols., 1872).
The Religions of the World (1847).
Theological Essays (1853).
What is Revelation? (1859).

BIOGRAPHY AND CRITICISM

Frederick Maurice, ed., *The Life of Frederick Denison Maurice Chiefly Told in His Own Letters* (1884).
C. F. G. Masterman, *Frederick Denison Maurice* (1907).
Florence M. G. Higham, *Frederick Dension Maurice* (1947).
H. G. Wood, *Frederick Denison Maurice* (1950).
Arthur Michael Ramsay, *F. D. Maurice and the Conflicts of Modern Theology* (1951).
Basil Willey, *More Nineteenth Century Studies: A Group of Honest Doubters* (1956).
A. O. J. Cockshut, *Anglican Attitudes: A Study of Victorian Religious Controversies* (1959).
W. Merlin Davies, *An Introduction to F. D. Maurice's Theology* (1964).
Olive J. Brose, *Frederick Denison Maurice, Rebellious Conformist* (1971).

---

from The Kingdom of Christ

Like many Victorians, Maurice was a champion of ideas of religious unity. The Kingdom of Christ is his appeal for such unity. It has proved to be his most popular work. It was first published in 1838 and in an expanded edition in 1842. The passage offered below, "The

Modern Statesman," is Section V from Volume Two. Maurice is here endeavoring to reconcile the role of the state and the role of religion, especially of the family, which he saw as divinely ordained.

The Modern Statesman

SUCH statements as these, however unacceptable to many Churchmen, will not avail to conciliate modern politicians, or to remove the fears which they entertain of ecclesiastical influence. Perhaps they will be inclined to say that the power which I claim for the spiritual body is really a more dangerous one than that which I renounce. "To admit the existence of a dominant hierarchy is the necessity of a statesman's position; nay, he has not much right to complain of the necessity; it helps in common times to keep other sects quiet, and clergymen indifferent. But when you say that this hierarchy is the proper educator of the land, you are not content that it should be entertained with a bauble. You wish it to become practically and politically mischievous. That power which can educate a land must rule over its families, over its arts, its literature, its science, its ethics, its philosophy, nay, in one sense, as the head of the professional classes, over its law and its medicine. These are pretensions which no government in this day can tolerate further than as it is compelled to tolerate them by circumstances. The religious bodies in every country must undoubtedly affect its education for good or for evil; but they are happily broken into fragments, and it is the statesman's business to see that they act, one and all of them, as religious bodies, and in no other character. The general education of the land he must gradually (for unquestionably there are many difficulties from old prejudices and institutions which he must remove before he can fully accomplish his desire) take under his own direction. If he allows it to be superintended by any ecclesiastical body, that body becomes just as dangerous as the Jesuits have ever been. For where has lain the real power of the Jesuits? Not in their government over courts, but over schools; not in the poison they have been able to infuse into the ears of monarchs, half so much as in the maxims of ecclesiastical submission and craft which they have communicated to children along with their primers and their grammars."

In the first division of this work I have endeavoured to trace the history of some of those political and philosophical movements, which have led men in our day to contemplate education as the only adequate means of preserving government and society. I showed that the course of thought by which we had arrived at this opinion was altogether at variance with the practical results to which it seemed to be leading. The statesman demands education as a power for acting upon the spirits of men. But the statesman of our day has distinctly and formally repudiated the notion that he can deal with the spirits of men; he has blamed his forefathers for assuming any such authority. It seemed to us, therefore, that when the statesman claimed himself to be the educator of his land, he was involved in a strange contradiction. Yet it was a contradiction into which he had fallen most naturally. He found that a set of warring religious bodies were not competent to exercise the kind of influence over his subjects which he feels to be necessary for them. He wants them to be united and harmonised; a sect-educator sets them at strife. He will therefore do what he can. He will leave to these religious bodies the right of teaching their own dogmas; whatever else is included in the idea of education must be taken under his own immediate cognisance. And this course, awkward and inconvenient as it evidently is, nay, destructive of the very idea of education, seemed to us the only one which is left for the modern statesman, unless there were some spiritual body existing in the heart of his nation, which was as organic as the civil body, and able to perform those functions which by its own confession the civil body is incompetent to perform. Our subsequent inquiries have led us to believe that there is such a body; that it has established itself in the heart of every European nation; that it has been the teacher of every nation; that it has incorporated itself with the civil society; that the statesman finds the society with which he has to deal everywhere bearing witness of its existence; that he is obliged to depose this body from its functions before he can commence schoolmaster for himself. Such is the state of the question at present. I shall not enter into it at large, because it has been discussed elsewhere. But it is necessary for our present purpose that I should offer some indications of the difference between the effects of an education given by a national Church which understands its own powers and responsibilities, and one given—first, by the State; secondly, by a set of different sects; thirdly, by an ecclesiastical extra-national order, like that of the Jesuits. That I may follow the method in which I have supposed the objection to arise, I will speak very shortly of these kinds of education as they affect family life, science, art and literature, popular ethics, and philosophy.

I. 1. I have already had occasion to speak more than once on the first of these subjects. I have shown that a mere religious body, such as that of the Quakers, of the Calvinists, etc., though it may regard family life with reverence, though, at certain stages of its existence, it may even have preserved family life in great purity, cannot connect the institution of the family, as such, with its religion. The religious man is one who chooses for himself; who at a certain time has been led to seek for a new life, and a new fellowship expressive of this new life. Such is the notion in which a sect begins. It becomes exceedingly modified when the sect has established itself. Hereditary feelings and sympathies develop themselves; to desert the faith of forefathers begins to be spoken of as an evil. But still the religious society subsists upon this principle. Those who are admitted into its privileges do not grow into them. The religious body is looked upon as something different in kind from the family. And therefore it is the common complaint in all sects, that wherever the hereditary habit has begun to prevail, the religion becomes a matter of course, its power is exhausted; some violent efforts must be made to revive it. Now such influences as these, I maintain, cannot by possibility cultivate the family life of a nation. They do not bring the spiritual life into any direct relation with the life of natural kinsmanship. And in a day when so many influences are threatening household sanctities, when so many schemes of universal society exist which cast them aside altogether, the statesman who has no better means of protecting them than that which is afforded by the teaching of religious sects, must be prepared to see them perish altogether. Where there are no political influences and motives at work, no trade-temper, no grand philosophical generalisations, the religious men in the sects may hope to keep alive the habit of respect and attachment among their children. Where these are abroad, they must tremble; at all events, he who believes that the existence of the nation depends upon the preservation of domestic relations must tremble if these be their only guardians.

2. But what can the statesman himself do by his education to protect these relations? Nothing whatever. Ought I not rather to say, that of necessity he must do much to shake the confidence in them, and to impair their sacredness? It is no fault of his, it is the necessity of his position, a part of his duty, that he should aim at making men citizens. He cannot teach them to be sons and brothers, he is obliged to interfere with the duties which belong to them in these capacities. He must have his schools established upon the express principle, that the parents are not competent to teach, or to choose teachers themselves. He must treat the authority of the father as if its sacredness depended upon the authority of the law. All wise statesmen of antiquity felt this difficulty, and rejoiced to avail themselves of such means as they had of escaping from it. Modern statesmen should surely ask themselves with some earnestness, whether any helps for this purpose are within their reach.

3. That the Jesuit is not exactly the person to whom one can safely confide the custody of family life and relations, most of the persons with whom I am now arguing will acknowledge. And perhaps they will agree with me in thinking, nay, may wonder that I should make such a concession, that the evil of the Jesuit's influence does not arise solely, or perhaps chiefly, from the particular opinions which he inculcates; that if there could be a Protestant order of the same kind, it would be almost equally mischievous. And wherein, then, upon my principle, does its evil consist? Precisely in this: I believe God has established a universal Church in the world, which grew out of a family, which embodied the idea of family life in its highest possible expansion. That idea, I believe, is preserved in freshness and reality, just so long as a strict unbroken connexion is kept up between its highest form and its lowest; so long as the application of the word Father to Him who was, who is, and who is to come, is felt to be no figurative abuse, but rather the only possible explanation of its most ordinary application. And I believe that Ignatius Loyola established a universal order of his own upon a principle altogether different from this Divine principle, nay, subversive of it; that such an order cannot be the means of preserving any part of the true constitution of society; that it must be continually interfering with it, and substituting something else in the place of it; that, above all, family order and this pseudo-ecclesiastical order must be perpetual, irreconcilable enemies.

4. If this be the case, I need not spend any words in proving that the spiritual and universal

society of which we have discovered the signs, seeing that it assumes the family to be taken by baptism into God's family, seeing that it supposes all civil duties and relations to grow naturally out of these first duties and relations, and seeing that it looks upon the highest ecclesiastical duties and relations as connected with the ordinary social duties, should be the great instrument for accomplishing that object which divided sects, the civil power, a seemingly universal fellowship cannot accomplish, that of building up and sanctifying the domestic society of every nation.

II. 1. How far religious bodies or sects can be trusted with the *scientific* education of a nation, may be judged from the difference of the feelings with which they have regarded science at different stages of their history. Almost without exception, the impulse of every sect, when its religious faith and sympathies were most strong, has been to look at science as something wholly alien from the nature of faith and not to be reconciled with it. Whether this has arisen from a Manichæan horror of the outward world, or from a dread of it as something too holy to be touched, or merely from a dislike of the slow and cold methods by which a knowledge of its secrets is obtained, or, as in the case of the Quakers, from a certain dim intuition of a link between the laws of physical and spiritual investigation which ordinary philosophers had overlooked, the result has been the same. In a generation or two the case becomes altogether changed, at least to all outward appearance. Persons arise out of these sects who show a genius for physical speculation, and devote themselves wholly to it; a notion pervades the members of the body generally that such pursuits can no longer be discouraged, as they were in the days of their fathers; a few sturdy Protestants still remain to warn younger men against perils which a sure instinct tells them are most real; others, who fancy themselves more wise and enlightened, and yet withal very religious, explain what lessons respecting the Divine wisdom and goodness may be gathered from natural discoveries. This last change strikes some as a very promising one; to me it seems that the old state of things was far better. The old teachers were acting out a principle; they believed that the business of man's life is to acquaint himself with his Creator, and to do His will; they did not see what these studies had to do with this great end, therefore they rejected them. Their descendants, when they first enter upon these pursuits, do not complain that the application of the maxim was narrow, they complain

that the maxim itself was narrow; that men, if they attend properly to their religious duties, may bestow a fair portion of their time upon pursuits which have a different aim and motive. Soon, of course, these pursuits are felt to be genuine and real, the religious duties artificial and traditional; if the former are not wholly followed, and the latter neglected, there is, at all events, no sympathy between them. Then if there should come a religious revival, and the feelings which are embodied in the different sects should be able to influence public opinion, and to create what is called a religious world, the expedient is resorted to, of making sciences tell a tale about the truth of the Scriptures, and the being and attributes of God. A moral is wrung out of its facts, by fair means or by foul, often by most dishonest construction of evidence, often by positive suppression of that which has been proved. If any fact is brought to light which opposes a current notion in theology or a current interpretation of the Scriptures, it must not be fairly looked at; the question is raised whether there ought to be such a fact, and, therefore, whether we may recognise it supposing it should be one. The scientific men are rightly disgusted. They see that not only the cause of science but also of honesty is at stake; they begin to suspect an hypothesis the more for its gratifying religious feelings.

2. And here comes in the civil power, and says, "This we cannot permit; our subjects must be taught science fairly and truly. We must have railways and steam-engines. In the present state of society, our very handicraftsmen must understand something of the regulations of that machinery which they have to work; the knowledge of a multitude of subjects unknown to their ancestors is needful for them; your religious men may impart what corrections or draw what inferences you please, we must teach the things, we must give our countrymen a scientific culture."

I have nothing to say in answer to this determination, but that I believe it will defeat itself. This teaching of a multitude of things is not, I fancy, scientific culture, but is fatal to it. The favourite name with those who defend this sort of education is the name of Bacon. Oh, that they would devote some real pains to the study of Bacon! They would find him denouncing as one of the main hindrances to scientific knowledge and scientific progress, the desire for facts which should be "fructiferous" and not "luciferous," which should lead to mere results, and not to the search for higher principles. The whole object of his writings was to teach how in facts one may seek for laws; not how, out of a heap of observations, one may make first a theory and then a machine. To the passion for mere effects, and what are called practical results, he attributed most of the delusions and crimes of the alchymists. And unquestionably, if he were to re-appear in our day, and were to hear himself eulogised as the man who had taught how much nobler a thing it is to make shoes than to seek for principles, he would believe that the very mischiefs out of which he had been the means of delivering his countrymen, were coming back upon them through the abuse of his own wisdom. Yet this is the doctrine which the statesman, who is merely a statesman, does inevitably adopt; this has ever been, and must ever be, the maxim of a State education.

3. The Jesuits cannot be accused of neglecting to give information on physical subjects to their scholars. Nor does it appear that they have attempted to restore old theories on these matters, or to teach any other opinions than those which had the general sanction of philosophers in their day. As the Dominicans and the Franciscans were the means of reversing the papal decree against Aristotle, so it seems as if the Jesuits had practically reversed the decree against Galileo, rather eagerly availing themselves of the direction which men's minds were taking towards physical inquiries, to turn them away from inquiries into subjects more immediately concerning themselves. Here, as everywhere, their instruction proceeded upon one principle, and in one regular, coherent system. Teach everything, be it physics, history, or philosophy, in such wise that the student shall feel he is not apprehending a truth, but only receiving a maxim upon trust, or studying a set of probabilities. Acting upon this rule, they could publish an edition of the "Principia,"[1] mentioning that the main doctrine of it had been denounced by the Pope, and was therefore to be rejected; but, at the same time, recommending the study of the book as containing a series of very ingenious arguments and apparent demonstrations. There was no curl of the lip in this utterance, strange as it may seem to us, nor, in the sense we commonly give to the word, any dishonesty. The editors did not believe that Newton *had* proved his point. They had not enough of the feeling of certainty in their minds, to think that anything could be proved. All is one sea of doubts, perplexities, possibilities; the

great necessity is to feel that we cannot arrive at truth, and that therefore we must submit ourselves to an infallible authority. This was the habit of their mind; whether it was a true one or no the religious man will be able to resolve when he has considered its effects in producing the scepticism of the eighteenth century; the scientific man, when he thinks how hopeless of progression those who cherish it must be.

4. Now a national Church, which believes that it exists for the purpose of cultivating the inward man, just as the civil power exists for the sake of the outward man, which believes that it has a commission and vocation for this end, must be a continual witness against all these notions of education. She cannot tolerate for an instant the sectarian notion, that the study of the laws according to which God has framed this universe is not a solemn and religious work, to be carried on reverently, in connexion with the study of the laws upon which He has constructed the moral universe. As she believes that there is a method for arriving at the knowledge of the one constitution, so she believes that there is a method for arriving at the knowledge of the other. There may be a connexion between these two methods, but they cannot be the same. The spiritual method is not honoured when you compel the physical facts into obedience to it; you are certain that they cannot contradict it; you are sure they will, at all events, illustrate it ten thousand-fold more than all your moralities about them ever can. A national Church must believe in the highest sense that what *is* is right. This is the pillar of her own existence; this is what she opposes to the maxim of the world, that things are right which we make so by our rules and conventions; therefore she must teach her children to ask bravely and boldly, "What is?" encouraging them by all means to expect an answer; teaching them in what frame of mind to wait for it, to receive it, to give thanks for it.

But this lesson is very unlike that one which the civil power seeks to inculcate in its education. The spiritual teacher in his own sphere is occupied in leading men into the secret heart of things, in teaching them the laws of their own being, and their direct relation to the Creator. In this sphere of physical science he must act upon the same principle. He cannot merely teach facts and opinions, he must seek to guide his pupil into the knowledge of laws. This method he will follow

---

[1] Newton's *Principia Mathematica* (1687).

with the higher or professional classes who are submitted to his discipline. He cannot change it, though he may alter altogether his scheme of instruction, when he is occupied with the lowest classes. For these, too, consist of men; of men who want to know, and who have a right to know, what that order is in which they are placed; what the meaning of the things which they are doing is; who must not merely be taught what they are to do, or merely be furnished with rules for doing it.

And therefore it is almost needless to say that such a teacher looks upon authority, not in the way in which the Jesuit does, as a substitute for truth, but as that which is to put us in the right way of searching after it. A national Church believes that she is set in the midst of a nation by Him, "who for this end was born, and for this end came into the world, that He might bear witness to the truth," in order that she may bear witness of it, and may rebuke the slavish and godless tempers which hinder men in any direction from seeking it; and that be leading them to know it she may make them free.

III. The treatment which literature and art are likely to receive from these different classes may be conjectured from the remarks which have been just made. Sects in their infancy reject both as worldly and heathenish, in their manhood and decline to tolerate them as necessary indulgences, or endeavour to make them religious by sugaring them over with a Christian phraseology. The civil power encourages both, because they furnish certain measures of diversion and entertainment to different classes of the community; but determines their value by the degree in which they minister to immediate utility. The Jesuit favours all that kind of literary diligence which exhibits itself in laborious compilations, annals, chronologies, etc; all that kind of art which may help to connect devotion more closely with the senses. So that in each of these forms of education, there is from different causes the same tendency to give to human uterances, whether in books, or pictures, or sculpture, or music, or architecture, an artificial, outward, fictitious character: to make them insincere expressions of that which is actually in the hearts of men; or else to make those hearts themselves insincere, by leading them constantly to aim at the production of some effect to which the names, "moral, useful, religious," by a great abuse of language are applied. But if there be any body which really believes that it has a commission to cultivate the mind and spirit of a nation; to call

forth in it that which is truest and noblest; to awaken the reason, the understanding, the affections; to give them their key-note, to bring out their different harmonies; such a body will feel that the men to whom God has given the power of expressing their own minds and the minds of their age, whether in words or in sensible forms, have a high vocation and a mighty responsbility; that the influences of the world are likely to choke their powers and prevent them from freely and happily expanding; that the spiritual mother is to brood over them with tender and affectionate care; to cheer them on amid outward and inward discouragements; to give them the soothing food and medicine of peaceful devotions and outward images of serenity and quietness; to stir them up by heroical examples, to make them conscious of their relation to the past and the future; to hold forth high and distant ends, that they may not be crushed by the influences of their age, or be tempted to court its approbation; to humble them that they may be exalted; to teach them how they may discover the invisible in the visible, instead of confounding them and bringing the higher under the conditions of the lower. While thus training the more illustrious citizens of the commonwealth, she is really marking out the course by which all should be trained who are to be citizens indeed; for to each God has committed some trust, which may be fulfilled for His glory and for the good of the land.

IV. 1. I will conclude this subject with a few words upon the subject of ethics. Strictly speaking, the sectarian does not recognise the existence of such a study. For he looks upon the religious man as taken into a position altogether different from that which other men occupy. He and they are not under the same law. There is a set of rules and maxims which they must observe, in order that they may be members of the family and citizens of the community to which they belong. The religious man submits to these, but he is subject to another set of Gospel influences, with which the ordinary man has nothing to do. Christian ethics mean the religion of the heart according to the Bible, they apply only to the converted; worldly ethics mean the regulation of the conduct according to the rules and maxims which are received among worldly men: these apply to the unconverted. Upon this showing a morality for man as man does not exist.

2. Accordingly the statesman interferes, and says in this case as in the others, "Then you shall teach that morality which belongs to your posi-

tion; I will teach that which belongs to mine. Men must acknowledge some rule of life. These subjects of mine, call them converted or un-converted, must be trained to some sense of their relations to each other. Mere legal penalties are not sufficient for them, they must be taught some reason for their conduct, some method of self-government." Of course these reasons and these methods must turn upon maxims of self-interest. How can they turn upon any other maxims? The statesman has been warned off the religious ground, this is all that remains to him.

3. Of Jesuit ethics I need not speak at length; they are in sufficiently bad odour among us, and probably in most nations of the Continent. What I wish to remark is, that all the evil which is in them has flowed from that first principle of establishing a universal order upon a human calculation of what is expedient for the preserva-tion of the Church and of religion. Once con-struct a society of such power and of such co-herency as the Jesuit society, and it is impossible, in the nature of things, that the preservation of this order should not begin to be regarded as the one great end, to which every other is subordinate. To keep this great machine in motion, to make it effective, everything must be sacrificed. I do not think that there is one pernicious maxim in the Constitutions which may not be legitimately deduced from this primary assumption. The Jesuits feel about morality, as about science, not that it *is* but that it *has been made*, and therefore, that it may be remade for a higher object. The world has framed its maxims to keep itself alive; he may frame his maxims in order to keep the holy religious order alive. The object is surely better; the ways in both cases are determined by arrangement and convention.

4. Once again I say a national Church exists to protest against these outrages upon that which is the very ground of a nation's existence. It affirms morality to be universal, in its highest form to be meant for all men and to be attainable by all men, seeing that the covenant of Baptism takes all who will receive it into the highest state which a man on earth can enjoy; the state in which he has all helps for resisting the powers of the flesh, the world, and the devil, which are seeking to rob him of his human privilege. It affirms morality to be in direct opposition to selfishness, not in its highest forms merely, but in its lowest; the penalties of the lawgiver, the prayers of the Church, being alike directed against this sin; one denouncing its outward effects, the other aiming at the extirpation of the

internal disease. It declares morality, not in its highest forms only but in its lowest, to be ground-ed upon the character and will of God; subjection to that will being the lesson inculcated by the law, conformity to that character being the effect produced by the power of the Gospel. And, there-fore, of necessity it must hate and curse all such schemes of morality as the Jesuits have sanctioned, schemes which pervert the truth that each in-dividual case has peculiar points and delicate complications of its own which require wisdom and refinement and a freedom from rash habits of judging in the person who deals in them, into the confounding doctrine that there is no common law of right and wrong, or that no conscience for perceiving that law exists in the creatures to whom it is addressed.

I have but two remarks to make before I conclude this head of my subject. The first is, that I believe all the defects in national Churches, and in the education which they have communi-cated, may be traced to a notion which has pre-vailed far too generally in the members and ministers of them: either that their position is sectarian, that they are merely civil bodies con-structed for certain civil ends; or, on the other hand, that they are merely parts of a religious society or order existing for purposes wholly foreign to those for which the civil power exists. Should therefore any opponent produce facts which illustrate the weakness and inefficiency of these Churches, or of any one of them, I shall be most willing to consider his statements. I am satisfied they will all tend to the confirmation of mine, that they will all tend to prove the inherent viciousness of those schemes of education which have at different periods suggested themselves as most plausible and satisfactory, that they will furnish another reason why every national Church should understand its own high position, and should zealously assert it. My other remark is addressed to the statesman. He has felt in most countries of Europe, he feels still, the peril of Jesuit influence, and the necessity of guarding himself against it. But what can he do? If he tries to get rid of the idea that there is one Catholic Church in the world, and treats religion as if it were merely a matter of private sectarian opinion, he will not hinder the Jesuits from entering his dominions and becoming masters of his schools. His tolerant maxims will make their settlement more easy; the earnest cry which will be raised throughout a land left to sectarian in-fluence for some united body, some organic fellowship, will cause their appearance to be hailed with delight. Will he, then, in despair, resort to his own peculiar powers? Will he proscribe and banish the intruders, or put them to death? These methods, he knows, have been tried and tried in vain; the crushed order has risen again with all its other influences made stronger by the credit of persecution and of martyrdom. One barrier, and one alone, this subtle and Protean society knows that it cannot break through. A national Church, strong in the conviction of its own distinct powers, paying respectful homage to those of the State, educating all classes to be citizens by making them men; this is a spectacle which the Jesuit regards with wonder and despair. Where there is such a national Church he may be safely allowed to walk up and down in the land; the sting of his order is taken away; he may become a worthy and respectable member of the commonwealth. If the statesman be convinced that the maiming and ultimate suppression of such a Church is the true object of his policy, he must invent some new charm for laying this enemy. None has yet been discovered.

John Stuart Mill

1806-1873

As the standard bearer in the Victorian age for the philosophy of utilitarianism, John Stuart Mill was carrying on the work of his father James Mill (1773–1836) and of his godfather Jeremy Bentham (1748–1832), the founder of utilitarianism. At the same time John Stuart Mill brought humanizing dimensions to utilitarianism that it lacked in its pure Benthamite formulation. Consequently, Mill has survived as a philosophical and literary figure far richer and more complex than the mechanical creation James Mill sought to produce by the rigid application of Benthamite educational methods. He is recognized indeed, far more than Bentham or James Mill, as the finest example of nineteenth-century liberalism.

John Stuart Mill was born in London, the eldest son of James Mill's nine children. His father took special care to educate John personally. Working as he was with an extremely gifted child, James Mill was able to teach John Greek at age three, Latin and arithmetic at eight, logic at twelve, and economics at thirteen. James Mill's methods involved demanding reading assignments and rigorous daily oral examinations. This course of education made an extraordinarily learned man of the child prodigy John Stuart Mill at the same time that it neglected most aspects of literature and the fine arts, except as they were useful for purely rational learning. Thus Mill read Greek and Roman history at an early age, but solely for the mastering of historical and linguistic knowledge.

The course of Mill's educational experience is best told by Mill himself in his posthumously published *Autobiography*. Although he endeavors there to be fair to the memory of his father, his dissatisfactions with the aridity of Benthamite educational methods inevitably emerge. The telling moment occurs in Mill's twentieth year when he passed through what he calls "a crisis in my mental history," something akin to a breakdown. Although he recovered, partly through the discovery of Wordsworth and Coleridge and the romantic impulse, Mill's crisis deeply affected his view of life and the world and contributed to the greater breadth and resonance of his treatment of utilitarianism than that of his father and Bentham.

Most of Mill's adult life was spent as a career civil servant in the offices of the East India Company, an organization that managed British interests in India until the establishment of the India Council in 1858. His father had occupied a post in the East India Company that gave him control of all the departments of Indian administration, and it was he who brought Mill into the organization in 1823. Mill remained with the East India Company until it was dissolved in 1858, when he retired with a pension from the headship of the office of The Examiner of Indian Correspondence. Subsequently he served in Parliament, 1865–68, as representative for Westminster during the period of the Second Reform Bill.

Throughout Mill's life of service for the East India Company he pursued an active literary and political career as well. His father had shaped him to assume the leadership of the utilitarians, or philosophic radicals, as they were also known, and as early as 1823 Mill became a member of a utilitarian society that met at the home of Jeremy Bentham. He was also active in the London Debating Society and as a frequent contributor to the *Westminster Review*, the organ of the philosophical radicals, founded in 1823 by Bentham. In 1835 Mill himself founded and edited the *London Review*, later the *London and Westminster Review*. Mill knew the leading intellectual figures of the day, and even maintained a longtime friendship with Thomas Carlyle, so unlike him in most ways, that was not broken until political differences drove them completely apart. Mill's essays of the eighteen-thirties on such figures as Carlyle, Tennyson, Browning, and Coleridge reflect these literary interests and associations.

Above all, however, Mill was concerned with questions of government, economics, and philosophy. His *System of Logic* (1843) and his *Principles of Political Economy* (1848) were highly regarded in Mill's own day and long remained standard treatises. But it is his philosophic treatise *On Liberty* (1859) that has secured Mill's subsequent reputation as the champion of individual freedom. His *Considerations on Representative Government* (1861) and *On the Subjection of Women* (1869) confirmed his position as the most eloquent spokesman for individual rights in the Victorian age.

Although Mill's fundamental views were formed by his schooling at the hands of his father and his lifetime association with the utilitarian school, two circumstances contributed to making Mill's position different from that of other utilitarians. The first was Mill's mental crisis in 1826–27, which opened his eyes to dimensions of life not adequately accounted for by utilitarianism. The second was his longtime association with Mrs. Harriet Taylor. Mill first met Mrs. Taylor in 1830. She was the intensely intellectual wife of the London merchant John Taylor who exhibited an attitude of exceptional tolerance toward her romance with Mill. Two years after Mr. Taylor's death in 1849, Mill and Harriet Taylor married. She died nine years later, but she is credited with having arrested Mill's movement away from strict utilitarianism and with having inspired views on the marriage relationship and women's rights. In his *Autobiography*, Mill speaks of Harriet Taylor as of a superior mind, but such a view may be attributed to his feelings of affection, rather than to sound intellectual judgment.

After his retirement from the East India Company in 1858 Mill spent much time in France, near Avignon, usually spending six months of each year there. He served in Parliament for three years and he was elected Lord Rector of St. Andrews University in Scotland in 1867. He also stood as "secular godfather" to Bertrand Russell, who was later to become one of the leading twentieth-century philosophers of the empiricist school to which Mill belonged. Mill died in 1873 and was buried at Avignon.

Although Mill's work in philosophy continues to occupy the attention of modern students of the subject, particularly students of the history of British empiricism, his enduring claims to literary attention rest on his social treatises, especially *On Liberty*, on his brilliant assessments of some of his contemporaries, especially Bentham and Coleridge, and increasingly on his subtly effective *Autobiography*.

As the inheritor of the rationalist utilitarian method, Mill exhibits in all his works a stunning command of logic, a subject he did much to revitalize with his *System of Logic*. Operating on the utilitarian assumption that the test of social and political action was that of utility, or in the catchphrase, of "the greatest good of the greatest number," Mill subjected all social conduct to the utilitarian measure. But Mill rose above the prosaic applications of this principle by his father and Bentham (the latter of whom is remembered for having seriously affirmed that "push pin [a game like pinball] is as good as poetry") in his awareness of the difficulties in defining "good" so as to go beyond mere hedonism. Unlike many utilitarians, Mill made qualitative distinctions among pleasures, even as he sought to affirm the traditional utilitarian premise that happiness alone is good and that right action is that which conduces to happiness.

In *On Liberty* Mill endeared himself to proponents of individual liberty by asserting that the individual need not justify his conduct to society when that conduct concerns no one but himself. Mill thus opposed not only the tyranny of government, but the tyranny of custom and tradition. As though to demonstrate his own willingness to follow the consequences of his thought, Mill affirmed the desirability of the same rights of individual freedom for women as for men, a proposition far more radical in his day than in ours.

Yet, with all Mill's commitment to the freedom of the individual and the test of pure utility, there remains in his most deeply pondered works the trace of a yearning to comprehend more than is dreamed of in utilitarian philosophy. In the *Autobiography* Mill clearly affirms a longing for art, poetry, and the emotions that is never fully accounted for in even his widened utilitarian system. Something of the same yearning comes through in his comparison essays on Bentham and Coleridge, which students of the subject have seen as favoring Coleridge at the expense of Mill's own mentor, Bentham. And in the posthumously published essays on religion and nature, Mill inclines toward transcendental views that seem to lead but to God, albeit a God not of Christian orthodoxy but rather one seeking the cooperation of man in the evolutionary process.

It is precisely through the admixture of Mill's hesitantly transcendental metaphysics with the clear, logical, rational utilitarianism of his dominant thought that his writings gain their greatest power and intensity. When the normally suppressed personal element is permitted to color Mill's admirably rigorous thinking, the result is writing that leaves the realm of the mere treatise and enters that of literature.

CHRONOLOGY

1806	Born 20 May in London.
1809–20	Educated at home by his father.
1820–21	Spends year in France.
1823	Joins office of the East India Company under his father.

1826–27 Crisis in his mental life.
1830   Meets Harriet Taylor.
1831   Meets Carlyle.
1832   Death of Jeremy Bentham. First Reform Bill.
1835–40 Founds and edits the *London Review*, later *London and Westminster Review*.
1836   Death of James Mill.
1843   *A System of Logic.*
1848   *Principles of Political Economy.*
1851   Marries Harriet Taylor.
1858   Retires from East India Company. Death of Harriet Taylor.
1859   *On Liberty.*
1863   *Utilitarianism.*
1865–68 Member of Parliament for Westminster.
1867   *Inaugural Address at St. Andrew's.* Second Reform Bill.
1869   *On the Subjection of Women.*
1873   Dies in Avignon, 7 May; buried at Avignon. *Autobiography* published.

EDITIONS

The Collected Works of John Stuart Mill, ed. F. E. L. Priestly, and John Robson (10 vols., 1963—in progress). [Will be the standard edition. Also contains the letters.]

Autobiography, ed. H. J. Laski (1924), J. J. Coss (1924), J. Stillinger (1969).

The Early Draft of John Stuart Mill's "Autobiography," ed. Jack Stillinger (1961).

John Mill's Boyhood Visit to France; Being a Journal and Notebook Written by John Stuart Mill in France, 1820–21, ed. Anna J. Mill (1960).

John Stuart Mill: Literary Essays, ed. Edward Alexander (1967).

John Stuart Mill: A Selection of His Works, ed. John M. Robson (1966).

Mill's Essays in Literature and Society, ed. J. B. Schneewind (1965).

The Spirit of the Age, ed. Frederick A. von Hayek (1942).

BIOGRAPHY AND CRITICISM

Edward Alexander, *Matthew Arnold and John Stuart Mill* (1965).

R. P. Anschutz, *The Philosophy of J. S. Mill* (1953).

Alexander Bain, *John Stuart Mill* (1882).

Karl Britton, *John Stuart Mill* (1953).

Élie Halévy, *The Growth of Philosophic Radicalism,* trans. Mary Morris (1928).

Joseph Hamburger, *Intellectuals in Politics: John Stuart Mill and the Philosophic Radicals* (1965).

F. A. von Hayek, *John Stuart Mill and Harriet Taylor* (1951).

Gertrude Himmelfarb, *On Liberty and Liberalism: The Case of John Stuart Mill* (1974).

Ney MacMinn, J. R. Hainds, and James M. McCrimmon, eds., *Bibliography of the Published Writings of John Stuart Mill* (1945).

H. J. McCloskey, *John Stuart Mill: A Critical Study* (1971).

Emery Neff, *Carlyle and Mill: Mystic and Utilitarian* (1924, rev. 1926).

Michael St. John Packe, *The Life of John Stuart Mill* (1954).

H. O. Pappe, *John Stuart Mill and the Harriet Taylor Myth* (1960).

John M. Robson, *The Improvement of Mankind: The Social and Political Thought of John Stuart Mill* (1968).
———, "John Stuart Mill," in *Victorian Prose: A Guide to Research* (1973).
Alan Ryan, *John Stuart Mill* (1970).
F. P. Sharpless, *The Literary Criticism of John Stuart Mill* (1967).
Leslie Stephen, *The English Utilitarians* (3 vols., 1900).

Bentham

Together with Mill's "Coleridge" essay that follows, "Bentham" provides one of the most illuminating statements in the nineteenth century of the two dominant modes of thought in the age. Mill was himself the leading Benthamite of the age, but his assessment of Bentham's intellectual position is nevertheless just and penetrating and, in the view of many, less favorable toward Bentham than the companion essay is toward Coleridge. The essay first appeared as a review of Bentham's Works *in Mill's* London and Westminster Review *in 1838.*

THERE are two men, recently deceased,[1] to whom their country is indebted not only for the greater part of the important ideas which have been thrown into circulation among its thinking men in their time, but for a revolution in its general modes of thought and investigation. These men, dissimilar in almost all else, agreed in being closet-students—secluded in a peculiar degree, by circumstances and character, from the business and intercourse of the world: and both were, through a large portion of their lives, regarded by those who took the lead in opinion (when they happened to hear of them) with feelings akin to contempt. But they were destined to renew a lesson given to mankind by every age, and always disregarded—to show that speculative philosophy, which to the superficial appears a thing so remote from the business of life and the outward interests of men, is in reality the thing on earth which most influences them, and in the long run overbears every other influence save those which it must itself obey. The writers of whom we speak have never been read by the multitude; except for the more slight of their works, their readers have been few: but they have been the teachers of the teachers; there is hardly to be found in England an individual of any importance in the world of mind, who (whatever opinions he may have afterwards adopted) did not first learn to think from one of these two; and though their influences have but begun to diffuse themselves through these intermediate channels over society at large, there is already scarcely a publication of any consequence addressed to the educated classes, which, if these persons had not existed, would not have been different from what it is. These men are, Jeremy Bentham and Samuel Taylor Coleridge—the two great seminal minds of England in their age.

No comparison is intended here between the minds or influences of these remarkable men: this were impossible unless there were first formed a complete judgment of each, considered apart. It is our intention to attempt, on the present occasion, an estimate of one of them; the only one, a complete edition of those works is yet in progress, and who, in the classification which may be made of all writers into Progressive and Conservative, belongs to the same division with ourselves. For although they were far too great men to be correctly designated by either appellation exclusively, yet in the main, Bentham was a Progressive philosopher, Coleridge a Conservative one. The influence of the former has made itself felt chiefly on minds of the Progressive class;

---

[1] Jeremy Bentham died in 1832; S. T. Coleridge in 1834.

of the latter, on those of the Conservative: and the two systems of concentric circles which the shock given by them is spreading over the ocean of mind, have only just begun to meet and intersect. The writings of both contain severe lessons to their own side, on many of the errors and faults they are addicted to: but to Bentham it was given to discern more particularly those truths with which existing doctrines and institutions were at variance; to Coleridge, the neglected truths which lay *in* them.

A man of great knowledge of the world, and of the highest reputation for practical talent and sagacity among the official men of his time (himself no follower of Bentham, nor of any partial or exclusive school whatever) once said to us, as the result of his observation, that to Bentham more than to any other source might be traced the questioning spirit, the disposition to demand the *why* of everything, which had gained so much ground and was producing such important consequences in these times. The more this assertion is examined, the more true it will be found. Bentham has been in this age and country the great questioner of things established. It is by the influence of the modes of thought with which his writings inoculated a considerable number of thinking men, that the yoke of authority has been broken, and innumerable opinions, formerly received on tradition as incontestable, are put upon their defence, and required to give an account of themselves. Who, before Bentham (whatever controversies might exist on points of detail), dared to speak disrespectfully, in express terms, of the British Constitution, of the English Law? He did so; and his arguments and his example together encouraged others. We do not mean that his writings caused the Reform Bill, or that the Appropriation Clause[2] owns him as its parent: the changes which have been made, and the greater changes which will be made, in our institutions, are not the work of philosophers, but of the interests and instincts of large portions of society recently grown into strength. But Bentham gave voice to those interests and instincts: until he spoke out, those who found our institutions unsuited to them did not dare to say so, did not dare consciously to think so; they had never heard the excellence of those institutions questioned by cultivated men, by men of acknowledged intellect; and it is not in the nature of uninstructed minds to resist the united authority

of the instructed. Bentham broke the spell. It was not Bentham by his own writings; it was Bentham through the minds and pens which those writings fed—through the men in more direct contact with the world, into whom his spirit passed. If the superstition about ancestorial wisdom has fallen into decay; if the public are grown familiar with the idea that their laws and institutions are in great part not the product of intellect and virtue, but of modern corruption grafted upon ancient barbarism; if the hardiest innovation is no longer scouted because it is an innovation—establishments no longer considered sacred because they are establishments—it will be found that those who have accustomed the public mind to these ideas have learnt them in Bentham's school, and that the assault on ancient institutions has been, and is, carried on for the most part with his weapons. It matters not although these thinkers, or indeed thinkers of any description, have been but scantily found among the persons prominently and ostensibly at the head of the Reform movement. All movements, except directly revolutionary ones, are headed, not by those who originate them but by those who know best how to compromise between the old opinions and the new. The father of English innovation, both in doctrines and in institutions, is Bentham: he is the great *subversive,* or, in the language of continental philosophers, the great *critical,* thinker of his age and country.

We consider this, however, to be not his highest title to fame. Were this all, he were only to be ranked among the lowest order of the potentates of mind—the negative, or destructive philosophers; those who can perceive what is false, but not what is true; who awaken the human mind to the inconsistencies and absurdities of time-sanctioned opinions and institutions, but substitute nothing in the place of what they take away. We have no desire to undervalue the services of such persons: mankind have been deeply indebted to them; nor will there ever be a lack of work for them, in a world in which so many false things are believed, in which so many which have been true, are believed long after they have ceased to be true. The qualities, however, which fit men for perceiving anomalies, without perceiving the truths which would rectify them, are not among the rarest of endowments. Courage, verbal acuteness, command over the forms of argumentation, and a popular style, will make, out of the shallowest man, with a sufficient

[2] A measure to apportion a part of the revenues of the Church of Ireland for civil purposes.

lack of reverence, a considerable negative philosopher. Such men have never been wanting in periods of culture; and the period in which Bentham formed his early impressions was emphatically their reign, in proportion to its barrenness in the more noble products of the human mind. An age of formalism in the Church and corruption in the State, when the most valuable part of the meaning of traditional doctrines had faded from the minds even of those who retained from habit a mechanical belief in them, was the time to raise up all kinds of sceptical philosophy. Accordingly, France had Voltaire, and his school of negative thinkers, and England (or rather Scotland) had the profoundest negative thinker on record, David Hume: a man, the peculiarities of whose mind qualified him to detect failure of proof, and want of logical consistency, at a depth which French sceptics, with their comparatively feeble powers of analysis and abstraction, stopt far short of, and which German subtlety alone could thoroughly appreciate, or hope to rival.

If Bentham had merely continued the work of Hume, he would scarcely have been heard of in philosophy; for he was far inferior to Hume in Hume's qualities, and was in no respect fitted to excel as a metaphysician. We must no look for subtlety, or the power of recondite analysis, among his intellectual characteristics. In the former quality, few great thinkers have ever been so deficient; and to find the latter, in any considerable measure, in a mind acknowledging any kindred with his, we must have recourse to the late Mr. Mill[3]—a man who united the great qualities of the metaphysicians of the eighteenth century, with others of a different complexion, admirably qualifying him to complete and correct their work. Bentham had not these peculiar gifts; but he possessed others, not inferior, which were not possessed by any of his precursors; which have made him a source of light to a generation which has far outgrown their influence, and, as we called him, the chief subversive thinker of an age which has long lost all that they could subvert.

To speak of him first as a merely negative philosopher—as one who refutes illogical arguments, exposes sophistry, detects contradiction and absurdity, even in that capacity there was a wide field left vacant for him by Hume, and which he has occupied to an unprecedented extent; the field of practical abuses. This was Bentham's peculiar province: to this he was called by the whole bent of his disposition: to carry the warfare against absurdity into things practical. He was an essentially practical mind. It was by practical abuses that his mind was first turned to speculation—by the abuses of the profession which was chosen for him, that of the law. He has himself stated what particular abuse first gave that shock to his mind, the recoil of which has made the whole mountain of abuse totter; it was the custom of making the client pay for three attendances in the office of a Master in Chancery, when only one was given. The law, he found, on examination, was full of such things. But were these discoveries of his? No; they were known to every lawyer who practised, to every judge who sat on the bench, and neither before nor for long after did they cause any apparent uneasiness to the consciences of these learned persons, nor hinder them from asserting, whenever occasion offered, in books, in parliament, or on the bench, that the law was the perfection of reason. During so many generations, in each of which thousands of educated young men were successively placed in Bentham's position and with Bentham's opportunities, he alone was found with sufficient moral sensibility and self-reliance to say to himself that these things, however profitable they might be, were frauds, and that between them and himself there should be a gulf fixed. To this rare union of self-reliance and moral sensibility we are indebted for all that Bentham has done. Sent to Oxford by his father at the unusually early age of fifteen[4]— required, on admission, to declare his belief in the Thirty-nine Articles—he felt it necessary to examine them; and the examination suggested scruples, which he sought to get removed, but instead of the satisfaction he expected, was told that it was not for boys like him to set up their judgment against the great men of the Church. After a struggle, he signed; but the impression that he had done an immoral act, never left him; he considered himself to have committed a falsehood, and throughout life he never relaxed in his indignant denunciations of all laws which commanded such falsehoods, all institutions which attach rewards to them.

By thus carrying the war of criticism and refutation, the conflict with falsehood and absurdity, into the field of practical evils, Bentham, even if he had done nothing else, would have earned an important place in the history of intellect. He

---

[3] Mill's father, James Mill, who died in 1836.
[4] Bentham actually completed his Oxford degree at age fifteen.

carried on the warfare without intermission. To this, not only many of his most piquant chapters, but some of the most finished of his entire works, are entirely devoted: the "Defence of Usury"; the "Book of Fallacies"; and the onslaught upon Blackstone, published anonymously under the title of "A Fragment on Government," which, though a first production, and of a writer afterwards so much ridiculed for his style, excited the highest admiration no less for its composition than for its thoughts, and was attributed by turns to Lord Mansfield, to Lord Camden, and (by Dr. Johnson) to Dunning, one of the greatest masters of style among the lawyers of his day.[5] These writings are altogether original; though of the negative school, they resemble nothing previously produced by negative philosophers; and would have sufficed to create for Bentham, among the subversive thinkers of modern Europe, a place peculiarly his own. But it is not these writings that constitute the real distinction between him and them. There was a deeper difference. It was that they were purely negative thinkers, he was positive: they only assailed error, he made it a point of conscience not to do so until he thought he could plant instead the corresponding truth. Their character was exclusively analytic, his was synthetic. They took for their starting-point the received opinion on any subject, dug round it with their logical implements, pronounced its foundations defective, and condemned it: he began *de novo*,[6] laid his own foundations deeply and firmly, built up his own structure, and bade mankind compare the two; it was when he had solved the problem himself, or thought he had done so, that he declared all other solutions to be erroneous. Hence, what they produced will not last; it must perish, much of it has already perished, with the errors which it exploded: what he did has its own value, by which it must outlast all errors to which it is opposed. Though we may reject, as we often must, his practical conclusions, yet his premises, the collections of facts and observations from which his conclusions were drawn, remain for ever, a part of the materials of philosophy.

A place, therefore, must be assigned to Bentham among the masters of wisdom, the great teachers and permanent intellectual ornaments of the human race. He is among those who have enriched mankind with imperishable gifts; and although these do not transcend all other gifts, nor entitle him to those honours "above all Greek, above all Roman fame," which by a natural reaction against the neglect and contempt of the ignorant, many of his admirers were once disposed to accumulate upon him, yet to refuse an admiring recognition of what he was, on account of what he was not, is a much worse error, and one which, pardonable in the vulgar, is no longer permitted to any cultivated and instructed mind.

If we were asked to say, in the fewest possible words, what we conceive to be Bentham's place among these great intellectual benefactors of humanity; what he was, and what he was not; what kind of service he did and did not render to truth; we should say—he was not a great philosopher, but he was a great reformer in philosophy. He brought into philosophy something which it greatly needed, and for want of which it was at a stand. It was not his doctrines which did this, it was his mode of arriving at them. He introduced into morals and politics those habits of thought and modes of investigation, which are essential to the idea of science; and the absence of which made those departments of inquiry, as physics had been before Bacon, a field of interminable discussion, leading to no result. It was not his opinions, in short, but his method, that constituted the novelty and the value of what he did; a value beyond all price, even though we should reject the whole, as we unquestionably must a large part, of the opinions themselves.

Bentham's method may be shortly described as the method of detail; of treating wholes by separating them into their parts, abstractions by resolving them into Things,—classes and generalities by distinguishing them into the individuals of which they are made up; and breaking every question into pieces before attempting to solve it. The precise amount of originality of this process, considered as a logical conception—its degree of connexion with the methods of physical science, or with the previous labours of Bacon, Hobbes, or Locke—is not an essential consideration in this place. Whatever originality there was in the method—in the subjects he applied it to, and in the rigidity with which he adhered to it, there was the greatest. Hence his interminable classifications. Hence his elaborate demonstrations of the most acknowledged truths. That murder, incendiarism, robbery, are mischievous actions, he will not take for granted without

---

[5] William Murray, Earl of Mansfield, a noted jurist; Charles Pratt, Earl Camden, the Lord Chancellor; John Dunning, Baron Ashburton, a leading member of Parliament.

[6] Anew, from the beginning.

proof; let the thing appear ever so self-evident, he will know the why and the how of it with the last degree of precision; he will distinguish all the different mischiefs of a crime, whether of the *first*, the *second*, or the *third* order, namely, 1. the evil to the sufferer, and to his personal connexions; 2. the *danger* from example, and the *alarm* or painful feeling of insecurity; and 3. the discouragement to industry and useful pursuits arising from the *alarm*, and the trouble and resources which must be expended in warding off the *danger*. After this enumeration, he will prove from the laws of human feeling, that even the first of these evils, the sufferings of the immediate victim, will on the average greatly outweigh the pleasure reaped by the offender; much more when all the other evils are taken into account. Unless this could be proved, he would account the infliction of punishment unwarrantable; and for taking the trouble to prove it formally, his defence is, "there are truths which it is necessary to prove, not for their own sakes, because they are acknowledged, but that an opening may be made for the reception of other truths which depend upon them. It is in this manner we provide for the reception of first principles, which, once received, prepare the way for admission of all other truths."[7] To which may be added, that in this manner also we discipline the mind for practising the same sort of dissection upon questions more complicated and of more doubtful issue.

It is a sound maxim, and one which all close thinkers have felt, but which no one before Bentham ever so consistently applied, that error lurks in generalities: that the human mind is not capable of embracing a complex whole, until it has surveyed and catalogued the parts of which that whole is made up; that abstractions are not realities *per se*, but an abridged mode of expressing facts, and that the only practical mode of dealing with them is to trace them back to the facts (whether of experience or of consciousness) of which they are the expression. Proceeding on this principle, Bentham makes short work with the ordinary modes of moral and political reasoning. These, it appeared to him, when hunted to their source, for the most part terminated in *phrases*. In politics, liberty, social order, constitution, law of nature, social compact, &c., were the catchwords: ethics had its analogous ones. Such were the arguments on which the gravest questions of morality and policy were made to turn; not reasons, but allusions to reasons; sacramental

expressions, by which a summary appeal was made to some general sentiment of mankind, or to some maxim in familiar use, which might be true or not, but the limitations of which no one had ever critically examined. And this satisfied other people; but not Bentham. He required something more than opinion as a reason for opinion. Whenever he found a *phrase* used as an argument for or against anything, he insisted upon knowing what it meant; whether it appealed to any standard, or gave intimation of any matter of fact relevant to the question; and if he could not find that it did either, he treated it as an attempt on the part of the disputant to impose his own individual sentiment on other people, without giving them a reason for it; a "contrivance for avoiding the obligation of appealing to any external standard, and for prevailing upon the reader to accept of the author's sentiment and opinion as a reason, and that a sufficient one, for itself." Bentham shall speak for himself on this subject: the passage is from his first systematic work, "Introduction to the Principles of Morals and Legislation," and we could scarcely quote anything more strongly exemplifying both the strength and weakness of his mode of philosophizing.

"It is curious enough to observe the variety of inventions men have hit upon, and the variety of phrases they have brought forward, in order to conceal from the world, and, if possible, from themselves, this very general and therefore very pardonable self-sufficiency.

"1. One man says, he has a thing made on purpose to tell him what is right and what is wrong; and that is called a 'moral sense': and then he goes to work at his ease, and says, such a thing is right, and such a thing is wrong—why? 'Because my moral sense tells me it is.'

"2. Another man comes and alters the phrase: leaving out *moral*, and putting in *common* in the room of it. He then tells you that his common sense tells him what is right and wrong, as surely as the other's moral sense did; meaning by common sense a sense of some kind or other, which, he says, is possessed by all mankind: the sense of those whose sense is not the same as the author's being struck out as not worth taking. This contrivance does better than the other; for a moral sense being a new thing, a man may feel about him a good while without being able to find it out: but common sense is as old as the creation; and there is no man but would be ashamed to be thought not to have as much of it as his neighbours. It has another great advantage: by appearing to share power, it lessens

---

[7] Part I, pp. 161–62, of the collected edition. [Mill's note]

envy; for when a man gets up upon this ground, in order to anathematize those who differ from him, it is not by a *sic volo sic jubeo,* but by a *velitis jubeatis.*[8]

"3. Another man comes, and says, that as to a moral sense indeed, he cannot find that he has any such thing: that, however, he has an *understanding,* which will do quite as well. This understanding, he says, is the standard of right and wrong: it tells him so and so. All good and wise men understand as he does: if other men's understandings differ in any part from his, so much the worse for them: it is sure sign they are either defective or corrupt.

"4. Another man says, that there is an eternal and immutable Rule of Right: that that rule of right dictates so and so: and then he begins giving you his sentiments upon anything that comes uppermost: and these sentiments (you are to take for granted) are so many branches of the eternal rule of right.

"5. Another man, or perhaps the same man (it is no matter), says that there are certain practices conformable, and others repugnant, to the Fitness of Things; and then he tells you, at his leisure, what practices are conformable, and what repugnant: just as he happens to like a practice or dislike it.

"6. A great multitude of people are continually talking of the Law of Nature; and then they go on giving you their sentiments about what is right and what is wrong: and these sentiments, you are to understand, are so many chapters and sections of the Law of Nature.

"7. Instead of the phrase, Law of Nature, you have sometimes Law of Reason, Right Reason, Natural Justice, Natural Equity, Good Order. Any of them will do equally well. This latter is most used in politics. The three last are much more tolerable than the others, because they do not very explicitly claim to be anything more than phrases: they insist but feebly upon the being looked upon as so many positive standards of themselves, and seem content to be taken, upon occasion, for phrases expressive of the conformity of the thing in question to the proper standard, whatever that may be. On most occasions, however, it will be better to say *utility: utility* is clearer, as referring more explicitly to pain and pleasure.

"8. We have one philosopher, who says, there is no harm in anything in the world but in telling a lie; and that if, for example, you were to murder your own father, this would only be a particular way of saying, he was not your father. Of course when this philosopher sees anything that he does not like, he says, it is a particular way of telling a lie. It is saying, that the act ought to be done, or may be done, when, *in truth,* it ought not to be done.

"9. The fairest and openest of them all is that sort of man who speaks out, and says, I am of the number of the Elect: now God himself takes care to inform the Elect what is right: and that with so good effect, that let them strive ever so, they cannot help not only knowing it but practising it. If therefore a man wants to know what is right and what is wrong, he has nothing to do but to come to me."

Few will contend that this is a perfectly fair representation of the *animus* of those who employ the various phrases so amusingly animadverted on; but that the phrases contain no argument, save what is grounded on the very feelings they are adduced to justify, is a truth which Bentham had the eminent merit of first pointing out.

It is the introduction into the philosophy of human conduct, of this method of detail—of this practice of never reasoning about wholes until they have been resolved into their parts, nor about abstractions until they have been translated into realities—that constitutes the originality of Bentham in philosophy, and makes him the great reformer of the moral and political branch of it. To what he terms the "exhaustive method of classification," which is but one branch of this more general method, he himself ascribes everything original in the systematic and elaborate work from which we have quoted. The generalities of his philosophy itself have little or no novelty: to ascribe any to the doctrine that general utility is the foundation of morality, would imply great ignorance of the history of philosophy, of general literature, and of Bentham's own writings. He derived the idea, as he says himself, from Helvetius; and it was the doctrine no less, of the religious philosophers of that age, prior to Reid and Beattie. We never saw an abler defence of the doctrine of utility than in a book written in refutation of Shaftesbury, and now little read— Brown's[9] "Essays on the Characteristics"; and in Johnson's celebrated review of Soame Jenyns, the same doctrine is set forth as that both of the author and of the reviewer. In all ages of philosophy one of its schools has been utilitarian—not only from the time of Epicurus, but long before. It was by mere accident that this opinion became connected in Bentham with his peculiar method. The utilitarian philosophers antecedent to him had no more claims to the method than their antagonists. To refer, for instance, to the Epicurean philosophy, according to the most complete view we have of the moral part of it, by the most accomplished scholar of antiquity, Cicero; we ask any one who has read his philosophical

---

[8] "Thus I intend and command," but by a "May it be pleasing to you."

[9] Author of another book which made no little sensation when it first appeared—*An Estimate of the Manners of the Times.* [Mill's note]

writings, the "De Finibus" for instance, whether the arguments of the Epicureans do not, just as much as those of the Stoics or Platonists, consist of mere rhetorical appeals to common notions, to ἐικότα and σημεῖα instead of τεκμήρια,[10] notions picked up as it were casually, and when true at all, never so narrowly looked into as to ascertain in what sense and under what limitations they are true. The application of a real inductive philosophy to the problems of ethics, is as unknown to the Epicurean moralists as to any of the other schools; they never take a question to pieces, and join issue on a definite point. Bentham certainly did not learn his sifting and anatomizing method from them.

This method Bentham has finally installed in philosophy; has made it henceforth imperative on philosophers of all schools. By it he has formed the intellects of many thinkers, who either never adopted, or have abandoned, many of his peculiar opinions. He has taught the method to men of the most opposite schools to his; he has made them perceive that if they do not test their doctrines by the method of detail, their adversaries will. He has thus, it is not too much to say, for the first time introduced precision of thought into moral and political philosophy. Instead of taking up their opinions by intuition, or by ratiocination from premises adopted on a mere rough view, and couched in language so vague that it is impossible to say exactly whether they are true or false, philosophers are now forced to understand one another, to break down the generality of their propositions, and join a precise issue in every dispute. This is nothing less than a revolution in philosophy. Its effect is gradually becoming evident in the writings of English thinkers of every variety of opinion, and will be felt more and more in proportion as Bentham's writings are diffused, and as the number of minds to whose formation they contribute is multiplied.

It will naturally be presumed that of the fruits of this great philosophical improvement some portion at least will have been reaped by its author. Armed with such a potent instrument, and wielding it with such singleness of aim; cultivating the field of practical philosophy with such unwearied and such consistent use of a method right in itself, and not adopted by his predecessors; it cannot be but that Bentham by his own inquiries must have accomplished something considerable. And so, it will be found, he has; something not only considerable, but extraordinary; though but little compared with what he has left undone, and far short of what his sanguine and almost boyish fancy made him flatter himself that he had accomplished. His peculiar method, admirably calculated to make clear thinkers, and sure ones to the extent of their materials, has not equal efficacy for making those materials complete. It is a security for accuracy, but not for comprehensiveness; or rather, it is a security for one sort of comprehensiveness, but not for another.

Bentham's method of laying out his subject is admirable as a preservative against one kind of narrow and partial views. He begins by placing before himself the whole of the field of inquiry to which the particular question belongs, and divides down till he arrives at the thing he is in search of; and thus by successively rejecting all which is not the thing, he gradually works out a definition of what it is. This, which he calls the exhaustive method, is as old as philosophy itself. Plato owes everything to it, and does everything by it; and the use made of it by that great man in his Dialogues, Bacon, in one of those pregnant logical hints scattered through his writings, and so much neglected by most of his pretended followers, pronounces to be the nearest approach to a true inductive method in the ancient philosophy. Bentham was probably not aware that Plato had anticipated him in the process to which he too declared that he owed everything. By the practice of it, his speculations are rendered eminently systematic and consistent; no question, with him, is ever an insulated one; he sees every subject in connexion with all the other subjects with which in his view it is related, and from which it requires to be distinguished; and as all that he knows, in the least degree allied to the subject, has been marshalled in an orderly manner before him, he does not, like people who use a looser method, forget and overlook a thing on one occasion to remember it on another. Hence there is probably no philosopher of so wide a range, in whom there are so few inconsistencies. If any of the truths which he did not see, had come to be seen by him, he would have remembered it everywhere and at all times, and would have adjusted his whole system to it. And this is another admirable quality which he has impressed upon the best of the minds trained in his habits of thought: when those minds open to admit new truths, they digest them as fast as they receive them.

[10] Aristotelean terms for "probabilities," "particular signs," and "conclusive signs."

But this system, excellent for keeping before the mind of the thinker all that he knows, does not make him know enough; it does not make a knowledge of some of the properties of a thing suffice for the whole of it, nor render a rooted habit of surveying a complex object (though ever so carefully) in only one of its aspects, tantamount to the power of contemplating it in all. To give this last power, other qualities are required: whether Bentham possessed those other qualities we now have to see.

Bentham's mind, as we have already said, was eminently synthetical. He begins all his inquiries by supposing nothing to be known on the subject, and reconstructs all philosophy *ab initio*, without reference to the opinions of his predecessors. But to build either a philosophy or anything else, there must be materials. For the philosophy of matter, the materials are the properties of matter; for moral and political philosophy, the properties of man, and of man's position in the world. The knowledge which any inquirer possesses of these properties, constitutes a limit beyond which, as a moralist or a political philosopher, whatever be his powers of mind, he cannot reach. Nobody's synthesis can be more complete than his analysis. If in his survey of human nature and life he has left any element out, then, wheresoever that element exerts any influence, his conclusions will fail, more or less, in their application. If he has left out many elements, and those very important, his labours may be highly valuable; he may have largely contributed to that body of partial truths which, when completed and corrected by one another, constitute practical truth; but the applicability of his system to practice in its own proper shape will be of an exceedingly limited range.

Human nature and human life are wide subjects, and whoever would embark in an enterprise requiring a thorough knowledge of them, has need both of large stores of his own, and of all aids and appliances from elsewhere. His qualifications for success will be proportional to two things: the degree in which his own nature and circumstances furnish him with a correct and complete picture of man's nature and circumstances; and his capacity of deriving light from other minds.

Bentham failed in deriving light from other minds. His writings contain few traces of the accurate knowledge of any schools of thinking but his own; and many proofs of his entire conviction that they could teach him nothing worth knowing.

For some of the most illustrious of previous thinkers, his contempt was unmeasured. In almost the only passage of the "Deontology"[11] which, from its style, and from its having before appeared in print, may be known to be Bentham's, Socrates and Plato are spoken of in terms distressing to his greatest admirers; and the incapacity to appreciate such men, is a fact perfectly in unison with the general habits of Bentham's mind. He had a phrase, expressive of the view he took of all moral speculations to which his method had not been applied, or (which he considered as the same thing) not founded on a recognition of utility as the moral standard; this phrase was "vague generalities." Whatever presented itself to him in such a shape, he dismissed as unworthy of notice, or dwelt upon only to denounce as absurd. He did not heed, or rather the nature of his mind prevented it from occurring to him, that these generalities contained the whole unanalysed experience of the human race.

Unless it can be asserted that mankind did not know anything until logicians taught it to them—that until the last hand has been put to a moral truth by giving it a metaphysically precise expression, all the previous rough-hewing which it has undergone by the common intellect at the suggestion of common wants and common experience is to go for nothing; it must be allowed, that even the originality which can, and the courage which dares, think for itself, is not a more necessary part of the philosophical character than a thoughtful regard for previous thinkers, and for the collective mind of the human race. What has been the opinion of mankind, has been the opinion of persons of all tempers and dispositions, of all partialities and prepossessions, of all varieties in position, in education, in opportunities of observation and inquiry. No one inquirer is all this; every inquirer is either young or old, rich or poor, sickly or healthy, married or unmarried, meditative or active, a poet or a logician, an ancient or a modern, a man or a woman; and if a thinking person, has, in addition, the accidental peculiarities of his individual modes of thought. Every circumstance which gives a character to the life of a human being, carries with it its peculiar biases; its peculiar facilities for perceiving some things, and for missing or forgetting others. But, from points of view different from his, different things are perceptible; and none are more likely to have seen what he does not

---

[11] Bentham's *Deontology* is a collection of Bentham's fragments gathered together by his editor, John Bowring.

see, than those who do not see what he sees. The general opinion of mankind is the average of the conclusions of all minds, stripped indeed of their choicest and most recondite thoughts, but freed from their twists and partialities: a net result, in which everybody's particular point of view is represented, nobody's predominant. The collective mind does not penetrate below the surface, but it sees all the surface; which profound thinkers, even by reason of their profundity, often fail to do: their intenser view of a thing in some of its aspects diverting their attention from others.

The hardiest assertor, therefore, of the freedom of private judgment—the keenest detector of the errors of his predecessors, and of the inaccuracies of current modes of thought—is the very person who most needs to fortify the weak side of his own intellect, by study of the opinions of mankind in all ages and nations, and of the speculations of philosophers of the modes of thought most opposite to his own. It is there that he will find the experiences denied to himself—the remainder of the truth of which he sees but half—the truths, of which the errors he detects are commonly but the exaggerations. If, like Bentham, he brings with him an improved instrument of investigation, the greater is the probability that he will find ready prepared a rich abundance of rough ore, which was merely waiting for that instrument. A man of clear ideas errs grievously if he imagines that whatever is seen confusedly does not exist: it belongs to him, when he meets with such a thing, to dispel the mist, and fix the outlines of the vague form which is looming through it.

Bentham's contempt, then, of all other schools of thinkers; his determination to create a philosophy wholly out of the materials funished by his own mind, and by minds like his own; was his first disqualification as a philosopher. His second, was the incompleteness of his own mind as a representative of universal human nature. In many of the most natural and strongest feelings of human nature he had no sympathy; from many of its graver experiences he was altogether cut-off; and the faculty by which one mind understands a mind different from itself, and throws itself into the feelings of that other mind, was denied him by his deficiency of Imagination.

With Imagination in the popular sense, command of imagery and metaphorical expression, Bentham was, to a certain degree endowed. For want, indeed, of poetical culture, the images with which his fancy supplied him were seldom beautiful, but they were quaint and humorous, or bold, forcible, and intense: passages might be quoted from him of playful irony, and of declamatory eloquence, seldom surpassed in the writings of philosophers. The Imagination which he had not, was that to which the name is generally appropriated by the best writers of the present day; that which enables us, by a voluntary effort, to conceive the absent as if it were present, the imaginary as if it were real, and to clothe it in the feelings which, if it were indeed real, it would bring along with it. This is the power by which one human being enters into the mind and circumstances of another. This power constitutes the poet, in so far as he does anything but melodiously utter his own actual feelings. It constitutes the dramatist entirely. It is one of the constituents of the historian; by it we understand other times; by it Guizot interprets to us the middle ages; Nisard, in his beautiful Studies on the later Latin poets, places us in the Rome of the Cæsars; Michelet disengages the distinctive characters of the different races and generations of mankind from the facts of their history.[12] Without it nobody knows even his own nature, further than circumstances have actually tried it and called it out; nor the nature of his fellow-creatures, beyond such generalizations as he may have been enabled to make from his observation of their outward conduct.

By these limits, accordingly, Bentham's knowledge of human nature is bounded. It is wholly empirical; and the empiricism of one who has had little experience. He had neither internal experience nor external; the quiet, even tenor of his life, and his healthiness of mind, conspired to exclude him from both. He never knew prosperity and adversity, passion nor satiety: he never had even the experiences which sickness gives; he lived from childhood to the age of eighty-five in boyish health. He knew no dejection, no heaviness of heart. He never felt life a sore and a weary burthen. He was a boy to the last. Self-consciousness, that dæmon of the men of genius of our time, from Wordsworth to Byron, from Goethe to Chateaubriand[13] and to which this age owes so much both of its cheerful and its mournful wisdom, never was awakened in him. How much of human nature slumbered in him he knew not, neither can

[12] François Pierre Guillaume Guizot (1787–1874), French historian and statesman; Désiré Nisard (1806–88), French journalist and literary critic; Jules Michelet (1798–1874), French historian.
[13] Vicomte François René de Chateaubriand (1768–1848), French writer and statesman.

we know. He had never been made alive to the unseen influences which were acting on himself, nor consequently on his fellow-creatures. Other ages and other nations were a blank to him for purposes of instruction. He measured them but by one standard; their knowledge of facts, and their capability to take correct views of utility, and merge all other objects in it. His own lot was cast in a generation of the leanest and barrenest men whom England had yet produced, and he was an old man when a better race came in with the present century. He saw accordingly in man little but what the vulgarest eye can see; recognised no diversities of character but such as he who runs may read. Knowing so little of human feelings, he knew still less of the influences by which those feelings are formed: all the more subtle workings both of the mind upon itself, and of external things upon the mind, escaped him; and no one, probably, who, in a highly instructed age, ever attempted to give a rule to all human conduct, set out with a more limited conception either of the agencies by which conduct *is*, or of those by which it *should* be, influenced.

This, then, is our idea of Bentham. He was a man both of remarkable endowments for philosophy, and of remarkable deficiencies for it: fitted, beyond almost any man, for drawing from his premises, conclusions not only correct, but sufficiently precise and specific to be practical: but whose general conception of human nature and life, furnished him with an unusually slender stock of premises. It is obvious what would be likely to be achieved by such a man; what a thinker, thus gifted and thus disqualified, could do in philosophy. He could, with close and accurate logic, hunt half-truths to their consequences and practical applications, on a scale both of greatness and of minuteness not previously exemplified; and this is the character which posterity will probably assign to Bentham.

We express our sincere and well-considered conviction when we say, that there is hardly anything positive in Bentham's philosophy which is not true: that when his practical conclusions are erroneous, which in our opinion they are very often, it is not because the considerations which he urges are not rational and valid in themselves, but because some more important principle, which he did not perceive, supersedes those considerations, and turns the scale. The bad part of his writings is his resolute denial of all that he does not see, of all truths but those which he recognises. By that alone has he exercised any bad influence upon his age; by that he has, not created a school

of deniers, for this is an ignorant prejudice, but put himself at the head of the school which exists always, though it does not always find a great man to give it the sanction of philosophy: thrown the mantle of intellect over the natural tendency of men in all ages to deny or disparage all feelings and mental states of which they have no consciousness in themselves.

The truths which are not Bentham's, which his philosophy takes no account of, are many and important; but his non-recognition of them does not put them out of existence; they are still with us, and it is a comparatively easy task that is reserved for us, to harmonize those truths with his. To reject his half of the truth because he overlooked the other half, would be to fall into his error without having his excuse. For our own part, we have a large tolerance for one-eyed men, provided their one eye is a penetrating one: if they saw more, they probably would not see so keenly, nor so eagerly pursue one course of inquiry. Almost all rich veins of original and striking speculation have been opened by systematic half-thinkers: though whether these new thoughts drive out others as good, or are peacefully superadded to them, depends on whether these half-thinkers are or are not followed in the same track by complete-thinkers. The field of man's nature and life cannot be too much worked, or in too many directions; until every clod is turned up the work is imperfect; no whole truth is possible but by combining the points of view of all the fractional truths, nor, therefore, until it has been fully seen what each fractional truth can do by itself.

What Bentham's fractional truths could do, there is no such good means of showing as by a review of his philosophy: and such a review, though inevitably a most brief and general one, it is now necessary to attempt.

The first question in regard to any man of speculation is, what is his theory of human life? In the minds of many philosophers, whatever theory they have of this sort is latent, and it would be a revelation to themselves to have it pointed out to them in their writings as others can see it, unconsciously moulding everything to its own likeness. But Bentham always knew his own premises, and made his reader know them: it was not his custom to leave the theoretic grounds of his practical conclusions to conjecture. Few great thinkers have afforded the means of assigning with so much certainty the exact conception which they had formed of man and of man's life.

Man is conceived by Bentham as a being susceptible of pleasures and pains, and governed in all his conduct partly by the different modifications of self-interest, and the passions commonly classed as selfish, partly by sympathies, or occasionally antipathies, towards other beings. And here Bentham's conception of human nature stops. He does not exclude religion; the prospect of divine rewards and punishments he includes under the head of "self-regarding interest," and the devotional feeling under that of sympathy with God. But the whole of the impelling or restraining principles, whether of this or of another world, which he recognises, are either self-love, or love or hatred towards other sentient beings. That there might be no doubt of what he thought on the subject, he has not left us to the general evidence of his writings, but has drawn out a "Table of the Springs of Action," an express enumeration and classification of human motives, with their various names, laudatory, vituperative, and neutral: and this table, to be found in Part I of his collected works, we recommend to the study of those who would understand his philosophy.

Man is never recognised by him as a being capable of pursuing spiritual perfection as an end; of desiring, for its own sake, the conformity of his own character to his standard of excellence, without hope of good or fear of evil from other source than his own inward consciousness. Even in the more limited form of Conscience, this great fact in human nature escapes him. Nothing is more curious than the absence of recognition in any of his writings of the existence of conscience, as a thing distinct from philanthropy, from affection for God or man, and from self-interest in this world or in the next. There is a studied abstinence from any of the phrases which, in the mouths of others, import the acknowledgment of such a fact.[14] If we find the words "Conscience," "Principle," "Moral Rectitude," "Moral Duty," in his Table of the Springs of Action, it is among the synonymes of the "love of reputation"; with an intimation as to the two former phrases, that they are also sometimes synonymous with the *religious* motive, or the motive of *sympathy*. The feeling of moral approbation or disapprobation properly so called, either towards ourselves or our fellow-creatures, he seems unaware of the existence of; and neither the word *self-respect*, nor the idea to which that word

is appropriated, occurs even once, so far as our recollection serves us, in his whole writings.

Nor is it only the moral part of man's nature, in the strict sense of the term—the desire of perfection, or the feeling of an approving or of an accusing conscience—that he overlooks; he but faintly recognises, as a fact in human nature, the pursuit of any other ideal end for its own sake. The sense of *honour*, and personal dignity—that feeling of personal exaltation and degradation which acts independently of other people's opinion, or even in defiance of it; the love of *beauty*, the passion of the artist; the love of *order*, of congruity, of consistency in all things, and conformity to their end; the love of *power*, not in the limited form of power over other human beings, but abstract power, the power of making our volitions effectual; the love of *action*, the thirst for movement and activity, a principle scarcely of less influence in human life than its opposite, the love of ease:—None of these powerful constituents of human nature are thought worthy of a place among the "Springs of Action"; and though there is possibly no one of them of the existence of which an acknowledgment might not be found in some corner of Bentham's writings, no conclusions are ever founded on the acknowledgment. Man, that most complex being, is a very simple one in his eyes. Even under the head of *sympathy*, his recognition does not extend to the more complex forms of the feeling—the love of *loving*, the need of a sympathising support, or of objects of admiration and reverence. If he thought at all of any of the deeper feelings of human nature, it was but as idiosyncrasies of taste, with which the moralist no more than the legislator had any concern, further than to prohibit such as were mischievous among the actions to which they might chance to lead. To say either that man should, or that he should not, take pleasure in one thing, displeasure in another, appeared to him as much an act of despotism in the moralist as in the political ruler.

It would be most unjust to Bentham to surmise (as narrow-minded and passionate adversaries are apt in such cases to do) that this picture of human nature was copied from himself; that all those constituents of humanity which he rejected from his table of motives, were wanting in his own breast. The unusual strength of his early feelings of virtue, was, as we have seen, the

---

[14] In a passage in the last volume of his book on Evidence, and possibly in one or two other places, the "love of justice" is spoken of as a feeling inherent in almost all mankind. It is impossible, without explanations now unattainable, to ascertain what sense is to be put upon casual expressions so inconsistent with the general tenor of his philosophy. [Mill's note]

original cause of all his speculations; and a noble sense of morality, and especially of justice, guides and pervades them all. But having been early accustomed to keep before his mind's eye the happiness of mankind (or rather of the whole sentient world), as the only thing desirable in itself, or which rendered anything else desirable, he confounded all disinterested feelings which he found in himself, with the desire of general happiness: just as some religious writers, who loved virtue for its own sake as much as perhaps as men could do, habitually confounded their love of virtue with their fear of hell. It would have required greater subtlety than Bentham possessed, to distinguish from each other, feelings which, from long habit, always acted in the same direction; and his want of imagination prevented him from reading the distinction, where it is legible enough, in the hearts of others.

Accordingly, he has not been followed in this grand oversight by any of the able men who, from the extent of their intellectual obligations to him, have been regarded as his disciples. They may have followed him in his doctrine of utility, and in his rejection of a moral sense as the test of right and wrong: but while repudiating it as such, they have endeavoured to account for it, to assign its laws: nor are they justly chargeable either with undervaluing this part of our nature, or with any disposition to throw it into the background of their speculations. If any part of the influence of this cardinal error has extended itself to them, it is circuitously, and through the effect on their minds of other parts of Bentham's doctrines.

Sympathy, the only disinterested motive which Bentham recognised, he felt the inadequacy of, except in certain limited cases, as a security for virtuous action. Personal affection, he knew well, is as liable to operate to the injury of third parties, and requires as much to be kept under government, as any other feeling whatever: and general philanthropy, considered as a motive influencing mankind in general, he estimated at its true value when divorced from the feeling of duty—as the very weakest and most unsteady of all feelings. There remained, as a motive by which mankind are influenced, and by which they may be guided to their good, only personal interest. Accordingly, Bentham's idea of the world is that of a collection of persons pursuing each his separate interest or pleasure, and the prevention of whom from jostling one another more than is unavoidable, may be attempted by hopes and fears derived from three sources—the law, religion, and public opinion. To these three powers, considered as binding human conduct, he gave the name of *sanctions*: the *political* sanction, operating by the rewards and penalties of the law; the *religious* sanction, by those expected from the Ruler of the Universe; and the *popular*, which he characteristically calls also the *moral* sanction, operating through the pains and pleasures arising from the favour or disfavour of our fellow-creatures.

Such is Bentham's theory of the world. And now, in a spirit neither of apology nor of censure, but of calm appreciation, we are to inquire how far this view of human nature and life will carry any one:—how much it will accomplish in morals, and how much in political and social philosophy: what it will do for the individual, and what for society.

It will do nothing for the conduct of the individual, beyond prescribing some of the more obvious dictates of worldly prudence, and outward probity and beneficence. There is no need to expatiate on the deficiencies of a system of ethics which does not pretend to aid individuals in the formation of their own character; which recognises no such wish as that of self-culture, we may even say no such power, as existing in human nature; and if it did recognise, could furnish little assistance to that great duty, because it overlooks the existence of about half of the whole number of mental feelings which human beings are capable of, including all those of which the direct objects are states of their own mind.

Morality consists of two parts. One of these is self-education; the training, by the human being himself, of his affections and will. That department is a blank in Bentham's system. The other and coequal part, the regulation of his outward actions, must be altogether halting and imperfect without the first; for how can we judge in what manner many an action will affect even the worldly interests of ourselves or others, unless we take in, as part of the question its influence, on the regulation of our, or their, affections and desires? A moralist on Bentham's principles may get as far as this, that he ought not to slay, burn, or steal; but what will be his qualifications for regulating the nicer shades of human behaviour, or for laying down even the greater moralities as to those facts in human life which tend to influence the depths of the character quite independently of any influence on worldly circumstances—such, for instance, as the sexual relations, or those of family in general, or any other social and sympathetic connexions of an intimate kind? The moralities of these questions depend essentially on considerations which Bentham never so much as took into the account; and when he happened to be in the right, it was always, and necessarily, on wrong or insufficient grounds.

It is fortunate for the world that Bentham's taste lay rather in the direction of jurisprudential than of properly ethical inquiry. Nothing expressly of the latter kind has been published under his name, except the "Deontology"—a book scarcely ever, in our experience, alluded to by any admirer of Bentham without deep regret that it ever saw the light. We did not expect from Bentham correct systematic views of ethics, or a sound treatment of any question the moralities of which require a profound knowledge of the human heart; but we did anticipate that the greater moral questions would have been boldly plunged into, and at least a searching criticism produced of the received opinions; we did not expect that the *petite morale* almost alone would have been treated, and that with the most pedantic minuteness, and on the *quid pro quo* principles which regulate trade. The book has not even the value which would belong to an authentic exhibition of the legitimate consequences of an erroneous line of thought; for the style proves it to have been so entirely rewritten, that it is impossible to tell how much or how little of it is Bentham's. The collected edition, now in progress, will not, it is said, include Bentham's religious writings; these, although we think most of them of exceedingly small value, are at least his, and the world has a right to whatever light they throw upon the constitution of his mind. But the omission of the "Deontology" would be an act of editorial discretion which we should deem entirely justifiable.

If Bentham's theory of life can do so little for the individual, what can it do for society?

It will enable a society which has attained a certain state of spiritual development, and the maintenance of which in that state is otherwise provided for, to prescribe the rules by which it may protect its material interests. It will do nothing (except sometimes as an instrument in the hands of a higher doctrine) for the spiritual interests of society; nor does it suffice of itself even for the material interests. That which alone causes any material interests to exist, which alone enables any body of human beings to exist as a society, is national character: *that* it is, which causes one nation to succeed in what it attempts, another to fail: one nation to understand and aspire to elevated things, another to grovel in mean ones; which makes the greatness of one

nation lasting, and dooms another to early and rapid decay. The true teacher of the fitting social arrangements for England, France or America, is the one who can point out how the English, French, or American character can be improved, and how it has been made what it is. A philosophy of laws and institutions, not founded on a philosophy of national character, is an absurdity. But what could Bentham's opinion be worth on national character? How could he, whose mind contained so few and so poor types of individual character, rise to that higher generalization? All he can do is but to indicate means by which, in any given state of the national mind, the material interests of society can be protected; saving the question, of which others must judge, whether the use of those means would have, on the national character, any injurious influence.

We have arrived, then, at a sort of estimate of what a philosophy like Bentham's can do. It can teach the means of organizing and regulating the merely *business* part of the social arrangements. Whatever can be understood or whatever done without reference to moral influences, his philosophy is equal to; where those influences require to be taken into account, it is at fault. He committed the mistake of supposing that the business part of human affairs was the whole of them; all at least that the legislator and the moralist had to do with. Not that he disregarded moral influences when he perceived them; but his want of imagination, small experience of human feelings, and ignorance of the filiation and connexion of feelings with one another, made this rarely the case.

The business part is accordingly the only province of human affairs which Bentham has cultivated with any success; into which he has introduced any considerable number of comprehensive and luminous practical principles. That is the field of his greatness; and there he is indeed great. He has swept away the accumulated cobwebs of centuries—he has untied knots which the efforts of the ablest thinkers, age after age, had only drawn tighter; and it is no exaggeration to say of him that over a great part of the field he was the first to shed the light of reason.

We turn with pleasure from what Bentham could not do, to what he did. It is an ungracious task to call a great benefactor of mankind to account for not being a greater—to insist upon the errors of a man who has originated more new truths, has given to the world more sound practical lessons, than it ever received, except in a few glorious instances, from any other individual. The unpleasing part of our work is ended. We are now to show the greatness of the man; the grasp which his intellect took of the subjects with which it was fitted to deal; the giant's task which was before him, and the hero's courage and strength with which he achieved it. Nor let that which he did be deemed of small account because its province was limited: man has but the choice to go a little way in many paths, or a great way in only one. The field of Bentham's labours was like the space between two parallel lines; narrow to excess in one direction, in another it reached to infinity.

Bentham's speculations, as we are already aware, began with law; and in that department he accomplished his greatest triumphs. He found the philosophy of law a chaos, he left it a science: he found the practice of the law an Augean stable, he turned the river into it which is mining and sweeping away mound after mound of its rubbish.

Without joining in the exaggerated invectives against lawyers, which Bentham sometimes permitted to himself, or making one portion of society alone accountable for the fault of all, we may say that circumstances had made English lawyers in a peculiar degree liable to the reproach of Voltaire, who defines lawyers the "conservators of ancient barbarous usages." The basis of the English law was, and still is, the feudal system. That system, like all those which existed as custom before they were established as law, possessed a certain degree of suitableness to the wants of the society among whom it grew up— that is to say, of a tribe of rude soldiers, holding a conquered people in subjection, and dividing its spoils among themselves. Advancing civilization had, however, converted this armed encampment of barbarous warriors in the midst of enemies reduced to slavery, into an industrious commercial, rich, and free people. The laws which were suitable to the first of these states of society, could have no manner of relation to the circumstances of the second; which could not even have come into existence unless something had been done to adapt those laws to it. But the adaptation was not the result of thought and design; it arose not from any comprehensive consideration of the new state of society and its exigencies. What was done, was done by a struggle of centuries between the old barbarism and the new civilization; between the feudal aristocracy of conquerors, holding fast to the rude system they had established, and the conquered effecting their emancipation. The

last was the growing power, but was never strong enough to break its bonds, though ever and anon some weak point gave way. Hence the law came to be like the costume of a full-grown man who had never put off the clothes made for him when he first went to school. Band after band had burst, and, as the rent widened, then, without removing anything except what might drop off itself, the hole was darned, or patches of fresh law were brought from the nearest shop and stuck on. Hence all ages of English history have given one another rendezvous in English law; their several products may be seen all together, not interfused, but heaped one upon another, as many different ages of the earth may be read in some perpendicular section of its surface—the deposits of each successive period not substituted but superimposed on those of the preceding. And in the world of law no less than in the physical world, every commotion and conflict of the elements has left its mark behind in some break or irregularity of the strata: every struggle which ever rent the bosom of society is apparent in the disjointed condition of the part of the field of law which covers the spot: nay, the very traps and pitfalls which one contending party set for another are still standing, and the teeth not of hyenas only, but of foxes and all cunning animals, are imprinted on the curious remains found in these antediluvian caves.

In the English law, as in the Roman before it, the adaptations of barbarous laws to the growth of civilized society were made chiefly by stealth. They were generally made by the courts of justice, who could not help reading the new wants of mankind in the cases between man and man which came before them; but who, having no authority to make new laws for those new wants, were obliged to do the work covertly, and evade the jealousy and opposition of an ignorant, prejudiced, and for the most part brutal and tyrannical legislature. Some of the most necessary of these improvements, such as the giving force of law to trusts, and the breaking up of entails, were effected in actual opposition to the strongly-declared will of Parliament, whose clumsy hands, no match for the astuteness of judges, could not, after repeated trials, manage to make any law which the judges could not find a trick for rendering inoperative. The whole history of the contest about trusts may still be read in the words of a conveyance, as could the contest about entails, till the abolition of fine and recovery by a bill of the present Attorney-

General,[15] but dearly did the client pay for the cabinet of historical curiosities which he was obliged to purchase every time that he made a settlement of his estate. The result of this mode of improving social institutions was, that whatever new things were done had to be done in consistency with old forms and names; and the laws were improved with much the same effect as if, in the improvement of agriculture, the plough could only have been introduced by making it look like a spade; or as if, when the primeval practice of ploughing by the horse's tail gave way to the innovation of harness, the tail, for form's sake, had still remained attached to the plough.

When the conflicts were over, and the mixed mass settled down into something like a fixed state, and that state a very profitable and therefore a very agreeable one to lawyers, they, following the natural tendency of the human mind, began to theorize upon it, and, in obedience to necessity, had to digest it and give it a systematic form. It was from this thing of shreds and patches, in which the only part that approached to order or system was the early barbarous part, already more than half superseded, that English lawyers had to construct, by induction and abstraction, their philosophy of law; and without the logical habits and general intellectual cultivation which the lawyers of the Roman empire brought to a similar task. Bentham found the philosophy of law what English practising lawyers had made it; a jumble, in which *real* and *personal* property, *law* and *equity, felony, præmunire, misprison,* and *misdemeanour,* words without a vestige of meaning when detached from the history of English institutions—mere tide-marks to point out the line which the sea and the shore, in their secular struggles, had adjusted as their mutual boundary—all passed for distinctions inherent in the nature of things; in which every absurdity, every lucrative abuse, had a reason found for it—a reason which only now and then even pretended to be drawn from expediency; most commonly a technical reason, one of mere form, derived from the old barbarous system. While the theory of the law was in this state, to describe what the practice of it was would require the pen of a Swift, or of Bentham himself. The whole progress of a suit at law seemed like a series of contrivances for lawyers' profit, in which the suitors were regarded as the prey; and if the poor were not the helpless victims of every Sir Giles Overreach[16] who could pay the price, they might thank opinion and manners for it, not the law.

It may be fancied by some people that Bentham did an easy thing in merely calling all this absurd, and proving it to be so. But he began the contest a young man, and he had grown old before he had any followers. History will one day refuse to give credit to the intensity of the superstition which, till very lately, protected this mischievous mess from examination of doubt—passed off the charming representations of Blackstone for a just estimate of the English law, and proclaimed the shame of human reason to be the perfection of it. Glory to Bentham that he has dealt to this superstition its deathblow—that he has been the Hercules of this hydra, the St. George of this pestilent dragon! The honour is all his—nothing but his peculiar qualities could have done it. There were wanted his indefatigable perseverance, his firm self-reliance, needing no support from other men's opinion; his intensely practical turn of mind, his synthetical habits—above all, his peculiar method. Metaphysicians, armed with vague generalities, had often tried their hands at the subject, and left it no more advanced than they found it. Law is a matter of business; means and ends are the things to be considered in it, not abstractions: vagueness was not to be met by vagueness, but by definiteness and precision: details were not to be encountered with generalities, but with details. Nor could any progress be made, on such a subject, by merely showing that existing things were bad; it was necessary also to show how they might be made better. No great man whom we read of was qualified to do this thing except Bentham. He has done it, once and for ever.

Into the particulars of what Bentham has done we cannot enter: many hundred pages would be required to give a tolerable abstract of it. To sum up our estimate under a few heads. First: he has expelled mysticism from the philosophy of law, and set the example of viewing laws in a practical light, as means to certain definite and precise ends. Secondly: he has cleared up the confusion and vagueness attaching to the idea of law in general, to the idea of a body of laws, and the various general ideas therein involved. Thirdly: he demonstrated the necessity and practicability of *codification,* or the

---

[15] John Campbell, 1st Baron Campbell (1779–1861), subsequently Lord Chancellor.
[16] Offensive character in Philip Massinger's *A New Way to Pay Old Debts.*

conversion of all law into a written and systematically arranged code: not like the Code Napoleon, a code without a single definition, requiring a constant reference to anterior precedent for the meaning of its technical terms; but one containing within itself all that is necessary for its own interpretation, together with a perpetual provision for its own emendation and improvement. He has shown of what parts such a code would consist; the relation of those parts to one another; and by his distinctions and classifications has done very much towards showing what should be, or might be, its nomenclature and arrangement. What he has left undone, he has made it comparatively easy for others to do. Fourthly: he has taken a systematic view[17] of the exigencies of society for which the civil code is intended to provide, and of the principles of human nature by which its provisions are to be tested: and this view, defective (as we have already intimated) wherever spiritual interests require to be taken into account, is excellent for that large portion of the laws of any country which are designed for the protection of material interests. Fifthly: (to say nothing of the subject of punishment, for which something considerable had been done before) he found the philosophy of judicial procedure, including that of judicial establishments and of evidence, in a more wretched state than even any other part of the philosophy of law; he carried it at once almost to perfection. He left it with every one of its principles established, and little remaining to be done even in the suggestion of practical arrangements.

These assertions in behalf of Bentham may be left, without fear for the result, in the hands of those who are competent to judge of them. There are now even in the highest seats of justice, men to whom the claims made for him will not appear extravagant. Principle after principle of those propounded by him is moreover making its way by infiltration into the understandings most shut against his influence, and driving nonsense and prejudice from one corner of them to another. The reform of the laws of any country according to his principles, can only be gradual, and may be long ere it is accomplished; but the work is in progress, and both parliament and the judges are every year doing something, and often something not inconsiderable, towards the forwarding of it.

It seems proper here to take notice of an accusation sometimes made both against Bentham and against the principle of codification—as if they required one uniform suit of ready-made laws for all times and all states of society. The doctrine of codification, as the word imports, relates to the form only of the laws, not their substance; it does not concern itself with what the laws should be, but declares that whatever they are, they ought to be systematically arranged, and fixed down to a determinate form of words. To the accusation, so far as it affects Bentham, one of the essays in the collection of his works (then for the first time published in English) is a complete answer: that "On the Influence of Time and Place in Matters of Legislation." It may there be seen that the different exigencies of different nations with respect to law, occupied his attention as systematically as any other portion of the wants which render laws necessary: with the limitations, it is true, which were set to all his speculations by the imperfections of his theory of human nature. For, taking, as we have seen, next to no account of national character and the causes which form and maintain it, he was precluded from considering, except to a very limited extent, the laws of a country as an instrument of national culture: one of their most important aspects, and in which they must of course vary according to the degree and kind of culture already attained; as a tutor gives his pupil different lessons according to the progress already made in his education. The same laws would not have suited our wild ancestors, accustomed to rude independence, and a people of Asiatics bowed down by military despotism: the slave needs to be trained to govern himself, the savage to submit to the government of others. The same laws will not suit the English, who distrust everything which emanates from general principles, and the French, who distrust whatever does not so emanate. Very different institutions are needed to train to the perfection of their nature, or to constitute into a united nation and social polity, an essentially *subjective* people like the Germans, and an essentially *objective* people like those of Northern and Central Italy; the one affectionate and dreamy, the other passionate and worldly; the one trustful and loyal, the other calculating and suspicious; the one not practical enough, the other overmuch; the one wanting individuality, the other fellow-feeling; the one failing for want of exacting enough for itself, the other for want of conceding enough to others.

---

[17] See the *Principles of Civil Law,* contained in Part II of his collected works. [Mill's note]

Bentham was little accustomed to look at institutions in their relation to these topics. The effects of this oversight must of course be perceptible throughout his speculations, but we do not think the errors into which it led him very material in the greater part of civil and penal law: it is in the department of constitutional legislation that they were fundamental.

The Benthamic theory of government has made so much noise in the world of late years; it has held such a conspicuous place among Radical philosophies, and Radical modes of thinking have participated so much more largely than any others in its spirit, that many worthy persons imagine there is no other Radical philosophy extant. Leaving such people to discover their mistake as they may, we shall expend a few words in attempting to discriminate between the truth and error of this celebrated theory.

There are three great questions in government. First, to what authority is it for the good of the people that they should be subject? Secondly, how are they to be induced to obey that authority? The answers to these two questions vary indefinitely, according to the degree and kind of civilization and cultivation already attained by a people, and their peculiar aptitudes for receiving more. Comes next a third question, not liable to so much variation, namely, by what means are the abuses of this authority to be checked? This third question is the only one of the three to which Bentham seriously applies himself, and he gives it the only answer it admits of—Responsibility: responsibility to persons whose interest, whose obvious and recognisable interest, accords with the end in view—good government. This being granted, it is next to be asked, in what body of persons this identity of interest with good government, that is, with the interest of the whole community, is to be found? In nothing less, says Bentham, than the numerical majority: nor, say we, even in the numerical majority itself; of no portion of the community less than all, will the interest coincide, at all times and in all respects, with the interest of all. But, since power given to all, by a representative government, is in fact given to a majority; we are obliged to fall back upon the first of our three questions, namely, under what authority is it for the good of the people that they be placed? And if to this the answer be, under that of a majority among themselves, Bentham's system cannot be questioned. This one assumption being made, his "Constitutional Code" is admirable. That extra-

ordinary power which he possessed, of at once seizing comprehensive principles, and scheming out minute details, is brought into play with surpassing vigour in devising means for preventing rulers from escaping from the control of the majority; for enabling and inducing the majority to exercise that control unremittingly; and for providing them with servants of every desirable endowment, moral and intellectual, compatible with entire subserviency to their will.

But *is* this fundamental doctrine of Bentham's political philosophy an universal truth? Is it, at all times and places, good for mankind to be under the absolute authority of the majority of themselves? We say the authority, not the political authority merely, because it is chimerical to suppose that whatever has absolute power over men's bodies will not arrogate it over their minds—will not seek to control (not perhaps by legal penalties, but by the persecutions of society) opinions and feelings which depart from its standard; will not attempt to shape the education of the young by its model, and to extinguish all books, all schools, all combinations of individuals for joint action upon society, which may be attempted for the purpose of keeping alive a spirit at variance with its own. Is it, we say, the proper condition of man, in all ages and nations, to be under the despotism of Public Opinion?

It is very conceivable that such a doctrine should find acceptance from some of the noblest spirits, in a time of reaction against the aristocratic governments of modern Europe; governments founded on the entire sacrifice (except so far as prudence, and sometimes humane feeling interfere) of the community generally, to the self-interest and ease of a few. European reformers have been accustomed to see the numerical majority everywhere unjustly depressed, everywhere trampled upon, or at the best overlooked, by governments; nowhere possessing power enough to extort redress of their most positive grievances, provision for their mental culture, or even to prevent themselves from being taxed avowedly for the pecuniary profit of the ruling classes. To see these things, and to seek to put an end to them, by means (among other things) of giving more political power to the majority, constitutes Radicalism; and it is because so many in this age have felt that the realization of it was an object worthy of men's devoting their lives to it, that such a theory of government as Bentham's has found favour with them. But, though to pass from one form of bad government to another be the ordinary fate of mankind, philosophers ought not to make themselves parties to it, by sacrificing one portion of important truth to another.

The numerical majority of any society whatever, must consist of persons all standing in the same social position, and having, in the main, the same pursuits, namely, unskilled manual labourers; and we mean no disparagement to them: whatever we say to their disadvantage, we say equally of a numerical majority of shop-keepers, or of squires. Where there is identity of position and pursuits, there also will be identity of partialities, passions, and prejudices; and to give to any one set of partialities, passions, and prejudices, absolute power, without counterbalance from partialities, passions, and prejudices of a different sort, is the way to render the correction of any of those imperfections hopeless; to make one narrow, mean type of human nature universal and perpetual, and to crush every influence which tends to the further improvement of man's intellectual and moral nature. There must, we know, be some paramount power in society; and that the majority should be that power, is on the whole right, not as being just in itself, but as being less unjust than any other footing on which the matter can be placed. But it is necessary that the institutions of society should make provision for keeping up, in some form or other, as a corrective to partial views, and a shelter for freedom of thought and individuality of character, a perpetual and standing Opposition to the will of the majority. All countries which have long continued progressive, or been durably great, have been so because there has been an organized opposition to the ruling power, of whatever kind that power was: plebeians to patricians, clergy to kings, free-thinkers to clergy, kings to barons, commons to king and aristocracy. Almost all the greatest men who ever lived have formed part of such an Opposition. Wherever some such quarrel has not been going on—wherever it has been terminated by the complete victory of one of the contending principles, and no new contest has taken the place of the old—society has either hardened into Chinese stationariness, or fallen into dissolution. A centre of resistance, round which all the moral and social elements which the ruling power views with disfavour may cluster themselves, and behind whose bulwarks they may find shelter from the attempts of that power

to hunt them out of existence, is as necessary where the opinion of the majority is sovereign, as where the ruling power is a hierarchy or an aristocracy. Where no such *point d'appui*[18] exists, there the human race will inevitably degenerate; and the question, whether the United States, for instance, will in time sink into another China (also a most commercial and industrious nation), resolves itself; to us, into the question, whether such a centre of resistance will gradually evolve itself or not.

These things being considered, we cannot think that Bentham made the most useful employment which might have been made of his great powers, when, not content with enthroning the majority as sovereign, by means of universal suffrage without king or house of lords, he exhausted all the resources of ingenuity in devising means for riveting the yoke of public opinion closer and closer round the necks of all public functionaries, and excluding every possibility of the exercise of the slightest or most temporary influence either by a minority, or by the functionary's own notions of right. Surely when any power has been made the strongest power, enough has been done for it; care is thenceforth wanted rather to prevent that strongest power from swallowing up all others. Wherever all the forces of society act in one single direction, the just claims of the individual human being are in extreme peril. The power of the majority is salutary so far as it is used defensively, not offensively—as its exertion is tempered by respect for the personality of the individual, and deference to superiority of cultivated intelligence. If Bentham had employed himself in pointing out the means by which institutions fundamentally democratic might be best adapted to the preservation and strengthening of those two sentiments, he would have done something more permanently valuable, and more worthy of his great intellect. Montesquieu, with the lights of the present age, would have done it; and we are possibly destined to receive this benefit from the Montesquieu of our own times, M. de Tocqueville.

Do we then consider Bentham's political speculations useless? Far from it. We consider them only one-sided. He has brought out into a strong light, has cleared from a thousand confusions and misconceptions, and pointed out with admirable skill and best means of promoting, one of the ideal qualities of a perfect government —identity of interest between the trustees and the community for whom they hold their power in trust. This quality is not attainable in its ideal perfection, and must moreover be striven for with a perpetual eye to all other requisites; but those other requisites must still more be striven for without losing sight of this: and when the slightest postponement is made of it to any other end, the sacrifice, often necessary, is never unattended with evil. Bentham has pointed out how complete this sacrifice is in modern European societies: how exclusively, partial and sinister interests are the ruling power there, with only such check as is imposed by public opinion—which being thus, in the existing order of things, perpetually apparent as a source of good, he was led by natural partiality to exaggerate its intrinsic excellence. This sinister interest of rulers Bentham hunted through all its disguises, and especially through those which hide it from the men themselves who are influenced by it. The greatest service rendered by him to the philosophy of universal human nature, is, perhaps, his illustration of what he terms "interest-begotten prejudice"—the common tendency of man to make a duty and a virtue of following his self-interest. The idea, it is true, was far from being peculiarly Bentham's: the artifices by which we persuade ourselves that we are not yielding to our selfish inclinations when we are, had attracted the notice of all moralists, and had been probed by religious writers to a depth as much below Bentham's, as their knowledge of the profundities and windings of the human heart was superior to his. But it is selfish interest in the form of class-interest, and the class morality founded thereon, which Bentham has illustrated: the manner in which any set of persons who mix much together, and have a common interest, are apt to make that common interest their standard of virtue, and the social feelings of the members of the class are made to play into the hands of their selfish ones; whence the union so often exemplified in history, between the most heroic personal disinterestedness and the most odious class-selfishness. This was one of Bentham's leading ideas, and almost the only one by which he contributed to the elucidation of history: much of which, except so far as this explained it, must have been entirely inexplicable to him. The idea was given him by Helvetius, whose book, "De l'Esprit," is one continued and most acute commentary on it; and, together with the other great idea of Helvetius, the influence of circumstances on character, it will make his name live by the side of Rousseau, when most of the other French metaphysicians of the eighteenth century will be extant as such only in literary history.

In the brief view which we have been able to give of Bentham's philosophy, it may surprise the reader that we have said so little about the first principle of it, with which his name is more identified than with anything else; the "principle of utility," or, as he afterwards named it, "the greatest-happiness principle." It is a topic on which much were to be said, if there were room, or if it were in reality necessary for the just estimation of Bentham. On an occasion more suitable for a discussion of the metaphysics of morality, or on which the elucidations necessary to make an opinion on so abstract a subject intelligible could be conveniently given, we should be fully prepared to state what we think on this subject. At present we shall only say, that while, under proper explanations, we entirely agree with Bentham in his principle, we do not hold with him that all right thinking on the details of morals depends on its express assertion. We think utility, or happiness, much too complex and indefinite an end to be sought except through the medium of various secondary ends, concerning which there may be, and often is, agreement among persons who differ in their ultimate standard; and about which there does in fact prevail a much greater unanimity among thinking persons, than might be supposed from their diametrical divergence on the great questions of moral metaphysics. As mankind are much more nearly of one nature, than of one opinion about their own nature, they are more easily brought to agree in their intermediate principles, *vera illa et media axiomata,* as Bacon says, than in their first principles: and the attempt to make the bearings of actions upon the ultimate end more evident than they can be made by referring them to the intermediate ends, and to estimate their value by a direct reference to human happiness, generally terminates in attaching most importance, not to those effects which are really the greatest, but to those which can most easily be pointed to and individually identified. Those who adopt utility as a standard can seldom apply it truly except through the secondary principles; those who reject it, generally do no more than erect those secondary principles into first principles. It is when two or more of the secondary principles conflict, that a direct appeal to some first principle becomes necessary; and then commences the practical importance of the utilitarian controversy; which is, in other respects, a question of arrangement and logical subordination rather than of practice; important principally in a purely scientific point of view, for the sake of the systematic unity and coherency of ethical philosophy. It is probable, however, that to the principle of utility we owe all that Bentham did; that it was necessary to him to find a first principle which he could receive as self-evident, and to which he could attach all his other doctrines as logical consequences: that to him systematic unity was an indispensable condition of his confidence in his own intellect. And there is something further to be remarked. Whether happiness be or be not the end to which morality should be referred—that it be referred to an *end* of some sort, and not left in the dominion of vague feeling or inexplicable internal conviction, that it be made a matter of reason and calculation, and not merely of sentiment, is essential to the very idea of moral philosophy; is, in fact, what renders argument or discussion on moral questions possible. That the morality of actions depends on the consequences which they tend to produce, is the doctrine of rational persons of all schools; that the good or evil of those consequences is measured solely by pleasure or pain, is all of the doctrine of the school of utility, which is peculiar to it.

In so far as Bentham's adoption of the principle of utility induced him to fix his attention upon the consequences of actions as the consideration determining their morality, so far he was indisputably in the right path: though to go far in it without wandering, there was needed a greater knowledge of the formation of character, and of the consequences of actions upon the agent's own frame of mind, than Bentham possessed. His want of power to estimate this class of consequences, together with his want of the degree of modest deference which, from those who have not competent experience of their own, is due to the experience of others on that part of the subject, greatly limit the value of his speculations on questions of practical ethics.

He is chargeable also with another error, which it would be improper to pass over, because nothing has tended more to place him in opposition to the common feelings of mankind, and to give to his philosophy that cold, mechanical, and ungenial air which characterizes the popular idea of a Benthamite. This error, or rather one-sidedness, belongs to him not as a utilitarian, but as a moralist by profession, and in common with almost all professed moralists, whether religious or philosophical: it is that of treating the *moral* view of actions and characters, which is unquestionably the first and most important mode of looking at them, as if it were the sole one: whereas it is only one of three, by all of which our sentiments towards the human being may be, ought to be, and without entirely crushing our own nature cannot but be, materially influenced. Every human action has three aspects: its *moral* aspect, or that of its *right* and *wrong;* its *æsthetic* aspect, or that of its *beauty;* its *sympathetic* aspect, or that of its *loveableness.* The first addresses itself to our reason and conscience; the second to our imagination; the third to our human fellow-feeling. According to the first, we approve or disapprove; according to the second, we admire or despise; according to the third, we love, pity, or dislike. The morality of an action depends on its foreseeable consequences; its beauty, and its loveableness, or the reverse, depend on the qualities which it is evidence of. Thus, a lie is *wrong,* because its effect is to mislead, and because it tends to destroy the confidence of man in man; it is also *mean,* because it is cowardly—because it proceeds from not daring to face the consequences of telling the truth—or at best is evidence of want of that *power* to compass our ends by straightforward means, which is conceived as properly belonging to every person not deficient in energy or in understanding. The action of Brutus in sentencing his sons[19] was *right,* because it was executing a law essential to the freedom of his country, against persons of whose guilt there was no doubt: it was *admirable,* because it evinced a rare degree of patriotism, courage, and self-control; but there was nothing *loveable* in it; it affords either no presumption in regard to loveable qualities, or a presumption of their deficiency. If one of the sons had engaged in the conspiracy from affection for the other, his action would have been loveable, though neither moral nor admirable. It is not possible for any sophistry to confound these three modes of viewing an action; but it is very possible to adhere to one of them exclusively, and lose sight of the rest. Sentimentality consists in setting the last two of the three above the first; the error of moralists in general, and of Bentham, is to sink the two latter entirely. This is pre-eminently the case with Bentham: he both wrote and felt as

---

[19] Brutus' sons conspired to restore the Tarquins to power.

if the moral standard ought not only to be paramount (which it ought), but to be alone; as if it ought to be the sole master of all our actions, and even of all our sentiments; as if either to admire or like, or despise or dislike a person for any action which neither does good not harm, or which does not do a good or a harm proportioned to the sentiment entertained, were an injustice and a prejudice. He carried this so far, that there were certain phrases which, being expressive of what he considered to be this groundless liking or aversion, he could not bear to hear pronounced in his presence. Among these phrases were those of *good* and *bad taste*. He thought it an insolent piece of dogmatism in one person to praise or condemn another in a matter of taste: as if men's likings and dislikings, on things in themselves indifferent, were not full of the most important inferences as to every point of their character; as if a person's tastes did not show him to be wise or a fool, cultivated or ignorant, gentle or rough, sensitive or callous, generous or sordid, benevolent or selfish, conscientious or depraved.

Connected with the same topic are Bentham's peculiar opinions on poetry. Much more has been said than there is any foundation for, about his contempt for the pleasures of imagination, and for the fine arts. Music was throughout life his favourite amusement; painting, sculpture, and the other arts addressed to the eye, he was so far from holding in any contempt, that he occasionally recognizes them as means employable for important social ends; though his ignorance of the deeper springs of human character prevented him (as it prevents most Englishmen) from suspecting how profoundly such things enter into the moral nature of man, and into the education both of the individual and of the race. But towards poetry in the narrower sense, that which employs the language of words, he entertained no favour. Words, he thought, were perverted from their proper office when they were employed in uttering anything but precise logical truth. He says, somewhere in his works, that, "quantity of pleasure being equal, push-pin is as good as poetry": but this is only a paradoxical way of stating what he would equally have said of the things which he most valued and admired. Another aphorism is attributed to him, which is much more characteristic of his view of this subject: "All poetry is misrepresentation." Poetry, he thought, consisted essentially in exaggeration for effect: in proclaiming some one view of a thing very emphatically, and suppressing all the limitations and qualifications. This trait of character seems to us a curious example of what Mr. Carlyle strikingly calls "the completeness of limited men." Here is a philosopher who is happy within his narrow boundary as no man of indefinite range ever was: who flatters himself that he is so completely emancipated from the essential law of poor human intellect, by which it can only see one thing at a time well, that he can even turn round upon the imperfection and lay a solemn interdict upon it. Did Bentham really suppose that it is in poetry only that propositions cannot be exactly true, cannot contain in themselves all the limitations and qualifications with which they require to be taken when applied to practice? We have seen how far his own prose propositions are from realizing this Utopia: and even the attempt to approach it would be incompatible not with poetry merely, but with oratory, and popular writing of every kind. Bentham's charge is true to the fullest extent; all writing which undertakes to make men feel truths as well as see them, does take up one point at a time, does seek to impress that, to drive that home, to make it sink into and colour the whole mind of the reader or hearer. It is justified in doing so, if the portion of truth which it thus enforces be that which is called for by the occasion. All writing addressed to the feelings has a natural tendency to exaggeration; but Bentham should have remembered that in this, as in many things, we must aim at too much, to be assured of doing enough.

From the same principle in Bentham came the intricate and involved style, which makes his later writings books for the student only, not the general reader. It was from his perpetually aiming at impracticable precision. Nearly all his earlier, and many parts of his later writings, are models, as we have already observed, of light, playful, and popular style: a Benthamiana might be made of passages worthy of Addison or Goldsmith. But in his later years and more advanced studies, he fell into a Latin or German structure of sentence, foreign to the genius of the English language. He could not bear, for the sake of clearness and the reader's ease, to say, as ordinary men are content to do, a little more than the truth in one sentence, and correct it in the next. The whole of the qualifying remarks which he intended to make, he insisted upon imbedding as parentheses in the very middle of the sentence itself. And thus the sense being so long suspended, and attention being required to the accessory ideas before the principal idea had been properly seized, it became difficult, without some practice, to make out the train of thought. It is fortunate that so many of the most important parts of his writings are free from this defect. We regard it as a *reductio ad absurdum* of his objection to poetry. In trying to write in a manner against which the same objection should not lie, he could stop nowhere short of utter unreadableness, and after all attained no more accuracy than is compatible with opinions as imperfect and one-sided as those of any poet or sentimentalist breathing. Judge then in what state literature and philosophy would be, and what chance they would have of influencing the multitude, if his objection were allowed, and all styles of writing banished which would not stand his test.

We must here close this brief and imperfect view of Bentham and his doctrines; in which many parts of the subject have been entirely untouched, and no part done justice to, but which at least proceeds from an intimate familiarity with his writings, and is nearly the first attempt at an impartial estimate of his character as a philosopher, and of the result of his labours to the world.

After every abatement, and it has been seen whether we have made our abatements sparingly —there remains to Bentham an indisputable place among the great intellectual benefactors of mankind. His writings will long form an indispensable part of the education of the highest order of practical thinkers; and the collected edition of them ought to be in the hands of every one who would either understand his age, or take any beneficial part in the great business of it.

Coleridge

The following essay first appeared in the London and Westminster Review *in 1840 as a review of several works by Coleridge, who had died in 1834. Mill here demonstrates a high degree of sympathy for Coleridge and a genuine insight into the strengths of Coleridge's philosophy, which he recognized as more comprehensive than Bentham's. Coleridge is seen by Mill as representing the other and complementary mode of thought in the nineteenth century to Bentham's. (The ellipses are Mill's.)*

THE name of Coleridge is one of the few English names of our time which are likely to be oftener pronounced, and to become symbolical of more important things, in proportion as the inward workings of the age manifest themselves more and more in outward facts. Bentham excepted, no Englishman of recent date has left his impress so deeply in the opinions and mental tendencies of those among us who attempt to enlighten their practice by philosophical meditation. If it be true, as Lord Bacon affirms, that a knowledge of the speculative opinions of the men between twenty and thirty years of age is the great source of political prophecy, the existence of Coleridge will show itself by no slight or ambiguous traces in the coming history of our country; for no one has contributed more to shape the opinions of those among its younger men, who can be said to have opinions at all.

The influence of Coleridge, like that of Bentham, extends far beyond those who share in the peculiarities of his religious or philosophical creed. He has been the great awakener in this country of the spirit of philosophy, within the bounds of traditional opinions. He has been, almost as truly as Bentham, "the great questioner of things established";[1] for a questioner needs not necessarily be an enemy. By Bentham, beyond all others, men have been led to ask themselves, in regard to any ancient or received opinion, Is it true? and by Coleridge, What is the meaning of it? The one took his stand outside the received opinion, and surveyed it as an entire stranger to it: the other looked at it from within, and endeavoured to see it with the eyes of a believer in it; to discover by what apparent facts it was at first suggested, and by what appearances it has ever since been rendered continually credible—has seemed, to a succession of persons, to be a faithful interpretation of their

[1] Mill is quoting from his own essay on Bentham.

experience. Bentham judged a proposition true or false as it accorded or not with the result of his own inquiries; and did not search very curiously into what might be meant by the proposition, when it obviously did not mean what he thought true. With Coleridge, on the contrary, the very fact that any doctrine had been believed by thoughtful men, and received by whole nations or generations of mankind, was part of the problem to be solved, was one of the phenomena to be accounted for. And as Bentham's short and easy method of referring all to the selfish interests of aristocracies, or priests, or lawyers, or some other species of imposters, could not satisfy a man who saw so much farther into the complexities of the human intellect and feelings—he considered the long or extensive prevalence of any opinion as a presumption that it was not altogether a fallacy; that, to its first authors at least, it was the result of a struggle to express in words something which had a reality to them, though perhaps not to many of those who have since received the doctrine by mere tradition. The long duration of a belief, he thought, is at least proof of an adaptation in it to some portion or other of the human mind; and if, on digging down to the root, we do not find, as is generally the case, some truth, we shall find some natural want or requirement of human nature which the doctrine in question is fitted to satisfy: among which wants the instincts of selfishness and of credulity have a place, but by no means an exclusive one. From this difference in the points of view of the two philosophers, and from the too rigid adherence of each to his own, it was to be expected that Bentham should continually miss the truth which is in the traditional opinions, and Coleridge that which is out of them, and at variance with them. But it was also likely that each would find, or show the way to finding, much of what the other missed.

It is hardly possible to speak of Coleridge, and his position among his contemporaries, without reverting to Bentham: they are connected by two of the closest bonds of association—resemblance and contrast. It would be difficult to find two persons of philosophic eminence more exactly the contrary of one another. Compare their modes of treatment of any subject, and you might fancy them inhabitants of different worlds. They seem to have scarcely a principle or a premise in common. Each of them sees scarcely anything but what the other does not see.

Bentham would have regarded Coleridge with a peculiar measure of the good-humoured contempt with which he was accustomed to regard all modes of philosophizing different from his own. Coleridge would probably have made Bentham one of the exceptions to the enlarged and liberal appreciation which (to the credit of *his* mode of philosophizing) he extended to most thinkers of any eminence, from whom he differed. But contraries, as logicians say, are but *quæ in eodem genere maxime distant*, the things which are farthest from one another in the same kind. These two agreed in being the men who, in their age and country, did most to enforce, by precept and example, the necessity of a philosophy. They agreed in making it their occupation to recall opinions to first principles; taking no proposition for granted without examining into the grounds of it, and ascertaining that it possessed the kind and degree of evidence suitable to its nature. They agreed in recognising that sound theory is the only foundation for sound practice, and that whoever despises theory, let him give himself what airs of wisdom he may, is self-convicted of being a quack. If a book were to be compiled containing all the best things ever said on the rule-of-thumb school of political craftsmanship, and on the insufficiency for practical purposes of what the mere practical man calls experience, it is difficult to say whether the collection would be more indebted to the writings of Bentham or of Coleridge. They agreed, too, in perceiving that the groundwork of all other philosophy must be laid in the philosophy of the mind. To lay this foundation deeply and strongly, and to raise a superstructure in accordance with it; were the objects to which their lives were devoted. They employed, indeed, for the most part, different materials; but as the materials of both were real observations, the genuine product of experience—the results will in the end be found not hostile, but supplementary, to one another. Of their methods of philosophizing, the same thing may be said: they were different, yet both were legitimate logical processes. In every respect the two men are each other's "completing counterpart": the strong points of each correspond to the weak points of the other. Whoever could master the premises and combine the methods of both, would possess the entire English philosophy of their age. Coleridge used to say that every one is born either a Platonist or an Aristotelian:[2] it may be similarly affirmed,

---

[2] From Coleridge's *Table Talk*, entry for 2 July 1830.

that every Englishman of the present day is by implication either a Benthamite or a Coleridgian; holds views of human affairs which can only be proved true on the principles either of Bentham or of Coleridge. In one respect, indeed, the paralell fails. Bentham so improved and added to the system of philosophy he adopted, that for his successors he may almost be accounted its founder; while Coleridge, though he has left on the system he inculcated, such traces of himself as cannot fail to be left by any mind of original powers, was anticipated in all the essentials of his doctrine by the great Germans of the latter half of the last century, and was accompanied in it by the remarkable series of their French expositors and followers. Hence, although Coleridge is to Englishmen the type and the main source of that doctrine, he is the creator rather of the shape in which it has appeared among us, than of the doctrine itself.

The time is yet far distant when, in the estimation of Coleridge, and of his influence upon the intellect of our time, anything like unanimity can be looked for. As a poet, Coleridge has taken his place. The healthier taste, and more intelligent canons of poetic criticism, which he was himself mainly instrumental in diffusing, have at length assigned to him his proper rank, as one among the great, and (if we look to the powers shown rather than to the amount of actual achievement) among the greatest, names in our literature. But as a philosopher, the class of thinkers has scarcely yet arisen by whom he is to be judged. The limited philosophical public of this country is as yet too exclusively divided between those to whom Coleridge and the views which he promulgated or defended are everything, and those to whom they are nothing. A true thinker can only be justly estimated when his thoughts have worked their way into minds formed in a different school; have been wrought and moulded into consistency with all other true and relevant thoughts; when the noisy conflict of half-truths, angrily denying one another, has subsided, and ideas which seemed mutually incompatible, have been found only to require mutual limitations. This time has not yet come for Coleridge. The spirit of philosophy in England, like that of religion, is still rootedly sectarian. Conservative thinkers and Liberals, transcen-

dentalists and admirers of Hobbes and Locke, regard each other as out of the pale of philosophical intercourse; look upon each other's speculations as vitiated by an original taint, which makes all study of them, except for purposes of attack, useless if not mischievous. An error much the same as if Kepler had refused to profit by Ptolemy's or Tycho's observations, because those astronomers believed that the sun moved round the earth; or as if Priestley and Lavoisier, because they differed on the doctrine of phlogiston, had rejected each other's chemical experiments.[3] It is even a still greater error than either of these. For, among the truths long recognised by Continental philosophers, but which very few Englishmen have yet arrived at, one is, the importance, in the present imperfect state of mental and social science, of antagonist modes of thought: which, it will one day be felt, are as necessary to one another in speculation, as mutually checking powers are in a political constitution. A clear insight, indeed, into this necessity is the only rational or enduring basis of philosophical tolerance; the only condition under which liberality in matters of opinion can be anything better than a polite synonym for indifference between one opinion and another.

All students of man and society who possess that first requisite for so difficult a study, a due sense of its difficulties, are aware that the besetting danger is not so much of embracing falsehood for truth, as of mistaking part of the truth for the whole. It might be plausibly maintained that in almost every one of the leading controversies, past or present, in social philosophy, both sides were in the right in what they affirmed, though wrong in what they denied; and that if either could have been made to take the other's views in addition to its own, little more would have been needed to make its doctrine correct. Take for instance the question how far mankind have gained by civilization. One observer is forcibly struck by the multiplication of physical comforts; the advancement and diffusion of knowledge; the decay of superstition; the facilities of mutual intercourse; the softening of manners; the decline of war and personal conflict; the progressive limitation of the tyranny of the strong over the weak; the great works accomplished throughout the globe by the

---

[3] Johannes Kepler (1571–1630), German astronomer; Ptolemy (5th century A.D.), astronomer, geographer, and mathematician; Joseph Priestley (1733–1804), English clergyman and chemist who supported the phlogistic theory of combustion—that is, fire was an element that involved the release of a substance called phlogiston; Antoine Lavoisier (1743–94), French chemist, father of modern chemistry, who disproved the phlogistic theory.

co-operation of multitudes: and he becomes that very common character, the worshipper of "our enlightened age." Another fixes his attention, not upon the value of these advantages, but upon the high price which is paid for them; the relaxation of individual energy and courage; the loss of proud and self-relying independence; the slavery of so large a portion of mankind to artificial wants; their effeminate shrinking from even the shadow of pain; the dull unexciting monotony of their lives, and the passionless insipidity, and absence of any marked individuality, in their characters; the contrast between the narrow mechanical understanding, produced by a life spent in executing by fixed rules a fixed task, and the varied powers of the man of the woods, whose subsistence and safety depend at each instant upon his capacity of extemporarily adapting means to ends; the demoralizing effect of great inequalities in wealth and social rank; and the sufferings of the great mass of the people of civilized countries, whose wants are scarcely better provided for than those of the savage, while they are bound by a thousand fetters in lieu of the freedom and excitement which are his compensations. One who attends to these things, and to these exclusively, will be apt to infer that savage life is preferable to civilized; that the work of civilization should as far as possible be undone; and from the premises of Rousseau, he will not improbably be led to the practical conclusions of Rousseau's disciple, Robespierre.[4] No two thinkers can be more entirely at variance than the two we have supposed—the worshippers of Civilization and of Independence, of the present and of the remote past. Yet all that is positive in the opinions of either of them is true; and we see how easy it would be to choose one's path, if either half of the truth were the whole of it, and how great may be the difficulty of framing, as it is necessary to do, a set of practical maxims which combine both.

So again, one person sees in a very strong light the need which the great mass of mankind have of being ruled over by a degree of intelligence and virtue superior to their own. He is deeply impressed with the mischief done to the uneducated and uncultivated by weaning them of all habits of reverence, appealing to them as a competent tribunal to decide the most intricate questions, and making them think themselves capable, not only of being a light to themselves, but of giving the law to their superiors in culture. He sees, further, that cultivation, to be carried beyond a certain point, requires leisure; that leisure is the natural attribute of a hereditary aristocracy; that such a body has all the means of acquiring intellectual and moral superiority; and he needs be at no loss to endow them with abundant motives to it. An aristocracy indeed, being human, are, as he cannot but see, not exempt, any more than their inferiors, from the common need of being controlled and enlightened by a still greater wisdom and goodness than their own. For this, however, his reliance is upon reverence for a Higher above them, sedulously inculcated and fostered by the course of their education. We thus see brought together all the elements of a conscientious zealot for an aristocratic government, supporting and supported by an established Christian church. There is truth, and important truth, in this thinker's premises. But there is a thinker of a very different description, in whose premises there is an equal portion of truth. This is he who says, that an average man, even an average member of an aristocracy, if he can postpone the interests of other people to his own calculations or instincts of self-interest, will do so; that all governments in all ages have done so, as far as they were permitted, and generally to a ruinous extent; and that the only possible remedy is a pure democracy, in which the people are their own governors, and can have no selfish interest in oppressing themselves.

Thus it is in regard to every important partial truth; there are always two conflicting modes of thought, one tending to give to that truth too large, the other to give it too small, a place: and the history of opinion is generally an oscillation between these extremes. From the imperfection of the human faculties, it seldom happens that, even in the minds of eminent thinkers, each partial view of their subject passes for its worth, and none for more than its worth. But even if this just balance exist in the mind of the wiser teacher, it will not exist in his disciples, still less in the general mind. He cannot prevent that which is new in his doctrine, and on which, being

---

[4] Jean Jacques Rousseau (1712–78), French philosopher, author of *Émile,* upholding his belief that man was a being who was naturally good and was corrupted by civilization, and author of *The Social Contract,* upholding the doctrine of a government based on the consent of the governed, or the "general will" as he called it; Maximilien Robespierre (1758–94), French revolutionary leader who followed Rousseau's theories.

ncw, he is forced to insist the most strongly, from making a disproportionate impression. The impetus necessary to overcome the obstacles which resist all novelties of opinion, seldom fails to carry the public mind almost as far on the contrary side of the perpendicular. Thus every excess in either direction determines a corresponding reaction; improvement consisting only in this, that the oscillation, each time, departs rather less widely from the centre, and an ever-increasing tendency is manifested to settle finally in it.

Now the Germano-Coleridgian doctrine is, in our view of the matter, the result of such a reaction. It expresses the revolt of the human mind against the philosophy of the eighteenth century. It is ontological, because that was experimental; conservative, because that was innovative; religious, because so much of that was infidel; concrete and historical, because that was abstract and metaphysical; poetical, because that was matter-of-fact and prosaic. In every respect it flies off in the contrary direction to its predecessor; yet faithful to the general law of improvement last noticed, it is less extreme in its opposition, it denies less of what is true in the doctrine it wars against, than had been the case in any previous philosophic reaction; and in particular, far less than when the philosophy of the eighteenth century triumphed, and so memorably abused its victory, over that which preceded it.

We may begin our consideration of the two systems either at one extreme or the other; with their highest philosophical generalizations, or with their practical conclusions. The former seems preferable, because it is in their highest generalities that the difference between the two systems is most familiarly known.

Every consistent scheme of philosophy requires as its starting-point, a theory respecting the sources of human knowledge, and the objects which the human faculties are capable of taking cognizance of. The prevailing theory in the eighteenth century, on this most comprehensive of questions, was that proclaimed by Locke, and commonly attributed to Aristotle—that all knowledge consists of generalizations from experience. Of nature, or anything whatever external to ourselves, we know, according to this theory, nothing, except the facts which present themselves to our senses, and such other facts as may, by analogy, be inferred from these. There is no knowledge *à priori;* no truths cognizable by the mind's inward light, and grounded on intuitive evidence. Sensation, and the mind's consciousness of its own acts, are not only the exclusive sources, but the sole materials of our knowledge. From this doctrine, Coleridge, with the German philosophers since Kant (not to go farther back) and most of the English since Reid,[5] strongly dissents. He claims for the human mind a capacity, within certain limits, of perceiving the nature and properties of "Things in themselves." He distinguishes in the human intellect two faculties, which, in the technical language common to him with the Germans, he calls Understanding and Reason. The former faculty judges of phenomena, or the appearances of things, and forms generalizations from these: to the latter it belongs, by direct intuition, to perceive things, and recognise truths, not cognizable by our senses. These perceptions are not indeed innate, nor could ever have been awakened in us without experience; but they are not copies of it: experience is not their prototype, it is only the occasion by which they are irresistibly suggested. The appearances in nature excite in us, by an inherent law, ideas of those invisible things, which are the causes of the visible appearances, and on whose laws those appearances depend: and we then perceive that these things must have pre-existed to render the appearances possible; just as (to use a frequent illustration of Coleridge's) we see, before we know that we have eyes; but when once this is known to us, we perceive that eyes must have pre-existed to enable us to see. Among the truths which are thus known *à priori,* by occasion of experience, but not themselves the subjects of experience, Coleridge includes the fundamental doctrines of religion and morals, the principles of mathematics, and the ultimate laws even of physical nature; which he contends cannot be proved by experience, though they must necessarily be consistent with it, and would, if we knew them perfectly, enable us to account for all observed facts, and to predict all those which are as yet unobserved.

It is not necessary to remind any one who concerns himself with such subjects, that between

---

[5] Thomas Reid (1710–96), Scottish philosopher and founder of the Common Sense school of philosophy, exponent of the doctrine of natural realism: the objects of the external world are exactly as they are perceived.

the partisans of these two opposite doctrines there reigns a *bellum internecinum*.[6] Neither side is sparing in the imputation of intellectual and moral obliquity to the perceptions, and of pernicious consequences to the creed, of its antagonists. Sensualism is the common term of abuse for the one philosophy, mysticism for the other. The one doctrine is accused of making men beasts, the other lunatics. It is the unaffected belief of numbers on one side of the controversy, that their adversaries are actuated by a desire to break loose from moral and religious obligation; and of numbers on the other that their opponents are either men fit for Bedlam, or who cunningly pander to the interests of hierarchies and aristocracies, by manufacturing superfine new arguments in favour of old prejudices. It is almost needless to say that those who are freest with these mutual accusations, are seldom those who are most at home in the real intricacies of the question, or who are best acquainted with the argumentative strength of the opposite side, or even of their own. But without going to these extreme lengths, even sober men on both sides take no charitable view of the tendencies of each other's opinions.

It is affirmed that the doctrine of Locke and his followers, that all knowledge is experience generalized, leads by strict logical consequence to atheism: that Hume and other sceptics were right when they contended that it is impossible to prove a God on grounds of experience; and Coleridge (like Kant) maintains positively, that the ordinary argument for a Deity, from marks of design in the universe, or, in other words, from the resemblance of the order in nature to the effects of human skill and contrivance, is not tenable. It is further said that the same doctrine annihilates moral obligation; reducing morality either to the blind impulses of animal sensibility, or to a calculation of prudential consequences, both equally fatal to its essence. Even science, it is affirmed, loses the character of science in this view of it, and becomes empiricism; a mere enumeration and arrangement of facts, not explaining nor accounting for them: since a fact is only then accounted for when we are made to see in it the manifestation of laws, which, as soon as they are perceived at all, are perceived to be *necessary*. These are the charges brought by the transcendental philosophers against the school

of Locke, Hartley,[7] and Bentham. They in their turn allege that the transcendentalists make imagination, and not observation, the criterion of truth; that they lay down principles under which a man may enthrone his wildest dreams in the chair of philosophy, and impose them on mankind as institutions of the pure reason: which has, in fact, been done in all ages, by all manner of mystical enthusiasts. And even if, with gross inconsistency, the private revelations of any individual Böhme or Swedenborg[8] be disowned, or, in other words, outvoted (the only means of discrimination which, it is contended, the theory admits of), this is still only substituting, as the test of truth, the dreams of the majority for the dreams of each individual. Whoever form a strong enough party, may at any time set up the immediate perceptions of *their* reason, that is to say, any reigning prejudice, as a truth independent of experience; a truth not only requiring no proof, but to be believed in opposition to all that appears proof to the mere understanding; nay, the more to be believed, because it cannot be put into words and into the logical form of a proposition without a contradiction in terms: for no less authority than this is claimed by some transcendentalists for their *à priori* truths. And thus a ready mode is provided, by which whoever is on the strongest side may dogmatize at his ease, and instead of proving his propositions, may rail at all who deny them, as bereft of "the vision and the faculty divine," or blinded to its plainest revelations by a corrupt heart.

This is a very temperate statement of what is charged by these two classes of thinkers against each other. How much of either representation is correct, cannot conveniently be discussed in this place. In truth, a system of consequences from an opinion, drawn by an adversary, is seldom of much worth. Disputants are rarely sufficiently masters of each other's doctrines, to be good judges what is fairly deducible from them, or how a consequence which seems to flow from one part of the theory may or may not be defeated by another part. To combine the different parts of a doctrine with one another, and with all admitted truths, is not indeed a small trouble, nor one which a person is often inclined to take for other people's opinions. Enough if each does it for his own, which he has a greater interest in, and is more disposed to be just to. Were we to

[6] Internecine war.

[7] David Hartley (1705–57), English philosopher, exponent of the doctrine of associational psychology.

[8] Jakob Boehme (1575–1624), German mystic; Emmanuel Swedenborg (1688–1772), Swedish mystic philosopher.

search among men's recorded thoughts for the choicest manifestations of human imbecility and prejudice, our specimens would be mostly taken from their opinions of the opinions of one another. Imputations of horrid consequences ought not to bias the judgement of any person capable of independent thought. Coleridge himself says (in the 25th Aphorism of his "Aids to Reflection"), "He who begins by loving Christianity better than truth, will proceed by loving his own sect or church better than Christianity, and end in loving himself better than all."

As to the fundamental difference of opinion respecting the sources of our knowledge (apart from the corollaries which either party may have drawn from its own principle, or imputed to its opponent's), the question lies far too deep in the recesses of psychology for us to discuss it here. The lists having been open ever since the dawn of philosophy, it is not wonderful that the two parties should have been forced to put on their strongest armour, both of attack and of defence. The question would not so long have remained a question, if the more obvious arguments on either side had been unanswerable. Each party has been able to urge in its own favour numerous and striking facts, to reconcile which with the opposite theory has required all the metaphysical resources which that theory could command. It will not be wondered at, then, that we here content ourselves with a bare statement of our opinion. It is, that the truth, on this much-debated question, lies with the school of Locke and of Bentham. The nature and laws of Things in themselves, or of the hidden causes of the phenomena which are the objects of experience, appear to us radically inaccessible to the human faculties. We see no ground for believing that anything can be the object of our knowledge except our experience, and what can be inferred from our experience by the analogies of experience itself; not that there is any idea, feeling, or power in the human mind, which, in order to account for it, requires that its origin should be referred to any other source. We are therefore at issue with Coleridge on the central idea of his philosophy; and we find no need of, and no use for, the peculiar technical terminology which he and his masters the Germans have introduced into philosophy, for the double purpose of giving logical precision to doctrines which we

do not admit, and of marking a relation between those abstract doctrines and many concrete experimental truths, which this language, in our judgment, serves not to elucidate, but to disguise and obscure. Indeed, but for these peculiarities of language, it would be difficult to understand how the reproach of mysticism (by which nothing is meant in common parlance but unintelligibleness) has been fixed upon Coleridge and the Germans in the minds of many, to whom doctrines substantially the same, when taught in a manner more superficial and less fenced round against objections, by Reid and Dugald Stewart,[9] have appeared the plain dictates of "common sense," successfully asserted against the subtleties of metaphysics.

Yet, though we think the doctrines of Coleridge and the Germans, in the pure science of mind, erroneous, and have no taste for their peculiar terminology, we are far from thinking that even in respect of this, the least valuable part of their intellectual exertions, those philosophers have lived in vain. The doctrines of the school of Locke stood in need of an entire renovation: to borrow a physiological illustration from Coleridge, they required, like certain secretions of the human body, to be reabsorbed into the system and secreted afresh. In what form did that philosophy generally prevail throughout Europe? In that of the shallowest set of doctrines which perhaps were ever passed off upon a cultivated age as a complete psychological system—the ideology of Condillac[10] and his school; a system which affected to resolve all the phenomena of the human mind into sensation, by a process which essentially consisted in merely *calling* all states of mind, however heterogeneous, by that name; a philosophy now acknowledged to consist solely of a set of verbal generalizations, explaining nothing, distinguishing nothing, leading to nothing. That men should begin by sweeping this away, was the first sign that the age of real psychology was about to commence. In England the case, though different, was scarcely better. The philosophy of Locke, as a popular doctrine, had remained nearly as it stood in his own book; which, as its title implies, did not pretend to give an account of any but the intellectual part of our nature; which, even within that limited sphere, was but the commencement of a system, and though its errors and defects as such have been

---

[9] Dugald Stewart (1753–1828), Scottish philosopher, student of Thomas Reid (see note 5 above) who for the most part applied himself to the exposition of Reid's philosophy of natural realism.

[10] Étienne Bonnot de Condillac (1715–80), French philosopher, exponent of the system of psychology upholding the theory that all knowledge is derived from sensations.

exaggerated beyond all just bounds, it did expose many vulnerable points to the searching criticism of the new school. The least imperfect part of it, the purely logical part, had almost dropped out of sight. With respect to those of Locke's doctrines which are properly meta-physical; however the sceptical part of them may have been followed up by others, and carried beyond the point at which he stopped; the only one of his successors who attempted, and achieved, any considerable improvement and extension of the analytical part, and thereby added anything to the explanation of the human mind on Locke's principles, was Hartley. But Hartley's doctrines, so far as they are true, were so much in advance of the age, and the way had been so little prepared for them by the general tone of thinking which yet prevailed, even under the influence of Locke's writings, that the philosophic world did not deem them worthy of being atten-ded to. Reid and Stewart were allowed to run them down uncontradicted: Brown,[11] though a man of a kindred genius, had evidently never read them; and but for the accident of their being taken up by Priestley, who transmitted them as a kind of heirloom to his Unitarian followers, the name of Hartley might have perished, or survived only as that of a visionary physician, the author of an exploded physiological hypothesis. It perhaps required all the violence of the assaults made by Reid and the German school upon Locke's system, to recall men's minds to Hartley's principles, as alone adequate to the solution, upon that system, of the peculiar difficulties which those assailants pressed upon men's attention as altogether insoluble by it. We may here notice that Coleridge, before he adopted his later philosophical views, was an enthusiastic Hartleian; so that his abandonment of the philosophy of Locke cannot be imputed to unacquaintance with the highest form of that philosophy which had yet appeared. That he should pass through that highest form without stopping at it, is itself a strong presumption that there were more difficulties in the question than Hartley had solved. That anything has since been done to solve them we probably owe to the revolution in opinion, of which Coleridge was one of the organs; and even in abstract metaphysics his writings, and those of his school of thinkers, are one of the richest mines from whence the opposite school can draw the materials

for what has yet to be done to perfect their own theory.

If we now pass from the purely abstract to the concrete and practical doctrines of the two schools, we shall see still more clearly the necessity of the reaction, and the great service rendered to philosophy by its authors. This will be best manifested by a survey of the state of practical philosophy in Europe, as Coleridge and his compeers found it, towards the close of the last century.

The state of opinion in the latter half of the eighteenth century was by no means the same on the Continent of Europe and in our own island; and the difference was still greater in appearance than it was in reality. In the more advanced nations of the Continent, the prevailing philos-ophy had done its work completely: it had spread itself over every department of human knowledge; it had taken possession of the whole Continental mind: and scarcely one educated person was left who retained any allegiance to the opinions or the institutions of ancient times. In England, the native country of compromise, things had stopped far short of this; the philo-sophical movement had been brought to a halt in an early stage, and a peace had been patched up by concessions on both sides, between the philosophy of the time and its traditional insti-tutions and creeds. Hence the aberrations of the age were generally, on the Continent, at that period, the extravagances of new opinions; in England, the corruptions of old ones.

To insist upon the deficiences of the Continen-tal philosophy of the last century, or, as it is commonly termed, the French philosophy, is almost superfluous. That philosophy is indeed as unpopular in this country as its bitterest enemy could desire. If its faults were as well understood as they are much railed at, criticism might be considered to have finished its work. But that this is not yet the case, the nature of the imputations currently made upon the French philosophers, sufficiently proves; many of these being as in-consistent with a just philosophic comprehension of their system of opinions, as with charity towards the men themselves. It is not true, for example, that any of them denied moral obliga-tion, or sought to weaken its force. So far were they from meriting this accusation, that they could not even tolerate the writers who, like

---

[11] Thomas Brown (1778–1820), fellow worker of Dugald Stewart (see note 9 above).

Helvetius, ascribed a selfish origin to the feelings of morality, resolving them into a sense of interest. Those writers were as much cried down among the *philosophes* themselves, and what was true and good in them (and there is much that is so) met with as little appreciation, then as now. The error of the philosophers was rather that they trusted too much to those feelings; believed them to be more deeply rooted in human nature than they are; to be not so dependent, as in fact they are, upon collateral influences. They thought them the natural and spontaneous growth of the human heart; so firmly fixed in it, that they would subsist unimpaired, nay invigorated, when the whole system of opinions and observances with which they were habitually intertwined was violently torn away.

To tear away was, indeed, all that these philosophers, for the most part, aimed at: they had no conception that anything else was needful. At their millennium, superstition, priestcraft, error and prejudice of every kind, were to be annihilated; some of them gradually added that despotism and hereditary privileges must share the same fate; and, this accomplished, they never for a moment suspected that all the virtues and graces of humanity could fail to flourish, or that when the noxious weeds were once rooted out, the soil would stand in any need of tillage.

In this they committed the very common error, of mistaking the state of things with which they had always been familiar, for the universal and natural condition of mankind. They were accustomed to see the human race agglomerated in large nations, all (except here and there a madman or a malefactor) yielding obedience more or less strict to a set of laws prescribed by a few of their own number, and to a set of moral rules prescribed by each other's opinion; renouncing the exercise of individual will and judgment, except within the limits imposed by these laws and rules; and acquiescing in the sacrifice of their individual wishes when the point was decided against them by lawful authority; or persevering only in hopes of altering the opinion of the ruling powers. Finding matters to be so generally in this condition, the philosophers apparently concluded that they could not possibly be in any other; and were ignorant, by what a host of civilizing and restraining influences a state of things so repugnant to man's self-will and love of inde-

pendence has been brought about, and how imperatively it demands the continuance of those influences as the condition of its own existence. The very first element of the social union, obedience to a government of some sort, has not been found so easy a thing to establish in the world. Among a timid and spiritless race, like the inhabitants of the vast plains of tropical countries, passive obedience may be of natural growth; though even there we doubt whether it has ever been found among any people with whom fatalism, or in other words, submission to the pressure of circumstances as the decree of God, did not prevail as a religious doctrine. But the difficulty of inducing a brave and warlike race to submit their individual *arbitrium*[12] to any common umpire, has always been felt to be so great, that nothing short of supernatural power has been deemed adequate to overcome it; and such tribes have always assigned to the first institution of civil society a divine origin. So differently did those judge who knew savage man by actual experience, from those who had no acquaintance with him except in the civilized state. In modern Europe itself, after the fall of the Roman empire, to subdue the feudal anarchy and bring the whole people of any European nation into subjection to government (although Christianity in the most concentrated form of its influence was co-operating in the work) required thrice as many centuries as have elapsed since that time.

Now if these philosophers had known human nature under any other type than that of their own age, and of the particular classes of society among them they lived, it would have occurred to them, that wherever this habitual submission to law and government has been firmly and durably established, and yet the vigour and manliness of character which resisted its establishment have been in any degree preserved, certain requisites have existed, certain conditions have been fulfilled, of which the following may be regarded as the principal.

First: There has existed, for all who were accounted citizens,—for all who were not slaves, kept down by brute force,—a system of *education*, beginning with infancy and continued through life, of which, whatever else it might include, one main and incessant ingredient was *restraining discipline*. To train the human being in the habit, and thence the power, of subordinating his

---

[12] Judgment.

personal impulses and aims, to what were considered the ends of society; of adhering, against all temptation, to the course of conduct which those ends prescribed; of controlling in himself all the feelings which were liable to militate against those ends, and encouraging all such as tended towards them; this was the purpose, to which every outward motive that the authority directing the system could command, and every inward power or principle which its knowledge of human nature enabled it to evoke, were endeavoured to be rendered instrumental. The entire civil and military policy of the ancient commonwealths was such a system of training: in modern nations its place has been attempted to be supplied principally by religious teaching. And whenever and in proportion as the strictness of the restraining discipline was relaxed, the natural tendency of mankind to anarchy reasserted itself; the State became disorganized from within; mutual conflict for selfish ends, neutralized the energies which were required to keep up the contest against natural causes of evil; and the nation, after a longer or briefer interval of progressive decline, became either the slave of a despotism, or the prey of a foreign invader.

The second condition of permanent political society has been found to be, the existence, in some form or other, of the feeling of allegiance, or loyalty. This feeling may vary in its objects, and is not confined to any particular form of government; but whether in a democracy or in a monarchy, its essence is always the same; viz. that there be in the constitution of the State *something* which is settled, something permanent, and not be be called in question; something which, by general agreement, has a right to be where it is, and to be secure against disturbance, whatever else may change. This feeling may attach itself, as among the Jews (and indeed in most of the commonwealths of antiquity), to a common God or gods, the protectors and guardians of their State. Or it may attach itself to certain persons, who are deemed to be, whether by divine appointment, by long prescription, or by the general recognition of their superior capacity and worthiness, the rightful guides and guardians of the rest. Or it may attach itself to laws; to ancient liberties, or ordinances. Or finally (and this is the only shape in which the feeling is likely to exist hereafter) it may attach itself to the principles of individual freedom and political and social equality, as realized in institutions which as yet exist nowhere, or exist only in a rudimentary state. But

in all political societies which have had a durable existence, there has been some fixed point; something which men agreed in holding sacred; which, wherever freedom of discussion was a recognised principle, it was of course lawful to contest in theory, but which no one could either fear or hope to see shaken in practice; which, in short (except perhaps during some temporary crisis), was in the common estimation placed beyond discussion. And the necessity of this may easily be made evident. A State never is, nor, until mankind are vastly improved, can hope to be, for any long time exempt from internal dissension; for there neither is, nor has ever been, any state of society in which collisions did not occur between the immediate interests and passions of powerful sections of the people. What, then, enables society to weather these storms, and pass through turbulent times without any permanent weakening of the securities for peaceable existence? Precisely this—that however important the interests about which men fell out, the conflict did not affect the fundamental principles of the system of social union which happened to exist; nor threaten large portions of the community with the subversion of that on which they had built their calculations, and with which their hopes and aims had become identified. But when the questioning of these fundamental principles is (not the occasional disease, or salutary medicine, but) the habitual condition of the body politic, and when all the violent animosities are called forth, which spring naturally from such a situation, the State is virtually in a position of civil war; and can never long remain free from it in act and fact.

The third essential condition of stability in political society, is a strong and active principle of cohesion among the members of the same community or state. We need scarcely say that we do not mean nationality in the vulgar sense of the term; a senseless antipathy to foreigners; an indifference to the general welfare of the human race, or an unjust preference of the supposed interests of our own country; a cherishing of bad peculiarities because they are national; or a refusal to adopt what has been found good by other countries. We mean a principle of sympathy, not of hostility; of union, not of separation. We mean a feeling of common interest among those who live under the same government, and are contained within the same natural or historical boundaries. We mean, that one part of the community do not consider themselves as foreigners with regard to another part; that they set a value on their connexion; feel that they are one people, that their lot is cast together, that evil to any of their fellow-countrymen is evil to themselves; and do not desire selfishly to free themselves from their share of any common inconvenience by severing the connexion. How strong this feeling was in those ancient commonwealths which attained any durable greatness, every one knows. How happily Rome, in spite of all her tyranny, succeeded in establishing the feeling of a common country among the provinces of her vast and divided empire, will appear when any one who has given due attention to the subject shall take the trouble to point it out.[13] In modern times the countries which have had that feeling in the strongest degree have been the most powerful countries; England, France, and, in proportion to their territory and resources, Holland and Switzerland; while England in her connexion with Ireland, is one of the most signal examples of the consequences of its absence. Every Italian knows why Italy is under a foreign yoke; every German knows what maintains despotism in the Austrian empire; the evils of Spain flow as much from the absence of nation-ality among the Spaniards themselves, as from the presence of it in their relations with foreigners; while the completest illustration of all is afforded by the republics of South America, where the parts of one and the same state adhere so slightly together, that no sooner does any province think itself aggrieved by the general government, than it proclaims itself a separate nation.

These essential requisites of civil society the French philosophers of the eighteenth century unfortunately overlooked. They found, indeed, all three—at least the first and second, and most of what nourishes and invigorates the third—already undermined by the vices of the institutions, and of the men, that were set up as the guardians and bulwarks of them. If innovators, in their theories, disregarded the elementary principles of the social union, Conservatives, in their practice, had set the first example. The existing order of things had ceased to realize those first principles: from the force of circumstances, and from the short-sighted selfishness of its administrators, it had ceased to possess the

---

[13] We are glad to quote a striking passage from Coleridge on this very subject. He is speaking of the misdeeds of England in Ireland; towards which misdeeds this Tory, as he is called (for the Tories, who neglected him in his lifetime, show no little eagerness to give themselves the credit of his name after his death), entertained feelings scarcely surpassed by those which are excited by the masterly exposure for which we have recently been indebted to M. de Beaumont.

"Let us discharge," he says, "what may well be deemed a debt of justice from every well-educated Englishman to his Roman Catholic fellow-subjects of the Sister Island. At least, let us ourselves understand the true cause of the evil as it now exists. To what and to whom is the present state of Ireland mainly to be attributed? This should be the question: and to this I answer aloud, that it is mainly attributable to those who, during a period of little less than a whole century, used as a substitute what Providence had given into their hand as an opportunity; who chose to consider as superseding the most sacred duty, a code of law, which could be excused only on the plea that it enabled them to perform it. To the sloth and improvidence, the weakness and wickedness, of the gentry, clergy, and governors of Ireland, who persevered in preferring intrigue, violence, and selfish expatriation to a system of preventive and remedial measures, the efficacy of which had been warranted for them alike by the whole provincial history of ancient Rome, *cui pacare subactos summa erat sapientia* [whose highest wisdom was to pacify the conquered], and by the happy results of the few exceptions to the contrary scheme unhappily pursued by their and our ancestors.

"I can imagine no work of genius that would more appropriately decorate the dome or wall of a Senate-house, than an abstract of Irish history from the landing of Strongbow to the battle of the Boyne, or to a yet later period, embodied in intelligible emblems—an allegorical history-piece designed in the spirit of a Rubens or a Buonarotti, and with the wild lights, portentous shades, and saturated colours of a Rembrandt, Caravaggio, and Spagnoletti. To complete the great moral and political lesson by the historic contrast, nothing more would be required than by some equally effective means to possess the mind of the spectator with the state and condition of ancient Spain, at less than half a century from the final conclusion of an obstinate and almost unremitting conflict of two hundred years by Agrippa's subjugation of the Cantabrians, *omnibus Hispaniæ populis devictis et pacatis* [all the peoples of Spain having been defeated and pacified]. At the breaking up of the empire the West Goths conquered the country, and made division of the lands. Then came eight centuries of Moorish domination. Yet so deeply had Roman wisdom impressed the fairest characters of the Roman mind, that at this very hour, if we except a comparatively insignificant portion of Arabic derivatives, the natives throughout the whole Peninsula speak a language less differing from the *Romana rustica,* or provincial Latin of the times of Lucan and Seneca, than any two of its dialects from each other. The time approaches, I trust, when our political economists may study the science of the provincial policy of the ancients in detail, under the auspices of hope, for immediate and practical purposes."—*Church and State,* p. 161. [Mill's note]

essential conditions of permanent society, and was therefore tottering to its fall. But the philosophers did not see this. Bad as the existing system was in the days of its decrepitude, according to them it was still worse when it actually did what it now only pretended to do. Instead of feeling that the effect of a bad social order in sapping the necessary foundations of society itself, is one of the worst of its many mischiefs, the philosophers saw only, and saw with joy, that it was sapping its own foundations. In the weakening of all government they saw only the weakening of bad government; and thought they could not better employ themselves that in finishing the task so well begun—in discrediting all that still remained of restraining discipline, because it rested on the ancient and decayed creeds against which they made war; in unsettling everything which was still considered settled, making men doubtful of the few things of which they still felt certain; and in uprooting what little remained in the people's minds of reverence for anything above them, of respect to any of the limits which custom and prescription had set to the indulgence of each man's fancies or inclinations, or of attachment to any of the things which belonged to them as a nation, and which made them feel their unity as such.

Much of all this was, no doubt, unavoidable, and not justly matter of blame. When the vices of all constituted authorities, added to natural causes of decay, have eaten the heart out of old institutions and beliefs, while at the same time the growth of knowledge, and the altered circumstances of the age, would have required institutions and creeds different from these even if they had remained uncorrupt, we are far from saying that any degree of wisdom on the part of speculative thinkers could avert the political catastrophes, and the subsequent moral anarchy and unsettledness, which we have witnessed and are witnessing. Still less do we pretend that those principles and influences which we have spoken of as the conditions of the permanent existence of the social union, once lost, can ever be, or should be attempted to be, revived in connexion with the same institutions or the same doctrines as before. When society requires to be rebuilt, there is no use in attempting to rebuild it on the old plan. By the union of the enlarged views and analytic powers of speculative men with the observation and contriving sagacity of men of practice, better institutions and better doctrines must be elaborated; and until this is done we cannot hope for much improvement in our present condition. The effort to do it in the eighteenth century would have been premature, as the attempts of the Economistes (who, of all persons then living, came nearest to it, and who were the first to form clearly the idea of a Social Science), sufficiently testify. The time was not ripe for doing effectually any other work than that of destruction. But the work of the day should have been so performed as not to impede that of the morrow. No one can calculate what struggles, which the cause of improvement has yet to undergo, might have been spared if the philosophers of the eighteenth century had done anything like justice to the Past. Their mistake was, that they did not acknowledge the historical value of much which had ceased to be useful, nor saw that institutions and creeds, now effete, had rendered essential services to civilization, and still filled a place in the human mind, and in the arrangements of society, which could not without great peril, be left vacant. Their mistake was, that they did not recognise in many of the errors which they assailed, corruptions of important truths, and in many of the institutions most cankered with abuse, necessary elements of civilized society, though in a form and vesture no longer suited to the age; and hence they involved, as far as in them lay, many great truths, in a common discredit with the errors which had grown up around them. They threw away the shell without preserving the kernel; and attempting to new-model society without the binding forces which hold society together, met with such success as might have been anticipated.

Now we claim, in behalf of the philosophers of the reactionary school—of the school to which Coleridge belongs—that exactly what we blame the philosophers of the eighteenth century for not doing, they have done.

Every reaction in opinion, of course brings into view that portion of the truth which was overlooked before. It was natural that a philosophy which anathematized all that had been going on in Europe from Constantine to Luther, or even to Voltaire, should be succeeded by another, at once a severe critic of the new tendencies of society, and an impassioned vindicator of what was good in the past. This is the easy merit of all Tory and Royalist writers. But the peculiarity of the Germano-Coleridgian school is, that they saw beyond the immediate controversy, to the fundamental principles involved in all such controversies. They were the first (except a solitary thinker here and there) who inquired with any comprehensiveness or depth into the inductive laws of the existence and growth of human society. They were the first to bring prominently forward the three requisites which we have enumerated, as essential principles of all permanent forms of social existence, as principles, we say, and not as mere accidental advantages inherent in the particular polity or religion which the writer happened to patronize. They were the first who pursued, philosophically and in the spirit of Baconian investigation, not only this inquiry, but others ulterior and collateral to it. They thus produced, not a piece of party advocacy, but a philosophy of society, in the only form in which it is yet possible, that of a philosophy of history; not a defence of particular ethical or religious doctrines, but a contribution, the largest yet made by any class of thinkers, towards the philosophy of human culture.

The brilliant light which has been thrown upon history during the last half century, has proceeded almost wholly from this school. The disrespect in which history was held by the *philosophes* is notorious; one of the soberest of them, D'Alembert we believe, was the author of the wish that all record whatever of past events could be blotted out. And indeed the ordinary mode of writing history, and the ordinary mode of drawing lessons from it, were almost sufficient to excuse this contempt. But the *philosophes* saw, as usual, what was not true, not what was. It is no wonder that they who looked on the greater part of what had been handed down from the past, as sheer hindrances to man's attaining a well-being which would otherwise be of easy attainment, should content themselves with a very superficial study of history. But the case was otherwise with those who regarded the maintenance of society at all, and especially its maintenance in a state of progressive advancement, as a very difficult task, actually achieved, in

however imperfect a manner, for a number of centuries, against the strongest obstacles. It was natural that they should feel a deep interest in ascertaining how this had been effected; and should be led to inquire, both what were the requisites of the permanent existence of the body politic, and what were the conditions which had rendered the preservation of these permanent requisites compatible with perpetual and progressive improvement. And hence that series of great writers and thinkers, from Herder to Michelet,[14] by whom history, which was till then "a tale told by an idiot, full of sound and fury, signifying nothing,"[15] has been made a science of causes and effects; who, by making the facts and events of the past have a meaning and an intelligible place in the gradual evolution of humanity, have at once given history, even to the imagination, an interest like romance, and afforded the only means of predicting and guiding the future, by unfolding the agencies which have produced and still maintain the Present.[16]

The same causes have naturally led the same class of thinkers to do what their predecessors never could have done, for the philosophy of human culture. For the tendency of their speculations compelled them to see in the character of the national education existing in any political society, at once the principal cause of its permanence as a society, and the chief source of its progressiveness: the former by the extent to which that education operated as a system of restraining discipline; the latter by the degree in which it called forth and invigorated the active faculties. Besides, not to have looked upon the culture of the inward man as the problem of problems, would have been incompatible with the belief which many of these philosophers entertained in Christianity, and the recognition by all of them of its historical value, and the prime part which

---

[14] Johann Gottfried von Herder (1744–1803), German philosopher and man of letters; Jules Michelet (1798–1874), French historian.

[15] *Macbeth*, V, v, 26–28.

[16] There is something at once ridiculous and discouraging in the signs which daily meet us, of the Cimmerian darkness still prevailing in England (wherever recent foreign literature or the speculations of the Coleridgians have not penetrated) concerning the very existence of the views of general history, which have been received throughout the Continent of Europe for the last twenty or thirty years. A writer in Blackwood's Magazine, certainly not the least able publication of our day, nor this the least able writer in it, lately announced, with all the pomp and heraldry of triumphant genius, a discovery which was to disabuse the world of an universal prejudice, and create "the philosophy of Roman history." This is, that the Roman empire perished not from outward violence, but from inward decay; and that the barbarian conquerors were the renovators, not the destroyers of its civilization. Why, there is not a schoolboy in France or Germany who did not possess this writer's discovery before him; the contrary opinion has receded so far into the past, that it must be rather a learned Frenchman or German who remembers that it was ever held. If the writer in Blackwood had read a line of Guizot (to go no further than the most obvious sources), he would probably have abstained from making himself very ridiculous, and his country, so far as depends upon him, the laughing-stock of Europe. [Mill's note]

it has acted in the progress of mankind. But here, too, let us not fail to observe, they rose to principles, and did not stick in the particular case. The culture of the human being had been carried to no ordinary height, and human nature had exhibited many of its noblest manifestations, not in Christian countries only, but in the ancient world, in Athens, Sparta, Rome; nay, even barbarians, as the Germans, or still more unmitigated savages, the wild Indians, and again the Chinese, the Egyptians, the Arabs, all had their own education, their own culture; a culture which, whatever might be its tendency upon the whole, had been successful in some respect or other. Every form of polity, every condition of society, whatever else it had done, had formed its type of national character. What that type was, and how it had been made what it was, were questions which the metaphysician might overlook, the historical philosopher could not. Accordingly, the views respecting the various elements of human culture and the causes influencing the formation of national character, which pervade the writings of the Germano-Coleridgian school, throw into the shade everything which had been effected before, or which has been attempted simultaneously by any other school. Such views are, more than anything else, the characteristic feature of the Goethian period of German literature; and are richly diffused through the historical and critical writings of the new French school, as well as of Coleridge and his followers.

In this long, though most compressed, dissertation on the Continental philosophy preceding the reaction, and on the nature of the reaction, so far as directed against that philosophy, we have unavoidably been led to speak rather of the movement itself, than of Coleridge's particular share in it; which, from his posteriority in date, was necessarily a subordinate one. And it would be useless, even did our limits permit, to bring together from the scattered writings of a man who produced no systematic work, any of the fragments which he may have contributed to an edifice still incomplete, and even the general character of which, we can have rendered very imperfectly intelligible to those who are not acquainted with the thing itself. Our object is to invite to the study of the original sources, not to supply the place of such a study. What was peculiar to Coleridge will be better manifested, when we now proceed to review the state of popular philosophy immediately preceding him

in our own island; which was different, in some material respects, from the contemporaneous Continental philosophy.

In England, the philosophical speculations of the age had not, except in a few highly metaphysical minds (whose example rather served to deter than to invite others), taken so audacious a flight, nor achieved anything like so complete a victory over the counteracting influences, as on the Continent. There is in the English mind, both in speculation and in practice, a highly salutary shrinking from all extremes. But as this shrinking is rather an instinct of caution than a result of insight, it is too ready to satisfy itself with any medium, merely because it is a medium, and to acquiesce in a union of the disadvantages of both extremes instead of their advantages. The circumstances of the age, too, were unfavourable to decided opinions. The repose which followed the great struggles of the Reformation and the Commonwealth; the final victory over Popery and Puritanism, Jacobitism and Republicanism, and the lulling of the controversies which kept speculation and spiritual consciousness alive; the lethargy which came upon all governors and teachers, after their position in society became fixed; and the growing absorption of all classes in material interests—caused a character of mind to diffuse itself, with less of deep inward workings, and less capable of interpreting those it had, than had existed for centuries. The age seemed smitten with an incapacity of producing deep or strong feeling, such as at least could ally itself with meditative habits. There were few poets, and none of a high order; and philosophy fell mostly into the hands of men of a dry prosaic nature, who had not enough of the materials of human feeling in them to be able to imagine any of its more complex and mysterious manifestations; all of which they either left out of their theories, or introduced them with such explanations as no one who had experienced the feelings could receive as adequate. An age like this, an age without earnestness, was the natural era of compromises and half-convictions.

To make out a case for the feudal and ecclesiastical institutions of modern Europe was by no means impossible: they had a meaning, had existed for honest ends, and an honest theory of them might be made. But the administration of those institutions had long ceased to accord with any honest theory. It was impossible to justify them in principle, except on grounds which condemned them in practice; and grounds of which there was at any rate little or no recognition in the philosophy of the eighteenth century. The natural tendency, therefore, of that philosophy, everywhere but in England, was to seek the extinction of those institutions. In England it would doubtless have done the same, had it been strong enough: but as this was beyond its strength, an adjustment was come to between the rival powers. What neither party cared about, the *ends* of existing institutions, the work that was to be done by teachers and governors, was flung overboard. The wages of that work the teachers and governors did care about, and those wages were secured to them. The existing institutions in Church and State were to be preserved inviolate, in outward semblance at least, but were required to be, practically, as much a nullity as possible. The Church continued to "rear her mitred front in courts and palaces," but not as in the days of Hildebrand or Becket, as the champion of arts against arms, of the serf against the seigneur, peace against war, or spiritual principles and powers against the domination of animal force. Nor even (as in the days of Latimer and John Knox[17]) as a body divinely commissioned to train the nation in a knowledge of God and obedience to his laws, whatever became of temporal principalities and powers, and whether this end might most effectually be compassed by their assistance or by trampling them under foot. No; but the people of England liked old things, and nobody knew how the place might be filled which the doing away with so conspicuous an institution would leave vacant, and *quieta ne movere*[18] was the favourite doctrine of those times; therefore, on condition of not making too much noise about religion, or taking it too much in earnest, the church was supported, even by philosophers—as a "bulwark against fanaticism," a sedative to the religious spirit, to prevent it from disturbing the harmony of society or the tranquillity of states. The clergy of the establishment thought they had a good bargain on these terms, and kept its conditions very faithfully.

The State, again, was no longer considered, according to the old ideal, as a concentration of the force of all the individuals of the nation in the hands of certain of its members, in order to the accomplishment of whatever could be best accomplished by systematic co-operation. It was found that the State was a bad judge of the wants of society; that it in reality cared very little for them; and when it attempted anything beyond that police against crime, and arbitration of disputes, which are indispensable to social existence, the private sinister interest of some class or individual was usually the prompter of its proceedings. The natural inference would have been that the constitution of the State was somehow not suited to the existing wants of society; having indeed descended, with scarcely any modifications that could be avoided, from a time when the most prominent exigencies of society were quite different. This conclusion, however, was shrunk from; and it required the peculiarities of very recent times, and the speculations of the Bentham school, to produce even any considerable tendency that way. The existing Constitution, and all the arrangements of existing society, continued to be applauded as the best possible. The celebrated theory of the three powers was got up, which made the excellence of our Constitution consist in doing less harm than would be done by any other form of government. Government altogether was regarded as a necessary evil, and was required to hide itself, to make itself as little felt as possible. The cry of the people was not "help us," "guide us," "do for us the things we cannot do, and instruct us, that we may do well those which we can"—and truly such requirements from such rulers would have been a bitter jest: the cry was "let us alone." Power to decide questions of *meum* and *tuum*,[19] to protect society from open violence, and from some of the most dangerous modes of fraud, could not be withheld; these functions the Government was left in possession of, and to these it became the expectation of the public that it should confine itself.

Such was the prevailing tone of English belief in temporals; what was it in spirituals? Here too a similar system of compromise had been at work. Those who pushed their philosophical speculations to the denial of the received religious belief, whether they went to the extent of infidelity or only of heterodoxy, met with little encouragement: neither religion itself, nor the received forms of it, were at all shaken by the few attacks which were made upon them from without. The philosophy, however, of the time,

---

[17] Hugh Latimer (1485?–1555), English supporter of Reformation and Protestant martyr, John Knox (1505–72), Scottish reformer, writer, and statesman, involved in the religious issue of Protestantism during the reigns of Mary Tudor, Mary Queen of Scots, and Queen Elizabeth I.

[18] Do not stir up that which is quiet.

[19] Mine and Thine.

made itself felt as effectually in another fashion; it pushed its way *into* religion. The *à priori* arguments for a God were first dismissed. This was indeed inevitable. The internal evidences of Christianity shared nearly the same fate; if not absolutely thrown aside, they fell into the background, and were little thought of. The doctrine of Locke, that we have no *innate* moral sense, perverted into the doctrine that we have no moral sense at all, made it appear that we had not any capacity of judging from the doctrine itself, whether it was worthy to have come from a righteous Being. In forgetfulness of the most solemn warnings of the Author of Christianity, as well as of the Apostle who was the main diffuser of it through the world, belief in his religion was left to stand upon miracles—a species of evidence which, according to the universal belief of the early Christians themselves was by no means peculiar to true religion: and it is melancholy to see on what frail reeds able defenders of Christianity preferred to rest, rather than upon that better evidence which alone gave to their so-called evidences any value as a collateral confirmation, In the interpretation of Christianity, the palpablest *bibliolatry* prevailed: if (with Coleridge) we may so term that superstitious worship of particular texts, which persecuted Galileo, and, in our own day, anathematized the discoveries of geology. Men whose faith in Christianity rested on the literal infallibility of the sacred volume, shrank in terror from the idea that it could have been included in the scheme of Providence that the human opinions and mental habits of the particular writers should be allowed to mix with and colour their mode of conceiving and of narrating the divine transactions. Yet this slavery to the letter has not only raised every difficulty which envelopes the most unimportant passage in the Bible, into an objection to revelation, but has paralysed many a well-meant effort to bring Christianity home, as a consistent scheme, to human experience and capacities of apprehension; as if there was much of it which it was more prudent to leave *in nubibus*,[20] lest, in the attempt to make the mind seize hold of it as a reality, some text might be found to stand in the way. It might have been expected that this idolatry of the words of Scripture would at least have saved its doctrines from being tampered with by human notions: but the contrary proved to be the effect; for the vague and sophistical mode of inter-

preting texts, which was necessary in order to reconcile what was manifestly irreconcilable, engendered a habit of playing fast and loose with Scripture, and finding in, or leaving out of it, whatever one pleased. Hence, while Christianity was, in theory and in intention, received and submitted to, with even "prostration of the understanding" before it, much alacrity was in fact displayed in *accommodating* it to the received philosophy, and even to the popular notions of the time. To take only one example, but so signal a one as to be *instar omnium*.[21] If there is any one requirement of Christianity less doubtful than another, it is that of being spiritually-minded; of loving and practising good from a pure love, simply because it is good. But one of the crotchets of the philosophy of the age was, that all virtue is self-interest; and accordingly, in the text-book adopted by the Church (in one of its universities) for instruction in moral philosophy, the reason for doing good is declared to be, that God is stronger than we are, and is able to damn us if we do not. This is no exaggeration of the sentiments of Paley, and hardly even of the crudity of his language.

Thus, on the whole, England had neither the benefits, such as they were, of the new ideas nor of the old. We were just sufficiently under the influences of each, to render the other powerless. We had a Government, which we respected too much to attempt to change it, but not enough to trust it with any power, or look to it for any services that were not compelled. We had a Church, which had ceased to fulfil the honest purposes of a church, but which we made a great point of keeping up as the pretence or *simulacrum* of one. We had a highly spiritual religion (which we were instructed to obey from selfish motives), and the most mechanical and worldly notions on every other subject; and we were so much afraid of being wanting in reference to each particular syllable of the book which contained our religion, that we let its most important meanings slip through our fingers, and entertained the most grovelling conceptions of its spirit and general purposes. This was not a state of things which could recommend itself to any earnest mind. It was sure in no great length of time to call forth two sorts of men—the one demanding the extinction of the institutions and creeds which had hitherto existed; the other that they be made a reality: the one pressing the new doctrines to their utmost consequences; the other

----

[20] In the clouds.   [21] Representative of all.

reasserting the best meaning and purposes of the old. The first type attained its greatest height in Bentham; the last in Coleridge.

We hold that these two sorts of men, who seem to be, and believe themselves to be, enemies, are in reality allies. The powers they wield are opposite poles of one great force of progression. What was really hateful and contemptible was the state which preceded them, and which each, in its way, has been striving now for many years to improve. Each ought to hail with rejoicing the advent of the other. But most of all ought an enlightened Radical or Liberal to rejoice over such a Conservative as Coleridge. For such a Radical must know, that the Constitution and Church of England, and the religious opinions and political maxims professed by their supporters, are not mere frauds, nor sheer nonsense— have not been got up originally, and all along maintained, for the sole purpose of picking people's pockets; without aiming at, or being found conducive to, any honest end during the whole process. Nothing, of which this is a sufficient account, would have lasted a tithe of five, eight, or ten centuries, in the most improving period and (during much of that period) the most improving nation in the world. These things, we may depend upon it, were not always without much good in them, however little of it may now be left: and Reformers ought to hail the man as a brother Reformer who points out what this good is; what it is which we have a right to expect from things established—which they are bound to do for us, as the justification of their being established: so that they may be recalled to it and compelled to do it, or the impossibility of their any longer doing it may be conclusively manifested. What is any case for reform good for, until it has passed this test? What mode is there of determining whether a thing is fit to exist, without first considering what purposes it exists for, and whether it be still capable of fulfilling them?

We have not room here to consider Coleridge's Conservative philosophy in all its aspects, or in relation to all the quarters from which objections might be raised against it. We shall consider it with relation to Reformers, and especially to Benthamites. We would assist them to determine whether they would have to do with Conservative philosophers or with Conservative dunces; and whether, since there are Tories, it be better that they should learn their Toryism from

Lord Eldon,[22] or even Sir Robert Peel, or from Coleridge.

Take, for instance, Coleridge's view of the grounds of a Church Establishment. His mode of treating any institution is to investigate what he terms the Idea of it, or what in common parlance would be called the principle involved in it. The idea or principle of a national church, and of the Church of England in that character, is, according to him, the reservation of a portion of the land, or of a right to a portion of its produce, as a fund—for what purpose? For the worship of God? For the performance of religious ceremonies? No; for the advancement of knowledge, and the civilization and cultivation of the community. This fund he does not term Church-property, but "the nationality," or national property. He considers it as destined for "the support and maintenance of a permanent class or order, with the following duties. A certain smaller number were to remain at the fountain-heads of the humanities, in cultivating and enlarging the knowledge already possessed, and in watching over the interests of physical and moral science; being likewise the instructors of such as constituted, or were to constitute, the remaining more numerous classes of the order. The members of this latter and far more numerous body were to be distributed throughout the country, so as not to leave even the smallest integral part or division without a resident guide, guardian, and instructor; the objects and final intention of the whole order being these—to preserve the stores and to guard the treasures of past civilization, and thus to bind the present with the past; to perfect and add to the same, and thus to connect the present with the future; but especially to diffuse through the whole community, and to every native entitled to its laws and rights, that quantity and quality of knowledge which was indispensable both for the understanding of those rights, and for the performance of the duties correspondent; finally, to secure for the nation, if not a superiority over the neighbouring states, yet an equality at least, in that character of general civilization, which equally with, or rather more than, fleets, armies, and revenue, forms the ground of its defensive and offensive power."

This organized body, set apart and endowed for the cultivation and diffusion of knowledge, is not, in Coleridge's view, necessarily a religious corporation. "Religion may be an indispensable

----

[22] John Scott, 1st Earl of Eldon (1751–1838), Tory opponent of reform.

ally, but is not the essential constitutive end, of that national institute, which is unfortunately, at least improperly, styled the Church; a name which, in its best sense, is exclusively appropriate to the Church of Christ. . . . The *clerisy* of the nation, or national church in its primary acceptation and original intention, comprehended the learned of all denominations, the sages and professors of the law and jurisprudence, of medicine and physiology, of music, of military and civil architecture, with the mathematical as the common organ of the preceding; in short, all the so-called liberal arts and sciences, the possession and application of which constitute the civilization of a country, as well as the theological. The last was, indeed, placed at the head of all; and of good right did it claim the precedence. But why? Because under the name of theology or divinity were contained the interpretation of languages, the conservation and tradition of past events, the momentous epochs and revolutions of the race and nation, the continuation of the records, logic, ethics, and the determination of ethical science, in application to the rights and duties of men in all their various relations, social and civil; and lastly, the ground-knowledge, the *prima scientia,*[23] as it was named,—philosophy, or the doctrine and discipline of ideas.

"Theology formed only a part of the objects, the theologians formed only a portion of the clerks or clergy, of the national Church. The theologi al order had precedency indeed, and deservedly; but not because its members were priests, whose office was to conciliate the invisible powers, and to superintend the interests that survive the grave; nor as being exclusively, or even principally, sacerdotal or templar, which, when it did occur, is to be considered as an accident of the age, a misgrowth of ignorance and oppression, a falsification of the constitutive principle, not a constituent part of the same. No; the theologians took the lead, because the science of theology was the root and the trunk of the knowledge of civilized man: because it gave unity and the circulating sap of life to all other sciences, by virtue of which alone they could be contemplated as forming collectively the living tree of knowledge. It had the precedency because, under the name theology, were comprised all the main aids, instruments, and materials of national education, the *nisus formativus*[24] of the body politic, the shaping and informing spirit, which,

educing or eliciting the latent man in all the natives of the soil, trains them up to be citizens of the country, free subjects of the realm. And, lastly, because to divinity belong those fundamental truths which are the common groundwork of our civil and our religious duties, not less indispensable to a right view of our temporal concerns than to a rational faith respecting our immortal well-being. Not without celestial observations can even terrestrial charts be accurately constructed."—*Church and State,* chap. v.

The nationality, or national property, according to Coleridge, "cannot rightfully, and without foul wrong to the nation never has been, alienated from its original purposes," from the promotion of "a continuing and progressive civilization," to the benefit of individuals, or any public purpose of merely economical or material interest. But the State may withdraw the fund from its actual holders, for the better execution of its purposes. There is no sanctity attached to the means, but only to the ends. The fund is not dedicated to any particular scheme of religion, nor even to religion at all; religion has only to do with it in the character of an instrument of civilization, and in common with all the other instruments. "I do not assert that the proceeds from the nationality cannot be rightfully vested, except in what we now mean by clergymen and the established clergy. I have everywhere implied the contrary. . . . In relation to the national church, Christianity, or the Church of Christ, is a blessed accident, a providential boon, a grace of God. . . . As the olive tree is said in its growth to fertilize the surrounding soil, to invigorate the roots of the vines in its immediate neighbourhood, and to improve the strength and flavour of the wines; such is the relation of the Christian and the national Church. But as the olive is not the same plant with the vine, or with the elm or poplar (that is, the State) with which the vine is wedded; and as the vine, with its prop, may exist, though in less perfection, without the olive, or previously to its implantation; even so is Christianity, and *à fortiori* any particular scheme of theology derived, and supposed by its partisans to be deduced, from Christianity, no essential part of the being of the national Church, however conducive or even indispensable it may be to its well-being."—chap. vi.

What would Sir Robert Inglis, or Sir Robert Peel, or Mr. Spooner[25] say to such a doctrine

[23] First knowledge.   [24] Shaping force.
[25] These were all contemporary opponents of Church reform.

as this? Will they thank Coleridge for this advocacy of Toryism? What would become of the three years' debates on the Appropriation Clause, which so disgraced this country before the face of Europe? Will the ends of practical Toryism be much served by a theory under which the Royal Society might claim a part of the Church property with as good right as the bench of bishops, if, by endowing that body like the French Institute, science could be better promoted? a theory by which the State, in the conscientious exercise of its judgment, having decided that the Church of England does not fulfil the object for which the nationalty was intended, might transfer its endowments to any other ecclesiastical body, or to any other body not ecclesiastical, which it deemed more competent to fulfil those objects; might establish any other sect, or all sects, or no sect at all, if it should deem that in the divided condition of religious opinion in this country, the State can no longer with advantage attempt the complete religious instruction of its people, but must for the present content itself with providing secular instruction, and such religious teaching, if any, as all can take part in; leaving each sect to apply to its own communion that which they all agree in considering as the keystone of the arch? We believe this to be the true state of affairs in Great Britain at the present time. We are far from thinking it other than a serious evil. We entirely acknowledge, that in any person fit to be a teacher, the view he takes of religion will be intimately connected with the view he will take of all the greatest things which he has to teach. Unless the same teachers who give instruction on those other subjects, are at liberty to enter freely on religion, the scheme of education will be, to a certain degree, fragmentary and incoherent. But the State at present has only the option of such an imperfect scheme, or of entrusting the whole business to perhaps the most unfit body for the exclusive charge of it that could be found among persons of any intellectual attainments, namely, the established clergy as at present trained and composed. Such a body would have no chance of being selected as the exclusive administrators of the nationalty, on any foundation but that of divine right; the ground avowedly taken by the only other school of Conservative philosophy which is attempting to raise its head in this country—that of the new Oxford theologians.[26]

Coleridge's merit in this matter consists, as it seems to us, in two things. First, that by setting in a clear light what a national church establishment ought to be, and what, by the very fact of its existence, it must be held to pretend to be, he has pronounced the severest satire upon what in fact it is. There is some difference, truly, between Coleridge's church, in which the schoolmaster forms the first step in the hierarchy "who, in due time, and under condition of a faithful performance of his arduous duties, should succeed to the pastorate,"[27] and the Church of England such as we now see. But to say the Church, and mean only the clergy, "constituted," according to Coleridge's conviction, "the first and fundamental apostasy."[28] He, and the thoughts which have proceeded from him, have done more than would have been effected in thrice the time by Dissenters and Radicals, to make the Church ashamed of the evil of her ways, and to determine that movement of improvement from within, which has begun where it ought to begin, at the Universities and among the younger clergy, and which, if this sect-ridden country is ever to be really taught, must proceed *pari passu* with the assault carried on from without.

Secondly, we honour Coleridge for having rescued from the discredit in which the corruptions of the English Church had involved everything connected with it, and for having vindicated against Bentham and Adam Smith and the whole eighteenth century, the principle of an endowed class, for the cultivation of learning, and for diffusing its results among the community. That such a class is likely to be behind, instead of before, the progress of knowledge is an induction erroneously drawn from the peculiar circumstances of the last two centuries, and in contradiction to all the rest of modern history. If we have seen much of the abuses of endowments, we have not seen what this country might be made by a proper administration of them, as we trust we shall not see what it would be without them. On this subject we are entirely at one with Coleridge, and with the other great defender of endowed establishments, Dr. Chalmers,[29] and we consider the definitive establishment of this fundamental principle, to be one of the permanent benefits which political science owes to the Conservative philosophers.

Coleridge's theory of the Constitution is not

---

[26] The Oxford Movement. [27] *Church and State*, p. 57. [Mill's note]
[28] *Literary Remains*, III, 386. [Mill's note]
[29] Thomas Chalmers (1780–1847), Scottish divine, defender of the principle of state churches.

less worthy of notice than his theory of the Church. The Delolme and Blackstone doctrine,[30] the balance of the three powers, he declares he never could elicit one ray of common sense from, no more than from the balance of trade.[31] There is, however, according to him, an Idea of the Constitution, of which he says—

"Because our whole history, from Alfred onwards, demonstrates the continued influence of such an idea, or ultimate aim, in the minds of our forefathers, in their characters and functions as public men, alike in what they resisted and what they claimed; in the institutions and forms of polity which they established, and with regard to those against which they more or less successfully contended; and because the result has been a progressive, though not always a direct or equable, advance in the gradual realization of the idea; and because it is actually, though (even because it is an idea) not adequately, represented in a correspondent scheme of means really existing; we speak, and have a right to speak, of the idea itself as actually existing, that is, as a principle existing in the only way in which a principle can exist—in the minds and consciences of the persons whose duties it prescribes, and whose rights it determines."[32] This fundamental idea "is at the same time the final criterion by which all particular frames of government must be tried: for here only can we find the great constructive principles of our representative system: those principles in the light of which it can alone be ascertained what are excrescences, symptoms of distemperature, and marks of degeneration, and what are native growths, or changes naturally attendant on the progressive development of the original germ, symptoms of immaturity, perhaps, but not of disease; or, at worst, modifications of the growth by the defective or faulty, but remediless or only gradually remediable, qualities of the soil and surrounding elements."[33]

Of these principles he gives the following account:—

"It is the chief of many blessings derived from the insular character and circumstances of our country, that our social institutions have formed themselves out of our proper needs and interests; that long and fierce as the birth-struggle and growing pains have been, the antagonist powers have been of our own system, and have been allowed to work out their final balance with less disturbance from external forces than was possible in the Continental States. . . . Now, in every country of civilized men, or acknowledging the rights of property, and by means of determined boundaries and common laws united into one people or nation, the two antagonist powers or opposite interests of the State, under which all other State interests are comprised, are those of *permanence* and of *progression.*"

The interest of permanence, or the Conservative interest, he considers to be naturally connected with the land, and with landed property. This doctrine, false in our opinion as an universal principle, is true of England, and of all countries where landed property is accumulated in large masses.

"On the other hand," he says, "the progression of a State, in the arts and comforts of life, in the diffusion of the information and knowledge useful or necessary for all; in short, all advances in civilization, and the rights and privileges of citizens, are especially connected with, and derived from, the four classes,—the mercantile, the manufacturing, the distributive, and the professional."[34] (We must omit the interesting historical illustrations of this maxim.) "These four last-mentioned classes I will designate by the name of the Personal Interest, as the exponent of all moveable and personal possessions, including skill and acquired knowledge, the moral and intellectual stock in trade of the professional man and the artist, no less than the raw materials, and the means of elaborating, transporting, and distributing them."[35]

The interest of permanence, then, is provided for by a representation of the landed proprietors; that of progression, by a representation of personal property and of intellectual acquirement: and while one branch of the Legislature, the Peerage, is essentially given over to the former, he considers it a part both of the general theory and of the actual English constitution, that the representatives of the latter should form "the clear and effectual majority of the Lower House"; or if not, that at least, by the added influence of public opinion, they should exercise an effective preponderance there. That "the very weight intended for the effectual counterpoise of the

---

[30] Found in Blackstone's *Commentaries* (1765–69) and in John Louis DeLolme's *The Constitution of England* (1775).
[31] *The Friend,* first collected edition (1818), II, 75. [Mill's note]
[32] *Church and State,* pp. 18–19. [Mill's note]   [33] *Church and State,* pp. 19–20. [Mill's note]
[34] *Church and State,* pp. 23–24. [Mill's note]   [35] *Church and State,* pp. 29–30. [Mill's note]

great landholders" has "in the course of events, been shifted into the opposite scale"; that the members for the towns "now constitute a large proportion of the political power and influence of the very class of men whose personal cupidity and whose partial views of the landed interest at large they were meant to keep in check";— these things he acknowledges: and only suggests a doubt, whether roads, canals, machinery, the press, and other influences favourable to the popular side, do not constitute an equivalent force to supply the deficiency.[36]

How much better a Parliamentary Reformer, then, is Coleridge, than Lord John Russell,[37] or any Whig who stickles for maintaining this unconstitutional omnipotence of the landed interest. If these became the principles of Tories, we should not wait long for further reform, even in our organic institutions. It is true Coleridge disapproved of the Reform Bill, or rather of the principle, or the no-principle, on which it was supported. He saw in it (as we may surmise) the dangers of a change amounting almost to a revolution, without any real tendency to remove those defects in the machine, which alone could justify a change so extensive. And that this is nearly a true view of the matter, all parties seem to be now agreed. The Reform Bill was not calculated greatly to improve the general composition of the Legislature. The good it has done, which is considerable, consists chiefly in this, that being so great a change, it has weakened the superstitious feeling against great changes. Any good, which is contrary to the selfish interest of the dominant class, is still only to be effected by a long and arduous struggle: but improvements which threaten no powerful body in their social importance or in their pecuniary emoluments, are no longer resisted, as they once were, because of their greatness—because of the very benefit which they promised. Witness the speedy passing of the Poor Law Amendment and the Penny Postage Acts.[38]

Meanwhile, though Coleridge's theory is but a mere commencement, not amounting to the first lines of a political philosophy, has the age produced any other theory of government which can stand a comparison with it as to its first principles? Let us take, for example, the Benthamic theory. The principle of this may be said to be, that since the general interest is the object

of government, a complete control over the government ought to be given to those whose interest is identical with the general interest. The authors and propounders of this theory were men of extraordinary intellectual powers, and the greater part of what they meant by it is true and important. But when considered as the foundation of a science, it would be difficult to find among theories proceeding from philosophers one less like a philosophical theory, or, in the works of analytical minds, anything more entirely unanalytical. What can a philosopher make of such complex notions as "interest" and "general interest," without breaking them down into the elements of which they are composed? If by men's interest be meant what would appear such to a calculating bystander, judging what would be good for a man during his whole life, and making no account, or but little, of the gratification of his present passions, his pride, his envy, his vanity, his cupidity, his love of pleasure, his love of ease—it may be questioned whether, in this sense, the interest of an aristocracy, and still more that of a monarch, would not be as accordant with the general interest as that of either the middle or the poorer classes; and if men's interest, in this understanding of it, usually governed their conduct, absolute monarchy would probably be the best form of government. But since men usually do what they like, often being perfectly aware that it is not for their ultimate interest, still more often that it is not for the interest of their posterity; and when they do believe that the object they are seeking is permanently good for them, almost always overrating its value; it is necessary to consider, not who are they whose permanent interest, but who are they whose immediate interests and habitual feelings, are likely to be most in accordance with the end we seek to obtain. And as that end (the general good) is a very complex state of things, comprising as its component elements many requisites which are neither of one and the same nature, nor attainable by one and the same means—political philosophy must begin by a classification of these elements, in order to distinguish those of them which go naturally together (so that the provision made for one will suffice for the rest), from those which are ordinarily in a state of antagonism, or at least of separation, and require to be provided for

---

[36] *Church and State*, pp. 30, 31–32. [Mill's note]
[37] John Russell, 1st Earl Russell (1792–1878), Whig statesman.
[38] In 1834 and in 1840.

apart. This preliminary classification being supposed, things would, in a perfect government, be so ordered, that corresponding to each of the great interests of society, there would be some branch or some integral part of the governing body, so constituted that it should not be merely deemed by philosophers, but should actually and constantly deem itself, to have its strongest interests involved in the maintenance of that one of the ends of society which it is intended to be the guardian of. This, we say, is the thing to be aimed at, the type of perfection in a political constitution. Not that there is a possibility of making more than a limited approach to it in practice. A government must be composed out of the elements already existing in society, and the distribution of power in the constitution cannot vary much or long from the distribution of it in society itself. But wherever the circumstances of society allow any choice, wherever wisdom and contrivance are at all available, this, we conceive, is the principle of guidance; and whatever anywhere exists is imperfect and a failure, just so far as it recedes from this type.

Such a philosophy of government, we need hardly say, is in its infancy: the first step to it, the classification of the exigencies of society, has not been made. Bentham, in his "Principles of Civil Law," has given a specimen, very useful for many other purposes, but not available, nor intended to be so, for founding a theory of representation upon it. For that particular purpose we have seen nothing comparable as far as it goes, notwithstanding its manifest insufficiency, to Coleridge's division of the interests of society into the two antagonist interests of Permanence and Progression. The Continental philosophers have, by a different path, arrived at the same division; and this is about as far, probably, as the science of political institutions has yet reached.

In the details of Coleridge's political opinions there is much good, and much that is questionable, or worse. In political economy especially he writes like an arrant driveller, and it would have been well for his reputation had he never meddled

with the subject.[39] But this department of knowledge can now take care of itself. On other points we meet with far-reaching remarks, and a tone of general feeling sufficient to make a Tory's hair stand on end. Thus, in the work from which we have most quoted, he calls the State policy of the last half-century "a Cyclops with one eye, and that in the back of the head"—its measures "either a series of anachronisms, or a truckling to events instead of the science that should command them."[40] He styles the great Commonwealthsmen "the stars of that narrow interspace of blue sky between the black clouds of the First and Second Charles's reigns."[41] The "Literary Remains" are full of disparaging remarks on many of the heroes of Toryism and Church-of-Englandism. He sees, for instance, no difference between Whitgift and Bancroft, and Bonner and Gardiner, except that the last were the most consistent—that the former sinned against better knowledge,[42] and one of the most poignant of his writings is a character of Pitt, the very reverse of panegyrical.[43] As a specimen of his practical views, we have mentioned his recommendation that the parochial clergy should begin by being schoolmasters. He urges "a different division and subdivision of the kingdom" instead of "the present barbarism, which forms an obstacle to the improvement of the country of much greater magnitude than men are generally aware."[44] But we must confine ourselves to instances in which he has helped to bring forward great principles, either implied in the old English opinions and institutions, or at least opposed to the new tendencies.

For example, he is at issue with the *let alone* doctrine, or the theory that governments can do no better than to do nothing; a doctrine generated by the manifest selfishness and incompetence of modern European governments, but of which, as a general theory, we may now be permitted to say, that one half of it is true, and the other half false. All who are on a level with their age now readily admit that government ought not to *interdict* men from publishing their opinions, pursuing their employments, or buying

---

[39] Yet even on this subject he has occasionally a just thought, happily expressed; as this: "Instead of the position that all things find, it would be less equivocal and far more descriptive of the fact to say, that things are always finding their level; which might be taken as the paraphrase or ironical definition of a storm."—*Second Lay Sermon*, p. 403. [Mill's note]

[40] *Church and State*, p. 69. [Mill's note]

[41] *Church and State*, p. 102. [Mill's note]

[42] *Literary Remains*, II, 388. [Mill's note]

[43] Written in the Morning Post, and now (as we rejoice to see) reprinted in Mr. Gillman's biographical memoir. [Mill's note]

[44] *Church and State*, p. 56. [Mill's note]

and selling their goods, in whatever place or manner they deem the most advantageous. Beyond suppressing force and fraud, governments can seldom, without doing more harm than good, attempt to chain up the free agency of individuals. But does it follow from this that government cannot exercise a free agency of its own?—that it cannot beneficially employ its powers, its means of information, and its pecuniary resources (so far surpassing those of any other association, or of any individual), in promoting the public welfare by a thousand means which individuals would never think of, would have no sufficient motives to attempt, or no sufficient power to accomplish? To confine ourselves to one, and that a limited view of the subject: a State ought to be considered as a great benefit society, or mutual insurance company, for helping (under the necessary regulations for preventing abuse) that large proportion of its members who cannot help themselves.

"Let us suppose," says Coleridge, "the negative ends of a State already attained, namely, its own safety by by means of its own strength, and the protection of person and property for all its members; there will then remain its positive ends:—1. To make the means of subsistence more easy to each individual: 2. To secure to each of its members the hope of bettering his own condition or that of his children: 3. The development of those faculties which are essential to his humanity, that is, to his rational and moral being."[45]

In regard to the two former ends, he of course does not mean that they can be accomplished merely by making laws to that effect; or that, according to the wild doctrines now afloat, it is the fault of the government if every one has not enough to eat and drink. But he means that government can do something directly, and very much indirectly, to promote even the physical comfort of the people; and that if, besides making a proper use of its own powers, it would exert itself to teach the people what is in theirs, indigence would soon disappear from the face of the earth.

Perhaps, however, the greatest service which Coleridge has rendered to politics in his capacity of a Conservative philosopher, though its fruits are mostly yet to come, is in reviving the idea of a *trust* inherent in landed property. The land, the gift of nature, the source of subsistence to all, and the foundation of everything that influences

our physical well-being, cannot be considered a subject of property, in the same absolute sense in which men are deemed proprietors of that in which no one has any interest but themselves— that which they have actually called into existence by their own bodily exertion. As Coleridge points out, such a notion is altogether of modern growth.

"The very idea of individual or private property in our present acceptation of the term, and according to the current notion of the right to it, was originally confined to moveable things; and the more moveable, the more susceptible of the nature of property,"[46]

By the early institutions of Europe, property in land was a public function, created for certain public purposes, and held under condition of their fulfilment; and as such, we predict, under the modifications suited to modern society, it will again come to be considered. In this age, when everything is called in question, and when the foundation of private property itself needs to be argumentatively maintained against plausible and persuasive sophisms, one may easily see the danger of mixing up what is not really tenable with what is—and the impossibility of maintaining an absolute right in an individual to an unrestricted control, a *jus utendi et abutendi*,[47] over an unlimited quantity of the mere raw material of the globe, to which every other person could originally make out as good a natural title as himself. It will certainly not be much longer tolerated that agriculture should be carried on (as Coleridge expresses it) on the same principles as those of trade; "that a gentleman should regard his estate as a merchant his cargo, or a shopkeeper his stock";[48] that he should be allowed to deal with it as if it only existed to yield rent to him, not food to the numbers whose hands till it; and should have a right, and a right possessing all the sacredness of property, to turn them out by hundreds and make them perish on the high road, as has been done before now by Irish landlords. We believe it will soon be thought, that a mode of property in land which has brought things to this pass, has existed long enough.

We shall not be suspected (we hope) of recommending a general resumption of landed possessions, or the depriving any one, without compensation, of anything which the law gives him. But we say that when the State allows any

---

[45] *Second Lay Sermon*, pp. 414–15. [Mill's note]
[47] The right to use and dispose of property.
[46] *Second Lay Sermon*, p. 413. [Mill's note]
[48] *Second Lay Sermon*, p. 413. [Mill's note]

one to exercise ownership over more land than suffices to raise by his own labour his subsistence and that of his family, it confers on him power over other human beings—power affecting them in their most vital interests; and that no notion of private property can bar the right which the State inherently possesses, to require that the power which it has so given shall not be abused. We say, also, that, by giving this direct power over so large a portion of the community, indirect power is necessarily conferred over all the remaining portion; and this, too, it is the duty of the State to place under proper control. Further, the tenure of land, the various rights connected with it, and the system on which its cultivation is carried on, are points of the utmost importance both to the economical and to the moral well-being of the whole community. And the State fails in one of its highest obligations, unless it takes these points under its particular superintendence; unless, to the full extent of its power, it takes means of providing that the manner in which land is held, the mode and degree of its division, and every other peculiarity which influences the mode of its cultivation, shall be the most favourable possible for making the best use of the land: for drawing the greatest benefit from its productive resources, for securing the happiest existence to those employed on it, and for setting the greatest number of hands free to employ their labour for the benefit of the community in other ways. We believe that these opinions will become, in no very long period, universal throughout Europe. And we gratefully bear testimony to the fact, that the first among us who has given the sanction of philosophy to so great a reform in the popular and current notions, is a Conservative philosopher.

Of Coleridge as a moral and religious philosopher (the character which he presents most prominently in his principal works), there is neither room, nor would it be expedient for us to speak more than generally. On both subjects, few men have ever combined so much earnestness with so catholic and unsectarian a spirit. "We have imprisoned," says he, "our own conceptions by the lines which we have drawn in order to exclude the conceptions of others. *J'ai trouvé que la plupart des sectes ont raison dans une bonne partie de ce qu'elles avancent, mais non pas tant en ce qu'elles nient.*"[49] That almost all sects, both

in philosophy and religion, are right in the positive part of their tenets, though commonly wrong in the negative, is a doctrine which he professes as strongly as the eclectic school in France. Almost all errors he holds to be "truths misunderstood," "half-truths taken as the whole," though not the less, but the more dangerous on that account.[50] Both the theory and practice of enlightened tolerance in matters of opinion, might be exhibited in extracts from his writings more copiously than in those of almost any other writer we know; though there are a few (and but a few) exceptions to his own practice of it. In the theory of ethics, he contends against the doctrine of general consequences, and holds that, *for man*, "to obey the simple unconditional commandment of eschewing every act that implies a self-contradiction"—so to act as to "be able, without involving any contradiction, to will that the maxim of thy conduct should be the law of all intelligent beings,—is the one universal and sufficient principle and guide of morality."[51] Yet even a utilitarian can have little conplaint to make of a philosopher who lays it down that "the *outward* object of virtue" is "the greatest producible sum of happiness of all men," and that "happiness in its proper sense is but the continuity and sum-total of the pleasure which is allotted or happens to a man."[52]

But his greatest object was to bring into harmony Religion and Philosophy. He laboured incessantly to establish that "the Christian faith—in which," says he, "I include every article of belief and doctrine professed by the first reformers in common"—is not only divine truth, but also "the perfection of Human Intelligence."[53] All that Christianity has revealed, philosophy, according to him, can prove, though there is much which it could never have discovered; human reason, once strengthened by Christianity, can evolve all the Christian doctrines from its own sources.[54] Moreover, "if infidelity is not to overspread England as well as France,"[55] the Scripture, and every passage of Scripture, must be submitted to this test; inasmuch as "the compatibility of a document with the conclusions of self-evident reason, and with the laws of conscience, is a condition *à priori* of any evidence adequate to the proof of its having been revealed by God"; and this, he says, is no philosophic

49 *Biographia Literaria* (1817), I, 249. [Mill's note]. Coleridge's citation from Leibniz reads: "I have found that most sects are correct in a good part of what they assert, but not so much in what they deny."
50 *Literary Remains*, III, 145. [Mill's note]   51 *The Friend* (1818), I, 256 and 340. [Mill's note]
52 *Aids to Reflection*, pp. 37 and 39. [Mill's note]   53 Preface to the *Aids to Reflection*. [Mill's note]
54 *Literary Remains*, I, 388. [Mill's note]   55 *Literary Remains*, III, 263. [Mill's note]

novelty, but a principle "clearly laid down both by Moses and St. Paul."[56] He thus goes quite as far as the Unitarians in making man's reason and moral feelings a test of revelation; but differs *toto cælo*[57] from them in their rejection of its mysteries, which he regards as the highest philosophic truths, and says that "the Christian to whom, after a long profession of Christianity, the mysteries remain as much mysteries as before, is in the same state as a school-boy with regard to his arithmetic, to whom the *facit* at the end of the examples in his cyphering-book is the whole ground for his assuming that such and such figures amount to so and so."

These opinions are not likely to be popular in the religious world, and Coleridge knew it: "I quite calculate,"[58] said he once, "on my being one day or other holden in worse repute by many Christians than the Unitarians" and even "Infidels." "It must be undergone by every one who loves the truth for its own sake beyond all other things." For our part, we are not bound to defend him; and we must admit that, in his attempt to arrive at theology by way of philosophy, we see much straining, and most frequently, as it appears to us, total failure. The question, however, is not whether Coleridge's attempts are successful, but whether it is desirable or not that such attempts should be made. Whatever some religious people may think, philosophy will and must go on, ever seeking to understand whatever can be made understandable; and, whatever some philosophers may think, there is little prospect at present that philosophy will take the place of religion, or that any philosophy will be speedily received in this country, unless supposed not only to be consistent with, but even to yield collateral support to, Christianity. What is the use, then, of treating with contempt the idea of a religious philosophy? Religious philosophies are among the things to be looked for, and our main hope ought to be that they may be such as fulfil the conditions of a philosophy—the very foremost of which is, unrestricted freedom of thought. There is no philosophy possible where fear of consequences is a stronger principle than love of truth; where speculation is paralyzed, either by the belief that conclusions honestly arrived at will be punished by a just and good Being with eternal damnation, or by seeing in every text of Scripture a foregone conclusion, with which the results of inquiry must, at any expense of sophistry and self-deception, be made to quadrate.

From both these withering influences, that have so often made the acutest intellects exhibit specimens of obliquity and imbecility in their theological speculations which have excited the pity of subsequent generations, Coleridge's mind was perfectly free. Faith—the faith which is placed among religious duties—was, in his view, a state of the will and of the affections, not of the understanding. Heresy, in "the literal sense and scriptural import of the word," is, according to him, "wilful error, or belief originating in some perversion of the will"; he says, therefore, that there may be orthodox heretics, since indifference to truth may as well be shown on the right side of the question as on the wrong; and denounces, in strong language, the contrary doctrine of the "pseudo-Athanasius," who "interprets Catholic faith by belief,"[59] an act of the understanding alone. The true Lutheran doctrine," he says, is, that "neither will truth, as a mere conviction of the understanding, save, nor error condemn. To love truth sincerely is spiritually to have truth; and an error becomes a personal error, not by its aberration from logic or history, but so far as the causes of such error are in the heart, or may be traced back to some antecedent unchristian wish or habit."[60] "The unmistakable passions of a factionary and a schismatic, the ostentatious display, the ambitions and dishonest arts of a sect-founder, must be superinduced on the false doctrine before the heresy makes the man a heretic."[61]

Against the other terror, so fatal to the unshackled exercise of reason on the greatest questions, the view which Coleridge took of the authority of the Scriptures was a preservative. He drew the strongest distinction between the inspiration which he owned in the various writers, and an express dictation by the Almighty of every word they wrote. "The notion of the absolute truth and divinity of every syllable of the text of the books of the Old and New Testament as we have it," he again and again asserts to be unsupported by the Scripture itself; to be one of those superstitions in which "there is a heart of unbelief";[62] to be, "if possible, still more extravagant" than the Papal infallibility; and

---

[56] *Literary Remains*, III, 293. [Mill's note]
[57] Completely, entirely.
[58] *Table Talk*, 2nd ed., p. 91. [Mill's note]
[59] *Literary Remains*, IV, 193. [Mill's note]
[60] *Literary Remains*, III, 359. [Mill's note]
[61] *Literary Remains*, IV, 245. [Mill's note]
[62] *Literary Remains*, III, 220; see also pp. 254, 323, and many other passages in the third and fourth volumes. [Mill's note]

declares that the very same arguments are used for both doctrines.[63] God, he believes, informed the minds of the writers with the truths he meant to reveal, and left the rest to their human faculties. He pleaded most earnestly, says his nephew and editor, for this liberty of criticism with respect to the Scriptures, as "the only middle path of safety and peace between a godless disregard of the unique and transcendent character of the Bible, taken generally, and that scheme of interpretation, scarcely less adverse to the pure spirit of Christian wisdom, which wildly arrays our faith in opposition to our reason, and inculcates the sacrifice of the latter to the former; for he threw up his hands in dismay at the language of some of our modern divinity on this point, as if a faith not founded on insight were aught else than a specious name for wilful positiveness; as if the Father of Lights could require, or would accept, from the only one of his creatures whom he had endowed with reason, the sacrifice of fools! . . . Of the aweless doctrine that God might, if he had so pleased, have given to man a religion which to human intelligence should not be rational, and exacted his faith in it, Coleridge's whole middle and later life was one deep and solemn denial."[64] He bewails "bibliolatry" as the pervading error of modern Protestant divinity, and the great stumbling-block of Christianity, and exclaims,[65] "O might I live but to utter all my meditations on this most concerning point . . . in what sense the Bible may be called the word of God, and how and under what conditions the unity of the Spirit is translucent through the letter, which, read as the letter merely, is the word of this and that pious, but fallible and imperfect, man." It is known that he did live to write down these meditations; and speculations so important will one day, it is devoutly to be hoped, be given to the world.[66]

Theological discussion is beyond our province, and it is not for us, in this place, to judge these sentiments of Coleridge; but it is clear enough that they are not the sentiments of a bigot, or of one who is to be dreaded by Liberals, lest he should illiberalize the minds of the rising generation of Tories and High-Churchmen. We think the danger is rather lest they should find him vastly too liberal. And yet, now when the most orthodox divines, both in the Church and out of it, find it necessary to explain away the obvious sense of the whole first chapter of Genesis, or failing to do that, consent to disbelieve it provisionally, on the speculation that there may hereafter be discovered a sense in which it can be believed, one would think the time gone by for expecting to learn from the Bible what it never could have been intended to communicate, and to find in all its statements a literal truth neither necessary nor conducive to what the volume itself declares to be the ends of revelation. Such at least was Coleridge's opinion; and whatever influence such an opinion may have over Conservatives, it cannot do other than make them less bigots, and better philosophers.

But we must close this long essay: long in itself, though short in its relation to its subject, and to the multitude of topics involved in it. We do not pretend to have given any sufficient account of Coleridge; but we hope we may have proved to some, not previously aware of it, that there is something both in him, and in the school to which he belongs, not unworthy of their better knowledge. We may have done something to show that a Tory philosopher cannot be wholly a Tory, but must often be a better Liberal than Liberals themselves; while he is the natural means of rescuing from oblivion truths which Tories have forgotten, and which the prevailing schools of Liberalism never knew.

And even if a Conservative philosophy were an absurdity, it is well calculated to drive out a hundred absurdities worse than itself. Let no one think that it is nothing, to accustom people to give a reason for their opinion, be the opinion ever so untenable, the reason ever so insufficient. A person accustomed to submit his fundamental tenets to the test of reason, will be more open to the dictates of reason on every other point. Not from him shall we have to apprehend the owl-like dread of light, the drudge-like aversion to change, which were the characteristics of the old unreasoning race of bigots. A man accustomed to contemplate the fair side of Toryism (the side that every attempt at a philosophy of it must bring to view), and to defend the existing system by the display of its capabilities as an

---

[63] *Literary Remains*, II, 385. [Mill's note]

[64] Preface to the third volume of the *Literary Remains*. [Mill's note]

[65] *Literary Remains*, IV, 6. [Mill's note]

[66] This wish has, to a certain extent, been fulfilled by the publication of the series of letters on the Inspiration of the Scriptures, which bears the not very appropriate name of *Confessions of an Inquiring Spirit*. [Mill's note]

engine of public good,—such a man, when he comes to administer the system, will be more anxious than another person to realize those capabilities, to bring the fact a little nearer to the specious theory. "Lord, enlighten thou our enemies," should be the prayer of every true Reformer; sharpen their wits, give acuteness to their perceptions, and consecutiveness and clearness to their reasoning powers: we are in danger from their folly, not from their wisdom; their weakness is what fills us with apprehension, not their strength.

For ourselves, we are not so blinded by our particular opinions as to be ignorant that in this and in every other country of Europe, the great mass of the owners of large property, and of all the classes intimately connected with the owners of large property, are, and must be expected to be, in the main, Conservative. To suppose that so mighty a body can be without immense influence in the commonwealth, or to lay plans for effecting great changes, either spiritual or temporal, in which they are left out of the question, would be the height of absurdity. Let those who desire such changes, ask themselves if they are content that these classes should be, and remain, to a man, banded against them; and what progress they expect to make, or by what means, unless a process of preparation shall be going on in the minds of these very classes; not by the impracticable method of converting them from Conservatives into Liberals, but by their being led to adopt one liberal opinion after another, as a part of Conservatism itself. The first step to this, is to inspire them with the desire to systematize and rationalize their own actual creed: and the feeblest attempt to do this has an intrinsic value; far more, then, one which has so much in it, both of moral goodness and true insight, as the philosophy of Coleridge.

from On Liberty

Mill's reputation in the twentieth century rests as much on his On Liberty *as on any other of his works. It has become the classic affirmation of individual liberty against encroachment by the civil power or by the power of custom. It represents the highest thinking on the subject by the greatest representative of nineteenth-century liberalism. The work was published in 1859, the same year as Darwin's* Origin of the Species. *The entire work is divided into five chapters, of which the first two are given complete below.*

CHAPTER I

Introductory

THE subject of this Essay is not the so-called Liberty of the Will, so unfortunately opposed to the misnamed doctrine of Philosophical Necessity; but Civil, or Social Liberty: the nature and limits of the power which can be legitimately exercised by society over the individual. A question seldom stated, and hardly ever discussed, in general terms, but which profoundly influences the practical controversies of the age by its latent presence, and is likely soon to make itself recognised as the vital question of the future. It is so far from being new, that in a certain sense, it has divided mankind, almost from the remotest ages; but in the stage of progress into which the more civilized portions of the species have now entered, it presents itself under new conditions, and requires a different and more fundamental treatment.

The struggle between Liberty and Authority is the most conspicuous feature in the portions of history with which we are earliest familiar, particularly in that of Greece, Rome, and England. But in old times this contest was between subjects, or some classes of subjects, and the government. By liberty, was meant protection against the tyranny of the political rulers. The rulers were conceived (except in some of the popular governments of Greece) as in a necessarily antagonistic position to the people whom they ruled. They consisted of a governing One, or a governing tribe or caste, who derived their authority from inheritance or conquest, who, at all events, did not hold it at the pleasure of the governed, and whose supremacy men did not venture, perhaps did not desire, to contest, whatever precautions might be taken against its oppressive exercise. Their power was regarded as necessary, but also as highly dangerous; as a weapon which they would attempt to use against their subjects, no less than against external enemies. To prevent the weaker members of the community from being preyed upon by innumerable vultures, it was needful that there should be an animal of prey stronger than the rest, commissioned to keep them down. But as the king of the vultures would be no less bent upon preying on the flock, than any of the minor harpies, it was indispensable to be in a perpetual attitude of defence against his beak and claws. The aim, therefore, of patriots, was to set limits to the power which the ruler should be suffered to exercise over the community; and this limitation was what they meant by liberty. It was attempted in two ways. First, by obtaining a recognition of certain immunities, called political liberties or rights, which it was to be regarded as a breach of duty in the ruler to infringe, and which if he did infringe, specific resistance, or general rebellion, was held to be justifiable. A second, and generally a later expedient, was the establishment of constitutional checks; by which the consent of the community, or of a body of some sort, supposed to represent its interests, was made a necessary condition to some of the more important acts of the governing power. To the first of these modes of limitation, the ruling power, in most European countries, was compelled, more or less, to submit. It was not so with the second; and to attain this, or when already in some degree possessed, to attain it more completely, became everywhere the principal object of the lovers of liberty. And so long as mankind were content to combat one enemy by another, and to be ruled by a master, on condition of being guaranteed more or less efficaciously against his tyranny, they did not carry their aspirations beyond this point.

A time, however, came, in the progress of human affairs, when men ceased to think it a necessity of nature that their governors should be an independent power, opposed in interest to themselves. It appeared to them much better that the various magistrates of the State should be their tenants or delegates, revocable at their pleasure. In that way alone, it seemed, could they have complete security that the powers of government would never be abused to their disadvantage. By degrees, this new demand for elective and temporary rulers became the prominent object of the exertions of the popular party, wherever any such party existed; and superseded, to a considerable extent, the previous efforts to limit the power of rulers. As the struggle proceeded for making the ruling power emanate from the periodical choice of the ruled, some persons began to think that too much importance had been attached to the limitation of the power itself. *That* (it might seem) was a resource against rulers whose interests were habitually opposed to those of the people. What was now wanted was, that the rulers should be identified with the people; that their interest and will should be the interest and will of the nation. The nation did not need to be protected against its own will. There was no fear of its tyrannizing over itself. Let the rulers be effectually responsible to it, promptly removable by it, and it could afford to trust them with power of which it could itself dictate the use to be made. Their power was but the nation's own power, concentrated, and in a form convenient for exercise. This mode of thought, or rather perhaps of feeling, was common among the last generation of European liberalism, in the Continental section of which, it still apparently predominates. Those who admit any limit to what a government may do, except in the case of such governments as they think ought not to exist, stand out as brilliant exceptions among the political thinkers of the Continent. A similar tone of sentiment might by this time have been prevalent in our own country, if the circumstances which for a time encouraged it, had continued unaltered.

But, in political and philosophical theories, as well as in persons, success discloses faults and infirmities which failure might have concealed from observation. The notion, that the people have no need to limit their power over themselves, might seem axiomatic, when popular government was a thing only dreamed about, or read of as having existed at some distant period of the past. Neither was that notion necessarily disturbed by such temporary aberrations as those of the French Revolution, the worst of which were the work of an usurping few, and which, in any case, belonged, not to the permanent working of popular institutions, but to a sudden and convulsive outbreak against monarchical and aristocratic despotism. In time, however, a democratic republic came to occupy a large portion of the earth's surface, and made itself felt as one of the most powerful members of the community of nations; and elective and responsible government became subject to the observations and criticisms which wait upon a great existing fact. It was now perceived that such phrases as "self-government," and "the power of the people over themselves," do not express the true state of the case. The "people" who exercise the power, are not always the same people with those over whom it is exercised; and the "self-government" spoken of, is not the government of each by himself, but of each by all the rest. The will of the people, moreover, practically means, the will of the most numerous or the most active *part* of the people; the majority, or those who succeed in making themselves accepted as the majority: the people, consequently, *may* desire to oppress a part of their number; and precautions are as much needed against this, as against any other abuse of power. The limitation, therefore, of the power of government over individuals, loses none of its importance when the holders of power are regularly accountable to the community, that is, to the strongest party therein. This view of things, recommending itself equally to the intelligence of thinkers and to the inclination of those important classes in European society to whose real or supposed interests democracy is adverse, has had no difficulty in establishing itself; and in political speculations "the tyranny of the majority" is now generally included among the evils against which society requires to be on its guard.

Like other tyrannies, the tyranny of the majority was at first, and is still vulgarly, held in dread, chiefly as operating through the acts of the public authorities. But reflecting persons perceived that when society is itself the tyrant— society collectively, over the separate individuals who compose it—its means of tyrannizing are not restricted to the acts which it may do by the hands of its political functionaries. Society can and does execute its own mandates: and if it issues wrong mandates instead of right, or any mandates at all in things with which it ought not to meddle, it practises a social tyranny more formidable than many kinds of political oppression, since, though not usually upheld by such extreme penalties, it leaves fewer means of escape, penetrating much more deeply into the details of life, and enslaving the soul itself. Protection, therefore, against the tyranny of the magistrate is not enough: there needs protection also against the tyranny of the prevailing opinion and feeling; against the tendency of society to impose, by other means than civil penalties, its own ideas and practices as rules of conduct on those who dissent from them; to fetter the development, and, if possible, prevent the formation, of any individuality not in harmony with its ways, and compel all characters to fashion themselves upon the model of its own. There is a limit to the legitimate interference of collective opinion with individual independence: and to find that limit, and maintain it against encroachment, is as indispensable to a good condition of human affairs, as protection against political despotism.

But though this proposition is not likely to be contested in general terms, the practical question, where to place the limit—how to make the fitting adjustment between individual independence and social control—is a subject on which nearly everything remains to be done. All that makes existence valuable to any one, depends on the enforcement of restraints upon the actions of other people. Some rules of conduct, therefore, must be imposed, by law in the first place, and by opinion on many things which are not fit subjects for the operation of law. What these rules should be, is the principal question in human affairs; but if we except a few of the most obvious cases, it is one of those which least progress has been made in resolving. No two ages, and scarcely any two countries, have decided it alike; and the decision of one age or country is a wonder to another. Yet the people of any given age and country no more suspect any difficulty in it, than if it were a subject on which mankind had always been agreed. The rules which obtain among themselves appear to them self-evident and self-justifying. This all but universal illusion is one of the examples of the magical influence of custom, which is not only, as the proverb says, a second nature, but is continually mistaken for the first. The effect of custom, in preventing any misgiving respecting the rules of conduct which mankind impose on one another, is all the more complete because the subject is one on which it is not generally considered necessary that reasons should be given, either by one person to others, or by each to himself. People are accustomed to believe, and have been encouraged in the belief by some who aspire to the character of philosophers, that their feelings, on subjects of this nature, are better than reasons, and render reasons unnecessary. The practical principle which guides them to their opinions on the regulation of human conduct, is the feeling in each person's mind that everybody should be required to act as he, and those with whom he sympathizes, would like them to act. No one, indeed, acknowledges to himself that his standard of judgment is his own liking; but an opinion on a point of conduct, not supported by reasons, can only count as one person's preference; and if the reasons, when given, are a mere appeal to a similar preference felt by other people, it is still only many people's liking instead of one. To an ordinary man, how- ever, his own preference, thus supported, is not only a perfectly satisfactory reason, but the only one he generally has for any of his notions of morality, taste, or propriety, which are not expressly written in his religious creed; and his chief guide in the interpretation even of that. Men's opinions, accordingly, on what is laud- able or blameable, are affected by all the multifarious causes which influence their wishes in regard to the conduct of others, and which are as numerous as those which determine their wishes on any other subject. Sometimes their reason—at other times their prejudices or superstitions: often their social affections, not seldom their antisocial ones, their envy or jealousy, their arrogance or contemptuousness: but most commonly, their desires or fears for themselves—their legitimate or illegitimate self-interest. Wherever there is an ascendant class, a large portion of the morality of the country emanates from its class interests, and its feelings of class superiority. The morality between Spartans and Helots, between planters and negroes, between princes and subjects, between nobles and roturiers, between men and women, has been for the most part the creation of these class interests and feelings: and the sentiments thus generated, react in turn upon the moral feelings of the members of the ascendant class, in their relations among themselves. Where, on the other hand, a class, formerly ascendant, has lost its ascendancy, or where its ascendancy is unpopular, the prevailing moral sentiments frequently bear the impress of an impatient dislike of superiority. Another grand determining principle of the rules of conduct, both in act and forbearance, which have been enforced by law or opinion, has been the servility of mankind towards the supposed preferences or aversions of their temporal masters, or of their gods. This servility, though essentially selfish, is not hypoc- risy; it gives rise to perfectly genuine sentiments of abhorrence; it made men burn magicians and heretics. Among so many baser influences, the

general and obvious interests of society have of course had a share, and a large one, in the direction of the moral sentiments: less, however, as a matter of reason, and on their own account, than as a consequence of the sympathies and antipathies which grew out of them: and sym- pathies and antipathies which had little or nothing to do with the interests of society, have made themselves felt in the establishment of moralities with quite as great force.

The likings and dislikings of society, or of some powerful portion of it, are thus the main thing which has practically determined the rules laid down for general observance, under the penalties of law or opinion. And in general, those who have been in advance of society in thought and feeling, have left this condition of things unassailed in principle, however they may have come into conflict with it in some of its details. They have occupied themselves rather in inquiring what things society ought to like or dislike, than in questioning whether its likings or dislikings should be a law to individuals. They preferred en- deavouring to alter the feelings of mankind on the particular points on which they were them- selves heretical, rather than make common cause in defence of freedom, with heretics generally. The only case in which the higher ground has been taken on principle and main- tained with consistency, by any but an individual here and there, is that of religious belief: a case instructive in many ways, and not least so as forming a most striking instance of the fallibility of what is called the moral sense: for the *odium theologicum*,[1] in a sincere bigot, is one of the most unequivocal cases of moral feeling. Those who first broke the yoke of what called itself the Universal Church, were in general as little willing to permit difference of religious opinion as that church itself. But when the heat of the conflict was over, without giving a complete victory to any party, and each church or sect was reduced to limit its hopes to retaining possession of the ground it already occupied; minorities, seeing that they had no chance of becoming majorities, were under the necessity of pleading to those whom they could not convert, for permission to differ. It is accordingly on this battle field, almost solely, that the rights of the individual against society have been asserted on broad grounds of principle, and the claim of society to exercise authority over dissentients, openly controverted. The great writers to whom the world owes

---

[1] The rancor associated with theological disputes.

what religious liberty it possesses, have mostly asserted freedom of conscience as an indefeasible right, and denied absolutely that a human being is accountable to others for his religious belief. Yet so natural to mankind is intolerance in whatever they really care about, that religious freedom has hardly anywhere been practically realized, except where religious indifference, which dislikes to have its peace disturbed by theological quarrels, has added its weight to the scale. In the minds of almost all religious persons, even in the most tolerant countries, the duty of toleration is admitted with tacit reserves. One person will bear with dissent in matters of church government, but not of dogma; another can tolerate everybody, short of a Papist or an Unitarian; another, every one who believes in revealed religion; a few extend their charity a little further, but stop at the belief in a God and in a future state. Wherever the sentiment of the majority is still geniune and intense, it is found to have abated little of its claim to be obeyed.

In England, from the peculiar circumstances of our political history, though the yoke of opinion is perhaps heavier, that of law is lighter, than in most other countries of Europe; and there is considerable jealousy of direct interference, by the legislative or the executive power, with private conduct; not so much from any just regard for the independence of the individual, as from the still subsisting habit of looking on the government as representing an opposite interest to the public. The majority have not yet learnt to feel the power of the government their power, or its opinions their opinions. When they do so, individual liberty will probably be as much exposed to invasion from the government, as it already is from public opinion. But, as yet, there is a considerable amount of feeling ready to be called forth against any attempt of the law to control individuals in things in which they have not hitherto been accustomed to be controlled by it; and this with very little discrimination as to whether the matter is, or is not, within the legitimate sphere of legal control; insomuch that the feeling, highly salutary on the whole, is perhaps quite as often misplaced as well grounded in the particular instances of its application. There is, in fact, no recognised principle by which the propriety of impropriety of government interference is customarily tested. People decide according to their personal preferences. Some, whenever they see any good to be done, or evil to be remedied, would willingly instigate the government to undertake the business; while others prefer to bear almost any amount of social evil, rather than add one to the departments of human interests amenable to governmental control. And men range themselves on one or the other side in any particular case, according to this general direction of their sentiments; or according to the degree of interest which they feel in the particular thing which it is proposed that the government should do, or according to the belief they entertain that the government would, or would not, do it in the manner they prefer; but very rarely on account of any opinion to which they consistently adhere, as to what things are fit to be done by a government. And it seems to me that in consequence of this absence of rule or principle, one side is at present as often wrong as the other; the interference of government is, with about equal frequency, improperly invoked and improperly condemned.

The object of this Essay is to assert one very simple principle, as entitled to govern absolutely the dealings of society with the individual in the way of compulsion and control, whether the means used be physical force in the form of legal penalties, or the moral coercion of public opinion. That principle is, that the sole end for which mankind are warranted, individually or collectively, in interfering with the liberty of action of any of their number, is self-protection. That the only purpose for which power can be rightfully exercised over any member of a civilized community, against his will, is to prevent harm to others. His own good, either physical or moral, is not a sufficient warrant. He cannot rightfully be compelled to do or forbear because it will be better for him to do so, because it will make him happier, because, in the opinions of others, to do so would be wise, or even right. These are good reasons for remonstrating with him, or reasoning with him, or persuading him, or entreating him, but not for compelling him, or visiting him with any evil in case he do otherwise. To justify that, the conduct from which it is desired to deter him, must be calculated to produce evil to some one else. The only part of the conduct of any one, for which he is amenable to society, is that which concerns others. In the part which merely concerns himself, his independence is, of right, absolute. Over himself, over his own body and mind, the individual is sovereign.

It is, perhaps, hardly necessary to say that this doctrine is meant to apply only to human beings in the maturity of their faculties. We are not speaking of children, or of young persons below the age which the law may fix as that of manhood or womanhood. Those who are still in a state to require being taken care of by others, must be protected against their own actions as well as against external injury. For the same reason, we may leave out of consideration those backward states of society in which the race itself may be considered as in its nonage. The early difficulties in the way of spontaneous progress are so great, that there is seldom any choice of means for overcoming them; and a ruler full of the spirit of improvement is warranted in the use of any expedients that will attain an end, perhaps otherwise unattainable. Despotism is a legitimate mode of government in dealing with barbarians, provided the end be their improvement, and the means justified by actually effecting that end. Liberty, as a principle, has no application to any state of things anterior to the time when mankind have become capable of being improved by free and equal discussion. Until then, there is nothing for them but implicit obedience to an Akbar or a Charlemagne, if they are so fortunate as to find one. But as soon as mankind have attained the capacity of being guided to their own improvement by conviction or persuasion (a period long since reached in all nations with whom we need here concern ourselves), compulsion, either in the direct form or in that of pains and penalties for non-compliance, is no longer admissible as a means to their own good, and justifiable only for the security of others.

It is proper to state that I forego any advantage which could be derived to my argument from the idea of abstract right, as a thing independent of utility. I regard utility as the ultimate appeal on all ethical questions; but it must be utility in the largest sense, grounded on the permanent interests of man as a progressive being. Those interests, I contend, authorize the subjection of individual spontaneity to external control, only in respect to those actions of each, which concern the interest of other people. If any one does an act hurtful to others, there is a *primâ facie* case for punishing him, by law, or, where legal penalties are not safely applicable, by general disapprobation. There are also many positive acts for the benefit of others, which he may rightfully be compelled to perform; such as, to give evidence in a court of justice; to bear his fair share in the common defence, or in any other joint work necessary to the interest of the society of which he enjoys the protection; and to perform certain acts of individual beneficence, such as saving a fellow-creature's life, or interposing to protect the defenceless against ill-usage, things which whenever it is obviously a man's duty to do, he may rightfully be made responsible to society for not doing. A person may cause evil to others not only by his actions but by his inaction, and in either case he is justly accountable to them for the injury. The latter case, it is true, requires a much more cautious exercise of compulsion than the former. To make any one answerable for doing evil to others, is the rule; to make him answerable for not preventing evil, is, comparatively speaking, the exception. Yet there are many cases clear enough and grave enough to justify that exception. In all things which regard the external relations of the individual, he is *de jure* amenable to those whose interests are concerned, and if need be, to society as their protector. There are often good reasons for not holding him to the responsibility; but these reasons must arise from the special expediences of the case: either because it is a kind of case in which he is on the whole likely to act better, when left to his own discretion, than when controlled in any way in which society have it in their power to control him; or because the attempt to exercise control would produce other evils, greater than those which it would prevent. When such reasons as these preclude the enforcement of responsibility, the conscience of the agent himself should step into the vacant judgment seat, and protect those interests of others which have no external protection; judging himself all the more rigidly, because the case does not admit of his being made accountable to the judgment of his fellow-creatures.

But there is a sphere of action in which society, as distinguished from the individual, has, if any, only an indirect interest; comprehending all that portion of a person's life and conduct which affects only himself, or if it also affects others, only with their free, voluntary, and undeceived consent and participation. When I say only himself, I mean directly, and in the first instance: for whatever affects himself, may affect others *through* himself; and the objection which may be grounded on this contingency, will receive consideration in the sequel. This, then, is the appropriate region of human liberty. It comprises, first, the inward domain of consciousness; demanding liberty of conscience, in the most comprehensive sense; liberty of thought and feeling; absolute freedom of opinion and sentiment on all subjects, practical or speculative, scientific, moral, or theological. The liberty of expressing and publishing opinions may seem to fall under a different principle, since it belongs to that part of the conduct of an individual which concerns other people; but, being almost of as much importance as the liberty of thought itself, and resting in great part on the same reasons, is practically inseparable from it. Secondly, the principle requires liberty of tastes and pursuits; of framing the plan of our life to suit our own character; of doing as we like, subject to such consequences as may follow: without impediment from our fellow-creatures, so long as what we do does not harm them, even though they should think our conduct foolish, perverse, or wrong. Thirdly, from this liberty of each individual, follows the liberty, within the same limits, of combination among individuals; freedom to unite, for any purpose not involving harm to others: the persons combining being supposed to be of full age, and not forced or deceived.

No society in which these liberties are not, on the whole, respected, is free, whatever may be its form of government; and none is completely free in which they do not exist absolute and unqualified. The only freedom which deserves the name, is that of pursuing our own good in our own way, so long as we do not attempt to deprive others of theirs, or impede their efforts to obtain it. Each is the proper guardian of his own health, whether bodily, or mental and spiritual. Mankind are greater gainers by suffering each other to live as seems good to themselves, than by compelling each to live as seems good to the rest.

Though this doctrine is anything but new, and, to some persons, may have the air of a truism, there is no doctrine which stands more directly opposed to the general tendency of existing opinion and practice. Society has expended fully as much effort in the attempt (according to its lights) to compel people to conform to its notions of personal, as of social excellence. The ancient commonwealths thought themselves entitled to practise, and the ancient philosophers countenanced, the regulation of every part of private conduct by public authority, on the ground that the State had a deep interest in the whole bodily and mental discipline of every one of its citizens; a mode of thinking which may have been admissible in small republics surrounded by powerful enemies, in constant peril of being subverted by foreign attack or internal commotion, and to which even a short interval of relaxed energy and self-command might so easily be fatal, that they could not afford to wait for the salutary permanent effects of freedom. In the modern world, the greater size of political communities, and above all, the separation between spiritual and temporal authority (which placed the direction of men's consciences in other hands than those which controlled their worldly affairs), prevented so great an interference by law in the details of private life; but the engines of moral repression have been wielded more strenuously against divergence from the reigning opinion in self-regarding, than even in social matters; religion, the most powerful of the elements which have entered into the formation of moral feeling, having almost always been governed either by the ambition of a hierarchy, seeking control over every department of human conduct, or by the spirit of Puritanism. And some of those modern reformers who have placed themselves in strongest opposition to the religions of the past, have been noway behind either churches or sects in their assertion of the right of spiritual domination: M. Comte, in particular, whose social system, as unfolded in his *Système de Politique Positive*,[2] aims at establishing (though by moral more than by legal appliances) a despotism of society over the individual, surpassing anything contemplated in the political ideal of the most rigid disciplinarian among the ancient philosophers.

Apart from the peculiar tenets of individual thinkers, there is also in the world at large an increasing inclination to stretch unduly the powers of society over the individual, both by the force of opinion and even by that of legislation: and as the tendency of all the changes taking place in the world is to strengthen society, and diminish the power of the individual, this encroachment is not one of the evils which tend spontaneously to disappear, but, on the contrary, to grow more and more formidable. The disposition of mankind, whether as rulers or as fellow-citizens, to impose their own opinions and inclinations as a rule of conduct on others, is so energetically supported by some of the best and by some of the worst feelings incident to human nature, that it is hardly ever kept under restraint by anything but want of power; and as the power is not declining, but growing, unless a strong barrier of moral conviction can be raised against the mischief, we must expect, in the present circumstances of the world, to see it increase.

It will be convenient for the argument, if, instead of at once entering upon the general

---

[2] August Comte (1798–1857), author of *Système de politique positive* (1851–54), the chief document of the philosophy of positivism.

thesis, we confine ourselves in the first instance to a single branch of it, on which the principle here stated is, if not fully, yet to a certain point, recognised by the current opinions. This one branch is the Liberty of Thought; from which it is impossible to separate the cognate liberty of speaking and of writing. Although these liberties, to some considerable amount, form part of the political morality of all countries which profess religious toleration and free institutions, the grounds, both philosophical and practical, on which they rest, are perhaps not so familiar to the general mind, nor so thoroughly appreciated by many even of the leaders of opinion, as might have been expected. Those grounds, when rightly understood, are of much wider application than to only one division of the subject, and a thorough consideration of this part of the question will be found the best introduction to the remainder. Those to whom nothing which I am about to say will be new, may therefore, I hope, excuse me, if on a subject which for now three centuries has been so often discussed, I venture on one discussion more.

CHAPTER II

Of The Liberty of Thought and Discussion

THE time, it is to be hoped, is gone by, when any defence would be necessary of the "liberty of the press" as one of the securities against corrupt or tyrannical government. No argument, we may suppose, can now be needed, against permitting a legislature or an executive, not identified in interest with the people, to prescribe opinions to them, and determine what doctrines or what arguments they shall be allowed to hear. This aspect of the question, besides, has been so often and so triumphantly enforced by preceding writers, that it needs not be specially insisted on in this place. Though the law of England, on the subject of the press, is as servile to this day as it was in the time of the Tudors, there is little danger of its being actually put in force against political discussion, except during some temporary panic, when fear of insurrection drives ministers and judges from their propriety,[1] and, speaking generally, it is not, in constitutional countries, to be apprehended that the government, whether completely responsible to the people or not, will often attempt to control the expression of opinion, except when in doing so it makes itself the organ of the general intolerance of the public. Let us suppose, therefore, that the government is entirely at one with the people, and never thinks of exerting any power of coercion unless in agreement with what it conceives to be their voice. But I deny the right of the people to exercise such coercion, either by themselves or by their government. The power itself is illegitimate. The best government has no more title to it than the worst. It is as noxious, or more noxious, when exerted in accordance with public opinion, than when in opposition to it. If all mankind minus one, were of one opinion, and only one person were of the contrary opinion, mankind would be no more justified in silencing that one person, than he, if he had the power, would be justified in silencing mankind. Were an opinion a personal possession of no value except to the owner; if to be obstructed in the enjoyment of it were simply a private injury, it would make some difference whether the injury was inflicted only on a few persons or on

---

[1] These words had scarcely been written, when, as if to give them an emphatic contradiction, occurred the Government Press Prosecutions of 1858. That ill-judged interference with the liberty of public discussion has not, however, induced me to alter a single word in the text, nor has it at all weakened my conviction that, moments of panic excepted, the era of pains and penalties for political discussion has, in our own country, passed away. For, in the first place, the prosecutions were not persisted in; and, in the second, they were never, properly speaking, political prosecutions. The offence charged was not that of criticising institutions, or the acts or persons of rulers, but of circulating what was deemed an immoral doctrine, the lawfulness of Tyrannicide.

If the arguments of the present chapter are of any validity, there ought to exist the fullest liberty of professing and discussing, as a matter of ethical conviction, any doctrine, however immoral it may be considered. It would, therefore, be irrelevant and out of place to examine here, whether the doctrine of Tyrannicide deserves that title. I shall content myself with saying, that the subject has been at all times one of the open questions of morals; that the act of a private citizen in striking down a criminal, who, by raising himself above the law, has placed himself beyond the reach of legal punishment or control, has been accounted by whole nations, and by some of the best and wisest of men, not a crime, but an act of exalted virtue; and that, right or wrong, it is not of the nature of assassination, but of civil

many. But the peculiar evil of silencing the expression of an opinion is, that it is robbing the human race; posterity as well as the existing generation; those who dissent from the opinion, still more than those who hold it. If the opinion is right, they are deprived of the opportunity of exchanging error for truth: if wrong, they lose, what is almost as great a benefit, the clearer perception and livelier impression of truth, produced by its collision with error.

It is necessary to consider separately these two hypotheses, each of which has a distinct branch of the argument corresponding to it. We can never be sure that the opinion we are endeavouring to stifle is a false opinion; and if we were sure, stifling it would be an evil still.

First: the opinion which it is attempted to suppress by authority may possibly be true. Those who desire to suppress it, of course deny its truth; but they are not infallible. They have no authority to decide the question for all mankind, and exclude every other person from the means of judging. To refuse a hearing to an opinion, because they are sure that it is false, is to assume that *their* certainty is the same thing as *absolute* certainty. All silencing of discussion is an assumption of infallibility. Its condemnation may be allowed to rest on this common argument, not the worse for being common.

Unfortunately for the good sense of mankind, the fact of their fallibility is far from carrying the weight in their practical judgment, which is always allowed to it in theory; for while every one well knows himself to be fallible, few think it necessary to take any precautions against their own fallibility, or admit the supposition that any opinion, of which they feel very certain, may be one of the examples of the error to which they acknowledge themselves to be liable. Absolute princes, or others who are accustomed to unlimited deference, usually feel this complete confidence in their own opinions on nearly all subjects. People more happily situated, who sometimes hear their opinions disputed, and are not wholly unused to be set right when they are wrong, place the same unbounded reliance only on such of their opinions as are shared by all who surround them, or to whom they habitually

defer: for in proportion to a man's want of confidence in his own solitary judgment, does he usually repose, with implicit trust, on the infallibility of "the world" in general. And the world, to each individual, means the part of it with which he comes in contact; his party, his sect, his church, his class of society: the man may be called, by comparison, almost liberal and large-minded to whom it means anything so comprehensive as his own country or his own age. Nor is his faith in this collective authority at all shaken by his being aware that other ages, countries, sects, churches, classes, and parties have thought, and even now think, the exact reverse. He devolves upon his own world the responsibility of being in the right against the dissentient worlds of other people; and it never troubles him that mere accident has decided which of these numerous worlds is the object of his reliance, and that the same causes which make him a Churchman in London, would have made him a Buddhist or a Confucian in Pekin. Yet it is as evident in itself, as any amount of argument can make it, that ages are no more infallible than individuals; every age having held many opinions which subsequent ages have deemed not only false but absurd; and it is as certain that many opinions, now general, will be rejected by future ages, as it is that many, once general, are rejected by the present.

The objection likely to be made to this argument, would probably take some such form as the following. There is no greater assumption of infallibility in forbidding the propagation of error, than in any other thing which is done by public authority on its own judgment and responsibility. Judgment is given to men that they may use it. Because it may be used erroneously, are men to be told that they ought not to use it at all? To prohibit what they think pernicious, is not claiming exemption from error, but fulfilling the duty incumbent on them, although fallible, of acting on their conscientious conviction. If we were never to act on our opinions, because those opinions may be wrong, we should leave all our interests uncared for, and all our duties unperformed. An objection which applies to all conduct, can be no valid objection to any conduct in particular. It is the duty of governments, and

---

war. As such, I hold that the instigation to it, in a specific case, may be a proper subject of punishment, but only if an overt act has followed, and at least a probable connexion can be established between the act and the instigation. Even then, it is not a foreign government, but the very government assailed, which alone, in the exercise of self-defence, can legitimately punish attacks directed against its own existence. [Mill's note]

of individuals, to form the truest opinions they can; to form them carefully, and never impose them upon others unless they are quite sure of being right. But when they are sure (such reasoners may say), it is not conscientiousness but cowardice to shrink from acting on their opinions, and allow doctrines which they honestly think dangerous to the welfare of mankind, either in this life or in another, to be scattered abroad without restraint, because other people, in less enlightened times, have persecuted opinions now believed to be true. Let us take care, it may be said, not to make the same mistake: but governments and nations have made mistakes in other things, which are not denied to be fit subjects for the exercise of authority: they have laid on bad taxes, made unjust wars. Ought we therefore to lay on no taxes, and, under whatever provocation, make no wars? Men, and governments, must act to the best of their ability. There is no such thing as absolute certainty, but there is assurance sufficient for the purposes of human life. We may, and must, assume our opinion to be true for the guidance of our own conduct: and it is assuming no more when we forbid bad men to pervert society by the propagation of opinions which we regard as false and pernicious.

I answer, that it is assuming very much more. There is the greatest difference between presuming an opinion to be true, because, with every opportunity for contesting it, it has not been refuted, and assuming its truth for the purpose of not permitting its refutation. Complete liberty of contradicting and disproving our opinion, is the very condition which justifies us in assuming its truth for purposes of action; and on no other terms can a being with human faculties have any rational assurance of being right.

When we consider either the history of opinion, or the ordinary conduct of human life, to what is it to be ascribed that the one and the other are no worse than they are? Not certainly to the inherent force of the human understanding; for, on any matter not self-evident, there are ninety-nine persons totally incapable of judging of it, for one who is capable; and the capacity of the hundredth person is only comparative; for the majority of the eminent men of every past generation held many opinions now known to be erroneous, and did or approved numerous things which no one will now justify. Why is it, then, that there is on the whole a preponderance among mankind of rational opinions and rational conduct? If there really is this preponderance—which there must be, unless human affairs are, and have always been, in an almost desperate state—it is owing to a quality of the human mind, the source of everything respectable in man either as an intellectual or as a moral being, namely, that his errors are corrigible. He is capable of rectifying his mistakes, by discussion and experience. Not by experience alone. There must be discussion, to show how experience is to be interpreted. Wrong opinions and practices gradually yield to fact and argument: but facts and arguments, to produce any effect on the mind, must be brought before it. Very few facts are able to tell their own story, without comments to bring out their meaning. The whole strength and value, then, of human judgment, depending on the one property, that it can be set right when it is wrong, reliance can be placed on it only when the means of setting it right are kept constantly at hand. In the case of any person whose judgment is really deserving of confidence, how has it become so? Because he has kept his mind open to criticism of his opinions and conduct. Because it has been his practice to listen to all that could be said against him; to profit by as much of it as was just, and expound to himself, and upon occasion to others, the fallacy of what was fallacious. Because he has felt, that the only way in which a human being can make some approach to knowing the whole of a subject, is by hearing what can be said about it by persons of every variety of opinion, and studying all modes in which it can be looked at by every character of mind. No wise man ever acquired his wisdom in any mode but this; nor is it in the nature of human intellect to become wise in any other manner. The steady habit of correcting and completing his own opinion by collating it with those of others, so far from causing doubt and hesitation in carrying it into practice, is the only stable foundation for a just reliance on it: for, being cognisant of all that can, at least obviously, be said against him, and having taken up his position against all gainsayers—knowing that he has sought for objections and difficulties, instead of avoiding them, and has shut out no light which can be thrown upon the subject from any quarter—he has a right to think his judgment better than that of any person, or any multitude, who have not gone through a similar process.

It is not too much to require that what the wisest of mankind, those who are best entitled to trust their own judgment, find necessary to warrant their relying on it, should be submitted to by that miscellaneous collection of a few wise and many foolish individuals, called the public. The most intolerant of churches, the Roman Catholic Church, even at the canonization of a saint, admits, and listens patiently to, a "devil's advocate." The holiest of men, it appears, cannot be admitted to posthumous honours, until all that the devil could say against him is known and weighed. If even the Newtonian philosophy were not permitted to be questioned, mankind could not feel as complete assurance of its truth as they now do. The beliefs which we have most warrant for, have no safeguard to rest on, but a standing invitation to the whole world to prove them unfounded. If the challenge is not accepted, or is accepted and the attempt fails, we are far enough from certainty still; but we have done the best that the existing state of human reason admits of; we have neglected nothing that could give the truth a chance of reaching us: if the lists are kept open, we may hope that if there be a better truth, it will be found when the human mind is capable of receiving it; and in the meantime we may rely on having attained such approach to truth, as is possible in our own day. This is the amount of certainty attainable by a fallible being, and this the sole way of attaining it.

Strange it is, that men should admit the validity of the arguments for free discussion, but object to their being "pushed to an extreme"; not seeing that unless the reasons are good for an extreme case, they are not good for any case. Strange that they should imagine that they are not assuming infallibility, when they acknowledge that there should be free discussion on all subjects which can possibly be *doubtful*, but think that some particular principle or doctrine should be forbidden to be questioned because it is *so certain*, that is, because *they are certain* that it is certain. To call any proposition certain, while there is any one who would deny its certainty if permitted, but who is not permitted, is to assume that we ourselves, and those who agree with us, are the judges of certainty, and judges without hearing the other side.

In the present age—which has been described as "destitute of faith, but terrified at scepticism"[2] —in which people feel sure, not so much that their opinions are true, as that they should not know what to do without them—the claims of an opinion to be protected from public attack are rested not so much on its truth, as on its

importance to society. There are, it is alleged, certain beliefs, so useful, not to say indispensable to well-being, that it is as much the duty of governments to uphold those beliefs, as to protect any other of the interests of society. In a case of such necessity, and so directly in the line of their duty, something less than infallibility may, it is maintained, warrant, and even bind, governments, to act on their own opinion, confirmed by the general opinion of mankind. It is also often argued, and still oftener thought, that none but bad men would desire to weaken these salutary beliefs; and there can be nothing wrong, it is thought, in restraining bad men, and prohibiting what only such men would wish to practise. This mode of thinking makes the justification of restraints on discussion not a question of the truth of doctrines, but of their usefulness; and flatters itself by that means to escape the responsibility of claiming to be an infallible judge of opinions. But those who thus satisfy themselves, do not perceive that the assumption of infallibility is merely shifted from one point to another. The usefulness of an opinion is itself matter of opinion: as disputable, as open to discussion, and requiring as much, as the opinion itself There is the same need of an infallible judge of opinions to decide an opinion to be noxious, as to decide it to be false, unless the opinion condemned has full opportunity of defending itself. And it will not do to say that the heretic may be allowed to maintain the utility or harmlessness of his opinion, though forbidden to maintain its truth. The truth of an opinion is part of its utility. If we would know whether or not it is desirable that a proposition should be believed, is it possible to exclude the consideration of whether or not it is true? In the opinion, not of bad men, but of the best men, no belief which is contrary to truth can be really useful: and can you prevent such men from urging that plea, when they are charged with culpability for denying some doctrine which they are told is useful, but which they believe to be false? Those who are on the side of received opinions, never fail to take all possible advantage of this plea; you do not find *them* handling the question of utility as if it could be completely abstracted from that of truth: on the contrary, it is, above all, because their doctrine is "the truth," that the knowledge or the belief of it is held to be so indispensable. There can be no fair discussion of the question of usefulness, when an argument so vital may be employed

_____
[2] By Carlyle.

on one side, but not on the other. And in point of fact, when law or public feeling do not permit the truth of an opinion to be disputed, they are just as little tolerant of a denial of its usefulness. The utmost they allow is an extenuation of its absolute necessity, or of the positive guilt of rejecting it.

In order more fully to illustrate the mischief of denying a hearing to opinions because we, in our own judgment, have condemned them, it will be desirable to fix down the discussion to a concrete case; and I choose, by preference, the cases which are least favourable to me—in which the argument against freedom of opinion, both on the score of truth and on that of utility, is considered the strongest. Let the opinions impugned be the belief in a God and in a future state, or any of the commonly received doctrines of morality. To fight the battle on such ground, gives a great advantage to an unfair antagonist; since he will be sure to say (and many who have no desire to be unfair will say it internally), Are these the doctrines which you do not deem sufficiently certain to be taken under the protection of law? Is the belief in a God one of the opinions, to feel sure of which, you hold to be assuming infallibility? But I must be permitted to observe, that it is not the feeling sure of a doctrine (be it what it may) which I call an assumption of infallibility. It is the undertaking to decide that question *for others*, without allowing them to hear what can be said on the contrary side. And I denounce and reprobate this pretension not the less, if put forth on the side of my most solemn convictions. However positive any one's persuasion may be, not only of the falsity, but of the pernicious consequences—not only of the pernicious consequences, but (to adopt expressions which I altogether condemn) the immorality and impiety of an opinion; yet if, in pursuance of that private judgment, though backed by the public judgment of his country or his contemporaries, he prevents the opinion from being heard in its defence, he assumes infallibility. And so far from the assumption being less objectionable or less dangerous because the opinion is called immoral or impious, this is the case of all others in which it is most fatal. These are exactly the occasions on which the men of one generation commit those dreadful mistakes, which excite the astonishment and horror of posterity. It is among such that we find the instances memorable in history, when the arm of the law has been employed to root out the best men and the noblest doctrines; with deplorable success as to the men, though some of the doctrines have survived to be (as if in mockery) invoked, in defence of similar conduct towards those who dissent from *them*, or from their received interpretation.

Mankind can hardly be too often reminded, that there was once a man named Socrates, between whom and the legal authorities and public opinion of his time, there took place a memorable collision. Born in an age and country abounding in individual greatness, this man has been handed down to us by those who best knew both him and the age, as the most virtuous man in it; while *we* know him as the head and prototype of all subsequent teachers of virtue, the source equally of the lofty inspiration of Plato and the judicious utilitarianism of Aristotle, "*i maëstri di color che sanno,*"[3] the two headsprings of ethical as of all other philosophy. This acknowledged master of all the eminent thinkers who have since lived—whose fame, still growing after more than two thousand years, all but outweighs the whole remainder of the names which make his native city illustrious—was put to death by his countrymen, after a judicial conviction, for impiety and immorality. Impiety, in denying the gods recognised by the State; indeed his accuser asserted (see the "Apologia") that he believed in no gods at all. Immorality, in being, by his doctrines and instructions, a "corruptor of youth." Of these charges the tribunal, there is every ground for believing, honestly found him guilty, and condemned the man who probably of all then born had deserved best of mankind, to be put to death as a criminal.

To pass from this to the only other instance of judicial iniquity, the mention of which, after the condemnation of Socrates, would not be an anticlimax: the event which took place on Calvary rather more than eighteen hundred years ago. The man who left on the memory of those who witnessed his life and conversation, such an impression of his moral grandeur, that eighteen subsequent centuries have done homage to him as the Almighty in person, was ignominiously put to death, as what? As a blasphemer. Men did not merely mistake their benefactor; they mistook him for the exact contrary of what he was, and treated him as that prodigy of impiety, which they themselves are now held to be, for their treatment of him. The feelings with which man-

---

[3] "The Masters of those who know" (Dante).

kind now regard these lamentable transactions, especially the later of the two, render them extremely unjust in their judgment of the unhappy actors. These were, to all appearance, not bad men—not worse than men commonly are, but rather the contrary; men who possessed in a full, or somewhat more than a full measure, the religious, moral, and patriotic feelings of their time and people: the very kind of men who, in all times, our own included, have every chance of passing through life blameless and respected. The high-priest who rent his garments when the words were pronounced, which, according to all the ideas of his country, constituted the blackest guilt, was in all probability quite as sincere in his horror and indignation, as the generality of respectable and pious men now are in the religious and moral sentiments they profess; and most of those who now shudder at his conduct, if they had lived in his time, and been born Jews, would have acted precisely as he did. Orthodox Christians who are tempted to think that those who stoned to death the first martyrs must have been worse men than they themselves are, ought to remember that one of those persecutors was Saint Paul.

Let us add one more example, the most striking of all, if the impressiveness of an error is measured by the wisdom and virtue of him who falls into it. If ever any one, possessed of power, had grounds for thinking himself the best and most enlightened among his contemporaries, it was the Emperor Marcus Aurelius. Absolute monarch of the whole civilized world, he preserved through life not only the most unblemished justice, but what was less to be expected from his Stoical breeding, the tenderest heart. The few failings which are attributed to him, were all on the side of indulgence: while his writings, the highest ethical product of the ancient mind, differ scarcely perceptibly, if they differ at all, from the most characteristic teachings of Christ. This man, a better Christian in all but the dogmatic sense of the word, than almost any of the ostensibly Christian sovereigns who have since reigned, persecuted Christianity. Placed at the summit of all the previous attainments of humanity, with an open, unfettered intellect, and a character which led him of himself to embody in his moral writings the Christian ideal, he yet failed to see that Christianity was to be a good and not an evil to the world, with his duties to which he was so deeply penetrated. Existing society he knew to be in a deplorable state. But such as it was, he saw, or thought he saw, that it was held to-gether, and prevented from being worse, by belief and reverence of the received divinities. As a ruler of mankind, he deemed it his duty not to suffer society to fall in pieces; and saw not how, if its existing ties were removed, any others could be formed which could again knit it together. The new religion openly aimed at dissolving these ties: unless, therefore, it was his duty to adopt that religion, it seemed to be his duty to put it down. Inasmuch then as the theology of Christianity did not appear to him true or of divine origin; inasmuch as this strange history of a crucified God was not credible to him, and a system which purported to rest entirely upon a foundation to him so wholly unbelievable, could not be forseen by him to be that renovating agency which, after all abatements, it has in fact proved to be; the gentlest and most amiable of philosophers and rulers, under a solemn sense of duty, authorized the persecution of Christianity. To my mind this is one of the most tragical facts in all history. It is a bitter thought, how different a thing the Christianity of the world might have been, if the Christian faith had been adopted as the religion of the empire under the auspices of Marcus Aurelius instead of those of Constantine. But it would be equally unjust to him and false to truth, to deny, that no one plea which can be for punishing anti-Christian teaching, was wanting to Marcus Aurelius for punishing, as he did, the propagation of Christianity. No Christian more firmly believes that Atheism is false, and tends to the dissolution of society, than Marcus Aurelius believed the same things of Christianity; he who, of all men then living, might have been thought the most capable of appreciating it. Unless any one who approves of punishment for the promulgation of opinions, flatters himself that he is a wiser and better man than Marcus Aurelius—more deeply versed in the wisdom of his time, more elevated in his intellect above it— more earnest in his search for truth, or more single-minded in his devotion to it when found;— let him abstain from that assumption of the joint infallibility of himself and the multitude, which the great Antoninus made with so unfortunate a result.

Aware of the impossibility of defending the use of punishment for restraining irreligious opinions, by any argument which will not justify Marcus Antoninus, the enemies of religious freedom, when hard pressed, occasionally accept this consequence, and say, with Dr. Johnson, that the persecutors of Christianity were in the right," that persecution is an ordeal through which truth ought to pass, and always passes successfully, legal penalties being, in the end, powerless against truth, though sometimes beneficially effective against mischievous errors. This is a form of the argument for religious intolerance, sufficiently remarkable not to be passed without notice.

A theory which maintains that truth may justifiably be persecuted because persecution cannot possibly do it any harm, cannot be charged with being intentionally hostile to the reception of new truths; but we cannot commend the generosity of its dealing with the persons to whom mankind are indebted for them. To discover to the world something which deeply concerns it, and of which it was previously ignorant; to prove to it that it had been mistaken on some vital point of temporal or spiritual interest, is as important a service as a human being can render to his fellow-creatures, and in certain cases, as in those of the early Christians and of the Reformers, those who think with Dr. Johnson believe it to have been the most precious gift which could be bestowed on mankind. That the authors of such splendid benefits should be requited by martyrdoms; that their reward should be to be dealt with as the vilest of criminals, is not, upon this theory, a deplorable error and misfortune, for which humanity should mourn in sackcloth and ashes, but the normal and justifiable state of things. The propounder of a new truth, according to this doctrine, should stand, as stood, in the legislation of the Locrians, the proposer of a new law, with a halter round his neck, to be instantly tightened if the public assembly did not, on hearing his reasons, then and there adopt his proposition. People who defend this mode of treating benefactors, cannot be supposed to set much value on the benefit; and I believe this view of the subject is mostly confined to the sort of persons who think that new truths may have been desirable once, but that we have had enough of them now.

But, indeed, the dictum that truth always triumphs over persecution, is one of those pleasant falsehoods which men repeat after one another till they pass into commonplaces, but which all experience refutes. History teems with instances of truth put down by persecution. If not suppressed for ever, it may be thrown back for centuries. To speak only of religious opinions:

the Reformation broke out at least twenty times before Luther, and was put down. Arnold of Brescia was put down. Fra Dolcino was put down. Savonarola was put down.[4] The Albigeois were put down. The Vaudois were put down. The Lollards were put down. The Hussites were put down. Even after the era of Luther, wherever persecution was persisted in, it was successful. In Spain, Italy, Flanders, the Austrian empire, Protestantism was rooted out; and, most likely, would have been so in England, had Queen Mary lived, or Queen Elizabeth died. Persecution has always succeeded, save where the heretics were too strong a party to be effectually persecuted. No reasonable person can doubt that Christianity might have been extirpated in the Roman Empire. It spread, and became predominant, because the persecutions were only occasional, lasting but a short time, and separated by long intervals of almost undisturbed propagandism. It is a piece of idle sentimentality that truth, merely as truth, has any inherent power denied to error, of prevailing against the dungeon and the stake. Men are not more zealous for truth than they often are for error, and a sufficient application of legal or even of social penalties will generally succeed in stopping the propagation of either. The real advantage which truth has, consists in this, that when an opinion is true, it may be extinguished once, twice, or many times, but in the course of ages there will generally be found persons to rediscover it, until some one of its reappearances falls on a time when from favourable circumstances it escapes persecution until it has made such head as to withstand all subsequent attempts to suppress it.

It will be said, that we do not now put to death the introducers of new opinions: we are not like our fathers who slew the prophets, we even build sepulchres to them. It is true we no longer put heretics to death; and the amount of penal infliction which modern feeling would probably tolerate, even against the most obnoxious opinions, is not sufficient to extirpate them. But let us not flatter ourselves that we are yet free from the stain even of legal persecution. Penalties for opinion, or at least for its expression, still exist by law; and their enforcement is not, even in these times, so unexampled as to make it at all incredible that they may some day be revived in full force. In the year 1857, at the assizes of the county of Cornwall, an unfortunate

---

[4] Italian religious reformers of the twelfth, fourteenth, and fifteenth centuries, respectively.

man,[5] said to be of unexceptionable conduct in all relations of life, was sentenced to twenty-one months imprisonment, for uttering, and writing on a gate, some offensive words concerning Christianity. Within a month of the same time, at the Old Bailey, two persons, on two separate occasions,[6] were rejected as jurymen, and one of them grossly insulted by the judge and by one of the counsel, because they honestly declared that they had no theological belief; and a third, a foreigner,[7] for the same reason, was denied justice against a thief. This refusal of redress took place in virtue of the legal doctrine, that no person can be allowed to give evidence in a court of justice, who does not profess belief in a God (any god is sufficient) and in a future state; which is equivalent to declaring such persons to be outlaws, excluded from the protection of the tribunals; who may not only be robbed or assaulted with impunity, if no one but themselves, or persons of similar opinions, be present, but any one else may be robbed or assaulted with impunity, if the proof of the fact depends on their evidence. The assumption on which this is grounded, is that the oath is worthless, of a person who does not believe in a future state; a proposition which betokens much ignorance of history in those who assent to it (since it is historically true that a large proportion of infidels in all ages have been persons of distinguished integrity and honour); and would be maintained by no one who had the smallest conception how many of the persons in greatest repute with the world, both for virtues and for attainments, are well known, at least to their intimates, to be unbelievers. The rule, besides, is suicidal, and cuts away its own foundation. Under pretence that atheists must be liars, it admits the testimony of all atheists who are willing to lie, and rejects only those who brave the obloquy of publicly confessing a detested creed rather than affirm a falsehood. A rule thus self-convicted of absurdity so far as regards its professed purpose, can be kept in force only as a badge of hatred, a relic of persecution; a persecution, too, having the peculiarity, that the qualification for undergoing it, is the being clearly proved not to deserve it. The rule, and the theory it implies, are hardly less insulting to believers than to infidels. For if he who does not believe in a future state, necessarily lies, it follows that they who do believe are only prevented from lying, if prevented they are, by the fear of hell. We will not do the authors and abettors of the rule the injury of supposing, that the conception which they have formed of Christian virtue is drawn from their own consciousness.

These, indeed, are but rags and remnants of persecution, and may be thought to be not so much an indication of the wish to persecute, as an example of that very frequent infirmity of English minds, which makes them take a preposterous pleasure in the assertion of a bad principle, when they are no longer bad enough to desire to carry it really into practice. But unhappily there is no security in the state of the public mind, that the suspension of worse forms of legal persecution, which has lasted for about the space of a generation, will continue. In this age the quiet surface of routine is as often ruffled by attempts to resuscitate past evils, as to introduce new benefits. What is boasted of at the present time as the revival of religion, is always, in narrow and uncultivated minds, at least as much the revival of bigotry; and where there is the strong permanent leaven of intolerance in the feelings of a people, which at all times abides in the middle classes of this country, it needs but little to provoke them into actively persecuting those whom they have never ceased to think proper objects of persecution.[8] For it is this—it is the opinions men entertain, and the feelings they cherish, respecting those who disown the beliefs they deem important, which

---

[5] Thomas Pooley, Bodmin Assizes, July 31, 1857. In December following, he received a free pardon from the Crown. [Mill's note]

[6] George Jacob Holyoake, August 17, 1857; Edward Truelove, July, 1857. [Mill's note]

[7] Baron de Gleichen, Marlborough-street Police Court, August 4, 1857. [Mill's note]

[8] Ample warning may be drawn from the large infusion of the passions of a persecutor, which mingled with the general display of the worst parts of our national character on the occasion of the Sepoy insurrection. The ravings of fanatics or charlatans from the pulpit may be unworthy of notice; but the heads of the Evangelical party have announced as their principle, for the government of Hindoos and Mahomedans, that no schools be supported by public money in which the Bible is not taught, and by necessary consequence that no public employment be given to any but real or pretended Christians. An Under-Secretary of State, in a speech delivered to his constituents on the 12th of November, 1857, is reported to have said: "Toleration of their faith" (the faith of a hundred millions of British subjects), "the superstition which they called religion, by the British Government, had had the effect of retarding the ascendancy of the British name, and preventing the salutary growth of Christianity

makes this country not a place of mental freedom. For a long time past, the chief mischief of the legal penalties is that they strengthen the social stigma. It is that stigma which is really effective, and so effective is it, that the profession of opinions which are under the ban of society is much less common in England, than is, in many other countries, the avowal of those which incur risk of judicial punishment. In respect to all persons but those whose pecuniary circumstances make them independent of the good will of other people, opinion, on this subject, is as efficacious as law; men might as well be imprisoned, as excluded from the means of earning their bread. Those whose bread is already secured, and who desire no favours from men in power, or from bodies of men, or from the public, have nothing to fear from the open avowal of any opinions, but to be ill-thought of and ill-spoken of, and this it ought not to require a very heroic mould to enable them to bear. There is no room for any appeal *ad misericordiam*[9] in behalf of such persons. But though we do not now inflict so much evil on those who think differently from us, as it was formerly our custom to do, it may be that we do ourselves as much evil as ever by our treatment of them. Socrates was put to death, but the Socratic philosophy rose like the sun in heaven, and spread its illumination over the whole intellectual firmament. Christians were cast to the lions, but the Christian church grew up a stately and spreading tree, overtopping the older and less vigorous growths, and stifling them by its shade. Our merely social intolerance kills no one, roots out no opinions, but induces men to disguise them, or to abstain from any active effort for their diffusion. With us, heretical opinions do not perceptibly gain, or even lose, ground in each decade or generation; they never blaze out far and wide, but continue to smoulder in the narrow circles of thinking and studious persons among whom they originate, without ever lighting up the general affairs of mankind with either a true or a deceptive light. And thus is kept up a state of things very satisfactory to some minds, because, without the unpleasant process of fin-

ing or imprisoning anybody, it maintains all prevailing opinions outwardly undisturbed, while it does not absolutely interdict the exercise of reason by dissentients afflicted with the malady of thought. A convenient plan for having peace in the intellectual world, and keeping all things going on therein very much as they do already. But the price paid for this sort of intellectual pacification, is the sacrifice of the entire moral courage of the human mind. A state of things in which a large portion of the most active and inquiring intellects find it advisable to keep the genuine principles and grounds of their convictions within their own breasts, and attempt, in what they address to the public, to fit as much as they can of their own conclusions to premises which they have internally renounced, cannot send forth the open, fearless characters, and logical, consistent intellects who once adorned the thinking world. The sort of men who can be looked for under it, are either mere conformers to commonplace, or time-servers for truth, whose arguments on all great subjects are meant for their hearers, and are not those which have convinced themselves. Those who avoid this alternative, do so by narrowing their thoughts and interest to things which can be spoken of without venturing within the region of principles, that is, to small practical matters, which would come right of themselves, if but the minds of mankind were strengthened and enlarged, and which will never be made effectually right until then: while that which would strengthen and enlarge men's minds, free and daring speculation on the highest subjects, is abandoned.

Those in whose eyes this reticence on the part of heretics is no evil, should consider in the first place, that in consequence of it there is never any fair and thorough discussion of heretical opinions; and that such of them as could not stand such a discussion, though they may be prevented from spreading, do not disappear. But it is not the minds of heretics that are deteriorated most, by the ban placed on all inquiry which does not end in the orthodox conclusions. The greatest harm done is to those who are not

---

.... Toleration was the great cornerstone of the religious liberties of this country; but do not let them abuse that precious word toleration. As he understood it, it meant the complete liberty to all, freedom of worship, *among Christians, who worshipped upon the same foundation.* It meant toleration of all sects and denominations of *Christians who believed in the one mediation.*" I desire to call attention to the fact, that a man who has been deemed fit to fill a high office in the government of this country, under a liberal Ministry, maintains the doctrine that all who do not believe in the divinity of Christ are beyond the pale of toleration. Who, after this imbecile display, can indulge the illusion that religious persecution has passed away, never to return? [Mill's note].

[9] To compassion or mercy.

heretics, and whose whole mental development is cramped, and their reason cowed, by the fear of heresy. Who can compute what the world loses in the multitude of promising intellects combined with timid characters, who dare not follow out any bold, vigorous, independent train of thought, lest it should land them in something which would admit of being considered irreligious or immoral? Among them we may occasionally see some man of deep conscientiousness, and subtle and refined understanding, who spends a life in sophisticating with an intellect which he cannot silence, and exhausts the resources of ingenuity in attempting to reconcile the promptings of his conscience and reason with orthodoxy, which yet he does not, perhaps, to the end succeed in doing. No one can be a great thinker who does not recognise, that as a thinker it is his first duty to follow his intellect to whatever conclusions it may lead. Truth gains more even by the errors of one who, with due study and preparation, thinks for himself, than by the true opinions of those who only hold them because they do not suffer themselves to think. Not that it is solely, or chiefly, to form great thinkers, that freedom of thinking is required. On the contrary, it is as much, and even more indispensable, to enable average human beings to attain the mental stature which they are capable of. There have been, and may again be, great individual thinkers, in a general atmosphere of mental slavery. But there never has been, nor ever will be, in that atmosphere, an intellectually active people. Where any people has made a temporary approach to such a character, it has been because the dread of heterodox speculation was for a time suspended. Where there is a tacit convention that principles are not to be disputed; where the discussion of the greatest questions which can occupy humanity is considered to be closed, we cannot hope to find that generally high scale of mental activity which has made some periods of history so remarkable. Never when controversy avoided the subjects which are large and important enough to kindle enthusiasm, was the mind of a people stirred up from its foundations, and the impulse given which raised even persons of the most ordinary intellect to something of the dignity of thinking beings. Of such we have had an example in the condition of Europe during the times immediately following the Reformation; another, though limited to the Continent and to a more cultivated class, in the speculative movement of the latter half of the eighteenth century;

and a third, of still briefer duration, in the intellectual fermentation of Germany during the Goethian and Fichtean period. These periods differed widely in the particular opinions which they developed; but were alike in this, that during all three the yoke of authority was broken. In each, an old mental despotism had been thrown off, and no new one had yet taken its place. The impulse given at these three periods has made Europe what it now is. Every single improvement which has taken place either in the human mind or in institutions, may be traced distinctly to one or other of them. Appearances have for some time indicated that all three impulses are well nigh spent; and we can expect no fresh start, until we again assert our mental freedom.

Let us now pass to the second division of the argument, and dismissing the supposition that any of the received opinions may be false, let us assume them to be true, and examine into the worth of the manner in which they are likely to be held, when their truth is not freely and openly canvassed. However unwillingly a person who has a strong opinion may admit the possibility that his opinion may be false, he ought to be moved by the consideration that however true it may be, if it is not fully, frequently, and fearlessly discussed, it will be held as a dead dogma, not a living truth.

There is a class of persons (happily not quite so numerous as formerly) who think it enough if a person assents undoubtingly to what they think true, though he has no knowledge whatever of the grounds of the opinion, and could not make a tenable defence of it against the most superficial objections. Such persons, if they can once get their creed taught from authority, naturally think that no good, and some harm, comes of its being allowed to be questioned. Where their influence prevails, they make it nearly impossible for the received opinion to be rejected wisely and considerately, though it may still be rejected rashly and ignorantly; for to shut out discussion entirely is seldom possible, and when it once gets in, beliefs not grounded on conviction are apt to give way before the slightest semblance of an argument. Waving, however, this possibility— assuming that the true opinion abides in the mind, but abides as a prejudice, a belief independent of, and proof against, argument—this is not the way in which truth ought to be held by a rational being. This is not knowing the truth. Truth, thus held, is but one superstition the more, accidentally clinging to the words which enunciate a truth.

If the intellect and judgment of mankind ought to be cultivated, a thing which Protestants at least do not deny, on what can these faculties be more appropriately exercised by any one, than on the things which concern him so much that it is considered necessary for him to hold opinions on them? If the cultivation of the understanding consists in one thing more than in another, it is surely in learning the grounds of one's own opinions. Whatever people believe, on subjects on which it is of the first importance to believe rightly, they ought to be able to defend against at least the common objections. But, some one may say, "Let them be *taught* the grounds of their opinions. It does not follow that opinions must be merely parroted because they are never heard controverted. Persons who learn geometry do not simply commit the theorems to memory, but understand and learn likewise the demonstrations; and it would be absurd to say that they remain ignorant of the grounds of geometrical truths, because they never hear any one deny, and attempt to disprove them." Undoubtedly: and such teaching suffices on a subject like mathematics, where there is nothing at all to be said on the wrong side of the question. The peculiarity of the evidence of mathematical truths is, that all the argument is on one side. There are no objections, and no answers to objections. But on every subject on which difference of opinion is possible, the truth depends on a balance to be struck between two sets of conflicting reasons. Even in natural philosophy, there is always some other explanation possible of the same facts; some geocentric theory instead of heliocentric, some phlogiston instead of oxygen; and it has to be shown why that other theory cannot be the true one: and until this is shown, and until we know how it is shown, we do not understand the grounds of our opinion. But when we turn to subjects infinitely more complicated, to morals, religion, politics, social relations, and the business of life, three-fourths of the arguments for every disputed opinion consist in dispelling the appearances which favour some opinion different from it. The greatest orator, save one, of antiquity[10], has left it on record that he always studied his adversary's case with as great, if not with still greater, intensity than even his own. What Cicero practised as the means of forensic success, requires to be imitated by all who study any subject in order to arrive at the truth. He who knows only his own side of the case, knows little of that. His reasons may be good, and no one may have been able to refute them. But if he is equally unable to refute the reasons on the opposite side; if he does not so much as know what they are, he has no ground for preferring either opinion. The rational position for him would be suspension of judgment, and unless he contents himself with that, he is either led by authority, or adopts, like the generality of the world, the side to which he feels most inclination. Nor is it enough that he should hear the arguments of adversaries from his own teachers, presented as they state them, and accompanied by what they offer as refutations That is not the way to do justice to the arguments, or bring them into real contact with his own mind. He must be able to hear them from persons who actually believe them; who defend them in earnest, and do their very utmost for them. He must know them in their most plausible and persuasive form; he must feel the whole force of the difficulty which the true view of the subject has to encounter and dispose of; else he will never really possess himself of the portion of truth which meets and removes that difficulty. Ninety-nine in a hundred of what are called educated men are in this condition; even of those who can argue fluently for their opinions. Their conclusion may be true, but it might be false for anything they know: they have never thrown themselves into the mental position of those who think differently from them, and considered what such persons may have to say; and consequently they do not, in any proper sense of the word, know the doctrine which they themselves profess. They do not know those parts of it which explain and justify the remainder; the considerations which show that a fact which seemingly conflicts with another is reconcilable with it, or that, of two apparently strong reasons, one and not the other ought to be preferred. All that part of the truth which turns the scale, and decides the judgment of a completely informed mind, they are strangers to; nor is it ever really known, but to those who have attended equally and impartially to both sides, and endeavoured to see the reasons of both in the strongest light. So essential is this discipline to a real understanding of moral and human subjects, that if opponents of all important truths do not exist, it is indispensable to imagine them, and

---

[10] Cicero. The other great orator was Demosthenes.

supply them with the strongest arguments which the most skilful devil's advocate can conjure up.

To abate the force of these considerations, an enemy of free discussion may be supposed to say, that there is no necessity for mankind in general to know and understand all that can be said against or for their opinions by philosophers and theologians. That it is not needful for common men to be able to expose all the misstatements or fallacies of an ingenious opponent. That it is enough if there is always somebody capable of answering them, so that nothing likely to mislead uninstructed persons remains unrefuted. That simple minds, having been taught the obvious grounds of the truths inculcated on them, may trust to authority for the rest, and being aware that they have neither knowledge nor talent to resolve every difficulty which can be raised, may repose in the assurance that all those which have been raised have been or can be answered, by those who are specially trained to the task.

Conceding to this view of the subject the utmost that can be claimed for it by those most easily satisfied with the amount of understanding of truth which ought to accompany the belief of it; even so, the argument for free discussion is no way weakened. For even this doctrine acknowledges that mankind ought to have a rational assurance that all objections have been satisfactorily answered; and how are they to be answered if that which requires to be answered is not spoken? or how can the answer be known to be satisfactory, if the objectors have no opportunity of showing that it is unsatisfactory? If not the public, at least the philosophers and theologians who are to resolve the difficulties, must make themselves familiar with those difficulties in their most puzzling form; and this cannot be accomplished unless they are freely stated, and placed in the most advantageous light which they admit of. The Catholic Church has its own way of dealing with this embarrassing problem. It makes a broad separation between those who can be permitted to receive its doctrines on conviction, and those who must accept them on trust. Neither, indeed, are allowed any choice as to what they will accept; but the clergy, such at least as can be fully confided in, may admissibly and meritoriously make themselves acquainted with the arguments of opponents, in order to answer them, and may, therefore, read heretical books; the laity, not unless by special permission,

hard to be obtained. This discipline recognises a knowledge of the enemy's case as beneficial to the teachers, but finds means, consistent with this, of denying it to the rest of the world: thus giving to the *élite* more mental culture, though not more mental freedom, than it allows to the mass. By this device it succeeds in obtaining the kind of mental superiority which its purposes require; for though culture without freedom never made a large and liberal mind, it can make a clever *nisi prius* advocate of a cause.[11] But in countries professing Protestantism, this resource is denied; since Protestants hold, at least in theory, that the responsibility for the choice of a religion must be borne by each for himself, and cannot be thrown off upon teachers. Besides, in the present state of the world, it is practically impossible that writings which are read by the instructed can be kept from the uninstructed. If the teachers of mankind are to be cognisant of all that they ought to know, everything must be free to be written and published without restraint.

If, however, the mischievous operation of the absence of free discussion, when the received opinions are true, were confined to leaving men ignorant of the grounds of those opinions, it might be thought that this, if an intellectual, is no moral evil, and does not affect the worth of the opinions, regarded in their influence on the character. The fact, however, is, that not only the grounds of the opinion are forgotten in the absence of discussion, but too often the meaning of the opinion itself. The words which convey it, cease to suggest ideas, or suggest only a small portion of those they were originally employed to communicate. Instead of a vivid conception and a living belief, there remain only a few phrases retained by rote; or, if any part, the shell and husk only of the meaning is retained, the finer essence being lost. The great chapter in human history which this fact occupies and fills, cannot be too earnestly studied and meditated on.

It is illustrated in the experience of almost all ethical doctrines and religious creeds. They are all full of meaning and vitality to those who originate them, and to the direct disciples of the originators. Their meaning continues to be felt in undiminished strength, and is perhaps brought out into even fuller consciousness, so long as the struggle lasts to give the doctrine or creed an ascendancy over other creeds. At last it either

[11] *Nisi prius*, lit. "unless before," arguments and courts having to do with prior validity or invalidity of a case.

prevails, and becomes the general opinion, or its progress stops; it keeps possession of the ground it has gained, but ceases to spread further. When either of these results has become apparent, controversy on the subject flags, and gradually dies away. The doctrine has taken its place, if not as a received opinion, as one of the admitted sects or divisions of opinion: those who hold it have generally inherited, not adopted it; and conversion from one of these doctrines to another, being now an exceptional fact, occupies little place in the thoughts of their professors. Instead of being, as at first, constantly on the alert either to defend themselves against the world, or to bring the world over to them, they have subsided into acquiescence, and neither listen, when they can help it, to arguments against their creed, nor trouble dissentients (if there be such) with arguments in its favour. From this time may usually be dated the decline in the living power of the doctrine. We often hear the teachers of all creeds lamenting the difficulty of keeping up in the minds of believers a lively apprehension of the truth which they nominally recognise, so that it may penetrate the feelings, and acquire a real mastery over the conduct. No such difficulty is complained of while the creed is still fighting for its existence: even the weaker combatants then know and feel what they are fighting for, and the difference between it and other doctrines; and in that period of every creed's existence, not a few persons may be found, who have realized its fundamental principles in all the forms of thought, have weighed and considered them in all their important bearings, and have experienced the full effect on the character, which belief in that creed ought to produce in a mind thoroughly imbued with it. But when it has come to be an hereditary creed, and to be received passively, not actively—when the mind is no longer compelled, in the same degree as at first, to exercise its vital powers on the questions which its belief presents to it, there is a progressive tendency to forget all of the belief except the formularies, or to give it a dull and torpid assent, as if accepting it on trust dispensed with the necessity of realizing it in consciousness, or testing it by personal experience; until it almost ceases to connect itself at all with the inner life of the human being. Then are seen the cases, so frequent in this age of the world as almost to form the majority, in which the creed remains as it were outside the mind, encrusting and petrifying it against all other influences addressed to the higher parts of our nature; manifesting its power

by not suffering any fresh and living conviction to get in, but itself doing nothing for the mind or heart, except standing sentinel over them to keep them vacant.

To what an extent doctrines intrinsically fitted to make the deepest impression upon the mind may remain in it as dead beliefs, without being ever realized in the imagination, the feelings, or the understanding, is exemplified by the manner in which the majority of believers hold the doctrines of Christianity. By Christianity I here mean what is accounted such by all churches and sects—the maxims and precepts contained in the New Testament. These are considered sacred, and accepted as laws, by all professing Christians. Yet it is scarcely too much to say that not one Christian in a thousand guides or tests his individual conduct by reference to those laws. The standard to which he does refer it, is the custom of his nation, his class, or his religious profession. He has thus, on the one hand, a collection of ethical maxims, which he believes to have been vouchsafed to him by infallible wisdom as rules for his government; and on the other, a set of every-day judgments and practices, which go a certain length with some of those maxims, not so great a length with others, stand in direct opposition to some, and are, on the whole, a compromise between the Christian creed and the interests and suggestions of worldly life. To the first of these standards he gives his homage; to the other his real allegiance. All Christians believe that the blessed are the poor and humble, and those who are ill-used by the world; that it is easier for a camel to pass through the eye of a needle than for a rich man to enter the kingdom of heaven; that they should judge not, lest they be judged; that they should swear not at all; that they should love their neighbour as themselves; that if one take their cloak, they should give him their coat also; that they should take no thought for the morrow; that if they would be perfect, they should sell all that they have and give it to the poor. They are not insincere when they say that they believe these things. They do believe them, as people believe what they have always heard lauded and never discussed. But in the sense of that living belief which regulates conduct, they believe these doctrines just up to the point to which it is usual to act upon them. The doctrines in their integrity are serviceable to pelt adversaries with; and it is understood that they are to be put forward (when possible) as the reasons for whatever people do that they think laudable.

But any one who reminded them that the maxims require an infinity of things which they never even think of doing, would gain nothing but to be classed among those very unpopular characters who affect to be better than other people. The doctrines have no hold on ordinary believers —are not a power in their minds. They have an habitual respect for the sound of them, but no feeling which spreads from the words to the things signified, and forces the mind to take *them* in, and make them conform to the formula. Whenever conduct is concerned, they look round for Mr. A and B to direct them how far to go in obeying Christ.

Now we may be well assured that the case was not thus, but far otherwise, with the early Christians. Had it been thus, Christianity never would have expanded from an obscure sect of the despised Hebrews into the religion of the Roman empire. When their enemies said, "See how these Christians love one another" (a remark not likely to be made by anybody now), they assuredly had a much livelier feeling of the meaning of their creed than they have ever had since. And to this cause, probably, it is chiefly owing that Christianity now makes so little progress in extending its domain, and after eighteen centuries, is still nearly confined to Europeans and the descendants of Europeans. Even with the strictly religious, who are much in earnest about their doctrines, and attach a greater amount of meaning to many of them than people in general, it commonly happens that the part which is thus comparatively active in their minds is that which was made by Calvin, or Knox, or some such person much nearer in character to themselves. The sayings of Christ coexist passively in their minds, producing hardly any effect beyond what is caused by mere listening to words so amiable and bland. There are many reasons, doubtless, why doctrines which are the badge of a sect retain more of their vitality than those common to all recognised sects, and why more pains are taken by teachers to keep their meaning alive; but one reason certainly is, that the peculiar doctrines are more questioned, and have to be oftener defended against open gainsayers. Both teachers and learners go to sleep at their post, as soon as there is no enemy in the field.

The same thing holds true, generally speaking, of all traditional doctrines—those of prudence and knowledge of life, as well as of morals or religion. All languages and literatures are full of general observations on life, both as to what it is, and how to conduct oneself in it; observations which everybody knows, which everybody repeats, or hears with acquiescence, which are received as truisms, yet of which most people first truly learn the meaning, when experience, generally of a painful kind, has made it a reality to them. How often, when smarting under some unforeseen misfortune or disappointment, does a person call to mind some proverb or common saying, familiar to him all his life, the meaning of which, if he had ever before felt it as he does now, would have saved him from the calamity. There are indeed reasons for this, other than the absence of discussion: there are many truths of which the full meaning *cannot* be realized, until personal experience has brought it home. But much more of the meaning even of these would have been understood, and what was understood would have been far more deeply impressed on the mind, if the man had been accustomed to hear it argued *pro* and *con* by people who did understand it. The fatal tendency of mankind to leave off thinking about a thing when it is no longer doubtful, is the cause of half their errors. A contemporary author has well spoken of "the deep slumber of a decided opinion."[12]

But what! (it may be asked) Is the absence of unanimity an indispensable condition of true knowledge? Is it necessary that some part of mankind should persist in error, to enable any to realize the truth? Does a belief cease to be real and vital as soon as it is generally received— and is a proposition never thoroughly understood and felt unless some doubt of it remains? As soon as mankind have unanimously accepted a truth, does the truth perish within them? The highest aim and best result of improved intelligence, it has hitherto been thought, is to unite mankind more and more in the acknowledgment of all important truths: and does the intelligence only last as long as it has not achieved its object? Do the fruits of conquest perish by the very completeness of the victory?

I affirm no such thing. As mankind improve, the number of doctrines which are no longer disputed or doubted will be constantly on the increase: and the well-being of mankind may almost be measured by the number and gravity of the truths which have reached the point of being uncontested. The cessation, on one question after another, of serious controversy, is one

---

[12] Arthur Helps, *Thoughts in the Cloister and the Crowd* (1835).

of the necessary incidents of the consolidation of opinion; a consolidation as salutary in the case of true opinions, as it is dangerous and noxious when the opinions are erroneous. But though this gradual narrowing of the bounds of diversity of opinion is necessary in both senses of the term, being at once inevitable and indispensable, we are not therefore obliged to conclude that all its consequences must be beneficial. The loss of so important an aid to the intelligent and living apprehension of a truth, as is afforded by the necessity of explaining it to, or defending it against, opponents, though not sufficient to outweigh, is no trifling drawback from, the benefit of its universal recognition. Where this advantage can no longer be had, I confess I should like to see the teachers of mankind endeavouring to provide a substitute for it; some contrivance for making the difficulties of the question as present to the learner's consciousness, as if they were pressed upon him by a dissentient champion, eager for his conversion.

But instead of seeking contrivances for this purpose, they have lost those they formerly had. The Socratic dialectics, so magnificently exemplified in the dialogues of Plato, were a contrivance of this description. They were essentially a negative discussion of the great questions of philosophy and life, directed with consummate skill to the purpose of convincing any one who had merely adopted the commonplaces of received opinion, that he did not understand the subject—that he as yet attached no definite meaning to the doctrines he professed; in order that, becoming aware of his ignorance, he might be put in the way to attain a stable belief, resting on a clear apprehension both of the meaning of doctrines and of their evidence. The school disputations of the middle ages had a somewhat similar object. They were intended to make sure that the pupil understood his own opinion, and (by necessary correlation) the opinion opposed to it, and could enforce the grounds of the one and confute those of the other. These last-mentioned contests had indeed the incurable defect, that the premises appealed to were taken from authority, not from reason; and, as a discipline to the mind, they were in every respect inferior to the powerful dialectics which formed the intellects of the "Socratici viri":[13] but the modern mind owes far more to both than it is generally willing to admit, and the present modes of education contain nothing which in the smallest

degree supplies the place either of the one or of the other. A person who derives all his instruction from teachers or books, even if he escape the besetting temptation of contenting himself with cram, is under no compulsion to hear both sides; accordingly it is far from a frequent accomplishment, even among thinkers, to know both sides; and the weakest part of what everybody says in defence of his opinion, is what he intends as a reply to antagonists. It is the fashion of the present time to disparage negative logic—that which points out weaknesses in theory or errors in practice, without establishing positive truths. Such negative criticism would indeed be poor enough as an ultimate result; but as a means to attaining any positive knowledge or conviction worthy the name, it cannot be valued too highly; and until people are again systematically trained to it, there will be few great thinkers, and a low general average of intellect, in any but the mathematical and physical departments of speculation. On any other subject no one's opinions deserve the name of knowledge, except so far as he has either had forced upon him by others, or gone through of himself, the same mental process which would have been required of him in carrying on an active controversy with opponents. That, therefore, which when absent, it is so indispensable, but so difficult, to create, how worse than absurd is it to forego, when spontaneously offering itself! If there are any persons who contest a received opinion, or who will do so if law or opinion will let them, let us thank them for it, open our minds to listen to them, and rejoice that there is some one to do for us what we otherwise ought, if we have any regard for either the certainty or the vitality of our convictions, to do with much greater labour for ourselves.

It still remains to speak of one of the principal causes which make diversity of opinion advantageous, and will continue to do so until mankind shall have entered a stage of intellectual advancement which at present seems at an incalculable distance. We have hitherto considered only two possibilities: that the received opinion may be false, and some other opinion, consequently, true; or that, the received opinion being true, a conflict with the opposite error is essential to a clear apprehension and deep feeling of its truth. But there is a commoner case than either of these; when the conflicting doctrines, instead

[13] The Socratics or followers of Socrates.

of being one true and the other false, share the truth between them; and the nonconforming opinion is needed to supply the remainder of the truth, of which the received doctrine embodies only a part. Popular opinions, on subjects not palpable to sense, are often true, but seldom or never the whole truth. They are a part of the truth; sometimes a greater, sometimes a smaller part, but exaggerated, distorted, and disjoined from the truths by which they ought to be accompanied and limited. Heretical opinions, on the other hand, are generally some of these suppressed and neglected truths, bursting the bonds which kept them down, and either seeking reconciliation with the truth contained in the common opinion, or fronting it as enemies, and setting themselves up, with similar exclusiveness, as the whole truth. The latter case is hitherto the most frequent, as, in the human mind, one-sidedness has always been the rule, and many-sidedness the exception. Hence even in revolutions of opinion, one part of the truth usually sets while another rises. Even progress, which ought to superadd, for the most part only substitutes one partial and incomplete truth for another; improvement consisting chiefly in this, that the new fragment of truth is more wanted, more adapted to the needs of the time, than that which it displaces. Such being the partial character of prevailing opinions, even when resting on a true foundation; every opinion which embodies somewhat of the portion of truth which the common opinion omits, ought to be considered precious, with whatever amount of error and confusion that truth may be blended. No sober judge of human affairs will feel bound to be indignant because those who force on our notice truths which we should otherwise have overlooked, overlook some of those which we see. Rather, he will think that so long as popular truth is onesided, it is more desirable than otherwise that unpopular truth should have one-sided asserters too; such being usually the most energetic, and the most likely to compel reluctant attention to the fragment of wisdom which they proclaim as if it were the whole.

Thus, in the eighteenth century, when nearly all the instructed, and all those of the uninstructed who were led by them, were lost in admiration of what is called civilization, and of the marvels of modern science, literature, and philosophy, and while greatly overrating the amount of unlikeness between the men of modern and those of ancient times, indulged the belief that the whole of the difference was in their own

favour; with what a salutary shock did the paradoxes of Rousseau explode like bombshells in the midst, dislocating the compact mass of onesided opinion, and forcing its elements to recombine in a better form and with additional ingredients. Not that the current opinions were on the whole farther from the truth than Rousseau's were; on the contrary they were nearer to it; they contained more of positive truth, and very much less of error. Nevertheless there lay in Rousseau's doctrine, and has floated down the stream of opinion along with it, a considerable amount of exactly those truths which the popular opinion wanted; and these are the deposit which was left behind when the flood subsided. The superior worth of simplicity of life, the enervating and demoralizing effect of the trammels and hypocrisies of artificial society, are ideas which have never been entirely absent from cultivated minds since Rousseau wrote; and they will in time produce their due effect, though at present needing to be asserted as much as ever, and to be asserted by deeds, for words, on this subject, have nearly exhausted their power.

In politics, again, it is almost a commonplace, that a party of order or stability, and a party of progress or reform, are both necessary elements of a healthy state of political life; until the one or the other shall have so enlarged its mental grasp as to be a party equally of order and of progress, knowing and distinguishing what is fit to be preserved from what ought to be swept away. Each of these modes of thinking derives its utility from the deficiencies of the other; but it is in a great measure the opposition of the other that keeps each within the limits of reason and sanity. Unless opinions favourable to democracy and to aristocracy, to property and to equality, to co-operation and to competition, to luxury and to abstinence, to sociality and individuality, to liberty and discipline, and all the other standing antagonisms of practical life, are expressed with equal freedom, and enforced and defended with equal talent and energy, there is no chance of both elements obtaining their due; one scale is sure to go up, and the other down. Truth, in the great practical concerns of life, is so much a question of the reconciling and combining of opposites, that very few have minds sufficiently capacious and impartial to make the adjustment with an approach to correctness, and it has to be made by the rough process of a struggle between combatants fighting under hostile banners. On any of the great open questions just enumerated, if either of the two opinions has a better claim than the other, not merely to be tolerated, but to be encouraged and countenanced, it is the one which happens at the particular time and place to be in a minority. That is the opinion which, for the time being, represents the neglected interests, the side of human well-being which is in danger of obtaining less than its share. I am aware that there is not, in this country, any intolerance of differences of opinion on most of these topics. They are adduced to show, by admitted and multiplied examples, the universality of the fact, that only through diversity of opinion is there, in the existing state of human intellect, a chance of fair play to all sides of the truth. When there are persons to be found, who form an exception to the apparent unanimity of the world on any subject, even if the world is in the right, it is always probable that dissentients have something worth hearing to say for themselves, and that truth would lose something by their silence.

It may be objected, "But *some* received principles, especially on the highest and most vital subjects, are more than half-truths. The Christian morality, for instance, is the whole truth on that subject, and if any one teaches a morality which varies from it, he is wholly in error." As this is of all cases the most important in practice, none can be fitter to test the general maxim. But before pronouncing what Christian morality is or is not, it would be desirable to decide what is meant by Christian morality. If it means the morality of the New Testament, I wonder that any one who derives his knowledge of this from the book itself, can suppose that it was announced, or intended, as a complete doctrine of morals. The Gospel always refers to a pre-existing morality, and confines its precepts to the particulars in which that morality was to be corrected, or superseded by a wider and higher; expressing itself, moreover, in terms most general, often impossible to be interpreted literally, and possessing rather the impressiveness of poetry of eloquence than the precision of legislation. To extract from it a body of ethical doctrine, has never been possible without eking it out from the Old Testament, that is, from a system elaborate indeed, but in many respects barbarous, and intended only for a barbarous people. St. Paul, a declared enemy to this Judaical mode of interpreting the doctrine and filling up the scheme of his Master, equally assumes a pre-existing morality, namely that of the Greeks and Romans; and his advice to Christians is in a great measure a system of accommodation to that; even to the extent of giving an apparent sanction to slavery. What is called Christian, but should rather be termed theological, morality, was not the work of Christ or the Apostles, but is of much later origin, having been gradually built up by the Catholic church of the first five centuries, and though not implicitly adopted by moderns and Protestants, has been much less modified by them than might have been expected. For the most part, indeed, they have contented themselves with cutting off the additions which had been made to it in the middle ages, each sect supplying the place by fresh additions, adapted to its own character and tendencies. That mankind owe a great debt to this morality, and to its early teachers, I should be the last person to deny; but I do not scruple to say of it, that it is, in many important points, incomplete and onesided, and that unless ideas and feelings, not sanctioned by it, had contributed to the formation of European life and character, human affairs would have been in a worse condition than they now are. Christian morality (so called) has all the characters of a reaction; it is, in great part, a protest against Paganism. Its ideal is negative rather than positive; passive rather than active; Innocence rather than Nobleness; Abstinence from Evil, rather than energetic Pursuit of Good: in its precepts (as has been well said) "thou shalt not" predominates unduly over "thou shalt." In its horror of sensuality, it made an idol of asceticism, which has been gradually compromised away into one of legality. It holds out the hope of heaven and the threat of hell, as the appointed and appropriate motives to a virtuous life: in this falling far below the best of the ancients, and doing what lies in it to give to human morality an essentially selfish character, by disconnecting each man's feelings of duty from the interests of his fellow-creatures, except so far as a self-interested inducement is offered to him for consulting them. It is essentially a doctrine of passive obedience; it inculcates submission to all authorities found established; who indeed are not to be actively obeyed when they command what religion forbids, but who are not to be resisted, far less rebelled against, for any amount of wrong to ourselves. And while, in the morality of the best Pagan nations, duty to the state holds even a disproportionate place, infringing on the just liberty of the individual; in purely Christian ethics, that grand department of duty is scarcely noticed or acknowledged. It is in the Koran, not the New Testament, that we read the maxim—"A ruler who appoints any man to an office, when there is in his dominions another man better qualified for it, sins against God and against the State." What little recognition the idea of obligation to the public obtains in modern morality, is derived from Greek and Roman sources, not from Christian; as, even in the morality of private life, whatever exists of magnanimity, highmindedness, personal dignity, even the sense of honour, is derived from the purely human, not the religious part of our education, and never could have grown out of a standard of ethics in which the only worth, professedly recognised, is that of obedience.

I am as far as any one from pretending that these defects are necessarily inherent in the Christian ethics, in every manner in which it can be conceived, or that the many requisites of a complete moral doctrine which it does not contain, do not admit of being reconciled with it. Far less would I insinuate this of the doctrines and precepts of Christ himself. I believe that the sayings of Christ are all that I can see any evidence of their having been intended to be; that they are irreconcileable with nothing which a comprehensive morality requires; that everything which is excellent in ethics may be brought within them, with no greater violence to their language than has been done to it by all who have attempted to deduce from them any practical system of conduct whatever. But it is quite consistent with this, to believe that they contain, and were meant to contain, only a part of the truth; that many essential elements of the highest morality are among the things which are not provided for, nor intended to be provided for, in the recorded deliverances of the Founder of Christianity, and which have been entirely thrown aside in the system of ethics erected on the basis of those deliverances by the Christian Church. And this being so, I think it a great error to persist in attempting to find in the Christian doctrine that complete rule for our guidance, which its author intended it to sanction and enforce, but only partially to provide. I believe, too, that this narrow theory is becoming a grave practical evil, detracting greatly from the value of the moral training and instruction, which so many well-meaning persons are now at length exerting themselves to promote. I much fear that by attempting to form the mind and feelings on an exclusively religious type, and discarding those secular standards (as for want of a better name they may be called) which heretofore

co-existed with and supplemented the Christian ethics, receiving some of its spirit, and infusing into it some of theirs, there will result, and is even now resulting, a low, abject, servile type of character, which, submit itself as it may to what it deems the Supreme Will, is incapable of rising to or sympathizing in the conception of Supreme Goodness. I believe that other ethics than any which can be evolved from exclusively Christian sources, must exist side by side with Christian ethics to produce the moral regeneration of mankind; and that the Christian system is no exception to the rule, that in an imperfect state of the human mind, the interests of truth require a diversity of opinions. It is not necessary that in ceasing to ignore the moral truths not contained in Christianity, men should ignore any of those which it does contain. Such prejudice, or oversight, when it occurs, is altogether an evil; but it is one from which we cannot hope to be always exempt, and must be regarded as the price paid for an inestimable good. The exclusive pretension made by a part of the truth to be the whole, must and ought to be protested against, and if a reactionary impulse should make the protestors unjust in their turn, this onesidedness, like the other, may be lamented, but must be tolerated. If Christians would teach infidels to be just to Christianity, they should themselves be just to infidelity. It can do truth no service to blink the fact, known to all who have the most ordinary acquaintance with literary history, that a large portion of the noblest and most valuable moral teaching has been the work, not only of men who did not know, but of men who knew and rejected, the Christian faith.

I do not pretend that the most unlimited use of the freedom of enunciating all possible opinions would put an end to the evils of religious or philosophical sectarianism. Every truth which men of narrow capacity are in earnest about, is sure to be asserted, inculcated, and in many ways even acted on, as if no other truth existed in the world, or at all events none that could limit or qualify the first. I acknowledge that the tendency of all opinions to become sectarian is not cured by the freest discussion, but is often heightened and exacerbated thereby; the truth which ought to have been, but was not, seen, being rejected all the more violently because proclaimed by persons regarded as opponents. But it is not on the impassioned partisan, it is on the calmer and more disinterested bystander, that this collision of opinions works its salutary effect. Not the violent conflict between parts of the truth, but the quiet suppression of half of it, is the formidable evil: there is always hope when people are forced to listen to both sides; it is when they attend only to one that errors harden into prejudices, and truth itself ceases to have the effect of truth, by being exaggerated into falsehood. And since there are few mental attributes more rare than that judicial faculty which can sit in intelligent judgment between two sides of a question, of which only one is represented by an advocate before it, truth has no chance but in proportion as every side of it, every opinion which embodies any fraction of the truth, not only finds advocates, but is so advocated as to be listened to.

We have now recognised the necessity to the mental well-being of mankind (on which all their other well-being depends) of freedom of opinion, and freedom of the expression of opinion, on four distinct grounds; which we will now briefly recapitulate.

First, if any opinion is compelled to silence, that opinion may, for aught we can certainly know, be true. To deny this is to assume our own infallibility.

Secondly, though the silenced opinion be an error, it may, and very commonly does, contain a portion of truth; and since the general or prevailing opinion on any subject is rarely or never the whole truth, it is only by the collision of adverse opinions that the remainder of the truth has any chance of being supplied.

Thirdly, even if the received opinion be not only true, but the whole truth; unless it is suffered to be, and actually is, vigorously and earnestly contested, it will, by most of those who receive it, be held in the manner of a prejudice, with little comprehension or feeling of its rational grounds. And not only this, but, fourthly, the meaning of the doctrine itself will be in danger of being lost, or enfeebled, and deprived of its vital effect on the character and conduct: the dogma becoming a mere formal profession, inefficacious for good, but cumbering the ground, and preventing the growth of any real and heart-felt conviction, from reason or personal experience.

Before quitting the subject of freedom of opinion, it is fit to take some notice of those who say, that the free expression of all opinions should be permitted, on condition that the manner be temperate, and do not pass the bounds of fair discussion. Much might be said on the impossibility of fixing where these supposed bounds are

to be placed; for if the test be offence to those whose opinion is attacked, I think experience testifies that this offence is given whenever the attack is telling and powerful, and that every opponent who pushes them hard, and whom they find it difficult to answer, appears to them, if he shows any strong feeling on the subject, an intemperate opponent. But this, though an important consideration in a practical point of view, merges in a more fundamental objection. Undoubtedly the manner of asserting an opinion, even though it be a true one, may be very objectionable, and may justly incur severe censure. But the principal offences of the kind are such as it is mostly impossibly, unless by accidental self-betrayal, to bring home to conviction. The gravest of them is, to argue sophistically, to suppress facts or arguments, to misstate the elements of the case, or misrepresent the opposite opinion. But all this, even to the most aggravated degree, is so continually done in perfect good faith, by persons who are not considered, and in many other respects may not deserve to be considered, ignorant or incompetent, that it is rarely possible on adequate grounds conscientiously to stamp the misrepresentation as morally culpable; and still less could law presume to interfere with this kind of controversial misconduct. With regard to what is commonly meant by intemperate discussion, namely invective, sarcasm, personality, and the like, the denunciation of these weapons would deserve more sympathy if it were ever proposed to interdict them equally to both sides; but it is only desired to restrain the employment of them against the prevailing opinion: against the unprevailing they may not only be used without general disapproval, but will be likely to obtain for him who uses them the praise of honest zeal and righteous indignation. Yet whatever mischief arises from their use, is greatest when they are employed against the comparatively defenceless; and whatever unfair advantage can be derived by any opinion from this mode of asserting it, accrues almost exclusively to received opinions. The worst offence of this kind which can be committed by a polemic, is to stigmatize those who hold the contrary opinion as bad and immoral men. To calumny of this sort, those who hold any unpopular opinion are peculiarly exposed, because they are in general few and uninfluential, and nobody but themselves feels much interest in seeing justice done them; but this weapon is, from the nature of the case, denied to those who attack a prevailing opinion:

they can neither use it with safety to themselves, nor, if they could, would it do anything but recoil on their own cause. In general, opinions contrary to those commonly received can only obtain a hearing by studied moderation of language, and the most cautious avoidance of unnecessary offence, from which they hardly ever deviate even in a slight degree without losing ground: while unmeasured vituperation employed on the side of the prevailing opinion, really does deter people from professing contrary opinions, and from listening to those who profess them. For the interest, therefore, of truth and justice, it is far more important to restrain this employment of vituperative language than the other; and, for example, if it were necessary to choose, there would be much more need to discourage offensive attacks on infidelity, than on religion. It is, however, obvious that law and authority have no business with restraining either, while opinion ought, in every instance, to determine its verdict by the circumstances of the individual case; condemning every one, on whichever side of the argument he places himself, in whose mode of advocacy either want of candour, or malignity, bigotry, or intolerance of feeling manifest themselves; but not inferring these vices from the side which a person takes, though it be the contrary side of the question to our own: and giving merited honour to every one, whatever opinion he may hold, who has calmness to see and honesty to state what his opponents and their opinions really are, exaggerating nothing to their discredit, keeping nothing back which tells, or can be supposed to tell, in their favour. This is the real morality of public discussion; and if often violated, I am happy to think that there are many controversialists who to a great extent observe it, and a still greater number who conscientiously strive towards it.

Thoughts on Poetry and Its Varieties

The following essay first appeared in 1833 in the Monthly Repository *as two separate essays. These were combined and revised by Mill and issued under the new title in 1859. In this essay Mill considers a subject generally neglected by the utilitarian school, demonstrating early in his career the breadth of interest that distinguishes him from most of the philosophic radicals.*

1

IT HAS often been asked, What is Poetry? And many and various are the answers which have been returned. The vulgarest of all—one with which no person possessed of the faculties to which poetry addresses itself can ever have been satisfied—is that which confounds poetry with metrical composition: yet to this wretched mockery of a definition, many had been led back, by the failure of all their attempts to find any other that would distinguish what they have been accustomed to call poetry, from much which they have known only under other names.

That, however, the word poetry imports something quite peculiar in its nature, something which may exist in what is called prose as well as in verse, something which does not even require the instrument of words, but can speak through the other audible symbols called musical sounds, and even through the visible ones which are the language of sculpture, painting, and architecture; all this, we believe, is and must be felt, though perhaps indistinctly, by all upon whom poetry in any of its shapes produces any impression beyond that of tickling the ear. The distinction between poetry and what is not poetry, whether explained or not, is felt to be fundamental: and where every one feels a difference, a difference there must be. All other appearances may be fallacious, but the appearance of a difference is a real difference. Appearances too, like other things, must have a cause, and that which can cause anything, even an illusion, must be a reality. And hence, while a half-philosophy disdains the classifications and distinctions indicated by popular language, philosophy carried to its highest point frames new ones, but rarely sets aside the old, content with correcting and regularizing them. It cuts fresh channels for thought, but does not fill up such as it finds ready-made; it traces, on the contrary, more deeply, broadly, and distinctly, those into which the current has spontaneously flowed.

Let us then attempt, in the way of modest inquiry, not to coerce and confine nature within the bounds of an arbitrary definition, but rather to find the boundaries which she herself has set, and erect a barrier round them; not calling mankind to account for having misapplied the word poetry, but attempting to clear up the conception which they already attach to it, and to bring forward as a distinct principle that which, as a vague feeling, has really guided them in their employment of the term.

The object of poetry is confessedly to act upon the emotions; and therein is poetry sufficiently distinguished from what Wordsworth affirms to be its logical opposite, namely, not prose, but matter of fact or science. The one addresses itself to the belief, the other to the feelings. The one does its work by convincing or persuading, the other by moving. The one acts by presenting a proposition to the understanding, the other by offering interesting objects of contemplation to the sensibilities.

This, however, leaves us very far from a definition of poetry. This distinguishes it from one thing, but we are bound to distinguish it from everything. To bring thoughts or images before the mind for the purpose of acting upon the emotions, does not belong to poetry alone. It is equally the province (for example) of the novelist: and yet the faculty of the poet and that of the novelist are as distinct as any other two faculties; as the faculties of the novelist and of the orator, or of the poet and the metaphysician. The two characters may be united, as characters the most disparate may; but they have no natural connexion.

Many of the greatest poems are in the form of fictitious narratives, and in almost all good serious fictions there is true poetry. But there is a radical distinction between the interest felt in a story as such, and the interest excited by poetry; for the one is derived from incident, the other from the representation of feeling. In one, the source of the emotion excited is the exhibition of a state or states of human sensibility; in the other, of a series of states of mere outward circumstances. Now, all minds are capable of being affected more or less by representations of the latter kind, and all, or almost all, by those of the former; yet the two sources of interest correspond to two distinct, and (as respects their greatest development) mutually exclusive, characters of mind.

At what age is the passion for a story, for almost any kind of story, merely as a story, the most intense? In childhood. But that also is the age at which poetry, even of the simplest description, is least relished and least understood; because the feelings with which it is especially conversant are yet undeveloped, and not having been even in the slightest degree experienced, cannot be sympathized with. In what stage of the progress of society, again, is story-telling most valued, and the story-teller in greatest request and honour?—In a rude state, like that of the Tartars and Arabs at this day, and of almost all nations in the earliest ages. But in this state of society there is little poetry except ballads, which are mostly narrative, that is, essentially stories, and derive their principal interest from the incidents. Considered as poetry, they are of the lowest and most elementary kind: the feelings depicted, or rather indicated, are the simplest our nature has; such joys and griefs as the immediate pressure of some outward event excites in rude minds, which live wholly immersed in outward things, and have never, either from choice or a force they could not resist, turned themselves to the contemplation of the world within. Passing now from childhood, and from the childhood of society, to the grown-up men and women of this most grown-up and unchildlike age—the minds and hearts of greatest depth and elevation are commonly those which take greatest delight in poetry; the shallowest and emptiest, on the contrary, are, at all events, not those least addicted to novel-reading. This accords, too, with all analogous experience of human nature. The sort of persons whom not merely in books, but in their lives, we find perpetually engaged in hunting for excitement from without, are invariably those who do not possess, either in the vigour of their intellectual powers or in the depth of their sensibilities, that which would enable them to find ample excitement nearer home. The most idle and frivolous persons take a natural delight in fictitious narrative; the excitement it affords is of the kind which comes from without. Such persons are rarely lovers of poetry, though they may fancy themselves so, because they relish novels in verse. But poetry, which is the delineation of the deeper and more secret workings of human emotion, is interesting only to those to whom it recalls what they have felt, or whose imagination it stirs up to conceive what they could feel, or what they might have been able to feel had their outward circumstances been different.

Poetry, when it is really such, is truth; and fiction also, if it is good for anything, is truth: but they are different truths. The truth of poetry is to paint the human soul truly: the truth of fiction is to give a true picture of life. The two kinds of knowledge are different, and come by different ways, come mostly to different persons. Great poets are often proverbially ignorant of life. What they know has come by observation of themselves; they have found within them one highly delicate and sensitive specimen of human nature on which the laws of emotion are written in large characters, such as can be read off without much study. Other knowledge of mankind, such as comes to men of the world by outward experience, is not indispensable to them as poets: but to the novelist such knowledge is all in all; he has to describe outward things, not the inward man; actions and events, not feelings; and it will not do for him to be numbered among those who, as Madame Roland said of Brissot, know man but not men.[1]

All this is no bar to the possibility of combining both elements, poetry and narrative or incident, in the same work, and calling it either a novel or a poem; but so may red and white combine on the same human features, or on the same canvas. There is one order of composition which requires the union of poetry and incident, each in its highest kind—the dramatic. Even there the two elements are perfectly distinguishable, and may exist of unequal quality, and in the most various proportion. The incidents of a dramatic poem may be scanty and ineffective, though the delineation of passion and character may be of the highest order; as in Goethe's admirable Torquato Tasso: or again, the story as a mere story may be well got up for effect, as is the case with some of the most trashy productions of the Minerva press:[2] it may even be, what those are not, a coherent and probable series of events, though there be scarcely a feeling exhibited which is not represented falsely, or in a manner absolutely commonplace. The combination of the two excellencies is what renders Shakespeare so generally acceptable, each sort of readers finding in him what is suitable to their faculties. To the many he is great as a story-teller, to the few as a poet.

In limiting poetry to the delineation of states of feeling, and denying the name where nothing is delineated but outward objects, we may be thought to have done what we promised to avoid—to have not found, but made a definition, in opposition to the usage of language, since it is established by common consent that there is a poetry called descriptive. We deny the charge. Description is not poetry because there is descriptive poetry, no more than science is poetry because there is such a thing as a didactic poem. But an object which admits of being described, or a truth which may fill a place in a scientific treatise, may also furnish an occasion for the generation of poetry, which we thereupon choose to call descriptive or didactic. The poetry is not in the object itself, nor in the scientific truth itself, but in the state of mind in which the one and the other may be contemplated. The mere delineation of the dimensions and colours of external objects is not poetry, no more than a geometrical ground-plan of St. Peter's or Westminster Abbey is painting. Descriptive poetry consists, no doubt, in description, but in description of things as they appear, not as they are; and it paints them not in their bare and natural lineaments, but seen through the medium and arrayed in the colours of the imagination set in action by the feelings. If a poet describes a lion, he does not describe him as a naturalist would, nor even as a traveller would, who was intent upon stating the truth, the whole truth, and nothing but the truth. He describes him by imagery, that is, by suggesting the most striking likenesses and contrasts which might occur to a mind contemplating the lion, in the state of awe, wonder, or terror, which the spectacle naturally excites, or is, on the occasion, supposed to excite. Now this is describing the lion professedly, but the state of excitement of the spectator really. The lion may be described falsely or with exaggeration, and the poetry be all the better; but if the human emotion be not painted with scrupulous truth, the poetry is bad poetry, *i.e.* is not poetry at all, but a failure.

Thus far our progress towards a clear view of the essentials of poetry has brought us very close to the last two attempts at a definition of poetry which we happen to have seen in print, both of them by poets and men of genius. The one is by Ebenezer Elliott, the author of "Corn-

---

[1] Mme. Marie Roland (1754–93), author of *Mémoires de Madame Roland* (1795); Jacques Pierre Brissot de Warville (1754–93), leader of the Girondists in the French Revolution. Both were guillotined.
[2] Publishing house for sensational novels.

Law Rhymes," and other poems of still greater merit. "Poetry," says he, "is impassioned truth." The other is by a writer in Blackwood's Magazine, and comes, we think, still nearer the mark. He defines poetry, "man's thoughts tinged by his feelings."[3] There is in either definition a near approximation to what we are in search of. Every truth which a human being can enunciate, every thought, even every outward impression, which can enter into his consciousness, may become poetry when shown through any impassioned medium, when invested with the colouring of joy, or grief, or pity, or affection, or admiration, or reverence, or awe, or even hatred or terror: and, unless so coloured, nothing, be it as interesting as it may, is poetry. But both these definitions fail to discriminate between poetry and eloquence. Eloquence, as well as poetry, is impassioned truth; eloquence, as well as poetry, is thoughts coloured by the feelings. Yet common apprehension and philosophic criticism alike recognise a distinction between the two: there is much that every one would call eloquence, which no one would think of classing as poetry. A question will sometimes arise, whether some particular author is a poet; and those who maintain the negative commonly allow, that though not a poet, he is a highly eloquent writer. The distinction between poetry and eloquence appears to us to be equally fundamental with the distinction between poetry and narrative, or between poetry and description, while it is still farther from having been satisfactorily cleared up than either of the others.

Poetry and eloquence are both alike the expression or utterance of feeling. But if we may be excused the antithesis, we should say that eloquence is *heard*, poetry is *over*heard. Eloquence supposes an audience; the peculiarity of poetry appears to us to lie in the poet's utter unconsciousness of a listener. Poetry is feeling, confessing itself to itself in moments of solitude, and embodying itself in symbols, which are the nearest possible representations of the feeling in the exact shape in which it exists in the poet's mind. Eloquence is feeling pouring itself out to other minds, courting their sympathy, or endeavouring to influence their belief, or move them to passion or to action.

All poetry is of the nature of soliloquy. It may be said that poetry which is printed on hot-pressed paper and sold at a book-seller's shop, is a soliloquy in full dress, and on the stage. It is so; but there is nothing absurd in the idea of such a mode of soliloquizing. What we have said to ourselves, we may tell to others afterwards; what we have said or done in solitude, we may voluntarily reproduce when we know that other eyes are upon us. But no trace of consciousness that any eyes are upon us must be visible in the work itself. The actor knows that there is an audience present; but if he act as though he knew it, he acts ill. A poet may write poetry not only with the intention of printing it, but for the express purpose of being paid for it; that it should *be* poetry, being written under such influences, is less probable; not, however, impossible; but no otherwise possible than if he can succeed in excluding from his work every vestige of such lookings-forth into the outward and every-day world, and can express his emotions exactly as he has felt them in solitude, or as he is conscious that he should feel them though they were to remain for ever unuttered, or (at the lowest) as he knows that others feel them in similar circumstances of solitude. But when he turns round and addresses himself to another person; when the act of utterance is not itself the end, but a means to an end—viz. by the feelings he himself expresses, to work upon the feelings, or upon the belief, or the will, of another, —when the expression of his emotions, or of his thoughts tinged by his emotions, is tinged also by that purpose, by that desire of making an impression upon another mind, then it ceases to be poetry, and becomes eloquence.

Poetry, accordingly, is the natural fruit of solitude and meditation; eloquence, of intercourse with the world. The persons who have most feeling of their own, if intellectual culture has given them a language in which to express it, have the highest faculty of poetry; those who best understand the feelings of others, are the most eloquent. The persons, and the nations, who commonly excel in poetry, are those whose character and tastes render them least dependent upon the applause, or sympathy, or concurrence of the world in general. Those to whom that applause, that sympathy, that concurrence are most necessary, generally excel most in eloquence. And hence, perhaps, the French, who are the least poetical of all great and intellectual nations, are among the most eloquent: the French, also, being the most sociable, the vainest, and the least self-dependent.

---

[3] Ebenezer Elliot (1781–1849), opponent of the Corn Laws and author of *Corn Law Rhymes*.

If the above be, as we believe, the true theory of the distinction commonly admitted between eloquence and poetry; or even though it be not so, yet if, as we cannot doubt, the distinction above stated be a real *bonâ fide* distinction, it will be found to hold, not merely in the language of words, but in all other language, and to intersect the whole domain of art.

Take, for example, music: we shall find in that art, so peculiarly the expression of passion, two perfectly distinct styles; one of which may be called the poetry, the other the oratory of music. This difference, being seized, would put an end to much musical sectarianism. There has been much contention whether the music of the modern Italian school, that of Rossini and his successors, be impassioned or not. Without doubt, the passion it expresses is not the musing, meditative tenderness, or pathos, or grief of Mozart or Beethoven. Yet it is passion, but garrulous passion—the passion which pours itself into other ears; and therein the better calculated for dramatic effect, having a natural adaptation for dialogue. Mozart also is great in musical oratory; but his most touching compositions are in the opposite style—that of soliloquy. Who can imagine "Dove sono"[4] *heard?* We imagine it *over*heard.

Purely pathetic music commonly partakes of soliloquy. The soul is absorbed in its distress, and though there may be bystanders, it is not thinking of them. When the mind is looking within, and not without, its state does not often or rapidly vary; and hence the even, uninterrupted flow, approaching almost to monotony, which a good reader, or a good singer, will give to words or music of a pensive or melancholy cast. But grief taking the form of a prayer, or of a complaint, becomes oratorical; no longer low, and even, and subdued, it assumes a more emphatic rhythm, a more rapidly returning accent; instead of a few slow equal notes, following one after another at regular intervals, it crowds note upon note, and often assumes a hurry and bustle like joy. Those who are familiar with some of the best of Rossini's serious compositions, such as the air "Tu che i miseri conforti," in the opera of "Tancredi," or the duet "Ebben per mia memoria," in "La Gazza Ladra," will at once understand and feel our meaning. Both are highly tragic and passionate; the passion of both is that of oratory, not poetry. The like

may be said of that most moving invocation in Beethoven's "Fidelio"—

'Komm, Hoffnung, lass den letzen Stern
Der Müden nicht erbleichen";[5]

in which Madame Schröder Devrient exhibited such consummate powers of pathetic expression. How different from Winter's beautiful "Paga fui," the very soul of melancholy exhaling itself in solitude; fuller of meaning, and, therefore, more profoundly poetical than the words for which it was composed—for it seems to express not simple melancholy, but the melancholy of remorse.

If, from vocal music, we now pass to instrumental, we may have a specimen of musical oratory in any fine military symphony or march: while the poetry of music seems to have attained its consummation in Beethoven's Overture to Egmont, so wonderful in its mixed expression of grandeur and melancholy.

In the arts which speak to the eye, the same distinctions will be found to hold, not only between poetry and oratory, but between poetry, oratory, narrative, and simple imitation or description.

Pure description is exemplified in a mere portrait or a mere landscape—productions of art, it is true, but of the mechanical rather than of the fine arts, being works of simple imitation, not creation. We say, a mere portrait, or a mere landscape, because it is possible for a portrait or a landscape, without ceasing to be such, to be also a picture; like Turner's landscapes, and the great portraits by Titian or Vandyke.

Whatever in painting or sculpture expresses human feeling—or character, which is only a certain state of feeling grown habitual—may be called, according to circumstances, the poetry, or the eloquence, of the painter's or the sculptor's art: the poetry, if the feeling declares itself by such signs as escape from us when we are unconscious of being seen; the oratory, if the signs are those we use for the purpose of voluntary communication.

The narrative style answers to what is called historical painting, which it is the fashion among connoisseurs to treat as the climax of the pictorial art. That it is the most difficult branch of the art we do not doubt, because, in its perfection, it includes the perfection of all the other branches: as in like manner an epic poem, though in so

---

[4] From *The Marriage of Figaro.*
[5] "Come, Hope, let not the last star fade from the weary one."

far as it is epic (*i.e.* narrative) it is not poetry at all, is yet esteemed the greatest effort of poetic genius, because there is no kind whatever of poetry which may not appropriately find a place in it. But an historical picture as such, that is, as the representation of an incident, must necessarily, as it seems to us, be poor and ineffective. The narrative powers of painting are extremely limited. Scarcely any picture, scarcely even any series of pictures, tells its own story without the aid of an interpreter. But it is the single figures which, to us, are the great charm even of an historical picture. It is in these that the power of the art is really seen. In the attempt to narrate, visible and permanent signs are too far behind the fugitive audible ones, which follow so fast one after another, while the faces and figures in a narrative picture, even though they be Titian's, stand still. Who would not prefer one Virgin and Child of Raphael, to all the pictures which Rubens, with his fat, frouzy Dutch Venuses, ever painted? Though Rubens, besides excelling almost every one in his mastery over the mechanical parts of his art, often shows real genius in grouping his figures, the peculiar problem of historical painting. But then, who, except a mere student of drawing and colouring, ever cared to look twice at any of the figures themselves? The power of painting lies in poetry, of which Rubens had not the slightest tincture—not in narrative, wherein he might have excelled.

The single figures, however, in an historical picture, are rather the eloquence of painting than the poetry: they mostly (unless they are quite out of place in the picture) express the feelings of one person as modified by the presence of others. Accordingly the minds whose bent leads them rather to eloquence than to poetry, rush to historical painting. The French painters, for instance, seldom attempt, because they could make nothing of, single heads, like those glorious ones of the Italian masters, with which they might feed themselves day after day in their own Louvre. They must all be historical; and they are, almost to a man, attitudinizers. If we wished to give any young artist the most impressive warning our imagination could devise against that kind of vice in the pictorial, which corresponds to rant in the histrionic art, we would advise him to walk once up and once down the gallery of the Luxembourg. Every figure in French painting or statuary seems to be showing

itself off before spectators: they are not poetical, but in the worst style of corrupted eloquence.

II

NASCITUR POËTA[6] is a maxim of classical antiquity, which has passed to these latter days with less questioning than most of the doctrines of that early age. When it originated, the human faculties were occupied, fortunately for posterity, less in examining how the works of genius are created, than in creating them: and the adage, probably, had no higher source than the tendency common among mankind to consider all power which is not visibly the effect of practice, all skill which is not capable of being reduced to mechanical rules, as the result of a peculiar gift. Yet this aphorism, born in the infancy of psychology, will perhaps be found, now when that science is in its adolescence, to be as true as an epigram ever is, that is, to contain some truth: truth, however, which has been so compressed and bent out of shape, in order to tie it up into so small a knot of only two words, that it requires an almost infinite amount of unrolling and laying straight, before it will resume its just proportions.

We are not now intending to remark upon the grosser misapplications of this ancient maxim, which have engendered so many races of poetasters. The days are gone by, when every raw youth whose borrowed phantasies have set themselves to a borrowed tune, mistaking, as Coleridge says, an ardent desire of poetic reputation for poetic genius, while unable to disguise from himself that he had taken no means whereby he might become a poet, could fancy himself a born one. Those who would reap without sowing, and gain the victory without fighting the battle, are ambitious now of another sort of distinction, and are born novelists, or public speakers, not poets. And the wiser thinkers understand and acknowledge that poetic excellence is subject to the same necessary conditions with any other mental endowment; and that to no one of the spiritual benefactors of mankind is a higher or a more assiduous intellectual culture needful than to the poet. It is true, he possesses this advantage over others who use the "instrument of words," that, of the truths which he utters, a large proportion are derived from personal consciousness, and a smaller from philosophic investigation. But the power itself of discriminating between what really is consciousness, and what is only a process of inference completed in a

---

[6] From the expression "Poeta nascitur, non fit" (the poet is born, not made).

single instant—and the capacity of distinguishing whether that of which the mind is conscious be an eternal truth, or but a dream—are among the last results of the most matured and perfect intellect. Not to mention that the poet, no more than any other person who writes, confines himself altogether to intuitive truths, nor has any means of communicating even these but by words, every one of which derives all its power of conveying a meaning, from a whole host of acquired notions, and facts learnt by study and experience.

Nevertheless, it seems undeniable in point of fact, and consistent with the principles of a sound metaphysics, that there are poetic *natures*. There is a mental and physical constitution or temperament, peculiarly fitted for poetry. This temperament will not of itself make a poet, no more than the soil will the fruit; and as good fruit may be raised by culture from indifferent soils, so may good poetry from naturally un-poetical minds. But the poetry of one who is a poet by nature, will be clearly and broadly distinguishable from the poetry of mere culture. It may not be truer; it may not be more useful; but it will be different: fewer will appreciate it, even though many should affect to do so; but in those few it will find a keener sympathy, and will yield them a deeper enjoyment.

One may write genuine poetry, and not be a poet; for whosoever writes out truly any human feeling, writes poetry. All persons, even the most unimaginative, in moments of strong emotion, speak poetry; and hence the drama is poetry, which else were always prose, except when a poet is one of the characters. What is poetry, but the thoughts and words in which emotion spontaneously embodies itself? As there are few who are not, at least for some moments and in some situations, capable of some strong feeling, poetry is natural to most persons at some period of their lives. And any one whose feelings are genuine, though but of the average strength—, if he be not diverted by uncongenial thoughts or occupations from the indulgence of them, and if he acquire by culture, as all persons may, the faculty of delineating them correctly,—has it in his power to be a poet, so far as a life passed in writing unquestionable poetry may be considered to confer that title. But ought it to do so? Yes, perhaps, in a collection of "British Poets." But "poet" is the name also of a variety of man, not solely of the author of a particular variety of book: now, to have written whole volumes of real poetry, is possible to almost all kinds of

characters, and implies no greater peculiarity of mental construction than to be the author of a history or a novel.

Whom, then, shall we call poets? Those who are so constituted, that emotions are the links of association by which their ideas, both sensuous and spiritual, are connected together. This constitution belongs (within certain limits) to all in whom poetry is a pervading principle. In all others, poetry is something extraneous and superinduced: something out of themselves, foreign to the habitual course of their every-day lives and characters; a world to which they may make occasional visits, but where they are sojourners, not dwellers, and which, when out of it, or even when in it, they think of, peradventure, but as a phantom-world, a place of *ignes fatui* and spectral illusions. Those only who have the peculiarity of association which we have mentioned, and which is a natural though not an universal consequence of intense sensibility, instead of seeming not themselves when they are uttering poetry, scarcely seem themselves when uttering anything to which poetry is foreign. Whatever be the thing which they are contemplating, if it be capable of connecting itself with their emotions, the aspect under which it first and most naturally paints itself to them, is its poetic aspect. The poet of culture sees his object in prose, and describes it in poetry; the poet of nature actually sees it in poetry.

This point is perhaps worth some little illustration; the rather, as metaphysicians (the ultimate arbiters of all philosophical criticism), while they have busied themselves for two thousand years, more or less, about the few universal laws of human nature, have strangely neglected the analysis of its diversities. Of these, none lie deeper or reach fruther than the varieties which difference of nature and of education makes in what may be termed the habitual bond of association. In a mind entirely uncultivated, which is also without any strong feelings, objects, whether of sense or of intellect, arrange themselves in the mere casual order in which they have been seen, heard, or otherwise perceived. Persons of this sort may be said to think chronologically. If they remember a fact, it is by reason of a fortuitous coincidence with some trifling incident or circumstance which took place at the very time. If they have a story to tell, or testimony to deliver in a witness-box, their narrative must follow the exact order in which the events took place: *dodge* them, and the thread of association is broken; they cannot go on. Their associations, to use the language of philosophers, are chiefly of the successive, not the synchronous kind, and whether successive or synchronous, are mostly casual.

To the man of science, again, or of business, objects group themselves according to the artificial classifications which the understanding has voluntarily made for the convenience of thought or of practice. But where any of the impressions are vivid and intense, the associations into which these enter are the ruling ones: it being a well-known law of association, that the stronger a feeling is, the more quickly and strongly it associates itself with any other object or feeling. Where, therefore, nature has given strong feelings, and education has not created factitious tendencies stronger than the natural ones, the prevailing associations will be those which connect objects and ideas with emotions, and with each other through the intervention of emotions. Thoughts and images will be linked together, according to the similarity of the feelings which cling to them. A thought will introduce a thought by first introducing a feeling which is allied with it. At the centre of each group of thoughts or images will be found a feeling; and the thoughts or images will be there only because the feeling was there. The combinations which the mind puts together, the pictures which it paints, the wholes which imagination constructs out of the materials supplied by fancy, will be indebted to some dominant feeling, not as in other natures to a dominant thought, for their unity and consistency of character—for what distinguishes them from incoherencies.

The difference, then, between the poetry of a poet, and the poetry of a cultivated but not naturally poetic mind, is, that in the latter, with however bright a halo of feeling the thought may be surrounded and glorified, the thought itself is always the conspicuous object; while the poetry of a poet is feeling itself, employing thought only as the medium of its expression. In the one, feeling waits upon thought; in the other, thought upon feeling. The one writer has a distinct aim, common to him with any other didactic author; he desires to convey the thought, and he conveys it clothed in the feelings which it excites in himself, or which he deems most appropriate to it. The other merely pours forth the overflowing of his feelings; and all the thoughts which those feelings suggest are floated promiscuously along the stream.

It may assist in rendering our meaning intelligible, if we illustrate it by a parallel between the two English authors of our own day who have produced the greatest quantity of true and enduring poetry, Wordsworth and Shelley. Apter instances could not be wished for; the one might be cited as the type, the *exemplar*, of what the poetry of culture may accomplish; the other as perhaps the most striking example ever known of the poetic temperament. How different, accordingly, is the poetry of these two great writers. In Wordsworth, the poetry is almost always the mere setting of a thought. The thought may be more valuable than the setting, or it may be less valuable, but there can be no question as to which was first in his mind: what he is impressed with, and what he is anxious to impress, is some proposition, more or less distinctly conceived; some truth, or something which he deems such. He lets the thought dwell in his mind, till it excites, as is the nature of thought, other thoughts, and also such feelings as the measure of his sensibility is adequate to supply. Among these thoughts and feelings, had he chosen a different walk of authorship (and there are many in which he might equally have excelled), he would probably have made a different selection of media for enforcing the parent thought: his habits, however, being those of poetic composition, he selects in preference the strongest feelings, and the thoughts with which most of feeling is naturally or habitually connected. His poetry, therefore, may be defined to be, his thoughts, coloured by, and impressing themselves by means of, emotions. Such poetry, Wordsworth has occupied a long life in producing. And well and wisely has he so done. Criticisms, no doubt, may be made occasionally both upon the thoughts themselves, and upon the skill he has demonstrated in the choice of his media: for, an affair of skill and study, in the most rigorous sense, it evidently was. But he has not laboured in vain: he has exercised, and continues to exercise, a powerful, and mostly a highly beneficial influence over the formation and growth of not a few of the most cultivated and vigorous of the youthful minds of our time, over whose heads poetry of the opposite description would have flown, for want of an original organization, physical or mental, in sympathy with it.

On the other hand, Wordsworth's poetry is never bounding, never ebullient; has little even of the appearance of spontaneousness: the well is never so full that it overflows. There is an air of calm deliberateness about all he writes, which is not characteristic of the poetic temperament: his poetry seems one thing, himself another;

he seems to be poetical because he wills to be so, not because he cannot help it: did he will to dismiss poetry, he need never again, it might almost seem, have a poetical thought. He never seems *possessed* by any feeling; no emotion seems ever so strong as to have entire sway, for the time being, over the current of his thoughts. He never, even for the space of a few stanzas, appears entirely given up to exultation, or grief, or pity, or love, or admiration, or devotion, or even animal spirits. He now and then, though seldom, attempts to write as if he were; and never, we think, without leaving an impression of poverty: as the brook which on nearly level ground quite fills its banks, appears but a thread when running rapidly down a precipitous declivity. He has feeling enough to form a decent, graceful, even beautiful decoration to a thought which is in itself interesting and moving; but not so much as suffices to stir up the soul by mere sympathy with itself in its simplest manifestation, nor enough to summon up that array of "thoughts of power" which in a richly stored mind always attends the call of really intense feeling. It is for this reason, doubtless, that the genius of Wordsworth is essentially unlyrical. Lyric poetry, as it was the earliest kind, is also, if the view we are now taking of poetry be correct, more eminently and peculiarly poetry than any other: it is the poetry most natural to a really poetic temperament, and least capable of being successfully imitated by one not so endowed by nature.

Shelley is the very reverse of all this. Where Wordsworth is strong, he is weak; where Wordsworth is weak, he is strong. Culture, that culture by which Wordsworth has reared from his own inward nature the richest harvest ever brought forth by a soil of so little depth, is precisely what was wanting to Shelley: or let us rather say, he had not, at the period of his deplorably early death, reached sufficiently far in that intellectual progression of which he was capable, and which, if it has done so much for greatly inferior natures, might have made of him the most perfect, as he was already the most gifted, of our poets. For him, voluntary mental discipline had done little: the vividness of his emotions and of his sensations had done all. He seldom follows up an idea; it starts into life, summons from the fairy-land of his inexhaustible fancy some three or four bold images, then vanishes, and straight he is off on the wings of some casual association into quite another sphere. He had scarcely yet acquired the consecutiveness of thought necessary for a long poem; his more ambitious compositions too often resemble the scattered fragments of a mirror; colours brilliant as life, single images without end, but no picture. It is only when under the overruling influence of some one state of feeling, either actually experienced, or summoned up in the vividness of reality by a fervid imagination, that he writes as a great poet; unity of feeling being to him the harmonizing principle which a central idea is to minds of another class, and supplying the coherency and consistency which would else have been wanting. Thus it is in many of his smaller, and especially his lyrical poems. They are obviously written to exhale, perhaps to relieve, a state of feeling, or of conception of feeling, almost oppressive from its vividness. The thoughts and imagery are suggested by the feeling, and are such as it finds unsought. The state of feeling may be either of soul or of sense, or oftener (might we not say invariably?) of both: for the poetic temperament is usually, perhaps always, accompanied by exquisite senses. The exciting cause may be either an object or an idea. But whatever of sensation enters into the feeling, must not be local, or consciously organic; it is a condition of the whole frame, not of a part only. Like the state of sensation produced by a fine climate, or indeed like all strongly pleasurable or painful sensations in an impassioned nature, it pervades the entire nervous system. States of feeling, whether sensuous or spiritual, which thus possess the whole being, are the fountains of that which we have called the poetry of poets; and which is little else than a pouring forth of the thoughts and images that pass across the mind while some permanent state of feeling is occupying it.

To the same original fineness of organization, Shelley was doubtless indebted for another of his rarest gifts, that exuberance of imagery, which when unrepressed, as in many of his poems it is, amounts to a fault. The susceptibility of his nervous system, which made his emotions intense, made also the impressions of his external senses deep and clear: and agreeably to the law of association by which, as already remarked, the strongest impressions are those which associate themselves the most easily and strongly, these vivid sensations were readily recalled to mind by all objects or thoughts which had coexisted with them, and by all feelings which in any degree resembled them. Never did a fancy so teem with sensuous imagery as Shelley's. Wordsworth economizes an image, and detains it until he has distilled all the poetry out of it, and it will not yield a drop more: Shelley lavishes his with a profusion which is unconscious because it is inexhaustible.

If, then, the maxim *Nascitur poëta*, mean, either that the power of producing poetical compositions is a peculiar faculty which the poet brings into the world with him, which grows with his growth like any of his bodily powers, and is as independent of culture as his height, and his complexion; or that any natural peculiarity whatever is implied in producing poetry, real poetry, and in any quantity—such poetry too, as, to the majority of educated and intelligent readers, shall appear quite as good as, or even better than, any other; in either sense the doctrine is false. And nevertheless, there *is* poetry which could not emanate but from a mental and physical constitution peculiar, not in the kind, but in the degree of its susceptibility: a constitution which makes its possessor capable of greater happiness than mankind in general, and also of greater unhappiness; and because greater, so also more various. And such poetry, to all who know enough of nature to own it as being in nature, is much more poetry, is poetry in a far higher sense, than any other; since the common element of all poetry, that which constitutes poetry, human feeling, enters far more largely into this than into the poetry of culture. Not only because the natures which we have called poetical, really feel more, and consequently have more feeling to express; but because, the capacity of feeling being so great, feeling, when excited and not voluntarily resisted, seizes the helm of their thoughts, and the succession of ideas and images becomes the mere utterance of an emotion; not, as in other natures, the emotion a mere ornamental colouring of the thought.

Ordinary education and the ordinary course of life are constantly at work counteracting this quality of mind, and substituting habits more suitable to their own ends: if instead of substituting, they were content to superadd, there would be nothing to complain of. But when will education consist, not in repressing any mental faculty or power, from the uncontrolled action of which danger is apprehended, but in training up to its proper strength the corrective and antagonist power?

In whomsoever the quality which we have described exists, and is not stifled, that person is a poet. Doubtless he is a greater poet in proportion as the fineness of his perceptions, whether of sense or of internal consciousness, furnishes him with an ampler supply of lovely images—the vigour and richness of his intellect with a greater abundance of moving thoughts. For it is through these thoughts and images that the feeling speaks, and through their impressiveness that it impresses itself, and finds response in other hearts; and from these media of transmitting it (contrary to the laws of physical nature) increase of intensity is reflected back upon the feeling itself. But all these it is possible to have, and not be a poet; they are mere materials, which the poet shares in common with other people. What constitutes the poet is not the imagery nor the thoughts, nor even the feelings, but the law according to which they are called up. He is a poet, not because he has ideas of any particular kind, but because the succession of his ideas is subordinate to the course of his emotions.

Many who have never acknowledged this in theory, bear testimony to it in their particular judgments. In listening to an oration, or reading a written discourse not professedly poetical, when do we begin to feel that the speaker or author is putting off the character of the orator or the prose writer, and is passing into the poet? Not when he begins to show strong feeling; then we merely say, he is in earnest, he feels what he says; still less when he expresses himself in imagery; then, unless illustration be manifestly his sole object, we are apt to say, this is affectation. It is when the feeling (instead of passing away, or, if it continue, letting the train of thoughts run on exactly as they would have done if there were no influence at work but the mere intellect) becomes itself the originator of another train of association, which expels, or blends with, the former; when (for example) either his words, or the mode of their arrangement, are such as we spontaneously use only when in a state of excitement, proving that the mind is at least as much occupied by a passive state of its own feelings, as by the desire of attaining the premeditated end which the discourse has in view.[7]

Our judgments of authors who lay actual claim

[7] And this, we may remark by the way, seems to point to the true theory of poetic diction; and to suggest the true answer to as much as is erroneous of Wordsworth's celebrated doctrine on that subject. For one the one hand, all language which is the natural expression of feeling, is really poetical, and will be felt as such, apart from conventional associations; but on the other, whenever intellectual culture has

to the title of poets, follow the same principle. Whenever, after a writer's meaning is fully understood, it is still matter of reasoning and discussion whether he is a poet or not, he will be found to be wanting in the characteristic peculiarity of association so often adverted to. When, on the contrary, after reading or hearing one or two passages, we instinctively and without hesitation cry out, This is a poet, the probability is, that the passages are strongly marked with this peculiar quality. And we may add that in such case, a critic who, not having sufficient feeling to respond to the poetry, is also without sufficient philosophy to understand it though he feel it not, will be apt to pronounce, not "this is prose," but "this is exaggeration," "this is mysticism," or, "this is nonsense."

Although a philosopher cannot, by culture, make himself, in the peculiar sense in which we now use the term, a poet, unless at least he have that peculiarity of nature which would probably have made poetry his earliest pursuit; a poet may always, by culture, make himself a philosopher. The poetic laws of association are by no means incompatible with the more ordinary laws; are by no means such as must have their course, even though a deliberate purpose require their suspension. If the pecularities of the poetic temperament were uncontrollable in any poet, they might be supposed so in Shelley; yet how powerfully, in the Cenci, does he coerce and restrain all the characteristic qualities of his genius; what severe simplicity, in place of his usual barbaric splendour; how rigidly does he keep the feelings and the imagery in subordination to the thought.

The investigation of nature requires no habits or qualities of mind, but such as may always be acquired by industry and mental activity. Because at one time the mind may be so given up to a state of feeling, that the succession of its ideas is determined by the present enjoyment or suffering which pervades it, this is no reason but that in the calm retirement of study, when under no peculiar excitement either of the outward or of the inward sense, it may form any combinations, or pursue any trains of ideas, which are most conducive to the purposes of philosophic inquiry; and may, while in that state, form deliberate convictions, from which no excitement will afterwards make it swerve.

Might we not go even further than this? We shall not pause to ask whether it be not a misunderstanding of the nature of passionate feeling to imagine that it is inconsistent with calmness; whether they who so deem of it, do not mistake passion in the militant or antagonistic state, for the type of passion universally; do not confound passion struggling towards an outward object, with passion brooding over itself. But without entering into this deeper investigation; that capacity of strong feeling, which is supposed necessarily to disturb the judgment, is also the material out of which all *motives* are made; the motives, consequently, which lead human beings to the pursuit of truth. The greater the individual's capability of happiness and of misery, the stronger interest has that individual in arriving at truth; and when once that interest is felt, an impassioned nature is sure to pursue this, as to pursue any other object, with greater ardour; for energy of character is commonly the offspring of strong feeling. If, therefore, the most impassioned natures do not ripen into the most powerful intellects, it is always from defect of culture, or something wrong in the circumstances by which the being has originally or successively been surrounded. Undoubtedly strong feelings require a strong intellect to carry them, as more sail requires more ballast: and when, from neglect, or bad education, that strength is wanting, no wonder if the grandest and swiftest vessels make the most utter wreck.

Where, as in some of our older poets, a poetic nature has been united with logical and scientific culture, the peculiarity of association arising from the finer nature so perpetually alternates with the associations attainable by commoner natures trained to high perfection, that its own particular law is not so conspicuously characteristic of the result produced, as in a poet like Shelley, to whom systematic intellectual culture, in a measure proportioned to the intensity of his own nature, has been wanting. Whether the superiority will naturally be on the side of the philosopher-poet or of the mere poet—whether the writings of the one ought, as a whole, to be truer, and their influence more beneficent, than those of the other—is too obvious in principle to need statement: it would be absurd to doubt whether two endowments are better than one; whether truth is more certainly arrived at by

---

afforded a choice between several modes of expressing the same emotion, the stronger the feeling is, the more naturally and certainly will it prefer the language which is most peculiarly appropriated to itself, and kept sacred from the contact of more vulgar objects of contemplation. [Mill's note].

two processes, verifying and correcting each other, than by one alone. Unfortunately, in practice the matter is not quite so simple; there the question often is, which is least prejudicial to the intellect, uncultivation or malcultivation. For, as long as education consists chiefly of the mere inculcation of traditional opinions, many of which, from the mere fact that the human intellect has not yet reached perfection, must necessarily be false; so long as even those who are best taught, are rather taught to know the thoughts of others than to think, it is not always clear that the poet of acquired ideas has the advantage over him whose feeling has been his sole teacher. For, the depth and durability of wrong as well as of right impressions, is propor-

tional to the fineness of the material; and they who have the greatest capacity of natural feeling are generally those whose artificial feelings are the strongest. Hence, doubtless, among other reasons, it is, that in an age of revolutions in opinion, the contemporary poets, those at least who deserve the name, those who have any individuality of character, if they are not before their age, are almost sure to be behind it. An observation curiously verified all over Europe in the present century. Nor let it be thought disparaging. However urgent may be the necessity for a breaking up of old modes of belief, the most strong-minded and discerning, next to those who head the movement, are generally those who bring up the rear of it.

from The Subjection of Women

Mill's least popular work in his own day, The Subjection of Women, *has recently come in for renewed attention and admiration, and Mill has been recognized as a pioneer in campaigning for the rights of women. He was also engaging in one of many continuing Victorian social debates This one reached a culmination in the twentieth century with the women's suffrage movement and the subsequent women's liberation movement.* The Subjection of Women *first appeared in 1869. The work is divided into four chapters of which the first is given complete here. Mill attributed much of his thinking on the woman question to the influence of Harriet Taylor.*

Chapter 1

T HE object of this Essay is to explain, as clearly as I am able, the grounds of an opinion which I have held from the very earliest period when I had formed any opinions at all on social or political matters, and which, instead of being weakened or modified, has been constantly growing stronger by the progress of reflection and the experience of life: That the principle which regulates the existing social relations between the two sexes—the legal subordination of one sex to the other—is wrong in itself, and now one of the chief hindrances to human improvement; and that it ought to be replaced by a principle of perfect equality, admitting no power or privilege on the one side, nor disability on the other.

The very words necessary to express the task I have undertaken, show how arduous it is. But it would be a mistake to suppose that the difficulty

of the case must lie in the insufficiency or obscurity of the grounds of reason on which my conviction rests. The difficulty is that which exists in all cases in which there is a mass of feeling to be contended against. So long as an opinion is strongly rooted in the feelings, it gains rather than loses in stability by having a preponderating weight of argument against it. For if it were accepted as a result of argument, the refutation of the argument might shake the solidity of the conviction; but when it rests solely on feeling, the worst it fares in argumentative contest, the more persuaded its adherents are that their feeling must have some deeper ground, which the arguments do not reach; and while the feeling remains, it is always throwing up fresh intrenchments of argument to repair any breach made in the old. And there are so many causes tending to make the feelings connected with this subject the most intense and most deeply rooted of all those which gather round and protect old institutions and customs, that we need not wonder to find them as yet less under-mined and loosened than any of the rest by the progress of the great modern spiritual and social transition; nor suppose that the barbarisms to which men cling longest must be less bar-barisms than those which they earlier shake off.

In every respect the burden is hard on those who attack an almost universal opinion. They must be very fortunate, as well as unusually capable, if they obtain a hearing at all. They have more difficulty in obtaining a trial, than any other litigants have in getting a verdict. If they do extort a hearing, they are subjected to a set of logical requirements totally different from those exacted from other people. In all other cases, the burden of proof is supposed to lie with the affirmative. If a person is charged with a murder, it rests with those who accuse him to give proof of his guilt, not with himself to prove his inno-cence. If there is a difference of opinion about the reality of any alleged historical event, in which the feelings of men in general are not much interested, as the Siege of Troy for example, those who maintain that the event took place are expected to produce their proofs, before those who take the other side can be required to say anything; and at no time are these re-quired to do more than show that the evidence produced by the others is of no value. Again, in practical matters, the burden of proof is supposed to be with those who are against liberty; who contend for any restriction or prohibition; either any limitation of the general freedom of human action, or any disqualification or disparity of privilege affecting one person or kind of persons, as compared with others. The *à priori* presumption is in favor of freedom and impartiality. It is held that there should be no restraint not required by the general good, and that the law should be no respecter of per-sons, but should treat all alike, save where dissimilarity of treatment is required by positive reasons, either of justice or of policy. But of none of these rules of evidence will the benefit be allowed to those who maintain the opinion I profess. It is useless for me to say that those who maintain the doctrine that men have a right to command and women are under an obligation to obey, or that men are fit for govern-ment and women unfit, are on the affirmative side of the question, and that they are bound to show positive evidence for the assertions, or submit to their rejection. It is equally unavailing for me to say that those who deny to women any freedom or privilege rightly allowed to men,

having the double presumption against them that they are opposing freedom and recommend-ing partiality, must be held to the strictest proof of their case, and unless their success be such as to exclude all doubt, the judgment ought to go against them. These would be thought good pleas in any common case; but they will not be thought so in this instance. Before I could hope to make any impression, I should be expected not only to answer all that has ever been said by those who take the other side of the question, but to imagine all that could be said by them—to find them in reasons, as well as answer all I find: and besides refuting all arguments for the affirmative, I shall be called upon for invincible positive arguments to prove a negative. And even if I could do all this, and leave the opposite party with a host of unanswered arguments against them, and not a single un-refuted one on their side, I should be thought to have done little; for a cause supported on the one hand by universal usage, and on the other by so great a preponderance of popular senti-ment, is supposed to have a presumption in its favor, superior to any conviction which an ap-peal to reason has power to produce in any intellects but those of a high class.

I do not mention these difficulties to complain of them: first, because it would be useless; they are inseparable from having to contend through people's understandings against the hostility of their feelings and practical tendencies: and truly the understandings of the majority of mankind would need to be much better culti-vated than has ever yet been the case, before they can be asked to place such reliance in their own power of estimating arguments, as to give up practical principles in which they have been born and bred and which are the basis of much of the existing order of the workd, at the first argumentative attack which they are not capable of logically resisting. I do not therefore quarrel with them for having too little faith in argument, but for having too much faith in custom and the general feeling. It is one of the characteristic prejudices of the reaction of the nineteenth century against the eighteenth, to accord to the unreasoning elements in human nature the infallibility which the eighteenth century is supposed to have ascribed to the reason-ing elements. For the apotheosis of Reason we have substituted that of Instinct; and we call everything instinct which we find in ourselves and for which we cannot trace any rational foundation. This idolatry, infinitely more degrading than the other, and the most pernicious of the false worships of the present day, of all of which it is now the main support, will probably hold its ground until it gives way before a sound psychology, laying bare the real root of much that is bowed down to as the intention of Nature and the ordinance of God. As regards the present question, I am willing to accept the unfavorable conditions which the prejudice assigns to me. I consent that established custom, and the general feeling, should be deemed conclusive against me, unless that custom and feeling from age to age can be shown to have owed their existence to other causes than their soundness, and to have derived their power from the worse rather than the better parts of human nature. I am willing that judgment should go against me, unless I can show that my judge has been tampered with. The concession is not so great as it might appear; for to prove this is by far the easiest portion of my task.

The generality of a practice is in some cases a strong presumption that it is, or at all events once was, conducive to laudable ends. This is the case, when the practice was first adopted, or afterward kept up, as a means to such ends, and was grounded on experience of the mode in which they could be most effectually attained. If the authority of men over women, when first established, had been the result of conscientious comparison between different modes of constituting the government of society; if, after trying various other modes of social organization—the government of women over men, equality between the two, and such mixed and divided modes of government as might be invented—it had been decided, on the testimony of experience, that the mode in which women are wholly under the rule of men, having no share at all in public concerns, and each in private being under the legal obligation of obedience to the man with whom she has associated her destiny, was the arrangement most conducive to the happiness and well-being of both; its general adoption might then be fairly thought to be some evidence that, at the time when it was adopted, it was the best: though even then the considerations which recommended it may, like so many other primeval social facts of the greatest importance, have subsequently, in the course of ages, ceased to exist. But the state of the case is in every respect the reverse of this. In the first place, the opinion in favor of the present system, which entirely subordinates the weaker sex to the stronger, rests upon theory only; for there never has been trial made of any other: so that experience, in the sense in which it is vulgarly opposed to theory, cannot be pretended to have pronounced any verdict. And in the second place, the adoption of this system of inequality never was the result of deliberation, or forethought, or any social ideas, or any notion whatever of what conduced to the benefit of humanity or the good order of society. It arose simply from the fact that from the very earliest twilight of human society, every woman (owing to the value attached to her by men, combined with her inferiority in muscular strength) was found in a state of bondage to some man. Laws and systems of polity always begin by recognizing the relations they find already existing between individuals. They convert what was a mere physical fact into a legal right, give it the sanction of society, and principally aim at the substitution of public and organized means of asserting and protecting these rights, instead of the irregular and lawless conflict of physical strength. Those who had already been compelled to obedience became in this manner legally bound to it. Slavery, from being a mere affair of force between the master and the slave, became regularized and a matter of compact among the masters, who, binding themselves to one another for common protection, guaranteed by their collective strength the private possessions of each, including his slaves. In early times, the great majority of the male sex were slaves, as well as the whole of the female. And many ages elapsed, some of them ages of high cultivation, before any thinker was bold enough to question the rightfulness, and the absolute social necessity, either of the one slavery or of the other. By degrees such thinkers did arise: and (the general progress of society assisting) the slavery of the male sex has, in all the countries of Christian Europe at least (though, in one of them, only within the last few years), been at length abolished, and that of the female sex has been gradually changed into a milder form of dependence. But this dependence, as it exists at present, is not an original institution, taking a fresh start from considerations of justice and social expediency—it is the primitive state of slavery lasting on, through successive mitigations and modifications occasioned by the same causes which have softened the general manners, and brought all human relations more under the control of justice and the influence of humanity. It has not lost the taint of its brutal origin. No presumption in its favor, therefore, can be drawn from the fact of its existence. The only such presumption which it could be supposed to have, must be grounded on its having lasted till now, when so many other things which came down from the same odious source have been done away with. And this, indeed, is what makes it strange to ordinary ears, to hear it asserted that the inequality of rights between men and women has no other source than the law of the strongest.

That this statement should have the effect of a paradox, is in some respects creditable to the progress of civilization, and the improvement of the moral sentiments of mankind. We now live —that is to say, one or two of the most advanced nations of the world now live—in a state in which the law of the strongest seems to be entirely abandoned as the regulating principle of the world's affairs: nobody professes it, and, as regards most of the relations between human beings, nobody is permitted to practice it. When anyone succeeds in doing so, it is under cover of some pretext which gives him the semblance of having some general social interest on his side. This being the ostensible state of things, people flatter themselves that the rule of mere force is ended; that the law of the strongest cannot be the reason of existence of anything which has remained in full operation down to the present time. However any of our present institutions may have begun, it can only, they think, have been preserved to this period of advanced civilization by a well-grounded feeling of its adaptation to human nature, and conduciveness to the general good. They do not understand the great vitality and durability of institutions which place right on the side of might; how intensely they are clung to; how the good as well as the bad propensities and sentiments of those who have power in their hands, become identified with retaining it; how slowly these bad institutions give way, one at a time, the weakest first, beginning with those which are least interwoven with the daily habits of life; and how very rarely those who have obtained legal power because they first had physical, have ever lost their hold of it until the physical power had passed over to the other side. Such shifting of the physical force not having taken place in the case of women; this fact, combined with all the peculiar and characteristic features of the particular case, made it certain from the first that this branch of the system of right founded on might, though softened in its most atrocious features at an earlier period than several of the others, would be the very last to disappear. It was

inevitable that this one case of a social relation grounded on force, would survive through generations of institutions grounded on equal justice, an almost solitary exception to the general character of their laws and customs; but which, so long as it does not proclaim its own origin, and as discussion has not brought out its true character, is not felt to jar with modern civilization, any more than domestic slavery among the Greeks jarred with their notion of themselves as a free people.

The truth is, that people of the present and the last two or three generations have lost all practical sense of the primitive conditions of humanity; and only the few who have studied history accurately, or have much frequented the parts of the world occupied by the living representatives of ages long past, are able to form any mental picture of what society then was. People are not aware how entirely, in former ages, the law of superior strength was the rule of life; how publicly and openly it was avowed, I do not say cynically or shamelessly—for these words imply a feeling that there was something in it to be ashamed of, and no such notion could find a place in the faculties of any person in those ages, except a philosopher or a saint. History gives a cruel experience of human nature, in showing how exactly the regard due to the life, possessions, and entire earthly happiness of any class of persons, was measured by what they had the power of enforcing; how all who made any resistance to authorities that had arms in their hands, however dreadful might be the provocation, had not only the law of force but all other laws, and all the notions of social obligation against them; and in the eyes of those whom they resisted, were not only guilty of crime, but of the worst of all crimes, deserving the most cruel chastisement which human beings could inflict. The first small vestige of a feeling of obligation in a superior to acknowledge any right in inferiors, began when he had been induced, for convenience to make some promise to them. Though these promises, even when sanctioned by the most solemn oaths, were for many ages revoked or violated on the most trifling provocation or temptation, it is probable that this, except by persons of still worse than the average morality, was seldom done without some twinges of conscience. The ancient republics, being mostly grounded from the first upon some kind of mutual compact, or at any rate formed by a union of persons not very unequal in strength, afforded, in consequence, the first instance of a portion of human relations fenced round, and placed under the dominion of another law than that of force. And though the original law of force remained in full operation between them and their slaves, and also (except so far as limited by express compact) between a commonwealth and its subjects, or other independent commonwealths; the banishment of that primitive law, even from so narrow a field, commenced the regeneration of human nature, by giving birth to sentiments of which experience soon demonstrated the immense value even for material interests, and which thenceforward only required to be enlarged, not created. Though slaves were no part of the commonwealth, it was in the free states that slaves were first felt to have rights as human beings. The Stoics were, I believe, the first (except so far as the Jewish law constitutes an exception) who taught as a part of morality that men were bound by moral obligations to their slaves. No one, after Christianity became ascendant, could ever again have been a stranger to this belief, in theory; nor, after the rise of the Catholic Church, was it ever without persons to stand up for it. Yet to enforce it was the most arduous task which Christianity ever had to perform. For more than a thousand years the Church kept up the contest, with hardly any perceptible success. It was not for want of power over men's minds. Its power was prodigious. It could make kings and nobles resign their most valued possessions to enrich the Church. It could make thousands, in the prime of life and the height of worldly advantages, shut themselves up in convents to work out their salvation by poverty, fasting, and prayer. It could send hundreds of thousands across land and sea, Europe and Asia, to give their lives for the deliverance of the Holy Sepulcher. It could make kings relinquish wives who were the object of their passionate attachment, because the Church declared that they were within the seventh (by our calculation the fourteenth) degree of relationship. All this it did; but it could not make men fight less with one another, nor tryannize less cruelly over the serfs, and when they were able, over burgesses. It could not make them renounce either of the applications of force; force militant, or force triumphant. This they could never be induced to do until they were themselves in their turn compelled by superior force. Only by the growing power of kings was an end put to fighting except between kings, or competitors for kingship; only by the growth of a wealthy and warlike bourgeoisie in the fortified towns, and of a ple-

beian infantry which proved more powerful in the field than the undisciplined chivalry, was the insolent tyranny of the nobles over the bourgeoisie and peasantry brought within some bounds. It was persisted in not only until, but long after, the oppressed had obtained a power enabling them often to take conspicuous vengenance; and on the Continent much of it continued to the time of the French Revolution, though in England the earlier and better organization of the democratic classes put an end to it sooner, by establishing equal laws and free national institutions.

If people are mostly so little aware how completely, during the greater part of the duration of our species, the law of force was the avowed rule of general conduct, any other being only a special and exceptional consequence of peculiar ties—and from how very recent a date it is that the affairs of society in general have been even pretended to be regulated according to any moral; as little do people remember or consider how institutions and customs which never had any ground but the law of force, last on into ages and states of general opinion which never would have permitted their first establishment. Less than forty years ago, Englishmen might still by law hold human beings in bondage as salable property: within the present century they might kidnap them and carry them off, and work them literally to death. This absolutely extreme case of the law of force, condemned by those who can tolerate almost every other form of arbitrary power, and which, of all others, presents features the most revolting to the feelings of all who look at it from an impartial position, was the law of civilized and Christian England within the memory of persons now living: and in one-half of Anglo-Saxon America three or four years ago, not only did slavery exist, but the slave-trade, and the breeding of slaves expressly for it, was a general practice between slave states. Yet not only was there a greater strength of sentiment against it, but, in England at least, a less amount either of feeling or of interest in favor of it, than of any other of the customary abuses of force: for its motive was the love of gain, unmixed and undisguised; and those who profited by it were a very small numerical fraction of the country, while the natural feeling of all who were not personally interested in it, was unmitigated abhorrence. So extreme an instance makes it almost superfluous to refer to any other: but consider the long duration of absolute monarchy. In England at present it is the almost universal conviction that military despotism is a case of the law of force, having no other origin or justification. Yet in all the great nations of Europe except England it either still exists, or has only just ceased to exist, and has even now a strong party favorable to it in all ranks of the people, especially among persons of station and consequence. Such is the power of an established system, even when far from universal; when not only in almost every period of history there have been great and well-known examples of the contrary system, but these have almost invariably been afforded by the most illustrious and most prosperous communities. In this case too, the possessor of the undue power, the person directly interested in it, is only one person, while those who are subject to it and suffer from it are literally all the rest. The yoke is naturally and necessarily humiliating to all persons, except the one who is on the throne, together with, at most, the one who expects to succeed to it. How different are these cases from that of the power of men over women! I am not now prejudging the question of its justifiableness. I am showing how vastly more permanent it could not but be, even if not justifiable, than these other dominations which have nevertheless lasted down to our own time. Whatever gratification of pride there is in the possession of power, and whatever personal interest in its exercise, is in this case not confined to a limited class, but common to the whole male sex. Instead of being, to most of its supporters, a thing desirable chiefly in the abstract, or, like the political ends usually contended for by factions, of little private importance to any but the leaders; it comes home to the person and hearth of every male head of a family, and of everyone who looks forward to being so. The clodhopper exercises, or is to exercise, his share of the power equally with the highest nobleman. And the case is that in which the desire of power is the strongest: for everyone who desires power, desires it most over those who are nearest to him, with whom his life is passed, with whom he has most concerns in common, and in whom any independence of his authority is oftenest likely to interfere with his individual preferences. If, in the other cases specified, powers manifestly grounded only on force, and having so much less to support them, are so slowly and with so much difficulty got rid of, much more must it be so with this, even if it rests on no better foundation than those. We must consider, too, that the possessors of the power have facilities in this case, greater than in any other, to prevent any up-rising against it. Every one of the subjects lives under the very eye, and almost, it may be said, in the hands, of one of the masters—in closer intimacy with him than with any of her fellow-subjects; with no means of combining against him, no power of even locally overmastering him, and, on the other hand, with the strongest motives for seeking his favor and avoiding to give him offense. In struggles for political emancipation, everybody knows how often its champions are bought off by bribes, or daunted by terrors. In the case of women, each individual of the subject-class is in a chronic state of bribery and intimidation combined. In setting up the standard of resistance, a large number of the leaders, and still more of the followers, must make an almost complete sacrifice of the pleasures or the alleviations of their own individual lot. If ever any system of privilege and enforced subjection had its yoke tightly riveted on the necks of those who are kept down by it, this has. I have not yet shown that it is a wrong system; but everyone who is capable of thinking on the subject must see that even if it is, it was certain to outlast all other forms of unjust authority. And when some of the grossest of the other forms still exist in many civilized countries, and have only recently been got rid of in others, it would be strange if that which is so much the deepest rooted had yet been perceptibly shaken anywhere. There is more reason to wonder that the protests and testimonies against it should have been so numerous and so weighty as they are.

Some will object, that a comparison cannot fairly be made between the government of the male sex and the forms of unjust power which I have adduced in illustration of it, since these are arbitrary, and the effect of mere usurpation, while it on the contrary is natural. But was there ever any domination which did not appear natural to those who possessed it? There was a time when the division of mankind into two classes, a small one of masters and a numerous one of slaves, appeared, even to the most cultivated minds, to be a natural, and the only natural, condition of the human race. No less an intellect, and one which contributed no less to the progress of human thought, than Aristotle, held this opinion without doubt or misgiving; and rested it on the same premises on which the same assertion in regard to the dominion of men over women is usually based, namely, that there are different natures among mankind, free natures, and slave natures; that the Greeks were of a free nature, the barbarian races of Thracians and Asiatics of a slave nature. But why need I go back to Aristotle? Did not the slave-owners of the Southern United States maintain the same doctrine, with all the fanaticism with which men cling to the theories that justify their passions and legitimate their personal interests? Did they not call heaven and earth to witness that the dominion of the white man over the black is natural, that the black race is by nature incapable of freedom, and marked out for slavery?—some even going so far as to say that the freedom of manual laborers is an unnatural order of things anywhere. Again, the theorists of absolute monarchy have always affirmed it to be the only natural form of government; issuing from the patriarchal, which was the primitive and spontaneous form of society, framed on the model of the paternal, which is anterior to society itself, and, as they contend, the most natural authority of all. Nay, for that matter, the law of force itself, to those who could not plead any other, has always seemed the most natural of all grounds for the exercise of authority. Conquering races hold it to be Nature's own dictate that the conquered should obey the conquerors, or, as they euphoniously paraphrase it, that the feebler and more unwarlike races should submit to the braver and manlier. The smallest acquaintance with human life in the middle ages, shows how supremely natural the dominion of the feudal nobility over men of low condition appeared to the nobility themselves, and how unnatural the conception seemed, of a person of the inferior class claiming equality with them, or exercising authority over them. It hardly seemed less so to the class held in subjection. The emancipated serfs and burgesses, even in their most vigorous struggles, never made any pretension to a share of authority; they only demanded more or less limitation to the power of tyrannizing over them. So true is it that unnatural generally means only uncustomary, and that everything which is usual appears natural. The subjection of women to men being a universal custom, any departure from it quite naturally appears unnatural. But how entirely, even in this case, the feeling is dependent on custom, appears by ample experience. Nothing so much astonishes the people of distant parts of the world, when they first learn anything about England, as to be told that it is under a queen: the thing seems to them so unnatural as to be almost incredible. To Englishmen this does not seem in the least degree unnatural, because they are used to it; but they do feel it unnatural that women should be soldiers or members of Parliament. In the feudal ages, on the contrary war and politics were not thought unnatural to women, because not unusual; it seemed natural that women of the privileged classes should be of manly character, inferior in nothing but bodily strength to their husbands and fathers. The independence of women seemed rather less unnatural to the Greeks than to other ancients, on account of the fabulous Amazons (whom they believed to be historical), and the partial example afforded by the Spartan women; who, though no less subordinate by law than in other Greek states, were more free in fact; and being trained to bodily exercises in the same manner with men, gave ample proof that they were not naturally disqualified for them. There can be little doubt that Spartan experience suggested to Plato, among many other of his doctrines, that of the social and political equality of the two sexes.

But, it will be said, the rule of men over women differs from all these others in not being a rule of force: it is accepted voluntarily; women make no complaint, and are consenting parties to it. In the first place, a great number of women do not accept it. Ever since there have been women able to make their sentiments known by their writings (the only mode of publicity which society permits to them), an increasing number of the them have recorded protests against their present social condition: and recently many thousands of them, headed by the most eminent women known to the public, have petitioned Parliament for their admission to the Parliamentary Suffrage. The claim of women to be educated as solidly, and in the same branches of knowledge, as men, is urged with growing intensity, and with a great prospect of success; while the demand for their admission into professions and occupations hitherto closed against them, becomes every year more urgent. Though there are not in this country, as there are in the United States, periodical Conventions and an organized party to agitate for the Rights of Women, there is a numerous and active Society organized and managed by women, for the more limited object of obtaining the political franchise. Nor is it only in our own country and in America that women are beginning to protest, more or less collectively, against the disabilities under which they labor. France and Italy, and Switzerland, and Russia now afford examples of the same thing. How many more women there are who silently cherish similar aspirations, no one can possibly know; but there are abundant tokens how many *would* cherish them, were they not so strenuously taught to repress them as contrary to the proprieties of their sex. It must be remembered, also, that no enslaved class ever asked for complete liberty at once. When Simon de Montfort[1] called the deputies of the commons to sit for the first time in Parliament, did any of them dream of demanding that an assembly, elected by their constituents, should make and destroy ministries, and dictate to the king in affairs of state? No such thought entered into the imagination of the most ambitious of them. The nobility had already these pretensions; the commons pretended to nothing but to be exempt from arbitrary taxation, and from the gross individual oppression of the king's officers. It is a political law of nature that those who are under any power of ancient origin, never begin by complaining of the power itself, but only of its oppressive exercise. There is never any want of women who complain of ill usage by their husbands. There would be infinitely more, if complaint were not the greatest of all provocatives to a repetition and increase of the ill usage. It is this which frustrates all attempts to maintain the power but protect the woman against its abuses. In no other case (except that of a child) is the person who has been proved judicially to have suffered an injury, replaced under the physical power of the culprit who inflicted it. Accordingly wives, even in the most extreme and protracted cases of bodily ill usage, hardly ever dare avail themselves of the laws made for their protection; and if, in a moment of irrepressible indignation, or by the interference of neighbors, they are induced to do so, their whole effort afterward is to disclose as little as they can, and to beg off their tyrant from his merited chastisement.

All causes, social and natural, combine to make it unlikely that women should be collectively rebellious to the power of men. They are so far in a position different from all other subject classes, that their masters require something more from them than actual service. Men do not want solely the obedience of women, they want their sentiments. All men, except the most brutish, desire to have, in the woman most nearly connected with them, not a forced slave but a willing one, not a slave merely, but a favorite. They have therefore put everything in practice to enslave their minds. The masters of all other slaves rely, for maintaining obedience, on fear,—either fear of themselves, or religious fears. The masters of women wanted more than simple obedience, and they turned the whole force of education to effect their purpose. All women are brought up from the very earliest years in the belief that their ideal of character is the very opposite to that of men; not self-will and government by self-control, but submission and yielding to the control of others. All the moralities tell them that it is the duty of women, and all the current sentimentalities that it is their nature, to live for others, to make complete abnegation of themselves, and to have no life but in their affections. And by their affections are meant the only ones they are allowed to have—those to the men with whom they are connected, or to the children who constitute an additional and indefeasible tie between them and a man. When we put together three things—first, the natural attraction between opposite sexes; secondly, the wife's entire dependence on the husband, every privilege or pleasure she has being either his gift, or depending entirely on his will; and lastly, that the principal object of human pursuit, consideration, and all objects of social ambition, can in general be sought or obtained by her only through him, it would be a miracle if the object of being attractive to men had not become the polar star of feminine education and formation of character. And this great means of influence over the minds of women having been acquired, an instinct of selfishness made men avail themselves of it to the utmost as a means of holding women in subjection, by representing to them meekness, submissiveness, and resignation of all individual will into the hands of a man, as an essential part of sexual attractiveness. Can it be doubted that any of the other yokes which mankind have succeeded in breaking, would have subsisted till now if the same means had existed, and had been as sedulously used, to bow down their minds to it? If it had been made the object of the life of every young plebeian to find personal favor in the eyes of some patrician of every young serf with some seigneur; if domestication with him, and a share of his personal affections, had been held out as the prize which they all should look out for, the most gifted and aspiring being able to reckon on the most desirable prizes; and if, when this prize had been obtained, they had been shut out by a wall of brass from all interests not centering in him, all feelings and desires but those which he shared or inculcated; would not serfs and seig-

---

[1] Simon de Monfort (c. 1208–65), leader of the barons against Henry III.

neurs, plebeians and patricians, have been as broadly distinguished at this day as men and women are? And would not all but a thinker here and there have believed the distinction to be a fundamental and unalterable fact in human nature?

The preceding considerations are amply sufficient to show that custom, however universal it may be, affords in this case no presumption, and ought not to create any prejudice, in favor of the arrangements which place women in social and political subjection to men. But I may go further, and maintain that the course of history, and the tendencies of progressive human society, afford not only no presumption in favor of this system of inequality of rights, but a strong one against it; and that, so far as the whole course of human improvement up to this time, the whole stream of modern tendencies, warrants any inference on the subject, it is, that this relic of the past is discordant with the future, and must necessarily disappear.

For, what is the peculiar character of the modern world—the difference which chiefly distinguishes modern institutions, modern social ideas, modern life itself, from those of times long past? It is, that human beings are no longer born to their place in life, and chained down by an inexorable bond to the place they are born to, but are free to employ their faculties, and such favorable chances as offer, to achieve the lot which may appear to them most desirable. Human society of old was constituted on a very different principle. All were born to a fixed social position, and were mostly kept in it by law, or interdicted from any means by which they could emerge from it. As some men are born white and others black, so some were born slaves and others freemen and citizens; some were born patricians, others plebeians; some were born feudal nobles, others commoners and *roturiers*.[2] A slave or serf could never make himself free, nor, except by the will of his master, become so. In most European countries it was not till toward the close of the middle ages, and as a consequence of the growth of regal power, that commoners could be ennobled. Even among nobles, the eldest son was born the exclusive heir to the paternal possessions, and a long time elapsed before it was fully established that the father could disinherit him. Among the industrious classes, only those who were born members of a guild, or were admitted into it by its members, could lawfully

practice their calling within its local limits; and nobody could practice any calling deemed important, in any but the legal manner—by processes authoritatively prescribed. Manufacturers have stood in the pillory for presuming to carry on their business by new and improved methods. In modern Europe, and most in those parts of it which have participated most largely in all other modern improvements, diametrically opposite doctrines now prevail. Law and government do not undertake to prescribe by whom any social or industrial operation shall or shall not be conducted, or what modes of conducting them shall be lawful. These things are left to the unfettered choice of individuals. Even the laws which required that workmen should serve an apprenticeship, have in this country been repealed: there being ample assurance that in all cases in which an apprenticeship is necessary, its necessity will suffice to enforce it. The old theory was, that the least possible should be left to the choice of the individual agent; that all he had to do should, as far as practicable, be laid down for him by superior wisdom. Left to himself he was sure to go wrong. The modern conviction, the fruit of a thousand years of experience, is, that things in which the individual is the person directly interested, never go right but as they are left to his own discretion; and that any regulation of them by authority, except to protect the rights of others, is sure to be mischievous. This conclusion, slowly arrived at, and not adopted until almost every possible application of the contrary theory had been made with disastrous result, now (in the industrial department) prevails universally in the most advanced countries, almost universally in all that have pretensions to any sort of advancement. It is not that all processes are supposed to be equally good, or all persons to be equally qualified for everything; but that freedom of individual choice is now known to be the only thing which procures the adoption of the best processes, and throws each operation into the hands of those who are best qualified for it. Nobody thinks it necessary to make a law that only a strong-armed man shall be a blacksmith. Freedom and competition suffice to make blacksmiths strong-armed men, because the weak-armed can earn more by engaging in occupations for which they are more fit. In consonance with this doctrine, it is felt to be an overstepping of the proper bounds of authority to fix beforehand, on some general presumption, that certain

_____
[2] Plebeians.

persons are not fit to do certain things. It is now thoroughly known and admitted that if some such presumptions exist, no such presumption is infallible. Even if it be well grounded in a majority of cases, which it is very likely not to be, there will be a minority of exceptional cases in which it does not hold: and in those it is both an injustice to the individuals, and a detriment to society, to place barriers in the way of their using their faculties for their own benefit and for that of others. In the cases, on the other hand, in which the unfitness is real, the ordinary motives of human conduct will on the whole suffice to prevent the incompetent person from making, or from persisting in, the attempt.

If this general principle of social and economical science is not true; if individuals, with such help as they can derive from the opinion of those who know them, are not better judges than the law and the government, of their own capacities and vocation; the world cannot too soon abandon this principle, and return to the old system of regulations and disabilities. But if the principle is true, we ought to act as if we believed it, and not to ordain that to be born a girl instead of a boy, any more than to be born black instead of white, or a commoner instead of a nobleman, shall decide the person's position through all life —shall interdict people from all the more elevated social positions, and from all, except a few, respectable occupations. Even were we to admit the utmost that is ever pretended as to the superior fitness of men for all the functions now reserved to them, the same argument applies which forbids a legal qualification for members of Parliament. If only once in a dozen years the conditions of eligibility exclude a fit person, there is a real loss, while the exclusion of thousands of unfit persons is no gain; for if the constitution of the electoral body disposes them to choose unfit persons, there are always plenty of such persons to choose from. In all things of any difficulty and importance, those who can do them well are fewer than the need, even with the most unrestricted latitude of choice; and any limitation of the field of selection deprives society of some chances of being served by the competent, without ever saving it from the incompetent.

At present, in the more improved countries, the disabilities of women are the only case, save one, in which laws and institutions take persons at their birth, and ordain that they shall never in all their lives be allowed to compete for certain things. The one exception is that of royalty. Persons still are born to the throne; no one, not of the reigning family, can ever occupy it, and no one even of that family can, by any means but the course of hereditary succession, attain it. All other dignities and social advantages are open to the whole male sex; many indeed are only attainable by wealth, but wealth may be striven for by anyone, and is actually obtained by many men of the very humblest origin. The difficulties, to the majority, are indeed insuperable without the aid of fortunate accidents; but no male human being is under any legal ban; neither law nor opinion superadd artificial obstacles to the natural ones. Royalty, as I have said, is excepted; but in this case everyone feels it to be an exception—an anomaly in the modern world, in marked opposition to its customs and principles, and to be justified only by extraordinary special expediencies, which, though individuals and nations differ in estimating their weight, unquestionably do in fact exist. But in this exceptional case, in which a high social function is, for important reasons, bestowed on birth instead of being put up to competition, all free nations contrive to adhere in substance to the principle from which they nominally derogate; for they circumscribe this high function by conditions avowedly intended to prevent the person to whom it ostensibly belongs from really performing it; while the person by whom it is performed, the responsible minister, does obtain the post by a competition from which no fullgrown citizen of the male sex is legally excluded. The disabilities, therefore, to which women are subject from the mere fact of their birth, are the solitary examples of the kind in modern legislation. In no instance except this, which comprehends half the human race, are the higher social functions closed against anyone by a fatality of birth which no exertions, and no change of circumstances can overcome; for even religious disabilities (besides that in England and in Europe they have practically almost ceased to exist) do not close any career to the disqualified person in case of conversion.

The social subordination of women thus stands out an isolated fact in modern social institutions; a solitary breach of what has become their fundamental law; a single relic of an old world of thought and practice exploded in everything else, but retained in the one thing of most universal interest; as if a gigantic dolmen, or a vast temple of Jupiter Olympius, occupied the site of St. Paul's and received daily worship, while the surrounding Christian churches were only resorted to on fasts and festivals. This entire discrepancy between one social fact and all those which accompany it, and the radical opposition between its nature and the progressive movement which is the boast of the modern world, and which has successively swept away everything else of an analogous character, surely affords, to a conscientious observer of human tendencies, serious matter for reflection. It raises a prima facie presumption on the unfavorable side, far outweighing any which custom and usage could in such circumstances create on the favorable; and should at least suffice to make this, like the choice between republicanism and royalty, a balanced question.

The least that can be demanded is, that the question should not be considered as prejudged by existing fact and existing opinion, but open to discussion on its merits, as a question of justice and expediency; the decision on this, as on any of the other social arrangements of mankind, depending on what an enlightened estimate of tendencies and consequences may show to be most advantageous to humanity in general, without distinction of sex. And the discussion must be a real discussion, descending to foundations, and not resting satisfied with vague and general assertions. It will not do, for instance, to assert in general terms, that the experience of mankind has pronounced in favor of the existing system. Experience cannot possibly have decided between two courses, so long as there had only been experience of one. If it be said that the doctrine of the equality of the sexes rests only on theory, it must be remembered that the contrary doctrine also has only theory to rest upon. All that is proved in its favor by direct experience, is that mankind have been able to exist under it, and to attain the degree of improvement and prosperity which we now see; but whether that prosperity has been attained sooner, or is now greater, than it would have been under the other system, experience does not say. On the other hand, experience does say, that every step in improvement has been so invariably accompanied by a step made in raising the social position of women, that historians and philosophers have been led to adopt their elevation or debasement as on the whole the surest test and most correct measure of the civilization of a people or an age. Through all the progressive period of human history, the condition of women has been approaching nearer to equality with men. This does not of itself prove that the assimilation must go on to complete equality; but it assuredly affords some presumption that such is the case.

Neither does it avail anything to say that the *nature* of the two sexes adapts them to their present functions and position, and renders these appropriate to them. Standing on the ground of common sense and the constitution of the human mind, I deny that anyone knows, or can know, the nature of the two sexes, as long as they have only been seen in their present relation to one another. If men had ever been found in society without women, or women without men, or if there had been a society of men and women in which the women were not under the control of the men, something might have been positively known about the mental and moral differences which may be inherent in the nature of each. What is now called the nature of women is an eminently artificial thing—the result of forced repression in some directions, unnatural stimulation in others. It may be asserted without scruple, that no other class of dependents have had their character so entirely distorted from its natural proportions by their relation with their masters; for, if conquered and slave races have been, in some respects, more forcibly repressed, whatever in them has not been crushed down by an iron heel has generally been let alone, and if left with any liberty of development it has developed itself according to its own laws; but in the case of women, a hot-house and stove cultivation has always been carried on of some of the capabilities of their nature, for the benefit and pleasure of their masters. Then, because certain products of the general vital force sprout luxuriantly and reach a great development in this heated atmosphere and under this active nurture and watering, while other shoots from the same root, which are left outside in the wintry air, with ice purposely heaped all round them, have a stunted growth, and some are burnt off with fire and disappear; men, with that inability to recognize their own work which distinguishes the unanalytic mind, indolently believe that the tree grows of itself in the way they have made it grow, and that it would die if one-half of it were not kept in a vapor-bath and the other half in the snow.

Of all difficulties which impede the progress of thought, and the formation of well-grounded opinions on life and social arrangements, the greatest is now the unspeakable ignorance and inattention of mankind in respect to the influences which form human character. Whatever any portion of the human species now are, or seem to be, such, it is supposed, they have a natural tendency to be: even when the most elementary knowledge of the circumstances in which they have been placed, clearly points out the causes that made them what they are. Because a cotter deeply in arrears to his landlord is not industrious, there are people who think that the Irish are naturally idle. Because constitutions can be overthrown when the authorities appointed to execute them turn their arms against them, there are people who think the French incapable of free government. Because the Greeks cheated the Turks, and the Turks only plundered the Greeks, there are persons who think that the Turks are naturally more sincere: and because women, as is often said, care nothing about politics except their personalities, it is supposed that the general good is naturally less interesting to women than to men. History, which is now so much better understood than formerly, teaches another lesson: if only by showing the extraordinary susceptibility of human nature to external influences, and the extreme variableness of those of its manifestations which are supposed to be most universal and uniform. But in history, as in traveling, men usually see only what they already had in their own minds; and few learn much from history, who do not bring much with them to its study.

Hence, in regard to that most difficult question, what are the natural differences between the two sexes—a subject on which it is impossible in the present state of society to obtain complete and correct knowledge—while almost everybody dogmatizes upon it, almost all neglect and make light of the only means by which any partial insight can be obtained into it. This is, an analytic study of the most important department of psychology, the laws of the influence of circumstances on character. For, however great and apparently ineradicable the moral and intellectual differences between men and women might be, the evidence of their being natural differences could only be negative. Those only could be inferred to be natural which could not possibly be artificial—the residuum, after deducting every characteristic of either sex which can admit of being explained from education or external circumstances. The profoundest knowledge of the laws of the formation of character is indispensable to entitle anyone to affirm even that there is any difference, much more what the difference is, between the two sexes considered as moral and rational beings; and since no one, as yet, has that knowledge (for there is hardly any subject which, in proportion to its importance, has been so little studied), no one is thus far entitled to any positive opinion on the subject. Conjectures are all that can at present be made; conjectures more or less probable, according as more or less authorized by such knowledge as we yet have of the laws of psychology, as applied to the formation of character.

Even the preliminary knowledge, what the differences between the sexes now are, apart from all question as to how they are made what they are, is still in the crudest and most incomplete state. Medical practitioners and physiologists have ascertained, to some extent, the differences in bodily constitution; and this is an important element to the psychologist; but hardly any medical practitioner is a psychologist. Respecting the mental characteristics of women, their observations are of no more worth than those of common men. It is a subject on which nothing final can be known, so long as those who alone can really know it, women themselves, have given but little testimony, and that little, mostly suborned. It is easy to know stupid women. Stupidity is much the same all the world over. A stupid person's notions and feelings may confidently be inferred from those which prevail in the circle by which the person is surrounded. Not so with those whose opinions and feelings are an emanation from their own nature and faculties. It is only a man here and there who has any tolerable knowledge of the character even of the women of his own family. I do not mean, of their capabilities; these nobody knows, not even themselves, because most of them have never been called out. I mean their actually existing thoughts and feelings. Many a man thinks he perfectly understands women, because he has had amatory relations with several, perhaps with many of them. If he is a good observer, and his experience extends to quality as well as quantity, he may have learnt something of one narrow department of their nature—an important department, no doubt. But of all the rest of it, few persons are generally more ignorant, because there are few from whom it is so carefully hidden. The most favorable case which a man can generally have for studying the character of a woman, is that of his own wife: for the opportunities are greater, and the cases of complete sympathy not so unspeakably rare. And in fact, this is the source from which any knowledge worth having on the subject has, I believe, generally come. But most men have not had the opportunity of studying in this way more than a single case; accordingly one can, to an almost laughable degree, infer what a man's wife is like, from his opinions about women in general. To make even this one case yield any result, the woman must be worth knowing, and the man not only a competent judge, but of a character so sympathetic in itself, and so well adapted to hers, that he can either read her mind by sympathetic intuition, or has nothing in himself which makes her shy of disclosing it. Hardly anything, I believe, can be more rare than this conjunction. It often happens that there is the most complete unity of feeling and community of intersts as to all external things, yet the one has as little admission into the internal life of the other as if they were common acquaintance. Even with true affection, authority on the one side and subordination on the other prevent perfect confidence. Though nothing may be intentionally withheld, much is not shown. In the analogous relation of parent and child, the corresponding phenomenon must have been in the observation of everyone. As between father and son, how many are the cases in which the father, in spite of real affection on both sides, obviously to all the world does not know, nor suspect, parts of the son's character familiar to his companions and equals. The truth is, that the position of looking up to another is extremely unpropitious to complete sincerity and openness with him. The fear of losing ground in his opinion or in his feelings is so strong that even in an upright character, there is an unconscious tendency to show only the best side, or the side which, though not the best, is that which he most likes to see; and it may be confidently said that thorough knowledge of one another hardly exists, but between persons who, besides being intimates, are equals. How much more true, then, must all this be, when the one is not only under the authority of the other, but has it inculcated on her as a duty to reckon everything else subordinate to his comfort and pleasure, and to let him neither see nor feel anything coming from her, except what is agreeable to him. All these difficulties stand in the way of a man's obtaining any thorough knowledge even of the one woman whom alone, in general, he has sufficient opportunity of studying. When we further consider that to understand one woman is not necessarily to understand any other woman; that even if he could study many women of one rank, or of one country, he would not thereby understand women of other ranks or countries; and even if he did, they are still only the women of a single period of history; we may safely assert that the knowledge which men can acquire of

women, even as they have been and are, without reference to what they might be, is wretchedly imperfect and superficial, and always will be so, until women themselves have told all that they have to tell.

And this time has not come; nor will it come otherwise than gradually. It is but of yesterday that women have either been qualified by literary accomplishments, or permitted by society, to tell anything to the general public. As yet very few of them dare tell anything, which men, on whom their literary success depends, are unwilling to bear. Let us remember in what manner, up to a very recent time, the expression, even by a male author, of uncustomary opinions, or what are deemed eccentric feelings, usually was, and in some degree still is, received; and we may form some faint conception under what impediments a woman, who is brought up to think custom and opinion her sovereign rule, attempts to express in books anything drawn from the depths of her own nature. The greatest woman who has left writings behind her sufficient to give her an eminent rank in the literature of her country, thought it necessary to prefix as a motto to her boldest work, *"Un homme peut braver l'opinion; une femme doit s'y soumettre."*[3] The greater part of what women write about women is mere sycophancy to men. In the case of unmarried women, much of it seems only intended to increase their chance of a husband. Many, both married and unmarried, overstep the mark, and inculcate a servility beyond what is desired or relished by any man, except the very vulgarest. But this is not so often the case as, even at a quite late period, it still was. Literary women are becoming more free-spoken, and more willing to express their real sentiments. Unfortunately, in this country especially, they are themselves such artificial products, that their sentiments are compounded of a small element of individual observation and consciousness, and a very large one of acquired associations. This will be less and less the case, but it will remain true to a great extent, as long as social institutions do not admit the same free development of originality in women which is possible to men. When that time comes, and not before, we shall see, and not merely hear, as much as it is necessary to know of the nature of women, and the adaptation of other things to it.

I have dwelt so much on the difficulties which at present obstruct any real knowledge by men of

---

[3] "A man can brave opinion; a woman must submit to it" (Madame de Staël, *Delphine*).

the true nature of women, because in this as in so many other things "*opinio copiæ inter maximas causas inopiæ est;*"[4] and there is little chance of reasonable thinking on the matter, while people flatter themselves that they perfectly understand a subject of which most men know absolutely nothing, and of which it is at present impossible that any man, or all men taken together, should have knowledge which can qualify them to lay down the law to women as to what is, or is not, their vocation. Happily, no such knowledge is necessary for any practical purpose connected with the position of women in relation to society and life. For, according to all the principles involved in modern society, the question rests with women themselves,—to be decided by their own experience, and by the use of their own faculties. There are no means of finding what either one person or many can do, but by trying, —and no means by which anyone else can discover for them what it is for happiness to do or leave undone.

One thing we may be certain of,—that what is contrary to women's nature to do, they never will be made to do by simply giving their nature free play. The anxiety of mankind to interfere in behalf of nature, for fear lest nature should not succeed in effecting its purpose, is an altogether unnecessary solicitude. What women by nature cannot do, it is quite superfluous to forbid them from doing. What they can do, but not so well as the men who are their competitors, competition suffices to exclude them from; since nobody asks for protective duties and bounties in favor of women; it is only asked that the present bounties and protective duties in favor of men should be recalled. If women have a greater natural inclination for some things than for others, there is no need of laws or social inculcation to make the majority of them do the former in preference to the latter. Whatever women's services are most wanted for, the free play of competition will hold out the strongest inducements to them to undertake. And, as the words imply, they are most wanted for the things for which they are most fit; by the apportionment of which to them, the collective faculties of the two sexes can be applied on the whole with the greatest sum of valuable result.

The general opinion of men is supposed to be, that the natural vocation of a woman is that of a wife and mother. I say, is supposed to be, because, judging from acts—from the whole of the present constitution of society—one might infer that their opinion was the direct contrary. They might be supposed to think that the alleged natural vocation of women was of all things the most repugnant to their nature; insomuch that if they are free to do anything else—if any other means of living, or occupation of their time and faculties, is open, which has any chance of appearing desirable to them—there will not be enough of them who will be willing to accept the condition said to be natural to them. If this is the real opinion of men in general it would be well that it should be spoken out. I should like to hear somebody openly enunciating the doctrine (it is already implied in much that is written on the subject)— "It is necessary to society that women should marry and produce children. They will not do so unless they are compelled. Therefore it is necessary to compel them." The merits of the case would then be clearly defined. It would be exactly that of the slave-holders of South Carolina and Louisiana. "It is necessary that cotton and sugar should be grown. White men cannot produce them. Negroes will not, for any wages which we choose to give. *Ergo* they must be compelled." An illustration still closer to the point is that of impressment. Sailors must absolutely be had to defend the country. It often happens that they will not voluntarily enlist. Therefore there must be the power of forcing them. How often has this logic been used! and, but for one flaw in it, without doubt it would have been successful up to this day. But it is open to the retort—First pay the sailors the honest value of their labor. When you have made it as well worth their while to serve you, as to work for other employers, you will have no more difficulty than others have in obtaining their services. To this there is no logical answer except "I will not:" and as people are now not only ashamed, but are not desirous, to rob the laborer of his hire, impressment is no longer advocated. Those who attempt to force women into marriage by closing all other doors against them, lay themselves open to a similar retort. If they mean what they say, their opinion must evidently be, that men do not render the married condition so desirable to women, as to induce them to accept it for its own recommendations. It is not a sign of one's thinking the boon one offers very attractive, when one allows only Hobson's choice, "that or none." And here, I believe, is the clew to the feelings of those men who have a real antipathy

---

[4] "The opinion of the multitude in important matters is useless."

to the equal freedom of women. I believe they are afraid, not lest women should be unwilling to marry, for I do not think that anyone in reality has that apprehension; but lest they should insist that marriage should be on equal conditions; lest all women of spirit and capacity should prefer doing almost anything else, not in their own eyes degrading, rather than marry, when marrying is giving themselves a master, and a master too of all their earthly possessions. And truly, if this consequence were necessarily incident to marriage, I think that the apprehension would be very well founded. I agree in thinking it probable that few women, capable of anything else, would, unless under an irresistible *entrainement*, rendering them for the time insensible to any-

thing but itself, choose such a lot, when any other means were open to them of filling a conventionally honorable place in life: and if men are determined that the law of marriage shall be a law of despotism, they are quite right, in point of mere policy, in leaving to women only Hobson's choice. But, in that case, all that has been done in the modern world to relax the chain on the minds of women, has been a mistake. They never should have been allowed to receive a literary education. Women who read, much more women who write, are, in the existing constitution of things, a contradiction and a disturbing element: and it was wrong to bring women up with any acquirements but those of an odalisque, or of a domestic servant.

from Autobiography

Mill began writing his autobiography in the mid-eighteen-fifties when he was concerned that both he and Harriet Taylor would soon die. She lived to 1858, time enough for her to go over the draft making suggestions and corrections, many of which Mill adopted in the final version. The work, however, was not published until 1873 just after Mill's death when it was seen through the press by Harriet Taylor's daughter Helen. Although Mill's onetime friend Carlyle called the work the "autobiography of a steam-engine," there is more passion in it than such a description would suggest. Mill strives as always to maintain a sober and judicious stance, but some of the intensity of his experiences comes through, nowhere more powerfully than in Chapter V, "A Crisis in My Mental History," given below. Here, the Saint of Rationalism, as Mill came to be known, reveals the spiritual deficiencies of the utilitarian philosophy in which he was raised, and how he succeeded in coming through an experience similar to loss of faith with his creed intact but enriched.

CHAPTER V

A Crisis in My Mental History, One Stage Onward

FOR some years after this time[1] I wrote very little, and nothing regularly, for publication: and great were the advantages which I derived from the intermission. It was of no common importance to me, at this period, to be able to digest and mature my thoughts for my own mind only, without any immediate call for giving them

out in print. Had I gone on writing, it would have much disturbed the important transformation in my opinions and character, which took place during those years. The origin of this transformation, or at least the process by which I was prepared for it, can only be explained by turning some distance back.

From the winter of 1821, when I first read Bentham, and especially from the commencement of the Westminster Review, I had what might truly be called an object in life; to be a reformer of the world. My conception of my own happiness was entirely identified with this object. The personal sympathies I wished for were those of fellow labourers in this enterprise. I endeavoured

[1] I.e., after 1828.

to pick up as many flowers as I could by the way; but as a serious and permanent personal satisfaction to rest upon, my whole reliance was placed on this: and I was accustomed to felicitate myself on the certainty of a happy life which I enjoyed, through placing my happiness in something durable and distant, in which some progress might be always making, while it could never be exhausted by complete attainment. This did very well for several years, during which the general improvement going on in the world and the idea of myself as engaged with others in struggling to promote it, seemed enough to fill up an interesting and animated existence. But the time came when I awakened from this as from a dream. It was in the autumn of 1826. I was in a dull state of nerves, such as everybody is occasionally liable to; unsusceptible to enjoyment or pleasurable excitement; one of those moods when what is pleasure at other times, becomes insipid or indifferent; the state, I should think, in which converts to Methodism usually are, when smitten by their first "conviction of sin." In this frame of mind it occurred to me to put the question directly to myself, "Suppose that all your objects in life were realized; that all the changes in institutions and opinions which you are looking forward to, could be completely effected at this very instant: would this be a great joy and happiness to you?" And an irrepressible self-consciousness distinctly answered, "No!" At this my heart sank within me: the whole foundation on which my life was constructed fell down. All my happiness was to have been found in the continual pursuit of this end. The end had ceased to charm, and how could there ever again be any interest in the means? I seemed to have nothing left to live for.

At first I hoped that the cloud would pass away of itself; but it did not. A night's sleep, the sovereign remedy for the smaller vexations of life, had no effect on it. I awoke to a renewed consciousness of the woful fact. I carried it with me into all companies, into all occupations. Hardly anything had power to cause me even a few minutes oblivion of it. For some months the cloud seemed to grow thicker and thicker. The lines in Coleridge's "Dejection"—I was not then acquainted with them—exactly describe my case:

> A grief without a pang, void, dark and drear,
> A drowsy, stifled, unimpassioned grief,
> Which finds no natural outlet or relief
> In word, or sigh, or tear.

In vain I sought relief from my favourite books; those memorials of past nobleness and greatness, from which I had always hitherto drawn strength and animation. I read them now without feeling, or with the accustomed feeling *minus* all its charm; and I became persuaded, that my love of mankind, and of excellence for its own sake, had worn itself out. I sought no comfort by speaking to others of what I felt. If I had loved any one sufficiently to make confiding my griefs a necessity, I should not have been in the condition I was. I felt, too, that mine was not an interesting, or in any way respectable distress. There was nothing in it to attract sympathy. Advice, if I had known where to seek it, would have been most precious. The words of Macbeth to the physician often occurred to my thoughts.[2] But there was no one on whom I could build the faintest hope of such assistance. My father, to whom it would have been natural to me to have recourse in any practical difficulties, was the last person to whom, in such a case as this, I looked for help. Everything convinced me that he had no knowledge of any such mental state as I was suffering from, and that even if he could be made to understand it, he was not the physician who could heal it. My education, which was wholly his work, had been conducted without any regard to the possibility of its ending in this result; and I saw no use in giving him the pain of thinking that his plans had failed, when the failure was probably irremediable, and at all events, beyond the power of *his* remedies. Of other friends, I had at that time none to whom I had any hope of making my condition intelligible. It was however abundantly intelligible to myself; and the more I dwelt upon it, the more hopeless it appeared.

My course of study had led me to believe, that all mental and moral feelings and qualities, whether of a good or of a bad kind, were the results of association; that we love one thing and hate another, take pleasure in one sort of action or contemplation, and pain in another sort, through the clinging of pleasurable or painful ideas to those things, from the effect of education or of experience. As a corollary from this, I had always heard it maintained by my father, and was myself convinced, that the object of education should be to form the strongest possible associations of the salutary class; associations of pleasure with all things beneficial to the great whole, and of pain with all things hurtful to it. This doctrine appeared inexpugnable; but it now seemed to me

---

[2] "Canst thou not minister to a mind diseas'd," etc. (*Macbeth*, V, ii, 40 ff.).

on retrospect, that my teachers had occupied themselves but superficially with the means of forming and keeping up these salutary associations. They seemed to have trusted altogether to the old familiar instruments, praise and blame, reward and punishment. Now I did not doubt that by these means, begun early and applied unremittingly, intense associations of pain and pleasure, especially of pain, might be created, and might produce desires and aversions capable of lasting undiminished to the end of life. But there must always be something artificial and casual in associations thus produced. The pains and pleasures thus forcibly associated with things, are not connected with them by any natural tie; and it is therefore, I thought, essential to the durability of these associations, that they should have become so intense and inveterate as to be practically indissoluble, before the habitual exercise of the power of analysis had commenced. For I now saw, or thought I saw, what I had always before received with incredulity—that the habit of analysis has a tendency to wear away the feelings: as indeed it has when no other mental habit is cultivated, and the analysing spirit remains without its natural complements and correctives. The very excellence of analysis (I argued) is that it tends to weaken and undermine whatever is the result of prejudice; and it enables us mentally to separate ideas which have only casually clung together: and no associations whatever could ultimately resist this dissolving force, were it not that we owe to analysis our clearest knowledge of the permanent sequences in nature; the real connexions between Things, not dependent on our will and feelings; natural laws, by virtue of which, in many cases, one thing is inseparable from another in fact; which laws, in proportion as they are clearly perceived and imaginatively realized, cause our ideas of things which are always joined together in Nature, to cohere more and more closely in our thoughts. Analytic habits may thus even strengthen the associations between causes and effects, means and ends, but tend altogether to weaken those which are, to speak familiarly, a *mere* matter of feeling. They are therefore (I thought) favourable to prudence and clear-sightedness, but a perpetual worm at the root both of the passions and of the virtues; and above all, fearfully undermine all desires, and all pleasures, which are the effects of association, that is, according to the theory I held, all except the purely physical and organic; of the entire insufficiency of which to make life desirable, no

one had a stronger conviction than I had. These were the laws of human nature by which, as it seemed to me, I had been brought to my present state. All those to whom I looked up, were of opinion that the pleasure of sympathy with human beings, and the feelings which made the good of others, and especially of mankind on a large scale, the object of existence, were the greatest and surest sources of happiness. Of the truth of this I was convinced, but to know that a feeling would make me happy if I had it, did not give me the feeling. My education, I thought, had failed to create these feelings in sufficient strength to resist the dissolving influence of analysis, while the whole course of my intellectual cultivation had made precocious and premature analysis the inveterate habit of my mind. I was thus, as I said to myself, left stranded at the commencement of my voyage, with a well equipped ship and a rudder, but no sail; without any real desire for the ends which I had been so carefully fitted out to work for: no delight in virtue or the general good, but also just as little in anything else. The fountains of vanity and ambition seemed to have dried up within me, as completely as those of benevolence. I had had (as I reflected) some gratification of vanity at too early an age: I had obtained some distinction, and felt myself of some importance, before the desire of distinction and of importance had grown into a passion: and little as it was which I had attained, yet having been attained too early, like all pleasures enjoyed too soon, it had made me *blasé* and indifferent to the pursuit. Thus neither selfish nor unselfish pleasures were pleasures to me. And there seemed no power in nature sufficient to begin the formation of my character anew, and create in a mind now irretrievably analytic, fresh associations of pleasure with any of the objects of human desire.

These were the thoughts which mingled with the dry heavy dejection of the melancholy winter of 1826–7. During this time I was not incapable of my usual occupations. I went on with them mechanically, by the mere force of habit. I had been so drilled in a certain sort of mental exercise, that I could still carry it on when all the spirit had gone out of it. I even composed and spoke several speeches at the debating society, how, or with what degree of success I know not. Of four years continual speaking at that society, this is the only year of which I remember next to nothing. Two lines of Coleridge, in whom alone of all writers I have found a true description of what I felt, were often in my thoughts, not at this time (for I had never read them), but in a later period of the same mental malady:

> Work without hope draws nectar in a sieve,
> And hope without an object cannot live.[3]

In all probability my case was by no means so peculiar as I fancied it, and I doubt not that many others have passed through a similar state; but the idiosyncracies of my education had given to the general phenomenon a special character, which made it seem the natural effect of causes that it was hardly possible for time to remove. I frequently asked myself, if I could, or if I was bound to go on living, when life must be passed in this manner. I generally answered to myself, that I did not think I could possibly bear it beyond a year. When, however, not more than half that duration of time had elapsed, a small ray of light broke in upon my gloom. I was reading, accidentally, Marmontel's Memoirs,[4] and came to the passage which relates his father's death, the distressed position of the family, and the sudden inspiration by which he, then a mere boy, felt and made them feel that he would be everything to them—would supply the place of all that they had lost. A vivid conception of the scene and its feelings came over me, and I was moved to tears. From this moment my burthen grew lighter. The oppression of the thought that all feeling was dead within me, was gone. I was no longer hopeless: I was not a stock or a stone. I had still, it seemed, some of the material out of which all worth of character, and all capacity for happiness, are made. Relieved from my ever present sense of irremediable wretchedness, I gradually found that the ordinary incidents of life could again give me some pleasure; that I could again find enjoyment, not intense, but sufficient for cheerfulness, in sunshine and sky, in books, in conversation, in public affairs; and that there was, once more, excitement, though of a moderate kind, in exerting myself for my opinions, and for the public good. Thus the cloud gradually drew off, and I again enjoyed life: and though I had several relapses, some of which lasted many months, I never again was as miserable as I had been.

The experiences of this period had two very marked effects on my opinions and character. In the first place, they led me to adopt a theory of life, very unlike that on which I had before acted, and having much in common with what at that time I certainly had never heard of, the anti-self-consciousness theory of Carlyle.[5] I never, indeed, wavered in the conviction that happiness is the test of all rules of conduct, and the end of life. But I now thought that this end was only to be attained by not making it the direct end. Those only are happy (I thought) who have their minds fixed on some object other than their own happiness; on the happiness of others, on the improvement of mankind, even on some art or pursuit, followed not as a means, but as itself an ideal end. Aiming thus at something else, they find happiness by the way. The enjoyments of life (such was now my theory) are sufficient to make it a pleasant thing, when they are taken *en passant,* without being made a principal object. Once make them so, and they are immediately felt to be insufficient. They will not bear a scrutinizing examination. Ask yourself whether you are happy, and you cease to be so. The only chance is to treat, not happiness, but some end external to it, as the purpose of life. Let your self-consciousness, your scrutiny, your self-interrogation, exhaust themselves on that; and if otherwise fortunately circumstanced you will inhale happiness with the air you breathe, without dwelling on it or thinking about it, without either forestalling it in imagination, or putting it to flight by fatal questioning. This theory now became the basis of my philosophy of life. And I still hold to it as the best theory for all those who have but a moderate degree of sensibility and of capacity for enjoyment, that is, for the great majority of mankind.

The other important change which my opinions at this time underwent, was that I, for the first time, gave its proper place, among the prime necessities of human well-being, to the internal culture of the individual. I ceased to attach almost exclusive importance to the ordering of outward circumstances, and the training of the human being for speculation and for action. I had now learnt by experience that the passive susceptibilities needed to be cultivated as well as the active capacities, and required to be nourished and enriched as well as guided. I did not, for an instant, lose sight of, or undervalue, that part of the truth which I had seen before; I never turned recreant to intellectual culture, or ceased to consider the power and practice of

---

[3] Coleridge's "Work Without Hope," ll., 13–14.
[4] Jean François Marmontel (1723–99), author of *Mémoires d'un père.*
[5] See especially Carlyle's "Characteristics," in this volume.

analysis as an essential condition both of individual and of social improvement. But I thought that it had consequences which required to be corrected, by joining other kinds of cultivation with it. The maintenance of a due balance among the faculties, now seemed to me of primary importance. The cultivation of the feelings became one of the cardinal points in my ethical and philosophical creed. And my thoughts and inclinations turned in an increasing degree towards whatever seemed capable of being instrumental to that object.

I now began to find meaning in the things which I had read or heard about the importance of poetry and art as instruments of human culture. But it was some time longer before I began to know this by personal experience. The only one of the imaginative arts in which I had from childhood taken great pleasure, was music; the best effect of which (and in this it surpasses perhaps every other art) consists in exciting enthusiasm; in winding up to a high pitch those feelings of an elevated kind which are already in the character, but to which this excitement gives a glow and a fervour, which though transitory at its utmost height, is precious for sustaining them at other times. This effect of music I had often experienced; but, like all my pleasurable susceptibilities, it was suspended during the gloomy period. I had sought relief again and again from this quarter, but found none. After the tide had turned, and I was in process of recovery, I had been helped forward by music, but in a much less elevated manner. I at this time first became acquainted with Weber's Oberon,[6] and the extreme pleasure which I drew from its delicious melodies did me good, by shewing me a source of pleasure to which I was as susceptible as ever. The good however was much impaired by the thought, that the pleasure of music (as is quite true of such pleasure as this was, that of mere tune) fades with familiarity, and requires either to be revived by intermittence, or fed by continual novelty. And it is very characteristic both of my then state, and of the general tone of my mind at this period of my life, that I was seriously tormented by the thought of the exhaustibility of musical combinations. The octave consists only of five tones and two semitones, which can be put together in only a limited number of ways, of

which but a small proportion are beautiful: most of these, it seemed to me, must have been already discovered, and there could not be room for a long succession of Mozarts and Webers, to strike out as these had done, entirely new and surpassingly rich veins of musical beauty. This source of anxiety may perhaps be thought to resemble that of the philosophers of Laputa, who feared lest the sun should be burnt out.[7] It was, however, connected with the best feature in my character, and the only good point to be found in my very unromantic and in no way honorable distress. For though my dejection, honestly looked at, could not be called other than egotistical, produced by the ruin, as I thought, of my fabric of happiness, yet the destiny of mankind in general was ever in my thoughts, and could not be separated from my own. I felt that the flaw in my life, must be a flaw in life itself; that the question was, whether, if the reformers of society and government could succeed in their objects, and every person in the community were free and in a state of physical comfort, the pleasures of life, being no longer kept up by struggle and privation, would cease to be pleasures. And I felt that unless I could see my way to some better hope than this for human happiness in general, my dejection must continue; but that if I could see such an outlet, I should then look on the world with pleasure; content as far as I was myself concerned, with any fair share of the general lot.

This state of my thoughts and feelings made the fact of my reading Wordsworth for the first time (in the autumn of 1828) an important event in my life. I took up the collection of his poems from curiosity, with no expectation of mental relief from it, though I had before resorted to poetry with that hope. In the worst period of my depression I had read through the whole of Byron (then new to me) to try whether a poet, whose peculiar department was supposed to be that of the intenser feelings, could rouse any feeling in me. As might be expected, I got no good from this reading, but the reverse. The poet's state of mind was too like my own. His was the lament of a man who had worn out all pleasures, and who seemed to think that life, to all who possess the good things of it, must necessarily be the vapid uninteresting thing which I

---

[6] Carl Maria Friedrich von Weber (1786–1826), German composer; his *Oberon* was first produced in London in 1826.
[7] Reference to Swift's *Gulliver's Travels*.

found it. His Harold and Manfred had the same burthen on them which I had; and I was not in a frame of mind to derive any comfort from the vehement sensual passion of his Giaours, or the sullenness of his Laras. But while Byron was exactly what did not suit my condition, Wordsworth was exactly what did. I had looked into the Excursion two or three years before, and found little in it; and should probably have found as little, had I read it at this time. But the miscellaneous poems, in the two-volume edition of 1815 (to which little of value was added in the latter part of the author's life), proved to be the precise thing for my mental wants at that particular juncture.

In the first place, these poems addressed themselves powerfully to one of the strongest of my pleasurable susceptibilities, the love of rural objects and natural scenery; to which I had been indebted not only for much of the pleasure of my life, but quite recently for relief from one of my longest relapses into depression. In this power of rural beauty over me, there was a foundation laid for taking pleasure in Wordsworth's poetry; the more so, as his scenery lies mostly among mountains, which, owing to my early Pyrenean excursion, were my ideal of natural beauty. But Wordsworth would never have had any great effect on me, if he had merely placed before me beautiful pictures of natural scenery. Scott does this still better than Wordsworth, and a very second-rate landscape does it more effectually than any poet. What made Wordsworth's poems a medicine for my state of mind, was that they expressed, not mere outward beauty, but states of feeling, and of thought coloured by feeling, under the excitement of beauty. They seemed to be the very culture of the feelings, which I was in quest of. In them I seemed to draw from a source of inward joy, of sympathetic and imaginative pleasure, which could be shared in by all human beings; which had no connexion with struggle or imperfection, but would be made richer by every improvement in the physical or social condition of mankind. From them I seemed to learn what would be the perennial sources of happiness, when all the greater evils of life shall have been removed. And I felt myself at once better and happier as I came under their influence. There have certainly been, even in our own age, greater poets than Wordsworth; but poetry of deeper and loftier feeling could not have done for me at that time what his did. I needed to be made to feel that there was real, permanent happiness in tranquil contemplation. Wordsworth taught me this, not only without turning away from, but with a greatly increased interest in, the common feelings and common destiny of human beings. And the delight which these poems gave me, proved that with culture of this sort, there was nothing to dread from the most confirmed habit of analysis. At the conclusion of the Poems came the famous Ode, falsely called Platonic, "Intimations of Immortality": in which, along with more than his usual sweetness of melody and rhythm, and along with the two passages of grand imagery but bad philosophy so often quoted, I found that he too had had similar experience to mine; that he also had felt that the first freshness of youthful enjoyment of life was not lasting; but that he had sought for compensation, and found it, in the way in which he was now teaching me to find it. The result was that I gradually, but completely, emerged from my habitual depression, and was never again subject to it. I long continued to value Wordsworth less according to his intrinsic merits, than by the measure of what he had done for me. Compared with the greatest poets, he may be said to be the poet of unpoetical natures, possessed of quiet and contemplative tastes. But unpoetical natures are precisely those which require poetic cultivation. This cultivation Wordsworth is much more fitted to give, than poets who are intrinsically far more poets than he.

It so fell out that the merits of Wordsworth were the occasion of my first public declaration of my new way of thinking, and separation from those of my habitual companions who had not undergone a similar change. The person with whom at that time I was most in the habit of comparing notes on such subjects was Roebuck, and I induced him to read Wordsworth, in whom he also at first seemed to find much to admire: but I, like most Wordsworthians, threw myself into strong antagonism to Byron, both as a poet and to his influence on the character. Roebuck, all whose instincts were those of action and struggle, had, on the contrary, a strong relish and great admiration of Byron, whose writings he regarded as the poetry of human life, while Wordsworth's, according to him, was that of flowers and butterflies. We agreed to have the fight out at our Debating Society, where we accordingly discussed for two evenings the comparative merits of Byron and Wordsworth, propounding and illustrating by long recitations our respective theories of poetry: Sterling also, in a brilliant speech, putting forward his particular theory.[8] This was the first debate on any weighty subject in which Roebuck and I had been on opposite sides. The schism between us widened from this time more and more, though we continued for some years longer to be companions. In the beginning, our chief divergence related to the cultivation of the feelings. Roebuck was in many respects very different from the vulgar notion of a Benthamite or Utilitarian. He was a lover of poetry and of most of the fine arts. He took great pleasure in music, in dramatic performances, especially in painting, and himself drew and designed landscapes with great facility and beauty. But he never could be made to see that these things have any value as aids in the formation of character. Personally, instead of being, as Benthamites are supposed to be, void of feeling, he had very quick and strong sensibilities. But, like most Englishmen who have feelings, he found his feelings stand very much in his way. He was much more susceptible in the painful sympathies than to the pleasurable, and looking for his happiness elsewhere, he wished that his feelings should be deadened rather than quickened. And in truth the English character, and English social circumstances, make it so seldom possible to derive happiness from the exercise of the sympathies, that it is not wonderful if they count for little in an Englishman's scheme of life. In most other countries the paramount importance of the sympathies as a constituent of individual happiness is an axiom, taken for granted rather than needing any formal statement; but most English thinkers almost seem to regard them as necessary evils, required for keeping men's actions benevolent and compassionate. Roebuck was, or appeared to be, this kind of Englishman. He saw little good in any cultivation of the feelings, and none at all in cultivating them through the imagination, which he thought was only cultivating illusions. It was in vain I urged on him that the imaginative emotion which an idea when vividly conceived excites in us, is not an illusion but a fact, as real as any of the other qualities of objects; and far from implying anything erroneous and delusive in our mental apprehension of the object, is quite consistent with the most accurate knowledge and most perfect practical recognition of all its physical and intellectual laws and relations. The intensest feeling of the beauty of a cloud lighted by the setting sun, is no hindrance to my knowing that the cloud is vapour of water, subject to all the laws of vapours in a state of suspension; and I am just as likely to allow for, and act on, these physical laws whenever there is occasion to do so, as if I had been incapable of perceiving any distinction between beauty and ugliness.

While my intimacy with Roebuck diminished, I fell more and more into friendly intercourse with our Coleridgian adversaries in the Society, Frederick Maurice and John Sterling,[9] both subsequently so well known, the former by his writings, the latter through the biographies by Hare and Carlyle. Of these two friends, Maurice was the thinker, Sterling the orator, and impassioned expositor of thoughts which, at this period, were almost entirely formed for him by Maurice. With Maurice I had for some time been acquainted through Eyton Tooke,[10] who had known him at Cambridge, and though my discussions with him were almost always disputes, I had carried away from them much that helped to build up my new fabric of thought, in the same way as I was deriving much from Coleridge, and from the writings of Goethe and other German authors which I read during those years. I have so deep a respect for Maurice's character and purposes, as well as for his great mental gifts, that it is with some unwillingness I say anything which may seem to place him on a less high eminence than I would gladly be able to accord to him. But I have always thought that there was more intellectual power wasted in Maurice than in any other of my co-temporaries. Few of them certainly have had so much to waste. Great powers of generalization, rare ingenuity and subtlety, and a wide perception of important and unobvious truths, served him not for putting something better into the place of the worthless heap of received opinions on the great subjects of thought, but for proving to his own mind that the Church of England had known everything from the first, and that all the truths on the ground of which the Church and orthodoxy have been attacked (many of which he saw as clearly as any one) are not only consistent with the Thirty-nine articles, but are better understood and expressed in those articles than by any one who rejects them. I have never been able to find any other explanation of this, then by attributing it to that timidity of

---

[8] John Arthur Roebuck (1801–79) and John Sterling (1806–44), members of Mill's debating society.
[9] Frederick Denison Maurice (1805–72); see selections in this volume. Sterling was later the subject of a biography by Carlyle.
[10] William Eyton Tooke (1806–30), son of the economist Thomas Tooke.

conscience, combined with original sensitiveness of temperament, which has so often driven highly gifted men into Romanism from the need of a firmer support than they can find in the independent conclusions of their own judgment. Any more vulgar kind of timidity no one who knew Maurice would ever think of imputing to him, even if he had not given public proof of his freedom from it, by his ultimate collision with some of the opinions commonly regarded as orthodox, and by his noble origination of the Christian Socialist movement. The nearest parallel to him, in a moral point of view, is Coleridge, to whom, in merely intellectual power, apart from poetical genius, I think him decidedly superior. At this time, however, he might be described as a disciple of Coleridge, and Sterling as a disciple of Coleridge and of him. The modifications which were taking place in my old opinions gave me some points of contact with them; and both Maurice and Sterling were of considerable use to my development. With Sterling I soon became very intimate, and was more attached to him than I have ever been to any other man. He was indeed one of the most loveable of men. His frank, cordial, affectionate and expansive character; a love of truth alike conspicuous in the highest things and the humblest; a generous and ardent nature which threw itself with impetuosity into the opinions it adopted, but was as eager to do justice to the doctrines and the men it was opposed to, as to make war on what it thought their errors; and an equal devotion to the two cardinal points of Liberty and Duty, formed a combination of qualities as attractive to me, as to all others who knew him as well as I did. With his open mind and heart, he found no difficulty in joining hands with me across the gulf which as yet divided our opinions. He told me how he and others had looked upon me (from hearsay information) as a "made" or manufactured man, having had a certain impress of opinion stamped on me which I could only reproduce; and what a change took place in his feelings when he found, in the discussion on Wordsworth and Byron, that Wordsworth, and all which that name implies, "belonged" to me as much as to him and his friends. The failure of his health soon scattered all his plans of life, and compelled him to live at a distance from London, so that after the first year or two of our acquaintance we only saw each other at distant intervals. But (as he said himself in one of his letters to Carlyle) when we did meet it was like brothers. Though he was never, in the full sense of the word, a profound thinker, his openness of mind, and the moral courage in which he greatly surpassed Maurice, made him outgrow the dominion which Maurice and Coleridge had once exercised over his intellect; though he retained to the last a great but discriminating admiration of both, and towards Maurice a warm affection. Except in that short and transitory phasis of his life, during which he made the mistake of becoming a clergyman, his mind was ever progressive; and the advance he always seemed to have made when I saw him after an interval, made me apply to him what Goethe said of Schiller, "Er hatte eine fürchterliche Fortschreitung."[11] He and I started from intellectual points almost as wide apart as the poles, but the distance between us was always diminishing: if I made steps towards some of his opinions, he, during his short life, was constantly approximating more and more to several of mine: and if he had lived, and had health and vigour to prosecute his ever assiduous self-culture, there is no knowing how much further this spontaneous assimilation might have proceeded.

After 1829 I withdrew from attendance on the Debating Society. I had had enough of speech-making, and was glad to carry on my private studies and meditations without any immediate call for outward assertion of their results. I found the fabric of my old and taught opinions giving way in many fresh places, and I never allowed it to fall to pieces, but was incessantly occupied in weaving it anew. I never, in the course of my transition, was content to remain, for ever so short a time, confused and unsettled. When I had taken in any new idea, I could not rest till I had adjusted its relation to my old opinions, and ascertained exactly how far its effect ought to extend in modifying or superseding them.

The conflicts which I had so often had to sustain in defending the theory of government laid down in Bentham's and my father's writings, and the acquaintance I had obtained with other schools of political thinking, made me aware of many things which that doctrine, professing to be a theory of government in general, ought to have made room for, and did not. But these things, as yet, remained with me rather as corrections to be made in applying the theory to practice, than as

[11] "He had a formidable rate of development."

defects in the theory. I felt that politics could not be a science of specific experience; and that the accusations against the Benthamic theory of *being* a theory, of proceeding *à priori*, by way of general reasoning, instead of Baconian experiment, shewed complete ignorance of Bacon's principles, and of the necessary conditions of experimental investigation. At this juncture appeared, in the Edinburgh Review, Macaulay's famous attack on my father's Essay on Government.[12] This gave me much to think about. I saw that Macaulay's conception of the logic of politics was erroneous; that he stood up for the empirical mode of treating political phenomena, against the philosophical; that even in physical science, his notion of philosophizing might have recognized Kepler, but would have excluded Newton and Laplace. But I could not help feeling, that though the tone was unbecoming (an error for which the writer, at a later period, made the most ample and honorable amends), there was truth in several of his strictures on my father's treatment of the subject; that my father's premises were really too narrow, and included but a small number of the general truths, on which, in politics, the important consequences depend. Identity of interest between the governing body and the community at large, is not, in any practical sense which can be attached to it, the only thing on which good government depends; neither can this identity of interest be secured by the mere conditions of election. I was not at all satisfied with the mode in which my father met the criticisms of Macaulay. He did not, as I thought he ought to have done, justify himself by saying, "I was not writing a scientific treatise on politics. I was writing an argument for parliamentary reform." He treated Macaulay's argument as simply irrational; an attack upon the reasoning faculty; an example of the saying of Hobbes, that when reason is against a man, a man will be against reason. This made me think that there was really something more fundamentally erroneous in my father's conception of philosophical Method, as applicable to politics, than I had hitherto supposed there was. But I did not at first see clearly what the error might be. At last it flashed upon me all at once in the course of other studies. In the early part of 1830 I had begun to put on paper the ideas on Logic (chiefly on the distinctions among Terms, and the import of Propositions) which had been suggested and in part worked out in the morning conversations already spoken of. Having secured these thoughts from being lost, I pushed on into the other parts of the subject, to try whether I could do anything further towards clearing up the theory of Logic generally. I grappled at once with the problem of Induction, postponing that of Reasoning, on the ground that it is necessary to obtain premises before we can reason from them. Now, Induction is mainly a process for finding the causes of effects: and in attempting to fathom the mode of tracing causes and effects in physical science, I soon saw that in the more perfect of the sciences, we ascend, by generalization from particulars, to the tendencies of causes considered singly, and then reason downward from those separate tendencies, to the effect of the same causes when combined. I then asked myself, what is the ultimate analysis of this deductive process; the common theory of the syllogism evidently throwing no light upon it. My practice (learnt from Hobbes and my father) being to study abstract principles by means of the best concrete instances I could find, the Composition of Forces, in dynamics, occurred to me as the most complete example of the logical process I was investigating. On examining, accordingly, what the mind does when it applies the principle of the Composition of Forces, I found that it performs a simple act of addition. It adds the separate effect of the one force to the separate effect of the other, and puts down the sum of these separate effects as the joint effect. But is this a legitimate process? In dynamics, and in all the mathematical branches of physics, it is; but in some other cases, as in chemistry, it is not; and I then recollected that something not unlike this was pointed out as one of the distinctions between chemical and mechanical phenomena, in the introduction to that favourite of my boyhood, Thomson's System of Chemistry.[13] This distinction at once made my mind clear as to what was perplexing me in respect to the philosophy of politics. I now saw, that a science is either deductive or experimental, according as, in the province it deals with, the effects of causes when conjoined, are or are not the sums of the effects which the same causes produce when separate. It followed that politics must be a deductive science. It thus appeared, that both Macaulay and my father were wrong; the one in assimilating the method of philosophizing in politics to the purely experimental

[12] In the *Edinburgh Review* for March 1829.
[13] Thomas Thomson (1773–1852), author of *System of Chemistry* (1802).

method of chemistry; while the other, though right in adopting a deductive method, had made a wrong selection of one, having taken as the type of deduction, not the appropriate process, that of the deductive branches of natural philosophy, but the inappropriate one of pure geometry, which not being a science of causation at all, does not require or admit of any summing-up of effects. A foundation was thus laid in my thoughts for the principal chapters of what I afterwards published on the Logic of the Moral Sciences; and my new position in respect to my old political creed, now became perfectly definite.

If I am asked what system of political philosophy I substituted for that which, as a philosophy, I had abandoned, I answer, no system: only a conviction, that the true system was something much more complex and many sided than I had previously had any idea of, and that its office was to supply, not a set of model institutions, but principles from which the institutions suitable to any given circumstances might be deduced. The influences of European, that is to say, Continental, thought, and especially those of the reaction of the nineteenth century against the eighteenth, were now streaming in upon me. They came from various quarters: from the writings of Coleridge, which I had begun to read with interest even before the change in my opinions; from the Coleridgians with whom I was in personal intercourse; from what I had read of Goethe; from Carlyle's early articles in the Edinburgh and Foreign Reviews, though for a long time I saw nothing in these (as my father saw nothing in them to the last) but insane rhapsody. From these sources, and from the acquaintance I kept up with the French literature of the time, I derived, among other ideas which the general turning upside down of the opinions of European thinkers had brought uppermost, these in particular: That the human mind has a certain order of possible progress, in which some things must precede others, an order which governments and public instructors can modify to some, but not to an unlimited extent: That all questions of political institutions are relative, not absolute, and that different stages of human progress not only *will* have, but *ought* to have, different institutions: That government is always either in the hands, or passing into the hands, of whatever is the strongest power in society, and that what this power is, does not depend on institutions, but institutions on it: That any general theory or philosophy of politics supposes a previous theory of human progress, and that this is the same thing

with a philosophy of history. These opinions, true in the main, were held in an exaggerated and violent manner by the thinkers with whom I was now most accustomed to compare notes, and who, as usual with a reaction, ignored that half of the truth which the thinkers of the eighteenth century saw. But though, at one period of my progress, I for some time undervalued that great century, I never joined in the reaction against it, but kept as firm hold of one side of the truth as I took of the other. The fight between the nineteenth century and the eighteenth always reminded me of the battle about the shield, one side of which was white and the other black. I marvelled at the blind rage with which the combatants rushed against one another. I applied to them, and to Coleridge himself, many of Coleridge's sayings about half truths; and Goethe's device, "many-sidedness," was one which I would most willingly, at this period, have taken for mine.

The writers by whom, more than by any others, a new mode of political thinking was brought home to me, were those of the St. Simonian school in France. In 1829 and 1830 I became acquainted with some of their writings. They were then only in the earlier stages of their speculations. They had not yet dressed out their philosophy as a religion, nor had they organized their scheme of Socialism. They were just beginning to question the principle of hereditary property. I was by no means prepared to go with them even this length; but I was greatly struck with the connected view which they for the first time presented to me, of the natural order of human progress; and especially with their division of all history into organic periods and critical periods. During the organic periods (they said) mankind accept with firm conviction some positive creed, claiming jurisdiction over all their actions, and containing more or less of truth and adaptation to the needs of humanity. Under its influence they make all the progress compatible with the creed, and finally outgrow it; when a period follows of criticism and negation, in which mankind lose their old convictions without acquiring any new ones, of a general or authoritative character, except the conviction that the old are false. The period of Greek and Roman polytheism, so long as really believed in by instructed Greeks and Romans, was an organic period, succeeded by the critical or sceptical period of the Greek philosophers. Another organic period came in with Christianity. The corresponding critical period began with the

Reformation, has lasted ever since, still lasts, and cannot altogether cease until a new organic period has been inaugurated by the triumph of a yet more advanced creed. These ideas, I knew, were not peculiar to the St. Simonians; on the contrary, they were the general property of Europe, or at least of Germany and France, but they had never, to my knowledge, been so completely systematized as by these writers, nor the distinguishing characteristics of a critical period so powerfully set forth; for I was not then acquainted with Fichte's Lectures on "the Characteristics of the Present Age." In Carlyle, indeed, I found bitter denunciations of an "age of unbelief," and of the present age as such, which I, like most people at that time, supposed to be passionate protests in favour of the old modes of belief. But all that was true in these denunciations I thought that I found more calmly and philosophically stated by the St. Simonians. Among their publications, too, there was one which seemed to me far superior to the rest; in which the general idea was matured into something much more definite and instructive. This was an early work of Auguste Comte, who then called himself, and even announced himself in the title page as, a pupil of Saint-Simon.[14] In this tract M. Comte first put forth the doctrine which he afterwards so copiously illustrated, of the natural succession of three stages in every department of human knowledge: first the theological, next the metaphysical, and lastly, the positive stage; and contended, that social science must be subject to the same law; that the feudal and Catholic system was the concluding phasis of the theological state of the social science, Protestantism the commencement and the doctrines of the French Revolution the consummation of the metaphysical, and that its positive state was yet to come. This doctrine harmonized well with my existing notions, to which it seemed to give a scientific shape. I already regarded the methods of physical science as the proper models for political. But the chief benefit which I derived at this time from the trains of thought suggested by the St. Simonians and by Comte, was, that I obtained a clearer conception than ever before of the peculiarities of an era of transition in opinion, and ceased to mistake the moral and intellectual characteristics of such an era, for the normal attributes of

humanity. I looked forward, through the present age of loud disputes but generally weak convictions, to a future which shall unite the best qualities of the critical with the best qualities of the organic periods; unchecked liberty of thought, unbounded freedom of individual action in all modes not hurtful to others; but also, convictions as to what is right and wrong, useful and pernicious, deeply engraven on the feelings by early education and general unanimity of sentiment, and so firmly grounded in reason and in the true exigencies of life, that they shall not, like all former and present creeds, religious, ethical, and political, require to be periodically thrown off and replaced by others.

M. Comte soon left the St. Simonians, and I lost sight of him and his writings for a number of years. But the St. Simonians I continued to cultivate. I was kept *au courant* of their progress by one of their most enthusiastic disciples, M. Gustave d'Eichthal, who about that time passed a considerable interval in England. I was introduced to their chiefs, Bazard and Enfantin, in 1830; and as long as their public teachings and proselytism continued, I read nearly everything they wrote. Their criticisms on the common doctrines of Liberalism seemed to me full of important truth; and it was partly by their writings that my eyes were opened to the very limited and temporary value of the old political economy, which assumed private property and inheritance as indefeasible facts, and freedom of production and exchange as the *dernier mot*[15] of social improvement. The scheme gradually unfolded by the St. Simonians, under which the labour and capital of society would be managed for the general account of the community, every individual being required to take a share of labour, either as thinker, teacher, artist, or producer, all being classed according to their capacity, and remunerated according to their works, appeared to me a far superior description of Socialism to Owen's.[16] Their aim seemed to me desirable and rational, however their means might be inefficacious; and though I neither believed in the practicability, nor in the beneficial operation of their social machinery, I felt that the proclamation of such an ideal of human society could not but tend to give a beneficial direction to the efforts of others to bring society, as at present constituted, nearer to some ideal standard.

---

[14] Comte was a follower of Claude Henri Saint-Simon (1760–1825), founder of French socialism.
[15] The last word.
[16] Robert Owen (1771–1858), British social experimenter and reformer.

I honoured them most of all for what they have been most cried down for—the boldness and freedom from prejudice with which they treated the subject of family, the most important of any, and needing more fundamental alterations than remain to be made in any other great social institution, but on which scarcely any reformer has the courage to touch. In proclaiming the perfect equality of men and women, and an entirely new order of things in regard to their relations with one another, the St. Simonians in common with Owen and Fourier[17] have entitled themselves to the grateful remembrance of future generations.

In giving an account of this period of my life, I have only specified such of my new impressions as appeared to me, both at the time and since, to be a kind of turning point, marking a definite progress in my mode of thought. But these few selected points give a very insufficient idea of the quantity of thinking which I carried on respecting a host of subjects during these years of transition. Much of this, it is true, consisted in rediscovering things known to all the world, which I had previously disbelieved, or disregarded. But the rediscovery was to me a discovery, giving me plenary possession of the truths not as traditional platitudes but fresh from their source: and it seldom failed to place them in some new light, by which they were reconciled with, and seemed to confirm while they modified, the truths less generally known which lay in my early opinions, and in no essential part of which I at any time wavered. All my new thinking only laid the foundation of these more deeply and strongly, while it often removed misapprehension and confusion of ideas which had perverted their effect. For example, during the later returns of my dejection, the doctrine of what is called Philosophical Necessity weighed on my existence like an incubus. I felt as if I was scientifically proved to be the helpless slave of antecedent circumstances; as if my character and that of all others had been formed for us by agencies beyond our control, and was wholly out of our own power. I often said to myself, what a relief it would be if I could disbelieve the doctrine of the formation of character by circumstances; and remembering the wish of Fox respecting the doctrine of resistance to governments, that it might never be forgotten by kings, nor remembered by subjects, I said that it would be a blessing if the doctrine

of necessity could be believed by all *quoad*[18] the characters of others, and disbelieved in regard to their own. I pondered painfully on the subject, till gradually I saw light through it. I perceived, that the word Necessity, as a name for the doctrine of Cause and Effect applied to human action, carried with it a misleading association; and that this association was the operative force in the depressing and paralysing influence which I had experienced. I saw that though our character is formed by circumstances, our own desires can do much to shape those circumstances; and that what is really inspiriting and ennobling in the doctrine of freewill, is the conviction that we have real power over the formation of our own character; that our will, by influencing some of our circumstances, can modify our future habits or capabilities of willing. All this was entirely consistent with the doctrine of circumstances, or rather, was that doctrine itself, properly understood. From that time I drew, in my own mind, a clear distinction between the doctrine of circumstances, and Fatalism; discarding altogether the misleading word Necessity. The theory, which I now for the first time rightly apprehended, ceased altogether to be discouraging, and besides the relief to my spirits, I no longer suffered under the burthen, so heavy to one who aims at being a reformer in opinions, of thinking one doctrine true, and the contrary doctrine morally beneficial. The train of thought which had extricated me from this dilemma, seemed to me, in after years, fitted to render a similar service to others; and it now forms the chapter on Liberty and Necessity in the concluding Book of my "System of Logic."

Again, in politics, though I no longer accepted the doctrine of the Essay on Government as a scientific theory; though I ceased to consider representative democracy as an absolute principle, and regarded it as a question of time, place, and circumstance; though I now looked upon the choice of political institutions as a moral and educational question more than one of material interests, thinking that it ought to be decided mainly by the consideration, what great improvement in life and culture stands next in order for the people concerned, as the condition of their further progress, and what institutions are most likely to promote that; nevertheless this change in the premises of my political philosophy did not alter my practical political creed as to the

---

[17] Charles Fourier (1772–1837), French advocate of communal living and property.
[18] With respect to.

requirements of my own time and country. I was as much as ever a radical and democrat, for Europe, and especially for England. I thought the predominance of the aristocratic classes, the noble and the rich, in the English Constitution, an evil worth any struggle to get rid of; not on account of taxes, or any such comparatively small inconvenience, but as the great demoralizing agency in the country. Demoralizing, first, because it made the conduct of the government an example of gross public immorality, through the predominance of private over public interests in the State, and the abuse of the power of legislation for the advantage of classes. Secondly, and in a still greater degree, because the respect of the multitude always attaching itself principally to that which, in the existing state of society, is the chief passport to power; and under English institutions, riches, hereditary or acquired, being the almost exclusive source of political importance; riches, and the signs of riches, were almost the only things really respected, and the life of the people was mainly devoted to the pursuit of them. I thought, that while the higher and richer classes held the power of government, the instruction and improvement of the mass of the people were contrary to the self interest of those classes, because tending to render the people more powerful for throwing off the yoke: but if the democracy obtained a large, and perhaps the principal, share in the governing power, it would become the interest of the opulent classes to promote their education, in order to ward off really mischievous errors, and especially those which would lead to unjust violations of property. On these grounds I was not only as ardent as ever for democratic institutions, but earnestly hoped that Owenite, St. Simonian, and all other anti-property doctrines might spread widely among the poorer classes; not that I thought those doctrines true, or desired that they should be acted on, but in order that the higher classes might be made to see that they had more to fear from the poor when uneducated, than when educated.

In this frame of mind the French Revolution of July[19] found me. It roused my utmost enthusiasm, and gave me, as it were, a new existence. I went at once to Paris, was introduced to Lafayette, and laid the groundwork of the intercourse I afterwards kept up with several of the active chiefs of the extreme popular party. At every return I entered warmly, as a writer, into the political discussions of the time; which soon became still more exciting, by the coming in of Lord Grey's ministry, and the proposing of the Reform Bill.[20] For the next few years I wrote copiously in newspapers. It was about this time that Fonblanque,[21] who had for some time written the political articles in the Examiner, became the proprietor and editor of the paper. It is not forgotten with what verve and talent, as well as fine wit, he carried it on, during the whole period of Lord Grey's ministry, and what importance it assumed as the principal representative, in the newspaper press, of radical opinions. The distinguishing character of the paper was given to it entirely by his own articles, which formed at least three fourths of all the original writing contained in it: but of the remaining fourth I contributed during those years a much larger share than any one else. I write nearly all the articles on French subjects, including a weekly summary of French politics, often extending to considerable length; together with many leading articles on general politics, commercial and financial legislation, and any miscellaneous subjects in which I felt interested, and which were suitable to the paper, including occasional reviews of books. Mere newspaper articles on the occurrences or questions of the moment gave no opportunity for the development of any general mode of thought; but I attempted, in the beginning of 1831, to embody in a series of articles, headed "The Spirit of the Age," some of my new opinions, and especially to point out in the character of the present age, the anomalies and evils characteristic of the transition from a system of opinions which had worn out, to another only in process of being formed. These articles were, I fancy, lumbering in style and not lively or striking enough to be at any time acceptable to newspaper readers; but had they been far more attractive, still, at that particular moment, when great political changes were impending, and engrossing all minds, these discussions were ill timed, and missed fire altogether. The only effect which I know to have been produced by them, was that Carlyle, then living in a secluded part of Scotland, read them in his solitude, and saying to himself (as he

---

[19] 1830.
[20] The First Reform Bill of 1832, passed during the ministry of Lord Grey.
[21] Albany Fonblanque (1793–1872), journalist, editor of the *Examiner* from 1830 to 1847.

afterwards told me) "here is a new Mystic," enquired on coming to London that autumn respecting their authorship; an enquiry which was the immediate cause of our becoming personally acquainted.

I have already mentioned Carlyle's earlier writings as one of the channels through which I received the influences which enlarged my early narrow creed; but I do not think that those writings, by themselves, would ever have had any effect on my opinions. What truths they contained, though of the very kind which I was already receiving from other quarters, were presented in a form and vesture less suited than any other to give them access to a mind trained as mine had been. They seemed a haze of poetry and German metaphysics, in which almost the only clear thing was a strong animosity to most of the opinions which were the basis of my mode of thought; religious scepticism, utilitarianism, the doctrine of circumstances, and the attaching any importance to democracy, logic, or political economy. Instead of my having been taught anything, in the first instance, by Carlyle, it was only in proportion as I came to see the same truths, through media more suited to my mental constitution, that I recognized them in his writings. Then, indeed, the wonderful power with which he put them forth made a deep impression upon me, and I was during a long period one of his most fervent admirers; but the good his writings did me, was not as philosophy to instruct, but as poetry to animate. Even at the time when our acquaintance commenced, I was not sufficiently advanced in my new modes of thought, to appreciate him fully; a proof of which is, that on his shewing me the manuscript of Sartor Resartus, his best and greatest work, which he just then finished, I made little of it; though when it came out about two years afterwards in Fraser's Magazine, I read it with enthusiastic admiration and the keenest delight.[22] I did not seek and cultivate Carlyle less on account of the fundamental differences in our philosophy. He soon found out that I was not "another mystic," and when for the sake of my own integrity I wrote to him a distinct profession of all those of my opinions which I knew he most disliked, he replied that the chief difference between us was that I "was as yet consciously nothing of a mystic." I do not know at what period he gave up the expectation that I was destined to become one; but though both his and my opinions underwent in subsequent years considerable changes, we never approached much nearer to each other's modes of thought than we were in the first years of our acquaintance. I did not, however, deem myself a competent judge of Carlyle. I felt that he was a poet, and that I was not; that he was a man of intuition, which I was not; and that as such, he not only saw many things long before me, which I could only, when they were pointed out to me, hobble after and prove, but that it was highly probable he could see many things which were not visible to me even after they were pointed out. I knew that I could not see round him, and could never be certain that I saw over him; and I never presumed to judge him with any definiteness, until he was interpreted to me by one greatly the superior of us both[23]—who was more a poet than he, and more a thinker than I—whose own mind and nature included his, and infinitely more.

Among the persons of intellect whom I had known of old, the one with whom I had now most points of agreement was the elder Austin.[24] I have mentioned that he always set himself in opposition to our early sectarianism; and latterly he had, like myself, come under new influences. Having been appointed Professor of Jurisprudence in the London University (now University College), he had lived for some time at Bonn to study for his Lectures; and the influences of German literature and of the German character and state of society had made a very perceptible change in his views of life. His personal disposition was much softened; he was less militant and polemic; his tastes had begun to turn themselves towards the poetic and contemplative. He attached much less importance than formerly to outward changes, unless accompanied by a better cultivation of the inward nature. He had a strong distaste for the general meanness of English life, the absence of enlarged thoughts and unselfish desires, the low objects on which the faculties of all classes of the English are intent. Even the kind of public interests which Englishmen care for, he held in very little esteem. He thought that there was more practical good government, and (which is true enough) infinitely more care for the education and mental improvement of all ranks of the people, under the

[22] *Sartor Resartus* was serialized in *Fraser's* in 1833–34.
[23] Harriet Taylor.
[24] John Austin (1790–1859), author of *Lectures on Jurisprudence* (1863).

Prussian monarchy, than under the English representative government: and he held, with the French Economistes, that the real security for good government is "un peuple éclairé,"[25] which is not always the fruit of popular institutions, and which if it could be had without them, would do their work better than they. Though he approved of the Reform Bill, he predicted, what in fact occurred, that it would not produce the great immediate improvements in government, which many expected from it. The men, he said, who could do these great things, did not exist in the country. There were many points of sympathy between him and me, both in the new opinions he had adopted and in the old ones which he retained. Like me, he never ceased to be an utilitarian, and with all his love of the Germans, and enjoyment of their literature, never became in the smallest degree reconciled to the innate-principle metaphysics. He cultivated more and more a kind of German religion, a religion of poetry and feeling with little if anything of positive dogma; while, in politics (and here it was that I most differed with him) he acquired an indifference, bordering on contempt, for the progress of popular institutions: though he rejoiced in that of Socialism, as the most effectual means of compelling the powerful classes to educate the people, and to impress on them the only real means of permanently improving their material condition, a limitation of their numbers. Neither was he, at this time, fundamentally opposed to Socialism in itself, as an ultimate result of improvement. He professed great disrespect for what he called "the universal principles of human nature of the political economists," and insisted on the evidence which history and daily experience afford of the "extraordinary pliability of human nature" (a phrase which I have somewhere borrowed from him); nor did he think it possible to set any positive bounds to the moral capabilities which might unfold themselves in mankind, under an enlightened direction of social and educational influences. Whether he retained all these opinions to the end of life I know not. Certainly the modes of thinking of his later years and especially of his last publication were much more Tory in their general character, than those which he held at this time.

My father's tone of thought and feeling, I now felt myself at a great distance from: greater, indeed, than a full and calm explanation and reconsideration on both sides, might have shewn to exist in reality. But my father was not one with whom calm and full explanations on fundamental points of doctrine could be expected, at least with one whom he might consider as, in some sort, a deserter from his standard. Fortunately we were almost always in strong agreement on the political questions of the day, which engrossed a large part of his interest and of his conversation. On those matters of opinion on which we differed, we talked little. He knew that the habit of thinking for myself, which his mode of education had fostered, sometimes led me to opinions different from his, and he perceived from time to time that I did not always tell him *how* different. I expected no good, but only pain to both of us, from discussing our differences: and I never expressed them but when he gave utterance to some opinion or feeling repugnant to mine, in a manner which would have made it disingenuousness on my part to remain silent.

It remains to speak of what I wrote during these years, which, independently of my contributions to newspapers, was considerable. In 1830 and 1831 I wrote the five Essays since published under the title of "Essays on some Unsettled Questions of Political Economy," almost as they now stand, except that in 1833 I partially rewrote the fifth Essay. They were written with no immediate purpose of publication; and, when, some years later, I offered them to a publisher, he declined them. They were only printed in 1844, after the success of the "System of Logic." I also resumed my speculations on this last subject, and puzzled myself, like others before me, with the great paradox of the discovery of new truths by general reasoning. As to the fact, there could be no doubt. As little could it be doubted, that all reasoning is resolvable into syllogisms, and that in every syllogism the conclusion is actually contained and implied in the premises. How, being so contained and implied, it could be new truth, and how the theorems of geometry, so different, in appearance, from the definitions and axioms, could be all contained in these, was a difficulty which no one, I thought, had sufficiently felt, and which at all events no one had succeeded in clearing up. The explanations offered by Whately[26] and others, though they might give a temporary satisfaction, always, in my mind, left a mist still hanging over the subject. At last, when

---

[25] An enlightened people.
[26] Richard Whately (1787–1863), author of *Logic* (1826).

reading a second or third time the chapters on Reasoning in the second volume of Dugald Stewart,[27] interrogating myself on every point, and following out as far as I knew how, every topic of thought which the book suggested, I came upon an idea of his respecting the use of axioms in ratiocination, which I did not remember to have before noticed, but which now, in meditating on it, seemed to me not only true of axioms, but of all general propositions whatever, and to be the key of the whole perplexity. From this germ grew the theory of the Syllogism propounded in the second Book of the Logic; which I immediately fixed by writing it out. And now, with greatly increased hope of being able to produce a work on Logic, of some originality and value, I proceeded to write the First Book, from the rough and imperfect draft I had already made. What I now wrote became the basis of that part of the subsequent Treatise; except that it did not contain the Theory of Kinds, which was a later addition, suggested by otherwise inextricable difficulties which met me in my first attempt to work out the subject of some of the concluding chapters of the Third Book. At the point which I have now reached I made a halt, which lasted five years. I had come to the end of my tether; I could make nothing satisfactory of Induction, at this time. I continued to read any book which seemed to promise light on the subject, and appropriated, as well as I could, the results; but for a long time I found nothing which seemed to open to me any very important vein of meditation.

In 1832 I wrote several papers for the first series of Tait's Magazine, and one for a quarterly periodical called the Jurist, which had been founded and for a short time carried on by a set of friends, all lawyers and law reformers, with several of whom I was acquainted. The paper in question is the one on the rights and duties of the State respecting Corporation and Church Property, now standing first among the collected "Dissertations and Discussions"; where one of my articles in Tait, "The Currency Juggle," also appears. In the whole mass of what I wrote previous to these, there is nothing of sufficient permanent value to justify reprinting. The paper in the Jurist, which I still think a very complete discussion of the rights of the State over Foundations, shewed both sides of my opinions, asserting as firmly as I should have done at any time, the doctrine that all endowments are national property, which the government may and ought to control; but not, as I should once have done, condemning endowments in themselves, and proposing that they should be taken to pay off the national debt. On the contrary, I urged strenuously the importance of having a provision for education, not dependent on the mere demand of the market, that is, on the knowledge and discernment of average parents, but calculated to establish and keep up a higher standard of instruction than is likely to be spontaneously demanded by the buyers of the article. All these opinions have been confirmed and strengthened by the whole course of my subsequent reflections.

---

[27] Dugald Stewart (1753–1828), Scottish philosopher, author of *Outlines of Moral Philosophy* (1793).

Charles Robert Darwin

1809-1882

THE QUIET, retiring gentleman scientist, Charles Darwin, made an impact on his and succeeding ages scarcely matched by any of his contemporaries, for he promulgated and gained acceptance for the theory of natural selection that revolutionized biology and most other scientific and historical studies as well. In doing so he helped to shape the modern world view.

Darwin was born at Shrewsbury, son of a physician and grandson of the eighteenth-century botanist and poet Erasmus Darwin, and descended on his mother's side from the Wedgwoods of pottery fame. He was educated at Shrewsbury, Edinburgh University, and Christ's College, Cambridge. Upon taking his B.A., Darwin embarked on a five-year-long voyage around the world on the H.M.S. *Beagle*. His extensive scientific observations and specimens from this trip provided much of the material for his wide knowledge of botany, geology, and zoology. Before writing his great work on natural selection, he had published various works relating to his scientific findings from the *Beagle* voyage.

From 1842 Darwin lived the life of a country gentleman and private student of science. He had formulated the germ of his theories on natural selection by the early eighteen-forties, but it was not until a theory identical with his had been advanced in a letter to him from the scientist Alfred Russel Wallace that he was impelled to set forth his findings at full length. The result was *The Origin of the Species by Means of Natural Selection* in 1859, far from the first but certainly the most influential of the evolutionary theories that proliferated widely throughout the nineteenth century.

Darwin's book caused an international sensation, for it challenged traditional theories of the origin of man and animals, proposed a vastly extended time frame for development on earth, and seemed to posit a universe devoid of any shade of benevolence. He was violently attacked in some quarters and almost equally violently defended in others, most notably in defense by Thomas Henry Huxley who became Darwin's special advocate. Subsequently social and even aesthetic theories were propounded that claimed Darwinism as their parent. Darwin himself continued to publish extensively on biology and evolution, including *The Descent of Man* (1871), until his death in 1882.

Darwin's writings are almost exclusively scientific and, despite the inherent interest of some of their subjects, they rarely rise above the factual and prosaic in style. His autobiography, however, although still restrained and unremarkable in tone, is a document of considerable interest in that it sheds light on the age and on the development and background of the most distinguished scientist the age produced.

CHRONOLOGY

1809	Born 12 February at Shrewsbury.
1825–27	Studies medicine at Edinburgh University.
1828–31	Studies at Christ's College, Cambridge.
1831	Sets sail on H.M.S. *Beagle*.
1831–36	Voyage of the *Beagle*.
1839	Marries his cousin Emma Wedgwood.
1842	Settles at Down, Kent.
1859	*The Origin of the Species*.
1871	*The Descent of Man*.
1882	Dies 19 April; buried in Westminster Abbey.

EDITIONS

There are numerous editions of Darwin's scientific writings. Titles below, by date, are those that would be of interest to students of literature.

Diary of the Voyage of H.M.S. Beagle, ed. Nora Barlow (1933).
The Living Thoughts of Darwin, ed. Julian Huxley and U. Fisher (1939).
Darwin and the Voyage of the Beagle, ed. Nora Barlow (1945).
The Darwin Reader, ed. N. Bates and P. S. Humphrey (1957).
On the Origin of the Species: A Variorum Text, ed. Morse Peckham (1959).
Darwin for Today: The Essence of his Works, ed. Stanley Edgar Hyman (1963).
The Autobiography of Charles Darwin, ed. Nora Barlow (1969).
Darwin, ed. Philip Appleman (1970). [Also contains writings by others.]

BIOGRAPHY AND CRITICISM

Francis Darwin, *The Life and Letters of Charles Darwin* (3 vols, 1887).
Leonard Huxley, *Charles Darwin* (1921).
Lionel Stevenson, *Darwin Among the Poets* (1932).
L. J. Henkin, *Darwinism in the English Novel* (1940).
Jacques Barzun, *Darwin, Marx, Wagner* (1941).
Richard Hofstadter, *Social Darwinism in American Thought* (1941).
D. C. Darlington, *Darwin's Place in History* (1959).
Loren Eisley, *Darwin's Century* (1959).
Gertrude Himmelfarb, *Darwin and the Darwinian Evolution* (1959).
B. J. Loewenberg, *Darwin, Wallace, and the Theory of Natural Selection* (1959).
Basil Willey, *Darwin and Butler: Two Versions of Evolution* (1960).
J. C. Greene, *Darwin and the Modern World* (1961).
Stanley Edgar Hyman, *The Tangled Bank* (1962).
R. B. Freeman, *The Works of Darwin: An Annotated Bibliographical Handlist* (1965).

from Francis Darwin,
The Life and Letters of Charles Darwin

Darwin's "autobiography" is in fact a brief series of what his son called "autobiographical recollections." It was first published five years after the author's death in his son's edition of his Life and Letters. *Darwin wrote his recollection in 1876, six years before his death, and he never expected publication of the work. The first portion of the autobiography contains the greatest interest, for by Darwin's own account most of his adult life was so wholly devoted to science that he ceased to take much pleasure in aesthetic matters or to have much to report except the publication of successive scientific studies.*

Charles Darwin's Autobiography

A GERMAN editor having written to me for an account of the development of my mind and character with some sketch of my autobiography, I have thought that the attempt would amuse me, and might possibly interest my children or their children. I know that it would have interested me greatly to have read even so short and dull a sketch of the mind of my grandfather, written by himself, and what he thought and did, and how he worked. I have attempted to write the following account of myself, as if I were a dead man in another world looking back at my own life. Nor have I found this difficult, for life is nearly over with me. I have taken no pains about my style of writing.

I was born at Shrewsbury on February 12th, 1809, and my earliest recollection goes back only to when I was a few months over four years old, when we went to near Abergele for seabathing, and I recollect some events and places there with some little distinctness.

My mother died in July 1817, when I was a little over eight years old, and it is odd that I can remember hardly anything about her except her death-bed, her black velvet gown, and her curiously constructed work-table. In the spring of this same year I was sent to a day-school in Shrewsbury, where I stayed a year. I have been told that I was much slower in learning than my younger sister Catherine, and I believe that I was in many ways a naughty boy.

By the time I went to this day-school my taste for natural history, and more especially for collecting, was well developed. I tried to make out the names of plants, and collected all sorts of things, shells, seals, franks, coins, and minerals. The passion for collecting which leads a man to be a systematic naturalist, a virtuoso, or a miser, was very strong in me, and was clearly innate, as none of my sisters or brother ever had this taste.

One little event during this year has fixed itself very firmly in my mind, and I hope that it has done so from my conscience having been afterwards sorely troubled by it; it is curious as showing that apparently I was interested at this early age in the variability of plants! I told another little boy (I believe it was Leighton, who afterwards became a well-known lichenologist and botanist) that I could produce variously coloured polyanthuses and primroses by watering then with certain coloured fluids, which was of course a monstrous fable, and had never been tried by me. I may here also confess that as a little boy I was much given to inventing deliberate falsehoods, and this was always done for the sake of causing excitement. For instance, I once gathered much valuable fruit from my father's trees and hid it in the shrubbery, and then ran in breathless haste to spread the news that I had discovered a hoard of stolen fruit.

I must have been a very simple little fellow when I first went to the school. A boy of the name of Garnett took me into a cake shop one day, and bought some cakes for which he did not pay, as the shopman trusted him. When we came out I asked him why he did not pay for them, and he instantly answered, "Why, do you not know that my uncle left a great sum of money to the town on condition that every tradesman should give whatever was wanted without payment to any one who wore his old hat and moved [it] in a particular manner?" and he then showed me how it was moved. He then went into another shop where he was trusted, and asked for some small article, moving his hat in the proper manner, and of course obtained it without payment. When we came out he said, "Now if you like to go by yourself into that cake-shop (how well I remember its exact position) I will lend you my hat, and you can get whatever you like if you move the hat on your head properly." I gladly accepted the generous offer, and went in and asked for some cakes, moved the old hat and was walking out of the shop, when the shopman made a rush at me, so I dropped the cakes and ran for dear life, and was astonished by being greeted with shouts of laughter by my false friend Garnett.

I can say in my own favour that I was as a boy humane, but I owed this entirely to the instruction and example of my sisters. I doubt indeed whether humanity is a natural or innate quality. I was very fond of collecting eggs, but I never took more than a single egg out of a bird's nest, except on one single occasion, when I took all, not for their value, but from a sort of bravado.

I had a strong taste for angling, and would sit for any number of hours on the bank of a river or pond watching the float; when at Maer[1] I was told that I could kill the worms with salt and water, and from that day I never spitted a living worm, though at the expense probably of some loss of success.

Once as a very little boy whilst at the day school, or before that time, I acted cruelly, for I beat a puppy, I believe, simply from enjoying the sense of power; but the beating could not have been severe, for the puppy did not howl, of which I feel sure, as the spot was near the house. This act lay heavily on my conscience, as is shown by my remembering the exact spot where the crime was committed. It probably lay all the heavier from my love of dogs being then, and for a long time afterwards, a passion. Dogs seemed to know this, for I was an adept in robbing their love from their masters.

I remember clearly only one other incident during this year whilst at Mr. Case's daily school,—namely, the burial of a dragoon soldier; and it is surprising how clearly I can still see the horse with the man's empty boots and carbine suspended to the saddle, and the firing over the grave. This scene deeply stirred whatever poetic fancy there was in me.

In the summer of 1818 I went to Dr. Butler's great school in Shrewsbury,[2] and remained there for seven years till mid-summer 1825, when I was sixteen years old. I boarded at this school, so that I had the great advantage of living the life of a true schoolboy; but as the distance was hardly more than a mile to my home, I very often ran there in the longer intervals between the callings over and before locking up at night. This, I think, was in many ways advantageous to me by keeping up home affections and interests. I remember in the early part of my school life that I often had to run very quickly to be in time, and from being a fleet runner was generally successful; but when in doubt I prayed earnestly to God to help me, and I well remember that I attribute my success to the prayers and not to my quick running, and marvelled how generally I was aided.

I have heard my father and elder sister say that I had, as a very young boy, a strong taste for long solitary walks; but what I thought about I know not. I often became quite absorbed, and once, whilst returning to school on the summit of the old fortifications round Shrewsbury, which had been converted into a public foot-path with no parapet on one side, I walked off and fell to the ground, but the height was only seven or eight feet. Nevertheless the number of thoughts which passed through my mind during this very short, but sudden and wholly unexpected fall, was astonishing, and seem hardly compatible with what physiologists have, I believe, proved about each thought requiring quite an appreciable amount of time.

Nothing could have been worse for the development of my mind than Dr. Butler's school, as it was strictly classical, nothing else being taught except a little ancient geography and history. The school as a means of education to me was simply a blank. During my whole life I have been singularly incapable of mastering any language. Especial attention was paid to verse-making, and this I could never do well. I had many friends, and got together a good collection of old verses, which by patching together, sometimes aided by other boys, I could work into any subject. Much attention was paid to learning by heart the lessons of the previous day; this I could effect with great facility, learning forty or fifty lines of Virgil or Homer, whilst I was in morning chapel; but this exercise was utterly useless, for every verse was

---

[1] The house of Darwin's uncle, Josiah Wedgwood.

[2] Shrewsbury School under the headmastership of Dr. Samuel Butler (1774–1839), grandfather of the novelist and essayist Samuel Butler.

forgotten in forty-eight hours. I was not idle, and with the exception of versification, generally worked conscientiously at my classics, not using cribs. The sole pleasure I ever received from such studies was from some of the odes of Horace, which I admired greatly.

When I left the school I was for my age neither high nor low in it; and I believe that I was considered by all my masters and by my father as a very ordinary boy, rather below the common standard in intellect. To my deep mortification my father once said to me, "You care for nothing but shooting, dogs, and rat-catching, and you will be a disgrace to yourself and all your family." But my father, who was the kindest man I ever knew and whose memory I love with all my heart, must have been angry and somewhat unjust when he used such words.

Looking back as well as I can at my character during my school life, the only qualities which at this period promised well for the future were, that I had strong and diversified tastes, much zeal for whatever interested me, and a keen pleasure in understanding any complex subject or thing. I was taught Euclid by a private tutor, and I distinctly remember the intense satisfaction which the clear geometrical proofs gave me. I remember, with equal distinctness, the delight which my uncle gave me (the father of Francis Galton) by explaining the principle of the vernier of a barometer. With respect to diversified tastes, independently of science, I was fond of reading various books, and I used to sit for hours reading the historical plays of Shakespeare, generally in an old window in the thick walls of the school. I read also other poetry, such as Thomson's *Seasons*, and the recently published poems by Byron and Scott. I mention this because later in life I wholly lost, to my great regret, all pleasure from poetry of any kind, including Shakespeare. In connection with pleasure from poetry, I may add that in 1822 a vivid delight in scenery was first awakened in my mind, during a riding tour on the borders of Wales, and this has lasted longer than any other æsthetic pleasure.

Early in my school days a boy had a copy of the *Wonders of the World*, which I often read, and disputed with other boys about the veracity of some of the statements; and I believe that this book first gave me a wish to travel in remote countries, which was ultimately fulfilled by the voyage of the *Beagle*. In the latter part of my school life I became passionately fond of shooting; I do not believe that any one could have shown more zeal for the most holy cause than I did for shooting birds. How well I remember killing my first snipe, and my excitement was so great that I had much difficulty in reloading my gun from the trembling of my hands. This taste long continued, and I became a very good shot. When at Cambridge I used to practise throwing up my gun to my shoulder before a looking-glass to see that I threw it up straight. Another and better plan was to get a friend to wave about a lighted candle, and then to fire at it with a cap on the nipple, and if the aim was accurate the little puff of air would blow out the candle. The explosion of the cap caused a sharp crack, and I was told that the tutor of the college remarked, "What an extraordinary thing it is, Mr. Darwin seems to spend hours in cracking a horse-whip in his room, for I often hear the crack when I pass under his windows."

I had many friends amongst the schoolboys, whom I loved dearly, and I think that my disposition was then very affectionate.

With respect to science, I continued collecting minerals with much zeal, but quite unscientifically—all that I cared about was a new-*named* mineral, and I hardly attempted to classify them. I must have observed insects with some little care, for when ten years old (1819) I went for three weeks to Plas Edwards on the sea-coast in Wales, I was very much interested and surprised at seeing a large black and scarlet Hemipterous insect, many moths (Zygæna), and a Cicindela which are not found in Shropshire. I almost made up my mind to begin collecting all the insects which I could find dead, for on consulting my sister I concluded that it was not right to kill insects for the sake of making a collection. From reading White's *Selborne*, I took much pleasure in watching the habits of birds, and even made notes on the subject. In my simplicity I remember wondering why every gentleman did not become an ornithologist.

Towards the close of my school life, my brother worked hard at chemistry, and made a fair laboratory with proper apparatus in the tool-house in the garden, and I was allowed to aid him as a servant in most of his experiments. He made all the gases and many compounds, and I read with great care several books on chemistry, such as Henry and Parkes' *Chemical Catechism*. The subject interested me greatly; and we often used to go on working till rather late at night. This was the best part of my education at school, for it showed me practically the meaning of experimental science. The fact that we worked at chemistry somehow got known at school, and as it was an unprecedented fact, I was nicknamed "Gas." I was also once publicly rebuked by the headmaster, Dr. Butler, for thus wasting my time on such useless subjects; and he called me very unjustly a "poco curante," and as I did not understand what he meant, it seemed to me a fearful reproach.

As I was doing no good at school, my father wisely took me away at a rather earlier age than usual, and sent me (Oct. 1825) to Edinburgh University with my brother, where I stayed for two years or sessions. My brother was completing his medical studies, though I do not believe he ever really intended to practice, and I was sent there to commence them. But soon after this period I became convinced from various small circumstances that my father would leave me property enough to subsist on with some comfort, though I never imagined that I should be so rich a man as I am; but my belief was sufficient to check any strenuous efforts to learn medicine.

The instruction at Edinburgh was altogether by lectures, and these were intolerably dull, with the exception of those on chemistry by Hope; but to my mind there are no advantages and many disadvantages in lectures compared with reading. Dr. Duncan's lectures on Materia Medica at 8 o'clock on a winter's morning are something fearful to remember. Dr. Munro made his lecture on human anatomy as dull as he was himself, and the subject disgusted me. It has proved one of the greatest evils in my life that I was not urged to practice dissection, for I should soon have got over my disgust; and the practice would have been invaluable for all my future work. This has been an irremediable evil, as well as my incapacity to draw. I also attended regularly the clinical wards in the hospital. Some of the cases distressed me a good deal, and I still have vivid pictures before me of some of them; but I was not so foolish as to allow this to lessen my attendance. I cannot understand why this part of my medical course did not interest me in a greater degree; for during the summer before coming to Edinburgh I began attending some of the poor people, chiefly children and women in Shrewsbury: I wrote down as full an account as I could of the case with all the symptoms, and read them aloud to my father, who suggested further inquiries and advised me what medicines to give, which I made up myself. At one time I had at

least a dozen patients, and I felt a keen interest in the work. My father, who was by far the best judge of character whom I ever knew, declared that I should make a successful physician,— meaning by this one who would get many patients. He maintained that the chief element of success was exciting confidence; but what he saw in me which convinced him that I should create confidence I know not. I also attended on two occasions the operating theatre in the hospital at Edinburgh, and saw two very bad operations, one on a child, but I rushed away before they were completed. Nor did I ever attend again, for hardly any inducement would have been strong enough to make me do so; this being long before the blessed days of chloroform. The two cases fairly haunted me for many a long year.

My brother stayed only one year at the University, so that during the second year I was left to my own resources; and this was an advantage, for I became well acquainted with several young men fond of natural science. One of these was Ainsworth, who afterwards published his travels in Assyria; he was a Wernerian geologist, and knew a little about many subjects. Dr. Coldstream was a very different young man, prim, formal, highly religious, and most kind-hearted; he afterwards published some good zoological articles. A third young man was Hardie, who would, I think, have made a good botanist, but died early in India. Lastly, Dr. Grant, my senior by several years, but how I became acquainted with him I cannot remember; he published some first-rate zoological papers, but after coming to London as Professor in University College, he did nothing more in science, a fact which has always been inexplicable to me. I knew him well; he was dry and formal in manner, with much enthusiasm beneath this outer crust. He one day, when we were walking together, burst forth in high admiration of Lamarck and his views on evolution. I listened in silent astonishment, and as far as I can judge without any effect on my mind. I had previously read the *Zoonomia* of my grandfather,[3] in which similar views are maintained, but without producing any effect on me. Nevertheless it is probable that the hearing rather early in life such views maintained and praised may have favoured my upholding them under a different form in my *Origin of Species*. At this time I admired greatly the *Zoonomia*; but on reading it a second time after an interval of ten or fifteen

[3] Erasmus Darwin (1731–1802), Charles Darwin's grandfather, author of *Zoonomia* (1794–96), which advances the Lamarckian view of the inheritability of acquired characteristics.

years, I was much disappointed; the proportion of speculation being so large to the facts given.

Drs. Grant and Coldstream attended much to marine Zoology, and I often accompanied the former to collect animals in the tidal pools, which I dissected as well as I could. I also became friends with some of the Newhaven fishermen, and sometimes accompanied them when they trawled for oysters, and thus got many specimens. But from not having had any regular practice in dissection, and from possessing only a wretched microscope, my attempts were very poor. Nevertheless I made one interesting little discovery, and read, about the beginning of the year 1826, a short paper on the subject before the Plinian Society. This was that the so-called ova of Flustra had the power of independent movement by means of cilia, and were in fact larvæ. In another short paper I showed that the little globular bodies which had been supposed to be the young state of *Fucus loreus* were the egg-cases of the wormlike *Pontobdella muricata*.

The Plinian Society was encouraged and, I believe, founded by Professor Jameson: it consisted of students and met in an underground room in the University for the sake of reading papers on natural science and discussing them. I used regularly to attend, and the meeting had a good effect on me in stimulating my zeal and giving me new congenial acquaintances. One evening a poor young man got up, and after stammering for a prodigious length of time, blushing crimson, he at last slowly got out the words, "Mr. President, I have forgotten what I was going to say." The poor fellow looked quite overwhelmed, and all the members were so surprised that no one could think of a word to say to cover his confusion. The papers which were read to our little society were not printed, so that I had not the satisfaction of seeing my paper in print; but I believe Dr. Grant noticed my small discovery in his excellent memoir on Flustra.

I was also a member of the Royal Medical Society, and attended pretty regularly; but as the subjects were exclusively medical, I did not much care about them. Much rubbish was talked there, but there were some good speakers, of whom the best was the present Sir J. Kay-Shuttleworth. Dr. Grant took me occasionally to the meetings of the Wernerian Society, where various papers on natural history were read, discussed, and afterwards published in the *Transactions*. I heard Audubon deliver there some interesting discourses on the habits of N. American birds, sneering somewhat unjustly at Waterton. By the

way, a Negro lived in Edinburgh, who had travelled with Waterton, and gained his livelihood by stuffing birds, which he did excellently: he gave me lessons for payment, and I used often to sit with him, for he was a very pleasant and intelligent man.

Mr. Leonard Horner also took me once to a meeting of the Royal Society of Edinburgh, where I saw Sir Walter Scott in the chair as President, and he apologised to the meeting as not feeling fitted for such a position. I looked at him and at the whole scene with some awe and reverence, and I think it was owing to this visit during my youth, and to my having attended the Royal Medical Society, that I felt the honour of being elected a few years ago an honorary member of both these Societies, more than any other similar honour. If I had been told at that time that I should one day have been thus honoured, I declare that I should have thought it as ridiculous and improbable, as if I had been told that I should be elected King of England.

During my second year at Edinburgh I attended Jameson's lectures on Geology and Zoology, but they were incredibly dull. The sole effect they produced on me was the determination never as long as I lived to read a book on Geology, or in any way to study the science. Yet I feel sure that I was prepared for a philosophical treatment of the subject; for an old Mr. Cotton in Shropshire, who knew a good deal about rocks, had pointed out to me two or three years previously a well-known large erratic boulder in the town of Shrewsbury, called the "bell-stone"; he told me that there was no rock of the same kind nearer than Cumberland or Scotland, and he solemnly assured me that the world would come to an end before any one would be able to explain how this stone came where it now lay. This produced a deep impression on me, and I meditated over this wonderful stone. So I felt the keenest delight when I first read of the action of icebergs in transporting boulders, and I gloried in the progress of Geology. Equally striking is the fact that I, though now only sixty-seven years old, heard the Professor, in a field lecture at Salisbury Craigs, discoursing on a trap-dyke, with amygdaloidal margins and the strata indurated on each side, with volcanic rocks all around us, say that it was a fissure filled with sediment from above, adding with a sneer that there were men who maintained that it had been injected from beneath in a molten condition. When I think of this lecture, I do not wonder that I determined never to attend to Geology.

From attending Jameson's lectures, I became acquainted with the curator of the museum, Mr. Macgillivray, who afterwards published a large and excellent book on the birds of Scotland. I had much interesting natural-history talk with him, and he was very kind to me. He gave me some rare shells, for I at that time collected marine mollusca, but with no great zeal.

My summer vacations during these two years were wholly given up to amusements, though I always had some book in hand, which I read with interest. During the summer of 1826 I took a long walking tour with two friends with knapsacks on our backs through North Wales. We walked thirty miles most days, including one day the ascent of Snowdon. I also went with my sister a riding tour in North Wales, a servant with saddle-bags carrying our clothes. The autumns were devoted to shooting chiefly at Mr. Owens', at Woodhouse, and at my Uncle Jos's, at Maer. My zeal was so great that I used to place my shooting-boots open by my bed-side when I went to bed, so as not to lose half a minute in putting them on in the morning; and on one occasion I reached a distant part of the Maer estate, on the 20th of August for black-game shooting, before I could see: I then toiled on with the game-keeper the whole day through thick heath and young Scotch firs.

I kept an exact record of every bird which I shot throughout the whole season. One day when shooting at Woodhouse with Captain Owen, the eldest son, and Major Hill, his cousin, afterwards Lord Berwick, both of whom I liked very much, I thought myself shamefully used, for every time after I had fired and thought that I had killed a bird, one of the two acted as if loading his gun, and cried out, "You must not count that bird, for I fired at the same time," and the game-keeper, perceiving the joke, backed them up. After some hours they told me the joke, but it was no joke to me, for I had shot a large number of birds, but did not know how many, and could not add them to my list, which I used to do by making a knot in a piece of string tied to a button-hole. This my wicked friends had perceived.

How I did enjoy shooting! but I think that I must have been half-consciously ashamed of my zeal, for I tried to persuade myself that shooting was almost an intellectual employment; it required so much skill to judge where to find most game and to hunt the dogs well.

One of my autumnal visits to Maer in 1827 was memorable from meeting there Sir J. Mackintosh, who was the best converser I ever listened to. I heard afterwards with a glow of pride that he had said, "There is something in that young man that interests me." This must have been chiefly due to his perceiving that I listened with much interest to everything which he said, for I was as ignorant as a pig about his subjects of history, politics, and moral philosophy. To hear of praise from an eminent person, though no doubt apt or certain to excite vanity, is, I think, good for a young man, as it helps to keep him in the right course.

My visits to Maer during these two or three succeeding years were quite delightful, inde-pendently of the autumnal shooting. Life there was perfectly free; the country was very pleasant for walking or riding; and in the evening there was much very agreeable conversation, not so personal as it generally is in large family parties, together with music. In the summer the whole family used often to sit on the steps of the old portico, with the flower-garden in front, and with the steep wooded bank opposite the house reflected in the lake, with here and there a fish rising or a water-bird paddling about. Nothing has left a more vivid picture on my mind than these evenings at Maer. I was also attached to and greatly revered my Uncle Jos; he was silent and reserved, so as to be a rather awful man; but he sometimes talked openly with me. He was the very type of an upright man, with the clearest judgment. I do not believe that any power on earth could have made him swerve an inch from what he considered the right course. I used to apply to him in my mind the well-known ode of Horace, now forgotten by me, in which the words "nec vultus tyranni, &c.," come in.

Cambridge 1828–1831.—After having spent two sessions in Edinburgh, my father perceived, or he heard from my sisters, that I did not like the thought of being a physician, so he proposed that I should become a clergyman. He was very properly vehement against my turning into an idle sporting man, which then seemed my probable destination. I asked for some time to consider, as from what little I had heard or thought on the subject I had scruples about declaring my belief in all the dogmas of the Church of England; though otherwise I liked the thought of being a country clergyman. Accord-ingly I read with care Pearson on the *Creed*, and a few other books on divinity; and as I did not then in the least doubt the strict and literal truth of every word in the Bible, I soon persuaded my-self that our Creed must be fully accepted.

Considering how fiercely I have been attacked by the orthodox, it seems ludicrous that I once intended to be a clergyman. Nor was this intention and my father's wish ever formally given up, but died a natural death when, on leaving Cambridge, I joined the *Beagle* as naturalist. If the phrenologists are to be trusted, I was well fitted in one respect to be a clergyman. A few years ago the secretaries of a German psychological society asked me earnestly by letter for a photograph of myself; and some time afterwards I received the proceedings of one of the meetings, in which it seemed that the shape of my head had been the subject of a public discussion, and one of the speakers declared that I had the bump of reverence developed enough for ten priests.

As it was decided that I should be a clergyman, it was necessary that I should go to one of the English universities and take a degree; but as I had never opened a classical book since leaving school, I found to my dismay, that in the two intervening years I had actually forgotten, incredible as it may appear, almost everything which I had learned, even to some few of the Greek letters. I did not therefore proceed to Cambridge at the usual time in October, but worked with a private tutor in Shrewsbury, and went to Cambridge after the Christmas vacation, early in 1828. I soon recovered my school standard of knowledge, and could translate easy Greek books, such as Homer and the Greek Testament, with moderate facility.

During the three years which I spent at Cambridge my time was wasted, as far as the academical studies were concerned, as completely as at Edinburgh and at school. I attempted mathematics, and even went during the summer of 1828 with a private tutor (a very dull man) to Barmouth, but I got on very slowly. The work was repugant to me, chiefly from my not being able to see any meaning in the early steps in algebra. This impatience was very foolish, and in after years I have deeply regretted that I did not proceed far enough at least to understand something of the great leading principles of mathematics, for men thus endowed seem to have an extra sense. But I do not believe that I should ever have succeeded beyond a very low grade. With respect to Classics I did nothing except attend a few compulsory college lectures, and the attendance was almost nominal. In my second year I had to work for a month or two to pass the Little-Go,[4] which I did easily. Again, in my last year I worked with some earnestness for my final

degree of B.A., and brushed up my Classics, together with a little Algebra and Euclid, which latter gave me much pleasure, as it did at school. In order to pass the B.A. examination, it was also necessary to get up Paley's *Evidences of Christianity*, and his *Moral Philosophy*. This was done in a thorough manner, and I am convinced that I could have written out the whole of the *Evidences* with perfect correctness, but not of course in the clear language of Paley. The logic of this book and, as I may add, of his *Natural Theology*, gave me as much delight as did Euclid. The careful study of these works, without attempting to learn any part by rote, was the only part of the academical course which, as I then felt and as I still believe, was of the least use to me in the education of my mind. I did not at that time trouble myself about Paley's premises; and taking these on trust, I was charmed and convinced by the long line of argumentation. By answering well the examination questions in Paley, by doing Euclid well, and by not failing miserably in Classics, I gained a good place among the hoi polloi or crowd of men who do not go in for honours. Oddly enough, I cannot remember how high I stood, and my memory fluctuates between the fifth, tenth, or twelfth, name on the list.[5]

Public lectures on several branches were given in the University, attendance being quite voluntary; but I was so sickened with lectures at Edinburgh that I did not even attend Sedgwick's eloquent and interesting lectures. Had I done so I should probably have become a geologist earlier than I did. I attended, however, Henslow's lectures on Botany, and liked them much for their extreme clearness, and the admirable illustrations; but I did not study botany. Henslow used to take his pupils, including several of the older members of the University, field excursions, on foot or in coaches, to distant places, or in a barge down the river, and lectured on the rarer plants and animals which were observed. These excursions were delightful.

Although, as we shall presently see, there were some redeeming features in my life at Cambridge, my time was sadly wasted there, and worse than wasted. From my passion for shooting and for hunting, and, when this failed, for riding across country, I got into a sporting set, including some dissipated low-minded young men. We used often to dine together in the evening, though these

---

[4] The first examination for the B.A. degree.
[5] Darwin's son and editor says the name stood tenth on the list.

dinners often included men of a higher stamp, and we sometimes drank too much, with jolly singing and playing at cards afterwards. I know that I ought to feel ashamed of days and evenings thus spent, but as some of my friends were very pleasant, and we were all in the highest spirits, I cannot help looking back to these times with much pleasure.

But I am glad to think that I had many other friends of a widely different nature. I was very intimate with Whitley,[6] who was afterwards Senior Wrangler, and we used continually to take long walks together. He innoculated me with a taste for pictures and good engravings, of which I bought some. I frequently went to the Fitzwilliam Gallery, and my taste must have been fairly good, for I certainly admired the best pictures, which I discussed with the old curator. I read also with much interest Sir Joshua Reynolds' book. This taste, though not natural to me, lasted for several years, and many of the pictures in the National Gallery in London gave me much pleasure; that of Sebastian del Piombo exciting in me a sense of sublimity.

I also got into a musical set, I believe by means of my warm-hearted friend, Herbert,[7] who took a high wrangler's degree. From associating with these men, and hearing them play, I acquired a strong taste for music, and used very often to time my walks so as to hear on week days the anthem in King's College Chapel. This gave me intense pleasure, so that my backbone would sometimes shiver. I am sure that there was no affectation or mere imitation in this taste, for I used generally to go by myself to King's College, and I sometimes hired the chorister boys to sing in my rooms. Nevertheless I am so utterly destitute of an ear, that I cannot perceive a discord, or keep time and hum a tune correctly; and it is a mystery how I could possibly have derived pleasure from music.

My musical friends soon perceived my taste, and sometimes amused themselves by making me pass an examination, which consisted in ascertaining how many tunes I could recognise when they were played rather more quickly or slowly than usual. "God save the King," when thus played, was a sore puzzle. There was another man with almost as bad an ear as I had, and strange to say he played a little on the flute. Once I had the triumph of beating him in one of our musical examinations.

But no pursuit at Cambridge was followed with nearly so much earnestness or gave me so much pleasure as collecting beetles. It was the mere passion for collecting, for I did not dissect them, and rarely compared their external characters with published descriptions, but got them named anyhow. I will give a proof of my zeal: one day, on tearing off some old bark, I saw two rare beetles, and seized one in each hand; then I saw a third and new kind, which I could not bear to lose, so that I popped the one which I held in my right hand into my mouth. Alas! it ejected some intensely acrid fluid, which burnt my tongue so that I was forced to spit the beetle out, which was lost, as was the third one.

I was very successful in collecting, and invented two new methods; I employed a labourer to scrape during the winter, moss off old trees and place it in a large bag, and likewise to collect the rubbish at the bottom of the barges in which reeds are brought from the fens, and thus I got some very rare species. No poet ever felt more delighted at seeing his first poem published than I did at seeing, in Stephens' *Illustrations of British Insects*, the magic words, "captured by C. Darwin, Esq." I was introduced to entomology by my second cousin, W. Darwin Fox, a clever and most pleasant man, who was then at Christ's College, and with whom I became extremely intimate. Afterwards I became well acquainted, and went out collecting, with Albert Way of Trinity, who in after years became a well-known archæologist; also with H. Thompson of the same College, afterwards a leading agriculturist, chairman of a great railway, and Member of Parliament. It seems therefore that a taste for collecting beetles is some indication of future success in life!

I am surprised what an indelible impression many of the beetles which I caught at Cambridge have left on my mind. I can remember the exact appearance of certain posts, old trees and banks where I made a good capture. The pretty *Panagæus crux-major* was a treasure in those days, and here at Down I saw a beetle running across a walk, and on picking it up instantly perceived that it differed slightly from *P. crux-major*, and it turned out to be *P. quadripunctatus*, which is only a variety or closely allied species, differing from it very slightly in outline. I had never seen in those old days Licinus alive, which to an uneducated eye hardly differs from many of the black

---

[6] Rev. C. Whitley, Hon. Canon of Durham, formerly Reader in Natural Philosophy in Durham University. [Francis Darwin's note]

[7] The late John Maurice Herbert, County Court Judge of Cardiff and the Monmouth Council. [Francis Darwin's note]

Carabidous beetles; but my sons found here a specimen, and I instantly recognized that it was new to me; yet I had not looked at a British beetle for the last twenty years.

I have not as yet mentioned a circumstance which influenced my whole career more than any other. This was my friendship with Professor Henslow. Before coming up to Cambridge, I had heard of him from my brother as a man who knew every branch of science, and I was accordingly prepared to reverence him. He kept open house once every week when all undergraduates, and some older members of the University, who were attached to science, used to meet in the evening. I soon got, through Fox, an invitation, and went there regularly. Before long I became well acquainted with Henslow, and during the latter half of my time at Cambridge took long walks with him on most days; so that I was called by some of the dons "the man who walks with Henslow"; and in the evening I was very often asked to join his family dinner. His knowledge was great in botany, entomology, chemistry, mineralogy, and geology. His strongest taste was to draw conclusions from long-continued minute observations. His judgment was excellent, and his whole mind well balanced; but I do not suppose that any one would say that he possessed much original genius. He was deeply religious, and so orthodox that he told me one day he should be grieved if a single word of the Thirty-nine Articles were altered. His moral qualities were in every way admirable. He was free from every tinge of vanity or other petty feeling; and I never saw a man who thought so little about himself or of his own concerns. His temper was imperturbably good, with the most winning and courteous manners; yet, as I have seen, he could be roused by any bad action to the warmest indignation and prompt action.

I once saw in his company in the streets of Cambridge almost as horrid a scene as could have been witnessed during the French Revolution. Two body-snatchers had been arrested, and whilst being taken to prison had been torn from the constable by a crowd of the roughest men, who dragged them by their legs along the muddy and stony road. They were covered from head to foot with mud, and their faces were bleeding either from having been kicked or from the stones; they looked like corpses, but the crowd was so dense that I got only a few momentary glimpses of the wretched creatures. Never in my life have I seen such wrath painted on a man's face as was shown by Henslow at this horrid scene. He tried repeatedly to penetrate the mob; but it was simply impossible. He then rushed away to the mayor, telling me not to follow him but to get more policemen. I forget the issue, except that the two men were got into prison without being killed.

Henslow's benevolence was unbounded, as he proved by his many excellent schemes for his poor parishioners, when in after years he held the living of Hitcham. My intimacy with such a man ought to have been, and I hope was, an inestimable benefit. I cannot resist mentioning a trifling incident, which showed his kind consideration. Whilst examining some pollen-grains on a damp surface, I saw the tubes exserted, and instantly rushed off to communicate my surprising discovery to him. Now I do not suppose any other professor of botany could have helped laughing at my coming in such a hurry to make such a communication. But he agreed how interesting the phenomenon was, and explained its meaning, but made me clearly understand how well it was known; so I left him not in the least mortified, but well pleased at having discovered for myself so remarkable a fact, but determined not to be in such a hurry again to communicate my discoveries.

Dr. Whewell was one of the older and distinguished men who sometimes visited Henslow, and on several occasions I walked home with him at night. Next to Sir J. Mackintosh he was the best converser on grave subjects to whom I ever listened. Leonard Jenyns, who afterwards published some good essays in Natural History, often stayed with Henslow, who was his brother-in-law. I visited him at his parsonage on the borders of the Fens [Swaffham Bulbeck,] and had many a good walk and talk with him about Natural History. I became also acquainted with several other men older than me, who did not care much about science, but were friends of Henslow. One was a Scotchman, brother of Sir Alexander Ramsay, and tutor of Jesus College; he was a delightful man, but did not live for many years. Another was Dr. Dawes, afterwards Dean of Hereford, and famous for his success in the education of the poor. These men and others of the same standing, together with Henslow, used sometimes to take distant excursions into the country, which I was allowed to join, and they were most agreeable.

Looking back, I infer that there must have been something in me a little superior to the common run of youths, otherwise the above-mentioned men, so much older than me and higher in academical position, would never have allowed me to associate with them. Certainly I was not aware of any such superiority, and I remember one of my sporting friends, Turner, who saw me at work with my beetles, saying that I should some day be a Fellow of the Royal Society, and the notion seemed to me preposterous.

During my last year at Cambridge, I read with care and profound interest Humboldt's *Personal Narrative*. This work, and Sir J. Herschel's *Introduction to the Study of Natural Philosophy*, stirred up in me a burning zeal to add even the most humble contribution to the noble structure of Natural Science. No one or a dozen other books influenced me nearly so much as these two. I copied out from Humboldt long passages about Teneriffe, and read them aloud on one of the above-mentioned excursions, to (I think) Henslow, Ramsay, and Dawes, for on a previous occasion I had talked about the glories of Teneriffe, and some of the party declared they would endeavour to go there; but I think that they were only half in earnest. I was, however, quite in earnest, and got an introduction to a merchant in London to enquire about ships; but the scheme was, of course, knocked on the head by the voyage of the *Beagle*.

My summer vacations were given up to collecting beetles, to some reading, and short tours. In the autumn my whole time was devoted to shooting, chiefly at Woodhouse and Maer, and sometimes with young Eyton of Eyton. Upon the whole the three years which I spent at Cambridge were the most joyful in my happy life; for I was then in excellent health, and almost always in high spirits.

As I had at first come up to Cambridge at Christmas, I was forced to keep two terms after passing my final examination, at the commencement of 1831; and Henslow then persuaded me to begin the study of geology. Therefore on my return to Shropshire I examined sections, and coloured a map of parts round Shrewsbury. Professor Sedgwick intended to visit North Wales in the beginning of August to pursue his famous geological investigations amongst the older rocks, and Henslow asked him to allow me to accompany him. Accordingly he came and slept at my father's house.

A short conversation with him during this evening produced a strong impression on my mind. Whilst examining an old gravel-pit near Shrewsbury, a labourer told me that he had found in it a large worn tropical Volute shell, such as may be seen on the chimney-pieces of cottages; and as he would not sell the shell, I was convinced that he had really found it in the pit. I told Sedgwick of the fact, and he at once said (no doubt truly) that it must have been thrown away by some one into the pit; but then added, if really embedded there it would be the greatest misfortune to geology, as it would overthrow all that we know about the superficial deposits of the Midland Counties. These gravel-beds belong in fact to the glacial period, and in after years I found in them broken arctic shells. But I was then utterly astonished at Sedgwick not being delighted at so wonderful a fact as a tropical shell being found near the surface in the middle of England. Nothing before had ever made me thoroughly realise, though I had read various scientific books, that science consists in grouping facts so that general laws or conclusions may be drawn from them.

Next morning we started for Llangollen, Conway, Bangor, and Capel Curig. This tour was of decided use in teaching me a little how to make out the geology of a country. Sedgwick often sent me on a line parallel to his, telling me to bring back specimen of the rocks and to mark the stratification on a map. I have little doubt that he did this for my good, as I was too ignorant to have aided him. On this tour I had a striking instance of how easy it is to overlook phenomena, however conspicuous, before they have been observed by any one. We spent many hours in Cwm Idwal, examining all the rocks with extreme care, as Sedgwick was anxious to find fossils in them; but neither of us saw a trace of the wonderful glacial phenomena all around us; we did not notice the plainly scored rocks, the perched boulders, the lateral and terminal moraines. Yet these phenomena are so conspicuous that, as I declared in a paper published many years afterwards in the *Philosophical Magazine*, a house burnt down by fire did not tell its story more plainly than did this valley. If it had still been filled by a glacier, the phenomena would have been less distinct than they now are.

At Capel Curig I left Sedgwick and went in a straight line by compass and map across the mountains to Barmouth, never following any track unless it coincided with my course. I thus came on some strange wild places, and enjoyed much this manner of travelling. I visited Barmouth to see some Cambridge friends who were reading there, and thence returned to Shrewsbury and to Maer for shooting; for at that time I should have thought myself mad to give up the first days of partridge-shooting for geology or any other science.

VOYAGE OF THE "BEAGLE" FROM DECEMBER 27, 1831, TO OCTOBER 2, 1836

On returning home from my short geological tour in North Wales, I found a letter from Henslow, informing me that Captain Fitz-Roy was willing to give up part of his own cabin to any young man who would volunteer to go with him without pay as a naturalist to the voyage of the *Beagle*. I have given, as I believe, in my MS. Journal an account of all the circumstances which then occurred; I will here only say that I was instantly eager to accept the offer, but my father strongly objected, adding the words, fortunate for me, "If you can find any man of common sense who advises you to go I will give my consent." So I wrote that evening and refused the offer. On the next morning I went to Maer to be ready for September 1st, and, whilst out shooting, my uncle sent for me, offering to drive me over to Shrewsbury and talk with my father, as my uncle thought it would be wise in me to accept the offer. My father always maintained that he was one of the most sensible men in the world, and he at once consented in the kindest manner. I had been rather extravagant at Cambridge, and to console my father, said, "that I should be deuced clever to spend more than my allowance whilst on board the *Beagle*"; but he answered with a smile, "But they tell me you are very clever."

Next day I started for Cambridge to see Henslow, and thence to London to see Fitz-Roy, and all was soon arranged. Afterwards, on becoming very intimate with Fitz-Roy, I heard that I had run a very narrow risk of being rejected, on account of the shape of my nose! He was an ardent disciple of Lavater, and was convinced that he could judge of a man's character by the outline of his features; and he doubted whether any one with my nose could possess sufficient energy and determination for the voyage. But I think he was afterwards well satisfied that my nose had spoken falsely.

Fitz-Roy's character was a singular one, with very many noble features: he was devoted to his duty, generous to a fault, bold, determined, and indomitably energetic, and an ardent friend to all under his sway. He would undertake any sort of trouble to assist those whom he thought deserved assistance. He was a handsome man, strikingly like a gentleman, with highly courteous manners, which resembled those of his maternal uncle, the famous Lord Castlereagh, as I was told by the Minister at Rio. Nevertheless he must have inherited much in his appearance from Charles II, for Dr. Wallich gave me a collection of photographs which he had made, and I was struck with the resemblance of one to Fitz-Roy; and on looking at the name, I found it Ch. E. Sobieski Stuart, Count d'Albanie, a descendant of the same monarch.

Fitz-Roy's temper was a most unfortunate one. It was usually worst in the early morning, and with his eagle eye he could generally detect something amiss about the ship, and was then unsparing in his blame. He was very kind to me, but was a man very difficult to live with on the intimate terms which necessarily followed from our messing by ourselves in the same cabin. We had several quarrels; for instance, early in the voyage at Bahia, in Brazil, he defended and praised slavery, which I abominated, and told me that he had just visited a great slave-owner, who had called up many of his slaves and asked them whether they were happy, and whether they wished to be free, and all answered "No." I then asked him, perhaps with a sneer, whether he thought that the answer of slaves in the presence of their master was worth anything? This made him excessively angry, and he said that as I doubted his word we could not live any longer together. I thought that I should have been compelled to leave the ship; but as soon as the news spread, which it did quickly, as the captain sent for the first lieutenant to assuage his anger by abusing me, I was deeply gratified by receiving an invitation from all the gun-room officers to mess with them. But after a few hours Fitz-Roy showed his actual magnanimity by sending an officer to me with an apology and a request that I would continue to live with him.

His character was in several respects one of the most noble which I have ever known.

The voyage of the *Beagle* has been by far the most important event in my life, and has determined my whole career; yet it depended on so small a circumstance as my uncle offering to drive me thirty miles to Shrewsbury, which few uncles would have done, and on such a trifle as the shape of my nose. I have always felt that I owe to the voyage the first real training or education of my mind; I was led to attend closely to several branches of natural history, and thus my powers of observation were improved, though they were always fairly developed.

The investigation of the geology of all the places visited was far more important, as reasoning here comes into play. On first examining a new district nothing can appear more hopeless than the chaos of rocks; but by recording the stratification and nature of the rocks and fossils at many points, always reasoning and predicting what will be found elsewhere, light soon begins to dawn on the district, and the structure of the whole becomes more or less intelligible. I had brought with me the first volume of Lyell's *Principles of Geology*, which I studied attentively; and the book was of the highest service to me in many ways. The very first place which I examined, namely St. Jago in the Cape de Verde islands, showed me clearly the wonderful superiority of Lyell's manner of treating geology, compared with that of any other author whose works I had with me or ever afterwards read.

Another of my occupations was collecting animals of all classes, briefly describing and roughly dissecting many of the marine ones; but from not being able to draw, and from not having sufficient anatomical knowledge, a great pile of MS. which I made during the voyage has proved almost useless. I thus lost much time, with the exception of that spent in acquiring some knowledge of the Crustaceans, as this was of service when in after years I undertook a monograph of the Cirripedia.

During some part of the day I wrote my Journal, and took much pains in describing carefully and vividly all that I had seen; and this was good practice. My Journal served also, in part, as letters to my home, and portions were sent to England whenever there was an opportunity.

The above various special studies were, however, of no importance compared with the habit of energetic industry and of concentrated attention to whatever I was engaged in, which I then acquired. Everything about which I thought or read was made to bear directly on what I had seen or was likely to see; and this habit of mind was continued during the five years of the voyage. I feel sure that it was this training which has enabled me to do whatever I have done in science.

Looking backwards, I can now perceive how my love for science gradually preponderated over every other taste. During the first two years my old passion for shooting survived in nearly full force, and I shot myself all the birds and animals for my collection; but gradually I gave up my gun more and more, and finally altogether, to my servant, as shooting interfered with my work, more especially with making out the geological structure of a country. I discovered, though unconsciously and insensibly, that the pleasure of observing and reasoning was a much higher one than that of skill and sport. That my mind became developed through my pursuits during the voyage is rendered probable by a remark made by my father, who was the most acute observer whom I ever saw, of a sceptical disposition, and far from being a believer in phrenology; for on first seeing me after the voyage, he turned round to my sisters, and exclaimed, "Why, the shape of his head is quite altered."

To return to the voyage. On September 11th (1831), I paid a flying visit with Fitz-Roy to the *Beagle* at Plymouth. Thence to Shrewsbury to wish my father and sisters a long farewell. On October 24th I took up my residence at Plymouth, and remained there until December 27th, when the *Beagle* finally left the shores of England for her circumnavigation of the world. We made two earlier attempts to sail, but were driven back each time by heavy gales. These two months at Plymouth were the most miserable which I ever spent, though I exerted myself in various ways. I was out of spirits at the thought of leaving all my family and friends for so long a time, and the weather seemed to me inexpressibly gloomy. I was also troubled with palpitation and pain about the heart, and like many a young ignorant man, especially one with a smattering of medical knowledge, was convinced that I had heart disease. I did not consult any doctor, as I fully expected to hear the verdict that I was not fit for the voyage, and I was resolved to go at all hazards.

I need not here refer to the events of the voyage—where we went and what we did—as I have given a sufficiently full account in my published Journal. The glories of the vegetation of the Tropics rise before my mind at the present time more vividly than anything else; through the sense of sublimity, which the great deserts of Patagonia and the forest-clad mountains of Tierra del Fuego excited in me, has left an indelible impression on my mind. The sight of a naked savage in his native land is an event which can never be forgotten. Many of my excursions on horseback through wild countries, or in the boats, some of which lasted several weeks, were deeply interesting: their discomfort and some degree of danger were at that time hardly a drawback, and none at all afterwards. I also reflect with high satisfaction on some of my scientific work, such as solving the problem of coral islands, and making out the geological structure of certain islands, for instance, St. Helena. Nor must I pass over the discovery of the singular relations of the animals and plants inhabiting the several islands of the Galapagos archipelago, and of all of them to the inhabitants of South America.

As far as I can judge of myself, I worked to the utmost during the voyage from the mere pleasure of investigation, and from my strong desire to add a few facts to the great mass of facts in Natural Science. But I was also ambitious to take a fair place among scientific men,—whether more ambitious or less so than most of my fellow-workers, I can form no opinion.

The geology of St. Jago is very striking, yet simple: a stream of lava formerly flowed over the bed of the sea, formed of triturated recent shells and corals, which it has baked into a hard white rock. Since then the whole island has been up-heaved. But the line of white rock revealed to me a new and important fact, namely, that there had been afterwards subsidence round the craters, which had since been in action, and had poured forth lava. It then first dawned on me that I might perhaps write a book on the geology of the various countries visited, and this made me thrill with delight. That was a memorable hour to me, and how distinctly I can call to mind the low cliff of lava beneath which I rested, with the sun glaring hot, a few strange desert plants growing near, and with living corals in the tidal pools at my feet. Later in the voyage, Fitz-Roy asked me to read some of my Journal, and declared it would be worth publishing; so here was a second book in prospect!

Towards the close of our voyage I received a letter whilst at Ascension, in which my sisters told me that Sedgwick had called on my father, and said that I should take a place among the leading scientific men. I could not at the time understand how he could have learnt anything of my proceedings, but I heard (I believe after-wards) that Henslow had read some of the letters which I wrote to him before the Philosophical Society of Cambridge, and had printed them for private distribution. My collection of fossil bones, which had been sent to Henslow, also excited considerable attention amongst palæontologists. After reading this letter, I clambered over the mountains of Ascension with a bounding step,

and made the volcanic rocks resound under my geological hammer. All this shows how ambitious I was; but I think that I can say with truth that in after years, though I cared in the highest degree for the approbation of such men as Lyell and Hooker, who were my friends, I did not care much about the general public. I do not mean to say that a favourable review or a large sale of my books did not please me greatly, but the pleasure was a fleeting one, and I am sure that I have never turned one inch out of my course to gain fame.

FROM MY RETURN TO ENGLAND (OCTOBER 2, 1836) TO MY MARRIAGE (JANUARY 29, 1839)

These two years and three months were the most active ones which I ever spent, though I was occasionally unwell, and so lost some time. After going backwards and forwards several times between Shrewsbury, Maer, Cambridge, and London, I settled in lodgings at Cambridge on December 13th, where all my collections were under the care of Henslow. I stayed here three months, and got my minerals and rocks examined by the aid of Professor Miller.

I began preparing my *Journal of Travels*, which was not hard work, as my MS. Journal had been written with care, and my chief labour was making an abstract of my more interesting scientific results. I sent also, at the request of Lyell, a short account of my observations on the elevation of the coast of Chile to the Geological Society.

On March 7th, 1837, I took lodgings in Great Marlborough Street in London, and remained there for nearly two years, until I was married. During these two years I finished my Journal, read several papers before the Geological Society, began preparing the MS. for my *Geological Observations*, and arranged for the publication of the *Zoology of the Voyage of the Beagle*. In July I opened my first note-book for facts in relation to the *Origin of Species*, about which I had long reflected, and never ceased working for the next twenty years.

During these two years I also went a little into society, and acted as one of the honorary secretaries of the Geological Society. I saw a great deal of Lyell. One of his chief characteristics was his sympathy with the work of others, and I was as much astonished as delighted at the interest which he showed when, on my return to England,

I explained to him my views on coral reefs. This encouraged me greatly, and his advice and example had much influence on me. During this time I saw also a good deal of Robert Brown; I used often to call and sit with him during his breakfast on Sunday mornings, and he poured forth a rich treasure of curious observations and acute remarks, but they almost always related to minute points, and he never with me discussed large or general questions in science.

During these two years I took several short excursions as a relaxation, and one longer one to the Parallel Roads of Glen Roy, an account of which was published in the *Philosophical Transactions*. This paper was a great failure, and I am ashamed of it. Having been deeply impressed with what I had seen of the elevation of the land of South America, I attributed the parallel lines to the action of the sea; but I had to give up this view when Agassiz propounded his glacier-lake theory. Because no other explanation was possible under our then state of knowledge, I argued in favor of sea-action; and my error has been a good lesson to me never to trust in science to the principle of exclusion.

As I was not able to work all day at science, I read a good deal during these two years on various subjects, including some metaphysical books; but I was not well fitted for such studies. About this time I took much delight in Wordsworth's and Coleridge's poetry; and can boast that I read the *Excursion* twice through. Formerly Milton's *Paradise Lost* had been my chief favourite, and in my excursions during the voyage of the *Beagle*, when I could take only a single volume, I always chose Milton.

William Ewart Gladstone

1809-1889

LTHOUGH he began his political career as a Tory, W. E.
Gladstone is remembered as the great Liberal prime minister of the
Victorian age. As a liberal, he served in numerous parliamentary
capacities and headed the government in no fewer than four
administrations. He superintended the passage of more successful legislation
than any other prime minister, and he won the reputation for being perhaps
the greatest of all parliamentary debaters.

Gladstone was born in Liverpool, the fourth son and fifth child of a very
prosperous Liverpool merchant originally from Scotland. He was educated at
Eton and Christ Church, Oxford, from which he was graduated with unusual
double first-class honors. Almost immediately he embarked on a political
career, serving in Parliament for the first time in 1832. His parliamentary
service, though interrupted at various times, did not cease until old age forced
him to resign in 1894, a record of more than sixty years in public life.

In his parliamentary career Gladstone served variously as representative
from Newark, the University of Oxford, South Lancashire, and Midlothian.
During his first thirty years in government the old Tory party divided on the
issue of free trade, with Disraeli taking the leadership of the opponents of free
trade and Gladstone the leadership of the proponents. Disraeli, though later
changing his views, remained a Tory, while Gladstone and his supporters
evolved into the Liberal Party.

Gladstone's first administration began in 1868, the Liberals having been
brought to power largely by the voters newly enfranchised by the Second
Reform Bill that Disraeli had seen through Parliament. For the next twenty-
five years Gladstone was to alternate the prime minister-ship, first with Disraeli,
then with Lord Salisbury. During the second Gladstone administration the
Third Reform Bill was passed, extending the franchise to agricultural workers;
and under Gladstone's leadership various measures of social and educational
reform were passed, including the first universal education act. Gladstone
failed, however, to secure home rule for Ireland, though he labored through
several administrations to resolve the Irish question. He died in 1898 at
Hawarden, his estate in Wales.

When not in power Gladstone occupied himself with literary studies,
producing works on religion (he was a devoted High Churchman), classical
literature, and statecraft. He left a substantial body of writing that alone

would qualify him for some attention from literary historians, especially for his Homeric studies and translations and his *The State in Its Relations with the Church*. Gladstone stands as an especially high-minded example of a cultivated intellect in the service of the state.

CHRONOLOGY

1809	Born 29 December in Liverpool.
1821–28	Attends Eton.
1828–31	Attends Christ Church, Oxford; graduates with double first-class honors.
1832	Enters Parliament.
1839	Marries Catherine Glynne of Hawarden, Flintshire.
1868	Prime Minister, first administration.
1880	Prime Minister, second administration.
1886	Prime Minister, third administration.
1892	Prime Minister, fourth administration.
1898	Dies 19 May; buried in Westminster Abbey.

EDITIONS

The State in Its Relations with the Church (1838, rev. 1841).
Studies on Homer and the Homeric Age (3 vols., 1858).
Juventus Mundi: The Gods and Men of the Heroic Age (1869).
Speeches on Great Questions of the Day (1870).
Gleanings of Past Years (7 vols., 1879).
Later Gleanings (1898).
Correspondence on Church and Religion of W. E. Gladstone, ed. D. C. Lathbury (2 vols., 1910).
Gladstone's Speeches, ed. A. Tilney Bassett (1916).

BIOGRAPHY AND CRITICISM

H. W. Paul, *The Life of W. E. Gladstone* (1901).
John Morley, *The Life of Gladstone* (3 vols., 1903).
Francis Birrell, *Gladstone* (1933).
Osburt Burdett, *Gladstone* (1933).
G. M. Young, *Mr. Gladstone* (1944).
Alec R. Vidler, *The Orb and the Cross* (1945).
J. L. Hammond and M. R. D. Foot, *Gladstone and Liberalism* (1952).
Philip Magnus, *Gladstone* (1954).

---

from Gleanings of the Past Years

Gladstone's Gleanings *is a collection of miscellaneous addresses and literary and political pieces composed over a period of some sixty years. The essay below, "Death of the Prince Consort," was Gladstone's response to the death in December of 1861 of Prince Albert of Saxe-Coburg,*

Victoria's husband. The event was a landmark in Victorian life, for after it Queen Victoria became the public widow of later fame. Gladstone first presented the piece as a talk on 23 April 1862 to the Lancashire and Cheshire Mechanics' Institute. It was published in 1862 and gathered in the first volume of Gleanings.

Death of the Prince Consort

Ladies and Gentlemen,—Although the duty in which we have just been engaged is a cheerful one, the season at which I come among you is, but too notoriously, a season of gloom in the district, and even in the city. In this busy region, all the forms of human industry are grouped around one central stock, which gives them their vitality; and they droop and come near to dying when, as now, the great cotton harvest is no longer wafted over the Atlantic to employ and feed the people. If the positive signs of distress do not glare in your streets, it is, I apprehend, because the manly and independent character of the Lancashire workman makes him unwilling to parade, or even to disclose, his sufferings before his fellow-men. None can doubt the existence of a torpor scarcely ever equalled in its intensity, and wholly without parallel in its cause. At points of the horizon in these counties, the eye suggests regret even for the unwonted thinness of the canopy of smoke, which bears witness to the partial slumber of the giant forces enlisted in your ordinary service. Rarely within living memory has so much of skill lain barren, so much of willing strength been smitten as with palsy; or has so much of poverty and want forced its way into homes that had long been wont to smile with comfort and abundance. Nor is the promise of to-morrow a compensation for the pressure of to-day. On the contrary, if the present be dark, the signs of the immediate future may seem darker still.

In times like these the human mind, and still more the human heart, searches all around for consolation and support. Of that support one kind is to be found in observing that trials the most severe and piercing are the lot not of one station only but of all. And perhaps in the wise counsels of Providence it was decreed that that crushing sorrow which came down as sudden as the hurricane, scarcely yet four months ago, upon the august head of our Sovereign, should serve, among other uses, that of teaching and helping her subjects to bear up under the sense of affliction and desolation, and should exhibit by conspicuous example the need and the duty both of mutual sympathy and mutual help. In many a humble cottage, darkened by the calamity of the past winter, the mourning inhabitants may have checked their own impatience by reflecting that, in the ancient Palace of our Kings, a Woman's heart lay bleeding; and that to the supreme place in birth, in station, in splendour, and in power, was now added another and sadder title of pre-eminence in grief.

For perhaps no sharper stroke ever cut human lives asunder than that which in December last parted, so far as this world of sense is concerned, the lives of the Queen of England and of her chosen Consort. It had been obvious to us all, though necessarily in different degrees, that they were blest with the possession of the secret of reconciling the discharge of incessant and wearing public duty with the cultivation of the inner and domestic life. The attachment that binds together wife and husband was known to be in their case, and to have been from the first, of an unusual force. Through more than twenty years, which flowed past like one long unclouded summer day, that attachment was cherished, exercised, and strengthened by all the forms of family interest, by all the associated pursuits of highly cultivated minds, by all the cares and responsibilities which surround the Throne, and which the Prince was called, in his own sphere, both to alleviate and to share. On the one side, such love is rare, even in the annals of the love of woman; on the other, such service can hardly find a parallel, for it is hard to know how a husband could render it to a wife, unless that wife were also Queen.

So, then, She, whom you have seen in your streets a source of joy to you all, and herself drinking in with cordial warmth the sights and the sounds of your enthusiastic loyalty, is now to be thought of as the first of English widows, lonely in proportion to her elevation and her cares. Nor let it be thought that those who are never called to suffer in respect of bodily wants therefore do not suffer sharply. Whereas, on the contrary, it is well established, not only that though the form of sorrow may be changed with a change in the sphere of life, the essence and power of it remain, but also that, as that sphere enlarges, the capacity of suffering deepens along with it, no less than the opportunities of enjoyment are multiplied. Therefore all the land, made aware, through the transparent manner of it, what was the true character of her life, has acknowledged in the Queen not only a true, but a signally afflicted mourner. And rely upon it that, even in the midst of desolation, she is conscious of our sympathy, and has thrilled more deeply to the signs of her people's grief on her behalf than ever, in other days, to their loudest and most heart-stirring acclamations.

And you, my friends, such of you in particular as have felt by your firesides the touch of this most trying time: if perchance many among you, turning in the day of need and trouble to the Father of all Mercies, have mingled with your prayers for your own relief another prayer, that She may be consoled in her sorrow and strengthened for her work during what we hope will be the long remainder of her days, that loyal prayer will come back with blessing into your own bosom, and in the effort to obtain comfort for another you will surely be comforted yourselves.

If the mourning of the nation for the Prince Consort's death was universal, yet within certain precincts it was also special. One of those precincts surely must have been the Association to promote whose purposes we are gathered here to-night. You had in him a Head; and a Head standing towards you in no merely titular relation, but one who, as his manner was, gave reality to every attribute of his station, and, in lending you his name, imparted to you freely of his thought and care to boot. His comprehensive gaze ranged to and fro between the base and the summit of society, and examined the interior forces by which it is kept at once in balance and in motion. In his well-ordered life there seemed to be room for all things—for every manly exercise, for the study and practice of art, for the exacting cares of a splendid Court, for minute attention to every domestic and paternal duty, for advice and aid towards the discharge of public business in its innumerable forms, and for meeting the voluntary calls of an active philanthropy: one day in considering the best form for the dwellings of the people; another day in bringing his just and gentle influence to bear on the relations of master and domestic servant; another in suggesting and supplying the means of culture for the most numerous classes; another in some good work of almsgiving or religion. Nor was it a merely external activity which he displayed. His mind, it is evident, was too deeply earnest to be satisfied

in anything, smaller or greater, with resting on the surface. With a strong grasp on practical life in all its forms, he united a habit of thought eminently philosophic; ever referring facts to their causes, and pursuing action to its consequences. Gone though he be from among us, he, like other worthies of mankind who have preceded him, is not altogether gone; for, in the words of the poet—

> "Your heads must come
>   To the cold tomb;
>   Only the actions of the just
>   Smell sweet and blossom in their dust."[1]

So he has left for all men, in all classes, many a useful lesson, to be learnt from the record of his life and character.

For example, it would, I believe, be difficult to find anywhere a model of a life more highly organised, more thoroughly and compactly ordered. Here in Manchester, if anywhere in the world, you know what order is, and what a power it holds. Here we see at work the vast systems of machinery, where ten thousand instruments are ever labouring, each in its own proper place, each with its own proper duty, but all obedient to one law, and all co-operating for one end. Scarcely in one of these your own great establishments are the principles of order and its power more vividly exemplified, than they were in the mind and life of the Prince Consort. Now this way of excelling is one that we all may follow. There is not one among us all here gathered who may not, if he will, especially if he be still young, by the simple specific of giving method to his life, greatly increase its power and efficacy for good.

But he would be a sorry imitator of the Prince who should suppose that this process could be satisfactorily performed as a mechanical process, in a presumptuous or in a servile spirit, and with a view to selfish or to worldly ends. A life that is to be active like his ought to find refreshment even in the midst of labours; nay, to draw refreshment from them. But this it cannot do, unless the man can take up the varied employments of the world with something of a childlike freshness. Few are they who carry on with them that childlike freshness of the earliest years into after-life. It is that especial light of Heaven, described by Wordsworth in his immortal 'Ode on the Recollections of Childhood': that light—

> "which lies about us in our infancy,"

---

[1] From James Shirley's *Ajax and Ulysses*.

which attends even the youth upon his way; but at length—

> "the Man perceives it die away,
> And fade into the light of common day."

Its radiance still plays about a favoured few: they are those few who, like the Prince, strive earnestly to keep themselves unspotted from the world, and are victors in the strife.

In beseeching, especially, the young to study the application to their daily life of that principle of order which both engenders diligence and strength of will, and likewise so greatly multiplies their power, I am well assured that they will find this to be not only an intellectual but a moral exercise. Every real and searching effort at self-improvement is of itself a lesson of profound humility. For we cannot move a step without learning and feeling the waywardness, the weakness, the vacillation of our movements, or without desiring to be set up upon the Rock that is higher than ourselves. Nor, again, is it likely that the self-denial and self-discipline which these efforts undoubtedly involve will often be cordially undergone, except by those who elevate and extend their vision beyond the narrow scope of the years—be they what we admit to be few, or what we think to be many—that are prescribed for our career on earth. An untiring sense of duty, an active consciousness of the perpetual presence of Him who is its author and its law, and a lofty aim beyond the grave—these are the best and most efficient parts, in every sense, of that apparatus wherewith we should be armed, when with full purpose of heart we address ourselves to the life-long work of self-improvement. And I believe that the lesson which I have thus, perhaps at once too boldly and too feebly, presumed to convey to you in words, is the very lesson which was taught us for twenty years, and has been bequeathed to us for lasting memory, by the Prince Consort, in the nobler form of action, in the silent witness of an earnest, manful, and devoted life.

But, although this world embraces no more than a limited part of our existence, and although it is certain that we ought to tread its floor with an upward and not with a downward eye, yet sometimes a strong reaction from the dominion of things visible and carnal begets the opposite excess. A strain of language may sometimes be heard among us which, if taken strictly, would imply that the Almighty had abandoned the earth and the creatures He had made; or, at the least, that if He retained any care at all for some portion of those creatures while continuing to be inhabitants of the world, it was only care how to take them out of it. It is sometimes said that this world is a world only of shadows and of phantoms. We may safely reply that, whatever it is, a world of shadows and of phantoms it can never truly be; for by shadows and by phantoms we mean vague existences, which neither endure nor act: creatures of the moment, which may touch the fancy, but which the understanding does not recognise; passing illusions, without heralds before them, without results or traces after them. With such a description as this, I say, our human life, in whatever state or station, can never correspond. It may be something better than this; it may be something worse, but this it can never be. Our life may be food to us, or may, if we will have it so, be poison; but one or the other it must be. Whichever and whatever it is, beyond all doubt it is eminently real. So surely as the day and the night alternately follow one another, does every day when it yields to darkness, and every night when it passes into dawn, bear with it its own tale of the results which it has silently wrought upon each of us, for evil or for good. The day of diligence, duty, and devotion leaves us richer than it found us; richer sometimes, and even commonly, in our circumstances; richer always in ourselves. But the day of aimless lethargy, the day of passionate and rebellious disorder, or of a merely selfish and perverse activity, as surely leaves us poorer at its close than we were at its beginning. The whole experience of life, in small things and in great, what is it? It is an aggregate of real forces, which are always acting upon us, we also reacting upon them. It is in the nature of things impossible that, in their contact with our plastic and susceptible natures, they should leave us as we were; and to deny the reality of their daily and continual influence, merely because we cannot register its results, as we note the changes of the barometer, from hour to hour, would be just as rational as to deny that the sea acts upon the beach because the eye will not tell us to-morrow that it is altered from what it has been to-day. If we fail to measure the results that are thus hourly wrought on shingle and in sand, it is not because those results are unreal, but because our vision is too limited in its powers to discern them. When, instead of comparing day with day, we compare century with century, then we may often find that land has become sea, and sea has become land. Even so we can perceive, at least in our neighbours—towards whom the eye is more impartial and discerning than towards ourselves— that, under the steady pressure of the experience of life, human characters are continually being determined for good or evil; are developed, confirmed, modified, altered, or undermined. It is the office of good sense, no less than of faith, to realise this great truth before we see it, and to live under the conviction, that our life from day to day is a true, powerful, and searching discipline, moulding us and making us, whether it be for evil or for good.

Nor are these real effects wrought by unreal instruments. Life and the world, their interests, their careers, the varied gifts of our nature, the traditions of our forefathers, the treasures of laws, institutions, usages, of languages, of literature, and of art; all the beauty, glory, and delight with which the Almighty Father has clothed this earth for the use and profit of His children, and which Evil, though it has defaced, has not been able utterly to destroy; all these are not merely allowable, but ordained and appointed instruments for the training of mankind. They are instruments true and efficient in themselves, though without doubt auxiliary and subordinate to that highest instrument of all which God has prepared to be the means of our recovery and final weal, by the revelation of Himself.

Thus, then, we arrive at a point which plainly exhibits the ennobling tendencies and high moral aims of an institution such as this, when it is worked in the spirit that alone befits our nature and condition.

Let me now address to you a few words on a marked feature of the institution—that feature with which in particular we are to-night concerned—I mean its examinations, to which reference is made in the eighth paragraph of its printed list of its objects. They evidently form not only a living and chief portion of its practice, but also a test of its power over the people; and it is manifest, from the results they have produced—from such results as with our own eyes we have witnessed in this hall to-night—that they have struck deep root in the mind of the community around you, and are likely to exercise in future a material influence upon conduct.

The use of examinations in this country, not alone, but with honours and prizes variously attached to them, as a main stimulus and support to mental cultivation, is in a very great degree peculiar to the present century. Examination on

trial, in one form or another, may be said to have constituted, nearly from its commencement, the basis of the practical system of our ancient Universities of Oxford and Cambridge. Perhaps those Universities have been the means of commending to the country the example it has so largely followed. These examinations have acquired progressively more and more of weight in our famous public schools. They now supply the only passport to the Civil Service of India, richly endowed as it is with emoluments, and heavily charged with duties and responsibilities. Admission to the Civil Service at home had been long the subject only of a political patronage which was, erroneously as I think, believed to be an essential part of the machinery of the Constitution, and the sole effectual substitute for the ruder methods of government formerly in use by prerogative or force. But it is now in some degree admitted that the privilege of entering the Civil Service of the country—and, indeed, the service of the country generally ought to be thrown open, as widely as may be, to its youth at large. And some progress has been made, by the method of examinations, both in securing the State against the intrusion of the unworthy, and in widening the way of access for those who aspire to prove themselves worthy of the honours and rewards of civil office. The like engine of competitive examination has been more freely applied to the highest—I mean the scientific—department of the army. At about the same time with the adoption of these last-mentioned improvements, the University of Oxford instituted, with great wisdom and forethought, that system of circuits for local examinations throughout the country which met at once with public acknowledgment and approval, and which was speedily and happily imitated from one or more other quarters. But none of these efforts touched the great masses of the people. They too, however, have been at least partially reached by the widening circles of the movement. A proposal is, as you know, under the consideration of Parliament, which aims at the establishment of the principle, that the merit of the pupils proved by elementary examination shall henceforth be, if not the sole, yet the main condition on which the money of the State, supplied by the taxes of the country, shall be dispensed in aid of primary schools. This, it may be said, is still prospective. But at least we have, in the Association of Lancashire and Cheshire Mechanics' Institutes, one living proof of the progress made, without aid either from old endowment or from the public purse, by the principle of examinations, with the condition of competition, and with the attraction of honour or reward. How strictly true is this assertion must be more familiarly known to many among you than to me.

I will not attempt to draw here, and now, a full picture of the association, but will only give in proof of what I have said a very few facts and figures. First, as regards the general condition of the district. We find that the involuntary leisure forced on the population by the contraction of the cotton trade has been attended by a decrease of crime. In Blackburn, for instance, where the crisis is felt with the utmost severity, the charges heard by the borough magistrates in the first quarter of the year 1857 were 721; in the first quarter of the year 1862, although the population must have grown, the charges were only 524. Now, we may naturally expect a decrease of drunkenness to accompany popular distress, because the means of indulgence have been contracted. But, on the other hand, we might not be greatly surprised if there were a positive increase of those offences to which men are tempted in a principal degree by want. Applying these considerations to the case of Blackburn, we find the following results. The charges other than for drunkenness in the first quarter of 1857 were 464; in 1862 they were 380. There is, my friends, consolation in these facts, which I hope will long survive the painful occasion that has brought them into view.

It also appears from the returns, that, speaking generally, while crime has decreased, the attendance upon classes, and the use of the means of mental culture, have increased. Now, my friends, there are beautiful and famous passages in ancient writers, where statesmen and orators describe the refreshment with which literature had supplied them, amid the cares of life and the pressure of public affairs. Without any disparagement to such representations, it is a far more touching picture to behold the labouring man, shut out by no fault of his own from the occupation that gives him bread, yet unconquered in spirit and resource, and turning to account his vacant hours in pursuits which strengthen and enlarge the faculties of his mind.

It would, however, be unjust to set down to the credit of this Association, or of those institutes which it binds together, more than a modest share in the general improvement of your social state. But let us observe more closely their actual progress. The members, formerly 2000, are now from 6000 to 8000. Four years ago, 500 persons passed the preliminary examinations; this year there are 1500. Four years ago, 214 passed the public and final examination; this year there are 730. What is more remarkable than all the rest is the fact that, of 180 persons who have to-night received honours and certificates, the number who draw their subsistence from weekly wages is no less than 177. Two of these are wholly unemployed; 83, between men and women, are weavers; fully 150 appear to belong, in the very strictest sense, to the labouring class. Again I say, here are the signs, for that class especially, of hope and real progress; of hope which will, I trust, bear its fruit, and abide with them when ripened into certainty, long after the clouds of the present visitation shall, if it please God, have passed away.

I have said to you, my friends, that the extended use of the instrument of examinations is eminently characteristic of the age in which we live. I would almost venture to say that, amid all the material and all the social changes by which the period has been distinguished, there have been few that are greater or more peculiar than this. The older methods of education, which had been in use in European countries, generally invited from students, with more or less of strictness, voluntary performances, which were intended to afford general evidence of competency; and which, where they were regularly exacted, were made conditions of the certificates of proficiency given by Universities and other learned bodies, and by them called Degrees. These exercises and exhibitions were the invention of remote ages, and were in all probability well adapted to the exigencies of those periods. But in the time of your immediate ancestors they had become generally and even grossly ineffective; and the instinct, so to speak, of the present age has prompted it, instead of reviving the ancient forms which had died out, to have recourse to the new method of examinations.

These examinations are in a great number of instances competitive; that is, they offer to the candidates one or more specific prizes, the possession of which by particular competitors involves the exclusion of others. This form of examination has great advantages. It raises to a *maximum* that stimulus which acts insensibly but powerfully upon the minds of students, as it were, from behind; and becomes an auxiliary force augmenting their energies, and helping them, almost without their knowledge, to surmount their difficulties. It is not found in practice, so far as I know, to be open to an objection which is popularly urged against it; this, namely, that it may elicit evil passions among the candidates, because it makes the gain of one the loss of another. I believe that, on the contrary, the pursuit of knowledge is found to carry with it, in this respect, its own preservatives and safeguards. Even in athletic sports, the loser does not resent or grudge the fairly won honours of the winner; and, in the race of minds, those who are behind, having confidence in the perfect fairness of the award, are not so blindly and basely selfish as to cherish resentment against others for being better than themselves. Again, it is a recommendation of purely competitive examinations that they bring the matter to the simplest issue; for, in nice cases, it is a much easier and safer task for the examiner to compare the performances of a candidate with those of another candidate, than to compare them with some more abstract standard, existing only in his own mind. On the other hand, it is a disadvantage of this system that the honours given at different times, purporting to be equal, are given to unequal merit: for the number and excellence of the competitors varies from one occasion to another; and the winner of one year may, on this account, be inferior to the loser of another.

Much may, in truth, be said in praise or in disparagement of one method of examination as compared with another. Into controversy of this kind I do not propose to enter, further than to say that I think the highest value belongs to the competitive species in cases like that of admission to the Civil Service of the State, where a main object is to bar the way against the action of corrupt or inferior motives in those who appoint. In the long-run, the simple, clear, and self-acting method of an open competition will probably be found more adequate than any other agency to contend against the wakeful energies of human selfishness, ever on the alert, first to prevent the adoption of improvements, and then to neutralise and mar their operation.

But what I would, on the present occasion, specially endeavour to bring to your attention is the general character of this instrument of examination, as it is understood and as it is applied in the present century, and in the institution with which we have now to deal. The essential character of it I take to be this—that the candidate, instead of himself producing a piece of work, and asking to be judged by it, offers and opens his mind to the examining authority to be tested, searched, and, so to speak, even ransacked, in such manner, and by such questions and processes, as that examining authority shall choose. The adoption, or wide extension, of such a method as this marks an epoch in the history of study. It shows that we have overlived the time when the greater part of those who engaged in the pursuit of knowledge were enamoured of its beauty, and loved it for its own sake, with a devout and tender love. In the childhood of mental culture, it was the prerogative of a few, and the mere possession of it constituted a high distinction. So, likewise, as in those days legal rights were ill defined and protected, commerce was circumscribed, nations were sharply severed, and but few of the careers of active life were open, it naturally happened that, in the case of many persons, mental culture had little to compete with for their regard. In circumstances like these, it might not be needful constantly to apply a strong stimulus from without. The very novelty and freshness of knowledge, in ages just emerging from darkness and disorder, gave it a powerful charm for the imagination, over and above its hold upon the intellect; it was pursued by a spontaneous movement from within, with passion as well as with conviction; and those who so pursue it do not need to be goaded in their onward course; their service is a service of love, and, like the love of youth for maiden, it is its own incentive and its own reward.

But when society has passed into what is distinctively, and in many respects truly, termed a progressive state; when the personal rights of men are as secure in the outer world as in the closest retirement; when a thousand new careers of external life are opened, and its attractions in a thousand forms are indefinitely multiplied; when large numbers can engage, not merely in labour for subsistence, but in the pursuit of wealth; and when a desire to rise upon the social ladder takes possession of whole classes, if not on their own behalf, at least on behalf of their children; then there arises a compound danger. First, lest the value of knowledge for its own sake should be wholly forgotten; and, secondly, lest even its utility in innumerable respects for the comfort and advancement of life should pass, in great measure, out of view.

Now, my friends, it is in such an age as this that we are living. That same attraction or necessity of wages, which takes the poorer child, either in town or village, from school at too early a period, is but the exhibition for one class of a pressure felt by all. With the wealthier it is pleasure, with the needier it is gain; but all classes and all circles are alike in this, that our youth are in danger of undervaluing solid mental culture, and of either neglecting or shortening its pursuit by reason of the increased allurements, or the more urgent calls, of the outer sphere of life. Although knowledge is in so many ways auxiliary to art and to commerce, yet this is a matter not so palpable to the individual that we can rely on it to enable him, as it were, to speculate upon a distant benefit, which concerns others as well as, or it may be more than, himself; and to forego for its sake advantages which lie nearer at hand, which appertain directly to his own career, and which are on the level of every man's understanding. Long, accordingly, after trade and manufactures had begun, one hundred years ago, their upward spring, education and art seemed rather to decline than to advance among us. At length a day of awakening came. Christian philanthropy, we may do well to remember, was first in the field on behalf of the masses of the people; but after a while, it found itself in partnership with an enlightened self-interest on the part of individuals, and with the political prudence of the Government. Now, for a long course of years, all three have prosecuted their work in remarkable harmony one with another. Long may their union continue, and its golden fruits teem and glow over all the surface of the land!

A principal form, in which they have well developed their united activity, has been the form of examinations; and I must in candour say that, among all the particular applications of this principle, I have seen none more remarkable than that which we have met to-night to commemorate and to encourage. For here it is not leisure, wealth, and ease which come to disport themselves as athletes in intellectual games: it is the hard hand of the worker, which his yet stronger will has taught to wield the pen; it is Labour, gathering up with infinite care and sacrifice the fragments of time, stealing them, many a one, from rest and sleep, and offering them up, like so many widows' mites, in the honest devotion of an effort at self-improvement.

There are those, my friends, who tell us that examinations, and especially that competitive examinations, are of no real value; that they produce the pretence and not the reality of knowledge; that they give us, not solid progress, but conceit and illusion. I freely admit that this modern method is likely to rear, as far as we can judge, no greater prodigies of learning than did the simple and spontaneous devotion of the olden time; perhaps, if we are to look only at individual cases of pre-eminence, none so great. But I say that the true way to imitate the wisdom of the olden time is this: to watch the conditions of the age in which we live; to accept them thankfully and freely, as at once the law of Providence for our guidance, and the gift for our encouragement: and when we learn by experience that the tools with which other generations wrought are not suited for the work that is given us to do, then to find, if we can, some other tools which are.

It is not too much to say that the experience of half a century, as well in the Universities as elsewhere, appears to have shown that the method of examinations is the best, and perhaps the only, method by which, in the England of the nineteenth century, any due efficiency can be imparted to the general business of education. I do not, indeed, deny that a certain trick or craft may be practised in them; that some may think more of the manner of displaying their knowledge to a momentary advantage, like goods in a shop-window, than of laying hold upon the substance. But I say that these abusive cases will be the exceptions, not the rule. I say that those who so unjustly plead them against the system forget that this very faculty, of the ready command and easy use of our knowledge, is in itself of immense value. It means clear perception, it means orderly arrangement. And, above all, they forget what I take to be the specific and peculiar virtue of the system of examinations, namely this, that they require us to concentrate all the faculties of the mind, with all their strength, upon a point. In and by the efforts necessary for that concentration, the mind itself, obtaining at once breadth of grasp and increased pliability and force, becomes more able to grapple with great occasions in the subsequent experience of life.

Therefore, my friends, again I say let us accept frankly and cheerfully the conditions of the age in which our lot is cast, and let us write among its titles this—that as it is the age of humane and liberal laws, the age of extended franchises, the age of warmer loyalty and more firmly established order, the age of free trade, the age of steam and railways; so it is likewise, even if last and least, the age of examinations. Let me add, it is the age in which this powerful instrument of good, formerly the exclusive privilege of the more opulent, has been extended, perhaps most conspicuously of all by this group of institutions, to the people. And I give you this for my concluding word; that, if that Prince of whose bright career and character I lately spoke were now among us, none, we may be sure, would more cordially than he claim honour for a system which, in such thorough harmony with the whole spirit of English laws and institutions, aims at enabling every one, in every rank of the social scale, the lowest like the highest, to give proof of what mettle he is made, and to turn to the best account the gifts with which, by the bounty of his Heavenly Father, his mind has been endowed.

William Makepeace Thackeray

1811-1863

A GREAT novelist in an age of great novelists, William Makepeace Thackeray needs no introduction as a writer of fiction. But Thackeray began and served a long apprenticeship as a journalist, satirist, and observer of social behavior in works of nonfiction. Although overshadowed by the novels, his nonfiction works display his considerable skills as a satirist, critic, and essayist.

Thackeray was born in Calcutta while his father was serving for the East India Company. His father died five years after Thackeray's birth and the youth was sent back to England. He attended Charterhouse School and Trinity Hall, Cambridge, but he left the university without taking a degree and spent some years in foreign travel. Financial necessity drove him to seek his fortune through journalism, and he contributed to various publications, including *Fraser's Magazine,* demonstrating from the start a turn for the satiric and comic. Domestic difficulties in the form of his wife's insanity spurred him to further writing for financial reasons. He began with sketches, comic pieces, and short stories, often under pseudonyms, finally moving to the full-scale novels of the later eighteen-forties and fifties that established his fame.

In addition to writing such celebrated novels as *Vanity Fair* (1847–48), *Pendennis* (1848), *Henry Esmond* (1852), and *The Newcomers* (1853–55), Thackeray edited the humorous magazine *Punch* and later the *Cornhill Magazine*. He also lectured widely, including in the United States, and wrote both comic and serious works of nonfiction, such as *The English Humourists of the Eighteenth-Century* (1853) and *The Four Georges* (1860), and various ballads and comic verses. He died in 1863.

As a writer of nonfiction Thackeray is always entertaining and perceptive. His special strengths are sketches and short essays, especially those of a satiric cast. *The Book of Snobs* is an unjustly neglected work of comic brilliance, and *The Roundabout Papers,* an important contribution to the development of the familiar essay in the nineteenth century that shows Thackeray to be the heir of Montaigne, Lamb, and Hazlitt.

CHRONOLOGY

1811   Born 18 July in Calcutta, India.
1816   Father dies; Thackeray sent back to England.
1822–28   Attends Charterhouse School
1829–30   Attends Trinity Hall, Cambridge.
1835   Studies art in Paris.
1836   Marries Isabella Shawe.
1840   Separates from wife.
1842   Begins association with *Punch*.
1847–48   *The Book of Snobs; Vanity Fair.*
1854   Retires from *Punch*.
1860   Becomes editor of the *Cornhill*.
1860–63   *The Roundabout Papers.*
1863   Dies 24 December; buried at Kensal Green Cemetery, London.

EDITIONS

Except for the initial citation of *Works*, no attempt is made to list Thackeray's novels, which exist in many modern editions.

Works, ed. Anne Thackeray Ritchie, Centenary Biographical Edition (26 volumes, 1910–11).

The Yellowplush Correspondence [subsequently known as *The Yellowplush Papers*] (1837–38).

The Paris Sketchbook (2 vols., 1840).

Miscellanies (2 vols., 1849–51; 6 vols., 1864).

The English Humourists of the Eighteenth Century, ed. E. Regel (1885–91), W. L. Phelps (1900).

The Snobs of England [subsequently known as *The Book of Snobs*], ed. G. K. Chesterton (1911).

Roundabout Papers, ed. J. E. Wells (1925).

The Letters and Private Papers of W. M. Thackeray, ed. Gordon N. Ray (4 vols., 1945–46).

BIOGRAPHY AND CRITICISM

Anthony Trollope, *Thackeray* (1879).

Lewis Melville, *Thackeray: A Biography* (2 vols., 1910).

W. C. Brownell, *Victorian Prose Masters* (1901).

Harold S. Gulliver, *Thackeray's Literary Apprenticeship* (1934).

Gordon N. Ray, *Thackeray: The Uses of Adversity* and *The Age of Wisdom* (1955–58).

Mr. Macaulay's Essays

Thackeray's veneration for that most Victorian of vocations, the man of letters, is given expression in the following essay that he published originally in the Pictorial Times *on 1 April 1843 as a review, or more properly a notice, of Macaulay's* Edinburgh Review *essays titled* Critical and Historical Essays *(1843). The volumes contained Macaulay's essays on Milton, Southey, and Samuel Johnson, among others.*

WE HAVE but a word or two to say this week as a welcome to the reappearance of these noble essays. No critic has a right to judge them hurriedly, and we hope that they may afford to the readers of this paper many hours of entertainment yet. For power and variety of memory, for vividness of painting, and for delightful grace of scholarship, there is no English author of our days who has equalled Mr. Macaulay; and the charm of his style is, that it is as warm and kindly as it is bright, and engages the reader's heart by its affectionate sympathy, as it delights his taste by its brilliancy, poetry, and wit.

Of course, in volumes embracing such a vast range of reading, and treating of little less than literature and history from their beginning until now, every reader who, in the course of his own humble pursuits, may encounter this active, untiring, bright-eyed inquirer, may have many a point to argue with him, and may not subscribe to many of the opinions which with such astounding prodigality are poured from him. But, whether one agree or not, one is always forced to admire; and the most uninformed reader of Mr. Macaulay's works will do this as well as the gravest student. It requires no more science than may be had from a circulating library or a Scott's novel to be delighted with narratives not less exciting than the best fictions of the novelist; while the reader who seeks for profit and study more than amusement, will better see the extraordinary powers of this brilliant intellect and the amazing variety and extent of learning which must have gone to the preparation of essays which all may so easily read.

And no small thanks are due to this accomplished scholar from the unlettered public, that,—unlike many a pedant, whose reputation is founded upon a tithe of Mr. Macaulay's learning, who fences round his stock of scholarship with hard words and dull phrases and old scholastic impediments, and from his old-world lore has a huge college gate to keep the public out, and a watchful porter with a cane to drive the vulgar from the prim old walks and grass-plats of his college-garden,—no small thanks do we owe Mr. Macaulay for laying open his learning to all, and bidding the humble and the great alike welcome to it.

This generous and kindly system characterizes his political as well as his literary career.

A man of letters and of the world, too, there is no man whose public life has better shown how the one and the other pursuit may be followed to the advantage of both; and his very success is as useful to both the causes which he has at heart as his talents and character have been. He had no other friend at the commencement of his career but his own genius; he never became the follower of any patron, or truckled to great man or mob; he never swerved from any principle with which he set out; he made no party sacrifice to win his honours; and the very publication of these volumes shows how he bears them. Allied with a party, he always bore himself above it; and has made his reputation and calling as a man of letters his title to honour, as others do their birth, their influence, or their money.

He is the first literary man in this country who has made himself honourably and worthily the equal of the noblest and wealthiest in it; this may be no cause for respect with the reader, perhaps, but with every *writer* it should be, who is glad to see in another his own profession advanced, and success and honour bestowed at last upon one of a body of men who were but a few score years since begging guineas from my lord for a dedication; the bye-word for poverty, the theme for sneering wits.

But the review, the newspaper addressed to no party merely, a clique of *literati* or politicians, have made the nation and the man of letters directly acquainted; and it begins to reward him as it does all the rest of its servants. As it receives instruction from him, it will take care that at least he shall be respected, and will treat him as it does any other man of any other liberal profession who labours in its advantage. And it is as a proof that the literary man's claim is a good one, and at last an acknowledged one, too, that we the more gladly welcome Mr. Macaulay's success. What was done once may be done again, and what his genius attained for itself his precedent and example will make easier for others. The mere party man has some reason to be grateful to Mr. Macaulay. He has made more converts to Liberalism than any mere politician ever could. He has brought thousands and thousands to interest themselves with literature,

to sympathize, that is, with truth, wherever it comes from, or from what rank of men; and to acknowledge (as who shall not that ever read in a history book?) the constant progress of the world, and how at the close of every century, it is in something, at least, more free, wise, or happy than at the beginning. The bitterest attack on its opponents will not bring so many recruits to the Liberal party, nor will the best places be given away.

And this is the part of the work of progress that is to be done *by the man of letters*; the rest is but the humble duty of officials and tape-men.

from The Book of Snobs

Thackeray's Book of Snobs *first appeared as a series of satirical sketches in* Punch *in 1847–48 just before the beginning of the serial appearance of* Vanity Fair. *The original title was* The Snobs of England, *but it was subsequently published and has been since known as* The Book of Snobs. *Thackeray's special gifts as a cunning and acute observer of the vagaries of English social life, especially its widespread snobbery, are here given full range. The selections below represent only a few of the kinds of snobs that are still encountered today.*

On University Snobs

I SHOULD like to fill several volumes with accounts of various University Snobs; so fond are my reminiscences of them, and so numerous are they. I should like to speak, above all, of the wives and daughters of some of the Professor-Snobs; their amusements, habits, jealousies; their innocent artifices to entrap young men; their pic-nics, concerts, and evening-parties. I wonder what has become of Emily Blades, daughter of Blades, the Professor of the Mandingo language? I remember her shoulders to this day, as she sat in the midst of a crowd of about seventy young gentlemen, from Corpus and Catherine Hall, entertaining them with ogles and French songs on the guitar. Are you married, fair Emily of the shoulders? What beautiful ringlets those were that used to dribble over them!—what a waist!— what a killing sea-green shot-silk gown!—what a cameo, the size of a muffin! There were thirty-six young men of the University in love at one time with Emily Blades: and no words are sufficient to describe the pity, the sorrow, the

deep, deep commiseration—the rage, fury, and uncharitableness, in other words—with which the Miss Trumps (daughter of Trumps, the Professor of Phlebotomy) regarded her, because she *didn't* squint, and because she *wasn't* marked with the small-pox.

As for the young University Snobs, I am getting too old, now, to speak of such very familiarly. My recollections of them lie in the far, far past— almost as far back as Pelham's time.

We *then* used to consider Snobs raw-looking lads, who never missed chapel; who wore high-lows and no straps; who walked two hours on the Trumpington road every day of their lives; who carried off the college scholarships, and who overrated themselves in hall. We were premature in pronouncing our verdict of youthful Snobbishness. The man without straps fulfilled his destiny and duty. He eased his old governor, the curate in Westmoreland, or helped his sisters to set up the Ladies' School. He wrote a "Dictionary," or a "Treatise on Conic Sections," as his nature and genius prompted. He got a fellowship: and then took to himself a wife, and a living. He presides over a parish now, and thinks it rather a dashing thing to belong to the "Oxford and Cambridge Club;" and his parishioners love him, and snore under his sermons. No, no, *he* is not a Snob. It is not straps that make the gentleman, or highlows that unmake him, be they ever so thick. My son, it is you who are the Snob if you lightly despise a man for doing his duty, and refuse to shake an honest man's hand because it wears a Berlin glove.

We then used to consider it not the least vulgar for a parcel of lads who had been whipped three months previous, and were not allowed more than three glasses of port at home, to sit down to pine-apples and ices at each other's rooms, and fuddle themselves with champagne and claret.

One looks back to what was called "a wine-party" with a sort of wonder. Thirty lads round a table covered with bad sweetmeats, drinking bad wines, telling bad stories, singing bad songs over and over again. Milk-punch—smoking—ghastly headache—frightful spectacle of dessert-table next morning, and smell of tobacco—your guardian, the clergyman, dropping in, in the midst of this—expecting to find you deep in Algebra, and discovering the Gyp administering soda-water.

There were young men who despised the lads who indulged in the coarse hospitalities of wine-parties, who prided themselves in giving *recherché* little French dinners. Both wine-party-givers and dinner-givers were Snobs.

There were what used to be called "dressy Snobs"—Jimmy, who might be seen at five o'clock elaborately rigged out, with a camellia in his button-hole, glazed boots, and fresh kid-gloves twice a day;—Jessamy, who was con-spicuous for his "jewelry,"—a young donkey, glittering all over with chains, rings, and shirt-studs;—Jacky, who rode every day solemnly on the Blenheim Road, in pumps and white silk stockings, with his hair curled,—all three of whom flattered themselves they gave laws to the University about dress—all three most odious varieties of Snobs.

Sporting Snobs of course there were, and are always—those happy beings in whom Nature has implanted a love of slang: who loitered about the horsekeeper's stables, and drove the London coaches—a stage in and out—and might be seen swaggering through the courts in pink of early mornings, and indulged in dice and blind-hookey at nights, and never missed a race or a boxing-match; and rode flat-races, and kept bull-

terriers. Worse Snobs even than these were poor miserable wretches who did not like hunting at all, and could not afford it, and were in mortal fear at a two-foot ditch; but who hunted because Glenlivat and Cinqbars hunted. The Billiard Snob and the Boating Snob were varieties of these, and are to be found elsewhere than in Universities.

Then there were Philosophical Snobs, who used to ape statesmen at the spouting-clubs, and who believed as a fact that Government always had an eye on the University for the selection of orators for the House of Commons. There were audacious young free-thinkers, who adored nobody or nothing, except perhaps Robespierre and the Koran, and panted for the day when the pale name of priest should shrink and dwindle away before the indignation of an enlightened world.

But the worst of all University Snobs are those unfortunates who go to rack and ruin from their desire to ape their betters. Smith becomes acquainted with great people at college, and is ashamed of his father the tradesman. Jones has fine acquaintances, and lives after their fashion like a gay free-hearted fellow as he is, and ruins his father, and robs his sister's portion, and cripples his younger brother's outset in life, for the pleasure of entertaining my lord, and riding by the side of Sir John. And though it may be very good fun for Robinson to fuddle himself at home as he does at College, and to be brought home by the policeman he has just been trying to knock down—think what fun it is for the poor old soul his mother!—the half-pay captain's widow, who has been pinching herself all her life long, in order that that jolly young fellow might have a University education.

On Literary Snobs

WHAT will he say about Literary Snobs? has been a question, I make no doubt, often asked by the public. How can he let off his own profession? Will that truculent and un-sparing monster who attacks the nobility, the clergy, the army, and the ladies, indiscriminately, hesitate when the turn comes to *égorger* his own flesh and blood?[1]

---

[1] *Égorger*, slaughter.

"Ludgate Hill" *by Gustave Doré*

from *London: A Pilgrimage* by Gustave Doré and Blanchard Jerrold (London, 1872).

John Keble *by George Richmond*

Courtesy National Portrait Gallery, London

Thomas Babington Macaulay
by J. Partridge

Courtesy National Portrait Gallery,
London

Thomas Carlyle *by Daniel Maclise*

from *Fraser's Magazine, 1833*

Thomas Carlyle *by John Everett Millais*

Courtesy National Portrait Gallery, London

Harriet Martineau *by Daniel Maclise*

from *Fraser's Magazine, 1833*

William Makepeace Thackeray
by Samuel Lawrence

Courtesy National Portrait Gallery,
London

The Crystal Palace

from *Official Descriptive and Illustrated Catalogue of the Great Exhibition* (London, 1851)

Central Court of the Crystal Palace

from *Illustrated London News*, 24 May 1851

"Holland House—A Garden Party"
by Gustave Doré

from *London: A Pilgrimage*
by Gustave Doré and Blanchard Jerrold
(London, 1872)

"Wentworth Street, Whitechapel"
by Gustave Doré

from *London: A Pilgrimage*
by Gustave Doré and Blanchard Jerrold
(London, 1872)

John Henry Newman *by George Richmond*

Courtesy National Portrait Gallery, London

John Henry Cardinal Newman
by Emmeline Dearne

Courtesy National Portrait Gallery, London

King's Cross, Battle Bridge

Chichester Cross

Contrasted Medieval
and Modern Crosses
by A. W. N. Pugin

from *Contrasts*
(2nd. ed., London, 1841)

Matthew Arnold
by G. F. Watts

Courtesy National Portrait
Gallery, London

Benjamin Disraeli *by John Everett Millais*

Courtesy National Portrait Gallery, London

William Ewart Gladstone
by John Everett Millais

Courtesy National Portrait Gallery, London

Queen Victoria in 1899 *by H. von Angeli*

Courtesy National Portrait Gallery, London

Albert, Prince Consort, in 1859
by F. Z. Winterhalter

Courtesy National Portrait Gallery, London

John Ruskin *by George Richmond*

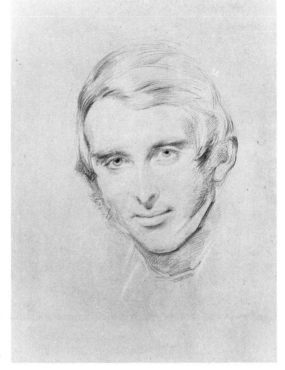

John Ruskin *by Sir Hubert von Herkomer*

Drawing by Ruskin for
The Seven Lamps of Architecture, 1849

[Tracery from the Campanile of Giotto, at Florence.]

Charles Robert Darwin *by Hon. John Collier*

Courtesy National Portrait Gallery, London

John Stuart Mill *by G. F. Watts*

Courtesy National Portrait Gallery, London

George Eliot (Mary Ann Evans)
by Sir F. W. Barton

Courtesy National Portrait Gallery, London

William Morris *by G. F. Watts*

Courtesy National Portrait Gallery, London

Robert Louis Stevenson
by W. B. Richmond

Courtesy National Portrait Gallery, London

Oscar Wilde *by C. Pellegrini*

Courtesy National Portrait Gallery, London

A Victorian Picnic at Ascot

from *Illustrated London News,* 8 June 1844

"Dudley Street, Seven Dials" *by Gustave Doré*

from *London: A Pilgrimage* by Gustave Doré and
Blanchard Jerrold (London, 1872)

The Albert Memorial, London

from *The Graphic,* 13 July 1872

My dear and excellent querist, whom does the schoolmaster flog so resolutely as his own son? Didn't Brutus chop his offspring's head off? You have a very bad opinion indeed of the present state of literature and of literary men, if you fancy that any one of us would hesitate to stick a knife into his neighbor penman, if the latter's death could do the State any service.

But the fact is, that in the literary profession THERE ARE NO SNOBS. Look round at the whole body of British men of letters, and I defy you to point out among them a single instance of vulgarity, or envy, or assumption.

Men and women, as far as I have known them, they are all modest in their demeanor, elegant in their manners, spotless in their lives, and honorable in their conduct to the world and to each other. You *may*, occasionally, it is true, hear one literary man abusing his brother; but why? Not in the least out of malice; not at all from envy; merely from a sense of truth and public duty. Suppose, for instance, I good-naturedly point out a blemish in my friend *Mr. Punch's* person, and say, *Mr. P.* has a hump-back, and his nose and chin are more crooked than those features in the Apollo or Antinous, which we are accustomed to consider as our standards of beauty; does this argue malice on my part towards *Mr. Punch*? Not in the least. It is the critic's duty to point out defects as well as merits, and he invariably does his duty with the utmost gentleness and candour.

An intelligent foreigner's testimony about our manners is always worth having, and I think, in this respect, the work of an eminent American, Mr. N. P. Willis,[2] is eminently valuable and impartial. In his "History of Ernest Clay," a crack magazine-writer, the reader will get an exact account of the life of a popular man of letters in England. He is always the great lion of society.

He takes the *pas* of dukes and earls; all the nobility crowd to see him: I forget how many baronesses and duchesses fall in love with him. But on this subject let us hold our tongues. Modesty forbids that we should reveal the names of the heart-broken countesses and dear marchionesses who are pining for every one of the contributors in *Punch*.

If anybody wants to know how intimately authors are connected with the fashionable world, they have but to read the genteel novels.[3] What refinement and delicacy pervades the works of Mrs. Barnaby! What delightful good company do you meet with in Mrs. Armytage! She seldom introduces you to anybody under a marquis! I don't know anything more delicious than the pictures of genteel life in "Ten Thousand a Year," except perhaps the "Young Duke," and "Coningsby." There's a modest grace about *them*, and an air of easy high fashion, which only belongs to blood, my dear Sir—to true blood.

And what linguists many of our writers are! Lady Bulwer, Lady Londonderry, Sir Edward himself—they write the French language with a luxurious elegance and ease which sets them far above their continental rivals, of whom not one (except Paul de Kock) knows a word of English.

And what Briton can read without enjoyment the works of James, so admirable for terseness; and the playful humor and dazzling off-hand lightness of Ainsworth? Among other humorists, one might glance at a Jerrold, the chivalrous advocate of Toryism and Church and State; an à Beckett, with a lightsome pen, but a savage earnestness of purpose; a Jeames, whose pure style, and wit unmingled with buffoonery, was relished by a congenial public.

Speaking of critics, perhaps there never was a review that has done so much for literature as the admirable *Quarterly*.[4] It has its prejudices, to be sure, as which of us have not? It goes out of its way to abuse a great man, or lays mercilessly on to such pretenders as Keats and Tennyson; but, on the other hand, it is the friend of all young authors, and has marked and nurtured all the rising talent of the country. It is loved by everybody. There, again, is *Blackwood's Magazine*—conspicuous for modest elegance and amiable satire; that review never passes the bounds of politeness in a joke. It is the arbiter of manners; and, while gently exposing the foibles of Londoners (for whom the *beaux esprits* of Edinburgh entertain a justifiable contempt), it is never coarse in its fun. The fiery enthusiasm of the *Athenæum* is well known: and the bitter wit of the too difficult *Literary Gazette*. The *Examiner* is perhaps too timid, and the *Spectator* too boisterous in its praise—but who can carp at these minor faults? No, no; the critics of England and the

---

[2] Nathaniel Parker Willis (1806–67), American editor and writer. His *Inklings of Adventure* (1836) contains his contributions to the *New Monthly Magazine* in London.
[3] Throughout the following paragraphs Thackeray is referring to fashionable novels and novelists of the "Silver-Fork School," which included Disraeli and Edward Bulwer-Lytton.
[4] Thackeray is cataloguing in an arch manner the leading critical journals of the day.

authors of England are unrivalled as a body; and hence it becomes impossible for us to find fault with them.

Above all, I never knew a man of letters *ashamed of his profession.* Those who know us, know what an affectionate and brotherly spirit there is among us all. Sometimes one of us rises in the world: we never attack him or sneer at him under those circumstances, but rejoice to a man at his success. If Jones dines with a lord, Smith never says Jones is a courtier and cringer. Nor, on the other hand, does Jones, who is in the habit of frequenting the society of great people, give himself any airs on account of the company he keeps; but will leave a duke's arm in Pall Mall to come over and speak to poor Brown, the young penny-a-liner.

That sense of equality and fraternity amongst authors has always struck me as one of the most amiable characteristics of the class. It is because we know and respect each other, that the world respects us so much; that we hold such a good position in society, and demean ourselves so irreproachably when there.

Literary persons are held in such esteem by the nation, that about two of them have been absolutely invited to court during the present reign; and it is probable that towards the end of the season, one or two will be asked to dinner by Sir Robert Peel.

They are such favorites with the public, that they are continually obliged to have their pictures taken and published; and one or two could be pointed out, of whom the nation insists upon having a fresh portrait every year. Nothing can be more gratifying than this proof of the affectionate regard which the people has for its instructors.

Literature is held in such honor in England, that there is a sum of near twelve hundred pounds per annum set apart to pension deserving persons following that profession. And a great compliment this is, too, to the professors, and a proof of their generally prosperous and flourishing condition. They are generally so rich and thrifty, that scarcely any money is wanted to help them.

If every word of this is true, how, I should like to know, am I to write about Literary Snobs.

from The Roundabout Papers

This collection of wide-ranging personal essays first appeared in installments between 1860 and 1861 in the Cornhill Magazine, *in part during Thackeray's editorship, and at the same time that he was completing his last short pieces of fiction. The subjects covered in this collection include such varied matters as literary criticism, social and character sketches, and above all the short reflective essay that descends ultimately from Montaigne. The selections below reflect Thackeray's work in this genre of the personal essay. His "Nil Nisi Bonum" should be compared with his earlier notice of Macaulay; both reflect Thackeray's commitment to the Roman proverb "De mortuis nil nisi bonum"—speak nothing but good of the dead. "The Last Sketch," on Charlotte Brontë, is also imbued with Thackeray's awareness of the transitoriness of life.*

Nil Nisi Bonum

Almost the last words which Sir Walter spoke to Lockhart,[1] his biographer, were, 'Be a good man, my dear!' and with the last flicker of breath on his dying lips, he sighed a farewell to his family, and passed away blessing them.

Two men, famous, admired, beloved, have just left us, the Goldsmith and the Gibbon of our time.[2] Ere a few weeks are over, many a critic's pen will be at work, reviewing their lives, and passing judgment on their works. This is no review, or history, or criticism: only a word in testimony of respect and regard from a man of letters, who owes to his own professional labour the honour of becoming acquainted with these

---

[1] I.e., Sir Walter Scott speaking to his biographer, John Gibson Lockhart.
[2] The "Goldsmith and Gibbon of our time" are respectively Washington Irving, who died 28 November 1859, and Thomas Babington Macaulay, who died 28 December 1859.

two eminent literary men. One was the first ambassador whom the New World of Letters sent to the Old. He was born almost with the republic; the *pater patriæ*[3] had laid his hand on the child's head. He bore Washington's name: he came amongst us bringing the kindest sympathy, the most artless, smiling goodwill. His new country (which some people here might be disposed to regard rather superciliously) could send us, as he showed in his own person, a gentleman, who, though himself born in no very high sphere, was most finished, polished, easy, witty, quiet; and, socially, the equal of the most refined Europeans. If Irving's welcome in England was a kind one, was it not also gratefully remembered? If he ate our salt, did he not pay us with a thankful heart? Who can calculate the amount of friendliness and good feeling for our country which this writer's generous and untiring regard for us disseminated in his own? His books are read by millions of his countrymen, whom he has taught to love England, and why to love her. It would have been easy to speak otherwise than he did: to inflame national rancours, which, at the time when he first became known as a public writer, war had just renewed: to cry down the old civilization at the expense of the new: to point out our faults, arrogance, shortcomings, and give the republic to infer how much she was the parent state's superior. There are writers enough in the United States, honest and otherwise, who preach that kind of doctrine. But the good Irving, the peaceful, the friendly, had no place for bitterness in his heart, and no scheme but kindness. Received in England with extraordinary tenderness and friendship (Scott, Southey, Byron, a hundred others have borne witness to their liking for him), he was a messenger of goodwill and peace between his country and ours. 'See, friends!' he seems to say, 'these English are not so wicked, rapacious, callous, proud, as you have been taught to believe them. I went amongst them a humble man; won my way by my pen; and, when known, found every hand held out to me with kindliness and welcome.

Scott is a great man, you acknowledge. Did not Scott's king of England give a gold medal to him, and another to me, your countryman, and a stranger?'

Tradition in the United States still fondly retains the history of the feasts and rejoicings which awaited Irving on his return to his native country from Europe. He had a national welcome; he stammered in his speeches, hid himself in confusion, and the people loved him all the better. He had worthily represented America in Europe. In that young community a man who brings home with him abundant European testimonials is still treated with respect (I have found American writers, of wide-world reputation, strangely solicitous about the opinions of quite obscure British critics, and elated or depressed by their judgments); and Irving went home medalled by the king, diplomatized by the university, crowned and honoured and admired. He had not in any way intrigued for his honours, he had fairly won them; and, in Irving's instance, as in others, the old country was glad and eager to pay them.

In America the love and regard for Irving was a national sentiment. Party wars are perpetually raging there, and are carried on by the press with a rancour and fierceness against individuals which exceed British, almost Irish, virulence. It seemed to me, during a year's travel in the country, as if no one ever aimed a blow at Irving. All men held their hand from that harmless, friendly peacemaker. I had the good fortune to see him at New York, Philadelphia, Baltimore and Washington,[4] and remarked how in every place he was honoured and welcome. Every large city has its 'Irving House.' The country takes pride in the fame of its men of letters. The gate of his own charming little domain on the beautiful Hudson River was for ever swinging before visitors who came to him. He shut out no one.[5] I had seen many pictures of his house, and read descriptions of it, in both of which it was treated with a not unusual American exaggeration. It was but a pretty

---

[3] Father of his country.

[4] At Washington, Mr. Irving came to a lecture given by the writer, which Mr. Fillmore and General Pierce, the president and president elect, were also kind enough to attend together. "Two kings of Brentford smelling at one rose," says Irving with his good-humoured smile. [Thackeray's note]

[5] Mr. Irving described to me, with that humour and good humour which he always kept, how, amongst other visitors, a member of the British press who had carried his distinguished pen to America (where he employed it in vilifying his own country) came to Sunnyside, introduced himself to Irving, partook of his wine and luncheon, and in two days described Mr. Irving, his house, his nieces, his meal, and his manner of dozing afterwards, in a New York paper. On another occasion, Irving said, laughing, "Two persons came to me, and one held me in conversation whilst the other miscreant took my portrait!" [Thackeray's note]

little cabin of a place; the gentleman of the press who took notes of the place, whilst his kind old host was sleeping, might have visited the whole house in a couple of minutes.

And how came it that this house was so small, when Mr. Irving's books were sold by hundreds of thousands, nay, millions, when his profits were known to be large, and the habits of life of the good old bachelor were notoriously modest and simple? He had loved once in his life. The lady he loved died; and he, whom all the world loved, never sought to replace her. I can't say how much the thought of that fidelity has touched me. Does not the very cheerfulness of his after life add to the pathos of that untold story? To grieve always was not in his nature; or, when he had his sorrow, to bring all the world in to condole with him and bemoan it. Deep and quiet he lays the love of his heart, and buries it; and grass and flowers grow over the scarred ground in due time.

Irving had such a small house and such narrow rooms, because there was a great number of people to occupy them. He could only afford to keep one old horse (which, lazy and aged as it was, managed once or twice to run away with that careless old horseman). He could only afford to give plain sherry to that amiable British paragraph-monger from New York, who saw the patriarch asleep over his modest, blameless cup, and fetched the public into his private chamber to look at him. Irving could only live very modestly, because the wifeless, childless man had a number of children to whom he was as a father. He had as many as nine nieces, I am told—I saw two of these ladies at his house—with all of whom the dear old man had shared the produce of his labour and genius.

'*Be a good man, my dear.*' One can't but think of these last words of the veteran Chief of Letters, who had tasted and tested the value of worldly success, admiration, prosperity. Was Irving not good, and, of his works, was not his life the best part? In his family, gentle, generous, good-humoured, affectionate, self-denying: in society, a delightful example of complete gentlemenhood; quite unspoiled by prosperity; never obsequious to the great (or, worse still, to the base and mean, as some public men are forced to be in his and other countries); eager to acknowledge every contemporary's merit; always kind and affable

to the young members of his calling; in his professional bargains and mercantile dealings delicately honest and grateful; one of the most charming masters of our lighter language; the constant friend to us and our nation; to men of letters doubly dear, not for his wit and genius merely, but as an exemplar of goodness, probity, and pure life:—I don't know what sort of testimonial will be raised to him in his own country, where generous and enthusiastic acknowledgment of American merit is never wanting: but Irving was in our service as well as theirs; and as they have placed a stone at Greenwich yonder in memory of that gallant young Bellot,[6] who shared the perils and fate of some of our Arctic seamen, I would like to hear of some memorial raised by English writers and friends of letters in affectionate remembrance of the dear and good Washington Irving.

As for the other writer,[7] whose departure many friends, some few most dearly-loved relatives, and multitudes of admiring readers deplore, our republic has already decreed his statue, and he must have known that he had earned this posthumous honour. He is not a poet and man of letters merely, but citizen, statesman, a great British worthy. Almost from the first moment when he appears, amongst boys, amongst college students, amongst men, he is marked, and takes rank as a great Englishman. All sorts of successes are easy to him: as a lad he goes down into the arena with others, and wins all the prizes to which he has a mind. A place in the senate is straightway offered to the young man. He takes his seat there; he speaks, when so minded, without party anger or intrigue, but not without party faith and a sort of heroic enthusiasm for his cause. Still he is poet and philosopher even more than orator. That he may have leisure and means to pursue his darling studies, he absents himself for a while, and accepts a richly-remunerative post in the East. As learned a man may live in a cottage or a college common-room; but it always seemed to me that ample means and recognized rank were Macaulay's as of right. Years ago there was a wretched outcry raised because Mr. Macaulay dated a letter from Windsor Castle, where he was staying. Immortal gods! Was this man not a fit guest for any palace in the world? or a fit companion for any man or woman in it?

---

[6] Reference to Joseph René Bellot (1826–53), French explorer, who perished on a British expedition in the Arctic.
[7] Macaulay.

I daresay, after Austerlitz, the old K. K.[8] court officials and footmen sneered at Napoleon for dating from Schönbrunn. But that miserable 'Windsor Castle' outcry is an echo out of fast-retreating old-world remembrances. The place of such a natural chief was amongst the first of the land; and that country is best, according to our British notion, at least, where the man of eminence has the best chance of investing his genius and intellect.

If a company of giants were got together, very likely one or two of the mere six-feet-six people might be angry at the incontestable superiority of the very tallest of the party: and so I have heard some London wits, rather peevish at Macaulay's superiority, complain that he occupied too much of the talk, and so forth. Now that wonderful tongue is to speak no more, will not many a man grieve that he no longer has the chance to listen? To remember the talk is to wonder: to think not only of the treasures he had in his memory, but of the trifles he had stored there, and could produce with equal readiness. Almost on the last day I had the fortune to see him, a conversation happened suddenly to spring up about senior wranglers, and what they had done in after life. To the almost terror of the persons present, Macaulay began with the senior wrangler of 1801-2-3-4, and so on, giving the name of each, and relating his subsequent career and rise. Every man who has known him has his story regarding that astonishing memory. It may be that he was not ill-pleased that you should recognize it; but to those prodigious intellectual feats, which were so easy to him, who would grudge his tribute of homage? His talk was, in a word, admirable, and we admired it.

Of the notices which have appeared regarding Lord Macaulay, up to the day when the present lines are written (the 9th of January), the reader should not deny himself the pleasure of looking especially at two. It is a good sign of the times when such articles as these (I mean the articles in *The Times* and *Saturday Review*) appear in our public prints about our public men. They educate us, as it were, to admire rightly. An uninstructed person in a museum or at a concert may pass by without recognizing a picture or a passage of music, which the connoisseur by his side may show him is a masterpiece of harmony, or a wonder of artistic skill. After reading these papers you like and respect more the person you have admired so much already. And so with regard to Macaulay's style there may be faults of course—what critic can't point them out? But for the nonce we are not talking about faults: we want to say *nil nisi bonum*. Well—take at hazard any three pages of the *Essays* or *History;*—and, glimmering below the stream of the narrative, as it were, you, an average reader, see one, two, three, a half-score of allusions to other historic facts, characters, literature, poetry, with which you are acquainted. Why is this epithet used? Whence is that simile drawn? How does he manage, in two or three words, to paint an individual, or to indicate a landscape? Your neighbour, who has *his* reading, and his little stock of literature stowed away in his mind, shall detect more points, allusions, happy touches, indicating not only the prodigious memory and vast learning of this master, but the wonderful industry, the honest, humble previous toil of this great scholar. He reads twenty books to write a sentence; he travels a hundred miles to make a line of description.

Many Londoners—not all—have seen the British Museum Library. I speak *à cœur ouvert,*[9] and pray the kindly reader to bear with me. I have seen all sorts of domes of Peters and Pauls, Sophia, Pantheon,—what not?—and have been struck by none of them so much as by that catholic dome in Bloomsbury, under which our million volumes are housed. What peace, what love, what truth, what beauty, what happiness for all, what generous kindness for you and me, are here spread out! It seems to me one cannot sit down in that place without a heart full of grateful reverence. I own to have said my grace at the table, and to have thanked heaven for this my English birthright, freely to partake of these bountiful books, and to speak the truth I find there. Under the dome which held Macaulay's brain, and from which his solemn eyes looked out on the world but a fortnight since, what a vast, brilliant, and wonderful store of learning was ranged! what strange lore would he not fetch for you at your bidding! A volume of law, or history, a book of poetry familiar or forgotten (except by himself who forgot nothing), a novel ever so old, and he had it at hand. I spoke to him once about *Clarissa.*[10] 'Not read *Clarissa*!' he cried out. 'If you have once thoroughly entered on *Clarissa,*

---

[8] K. K., "Kaiserlich und Königlich," Imperial and regal, term used in connection with the Hapsburg court.

[9] With open heart. [10] Samuel Richardson's novel *Clarissa* (1748).

and are infected by it, you can't leave it. When I was in India, I passed one hot season at the hills, and there were the governor-general, and the secretary of government, and the commander-in-chief, and their wives. I had *Clarissa* with me: and, as soon as they began to read, the whole station was in a passion of excitement about Miss Harlowe and her misfortunes, and her scoundrelly Lovelace! The governor's wife seized the book, and the secretary waited for it, and the chief justice could not read it for tears!' He acted the whole scene: he paced up and down the Athenæum library: I daresay he could have spoken pages of the book—of that book, and of what countless piles of others!

In this little paper let us keep to the text of *nil nisi bonum*. One paper I have read regarding Lord Macaulay says 'he had no heart.' Why, a man's books may not always speak the truth, but they speak his mind in spite of himself: and it seems to me this man's heart is beating through every page he penned. He is always in a storm of revolt and indignation against wrong, craft, tyranny. How he cheers heroic resistance; how he backs and applauds freedom struggling for its own; how he hates scoundrels, ever so victorious and successful; how he recognizes genius, though selfish villains possess it! The critic who says Macaulay had no heart, might say that Johnson had none: and two men more generous, and more loving, and more hating, and more partial, and more noble, do not live in our history. Those who knew Lord Macaulay knew how admirably tender, and generous,[11] and affectionate he was. It was not his business to bring his family before the theatre footlights, and call for bouquets from the gallery as he wept over them.

If any young man of letters reads this little sermon—and to him, indeed, it is addressed—I would say to him, 'Bear Scott's words in your mind, and *"be good, my dear."* ' Here are two literary men gone to their account, and, *laus Deo,*[12] as far as we know, it is fair, and open, and clean. Here is no need of apologies for shortcomings, or explanations of vices which would have been virtues but for unavoidable &c. Here are two examples of men most differently gifted: each pursuing his calling; each speaking his truth as God bade him; each honest in his life; just and irreproachable in his dealings; dear to his friends; honoured by his country; beloved at his fireside. It has been the fortunate lot of both to give incalculable happiness and delight to the world, which thanks them in return with an immense kindliness, respect, affection. It may not be our chance, brother scribe, to be endowed with such merit, or rewarded with such fame. But the rewards of these men are rewards paid to *our service*. We may not win the baton or epaulettes; but God give us strength to guard the honour of the flag!

The Last Sketch

NOT many days since I went to visit a house where in former years I had received many a friendly welcome. We went in to the owner's—an artist's—studio. Prints, pictures, and sketches hung on the walls as I had last seen and remembered them. The implements of the painter's art were there. The light which had shone upon so many, many hours of patient and cheerful toil, poured through the northern window upon print and bust, lay figure and sketch, and upon the easel before which the good, the gentle, the beloved Leslie laboured. In this room the busy brain had devised, and the skilful hand executed, I know not how many of the noble works which have delighted the world with their beauty and charming humour. Here the poet called up into pictorial presence, and informed with life, grace, beauty, infinite friendly mirth and wondrous naturalness of expression, the people of whom his dear books told him the stories,—his Shakspeare, his Cervantes, his Molière, his Le Sage. There was his last work on the easel—a beautiful fresh smiling shape of Titania, such as his sweet guileless fancy imagined the *Midsummer Night's* queen to be. Gracious, and pure, and bright, the sweet smiling image glimmers on the canvas. Fairy elves, no doubt, were to have been grouped around their mistress in laughing clusters. Honest Bottom's grotesque head and form are indicated as reposing by the side of the consummate beauty. The darkling forest would have grown around them, with the stars glittering from the midsummer sky: the flowers at the queen's feet, and the boughs and

---

[11] Since the above was written, I have been informed that it has been found, on examining Lord Macaulay's papers, that he was in the habit of giving away *more than a fourth part* of his annual income. [Thackeray's note]

[12] Praise to the Lord.

foliage about her, would have been peopled with gambolling sprites and fays. They were dwelling in the artist's mind no doubt, and would have been developed by that patient, faithful, admirable genius: but the busy brain stopped working, the skilful hand fell lifeless, the loving, honest heart ceased to beat. What was she to have been—that fair Titania—when perfected by the patient skill of the poet, who in imagination saw the sweet innocent figure, and with tender courtesy and caresses, as it were, posed and shaped and traced the fair form? Is there record kept anywhere of fancies conceived, beautiful, unborn? Some day will they assume form in some yet undeveloped light? If our bad unspoken thoughts are registered against us, and are written in the awful account, will not the good thoughts unspoken, the love and tenderness, the pity, beauty, charity, which pass through the breast, and cause the heart to throb with silent good, find a remembrance, too? A few weeks more, and this lovely offspring of the poet's conception would have been complete—to charm the world with its beautiful mirth. May there not be some sphere unknown to us where it may have an existence? They say our words, once out of our lips, go travelling *in omne ævum,* reverberating for ever and ever. If our words, why not our thoughts? If the Has Been, why not the Might Have Been?

Some day our spirits may be permitted to walk in galleries of fancies more wondrous and beautiful than any achieved works which at present we see, and our minds to behold and delight in masterpieces which poets' and artists' minds have fathered and conceived only.

With a feeling much akin to that with which I looked upon the friend's—the admirable artist's—unfinished work, I can fancy many readers turning to these—the last pages which were traced by Charlotte Brontë's hand.[1] Of the multitude that has read her books, who has not known and deplored the tragedy of her family, her own most sad and untimely fate? Which of her readers has not become her friend? Who that has known her books has not admired the artist's noble English, the burning love of truth, the bravery, the simplicity, the indignation at wrong, the eager sympathy, the pious love and reverence, the passionate honour, so to speak, of the woman? What a story is that of that family of poets in their solitude yonder on the gloomy northern moors! At nine o'clock at night, Mrs. Gaskell tells,[2] after evening prayers, when their guardian and relative had gone to bed, the three poetesses—the three maidens, Charlotte, and Emily, and Anne—Charlotte being the 'motherly friend and guardian to the other two'—'began, like restless wild animals, to pace up and down their parlour, "making out," their wonderful stories, talking over plans and projects, and thoughts of what was to be their future life.'

One evening, at the close of 1854, as Charlotte Nicholls sat with her husband by the fire, listening to the howling of the wind about the house, she suddenly said to her husband, 'If you had not been with me, I must have been writing now.' She then ran upstairs, and brought down, and read aloud, the beginning of a new tale. When she had finished, her husband remarked, 'The critics will accuse you of repetition.' She replied, 'Oh! I shall alter that. I always begin two or three times before I can please myself.' But it was not to be. The trembling little hand was to write no more. The heart, newly awakened to love and happiness, and throbbing with maternal hope, was soon to cease to beat; that intrepid outspeaker and champion of truth, that eager, impetuous redresser of wrong, was to be called out of the world's fight and struggle, to lay down the shining arms, and to be removed to a sphere where even a noble indignation *cor ulterius nequit lacerare,*[3] and where truth complete, and right triumphant, no longer need to wage war.

I can only say of this lady, *vidi tantum.*[4] I saw her first just as I rose out of an illness from which I had never thought to recover. I remember the trembling little frame, the little hand, the great honest eyes. An impetuous honesty seemed to me to characterize the woman. Twice I recollect she took me to task for what she held to be errors in doctrine. Once about Fielding we had a disputation. She spoke her mind out. She jumped too rapidly to conclusions. (I have smiled at one or two passages in the *Biography,* in which my own disposition or behaviour forms the subject of talk.) She formed conclusions that might be wrong, and built up whole theories of character upon them. New to the London world, she entered it with an independent, indomitable spirit of her own; and judged of contemporaries, and especially spied out arrogance or affectation,

---

[1] Charlotte Brontë at her death in 1854 left the fragment of an unfinished novel, *Emma.*
[2] Reference to the *Life of Charlotte Brontë* by Elizabeth Gaskell, published in 1857.
[3] "Can no longer lacerate her heart," an adaptation of the epitaph on Jonathan Swift's grave.
[4] I have seen so much.

with extraordinary keenness of vision. She was angry with her favourites if their conduct or conversation fell below her ideal. Often she seemed to me to be judging the London folk prematurely: but perhaps the city is rather angry at being judged. I fancied an austere little Joan of Arc marching in upon us, and rebuking our easy lives, our easy morals. She gave me the impression of being a very pure, and lofty, and high-minded person. A great and holy reverence of right and truth seemed to be with her always. Such, in our brief interview, she appeared to me. As one thinks of that life so noble, so lonely—of that passion for truth—of those nights and nights of eager study, swarming fancies, invention, depression, elation, prayer; as one reads the necessarily incomplete, though most touching and admirable history of the heart that throbbed in this one little frame—of this one amongst the myriads of souls that have lived and died on this great earth—this great earth?—this little speck in the infinite universe of God,—with what wonder do we think of to-day, with what awe await to-morrow, when that which is now but darkly seen shall be clear! As I read this little fragmentary sketch, I think of the rest. Is it? And where is it? Will not the leaf be turned some day, and the story be told? Shall the deviser of the tale somewhere perfect the history of little EMMA's griefs and troubles? Shall TITANIA come forth complete with her sportive court, with the flowers at her feet, the forest around her, and all the stars of summer glittering overhead?

How well I remember the delight, and wonder, and pleasure with which I read *Jane Eyre*, sent to me by an author whose name and sex were then alike unknown to me; the strange fascinations of the book; and how with my own work pressing upon me, I could not, having taken the volumes up, lay them down until they were read through! Hundreds of those who, like myself, recognized and admired that master-work of a great genius, will look with a mournful interest and regard and curiosity upon this, the last fragmentary sketch from the noble hand which wrote *Jane Eyre*.

Henry Mayhew

1812-1887

H ENRY MAYHEW, editor, comic writer, sometime joint novelist with his brother, captured contemporary attention and that of posterity by his extensive social survey of life in working-class London, and it is as the chronicler of that life that he has survived in literature.

Mayhew was born in London, the son of a solicitor, and educated at Westminster School, but he ran away from school to go to sea. Upon his return he first studied law, but he abandoned that to pursue a varied literary and journalistic career. In 1841 he was one of the founders and coeditors of *Punch* with Mark Lemon (1809–70). Lemon later edited *Punch* alone and Mayhew went on to collaborate in the writing of popular novels with his younger brother Augustus. Together they wrote five successful works of fiction, including *The Good Genius that Turns Everything to Gold* (1847) and *Whom to Marry* (1848). Augustus Mayhew subsequently wrote novels on his own, though his most arresting work, *Paved with Gold, or The Romance and Reality of the London Streets,* was originally begun as a collaboration with Henry and owes much of its realism to the investigations of London low life undertaken by Henry and Augustus in research for *London Labour and London Poor.*

Henry Mayhew began his study of London life for the *Morning Chronicle* in 1849, and when he left the *Chronicle* he continued his researches, aided by his brother Augustus. Indeed, Augustus credits himself with the section on crossing-sweepers, much of which is incorporated into *Paved with Gold.*

Henry Mayhew went on to write other studies of London life, biographies, travel literature, and works of humor, but nothing from his pen has been held equal to his *London Labour.* He died in 1887.

Although Mayhew was only one, albeit a very early one, of a number of investigators into the severe conditions of urban life in the Victorian age—there were novelists who depicted such matters, as well as later official government reports and the investigations of other journalists—Mayhew's account has remained the classic work on the subject because of its wealth of detail and vivid observation. From Mayhew's reportage it is easy to see why novelists like Dickens quarried London slum life for some of their most effective passages.

CHRONOLOGY

1812   Born in London.
1822   Attends Westminster School.
1826   Runs away from school .
1841   Helps to found *Punch*.
1849   Begins investigation of labor and the poor for *Morning Chronicle*.
1851–52   Serial publication of "London Labour and London Poor."
1861–62   Book publication of *London Labour and London Poor*.
1862   Visits Germany.
1887   Dies 25 July; buried at Kensal Green Cemetery, London.

EDITIONS

London Labour and London Poor (4 vols., 1861–62)
The Rhine and its Picturesque Scenery (1856).
The Great World of London (in part) (1856).
Young Benjamin Franklin (1861).
German Life and Manners (2 vols., 1864).
The Comic Almanack (2 vols., 1871).
Mayhew's London, ed. Peter Quennell (1949).
London's Underworld, ed. Peter Quennell (1950).
Mayhew's Characters, ed. Peter Quennell (1951).
Selections from London Labour and London Poor, ed. John L. Bradley (1965).

---

from London Labour and London Poor

Mayhew's comprehensive survey of the life of London's poor is especially rich in freshly observed detail about the many occupations that gave paltry sustenance to London workers. Below is printed the section from volume two on crossing-sweepers, that Victorian occupation whereby men of all ages, including young boys like Dickens' Jo in Bleak House, *were employed to sweep lanes and intersections of London streets.*

Crossing-Sweepers

THAT portion of the London street-folk who earn a scanty living by sweeping crossings constitute a large class of the Metropolitan poor. We can scarcely walk along a street of any extent, or pass through a square of the least pretensions to 'gentility,' without meeting one or more of these private scavengers. Crossing-sweeping seems to be one of those occupations which are resorted to as an excuse for begging; and, indeed, as many expressed it to me, 'it was the last chance left of obtaining an honest crust.'

The advantages of crossing-sweeping as a means of livelihood seem to be:

1st, the smallness of the capital required in order to commence the business;

2ndly, the excuse the apparent occupation affords for soliciting gratuities without being considered in the light of a street-beggar;

And 3rdly, the benefits arising from being constantly seen in the same place, and thus exciting the sympathy of the neighbouring householders, till small weekly allowances or 'pensions' are obtained.

The first curious point in connexion with this subject is what constitutes the '*property*,' so to speak, in a crossing, or the *right* to sweep a pathway across a certain thoroughfare. A nobleman, who has been one of Her Majesty's Ministers, whilst conversing with me on the subject of crossing-sweepers, expressed to me the curiosity he felt on the subject, saying that he had noticed some of the sweepers in the same place for years. 'What were the rights of property,' he asked, 'in such cases, and what constituted the title that such a man had to a particular crossing? Why did not the stronger sweeper supplant the weaker? Could a man bequeath a crossing to a son, or present it to a friend? How did he first obtain the spot?'

The answer is, that crossing-sweepers are, in a measure, under the protection of the police. If the accommodation afforded by a well-swept pathway is evident, the policeman on that district will protect the original sweeper of the crossing from the intrusion of a rival. I have, indeed, met with instances of men who, before taking to a crossing, have asked for and obtained permission of the police; and one sweeper, who gave me his statement, had even solicited the authority of the inhabitants before he applied to the inspector at the station-house.

If a crossing have been vacant for some time, another sweeper may take to it; but should the original proprietor again make his appearance, the officer on duty will generally re-establish him. One man to whom I spoke, had fixed himself on a crossing which for years another sweeper had kept clean on the Sunday morning only. A dispute ensued; the one claimant pleading his long Sabbath possession, and the other his continuous everyday service. The quarrel was referred to the police, who decided that he who was oftener on the ground was the rightful owner; and the option was given to the former possessor, that if he would sweep there every day the crossing should be his.

I believe there is only one crossing in London which is in the gift of a householder, and this proprietorship originated in a tradesman having, at his own expense, caused a paved footway to be laid down over the macadamized road in front of his shop, so that his customers might run less chance of dirtying their boots when they crossed over to give their orders.

Some bankers, however, keep a crossing-sweeper, not only to sweep a clean path for the 'clients' visiting house, but to open and shut the doors of the carriages calling at the house.

Concerning the *causes which lead or drive* people to this occupation, they are various. People take to crossing-sweeping either on account of their bodily afflictions, depriving them of the power of performing ruder work, or because the occupation is the last resource left open to them of earning a living, and they considered even the scanty subsistence it yields preferable to that of the work-house. The greater proportion of crossing-sweepers are those who, from some bodily infirmity or injury, are prevented from a more laborious mode of obtaining their living. Among the bodily infirmities the chief old age, asthma, and rheumatism; and the injuries mostly consist of loss of limbs. Many of the rheumatic sweepers have been bricklayers' labourers.

The classification of crossing-sweepers is not very complex. They may be divided into the *casual* and the *regular*.

By the casual I mean such as pursue the occupation only on certain days in the week, as, for instance, those who make their appearance on the Sunday morning, as well as the boys who, broom in hand, travel about the streets, sweeping before the foot-passengers or stopping an hour at one place, and then, if not fortunate, moving on to another.

The regular crossing-sweepers are those who have taken up their posts at the corners of streets or squares; and I have met with some who have kept to the same spot for more than forty years.

The crossing-sweepers in the squares may be reckoned among the most fortunate of the class. With them the crossing is a kind of stand, where any one requiring their services knows they may be found. These sweepers are often employed by the butlers and servants in the neighbouring mansions for running errands, posting letters, and occasionally helping in the packing-up and removal of furniture or boxes when the family goes out of town. I have met with other sweepers who, from being known for years to the inhabitants, have at last got to be regularly employed at some of the houses to clean knives, boots, windows, &c.

It is not at all an unfrequent circumstance, however, for a sweeper to be in receipt of a weekly sum from some of the inhabitants in the district. The crossing itself is in these cases but of little value for chance customers, for were it not for the regular charity of the householders, it would be deserted. Broken victuals and old clothes also form part of a sweeper's means of living; nor are the clothes always old ones, for one or two of this class have for years been in the habit of having new suits presented to them by the neighbours at Christmas.

The irregular sweepers mostly consist of boys and girls who have formed themselves into a kind of company, and come to an agreement to work together on the same crossings. The principal resort of these is about Trafalgar-square, where they have seized upon some three or four crossings, which they visit from time to time in the course of the day.

One of these gangs I found had appointed its king and captain, though the titles were more honorary than privileged. They had framed their own laws respecting each one's right to the money he took, and the obedience to these laws was enforced by the strength of the little fraternity.

One or two girls whom I questioned, told me that they mixed up ballad-singing or lace-selling with crossing-sweeping, taking to the broom only when the streets were wet and muddy. These children are usually sent out by their parents, and have to carry home at night their earnings. A few of them are orphans with a longing-house for a home.

Taken as a class, crossing-sweepers are among the most honest of the London poor. They all tell you that, without a good character and 'the respect of the neighbourhood,' there is not a living to be got out of the broom. Indeed, those whom I found best-to-do in the world were those who had been longest at their posts.

Among them are many who have been servants until sickness or accident deprived them of their situations, and nearly all of them have had their minds so subdued by affliction, that they have been tamed so as to be incapable of mischief.

The *earnings*, or rather '*takings*,' of crossing-sweepers are difficult to estimate—generally speaking—that is, to strike the average for the entire class. An erroneous idea prevails that crossing-sweeping is a lucrative employment. All whom I have spoken with agree in saying, that some thirty years back it was a good living; but they bewail piteously the spirit of the present generation. I have met with some who, in former days, took their 3*l.* weekly; and there are but few I have spoken to who would not, at one period, have considered fifteen shillings a bad week's work. But now 'the takings' are very much reduced. The man who was known to this class as having been the most prosperous of all—for from one nobleman alone he received an allowance of seven shillings and sixpence weekly—assured me

that twelve shillings a-week was the average of his present gains, taking the year round; whilst the majority of the sweepers agree that a shilling is a good day's earnings.

A shilling a-day is the very limit of the average incomes of the London sweepers, and this is rather an over than an under calculation; for, although a few of the more fortunate, who are to be found in the squares or main thoroughfares or opposite the public buildings, may earn their twelve or fifteen shillings a-week, yet there are hundreds who are daily to be found in the by-streets of the metropolis who assert that eighteenpence a-day is their average taking; and, indeed, in proof of their poverty, they refer you to the work-house authorities, who allow them certain quartern-loaves weekly. The old stories of delicate suppers and stockings full of money have in the present day no foundation of truth.

The black crossing-sweeper, who bequeathed 500*l.* to Miss Waithman, would almost seem to be the last of the class whose earnings were above his positive necessities.

Lastly, concerning the *numbers* belonging to this large class, we may add that it is difficult to reckon up the number of crossing-sweepers in London. There are few squares without a couple of these pathway scavengers; and in the more respectable squares, such as Cavendish or Portman, every corner has been seized upon. Again, in the principal thoroughfares, nearly every street has its crossing and attendant.

· · ·

Juvenile Crossing-Sweepers

BOY CROSSING-SWEEPERS AND TUMBLERS

A REMARKABLY intelligent lad, who, on being spoken to, at once consented to give all the information in his power, told me the following story of his life.

It will be seen from this boy's account, and the one or two following that a kind of partnership exists among some of these young sweepers. They have associated themselves together, appropriated several crossings to their use, and appointed a captain over them. They have their forms of trial, and 'jury-house' for the settlement of disputes; laws have been framed, which govern their commercial proceedings, and a kind of language adopted by the society for its better protection from the arch-enemy, the policeman.

I found the lad who first gave me an insight into the proceedings of the associated crossing-sweepers crouched on the stone steps of a door in Adelaide-street, Strand; and when I spoke to him he was preparing to settle down in a corner and go to sleep—his legs and body being curled round almost as closely as those of a cat on a hearth. The moment he heard my voice he was upon his feet, asking me to 'give a halfpenny to poor little Jack.'

He was a good-looking lad, with a pair of large mild eyes, which he took good care to turn up with an expression of supplication as he moaned for a halfpenny.

A cap, or more properly a stuff bag, covered a crop of hair which had matted itself into the form of so many paint-brushes, while his face, from its roundness of feature and the complexion of dirt, had an almost Indian look about it; the colour of his hands, too, was such that you could imagine he had been shelling walnuts.

He ran before me, treading cautiously with his naked feet, until I reached a convenient spot to take down his statement, which was as follows:—

'I've got no mother or father; mother has been dead for two years, and father's been gone for more than that—more nigh five years—he died at Ipswich, in Suffolk. He was a perfumer by trade, and used to make hair-dye, and scent, and pomatum, and all kinds of scents. He didn't keep a shop himself, but he used to serve them as did; he didn't hawk his goods about, neether, but had regular customers, what used to send him a letter, and then he'd take them what they wanted. Yes, he used to serve some good shops: there was H——'s, of London Bridge, what's a large chemist's. He used to make a good deal of money, but he lost it betting; and so his brother, my uncle, did all his. He used to go up to High Park, and then go round by the Hospital, and then turn up a yard, where all the men are who play for money [Tattersall's]; and there he'd lose his money, or sometimes win,—but that wasn't often. I remember he used to come home tipsy, and say he'd lost on this or that horse, naming wot one he'd laid on; and then mother would coax him to bed, and afterwards sit down and begin to cry.

'Ah! she was a very good, kind mother, and very fond of both of us; though father wasn't, for he'd always have a noise with mother when he come home, only he was seldom with us when he was making his goods.

'After mother died, sister still kept on making nets, and I lived with her for some time. But she was keeping company with a young man, and one day they went out, and came back and said they'd been and got married. It was him as got rid of me.

'He was kind to me for the first two or three months, while he was keeping her company; but before he was married he got a little cross, and after he was married he begun to get more cross, and used to send me to play in the streets, and tell me not to come home again till night. One day he hit me, and I said I wouldn't be hit about by him, and then at tea that night sister gave me three shillings, and told me I must go and get my own living. So I bought a box and brushes (they cost me just the money) and went cleaning boots, and I done pretty well with them, till my box was stole from me by a boy where I was lodging. He's in prison now—got six calendar for picking pockets.

'I was fifteen the 24th of last May, sir, and I've been sweeping crossings now near upon two years. There's party of six of us, and we have the crossings from St. Martin's Church as far as Pall Mall. I always go along with them as lodges in the same place as I do. In the daytime, if it's dry, we do anythink we can—open cabs, or anythink; but if it's wet, we separate, and I an' another gets a crossing—those who gets on it first, keeps it,—and we stand on each side and take our chance.

'We do it this way:—if I was to see two gentlemen coming, I should cry out, "Two toffs!" and then they are mine; and whether they give me anythink or not they are mine, and my mate is bound not to follow them; for if he did he would get a hiding from the whole lot of us. If we both cry out together, then we share. If it's a lady and a gentleman, then we cries, "A toff and a doll!" Sometimes we are caught out in this way. Perhaps it is a lady and gentleman and a child; and if I was to see them, and only say, "A toff and a doll," and leave out the child, then my mate can add the child; and as he is right and I wrong, then it's his party.

'When we see the rain we say together, "Oh! there's a jolly good rain! we'll have a good day to-morrow." If a shower comes on, and we are at our room, which we general are about three o'clock, to get somethink to eat—besides, we general go there to see how much each other's taken in the day—why, out we run with our brooms.

'At night-time we tumbles—that is, if the policeman ain't nigh. We goes general to Waterloo-place when the Opera's on. We sends on one of us ahead, as a looker-out, to look for the policeman, and then we follows. It's no good tumbling to gentlemen *going* to the Opera; it's when they're coming back they gives us money. When they've got a young lady on their arm they laugh at us tumbling; some will give us a penny, others threepence, sometimes a sixpence or a shilling, and sometimes a halfpenny. We either do the cat'unwhell, or else we keep before the gentleman and lady, turning head-over-heels, putting our broom on the ground and then turning over it.

'After the Opera we go into the Haymarket, where all the women are who walk the streets all night. They don't give us no money, but they tell the gentlemen to. Sometimes, when they are talking to the gentlemen, they say, "Go away,

you young rascal!" and if they are saucy, then we say to them, "We're not talking to you, my doxy, we're talking to the gentleman,"—but that's only if they're rude, for if they speak civil we always goes. They knows what "doxy" means. What is it? Why that they are no better than us! If we are on the crossing, and we says to them as they go by, "Good luck to you!" they always give us somethink either that night or the next. There are two with bloomer bonnets, who always give us something if we says "Good luck."

'When we are talking together we always talk in a kind of slang. Each policeman we gives a regular name—there's "Bull's Head," "Bandy Shanks," and "Old Cherry Legs," and "Dot-and-carry-one;" they all knows their names as well as us. We never talks of crossings, but "fakes." We don't make no slang of our own, but uses the regular one.

'A broom doesn't last us more than a week in wet weather, and they costs us twopence half-penny each; but in dry weather they are good a fortnight.'

Augustus Welby Northmore Pugin

1812-1852

THE ARCHITECT Pugin was the son of a French architect and emigré, Auguste Pugin, and it was in his father's office that he learned his trade by, among other things, making illustrations for his father's books on Gothic architecture. He went on to become one of the earliest and certainly the most insistent champion of the Gothic style in Victorian England.

Pugin was born in London and studied at Christ's Hospital. After that most of his education came from work in his father's architectural office. Although he was early attracted to the Gothic style, his devotion to it became an article of faith after he converted to the Roman Catholic Church in 1834. Most of the design and visible decoration for the then new Houses of Parliament in 1836–37 came from Pugin's hand while he was working with Sir Charles Barry, although the exact division of labor was long a matter of dispute. But most of Pugin's subsequent architectural designs were ecclesiastical structures, mainly but not exclusively Roman Catholic. The most notable of these is the Roman Catholic Cathedral at Birmingham, but many London area Gothic revival churches were also the work of Pugin.

Pugin was not content only to design Gothic style buildings; his industry in stained glass work and ornament was prodigious. He believed firmly, even fanatically, in what seemed to him to be the moral superiority of Gothic architecture. He did much to popularize the rise of Victorian Gothic (already under way from various other sources) in such works as *Contrasts* (1836) and the *True Principles of Christian Architecture* (1841). In these works Pugin inveighed against contemporary Victorian architecture, especially industrial architecture, and advocated the return to a Gothic style, not only in buildings but in matters of faith and belief. Pugin has been recognized as anticipating and influencing Ruskin (though Ruskin denied it) in discerning the relationship between the ideas and beliefs of a society and the style of architecture in which it constructs its buildings.

After about 1851 Pugin suffered increasingly from mental derangement, partly as a result of his frantic pace of work. His son, Edward Welby Pugin

(1834–75), completed a good deal of his father's work after Pugin's mind gave way entirely in the spring of 1852. He was removed to a mental institution, but he died at home in Ramsgate in September of that year.

As an author Pugin's most impressive work is *Contrast's* both for its wealth of illustrations from his own hand and for its earnestly argued thesis that the architecture of the fourteenth and fifteenth centuries reflected a sounder attitude toward life than that of the nineteenth. Although his interests were specifically ecclesiastical and architectural, Pugin anticipates not only Ruskin but other Victorians, such as Carlyle, who found instructive the comparison of Victorian England to medieval England.

CHRONOLOGY

1812	Born 1 March in London.
1825	Studies at Christ's Hospital.
1834	Converts to Roman Catholicism.
1836	*Contrasts.*
1836–37	Helps design the new Houses of Parliament.
1837	Professor of Architecture at Oscott College.
1841	*True Principles of Christian Architecture.*
1852	Dies 14 September at Ramsgate.

EDITIONS

Contrasts between the Architecture of the Fifteenth and Nineteenth Centuries (1836; 2nd ed., 1840).
True Principles of Pointed or Christian Architecture (1841).
Apology for the Revival of Christian Architecture (1843).
Glossary of Ecclesiastical Ornament and Costume (1844).
Chancel Screens (1851).

BIOGRAPHY AND CRITICISM

B. Ferrey, *Recollections of A. W. N. Pugin and his Father* (1861).
Kenneth Clark, *The Gothic Revival* (1928).
Michael Trappes-Lomax, *Pugin: A Mediaeval Victorian* (1932).
H. E. G. Rope, *Pugin* (1935).
Dennis Gwynn, *Lord Shrewsbury, Pugin, and the Catholic Revival* (1946).

from Contrasts

Or a Parallel between the Noble Edifices of the Fourteenth and Fifteenth Centuries and Similar Buildings of the Present Day, Shewing the Present Decay of Taste

The long title of this work tells its thesis. Pugin was unable to find a publisher for it, so he published it with his own funds in 1836. Although he made no money from the sale of the book, he made his reputation and was thenceforth much sought after as designer for Roman Catholic and high Anglican ecclesiastical commissions. The selection below is all of Chapter One and the Conclusion, from the second edition, 1840. (The ellipses in the "Conclusion" are Pugin's.)

CHAPTER ONE

On the Feelings Which Produced the Great Edifices of the Middle Ages

ON comparing the Architectural Works of the last three Centuries with those of the Middle Ages, the wonderful superiority of the latter must strike every attentive observer; and the mind is naturally led to reflect on the causes which have wrought this mighty change, and to endeavour to trace the fall of Architectural taste, from the period of its first decline to the present day; and this will form the subject of the following pages.

It will be readily admitted, that the great test of Architectural beauty is the fitness of the design to the purpose for which it is intended, and that the style of a building should so correspond with its use that the spectator may at once perceive the purpose for which it was erected.

Acting on this principle, different nations have given birth to so many various styles of Architecture, each suited to their climate, customs, and religion; and as it is among edifices of this latter class that we look for the most splendid and lasting monuments, there can be little doubt that the religious ideas and ceremonies of these different people had by far the greatest influence in the formation of their various styles of Architecture.

The more closely we compare the temples of the Pagan nations with their religious rites and mythologies, the more shall we be satisfied with the truth of this assertion.

In them every ornament, every detail had a mystical import. The pyramid and obelisk of Egyptian Architecture, its Lotus capitals, its gigantic sphynxes and multiplied hieroglyphics, were not mere fanciful Architectural combinations and ornaments, but emblems of the philosophy and mythology of that nation.

In classic Architecture again, not only were the forms of the temples dedicated to different deities varied, but certain capitals and orders of Architecture were peculiar to each; and the very foliage ornaments of the friezes were symbolic. The same principle, of Architecture resulting from religious belief, may be traced from the caverns of Elora, to the Druidical remains of Stonehenge and Avebury; and in all these works of Pagan antiquity, we shall invariably find that both the plan and decoration of the building is mystical and emblematic.

And is it to be supposed that Christianity alone, with its sublime truths, with its stupendous mysteries, should be deficient in this respect, and not possess a symbolical architecture for her temples which would embody her doctrines and instruct her children? surely not,—nor is it so: from Christianity has arisen an architecture so glorious, so sublime, so perfect, that all the productions of ancient paganism sink, when compared before it, to a level with the false and corrupt systems from which they originated.

Pointed or Christian Architecture has far higher claims on our admiration than mere beauty or antiquity; the former may be regarded as a matter of opinion,—the latter, in the abstract, is no proof of excellence, but in it alone we find *the faith of Christianity embodied, and its practices illustrated.*

The three great doctrines, of the redemption of man by the sacrifice of our Lord on the cross; the three equal persons united in one God-head; and the resurrection of the dead,—are the foundation of Christian Architecture.

The first—the cross—is not only the very plan and form of a Catholic church, but it terminates each spire and gable, and is imprinted as a seal of faith on the very furniture of the altar.

The second is fully developed in the triangular form and arrangement of arches, tracery, and even subdivisions of the buildings themselves.

The third is beautifully exemplified by great height and vertical lines, which have been considered by the Christians, from the earliest period, as the emblem of the resurrection. According to ancient tradition, the faithful prayed in a standing position, both on Sundays and during the pascal time, in allusion to this great mystery. This is mentioned by Tertullian and by St. Augustine. *Stantes oramus, quod est signum resurrectionis;*[1] and, by the last council of Nice, it was forbidden to kneel on Sundays, or from Easter to Pentecost. The vertical principal being an acknowledged emblem of the resurrection, we may readily account for the adoption of the pointed arch by the Christians, for the purpose of gaining greater height with a given width. I say adoption, because the mere form of the pointed arch is of great antiquity; and Euclid himself must have been perfectly acquainted with it. But there was nothing to call it into use, till the vertical principle was established. The Christian churches had previously been built with the view to internal height: triforia and clerestories existed in the Saxon churches. But lofty as were these buildings, when compared with the flat and depressed temples of classic antiquity, still the introduction of the pointed arch[2] enabled the builders to obtain nearly double the elevation with the same width, as is clearly seen in the annexed cut. But do not all the features and details of the churches erected during the middle ages, set forth their origin, and, at the same time, exhibit the triumphs of Christian truth? Like the religion itself, their foundations are in the cross, and they rise from it

in majesty and glory. The lofty nave and choir, with still loftier towers, crowned by clusters of pinnacles and spires, all directed towards heaven, beautiful emblems of the Christian's brightest hope, the shame of the Pagan; the cross, raised on high in glory,—a token of mercy and forgiveness,—crowning the sacred edifice, and placed between the anger of God and the sins of the city.

The images of holy martyrs, each bearing the instrument of the cruel death by which Pagan foolishness hoped to exterminate, with their lives, the truths they witnessed, fill every niche that line the arched recesses of the doorways. Above them are forms of cherubims and the heavenly host, mingled with patriarchs and prophets. Over the great entrance, is the dome or final judgment, the divine majesty, the joys of the blessed spirits, the despair of the condemned. What subjects for contemplation do not these majestic portals present to the Christian, as he approaches the house of prayer! and well are they calculated to awaken those sentiments of reverence and devotion, suited to the holy place. But if the exterior of the temple be so soul-stirring, what a burst of glory meets the eye, on entering a long majestic line of pillars rising into lofty and fretted vaulting! The eye is lost in the intricacies of the aisles and lateral chapels; each window beams with sacred instructions, and sparkles with glowing and sacred tints; the pavement is a rich enamel, interspersed with brass memorials of departed souls. Every capital and base are fashioned to represent some holy mystery; the great rood loft, with its lights and images, through the centre arch of which, in distant perspective, may be seen the high altar blazing with gold and jewels, surmounted by a golden dove, the early tabernacle of the Highest; before which, burn three unextinguished lamps. It is, indeed, a sacred place; the modulated light, the gleaming tapers, the tombs of the faithful, the various altars, the venerable images of the just,—all conspire to fill the mind with veneration, and to impress it with the sublimity of Christian worship. And when the deep intonations of the bells from the lofty campaniles, which summon the people to the house of prayer, have ceased, and the solemn chant of the choir swells through the vast edifice,—cold, indeed, must be the heart

---

[1] We pray standing because it is the sign of the Resurrection.
[2] We may consider the introduction of the depressed or four-centered arch as the first symptom of the decline of Christian Architecture, the leading character of which was the vertical or pointed principle. [Pugin's note]

of that man who does not cry out with the Psalmist, Domine dileri decorem domus tuae, et locum habitationis gloriae tuae.[3]

Such effects as these can only be produced on the mind by buildings, the composition of which has emanated from men who were thoroughly embued with devotion for, and faith in, the religion for whose worship they were erected.

Their whole energies were directed towards attaining excellence; they were actuated by far nobler motives than the hopes of pecuniary reward, or even the applause and admiration of mankind. They felt they were engaged in one of the most glorious occupations that can fall to the lot of man—that of raising a temple to the worship of the true and living God.

It was this feeling that operated alike on the master-mind that planned the edifice, and on the patient sculptor whose chisel wrought each varied and beautiful detail. It was this feeling that enabled the ancient masons, in spite of labour, danger, and difficulties, to persevere till they had raised their gigantic spires into the very regions of the clouds. It was this feeling that induced the ecclesiastics of old to devote their revenues to this pious purpose, and to labour with their own hands in the accomplishment of the work; and it is a feeling that may be traced throughout the whole of the numerous edifices of the middle ages, and which, amidst the great variety of genius which their varied decorations display, still bespeaks the unity of purpose which influenced their builders and artists.

They borrowed their ideas from no heathen rites, nor sought for decorations from the idolatrous emblems of a strange people. The foundation and progress of the Christian faith, and the sacraments and ceremonies of the church, formed an ample and noble field for the exercise of their talents; and it is an incontrovertible fact, that every class of artists, who flourished during those glorious periods, selected their subjects from this inexhaustible source, and devoted their greatest efforts towards the embellishment of ecclesiastical edifices.

Yes, it was, indeed, the faith, the zeal, and above all, the unity, of our ancestors, that enabled them to conceive and raise those wonderful fabrics that still remain to excite our wonder and admiration. They were erected for the most solemn rites of Christian worship, when the term Christian had but one signification throughout the world; when the glory of the house of God formed an important consideration with mankind, when men were zealous for religion, liberal in their gifts, and devoted to her cause. I am well aware that modern writers have attributed the numerous churches erected during the middle ages to the effect of superstition. But if we believe the great principle of Christian truth, that this life is merely a preparation for a future state, and that the most important occupation of man in this world is to prepare for the next, the multiplicity of religious establishments during the ages of faith, may be accounted for on far nobler motives than have been generally ascribed to them.

It may be objected, and with some apparent reason, that if pointed Architecture had been the result of Christian faith, it would have been introduced earlier. But if we examine the history of the Church, we shall find that the long period which intervened between the establishment of Christianity and the full development of Christian art, can be most satisfactorily accounted for. When the Catholic faith was first preached, *all art was devoted to the service of error and impurity.* Then the great and terrible persecutions of the first centuries, utterly precluded its exercise among the early Christians. The convulsion consequent on the overthrow of the Roman empire, which destroyed, for a time, all the practical resources of art, was a sufficient cause for the barbarous state of Architecture at that period: but when Christianity had over-spread the whole of western Europe, and infused her salutary and ennobling influence in the hearts of the converted nations, art arose purified and glorious; and as it had been previously devoted to the gratification of the senses, then it administered to the soul: and exalted by the grandeur of the Christian mysteries, ennobled by its sublime virtues, it reached a point of excellence far beyond any it had previously attained; and instead of being confined to what was sensual or human, it was devoted to the spiritual and divine. Christian art was the natural result of the progress of Catholic feeling and devotion; and its decay was consequent on that of the faith itself; and all revived classic buildings, whether erected in Catholic or Protestant countries, are evidences of a lamentable departure from true Catholic principles and feelings, as will be shown in the ensuing chapter.

---

[3] Lord, I have loved the habitation of thy house, and the place where thine honour dwelleth (Psalms 26:8).

CONCLUSION

Reflections on the Probable State of the English Churches, Had This Country Remained in Communion with the Catholic Church

HAVING now shown the disastrous effects of the Protestant or destructive principle, on Catholic art and architecture in England, it may not be uninstructive to take into consideration the probable results which would have befallen the ancient churches, had Protestantism never been established in this country. Judging from what has occurred during the last three centuries on the Continent, it would be presuming far too much to suppose that England alone would have escaped the pestilential influence of Pagan ideas and taste which was spreading over Europe at the period of England's schism, and of which even some indications were perceptible[1] in the latter pointed erections; and there is but too great reason to believe that had the destructive spirit been suppressed, the restorative or classic rage would have been almost as fatal to Catholic art. As it is, everything glorious about the English churches is Catholic, everything debased and hideous, Protestant. This is certainly a melancholy superiority to the foreign churches, which present, in their solemn constructions, and paltry and incongruous fittings, a most lamentable contrast between the ancient spirit and modern practices of Catholicism, setting forth at one view the summit of excellence, and the lowest depth of degradation. A fine old Catholic church used for Protestant service, is indeed a melancholy sight, but scarcely less melancholy is it to see modern Catholics with their own hands polluting and disfiguring, by pagan emblems and theatrical trumpery, the glorious structures raised by their ancestors in the faith.[2] The consideration of modern degeneracy tends to alleviate the sorrow we feel at Protestant ravages. Far better is it to see the great abbeys of England, ruined and roofless as they are, than to behold them degraded into mere means of revenue, and held *in commendam* by some tonsured child, or converted into a luxurious abode for a few nominal monks. Our English monasteries were cut off in their glory, in the midst of boundless

---

[1] In Wolsey's palace of Hampton Court, the heads in terra-cotta on the turrets of the inner gatehouse, represent four of the Caesars. Bishop Gardner's tomb at Winchester exhibits a variety of debased or Italian features and details.

In the Countess of Salisbury's chantry in the Priory church of Christ's Church, Hampshire, are several details in what is termed the *renaissance* style. Many instances might be cited to prove that germs of the revived pagan style existed in England previous to the separation of the English Church from Catholic communion. [Pugin's note]

[2] What, indeed, can be more agonizing to a faithful Catholic, than to behold the clergy themselves (the legitimate guardians of these ancient fabrics, the successors of those holy and learned ecclesiastics who were at once the architects and ministers of the temple), filled with the most anti-Christian ideas of art, and united in the destruction of the venerable remains of Catholic dignity, to introduce the bastard pagan style, the very date of which is coeval with the decay of faith, and decline of their influence? Many churches in France have escaped the ravages of the Huguenots and Calvinists,—many the tremendous revolutions of 1790; but not one has been preserved from the innovating and paltry taste of the modern clergy. Were they to confine the display of their wretched ideas to mere fittings which could easily be removed, the case would not be so distressing, but the fabrics themselves are frequently mutilated past restoration, by these wholesale destructives. The Count de Montalembert gives a harrowing description of these barbarities, the truth of many of which I have confirmed by actual observation. Hundreds of stained windows have been either sold out, or destroyed, to be replaced by white panes; the most curious frescoes and rich painted ceilings have been mercilessly covered by thick coats of white and yellow wash, the usual modern decorations of ecclesiastical buildings. Every vestige of internal sculpture or ancient art has been destroyed, to be replaced by the odious productions of modern manufacturers—"*d'objets d'églises,*" while the new altars present every possible combination of outrageous architecture and paltry ornament, and these are not unfrequently placed in such a position as to conceal the most interesting portions of the original buildings. It is quite impossible to enter a French church without being thoroughly disgusted with the extreme contempt of antiquity and degraded taste which their fittings and ornaments display. The result of this is truly lamentable; for few men are sufficiently instructed in these matters, to discriminate between really Catholic productions, and the wretched externals of modern paganism, which disguise the solemnities of the Church, or to draw the vast distinction between the ancient solemn celebration of

hospitality and regular observance.[3] We can trace no sign of pagan novelties about their venerable ruins—all these breathe of faith, of charity, of contemplation, of austerity and prayer; and we can visit these solemn remains of ancient piety with unalloyed reverence and regret, but not so the abbatial remains of France, where the pointed arch and Christian sculpture of the St. Louis is mingled with the fantastic compositions of Francis the First, and the ultra-paganism of the "grand monarque." After the fatal Concordat, many of these once-famous houses lingered on till their final suppression in 1790. Large masses of hideous modern Italian buildings[4] filled with vast apartments of pagan design, had either been added to, *or even replaced* the conventual refectory and dormitory; and not unfrequently these degenerate monks had transformed their ancient and solemn church, as far as possible, into a semi-pagan or Italian building, by encasing the pillars with pilasters, inserting semies under the pointed arches, and disguising the original features by festoons, clouds, and similar monstrosities.

So fatal, indeed, has this rage for pagan novelties proved to Christian art, that after all the demolitions and destruction they have escaped, the old English churches have retained more of their original features, than most of those on the Continent. They have had all *the advantages of neglect,* and to Protestant apathy we are not a little indebted,—for both of these are

---

the Eucharistic Sacrifice, and the theatrical trumpery of a modern fête. Many devout and well-intentioned persons, who are conscious of the insufficiency of the Protestant system, and are favourably disposed towards Catholic truth, go abroad full of expectation, and return utterly disheartened by what they have beheld, and which they attribute to the effect of Catholicism, instead of being the result of the opposite principle. Could they but have seen one of these very churches, now so disfigured, as it appeared in all its venerable grandeur during the ages of faith, how different would have been the result produced on their mind; but while the present childish and tinsel ornaments are mixed up with the most sacred rites, and bedizened dolls exhibited as representations of our blessed Lady, it is impossible for a mere observer to receive any but unfavourable impressions from the externals of religion; and to this cause may we principally attribute the very small number of conversions among the numerous travellers who anually visit Catholic countries. [Pugin's note]

[3] In the very act by which the lesser monasteries were suppressed, the great houses were declared to be without blame.

It is truly edifying to see how exactly the rule was observed in Durham Abbey, one of the richest houses in England up to the time of its suppression. The vast wealth and possessions of the monks were entirely employed in charity, hospitality, and the advancement of learning and art, while they lived in a truly monastic state, sleeping in a common dormitory, rising at midnight to matins, remaining content with one fire in winter-time, and passing their whole time in devotion and study. I have printed some interesting extracts from a scarce book called *The Antiquities of Durham,* in the Appendix, which will fully illustrate these facts. [Pugin's note]

[4] At the abbey of St. Ouen, Rouen, a sort of palace, now the Hôtel de Ville, was erected for the residence of the few monks, which resided in that famous house during the seventeenth century, who having abandoned all regular observances of the cloister, resided in separate suites of spacious apartments; and while they expended an immense sum for their own personal luxury, suffered the western end of their unrivalled church to remain in the unfinished state in which it was left before the Concordat, and which the amount they squandered away in this irregular lodging, would have amply sufficed to complete. The contrast between the abbatial church of St. Denis, near Paris, and the conventual buildings erected during the reign of Louis XIV, is painfully striking. The former is a noble specimen of monastic architecture, raised under the auspices of the illustrious Suger; the latter, a mere classic sort of barrack, undistinguishable by its architecture and arrangement from the hôtels of that period. Even the venerable abbey of Jumièges was disfigured by similar erections, which are to be found in almost all the abbatial buildings of France. At St. Wandrille, an abbey near Candebec, on the Seine, whose foundations date of the highest Christian antiquity of Normandy, the whole of the conventual buildings, with the exception of the cloisters, were reconstructed during the seventeenth century, in the worst style of French architecture; and the ancient chapter-house, which contained the tombs of *several canonized abbots,* was demolished, to be replaced by a mere modern room, while the sacred remains of the illustrious and saintly dead were treated with almost Calvinistic irreverence, and scattered among the rubbish. I have printed a full account of this proceeding in the Appendix, No. 5. It is most interesting to observe the great similarity that exists between the proceedings of modern pagans and Protestants. The Protestant canons of Durham only a few years since demolished the magnificent chapter-house of that abbey, and erected a common sitting-room, such as might be found in any ordinary inn, in its stead. Both the chapter-houses of St. Wandrille and Durham were erected under the influence of the Catholic principle; the former was demolished by degenerate monks acting under the revived pagan ideas; the latter by degenerate canons instigated by Protestant principles. [Pugin's note]

great preservatives of antiquity, when compared to either modern innovation or restoration.

Salisbury Cathedral suffered more under its pretended restoration by Bishop Barrington, than during the three preceding centuries, including the reigns of Henry VIII, Edward VI, and the rule of the usurper Cromwell. It is not unfrequently remarked how glorious these ancient churches would appear if restored to Catholic worship; and glorious indeed would they be could we but revive the old solemnity; but, owing to the long persecution and other causes, to such a low ebb are the ancient ideas and feelings fallen, that I much question the probability of finding sufficient English Catholics in any one place who would understand the real use of one of these vast piles, much better than their Protestant possessors; and supposing they had them in their possession, it is not improbable that many choir screens would be demolished, stalls removed, and after a host of other barbarous innovations, as the people could not *see the high altar through a pillar, or hear the preacher* at the extreme end of the nave, the buildings would be condemned as inconvenient and uncomfortable, and by no means comparable to the new galleried assembly rooms used for Catholic worship at the present day, and which have even been built, as if in mockery, under the very walls of our venerable cathedrals.[5] Indeed a vast change must take place in the minds of many modern Catholics, to render them really worthy of these stupendous monuments of ancient piety, and heaven forbid that they should ever be restored to *anything less than their former glory;* for who could wish to see the cathedrals, where a St. Thomas or a St. Hugh celebrated the holy mysteries in ample chasuble and solemn chaunt, disgraced by buckram vestments of last Lyons cut, a semi-pagan altar, and the theatrical quaverings of a Warwick-street choir? It is a most melancholy truth that there does not exist much sympathy of idea between a great portion of the present Catholic body in England and their glorious ancestors, and they have frequently abandoned ancient traditions to follow the tide of innovations and paltry novelties. Is there a worldly hollow expedient started by some half-fledged sect of Protestants to collect cash,—it is often adopted. Does some hideous mass of modern deformity rise under the name of a church,—it is not unfrequently preferred to an ancient and appropriate model. Nay, the holy mysteries themselves have been made a vehicle for raising temporary supplies, and their celebration has been placarded about walls as affording a musical treat to the lovers of harmony, who are admitted at so much per head. Now, although these things may pass muster in these days of charitable balls and steam excursions, Methodist Centenaries, Christian societies, York festivals, and the like, yet how do they accord with ancient Catholic practices? and what an awful state of degeneracy do they attest among those who ought to be far in advance of all others in acting upon sound principle, and avoid even the semblance of modern expedience . . . Indeed, such is the total absence of solemnity in a great portion of modern Catholic buildings in England, that I do not hesitate to say, that a few crumbling walls and prostrate arches of a religious edifice raised during the days of faith, will convey a far stronger religious impression to the mind than the actual service of half the chapels in England.

Taking, therefore, these facts into consideration, as well as the prevailing rage for paganism during the last three centuries on the Continent, I do not think the architecture of our English churches would have fared much better under a Catholic hierarchy; for, independent of the almost certain destruction of every screen in England, we might have had the lantern of Ely terminated by a miniature dome, and a Doric portico to front the nave of York.

But let no one imagine for a moment that the preservation of the choir screens and other ancient arrangements, was owing to any love or veneration for antiquity[6] on the part of the

---

[5] Hereford presents two striking examples of modern Catholic and Protestant degeneracy; the new church built close to the cathedral, is an attempt to adapt pagan architecture to Christian purposes; and although it has cost double the sum required for a Catholic parish church, it is a miserable failure. The west end of the cathedral was rebuilt a few years since by James Wyatt, of Salisbury-destroying notoriety, and at the same time a large room was erected for concerts on the site of the west cloister, under the Protestant system,—both vile burlesques of the pointed style. It is difficult to say which of these works exhibit the greatest departure from true Catholic principles.

The new Catholic church at Bury St. Edmund's, is another semi-pagan abortion. Having occasion lately to inspect the glorious remains of ancient art in that venerable town, I could not avoid remarking, that, excepting the new hotel, it was the most uncatholic looking building in the whole place. [Pugin's note]

[6] The Protestant system of turning the cathedral choirs into pewed enclosures, has undoubtedly saved the rood screens at the entrance, and which have almost disappeared in the Continental churches,

Protestant clergy. The difference between them and their Catholic cotemporaries, is precisely this: they left many of the original features standing through indifference; the latter removed them through a false idea of improvement. When Protestantism did anything *of itself,* it was ten times worse than their extravagances, since it embodied the same wretched pagan ideas, without either the scale or richness of the foreign architecture of the same period. Queen's College, Oxford; the new quadrangle of Christ's Church; Radcliffe Library; St. Paul's Cathedral, London, and many other buildings of the same class, are utter departures from Catholic architecture, and meagre imitations of Italian paganism. It is most fortunate for English architecture, that during the greatest rage for classic art, the desire for church building was nearly extinct, in consequence of Protestant ascendancy. Hence many of our finest monuments remained comparatively safe in their neglect, while all the furor for the new style was diverted into mansions, palaces, and erections for luxury and temporal splendour.

And now I cannot dismiss this subject without a few remarks on those who seem to think, that, by restoring the details and accessories of pointed architecture, they are reviving Catholic art. Not at all. *Unless the ancient arrangement be restored,* and the *true principles carried out,* all mouldings, pinnacles, tracery, and details, be they ever so well executed, are a mere disguise. It is a great profanation to deck out Protestant monstrosities in the garb of Catholic antiquity; pew and gallery fronts with tracery panels; reading-desks with canopied tops, and carved communion-tables; for however elaborate the ornaments—however costly the execution, and however correct the details may be in the abstract, unless a church be built on the ancient traditional form, it must appear a miserable failure. A follower of John Knox himself, as in the Scotch conventicle in London, may build a meeting-house with pointed windows, arches, and tolerably good detail, but these will always look like the scattered leaves of a precious volume that have been bound up by an unskilful hand, without connexion or relation to their meaning.

To apply these venerable forms to any but their real intention, is a perfect prostitution of this glorious style; a Catholic church not only requires pillars, arches, windows, screens, and niches, but it *requires them to be disposed according to a certain traditional form;* it demands a chancel set apart for sacrifice, and screened off from the people; it requires a stone altar, a sacrarium sedilia for the officiating priests, and an elevated roodloft from whence the Holy Gospel may be chaunted to the assembled faithful; it requires chapels for penance and prayer, a sacristy to contain the sacred vessels, a font for the holy sacrament of baptism, a southern porch for penitents and catechumens, a stoup for hallowed water, and a tower for bells;—and unless a building destined for a church possess all these requisites, however correctly its details may be copied from ancient authorities, it is a mere modern conventicle, and cannot by any means be accounted a revival of Catholic art.

---

during the rage for innovation which prevailed during the last three centuries: and had not this miserable expedient of filling up the deserted stalls of the ecclesiastics been adopted, instead of the congregation being kept in their original place—the nave, it is most probable that the venerable images of saints and kings that still adorn the canopied and fretted screens of York and Canterbury, would long ere this have been demolished, *to throw the view of the church open,*—the reason assigned for the removal of screens by those modern churchmen who have destroyed this mystical separation between the people and the sacrifice that had existed for ages. The learned Father Thiers has written a most admirable dissertation on the use and antiquity of these screens, in which he appropriately designates the modern innovators as Ambonoclasts, and sets forth in most powerful language and argument, the heinous offence of departing from the approved traditions of the Church in these matters. [Pugin's note]

Samuel Smiles

1812-1904

OTH THE NAME and the character of Samuel Smiles sound as though invented to provide industrious Victorian children with a model of optimistic diligence rewarded by success. But it was not only Victorian children who felt uplifted by the numerous didactic biographies and manuals of good conduct that issued from Samuel Smiles's pen. Nor were the name and character invented; they belonged to a long-lived Scottish surgeon and writer whose works have come to symbolize Victorian bourgeois respectability and morality.

Samuel Smiles was born in Haddington, Scotland, eleven years after the birth there of Jane Welsh Carlyle. He was one of eleven children. He was educated at Haddington Grammar School and at Edinburgh University, where he studied to be a doctor. Early in his medical career he published *Physical Education* (1838). He practised medicine, first in Haddington, then in Leeds. But his literary impulses soon took command, and he became the editor of the *Leeds Times* and much involved with the burgeoning railways of Victorian England. He wrote a life of George Stephenson (1857), the inventor of the locomotive, and then a series of *Lives of the Engineers* (1861–62). The typical Smiles biography showed industry and thrift rewarded by financial success.

But it is as the author of various homiletic works with revealingly pithy titles that Smiles is best remembered. His greatest success, *Self-Help,* appeared in 1859. By the time of his death it had sold over 120,000 copies. It was followed by *Character* (1871), *Thrift* (1875), *Duty* (1880), and *Life and Labour* (1887). In these works Smiles advocated the traditional middle-class virtues and also expressed the political and social views of the Manchester school of liberal economics. His works were enormously successful with earnest Victorians and frequently given as school prizes to diligent students.

In the seventies and eighties Smiles traveled extensively in Europe, but he spent his last years in Kensington, London, dying in 1904, one of the longest-lived of all the Victorians.

The historian Asa Briggs has condensed Smiles's work into a sentence by writing, "What Carlyle prophesied, Samuel Smiles turned to homilies." Smiles's works often do represent the popularization of certain Victorian high ideals, such as those of duty and self-help. He was also especially attracted to worldly success, and his biographies of great men are almost always of those who were self-made and frequently self-taught. The writings of Smiles offer an exceptionally straightforward treatment for the popular mind of certain cherished Victorian platitudes.

CHRONOLOGY

1812   Born 23 December in Haddington, Scotland.
1829   Enters Edinburgh University.
1832   Takes M.D. degree at Edinburgh.
1838   Settles at Leeds; becomes editor of *Leeds Times*.
1854   Moves to London as secretary of South Eastern Railway.
1857   *Life of George Stephenson.*
1859   *Self-Help.*
1861–62 *Lives of the Engineers.*
1904   Dies 16 April at Kensington; buried in Brompton Cemetery, London.

EDITIONS, BIOGRAPHY, CRITICISM

Autobiography, ed. Thomas Mackay (1905).
Self-Help, ed. Asa Briggs (1958).
T. Bowden Green, *Samuel Smiles: His Life and Work* (1904).
Asa Briggs, *Victorian People* (1955).
Aileen Smiles, *Life of Samuel Smiles* (1956).

---

from Self-Help

With Illustrations of Conduct and Perseverance

Smiles's popular Self-Help *first appeared in 1859. The work is divided into thirteen chapters with such titles as "Self-Help: National and Individual," "Application and Perseverance," "Energy and Courage," "Self-Culture: Facilities and Difficulties." Throughout, the main theme is teaching by example, so the book is filled with the stories of men who exhibit the qualities Smiles prizes. Two selections are offered below.*

Self-Help: National and Individual

'HEAVEN helps those who help themselves' is a well-tried maxim, embodying in a small compass the results of vast human experience. The spirit of self-help is the root of all genuine growth in the individual; and, exhibited in the lives of many, it constitutes the true source of national vigour and strength. Help from without is often enfeebling in its effects, but help from within invariably invigorates. Whatever is done *for* men or classes, to a certain extent takes away the stimulus and necessity of doing for themselves; and where men are subjected to over-guidance and over-government, the inevitable tendency is to render them comparatively helpless.

Even the best institutions can give a man no active help. Perhaps the most they can do is to leave him free to develop himself and improve his individual condition. But in all times men have been prone to believe that their happiness and well-being were to be secured by means of institutions rather than by their own conduct. Hence the value of legislation as an agent in human advancement has usually been much over-estimated. To constitute the millionth part of a Legislature, by voting for one or two men once in three or five years, however conscientiously this duty may be performed, can exercise but little active influence upon any man's life and character. Moreover, it is every day becoming more clearly understood, that the function of Government is negative and restrictive, rather than positive and active; being resolvable principally into protection—protection of life, liberty and property. Laws, wisely administered, will secure men in the enjoyment of the fruits of their labour, whether of mind or body, at a comparatively small personal sacrifice; but no laws, however stringent, can make the idle industrious, the thriftless provident, or the drunken sober. Such reforms can only be effected by means of individual action, economy, and self-denial, by better habits, rather than by greater rights.

The Government of a nation itself is usually found to be but the reflex of the individuals composing it. The Government that is ahead of the people will inevitably be dragged down to their level, as the Government that is behind them will in the long run be dragged up. In the order of nature, the collective character of a nation will as surely find its befitting results in its law and government, as water finds its own level. The noble people will be nobly ruled, and the ignorant and corrupt ignobly. Indeed, all experience serves to prove that the worth and strength of a State depend far less upon the form of its institutions than upon the character of its men. For the nation is only an aggregate of individual conditions, and civilization itself is but a question of the personal improvement of the men, women, and children of whom society is composed.

National progress is the sum of individual industry, energy, and uprightness, as national decay is of individual idleness, selfishness and vice. What we are accustomed to decry as great social evils, will, for the most part, be found to be but the outgrowth of man's own perverted life; and though we may endeavour to cut them down and extirpate them by means of Law, they will only spring up again with fresh luxuriance in some other form, unless the conditions of personal life and character are radically improved. If this view be correct, then it follows that the highest patriotism and philanthropy consist, not so much in altering laws and modifying institutions, as in helping and stimulating men to elevate and improve themselves by their own free and independent individual action.

It may be of comparatively little consequence how a man is governed from without, whilst everything depends upon how he governs himself from within. The greatest slave is not he who is ruled by a despot, great though that evil be, but he who is the thrall of his own moral ignorance, selfishness, and vice. Nations who are thus enslaved at heart cannot be freed by any mere changes of masters or of institutions; and so long as the fatal delusion prevails, that liberty solely depends upon and consists in government, so long will such changes, no matter at what cost they may be effected, have as little practical and lasting result as the shifting of the figures in a phantasmagoria. The solid foundations of liberty must rest upon individual character; which is also the only sure guarantee for social security and national progress. John Stuart Mill truly observes that 'even despotism does not produce its worst effects so long as individuality exists under it; and whatever crushes individuality *is* despotism, by whatever name it be called.'

Old fallacies as to human progress are constantly turning up. Some call for Caesars, others for Nationalities, and others for Acts of Parliament. We are to wait for Caesars, and when they are found, 'happy the people who recognize and follow them'.[1] This doctrine shortly means, everything *for* the people, nothing *by* them,—a doctrine which, if taken as a guide, must, by destroying the free conscience of a community, speedily prepare the way for any form of despotism. Caesarism is human idolatry in its worst form—a worship of mere power, as degrading in its effects as the worship of mere wealth would be. A far healthier doctrine to inculcate among the nations would be that of Self-Help; and so soon as it is thoroughly understood and carried into action, Caesarism will be no more. The two principles are directly antagonistic; and what Victor Hugo said of the Pen and the Sword alike applies to them. 'Ceci tuera cela.'[2]

The power of Nationalities and Acts of

[1] Napoleon III, *Life of Caesar*. [Smiles's note]

[2] This will kill that.

Parliament is also a prevalent superstition. What William Dargan, one of Ireland's truest patriots, said at the closing of the first Dublin Industrial Exhibition, may well be quoted now. 'To tell the truth,' he said, 'I never heard the word independence mentioned that my own country and my own fellow townsmen did not occur to my mind. I have heard a great deal about the independence that we were to get from this, that, and the other place, and of the great expectations we were to have from persons from other countries coming amongst us. Whilst I value as much as any man the great advantages that must result to us from that intercourse, I have always been deeply impressed with the feeling that our industrial independence is dependent upon ourselves. I believe that with simple industry and careful exactness in the utilization of our energies, we never had a fairer chance nor a brighter prospect than the present. We have made a step, but perseverance is the great agent of success; and if we but go on zealously, I believe in my conscience that in a short period we shall arrive at a position of equal comfort, of equal happiness, and of equal independence, with that of any other people.'

All nations have been made what they are by the thinking and the working of many generations of men. Patient and persevering labourers in all ranks and conditions of life, cultivators of the soil and explorers of the mine, inventors and discoverers, manufacturers, mechanics and artisans, poets, philosophers, and politicians, all have contributed towards the grand result, one generation building upon another's labours, and carrying them forward to still higher stages. This constant succession of noble workers—the artisans of civilization—has served to create order out of chaos in industry, science, and art; and the living race has thus, in the course of nature, become the inheritor of the rich estate provided by the skill and industry of our forefathers, which is placed in our hands to cultivate, and to hand down, not only unimpaired but improved, to our successors.

The spirit of self-help, as exhibited in the energetic action of individuals, has in all times been a marked feature in the English character, and furnishes the true measure of our power as a nation. Rising above the heads of the mass there were always to be found a series of individuals distinguished beyond others, who commanded the public homage. But our progress has also been owing to multitudes of smaller and less known men. Though only the generals' names

may be remembered in the history of any great campaign, it has been in a great measure through the individual valour and heroism of the privates that victories have been won. And life, too, is 'a soldiers' battle',—men in the ranks having in all times been amongst the greatest of workers. Many are the lives of men unwritten, which have nevertheless as powerfully influenced civilization and progress as the more fortunate Great whose names are recorded in biography. Even the humblest person, who sets before his fellows an example of industry, sobriety, and upright honesty of purpose in life, has a present as well as a future influence upon the well-being of his country; for his life and character pass unconsciously into the lives of others, and propagate good example for all time to come.

Daily experience shows that it is energetic individualism which produces the most powerful effects upon the life and action of others, and really constitutes the best practical education. Schools, academies, and colleges, give but the merest beginnings of culture in comparison with it. Far more influential is the life-education daily given in our homes, in the streets, behind counters, in workshops, at the loom and the plough, in counting-houses and manufactories, and in the bushy haunts of men. This is that finishing instruction as members of society, which Schiller designated 'the education of the human race', consisting in action, conduct, self-culture, self-control,—all that tends to discipline a man truly, and fit him for the proper performance of the duties and business of life,—a kind of education not to be learnt from books, or acquired by any amount of mere literary training. With his usual weight of words Bacon observes, that 'Studies teach not their own use; but there is a wisdom without them, and above them, won by observation'; a remark that holds true of actual life, as well as of the cultivation of the intellect itself. For all experience serves to illustrate and enforce the lesson, that a man perfects himself by work more than by reading,— that it is life rather than literature, action rather than study, and character rather than biography, which tend perpetually to renovate mankind.

Biographies of great, but especially of good men, are nevertheless most instructive and useful, as helps, guides, and incentives to others. Some of the best are almost equivalent to gospels—teaching high living, high thinking, and energetic action for their own and the world's good. The valuable examples which they furnish of the power of self-help, of patient purpose, resolute working, and steadfast integrity, issuing in the formation of truly noble and manly character, exhibit, in language not to be misunderstood, what it is in the power of each to accomplish for himself; and eloquently illustrate the efficacy of self-respect and self-reliance in enabling men of even the humblest rank to work out for themselves an honourable competency and a solid reputation.

Great men of science, literature, and art—apostles of great thoughts and lords of the great heart—have belonged to no exclusive class nor rank in life. They have come alike from colleges, workshops, and farmhouses,—from the huts of poor men and the mansions of the rich. Some of God's greatest apostles have come from 'the ranks'. The poorest have sometimes taken the highest places; nor have difficulties apparently the most insuperable proved obstacles in their way. Those very difficulties, in many instances, would ever seem to have been their best helpers, by evoking their powers of labour and endurance, and stimulating into life faculties which might otherwise have lain dormant. The instances of obstacles thus surmounted, and of triumphs thus achieved, are indeed so numerous, as almost to justify the proverb that 'with Will one can do anything'. Take, for instance, the remarkable fact, that from the barber's shop came Jeremy Taylor, the most poetical of divines; Sir Richard Arkwright, the inventor of the spinning jenny and founder of the cotton manufacture; Lord Tenterden, one of the most distinguished of Lord Chief Justices;[3] and Turner, the greatest among landscape painters.

No one knows to a certainty what Shakespeare was; but it is unquestionable that he sprang from a humble rank. His father was a butcher and grazier; and Shakespeare himself is supposed to have been in early life a woolcomber; whilst others aver that he was an usher in a school and afterwards a scrivener's clerk. He truly seems to have been 'not one, but all mankind's epitome.' For such is the accuracy of his sea phrases that a naval writer alleges that he must have been a sailor; whilst a clergyman infers, from internal evidence in his writings, that he was probably a parson's clerk; and a distinguished judge of horse-flesh insists that he must have been a horse-dealer. Shakespeare was certainly an actor, and in the course of his life 'played many parts', gathering his wonderful stores of knowledge from a wide field of experience and observation. In any event, he must have been a close student and a hard worker; and to this day his writings continue to exercise a powerful influence on the formation of English character.

Character: The True Gentleman

THE crown and glory of life is Character. It is the noblest possession of a man, constituting a rank in itself, and an estate in the general goodwill; dignifying every station, and exalting every position in society. It exercises a greater power than wealth, and secures all the honour without the jealousies of fame. It carries with it an influence which always tells; for it is the result of proved honour, rectitude, and consistency—qualities which, perhaps more than any other, command the general confidence and respect of mankind.

Character is human nature in its best form. It is moral order embodied in the individual. Men of character are not only the conscience of society, but in every well-governed State they are its best motive power; for it is moral qualities in the main which rule the world. Even in war, Napoleon said the moral is to the physical as ten to one. The strength, the industry, and the civilization of nations—all depend upon individual character; and the very foundations of civil security rest upon it. Laws and institutions are but its outgrowth. In the just balance of nature, individuals, nations, and races will obtain just so much as they deserve, and no more. And as effect finds its cause, so surely does quality of character amongst a people produce its befitting results.

Though a man have comparatively little culture, slender abilities, and but small wealth, yet, if his character be of sterling worth, he will always command an influence, whether it be in the workshop, the counting-house, the mart, or the senate. Canning wisely wrote in 1801, 'My road must be through Character to power; I will try no other course; and I am sanguine enough to believe that this course, though not perhaps

---

[3] Jeremy Taylor (1613–67), English divine and author; Richard Arkwright (1732–92), inventor; Charles Abbott, 1st Baron Tenterden (1762–1832), English lawyer and Chief Justice.

the quickest, is the surest.' You may admire men of intellect; but something more is necessary before you will trust them. Hence Lord John Russell once observed in a sentence full of truth, 'It is the nature of party in England to ask the assistance of men of genius, but to follow the guidance of men of character.' This was strikingly illustrated in the career of Francis Horner—a man of whom Sydney Smith said that the Ten Commandments were stamped upon his countenance. 'The valuable and peculiar light,' says Lord Cockburn,[1] in which his history is calculated to inspire every right-minded youth, is this. He died at the age of thirty-eight; possessed of greater public influence than any other private man; and admired, beloved, trusted, and deplored by all, except the heartless or the base. No greater homage was ever paid in Parliament to any deceased member. Now let every young man ask—how was this attained? By rank? He was the son of an Edinburgh merchant. By wealth? Neither he, nor any of his relations, ever had a superfluous sixpence. By office? He held but one, and only for a few years, of no influence, and with very little pay. By talents? His were not splendid, and he had no genius. Cautious and slow, his only ambition was to be right. By eloquence? He spoke in calm, good taste, without any of the oratory that either terrifies or seduces. By any fascination of manner? His was only correct and agreeable. By what, then, was it? Merely by sense, industry, good principles, and a good heart—qualities which no well-constituted mind need ever despair of attaining. It was the force of his character that raised him; and this character not impressed upon him by nature, but formed, out of no peculiarly fine elements, by himself. There were many in the House of Commons of far greater ability and eloquence. But no one surpassed him in the combination of an adequate portion of these with moral worth. Horner was born to show what moderate powers, unaided by anything whatever except culture and goodness, may achieve, even when these powers are displayed amidst the competition and jealousy of public life.'

Franklin, also, attributed his success as a public man, not to his talents or his powers of speaking—for these were but moderate—but to his known integrity of character. Hence it was, he says, 'that I had so much weight with my fellow-citizens. I was but a bad speaker, never eloquent, subject to much hesitation in my choice of words, hardly correct in language, and yet I generally carried my point.' Character creates confidence in men of high station as well as in humble life. It was said of the first Emperor Alexander of Russia, that his personal character was equivalent to a constitution. During the wars of the Fronde, Montaigne was the only man amongst the French gentry who kept his castle gates unbarred; and it was said of him, that his personal character was a better protection for him than a regiment of horse would have been.

That character is power, is true in a much higher sense than that knowledge is power. Mind without heart, intelligence without conduct, cleverness without goodness, are powers in their way, but they may be powers only for mischief. We may be instructed or amused by them; but it is sometimes as difficult to admire them as it would be to admire the dexterity of a pickpocket or the horsemanship of a highwayman.

Truthfulness, integrity, and goodness—qualities that hang not on any man's breath—form the essence of manly character, or, as one of our old writers has it, 'that inbred loyalty unto Virtue which can serve her without a livery'. He who possesses these qualities, united with strength of purpose, carries with him a power which is irresistible. He is strong to do good, strong to resist evil, and strong to bear up under difficulty and misfortune. When Stephen of Colonna fell into the hands of his base assailants, and they asked him in derision, 'Where is now your fortress?' 'Here', was his bold reply, placing his hand upon his heart. It is in misfortune that the character of the upright man shines forth with the greatest lustre; and when all else fails, he takes stand upon his integrity and his courage.

The rules of conduct followed by Lord Erskine[2]—a man of sterling independence of principle and scrupulous adherence to truth—are worthy of being engraven on every young man's heart. 'It was a first command and counsel of my earliest youth', he said, 'always to do what my conscience told me to be a duty, and to leave the consequence to God. I shall carry with me the memory, and I trust the practice, of this parental lesson to the grave. I have hitherto followed it, and I have no reason to complain that my obedience to it has been a temporal sacrifice. I

---

[1] Lord John Russell (1792–1878), British statesman and Prime Minister; Francis Horner (1778–1812), British economist; Sydney Smith (1771–1845), English journalist, cofounder of the *Edinburgh Review;* Henry Cockburn (1779–1854), Scottish judge.

[2] Thomas Erskine (1750–1823), Scottish statesman.

have found it, on the contrary, the road to prosperity and wealth, and I shall point out the same path to my children for their pursuit.'

Every man is bound to aim at the possession of a good character as one of the highest objects of life. The very effort to secure it by worthy means will furnish him with a motive for exertion; and his idea of manhood, in proportion as it is elevated, will steady and animate his motive. It is well to have a high standard of life, even though we may not be able altogether to realize it. 'The youth', says Mr. Disraeli, 'who does not look up will look down; and the spirit that does not soar is destined perhaps to grovel.' George Herbert wisely writes:

> Pitch thy behaviour low, thy projects high,
>   So shalt thou humble and magnanimous be.
> Sink not in spirit: who aimeth at the sky
>   Shoots higher much than he that means a tree.

He who has a high standard of living and thinking will certainly do better than he who has none at all. 'Pluck at a gown of gold', says the Scotch proverb, 'and you may get a sleeve o't.' Whoever tries for the highest results cannot fail to reach a point far in advance of that from which he started; and though the end attained may fall short of that proposed, still, the very effort to rise, of itself, cannot fail to prove permanently beneficial.

There are many counterfeits of character, but the genuine article is difficult to be mistaken. Some, knowing its money value, would assume its disguise for the purpose of imposing upon the unwary. Colonel Charteris[3] said to a man distinguished for his honesty, 'I would give a thousand pounds for your good name.' 'Why?' 'Because I could make ten thousand by it,' was the knave's reply.

Integrity in word and deed is the backbone of character; and loyal adherence to veracity its most prominent characteristic. One of the finest testimonies to the character of Sir Robert Peel[4] was that borne by the Duke of Wellington in the House of Lords, a few days after the great statesman's death. 'Your lordships', he said, 'must all feel the high and honourable character of the late Sir Robert Peel. I was long connected with him in public life. We were both in the councils of our Sovereign together, and I had long the honour to enjoy his private friendship.

In all the course of my acquaintance with him I never knew a man in whose truth and justice I had greater confidence, or in whom I saw a more invariable desire to promote the public service. In the whole course of my communication with him, I never knew an instance in which he did not show the strongest attachment to truth; and I never saw in the whole course of my life the smallest reason for suspecting that he stated anything which he did not firmly believe to be the fact.'

There is a truthfulness in action as well as in words, which is essential to uprightness of character. A man must really be what he seems or purposes to be. When an American gentleman wrote to Granville Sharp,[5] that from respect for his great virtues he had named one of his sons after him, Sharp replied: 'I must request you to teach him a favourite maxim of the family whose name you have given him—*Always endeavour to be really what you would wish to appear*. This maxim, as my father informed me, was carefully and humbly practised by *his* father, whose sincerity, as a plain and honest man, thereby became the principal feature of his character, both in public and private life.' Every man who respects himself, and values the respect of others, will carry out the maxim in act—doing honestly what he proposes to do—putting the highest character into his work, scamping nothing, but priding himself upon his integrity and conscientiousness. Once Cromwell said to Bernard—a clever but somewhat unscrupulous lawyer—'I understand that you have lately been vastly wary in your conduct; do not be too confident of this; subtlety may deceive you, integrity never will.' Men whose acts are at direct variance with their words command no respect, and what they say has but little weight; even truths, when uttered by them, seem to come blasted from their lips.

The true character acts rightly, whether in secret or in the sight of men. That boy was well trained who, when asked why he did not pocket some pears, for nobody was there to see, replied, 'Yes, there was: I was there to see myself; and I don't intend ever to see myself do a dishonest thing.' This is a simple but not inappropriate illustration of principle, or conscience, dominating in the character, and exercising a noble protectorate over it; not merely a passive influence, but an active power regulating the life. Such a

---

[3] Francis Charteris (1675–1732), noted gambler and scoundrel.
[4] Sir Robert Peel (1788–1850), English statesman and Prime Minister.
[5] Granville Sharp (1735–1813), English abolitionist.

principle goes on moulding the character hourly and daily, growing with a force that operates every movement. Without this dominating influence, character has no protection, but is constantly liable to fall away before temptation; and every such temptation succumbed to, every act of meanness or dishonesty, however slight, causes self-degradation. It matters not whether the act be successful or not, discovered or concealed; the culprit is no longer the same, but another person; and he is pursued by a secret uneasiness, by self-reproach, or the workings of what we call conscience, which is the inevitable doom of the guilty.

And here it may be observed how greatly the character may be strengthened and supported by the cultivation of good habits. Man, it has been said, is a bundle of habits; and habit is second nature. Metastasio entertained so strong an opinion as to the power of repetition in act and thought, that he said, 'All is habit in mankind, even virtue itself.' Butler,[6] in his *Analogy*, impresses the importance of careful self-discipline and firm resistance to temptation, as tending to make virtue habitual, so that at length it may become more easy to be good than to give way to sin. 'As habits belonging to the body', he says, 'are produced by external acts, so habits of the mind are produced by the execution of inward practical purposes, *i.e.* carrying them into act, or acting upon them—the principles of obedience, veracity, justice and charity.' It is a fine remark of a Russian writer, that 'Habits are a necklace of pearls: untie the knot, and the whole unthreads.'

It is indeed scarcely possible to over-estimate the importance of training the young to virtuous habits. In them they are the easiest formed, and when formed they last for life; like letters cut on the bark of a tree, they grow and widen with age. 'Train up a child in the way he should go, and when he is old he will not depart from it.' The beginning holds within it the end; the first start on the road of life determines the direction and the destination of the journey; *ce n'est que le premier pas qui coûte*.[7] 'Remember,' said Lord Collingwood[8] to a young man whom he loved, 'before you are five-and-twenty you must establish a character that will serve you all your life.' As habit strengthens with age, and character

becomes formed, any turning into a new path becomes more and more difficult. Hence, it is often harder to unlearn than to learn; and for this reason the Grecian flute-player was justified who charged double fees to those pupils who had been taught by an inferior master. To uproot an old habit is sometimes a more painful thing, and vastly more difficult, than to wrench out a tooth. Hence, as Mr. Lynch observes, 'the wisest habit of all is the habit of care in the formation of good habits'.

Even happiness itself may become habitual. There is a habit of looking at the bright side of things, and also of looking at the dark side. Dr. Johnson has said that the habit of looking at the best side of a thing is worth more to a man than a thousand pounds a year. And we possess the power, to a great extent, of so exercising the will as to direct the thoughts upon objects calculated to yield happiness and improvement rather than their opposites. In this way the habit of happy thought may be made to spring up like any other habit. And to bring up men or women with a genial nature of this sort, a good temper, and a happy frame of mind, is perhaps of even more importance, in many cases, than to perfect them in much knowledge and many accomplishments.

As daylight can be seen through very small holes, so little things will illustrate a person's character. Indeed, character consists in little acts, well and honourably performed; daily life being the quarry from which we build it up, and rough-hew the habits which form it. One of the most marked tests of character is the manner in which we conduct ourselves towards others. A graceful behaviour towards superiors, inferiors, and equals is a constant source of pleasure. It pleases others because it indicates respect for their personality; but it gives tenfold more pleasure to ourselves. Every man may to a large extent be a self-educator in good behaviour, as in everything else; he can be civil and kind, if he will, though he have not a penny in his purse. Gentleness in society is like the silent influence of light, which gives colour to all nature; it is far more powerful than loudness or force, and far more fruitful. It pushes its way quietly and persistently, like the tiniest daffodil in spring, which raises the clod and thrusts it aside by the simple persistency of growing.

---

[6] Joseph Butler (1692–1725), English divine, author of the *Analogy of Religion*.
[7] "It is not only the first step that is an effort."
[8] Cuthbert Collingwood (1750–1810), English admiral.

James Anthony Froude

1818-1894

J AMES ANTHONY FROUDE was the younger brother of the
Tractarian Richard Hurrell Froude (see selection by R. H. Froude in
this volume) and was himself for a time a supporter of Tractarian ideals,
but he gained his chief fame as an historian of England and as the
literary executor and biographer of Thomas Carlyle.

Like his brother, Froude was born at Dartington, Devon, but fifteen years
later than brother Hurrell, eight years later than the middle son William.
He was educated at Westminster School and at Oriel College, Oxford. He
became a fellow of Exeter College, Oxford, and in 1844 he took Deacon's
orders in the Church of England. He had been much under the influence of
Newman and the Tractarians in his undergraduate years, but with Newman's
secession to Rome, he moved toward skepticism. The change in view was made
public with his two thinly disguised novels, *Shadows of the Clouds* (1847, suppressed) and *The Nemesis of Faith* (1848). These cost Froude his fellowship, and
he left teaching for writing.

For several years he wrote for *Fraser's Magazine,* and the *Westminster Review.*
Later he edited *Fraser's.* He made the acquaintance of such literary lights as
Carlyle and Charles Kingsley, becoming Carlyle's disciple and ultimately his
literary executor. His frank biography of Carlyle and his handling of the
Carlyle papers caused a literary scandal that did not die down until this
century. But it is Froude's work as historian that most commanded the attention
of his contemporaries before the Carlyle controversy. He published his *History
of England,* dealing with the sixteenth century, in twelve volumes between 1856
and 1869. He was likened to Macaulay in his power of vivid portrayal and
also in his clear partisanship in historical issues. Froude clearly took the side of
Henry VIII and the emergent nationalism of sixteenth-century England over
that of the Papacy and the old religion, a position perhaps influenced by his
rejection of Tractarianism. As was to occur later with the Carlyle biography,
controversy arose over Froude's historical accuracy. Subsequent opinion has
allowed that Froude permitted his zeal to color his treatment of the facts but
that he was not maliciously inaccurate.

In the eighteen-seventies and eighties Froude traveled extensively, to
South Africa, Australia, and the West Indies, and wrote various books based
on his travels. He was appointed Regius Professor of Modern History at
Oxford in 1892. He died in 1894.

Froude's history continues to be read as a colorful panorama of sixteenth-century England from a highly partisan nineteenth-century imperialist stance. His various miscellaneous writings contain entertaining and informative essays on a wide variety of subjects of interest to the student of the Victorian age. His biography of Carlyle continues to be indispensable to the study of that literary figure.

CHRONOLOGY

1818	Born 23 April at Dartington, Devon.
1830–33	Attends Winchester School.
1835–40	Attends Oriel College, Oxford.
1844	Takes Deacon's order in Church of England.
1849	Meets Thomas Carlyle.
1856–70	*History of England.*
1860–74	Edits *Fraser's Magazine.*
1869	Elected Rector of St. Andrews University.
1874–75	Visits South Africa.
1882–84	*Life of Carlyle.*
1884–85	Visits Australia.
1886–87	Visits West Indies.
1892	Appointed Regius Professor of Modern History at Oxford.
1894	Dies 20 October at Salcombe, Devon; buried at Salcombe.

EDITIONS

History of England from the Fall of Wolsey to the Death of Elizabeth (12 vols., 1856–70); also as *History of England from the Fall of Wolsey to the Defeat of the Spanish Armada,* ed. W. L. Williams (10 vols., 1909–12).

Short Studies on Great Subjects (3 vols., 1827), ed. H. Belloc (1915), David Ogg (1967).

Thomas Carlyle (4 vols., 1881–84).

Historical and Other Sketches, ed. D. H. Wheeler (1883).

Lord Beaconsfield (1890).

Selected Essays, ed. H. G. Rawlinson (1900).

BIOGRAPHY AND CRITICISM

D. A. Wilson, *Mr. Froude and Carlyle* (1898).

Herbert Paul, *The Life of Froude* (1905).

Waldo Hilary Dunn, *Froude and Carlyle* (1930).

———, *Froude* (2 vols., 1961–63).

Basil Willey, *More Nineteenth-Century Studies* (1956).

L. M. Angus-Butterworth, *Ten Master Historians* (1961).

Words About Oxford

Froude's essay on Oxford was first published in Fraser's Magazine *in March 1850 and later collected in various editions of Froude's miscellaneous essays. In this characteristic piece from the hand of a leading Victorian man of letters one sees a view of Oxford that should be compared with that offered by Newman in his* Apologia *as an illustration of the way in which Oxford captured and held the imagination of men of all shades of opinion.*

MANY long years had passed since I visited Oxford,—some twenty-eight or more.[1] I had friends among the resident members of that venerable domicile of learning. Pleasant had been the time that I had spent there, of which intervening years had not diminished the remembrance—perhaps heightened the tone of its colouring. On many accounts I regarded that beautiful city with affectionate veneration. There were more than local attractions to render it interesting. There were the recollections of those who ceased in the interval to be denizens of this world. These could not but breathe sadness over the noble edifices that recalled men, conversations, and convivialities which, however long departed, shadowed upon the mind its own inevitable destiny. Again were those venerable buildings before me in their architectural richness. There were tower, and roof, and gateway, in all their variety of outline, defined with the sharp light and shade peculiar to ecclesiastical architecture. There were tufted groves overshadowing the haunts of learning; and there, too, was old Magdalen, which used to greet our sight so pleasantly upon our approach to the city. I began to fancy I had leaped no gulf of time since, for the Cherwell ran on as of old. I felt that the happy allusion of Quevedo to the Tiber was not out of place here, "The fugitive is alone permanent." The same river ran on as it had run on before, but the cheerful faces that had been once reflected in its stream had passed away. I saw things once familiar as I saw them before; but "the fathers, where were they?" I was in this respect like one awaked from the slumber of an age, who found himself a stranger in his own land.

I walked through High Street. I entered All Souls' and came out quickly, for the quadrangle, or rather one glance round it, was sufficient to put "the past to pain." I went over the different sites, and even paced Christ Church meadows. But I could not deceive myself for a moment. There was an indescribable vacuum somewhere that indicated there was no mode of making the past the present. What had become of the pleasant faces, the cheerful voices, the animal spirits, which seemed in my eyes to give a soul to those splendid donations of our forefathers to learning in years gone by? That instinct—soul, spirit, whatever it be—which animates and vivifies everything, and without which the palace is not comparable to the hovel possessing it,—that instinct or spirit was absent for me, at least. At length I adjourned to the Star, somewhat moody, more than half wishing I had not entered the city. I ordered my solitary meal, and began ruminating, as we all do, over the thousandth-time told tale of human destiny by generation after generation. I am not sure I did not greet with sullen pleasure a heavy, dark, dense mass of cloud that at that moment canopied the city. The mind finds all kinds of congenialities grateful at such moments. Some drops of rain fell; then a shower, tolerably heavy. I could not go out again as I intended doing. I sat and sipped my wine, thinking of the fate of cities,—of Nineveh the renowned, of the marbles lately recovered from thence with the mysterious arrow-headed characters. I thought that some future Layard might exhume the cornices of the Oxford temples. The deaths of cities were as inevitable as those of men. I felt that my missing friends had only a priority in mortality, and that the law of the Supreme existed to be obeyed without man's questionings.

But a sun-burst took place, the shower ceased, all became fresh and clear. I saw several gownsmen pass down the street, and I sallied forth again. Several who were in front of me, so full was

---

[1] Froude is here adopting a persona: he had left Oxford in 1848, only two years before this article appeared under the nom de plume of "Zeta."

I of old imaginings, I thought might be old friends whom I should recognize. How idle! I strolled to the Isis. It was all glitter and gaiety. The sun shone out warmly and covered the surface of the river with gold. Numerous skiffs of the university-men were alive on the water, realizing the lines,—

"Some lightly o'er the current swim,
Some show their gaily gilded trim
Quick glancing to the sun."

Here was the repetition of an old performance, but the actors were new. I too had once floated over that glittering water, or lain up by the bank in conversation, or reciting verses, or, perhaps, in that silent, dreamy vacancy, in which the mind ruminates or rests folded up within itself in the consciousness of its own immortality.

Here I must place a word or two in regard to the censures cast upon this magnificent foundation of learning relative to the extravangances of young collegians. Let it be granted, as it is asserted by some, that there is too much exclusiveness, and that there are improvements to be recommended in some of the details of an organization so ancient. It may be true to a certain extent, for what under heaven is perfect? But a vast mass of good is to be brought to bear on the other hand. I cannot, therefore, agree in those censures which journalism has cast upon the officers of the university, as if they encouraged, or, at all events, did not control, the vicious extravagance of young men. I am expressing only an individual opinion, it is true; and this may be a reason why it may be undervalued, when the justice of a question is not the criterion by which it is judged. All that such a foundation can be expected to do is to render the advantages of learning as accessible as possible, upon reasonable terms, that genius, not wealth alone, may be able to avail itself of its advantages. If the present sum be too high, let its reduction be considered with a view to any practicable change. The pecuniary resources of the collegian it becomes no part of the duty of the university to control, beyond the demands necessary for the main object of instruction. As the circumstances of parents vary, so will the pecuniary allowance made to their offspring. It would be a task neither practicable nor justifiable for the university to regulate the outlay of the collegian, or, in fact, become the paymaster of his *menus plaisirs*.[2] Only let such a task be imagined in its enormity

of control, from the son of the nobleman with an allowance of a thousand a year to one of a hundred and fifty pounds. It is not in the college, but prior to the arrival there of the youth, that he should be instructed in the views his relations have in sending him, and be taught that he must not ape the outlay and show of those who have larger means. If a youth orders a dozen coats within a time for which one only would be found adequate, I do not see what his college has to do with it. Youths entering the navy and army are left in a much more extended field of temptation. No time-hallowed walls shelter them. No salutary college rules remind them of their moral duties, daily and almost hourly. They go up and down the world under their own guardianship, exposed to every sinister influence, and with inclinations only restrained by their own monitorship. The college discipline, even if it extend not beyond college duties, is a perpetual remembrancer of the high moral end for which the student is placed within its precincts. His only allurement to extravagance is the desire of vying with those who make a greater display than himself, or else it arises from, if possible, a less defensible motive, namely, that of becoming himself an object of emulation to others. It is not the duty of the college authorities to compensate by their watchfulness the effects of a weak understanding, or that lax principle, or the want of self-command, of which the neglect of the parent or guardian has been the cause. If the freshman is destitute of self-dependence and self-restraint he must suffer from the consequences. Not only in the navy and army is youth exposed to temptations very far beyond the collegian, but in the inns of court young men are left to take care of themselves, in the midst of a great capital, without any surveillance whatever. From these youths arise excellent men of business. Most assuredly under the surveillance of a college in smaller cities, and where many heads of expense are from the nature of their position wholly out of the question, it does seem singular that such complaints should arise. It is true, display is the vice of modern society among the old as well as the young, and in both cases most dishonest means are had recourse to to sustain those appearances, which are all the world looks to. It is possible, therefore, that little efforts have been made to initiate youth, prior to entering the universities, in that path of self-denial and high-mindedness which are the safeguard from vicious prodigality. They

---

[2] Pocket money.

bring with them the vices of their caste, whatever that caste may be. Youth is imitative, and seldom a clumsy copyist, of the faults of its elders, provided those faults are fashionable faults, however unprincipled. However this may be, I must protest against the universities being made answerable for these doings. Attempts have been made, and failed, in respect to manners and to credit; and have failed clearly because they were impracticable, and, more than that, better left alone. The university ought not to be answerable in such cases, any more than the benchers for the Temple students. It cannot be expected that the noble quadrangles of our colleges are to become something like poor-law prisons, and the regulations of the night be extended over the day. The very existence of the collegian, as such, implies something like freedom, both mental and bodily. Learning that is converted into a tyranny will never bring forth good fruit. It is the duty of parents and schoolmasters to impress upon the mind of youth that a seat of learning is the home of an easy frugality rather than of prodigal rivalry; that the university will only give degrees and honours where there is industry and good moral conduct. It is to be feared that youth, quitting the discipline of the school, looks upon the university as the place where he may indulge in his own wayward will, and be as idle and indolent as he please. If this be the case the university is not to blame for such lapses, but a bad prior apprehension of duty, and a defective, ill-directed education.

It is impossible to read the biographies of some of our most celebrated men, and not to see that with means scanty enough they were enabled to keep their terms with honour, and in the end confer additional celebrity upon the noble foundations where they had studied. If such be the case, we have only the result of personal good or ill conduct to explain the whole of the affair. But enough on this subject.

But it is not the venerable appearance of University College, hallowed by the associations of so many centuries in age, nor Queen's opposite, nor All Souls', nor any other of the colleges as mere buildings, that so connect them with our feelings. We must turn the mind from stone and wood to the humanity in connection with them. It is that which casts over them the "religious light," speaking so sadly and sweetly to the heart. In University College we see the glorious name of Alfred, and nearly a thousand years,

with their perished annals, point to it as the witness of their departed successions. Who on seeing New College does not recall William of Wykeham? and then, what a roll of proud names own this renowned university for their *Alma Mater*. The very stones "prate of the whereabout" of things connected with the development of great minds, and while we look without fatigue at the gorgeous mass of buildings in this university, we feel we are contemplating what carries an intimate connexion, in object at least, with that all of man which marches in the track of eternity. It is not mere antiquity, therefore, on which our reverence for a great seminary of learning is founded. Priority of existence has no solid claims to our regard, except for that *verde antique*[3] which covers it, as it covers all things past, good or indifferent; it is the connexion of the foundation with the history of man—with the names that, like the flowers called "immortals," bloom amid the wrecks and desolateness with which the flood of ages strew the rearway of humankind.

Of late there has been small response to feelings such as these in the great world, for we have not been looking much toward what is above us, nor discriminating from meaner things those which approach to heroic natures. We must abandon Mammon, politics, and polemics, when we would approach the threshold of elevated meditation—when we dwell on the illustrious names of the past, and tread over the stones which they trod. I never wandered along the banks of the sedgy Cam, at that lone, twilight hour, when the dimness of external objects tends most to concentrate the faculties upon the immediate object of contemplation, but I have fancied the shades of Bacon, Milton, or Locke, to be near me, as the Indian fancies the shades of his fathers haunt the old hunting-grounds of his race. I know that these are heterodox feelings in the present day. I know that he who speaks of Homer or Milton, for example, is continually answered by the question, "Who reads them now?" The truth being, perhaps, that we are getting too far below them to relish their superior standard in sterling merit. But there are still in our universities, if not elsewhere, some who are content to be the last of the Goths in the estimation of the multitude, who cannot see the Isis, or Cherwell, or the reedy Cam, without feelings of which the crowd knows nothing; who can dream away an hour in the avenue of Christ Church, and almost conjure spirits from the depths of the

[3] Ancient green.

grave to realize the pictures of imagination, which are there always invested with purity and holiness, so much do external things impress their character on our imaginings. This is the true poetry of life, neither found in the haunts of fashion, nor among the denizens of Cornhill or St. Giles'. The good and deep things of the mind, the search into the secrets of nature, the sublimest truth, the purest philosophy of which man has to boast, has proceeded from those who were inhabitants of such seats of learning. It is impossible to state the precise amount of assistance which genius and learning may derive from the ease and peace enjoyed in such a university. They are inestimable to the student from association, tranquillity, and convenience. The very "dim religious light" of college rooms are solicitations to reflection. Then there are the conveniences of first-rate professors, and access to the writings of the learned in all ages. Thus some who professed a distaste for a university life, have returned to it again, and made it the arena where they have conquered a lasting reputation—such, for example, was the case with Gray the poet.

The increase of knowledge, and consequently of morality, is the great aim of such a noble establishment as this; and the rewards and honours dispensed there are bestowed in proportion to the industry and good conduct of those who receive them. If the offences of freshmen outside the walls be unvisited by the university from wariness in the offenders, or the impossibility of controlling them, they are certain to meet with a just estimation of their demerit here; and, as before noticed, this is perhaps the best mode of repressing them. The assistance derived by the industrious student from the university itself is invaluable. The very locality is an aid to progress. Where can there be places more favourable for thought than those noble buildings, ancient halls, and delightful walks? Everything invites to contemplation. Magdalen always seemed to me as if soliciting the student's presence in a peculiar manner. A favourite resort of mine, at certain times, was the road passing the Observatory, leading to Woodstock. But of all the college walks, those of Magdalen were the more impressive and attractive. It appeared to embody the whole of the noble city in its own personification, as a single word will sometimes express the pith of an entire sentence. The "Mighty Tom" in the olden time, even of Walter de Mapes,[4] if its metal was then out of the ore, never sounded

(then perhaps not nine) but the midnight hour, to that worthy archdeacon, with more of the character of its locality, than the visual aspect of Magdalen represents the beautiful city to one in its entirety. It seems a sort of metonymy; Maudlin put for Oxford. The walk is, after all, but a sober path, worthy by association with one of the walks of Eden. Yet it shows no gay foliage, nor "shade above shade a woody theatre," such as is seen on a mountain declivity. It is a simple shadowy walk—shadowy to richness, cool, tranquil, redolent of freshness. There the soul feels "private, inactive, clam, contemplative," linked to things that were and are not. The mellow hue of time, not yet stricken by decay, clothes the buildings of this college, which, compared with other edifices more steeped in maturity of years, occupies, as it were, a middle term in existence.

The variety of building in this city is amazing, and would occupy a very considerable time to study even imperfectly. At a little distance no place impresses the mind more justly with its own lofty pretensions. The towers, steeples, and domes, rising over the masses of foliage beneath, which conceal the bodies of the edifices, seen at the break of morning or at sunset, appear in great beauty. Bathed in light, although not the "alabaster tipped with golden spires" of the poet, for even the climate of Oxford is no exception to the defacement of nature's colouring, everywhere that coal smoke ascends; but the *tout ensemble* is truly poetical and magnificent.

Oriel still, they say, maintains its precedency of teaching its students how to conduct themselves with a view to university honours, and to the world's respect. The preliminary examinations there have proved a touchstone of merit, and elevated Oriel College into something near the envy of every other in this country. Worthy Oriel, the star of Oxford. "I don't know how it is," said the Rev. C. C., walking down High Street one day, "but Oriel College is all I envy Oxford. It is the richest gem in the ephod of the high-priest (vice-chancellor) of this university. I should like to steal and transplant it to my *Alma Mater* among the fens."[5]

There was formerly a Welsh harper in Oxford, whom the collegians sometimes denominated King David. He was the first of the Cymri brotherhood I ever heard perform. Since that distant day I have often heard those minstrels in their native land, particularly in North Wales, at Bedd Gelert, Caernarvon, and other places, but I

---

[4] Walter Map or Mapes (c. 1137–1209), Welsh poet.   [5] I.e., to Cambridge.

confess I never was so much struck as by this Oxford harper. He often played at the Angel, where the university men used to group round him, for he excited general admiration. His music was not of so plaintive a character as that in his own land, or else the scenery of the latter had some effect in saddening the music there through association—perhaps this difference was, after all, only in fancy.

Christchurch, the noblest of the churches! How have I heard with delight its merry peal of bells, and the deep resonance of the "Mighty Tom," that sounds with no "friendly voice" the call home of the students still, I presume, as it did so many years ago! There is a long list of names, of no mean reputation, educated here, since the rapacious Henry VIII. seized the foundations, which had belonged to Cardinal Wolsey. The gratitude of posterity, never very strong, has in the present case preserved the remembrance of Wolsey, if I recollect aright, by a statue of the proud man in his cardinal's robes. The grove of trees belonging to Christchurch, and the scenery accompanying the entire buildings, are eminently impressive. Here, when divine service is celebrating, there is a peculiar propriety, or rather adaptation of the architecture to the feeling; the trees, and every accompaniment, are suitable to the end. There is religion or its sentiment addressing the mind here through every sense. All that can raise devotion in external appliances, combines in a wonderful manner; and when the sound of the organ is reverberated deeply along the vaulted roofs and walls, the effect was indescribably fine. Christchurch walk or meadow is an adjunct to this college, such as few places possess. I have trod it with those who will never tread it again. I have skimmed over its smooth shaven surface when life seemed a vista of unmeasured years. Its very beauty touches upon a melancholy chord, since it vibrates the sound of time passed away with those who lie in dust in distant climates, of whom memory alone is now the only record that they were and are not.

I remember being told by an eminent, but aged doctor in divinity, who had been the better part of his life employed in the education of youth, that he had kept an account of the history of all his pupils as far as he could obtain it, and they were very numerous. From his own tuition—and there were some celebrated names amongst them—he traced them to the university, or to professions of a more active nature than a sojourn at the university would allow. To Oxford he had sent the larger number of his pupils. "And

afterwards, doctor?" "Some came off nobly there; others I heard of in distant parts of the globe in their country's service: but it is the common tale with nearly all of them—they are dead." What hosts, I often thought, who had moved among the deep shades of this university until it became entwined with their earliest affections—who had studied within those embattled walls until the sight of them became almost a part of his existence—what hosts of such have but served to swell the waters of oblivion, and press the associations of a common mortality upon the mind in the reflection on this very truism! The late Sir Egerton Brydges—a writer whose talents, though admitted, were never received as they merited to have been by the world, owing, perhaps, to an untoward disposition in other respects—was of opinion that the calmness and seclusion of a university were not best adapted for calling forth the efforts of genius; but that adversity and some struggling were necessary to bring out greatness of character. He thought that praise enervated the mind, and that to bear it required a much greater degree of fortitude than to withstand censure. The consequence of this would be, that the honours decreed in a university must be pernicious to youth. This cannot be conceded. Sir Egerton's notion may be just in relation to himself, or to one or two temperaments irregularly constituted; but a university exists not for the exceptions, but for the many. How numerous is the list of those who, but for the fostering care of Oxford or Cambridge, would have never been known as the ornament and delight of their fellow-men! How much more numerous is the list of those, whose abilities not rising beyond the circle of social usefulness have lived "obscure to fame," yet owe the pleasure they imparted to their friends, and the beguilement of many troubles inseparable from mortality, to the fruits of their university studies, and to a partial unrolling before them of that map of knowledge, which before those of loftier claims and some hold upon fame had been more amply displayed! In this view of the matter, the justness of which cannot be contested, the utility of such foundations is boundless. The effect upon the social body—I do not speak of polemics, but of the sound instruction thus made available—cannot be estimated. In the midst of fluctuating systems of instruction, it is something to have a standard by which to test the measure of knowledge imparted to youth. If accused of being restricted in variety of knowledge, the perfection and mastery in what is taught must be conceded to Oxford and Cambridge. Perhaps there is too much reason to fear, that without these foundations we should speedily fall into a very superficial knowledge, indeed, of the classical languages of antiquity. This would be to exclude ourselves from an acquaintance with all past time, except in monkish fiction and the feudal barbarism of the Goths of the north.

There are, I verily believe, or I should rather say there were, imbibed at the university so many attachments at one time to words in place of things, that the collegian in after life became liable to reproach upon this head. Pedants are bred everywhere out of literature, and the variety in verbiage once exhibited by some university men has been justly condemned. But while such word-worms were crawling here and there out of the porches of our colleges, giants in acquirement were striding over them in their petty convolutions. Their intertwinings attracted the attention of the mere gazer, who is always more stricken with any microcosmic object that comes casually in the way and is embraced at a glance, than with objects the magnitude of which demand repeated examinations. But all this while the great and glorious spring of knowledge was unpolluted. The reign of mere verbiage passed away; the benefits of the universities had never ceased to be imparted the whole time. The key to the better stores of knowledge was placed in the hands of every one who chose to avail himself of its advantages. The minds of the collegians were filled with an affection for the works of the writers of antiquity, which have been the guide, solace, and pleasure of the greatest and most accomplished men since the Christian era commenced. Studies will teach their own use in after life "by the wisdom that is about them and above them, won by observation," as a great writer observes; but then there *must be* the studies.

There seems of late years much less of that feeling for poetry than once existed; the same may be observed in respect to classical learning. Few now regard how perished nations lived and passed away,—how men thought, acted, and were moved, for example, in the time of Pericles or the Roman Augustus. What are they to us? What is blind Meonides to us, or that Roman who wrote odes so beautifully—who understood so well the philosophy of life and the poetry of life at the spring of Bardusia? In the past generation, a part of the adolescent being and of manhood extended a kindly feeling towards them. We hear no admiration of those immortal strains now. We must turn for them to our universities. People are getting shy of them, as rich men shirk poor friends. Are we in the declining state, that of "mechanical arts and merchandize," to use Lord Bacon's phrase, and is our middle age of learning past? Even then, thank Heaven, we have our universities still, where we may, for a time at least, enter and converse with the spirits of the good, that "sit in the clouds and mock" the rest of the greedy world. They will last our time—glorious mementos of the anxiety of our forefathers for the preservation of learning; hallowed by grateful recollections, by time, renown, virtue, conquests over ignorance, imperishable gratitude, a proud roll of mighty names in their sons, and the prospect of continuing to be monuments of glory to unborn generations. Long may Oxford and Cambridge stand and brighten with years, though to some they may not, as they do to me, exhibit a title to the gratitude and admiration of Old England, to which it would be difficult to point out worthy rivals.

John Ruskin

1819-1900

IF ONE HAD to choose a single Victorian prose writer whose works embodied all the variety, and all the contradictions, of Victorianism, that writer would surely be John Ruskin. An art critic who turned to social reforming, an evangelical who "unconverted" but remained convinced of the religious basis of culture, a "Tory of the old school" (to use his own words) who became a kind of Christian socialist, Ruskin is the most protean of the prose writers of the age.

Ruskin's life is as interesting and as problematical as any of his works, and it has beguiled many a student of the age away from those works. Ruskin was an only child of first cousins, John James and Margaret Ruskin, who reared him with considerable severity in such matters as playthings and companions (he had none of either), and with intense Evangelical zeal, but who at the same time provided him with frequent trips around the country and abroad in connection with his father's wine business, a partnership with the Domecq family. Before entering the university Ruskin was educated at home through wide reading, including memorization for his mother of vast stretches of the Bible, frequent tours of art galleries and private collections, and even private tutoring in art.

When he was seventeen Ruskin fell in love with Adèle Domecq, daughter of his father's partner, but his affection was not returned. In 1837 he entered Christ Church, Oxford. His father's hopes for an ecclesiastical career for his son were not to be realized. Ruskin's schooling at Oxford remained somewhat desultory, partly perhaps because his mother took up residence in Oxford with him in order to supervise his health and conduct. Although he gained some distinction at the university, winning the Newdigate prize for poetry in 1839, he frequently interrupted his education for tours with his parents. In 1840 he went abroad for his health, traveling with his parents.

It was in 1840 that Ruskin met the great landscape painter J. M. W. Turner and conceived the idea of restoring Turner's damaged reputation. In the following year he made the acquaintance of Euphemia Chalmers Gray whose parents were old friends of the senior Ruskins. For her he wrote the popular fairy tale *The King of the Golden River*. He returned to Oxford and took his degree in 1842, then toured the Continent with his parents. Until this time the Ruskins had lived at Herne Hill near Dulwich outside London. In 1842 they moved to Denmark Hill, a more fashionable suburb.

Ruskin published the first volume of *Modern Painters* in 1843. It was begun as a defense of Turner, but subsequent volumes were to include a much larger field. Frequently interrupted for work on other projects, *Modern Painters* was not completed until 1860. Although the response to the first volume of *Modern Painters* was mixed, the reading public proved enthusiastic, for it seemed to make art comprehensible to the layman and it firmly linked art to morality. For the next several years Ruskin toured the Continent, at times alone, at times with his parents. He made a deep study of Italian art and important advances in his recognition of the virtues of Gothic art.

Following arrangements by both sets of parents, Ruskin was married to Euphemia (Effie) Gray on 10 April 1848. Although at first they toured happily together—Ruskin lionized as the great writer, Effie as a great social success—the marriage was in the long run a failure. By 1853 Effie had encountered the painter John Everett Millais and these two embarked on a romance that was to end in the following year with the dissolution of Ruskin's marriage and the subsequent marriage of Effie to Millais. The grounds for annulment were nonconsummation of the marriage, a matter that caused no little gossip at the time and that has provided fuel for much of the subsequent biographical speculations about Ruskin.

Despite the disintegration of the Ruskin marriage in the early fifties, Ruskin's literary industry never flagged. He interrupted *Modern Painters* for the research that issued in *The Seven Lamps of Architecture* (1849) and the three volumes of his extraordinary *Stones of Venice* (1851–53). In the second half of the same decade he completed Volumes III, IV, and V of *Modern Painters* (1856–60), the *Elements of Drawing* (1856), and the *Political Economy of Art* (1857). In 1858 in a chapel in Turin he underwent a spiritual "unconversion" away from his early evangelicalism.

By the beginning of the eighteen-sixties Ruskin's interests had turned sharply to social and economic questions. The germ of such interest had been clear in his earlier works on art and architecture, especially the *Stones of Venice* in which Ruskin examined the relationship between the architecture and the religious and cultural fabric of society. After the success of the first volume of this work he had met Carlyle, whom he revered as a thinker and social critic, and such earnest reformers as F. D. Maurice, and he had begun lecturing at Maurice's Working Man's College. By 1860 Ruskin turned his longtime interest in economics directly to account in his *Unto This Last*, a bitter attack on the contemporary economic system. Thackeray had accepted the series for the *Cornhill Magazine,* but felt compelled to cut it short when it met with such an unfavorable response from the public. Something of the same sort occurred with the essays later known as *Munera Pulveris*. These appeared in part in 1862–63 in *Fraser's* under the editorship of James Anthony Froude, but had to be discontinued owing to the public outcry.

With his turn to social reform Ruskin saw his own popularity decrease. As an art critic he had gained enormous prestige with the Victorian public. His favorable word was a seal of approval. He used it not only in the defense of Turner (a defense Turner himself was not sure he was in need of), but later in 1851 in defense of the Pre-Raphaelites, thus forging another link between his ideas and those of the later Aesthetic Movement. But when Ruskin sought to transfer that prestige to questions of political economy, as the Victorians called economics, he found it not transferable. He was still listened to and still honored as an art critic, but he was not heeded as a social critic, and he began to develop the sense of frustration common to such Victorian prophets as his master Carlyle. Some of his doctrines later bore fruit, however, in the ideas of the British Labour Party.

Ruskin's father died in 1864, a loss he greatly mourned, but one that seemed to release him for more frenzied activity. He delivered the lectures that became *Sesame and Lilies,* published *Ethics of the Dust* and the *Crown of Wild Olive,* all based on lectures delivered to various groups, not infrequently to young ladies. By 1865 Ruskin's health, physical and mental, was beginning to fail him, though there are indications that his mental instability was of long standing. As early as 1858 he had met Rose La Touche, then ten years old, when her mother engaged Ruskin as an art tutor for her daughter. Ruskin fell hopelessly in love with the young child and by 1866, despite the thirty years difference in their ages, he had proposed marriage. The proposal was rejected, partly on religious grounds, for Rose was intensely devout, and for a period of time Ruskin was prevented from communicating with Rose at all. The affair heightened Ruskin's mental disturbance and contributed to his obsession with rose imagery in his writings.

By the eighteen-seventies Ruskin's mental health was seriously weakening, and he suffered from spells of deep melancholy. He had accepted the post of the first Slade Professor of Art at Oxford in 1869 and gave his first lectures in 1870; he also began the series of letters later published as *Fors Clavigera.* But at the same time his religious faith was weakening in a repeat of doubts earlier experienced, and he greatly mourned the death in 1870 of his mother, despite the fact that she had continued to govern his domestic life with a firm hand until almost the end of her long life. Also in 1870 Ruskin bought Brantwood on Coniston Lake near the Lake District. It was to be his home for the rest of his life.

Even in the troubled decade of the seventies Ruskin did not cease to publish widely, or to tour frequently on the Continent, or to engage in numerous social ventures, such as the Guild of St. George (1871), an unsuccessful cooperative to which he gave great sums of money. But in 1875 Rose La Touche died, after years of great mental distress, and Ruskin began suffering from psychological disturbances that were usually referred to as attacks of mania. He resigned the Slade Professorship to which he had been reelected in 1876, but he accepted reelection again in 1883, even though a second mental attack had intervened in 1881.

Up to about 1885 Ruskin continued his vigorous course of public lectures, foreign tours, and indefatigable writing. The writing included his brooding and prophetic *Storm-Cloud of the Nineteenth Century* (1884), *The Bible of Amiens* (1885), and the beginning of his hauntingly beautiful autobiography *Præterita.* This last work he undertook in 1885, but he suffered yet another mental breakdown in July of that year and was obliged to resign the Slade Professorship and reduce his public commitments. His last public attack occurred in Paris in 1888, and following it he was taken to Brantwood. There, in the care of his cousin, Joan Severn, he continued to write at *Præterita* in his infrequent spells of sanity until 1889, after which the lucid periods became too infrequent to count. He lived on in this twilight for more than a decade and died of influenza in 1900.

Ruskin's extraordinary career can be described as moving in stages, from a consideration of art, to architecture, to economics and society, to a final inward turning on the self. But it is important to stress that such a movement is not a series of isolated, changing interests, but rather an unfolding of interrelated interests that modify and enrich each other. At the time of his greatest concern for art and architecture Ruskin was also deeply involved in the question of the relation of art to society; and at the time of his most unremitting concern for social and economic questions, Ruskin held forth the idea of the need for art to be part of life and part of the genuine expression of the work of the humblest laborer. His multiple interests were to make Ruskin an influence on such varied fields as art criticism, social theory, the Aesthetic Movement, and the arts and crafts movement.

As a writer Ruskin has long been noted for his superb power at word painting. His prose on art and architecture was and is prized for the passages of brilliant description that rival in words the works of visual art that he was concerned to exalt. Ruskin himself regretted that the response to his works was sometimes a response merely to the literary beauties of his brilliant descriptive passages. His writing after 1860 tends to be deliberately less pictorial, but his literary gifts were so insistent and various that his writings on political economy and society have a power and a beauty all their own. And in his final work, *Præterita,* the command of the visual through words is as poignantly manifest as it is in any of his early works. Some of Ruskin's verbal skill can be traced to his close attention to the visual arts (he was himself a gifted amateur sketcher and painter), some to his rigorous childhood schooling in the rhythms and sonorities of the King James Bible, and some to his wide reading and equally wide lecturing. From these and other sources and his own native genius Ruskin created one of the greatest prose styles in all English literature.

One of the characteristic Victorian insights, promulgated most powerfully by Carlyle, but deriving from Coleridge and the Romantic movement, was the awareness of the interrelatedness of all life, an awareness made the more keen by the progressive alienation of man from his environment, and of social classes from each other. No writer of any genre expresses and exemplifies this awareness more vividly than does Ruskin. His works are a microcosm (given their extent, some would say a macrocosm) of Victorian interests in art, morality, society, literature, religion, culture, economics, and the role of the self in the nineteenth century. That they are riddled with contradictions and dogmatisms, with interminable digressions and impenetrable obscurities, cannot be denied. But in their bulk and power they convey as movingly as the work of anyone in the age what it meant to be alive and concerned with life in Victorian England.

CHRONOLOGY

1819   Born 8 February in London.
1823   Takes first of many tours with parents.
1836   Falls in love with Adèle Domecq.
1837–42   Attends Christ Church, Oxford.
1843–46   *Modern Painters,* I and II.
1848   Marries Euphemia Chalmers Gray.
1849   *The Seven Lamps of Architecture.*

1851–53   *The Stones of Venice.*
1854   Marriage annulled.
1856–60   *Modern Painters,* III, IV, and V.
1858   Meets Rose La Touche; spiritual crisis in Turin.
1860   *Unto This Last.*
1864   Father dies.
1865–66   *Sesame and Lilies; Ethics of the Dust; Crown of Wild Olive.*
1867   *Time and Tide.*
1869   *The Queen of the Air;* appointed Slade Professor of Fine Art.
1870   Mother dies.
1871   Forms Guild of St. George.
1871–84   *Fors Clavigera.*
1872   *The Eagle's Nest.*
1875   Death of Rose La Touche.
1878   Mental breakdown; resigns Slade Professorship.
1883   Reelected Slade Professor.
1884   *The Storm-Cloud of the Nineteenth Century.*
1885   Resigns Slade Professorship; begins *Præterita.*
1888   Experiences severe mental attack; taken to Brantwood.
1900   Dies 20 January; buried in Coniston Churchyard.

EDITIONS

The Works of John Ruskin, Library Edition, ed. E. T. Cook and A. Wedderburn (39 vols., 1903–13) [The standard edition].
Art Criticism of John Ruskin, ed. Robert L. Herbert (1964).
The Genius of John Ruskin, ed. John Rosenberg (1963).
The Lamp of Beauty: Writings on Art by John Ruskin, ed. Joan Evans (1958).
The Literary Criticism of John Ruskin, ed. Harold Bloom (1965).
Præterita, ed. Kenneth Clark (1949).
Ruskin Today, ed. Kenneth Clark (1964).
Selected Writings of John Ruskin, ed. Peter Quennell (1952).
The Stones of Venice, ed. and abrgd. J. G. Lincks (1960).
Unto This Last, ed. John L. Bradley (1967).

BIOGRAPHY AND CRITICISM

Edward Alexander, *Matthew Arnold, John Ruskin and The Modern Temper* (1973)
Quentin Bell, *Ruskin* (1963).
J. L. Bradley, *An Introduction to John Ruskin* (1971).
W. G. Collingwood, *The Life and Work of John Ruskin* (1893, 1900).
E. T. Cook, *The Life of John Ruskin* (2 vols., 1911).
Joan Evans, *John Ruskin* (1954).
John T. Fain, *Ruskin and the Economists* (1956).
Luke Hermann, *Ruskin and Turner* (1969).
John A. Hobson, *John Ruskin: Social Reformer* (1898).
Graham Hough, *The Last Romantics* (1949).
Henry Ladd, *The Victorian Morality of Art* (1932).
George Landow, *The Aesthetic and Critical Theories of John Ruskin* (1971).
Derrick Leon, *Ruskin, The Great Victorian* (1949).
Benjamin E. Lippincott, *Victorian Critics of Democracy* (1938).

Peter Quennell, *John Ruskin, Portrait of a Prophet* (1949).

John D. Rosenberg, *The Darkening Glass* (1961).

James Clark Sherburne, *John Ruskin, or the Ambiguities of Abundance* (1972).

Roger B. Stein, *John Ruskin and Aesthetic Thought in America* (1967).

Francis G. Townsend, "John Ruskin," in *Victorian Prose: A Guide to Research* (1973).

Helen Gill Viljoen, *Ruskin's Scottish Heritage: A Prelude* (1956).

R. H. Wilenski, *John Ruskin* (1933).

---

from Modern Painters

The five volumes of Modern Painters, *published intermittently and with interruptions for other works between 1843 and 1860, contain such a wealth of observations on art and on the multitude of subjects Ruskin found related to art that the volumes by themselves constitute a storehouse of Ruskinian lore and insights. The selections below represent a small sampling of Ruskin's remarks on subjects ranging from Turner to the celebrated chapter on the Grand Style.*

FROM VOLUME I

General Remarks Respecting the Truth of Turner

WE HAVE now arrived at some general conception of the extent of Turner's knowledge, and the truth of his practice, by the deliberate examination of the characteristics of the four great elements of landscape,—sky, earth, water, and vegetation. I have not thought it necessary to devote a chapter to architecture, because enough has been said on this subject in Part II. Sec. I. Chap. VII.; and its general truths, which are those with which the landscape painter, as such, is chiefly concerned, require only a simple and straightforward application of those rules of which every other material object of a landscape has required a most difficult and complicated application. Turner's knowledge of perspective probably adds to his power in the arrangement of every order of subject; but ignorance on this head is rather disgraceful than knowledge

meritorious. It is disgraceful, for instance, that any man should commit such palpable and atrocious errors in ordinary perspective as are seen in the quay in Claude's[1] sea-piece, No. 14 National Gallery, or in the curved portico of No. 30; but still these are not points to be taken into consideration as having anything to do with artistical rank, just as, though we should say it was disgraceful if a great poet could not spell, we should not consider such a defect as in any way taking from his poetical rank. Neither is there anything particularly belonging to architecture, as such, which it is any credit to an artist to observe or represent; it is only a simple and clear field for the manifestation of his knowledge of general laws. Any surveyor or engineer could have drawn the steps and balustrade in the Hero and Leander, as well as Turner has; but there is no man living but himself who could have thrown the accidental shadows upon them. I may, however, refer, for general illustration of Turner's power as an architectural draughtsman, to the front of Rouen Cathedral, engraved in the Rivers of France, and to the Ely in the England. I know nothing in art which can be set beside the former of these for overwhelming grandeur

---

[1] Claude Lorraine (1600–1682), French landscape painter.

and simplicity of effect, and inexhaustible intricacy of parts. I have then only a few remarks farther to offer respecting the general character of all those truths which we have been hitherto endeavouring to explain and illustrate.

The difference in accuracy between the lines of the Torso of the Vatican (the "Master" of M. Angelo)[2] and those in one of M. Angelo's finest works, could perhaps scarcely be appreciated by any eye or feeling undisciplined by the most perfect and practical anatomical knowledge. It rests on points of so traceless and refined delicacy, that though we feel them in the result, we cannot follow them in the details. Yet they are such and so great as to place the Torso alone in art, solitary and supreme; while the finest of M. Angelo's works, considered with respect to truth alone, are said to be only on a level with antiques of the second class, under the Apollo and Venus, that is, two classes or grades below the Torso. But suppose the best sculptor in the world, possessing the most entire appreciation of the excellence of the Torso, were to sit down, pen in hand, to try and tell us wherein the peculiar truth of each line consisted. Could any words that he could use make us feel the hair's-breadth of depth and curve on which all depends; or end in anything more than bare assertions of the inferiority of this line to that, which, if we did not perceive for ourselves, no explanation could ever illustrate to us? He might as well endeavour to explain to us by words some scent or flavour, or other subject of sense, of which we had no experience. And so it is with all truths of the highest order; they are separated from those of average precision by points of extreme delicacy, which none but the cultivated eye can in the least feel, and to express which, all words are absolutely meaningless and useless. Consequently, in all that I have been saying of the truth of artists, I have been able to point out only coarse, broad, and explicable matters; I have been perfectly unable to express (and indeed I have made no endeavour to express) the finely drawn and distinguished truth in which all the real excellence of art consists. All those truths which I have been able to explain and demonstrate in Turner, are such as any artist of ordinary powers of observation ought to be capable of rendering. It is disgraceful to omit them; but it is no very great credit to observe them. I have indeed proved that they have been neglected, and disgracefully so, by those men who are commonly considered

the Fathers of Art; but in showing that they have been observed by Turner, I have only proved him to be *above* other men in knowledge of truth, I have not given any conception of his own positive rank as a Painter of Nature. But it stands to reason, that the men, who in broad, simple, and demonstrable matters are perpetually violating truth, will not be particularly accurate or careful in carrying out delicate and refined and undemonstrable matters; and it stands equally to reason that the man, who, as far as argument or demonstration can go, is found invariably truthful, will, in all probability, be truthful to the last line, and shadow of a line. And such is, indeed, the case with every touch of this consummate artist; the essential excellence, all that constitutes the real and exceeding value of his works, is beyond and above expression: it is a truth inherent in every line, and breathing in every hue, too delicate and exquisite to admit of any kind of proof, nor to be ascertained except by the highest of tests, the keen feeling attained by extended knowledge and long study. Two lines are laid on canvas; one is right and another wrong. There is no difference between them appreciable by the compasses, none appreciable by the ordinary eye, none which can be pointed out, if it is not seen. One person feels it, another does not; but the feeling or sight of the one can by no words be communicated to the other:— that feeling and sight have been the reward of years of labour. There is no test of our acquaintance with nature so absolute and unfailing, as the degree of admiration we feel for Turner's painting. Precisely as we are shallow in our knowledge, vulgar in our feeling, and contracted in our views of principles, will the works of this artist be stumbling-blocks or foolishness to us: precisely in the degree in which we are familiar with nature, constant in our observation of her, and enlarged in our understanding of her, will they expand before our eyes into glory and beauty. In every new insight which we obtain into the works of God, in every new idea which we receive from His creation, we shall find ourselves possessed of an interpretation and a guide to something in Turner's works which we had not before understood. We may range over Europe, from shore to shore; and from every rock that we tread upon, every sky that passes over our heads, every local form of vegetation or of soil, we shall receive fresh illustration of his principles, fresh confirmation of his facts.

[2] The Torso of Heracles, also known as the Belvedere Torso. M. Angelo is Michelangelo.

We shall feel, wherever we go, that he has been there before us: whatever we see, that he has seen and seized before us: and we shall at last cease the investigation, with a well-grounded trust, that whatever we have been unable to account for, and what we still dislike in his works, has reason for it, and foundation like the rest; and that even where he has failed or erred, there is a beauty in the failure which none are able to equal, and a dignity in the error which none are worthy to reprove.

There has been marked and constant progress in his mind; he has not, like some few artists, been without childhood; his course of study has been as evidently, as it has been swiftly, progressive; and in different stages of the struggle, sometimes one order of truth, sometimes another, has been aimed at or omitted. But, from the beginning to the height of his career, he never sacrificed a greater truth to a less. As he advanced, the previous knowledge or attainment was absorbed in what succeeded, or abandoned only if incompatible, and never abandoned without a gain; and his last works presented the sum and perfection of his accumulated knowledge, delivered with the impatience and passion of one who feels too much, and knows too much, and has too little time to say it in, to pause for expression, or ponder over his syllables. There was in them the obscurity, but the truth, of prophecy; the instinctive and burning language which would express less if it uttered more, which is indistinct only by its fulness, and dark with its abundant meaning. He felt now, with long-trained vividness and keenness of sense, too bitterly the impotence of the hand, and the vainness of the colour, to catch one shadow or one image of the glory which God had revealed to him. "I cannot gather the sunbeams out of the east, or I would make *them* tell you what I have seen; but read this, and interpret this, and let us remember together. I cannot gather the gloom out of the night sky, or I would make that teach you what I have seen; but read this, and interpret this, and let us feel together. And if you have not that within you which I can summon to my aid, if you have not the sun in your spirit, and the passion in your heart, which my words may awaken, though they be indistinct and swift, leave me; for I will give you no patient mockery, no laborious insult of that glorious nature, whose I am and whom I serve. Let other servants imitate the voice and the gesture of their master,

while they forget his message. Hear that message from me; but remember that the teaching of Divine truth must still be a mystery."

FROM VOLUME II

Of Purity, or the Type of Divine Energy

IT MAY at first appear strange that I have not, in my enumeration of the Types of Divine attributes, included that which is certainly the most visible and evident of all, as well as the most distinctly expressed in Scripture; "God is light, and in Him is no darkness at all."[1] But I could not logically class the presence of an actual substance or motion with mere conditions and modes of being; neither could I logically separate from any of these, that which is evidently necessary to the perception of all. And it is also to be observed, that, though the love of light is more instinctive in the human heart than any other of the desires connected with beauty, we can hardly separate its agreeableness in its own nature from the sense of its necessity and value for the purposes of life; neither the abstract painfulness of darkness from the sense of danger and powerlessness connected with it. And note also that it is not *all* light, but light possessing the universal qualities of beauty, diffused or infinite rather than in points; tranquil, not startling and variable; pure, not sullied or oppressed; which is indeed pleasant and perfectly typical of the Divine nature.

Observe, however, that there is one quality, the idea of which has been just introduced in connection with light, which might have escaped us in the consideration of mere matter, namely Purity: and yet I think that the original notion of this quality is altogether material, and has only been attributed to colour when such colour is suggestive of the condition of matter from which we originally received the idea. For I see not in the abstract how one colour should be considered *purer* than another, except as more or less compounded: whereas there is certainly a sense of purity or impurity in the most compound and neutral colours, as well as in the simplest; a

---

[1] I John 1:5.

quality difficult to define, and which the reader will probably be surprised by my calling the type of Energy, with which it has certainly little traceable connection in the mind.

I believe, however, if we carefully analyze the nature of our ideas of impurity in general, we shall find them refer especially to conditions of matter in which its various elements are placed in a relation incapable of healthy or proper operation; and most distinctly to conditions in which the negation of vital or energetic action is most evident; as in corruption and decay of all kinds, wherein particles which once, by their operation on each other, produced a living and energetic whole, are reduced to a condition of perfect passiveness, in which they are seized upon and appropriated, one by one, piecemeal, by whatever has need of them, without any power of resistance or energy of their own. And thus there is a peculiar painfulness attached to any associations of inorganic with organic matter, such as appear to involve the inactivity and feebleness of the latter; so that things which are not felt to be foul in their own nature become so in association with things of greater inherent energy: as dust or earth, which in a mass excites no painful sensation, excites a most disagreeable one when strewing or staining an animal's skin; because it implies a decline and deadening of the vital and healthy power of the skin. But all reasoning about this impression is rendered difficult, because the ocular sense of impurity connected with corruption is enhanced by the offending of other senses and by the grief and horror of it in its own nature, as the special punishment and evidence of sin: and on the other hand, the ocular delight in purity is mingled, as I before observed, with the love of the mere element of light, as a type of wisdom and of truth; whence it seems to me that we admire the transparency of bodies; though probably it is still rather owing to our sense of more perfect order and arrangement of particles, and not to our love of light, that we look upon a piece of rock crystal as purer than a piece of marble, and on the marble as purer than a piece of chalk. And let it be observed, also, that the most lovely objects in nature are only partially transparent. I suppose the utmost possible sense of beauty is conveyed by a feebly translucent, smooth, but not lustrous surface of white, and pale warm red, subdued by the most pure and delicate greys, as in the finer portions of the human frame; in wreaths of snow, and in white plumage under rose light,[2] so Viola of Olivia in *Twelfth Night*, and Homer of Atrides wounded.[3] And I think that transparency and lustre, both beautiful in themselves, are incompatible with the highest beauty; because they destroy form, on the full perception of which more of the divinely typical character of the object depends than upon its colour. Hence in the beauty of snow and of flesh, so much translucency is allowed as is consistent with the full explanation of the forms; while we are suffered to receive more intense impressions of light and transparency from other objects, which nevertheless, owing to their necessarily unperceived form, are not perfectly nor affectingly beautiful. A fair forehead outshines its diamond diadem. The sparkle of the cascade withdraws not our eyes from the snowy summits in their evening silence.

---

[2] The reader will observe that I am speaking at present of mere material qualities. If he would obtain perfect ideas respecting loveliness of luminous surface, let him closely observe a swan with its wings expanded in full light five minutes before sunset. The human cheek or the rose leaf is perhaps hardly so pure, and the forms of snow, though individually as beautiful, are less exquisitely combined. [Ruskin's note]

[3] (ὡς δ' ὅτε τίς τ' ἐλέφαντα γυνὴ φοίνικι μιήνη Μῄονὶς.)
So Spenser of Shamefacedness, an exquisite piece of glowing colour, and (sweetly of Belphœbe; so the roses and lilies of all poets. Compare) the making of the image of Florimel:

> "The substance whereof she the body made
> Was purest snow, in mossy mould congealed,
> Which she had gathered in a shady glade
> Of the Riphæan hills.
> The same she tempered with fine mercury,
> And mingled them with perfect vermily."

With Una he perhaps overdoes the white a little. She is two degrees of comparison above snow. Compare his questioning in the Hymn to Beauty, about that mixture made of colours fair; (and goodly temperament of pure complexion):

> "Hath white and red in it such wondrous power
> That it can pierce through the eyes into the heart?"

(Where the distinction between typical and vital beauty is very gloriously carried out.) [Ruskin's note]

It may seem strange to many readers that I have not spoken of purity in that sense in which it is most frequently used, as a type of sinlessness. I do not deny that the frequent metaphorical use of it in Scripture may have, and ought to have, much influence on the sympathies with which we regard it; and that probably the immediate agreeableness of it to most minds arises far more from this source[4] than from that to which I have chosen to attribute it. But, in the first place, if it be indeed in the signs of Divine and not of human attributes that beauty consists, I see not how the idea of sin can be formed with respect to the Deity; for it is an idea of a relation borne by us to Him, and not in any way to be attached to His abstract nature: while the Love, Mercifulness, and Justice of God I have supposed to be symbolized by other qualities of beauty, and I cannot trace any rational connection between them and the idea of Spotlessness in matter; nor between this idea and any of the virtues which make up the righteousness of man, except perhaps those of truth and openness, which have been above spoken of as more expressed by the transparency than the mere purity of matter. So that I conceive the use of the terms purity, spotlessness, etc., in moral subjects, to be merely metaphorical; and that it is rather that we illustrate these virtues by the desirableness of material purity than that we desire material purity because it is illustrative of these virtues.[5]

I repeat, then, that the only idea which I think can be legitimately connected with purity of matter, is this of vital and energetic connection among its particles; as that of foulness is essentially connected with dissolution and death. Thus the purity of the rock, contrasted with the foulness of dust or mould, is expressed by the epithet "living," very singularly given to rock, in almost all languages (singularly, because life is almost the last attribute one would ascribe to stone, but for this visible energy and connection of its particles); and so to flowing water, opposed to stagnant. And I do not think that,

however pure a powder or dust may be, the idea of beauty is ever connected with it; for it is not the mere purity, but the *active* condition of the substance which is desired;[6] so that as soon as it shoots into crystals, or gathers into efflorescence, a sensation of active or real purity is received which was not felt in the calcined caput mortuum.

And again, in colour, I imagine that the quality which we term purity is dependent on the full energizing of the rays that compose it; of which if in compound hues any are overpowered and killed by the rest, so as to be of no value nor operation, foulness is the consequence; while so long as all act together, whether side by side, or from pigments seen one through the other, so that all the colouring matter employed may come into play in the harmony desired, and none be quenched nor killed, purity results.[7] And so in all cases I suppose that pureness is made to us desirable, because expressive of that constant presence and energizing of the Deity by which all things live and move, and have their being;[8] and that foulness is painful as the accompaniment of disorder and decay, and always indicative of the withdrawal of Divine support. And the practical analogies of life, the invariable connection of outward foulness with mental sloth and degradation, as well as with bodily lethargy and disease, together with the contrary indications of freshness and purity belonging to every healthy and active organic frame (singularly seen in the effort of the young leaves when first their inward energy prevails over the earth, pierces its corruption, and shakes its dust away from their own white purity of life), all these circumstances strengthen the instinct by associations countless and irresistible. And then, finally, with the idea of purity comes that of spirituality; for the essential characteristic of matter is its inertia, whence, by adding to its purity of energy, we may in some measure spiritualize even matter itself. Thus in the Apocalyptic descriptions, it is the purity of every substance that fits it for its place in

---

[4] I cannot but wonder more and more at the obstinacy of the public in calling these books my best writing. The hissing of these two lines, after "immediate," might be made a warning example in public schools. [Ruskin's note]

[5] This uncertain and unsatisfactory paragraph enters on subjects far out of its grasp, and misses the things close at hand, which needed chief consideration. See final note to this chapter. [Ruskin's note]

[6] Well observed, but not conclusively. Snow is a powder, practically, in hard frost; and it is perhaps easier to attach the idea of purity to flour than to bread. [Ruskin's note]

[7] Again well said; and the statement should have been farther enforced. The essential difference between painting and daubing is that a *painter* lays not a grain more colour than is needed. [Ruskin's note]

[8] Acts 27:28.

heaven; the river of the water of life, that proceeds out of the throne of the Lamb, is clear as crystal,[9] and the pavement of the city is pure gold "like unto clear glass."[10]

FROM VOLUME III

Of the Received Opinions Touching the "Grand Style"

IN TAKING up the clue of an inquiry, now intermitted for nearly ten years,[1] it may be well to do as a traveller would, who had to recommence an interrupted journey in a guideless country; and, ascending, as it were, some little hill beside our road, note how far we have already advanced, and what pleasantest ways we may choose for farther progress.

I endeavoured, in the beginning of the first volume, to divide the sources of pleasure open to us in Art into certain groups, which might conveniently be studied in succession. After some preliminary discussion, it was concluded (Part I. Sec. II. Chap. III § 6,) that these groups were, in the main, three; consisting, first, of the pleasures taken in perceiving simple resemblance to Nature (Ideas of Truth); secondly, of the pleasures taken in the beauty of the things chosen to be painted (Ideas of Beauty); and, lastly, of pleasures taken in the meanings and relations of these things (Ideas of Relation).

The first volume, treating of the Ideas of Truth, was chiefly occupied with an inquiry into the various success with which different artists had represented the facts of Nature,—an inquiry necessarily conducted very imperfectly, owing to the want of pictorial illustration.

The second volume merely opened the inquiry into the nature of ideas of Beauty and Relation, by analysing (as far as I was able to do so) the two faculties of the human mind which mainly seized such ideas; namely, the contemplative and imaginative faculties.

It remains for us to examine the various success of artists, especially of the great landscape-painter whose works have been throughout our principal subject, in addressing these faculties of the human mind, and to consider who among them has conveyed the noblest ideas of beauty, and touched the deepest sources of thought.

I do not intend, however, now to pursue the inquiry in a method so laboriously systematic; for the subject may, it seems to me, be more usefully treated by pursuing the different questions which arise out of it just as they occur to us, without too great scrupulousness in marking connections, or insisting on sequences. Much time is wasted by human beings, in general, on establishment of systems; and it often takes more labour to master the intricacies of an artificial

---

[9] Revelation 22:1, 21:18–21.

[10] I have not spoken here of any of the associations connected with warmth or coolness of colour; they are partly connected with Vital beauty, compare Chap. XIV. §§ 21, 22, and partly with impressions of the sublime, the discussion of which is foreign to the present subject: purity, however, it is which gives colour to both; for neither warm nor cool colour can be beautiful, if impure.

Neither have I spoken of any questions relating to melodies of colour; a subject of separate science, whose general principle has been already stated in the Seventh Chapter respecting unity of Sequence. Those qualities only are here noted which give absolute beauty, whether to separate colour or to melodies of it: for all melodies of it are not beautiful, but only those which are expressive of certain pleasant or solemn emotion; the rest are startling, or curious, or cheerful, or exciting, or sublime, but not beautiful; and so in music. And all questions relating to this grandeur, cheerfulness, or other characteristic impression of colour, must be considered under the head of Ideas of Relation.** [Ruskin's note to first edition]

** I used then to slip things out of my way from one chapter to another, partly with a notion of being systematic, partly because I was tired; until at last they often slipped out of my head altogether. Thus in the sixth paragraph, the quite primary difficulty of saying whether *spots* are pretty or ugly; whether a fallow-deer is the worse for dappling, or a mackerel for mottling, or a fox-glove for speckling, is wholly lost sight of; and, throughout the chapter, the question why we like gold-yellow better than brass-yellow—or rose-colour better than brown—or in general any colour better than any other. I believe there is something said on these points farther on in the book: if not, I'll say something about them where I think it will be useful; only in the meantime, observe that we like gold because it is of a pretty and permanent yellow; and not the yellow colour because it is like gold. I overwork the epithet "golden" in most of my descriptions; not because I like guineas, but because I like buttercups and broom. [Ruskin's note to edition of 1883]

[1] Volume II of *Modern Painters* had appeared in 1846; Volume III was published in 1856.

connection, than to remember the separate facts which are so carefully connected. I suspect that system-makers, in general, are not of much more use, each in his own domain, than, in that of Pomona, the old women who tie cherries upon sticks, for the more convenient portableness of the same. To cultivate well, and choose well, your cherries, is of some importance; but if they can be had in their own wild way of clustering about their crabbed stalk, it is a better connection for them than any other; and, if they cannot, then, so that they be not bruised, it makes to a boy of a practical disposition not much difference whether he gets them by handfuls, or in beaded symmetry on the exalting stick. I purpose, therefore, henceforward to trouble myself little with sticks or twine, but to arrange my chapters with a view to convenient reference, rather than to any careful division of subjects, and to follow out, in any by-ways that may open, on right hand or left, whatever question it seems useful at any moment to settle.

And, in the outset, I find myself met by one which I ought to have touched upon before—one of especial interest in the present state of the Arts. I have said that the art is greatest which includes the greatest ideas; but I have not endeavoured to define the nature of this greatness in the ideas themselves. We speak of great truths, of great beauties, great thoughts. What is it which makes one truth greater than another, one thought greater than another? This question is, I repeat, of peculiar importance at the present time; for, during a period now of some hundred and fifty years, all writers on Art who have pretended to eminence, have insisted much on a supposed distinction between what they call the Great and the Low Schools; using the terms "High Art," "Great or Ideal Style," and other such, as descriptive of a certain noble manner of painting, which it was desirable that all students of Art should be early led to reverence and adopt; and characterising as "vulgar," or "low," or "realist," another manner of painting and conceiving, which it was equally necessary that all students should be taught to avoid.

But lately this established teaching, never very intelligible, has been gravely called in question. The advocates and self-supposed practisers of "High Art" are beginning to be looked upon with doubt, and their peculiar phraseology to be treated with even a certain degree of ridicule.

And other forms of Art are partly developed among us, which do not pretend to be high, but rather to be strong, healthy, and humble. This matter of "highness" in Art, therefore, deserves our most careful consideration. Has it been, or is it, a true highness, a true princeliness, or only a show of it, consisting in courtly manners and robes of state? Is it rocky height or cloudy height, adamant or vapour, on which the sun of praise so long has risen and set? It will be well at once to consider this.

And first, let us get, as quickly as may be, at the exact meaning with which the advocates of "High Art" use that somewhat obscure and figurative term.

I do not know that the principles in question are anywhere more distinctly expressed than in two papers in the *Idler*, written by Sir Joshua Reynolds,[2] of course under the immediate sanction of Johnson; and which may thus be considered as the utterance of the views then held upon the subject by the artists of chief skill, and critics of most sense, arranged in a form so brief and clear, as to admit of their being brought before the public for a morning's entertainment. I cannot, therefore, it seems to me, do better than quote these two letters, or at least the important parts of them, examining the exact meaning of each passage as it occurs. There are, in all, in the *Idler* three letters on painting, Nos. 76, 79, and 82; of these, the first is directed only against the impertinences of pretended connoisseurs, and is as notable for its faithfulness, as for its wit, in the description of the several modes of criticism in an artificial and ignorant state of society: it is only, therefore, in the two last papers that we find the expression of the doctrines which it is our business to examine.

No. 79 (Saturday, Oct. 20th, 1759) begins, after a short preamble, with the following passage:—

"Amongst the Painters, and the writers on Painting, there is one maxim universally admitted and continually inculcated. *Imitate nature* is the invariable rule; but I know none who have explained in what manner this rule is to be understood; the consequence of which is, that every one takes it in the most obvious sense—that objects are represented naturally, when they have such relief that they seem real. It may appear strange, perhaps, to hear this sense of the

---

[2] Sir Joshua Reynolds (1723–92) contributed essays to Samuel Johnson's *Idler* which ran between 1758 and 1760.

rule disputed; but it must be considered, that, if the excellency of a Painter consisted only in this kind of imitation, Painting must lose its rank, and be no longer considered as a liberal art, and sister to Poetry: this imitation being merely mechanical, in which the slowest intellect is always sure to succeed best; for the Painter of genius cannot stoop to drudgery, in which the understanding has no part; and what pretence has the Art to claim kindred with Poetry, but by its power over the imagination? To this power the Painter of genius directs him; in this sense he studies Nature, and often arrives at his end, even by being unnatural in the confined sense of the word.

"The grand style of Painting requires this minute attention to be carefully avoided, and must be kept as separate from it as the style of Poetry from that of History. (Poetical ornaments destroy that air of truth and plainness which ought to characterise History; but the very being of Poetry consists in departing from this plain narrative, and adopting every ornament that will warm the imagination.[3]) To desire to see the excellences of each style united— to mingle the Dutch with the Italian school, is to join contrarieties which cannot subsist together, and which destroy the efficacy of each other."

We find, first, from this interesting passage, that the writer considers the Dutch and Italian masters as severally representative of the low and high schools; next, that he considers the Dutch painters as excelling in a mechanical imitation, "in which the slowest intellect is always sure to succeed best;" and, thirdly, that he considers the Italian painters as excelling in a style which corresponds to that of imaginative poetry in literature, and which has an exclusive right to be called the grand style.

I wish that it were in my power entirely to concur with the writer, and to enforce this opinion thus distinctly stated. I have never been a zealous partisan of the Dutch school, and should rejoice in claiming Reynolds's authority for the assertion, that their manner was one "in which the slowest intellect is always sure to succeed best." But before his authority can be so claimed, we must observe exactly the meaning of the assertion itself, and separate it from the company

of some others not perhaps so admissible. First, I say, we must observe Reynolds's exact meaning, for (though the assertion may at first appear singular) a man who uses accurate language is always more liable to misinterpretation than one who is careless in his expressions. We may assume that the latter means very nearly what we at first suppose him to mean, for words which have been uttered without thought may be received without examination. But when a writer or speaker may be fairly supposed to have considered his expressions carefully, and, after having revolved a number of terms in his mind, to have chosen the one which *exactly* means the thing he intends to say, we may be assured that what costs him time to select, will require from us time to understand; and that we shall do him wrong, unless we pause to reflect how the word which he has actually employed differs from other words which it seems he *might* have employed. It thus constantly happens that persons themselves unaccustomed to think clearly, or speak correctly, misunderstand a logical and careful writer, and are actually in more danger of being misled by language which is measured and precise, than by that which is loose and inaccurate.

Now, in the instance before us, a person not accustomed to good writing might very rashly conclude that when Reynolds spoke of the Dutch School as one "in which the slowest intellect was sure to succeed best," he meant to say that every successful Dutch painter was a fool. We have no right to take his assertion in that sense. He says, the *slowest* intellect. We have no right to assume that he meant the *weakest*. For it is true, that in order to succeed in the Dutch style, a man has need of qualities of mind eminently deliberate and sustained. He must be possessed of patience rather than of power; and must feel no weariness in contemplating the expression of a single thought for several months together. As opposed to the changeful energies of the imagination, these mental characters may be properly spoken of as under the general term—slowness of intellect. But it by no means follows that they are necessarily those of weak or foolish men.

We observe, however, farther, that the imitation which Reynolds supposes to be characteristic of the Dutch School is that which gives to objects such relief that they seem real, and that he then

---

[3] I have put this sentence in a parenthesis, because it is inconsistent with the rest of the statement, and with the general teaching of the paper; since that which "attends only to the invariable," cannot certainly adopt "every ornament that will warm the imagination." [Ruskin's note]

speaks of this art of realistic imitation as corresponding to *history* in literature.

Reynolds, therefore, seems to class these dull works of the Dutch School under a general head, to which they are not commonly referred— that of *Historical* painting; while he speaks of the works of the Italian School not as historical, but as *poetical* painting. His next sentence will farther manifest his meaning.

"The Italian attends only to the invariable, the great and general ideas which are fixed and inherent in universal Nature; the Dutch, on the contrary, to literal truth, and a minute exactness in the detail, as I may say, of Nature modified by accident. The attention to these petty peculiarities is the very cause of this naturalness so much admired in the Dutch pictures, which, if we suppose it to be a beauty, is certainly of a lower order, which ought to give place to a beauty of a superior kind, since one cannot be obtained but by departing from the other.

"If my opinion were asked concerning the works of Michael Angelo, whether they would receive any advantage from possessing this mechanical merit, I should not scruple to say, they would not only receive no advantage, but would lose, in a great measure, the effect which they now have on every mind susceptible of great and noble ideas. His works may be said to be all genius and soul; and why should they be loaded with heavy matter, which can only counteract his purpose by retarding the progress of the imagination?"

Examining carefully this and the preceding passage, we find the author's unmistakable meaning to be, that Dutch painting is *history;* attending to literal truth and "minute exactness in the details of nature modified by accident." That Italian painting is *poetry*, attending only to the invariable; and that works which attend only to the invariable are full of genius and soul; but that literal truth and exact detail are "heavy matter which retards the progress of the imagination."

This being then indisputably what Reynolds means to tell us, let us think a little whether he is in all respects right. And first, as he compares his two kinds of painting to history and poetry, let us see how poetry and history themselves differ, in their use of *variable* and *invariable* details. I am writing at a window which commands a view of the head of the Lake of Geneva; and as I look up from my paper, to consider this point, I see, beyond it, a blue breadth of softly moving water, and the outline of the mountains above Chillon, bathed in morning mist. The first verses which naturally come into my mind are—

> "A thousand feet in depth below
> The massy waters meet and flow;
> So far the fathom line was sent
> From Chillon's snow-white battlement."[4]

Let us see in what manner this poetical statement is distinguished from a historical one.

It is distinguished from a truly historical statement, first, in being simply false. The water under the Castle of Chillon is not a thousand feet deep, nor anything like it.[5] Herein, certainly, these lines fulfil Reynolds's first requirement in poetry, "that it should be inattentive to literal truth and minute exactness in detail." In order, however, to make our comparison more closely in other points, let us assume that what is stated is indeed a fact, and that it was to be recorded, first historically, and then poetically.

Historically stating it, then, we should say: "The lake was sounded from the walls of the Castle of Chillon, and found to be a thousand feet deep."

Now, if Reynolds be right in his idea of the difference between history and poetry, we shall find that Byron leaves out of this statement certain *un*necessary details, and retains only the invariable,—that is to say, the points which the Lake of Geneva and Castle of Chillon have in common with all other lakes and castles.

Let us hear, therefore.

"A thousand feet in depth below."

"Below?" Here is, at all events, a word added (instead of anything being taken away); invariable, certainly in the case of lakes, but not absolutely necessary.

"The massy waters meet and flow."

"Massy!" why massy? Because deep water is

[4] Byron's "Prisoner of Chillon," stanza vi, slightly misquoted.
[5] "MM. Mallet et Pictet, se trouvant sur le lac auprès du château de Chillon, le 6 Août, 1774, plongèrent à la profondeur de 312 pieds un thermomètre, "etc.—SAUSSURE, *Voyages dans les Alpes*, chap. ii. § 33. It appears from the next paragraph that the thermometer was "au fond du lac." [Ruskin's note]

heavy. The word is a good word, but it is assuredly an added detail, and expresses a character, not which the Lake of Geneva has in common with all other lakes, but which it has in distinction from those which are narrow, or shallow.

"Meet and flow." Why meet and flow? Partly to make up a rhyme; partly to tell us that the waters are forceful as well as massy, and changeful as well as deep. Observe, a farther addition of details, and of details more or less peculiar to the spot, or, according to Reynolds's definition, of "heavy matter, retarding the progress of the imagination."

"So far the fathom line was sent."

Why fathom line? All lines for sounding are not fathom lines. If the lake was ever sounded from Chillon, it was probably sounded in mètres, not fathoms. This is an addition of another particular detail, in which the only compliance with Reynolds's requirement is, that there is some chance of its being an inaccurate one.

"From Chillon's snow-white battlement."

Why snow-white? Because castle battlements are not usually snow-white. This is another added detail, and a detail quite peculiar to Chillon, and therefore exactly the most striking word in the whole passage.

"Battlement!" Why battlement? Because all walls have not battlements, and the addition of the term marks the castle to be not merely a prison, but a fortress.

This is a curious result. Instead of finding, as we expected, the poetry distinguished from the history by the omission of details, we find it consist entirely in the *addition* of details; and instead of being characterised by regard only of the invariable, we find its whole power to consist in the clear expression of what is singular and particular!

The reader may pursue the investigation for himself in other instances. He will find in every case that a poetical is distinguished from a merely historical statement, not by being more vague, but more specific; and it might, therefore, at first appear that our author's comparison should be simply reversed, and that the Dutch School should be called poetical, and the Italian historical. But the term poetical does not appear very applicable to the generality of Dutch painting; and a little reflection will show us, that if the Italians represent only the invariable, they cannot be properly compared even to historians. For that which is incapable of change has no

history, and records which state only the invariable need not be written, and could not be read.

It is evident, therefore, that our author has entangled himself in some grave fallacy, by introducing this idea of invariableness as forming a distinction between poetical and historical art. What the fallacy is, we shall discover as we proceed; but as an invading army should not leave an untaken fortress in its rear, we must not go on with our inquiry into the views of Reynolds until we have settled satisfactorily the question already suggested to us, in what the essence of poetical treatment really consists. For though, as we have seen, it certainly involves the addition of specific details, it cannot be simply that addition which turns the history into poetry. For it is perfectly possible to add any number of details to a historical statement, and to make it more prosaic with every added word. As, for instance, "The lake was sounded out of a flat-bottomed boat, near the crab-tree at the corner of the kitchen-garden, and was found to be a thousand feet nine inches deep, with a muddy bottom." It thus appears that it is not the multiplication of details which constitutes poetry; nor their subtraction which constitutes history, but that there must be something either in the nature of the details themselves, or the method of using them, which invests them with poetical power or historical propriety.

It seems to me, and may seem to the reader, strange that we should need to ask the question, "What is poetry?" Here is a word we have been using all our lives, and, I suppose, with a very distinct idea attached to it; and when I am now called upon to give a definition of this idea, I find myself at a pause. What is more singular, I do not at present recollect hearing the question often asked, though surely it is a very natural one; and I never recollect hearing it answered, or even attempted to be answered. In general, people shelter themselves under metaphors, and while we hear poetry described as an utterance of the soul, an effusion of Divinity, or voice of nature, or in other terms equally elevated and obscure, we never attain anything like a definite explanation of the character which actually distinguishes it from prose.

I come, after some embarrassment, to the conclusion, that poetry is "the suggestion, by the imagination, of noble grounds for the noble emotions." I mean, by the noble emotions, those four principal sacred passions—Love, Veneration, Admiration, and Joy (this latter especially, if unselfish); and their opposites—

Hatred, Indignation (or Scorn), Horror, and Grief—this last, when unselfish, becoming Compassion. These passions in their various combinations constitute what is called "poetical feeling," when they are felt on noble grounds, that is, on great and true grounds. Indignation, for instance, is a poetical feeling, if excited by serious injury; but it is not a poetical feeling if entertained on being cheated out of a small sum of money. It is very possible the manner of the cheat may have been such as to justify considerable indignation; but the feeling is nevertheless not poetical unless the grounds of it be large as well as just. In like manner, energetic admiration may be excited in certain minds by a display of fireworks, or a street of handsome shops; but the feeling is not poetical, because the grounds of it are false, and therefore ignoble. There is in reality nothing to deserve admiration either in the firing of packets of gunpowder, or in the display of the stocks of warehouses. But admiration excited by the budding of a flower is a poetical feeling, because it is impossible that this manifestation of spiritual power and vital beauty can ever be enough admired.

Farther, it is necessary to the existence of poetry that the grounds of these feelings should be *furnished by the imagination*. Poetical feeling, that is to say, mere noble emotion, is not poetry.

It is happily inherent in all human nature deserving the name and, is found often to be purest in the least sophisticated. But the power of assembling, by *the help of the imagination*, such images as will excite these feelings, is the power of the poet or literally of the "Maker."[6]

Now this power of exciting the emotions depends of course on the richness of the imagination, and on its choice of those images which, in combination, will be most effective, or, for the particular work to be done, most fit. And it is altogether impossible for a writer not endowed with invention to conceive what tools a true poet will make use of, or in what way he will apply them, or what unexpected results he will bring out by them; so that it is vain to say that the details of poetry ought to possess, or ever do possess, any *definite* character. Generally speaking, poetry runs into finer and more delicate details than prose; but the details are not poetical because they are more delicate, but because they are employed so as to bring out an affecting result. For instance, no one but a true poet would have thought of exciting our pity for a bereaved father by describing his way of locking the door of his house:

"Perhaps to himself at that moment he said,
'The key I must take, for my Ellen is dead.'

---

[6] Take, for instance, the beautiful stanza in the "Affliction of Margaret":

"I look for ghosts, but none will force
    Their way to me. 'Tis falsely said
That ever there was intercourse
    Between the living and the dead;
For, surely, then, I should have sight
Of him I wait for, day and night,
With love and longing infinite."

This we call Poetry, because it is invented or *made* by the writer, entering into the mind of a supposed person. Next, take an instance of the actual feeling truly experienced and simply expressed by a real person.

"Nothing surprised me more than a woman of Argentière, whose cottage I went into to ask for milk, as I came down from the glacier of Argentière, in the month of March, 1764. An epidemic dysentery had prevailed in the village, and, a few months before, had taken away from her, her father, her husband, and her brothers, so that she was left alone, with three children in the cradle. Her face had something noble in it, and its expression bore the seal of a calm and profound sorrow. After having given me milk, she asked me whence I came, and what I came there to do, so early in the year. When she knew that I was of Geneva, she said to me, 'she could not believe that all Protestants were lost souls; that there were many honest people among us, and that God was too good and too great to condemn all without distinction.' Then, after a moment of reflection, she added, in shaking her head, 'But that which is very strange is that of so many who have gone away, none have ever returned. I,' she added, with an expression of grief, 'who have so mourned my husband and my brothers, who have never ceased to think of them, who every night conjure them with beseechings to tell me where they are, and in what state they are! Ah, surely, if they lived anywhere, they would not leave me thus! But, perhaps,' she added, 'I am not worthy of this kindness, perhaps the pure and innocent spirits of these children,' and she looked at the cradle, 'may have their presence, and the joy which is denied to me.' "—SAUSSURE, *Voyages dans les Alpes,* chap. xxiv.

This we do not call Poetry, merely because it is not invented, but the true utterance of a real person. [Ruskin's note]

But of this in my ears not a word did he speak;
And he went to the chase with a tear on his cheek."[7]

In like manner, in painting, it is altogether impossible to say beforehand what details a great painter may make poetical by his use of them to excite noble emotions: and we shall, therefore, find presently that a painting is to be classed in the great or inferior schools, not according to the kind of details which it represents, but according to the uses for which it employs them.

It is only farther to be noticed, that infinite confusion has been introduced into this subject by the careless and illogical custom of opposing painting to poetry, instead of regarding poetry as consisting in a noble use, whether of colours or words. Painting is properly to be opposed to *speaking* or *writing*, but not to *poetry*. Both painting and speaking are methods of expression. Poetry is the employment of either for the noblest purposes.

This question being thus far determined, we may proceed with our paper in the *Idler*.

"It is very difficult to determine the exact degree of enthusiasm that the arts of Painting and Poetry may admit. There may, perhaps, be too great an indulgence as well as too great a restraint of imagination; if the one produces incoherent monsters, the other produces what is full as bad, lifeless insipidity. An intimate knowledge of the passions, and good sense, but not common sense, must at last determine its limits. It has been thought, and I believe with reason, that Michael Angelo sometimes transgressed those limits; and, I think, I have seen figures of him of which it was very difficult to determine whether they were in the highest degree sublime or extremely ridiculous. Such faults may be said to be the ebullitions of genius; but at least he had this merit, that he never was insipid; and whatever passion his works may excite, they will always escape contempt.

"What I have had under consideration is the sublimest style, particularly that of Michael Angelo, the Homer of painting. Other kinds may admit of this naturalness, which of the lowest kind is the chief merit; but in painting, as in poetry, the highest style has the least of common nature."

From this passage we gather three important indications of the supposed nature of the Great Style. That it is the work of men in a state of enthusiasm. That it is like the writing of Homer; and that it has as little as possible of "common nature" in it.

First, it is produced by men in a state of enthusiasm. That is, by men who feel *strongly* and *nobly;* for we do not call a strong feeling of envy, jealousy, or ambition, enthusiasm. That is, therefore, by men who feel poetically. This much we may admit, I think, with perfect safety. Great art is produced by men who feel acutely and nobly; and it is in some sort an expression of this personal feeling. We can easily conceive that there may be a sufficiently marked distinction between such art, and that which is produced by men who do not feel at all, but who reproduce, though ever so accurately, yet coldly, like human mirrors, the scenes which pass before their eyes.

Secondly, Great Art is like the writing of Homer, and this chiefly because it has little of "common nature" in it. We are not clearly informed what is meant by common nature in this passage. Homer seems to describe a great deal of what is common:—cookery, for instance, very carefully in all its processes[8]. I suppose the passage in the *Iliad* which, on the whole, has excited most admiration, is that which describes a wife's sorrow at parting from her husband, and a child's fright at its father's helmet;[9] and I hope, at least, the former feeling may be considered "common nature." But the true greatness of Homer's style is, doubtless, held by our author to consist in his imaginations of things not only uncommon but impossible (such as spirits in brazen armour, or monsters with heads of men and bodies of beasts), and in his occasional delineations of the human character and form in their utmost, or heroic, strength and beauty. We gather then on the whole, that a painter in the Great Style must be enthusiastic, or full of emotion, and must paint the human form in its utmost strength and beauty, and perhaps certain impossible forms besides, liable by persons not in an equally enthusiastic state of mind to be looked upon as in some degree absurd. This I presume to be Reynolds's meaning, and to be all that he intends us to gather from his comparison of the Great Style with the writings of Homer. But if that comparison be a just one in all respects, surely two other corollaries ought to be drawn from it, namely,—first, that these Heroic or

---

[7] Wordsworth's "The Childless Father," last stanza.   [8] *Iliad*, I, 463 ff.   [9] *Iliad*, VI, 468.

Impossible images are to be mingled with others very unheroic and very possible; and, secondly, that in the representation of the Heroic or Impossible forms, the greatest care must be taken in *finishing the details*, so that a painter must not be satisfied with painting well the countenance and the body of his hero, but ought to spend the greatest part of his time (as Homer the greatest numbers of verses) in elaborating the sculptured pattern on his shield.

Let us, however, proceed with our paper.

"One may very safely recommend a little more enthusiasm to the modern Painters; too much is certainly not the vice of the present age. The Italians seem to have been continually declining in this respect from the time of Michael Angelo to that of Carlo Maratti,[10] and from thence to the very bathos of insipidity to which they are now sunk; so that there is no need of remarking, that where I mentioned the Italian painters in opposition to the Dutch, I mean not the moderns, but the heads of the old Roman and Bolognian Schools; nor did I mean to include, in my idea of an Italian painter, the Venetian school, *which may be said to be the Dutch part of the Italian genius*. I have only to add a word of advice to the Painters,—that, however excellent they may be in painting naturally, they would not flatter themselves very much upon it; and to the Connoisseurs, that when they see a cat or a fiddle painted so finely, that, as the phrase is, it looks as if you could take it up, they would not for that reason immediately compare the Painter to Raffaelle and Michael Angelo."

In this passage there are four points chiefly to be remarked. The first, that in the year 1759 the Italian painters were, in our author's opinion, sunk in the very bathos of insipidity. The second, that the Venetian painters, *i.e.,* Titian, Tintoret, and Veronese, are, in our author's opinion, to be classed with the Dutch; that is to say, are painters in a style "in which the slowest intellect is always sure to succeed best." Thirdly, that painting naturally is not a difficult thing, nor one on which a painter should pride himself. And, finally, that connoisseurs, seeing a cat or a fiddle successfully painted, ought not therefore immediately to compare the painter to Raphael or Michael Angelo.

Yet Raphael painted fiddles very carefully in the foreground of his St. Cecilia,—so carefully, that they quite look as if they might be taken up. So carefully, that I never yet looked at the picture without wishing that somebody *would* take them up, and out of the way. And I am under a very strong persuasion that Raphael did not think painting "naturally" an easy thing. It will be well to examine into this point a little; and for the present, with the reader's permission, we will pass over the first two statements in this passage (touching the character of Italian art in 1759, and of Venetian art in general), and immediately examine some of the evidence existing as to the real dignity of "natural" painting—that is to say, of painting carried to the point at which it reaches a deceptive appearance of reality.

FROM VOLUME V

The Dark Mirror

IN THE course of our inquiry into the moral of landscape (Vol. III., Chap. XVII.), we promised at the close of our work to seek for some better, or at least clearer, conclusions than were then possible to us. We confined ourselves in that chapter to the vindication of the probable utility of the *love* of natural scenery. We made no assertion of the usefulness of *painting* such scenery. It might be well to delight in the real country, or admire the real flowers and true mountains. But it did not follow that it was advisable to paint them.

Far from it. Many reasons might be given why we should not paint them. All the purposes of good which we saw that the beauty of Nature could accomplish, may be better fulfilled by the meanest of her realities, than by the brightest of imitations. For prolonged entertainment, no picture can be compared with the wealth of interest which may be found in the herbage of the poorest field, or blossoms of the narrowest copse. As suggestive of supernatural power, the passing away of a fitful raincloud, or opening of dawn, are in their change and mystery more pregnant than any pictures. A child would, I suppose, receive a religious lesson from a flower more willingly than from a print of one; and

[10] Carlo Maratti (1625–1713), Italian baroque painter.

might be taught to understand the nineteenth
Psalm,[1] on a starry night, better than by diagrams of the constellations.

Whence it might seem a waste of time to draw
landscape at all.

I believe it is;—to draw landscape mere and
solitary, however beautiful (unless it be for the
sake of geographical or other science, or of
historical record). But there *is* a kind of landscape
which it is not inexpedient to draw. What kind,
we may probably discover by considering that
which mankind has thitherto contented itself
with painting.

We may arrange nearly all existing landscape
under the following heads:—

I. Heroic. Representing an imaginary world,
inhabited by men not perhaps perfectly civilized,
but noble, and usually subjected to severe
trials, and by spiritual powers of the highest order.
It is frequently without architecture; never
without figure-action, or emotion. Its principal
master is Titian.

II. Classical. Representing an imaginary world,
inhabited by perfectly civilized men, and by
spiritual powers of an inferior order.

It generally assumes this condition of things
to have existed among the Greek and Roman
nations. It contains usually architecture of an
elevated character, and always incidents of
figure-action, or emotion. Its principal master
is Nicolo Poussin.

III. Pastoral. Representing peasant life and its
daily work, or such scenery as may naturally
be suggestive of it, consisting usually of simple
landscape, in part subjected to agriculture, with
figures, cattle, and domestic buildings. No supernatural being is ever visibly present. It does not
in ordinary cases admit architecture of an elevated
character nor exciting incident. Its principal
master is Cuyp.

IV. Contemplative. Directed principally to the
observance of the powers of Nature, and record
of the historical associations connected with
landscape, illustrated by, or contrasted with,
existing states of human life. No supernatural
being is visibly present. It admits every variety of
subject, and requires, in general, figure incident,

but not of an exciting character. It was not
developed completely until recent times. Its
principal master is Turner.[2]

These are the four true orders of landscape,
not of course distinctly separated from each
other in all cases, but very distinctly in typical
examples. Two spurious forms require separate
note.

(*a*) *Picturesque.* This is indeed rather the degradation (or sometimes the undeveloped state)
of the contemplative, than a distinct class; but
it may be considered generally as including
pictures meant to display the skill of the artist,
and his powers of composition; or to give agreeable forms and colours, irrespective of sentiment.
It will include much modern art, with the street
views and church interiors of the Dutch, and the
works of Canaletto, Guardi, Tempesta, and the
like.

(*b*) *Hybrid.* Landscape in which the painter
endeavours to unite the irreconcilable sentiment
of two or more of the above-named classes. Its
principal masters are Berghem and Wouvermans.

Passing for the present by these inferior schools,
we find that all true landscape, whether simple
or exalted, depends primarily for its interest on
connection with humanity, or with spiritual
powers. Banish your heroes and nymphs from
the classical landscape—its laurel shades will
move you no more. Show that the dark clefts
of the most romantic mountain are uninhabited
and untraversed; it will cease to be romantic.
Fields without shepherds and without fairies
will have no gaiety in their green, nor will the
noblest masses of ground or colours of cloud
arrest or raise your thoughts, if the earth has
no life to sustain, and the heaven none to
refresh.

It might perhaps be thought that, since from
scenes in which the figure was principal, and
landscape symbolical and subordinate (as in the
art of Egypt), the process of ages had led us to
scenes in which landscape was principal and the
figure subordinate,—a continuance in the same
current of feeling might bring forth at last an
art from which humanity and its interests should
wholly vanish, leaving us to the passionless

---

[1] The Psalm beginning "The heavens declare the glory of God: and the firmament sheweth his
handiwork."

[2] I have been embarrassed in assigning the names to these orders of art, the term "Contemplative"
belonging in justice nearly as much to the romantic and pastoral conception as to the modern landscape. I intended, originally, to call the four schools—Romantic, Classic, Georgic, and Theoretic—
which would have been more accurate; and more consistent with the nomenclature of the second
volume; but would not have been pleasant in sound, nor, to the general reader, very clear in sense.
[Ruskin's note]

admiration of herbage and stone. But this will not, and cannot be. For observe the parallel instance in the gradually increasing importance of dress. From the simplicity of Greek design, concentrating, I suppose, its skill chiefly on the naked form, the course of time developed conditions of Venetian imagination which found nearly as much interest, and expressed nearly as much dignity, in folds of dress and fancies of decoration as in the faces of the figures themselves: so that if from Veronese's Marriage in Cana we remove the architecture and the gay dresses, we shall not in the faces and hands remaining, find a satisfactory abstract of the picture. But try it the other way. Take out the faces; leave the draperies, and how then? Put the fine dresses and jewelled girdles into the best group you can; paint them with all Veronese's skill: will they satisfy you?

Not so. As long as they are in their due service and subjection—while their folds are formed by the motion of men, and their lustre adorns the nobleness of men—so long the lustre and the folds are lovely. But cast them from the human limbs;—golden circlet and silken tissue are withered; the dead leaves of autumn are more precious than they.

This is just as true, but in a far deeper sense, of the weaving of the natural robe of man's soul. Fragrant tissue of flowers, golden circlets of clouds, are only fair when they meet the fondness of human thoughts, and glorify human visions of heaven.

It is the leaning on this truth which, more than any other, has been the distinctive character of all my own past work. And in closing a series of Art-studies, prolonged during so many years it may be perhaps permitted me to point out this specialty—the rather that it has been, of all their characters, the one most denied. I constantly see that the same thing takes place in the estimation formed by the modern public of the work of almost any true person, living or dead. It is not needful to state here the causes of such error; but the fact is indeed so, that precisely the distinctive root and leading force of any true man's work and way are the things denied concerning him.

And in these books of mine, their distinctive character, as essays on art, is their bringing everything to a root in human passion or human hope. Arising first not in any desire to explain the principles of art, but in the endeavour to defend an individual painter from injustice, they have been coloured throughout,—nay,

continually altered in shape, and even warped and broken, by digressions respecting social questions, which had for me an interest tenfold greater than the work I had been forced into undertaking. Every principle of painting which I have stated is traced to some vital or spiritual fact; and in my works on architecture the preference accorded finally to one school over another, is founded on a comparison of their influences on the life of the workman—a question by all other writers on the subject of architecture wholly forgotten or despised.

The essential connection of the power of landscape with human emotion is not less certain, because in many impressive pictures the link is slight or local. That the connection should exist at a single point is all that we need. The comparison with the dress of the body may be carried out into the extremest parallelism. It may often happen that no part of the figure wearing the dress is discernible, nevertheless, the perceivable fact that the drapery is worn by a figure makes all the difference. In one of the most sublime figures in the world this is actually so: one of the fainting Maries in Tintoret's Crucifixion has cast her mantle over her head, and her face is lost in its shade, and her whole figure veiled in folds of gray. But what the difference is between that gray woof, that gathers round her as she falls, and the same folds cast in a heap upon the ground, that difference, and more, exists between the power of Nature through which humanity is seen, and her power in the desert—whether of leaf or sand—true desertness is not in the want of leaves, but of life. Where humanity is not, and was not, the best natural beauty is more than vain. It is even terrible; not as the dress cast aside from the body; but as an embroidered shroud hiding a skeleton.

And on each side of a right feeling in this matter there lie, as usual, two opposite errors.

The first, that of caring for man only; and for the rest of the universe, little, or not at all, which, in a measure, was the error of the Greeks and Florentines; the other, that of caring for the universe only;—for man, not at all—which, in a measure, is the error of modern science, and of the Art connecting itself with such science.

The degree of power which any man may ultimately possess in landscape-painting will depend finally on his perception of this influence. If he has to paint the desert, its awfulness—if the garden, its gladsomeness—will arise simply and only from his sensibility to the story of life. Without this he is nothing but a scientific mechanist; this, though it cannot make him yet a painter, raises him to the sphere in which he may become one. Nay, the mere shadow and semblance of this have given dangerous power to works in all other respects unnoticeable; and the least degree of its true presence has given value to work in all other respects vain.

The true presence, observe, of sympathy with the spirit of man. Where this is not, sympathy with any higher spirit is impossible.

For the directest manifestation of Deity to man is in His own image, that is, in man.

"In His own image. After His likeness." *Ad imaginem et Similitudinem Suam.* [3] I do not know what people in general understand by those words. I suppose they ought to be understood. The truth they contain seems to lie at the foundation of our knowledge both of God and man; yet do we not usually pass the sentence by, in dull reverence, attaching no definite sense to it at all? For all practical purpose, might it not as well be out of the text?

I have no time, nor much desire, to examine the vague expressions of belief with which the verse has been encumbered. Let us try to find its only possible plain significance.

It cannot be supposed that the bodily shape of man resembles, or resembled, any bodily shape in Deity. The likeness must therefore be, or have been, in the soul. Had it wholly passed away, and the divine soul been altered into a soul brutal or diabolic, I suppose we should have been told of the change. But we are told nothing of the kind. The verse still stands as if for our use and trust. It was only death which was to be our punishment. Not *change.* So far as we live, the image is still there; defiled, if you will; broken, if you will; all but effaced, if you will, by death and the shadow of it. But not changed. We are not made now in any other image than God's. There are, indeed, the two states of this image—the earthly and heavenly, but both Adamite, both human, both the same likeness; only one defiled, and one pure. So that the soul of man is still a mirror, wherein may be seen, darkly, the image of the mind of God. [4]

These may seem daring words. I am sorry that they do; but I am helpless to soften them. Discover any other meaning of the text if you are able;—but be sure that it *is* a meaning—a meaning in your head and heart;—not a subtle gloss, nor a shifting of one verbal expression into another, both idealess. I repeat that, to me, the verse has, and can have, no other signification than this—that the soul of man is a mirror of the mind of God. A mirror, dark, distorted, broken, use what blameful words you please of its state; yet in the main, a true mirror, out of which alone, and by which alone, we can know anything of God at all.

"How?" the reader, perhaps, answers indignantly. "I know the nature of God by revelation, not by looking into myself."

Revelation to what? To a nature incapable of receiving truth? That cannot be; for only to a nature capable of truth, desirous of it, distinguishing it, feeding upon it, revelation is possible. To a being undesirous of it, and hating it, revelation is impossible. There can be none to a brute, or fiend. In so far, therefore, as you love truth, and live therein, in so far revelation can exist for you;—and in so far, your mind is the image of God's.

But consider, farther, not only *to* what, but *by* what, is the revelation. By sight? or word? If by sight, then to eyes which see justly. Otherwise, no sight would be revelation. So far, then, as your sight is just, it is the image of God's sight.

If by words,—how do you know their meanings, Here is a short piece of precious word revelation for instance. "God is love." [5]

Love! yes. But what is *that?* The revelation does not tell you that, I think. Look into the mirror, and you will see. Out of your own heart, you may know what love is. In no other possible way,—by no other help or sign. All the words and sounds ever uttered, all the revelations of cloud, or flame, or crystal, are utterly powerless. They cannot tell you, in the smallest point, what love means. Only the broken mirror can.

Here is more revelation. "God is just!" [6] Just! What is that? The revelation cannot help you to discover. You say it is dealing equitably or equally. But how do you discern the equality? Not by inequality of mind; not by a mind incapable of weighing, judging, or distributing. If the lengths seem unequal in the broken mirror, for you they are unequal; but if they seem equal, then the mirror is true. So far as you recognize equality, and your conscience tells you what is just, so far your mind is the image of God's; and so far as you do *not* discern this nature of justice or equality, the words "God is just" bring no revelation to you.

---

[3] Genesis 1:26.   [4] I Corinthians 13:12.   [5] I John 4:16.
[6] Deuteronomy 32:4.

"But His thoughts are not as our thoughts."[7] No; the sea is not as the standing pool by the wayside. Yet when the breeze crisps the pool, you may see the image of the breakers, and a likeness of the foam. Nay, in some sort, the same foam. If the sea is for ever invisible to you, something you may learn of it from the pool. Nothing, assuredly, any otherwise.

"But this poor miserable Me! Is *this*, then, all the book I have got to read about God in?" Yes, truly so. No other book nor fragment of book, than that, will you ever find; no velvet-bound missal, nor frankincensed manuscript;— nothing hieroglyphic nor cuneiform; papyrus and pyramid are alike silent on this matter;— nothing in the clouds above, nor in the earth beneath.[8] That flesh-bound volume is the only revelation that is, that was, or that can be. In that is the image of God painted; in that is the law of God written; in that is the promise of God

revealed. Know thyself; for through thyself only thou canst know God.

Through the glass, darkly.[9] But, except through the glass, in nowise.

A tremulous crystal, waved as water, poured out upon the ground;—you may defile it, despise it, pollute it, at your pleasure and at your peril; for on the peace of those weak waves must all the heaven you shall ever gain be first seen; and through such purity as you can win for those dark waves, must all the light of the risen Sun of Righteousness be bent down, by faint refraction. Cleanse them, and calm them, as you love your life.

Therefore it is that all the power of nature depends on subjection to the human soul. Man is the sun of the world; more than the real sun. The fire of his wonderful heart is the only light and heat worth gauge or measure. Where he is, are the tropics; where he is not, the ice-world.

from The Seven Lamps of Architecture

The famous Ruskinian discursiveness and tendency to digression are largely curbed in his most tightly organized work, The Seven Lamps of Architecture. *In it Ruskin advances the thesis, later elaborated and sustained by abundant specific example in* The Stones of Venice, *that the communal art of architecture is the public record of the soul and spirit of the people producing it. Although many of his remarks in this work are highly technical, the principle of organization around the seven "lamps" or guiding principles of architecture is broad and comprehensive, as shown by the titles of the seven lamps: Sacrifice, Truth, Power, Beauty, Life, Memory, and Obedience. The final chapter, "The Lamp of Obedience," is given below. The work was first published in 1849.*

CHAPTER VII

The Lamp of Obedience

IT HAS been my endeavour to show in the preceding pages how every form of noble architecture is in some sort the embodiment of the Polity, Life, History, and Religious Faith of nations. Once or twice in doing this, I have named a principle to which I would now assign a definite place among those which direct that embodiment; the last place, not only as that to which its own humility would incline, but rather

as belonging to it in the aspect of the crowning grace of all the rest; that principle, I mean, to which Polity owes its stability, Life its happiness, Faith its acceptance, Creation its continuance,— Obedience.

Nor is it the least among the sources of more serious satisfaction which I have found in the pursuit of a subject that at first appeared to bear but slightly on the grave interests of mankind, that the conditions of material perfection which it leads me in conclusion to consider, furnish a strange proof how false is the conception, how frantic the pursuit, of that treacherous phantom which men call Liberty: most treacherous, indeed, of all phantoms; for the feeblest ray of reason

---

[7] Isaiah 55:8.   [8] Exodus 20:4.   [9] I Corinthians 13:12.

might surely show us, that not only its attainment, but its being, was impossible. There is no such thing in the universe. There can never be. The stars have it not; the earth has it not; the sea has it not; and we men have the mockery and semblance of it only for our heaviest punishment.

In one of the noblest poems for its imagery and its music belonging to the recent school of our literature, the writer has sought in the aspect of inanimate nature the expression of that Liberty which, having once loved, he has seen among men in its true dyes of darkness. But with what strange fallacy of interpretation! since in one noble line of his invocation he has contradicted the assumptions of the rest, and acknowledged the presence of a subjection, surely not less severe because eternal. How could he otherwise? since if there be any one principle more widely than another confessed by every utterance, or more sternly than another imprinted on every atom, of the visible creation, that principle is not Liberty, but Law.

The enthusiast would reply that by Liberty he meant the Law of Liberty. Then why use the single and misunderstood word? If by liberty you mean chastisement of the passions, discipline of the intellect, subjection of the will; if you mean the fear of inflicting, the shame of committing a wrong; if you mean respect for all who are in authority, and consideration for all who are in dependence; veneration for the good, mercy to the evil, sympathy with the weak; if you mean watchfulness over all thoughts, temperance in all pleasures, and perseverance in all toils; if you mean, in a word, that Service which is defined in the liturgy of the English Church to be perfect Freedom,[1] why do you name this by the same word by which the luxurious mean license, and the reckless mean change; by which the rogue means rapine, and the fool, equality; by which the proud mean anarchy, and the malignant mean violence? Call it by any name rather than this, but its best and truest is Obedience. Obedience is, indeed, founded on a kind of freedom, else it would become mere subjugation, but that freedom is only granted that obedience may be more perfect; and thus, while a measure of license is necessary to exhibit the individual energies of things, the fairness and pleasantness and perfection of them all consist in their Restraint. Compare a river that has burst its banks with one that is bound by them, and the clouds that are scattered over the face of the whole heaven with those that are marshalled into ranks and orders by its winds. So that though restraint, utter and unrelaxing, can never be comely, this is not because it is in itself an evil, but only because, when too great, it overpowers the nature of the thing restrained, and so counteracts the other laws of which that nature is itself composed. And the balance wherein consists the fairness of creation is between the laws of life and being in the things governed, and the laws of general sway to which they are subjected; and the suspension or infringement of either kind of law, or, literally, disorder, is equivalent to, and synonymous with, disease; while the increase of both honour and beauty is habitually on the side of restraint (or the action of superior law) rather than of character (or the action of inherent law). The noblest word in the catalogue of social virtue is "Loyalty," and the sweetest which men have learned in the pastures of the wilderness is "Fold."

Nor is this all; but we may observe, that exactly in proportion to the majesty of things in the scale of being, is the completeness of their obedience to the laws that are set over them. Gravitation is less quietly, less instantly obeyed by a grain of dust than it is by the sun and moon; and the ocean falls and flows under influences which the lake and river do not recognize. So also in estimating the dignity of any action or occupation of men, there is perhaps no better test than the question "are its laws strait?" For their severity will probably be commensurate with the greatness of the numbers whose labour it concentrates or whose interest it concerns.

This severity must be singular, therefore, in the case of that art, above all others, whose productions are the most vast and the most common; which requires for its practice the co-operation of bodies of men, and for its perfection the perseverance of successive generations. And, taking into account also what we have before so often observed of Architecture, her continual influence over the emotions of daily life, and her realism, as opposed to the two sister arts which are in comparison but the picturing of stories and of dreams, we might beforehand expect that we should find her healthy state and action dependent on far more severe laws than theirs: that the license which they extend to the workings of individual mind would be withdrawn by her; and that, in assertion of the relations which she holds with all that is universally important to man, she

---

[1] Book of Common Prayer, Second Collect in the Order for Morning Prayer.

would set forth, by her own majestic subjection, some likeness of that on which man's social happiness and power depend. We might, therefore, without the light of experience, conclude, that Architecture never could flourish except when it was subjected to a national law as strict and as minutely authoritative as the laws which regulate religion, policy, and social relations; nay, even more authoritative than these, because both capable of more enforcement, as over more passive matter; and needing more enforcement, as the purest type not of one law nor of another, but of the common authority of all. But in this matter experience speaks more loudly than reason. If there be any one condition which, in watching the progress of architecture, we see distinct and general; if, amidst the counter-evidence of success attending opposite accidents of character and circumstance, any one conclusion may be constantly and indisputably drawn, it is this; that the architecture of a nation is great only when it is as universal and as established as its language; and when provincial differences of style are nothing more than so many dialects. Other necessities are matters of doubt: nations have been alike successful in their architecture in times of poverty and of wealth; in times of war and of peace; in times of barbarism and of refinement; under governments the most liberal or the most arbitrary; but this one condition has been constant, this one requirement clear in all places and at all times, that the work shall be that of a *school*, that no individual caprice shall dispense with, or materially vary, accepted types and customary decorations; and that from the cottage to the palace, and from the chapel to the basilica, and from the garden fence to the fortress wall, every member and feature of the architecture of the nation shall be as commonly current, as frankly accepted, as its language or its coin.

A day never passes without our hearing our English architects called upon to be original, and to invent a new style: about as sensible and necessary an exhortation as to ask of a man who has never had rags enough on his back to keep out cold, to invent a new mode of cutting a coat. Give him a whole coat first, and let him concern himself about the fashion of it afterwards. We want no new style of architecture. Who wants a new style of painting or sculpture? But we want *some* style. It is of marvellously little importance, if we have a code of laws and they be good laws, whether they be new or old, foreign or native, Roman or Saxon, or Norman, or English laws. But it is of considerable importance that we

should have a code of laws of one kind or another, and that code accepted and enforced from one side of the island to another, and not one law made ground of judgment at York and another in Exeter. And in like manner it does not matter one marble splinter whether we have an old or new architecture, but it matters everything whether we have an architecture truly so called or not; that is, whether an architecture whose laws might be taught at our schools from Cornwall to Northumberland, as we teach English spelling and English grammar, or an architecture which is to be invented fresh every time we build a workhouse or a parish school. There seems to me to be a wonderful misunderstanding among the majority of architects of the present day as to the very nature and meaning of Originality, and of all wherein it consists. Originality in expression does not depend on invention of new words; nor originality in poetry on invention of new measures; nor, in painting, on invention of new colours, or new modes of using them. The chords of music, the harmonies of colour, the general principles of the arrangement of sculptural masses, have been determined long ago, and, in all probability, cannot be added to any more than they can be altered. Granting that they may be, such additions or alterations are much more the work of time and of multitudes than of individual inventors. We may have one Van Eyck, who will be known as the introducer of a new style once in ten centuries, but he himself will trace his invention to some accidental by-play or pursuit; and the use of that invention will depend altogether on the popular necessities or instincts of the period. Originality depends on nothing of the kind. A man who has the gift, will take up any style that is going, the style of his day, and will work in that, and be great in that, and make everything that he does in it look as fresh as if every thought of it had just come down from heaven. I do not say that he will not take liberties with his materials, or with his rules: I do not say that strange changes will not sometimes be wrought by his efforts, or his fancies, in both. But those changes will be instructive, natural, facile, though sometimes marvellous; they will never be sought after as things necessary to his dignity or to his independence; and those liberties will be like the liberties that a great speaker takes with the language, not a defiance of its rules for the sake of singularity; but inevitable, uncalculated, and brilliant consequences of an effort to express what the language, without such infraction, could not. There may be times when, as I have above described, the life of an art is manifested in its changes, and in its refusal of ancient limitations: so there are in the life of an insect; and there is great interest in the state of both the art and the insect at those periods when, by their natural progress and constitutional power, such changes are about to be wrought. But as that would be both an uncomfortable and foolish caterpillar which, instead of being contented with a caterpillar's life and feeding on caterpillar's food, was always striving to turn itself into a chrysalis; and as that would be an unhappy chrysalis which should lie awake at night and roll restlessly in its cocoon, in efforts to turn itself prematurely into a moth; so will that art be unhappy and unprosperous which, instead of supporting itself on the food, and contenting itself with the customs, which have been enough for the support and guidance of other arts before it and like it, is struggling and fretting under the natural limitations of its existence, and striving to become something other than it is. And though it is the nobility of the highest creatures to look forward to, and partly to understand the changes which are appointed for them, preparing for them beforehand; and if, as is usual with *appointed* changes, they be into a higher state, even desiring them, and rejoicing in the hope of them, yet it is the strength of every creature, be it changeful or not, to rest, for the time being, contented with the conditions of its existence, and striving only to bring about the changes which it desires, by fulfilling to the uttermost the duties for which its present state is appointed and continued.

Neither originality, therefore, nor change, good though both may be, and this is commonly a most merciful and enthusiastic supposition with respect to either, is ever to be sought in itself, or can ever be healthily obtained by any struggle or rebellion against common laws. We want neither the one nor the other. The forms of architecture already known are good enough for us, and for far better than any of us: and it will be time enough to think of changing them for better when we can use them as they are. But there are some things which we not only want, but cannot do without; and which all the struggling and raving in the world, nay more, which all the real talent and resolution in England, will never enable us to do without: and these are Obedience, Unity, Fellowship, and Order. And all our schools of design, and committees of taste; all our academies and lectures, and journalisms, and essays; all the sacrifices which

we are beginning to make, all the truth which there is in our English nature, all the power of our English will, and the life of our English intellect, will in this matter be as useless as efforts and emotions in a dream, unless we are contented to submit architecture and all art, like other things, to English law.

I say architecture and all art; for I believe architecture must be the beginning of arts, and that the others must follow her in their time and order; and I think the prosperity of our schools of painting and sculpture, in which no one will deny the life, though many the health, depends upon that of our architecture. I think that all will languish until that takes the lead, and (this I do not *think*, but I proclaim, as confidently as I would assert the necessity, for the safety of society, of an understood and strongly administered legal government) our architecture *will* languish, and that in the very dust, until the first principle of common sense be manfully obeyed, and an universal system of form and workmanship be everywhere adopted and enforced. It may be said that this is impossible. It may be so—I fear it is so: I have nothing to do with the possibility or impossibility of it; I simply know and assert the necessity of it. If it be impossible, English art is impossible. Give it up at once. You are wasting time, and money, and energy upon it, and though you exhaust centuries and treasuries, and break hearts for it, you will never raise it above the merest dilettanteism. Think not of it. It is a dangerous vanity, a mere gulph in which genius after genius will be swallowed up, and it will not close. And so it will continue to be, unless the one bold and broad step be taken at the beginning. We shall not manufacture art out of pottery and printed stuffs: we shall not reason out art by our philosophy; we shall not stumble upon art by our experiments, nor create it by our fancies: I do not say that we can even build it out of brick and stone; but there is a chance for us in these, and there is none else; and that chance rests on the bare possibility of obtaining the consent, both of architects and of the public, to choose a style, and to use it universally.

How surely its principles ought at first to be limited, we may easily determine by the consideration of the necessary modes of teaching any other branch of general knowledge. When we begin to teach children writing, we force them to absolute copyism, and require absolute accuracy in the formation of the letters; as they obtain command of the received modes of literal expression, we cannot prevent their falling into such variations as are consistent with their feeling, their circumstances, or their characters. So, when a boy is first taught to write Latin, an authority is required of him for every expression he uses; as he becomes master of the language he may take a license, and feel his right to do so without any authority, and yet write better Latin than when he borrowed every separate expression. In the same way our architects would have to be taught to write the accepted style. We must first determine what buildings are to be considered Augustan in their authority; their modes of construction and laws of proportion are to be studied with the most penetrating care; then the different forms and uses of their decorations are to be classed and catalogued, as a German grammarian classes the powers of prepositions; and under this absolute, irrefragable authority, we are to begin to work; admitting not so much as an alteration in the depth of a cavetto, or the breadth of a fillet. Then, when our sight is once accustomed to the grammatical forms and arrangements, and our thoughts familiar with the expression of them all; when we can speak this dead language naturally, and apply it to whatever ideas we have to render, that is to say, to every practical purpose of life; then, and not till then, a license might be permitted, and individual authority allowed to change or to add to the received forms, always within certain limits; the decorations, especially, might be made subjects of variable fancy, and enriched with ideas either original or taken from other schools. And thus, in process of time, and by a great national movement, it might come to pass that a new style should arise, as language itself changes; we might perhaps come to speak Italian instead of Latin, or to speak modern instead of old English; but this would be a matter of entire indifference, and a matter, besides, which no determination or desire could either hasten or prevent. That alone which it is in our power to obtain, and which it is our duty to desire, is an unanimous style of some kind, and such comprehension and practice of it as would enable us to adapt its features to the peculiar character of every several building, large or small, domestic, civil, or ecclesiastical. I have said that it was immaterial what style was adopted, so far as regards the room for originality which its development would admit: it is not so, however, when we take into consideration the far more important questions of the facility of adaptation to general purposes, and of the sympathy with which this or that style would

be popularly regarded. The choice of Classical or Gothic, again using the latter term in its broadest sense, may be questionable when it regards some single and considerable public building; but I cannot conceive it questionable, for an instant, when it regards modern uses in general: I cannot conceive any architect insane enough to project the vulgarization of Greek architecture. Neither can it be rationally questionable whether we should adopt early or late, original or derivative Gothic; if the latter were chosen, it must be either some impotent and ugly degradation, like our own Tudor, or else a style whose grammatical laws it would be nearly impossible to limit or arrange, like the French Flamboyant. We are equally precluded from adopting styles essentially infantine or barbarous, however Herculean their infancy, or majestic their outlawry, such as our own Norman, or the Lombard Romanesque. The choice would lie I think between four styles:—1. The Pisan Romanesque; 2. The early Gothic of the Western Italian Republics, advanced as far and as fast as our art would enable us to the Gothic of Giotto; 3. The Venetian Gothic in its purest development; 4. The English earliest decorated. The most natural, perhaps the safest choice, would be of the last, well fenced from chance of again stiffening into the perpendicular; and perhaps enriched by some mingling of decorative elements from the exquisite decorated Gothic of France, of which, in such cases, it would be needful to accept some well-known examples, as the North door of Rouen and the church of St. Urbain at Troyes, for final and limiting authorities on the side of decoration.

It is almost impossible for us to conceive, in our present state of doubt and ignorance, the sudden dawn of intelligence and fancy, the rapidly increasing sense of power and facility, and, in its *proper sense*, of Freedom, which such wholesome restraint would instantly cause throughout the whole circle of the arts. Freed from the agitation and embarrassment of that liberty of choice which is the cause of half the discomforts of the world; freed from the accompanying necessity of studying all past, present, or even possible styles; and enabled, by concentration of individual, and co-operation of multitudinous energy, to penetrate into the uttermost secrets of the adopted style, the architect would find his whole understanding enlarged, his practical knowledge certain and ready to hand, and his imagination playful and vigorous, as a child's would be within a walled garden, who would sit down and shudder if he were left free in a fenceless plain. How many and how bright would be the results in every direction of interest, not to the arts merely, but to national happiness and virtue, it would be as difficult to preconceive as it would seem extravagant to state: but the first, perhaps the least, of them would be an increased sense of fellowship among ourselves, a cementing of every patriotic bond of union, a proud and happy recognition of our affection for and sympathy with each other, and our willingness in all things to submit ourselves to every law that could advance the interest of the community; a barrier, also, the best conceivable, to the unhappy rivalry of the upper and middle classes, in houses, furniture, and establishments; and even a check to much of what is as vain as it is painful in the oppositions of religious parties respecting matters of ritual. These, I say, would be the first consequences. Economy increased tenfold, as it would be by the simplicity of practice; domestic comforts uninterfered with by the caprice and mistakes of architects ignorant of the capacities of the styles they use, and all the symmetry and sightliness of our harmonized streets and public buildings, are things of slighter account in the catalogue of benefits. But it would be mere enthusiasm to endeavour to trace them farther.[2] I have suffered myself too long to indulge in the speculative statement of requirements which perhaps we have more immediate and more serious work than to supply, and of feelings which it may be only contingently in our power to recover. I should be unjustly thought unaware of the difficulty of what I have proposed, or of the unimportance of the whole subject as compared with many which are brought home to our interests and fixed upon our consideration by the wild course of the present century. But of difficulty and of importance it is for others to judge. I have limited myself to the simple statement of what, if we desire to have architecture, we MUST primarily endeavour to feel and do: but then it may not be desirable for us to have architecture at all. There are many who feel it to be so; many who sacrifice much to that end; and I am sorry to see their energies wasted and their lives disquieted in vain. I have stated, therefore, the only ways in which that end is

attainable, without venturing even to express an opinion as to its real desirableness. I have an opinion, and the zeal with which I have spoken may sometimes have betrayed it, but I hold to it with no confidence. I know too well the undue importance which the study that every man follows must assume in his own eyes, to trust my own impressions of the dignity of that of Architecture; and yet I think I cannot be utterly mistaken in regarding it as at least useful in the sense of a National employment. I am confirmed in this impression by what I see passing among the states of Europe at this instant. All the horror, distress, and tumult which oppress the foreign nations, are traceable, among the other secondary causes through which God is working out His will upon them, to the simple one of their not having enough to do. I am not blind to the distress among their operatives; nor do I deny the nearer and visibly active causes of the movement: the recklessness of villainy in the leaders of revolt, the absence of common moral principle in the upper classes, and of common courage and honesty in the heads of governments. But these causes themselves are ultimately traceable to a deeper and simpler one: the recklessness of the demagogue, the immorality of the middle class, and the effeminacy and treachery of the noble, are traceable in all these nations to the commonest and most fruitful cause of calamity in households —idleness. We think too much in our benevolent efforts, more multiplied and more vain day by day, of bettering men by giving them advice and instruction. There are few who will take either: the chief thing they need is occupation. I do not mean work in the sense of bread,—I mean work in the sense of mental interest; for those who either are placed above the necessity of labour for their bread, or who will not work although they should. There is a vast quantity of idle energy among European nations at this time, which ought to go into handicrafts; there are multitudes of idle semi-gentlemen who ought to be shoemakers and carpenters; but since they will not be these so long as they can help it, the business of the philanthropist is to find them some other employment than disturbing governments. It is of no use to tell them they are fools, and that they will only make themselves miserable

---

[2] I am well content to close my thirty-three aphorisms with this most comprehensive one;—and my fifty-five notes with this still more comprehensive reduction of them to practice for the modern reader:— Build nothing that you can possibly help,—and let no land on building leases. [Ruskin's note]

The aphorisms to which Ruskin refers were scattered in the margins throughout *The Seven Lamps of Architecture*. There were two in the final chapter, "The Lamp of Obedience": aphorism 32: "There is no such thing as liberty," and aphorism 33: "The glory and use of restraint."

in the end as well as others: if they have nothing else to do, they will do mischief; and the man who will not work, and who has no means of intellectual pleasure, is as sure to become an instrument of evil as if he had sold himself bodily to Satan. I have myself seen enough of the daily life of the young educated men of France and Italy, to account for, as it deserves, the deepest national suffering and degradation; and though, for the most part, our commerce and our national habits of industry preserve us from a similar paralysis, yet it would be wise to consider whether the forms of employment which we chiefly adopt or promote, are as well calculated as they might be to improve and elevate us.

We have just spent, for instance, a hundred and fifty millions, with which we have paid men for digging ground from one place and depositing it in another. We have formed a large class of men, the railway navvies, especially reckless, unmanageable, and dangerous. We have maintained besides (let us state the benefits as fairly as possible) a number of ironfounders in an unhealthy and painful employment; we have developed (this is at least good) a very large amount of mechanical ingenuity; and we have, in fine, attained the power of going fast from one place to another. Meantime we have had no mental interest or concern ourselves in the operations we have set on foot, but have been left to the usual vanities and cares of our existence. Suppose, on the other hand, that we had employed the same sums in building beautiful houses and churches. We should have maintained the same number of men, not in driving wheelbarrows, but in a distinctly technical, if not intellectual employment; and those who were more intelligent among them would have been especially happy in that employment, as having room in it for the development of their fancy, and being directed by it to that observation of beauty which, associated with the pursuit of natural science, at present forms the enjoyment of many of the more intelligent manufacturing operatives. Of mechanical ingenuity, there is, I imagine, at least as much required to build a cathedral as to cut a tunnel or contrive a locomotive: we should, therefore, have developed as much science, while the artistical element of intellect would have been added to the gain. Meantime we should ourselves have been made happier and wiser by the interest we should have taken in the work with which we were personally concerned; and when all was done, instead of the very doubtful advantage of the power of going fast from place to place, we should have had the certain advantage of increased pleasure in stopping at home.

There are many other less capacious, but more constant, channels of expenditure, quite as disputable in their beneficial tendency; and we are, perhaps, hardly enough in the habit of inquiring, with respect to any particular form of luxury or any customary appliance of life, whether the kind of employment it gives to the operative or the dependant be as healthy and fitting an employment as we might otherwise provide for him. It is not enough to find men absolute subsistence; we should think of the manner of life which our demands necessitate; and endeavour, as far as may be, to make all our needs such as may, in the supply of them, raise, as well as feed, the poor. It is far better to give work which is above the men, than to educate the men to be above their work. It may be doubted, for instance, whether the habits of luxury, which necessitate a large train of men servants, be a wholesome form of expenditure; and more, whether the pursuits which have a tendency to enlarge the class of the jockey and the groom be a philanthropic form of mental occupation. So again, consider the large number of men whose lives are employed by civilised nations in cutting facets upon jewels. There is much dexterity of hand, patience and ingenuity thus bestowed, which are simply burned out in the blaze of the tiara, without, so far as I see, bestowing any pleasure upon those who wear or who behold, at all compensatory for the loss of life and mental power which are involved in the employment of the workman. He would be far more healthily and happily sustained by being set to carve stone; certain qualities of his mind, for which there is no room in his present occupation, would develope themselves in the nobler; and I believe that most women would, in the end, prefer the pleasure of having built a church, or contributed to the adornment of a cathedral, to the pride of bearing a certain quantity of adamant on their foreheads.

I could pursue this subject willingly, but I have some strange notions about it which it is perhaps wiser not loosely to set down. I content myself with finally reasserting, what has been throughout the burden of the preceding pages, that whatever rank, or whatever importance, may be attributed or attached to their immediate subject, there is at least some value in the analogies with which its pursuit has presented us, and some instruction in the frequent reference of its commonest necessities to the mighty laws, in the sense and scope of which all men are Builders, whom every hour sees laying the stubble or the stone.

I have paused, not once nor twice, as I wrote, and often have checked the course of what might otherwise have been importunate persuasion, as the thought has crossed me, how soon all Architecture may be vain, except that which is not made with hands.[3] There is something ominous in the light which has enabled us to look back with disdain upon the ages among whose lovely vestiges we have been wandering. I could smile when I hear the hopeful exultation of many, at the new reach of worldly science, and vigour of worldly effort; as if we were again at the beginning of days. There is thunder on the horizon as well as dawn. The sun was risen upon the earth when Lot entered into Zoar.[4]

from The Stones of Venice

This is perhaps Ruskin's most widely acclaimed work, for in it he combines his surpassing knowledge of art and history to enunciate his theory of the interaction between the life of a society and the works of architecture that it produces. In three well-organized volumes he traces the origin, rise, and fall of Venice as shown through its architecture. Here too Ruskin makes his impassioned plea for the superiority of Gothic architecture over what he saw as the debased architecture of the Renaissance and subsequent periods. His glorification of Gothic gave an enormous boost to the already burgeoning Gothic revival of Victorian England. The bulk of the chapter on the nature of Gothic is reproduced below. The work was published in three volumes over the period 1851 to 1853.

Second, or Gothic, Period

CHAPTER VI

The Nature of Gothic

§ 1. If the reader will look back to the division of our subject which was made in the first chapter of the first volume, he will find that we are now about to enter upon the examination of that school of Venetian architecture which forms an intermediate step between the Byzantine and Gothic forms; but which I find may be conveniently considered in its connexion with the latter style. In order that we may discern the tendency of each step of this change, it will be wise in the outset to endeavour to form some general idea of its final result. We know already what the Byzantine architecture is from which the transition was made, but we ought to know something of the Gothic architecture into which it led. I shall endeavour therefore to give the reader in this chapter an idea, at once broad and definite, of the true nature of *Gothic* architecture, properly so called; not of that of Venice only, but of universal Gothic: for it will be one of the most interesting parts of our subsequent inquiry to find out how far Venetian architecture reached the universal or perfect type of Gothic, and how far it either fell short of it, or assumed foreign and independent forms.

§ 2. The principal difficulty in doing this arises from the fact that every building of the Gothic period differs in some important respect from every other; and many include features which, if they occurred in other buildings, would not be considered Gothic at all; so that all we have to reason upon is merely, if I may be allowed so to express it, a greater or less degree of *Gothicness* in each building we examine. And it is this Gothicness,—the character which, according as it is found more or less in a building, makes it more or less Gothic—of which I want to define the nature; and I feel the same kind of difficulty in doing so which would be encountered by any one who undertook to explain, for instance, the nature of Redness, without any actually red thing to point to, but only orange and purple

---

[3] 2 Corinthians 5:1.   [4] Genesis 19:23.

things. Suppose he had only a piece of heather and a dead oak-leaf to do it with. He might say, the colour which is mixed with the yellow in this oak-leaf, and with the blue in this heather, would be red, if you had it separate; but it would be difficult, nevertheless, to make the abstraction perfectly intelligible: and it is so in a far greater degree to make the abstraction of the Gothic character intelligible, because that character itself is made up of many mingled ideas, and can consist only in their union. That is to say, pointed arches do not constitute Gothic, nor vaulted roofs, nor flying buttresses, nor grotesque sculptures; but all or some of these things, and many other things with them, when they come together so as to have life.

§ 3. Observe also, that, in the definition proposed, I shall only endeavour to analyze the idea which I suppose already to exist in the reader's mind. We all have some notion, most of us a very determined one, of the meaning of the term Gothic, but I know that many persons have this idea in their minds without being able to define it: that is to say, understanding generally that Westminster Abbey is Gothic, and St. Paul's is not, that Strasburg Cathedral is Gothic, and St. Peter's is not, they have, nevertheless, no clear notion of what it is that they recognize in the one or miss in the other, such as would enable them to say how far the work at Westminster or Strasburg is good and pure of its kind; still less to say of any nondescript building, like St. James's Palace or Windsor Castle, how much right Gothic element there is in it, and how much wanting. And I believe this inquiry to be a pleasant and profitable one; and that there will be found something more than usually interesting in tracing out this grey, shadowy, many-pinnacled image of the Gothic spirit within us; and discerning what fellowship there is between it and our Northern hearts. And if, at any point of the inquiry, I should interfere with any of the reader's previously formed conceptions, and use the term Gothic in any sense which he would not willingly attach to it, I do not ask him to accept, but only to examine and understand, my interpretation, as necessary to the intelligibility of what follows in the rest of the work.

§ 4. We have, then, the Gothic character submitted to our analysis, just as the rough mineral is submitted to that of the chemist, entangled with many other foreign substances, itself perhaps in no place pure, or ever to be obtained or seen in purity for more than an instant; but nevertheless a thing of definite and separate nature, however inextricable or confused in appearance. Now observe: the chemist defines his mineral by two separate kinds of character; one external, its crystalline form, hardness, lustre, etc.; the other internal, the proportions and nature of its constituent atoms. Exactly in the same manner, we shall find that Gothic architecture has external forms and internal elements. Its elements are certain mental tendencies of the builders, legibly expressed in it; as fancifulness, love of variety, love of richness, and such others. Its external forms are pointed arches, vaulted roofs, etc. And unless both the elements and the forms are there, we have no right to call the style Gothic. It is not enough that it has the Form, if it have not also the power and life. It is not enough that it has the Power, if it have not the form. We must therefore inquire into each of these characters successively; and determine first, what is the Mental Expression, and secondly, what the Material Form of Gothic architecture, properly so called.

1st. Mental Power or Expression. What characters, we have to discover, did the Gothic builders love, or instinctively express in their work, as distinguished from all other builders?

§ 5. Let us go back for a moment to our chemistry, and note that, in defining a mineral by its constituent parts, it is not one nor another of them, that can make up the mineral, but the union of all: for instance, it is neither in charcoal, nor in oxygen, nor in lime, that there is the making of chalk, but in the combination of all three in certain measures; they are all found in very different things from chalk, and there is nothing like chalk either in charcoal or in oxygen, but they are nevertheless necessary to its existence.

So in the various mental characters which make up the soul of Gothic. It is not one nor another that produces it; but their union in certain measures. Each one of them is found in many other architectures beside Gothic; but Gothic cannot exist where they are not found, or, at least, where their place is not in some way supplied. Only there is this great difference between the composition of the mineral and of the architectural style, that if we withdraw one of its elements from the stone, its form is utterly changed, and its existence as such and such a mineral is destroyed; but if we withdraw one of its mental elements from the Gothic style, it is only a little less Gothic than it was before, and the union of two or three of its elements is enough already to bestow a certain Gothicness of character, which gains in intensity as we add the others, and loses as we again withdraw them.

§ 6. I believe, then, that the characteristic or moral elements of Gothic are the following, placed in the order of their importance:

1. Savageness.
2. Changefulness.
3. Naturalism.
4. Grotesqueness.
5. Rigidity.
6. Redundance.

These characters are here expressed as belonging to the building; as belonging to the builder, they would be expressed thus:—1. Savageness or Rudeness. 2. Love of Change. 3. Love of Nature. 4. Disturbed Imagination. 5. Obstinacy. 6. Generosity. And I repeat, that the withdrawal of any one, or any two, will not at once destroy the Gothic character of a building, but the removal of a majority of them will. I shall proceed to examine them in their order.

§ 7. (1.) SAVAGENESS. I am not sure when the word "Gothic" was first generically applied to the architecture of the North; but I presume that, whatever the date of its original usage, it was intended to imply reproach, and express the barbaric character of the nations among whom that architecture arose. It never implied that they were literally of Gothic lineage, far less that their architecture had been originally invented by the Goths themselves; but it did imply that they and their buildings together exhibited a degree of sternness and rudeness, which, in contradistinction to the character of Southern and Eastern nations, appeared like a perpetual reflection of the contrast between the Goth and the Roman in their first encounter. And when that fallen Roman, in the utmost impotence of his luxury, and insolence of his guilt, became the model for the imitation of civilized Europe, at the close of the so-called Dark ages, the word Gothic became a term of unmitigated contempt, not unmixed with aversion. From that contempt, by the exertion of the antiquaries and architects of this century, Gothic architecture has been sufficiently vindicated; and perhaps some among us, in our admiration of the magnificent science of its structure, and sacredness of its expression, might desire that the term of ancient reproach should be withdrawn, and some other, of more apparent honourableness, adopted in its place. There is no chance, as there is no need, of such a substitution. As far as the epithet was used scornfully, it was used falsely; but there is no reproach in the word, rightly understood; on

the contrary, there is a profound truth, which the instinct of mankind almost unconsciously recognizes. It is true, greatly and deeply true, that the architecture of the North is rude and wild; but it is not true, that, for this reason, we are to condemn it, or despise. Far otherwise: I believe it is in this very character that it deserves our profoundest reverence.

§ 8. The charts of the world which have been drawn up by modern science have thrown into a narrow space the expression of a vast amount of knowledge, but I have never yet seen any one pictorial enough to enable the spectator to imagine the kind of contrast in physical character which exists between Northern and Southern countries. We know the difference in detail, but we have not that broad glance and grasp which would enable us to feel them in their fulness. We know that gentians grow on the Alps, and olives on the Apennines; but we do not enough conceive for ourselves that variegated mosaic of the world's surface which a bird sees in its migration, that difference between the district of the gentian and of the olive which the stork and the swallow see far off, as they lean upon the sirocco wind. Let us, for a moment, try to raise ourselves even above the level of their flight, and imagine the Mediterranean lying beneath us like an irregular lake, and all its ancient promontories sleeping in the sun: here and there an angry spot of thunder, a grey stain of storm, moving upon the burning field; and here and there a fixed wreath of white volcano smoke, surrounded by its circle of ashes; but for the most part a great peacefulness of light, Syria and Greece, Italy and Spain, laid like pieces of a golden pavement into the sea-blue, chased, as we stoop nearer to them, with bossy beaten work of mountain chains, and glowing softly with terraced gardens, and flowers heavy with frankincense, mixed among masses of laurel, and orange, and plumy palm, that abate with their grey-green shadows the burning of the marble rocks, and of the ledges of porphyry sloping under lucent sand. Then let us pass farther towards the north, until we see the orient colours change gradually into a vast belt of rainy green, where the pastures of Switzerland, and poplar valleys of France, and dark forests of the Danube and Carpathians stretch from the mouths of the Loire to those of the Volga, seen through clefts in grey swirls of raincloud and flaky veils of the mist of the brooks, spreading low along the pasture lands: and then, farther north still, to see the earth heave into mighty masses of leaden rock and heathy moor, bordering with a broad waste of gloomy purple that belt of field and wood, and splintering into irregular and grisly islands amidst the northern seas, beaten by storm, and chilled by ice-drift, and tormented by furious pulses of contending tide, until the roots of the last forests fail from among the hill ravines, and the hunger of the north wind bites their peaks into barrenness; and, at last, the wall of ice, durable like iron, sets, death-like, its white teeth against us out of the polar twilight. And, having once traversed in thought this gradation of the zoned iris of the earth in all its material vastness, let us go down nearer to it, and watch the parallel change in the belt of animal life; the multitudes of swift and brilliant creatures that glance in the air and sea, or tread the sands of the southern zone; striped zebras and spotted leopards, glistening serpents, and birds arrayed in purple and scarlet. Let us contrast their delicacy and brilliancy of colour, and swift-ness of motion, with the frost-cramped strength, and shaggy covering, and dusky plumage of the northern tribes; contrast the Arabian horse with the Shetland, the tiger and leopard with the wolf and bear, the antelope with the elk, the bird of paradise with the osprey: and then, submissively acknowledging the great laws by which the earth and all that it bears are ruled throughout their being, let us not condemn, but rejoice in the expression by man of his own rest in the statues of the lands that gave him birth. Let us watch him with reverence as he sets side by side the burning gems, and smooths with soft sculpture the jasper pillars, that are to re-flect a ceaseless sunshine, and rise into a cloudless sky: but not with less reverence let us stand by him, when, with rough strength and hurried stroke, he smites an uncouth animation out of the rocks which he has torn from among the moss of the moorland, and heaves into the dark-ened air of the pile of iron buttress and rugged wall, instinct with a work of an imagination as wild and wayward as the northern sea; creations of ungainly shape and rigid limb, but full of wolfish life; fierce as the winds that beat, and changeful as the clouds that shade them.

There is, I repeat, no degradation, no reproach in this, but all dignity and honourableness: and we should err grievously in refusing either to recognize as an essential character of the existing architecture of the North, or to admit as a desirable character in that which it yet may be, this wildness of thought, and roughness of work; this look of mountain brotherhood between the cathedral and the Alp; this magnificence of sturdy power, put forth only the more energeti-cally because the fine finger-touch was chilled away by the frosty wind, and the eye dimmed by the moor-mist, or blinded by the hail; this out-speaking of the strong spirit of men who may not gather redundant fruitage from the earth, nor bask in dreamy benignity of sunshine, but must break the rock for bread, and cleave the forest for fire, and show, even in what they did for their delight, some of the hard habits of the arm and heart that grew on them as they swung the axe or pressed the plough.

§ 9. If, however, the savageness of Gothic architecture, merely as an expression of its origin among Northern nations, may be con-sidered, in some sort, a noble character, it pos-sesses a higher nobility still, when considered as an index, not of climate, but of religious principle.

In the 13th and 14th paragraphs of Chapter XXI of the first volume of this work, it was noticed that the systems of architectural orna-ment, properly so called, might be divided into three:—1. Servile ornament, in which the execution or power of the inferior workman is entirely subjected to the intellect of the higher;—2. Constitutional ornament, in which the execu-tive inferior power is, to a certain point, emanci-pated and independent, having a will of its own, yet confessing its inferiority and rendering obedience to higher powers;—and 3. Revolu-tionary ornament, in which no executive in-feriority is admitted at all. I must here explain the nature of these divisions at somewhat greater length.

Of Servile ornament, the principal schools are the Greek, Ninevite, and Egyptian; but their servility is of different kinds. The Greek master-workman was far advanced in knowledge and power above the Assyrian or Egyptian. Neither he nor those for whom he worked could endure the appearance of imperfection in anything; and, therefore, what ornament he appointed to be done by those beneath him was composed of mere geometrical forms,—balls, ridges, and perfectly symmetrical foliage,—which could be executed with absolute precision by line and rule, and were as perfect in their way, when completed, as his own figure sculpture. The Assyrian and Egyptian, on the contrary, less cognisant of accurate form in anything, were content to allow their figure sculpture to be executed by inferior workmen, but lowered the method of its treatment to a standard which every workman could reach, and then trained him by discipline so rigid, that there was no chance of his falling beneath the standard appointed. The Greek gave to the lower workman no subject which he could not perfectly execute. The Assyrian gave him subjects which he could only execute imperfectly, but fixed a legal standard for his imperfection. The workman was, in both systems, a slave.[1]

§ 10. But in the mediæval, or especially Christian, system of ornament, this slavery is done away with altogether; Christianity having recognized, in small things as well as great, the individual value of every soul. But it not only recognizes its value; it confesses its imperfection, in only bestowing dignity upon the acknowledgment of unworthiness. That admission of lost power and fallen nature, which the Greek or Ninevite felt to be intensely painful, and, as far as might be, altogether refused, the Christian makes daily and hourly, contemplating the fact of it without fear, as tending, in the end, to God's greater glory. Therefore, to every spirit which Christianity summons to her service, her exhortation is: Do what you can, and confess frankly what you are unable to do; neither let your effort be shortened for fear of failure, nor your confession silenced for fear of shame. And it is, perhaps, the principal admirableness of the Gothic schools of architecture, that they thus receive the results of the labour of inferior minds; and out of fragments full of imperfection, and betraying that imperfection in every touch, indulgently raise up a stately and unaccusable whole.

§ 11. But the modern English mind has this much in common with that of the Greek, that it intensely desires, in all things, the utmost completion or perfection compatible with their nature. This is a noble character in the abstract, but becomes ignoble when it causes us to forget the relative dignities of that nature itself, and to prefer the perfectness of the lower nature to the imperfection of the higher; not considering that as, judged by such a rule, all the brute animals would be preferable to man, because more perfect in their functions and kind, and yet are always held inferior to him, so also in the works of man, those which are more perfect in their

kind are always inferior to those which are, in their nature, liable to more faults and shortcomings. For the finer the nature, the more flaws it will show through the clearness of it; and it is a law of this universe, that the best things shall be seldomest seen in their best form. The wild grass grows well and strongly, one year with another: but the wheat is, according to the greater nobleness of its nature, liable to the bitterer blight. And therefore, while in all things that we see or do, we are to desire perfection, and strive for it, we are nevertheless not to set the meaner thing, in its narrow accomplishment, above the nobler thing, in its mighty progress; not to esteem smooth minuteness above shattered majesty; not to prefer mean victory to honourable defeat; not to lower the level of our aim, that we may the more surely enjoy the complacency of success. But, above all, in our dealings with the souls of other men, we are to take care how we check, by severe requirement or narrow caution, efforts which might otherwise lead to a noble issue; and, still more, how we withhold our admiration from great excellencies, because they are mingled with rough faults. Now, in the make and nature of every man, however rude or simple, whom we employ in manual labour, there are some powers for better things; some tardy imagination, torpid capacity of emotion; tottering steps of thought, there are, even at the worst; and in most cases it is all our own fault that they *are* tardy or torpid. But they cannot be strengthened, unless we are content to take them in their feebleness, and unless we prize and honour them in their imperfection above the best and most perfect manual skill. And this is what we have to do with all our labourers; to look for the *thoughtful* part of them, and get that out of them, whatever we lose for it, whatever faults and errors we are obliged to take with it. For the best that is in them cannot manifest itself, but in company with much error. Understand this clearly: You can teach a man to draw a straight line, and to cut one; to strike a curved line, and to carve it; and to copy and carve any number of given lines or forms, with admirable speed and perfect precision: and you find his work perfect of its kind: but if you ask him to think about any of those forms, to con-

---

[1] The third kind of ornament, the Renaissance, is that in which the inferior detail becomes principal, the executor of every minor portion being required to exhibit skill and possess knowledge as great as that which is possessed by the master of the design; and in the endeavour to endow him with this skill and knowledge, his own original power is overwhelmed, and the whole building becomes a wearisome exhibition of well-educated imbecility. We must fully inquire into the nature of this form of error, when we arrive at the examination of the Renaissance schools. [Ruskin's note]

sider if he cannot find any better in his own head, he stops; his execution becomes hesitating; he thinks, and ten to one he thinks wrong; ten to one he makes a mistake in the first touch he gives to his work as a thinking being. But you have made a man of him for all that. He was only a machine before, an animated tool.

§ 12. And observe, you are put to stern choice in this matter. You must either make a tool of the creature, or a man of him. You cannot make both. Men were not intended to work with the accuracy of tools, to be precise and perfect in all their actions. If you will have that precision out of them, and make their fingers measure degrees like cog-wheels, and their arms strike curves like compasses, you must unhumanize them. All the energy of their spirits must be given to make cogs and compasses of themselves. All their attention and strength must go to the accomplishment of the mean act. The eye of the soul must be bent upon the finger-point, and the soul's force must fill all the invisible nerves that guide it, ten hours a day, that it may not err from its steely precision, and so soul and sight be worn away, and the whole human being be lost at last—a heap of sawdust, so far as its intellectual work in this world is concerned: saved only by its Heart, which cannot go into the form of cogs and compasses, but expands, after the ten hours are over, into fireside humanity. On the other hand, if you will make a man of the working creature, you cannot make a tool. Let him but begin to imagine, to think, to try to do anything worth doing; and the engine-turned precision is lost at once. Out come all his roughness, all his dulness, all his incapability; shame upon shame, failure upon failure, pause after pause: but out comes the whole majesty of him also; and we know the height of it only when we see the clouds settling upon him. And, whether the clouds be bright or dark, there will be transfiguration behind and within them.

§ 13. And now, reader, look round this English room of yours, about which you have been proud so often, because the work of it was so good and strong, and the ornaments of it so finished. Examine again all those accurate mouldings, and perfect polishings, and unerring adjustments of the seasoned wood and tempered steel. Many a time you have exulted over them, and thought how great England was, because her slightest work was done so thoroughly. Alas! if read rightly, these perfectnesses are signs of a slavery in our

England a thousand times more bitter and more degrading than that of the scourged African, or helot Greek. Men may be beaten, chained, tormented, yoked like cattle, slaughtered like summer flies, and yet remain in one sense, and the best sense, free. But to smother their souls with them, to blight and hew into rotting pollards the suckling branches of their human intelligence, to make the flesh and skin which, after the worm's work on it, is to see God, into leathern thongs to yoke machinery with,—this is to be slave-masters indeed; and there might be more freedom in England, though her feudal lords' lightest words were worth men's lives, and though the blood of the vexed husbandman dropped in the furrows of her fields, than there is while the animation of her multitudes is sent like fuel to feed the factory smoke, and the strength of them is given daily to be wasted into the fineness of a web, or racked into the exactness of a line.

§ 14. And, on the other hand, go forth again to gaze upon the old cathedral front, where you have smiled so often at the fantastic ignorance of the old sculptors: examine once more those ugly goblins, and formless monsters, and stern statues, anatomiless[2] and rigid; but do not mock at them, for they are signs of the life and liberty of every workman who struck the stone; a freedom of thought, and rank in scale of being, such as no laws, no charters, no charities can secure: but which it must be the first aim of all Europe at this day to regain for her children.

§ 15. Let me not be thought to speak wildly or extravagantly. It is verily this degradation of the operative into a machine, which, more than any other evil of the times, is leading the mass of the nations everywhere into vain, incoherent, destructive struggling for a freedom of which they cannot explain the nature to themselves. Their universal outcry against wealth, and against nobility, is not forced from them either by the pressure of famine, or the sting of mortified pride. These do much, and have done much in all ages; but the foundations of society were never yet shaken as they are at this day. It is not that men are ill fed, but that they have no pleasure in the work by which they make their bread, and therefore look to wealth as the only means of pleasure. It is not that men are pained by the scorn of the upper classes, but they cannot endure their own; for they feel that the kind of labour to which they are condemned is verily a degrading one, and makes them less

---

[2] The word appears to be a Ruskin coinage.

than men. Never had the upper classes so much sympathy with the lower, or charity for them, as they have at this day, and yet never were they so much hated by them: for, of old, the separation between the noble and the poor was merely a wall built by law; now it is a veritable difference in level of standing, a precipice between upper and lower grounds in the field of humanity, and there is pestilential air at the bottom of it. I know not if a day is ever to come when the nature of right freedom will be understood, and when men will see that to obey another man, to labour for him, yield reverence to him or to his place, is not slavery. It is often the best kind of liberty,—liberty from care. The man who says to one, Go, and he goeth, and to another, Come, and he cometh,[3] has, in most cases, more sense of restraint and difficulty than the man who obeys him. The movements of the one are hindered by the burden on his shoulder; of the other by the bridle on his lips: there is no way by which the burden may be lightened; but we need not suffer from the bridle if we do not champ at it. To yield reverence to another, to hold ourselves and our likes at his disposal, is not slavery; often it is the noblest state in which a man can live in this world. There is, indeed, a reverence which is servile, that is to say, irrational or selfish: but there is also noble reverence, that is to say, reasonable and loving; and a man is never so noble as when he is reverent in this kind; nay, even if the feeling pass the bounds of mere reason, so that it be loving, a man is raised by it. Which had, in reality, most of the serf nature in him,—the Irish peasant who was lying in wait yesterday for his landlord, with his musket muzzle thrust through the ragged hedge; or that old mountain servant, who 200 years ago, at Inverkeithing, gave up his own life and the lives of his seven sons for his chief?—as each fell, calling forth his brother to the death, "Another for Hector!"[4] And therefore, in all ages and all countries, reverence has been paid and sacrifice made by men to each other, not only without complaint, but rejoicingly; and famine, and peril, and sword, and all evil, and all shame, have been borne willingly in the causes of masters and kings; for all these gifts of the heart ennobled the men who gave, not less than the men who received them, and nature prompted, and God rewarded the sacrifice. But to feel their souls withering within them, unthanked, to find their whole being sunk into an unrecognized

abyss, to be counted off into a heap of mechanism numbered with its wheels, and weighed with its hammer strokes—this, nature bade not,—this, God blesses not,—this, humanity for no long time is able to endure.

§ 16. We have much studied and much perfected, of late, the great civilized invention of the division of labour; only we give it a false name. It is not, truly speaking, the labour that is divided; but the men:—Divided into mere segments of men—broken into small fragments and crumbs of life; so that all the little piece of intelligence that is left in a man is not enough to make a pin, or a nail, but exhausts itself in making the point of a pin or the head of a nail. Now it is a good and desirable thing, truly, to make many pins in a day; but if we could only see with what crystal sand their points were polished,—sand of human soul, much to be magnified before it can be discerned for what it is—we should think there might be some loss in it also. And the great cry that rises from all our manufacturing cities, louder than their furnace blast, is all in very deed for this,—that we manufacture everything there except men; we blanch cotton, and strengthen steel, and refine sugar, and shape pottery; but to brighten, to strengthen, to refine, or to form a single living spirit, never enters into our estimate of advantages. And all the evil to which that cry is urging our myriads can be met only in one way: not by teaching nor preaching, for to teach them is but to show them their misery, and to preach to them, if we do nothing more than preach, is to mock at it. It can be met only by a right understanding, on the part of all classes, of what kinds of labour are good for men, raising them, and making them happy; by a determined sacrifice of such convenience, or beauty, or cheapness as is to be got only by the degradation of the workman; and by equally determined demand for the products and results of healthy and ennobling labour.

§ 17. And how, it will be asked, are these products to be recognized, and this demand to be regulated? Easily: by the observance of three broad and simple rules:

1. Never encourage the manufacture of any article not absolutely necessary, in the production of which *Invention* has no share.

2. Never demand an exact finish for its own sake, but only for some practical or noble end.

3. Never encourage imitation or copying of

---

[3] Matthew 8:9.   [4] Vide Preface to *Fair Maid of Perth*. [Ruskin's note]

any kind, except for the sake of preserving records of great works.

The second of these principles is the only one which directly rises out of the consideration of our immediate subject; but I shall briefly explain the meaning and extent of the first also, reserving the enforcement of the third for another place.

1. Never encourage the manufacture of anything not necessary, in the production of which invention has no share.

For instance. Glass beads are utterly unnecessary, and there is no design or thought employed in their manufacture. They are formed by first drawing out the glass into rods; these rods are chopped up into fragments of the size of beads by the human hand, and the fragments are then rounded in the furnace. The men who chop up the rods sit at their work all day, their hands vibrating with a perpetual and exquisitely timed palsy, and the beads dropping beneath their vibration like hail. Neither they, nor the men who draw out the rods or fuse the fragments, have the smallest occasion for the use of any single human faculty; and every young lady, therefore, who buys glass beads is engaged in the slave-trade, and in a much more cruel one than that which we have so long been endeavouring to put down.

But glass cups and vessels may become the subjects of exquisite invention; and if in buying these we pay for the invention, that is to say, for the beautiful form, or colour, or engraving, and not for mere finish of execution, we are doing good to humanity.

§ 18. So, again, the cutting of precious stones, in all ordinary cases, requires little exertion of any mental faculty; some tact and judgment in avoiding flaws, and so on, but nothing to bring out the whole mind. Every person who wears cut jewels merely for the sake of their value is, therefore, a slave-driver.

But the working of the goldsmith, and the various designing of grouped jewellery and enamel-work, may become the subject of the most noble human intelligence. Therefore, money spent in the purchase of well-designed plate, of precious engraved vases, cameos, or enamels, does good to humanity; and, in work of this kind, jewels may be employed to heighten its splendour; and their cutting is then a price paid for the attainment of a noble end, and thus perfectly allowable.

§ 19. I shall perhaps press this law farther elsewhere, but our immediate concern is chiefly with the second, namely, never to demand an exact finish, when it does not lead to a noble end. For observe, I have only dwelt upon the rudeness of Gothic, or any other kind of imperfectness, as admirable, where it was impossible to get design or thought without it. If you are to have the thought of a rough and untaught man, you must have it in a rough and untaught way; but from an educated man, who can without effort express his thoughts in an educated way, take the graceful expression, and be thankful. Only *get* the thought, and do not silence the peasant because he cannot speak good grammar, or until you have taught him his grammar. Grammar and refinement are good things, both, only be sure of the better thing first. And thus in art, delicate finish is desirable from the greatest masters, and is always given by them. In some places Michael Angelo, Leonardo, Phidias, Pèrugino, Turner, all finished with the most exquisite care; and the finish they give always leads to the fuller accomplishment of their noble purposes. But lower men than these cannot finish, for it requires consummate knowledge to finish consummately, and then we must take their thoughts as they are able to give them. So the rule is simple: Always look for invention first, and after that, for such execution as will help the invention, and as the inventor is capable of without painful effort, and *no more*. Above all, demand no refinement of execution where there is no thought, for that is slaves' work, unredeemed. Rather choose rough work than smooth work, so only that the practical purpose be answered, and never imagine there is reason to be proud of anything that may be accomplished by patience and sand-paper.

§ 20. I shall only give one example, which however will show the reader what I mean, from the manufacture already alluded to, that of glass. Our modern glass is exquisitely clear in its substance, true in its form, accurate in its cutting. We are proud of this. We ought to be ashamed of it. The old Venice glass was muddy, inaccurate in all its forms, and clumsily cut, if at all. And the old Venetian was justly proud of it. For there is this difference between the English and Venetian workman, that the former thinks only of accurately matching his patterns, and getting his curves perfectly true and his edges perfectly sharp, and becomes a mere machine for rounding curves and sharpening edges; while the old Venetian cared not a whit whether his edges were sharp or not, but he invented a new design for every glass that he made, and never moulded a handle or a lip without a new fancy in it.

And therefore, though some Venetian glass is ugly and clumsy enough when made by clumsy and uninventive workmen, other Venetian glass is so lovely in its forms that no price is too great for it; and we never see the same form in it twice. Now you cannot have the finish and the varied form too. If the workman is thinking about his edges, he cannot be thinking of his design; if of his design, he cannot think of his edges. Choose whether you will pay for the lovely form or the perfect finish, and choose at the same moment whether you will make the worker a man or a grindstone.

§ 21. Nay, but the reader interrupts me,— "If the workman can design beautifully, I would not have him kept at the furnace. Let him be taken away and made a gentleman, and have a studio, and design his glass there, and I will have it blown and cut for him by common workmen, and so I will have my design and my finish too."

All ideas of this kind are founded upon two mistaken suppositions: the first, that one man's thoughts can be, or ought to be, executed by another man's hands; the second, that manual labour is a degradation, when it is governed by intellect.

On a large scale, and in work determinable by line and rule, it is indeed both possible and necessary that the thoughts of one man should be carried out by the labour of others; in this sense I have already defined the best architecture to be the expression of the mind of manhood by the hands of childhood. But on a smaller scale, and in a design which cannot be mathematically defined, one man's thoughts can never be expressed by another: and the difference between the spirit of touch of the man who is inventing, and of the man who is obeying directions, is often all the difference between a great and a common work of art. How wide the separation is between original and second-hand execution, I shall endeavour to show elsewhere; it is not so much to our purpose here as to mark the other and more fatal error of despising manual labour when governed by intellect; for it is no less fatal an error to despise it when thus regulated by intellect, than to value it for its own sake. We are always in these days endeavouring to separate the two; we want one man to be always thinking, and another to be always working, and we call one a gentleman, and the other an operative; whereas the workman ought often to be thinking, and the thinker often to be working, and both should be gentlemen, in the best sense. As it is,

we make both ungentle, the one envying, the other despising, his brother; and the mass of society is made up of morbid thinkers, and miserable workers. Now it is only by labour that thought can be made healthy, and only by thought that labour can be made happy, and the two cannot be separated with impunity. It would be well if all of us were good handicraftsmen in some kind, and the dishonour of manual labour done away with altogether; so that though there should still be a trenchant distinction of race between nobles and commoners, there should not, among the latter, be a trenchant distinction of employment, as between idle and working men, or between men of liberal and illiberal professions. All professions should be liberal, and there should be less pride in peculiarity of employment, and more in excellence of achievement. And yet more, in each several profession, no master should be too proud to do its hardest work. The painter should grind his own colours; the architect work in the mason's yard with his men; the master-manufacturer be himself a more skilful operative than any man in his mills; and the distinction between one man and another be only in experience and skill, and the authority and wealth which these must naturally and justly obtain.

§ 22. I should be led far from the matter in hand, if I were to pursue this interesting subject. Enough, I trust, has been said to show the reader that the rudeness or imperfection which at first rendered the term "Gothic" one of reproach is indeed, when rightly understood, one of the most noble characters of Christian architecture, and not only a noble but an *essential* one. It seems a fantastic paradox, but it is nevertheless a most important truth, that no architecture can be truly noble which is *not* imperfect. And this is easily demonstrable. For since the architect, whom we will suppose capable of doing all in perfection, cannot execute the whole with his own hands, he must either make slaves of his workmen in the old Greek, and present English fashion, and level his work to a slave's capacities, which is to degrade it; or else he must take his workmen as he finds them, and let them show their weaknesses together with their strength, which will involve the Gothic imperfection, but render the whole work as noble as the intellect of the age can make it.

§ 23. But the principle may be stated more broadly still. I have confined the illustration of it to architecture, but I must not leave it as if true of architecture only. Hitherto I have used the words imperfect and perfect merely to distinguish between work grossly unskilful, and work executed with average precision and science; and I have been pleading that any degree of unskilfulness should be admitted, so only that the labourer's mind had room for expression. But, accurately speaking, no good work whatever can be perfect, and *the demand for perfection is always a sign of a misunderstanding of the ends of art.*

§ 24. This for two reasons, both based on everlasting laws. The first, that no great man ever stops working till he has reached his point of failure: that is to say, his mind is always far in advance of his powers of execution, and the latter will now and then give way in trying to follow it; besides that he will always give to the inferior portions of his work only such inferior attention as they require; and according to his greatness he becomes so accustomed to the feeling of dissatisfaction with the best he can do, that in moments of lassitude or anger with himself he will not care though the beholder be dissatisfied also. I believe there has only been one man who would not acknowledge this necessity, and strove always to reach perfection, Leonardo; the end of his vain effort being merely that he would take ten years to a picture and leave it unfinished. And therefore, if we are to have great men working at all, or less men doing their best, the work will be imperfect, however beautiful. Of human work none but what is bad can be perfect, in its own bad way.[5]

§ 25. The second reason is, that imperfection is in some sort essential to all that we know of life. It is the sign of life in a mortal body, that is to say, of a state of progress and change. Nothing that lives is, or can be, rigidly perfect; part of it is decaying, part nascent. The foxglove blossom,—a third part bud, a third part past, a third part in full bloom,—is a type of the life of this world. And in all things that live there are certain irregularities and deficiencies which are not only signs of life, but sources of beauty. No human face is exactly the same in its lines on each side, no leaf perfect in its lobes, no branch in its symmetry. All admit irregularity as they imply change; and to banish imperfection is to destroy expression, to check exertion, to paralyze vitality. All things are literally better, lovelier,

and more beloved for the imperfections which have been divinely appointed, that the law of human life may be Effort, and the law of human judgment, Mercy.

Accept this then for a universal law, that neither architecture nor any other noble work of man can be good unless it be imperfect; and let us be prepared for the otherwise strange fact, which we shall discern clearly as we approach the period of the Renaissance, that the first cause of the fall of the arts of Europe was a relentless requirement of perfection, incapable alike either of being silenced by veneration for greatness, or softened into forgiveness of simplicity.

Thus far then of the Rudeness or Savageness, which is the first mental element of Gothic architecture. It is an element in many other healthy architectures also, as the Byzantine and Romanesque; but true Gothic cannot exist without it.

§ 26. The second mental element above named was CHANGEFULNESS, or Variety.

I have already enforced the allowing independent operation to the inferior workman, simply as a duty *to him*, and as ennobling the architecture by rendering it more Christian. We have now to consider what reward we obtain for the performance of this duty, namely, the perpetual variety of every feature of the building.

Wherever the workman is utterly enslaved, the parts of the building must of course be absolutely like each other; for the perfection of his execution can only be reached by exercising him in doing one thing, and giving him nothing else to do. The degree in which the workman is degraded may be thus known at a glance, by observing whether the several parts of the building are similar or not; and if, as in Greek work, all the capitals are alike, and all the mouldings unvaried, then the degradation is complete; if, as in Egyptian or Ninevite work, though the manner of executing certain figures is always the same, the order of design is perpetually varied, the degradation is less total; if, as in Gothic work, there is perpetual change both in design and execution, the workman must have been altogether set free.

§ 27. How much the beholder gains from the liberty of the labourer may perhaps be questioned in England, where one of the strongest instincts

---

[5] The Elgin marbles are supposed by many persons to be "perfect." In the most important portions they indeed approach perfection, but only there. The draperies are unfinished, the hair and wool of the animals are unfinished, and the entire bas-reliefs of the frieze are roughly cut. [Ruskin's note]

in nearly every mind is that Love of Order which makes us desire that our house windows should pair like our carriage horses, and allows us to yield our faith unhesitatingly to architectural theories which fix a form for everything, and forbid variation from it. I would not impeach love of order: it is one of the most useful elements of the English mind; it helps us in our commerce and in all purely practical matters; and it is in many cases one of the foundation stones of morality. Only do not let us suppose that love of order is love of art. It is true that order, in its highest sense, is one of the necessities of art, just as time is a necessity of music; but love of order has no more to do with our right enjoyment of architecture or painting, than love of punctuality with the appreciation of an opera. Experience, I fear, teaches us that accurate and methodical habits in daily life are seldom characteristic of those who either quickly perceive, or richly possess, the creative powers of art; there is, however, nothing inconsistent between the two instincts, and nothing to hinder us from retaining our business habits, and yet fully allowing and enjoying the noblest gifts of Invention. We already do so, in every other branch of art except architecture, and we only do *not* so there because we have been taught that it would be wrong. Our architects gravely inform us that, as there are four rules of arithmetic, there are five orders of architecture; we, in our simplicity, think that this sounds consistent, and believe them. They inform us also that there is one proper form for Corinthian capitals, another for Doric, and another for Ionic. We, considering that there is also a proper form for the letters A, B, and C, think that this also sounds consistent, and accept the proposition. Understanding, therefore, that one form of the said capitals is proper, and no other, and having a conscientious horror of all impropriety, we allow the architect to provide us with the said capitals, of the proper form, in such and such a quantity, and in all other points to take care that the legal forms are observed; which having done, we rest in forced confidence that we are well housed.

§ 28. But our higher instincts are not deceived. We take no pleasure in the building provided for us, resembling that which we take in a new book or a new picture. We may be proud of its size, complacent in its correctness, and happy in its convenience. We may take the same pleasure in its symmetry and workmanship as in a well-ordered room, or a skilful piece of manufacture. And this we suppose to be all the pleasure that

architecture was ever intended to give us. The idea of reading a building as we would read Milton or Dante, and getting the same kind of delight out of the stones as out of the stanzas, never enters our mind for a moment. And for good reason;—There is indeed rhythm in the verses, quite as strict as the symmetries or rhythm of the architecture, and a thousand times more beautiful, but there is something else than rhythm. The verses were neither made to order, nor to match, as the capitals were; and we have therefore a kind of pleasure in them other than a sense of propriety. But it requires a strong effort of common sense to shake ourselves quit of all that we have been taught for the last two centuries, and wake to the perception of a truth just as simple and certain as it is new: that great art, whether expressing itself in words, colours, or stones, does *not* say the same thing over and over again; that the merit of architectural, as of every other art, consists in its saying new and different things; that to repeat itself is no more a characteristic of genius in marble than it is of genius in print; and that we may, without offending any laws of good taste, require of an architect, as we do of a novelist, that he should be not only correct, but entertaining.

Yet all this is true, and self-evident; only hidden from us, as many other self-evident things are, by false teaching. Nothing is a great work of art, for the production of which either rules or models can be given. Exactly so far as architecture works on known rules, and from given models, it is not an art, but a manufacture; and it is, of the two procedures, rather less rational (because more easy) to copy capitals or mouldings from Phidias, and call ourselves architects, than to copy heads and hands from Titian, and call ourselves painters.

§ 29. Let us then understand at once that change or variety is as much a necessity to the human heart and brain in buildings as in books; that there is no merit, though there is some occasional use, in monotony; and that we must no more expect to derive either pleasure or profit from an architecture whose ornaments are of one pattern, and whose pillars are of one proportion, than we should out of a universe in which the clouds were all of one shape, and the trees all of one size.

§ 30. And this we confess in deeds, though not in words. All the pleasure which the people of the nineteenth century take in art, is in pictures, sculpture, minor objects of virtù, or mediæval architecture, which we enjoy under the term picturesque: no pleasure is taken anywhere in modern buildings, and we find all men of true feeling delighting to escape out of modern cities into natural scenery: hence, as I shall hereafter show, that peculiar love of landscape, which is characteristic of the age. It would be well, if in all other matters, we were as ready to put up with what we dislike, for the sake of compliance with established law, as we are in architecture.

§ 31. How so debased a law ever came to be established, we shall see when we come to describe the Renaissance schools; here we have only to note, as a second most essential element of the Gothic spirit, that it broke through that law wherever it found it in existence; it not only dared, but delighted in, the infringement of every servile principle; and invented a series of forms of which the merit was, not merely that they were new, but that they were *capable of perpetual novelty*. The pointed arch was not merely a bold variation from the round, but it admitted of millions of variations in itself; for the proportions of a pointed arch are changeable to infinity, while a circular arch is always the same. The grouped shaft was not merely a bold variation from the single one, but it admitted of millions of variations in its grouping, and in the proportions resultant from its grouping. The introduction of tracery was not only a startling change in the treatment of window lights, but admitted endless changes in the interlacement of the tracery bars themselves. So that, while in all living Christian architecture the love of variety exists, the Gothic schools exhibited that love in culminating energy; and their influence, wherever it extended itself, may be sooner and farther traced by this character than by any other; the tendency to the adoption of Gothic types being always first shown by greater irregularity, and richer variation in the forms of architecture it is about to supersede, long before the appearance of the pointed arch or of any other recognizable *outward* sign of the Gothic mind.

§ 32. We must, however, herein note carefully what distinction there is between a healthy and a diseased love of change; for as it was in healthy love of change that the Gothic architecture rose, it was partly in consequence of diseased love of change that it was destroyed. In order to understand this clearly, it will be necessary to consider the different ways in which change and monotony are presented to us in nature; both having their use, like darkness and light, and the one incapable of being enjoyed without the other: change being most delightful after some prolongation of monotony, as light appears most brilliant after the eyes have been for some time closed.

§ 33. I believe that the true relations of monotony and change may be most simply understood by observing them in music. We may therein notice first, that there is a sublimity and majesty in monotony, which there is not in rapid or frequent variation. This is true throughout all nature. The greater part of the sublimity of the sea depends on its monotony; so also that of desolate moor and mountain scenery; and especially the sublimity of motion, as in the quiet, unchanged fall and rise of an engine beam. So also there is sublimity in darkness which there is not in light.

§ 34. Again, monotony after a certain time, or beyond a certain degree, becomes either uninteresting or intolerable, and the musician is obliged to break it in one of two ways: either while the air or passage is perpetually repeated, its notes are variously enriched and harmonized; or else, after a certain number of repeated passages, an entirely new passage is introduced, which is more or less delightful according to the length of the previous monotony. Nature, of course, uses both these kinds of variation perpetually. The sea-waves, resembling each other in general mass, but none like its brother in minor divisions and curves, are a monotony of the first kind; the great plain, broken by an emergent rock or clump of trees, is a monotony of the second.

§ 35. Farther: in order to the enjoyment of the change in either case, a certain degree of patience is required from the hearer or observer. In the first case, he must be satisfied to endure with patience the recurrence of the great masses of sound or form, and to seek for entertainment in a careful watchfulness of the minor details. In the second case, he must bear patiently the infliction of the monotony for some moments, in order to feel the full refreshment of the change. This is true even of the shortest musical passage in which the element of monotony is employed. In cases of more majestic monotony, the patience required is so considerable that it becomes a kind of pain,—a price paid for the future pleasure.

§ 36. Again: the talent of the composer is not in the monotony, but in the changes: he may show feeling and taste by his use of monotony in certain places or degrees; that is to say, by his *various* employment of it; but it is always in the new arrangement or invention that his intellect is shown, and not in the monotony which relieves it.

Lastly: if the pleasure of change be too often repeated, it ceases to be delightful, for then change itself becomes monotonous, and we are driven to seek delight in extreme and fantastic degree of it. This is the diseased love of change of which we have above spoken.

§ 37. From these facts we may gather generally that monotony is, and ought to be, in itself painful to us, just as darkness is; that an architecture which is altogether monotonous is a dark or dead architecture; and of those who love it, it may be truly said, "they love darkness rather than light."[6] But monotony in certain measure, used in order to give value to change, and above all, that *transparent* monotony, which, like the shadows of a great painter, suffers all manner of dimly suggested form to be seen through the body of it, is an essential in architectural as in all other composition; and the endurance of monotony has about the same place in a healthy mind that the endurance of darkness has: that is to say, as a strong intellect will have pleasure in the solemnities of storm and twilight, and in the broken and mysterious lights that gleam among them, rather than in mere brilliancy and glare, while a frivolous mind will dread the shadow and the storm; and as a great man will be ready to endure much darkness of fortune in order to reach greater eminence of power or felicity, while an inferior man will not pay the price; exactly in like manner a great mind will accept, or even delight in, monotony which would be wearisome to an inferior intellect, because it has more patience and power of expectation, and is ready to pay the full price for the great future pleasure of change. But in all cases it is not that the noble nature loves monotony, any more than it loves darkness or pain. But it can bear with it, and receive a high pleasure in the endurance or patience, a pleasure necessary to the well-being of this world; while those who will not submit to the temporary sameness, but rush from one change to another, gradually dull the edge of change itself, and bring a shadow and weariness over the whole world from which there is no more escape.

§ 38. From these general uses of variety in the economy of the world, we may at once understand its use and abuse in architecture. The variety of the Gothic schools is the more healthy and beautiful, because in many cases it is en-tirely unstudied, and results, not from mere love of change, but from practical necessities. For in one point of view Gothic is not only the best, but the *only rational* architecture, as being that which can fit itself most easily to all services, vulgar or noble. Undefined in its slope of roof, height of shaft, breadth of arch, or disposition of ground plan, it can shrink into a turret, expand into a hall, coil into a staircase, or spring into a spire, with undegraded grace and unexhausted energy; and whenever it finds occasion for change in its form or purpose, it submits to it without the slightest sense of loss either to its unity or majesty,—subtle and flexible like a fiery serpent, but ever attentive to the voice of the charmer. And it is one of the chief virtues of the Gothic builders, that they never suffered ideas of outside symmetries and consistencies to interfere with the real use and value of what they did. If they wanted a window, they opened one; a room, they added one; a buttress, they built one; utterly regardless of any established conventionalities of external appearance, knowing (as indeed it always happened) that such daring interruptions of the formal plan would rather give additional interest to its symmetry than injure it. So that, in the best times of Gothic, a useless window would rather have been opened in an unexpected place for the sake of the surprise, than a useful one forbidden for the sake of symmetry. Every successive architect, employed upon a great work, built the pieces he added in his own way, utterly regardless of the style adopted by his predecessors; and if two towers were raised in nominal correspondence at the sides of a cathedral front, one was nearly sure to be different from the other, and in each the style at the top to be different from the style at the bottom.[7]

§39. These marked variations were, however, only permitted as part of the great system of perpetual change which ran through every member of Gothic design, and rendered it as endless a field for the beholder's inquiry as for the builder's imagination: change, which in the best schools is subtle and delicate, and rendered more delightful by intermingling of a noble monotony; in the more barbaric schools is somewhat fantastic and redundant; but, in all, a necessary and constant condition of the life of the school. Sometimes the variety is in one feature, some-

---

[6] John 3:19.

[7] In the eighth chapter we shall see a remarkable instance of this sacrifice of symmetry to convenience in the arrangement of the windows of the Ducal Palace. [Ruskin's note]

times in another; it may be in the capitals or crockets, in the niches or the traceries, or in all together, but in some one or other of the features it will be found always. If the mouldings are constant, the surface sculpture will change; if the capitals are of a fixed design, the traceries will change; if the traceries are monotonous, the capitals will change; and if even, as in some fine schools, the early English for example, there is the slightest approximation to an unvarying type of mouldings, capitals, and floral decoration, the variety is found in the disposition of the masses, and in the figure sculpture.

§ 40. I must now refer for a moment, before we quit the consideration of this, the second mental element of Gothic, to the opening of the third chapter of the *Seven Lamps of Architecture*, in which the distinction was drawn (§ 2) between man gathering and man governing; between his acceptance of the sources of delight from nature, and his development of authoritative or imaginative power in their arrangement: for the two mental elements, not only of Gothic, but of all good architecture, which we have just been examining, belong to it, and are admirable in it, chiefly as it is, more than any other subject of art, the work of man, and the expression of the average power of man. A picture or poem is often little more than a feeble utterance of man's admiration of something out of himself; but architecture approaches more to a creation of his own, born of his necessities, and expressive of his nature. It is also, in some sort, the work of the whole race, while the picture or statue is the work of one only, in most cases more highly gifted than his fellows. And therefore we may expect that the first two elements of good architecture should be expressive of some great truths commonly belonging to the whole race, and necessary to be understood or felt by them in all their work that they do under the sun. And observe what they are: the confession of Imperfection, and the confession of Desire of Change. The building of the bird and the bee needs not express anything like this. It is perfect and unchanging. But just because we are something better than birds or bees, our building must confess that we have not reached the perfection we can imagine, and cannot rest in the condition we have attained. If we pretend to have reached either perfection or satisfaction, we have degraded ourselves and our work. God's work only may express that; but ours may never have that

sentence written upon it,— "And behold, it was very good."[8] And, observe again, it is not merely as it renders the edifice a book of various knowledge, or a mine of precious thought, that variety is essential to its nobleness. The vital principle is not the love of *Knowledge*, but the love of *Change*. It is that strange *disquietude* of the Gothic spirit that is its greatness; that restlessness of the dreaming mind, that wanders hither and thither among the niches, and flickers feverishly around the pinnacles, and frets and fades in labyrinthine knots and shadows along wall and roof, and yet is not satisfied, nor shall be satisfied. The Greek could stay in his triglyph furrow, and be at peace; but the work of the Gothic heart is fretwork still, and it can neither rest in, nor from, its labour, but must pass on, sleeplessly, until its love of change shall be pacified for ever in the change that must come alike on them that wake and them that sleep.

§ 41. The third constituent element of the Gothic mind was stated to be NATURALISM; that is to say, the love of natural objects for their own sake, and the effort to represent them frankly, unconstrained by artistical laws.

This characteristic of the style partly follows in necessary connection with those named above. For, so soon as the workman is left free to represent what subjects he chooses, he must look to the nature that is round him for material, and will endeavour to represent it as he sees it, with more or less accuracy according to the skill he possesses, and with much play of fancy, but with small respect for law. There is, however, a marked distinction between the imaginations of the Western and Eastern races, even when both are left free; the Western, or Gothic, delighting most in the representation of facts, and the Eastern (Arabian, Persian, and Chinese) in the harmony of colours and forms. Each of these intellectual dispositions has its particular forms of error and abuse, which, though I have often before stated, I must here again briefly explain; and this the rather, because the word Naturalism is, in one of its senses, justly used as a term of reproach, and the questions respecting the real relations of art and nature are so many and so confused throughout all the schools of Europe at this day, that I cannot clearly enunciate any single truth without appearing to admit, in fellowship with it, some kind of error, unless the reader will bear with me in entering into such an analysis of the subject as will serve us for general guidance.

[8] Genesis 1:31.

§ 42. We are to remember, in the first place, that the arrangement of colours and lines is an art analogous to the composition[9] of music, and entirely independent of the representation of facts. Good colouring does not necessarily convey the image of anything but itself. It consists in certain proportions and arrangements of rays of light, but not in likenesses to anything. A few touches of certain greys and purples laid by a master's hand on white paper will be good colouring; as more touches are added beside a dove's neck, and we may praise, as the drawing advances, the perfect imitation of the dove's neck. But the good colouring does not consist in that imitation, but in the abstract qualities and relations of the grey and purple.

In like manner, as soon as a great sculptor begins to shape his work out of the block, we shall see that its lines are nobly arranged, and of noble character. We may not have the slightest idea for what the forms are intended, whether they are of man or beast, of vegetation or drapery. Their likeness to anything does not effect their nobleness. They are magnificent forms, and that is all we need care to know of them, in order to say whether the workman is a good or bad sculptor.

§ 43. Now the noblest art is an exact unison of the abstract value, with the imitative power, of forms and colours. It is the noblest composition, used to express the noblest facts. But the human mind cannot in general unite the two perfections: it either pursues the fact to the neglect of the composition, or pursues the composition to the neglect of the fact.

§ 44. And it is intended by the Deity that it *should* do this: the best art is not always wanted. Facts are often wanted without art, as in a geological diagram; and art often without facts, as in a Turkey carpet. And most men have been made capable of giving either one or the other, but not both; only one or two, the very highest, can give both.

Observe then. Men are universally divided, as

respects their artistical qualifications, into three great classes; a right, a left, and a centre. On the right side are the men of facts, on the left the men of design,[10] in the centre the men of both.

The three classes of course pass into each other by imperceptible gradations. The men of facts are hardly ever altogether without powers of design; the men of design are always in some measure cognizant of facts; and as each class possesses more or less of the powers of the opposite one, it approaches to the character of the central class. Few men, even in that central rank, are so exactly throned on the summit of the crest that they cannot be perceived to incline in the least one way or the other, embracing both horizons with their glance. Now each of these classes has, as I above said, a healthy function in the world, and correlative diseases or unhealthy functions; and, when the work of either of them is seen in its morbid condition, we are apt to find fault only with the class of workmen, instead of finding fault with the particular abuse which has perverted their action.

§ 45. Let us first take an instance of the healthy action of the three classes on a simple subject, so as fully to understand the dinstinction between them, and then we shall more easily examine the corruptions to which they are liable. Fig. 1 in Plate 6 is a spray of vine with a bough of cherry-tree, which I have outlined from nature as accurately as I could, without in the least endeavouring to compose or arrange the form. It is a simple piece of fact-work, healthy and good as such, and useful to any one who wanted to know plain truths about tendrils of vines, but there is no attempt at design in it. Plate 19 below, represents a branch of vine used to decorate the angle of the Ducal Palace. It is faithful as a representation of vine, and yet so designed that every leaf serves an architectural purpose, and could not be spared from its place without harm. This is central work; fact and design together. Fig. 2 in Plate 6 is a spandril from St. Mark's, in which the forms of the vine

[9] I am always afraid to use this word "Composition;" it is so utterly misused in the general parlance respecting art. Nothing is more common than to hear divisions of art into "form, composition, and colour," or "light and shade and composition," or "sentiment and composition," or it matters not what else and composition; the speakers in each case attaching a perfectly different meaning to the word, generally an indistinct one, and always a wrong one. Composition is, in plain English, "putting together," and it means the putting together of lines, of forms, of colours, of shades, or of ideas. Painters compose in colour, compose in thought, compose in form, and compose in effect; the word being of no use merely in order to express a scientific, disciplined, and inventive arrangement of any of these, instead of a merely natural or accidental one. [Ruskin's note]

[10] Design is used in this place as expressive of the power to arrange lines and colours nobly. By facts, I mean facts perceived by the eye and mind, not facts accumulated by knowledge. See the chapter on Roman Renaissance (Vol. III Chap. II) for this distinction. [Ruskin's note]

are dimly suggested, the object of the design being merely to obtain graceful lines, and well-proportioned masses upon the gold ground. There is not the least attempt to inform the spectator of any facts about the growth of the vine; there are no stalks or tendrils,—merely running bands with leaves emergent from them, of which nothing but the outline is taken from the vine, and even that imperfectly. This is design, unregardful of facts.

Now the work is, in all these three cases, perfectly healthy. Fig. 1 is not bad work because it has not design, nor Fig. 2 bad work because it has not facts. The object of the one is to give pleasure through truth, and of the other to give pleasure through composition. And both are right.

What, then, are the diseased operations to which the three classes of workmen are liable?

§ 46. Primarily, two; affecting the two inferior classes;

    1st, When either of those two classes Despises the other;

    2nd, When either of the two classes Envies the other; producing, therefore, four forms of dangerous error.

First, when the men of facts despise design. This is the error of the common Dutch painters, of merely imitative painters of still life, flowers, etc., and other men who, having either the gift of accurate imitation or strong sympathies with nature, suppose that all is done when the imitation is perfected or sympathy expressed. A large body of English landscapists come into this class, including most clever sketchers from nature, who fancy that to get a sky of true tone, and a gleam of sunshine or sweep of shower faithfully expressed, is all that can be required of art. These men are generally themselves answerable for much of their deadness of feeling to the higher qualities of composition. They probably have not originally the high gifts of design, but they lose such powers as they originally possessed by despising, and refusing to study, the results of great power of design in others. Their knowledge, as far as it goes, being accurate, they are usually presumptuous and self-conceited, and gradually become incapable of admiring anything but what is like their own works. They see nothing in the works of great designers but the faults, and do harm almost incalculable in the European

society of the present day by sneering at the compositions of the greatest men of the earlier ages,[11] because they do not absolutely tally with their own ideas of "Nature."

§ 47. The second form of error is when the men of design despise facts. All noble design must deal with facts to a certain extent, for there is no food for it but in nature. The best colourist invents best by taking hints from natural colours; from birds, skies, or groups of figures. And if, in the delight of inventing fantastic colour and form, the truths of nature are wilfully neglected, the intellect becomes comparatively decrepit, and that state of art results which we find among the Chinese. The Greek designers delighted in the facts of the human form, and became great in consequence; but the facts of lower nature were disregarded by them, and their inferior ornament became, therefore, dead and valueless.

§ 48. The third form of error is when the men of facts envy design; that is to say, when, having only imitative powers, they refuse to employ those powers upon the visible world around them; but, having been taught that composition is the end of art, strive to obtain the inventive powers which nature has denied them, study nothing but the works of reputed designers, and perish in a fungous growth of plagiarism and laws of art.

Here was the error of the beginning of this century; it is the error of the meanest kind of men that employ themselves in painting, and it is the most fatal of all, rendering those who fall into it utterly useless, incapable of helping the world with either truth or fancy, while, in all probability, they deceive it by base resemblances of both, until it hardly recognizes truth or fancy when they really exist.

§ 49. The fourth form of error is when the men of design envy facts; that is to say, when the temptation of closely imitating nature leads them to forget their own proper ornamental function, and when they lose the power of the composition for the sake of graphic truth; as, for instance, in the hawthorn moulding so often spoken of round the porch of Bourges Cathedral, which, though very lovely, might perhaps, as we saw above, have been better, if the old builder, in his excessive desire to make it look like hawthorn, had not painted it green.

§ 50. It is, however, carefully to be noted, that the two morbid conditions to which the men of

---

[11] "Earlier," that is to say, pre-Raphaelite ages. Men of this stamp will praise Claude, and such other comparatively debased artists; but they cannot taste the work of the thirteenth century. [Ruskin's note]

facts are liable are much more dangerous and harmful than those to which the men of design are liable. The morbid state of men of design injures themselves only; that of the men of facts injures the whole world. The Chinese porcelain-painter is, indeed, not so great a man as he might be, but he does not want to break everything that is not porcelain: but the modern English fact-hunter, despising design, wants to destroy everything that does not agree with his own notions of truth, and becomes the most dangerous and despicable of iconoclasts, excited by egotism instead of religion. Again: the Bourges sculptor, painting his hawthorns green, did indeed somewhat hurt the effect of his own beautiful design, but did not prevent any one from loving hawthorn: but Sir George Beaumont, trying to make Constable paint grass brown *instead* of green,[12] was setting himself between Constable and nature, blinding the painter, and blaspheming the work of God.

§ 51. So much, then, of the diseases of the inferior classes, caused by their envying or despising each other. It is evident that the men of the central class cannot be liable to any morbid operation of this kind, they possessing the powers of both.

But there is another order of diseases which affect all the three classes, considered with respect to their pursuit of facts. For observe, all the three classes are in some degree pursuers of facts; even the men of design not being in any case altogether independent of external truth. Now, considering them *all* as more or less searchers after truth, there is another triple division to be made of them. Everything presented to them in nature has good and evil mingled in it: and artists, considered as searchers after truth, are again to be divided into three great classes, a right, a left, and a centre. Those on the right perceive, and pursue, the good, and leave the evil: those in the centre, the greatest, perceive and pursue the good and evil together, the whole thing as it verily is: those on the left perceive and pursue the evil, and leave the good.

§ 52. The first class, I say, take the good and leave the evil. Out of whatever is presented to them, they gather what it has of grace, and life, and light, and holiness, and leave all, or at least as much as possible, of the rest undrawn. The faces of their figures express no evil passions; the skies of their landscapes are without storm; the prevalent character of their colour is brightness, and of their chiaroscuro fulness of light. The early Italian and Flemish painters, Angelico and Hemling, Perugino, Francia, Raffaelle in his best time, John Bellini, and our own Stothard,[13] belong eminently to this class.

§ 53. The second, or greatest class, render all that they see in nature unhesitatingly, with a kind of divine grasp and government of the whole, sympathizing with all the good, and yet confessing, permitting, and bringing good out of the evil also. Their subject is infinite as nature, their colour equally balanced between splendour and sadness, reaching occasionally the highest degrees of both, and their chiaroscuro equally balanced between light and shade.

The principal men of this class are Michael Angelo, Leonardo, Giotto, Tintoret, and Turner. Raffaelle in his second time, Titian, and Rubens are transitional; the first inclining to the eclectic, and the last two to the impure class, Raffaelle rarely giving all the evil, Titian and Rubens rarely all the good.

§ 54. The last class perceive and imitate evil only. They cannot draw the trunk of a tree without blasting and shattering it, nor a sky except covered with stormy clouds; they delight in the beggary and brutality of the human race; their colour is for the most part subdued or lurid, and the greater spaces of their pictures are occupied by darkness.

Happily the examples of this class are seldom seen in perfection. Salvator Rosa and Caravaggio are the most characteristic: the other men belonging to it approach towards the central rank by imperceptible gradations, as they perceive and represent more and more of good. But Murillo, Zurbaran, Camillo Procaccini, Rembrandt, and Teniers, all belong naturally to this lower class.

§ 55. Now, observe: the three classes into which artists were previously divided, of men of fact, men of design, and men of both, are all of Divine institution; but of these latter three, the last is in nowise of Divine institution. It is entirely human, and the men who belong to it have sunk into it by their own faults. They are, so far forth, either useless or harmful men. It is indeed good that evil should be occasionally represented, even in its worst forms, but never

---

[12] Sir George Beaumont (1753–1827) and John Constable (1776–1837), English landscape painters, Constable the more highly regarded of the two.

[13] Thomas Stothard (1775–1834), English painter and engraver, frequent illustrator of works of fiction.

that it should be taken delight in: and the mighty men of the central class will always give us all that is needful of it; sometimes, as Hogarth did, dwelling upon it bitterly as satirists,—but this with the more effect, because they will neither exaggerate it, nor represent it mercilessly, and without the atoning points that all evil shows to a Divinely guided glance, even at its deepest. So then, though the third class will always, I fear, in some measure exist, the two necessary classes are only the first two: and this is so far acknowledged by the general sense of men, that the basest class has been confounded with the second; and painters have been divided commonly only into two ranks, now known, I believe, throughout Europe by the names which they first received in Italy, "Puristi and Naturalisti."[14] Since, however, in the existing state of things, the degraded or evil-loving class, though less defined than that of the Puristi, is just as vast as it is indistinct, this division has done infinite dishonour to the great faithful painters of nature: and it has long been one of the objects I have had most at heart to show that, in reality, the Purists, in their sanctity, are less separated from these natural painters than the Sensualists in their foulness; and that the difference, though less discernible, is in reality greater, between the man who pursues evil for its own sake, and him who bears with it for the sake of truth, than between this latter and the man who will not endure it at all.

§ 56. Let us, then, endeavour briefly to mark the real relations of these three vast ranks of men, whom I shall call, for convenience in speaking of them, Purists, Naturalists, and Sensualists; not that these terms express their real characters, but I know no word, and cannot coin a convenient one, which would accurately express the opposite of Purist; and I keep the terms Purist and Naturalist in order to comply, as far as possible, with the established usage of language on the Continent. Now, observe: in saying that nearly everything presented to us in nature has mingling in it of good and evil, I do not mean that nature is conceivably improvable, or that anything that God has made could be called evil, if we could see far enough into its uses, but that, with respect to immediate effects or appearances, it may be so, just as the hard rind or bitter kernel or a fruit may be an evil to the eater, though in the one is the protection of the fruit, and in the other its continuance. The Purist, therefore, does not mend nature, but receives from nature and from God

that which is good for him; while the Sensualist fills himself "with the husks that the swine did eat." Luke xv. 16.

The three classes may, therefore, be likened to men reaping wheat, of which the Purists take the fine flour, and the Sensualists the chaff and straw, but the Naturalists take all home, and make their cake of the one, and their couch of the other.

§ 57. For instance. We know more certainly every day that whatever appears to us harmful in the universe has some beneficent or necessary operation; that the storm which destroys a harvest brightens the sunbeams for harvests yet unsown, and that the volcano which buries a city preserves a thousand from destruction. But the evil is not for the time less fearful, because we have learned it to be necessary; and we easily understand the timidity or the tenderness of the spirit which would withdraw itself from the presence of destruction, and create in its imagination a world of which the peace should be unbroken, in which the sky should not darken nor the sea rage, in which the leaf should not change nor the blossom wither. That man is greater, however, who contemplates with an equal mind the alternations of terror and of beauty; who, not rejoicing less beneath the sunny sky, can bear also to watch the bars of twilight narrowing on the horizon; and, not less sensible to the blessing of the peace of nature, can rejoice in the magnificence of the ordinances by which that peace is protected and secured. But separated from both by an immeasurable distance would be the man who delighted in convulsion and disease for their own sake; who found his daily food in the disorder of nature mingled with the suffering of humanity; and watched joyfully at the right hand of the Angel whose appointed work is to destroy as well as to accuse, while the corners of the house of feasting were struck by the wind from the wilderness.

§ 58. And far more is this true, when the subject of contemplation is humanity itself. The passions of mankind are partly protective, partly beneficent, like the chaff and grain of the corn; but none without their use, none without nobleness when seen in balanced unity with the rest of the spirit which they are charged to defend. The passions of which the end is the continuance of the race: the indignation which is to arm it against injustice, or strengthen it to resist wanton

---

[14] Purists and naturalists.

injury; and the fear[15] which lies at the root of prudence, reverence, and awe, are all honourable and beautiful, so long as man is regarded in his relations to the existing world. The religious Purist, striving to conceive him withdrawn from those relations, effaces from the countenance the traces of all transitory passion, illumines it with holy hope and love, and seals it with the serenity of heavenly peace; he conceals the forms of the body by the deep-folded garment, or else represents them under severely chastened types, and would rather paint them emaciated by the fast, or pale from the torture, than strengthened by exertion, or flushed by emotion. But the great Naturalist takes the human being in its wholeness, in its mortal as well as its spiritual strength. Capable of sounding and sympathizing with the whole range of its passions, he brings one majestic harmony out of them all; he represents it fearlessly in all its acts and thoughts, in its haste, its anger, its sensuality, and its pride, as well as in its fortitude or faith, but makes it noble in them all; he casts aside the veil from the body, and behonds the mysteries of its form like an angel looking down on an inferior creature: there is nothing which he is reluctant to behold, nothing that he is ashamed to confess; with all that lives, triumphing, falling, or suffering, he claims kindred, either in majesty or in mercy, yet standing, in a sort, afar off, unmoved even in the deepness of his sympathy; for the spirit within him is too thoughtful to be grieved, too brave to be appalled, and too pure to be polluted.

§ 59. How far beneath these two ranks of men shall we place, in the scale of being, those whose pleasure is only in sin or in suffering; who habitually contemplate humanity in poverty or decrepitude, fury or sensuality; whose works are either temptations to its weakness, or triumphs over its ruin, and recognize no other subjects for thought or admiration than the subtlety of the robber, the rage of the soldier, or the joy of the Sybarite? It seems strange, when thus definitely stated, that such a school should exist. Yet consider a little what gaps and blanks would disfigure our gallery and chamber walls, in places that we have long approached with reverence, if every picture, every statue, were removed from them, of which the subject was either the vice or the misery of mankind, portrayed without any moral purpose; consider the innumerable groups having reference merely to various forms of passion, low or high: drunken revels and brawls among peasants, gambling or fighting scenes among soldiers, amours and intrigues among every class, brutal battle pieces, banditti subjects, gluts of torture and death in famine, wreck, or slaughter, for the sake merely of the excitement,—that quickening and suppling of the dull spirit that cannot be gained for it but by bathing it in blood, afterward to wither back into stained and stiffened apathy; and then that whole vast false heaven of sensual passion, full of nymphs, satyrs, graces, goddesses, and I know not what, from its high seventh circle in Correggio's Antiope, down to the Grecized ballet-dancers and smirking Cupids of the Parisian upholsterer. Sweep away all this, remorselessly, and see how much art we should have left.

§ 60. And yet these are only the grossest manifestations of the tendency of the school. There are subtler, yet not less certain, signs of it in the works of men who stand high in the world's list of sacred painters. I doubt not that the reader was surprised when I named Murillo among the men of this third rank. Yet, go into the Dulwich Gallery, and meditate for a little over that much celebrated picture of the two beggar boys, one eating, lying on the ground, the other standing beside him. We have among our own painters one who cannot indeed be set beside Murillo as a painter of Madonnas, for he is a pure Naturalist, and, never having seen a Madonna, does not paint any; but who, as a painter of beggar or peasant boys, may be set beside Murillo, or any one else,—W. Hunt.[16] He loves peasant boys, because he finds them more roughly and picturesquely dressed, and more healthily coloured, than others. And he paints all that he sees in them fearlessly; all the health and humour, and freshness and vitality, together with such awkwardness and stupidity, and what else of negative or positive harm there may be in the creature; but yet so that on the whole we love it, and find it perhaps even beautiful, or if not, at least we see that there is capability of good in it, rather than of evil; and all is lighted up by a sunshine and sweet colour that makes the smock frock as precious as cloth of gold. But look at those two ragged and vicious vagrants that Murillo has gathered out of the street. You smile at first, because they are eating so naturally, and their

---

[15] Not selfish fear, caused by want of trust in God, or of resolution in the soul. Compare *Modern Painters*, vol. ii, pt. iii section 1, chap. xiv. [Ruskin's note]
[16] William Henry Hunt (1790–1864), English watercolorist.

roguery is so complete. But is there anything else than roguery there, or was it well for the painter to give his time to the painting of those repulsive and wicked children? Do you feel moved with any charity towards children as you look at them? Are we the least more likely to take any interest in ragged schools, or to help the next pauper child that comes in our way, because the painter has shown us a cunning beggar feeding greedily? Mark the choice of the act. He might have shown hunger in other ways, and given interest to even this act of eating, by making the face wasted, or the eye wistful. But he did not care to do this. He delighted merely in the disgusting manner of eating, the food filling the cheek; the boy is not hungry, else he would not turn round to talk and grin as he eats.

§ 61. But observe another point in the lower figure. It lies so that the sole of the foot is turned towards the spectator; not because it would have lain less easily in another attitude, but that the painter may draw, and exhibit, the grey dust engrained in the foot. Do not call this the painting of nature: it is mere delight in foulness. The lesson, if there be any, in the picture, is not one whit the stronger. We all know that a beggar's bare foot cannot be clean; there is no need to thrust its degradation into the light, as if no human imagination were vigorous enough for its conception.

§ 62. The position of the Sensualists, in treatment of landscape, is less distinctly marked than in that of the figure, because even the wildest passions of nature are noble: but the inclination is manifested by carelessness in marking generic form in trees and flowers: by their preferring confused and irregular arrangements of foliage or foreground to symmetrical and simple grouping: by their general choice of such picturesqueness as results from decay, disorder, and disease, rather than of that which is consistent with the perfection of the things in which it is found; and by their imperfect rendering of the elements of strength

and beauty in all things. I propose to work out this subject fully in the last volume of *Modern Painters;* but I trust that enough has been here said to enable the reader to understand the relations of the three great classes of artists, and therefore also the kinds of morbid condition into which the two higher (for the last has no other than a morbid condition) are liable to fall. For, since the function of the Naturalists is to represent, as far as may be, the whole of nature, and of the Purists to represent what is absolutely good for some special purpose or time, it is evident that both are liable to err from shortness of sight, and the last also from weakness of judgment. I say, in the first place, both may err from shortness of sight, from not seeing all that there is in nature; seeing only the outside of things, or those points of them which bear least on the matter in hand. For instance, a modern continental Naturalist sees the anatomy of a limb thoroughly, but does not see its colour against the sky, which latter fact is to a painter far the more important of the two. And because it is always easier to see the surface than the depth of things, the full sight of them requiring the highest powers of penetration, sympathy, and imagination, the world is full of vulgar Naturalists: not Sensualists observe, not men who delight in evil; but men who never see the deepest good, and who bring discredit on all painting of Nature by the little that they discover in her. And the Purist, besides being liable to this same shortsightedness, is liable also to fatal errors of judgment; for he may think that good which is not so, and that the highest good which is the least. And thus the world is full of vulgar Purists,[17] who bring discredit on all selection by the silliness of their choice; and this the more, because the very becoming a Purist is commonly indicative of some slight degree of weakness, readiness to be offended, or narrowness of understanding of the ends of things: the greatest men being, in all times of art, Naturalists, without any exception; and the greatest Purists being

<hr />

[17] I reserve for another place the full discussion of this interesting subject, which here would have led me too far; but it must be noted, in passing, that this vulgar Purism, which rejects truth, not because it is vicious, but because it is humble, and consists not in choosing what is good, but in disguising what is rough, extends itself into every species of art. The most definite instance of it is the dressing of characters of peasantry in an opera or ballet scene; and the walls of our exhibitions are full of works of art which "exalt nature" in the same way, not by revealing what is great in the heart, but by smoothing what is coarse in the complexion. There is nothing, I believe, so vulgar, so hopeless, so indicative of an irretrievably base mind, as this species of Purism. Of healthy Purism carried to the utmost endurable length in this direction, exalting the heart first, and the features with it, perhaps the most characteristic instance I can give is Stothard's vignette to "Jorasse," in Rogers's *Italy:* at least it would be so if it could be seen beside a real group of Swiss girls. The poems of Rogers, compared with those of Crabbe, are admirable instances of the healthiest Purism and healthiest Naturalism in poetry. The first great Naturalists of Christian art were Orcagna and Giotto. [Ruskin's note]

those who approach nearest to the Naturalists, as Benozzo Gozzoli and Perugino. Hence there is a tendency in the Naturalists to despise the Purists, and in the Purists to be offended with the Naturalists (not understanding them, and confounding them with the Sensualists); and this is grievously harmful to both.

§ 63. Of the various forms of resultant mischief it is not here the place to speak; the reader may already be somewhat wearied with a statement which has led us apparently so far from our immediate subject. But the digression was necessary, in order that I might clearly define the sense in which I use the word Naturalism when I state it to be the third most essential characteristic of Gothic architecture. I mean that the Gothic builders belong to the central or greatest rank in *both* the classifications of artists which we have just made; that considering all artists as either men of design, men of facts, or men of both, the Gothic builders were men of both; and that again, considering all artists as either Purists, Naturalists, or Sensualists, the Gothic builders were Naturalists.

§ 64. I say first, that the Gothic builders were of that central class which unites fact with design; but that the part of the work which was more especially their own was the truthfulness. Their power of artistical invention or arrangement was not greater than that of Romanesque and Byzantine workmen: by those workmen they were taught the principles, and from them received their models, of design; but to the ornamental feeling and rich fancy of the Byzantine the Gothic builder added a love of *fact* which is never found in the South. Both Greek and Roman used conventional foliage in their ornament, passing into something that was not foliage at all, knotting itself into strange cup-like buds or clusters, and growing out of lifeless rods instead of stems; the Gothic sculptor received these types, at first, as things that ought to be, just as we have a second time received them; but he could not rest in them. He saw there was no veracity in them, no knowledge, no vitality. Do what he would, he could not help liking the true leaves better; and cautiously, a little at a time, he put more of nature into his work, until at last it was all true, retaining, nevertheless, every valuable character of the original well-disciplined and designed arrangement.[18]

§ 65. Nor is it only in external and visible subject that the Gothic workman wrought for truth: he is as firm in his rendering of imaginative as of actual truth; that is to say, when an idea would have been by a Roman, or Byzantine, symbolically represented, the Gothic mind realizes it to the utmost. For instance, the purgatorial fire is represented in the mosaic of Torcello (Romanesque) as a red stream, longitudinally striped like a riband, descending out of the throne of Christ, and gradually extending itself to envelope the wicked. When we are once informed what this means, it is enough for its purpose; but the Gothic inventor does not leave the sign in need of interpretation. He makes the fire as like real fire as he can; and in the porch of St. Maclou at Rouen the sculptured flames burst out of the Hades gate, and flicker up, in writhing tongues of stone, through the interstices of the niches, as if the church itself were on fire. This is an extreme instance, but it is all the more illustrative of the entire difference in temper and thought between the two schools of art, and of the intense love of veracity which influenced the Gothic design.

§ 66. I do not say that this love of veracity is always healthy in its operation. I have above noticed the errors into which it falls from despising design; and there is another kind of error noticeable in the instance just given, in which the love of truth is too hasty, and seizes on a surface truth instead of an inner one. For in representing the Hades fire, it is not the mere *form* of the flame which needs most to be told, but its unquenchableness, its Divine ordainment and limitation, and its inner fierceness, not physical and material, but in being the expression of the wrath of God. And these things are not to be told by imitating the fire that flashes out of a bundle of sticks. If we think over his symbol a little, we shall perhaps find that the Romanesque builder told more truth in that likeness of a blood-red stream, flowing between definite shores, and out of God's throne, and expanding, as if fed by a perpetual current, into the lake wherein the wicked are cast, than the Gothic builder in those torch-flickerings about his niches. But this is not to our immediate purpose; I am not at present to insist upon the faults into which the love of truth was led in the later Gothic times, but on the feeling itself, as a glorious and pecu-

---

[18] The reader will understand this in a moment by glancing at Plate 20, the last in this volume, where the series 1 to 12 represents the change in one kind of leaf, from the Byzantine to the perfect Gothic. [Ruskin's note]

liar characteristic of the Northern builders. For, observe, it is not, even in the above instance, love of truth, but want of thought, which *causes* the fault. The love of truth, as such, is good, but when it is misdirected by thoughtlessness or over-excited by vanity, and either seizes on facts of small value, or gathers them chiefly that it may boast of its grasp and apprehension, its work may well become dull or offensive. Yet let us not, therefore, blame the inherent love of facts, but the incautiousness of their selection, and impertinence of their statement.

§ 67. I said, in the second place, that Gothic work, when referred to the arrangement of all art, as purist, naturalist, or sensualist, was naturalist. This character follows necessarily on its extreme love of truth, prevailing over the sense of beauty, and causing it to take delight in portraiture of every kind, and to express the various characters of the human countenance and form, as it did the varieties of leaves and the ruggedness of branches. And this tendency is both increased and ennobled by the same Christian humility which we saw expressed in the first character of Gothic work, its rudeness. For as that resulted from a humility which confessed the imperfection of the *workman,* so this naturalist portraiture is rendered more faithful by the humility which confesses the imperfection of the *subject.* The Greek sculptor could neither bear to confess his own feebleness, nor to tell the faults of the forms that he portrayed. But the Christian workman, believing that all is finally to work together for good,[19] freely confesses both, and neither seeks to disguise his own roughness of work, nor his subject's roughness of make. Yet this frankness being joined, for the most part, with depth of religious feeling in other directions, and especially with charity, there is sometimes a tendency to Purism in the best Gothic sculpture; so that it frequently reaches great dignity of form and tenderness of expression, yet never so as to lose the veracity of portraiture wherever portraiture is possible: not exalting its kings into demi-gods, nor its saints into archangels, but giving what kingliness and sanctity was in them, to the full, mixed with due record of their faults; and this in the most part with a great indifference like that of Scripture

history, which sets down, with unmoved and unexcusing resoluteness, the virtues and errors of all men of whom it speaks, often leaving the reader to form his own estimate of them, without an indication of the judgment of the historian. And this veracity is carried out by the Gothic sculptors in the minuteness and generality, as well as the equity, of their delineation: for they do not limit their art to the portraiture of saints and kings, but introduce the most familiar scenes and most simple subjects: filling up the backgrounds of Scripture histories with vivid and curious representations of the commonest incidents of daily life, and availing themselves of every occasion in which, either as a symbol, or an explanation of a scene or time, the things familiar to the eye of the workmen could be introduced and made of account. Hence Gothic sculpture and painting are not only full of valuable portraiture of the greatest men, but copious records of all the domestic customs and inferior arts of the ages in which it flourished.[20]

§ 68. There is, however, one direction in which the Naturalism of the Gothic workmen is peculiarly manifested; and this direction is even more characteristic of the school than the Naturalism itself; I mean their peculiar fondness for the forms of Vegetation. In rendering the various circumstances of daily life, Egyptian and Ninevite sculpture is as frank and as diffuse as the Gothic. From the highest pomps of state or triumphs of battle, to the most trivial domestic arts and amusements, all is taken advantage of to fill the field of granite with the perpetual interest of a crowded drama; and the early Lombardic and Romanesque sculpture is equally copious in its description of the familiar circumstances of war and the chase. But in all the scenes portrayed by the workmen of these nations, vegetation occurs only as an explanatory accessary; the reed is introduced to mark the course of the river, or the tree to mark the covert of the wild beast, or the ambush of the enemy, but there is no especial interest in the forms of the vegetation strong enough to induce them to make it a subject of separate and accurate study. Again, among the nations who followed the arts of design exclusively, the forms of foliage introduced were meagre and general, and their real intricacy

---

[19] Romans 8:28.

[20] The best art either represents the facts of its own day, or, if fact of the past, expresses them with accessories of the time in which the work was done. All good art, representing past events, is therefore full of the most frank anachronism, and always *ought* to be. No painter has any business to be an antiquarian. We do not want his impressions or suppositions respecting things that are past. We want his clear assertions respecting things present. [Ruskin's note]

and life were neither admired nor expressed. But to the Gothic workman the living foliage became a subject of intense affection, and he struggled to render all its characters with as much accuracy as was compatible with the laws of his design and the nature of his material, not unfrequently tempted in his enthusiasm to transgress the one and disguise the other.

§ 69. There is a peculiar significance in this, indicative both of higher civilization and gentler temperament, than had before been manifested in architecture. Rudeness, and the love of change, which we have insisted upon as the first elements of Gothic, are also elements common to all healthy schools. But here is a softer element mingled with them, peculiar to the Gothic itself. The rudeness or ignorance which would have been painfully exposed in the treatment of the human form, are still not so great as to prevent the successful rendering of the wayside herbage; and the love of change, which becomes morbid and feverish in following the haste of the hunter and the rage of the combatant, is at once soothed and satisfied as it watches the wandering of the tendril, and the budding of the flower. Nor is this all: the new direction of mental interest marks an infinite change in the means and the habits of life. The nations whose chief support was in the chase, whose chief interest was in the battle, whose chief pleasure was in the banquet, would take small care respecting the shapes of leaves and flowers; and notice little in the forms of the forest trees which sheltered them, except the signs indicative of the wood which would make the toughest lance, the closest roof, or the clearest fire. The affectionate observation of the grace and outward character of vegetation is the sure sign of a more tranquil and gentle existence, sustained by the gifts, and gladdened by the splendour, of the earth. In that careful distinction of species, and richness of delicate and undisturbed organization, which characterize the Gothic design, there is the history of rural and thoughtful life, influenced by habitual tenderness, and devoted to subtle inquiry; and every discriminating and delicate touch of the chisel, as it rounds the petal or guides the branch, is a prophecy of the development of the entire body of the natural sciences, beginning with that of medicine, of the recovery of literature, and the establishment of the most necessary principles of domestic wisdom and national peace.

§ 70. I have before alluded to the strange and

vain supposition, that the original conception of Gothic architecture had been derived from vegetation,—from the symmetry of avenues, and the interlacing of branches. It is a supposition which never could have existed for a moment in the mind of any person acquainted with early Gothic; but, however idle as a theory, it is most valuable as a testimony to the character of the perfected style. It is precisely because the reverse of this theory is the fact, because the Gothic did not arise out of, but develope itself into, a resemblance to vegetation, that this resemblance is so instructive as an indication of the temper of the builders. It was no chance suggestion of the form of an arch from the bending of a bough, but a gradual and continual discovery of a beauty in natural forms which could be more and more perfectly transferred into those of stone, that influenced at once the heart of the people, and the form of the edifice. The Gothic architecture arose in massy and mountainous strength, axe-hewn, and iron-bound, block heaved upon block by the monk's enthusiasm and the soldier's force; and cramped and stanchioned into such weight of grisly wall, as might bury the anchoret in darkness, and beat back the utmost storm of battle, suffering but by the same narrow crosslet the passing of the sunbeam, or of the arrow. Gradually, as that monkish enthusiasm became more thoughtful, and as the sound of war became more and more intermittent beyond the gates of the convent or the keep, the stony pillar grew slender and the vaulted roof grew light, till they had wreathed themselves into the semblance of the summer woods at their fairest, and of the dead field-flowers, long trodden down in blood, sweet monumental statues were set to bloom for ever, beneath the porch of the temple, or the canopy of the tomb.

§ 71. Nor is it only as a sign of greater gentleness or refinement of mind, but as a proof of the best possible direction of this refinement, that the tendency of the Gothic to the expression of vegetative life is to be admired. That sentence of Genesis, "I have given thee every green herb for meat,"[21] like all the rest of the book, has a profound symbolical as well as a literal meaning. It is not merely the nourishment of the body, but the food of the soul, that is intended. The green herb is, of all nature, that which is most essential to the healthy spiritual life of man. Most of us do not need fine scenery; the precipice and the mountain peak are not intended to be seen by all

---

[21] Genesis 1:30.

men,—perhaps their power is greatest over those who are unaccustomed to them. But trees and fields and flowers were made for all, and are necessary for all. God has connected the labour which is essential to the bodily sustenance with the pleasures which are healthiest for the heart; and while He made the ground stubborn, He made its herbage fragrant, and its blossoms fair. The proudest architecture that man can build has no higher honour than to bear the image and recall the memory of that grass of the field which is, at once, the type and the support of his existence; the goodly building is then most glorious when it is sculptured into the likeness of the leaves of Paradise; and the great Gothic spirit, as we showed it to be noble in its disquietude, is also noble in its hold of nature; it is, indeed, like the dove of Noah, in that she found no rest upon the face of the waters,—but like her in this also, "Lo, IN HER MOUTH WAS AN OLIVE BRANCH, PLUCKED OFF." [22]

§ 72. The fourth essential element of the Gothic mind was above stated to be the sense of the GROTESQUE; but I shall defer the endeavour to define this most curious and subtle character until we have occasion to examine one of the divisions of the Renaissance schools, which was morbidly influenced by it (Vol. III. Chap. III.). It is the less necessary to insist upon it here, because every reader familiar with Gothic architecture must understand what I mean, and will, I believe, have no hesitation in admitting, that the tendency to delight in fantastic and ludicrous, as well as in sublime, images, is a universal instinct of the Gothic imagination.

§ 73. The fifth element above named was RIGIDITY; and this character I must endeavour carefully to define, for neither the word I have used, nor any other that I can think of, will express it accurately. For I mean, not merely stable, but *active* rigidity; the peculiar energy which gives tension to movement, and stiffness to resistance, which makes the fiercest lightning forked rather than curved, and the stoutest oak-branch angular rather than bending, and is as much seen in the quivering of the lance as in the glittering of the icicle.

§ 74. I have before had occasion (Vol. I. Chap. XIII. § 7) to note some manifestations of this energy or fixedness; but it must be still more attentively considered here, as it shows itself throughout the whole structure and decoration of Gothic work. Egyptian and Greek build-

ings stand, for the most part, by their own weight and mass, one stone passively incumbent on another; but in the Gothic vaults and traceries there is a stiffness analogous to that of the bones of a limb, or fibres of a tree; an elastic tension and communication of force from part to part, and also a studious expression of this throughout every visible line of the building. And, in like manner, the Greek and Egyptian ornament is either mere surface engraving, as if the face of the wall had been stamped with a seal, or its lines are flowing, lithe, and luxuriant; in either case, there is no expression of energy in the framework of the ornament itself. But the Gothic ornament stands out in prickly independence, and frosty fortitude, jutting into crockets, and freezing into pinnacles; here starting up into a monster, there germinating into a blossom, anon knitting itself into a branch, alternately thorny, bossy, and bristly, or writhed into every form of nervous entanglement; but, even when most graceful, never for an instant languid, always quickset: erring, if at all, ever on the side of brusquerie.

§ 75. The feelings or habits in the workman which give rise to this character in the work, are more complicated and various than those indicated by any other sculptural expression hitherto named. There is, first, the habit of hard and rapid working; the industry of the tribes of the North, quickened by the coldness of the climate, and giving an expression of sharp energy to all they do (as above noted, Vol. I. Chap. XIII. § 7), as opposed to the langour of the Southern tribes, however much of fire there may be in the heart of that langour, for lava itself may flow languidly. There is also the habit of finding enjoyment in the signs of cold, which is never found, I believe, in the inhabitants of countries south of the Alps. Cold is to them an unredeemed evil, to be suffered and forgotten as soon as may be; but the long winter of the North forces the Goth (I mean the Englishman, Frenchman, Dane, or German), if he would lead a happy life at all, to find sources of happiness in foul weather as well as fair, and to rejoice in the leafless as well as in the shady forest. And this we do with all our hearts; finding perhaps nearly as much contentment by the Christmas fire as in the summer sunshine, and gaining health and strength on the ice-fields of winter, as well as among the meadows of spring. So that there is nothing adverse or painful to our feelings in the cramped and stiffened structure of vegetation

---

[22] Genesis 8:9–11.

checked by cold; and instead of seeking, like the Southern sculpture, to express only the softness of leafage nourished in all tenderness, and tempted into all luxuriance by warm winds and glowing rays, we find pleasure in dwelling upon the crabbed, perverse, and morose animation of plants that have known little kindness from earth or heaven, but, season after season, have had their best efforts palsied by frost, their brightest buds buried under snow, and their goodliest limbs lopped by tempest.

§ 76. There are many subtle sympathies and affections which join to confirm the Gothic mind in this peculiar choice of subject; and when we add to the influence of these, the necessities consequent upon the employment of a rougher material, compelling the workman to seek for vigour of effect, rather than refinement of texture or accuracy of form, we have direct and manifest causes for much of the difference between the Northern and Southern cast of conception: but there are indirect causes holding a far more important place in the Gothic heart, though less immediate in their influence on design. Strength of will, independence of character, resoluteness of purpose, impatience of undue control, and that general tendency to set the individual reason against authority, and the individual deed against destiny, which, in the Northern tribes, has opposed itself throughout all ages, to the languid submission, in the Southern, of thought to tradition, and purpose to fatality, are all more or less traceable in the rigid lines, vigorous and various masses, and daringly projecting and independent structure of the Northern Gothic ornament: while the opposite feelings are in like manner legible in the graceful and softly guided waves and wreathed bands, in which Southern decoration is constantly disposed; in its tendency to lose its independence, and fuse itself into the surface of the masses upon which it is traced; and in the expression seen so often, in the arrangement of those masses themselves, of an abandonment of their strength to an inevitable necessity, or a listless repose.

§ 77. There is virtue in the measure, and error in the excess, of both these characters of mind, and in both of the styles which they have created; the

best architecture, and the best temper, are those which unite them both; and this fifth impulse of the Gothic heart is therefore that which needs most caution in its indulgence. It is more definitely Gothic than any other, but the best Gothic building is not that which is *most* Gothic: it can hardly be too frank in its confession of rudeness, hardly too rich in its changefulness, hardly too faithful in its naturalism; but it may go too far in its rigidity, and, like the great Puritan spirit in its extreme, lose itself either in frivolity of division, or perversity of purpose.[23] It actually did so in its later times; but it is gladdening to remember that in its utmost nobleness, the very temper which has been thought most adverse to it, the Protestant spirit of self-dependence and inquiry, was expressed in its every line. Faith and aspiration there were, in every Christian ecclesiastical building, from the first century to the fifteenth; but the moral habits to which England in this age owes the kind of greatness that she has,—the habits of philosophical investigation, of accurate thought, of domestic seclusion and independence, of stern self-reliance and sincere upright searching into religious truth.—were only traceable in the features which were the distinctive creation of the Gothic schools, in the veined foliage, and thorny fretwork, and shadowy niche, and buttressed pier, and fearless height of subtle pinnacle and crested tower, sent like an "unperplexed question up to Heaven."[24]

§ 78. Last, because the least essential, of the constituent elements of this noble school, was placed that of REDUNDANCE,—the uncalculating bestowal of the wealth of its labour. There is, indeed, much Gothic, and that of the best period, in which this element is hardly traceable, and which depends for its effect almost exclusively on loveliness of simple design and grace of uninvolved proportion; still, in the most characteristic buildings, a certain portion of their effect depends upon accumulation of ornament; and many of those which have most influence on the minds of men, have attained it by means of this attitude alone. And although, by careful study of the school, it is possible to arrive at a condition of taste which shall be better contented by a few perfect lines than by a whole façade covered with

---

[23] See the account of the meeting at Talla Linns, in 1682, given in the fourth chapter of the *Heart of Midlothian*. At length they arrived at the conclusion that "they who owned (or allowed) such names as Monday, Tuesday, January, February, and so forth, served themselves heirs to the same if not greater punishment than had been denounced against the idolaters of old." [Ruskin's note]

[24] See the beautiful description of Florence in Elizabeth Browning's Casa Guidi Windows, which is not only a noble poem, but the only book I have seen which, favouring the Liberal cause in Italy, gives a just account of the incapacities of the modern Italian. [Ruskin's note]

fretwork, the building which only satisfies such a taste is not to be considered the best. For the very first requirement of Gothic architecture being, as we saw above, that it shall both admit the aid, and appeal to the admiration, of the rudest as well as the most refined minds, the richness of the work is, paradoxical as the statement may appear, a part of its humility. No architecture is so haughty as that which is simple; which refuses to address the eye, except in a few clear and forceful lines; which implies, in offering so little to our regards, that all it has offered is perfect; and disdains, either by the complexity or the attractiveness of its features, to embarrass our investigation, or betray us into delight. That humility, which is the very life of the Gothic school, is shown not only in the imperfection, but in the accumulation, of ornament. The inferior rank of the workman is often shown as much in the richness, as the roughness, of his work; and if the co-operation of every hand, and the sympathy of every heart, are to be received, we must be content to allow the redundance which disguises the failure of the feeble, and wins the regard of the inattentive. There are, however, far nobler interests mingling, in the Gothic heart, with the rude love of decorative accumulation: a magnificent enthusiasm, which feels as if it never could do enough to reach the fulness of its ideal; an unselfishness of sacrifice, which would rather cast fruitless labour before the altar than stand idle in the market; and, finally, a profound sympathy with the fulness and wealth of the material universe, rising out of that Naturalism whose operation we have already endeavoured to define. The sculptor who sought for his models among the forest leaves, could not but quickly and deeply feel that complexity need not involve the loss of grace, nor richness that of repose; and every hour which he spent in the study of the minute and various work of Nature, made him feel more forcibly the barrenness of what was best in that of man: nor is it to be wondered at, that, seeing her perfect and exquisite creations poured forth in a profusion which conception could not grasp nor calculation sum, he should think that it ill became him to be niggardly of his own rude craftsmanship; and where he saw throughout the universe a faultless beauty lavished on measureless spaces of broidered field and blooming mountain, to grudge his poor and imperfect labour to the few stones that he had raised one upon another, for habitation or memorial. The years of his life passed away before his task was accomplished; but generation succeeded generation with unwearied enthusiasm, and the cathedral front was at last lost in the tapestry of its traceries, like a rock among the thickets and herbage of spring.

§ 79. We have now, I believe, obtained a view approaching to completeness of the various moral or imaginative elements which composed the inner spirit of Gothic architecture. We have, in the second place, to define its outward form . . . [25]

·   ·   ·

§ 103. Now observe: it is not, at present, the question, whether the form of the Veronese niche, and the design of its flower-work, be as good as they might have been; but simply, which of the two architectural principles is the greater and better. And this we cannot hesitate for an instant in deciding. The Veronese Gothic is strong in its masonry, simple in its masses, but perpetual in its variety. The late French Gothic is weak in masonry, broken in mass, and repeats the same idea continually. It is very beautiful, but the Italian Gothic is the nobler style.

§ 104. Yet, in saying that the French Gothic repeats one idea, I mean merely that it depends too much upon the foliation of its traceries. The disposition of the traceries themselves is endlessly varied and inventive; and, indeed, the mind of the French workman was, perhaps, even richer in fancy than that of the Italian, only he had been taught a less noble style. This is especially to be remembered with respect to the subordination of figure sculpture above noticed as characteristic of the later Gothic.

It is not that such sculpture is wanting; on the contrary, it is often worked into richer groups, and carried out with a perfection of execution, far greater than those which adorn the earlier buildings: but, in the early work, it is vigorous, prominent, and essential to the beauty of the whole; in the late work it is enfeebled, and shrouded in the veil of tracery, from which it may often be removed with little harm to the general effect. [26]

§ 105. Now the reader may rest assured that no principle of art is more absolute than this,—

[25] Paragraphs 80 through 102, presenting in extensive detail the outward form of Gothic architecture as seen by Ruskin, have been omitted.

[26] In many of the best French Gothic Churches, the groups of figures have been all broken away at the Revolution, without much harm to the picturesqueness, though with grievous loss to the

that a composition from which anything can be removed without doing mischief, is always so far forth inferior. On this ground, therefore, if on no other, there can be no question, for a moment, which of the two schools is the greater; although there are many most noble works in the French traceried Gothic, having a sublimity of their own, dependent on their extreme richness and grace of line, and for which we may be most grateful to their builders. And, indeed, the superiority of the Surface Gothic cannot be completely felt, until we compare it with the more degraded Linear schools, as, for instance, with our own English perpendicular. The ornaments of the Veronese niche, which we have used for our example, are by no means among the best of their school, yet they will serve our purpose for such a comparison. That of its pinnacle is composed of a single upright flowering plant, of which the stem shoots up through the centres of the leaves, and bears a pendant blossom, somewhat like that of the imperial lily. The leaves are thrown back from the stem with singular grace and freedom, and foreshortened, as if by a skilful painter, in the shallow marble relief . . . and if the reader will simply try the experiment for himself,—first, of covering a piece of paper with crossed lines, as if for accounts, and filling all the interstices with any foliation that comes into his head . . . and then, of trying to fill the point of a gable with a piece of leafage . . . putting the figure itself aside,—he will presently find that more thought and invention are required to design this single minute pinnacle, than to cover acres of ground with English perpendicular.

§ 106. We have now, I believe, obtained a sufficiently accurate knowledge both of the spirit and form of Gothic architecture; but it may, perhaps, be useful to the general reader, if, in conclusion, I set down a few plain and practical rules for determining, in every instance, whether a given building be good Gothic or not, and, if not Gothic, whether its architecture is of a kind which will probably reward the pains of careful examination.

§ 107. First, Look if the roof rises in a steep gable, high above the walls. If it does not do this, there is something wrong: the building is not quite pure Gothic, or has been altered.

§ 108. Secondly, Look if the principal windows and doors have pointed arches with gables over

them. If not pointed arches, the building is not Gothic; if they have not any gables over them, it is either not pure, or not first-rate.

If, however, it has the steep roof, the pointed arch, and gable all united, it is nearly certain to be a Gothic building of a very fine time.

§ 109. Thirdly, Look if the arches are cusped, or apertures foliated. If the building has met the first two conditions, it is sure to be foliated somewhere; but if not everywhere, the parts which are unfoliated are imperfect, unless they are large bearing arches, or small and sharp arches in groups, forming a kind of foliation by their own multiplicity, and relieved by sculpture and rich mouldings. The upper windows, for instance, in the east end of Westminster Abbey are imperfect for want of foliation. If there be no foliation anywhere, the building is assuredly imperfect Gothic.

§ 110. Fourthly, If the building meets all the first three conditions, look if its arches in general, whether of windows and doors, or of minor ornamentation, are carried on *true shafts with bases and capitals*. If they are, then the building is assuredly of the finest Gothic style. It may still, perhaps, be an imitation, a feeble copy, or a bad example, of a noble style; but the manner of it, having met all these four conditions, is assuredly first-rate.

If its apertures have not shafts and capitals, look if they are plain openings in the walls, studiously simple, and unmoulded at the sides. . . . If so, the building may still be of the finest Gothic adapted to some domestic or military service. But if the sides of the window be moulded, and yet there are no capitals at the spring of the arch, it is assuredly of an inferior school.

This is all that is necessary to determine whether the building be of a fine Gothic style. The next tests to be applied are in order to discover whether it be good architecture or not; for it may be very impure Gothic, and yet very noble architecture; or it may be very pure Gothic, and yet if a copy, or originally raised by an ungifted builder, very bad architecture.

If it belong to any of the great schools of colour, its criticism becomes as complicated, and needs as much care, as that of a piece of music, and no general rules for it can be given: but if not—

§ 111. First, See if it looks as if it had been built by strong men; if it has the sort of rough-

---

historical value of the architecture: whereas, if from the niche at Verona we were to remove its floral ornaments, and the statue beneath it, nothing would remain but a rude square trefoiled sheet, utterly valueless, or even ugly. [Ruskin's note]

ness, and largeness, and nonchalance, mixed in places with the exquisite tenderness which seems always to be the sign-manual of the broad vision, and massy power of men, who can see *past* the work they are doing, and betray here and there something like disdain for it. If the building has this character, it is much already in its favour; it will go hard but it proves a noble one. If it has not this, but is altogether accurate, minute, and scrupulous, in its workmanship, it must belong to either the very best or the very worst of schools: the very best, in which exquisite design is wrought out with untiring and conscientious care, as in the Giottesque Gothic; or the very worst, in which mechanism has taken the place of design. It is more likely, in general, that it should belong to the worst than the best: so that, on the whole, very accurate workmanship is to be esteemed a bad sign; and if there is nothing remarkable about the building but its precision, it may be passed at once with contempt.

§ 112. Secondly, Observe if it be irregular, its different parts fitting themselves to different purposes, no one caring what becomes of them, so that they do their work. If one part always answers accurately to another part, it is sure to be a bad building; and the greater and more conspicuous the irregularities, the greater the chances are that it is a good one. For instance, in the Ducal Palace . . . the general idea is sternly symmetrical; but two windows are lower than the rest of the six; and if the reader will count the arches of the small arcade as far as to the great balcony, he will find it is not in the centre, but set to the right-hand side by the whole width of one of those arches. We may be pretty sure that the building is a good one; none but a master of his craft would have ventured to do this.

§ 113. Thirdly, Observe if all the traceries, capitals, and other ornaments are of perpetually varied design. If not, the work is assuredly bad.

§ 114. Lastly, *Read* the sculpture. Preparatory to reading it, you will have to discover whether it is legible (and, if legible, it is nearly certain to be worth reading). On a good building, the sculpture is *always* so set, and on such a scale, that at the ordinary distance from which the edifice is seen, the sculpture shall be thoroughly intelligible and interesting. In order to accomplish this, the uppermost statues will be ten or twelve feet high, and the upper ornamentation will be colossal, increasing in fineness as it descends, till on the foundation it will often be wrought as if for a precious cabinet in a king's chamber; but the spectator will not notice that the upper sculptures are colossal. He will merely feel that he can see them plainly, and make them all out at his ease.

And having ascertained this, let him set himself to read them. Thenceforward the criticism of the building is to be conducted precisely on the same principles as that of a book; and it must depend on the knowledge, feeling, and not a little on the industry and perseverance of the reader, whether, even in the case of the best works, he either perceive them to be great, or feel them to be entertaining.

The Opening of the Crystal Palace

Considered in Some of Its Relations to the Prospects of Art

The Great Exhibition of 1851, or the Crystal Palace Exhibition as it is more often called, was in effect the first world's fair. The massive iron and glass structure built in Hyde Park to house the exhibition of British manufacturing and industrial glory roused the admiration of the multitude and the ire of some critics. Carlyle for one called it a "gigantic soap-bubble." Ruskin, often an enthusiast for the use of contemporary and native materials, was not impressed in the case of the Crystal Palace. He takes the occasion of his essay on the structure to make a plea for the preservation of earlier art. This essay was published in 1854 after the opening of the Crystal Palace at its new location in Sydenham where it remained until destroyed by fire in 1936.

1. I READ the account in the *Times* newspaper of the opening of the Crystal Palace at Sydenham as I ascended the hill between Vevay and Châtel St. Denis,[1] and the thoughts which it called up haunted me all day long, as my road wound among the grassy slopes of the Simmenthal. There was a strange contrast between the image of that mighty palace, raised so high above the hills on which it is built as to make them seem little less that a basement for its glittering stateliness, and those low larch huts, half hidden beneath their coverts of forest, and scattered like grey stones along the masses of far-away mountain. Here, man contending with the powers of Nature for his existence; there commanding them for his recreation: here, a feeble folk nested among the rocks with the wild goat and the coney, and retaining the same quiet thoughts from generation to generation; there, a great multitude triumphing in the splendour of immeasurable habitation, and haughty with hope of endless progress and irresistible power.

2. It is indeed impossible to limit, in imagination, the beneficent results which may follow from the undertaking thus happily begun. For the first time in the history of the world, a national museum is formed in which a whole nation is interested; formed on a scale which permits the exhibition of monuments of art in unbroken symmetry, and of the productions of nature in unthwarted growth,—formed under the auspices of science which can hardly err, and of wealth which can hardly be exhausted; and placed in the close neighbourhood of a metropolis overflowing with a population weary of labour, yet thirsting for knowledge, where contemplation may be consistent with rest, and instruction with enjoyment. It is impossible, I repeat, to estimate the influence of such an institution on the minds of the working-classes. How many hours once wasted may now be profitably dedicated to pursuits in which interest was first awakened by some accidental display in the Norwood palace; how many constitutions, almost broken, may be restored by the healthy temptation into the country air,—how many intellects, once dormant, may be roused into activity within the crystal walls, and how these noble results may go on multiplying and increasing and bearing fruit seventy times seven-fold, as the nation pursues its career,—are questions as full of hope as incapable

of calculation. But with all these grounds for hope there are others for despondency, giving rise to a group of melancholy thoughts, of which I can neither repress the importunity nor forbear the expression.

3. For three hundred years, the art of architecture has been the subject of the most curious investigation; its principles have been discussed with all earnestness and acuteness; its models in all countries and of all ages have been examined with scrupulous care, and imitated with unsparing expenditure. And of all this refinement of inquiry,—this lofty search after the ideal,—this subtlety of investigation and sumptuousness of practice,—the great result, the admirable and long-expected conclusion is, that in the centre of the nineteenth century, we suppose ourselves to have invented a new style of architecture, when we have magnified a conservatory!

4. In Mr. Laing's speech,[2] at the opening of the Palace, he declares that *"an entirely novel order of architecture,* producing, by means of unrivalled mechanical ingenuity, the most marvellous and beautiful effects, sprang into existence to provide a building."[3] In these words, the speaker is not merely giving utterance to his own feelings. He is expressing the popular view of the facts, nor that a view merely popular, but one which has been encouraged by nearly all the professors of art of our time.

It is to this, then, that our Doric and Palladian pride is at last reduced! We have vaunted the divinity of the Greek ideal—we have plumed ourselves on the purity of our Italian taste—we have cast our whole souls into the proportions of pillars and the relations of orders—and behold the end! Our taste, thus exalted and disciplined, is dazzled by the lustre of a few rows of panes of glass; and the first principles of architectural sublimity, so far sought, are found all the while to have consisted merely in sparkling and in space.

Let it not be thought that I would depreciate (were it possible to depreciate) the mechanical ingenuity which has been displayed in the erection of the Crystal Palace, or that I underrate the effect which its vastness may continue to produce on the popular imagination. But mechanical ingenuity is *not* the essence either of painting or architecture, and largeness of dimension does not necessarily involve nobleness of design. There is assuredly as much ingenuity

---

[1] Ruskin was vacationing in Switzerland with his parents at the time of the removal of the Crystal Palace to Sydenham.

[2] Samuel Laing (1812–97), chairman of the Crystal Palace Company.

[3] See the *Times* of Monday, June 12th. [Ruskin's note]

required to build a screw frigate, or a tubular bridge, as a hall of glass;—all these are works characteristic of the age; and all, in their several ways, deserve our highest admiration, but not admiration of the kind that is rendered to poetry or to art. We may cover the German Ocean with frigates, and bridge the Bristol Channel with iron, and roof the county of Middlesex with crystal, and yet not possess one Milton, or Michael Angelo.

5. Well, it may be replied, we need our bridges, and have pleasure in our palaces; but we do not want Miltons, nor Michael Angelos.

Truly, it seems so; for, in the year in which the first Crystal Palace was built, there died among us a man whose name, in after-ages, will stand with those of the great of all time. Dying, he bequeathed to the nation the whole mass of his most cherished works; and for these three years, while we have been building this colossal receptacle for casts and copies of the art of other nations, these works of our own greatest painter have been left to decay in a dark room near Cavendish Square,[4] under the custody of an aged servant.

This is quite natural. But it is also memorable.

6. There is another interesting fact connected with the history of the Crystal Palace as it bears on that of the art of Europe, namely, that in the year 1851, when all that glittering roof was built, in order to exhibit the paltry arts of our fashionable luxury—the carved bedsteads of Vienna, and glued toys of Switzerland, and gay jewellery of France—in that very year, I say, the greatest pictures of the Venetian masters were rotting at Venice in the rain, for want of roof to cover them, with holes made by cannon shot through their canvass.

There is another fact, however, more curious than either of these, which will hereafter be connected with the history of the palace now in building; namely, that at the very period when Europe is congratulated on the invention of a new style of architecture, because fourteen acres of ground have been covered with glass, the greatest examples in existence of true and noble Christian architecture are being resolutely destroyed; and destroyed by the effects of the very interest which was beginning to be excited by them.

7. Under the firm and wise government of the third Napoleon,[5] France has entered on a new epoch of prosperity, one of the signs of which is a zealous care for the preservation of her noble public buildings. Under the influence of this healthy impulse, repairs of the most extensive kind are at this moment proceeding, on the cathedrals of Rheims, Amiens, Rouen, Chartres, and Paris; (probably also in many other instances unknown to me). These repairs were, in many cases, necessary up to a certain point; and they have been executed by architects as skilful and learned as at present exist,—executed with noble disregard of expense, and sincere desire on the part of their superintendents that they should be completed in a manner honourable to the country.

8. They are, nevertheless, more fatal to the monuments they are intended to preserve, than fire, war, or revolution. For they are undertaken, in the plurality of instances, under an impression, which the efforts of all true antiquaries have as yet been unable to remove, that it is possible to reproduce the mutilated sculpture of past ages in its original beauty.

"Reproduire avec une exactitude mathematique," are the words used, by one of the most intelligent writers on this subject,[6] of the proposed regeneration of the statue of Ste. Modeste, on the north porch of the Cathedral of Chartres.

Now it is not the question at present, whether thirteenth century sculpture be of value, or not. Its value is assumed by the authorities who have devoted sums so large to its so-called restoration, and may therefore be assumed in my argument. The worst state of the sculptures whose restoration is demanded may be fairly represented by that of the celebrated group of the Fates, among the Elgin Marbles in the British Museum. With what favour would the guardians of those marbles, or any other persons interested in Greek art, receive a proposal from a living sculptor to "reproduce with mathematical exactitude" the group of the Fates, in a perfect form, and to destroy the original? For with exactly such favour, those who are interested in Gothic art should receive proposals to reproduce the sculpture of Chartres or Rouen.

9. In like manner, the state of the architecture which it is proposed to restore may, at its worst, be fairly represented to the British public by that of the best preserved portions of Melrose Abbey. With what encouragement would those among

---

[4] Reference to paintings left after the death of Turner.

[5] Napoleon III (1808–73), at this time ruler of France.

[6] M. l'Abbé Bulteau, *Description de la Cathédrale de Chartres* (8vo, Paris, Sagnier et Bray, 1850), p. 98, *note*. [Ruskin's note]

us who are sincerely interested in history, or in art, receive a proposal to pull down Melrose Abbey, and "reproduce it mathematically"? There can be no doubt of the answer which, in the instances supposed, it would be proper to return. "By all means, if you can, reproduce mathematically, elsewhere, the group of the Fates, and the Abbey of Melrose. But leave unharmed the original fragment, and the existing ruin." And an answer of the same tenour ought to be given to every proposal to restore a Gothic sculpture or building. Carve or raise a model of it in some other part of the city; but touch not the actual edifice, except only so far as may be necessary to sustain, to protect it. I said above that repairs were in many instances necessary. These necessary operations consist in substituting new stones for decayed ones, where they are absolutely essential to the stability of the fabric; in propping, with wood or metal, the portions likely to give way; in binding or cementing into their places the sculptures which are ready to detach themselves; and in general care to remove luxuriant weeds and obstructions of the channels for the discharge of the rain. But no modern or imitative sculpture ought *ever,* under any circumstances, to be mingled with the ancient work.

10. Unfortunately, repairs thus conscientiously executed are always unsightly, and meet with little approbation from the general public; so that a strong temptation is necessarily felt by the superintendents of public works to execute the required repairs in a manner which, though indeed fatal to the monument, may be, in appearance, seemly. But a far more cruel temptation is held out to the architect. He who should propose to a municipal body to build in the form of a new church, to be erected in some other part of their city, models of such portions of their cathedral as were falling into decay, would be looked upon as merely asking for employment, and his offer would be rejected with disdain. But let an architect declare that the existing fabric stands in need of repairs, and offer to restore it to its original beauty, and he is instantly regarded as a lover of his country, and has a chance of obtaining a commission which will furnish him with a large and ready income, and enormous patronage, for twenty or thirty years to come.

11. I have great respect for human nature. But I would rather leave it to others than myself to pronounce how far such a temptation is always likely to be resisted, and how far, when repairs

are once permitted to be undertaken, a fabric is likely to be spared from mere interest in its beauty, when its destruction, under the name of restoration, has become permanently remunerative to a large body of workmen.

Let us assume, however, that the architect is always conscientious—always willing, the moment he has done what is strictly necessary for the safety and decorous aspect of the building, to abandon his income, and declare his farther services unnecessary. Let us presume, also, that every one of the two or three hundred workmen who must be employed under him is equally conscientious, and, during the course of years of labour, will never destroy in carelessness what it may be inconvenient to save, or in cunning what it is difficult to imitate. Will all this probity of purpose preserve the hand from error, and the heart from weariness? Will it give dexterity to the awkward—sagacity to the dull—and at once invest two or three hundred imperfectly educated men with the feeling, intention, and information of the freemasons of the thirteenth century? Grant that it can do all this, and that the new building is both equal to the old in beauty, and precisely correspondent to it in detail. Is it, therefore, altogether *worth* the old building? Is the stone carved to-day in their masons' yards altogether the same in value to the hearts of the French people as that which the eyes of St. Louis saw lifted to its place? Would a loving daughter, in mere desire for gaudy dress, ask a jeweller for a bright facsimile of the worn cross which her mother bequeathed to her on her deathbed?—would a thoughtful nation, in mere fondness for splendour of streets, ask its architects to provide for it facsimiles of the temples which for centuries had given joy to its saints, comfort to its mourners, and strength to its chivalry?

12. But it may be replied, that all this is already admitted by the antiquaries of France and England; and that it is impossible that works so important should now be undertaken without due consideration and faithful superintendence.

I answer, that the men who justly feel these truths are rarely those who have much influence in public affairs. It is the poor abbé, whose little garden is sheltered by the mighty buttresses from the north wind, who knows the worth of the cathedral. It is the bustling mayor and the prosperous architect who determine its fate.

I answer farther, by the statement of a simple fact. I have given many years, in many cities, to the study of Gothic architecture; and of all that I know, or knew, the entrance to the north transept of Rouen Cathedral was, on the whole, the most beautiful—beautiful, not only as an elaborate and faultless work of the finest time of Gothic art, but yet more beautiful in the partial, though not dangerous, decay which had touched its pinnacles with pensive colouring, and softened its severer lines with unexpected change and delicate fracture, like sweet brakes in a distant music. The upper part of it has been already restored to the white accuracies of novelty; the lower pinnacles, which flanked its approach, far more exquisite in their partial ruin than the loveliest remains of our English abbeys, have been entirely destroyed, and rebuilt in rough blocks, now in process of sculpture. This restoration, so far as it has gone, has been executed by peculiarly skilful workmen; it is an unusually favourable example of restoration, especially in the care which has been taken to preserve intact the exquisite, and hitherto almost uninjured sculptures which fill the quatrefoils of the tracery above the arch. But I happened myself to have made, five years ago, detailed drawings of the buttress decorations on the right and left of this tracery, which are part of the work that has been completely restored. And I found the restorations as inaccurate as they were unnecessary.

13. If this is the case in a most favourable instance, in that of a well-known monument, highly esteemed by every antiquary in France, what, during the progress of the now almost universal repair, is likely to become of architecture which is unwatched and despised?

Despised! and more than despised—even hated! It is a sad truth, that there is something in the solemn aspect of ancient architecture which, in rebuking frivolity and chastening gaiety, has become at this time literally *repulsive* to a large majority of the population of Europe. Examine the direction which is taken by all the influences of fortune and of fancy, wherever they concern themselves with art, and it will be found that the real, earnest effort of the upper classes of European society is to make every place in the world as much like the Champs Elysées of Paris as possible. Wherever the influence of that educated society is felt, the old buildings are relentlessly destroyed; vast hotels, like barracks, and rows of high, square-windowed dwelling-houses, thrust themselves forward to conceal the hated antiquities of the great cities of France and Italy. Gay promenades, with fountains and statues,

prolong themselves along the quays once dedicated to commerce; ball-rooms and theatres rise upon the dust of desecrated chapels, and thrust into darkness the humility of domestic life. And when the formal street, in all its pride of perfumery and confectionery, has successfully consumed its way through wrecks of historical monuments, and consummated its symmetry in the ruin of all that once prompted a reflection, or pleaded for regard, the whitened city is praised for its splendour, and the exulting inhabitants for their patriotism—patriotism which consists in insulting their fathers with forgetfulness, and surrounding their children with temptation.

14. I am far from intending my words to involve any disrespectful allusion to the very noble improvements in the city of Paris itself, lately carried out under the encouragement of the Emperor. Paris, in its own peculiar character of bright magnificence, had nothing to fear, and everything to gain, from the gorgeous prolongations of the Rue Rivoli. But I speak of the general influence of the rich travellers and proprietors of Europe on the cities which they pretend to admire, or endeavour to improve. I speak of the changes wrought during my own lifetime on the cities of Venice, Florence, Geneva, Lucerne, and chief of all on Rouen, a city altogether inestimable for its retention of mediæval character in the infinitely varied streets in which one half of the existing and inhabited houses date from the fifteenth or early sixteenth century, and the only town left in France in which the effect of old French domestic architecture can yet be seen in its collective groups. But when I was there, this last spring, I heard that these noble old Norman houses are all, as speedily as may be, to be stripped of the dark slates which protected their timbers, and deliberately whitewashed over all their sculptures and ornaments, in order to bring the interior of the town into some conformity with the "handsome fronts" of the hotels and offices on the quay.

Hotels and offices, and "handsome fronts" in general—they can be built in America or Australia—built at any moment, and in any height of splendour. But who shall give us back, when once destroyed, the habitations of the French chivalry and bourgeoisie, in the days of the Field of the Cloth of Gold?

15. It is strange that no one seems to think of this! What do men travel for, in this Europe of ours? Is it only to gamble with French dies[7]—to

---

[7] I.e., dice.

drink coffee out of French porcelain—to dance to the beat of German drums, and sleep in the soft air of Italy? Are the ball-room, the billiard-room, and the Boulevard, the only attractions that win us into wandering, or tempt us to repose? And when the time is come, as come it will, and that shortly, when the parsimony—or lassitude—which, for the most part, are the only protectors of the remnants of elder time, shall be scattered by the advance of civilization—when all the monuments, preserved only because it was too costly to destroy them, shall have been crushed by the energies of the new world, will the proud nations of the twentieth century, looking round on the plains of Europe, disencumbered of their memorial marbles,—will those nations indeed stand up with no other feeling than one of triumph, freed from the paralysis of precedent and the entanglement of memory, to thank us, the fathers of progress, that no saddening shadows can any more trouble the enjoyments of the future,—no moments of reflection retard its activities; and that the new-born population of a world without a record and without a ruin may, in the fulness of ephemeral felicity, dispose itself to eat, and to drink, and to die?

16. Is this verily the end at which we aim, and will the mission of the age have been then only accomplished, when the last castle has fallen from our rocks, the last cloisters faded from our valleys, the last streets, in which the dead have dwelt, been effaced from our cities, and re-generated society is left in luxurious possession of towns composed only of bright saloons, over-looking gay parterres? If this be indeed our end, yet why must it be so laboriously accomplished? Are there no new countries on the earth, as yet uncrowned by Thorns of cathedral spires, untenanted by the consciousness of a past? Must this little Europe—this corner of our globe, gilded with the blood of old battles, and grey with the temples of old pieties—this narrow piece of the world's pavement, worn down by so many pilgrims' feet, be utterly swept and garnished for the masque of the Future? Is America not wide enough for the elasticities of our humanity? Asia not rich enough for its pride? or among the quiet meadow-lands and solitary hills of the old land, is there not yet room enough for the spreadings of power, or the indulgences of magnificence, with-out founding all glory upon ruin, and prefacing all progress with obliteration?

17. We must answer these questions speedily, or we answer them in vain. The peculiar charac-ter of the evil which is being wrought by this age

is its utter irreparableness. Its newly formed schools of art, its extending galleries, and well-ordered museums will assuredly bear some fruit in time, and give once more to the popular mind the power to discern what is great, and the disposition to protect what is precious. But it will be too late. We shall wander through our palaces of crystal, gazing sadly on copies of pictures torn by cannon-shot, and on casts of sculpture dashed to pieces long ago. We shall gradually learn to distinguish originality and sincerity from the decrepitudes of imitation and palsies of repetition; but it will be only in hopelessness to recognize the truth, that archi-tecture and painting can be "restored" when the dead can be raised,—and not till then.

18. Something might yet be done, if it were but possible thoroughly to awaken and alarm the men whose studies of archæology have enabled them to form an accurate judgment of the importance of the crisis. But it is one of the strange characters of the human mind, necessary indeed to its peace, but infinitely destructive of its power, that we never thoroughly feel the evils which are not actually set before our eyes. If, suddenly, in the midst of the enjoyments of the palate and lightnesses of heart of a London dinner-party, the walls of the chamber were parted, and through their gap, the nearest human beings who were famishing, and in misery, were borne into the midst of the company—feasting and fancy-free—if, pale with sickness, horrible in destitution, broken by despair, body by body, they were laid upon the soft carpet, one beside the chair of every guest, would only the crumbs of the dainties be cast to them—would only a passing glance, a passing thought be vouchsafed to them? Yet the actual facts, the real relations of each Dives and Lazarus, are not altered by the intervention of the house wall between the table and the sick-bed—by the few feet of ground (how few!) which are indeed all that separate the merriment from the misery.

19. It is the same in the matters of which I have hitherto been speaking. If every one of us, who knows what food for the human heart there is in the great works of elder time, could indeed see with his own eyes their progressive ruin; if every earnest antiquarian, happy in his well-ordered library, and in the sense of having been useful in preserving an old stone or two out of his parish church, and an old coin or two out of a furrow in the next ploughed field, could indeed behold, each morning as he awaked, the mightiest works of departed nations mouldering to the ground in

disregarded heaps; if he could always have in clear phantasm before his eyes the ignorant monk trampling on the manuscript, the village mason striking down the monument, the court painter daubing the despised and priceless masterpiece into freshness of fatuity, he would not always smile so complacently in the thoughts of the little learnings and petty preservations of his own immediate sphere. And if every man, who has the interest of Art and of History at heart, would at once devote himself earnestly—not to enrich his own collection—not even to enlighten his own neighbours or investigate his own parish-territory —but to far-sighted and *fore*-sighted endeavour in the great field of Europe, there is yet time to do much. An association might be formed,[8] thoroughly organized so as to maintain active watchers and agents in every town of importance, who, in the first place, should furnish the society with a *perfect* account of every monument of interest in its neighbourhood, and then with a yearly or half-yearly report of the state of such monuments, and of the changes proposed to be made upon them; the society then furnishing funds, either to buy, freehold, such buildings or other works of untransferable art as at any time might be offered for sale, or to assist their proprietors, whether private individuals or public bodies, in the maintenance of such guardianship as was really necessary for their safety; and exerting itself, with all the influence which such an association would rapidly command, to prevent unwise restoration and unnecessary destruction.

20. Such a society would of course be rewarded only by the consciousness of its usefulness. Its funds would have to be supplied, in pure self-denial, by its members, who would be required, so far as they assisted it, to give up the pleasure of purchasing prints or pictures for their own walls, that they might save pictures which in their lifetime they might never behold;—they would have to forego the enlargement of their own estates, that they might buy, for a European property, ground on which their feet might never tread. But is it absurd to believe that men are capable of doing this? Is the love of art altogether a selfish principle in the heart? and are its emotions altogether incompatible with the exertions of self-denial, or enjoyments of generosity?

21. I make this appeal at the risk of incurring only contempt for my Utopianism. But I should for ever reproach myself if I were prevented from making it by such a risk; and I pray those who may be disposed in any wise to favour it to remember that it must be answered at once or never. The next five years determine what is to be saved—what destroyed. The restorations have actually begun like cancers on every important piece of Gothic architecture in Christendom; the question is only how much can yet be saved. All projects, all pursuits, having reference to art, are at this moment of less importance than those which are simply protective. There is time enough for everything else. Time enough for teaching—time enough for criticising—time enough for inventing. But time little enough for saving. Hereafter we can create, but it is now only that we can preserve. By the exertion of great national powers, and under the guidance of enlightened monarchs, we may raise magnificent temples and gorgeous cities; we may furnish labour for the idle, and interest for the ignorant. But the power neither of emperors, nor queens, nor kingdoms, can ever print again upon the sands of time the effaced footsteps of departed generations, or gather together from the dust the stones which had been stamped with the spirit of our ancestors.

Unto This Last

The year 1860 is often said to mark the turning point in Ruskin's intellectual life, for it was the year of the publication of Unto This Last *in which Ruskin lashed out at the dominant laissez-faire economics of the day and at what he saw as its impoverishment of the many for the benefit of the few. The work was begun in installments in the* Cornhill Magazine, *but Ruskin was obliged to bring it to an early conclusion because of public disapproval. The four essays that constitute the work nevertheless form a coherent whole and a work that Ruskin himself regarded as the most likely of all his works to endure. The entire work is reproduced below.*

[8] In 1877 William Morris organized the Society for the Protection of Ancient Buildings.

ESSAY I

The Roots of Honour

1. AMONG the delusions which at different periods have possessed themselves of the minds of large masses of the human race, perhaps the most curious—certainly the least creditable—is the modern *soi-disant* science of political economy, based on the idea that an advantageous code of social action may be determined irrespectively of the influence of social affection.

Of course, as in the instances of alchemy, astrology, witchcraft, and other such popular creeds, political economy has a plausible idea at the root of it. "The social affections," says the economist, "are accidental and disturbing elements in human nature; but avarice and the desire of progress are constant elements. Let us eliminate the inconstants, and, considering the human being merely as a covetous machine, examine by what laws of labour, purchase, and sale, the greatest accumulative result in wealth is obtainable. Those laws once determined, it will be for each individual afterwards to introduce as much of the disturbing affectionate element as he chooses, and to determine for himself the result on the new conditions supposed."

2. This would be a perfectly logical and successful method of analysis, if the accidentals afterwards to be introduced were of the same nature as the powers first examined. Supposing a body in motion to be influenced by constant and inconstant forces, it is usually the simplest way of examining its course to trace it first under the persistent conditions, and afterwards introduce the causes of variation. But the disturbing elements in the social problem are not of the same nature as the constant ones: they alter the essence of the creature under examination the moment they are added; they operate, not mathematically, but chemically, introducing conditions which render all our previous knowledge unavailable. We made learned experiments upon pure nitrogen, and have convinced ourselves that it is a very manageable gas: but, behold! the thing which we have practically to deal with is its chloride; and this, the moment we touch it on our established principles, sends us and our apparatus through the ceiling.

3. Observe, I neither impugn nor doubt the conclusion of the science if its terms are accepted. I am simply uninterested in them, as I should be in those of a science of gymnastics which assumed that men had no skeletons. It might be shown, on that supposition, that it would be advantageous to roll the students up into pellets, flatten them into cakes, or stretch them into cables; and that when these results were effected, the re-insertion of the skeleton would be attended with various inconveniences to their constitution. The reasoning might be admirable, the conclusions true, and the science deficient only in applicability. Modern political economy stands on a precisely similar basis. Assuming, not that the human being has no skeleton, but that is is all skeleton, it founds an ossifiant theory of progress on this negation of a soul; and having shown the utmost that may be made of bones, and constructed a number of interesting geometrical figures with death's-head and humeri, successfully proves the inconvenience of the reappearance of a soul among these corpuscular structures. I do not deny the truth of this theory: I simply deny its applicability to the present phase of the world.

4. This inapplicability has been curiously manifested during the embarassment caused by the late strikes of our workmen.[1] Here occurs one of the simplest cases, in a pertinent and positive form, of the first vital problem which political economy has to deal with (the relation between employer and employed); and, at a severe crisis, when lives in multitudes and wealth in masses are at stake, the political economists are helpless—practically mute: no demonstrable solution of the difficulty can be given by them, such as may convince or calm the opposing parties. Obstinately the masters take one view of the matter; obstinately the operatives another; and no political science can set them at one.

5. It would be strange if it could, it being not by "science" of any kind that men were ever intended to be set at one. Disputant after disputant vainly strives to show that the interests of the masters are, or are not, antagonistic to those of the men: none of the pleaders ever seeming to remember that it does not absolutely or always follow that the persons must be antagonistic because their interests are. If there is only a crust of bread in the house, and mother and children are starving, their interests are not the same. If the mother eats it, the children want it; if the children eat it, the mother must go hungry

---

[1] There was a builders' strike in the fall of 1859.

to her work. Yet it does not necessarily follow that there will be "antagonism" between them, that they will fight for the crust, and that the mother, being strongest, will get it, and eat it. Neither, in any other case, whatever the relations of the persons may be, can it be assumed for certain that, because their interests are diverse, they must necessarily regard each other with hostility, and use violence or cunning to obtain the advantage.

6. Even if this were so, and it were as just as it is convenient to consider men as actuated by no other moral influences that those which affect rats or swine, the logical conditions of the question are still indeterminable. It can never be shown generally either that the interests of master and labourer are alike, or that they are opposed; for, according to circumstances, they may be either. It is, indeed, always the interest of both that the work should be rightly done, and a just price obtained for it; but, in the division of profits, the gain of the one may or may not be the loss of the other. It is not the master's interest to pay wages so low as to leave the men sickly and depressed, nor the workman's interest to be paid high wages if the smallness of the master's profit hinders him from enlarging his business, or conducting it in a safe and liberal way. A stoker ought not to desire high pay if the company is too poor to keep the engine-wheels in repair.

7. And the varieties of circumstance which influence these reciprocal interests are so endless, that all endeavour to deduce rules of action from balance of expediency is in vain. And it is meant to be in vain. For no human actions ever were intended by the Maker of men to be guided by balances of expediency, but by balances of justice. He has therefore rendered all endeavours to determine expediency futile for evermore. No man ever knew, or can know, what will be the ultimate result to himself, or to others, of any given line of conduct. But every man may know, and most of us do know, what is a just and unjust act. And all of us may know also, that the consequences of justice will be ultimately the best possible, both to others and ourselves, though we can neither say what *is* best, or how it is likely to come to pass.

I have said balances of justice, meaning, in the term justice, to include affection,—such affection as one man *owes* to another. All right relations between master and operative, and all their best interests, ultimately depend on these.

8. We shall find the best and simplest illus-tration of the relations of master and operative in the position of domestic servants.

We will suppose that the master of a household desires only to get as much work out of his servants as he can, at the rate of wages he gives. He never allows them to be idle; feeds them as poorly and lodges them as ill as they will endure, and in all things pushes his requirements to the exact point beyond which he cannot go without forcing the servant to leave him. In doing this, there is no violation on his part of what is commonly called "justice." He agrees with the domestic for his whole time and service, and takes them;—the limits of hardship in treatment being fixed by the practice of other masters in his neighbourhood; that is to say, by the current rate of wages for domestic labour. If the servant can get a better place, he is free to take one, and the master can only tell what is the real market value of his labour, by requiring as much as he will give.

This is the politico-economical view of the case, according to the doctors of that science; who assert that by this procedure the greatest average of work will be obtained from the servant, and therefore the greatest benefit to the community, and through the community, by reversion, to the servant himself.

That, however, is not so. It would be so if the servant were an engine of which the motive power was steam, magnetism, gravitation, or any other agent of calculable force. But he being, on the contrary, an engine whose motive power is a Soul, the force of this very peculiar agent, as an unknown quantity, enters into all the political economist's equations, without his knowledge, and falsifies every one of their results. The largest quantity of work will not be done by this curious engine for pay, or under pressure, or by help of any kind of fuel which may be supplied by the chaldron. It will be done only when the motive force, that is to say, the will or spirit of the creature, is brought to its greatest strength by its own proper fuel: namely, by the affections.

9. It may indeed happen, and does happen often, that if the master is a man of sense and energy, a large quantity of material work may be done under mechanical pressure, enforced by strong will and guided by wise method; also it may happen, and does happen often, that if the master is indolent and weak (however good-natured), a very small quantity of work, and that bad, may be produced by the servant's undirected strength, and contemptuous gratitude. But the universal law of the matter is that,

assuming any given quantity of energy and sense in master and servant, the greatest material result obtainable by them will be, not through antagonism to each other, but through affection for each other; and that, if the master, instead of endeavouring to get as much work as possible from the servant, seeks rather to render his appointed and necessary work beneficial to him, and to forward his interests in all just and wholesome ways, the real amount of work ultimately done, or of good rendered, by the person so cared for, will indeed be the greatest possible.

Observe, I say, "of good rendered," for a servant's work is not necessarily or always the best thing he can give his master. But good of all kinds, whether in material service, in protective watchfulness of his master's interest and credit, or in joyful readiness to seize unexpected an irregular occasions of help.

Nor is this one whit less generally true because indulgence will be frequently abused, and kindness met with ingratitude. For the servant who, gently treated, is ungrateful, treated ungently, will be revengeful; and the man who is dishonest to a liberal master will be injurious to an unjust one.

10. In any case, and with any person, this unselfish treatment will produce the most effective return. Observe, I am here considering the affections wholly as a motive power; not at all as things in themselves desirable or noble, or in any other way abstractedly good. I look at them simply as an anomalous force, rendering every one of the ordinary political economist's calculations nugatory; while, even if he desired to introduce this new element into his estimates, he has no power of dealing with it; for the affections only become a true motive power when they ignore every other motive and condition of political economy. Treat the servant kindly, with the idea of turning his gratitude to account, and you will get, as you deserve, no gratitude, nor any value for your kindness; but treat him kindly without any economical purpose, and all economical purposes will be answered; in this, as in all other matters, whosoever will save his life shall lose it, whoso loses it shall find it. [2]

11. The next clearest and simplest example of relation between master and operative is that which exists between the commander of a regiment and his men.

Supposing the officer only desires to apply the rules of discipline so as, with least trouble to himself, to make the regiment most effective, he will not be able, by any rules or administration of rules, on this selfish principle, to develop the full strength of his subordinates. If a man of sense and firmness, he may, as in the former instance, produce a better result than would be obtained by the irregular kindness of a weak officer; but let the sense and firmness be the same in both cases, and assuredly the officer who has the most direct personal relations with his men, the most care for their interests, and the most value for their lives, will develop their effective strength, through their affection for his own person, and trust in his character, to a degree wholly unattainable by other means. This law applies still more stringently as the numbers concerned are larger: a charge may often be successful, though the men dislike their officers; a battle has rarely been won, unless they loved their general.

[2] The difference between the two modes of treatment, and between their effective material results, may be seen very accurately by a comparison of the relations of Esther and Charlie in *Bleak House* with those of Miss Brass and the Marchioness in *Master Humphrey's Clock*.

The essential value and truth of Dickens's writings have been unwisely lost sight of by many thoughtful persons, merely because he presents his truth with some colour of caricature. Unwisely, because Dickens's caricature, though often gross, is never mistaken. Allowing for his manner of telling them, the things he tells us are always true. I wish that he could think it right to limit his brilliant exaggeration to works written only for public amusement; and when he takes up a subject of high national importance, such as that which he handled in *Hard Times,* that he would use severer and more accurate analysis. The usefulness of that work (to my mind, in several respects the greatest he has written) is with many persons seriously diminished because Mr. Bounderby is a dramatic monster, instead of a characteristic example of a worldly master; and Stephen Blackpool a dramatic perfection, instead of a characteristic example of an honest workman. But let us not lose the use of Dickens's wit and insight, because he chooses to speak in a circle of stage fire. He is entirely right in his main drift and purpose in every book he has written; and all of them, but expecially *Hard Times,* should be studied with close and earnest care by persons interested in social questions. They will find much that is partial, and, because partial, apparently unjust; but if they examine all the evidence on the other side, which Dickens seems to overlook, it will appear, after all their trouble, that his view was the finally right one, grossly and sharply told. [Ruskin's note]

12. Passing from these simple examples to the more complicated relations existing between a manufacturer and his workmen, we are met first by certain curious difficulties, resulting, apparently, from a harder and colder state of moral elements. It is easy to imagine an enthusiastic affection existing among soldiers for the colonel. Not so easy to imagine an enthusiastic affection among cotton-spinners for the proprietor of the mill. A body of men associated for purposes of robbery (as a Highland clan in ancient times) shall be animated by perfect affection, and every member of it be ready to lay down his life for the life of his chief. But a band of men associated for purposes of legal production and accumulation is usually animated, it appears, by no such emotions, and none of them are in any wise willing to give his life for the life of his chief. Not only are we met by this apparent anomaly, in moral matters, but by others connected with it, in administration of system. For a servant or a soldier is engaged at a definite rate of wages, for a definite period; but a workman at a rate of wages variable according to the demand for labour, and with the risk of being at any time thrown out of his situation by chances of trade. Now, as, under these contingencies, no action of the affections can take place, but only an explosive action of *dis*affections, two points offer themselves for consideration in the matter.

The first—How far the rate of wages may be so regulated as not to vary with the demand for labour.

The second—How far it is possible that bodies of workmen may be engaged and maintained at such fixed rate of wages (whatever the state of trade may be), without enlarging or diminishing their number, so as to give them permanent interest in the establishment with which they are connected, like that of the domestic servants in an old family, or an *esprit de corps,* like that of the soldiers in a crack regiment.

13. The first question is, I say, how far it may be possible to fix the rate of wages, irrespectively of the demand for labour.

Perhaps one of the most curious facts in the history of human error is the denial by the common political economist of the possibility of thus regulating wages; while, for all the important, and much of the unimportant, labour, on the earth, wages are already so regulated.

We do not sell our prime-ministership by Dutch auction;[3] nor, on the decease of a bishop, whatever may be the general advantages of simony, do we (yet) offer his diocese to the clergyman who will take the episcopacy at the lowest contract. We (with exquisite sagacity of political economy!) do indeed sell commissions; but not openly, generalships: sick, we do not inquire for a physician who takes less than a guinea; litigious, we never think of reducing six-and-eightpence to four-and-sixpence; caught in a shower, we do not canvass the cabmen, to find one who values his driving at less than sixpence a mile.

It is true that in all these cases there is, and in every conceivable case there must be, ultimate reference to the presumed difficulty of the work, or number of candidates for the office. If it were thought that the labour necessary to make a good physician would be gone through by a sufficient number of students with the prospect of only half-guinea fees, public consent would soon withdraw the unnecessary half-guinea. In this ultimate sense, the price of labour is indeed always regulated by the demand for it; but, so far as the practical and immediate administration of the matter is regarded, the best labour always has been, and is, as *all* labour ought to be, paid by an invariable standard.

14. "What!" the reader perhaps answers amazedly: "pay good and bad workmen alike?"

Certainly. The difference between one prelate's sermons and his successor's—or between one physician's opinion and another's,—is far greater, as respects the qualities of mind involved, and far more important in result to you personally, than the difference between good and bad laying of bricks (though that is greater than most people suppose). Yet you pay with equal fee, contentedly, the good and bad workmen upon your soul, and the good and bad workmen upon your body; much more may you pay, contentedly, with equal fees, the good and bad workmen upon your house.

"Nay, but I choose my physician, and (?) my clergyman, thus indicating my sense of the quality of their work." By all means, also, choose your bricklayer; that is the proper reward of the good workman, to be "chosen." The natural and right system respecting all labour is, that it should be paid at a fixed rate, but the good workman employed, and the bad workman unemployed. The false, unnatural, and destruc-

[3] An auction where prices start above the value of the items and are lowered until a sale is made.

tive system is when the bad workman is allowed to offer his work at half-price, and either take the place of the good, or force him by his competition to work for an inadequate sum.

15. This equality of wages, then, being the first object towards which we have to discover the directest available road, the second is, as above stated, that of maintaining constant numbers of workmen in employment, whatever may be the accidental demand for the article they produce.

I believe the sudden and extensive inequalities of demand, which necessarily arise in the mercantile operations of an active nation, constitute the only essential difficulty which has to be overcome in a just organization of labour.

The subject opens into too many branches to admit of being investigated in a paper of this kind; but the following general facts bearing on it may be noted.

The wages which enable any workman to live are necessarily higher, if his work is liable to intermission, than if it is assured and continuous; and however severe the struggle for work may become, the general law will always hold, that men must get more daily pay if, on the average, they can only calculate on work three days a week than they would require if they were sure of work six days a week. Supposing that a man cannot live on less than a shilling a day, his seven shillings he must get, either for three days' violent work, or six days' deliberate work. The tendency of all modern mercantile operations is to throw both wages and trade into the form of a lottery, and to make the workman's pay depend on intermittent exertion, and the principal's profit on dexterously used chance.

16. In what partial degree, I repeat, this may be necessary in consequence of the activities of modern trade, I do not here investigate; contenting myself with the fact that in its fatallest aspects it is assuredly unnecessary, and results merely from love of gambling on the part of the masters, and from ignorance and sensuality in the men. The masters cannot bear to let any opportunity of gain escape them, and frantically rush at every gap and breach in the walls of Fortune, raging to be rich, and affronting, with impatient covetousness, every risk of ruin, while the men prefer three days of violent labour, and three days of drunkenness, to six days of moderate work and wise rest. There is no way in which a principal, who really desires to help his workmen, may do it more effectually than by checking these disorderly habits both in himself and them;

keeping his own business operations on a scale which will enable him to pursue them securely, not yielding to temptations of precarious gain; and at the same time, leading his workmen into regular habits of labour and life, either by inducing them rather to take low wages, in the form of a fixed salary, than high wages, subject to the chance of their being thrown out of work; or, if this be impossible, by discouraging the system of violent exertion for nominally high day wages, and leading the men to take lower pay for more regular labour.

In effecting any radical changes of this kind, doubtless there would be great inconvenience and loss incurred by all the originators of the movement. That which can be done with perfect convenience and without loss, is not always the thing that most needs to be done, or which we are most imperatively required to do.

17. I have already alluded to the difference hitherto existing between regiments of men associated for purposes of violence, and for purposes of manufacture; in that the former appear capable of self-sacrifice—the latter, not; which singular fact is the real reason of the general lowness of estimate in which the profession of commerce is held, as compared with that of arms. Philosophically, it does not, at first sight, appear reasonable (many writers have endeavoured to prove it unreasonable) that a peaceable and rational person, whose trade is buying and selling, should be held in less honour than an unpeaceable and often irrational person, whose trade is slaying. Nevertheless, the consent of mankind has always, in spite of the philosophers, given precedence to the soldier.

And this is right.

For the soldier's trade, verily and essentially, is not slaying, but being slain. This, without well knowing its own meaning, the world honours it for. A bravo's trade is slaying; but the world has never respected bravos more than merchants: the reason it honours the soldier is, because he holds his life at the service of the State. Reckless he may be—fond of pleasure or of adventure—all kinds of bye-motives and mean impulses may have determined the choice of his profession, and may affect (to all appearance exclusively) his daily conduct in it; but our estimate of him is based on this ultimate fact—of which we are well assured—that put him in a fortress breach, with all the pleasures of the world behind him, and only death and his duty in front of him, he will keep his face to the front; and he knows that his choice may be put to him at any moment—and has beforehand taken his part—virtually takes such part continually—does, in reality, die daily.[4]

18. Not less is the respect we pay to the lawyer and physician, founded ultimately on their self-sacrifice. Whatever the learning or acuteness of a great lawyer, our chief respect for him depends on our belief that, set in a judge's seat, he will strive to judge justly, come of it what may. Could we suppose that he would take bribes, and use his acuteness and legal knowledge to give plausibility to iniquitous decisions, no degree of intellect would win for him our respect. Nothing will win it, short of our tacit conviction, that in all important acts of his life justice is first with him; his own interest, second.

In the case of a physician, the ground of the honour we render him is clearer still. Whatever his science, we would shrink from him in horror if we found him regard his patients merely as subjects to experiment upon; much more, if we found that, receiving bribes from persons interested in their deaths, he was using his best skill to give poison in the mask of medicine.

Finally, the principle holds with utmost clearness as it respects clergymen. No goodness of disposition will excuse want of science in a physician, or of shrewdness in an advocate; but a clergymen, even though his power of intellect be small, is respected on the presumed ground of his unselfishness and serviceableness.

19. Now, there can be no question but that the tact, foresight, decision, and other mental powers, required for the successful management of a large mercantile concern, if not such as could be compared with those of a great lawyer, general, or divine, would at least match the general conditions of mind required in the subordinate officers of a ship, or of a regiment, or in the curate of a country parish. If, therefore, all the efficient members of the so-called liberal professions are still, somehow, in public estimate of honour, preferred before the head of a commercial firm, the reason must lie deeper than in the measurement of their several powers of mind.

And the essential reason for such preference will be found to lie in the fact that the merchant is presumed to act always selfishly. His work may be very necessary to the community; but the motive of it is understood to be wholly personal. The merchant's first object in all his dealings must be (the public believe) to get as much for himself, and leave as little to his neighbour (or customer) as possible. Enforcing this upon him, by political statute, as the necessary principle of his action; recommending it to him on all occasions, and themselves reciprocally adopting it, proclaiming vociferously, for law of the universe, that a buyer's function is to cheapen, and a seller's to cheat,—the public, nevertheless, involuntarily condemn the man of commerce for his compliance with their own statement, and stamp him for ever as belonging to an inferior grade of human personality.

20. This they will find, eventually, they must give up doing. They must not cease to condemn selfishness; but they will have to discover a kind of commerce which is not exclusively selfish. Or, rather, they will have to discover that there never was, or can be, any other kind of commerce; that this which they have called commerce was not commerce at all, but cozening; and that a true merchant differs as much from a merchant according to laws of modern political economy, as the hero of the *Excursion* from Autolycus.[5] They will find that commerce is an occupation which gentlemen will every day see more need to engage in, rather than in the business of talking to men, or slaying them; that, in true commerce, as in true preaching, or true fighting, it is necessary to admit the idea of occasional voluntary loss;—that sixpences have to be lost, as well as lives, under a sense of duty; that the market may have its martyrdoms as well as the pulpit; and trade its heroisms as well as war.

May have—in the final issue, must have—and only has not had yet, because men of heroic temper have always been misguided in their youth into other fields; not recognizing what is in our days, perhaps, the most important of all fields; so that, while many a zealous person loses his life in trying to teach the form of a gospel, very few will lose a hundred pounds in showing the practice of one.

21. The fact is, that people never have had clearly explained to them the true functions of a merchant with respect to other people. I should like the reader to be very clear about this.

Five great intellectual professions, relating to daily necessities of life, have hitherto existed—three exist necessarily, in every civilized nation:

The Soldier's profession is to *defend* it.

---

[4] I Corinthians 15:31.

[5] The hero of Wordsworth's *Excursion* (1814) is the Wanderer; Autolycus in Shakespeare's *Winter's Tale* is a peddler.

The Pastor's to *teach* it.

The Physician's to *keep it in health*.

The Lawyer's to *enforce justice* in it.

The Merchant's to *provide* for it.

And the duty of all these men is, on due occasion, to *die* for it.

"On due occasion," namely:—

The Soldier, rather than leave his post in battle.

The Physician, rather than leave his post in plague.

The Pastor, rather than teach Falsehood.

The Lawyer, rather than countenance Injustice.

The Merchant—what is *his* "due occasion" of death?

22. It is the main question for the merchant, as for all of us. For, truly, the man who does not know when to die, does not know how to live.

Observe, the merchant's function (or manufacturer's, for in the broad sense in which it is here used the word must be understood to include both) is to provide for the nation. It is no more his function to get profit for himself out of that provision than it is a clergyman's function to get his stipend. This stipend is a due and necessary adjunct, but not the object of his life, if he be a true clergyman, any more than his fee (or honorarium) is the object of life to a true physician. Neither is his fee the object of life to a true merchant. All three, if true men, have a work to be done irrespective of fee—to be done even at any cost, or for quite the contrary of fee; the pastor's function being to teach, the physician's to heal, and the merchant's, as I have said, to provide. That is to say, he had to understand to their very root the qualities of the thing he deals in, and the means of obtaining or producing it; and he has to apply all his sagacity and energy to the producing or obtaining it in perfect state, and distributing it at the cheapest possible price where it is most needed.

And because the production or obtaining of any commodity involves necessarily the agency of many lives and hands, the merchant becomes in the course of his business the master and governor of large masses of men in a more direct, though less confessed way, than a military officer or pastor; so that on him falls, in great part, the responsibility for the kind of life they lead: and it becomes his duty, not only to be always considering how to produce what he sells, in the purest and cheapest forms, but how to make the various employments involved in the production, or transference of it, most beneficial to the men employed.

23. And as into these two functions, requiring for their right exercise the highest intelligence, as well as patience, kindness, and tact, the merchant is bound to put all his energy, so for their just discharge he is bound, as soldier or physician is bound, to give up, if need be, his life, in such way as it be demanded of him. Two main points he has in his providing function to maintain: first, his engagements (faithfulness to engagements being the real root of all possibilities, in commerce); and, secondly, the prefectness and purity of the thing provided; so that, rather than fail in any engagement, or consent to any deterioration, adulteration, or unjust and exorbitant price of that which he provides, he is bound to meet fearlessly any form of distress, poverty, or labour, which may, through maintenance of these points, come upon him.

24. Again: in his office as governor of the men employed by him, the merchant or manufacturer is invested with a distinctly paternal authority and responsibility. In most cases, a youth entering a commercial establishment is withdrawn altogether from home influence; his master must become his father, else he has, for practical and constant help, no father at hand: in all cases the master's authority, together with the general tone and atmosphere of his business, and the character of the men with whom the youth is compelled in the course of it to associate, have more immediate and pressing weight than the home influence, and will usually neutralize it either for good or evil; so that the only means which the master has of doing justice to the men employed by him is to ask himself sternly whether he is dealing with such subordinate as he would with his own son, if compelled by circumstances to take such a position.

Supposing the captain of a frigate saw it right, or were by any chance obliged, to place his own son in the position of a common sailor: as he would then treat his son, he is bound always to treat every one of the men under him. So, also, supposing the master of a manufactory saw it right, or were by any chance obliged, to place his own son in the position of an ordinary workman; as he would then treat his son, he is bound always to treat every one of his men. This is the only effective, true, or practical RULE which can be given on this point of political economy.

And as the captain of a ship is bound to be the last man to leave his ship in case of wreck, and to share his last crust with the sailors in case of famine, so the manufacturer, in any commercial crisis or distress, is bound to take the suffering of it with his men, and even to take more of it for himself than he allows his men to feel; as a father would in a famine, shipwreck, or battle, sacrifice himself for his son.

25. All which sounds very strange: the only real strangeness in the matter being, nevertheless, that it should so sound. For all this is true, and that not partially nor theoretically, but everlastingly and practically; all other doctrine than this respecting matters political being false in premises, absurd in deduction, and impossible in practice, consistently with any progressive state of national life; all the life which we now possess as a nation showing itself in the resolute denial and scorn, by a few strong minds and faithful hearts, of the economic principles taught to our multitudes, which principles, so far as accepted, lead straight to national destruction. Respecting the modes and forms of destruction to which they lead, and, on the other hand, respecting the farther practical working of true polity, I hope to reason farther in a following paper.

The Veins of Wealth

26. The answer which would be made by any ordinary political economist to the statements contained in the preceding paper, is in few words as follows:—

"It is indeed true that certain advantages of a general nature may be obtained by the development of social affections. But political economists never professed, nor profess, to take advantages of a general nature into consideration. Our science is simply the science of getting rich. So far from being a fallacious or visionary one, it is found by experience to be practically effective. Persons who follow its precepts do actually become rich, and persons who disobey them become poor. Every capitalist of Europe has acquired his fortune by following the known laws of our science, and increases his capital daily by an adherence to them. It is vain to bring forward tricks of logic, against the force of accomplished facts. Every man of business knows by experience how money is made, and how it is lost."

Pardon me. Men of business do indeed know how they themselves made their money, or how, on occasion, they lost it. Playing a long-practised game, they are familiar with the chances of its cards, and can rightly explain their losses and gains. But they neither know who keeps the bank of the gambling-house, nor what other games may be played with the same cards, nor what other losses and gains, far away among the dark streets, are essentially, though invisibly, dependent on theirs in the lighted rooms. They have learned a few, and only a few, of the laws of mercantile economy; but not one of those of political economy.

27. Primarily, which is very notable and curious, I observe that men of business rarely know the meaning of the word "rich." At least, if they know, they do not in their reasonings allow for the fact, that it is a relative word, implying its opposite "poor" as positively as the word "north" implies its opposite "south." Men nearly always speak and write as if riches were absolute, and it were possible, by following certain scientific precepts, for everybody to be rich. Whereas riches are a power like that of electricity, acting only through inequalities or negations of itself. The force of the guinea you have in your pocket depends wholly on the default of a guinea in your neighbour's pocket. If he did not want it, it would be of no use to you; the degree of power it possesses depends accurately upon the need or desire he has for it,—and the art of making yourself rich, in the ordinary mercantile economist's sense, is therefore equally and necessarily the art of keeping your neighbour poor.

I would not contend in this matter (and rarely in any matter) for the acceptance of terms. But I wish the reader clearly and deeply to understand the difference between the two economies, to which the terms "Political" and "Mercantile" might not unadvisedly be attached.

28. Political economy (the economy of a State, or of citizens) consists simply in the production, preservation, and distribution, at fittest time and place, of useful or pleasurable things. The farmer who cuts his hay at the right time; the shopwright who drives his bolts well home in sound wood; the builder who lays good bricks in welltempered mortar; the housewife who takes care of her furniture in the parlour, and guards against all waste in her kitchen; and the singer who rightly disciplines, and never overstrains her voice, are all political economists in the true and final sense: adding continually to the riches and well-being of the nation to which they belong.

But mercantile economy, the economy of "merces" or of "pay," signifies the accumulation, in the hands of individuals of legal or moral claim upon, or power over, the labour of others; every such claim implying precisely as much poverty or debt on one side, as it implies riches or right on the other.

It does not, therefore, necessarily involve an addition to the actual property, or well-being of the State in which it exists. But since this commercial wealth, or power over labour, is nearly always convertible at once into real property, while real property is not always convertible at once into power over labour, the idea of riches among active men in civilized nations generally refers to commercial wealth; and in estimating their possessions, they rather calculate the value of their horses and fields by the number of guineas they could get for them, than the value of their guineas by the number of horses and fields they could buy with them.

29. There is, however, another reason for this habit of mind; namely, that an accumulation of real property is of little use to its owner, unless, together with it, he has commercial power over labour. Thus, suppose any person to be put in possession of a large estate of fruitful land, with rich beds of gold in its gravel; countless herds of cattle in its pastures; houses, and gardens, and storehouses full of useful stores: but suppose, after all, that he could get no servants? In order that he may be able to have servants, some one in his neighbourhood must be poor, and in want of his gold—or his corn. Assume that no one is in want of either, and that no servants are to be had. He must, therefore, bake his own bread, make his own clothes, plough his own ground, and shepherd his own flocks. His gold will be as useful to him as any other yellow pebbles on his estate. His stores must rot, for he cannot consume them. He can eat no more than another man could eat, and wear no more than another man could wear. He must lead a life of severe and common labour to procure even ordinary comforts; he will be ultimately unable to keep either houses in repair, or fields in cultivation; and forced to content himself with a poor man's portion of cottage and garden, in the midst of a desert of waste land, trampled by wild cattle, and encumbered by ruins of palaces, which he will hardly mock at himself by calling "his own."

30. The most covetous of mankind would, with small exultation, I presume, accept riches of this kind on these terms. What is really desired, under the name of riches, is, essentially, power over men; in its simplest sense, the power of obtaining for our own advantage the labour of servant, tradesman, and artist; in wider sense, authority of directing large masses of the nation to various ends (good, trivial, or hurtful, according to the mind of the rich person). And this power of wealth of course is greater or less in direct proportion to the poverty of the men ever whom it is exercised, and in inverse proportion to the number of persons who are as rich as ourselves, and who are ready to give the same price for an article of which the supply is limited. If the musician is poor, he will sing for small pay, as long as there is only one person who can pay him; but if there be two or three, he will sing for the one who offers him most. And thus the power of the riches of the patron (always imperfect and doubtful, as we shall see presently even when most authoritative) depends first on the poverty of the artist, and then on the limitation of the number of equally wealthy persons, who also want seats at the concert. So that, as above stated, the art of becoming "rich," in the common sense, is not absolutely nor finally the art of accumulating much money for ourselves, but also of contriving that our neighbours shall have less. In accurate terms, it is "the art of establishing the maximum inequality in our own favour."

31. Now, the establishment of such inequality cannot be shown in the abstract to be either advantageous or disadvantageous to the body of the nation. The rash and absurd assumption that such inequalities are necessarily advantageous, lies at the root of most of the popular fallacies on the subject of political economy. For the eternal and inevitable law in this matter is, that the beneficialness of the inequality depends, first, on the methods by which it was accomplished; and, secondly, on the purposes to which it is applied. Inequalities of wealth, unjustly established, have assuredly injured the nation in which they exist during their establishment; and, unjustly directed, injure it yet more during their existence. But inequalities of wealth, justly established, benefit the nation in the course of their establishment; and, nobly used, aid it yet more by their existence. That is to say, among every active and well-governed people, the various strength of individuals, tested by full exertion and specially applied to various need, issues in unequal, but harmonious results, receiving reward or authority according to its class and service; while, in the inactive or ill-governed nation, the gradations of decay and the victories of treason work out also their own

rugged system of subjection and success; and substitute, for the melodious inequalities of concurrent power, the iniquitous dominances and depressions of guilt and misfortune.

32. Thus the circulation of wealth in a nation resembles that of the blood in the natural body. There is one quickness of the current which comes of cheerful emotion or wholesome exercise; and another which comes of shame or of fever. There is a flush of the body which is full of warmth and life; and another which will pass into putrefaction.

The analogy will hold down even to minute particulars. For as diseased local determination of the blood involves depression of the general health of the system, all morbid local action of riches will be found ultimately to involve a weakening of the resources of the body politic.

The mode in which this is produced may be at once understood by examining one or two instances of the development of wealth in the simplest possible circumstances.

33. Suppose two sailors cast away on an uninhabited coast, and obliged to maintain themselves there by their own labour for a series of years.

If they both kept their health, and worked steadily and in amity with each other, they might build themselves a convenient house, and in time come to possess a certain quantity of cultivated land, together with various stores laid up for future use. All these things would be real riches or property; and, supposing the men both to have worked equally hard, they would each have right to equal share or use of it. Their political economy would consist merely in careful preservation and just division of these possessions. Perhaps, however, after some time one or other might be dissatisfied with the results of their common farming; and they might in consequence agree to divide the land they had brought under the spade into equal shares, so that each might thenceforward work in his own field, and live by it. Suppose that after this arrangement had been made, one of them were to fall ill, and be unable to work on his land at a critical time—say of sowing or harvest.

He would naturally ask the other to sow or reap for him.

Then his companion might say, with perfect justice, "I will do this additional work for you; but if I do it, you must promise to do as much for me at another time. I will count how many hours I spend on your ground, and you shall give me a written promise to work for the same

number of hours on mine, whenever I need your help, and you are able to give it."

34. Suppose the disabled man's sickness to continue, and that under various circumstances, for several years, requiring the help of the other, he on each occasion gave a written pledge to work, as soon as he was able, at his companion's orders, for the same number of hours which the other had given up to him. What will the positions of the two men be when the invalid is able to resume work?

Considered as a "Polis," or state, they will be poorer than they would have been otherwise: poorer by the withdrawal of what the sick man's labour would have produced in the interval. His friend may perhaps have toiled with an energy quickened by the enlarged need, but in the end his own land and property must have suffered by the withdrawal of so much of his time and thought from them: and the united property of the two men will be certainly less than it would have been if both had remained in health and activity.

But the relations in which they stand to each other are also widely altered. The sick man has not only pledged his labour for some years, but will probably have exhausted his own share of the accumulated stores, and will be in consequence for some time dependent on the other for food, which he can only "pay" or reward him for by yet more deeply pledging his own labour.

Supposing the written promises to be held entirely valid (among civilized nations their validity is secured by legal measures), the person who had hitherto worked for both might now, if he chose, rest altogether, and pass his time in idleness, not only forcing his companion to redeem all the engagements he had already entered into, but exacting from him pledges for further labour, to an arbitrary amount, for what food he had to advance to him.

35. There might not, from first to last, be the least illegality (in the ordinary sense of the word) in the arrangement; but if a stranger arrived on the coast at this advanced epoch of their political economy, he would find one man commercially Rich; the other commercially Poor. He would see, perhaps, with no small surprise, one passing his days in idleness; the other labouring for both, and living sparely, in the hope of recovering his independence at some distant period.

This is, of course, an example of one only out of many ways in which inequality of possession may be established between different persons, giving rise to the Mercantile forms of Riches and

Poverty. In the instance before us, one of the men might from the first have deliberately chosen to be idle, and to put his life in pawn for present ease; or he might have mismanaged his land, and been compelled to have recourse to his neighbour for food and help, pledging his future labour for it. But what I want the reader to note especially is the fact, common to a large number of typical cases of this kind, that the establishment of the mercantile wealth which consists in a claim upon labour, signifies a political diminution of the real wealth which consists in substantial possessions.

36. Take another example, more consistent with the ordinary course of affairs of trade. Suppose that three men, instead of two, formed the little isolated republic, and found themselves obliged to separate, in order to farm different pieces of land at some distance from each other along the coast: each estate furnishing a distinct kind of produce, and each more or less in need of the material raised on the other. Suppose that the third man, in order to save the time of all three, undertakes simply to superintend the transference of commodities from one farm to the other; on condition of receiving some sufficiently remunerative share of every parcel of goods conveyed, or of some other parcel received in exchange for it.

If this carrier or messenger always brings to each estate, from the other, what is chiefly wanted, at the right time, the operations of the two farmers will go on prosperously, and the largest possible result in produce, or wealth, will be attained by the little community. But suppose no intercourse between the landowners is possible, except through the travelling agent; and that, after a time; this agent, watching the course of each man's agriculture, keeps back the articles with which he has been entrusted until there comes a period of extreme necessity for them, on one side or other, and then extracts in exchange for them all that the distressed farmer can spare of other kinds of produce: it is easy to see that by ingeniously watching his opportunities, he might possess himself regularly of the greater part of the superfluous produce of the two estates, and at last, in some year of severest trial or scarcity, purchase both for himself and maintain the former proprietors thenceforward as his labourers or servants.

37. This would be a case of commercial wealth acquired on the exactest principles of modern

political economy. But more distinctly even than in the former instance, it is manifest in this that the wealth of the State, or of the three men considered as a society, is collectively less than it would have been had the merchant been content with juster profit. The operations of the two agriculturists have been cramped to the utmost; and the continual limitations of the supply of things they wanted at critical times, together with the failure of courage consequent on the prolongation of a struggle for mere existence, without any sense of permanent gain, must have seriously diminished the effective results of their labour; and the stores finally accumulated in the merchant's hand will not in any wise be of equivalent value to those which, had his dealings been honest, would have filled at once the granaries of the farmers and his own. The whole question, therefore, respecting not only the advantage, but even the quantity, of national wealth, resolves itself finally into one of abstract justice. It is impossible to conclude, of any given mass of acquired wealth, merely by the fact of its existence, whether it signifies good or evil to the nation in the midst of which it exists. Its real value depends on the moral sign attached to it, just as sternly as that of a mathematical quantity depends on the algebraical sign attached to it. Any given accumulation of commercial wealth may be indicative, on the one hand, of faithful industries, progressive energies, and productive ingenuities: or, on the other, it may be indicative of mortal luxury, merciless tyranny, ruinous chicane. Some treasures are heavy with human tears, as an ill-stored harvest with untimely rain; and some gold is brighter in sunshine than it is in substance.

38. And these are not, observe, merely moral or pathetic attributes of riches, which the seeker of riches may, if he chooses, despise; they are, literally and sternly, material attributes of riches, depreciating or exalting, incalculably, the monetary signification of the sum in question. One mass of money is the outcome of action which has created,—another, of action which has annihilated,—ten times as much in the gathering of it; such and such strong hands have been paralyzed, as if they had been numbed by nightshade: so many strong men's courage broken, so many productive operations hindered; this, and the other false direction given to labour, and lying image of prosperity set up, on Dura plains[1] dug into seven-times-heated furnaces.

---

[1] Daniel 3:1.

That which seems to be wealth may in verity be only the gilded index of far-reaching ruin; a wrecker's handful of coin gleaned from the beach to which he has beguiled an argosy; a camp-follower's bundle of rags unwrapped from the breasts of goodly soldiers dead; the purchase-pieces of potter's fields, wherein shall be buried together the citizen and the stranger.[2]

And therefore, the idea that directions can be given for the gaining of wealth, irrespectively of the consideration of its moral sources, or that any general or technical law of purchase and gain can be set down for national practice, is perhaps the most insolently futile of all that ever beguiled men through their vices. So far as I know, there is not in history record of anything so disgraceful to the human intellect as the modern idea that the commercial text, "Buy in the cheapest market and sell in the dearest," represents, or under any circumstances could represent, and available principle of national economy. Buy in the cheapest market?—yes; but what made your market cheap? Charcoal may be cheap among your roof timbers after a fire, and bricks may be cheap in your streets after an earthquake; but fire and earthquake may not therefore be national benefits. Sell in the dearest?—yes, truly; but what made your market dear? You sold your bread well to-day: was it to a dying man who gave his last coin for it, and will never need bread more; or to a rich man who to-morrow will buy your farm over your head; or to a soldier on his way to pillage the bank in which you have put your fortune?

None of these things you can know. One thing only you can know: namely, whether this dealing of yours is a just and faithful one, which is all you need concern yourself about respecting it; sure thus to have done your own part in bringing about ultimately in the world a state of things which will not issue in pillage or in death. And thus every question concerning these things merges itself ultimately in the great question of justice, which, the ground being thus far cleared for it, I will enter upon in the next paper, leaving only, in this, three final points for the reader's consideration.

39. It has been shown that the chief value and virtue of money consists in its having power over human beings; that, without this power, large material possessions are useless, and to any person possessing such power, comparatively unnecessary. But power over human beings is attainable by other means than by money. As I said a few pages back, the money power is always imperfect and doubtful; there are many things which cannot be reached with it, others which cannot be retained by it. Many joys may be given to men which cannot be bought for gold, and many fidelities found in them which cannot be rewarded with it.

Trite enough,—the reader thinks. Yes: but it is not so trite,—I wish it were,—that in this moral power, quite inscrutable and immeasurable though it be, there is a monetary value just as real as that represented by more ponderous currencies. A man's hand may be full of invisible gold, and the wave of it, or the grasp, shall do more than another's with a shower of bullion. This invisible gold, also, does not necessarily diminish in spending. Political economists will do well some day to take heed of it, though they cannot take measure.

But farther. Since the essence of wealth consists in its authority over men, if the apparent or nominal wealth fail in this power, it fails in essence; in fact, ceases to be wealth at all. It does not appear lately in England, that our authority over men is absolute. The servants show some disposition to rush riotously upstairs, under an impression that their wages are not regularly paid. We should augur ill of any gentleman's property to whom this happened every other day in his drawing-room.

So, also, the power of our wealth seems limited as respects the comfort of the servants, no less than their quietude. The persons in the kitchen appear to be ill-dressed, squalid, half-starved. One cannot help imagining that the riches of the establishment must be of a very theoretical and documentary character.

40. Finally. Since the essence of wealth consists in power over men, will it not follow that the nobler and the more in number the persons are over whom it has power, the greater the wealth? Perhaps it may even appear, after some consideration, that the persons themselves *are* the wealth—that these pieces of gold with which we are in the habit of guiding them, are, in fact, nothing more than a kind of Byzantine harness or trappings, very glittering and beautiful in barbaric sight, wherewith we bridle the creatures; but that if these same living creatures could be guides without the fretting and jingling of the Byzants[3] in their mouths and ears, they might themselves be more valuable than their bridles.

---

[2] Matthew 27:6–7.   [3] Golden coins.

In fact, it may be discovered that the true veins of wealth are purple—and not in Rock, but in Flesh—perhaps even that the final outcome and consummation of all wealth is in the producing as many as possible full-breathed, bright-eyed, and happy-hearted human creatures. Our modern wealth, I think, has rather a tendency the other way;—most political economists appearing to consider multitudes of human creatures not conducive to wealth, or at best conducive to it only by remaining in a dim-eyed and narrow-chested state of being.

41. Nevertheless, it is open, I repeat, to serious question, which I leave to the reader's pondering, whether, among national manufactures, that of Souls of a good quality may not at last turn out a quite leadingly lucrative one? Nay, in some far-away and yet undreamt-of hour, I can even imagine that England may cast all thoughts of possessive wealth back to the barbaric nations among whom they first arose; and that, while the sands of the Indus and adamant of Golconda may yet stiffen the housings of the charger, and flash from the turban of a slave, she, as a Christian mother, may at last attain to the virtues and the treasures of a Heathen one, and be able to lead forth her Sons, saying,—

"These are MY Jewels."

ESSAY III

Qui Judicatis Terram?[1]

42. Some centuries before the Christian era, a Jew merchant, largely engaged in business on the Gold Coast, and reported to have made one of the largest fortunes of his time (held also in repute for much practical sagacity), left among his ledgers some general maxims concerning wealth, which have been preserved, strangely enough, even to our own days. They were held in considerable respect by the most active traders of the Middle Ages, especially by the Venetians, who even went so far in their admiration as to place a statue of the old Jew on the angle of one of their principle public buildings.[2] Of late years these writings

have fallen into disrepute, being opposed in every particular to the spirit of modern commerce. Nevertheless I shall reproduce a passage or two from them here, partly because they may interest the reader by their novelty; and chiefly because they will show him that it is possible for a very practical and acquisitive tradesman to hold, through a not unsuccessful career, that principle of distinction between well-gotten and ill-gotten wealth, which, partially insisted on in my last paper, it must be our work more completely to examine in this.

43.[3] He says, for instance, in one place: "The getting of treasures by a lying tongue is a vanity tossed to and fro of them that seek death"; adding in another, with the same meaning (he has a curious way of doubling his sayings): "Treasures of wickedness profit nothing: but justice delivers from death." Both these passages are notable for their assertions of death as the only real issue and sum of attainment by any unjust scheme of wealth. If we read, instead of "lying tongue," "lying label, title, pretence, or advertisement," we shall more clearly perceive the bearing of the words on modern business. The seeking of death is a grand expression of the true course of men's toil in such business. We usually speak as if death pursued us, and we fled from him; but that is only so in rare instances. Ordinarily he masks himself—makes himself beautiful—all-glorious; not like the King's daughter, all-glorious within, but outwardly: his clothing of wrought gold. We pursue him frantically all our days, he flying or hiding from us. Our crowning success at three-score and ten is utterly and perfectly to seize, and hold him in his eternal integrity—robes, ashes, and sting.

Again: the merchant says, "He that oppresseth the poor to increase his riches, shall surely come to want." And again, more strongly: "Rob not the poor because he is poor; neither oppress the afflicted in the place of business. For God shall spoil the soul of those that spoiled them."

This "robbing the poor because he is poor," is especially the mercantile form of theft, consisting in taking advantage of a man's necessities in order to obtain his labour or property at a reduced price. The ordinary highwayman's opposite form of robbery—of the rich, because he

---

[1] Ruskin explains the title of this essay in paragraph 46.
[2] The statue of Solomon on the Ducal Palace in Venice.
[3] Throughout this section Ruskin interweaves biblical quotations into his argument.

is rich—does not appear to occur so often to the old merchant's mind; probably because being less profitable and more dangerous than the robbery of the poor, it is rarely practised by persons of discretion.

44. But the two most remarkable passages in their deep general significance are the following:—

"The rich and the poor have met. God is their maker."

"The rich and the poor have met. God is their light."

They "have met": more literally, have stood in each other's way *(obviaverunt)*. That is to say, as long as and the world lasts, the action and counteraction of wealth and poverty, the meeting, face to face, of rich and poor, is just as appointed and necessary a law of that world as the flow of stream to sea, or the interchange of power among the electric clouds:—"God is their maker." But, also, this action may be either gentle and just, or convulsive and destructive: it may be by rage of devouring flood, or by lapse of serviceable wave;—in blackness of thunderstroke, or continual force of vital fire, soft, and shapeable into love-syllables from far away. And which of these it shall be, depends on both rich and poor knowing that God is their light; that in the mystery of human life, there is no other light than this by which they can see each other's faces, and live;—light, which is called in another of the books among which the merchant's maxims have been preserved, the "sun of justice," of which it is promised that it shall rise at last with "healing" (health-giving or helping, making whole or setting at one) in its wings. For truly this healing is only possible by means of justice; no love, no faith, no hope will do it; men will be unwisely fond—vainly faithful,—unless primarily they are just; and the mistake of the best men through generation after generation, has been that great one of thinking to help the poor by almsgiving, and by preaching of patience or of hope, and by every other means, emollient or consolatory, except the one thing which God orders for them, justice. But this justice, with its accompanying holiness or helpfulness, being even by the best man denied in its trial time, is by the mass of men hated wherever it appears: so that, when the choice was one day fairly put to them, they denied the Helpful One and the Just; and desired a murderer, sedition-raiser, and robber, to be granted to them;—the murderer instead of the Lord of Life, the sedition-raiser instead of the Prince of Peace, and the robber instead of the Just Judge of all the world.

45. I have just spoken of the flowing of streams to the sea as a partial image of the action of wealth. In one respect it is not a partial, but a perfect image. The popular economist thinks himself wise in having discovered that wealth, or the forms of property in general, must go where they are required; that where demand is, supply must follow. He farther declares that this course of demand and supply cannot be forbidden by human laws. Precisely in the same sense, and with the same certainty, the waters of the world go where they are required. Where the land falls, the water flows. The course neither of clouds nor rivers can be forbidden by human will. But the disposition and administration of them can be altered by human forethought. Whether the stream shall be a curse or a blessing, depends upon man's labour, and administering intelligence. For centuries after centuries, great districts of the world, rich in soil, and favoured in climate, have lain desert under the rage of their own rivers; nor only desert, but plague-struck. The stream which, rightly directed, would have flowed in soft irrigation from field to field— would have purified the air, given food to man and beast, and carried their burdens for them on its bosom—now overwhelms the plain and poisons the wind; its breath pestilence, and its work famine. In like manner this wealth "goes where it is required." No human laws can withstand its flow. They can only guide it: but this, the leading trench and limiting mound can do so thoroughly, that it shall become water of life—the riches of the hand of wisdom; or, on the contrary, by leaving it to its own lawless flow, they may make it, what it has been too often, the last and deadliest of national plagues: water of Marah[4]—the water which feeds the roots of all evil.

The necessity of these laws of distribution or restaint is curiously overlooked in the ordinary political economist's definition of his own "science." He calls it, shortly, the "science of getting rich." But there are many sciences, as well as many arts, of getting rich. Poisoning people of large estates, was one employed largely in the Middle Ages; adulteration of food of people of small estates, is one employed largely now. The ancient and honourable Highland method of black mail; the more modern and less honourable system of obtaining goods on credit, and the

---

[4] Exodus 15:23.

other variously improved methods of appropriation—which, in major and minor scales of industry, down to the most artistic pocket-picking, we owe to recent genius,—all come under the general head of sciences, or arts, of getting rich.

46. So that it is clear the popular economist, in calling his science the science par excellence of getting rich, must attach some peculiar ideas of limitation to its character. I hope I do not misrepresent him, by assuming that he means *his* science to be the science of "getting rich by legal or just means." In this definition, is the word "just", or "legal," finally to stand? For it is possible among certain nations, or under certain rulers, or by help of certain advocates, that proceedings may be legal which are by no means just. If, therefore, we leave at last only the word "just" in that place of our definition, the insertion of this solitary and small word will make a notable difference in the grammar of our science. For then it will follow that in order to grow rich scientifically, we must grow rich justly; and, therefore, know what is just; so that our economy will no longer depend merely on prudence, but on jurisprudence—and that of divine, not human law. Which prudence is indeed of no mean order, holding itself, as it were, high in the air of heaven, and gazing for ever on the light of the sun of justice; hence the souls which have excelled in it are represented by Dante as stars forming in heaven for ever the figure of the eye of an eagle,[5] they having been in life the discerners of light from darkness; or to the whole human race, as the light of the body, which is the eye,[6] while those souls which form the wings of the bird (giving power and dominion to justice, "healing in its wings") trace also in light the inscription in heaven: "DILIGITE JUSTITIAM QUI JUDICATIS TERRAM." "Ye who judge the earth, give" (not, observe, merely love, but) "diligent love to justice": the love which seeks diligently, that is to say, choosingly, and by preference to all things else. Which judging or doing judgment in the earth is, according to their capacity and position, required not of judges only, not of rulers only, but of all men: a truth sorrowfully lost sight of even by those who are ready enough to apply to themselves passages in which Christian men are spoken of as called to be "saints" (*i.e.,* to helpful or healing functions); and "chosen to be kings" (*i.e.,* to knowing or directing functions); the true

meaning of these titles having been long lost through the pretences of unhelpful and unable persons to saintly and kingly character; also through the once popular idea that both the sanctity and royalty are to consist in wearing long robes and high crowns, instead of in mercy and judgment; whereas all true sanctity is saving power, as all true royalty is ruling power; and injustice is part and parcel of the denial of such power, which "makes men as the creeping things, as the fishes of the sea, that have no ruler over them."

47. Absolute justice is indeed no more attainable than absolute truth; but the righteous man is distinguished from the unrighteous by his desire and hope of justice, as the true man from the false by his desire and hope of truth. And though absolute justice be unattainable, as much justice as we need for all practical use is attainable by all those who make it their aim.

We have to examine, then, in the subject before us, what are the laws of justice respecting payment of labour—no small part, these, of the foundations of all jurisprudence.

I reduced, in my last paper, the idea of money payment to its simplest or radical terms. In those terms its nature, and the conditions of justice respecting it, can be best ascertained.

Money payment, as there stated, consists radically in a promise to some person working for us, that for the time and labour he spends in our service to-day we will give or procure equivalent time and labour in his service at any future time when he may demand it.

If we promise to give him less labour than he has given us, we under-pay him. If we promise to give him more labour than he has given us, we over-pay him. In practice, according to the laws of demand and supply, when two men are ready to do the work, and only one man wants to have it done, the two men underbid each other for it; and the one who gets it to do, is under-paid. But when two men want the work done, and there is only one man ready to do it, the two men who want it done overbid each other, and the workman is over-paid.

48. I will examine these two points of injustice in succession; but first I wish the reader to clearly understand the central principle, lying between the two, of right or just payment.

When we ask a service of any man, he may either give it us freely, or demand payment for it. Respecting free gift of service, there is no question

---

[5] *Paradiso,* canto 18.   [6] Matthew 6:22.

at present, that being a matter of affection—not of traffic. But if he demand payment for it, and we wish to treat him with absolute equity, it is evident that this equity can only consist in giving time for time, strength for strength, and skill for skill. If a man works an hour for us, and we only promise to work half an hour for him in return, we obtain an unjust advantage. If, on the contrary, we promise to work an hour and a half for him in return, he has an unjust advantage. The justice consists in absolute exchange; or, if there be any respect to the stations of the parties, it will not be in favour of the employer: there is certainly no equitable reason in a man's being poor, that if he give me a pound of bread to-day, I should return him less than a pound of bread to-morrow; or any equitable reason in a man's being uneducated, that if he uses a certain quantity of skill and knowledge in my service, I should use a less quantity of skill and knowledge in his. Perhaps, ultimately, it may appear desirable, or, to say the least, gracious, that I should give in return somewhat more than I received. But at present, we are concerned on the law of justice only, which is that of perfect and accurate exchange;—one circumstance only interfering with the simplicity of this radical idea of just payment—that insamuch as labour (rightly directed) is fruitful just as seed is, the fruit (or "interest," as it is called) of the labour first given, or "advanced," ought to be taken into account, and balanced by an additional quantity of labour in the subsequent repayment. Supposing the repayment to take place at the end of the year, or of any other given time, this calculation could be approximately made, but as money (that is to say, cash) payment involves no reference to time (it being optional with the person paid to spend what he receives at once or after any number of years), we can only assume, generally, that some slight advantage must in equity be allowed to the person who advances the labour, so that the typical form of bargain will be: if you give me an hour to-day, I will give you an hour and five minutes on demand. If you give me a pound of bread to-day, I will give you seventeen ounces on demand, and so on. All that is necessary for the reader to note is, that the amount returned is at least in equity not to be *less* than the amount given.

The abstract idea, then, of just or due wages, as respects the labourer, is that they will consist in a sum of money which will at any time procure for him at least as much labour as he has given, rather more than less. And this equity or justice of payment is, observe, wholly independent of any reference to the number of men who are willing to do the work. I want a horseshoe for my horse. Twenty smiths, or twenty thousand smiths, may be ready to forge it; their number does not in one atom's weight affect the question of the equitable payment of the one who *does* forge it. It costs him a quarter of an hour of his life, and so much skill and strength of arm, to make that horseshoe for me. Then at some future time I am bound in equity to give a quarter of an hour, and some minutes more, of my life (or of some other person's at my disposal), and also as much strength of arm and skill, and a little more, in making or doing what the smith may have need of.

49. Such being the abstract theory of just remunerative payment, its application is practically modified by the fact that the order for labour, given in payment, is general, while the labour received is special. The current coin or document is practically an order on the nation for so much work of any kind; and this universal applicability to immediate need renders it so much more valuable than special labour can be, that an order for a less quantity of this general toil will always be accepted as a just equivalent for a greater quantity of special toil. Any given craftsman will always be willing to give an hour of his own work in order to receive command over half an hour, or even much less, of national work. This source of uncertainty, together with the difficulty of determining the monetary value of skill, render the ascertainment (even approximate) of the proper wages of any given labour in terms of a currency, matter of considerable complexity. But they do not affect the principle of exchange. The worth of the work may not be easily known; but it *has* a worth, just as fixed and real as the specific gravity of a substance, though such specific gravity may not be easily ascertainable when the substance is united with many others. Nor is there so much difficulty or chance in determining it, as in determining the ordinary maxima and minima of vulgar political economy. There are few bargains in which the buyer can ascertain with anything like precision that the seller would have taken no less;—or the seller acquire more than a comfortable faith that the purchaser would have given no more. This impossibility of precise knowledge prevents neither from striving to attain the desired point of greatest vexation and injury to the other, nor from accepting it for a scientific principle that he is to buy for the least and sell for

the most possible, though what the real least or most may be he cannot tell. In like manner, a just person lays it down for a scientific principle that he is to pay a just price, and, without being able precisely to ascertain the limits of such a price, will nevertheless strive to attain the closest possible approximation to them. A practically serviceable approximation he *can* obtain. It is easier to determine scientifically what a man ought to have for his work, than what his necessities will compel him to take for it. His necessities can only be ascertained by empirical, but his due by analytical, investigation. In the one case, you try your answer to the sum like a puzzled schoolboy—till you find one that fits; in the other, you bring our your result within certain limits, by process of calculation.

50. Supposing, then, the just wages of any quantity of given labour to have been ascertained, let us examine the first results of just and unjust payment, when in favour of the purchaser or employer: *i.e.*, when two men are ready to do the work, and only one wants to have it done.

The unjust purchaser forces the two to bid against each other till he has reduced their demand to its lowest terms. Let us assume that the lowest bidder offers to do the work at half its just price.

The purchaser employs him, and does not employ the other. The first or *apparent* result is, therefore, that one of the two men is left out of employ, or to starvation, just as definitely as by the just procedure of giving fair price to the best workman. The various writers who endeavoured to invalidate the positions of my first paper never saw this, and assumed that the unjust hirer employed *both*. He employs both no more than the just hirer. The only difference (in the outset) is that the just man pays sufficiently, the unjust man insufficiently, for the labour of the single person employed.

I say, "in the outset"; for this first or apparent difference is not the actual difference. By the unjust procedure, half the proper price of the work is left in the hand of the employer. This enables him to hire another man at the same unjust rate, on some other kind of work; and the final result is that he has two men working for him at half-price, and two are out of employ.

51. By the just procedure, the whole price of the first piece of work goes into the hands of the man who does it. No surplus being left in the employer's hands, *he* cannot hire another man for another piece of labour. But by precisely so much as his power is diminished, the hired workman's

power is increased: that is to say, by the additional half of the price he has received; which additional half *he* has the power of using to employ another man in *his* service. I will suppose, for the moment, the least favourable, though quite probable, case—that, though justly treated himself, he yet will act unjustly to his subordinate; and hire at half-price if he can. The final result will then be, that one man works for the employer, at just price; one for the workman, at half-price; and two, as in the first case, are still out of employ. These two, as I said before, are out of employ in *both* cases. The difference between the just and unjust procedure does not lie in the number of men hired, but in the price paid to them, and the *persons by whom* it is paid. The essential difference, that which I want the reader to see clearly, is, that in the unjust case, two men work for one, the first hirer. In the just case, one man works for the first hirer, one for the person hired, and so on, down or up through the various grades of service; the influence being carried forward by justice, and arrested by injustice. The universal and constant action of justice in this matter is therefore to diminish the power of wealth, in the hands of one individual, over masses of men, and to distribute it through a chain of men. The actual power exerted by the wealth is the same in both cases; but by injustice it is put all into one man's hands, so that he directs at once and with equal force the labour of a circle of men about him; by the just procedure, he is permitted to touch the nearest only, through whom, with diminished force, modified by new minds, the energy of the wealth passes on to others, and so till it exhausts itself.

52. The immediate operation of justice in this respect is therefore to diminish the power of wealth, first, in acquisition of luxury, and secondly, in exercise of moral influence. The employer cannot concentrate so multitudinous labour on his own interests, nor can he subdue so multitudinous mind to his own will. But the secondary operation of justice is not less important. The insufficient payment of the group of men working for one, places each under a maximum of difficulty in rising above his position. The tendency of the system is to check advancement. But the sufficient or just payment, distributed through a descending series of offices or grades of labour, gives each subordinated person fair and sufficient means of rising in the social scale, if he chooses to use them; and thus not only diminishes the immediate power of wealth, but removes the worst disabilities of poverty.

53. It is on this vital problem that the entire destiny of the labourer is ultimately dependent. Many minor interests may sometimes appear to interfere with it, but all branch from it. For instance, considerable agitation is often caused in the minds of the lower classes when they discover the share which they nominally, and to all appearance, actually, pay out of their wages in taxation (I believe thirty-five or forty per cent). This sounds very grievous; but in reality the labourer does not pay it, but his employer. If the workman had not to pay it, his wages would be less by just that sum; competition would still reduce them to the lowest rate at which life was possible. Similarly the lower orders agitated for the repeal of the corn laws, thinking they would be better off if bread were cheaper; never perceiving that as soon as bread was permanently cheaper, wages would permanently fall in precisely that proportion. The corn laws were rightly repealed; not, however, because they directly oppressed the poor, but because they indirectly oppressed them in causing a large quantity of their labour to be consumed unproductively. So also unnecessary taxation oppresses them, through destruction of capital; but the destiny of the poor depends primarily always on this one question of the dueness of wages. Their distress (irrespectively of that caused by sloth, minor error, or crime) arises on the grand scale from the two reacting forces of competition and oppression. There is not yet, nor will yet for ages be, any real over-population in the world; but a local over-population, or, more accurately, a degree of population locally unmanageable under existing circumstances for want of forethought and sufficient machinery, necessarily shows itself by pressure of competition; and the taking advantage of this competition by the purchaser to obtain their labour unjustly cheap, consummates at once their suffering and his own; for in this (as I believe in every other kind of slavery) the oppressor suffers at last more than the oppressed, and those magnificent lines of Pope, even in all their force, fall short of the truth:—

"Yet, to be just to these poor men of pelf.
  Each does but HATE HIS NEIGHBOUR AS
    HIMSELF:
  Damned to the mines, an equal fate betides
  The slave that digs it, and the slave that hides."[7]

54. The collateral and reversionary operations of justice in this matter I shall examine hereafter (it being needful first to define the nature of value); proceeding then to consider within what practical terms a juster system may be established; and ultimately the vexed question of the destinies of the unemployed workmen. Lest, however, the reader should be alarmed at some of the issues to which our investigations seem to be tending, as if in their bearing against the power of wealth they had something in common with those of socialism, I wish him to know, in accurate terms, one or two of the main points which I have in view.

Whether socialism has made more progress among the army and navy (where payment is made on my principles) or among the manufacturing operatives (who are paid on my opponents' principles), I leave it to those opponents to ascertain and declare. Whatever their conclusion may be, I think it necessary to answer for myself only this: that if there be any one point insisted on throughout my works more frequently than another, that one point is the impossibility of Equality. My continual aim has been to show the eternal superiority of some men to others, sometimes even of one man to all others; and to show also the advisability of appointing such persons or person to guide, to lead, or on occasion even to compel and subdue, their inferiors according to their own better knowledge and wiser will. My principles of Political Economy were all involved in a single phrase spoken three years ago at Manchester: "Soldiers of the Ploughshare as well as Soldiers of the Sword";[8] and they were all summed in a single sentence in the last volume of *Modern Painters*—"Government and co-operation are in all things the Laws of Life; Anarchy and competition the Laws of Death."

And with respect to the mode in which these general principles affect the secure possession of property, so far am I from invalidating such security, that the whole gist of these papers will be found ultimately to aim at an extension in its range; and whereas it has long been known and declared that the poor have no right to the property of the rich, I wish it also to be known and declared that the rich have no right to the property of the poor.

55. But that the working of the system which I have undertaken to develop would in many ways shorten the apparent and direct, though not the unseen and collateral, power, both of wealth, as

---

[7] Pope, *Moral Essays*, Epistle III.   [8] From a Lecture Ruskin delivered on 10 July 1857.

the Lady of Pleasure, and of capital as the Lord of Toil, I do not deny: on the contrary, I affirm it in all joyfulness; knowing that the attraction of riches is already too strong, as their authority is already too weighty, for the reason of mankind. I said in my last paper[9] that nothing in history had ever been so disgraceful to human intellect as the acceptance among us of the common doctrines of political economy as a science. I have many grounds for saying this, but one of the chief may be given in few words. I know no previous instance in history of a nation's establishing a systematic disobedience to the first principles of its professed religion. The writings which we (verbally) esteem as divine, not only denounce the love of money as the source of all evil, and as an idolatry abhorred of the Deity, but declare mammon service to be the accurate and irreconcileable opposite of God's service: and, whenever they speak of riches absolute, and poverty absolute, declare woe to the rich, and blessing to the poor. Whereupon we forthwith investigate a science of becoming rich, as the shortest road to national prosperity.

"Tai Cristian dannerà l'Etiòpe,
  Quando so partiranno i due collegi,
  L'UNO IN ETERNO RICCO, E L'ALTRO INÒPE."[10]

ESSAY IV

Ad Valorem

56. In the last paper we saw that just payment of labour consisted in a sum of money which would approximately obtain equivalent labour at a future time: we have now to examine the means of obtaining such equivalence. Which question involves the definition of Value, Wealth, Price, and Produce.

None of these terms are yet defined so as to be understood by the public. But the last, Produce, which one might have thought the clearest of all,

is, in use, the most ambiguous; and the examination of the kind of ambiguity attendant on its present employment will best open the way to our work.

In his chapter on Capital,[1] Mr. J. S. Mill instances, as a capitalist, a hardware manufacturer, who, having intended to spend a certain portion of the proceeds of his business in buying plate and jewels, changes his mind, and "pays it as wages to additional workpeople." The effect is stated by Mr. Mill to be, that "more food is appropriated to the consumption of productive labourers."

57. Now I do not ask, though, had I written this paragraph, it would surely have been asked of me, What is to become of the silversmiths? If they are truly unproductive persons, we will acquiesce in their extinction. And though in another part of the same passage, the hardware merchant is supposed also to dispense with a number of servants, whose "food is thus set free for productive purposes," I do not inquire what will be the effect, painful or otherwise, upon the servants, of this emancipation of their food. But I very seriously inquire why ironware is produce, and silverware is not? That the merchant consumes the one, and sells the other, certainly does not constitute the difference, unless it can be shown (which, indeed, I perceive it to be becoming daily more and more the aim of tradesmen to show) that commodities are made to be sold, and not to be consumed. The merchant is an agent of conveyance to the consumer in one case, and is himself the consumer in the other: but the labourers are in either case equally productive, since they have produced goods to the same value, if the hardware and the plate are both goods.

And what distinction separates them? It is indeed possible that in the "comparative estimate of the moralist," with which Mr. Mill says political economy has nothing to do (III. i. 2), a steel fork might appear a more substantial production than a silver one: we may grant also that knives, no less than forks, are good produce; and scythes and ploughshares serviceable articles. But, how of bayonets? Supposing the hardware merchant to effect large sales of *these*, by help

---

[9] Correctly in the first essay, "The Roots of Honour."

[10] Christians like these the Aethiop shall condemn:
  When that the two assemblages shall part;
  One rich eternally, the other poor.

  (*Divine Comedy*, Paradiso, canto 19).

[1] In his *Principles of Political Economy*, Bk. I, chap. iv., Ruskin refers repeatedly in this essay to the theories of economics espoused by Mill and others of the laissez-faire school.

of the "setting free" of the food of his servants and his silversmith,—is he still employing productive labourers, or, in Mr. Mill's words, labourers who increase "the stock of permanent means of enjoyment" (I. iii. 4)? Or if, instead of bayonets, he supply bombs, will not the absolute and final "enjoyment" of even these energetically productive articles (each of which costs ten pounds) be dependent on a proper choice of time and place for their *enfantement;* choice, that is to say, depending on those philosophical considerations with which political economy has nothing to do?

58. I should have regretted the need of pointing out inconsistency in any portion of Mr. Mill's work, had not the value of his work proceeded from its inconsistencies. He deserves honour among economists by inadvetently disclaiming the principles which he states, and tacitly introducing the moral considerations with which he declares his science has no connection. Many of his chapters are, therefore, true and valuable; and the only conclusions of his which I have to dispute are those which follow from his premises.

Thus, the idea which lies at the root of the passage we have just been examining, namely, that labour applied to produce luxuries will not support so many persons as labour applied to produce useful articles, is entirely true; but the instance given fails—and in four directions of failure at once—because Mr. Mill has not defined the real meaning of usefulness. The definition which he has given— "capacity to satisfy a desire, or serve a purpose" (III. i. 2)—applies equally to the iron and silver; while the true definition—which he has not given, but which nevertheless underlies the false verbal definition in his mind, and comes out once or twice by accident (as in the words "any support to life or strength" in I. iii. 5)—applies to some articles of iron, but not to others, and to some articles of silver, but not to others. It applies to ploughs, but not to bayonets; and to forks, but not to filigree.

59. The eliciting of the true definitions will give us the reply to our first question, "What is value?" respecting which, however, we must first hear the popular statements.

"The word 'value,' when used without adjunct, always means, in political economy, value in exchange (Mill, III. i. 2). So that, if two ships cannot exchange their rudders, their rudders are,

in politico-economic language, of no value to either.

But "the subject of political economy is wealth."—(Preliminary remarks, page 1.)

And wealth "consists of all useful and agreeable objects which possess exchangeable value."—(Preliminary remarks, page 10.)

It appears, then, according to Mr. Mill, that usefulness and agreeableness underlie the exchange value, and must be ascertained to exist in the thing, before we can esteem it an object of wealth.

Now, the economical usefulness of a thing depends not merely on its own nature, but on the number of people who can and will use it. A horse is useless, and therefore unsaleable, if no one can ride,—a sword, if no one can strike, and meat, if no one can eat. Thus every material utility depends on its relative human capacity.

Similarly: The agreeableness of a thing depends not merely on its own likeableness, but on the number of people who can be got to like it. The relative agreeableness, and therefore saleableness, of "a pot of the smallest ale," and of "Adonis painted by a running brook," depends virtually on the opinion of Demos, in the shape of Christopher Sly.[2] That is to say, the agreeableness of a thing depends on its relatively human disposition. Therefore, political economy, being a science of wealth, must be a science respecting human capacities and dispositions. But moral considerations have nothing to do with political economy (III. i. 2). Therefore, moral considerations have nothing to do with human capacities and dispositions.

60. I do not wholly like the look of this conclusion from Mr. Mill's statements:—let us try Mr. Ricardo's[3]

"Utility is not the measure of exchangeable value, though it is absolutely essential to it."—(Chap. I. sect. i.) Essential in what degree, Mr. Ricardo? There may be greater and less degrees of utility. Meat, for instance, may be so good as to be fit for any one to eat, or so bad as to be fit for no one to eat. What is the exact degree of goodness which is "essential" to its exchangeable value, but not "the measure" of it? How good must the meat be, in order to possess any exchangeable value? and how bad must it be—(I wish this were a settled question in London markets)—in order to possess none?

There appears to be some hitch, I think, in the working even of Mr. Ricardo's principles;

---

[2] *Taming of the Shrew.*   [3] David Ricardo's *Principles of Political Economy and Taxation* (1817).

but let him take his own example: "Suppose that in the early stages of society the bows and arrows of the hunter were of equal value with the implements of the fisherman. Under such circumstances the value of the deer, the produce of the hunter's day's labour, would be *exactly*" (italics mine) "equal to the value of the fish, the product of the fisherman's day's labour. The comparative value of the fish and game would be *entirely* regulated by the quantity of labour realized in each." (Ricardo, chap. iii. On Value.)

Indeed! Therefore, if the fisherman catches one sprat, and the huntsman one deer, one sprat will be equal in value to one deer; but if the fisherman catch no sprat and the hutsman two deer, no sprat will be equal in value to two deer?

Nay; but—Mr. Ricardo's supporters may say—he means, on an average;—if the average product of a day's work of fisher and hunter be one fish and one deer, the one fish will always be equal in value to the one deer.

Might I inquire the species of fish? Whale? or whitebait?

It would be waste of time to pursue these fallacies farther; we will seek for a true definition.

61. Much store has been set for centuries upon the use of our English classical education. It were to be wished that our well-educated merchants recalled to mind always this much of their Latin schooling,—that the nominative of *valorem* (a word already sufficiently familiar to them) is *valor;* a word which, therefore, ought to be familiar to them. *Valor*, from valere, to be well or strong (ὑγιαίνω);—strong, *in* life (if a man), or valiant; strong, *for* life (if a thing), or valuable. To be "valuable," therefore, is to "avail towards life." A truly valuable or availing thing is that which leads to life with its whole strength. In proportion as it does not lead to life, or as its strength is broken, it is less valuable; in proportion as it leads away from life, it is unvaluable or malignant.

The value of a thing, therefore, is independent of opinion, and of quantity. Think what you will of it, gain how much you may of it, the value of the thing itself is neither greater nor less. For ever it avails, or avails not; no estimate can raise, no disdain repress, the power which it holds from the Maker of things and men.

The real science of political economy, which has yet to be distinguished from the bastard science, as medicine from witchcraft, and astron-omy from astrology, is that which teaches nations to desire and labour for the things that lead to life; and which teaches them to scorn and destroy the things that lead to destruction. And if, in a state of infancy, they supposed indifferent things, such as excrescences of shell-fish, and pieces of blue and red stone, to be valuable, and spent large measures of the labour which ought to be employed for the extension and ennobling of life, in diving or digging for them, and cutting them into various shapes,—or if, in the same state of infancy, they imagine precious and beneficient things, such as air, light, and cleanliness, to be valueless,—or if, finally, they imagine the conditions of their own existence, by which alone they can truly possess or use anything, such, for instance, as peace, trust, and love, to be prudently exchangeable, when the markets offer, for gold, iron, or excrescences of shells—the great and only science of Political Economy teaches them, in all these cases, what is vanity, and what substance; and how the service of Death, the Lord of Waste, and of eternal emptiness, differs from the service of Wisdom, the Lady of Saving, and of eternal fullness; she who has said, "I will cause those that love me to inherit SUBSTANCE; and I will FILL their treasures."[4]

The "Lady of Saving," in a profounder sense than that of the savings bank, though that is a good one: Madonna della Salute,—Lady of Health,—which, though commonly spoken of as if separate from wealth, is indeed a part of wealth. This word, "wealth," it will be remembered, is the next we have to define.

62. "To be wealthy," says Mr. Mill, "is to have a large stock of useful articles."

I accept this definition. Only let us perfectly understand it. My opponents often lament my not giving them enough logic: I fear I must at present use a little more than they will like; but this business of Political Economy is no light one, and we must allow no loose terms in it.

We have, therefore, to ascertain in the above definition, first, what is the meaning of "having," or the nature of Possession. Then what is the meaning of "useful," or the nature of Utility.

And first of possession. At the crossing of the transepts of Milan Cathedral has lain, for three hundred years, the embalmed body of St. Carlo Borromeo. It holds a golden crosier, and has a cross of emeralds on its breast. Admitting the crosier and emeralds to be useful articles, is the

---

4 Proverbs 8:21.

body to be considered as "having" them? Do they, in the politico-economical sense of property, belong to it? If not, and if we may, therefore, conclude generally that a dead body cannot possess property, what degree and period of animation in the body will render possession possible?

As thus: lately in a wreck of a Californian ship, one of the passengers fastened a belt about him with two hundred pounds of gold in it, with which he was found afterwards at the bottom. Now, as he was sinking—had he the gold? or had the gold him?

And if, instead of sinking him in the sea by its weight, the gold had struck him on the forehead, and thereby caused incurable disease—suppose palsy or insanity,—would the gold in that case have been more a "possession" than in the first? Without pressing the inquiry up through instances of gradually increasing vital power over the gold (which I will, however, give, if they are asked for), I presume the reader will see that possession, or "having," is not an absolute, but a gradated, power; and consists not only in the quantity or nature of the thing possessed, but (and in a greater degree) in its suitableness to the person possessing it and in his vital power to use it.

And our definition of Wealth, expanded, becomes: "The possession of useful articles, *which we can use.*" This is a very serious change. For wealth, instead of depending merely on a "have," is thus seen to depend on a "can." Gladiator's death, on a "habet"; but soldier's victory, and State's salvation, on a "quo plurimum posset." (Liv. VII. 6)[5] And what we reasoned of only as accumulation of material, is seen to demand also accumulation of capacity.

63. So much for our verb. Next for our adjective. What is the meaning of "useful"?

The inquiry is closely connected with the last. For what is capable of use in the hands of some persons, is capable, in the hands of others, of the opposite of use, called commonly "from-use," or "ab-use." And it depends on the person, much more than on the article, whether its usefulness or ab-usefulness will be the quality developed in it. Thus, wine, which the Greeks, in their Bacchus, made rightly the type of all passion and which, when used, "cheereth god and man"[6] (that is to say, strengthens both the divine life, or reasoning power, and the earthy, or carnal power, of man); yet, when abused, becomes

"Dionusos," hurtful especially to the divine part of man, or reason. And again, the body itself, being equally liable to use and to abuse, and, when rightly disciplined, serviceable to the State, both for war and labour;—but when not disciplined, or abused, valueless to the State, and capable only of continuing the private or single existence of the individual (and that but feebly)— the Greeks called such a body an "idiotic" or "private" body, from their word signifying a person employed in no way directly useful to the State, whence finally, our "idiot," meaning a person entirely occupied with his own concerns.

Hence, it follows that if a thing is to be useful, it must be not only of an availing nature, but in availing hands. Or, in accurate terms, usefulness is value in the hands of the valiant; so that this science of wealth being, as we have just seen, when regarded as the science of Accumulation, accumulative of capacity as well as of material,— when regarded as the Science of Distribution, is distribution not absolute, but discriminate; not of every thing to every man, but of the right thing to the right man. A difficult science, dependent on more than arithmetic.

64. Wealth, therefore, is "THE POSSESSION OF THE VALUABLE BY THE VALIANT"; and in considering it as a power existing in a nation, the two elements, the value of the thing, and the valour of its possessor, must be estimated together. Whence it appears that many of the persons commonly considered wealthy, are in reality no more wealthy than the locks of their own strong boxes are, they being inherently and eternally incapable of wealth; and operating for the nation, in an economical point of view, either as pools of dead water, and eddies in a stream (which, so long as the stream flows, are useless, or serve only to drown people, but may become of importance in a state of stagnation should the stream dry); or else, as dams in a river, of which the ultimate service depends not on the dam, but the miller; or else, as mere accidental stays and impediments, acting not as wealth but (for we ought to have a correspondent term) as "illth," causing various devastation and trouble around them in all directions; or lastly, act not at all, but are merely animated conditions of delay, (no use being possible of anything they have until they are dead,) in which last condition they are nevertheless often useful *as* delays, and "impedimenta," if a nation is apt to move too fast.

---

[5] Livy, *History of Rome.*   [6] Judges 9:13.

65. This being so, the difficulty of the true science of Political Economy lies not merely in the need of developing manly character to deal with material value, but in the fact, that while the manly character and material value only form wealth by their conjunction, they have nevertheless a mutually destructive operation on each other. For the manly character is apt to ignore, or even cast away, the material value:—whence that of Pope:—

> "Sure, of qualities demanding praise,
> More go to ruin fortunes, than to raise."[7]

And on the other hand, the material value is apt to undermine the manly character; so that it must be our work, in the issue, to examine what evidence there is of the effect of wealth on the minds of its possessors; also, what kind of person it is who usually sets himself to obtain wealth, and succeeds in doing so; and whether the world owes more gratitude to rich or to poor men, either for their moral indifference upon it, or for chief goods, discoveries, and practical advancements. I may, however, anticipate future conclusions, so far as to state that in a community regulated only by laws of demand and supply, but protected from open violence, the persons who become rich are, generally speaking, industrious, resolute, proud, covetous, prompt, methodical, sensible, unimaginative, insensitive, and ignorant. The persons who remain poor are the entirely foolish, the entirely wise, the idle, the reckless, the humble, the thoughtful, the dull, the imaginative, the sensitive, the well-informed, the improvident, the irregularly and impulsively wicked, the clumsy knave, the open thief, and the entirely merciful, just, and godly person.

66. Thus far, then, of wealth. Next, we have to ascertain the nature of PRICE; that is to say, of exchange value, and its expression by currencies.

Note first, of exchange, there can be no *profit* in it. It is only in labour there can be profit—that is to say, a "making in advance," or "making in favour of" (from proficio). In exchange, there is only advantage, *i.e.*, a bringing of vantage or power to the exchanging persons. Thus, one man by sowing and reaping, turns one measure of corn into two measures. That is Profit. Another, by digging and forging, turns one spade into two spades. That is Profit. But the man who has two measures of corn wants sometimes to dig; and the man who has two spades wants sometimes to eat:—They exchange the gained grain for the gained tool; and both are the better for the exchange; but though there is much advantage in the transaction, there is no profit. Nothing is constructed or produced. Only that which had been before constructed is given to the person by whom it can be used. If labour is necessary to effect the exchange, that labour is in reality involved in the production, and, like all other labour, bears profit. Whatever number of men are concerned in the manufacture, or in the conveyance, have share in the profit; but neither the manufacture nor the conveyance are the exchange, and in the exchange itself there is no profit.

There may, however, be acquisition, which is a very different thing. If, in the exchange, one man is able to give what cost him little labour for what has cost the other much, he "acquires" a certain quantity of the produce of the other's labour. And precisely what he acquires, the other loses. In mercantile language, the person who thus acquires is commonly said to have "made a profit"; and I believe that many of our merchants are seriously under the impression that it is possible for everybody, somehow, to make a profit in this manner. Whereas, by the unfortunate constitution of the world we live in, the laws both of matter and motion have quite rigorously forbidden universal acquisition of this kind. Profit, or material gain, is attainable only by construction or by discovery; not by exchange. Whenever material gain follows exchange, for every *plus* there is a precisely equal *minus*.

Unhappily for the progress of the science of Political Economy, the plus quantities, or—if I may be allowed to coin an awkward plural—the pluses, make a very positive and venerable appearance in the world, so that every one is eager to learn the science which produces results so magnificent; whereas the minuses have, on the other hand, a tendency to retire into back streets, and other places of shade,—or even to get themselves wholly and finally put out of sight in graves: which renders the algebra of this science peculiar, and difficulty legible; a large number of its negative signs being written by the account-keeper in a kind of red ink, which starvation thins, and makes strangely pale, or even quite invisible ink, for the present.

---

[7] Pope's *Moral Essays*, Epistle III, quoted slightly inaccurately.

67. The Science of Exchange, or as I hear it has been proposed to call it, of "Catallactics,"[8] considered as one of gain, is, therefore, simply nugatory; but considered as one of acquisition, it is a very curious science, differing in its data and basis from every other science known. Thus:—If I can exchange a needle with a savage for a diamond, my power of doing so depends either on the savage's ignorance of social arrangements in Europe, or on his want of power to take advantage of them, by selling the diamond to any one else for more needles, If, farther, I make the bargain as completely advantageous to myself as possible, by giving to the savage a needle with no eye in it (reaching, thus a sufficiently satisfactory type of the perfect operation of catallactic science), the advantage to me in the entire transaction depends wholly upon the ignorance, powerlessness, or heedlessness of the person dealt with. Do away with these, and catallactic advantage becomes impossible. So far, therefore, as the science of exchange relates to the advantage of one of the exchanging persons only, it is founded on the ignorance or incapacity of the opposite person. Where these vanish, it also vanishes. It is therefore a science founded on nescience, and an art founded on artlessness. But all other sciences and arts, except this, have for their object the doing away with their opposite nescience and artlessness. This science, alone of sciences, must, by all available means, promulgate and prolong its opposite nescience; otherwise the science itself is impossible. It is, therefore, peculiarly and alone the science of darkness; probably a bastard science—not by any means a *divina scientia*, but one begotten of another father, that father who, advising his children to turn stones into bread, is himself employed in turning bread into stones, and who, if you ask a fish of him (fish not being producible on his estate), can but give you a serpent.

68. The general law, then, respecting just or economical exchange, is simply this:—There must be advantage on both sides (or if only advantage on one, at least no disadvantage on the other) to the persons exchanging; and just payment for this time, intelligence, and labour, to any intermediate person effecting the transaction (commonly called a merchant); and whatever advantage there is on either side, and

whatever pay is given to the intermediate person, should be thoroughly known to all concerned. All attempt at concealment implies some practice of the opposite, or undivine science, founded on nescience. Whence another saying of the Jew merchant's—"As a nail between the stone joints, so doth sin stick fast between buying and selling."[9] Which peculiar riveting of stone and timber, in men's dealings with each other, is again set forth in the house which was to be destroyed—timber and stones together—when Zechariah's roll (more probably "curved sword")[10] flew over it: "the curse that goeth forth over all the earth upon every one that stealeth and holdeth himself guiltless," instantly followed by the vision of the Great Measure;—the measure "of the injustice of them in all the earth" (αὔτη ἡ ἀδικία αὐτῶν ἐν πά σῆ τῆ γῆ), with the weight of lead for its lid, and the woman, the spirit of wickedness, within it;—that is to say, Wickedness hidden by dulness, and formalized, outwardly, into ponderously established cruelty. "It shall be set upon its own base in the land of Babel."

69. I have hitherto carefully restricted myself, in speaking of exchange, to the use of the term "advantage"; but the term includes two ideas: the advantage, namely, of getting what we *need*, and that of getting what we *wish for*. Three-forths of the demands existing in the world are romantic; founded on visions, idealisms, hopes, and affections; and the regulation of the purse is, in its essence, regulation of the imagination and the heart. Hence, the right discussion of the nature of price is a very high metaphysical and psychical problem; sometimes to be solved only in a passionate manner, as by David in his counting the price of the water of the well by the gate of Bethlehem;[11] but its first conditions are the following:—The price of anything is the quantity of labour given by the person desiring it, in order to obtain possession of it. This price depends on four variable quantities. *A.* The quantity of wish the purchaser has for the thing; opposed to *a,* the quantity of wish the seller has to keep it. *B.* The quantity of labour the purchaser can afford, to obtain the thing; opposed to *β,* the quantity of labour the seller can afford to keep it. These quantities are operative only in excess; *i.e.,* the quantity of wish (*A*) means the quantity of wish for this thing, above wish for other things;

---

[8] So named in Richard Whately's *Lectures on Political Economy.*   [9] Ecclesiasticus 27:2.
[10] Zechariah 5:12. Following quotations in the passage also derive from Zechariah.
[11] II Samuel 23:15–16.

and the quantity of work (*B*) means the quantity which can be spared to get this thing from the quantity needed to get other things.

Phenomena of price, therefore, are intensely complex, curious, and interesting—too complex, however, to be examined yet; every one of them, when traced far enough, showing itself at last as a part of the bargain of the Poor of the Flock (or "flock of slaughter"), "If ye think good, give ME my price, and if not, forbear"—Zech. xi. 12; but as the price of everything is to be calculated finally in labour, it is necessary to define the nature of that standard.

70. Labour is the contest of the life of man with and opposite;—the term "life" including his intellect, soul, and physical power, contending with question, difficulty, trial, or material force.

Labour is of a higher or lower order, as it includes more or fewer of the elements of life: and labour of good quality, in any kind, includes always as much intellect and feeling as will fully and harmoniously regulate the physical force.

In speaking of the value and price of labour, it is necessary always to understand labour of a given rank and quality, as we should speak of gold or silver of a given standard. Bad (that is, heartless, inexperienced, or senseless) labour cannot be valued; it is like gold of uncertain alloy, or flawed iron.

The quality and kind of labour being given, its value, like that of all other valuable things, is invariable. But the quantity of it which must be given for other things is variable: and in estimating this variation, the price of other things must always be counted by the quantity of labour; not the price of labour by the quantity of other things.

71. Thus, if we want to plant an apple sapling in rocky ground, it may take two hours' work; in soft ground, perhaps only half an hour. Grant the soil equally good for the tree in each case. Then the value of the sapling planted by two hours' work is nowise greater than that of the sapling planted in half an hour. One will bear no more fruit than the other. Also, one half-hour of work is as valuable as another half-hour; nevertheless, the one sapling has cost four such pieces of work, the other only one. Now, the proper statement of this fact is, not the labour on the hard ground is cheaper than on the soft; but that the tree is dearer. The exchange value may, or may not, afterwards depend on this fact. If other people have plenty of soft ground to plant in, they will take no cognizance of our two hours' labour in the price they will offer for the plant on the rock. And if, through want of sufficient botanical science, we have planted an upas-tree instead of an apple, the exchange value will be a negative quantity; still less proportionate to the labour expended.

What is commonly called cheapness of labour, signifies, therefore, in reality, that many obstacles have to be overcome by it; so that much labour is required to produce a small result. But this should never be spoken of as cheapness of labour, but as dearness of the object wrought for. It would be just as rational to say that walking was cheap, because we had ten miles to walk home to our dinner, as that labour was cheap, because we had to work ten hours to earn it.

72. The last word which we have to define is "Production."

I have hitherto spoken of all labour as profitable; because it is impossible to consider under one head the quality or value of labour, and its aim. But labour of the best quality may be various in aim. It may be either constructive ("gathering," from con and struo), as agriculture; nugatory, as jewel-cutting; or destructive ("scattering," from de and struo), as war. It is not, however, always easy to prove labour, apparently nugatory, to be actually so; generally, the formula holds good: "he that gathereth not, scattereth";[12] thus, the jeweller's art is probably very harmful in its ministering to a clumsy and inelegant pride. So that, finally, I believe nearly all labour may be shortly divided into positive and negative labour: positive, that which produces life; negative, that which produces death; the most directly negative labour being murder, and the most directly positive, the bearing and rearing of children: so that in the precise degree in which murder is hateful, on the negative side of idleness, in that exact degree child-rearing is admirable, on the positive side of idleness. For which reason, and because of the honour that there is in rearing children, while the wife is said to be as the vine (for cheering), the children are as the olive branch[13] for praise: nor for praise only, but for peace (because large families can only be reared in times of peace): though since, in their spreading and voyaging in various directions, they distribute strength, they are, to the home strength, as arrows in the hand of the giant[14]—striking here and there far away.

Labour being thus various in its result, the

---

[12] Matthew 12:30.   [13] Psalms 128:3.   [14] Psalms 127:4.

prosperity of any nation is in exact proportion to the quantity of labour which it spends in obtaining and employing means of life. Observe,— I say, obtaining and employing; that is to say, not merely wisely producing, but wisely distributing and consuming. Economists usually speak as if there were no good in consumption absolute. So far from this being so, consumption absolute is the end, crown, and perfection of production; and wise consumption is a far more difficult art than wise production. Twenty people can gain money for one who can use it; and the vital question, for individual and for nation, is, never "how much do they make?" but "to what purpose do they spend?"

73. The reader may, perhaps, have been surprised at the slight reference I have hitherto made to "capital," and its functions. It is here the place to define them.

Capital signifies "head, or source, or root material"—it is material by which some derivative or secondary good is produced. It is only capital proper (caput vivum, not caput mortuum) when it is thus producing something different from itself. It is a root, which does not enter into vital function till it produces something else than a root: namely, fruit. That fruit will in time again produce roots; and so all living capital issues in reproduction of capital; but capital which produces nothing but capital is only root producing root; bulb issuing in bulb, never in tulip; seed issuing in seed, never in bread. The Political Economy of Europe has hitherto devoted itself wholly to the multiplication, or (less even) the aggregation, of bulbs. It never saw, nor conceived, such a thing as a tulip. Nay, boiled bulbs they might have been—glass bulbs—Prince Rupert's drops,[15] consummated in powder (well, if it were glass-powder and not gunpowder), for any end or meaning the economists had in defining the laws of aggregation. We will try and get a clearer notion of them.

The best and simplest general type of capital is a well-made ploughshare. Now, if that ploughshare did nothing but beget other ploughshares, in a polypous manner,—however the great cluster of polypous plough might glitter in the sun, it would have lost its function of capital. It becomes true capital only by another kind of splendour,— when it is seen "splendescere sulco,"[16] to grow bright in the furrow; rather with diminution

of its substance, than addition, by the noble friction. And the true home question, to every capitalist and to every nation, is not, "how many ploughs have you?" but, "where are your furrows?" not—"how quickly will this capital reproduce itself?"—but, "what will it do during reproduction?" What substance will it furnish, good for life? what work construct, protective of life? if none, its own reproduction is useless—if worse than none,—(for capital may destroy life as well as support it), its own reproduction is worse than useless; it is merely an advance from Tisiphone,[17] on mortgage—not a profit by any means.

74. Not a profit, as the ancients truly saw, and showed in the type of Ixion;—for capital is the head, or fountain head, of wealth—the "wellhead" of wealth, as the clouds are the well-heads of rain; but when clouds are without water, and only beget clouds, they issue in wrath at last, instead of rain, and in lightning instead of harvest; whence Ixion is said first to have invited his guests to a banquet, and then made them fall into a pit filled with fire; which is the type of the temptation of riches issuing in imprisoned torment,— torment in a pit, (as also Demas' silver mine,)[18] after which, to show the rage of riches passing from lust of pleasure to lust of power, yet power not truly understood, Ixion is said to have desired Juno, and instead, embracing a cloud (or phantasm), to have begotten the Centaurs; the power of mere wealth being, in itself, as the embrace of a shadow,—comfortless, (so also "Ephraim feedeth on wind and followeth after the east wind";[19] or "that which is not"—Prov. xxiii, 5; and again Dante's Geryon,[20] the type of avaricious fraud, as he flies, gathers the *air* up with retractile claws,—"l'aer a se raccolse,") but in its offspring, a mingling of the brutal with the human nature: human in sagacity—using both intellect and arrow; but brutal in its body and hoof, for consuming, and trampling down. For which sin Ixion is at last bound upon a wheel—fiery and toothed, and rolling perpetually in the air;—the type of human labour when selfish and fruitless (kept far into the Middle Ages in their wheel of fortune); the wheel which has in it no breath or spirit, but is whirled by chance only; whereas of all true work the Ezekiel vision is true, that the Spirit of the living creature is in the wheels, and where the angels go, the wheels go by them[21] but move no otherwise.

---

[15] A toy for children.   [16] Virgil, *Georgics*.   [17] One of the Eumenides.
[18] *Pilgrim's Progress*, part 1.   [19] Hosea 12:1.   [20] *Divine Comedy,* Inferno, canto 17.
[21] Ezekiel 1:15.

75. This being the real nature of capital, it follows that there are two kinds of true production, always going on in an active State: one of seed, and one of food; or production for the Ground, and for the Mouth; both of which are by covetous persons thought to be production only for the granary; whereas the function of the granary is but intermediate and conservative, fulfilled in distribution; else it ends in nothing but mildew, and nourishment of rats and worms. And since production for the Ground is only useful with future hope of harvest, all *essential* production is for the Mouth; and is finally measured by the mouth; hence, as I said above, consumption is the crown of production; and the wealth of a nation is only to be estimated by what it consumes.

The want of any clear sight of this fact is the capital error, issuing in rich interest and revenue of error among the political economists. Their minds are continually set on money-gain, not on mouth-gain; and they fall into every sort of net and snare, dazzled by the coin-glitter as birds by the fowler's glass; or rather (for there is not much else like birds in them) they are like children trying to jump on the heads of their own shadows; the money-gain being only the shadow of the true gain, which is humanity.

76. The final object of political economy, therefore, is to get good method of consumption, and great quantity of consumption: in other words, to use everything, and to use it nobly; whether it be substance, service, or service perfecting substance. The most curious error in Mr. Mill's entire work, (provided for him originally by Ricardo,) is his endeavour to distinguish between direct and indirect service, and consequent assertion that a demand for commodities is not demand for labour (I. v. 9, *et seq.*). He distinguishes between labourers employed to lay out pleasure grounds, and to manufacture velvet; declaring that it makes material difference to the labouring classes in which of these two ways a capitalist spends his money; because the employment of the gardeners is a demand for labour, but the purchase of velvet is not. Error colossal, as well as strange. It will, indeed, make a difference to the labourer whether we bid him swing his scythe in the spring winds, or drive the loom in pestilential air; but, so far as his pocket is concerned, it makes to him absolutely no difference whether we order him to make green velvet, with seed and a scythe, or red velvet, with silk and scissors. Neither does it anywise concern him whether, when the velvet is made, we consume it by walking on it, or wearing it, so long as our consumption of it is wholly selfish. But if our consumption is to be in anywise unselfish, not only our mode of consuming the articles we require interests him, but also the *kind* of article we require with a view to consumption. As thus (returning for a moment to Mr. Mill's great hardware theory) it matters, so far as the labourer's immediate profit is concerned, not an iron filing whether I employ him in growing a peach, or forging a bombshell; but my probable mode of consumption of those articles matters seriously. Admit that it is to be in both cases 'unselfish,'' and the difference, to him, is final, whether when his child is ill, I walk into his cottage and give it the peach or, drop the shell down his chimney, and blow his roof off.

The worst of it, for the peasant, is, that the capitalist's consumption of the peach is apt to be selfish, and of the shell, distributive; but, in all cases, this is the broad and general fact, that on due catallactic commercial principles, *somebody's* roof must go off in fulfilment of the bomb's destiny. You may grow for your neighbour, at your liking, grapes, or grape-shot; he will also catallactically, grow grapes or grape-shot for you, and you will each reap what you have sown.

77. It is, therefore, the manner and issue of consumption which are the real tests of production. Production does not consist in things laboriously made, but in things serviceably consumable; and the question for the nation is not how much labour it employs, but how much life it produces. For as consumption is the end and aim of production, so life is the end and aim of consumption.

I left this question to the reader's thought two months ago, choosing rather that he should work it out for himself than have it sharply stated to him. But now, the ground being sufficiently broken (and the details into which the several questions, here opened, must lead us, being too complex for discussion in the pages of a periodical, so that I must pursue them elsewhere), I desire, in closing the series of introductory papers, to leave this one great fact clearly stated. THERE IS NO WEALTH BUT LIFE. Life, including all its powers of love, of joy, and of admiration. That country is the richest which nourishes the greatest number of noble and happy human beings; that man is richest who, having perfected the functions of his own life to the utmost, has also the widest helpful influence, both personal, and by means of his possessions, over the lives of others.

A strange political economy; the only one, nevertheless, that ever was or can be: all political economy founded on self-interest being but the fulfilment of that which once brought schism into the Policy of angels, and ruin into the Economy of Heaven.

78. "The greatest number of human beings noble and happy." But is the nobleness consistent with the number? Yes, not only consistent with it, but essential to it. The maximum of life can only be reached by the maximum of virtue. In this respect the law of human population differs wholly from that of animal life. The multiplication of animals is checked only by want of food, and by the hostility of races; the population of the gnat is restrained by the hunger of the swallow, and that of the swallow by the scarcity of gnats. Man, considered as an animal, is indeed limited by the same laws: hunger, or plague, or war, are the necessary and only restraints upon his increase,—effectual restraints hitherto,—his principal study having been how most swiftly to destroy himself, or ravage his dwelling-places, and his highest skill directed to give range to the famine, seed to the plague, and sway to the sword. But, considered as other than an animal, his increase is not limited by these laws. It is limited only by the limits of his courage and his love. Both of these *have* their bounds; and ought to have; his race has its bounds also; but these have not yet been reached, nor will be reached for ages.

79. In all the ranges of human thought I know none so melancholy as the speculations of political economists on the population question. It is proposed to better the condition of the labourer by giving him higher wages. "Nay," says the economist,—"if you raise his wages, he will either people down to the same point of misery at which you found him, or drink your wages away." He will. I know it. Who gave him this will? Suppose it were your own son of whom you spoke, declaring to me that you dared not take him into your firm, nor even give him his just labourer's wages, because if you did he would die of drunkenness, and leave half a score of children to the parish. "Who gave your son these dispositions?"—I should enquire. Has he them by inheritance or by education? By one or other they *must* come; and as in him, so also in the poor. Either these poor are of a race essentially different from ours, and unredeemable (which, however often implied, I have heard none yet openly say),

or else by such care as we have ourselves received, we may make them continent and sober as ourselves—wise and dispassionate as we are—models arduous of imitation. "But," it is answered, "they cannot receive education." Why not? That is precisely the point at issue. Charitable persons suppose the worst fault of the rich is to refuse the people meat; and the people cry for their meat, kept back by fraud, to the Lord of Multitudes.[22] Alas! it is not meat of which the refusal is cruelest, or to which the claim is validest. The life is more than the meat.[23] The rich not only refuse food to the poor; they refuse wisdom; they refuse virtue; they refuse salvation. Ye sheep without shepherd, it is not the pasture that has been shut from you, but the Presence. Meat! perhaps your right to that may be pleadable; but other rights have to be pleaded first. Claim your crumbs from the table if you will; but claim them as children, not as dogs; claim your right to be fed, but claim more loudly your right to be holy, perfect, and pure.

Strange words to be used of working people! "What! holy; without any long robes or anointing oils; these rough-jacketed, rough-worded persons; set to nameless, dishonoured service? Perfect!—these, with dim eyes and cramped limbs, and slowly wakening minds? Pure!—these, with sensual desire and grovelling thought; foul of body and coarse of soul?" It may be so; nevertheless, such as they are, they are the holiest, perfectest, purest persons the earth can at present show. They may be what you have said; but if so, they yet are holier than we who have left them thus.

But what can be done for them? Who can clothe—who teach—who restrain their multitudes? What end can there be for them at last, but to consume one another?

I hope for another end, though not, indeed, from any of the three remedies for over-population commmonly suggested by economists.

80. These three are, in brief—Colonization; Bringing in of waste lands; or Discouragement of Marriage.

The first and second of these expedients merely evade or delay the question. It will, indeed, be long before the world has been all colonized, and its deserts all brought under cultivation. But the radical question is, not how much habitable land is in the world, but how many human beings ought to be maintained on a given space of habitable land.

---

[22] James 5:4.   [23] Matthew 6:25.

Observe, I say, *ought* to be, not how many *can* be. Ricardo, with his usual inaccuracy, defines what he calls the "natural rate of wages" as "that which will maintain the labourer." Maintain him! yes; but how?—the question was instantly thus asked of me by a working girl, to whom I read the passage. I will amplify her question for her. "Maintain him, how?" As, first, to what length of life? Out of a given number of fed persons, how many are to be old—how many young? that is to say, will you arrange their maintenance so as to kill them early—say at thirty or thirty-five on the average, including deaths of weakly or ill-fed children?—or so as to enable them to live out a natural life? You will feed a greater number, in the first case, by rapidity of succession; probably a happier number in the second: which does Mr. Ricardo mean to be their natural state, and to which state belongs the natural rate of wages?

Again: A piece of land which will only support ten idle, ignorant, and improvident persons, will support thirty or forty intelligent and industrious ones. Which of these is their natural state, and to which of them belongs the natural rate of wages?

Again: If a piece of land support forty persons in industrious ignorance; and if, tired of this ignorance, they set apart ten of their number to study the properties of cones, and the sizes of stars; the labour of these ten being withdrawn from the ground, must either tend to the increase of food in some transitional manner, or the persons set apart for sidereal and conic purposes must starve, or some one else starve instead of them. What is, therefore, the natural rate of wages of the scientific persons, and how does this rate relate to, or measure, their reverted or transitional productiveness?

Again: If the ground maintains, at first, forty labourers in a peaceable and pious state of mind, but they become in a few years so quarrelsome and impious that they have to set apart five, to meditate upon and settle their disputes;—ten, armed to the teeth with costly instruments, to enforce the decisions; and five to remind everybody in an eloquent manner of the existence of God;—what will be the result upon the general power of production, and what is the "natural rate of wages" of the meditative, muscular, and oracular labourers?

81. Leaving these questions to be discussed, or waived, at their pleasure, by Mr. Ricardo's followers, I proceed to state the main facts bearing on that probable future of the labouring classes which has been partially glanced at by

Mr. Mill. That chapter and the preceding one differ from the common writing of political economists in admitting some value in the aspect of nature, and expressing regret at the probability of the destruction of natural scenery. But we may spare our anxieties on this head. Men can neither drink steam, nor eat stone. The maximum of population on a given space of land implies also the relative maximum of edible vegetable, whether for men or cattle; it implies a maximum of pure air, and of pure water. Therefore: a maximum of wood, to transmute the air, and of sloping ground, protected by herbage from the extreme heat of the sun, to feed the streams. All England may, if it so chooses, become one manufacturing town; and Englishmen, sacrificing themselves to the good of general humanity, may live diminished lives in the midst of noise, of darkness, and of deadly exhalation. But the world cannot become a factory nor a mine. No amount of ingenuity will ever make iron digestible by the million, nor substitute hydrogen for wine. Neither the avarice nor the rage of men will ever feed them; and however the apple of Sodom and the grape of Gomorrah may spread their table for a time with dainties of ashes, and nectar of asps,—so long as men live by bread, the far away valleys must laugh as they are covered with the gold of God, and the shouts of His happy multitudes ring round the winepress and the well.

82. Nor need our more sentimental economists fear the too wide spread of the formalities of a mechanical agriculture. The presence of a wise population implies the search for felicity as well as for food; nor can any population reach its maximum but through that wisdom which "rejoices" in the habitable parts of the earth. The desert has its appointed place and work; the eternal engine, whose beam is the earth's axle, whose beat is its year, and whose breath is its ocean, will still divide imperiously to their desert kingdoms bound with unfurrowable rock, and swept by unarrested sand, their powers of frost and fire: but the zones and lands between, habitable, will be loveliest in habitation. The desire of the heart is also the light of the eyes. No scene is continually and untiringly loved, but one rich by joyful human labour; smooth in field; fair in garden; full in orchard; trim, sweet, and frequent in homestead; ringing with voices of vivid existence. No air is sweet that is silent; it is only sweet when full of low currents of under sound—triplets of birds, and murmur and chirp of insects, and deep-toned words of men, and wayward trebles of childhood. As the art of life

is learned, it will be found at last that all lovely things are also necessary:—the wild flower by the wayside, as well as the tended corn; and the wild birds and creatures of the forest, as well as the tended cattle; because man doth not live by bread only[24] but also by the desert manna; by every wondrous word and unknowable work of God. Happy, in that he knew them not, nor did his fathers know; and that round about him reaches yet into the infinite, the amazement of his existence.

83. Note, finally, that all effectual advancement towards this true felicity of the human race must be by individual, not public effort. Certain general measures may aid, certain revised laws guide, such advancement; but the measure and law which have first to be determined are those of each man's home. We continually hear it recommended by sagacious people to complaining neighbours (usually less well placed in the world than themselves), that they should "remain content in the station in which Providence has placed them." There are perhaps some circumstances of life in which Providence has no intention that people *should* be content. Nevertheless, the maxim is on the whole a good one; but it is peculiarly for home use. That your neighbour should, or should not, remain content with *his* position, is not your business; but it is very much your business to remain content with your own. What is chiefly needed in England at the present day is to show the quantity of pleasure that may be obtained by a consistent, well-administered competence, modest, confessed, and laborious. We need examples of people who, leaving Heaven to decide whether they are to rise in the world, decide for themselves that they will be happy in it, and have resolved to seek—not greater wealth, but simpler pleasure; not higher fortune, but deeper felicity; making the first of possessions, self-possession; and honouring themselves in the harmless pride and calm pursuits of peace.

Of which lowly peace it is written that "justice and peace have kissed each other"; and that the fruit of justice is "sown in peace of them that make peace";[25] not "peace-makers" in the common understanding—reconcilers of quarrels; (though that function also follows on the greater one;) but peace-Creators; Givers of Calm. Which you cannot give, unless you first gain; nor is this gain one which will follow assuredly on any course of business, commonly so called.

No form of gain is less probable, business being (as is shown in the language of all nations—πωλεῖν from πέλω, πρᾶρις from περάω, venire, vendre, and venal, from venio, etc.) essentially restless—and probably contentious;—having a raven-like mind to the motion to and fro, as to the carrion food; whereas the olive-feeding and bearing birds look for rest for their feet; thus it is said of Wisdom that she "hath builded her house, and hewn out her seven pillars";[26] and even when, though apt to wait long at the doorposts, she has to leave her house and go abroad, her paths are peace also.

84. For us, at all events, her work must begin at the entry of the doors: all true economy is "Law of the house." Strive to make that law strict, simple, generous: waste nothing, and grudge nothing. Care in no-wise to make more of money, but care to make much of it; remembering always the great, palpable, inevitable fact—the rule and root of all economy—that what one person has, another cannot have; and that every atom of substance, of whatever kind, used or consumed, is so much human life spent; which, if it issue in the saving present life, or gaining more, is well spent, but if not is either so much life prevented, or so much slain. In all buying, consider, first, what condition of existence you cause in the producers of what you buy; secondly, whether the sum you have paid is just to the producer, and in due proportion, lodged in his hands; thirdly, to how much clear use, for food, knowledge, or joy, this that you have bought can be put; and fourthly, to whom and in what way it can be most speedily and serviceably distributed; in all dealings whatsoever insisting on entire openness and stern fulfilment; and in all doings on perfection and loveliness of accomplishment; especially on fineness and purity of all marketable commodity: watching at the same time for all ways of gaining, or teaching, powers of simple pleasure; and of showing "ὅσον ἐν ἀσφοδέλῳ μέγ ὄνειαρ"[27]—the sum of enjoyment depending not on the quantity of things tasted, but on the vivacity and patience of taste.

85. And if, on due and honest thought over these things, it seems that the kind of existence to which men are now summoned by every plea of pity and claim of right, may, for some time at least, not be a luxurious one;—consider whether, even supposing it guiltless, luxury would be desired by any of us, if we saw clearly at our sides the suffering which accompanies

---

[24] Deuteronomy 8:3.   [25] Psalms 85:10.   [26] Proverbs 9:1.   [27] Hesiod, *Works and Days.*

it in the world. Luxury is indeed possible in the future—innocent and exquisite; luxury for all, and by the help of all; but luxury at present can only be enjoyed by the ignorant; the cruelest man living could not sit at his feast, unless he sat blindfold. Raise the veil boldly; face the light, and if, as yet, the light of the eye can only be through tears, and the light of the body through sackcloth, go thou forth weeping, bearing precious seed, until the time come, and the kingdom, when Christ's gift of bread, and bequest of peace, shall be "Unto this last as unto thee",[28] and when, for earth's severed multitudes of the wicked and the weary, there shall be holier reconciliation than that of the narrow home, and calm economy, where the Wicked cease—not from trouble, but from troubling—and the Weary are at rest.[29]

from Sesame and Lilies

Originally a series of lectures to young ladies instructing them on their duties and opportunities in a manner that strikes some modern readers as excessively Victorian, Sesame and Lilies *nevertheless contains some of Ruskin's most moving tributes to the glories of literature. It was published in 1865. "The Mystery of Life and Its Arts" is an essay delivered in 1868 in Dublin during a time of acute difficulties over Rose La Touche. It was later published with* Sesame and Lilies, *then suppressed by Ruskin for what seemed to him signs of religious uncertainty in it, then subsequently regularly included in editions of* Sesame and Lilies. *Whatever the case regarding the religious questions, the essay has proved to be one of Ruskin's most enduring and one of the most beautiful of all his writings.*

LECTURE III

The Mystery of Life and Its Arts

WHEN I accepted the privilege of addressing you today, I was not aware of a restriction with respect to the topics of discussion which may be brought before this Society[1]—a restriction which, though entirely wise and right under the circumstances contemplated in its introduction, would necessarily have disabled me, thinking as I think, from preparing any lecture for you on the subject of art in a form which might be permanently useful. Pardon me, therefore, in so far as I must transgress such limitation; for indeed my infringement will be of the letter—not of the spirit—of your commands. In whatever I may say touching the religion which has been the foundation of art, or the policy which has contributed to its power, if I offend one, I shall offend all; for I shall take no note of any separations in creeds, or antag-onisms in parties: neither do I fear that ultimately I shall offend any, by proving—or at least stating as capable of positive proof—the connection of all that is best in the crafts and arts of man, with the simplicity of his faith, and the sincerity of his patriotism.

But I speak to you under another disadvantage, by which I am checked in frankness of utterance, not here only, but everywhere: namely, that I am never fully aware how far my audiences are disposed to give me credit for real knowledge of my subject, or how far they grant me attention only because I have been sometimes thought an ingenious or pleasant essayist upon it. For I have had what, in many respects, I boldly call the misfortune, to set my words sometimes prettily together; not without a foolish vanity in the poor knack that I had of doing so: until I was heavily punished for this pride, by finding that many people thought of the words only, and cared nothing for their meaning. Happily, therefore, the power of using such pleasant language—if indeed it ever were mine—is passing away from me; and whatever I am now able to say at all,

[28] Matthew 20:14.   [29] Job 3:17.
[1] That no reference should be made to religious questions. [Ruskin's note]

I find myself forced to say with great plainness. For my thoughts have changed also, as my words have; and whereas in earlier life, what little influence I obtained was due perhaps chiefly to the enthusiasm with which I was able to dwell on the beauty of the physical clouds, and of their colours in the sky; so all the influence I now desire to retain must be due to the earnestness with which I am endeavouring to trace the form and beauty of another kind of cloud than those; the bright cloud of which it is written—"What is your life? It is even as a vapour that appeareth for a little time, and then vanisheth away."[2]

I suppose few people reach the middle or latter period of their age, without having, at some moment of change or disappointment, felt the truth of those bitter words; and been startled by the fading of the sunshine from the cloud of their life into the sudden agony of the knowledge that the fabric of it was as fragile as a dream, and the endurance of it as transient as the dew. But it is not always that, even at such times of melancholy surprise, we can enter into any true perception that this human life shares in the nature of it, not only the evanescence, but the mystery of the cloud; that its avenues are wreathed in darkness, and its forms and courses no less fantastic, than spectral and obscure; so that not only in the vanity which we cannot grasp, but in the shadow which we cannot pierce, it is true of this cloudy life of ours, that "man walketh in a vain shadow, and disquieteth himself in vain."[3]

And least of all, whatever may have been the eagerness of our passions, or the height of our pride, are we able to understand in its depth the third and most solemn character in which our life is like those clouds of heaven; that to it belongs not only their transience, not only their mystery, but also their power; that in the cloud of the human soul there is a fire stronger than the lightning, and a grace more precious than the rain; and that though of the good and evil it shall one day be said alike, that the place that knew them knows them no more, there is an infinite separation between those whose brief presence had there been a blessing, like the mist of Eden that went up from the earth to water the garden,[4] and those whose place knew them only as a drifting and changeful shade, of whom the heavenly sentence is, that they are "wells without water; clouds that are carried with a tempest, to whom the mist of darkness is reserved for ever."[5]

To those among us, however, who have lived long enough to form some just estimate of the rate of the changes which are, hour by hour in accelerating catastrophe, manifesting themselves in the laws, the arts, and the creeds of men, it seems to me, that now at least, if never at any former time, the thoughts of the true nature of our life, and of its powers and responsibilities, should present themselves with absolute sadness and sternness. And although I know that this feeling is much deepened in my own mind by disappointment, which, by chance, has attended the greater number of my cherished purposes, I do not for that reason distrust the feeling itself, though I am on my guard against an exaggerated degree of it: nay, I rather believe that in periods of new effort and violent change, disappointment is a wholesome medicine; and that in the secret of it, as in the twilight so beloved by Titian, we may see the colours of things with deeper truth than in the most dazzling sunshine. And because these truths about the works of men, which I want to bring to-day before you, are most of them sad ones, though at the same time helpful; and because also I believe that your kind Irish hearts will answer more gladly to the truthful expression of a personal feeling, than to the exposition of an abstract principle, I will permit myself so much unreserved speaking of my own causes of regret, as may enable you to make just allowance for what, according to your sympathies, you will call either the bitterness, or the insight, of a mind which has surrendered its best hopes, and been foiled in its favourite aims.

I spent the ten strongest years of my life, (from twenty to thirty,) in endeavouring to show the excellence of the work of the man whom I believed, and rightly believed, to be the greatest painter of the schools of England since Reynolds. I had then perfect faith in the power of every great truth of beauty to prevail ultimately, and take its right place in usefulness and honour; and I strove to bring the painter's work into this due place, while the painter was yet alive. But he knew, better than I, the uselessness of talking about what people could not see for themselves. He always discouraged me scornfully, even when he thanked me—and he died before even the superficial effect of my work was visible. I went on, however, thinking I could at least be of use to the public, if not to him, in proving his power. My books got talked about a little. The prices of modern pictures, generally, rose, and I was

[2] James 4:14.   [3] Psalms 39:7.   [4] Genesis 2:6.   [5] II Peter 2:17.

beginning to take some pleasure in a sense of gradual victory, when, fortunately or unfortunately, an opportunity of perfect trial undeceived me at once, and for ever. The Trustees of the National Gallery commissioned me to arrange the Turner drawings there, and permitted me to prepare three hundred examples of his studies from nature, for exhibition at Kensington. At Kensington they were, and are, placed for exhibition; but they are not exhibited, for the room in which they hang is always empty.

Well—this showed me at once, that those ten years of my life had been, in their chief purpose, lost. For that, I did not so much care; I had, at least, learned my own business thoroughly, and should be able, as I fondly supposed, after such a lesson, now to use my knowledge, with better effect. But what I did care for was the—to me frightful—discovery, that the most splendid genius in the arts might be permitted by Providence to labour and perish uselessly; that in the very fineness of it there might be something rendering it invisible to ordinary eyes; but that, with this strange excellence, faults might be mingled which would be as deadly as its virtues were vain; that the glory of it was perishable, as well as invisible, and the gift and grace of it might be to us as snow in summer and as rain in harvest.

That was the first mystery of life to me. But, while my best energy was given to the study of painting, I had put collateral effort, more prudent if less enthusiastic, into that of architecture; and in this I could not complain of meeting with no sympathy. Among several personal reasons which caused me to desire that I might give this, my closing lecture on the subject of art here, in Ireland, one of the chief was, that in reading it, I should stand near the beautiful building,—the engineer's school of your college,— which was the first realization I had the joy to see, of the principles I had, until then, been endeavouring to teach! but which, alas, is now, to me, no more than the richly canopied monument of one of the most earnest souls that ever gave itself to the arts, and one of my truest and most loving friends, Benjamin Woodward.[6] Nor was it here in Ireland only that I received the help of Irish sympathy and genius. When to another friend, Sir Thomas Deane,[7] with Mr. Woodward, was entrusted the building of the museum at Oxford, the best details of the work

were executed by sculptors who had been born and trained here; and the first window of the façade of the building, in which was inaugurated the study of natural science in England, in true fellowship with literature, was carved from my design by an Irish sculptor.

You may perhaps think that no man ought to speak of disappointment, to whom, even in one branch of labour, so much success was granted. Had Mr. Woodward now been beside me, I had not so spoken; but his gentle and passionate spirit was cut off from the fulfilment of its purposes, and the work we did together is now become vain. It may not be so in future; but the architecture we endeavoured to introduce is inconsistent alike with the reckless luxury, the deforming mechanism, and the squalid misery of modern cities; among the formative fashions of the day, aided, especially in England, by ecclesiastical sentiment, it indeed obtained notoriety; and sometimes behind an engine furnace, or a railroad bank, you may detect the pathetic discord of its momentary grace, and, with toil, decipher its floral carvings choked with soot. I felt answerable to the schools I loved, only for their injury. I perceived that this new portion of my strength had also been spent in vain; and from amidst streets of iron, and palaces of crystal,[8] shrank back at last to the carving of the mountain and colour of the flower.

And still I could tell of failure, and failure repeated, as years went on; but I have trespassed enough on your patience to show you, in part, the causes of my discouragement. Now let me more deliberately tell you its results. You know there is a tendency in the minds of many men, when they are heavily disappointed in the main purposes of their life, to feel, and perhaps in warning, perhaps in mockery, to declare, that life itself is a vanity. Because it has disappointed them, they think its nature is of disappointment always, or at best, of pleasure that can be grasped by imagination only; that the cloud of it has no strength nor fire within; but is a painted cloud only, to be delighted in, yet despised. You know how beautifully Pope has expressed this particular phase of thought:—

> "Meanwhile opinion gilds, with varying rays,
> These painted clouds that beautify our days;
> Each want of happiness by hope supplied,
> And each vacuity of sense, by pride.

[6] Benjamin Woodward (1815–61), architect and friend of the Pre-Raphaelites.
[7] Sir Thomas Deane (1792–1871), architect and builder in Cork.
[8] Reference to the Crystal Palace. See Ruskin's essay on the subject in this volume.

Hope builds as fast as Knowledge can destroy;
In Folly's cup, still laughs the bubble joy.
One pleasure past, another still we gain,
And not a vanity is given in vain."[9]

But the effect of failure upon my own mind has been just the reverse of this. The more that my life disappointed me, the more solemn and wonderful it became to me. It seemed, contrarily to Pope's saying, that the vanity of it *was* indeed given in vain; but that there was something behind the veil of it, which was not vanity. It became to me not a painted cloud, but a terrible and impenetrable one: not a mirage, which vanished as I drew near, but a pillar of darkness, to which I was forbidden to draw near. For I saw that both my own failure, and such success in petty things as in its poor triumph seemed to me worse than failure, came from the want of sufficiently earnest effort to understand the whole law and meaning of existence, and to bring it to noble and due end; as, on the other hand, I saw more and more clearly that all enduring success in the arts, or in any other occupation, had come from the ruling of lower purposes, not by a conviction of their nothingness, but by a solemn faith in the advancing power of human nature, or in the promise, however dimly apprehended, that the mortal part of it would one day be swallowed up in immortality; and that, indeed, the arts themselves never had reached any vital strength or honour, but in the effort to proclaim this immortality, and in the service either of great and just religion, or of some unselfish patriotism, and law of such national life as must be the foundation of religion.

Nothing that I have ever said is more true or necessary—nothing has been more misunderstood or misapplied—than my strong assertion that the arts can never be right themselves, unless their motive is right. It is misunderstood this way: weak painters, who have never learned their business, and cannot lay a true line, continually come to me, crying out—"Look at this picture of mine; it *must* be good, I had such a lovely motive. I have put my whole heart into it, and taken years to think over its treatment." Well, the only answer for these people is—if one had the cruelty to make it—"Sir, you cannot think over *any*thing in any number of years,—you haven't the head to do it; and though you had fine motives, strong enough to make you burn yourself in a slow fire, if only first you could

paint a picture, you can't paint one, nor half an inch of one; you haven't the hand to do it."

But, far more decisively we have to say to the men who *do* know their business, or may know it if they choose—"Sir, you have this gift, and a mighty one; see that you serve your nation faithfully with it. It is a greater trust than ships and armies: you might cast *them* away, if you were their captain, with less treason to your people than in casting your own glorious power away, and serving the devil with it instead of men. Ships and armies you may replace if they are lost, but a great intellect, once abused, is a curse to the earth for ever."

This, then, I meant by saying that the arts must have noble motive. This also I said respecting them, that they never had prospered, nor could prosper, but when they had such true purpose, and were devoted to the proclamation of divine truth or law. And yet I saw also that they had always failed in this proclamation— that poetry, and sculpture, and painting, though only great when they strove to teach us something about the gods, never had taught us anything trustworthy about the gods, but had always betrayed their trust in the crisis of it, and, with their powers at the full reach, became ministers to pride and to lust. And I felt also, with increasing amazement, the unconquerable apathy in ourselves and hearers, no less than in these the teachers; and that while the wisdom and rightness of every act and art of life could only be consistent with a right understanding of the ends of life, we were all plunged as in a languid dream —our hearts fat, and our eyes heavy, and our ears closed, lest the inspiration of hand or voice should reach us—lest we should see with our eyes, and understand with our hearts, and be healed.[10]

This intense apathy in all of us is the first great mystery of life; it stands in the way of every perception, every virtue. There is no making ourselves feel enough astonishment at it. That the occupations or pastimes of life should have no motive, is understandable; but—That life itself should have no motive—that we neither care to find out what it may lead to, nor to guard against its being for ever taken away from us— here is a mystery indeed. For just suppose I were able to call at this moment to any one in this audience by name, and to tell him positively that I knew a large estate had been lately left to him on some curious conditions; but that

[9] Pope's *Essay on Man*, II, 283–90.
[10] Isaiah 6:10.

though I knew it was large, I did not know how large, nor even where it was—whether in the East Indies or the West, or in England, or at the Antipodes. I only knew it was a vast estate, and that there was a chance of his losing it altogether if he did not soon find out on what terms it had been left to him. Suppose I were able to say this positively to any single man in this audience, and he knew that I did not speak without warrant, do you think that he would rest content with that vague knowledge, if it were anywise possible to obtain more? Would he not give every energy to find some trace of the facts, and never rest till he had ascertained where this place was, and what it was like? And suppose he were a young man, and all he could discover by his best endeavour was that the estate was never to be his at all, unless he persevered, during certain years of probation, in an orderly and industrious life; but that, according to the rightness of his conduct, the portion of the estate assigned to him would be greater or less, so that it literally depended on his behaviour from day to day whether he got ten thousand a year, or thirty thousand a year, or nothing whatever—would you not think it strange if the youth never troubled himself to satisfy the conditions in any way, nor even to know what was required of him, but lived exactly as he chose, and never inquired whether his chances of the estate were increasing or passing away? Well, you know that this is actually and literally so with the greater number of the educated persons now living in Christian countries. Nearly every man and woman in any company such as this, outwardly professes to believe—and a large number unquestionably think they believe—much more than this; not only that a quite unlimited estate is in prospect for them if they please the Holder of it, but that the infinite contrary of such a possession—an estate of perpetual misery—is in store for them if they displease this great Land-Holder, this great Heaven-Holder. And yet there is not one in a thousand of these human souls that cares to think, for ten minutes of the day, where this estate is or how beautiful it is, or what kind of life they are to lead in it, or what kind of life they must lead to obtain it.

You fancy that you care to know this: so little do you care that, probably, at this moment many of you are displeased with me for talking of the matter! You came to hear about the Art of this world, not about the Life of the next, and you are provoked with me for talking of what you can hear any Sunday in church. But do not be afraid. I will tell you something before you go about pictures, and carvings, and pottery, and what else you would like better to hear of than the other world. Nay, perhaps you say, "We want you to talk of pictures and pottery, because we are sure that you know something of them, and you know nothing of the other world." Well —I don't. That is quite true. But the very strangeness and mystery of which I urge you to take notice, is in this—that I do not;—nor you either. Can you answer a single bold question unflinchingly about that other world?—Are you sure there is a heaven? Sure there is a hell? Sure that men are dropping before your faces through the pavements of these streets into eternal fire, or sure that they are not? Sure that at your own death you are going to be delivered from all sorrow, to be endowed with all virtue, to be gifted with all felicity, and raised into perpetual companionship with a King, compared to whom the kings of the earth are as grasshoppers, and the nations as the dust of His feet?[11] Are you sure of this? or, if not sure, do any of us so much as care to make it sure? and, if not, how can anything that we do be right—how can anything we think be wise? what honour can there be in the arts that amuse us, or what profit in the possessions that please?

Is not this a mystery of life?

But farther, you may, perhaps, think it a beneficent ordinance for the generality of men that they do not, with earnestness or anxiety, dwell on such questions of the future because the business of the day could not be done if this kind of thought were taken by all of us for the morrow. Be it so: but at least we might anticipate that the greatest and wisest of us, who were evidently the appointed teachers of the rest, would set themselves apart to seek out whatever could be surely known of the future destinies of their race; and to teach this in no rhetorical or ambiguous manner, but in the plainest and most severely earnest words.

Now, the highest representatives of men who have thus endeavoured, during the Christian era, to search out these deep things, and relate them, are Dante and Milton. There are none who for earnestness of thought, for mastery of word, can be classed with these. I am not at present, mind you, speaking of persons set apart in any priestly or pastoral office, to deliver creeds to us, or doctrines; but of men who try to discover and set forth, as far as by human intellect is possible, the facts of the other world. Divines may perhaps teach us how to arrive there, but only these two poets have in any powerful manner striven to discover, or in any definite words professed to tell, what we shall see and become there; or how those upper and nether worlds are, and have been, inhabited.

And what have they told us? Milton's account of the most important event in his whole system of the universe, the fall of the angels, is evidently unbelievable to himself; and the more so, that it is wholly founded on, and in a great part spoiled and degraded from, Hesiod's account of the decisive war of the younger gods with the Titans.[12] The rest of his poem is a picturesque drama, in which every artifice of invention is visibly and consciously employed; not a single fact being, for an instant, conceived as tenable by any living faith. Dante's conception is far more intense, and, by himself, for the time, not to be escaped from; it is indeed a vision, but a vision only, and that one of the wildest that ever entranced a soul—a dream in which every grotesque type or phantasy of heathen tradition is renewed, and adorned; and the destinies of the Christian Church, under their most sacred symbols, become literally subordinate to the praise, and are only to be understood by the aid, of one dear Florentine maiden.

I tell you truly that, as I strive more with this strange lethargy and trance in myself, and awake to the meaning and power of life, it seems daily more amazing to me that men such as these should dare to play with the most precious truths, (or the most deadly untruths,) by which the whole human race listening to them could be informed, or deceived;—all the world their audiences for ever, with pleased ear, and passionate heart;—and yet, to this submissive infinitude of souls, and evermore succeeding and succeeding multitude, hungry for bread of life, they do but play upon sweetly modulated pipes; with pompous nomenclature adorn the councils of hell; touch a troubadour's guitar to the courses of the suns; and fill the openings of eternity, before which prophets have veiled their faces, and which angels desire to look into,[13] with idle puppets of their scholastic imagination, and melancholy lights of frantic faith in their lost mortal love.

Is not this a mystery of life?

But more. We have to remember that these two great teachers were both of them warped in their temper, and thwarted in their search for truth. They were men of intellectual war, unable, through darkness of controversy, or stress of personal grief, to discern where their own ambition modified their utterances of the moral law; or their own agony mingled with their anger at its violation. But greater men than these have been—innocent-hearted—too great for contest. Men, like Homer and Shakespeare, of so unrecognized personality, that it disappears in future ages, and becomes ghostly, like the tradition of a lost heathen god. Men, therefore, to whose unoffended, uncondemning sight, the whole of human nature reveals itself in a pathetic weakness, with which they will not strive; or in mournful and transitory strength, which they dare not praise. And all Pagan and Christian Civilization thus becomes subject to them. It does not matter how little, or how much, any of us have read, either of Homer or Shakespeare; everything round us, in substance, or in thought, has been moulded by them. All Greek gentlemen were educated under Homer. All Roman gentlemen, by Greek literature. All Italian, and French, and English gentlemen, by Roman literature, and by its principles. Of the scope of Shakespeare, I will say only, that the intellectual measure of every man since born, in the domains of creative thought, may be assigned to him, according to the degree in which he has been taught by Shakespeare. Well, what do these two men, centres of mortal intelligence, deliver to us of conviction respecting what it most behoves that intelligence to grasp? What is their hope—their crown of rejoicing?[14] what manner of exhortation have they for us, or of rebuke? what lies next their own hearts, and dictates their undying words? Have they any peace to promise to our unrest—any redemption to our misery?

Take Homer first, and think if there is any sadder image of human fate than the great Homeric story. The main features in the character of Achilles are its intense desire of justice, and its tenderness of affection. And in that bitter song of the *Iliad*, this man, though aided continually by the wisest of the gods, and burning with the desire of justice in his heart, becomes yet, through ill-governed passion, the most unjust of men: and, full of the deepest tenderness

---

[12] Hesiod's *Theogony*. [13] Isaiah 6:2; I Peter 1:12. [14] I Thessalonians 2:19.

in his heart, becomes yet, through ill-governed passion, the most cruel of men. Intense alike in love and in friendship, he loses, first his mistress, and then his friend; for the sake of the one, he surrenders to death the armies of his own land; for the sake of the other, he surrenders all. Will a man lay down his life for his friend?[15] Yea—even for his *dead* friend, this Achilles, though goddess-born, and goddess-taught, gives up his kingdom, his country, and his life—casts alike the innocent and guilty, with himself, into one gulf of slaughter, and dies at last by the hand of the basest of his adversaries.

Is not this a mystery of life?

But what, then, is the message to us of our own poet, and searcher of hearts, after fifteen hundred years of Christian faith have been numbered over the graves of men? Are his words more cheerful than the Heathen's—is his hope more near—his trust more sure—his reading of fate more happy? Ah, no! He differs from the Heathen poet chiefly in this—that he recognizes, for deliverance, no gods nigh at hand; and that, by petty chance—by momentary folly—by broken message—by fool's tyranny—or traitor's snare, the strongest and most righteous are brought to their ruin, and perish without word of hope. He indeed, as part of his rendering of character, ascribes the power and modesty of habitual devotion to the gentle and the just. The death-bed of Katharine is bright with visions of angels; and the great soldier-king, standing by his few dead,[16] acknowledges the presence of the Hand that can save alike by many or by few.[17] But observe that from those who with deepest spirit, meditate, and with deepest passion, mourn, there are no such words as these; nor in their hearts are any such consolations. Instead of the perpetual sense of the helpful presence of the Deity, which, through all heathen tradition, is the source of heroic strength, in battle, in exile, and in the valley of the shadow of death,[18] we find only in the great Christian poet, the consciousness of a moral law, through which "the gods are just, and of our pleasant vices make instruments to scourge us";[19] and of the resolved arbitration of the destinies, that conclude into precision of doom what we feebly and blindly began; and force us, when our indiscretion serves us, and our deepest plots do pall, to the confession, that "there's a divinity that shapes our ends, rough hew them how we will."[20]

Is not this a mystery of life?

Be it so, then. About this human life that is to be, or that is, the wise religious men tell us nothing that we can trust; and the wise contemplative men, nothing that can give us peace. But there is yet a third class, to whom we may turn—the wise practical men. We have sat at the feet of the poets who sang of heaven, and they have told us their dreams. We have listened to the poets who sang of earth, and they have chanted to us dirges and words of despair. But there is one class of men more:—men, not capable of vision, nor sensitive to sorrow, but firm of purpose—practised in business; learned in all that can be, (by handling,) known. Men, whose hearts and hopes are wholly in this present world, from whom, therefore, we may surely learn, at least, how, at present, conveniently to live in it. What will *they* say to us, or show us by example? These kings—these councillors—these statesmen and builders of kingdoms—these capitalists and men of business, who weigh the earth, and the dust of it, in a balance.[21] They know the world, surely; and what is the mystery of life to us, is none to them. They can surely show us how to live, while we live, and to gather out of the present world what is best.

I think I can best tell you their answer, by telling you a dream I had once. For though I am no poet, I have dreams sometimes:—I dreamed I was at a child's May-day party, in which every means of entertainment had been provided for them, by a wise and kind host. It was in a stately house, with beautiful gardens attached to it; and the children had been set free in the rooms and gardens, with no care whatever but how to pass their afternoon rejoicingly. They did not, indeed, know much about what was to happen next day; and some of them, I thought, were a little frightened, because there was a chance of their being sent to a new school where there were examinations; but they kept the thoughts of that out of their heads as well as they could, and resolved to enjoy themselves. The house, I said, was in a beautiful garden, and in the garden were all kinds of flowers; sweet, grassy banks for rest; and smooth lawns for play; and pleasant streams and woods; and rocky places for climbing. And the children were happy for a little while, but presently they separated themselves into parties; and then each party declared it would have a

---

[15] John 13:15.   [16] *Henry V*, IV, viii.   [17] I Samuel 14:6.   [18] Psalms 23:4.
[19] *King Lear*, V, iii, 170–71.   [20] *Hamlet*, V, ii, 7–10.   [21] Isaiah, 40:12.

piece of the garden for its own, and that none of the others should have anything to do with that piece. Next, they quarrelled violently which pieces they would have; and at last the boys took up the thing, as boys should do, "practically," and fought in the flower-beds till there was hardly a flower left standing; then they trampled down each other's bits of the garden out of spite; and the girls cried till they could cry no more; and so they all lay down at last breathless in the ruin, and waited for the time when they were to be taken home in the evening.[22]

Meanwhile, the children in the house had been making themselves happy also in their manner. For them, there had been provided every kind of indoor pleasure: there was music for them to dance to; and the library was open, with all manner of amusing books; and there was a museum full of the most curious shells, and animals, and birds; and there was a workshop, with lathes and carpenter's tools, for the ingenious boys; and there were pretty fantastic dresses, for the girls to dress in; and there were microscopes, and kaleidoscopes; and whatever toys a child could fancy; and a table, in the dining-room, loaded with everything nice to eat.

But, in the midst of all this, it struck two or three of the more "practical" children, that they would like some of the brass-headed nails that studded the chairs; and so they set to work to pull them out. Presently, the others, who were reading, or looking at shells, took a fancy to do the like; and, in a little while, all the children, nearly, were spraining their fingers, in pulling out brass-headed nails. With all that they could pull out, they were not satisfied; and then, everybody wanted some of somebody else's. And at last, the really practical and sensible ones declared, that nothing was of any real consequence, that afternoon, except to get plenty of brass-headed nails; and that the books, and the cakes, and the microscopes were of no use at all in themselves, but only, if they could be exchanged for nail-heads. And at last they began to fight for nail-heads, as the others fought for the bits of garden. Only here and there, a despised one shrank away into a corner, and tried to get a little quiet with a book, in the midst of the noise; but all the practical ones thought of nothing else but counting nail-heads all the afternoon—

even though they knew they would not be allowed to carry so much as one brass knob away with them. But no—it was—"Who has most nails? I have a hundred, and you have fifty; or, I have a thousand, and you have two. I must have as many as you before I leave the house, or I cannot possibly go home in peace." At last, they made so much noise that I awoke, and thought to myself, "What a false dream that is, of *children!*" The child is the father of the man;[23] and wiser. Children never do such foolish things. Only men do.

But there is yet one last class of persons to be interrogated. The wise religious men we have asked in vain; the wise contemplative men, in vain; the wise worldly men, in vain. But there is another group yet. In the midst of this vanity of empty religion—of tragic contemplation—of wrathful and wretched ambition, and dispute for dust, there is yet one great group of persons, by whom all these disputers live—the persons who have determined, or have had it by a beneficent Providence determined for them, that they will do something useful; that whatever may be prepared for them hereafter, or happen to them here, they will, at least, deserve the food that God gives them by winning it honourably: and that, however fallen from the purity, or far from the peace, of Eden, they will carry out the duty of human dominion, though they have lost its felicity; and dress and keep[24] the wilderness, though they no more can dress or keep the garden.

These,—hewers of wood, and drawers of water,[25]—these, bent under burdens, or torn of scourges—these, that dig and weave—that plant and build; workers in wood, and in marble, and in iron—by whom all food, clothing, habitation, furniture, and means of delight are produced, for themselves, and for all men beside; men, whose deeds are good, though their words may be few; men, whose lives are serviceable, be they never so short, and worthy of honour, be they never so humble;—from these, surely, at least, we may receive some clear message of teaching; and pierce, for an instant, into the mystery of life, and of its arts.

Yes; from these, at last, we do receive a lesson. But I grieve to say, or rather—for that is the deeper truth of the matter—I rejoice to say—this

[22] I have sometimes been asked what this means. I intended it to set forth the wisdom of men in war contending for kingdoms, and what follows to set forth their wisdom in peace, contending for wealth. [Ruskin's note]
[23] Wordsworth's "My Heart Leaps Up."
[24] Genesis 2:15.   [25] Joshua 9:21.

message of theirs can only be received by joining them—not by thinking about them.

You sent for me to talk to you of art; and I have obeyed you in coming. But the main thing I have to tell you is,—that art must not be talked about. The fact that there is talk about it at all, signifies that it is ill done, or cannot be done. No true painter ever speaks, or ever has spoken, much of his art. The greatest speak nothing. Even Reynolds is no exception, for he wrote of all that he could not himself do, and was utterly silent respecting all that he himself did.

The moment a man can really do his work he becomes speechless about it. All words become idle to him—all theories.

Does a bird need to theorize about building its nest, or boast of it when built? All good work is essentially done that way—without hesitation, without difficulty, without boasting; and in the doers of the best, there is an inner and involuntary power which approximates literally to the instinct of an animal—nay, I am certain that in the most perfect human artists, reason does *not* supersede instinct, but is added to an instinct as much more divine than that of the lower animals as the human body is more beautiful than theirs; that a great singer sings not with less instinct than the nightingale, but with more— only more various, applicable, and governable; that a great architect does not build with less instinct than the beaver or the bee, but with more—with an innate cunning of proportion that embraces all beauty, and a divine ingenuity of skill that improvises all construction. But be that as it may—be the instinct less or more than that of inferior animals—like or unlike theirs, still the human art is dependent on that first, and then upon an amount of practice, of science, —and of imagination disciplined by thought, which the true possessor of it knows to be incommunicable, and the true critic of it, inexplicable, except through long process of laborious years. That journey of life's conquest, in which hills over hills, and Alps on Alps arose, and sank,— do you think you can make another trace it painlessly, by talking? Why, you cannot even carry us up an Alp, by talking. You can guide us up it, step by step, no otherwise—even so, best silently. You girls, who have been among the hills, know how the bad guide chatters and gesticulates, and it is "Put your foot here"; and "Mind how you balance yourself there"; but the good guide walks on quietly, without a word, only with his eyes on you when need is, and his arm like an iron bar, if need be.

In that slow way, also, art can be taught— if you have faith in your guide, and will let his arm be to you as an iron bar when need is. But in what teacher of art have you such faith? Certainly not in me; for, as I told you at first, I know well enough it is only because you think I can talk, not because you think I know my business, that you let me speak to you at all. If I were to tell you anything that seemed to you strange you would not believe it, and yet it would only be in telling you strange things that I could be of use to you. I could be of great use to you—infinite use—with brief saying, if you would believe it; but you would not, just because the thing that would be of real use would displease you. You are all wild, for instance, with admiration of Gustave Doré.[26] Well, suppose I were to tell you, in the strongest terms I could use, that Gustave Doré's art was bad—bad, not in weakness,—not in failure,—but bad with dreadful power—the power of the Furies and the Harpies mingled, enraging, and polluting; that so long as you looked at it, no perception of pure or beautiful art was possible for you. Suppose I were to tell you that! What would be the use? Would you look at Gustave Doré less? Rather, more, I fancy. On the other hand, I could soon put you into good humour with me, if I chose. I know well enough what you like, and how to praise it to your better liking. I could talk to you about moonlight, and twilight, and spring flowers, and autumn leaves, and the Madonnas of Raphael—how motherly! and the Sibyls of Michael Angelo—how majestic! and the Saints of Angelico—how pious! and the Cherubs of Correggio—how delicious! Old as I am, I could play you a tune on the harp yet, that you would dance to. But neither you nor I should be a bit the better or wiser; or, if we were, our increased wisdom could be of no practical effect. For, indeed, the arts, as regards teachableness, differ from the sciences also in this, that their power is founded not merely on facts which can be communicated, but on dispositions which require to be created. Art is neither to be achieved by effort of thinking, nor explained by accuracy of speaking. It is the instinctive and necessary result of power, which can only be developed through the mind of successive generations, and which finally burst into life under social conditions as slow of growth as the faculties

---

[26] Gustave Doré (1833–83), French painter, frequent illustrator of literary texts.

they regulate. Whole æras of mighty history are summed, and the passions of dead myriads are concentrated, in the existence of a noble art; and if that noble art were among us, we should feel it and rejoice; not caring in the least to hear lectures on it; and since it is not among us, be assured we have to go back to the root of it, or, at least, to the place where the stock of it is yet alive, and the branches began to die.

And now, may I have your pardon for pointing out, partly with reference to matters which are at this time of greater moment than the arts— that if we undertook such recession to the vital germ of national arts that have decayed, we should find a more singular arrest of their power in Ireland than in any other European country? For in the eighth century Ireland possessed a school of art in her manuscripts and sculpture, which, in many of its qualities—apparently in all essential qualities of decorative invention— was quite without rival; seeming as if it might have advanced to the highest triumphs in architecture and in painting. But there was one fatal flaw in its nature, by which it was stayed, and stayed with a conspicuousness of pause to which there is no parallel: so that, long ago, in tracing the progress of European schools from infancy to strength, I chose for the students of Kensington, in a lecture since published, two characteristic examples of early art, of equal skill; but in the one case, skill which was progressive—in the other, skill which was at pause. In the one case, it was work receptive of correction—hungry for correction; and in the other, work which inherently rejected correction. I chose for them a corrigible Eve, and an incorrigible Angel, and I grieve to say that the incorrigible Angel was also an Irish Angel![27]

And the fatal difference lay wholly in this. In both pieces of art there was an equal falling short of the needs of fact; but the Lombardic Eve knew she was in the wrong, and the Irish Angel thought himself all right. The eager Lombardic sculptor, though firmly insisting on his childish idea, yet showed in the irregular broken touches of the features, and the imperfect struggle for softer lines in the form, a perception of beauty and law that he could not render; there was the strain of effort, under conscious imperfection, in every line. But the Irish missal-painter had drawn his angel with no sense of failure, in happy complacency, and put red dots into the palm of each hand, and rounded the eyes into perfect circles, and, I regret to say, left the mouth out altogether, with perfect satisfaction to himself.

May I without offence ask you to consider whether this mode of arrest in ancient Irish art may not be indicative of points of character which even yet, in some measure, arrest your national power? I have seen much of Irish character, and have watched it closely, for I have also much loved it. And I think the form of failure to which it is most liable is this,—that being generous-hearted, and wholly intending always to do right, it does not attend to the external laws of right, but thinks it must necessarily do right because it means to do so, and therefore does wrong without finding it out; and then, when the consequences of its wrong come upon it, or upon others connected with it, it cannot conceive that the wrong is in anywise of its causing or of its doing, but flies into wrath, and a strange agony of desire for justice, as feeling itself wholly innocent, which leads it farther astray, until there is nothing that it is not capable of doing with a good conscience.

But mind, I do not mean to say that, in past or present relations between Ireland and England, you have been wrong, and we right. Far from that, I believe that in all great questions of principle, and in all details of administration of law, you have been usually right, and we wrong; sometimes in misunderstanding you, sometimes in resolute iniquity to you. Nevertheless, in all disputes between states, though the stronger is nearly always mainly in the wrong, the weaker is often so in a minor degree; and I think we sometimes admit the possibility of our being in error, and you never do.

And now, returning to the broader question, what these arts and labours of life have to teach us of its mystery, this is the first of their lessons— that the more beautiful the art, the more it is essentially the work of people who *feel themselves wrong;*—who are striving for the fulfilment of a law, and the grasp of a loveliness, which they have not yet attained, which they feel even farther and farther from attaining the more they strive for it. And yet, in still deeper sense, it is the work of people who know also that they are right. The very sense of inevitable error from their purpose marks the perfectness of that purpose, and the continued sense of failure arises from the continued opening of the eyes more clearly to all the sacredest laws of truth.

[27] See *The Two Paths,* paragraphs 28 *et seq.* [Ruskin's note]

This is one lesson. The second is a very plain, and greatly precious one: namely—that whenever the arts and labours of life are fulfilled in this spirit of striving against misrule, and doing whatever we have to do, honourably and perfectly, they invariably bring happiness, as much as seems possible to the nature of man. In all other paths by which that happiness is pursued there is disappointment, or destruction: for ambition and for passion there is no rest—no fruition; the fairest pleasures of youth perish in a darkness greater than their past light: and the loftiest and purest love too often does but inflame the cloud of life with endless fire of pain. But, ascending from lowest to highest, through every scale of human industry, that industry worthily followed, gives peace. Ask the labourer in the field, at the forge, or in the mine; ask the patient, delicate-fingered artisan, or the strong-armed, fiery-hearted worker in bronze, and in marble, and with the colours of light; and none of these, who are true workmen, will ever tell you, that they have found the law of heaven an unkind one—that in the sweat of their face they should eat bread, till they return to the ground;[28] nor that they ever found it an unrewarded obedience, if, indeed, it was rendered faithfully to the command—"Whatsoever thy hand findeth to do—do it with thy might."[29]

These are the two great and constant lessons which our labourers teach us of the mystery of life. But there is another, and a sadder one, which they cannot teach us, which we must read on their tombstones.

"Do it with thy might." There have been myriads upon myriads of human creatures who have obeyed this law—who have put every breath and nerve of their being into its toil—who have devoted every hour, and exhausted every faculty —who have bequeathed their unaccomplished thoughts at death—who, being dead, have yet spoken,[30] by majesty of memory, and strength of example. And, at last, what has all this "Might" of humanity accomplished, in six thousand years of labour and sorrow? What has it *done?* Take the three chief occupations and arts of men, one by one, and count their achievements. Begin with the first—the lord of them all— Agriculture. Six thousand years have passed since we were set to till the ground, from which we were taken. How much of it is tilled? How

much of that which is, wisely or well? In the very centre and chief garden of Europe—where the two forms of parent Christianity have had their fortresses—where the noble Catholics of the Forest Cantons, and the noble Protestants of the Vaudois valleys, have maintained, for dateless ages, their faiths and liberties—there the unchecked Alpine rivers yet run wild in devastation; and the marshes, which a few hundred men could redeem with a year's labour, still blast their helpless inhabitants into fevered idiotism. That is so, in the centre of Europe! While, on the near coast of Africa, once the Garden of the Hesperides, an Arab woman, but a few sunsets since, ate her child, for famine. And, with all the treasures of the East at our feet, we, in our own dominion, could not find a few grains of rice, for a people that asked of us no more; but stood by, and saw five hundred thousand of them perish of hunger.

Then, after agriculture, the art of kings, take the next head of human arts—Weaving; the art of queens, honoured of all noble Heathen women, in the person of their virgin goddess[31]—honoured of all Hebrew women, by the word of their wisest king—"She layeth her hands to the spindle, and her hands hold the distaff; she stretcheth out her hand to the poor. She is not afraid of the snow for her household, for all her household are clothed with scarlet. She maketh herself covering of tapestry; her clothing is silk and purple. She maketh fine linen, and selleth it, and delivereth girdles to the merchant."[32] What have we done in all these thousands of years with this bright art of Greek maid and Christian matron? Six thousand years of weaving, and have we learned to weave? Might not every naked wall have been purple with tapestry, and every feeble breast fenced with sweet colours from the cold? What have we done? Our fingers are too few, it seems, to twist together some poor covering for our bodies. We set our streams to work for us, and choke the air with fire, to turn our spinning-wheels—and, —*are we yet clothed?* Are not the streets of the capitals of Europe foul with sale of cast clouts and rotten rags?[33] Is not the beauty of your sweet children left in wretchedness of disgrace, while, with better honour, nature clothes the brood of the bird in its nest, and the suckling of the wolf in her den? And does not every win-

---

[28] Genesis 3:19.   [29] Ecclesiastes 9:10.   [30] Hebrews 11:4.
[31] Athena, goddess of wisdom, was also goddess of such arts as weaving.
[32] Proverbs 31:19–22.   [33] Jeremiah 38:11.

ter's snow robe what you have not robed, and shroud what you have not shrouded; and every winter's wind bear up to heaven its wasted souls, to witness against you hereafter, by the voice of their Christ,—"I was naked, and ye clothed me not"?[34]

Lastly—take the Art of Building—the strongest —proudest—most orderly—most enduring of the arts of man; that of which the produce is in the surest manner accumulative, and need not perish, or be replaced; but if once well done, will stand more strongly than the unbalanced rocks—more prevalently than the crumbling hills. The art which is associated with all civic pride and sacred principle; with which men record their power—satisfy their enthusiasm— make sure their defence—define and make dear their habitation. And in six thousand years of building, what have we done? Of the greater part of all that skill and strength, *no* vestige is left, but fallen stones, that encumber the fields and impede the streams. But, from this waste of disorder, and of time, and of rage, what *is* left to us? Constructive and progressive creatures that we are, with ruling brains, and forming hands, capable of fellowship, and thirsting for fame, can we not contend, in comfort, with the insects of the forest, or, in achievement, with the worm of the sea? The white surf rages in vain against the ramparts built by poor atoms of scarcely nascent life; but only ridges of formless ruin mark the places where once dwelt our noblest multitudes. The ant and the moth have cells for each of their young, but our little ones lie in festering heaps, in homes that consume them like graves; and night by night, from the corners of our streets, rises up the cry of the homeless—"I was a stranger, and ye took me not in."[35]

Must it be always thus? Is our life for ever to be without profit—without possession? Shall the strength of its generations be as barren as death; or cast away their labour, as the wild fig-tree casts her untimely figs? Is it all a dream then— the desire of the eyes and the pride of life— or, if it be, might we not live in nobler dream than this? The poets and prophets, the wise men, and the scribes, though they have told us nothing about a life to come, have told us much about the life that is now. They have had—they also,— their dreams, and we have laughed at them. They have dreamed of mercy, and of justice;

they have dreamed of peace and good-will; they have dreamed of labour undisappointed, and of rest undisturbed; they have dreamed of fulness in harvest, and overflowing in store; they have dreamed of wisdom in council, and of providence in law; of gladness of parents, and strength of children, and glory of grey hairs. And at these visions of theirs we have mocked, and held them for idle and vain, unreal and un-accomplishable. What have we accomplished with our realities? Is this what has come of our worldly wisdom, tried against their folly? this, our mightiest possible, against their impotent ideal? or, have we only wandered among the spectra of a baser felicity, and chased phantoms of the tombs, instead of visions of the Almighty; and walked after the imaginations of our evil hearts,[36] instead of after the counsels of Eternity, until our lives— not in the likeness of the cloud of heaven, but of the smoke of hell—have become "as a vapour, that appeareth for a little time, and then vanisheth away"?

Does it vanish then? Are you sure of that?— sure, that the nothingness of the grave will be a rest from this troubled nothingness; and that the coiling shadow, which disquiets itself in vain, cannot change into the smoke of the torment that ascends for ever?[37] Will any answer that they *are* sure of it, and that there is no fear, nor hope, nor desire, nor labour, whither they go? Be it so: will you not, then, make as sure of the Life that now is, as you are of the Death that is to come? Your hearts are wholly in this world— will you not give them to it wisely, as well as perfectly? And see, first of all, that you *have* hearts, and sound hearts, too, to give. Because you have no heaven to look for, is that any reason that you should remain ignorant of this wonderful and infinite earth, which is firmly and instantly given you in possession? Although your days are numbered, and the following darkness sure, is it necessary that you should share the degradation of the brute, because you are condemned to its mortality; or live the life of the moth, and of the worm, because you are to companion them in the dust? Not so; we may have but a few thousands of days to spend, perhaps hundreds only—perhaps tens; nay, the longest of our time and best, looked back on, will be but as a moment, as the twinkling of an eye;[38] still we are men, not insects; we are living spirits, not passing clouds. "He maketh the winds His messengers;

---

[34] Matthew 25:43. [35] Matthew 25:43. [36] Jeremiah 11:8. [37] Psalms 39:7.
[38] I Corinthians 15:52.

the momentary fire, His minister;[39] and shall we do less than *these?* Let us do the work of men while we bear the form of them; and, as we snatch our narrow portion of time out of Eternity, snatch also our narrow inheritance of passion out of Immortality—even though our lives *be* as a vapour, that appeareth for a little time, and then vanisheth away.

But there are some of you who believe not this—who think this cloud of life has no such close—that it is to float, revealed and illumined, upon the floor of heaven, in the day when He cometh with clouds, and every eye shall see Him.[40] Some day, you believe, within these five, or ten, or twenty years, for every one of us the judgment will be set, and the books opened.[41] If that be true, far more than that must be true. Is there but one day of judgment? Why, for us every day is a day of judgment—every day is a Dies Iræ, and writes its irrevocable verdict in the flame of its West. Think you that judgment waits till the doors of the grave are opened? It waits at the doors of your houses—it waits at the corners of your streets; we are in the midst of judgment—the insects that we crush are our judges—the moments we fret away are our judges—the elements that feed us, judge, as they minister—and the pleasures that deceive us, judge, as they indulge. Let us, for our lives, do the work of Men while we bear the form of them, if indeed those lives are *Not* as a vapour, and do *Not* vanish away.

"The work of men"—and what is that? Well, we may any of us know very quickly, on the condition of being wholly ready to do it. But many of us are for the most part thinking, not of what we are to do, but of what we are to get; and the best of us are sunk into the sin of Ananias,[42] and it is a mortal one—we want to keep back part of the price; and we continually talk of taking up our cross, as if the only harm in a cross was the *weight* of it—as if it was only a thing to be carried, instead of to be—crucified upon. "They that are His have crucified the flesh, with the affections and lusts." Does that mean, think you, that in time of national distress, of religious trial, of crisis for every interest and hope of humanity—none of us will cease jesting, none cease idling, none put themselves to any wholesome work, none take so much as a tag of lace off their footmen's coats, to save the world?

Or does it rather mean, that they are ready to leave houses, lands, and kindreds—yes, and life if need be? Life!—some of us are ready enough to throw that away, joyless as we have made it. But "*station* in Life"—how many of us are ready to quit *that?* Is it not always the great objection, where there is question of finding something useful to do—"We cannot leave our stations in Life"?

Those of us who really cannot—that is to say, who can only maintain themselves by continuing in some business or salaried office, have already something to do; and all that they have to see to is, that they do it honestly and with all their might. But with most people who use that apology, "remaining in the station of life to which Providence has called them" means keeping all the carriages, and all the footmen and large houses they can possibly pay for; and, once for all, I say that if ever Providence *did* put them into stations of that sort—which is not at all a matter of certainty—Providence is just now very distinctly calling them out again. Levi's station in life was the receipt of custom; and Peter's, the shore of Galilee; and Paul's, the antechambers of the High Priest,—which "station in life" each had to leave, with brief notice.

And, whatever our station in life may be, at this crisis, those of us who mean to fulfil our duty ought first to live on as little as we can; and, secondly, to do all the wholesome work for it we can, and to spend all we can spare in doing all the sure good we can.

And sure good is, first in feeding people, then in dressing people, then in lodging people, and lastly in rightly pleasing people, with arts, or sciences, or any other subject of thought.

I say first in feeding; and, once for all, do not let yourselves be deceived by any of the common talk of "indiscriminate charity." The order to us is not to feed the deserving hungry, nor the industrious hungry, nor the amiable and well-intentioned hungry, but simply to feed the hungry.[43] It is quite true, infallibly true, that if any man will not work, neither should he eat[44]—think of that, and every time you sit down to your dinner, ladies and gentlemen, say solemnly, before you ask a blessing, "How much work have I done to-day for my dinner?" But the proper way to enforce that order on those below you, as well as on yourselves, is not to leave

[39] Psalms 104:42. [40] Revelation 1:7. [41] Daniel 7:10. [42] Acts 5:1-2. [43] Isaiah 58:6-7.
[44] II Thessalonians 3:10.

vagabonds and honest people to starve together, but very distinctly to discern and seize your vagabond; and shut your vagabond up out of honest people's way, and very sternly then see that, until he has worked, he does *not* eat. But the first thing is to be sure you have the food to give; and, therefore, to enforce the organization of vast activities in agriculture and in commerce, for the production of the wholesomest food, and proper storing and distribution of it, so that no famine shall any more be possible among civilized beings. There is plenty of work in this business alone, and at once, for any number of people who like to engage in it.

Secondly, dressing people—that is to say, urging every one within reach of your influence to be always neat and clean, and giving them means of being so. In so far as they absolutely refuse, you must give up the effort with respect to them, only taking care that no children within your sphere of influence shall any more be brought up with such habits; and that every person who is willing to dress with propriety shall have encouragement to do so. And the first absolutely necessary step towards this is the gradual adoption of a consistent dress for different ranks of persons, so that their rank shall be known by their dress; and the restriction of the changes of fashion within certain limits. All which appears for the present quite impossible; but it is only so far even difficult as it is difficult to conquer our vanity, frivolity, and desire to appear what we are not. And it is not, nor ever shall be, creed of mine, that these mean and shallow vices are unconquerable by Christian women.

And then, thirdly, lodging people, which you may think should have been put first, but I put it third, because we must feed and clothe people where we find them, and lodge them afterwards. And providing lodgment for them means a great deal of vigorous legislature, and cutting down of vested interests that stand in the way, and after that, or before that, so far as we can get it, thorough sanitary and remedial action in the houses that we have; and then the building of more, strongly, beautifully, and in groups of limited extent, kept in proportion to their streams, and walled round, so that there may be no festering and wretched suburb anywhere, but clean and busy street within, and the open country without, with a belt of beautiful garden and orchard round the walls, so that from any part of the city perfectly fresh air and grass, and sight of far horizon, might be reachable in a few minutes' walk. This the final aim; but in immediate action every minor and possible good to be instantly done, when, and as, we can; roofs mended that have holes in them—fences patched that have gaps in them—walls buttressed that totter—and floors propped that shake; cleanliness and order enforced with our own hands and eyes, till we are breathless, every day. And all the fine arts will healthily follow. I myself have washed a flight of stone stairs all down, with bucket and broom, in a Savoy inn, where they hadn't washed their stairs since they first went up them; and I never made a better sketch than that afternoon.

These, then, are the three first needs of civilized life; and the law for every Christian man and woman is, that they shall be in direct service towards one of these three needs, as far as is consistent with their own special occupation, and if they have no special business, then wholly in one of these services. And out of such exertion in plain duty all other good will come; for in this direct contention with material evil, you will find out the real nature of all evil; you will discern by the various kinds of resistance, what is really the fault and main antagonism to good; also you will find the most unexpected helps and profound lessons given, and truths will come thus down to us which the speculation of all our lives would never have raised us up to. You will find nearly every educational problem solved, as soon as you truly want to do something; everybody will become of use in their own fittest way, and will learn what is best for them to know in that use. Competitive examination will then, and not till then, be wholesome, because it will be daily, and calm, and in practice; and on these familiar arts, and minute, but certain and serviceable knowledges, will be surely edified and sustained the greater arts and splendid theoretical sciences.

But much more than this. On such holy and simple practice will be founded, indeed, at last, an infallible religion. The greatest of all the mysteries of life, and the most terrible, is the corruption of even the sincerest religion, which is not daily founded on rational, effective, humble, and helpful action, Helpful action, observe! for there is just one law, which, obeyed, keeps all religions pure—forgotten, makes them all false. Whenever in any religious faith, dark or bright, we allow our minds to dwell upon the points in which we differ from other people, we are wrong, and in the devil's power. That is the essence of the Pharisee's thanksgiving—"Lord, I thank Thee that I am not as other men are."[45] At every moment of our lives we should be trying to find out, not in what we differ from other people, but in what we agree with them; and the moment we find we can agree as to anything that should be done, kind or good, (and who but fools couldn't?) then do it; push at it together: you can't quarrel in a side-by-side push; but the moment that even the best men stop pushing, and begin talking, they mistake their pugnacity for piety, and it's all over. I will not speak of the crimes which in past times have been committed in the name of Christ, nor of the follies which are at this hour held to be consistent with obedience to Him; but I *will* speak of the morbid corruption and waste of vital power in religious sentiment, by which the pure strength of that which should be the guiding soul of every nation, the splendour of its youthful manhood, and spotless light of its maidenhood, is averted or cast away. You may see continually girls who have never been taught to do a single useful thing thoroughly; who cannot sew, who cannot cook, who cannot cast an account, nor prepare a medicine, whose whole life has been passed either in play or in pride; you will find girls like these, when they are earnest-hearted, cast all their innate passion of religious spirit, which was meant by God to support them through the irksomeness of daily toil, into grievous and vain meditation over the meaning of the great Book, of which no syllable was ever yet to be understood but through a deed; all the instinctive wisdom and mercy of their womanhood made vain, and the glory of their pure consciences warped into fruitless agony concerning questions which the laws of common serviceable life would have either solved for them in an instant, or kept out of their way. Give such a girl any true work that will make her active in the dawn, and weary at night, with the consciousness that her fellow-creatures have indeed been the better for her day, and the powerless sorrow of her enthusiasm will transform itself into a majesty of radiant and beneficent peace.

So with our youths. We once taught them to make Latin verses, and called them educated; now we teach them to leap and to row, to hit a ball with a bat, and call them educated. Can they plough, can they sow, can they plant at the right time, or build with a steady hand? Is it the effort of their lives to be chaste, knightly, faithful, holy in thought, lovely in word and deed? Indeed it is, with some, nay, with many, and the strength of England is in them, and the hope; but we have to turn their courage from the toil of war to the toil of mercy; and their intellect from dispute of words to discernment of things; and their knighthood from the errantry of adventure to the state and fidelity of a kingly power. And then, indeed, shall abide, for them and for us, an incorruptible felicity, and an infallible religion; shall abide for us Faith, no more to be assailed by temptation, no more to be defended by wrath and by fear;—shall abide with us Hope, no more to be quenched by the years that overwhelm, or made ashamed by the shadows that betray:—shall abide for us, and with us, the greatest of these; the abiding will, the abiding name of our Father. For the greatest of these is Charity.[46]

from The Storm-Cloud
of the Nineteenth Century

By the time Ruskin came to write The Storm-Cloud *(1884), his mind had already suffered several severe attacks, and his eccentricities had in many cases reached the point of obsessions. There is some evidence of mental unbalance in the full text of* The Storm-Cloud, *but at the same time there is much evidence of Ruskin's prescient concern for the impact of industrialization on the physical condition of England, a concern that has made him a forerunner of the modern ecology movement. Ruskin's acute observations of natural phenomena, coupled with his unrivaled power of denunciation, make this his most menacing and sobering work.*

[45] Luke 18:11–12.   [46] I Corinthians 13:13.

Lecture I

1. Let me first assure my audience that I have no *arrière pensée* in the title chosen for this lecture. I might, indeed, have meant, and it would have been only too like me to mean, any number of things by such a title;—but, to-night, I mean simply what I have said, and propose to bring to your notice a series of cloud phenomena, which, so far as I can weigh existing evidence, are peculiar to our own times; yet which have not hitherto received any special notice or description from meteorologists.

2. So far as the existing evidence, I say, of former literature can be interpreted, the storm-cloud—or more accurately plague-cloud, for it is not always stormy—which I am about to describe to you, never was seen but by now living, or *lately* living eyes. It is not yet twenty years that this—I may well call it, wonderful—cloud has been, in its essence, recognizable. There is no description of it, so far as I have read, by any ancient observer. Neither Homer nor Virgil, neither Aristophanes nor Horace, acknowledge any such clouds among those compelled by Jove. Chaucer has no word of them, nor Dante; Milton none, nor Thomson. In modern times, Scott, Wordsworth, and Byron are alike unconscious of them; and the most observant and descriptive of scientific men, De Saussure, is utterly silent concerning them. Taking up the traditions of air from the year before Scott's death, I am able, by my own constant and close observation, to certify you that in the forty following years (1831 to 1871 approximately—for the phenomena in question came on gradually)—no such clouds as these are, and are now often for months without intermission, were ever seen in the skies of England, France, or Italy.

3. In those old days, when weather was fine, it was luxuriously fine; when it was bad—it was often abominably bad, but it had its fit of temper and was done with it—it didn't sulk for three months without letting you see the sun,—nor send you one cyclone inside out, every Saturday afternoon, and another outside in, every Monday morning.

In fine weather the sky was either blue or clear in its light; the clouds, either white or golden, adding to, not abating, the lustre of the sky. In wet weather, there were two different species of clouds,—those of beneficent rain, which

for distinction's sake I will call the non-electric rain-cloud, and those of storm, usually charged highly with electricity. The beneficent rain-cloud was indeed often extremely dull and grey for days together, but gracious nevertheless, felt to be doing good, and often to be delightful after drought; capable also of the most exquisite colouring, under certain conditions; and continually traversed in clearing by the rainbow:—and, secondly, the storm-cloud, always majestic, often dazzlingly beautiful, and felt also to be beneficent in its own way, affecting the mass of the air with vital agitation, and purging it from the impurity of all morbific elements.

4. In the entire system of the Firmament, thus seen and understood, there appeared to be, to all the thinkers of those ages, the incontrovertible and unmistakable evidence of a Divine Power in creation, which had fitted, as the air for human breath, so the clouds for human sight and nourishment;—the Father who was in heaven feeding day by day the souls of His children with marvels, and satisfying them with bread, and so filling their hearts with food and gladness.[1]

Their *hearts,* you will observe, it is said, not merely their bellies,—or indeed not at all, in this sense, their bellies—but the heart itself, with its blood for this life, and its faith for the next. The opposition between this idea and the notions of our own time may be more accurately expressed by modification of the Greek than of the English sentence. The old Greek is—

ἐμπιπλῶν τροφῆς καὶ εὐφροσύνης τὰς καρδίας ἡμῶν.

filling with meat, and cheerfulness, our hearts. The modern Greek should be—

ἐμπιπλῶν ἀνέμου καὶ ἀφροσύνης τὰς γαστέρας ἡμῶν.

filling with wind, and foolishness, our stomachs.

5. You will not think I waste your time in giving you two cardinal examples of the sort of evidence which the higher forms of literature furnish respecting the cloud-phenomena of former times.

When, in the close of my lecture on landscape last year at Oxford, I spoke of stationary clouds as distinguished from passing ones, some blockheads wrote to the papers to say that clouds never were stationary. Those foolish letters were so far useful in causing a friend to write me the pretty one I am about to read to you, quoting a passage about clouds in Homer which I had

[1] Acts 14:17.

myself never noticed, though perhaps the most beautiful of its kind in the *Iliad*. In the fifth book, after the truce is broken, and the aggressor Trojans are rushing to the onset in a tumult of clamour and charge, Homer says that the Greeks, abiding them, "stood like clouds." My correspondent, giving the passage, writes as follows:—

"SIR,—Last winter when I was at Ajaccio, I was one day reading Homer by the open window, and came upon the lines—

'Αλλ' ἔμενον, νεφέλησιν ἐοικότες, ἅς τε Κρονίων
Νηνεμίης ἔστησεν ἐπ' ἀκροπόλοισιν ὄρεσσιν,
'Ατρέμας, ὄφρ' εὕδησι μένος Βορέαο καὶ ἄλλων
Ζαχρηῶν ἀνέμων, οἵτε νέφεα σκιόεντα
Πνοιῇσιν λιγυρῇσι διασκιδνᾶσιν ἀέντες
'Ὡς Δαναοὶ Τρῶας μένον ἔμπεδον, οὐδὲ φέβοντο.²

'But they stood, like the clouds which the Son of Kronos establishes in calm upon the mountains, motionless, when the rage of the North and of all the fiery winds is asleep.' As I finished these lines, I raised my eyes, and looking across the gulf, saw a long line of clouds resting on the top of its hills. The day was windless, and there they stayed, hour after hour, without any stir or motion. I remember how I was delighted at the time, and have often since that day thought on the beauty and the truthfulness of Homer's simile.

"Perhaps this little fact may interest you, at a time when you are attacked for your description of clouds.

"I am, sir, yours faithfully,

"G. B. HILL."³

6. With this bit of noonday from Homer, I will read you a sunset and a sunrise from Byron. That will enough express to you the scope and sweep of all glorious literature, from the orient of Greece herself to the death of the last Englishman who loved her. I will read you from *Sardanapalus* the address of the Chaldean priest Beleses to the sunset, and of the Greek slave, Myrrha, to the morning.

"The sun goes down: methinks he sets more slowly,
Taking his last look of Assyria's empire.
How red he glares amongst those deepening clouds,
Like the blood he predicts If not in vain,
Thou sun that sinkest, and ye stars which rise,
I have outwatch'd ye, reading ray by ray
The edicts of your orbs, which make Time tremble
For what he brings the nations, 't is the furthest
Hour of Assyria's years. And yet how calm!
An earthquake should announce so great a fall—
A summer's sun discloses it. Yon disk

To the star-read Chaldean, bears upon
Its everlasting page the end of what
Seem'd everlasting; but oh! thou TRUE sun!
The burning oracle of all that live,
As fountain of all life, and *symbol of*
Him who bestows it, wherefore dost thou limit
Thy lore unto calamity? Why not
Unfold the rise of days more worthy thine
All-glorious burst from ocean? why not dart
A beam of hope athwart the future years,
As of wrath to its days? Hear me! oh, hear me!
I am thy worshipper, thy priest, thy servant—
I have gazed on thee at thy rise and fall,
And bow'd my head beneath thy mid-day beams,
When my eye dared not meet thee. I have watch'd
For thee, and after thee, and pray'd to thee,
And sacrificed to thee, and read, and fear'd thee,
And ask'd of thee, and thou hast answer'd—but
Only to thus much. While I speak, he sinks—
Is gone—and leaves his beauty, not his knowledge,
To the delighted west, which revels in
Its hues of dying glory. Yet what is
Death, so it be but glorious? 'T is a sunset;
And mortals may be happy to resemble
The gods but in decay."⁴

Thus the Chaldean priest, to the brightness of the setting sun. Hear now the Greek girl, Myrrha, of his rising:—

"The day at last has broken. What a night
Hath usher'd it! How beautiful in heaven!
Though varied with a transitory storm,
More beautiful in that variety:
How hideous upon earth! where peace, and hope,
And love, and revel, in an hour were trampled
By human passions to a human chaos,
Not yet resolved to separate elements:—
'T is warring still! And can the sun so rise,
So bright, so rolling back the clouds into
Vapours more lovely than the unclouded sky,
With golden pinnacles, and snowy mountains,
And billows purpler than the ocean's, making
In heaven a glorious mockery of the earth,
So like,—we almost deem it permanent;
So fleeting,—we can scarcely call it aught
Beyond a vision, 't is so transiently
Scatter'd along the eternal vault: and yet
It dwells upon the soul, and soothes the soul,
And blends itself into the soul, until
Sunrise and sunset form the haunted epoch
Of sorrow and of love."⁵

How often *now*—young maids of London,—do you make *sunrise* the "haunted epoch" of either?

7. Thus much, then, of the skies that used to be, and clouds "more lovely than the unclouded

---

² *Iliad*, Bk. 5.
³ George Birkbeck Hill (1835–1903), English author, specialist on the life and works of Samuel Johnson.
⁴ Byron's *Sardanapalus*, Act II, scene 1. ⁵ Act V, scene 1.

sky," and of the temper of their observers. I pass to the account of clouds that *are*, and—I say it with sorrow—of the *dis*temper of *their* observers.

But the general division which I have instituted between bad-weather and fair-weather clouds must be more carefully carried out in the sub-species, before we can reason of it farther: and before we begin talk either of the sub-genera and sub-species, or super-genera and super-species of cloud, perhaps we had better define what *every* cloud is, and must be, to begin with.

Every cloud that can be, is thus primarily definable: "Visible vapour of water floating at a certain height in the air." The second clause of this definition, you see, at once implies that there is such a thing as visible vapour of water which does *not* float at a certain height in the air. You are all familiar with one extremely cognizable variety of that sort of vapour—London Particular;[6] but that especial blessing of metropolitan society is only a strongly-developed and highly-seasoned condition of a form of watery vapour which exists just as generally and widely at the bottom of the air, as the clouds do—on what, for convenience' sake, we may call the top of it;—only as yet, thanks to the sagacity of scientific men, we have got no general name for the bottom cloud, though the whole question of cloud nature begins in this broad fact, that you have one kind of vapour that lies to a certain depth on the ground, and another that floats at a certain height in the sky. Perfectly definite, in both cases, the surface level of the earthly vapour, and the roof level of the heavenly vapour, are each of them drawn within the depth of a fathom. Under *their* line, drawn for the day and for the hour, the clouds will not stoop, and above *theirs,* the mists will not rise. Each in their own region, high or deep, may expatiate at their pleasure; within that, they climb, or decline,—within that they congeal or melt away; but below their assigned horizon the surges of the cloud sea may not sink, and the floods of the mist lagoon may not be swollen.

8. That is the first idea you have to get well into your minds concerning the abodes of this visible vapour; next, you have to consider the manner of its visibility. Is it, you have to ask, with cloud vapour, as with most other things, that they are seen when they are there, and not seen when they are not there? or has cloud vapour so much of the ghost in it, that it can be visible or invisible as it likes, and may perhaps be all unpleasantly and malignantly there, just as much when we don't see it, as when we do? To which I answer, comfortably and generally, that, on the whole, a cloud is where you see it, and isn't where you don't; that, when there's an evident and honest thunder-cloud in the north-east, you needn't suppose there's a surreptitious and slinking one in the north-west;—when there's a visible fog at Bermondsey, it doesn't follow there's a spiritual one, more than usual, at the West End: and when you get up to the clouds, and can walk into them or out of them, as you like, you find when you're in them they wet your whiskers, or take out your curls, and when you're out of them, they don't; and therefore you may with probability assume—not with certainty, observe, but with probability—that there's more water in the air where it damps your curls than where it doesn't. If it gets much denser than that, it will begin to rain; and then you may assert, certainly with safety, that there is a shower in one place, and not in another; and not allow the scientific people to tell you that the rain is everywhere, but palpable in Tooley Street, and impalpable in Grosvenor Square.

9. That, I say, is broadly and comfortably so on the whole,—and yet with this kind of qualification and farther condition in the matter. If you watch the steam coming strongly out of an engine-funnel,—at the top of the funnel it is transparent,—you can't see it, though it is more densely and intensely there than anywhere else. Six inches out of the funnel it becomes snow white,—you see it, and you see it, observe, exactly where it is,—it is then a real and proper cloud. Twenty yards off the funnel it scatters and melts away; a little of it sprinkles you with rain if you are underneath it, but the rest disappears; yet it is still there;—the surrounding air does not absorb it all into space in a moment; there is a gradually diffusing current of invisible moisture at the end of the visible stream—an invisible, yet quite substantial, vapour; but not, according to our definition, a cloud, for a cloud is vapour *visible.*

10. Then the next bit of the question, of course, is, What makes the vapour visible, when it is so? Why is the compressed steam transparent, the loose steam white, the dissolved steam transparent again?

The scientific people tell you that the vapour becomes visible, and chilled, as it expands. Many thanks to them; but can they show us any reason

[6] The name for a heavy London fog.

why particles of water should be more opaque when they are separated than when they are close together, or give us any idea of the difference of the state of a particle of water, which won't *sink* in the air, from that of one that won't *rise* in it?

11. And here I must parenthetically give you a little word of, I will venture to say, extremely useful, advice about scientific people in general. Their first business is, of course, to tell you things that are so, and do happen,—as that, if you warm water, it will boil; if you cool it, it will freeze; and if you put a candle to a cask of gun-powder, it will blow you up. Their second, and far more important business, is to tell you what you had best do under the circumstances,—put the kettle on in time for tea; powder your ice and salt, if you have a mind for ices; and obviate the chance of explosion by not making the gun-powder. But if, beyond this safe and beneficial business, they ever try to *explain* anything to you, you may be confident of one of two things,— either that they know nothing (to speak of) about it, or that they have only seen one side of it—and not only haven't seen, but usually have no mind to see, the other. When, for instance, Professor Tyndall[7] explains the twisted beds of the Jungfrau to you by intimating that the Matterhorn is growing flat; or the clouds on the lee side of the Matterhorn by the wind's rubbing against the windward side of it,—you may be pretty sure the scientific people don't know much (to speak of) yet, either about rock-beds, or cloud-beds. And even if the explanation, so to call it, be sound on one side, windward or lee, you may, as I said, be nearly certain it won't do on the other. Take the very top and centre of scientific interpretation by the greatest of its masters: Newton explained to you—or at least was once supposed to have explained—why an apple fell; but he never thought of explaining the exactly correlative, but infinitely more difficult question, how the apple got up there!

You will not, therefore, so please you, expect me to explain anything to you,—I have come solely and simply to put before you a few facts, which you can't see by candlelight, or in railroad tunnels, but which are making themselves now so very distinctly felt as well as seen, that you may perhaps have to roof, if not wall, half London afresh before we are many years older.

12. I go back to my point—the way in which clouds, as a matter of fact, become visible. I have defined the floating or sky cloud, and defined the falling or earth cloud. But there's a sort of thing between the two, which needs a third definition: namely, Mist. In the 22nd page of his *Glaciers of the Alps,* Professor Tyndall says that "the marvellous blueness of the sky in the earlier part of the day indicated that the air was charged, almost to saturation, with transparent aqueous vapour." Well, in certain weather that is true. You all know the peculiar clearness which precedes rain,—when the distant hills are looking nigh. I take it on trust from the scientific people that there is then a quantity—almost to saturation—of aqueous vapour in the air, but it is aqueous vapour in a state which makes the air more transparent than it would be without it. What state of aqueous molecule is that, absolutely unreflective of light—perfectly transmissive of light, and showing at once the colour of blue water and blue air on the distant hills?

13. I put the questions—and pass round to the other side. Such a clearness, though a certain forerunner of rain, is not always its forerunner. Far the contrary. Thick air is a much more frequent forerunner of rain than clear air. In cool weather, you will often get the transparent prophecy: but in hot weather, or in certain not hitherto defined states of atmosphere, the forerunner of rain is mist. In a general way, after you have had two or three days of rain, the air and sky are healthily clear, and the sun bright. If it is hot also, the next day is a little mistier—the next misty and sultry,—and the next and the next, getting thicker and thicker, end in another storm, or period of rain.

14. I suppose the thick air, as well as the transparent, is in both cases saturated with aqueous vapour;—but also in both, observe, vapour that floats everywhere, as if you mixed mud with the sea; and it takes no shape any-where: you may have it with calm, or with wind, it makes no difference to it. You have a nasty haze with a bitter east wind, or a nasty haze with not a leaf stirring, and you may have the clear blue vapour with a fresh rainy breeze, or the clear blue vapour as still as the sky above. What difference is there between *these* aqueous mol-ecules that are clear, and those that are muddy, *these* that must sink or rise, and those that must stay where they are, *these* that have form and stature, that are bellied like whales and backed

---

[7] John Tyndall (1820–93), Irish scientist and physicist, collaborated with T. H. Huxley on *The Glaciers of the Alps* (1860).

like weasels, and those that have neither backs nor fronts, nor feet nor faces, but are a mist—and no more—over two or three thousand square miles?

I again leave the questions with you, and pass on.

15. Hitherto I have spoken of all aqueous vapour as if it were either transparent or white— visible by becoming opaque like snow, but not by any accession of colour. But even those of us who are least observant of skies, know that, irrespective of all supervening colours from the sun, there are white clouds, brown clouds, grey clouds, and black clouds. Are these indeed—what they appear to be—entirely distinct monastic disciplines of cloud: Black Friars, and White Friars, and Friars of Orders Grey? Or is it only their various nearness to us, their denseness, and the failing of the light upon them, that makes some clouds look black and others snowy?

I can only give you qualified and cautious answer. There are, by differences in their own character, Dominican clouds, and there are Franciscan;—there are the Black Hussars of the Bandiera della Morte, and there are the Scots Greys whose horses *can* run upon the rock.[8] But if you ask me, as I would have you ask me, why argent and why sable, how baptized in white like a bride or a novice and how hooded with blackness like a Judge of the Vehmgericht Tribunal,—I leave these questions with you, and pass on.

16. Admitting degrees of darkness, we have next to ask what colour from sunshine can the white cloud receive, and what the black?

You won't expect me to tell you all that, or even the little that is accurately known about that, in a quarter of an hour; yet note these main facts on the matter.

On any pure white, and practically opaque, cloud, or thing like a cloud, as an Alp, or Milan Cathedral, you can have cast by rising or setting sunlight, any tints of amber, orange, or moderately deep rose—you can't have lemon yellows, or any kind of green except in negative hue by opposition; and though by storm-light you may sometimes get the reds cast very deep, beyond a certain limit you cannot go,—the Alps are never vermilion colour, nor flamingo colour, nor canary colour; nor did you ever see a full scarlet cumulus of thunder-cloud.

On opaque white vapour, then, remember, you can get a glow or a blush of colour, never a flame of it.

17. But when the cloud is transparent as well as pure, and can be filled with light through all the body of it, you then can have by the light reflected from its atoms any force conceivable by human mind of the entire group of the golden and ruby colours, from intensely burnished gold colour, through a scarlet for whose brightness there are no words, into any depth and any hue of Tyrian crimson and Byzantine purple. These with full blue breathed between them at the zenith, and green blue nearer the horizon, form the scales and chords of colour possible to the morning and evening sky in pure and fine weather; the keynote of the opposition being vermilion against green blue, both of equal tone, and at such a height and acme of brilliancy that you cannot see the line where their edges pass into each other.

18. No colours that can be fixed in earth can ever represent to you the lustre of these cloudy ones. But the actual tints may be shown you in a lower key, and to a certain extent their power and relation to each other.

I have painted the diagram here shown you with colours prepared for me lately by Messrs. Newman, which I find brilliant to the height that pigments can be; and the ready kindness of Mr. Wilson Barrett[9] enables me to show you their effect by a white light as pure as that of the day. The diagram is enlarged from my careful sketch of the sunset of 1st October, 1868, at Abbeville, which was a beautiful example of what, in fine weather about to pass into storm, a sunset could then be, in the districts of Kent and Picardy unaffected by smoke. In reality, the ruby and vermilion clouds were, by myriads, more numerous than I have had time to paint: but the general character of their grouping is well enough expressed. All the illumined clouds are high in the air, and nearly motionless; beneath them, electric storm-cloud rises in a threatening cumulus on the right, and drifts in dark flakes across the horizon, casting from its broken masses radiating shadows on the upper clouds. These shadows are traced, in the first place by making the misty blue of the open sky more transparent, and therefore darker; and secondly, by entirely intercepting the sunbeams on the bars of cloud, which, within the shadowed spaces, show dark on the blue instead of light.

---

[8] Amos 6:12.
[9] Wilson Barratt (1846–1904), English actor and theatre manager.

But, mind, all that is done by reflected light—and in that light you never get a *green* ray from the reflecting cloud; there is no such thing in nature as a green lighted cloud relieved from a red sky,—the cloud is always red, and the sky green, and green, observe, by transmitted, not reflected light.

19. But now note, there is another kind of cloud, pure white, and exquisitely delicate; which acts not by reflecting, nor by refracting, but, as it is now called, *dif* fracting, the sun's rays. The particles of this cloud are said—with what truth I know not—to send the sunbeams round them instead of through them; somehow or other, at any rate, they resolve them into their prismatic element; and then you have literally a kaleidoscope in the sky, with every colour of the prism in absolute purity; but above all in force, now, the ruby red and the *green*,—with purple, and violet-blue, in a virtual equality, more definite than that of the rainbow. The red in the rainbow is mostly brick red, the violet, though beautiful, often lost at the edge; but in the prismatic cloud the violet, the green, and the ruby are all more lovely than in any precious stones, and they are varied as in a bird's breast, changing their places, depths, and extent at every instant;—the main cause of this change being, that the prismatic cloud itself is always in rapid, and generally in fluctuating motion.

"A light veil of clouds had drawn itself," says Professor Tyndall, in describing his solitary ascent of Monte Rosa, "between me and the sun, and this was flooded with the most brilliant dyes. Orange, red, green, blue—all the hues produced by diffraction—were exhibited in the utmost splendour.

"Three times during my ascent (the short ascent of the last peak) similar veils drew themselves across the sun, and at each passage the spendid phenomena were renewed. There seemed a tendency to form circular zones of colour round the sun; but the clouds were not sufficiently uniform to permit of this, and they were consequently broken into spaces, each steeped with the colour due to the condition of the cloud at the place."[10]

Three times, you observe, the veil passed, and three times another came, or the first faded and another formed; and so it is always, as far as I have registered prismatic cloud: and the most beautiful colours I ever saw were on those that flew fastest.

20. This second diagram is enlarged admirably by Mr. Arthur Severn from my sketch of the sky in the afternoon of the 6th of August, 1880, at

[10] In Tyndall's *Glaciers of the Alps*, p. 154.

Brantwood, two hours before sunset. You are looking west by north, straight towards the sun, and nearly straight towards the wind. From the west the wind blows fiercely towards you out of the blue sky. Under the blue space is a flattened dome of earth-cloud clinging to, and altogether masquing the form of, the mountain, known as the Old Man of Coniston.

The top of that dome of cloud is two thousand eight hundred feet above the sea, the mountain two thousand six hundred, the cloud lying two hundred feet deep on it. Behind it, westward and seaward, all's clear; but when the wind out of that blue clearness comes over the ridge of the earth-cloud, at that moment and that line, its own moisture congeals into these white—I believe, *ice*-clouds; threads, and meshes, and tresses, and tapestries, flying, failing, melting, reappearing; spinning and unspinning themselves, coiling and uncoiling, winding and unwinding, faster than eye or thought can follow: and through all their dazzling maze of frosty filaments shines a painted window in palpitation; its pulses of colour interwoven in motion, intermittent in fire,—emerald and ruby and pale purple and violet melting into a blue that is not of the sky, but of the sunbeam;—purer than the crystal, softer than the rainbow, and brighter than the snow.

But you must please here observe that while my first diagram did with some adequateness represent to you the colour facts there spoken of, the present diagram can only *explain*, not reproduce them. The bright reflected colours of clouds *can* be represented in painting, because they are relieved against darker colours, or, in many cases, *are* dark colours, the vermilion and ruby clouds being often much darker than the green or blue sky beyond them. But in the case of the phenomena now under your attention, the colours are all *brighter than pure white*,—the entire body of the cloud in which they show themselves being white by transmitted light, so that I can only show you what the colours are, and where they are,—but leaving them dark on the white ground. Only artificial, and very high illumination would give the real effect of them,—painting cannot.

21. Enough, however, is here done to fix in your minds the distinction between those two species of cloud,—one, either stationary, or slow in motion, *reflecting unresolved* light; the other, fast-flying, and *transmitting resolved* light. What

difference is there in the nature of the atoms, between those two kinds of clouds? I leave the question with you for to-day, merely hinting to you my suspicion that the prismatic cloud is of finely-comminuted water, or ice, instead of aqueous vapour; but the only clue I have to this idea is in the purity of the rainbow formed in frost mist, lying close to water surfaces. Such mist, however, only becomes prismatic as common rain does, when the sun is behind the spectator, while prismatic clouds are, on the contrary, always between the spectator and the sun.

22. The main reason, however, why I can tell you nothing yet about these colours of diffraction or interference, is that, whenever I try to find anything firm for you to depend on, I am stopped by the quite frightful inaccuracy of the scientific people's terms, which is the consequence of their always trying to write mixed Latin and English, so losing the grace of the one and the sense of the other. And, in this point of the diffraction of light I am stopped dead by their confusion of idea also, in using the words undulation and vibration as synonyms. "When," says Professor Tyndall, "you are told that the atoms of the sun *vibrate* at different rates, and produce *waves* of different sizes,—your experience of water-waves will enable you to form a tolerably clear notion of what is meant."

"Tolerably clear"!—your toleration must be considerable, then. Do you suppose a water-wave is like a harp-string? Vibration is the movement of a body in a state of tension,—undulation, that of a body absolutely lax. In vibration, not an atom of the body changes its place in relation to another,—in undulation, not an atom of the body remains in the same place with regard to another. In vibration, every particle of the body ignores gravitation, or defies it,—in undulation, every particle of the body is slavishly submitted to it. In undulation, not one wave is like another; in vibration, every pulse is alike. And of undulation itself, there are all manner of visible conditions, which are not true conditions. A flag ripples in the wind, but it does not undulate as the sea does,—for in the sea, the water is taken from the trough to put on to the ridge, but in the flag, though the motion is progressive, the bits of bunting keep their place. You see a field of corn undulating as if it was water,—it is different from the flag, for the ears of corn bow out of their places and return to them,—and yet, it is no more like the undulation of the sea, than the shaking of

an aspen leaf in a storm, or the lowering of the lances in a battle.

And the best of the jest is, that after mixing up these two notions in their heads inextricably, the scientific people apply both when neither will fit; and when all undulation known to us presumes weight, and all vibration, impact,—the undulating theory of light is proposed to you concerning a medium which you can neither weigh nor touch!

All *communicable* vibration—of course I mean—and in dead matter: *You* may fall a-shivering on your own account, if you like, but you can't get a billiard-ball to fall a-shivering on *its* own account.

23. Yet observe that in thus signalizing the inaccuracy of the terms in which they are taught, I neither accept, nor assail, the conclusions respecting the oscillatory states of light, heat, and sound, which have resulted from the postulate of an elastic, though impalpable and imponderable ether, possessing the elasticity of air. This only I desire you to mark with attention,—that both light and sound are *sensations* of the animal frame, which remain, and must remain, wholly inexplicable, whatever manner of force, pulse, or palpitation may be instrumental in producing them: nor does any such force *become* light or sound, except in its rencontre with an animal. The leaf hears no murmur in the wind to which it wavers on the branches, nor can the clay discern the vibration by which it is thrilled into a ruby. The Eye and the Ear are the creators alike of the ray and the tone; and the conclusion follows logically from the right conception of their living power,—"He that planted the Ear, shall He not hear? He that formed the Eye, shall not He see?"[11]

24. For security, therefore, and simplicity of definition of light, you will find no possibility of advancing beyond Plato's "the power that through the eye manifests colour," but on that definition, you will find, alike by Plato and all great subsequent thinkers, a *moral* Science of Light founded, far and away more important to you than all the physical laws ever learned by vitreous revelation. Concerning which I will refer you to the sixth lecture which I gave at Oxford in 1872, on the relation of Art to the Science of Light (*Eagle's Nest,* § 97), reading now only the sentence introducing its subject:—

"The 'Fiat lux' of creation is therefore, in the deep sense, 'fiat anima,' and is as much, when you understand it, the ordering of Intelligence as the ordering

[11] Psalms 94:9.

of Vision. It is the appointment of change of what had been else only a mechanical effluence from things unseen to things unseeing,—from Stars, that did not shine, to Earth, that did not perceive,—the change, I say, of that blind vibration into the glory of the Sun and Moon for human eyes: so making possible the communication out of the unfathomable truth of that portion of truth which is good for us, and animating to us, and is set to rule over the day and over the night of our joy and our sorrow."

25. Returning now to our subject at the point from which I permitted myself, I trust not without your pardon, to diverge; you may incidentally, but carefully, observe, that the effect of such a sky as that represented in the second diagram, so far as it can be abstracted or conveyed by painting at all, implies the total absence of any pervading warmth of tint, such as artists usually call "tone." Every tint must be the purest possible, and above all the white. Partly, lest you should think, from my treatment of these two phases of effect, that I am insensible to the quality of tone,—and partly to complete the representation of states of weather undefiled by plague-cloud, yet capable of the most solemn dignity in saddening colour, I show you, Diagram 3, the record of an autumn twilight of the year 1845,—sketched while I was changing horses between Verona and Brescia. The distant sky in this drawing is in the glowing calm which is always taken by the great Italian painters for the background of their sacred pictures; a broad field of cloud is advancing upon it overhead, and meeting others enlarging in the distance; these are rain-clouds, which will certainly close over the clear sky, and bring on rain before midnight: but there is no power in them to pollute the sky beyond and above them: they do not darken the air, nor defile it, nor in any way mingle with it; their edges are burnished by the sun like the edges of golden shields, and their advancing march is as deliberate and majestic as the fading of the twilight itself into a darkness full of stars.

26. These three instances are all I have time to give of the former conditions of serene weather, and of non-electric rain-cloud. But I must yet, to complete the sequence of my subject, show you one example of a good, old-fashioned, healthy, and mighty, storm.

In Diagram 4, Mr. Severn has beautifully enlarged my sketch of a July thunder-cloud of the year 1858, on the Alps of the Val d'Aosta, seen from Turin, that is to say, some twenty-five or thirty miles distant. You see that no mistake is possible here about what is good weather and

what bad, or which is cloud and which is sky; but I show you this sketch especially to give you the scale of heights for such clouds in the atmosphere. These thunder cumuli entirely *hide* the higher Alps. It does not, however, follow that they have buried them, for most of their own aspect of height is owing to the approach of their nearer masses; but at all events, you have cumulus there rising from its base, at about three thousand feet above the plain, to a good ten thousand in the air.

White cirri, in reality parallel, but by perspective radiating, catch the sunshine above, at a height of from fifteen to twenty thousand feet; but the storm on the mountains gathers itself into a full mile's depth of massy cloud,—every fold of it involved with thunder, but every form of it, every action, every colour, magnificent:—doing its mighty work in its own hour and its own dominion, nor snatching from you for an instant, not defiling with a stain, the abiding blue of the transcendent sky, or the fretted silver of its passionless clouds.

27. We so rarely now see cumulus cloud of this grand kind, that I will yet delay you by reading the description of its nearer aspect, in the 130th page of *Eagle's Nest:*—

"The rain which flooded our fields the Sunday before last, was followed, as you will remember, by bright days, of which Tuesday the 20th (February, 1872) was, in London, notable for the splendour, towards the afternoon, of its white cumulus clouds. There has been so much black east wind lately, and so much fog and artificial gloom, besides, that I find it is actually some two years since I last saw a noble cumulus cloud under full light. I chanced to be standing under the Victoria Tower at Westminster, when the largest mass of them floated past, that day, from the north-west; and I was more impressed than ever yet by the awfulness of the cloud-form, and its unaccountableness, in the present state of our knowledge. The Victoria Tower, seen against it, had no magnitude: it was like looking at Mont Blanc over a lamp-post. The domes of cloud-snow were heaped as definitely: their broken flanks were as grey and firm as rocks, and the whole mountain, of a compass and height in heaven which only became more and more inconceivable as the eye strove to ascend it, was passing behind the tower with a steady march, whose swiftness must in reality have been that of a tempest: yet, along all the ravines of vapour, precipice kept pace with precipice, and not one thrust another.

"What is it that hews them out? Why is the blue sky pure there,—the cloud solid here; and edged like marble: and why does the state of the blue sky pass into the state of cloud, in that calm advance?

"It is true that you can more or less imitate the forms of cloud with explosive vapour or steam; but the steam melts instantly, and the explosive vapour dissipates itself. The cloud, of perfect form, proceeds unchanged. It is not an explosion, but an enduring and advancing presence. The more you think of it, the less explicable it will become to you."

28. Thus far then of clouds that were once familiar; now at last, entering on my immediate subject, I shall best introduce it to you by reading an entry in my diary which gives progressive description of the most gentle aspect of the modern plague-cloud.

"BOLTON ABBEY, *4th July,* 1875.

"Half-past eight, morning; the first bright morning for the last fortnight.

"At half-past five it was entirely clear, and entirely calm; the moorlands glowing, and the Wharfe glittering in sacred light, and even the thin-stemmed field-flowers quiet as stars, in the peace in which—

> "'All trees and simples, great and small,
> That balmy leaf do bear,
> Than they were painted on a wall,
> No more to move, nor steir.'[12]

But, an hour ago, the leaves at my window first shook slightly. They are now trembling *continuously,* as those of all the trees, under a gradually rising wind, of which the tremulous action scarcely permits the direction to be defined,—but which falls and returns in fits of varying force, like those which precede a thunderstorm—never wholly ceasing: the direction of its upper current is shown by a few ragged white clouds, moving fast from the north, which rose, at the time of the first leaf-shaking, behind the edge of the moors in the east.

"This wind is the plague-wind of the eighth decade of years in the nineteenth century; a period which will assuredly be recognized in future meteorological history as one of phenomena hitherto unrecorded in the courses of nature, and characterized pre-eminently by the almost ceaseless action of this calamitous wind. While I have been writing these sentences, the white clouds above specified have increased to twice the size they had when I began to write; and in about two hours from this time—say by eleven o'clock, if the wind continue,—the whole sky will be dark with them, as it was yesterday, and has been through prolonged periods during the last five years. I first noticed the definite character of this wind, and of the clouds it brings with it, in the year 1871, describing it then in the July number

of *Fors Clavigera;* but little, at that time, apprehending either its universality, or any probability of its annual continuance. I am able now to state positively that its range of power extends from the North of England to Sicily; and that it blows more or less during the whole of the year, except the early autumn. This autumnal abdication is, I hope, beginning: it blew but feebly yesterday, though without intermission, from the north, making every shady place cold, while the sun was burning; its effect on the sky being only to dim the blue of it between masses of ragged cumulus. To-day it has entirely fallen; and there seems hope of bright weather, the first for me since the end of May, when I had two fine days at Aylesbury; the third, May 28th, being black again from morning to evening. There seems to be some reference to the blackness caused by the prevalence of this wind in the old French name of Bise, '*grey* wind'; and, indeed, one of the darkest and bitterest days of it I ever saw was at Vevay in 1872."

29. The first time I recognized the clouds brought by the plague-wind as distinct in character was in walking back from Oxford, after a hard day's work, to Abingdon, in the early spring of 1871: it would take too long to give you any account this evening of the particulars which drew my attention to them; but during the following months I had too frequent opportunities of verifying my first thoughts of them, and on the first of July in that year wrote the description of them which begins the *Fors Clavigera* of August, thus:—

"It is the first of July, and I sit down to write by the dismallest light that ever yet I wrote by; namely, the light of this midsummer morning, in mid-England (Matlock, Derbyshire), in the year 1871.

"For the sky is covered with grey cloud;—not rain-cloud, but a dry black veil, which no ray of sunshine can pierce; partly diffused in mist, feeble mist, enough to make distant objects unintelligible, yet without any substance, or wreathing, or colour of its own. And everywhere the leaves of the trees are shaking fitfully, as they do before a thunderstorm; only not violently, but enough to show the passing to and fro of a strange, bitter, blighting wind. Dismal enough, had it been the first morning of its kind that summer had sent. But during all this spring, in London, and at Oxford, through meagre March, through changelessly sullen April, through despondent May, and darkened June, morning after morning has come grey-shrouded thus.

"And it is a new thing to me, and a very dreadful one. I am fifty years old, and more; and since I was five,

[12] Alexander Hume, *Hymnes, or Sacred Songs* (1599).

have gleaned the best hours of my life in the sun of spring and summer mornings; and I never saw such as these, till now.

"And the scientific men are busy as ants, examining the sun and the moon, and the seven stars, and can tell me all about *them*, I believe, by this time; and how they move, and what they are made of.

"And I do not care, for my part, two copper spangles how they move, nor what they are made of. I can't move them any other way than they go, nor make them of anything else, better than they are made. But I would care much and give much, if I could be told where this bitter wind comes from, and what *it* is made of.

"For, perhaps, with forethought, and fine laboratory science, one might make it of something else.

"It looks partly as if it were made of poisonous smoke; very possibly it may be: there are at least two hundred furnace chimneys in a square of two miles on every side of me. But mere smoke would not blow to and fro in that wild way. It looks more to me as if it were made of dead men's souls—such of them as are not gone yet where they have to go, and may be flitting hither and thither, doubting, themselves, of the fittest place for them.

"You know, if there *are* such things as souls, and if ever any of them haunt places where they have been hurt, there must be many above us, just now, displeased enough!"

The last sentence refers of course to the battles of the Franco-German campaign, which was especially horrible to me, in its digging, as the Germans should have known, a moat flooded with waters of death between the two nations for a century to come.

30. Since that Midsummer day, my attention, however otherwise occupied, has never relaxed in its record of the phenomena characteristic of the plague-wind; and I now define for you, as briefly as possible, the essential signs of it.

(1.) It is a wind of darkness,—all the former conditions of tormenting winds, whether from the north or east, were more or less capable of co-existing with sunlight, and often with steady and bright sunlight; but whenever, and wherever the plague-wind blows, be it but for ten minutes, the sky is darkened instantly.

31. (2.) It is a malignant *quality* of wind, unconnected with any one quarter of the compass; it blows indifferently from all, attaching its own bitterness and malice to the worst characters of the proper winds of each quarter. It will blow either with drenching rain, or dry rage, from the south,—with ruinous blasts from the west,—with bitterest chills from the north,—and with venomous blight from the east.

Its own favourite quarter, however, is the south-west, so that it is distinguished in its malignity equally from the Bise of Provence, which is a north wind always, and from our own old friend, the east.

32. (3.) It always blows *tremulously*, making the leaves of the trees shudder as if they were all aspens, but with a peculiar fitfulness which gives them—and I watch them this moment as I write—an expression of anger as well as of fear and distress. You may see the kind of quivering, and hear the ominous whimpering, in the gusts that precede a great thunderstorm; but plague-wind is more panic-struck, and feverish; and its sound is a hiss instead of a wail.

When I was last at Avallon, in South France, I went to see *Faust* played at the little country theatre: it was done with scarcely any means of pictorial effect, except a few old curtains, and a blue light or two. But the night on the Brocken was nevertheless extremely appalling to me,—a strange ghastliness being obtained in some of the witch scenes merely by fine management of gesture and drapery; and in the phantom scenes, by the half-palsied, half-furious, faltering or fluttering past of phantoms stumbling as into graves; as if of not only soulless, but senseless, Dead, moving with the very action, the rage, the decrepitude, and the trembling of the plague-wind.

33. (4.) Not only tremulous at every moment, it is also *intermittent* with a rapidity quite unexampled in former weather. There are, indeed, days—and weeks, on which it blows without cessation, and is as inevitable as the Gulf Stream; but also there are days when it is contending with healthy weather, and on such days it will remit for half an hour, and the sun will begin to show itself, and then the wind will come back and cover the whole sky with clouds in ten minutes; and so on, every half-hour, through the whole day; so that it is often impossible to go on with any kind of drawing in colour, the light being never for two seconds the same from morning till evening.

34. (5.) It degrades, while it intensifies, ordinary storm; but before I read you any description of its efforts in this kind, I must correct an impression which has got abroad through the papers, that I speak as if the plague-wind blew now always, and there were no more any natural weather. On the contrary, the winter of 1878–9 was one of the most healthy and lovely I ever saw ice in;—Coniston lake shone under the calm clear frost in one marble field, as strong as the floor of Milan Cathedral, half a mile across and

four miles down; and the first entries in my diary which I read you shall be from the 22nd to 26th June, 1876, of perfectly lovely and natural weather:—

"Sunday, 25th June, 1876.

"Yesterday, an entirely glorious sunset, unmatched in beauty since that at Abbeville,—deep scarlet, and purest rose, on purple grey, in bars; and stationary, plumy, sweeping filaments above in upper sky, like *'using up the brush,'* said Joanie; remaining in glory, every moment best, changing from one good into another, (but only in colour or light—*form steady,*) for half an hour full, and the clouds afterwards fading into the grey against amber twilight, *stationary in the same form for about two hours,* at least. The darkening rose tint remained till half-past ten, the grand time being at nine.

"The day had been fine,—exquisite green light on afternoon hills."

"Monday, 26th June, 1876.

"Yesterday an entirely perfect summer light on the Old Man; Lancaster Bay all clear; Ingleborough and the great Pennine fault as on a map. Divine beauty of western colour on thyme and rose,—then twilight of clearest *warm* amber far into night, of *pale* amber all night long; hills dark-clear against it.

"And so it continued, only growing more intense in blue and sunlight, all day. After breakfast, I came in from the well under strawberry bed, to say I had never seen anything like it, so pure or intense, in Italy; and so it went glowing on, cloudless, with soft north wind, all day."

"16th July.

"The sunset almost too bright *through the blinds* for me to read Humboldt at tea by,—finally, new moon like a lime-light, reflected on breeze-struck water; traces, across dark calm, of reflected hills."

35. These extracts are, I hope, enough to guard you against the absurdity of supposing that it all only means that I am myself soured, or doting, in my old age, and always in an ill humour. Depend upon it, when old men are worth anything, they are better-humoured than young ones; and have learned to see what good there is, and pleasantness, in the world they are likely so soon to have orders to quit.

---

13 I.e., his sailboat on Coniston Lake.

Now then—take the following sequences of accurate description of thunderstorm, *with* plague-wind.

"22nd June, 1876.

"Thunderstorm; pitch dark, with no *blackness,*—but deep, high, *filthiness* of lurid, yet not sublimely lurid, smoke-cloud; dense manufacturing mist; fearful squalls of shivery wind, making Mr. Severn's sail[13] quiver like a man in a fever fit—all about four, afternoon—but only two or three claps of thunder, and feeble, though near, flashes. I never saw such a dirty, weak, foul storm. It cleared suddenly after raining all afternoon, at half-past eight to nine, into pure, natural weather,—low rain-clouds on quite clear, green, wet hills."

"Brantwood, 13th August, 1879.

"The most terrific and horrible thunderstorm, this morning, I ever remember. It waked me at six, or a little before—then rolling incessantly, like railway luggage trains, quite ghastly in its mockery of them—the air one loathsome mass of sultry and foul fog, like smoke; scarcely raining at all, but increasing to heavier rollings, with flashes quivering vaguely through all the air, and at last terrific double streams of reddish-violet fire, not forked or zigzag, but rippled rivulets—two at the same instant some twenty to thirty degrees apart, and lasting on the eye at least half a second, with grand artillery-peals following; not rattling crashes, or irregular cracklings, but delivered volleys. It lasted an hour, then passed off, clearing a little, without rain to speak of,—not a glimpse of blue,—and now, half-past seven, seems settling down again into Manchester devil's darkness.

"Quarter to eight, morning.—Thunder returned, all the air collapsed into one black fog, the hills invisible, and scarcely visible the opposite shore; heavy rain in short fits, and frequent, though less formidable, flashes, and shorter thunder. While I have written this sentence the cloud has again dissolved itself, like a nasty solution in a bottle, with miraculous and unnatural rapidity, and the hills are in sight again; a double-forked flash—rippled, I mean, like the others—starts into its frightful ladder of light between me and Wetherlam, as I raise my eyes. All black above, a rugged spray cloud on the Eaglet. (The 'Eaglet' is my own name for the bold and elevated crag to the west of the little lake above Coniston mines. It had no name among the country people, and is one of the most conspicuous features of the mountain chain, as seen from Brantwood.)

"Half-past eight.—Three times light and three times dark since last I wrote, and the darkness seeming each time as it settles more loathsome, at last stopping my reading in mere blindness. One lurid gleam of white cumulus in upper lead-blue sky, seen for half a minute through the sulphurous chimney-pot vomit of blackguardly cloud beneath, where its rags were thinnest."

"Thursday, 22nd Feb., 1883.

"Yesterday a fearfully dark mist all afternoon, with steady, south plague-wind of the bitterest, nastiest, poisonous blight, and fretful flutter. I could scarcely stay in the wood for the horror of it. To-day, really rather bright blue, and bright semi-cumuli, with the frantic Old Man blowing sheaves of lancets and chisels across the lake—not in strength enough, or whirl enough, to raise it in spray, but tracing every squall's outline in black on the silver grey waves, and whistling meanly, and as if on a flute made of a file."

"Sunday, 17th August, 1879.

"Raining in foul drizzle, slow and steady; sky pitch-dark, and I just get a little light by sitting in the bow-window; diabolic clouds over everything: and looking over my kitchen garden yesterday, I found it one miserable mass of weeds gone to seed, the roses in the higher garden putrefied into brown sponges, feeling like dead snails; and the half-ripe strawberries all rotten at the stalks."

36. (6.) And now I come to the most important sign of the plague-wind and the plague-cloud: that in bringing on their peculiar darkness, they *blanch* the sun instead of reddening it. And here I must note briefly to you the uselessness of observation by instruments, or machines, instead of eyes. In the first year when I had begun to notice the specialty of the plague-wind, I went of course to the Oxford observatory to consult its registrars. They have their anemometer always on the twirl, and can tell you the force, or at least the pace, of a gale, by day or night. But the anemometer can only record for you how often it has been driven round, not at all whether it went round *steadily,* or went round *trembling.* And on that point depends the entire question whether it is a plague breeze or a healthy one: and what's the use of telling you

whether the wind's strong or not, when it can't tell you whether it's a strong medicine, or a strong poison?

But again—you have your *sun*-measure, and can tell exactly at any moment how strong, or how weak, or how wanting, the sun is. But the sun-measurer can't tell you whether the rays are stopped by a dense *shallow* cloud, or a thin *deep* one. In healthy weather, the sun is hidden behind a cloud, as it is behind a tree; and, when the cloud is past, it comes out again, as bright as before. But in plague-wind, the sun is choked out of the whole heaven, all day long, by a cloud which may be a thousand miles square and five miles deep.

And yet observe: that thin, scraggy, filthy, mangy, miserable cloud, for all the depth of it, can't turn the sun red, as a good, business-like fog does with a hundred feet or so of itself. By the plague-wind every breath of air you draw is polluted, half round the world; in a London fog the air itself is pure, though you choose to mix up dirt with it, and choke yourself with your own nastiness.

37. Now I'm going to show you a diagram of a sunset in entirely pure weather, above London smoke. I saw it and sketched it from my old post of observation—the top garret of my father's house at Herne Hill. There, when the wind is south, we are outside of the smoke and above it; and this diagram, admirably enlarged from my own drawing by my, now in all things best aide-de-camp, Mr. Collingwood, shows you an old-fashioned sunset—the sort of thing Turner and I used to have to look at,—(nobody else ever would) constantly. Every sunset and every dawn, and fine weather, had something of the sort to show us. This is one of the last pure sunsets I ever saw, about the year 1876,—and the point I want you to note in it is, that the air being pure, the smoke on the horizon, though at last it hides the sun, yet hides it through gold and vermilion. Now, don't go away fancying there's any exaggeration in that study. The *prismatic* colours, I told you, were simply impossible to paint; these, which are transmitted colours, can indeed be suggested, but no more. The brightest pigment we have would look dim beside the truth.

38. I should have liked to have blotted down for you a bit of plague-cloud to put beside this; but Heaven knows, you can see enough of it nowadays without any trouble of mine; and if you want, in a hurry, to see what the sun looks like through it, you've only to throw a bad half-crown into a basin of soap and water.

Blanched Sun, —blighted grass,—blinded man. —If, in conclusion, you ask me for any conceivable cause or meaning of these things—I can tell you none, according to your modern beliefs; but I can tell you what meaning it would have borne to the men of old time. Remember, for the last twenty years, England, and all foreign nations, either tempting her, or following her, have blasphemed the name of God deliberately and openly; and have done iniquity by proclamation, every man doing as much injustice to his brother as it is in his power to do. Of states in such moral gloom every seer of old predicted the physical gloom, saying, "The light shall be darkened in the heavens thereof, and the stars shall withdraw their shining."[14] All Greek, all Christian, all Jewish prophecy insists on the same truth through a thousand myths; but of all the chief, to former thought, was the fable of the Jewish warrior and prophet, for whom the sun hasted not to go down, with which I leave you to compare at leisure the physical result of your own wars and prophecies, as declared by your own elect journal not fourteen days ago,—that the Empire of England, on which formerly the sun never set, has become one on which he never rises.

39. What is best to be done, do you ask me? The answer is plain. Whether you can affect the signs of the sky or not, you *can* the signs of the times.[15] Whether you can bring the *sun* back or not, you can assuredly bring back your own cheerfulness, and your own honesty. You may not be able to say to the winds, "Peace; be still," but you can cease from the insolence of your own lips, and the troubling of your own passions. And all *that* it would be extremely well to do, even though the day *were* coming when the sun should be as darkness, and the moon as blood. But, the paths of rectitude and piety once regained, who shall say that the promise of old time would not be found to hold for us also?—"Bring ye all the tithes into my storehouse, and prove me now herewith, saith the Lord God, if I will not open you the windows of heaven, and pour you out a blessing, that there shall not be room enough to receive it."

from Præterita

The uncompleted autobiography Præterita *(meaning "the past") was begun as early as 1885. Until 1889 Ruskin wrote at the work in his lucid periods, relapsing intermittently into inaccessible melancholy. The work was issued in parts between 1885 and 1889 with additional portions published after his death. Although what Ruskin chose to remember of the past is highly selective (he omits all mention of his marriage for instance) and mainly of his early life, it is nevertheless glowingly re-created, making this in the view of many Ruskin's most moving work. Three passages from the volume are given below, two dealing with Ruskin's early life and the final selection, "Joanna's Care," dealing with his cousin Joan Agnew Severn, who had taken care of him as a child and who was to minister to him in his last tragic decade.*

CHAPTER I

The Springs of Wandel

(The reader must be advised that the first two chapters are reprinted, with slight revision, from "Fors Clavigera," having been written there chiefly for the political lessons, which appear now introduced somewhat violently.)

1. I am, and my father was before me, a violent Tory of the old school;—Walter Scott's school, that is to say, and Homer's. I name these two out of the numberless great Tory writers, because they were my own two masters. I had Walter Scott's novels, and the *Iliad* (Pope's translation), for constant reading when I was a child, on weekdays: on Sunday, their effect was tempered by *Robinson Crusoe* and the *Pilgrim's Progress;* my mother having it deeply in her heart to make an

---

[14] Joel 2:10.
[15] Matthew 16:3, followed by references to Mark 4:39, Job 3:17; Joel 2:31; and Malachi 3:10.

evangelical clergyman of me. Fortunately, I had an aunt more evangelical than my mother; and my aunt gave me cold mutton for Sunday's dinner, which—as I much preferred it hot—greatly diminished the influence of the *Pilgrim's Progress;* and the end of the matter was, that I got all the noble imaginative teaching of Defoe and Bunyan, and yet—am not an evangelical clergyman.

2. I had, however, still better teaching than theirs, and that compulsorily, and every day of the week.

Walter Scott and Pope's Homer were reading of my own election, and my mother forced me, by steady daily toil, to learn long chapters of the Bible by heart; as well as to read it every syllable through, aloud, hard names and all, from Genesis to the Apocalypse, about once a year: and to that discipline—patient, accurate, and resolute—I owe, not only a knowledge of the book, which I find occasionally serviceable, but much of my general power of taking pains, and the best part of my taste in literature. From Walter Scott's novels I might easily, as I grew older, have fallen to other people's novels; and Pope might, perhaps, have led me to take Johnson's English, or Gibbon's, as types of language; but, once knowing the 32nd of Deuteronomy, the 119th Psalm, the 15th of 1st Corinthians, the Sermon on the Mount, and most of the Apocalypse, every syllable by heart, and having always a way of thinking with myself what words meant, it was not possible for me, even in the foolishest times of youth, to write entirely superficial or formal English; and the affectation of trying to write like Hooker and George Herbert was the most innocent I could have fallen into.

3. From my own chosen masters, then, Scott and Homer, I learned the Toryism which my best after-thought has only served to confirm.

That is to say, a most sincere love of kings, and dislike of everybody who attempted to disobey them. Only, both by Homer and Scott, I was taught strange ideas about kings, which I find for the present much obsolete; for, I perceived that both the author of the *Iliad* and the author of *Waverley* made their kings, or king-loving persons, do harder work than anybody else. Tydides or Idomeneus always killed twenty Trojans to other people's one, and Redgauntlet speared more salmon than any of the Solway fishermen; and—which was particularly a subject of admiration to me—I observed that they not only did more, but in proportion to their doings *got* less, than other people—nay, that the best of them were even ready to govern for nothing! and let their followers divide any quantity of spoil or profit. Of late it has seemed to me that the idea of a king has become exactly the contrary of this, and that it has been supposed the duty of superior persons generally to govern less, and get more, than anybody else. So that it was, perhaps, quite as well that in those early days my contemplation of existent kingship was a very distant one.

4. The aunt who gave me cold mutton on Sundays was my father's sister:[1] she lived at Bridge-end, in the town of Perth, and had a garden full of gooseberry-bushes, sloping down to the Tay, with a door opening to the water, which ran past it, clear-brown over the pebbles three or four feet deep; swift-eddying,—an infinite thing for a child to look down into.

5. My father began business as a wine-merchant, with no capital, and a considerable amount of debts bequeathed him by my grandfather.[2] He accepted the bequest, and paid them all before he began to lay by anything for himself,—for which his best friends called him a fool, and I, without expressing any opinion as to his wisdom, which I knew in such matters to be at least equal to mine, have written on the granite slab over his grave that he was "an entirely honest merchant." As days went on he was able to take a house in Hunter Street, Brunswick Square, No. 54, (the windows of it, fortunately for me, commanded a view of a marvellous iron post, out of which the water-carts were filled through beautiful little trap-doors, by pipes like boa-constrictors; and I was never weary of contemplating that mystery, and the delicious dripping consequent); and as years went on, and I came to be four or five years old, he could command a postchaise and pair for two months in the summer, by help of which, with my mother and me, he went the round of his country customers (who liked to see the principal of the house his own traveller); so that, at a jog-trot pace, and through the panoramic opening of the four windows of a post-chaise, made more panoramic still to me because my seat was a little bracket in front, (for we used to hire the chaise regularly for the two months out of Long Acre, and so could have it bracketed and pocketed as we liked,) I saw all the high-roads, and most of the cross ones, of England and Wales; and great

---

[1] Jessie Ruskin, who married Peter Richardson of Perth.
[2] John Thomas Ruskin of Edinburgh (1761–1817?).

part of lowland Scotland, as far as Perth, where every other year we spent the whole summer: and I used to read the *Abbot* at Kinross, and the *Monastery* in Glen Farg, which I confused with "Glendearg," and thought that the White Lady had as certainly lived by the streamlet in that glen of the Ochils, as the Queen of Scots in the island of Loch Leven.

6. To my farther great benefit, as I grew older, I thus saw nearly all the noblemen's houses in England; in reverent and healthy delight of un-covetous admiration,—perceiving, as soon as I could perceive any political truth at all, that it was probably much happier to live in a small house, and have Warwick Castle to be astonished at, than to live in Warwick Castle and have nothing to be astonished at; but that, at all events it would not make Brunswick Square in the least more pleasantly habitable, to pull Warwick Castle down. And at this day, though I have kind invitations enough to visit America, I could not, even for a couple of months, live in a country so miserable as to possess no castles.

7. Nevertheless, having formed my notion of kinghood chiefly from the FitzJames of the *Lady of the Lake*, and of noblesse from the Douglas there, and the Douglas in *Marmion*, a painful wonder soon arose in my child-mind, why the castles should now be always empty. Tantallon was there; but no Archibald of Angus:—Stirling, but no Knight of Snowdoun. The galleries and gar-dens of England were beautiful to see—but his Lordship and her Ladyship were always in town, said the housekeepers and gardeners. Deep yearn-ing took hold of me for a kind of "Restoration," which I began slowly to feel that Charles the Second had not altogether effected, though I always wore a gilded oak-apple very piously in my button-hole on the 29th of May. It seemed to me that Charles the Second's Restoration had been, as compared with the Restoration I wanted, much as that gilded oak-apple to a real apple. And as I grew wiser, the desire for sweet pippins instead of bitter ones, and Living Kings instead of dead ones, appeared to me rational as well as romantic; and gradually it has become the main purpose of my life to grow pippins, and its chief hope, to see Kings.[3]

8. I have never been able to trace these pre-judices to any royalty of descent: of my father's ancestors I know nothing, nor of my mother's more than that my maternal grandmother was the landlady of the Old King's Head in Market Street, Croydon; and I wish she were alive again, and I could paint her Simone Memmi's King's Head,[4] for a sign.

My maternal grandfather was, as I have said, a sailor, who used to embark, like Robinson Crusoe, at Yarmouth, and come back at rare intervals, making himself very delightful at home. I have an idea he had something to do with the herring business, but am not clear on that point; my mother never being much communicative concerning it. He spoiled her, and her (younger) sister, with all his heart, when he was at home; unless there appeared any tendency to equivoca-tion, or imaginative statements, on the part of the children, which were always unforgiveable. My mother being once perceived by him to have distinctly told him a lie, he sent the servant out forthwith to buy an entire bundle of new broom twigs to whip her with. "They did not hurt me so much as one" (twig) "would have done," said my mother, "but I *thought* a good deal of it."

9. My maternal grandfather was killed at two-and-thirty, by trying to ride, instead of walk, into Croydon; he got his leg crushed by his horse against a wall; and died of the hurt's mortifying. My mother was then seven or eight years old, and, with her sister, was sent to quite a fashionable (for Croydon) day-school, Mrs. Rice's: where my mother was taught evangelical principles, and became the pattern girl and best needlewoman in the school; and where my aunt absolutely refused evangelical principles, and became the plague and pet of it.

10. My mother, being a girl of great power, with not a little pride, grew more and more exemplary in her entirely conscientious career, much laughed at, though much beloved, by her sister; who had more wit, less pride, and no con-science. At last my mother, formed into a consum-mate housewife, was sent for to Scotland to take care of my paternal grandfather's house; who was gradually ruining himself; and who at last effec-tually ruined, and killed, himself. My father came up to London; was a clerk in a merchant's house for nine years, without a holiday; then began business on his own account; paid his father's debts; and married his exemplary Croydon cousin.

11. Meantime my aunt[5] had remained in Croydon, and married a baker. By the time I was

---

[3] The St. George's Company was founded for the promotion of agricultural instead of town life: and my only hope of prosperity for England, or any other country, in whatever life they lead, is in their discovering and obeying men capable of Kinghood. [Ruskin's note]

[4] On a fresco in Florence.   [5] Bridget Cox, sister of Ruskin's mother.

four years old, and beginning to recollect things,—my father rapidly taking higher commercial position in London,—there was traceable—though to me, as a child, wholly incomprehensible,—just the least possible shade of shyness on the part of Hunter Street, Brunswick Square, towards Market Street, Croydon. But whenever my father was ill, —and hard work and sorrow had already set their mark on him,—we all went down to Croydon to be petted by my homely aunt; and walk on Duppas Hill, and on the heather of Addington.

12. My aunt lived in the little house still standing—or which was so four months ago—the fashionablest in Market Street, having actually two windows over the shop, in the second story; but I never troubled myself about that superior part of the mansion, unless my father happened to be making drawings in Indian ink, when I would sit reverently by and watch; my chosen domains being, at all other times, the shop, the bakehouse, and the stones round the spring of crystal water at the back door (long since let down into the modern sewer); and my chief companion, my aunt's dog, Towzer, whom she had taken pity on when he was a snappish, starved vagrant; and made a brave and affectionate dog of: which was the kind of thing she did for every living creature that came in her way, all her life long.

13. Contented, by help of these occasional glimpses of the rivers of Paradise, I lived until I was more than four years old in Hunter Street, Brunswick Square, the greater part of the year; for a few weeks in the summer breathing country air by taking lodgings in small cottages (real cottages, not villas, so-called) either about Hampstead, or at Dulwich, at "Mrs. Ridley's," the last of a row in a lane which led out into the Dulwich fields on one side, and was itself full of buttercups in spring, and blackberries in autumn. But my chief remaining impressions of those days are attached to Hunter Street. My mother's general principles of first treatment were, to guard me with steady watchfulness from all avoidable pain or danger; and, for the rest, to let me amuse myself as I liked, provided I was neither fretful nor troublesome. But the law was, that I should find my own amusement. No toys of any kind were at first allowed;—and the pity of my Croydon aunt for my monastic poverty in this respect was boundless. On one of my birthdays, thinking to overcome my mother's resolution by splendour of temptation, she brought the most radiant Punch and Judy she could find in all the Soho bazaar— as big as a real Punch and Judy, all dressed in scarlet and gold, and that would dance, tied to the leg of a chair. I must have been greatly impressed, for I remember well the look of the two figures, as my aunt herself exhibited their virtues. My mother was obliged to accept them; but afterwards quietly told me it was not right that I should have them; and I never saw them again.

14. Nor did I painfully wish, what I was never permitted for an instant to hope, or even imagine, the possession of such things as one saw in toyshops. I had a bunch of keys to play with, as long as I was capable only of pleasure in what glittered and jingled; as I grew older, I had a cart, and a ball; and when I was five or six years old, two boxes of well-cut wooden bricks. With these modest, but, I still think, entirely sufficient possessions, and being always summarily whipped if I cried, did not do as I was bid, or tumbled on the stairs, I soon attained serene and secure methods of life and motion; and could pass my days contentedly in tracing the squares and comparing the colours of my carpet;—examining the knots in the wood of the floor, or counting the bricks in the opposite houses; with rapturous intervals of excitement during the filling of the water-cart, through its leathern pipe, from the dripping iron post at the pavement edge; or the still more admirable proceedings of the turncock, when he turned and turned till a fountain sprang up in the middle of the street. But the carpet, and what patterns I could find in bed-covers, dresses, or wall-papers to be examined, were my chief resources, and my attention to the particulars in these was soon so accurate, that when at three and a half I was taken to have my portrait painted by Mr. Northcote, I had not been ten minutes alone with him before I asked him why there were holes in his carpet. The portrait in question represents a very pretty child with yellow hair, dressed in a white frock like a girl, with a broad light-blue sash and blue shoes to match; the feet of the child wholesomely large in proportion to its body; and the shoes still more wholesomely large in proportion to the feet.

15. These articles of my daily dress were all sent to the old painter for perfect realization; but they appear in the picture more remarkable than they were in my nursery, because I am represented as running in a field at the edge of a wood with the trunks of its trees striped across in the manner of Sir Joshua Reynolds; while two rounded hills, as blue as my shoes, appear in the distance, which were put in by the painter at my own request; for I had already been once, if not twice, taken to Scotland; and my Scottish nurse having always

sung to me as we approached the Tweed or Esk,—

"For Scotland, my darling, lies in thy view,
  With her barefooted lassies, and mountains so blue,"

the idea of distant hills was connected in my mind with approach to the extreme felicities of life, in my Scottish aunt's garden of gooseberry bushes, sloping to the Tay. But that, when old Mr. Northcote asked me (little thinking, I fancy, to get any answer so explicit) what I would like to have in the distance of my picture, I should have said "blue hills" instead of "gooseberry bushes," appears to me—and I think without any morbid tendency to think over-much of myself—a fact sufficiently curious, and not without promise, in a child of that age.

16. I think it should be related also that having, as aforesaid, been steadily whipped if I was troublesome, my formed habit of serenity was greatly pleasing to the old painter; for I sat contentedly motionless, counting the holes in his carpet, or watching him squeeze his paint out of its bladders,—a beautiful operation, indeed, to my thinking;—but I do not remember taking any interest in Mr. Northcote's application of the pigments to the canvas; my ideas of delightful art, in that respect, involving indispensably the possession of a large pot, filled with paint of the brightest green, and of a brush which would come out of it soppy. But my quietude was so pleasing to the old man that he begged my father and mother to let me sit to him for the face of a child which he was painting in a classical subject; where I was accordingly represented as reclining on a leopard skin, and having a thorn taken out of my foot by a wild man of the woods.

17. In all these particulars, I think the treatment, or accidental conditions, of my childhood, entirely right, for a child of my temperament: but the mode of my introduction to literature appears to me questionable, and I am not prepared to carry it out in St. George's schools, without much modification. I absolutely declined to learn to read by syllables; but would get an entire sentence by heart with great facility, and point with accuracy to every word in the page as I repeated it. As, however, when the words were once displaced, I had no more to say, my mother gave up, for the time, the endeavour to teach me to read, hoping only that I might consent, in process of years, to adopt the popular system of syllabic study. But I went on to amuse myself, in my own way, learnt whole words at a time, as I

did patterns; and at five years old was sending for my "second volumes" to the circulating library.

18. This effort to learn the words in their collective aspect, was assisted by my real admiration of the look of printed type, which I began to copy for my pleasure, as other children draw dogs and horses. The following inscription, facsimile'd from the fly-leaf of my *Seven Champions of Christendom* (judging from the independent views taken in it of the character of the letter L, and the relative elevation of G,) I believe to be an extremely early art study of this class; and as by the will of Fors, the first lines of the note, written after an interval of fifty years, underneath my copy of it, in direction to Mr. Burgess, presented some notable points of correspondence with it, I thought it well he should engrave them together, as they stood.

19. My mother had, as she afterwards told me, solemnly "devoted me to God" before I was born; in imitation of Hannah.[6]

Very good women are remarkably apt to make away with their children prematurely, in this manner: the real meaning of the pious act being, that, as the sons of Zebedee are not (or at least they hope not), to sit on the right and left of Christ, in His Kingdom, their own sons may perhaps, they think, in time be advanced to that respectable position in eternal life; especially if they ask Christ very humbly for it every day: and they always forget in the most naïve way that the position is not His to give![7]

20. "Devoting me to God," meant, as far as my mother knew herself what she meant, that she would try to send me to college, and make a clergyman of me: and I was accordingly bred for "the Church." My father, who—rest be to his soul—had the exceedingly bad habit of yielding to my mother in large things and taking his own way in little ones, allowed me, without saying a word, to be thus withdrawn from the sherry trade as an unclean thing; not without some pardonable participation in my mother's ultimate views for me. For, many and many a year afterwards, I remember, while he was speaking to one of our artist friends, who admired Raphael, and greatly regretted my endeavours to interfere with that popular taste,—while my father and he were condoling with each other on my having been impudent enough to think I could tell the public about Turner and Raphael,—instead of contenting myself, as I ought, with explaining the way of

---

[6] I Samuel 1:11.   [7] Matthew 20:20–23.

their souls' salvation to them—and what an amiable clergyman was lost in me,—"Yes," said my father, with tears in his eyes—(true and tender tears, as ever father shed,) "he would have been a Bishop."

21. Luckily for me, my mother, under these distinct impressions of her own duty, and with such latent hopes of my future eminence, took me very early to church;—where, in spite of my quiet habits, and my mother's golden vinaigrette, always indulged to me there, and there only, with its lid unclasped that I might see the wreathed open pattern above the sponge, I found the bottom of the pew so extremely dull a place to keep quiet in, (my best storybooks being also taken away from me in the morning,) that, as I have somewhere said before, the horror of Sunday used even to cast its prescient gloom as far back in the week as Friday—and all the glory of Monday, with church seven days removed again, was no equivalent for it.

22. Notwithstanding, I arrived at some abstract in my own mind of the Rev. Mr. Howell's sermons; and occasionally, in imitation of him, preached a sermon at home over the red sofa cushions;—this performance being always called for by my mother's dearest friends, as the great accomplishment of my childhood. The sermon was, I believe, some eleven words long; very exemplary, it seems to me, in that respect—and I still think must have been the purest gospel, for I know it began with, "People, be good."

23. We seldom had company, even on week days; and I was never allowed to come down to dessert, until much later in life—when I was able to crack nuts neatly. I was then permitted to come down to crack other people's nuts for them—(I hope they liked the ministration)—but never to have any myself; nor anything else of dainty kind, either then or at other times. Once at Hunter Street, I recollect my mother giving me three raisins, in the forenoon, out of the store cabinet; and I remember perfectly the first time I tasted custard, in our lodgings in Norfolk Street—where we had gone while the house was being painted, or cleaned, or something. My father was dining in the front room, and did not finish his custard; and my mother brought me the bottom of it into the back room.

24. But for the reader's better understanding of such further progress of my poor little life as I may trespass on his patience in describing, it is now needful that I give some account of my father's mercantile position in London.

The firm of which he was head partner may be yet remembered by some of the older city houses, as carrying on their business in a small counting-house on the first floor of narrow premises, in as narrow a thoroughfare of East London,—Billiter Street, the principal traverse from Leadenhall Street into Fenchurch Street.

The names of the three partners were given in full on their brass plate under the counting-house bell,—Ruskin, Telford, and Domecq.

25. Mr. Domecq's name should have been the first, by rights, for my father and Mr. Telford were only his agents. He was the sole proprietor of the estate which was the main capital of the firm—the vineyard of Macharnudo, the most precious hillside, for growth of white wine, in the Spanish peninsula. The quality of the Machar-nudo vintage essentially fixed the standard of Xeres "sack," or "dry"—secco—sherris, or sherry, from the days of Henry the Fifth to our own;—the unalterable and unrivalled chalk-marl of it putting a strength into the grape which age can only enrich and darken,—never impair.

26. Mr. Peter Domecq was, I believe, Spanish born; and partly French, partly English bred; a man of strictest honour, and kindly disposition; how descended, I do not know; how he became possessor of his vineyard, I do not know; what position he held, when young, in the firm of Gordon, Murphy, and Company, I do not know; but in their house he watched their head clerk, my father, during his nine years of duty, and when the house broke up, asked him to be his own agent in England. My father saw that he could fully trust Mr. Domecq's honour, and feeling;—but, not so fully either his sense, or his industry; and insisted, though taking only his agent's commission, on being both nominally, and practically, the head-partner of the firm.

27. Mr. Domecq lived chiefly in Paris; rarely visiting his Spanish estate, but having perfect knowledge of the proper processes of its cultivation, and authority over its labourers almost like a chief's over his clan. He kept the wines at the highest possible standard; and allowed my father to manage all matters concerning their sale, as he thought best. The second partner, Mr. Henry Telford, brought into the business what capital was necessary for its London branch. The premises in Billiter Street belonged to him; and he had a pleasant country house at Widmore, near Bromley; a quite far-away Kentish village in those days.

He was a perfect type of an English country gentleman of moderate fortune; unmarried, living with three unmarried sisters,—who, in the refinement of their highly educated, unpretending, benevolent, and felicitous lives, remain in my memory more like the figures in a beautiful story than realities. Neither in story, nor in reality, have I ever again heard of, or seen, anything like Mr. Henry Telford:—so gentle, so humble, so affectionate, so clear in common sense, so fond of horses,—and so entirely incapable of doing, thinking, or saying, anything that had the slightest taint in it of the racecourse or the stable.

28. Yet I believe he never missed any great race; passed the greater part of his life on horseback; and hunted during the whole Leicestershire season; but never made a bet, never had a serious fall, and never hurt a horse. Between him and my father there was absolute confidence, and the utmost friendship that could exist without community of pursuit. My father was greatly proud of Mr. Telford's standing among the country gentlemen; and Mr. Telford was affectionately respectful to my father's steady industry and infallible commercial instinct. Mr. Telford's actual part in the conduct of the business was limited to attendance in the counting-house during two months at Midsummer, when my father took his holiday, and sometimes for a month at the beginning of the year, when he travelled for orders. At these times Mr. Telford rode into London daily from Widmore, signed what letters and bills needed signature, read the papers, and rode home again; any matters needing deliberation were referred to my father, or awaited his return. All the family at Widmore would have been limitlessly kind to my mother and me, if they had been permitted any opportunity; but my mother always felt, in cultivated society,—and was too proud to feel with patience, —the defects of her own early education; and therefore (which was the true and fatal sign of such defect) never familiarly visited any one whom she did not feel to be, in some sort, her inferior.

Nevertheless, Mr. Telford had a singularly important influence in my education. By, I believe, his sisters' advice, he gave me, as soon as it was published, the illustrated edition of Rogers's *Italy*.[8] This book was the first means I had of looking carefully at Turner's work: and I might, not without some appearance of reason, attribute to the gift the entire direction of my life's energies. But it is the great error of thoughtless biographers to attribute to the accident which introduces some new phase of character, all the circumstances of character which gave the accident importance. The essential point to be noted, and accounted for, was that I could understand Turner's work, when I saw it;—not what chance, or in what year, it was first seen. Poor Mr. Telford, nevertheless, was always held by papa and mamma primarily responsible for my Turner insanities.

29. In a more direct, though less intended way, his help to me was important. For, before my father thought it right to hire a carriage for the above-mentioned Mid-summer holiday, Mr. Telford always lent us his own travelling chariot.

Now the old English chariot is the most luxurious of travelling carriages, for two persons, or even for two persons and so much of third personage as I possessed at three years old. The one in question was hung high, so that we could see well over stone dykes and average hedges out of it; such elevation being attained by the old-fashioned folding-steps, with a lovely padded cushion fitting into the recess of the door,—steps which it was one of my chief travelling delights to see the hostlers fold up and down; though my delight was painfully alloyed by envious ambition to be allowed to do it myself:—but I never was,—lest I should pinch my fingers.

30. The "dickey,"—(to think that I should never till this moment have asked myself the derivation of that word, and now be unable to get at it!)—being, typically, that commanding seat in her Majesty's mail, occupied by the Guard; and classical, even in modern literature, as the scene of Mr. Bob Sawyer's arrangements with Sam,[9]—was thrown far back in Mr. Telford's chariot, so as to give perfectly comfortable room for the legs (if one chose to travel outside on fine days), and to afford beneath it spacious area to the boot, a storehouse of rearward miscellaneous luggage. Over which—with all the rest of forward and superficial luggage—my nurse Anne presided, both as guard and packer; unrivalled, she, in the flatness and precision of her in-laying of dresses, as in turning of pancakes; the fine precision, observe, meaning also the easy wit and invention of her art; for, no more in packing a trunk than commanding a campaign, is precision possible without foresight.

31. Among the people whom one must miss out of one's life, dead, or worse than dead, by the time one is past fifty, I can only say for my own part, that the one I practically and truly miss most next to father and mother, (and putting

[8] Samuel Rogers (1763–1855), English poet, author of the blank verse poem *Italy* (1822–28).
[9] *Pickwick Papers*, chap. 1.

losses of imaginary good out of the question,) is this Anne, my father's nurse, and mine. She was one of our "many,"[10] (our many being always but few,) and from her girlhood to her old age, the entire ability of her life was given to serving us. She had a natural gift and speciality for doing disagreeable things; above all, the service of a sick room; so that she was never quite in her glory unless some of us were ill. She had also some parallel speciality for *saying* disagreeable things; and might be relied upon to give the extremely darkest view of any subject, before proceeding to ameliorative action upon it. And she had a very creditable and republican aversion to doing immediately, or in set terms as she was bid; so that when my mother and she got old together, and my mother became very imperative and particular about having her teacup set on one side of her little round table, Anne would observantly and punctiliously put it always on the other; which caused my mother to state to me, every morning after breakfast, gravely, that if ever a woman in this world was possessed by the Devil, Anne was that woman. But in spite of these momentary and petulant aspirations to liberality and independence of character, poor Anne remained very servile in soul all her days; and was altogether occupied, from the age of fifteen to seventy-two, in doing other people's wills instead of her own, and seeking other people's good instead of her own: nor did I ever hear on any occasion of her doing harm to a human being, except by saving two hundred and some odd pounds for her relations; in consequence of which some of them, after her funeral, did not speak to the rest for several months.

32. The dickey then aforesaid, being indispensable for our guard Anne, was made wide enough for two, that my father might go outside also when the scenery and day were fine. The entire equipage was not a light one of its kind; but, the luggage being carefully limited, went gaily behind good horses on the then perfectly smooth mail roads; and posting, in those days, being universal, so that at the leading inns in every country town, the cry "Horses out!" down the yard, as one drove up, was answered, often instantly, always within five minutes, by the merry trot through the archway of the booted and bright-jacketed rider, with his caparisoned pair,—there was no driver's seat in front: and the four large, admirably fitting and sliding windows, admitting no drop of rain when they

were up, and never sticking as they were let down, formed one large moving oriel, out of which one saw the country round, to the full half of the horizon. My own prospect was more extended still, for my seat was the little box containing my clothes, strongly made, with a cushion on one end of it; set upright in front (and well forward), between my father and mother. I was thus not the least in their way, and my horizon of sight the widest possible. When no object of particular interest presented itself, I trotted, keeping time with the postboy on my trunk cushion for a saddle, and whipped my father's legs for horses; at first theoretically only, with dexterous motion of wrist; but ultimately in a quite practical and efficient manner, my father having presented me with a silver-mounted postillion's whip.

33. The Midsummer holiday, for better enjoyment of which Mr. Telford provided us with these luxuries, began usually on the fifteenth of May, or thereabouts;—my father's birthday was the tenth; on that day I was always allowed to gather the gooseberries for his first gooseberry pie of the year, from the tree between the buttresses on the north wall of the Herne Hill garden; so that we could not leave before that *festa*. The holiday itself consisted in a tour for orders through half the English counties; and a visit (if the counties lay northward) to my aunt in Scotland.

34. The mode of journeying was as fixed as that of our home life. We went from forty to fifty miles a day, starting always early enough in the morning to arrive comfortably to four o'clock dinner. Generally, therefore, getting off at six o'clock, a stage or two were done before breakfast, with the dew on the grass, and first scent from the hawthorns; if in the course of the midday drive there were any gentleman's house to be seen,—or, better still, a lord's—or, best of all, a duke's,—my father baited the horses, and took my mother and me reverently through the state rooms; always speaking a little under our breath to the housekeeper, major-domo, or other authority in charge; and gleaning worshipfully what fragmentary illustrations of the history and domestic ways of the family might fall from their lips.

35. In analyzing above, page 785, the effect on my mind of all this, I have perhaps a little antedated the supposed resultant impression that it was probably happier to live in a small house than a large one. But assuredly, while I never to this day pass a lattice-windowed cottage

---

[10] Formerly "Meinie," "attendant company." [Ruskin's note]

without wishing to be its cottager, I never yet saw the castle which I envied to its lord; and although, in the course of these many worshipful pilgrimages, I gathered curiously extensive knowledge, both of art and natural scenery, afterwards infinitely useful, it is evident to me in retrospect that my own character and affections were little altered by them; and that the personal feeling and native instinct of me had been fastened, irrevocably, long before, to things modest, humble, and pure in peace, under the low red roofs of Croydon, and by the cress-set rivulet in which the sand danced and minnows darted above the Springs of Wandel.

CHAPTER II

Herne-Hill Almond Blossoms

36. When I was about four years old my father found himself able to buy the lease of a house on Herne Hill, a rustic eminence four miles south of the "Standard in Cornhill"; of which the leafy seclusion remains, in all essential points of character, unchanged to this day: certain Gothic splendours, lately indulged in by our wealthier neighbours, being the only serious innovations; and these are so graciously concealed by the fine trees of their grounds, that the passing viator remains unappalled by them; and I can still walk up and down the piece of road between the Fox tavern and the Herne Hill station, imagining myself four years old.

37. Our house was the northernmost of a group which stand accurately on the top or dome of the hill, where the ground is for a small space level, as the snows are, (I understand,) on the dome of Mont Blanc; presently falling, however, in what may be, in the London clay formation, considered a precipitous slope, to our valley of Chamouni (or of Dulwich) on the east; and with a softer descent into Cold Harbour-lane[1] on the west: on the south, no less beautifully declining to the dale of the Effra, (doubtless shortened from Effrena, signifying the "Unbridled" river; recently, I regret to say, bricked over for the convenience of Mr. Biffin, chemist, and others); while on the

north, prolonged indeed with slight depression some half mile or so, and receiving, in the parish of Lambeth, the chivalric title of "Champion Hill," it plunges down at last to efface itself in the plains of Peckham, and the rural barbarism of Goose Green.

38. The group, of which our house was the quarter, consisted of two precisely similar partner-couples of houses, gardens and all to match; still the two highest blocks of buildings seen from Norwood on the crest of the ridge; so that the house itself, three-storied with garrets above, commanded, in those comparatively smokeless days, a very notable view from its garret windows, of the Norwood hills on one side, and the winter sunrise over them; and of the valley of the Thames on the other, with Windsor telescopically clear in the distance, and Harrow, conspicuous always in fine weather to open vision against the summer sunset. It had front and back garden in sufficient proportion to its size; the front, richly set with old evergreens, and well-grown lilac and laburnum; the back, seventy yards long by twenty wide, renowned over all the hill for its pears and apples, which had been chosen with extreme care by our predecessor, (shame on me to forget the name of a man to whom I owe so much!)—and possessing also a strong old mulberry tree, a tall white-heart cherry tree, a black Kentish one, and an almost unbroken hedge, all round, of alternate gooseberry and currant bush; decked, in due season, (for the ground was wholly beneficent,) with magical splendour of abundant fruit: fresh green, soft amber, and rough-bristled crimson bending the spinous branches; clustered pearl and pendant ruby joyfully discoverable under the large leaves that looked like vine.

39. The differences of primal importance which I observed between the nature of this garden, and that of Eden, as I had imagined it, were, that, in this one, *all* the fruit was forbidden; and there were no companionable beasts; in other respects the little domain answered every purpose of Paradise to me; and the climate, in that cycle of our years, allowed me to pass most of my life in it. My mother never gave me more to learn than she knew I could easily get learnt, if I set myself honestly to work, by twelve o'clock. She never allowed anything to disturb me when my task was set; if it was not said rightly by twelve o'clock, I was kept in till I knew it, and in general, even

---

[1] Said in the History of Croydon to be a name which has long puzzled antiquaries, and nearly always found near Roman military stations. [Ruskin's note]

when Latin Grammar came to supplement the Psalms, I was my own master for at least an hour before half-past one dinner, and for the rest of the afternoon.

40. My mother, herself finding her chief personal pleasure in her flowers, was often planting or pruning beside me, at least if I chose to stay beside *her*. I never thought of doing anything behind her back which I would not have done before her face; and her presence was therefore no restraint to me; but, also, no particular pleasure, for, from having always been left so much alone, I had generally my own little affairs to see after; and, on the whole, by the time I was seven years old, was already getting too independent, mentally, even of my father and mother; and, having nobody else to be dependent upon, began to lead a very small, perky, contented, conceited, Cock-Robinson-Crusoe sort of life, in the central point which it appeared to me, (as it must naturally appear to geometrical animals,) that I occupied in the universe.

41. This was partly the fault of my father's modesty; and partly of his pride. He had so much more confidence in my mother's judgment as to such matters than in his own, that he never ventured even to help, much less to cross her, in the conduct of my education; on the other hand, in the fixed purpose of making an ecclesiastical gentleman of me, with the superfinest of manners, and access to the highest circles of fleshly and spiritual society, the visits to Croydon, where I entirely loved my aunt, and young baker-cousins, became rarer and more rare: the society of our neighbours on the hill could not be had without breaking up our regular and sweetly selfish manner of living; and on the whole, I had nothing animate to care for, in a childish way, but myself, some nests of ants, which the gardener would never leave undisturbed for me, and a sociable bird or two; though I never had the sense or perseverance to make one really tame. But that was partly because, if ever I managed to bring one to be the least trustful of me, the cats got it.

Under these circumstances, what powers of imagination I possessed, either fastened themselves on inanimate things—the sky, the leaves, and pebbles, observable within the walls of Eden, —or caught at any opportunity of flight into regions of romance, compatible with the objective realities of existence in the nineteenth century, within a mile and a quarter of Camberwell Green.

42. Herein my father, happily, though with no definite intention other than of pleasing me, when he found he could do so without infringing any of my mother's rules, became my guide. I was particularly fond of watching him shave; and was always allowed to come into his room in the morning (under the one in which I am now writing), to be the motionless witness of that operation. Over his dressing-table hung one of his own water-colour drawings, made under the teaching of the elder Nasmyth; I believe, at the High School of Edinburgh. It was done in the early manner of tinting, which, just about the time when my father was at the High School, Dr. Munro was teaching Turner; namely, in grey under-tints of Prussian blue and British ink, washed with warm colour afterwards on the lights. It represented Conway Castle, with its Frith, and, in the foreground, a cottage, a fisherman, and a boat at the water's edge.[2]

43. When my father had finished shaving, he always told me a story about this picture. The custom began without any initial purpose of his, in consequence of my troublesome curiosity whether the fisherman lived in the cottage, and where he was going to in the boat. It being settled, for peace' sake, that he *did* live in the cottage, and was going in the boat to fish near the castle, the plot of the drama afterwards gradually thickened; and became, I believe, involved with that of the tragedy of *Douglas*, and of the *Castle Spectre*,[3] in both of which pieces my father had performed in private theatricals, before my mother, and a select Edinburgh audience, when he was a boy of sixteen, and she, at grave twenty, a model housekeeper, and very scornful and religiously suspicious of theatricals. But she was never weary of telling me, in later years, how beautiful my father looked in his Highland dress, with the high black feathers.

44. In the afternoons, when my father returned (always punctually) from his business, he dined, at half-past four, in the front parlour, my mother sitting beside him to hear the events of the day, and give counsel and encouragement with respect to the same;—chiefly the last, for my father was apt to be vexed if orders for sherry fell the least short of their due standard, even for a day or two. I was never present at this time, however, and only avouch what I relate by hearsay and probable conjecture; for between four and six it would have been a grave misdemeanour in me if I so much

---

[2] This drawing is still over the chimney-piece of my bedroom at Brantwood. [Ruskin's note]
[3] *Douglas*, a play by John Home (1757); *The Castle Spectre* (1798) by "Monk" Lewis.

as approached the parlour door. After that, in summer time, we were all in the garden as long as the day lasted; tea under the white-heart cherry tree; or in the winter and rough weather, at six o'clock in the drawing-room,—I having my cup of milk, and slice of bread-and-butter, in a little recess, with a table in front of it, wholly sacred to me; and in which I remained in the evenings as an Idol in a niche, while my mother knitted, and my father read to her,—and to me, so far as I chose to listen.

45. The series of the Waverley novels, then drawing towards its close, was still the chief source of delight in all households caring for literature; and I can no more recollect the time when I did not know them than when I did not know the Bible; but I have still a vivid remembrance of my father's intense expression of sorrow mixed with scorn, as he threw down *Count Robert of Paris*, after reading three or four pages; and knew that the life of Scott was ended: the scorn being a very complex and bitter feeling in him—partly, indeed, of the book itself, but chiefly of the wretches who were tormenting and selling the wrecked intellect, and not a little, deep down, of the subtle dishonesty which had essentially caused the ruin. My father never could forgive Scott his concealment of the Ballantyne partnership.

46. Such being the salutary pleasures of Herne Hill, I have next with deeper gratitude to chronicle what I owe to my mother for the resolutely consistent lessons which so exercised me in the Scriptures as to make every word of them familiar to my ear in habitual music,—yet in that familiarity reverenced, as transcending all thought, and ordaining all conduct.[4]

This she effected, not by her own sayings or personal authority; but simply by compelling me to read the book thoroughly, for myself. As soon as I was able to read with fluency, she began a course of Bible work with me, which never ceased till I went to Oxford. She read alternate verses with me, watching, at first, every intonation of my voice, and correcting the false ones, till she made me understand the verse, if within my reach, rightly, and energetically. It might be beyond me altogether; that she did not care about; but she made sure that as soon as I got hold of it at all, I should get hold of it by the right end.

In this way she began with the first verse of Genesis, and went straight through, to the last verse of the Apocalypse; hard names, numbers, Levitical law, and all; and began again at Genesis the next day. If a name was hard, the better the exercise in pronunciation,—if a chapter was tiresome, the better lesson in patience,—if loathesome, the better lesson in faith that there was some use in its being so outspoken. After our chapters, (from two to three a day, according to their length, the first thing after breakfast, and no interruption from servants allowed,—none from visitors, who either joined in the reading or had to stay upstairs,—and none from any visitings or excursions, except real travelling,) I had to learn a few verses by heart, or repeat, to make sure I had not lost, something of what was already known; and, with the chapters thus gradually possessed from the first word to the last, I had to learn the whole body of the fine old Scottish paraphrases, which are good, melodious, and forceful verse; and to which, together with the Bible itself, I owe the first cultivation of my ear in sound.

It is strange that of all the pieces of the Bible which my mother thus taught me, that which cost me most to learn, and which was, to my child's mind, chiefly repulsive—the 119th Psalm—has now become of all the most precious to me, in its overflowing and glorious passion of love for the Law of God, in opposition to the abuse of it by modern preachers of what they imagine to be His gospel.

47. But it is only by deliberate effort that I recall the long morning hours of toil, as regular as sunrise,—toil on both sides equal—by which, year after year, my mother forced me to learn these paraphrases, and chapters, (the eighth of 1st Kings being one—try it, good reader, in a leisure hour!) allowing not so much as a syllable to be missed or misplaced; while every sentence was required to said over and over again till she was satisfied with the accent of it. I recollect a struggle between us of about three weeks, concerning the accent of the "of" in the lines

"Shall any following spring revive
The ashes of the urn?—

I insisting, partly in childish obstinacy, and partly in true instinct for rhythm, (being wholly careless on the subject both of urns and their contents,) on reciting it with an accented *of*. It was not, I say, till after three week's labour, that my mother got the accent lightened on the "of" and laid on the ashes, to her mind. But had it taken three years she would have done it, having once under-

---

[4] Compare the 52nd paragraph of chapter iii. of *The Bible of Amiens*. [Ruskin's note]

taken to do it. And, assuredly, had she not done it,—well, there's no knowing what would have happened; but I'm very thankful she *did*.

48. I have just opened my oldest (in use) Bible,—a small, closely, and very neatly printed volume it is, printed in Edinburgh by Sir D. Hunter Blair and J. Bruce, Printers to the King's Most Excellent Majesty, in 1816. Yellow, now, with age; and flexible, but not unclean, with much use; except that the lower corners of the pages at 8th of 1st Kings and, 32nd Deuteronomy, are worn somewhat thin and dark, the learning of these two chapters having cost me much pains. My mother's list of the chapters with which, thus learned, she established my soul in life,[5] has just fallen out of it. I wil take what indulgence the incurious reader can give me, for printing the list thus accidentally occurrent:—

Exodus	chapters	15th and 20th.
2 Samuel	chapters	1st, from 17th verse to the end.
1 Kings	chapters	8th.
Psalms	chapters	23rd, 32nd, 90th, 91st, 103rd, 112th, 119th, 139th.
Proverbs	chapters	2nd, 3rd, 8th, 12th.
Isaiah	chapters	58th.
Matthew	chapters	5th, 6th, 7th.
Acts	chapters	26th.
1 Corinthians	chapters	13th, 15th.
James	chapters	4th.
Revelation	chapters	5th, 6th.

And truly, though I have picked up the elements of a little further knowledge—in mathematics, meteorology, and the like, in after life,—and owe not a little to the teaching of many people, this maternal installation of my mind in that property of chapters I count very confidently the most precious, and, on the whole, the one *essential* part of all my education.

And it is perhaps already time to mark what advantage and mischief, by the chances of life up to seven years old, had been irrevocably determined for me.

I will first count my blessings (as a not unwise friend once recommended me to do, continually; whereas I have a bad trick of always numbering the thorns in my fingers and not the bones in them).

And for best and truest beginning of all blessings, I had been taught the perfect meaning of Peace, in thought, act, and word.

I never had heard my father's or mother's voice once raised in any question with each other; nor seen an angry, or even slightly hurt or offended, glance in the eyes of either. I had never heard a servant scolded; nor even suddenly, passionately, or in any severe manner, blamed. I had never seen a moment's trouble or disorder in any household matter; nor anything whatever either done in a hurry, or undone in due time. I had no conception of such a feeling as anxiety; my father's occasional vexation in the afternoons, when he had only got an order for twelve butts after expecting one for fifteen, as I have just stated, was never manifested to *me*; and itself only to the question whether his name would be a step higher or lower in the year's list of sherry exporters; for he never spent more than half his income, and therefore found himself little incommoded by occasional variations in the total of it. I had never done any wrong that I knew of—beyond occasionally delaying the commitment to heart of some improving sentence, that I might watch a wasp on the window pane, or a bird in the cherry tree; and I had never seen any grief.

49. Next to this quite priceless gift of Peace, I had received the perfect understanding of the natures of Obedience and Faith. I obeyed word, or lifted finger, of father or mother, simply as a ship her helm; not only without idea of resistance, but receiving the direction as a part of my own life and force, and helpful law, as necessary to me in every moral action as the law of gravity in leaping. And my practice in Faith was soon complete: nothing was ever promised me that was not given; nothing ever threatened me that was not inflicted, and nothing ever told me that was not true.

Peace, obedience, faith; these three for chief good; next to these, the habit of fixed attention with both eyes and mind—on which I will not further enlarge at this moment, this being the main practical faculty of my life, causing Mazzini to say of me, in conversation authentically reported, a year or two before his death, that I had "the most analytic mind in Europe." An opinion in which, so far as I am acquainted with Europe, I am myself entirely disposed to concur.

Lastly, an extreme perfection in palate and all other bodily senses, given by the utter prohibition of cake, wine, comfits, or, except in carefullest

---

[5] This expression in *Fors* has naturally been supposed by some readers to mean that my mother at this time made me vitally and evangelically religious. The fact was far otherwise. I meant only that she gave me secure *grounds* for all future life, practical or spiritual. See the paragraph next following. [Ruskin's note]

restriction, fruit; and by fine preparation of what food was given to me. Such I esteem the main blessings of my childhood;—next, let me count the equally dominant calamities.

50. First, that I had nothing to love.

My parents were—in a sort—visible powers of nature to me, no more loved than the sun and the moon: only I should have been annoyed and puzzled if either of them had gone out; (how much, now, when both are darkened!)—still less did I love God; not that I had any quarrel with Him, or fear of Him; but simply found what people told me was His service, disagreeable; and what people told me was His book, not entertaining. I had no companions to quarrel with, neither; nobody to assist, and nobody to thank. Not a servant was ever allowed to do anything for me, but what it was their duty to do; and why should I have been grateful to the cook for cooking, or the gardener for gardening,—when the one dared not give me a baked potato without asking leave, and the other would not let my ants' nests alone, because they made the walks untidy? The evil consequence of all this was not, however, what might perhaps have been expected, that I grew up selfish or unaffectionate; but that, when affection did come, it came with violence utterly rampant and unmanageable, at least by me, who never before had anything to manage.

51. For (second of chief calamities) I had nothing to endure. Danger or pain of any kind I knew not: my strength was never exercised, my patience never tried, and my courage never fortified. Not that I was ever afraid of anything, either ghosts, thunder, or beasts; and one of the nearest approaches to insubordination which I was ever tempted into as a child, was in passionate effort to get leave to play with the lion's cubs in Wombwell's menagerie.

52. Thirdly. I was taught no precision nor etiquette of manners; it was enough if, in the little society we saw, I remained unobtrusive, and replied to a question without shyness: but the shyness came later, and increased as I grew conscious of the rudeness arising from the want of social discipline, and found it impossible to acquire, in advanced life, dexterity in any bodily exercise, skill in any pleasing accomplishment, or ease and tact in ordinary behaviour.

53. Lastly, and chief of evils. My judgment of right and wrong, and powers of independent action,[6] were left entirely undeveloped; because the bridle and blinkers were never taken off me.

Children should have their times of being off duty, like soldiers; and when once the obedience, if required, is certain, the little creature should be very early put for periods of practice in complete command of itself; set on the barebacked horse of its own will, and left to break it by its own strength. But the ceaseless authority exercised over my youth left me, when cast out at last into the world, unable for some time to do more than drift with its vortices.

54. My present verdict, therefore, on the general tenor of my education at that time, must be, that it was at once too formal and too luxurious; leaving my character, at the most important moment for its construction, cramped indeed, but not disciplined; and only by protection innocent, instead of by practice virtuous. My mother saw this herself, and but too clearly, in later years; and whenever I did anything wrong, stupid, or hard-hearted,—(and I have done many things that were all three,)—always said, "It is because you were too much indulged."

55. Thus far, with some omissions, I have merely reprinted the account of these times given in *Fors*: and I fear the sequel may be more trivial, because much is concentrated in the foregoing broad statement, which I have now to continue by slower steps;—and yet less amusing, because I tried always in *Fors* to say things, if I could, a little piquantly; and the rest of the things related in this book will be told as plainly as I can. But whether I succeeded in writing piquantly in *Fors* or not, I certainly wrote often obscurely; and the description above given of Herne Hill seems to me to need at once some reduction to plainer terms.

56. The actual height of the long ridge of Herne Hill, above Thames,—at least above the nearly Thames-level of its base at Camberwell Green, is, I conceive, not more than one hundred and fifty feet: but it gives the whole of this fall on both sides of it in about a quarter of a mile; forming, east and west, a succession of quite beautiful pleasure-ground and gardens, instantly dry after rain, and in which, for children, running down is pleasant play, and rolling a roller up, vigorous work. The view from the ridge on both sides was, before railroads came, entirely lovely: westward at evening, almost sublime, over softly wreathing distances of domestic wood;—Thames herself not visible, nor any fields except immediately beneath; but the tops of twenty square miles of politely inhabited groves. On the other

---

[6] *Action*, observe, I say here: in *thought* I was too independent, as I said above. [Ruskin's note]

side, east and south, the Norwood hills, partly rough with furze, partly wooded with birch and oak, partly in pure green bramble copse, and rather steep pasture, rose with the promise of all the rustic loveliness of Surrey and Kent in them, and with so much of space and height in their sweep, as gave them some fellowship with hills of true hill-districts. Fellowship now inconceivable, for the Crystal Palace, without ever itself attaining any true aspect of size, and possessing no more sublimity than a cucumber frame between two chimneys, yet by its stupidity of hollow bulk dwarfs the hills at once; so that now one thinks of them no more but as three long lumps of clay, on lease for building. But then, the Nor-wood, or North-wood, so called as it was seen from Croydon, in opposition to the South wood of the Surrey downs, drew itself in sweeping crescent good five miles round Dulwich to the south, broken by lanes of ascent, Gipsy Hill, and others; and, from the top, commanding views towards Dartford, and over the plain of Croydon,—in contemplation of which I one day frightened my mother out of her wits by saying "the eyes were coming out of my head!" She thought it was an attack of coup-de-soleil.

57. Central in such amphitheatre, the crowing glory of Herne Hill was accordingly, that, after walking along its ridge southward from London through a mile of chestnut, lilac, and apple trees, hanging over the wooden palings on each side—suddenly the trees stopped on the left, and out one came on the top of a field sloping down to the south into Dulwich valley—open field animate with cow and buttercup, and below, the beautiful meadows and high avenues of Dulwich; and beyond, all that crescent of the Norwood hills; a footpath, entered by a turnstile, going down to the left, always so warm that invalids could be sheltered there in March, then to walk elsewhere would have been death to them; and so quiet, that whenever I had anything difficult to compose or think of, I used to do it rather there than in our own garden. The great field was separated from the path and road only by light wooden open palings, four feet high, needful to keep the cows in. Since I last composed, or meditated there, various improvements have taken place; first the neighbourhood wanted a new church, and built a meagre Gothic one with a useless spire, for the fashion of the thing, at the side of the field; then they built a parsonage

behind it, the two stopping out half the view in that direction. Then the Crystal Palace came, for ever spoiling the view through all its compass, and bringing every show-day, from London, a flood of pedestrians down the footpath, who left it filthy with cigar ashes for the rest of the week: then the railroads came, and expatiating roughs by every excursion train, who knocked the palings about, roared at the cows, and tore down what branches of blossom they could reach over the palings on the enclosed side. Then the residents on the enclosed side built a brick wall to defend themselves. Then the path got to be insufferably hot as well as dirty, and was gradually abandoned to the roughs, with a policeman on watch at the bottom. Finally, this year, a six foot high close paling has been put down the other side of it, and the processional excursionist has the liberty of obtaining what notion of the country air and prospect he may, between the wall and that, with one bad cigar before him, another behind him, and another in his mouth.

58. I do not mean this book to be in any avoidable way disagreeable or querulous; but expressive generally of my native disposition— which, though I say it, is extremely amiable, when I'm not bothered: I will grumble elsewhere when I must, and only notice this injury alike to the resident and excursionist at Herne Hill, because questions of right-of-way are now of constant occurrence; and in most cases, the mere *path* is the smallest part of the old Right, truly understood. The Right is of the cheerful view and sweet air which the path commanded.

Also, I may note in passing, that for all their talk about Magna Charta, very few Englishmen are aware that one of the main provisions of it is that Law should not be sold;[7] and it seems to me that the law of England might preserve Banstead and other downs free to the poor of England, without charging me, as it has just done, a hundred pounds for its temporary performance of that otherwise unremunerative duty.

59. I shall have to return over the ground of these early years, to fill gaps, after getting on a little first; but will yet venture here the tediousness of explaining that my saying "in Herne Hill garden all fruit was forbidden," only meant, of course, forbidden unless under defined restriction; which made the various gatherings of each kind in its season a sort of harvest festival; and which had this further good in its apparent severity, that,

---

[7] "To no one will We sell, to no one will We deny or defer, Right, or Justice." [Ruskin's note]

although in the at last indulgent areas, the peach which my mother gathered for me when she was sure it was ripe, and the cherry pie for which I had chosen the cherries red all round, were, I suppose, of more ethereal flavour to me than they could have been to children allowed to pluck and eat at their will; still the unalloyed and long continuing pleasure given to me by our fruit-tree avenue was in its blossom, not in its bearing. For the general epicurean enjoyment of existence, potatoes well browned, green pease well boiled,—broad beans of the true bitter,—and the pots of damson and currant for whose annual filling we were dependent more on the greengrocer than the garden, were a hundredfold more important to me than the dozen or two of nectarines of which perhaps I might get the halves of three,—(the other sides mouldy)—or the bushel or two of pears which went directly to the store-shelf. So that, very early indeed in my thoughts of trees, I had got at the principle given fifty years afterwards in *Proserpina*, that the seeds and fruits of them were for the sake of the flowers, not the flowers for the fruit. The first joy of the year being in its snowdrops, the second, and cardinal one, was in the almond blossom,—every other garden and woodland gladness following from that in an unbroken order of kindling flower and shadowy leaf; and for many and many a year to come,—until indeed, the whole of life became autumn to me,—my chief prayer for the kindness of heaven, in its flowerful seasons, was that the frost might not touch the almond blossom.

CHAPTER IV

Joanna's Care

60. The mischances which have delayed the sequence of *Præterita*[1] must modify somewhat also its intended order. I leave Rosie's letter to tell what it can of the beginning of happiest days; but omit, for a little while, the further record of them,—of the shadows which gathered around them, and increased, in my father's illness; and of the lightning which struck him down in death[2]—so sudden, that I find it extremely difficult, in looking back, to realize the state of mind in which it left either my mother or me. My own principal feeling was certainly anxiety for her, who had been for so many years in every thought dependent on my father's wishes, and withdrawn from all other social pleasure as long as she could be *his* companion. I scarcely felt the power I had over her, myself; and was at first amazed to find my own life suddenly becoming to her another ideal; and that new hope and pride were possible to her, in seeing me take command of my father's fortune, and permitted by him, from his grave, to carry out the theories I had formed for my political work, with unrestricted and deliberate energy.

My mother's perfect health of mind, and vital religious faith, enabled her to take all the good that was left to her, in the world, while she looked in secure patience for the heavenly future: but there was immediate need for some companionship which might lighten the burden of the days to her.

61. I have never yet spoken of the members of my grandmother's family, who either remained in Galloway, or were associated with my early days in London. Quite one of the dearest of them at this time, was Mrs. Agnew, born Catherine Tweddale, and named Catherine after her aunt, my father's mother. She had now for some years been living in widowhood; her little daughter, Joan, only five years old when her father died, having grown up in their pretty old house at Wigtown,[3] in the simplicity of entirely natural and contented life: and, though again and again under the stress of domestic sorrow, untellable in the depth of the cup which the death-angels filled for the child, yet in such daily happiness as her own bright and loving nature secured in her relations with all those around her; and in the habits of childish play, or education, then common in the rural towns of South Scotland: of which, let me say at once that there was greater refinement in them, and more honourable pride, than probably, at that time, in any other district

---

[1] Ruskin is referring to the interruptions in the original serial publication of *Præterita*, occasioned by his mental condition.

[2] He died 3 March 1864.

[3] Now pulled down and the site taken for the new county buildings. The house as it once stood is seen in the center of the woodcut at page 6 of the Gordon Fraser's Guide, with the Stewartry hills in the distance. I have seldom seen a truer rendering of the look of an old Scottish town. [Ruskin's note]

of Europe;[4] a certain pathetic melody and power of tradition consecrating nearly every scene with some past light, either of heroism or religion.

62. And so it chanced, providentially, that at this moment, when my mother's thoughts dwelt constantly on the past, there should be this child near us,—still truly a child, in her powers of innocent pleasure, but already so accustomed to sorrow, that there was nothing that could farther depress her in my mother's solitude. I have not time to tell of the pretty little ways in which it came about, but they all ended in my driving to No. 1, Cambridge Street, on the 19th April, 1864: where her uncle (my cousin, John Tweddale) brought her up to the drawing-room to me, saying, "This is Joan."

I had seen her three years before, but not long enough to remember her distinctly: only I had a notion that she would be "nice,"[5] and saw at once that she *was* entirely nice, both in my mother's way, and mine; being now seventeen years and some—well, for example of accuracy and conscience—forty-five days, old. And I very thankfully took her hand out of her uncle's, and received her in trust, saying—I do not remember just what,—but certainly *feeling* much more strongly than either her uncle or she did, that the gift, both to my mother and me, was one which we should not easily bear to be again withdrawn. I put her into my father's carriage at the door, and drove her out to Denmark Hill.

63. Here is her own account of what followed between my mother and her:—

"I was received with great kindness by the dear old lady, who did not inspire *me*, as she did so many other people, with a feeling of awe! We were the best of friends, from the first. She, ever most considerate of what would please *me*, and make me happy; and I, (ever a lover of old ladies!) delighted to find it so easily possible to please *her*.

"Next morning she said, 'Now tell me frankly, child, what you like best to eat, and you shall have it. Don't hesitate; say what you'd really like,— for luncheon to-day, for instance.' I said, truthfully, 'Cold mutton, and oysters'; and this became a sort of standing order (in months with the letter *r*!)—Greatly to the cook's amusement.

"Of course I respectfully called the old lady '*Mrs. Ruskin*'; but in a day or two, she told me she didn't like it, and would I call her 'Aunt' or 'Auntie'? I readily did so.

"The days flew in that lovely garden, and as I had only been invited to stay a week, until Mr. Ruskin should return home,[6] I felt miserable when he did come, thinking I must go back to London streets, and noise; (though I was always very happy with my good uncle and aunts).

"So, when the last evening came, of my week, I said, with some hesitation, 'Auntie, I had better go back to my uncle's to-morrow!'

"She flung down her netting, and turned

---

[4] The following couple of pages, from *Redgauntlet,* put in very few words the points of difference between them and the fatally progressive follies and vanities of Edinburgh:—

" 'Come away, Mr. Fairford; the Edinburgh time is later than ours,' said the Provost.

" 'And come away, young gentleman,' said the Laird; 'I remember your father weel, at the Cross, thirty years ago. I reckon you are as late in Edinburgh as at London; *four* o'clock hours, eh?'

" 'Not quite so degenerate,' replied Fairford; 'but certainly many Edinburgh people are so ill-advised as to *postpone their dinner* till three, that they may have full time to answer their London correspondents.'

" 'London correspondents!' said Mr. Maxwell; 'and pray, what the devil have the people of Auld Reekie to do with London correspondents?'

" 'The tradesmen must have their goods,' said Fairford.

" 'Can they not buy our own Scottish manufactures, and pick their customers' pockets in a more patriotic manner?'

" 'Then the ladies must have fashions,' said Fairford.

" 'Can they not busk the plaid over their heads, as their mothers did? A tartan screen, and once a year a new cockernony from Paris, should serve a countess; but ye have not many of *them* left, I think. Mareschal, Airley, Winton, Wemyss, Balmerino—ay, ay, the countesses and ladies of quality will scarce take up too much of your ballroom floor with their quality hoops nowadays.'

" 'There is no want of crowding, however, sir,' said Fairford; 'they begin to talk of a new Assembly Room.'

" 'A new Assembly Room!' said the old Jacobite Laird. 'Umph—I mind quartering three hundred men in the Assembly Room you *have*. But, come, come: I'll ask no more questions—the answers all smell of new lords, new lands.' " [Ruskin's note]

[5] And the word means more, with me than with Sydney Smith (see his Memoirs); but it means *all* that *he* does, to begin with. [Ruskin's note]

[6] I must have been going away somewhere the day after I brought her to Denmark Hill. [Ruskin's note]

sharply round, saying, 'Are you unhappy, child?' 'Oh no!' said I, 'only my week is up, and I thought it was time——'

"I was not allowed to finish my sentence. She said, 'Never let me hear you say anything again about going; as long as you are happy here, stay, and we'll send for your clothes, and make arrangements about lessons, and everything else here.'

"And thus it came about that I stayed *seven years!*—till I married; going home now and then to Scotland, but always getting pathetic little letters there, telling me to 'come back as soon as my mother could spare me, that I was much missed, and nobody could ever fill my place.' And auntie was very old then (not that she ever could bear being called *old*, at ninety!), and I could not ever bear the thought of leaving her!"

64. Thus far Joanie; nor virtually have she and I ever parted since. I do not care to count how long it is since her marriage to Arthur Severn; only I think her a great deal prettier now than I did then: but other people thought her extremely pretty then, and I am certain that everybody *felt* the guileless and melodious sweetness of the face. Her first conquest was almost on our threshold; for half an hour or so after we had reached Denmark Hill, Carlyle rode up the front garden, joyfully and reverently received as always; and stayed the whole afternoon; even (Joan says) sitting with us during our early dinner at five. Many a day after that, he used to come; and one evening, "in describing with some rapture how he had once as a young man had a delightful trip into Galloway, 'where he was most hospitably entertained in the town of Wigtown by a Mr. Tweddale,' I (Joan) said quietly, 'I *am* so glad! That was my grandfather, and Wigtown is my native place!' He turned in a startled, sudden way, saying, 'Bless the child, is that so?' adding some very pretty compliments to my place and its people, which filled my heart with great pride. And, on another occasion, after he had been to meet the Queen at Dean Stanley's,[7] in describing to us some of the conversation, he made us laugh by telling how, in describing to Her Majesty the beauty of Galloway, that 'he believed there was no finer or more beautiful drive in her kingdom than the one round the shore of the Stewartry, by Gatehouse of Fleet,' he got so absorbed in his subject that, in drawing his chair closer to the Queen, he at last became aware he had fixed it on her dress, and that she could not move till he withdrew it! Do you think I may say farther"

(Of course, Joanic), "that Carlyle as a young man often went to my great aunt's (Mrs. Church) in Dumfriesshire; and he has several times told me that he considered *her* one of the most remarkable and kindest women he had ever known. On one occasion while there, he went to the little Cummertrees Church, where the then minister (as a joke sometimes called 'Daft Davie Gillespie') used to speak his mind very plainly from the pulpit, and while preaching a sermon on 'Youth and Beauty being laid in the grave,' something tickled Carlyle, and he was seen to smile; upon which Mr. Gillespie stopped suddenly, looked with a frown at Carlyle (who was sitting in my aunt's pew), and said, 'Mistake me not, young man; it is *youth alone* that *you* possess.' This was told to me, (Joan,) by an old cousin of mine who heard it, and was sitting next Carlyle at the time."

65. I am so glad to be led back by Joanie to the thoughts of Carlyle, as he showed himself to her, and to me, in those spring days, when he used to take pleasure in the quiet of the Denmark Hill garden, and to use all his influence with me to make me contented in my duty to my mother; which he, as, with even greater insistence, Turner, always told me was my first;—both of them seeing, with equal clearness, the happiness of the life that was possible to me in merely meeting my father's affection and hers, with the tranquil exertion of my own natural powers, in the place where God had set me.

Both at the time, and ever since, I have felt bitter remorse that I did not make Carlyle free of the garden, and his horse of the stables, whether we were at home or not; for the fresh air, and bright view of the Norwood hills, were entirely grateful and healing to him, when the little back garden at Cheyne Row was too hot, or the neighbourhood of it too noisy, for his comfort.

66. And at this time, nearly every opportunity of good, and peace, was granted in Joan's coming to help me to take care of my mother. She was perfectly happy, herself, in the seclusion of Denmark Hill; while yet the occasional evenings spent at George Richmond's, or with others of her London friends, (whose circle rapidly widened,) enabled her to bring back to my mother little bits of gossip which were entirely refreshing to both of us; for I used to leave my study whenever Joanie came back from these expeditions, to watch my mother's face in its glittering sympathy. I think I have said of her before, that although not witty herself, her strong sense gave her the

---

[7] Arthur Penrhyn Stanley (1815–81), Dean of Westminster.

keenest enjoyment of kindly humour, whether in saying or incident; and I have seen her laughing, partly *at* Joanie and partly *with* her, till the tears ran down her still brightly flushing cheeks. Joan was never tired of telling her whatever gave her pleasure, nor of reading to her, in quieter time, the books she delighted in, against which, girls less serenely—nay, less religiously, bred, would assuredly have rebelled,—any quantity, for instance, of Miss Edgeworth and Richardson.

(I interrupt myself for a moment to express, at this latter time of life, the deep admiration I still feel for Richardson. The follies of modern novel writing render it impossible for young people to understand the perfection of the human nature in his conception, and delicacy of finish in his dialogue, rendering all his greater scenes unsurpassable in their own manner of art. They belong to a time of the English language in which it could express with precision the most delicate phases of sentiment, necessarily now lost under American, Cockney, or scholastic slang.)

67. Joanie herself had real faculty and genius in all rightly girlish directions. She had an extremely sweet voice, whether in reading or singing; inventive wit, which was softly satirical, but never malicious; and quite a peculiar, and perfect, sense of clownish humour, which never for an instant diminished her refinement, but enabled her to sing either humorous Scotch, or the brightest Christy Minstrel carols, with a grace and animation which, within their gentle limits, could not be surpassed. She had a good natural faculty for drawing also, not inventive, but realistic; so that she answered my *first* lessons with serviceable care and patience; and was soon able to draw and paint flowers which were a great deal liker the flowers themselves than my own elaborate studies;—no one said of them, "What wonderful drawing!" but everybody said, "How like a violet, or a buttercup!" At that point, however, she stayed, and yet stays, to my sorrow, never having advanced into landscape drawing.

But very soon, also, she was able to help me in arranging my crystals; and the day divided itself between my mother's room, the mineral room, the garden, and the drawing-room, with busy pleasures for every hour.

68. Then, in my favourite readings, the deep interest which, in his period of entirely central power, Scott had taken in the scenery of the Solway, rendered everything that Joanie could tell me of her native bay and its hills, of the most living interest to me; and although, from my father's unerring tutorship, I had learned Scott's own Edinburgh accent with a precision which made the turn of every sentence precious to me, (and, I believe, my own rendering of it thoroughly interesting, even to a Scottish listener,)—yet every now and then Joanie could tell me something of old, classic, Galloway Scotch, which was no less valuable to me than a sudden light thrown on a chorus in Æschylus would be to a Greek scholar; —nay, only the other day I was entirely crushed by her interpreting to me, for the first time, the meaning of the name of the village of Captain Clutterbuck's residence,—Kennaquhair. [8]

69. And it has chiefly been owing to Joan's help,—and even so, only within the last five or six years,—that I have fully understood the power, not on Sir Walter's mind merely, but on the character of all good Scotchmen, (much more, good Scotchwomen,) of the two lines of coast from Holy Island to Edinburgh, and from Annan to the Mull of Galloway. Between them, if the reader will glance at any old map which gives rivers and mountains, instead of railroads and factories, he will find that all the highest intellectual and moral powers of Scotland were developed, from the days of the Douglases at Lochmaben, to those of Scott in Edinburgh,—Burns in Ayr,— and Carlyle at Ecclefechan, by the *pastoral* country, everywhere habitable, but only by hardihood under suffering, and patience in poverty; defending themselves always against the northern Pictish war of the Highlands, and the southern, of the English Edwards and Percys, in the days when whatever was loveliest and best of the

---

[8] "Ken na' where"! Note the cunning with which Scott himself throws his reader off the scent, in the first sentence of *The Monastery*, by quoting the learned Chalmers "for the derivation of the word 'Quhair,' from the winding course of the stream; a definition which coincides in a remarkable degree with the serpentine turns of the Tweed"! ("It's a *serpentine turn* of his own, I think!" says Joanie, as I show her the sentence,) while in the next paragraph he gives an apparently historical existence to "the village of which we speak," by associating it with Melrose, Jedburgh, and Kelso, in the "splendour of foundation by David I.," and concludes, respecting the lands with which the king endowed these wealthy fraternities, with a grave sentence, perhaps the most candid ever written by a Scotsman, of the centuries preceding the Reformation: "In fact, for several ages the possessions of these Abbeys were each a sort of Goshen, enjoying the calm light of peace and immunity, while the rest of the country, occupied by wild clans and marauding barons, was one dark scene of confusion, blood, and unremitted outrage." [Ruskin's note]

Catholic religion haunted still the—then *not* ruins,—of Melrose, Jedburgh, Dryburgh, Kelso, Dunblane, Dundrennan, New Abbey of Dumfries, and, above all, the most ancient Cave of Whithorn,—the Candida Casa of St. Ninian; while perfectly sincere and passionate forms of Evangelicalism purified and brightened the later characters of shepherd Cameronian life, being won, like all the great victories of Christianity, by martyrdoms, of which the memory remains most vivid by those very shores where Christianity was first planted in Scotland,—Whithorn is, I think, only ten miles south of Wigtown Bay; and in the churchyard of Wigtown, close to the old Agnew burying-ground, (where most of Joanie's family are laid,) are the graves of Margaret MacLachlan, and Margaret Wilson, over which in rhythm is recorded on little square tombstones the story of their martydom.

70. It was only, I repeat, since what became practically my farewell journey in Italy in 1882, that I recovered the train of old associations by re-visiting Tweedside, from Coldstream up to Ashestiel; and the Solway shores from Dumfries to Whithorn; and while what knowledge I had of southern and foreign history then arranged itself for final review, it seemed to me that this space of low mountain ground, with the eternal sublimity of its rocky seashores, of its stormy seas and dangerous sands; its strange and mighty crags, Ailsa and the Bass, and its pathless moorlands, haunted by the driving cloud, had been of more import in the true world's history than all the lovely countries of the South, except only Palestine. In my quite last journey to Venice I was, I think, justly and finally impressed with the sadness and even *weakness* of the Mediterranean coasts; and the temptation to human nature, there, to solace itself with debasing pleasures; while the very impossibility of either accumulating the treasurers, or multiplying the dreams, of art, among those northern waves and rocks, left the spirit of man strong to bear the hardships of the world, and faithful to obey the precepts of Heaven.

71. It is farther strange to me, even now, on reflection—to find how great the influence of this double ocean coast and Cheviot mountain border was upon Scott's imagination; and how salutary they were in withdrawing him from the morbid German fancies which proved so fatal to Carlyle: but there was this grand original difference between the two, that, with Scott, his story-telling and singing were all in the joyful admiration of that past with which he could re-people the scenery he gave the working part of his day to traverse, and all the sensibility of his soul to love;[9] while Carlyle's mind, fixed anxiously on the future, and besides embarrassed by the practical pinching, as well as the unconfessed shame, of poverty, saw and felt from his earliest childhood nothing but the faultfulness and gloom of the Present.

It has been impossible, hitherto, to make the modern reader understand the vastness of Scott's true historical knowledge, underneath its romantic colouring, nor the concentration of it in the production of his eternally great poems and romances. English ignorance of the Scottish dialect is at present nearly total; nor can it be without very earnest effort, that the melody of Scott's verse, or the meaning of his dialogue, can ever again be estimated. He must now be read with the care which we give to Chaucer; but with the greater reward, that what is only a dream in Chaucer, becomes to us, understood from Scott, a consummate historical morality and truth.

72. The first two of his great poems, *The Lay of the Last Minstrel* and *Marmion*, are the re-animation of Border legends, closing with the truest and grandest battle-piece that, so far as I know, exists in the whole compass of literature;[10]—the absolutely fairest in justice to both contending nations, the absolutely most beautiful in its conceptions of both. And that the palm in that conception remains with the Scotch, through the sorrow of their defeat, is no more than accurate justice to the national character, which rose from the fraternal branches of the Douglas of Tantallon and the Douglas of Dunkeld. But,—between Tantallon and Dunkeld,—what moor or mountain is there over which the purple cloud of Scott's imagination has not wrapt its light, in

---

[9] Yet, remember, so just and intense is his perception, and so stern his condemnation, of whatever is *corrupt* in the Scottish character, that while of distinctly evil natures—Varney, Rashleigh, or Lord Dalgarno—he takes world-wide examples,—the unpardonable baseness of so-called respectable or religious persons, and the cruelties of entirely selfish soldiers, are always Scotch. Take for the highest type the Lord Lindsay of *The Abbot,* and for the worst, Morton in *The Monastery,* then the terrible, *because* at first sincere, Balfour of Burleigh in *Old Mortality;* and in lower kind, the Andrew Fairservice and MacVittie of *Rob Roy,* the Peter Peebles of *Redgauntlet,* the Glossin of *Guy Mannering,* and the Saddletree of *The Heart of Midlothian.* [Ruskin's note]

[10] I include the literature of all foreign languages, so far as known to me: there is nothing to approach the finished delineation and flawless majesty of conduct in Scott's Flodden. [Ruskin's note]

those two great poems?—followed by the entirely heroic enchantment of *The Lady of the Lake*, dwelling on the Highland virtue which gives the strength of clanship, and the Lowland honour of knighthood, founded on the Catholic religion. Then came the series of novels, in which, as I have stated elsewhere, those which dealt with the history of other nations, such as *Ivanhoe, Kenilworth, Woodstock, Quentin Durward, Peveril of the Peak, The Betrothed*, and *The Crusaders*, however attractive to the general world, were continually weak in fancy, and false in prejudice; but the literally *Scotch* novels, *Waverley, Guy Mannering, The Antiquary, Old Mortality, The Heart of Midlothian, The Abbot, Redgauntlet*, and *The Fortunes of Nigel, are*, whatever the modern world may think of them, as faultless, throughout, as human work can be: and eternal examples of the ineffable art which is taught by the loveliest nature to her truest children.

Now of these, observe, *Guy Mannering, Redgauntlet*, a great part of *Waverley*, and the beautiful close of *The Abbot*, pass on the two coasts of Solway. The entire power of *Old Mortality* rises out of them, and their influence on Scott is curiously shown by his adoption of the name "Ochiltree" for his bedesman of Montrose, coming, not from the near hills, as one at first fancies, but from the Ochiltree Castle, which in Mercator's old map of 1637 I find in the centre of the archbishopric, then extending from Glasgow to Wigtown, and correspondent to that of St. Andrew's on the east,—the subordinate bishopric of Candida Casa, answering to that of Dunkeld, with the bishoprics of the isles of Sura, Mura, and Isla. It is also, Mercator adds in his note, called the "bishopric of Galloway."

73. "Even I," says Joanie, again, "remember old people who knew the real Old Mortality. He used to come through all the Galloway district to clean and re-cut the old worn gravestones of the martyrs; sometimes, I have been told, to the long since disused kirkyard of Kirkchrist, the place where my great aunt, Mrs. Church (Carlyle's friend, of whom I have spoken), began her married life. Kirkchrist is just on the opposite side from Kirkcudbright, overlooking the River Dee."

I must go back to a middle-aged map of 1773,

to find the noble river rightly traced from its source above Kenmure Castle to the winding bay which opens into Solway, by St. Mary's Isle; where Kirkchrist is marked as Christ K, with a cross, indicating the church then existing.

I was staying with Arthur and Joan, at Kenmure Castle itself in the year 1876, and remember much of its dear people: and, among the prettiest scenes of Scottish gardens, the beautiful trees on the north of that lawn on which the last muster met for King James; "and you know," says Joanie, "the famous song that used to inspire them all, of 'Kenmure's on and awa', Willie!' "[11] The thoughts come too fast upon me, for before Joanie said this, I was trying to recollect on what height above Solway, Darsie Latimer pauses with Wandering Willie, in whom Scott records for ever the glory,—not of Scottish music only, but of all *Music*, rightly so called,—which is a part of God's own creation, becoming an expression of the purest hearts.

74. I cannot pause now to find the spot,[12] and still less the churchyard in which, at the end of Wandering Willie's tale, his grandsire wakes: but, to the living reader, I have this to say very earnestly, that the whole glory and blessing of these sacred coasts depended on the rise and fall of their eternal sea, over sands which the sunset gilded with its withdrawing glow, from the measureless distances of the west, on the ocean horizon, or veiled in silvery mists, or shadowed with fast-flying storm, of which nevertheless every cloud was pure, and the winter snows blanched in the starlight. For myself, the impressions of the Solway sands are a part of the greatest teaching that ever I received during the joy of youth:—for Turner, they became the most pathetic that formed his character in the prime of life, and the five *Liber Studiorum* subjects, "Solway Moss," "Peat Bog, Scotland," "The Falls of Clyde," "Ben Arthur," and "Dunblane Abbey," remain more complete expressions of his intellect, and more noble monuments of his art, than all his mightiest after work, until the days of sunset in the west came for *it* also.

75. As *Redgauntlet* is, in its easily readable form, inaccessible, nowadays, I quote at once the two passages which prove Scott's knowledge of music, and the strong impression made on him by the

---

[11] "Lady Huntley plays Scotch tunes like a Highland angel. She ran a set of variations on 'Kenmure's on and awa',' which I told her were enough to raise a whole country-side. I never in my life heard such fire thrown into that sort of music."—*Sir Walter writing to his daughter Sophia. Lockhart's "Life,"* vol. iv. page 371. [Ruskin's note]

[12] It is on the highest bit of moor between Dumfries and Annan. Wandering Willie's "parishine" is only thus defined in *Redgauntlet*—"They ca' the place Primrose Knowe." [Ruskin's note]

scenery between Dumfries and Annan. Hear, first, of Darsie Latimer's escape from the simplicity of his Quaker friends to the open downs of the coast which had formerly seemed so waste and dreary:—

"The air I breathed felt purer and more bracing. The clouds, riding high upon a summer breeze, drove, in gay succession, over my head, now obscuring the sun, now letting its rays stream in transient flashes upon various parts of the landscape, and especially upon the broad mirror of the distant Firth of Solway."

A moment afterwards he catches the tune of "Old Sir Thom a Lyne," sung by three musicians "cosily niched into what you might call a *hunker*,[13] a little sandpit, dry and snug, surrounded by its banks, and a screen of furze in full bloom." Of whom the youngest, Benjie, at first

"somewhat dismayed at my appearance, but calculating on my placability, . . . almost in one breath assured the itinerants that I was 'a grand gentleman, and had plenty of money, and was very kind to poor folk,' and informed *me* that this was 'Willie Steenson, Wandering Willie, the best fiddler that ever kittled thairm (cat-gut) with horse-hair.' . . . I asked him if he was of this country. '*This* country!' replied the blind man, 'I am of every country in broad Scotland, and a wee bit of England to the boot. But yet I am in some sense of this country, *for I was born within hearing of the roar of Solway.*'"

76. I must pause again to tell the modern reader that no word is ever used by Scott in a hackneyed sense. For three hundred years of English commonplace, *roar* has rhymed to *shore,* as *breeze* to *trees*; yet in this sentence the word is as powerful as if it had never been written till now! for no other sound of the sea is for an instant comparable to the breaking of deep ocean, as it rises over great spaces of sand. In its rise and fall on a rocky coast, it is either perfectly silent, or, if it strike, it is with a crash, or a blow like that of a heavy gun. Therefore, under ordinary conditions, there may be either *splash,* or *crash,* or *sigh,* or *boom*; but not *roar.* But the hollow sound of the countless ranks of surfy breakers, rolling mile

after mile in ceaseless following, every one of them with the apparent anger and threatening of a fate which is assured death unless fled from,—the sound of this approach, over quicksands, and into inextricable gulfs of mountain bay, this, heard far out at sea, or heard far inland, through the peace of secure night—or stormless day, is still an eternal voice, with the harmony in it of a mighty law, and the gloom of a mortal warning.

The old man "preluded as he spoke . . . and then taking the old tune of 'Galashiels' for his theme, he graced it with a number of wild, complicated and beautiful variations; during which it was wonderful to observe how his sightless face was lighted up under the conscious pride and heartfelt delight in the exercise of his own very considerable powers."

"'What think you of that now, for threescore and twa?'"

77. I pause again to distinguish this noble pride of a man of unerring genius, in the power which all his life has been too short to attain, up to the point he conceives of,—from the base complacency of the narrow brain and dull heart, in their own chosen ways of indolence or error.

The feeling comes out more distinctly still, three pages forward, when his wife tells him, "'The gentleman is a gentleman, Willie; ye maunna speak that gate to him, hinnie.' 'The deevil I maunna!' said Willie,[14] 'and what for maunna I? If he was ten gentles, he *canna draw a bow like me, can he?*'"

78. I need to insist upon this distinction, at this time in England especially, when the names of artists, whose birth was an epoch in the world's history, are dragged through the gutters of Paris, Manchester, and New York, to decorate the last puffs written for a morning concert, or a monthly exhibition. I have just turned out of the house a book in which I am told by the modern picture dealer that Mr. A., B., C., D., or F. is "the Mozart of the nineteenth century"; the fact being that Mozart's birth wrote the laws of melody for all the world as irrevocably as if they had been set down by the waves of Solway; and as widely as

---

[13] This is a modern word, meaning, first, a large chest; then, a recess scooped in soft rock. [Ruskin's note]

[14] Joanie tells me she has often heard the fame of the *real* Wandering Willie spoken of: he was well known in travel from the Border right into Galloway, stopping to play in villages and at all sorts of out-of-the-way houses, and, strangely, succeeded by a *blind woman* fiddler, who used to come led by a sister; and the chief singing lessons in Joanie's young days were given through Galloway by a *blind man,* who played the fiddle to perfection; and his ear was so correct that if in a class of fifty voices one note was discordant, he would stop instantly, tap loudly on the fiddle with the back of his bow, fly to the spot where the wrong note came from, pounce on the person, and say, 'It was *you,* and it's no use denying it; if I can't *see,* I can *hear!*' and he'd make the culprit go over and over the phrase till it was conquered. He always opened the class with a sweeping scale, dividing off so many voices to each note, to follow in succession. [Ruskin's note]

the birth of St. Gregory in the sixth century fixed to *its* date for ever the establishment of the laws of musical expression. Men of perfect genius are known in all centuries by their perfect respect to all law, and love of past tradition; their work in the world is never innovation, but new creation; without disturbing for an instant the foundations which were laid of old time. One would have imagined—at least, any one but Scott would have imagined—that a Scottish blind fiddler would have been only the exponent of Scottish feeling and Scottish art; it was even with astonishment that I myself read the conclusion of his dialogue with Darsie Latimer:—

"'Are ye in the wont of drawing up wi' all the gangrel bodies that ye meet on the high road, or find cowering in a sand-bunker upon the links?' demanded Willie.

"'Oh, no! only with honest folks like yourself, Willie,' was my reply.

"'Honest folks like me! How do ye ken whether I am honest, or what I am? I may be the deevil himsell for what ye ken; for he has power to come disguised like an angel of light; and besides, he is a prime fiddler. He played a sonata to *Corelli*, ye ken.'"

79. This reference to the simplest and purest writer of Italian melody being not for the sake of the story, but because Willie's own art had been truly founded upon him, so that he had been really an angel of music, as well as light to him. See the beginning of the dialogue in the previous page:—

"'Do you ken the Laird?' said Willie, interrupting an overture of Corelli, of which he had whistled several bars with great precision."

I must pause again, to crowd together one or two explanations of the references to music in my own writings hitherto, which I can here sum by asking the reader to compare the use of the voice in war, beginning with the cry of Achilles on the Greek wall, down to what may be named as the two great instances of modern choral warsong: the singing of the known Church-hymn[15] at the Battle of Leuthen (*Friedrich*, vol. ii p. 259), in which "five-and-twenty thousand victor voices joined":

"Now thank God one and all,
With heart, with voice, with hands,

Who wonders great hath done
To us and to all lands;"—

and, on the counter side, the song of the Marseillaise on the march to Paris, which began the conquests of the French Revolution, in turning the tide of its enemies. Compare these, I say, with the debased use of modern military bands at dinners and dances, which inaugurate such victory as *we* had at the Battle of Balaclava, and the modern no-Battle of the Baltic, when our entire war fleet, a vast job of ironmongers, retreated, under Sir C. Napier, from before the Russian fortress of Cronstadt.

80. I preface with this question the repetition of what I have always taught, that the Voice is the eternal musical instrument of heaven and earth, from angels down to birds. Half way between them, my little Joanie sang me yesterday, 13th May, 1889, "Farewell, Manchester," and "Golden Slumbers," two pieces of consummate melody, which can only be expressed by the voice, and belonging to the group of like melodies which have been, not invented, but inspired, to all nations in the days of their loyalty to God, to their prince, and to themselves. That Manchester has since become the funnel of a volcano, which, not content with vomiting pestilence, gorges the whole rain of heaven, that falls over a district as distant as the ancient Scottish border,—is not indeed wholly Manchester's fault, nor altogether Charles Stuart's fault; the beginning of both faults is in the substitution of mercenary armies for the troops of nations *led* by their *kings*. Had Queen Mary led like Zenobia, at Langside; had Charles I. charged instead of Prince Rupert at Naseby; and Prince Edward bade Lochiel follow *him* at Culloden, we should not to-day have been debating who was to be our king at Birmingham or Glasgow. For the rest I take the bye-help that Fors gives me in this record of the power of a bird's voice only.[16]

81. But the distinction of the music of Scotland from every other is in its association with sweeter natural sounds, and filling a deeper silence. As Fors also ordered it, yesterday afternoon, before Joanie sang these songs to me, I had been, for for the first time since my return from Venice, down to the shore of my own lake, with her and her two youngest children, at the little promon-

---

[15] *Psalm,* I believe, rather; but see my separate notes on St. Louis' Psalter (now in preparation). [Ruskin's note]. The papers referred to have not been identified.

[16] "An extraordinary scene is to be witnessed every evening at Leicester in the freemen's allotment gardens, where a nightingale has established itself. The midnight songster was first heard a week ago, and every evening hundreds of people line the roads near the trees where the bird has his haunt. The crowds patiently wait till the music begins, and the bulk of the listeners remain till midnight, while a

tory of shingle thrown out into it by the only mountain brook on this eastern side, (Beck Leven,) which commands the windings of its wooded shore under Furness Fells, and the calm of its fairest expanse of mirror wave,—a scene which is in general almost melancholy in its perfect solitude; but, when the woods are in their gladness, and the green—how much purer, how much softer than ever emerald!—of their unsullied spring, and the light of dawning summer, possessing alike the clouds and mountains of the west,—it is, literally, one of the most beautiful and strange remnants of all that was once most sacred to this British land,—all to which we owe, whether the heart, or the voice, of the Douglas "tender and true," or the minstrel of the Eildons, or the bard of Plynlimmon, or the Ellen of the lonely Isle,— to whose lips Scott entrusted the most beautiful Ave Maria that was ever sung, and which can never be sung rightly again until it is remembered that the harp is the true ancient instrument of Scotland, as well as of Ireland.[17]

I am afraid of being diverted too far from Solway Moss, and must ask the reader to look back to my description of the Spirit of music in the Spanish chapel at Florence ("The Strait Gate," pages 134 and 135), remembering only this passage at the beginning of it, "After learning to reason, you will learn to sing: for you will want to. There is much reason for singing in the sweet world, when one thinks rightly of it. None for grumbling, provided always you *have* entered in at the strait gate. You will sing all along the road then, in a little while, in a manner pleasant for other people to hear."

82. I will only return to Scott for one half page more, in which he has contrasted with his utmost masterhood the impressions of English and Scottish landscape. Few scenes of the world have been oftener described, with the utmost skill and sincerity of authors, than the view from Richmond Hill sixty years since; but none can be compared with the ten lines in *The Heart of Midlothian*, edition of 1830, page 374:—

"A huge sea of verdure, with crossing and intersecting promontories of massive and tufted groves, was tenanted by numberless flocks and herds, which seemed to wander unrestrained, and unbounded, through the rich pastures. The Thames, here turreted with villas, and there garlanded with forests, moved on slowly and placidly, like the mighty monarch of the scene, to whom all its other beauties were but accessories, and bore on his bosom a hundred barks and skiffs, whose white sails and gaily fluttering pennons gave life to the whole.

"As the Duke of Argyle looked on this inimitable landscape, his thoughts naturally reverted to his own more grand and scarce less beautiful domains of Inveraray. 'This is a fine scene,' he said to his companion, curious perhaps to draw out her sentiments; 'we have nothing like it in Scotland.' 'It's braw rich feeding for the cows, and they have a fine breed o' cattle here,' replied Jeanie; 'but I like just as weel to look at the craigs of Arthur's Seat, and the sea coming in ayont them, as at a' thae muckle trees.'"

83. I do not know how often I have already vainly dwelt on the vulgarity and vainness of the pride in mere magnitude of timber which began in Evelyn's *Sylva*, and now is endlessly measuring, whether Californian pines or Parisian towers,— of which, though they could darken continents, and hide the stars, the entire substance, cost, and pleasure are not worth one gleam of leafage in Kelvin Grove, or glow of rowan tree by the banks

---

number of enthusiasts linger till one and two o'clock in the morning. Strange to say, the bird usually sings in a large thorn bush just over the mouth of the tunnel of the Midland main line, but the songster is heedless of noise, and smoke, and steam, his stream of song being uninterrupted for four or five hours every night. So large has been the throng of listeners that the chief constable has drafted a number of policemen to maintain order and prevent damage."—*Pall Mall Gazette*, May 11th, 1889. [Ruskin's note]

[17] Although the violin was known as early as 1270, and occurs again and again in French and Italian sculpture and illumination, its introduction, in superseding both the voice, the golden bell, and the silver trumpet, was entirely owing to the demoralization of the Spanish kingdom in Naples, of which Evelyn writes in 1644, "The building of the city is, for the size, the most magnificent in Europe. To it belongeth three thousand churches and monasteries, and those best built and adorned of any in Italy. They greatly affect the Spanish gravity in their habit, delight in good horses, the streets are full of gallants on horseback, and in coaches and sedans, from hence first brought into England by Sir Sanders Duncomb; the country people so jovial, and addicted to music, that the very husbandmen almost universally play on the guitar, singing and composing songs in praise of their sweethearts, and will commonly go to the field with their fiddle,—they are merry, witty, and genial, all which I attribute to the excellent quality of the air."

What Evelyn means by the *fiddle* is not quite certain, since he himself, going to study "in Padua, far beyond the sea," there learned to play on "ye theorba, taught by Signior Domenico Bassano, who had a daughter married to a doctor of laws, that played and sung *to nine* several instruments, with that skill and addresse as few masters in Italy exceeded her; she likewise composed divers excellent pieces. I had never seen any play on the *Naples viol* before." [Ruskin's note]

of Earn, or branch of wild rose of Hazeldean;—
but I may forget, unless I speak of it here, a walk
in Scott's own haunt of Rhymer's Glen,[18] where
the brook is narrowest in its sandstone bed, and
Mary Ker stopped to gather a wild rose for me.
Her brother, then the youngest captain in the
English navy, afterwards gave his pure soul up
to his Captain, Christ,—not like banished
Norfolk, but becoming a monk in the Jesuits'
College, Hampton.

84. And still I have not room enough to say
what I should like of Joanie's rarest, if not
chiefest merit, her beautiful dancing. *Real*
dancing, not jumping, or whirling, or trotting, or
jigging, but dancing,—like Green Mantle's in
Redgauntlet, winning applause from men and gods,
whether the fishermen and ocean Gods of Solway,
or the marchmen and mountain Gods of

Cheviot.[19] Rarest, nowadays, of all the gifts of
cultivated womankind. It *used* to be said of a
Swiss girl, in terms of commendation, she "prays
well and dances well"; but now, no human
creature can pray at the pace of our common
prayers, or dance at the pace of popular gavottes,
—more especially the last; for however fast the
clergyman may gabble, or the choir-boys yowl,
their psalms, an earnest reader can always *think*
his prayer, to the end of the verse; but no mortal
footing can give either the right accent, or the
due pause, in any beautiful step, at the pace of
modern waltz or polka music. Nay, even the last
quadrille I ever saw well danced, (and would
have given my wits to have joined hands in,) by
Jessie and Vicky Vokes, with Fred and Rosina,
was in truth *not* a quadrille, or four-square dance,
always dance everything *rightly*,[20] having not

---

[18] "Captain Adam Ferguson, who had written, from the lines of Torres Vedras, his hopes of finding,
when the war should be over, some sheltering cottage upon the Tweed, within a walk of Abbotsford,
was delighted to see his dreams realized; and the family took up their residence next spring at the new
house of Toftfield, on which Scott then bestowed, at the ladies' request, the name of *Huntley Burn;*—
this more harmonious designation being taken from the mountain brook which passes through its
grounds and garden,—the same famous in tradition as the scene of Thomas the Rhymer's interviews
with the Queen of Fairy.

"On completing this purchase, Scott writes to John Ballantyne:—'Dear John,—I have closed with
Usher for his beautiful patrimony, which makes me a great laird. I am afraid the people will take me
up for coining. Indeed these novels, while their attractions last, are something like it. I am very glad
of *your* good prospects. Still I cry, *Prudence! Prudence!* Yours truly, W. S.' "—*Lockhart's "Life,"* vol. iv. page
82. [Ruskin's notes]

[19] I must here once for all explain distinctly to the most matter-of-fact reader, the sense in which
throughout all my earnest writing of the last twenty years I use the plural word "gods." I mean by it,
the totality of spiritual powers, delegated by the Lord of the universe to do, in their several heights,
or offices, parts of His will respecting men, or the world that man is imprisoned in;—not as myself
knowing, or in security believing, that there are such, but in meekness accepting the testimony and
belief of all ages, to the presence, in heaven and earth, of angels, principalities, powers, thrones, and
the like,—with genii, fairies, or spirits ministering and guardian, or destroying or tempting; or aiding
good work and inspiring the mightiest. For all these, I take the general word "gods," as the best
understood in all languages, and the truest and widest in meaning, including the minor ones of seraph,
cherub, ghost, wraith, and the like; and myself knowing for an indisputable fact, that no true happiness
exists, nor is any good work ever done by human creatures, but in the sense or imagination of such
presences. The following passage from the first volume of *Fors Clavigera* gives example of the sense in
which I most literally and earnestly refer to them:—

"You think it a great triumph to make the sun draw brown landscapes for you! That was also a
discovery, and some day may be useful. But the sun had drawn landscapes before for you, not in brown,
but in green, and blue, and all imaginable colours, here in England. Not one of you ever looked at
them, then; not one of you cares for the loss of them, now, when you have shut the sun out with smoke,
so that he can draw nothing more, except brown blots through a hole in a box. There was a rocky
valley between Buxton and Bakewell, once upon a time, divine as the vale of Tempe; you might have
seen the gods there morning and evening,—Apollo and all the sweet Muses of the Light, walking in
fair procession on the lawns of it, and to and fro among the pinnacles of its crags. You cared neither
for gods nor grass, but for cash (which you did not know the way to get). You thought you could get
it by what the *Times* calls 'Railroad Enterprise.' You enterprised a railroad through the valley, you
blasted its rocks away, heaped thousands of tons of shale into its lovely stream. The valley is gone,
and the gods with it; and now, every fool in Buxton can be at Bakewell in half-an-hour, and every fool
in Bakewell at Buxton; which you think a lucrative process of exchange, you Fools everywhere!"
[Ruskin's note]

[20] Of *right* dancing, in its use on the stage, see the repeated notices in *Time and Tide*. Here is the
most careful one:—"She did it beautifully and simply, as a child ought to dance. She was not an
infant prodigy; there was no evidence, in the finish or strength of her motion, that she had been put
to continual torture through half her eight or nine years. She did nothing more than any child, well

only the brightest light and warmth of heart, but a faultless foot; faultless in freedom—never narrowed, or lifted into point or arch by its boot or heel, but level, and at ease, small, *almost* to a fault, and in its swiftest steps rising and falling with the gentleness which only Byron has found words for—

"Naked foot,
That shines like snow—and falls on earth as mute."

The modern artificial ideal being, on the contrary, expressed by the manner of stamp or tap, as in the Laureate's line—

"She tapped her tiny silken-sandalled foot."[21]

From which type the way is short, and has since been traversed quickly, to the conditions of patten, clog, golosh, and high-heeled bottines, with the real back of the foot thrown behind the ankle like a negress's, which have distressed alike, and disgraced, all feminine motion for the last quarter of a century,—the slight harebell having little chance enough of raising its head, once well under the hoofs of our proud maidenhood, decorate with dead robins, transfixed humming-birds, and hot-house flowers,—for its "Wedding March by Mendelssohn," To think that there is not enough love or praise in all Europe and America to invent one other tune for the poor things to strut to!

85. I draw back to my own home, twenty years ago, permitted to thank Heaven once more for the peace, and hope, and loveliness of it, and the Elysian walks with Joanie, and Paradisiacal with Rosie, under the peach-blossom branches by the little glittering stream which I had paved with crystal for them. I had built behind the highest cluster of laurels a reservoir, from which, on sunny afternoons, I could let a quite rippling

film of water run for a couple of hours down behind the hayfield, where the grass in spring still grew fresh and deep. There used to be always a corncake or two in it. Twilight after twilight I have hunted that bird, and never once got a glimpse of it: the voice was always at the other side of the field, or in the inscrutable air or earth. And the little stream had its falls, and pools, and imaginary lakes. Here and there it laid for itself lines of graceful sand; there and here it lost itself under beads of chalcedony. It wasn't the Liffey, nor the Nith, nor the Wandel; but the two girls were surely a little cruel to call it "The Gutter"! Happiest times, for all of us, that ever were to be; not but that Joanie and her Arthur are giddy enough, both of them yet, with their five little ones, but they have been sorely anxious about me, and I have been sorrowful enough for myself, since ever I lost sight of that peach-blossom avenue. "Eden-land" Rosie calls it sometimes in her letters. Whether its tiny river were of the waters of Abana,[22] or Euphrates, or Thamesis, I know not, but they were sweeter to my thirst than the fountains of Trevi or Branda.

86. How things bind and blend themselves together! The last time I saw the Fountain of Trevi, it was from Arthur's father's room— Joseph Severn's, where we both took Joanie to see him in 1872, and the old man made a sweet drawing of his pretty daughter-in-law, now in her schoolroom; he himself then eager in finishing his last picture of the Marriage in Cana, which he had caused to take place under a vine trellis, and delighted himself by painting the crystal and ruby glittering of the changing rivulet of water out of the Greek vase, glowing into wine. Fonte Branda I last saw with Charles Norton,[23] under the same arches where Dante saw it. We

---

taught, but painlessly, might do. She caricatured no older person,—attempted no curious or fantastic skill. She was dressed decently,—she moved decently,—she looked and behaved innocently,—and she danced her joyful dance with perfect grace, spirit, sweetness, and self-forgetfulness. And through all the vast theatre, full of English fathers and mothers and children, there was not one hand lifted to give her sign of praise but mine.

"Presently after this came on the forty thieves, who, as I told you, were girls; and there being no thieving to be presently done, and time hanging heavy on their hands, arms, and legs, the forty thief-girls proceeded to light forty cigars. Whereupon the British public gave them a round of applause.

"Whereupon I fell a-thinking; and saw little more of the piece, except as an ugly and disturbing dream." [Ruskin's note]

[21] Tennyson's *The Princess*, Prologue.   [22] II Kings 5:12.

[23] I must here say of Joanna and Charles Norton this much farther, that they were mostly of a mind in the advice they gave me about my books; and though Joan was, as it must have been already enough seen, a true-bred Jacobite, she curiously objected to my early Catholic opinions as roundly as either Norton or John P. Robinson. The three of them—not counting Lady Trevelyan or little Connie, (all together *five* opponent powers)—may be held practically answerable for my having never followed up the historic study begun in Val d'Arno, for it chanced that, alike in Florence, Siena, and Rome, all these friends, tutors, or enchantresses were at different times amusing themselves when I was at my

drank of it together, and walked together that evening on the hills above, where the fireflies among the scented thickets shone fitfully in the still undarkened air. *How* they shone! moving like fine-broken starlight through the purple leaves. How they shone! through the sunset that faded into thunderous night as I entered Siena three days before, the white edges of the mountainous clouds still lighted from the west, and the openly golden sky calm behind the Gate of Siena's heart, with its still golden words, "Cor magis tibi Sena pandit,"[24] and the fireflies everywhere in sky and cloud rising and falling, mixed with the lightning, and more intense than the stars.

---

hardest work; and many happy days were spent by all of us in somewhat luxurious hotel life, when by rights I should have been still under Padre Tino in the sacristy of Assisi, or Cardinal Agostini at Venice, or the Pope himself at Rome, with my much older friend than any of these, Mr. Rawdon Brown's perfectly faithful and loving servant Antonio. Of Joanna's and Connie's care of *me* some further history will certainly, if I live, be given in No. VII., "The Rainbows of Giessbach"; of Charles Norton's visit to me there also. [Ruskin's note]

[24] "Siena opens her great heart to you."

Queen Victoria

1819-1901

ALEXANDRINA VICTORIA, Queen of the United Kingdom of Great Britain and Ireland, Empress of India (after 1876), was the only child of the fourth son of King George III. George III's first and third sons preceded her to the throne, as Kings George IV and William IV, respectively. She ascended the throne on the death of the latter in 1837. Her reign of just under sixty-four years was to be the longest of any British monarch in history.

Trained from earliest childhood for royal responsibilities, Victoria proved to be firm-minded and an independent monarch when she took the throne. She displayed a preference for conservative prime ministers who often guided her judgment. The first of these was Lord Melbourne, who counseled her closely through the early years of her reign and formed something of an English counterbalance to the strong influence of her uncle, the King of Belgium.

In 1840 Victoria married Prince Albert of Saxe-Coburg and Gotha, thereby altering the name of the ruling house of England from Brunswick-Hanover to Saxe-Coburg. (It was subsequently changed by decree to Windsor by Victoria's successors.) With Albert Victoria had four sons and five daughters, thus exemplifying for Victorians a much admired pattern of domesticity. While he lived Albert worked closely with the Queen on matters of policy. He died in 1861, and for a long period Victoria remained in seclusion from public life.

The successful Disraeli administrations of the sixties and seventies, marked especially by the declaration of Victoria as Empress of India, returned her to the public arena and to the enduring affection of her subjects. Her relationship with Disraeli was particularly close and paralleled her earlier rapport with Melbourne. She made no secret of her preference for ministers like Disraeli over such as Gladstone and Palmerston. When she died in 1901, following Golden and Diamond Jubilees celebrated in 1887 and 1897, she was a venerated figure in England and the world at large and was already, through the marriages of her children, the grandmother of most of the royal houses of Europe.

Victoria was not a writer in any professional sense, but her extensive correspondence is of literary and of course historical interest, as is her record of life in the highlands. All of her writings reveal her solidly practical and sensible character, her seriousness of purpose, and indeed many of the qualities thought of today as quintessentially "Victorian."

CHRONOLOGY

1819   Born 24 May at Kensington Palace.
1837   Succeeds to throne 20 June on the death of William IV.
1840   Marries Prince Albert of Saxe-Coburg-Gotha.
1861   Death of Albert.
1876   Proclaimed Empress of India.
1887   Golden Jubilee.
1897   Diamond Jubilee.
1901   Dies 22 January; buried at Windsor Castle.

EDITIONS

Leaves from a Journal of Our Life in the Highlands, ed. Arthur Helps (1868).
More Leaves (1884).
Letters of Queen Victoria, 1837–61, first series, ed. A. C. Benson (1908).
Letters of Queen Victoria, 1861–1901, second and third series, ed. G. E. Buckle (6 vols., 1926–32).
Regina vs. Palmerston: Correspondence, ed. Brian Cornell (1962).
Victoria in the Highlands, ed. David Duff (1968).

BIOGRAPHY AND CRITICISMS

Sidney Lee, *Queen Victoria* (1903).
Lytton Strachey, *Queen Victoria* (1921).
Philip Guedalla, *The Queen and Mr. Gladstone* (1933).
Hector Bolitho, *The Reign of Queen Victoria* (1949).
Roger Fulford, *Hanover to Windsor* (1960).
Elizabeth Longford, *Victoria R.I.* (1964).
Winslow Ames, *Prince Albert and Victorian Taste* (1968).
David Duff, *Victoria Travels* (1970).
———, *Albert and Victoria* (1972).
Cecil Woodham-Smith, *Queen Victoria: Her Life and Times* (1972).

---

from Leaves from the Journal of
Our Life in the Highlands

The first publication of this work was a private one in 1867, but it was soon evident that general public interest attached to the Queen's observations. Accordingly the work was publicly issued in the following year. In 1884 an additional volume titled More Leaves *was published. The selections below are taken from the first volume of the Queen's journal and record her first experience of Balmoral, which, after purchase and new construction between 1848 and 1854, was to become one of her favorite residences and that of subsequent monarchs as well.*

BUILDING THE CAIRN ON CRAIG GOWAN, ETC.

Monday, October 11, 1852.

This day has been a very happy, lucky, and memorable one—our last! A fine morning.

Albert had to see Mr. Walpole, and therefore it was nearly eleven o'clock before we could go up to the top of *Craig Gowan,* to see the cairn built, which was to commemorate our taking possession of this dear place, the old cairn having been pulled down. We set off with all the children, ladies, gentlemen, and a few of the servants, including Macdonald and Grant, who had not already gone up; and at the *Moss House,* which is half way, Mackay met us, and preceded us, playing, Duncan and Donald Stewart[1] going before him, to the highest point of *Craig Gowan,* where were assembled all the servants and tenants, with their wives, and children, and old relations. All our little friends were there—Mary Symons and Lizzie Stewart, the four Grants, and several others.

I then placed the first stone, after which Albert laid one, then the children, according to their ages. All the ladies and gentlemen placed one; and then every one came forward at once, each person carrying a stone and placing it on the cairn. Mr. and Mrs. Anderson were there; Mackay played; and whisky was given to all. It took, I am sure, an hour building; and while it was going on, some merry reels were danced on a stone opposite. All the old people (even the gardener's wife from *Corbie Hall,* near *Abergeldie*) danced; and many of the children, Mary Symons and Lizzie Stewart especially, danced so nicely, the latter with her hair all hanging down. Poor dear old "Monk," Sir Robert Gordon's faithful old dog, was sitting there among us all. At last, when the cairn, which is, I think, seven or eight feet high, was nearly completed, Albert climbed up to the top of it, and placed the last stone, after which three cheers were given. It was a gay, pretty, and touching sight, and I felt almost inclined to cry. The view was so beautiful over the dear hills; the day so fine; the whole so *gemüthlich.* May God bless this place, and allow us yet to see it and enjoy it many a long year!

After luncheon, Albert decided to walk through the wood for the last time, to have a last chance, and allowed Vicky and me to go with him. At half past three o'clock we started, got out at Grant's, and walked up part of *Carrop,* intending to go along the upper path, when a stag was heard to roar, and we all turned into the wood. We crept along, and got into the middle path. Albert soon left us to go lower, and we sat down to wait for him; presently we heard a shot—then complete silence—and, after another pause of some little time, three more shots. This was again succeeded by complete silence. We sent some one to look, who shortly after returned, saying the stag had been twice hit, and they were after him. Macdonald next went in, and in about five minutes we heard "Solomon" give tongue, and knew he had the stag at bay. We listened a little while, and then began moving down, hoping to arrive in time; but the barking had ceased, and Albert had already killed the stag; and on the road he lay, a little way beyond *Invergelder*—the beauty that we had admired yesterday evening. He was a magnificent animal, and I sat down and scratched a little sketch of him on a bit of paper that Macdonald had in his pocket, which I put on a stone, while Albert and Vicky, with the others, built a little cairn to mark the spot. We heard, after I had finished my scrawl, and the carriage had joined us, that another stag had been seen near the road; and we had not gone as far as the "Irons"[2] before we saw one below the road, looking so handsome. Albert jumped out and fired—the animal fell, but rose again, and went on a little way, and Albert followed. Very shortly after, however, we heard a cry, and ran down and found Grant and Donald Stewart pulling up a stag with a very pretty head. Albert had gone on, Grant went after him, and I and Vicky remained with

---

[1] One of the keepers, whom we found here in 1848. He is an excellent man, and was much liked by the Prince; he always led the dogs when the Prince went out stalking. He lives in the Western Lodge, close to Grant's house, which was built for him by the Prince. [Victoria's note]

[2] These "Irons" are the levers of an old saw-mill which was pulled down, and they were left there to be sold—between thirty and forty years ago—and have remained there ever since, not being considered worth selling, on account of the immense trouble of transporting them. [Victoria's note]

Donald Stewart, the stag, and the dogs. I sat down to sketch, and poor Vicky unfortunately seated herself on a wasp's nest, and was much stung. Donald Stewart rescued her, for I could not, being myself too much alarmed. Albert joined us in twenty minutes, unaware of having killed the stag. What a delightful day! but sad that it should be the last day! Home by half past six. We found our beautiful stag had arrived, and admired him much.

LAYING THE FOUNDATION-STONE OF OUR NEW HOUSE.

September 28, 1853.

A fine morning early, but when we walked out at half past ten o'clock it began raining, and soon poured down without ceasing. Most fortunately it cleared up before two, and the sun shone brightly for the ceremony of laying the foundation-stone of the new house. Mamma and all her party arrived from *Abergeldie* a little before three. I annex the Programme of the Ceremony, which was strictly adhered to, and was really very interesting:

PROGRAMME

The stone being prepared and suspended over that upon which it is to rest (in which will be a cavity for the bottle containing the parchment and the coins),

The workmen will be placed in a semicircle at a little distance from the stone, and the women and home servants in an inner semicircle.

Her Majesty the Queen, and His Royal Highness the Prince, accompanied by the Royal Children, Her Royal Highness the Duchess of Kent, and attended by Her Majesty's guests and suite, will proceed from the house.

Her Majesty, the Prince, and the Royal Family will stand on the south side of the stone, the suite being behind and on each side of the Royal party.

The Rev. Mr. Anderson will then pray for a blessing on the work. Her Majesty will affix her signature to the parchment, recording the day upon which the foundation-stone was laid. Her Majesty's signature will be followed by that of the Prince and the Royal Children, the Duchess of Kent, and any others that Her Majesty may command, and the parchment will be placed in the bottle.

One of each of the current coins of the present reign will also be placed in the bottle, and the bottle, having been sealed up, will be placed in the cavity. The trowel will then be delivered to Her Majesty by Mr. Smith of Aberdeen, the architect, and the mortar having been spread, the stone will be lowered.

The level and square will then be applied, and their

correctness having been ascertained, the mallet will be delivered to Her Majesty by Mr. Stuart (the clerk of the works), when Her Majesty will strike the stone and declare it to be laid. The cornucopia will be placed upon the stone, and the oil and wine poured out by Her Majesty.

The pipes will play, and Her Majesty, with the Royal Family will retire.

As soon after as it can be got ready, the workmen will proceed to their dinner. After dinner, the following toasts will be given by Mr. Smith:

"The Queen."

"The Prince and the Royal Family."

"Prosperity to the house, and happiness to the inmates of Balmoral."

The workmen will then leave the dinner-room, and amuse themselves upon the green with Highland games till seven o'clock, when a dance will take place in the ballroom.

We walked round to the spot, preceded by Mackay. Mr. Anderson[3] made a very appropriate prayer. The wind was very high, but else every thing went off as well as could possibly be desired.

The workmen and people all gave a cheer when the whole was concluded. In about three quarters of an hour's time we went in to see the people at their dinner, and after this walked over to *Craig Gowan* for Albert to get a chance for black game.

We dressed early, and went for twenty minutes before dinner to see the people dancing in the ballroom, which they did with the greatest spirit.

THE KIRK.

October 29, 1854.

We went to Kirk, as usual, at twelve o'clock. The service was performed by the Rev. Norman McLeod, of *Glasgow*, son of Dr. McLeod, and any thing finer I never heard. The sermon, entirely extempore, was quite admirable; so simple, and yet so eloquent, and so beautifully argued and put. The text was from the account of the coming of Nicodemus to Christ by night; St. John, chapter iii. Mr. McLeod showed in the sermon how we *all* tried to please *self,* and live for *that,* and in so doing found no rest. Christ had come not only to die for us, but to show how we were to live. The second prayer was very touching; his allusions to us were so simple, saying, after his mention of us, "bless their children." It gave me a lump in my throat, as also when he prayed for "the dying, the wounded,

---

[3] The Minister of Carthie: he died November, 1866. [Victoria's note]

the widow, and the orphans." Every one came back delighted; and how satisfactory it is to come back from church with such feelings! The servants and the Highlanders—*all*—were equally delighted.

ARRIVAL AT THE NEW CASTLE AT BALMORAL.

September 7, 1855.

At a quarter past seven o'clock we arrived at dear *Balmoral*. Strange, very strange, it seemed to me to drive past, indeed *through* the old house, the connecting part between it and the offices being broken through. The new house looks beautiful. The tower and the rooms in the connecting part are, however, only half finished, and the offices are still unbuilt, therefore the gentlemen (except the Minister[4]) live in the old house, and so do most of the servants; there is a long wooden passage which connects the new house with the offices. An old shoe was thrown after us into the house, for good luck, when we entered the hall. The house is charming; the rooms delightful; the furniture, papers, every thing perfection.

IMPRESSIONS OF THE NEW CASTLE.

September 8, 1855.

The view from the windows of our rooms, and from the library, drawing-room, etc., below them, of the valley of the *Dee*, with the mountains in the background, which one never could see from the old house, is quite beautiful. We walked about, and alongside the river, and looked at all that has been done, and considered all that has to be done, and afterward we went over the poor dear old house, and to our rooms, which it was quite melancholy to see so deserted, and settled about things being brought over.

NEWS OF THE FALL OF SEVASTOPOL.

September 10, 1855.

Mamma, and her lady and gentleman, to dinner.

All were in constant expectation of more telegraphic dispatches. At half past ten o'clock two arrived—one for me, and one for Lord Granville. I began reading mine, which was from Lord Clarendon, with details from Marshal Pélissier of the farther destruction of the Russian ships; and Lord Granville said, "I have still better news;" on which he read, "From General Simpson—*Sevastopol is in the hands of the Allies.*" God be praised for it! Our delight was great; but we could hardly believe the good news, and, from having so long, so anxiously expected it, one could not realize the actual fact.

Albert said they should go at once and light the bonfire which had been prepared when the false report of the fall of the town arrived last year, and had remained ever since, waiting to be lit. On the 5th of November, the day of the battle of *Inkermann,* the wind upset it, strange to say; and now again, most strangely, it only seemed to *wait* for our return to be lit.

The new house seems to be lucky indeed, for, from the first moment of our arrival, we have had good news. In a few minutes Albert and all the gentlemen, in every species of attire, sallied forth, followed by all the servants, and gradually by all the population of the village—keepers, gillies, workmen—up to the top of the cairn. We waited, and saw them light it, accompanied by general cheering. The bonfire blazed forth brilliantly, and we could see the numerous figures surrounding it—some dancing, all shouting; Ross[5] playing his pipes, and Grant and Macdonald firing off guns continually; while poor old François d'Albertançon[6] lighted a number of squibs below, the greater part of which would not go off. About three quarters of an hour after, Albert came down, and said the scene had been wild and exciting beyond every thing. The people had been drinking healths in whisky, and were in great ecstasy. The whole house seemed in a wonderful state of excitement. The boys were with difficulty awakened, and when at last this was the case, they begged leave to go up to the top of the cairn.

We remained till a quarter to twelve; and, just as I was undressing, all the people came down under the windows, the pipes playing, the people singing, firing off guns, and cheering—first for me, then for Albert, the Emperor of the French, and the "downfall of *Sevastopol.*"

---

[4] The cabinet minister who was regularly in attendance upon the Queen.

[5] My Piper since 1854; he had served seventeen years in the 42d Highlanders—a very respectable, good man. [Victoria's note]

[6] An old servant of Sir R. Gordon's, who had charge of the house, and was a native of Alsace. He died in 1858. [Victoria's note]

THE BETROTHAL OF THE PRINCESS ROYAL.

September 29, 1855.

Our dear Victoria was this day engaged to
Prince Frederick William of Prussia, who had
been on a visit to us since the 14th. He had
already spoken to us, on the 20th, of his wishes
but we were uncertain, on account of her extreme
youth, whether he should speak to her himself, or
wait till he came back again. However, we felt
it was better he should do so; and during our
ride up *Craig-na-Ban* this afternoon, he picked a
piece of white heather (the emblem of "good
luck"), which he gave to her, and this enabled
him to make an allusion to his hopes and wishes
as they rode down *Glen Girnoch,* which led to this
happy conclusion.

George Eliot

[Mary Ann Evans Cross]

1819-1880

L IKE T HACKERAY, George Eliot was in the first instance a great
novelist of the Victorian age; but also like Thackeray and many
other novelists she engaged in literary criticism and in writing works
of nonfiction for intellectual journals.

George Eliot was born Mary Ann Evans near Nuneaton, Warwickshire.
she was well educated in several boarding schools in the area and later by visiting schoolmasters. She mastered German and Italian and developed a great
love of music. She was also intensely religious in her early years. Her mother
died when Mary Ann was seventeen, and she was obliged to take over the
management of the household. The family moved to Coventry in 1841, and
there she came under the influence of the writer Charles Bray and his brother-
in-law Charles Hennel, a well-known freethinker. Under the influence of the
Bray-Hennel circle she shed her fervent evangelicalism, and by 1844 she was
engaged in translating David Friedrich Strauss' *Leben Jesu* (Life of Jesus), a
skeptical inquiry into the nature of the historical Christ from the standpoint of
what was called the Higher Criticism.

Mary Ann Evans' father died in 1849. At first she traveled abroad with
the Brays, but in 1850 she returned to London and began writing for the *Westminster Review,* which in the following year she helped edit. She also translated
another skeptical German work, Feuerbach's *Essence of Christianity*. It was
during this period that she met George Henry Lewes with whom she was to
establish a relationship in 1854 that lasted until his death in 1878. In the late
eighteen-fifties she began writing stories and novels under the pseudonym
George Eliot. Eventually she devoted herself almost exclusively to this activity.
Of her many notable novels, including *Adam Bede* (1859), *The Mill on the Floss*
(1860), and *Silas Marner* (1861), the most highly regarded is *Middlemarch* (1871–
72), held by many critics to be the greatest novel of the Victorian era.

After Lewes' death in 1878 George Eliot was comforted by John Cross, an
old friend of Lewes and herself. She married him in May of 1880, but she died
within a few months of the marriage. She is buried in Highgate Cemetery in a
grave next to G. H. Lewes.

Intellectually George Eliot belongs to the rationalist tradition of the nineteenth century, and her criticism reflects the sobriety, clarity, and precision of that tradition. But George Eliot was never a narrow rationalist, and her criticism like her novels reflects a wider range of sympathy and understanding than is evident in other critics of the rationalist school. Her very exceptional intellectual brilliance is always at the service of a humanizing understanding of the need for traditions and values.

CHRONOLOGY

1819	Born 22 November near Nuneaton, Warwickshire.
1836	Mother dies.
1841	Family moves to Coventry.
1846	Translation of Strauss' *Leben Jesu*.
1849	Father dies; she travels abroad with the Brays.
1851	Becomes assistant editor of *Westminster Review;* meets G. H. Lewes.
1854	Forms lifelong union with Lewes.
1859	*Adam Bede.*
1871–72	*Middlemarch.*
1878	Death of Lewes.
1880	Marries John Cross. Dies 22 December; buried Highgate Cemetery, London.

EDITIONS

Except for the inclusion of *Works*, no attempt is made to list George Eliot's novels. These exist in many modern editions.

Works, The Cabinet Edition (2 vols., 1878–1885).
Impressions of Theophrastus Such (1879).
Essays of George Eliot, ed. Nathan Sheppard (1883).
Essays and Leaves from a Note-book, ed. C. L. Lewes (1884).
Essays and Reviews of George Eliot, ed. S. B. Herrick (1887).
The George Eliot Letters, ed. G. S. Haight (7 vols., 1954–55).
Essays of George Eliot, ed. Thomas Pinney (1963).

BIOGRAPHY AND CRITICISM

J. W. Cross, *George Eliot's Life and Letters* (1885).
Mary H. Deakin, *The Early Life of George Eliot* (1913).
Gerald Bullett, *George Eliot* (1947).
Joan Bennett, *George Eliot: Her Mind and Art* (1948).
Barbara Hardy, *The Novels of George Eliot* (1959).
W. J. Harvey, *The Art of George Eliot* (1961).
————, "George Eliot," in *Victorian Fiction: A Guide to Research* (1964).
Gordon S. Haight, *George Eliot: A Biography* (1968).
U. C. Knoepflmacher, *George Eliot's Early Novels* (1968).

Margaret Fuller and
Mary Wollstonecraft

George Eliot felt a special kinship with other woman writers of the nineteenth century, especially with the American Margaret Fuller. The following review, which appeared originally in the Leader *on 13 October 1855, was occasioned by the publication of Margaret Fuller's* Woman in the Nineteenth Century. *It also treats the celebrated independent woman Mary Wollstonecraft Shelley and her* Rights of Woman, *first published in 1792.*

THE DEARTH of new books just now gives us time to recur to less recent ones which we have hitherto noticed but slightly; and among these we choose the late edition of Margaret Fuller's *Woman in the Nineteenth Century*,[1] because we think it has been unduly thrust into the background by less comprehensive and candid productions on the same subject. Notwithstanding certain defects of taste and a sort of vague spiritualism and grandiloquence which belong to all but the very best American writers, the book is a valuable one: it has the enthusiasm of a noble and sympathetic nature, with the moderation and breadth and large allowance of a vigorous and cultivated understanding. There is no exaggeration of woman's moral excellence or intellectual capabilities; no injudicious insistance on her fitness for this or that function hitherto engrossed by men; but a calm plea for the removal of unjust laws and artificial restrictions, so that the possibilities of her nature may have room for full development, a wisely stated demand to disencumber her of the

> Parasitic forms
> That seem to keep her up, but drag her down—
> And leave her field to burgeon and to bloom
> From all within her, make herself her own
> To give or keep, to live and learn and be
> All that not harms distinctive womanhood.[2]

It is interesting to compare this essay of Margaret Fuller's published in its earliest form in 1843,[3] with a work on the position of woman, written between sixty and seventy years ago—we mean Mary Wollstonecraft's *Rights of Woman*.[4] The latter work was not continued beyond the first volume; but so far as this carries the subject, the comparison, at least in relation to strong

sense and loftiness of moral tone, is not at all disadvantageous to the woman of the last century. There is in some quarters a vague prejudice against the *Rights of Woman* as in some way or other a reprehensible book, but readers who go to it with this impression will be surprised to find it eminently serious, severely moral, and withal rather heavy—the true reason, perhaps, that no edition has been published since 1796, and that it is now rather scarce. There are several points of resemblance, as well as of striking difference, between the two books. A strong understanding is present in both; but Margaret Fuller's mind was like some regions of her own American continent, where you are constantly stepping from the sunny 'clearings' into the mysterious twilight of the tangled forest—she often passes in one breath from forcible reasoning to dreamy vagueness; moreover, her unusually varied culture gives her great command of illustration. Mary Wollstonecraft, on the other hand, is nothing if not rational; she had no erudition, and her grave pages are lit up by no ray of fancy. In both writers we discern, under the brave bearing of a strong and truthful nature, the beating of a loving woman's heart, which teaches them not to undervalue the smallest offices of domestic care of kindliness. But Margaret Fuller, with all her passionate sensibility, is more of the literary woman, who would not have been satisfied without intellectual production; Mary Wollstonecraft, we imagine, wrote not at all for writing's sake, but from the pressure of other motives. So far as the difference of date allows, there is a striking coincidence in their trains of thought; indeed, every important idea in the *Rights of Woman*, except the combination of home education with a common day-school for boys

---

[1] Published 1855.   [2] Tennyson's *The Princess*.
[3] *Woman in the Nineteenth Century* was an expansion of an earlier periodical article.
[4] The full title is *A Vindication of the Rights of Woman* (1792).

and girls, reappears in Margaret Fuller's essay.

One point on which they both write forcibly is the fact that, while men have a horror of such faculty or culture in the other sex as tends to place it on a level with their own, they are really in a state of subjection to ignorant and feeble-minded women. Margaret Fuller says:

Wherever man is sufficiently raised above extreme poverty or brutal stupidity, to care for the comforts of the fireside, or the bloom and ornamental of life, woman has always power enough, if she choose to exert it, and is usually disposed to do so, in proportion to her ignorance and childish vanity. Unacquainted with the importance of life and its purposes, trained to a selfish coquetry and love of petty power, she does not look beyond the pleasure of making herself felt at the moment, and governments are shaken and commence broken up to gratify the pique of a female favourite. The English shopkeeper's wife does not vote, but it is for her interest that the politician canvasses by the coarsest flattery.

Again:

All wives, bad or good, loved or unloved, inevitably influence their husbands from the power their position not merely gives, but necessitates of colouring evidence and infusing feelings in hours when the—patient, shall I call him?—is off his guard.

Hear now what Mary Wollstonecraft says on the same subject:

Women have been allowed to remain in ignorance and slavish dependence many, very many years, and still we hear of nothing but their fondness of pleasure and sway, their preference of rakes and soldiers, their childish attachment to toys, and the vanity that makes them value accomplishments more than virtues. History brings forward a fearful catalogue of the crimes which their cunning has produced, then the weak slaves have had sufficient address to over-reach their masters. . . . When, therefore, I call women slaves, I mean in a political and civil sense; for indirectly they obtain too much power, and are debased by their exertions to obtain illicit sway. . . . The libertinism, and even the virtues of superior men, will always give women of some description great power over them; and these weak women, under the influence of childish passions and selfish vanity, *will throw a false light over the objects which the very men view with their eyes who ought to enlighten their judgment.* Men of fancy, and those sanguine characters who mostly hold the helm of human affairs in general, relax in the society of women; and surely I need not cite to the most superficial reader of history the numerous examples of vice and oppression which the private intrigues of female favourites have produced; not to dwell on the mischief that naturally arises from the blundering interposition of well-meaning folly. *For in the transactions of business it is much better to have to deal with a knave than a fool, because a knave adheres to some plan, and any plan of reason may be seen through sooner than a sudden flight of folly.* The power which vile and foolish women have had over wise men who possessed sensibility is notorious.

There is a notion commonly entertained among men that an instructed woman, capable of having opinions, is likely to prove an impracticable yoke-fellow, always pulling one way when her husband wants to go the other, oracular in tone, and prone to give curtain lectures on metaphysics. But surely, so far as obstinacy is concerned, your unreasoning animal is the most unmanageable of creatures, where you are not allowed to settle the question by a cudgel, a whip and bridle, or even a string to the leg. For our own parts, we see no consistent or commodious medium between the old plan of corporal discipline and that thorough education of women which will make them rational beings in the highest sense of the word. Wherever weakness is not harshly controlled it must *govern*, as you may see when a strong man holds a little child by the hand, how he is pulled hither and thither, and wearied in his walk by his submission to the whims and feeble movements of his companion. A really cultured woman, like a really cultured man, will be ready to yield in trifles. So far as we see, there is no indissoluble connexion between infirmity of logic and infirmity of will, and a woman quite innocent of an opinion in philosophy, is as likely as not to have an indomitable opinion about the kitchen. As to airs of superiority, no woman ever had them in consequence of true culture, but only because her culture was shallow or unreal, only as a result of what Mrs. Malaprop well calls 'the ineffectual qualities in a woman'—mere acquisitions carried about, and not knowledge thoroughly assimilated so as to enter into the growth of the character.

To return to Margaret Fuller, some of the best things she says are on the folly of absolute definitions of woman's nature and absolute demarcations of woman's mission. 'Nature,' she says, 'seems to delight in varying the arrangements, as if to show that she will be fettered by no rule; and we must admit the same varieties that she admits.' Again: 'If nature is never bound down, nor the voice of inspiration stifled, that is enough. We are pleased that women should write and speak, if they feel need of it, from having something to tell; but silence for ages would be no misfortune, if that silence be from divine command, and not from man's tradition.' And here is a passage, the beginning of which has been often quoted:

If you ask me what offices they (women) may fill, I reply—any. I do not care what case you put; let them be sea-captains if you will. I do not doubt there are women well fitted for such an office, and, if so, I should be glad as to welcome the Maid of Saragossa, or the Maid of Missolonghi, or the Suliote heroine, or Emily Plater. I think women need, especially at this juncture, a much greater range of occupation than they have, to rouse their latent powers. . . . In families that I know, some little girls like to saw wood, other to use carpenter's tools. Where these tastes are indulged, cheerfulness and good-humour are promoted. Where they are forbidden, because 'such things are not proper for girls,' they grow sullen and mischievous. Fourier had observed these wants of women, as no one can fail to do who watches the desires of little girls, or knows the *ennui* that haunts grown women, except where they make to themselves a serene little world by art of some kind. He, therefore, in proposing a great variety of employments, in manufactures or the care of plants and animals, allows for one-third of women as likely to have a taste for masculine pursuits, one-third of men for feminine. . . . I have no doubt, however, that a large proportion of women would give themselves to the same employments as now, because there are circumstances that must lead them. Mothers will delight to make the nest soft and warm. Nature would take care of that; no need to clip the wings of any bird that wants to soar and sing, or finds in itself the strength of pinion for a migratory flight unusual to its kind. The difference would be that *all* need not be constrained to employments for which *some* are unfit.

A propos of the same subject, we find Mary Wollstonecraft offering a suggestion which the women of the United States have already begun to carry out. She says:

Women, in particular, all want to be ladies, Which is simply to have nothing to do, but listlessly to go they scarcely care where, for they cannot tell what. But what have women to do in society? I may be asked, but to loiter with easy grace; surely you would not condemn them all to suckle fools and chronicle small beer. No. *Women might certainly study the art of healing, and be physicians as well as nurses.* . . . Business of various kinds they might likewise pursue, if they were educated in a more orderly manner. . . . Women would not then marry for a support, as men accept of places under government, and neglect the implied duties.

Men pay a heavy price for their reluctance to encourage self-help and independent resources in women. The precious meridian years of many a man of genius have to be spent in the toil of routine, that an 'establishment' may be kept up

for a woman who can understand none of his secret yearnings, who is fit for nothing but to sit in her drawing-room like a doll-Madonna in her shrine. No matter. Anything is more endurable than to change our established formulæ about women, or to run the risk of looking up to our wives instead of looking down on them. *Sit divus, dummodo non sit vivus* (let him be a god, provided he be not living), said the Roman magnates of Romulus; and so men say of women, let them be idols, useless absorbents of precious things, provided we are not obliged to admit them to be strictly fellow-beings, to be treated, one and all, with justice and sober reverence.

On one side we hear that woman's position can never be improved until women themselves are better; and, on the other, that women can never become better until their position is improved—until the laws are made more just, and a wider field opened to feminine activity. But we constantly hear the same difficulty stated about the human race in general. There is a perpetual action and reaction between individuals and institutions; we must try and mend both by little and little—the only way in which human things can be mended. Unfortunately, many over-zealous champions of women assert their actual equality with men—nay, even their moral superiority to men —as a ground for their release from oppressive laws and restrictions. They lose strength immensely by this false position. If it were true, then there would be a case in which slavery and ignorance nourished virtue, and so far we should have an argument for the continuance of bondage. But we want freedom and culture for woman, because subjection and ignorance have debased her, and with her, Man; for—

If she be small, slight-natured, miserable,
How shall men grow?[5]

Both Margaret Fuller and Mary Wollstonecraft have too much sagacity to fall into this sentimental exaggeration. Their ardent hopes of what women may become do not prevent them from seeing and painting women as they are. On the relative moral excellence of men and women Mary Wollstonecraft speaks with the most decision:

Women are supposed to possess more sensibility, and even humanity, than men, and their strong attachments and instantaneous emotions of compassion are given as proofs; but the clinging affection of ignorance

[5] Tennyson's *The Princess*.

has seldom anything noble in it, and may mostly be resolved into selfishness, as well as the affection of children and brutes. I have known many weak women whose sensibility was entirely engrossed by their husbands; and as for their humanity, it was very faint indeed, or rather it was only a transient emotion of compassion. Humanity does not consist 'in a squeamish ear,' says an eminent orator. 'It belongs to the mind as well as to the nerves.' But this kind of exclusive affection, though it degrades the individual, should not be brought forward as a proof of the inferiority of the sex, because it is the natural consequence of confined views for even women of superior sense, having their attention turned to little employments and private plans, rarely rise to heroism, unless when spurred on by love! and love, as an heroic passion, like genius, appears but once in an age. I therefore agree with the moralist who asserts 'that women have seldom so much generosity as men;' and that their narrow affections, to which justice and humanity are often sacrificed, render the sex apparently inferior, expecially as they are commonly inspired by men; but I contend that the heart would expand as the understanding gained strength, if women were not depressed from their cradles.

We had marked several other passages of Margaret Fuller's for extract, but as we do not aim at an exhaustive treatment of our subject, and are only touching a few of its points, we have, perhaps, already claimed as much of the reader's attention as he will be willing to give to such desultory material.

Thomas Carlyle

This brief essay was a review of a volume of selections from Carlyle with a memoir, by Thomas Ballantyne, that appeared in 1855. George Eliot's review appeared originally in G. H. Lewes' Leader *for 27 October 1855. As she does elsewhere in letters and other writings, George Eliot here expresses something of her debt to Carlyle's writings and her awareness of their widespread influence in Victorian literature.*

IT HAS been well said that the highest aim in education is analogous to the highest aim in mathematics, namely, to obtain not *results* but *powers,* not particular solutions, but the means by which endless solutions may be wrought. He is the most effective educator who aims less at perfecting specific acquirements than at producing that mental condition which renders acquirements easy, and leads to their useful application; who does not seek to make his puplis moral by enjoining particular courses of action, but by bringing into activity the feelings and sympathies that must issue in noble action. On the same ground it may be said that the most effective writer is not he who announces a particular discovery, who convinces men of a particular conclusion, who demonstrates that this measure is right and that measure wrong; but he who rouses in others the activities that must issue in discovery, who awakes men from their indifference to the right and the wrong, who nerves their energies to seek for the truth and live up to it at whatever cost. The influence of such a writer is dynamic. He does not teach men how to use sword and musket, but he inspires their souls with courage and sends a strong will into their muscles. He does not, perhaps, enrich your stock of data, but he clears away the film from your eyes that you may search for data to some purpose. He does not, perhaps, convince you, but he strikes you, undeceives you, animates you. You are not directly fed by his books, but you are braced as by a walk up to an alpine summit, and yet subdued to calm and reverence as by the sublime things to be seen from that summit.

Such a writer is Thomas Carlyle. It is an idle question to ask whether his books will be read a century hence: if they were all burnt as the grandest of Suttees on his funeral pile, it would be only like cutting down an oak after its acorns have sown a forest. For there is hardly a superior or active mind of this generation that has not been modified by Carlyle's writings; there has hardly been an English book written for the last ten or twelve years that would not have been different if Carlyle had not lived. The character of his influence is best seen in the fact that many of the men who have the least agreement with his opinions are those to whom the reading of *Sartor Resartus* was an epoch in the history of their minds. The extent of his influence may be best seen in the fact that ideas which were startling novelties when he first wrote them are now become common-places. And we think few men will be found to say that this influence on the whole has not been for good. There are plenty who question the justice of Carlyle's estimates of past men and past times, plenty who quarrel with the exaggerations of the *Latter-Day Pamphlets,* and who are as far as possible from looking for an amendment of things from a Carlylian theocracy with the 'greatest man', as a Joshua who is to smite the wicked (and the stupid) till the going down of the sun. But for any large nature, those points of difference are quite incidental. It is not as a theorist, but as a great and beautiful human nature, that Carlyle influences us. You may meet a man whose wisdom seems unimpeachable, since you find him entirely in agreement with yourself; but this oracular man of unexceptionable opinions has a green eye, a wiry hand, and altogether a *Wesen,* or demeanour, that makes the world look blank to you, and whose unexceptionable opinions become a bore; while another man who deals in what you cannot but think 'dangerous paradoxes', warms your heart by the pressure of his hand, and looks out on the world with so clear and loving an eye, that nature seems to reflect the light of his glance upon your own feeling. So it is with Carlyle. When he is saying the very opposite of what we think, he says it so finely, with so hearty conviction—he makes the object about which we differ stand out in such grand relief under the clear light of his strong and honest intellect—he appeals so constantly to our sense of the manly and the truthful—that we are obliged to say 'Hear! hear'! to the writer before we can give the decorous 'Oh! oh'! to his opinions.

Much twaddling criticism has been spent on Carlyle's style. Unquestionably there are some genuine minds, not at all given to twaddle, to whom his style is antipathetic, who find it as unendurable as an English lady finds peppermint. Against antipathies there is no arguing; they are misfortunes. But instinctive repulsion apart, surely there is no one who can read and relish Carlyle without feeling that they could no more wish him to have written in another style than they could wish Gothic architecture not to be Gothic, or Raffaelle[1] not to be Raffaellesque. It is the fashion to speak of Carlyle almost exclusively as a philosopher; but, to our thinking, he is yet more of an artist than a philosopher. He glances deep down into human nature, and shows the causes of human actions; he seizes grand generalisations, and traces them in the particular with wonderful acumen; and in all this he is a philosopher. But, perhaps, his greatest power lies in concrete presentation. No novelist has made his creations live for us more thoroughly than Carlyle has made Mirabeau and the men of the French Revolution, Cromwell and the Puritans. What humour in his pictures! Yet what depth of appreciation, what reverence for the great and god-like under every sort of earthly mummery!

It is several years now since we read a work of Carlyle's *seriatim,* but this our long-standing impression of him as a writer we find confirmed by looking over Mr. Ballantyne's Selections. Such a volume as this is surely a benefit to the public, for alas! Carlyle's works are still dear, and many who would like to have them are obliged to forego the possession of more than a volume or two. Through this good service of Mr. Ballantyne's, however, they may now obtain for a moderate sum a large collection of extracts—if not the best that could have been made, still very precious ones.

To make extracts from a book of extracts may at first seem easy, and to make extracts from a writer so well known may seem superfluous. The *embarras de richesses* and the length of the passages make the first not easy; and as to the second, why, we have reread these passages so often in the volumes, and now again in Mr. Ballantyne's selection, that we cannot suppose any amount of repetition otherwise than agreeable. We will, however, be sparing.[2]

---

[1] I.e., Raphael.

[2] The remainder of the article, here omitted, consists of selections from Carlyle's writings.

Herbert Spencer

1820-1903

VICTORIAN LIBERALISM produced no more ambitious or industrious a spokesman than Herbert Spencer. With something like renaissance aspiration he undertook to set forth a systematic philosophy of all knowledge, but in this case based on purely rational and empirical principles, those that stood behind the thrust of utilitarianism, liberal political economy, and evolutionary Darwinism. Indeed it was evolution that underlay all of Spencer's thinking.

Herbert Spencer was born at Derby, eldest and only surviving of nine children. He was educated by an uncle at Hinton Charterhouse; later he became an engineer for various railways. He abandoned engineering for writing and philosophical study. He worked for a Birmingham newspaper and in 1848 became a subeditor of the *Economist,* a journal that advocated the laissez-faire economic principles that Spencer himself espoused. His support of this approach to economics was expressed in his *Social Statics* (1851), while his firm commitment to evolution even before Darwin was set forth in his *Principles of Psychology* (1855). Upon the appearance of the *Origin of the Species* Spencer found in it merely the practical application of the principles he had already advanced.

It is Spencer's "System of Synthetic Philosophy," begun in 1860, that represents his lifework. The system contains his *First Principles* (1862), *Principles of Biology* (1865–67), *Principles of Psychology* (1870–72, a revision of the earlier work), *Principles of Sociology* (1876–96), and *Principles of Ethics* (1879–93). In his system all phenomena are the result of an ultimately unknowable force that impels all things toward evolutionary change according to discernible laws. Spencer saw it as his mission to set forth the philosophy of those discernible laws and principles, leaving aside the question of the unknowable force. He even endeavored to derive a system of ethics from the known facts of science, though he admitted to finding less support here from Darwinism than he had anticipated. His educational theories ran heavily toward a scientific and anti-humanistic educational program.

Spencer spent the last forty years of the century working out his system, mainly in London, with occasional trips abroad, including one to the United States. His nerves gave way in his final decade and he moved to Brighton for his health. He died there in 1903; his *Autobiography* was published posthumously.

Spencer's writings had great currency in their day, but in the view of posterity his philosophy has not worn well, for it is seen as too deeply and limitingly involved in the now superseded science of his age. But as a supporter of the individualism characteristic of Victorian liberal thought Spencer is still recognized as speaking persuasively for the rights of the individual as opposed to the state. His writing is careful and pedantic, scientific rather than imaginative, but usually clear and sober and occasionally eloquent.

CHRONOLOGY

1820	Born 27 April at Derby.
1837	Civil engineer for London and Birmingham Railway.
1844	Subeditor of the Birmingham *Pilot*.
1848–53	Subeditor of the *Economist*.
1851	*Social Statics*.
1860–96	*A System of Synthetic Philosophy*.
1882	Visits America.
1898	Moves to Brighton.
1903	Dies in Brighton 8 December; ashes buried in Highgate Cemetery, London.

EDITIONS

Social Statics (1851).
Essays, Scientific, Political and Speculative (1858–1863).
Education: Intellectual, Moral and Physical (1861).
A System of Synthetic Philosophy (10 vols., 1860–96; 15 vols., 1900).
Philosophy of Style (1873).
The Man versus the State (1884).
Religion: A Retrospect and Prospect (1885).
Autobiography (2 vols., 1904).
Essays on Education and Kindred Subjects (1904; rpt. 1963).

BIOGRAPHY AND CRITICISM

William Henry Hudson, *Introduction to the Philosophy of Herbert Spencer* (1894).
J. Arthur Thomson, *Herbert Spencer* (1906).
David Duncan, *Life and Letters of Herbert Spencer* (1908).
William Henry Hudson, *Herbert Spencer* (1908).
Hugh Elliot, *Herbert Spencer* (1917).
J. Rumney, *Herbert Spencer's Sociology* (1934).
Rudolf Metz, *A Hundred Years of British Philosophy* (1938).
Richard Hofstadter, *Social Darwinism in American Thought* (1944).
T. Munro, *Evolution in the Arts* (1964).
A. O. J. Cockshut, *The Unbelievers* (1964).
J. W. Burrow, *Evolution and Society* (1966).

Use and Beauty

One of Spencer's many essays directed toward harmonizing what sometimes seem opposing principles, by seeing beauty as an after-effect of use, "Use and Beauty" was first published in The Leader *of 3 January 1852. It was later collected in his* Essays, Scientific, Political and Speculative *(1902).*

IN ONE of his essays, Emerson remarks, that what Nature at one time provides for use, she afterwards turns to ornament; and he cites in illustration the structure of a sea-shell, in which the parts that have for a while formed the mouth are at the next season of growth left behind, and become decorative nodes and spines.

Ignoring the implied teleology, which does not here concern us, it has often occurred to me that this same remark might be extended to the progress of Humanity. Here, too, the appliances of one era serve as embellishments to the next. Equally in institutions, creeds, customs, and superstitions, we may trace this evolution of beauty out of what was once purely utilitarian.

The contrast between the feeling with which we regard portions of the Earth's surface still left in their original state, and the feeling with which the savage regarded them, is an instance that comes first in order of time. If any one walking over Hampstead Heath, will note how strongly its picturesqueness is brought out by contrast with the surrounding cultivated fields and the masses of houses lying in the distance; and will further reflect that, had this irregular gorse-covered surface extended on all sides to the horizon, it would have looked dreary and prosaic rather than pleasing; he will see that to the primitive man a country so clothed presented no beauty at all. To him it was merely a haunt of wild animals, and a ground out of which roots might be dug. What have become for us places of relaxation and enjoyment—places for afternoon strolls and for gathering flowers—were his places for labour and food, probably arousing in his mind none but utilitarian associations.

Ruined castles afford obvious instances of this metamorphosis of the useful into the beautiful. To feudal barons and their retainers, security was the chief, if not the only end, sought in choosing the sites and styles of their strongholds. Probably they aimed as little at the picturesque as do the builders of cheap brick houses in our modern towns. Yet what were erected for shelter and safety, and what in those early days fulfilled an important function in the social economy, have now assumed a purely ornamental character. They serve as scenes for picnics; pictures of them decorate our drawing-rooms; and each supplies its surrounding districts with legends for Christmas Eve.

On following out the train of thought suggested by this last illustration, we may see that not only do the material exuviæ of past social states become the ornaments of our landscapes; but that past habits, manners, and arrangements, serve as ornamental elements in our literature. The tyrannies which, to the serfs who bore them, were harsh and dreary facts; the feuds which, to those who took part in them, were very practical life-and-death affairs; the mailed, moated, sentinelled security which was irksome to the nobles who needed it; the imprisonments, and tortures, and escapes, which were stern and quite prosaic realities to all concerned in them; have become to us material for romantic tales—material which, when woven into Ivanhoes and Marmions, serves for amusement in leisure hours, and becomes poetical by contrast with our daily lives.

Thus, also, is it with extinct creeds. Stonehenge, which in the hands of the Druids had a governmental influence over men, is in our day a place for antiquarian excursions; and its attendant priests are worked up into an opera. Greek sculptures, preserved for their beauty in our galleries of art, and copied for the decoration of pleasure grounds and entrance halls, once lived in men's minds as gods demanding obedience; as did also the grotesque idols that now amuse the visitors to our museums.

Equally marked is this change of function in the case of minor superstitions. The fairy lore, which in past times was matter of grave belief, and held sway over people's conduct, have since been transformed into ornament for *A Midsummer Night's Dream, The Tempest, The Fairy Queen,* and endless small tales and poems; and still affords subjects for children's storybooks, themes for ballets, and plots for Planché's burlesques. Gnomes, and genii, and afrits, losing their terrors, give piquancy to the woodcuts in our illustrated edition of the *Arabian Nights*. While ghost-stories, and tales of magic and witchcraft, after serving to amuse boys and girls in their leisure hours, become matter for jocose allusions that enliven tea-table conversation.

Even our serious literature and our speeches are relieved by ornaments drawn from such sources. A Greek myth is often used as a parallel by which to vary the monotony of some grave argument. The lecturer breaks the dead level of his practical discourse by illustrations drawn from byegone customs, events, or beliefs. And metaphors, similarly derived, give brilliancy to political orations, and to *Times* leading articles.

Indeed, on careful inquiry, I think it will be found that we turn to purposes of beauty most byegone phenomena which are at all conspicuous. The busts of great men in our libraries, and their tombs in our churches; the once useful but now purely ornamental heraldic symbols; the monks, nuns, and convents, which give interest to a certain class of novels; the bronze mediæval soldiers used for embellishing drawing-rooms; the gilt Apollos which recline on time-pieces; the narratives that serve as plots for our great dramas; and the events that afford subjects for historical pictures;—these and such like illustrations of the metamorphosis of the useful into the beautiful, are so numerous as to suggest that, did we search diligently enough, we should find that in some place, or under some circumstance, nearly every notable product of the past has assumed a decorative character.

And here the mention of historical pictures reminds me that an inference may be drawn from all this, bearing directly on the practice of art. It has of late years been a frequent criticism upon our historical painters, that they err in choosing their subjects from the past; and that, would they found a genuine and vital school, they must render on canvas the life and deeds and aims of our own time. If, however, there be any significance in the foregoing facts, it seems doubtful whether this criticism is a just one. For if it be the course of things that what has performed some active function in society during one era, becomes available for ornament in a subsequent one; it almost follows that, conversely, whatever is performing some active function now, or has very recently performed one, does not possess the ornamental character; and is, consequently, inapplicable to any purpose of which beauty is the aim, or of which it is a needful ingredient.

Still more reasonable will this conclusion appear, when we consider the nature of this process by which the useful is changed into the ornamental. An essential pre-requisite to all beauty is *contrast*. To obtain artistic effect, light must be put in juxtaposition with shade, bright colours with dull colours, a fretted surface with a plain one. *Forte* passages in music must have *piano* passages to relieve them; concerted pieces need interspersing with solos; and rich chords must not be continuously repeated. In the drama we demand contrast of characters, of scenes, of sentiment, of style. In prose composition an eloquent passage should have a comparatively plain setting; and in poems great effect is obtained by occasional change of versification. This general principle will, I think, explain the transformation of the bygone useful into the present beautiful. It is by virtue of their contrast with out present modes of life, that past modes of life look interesting and romantic. Just as a picnic, which is a temporary return to an aboriginal condition, derives, from its unfamiliarity, a certain poetry which it would not have were it habitual; so, everything ancient gains, from its relative novelty to us, an element of interest. Gradually as, by the growth of society, we leave behind the customs, manners, arrangements, and all the products, material and mental, of a bygone age—gradually as we recede from these so far that there arises a conscpiuous difference between them and those we are familiar with; so gradually do they begin to assume to us a poetical aspect, and become applicable for ornament. And hence it follows that things and events which are close to us, and which are accompanied by associations of ideas not markedly contrasted with our ordinary associations, are *relatively* inappropriate for purposes of art. I say relatively because an incident of modern life or even of daily life may acquire adequate fitness for art purposes by an unusualness of some other kind than that due to unlikeness between past and present.

from Principles of Ethics

Spencer's Principles of Ethics *appeared between 1879 and 1893. It was designed as the capstone of his "synthetic philosophy" and was supposed to bridge the gulf between ethical behavior and the impersonal findings of science so that the two would be shown to be part of the same philosophic whole. The primary principle that emerges, however, is that of individual liberty. The selection that follows illustrates Spencer's thinking on a question that was of absorbing interest to Victorians and continues to interest readers today.*

The Rights of Women

WHEN in certain preceding chapters the fundamental principle of justice was discussed, a relevant question which might have been raised, I decided to postpone, because I thought discussion of it would appropriately introduce the subject-matter of this chapter.

"Why," it might have been asked, "should not men have rights proportionate to their faculties? Why should not the sphere of action of the superior individual be greater than that of the inferior individual? Surely, as a big man occupies more space than a little man, so too does he need larger supplies of the necessaries of life; and so, too, does he need greater scope for the use of his powers. Hence it is unreasonable that the activities of great and small, strong and weak, high and low, should be severally restrained within limits too narrow for these and too wide for those."

The first reply is that the metaphors which we are obliged to use are misleading if interpreted literally. Though, as above, and as in previous chapters, men's equal liberties are figured as spaces surrounding each, which mutually limit one another, yet they cannot be truly represented in so simple a manner. The inferior man, who claims as great a right to bodily integrity as the superior man, does not by doing this trespass on the bodily integrity of the superior man. If he asserts like freedom with him to move about and to work, he does not thereby prevent him from moving about and working. And if he retains as his own whatever his activities have gained for him, he in no degree prevents the superior man from retaining the produce of his activities, which, by implication, are greater in amount.

The second reply is that denying to inferior faculty a sphere of action equal to that which superior faculty has, is to add an artificial hardship to a natural hardship. To be born with a dwarfed or deformed body, or imperfect senses, or a feeble constitution, or a low intelligence, or ill-balanced emotions, is in itself a pitiable fate. Could we charge Nature with injustice, we might fitly say it is unjust that some should have natural endowments so much lower than others have, and that they should thus be in large measure incapacitated for the battle of life. And if so, what shall we say to the proposal that, being already disadvantaged by having smaller powers, they should be further disadvantaged by having narrower spheres for the exercise of those powers? Sympathy might contrariwise urge that, by way of compensation for inherited disabilities, they should have extended opportunities. But, evidently the least that can be done is to allow them as much freedom as others to make the best of themselves.

A third reply is that, were it equitable to make men's liberties proportionate to their abilities, it would be impracticable; since we have no means by which either the one or the other can be measured. In the great mass of cases there is no difficulty in carrying out the principle of equality. If, (previous aggression being supposed absent,) A kills B, or knocks him down, or locks him up, it is clear that the liberties of action assumed by the two are unlike; or if C, having bought goods of D, does not pay the price agreed upon, it is clear that the contract having been fulfilled on one side and not on the other, the degrees of freedom used are not the same. But if liberties are to be proportioned to abilities, then the implication is that the relative amounts of each faculty, bodily and mental, must be ascertained; and the further implication is that the several kinds of freedom needed must be meted out. Neither of these things can be done; and therefore, apart from other reasons, the regard for practicability would require us to treat men's freedoms as equal, irrespective of their endowments.

With change of terms these arguments are applicable to the relation between the rights of men and the rights of women. This is not the place for comparing in detail the capacities of men and women. It suffices for present purposes to recognize the unquestionable fact that some women are physically stronger than some men, and that some women have higher mental endowments than some men—higher, indeed, than the great majority of men. Hence it results, as above, that were liberties to be adjusted to abilities, the adjustment, even could we make it, would have to be made irrespective of sex.

The difficulty reappears under another form, if we set out with the proposition that just as, disregarding exceptions, the average physical powers of women are less than the average physical powers of men, so too are their average mental powers. For we could not conform our plans to this truth: it would be impossible to ascertain the ratio between the two averages; and if would be impossible rightly to proportion the spheres of activity to them.

But, as above argued, generosity prompting equalization would direct that were any difference to be made it ought to be that, by way of compensation, smaller faculties should have greater facilities. Generosity aside however, justice demands the women, if they are not artificially advantaged, must not, at any rate, be artificially disadvantaged.

Hence, if men and women are severally ragarded as independent members of a society, each one of whom has to do the best for himself or herself, it results that no restraints can equitably be placed upon women in respect of the occupations, professions, or other careers which they may wish to adopt. They must have like freedom to prepare themselves, and like freedom to profit by such information and skill as they acquire.

But more involved questions arise when we take into account the relations of women to men in marriage, and the relations of women to men in the State.

Of these equal liberties with men which women should have before marriage, we must say that in equity they retain after marriage all those which are not necessarily interfered with by the marital relation—the rights to physical integrity, the rights to ownership of property earned and property given or bequeathed, the rights to free belief and free speech, &c. Their claims can properly be qualified only in so far as they are traversed by the understood or expressed terms of the contract voluntarily entered into; and as these terms vary in different places and times, the resulting qualifications must vary. Here, in default of definite measures, we must be content with approximations.

In respect of property, for instance, it may be reasonably held that where the husband is exclusively responsible for maintenance of the family, property which would otherwise belong to the wife may equitably be assigned to him—the use, at least, if not the possession; since, if not, it becomes possible for the wife to use her property or its proceeds for her personal benefit only, and refuse to contribute towards the expenses of the joint household. Only is she is equally responsible with him for family maintenance, does it seem right that she should have equally unqualified ownership of property. Yet, on the other hand, we cannot say that the responsibilities must be entirely reciprocal. For though, rights of ownership being supposed equal; it would at first sight appear that the one is as much bound as the other to maintain the two and their children; yet this is negatived by the existence on the one side of onerous functions which do not exist on the other, and which largely incapacitate for active life. Nothing more than a compromise, varying according to the circumstances, seems here possible. The discharge of domestic and maternal duties by the wife may ordinarily be held a fair equivalent for the earning of an income by the husband.

Respecting powers of control over one another's actions and over the household, the conclusions to be drawn are still more indefinite. The relative positions of the two as contributors of monies and services have to be taken into account, as well as their respective natures; and these factors in the problem are variable. When there arise conflicting wills of which both cannot be fulfilled, but one of which must issue in action, the law of equal freedom cannot, in each particular case, be conformed to; but can be conformed to only in the average of cases. Whether it should be conformed to in the average of cases must depend on circumstances. We may, however, say that since, speaking generally, man is more judicially-minded than woman, the balance of authority should incline to the side of the husband; especially as he usually provides the means which make possible the fulfilment of the will of either or the wills of both. But in respect of this relation reasoning goes for little: the characters of those concerned determine the form it takes. The only effect which ethical considerations are likely to have is that of moderating the use of such supremacy as eventually arises.

The remaining question, equally involved or more involved, concerns the possession and management of children. Decisions about management have to be made daily; and decisions about possession must be made in all cases of separation. What are the relative claims of husband and wife in such cases? On the one hand, it may be said of the direct physical claims, otherwise equal, that that of the mother is rendered far greater by the continued nutrition before and after birth, than that of the father. On the other hand, it may be urged on the part of the father, that in the normal order the food by which the mother has been supported and the nutrition of the infant made possible, has been provided by his labour. Whether this counter-claim be or be not equivalent, it must be admitted that the claim of the mother cannot well be less than that of the father. Of the compromise respecting management which justice thus appears to dictate, we may perhaps reasonably say that the power of the mother may fitly predominate during the earlier part of a child's life, and that of the father during the later part. The maternal nature is better adjusted to the needs of infancy and early childhood than the paternal nature; while for fitting children, and especially boys, for the battle of life, the father, who has had most experience of it, may be considered the best guide. But it seems alike inequitable and inexpedient that the power of either should at any time be exercised to the exclusion of the power of the other. Of the respective claims to possession where separation takes place, some guidance is again furnished by consideration of children's welfare; an equal division, where it is possible, being so made that the younger remain with the mother and the elder to with the father. Evidently, however, nothing is here possible but compromise based on consideration of the special circumstances.

Concerning the claims of women, as domestically associated with men, I may add that here in England, and still more in America, the need for urging them is not pressing. In some cases, indeed, there is a converse need. But there are other civilized societies in which their claims are very inadequately recognized: instance Germany.[1]

As in other cases, let us look now at the stages through which usage and law have grown into conformity with ethics.

Save among the few primitive peoples who do not preach the virtues called Christian but merely practise them—save among those absolutely peaceful tribes here and there found who, while admirable in their general conduct, treat their women with equity as well as kindness, uncivilized tribes at large have no more conception of the rights of women than of the rights of brutes. Such regard for women's claims as enables mothers to survive and rear offspring, of course exists; since tribes in which it is less than this disappear. But, frequently, the regard is not greater than is needful to prevent extinction.

When we read of a Fijian that he might kill and eat his wife if he pleased; of the Fuegians and wilder Australians that they sacrificed their old women for food; and of the many peoples among whom women are killed to accompany their dead husbands to the other world; we see that they are commonly denied even the first of all rights. The facts that in these low stages women, leading the lives of slaves, are also sold as slaves, and, when married, are either stolen or bought, prove that no liberties are recognized as belonging to them. And on remembering that where wives are habitually considered as property, the implication is that independent ownership of property by them can scarcely exist, we are shown that this further fundamental right is at the outset but very vaguely recognized. Though the matter is in many cases complicated and qualified by the system of descent in the female line, it is certain that, speaking generally, in rude societies where among men aggression is restrained only by fear of vengeance, the claims of women are habitually disregarded.

To trace up in this place the rising *status* of women is out of the question. Passing over those ancient societies in which descent in the female line gave to women a relatively high position, as it did among the Egyptians, it will suffice to

[1] With other reasons prompting this remark, is joined the remembrance of a conversation between two Germans residing in England, in which, with contemptuous laughter, they were describing how they had often seen, on a Sunday or other holiday, an English artizan relieving his wife by carrying the child they had with them. Their sneers produced in me a feeling of shame—but not for the artizan. [Spencer's note]

note that in societies which have arisen by aggregation of patriarchal groups, the rights of women, at first scarcely more recognized than among savages, have, during these two thousand years, gradually established themselves. Limiting our attention to the Aryans who overspread Europe, we see that save where, as indicated by Tacitus, women, by sharing in the dangers of war, gained a better position (a connexion of facts which we find among various peoples), they were absolutely subordinated. The primitive Germans bought their wives; and husbands might sell and even kill them. In the early Teutonic society, as in the early Roman society, there was perpetual tutelage of women, and consequent incapacity for independent ownership of property. A like state of things existed here in the old English period. Brides were purchased: their wills counting for nothing in the bargains. Mitigations gradually came. Among the Romans the requirement that a bride should be transferred to the bridegroom by legal conveyance, ceased to be observed. The life and death power came to an end: though sometimes reappearing, as when the early Angevin ruler, Fulc the Black, burnt his wife. Generalizing the facts we see that as life became less exclusively militant, the subjection of women to men became less extreme. How that decline of the system of *status* and rise of the system of contract, which characterizes industrialism, ameliorated, in early days, the position of women, is curiously shown by the occurrence of their signatures in the documents of guilds, while yet their position outside of the guilds remained much as before. This connexion has continued to be a general one. Both in England and in America, where the industrial type of organization is most developed, the legal *status* of women is higher than on the continent, where militancy is more pronounced. Add to which that among ourselves, along with the modern growth of free institutions characterizing predominant industrialism, the positions of women have been with increasing rapidity approximated to those of men.

Here again, then, ethical deductions harmonize with historical inductions. As in preceding chapters we saw that each of those corollaries from the law of equal freedom which we call a right, has been better established as fast as a higher social life has been reached; so here, we see that the general body of such rights, originally denied entirely to women, has, in the course of this same progress, been acquired by them.

There has still to be considered from the ethical point of view, the political position of women as compared with the political position of men; but until the last of these has been dealt with, we cannot in a complete way deal with the first. When, presently, we enter on the consideration of what are commonly called "political rights," we shall find need for changing, in essential ways, the current conceptions of them; and until this has been done the political rights of women cannot be adequately treated of. There is, however, one aspect of the matter which we may deal with now no less conveniently than hereafter.

Are the political rights of women the same as those of men? The assumption that they are the same is now widely made. Along with that identity of rights above set forth as arising from the human nature common to the two sexes, there is supposed to go an identity of rights in respect to the direction of public affairs. At first sight it seems that the two properly go together; but consideration shows that this is not so. Citizenship does not include only the giving of votes, joined now and again with the fulfilment of representative functions. It includes also certain serious responsibilities. But if so, there cannot be equality of citizenship unless along with the share of good there goes the share of evil. To call that equality of citizenship under which some have their powers *gratis,* while others pay for their powers by undertaking risks, is absurd. Now men, whatever political powers they may in any case possess, are at the same time severally liable to the loss of liberty, to the privation, and occasionally to the death, consequent on having to defend the country; and if women, along with the same political powers, have not the same liabilities, their position is not one of equality but one of supremacy.

Unless, therefore, women furnish contingents to the army and navy such as men furnish, it is manifest that, ethically considered, the question of the equal "political rights," so-called, of women, cannot be entertained until there is reached a state of permanent peace. Then only will it be possible (whether desirable or not) to make the political positions of men and women the same.

It should be added that of course this reason does not negative the claims of women to equal shares in local governments and administrations. If it is contended that these should be withheld, it must be for reasons of other kinds.

Matthew Arnold

1822-1888

EW ARE THE writers of any age who distinguish themselves in more than one literary genre. Matthew Arnold is among that select number, for he is one of the great poets and simultaneously one of the great prose writers of the Victorian age. As a poet Arnold is held to be among the most sympathetic of the major Victorian poets to the modern sensibility; as a prose writer he is recognized as standing in the latter part of the century in the commanding position earlier occupied by Coleridge.

Arnold was the son of Thomas Arnold of Rugby (see the selection by Thomas Arnold in this volume), himself a notable personality of the early Victorian period. Arnold was born at Laleham near Staines, the eldest of nine children. His godfather was John Keble, not then estranged from the Arnold circle by the Tractarian dispute. He was educated briefly at Winchester and chiefly at his father's own Rugby School. At the same time he did not appear in those years to be a characteristic example of the manly Rugbyite later immortalized as the typical product of Thomas Arnold's schooling in *Tom Brown's Schooldays*. Rather, Matthew appeared somewhat lighthearted and ironic in manner, and with more than a touch of the dandy. So at any rate he struck his Oxford contemporaries when he came up from Rugby.

Yet Matthew Arnold had not been by any means uninfluenced by his father, as his later career would show. At Oxford he won the Newdigate prize for poetry when he was an undergraduate at Balliol College. After graduation in 1844 he became a fellow of Oriel College, Newman's old college. During his Oxford years Arnold was acutely sensitive to the flow of ideas. He sensed some of the religious conflict that broke his friend Arthur Hugh Clough, and he received the twin influences of Carlyle and Newman, as his own later testimony affirms. Both of these great prose writers figure in Arnold's later thought and style.

For four years Arnold served as the private secretary to Lord Lansdowne, a liberal statesman who had earlier been instrumental in the passage of the First Reform Bill. In 1851 Arnold accepted the post of a lay inspector of schools. He held the job until he retired in 1886, serving in numerous official government capacities concerned with education. Thus, throughout his literary career, Arnold was also serving as a civil servant. His post required frequent travel in England and on the Continent and frequent reports on school conditions. Arnold became thereby, like his father, a figure in nineteenth-century educational reform. Through his work Arnold gained firsthand knowledge of the actual state of education and culture in Britain and abroad, and this knowledge contributed to his later social and educational thinking and thus to the ideas expressed in his prose treatises on culture and society.

When he took up his educational post in 1851 Arnold also married Frances Lucy Wightman, daughter of a judge. Three years before, he had experienced his thwarted first love with the French girl in Switzerland known to us only through his cycle of poems as "Marguerite." His marriage, however, was a happy one, although he was obliged to be often away on travels. However, three of his sons died before reaching adulthood; one daughter survived.

Arnold began his literary career as a poet and most of his fairly small output of poetry was written before 1853. Volumes appeared in 1849, 1852, 1853, and 1855, with one later volume in 1867. Arnold was appointed Poetry Professor at Oxford during the period 1857–1867, a post earlier held by his godfather Keble. Arnold broke with tradition by delivering his lectures in English, not Latin. Although his poetry shows a dominant note of melancholy and what we have come to call *Angst*—much of it the reflection of what Arnold called the *Zeitgeist*, or spirit of the times—Arnold's prose is of a generally more positive character. His shift indeed from poetry to prose can be accounted for by his desire to engage in a more encouraging and socially beneficial kind of literary endeavor.

Arnold's earliest important prose falls into the category of literary criticism and much of it stemmed from his lectures as poetry professor at Oxford. Other works of criticism were written as essays during the same period, the eighteen-sixties. Among the earliest of the Oxford lectures is the volume *On Translating Homer* (1861–62). Later there appeared *On the Study of Celtic Literature* (1867). And between these two Arnold published a collection of essays called *Essays in Criticism* (1865). Toward the end of his life he published a second series of *Essays in Criticism* (1888). With this later volume and the volumes published in the sixties the reader has the great bulk of Arnold's literary criticism.

The criticism Arnold produced is most notable for its breadth and cosmopolitanism. Arnold was unusually widely read, even for one schooled in the comprehensive course of humane letters that was his and so many others' Oxford program. His knowledge of classical literature was both deep and wide. He even wrote a classical drama in English verse, *Merope* (1858), that is at least technically of great purity. Moreover, his reading among modern literatures, especially German, French, and Italian, was astonishingly wide. He had absorbed much of Carlyle's message on German letters, but he went on to supplement it with his own. As a student of French letters, Arnold had few peers in the age. He has himself often been called the Sainte-Beuve of English criticism, not only for his wide knowledge of French and other non-English literatures, but for his subtlety and discrimination, his range and his sympathy. Arnold's cosmopolitanism as a literary critic is thus probably the most distinguishing mark of his outlook.

Arnold's critical message that literature should be a "criticism of life," that it should seek out and foster the "best that has been thought and said in the world," that it should harmonize the individual with society, is also the message that underlies Arnold's social views. For, like Ruskin and Carlyle before him, Arnold began with a concern for aesthetics but moved to a concern for society and the whole man. In that concern he carried with him the lessons of his study of literature and art.

Arnold's most important venture in social as opposed to literary criticism is his *Culture and Anarchy* (1869), written during the turmoil that attended the efforts to pass the Second Reform Bill in 1867, the same agitation that provoked Carlyle's forceful *Shooting Niagara*. In Arnold's work he expanded his definition of criticism and applied it to culture—"Getting to know on all the matters which most concern us, the best which has been thought and said in the world and, through this knowledge, turning a stream of fresh thought upon our own stock notions and habits." It was an ambitious and, of course, cosmopolitan prescription, one that Arnold recognized could not be applied wholly without pain. He does not therefore spare his intellectual opponents, chiefly the individualist liberals of the day, from some withering satire. But the vision Arnold holds out is one in which a large national consciousness will subsume the otherwise confused stirrings of the individual in a more uplifting design than can be offered by the liberals' goddess of Getting-On, to use Ruskin's pejorative phrase.

A more uplifting design for society, Arnold realized, can come only if that society has a shared and ennobling religion. That is to say, the drift of all Arnold's criticism, literary and social, was inevitably toward religion as the motivating force behind culture. As a literary critic Arnold sometimes seems to express the hope that literature will replace religion, a frequent nineteenth-century notion deriving from Goethe. Arnold never ceases to link religion and literature, but his study of society taught him that religion is more than literature alone. By the eighteen-seventies Arnold was writing directly on religious questions. In this area he showed himself the heir of his father as well as of Coleridge and the Broad Church movement, for Arnold sought in his religious writings, as he had in his literary and social ones, to enlarge the contemporary concept of religion. He wanted to rid Protestantism of its narrowness and sin-obsessed puritanism; at the same time he wanted to reduce High Church emphasis on ritual and dogma, thus opening the Church to secularists and others disaffected from religion. His three important treatises on religion, *St. Paul and Protestantism* (1870), *Literature and Dogma* (1873), and *God and the Bible* (1875), aroused much interest and some disapproval, but failed to win over either the rationalists or the traditionally pious.

In the eighteen-eighties Arnold was again concerning himself with literary questions, and his utterances on these matters are gathered in the second series of *Essays in Criticism*. The volume represents Arnold at his most gracious as a critic. Prior to the gathering of these essays, which occurred in Arnold's last year, he had visited the United States lecturing on such topics as democracy and education. These lectures were published as *Discourses in America* (1883), and contain his brilliant "Literature and Science," in which he takes issue with T. H. Huxley and the movement to decrease the traditional humanistic and literary education of the universities in favor of a more technical and scientific one. In this continuing debate Arnold's eloquent defense of the value of humane letters still bears serious consideration.

Arnold died suddenly in Liverpool in 1888. He was buried in Laleham churchyard in the town of his birth.

As a prose writer Matthew Arnold stands as one of the towering figures of the age. His style is urbane and gracious, though not without its full measure of irony and severity when aroused. He possessed some of the force of a Carlyle or a Ruskin and some of the elegance of a Newman. He has been accused of a certain disdain for the common and the everyday; yet no writer had a larger vision of literature, of society, of culture, even of religion, and no writer was more thoughtful in placing that large vision at the service of his contemporaries in an effort to bring them to share his breadth of learning and understanding. As a literary and social critic Arnold stands in a tradition that derives from Coleridge and moves in on our own century to T. S. Eliot. Following Carlyle and Ruskin, Arnold was the last of the great Victorian sages, and it is as an intellectual and cultural force, rather than as a systematic critic and philosopher, that Arnold makes his greatest impact.

CHRONOLOGY

1822	Born 24 December at Laleham.
1828	Family moves to Rugby.
1833–37	Lives at Fox How in Westmoreland.
1836	Attends Winchester School for one year.
1837	Visits France with parents; returns to Rugby.
1841	Enters Balliol College, Oxford.
1842	Death of Thomas Arnold.
1843	Wins Newdigate Prize for poetry.
1844	Graduates from Oxford.
1845	Elected Fellow of Oriel College.
1847–51	Secretary to Lord Lansdowne.
1848	Visits France; love affair with "Marguerite."
1851	Marries Frances Lucy Wightman; appointed inspector of schools.
1852	*Empedocles on Etna.*
1853	*Poems.*
1857–67	Professor of Poetry at Oxford.
1859	Visits France.
1861	*On Translating Homer.*
1865	*Essays in Criticism,* first series; visits Continent on school inspection tour.
1867	*On the Study of Celtic Literature; New Poems.*
1869	*Culture and Anarchy.*
1870	*St. Paul and Protestantism.*
1873	*Literature and Dogma.*
1875	*God and the Bible.*
1879	*Mixed Essays.*
1880	Visits Switzerland.
1883	Given government pension by Gladstone; tours America.
1885	*Discourses in America;* visits Germany.
1886	Retires as Inspector of Schools.
1888	*Essays in Criticism,* second series. Dies 15 April; buried in Laleham Churchyard.

EDITIONS

Except for the citation of *Works,* only works of prose are listed below.

Works, ed. G. W. E. Russell (15 vols., 1903–4).

Complete Prose of Matthew Arnold, ed. R. H. Super (10 vols., 1960—in progress).
   [Will be the standard edition of the prose.]

Arnold's Diaries, ed. W. G. Guthrie (1959).
Culture and Anarchy, ed. J. Dover Wilson (1932), Ian Gregor (1968).
Essays in Criticism, first series, ed. T. M. Hoctor (1958), K. Allott (1964).
Essays in Criticism, second series, ed. K. Allott (1964).
Essays in Criticism, third series, ed. E. J. O'Brien (1910).
Essays, Letters, and Reviews, ed. Fraser Neiman (1960).
Five Uncollected Essays, ed. K. Allott (1953).
Letters of Matthew Arnold, ed. G. W. E. Russell (2 vols., 1895).
Passages from the Prose Writings of Matthew Arnold, ed. M. Arnold (1880; rpt. 1963).
Poetry and Criticism of Matthew Arnold, ed. A. Dwight Culler (1961).
Thoughts on Education, ed. L. Huxley (1912).
Unpublished Letters, ed. A. Whitridge (1923).

BIOGRAPHY AND CRITICISM

Edward Alexander, *Matthew Arnold and John Stuart Mill* (1965).
———, *Matthew Arnold, John Ruskin and The Modern Temper* (1973).
Kenneth Allott, *Matthew Arnold* (1955).
Louis Bonnerot, *Matthew Arnold, poète* (1947).
E. K. Brown, *Studies in the Text of Matthew Arnold's Prose Works* (1935).
———, *Matthew Arnold: A Study in Conflict* (1948).
William E. Buckler, *Matthew Arnold's Books* (1958).
Douglas Bush, *Matthew Arnold* (1971).
W. F. Connell, *The Educational Thought and Influence of Matthew Arnold* (1950).
David J. DeLaura, *Hebrew and Hellene in Victorian England* (1969).
———, "Matthew Arnold" in *Victorian Prose; A Guide to Research* (1973).
John Eels, *The Touchstones of Matthew Arnold* (1955).
John Gross, *The Rise and Fall of the Man of Letters* (1969).
F. J. W. Harding, *Matthew Arnold: The Critic and France* (1964).
John Holloway, *The Victorian Sage* (1953).
D. G. James, *Matthew Arnold and the Decline of English Romanticism* (1961).
John D. Jump, *Matthew Arnold* (1955).
William E. Madden, *Matthew Arnold* (1967).
Patrick J. McCarthy, *Matthew Arnold and the Three Classes* (1964).
Fraser Neiman, *Matthew Arnold* (1968).
John Henry Raleigh, *Matthew Arnold and American Culture* (1957).
William Robbins, *The Ethical Idealism of Matthew Arnold* (1959).
Thomas B. Smart, *Bibliography of Matthew Arnold* (1892).
Lionel Trilling, *Matthew Arnold* (1949).
Fred G. Walcott, *The Origins of Culture and Anarchy* (1970).
Basil Willey, *Nineteenth Century Studies* (1949).

Preface to First Edition of Poems (1853)

This celebrated essay was prefixed to the edition of Arnold's poetry that contained, among others, "Sorhab and Rustum" and "The Scholar-Gypsy", along with the republication of his poems from 1849 to 1852. Here he explains his reasons for omitting Empedocles on Etna from this collection and in so doing sets forth a theory of poetry that anticipates his later critical views. The essay has been hailed as one of the most important critical utterances of the Victorian age.

IN TWO small volumes of Poems, published anonymously, one in 1849, the other in 1852, many of the poems which compose the present volume have already appeared.[1] The rest are now published for the first time.

I have, in the present collection, omitted the poem from which the volume published in 1852 took its title. I have done so, not because the subject of it was a Sicilian Greek born between two and three thousand years ago, although many persons would think this a sufficient reason. Neither have I done so because I had, in my own opinion, failed in the delineation which I intended to effect. I intended to delineate the feelings of one of the last of the Greek religious philosophers, one of the family of Orpheus and Musæus, having survived his fellows, living on into a time when the habits of Greek thought and feeling had begun fast to change, character to dwindle, the influence of the Sophists to prevail. Into the feelings of a man so situated there entered much that we are accustomed to consider as exclusively modern; how much the fragments of Empedocles himself which remain to us are sufficient at least to indicate. What those who are familiar only with the great monuments of early Greek genius suppose to be its exclusive characteristics, have disappeared; the calm, the cheerfulness, the disinterested objectivity have disappeared; the dialogue of the mind with itself has commenced; modern problems have presented themselves; we hear already the doubts, we witness the discouragement, of Hamlet and of Faust.

The representation of such a man's feelings must be interesting if consistently drawn. We all naturally take pleasure, says Aristotle, in any imitation or representation whatever; this is the basis of our love of poetry; and we take pleasure in them, he adds, because all knowledge is naturally agreeable to us; not to the philosopher only, but to mankind at large. Every representation, therefore, which is consistently drawn may be supposed to be interesting, inasmuch as it gratifies this natural interest in knowledge of all kinds. What is *not* interesting is that which does not add to our knowledge of any kind; that which is vaguely conceived and loosely drawn; a representation which is general, indeterminate, and faint, instead of being particular, precise, and firm.

Any accurate representation may therefore be expected to be interesting; but, if the representation be a poetical one, more than this is demanded. It is demanded not only that it shall interest, but also that it shall inspirit and rejoice the reader; that it shall convey a charm, and infuse delight. For the Muses, as Hesiod says,[2] were born that they might be 'a forgetfulness of evils, and a truce from cares': and it is not enough that the poet should add to the knowledge of men, it is required of him also that he should add to their happiness. 'All art,' says Schiller,[3] 'is dedicated to joy, and there is no higher and no more serious problem than how to make men happy. The right art is that alone which creates the highest enjoyment.'

A poetical work, therefore, is not yet justified when it has been shown to be an accurate and therefore interesting representation; it has to be shown also that it is a representation from which men can derive enjoyment. In presence of the most tragic circumstances, represented in a work of art, the feeling of enjoyment, as is well known, may still subsist; the representation of the most utter calamity, of the liveliest anguish, is not sufficient to destroy it; the more tragic the situation, the deeper becomes the enjoyment;

---

[1] *The Strayed Reveller* (1849) and *Empedocles on Etna* (1852). It is the title poem of the second volume that Arnold refers to in subsequent paragraphs.
[2] Hesiod's *Theogony*.   [3] In his *Die Braut von Messina*.

and the situation is more tragic in proportion as it becomes more terrible.

What then are the situations, from the representation of which, though accurate, no poetical enjoyment can be derived? They are those in which the suffering finds no vent in action; in which a continuous state of mental distress is prolonged, unrelieved by incident, hope, or resistance; in which there is everything to be endured, nothing to be done. In such situations there is inevitably something morbid, in the description of them something monotonous. When they occur in actual life they are painful, not tragic; the representation of them in poetry is painful also.

To this class of situations, poetically faulty as it appears to me, that of Empedocles, as I have endeavoured to represent him, belongs; and I have therefore excluded the poem from the present collection.

And why, it may be asked, have I entered into this explanation respecting a matter so unimportant as the admission or exclusion of the poem in question? I have done so, because I was anxious to avow that the sole reason for its exclusion was that which has been stated above; and that it has not been excluded in deference to the opinion which many critics of the present day appear to entertain against subjects chosen from distant times and countries: against the choice, in short, of any subjects but modern ones.

'The poet,' it is said,[4] and by an intelligent critic, 'the poet who would really fix the public attention must leave the exhausted past and draw his subjects from matters of present import, and *therefore* both of interest and novelty.'

Now this view I believe to be completely false. It is worth examining, inasmuch as it is a fair sample of a class of critical dicta everywhere current at the present day, having a philosophical form and air, but no real basis in fact; and which are calculated to vitiate the judgment of readers of poetry, while they exert, so far as they are adopted, a misleading influence on the practice of those who make it.

What are the eternal objects of poetry, among all nations, and at all times? They are actions; human actions; possessing an inherent interest in themselves, and which are to be communicated in an interesting manner by the art of the poet. Vainly will the latter imagine that he has everything in his own power; that he can make an intrinsically inferior action equally delightful with a more excellent one by his treatment of it. He may indeed compel us to admire his skill, but his work will possess, within itself, an incurable defect.

The poet, then, has in the first place to select an excellent action; and what actions are the most excellent? Those, certainly, which most powerfully appeal to the great primary human affections: to those elementary feelings which subsist permanently in the race, and which are independent of time. These feelings are permanent and the same; that which interests them is permanent and the same also. The modernness or antiquity of an action, therefore, has nothing to do with its fitness for poetical representation; this depends upon its inherent qualities. To the elementary part of our nature, to our passions, that which is great and passionate is eternally interesting; and interesting solely in proportion to its greatness and to its passion. A great human action of a thousand years ago is more interesting to it than a smaller human action of to-day, even though upon the representation of this last the most consummate skill may have been expended, and though it has the advantage of appealing by its modern language, familiar manners, and contemporary allusions, to all our transient feelings and interests. These, however, have no right to demand of a poetical work that it shall satisfy them; their claims are to be directed elsewhere. Poetical works belong to the domain of our permanent passions; let them interest these, and the voice of all subordinate claims upon them is at once silenced.

Achilles, Prometheus, Clytemnestra, Dido,—what modern poem presents personages as interesting, even to us moderns, as these personages of an 'exhausted past'? We have the domestic epic dealing with the details of modern life which pass daily under our eyes; we have poems representing modern personages in contact with the problems of modern life, moral, intellectual, and social; these works have been produced by poets the most distinguished of their nation and time; yet I fearlessly assert that *Hermann and Dorothea, Childe Harold, Jocelyn,* the *Excursion,* leave the reader cold in comparison with the effect produced upon him by the latter books of the *Iliad,* by the *Oresteia,* or by the episode of Dido. And why is this? Simply because in the three last-named cases the action

---

4. In the *Spectator* of April 2, 1853. The words quoted were not used with reference to poems of mine. [Arnold's note]

is greater, the personages nobler, the situations more intense: and this is the true basis of the interest in a poetical work, and this alone.

It may be urged, however, that past actions may be interesting in themselves, but that they are not to be adopted by the modern poet, because it is impossible for him to have them clearly present to his own mind, and he cannot therefore feel them deeply, nor represent them forcibly. But this is not necessarily the case. The externals of a past action, indeed, he cannot know with the precision of a contemporary; but his business is with its essentials. The outward man of Œdipus or of Macbeth, the houses in which they lived, the ceremonies of their courts, he cannot accurately figure to himself; but neither do they essentially concern him. His business is with their inward man; with their feelings and behaviour in certain tragic situations, which engage their passions as men; these have in them nothing local and casual; they are as accessible to the modern poet as to a contemporary.

The date of an action, then, signifies nothing; the action itself, its selection and construction, this is what is all-important. This the Greeks understood far more clearly than we do. The radical difference between their poetical theory and ours consists, as it appears to me, in this: that, with them, the poetical character of the action in itself, and the conduct of it, was the first consideration; with us, attention is fixed mainly on the value of the separate thoughts and images which occur in the treatment of an action. They regarded the whole; we regard the parts. With them the action predominated over the expression of it; with us the expression predominates over the action. Not that they failed in expression, or were inattentive to it; on the contrary, they are the highest models of expression, the unapproached masters of the *grand style*. But their expression is so excellent because it is so admirably kept in its right degree of prominence; because it is so simple and so well subordinated; because it draws its force directly from the pregnancy of the matter which it conveys. For what reason was the Greek tragic poet confined to so limited a range of subjects? Because there are so few actions which unite in themselves, in the highest degree, the conditions of excellence: and it was not thought that on any but an excellent subject could an excellent poem be constructed. A few actions, therefore,

eminently adapted for tragedy, maintained almost exclusive possession of the Greek tragic stage. Their significance appeared inexhaustible; they were as permanent problems, perpetually offered to the genius of every fresh poet. This, too, is the reason of what appears to us moderns a certain baldness of expression in Greek tragedy; of the triviality with which we often reproach the remarks of the chorus, where it takes part in the dialogue: that the action itself, the situation of Orestes, or Merope, or Alcmæon, was to stand the central point of interest, unforgotten, absorbing, principal; that no accessories were for a moment to distract the spectator's attention from this; that the tone of the parts was to be perpetually kept down, in order not to impair the grandiose effect of the whole. The terrible old mythic story on which the drama was founded stood, before he entered the theatre, traced in its bare outlines upon the spectator's mind; it stood in his memory as a group of statuary, faintly seen, at the end of a long and dark vista: then came the poet, embodying outlines, developing situations, not a word wasted, not a sentiment capriciously thrown in; stroke upon stroke, the drama proceeded; the light deepened upon the group; more and more it revealed itself to the riveted gaze of the spectator, until at last, when the final words were spoken, it stood before him in broad sunlight, a model of immortal beauty.

This was what a Greek critic demanded; this was what a Greek poet endeavoured to effect. It signified nothing to what time an action belonged. We do not find that the Persæ[5] occupied a particularly high rank among the dramas of Æschylus, because it represented a matter of contemporary interest; this was not what a cultivated Athenian required. He required that the permanent elements of his nature should be moved; and dramas of which the action, though taken from a long-distant mythic time, yet was calculated to accomplish this in a higher degree than that of the Persæ, stood higher in his estimation accordingly. The Greeks felt, no doubt, with their exquisite sagacity of taste, that an action of present times was too near them, too much mixed up with what was accidental and passing, to form a sufficiently grand, detached, and self-subsistent object for a tragic poem. Such objects belonged to the domain of the comic poet, and of the lighter kinds of poetry. For the more serious kinds, for *pragmatic* poetry, to use an excellent expression of Polybius,[6] they were

---

[5] Aeschylus, *The Persæ* (472 B.C.).   [6] Greek historian (205–123 B.C.).

more difficult and severe in the range of subjects which they permitted. Their theory and practice alike, the admirable treatise of Aristotle, and the unrivalled works of their poets, exclaim with a thousand tongues—'All depends upon the subject; choose a fitting action, penetrate yourself with the feeling of its situations; this done, everything else will follow.'

But for all kinds of poetry alike there was one point of which they were rigidly exacting: the adaptability of the subject to the kind of poetry selected, and the careful construction of the poem.

How different a way of thinking from this is ours! We can hardly at the present day understand what Menander[7] meant, when he told a man who inquired as to the progress of his comedy that he had finished it, not having yet written a single line, because he had constructed the action of it in his mind. A modern critic would have assured him that the merit of his piece depended on the brilliant things which arose under his pen as he went along. We have poems which seem to exist merely for the sake of single lines and passages; not for the sake of producing any total impression. We have critics who seem to direct their attention merely to detached expressions, to the language about the action, not to the action itself. I verily think, that the majority of them do not in their hearts believe that there is such a thing as a total impression to be derived from a poem at all, or to be demanded from a poet; they think the term a commonplace of metaphysical criticism. They will permit the poet to select any action he pleases, and to suffer that action to go as it will, provided he gratifies them with occasional bursts of fine writing, and with a shower of isolated thoughts and images. That is, they permit him to leave their poetical sense ungratified, provided that he gratifies their rhetorical sense and their curiosity. Of his neglecting to gratify these, there is little danger. He needs rather to be warned against the danger of attempting to gratify these alone; he needs rather to be perpetually reminded to prefer his action to everything else; so to treat this, as to permit its inherent excellences to develop themselves, without interruption from the intrusion of his personal peculiarities; most fortunate, when he most entirely succeeds in effacing himself, and in enabling a noble action to subsist as it did in nature.

But the modern critic not only permits a false practice; he absolutely prescribes false aims.

'A true allegory of the state of one's own mind in a representative history,' the poet is told, 'is perhaps the highest thing that one can attempt in the way of poetry.' And accordingly he attempts it. An allegory of the state of one's own mind, the highest problem of an art which imitates actions! No, assuredly, it is not, it never can be so: no great poetical work has ever been produced with such an aim. *Faust* itself, in which something of the kind is attempted, wonderful passages as it contains, and in spite of the unsurpassed beauty of the scenes which relate to Margaret, *Faust* itself, judged as a whole, and judged strictly as a poetical work, is defective: its illustrious author, the greatest poet of modern times, the greatest critic of all times, would have been the first to acknowledge it; he only defended his work, indeed, by asserting it to be 'something incommensurable.'

The confusion of the present times is great, the multitude of voices counselling different things bewildering, the number of existing works capable of attracting a young writer's attention and of becoming his models, immense. What he wants is a hand to guide him through the confusion, a voice to prescribe to him the aim which he should keep in view, and to explain to him that the value of the literary works which offer themselves to his attention is relative to their power of helping him forward on his road towards this aim. Such a guide the English writer at the present day will nowhere find. Failing this, all that can be looked for, all indeed that can be desired, is, that his attention should be fixed on excellent models; that he may reproduce, at any rate, something of their excellence, by penetrating himself with their works and by catching their spirit, if he cannot be taught to produce what is excellent independently.

Foremost among these models for the English writer stands Shakspeare: a name the greatest perhaps of all poetical names; a name never to be mentioned without reverence. I will venture, however, to express a doubt, whether the influence of his works, excellent and fruitful for the readers of poetry, for the great majority, has been of unmixed advantage to the writers of it. Shakspeare indeed chose excellent subjects; the world could afford no better than *Macbeth,* or *Romeo and Juliet,* or *Othello;* he had no theory respecting the necessity of choosing subjects of present import, or the paramount interest

---

[7] Greek dramatist (342–292 B.C.).

attaching to allegories of the state of one's own mind; like all great poets, he knew well what constituted a poetical action; like them, wherever he found such an action he took it; like them, too, he found his best in past times. But to these general characteristics of all great poets he added a special one of his own; a gift, namely, of happy, abundant, and ingenious expression, eminent and unrivalled: so eminent as irresistibly to strike the attention first in him, and even to throw into comparative shade his other excellences as a poet. Here has been the mischief. These other excellences were his fundamental excellences *as a poet;* what distinguishes the artist from the mere amateur, says Goethe, is *Architectonicè* in the highest sense; that power of execution, which creates, forms, and constitutes: not the profoundness of single thoughts, not the richness of imagery, not the abundance of illustration. But these attractive accessories of a poetical work being more easily seized than the spirit of the whole, and these accessories being possessed by Shakspeare in an unequalled degree, a young writer having recourse to Shakspeare as his model runs great risk of being vanquished and absorbed by them, and, in consequence, of reproducing, according to the measure of his power, these, and these alone. Of this preponderating quality of Shakspeare's genius, accordingly, almost the whole of modern English poetry has, it appears to me, felt the influence. To the exclusive attention on the part of his imitators to this it is in a great degree owing, that of the majority of modern poetical works the details alone are valuable, the composition worthless. In reading them one is perpetually reminded of that terrible sentence on a modern French poet:—*Il dit tout ce qu'il veut, mais malheureusement il n'a rien à dire.*[8]

Let me give an instance of what I mean. I will take it from the works of the very chief among those who seem to have been formed in the school of Shakspeare; of one whose exquisite genius and pathetic death render him for ever interesting. I will take the poem of *Isabella, or the Pot of Basil,* by Keats. I choose this rather than the *Endymion,* because the latter work (which a modern critic has classed with the *Faery Queen!*), although undoubtedly there blows through it the breath of genius, is yet, as a whole, so utterly incoherent, as not strictly to merit the name of a poem at all. The poem of *Isabella,* then, is a perfect treasure-house of graceful and felicitous words and images: almost in every stanza there occurs one of those vivid and picturesque turns of expression, by which the object is made to flash upon the eye of the mind, and which thrill the reader with a sudden delight. This one short poem contains, perhaps, a greater number of happy single expressions which one could quote than all the extant tragedies of Sophocles. But the action, the story? The action in itself is an excellent one; but so feebly is it conceived by the poet, so loosely constructed, that the effect produced by it, in and for itself, is absolutely null. Let the reader, after he has finished the poem of Keats, turn to the same story in the *Decameron:* he will then feel how pregnant and interesting the same action has become in the hands of a great artist, who above all things delineates his object; who subordinates expression to that which it is designed to express.

I have said that the imitators of Shakspeare, fixing their attention on his wonderful gift of expression, have directed their imitation to this, neglecting his other excellences. These excellences, the fundamental excellences of poetical art, Shakspeare no doubt possessed them,—possessed many of them in a splendid degree; but it may perhaps be doubted whether even he himself did not sometimes give scope to his faculty of expression to the prejudice of a higher poetical duty. For we must never forget that Shakspeare is the great poet he is from his skill in discerning and firmly conceiving an excellent action, from his power of intensely feeling a situation, of intimately associating himself with a character; not from his gift of expression, which rather even leads him astray, degenerating sometimes into a fondness for curiosity of expression, into an irritability of fancy, which seems to make it impossible for him to say a thing plainly, even when the press of the action demands the very directest language, or its level character the very simplest. Mr. Hallam,[9] than whom it is impossible to find a saner and more judicious critic, has had the courage (for at the present day it needs courage) to remark, how extremely and faultily difficult Shakspeare's language often is. It is so: you may find main scenes in some of his greatest tragedies, *King Lear,* for instance, where the language is so artificial, so curiously tortured, and so difficult, that every speech has to be read two or three

---

[8] "He says everything that he wants to say, but unfortunately he has nothing to say."
[9] Henry Hallam (1777–1859), historian, father of Arthur Henry Hallam, subject of *In Memorian*.

times before its meaning can be comprehended. This over-curiousness of expression is indeed but the excessive employment of a wonderful gift,— of the power of saying a thing in a happier way than any other man; nevertheless, it is carried so far that one understands what M. Guizot[10] meant, when he said that Shakspeare appears in his language to have tried all styles except that of simplicity. He has not the severe and scrupulous self-restraint of the ancients, partly, no doubt, because he had a far less cultivated and exacting audience. He has indeed a far wider range than they had, a far richer fertility of thought; in this respect he rises above them. In his strong conception of his subject, in the genuine way in which he is penetrated with it, he resembles them, and is unlike the moderns. But in the accurate limitation of it, the conscientious rejection of superfluities, the simple and rigorous development of it from the first line of his work to the last, he falls below them, and comes nearer to the moderns. In his chief works, besides what he has of his own, he has the elementary soundness of the ancients; he has their important action and their large and broad manner; but he has not their purity of method. He is therefore a less safe model; for what he has of his own is personal, and inseparable from his own rich nature; it may be imitated and exaggerated, it cannot be learned or applied as an art. He is above all suggestive; more valuable, therefore, to young writers as men than as artists. But clearness of arrangement, rigour of development, simplicity of style,— these may to a certain extent be learned; and these may, I am convinced, be learned best from the ancients, who, although infinitely less suggestive than Shakspeare, are thus, to the artist, more instructive.

What then, it will be asked, are the ancients to be our sole models? the ancients with their comparatively narrow range of experience, and their widely different circumstances? Not, certainly, that which is narrow in the ancients, nor that in which we can no longer sympathise. An action like the action of the *Antigone* of Sophocles, which turns upon the conflict between the heroine's duty to her brother's corpse and that to the laws of her country, is no longer one in which it is possible that we should feel a deep interest. I am speaking too, it will be remembered,

not of the best sources of intellectual stimulus for the general reader, but of the best models of instruction for the individual writer. This last may certainly learn of the ancients, better than anywhere else, three things which it is vitally important for him to know—the all-importance of the choice of a subject; the necessity of accurate construction; and the subordinate character of expression. He will learn from them how unspeakably superior is the effect of the one moral impression left by a great action treated as a whole, to the effect produced by the most striking single thought or by the happiest image. As he penetrates into the spirit of the great classical works, as he becomes gradually aware of their intense significance, their noble simplicity, and their calm pathos, he will be convinced that it is this effect, unity and profoundness of moral impression, at which the ancient poets aimed; that it is this which constitutes the grandeur of their works, and which makes them immortal. He will desire to direct his own efforts towards producing the same effect. Above all, he will deliver himself from the jargon of modern criticism, and escape the danger of producing poetical works conceived in the spirit of the passing time, and which partake of its transitoriness.

The present age makes great claims upon us; we owe it service, it will not be satisfied without our admiration. I know not how it is, but their commerce with the ancients appears to me to produce, in those who constantly practise it, a steadying and composing effect upon their judgment, not of literary works only, but of men and events in general. They are like persons who have had a very weighty and impressive experience; they are more truly than others under the empire of facts, and more independent of the language current among those with whom they live. They wish neither to applaud nor to revile their age; they wish to know what it is, what it can give them, and whether this is what they want. What they want, they know very well; they want to educe and cultivate what is best and noblest in themselves; they know, too, that this is no easy task—χαλεπὸν, as Pittacus said, χαλεπὸν ἐσθλὸν ἔμμεναι[11]—and they ask themselves sincerely whether their age and its literature can assist them in the attempt. If they are endeavouring to practise any art, they remember

---

[10] François Pierre Guillaume Guizot (1787–1874), French historian, author of *Shakespeare and His Times*.
   [11] "It is difficult to be excellent." Pittacus (c. 650–569 B.C.), Greek sage.

the plain and simple proceedings of the old artists, who attained their grand results by penetrating themselves with some noble and significant action, not by inflating themselves with a belief in the pre-eminent importance and greatness of their own times. They do not talk of their mission, nor of interpreting their age, nor of the coming poet; all this, they know, is the mere delirium of vanity; their business is not to praise their age, but to afford to the men who live in it the highest pleasure which they are capable of feeling. If asked to afford this by means of subjects drawn from the age itself, they ask what special fitness the present age has for supplying them. They are told that it is an era of progress, an age commissioned to carry out the great ideas of industrial development and social amelioration. They reply that with all this they can do nothing; that the elements they need for the exercise of their art are great actions, calculated powerfully and delightfully to affect what is permanent in the human soul; that so far as the present age can supply such actions, they will gladly make use of them; but that an age wanting in moral grandeur can with difficulty supply such, and an age of spiritual discomfort with difficulty be powerfully and delightfully affected by them.

A host of voices will indignantly rejoin that the present age is inferior to the past neither in moral grandeur nor in spiritual health. He who possesses the discipline I speak of will content himself with remembering the judgments passed upon the present age, in this respect, by the men of strongest head and widest culture whom it has produced; by Goethe and by Niebuhr.[12] It will be sufficient for him that he knows the opinions held by these two great men respecting the present age and its literature; and that he feels assured in his own mind that their aims and demands upon life were such as he would wish, at any rate, his own to be; and their judgment as to what is impeding and disabling such as he may safely follow. He will not, however, maintain a hostile attitude towards the false pretensions of his age: he will content himself with not being overwhelmed by them. He will esteem himself fortunate if he can succeed in banishing from his mind all feelings of contradiction, and irritation, and impatience; in order to delight himself with the contemplation of some noble action of a heroic time, and to enable others, through his representation of it, to delight in it also.

I am far indeed from making any claim, for myself, that I possess this discipline; or for the following poems, that they breathe its spirit. But I say, that in the sincere endeavour to learn and practise, amid the bewildering confusion of our times, what is sound and true in poetical art, I seemed to myself to find the only sure guidance, the only solid footing, among the ancients. They, at any rate, knew what they wanted in art, and we do not. It is this uncertainty which is disheartening, and not hostile criticism. How often have I felt this when reading words of disparagement or of cavil: that it is the uncertainty as to what is really to be aimed at which makes our difficulty, not the dissatisfaction of the critic, who himself suffers from the same uncertainty! *Non me tua fervida terrent Dicta; . . . Dii me terrent, et Jupiter hostis.*[13]

Two kinds of *dilettanti*, says Goethe, there are in poetry: he who neglects the indispensable mechanical part, and thinks he has done enough if he shows spirituality and feeling; and he who seeks to arrive at poetry merely by mechanism, in which he can acquire an artisan's readiness, and is without soul and matter. And he adds, that the first does most harm to art, and the last to himself. If we must be *dilettanti*: if it is impossible for us, under the circumstances amidst which we live, to think clearly, to feel nobly, and to delineate firmly: if we cannot attain to the mastery of the great artists;—let us, at least, have so much respect for our art as to prefer it to ourselves. Let us not bewilder our successors; let us transmit to them the practice of poetry, with its boundaries and wholesome regulative laws, under which excellent works may again, perhaps, at some future time, be produced, not yet fallen into oblivion through our neglect, not yet condemned and cancelled by the influence of their eternal enemy, caprice.

[12] Barthold Georg Niebuhr (1776–1831), German historian.
[13] "Your passionate words do not frighten me; . . . It is the gods who frighten me, and Jupiter as an enemy" *(Aeneid)*.

from Essays in Criticism, First Series

The essays gathered in this collection were in most cases initially lectures at Oxford, then essays published in various journals between 1863 and 1864. The whole volume in its final form contains ten essays, of which the first two are given below. The work established Arnold as one of the leading literary critics of the day upon its appearance in 1865.

"The Function of Criticism at the Present Time," the first and the major essay in the collection, was originally a lecture at Oxford after which it was published in the National Review *in November 1864. It is the essay in which Arnold lays down his critical principles and his lofty view of the rôle of criticism. The essence of his idea of criticism as advanced in this essay forms also the essence of the definition of culture in his later social-ethical writings.*

"The Literary Influence of Academies" was a lecture delivered first at Oxford, then published in the Cornhill Magazine *in April 1864. Although written before "The Function of Criticism at the Present Time," it can be seen as the application of the theory set forth in that later essay to the specific case of literary academies. It was printed second in the volume publication.*

The Function of Criticism at the Present Time

MANY objections have been made to a proposition which, in some remarks of mine on translating Homer, I ventured to put forth; a proposition about criticism, and its importance at the present day. I said: 'Of the literature of France and Germany, as of the intellect of Europe in general, the main effort, for now many years, has been a critical effort; the endeavour, in all branches of knowledge, theology, philosophy, history, art, science, to see the object as in itself it really is.' I added, that owing to the operation in English literature of certain causes, 'almost the last thing for which one would come to English literature is just that very thing which now Europe most desires,—criticism;' and that the power and value of English literature was thereby impaired. More than one rejoinder declared that the importance I here assigned to criticism was excessive, and asserted the inherent superiority of the creative effort of the human spirit over its critical effort. And the other day, having been led by a Mr. Shairp's excellent notice of Wordsworth[1] to turn again to his biography, I found, in the words of this great man, whom I, for one, must always listen to with the profoundest respect, a sentence passed on the critic's business, which seems to justify every possible disparagement of it. Wordsworth says in one of his letters.[2]—

'The writers in these publications' (the Reviews), 'while they prosecute their inglorious employment, cannot be supposed to be in a state of mind very favourable for being affected by the finer influences of a thing so pure as genuine poetry.'

And a trustworthy reporter of his conversation quotes a more elaborate judgment to the same effect:—

'Wordsworth holds the critical power very low, infinitely lower than the inventive; and he said to-day that if the quantity of time consumed in writing critiques on the works of others were given to original composition, of whatever kind it might be, it would be much better employed; it would make a man find out sooner his own level, and it would do infinitely less mischief. A false or malicious criticism may do much injury to the minds of others; a stupid invention, either in prose or verse, is quite harmless.'

---

[1] I cannot help thinking that a practice, common in England during the last century, and still followed in France, of printing a notice of this kind,—a notice by a competent critic,—to serve as an introduction to an eminent author's works, might be revived among us with advantage. To introduce all succeeding editions of Wordsworth, Mr. Shairp's notice might, it seems to me, excellently serve; it is written from the point of view of an admirer, nay, of a disciple, and that is right; but then the disciple must be also, as in this case he is, a critic, a man of letters, not, as too often happens, some relation or friend with no qualification for his task except affection for his author. [Arnold's note]

John Campbell Shairp (1819–85) was a Scottish critic and served later as Professor of Poetry at Oxford (1877–84).

[2] A letter from Wordsworth to the Quaker poet Bernard Barton (1784–1849).

It is almost too much to expect of poor human nature, that a man capable of producing some effect in one line of literature, should, for the greater good of society, voluntarily doom himself to impotence and obscurity in another. Still less is this to be expected from men addicted to the composition of the 'false or malicious criticism,' of which Wordsworth speaks. However, everybody would admit that a false or malicious criticism had better never have been written. Everybody, too, would be willing to admit, as a general proposition, that the critical faculty is lower than the inventive. But is it true that criticism is really, in itself, a baneful and injurious employment; is it true that all time given to writing critiques on the works of others would be much better employed if it were given to original composition, of whatever kind this may be? Is it true that Johnson had better have gone on producing more *Irenes*[3] instead of writing his *Lives of the Poets;* nay, is it certain that Wordsworth himself was better employed in making his Ecclesiastical Sonnets, than when he made his celebrated Preface, so full of criticism, and criticism of the works of others? Wordsworth was himself a great critic, and it is to be sincerely regretted that he has not left us more criticism; Goethe was one of the greatest of critics, and we may sincerely congratulate ourselves that he has left us so much criticism. Without wasting time over the exaggeration which Wordsworth's judgment on criticism clearly contains, or over an attempt to trace the causes,—not difficult I think to be traced,—which may have led Wordsworth to this exaggeration, a critic may with advantage seize an occasion for trying his own conscience, and for asking himself of what real service, at any given moment, the practice of criticism either is, or may be made, to his own mind and spirit, and to the minds and spirits of others.

The critical power is of lower rank than the creative. True; but in assenting to this proposition, one or two things are to be kept in mind. It is undeniable that the exercise of a creative power, that a free creative activity, is the highest function of man; it is proved to be so by man's finding in it his true happiness. But it is undeniable, also, that men may have the sense of exercising this free creative activity in other ways than in producing great works of literature or art; if it were not so, all but a very few men would be shut out from the true happiness of all men. They may have it in well-doing, they may have it in learning,

they may have it even in criticising. This is one thing to be kept in mind. Another is, that the exercise of the creative power in the production of great works of literature or art, however high this exercise of it may rank, is not at all epochs and under all conditions possible; and that therefore labour may be vainly spent in attempting it, which might with more fruit be used in preparing for it, in rendering it possible. This creative power works with elements, with materials; what if it has not those materials, those elements, ready for its use? In that case it must surely wait till they are ready. Now in literature,—I will limit myself to literature, for it is about literature that the question arises,—the elements with which the creative power works are ideas; the best ideas, on every matter which literature touches, current at the time. At any rate we may lay it down as certain that in modern literature no manifestation of the creative power not working with these can be very important or fruitful. And I say *current* at the time, not merely accessible at the time; for creative literary genius does not principally show itself in discovering new ideas; that is rather the business of the philosopher. The grand work of literary genius is a work of synthesis and exposition, not of analysis and discovery; its gift lies in the faculty of being happily inspired by a certain intellectual and spiritual atmosphere, by a certain order of ideas, when it finds itself in them; of dealing divinely with these ideas, presenting them in the most effective and attractive combinations,—making beautiful works with them, in short. But it must have the atmosphere, it must find itself amidst the order of ideas, in order to work freely; and these it is not so easy to command. This is why great creative epochs in literature are so rare, this is why there is so much that is unsatisfactory in the productions of many men of real genius;—because, for the creation of a masterwork of literature two powers must concur, the power of the man and the power of the moment, and the man is not enough without the moment; the creative power has, for its happy exercise, appointed elements, and those elements are not in its own control.

Nay, they are more within the control of the critical power. It is the business of the critical power, as I said in the words already quoted, 'in all branches of knowledge, theology, philosophy, history, art, science, to see the object as in itself it really is.' Thus it tends, at last, to

---

[3] An unsuccessful classical drama by Samuel Johnson.

make an intellectual situation of which the creative power can profitably avail itself. It tends to establish an order of ideas, if not absolutely true, yet true by comparison with that which it displaces; to make the best ideas prevail. Presently these new ideas reach society, the touch of truth is the touch of life, and there is a stir and growth everywhere; out of this stir and growth come the creative epochs of literature.

Or, to narrow our range, and quit these considerations of the general march of genius and of society, considerations which are apt to become too abstract and impalpable,—every one can see that a poet, for instance, ought to know life and the world before dealing with them in poetry; and life and the world being, in modern times, very complex things, the creation of a modern poet, to be worth much, implies a great critical effort behind it; else it must be a comparatively poor, barren, and short-lived affair. This is why Byron's poetry had so little endurance in it, and Goethe's so much; both Byron and Goethe had a great productive power, but Goethe's was nourished by a great critical effort providing the true materials for it, and Byron's was not; Goethe knew life and the world, the poet's necessary subjects, much more comprehensively and thoroughly than Byron. He knew a great deal more of them, and he knew them much more as they really are.

It has long seemed to me that the burst of creative activity in our literature, through the first quarter of this century, had about it, in fact, something premature; and that from this cause its productions are doomed, most of them, in spite of the sanguine hopes which accompanied and do still accompany them, to prove more lasting than the productions of far less splendid epochs. And this prematureness comes from its having proceeded without having its proper data, without sufficient materials to work with. In other words, the English poetry of the first quarter of this century, with plenty of energy, plenty of creative force, did not know enough. This makes Byron so empty of matter, Shelley so incoherent, Wordsworth even, profound as he is, yet so wanting in completeness and variety. Wordsworth cared little for books, and disparaged Goethe. I admire Wordsworth, as he is, so much that I cannot wish him different; and it is vain, no doubt, to imagine such a man different from what he is, to suppose that he *could* have been different. But surely the one thing wanting to make Wordsworth an even greater poet than he is,—his thought richer, and his influence of

wider application,—was that he should have read more books, among them, no doubt, those of that Goethe whom he disparaged without reading him.

But to speak of books and reading may easily lead to a misunderstanding here. It was not really books and reading that lacked to our poetry, at this epoch; Shelley had plenty of reading, Coleridge had immense reading. Pindar and Sophocles—as we all say so glibly, and often with so little discernment of the real import of what we are saying—had not many books; Shakspeare was no deep reader. True; but in the Greece of Pindar and Sophocles, in the England of Shakspeare; the poet lived in a current of ideas in the highest degree animating and nourishing to the creative power; society was, in the fullest measure, permeated by fresh thought, intelligent and alive. And this state of things is the true basis for the creative power's exercise, in this it finds its data, its materials, truly ready for its hand; all the books and reading in the world are only valuable as they are helps to this. Even when this does not actually exist, books and reading may enable a man to construct a kind of semblance of it in his own mind, a world of knowledge and intelligence in which he may live and work. This is by no means an equivalent, to the artist, for the nationally diffused life and thought of the epochs of Sophocles or Shakspeare; but, besides that it may be a means of preparation for such epochs, it does really constitute, if many share in it, a quickening and sustaining atmosphere of great value. Such an atmosphere the many-sided learning and the long and widely-combined critical effort of Germany formed for Goethe, when he lived and worked. There was no national glow of life and thought there, as in the Athens of Pericles, or the England of Elizabeth. That was the poet's weakness. But there was a sort of equivalent for it in the complete culture and unfettered thinking of a large body of Germans. That was his strength. In the England of the first quarter of this century, there was neither a national glow of life and thought, such as we had in the age of Elizabeth, nor yet a culture and a force of learning and criticism, such as were to be found in Germany. Therefore the creative power of poetry wanted, for success in the highest sense, materials and a basis; a thorough interpretation of the world was necessarily denied to it.

At first sight it seems strange that out of the immense stir of the French Revolution and its age should not have come a crop of works of genius equal to that which came out of the stir of the great productive time of Greece, or out of that of the Renascence with its powerful episode the Reformation. But the truth is that the stir of the French Revolution took a character which essentially distinguished it from such movements as these. These were, in the main, disinterestedly intellectual and spiritual movements; movements in which the human spirit looked for its satisfaction in itself and in the increased play of its own activity. The French Revolution took a political, practical character. The movement which went on in France under the old *régime*, from 1700 to 1789, was far more really akin than that of the Revolution itself to the movement of the Renascence; the France of Voltaire and Rousseau told far more powerfully upon the mind of Europe than the France of the Revolution. Goethe reproached this last expressly with having 'thrown quiet culture back.' Nay, and the true key to how much in our Byron, even in our Wordsworth, is this!—that they had their source in a great movement of feeling, not in a great movement of mind. The French Revolution, however,—that object of so much blind love and so much blind hatred,—found undoubtedly its motive-power in the intelligence of men and not in their practical sense;—this is what distinguishes it from the English Revolution of Charles the First's time. This is what makes it a more spiritual event than our Revolution, an event of much more powerful and world-wide interest, though practically less successful;—it appeals to an order of ideas which are universal, certain, permanent. 1789 asked of a thing, Is it rational? 1642 asked of a thing, Is it legal? or, when it went furthest, Is it according to conscience? This is the English fashion; a fashion to be treated within its own sphere, with the highest respect; for its success, within its own sphere, has been prodigious. But what is law in one place, is not law in another; what is law here to-day, is not law even here to-morrow; and as for conscience, what is binding on one man's conscience is not binding on another's. The old woman who threw her stool[4] at the head of the surpliced minister in St. Giles's Church at Edinburgh obeyed an impulse to which millions of the human race may be permitted to remain strangers. But the prescriptions of reason are absolute, unchanging, of universal validity; *to count by tens is the easiest way of counting*,—that is a proposition

of which every one, from here to the Antipodes, feels the force; at least, I should say so, if we did not live in a country where it is not impossible that any morning we may find a letter in the *Times* declaring that a decimal coinage is an absurdity: That a whole nation should have been penetrated with an enthusiasm for pure reason, and with an ardent zeal for making its prescriptions triumph, is a very remarkable thing, when we consider how little of mind, or anything so worthy and quickening as mind, comes into the motives which alone, in general, impel great masses of men. In spite of the extravagant direction given to this enthusiasm, in spite of the crimes and follies in which it lost itself, the French Revolution derives from the force, truth, and universality of the ideas which it took for its law, and from the passion with which it could inspire a multitude for these ideas, a unique and still living power; it is,—it will probably long remain,—the greatest, the most animating event in history. And, as no sincere passion for the things of the mind, even though it turn out in many respects an unfortunate passion, is ever quite thrown away and quite barren of good, France has reaped from hers one fruit,—the natural and legitimate fruit, though not precisely the grand fruit she expected; she is the country in Europe where *the people* is most alive.

But the mania for giving an immediate political and practical application to all these fine ideas of the reason was fatal. Here an Englishman is in his element: on this theme we can all go on for hours. And all we are in the habit of saying on it has undoubtedly a great deal of truth. Ideas cannot be too much prized in and for themselves, cannot be too much lived with; but to transport them abruptly into the world of politics and practice, violently to revolutionise this world to their bidding,—that is quite another thing. There is the world of ideas and there is the world of practice; the French are often for suppressing the one and the English the other; but neither is to be suppressed. A member of the House of Commons said to me the other day: 'That a thing is an anomaly, I consider to be no objection to it whatever.' I venture to think he was wrong; that a thing is an anomaly *is* an objection to it, but absolutely and in the sphere of ideas: it is not necessarily, under such and such circumstances, or at such and such a moment, an objection to it in the sphere of politics and practice.

---

[4] Jenny Geddes, who thereby began a riot at St. Giles on 23 July 1637 in protest against the religious service ordered by Charles I for Scotland.

Joubert[5] has said beautifully: 'C'est la force et le droit qui règlent toutes choses dans le monde; la force en attendant le droit.' (Force and right are the governors of this world; force till right is ready.) *Force till right is ready;* and till right is ready, force, the existing order of things, is justified, is the legitimate ruler. But right is something moral, and implies inward recognition, free assent of the will; we are not ready for right,— *right,* so far as we are concerned, *is not ready,*— until we have attained this sense of seeing it and willing it. The way in which for us it may change and transform force, the existing order of things, and become, in its turn, the legitimate ruler of the world, should depend on the way in which, when our time comes, we see it and will it. Therefore for other people enamoured of their own newly discerned right, to attempt to impose it upon us as ours, and violently to substitute their right for our force, is an act of tyranny, and to be resisted. It sets at nought the second great half of our maxim, *force till right is ready.* This was the grand error of the French Revolution; and its movement of ideas, by quitting the intellectual sphere and rushing furiously into the political sphere, ran, indeed, a prodigious and memorable course, but produced no such intellectual fruit as the movement of ideas of the Renascence, and created, in opposition to itself, what I may call an *epoch of concentration.* The great force of that epoch of concentration was England; and the great voice of that epoch of concentration was Burke. It is the fashion to treat Burke's writings on the French Revolution as super-annuated and con-quered by the event; as the eloquent but un-philosophical tirades of bigotry and prejudice. I will not deny that they are often disfigured by the violence and passion of the moment, and that in some directions Burke's view was bounded, and his observation therefore at fault. But on the whole, and for those who can make the needful corrections, what distinguishes these writings is their profound, permanent, fruitful, philosoph-ical truth. They contain the true philosophy of an epoch of concentration, dissipate the heavy atmosphere which its own nature is apt to en-gender round it, and make its resistance rational instead of mechanical.

But Burke is so great because, almost alone in England, he brings thought to bear upon politics, he saturates politics with thought. It is his acci-dent that his ideas were at the service of an epoch of concentration, not of an epoch of expansion; it is his characteristic that he so lived by ideas, and had such a source of them welling up within him, that he could float even an epoch of concentration and English Tory politics with them. It does not hurt him that Dr. Price[6] and the Liberals were enraged with him; it does not even hurt him that George the Third and the Tories were enchanted with him. His greatness is that he lived in a world which neither English Liberalism nor English Toryism is apt to enter;— the world of ideas, not the world of catchwords and party habits. So far is it from being really true of him that he 'to party gave up what was meant for mankind,' that at the very end of his fierce struggle with the French Revolution, after all his invectives against its false pretensions, hollowness, and madness, with his sincere con-viction of its mischievousness, he can close a memorandum on the best means of combating it, some of the last pages he ever wrote,—the *Thoughts on French Affairs,* in December 1791,— with these striking words:—

'The evil is stated, in my opinion, as it exists. The remedy must be where power, wisdom, and infor-mation, I hope, are more united with good intentions than they can be with me. I have done with this subject, I believe, for ever. It has given me many anx-ious moments for the last two years. *If a great change is to be made in human affairs, the minds of men will be fitted to it; the general opinions and feelings will draw that way. Every fear, every hope will forward it; and then they who persist in opposing this mighty current in human affairs, will appear rather to resist the decrees of Providence itself, than the mere designs of men. They will not be resolute and firm, but perverse and obstinate.'*

That return of Burke upon himself has always seemed to me one of the finest things in English literature, or indeed in any literature. That is what I call living by ideas: when one side of a question has long had your earnest support, when all your feelings are engaged, when you hear all round you no language but one, when your party talks this language like a steam-engine and can imagine no other,—still to be able to think, still to be irresistibly carried, if so it be, by the current of thought to the opposite side of the question, and, like Balaam, to be unable to speak anything *but what the Lord has put in your mouth.* I know nothing more striking, and I must add that I know nothing more un-English.

---

[5] Joseph Joubert (1754–1824), French critic.
[6] Richard Price (1723–91), dissenting minister, sympathetic to the French Revolution.

For the Englishman in general is like my friend the Member of Parliament, and believes, point-blank, that for a thing to be an anomaly is absolutely no objection to it whatever. He is like the Lord Auckland[7] of Burke's day, who, in a memorandum on the French Revolution, talks of 'certain miscreants, assuming the name of philosophers, who have presumed themselves capable of establishing a new system of society.' The Englishman has been called a political animal, and he values what is political and practical so much that ideas easily become objects of dislike in his eyes, and thinkers 'miscreants,' because ideas and thinkers have rashly meddled with politics and practice. This would be all very well if the dislike and neglect confined themselves to ideas transported out of their own sphere, and meddling rashly with practice; but they are inevitably extended to ideas as such, and to the whole life of intelligence; practice is everything, a free play of the mind is nothing. The notion of the free play of the mind upon all subjects being a pleasure in itself, being an object of desire, being an essential provider of elements without which a nation's spirit, whatever compensations it may have for them, must, in the long run, die of inanition, hardly enters into an Englishman's thoughts. It is noticeable that the word *curiosity*, which in other languages is used in a good sense, to mean, as a high and fine quality of man's nature, just this disinterested love of a free play of the mind on all subjects, for its own sake,—it is noticeable, I say, that this word has in our language no sense of the kind, no sense but a rather bad and disparaging one. But criticism, real criticism, is essentially the exercise of this very quality. It obeys an instinct prompting it to try to know the best that is known and thought in the world, irrespectively of practice, politics, and everything of the kind; and to value knowledge and thought as they approach this best, without the intrusion of any other considerations whatever. This is an instinct for which there is, I think, little original sympathy in the practical English nature, and what there was of it has undergone a long benumbing period of blight and suppression in the epoch of concentration which followed the French Revolution.

But epochs of concentration cannot well endure for ever; epochs of expansion, in the due course of things, follow them. Such an epoch of expansion seems to be opening in this country. In the first place all danger of a hostile forcible pressure of foreign ideas upon our practice has long disappeared; like the traveller in the fable, therefore, we begin to wear our cloak a little more loosely. Then, with a long peace, the ideas of Europe steal gradually and amicably in, and mingle, though in infinitesimally small quantities at a time, with our own notions. Then, too, in spite of all that is said about the absorbing and brutalising influence of our passionate material progress, it seems to me indisputable that this progress is likely, though not certain, to lead in the end to an apparition of intellectual life; and that man, after he has made himself perfectly comfortable and has now to determine what to do with himself next, may begin to remember that he has a mind, and that the mind may be made the source of great pleasure. I grant it is mainly the privilege of faith, at present, to discern this end to our railways, our business, and our fortune-making; but we shall see if, here as elsewhere, faith is not in the end the true prophet. Our ease, our travelling, and our unbounded liberty to hold just as hard and securely as we please to the practice to which our notions have given birth, all tend to beget an inclination to deal a little more freely with these notions themselves, to canvass them a little, to penetrate a little into their real nature. Flutterings of curiosity, in the foreign sense of the word, appear amongst us, and it is in these that criticism must look to find its account. Criticism first; a time of true creative activity, perhaps,—which, as I have said, must inevitably be preceded amongst us by a time of criticism,—hereafter, when criticism has done its work.

It is of the last importance that English criticism should clearly discern what rule for its course, in order to avail itself of the field now opening to it, and to produce fruit for the future, it ought to take. The rule may be summed up in one word,—*disinterestedness*. And how is criticism to show disinterestedness? By keeping aloof from what is called 'the practical view of things;' by resolutely following the law of its own nature, which is to be a free play of the mind on all subjects which it touches. By steadily refusing to lend itself to any of those ulterior, political, practical considerations about ideas, which plenty of people will be sure to attach to them, which perhaps ought often to be attached to them, which in this country at any rate are certain to be attached to them quite sufficiently, but which criticism has really nothing to do with.

[7] William Eden, 1st Baron Auckland (1744–1814), British statesman.

Its business is, as I have said, simply to know the best that is known and thought in the world, and by in its turn making this known, to create a current of true and fresh ideas. Its business is to do this with inflexible honesty, with due ability; but its business is to do no more, and to leave alone all questions of practical consequences and applications, questions which will never fail to have due prominence given to them. Else criticism, besides being really false to its own nature, merely continues in the old rut which it has hitherto followed in this country, and will certainly miss the chance now given to it. For what is at present the bane of criticism in this country? It is that practical considerations cling to it and stifle it. It subserves interests not its own. Our organs of criticism are organs of men and parties having practical ends to serve, and with them those practical ends are the first thing and the play of mind the second; so much play of mind as is compatible with the prosecution of those practical ends is all that is wanted. An organ like the *Revue des Deux Mondes*, having for its main function to understand and utter the best that is known and thought in the world, existing, it may be said, as just an organ for a free play of the mind, we have not. But we have the *Edinburgh Review*, existing as an organ of the old Whigs, and for as much play of the mind as may suit its being that; we have the *Quarterly Review*, existing as an organ of the Tories, and for as much play of mind as may suit its being that; we have the *British Quarterly Review*, existing as an organ of the political Dissenters, and for as much play of mind as may suit its being that; we have the *Times*, existing as an organ of the common, satisfied, well-to-do Englishman, and for as much play of mind as may suit its being that. And so on through all the various fractions, political and religious, of our society; every fraction has, as such, its organ of criticism, but the notion of combining all fractions in the common pleasure of a free disinterested play of mind meets with no favour. Directly this play of mind wants to have more scope, and to forget the pressure of practical considerations a little, it is checked, it is made to feel the chain. We saw this the other day in the extinction, so much to be regretted, of the *Home and Foreign Review*. Perhaps in no organ of criticism in this country was there so much knowledge, so much play of mind; but these could not save it. The *Dublin Review* subordinates

play of mind to the practical business of English and Irish Catholicism, and lives. It must needs be that men should act in sects and parties, that each of these sects and parties should have its organ, and should make this organ subserve the interests of its action; but it would be well, too, that there should be a criticism, not the minister of these interests, not their enemy, but absolutely and entirely independent of them. No other criticism will ever attain any real authority or make any real way towards its end,—the creating a current of true and fresh ideas.

It is because criticism has so little kept in the pure intellectual sphere, has so little detached itself from practice, has been so directly polemical and controversial, that it has so ill accomplished, in this country, its best spiritual work; which is to keep man from a self-satisfaction which is retarding and vulgarising, to lead him towards perfection, by making his mind dwell upon what is excellent in itself, and the absolute beauty and fitness of things. A polemical practical criticism makes men blind even to the ideal imperfection of their practice, makes them willingly assert its ideal perfection, in order the better to secure it against attack; and clearly this is narrowing and baneful for them. If they were reassured on the practical side, speculative considerations of ideal perfection they might be brought to entertain, and their spiritual horizon would thus gradually widen. Sir Charles Adderley[8] says to the Warwickshire farmers:—

'Talk of the improvement of breed! Why, the race we ourselves represent, the men and women, the old Anglo-Saxon race, are the best breed in the whole world. . . . The absence of a too enervating climate, too unclouded skies, and a too luxurious nature, has produced so vigorous a race of people, and has rendered us so superior to all the world.'

Mr. Roebuck[9] says to the Sheffield cutlers:—

'I look around me and ask what is the state of England? Is not property safe? Is not every man able to say what he likes? Can you not walk from one end of England to the other in perfect security? I ask you whether, the world over or in past history, there is anything like it? Nothing. I pray that our unrivalled happiness may last.'

Now obviously there is a peril for poor human nature in words and thoughts of such exuberant self-satisfaction, until we find ourselves safe in the streets of the Celestial City.

[8] Charles Bowyer Adderley, 1st Baron Norton (1814–1905), English politician.
[9] John Arthur Roebuck (1801–79), radical reformer, member of Parliament.

'Das wenige verschwindet leicht dem Blicke
Der vorwärts sieht, wie viel noch übrig bleibt[10]—'

says Goethe; 'the little that is done seems nothing when we look forward and see how much we have yet to do.' Clearly this is a better line of reflection for weak humanity, so long as it remains on this earthly field of labour and trial.

But neither Sir Charles Adderley nor Mr. Roebuck are by nature inaccessible to considerations of this sort. They only lose sight of them owing to the controversial life we all lead, and the practical form which all speculation takes with us. They have in view opponents whose aim is not ideal, but practical; and in their zeal to uphold their own practice against these innovators, they go so far as even to attribute to this practice an ideal perfection. Somebody has been wanting to introduce a six-pound franchise, or to abolish church-rates, or to collect agricultural statistics by force, or to diminish local self-government. How natural, in reply to such proposals, very likely improper or ill-timed, to go a little beyond the mark, and to say stoutly, 'Such a race of people as we stand, so superior to all the world! The old Anglo-Saxon race, the best breed in the whole world! I pray that our unrivalled happiness may last! I ask you whether, the world over or in past history, there is anything like it!' And so long as criticism answers this dithyramb by insisting that the old Anglo-Saxon race would be still more superior to all others if it had no church-rates, or that our unrivalled happiness would last yet longer with a six-pound franchise, so long will the strain, 'The best breed in the whole world!' swell louder and louder, everything ideal and refining will be lost out of sight, and both the assailed and their critics will remain in a sphere, to say the truth, perfectly unvital, a sphere in which spiritual progression is impossible. But let criticism leave church-rates and the franchise alone, and in the most candid spirit, without a single lurking thought of practical innovation, confront with our dithyramb this paragraph on which I stumbled in a newspaper immediately after reading Mr. Roebuck:—

'A shocking child murder has just been committed at Nottingham. A girl named Wragg left the workhouse there on Saturday morning with her young illegitimate child. The child was soon afterwards found dead on Mapperly Hills, having been strangled. Wragg is in custody.'

Nothing but that; but, in juxtaposition with the absolute eulogies of Sir Charles Adderley and Mr. Roebuck, how eloquent, how suggestive are those few lines! 'Our old Anglo-Saxon breed, the best in the whole world!'—how much that is harsh and ill-favoured there is in this best! *Wragg!* If we are to talk of ideal perfection, of 'the best in the whole world,' has any one reflected what a touch of grossness in our race, what an original shortcoming in the more delicate spiritual perceptions, is shown by the natural growth amongst us of such hideous names,—Higginbottom, Stiggins, Bugg! In Ionia and Attica they were luckier in this respect than 'the best race in the world;' by the Ilissus there was no Wragg, poor thing! And 'our unrivalled happiness;'—what an element of grimness, bareness, and hideousness mixes with it and blurs it; the workhouse, the dismal Mapperly Hills,—how dismal those who have seen them will remember;—the gloom, the smoke, the cold, the strangled illegitimate child! 'I ask you whether, the world over or in past history, there is anything like it?' Perhaps not, one is inclined to answer; but at any rate, in that case, the world is very much to be pitied. And the final touch,—short, bleak, and inhuman: *Wragg is in custody.* The sex lost in the confusion of our unrivalled happiness; or (shall I say?) the superfluous Christian name lopped off by the straightforward vigour of our old Anglo-Saxon breed! There is profit for the spirit in such contrasts as this; criticism serves the cause of perfection by establishing them. By eluding sterile conflict, by refusing to remain in the sphere where alone narrow and relative conceptions have any worth and validity, criticism may diminish its momentary importance, but only in this way has it a chance of gaining admittance for those wider and more perfect conceptions to which all its duty is really owed. Mr. Roebuck will have a poor opinion of an adversary who replies to his defiant songs of triumph only by murmuring under his breath, *Wragg is in custody;* but in no other way will these songs of triumph be induced gradually to moderate themselves, to get rid of what in them is excessive and offensive, and to fall into a softer and truer key.

It will be said that it is a very subtle and indirect action which I am thus prescribing for criticism, and that by embracing in this manner the Indian virtue of detachment and abandoning the sphere of practical life, it condemns itself to a

---

[10] In his *Iphigenia auf Tauris.* Arnold translates the passage in the next line.

slow and obscure work. Slow and obscure it may be, but it is the only proper work of criticism. The mass of mankind will never have any ardent zeal for seeing things as they are; very inadequate ideas will always satisfy them. On these inadequate ideas reposes, and must repose, the general practice of the world. That is as much as saying that whoever sets himself to see things as they are will find himself one of a very small circle; but it is only by this small circle resolutely doing its own work that adequate ideas will ever get current at all. The rush and roar of practical life will always have a dizzying and attracting effect upon the most collected spectator, and tend to draw him into its vortex; most of all will this be the case where that life is so powerful as it is in England. But it is only by remaining collected, and refusing to lend himself to the point of view of the practical man, that the critic can do the practical man any service; and it is only by the greatest sincerity in pursuing his own course, and by at last convincing even the practical man of his sincerity, that he can escape misunderstandings which perpetually threaten him.

For the practical man is not apt for fine distinctions, and yet in these distinctions truth and the highest culture greatly find their account. But it is not easy to lead a practical man,—unless you reassure him as to your practical intentions, you have no chance of leading him,—to see that a thing which he has always been used to look at from one side only, which he greatly values, and which, looked at from that side, quite deserves, perhaps, all the prizing and admiring which he bestows upon it,—that this thing, looked at from another side, may appear much less beneficent and beautiful, and yet retain all its claims to our practical allegiance. Where shall we find language innocent enough, how shall we make the spotless purity of our intentions evident enough, to enable us to say to the political Englishman that the British Constitution itself, which, seen from the practical side, looks such a magnificent organ of progress and virtue, seen from the speculative side,—with its compromises, its love of facts, its horror of theory, its studied avoidance of clear thoughts,—that, seen from this side, our august Constitution sometimes looks,—forgive me, shade of Lord Somers![11]—a colossal machine for the manufacture of Philistines? How is Cobbett[12] to say this and not be misunderstood, blackened as he is with the smoke of a life-long conflict in the field of political practice? how is Mr. Carlyle to say it and not be misunderstood, after his furious raid into this field with his *Latter-day Pamphlets?* how is Mr. Ruskin, after his pugnacious political economy? I say, the critic must keep out of the region of immediate practice in the political, social, humanitarian sphere, if he wants to make a beginning for that more free speculative treatment of things, which may perhaps one day make its benefits felt even in this sphere, but in a natural and thence irresistible manner.

Do what he will, however, the critic will still remain exposed to frequent misunderstandings, and nowhere so much as in this country. For here people are particularly indisposed even to comprehend that without this free disinterested treatment of things, truth and the highest culture are out of the question. So immersed are they in practical life, so accustomed to take all their notions from this life and its processes, that they are apt to think that truth and culture themselves can be reached by the processes of this life, and that it is an impertinent singularity to think of reaching them in any other. 'We are all *terrae filii*,'[13] cries their eloquent advocate; 'all Philistines together. Away with the notion of proceeding by any other course than the course dear to the Philistines; let us have a social movement, let us organise and combine a party to pursue truth and new thought, let us call it *the liberal party,* and let us all stick to each other, and back each other up. Let us have no nonsense about independent criticism, and intellectual delicacy, and the few and the many. Don't let us trouble ourselves about foreign thought; we shall invent the whole thing for ourselves as we go along. If one of us speaks well, applaud him; if one of us speaks ill, applaud him too; we are all in the same movement, we are all liberals, we are all in pursuit of truth.' In this way the pursuit of truth becomes really a social, practical, pleasurable affair, almost requiring a chairman, a secretary, and advertisements; with the excitement of an occasional scandal, with a little resistance to give the happy sense of difficulty overcome; but, in general, plenty of bustle and very little thought. To act is so easy, as Goethe says; to think is so hard! It is true that the critic has many temptations to go with the stream, to make one of the party of movement, one of these *terrae filii;* it seems ungracious to refuse to be a *terrae filius,* when so many excellent people are; but the

---

[11] John Somers, Baron Somers (1651–1716), English lawyer and statesman.
[12] William Cobbett (1762–1835), radical pamphleteer.   [13] "Sons of the earth."

critic's duty is to refuse, or, if resistance is vain, at least to cry with Obermann: *Périssons en résistant.*[14]

How serious a matter it is to try and resist, I had ample opportunity of experiencing when I ventured some time ago to criticise the celebrated first volume of Bishop Colenso.[15] The echoes of the storm which was then raised I still, from time to time, hear grumbling round me. That storm arose out of a misunderstanding almost inevitable. It is a result of no little culture to attain to a clear perception that science and religion are two wholly different things. The multitude will for ever confuse them; but happily that is of no great real importance, for while the multitude imagines itself to live by its false science, it does really live by its true religion. Dr. Colenso, however, in his first volume did all he could to strengthen the confusion,[16] and to make it dangerous. He did this with the best intentions, I freely admit, and with the most candid ignorance that this was the natural effect of what he was doing; but, says Joubert, 'Ignorance, which in matters of morals extenuates the crime, is itself, in intellectual matters, a crime of the first order.' I criticised Bishop Colenso's speculative confusion. Immediately there was a cry raised: 'What is this? here is a liberal attacking a liberal. Do not you belong to the movement? are not you a friend of truth? Is not Bishop Colenso in pursuit of truth? then speak with proper respect of his book. Dr. Stanley[17] is another friend of truth, and you speak with proper respect of his book; why make these invidious differences? both books are excellent, admirable, liberal; Bishop Colenso's perhaps the most so, because it is the boldest, and will have the best practical consequences for the liberal cause. Do you want to encourage to the attack of a brother liberal his, and your, and our implacable enemies, the *Church and State Review* or the *Record,*—the High Church rhinoceros and the Evangelical hyaena? Be silent, therefore; or rather speak, speak as loud as ever you can! and go into ecstasies over the eighty and odd pigeons.'

But criticism cannot follow this coarse and indiscriminate method. It is unfortunately possible for a man in pursuit of truth to write a book which reposes upon a false conception. Even the practical consequences of a book are to genuine criticism no recommendation of it, if the book is, in the highest sense, blundering. I see that a lady[18] who herself, too, is in pursuit of truth, and who writes with great ability, but a little too much, perhaps, under the influence of the practical spirit of the English liberal movement, classes Bishop Colenso's book and M. Renan's[19] together, in her survey of the religious state of Europe, as facts of the same order, works, both of them, of 'great importance;' 'great ability, power, and skill;' Bishop Colenso's, perhaps, the most powerful; at least, Miss Cobbe gives special expression to her gratitude that to Bishop Colenso 'has been given the strength to grasp, and the courage to teach, truths of such deep import.' In the same way, more than one popular writer has compared him to Luther. Now it is just this kind of false estimate which the critical spirit is, it seems to me, bound to resist. It is really the strongest possible proof of the low ebb at which, in England, the critical spirit is, that while the critical hit in the religious literature of Germany is Dr. Strauss's[20] book, in that of France M. Renan's book, the book of Bishop Colenso is the critical hit in the religious literature of England. Bishop Colenso's book reposes on a total misconception of the essential elements of the religious problem, as that problem is now presented for solution. To criticism, therefore, which seeks to have the best that is known and thought on this problem, it is, however well meant, of no

---

[14] "Let us die resisting!"

[15] So sincere is my dislike to all personal attack and controversy, that I abstain from reprinting, at this distance of time from the occasion which called them forth, the essays in which I criticised Dr. Colenso's book; I feel bound, however, after all that has passed, to make here a final declaration of my sincere impenitence for having published them. Nay, I cannot forbear repeating yet once more, for his benefit and that of his readers, this sentence from my original remarks upon him: *There is truth of science and truth of religion; truth of science does not become truth of religion till it is made religious.* And I will add: Let us have all the science there is from the men of science; from the men of religion let us have religion. [Arnold's note]

[16] It has been said I make it 'a crime against literary criticism and the higher culture to attempt to inform the ignorant.' Need I point out that the ignorant are not informed by being confirmed in a confusion? [Arnold's note]

[17] Arthur Penrhyn Stanley (1815–81), Dean of Westminster.

[18] Frances Power Cobbe (1822–1904) in her *Broken Lights* (1864).

[19] Ernest Renan (1823–92), French philosopher, author of *La Vie de Jésus* (1863).

[20] David Friedrich Strauss (1808–74), German biblical critic, author of *Das Leben Jesu* (1835).

importance whatever. M. Renan's book attempts a new synthesis of the elements furnished to us by the Four Gospels. It attempts, in my opinion, a synthesis, perhaps premature, perhaps impossible, certainly not successful. Up to the present time, at any rate, we must acquiesce in Fleury's sentence on such recastings of the Gospel story: *Quiconque s'imagine la pouvoir mieux écrire, ne l'entend pas.*[21] M. Renan had himself passed by anticipation a like sentence on his own work, when he said: 'If a new presentation of the character of Jesus were offered to me, I would not have it; its very clearness would be, in my opinion, the best proof of its insufficiency.' His friends may with perfect justice rejoin that at the sight of the Holy Land, and of the actual scene of the Gospel-story, all the current of M. Renan's thoughts may have naturally changed, and a new casting of that story irresistibly suggested itself to him; and that this is just a case for applying Cicero's maxim: Change of mind is not inconsistency—*nemo doctus unquam mutationem consilii inconstantiam dixit esse.*[22] Nevertheless, for criticism, M. Renan's first thought must still be the truer one, as long as his new casting so fails more fully to commend itself, more fully (to use Coleridge's happy phrase about the Bible) to *find* us. Still M. Renan's attempt is, for criticism, of the most real interest and importance, since, with all its difficulty, a fresh synthesis of the New Testament *data,*—not a making war on them, in Voltaire's fashion, not a leaving them out of mind, in the world's fashion, but the putting a new construction upon them, the taking them from under the old, traditional, conventional point of view and placing them under a new one,—is the very essence of the religious problem, as now presented; and only by efforts in this direction can it receive a solution.

Again, in the same spirit in which she judges Bishop Colenso, Miss Cobbe, like so many earnest liberals of our practical race, both here and in America, herself sets vigorously about a positive reconstruction of religion, about making a religion of the future out of hand, or at least setting about making it. We must not rest, she and they are always thinking and saying, in negative criticism, we must be creative and constructive; hence, we have such works as her recent *Religious Duty,* and works still more considerable, perhaps, by others, which will be in every one's mind. These works often have much ability; they often spring out of sincere convictions, and a sincere wish to do good; and they sometimes, perhaps, do good. Their fault is (if I may be permitted to say so) one which they have in common with the British College of Health, in the New Road. Every one knows the British College of Health; it is that building with the lion and the statue of the Goddess Hygeia before it; at least, I am sure about the lion, though I am not absolutely certain about the Goddess Hygeia. This building does credit, perhaps, to the resources of Dr. Morison[23] and his disciples; but it falls a good deal short of one's idea of what a British College of Health ought to be. In England, where we hate public interference and love individual enterprise, we have a whole crop of places like the British College of Health; the grand name without the grand thing. Unluckily, creditable to individual enterprise as they are, they tend to impair our taste by making us forget what more grandiose, noble, or beautiful character properly belongs to a public institution. The same may be said of the religions of the future of Miss Cobbe and others. Creditable, like the British College of Health, to the resources of their authors, they yet tend to make us forget what more grandiose, noble, or beautiful character properly belongs to religious constructions. The historic religions, with all their faults, have had this; it certainly belongs to the religious sentiment, when it truly flowers, to have this; and we impoverish our spirit if we allow a religion of the future without it. What then is the duty of criticism here? To take the practical point of view, to applaud the liberal movement and all its works,—its New Road religions of the future into the bargain,—for their general utility's sake? By no means; but to be perpetually dissatisfied with these works, while they perpetually fall short of a high and perfect ideal.

For criticism, these are elementary laws; but they never can be popular, and in this country they have been very little followed, and one meets with immense obstacles in following them. That is a reason for asserting them again and again. Criticism must maintain its independence of the practical spirit and its aims. Even with well-meant efforts of the practical spirit it must express dissatisfaction, if in the sphere of the ideal they seem impoverishing and limiting. It

[21] "Whoever thinks he is able to write it better doesn't understand it."
[22] "No learned person has ever said that changing one's mind is inconsistency."
[23] James Morison (1770–1840), creator and vendor of Morison's Pills, an alleged cure-all. He called himself the "Hygeist." See also Carlyle's *Past and Present.*

must not hurry on to the goal because of its practical importance. It must be patient, and know how to wait; and flexible, and know how to attach itself to things and how to withdraw from them. It must be apt to study and praise elements that for the fulness of spiritual perfection are wanted, even though they belong to a power which in the practical sphere may be maleficent. It must be apt to discern the spiritual short-comings or illusions of powers that in the practical sphere may be beneficent. And this without any notion of favouring or injuring, in the practical sphere, one power or the other; without any notion of playing off, in this sphere, one power against the other. When one looks, for instance, at the English Divorce Court,—an institution which perhaps has its practical conveniences, but which in the ideal sphere is so hideous; an institution which neither makes divorce im-possible nor makes it decent, which allows a man to get rid of his wife, or a wife of her husband, but makes them drag one another first, for the public edification, through a mire of unutterable infamy,—when one looks at this charming institution, I say, with its crowded trials, its newspaper-reports, and its money-compensations, this institution in which the gross unregenerate British Philistine has indeed stamped an image of himself,—one may be permitted to find the marriage-theory of Catholicism refreshing and elevating. Or when Protestantism, in virtue of its supposed rational and intellectual origin, gives the law to criticism too magisterially, criticism may and must remind it that its pretensions, in this respect, are illusive and do it harm; that the Reformation was a moral rather than an intellectual event; that Luther's theory of grace no more exactly reflects the mind of the spirit than Bossuet's[24] philosophy of history reflects it; and that there is no more antecedent probability of the Bishop of Durham's stock of ideas being agreeable to perfect reason than of Pope Pius the Ninth's. But criticism will not on that account forget the achievements of Pro-testantism in the practical and moral sphere; nor that, even in the intellectual sphere, Protes-tantism, though in a blind and stumbling manner, carried forward the Renascence, while Catho-licism threw itself violently across its path.

I lately heard a man of thought and energy contrasting the want of ardour and movement which he now found amongst young men in this country with what he remembered in his own youth, twenty years ago. 'What reformers we were then!' he exclaimed; 'what a zeal we had! how we canvassed every institution in Church and State, and were prepared to remodel them all on first principles!' He was inclined to regret, as a spiritual flagging, the lull which he saw. I am disposed rather to regard it as a pause in which the turn to a new mode of spiritual progress is being accomplished. Everything was long seen, by the young and ardent amongst us, in in-separable connection with politics and practical life. We have pretty well exhausted the benefits of seeing things in this connection, we have got all that can be got by so seeing them. Let us try a more disinterested mode of seeing them; let us betake ourselves more to the serener life of the mind and spirit. This life, too, may have its excesses and dangers; but they are not for us at present. Let us think of quietly enlarging our stock of true and fresh ideas, and not, as soon as we get an idea or half an idea, be running out with it into the street, and trying to make it rule there. Our ideas will, in the end, shape the world all the better for maturing a little. Perhaps in fifty years' time it will in the English House of Commons be an objection to an institution that it is an anomaly, and my friend the Member of Parliament will shudder in his grave. But let us in the meanwhile rather endeavour that in twenty years' time it may, in English literature, be an objection to a proposition that it is absurd. That will be a change so vast, that the imagina-tion almost fails to grasp it. *Ab integro saeclorum nascitur ordo.*[25]

If I have insisted so much on the course which criticism must take where politics and religion are concerned, it is because, where these burning matters are in question, it is most likely to go astray. I have wished, above all, to insist on the attitude which criticism should adopt towards things in general; on its right tone and temper of mind. But then comes another question as to the subject-matter which literary criticism should most seek. Here, in general, its course is deter-mined for it by the idea which is the law of its being; the idea of a disinterested endeavour to learn and propagate the best that is known and thought in the world, and thus to establish a current of fresh and true ideas. By the very

---

[24] Jacques Bossuet (1627–1704), French theologian and bishop, proclaimed that universal history had been directed for the benefit of Christianity.
[25] "From the renewal of the generations is born order" (Vergil, *Eclogues*).

nature of things, as England is not all the world, much of the best that is known and thought in the world cannot be of English growth, must be foreign; by the nature of things, again, it is just this that we are least likely to know, while English thought is streaming in upon us from all sides, and takes excellent care that we shall not be ignorant of its existence. The English critic of literature, therefore, must dwell much on foreign thought, and with particular heed on any part of it, which, while significant and fruitful in itself, is for any reason specially likely to escape him. Again, judging is often spoken of as the critic's one business; and so in some sense it is; but the judgment which almost insensibly forms itself in a fair and clear mind, along with fresh knowledge, is the valuable one; and thus knowledge, and ever fresh knowledge, must be the critic's great concern for himself. And it is by communicating fresh knowledge, and letting his own judgment pass along with it,—but insensibly, and in the second place, not the first, as a sort of companion and clue, not as an abstract lawgiver,—that the critic will generally do most good to his readers. Sometimes, no doubt, for the sake of establishing an author's place in literature, and his relation to a central standard (and if this is not done, how are we to get at our *best in the world?*) criticism may have to deal with a subject-matter so familiar that fresh knowledge is out of the question, and then it must be all judgment; an enunciation and detailed application of principles. Here the great safeguard is never to let oneself become abstract, always to retain an intimate and lively consciousness of the truth of what one is saying, and, the moment this fails us, to be sure that something is wrong. Still, under all circumstances, this mere judgment and application of principles is, in itself, not the most satisfactory work to the critic; like mathematics, it is tautological, and cannot well give us, like fresh learning, the sense of creative activity.

But stop, some one will say; all this talk is of no practical use to us whatever; this criticism of yours is not what we have in our minds when we speak of criticism; when we speak of critics and criticism, we mean critics and criticism of the current English literature of the day; when you offer to tell criticism its function, it is to this criticism that we expect you to address yourself. I am sorry for it, for I am afraid I must disappoint these expectations. I am bound by my own definition of criticism: *a disinterested endeavour to learn and propagate the best that is known and thought in the world*. How much of current English

literature comes into this 'best that is known and thought in the world?' Not very much, I fear; certainly less, at this moment, than of the current literature of France or Germany. Well, then, am I to alter my definition of criticism, in order to meet the requirements of a number of practising English critics, who, after all, are free in their choice of a business? That would be making criticism lend itself just to one of those alien practical considerations, which, I have said, are so fatal to it. One may say, indeed, to those who have to deal with the mass—so much better disregarded—of current English literature, that they may at all events endeavour, in dealing with this, to try it, so far as they can, by the standard of the best that is known and thought in the world; one may say, that to get anywhere near this standard, every critic should try and possess one great literature, at least, besides his own; and the more unlike his own, the better. But, after all, the criticism I am really concerned with,—the criticism which alone can much help us for the future, the criticism which, throughout Europe, is at the present day meant, when so much stress is laid on the importance of criticism and the critical spirit,—is a criticism which regards Europe as being, for intellectual and spiritual purposes, one great confederation, bound to a joint action and working to a common result; and whose members have, for their proper outfit, a knowledge of Greek, Roman, and Eastern antiquity, and of one another. Special, local, and temporary advantages being put out of account, that modern nation will in the intellectual and spiritual sphere make most progress, which most thoroughly carries out this programme. And what is that but saying that we too, all of us, as individuals, the more thoroughly we carry it out, shall make the more progress?

There is so much inviting us!—what are we to take? what will nourish us in growth towards perfection? That is the question which, with the immense field of life and of literature lying before him, the critic has to answer; for himself first, and afterwards for others. In this idea of the critic's business the essays brought together in the following pages have had their origin; in this idea, widely different as are their subjects, they have, perhaps, their unity.

I conclude with what I said at the beginning: to have the sense of creative activity is the great happiness and the great proof of being alive, and it is not denied to criticism to have it; but then criticism must be sincere, simple, flexible, ardent, ever widening its knowledge. Then it may have, in no contemptible measure, a joyful sense of creative activity; a sense which a man of insight and conscience will prefer to what he might derive from a poor, starved, fragmentary, inadequate creation. And at some epochs no other creation is possible.

Still, in full measure, the sense of creative activity belongs only to genuine creation; in literature we must never forget that. But what true man of letters ever can forget it? It is no such common matter for a gifted nature to come into possession of a current of true and living ideas, and to produce amidst the inspiration of them, that we are likely to underrate it. The epochs of Æschylus and Shakspeare make us feel their pre-eminence. In an epoch like those is, no doubt, the true life of a literature; there is the promised land, towards which criticism can only beckon. That promised land it will not be ours to enter, and we shall die in the wilderness; but to have desired to enter it, to have saluted it from afar, is already, perhaps, the best distinction among contemporaries; it will certainly be the best title to esteem with posterity.

The Literary Influence of Academies

IT IS impossible to put down a book like the history of the French Academy, by Pellisson and D'Olivet, which M. Charles Livet has lately re-edited,[1] without being led to reflect upon the absence, in our own country, of any institution like the French Academy, upon the probable causes of this absence, and upon its results. A thousand voices will be ready to tell us that this absence is a signal mark of our national superiority; that it is in great part owing to this absence that the exhilarating words of Lord Macaulay, lately given to the world by his very clever nephew, Mr. Trevelyan,[2] are so profoundly true: "It may safely be said that the literature now extant in the English language is of far greater value than all the literature which three hundred years ago was extant in all the languages of the world together." I daresay this

is so; only, remembering Spinoza's maxim that the two great banes of humanity are self-conceit and the laziness coming from self-conceit, I think it may do us good, instead of resting in our pre-eminence with perfect security, to look a little more closely why this is so, and whether it is so without any limitations.

But first of all I must give a very few words to the outward history of the French Academy. About the year 1629, seven or eight persons in Paris, fond of literature, formed themselves into a sort of little club to meet at one another's houses and discuss literary matters. Their meetings got talked of, and Cardinal Richelieu,[3] then minister and all-powerful, heard of them. He himself had a noble passion for letters, and for all fine culture; he was interested by what he heard of the nascent society. Himself a man in the grand style, if ever man was, he had the insight to perceive what a potent instrument of the grand style was here to his hand. It was the beginning of a great century for France, the seventeenth; men's minds were working, the French language was forming. Richelieu sent to ask the members of the new society whether they would be willing to become a body with a public character, holding regular meetings. Not without a little hesitation,—for apparently they found themselves very well as they were, and these seven or eight gentlemen of a social and literary turn were not perfectly at their ease as to what the great and terrible minister could want with them,—they consented. The favours of a man like Richelieu are not easily refused, whether they are honestly meant or no; but this favour of Richelieu's was meant quite honestly. The Parliament, however, had its doubts of this. The Parliament had none of Richelieu's enthusiasm about letters and culture; it was jealous of the apparition of a new public body in the State; above all, of a body called into existence by Richelieu. The King's letters-patent, establishing and authorising the new society, were granted early in 1635; but, by the old constitution of France, these letters-patent required the verification of the Parliament. It was two years and a half—towards the autumn of 1637—before the Parliament would give it; and it then gave it only after pressing solicitations, and earnest assurances of the innocent intentions of the young Academy. Jocose people said that this society, with its mission to purify and embellish

---

[1] *Histoire de l'Academie Française,* by Pellison and d'Olivet, was edited by Charles Livet in 1858.
[2] Sir George Otto Trevelyan (1838–1928).
[3] Armand Jean du Plessis, Cardinal Richelieu (1585–1642), French prelate and statesman.

the language, filled with terror a body of lawyers like the French Parliament, the stronghold of barbarous jargon and of chicane.

This improvement of the language was in truth the declared grand aim for the operations of the Academy. Its statutes of foundation, approved by Richelieu before the royal edict establishing it was issued, say expressly: "The Academy's principal function shall be to work with all the care and all the diligence possible at giving sure rules to our language, and rendering it pure, eloquent, and capable of treating the arts and sciences." This zeal for making a nation's great instrument of thought,—its language,— correct and worthy, is undoubtedly a sign full of promise,—a weighty earnest of future power. It is said that Richelieu had it in his mind that French should succeed Latin in its general ascendency, as Latin had succeeded Greek; if it was so, even this wish has to some extent been fulfilled. But, at any rate, the *ethical* influences of style in language,—its close relations, so often pointed out, with character,—are most important. Richelieu, a man of high culture, and, at the same time, of great character, felt them profoundly; and that he should have sought to regularise, strengthen, and perpetuate them by an institution for perfecting language, is alone a striking proof of his governing spirit and of his genius.

This was not all he had in his mind, however. The new Academy, now enlarged to a body of forty members, and meant to contain all the chief literary men of France, was to be a *literary tribunal.* The works of its members were to be brought before it previous to publication, were to be criticised by it, and finally, if it saw fit, to be published with its declared approbation. The works of other writers, not members of the Academy, might also, at the request of these writers themselves, be passed under the Academy's review. Besides this, in essays and discussions the Academy examined and judged works already published, whether by living or dead authors, and literary matters in general. The celebrated opinion on Corneille's *Cid,* delivered in 1637 by the Academy at Richelieu's urgent request, when this poem, which strongly occupied public attention, had been attacked by M. de Scudéry,[4] shows how fully Richelieu designed his new creation to do duty as a supreme court of literature, and how early it in fact began to exercise this function. One[5] who had known Richelieu declared, after the Cardinal's death, that he had projected a yet greater institution than the Academy, a sort of grand European college of art, science, and literature, a Prytaneum, where the chief authors of all Europe should be gathered together in one central home, there to live in security, leisure, and honour;— that was a dream which will not bear to be pulled about too roughly. But the project of forming a high court of letters for France was no dream; Richelieu in great measure fulfilled it. This is what the Academy, by its idea, really is; this is what it has always tended to become; this is what it has, from time to time, really been; by being, or tending to be this, far more than even by what it has done for the language, it is of such importance in France. To give the law, the tone to literature, and that tone a high one, is its business. "Richelieu meant it," says M. Sainte-Beuve, "to be a *haut jury,*"—a jury the most choice and authoritative that could be found on all important literary matters in question before the public; to be, as it in fact became in the latter half of the eighteenth century, "a sovereign organ of opinion." "The duty of the Academy is," says M. Renan, "*maintenir la délicatesse de l'esprit français*"—to keep the fine quality of the French spirit unimpaired; it represents a kind of "*maitrise en fait de bon ton*"—the authority of a recognised master in matters of tone and taste. "All ages," says M. Renan again, "have had their inferior literature; but the great danger of our time is that this inferior literature tends more and more to get the upper place. No one has the same advantage as the Academy for fighting against this mischief;" the Academy, which, as he says elsewhere, has even special facilities for "creating a form of intellectual culture *which shall impose itself on all around.*" M. Sainte-Beuve and M. Renan[6] are, both of them, very keen-sighted critics; and they show it signally by seizing and putting so prominently forward this character of the French Academy.

Such an effort to set up a recognised authority, imposing on us a high standard in matters of intellect and taste, has many enemies in human nature. We all of us like to go our own way, and not to be forced out of the atmosphere of commonplace habitual to most of us;—"*was uns alle bändigt,*" says Goethe, "*das Gemeine.*"[7] We like to

---

[4] George de Scudéry (1601–67), French dramatist.   [5] La Mesnardière. [Arnold's note]
[6] Charles Augustin Sainte-Beuve (1804–69), French critic, a favorite of Arnold's. For Renan see "Function of Criticism," note 19.
[7] "That which confines us all—the Commonplace."

be suffered to lie comfortably in the old straw of our habits, especially of our intellectual habits, even though this straw may not be very clean and fine. But if the effort to limit this freedom of our lower nature finds, as it does and must find, enemies in human nature, it finds also auxiliaries in it. Out of the four great parts, says Cicero, of the *honestum,* or good, which forms the matter on which *officium,* or human duty, finds employment, one is the fixing of a *modus* and an *ordo,* a measure and an order, to fashion and wholesomely constrain our action, in order to lift it above the level it keeps if left to itself, and to bring it nearer to perfection. Man alone of living creatures, he says, goes feeling after *"quid sit* ordo, *quid sid quod* deceat, *in factis dictisque qui* modus—the discovery of an *order,* a law of *good taste,* a *measure* for his words and actions."[8] Other creatures submissively follow the law of their nature; man alone has an impulse leading him to set up some other law to control the bent of his nature.

This holds good, of course, as to moral matters, as well as intellectual matters: and it is of moral matters that we are generally thinking when we affirm it. But it holds good as to intellectual matters too. Now, probably, M. Sainte-Beuve had not these words of Cicero in his mind when he made, about the French nation, the assertion I am going to quote; but, for all that, the assertion leans for support, one may say, upon the truth conveyed in those words of Cicero, and wonderfully illustrates and confirms them. "In France," says M. Sainte-Beuve, "the first consideration for us is not whether we are amused and pleased by a work of art or mind, nor is it whether we are touched by it. What we seek above all to learn is, whether *we were right* in being amused with it, and in applauding it, and in being moved by it." Those are very remarkable words, and they are, I believe, in the main quite true. A Frenchman has, to a considerable degree, what one may call a conscience in intellectual matters; he has an active belief that there is a right and a wrong in them, that he is bound to honour and obey the right, that he is disgraced by cleaving to the wrong. All the world has, or professes to have, this conscience in moral matters. The word *conscience* has become almost confined, in popular use, to the moral sphere, because this lively susceptibility of feeling is, in the moral sphere, so far more common than in the intellectual sphere; the livelier, in the moral sphere, this susceptibility

is, the greater becomes a man's readiness to admit a high standard of action, an ideal authoritatively correcting his everyday moral habits; here, such willing admission of authority is due to sensitiveness of conscience. And a like deference to a standard higher than one's own habitual standard in intellectual matters, a like respectful recognition of a superior ideal, is caused, in the intellectual sphere, by sensitiveness of intelligence. Those whose intelligence is quickest, openest, most sensitive, are readiest with this deference; those whose intelligence is less delicate and sensitive are less disposed to it. Well, now we are on the road to see why the French have their Academy and we have nothing of the kind.

What are the essential characteristics of the spirit of our nation? Not, certainly, an open and clear mind, not a quick and flexible intelligence. Our greatest admirers would not claim for us that we have these in a pre-eminent degree; they might say that we had more of them than our detractors gave us credit for; but they would not assert them to be our essential characteristics. They would rather allege, as our chief spiritual characteristics, energy and honesty; and, if we are judged favourably and positively, not invidiously and negatively, our chief characteristics are, no doubt, these:—energy and honesty, not an open and clear mind, not a quick and flexible intelligence. Openness of mind and flexibility of intelligence were very signal characteristics of the Athenian people in ancient times; everbody will feel that. Openness of mind and flexibility of intelligence are remarkable characteristics of the French people in modern times; at any rate, they strikingly characterise them as compared with us; I think everybody, or almost everybody, will feel that. I will not now ask what more the Athenian or the French spirit has than this, nor what shortcomings either of them may have as a set-off against this; all I want now to point out is that they have this, and that we have it in a much lesser degree.

Let me remark, however, that not only in the moral sphere, but also in the intellectual and spiritual sphere, energy and honesty are most important and fruitful qualities; that, for instance, of what we call genius energy is the most essential part. So, by assigning to a nation energy and honesty as its chief spiritual characteristics,—by refusing to it, as at all eminent characteristics, openness of mind and flexibility of intelligence,—

[8] Cicero's *De Officiis.*

we do not by any means, as some people might at first suppose, relegate its importance and its power of manifesting itself with effect from the intellectual to the moral sphere. We only indicate its probable special line of successful activity in the intellectual sphere, and, it is true, certain imperfections and failings to which, in this sphere, it will always be subject. Genius is mainly an affair of energy, and poetry is mainly an affair of genius; therefore, a nation whose spirit is characterised by energy may well be eminent in poetry;—and we have Shakspeare. Again, the highest reach of science is, one may say, an inventive power, a faculty of divination, akin to the highest power exercised in poetry; therefore, a nation whose spirit is characterised by energy may well be eminent in science;—and we have Newton. Shakspeare and Newton: in the intellectual sphere there can be no higher names. And what that energy, which is the life of genius, above everything demands and insists upon, is freedom; entire independence of all authority, prescription, and routine,—the fullest room to expand as it will. Therefore, a nation whose chief spiritual characteristic is energy, will not be very apt to set up, in intellectual matters, a fixed standard, an authority, like an academy. By this it certainly escapes certain real inconveniences and dangers, and it can, at the same time, as we have seen, reach undeniably splendid heights in poetry and science. On the other hand, some of the requisites of intellectual work are specially the affair of quickness of mind and flexibility of intelligence. The form, the method of evolution, the precision, the proportions, the relations of the parts to the whole, in an intellectual work, depend mainly upon them. And these are the elements of an intellectual work which are really most communicable from it, which can most be learned and adopted from it, which have, therefore, the greatest effect upon the intellectual performance of others. Even in poetry, these requisites are very important; and the poetry of a nation, not eminent for the gifts on which they depend, will, more or less, suffer by this shortcoming. In poetry, however, they are, after all, secondary, and energy is the first thing; but in prose they are of first-rate importance. In its prose literature, therefore, and in the routine of intellectual work generally, a nation with no particular gifts for these will not be so successful. These are what, as I have said, can to a certain degree be learned and appropriated, while the free activity of genius cannot. Academies conse-

crate and maintain them, and, therefore, a nation with an eminent turn for them naturally establishes academies. So far as routine and authority tend to embarrass energy and inventive genius, academies may be said to be obstructive to energy and inventive genius, and, to this extent, to the human spirit's general advance. But then this evil is so much compensated by the propagation, on a large scale, of the mental aptitudes and demands which an open mind and a flexible intelligence naturally engender, genius itself, in the long run, so greatly finds its account in this propagation, and bodies like the French Academy have such power for promoting it, that the general advance of the human spirit is perhaps, on the whole, rather furthered than impeded by their existence.

How much greater is our nation in poetry than prose! how much better, in general, do the productions of its spirit show in the qualities of genius than in the qualities of intelligence! One may constantly remark this in the work of individuals; how much more striking, in general, does any Englishman,—of some vigour of mind, but by no means a poet,—seem in his verse than in his prose! His verse partly suffers from his not being really a poet, partly, no doubt, from the very same defects which impair his prose, and he cannot express himself with thorough success in it. But how much more powerful a personage does he appear in it, by dint of feeling, and of originality and movement of ideas, than when he is writing prose! With a Frenchman of like stamp, it is just the reverse: set him to write poetry, he is limited, artificial, and impotent; set him to write prose, he is free, natural, and effective. The power of French literature is in its prose-writers, the power of English literature is in its poets. Nay, many of the celebrated French poets depend wholly for their fame upon the qualities of intelligence which they exhibit,— qualities which are the distinctive support of prose; many of the celebrated English prose-writers depend wholly for their fame upon the qualities of genius and imagination which they exhibit,—qualities which are the distinctive support of poetry. But, as I have said, the qualities of genius are less transferable than the qualities of intelligence; less can be immediately learned and appropriated from their product; they are less direct and stringent intellectual agencies, though they may be more beautiful and divine. Shakspeare and our great Elizabethan group were certainly more gifted writers than

Corneille and his group; but what was the sequel to this great literature, this literature of genius, as we may call it, stretching from Marlow to Milton? What did it lead up to in English literature? To our provincial and second-rate literature of the eighteenth century. What on the other hand, was the sequel to the literature of the French "great century," to this literature of intelligence, as, by comparison with our Elizabethan literature, we may call it; what did it lead up to? To the French literature of the eighteenth century, one of the most powerful and pervasive intellectual agencies that have ever existed,—the greatest European force of the eighteenth century. In science, again, we had Newton, a genius of the very highest order, a type of genius in science, if ever there was one. On the continent, as a sort of counterpart to Newton, there was Leibnitz; a man, it seems to me (though on these matters I speak under correction), of much less creative energy of genius, much less power of divination than Newton, but rather a man of admirable intelligence, a type of intelligence in science, if ever there was one. Well, and what did they each directly lead up to in science? What was the intellectual generation that sprang from each of them? I only repeat what the men of science have themselves pointed out. The man of genius was continued by the English analysts of the eighteenth century, comparatively powerless and obscure followers of the renowed master. The man of intelligence was continued by successors like Bernouilli, Euler, Lagrange, and Laplace,[9] the greatest names in modern mathematics.

What I want the reader to see is, that the question as to the utility of academies to the intellectual life of a nation is not settled when we say, for instance: "Oh, we have never had an academy, and yet we have, confessedly, a very great literature." It still remains to be asked: "What sort of a great literature? a literature great in the special qualities of genius, or great in the special qualities of intelligence?" If in the former, it is by no means sure that either our literature, or the general intellectual life of our nation, has got already, without academies, all that academies can give. Both the one and the other may very well be somewhat wanting in those qualities of intelligence out of a lively sense for which a body like the French Academy, as I have said, springs, and which such a body does a great deal to spread and confirm. Our literature, in spite of the genius manifested in it, may fall short in form, method, precision, proportions, arrangement,—all of them, I have said, things where intelligence proper comes in. It may be comparatively weak in prose, that branch of literature where intelligence proper is, so to speak, all in all. In this branch it may show many grave faults to which the want of a quick, flexible intelligence, and of the strict standard which such an intelligence tends to impose, makes it liable; it may be full of hap-hazard, crudeness, provincialism, eccentricity, violence, blundering. It may be a less stringent and effective intellectual agency, both upon our own nation and upon the world at large, than other literatures which show less genius, perhaps, but more intelligence.

The right conclusion certainly is that we should try, so far as we can, to make up our shortcomings; and that to this end, instead of always fixing our thoughts upon the points in which our literature, and our intellectual life generally, are strong, we should, from time to time, fix them upon those in which they are weak, and so learn to perceive clearly what we have to amend. What is our second great spiritual characteristic,—our honesty,—good for, if it is not good for this? But it will,—I am sure it will,—more and more, as time goes on, be found good for this.

Well, then, an institution like the French Academy,—an institution owing its existence to a national bent towards the things of the mind, towards culture, towards clearness, correctness, and propriety in thinking and speaking, and, in its turn, promoting this bent,—sets standards in a number of directions, and creates, in all these directions, a force of educated opinion, checking and rebuking those who fall below these standards, or who set them at nought. Educated opinion exists here as in France; but in France the Academy serves as a sort of centre and rallying-point to it, and gives it a force which it has not got here. Why is all the *journeyman-work* of literature, as I may call it, so much worse done here than it is in France? I do not wish to hurt any one's feelings; but surely this is so. Think of the difference between our books of reference and those of the French, between our biographical dictionaries (to take a striking instance) and theirs; think of the difference between the translations of the classics turned out for Mr. Bohn's library and those turned out for M.

---

[9] European mathematicians of the seventeenth to nineteenth centuries.

Nisard's collection![10] As a general rule, hardly any one amongst us, who knows French and German well, would use an English book of reference when he could get a French or German one; or would look at an English prose translation of an ancient author when he could get a French or German one. It is not that there do not exist in England, as in France, a number of people perfectly well able to discern what is good, in these things, from what is bad, and preferring what is good; but they are isolated, they form no powerful body of opinion, they are not strong enough to set a standard, up to which even the journeyman-work of literature must be brought, if it is to be vendible. Ignorance and charlatanism in work of this kind are always trying to pass off their wares as excellent, and to cry down criticism as the voice of an insignificant, over-fastidious minority; they easily persuade the multitude that this is so when the minority is scattered about as it is here; not so easily when it is banded together as in the French Academy. So, again, with freaks in dealing with language; certainly all such freaks tend to impair the power and beauty of language; and how far more common they are with us than with the French! To take a very familiar instance. Every one has noticed the way in which the *Times* chooses to spell the word "diocese;" it always spells it dioce*ss*,[11] deriving it, I suppose, from *Zeus* and *census*. The *Journal des Débats*[12] might just as well write "diocess" instead of "diocèse," but imagine the *Journal des Débats* doing so! Imagine an educated Frenchman indulging himself in an orthographical antic of this sort, in face of the grave respect with which the Academy and its dictionary invest the French language! Some people will say these are little things; they are not; they are of bad example. They tend to spread the baneful notion that there is no such thing as a high, correct standard in intellectual matters; that every one may as well take his own way; they are at variance with the severe discipline necessary for all real culture; they confirm us in habits of wilfulness and eccentricity, which hurt our minds, and damage our credit with serious people. The late Mr. Donaldson[13] was certainly a man of great

ability, and I, who am not an Orientalist, do not pretend to judge his *Jashar*: but let the reader observe the form which a foreign Orientalist's judgment of it naturally takes. M. Renan calls it a *tentative malheureuse,* a failure, in short; this it may be, or it may not be; I am no judge. But he goes on: "It is astonishing that a recent article" (in a French periodical, he means) "should have brought forward as the last word of German exegesis a work like this, composed by a doctor of the University of Cambridge, and universally condemned by German critics." You see what he means to imply: an extravagance of this sort could never have come from Germany, where there is a great force of critical opinion controlling a learned man's vagaries, and keeping him straight; it comes from the native home of intellectual eccentricity of all kinds,[14]—from England, from a doctor of the University of Cambridge:—and I daresay he would not expect much better things from a doctor of the University of Oxford. Again, after speaking of what Germany and France have done for the history of Mahomet: "America and England," M. Renan goes on, "have also occupied themselves with Mahomet." He mentions Washington Irving's *Life of Mahomet,*[15] which does not, he says, evince much of an historical sense, a *sentiment historique fort élevé;* "but," he proceeds, "this book shows a real progress, when one thinks that in 1829 Mr. Charles Forster published two thick volumes,[16] which enchanted the English *révérends,* to make out that Mahomet was the little horn of the he-goat that figures in the eighth chapter of Daniel, and that the Pope was the great horn. Mr. Forster founded on this ingenious parallel a whole philosophy of history, according to which the Pope represented the Western corruption of Christianity, and Mahomet the Eastern; thence the striking resemblances between Mahometanism and Popery." And in a note M. Renan adds: "This is the same Mr. Charles Forster who is the author of a mystification about the Sinaitic inscriptions, in which he declares he finds the primitive language." As much as to say: "It is an Englishman, be surprised at no extravagance." If these innuendoes had no ground, and were

---

[10] Henry George Bohn (1796–1884), bookseller; Désiré Nisard (1806–88), French editor, helped publish translations of classics.

[11] The *Times* has now (1868) abandoned this spelling and adopted the ordinary one. [Arnold's note]

[12] A Parisian newspaper.   [13] John William Donaldson (1811–61), philologist.

[14] A critic declares I am wrong in saying that M. Renan's language implies this. I still think that there is a shade, a *nuance* of expression, in M. Renan's language, which does imply this; but, I confess, the only person who can really settle such a question is M. Renan himself. [Arnold's note]

[15] Published 1850.   [16] *Mohametanism Unveiled!* (2 vols., 1829).

made in hatred and malice, they would not be worth a moment's attention; but they come from a grave Orientalist, on his own subject, and they point to a real fact;—the absence, in this country, of any force of educated literary and scientific opinion, making aberrations like those of the author of *The One Primeval Language* out of the question. Not only the author of such aberrations, often a very clever man, suffers by the want of check, by the not being kept straight, and spends force in vain on a false road, which, under better discipline, he might have used with profit on a true one; but all his adherents, both "reverends" and others, suffer too, and the general rate of information and judgment is in this way kept low.

In a production which we have all been reading lately, a production stamped throughout with a literary quality very rare in this country, and of which I shall have a word to say presently— *urbanity;* in this production, the work of a man never to be named by any son of Oxford without sympathy, a man who alone in Oxford of his generation, alone of many generations, conveyed to us in his genius that same charm, that same ineffable sentiment which this exquisite place itself conveys,—I mean Dr. Newman,—an expression is frequently used which is more common in theological than in literary language, but which seems to me fitted to be of general service; the *note* of so and so, the note of catholicity, the note of antiquity, the note of sanctity, and so on. Adopting this expressive word, I say that in the bulk of the intellectual work of a nation which has no centre, no intellectual metropolis like an academy, like M. Sainte-Beuve's "sovereign organ of opinion," like M. Renan's "recognised authority in matters of tone and taste,"—there is observable a *note of provinciality*. Now to get rid of provinciality is a certain stage of culture; a stage the positive result of which we must not make of too much importance, but which is, nevertheless, indispensable, for it brings us on to the platform where alone the best and highest intellectual work can be said fairly to begin. Work done after men have reached this platform is *classical;* and that is the only work which, in the long run, can stand. All the *scoriæ* in the work of men of great genius who have not lived on this platform are due to their not having lived on it. Genius raises them to it by moments, and the portions of their work which are immortal are done at these moments; but more of it would have been immortal if they had not reached this platform at moments only, if they had had the culture which makes men live there.

The less a literature has felt the influence of a supposed centre of correct information, correct judgment, correct taste, the more we shall find in it this note of provinciality. I have shown the note of provinciality as caused by remoteness from a centre of correct information. Of course the note of provinciality from the want of a centre of correct taste is still more visible, and it is also still more common. For here great—even the greatest –powers of mind most fail a man. Great powers of mind will make him inform himself thoroughly, great powers of mind will make him think profoundly, even with ignorance and platitude all round him; but not even great powers of mind will keep his taste and style perfectly sound and sure, if he is left too much to himself, with no "sovereign organ of opinion" in these matters near him. Even men like Jeremy Taylor[17] and Burke suffer here. Take this passage from Taylor's funeral sermon on Lady Carbery:—

"So have I seen a river, deep and smooth, passing with a still foot and a sober face, and paying to the *fiscus,* the great exchequer of the sea, a tribute large and full; and hard by it a little brook, skipping and making a noise upon its unequal and neighbour bottom; and after all its talking and bragged motion, it paid to its common audit no more than the revenues of a little cloud or a contemptible vessel: so have I sometimes compared the issues of her religion to the solemnities and famed outsides of another's piety."

That passage has been much admired, and, indeed, the genius in it is undeniable. I should say, for my part, that genius, the ruling divinity of poetry, had been too busy in it, and intelligence, the ruling divinity of prose, not busy enough. But can any one, with the best models of style in his head, help feeling the note of provinciality there, the want of simplicity, the want of measure, the want of just the qualities that make prose classical? If he does not feel what I mean, let him place beside the passage of Taylor this passage from the Panegyric of St. Paul, by Taylor's contemporary, Bossuet:[18]—

"Il ira, cet ignorant dans l'art de bien dire,

---

[17] Jeremy Taylor (1613-67), English divine and author.
[18] Jacques Bossuet (1627–1704). The passage reads: "He will go, this man ignorant of the art of fine speaking, with his crude discourse, with that phrase that has an air of the foreigner, he will go into

avec cette locution rude, avec cette phrase qui sent l'étranger il ira en cette Grèce polie, la mère des philosophes et des orateurs; et malgré la résistance du monde, il y établira plus d'Eglises que Platon n'y a gagné de disciples par cette éloquence qu'on a crue divine."

There we have prose without the note of provinciality—classical prose, prose of the centre.

Or take Burke, our greatest English prose-writer, as I think; take expressions like this:[19]—

"Blindfold themselves, like bulls that shut their eyes when they push, they drive, by the point of their bayonets, their slaves, blindfolded, indeed, no worse than their lords, to take their fictions for currencies, and to swallow down paper pills by thirty-four millions sterling at a dose."

Or this:—

"They used it" (the royal name) "as a sort of navel-string, to nourish their unnatural offspring from the bowels of royalty itself. Now that the monster can purvey for its own subsistence, it will only carry the mark about it, as a token of its having torn the womb it came from."

Or this:—

"Without one natural pang, he" (Rousseau) "casts away, as a sort of offal and excrement, the spawn of his disgustful amours, and sends his children to the hospital of foundlings."

Or this:—

"I confess I never liked this continual talk of resistance and revolution, or the practice of making the extreme medicine of the constitution its daily bread. It renders the habit of society dangerously valetudinary; it is taking periodical doses of mercury sublimate, and swallowing down repeated provocatives of cantharides to our love of liberty."

I say that is extravagant prose; prose too much suffered to indulge its caprices; prose at too great

a distance from the centre of good taste; prose, in short, with the note of provinciality. People may reply, it is rich and imaginative; yes, that is just it, it is *Asiatic* prose, as the ancient critics would have said; prose somewhat barbarously rich and overloaded. But the true prose is Attic prose.

Well, but Addison's prose is Attic prose. Where, then, it may be asked, is the note of provinciality in Addison? I answer, in the commonplace of his ideas.[20] This is a matter worth remarking. Addison claims to take leading rank as a moralist. To do that, you must have ideas of the first order on your subject—the best ideas, at any rate, attainable in your time—as well as be able to express them in a perfectly sound and sure style. Else you show your distance from the centre of ideas by your matter; you are provincial by your matter, though you may not be provincial by your style. It is comparatively a small matter to express oneself well, if one will be content with not expressing much, with expressing only trite ideas; the problem is to express new and profound ideas in a perfectly sound and classical style. He is the true classic, in every age, who does that. Now Addison has not, on his subject of morals, the force of ideas of the moralists of the first class—the classical moralists; he has not the best ideas attainable in or about his time, and which were, so to speak, in the air then, to be seized by the finest spirits; he is not to be compared for power, searchingness, or delicacy of thought to Pascal or La Bruyère or Vauvenargues; he is rather on a level, in this respect, with a man like Marmontel.[21] Therefore, I say, he has the note of provinciality as a moralist; he is provincial by his matter, though not by his style.

To illustrate what I mean by an example. Addison, writing as a moralist on fixedness in religious faith, says:—

this cultured Greece, mother of philosophers and orators; and in spite of the opposition of the world, he will establish there more churches than Plato won disciples by that eloquence which was believed to be divine."

[19] The first and fourth passage come from Burke's *Reflections on the Revolution in France;* the second and third come from his *Letter to a Member of the National Assembly.*

[20] A critic says this is paradoxical, and urges that many second-rate French academicians have uttered the most commonplace ideas possible. I agree that many second-rate French academicians have uttered the most commonplace ideas possible; but Addison is not a second-rate man. He is a man of the order, I will not say of Pascal, but at any rate of La Bruyère and Vauvenargues; why does he not equal them? I say because of the medium in which he finds himself, the atmosphere in which he lives and works; an atmosphere which tells unfavourably, or rather *tends* to tell unfavourably (for that is the truer way of putting it) either upon style or else upon ideas; tends to make even a man of great ability either a Mr. Carlyle or else a Lord Macaulay.

It is to be observed, however, that Lord Macaulay's style has in its turn suffered by his failure in ideas, and this cannot be said of Addison's. [Arnold's note]

[21] Blaise Pascal (1623–62), French philosopher; Jean de La Bruyère (1645–96), French essayist; Luc de Clapiers de Vauvenargues (1715–47), French philosopher; Jean François Marmontel (1723–99), French critic.

"Those who delight in reading books of controversy do very seldom arrive at a fixed and settled habit of faith. The doubt which was laid revives again, and shows itself in new difficulties; and that generally for this reason,—because the mind, which is perpetually tossed in controversies and disputes, is apt to forget the reasons which had once set it at rest, and to be disquieted with any former perplexity when it appears in a new shape, or is started by a different hand."

It may be said, that is classical English, perfect in lucidity, measure, and propriety. I make no objection; but, in my turn, I say that the idea expressed is perfectly trite and barren, and that it is a note of provinciality in Addison, in a man whom a nation puts forward as one of its great moralists, to have no profounder and more striking idea to produce on this great subject. Compare, on the same subject, these words of a moralist really of the first order, really at the centre by his ideas,—Joubert:—

"L'expérience de beaucoup d'opinions donne à l'esprit beaucoup de flexibilité et l'affermit dans celles qu'il croit les meilleures."[22]

With what a flash of light that touches the subject! how it sets us thinking! what a genuine contribution to moral science it is!

In short, where there is no centre like an academy, if you have genius and powerful ideas, you are apt not to have the best style going; if you have precision of style and not genius, you are apt not to have the best ideas going.

The provincial spirit, again, exaggerates the value of its ideas for want of a high standard at hand by which to try them. Or rather, for want of such a standard, it gives one idea too much prominence at the expense of others; it orders its ideas amiss; it is hurried away by fancies; it likes and dislikes too passionately, too exclusively. Its admiration weeps hysterical tears, and its disapprobation foams at the mouth. So we get the *eruptive* and the *aggressive* manner in literature; the former prevails most in our criticism, the latter in our newspapers. For, not having the lucidity of a large and centrally placed intelligence, the provincial spirit has not its graciousness; it does not persuade, it makes war; it has not urbanity, the tone of the city, of the centre, the tone which always aims at a spiritual and intellectual effect, and not excluding the use of banter, never disjoins banter itself from politeness,

from felicity. But the provincial tone is more violent, and seems to aim rather at an effect upon the blood and senses than upon the spirit and intellect; it loves hard-hitting rather than persuading. The newspaper, with its party spirit, its thorough-goingness, its resolute avoidance of shades and distinctions, its short, highly-charged, heavy-shotted articles, its style so unlike that style *lenis minimèque pertinax*—easy and not too violently insisting,—which the ancients so much admired, is its true literature; the provincial spirit likes in the newspaper just what makes the newspaper such bad food for it,—just what made Goethe say, when he was pressed hard about the immorality of Byron's poems, that, after all, they were not so immoral as the newspapers. The French talk of the *brutalité des journaux anglais*.[23] What strikes them comes from the necessary inherent tendencies of newspaper-writing not being checked in England by any centre of intelligent and urbane spirit, but rather stimulated by coming in contact with a provincial spirit. Even a newspaper like the *Saturday Review*, that old friend of all of us, a newspaper expressly aiming at an immunity from the common newspaper-spirit, aiming at being a sort of organ of reason,—and, by thus aiming, it merits great gratitude and has done great good,—even the *Saturday Review*, replying to some foreign criticism on our precautions against invasion, falls into a strain of this kind:—

"To do this" (to take these precautions) "seems to us eminently worthy of a great nation, and to talk of it as unworthy of a great nation, seems to us eminently worthy of a great fool."

There is what the French mean when they talk of the *brutalité des journaux anglais;* there is a style certainly as far removed from urbanity as possible,—a style with what I call the note of provinciality. And the same note may not unfrequently be observed even in the ideas of this newspaper, full as it is of thought and cleverness: certain ideas allowed to become fixed ideas, to prevail too absolutely. I will not speak of the immediate present, but, to go a little while back, it had the critic who so disliked the Emperor of the French; it had the critic who so disliked the subject of my present remarks— academies; it had the critic who was so fond of the German element in our nation, and, indeed, everywhere; who ground his teeth if one said

---

[22] "Acquaintance with many opinions gives the spirit a great deal of flexibility and strengthens it in those opinions which it believes to be the best." [Joubert's *Pensées*]
[23] "The brutality of English newspapers."

Charlemagne instead of *Charles the Great,* and, in short, saw all things in Teutonism, as Malebranche[24] saw all things in God. Certainly any one may fairly find faults in the Emperor Napoleon or in academies, and merit in the German element; but it is a note of the provincial spirit not to hold ideas of this kind a little more easily, to be so devoured by them, to suffer them to become crotchets.

In England there needs a miracle of genius like Shakspeare's to produce balance of mind, and a miracle of intellectual delicacy like Dr. Newman's to produce urbanity of style. How prevalent all round us is the want of balance of mind and urbanity of style! How much, doubtless, it is to be found in ourselves,—in each of us! but, as human nature is constituted, every one can see it clearest in his contemporaries. There, above all, we should consider it, because they and we are exposed to the same influences; and it is in the best of one's contemporaries that it is most worth considering, because one then most feels the harm it does, when one sees what they would be without it. Think of the difference between Mr. Ruskin exercising his genius, and Mr. Ruskin exercising his intelligence; consider the truth and beauty of this:—

"Go out, in the spring-time, among the meadows that slope from the shores of the Swiss lakes to the roots of their lower mountains. There, mingled with the taller gentians and the white narcissus, the grass grows deep and free; and as you follow the winding mountain paths, beneath arching boughs all veiled and dim with blossom, —paths that for ever droop and rise over the green banks and mounds sweeping down in scented undulation, steep to the blue water studded here and there with new-mown heaps, filling all the air with fainter sweetness,—look up towards the higher hills, where the waves of everlasting green roll silently into their long inlets among the shadows of the pines. . . . . ."

There is what the genius, the feeling, the temperament in Mr. Ruskin, the original and incommunicable part, has to do with; and how exquisite it is! All the critic could possibly suggest, in the way of objection, would be, perhaps, that Mr. Ruskin is there trying to make prose do more than it can perfectly do; that what he is there attempting he will never, except in poetry, be able to accomplish to his own entire

satisfaction: but he accomplishes so much that the critic may well hesitate to suggest even this. Place beside this charming passage another,—a passage about Shakspeare's names, where the intelligence and judgment of Mr. Ruskin, the acquired, trained, communicable part in him, are brought into play,—and see the difference:—

"Of Shakspeare's names I will afterwards speak at more length; they are curiously—often barbarously—mixed out of various traditions and languages. Three of the clearest in meaning have been already noticed. Desdemona—'δυσδαιμονία,' *miserable fortune*—is also plain enough. Othello is, I believe, 'the careful;' all the calamity of the tragedy arising from the single flaw and error in his magnificently collected strength. Ophelia, 'serviceableness,' the true, lost wife of Hamlet, is marked as having a Greek name by that of her brother, Laertes; and its signification is once exquisitely alluded to in that brother's last word of her, where her gentle preciousness is opposed to the uselessness of the churlish clergy:—'A *ministering* angel shall my sister be, when thou liest howling.' Hamlet is, I believe, connected in some way with 'homely,' the entire event of the tragedy turning on betrayal of home duty. Hermione (ἕρμα), 'pillar-like' (ἡ εἶδος ἔχε χρυσῆς Ἀφροδίτης); Titania (τιτήνη), 'the queen;' Benedick and Beatrice, 'blessed and blessing;' Valentine and Proteus, 'enduring or strong' (*valens*), and 'changeful.' Iago and Iachimo have evidently the same root—probably the Spanish Iago, Jacob, 'the supplanter.' "

Now, really, what a piece of extravagance all that is! I will not say that the meaning of Shakspeare's names (I put aside the question as to the correctness of Mr. Ruskin's etymologies) has no effect at all, may be entirely lost sight of; but to give it that degree of prominence is to throw the reins to one's whim, to forget all moderation and proportion, to lose the balance of one's mind altogether. It is to show in one's criticism, to the highest excess, the note of provinciality.

Again, there is Mr. Palgrave,[25] certainly endowed with a very fine critical tact: his *Golden Treasury* abundantly proves it. The plan of arrangement which he devised for that work, the mode in which he followed his plan out, nay, one might even say, merely the juxtaposition, in pursuance of it, of two such pieces as those of

---

[24] Nicolas de Malebranche (1638–1715), French philosopher.
[25] Francis Turner Palgrave (1824–97), poet, man of letters, editor of *The Golden Treasury* (1861), an anthology of poetry.

Wordsworth and Shelley which form the 285th and 286th in his collection, show a delicacy of feeling in these matters which is quite indisputable and very rare. And his notes are full of remarks which show it too. All the more striking, conjoined with so much justness of perception, are certain freaks and violences in Mr. Palgrave's criticism, mainly imputable, I think, to the critic's isolated position in this country, to his feeling himself too much left to take his own way, too much without any central authority representing high culture and sound judgment, by which he may be, on the one hand, confirmed as against the ignorant, on the other, held in respect when he himself is inclined to take liberties. I mean such things as this note on Milton's line,—

"The great Emathian conqueror bade spare" . . .

"When Thebes was destroyed, Alexander ordered the house of Pindar to be spared. *He was as incapable of appreciating the poet as Louis XIV. of appreciating Racine; but even the narrow and barbarian mind of Alexander could understand the advantage of a showy act of homage to poetry.*" A note like that I call a freak or a violence; if this disparaging view of Alexander and Louis XIV., so unlike the current view, is wrong,—if the current view is, after all, the truer one of them,—the note is a freak. But, even if its disparaging view is right, the note is a violence; for, abandoning the true mode of intellectual action—persuasion, the instilment of conviction,—it simply astounds and irritates the hearer by contradicting without a word of proof or preparation, his fixed and familiar notions; and this is mere violence. In either case, the fitness, the measure, the centrality, which is the soul of all good criticism, is lost, and the note of provinciality shows itself.

Thus, in the famous *Handbook*,[26] marks of a fine power of perception are everywhere discernible, but so, too, are marks of the want of sure balance, of the check and support afforded by knowing one speaks before good and severe judges. When Mr. Palgrave dislikes a thing, he feels no pressure constraining him either to try his dislike closely or to express it moderately; he does not mince matters, he gives his dislike all its own way; both his judgment and his style would gain if he were under more restraint. "The style

which has filled London with the dead monotony of Gower or Harley Streets, or the pale commonplace of Belgravia, Tyburnia, and Kensington; which has pierced Paris and Madrid with the feeble frivolities of the Rue Rivoli and the Strada de Toledo." He dislikes the architecture of the Rue Rivoli, and he puts it on a level with the architecture of Belgravia and Gower Street; he lumps them all together in one condemnation, he loses sight of the shade, the distinction, which is everything here; the distinction, namely, that the architecture of the Rue Rivoli expresses show, splendour, pleasure,—unworthy things, perhaps, to express alone and for their own sakes, but it expresses them; whereas the architecture of Gower Street and Belgravia merely expresses the impotence of the architect to express anything. Then, as to style: "sculpture which stands in a contrast with Woolner[27] hardly more shameful than diverting." . . . "passing from Davy or Faraday[28] to the art of the mountebank or the science of the spirit-rapper." . . . "it is the old, old story with Marochetti, the frog trying to blow himself out to bull dimensions. He may puff and be puffed, but he will never do it." We all remember that shower of amenities on poor M. Marochetti.[29] Now, here Mr. Palgrave himself enables us to form a contrast which lets us see just what the presence of an academy does for style; for he quotes a criticism by M. Gustave Planche[30] on this very M. Marochetti. M. Gustave Planche was a critic of the very first order, a man of strong opinions, which he expressed with severity; he, too, condemns M. Marochetti's work, and Mr. Palgrave calls him as a witness to back what he has himself said; certainly Mr. Palgrave's translation will not exaggerate M. Planche's urbanity in dealing with M. Marochetti, but, even in this translation, see the difference in sobriety, in measure, between the critic writing in Paris and the critic writing in London:—

"These conditions are so elementary, that I am at a perfect loss to comprehend how M. Marochetti has neglected them. There are soldiers here like the leaden playthings of the nursery: it is almost impossible to guess whether there is a body beneath the dress. We have here no question of style, not even of grammar; it is nothing beyond mere matter of the alphabet of art. To break

---

[26] Palgrave's *Handbook to the Fine Art Collection in the International Exhibition of 1862.*
[27] Thomas Woolner (1825–92), sculptor.
[28] Humphry Davy (1778–1829) and Michael Faraday (1791–1867), distinguished scientists.
[29] Carlo Marochetti (1801–68), Italian sculptor.
[30] Gustave Planche (1808–57), French critic.

these conditions is the same as to be ignorant of spelling."

That is really more formidable criticism than Mr. Palgrave's, and yet in how perfectly temperate a style! M. Planche's advantage is, that he feels himself to be speaking before competent judges, that there is a force of cultivated opinion for him to appeal to. Therefore, he must not be extravagant, and he need not storm; he must satisfy the reason and taste,—that is his business. Mr. Palgrave, on the other hand, feels himself to be speaking before a promiscuous multitude, with the few good judges so scattered through it as to be powerless; therefore, he has no calm confidence and no self-control; he relies on the strength of his lungs; he knows that big words impose on the mob, and that, even if he is outrageous, most of his audience are apt to be a great deal more so.[31]

Again, the first two volumes of Mr. Kinglake's *Invasion of the Crimea*[32] were certainly among the most successful and renowned English books of our time. Their style was one of the most renowned things about them, and yet how conspicuous a fault in Mr. Kinglake's style is this over-charge of which I have been speaking! Mr. James Gordon Bennett,[33] of the *New York Herald,* says, I believe, that the highest achievement of the human intellect is what he calls "a good editorial." This is not quite so; but, if it were so, on what a height would these two volumes by Mr. Kinglake stand! I have already spoken of the Attic and the Asiatic styles; besides these, there is the Corinthian style. That is the style for "a good editorial," and Mr. Kinglake has really reached perfection in it. It has not the warm glow, blithe movement, and soft pliancy of life, as the Attic style has; it has not the over-heavy richness and encumbered gait of the Asiatic style; it has glitter without warmth, rapidity without ease, effectiveness without charm. Its characteristic is, that it has no *soul;* all it exists for, is to get its ends, to make its points, to damage its adversaries, to be admired, to triumph. A style so bent on effect at the expense of soul, simplicity, and delicacy; a style so little studious of the charm of the great models; so far from classic truth and grace, must surely be said to have the note of provinciality. Yet Mr. Kinglake's talent is a really eminent one, and so in harmony with our intellectual habits and tendencies, that, to the great bulk of English people, the faults of his style seem its merits; all the more needful that criticism should not be dazzled by them.

We must not compare a man of Mr. Kinglake's literary talent with French writers like M. de Bazancourt. We must compare him with M. Thiers.[34] And what a superiority in style has M. Thiers from being formed in a good school, with severe traditions, wholesome restraining influences! Even in this age of Mr. James Gordon Bennett, his style has nothing Corinthian about it, its lightness and brightness make it almost Attic. It is not quite Attic, however; it has not the infallible sureness of Attic taste. Sometimes his head gets a little hot with the fumes of patriotism, and then he crosses the line, he loses perfect measure, he declaims, he raises a momentary smile. France condemned 'à être l'effroi du monde *dont elle pourrait être l'amour,*'[35]— Cæsar, whose exquisite simplicity M. Thiers so much admires, would not have written like that. There is, if I may be allowed to say so, the slightest possible touch of fatuity in such language,—of that failure in good sense which comes from too warm a self-satisfaction. But compare this language with Mr. Kinglake's Marshal St. Arnaud—"dismissed from the presence" of Lord Raglan or Lord Stratford,[36] "cowed and pressed down" under their "stern reproofs," or under "the majesty of the great Elchi's Canning brow and tight, merciless lips!" The failure in good sense and good taste there reaches far beyond what the French mean by *fatuity;* they would call it by another word, a word expressing blank defect of intelligence, a word for which we have no exact equivalent in English,—*bête.* It is the difference between a venial, momentary, good-tempered excess, in a

---

[31] When I wrote this I had before me the first edition of Mr. Palgrave's Handbook. I am bound to say that in the second edition much strong language has been expunged, and what remains, softened. [Arnold's note]

[32] Alexander William Kinglake (1809–91), traveler and historian. Volumes I and II of the *Invasion of the Crimea* appeared in 1863.

[33] James Gordon Bennett (1795–1872), American journalist, editor of the *New York Herald.*

[34] Cesar Lécat, Baron de Bazancourt (1810–65), French historian; Louis Adolphe Thiers (1797–1877), French historian and statesman.

[35] "To be the terror of the world of which she could be the beloved."

[36] Lord Raglan was commander of British forces in the Crimean War; Lord Stratford was British ambassador to Turkey at the time Arnold is referring to.

man of the world, of an amiable and social weakness,—vanity; and a serious, settled, fierce, narrow, provincial misconception of the whole relative value of one's own things and the things of others. So baneful to the style of even the cleverest man may be the total want of checks.

In all I have said, I do not pretend that the examples given prove my rule as to the influence of academies; they only illustrate it. Examples in plenty might very likely be found to set against them; the truth of the rule depends, no doubt, on whether the balance of all the examples is in its favour or not; but actually to strike this balance is always out of the question. Here, as everywhere else, the rule, the idea, if true, commends itself to the judicious, and then the examples make it clearer still to them. This is the real use of examples, and this alone is the purpose which I have meant mine to serve. There is also another side to the whole question,—as to the limiting and prejudicial operation which academies may have; but this side of the question it rather behoves the French, not us, to study.

The reader will ask for some practical conclusion about the establishment of an Academy in this country, and perhaps I shall hardly give him the one he expects. But nations have their own modes of acting, and these modes are not easily changed; they are even consecrated, when great things have been done in them. When a literature has produced Shakspeare and Milton, when it has even produced Barrow[37] and Burke, it cannot well abandon its traditions; it can

hardly begin, at this late time of day, with an institution like the French Academy. I think academies with a limited, special, scientific scope, in the various lines of intellectual work,—academies like that of Berlin,[38] for instance,—we with time may, and probably shall, establish. And no doubt they will do good; no doubt the presence of such influential centres of correct information will tend to raise the standard amongst us for what I have called the *journeyman-work* of literature, and to free us from the scandal of such biographical dictionaries as Chalmers's,[39] or such translations as a recent one of Spinoza, or perhaps, such philological freaks as Mr. Forster's about the one primeval language. But an academy quite like the French Academy, a sovereign organ of the highest literary opinion, a recognised authority in matters of intellectual tone and taste, we shall hardly have, and perhaps we ought not to wish to have it. But then every one amongst us with any turn for literature will do well to remember to what shortcomings and excesses, which such an academy tends to correct, we are liable; and the more liable, of course, for not having it. He will do well constantly to try himself in respect of these, steadily to widen his culture, severely to check in himself the provincial spirit; and he will do this the better the more he keeps in mind that all mere glorification by ourselves of ourselves or our literature, in the strain of what, at the beginning of these remarks, I quoted from Lord Macaulay, is both vulgar, and, besides being vulgar retarding.

from Culture and Anarchy

Very much an occasional work in that it was largely the result of Arnold's response to the agitations surrounding the passage of the Second Reform Bill in 1867, Culture and Anarchy is at the same time an enduring statement of the perennial issue between social order and individual license. The work was originally published as a series of articles in the Cornhill Magazine between July 1867 and August 1868, the period covering the passage of the bill and just preceding the first election under the new franchise. The first of the articles bore the title "Culture and Its Enemies," and later became the preface and the first chapter of the book. It had been Arnold's final lecture as Oxford Professor of Poetry. The other five articles bore the common title "Anarchy and Authority," and they became Chapters II through VI of the final work. The first edition with the new title—a blend of the titles of the magazine essays—appeared

[37] Isaac Barrow (1630–77), Anglican clergyman, noted orator.
[38] The Academy of Sciences, founded by Leibnitz in 1700.
[39] Alexander Chalmers (1759–1834), author of *General Biographical Dictionary* (1812–17).

in 1869. This is the edition used here. There were two more editions in Arnold's lifetime, and the work has been frequently reprinted since then.

To move from the Essays in Criticism, *First Series, to* Culture and Anarchy, *especially from "The Function of Criticism at the Present Time" to the chapter "Sweetness and Light," is to see at once the continuity of Arnold's literary and social thinking. His concept of criticism is sufficiently large-minded so that it contains in it the seeds of his concept of culture itself. The work should be compared with Mill's* On Liberty *as one of the most important Victorian statements on the role of the individual in relation to society.*

Excluding the Preface, the entire work is given below.

Introduction

I**N ONE** of his speeches a short time ago, that fine speaker and famous Liberal, Mr. Bright,[1] took occasion to have a fling at the friends and preachers of culture. "People who talk about what they call *culture!*" said he contemptuously; "by which they mean a smattering of the two dead languages of Greek and Latin." And he went on to remark, in a strain with which modern speakers and writers have made us very familiar, how poor a thing this culture is, how little good it can do to the world, and how absurd it is for its possessors to set much store by it. And the other day a younger Liberal than Mr. Bright, one of a school whose mission it is to bring into order and system that body of truth with which the earlier Liberals merely fumbled, a member of the University of Oxford, and a very clever writer, Mr. Frederic Harrison,[2] developed, in the systematic and stringent manner of his school, the thesis which Mr. Bright had propounded in only general terms. "Perhaps the very silliest cant of the day," said Mr. Frederic Harrison, "is the cant about culture. Culture is a desirable quality in a critic of new books, and sits well on a professor of *belles lettres;* but as applied to politics, it means simply a turn for small fault-finding, love of selfish ease, and indecision in action. The man of culture is in politics one of the poorest mortals alive. For simple pedantry and want of good sense no man is his equal. No assumption is too unreal, no end is too unpractical for him. But the active exercise of politics requires common sense, sympathy, trust, resolution and enthusiasm, qualities which your man of culture has carefully rooted up, lest they damage the delicacy of his critical olfactories. Perhaps they are the only class of responsible beings in the community who cannot with safety be entrusted with power."

Now for my part I do not wish to see men of culture asking to be entrusted with power; and, indeed, I have freely said, that in my opinion the speech most proper, at present, for a man of culture to make to a body of his fellow-countrymen who get him into a committee-room, is Socrates's: *Know thyself!* and this is not a speech to be made by men wanting to be entrusted with power. For this very indifference to direct political action I have been taken to task by the *Daily Telegraph,*[3] coupled, by a strange perversity of fate, with just that very one of the Hebrew prophets whose style I admire the least, and called "an elegant Jeremiah." It is because I say (to use the words which the *Daily Telegraph* puts in my mouth):—"You mustn't make a fuss because you have no vote,—that is vulgarity; you mustn't hold big meetings to agitate for reform bills and to repeal corn laws,—that is the very height of vulgarity,"—it is for this reason that I am called, sometimes an elegant Jeremiah, sometimes a spurious Jeremiah, a Jeremiah about the reality of whose mission the writer in the *Daily Telegraph* has his doubts. It is evident, therefore, that I have so taken my line as not to be exposed to the whole brunt of Mr. Frederic Harrison's censure. Still, I have often spoken in praise of culture, I have striven to make all my works and ways serve the interests of culture. I take culture to be something a great deal more than what Mr. Frederic Harrison and others call it: "a desirable quality in a critic of new books." Nay, even though to a certain extent I am disposed to agree with Mr. Frederic Harrison, that men of culture are just the class of responsible

---

[1] John Bright (1811–89), orator and Member of Parliament, active on behalf of the manufacturing class.

[2] Frederic Harrison (1831–1923), author, supporter of the working class.

[3] At that time a sensational newspaper. Arnold had criticized its reporter, G. A. Sala, in the "Preface" to *Culture and Anarchy*.

beings in this community of ours who cannot properly, at present, be entrusted with power, I am not sure that I do not think this the fault of our community rather than of the men of culture. In short, although, like Mr. Bright and Mr. Frederic Harrison, and the editor of the *Daily Telegraph*, and a large body of valued friends of mine, I am a Liberal, yet I am a Liberal tempered by experience, reflection, and renouncement, and I am, above all, a believer in culture. Therefore I propose now to try and enquire, in the simple unsystematic way which best suits both my taste and my powers, what culture really is, what good it can do, what is our own special need of it; and I shall seek to find some plain grounds on which a faith in culture—both my own faith in it and the faith of others—may rest securely.

CHAPTER I

Sweetness and Light

THE disparagers of culture make its motive curiosity; sometimes, indeed, they make its motive mere exclusiveness and vanity. The culture which is supposed to plume itself on a smattering of Greek and Latin is a culture which is begotten by nothing so intellectual as curiosity; it is valued either out of sheer vanity and ignorance, or else as an engine of social and class distinction, separating its holder, like a badge or title, from other people who have not got it. No serious man would call this *culture,* or attach any value to it, as culture, at all. To find the real ground for the very differing estimate which serious people will set upon culture, we must find some motive for culture in the terms of which may lie a real ambiguity; and such a motive the word *curiosity* gives us.

I have before now pointed out that we English do not, like the foreigners, use this word in a good sense as well as in a bad sense. With us the word is always used in a somewhat disapproving sense. A liberal and intelligent eagerness about the things of the mind may be meant by a foreigner when he speaks of curiosity, but with us the word always conveys a certain notion of frivolous and

unedifying activity. In the *Quarterly Review,* some little time ago,[1] was an estimate of the celebrated French critic, M. Sainte-Beuve, and a very inadequate estimate it in my judgment was. And its inadequacy consisted chiefly in this: that in our English way it left out of sight the double sense really involved in the word *curiosity,* thinking enough was said to stamp M. Sainte-Beuve with blame if it was said that he was impelled in his operations as a critic by curiosity, and omitting either to perceive that M. Sainte-Beuve himself, and many other people with him, would consider that this was praiseworthy and not blameworthy, or to point out why it ought really to be accounted worthy of blame and not of praise. For as there is a curiosity about intellectual matters which is futile, and merely a disease, so there is certainly a curiosity,—a desire after the things of the mind simply for their own sakes and for the pleasure of seeing them as they are,—which is, in an intelligent being, natural and laudable. Nay, and the very desire to see things as they are, implies a balance and regulation of mind which is not often attained without fruitful effort, and which is the very opposite of the blind and diseased impulse of mind which is what we mean to blame when we blame curiosity. Montesquieu[2] says:—"The first motive which ought to impel us to study is the desire to augment the excellence of our nature, and to render an intelligent being yet more intelligent." This is the true ground to assign for the genuine scientific passion, however manifested, and for culture, viewed simply as a fruit of this passion; and it is a worthy ground, even though we let the term *curiosity* stand to describe it.

But there is of culture another view, in which not solely the scientific passion, the sheer desire to see things as they are, natural and proper in an intelligent being, appears as the ground of it. There is a view in which all the love of our neighbour, the impulses towards action, help, and beneficence, the desire for removing human error, clearing human confusion, and diminishing human misery, the noble aspiration to leave the world better and happier than we found it,—motives eminently such as are called social,—come in as part of the grounds of culture, and the main and pre-eminent part. Culture is then properly described not as having its origin in curiosity, but as having its origin in the love of

---

[1] *Quarterly Review,* January 1866.
[2] Charles de Secondat, Baron de Montesquieu (1689–1755), author of *De l'esprit des lois* (1748).

perfection; it is *a study of perfection*. It moves by the force, not merely or primarily of the scientific passion for pure knowledge, but also of the moral and social passion for doing good. As, in the first view of it, we took for its worthy motto Montesquieu's words: "To render an intelligent being yet more intelligent!" so, in the second view of it, there is no better motto which it can have than these words of Bishop Wilson:[3] "To make reason and the will of God prevail!"

Only, whereas the passion for doing good is apt to be overhasty in determining what reason and the will of God say, because its turn is for acting rather than thinking, and it wants to be beginning to act; and whereas it is apt to take its own conceptions, which proceed from its own state of development and share in all the imperfections and immaturities of this, for a basis of action; what distinguishes culture is, that it is possessed by the scientific passion as well as by the passion of doing good; that it demands worthy notions of reason and the will of God, and does not readily suffer its own crude conceptions to substitute themselves for them. And knowing that no action or institution can be salutary and stable which is not based on reason and the will of God, it is not so bent on acting and instituting, even with the great aim of diminishing human error and misery ever before its thoughts, but that it can remember that acting and instituting are of little use, unless we know how and what we ought to act and to institute.

This culture is more interesting and more far-reaching than that other, which is founded solely on the scientific passion for knowing. But it needs times of faith and ardour, times when the intellectual horizon is opening and widening all round us, to flourish in. And is not the close and bounded intellectual horizon within which we have long lived and moved now lifting up, and are not new lights finding free passage to shine in upon us? For a long time there was no passage for them to make their way in upon us, and then it was of no use to think of adapting the world's action to them. Where was the hope of making reason and the will of God prevail among people who had a routine which they had christened reason and the will of God, in which they were inextricably bound, and beyond which they had no power of looking? But now the iron force of adhesion to the old routine,—social, political, religious,—has wonderfully yielded; the iron force of exclusion of all which is new has wonder-

fully yielded. The danger now is, not that people should obstinately refuse to allow anything but their old routine to pass for reason and the will of God, but either that they should allow some novelty or other to pass for these too easily, or else that they should underrate the importance of them altogether, and think it enough to follow action for its own sake, without troubling themselves to make reason and the will of God prevail therein. Now, then, is the moment for culture to be of service, culture which believes in making reason and the will of God prevail, believes in perfection, is the study and pursuit of perfection, and is no longer debarred, by a rigid invincible exclusion of whatever is new, from getting acceptance for its ideas, simply because they are new.

The moment this view of culture is seized, the moment it is regarded not solely as the endeavour to see things as they are, to draw towards a knowledge of the universal order which seems to be intended and aimed at in the world, and which it is a man's happiness to go along with or his misery to go counter to,—to learn, in short, the will of God,—the moment, I say, culture is considered not merely as the endeavour to *see* and *learn* this, but as the endeavour, also, to make it *prevail*, the moral, social, and beneficent character of culture becomes manifest. The mere endeavour to see and learn the truth for our own personal satisfaction is indeed a commencement for making it prevail, a preparing the way for this, which always serves this, and is wrongly, therefore, stamped with blame absolutely in itself and not only in its caricature and degeneration. But perhaps it has got stamped with blame, and disparaged with the dubious title of curiosity, because in comparison with this wider endeavour of such great and plain utility it looks selfish, petty, and unprofitable.

And religion, the greatest and most important of the efforts by which the human race has manifested its impulse to perfect itself,—religion, that voice of the deepest human experience,—does not only enjoin and sanction the aim which is the great aim of culture, the aim of setting ourselves to ascertain what perfection is and to make it prevail; but also, in determining generally in what human perfection consists, religion comes to a conclusion identical with that which culture,—culture seeking the determination of this question through *all* the voices of human experience which have been heard upon it, of

---

[3] Thomas Wilson (1663–1755), Bishop of Sodor and Man; from his *Sacra Privata*.

art, science, poetry, philosophy, history, as well as of religion, in order to give a greater fulness and certainty to its solution, —likewise reaches. Religion says: *The kingdom of God is within you,*[4] and culture, in like manner, places human perfection in an *internal* condition, in the growth and predominance of our humanity proper, as distinguished from our animality. It places it in the ever-increasing efficacy and in the general harmonious expansion of those gifts of thought and feeling which make the peculiar dignity, wealth, and happiness of human nature. As I have said on a former occasion: "It is in making endless additions to itself, in the endless expansion of its powers, in endless growth in wisdom and beauty, that the spirit of the human race finds its ideal. To reach this ideal, culture is an indispensable aid, and that is the true value of culture."[5] Not a having and a resting, but a growing and a becoming, is the character of perfection as culture conceives it; and here, too, it coincides with religion.

And because men are all members of one great whole, and the sympathy which is in human nature will not allow one member to be indifferent to the rest or to have a perfect welfare independent of the rest, the expansion of our humanity, to suit the idea of perfection which culture forms, must be a *general* expansion. Perfection, as culture conceives it, is not possible while the individual remains isolated. The individual is required, under pain of being stunted and enfeebled in his own development if he disobeys, to carry others along with him in his march towards perfection, to be continually doing all he can to enlarge and increase the volume of the human stream sweeping thitherward. And here, once more, culture lays on us the same obligation as religion, which says, as Bishop Wilson has admirably put it, that "to promote the kingdom of God is to increase and hasten one's own happiness."

But, finally, perfection,—as culture, from a thorough disinterested study of human nature and human experience learns to conceive it,—is a harmonious expansion of *all* the powers which make the beauty and worth of human nature, and is not consistent with the over-development of any one power at the expense of the rest. Here culture goes beyond religion, as religion is generally conceived by us.

If culture, then, is a study of perfection, and of harmonious perfection, general perfection, and

perfection which consists in becoming something rather than in having something, in an inward condition of the mind and spirit, not in an outward set of circumstances,—it is clear that culture, instead of being the frivolous and useless thing which Mr. Bright, and Mr. Frederic Harrison, and many other Liberals are apt to call it, has a very important function to fulfil for mankind. And this function is particularly important in our modern world, of which the whole civilisation is, to a much greater degree than the civilisation of Greece and Rome, mechanical and external, and tends constantly to become more so. But above all in our own country has culture a weighty part to perform, because here that mechanical character, which civilisation tends to take everywhere, is shown in the most eminent degree. Indeed nearly all the characters of perfection, as culture teaches us to fix them, meet in this country with some powerful tendency which thwarts them and sets them at defiance. The idea of perfection as an *inward* condition of the mind and spirit is at variance with the mechanical and material civilisation in esteem with us, and nowhere, as I have said, so much in esteem as with us. The idea of perfection as a *general* expansion of the human family is at variance with our strong individualism, our hatred of all limits to the unrestrained swing of the individual's personality, our maxim of "every man for himself." Above all the idea of perfection as a *harmonious* expansion of human nature is at variance with our want of flexibility, with our inaptitude for seeing more than one side of a thing, with our intense energetic absorption in the particular pursuit we happen to be following. So culture has a rough task to achieve in this country. Its preachers have, and are likely long to have, a hard time of it, and they will much oftener be regarded, for a great while to come, as elegant or spurious Jeremiahs, than as friends and benefactors. That, however, will not prevent their doing in the end good service if they persevere. And meanwhile, the mode of action they have to pursue, and the sort of habits they must fight against, ought to be made quite clear for every one to see who may be willing to look at the matter attentively and dispassionately.

Faith in machinery is, I said, our besetting danger; often in machinery most absurdly disproportioned to the end which this machinery, if it is to do any good at all, is to serve; but always in machinery, as if it had a value in and

---

[4] Luke 17:21.   [5] See Arnold's *A French Eton*.

for itself. What is freedom but machinery? what is population but machinery? what is coal but machinery? what are railroads but machinery? what is wealth but machinery? what are, even, religious organisations but machinery? Now almost every voice in England is accustomed to speak of these things as if they were precious ends in themselves, and therefore had some of the characters of perfection indisputably joined to them. I have before now noticed Mr. Roebuck's[6] stock argument for proving the greatness and happiness of England as she is, and for quite stopping the mouths of all gainsayers. Mr. Roebuck is never weary of reiterating this argument of his, so I do not know why I should be weary of noticing it. "May not every man in England say what he likes?"—Mr. Roebuck perpetually asks; and that, he thinks, is quite sufficient, and when every man may say what he likes, our aspirations ought to be satisfied. But the aspirations of culture, which is the study of perfection, are not satisfied, unless what men say, when they may say what they like, is worth saying,—has good in it, and more good than bad. In the same way the *Times*, replying to some foreign strictures on the dress, looks, and behaviour of the English abroad, urges that the English ideal is that every one should be free to do and to look just as he likes. But culture indefatigably tries, not to make what each raw person may like, the rule by which he fashions himself; but to draw ever nearer to a sense of what is indeed beautiful, graceful, and becoming, and to get the raw person to like that.

And in the same way with respect to railroads and coal. Every one must have observed the strange language current during the late discussions as to the possible failure of our supplies of coal. Our coal, thousands of people were saying, is the real basis of our national greatness; if our coal runs short, there is an end of the greatness of England. But what *is* greatness?—culture makes us ask. Greatness is a spiritual condition worthy to excite love, interest, and admiration; and the outward proof of possessing greatness is that we excite love, interest, and admiration. If England were swallowed up by the sea to-morrow, which of the two, a hundred years hence, would most excite the love, interest, and admiration of mankind,—would most, therefore, show the evidences of having possessed greatness,—the England of the last twenty years, or the England of Elizabeth, of a time of splendid spiritual effort, but when our coal, and our industrial operations depending on coal, were very little developed? Well, then, what an unsound habit of mind it must be which makes us talk of things like coal or iron as constituting the greatness of England, and how salutary a friend is culture, bent on seeing things as they are, and thus dissipating delusions of this kind and fixing standards of perfection that are real!

Wealth, again, that end to which our prodigious works for material advantage are directed,—the commonest of commonplaces tells us how men are always apt to regard wealth as a precious end in itself; and certainly they have never been so apt thus to regard it as they are in England at the present time. Never did people believe anything more firmly, than nine Englishmen out of ten at the present day believe that our greatness and welfare are proved by our being so very rich. Now, the use of culture is that it helps us, by means of its spiritual standard of perfection, to regard wealth as but machinery, and not only to say as a matter of words that we regard wealth as but machinery, but really to perceive and feel that it is so. If it were not for this purging effect wrought upon our minds by culture, the whole world, the future as well as the present, would inevitably belong to the Philistines. The people who believe most that our greatness and welfare are proved by our being very rich, and who most give their lives and thoughts to becoming rich, are just the very people whom we call Philistines. Culture says: "Consider these people, then, their way of life, their habits, their manners, the very tones of their voice; look at them attentively; observe the literature they read, the things which give them pleasure, the words which come forth out of their mouths, the thoughts which make the furniture of their minds; would any amount of wealth be worth having with the condition that one was to become just like these people by having it?" And thus culture begets a dissatisfaction which is of the highest possible value in stemming the common tide of men's thoughts in a wealthy and industrial community, and which saves the future, as one may hope, from being vulgarised, even if it cannot save the present.

Population, again, and bodily health and vigour, are things which are nowhere treated in such an unintelligent, misleading, exaggerated way as in England. Both are really machinery;

---

[6] John Arthur Roebuck (1801–79), radical reformer; see "The Function of Criticism at the Present Time" in this volume.

yet how many people all around us do we see rest in them and fail to look beyond them! Why, one has heard people, fresh from reading certain articles of the *Times* on the Registrar-General's returns of marriages and births in this country, who would talk of our large English families in quite a solemn strain, as if they had something in itself beautiful, elevating, and meritorious in them; as if the British Philistine would have only to present himself before the Great Judge with his twelve children, in order to be received among the sheep as a matter of right!

But bodily health and vigour, it may be said, are not to be classed with wealth and population as mere machinery; they have a more real and essential value. True; but only as they are more intimately connected with a perfect spiritual condition than wealth or population are. The moment we disjoin them from the idea of a perfect spiritual condition, and pursue them, as we do pursue them, for their own sake and as ends in themselves, our worship of them becomes as mere worship of machinery, as our worship of wealth or population, and as unintelligent and vulgarising a worship as that is. Every one with anything like an adequate idea of human perfection has distinctly marked this subordination to higher and spiritual ends of the cultivation of bodily vigour and activity. "Bodily exercise profiteth little; but godliness is profitable unto all things,"[7] says the author of the Epistle to Timothy. And the utilitarian Franklin says just as explicitly:—"Eat and drink such an exact quantity as suits the constitution of thy body, *in reference to the services of the mind*."[8] But the point of view of culture, keeping the mark of human perfection simply and broadly in view, and not assigning to this perfection, as religion or utilitarianism assign to it, a special and limited character,—this point of view, I say, of culture is best given by these words of Epictetus:[9]—"It is a sign of ἀφυΐα," says he,—that is, of a nature not finely tempered,—"to give yourselves up to things which relate to the body; to make, for instance, a great fuss about exercise, a great fuss about eating, a great fuss about drinking, a great fuss about walking, a great fuss about riding. All these things ought to be done merely by the way: the formation of the spirit and character must be our real concern." This is admirable; and, indeed, the Greek word εὐφυΐα, a finely tempered nature, gives exactly the notion of perfection as

culture brings us to conceive it: a harmonious perfection, a perfection in which the characters of beauty and intelligence are both present, which unites "the two noblest of things,"—as Swift, who of one of the two, at any rate, had himself all too little, most happily calls them in his *Battle of the Books*,—"the two noblest of things, *sweetness and light*." The εὐφυής is the man who tends towards sweetness and light; the ἀφυής, on the other hand, is our Philistine. The immense spiritual significance of the Greeks is due to their having been inspired with this central and happy idea of the essential character of human perfection; and Mr. Bright's misconception of culture, as a smattering of Greek and Latin, comes itself, after all, from this wonderful significance of the Greeks having affected the very machinery of our education, and is in itself a kind of homage to it.

In thus making sweetness and light to be characters of perfection, culture is of like spirit with poetry, follows one law with poetry. Far more than on our freedom, our population, and our industrialism, many amongst us rely upon our religious organisations to save us. I have called religion a yet more important manifestation of human nature than poetry, because it has worked on a broader scale for perfection, and with greater masses of men. But the idea of beauty and of a human nature perfect on all its sides, which is the dominant idea of poetry, is a true and invaluable idea, though it has not yet had the success that the idea of conquering the obvious faults of our animality, and of a human nature perfect on the moral side,—which is the dominant idea of religion,—has been enabled to have; and it is destined, adding to itself the religious idea of a devout energy, to transform and govern the other.

The best art and poetry of the Greeks, in which religion and poetry are one, in which the idea of beauty and of a human nature perfect on all sides adds to itself a religious and devout energy, and works in the strength of that, is on this account of such surpassing interest and instructiveness for us, though it was,—as, having regard to the human race in general, and, indeed, having regard to the Greeks themselves, we must own,—a premature attempt, an attempt which for success needed the moral and religious fibre in humanity to be more braced and developed than it had yet been. But Greece did not err in having the idea of beauty, harmony, and

---

[7] I Timothy 4:8.   [8] From *Poor Richard's Almanack* for December 1742.
[9] Epictetus (60?–120?), Roman philosopher.

complete human perfection, so present and paramount. It is impossible to have this idea too present and paramount; only, the moral fibre must be braced too. And we, because we have braced the moral fibre, are not on that account in the right way, if at the same time the idea of beauty, harmony, and complete human perfection, is wanting or misapprehended amongst us; and evidently it *is* wanting or misapprehended at present. And when we rely as we do on our religious organisations, which in themselves do not and cannot give us this idea, and think we have done enough if we make them spread and prevail, then, I say, we fall into our common fault of over-valuing machinery.

Nothing is more common than for people to confound the inward peace and satisfaction which follows the subduing of the obvious faults of our animality with what I may call absolute inward peace and satisfaction,—the peace and satisfaction which are reached as we draw near to complete spiritual perfection, and not merely to moral perfection, or rather to relative moral perfection. No people in the world have done more and struggled more to attain this relative moral perfection than our English race has. For no people in the world has the command to *resist the devil,* to *overcome the wicked one,*[10] in the nearest and most obvious sense of those words, had such a pressing force and reality. And we have had our reward, not only in the great worldly prosperity which our obedience to this command has brought us, but also, and far more, in great inward peace and satisfaction. But to me few things are more pathetic than to see people, on the strength of the inward peace and satisfaction which their rudimentary efforts towards perfection have brought them, employ, concerning their incomplete perfection and the religious organisations within which they have found it, language which properly applies only to complete perfection, and is a far-off echo of the human soul's prophecy of it. Religion itself, I need hardly say, supplies them in abundance with this grand language. And very freely do they use it; yet it is really the severest criticism of such an incomplete perfection as alone we have yet reached through our religious organisations.

The impulse of the English race towards moral development and self-conquest has nowhere so powerfully manifested itself as in Puritanism. Nowhere has Puritanism found so adequate an expression as in the religious organisation of the Independents. The modern Independents have a newspaper, the *Nonconformist,*[11] written with great sincerity and ability. The motto, the standard, the profession of faith which this organ of theirs carries aloft, is: "The Dissidence of Dissent and the Protestantism of the Protestant religion." There is sweetness and light, and an ideal of complete harmonious human perfection! One need not go to culture and poetry to find language to judge it. Religion, with its instinct for perfection, supplies language to judge it, language too which is in our mouths every day. "Finally, be of one mind, united in feeling," says St. Peter. There is an ideal which judges the Puritan ideal: "The Dissidence of Dissent and the Protestantism of the Protestant religion!" And religious organisations like this are what people believe in, rest in, would give their lives for! Such, I say, is the wonderful virtue of even the beginnings of perfection, of having conquered even the plain faults of our animality, that the religious organisation which has helped us to do it can seem to us something precious, salutary, and to be propagated, even when it wears such a brand of imperfection on its forehead as this. And men have got such a habit of giving to the language of religion a special application, of making it a mere jargon, that for the condemnation which religion itself passes on the shortcomings of their religious organisations they have no ear; they are sure to cheat themselves and to explain this condemnation away. They can only be reached by the criticism which culture, like poetry, speaking a language not to be sophisticated, and resolutely testing these organisations by the ideal of a human perfection complete on all sides, applies to them.

But men of culture and poetry, it will be said, are again and again failing, and failing conspicuously, in the necessary first stage to a harmonious perfection, in the subduing of the great obvious faults of our animality, which it is the glory of these religious organisations to have helped us to subdue. True, they do often so fail. They have often been without the virtues as well as the faults of the Puritan; it has been one of their dangers that they so felt the Puritan's faults that they too much neglected the practice of his virtues. I will not, however, exculpate them at the Puritan's expense. They have often failed in morality, and morality is indispensable. And

---

[10] James 4:7; Romans 12:21; Revelation 12:11.
[11] The *Nonconformist* was a Congregational weekly founded in 1841.

they have been punished for their failure, as the Puritan has been rewarded for his performance. They have been punished wherein they erred; but their ideal of beauty, of sweetness and light, and a human nature complete on all its sides, remains the true ideal of perfection still; just as the Puritan's ideal of perfection remains narrow and inadequate, although for what he did well he has been richly rewarded. Notwithstanding the mighty results of the Pilgrim Fathers' voyage, they and their standard of perfection are rightly judged when we figure to ourselves Shakespeare or Virgil,—souls in whom sweetness and light, and all that in human nature is most humane, were eminent,—accompanying them on their voyage, and think what intolerable company Shakespeare and Virgil would have found them! In the same way let us judge the religious organisations which we see all around us. Do not let us deny the good and the happiness which they have accomplished; but do not let us fail to see clearly that their idea of human perfection is narrow and inadequate, and that the Dissidence of Dissent and the Protestantism of the Protestant religion will never bring humanity to its true goal. As I said with regard to wealth: Let us look at the life of those who live in and for it,—so I say with regard to the religious organisations. Look at the life imaged in such a newspaper as the *Nonconformist*,—a life of jealousy of the Establishment,[12] disputes, tea-meetings, openings of chapels, sermons; and then think of it as an ideal of a human life completing itself on all sides, and aspiring with all its organs after sweetness, light, and perfection!

Another newspaper, representing, like the *Nonconformist*, one of the religious organisations of this country, was a short time ago giving an account of the crowd at Epsom on the Derby day, and of all the vice and hideousness which was to be seen in that crowd; and then the writer turned suddenly round upon Professor Huxley,[13] and asked him how he proposed to cure all this vice and hideousness without religion. I confess I felt disposed to ask the asker this question: and how do you propose to cure it with such a religion as yours? How is the ideal of a life so unlovely, so unattractive, so incomplete, so narrow, so far removed from a true and satisfying ideal of human perfection, as is the life of your religious organisation as you yourself

reflect it, to conquer and transform all this vice and hideousness? Indeed, the strongest plea for the study of perfection as pursued by culture, the clearest proof of the actual inadequacy of the idea of perfection held by the religious organisations,—expressing, as I have said, the most wide-spread effort which the human race has yet made after perfection,—is to be found in the state of our life and society with these in possession of it, and having been in possession of it I know not how many hundred years. We are all of us included in some religious organisation or other; we all call ourselves, in the sublime and aspiring language of religion which I have before noticed, *children of God*. Children of God;—it is an immense pretension!—and how are we to justify it? By the works which we do, and the words which we speak. And the work which we collective children of God do, our grand centre of life, our *city* which we have builded for us to dwell in, is London! London, with its unutterable external hideousness, and with its internal canker of *publicè egestas, privatim opulentia*,[14]—to use the words which Sallust puts into Cato's mouth about Rome,—unequalled in the world! The word, again, which we children of God speak, the voice which most hits our collective thought, the newspaper with the largest circulation in England, nay, with the largest circulation in the whole world, is the *Daily Telegraph*! I say that when our religious organisations,—which I admit to express the most considerable effort after perfection that our race has yet made,—land us in no better result than this, it is high time to examine carefully their idea of perfection, to see whether it does not leave out of account sides and forces of human nature which we might turn to great use; whether it would not be more operative if it were more complete. And I say that the English reliance on our religious organisations and on their ideas of human perfection just as they stand, is like our reliance on freedom, on muscular Christianity, on population, on coal, on wealth,—mere belief in machinery, and unfruitful; and that it is wholesomely counteracted by culture, bent on seeing things as they are, and on drawing the human race onwards to a more complete, a harmonious perfection.

Culture, however, shows its single-minded love of perfection, its desire simply to make reason and the will of God prevail, its freedom from

---

[12] I.e., the Church of England, "as by law established."
[13] T. H. Huxley; see selections by Huxley in this volume.
[14] "Publicly great want, privately great wealth."

fanaticism, by its attitude towards all this machinery, even while it insists that it *is* machinery. Fanatics, seeing the mischief men do themselves by their blind belief in some machinery or other,—whether it is wealth and industrialism, or whether it is the cultivation of bodily strength and activity, or whether it is a political organisation,—or whether it is a religious organisation,— oppose with might and main the tendency to this or that political and religious organisation, or to games and athletic exercises, or to wealth and industrialism, and try violently to stop it. But the flexibility which sweetness and light give, and which is one of the rewards of culture pursued in good faith, enables a man to see that a tendency may be necessary, and even, as a preparation for something in the future, salutary, and yet that the generations or individuals who obey this tendency are sacrificed to it, that they fall short of the hope of perfection by following it; and that its mischiefs are to be criticised, lest it should take too firm a hold and last after it has served its purpose.

Mr. Gladstone well pointed out, in a speech at Paris,[15]—and others have pointed out the same thing,—how necessary is the present great movement towards wealth and industrialism, in order to lay broad foundations of material well-being for the society of the future. The worst of these justifications is, that they are generally addressed to the very people engaged, body and soul, in the movement in question; at all events, that they are always seized with the greatest avidity by these people, and taken by them as quite justifying their life; and that thus they tend to harden them in their sins. Now, culture admits the necessity of the movement towards fortune-making and exaggerated industrialism, readily allows that the future may derive benefit from it; but insists, at the same time, that the passing generations of industrialists,—forming, for the most part, the stout main body of Philistinism,— are sacrificed to it. In the same way, the result of all the games and sports which occupy the passing generation of boys and young men may be the establishment of a better and sounder physical type for the future to work with. Culture does not set itself against the games and sports; it congratulates the future, and hopes it will make a good use of its improved physical basis; but it points out that our passing generation of boys and young men is, meantime, sacrificed. Puritanism

was perhaps necessary to develop the moral fibre of the English race, Nonconformity to break the yoke of ecclesiastical domination over men's minds and to prepare the way for freedom of thought in the distant future; still, culture points out that the harmonious perfection of generations of Puritans and Nonconformists has been, in consequence, sacrificed. Freedom of speech may be necessary for the society of the future, but the young lions of the *Daily Telegraph* in the meanwhile are sacrificed. A voice for every man in his country's government may be necessary for the society of the future, but meanwhile Mr. Beales and Mr. Bradlaugh are sacrificed.[16]

Oxford, the Oxford of the past, has many faults; and she has heavily paid for them in defeat, in isolation, in want of hold upon the modern world. Yet we in Oxford, brought up amidst the beauty and sweetness of that beautiful place, have not failed to seize one truth:—the truth that beauty and sweetness are essential characters of a complete human perfection. When I insist on this, I am all in the faith and tradition of Oxford. I say boldly that this our sentiment for beauty and sweetness, our sentiment against hideousness and rawness, has been at the bottom of our attachment to so many beaten causes, of our opposition to so many triumphant movements. And the sentiment is true, and has never been wholly defeated, and has shown its power even in its defeat. We have not won our political battles, we have not carried our main points, we have not stopped our adversaries' advance, we have not marched victoriously with the modern world; but we have told silently upon the mind of the country, we have prepared currents of feeling which sap our adversaries' position when it seems gained, we have kept up our own communications with the future. Look at the course of the great movement which shook Oxford to its centre some thirty years ago! It was directed, as any one who reads Dr. Newman's *Apology* may see, against what in one word may be called "Liberalism." Liberalism prevailed; it was the appointed force to do the work of the hour; it was necessary, it was inevitable that it should prevail. The Oxford movement was broken, it failed; our wrecks are scattered on every shore:—

Quæ regio in terris nostri non plena laboris?[17]

---

[15] At a speech on 31 January 1867 in connection with the Industrial Exhibition.
[16] Edmond Beales (1803–81), political reformer; Charles Bradlaugh (1833–91), reformer; see selection by Bradlaugh in this volume.
[17] "What part of the world is not full of the story of our labours and woes?" (*Aeneid*).

But what was it, this Liberalism, as Dr. Newman saw it, and as it really broke the Oxford movement? It was the great middle-class Liberalism, which had for the cardinal points of its belief the Reform Bill of 1832, and local self-government, in politics; in the social sphere, free-trade, unrestricted competition, and the making of large industrial fortunes; in the religious sphere, the Dissidence of Dissent and the Protestantism of the Protestant religion. I do not say that other and more intelligent forces than this were not opposed to the Oxford movement: but this was the force which really beat it; this was the force which Dr. Newman felt himself fighting with; this was the force which till only the other day seemed to be the paramount force in this country, and to be in possession of the future; this was the force whose achievements fill Mr. Lowe[18] with such inexpressible admiration, and whose rule he was so horror-struck to see threatened. And where is this great force of Philistinism now? It is thrust into the second rank, it is become a power of yesterday, it has lost the future. A new power has suddenly appeared, a power which it is impossible yet to judge fully, but which is certainly a wholly different force from middle-class Liberalism; different in its cardinal points of belief, different in its tendencies in every sphere. It loves and admires neither the legislation of middle-class Parliaments, nor the local self-government of middle-class vestries, nor the unrestricted competition of middle-class industrialists, nor the dissidence of middle-class Dissent and the Protestantism of middle-class Protestant religion. I am not now praising this new force, or saying that its own ideals are better; all I say is, that they are wholly different. And who will estimate how much the currents of feeling created by Dr. Newman's movement, the keen desire for beauty and sweetness which it nourished, the deep aversion it manifested to the hardness and vulgarity of middle-class Liberalism, the strong light it turned on the hideous and grotesque illusions of middle-class Protestantism, —who will estimate how much all these contributed to swell the tide of secret dissatisfaction which has mined the ground under the self-confident Liberalism of the last thirty years, and has prepared the way for its sudden collapse and supersession? It is in this manner that the sentiment of Oxford for beauty and sweetness conquers, and in this manner long may it continue to conquer!

In this manner it works to the same end as culture, and there is plenty of work for it yet to do. I have said that the new and more democratic force which is now superseding our old middle-class Liberalism cannot yet be rightly judged. It has its main tendencies still to form. We hear promises of its giving us administrative reform, law reform, reform of education, and I know not what; but those promises come rather from its advocates, wishing to make a good plea for it and to justify it for superseding middle-class Liberalism, than from clear tendencies which it has itself yet developed. But meanwhile it has plenty of well-intentioned friends against whom culture may with advantage continue to uphold steadily its ideal of human perfection; that this is *an inward spiritual activity, having for its characters increased sweetness, increased light, increased life, increased sympathy.* Mr. Bright, who has a foot in both worlds, the world of middle-class Liberalism and the world of democracy, but who brings most of his ideas from the world of middle-class Liberalism in which he was bred, always inclines to inculcate that faith in machinery to which, as we have seen, Englishmen are so prone, and which has been the bane of middle-class Liberalism. He complains with a sorrowful indignation of people who "appear to have no proper estimate of the value of the franchise;" he leads his disciples to believe,—what the Englishman is always too ready to believe,—that the having a vote, like the having a large family, or a large business, or large muscles, has in itself some edifying and perfecting effect upon human nature. Or else he cries out to the democracy,— "the men," as he calls them, "upon whose shoulders the greatness of England rests,"—he cries out to them: "See what you have done! I look over this country and see the cities you have built, the railroads you have made, the manufactures you have produced, the cargoes which freight the ships of the greatest mercantile navy the world has ever seen! I see that you have converted by your labours what was once a wilderness, these islands, into a fruitful garden; I know that you have created this wealth, and are a nation whose name is a word of power throughout all the world." Why, this is just the very style of laudation with which Mr. Roebuck or Mr. Lowe debauch the minds of the middle classes, and make such Philistines of them. It is the same fashion of teaching a man to value himself not on what he *is,* not on his progress in

---

[18] Robert Lowe (1811–92), Viscount Sherbrooke, opponent of the Reform Bill of 1867.

sweetness and light, but on the number of the railroads he has constructed, or the bigness of the tabernacle he has built. Only the middle classes are told they have done it all with their energy, self-reliance, and capital, and the democracy are told they have done it all with their hands and sinews. But teaching the democracy to put its trust in achievements of this kind is merely training them to be Philistines to take the place of the Philistines whom they are superseding; and they too, like the middle class, will be encouraged to sit down at the banquet of the future without having on a wedding garment, and nothing excellent can then come from them. Those who know their besetting faults, those who have watched them and listened to them, or those who will read the instructive account recently given of them by one of themselves, the *Journeyman Engineer*,[19] will agree that the idea which culture sets before us of perfection,—an increased spiritual activity, having for its characters increased sweetness, increased light, increased life, increased sympathy,—is an idea which the new democracy needs far more than the idea of the blessedness of the franchise, or the wonderfulness of its own industrial performances.

Other well-meaning friends of this new power are for leading it, not in the old ruts of middle-class Philistinism, but in ways which are naturally alluring to the feet of democracy, though in this country they are novel and untried ways. I may call them the ways of Jacobinism. Violent indignation with the past, abstract systems of renovation applied wholesale, a new doctrine drawn up in black and white for elaborating down to the very smallest details a rational society for the future,—these are the ways of Jacobinism. Mr. Frederic Harrison and other disciples of Comte,[20]—one of them, Mr. Congreve,[21] is an old friend of mine, and I am glad to have an opportunity of publicly expressing my respect for his talents and character,—are among the friends of democracy who are for leading it in paths of this kind. Mr. Frederic Harrison is very hostile to culture, and from a natural enough motive; for culture is the eternal opponent of the two things which are the signal marks of Jacobinism,—its fierceness, and its addiction to an abstract system. Culture is always assigning to system-makers and systems a smaller share in the bent of human destiny than their friends like. A current

in people's minds sets towards new ideas; people are dissatisfied with their old narrow stock of Philistine ideas, Anglo-Saxon ideas, or any other; and some man, some Bentham or Comte, who has the real merit of having early and strongly felt and helped the new current, but who brings plenty of narrowness and mistakes of his own into his feeling and help of it, is credited with being the author of the whole current, the fit person to be entrusted with its regulation and to guide the human race.

The excellent German historian of the mythology of Rome, Preller,[22] relating the introduction at Rome under the Tarquins of the worship of Apollo, the god of light, healing, and reconciliation, will have us observe that it was not so much the Tarquins who brought to Rome the new worship of Apollo, as a current in the mind of the Roman people which set powerfully at that time towards a new worship of this kind, and away from the old run of Latin and Sabine religious ideas. In a similar way, culture directs our attention to the natural current there is in human affairs, and to its continual working, and will not let us rivet our faith upon any one man and his doings. It makes us see, not only his good side, but also how much in him was of necessity limited and transient; nay, it even feels a pleasure, a sense of an increased freedom and of an ampler future, in so doing.

I remember, when I was under the influence of a mind to which I feel the greatest obligations, the mind of a man who was the very incarnation of sanity and clear sense, a man the most considerable, it seems to me, whom America has yet produced,—Benjamin Franklin,—I remember the relief with which, after long feeling the sway of Franklin's imperturbable common-sense, I came upon a project of his for a new version of the Book of Job, to replace the old version, the style of which, says Franklin, has become obsolete, and thence less agreeable. "I give," he continues, "a few verses, which may serve as a sample of the kind of version I would recommend." We all recollect the famous verse in our translation: "Then Satan answered the Lord and said: 'Doth Job fear God for nought?'" Franklin makes this: "Does Your Majesty imagine that Job's good conduct is the effect of mere personal attachment and affection?" I well remember how when first I read that, I drew a deep breath of

---

[19] The pseudonym of Thomas Wright, author of *Some Habits and Customs of the Working Classes* (1867).
[20] Auguste Comte (1798–1857), French positivist.
[21] Richard Congreve (1819–99), English positivist, translator of Comte.
[22] Ludwig Preller (1809–61), German author of *Roman Mythology* (1858).

relief, and said to myself: "After all, there is a stretch of humanity beyond Franklin's victorious good sense!" So, after hearing Bentham cried loudly up as the renovator of modern society, and Bentham's mind and ideas proposed as the rulers of our future, I open the *Deontology*.[23] There I read: "While Xenophon was writing his history and Euclid teaching geometry, Socrates and Plato were talking nonsense under pretence of talking wisdom and morality. This morality of theirs consisted in words; this wisdom of theirs was the denial of matters known to every man's experience." From the moment of reading that, I am delivered from the bondage of Bentham! the fanaticism of his adherents can touch me no longer; I feel the inadequacy of his mind and ideas for supplying the rule of human society, for perfection.

Culture tends always thus to deal with the men of a system, of disciples, of a school; with men like Comte or, the late Mr. Buckle, or Mr. Mill.[24] However much it may find to admire in these personages, or in some of them, it nevertheless remembers the text: "Be not ye called Rabbi!"[25] and it soon passes on from any Rabbi. But Jacobinism loves a Rabbi; it does not want to pass on from its Rabbi in pursuit of a future and still unreached perfection; it wants its Rabbi and his ideas to stand for perfection, that they may with the more authority recast the world; and for Jacobinism, therefore, culture,—eternally passing onwards and seeking,—is an impertinence and an offence. But culture, just because it resists this tendency of Jacobinism to impose on us a man with limitations and errors of his own along with the true ideas of which he is the organ, really does the world and Jacobinism itself a service.

So, too, Jacobinism, in its fierce hatred of the past and of those whom it makes liable for the sins of the past, cannot away with the inexhaustible indulgence proper to culture, the consideration of circumstances, the severe judgment of actions joined to the merciful judgment of persons. "The man of culture is in politics," cries Mr. Frederic Harrison, "one of the poorest mortals alive!" Mr. Frederic Harrison wants to be doing business, and he complains that the man of culture stops him with a "turn for small fault-finding, love of selfish ease, and indecision

in action." Of what use is culture, he asks, except for "a critic of new books or a professor of *belles lettres?*" Why, it is of use because, in presence of the fierce exasperation which breathes, or rather, I may say, hisses, through the whole production in which Mr. Frederic Harrison asks that question, it reminds us that the perfection of human nature is sweetness and light. It is of use because, like religion,—that other effort after perfection,—it testifies that, where bitter envying and strife are, there is confusion and every evil work.

The pursuit of perfection, then, is the pursuit of sweetness and light. He who works for sweetness works in the end for light also; he who works for light works in the end for sweetness also. But he who works for sweetness and light united, works to make reason and the will of God prevail. He who works for machinery, he who works for hatred, works only for confusion. Culture looks beyond machinery, culture hates hatred; culture has one great passion, the passion for sweetness and light. It has one even yet greater!—the passion for making them *prevail*. It is not satisfied till we *all* come to a perfect man; it knows that the sweetness and light of the few must be imperfect until the raw and unkindled masses of humanity are touched with sweetness and light. If I have not shrunk from saying that we must work for sweetness and light, so neither have I shrunk from saying that we must have a broad basis, must have sweetness and light for as many as possible. Again and again I have insisted how those are the happy moments of humanity, how those are the marking epochs of a people's life, how those are the flowering times for literature and art and all the creative power of genius, when there is a *national* glow of life and thought, when the whole of society is in the fullest measure permeated by thought, sensible to beauty, intelligent and alive. Only it must be *real* thought and *real* beauty; *real* sweetness and *real* light. Plenty of people will try to give the masses, as they call them, an intellectual food prepared and adapted in the way they think proper for the actual condition of the masses. The ordinary popular literature is an example of this way of working on the masses. Plenty of people will try to indoctrinate the masses with the set of ideas and judgments constituting the creed of

---

[23] The collection of Bentham's notes and observations brought together after Bentham's death by John Bowring.

[24] Henry Thomas Buckle (1821–62), author of *History of Civilisation in England* (1857–61); Mill is John Stuart Mill.

[25] Matthew 23:8.

their own profession or party. Our religious and political organisations give an example of this way of working on the masses. I condemn neither way; but culture works differently. It does not try to teach down to the level of inferior classes; it does not try to win them for this or that sect of its own, with ready-made judgments and watchwords. It seeks to do away with classes; to make the best that has been thought and known in the world current everywhere; to make all men live in an atmosphere of sweetness and light, where they may use ideas, as it uses them itself, freely,—nourished and not bound by them.

This is the *social idea;* and the men of culture are the true apostles of equality. The great men of culture are those who have had a passion for diffusing, for making prevail, for carrying from one end of society to the other, the best knowledge, the best ideas of their time; who have laboured to divest knowledge of all that was harsh, uncouth, difficult, abstract, professional, exclusive; to humanise it, to make it efficient outside the clique of the cultivated and learned, yet still remaining the *best* knowledge and thought of the time, and a true source, therefore, of sweetness and light. Such a man was Abelard in the Middle Ages, in spite of all his imperfections; and thence the boundless emotion and enthusiasm which Abelard excited. Such were Lessing and Herder[26] in Germany, at the end of the last century; and their services to Germany were in this way inestimably precious. Generations will pass, and literary monuments will accumulate, and works far more perfect than the works of Lessing and Herder will be produced in Germany; and yet the names of these two men will fill a German with a reverence and enthusiasm such as the names of the most gifted masters will hardly awaken. And why? Because they *humanised* knowledge; because they broadened the basis of life and intelligence; because they worked powerfully to diffuse sweetness and light, to make reason and the will of God prevail. With Saint Augustine they said: "Let us not leave Thee alone to make in the secret of thy knowledge, as thou didst before the creation of the firmament, the division of light from darkness; let the children of thy spirit, placed in their firmament, make their light shine upon the earth, mark the division of night and day, and

announce the revolution of the times; for the old order is passed, and the new arises; the night is spent, the day is come forth; and thou shalt crown the year with thy blessing, when thou shalt send forth labourers into thy harvest sown by other hands than theirs; when thou shalt send forth new labourers to new seed-times, whereof the harvest shall be not yet."

CHAPTER II

Doing As One Likes

I HAVE been trying to show that culture is, or ought to be, the study and pursuit of perfection; and that of perfection, as pursued by culture, beauty and intelligence, or, in other words, sweetness and light, are the main characters. But hitherto I have been insisting chiefly on beauty, or sweetness, as a character of perfection. To complete rightly my design, it evidently remains to speak also of intelligence, or light, as a character of perfection.

First, however, I ought perhaps to notice that, both here and on the other side of the Atlantic, all sorts of objections are raised against the "religion of culture," as the objectors mockingly call it, which I am supposed to be promulgating. It is said to be a religion proposing parmaceti, or some scented salve or other, as a cure for human miseries; a religion breathing a spirit of cultivated inaction, making its believer refuse to lend a hand at uprooting the definite evils on all sides of us, and filling him with antipathy against the reforms and reformers which try to extirpate them. In general, it is summed up as being not practical, or,—as some critics familiarly put it,— all moonshine. That Alcibiades,[1] the editor of the *Morning Star*,[2] taunts me, as its promulgator, with living out of the world and knowing nothing of life and men. That great austere toiler, the editor of the *Daily Telegraph*, upbraids me,—but kindly, and more in sorrow than in anger,—for trifling with æsthetics and poetical

---

[26] Peter Abelard (1079–1142), French scholastic philosopher; Gotthold Ephraim Lessing (1729–81), German critic and dramatist; Johann Gottfried von Herder (1744–1803), German critic and Romantic philosopher.

[1] Alcibiades (450?–404 B.C.), pupil of Socrates, and a type of the luxurious, morally flexible person.

[2] A vulgar newspaper for noncomformists and radicals.

fancies, while he himself, in that arsenal of his in Fleet Street, is bearing the burden and heat of the day. An intelligent American newspaper, the *Nation,* says that it is very easy to sit in one's study and find fault with the course of modern society, but the thing is to propose practical improvements for it. While, finally, Mr. Frederic Harrison, in a very good-tempered and witty satire,[3] which makes me quite understand his having apparently achieved such a conquest of my young Prussian friend, Arminius, at last gets moved to an almost stern moral impatience, to behold, as he says, "Death, sin, cruelty stalk among us, filling their maws with innocence and youth," and me, in the midst of the general tribulation, handing out my pouncet-box.

It is impossible that all these remonstrances and reproofs should not affect me, and I shall try my very best, in completing my design and in speaking of light as one of the characters of perfection, and of culture as giving us light, to profit by the objections I have heard and read, and to drive at practice as much as I can, by showing the communications and passages into practical life from the doctrine which I am inculcating.

It is said that a man with my theories of sweetness and light is full of antipathy against the rougher or coarser movements going on around him, that he will not lend a hand to the humble operation of uprooting evil by their means, and that therefore the believers in action grow impatient with them. But what if rough and coarse action, ill-calculated action, action with insufficient light, is, and has for a long time been, our bane? What if our urgent want now is, not to act at any price, but rather to lay in a stock of light for our difficulties? In that case, to refuse to lend a hand to the rougher and coarser movements going on round us, to make the primary need, both for oneself and others, to consist in enlightening ourselves and qualifying ourselves to act less at random, is surely the best and in real truth the most practical line our endeavours can take. So that if I can show what my opponents call rough or coarse action, but what I would rather call random and ill-regulated action,—action with insufficient light, action pursued because we like to be doing something and doing it as we please, and do not like the trouble of thinking and the severe constraint of any kind of rule,—if I can show this to be, at the present moment, a practical mischief and

dangerous to us, then I have found a practical use for light in correcting this state of things, and have only to exemplify how, in cases which fall under everybody's observation, it may deal with it.

When I began to speak of culture, I insisted on our bondage to machinery, on our proneness to value machinery as an end in itself, without looking beyond it to the end for which alone, in truth, it is valuable. Freedom, I said, was one of those things which we thus worshipped in itself, without enough regarding the ends for which freedom is to be desired. In our common notions and talk about freedom, we eminently show our idolatry of machinery. Our prevalent notion is,—and I quoted a number of instances to prove it,—that it is a most happy and important thing for a man merely to be able to do as he likes. On what he is to do when he is thus free to do as he likes, we do not lay so much stress. Our familiar praise of the British Constitution under which we live, is that it is a system of checks,—a system which stops and paralyses any power in interfering with the free action of individuals. To this effect Mr. Bright, who loves to walk in the old ways of the Constitution, said forcibly in one of his great speeches, what many other people are every day saying less forcibly, that the central idea of English life and politics is *the assertion of personal liberty.* Evidently this is so; but evidently, also, as feudalism, which with its ideas and habits of subordination was for many centuries silently behind the British Constitution, dies out, and we are left with nothing but our system of checks, and our notion of its being the great right and happiness of an Englishman to do as far as possible what he likes, we are in danger of drifting towards anarchy. We have not the notion, so familiar on the Continent and to antiquity, of *the State*—the nation in its collective and corporate character, entrusted with stringent powers for the general advantage, and controlling individual wills in the name of an interest wider than that of individuals. We say, what is very true, that this notion is often made instrumental to tyranny; we say that a State is in reality made up of the individuals who compose it, and that every individual is the best judge of his own interests. Our leading class is an aristocracy, and no aristocracy likes the notion of a State-authority greater than itself, with a stringent administrative machinery superseding the decorative inutilities of lord-lieutenancy, deputy-

---

[3] A criticism of Arnold by Harrison in the *Fortnightly Review* for November 1867.

lieutenancy, and the *posse comitatûs*,[4] which are all in its own hands. Our middle class, the great representative of trade and Dissent, with its maxims of every man for himself in business, every man for himself in religion, dreads a powerful administration which might somehow interfere with it; and besides, it has its own decorative inutilities of vestrymanship and guardianship, which are to this class what lord-lieutenancy and the county magistracy are to the aristocratic class, and a stringent administration might either take these functions out of its hands, or prevent its exercising them in its own comfortable, independent manner, as at present.

Then as to our working class. This class, pressed constantly by the hard daily compulsion of material wants, is naturally the very centre and stronghold of our national idea, that it is man's ideal right and felicity to do as he likes. I think I have somewhere related how M. Michelet[5] said to me of the people of France, that it was "a nation of barbarians civilised by the conscription." He meant that through their military service the idea of public duty and of discipline was brought to the mind of these masses, in other respects so raw and uncultivated. Our masses are quite as raw and uncultivated as the French; and so far from their having the idea of public duty and of discipline, superior to the individual's self-will, brought to their mind by a universal obligation of military service, such as that of the conscription,—so far from their having this, the very idea of a conscription is so at variance with our English notion of the prime right and blessedness of doing as one likes, that I remember the manager of the Clay Cross works in Derby-shire told me during the Crimean war, when our want of soldiers was much felt and some people were talking of a conscription, that sooner than submit to a conscription the population of that district would flee to the mines, and lead a sort of Robin Hood life under ground.

For a long time, as I have said, the strong feudal habits of subordination and deference continued to tell upon the working class. The modern spirit has now almost entirely dissolved those habits, and the anarchical tendency of our worship of freedom in and for itself, of our superstitious faith, as I say, in machinery, is becoming very manifest. More and more, because of this our blind faith in machinery,

because of our want of light to enable us to look beyond machinery to the end for which machinery is valuable, this and that man, and this and that body of men, all over the country, are beginning to assert and put in practice an Englishman's right to do what he likes; his right to march where he likes, meet where he likes, enter where he likes, hoot as he likes, threaten as he likes, smash as he likes. All this, I say, tends to anarchy; and though a number of excellent people, and particularly my friends of the Liberal or progressive party, as they call themselves, are kind enough to reassure us by saying that these are trifles, that a few transient outbreaks of rowdyism signify nothing, that our system of liberty is one which itself cures all the evils which it works, that the educated and intelligent classes stand in overwhelming strength and majestic repose, ready, like our military force in riots, to act at a moment's notice,—yet one finds that one's Liberal friends generally say this because they have such faith in themselves and their nostrums, when they shall return, as the public welfare requires, to place and power. But this faith of theirs one cannot exactly share, when one has so long had them and their nostrums at work, and sees that they have not prevented our coming to our present embarrassed condition. And one finds, also, that the outbreaks of rowdyism tend to become less and less of trifles, to become more frequent rather than less frequent; and that meanwhile our educated and intelligent classes remain in their majestic repose, and somehow or other, whatever happens, their overwhelming strength, like our military force in riots, never does act.

How, indeed, *should* their overwhelming strength act, when the man who gives an inflammatory lecture, or breaks down the park railings, or invades a Secretary of State's office, is only following an Englishman's impulse to do as he likes; and our own conscience tells us that we ourselves have always regarded this impulse as something primary and sacred? Mr. Murphy[6] lectures at Birmingham, and showers on the Catholic population of that town "words," says the Home Secretary, Mr. Hardy, "only fit to be addressed to thieves or murderers." What then? Mr. Murphy has his own reasons of several kinds. He suspects the Roman Catholic Church of designs upon Mrs. Murphy; and he says, if

---

[4] Literally, "power of the county," a group of men called by the sheriff to help enforce the law.
[5] Jules Michelet (1798–1874), French historian.
[6] An anti-Roman Catholic agitator.

mayors and magistrates do not care for their wives and daughters, he does. But, above all, he is doing as he likes; or, in worthier language, asserting his personal liberty. "I will carry out my lectures if they walk over my body as a dead corpse; and I say to the Mayor of Birmingham that he is my servant while I am in Birmingham, and as my servant he must do his duty and protect me." Touching and beautiful words, which find a sympathetic chord in every British bosom! The moment it is plainly put before us that a man is asserting his personal liberty, we are half disarmed; because we are believers in freedom, and not in some dream of a right reason to which the assertion of our freedom is to be subordinated. Accordingly, the Secretary of State had to say that although the lecturer's language was "only fit to be addressed to thieves or murderers," yet, "I do not think he is to be deprived, I do not think that anything I have said could justify the inference that he is to be deprived, of the right of protection in a place built by him for the purpose of these lectures; because the language was not language which afforded grounds for a criminal prosecution." No, nor to be silenced by Mayor, or Home Secretary, or any administrative authority on earth, simply on their notion of what is discreet and reasonable! This is in perfect consonance with our public opinion, and with our national love for the assertion of personal liberty.

In quite another department of affairs, an experienced and distinguished Chancery Judge relates an incident which is just to the same effect as this of Mr. Murphy. A testator bequeathed 300*l.* a year, to be for ever applied as a pension to some person who had been unsuccessful in literature, and whose duty should be to support and diffuse, by his writings, the testator's own views, as enforced in the testator's publications. The views were not worth a straw and the bequest was appealed against in the Court of Chancery on the ground of its absurdity; but, being only absurd, it was upheld, and the so-called charity was established. Having, I say, at the bottom of our English hearts a very strong belief in freedom, and a very weak belief in right reason, we are soon silenced when a man pleads the prime right to do as he likes, because this is the prime right for ourselves too; and even if we attempt now and then to mumble something about reason, yet we have ourselves thought so little about this and so much about liberty, that we are in conscience forced, when our brother Philistine with whom we are meddling turns boldly round upon us and asks: *Have you any light?*—to shake our heads ruefully, and to let him go his own way after all.

There are many things to be said on behalf of this exclusive attention of ours to liberty, and of the relaxed habits of government which it has engendered. It is very easy to mistake or to exaggerate the sort of anarchy from which we are in danger through them. We are not in danger from Fenianism,[7] fierce and turbulent as it may show itself; for against this our conscience is free enough to let us act resolutely and put forth our overwhelming strength the moment there is any real need for it. In the first place, it never was any part of our creed that the great right and blessedness of an Irishman, or, indeed, of anybody on earth except an Englishman, is to do as he likes; and we can have no scruple at all about abridging, if necessary, a non-Englishman's assertion of personal liberty. The British Constitution, its checks, and its prime virtues, are for Englishmen. We may extend them to others out of love and kindness; but we find no real divine law written on our hearts constraining us so to extend them. And then the difference between an Irish Fenian and an English rough is so immense, and the case, in dealing with the Fenian, so much more clear! He is so evidently desperate and dangerous, a man of a conquered race, a Papist, with centuries of ill-usage to inflame him against us, with an alien religion established in his country by us at his expense, with no admiration of our institutions, no love of our virtues, no talents for our business, no turn for our comfort! Show him our symbolical Truss Manufactory on the finest site in Europe, and tell him that British industrialism and individualism can bring a man to that, and he remains cold! Evidently, if we deal tenderly with a sentimentalist like this, it is out of pure philanthropy.

But with the Hyde Park rioter how different! He is our own flesh and blood; he is a Protestant; he is framed by nature to do as we do, hate what we hate, love what we love; he is capable of feeling the symbolical force of the Truss Manufactory;[8] the question of questions, for him, is a wages question. That beautiful sentence Sir Daniel Gooch[9] quoted to the Swindon workmen,

---

[7] Movement for Irish independence.
[8] A factory building in Trafalgar Square for the making of Cole's trusses.
[9] Sir Daniel Gooch (1816–89), a railway magnate and inventor.

and which I treasure as Mrs. Gooch's Golden Rule, or the Divine Injunction "Be ye Perfect"[10] done into British,—the sentence Sir Daniel Gooch's mother repeated to him every morning when he was a boy going to work: *"Ever remember, my dear Dan, that you should look forward to being some day manager of that concern!"*—this fruitful maxim is perfectly fitted to shine forth in the heart of the Hyde Park rough also, and to be his guiding-star through life. He has no visionary schemes of revolution and transformation, though of course he would like his class to rule, as the aristocratic class like their class to rule, and the middle class theirs. But meanwhile our social machine is a little out of order; there are a good many people in our paradisiacal centres of industrialism and individualism taking the bread out of one another's mouths. The rough has not yet quite found his groove and settled down to his work, and so he is just asserting his personal liberty a little, going where he likes, assembling where he likes, bawling as he likes, hustling as he likes. Just as the rest of us,—as the country squires in the aristocratic class, as the political dissenters in the middle class,—he has no idea of a *State,* of the nation in its collective and corporate character controlling, as government, the free swing of this or that one of its members in the name of the higher reason of all of them, his own as well as that of others. He sees the rich, the aristocratic class, in occupation of the executive government, and so if he is stopped from making Hyde Park a bear-garden or the streets impassable, he says he is being butchered by the aristocracy.

His apparition is somewhat embarrassing, because too many cooks spoil the broth; because, while the aristocratic and middle classes have long been doing as they like with great vigour, he has been too undeveloped and submissive hitherto to join in the game; and now, when he does come, he comes in immense numbers, and is rather raw and rough. But he does not break many laws, or not many at one time; and, as our laws were made for very different circumstances from our present (but always with an eye to Englishmen doing as they like), and as the clear letter of the law must be against our Englishman who does as he likes and not only the spirit of the law and public policy, and as Government must neither have any discretionary power nor act resolutely on its own interpretation of the law if any one disputes it, it is evident our laws give our playful giant, in doing as he likes, considerable advantage. Besides, even if he can be clearly proved to commit an illegality in doing as he likes, there is always the resource of not putting the law in force, or of abolishing it. So he has his way, and if he has his way he is soon satisfied for the time. However, he falls into the habit of taking it oftener and oftener, and at last begins to create by his operations a confusion of which mischievous people can take advantage, and which at any rate, by troubling the common course of business throughout the country, tends to cause distress, and so to increase the sort of anarchy and social disintegration which had previously commenced. And thus that profound sense of settled order and security, without which a society like ours cannot live and grow at all, sometimes seems to be beginning to threaten us with taking its departure.

Now, if culture, which simply means trying to perfect oneself, and one's mind as part of oneself, brings us light, and if light shows us that there is nothing so very blessed in merely doing as one likes, that the worship of the mere freedom to do as one likes is worship of machinery, that the really blessed thing is to like what right reason ordains, and to follow her authority, then we have got a practical benefit out of culture. We have got a much wanted principle, a principle of authority, to counteract the tendency to anarchy which seems to be threatening us.

But how to organise this authority, or to what hands to entrust the wielding of it? How to get your *State,* summing up the right reason of the community, and giving effect to it, as circumstances may require, with vigour? And here I think I see my enemies waiting for me with a hungry joy in their eyes. But I shall elude them.

The *State,* the power most representing the right reason of the nation, and most worthy, therefore, of ruling,—of exercising, when circumstances require it, authority over us all,—is for Mr. Carlyle the aristocracy.[11] For Mr. Lowe, it is the middle class with its incomparable Parliament. For the Reform League, it is the working class, the class with "the brightest powers of sympathy and readiest powers of action."[12] Now, culture, with its disinterested pursuit of perfection, culture, simply trying to see things as they are, in order to seize on the best and to make it prevail, is surely well fitted

---

[10] Matthew 5:28.　　[11] Reference to Carlyle's *Shooting Niagara.*
[12] Reference to an article by Frederic Harrison in the *Fortnightly Review* for March 1867.

to help us to judge rightly, by all the aids of observing, reading, and thinking, the qualifications and titles to our confidence of these three candidates for authority, and can thus render us a practical service of no mean value.

So when Mr. Carlyle, a man of genius to whom we have all at one time or other been indebted for refreshment and stimulus, says we should give rule to the aristocracy, mainly because of its dignity and politeness, surely culture is useful in reminding us, that in our idea of perfection the characters of beauty and intelligence are both of them present, and sweetness and light, the two noblest of things, are united. Allowing, therefore, with Mr. Carlyle, the aristocratic class to possess sweetness, culture insists on the necessity of light also, and shows us that aristocracies, being by the very nature of things inaccessible to ideas, unapt to see how the world is going, must be somewhat wanting in light, and must therefore be, at a moment when light is our great requisite, inadequate to our needs. Aristocracies, those children of the established fact, are for epochs of concentration. In epochs of expansion, epochs such as that in which we now live, epochs when always the warning voice is again heard: *Now is the judgment of this world*[13]—in such epochs aristocracies with their natural clinging to the established fact, their want of sense for the flux of things, for the inevitable transitoriness of all human institutions, are bewildered and helpless. Their serenity, their high spirit, their power of haughty resistance,—the great qualities of an aristocracy, and the secret of its distinguished manners and dignity,—these very qualities, in an epoch of expansion, turn against their possessors. Again and again I have said how the refinement of an aristocracy may be precious and educative to a raw nation as a kind of shadow of true refinement; how its serenity and dignified freedom from petty cares may serve as a useful foil to set off the vulgarity and hideousness of that type of life which a hard middle class tends to establish, and to help people to see this vulgarity and hideousness in their true colours. From such an ignoble spectacle as that of poor Mrs. Lincoln,—a spectacle to vulgarise a whole nation,—aristocracies undoubtedly preserve us. But the true grace and serenity is that of which Greece and Greek art suggest the admirable ideals of perfection,—a serenity which comes from having made order among ideas and harmonised them; whereas the serenity of

aristocracies, at least the peculiar serenity of aristocracies of Teutonic origin, appears to come from their never having had any ideas to trouble them. And so, in a time of expansion like the present, a time for ideas, one gets, perhaps, in regarding an aristocracy, even more than the idea of serenity, the idea of futility and sterility.

One has often wondered whether upon the whole earth there is anything so unintelligent, so unapt to perceive how the world is really going, as an ordinary young Englishman of our upper class. Ideas he has not, and neither has he that seriousness of our middle class which is, as I have often said, the great strength of this class, and may become its salvation. Why, a man may hear a young Dives of the aristocratic class, when the whim takes him to sing the praises of wealth and material comfort, sing them with a cynicism from which the conscience of the veriest Philistine of our industrial middle class would recoil in affright. And when, with the natural sympathy of aristocracies for firm dealing with the multitude, and his uneasiness at our feeble dealing with it at home, an unvarnished young Englishman of our aristocratic class applauds the absolute rulers on the Continent, he in general manages completely to miss the grounds of reason and intelligence which alone can give any colour of justification, any possibility of existence, to those rulers, and applauds them on grounds which it would make their own hair stand on end to listen to.

And all this time we are in an epoch of expansion; and the essence of an epoch of expansion is a movement of ideas, and the one salvation of an epoch of expansion is a harmony of ideas. The very principle of the authority which we are seeking as a defence against anarchy is right reason, ideas, light. The more, therefore, an aristocracy calls to its aid its innate forces,—its impenetrability, its high spirit, its power of haughty resistance,—to deal with an epoch of expansion, the graver is the danger, the greater the certainty of explosion, the surer the aristocracy's defeat; for it is trying to do violence to nature instead of working along with it. The best powers shown by the best men of an aristocracy at such an epoch are, it will be observed, non-aristocratical powers, powers of industry, powers of intelligence; and these powers, thus exhibited, tend really not to strengthen the aristocracy, but to take their owners out of it, to expose them to the dissolving agencies of thought and change, to

---

[13] John 12:31.

make them men of the modern spirit and of the future. If, as sometimes happens, they add to their non-aristocratical qualities of labour and thought, a strong dose of aristocratical qualities also,—of pride, defiance, turn for resistance—this truly aristocratical side of them, so far from adding any strength to them, really neutralises their force and makes them impracticable and ineffective.

Knowing myself to be indeed sadly to seek, as one of my many critics says,[14] in "a philosophy with coherent, interdependent, subordinate and derivative principles," I continually have recourse to a plain man's expedient of trying to make what few simple notions I have, clearer and more intelligible to myself, by means of example and illustration. And having been brought up at Oxford in the bad old times, when we were stuffed with Greek and Aristotle, and thought nothing of preparing ourselves by the study of modern languages,—as after Mr. Lowe's great speech at Edinburgh[15] we shall do,—to fight the battle of life with the waiters in foreign hotels, my head is still full of a lumber of phrases we learnt at Oxford from Aristotle, about virtue being in a mean, and about excess and defect, and so on. Once when I had had the advantage of listening to the Reform debates in the House of Commons, having heard a number of interesting speakers, and among them Lord Elcho and Sir Thomas Bateson,[16] I remember it struck me, applying Aristotle's machinery of the mean to my ideas about our aristocracy, that Lord Elcho was exactly the perfection, or happy mean, or virtue, of aristocracy, and Sir Thomas Bateson the excess; and I fancied that by observing these two we might see both the inadequacy of aristocracy to supply the principle of authority needful for our present wants, and the danger of its trying to supply it when it was not really competent for the business. On the one hand, in Lord Elcho, showing plenty of high spirit, but remarkable, far above and beyond his gift of high spirit, for the fine tempering of his high spirit, for ease, serenity, politeness,—the great virtues, as Mr. Carlyle says, of aristocracy,—in this beautiful and virtuous mean, there seemed evidently some insufficiency of light; while, on the other hand, Sir Thomas Bateson, in whom the high spirit of aristocracy, its impenetrability, defiant courage,

and pride of resistance, were developed even in excess, was manifestly capable, if he had his way given him, of causing us great danger, and, indeed, of throwing the whole commonwealth into confusion. Then I reverted to that old fundamental notion of mine about the grand merit of our race being really our honesty. And the very helplessness of our aristocratic or governing class in dealing with our perturbed social condition gave me a sort of pride and satisfaction; because I saw they were, as a whole, too honest to try and manage a business for which they did not feel themselves capable.

Surely, now, it is no inconsiderable boon which culture confers upon us, if in embarrassed times like the present it enables us to look at the ins and the outs of things in this way, without hatred and without partiality, and with a disposition to see the good in everybody all round. And I try to follow just the same course with our middle class as with our aristocracy. Mr. Lowe talks to us of this strong middle part of the nation, of the unrivalled deeds of our Liberal middle-class Parliament, of the noble, the heroic work it has performed in the last thirty years; and I begin to ask myself if we shall not, then, find in our middle class the principle of authority we want, and if we had not better take administration as well as legislation away from the weak extreme which now administers for us, and commit both to the strong middle part. I observe, too, that the heroes of middle-class Liberalism, such as we have hitherto known it, speak with a kind of prophetic anticipation of the great destiny which awaits them, and as if the future was clearly theirs. The advanced party, the progressive party, the party in alliance with the future, are the names they like to give themselves. "The principles which will obtain recognition in the future," says Mr. Miall,[17] a personage of deserved eminence among the political Dissenters, as they are called, who have been the backbone of middle-class Liberalism—"the principles which will obtain recognition in the future are the principles for which I have long and zealously laboured. I qualified myself for joining in the work of harvest by doing to the best of my ability the duties of seed time." These duties, if one is to gather them from the works of the great Liberal party in the last thirty years,

---

[14] Frederic Harrison.
[15] Ironic reference to a speech by Lowe at Edinburgh on 1 November 1867 urging replacement of Greek and Latin by the study of modern languages.
[16] Lord Elcho (1818–1914), conservative politician; Sir Thomas Bateson, a Member of Parliament.
[17] Edward Miall (1809–81), editor of the *Nonconformist*.

are, as I have elsewhere summed them up, the advocacy of free-trade, of parliamentary reform, of abolition of church-rates, of voluntaryism in religion and education, of non-interference of the State between employers and employed, and of marriage with one's deceased wife's sister.

Now I know, when I object that all this is machinery, the great Liberal middle class has by this time grown cunning enough to answer that it always meant more by these things than meets the eye; that it has had that within which passes show, and that we are soon going to see, in a Free Church and all manner of good things, what it was. But I have learned from Bishop Wilson (if Mr. Frederic Harrison will forgive my again quoting that poor old hierophant of a decayed superstition[18]): "If we would really know our heart let us impartially view our actions;" and I cannot help thinking that if our Liberals had had so much sweetness and light in their inner minds as they allege, more of it must have come out in their sayings and doings.

An American friend of the English Liberals says, indeed, that their Dissidence of Dissent has been a mere instrument of the political Dissenters for making reason and the will of God prevail (and no doubt he would say the same of marriage with one's deceased wife's sister); and that the abolition of a State Church is merely the Dissenter's means to this end, just as culture is mine. Another American defender of theirs says just the same of their industrialism and free-trade; indeed, this gentleman, taking the bull by the horns, proposes that we should for the future call industrialism culture, and the industrialists the men of culture, and then of course there can be no longer any misapprehension about their true character; and besides the pleasure of being wealthy and comfortable, they will have authentic recognition as vessels of sweetness and light.

All this is undoubtedly specious; but I must remark that the culture of which I talked was an endeavour to come at reason and the will of God by means of reading, observing, and thinking; and that whoever calls anything else culture, may, indeed, call it so if he likes, but then he talks of something quite different from what I talked of. And, again, as culture's way of working for reason and the will of God is by directly trying to know more about them, while the Dissidence of Dissent is evidently in itself no effort of this kind, nor is its Free Church, in fact,

a church with worthier conceptions of God and the ordering of the world than the State Church professes, but with mainly the same conceptions of these as the State Church has, only that every man is to comport himself as he likes in professing them,—this being so, I cannot at once accept the Nonconformity any more than the industrialism and the other great works of our Liberal middle class as proof positive that this class is in possession of light, and that here is the true seat of authority for which we are in search; but I must try a little further, and seek for other indications which may enable me to make up my mind.

Why should we not do with the middle class as we have done with the aristocratic class,—find in it some representative men who may stand for the virtuous mean of this class, for the perfection of its present qualities and mode of being, and also for the excess of them. Such men must clearly not be men of genius like Mr. Bright; for, as I have formerly said, so far as a man has genius he tends to take himself out of the category of class altogether, and to become simply a man. Mr. Bright's brother, Mr. Jacob Bright, would, perhaps, be more to the purpose; he seems to sum up very well in himself, without disturbing influences, the general liberal force of the middle class, the force by which it has done its great works of free-trade, parliamentary reform, voluntaryism, and so on, and the spirit in which it has done them. Now it is clear, from what has been already said, that there has been at least an apparent want of light in the force and spirit through which these great works have been done, and that the works have worn in consequence too much a look of machinery. But this will be clearer still if we take, as the happy mean of the middle class, not Mr. Jacob Bright, but his colleague in the representation of Manchester, Mr. Bazley.[19] Mr. Bazley sums up for us, in general, the middle class, its spirit and its works, at least as well as Mr. Jacob Bright; and he has given us, moreover, a famous sentence, which bears directly on the resolution of our present question,—whether there is light enough in our middle class to make it the proper seat of the authority we wish to establish. When there was a talk some little while ago about the state of middle-class education, Mr. Bazley, as the representative of that class, spoke some memorable words:—"There had been a cry that middle

---

[18] Reference to Harrison's well-known opposition to traditional Christianity.
[19] Sir Thomas Bazley (1797–1885), Manchester merchant.

class education ought to receive more attention. He confessed himself very much surprised by the clamour that was raised. He did not think that class need excite the sympathy either of the legislature or the public." Now this satisfaction of Mr. Bazley with the mental state of the middle class was truly representative, and makes good his claim to stand as the beautiful and virtuous mean of that class. But it is obviously at variance with our definition of culture, or the pursuit of light and perfection, which made light and perfection consist, not in resting and being, but in growing and becoming, in a perpetual advance in beauty and wisdom. So the middle class is by its essence, as one may say, by its incomparable self-satisfaction decisively expressed through its beautiful and virtuous mean, self-excluded from wielding an authority of which light is to be the very soul.

Clear as this is, it will be made clearer still if we take some representative man as the excess of the middle class, and remember that the middle class, in general, is to be conceived as a body swaying between the qualities of its mean and of its excess, and on the whole, of course, as human nature is constituted, inclining rather towards the excess than the mean. Of its excess no better representative can possibly be imagined than the Rev. W. Cattle,[20] a Dissenting minister from Walsall, who came before the public in connection with the proceedings at Birmingham of Mr. Murphy, already mentioned. Speaking in the midst of an irritated population of Catholics, the Rev. W. Cattle exclaimed:—"I say, then, away with the Mass! It is from the bottomless pit; and in the bottomless pit shall all liars have their part, in the lake that burneth with fire and brimstone." And again: "When all the praties[21] were black in Ireland, why didn't the priests say the hocus-pocus over them, and make them all good again?" He shared, too, Mr. Murphy's fears of some invasion of his domestic happiness: "What I wish to say to you as Protestant husbands is, *Take care of your wives!*" And, finally, in the true vein of an Englishman doing as he likes, a vein of which I have at some length pointed out the present dangers, he recommended for imitation the example of some churchwardens at Dublin, among whom, said he, "there was a Luther and also a Melancthon,"[22] who had made very short work with some ritualist or other, hauled him down from his pulpit, and kicked him out of church. Now it is manifest, as I said in the case of Sir Thomas Bateson, that if we let this excess of the sturdy English middle class, this conscientious Protestant Dissenter, so strong, so self-reliant, so fully persuaded in his own mind, have his way, he would be capable, with his want of light—or, to use the language of the religious world, with his zeal without knowledge—of stirring up strife which neither he nor any one else could easily compose.

And then comes in, as it did also with the aristocracy, the honesty of our race, and by the voice of another middle-class man, Alderman Wilson, Alderman of the City of London and Colonel of the City of London Militia, proclaims that it has twinges of conscience, and that it will not attempt to cope with our social disorders, and to deal with a business which it feels to be too high for it. Every one remembers how this virtuous Alderman-Colonel, or Colonel-Alderman, led his militia through the London streets; how the bystanders gathered to see him pass; how the London roughs, asserting an Englishman's best and most blissful right of doing what he likes, robbed and beat the bystanders; and how the blameless warrior-magistrate refused to let his troops interfere. "The crowd," he touchingly said afterwards, "was mostly composed of fine healthy strong men, bent on mischief; if he had allowed his soldiers to interfere they might have been overpowered, their rifles taken from them and used against them by the mob; a riot, in fact, might have ensued, and been attended with bloodshed, compared with which the assaults and loss of property that actually occurred would have been as nothing." Honest and affecting testimony of the English middle class to its own inadequacy for the authoritative part one's admiration would sometimes incline one to assign to it! "Who are we," they say by the voice of their Alderman-Colonel, "that we should not be overpowered if we attempt to cope with social anarchy, our rifles taken from us and used against us by the mob, and we, perhaps, robbed and beaten ourselves? Or what light have we, beyond a free-born Englishman's impulse to do as he likes, which could justify us in preventing, at the cost of bloodshed, other free-born Englishmen from doing as they like, and robbing and beating us as much as they please?"

This distrust of themselves as an adequate centre of authority does not mark the working

---

[20] W. Cattle, a Wesleyan minister.   [21] Potatoes.
[22] Philip Melancthon (1497–1560), German Protestant reformer.

class, as was shown by their readiness the other day in Hyde Park to take upon themselves all the functions of government. But this comes from the working class being, as I have often said, still an embryo, of which no one can yet quite foresee the final development; and from its not having the same experience and self-knowledge as the aristocratic and middle classes. Honesty it no doubt has, just like the other classes of Englishmen, but honesty in an inchoate and untrained state; and meanwhile its powers of action, which are, as Mr. Frederic Harrison says, exceedingly ready, easily run away with it. That it cannot at present have a sufficiency of light which comes by culture,—that is, by reading, observing, and thinking,—is clear from the very nature of its condition; and, indeed, we saw that Mr. Frederic Harrison, in seeking to make a free stage for its bright powers of sympathy and ready powers of action, had to begin by throwing overboard culture, and flouting it as only fit for a professor of *belles lettres*. Still, to make it perfectly manifest that no more in the working class than in the aristocratic and middle classes can one find an adequate centre of authority,—that is, as culture teaches us to conceive our required authority, of light,—let us again follow, with this class, the method we have followed with the aristocratic and middle classes, and try to bring before our minds representative men, who may figure to us its virtue and its excess.

We must not take, of course, men like the chiefs of the Hyde Park demonstration, Colonel Dickson or Mr. Beales; because Colonel Dickson, by his martial profession and dashing exterior, seems to belong properly, like Julius Cæsar and Mirabeau and other great popular leaders, to the aristocratic class, and to be carried into the popular ranks only by his ambition or his genius; while Mr. Beales belongs to our solid middle class, and, perhaps, if he had not been a great popular leader, would have been a Philistine. But Mr. Odger,[23] whose speeches we have all read, and of whom his friends relate, besides, much that is favourable, may very well stand for the beautiful and virtuous mean of our present working class; and I think everybody will admit that in Mr. Odger, as in Lord Elcho, there is manifestly, with all his good points, some insufficiency of light. The excess of the working class, in its present state of development, is perhaps best shown in Mr. Bradlaugh, the iconoclast, who seems to be almost for baptizing

us all in blood and fire into his new social dispensation, and to whose reflections, now that I have once been set going on Bishop Wilson's track, I cannot forbear commending this maxim of the good old man: "Intemperance in talk makes a dreadful havoc in the heart." Mr. Bradlaugh, like Sir Thomas Bateson and the Rev. W. Cattle, is evidently capable, if he had his head given him, of running us all into great dangers and confusion. I conclude, therefore—what, indeed, few of those who do me the honour to read this disquisition are likely to dispute,—that we can as little find in the working class as in the aristocratic or in the middle class our much-wanted source of authority, as culture suggests it to us.

Well, then, what if we tried to rise above the idea of class to the idea of the whole community, *the State*, and to find our centre of light and authority there? Every one of us has the idea of country, as a sentiment; hardly any one of us has the idea of *the State*, as a working power. And why? Because we habitually live in our ordinary selves, which do not carry us beyond the ideas and wishes of the class to which we happen to belong. And we are all afraid of giving to the State too much power, because we only conceive of the State as something equivalent to the class in occupation of the executive government, and are afraid of that class abusing power to its own purposes. If we strengthen the State with the aristocratic class in occupation of the executive government, we imagine we are delivering ourselves up captive to the ideas and wishes of our fierce aristocratical baronet Sir Thomas Bateson; if with the middle class in occupation of the executive government, to those of our truculent middle-class Dissenting minister, the Rev. W. Cattle; if with the working class, to those of its notorious tribune, Mr. Bradlaugh. And with much justice; owing to the exaggerated notion which we English, as I have said, entertain of the right and blessedness of the mere doing as one likes, of the affirming one-self, and oneself just as it is. People of the aristocratic class want to affirm their ordinary selves, their likings and dislikings; people of the middle class the same, people of the working class the same. By our every-day selves, however, we are separate, personal, at war; we are only safe from one another's tyranny when no one has any power; and this safety, in its turn, cannot save us from anarchy. And when, therefore, anarchy presents

---

[23] George Odger (1820–77), London shoemaker active in workingmen's associations.

itself as a danger to us, we know not where to turn.

But by our *best self* we are united, impersonal, at harmony. We are in no peril from giving authority to this, because it is the truest friend we all of us can have; and when anarchy is a danger to us, to this authority we may turn with sure trust. Well, and this is the very self which culture, or the study of perfection, seeks to develop in us; at the expense of our old untransformed self, taking pleasure only in doing what it likes or is used to do, and exposing us to the risk of clashing with every one else who is doing the same! So that our poor culture, which is flouted as so unpractical, leads us to the very ideas capable of meeting the great want of our present embarrassed times! We want an authority, and we find nothing but jealous classes, checks, and a deadlock; culture suggests the idea of *the State*. We find no basis for a firm State-power in our ordinary selves; culture suggests one to us in our *best self*.

It cannot but acutely try a tender conscience to be accused, in a practical country like ours, of keeping aloof from the work and hope of a multitude of earnest-hearted men, and of merely toying with poetry and æsthetics. So it is with no little sense of relief that I find myself thus in the position of one who makes a contribution in aid of the practical necessities of our times. The great thing, it will be observed, is to find our *best* self, and to seek to affirm nothing but that; not,—as we English with our over-value for merely being free and busy have been so accustomed to do,—resting satisfied with a self which comes uppermost long before our best self, and affirming that with blind energy. In short,—to go back yet once more to Bishop Wilson,—of these two excellent rules of Bishop Wilson's for a man's guidance: "Firstly, never go against the best light you have; secondly, take care that your light be not darkness," we English have followed with praiseworthy zeal the first rule, but we have not given so much heed to the second. We have gone manfully, the Rev. W. Cattle and the rest of us, according to the best light we have; but we have not taken enough care that this should be really the best light possible for us, that it should not be darkness. And, our honesty being very great, conscience has whispered to us that the light we were following, our ordinary self, was, indeed, perhaps, only an inferior self, only darkness; and that it would not do to impose this seriously on all the world.

But our best self inspires faith, and is capable of affording a serious principle of authority. For example. We are on our way to what the late Duke of Wellington, with his strong sagacity, foresaw and admirably described as "a revolution by due course of law." This is undoubtedly,—if we are still to live and grow, and this famous nation is not to stagnate and dwindle away on the one hand, or, on the other, to perish miserably in mere anarchy and confusion,—what we are on the way to. Great changes there must be, for a revolution cannot accomplish itself without great changes; yet order there must be, for without order a revolution cannot accomplish itself by due course of law. So whatever brings risk of tumult and disorder, multitudinous processions in the streets of our crowded towns, multitudinous meetings in their public places and parks,—demonstrations perfectly unnecessary in the present course of our affairs,—our best self, or right reason, plainly enjoins us to set our faces against. It enjoins us to encourage and uphold the occupants of the executive power, whoever they may be, in firmly prohibiting them. But it does this clearly and resolutely, and is thus a real principle of authority, because it does it with a free conscience; because in thus provisionally strengthening the executive power, it knows that it is not doing this merely to enable Sir Thomas Bateson to affirm himself as against Mr. Bradlaugh, or the Rev. W. Cattle to affirm himself as against both. It knows that it is stabilising *the State,* or organ of our collective best self, of our national right reason; and it has the testimony of conscience that it is stablishing the State on behalf of whatever great changes are needed, just as much as on behalf of order; stablishing it to deal just as stringently, when the time comes, with Sir Thomas Bateson's Protestant ascendency, or with the Rev. W. Cattle's sorry education of his children, as it deals with Mr. Bradlaugh's street-processions.

CHAPTER III

Barbarians, Philistines, Populace

FROM a man without a philosophy no one can expect philosophical completeness. Therefore I may observe without shame, that in trying to get a distinct notion of our aristocratic, our middle, and our working class, with a view of testing the claims of each of these classes to become a centre of authority, I have omitted, I find, to complete the old-fashioned analysis which I had the fancy of applying, and have not shown in these classes, as well as the virtuous mean and the excess, the defect also. I do not know that the omission very much matters. Still, as clearness is the one merit which a plain, unsystematic writer, without a philosophy, can hope to have, and as our notion of the three great English classes may perhaps be made clearer if we see their distinctive qualities in the defect, as well as in the excess and in the mean, let us try, before proceeding further, to remedy this omission.

It is manifest, if the perfect and virtuous mean of that fine spirit which is the distinctive quality of aristocracies, is to be found in Lord Elcho's chivalrous style, and its excess in Sir Thomas Bateson's turn for resistance, that its defect must lie in a spirit not bold and high enough, and in an excessive and pusillanimous unaptness for resistance. If, again, the perfect and virtuous mean of that force by which our middle class has done its great works, and of that self-reliance with which it contemplates itself and them, is to be seen in the performances and speeches of Mr. Bazley, and the excess of that force and of that self-reliance in the performances and speeches of the Rev. W. Cattle, then it is manifest that their defect must lie in a helpless inaptitude for the great works of the middle class, and in a poor and despicable lack of its self-satisfaction.

To be chosen to exemplify the happy mean of a good quality, or set of good qualities, is evidently a praise to a man; nay, to be chosen to exemplify even their excess, is a kind of praise. Therefore I could have no hesitation in taking Lord Elcho and Mr. Bazley, the Rev. W. Cattle and Sir Thomas Bateson, to exemplify, respectively, the mean and the excess of aristocratic and middle-class qualities. But perhaps there might be a want of urbanity in singling out this or that personage as the representative of defect. Therefore I shall leave the defect of aristocracy unillustrated by any representative man. But with oneself one may always, without impropriety, deal quite freely; and, indeed, this sort of plain-dealing with oneself has in it, as all the moralists tell us, something very wholesome.

So I will venture to humbly offer myself as an illustration of defect in those forces and qualities which make our middle class what it is. The too well-founded reproaches of my opponents declare how little I have lent a hand to the great works of the middle class; for it is evidently these works, and my slackness at them, which are meant, when I am said to "refuse to lend a hand to the humble operation of uprooting certain definite evils" (such as church-rates and others), and that therefore "the believers in action grow impatient" with me. The line, again, of a still unsatisfied seeker which I have followed, the idea of self-transformation, of growing towards some measure of sweetness and light not yet reached, is evidently at clean variance with the perfect self-satisfaction current in my class, the middle class, and may serve to indicate in me, therefore, the extreme defect of this feeling. But these confessions, though salutary, are bitter and unpleasant.

To pass, then, to the working class. The defect of this class would be the falling short in what Mr. Frederic Harrison calls those "bright powers of sympathy and ready powers of action," of which we saw in Mr. Odger the virtuous mean, and Mr. Bradlaugh the excess. The working class is so fast growing and rising at the present time, that instances of this defect cannot well be now very common. Perhaps Canning's "Needy Knife-Grinder"[1] (who is dead, and therefore cannot be pained at my taking him for an illustration) may serve to give us the notion of defect in the essential quality of a working class; or I might even cite (since, though he is alive in the flesh, he is dead to all heed of criticism) my poor old poaching friend, Zephaniah Diggs,[2] who, between his hare-snaring and his gin-drinking, has got his powers of sympathy quite dulled and his powers of action in any great movement of his class hopelessly impaired. But examples of this defect belong, as I have said, to a bygone age rather than to the present.

The same desire for clearness, which has led me thus to extend a little my first analysis of the three great classes of English society, prompts me also to improve my nomenclature for them a little, with a view to making it thereby more manageable. It is awkward and tiresome to be always saying the aristocratic class, the middle class, the working class. For the middle class, for that great body which, as we know, "has done all

---

[1] George Canning (1770–1827), statesman, author of a poem called "The Friend of Humanity and the Needy Knife-Grinder."
[2] A character created by Arnold in his *Friendship's Garland* to represent the crudest aspects of English country life.

the great things that have been done in all departments," and which is to be conceived as moving between its two cardinal points of Mr. Bazley, our commercial member of Parliament, and the Rev. W. Cattle, our fanatical Protestant Dissenter,—for this class we have a designation which now has become pretty well known, and which we may as well still keep for them, the designation of Philistines. What this term means I have so often explained that I need not repeat it here. For the aristocratic class, conceived mainly as a body moving between the two cardinal points of our chivalrous Lord Elcho and our definant baronet, Sir Thomas Bateson, we have as yet got no special designation. Almost all my attention has naturally been concentrated on my own class, the middle class, with which I am in closest sympathy, and which has been, besides, the great power of our day, and has had its praises sung by all speakers and newspapers.

Still the aristocratic class is so important in itself, and the weighty functions which Mr. Carlyle proposes at the present critical time to commit to it must add so much to its importance, that it seems neglectful, and a strong instance of that want of coherent philosophic method for which Mr. Frederic Harrison blames me, to leave the aristocratic class so much without notice and denomination. It may be thought that the characteristic which I have occasionally mentioned as proper to aristocracies,—their natural inaccessibility, as children of the established fact, to ideas,—points to our extending to this class also the designation of Philistines; the Philistine being, as is well known, the enemy of the children of light or servants of the idea. Nevertheless, there seems to be an inconvenience in thus giving one and the same designation to two very different classes; and besides, if we look into the thing closely, we shall find that the term Philistine conveys a sense which makes it more peculiarly appropriate to our middle class than to our aristocratic. For *Philistine* gives the notion of something particularly stiff-necked and perverse in the resistance to light and its children; and therein it specially suits our middle class, who not only do not pursue sweetness and light, but who even prefer to them that sort of machinery of business, chapels, tea-meetings, and addresses from Mr. Murphy and the Rev. W. Cattle, which makes up the dismal and illiberal life on which I have so often touched. But the aristocratic class has actually, as we have seen, in its well-known politeness, a kind of image or shadow of sweetness; and as for light, if it does not pursue

light, it is not that it perversely cherishes some dismal and illiberal existence in preference to light, but it is lured off from following light by those mighty and eternal seducers of our race which weave for this class their most irresistible charms,—by worldly splendour, security, power and pleasure. These seducers are exterior goods, but in a way they are goods; and he who is hindered by them from caring for light and ideas, is not so much doing what is perverse as what is too natural.

Keeping this in view, I have in my own mind often indulged myself with the fancy of employing, in order to designate our aristocratic class, the name of *The Barbarians*. The Barbarians, to whom we all owe so much, and who reinvigorated and renewed our worn-out Europe, had, as is well known, eminent merits; and in this country, where we are for the most part sprung from the Barbarians, we have never had the prejudice against them which prevails among the races of Latin origin. The Barbarians brought with them that staunch individualism, as the modern phrase is, and that passion for doing as one likes, for the assertion of personal liberty, which appears to Mr. Bright the central idea of English life, and of which we have, at any rate, a very rich supply. The stronghold and natural seat of this passion was in the nobles of whom our aristocratic class are the inheritors; and this class, accordingly, have signally manifested it, and have done much by their example to recommend it to the body of the nation, who already, indeed, had it in their blood. The Barbarians, again, had the passion for field-sports; and they have handed it on to our aristocratic class, who of this passion too, as of the passion for asserting one's personal liberty, are the great natural stronghold. The care of the Barbarians for the body, and for all manly exercises; the vigour, good looks, and fine complexion which they acquired and perpetuated in their families by these means,—all this may be observed still in our aristocratic class. The chivalry of the Barbarians, with its characteristics of high spirit, choice manners, and distinguished bearing,—what is this but the attractive commencement of the politeness of our aristocratic class? In some Barbarian noble, no doubt, one would have admired, if one could have been then alive to see it, the rudiments of Lord Elcho. Only, all this culture (to call it by that name) of the Barbarians was an exterior culture mainly. It consisted principally in outward gifts and graces, in looks, manners, accomplishments, prowess. The chief inward gifts which had part in it were the most exterior, so to speak, of inward gifts, those which come nearest to outward ones; they were courage, a high spirit, self-confidence. Far within, and unawakened, lay a whole range of powers of thought and feeling, to which these interesting productions of nature had, from the circumstances of their life, no access. Making allowances for the difference of the times, surely we can observe precisely the same thing now in our aristocratic class. In general its culture is exterior chiefly; all the exterior graces and accomplishments, and the more external of the inward virtues, seem to be principally its portion. It now, of course, cannot but be often in contact with those studies by which, from the world of thought and feeling, true culture teaches us to fetch sweetness and light; but its hold upon these very studies appears remarkably external, and unable to exert any deep power upon its spirit. Therefore the one insufficiency which we noted in the perfect mean of this class, Lord Elcho, was an insufficiency of light. And owing to the same causes, does not a subtle criticism lead us to make, even on the good looks and politeness of our aristocratic class, and of even the most fascinating half of that class, the feminine half, the one qualifying remark, that in these charming gifts there should perhaps be, for ideal perfection, a shade more *soul*?

I often, therefore, when I want to distinguish clearly the aristocratic class from the Philistines proper, or middle class, name the former, in my own mind, *the Barbarians*. And when I go through the country, and see this and that beautiful and imposing seat of theirs crowning the landscape, "There," I say to myself, "is a great fortified post of the Barbarians."

It is obvious that that part of the working class which, working diligently by the light of Mrs. Gooch's Golden Rule, looks forward to the happy day when it will sit on thrones with Mr. Bazley and other middle-class potentates, to survey, as Mr. Bright beautifully says, "the cities it has built, the railroads it has made, the manufactures it has produced, the cargoes which freight the ships of the greatest mercantile navy the world has ever seen,"—it is obvious, I say, that this part of the working class is, or is in a fair way to be, one in spirit with the industrial middle class. It is notorious that our middle-class Liberals have long looked forward to this consummation, when the working class shall join forces with them, aid them heartily to carry forward their great works, go in a body to their tea-meetings, and, in short, enable them to bring about their millennium. That part of the working class, therefore, which does really seem to lend itself to these great aims, may, with propriety, be numbered by us among the Philistines. That part of it, again, which so much occupies the attention of philanthropists at present,—the part which gives all its energies to organising itself, through trades' unions and other means, so as to constitute, first, a great working-class power, independent of the middle and aristocratic classes, and then, by dint of numbers, give the law to them, and itself reign absolutely,—this lively and interesting part must also, according to our definition, go with the Philistines; because it is its class and its class-instinct which it seeks to affirm, its ordinary self, not its best self; and it is a machinery, an industrial machinery, and power and pre-eminence and other external goods, which fill its thoughts, and not an inward perfection. It is wholly occupied, according to Plato's subtle expression, with the things of itself and not its real self, with the things of the State and not the real State. But that vast portion, lastly, of the working class which, raw and half-developed, has long lain half-hidden amidst its poverty and squalor, and is now issuing from its hiding-place to assert an Englishman's heaven-born privilege of doing as he likes, and is beginning to perplex us by marching where it likes, meeting where it likes, bawling what it likes, breaking what it likes,—to this vast residuum we may with great propriety give the name of *Populace*.

Thus we have got three distinct terms, *Barbarians, Philistines, Populace*, to denote roughly the three great classes into which our society is divided; and though this humble attempt at a scientific nomenclature falls, no doubt, very far short in precision of what might be required from a writer equipped with a complete and coherent philosophy, yet, from a notoriously unsystematic and unpretending writer, it will, I trust, be accepted as sufficient.

But in using this new, and, I hope, convenient division of English society, two things are to be borne in mind. The first is, that since, under all our class divisions, there is a common basis of human nature, therefore, in every one of us, whether we be properly Barbarians, Philistines, or Populace, there exists, sometimes only in germ and potentially, sometimes more or less developed, the same tendencies and passions which have made our fellow-citizens of other classes what they are. This consideration is very important, because it has great influence in begetting that spirit of indulgence which is a necessary part of sweetness, and which, indeed, when our culture is complete, is, as I have said, inexhaustible. Thus, an English Barbarian who examines himself will, in general, find himself to be not so entirely a Barbarian but that he has in him, also, something of the Philistine, and even something of the Populace as well. And the same with Englishmen of the two other classes.

This is an experience which we may all verify every day. For instance, I myself (I again take myself as a sort of *corpus vile* to serve for illustration in a matter where serving for illustration may not by every one be thought agreeable), I myself am properly a Philistine,—Mr. Swinburne would add, the son of a Philistine. And although, through circumstances which will perhaps one day be known if ever the affecting history of my conversion comes to be written, I have, for the most part, broken with the ideas and the tea-meetings of my own class, yet I have not, on that account, been brought much the nearer to the ideas and works of the Barbarians or of the Populace. Nevertheless, I never take a gun or a fishing-rod in my hands without feeling that I have in the ground of my nature the self-same seeds which, fostered by circumstances, do so much to make the Barbarian; and that, with the Barbarian's advantages, I might have rivalled him. Place me in one of his great fortified posts, with these seeds of a love for field-sports sown in my nature, with all the means of developing them, with all pleasures at my command, with most whom I met deferring to me, every one I met smiling on me, and with every appearance of permanence and security before me and behind me,—then I too might have grown, I feel, into a very passable child of the established fact, of commendable spirit and politeness, and, at the same time, a little inaccessible to ideas and light; not, of course, with either the eminent fine spirit of Lord Elcho, or the eminent power of resistance of Sir Thomas Bateson, but, according to the measure of the common run of mankind, something between the two. And as to the Populace, who, whether he be Barbarian or Philistine, can look at them without sympathy, when he remembers how often,—every time that we snatch up a vehement opinion in ignorance and passion, every time that we long to crush an adversary by sheer violence, every time that we are envious, every time that we are brutal, every time that we adore mere power or success, every time that we add our voice to swell a blind

clamour against some unpopular personage, every time that we trample savagely on the fallen,—he has found in his own bosom the eternal spirit of the Populace, and that there needs only a little help from circumstances to make it triumph in him untameably?

The second thing to be borne in mind I have indicated several times already. It is this. All of us, so far as we are Barbarians, Philistines, or Populace, imagine happiness to consist in doing what one's ordinary self likes. What one's ordinary self likes differs according to the class to which one belongs, and has its severer and its lighter side; always, however, remaining machinery, and nothing more. The graver self of the Barbarian likes honours and consideration; his more relaxed self, field-sports and pleasure. The graver self of one kind of Philistine likes fanaticism, business, and money-making; his more relaxed self, comfort and tea-meetings. Of another kind of Philistine, the graver self likes rattening; the relaxed self, deputations, or hearing Mr. Odger speak. The sterner self of the Populace likes bawling, hustling, and smashing; the lighter self, beer. But in each class there are born a certain number of natures with a curiosity about their best self, with a bent for seeing things as they are, for disentangling themselves from machinery, for simply concerning themselves with reason and the will of God, and doing their best to make these prevail;—for the pursuit, in a word, of perfection. To certain manifestations of this love for perfection mankind have accustomed themselves to give the name of genius; implying, by this name, something original and heaven-bestowed in the passion. But the passion is to be found far beyond those manifestations of it to which the world usually gives the name of genius, and in which there is, for the most part, a *talent* of some kind or other, a special and striking faculty of execution, informed by the heaven-bestowed ardour, or genius. It is to be found in many manifestations besides these, and may best be called, as we have called it, the love and pursuit of perfection; culture being the true nurse of the pursuing love, and sweetness and light the true character of the pursued perfection. Natures with this bent emerge in all classes,—among the Barbarians, among the Philistines, among the Populace. And this bent always tends to take them out of their class, and to make their distinguishing characteristic not their Barbarianism or their Philistinism, but their *humanity*. They have, in general, a rough time of it in their lives; but they are sown more abundantly than one might think, they appear where and when one least expects it, they set up a fire which enfilades, so to speak, the class with which they are ranked; and, in general, by the extrication of their best self as the self to develop, and by the simplicity of the ends fixed by them as paramount, they hinder the unchecked predominance of that class-life which is the affirmation of our ordinary self, and seasonably disconcert mankind in their worship of machinery.

Therefore, when we speak of ourselves as divided into Barbarians, Philistines, and Populace, we must be understood always to imply that within each of these classes there are a certain number of *aliens*, if we may so call them,—persons who are mainly led, not by their class spirit, but by a general *humane* spirit, by the love of human perfection; and that this number is capable of being diminished or augmented. I mean, the number of those who will succeed in developing this happy instinct will be greater or smaller, in proportion both to the force of the original instinct within them, and to the hindrance or encouragement which it meets with from without. In almost all who have it, it is mixed with some infusion of the spirit of an ordinary self, some quantity of class-instinct, and even, as has been shown, of more than one class-instinct at the same time; so that, in general, the extrication of the best self, the predominance of the *humane* instinct, will very much depend upon its meeting, or not, with what is fitted to help and elicit it. At a moment, therefore, when it is agreed that we want a source of authority, and when it seems probable that the right source is our best self, it becomes of vast importance to see whether or not the things around us are, in general, such as to help and elicit our best self, and if they are not, to see why they are not, and the most promising way of mending them.

Now, it is clear that the very absence of any powerful authority amongst us, and the prevalent doctrine of the duty and happiness of doing as one likes, and asserting our personal liberty, must tend to prevent the erection of any very strict standard of excellence, the belief in any very paramount authority of right reason, the recognition of our best self as anything very recondite and hard to come at. It may be, as I have said, a proof of our honesty that we do not attempt to give to our ordinary self, as we have it in action, predominant

authority, and to impose its rule upon other people. But it is evident, also, that it is not easy, with our style of proceeding, to get beyond the notion of an ordinary self at all, or to get the paramount authority of a commanding best self, or right reason, recognized. The learned Martinus Scriblerus[3] well says:—"The taste of the bathos is implanted by nature itself in the soul of man; till, perverted by custom or example, he is taught, or rather compelled, to relish the sublime." But with us everything seems directed to prevent any such perversion of us by custom or example as might compel us to relish the sublime; by all means we are encouraged to keep our natural taste for the bathos unimpaired.

I have formerly pointed out how in literature the absence of any authoritative centre, like an Academy, tends to do this. Each section of the public has its own literary organ, and the mass of the public is without any suspicion that the value of these organs is relative to their being nearer a certain ideal centre of correct information, taste, and intelligence, or farther away from it. I have said that within certain limits, which any one who is likely to read this will have no difficulty in drawing for himself, my old adversary, the *Saturday Review*,[4] may, on matters of literature and taste, be fairly enough regarded, relatively to the mass of newspapers which treat these matters, as a kind of organ of reason. But I remember once conversing with a company of Nonconformist admirers of some lecturer who had let off a great firework, which the *Saturday Review* said was all noise and false lights, and feeling my way as tenderly as I could about the effect of this unfavourable judgment upon those with whom I was conversing. "Oh," said one who was their spokesman, with the most tranquil air of conviction, "it is true the *Saturday Review* abuses the lecture, but the *British Banner*"[5] (I am not quite sure it was the *British Banner,* but it was some newspaper of that stamp) "says that the *Saturday Review* is quite wrong." The speaker had evidently no notion that there was a scale of value for judgments on these topics, and that the judgments of the *Saturday Review* ranked high on this scale, and those of the *British Banner* low; the taste of the bathos implanted by nature in the literary judgments of man had never, in my friend's case, encountered any let or hindrance.

Just the same in religion as in leterature. We

---

[3] "The Memoirs of Martinus Scriblerus," mostly written by John Arbuthnot (1667–1735).

[4] Reference to an unfavorable review of Arnold's *Essays in Criticism* in the *Saturday Review* in February 1865.

[5] A nonconformist weekly founded in 1847.

have most of us little idea of a high standard to choose our guides by, of a great and profound spirit, which is an authority, while inferior spirits are none. It is enough to give importance to things that this or that person says them decisively, and has a large following of some strong kind when he says them. This habit of ours is very well shown in that able and interesting work of Mr. Hepworth Dixon's,[6] which we were all reading lately, *The Mormons, by One of Themselves*. Here, again, I am not quite sure that my memory serves me as to the exact title, but I mean the well-known book in which Mr. Hepworth Dixon described the Mormons, and other similar religious bodies in America, with so much detail and such warm sympathy. In this work it seems enough for Mr. Dixon that this or that doctrine has its Rabbi, who talks big to him, has a staunch body of disciples, and, above all, has plenty of rifles. That there are any further stricter tests to be applied to a doctrine, before it is pronounced important, never seems to occur to him. "It is easy to say," he writes of the Mormons, "that these saints are dupes and fanatics, to laugh at Joe Smith and his church, but what then? *The great facts remain.* Young and his people are at Utah; a church of 200,000 souls; an army of 20,000 rifles." But if the followers of a doctrine are really dupes, or worse, and its promulgators are really fanatics, or worse, it gives the doctrine no seriousness or authority the more that there should be found 200,000 souls,—200,000 of the innumerable multitude with a natural taste for the bathos,—to hold it, and 20,000 rifles to defend it. And again, of another religious organisation in America: "A fair and open field is not to be refused when hosts so mighty throw down wager of battle on behalf of what they hold to be true, however strange their faith may seem." A fair and open field is not to be refused to any speaker; but this solemn way of heralding him is quite out of place, unless he has, for the best reason and spirit of man, some significance. "Well, but," says Mr. Hepworth Dixon, "a theory which has been accepted by men like Judge Edmonds, Dr. Hare, Elder Frederick, and Professor Bush!" And again: "Such are, in brief, the bases of what Newman Weeks, Sarah Horton, Deborah Butler, and the associated brethren, proclaimed in Rolt's Hall as the new covenant!" If he was summing up an account of the doctrine of Plato or of St. Paul,

and of its followers, Mr. Hepworth Dixon could not be more earnestly reverential. But the question is, Have personages like Judge Edmonds, and Newman Weeks, and Elderess Polly, and Elderess Antoinette, and the rest of Mr. Hepworth Dixon's heroes and heroines, anything of the weight and significance for the best reason and spirit of man that Plato and St. Paul have? Evidently they, at present, have not; and a very small taste of them and their doctrines ought to have convinced Mr. Hepworth Dixon that they never could have. "But," says he, "the magnetic power which Shakerism is exercising on American thought would of itself compel us,"—and so on. Now as far as real thought is concerned,—thought which affects the best reason and spirit of man, the scientific or the imaginative thought of the world, the only thought which deserves speaking of in this solemn way,—America has up to the present time been hardly more than a province of England, and even now would not herself claim to be more than abreast of England; and of this only real human thought, English thought itself is not just now, as we must all admit, the most significant factor. Neither, then, can American thought be; and the magnetic power which Shakerism exercises on American thought is about as important, for the best reason and spirit of man, as the magnetic power which Mr. Murphy exercises on Birmingham Protestantism. And as we shall never get rid of our natural taste for the bathos in religion,—never get access to a best self and right reason which may stand as a serious authority,—by treating Mr. Murphy as his own disciples treat him, seriously, and as if he was as much an authority as any one else: so we shall never get rid of it while our able and popular writers treat their Joe Smiths and Deborah Butlers, with their so many thousand souls and so many thousand rifles, in the like exaggerated and misleading manner, and so do their best to confirm us in a bad mental habit to which we are already too prone.

If our habits make it hard for us to come at the idea of a high best self, of a paramount authority, in literature or religion, how much more do they make this hard in the sphere of politics! In other countries the governors, not depending so immediately on the favour of the governed, have everything to urge them, if they know anything of right reason (and it is at least supposed that governors should know more of this than the

---

[6] William Hepworth Dixon (1821–79), author of *New America* (1867). Subsequent references are to the founders of Mormonism, Joseph Smith and Brigham Young.

mass of the governed), to set it authoritatively before the community. But our whole scheme of government being representative, every one of our governors has all possible temptation, instead of setting up before the governed who elect him, and on whose favour he depends, a high standard of right reason, to accommodate himself as much as possible to their natural taste for the bathos; and even if he tries to go counter to it, to proceed in this with so much flattering and coaxing, that they shall not suspect their ignorance and prejudices to be anything very unlike right reason, or their natural taste for the bathos to differ much from a relish for the sublime. Every one is thus in every possible way encouraged to trust in his own heart; but "he that trusteth in his own heart," says the Wise Man, "is a fool;"[7] and at any rate this, which Bishop Wilson says, is undeniably true: "The number of those who need to be awakened is far greater than that of those who need comfort."

But in our political system everybody is comforted. Our guides and governors who have to be elected by the influence of the Barbarians, and who depend on their favour, sing the praises of the Barbarians, and say all the smooth things that can be said of them. With Mr. Tennyson, they celebrate "the great broad-shouldered genial Englishman," with his "sense of duty," his "reverence for the laws," and his "patient force," who saves us from the "revolts, republics, revolutions, most no graver than a schoolboy's barring out,"[8] which upset other and less broad-shouldered nations. Our guides who are chosen by the Philistines and who have to look to their favour, tell the Philistines how "all the world knows that the great middle class of this country supplies the mind, the will, and the power requisite for all the great and good things that have to be done," and congratulate them on their "earnest good sense, which penetrates though sophisms, ignores commonplaces, and gives to conventional illusions their true value." Our guides who look to the favour of the Populace, tell them that "theirs are the brightest powers of sympathy, and the readiest powers of action."

Harsh things are said too, no doubt, against all the great classes of the community; but these things so evidently come from a hostile class, and are so manifestly dictated by the passions and prepossessions of a hostile class, and not by right reason, that they make no serious impression on those at whom they are launched, but slide easily off their minds. For instance, when the Reform League orators inveigh against our cruel and bloated aristocracy, these invectives so evidently show the passions and point of view of the Populace, that they do not sink into the minds of those at whom they are addressed, or awaken any thought or self-examination in them. Again, when Sir Thomas Bateson describes the Philistines and the Populace as influenced with a kind of hideous mania for emasculating the aristocracy, that reproach so clearly comes from the wrath and excited imagination of the Barbarians, that it does not much set the Philistines and the Populace thinking. Or when Mr. Lowe calls the Populace drunken and venal, he so evidently calls them this in an agony of apprehension for his Philistine or middle-class Parliament, which has done so many great and heroic works, and is now threatened with mixture and debasement, that the Populace do not lay his words seriously to heart.

So the voice which makes a permanent impression on each of our classes is the voice of its friends, and this is from the nature of things, as I have said, a comforting voice. The Barbarians remain in the belief that the great broad-shouldered genial Englishman may be well satisfied with himself; the Philistines remain in the belief that the great middle class of this country, with its earnest common-sense penetrating through sophisms and ignoring commonplaces, may be well satisfied with itself; the Populace, that the working man with his bright powers of sympathy and ready powers of action, may be well satisfied with himself. What hope, at this rate, of extinguishing the taste of the bathos implanted by nature itself in the soul of man, or of inculcating the belief that excellence dwells among high and steep rocks, and can only be reached by those who sweat blood to reach her?

But it will be said, perhaps, that candidates for political influence and leadership, who thus caress the self-love of those whose suffrages they desire, know quite well that they are not saying the sheer truth as reason sees it, but that they are using a sort of conventional language, or what we call clap-trap, which is essential to the working of representative institutions. And therefore, I

---

[7] Proverbs 28:26.

[8] The quotations are from Tennyson's *The Princess*. "Barring out" was a practice in the public schools whereby schoolboys barred the master until demands were met.

suppose, we ought rather to say with Figaro: *Qui est-ce qu'on trompe ici?*[9] Now, I admit that often, but not always, when our governors say smooth things to the self-love of the class whose political support they want, they know very well that they are over-stepping, by a long stride, the bounds of truth and soberness; and while they talk, they in a manner, no doubt, put their tongue in their cheek. Not always; because, when a Barbarian appeals to his own class to make him their representative and give him political power, he, when he pleases their self-love by extolling broad-shouldered genial Englishmen with their sense of duty, reverence for the laws, and patient force, pleases his own self-love and extols himself, and is, therefore, himself ensnared by his own smooth words. And so, too, when a Philistine wants to be sent to Parliament by his brother Philistines, and extols the earnest good sense which characterises Manchester and supplies the mind, the will, and the power, as the *Daily News*[10] eloquently says, requisite for all the great and good things that have to be done, he intoxicates and deludes himself as well as his brother Philistines who hear him.

But it is true that a Barbarian often wants the political support of the Philistines; and he unquestionably, when he flatters the self-love of Philistinism, and extols, in the approved fashion, its energy, enterprise, and self-reliance, knows that he is talking clap-trap, and so to say, puts his tongue in his cheek. On all matters where Nonconformity and its catchwords are concerned, this insincerity of Barbarians needing Nonconformist support, and, therefore, flattering the self-love of Nonconformity and repeating its catchwords without the least real belief in them, is very noticeable. When the Nonconformists, in a transport of blind zeal, threw out Sir James Graham's[11] useful Education Clauses in 1843, one-half of their parliamentary advocates, no doubt, who cried aloud against "trampling on the religious liberty of the Dissenters by taking the money of Dissenters to teach the tenets of the Church of England," put their tongue in their cheek while they so cried out. And perhaps there is even a sort of motion of Mr. Frederic Harrison's tongue towards his cheek when he talks of "the shriek of superstition," and tells the working class that "theirs are the brightest powers of sympathy and the readiest powers of action." But the point on which I would insist is, that this involuntary tribute to truth and soberness on the part of certain of our governors and guides never reaches at all the mass of us governed, to serve as a lesson to us, to abate our self-love, and to awaken in us a suspicion that our favourite prejudices may be, to a higher reason, all nonsense. Whatever by-play goes on among the more intelligent of our leaders, we do not see it; and we are left to believe that, not only in our own eyes, but in the eyes of our representative and ruling men, there is nothing more admirable than our ordinary self, whatever our ordinary self happens to be, Barbarian, Philistine, or Populace.

Thus everything in our political life tends to hide from us that there is anything wiser than our ordinary selves, and to prevent our getting the notion of a paramount right reason. Royalty itself, in its idea the expression of the collective nation, and a sort of constituted witness to its best mind, we try to turn into a kind of grand advertising van, meant to give publicity and credit to the inventions, sound or unsound, of the ordinary self of individuals.

I remember, when I was in North Germany, having this very strongly brought to my mind in the matter of schools and their institution. In Prussia, the best schools are Crown patronage schools, as they are called; schools which have been established and endowed (and new ones are to this day being established and endowed) by the Sovereign himself out of his own revenues, to be under the direct control and management of him or of those representing him, and to serve as types of what schools should be. The Sovereign, as his position raises him above many prejudices and littlenesses, and as he can always have at his disposal the best advice, has evident advantages over private founders in well planning and directing a school; while at the same time his great means and his great influence secure, to a well-planned school of his, credit and authority. This is what, in North Germany, the governors do in the matter of education for the governed; and one may say that they thus give the governed a lesson, and draw out in them the idea of a right reason higher than the suggestions of an ordinary man's ordinary self.

But in England how different is the part which in this matter our governors are accustomed to play! The Licensed Victuallers or the Com-

---

9 "Who is being deceived here?"   10 Founded in 1846 by Charles Dickens.
     11 Sir James Graham (1792–1861), Home Secretary, proponent of an education act that included Anglican religious instruction.

mercial Travellers propose to make a school for their children; and I suppose, in the matter of schools, one may call the Licensed Victuallers or the Commercial Travellers ordinary men, with their natural taste for the bathos still strong; and a Sovereign with the advice of men like Wilhelm von Humboldt or Schleiermacher[12] may, in this matter, be a better judge, and nearer to right reason. And it will be allowed, probably, that right reason would suggest that, to have a sheer school of Licensed Victuallers' children, or a sheer school of Commercial Travellers' children, and to bring them all up, not only at home but at school too, in a kind of odour of licensed victualism or of bagmanism, is not a wise training to give to these children. And in Germany, I have said, the action of the national guides or governors is to suggest and provide a better. But, in England, the action of the national guides or governors is, for a Royal Prince or a great Minister to go down to the opening of the Licensed Victuallers' or of the Commercial Traveller's school, to take the chair, to extol the energy and self-reliance of the Licensed Victuallers or the Commercial Travellers, to be all of their way of thinking, to predict full success to their schools, and never so much as to hint to them that they are probably doing a very foolish thing, and that the right way to go to work with their children's education is quite different. And it is the same in almost every department of affairs. While, on the Continent, the idea prevails that it is the business of the heads and representatives of the nation, by virtue of their superior means, power, and information, to set an example and to provide suggestions of right reason, among us the idea is that the business of the heads and representatives of the nation is to do nothing of the kind, but to applaud the natural taste for the bathos showing itself vigorously in any part of the community, and to encourage its works.

Now I do not say that the political system of foreign countries has not inconveniences which may outweigh the inconveniences of our own political system; nor am I the least proposing to get rid of our own political system and to adopt theirs. But a sound centre of authority being what, in this disquisition, we have been led to seek and right reason, or our best self, appearing alone to offer such a sound centre of authority, it is necessary to take note of the chief impediments which hinder, in this country, the extri-

cation or recognition of this right reason as a paramount authority, with a view to afterwards trying in what way they can best be removed.

This being borne in mind, I proceed to remark how not only do we get no suggestions of right reason, and no rebukes of our ordinary self, from our governors, but a kind of philosophical theory is widely spread among us to the effect that there is no such thing at all as a best self and a right reason having claim to paramount authority, or, at any rate, no such thing ascertainable and capable of being made use of; and that there is nothing but an infinite number of ideas and works of our ordinary selves, and suggestions of our natural taste for the bathos, pretty nearly equal in value, which are doomed either to an irreconcilable conflict, or else to a perpetual give and take; and that wisdom consists in choosing the give and take rather than the conflict, and in sticking to our choice with patience and good humour.

And, on the other hand, we have another philosophical theory rife among us, to the effect that without the labour of perverting ourselves by custom or example to relish right reason, but by continuing all of us to follow freely our natural taste for the bathos, we shall, by the mercy of Providence, and by a kind of natural tendency of things, come in due time to relish and follow right reason.

The great promoters of these philosophical theories are our newspapers, which, no less than our parliamentary representatives, may be said to act the part of guides and governors to us; and these favourite doctrines of theirs I call,—or should call, if the doctrines were not preached by authorities I so much respect,—the first, a peculiarly British form of Atheism, the second, a peculiarly British form of Quietism. The first-named melancholy doctrine is preached in the *Times* with great clearness and force of style; indeed, it is well known, from the example of the poet Lucretius and others, what great masters of style the atheistic doctrine has always counted among its promulgators. "It is of no use," says the *Times,* "for us to attempt to force upon our neighbours our several likings and dislikings. We must take things as they are. Everybody has his own little vision of religious or civil perfection. Under the evident impossibility of satisfying everybody, we agree to take our stand on equal laws and on a system as open and liberal as is

[12] Wilhelm von Humboldt (1767–1835), German statesman and educator; Friedrich Schleiermacher (1768–1834), German philosopher.

possible. The result is that everybody has more liberty of action and of speaking here than anywhere else in the Old World." We come again here upon Mr. Roebuck's celebrated definition of happiness, on which I have so often commented: "I look around me and ask what is the state of England? Is not every man able to say what he likes? I ask you whether the world over, or in past history, there is anything like it? Nothing. I pray that our unrivalled happiness may last." This is the old story of our system of checks and every Englishman doing as he likes, which we have already seen to have been convenient enough so long as there were only the Barbarians and the Philistines to do what they liked, but to be getting inconvenient, and productive of anarchy, now that the Populace wants to to what it likes too.

But for all that, I will not at once dismiss this famous doctrine, but will first quote another passage from the *Times,* applying the doctrine to a matter of which we have just been speaking,— education. "The difficulty here" (in providing a national system of education), says the *Times,* "does not reside in any removable arrangements. It is inherent and native in the actual and inveterate state of things in this country. All these powers and personages, all these conflicting influences and varieties of character, exist, and have long existed among us; they are fighting it out, and will long continue to fight it out, without coming to that happy consummation when some one element of the British character is to destroy or to absorb all the rest." There it is; the various promptings of the natural taste for the bathos in this man and that amongst us are fighting it out; and the day will never come (and, indeed, why should we wish it to come?) when one man's particular sort of taste for the bathos shall tyrannise over another man's; nor when right reason (if that may be called an element of the British character) shall absorb and rule them all. "The whole system of this country, like the constitution we boast to inherit, and are glad to uphold, is made up of established facts, prescriptive authorities, existing usages, powers that be, persons in possession, and communities or classes that have won dominion for themselves, and will hold it against all comers." Every force in the world, evidently, except the one reconciling force, right reason! Sir Thomas Bateson here, the Rev. W. Cattle on this side, Mr. Bradlaugh on that!—pull devil, pull baker! Really, presented with the mastery of style of our leading journal,

the sad picture, as one gazes upon it, assumes the iron and inexorable solemnity of tragic Destiny.

After this, the milder doctrine of our other philosophical teacher, the *Daily News,* has, at first, something very attractive and assuaging. The *Daily News* begins, indeed, in appearance, to weave the iron web of necessity round us like the *Times.* "The alternative is between a man's doing what he likes and his doing what some one else, probably not one whit wiser than himself, likes." This points to the tacit compact, mentioned in my last paper, between the Barbarians and the Philistines, and into which it is hoped that the Populace will one day enter; the compact, so creditable to English honesty, that since each class has only the ideas and aims of its ordinary self to give effect to, none of them shall, if it exercise power, treat its ordinary self too seriously, or attempt to impose it on others; but shall let these others,—the Rev. W. Cattle, for instance, in his Papist-baiting, and Mr. Bradlaugh in his Hyde Park anarchy-mongering,—have their fling. But then the *Daily News* suddenly lights up the gloom of necessitarianism with bright beams of hope. "No doubt," it says, "the common reason of society ought to check the aberrations of individual eccentricity." This common reason of society looks very like our best self or right reason, to which we want to give authority, by making the action of the *State,* or nation in its collective character, the expression of it. But of this project of ours, the *Daily News,* with its subtle dialectics, makes havoc. "Make the State the organ of the common reason?"—it says "You may make it the organ of something or other, but how can you be certain that reason will be the quality which will be embodied in it?" You cannot be certain of it, undoubtedly, if you never try to bring the thing about; but the question is, the action of the State being the action of the collective nation and the action of the collective nation carrying naturally great publicity, weight, and force of example with it, whether we should not try to put into the action of the State as much as possible of right reason, or our best self, which may, in this manner, come back to us with new force and authority; may have visibility, form, and influence; and help to confirm us, in the many moments when we are tempted to be our ordinary selves merely, in resisting our natural taste of the bathos rather than in giving way to it?

But no! says our teacher: "It is better there should be an infinite variety of experiments in human action, because, as the explorers multiply, the true track is more likely to be discovered. The common reason of society can check the aberrations of individual eccentricity only by acting on the individual reason; and it will do so in the main sufficiently, if left to this natural operation." This is what I call the specially British form of Quietism, or a devout, but excessive reliance on an over-ruling Providence. Providence, as the moralists are careful to tell us, generally works in human affairs by human means; so when we want to make right reason act on individual inclination, our best self on our ordinary self, we seek to give it more power of doing so by giving it public recognition and authority, and embodying it, so far as we can, in the State. It seems too much to ask of Providence, that while we, on our part, leave our congenital taste for the bathos to is natural operation and its infinite variety of experiments, Providence should mysteriously guide it into the true track, and compel it to relish the sublime. At any rate, great men and great institutions have hitherto seemed necessary for producing any considerable effect of this kind. No doubt we have an infinite variety of experiments, and an ever-multiplying multitude of explorers. Even in these few chapters I have enumerated many: the *British Banner,* Judge Edmonds, Newman Weeks, Deborah Butler, Elderess Polly, Brother Noyes, the Rev. W. Cattle, the Licensed Victuallers, the Commercial Travellers, and I know not how many more; and the members of the noble army are swelling every day. But what a depth of Quietism, or rather, what an over-bold call on the direct interposition of Providence, to believe that these interesting explorers will discover the true track, or at any rate, "will do so in the main well enough" (whatever that may mean) if left to their natural operation; that is, by going on as they are! Philosophers say, indeed, that we learn virtue by performing acts of virtue; but to say that we shall learn virtue by performing any acts to which our natural taste for the bathos carries us, that the Rev. W. Cattle comes at his best self by Papist-baiting, or Newman Weeks and Deborah Butler at right reason by following their noses, this certainly does appear over-sanguine.

It is true, what we want is to make right reason act on individual reason, the reason of individuals; all our search for authority has that for its end and aim. The *Daily News* says, I observe, that all my argument for authority "has a non-intellectual root;" and from what I know of my own mind and its poverty I think this so probable, that I should be inclined easily to admit it, if it were not that, in the first place, nothing of this kind, perhaps, should be admitted without examination; and, in the second, a way of accounting for the charge being made, in this particular instance, without good grounds, appears to present itself. What seems to me to account here, perhaps, for the charge, is the want of flexibility of our race, on which I have so often remarked. I mean, it being admitted that the conformity of the individual reason of the Rev. W. Cattle or Mr. Bradlaugh with right reason is our true object, and not the mere restraining them, by the strong arm of the State, from Papist-baiting or railing-breaking,—admitting this, we English have so little flexibility that we cannot readily perceive that the State's restraining them from these indulgences may yet fix clearly in their minds that, to the collective nation, these indulgences appear irrational and unallowable, may make them pause and reflect, and may contribute to bringing, with time, their individual reason into harmony with right reason. But in no country, owing to the want of intellectual flexibility above mentioned, is the leaning which is our natural one, and, therefore, needs no recommending to us, so sedulously recommended, and the leaning which is not our natural one, and, therefore, does not need dispraising to us, so sedulously dispraised, as in ours. To rely on the individual being, with us, the natural leaning, we will hear of nothing but the good of relying on the individual; to act through the collective nation on the individual being not our natural leaning, we will hear nothing in recommendation of it. But the wise know that we often need to hear most of that to which we are least inclined, and even to learn to employ, in certain circumstances, that which is capable, if employed amiss, of being a danger to us.

Elsewhere this is certainly better understood than here. In a recent number of the *Westminster Review,* an able writer, but with precisely our national want of flexibility of which I have been speaking, has unearthed, I see, for our present needs, an English translation, published some years ago, of Wilhelm von Humboldt's book, *The Sphere and Duties of Government.*[13] Humboldt's

---

[13] Reference to an anonymous article in the *Westminster Review* of January 1868 reviewing Carlyle's *Shooting Niagara* and Humboldt's *Sphere and Duties of Government.*

object in this book is to show that the operation of government ought to be severely limited to what directly and immediately relates to the security of person and property. Wilhelm von Humboldt, one of the most beautiful souls that have ever existed, used to say that one's business in life was first to perfect oneself by all the means in one's power, and secondly to try and create in the world around one an aristocracy, the most numerous that one possible could, of talents and characters. He saw, of course, that, in the end, everything comes to this,—that the individual must act for himself, and must be perfect in himself; and he lived in a country, Germany, where people were disposed to act too little for themselves, and to rely too much on the Government. But even thus, such as his flexibility, so little was he in bondage to a mere abstract maxim, that he saw very well that for his purpose itself, of enabling the individual to stand perfect on his own foundations and to do without the State, the action of the State would for long, long years be necessary. And soon after he wrote his book on *The Sphere and Duties of Government,* Wilhelm von Humboldt became Minister of Education in Prussia; and from his ministry all the great reforms which give the control of Prussian education to the State,—the transference of the management of public schools from their old boards of trustees to the State, the obligatory State-examination for schools, the obligatory State-examination for schoolmasters, and the foundation of the great State-University of Berlin,—take their origin. This his English reviewer says not a word of. But, writing for a people whose dangers lie, as we have seen, on the side of their unchecked and unguided individual action, whose dangers none of them lie on the side of an over-reliance on the State, he quotes just so much of Wilhelm von Humboldt's example as can flatter them in their propensities, and do them no good; and just what might make them think, and be of use to them, he leaves on one side. This precisely recalls the manner, it will be observed, in which we have seen that our royal and noble personages proceed with the Licensed Victuallers.

In France the action of the State on individuals is yet more preponderant than in Germany; and the need which friends of human perfection feel for what may enable the individual to stand perfect on his own foundations is all the stronger. But what says one of the staunchest of these friends, M. Renan, on State action; and even State action in that very sphere where in France

is it most excessive, the sphere of education? Here are his words:—"A Liberal believes in liberty, and liberty signifies the non-intervention of the State. *But such an ideal is still a long way off from us, and the very means to remove it to an indefinite distance would be precisely the State's withdrawing its action too soon.*" And this, he adds, is even truer of education, than of any other department of public affairs.

We see, then, how indispensable to that human perfection which we seek is, in the opinion of good judges, some public recognition and establishment of our best self, or right reason. We see how our habits and practice oppose themselves to such a recognition, and the many inconveniences which we therefore suffer. But now let us try to go a little deeper, and to find, beneath our actual habits and practice, the very ground and cause out of which they spring.

CHAPTER IV

Hebraism and Hellenism

THIS fundamental ground is our preference of doing to thinking. Now this preference is a main element in our nature, and as we study it we find ourselves opening up a number of large questions on every side.

Let me go back for a moment to Bishop Wilson, who says:—"First, never go against the best light you have; secondly, take care that your light be not darkness." We show, as a nation, laudable energy and persistence in walking according to the best light we have, but are not quite careful enough, perhaps, to see that our light be not darkness. This is only another version of the old story that energy is our strong point and favourable characteristic rather than intelligence. But we may give to this idea a more general form still, in which it will have a yet larger range of application. We may regard this energy driving at practice, this paramount sense of the obligation of duty, self-control, and work, this earnestness in going manfully with the best light we have, as one force. And we may regard the intelligence driving at those ideas which are, after all, the basis of right practice, the ardent sense for all the new and changing combinations of them which man's development brings with it, the indomitable impulse to know and adjust them perfectly, as another force. And these two forces we may regard as in some sense rivals,— rivals not by the necessity of their own nature, but as exhibited in man and his history,—and rivals dividing the empire of the world between them. And to give these forces names from the two races of men who have supplied the most signal and splendid manifestations of them, we may call them respectively the forces of Hebraism and Hellenism. Hebraism and Hellenism,—between these two points of influence moves our world. At one time it feels more powerfully the attraction of one of them, at another time of the other; and it ought to be, though it never, is evenly and happily balanced between them.

The final aim of both Hellensim and Hebraism, as of all great spiritual disciplines, is no doubt the same: man's perfection or salvation. The very language which they both of them use in schooling us to reach this aim is often identical. Even when their language indicates by variation,— sometimes a broad variation, often a but slight and subtle variation,—the different courses of thought which are uppermost in each discipline, even then the unity of the final end and aim is still apparent. To employ the actual words of that discipline with which we ourselves are all of us most familiar, and the words of which, therefore, come most home to us, that final end and aim is "that we might be partakers of the divine nature."[1] These are the words of a Hebrew apostle, but of Hellenism and Hebraism alike this is, I say, the aim. When the two are confronted, as they very often are confronted, it is nearly always with what I may call a rhetorical purpose; the speaker's whole design is to exalt and enthrone one of the two, and he uses the other only as a foil and to enable him the better to give effect to his purpose. Obviously, with us, it is usually Hellenism which is thus reduced to minister to the triumph of Hebraism. There is a sermon on Greece and the Greek spirit by a man never to be mentioned without interest and respect, Frederick Robertson,[2] in which this rhetorical use of Greece and the Greek spirit, and the inadequate exhibition of them necessarily consequent upon this, is almost ludicrous, and would be censurable if it were not to be explained by the exigencies of a sermon. On the other hand, Heinrich Heine,[3] and other writers of his sort,

give us the spectacle of the tables completely turned, and of Hebraism brought in just as a foil and contrast to Hellenism, and to make the superiority of Hellenism more manifest. In both these cases there is injustice and misrepresentation. The aim and end of both Hebraism and Hellenism is, as I have said, one and the same, and this aim and end is august and admirable.

Still, they pursue this aim by very different courses. The uppermost idea with Hellenism is to see things as they really are; the uppermost idea with Hebraism is conduct and obedience. Nothing can do away with this ineffaceable difference. The Greek quarrel with the body and its desires is, that they hinder right thinking, the Hebrew quarrel with them is, that they hinder right acting. "He that keepeth the law, happy is he;" "Blessed is the man that feareth the Eternal, that delighteth greatly in his commandments,"[4] that is the Hebrew notion of felicity; and, pursued with passion and tenacity, this notion would not let the Hebrew rest till, as is well known, he had at last got out of the law a network of prescriptions to enwrap his whole life, to govern every moment of it, every impulse, every action. The Greek notion of felicity, on the other hand, is perfectly conveyed in these words of a great French moralist: *"C'est le bonheur des hommes"*— when? when they abhor that which is evil?—no; when they exercise themselves in the law of the Lord day and night?—no; when they die daily? —no; when they walk about the New Jerusalem with palms in their hands?—no; but when they think aright, when their thought hits: *"quand ils pensent juste."*[5] At the bottom of both the Greek and the Hebrew notion is the desire, native in man, for reason and the will of God, the feeling after the universal order,—in a word, the love of God. But, while Hebraism seizes upon certain plain, capital intimations of the universal order, and rivets itself, one may say, with unequalled grandeur of earnestness and intensity on the study and observance of them, the bent of Hellenism is to fellow, with flexible activity, the whole play of the universal order, to be apprehensive of missing any part of it, of sacrificing one part to another, to slip away from resting in this or that intimation of it, however capital. An unclouded clearness of mind, an unimpeded play of thought, is what this bent drives at.

---

[1] II Peter 1:4.   [2] Frederick William Robertson (1816–53), clergyman and noted preacher.
[3] Heinrich Heine (1797–1856), German poet.   [4] Proverbs 29:18; Psalms 112:1.
[5] "It is happiness for men when they think justly" (Sainte-Beuve).

The governing idea of Hellenism is *spontaneity of consciousness;* that of Hebraism, *strictness of conscience.*

Christianity changed nothing in this essential bent of Hebraism to set doing above knowing. Self-conquest, self-devotion, the following not our own individual will, but the will of God, *obedience,* is the fundamental idea of this form, also of the discipline to which we have attached the general name of Hebraism. Only as the old law and the network of prescriptions with which it enveloped human life were evidently a motive-power not driving and searching enough to produce the result aimed at,—patient continuance in well doing, self-conquest,—Christianity substituted for them boundless devotion to that inspiring and affecting pattern of self-conquest offered by Jesus Christ; and by the new motive-power, of which the essence was this, though the love and admiration of Christian churches have for centuries been employed in varying, amplifying, and adorning the plain description of it, Christianity, as St. Paul truly says, "establishes the law," and in the strength of the ampler power which she had thus supplied to fulfil it, has accomplished the miracles, which we all see, of her history.

So long as we do not forget that both Hellenism and Hebraism are profound and admirable manifestations of man's life, tendencies, and powers, and that both of them aim at a like final result, we can hardly insist too strongly on the divergence of line and of operation with which they proceed. It is a divergence so great that it most truly, as the prophet Zechariah says, "has raised up thy sons, O Zion, against thy sons, O Greece!"[6] The difference whether it is by doing or by knowing that we set most store, and the practical consequences which follow from this difference, leave their mark on all the history of our race and of its development. Language may be abundantly quoted from both Hellenism and Hebraism to make it seem that one follows the same current as the other towards the same goal. They are, truly, borne towards the same goal; but the currents which bear them are infinitely different. It is true, Solomon will praise knowing: "Understanding is a well-spring of life unto him that hath it." And in the New Testament, again, Jesus Christ is a "light," and "truth makes us free."[7] It is true, Aristotle will under-value knowing: "In what concerns virtue,"

says he, "three things are necessary—knowledge, deliberate will, and perseverance; but, whereas the two last are all-important, the first is a matter of little importance." It is true that with the same impatience with which St. James enjoins a man to be not a forgetful hearer, but a *doer of the work,* Epictetus exhorts us to *do* what we have demonstrated to ourselves we ought to do; or he taunts us with futility, for being armed at all points to prove that lying is wrong, yet all the time continuing to lie. It is true, Plato, in words which are almost the words of the New Testament or the Imitation,[8] calls life a learning to die. But underneath the superficial agreement the fundamental divergence still subsists. The understanding of Solomon is "the walking in the way of the commandments;" this is "the way of peace,"[9] and it is of this that blessedness comes. In the New Testament, the truth which gives us the peace of God and makes us free, is the love of Christ constraining us to crucify, as he did, and with a like purpose of moral regeneration, the flesh with its affections and lusts, and thus establishing, as we have seen, the law. To St. Paul it appears possible to "hold the truth in unrighteousness," which is just what Socrates judged impossible. The moral virtues, on the other hand, are with Aristotle but the porch and access to the intellectual, and with these last is blessedness. That partaking of the divine life, which both Hellenism and Hebraism, as we have said, fix as their crowning aim, Plato expressly denies to the man of practical virtue merely, of self-conquest with any other motive than that of perfect intellectual vision. He reserves it for the lover of pure knowledge, of seeing things as they really are, the φιλομαθής.[10]

Both Hellenism and Hebraism arise out of the wants of human nature, and address themselves to satisfying those wants. But their methods are so different, they lay stress on such different points, and call into being by their respective disciplines such different activities, that the face which human nature presents when it passes from the hands of one of them to those of the other, is no longer the same. To get rid of one's ignorance, to see things as they are, and by seeing them as they are to see them in their beauty, is the simple and attractive ideal which Hellenism holds out before human nature; and from the simplicity and charm of this ideal, Hellenism, and human life in the hands of

---

[6] Zechariah 9:13.   [7] Proverbs 16:22; John 1:4–9, 8:12; Luke 2:32; John 8:32.
[8] I.e., *The Imitation of Christ.*   [9] Proverbs 1 to 3.   [10] The lover of learning.

Hellenism, is invested with a kind of aërial ease, clearness, and radiancy; they are full of what we call sweetness and light. Difficulties are kept out of view, and the beauty and rationalness of the ideal have all our thoughts. "The best man is he who most tries to perfect himself, and the happiest man is he who most feels that he *is* perfecting himself,"—this account of the matter by Socrates, the true Socrates of the *Memorabilia*,[11] has something so simple, spontaneous, and unsophisticated about it, that it seems to fill us with clearness and hope when we hear it. But there is a saying which I have heard attributed to Mr. Carlyle about Socrates,—a very happy saying, whether it is really Mr. Carlyle's or not,—which excellently marks the essential point in which Hebraism differs from Hellenism. "Socrates," this saying goes, "is terribly *at ease in Zion.*" Hebraism,—and here is the source of its wonderful strength,—has always been severely pre-occupied with an awful sense of the impossibility of being at ease in Zion; of the difficulties which oppose themselves to man's pursuit or attainment of that perfection of which Socrates talks so hopefully, and, as from this point of view one might almost say, so glibly. It is all very well to talk of getting rid of one's ignorance, of seeing things in their reality, seeing them in their beauty; but how is this to be done when there is something which thwarts and spoils all our efforts?

This something is *sin;* and the space which sin fills in Hebraism, as compared with Hellenism, is indeed prodigious. This obstacle to perfection fills the whole scene, and perfection appears remote and rising away from earth, in the background. Under the name of sin, the difficulties of knowing oneself and conquering oneself which impede man's passage to perfection, become, for Hebraism, a positive, active entity hostile to man, a mysterious power which I heard Dr. Pusey[12] the other day, in one of his impressive sermons, compare to a hideous hunchback seated on our shoulders, and which it is the main business of our lives to hate and oppose. The discipline of the Old Testament may be summed up as a discpline teaching us to abhor and flee from sin; the discipline of the New Testament, as a discipline teaching us to die to it. As Hellenism speaks of thinking clearly, seeing things in their essence and beauty, as a grand and precious feat for man to achieve, so Hebraism speaks of becoming conscious of sin, of awakening to a sense of sin, as a feat of this kind. It is obvious to what wide divergence these differing tendencies, actively followed, must lead. As one passes and repasses from Hellenism to Hebraism, from Plato to St. Paul, one feels inclined to rub one's eyes and ask oneself whether man is indeed a gentle and simple being, showing the traces of a noble and divine nature; or an unhappy chained captive, labouring with groanings that cannot be uttered to free himself from the body of this death.

Apparently it was the Hellenic conception of human nature which was unsound, for the world could not live by it. Absolutely to call it unsound, however, is to fall into the common error of its Hebraising enemies; but it was unsound at that particular moment of man's development, it was premature. The indispensable basis of conduct and self-control, the platform upon which alone the perfection aimed at by Greece can come into bloom, was not to be reached by our race so easily; centuries of probation and discipline were needed to bring us to it. Therefore the bright promise of Hellenism faded, and Hebraism ruled the world. Then was seen that astonishing spectacle, so well marked by the often-quoted the world. Then was seen that astonishing words of the prophet Zechariah, when men of all languages and nations took hold of the skirt of him that was a Jew, saying:—"*We will go with you, for we have heard that God is with you.*"[13] And the Hebraism which thus received and ruled a world all gone out of the way and altogether become unprofitable, was, and could not but be, the later, the more spiritual, the more attractive development of Hebraism. It was Christianity; that is to say, Hebraism aiming at self-conquest and rescue from the thrall of vile affections, not by obedience to the letter of a law, but by conformity to the image of a self-sacrificing example. To a world stricken with moral enervation Christianity offered its spectacle of an inspired self-sacrifice; to men who refused themselves nothing, it showed one who refused himself everything;—"*my Saviour banished joy!*" says George Herbert.[14] When the *alma Venus,* the life-giving and joy-giving power of nature, so fondly cherished by the pagan world, could not save her followers from self-dissatisfaction and ennui, the severe words of the apostle came bracingly and refreshingly: "Let no man deceive you with vain words, for because of these things cometh the wrath of God upon the children of

---

[11] By Xenophon.   [12] Edward Bouverie Pusey (1800–82), leader of the Oxford Movement.
[13] Zechariah 8:23.   [14] Herbert's "The Size."

disobedience."[15] Through age after age and generation after generation, our race, or all that part of our race which was most living and progressive, was *baptized into a death*;[16] and endeavoured, by suffering in the flesh, to cease from sin. Of this endeavour, the animating labours and afflictions of early Christianity, the touching asceticism of mediæval Christianity, are the great historical manifestations. Literary monuments of it, each in its own way incomparable, remain in the Epistles of St. Paul, in St. Augustine's Confessions, and in the two original and simplest books of the Imitation.[17]

Of two disciplines laying their main stress, the one, on clear intelligence, the other, on firm obedience; the one, on comprehensively knowing the grounds of one's duty, the other, on diligently practising it; the one, on taking all possible care (to use Bishop Wilson's words again) that the light we have be not darkness, the other, that according to the best light we have we diligently walk,—the priority naturally belongs to that discipline which braces all man's moral powers, and founds for him an indispensable basis of character. And, therefore, it is justly said of the Jewish people, who were charged with setting powerfully forth that side of the divine order to which the words *conscience* and *self-conquest* point, that they were "entrusted with the oracles of God;"[18] as it is justly said of Christianity, which followed Judaism and which set forth this side with a much deeper effectiveness and a much wider influence, that the wisdom of the old Pagan world was foolishness compared to it. No words of devotion and admiration can be too strong to render thanks to these beneficent forces which have so borne forward humanity in its appointed work of coming to the knowledge and possession of itself; above all, in those great moments when their action was the wholesomest and the most necessary.

But the evolution of these forces, separately and in themselves, is not the whole evolution of humanity,—their single history is not the whole history of man; whereas their admirers are always apt to make it stand for the whole history. Hebraism and Hellenism are, neither of them, the *law* of human development, as their admirers are prone to make them; they are, each of them, *contributions* to human development,—august contributions, invaluable contributions; and each

showing itself to us more august, more invaluable, more preponderant over the other, according to the moment in which we take them, and the relation in which we stand to them. The nations of our modern world, children of that immense and salutary movement which broke up the Pagan world, inevitably stand to Hellenism in a relation which dwarfs it, and to Hebraism in a relation which magnifies it. They are inevitably prone to take Hebraism as the law of human development, and not as simply a contribution to it, however precious. And yet the lesson must perforce be learned, that the human spirit is wider than the most priceless of the forces which bear it onward, and that to the whole development of man Hebraism itself is, like Hellenism, but a contribution.

Perhaps we may help ourselves to see this clearer by an illustration drawn from the treatment of a single great idea which has profoundly engaged the human spirit, and has given it eminent opportunities for showing its nobleness and energy. It surely must be perceived that the idea of immortality, as this idea rises in its generality before the human spirit, is something grander, truer, and more satisfying, than it is in the particular forms by which St. Paul, in the famous fifteenth chapter of the Epistle to the Corinthians, and Plato, in the *Phædo*, endeavour to develop and establish it. Surely we cannot but feel that the argumentation with which the Hebrew apostle goes about to expound this great idea is, after all, confused and inconclusive; and that the reasoning, drawn from analogies of likeness and equality, which is employed upon it by the Greek philosopher, is over-subtle and sterile. Above and beyond the inadequate solutions which Hebraism and Hellenism here attempt, extends the immense and august problem itself, and the human spirit which gave birth to it. And this single illustration may suggest to us how the same thing happens in other cases also.

But meanwhile, by alternations of Hebraism and Hellenism, of a man's intellectual and moral impulses, of the effort to see things as they really are and the effort to win peace by self-conquest, the human spirit proceeds; and each of these two forces has its appointed hours of culmination and seasons of rule. As the great movement of Christianity was a triumph of Hebraism and man's moral impulses, so the great movement

---

[15] Ephesians 5:6.   [16] Romans 6:3.   [17] The first two books. [Arnold's note]
[18] Romans 3:2.

which goes by the name of the Renascence[19] was an uprising and re-instatement of man's intellectual impulses and of Hellenism. We in England, the devoted children of Protestantism, chiefly know the Renascence by its subordinate and secondary side of the Reformation. The Reformation has been often called a Hebraising revival, a return to the ardour and sincereness of primitive Christianity. No one, however, can study the development of Protestantism and of Protestant churches without feeling that into the Reformation too,—Hebraising child of the Renascence and offspring of its fervour, rather than its intelligence, as it undoubtedly was,—the subtle Hellenic leaven of the Renascence found its way, and that the exact respective parts, in the Reformation, of Hebraism and of Hellenism, are not easy to separate. But what we may with truth say is, that all which Protestantism was to itself clearly conscious of, all which it succeeded in clearly setting forth in words, had the characters of Hebraism rather than of Hellenism. The Reformation was strong, in that it was an earnest return to the Bible and to doing from the heart the will of God as there written. It was weak, in that it never consciously grasped or applied the central idea of the Renascence,—the Hellenic idea of pursuing, in all lines of activity, the law and science, to use Plato's words, of things as they really are. Whatever direct superiority, therefore, Protestantism had over Catholicism was a moral superiority, a superiority arising out of its greater sincerity and earnestness,—at the moment of its apparition at any rate,—in dealing with the heart and conscience. Its pretensions to an intellectual superiority are in general quite illusory. For Hellenism, for the thinking side in man as distinguished from the acting side, the attitude of mind of Protestantism towards the Bible in no respect differs from the attitude of mind of Catholicism towards the Church. The mental habit of him who imagines that Balaam's ass[20] spoke, in no respect differs from the mental habit of him who imagines that a Madonna of wood or stone winked; and the one, who says that God's Church makes him believe what he believes, and the other, who says that God's Word makes him believe what he believes, are for the philosopher perfectly alike in not really and truly knowing, when they say *God's Church* and *God's Word*, what it is they say, or whereof they affirm.

In the sixteenth century, therefore, Hellenism re-entered the world, and again stood in presence of Hebraism,—a Hebraism renewed and purged. Now, it has not been enough observed, how, in the seventeenth century, a fate befell Hellenism in some respects analogous to that which befell it at the commencement of our era. The Renascence, that great re-awakening of Hellenism, that irresistible return of humanity to nature and to seeing things as they are, which in art, in literature, and in physics, produced such splendid fruits, had, like the anterior Hellenism of the Pagan world, a side of moral weakness, and of relaxation or insensibility of the moral fibre, which in Italy showed itself with the most startling plainness, but which in France, England, and other countries, was very apparent too. Again this loss of spiritual balance, this exclusive preponderance given to man's perceiving and knowing side, this unnatural defect of his feeling and acting side, provoked a reaction. Let us trace that reaction where it most nearly concerns us.

Science has now made visible to everybody the great and pregnant elements of difference which lie in race, and in how signal a manner they make the genius and history of an Indo-European people vary from those of a Semitic people. Hellenism is of Indo-European growth, Hebraism is of Semitic growth; and we English, a nation of Indo-European stock, seem to belong naturally to the movement of Hellenism. But nothing more strongly marks the essential unity of man than the affinities we can perceive, in this point or that, between members of one family of peoples and members of another, and no affinity of this kind is more strongly marked than that likeness in the strength and prominence of the moral fibre, which, notwithstanding immense elements of difference, knits in some special sort the genius and history of us English, and our American descendants across the Atlantic, to the genius and history of the Hebrew people. Puritanism, which has been so great a power in the English nation, and in the strongest part of the English nation, was originally the reaction in the seventeenth century of the conscience and moral sense of our race, against the moral indifference and lax rule of conduct which in the sixteenth century came in

---

[19] I have ventured to give to the foreign word *Renaissance,*—destined to become of more common use amongst us as the movement which it denotes comes, as it will come, increasingly to interest us,—an English form. [Arnold's note]

[20] Numbers 22:22–35.

with the Renascence. It was a reaction of Hebraism against Hellenism; and it powerfully manifested itself, as was natural, in a people with much of what we call a Hebraising turn, with a signal affinity for the bent which was the master-bent of Hebrew life. Eminently Indo-European by its *humour,* by the power it shows, through this gift, of imaginatively acknowledging the multiform aspects of the problem of life, and of thus getting itself unfixed from its own over-certainty, of smiling at its own over-tenacity, our race has yet (and a great part of its strength lies here), in matters of practical life and moral conduct, a strong share of the assuredness, the tenacity, the intensity of the Hebrews. This turn manifested itself in Puritanism, and has had a great part in shaping our history for the last two hundred years. Undoubtedly it checked and changed amongst us that movement of the Renascence which we see producing in the reign of Elizabeth such wonderful fruits. Undoubtedly it stopped the prominent rule and direct development of that order of ideas which we call by the name of Hellenism, and gave the first rank to a different order of ideas. Apparently, too, as we said of the former defeat of Hellenism, if Hellenism was defeated, this shows that Hellenism was imperfect, and that its ascendency at that moment would not have been for the world's good. ·

Yet there is a very important difference between the defeat inflicted on Hellenism by Christianity eighteen hundred years ago, and the check given to the Renascence by Puritanism. The greatness of the difference is well measured by the difference in force, beauty, significance and usefulness, between primitive Christianity and Protestant-ism. Eighteen hundred years ago it was al-together the hour of Hebraism. Primitive Christianity was legitimately and truly the ascendant force in the world at that time, and the way of mankind's progress lay through its full development. Another hour in man's develop-ment began in the fifteenth century, and the main road of his progress then lay for a time through Hellenism. Puritanism was no longer the central current of the world's progress, it was a side stream crossing the central current and checking it. The cross and the check may have been necessary and salutary, but that does not do away with the essential difference between the main stream of man's advance and a cross or side stream. For more than two hundred years

the main stream of man's advance has moved towards knowing himself and the world, seeing things as they are, spontaneity of consciousness; the main impulse of a great part, and that the strongest part, of our nation has been towards strictness of conscience. They have made the secondary the principal at the wrong moment, and the principal they have at the wrong moment treated as secondary. This contravention of the natural order has produced, as such contra-vention always must produce, a certain con-fusion and false movement, of which we are now beginning to feel, in almost every direction, the inconvenience. In all directions our habitual courses of action seem to be losing efficaciousness, credit, and control, both with others and even with ourselves; everywhere we see the beginnings of confusion, and we want a clue to some sound order and authority. This we can only get by going back upon the actual instincts and forces which rule our life, seeing them as they really are, connecting them with other instincts and forces, and enlarging our whole view and rule of life.

CHAPTER V

Porro Unum Est Necessarium[1]

THE matter here opened is so large, and the trains of thought to which it gives rise are so manifold, that we must be careful to limit ourselves scrupulously to what has a direct bearing upon our actual discussion. We have found that at the bottom of our present unsettled state, so full of the seeds of trouble, lies the notion of its being the prime right and happiness, for each of us, to affirm himself, and his ordinary self; to be doing, and to be doing freely and as he likes. We have found at the bottom of it the disbelief in right reason as a lawful authority. It was easy to show from our practice and current history that this is so; but it was impossible to show why it is so without taking a somewhat wider sweep and going into things a little more deeply. Why, in fact, should good, well-meaning, energetic, sensible people, like the bulk of our countrymen, come to have such light belief in

---

[1] "For one thing is needful" (Luke 10:41–42).

right reason, and such an exaggerated value for their own independent doing, however crude? The answer is: because of an exclusive and excessive development in them, without due allowance for time, place, and circumstance, of that side of human nature, and that group of human forces, to which we have given the general name of Hebraism. Because they have thought their real and only important homage was owed to a power concerned with their obedience rather than with their intelligence, a power interested in the moral side of their nature almost exclusively. Thus they have been led to regard in themselves, as the one thing needful, *strictness of conscience*, the staunch adherence to some fixed law of doing we have got already, instead of *spontaneity of consciousness*, which tends continually to enlarge our whole law of doing. They have fancied themselves to have in their religion a sufficient basis for the whole of their life fixed and certain for ever, a full law of conduct and a full law of thought, so far as thought is needed, as well; whereas what they really have is a law of conduct, a law of unexampled power for enabling them to war against the law of sin in their members and not to serve it in the lusts thereof. The book which contains this invaluable law they call the Word of God, and attribute to it, as I have said, and as, indeed, is perfectly well known, a reach and sufficiency co-extensive with all the wants of human nature.

This might, no doubt, be so, if humanity were not the composite thing it is, if it had only, or in quite over-powering eminence, a moral side, and the group of instincts and powers which we call moral. But it has besides, and in notable eminence, an intellectual side, and the group of instincts and powers which we call intellectual. No doubt, mankind makes in general its progress in a fashion which gives at one time full swing to one of these groups of instincts, at another time to the other; and man's faculties are so intertwined, that when his moral side, and the current of force which we call Hebraism, is uppermost, this side will manage somehow to provide, or appear to provide, satisfaction for his intellectual needs; and when his intellectual side, and the current of force which we call Hellenism, is uppermost, this again will provide, or appear to provide, satisfaction for men's moral needs. But sooner or later it becomes a manifest that when the two sides of humanity proceed in this fashion of alternate preponderance, and not of mutual

understanding and balance, the side which is uppermost does not really provide in a satisfactory manner for the needs of the side which is undermost, and a state of confusion is, sooner or later, the result. The Hellenic half of our nature, bearing rule, makes a sort of provision for the Hebrew half, but it turns out to be an inadequate provision; and again the Hebrew half of our nature, bearing rule, makes a sort of provision for the Hellenic half, but this, too, turns out to be an inadequate provision. The true and smooth order of humanity's development is not reached in either way. And therefore, while we willingly admit with the Christian apostle that the world by wisdom,—that is, by the isolated preponderance of its intellectual impulses,—knew not God,[2] or the true order of things, it is yet necessary, also, to set up a sort of converse to this proposition, and to say likewise (what is equally true) that the world by Puritanism knew not God. And it is on this converse of the apostle's proposition that it is particularly needful to insist in our own country just at present.

Here, indeed, is the answer to many criticisms which have been addressed to all that we have said in praise of sweetness and light. Sweetness and light evidently have to do with the bent or side in humanity which we call Hellenic. Greek intelligence has obviously for its essence the instinct for what Plato calls the true, firm, intelligible law of things; the law of light, of seeing things as they are. Even in the natural sciences, where the Greeks had not time and means adequately to apply this instinct, and where we have gone a great deal further than they did, it is this instinct which is the root of the whole matter and the ground of all our success; and this instinct the world has mainly learnt of the Greeks, inasmuch as they are humanity's most signal manifestation of it. Greek art, again, Greek beauty, have their root in the same impulse to see things as they really are, inasmuch as Greek art and beauty rest on fidelity to nature,—the *best* nature,—and on a delicate discrimination of what this best nature is. To say we work for sweetness and light, then, is only another way of saying that we work for Hellenism. But, oh! cry many people, sweetness and light are not enough; you must put strength or energy along with them, and make a kind of trinity of strength, sweetness and light, and then, perhaps, you may do some good. That is to say, we are to join Hebraism, strictness of the moral conscience, and manful

[2] I Corinthians 1:22.

walking by the best light we have, together with Hellenism, inculcate both, and rehearse the praises of both.

Or, rather, we may praise both in conjunction, but we must be careful to praise Hebraism most. "Culture," says an acute, though somewhat rigid critic, Mr. Sidgwick,[3] "diffuses sweetness and light. I do not undervalue these blessings, but religion gives fire and strength, and the world wants fire and strength even more than sweetness and light." By religion, let me explain, Mr. Sidgwick here means particularly that Puritanism on the insufficiency of which I have been commenting and to which he says I am unfair. Now, no doubt, it is possible to be a fanatical partisan of light and the instincts which push us to it, a fanatical enemy of strictness of moral conscience and the instincts which push us to it. A fanaticism of this sort deforms and vulgarises the well-known work, in some respects so remarkable, of the late Mr. Buckle. Such a fanaticism carries its own mark with it, in lacking sweetness; and its own penalty, in that, lacking sweetness, it comes in the end to lack light too. And the Greeks,—the great exponents of humanity's bent for sweetness and light united, of its perception that the truth of things must be at the same time beauty,—singularly escaped the fanaticism which we moderns, whether we Hellenise or whether we Hebraise, are so apt to show. They arrived,—though failing, as has been said, to give adequate practical satisfaction to the claims of man's moral side,—at the idea of a comprehensive adjustment of the claims of both the sides in man, the moral as well as the intellectual, of a full estimate of both, and of a reconciliation of both; an idea which is philosophically of the greatest value, and the best of lessons for us moderns. So we ought to have no difficulty in conceding to Mr. Sidgwick that manful walking by the best light one has,— fire and strength as he calls it,—has its high value as well as culture, the endeavour to see things in their truth and beauty, the pursuit of sweetness and light. But whether at this or that time, and to this or that set of persons, one ought to insist most on the praises of fire and strength, or on the praises of sweetness and light, must depend, one would think, on the circumstances and needs of that particular time and those particular persons. And all that we have been saying, and indeed any glance at the world around us, shows that with us, with the most

respectable and strongest part of us, the ruling force is now, and long has been, a Puritan force,—the care for fire and strength, strictness of conscience, Hebraism, rather than the care for sweetness and light, spontaneity of consciousness, Hellenism.

Well, then, what is the good of our now rehearsing the praises of fire and strength to ourselves, who dwell too exclusively on them already? When Mr. Sidgwick says so broadly, that the world wants fire and strength even more than sweetness and light, is he not carried away by a turn for broad generalisation? does he not forget that the world is not all of one piece, and every piece with the same needs at the same time? It may be true that the Roman world at the beginning of our era, or Leo the Tenth's Court at the time of the Reformation, or French society in the eighteenth century, needed fire and strength even more than sweetness and light. But it can be said that the Barbarians who overran the empire needed fire and strength even more than sweetness and light; or that the Puritans needed them more; or that Mr. Murphy, the Birmingham lecturer, and the Rev. W. Cattle and his friends, need them more?

The Puritan's great danger is that he imagines himself in possession of a rule telling him the *unum necessarium,* or one thing needful, and that he then remains satisfied with a very crude conception of what this rule really is and what it tells him, thinks he has now knowledge and henceforth needs only to act, and, in this dangerous state of assurance and self-satisfaction, proceeds to give full swing to a number of the instincts of his ordinary self. Some of the instincts of his ordinary self he has, by the help of his rule of life, conquered; but others which he has not conquered by this help he is so far from perceiving to need subjugation, and to be instincts of an inferior self, that he even fancies it to be his right and duty, in virtue of having conquered a limited part of himself, to give unchecked swing to the remainder. He is, I say, a victim of Hebraism, of the tendency to cultivate strictness of conscience rather than spontaneity of consciousness. And what he wants is a larger conception of human nature, showing him the number of other points at which his nature must come to its best, besides the points which he himself knows and thinks of. There is no *unum necessarium,* or one thing needful, which can free human nature from the obligation of trying to come to its best

---

[3] Henry Sidgwick (1838–1900), Cambridge philosopher.

at all these points. The real *unum necessarium* for us is to come to our best at all points. Instead of our "one thing needful, justifying in us vulgarity, hideousness, ignorance, violence,—our vulgarity, hideousness, ignorance, violence, are really so many touchstones which try our one thing needful, and which prove that in the state, at any rate, in which we ourselves have it, it is not all we want. And as the force which encourages us to stand staunch and fast by the rule and ground we have is Hebraism, so the force which encourages us to go back upon this rule, and to try the very ground on which we appear to stand, is Hellenism,—a turn for giving our consciousness free play and enlarging its range. And what I say is, not that Hellenism is always for everybody more wanted than Hebraism, but that for the Rev. W. Cattle at this particular moment, and for the great majority of us his fellow-countrymen, it is more wanted.

Nothing is more striking than to observe in how many ways a limited conception of human nature, the notion of a one thing needful, a one side in us to be made uppermost, the disregard of a full and harmonious development of ourselves, tells injuriously on our thinking and acting. In the first place, our hold upon the rule or standard to which we look for our one thing needful, tends to become less and less near and vital, our conception of it more and more mechanical, and more and more unlike the thing itself as it was conceived in the mind where it originated. The dealings of Puritanism with the writings of St. Paul afford a noteworthy illustration of this. Nowhere so much as in the writings of St. Paul, and in that great apostle's greatest work, the Epistle to the Romans, has Puritanism found what seemed to furnish it with the one thing needful, and to give it canons of truth absolute and final. Now all writings, as has been already said, even the most precious writings and the most fruitful, must inevitably, from the very nature of things, be but contributions to human thought and human development, which extend wider than they do. Indeed, St. Paul, in the very Epistle of which we are speaking, shows, when he asks, "Who hath known the mind of the Lord?"—who hath known, that is, the true and divine order of things in its entirety,—that he himself acknowledges this fully. And we have already pointed out in another Epistle of St. Paul a great and vital idea of the human spirit,—the idea of immortality,—transcending and overlapping, so to speak, the expositor's power to give it adequate definition and expression.

But quite distinct from the question whether St. Paul's expression, or any man's expression, can be a perfect and final expression of truth, comes the question whether we rightly seize and understand his expression as it exists. Now, perfectly to seize another man's meaning, as it stood in his own mind, is not easy; especially when the man is separated from us by such differences of race, training, time, and circumstances at St. Paul. But there are degrees of nearness in getting at a man's meaning; and though we cannot arrive quite at what St. Paul had in his mind, yet we may come near it. And who, that comes thus near it, must not feel how terms which St. Paul employs, in trying to follow with his analysis of such profound power and originality some of the most delicate, intricate, obscure, and contradictory workings and states of the human spirit, are detached and employed by Puritanism, not in the connected and fluid way in which St. Paul employs them, and for which alone words are really meant, but in an isolated, fixed, mechanical way, as if they were talismans; and how all trace and sense of St. Paul's true movement of ideas, and sustained masterly analysis, is thus lost? Who, I say, that has watched Puritanism,—the force which so strongly Hebraises, which so takes St. Paul's writings as something absolute and final, containing the one thing needful,—handle such terms as *grace, faith, election, righteousness,* but must feel, not only that these terms have for the mind of Puritanism a sense false and misleading, but also that this sense is the most monstrous and grotesque caricature of the sense of St. Paul, and that his true meaning is by these worshippers of his words altogether lost?

Or to take another eminent example, in which not Puritanism only, but, one may say, the whole religious world, by their mechanical use of St. Paul's writings, can be shown to miss or change his real meaning. The whole religious world, one may say, use now the word *resurrection,*—a word which is so often in their thoughts and on their lips, and which they find so often in St. Paul's writings,—in one sense only. They use it to mean a rising again after the physical death of the body. Now it is quite true that St. Paul speaks of resurrection in this sense, that he tries to describe and explain it, and that he condemns those who doubt and deny it. But it is true, also, that in nine cases out of ten where St. Paul thinks and speaks of resurrection, he thinks and speaks of it in a sense different from this;—in the sense of a rising to a new life before the physical death of the body, and not after it. The idea on which we have already touched, the profound idea of being baptized into the death of the great exemplar of self-devotion and self-annulment, of repeating in our own person, by virtue of identification with our exemplar, his course of self-devotion and self-annulment, and of thus coming, within the limits of our present life, to a new life, in which, as in the death going before it, we are identified with our exemplar,—this is the fruitful and original conception of being *risen with Christ* which possesses the mind of St. Paul, and this is the central point round which, with such incomparable emotion and eloquence, all his teaching moves. For him, the life after our physical death is really in the main but a consequence and continuation of the inexhaustible energy of the new life thus originated on this side the grave. This grand Pauline idea of Christian resurrection is worthily rehearsed in one of the noblest collects of the Prayer-Book, and is destined, no doubt, to fill a more and more important place in the Christianity of the future. But meanwhile, almost as signal as the essentialness of this characteristic idea in St. Paul's teaching, is the completeness with which the worshippers of St. Paul's words as an absolute final expression of saving truth have lost it, and have substituted for the apostle's living and near conception of a resurrection now, their mechanical and remote conception of a resurrection hereafter.

In short, so fatal is the notion of possessing, even in the most precious words or standards, the one thing needful, of having in them, once for all, a full and sufficient measure of light to guide us, and of there being no duty left for us except to make our practice square exactly with them,—so fatal, I say, is this notion to the right knowledge and comprehension of the very words or standards we thus adopt, and to such strange distortions and perversions of them does it inevitably lead, that whenever we hear that commonplace which Hebraism, if we venture to inquire what a man knows, is so apt to bring out against us, in disparagement of what we call culture, and in praise of a man's sticking to the one thing needful,—*he knows*, says Hebraism, *his Bible!*—whenever we hear this said, we may, without any elaborate defence of culture, content ourselves with answering simply: "No man, who knows nothing else, knows even his Bible."

Now the force which we have so much neglected, Hellenism, may be liable to fail in moral strength and earnestness, but by the law of its nature,—the very same law which makes it sometimes deficient in intensity when intensity is required,—it opposes itself to the notion of cutting our being in two, of attributing to one part the dignity of dealing with the one thing needful, and leaving the other part to take its chance, which is the bane of Hebraism. Essential in Hellenism is the impulse to the development of the whole man, to connecting and harmonising all parts of him, perfecting all, leaving none to take their chance.

The characteristic bent of Hellenism, as has been said, is to find the intelligible law of things, to see them in their true nature and as they really are. But many things are not seen in their true nature and as they really are, unless they are seen as beautiful. Behaviour is not intelligible, does not account for itself to the mind and show the reason for its existing, unless it is beautiful. The same with discourse, the same with song, the same with worship, all of them modes in which man proves his activity and expresses himself. To think that when one produces in these what is mean, or vulgar, or hideous, one can be permitted to plead that one has that within which passes show; to suppose that the possession of what benefits and satisfies one part of our being can make allowable either discourse like Mr. Murphy's and the Rev. W. Cattle's, or poetry like the hymns we all hear, or places of worship like the chapels we all see,—this it is abhorrent to the nature of Hellenism to concede. And to be, like our honoured and justly honoured Faraday,[4] a great natural philosopher with one side of his being and a Sandemanian[5] with the other, would to Archimedes have been impossible.

It is evident to what a many-sided perfecting of man's powers and activities this demand of Hellenism for satisfaction to be given to the mind by everything which we do, is calculated to impel our race. It has its dangers, as has been fully granted. The notion of this sort of equipollency in man's modes of activity may lead to moral relaxation; what we do not make our one thing needful, we may come to treat not enough as if it were needful, though it is indeed very needful and at the same time very hard. Still, what side in us has not its dangers, and

---

[4] Michael Faraday (1791–1867), English chemist and electrical scientist.
[5] Sandemanians were a Scottish sect founded by Robert Sandeman. They believed in a literal interpretation of Scripture.

which of our impulses can be a talisman to give us perfection outright, and not merely a help to bring us towards it? Has not Hebraism, as we have shown, its dangers as well as Hellenism? or have we used so excessively the tendencies in ourselves to which Hellenism makes appeal, that we are now suffering from it? Are we not, on the contrary, now suffering because we have not enough used these tendencies as a help towards perfection?

For we see whither it has brought us, the long exclusive predominance of Hebraism,—the insisting on perfection in one part of our nature and not in all; the singling out the moral side, the side of obedience and action, for such intent regard; making strictness of the moral conscience so far the principal thing, and putting off for hereafter and for another world the care for being complete at all points, the full and harmonious development of our humanity. Instead of watching and following on its ways the desire which, as Plato says," for ever through all the universe tends towards that which is lovely," we think that the world has settled its accounts with this desire, knows what this desire wants of it, and that all the impulses of our ordinary self which do not conflict with the terms of this settlement, in our narrow view of it, we may follow unrestrainedly, under the sanction of some such text as "Not slothful in business," or "Whatsoever thy hand findeth to do, do it with all thy might," or something else of the same kind. And to any of these impulses we soon come to give that same character of a mechanical, absolute law, which we give to our religion; we regard it, as we do our religion, as an object for strictness of conscience, not for spontaneity of consciousness; for unremitting adherence on its own account, not for going back upon, viewing in its connection with other things, and adjusting to a number of changing circumstances. We treat it, in short, just as we treat our religion,—as machinery. It is in this way that the Barbarians treat their bodily exercises, the Philistines their business, Mr. Spurgeon his voluntaryism, Mr. Bright the assertion of personal liberty, Mr. Beales the right of meeting in Hyde Park. In all those cases what is needed is a freer play of consciousness upon the object of pursuit; and in all of them Hebraism, the valuing staunchness and earnestness more than this free play, the entire subordination of thinking to doing, has led to a mistaken and misleading treatment of things.

The newspapers a short time ago contained an account of the suicide of a Mr. Smith, secretary to some insurance company, who, it was said, "laboured under the apprehension that he would come to poverty, and that he was eternally lost," And when I read these words, it occurred to me that the poor man who came to such a mournful end was, in truth, a kind of type,—by the selection of his two grand objects of concern, by their isolation from everything else, and their juxtaposition to one another,—of all the strongest, most respectable, and most representative part of our nation. "He laboured under the apprehension that he would come to poverty, and that he was eternally lost." The whole middle class have a conception of things,—a conception which makes us call them Philistines,—just like that of this poor man; though we are seldom, of course, shocked by seeing it take the distressing, violently morbid, and fatal turn, which it took with him. But how generally, with how many of us, are the main concerns of life limited to these two: the concern for making money, and the concern for saving our souls! And how entirely does the narrow and mechanical conception of our secular business proceed from a narrow and mechanical conception of our religious business! What havoc do the united conceptions make of our lives! It is because the second-named of these two master-concerns presents to us the one thing needful in so fixed, narrow, and mechanical a way, that so ignoble a fellow master-concern to it as the first-named becomes possible; and, having been once admitted, takes the same rigid and absolute character as the other.

Poor Mr. Smith had sincerely the nobler master-concern as well as the meaner,—the concern for saving his soul (according to the narrow and mechanical conception which Puritanism has of what the salvation of the soul is), as well as the concern for making money. But let us remark how many people there are, especially outside the limits of the serious and conscientious middle class to which Mr. Smith belonged, who take up with a meaner master-concern,—whether it be pleasure, or field-sports, or bodily exercises, or business, or popular agitation,—who take up with one of these exclusively, and neglect Mr. Smith's nobler master-concern, because of the mechanical form which Hebraism has given to this noble master-concern. Hebraism makes it stand, as we have said, as something talismanic, isolated, and all-sufficient, justifying our giving our ordinary selves free play in bodily exercises, or business, or popular agitation, if we have made our account square with this master-concern; and, if we have not, rendering other things indifferent, and our ordinary self all we have to follow, and to follow with all the energy that is in us, till we do. Whereas the idea of perfection at all points, the encouraging in ourselves spontaneity of consciousness, the letting a free play of thought live and flow around all our activity, the indisposition to allow one side of our activity to stand as so all-important and all-sufficing that it makes other sides indifferent,—this bent of mind in us may not only check us in following unreservedly a mean master-concern of any kind, but may even, also, bring new life and movement into that side of us which alone Hebraism concerns itself, and awaken a healthier and less mechanical activity there. Hellenism may thus actually serve to further the designs of Hebraism.

Undoubtedly it thus served in the first days of Christianity. Christianity, as has been said, occupied itself, like Hebraism, with the moral side of man exclusively, with his moral affections and moral conduct; and so far it was but a continuation of Hebraism. But it transformed and renewed Hebraism by criticising a fixed rule, which had become mechanical, and had thus lost its vital motive-power; by letting the thought play freely around this old rule, and perceive its inadequacy; by developing a new motive-power, which men's moral consciousness could take living hold of, and could move in sympathy with. What was this but an importation of Hellenism, as we have defined it, into Hebraism? St. Paul used the contradiction between the Jew's profession and practice, his short-comings on that very side of moral affection and moral conduct which the Jew and St. Paul, both of them, regarded as all in all ("Thou that sayest a man should not steal, dost thou steal? thou that sayest a man should not commit adultery, dost thou commit adultery?"[6]), for a proof of the inadequacy of the old rule of life in the Jew's mechanical conception of it; and tried to rescue him by making his consciousness play freely around this rule,—that is, by a, so far, Hellenic treatment of it. Even so we too, when we hear so much said of the growth of commercial immorality in our serious middle class, of the melting away of habits of strict probity before the temptation to get quickly rich and to cut a figure in the world; when we see, at any rate, so much confusion of thought and of practice in this great representative class of our nation,—

may we not be disposed to say, that this confusion shows that his new motive-power of grace and imputed righteousness has become to the Puritan as mechanical, and with as ineffective a hold upon his practice, as the old motive-power of the law was to the Jew? and that the remedy is the same as that which St. Paul employed,—an importation of what we have called Hellenism into his Hebraism, a making his consciousness flow freely round his petrified rule of life and renew it? Only with this difference: that whereas St. Paul imported Hellenism within the limits of our moral part only, this part being still treated by him as all in all; and whereas he well-nigh exhausted, one may say, and used to the very uttermost, the possibilities of fruitfully importing it on that side exclusively; we ought to try and import it,—guiding ourselves by the ideal of a human nature harmoniously perfect in all points,—into all the lines of our activity. Only by so doing can we rightly quicken, refresh, and renew those very instincts, now so much baffled, to which Hebraism makes appeal.

But if we will not be warned by the confusion visible enough at present in our thinking and acting, that we are in a false line in having developed our Hebrew side so exclusively, and our Hellenic side so feebly and at random, in loving fixed rules of action so much more than the intelligible law of things, let us listen to a remarkable testimony which the opinion of the world around us offers. All the world now sets great and increasing value on three objects which have long been very dear to us, and pursues them in its own way, or tries to pursue them. These three objects are industrial enterprise, bodily exercises, and freedom. Certainly we have, before and beyond our neighbours, given ourselves to these three things with ardent passion and with high success. And this our neighbours cannot but acknowledge; and they must needs, when they themselves turn to these things, have an eye to our example, and take something of our practice.

Now, generally, when people are interested in an object or pursuit, they cannot help feeling an enthusiasm for those who have already laboured successfully at it, and for their success; not only do they study them, they also love and admire them. In this way a man who is interested in the art of war not only acquaints himself with the performance of great generals, but he has an admiration and enthusiasm for them. So, too,

---

[6] Romans 2:21-22.

one who wants to be a painter or a poet cannot help loving and admiring the great painters or poets, who have gone before him and shown him the way.

But it is strange with how little of love, admiration, or enthusiasm, the world regards us and our freedom, our bodily exercises, and our industrial prowess, much as these things themselves are beginning to interest it. And is not the reason because we follow each of these things in a mechanical manner, as an end in and for itself, and not in reference to a general end of human perfection; and this makes the pursuit of them uninteresting to humanity, and not what the world truly wants? It seems to them mere machinery that we can, knowingly, teach them to worship,—a mere fetish. British freedom, British industry, British muscularity, we work for each of these three things blindly, with no notion of giving each its due proportion and prominence, because we have no ideal of harmonious human perfection before our minds, to set our work in motion, and to guide it. So the rest of the world, desiring industry, or freedom, or bodily strength, yet desiring these not, as we do, absolutely, but as means to something else, imitate, indeed, of our practice what seems useful for them, but us, whose practice they imitate, they seem to entertain neither love nor admiration for.

Let us observe, on the other hand, the love and enthusiasm excited by others who have laboured for these very things. Perhaps of what we call industrial enterprise it is not easy to find examples in former times; but let us consider how Greek freedom and Greek gymnastics have attracted the love and praise of mankind, who give so little love and praise to ours. And what can be the reason of this difference? Surely because the Greeks pursued freedom and pursued gymnastics not mechanically, but with constant reference to some ideal of complete human perfection and happiness. And therefore, in spite of faults and failures they interest and delight by their pursuit of them all the rest of mankind, who instinctively feel that only as things are pursued with reference to this ideal are they valuable.

Here again, therefore, as in the confusion into which the thought and action of even the steadiest class amonst us is beginning to fall, we seem to have an admonition that we have fostered our Hebraising instincts, our preference of earnestness of doing to delicacy and flexibility of thinking, too exclusively, and have been landed by them in a mechanical and unfruitful routine. And again we seem taught that the development of our Hellenising instincts, seeking ardently the intelligible law of things, and making a stream of fresh thought play freely about our stock notions and habits, is what is most wanted by us at present.

Well, then, from all sides, the more we go into the matter, the currents seem to converge, and together to bear us along towards culture. If we look at the world outside us we find a disquieting absence of sure authority. We discover that only in right reason can we get a source of sure authority; and culture brings us towards right reason. If we look at our own inner world, we find all manner of confusion arising out of the habits of unintelligent routine and one-sided growth, to which a too exclusive worship of fire, strength, earnestness, and action, has brought us. What we want is a fuller harmonious development of our humanity, a free play of thought upon our routine notions, spontaneity of consciousness, sweetness and light; and these are just what culture generates and fosters. Proceeding from this idea of the harmonious perfection of our humanity, and seeking to help itself up towards this perfection by knowing and spreading the best which has been reached in the world—an object not to be gained without books and reading— culture has got its name touched, in the fancies of men, with a sort of air of bookishness and pedantry, cast upon it from the follies of the many bookmen who forget the end in the means, and use their books with no real aim at perfection. We will not stickle for a name, and the name of culture one might easily give up, if only those who decry the frivolous and pedantic sort of culture, but wish at bottom for the same things as we do, would be careful on their part, not, in disparaging and discrediting the false culture, to unwittingly disparage and discredit, among a people with little natural reverence for it, the true also. But what we are concerned for is the thing, not the name; and the thing, call it by what name we will, is simply the enabling ourselves, whether by reading, observing, or thinking, to come as near as we can to the firm intelligible law of things, and thus to get a basis for a less confused action and a more complete perfection than we have at present.

And now, therefore, when we are accused of preaching up a spirit of cultivated inaction, of provoking the earnest lovers of action, of refusing to lend a hand at uprooting certain definite evils, of despairing to find any lasting truth to minister to the diseased spirit of our time, we shall not be so much confounded and embarrassed what to answer for ourselves. We shall say boldly that we do not at all despair of finding some lasting truth to minister to the diseased spirit of our time; but that we have discovered the best way of finding this to be not so much by lending a hand to our friends and countrymen in their actual operations for the removal of certain definite evils, but rather in getting our friends and countrymen to seek culture, to let their consciousness play freely round their present operations and the stock notions on which they are founded, show what these are like, and how related to the intelligible law of things, and auxiliary to true human perfection.

CHAPTER VI

Our Liberal Practitioners

But an unpretending writer, without a philosophy based on inter-dependent, subordinate, and coherent principles, must not presume to indulge himself too much in generalities. He must keep close to the level ground of common fact, the only safe ground for understandings without a scientific equipment. Therefore, since I have spoken so slightingly of the practical operations in which my friends and countrymen are at this moment engaged for the removal of certain definite evils, I am bound to take, before concluding, some of those operations and to make them, if I can, show the truth of what I have advanced.

Probably I could hardly give a greater proof of my confessed inexpertness in reasoning and arguing, than by taking, for my first example of an operation of this kind, the proceedings for the disestablishment of the Irish Church, which we are now witnessing. It seems so clear that this is surely one of those operations for the uprooting of a certain definite evil in which one's Liberal friends engage, and have a right to complain, and to get impatient, and to reproach one with delicate Conservative scepticism and cultivated inaction, if one does not lend a hand to help them. This does, indeed, seem evident; and yet this operation comes so prominently before us at this moment,—it so challenges everybody's regard,— that one seems cowardly in blinking it. So let us venture to try and see whether this conspicuous operation is one of those round which we need to let our consciousness play freely and reveal what manner of spirit we are of in doing it; or whether it is one which by no means admits the application of this doctrine of ours, and one to which we ought to lend a hand immediately.

I

Now it seems plain that the present Church-establishment in Ireland is contrary to reason and justice, in so far as the Church of a very small minority of the people there takes for itself all the Church-property of the Irish people. And one would think, that property, assigned for the purpose of providing for a people's religious worship was one, the State should, when that worship is split into several forms, apportion between those several forms. But the apportionment should be made with due regard to circumstances, taking account only of great differences, which are likely to be lasting, and of considerable communions, which are likely to represent profound and widespread religious characteristics. It should overlook petty differences, which have no serious reason for lasting, and inconsiderable communions, which can hardly be taken to express any broad and necessary religious lineaments of our common nature. This is just in accordance with that maxim about the State which we have more than once used: *The State is of the religion of all its citizens without the fanaticism of any of them.* Those who deny this, either think so poorly of the State that they do not like to see religion condescend to touch the State, or they think so poorly of religion that they do not like to see the State condescend to touch religion. But no good statesman will easily think thus unworthily either of the State or of religion.

Our statesmen of both parties were inclined, one may say, to follow the natural line of the State's duty, and to make in Ireland some fair apportionment of Church-property between large and radically divided religious communions in that country. But then it was discovered that in Great Britain the national mind, as it is called, is grown averse to endowments for religion and will make no new ones; and though this in itself looks general and solemn enough, yet there were found political philosophers, like Mr. Baxter and Mr. Charles Buxton, to give it a look of more generality and more solemnity still, and to elevate, by their dexterous command of powerful and beautiful language, this supposed edict of the British national mind into a sort of formula for expressing a great law of religious transition and progress for all the world.

But we, who, having no coherent philosophy, must not let ourselves philosophise, only see that the English and Scotch Nonconformists have a great horror of establishments and endowments for religion, which, they assert, were forbidden by Jesus Christ when he said: "My kingdom is not of this world;"[1] and that the Nonconformists will be delighted to aid statesmen in disestablishing any church, but will suffer none to be established or endowed if they can help it. Then we see that the Nonconformists make the strength of the Liberal majority in the House of Commons; and that, therefore, the leading Liberal statesmen, to get the support of the Nonconformists, forsake the notion of fairly apportioning Church-property in Ireland among the chief religious communions, declare that the national mind has decided against new endowments, and propose simply to disestablish and disendow the present establishment in Ireland without establishing or endowing any other. The actual power, in short, by virtue of which the Liberal party in the House of Commons is now trying to disestablish the Irish Church, is not the power of reason and justice, it is the power of the Nonconformists' antipathy to Church establishments.

Clearly it is this; because Liberal statesmen, relying on the power of reason and justice to help them, proposed something quite different from what they now propose; and they proposed what they now propose, and talked of the decision of the national mind, because they had to rely on the English and Scotch Nonconformists. And clearly the Nonconformists are actuated by antipathy to establishments, not by antipathy to the injustice and irrationality of the present appropriation of Church-property in Ireland; because Mr. Spurgeon,[2] in his eloquent and memorable letter, expressly avowed that the would sooner leave things as they are in Ireland, that is, he would sooner let the injustice and irrationality of the present appropriation continue, than do anything to set up the Roman image,—that is, than give the Catholics their fair and reasonable share of Church-property. Most indisputably, therefore, we may affirm that the real moving power by which the Liberal party are now operating the overthrow of the Irish establishment is the antipathy of the Nonconformists to Church-establishments, and not the sense of reason or justice, except so far as reason and justice may be contained in this antipathy. And thus the matter stands at present.

Now surely we must all see many inconveniences in performing the operation of uprooting this evil, the Irish Church-establishment, in this particular way. As was said about industry and freedom and gymnastics, we shall never awaken love and gratitude by this mode of operation; for it is pursued, not in view of reason and justice and human perfection and all that enkindles the enthusiasm of men, but it is pursued in view of a certain stock notion, or fetish, of the Nonconformists, which proscribes Church-establishments. And yet, evidently, one of the main benefits to be got by operating on the Irish Church is to win the affections of the Irish people. Besides this, an operation performed in virtue of a mechanical rule, or fetish, like the supposed decision of the English national mind against new endowments, does not easily inspire respect in its adversaries, and make their opposition feeble and hardly to be persisted in, as an operation evidently done in virtue of reason and justice might. For reason and justice have in them something persuasive and irresistible; but a fetish or mechanical maxim, like this of the Nonconformists, has in it nothing at all to conciliate either the affections or the understanding. Nay, it provokes the counter-employment of other fetishes or mechanical maxims on the opposite side, by which the confusion and hostility already prevalent are heightened. Only in this way can be explained the apparition of such fetishes as are beginning to be set up on the Conservative side against the fetish of the Nonconformists:—*The Constitution in danger! The bulwark of British freedom menaced! The lamp of the Reformation put out! No Popery!*—and so on. To elevate these against an operation relying on reason and justice to back it, is not so easy, or so tempting to human infirmity, as to elevate them against an operation relying on the Nonconformists' antipathy to Church-establishments to back it. For after all, *No Popery!* is a rallying cry which touches the human spirit quite as vitally as *No Church-establishments!*—that is to say, neither the one nor the other, in themselves, touch the human spirit vitally at all.

Ought the believers in action, then, to be so impatient with us, if we say, that even for the sake of this operation of theirs itself and its satisfactory accomplishment, it is more important to make our consciousness play freely round the stock notion or habit on which their operation relies for aid, than to lend a hand to it straight away? Clearly they ought not; because nothing is so effectual for

---

[1] John 18:36.   [2] Charles Haddon Spurgeon (1834–92), popular nonconformist preacher.

operating as reason and justice, and a free play of thought will either disengage the reason and justice lying hid in the Nonconformist fetish, and make them effectual, or else it will help to get this fetish out of the way, and to let statesmen go freely where reason and justice take them.

So, suppose we take this absolute rule, this mechanical maxim of Mr. Spurgeon and the Nonconformists, that Church-establishments are bad things because Jesus Christ said: "My kingdom is not of this world." Suppose we try and make our consciousness bathe and float this piece of petrifaction,—for such it now is,—and bring it within the stream of the vital movement of our thought, and into relation with the whole intelligible law of things. An enemy and a disputant might probably say that much of the machinery which Nonconformists themselves employ,—the Liberation Society[3] which exists already, and the Nonconformist Union which Mr. Spurgeon desires to see existing,—come within the scope of Christ's words as well as Church-establishments. This, however, is merely a negative and contentious way of dealing with the Nonconformist maxim; whereas what we desire is to bring this maxim within the positive and vital movement of our thought. We say, therefore, that Jesus Christ's words mean that his religion is a force of inward persuasion acting on the soul, and not a force of outward constraint acting on the body; and if the Nonconformist maxim against Church-establishments and Church-endowments has warrant given to it from what Christ thus meant, then their maxim is good, even though their own practice in the matter of the Liberation Society may be at variance with it.

And here we cannot but remember what we have formerly said about religion, Miss Cobbe, and the British College of Health in the New Road.[4] In religion there are two parts, the part of thought and speculation, and the part of worship and devotion. Jesus Christ certainly meant his religion, as a force of inward persuasion acting on the soul, to employ both parts as perfectly as possible. Now thought and speculation is eminently an individual matter, and worship and devotion is eminently a collective matter. It does not help me to think a thing more clearly that thousands of other people are thinking the same; but it does help me to worship with more emotion that thousands of other people are worshipping

with me. The consecration of common consent, antiquity, public establishment, long-used rites, national edifices, is everything for religious worship. "Just what makes worship impressive,"says Joubert, "is its publicity, its external manifestation, its sound, its splendour, its observance universally and visibly holding its sway through all the details both of our outward and of our inward life." Worship, therefore, should have in it as little as possible of what divides us, and should be as much as possible a common and public act; as Joubert says again: "The best prayers are those which have nothing distinct about them, and which are thus of the nature of simple adoration." For, "the same devotion," as he says in another place, "unites men far more than the same thought and knowledge." Thought and knowledge, as we have said before, is eminently something individual, and of our own; the more we possess it as strictly of our own, the more power it has on us. Man worships best, therefore, with the community; he philosophises best alone.

So it seems that whoever would truly give effect to Jesus Christ's declaration that his religion is a force of inward persuasion acting on the soul, would leave our thought on the intellectual aspects of Christianity as individual as possible, but would make Christian worship as collective as possible. Worship, then, appears to be eminently a matter for public and national establishment; for even Mr. Bright, who, when he stands in Mr. Spurgeon's great Tabernacle, is so ravished with admiration, will hardly say that the great Tabernacle and its worship are in themselves, as a temple and service of religion, so impressive and affecting as the public and national Westminster Abbey, or Notre Dame, with their worship. And when, immediately after the great Tabernacle, one comes plump down to the mass of private and individual establishments of religious worship, establishments falling, like the British College of Health in the New Road, conspicuously short of what a public and national establishment might be, then one cannot but feel that Jesus Christ's command to make his religion a force of persuasion to the soul, is, so far as one main source of persuasion is concerned, altogether set at nought.

But perhaps the Nonconformists worship so unimpressively because they philosophise so keenly; and one part of religion, the part of

---

[3] Founded 1845 by Edward Miall for the separation of church and state.
[4] Frances Power Cobbe and the College of Health are discussed in Matthew Arnold's "Function of Criticism at the Present Time," included in this volume.

public national worship, they have subordinated to the other part, the part of individual thought and knowledge. This, however, their organisation in congregations forbids us to admit. They are members of congregations, not isolated thinkers; and a free play of individual thought is at least as much impeded by membership of a small congregation as by membership of a great Church. Thinking by batches of fifties is to the full as fatal to free thought as thinking by batches of thousands. Accordingly, we have had occasion already to notice that Nonconformity does not at all differ from the Established Church by having worthier or more philosophical ideas about God, and the ordering of the world, than the Established Church has. It has very much the same ideas about these as the Established Church has, but it differs from the Established Church in that its worship is a much less collective and national affair.

So Mr. Spurgeon and the Nonconformists seem to have misapprehended the true meaning of Christ's words, *My kingdom is not of this world.* Because, by these words, Christ meant that his religion was to work on the soul. And of the two parts of the soul on which religion works,—the thinking and speculative part, and the feeling and imaginative part,—Nonconformity satisfies the first no better than the Established Churches, which Christ by these words is supposed to have condemned, satisfy it; and the second part it satisfies even worse than the Established Churches. And thus the balance of advantage seems to rest with the Established Churches; and they seem to have apprehended and applied Christ's words, if not with perfect adequacy, at least, less inadequately than the Nonconformists.

Might it not, then, be urged with great force that the way to do good, in presence of this operation for uprooting the Church-establishment in Ireland by the power of the Nonconformists' antipathy to publicly establishing or endowing religious worship, is not be lending a hand straight away to the operation, and Hebraising, —that is, in this case, taking an uncritical interpretation of certain Bible words as our absolute rule of conduct,—with the Nonconformists! It may be very well for born Hebraisers, like Mr. Spurgeon, to Hebraise; but for Liberal statesmen to Hebraise is surely unsafe, and to see poor old Liberal hacks Hebraising, whose real self belongs to a kind of negative Hellenism,—a state of moral indifference without intellectual ardour,—is even painful. And when, by our Hebraising, we neither do what the better mind of statesmen prompted

them to do, nor win the affections of the people we want to conciliate, nor yet reduce the opposition of our adversaries but rather heighten it, surely it may not be unreasonable to Hellenise a little, to let our thought and consciousness play freely about our proposed operation and its motives, dissolve these motives if they are unsound,—which certainly they have some appearance, at any rate, of being,—and create in their stead, if they are, a set of sounder and more persuasive motives conducting to a more solid operation. May not the man who promotes this be giving the best help finding some lasting truth to minister to the diseased spirit of his time, and does he really deserve that the believers in action should grow impatient with him?

II

But now to take another operation which does not at this moment so excite people's feelings as the disestablishment of the Irish Church, but which, I suppose, would also be called exactly one of those operations of simple, practical, commonsense reform, aiming at the removal of some particular abuse, and rigidly restricted to that object, to which a Liberal ought to lend a hand, and deserves that other Liberals should grow impatient with him if he does not. This operation I had the great advantage of, with my own ears, hearing discussed in the House of Commons, and recommended by a powerful speech from that famous speaker, Mr. Bright. So that the effeminate horror which, it is alleged, I have of practical reforms of this kind, was put to a searching test; and if it survived, it must have, one would think, some reason or other to support it, and can hardly quite merit the stigma of its present name.

The operation I mean was that which the Real Estate Intestacy Bill aimed at accomplishing, and the discussion on this bill I heard in the House of Commons. The bill proposed, as every one knows, to prevent the land of a man who dies intestate from going, as it goes now, to his eldest son, and was thought, by its friends and by its enemies, to be a step towards abating the now almost exclusive possession of the land of this country by the people whom we call the Barbarians. Mr. Bright, and other speakers on his side, seemed to hold that there is a kind of natural law or fitness of things which assigns to all a man's children a right to equal shares in the enjoyment of his property after his death; and that if, without depriving a man of an English-man's prime privilege of doing what he likes by making what will he chooses, you provide that when he makes none his land shall be divided among his family, then you give the sanction of the law to the natural fitness of things, and inflict a sort of check on the present violation of this by the Barbarians.

It occurred to me, when I saw Mr. Bright and his friends proceeding in this way, to ask myself a question. If the almost exclusive possession of the land of this country by the Barbarians is a bad thing, is this practical operation of the Liberals, and the stock notion, on which it seems to rest, about the natural right of children to share equally in the enjoyment of their father's property after his death, the best and most effective means of dealing with it? Or is it best dealt with by letting one's thought and consciousness play freely and naturally upon the Barbarians, this Liberal operation, and the stock notion at the bottom of it, and trying to get as near as we can to the intelligible law of things as to each of them?

Now does any one, if he simply and naturally reads his consciousness, discover that he has any rights at all? For my part, the deeper I go in my own consciousness, and the more simply I abandon myself to it, the more it seems to tell me that I have no rights at all, only duties; and that men get this notion of rights from a process of abstract reasoning, inferring that the obligations they are conscious of towards others, others must be conscious of towards them, and not from any direct witness of consciousness at all. But it is obvious that the notion of a right, arrived at in this way, is likely to stand as a formal and petrified thing, deceiving and misleading us; and that the notions got directly from our consciousness ought to be brought to bear upon it, and to control it. So it is unsafe and misleading to say that our children have rights against us; what is true and safe to say is, that we have duties towards our children. But who will find among these natural duties, set forth to us by our consciousness, the obligation to leave to all our children an equal share in the enjoyment of our property? Or, though consciousness tell us we ought to provide for our children's welfare, whose consciousness tells him that the enjoyment of property is in itself welfare? Whether our children's welfare is best served by their all sharing equally in our property, depends on circumstances and on the state of the community in which we live. With this equal sharing, society could not, for example, have organised itself afresh out of the chaos left by the fall of the Roman Empire; and to have an organised society to live in is more for a child's

welfare than to have an equal share of his father's property.

So we see how little convincing force the stock notion on which the Real Estate Intestacy Bill was based,—the notion that in the nature and fitness of things all a man's children have a right to an equal share in the enjoyment of what he leaves,—really has; and how powerless, therefore, it must of necessity be to persuade and win any one who has habits and interests which disincline him to it. On the other hand, the practical operation proposed relies entirely, if it is to be effectual in altering the present practice of the Barbarians, on the power of truth and persuasiveness in the notion which it seeks to consecrate; for it leaves to the Barbarians full liberty to continue their present practice, to which all their habits and interests incline them, unless the promulgation of a notion, which we have seen to have no vital efficacy and hold upon our consciousness, shall hinder them.

Are we really to adorn an operation of this kind, merely because it proposes to *do* something, with all the favourable epithets of simple, practical, common-sense, definite; to enlist on its side all the zeal of the believers in action, and to call indifference to it an effeminate horror of useful reforms? It seems to me quite easy to show that a free disinterested play of thought on the Barbarians and their land-holding is a thousand times more really practical, a thousand times more likely to lead to some effective result, than an operation such as that of which we have been now speaking. For if, casting aside the impediments of stock notions and mechanical action, we try to find the intelligible law of things respecting a great land-owning class such as we have in this country, does not our consciousness readily tell us that whether the perpetuation of such a class is for its own real good and for the real good of the community, depends on the actual circumstances of this class and of the community? Does it not readily tell us that wealth, power, and consideration are,—and above all when inherited and not earned,—in themselves trying and dangerous things? as Bishop Wilson excellently says: "Riches are almost always abused without a very extraordinary grace." But this extraordinary grace was in great measure supplied by the circumstances of the feudal epoch, out of which our land-holding class, with its rules of inheritance, sprang. The labour and contentions of a rude, nascent, and struggling society supplied it. These perpetually were trying, chastising, and forming the class whose predominance was then needed by society to give it points of cohesion, and was not so harmful to themselves because they were thus sharply tried and exercised. But in a luxurious, settled, and easy society, where wealth offers the means of enjoyment a thousand times more, and the temptation to abuse them is thus made a thousand times greater, the exercising discipline is at the same time taken away, and the feudal class is left exposed to the full operation of the natural law well put by the French moralist: *Pouvoir sans savior est fort dangereux.*[5] And, for my part, when I regard the young people of this class, it is above all by the trial and shipwreck made of their own welfare by the circumstances in which they live that I am struck. How far better it would have been for nine out of every ten among them, if they had had their own way to make in the world, and not been tried by a condition for which they had not the extraordinary grace requisite!

This, I say, seems to be what a man's consciousness, simply consulted, would tell him about the actual welfare of our Barbarians themselves. Then, as to the effect upon the welfare of the community, how can that be salutary, if a class which, by the very possession of wealth, power and consideration, becomes a kind of ideal or standard for the rest of the community, is tried by ease and pleasure more than it can well bear, and almost irresistibly carried away from excellence and strenuous virtue? This must certainly be what Solomon meant when he said: "As he who putteth a stone in a sling, so is he that giveth honour to a fool."[6]

For any one can perceive how this honouring of a false ideal, not of intelligence and strenuous virtue, but of wealth and station, pleasure and ease, is as a stone from a sling to kill in our great middle class, in us who are called Philistines, the desire before spoken of, which by nature for ever carries all men towards that which is lovely; and to leave instead of it only a blind deteriorating pursuit, for ourselves also, of the false ideal. And in those among us Philistines whom the desire does not wholly abandon, yet, having no excellent ideal set forth to nourish and to steady it, it meets with that natural bent for the bathos which together with this desire itself is implanted at birth in the breast of man, and is by that force twisted awry, and borne at random hither and thither, and at last flung upon those grotesque and hideous forms of popular religion which the more respectable part among us Philistines mistake for the true goal of man's desire after all that is lovely. And for the Populace this false ideal is a stone which kills the desire before it can even arise; so impossible and unattainable for them do the conditions of that which is lovely appear according to this ideal to be made, so necessary to the reaching of them by the few seems the falling short of them by the many. So that, perhaps, of the actual vulgarity of our Philistines and brutality of our Populace, the Barbarians and their feudal habits of succession, enduring out of their due time and place, are involuntarily the cause in a great degree; and they hurt the welfare of the rest of the community at the same time that, as we have seen, they hurt their own.

But must not, now, the working in our minds of considerations like these, to which culture, that is, the disinterested and active use of reading, reflection, and observation, in the endeavour to know the best that can be known, carries us, be really much more effectual to the dissolution of feudal habits and rules of succession in land than an operation like the Real Estate Intestacy Bill, and a stock notion like that of the natural right of all a man's children to an equal share in the enjoyment of his property; since we have seen that this mechanical maxim is unsound, and that, if it is unsound, the operation relying upon it cannot possibly be effective? If truth and reason have, as we believe, any natural irresistible effect on the mind of man, it must. These considerations, when culture has called them forth and given them free course in our minds, will live and work. They will work gradually, no doubt, and will not bring us ourselves to the front to sit in high place and put them into effect; but so they will be all the more beneficial. Everything teaches us how gradually nature would have all profound changes brought about; and we can even see, too, where the absolute abrupt stoppage of feudal habits has worked harm. And appealing to the sense of truth and reason, these considerations will, without doubt, touch and move all those of even the Barbarians themselves, who are (as are some of us Philistines also, and some of the Populace) beyond their fellows quick of feeling for truth and reason. For indeed this is just one of the advantages of sweetness and light over fire and strength, that sweetness and light make a

---

[5] "Power without knowledge is highly dangerous." [6] Proverbs 26:8.

feudal class quietly and gradually drop its feudal habits because it sees them at variance with truth and reason, while fire and strength are for tearing them passionately off, because this class applauded Mr. Lowe when he called, or was supposed to call, the working class drunken and venal.

III

But when once we have begun to recount the practical operations by which our Liberal friends work for the removal of definite evils, and in which if we do not join them they are apt to grow impatient with us, how can we pass over that very interesting operation,—the attempt to enable a man to marry his deceased wife's sister? This operation, too, like that for abating the feudal customs of succession in land, I have had the advantage of myself seeing and hearing my Liberal friends labour at.

I was lucky enough to be present when Mr. Chambers[7] brought forward in the House of Commons his bill for enabling a man to marry his deceased wife's sister, and I heard the speech which Mr. Chambers then made in support of his bill. His first point was that God's law,—the name he always gave to the Book of Leviticus,— did not really forbid a man to marry his deceased wife's sister. God's law not forbidding it, the Liberal maxim, that a man's prime right and happiness is to do as he likes, ought at once to come into force, and to annul any such check upon the assertion of personal liberty as the prohibition to marry one's deceased wife's sister. A distinguished Liberal supporter of Mr. Chambers, in the debate which followed the introduction of the bill, produced a formula of much beauty and neatness for conveying in brief the Liberal notions on this head: "Liberty," said he, "is the law of human life." And, therefore, the moment it is ascertained that God's law, the Book of Leviticus, does not stop the way, man's law, the law of liberty, asserts its right, and makes us free to marry our deceased wife's sister.

And this exactly falls in with what Mr. Hepworth Dixon, who may almost be called the Colenso of love and marriage—such a revolution does he make in our ideas on these matters, just as Dr. Colenso does in our ideas on religion,—tells us of the notions and proceedings of our kinsmen in America. With that affinity of genius to the Hebrew genius which we have already noticed, and with the strong belief of our race that liberty is the law of human life, so far as that fixed, perfect, and paramount rule of conscience, the Bible, does not expressly control it, our American kinsmen go again, Mr. Hepworth Dixon tells us, to their Bible, the Mormons to the patriarchs and the Old Testament, Brother Noyes to St. Paul and the New, and having never before read anything else but their Bible, they now read their Bible over again, and make all manner of great discoveries there. All these discoveries are favourable to liberty, and in this way is satisfied that double craving so characteristic of our Philistine, and so eminently exemplified in that crowned Philistine, Henry the Eighth,—the craving for forbidden fruit and the craving for legality.

Mr. Hepworth Dixon's eloquent writings give currency, over here, to these important discoveries; so that now, as regards love and marriage, we seem to be entering, with all our sails spread, upon what Mr. Hepworth Dixon, its apostle and evangelist, calls a Gothic Revival, but what one of the many newspapers that so greatly admire Mr. Hepworth Dixon's lithe and sinewy style and form their own style upon it, calls, by a yet bolder and more striking figure, "a great sexual insurrection of our Anglo-Teutonic race." For this end we have to avert our eyes from everything Hellenic and fanciful, and to keep them steadily fixed upon the two cardinal points of the Bible and liberty. And one of those practical operations in which the Liberal party engage, and in which we are summoned to join them, directs itself entirely, as we have seen, to these cardinal points, and may almost be regarded, perhaps, as a kind of first instalment, or public and parliamentary pledge, of the great sexual insurrection of our Anglo-Teutonic race.

But here, as elsewhere, what we seek is the Philistine's perfection, the development of his best self, not mere liberty for his ordinary self. And we no more allow absolute validity to his stock maxim, *Liberty is the law of human life*, than we allow it to the opposite maxim, which is just as true, *Renouncement is the law of human life*. For we know that the only perfect freedom is, as our religion says, a service; not a service to any stock maxim, but an elevation of our best self, and a harmonising in subordination to this, and to the idea of a perfected humanity, all the multitudinous, turbulent, and blind impulses of our ordinary selves. Now, the Philistine's great defect being a defect in delicacy of perception, to cultivate in him this delicacy, to render it

---

[7] Sir Thomas Chambers (1814–91), Member of Parliament, introduced the bill Arnold is referring to.

independent of external and mechanical rule, and a law to itself, is what seems to make most for his perfection, his true humanity. And his true humanity, and therefore his happiness, appears to lie much more, so far as the relations of love and marriage are concerned, in becoming alive to the finer shades of feeling which arise within these relations, in being able to enter with tact and sympathy into the subtle instinctive propensions and repugnances of the person with whose life his own life is bound up, to make them his own, to direct and govern in harmony with them the arbitrary range of his personal action, and thus to enlarge his spiritual and intellectual life and liberty, than in remaining insensible to these finer shades of feeling and this delicate sympathy, in giving unchecked range, so far as he can, to his mere personal action, in allowing no limits or government to this except such as a mechanical external law imposes, and in thus really narrowing, for the satisfaction of his ordinary self, his spiritual and intellectual life and liberty.

Still more must this be so, when his fixed eternal rule, his God's law, is supplied to him from a source which is less fit, perhaps, to supply final and absolute instructions on this particular topic of love and marriage than on any other relation of human life. Bishop Wilson, who is full of examples of that fruitful Hellenising within the limits of Hebraism itself, of that renewing of the stiff and stark notions of Hebraism by turning upon them a stream of fresh thought and consciousness, which we have already noticed in St. Paul,—Bishop Wilson gives an admirable lesson to rigid Hebraisers, like Mr. Chambers, asking themselves: Does God's law (that is, the Book of Leviticus) forbid us to marry our wife's sister?—Does God's law (that is, again, the Book of Leviticus) allow us to marry our wife's sister?—when he says: "Christian duties are founded on reason, not on the sovereign authority of God commanding what he pleases; God cannot command us what is not fit to be believed or done, all his commands being founded in the necessities of our nature." And, immense as is our debt to the Hebrew race and its genius, incomparable as is its authority on certain profoundly important sides of our human nature, worthy as it is to be described as having uttered, for those sides, the voice of the deepest necessities of our nature, the statutes of the divine and eternal order of things, the law of God,—who, that is not manacled and hoodwinked by his Hebraism, can believe that, as to love and marriage, our reason and the necessities of our humanity have their true,

sufficient, and divine law expressed for them by the voice of any Oriental and polygamous nation like the Hebrews? Who, I say, will believe, when he really considers the matter, that where the feminine nature, the feminine ideal, and our relations to them, are brought into question, the delicate and apprehensive genius of the Indo-European race, the race which invented the Muses, and chivalry, and the Madonna, is to find its last word on this question in the institutions of a Semitic people, whose wisest king had seven hundred wives and three hundred concubines?

IV

If here again, therefore, we seem to minister better to the diseased spirit of our time by leading it to think about the operation our Liberal friends have in hand, than by lending a hand to this operation ourselves, let us see, before we dismiss from our view the practical operations of our Liberal friends, whether the same thing does not hold good as to their celebrated industrial and economical labours also. Their great work of this kind is, of course, their free-trade policy. This policy, as having enabled the poor man to eat untaxed bread, and as having wonderfully augmented trade, we are accustomed to speak of with a kind of thankful solemnity. It is chiefly on their having been our leaders in this policy that Mr. Bright founds for himself and his friends the claim, so often asserted by him, to be considered guides of the blind, teachers of the ignorant, benefactors slowly and laboriously developing in the Conservative party and in the country that which Mr. Bright is fond of calling *the growth of intelligence,*—the object, as is well known, of all the friends of culture also, and the great end and aim of the culture that we preach.

Now, having first saluted free-trade and its doctors with all respect, let us see whether even here, too, our Liberal friends do not pursue their operations in a mechanical way, without reference to any firm intelligible law of things, to human life as a whole, and human happiness; and whether it is not more for our good, at this particular moment at any rate, if, instead of worshipping free-trade with them Hebraistically, as a kind of fetish, and helping them to pursue it as an end in and for itself, we turn the free stream of our thought upon their treatment of it, and see how this is related to the intelligible law of human life, and to national well-being and happiness. In short, suppose we Hellenise a little with free-trade, as we Hellenised with the Real Estate Intestacy Bill, and with the disestablishment of the Irish Church by the power of the Nonconformists' antipathy to religious establishments and endowments, and see whether what our reprovers beautifully call ministering to the diseased spirit of our time is best done by the Hellenising method of proceeding, or by the other.

But first let us understand how the policy of free-trade really shapes itself for our Liberal friends, and how they practically employ it as an instrument of national happiness and salvation. For as we said that it seemed clearly right to prevent the Church-property of Ireland from being all taken for the benefit of the Church of a small minority, so it seems clearly right that the poor man should eat untaxed bread, and, generally, that restrictions and regulations which, for the supposed benefit of some particular person or class of persons, make the price of things artificially high here, or artificially low there, and interfere with the natural flow of trade and commerce, should be done away with. But in the policy of our Liberal friends free-trade means more than this, and is specially valued as a stimulant to the production of wealth, as they call it, and to the increase of the trade, business, and population of the country. We have already seen how these things,—trade, business, and population,—are mechanically pursued by us as ends precious in themselves, and are worshipped as what we call fetishes; and Mr. Bright, I have already said, when he wishes to give the working class a true sense of what makes glory and greatness, tells it to look at the cities it has built, the railroads it has made, the manufactures it has produced. So to this idea of glory and greatness the free-trade which our Liberal friends extol so solemnly and devoutly has served,—to the increase of trade, business, and population; and for this it is prized. Therefore, the untaxing of the poor man's bread has, with this view of national happiness, been used not so much to make the existing poor man's bread cheaper or more abundant, but rather to create more poor men to eat it; so that we cannot precisely say that we have fewer poor men than we had before free-trade, but we can say with truth that we have many more centres of industry, as they are called, and much more business, population, and manufactures. And if we are sometimes a little troubled by our multitude of poor men, yet we know the increase of manufactures and population to be such a salutary thing in itself, and our free-trade policy begets such an admirable movement, creating fresh centres of industry and fresh poor men here, while we were thinking about our poor men there, that we are quite dazzled and borne away, and more and more industrial movement is called for, and our social progress seems to become one triumphant and enjoyable course of what is sometimes called, vulgarly, outrunning the constable.

If, however, taking some other criterion of man's well-being than the cities he has built and the manufactures he has produced, we persist in thinking that our social progress would be happier if there were not so many of us so very poor, and in busying ourselves with notions of in some way or other adjusting the poor man and business one to the other, and not multiplying the one and the other mechanically and blindly, then our Liberal friends, the appointed doctors of free-trade, take us up very sharply. "Art is long," says the *Times*, "and life is short; for the most part we settle things first and understand them afterwards. Let us have as few theories as possible; what is wanted is not the light of speculation. If nothing worked well of which the theory was not perfectly understood, we should be in sad confusion. The relations of labour and capital, we are told, are not understood, yet trade and commerce, on the whole, work satisfactorily." I quote from the *Times* of only the other day. But thoughts like these, as I have often pointed out, are thoroughly British thoughts, and we have been familiar with them for years.

Or, if we want more of a philosophy of the matter than this, our free-trade friends have two axioms for us, axioms laid down by their justly esteemed doctors, which they think ought to satisfy us entirely. One is, that, other things being equal, the more population increases, the more does production increase to keep pace with it; because men by their numbers and contact call forth all manner of activities and resources in one another and in nature, which, when men are few and sparse, are never developed. The other is, that, although population always tends to equal the means of subsistence, yet people's notions of what subsistence is enlarge as civilisation advances, and take in a number of things beyond the bare necessaries of life; and thus, therefore, is supplied whatever check on population is needed. But the error of our friends is, perhaps, that they apply axioms of this sort as if they were self-acting laws which will put themselves into operation without trouble or planning on our part, if we will only pursue free-trade, business, and population zealously and staunchly. Whereas the real truth is, that, however the case might be under other circumstances, yet in fact, as we now manage the matter, the enlarged conception of what is included in *subsistence* does not operate to prevent the bringing into the world of numbers of people who but just attain to the barest necessaries of life or who even fail to attain to them; while, again, though production may increase as population increases, yet it seems that the production may be of such a kind, and so related, or rather non-related, to population, that the population may be little the better for it.

For instance, with the increase of population since Queen Elizabeth's time the production of silk-stockings has wonderfully increased, and silk-stockings have become much cheaper, and procurable in greater abundance by many more people, and tend perhaps, as population and manufactures increase, to get cheaper and cheaper, and at last to become, according to Bastiat's[8] favourite image, a common free property of the human race, like light and air. But bread and bacon have not become much cheaper with the increase of population since Queen Elizabeth's time, nor procurable in much greater abundance by many more people; neither do they seem at all to promise to become, like light and air, a common free property of the human race. And if bread and bacon have not kept pace with our population, and we have many more people in want of them now than in Queen Elizabeth's time, it seems vain to tell us that silk-stockings have kept pace with our population, or even more than kept pace with it, and that we are to get our comfort out of that.

In short, it turns out that our pursuit of free-trade, as of so many other things, has been too mechanical. We fix upon some object, which in this case is the production of wealth, and the increase of manufactures, population, and commerce through free-trade, as a kind of one thing needful or end in itself; and then we pursue it staunchly and mechanically, and say that it is our duty to pursue it staunchly and mechanically, not to see how it is related to the whole intelligible law of things and to full human perfection, or to treat it as the piece of machinery, of varying value as its relations to the intelligible law of things vary, which it really is.

So it is of no use to say to the *Times*, and to our Liberal friends rejoicing in the possession of their talisman of free-trade, that about one in nineteen of our population is a pauper, and that, this being so, trade and commerce can hardly be said to

prove by their satisfactory working that it matters nothing whether the relations between labour and capital are understood or not; nay, that we can hardly be said not to be in sad confusion. For here our faith in the staunch mechanical pursuit of a fixed object comes in, and covers itself with that imposing and colossal necessitarianism of the *Times* which we have before noticed. And this necessitarianism, taking for granted that an increase in trade and population is a good in itself, one of the chiefest of goods, tells us that disturbances of human happiness caused by ebbs and flows in the tide of trade and business, which, on the whole, steadily mounts, are inevitable and not to be quarrelled with. This firm philosophy I seek to call to mind when I am in the East of London, whither my avocations often lead me; and, indeed, to fortify myself against the depressing sights which on these occasions assail us, I have transcribed from the *Times* one strain of this kind, full of the finest economical doctrine, and always carry it about with me. The passage is this:—

"The East End is the most commerical, the most industrial, the most fluctuating region of the metropolis. It is always the first to suffer; for it is the creature of prosperity, and falls to the ground the instant there is no wind to bear it up. The whole of that region is covered with huge docks, shipyards, manufactories, and a wilderness of small houses, all full of life and happiness in brisk times, but in dull times withered and lifeless, like the deserts we read of in the East. Now their brief spring is over. There is no one to blame for this; it is the result of Nature's simplest laws!" We must all agree that it is impossible that anything can be firmer than this, or show a surer faith in the working of free-trade, as our Liberal friends understand and employ it.

But, if we still at all doubt whether the indefinite multiplication of manufactories and small houses can be such an absolute good in itself as to counterbalance the indefinite multiplication of poor people, we shall learn that this multiplication of poor people, too, is an absolute good in itself, and the result of divine and beautiful laws. This is indeed a favourite thesis with our Philistine friends, and I have already noticed the pride and gratitude with which they receive certain articles in the *Times*, dilating in thankful and solemn language on the majestic growth of our population. But I prefer to quote now, on this topic, the words of an ingenious young Scotch writer, Mr.

[8] Frederic Bastiat (1801–50), French economist.

Robert Buchanan,[9] because he invests with so much imagination and poetry this current idea of the blessed and even divine character which the multiplying of population is supposed in itself to have. "We move to multiplicity," says Mr. Robert Buchanan. "If there is one quality which seems God's, and his exclusively, it seems that divine philoprogenitiveness, that passionate love of distribution and expansion into living forms. Every animal added seems a new ecstasy to the Maker; every life added, a new embodiment of his love. He would *swarm* the earth with beings. There are never enough. Life, life, life,—faces gleaming, hearts beating, must fill every cranny. Not a corner is suffered to remain empty. The whole earth breeds, and God glories."

It is a little unjust, perhaps, to attribute to the Divinity exclusively this philoprogenitiveness, which the British Philistine, and the poorer class of Irish, may certainly claim to share with him; yet how inspiriting is here the whole strain of thought! and these beautiful words, too, I carry about with me in the East of London, and often read them there. They are quite in agreement with the popular language one is accustomed to hear about children and large families, which describes children as *sent*. And a line of poetry, which Mr. Robert Buchanan throws in presently after the poetical prose I have quoted,—

'Tis the old story of the fig-leaf time—

this fine line, too, naturally connects itself, when one is in the East of London, with the idea of God's desire to *swarm* the earth with beings; because the swarming of the earth with beings does indeed, in the East of London, so seem to revive *the old story of the fig-leaf time*, such a number of the people one meets there having hardly a rag to cover them; and the more the swarming goes on, the more it promises to revive this old story. And when the story is perfectly revived, the swarming quite completed, and every cranny choke full, then, too, no doubt, the faces in the East of London will be gleaming faces, which Mr. Robert Buchanan says it is God's desire they should be, and which every one must perceive they are not at present, but, on the contrary, very miserable.

But to prevent all this philosophy and poetry from quite running away with us, and making us think with the *Times*, and our practical Liberal free-traders, and the British Philistines generally,

that the increase of houses and manufactories, or the increase of population, are absolute goods in themselves, to be mechanically pursued, and to be worshipped like fetishes,—to prevent this, we have got that notion of ours immovably fixed, of which I have long ago spoken, the notion that culture, or the study of perfection, leads us to conceive of no perfection as being real which is not a *general* perfection, embracing all our fellow-men with whom we have to do. Such is the sympathy which binds humanity together, that we are indeed, as our religion says, members of one body, and if one member suffer, all the members suffer with it. Individual perfection is impossible so long as the rest of mankind are not perfected along with us. "The *multitude* of the wise is the welfare of the world,"[10] says the Wise Man. And to this effect that excellent and often quoted guide of ours, Bishop Wilson, has some striking words:—"It is not," says he, "so much our neighbour's interest as our own that we love him." And again he says: "Our salvation does in some measure depend upon that of others." And the author of the *Imitation* puts the same thing admirably when he says:— "*Obscurior etiam via ad cælum videbatur quando tam pauci regnum cælorum quærere curabant*; the fewer there are who follow the way to perfection, the harder that way is to find." So all our fellow-men, in the East of London and elsewhere, we must take along with us in the progress towards perfection, if we ourselves really, as we profess, want to be perfect; and we must not let the worship of any fetish, any machinery, such as manufactures or population,—which are not, like perfection, absolute goods in themselves, though we think them so,—create for us such a multitude of miserable, sunken, and ignorant human beings, that to carry them all along with us is impossible, and perforce they must for the most part be left by us in their degradation and wretchedness. But evidently the conception of free-trade, on which our Liberal friends vaunt themselves, and in which they think they have found the secret of national prosperity,—evidently, I say, the mere unfettered pursuit of the production of wealth, and the mere mechanical multiplying, for this end, of manufactures and population, threatens to create for us, if it has not created already, those vast, miserable, unmanageable masses of sunken people,—one pauper at the present moment, for every nineteen of us,—to the existence of which we are, as we have seen,

---

[9] Robert Buchanan (1841–1901), minor poet and critic, noted for his attack on D. G. Rossetti.
[10] Wisdom 6:24.

absolutely forbidden to reconcile ourselves, in spite of all that the philosophy of the *Times* and the poetry of Mr. Robert Buchanan may say to persuade us.

And though Hebraism, following its best and highest instinct,—identical, as we have seen, with that of Hellenism in its final aim, the aim of perfection,—teaches us this very clearly; and though from Hebraising counsellors,—the Bible, Bishop Wilson, the author of the *Imitation*,—I have preferred (as well I may, for from this rock of Hebraism we are all hewn!) to draw the texts which we use to bring home to our minds this teaching; yet Hebraism in general seems powerless, almost as powerless as our free-trading Liberal friends, to deal efficaciously with our ever-accumulating masses of pauperism, and to prevent their accumulating still more. Hebraism builds churches, indeed, for these masses, and sends missionaries among them; above all, it sets itself against the social necessitarianism of the *Times*, and refuses to accept their degradation as inevitable. But with regard to their ever-increasing accumulation, it seems to be led to the very same conclusions, though from a point of view of its own, as our free-trading Liberal friends. Hebraism, with that mechanical and misleading use of the letter of Scripture on which we have already commented, is governed by such texts as: *Be fruitful and multiply*[11], the edict of God's law, as Mr. Chambers would say; or by the declaration of what he would call God's word in the Psalms, that the man who has a great number of children is thereby made happy. And in conjunction with such texts as these, Hebraism is apt to place another text: *The poor shall never cease out of the land.*[12] Thus Hebraism is conducted to nearly the same notion as the popular mind and as Mr. Robert Buchanan, that children are *sent*, and that the divine nature takes a delight in swarming the East End of London with paupers. Only, when they are perishing in their helplessness and wretchedness, it asserts the Christian duty of succouring them, instead of saying, like the *Times*: "Now their brief spring is over; there is nobody to blame for this; it is the result of Nature's simplest laws!" But, like the *Times*, Hebraism despairs of any help from knowledge and says that "what is wanted is not the light of speculation."

I remember, only the other day, a good man looking with me upon a multitude of children who were gathered before us in one of the most miserable regions of London,—children eaten up with disease, half-sized, half-fed, half-clothed, neglected by their parents, without health, without home, without hope,—said to me: "The one thing really needful is to teach these little ones to succour one another, if only with a cup of cold water; but now, from one end of the country to the other, one hears nothing but the cry for knowledge, knowledge, knowledge!" And yet surely, so long as these children are there in these festering masses, without health, without home, without hope, and so long as their multitude is perpetually swelling, charged with misery they must still be for themselves, charged with misery they must still be for us, whether they help one another with a cup of cold water or no; and the knowledge how to prevent their acculumating is necessary, even to give their moral life and growth a fair chance!

May we not, therefore, say, that neither the true Hebraism of this good man, willing to *spend* and be spent for these sunken multitudes, nor what I may call the spurious Hebraism of our free-trading Liberal friends,—mechanically worshipping their fetish of the production of wealth and of the increase of manufactures and population, and looking neither to the right nor left so long as this increase goes on,—avail us much here; and that here, again, what we want is Hellenism, the letting our consciousness play freely and simply upon the facts before us, and listening to what it tells us of the intelligible law of things as concerns them? And surely what it tells us is, that a man's children are not really *sent*, any more than the pictures upon his wall, or the horses in his stable are *sent*; and that to bring people into the world, when one cannot afford to keep them and oneself decently and not too precariously, or to bring more of them into the world than one can afford to keep thus, is, whatever the *Times* and Mr. Robert Buchanan may say, by no means an accomplishment of the divine will or a fulfilment of Nature's simplest laws, but is just as wrong, just as contrary to reason and the will of God, as for a man to have horses, or carriages, or pictures, when he cannot afford them, or to have more of them than he can afford; and that, in the one case as in the other, the larger the scale on which the violation of reason's law is practised, and the longer it is persisted in, the greater must be the confusion and final trouble. Surely no laudations of free-trade, no meetings of bishops and clergy in the East End of London, no reading of papers and

11 Genesis 1:28.   12 Deuteronomy 15:11.

reports, can tell us anything about our social condition which it more concerns us to know than that! and not only to know, but habitually to have the knowledge present, and to act upon it as one acts upon the knowledge that water wets and fire burns! And not only the sunken populace of our great cities are concerned to know it, and the pauper twentieth of our population; we Philistines of the middle class, too, are concerned to know it, and all who have to set themselves to make progress in perfection.

But we all know it already! some one will say; it is the simplest law of prudence. But how little reality must there be in our knowledge of it; how little can we be putting it in practice; how little is it likely to penetrate among the poor and struggling masses of our population, and to better our condition, so long as an unintelligent Hebraism of one sort keeps repeating as an absolute eternal word of God the psalm-verse which says that the man who has a great many children is happy; or an unintelligent Hebraism of another sort—that is to say, a blind following of certain stock notions as infallible—keeps assigning as an absolute proof of national prosperity the multiplying of manufactures and population! Surely, the one set of Hebraisers have to learn that their psalm-verse was composed at the resettlement of Jerusalem after the Captivity, when the Jews of Jerusalem were a handful, an undermanned garrison, and every child was a blessing; and that the word of God, or the voice of the divine order of things, declares the possession of a great many children to be a blessing only when it really is so! And the other set of Hebraisers, have they not to learn that if they call their private acquaintances imprudent or unlucky when, with no means of support for them or with precarious means, they have a large family of children, then they ought not to call the State well managed and prosperous merely because its manufactures and its citizens multiply, if the manufactures, which bring new citizens into existence just as much as if they had actually begotten them, bring more of them into existence than they can maintain, or are too precarious to go on maintaining those whom for a while they maintained?

Hellenism, surely, or the habit of fixing our mind upon the intelligible law of things, is most salutary if it makes us see that the only absolute good, the only absolute and eternal object prescribed to us by God's law, or the divine order of things, is the progress towards perfection,—our own progress towards it and the progress of humanity. And therefore, for every individual man, and for every society of men, the possession and multiplication of children, like the possession and multiplication of horses and pictures, is to be accounted good or bad, not in itself, but with reference to this object and the progress towards it. And as no man is to be excused in having horses or pictures, if his having them hinders his own or others' progress towards perfection and makes them lead a servile and ignoble life, so is no man to be excused for having children if his having them makes him or other lead this. Plain thoughts of this kind are surely the spontaneous product of our consciousness, when it is allowed to play freely and disinterestedly upon the actual facts of our social condition, and upon our stock notions and stock habits in respect to it. Firmly grasped and simply uttered, they are more likely, one cannot but think, to better that condition, and to diminish our formidable rate of one pauper to every nineteen of us, than is the Hebraising and mechanical pursuit of free-trade by our Liberal friends.

V

So that, here as elsewhere, the practical operations of our Liberal friends, by which they set so much store, and in which they invite us to join them and to show what Mr. Bright calls a commendable interest, do not seem to us so practical for real good as they think; and our Liberal friends seem to us themselves to need to Hellenise, as we say, a little,—that is, to examine into the nature of real good, and to listen to what their consciousness tells them about it,—rather than to pursue with such heat and confidence their present practical operations. And it is clear that they have no just cause, so far as regards several operations of theirs which we have canvassed, to reproach us with delicate Conservative scepticism. For often by Hellenising we seem to subvert stock Conservative notions and usages more effectually than they subvert them by Hebraising. But, in truth, the free spontaneous play of consciousness with which culture tries to float our stock habits of thinking and acting, is by its very nature, as has been said, disinterested. Sometimes the result of floating them may be agreeable to this party, sometimes to that; now it may be unwelcome to our so-called Liberals, now to our so-called Conservatives; but what culture seeks is, above all, to *float* them, to prevent their being stiff and stark pieces of petrifaction any longer. It is mere Hebraising, if we stop short, and refuse to let our consciousness play freely, whenever we or our friends do not happen to like what it discovers to us. This is to make the Liberal party, or the Conservative party, our one thing needful, instead of human perfection; and we have seen what mischief arises from making an even greater thing than the Liberal or the Conservative party, —the predominance of the moral side in man,— our one thing needful. But wherever the free play of our consciousness leads us, we shall follow; believing that in this way we shall tend to make good at all points what is wanting to us, and so shall be brought nearer to our complete human perfection.

Thus we may often, perhaps, praise much that a so-called Liberal thinks himself forbidden to praise, and yet blame much that a so-called Conservative thinks himself forbidden to blame, because these are both of them partisans, and no partisan can afford to be thus disinterested. But we who are not partisans can afford it; and so, after we have seen what Nonconformists lose by being locked up in their New Road forms of religious institution, we can let ourselves see, on the other hand, how their ministers, in a time of movement of ideas like our present time, are apt to be more exempt than the ministers of a great Church establishment from that self-confidence, and sense of superiority to such a movement, which are natural to a powerful hierarchy; and which in Archdeacon Denison,[13] for instance, seem almost carried to such a pitch that they may become, one cannot but fear, his spiritual ruin. But seeing this does not dispose us, therefore, to lock up all the nation in forms of worship of the New Road type; but it points us to the quite new ideal, of combining grand and national forms of worship with an openness and movement of mind not yet found in any hierarchy. So, again, if we see what is called ritualism making conquests in our Puritan middle class, we may rejoice that portions of this class should have become alive to the æsthetical weakness of their position, even although they have not yet become alive to the intellectual weakness of it. In Puritanism, on the other hand, we can respect that idea of dealing sincerely with oneself, which is at once the great force of Puritanism,—Puritanism's great superiority over all products, like ritualism, of our Catholicising tendencies,—and also an idea rich in the latent seeds of intellectual promise. But we do this, without on that account hiding from ourselves that Puritanism has by Hebraising misapplied that idea, has as yet developed none or hardly one of those seeds, and that its triumph

at its present stage of development would be baneful.

Everything, in short, confirms us in the doctrine, so unpalatable to the believers in action, that our main business at the present moment is not so much to work away at certain crude reforms of which we have already the scheme in our own mind, as to create, through the help of that culture which at the very outset we began by praising and recommending, a frame of mind out of which the schemes of really fruitful reforms may with time grow. At any rate, we ourselves must put up with our friends' impatience and with their reproaches against cultivated inaction, and must still decline to lend a hand to their practical operations, until we, for our own part at least, have grown a little clearer about the nature of real good, and have arrived nearer to a condition of mind out of which really fruitful and solid operations may spring.

In the meanwhile, since our Liberal friends keep loudly and resolutely assuring us that their actual operations at present are fruitful and solid, let us in each case keep testing these operations in the simple way we have indicated, by letting the natural stream of our consciousness flow over them freely; and if they stand this test successfully, then let us give them our interest, but not else. For example. Our Liberal friends assure us, at the very top of their voices, that their present actual operation for the disestablishment of the Irish Church is fruitful and solid. But what if, on testing it, the truth appears to be, that the statesmen and reasonable people of both parties wished for much the same thing,—the fair apportionment of the church property of Ireland among the principal religious bodies there; but that, behind the statesmen and reasonable people, there was, on one side, a mass of Tory prejudice, and, on the other, a mass of Nonconformist prejudice, to which such an arrangement was unpalatable? Well, the natural way, one thinks, would have been for the statesmen and reasonable people of both sides to have united, and to have allayed and dissipated, so far as they could, the resistance of their respective extremes, and where they could not, to have confronted it in concert. But we see that, instead of this, Liberal statesmen waited to trip up their rivals, if they proposed the arrangement which both knew to be reasonable, by means of the prejudice of their own Nonconformist extreme; and then, themselves proposing an arrangement to flatter this prejudice, made the

---

[13] Archdeacon Denison (1805–96), prominent High Churchman.

other arrangement, which they themselves knew to be reasonable, out of the question; and drove their rivals in their turn to blow up with all their might, in the hope of baffling them, a great fire, among their own Tory extreme, of fierce prejudice and religious bigotry,—a fire which, once kindled, may always very easily spread further? If, I say, on testing the present operation of our Liberal friends for the disestablishment of the Irish Church, the truth about it appears to be very much this, then, I think,—even with a triumphant Liberal majority, and with our Liberal friends making impassioned appeals to us to take a commendable interest in their operation and them, and to rally round what Sir Henry Hoare (who may be described, perhaps, as a Barbarian converted to Philistinism, as I, on the other hand, seem to be a Philistine converted to culture) finely calls the conscientiousness of a Gladstone and the intellect of a Bright,—it is rather our duty to abstain, and, instead of lending a hand to the operation of our Liberal friends, to do what we can to abate and dissolve the mass of prejudice, Tory or Nonconformist, which makes so doubtfully begotten and equivocal an operation as the present, producible and possible.

Conclusion

AND SO we bring to an end what we had to say in praise of culture, and in evidence of its special utility for the circumstances in which we find ourselves, and the confusion which environs us. Through culture seems to lie our way, not only to perfection, but even to safety. Resolutely refusing to lend a hand to the imperfect operations of our Liberal friends, disregarding their impatience, taunts, and reproaches, firmly bent on trying to find in the intelligible law of things a firmer and sounder basis for future practice than any which we have at present, and believing this search and discovery to be, for our generation and circumstances, of yet more vital and pressing importance than practice itself, we nevertheless may do more, perhaps, we poor disparaged followers of culture, to make the actual present, and the frame of society in which we live, solid and seaworthy, than all which our bustling politicians can do.

For we have seen how much of our disorders and perplexities is due to the disbelief, among the classes and combinations of men, Barbarian or Philistine, which have hitherto governed our society, in right reason, in a paramount best self; to the inevitable decay and break-up of the organisations by which, asserting and expressing in these organisations their ordinary self only, they have so long ruled us; and to their irresolution, when the society, which their conscience tells them they have made and still manage not with right reason but with their ordinary self, is rudely shaken, in offering resistance to its subverters. But for us,—who believe in right reason, in the duty and possibility of extricating and elevating our best self, in the progress of humanity towards perfection,—for us the framework of society, that theatre on which this august drama has to unroll itself, is sacred; and whoever administers it, and however we may seek to remove them from their tenure of administration, yet, while they administer, we steadily and with undivided heart support them in repressing anarchy and disorder; because without order there can be no society, and without society there can be no human perfection.

With me, indeed, this rule of conduct is hereditary. I remember my father, in one of his unpublished letters written more than forty years ago, when the political and social state of the country was gloomy and troubled, and there were riots in many places, goes on, after strongly insisting on the badness and foolishness of the government, and on the harm and danger-ousness of our feudal and aristocratical con-stitution of society, and ends thus: "As for rioting, the old Roman way of dealing with *that* is always the right one; flog the rank and file, and fling the ring-leaders from the Tarpeian Rock!" And this opinion we can never forsake, however our Liberal friends may think a little rioting, and what they call popular demonstrations, useful sometimes to their own interests and to the interests of the valuable practical operations they have in hand, and however they may preach the right of an Englishman to be left to do as far as possible what he likes, and the duty of his government to indulge him and connive as much as possible and abstain from all harshness of repression. And even when they artfully show us operations which are undoubtedly precious, such as the abolition of the slave-trade, and ask us if, for their sake, foolish and obstinate governments may not wholesomely be frightened by a little disturbance, the good design in view and the difficulty of overcoming opposition to it being considered,—still we say no, and that monster processions in the streets and forcible irruptions into the parks, even in professed support of this good design, ought to be unflinchingly forbidden and repressed; and that far more is lost than is gained by permitting them. Because a State in which law is authoritative and sovereign, a firm and settled course of public order, is requisite if man is to bring to maturity anything precious and lasting now, or to found anything precious and lasting for the future.

Thus, in our eyes, the very framework and exterior order of the State, whoever may administer the State, is sacred; and culture is the most resolute enemy of anarchy, because of the great hopes and designs for the State which culture teaches us to nourish. But as, believing in right reason, and having faith in the progress of humanity towards perfection, and ever labouring for this end, we grow to have clearer sight of the ideas of right reason, and of the elements and helps of perfection, and come gradually to fill the framework of the State with them, to fashion its internal composition and all its laws and institutions conformably to them, and to make the State more and more the expression, as we say, of our best self, which is not manifold, and vulgar, and unstable, and contentious, and ever-varying, but one, and noble, and secure, and peaceful, and the same for all mankind,—with what aversion shall we not *then* regard anarchy, with what firmness shall we not check it, when there is so much that is so precious which it will endanger!

So that, for the sake of the present, but far more for the sake of the future, the lovers of culture are unswervingly and with a good conscience the opposers of anarchy. And not as the Barbarians and Philistines, whose honesty and whose sense of humour make them shrink, as we have seen, from treating the State as too serious a thing, and from giving it too much power,—for indeed the only State they know of, and think they administer, is the expression of their ordinary self. And though the headstrong and violent extreme among them might gladly arm this with full authority, yet their virtuous mean is, as we have said, pricked in conscience at doing this; and so our Barbarian Secretaries of State let the Park railings be broken down, and our Philistine Aldermen-Colonels let the London roughs rob and beat the bystanders. But we, beholding in the State no expression of our ordinary self, but even already, as it were, the appointed frame and prepared vessel of our best self, and, for the future, our best self's powerful, beneficent and

sacred expression and organ,—we are willing and resolved, even now, to strengthen against anarchy the trembling hands of our Barbarian Home Secretaries and the feeble knees of our Philistine Alderman-Colonels; and to tell them, that it is not really in behalf of their own ordinary self that they are called to protect the Park railings, and to suppress the London roughs, but in behalf of the best self both of themselves and of all of us in the future.

Nevertheless, though for resisting anarchy the lovers of culture may prize and employ fire and strength, yet they must, at the same time, bear constantly in mind that it is not at this moment true, what the majority of people tell us, that the world wants fire and strength more than sweetness and light, and that things are for the most part to be settled first and understood afterwards. We have seen how much of our present perplexities and confusion this untrue notion of the majority of people amongst us has caused, and tends to perpetuate. Therefore the true business of the friends of culture now is, to dissipate this false notion, to spread the belief in right reason and in a firm intelligible law of things, and to get men to allow their thought and consciousness to play on their stock notions and habits disinterestedly and freely; to get men to try, in preference to staunchly acting with imperfect knowledge, to obtain some sounder basis of knowledge on which to act. This is what the friends and lovers of culture have to do, however the believers in action may grow impatient with us for saying so, and may insist on our lending a hand to their practical operations and showing a commendable interest in them.

To this insistence we must indeed turn a deaf ear. But neither, on the other hand, must the friends of culture expect to take the believers in action by storm, or to be visibly and speedily important, and to rule and cut a figure in the world. Aristotle says that those for whom alone ideas and the pursuit of the intelligible law of things can, in general, have much attraction, are principally the young, filled with generous spirit and with a passion for perfection; but the mass of mankind, he says, follow seeming goods for real, bestowing hardly a thought upon true sweetness and light;—"and to *their* lives," he adds mournfully, "who can give another and a better rhythm?" But, although those chiefly attracted by sweetness and light will probably always be the young and enthusiastic, and culture must not hope to take the mass of mankind by storm, yet we will not therefore, for our own day and for our own people, admit and rest in the desponding sentence of Aristotle. For is not this the right crown of the long discipline of Hebraism, and the due fruit of mankind's centuries of painful schooling in self-conquest, and the just reward, above all, of the strenuous energy of our own nation and kindred in dealing honestly with itself and walking steadfastly according to the best light it knows,—that when in the fulness of time it has reason and beauty offered to it, and the law of things as they really are, it should at last walk by this true light with the same staunchness and zeal with which it formerly walked by its imperfect light? And thus man's two great natural forces, Hebraism and Hellenism, will no longer be dissociated and rival, but will be a joint force of right thinking and strong doing to carry him on towards perfection. This is what the lovers of culture may perhaps dare to augur for such a nation as ours.

Therefore, however great the changes to be accomplished, and however dense the array of Barbarians, Philistines, and Populace, we will neither despair on the one hand, nor, on the other, threaten violent revolution and change. But we will look forward cheerfully and hopefully to "a revolution," as the Duke of Wellington said, "by due course of law;" though not exactly such laws as our Liberal friends are now, with their actual lights, fond of offering to us.

But if despondency and violence are both of them forbidden to the believer in culture, yet neither, on the other hand, is public life and direct political action much permitted to him. For it is his business, as we have seen, to get the present believers in action, and lovers of political talking and doing, to make a return upon their own minds, scrutinise their stock notions and habits much more, value their present talking and doing much less; in order that, by learning to think more clearly, they may come at last to act less confusedly. But how shall we persuade our Barbarian to hold lightly to his feudal usages; how shall we persuade our Nonconformist that his time spent in agitating for the abolition of church-establishments would have been better spent in getting worthier ideas than churchmen have of God and the ordering of the world, or his time spent in battling for voluntaryism in education better spent in learning to value and found a public and national culture; how shall we persuade, finally, our Alderman-Colonel not to be content with sitting in the hall of judgment or marching at the head of his men of war, without some knowledge how to perform judg-

ment and how to direct men of war,—how, I say, shall we persuade all these of this, if our Alderman-Colonel sees that we want to get his leading-staff and his scales of justice for our own hands; or the Nonconformist, that we want for ourselves his platform; or the Barbarian, that we want for ourselves his pre-eminence and function? Certainly they will be less slow to believe, as we want them to believe, that the intelligible law of things has in itself something desirable and precious, and that all place, function, and bustle are hollow goods without it, if they see that we ourselves can content ourselves with this law, and find in it our satisfaction, without making it an instrument to give us for ourselves place, function, and bustle.

And although Mr. Sidgwick says that social usefulness really means "losing oneself in a mass of disagreeable, hard, mechanical details," and though all the believers in action are fond of asserting the same thing, yet, as to lose ourselves is not what we want, but to find ourselves through finding the intelligible law of things, this assertion too we shall not blindly accept, but shall sift and try it a little first. And if we see that because the believers in action, forgetting Goethe's maxim, "To act is easy, to think is hard," imagine there is some wonderful virtue in losing oneself in a mass of mechanical details, therefore they excuse themselves from much thought about the clear ideas which ought to govern these details, then we shall give our chief care and pains to seeking out those ideas and to setting them forth; being persuaded that if we have the ideas firm and clear, the mechanical details for their execution will come a great deal more simply and easily than we now suppose. And even in education, where our Liberal friends are now, with much zeal, bringing out their train of practical operations and inviting all men to lend them a hand; and where, since education is the road to culture, we might gladly lend them a hand with their practical operations if we could lend them one anywhere; yet, if we see that any German or Swiss or French law for education rests on very clear ideas about the citizen's claim, in this matter, upon the State, and the State's duty towards the citizen, but has its mechanical details comparatively few and simple, while an English law for the same concern is ruled by no clear idea about the citizen's claim and the State's duty, but has, in compensation, a mass of minute mechanical details about the number of members on a school-committee, and how many shall be a quorum, and how they shall be summoned and how often they shall meet,—then we must conclude that our nation stands in more need of clear ideas on the main matter than of laboured details about the accessories of the matter, and that we do more service by trying to help it to the ideas, than by lending it a hand with the details. So while Mr. Samuel Morley[1] and his friends talk of changing their policy on education not for the sake of modelling it on more sound ideas but "for fear the management of education should be taken out of their hands," we shall not much care for taking the management out of their hands and getting it into ours; but rather we shall try and make them perceive, that to model education on sound ideas is of more importance than to have the management of it in one's own hands ever so fully.

At this exciting juncture, then, while so many of the lovers of new ideas, somewhat weary, as we too are, of the stock performances of our Liberal friends upon the political stage, are disposed to rush valiantly upon this public stage themselves, we cannot at all think that for a wise lover of new ideas this stage is the right one. Plenty of people there will be without us,— country gentlemen in search of a club, demagogues in search of a tub, lawyers in search of a place, industrialists in search of gentility,—who will come from the east and from the west, and will sit down at that Thyestean banquet[2] of clap-trap which English public life for these many years past has been. And, so long as those old organisations, of which we have seen the insufficiency,—those expressions of our ordinary self, Barbarian or Philistine—have force anywhere, they will have force in Parliament. There, the man whom the Barbarians send, cannot but be impelled to please the Barbarians' ordinary self, and their natural taste for the bathos: and the man whom the Philistines send cannot but be impelled to please those of the Philistines. Parliamentary Conservatism will and must long mean this, that the Barbarians should keep their heritage; and Parliamentary Liberalism, that the Barbarians should pass away, as they will pass away, and that into their heritage the Philistines should enter. This seems, indeed, to be the true and authentic promise of which our Liberal friends and Mr. Bright believe themselves the heirs, and the goal of that great man's labours. Presently, perhaps, Mr. Odger and Mr. Bradlaugh will be there with their mission to oust both Barbarians and Philistines, and to get the heritage for the Populace.

We, on the other hand, are for giving the heritage neither to the Barbarians nor to the Philistines, nor yet to the Populace; but we are for the transformation of each and all of these according to the law of perfection. Through the length and breadth of our nation a sense,—vague and obscure as yet,—of weariness with the old organisations, of desire for this transformation, works and grows. In the House of Commons the old organisations must inevitably be most enduring and strongest, the transformation must inevitably be longest in showing itself; and it may truly be averred, therefore, that at the present juncture the centre of movement is not in the House of Commons. It is in the fermenting mind of the nation; and his is for the next twenty years the real influence who can address himself to this.

Pericles was perhaps the most perfect public speaker who ever lived, for he was the man who most perfectly combined thought and wisdom with feeling and eloquence. Yet Plato brings in Alcibiades declaring, that men went away from the oratory of Pericles, saying it was very fine, it was very good, and afterwards thinking no more about it; but they went away from hearing Socrates talk, he says, with the point of what he had said sticking fast in their minds, and they could not get rid of it. Socrates has drunk his hemlock, and is dead; but in his own breast does not every man carry about with him a possible Socrates, in that power of a disinterested play of consciousness upon his stock notions and habits, of which this wise and admirable man gave all through his lifetime the great example, and which was the secret of his incomparable influence? and he who leads men to call forth and exercise in themselves this power, and who busily calls it forth and exercises it in himself, is at the present moment, perhaps, as Socrates was in his time, more in concert with the vital working of men's minds, and more effectually significant, than any House of Commons' orator, or practical operator in politics.

Everyone is now boasting of what he has done to educate men's minds and to give things the course they are taking. Mr. Disraeli educates, Mr. Bright educates, Mr. Beales educates. We, indeed, pretend to educate no one, for we are still engaged in trying to clear and educate

---

[1] Samuel Morley was Member of Parliament for Nottingham.
[2] A banquet in classical mythology in which Thyestes unwittingly ate the flesh of his own sons.

ourselves. But we are sure that the endeavour to reach, through culture, the firm intelligible law of things,—we are sure that the detaching ourselves from our stock notions and habits,—that a more free play of consciousness, an increased desire for sweetness and light, and all the bent which we call Hellenising, is the master-impulse even now of the life of our nation and of humanity,—somewhat obscurely perhaps for this actual moment, but decisively and certainly for the immediate future; and that those who work for this are the sovereign educators.

Docile echoes of the eternal voice, pliant organs of the infinite will, such workers are going along with the esesntial movement of the world; and this is their strength, and their happy and divine fortune. For if the believers in action, who are so impatient with us and call us effeminate, had had the same good furtune, they would, no doubt, have surpassed us in this sphere of vital influence by all the superiority of their genius and energy over ours. But now we go the way the human race is going, while they abolish the Irish Church by the power of the Nonconformists' antipathy to establishments, or they enable a man to marry his deceased wife's sister.

from Literature and Dogma

Literature and Dogma is one of Arnold's most instructive ventures into the field of criticism on religion. It was published in 1873. After publishing St. Paul and Protestantism *in 1870 Arnold had taken up the study of Hebrew the better to grasp the literary excellence of the Bible, and it is as a literary-critical defense of the Bible that* Literature and Dogma *takes its stand. Its subtitle is "An Essay Towards a Better Apprehension of the Bible." Skeptical as Arnold was of both theology and metaphysics as means of advancing religion, he believed that a right reading of the Bible would do more for the spread of Christianity than any other approach. The volume* Literature and Dogma *grew out of essays Arnold published in the* Cornhill *in 1871. The Introduction, Chapter XII, and the Conclusion are given below. (Notes marked [A] are by Arnold.)*

Introduction

MR. DISRAELI, treating Hellenic things with the scornful negligence natural to a Hebrew, said the other day in a well-known book, that our aristocratic class, the polite flower of the nation, were truly Hellenic in this respect among others,—that they cared nothing for letters and never read. Now, there seems to be here some inaccuracy, if we take our standard of what is Hellenic from Hellas at its highest pitch of development. For the latest historian of Greece, Dr. Curtius,[1] tells us that in the Athens of Pericles 'reading was universally diffused'; and again, that 'what more than anything distinguishes the Greeks from the barbarians of ancient and modern times, is the idea of a culture comprehending body *and soul* in an equal measure.' And we have ourselves called our aristocratic class *Barbarians,* which is the contrary of Hellenes, from this very reason: because, with all their fine, fresh appearance, their open-air life, and their love of field-sports, for reading and thinking they have in general no great turn. But no doubt Mr. Disraeli was thinking of the primitive Hellenes of north-western Greece, from among whom the Dorians of Peloponnesus originally came, but who themselves remained in their old seats and did not migrate and develop like their more famous brethren. And of these primitive Hellenes, of Greeks like the Chaonians and Molossians, it is probably a very just account to give, that they lived in the open air, loved

---

[1] Ernst Curtius (1814–96), German scholar, author of *Griechische Geschichte* (1857–61).

field-sports, and never read. And, explained in this way, Mr. Disraeli's parallel of our aristocratic class with what he somewhat misleadingly calls the old Hellenic race, appears ingenious and sound. To those lusty northerners, the Molossian and Chaonian Greeks—Greeks untouched by the development which contradistinguishes the Hellene from the barbarian,—our aristocratic class, as he exhibits it, has a strong resemblance. At any rate, this class,—which from its great possessions, its beauty and attractiveness, the admiration felt for it by the Philistines or middle class, its actual power in the nation, and the still more considerable destinies to which its politeness, in Mr. Carlyle's opinion, entitles it, cannot but attract our notice pre-eminently,—shows at present a great and genuine disregard for letters.

And perhaps, if there is any other body of men which strikes one, even after looking at our aristocratic class, as being in the sunshine, as exercising great attraction, as being admired by the Philistines or middle class, and as having before it a future still more brilliant than its present, it is the friends of physical science. Now, their revolt against the tyranny of letters is notorious. To deprive letters of the too great place they have hitherto filled in men's estimation, and to substitute other studies for these, is the object of a sort of crusade with a body of people important in itself, but still more important because of the gifted leaders who march at its head.

Religion has always hitherto been a great power in England; and on this account, perhaps, whatever humiliations may be in store for religion in the future, the friends of physical science will not object to our saying that, after them and the aristocracy, the leaders of the religious world fill a prominent place in the public eye even now, and one cannot help noticing what their opinions and likings are. And it is curious how the feeling of the chief people in the religious world, too, seems to be just now against mere letters, which they slight as the vague and inexact instrument of shallow essayists and magazine-writers; and in favour of dogma, of a scientific and exact presentment of religious things, instead of a literary presentment of them. 'Dogmatic theology,' says the *Guardian*, speaking of our existing dogmatic theology,—'Dogmatic theology, *that is, precision and definiteness* of religious thought.' 'Maudlin sentimentalism,'

says the Dean of Norwich, 'with its miserable disparagements of any *definite* doctrine; a *nerveless* religion, without the *sinew* and *bone* of doctrine.' The distinguished Chancellor of the University of Oxford thought it needful to tell us on a public occasion lately, that 'religion is no more to be severed from dogma than light from the sun.' Every one, again, remembers the Bishops of Winchester[2] and Gloucester making in Convocation their remarkable effort 'to do something,' as they said, 'for the honour of Our Lord's Godhead,' and to mark their sense of 'that infinite separation for time and for eternity which is involved in rejecting the Godhead of the Eternal Son.' In the same way: 'To no teaching,' says one champion of dogma, 'can the appellation of Christian be truly given which does not involve the idea of a Personal God.' Another lays like stress on correct ideas about the Personality of the Holy Ghost. 'Our Lord unquestionably,' says a third, 'annexes eternal life to a right knowledge of the Godhead,'—that is, to a right speculative, dogmatic knowledge of it. A fourth appeals to history and human nature for proof that 'an undogmatic Church can no more satisfy the hunger of the soul, than a snowball, painted to look like fruit, would stay the hunger of the stomach.' And all these friends of theological science are, like the friends of physical science, though from another cause, severe upon letters. Attempts made at a literary treatment of religious history and ideas they call 'a subverting of the faith once delivered to the saints.' Those who make them they speak of as 'those who have made shipwreck of the faith'; and when they talk of 'the poison openly disseminated by infidels,' and describe the 'progress of infidelity,' which more and more, according to their account, 'denies God, rejects Christ, and lets loose every human passion,' though they have the audaciousness of physical science most in their eye, yet they have a direct aim, too, at the looseness and dangerous temerity of letters.

Keeping in remembrance what Scripture says about the young man who had great possessions, to be able to work a change of mind in our aristocratic class we never have pretended, we never shall pretend. But to the friends of physical science and to the friends of dogma we do feel emboldened, after giving our best consideration to the matter, to say a few words on behalf of letters, and in deprecation of the slight which, on

---

[2] The late Bishop Wilberforce. [A]

different grounds, they both put upon them. But particularly in reply to the friends of dogma do we wish to insist on the case for letters, because of the great issues which seem to us to be here involved. Therefore of the relation of letters to religion we are going now to speak; of their effect upon dogma, and of the consequences of this to religion. And so the subject of the present volume will be *literature and dogma*.

II

It is clear that dogmatists love religion;—for else why do they occupy themselves with it so much, and make it, most of them, the business, even the professional business, of their lives? And clearly religion seeks man's salvation. How distressing, therefore, must it be to them, to think that 'salvation is unquestionably annexed to a right knowledge of the Godhead,' and that a right knowledge of the Godhead depends upon reasoning, for which so many people have not much aptitude; and upon reasoning from ideas or terms such as substance, identity, causation, design, about which there is endless disagreement! It is true, a right knowledge of geometry also depends upon reasoning, and many people never get it; but then, in the first place, salvation is not annexed to a right knowledge of geometry; and in the second, the ideas or terms such as *point, line, angle,* from which we reason in geometry, are terms about which there is no ambiguity or disagreement. But as to the demonstrations and terms of theology we cannot comfort ourselves in this manner. How must this thought mar the Archbishop of York's enjoyment of such a solemnity as that in which, to uphold and renovate religion, he lectured lately to Lord Harrowby, Dean Payne Smith, and other kindred souls, upon the theory of causation! And what a consolation to us, who are so perpetually being taunted with our known inaptitude for abstruse reasoning, if we can find that for this great concern of religion, at any rate, abstruse reasoning does not seem to be the appointed help; and that as good or better a help,—for indeed there can hardly, to judge by the present state of things, be a worse,—may be something which is in an ordinary man's power.

For the good of letters is, that they require no extraordinary acuteness such as is required to handle the theory of causation like the Archbishop of York, or the doctrine of the Godhead of the Eternal Son like the Bishops of Winchester and Gloucester. The good of letters may be had

without skill in arguing, or that formidable logical apparatus, not unlike a guillotine, which Professor Huxley speaks of somewhere as the young man's best companion;—and so it *would* be, no doubt, if all wisdom were come at by hard reasoning. In that case, all who could not manage this apparatus (and only a few picked craftsmen can manage it) would be in a pitiable condition.

But the valuable thing in letters,—that is, in the acquainting oneself with the best which has been thought and said in the world,—is, as we have often remarked, the judgment which forms itself insensibly in a fair mind along with fresh knowledge; and this judgment almost any one with a fair mind, who will but trouble himself to try and make acquaintance with the best which has been thought and uttered in the world, may, if he is lucky, hope to attain to. For this judgment comes almost of itself; and what it displaces it displaces easily and naturally, and without any turmoil of controversial reasonings. The thing comes to look differently to us, as we look at it by the light of fresh knowledge. We are not beaten from our old opinion by logic, we are not driven off our ground;—our ground itself changes with us.

Far more of our mistakes come from want of fresh knowledge than from want of correct reasoning; and, therefore, letters meet a greater want in us than does logic. The idea of a triangle is a definite and ascertained thing, and to deduce the properties of a triangle from it is an affair of reasoning. There are heads unapt for this sort of work, and some of the blundering to be found in the world is from this cause. But how far more of the blundering to be found in the world comes from people fancying that some idea is a definite and ascertained thing, like the idea of a triangle, when it is not; and proceeding to deduce properties from it, and to do battle about them, when their first start was a mistake! And how liable are people with a talent for hard, abstruse reasoning, to be tempted to this mistake! and what can clear up such a mistake except a wide and familiar acquaintance with the human spirit and its productions, showing how ideas and terms arose, and what is their character? and this is letters and history, not logic.

So that minds with small aptitude for abstruse reasoning may yet, through letters, gain some hold on sound judgment and useful knowledge, and may even clear up blunders committed, out of their very excess of talent, by the athletes of logic.

CHAPTER XII

The True Greatness of Christianity

No; the *mystery* hidden from ages and genera-tions,[1] which none of the rulers of this world knew,[2] the mystery revealed finally by Jesus Christ and rejected by the Jews, was not the doctrine of the Trinity, nor anything specu-lative. It was the method and the secret of Jesus. Jesus did not change the object for men,—righteousness. He made clear what it was, and that it was this:—his *method* and his *secret*.

This was the *mystery*, and the Apostles had still the consciousness that it was. To 'learn Christ,' to 'be taught the truth as it is in Jesus,' was not, with them, to acquire certain tenets about One God in Trinity and Trinity in Unity. It was, *'to be renewed in the spirit of your mind, and to put on the new man which after God is created in righteousness and true holiness.'*[3] And this exactly amounts to the method and secret of Jesus.

For Catholic and for Protestant theology alike, this consciousness, which the Apostles had still preserved, was lost. For Catholic and Protestant theology alike, the truth as it is in Jesus, the mystery revealed in Christ, meant something totally different from his method and secret. But they recognised, and indeed the thing was so plain that they could not well miss it, they recognised that on all Christians the method and secret of Jesus were enjoined. So to this extent the method and secret of Jesus were preached and had their effect. To this extent true Chris-tianity has been known, and to the extent before stated it has been neglected. Now, as we say that the truth and grandeur of the Old Testament most comes out *experimentally,*—that is, by the whole course of the world establishing it, and confuting what is opposed to it— so it is with Christianity. Its grandeur and truth are far best brought out *experimentally;* and the thing is, to make people see this.

But there is this difference between the religion of the Old Testament and Christianity. Of the religion of the Old Testament we can pretty well

see to the end, we can trace fully enough the experimental proof of it in history. But of Chris-tianity the future is as yet almost unknown. For that the world cannot get on without righteous-ness we have the clear experience, and a grand and admirable experience it is. But what the world will become by the thorough use of that which is really righteousness, the method and the secret and the sweet reasonableness of Jesus, we have as yet hardly any experience at all. There-fore we, who in this essay limit ourselves to experience, shall speak here of Christianity and of its greatness very soberly. Yet Christianity is really all the grander for that very reason which makes us speak about it in this sober manner,—that it has such an immense development still before it, and that it has as yet so little shown all it contains, all it can do. Indeed, that Chris-tianity has already done so much as it has, is a witness to it; and that it has not yet done more, is a witness to it too. Let us observe how this is so.

II

Few things are more melancholy than to observe Christian apologists taunting the Jews with the failure of Hebraism to fulfil the splendid promises of prophecy, and Jewish apologists taunting Christendom with the like failure on the part of Christianity. Neither has yet fulfilled them, or could yet have fulfilled them. Certainly the resotration by Cyrus, the Second Temple, the Maccabean victories, are hardly more than the shadows of a fulfilment of the magnificent words: 'The sons of them that afflicted thee shall come bending unto thee, and all they that despised thee shall bow themselves down at the soles of thy feet; thy gates shall not be shut day nor night, that men may bring unto thee the treasures of the Gentiles, and that their kings may be brought.'[4] The Christianisation of all the leading nations of the world is, it is said, a much better fulfilment of that promise. Be it so. Yet does Christendom, let us ask, offer more than a shadow of the fulfilment of *this:* 'Violence shall no more be heard in thy land; the vile person shall no more be called liberal, nor the churl bountiful; thy people shall be *all* righteous; they shall *all* know me, from the least to the greatest; I will put my law in their inward parts, and write it in their hearts; the Eternal shall be thine everlasting light, and the days of thy mourning

---

[1] Colossians 1:26. [A]   [2] I Corinthians 2:8. [A]   [3] Ephesians 4:23–24. [A]
[4] Isaiah 40:14, 11. [A]

shall be ended'?[5] Manifestly it does not. Yet the two promises hang together; one of them is not truly fulfilled unless the other is.

The promises were made to *righteousness*, with all which the idea of righteousness involves. And it involves Christianity. They were made on the immediate prospect of a small triumph for righteousness, the restoration of the Jews after the captivity in Babylon; but they are not satisfied by that triumph. The prevalence of the profession of Christianity is a larger triumph; yet in itself it hardly satisfies them any better. What satisfies them is the prevailing of that which righteousness really is, and nothing else satisfies them. Now, Christianity is that which righteousness really is. Therefore, if something called Christianity prevails, and yet the promises are not satisfied, the inference is that this *something* is not that which righteousness really is, and therefore not really Christianity. And as the course of the world is perpetually establishing the pre-eminence of righteousness, and confounding whatever denies this pre-eminence, so, too, the course of the world is for ever establishing what righteousness really is,—that is to say, true Christianity,—and confounding whatever pretends to be true Christianity and is not.

Now, just as the constitution of things turned out to be against the great unrighteous kingdoms of the heathen world, and against all the brilliant Ishmaels we have seen since, so the constitution of things turns out to be against all false presentations of Christianity, such as the theology of the Fathers or Protestant theology. They do not work successfully, they do not reach the aim, they do not bring the world to the fruition of the promises made to righteousness. And the reason is, because they substitute for what is really righteousness something else. Catholic dogma or Lutheran justification by faith they substitute for the method and secret of Jesus.

Nevertheless, as all Christian Churches do recommend the method and the secret of Jesus, though not in the right way or in the right eminency, still the world is made partially acquainted with what righteousness really is, and the doctrine produces some effect, although the full effect is much thwarted and deadened by the false way in which the doctrine is presented. Still, the effect produced is great. For instance, the sum of individual happiness that has been caused by Christianity is, any one can see, enormous. But let us take the effect of Christianity on the world. And if we look at the thing closely, we shall find that its effect has been this: Christianity has brought the world, or at any rate all the leading part of the world, *to regard righteousness as only the Jews regarded it before the coming of Christ.* The world has accepted, so far as profession goes, that original revelation made to Israel: *the pre-eminence of righteousness.* The infinite truth and attractiveness of the method and secret and character of Jesus, however falsely surrounded, have prevailed with the world so far as this. And this is an immense gain, and a signal witness to Christianity. The world does homage to the pre-eminence of righteousness; and here we have one of those fulfilments of prophecy which are so real and so glorious. 'Glorious things are spoken of thee, O City of God! I will make mention of Rahab and Babylon as of them that know me! behold, the Philistines also, and Tyre, with the Ethiopians,—these were born *there!* And of Zion it shall be reported: This and that man was born in *her!*—and the Most High shall stablish her. The Eternal shall count, when he writeth up the people: This man was born *there!*'[6] That prophecy is at the present day abundantly fulfilled. The world's chief nations have now all come, we see, to reckon and profess themselves *born in Zion,*—born, that is, in the religion of Zion, *the city of righteousness.*

But there remains the question: *what* righteousness really is. The method and secret and sweet reasonableness of Jesus. But the world does not see this; for it puts, as righteousness, something else first and this second. So that here, too, as to seeing what righteousness really is, the world now is much in the same position in which the Jews, when Jesus Christ came, were. It is often said: If Jesus Christ came now, his religion would be rejected. And this is only another way of saying that the world now, as the Jewish people formerly, has something which thwarts and confuses its perception of what righteousness really is. It is so; and the thwarting cause is the same now as then:—the dogmatic system current, the so-called orthodox theology. This prevents now, as it did then, that which righteousness really is, the method and secret of Jesus, from being rightly received, from operating fully, and from accomplishing its due effect.

So true is this, that we have only to look at our own community to see the almost precise parallel, so far as religion is concerned, to the state of things presented in Judæa when Jesus

---

[5] Isaiah 40:18; 32:5; 40:21; Jeremiah 31:33, 34; Isaiah 40:20. [A]   [6] Psalms 87:3–6. [A]

Christ came. The multitudes are the same everywhere. The chief priests and elders of the people, and the scribes, are our bishops and dogmatists, with their pseudo-science of learned theology blinding their eyes, and always,—whenever simple souls are disposed to think that the method and secret of Jesus is true religion, and that the Great Personal First Cause and the Godhead of the Eternal Son have nothing to do with it,— eager to cry out: *This people that knoweth not the law are cursed!*[7] The Pharisees, with their genuine concern for religion, but total want of perception of what religion really is, and by their temper, attitude, and aims doing their best to make religion impossible, are the Protestant Dissenters. The Sadducees are our friends the philosophical Liberals, who believe neither in angel nor spirit but in Mr. Herbert Spencer. Even the Roman governor has his close parallel in our celebrated aristocracy, with its superficial good sense and good nature, its complete inaptitude for ideas, its profound helplessness in presence of all great spiritual movements. And the result is, that the splendid promises to righteousness made by the Hebrew prophets, claimed by the Jews as the property of Judaism, claimed by us as the property of Christianity, are almost as ludicrously inapplicable to our religious state now, as to theirs then.

And this, we say, is again a signal witness to Christianity. Jesus Christ came to reveal what righteousness, to which the promises belong, really is; and so long as this, though shown by Jesus, is not recognised by us, we may call ourselves Christendom as much as we please, the true character of a Christendom will be wanting to us, because the great promises of prophecy will be still without their fulfilment. Nothing will do except righteousness; and no other conception of righteousness will do, except Jesus Christ's conception of it:—his *method* and his *secret*.

III

Yes, the grandeur of Christianity and the imposing and impressive attestation of it, if we could but worthily bring the thing out, is here: in that immense experimental proof of the necessity of it, which the whole course of the world has steadily accumulated, and indicates to us as still continuing and extending. Men will not admit assumptions, the popular legend they

call a fairy-tale, the metaphysical demonstrations do not demonstrate, nothing but experimental proof will go down; and here is an experimental proof which never fails, and which at the same time is infinitely grander, by the vastness of its scale, the scope of its duration, the gravity of its results, than the machinery of the popular fairy-tale. Walking on the water, multiplying loaves, raising corpses, a heavenly judge appearing with trumpets in the clouds while we are yet alive,— what is this compared to the real experience offered as witness to us by Christianity? It is like the difference between the grandeur of an extravaganza and the grandeur of the sea or the sky,—immense objects which dwarf us, but where we are in contact with reality, and a reality of which we can gradually, though very slowly, trace the laws.

The more we trace the real law of Christianity's action, the grander it will seem. Certainly in the Gospels there is plenty of matter to call out our feelings. But perhaps this has been somewhat over-used and mis-used, applied, as it has been, chiefly so as to be subservient, as it has been, chiefly so as to be subservient to what we call the fairy-tale of the three Lord Shaftesburys,[8]—a story which we do not deny to have, like other products of the popular imagination, its pathos and power, but which we have seen to be no solid foundation to rest our faith in the Bible on. And perhaps, too, we do wrong, and inevitably fall into what is artificial and unnatural, in labouring so much to produce in ourselves now, as the one impulse determining us to use the method and secret of Jesus, that conscious ardent sensation of personal love to him, which we find the first generation of Christians feeling and professing, and which was the natural motor for those who were with him or near him, and, so to speak, touched him; and in making this our first object. At any rate, misemployed as this motor has often been, it might be well to forego or at least suspend its use for ourselves and others for a time, and to fix our minds exclusively on the recommendation given to the method and secret of Jesus by their being *true,* and by the whole course of things proving this.

Now, just as the best recommendation of the oracle committed to Israel, *Righteousness is salvation,* is found in our more and more discovering, in our own history and in the whole history of the world, that it *is* so, so we shall

---

[7] John 7:49. [A]

[8] Anthony Ashley Cooper, 7th Earl of Shaftesbury (1801–85), English philanthropist and reformer.

find it to be with the method and secret of Jesus. That this *is* the righteousness which is salvation, that the method and secret of Jesus, that is to say, conscience and self-renouncement, *are* righteousness, bring about the kingdom of God or the reign of righteousness,—this, which is the Christian revelation and what Jesus came to establish, is best impressed, for the present at any rate, by experiencing and showing again and again, in ourselves and in the course of the world, that it *is* so; that this is the righteousness which is saving, and that there is none other. Let us but well observe what comes, in ourselves or the world, of trying any other, of not being convinced that this is righteousness, and this only; and we shall find ourselves more and more, as by irresistible viewless hands, caught and drawn towards the Christian revelation, and made to desire more and more to serve it. No proof can be so solid as this experimental proof; and none, again, can be so grand, so fitted to fill us with awe, admiration, and gratitude. So that feeling and emotion will now well come in after it, though not before it. For the whole course of human things is really, according to this experience, leading up to the fulfilment of Jesus Christ's promise to his disciples: *Fear not, little flock! for it is your Father's good pleasure to give you the kingdom.*[9] And thus that comes out, after all, to be true, which St. Paul announced prematurely to the first generation of Christians: *When Christ, who is our life, shall appear, then shall ye also appear with him in glory.*[10] And the author of the Apocalypse, in like manner, foretold: *The kingdom of the world is become the kingdom of our Lord and his Christ.*[11] The kingdom of the Lord the world is already become, by its chief nations professing the religion of righteousness. The kingdom of Christ the world will have to become, it is on its way to become, because the profession of righteousness, except as Jesus Christ interpreted righteousness, is vain. We can see the process, we are ourselves part of it, and can in our measure help forward or keep back its completion.

When the prophet, indeed, says to Israel, on the point of being restored by Cyrus: '*The nation and kingdom that will not serve thee shall perish!*'[12] the promise, applied literally, fails. But extended to that idea of righteousness, of which Israel was the depositary and in which the real life of Israel lay, the promise is true,

and we can see it fulfilled. In like manner, when the Apostle says to the Corinthians or to the Colossians, instructed that the second advent would come in their own generation: '*We must all appear before the Judgment-seat of Christ!*'[13]— '*When Christ, who is our life, shall appear, then shall ye also appear with him in glory!*'[14] the promise, applied literally as the Apostle meant it and his converts understood it, fails. But divested of this *Aberglaube* or extra-belief, it is true; if indeed the world can be shown,—and it can,—to be moving necessarily towards the triumph of that Christ in whom the Corinthian and Colossian disciples lived, and whose triumph is the triumph of all his disciples also.

IV

Let us keep hold of this same experimental process in dealing with the promise of immortality; although here, if anywhere, *Aberglaube*, extra-belief, hope, anticipation, may well be permitted to come in. Still, what we need for our foundation is not *Aberglaube*, but *Glaube;* not extra-belief in what is beyond the range of possible experience, but belief in what can and should be known to be true.

By what futilities the demonstration of our immortality may be attempted, is to be seen in Plato's *Phædo.* Man's natural desire for continuance, however little it may be worth as a scientific proof of our immortality, is at least a proof a thousand times stronger than any such demonstration. The want of solidity in such argument is so palpable, that one scarcely cares to turn a steady regard upon it at all. And even of the common Christian conception of immortality the want of solidity is, perhaps, most conclusively shown, by the impossibility of so framing it as that it will at all support a steady regard turned upon it. In our English popular religion, for instance, the common conception of a future state of bliss is just that of the Vision of Mirza: 'Persons dressed in glorious habits with garlands on their heads, passing among the trees, lying down by the fountains, or resting on beds of flowers, amid a confused harmony of singing birds, falling waters, human voices, and musical instruments.' Or, even, with many, it is that of a kind of perfected middle-class home, with labour ended, the table spread, goodness all around, the lost ones restored, hymnody in-

---

[9] Luke 12:32. [A]   [10] Colossians 3:4. [A]
[11] Revelation 11:15. The Alexandrian manuscript is followed. [A]
[12] Isaiah 40:12. [A]   [13] II Corinthians 5:10. [A]   [14] Colossians 3:4. [A]

cessant. '*Poor fragments all of this low earth!*' Keble might well say.[15] That this conception of immortality cannot possibly be true, we feel, the moment we consider it seriously. And yet who can devise any conception of a future state of bliss, which shall bear close examination better?

Here, again, it is far best to take what is experimentally true, and nothing else, as our foundation, and afterwards to let hope and aspiration grow, if so it may be, out of this. Israel has said: 'In the way of righteousness is life, and in the pathway thereof there is no death.'[16] He had said: 'The righteous hath hope in his death.'[17] He had cried to his *Eternal that loveth righteousness:* 'Thou wilt not leave my soul in the grave, neither wilt thou suffer thy faithful servant to see corruption! thou wilt show me the path of life!'[18] And by a kind of short cut to the conclusion thus laid down, the Jews constructed their fairy-tale of an advent, judgment, and resurrection, as we find it in the Book of Daniel. Jesus, again, had said: 'If a man keep my word, he shall never see death.'[19] And by a kind of short cut to the conclusion thus laid down, Christians constructed their fairy-tale of the second advent, the resurrection of the body, the New Jerusalem. But instead of fairy-tales, let us begin, at least, with certainties.

And a certainty is the sense of *life,* of being truly *alive,* which accompanies righteousness. If this experimental sense does not rise to be stronger in us, does not rise to the sense of being inextinguishable, that is probably because our experience of righteousness is really so very small. Here, therefore, we may well permit ourselves to trust Jesus, whose practice and intuition both of them went, in these matters, so far deeper than ours. At any rate, we have in our experience this strong sense of *life from righteousness* to start with; capable of being developed, apparently, by progress in righteousness into something immeasurably stronger. Here is the true basis for all religious aspiration after immortality. And it is an experimental basis; and therefore, as to grandeur, it is again, when compared with the popular *Aberglaube,* grand with all the superior grandeur, on a subject of the highest seriousness, of reality over fantasy.

At present, the fantasy hides the grandeur of the reality. But when all the *Aberglaube* of the second advent, with its signs in the sky, sounding

trumpets and opening graves, is cleared away, then and not till then will come out the profound truth and grandeur of words of Jesus like these: 'The hour is coming, when they that are in the graves shall hear the voice of the Son of God; and they that hear shall *live.*'[20]

V

Finally, and above all. As, for the right inculcation of righteousness, we need the inspiring words of Israel's love for it, that is, we need the Bible; so, for the right inculcation of the method and secret of Jesus, we need the *epieikeia,* the sweet reasonableness, of Jesus. That is, in other words again, we need the *Bible;* for only through the Bible-records of Jesus can we get at his *epieikeia.* Even in these records, it is and can be presented but imperfectly; but only by reading and re-reading the Bible can we get at it at all.

Now, greatly as the failure, from the stress laid upon the pseudo-science of Church-dogma, to lay enough stress upon the method and secret of Jesus, has kept Christianity back from showing itself in its full power, it is probable that the failure to apply to the method and secret of Jesus, so far as these have at any rate been used, his sweet reasonableness or *epieikeia,* has kept it back even more. And the *infinite* of the religion of Jesus,—its immense capacity for ceaseless progress and farther development,— lies principally, perhaps, in the line of extricating more and more his sweet reasonableness, and applying it to his method and secret. For it is obvious from experience, how much our use of Christ's method and secret requires to be guided and governed by his *epieikeia.* Indeed, without this, his method and secret seem often of no use at all. The Flagellants imagined that they were employing his secret; and the Dissenters, with their 'spirit of watchful jealousy,' imagine that they are employing his method. To be sure, Mr. Bradlaugh imagines that the method and the secret of Jesus, nay, and Jesus himself too, are all baneful, and that the sooner we get rid of them all, the better. So far, then, the Flagellants and the Dissenters are in advance of Mr. Bradlaugh.[21] they value Christianity, and they profess the method and secret of Jesus. But they employ them so ill, that one is tempted to say they might nearly as well be without them. And this is

---

[15] John Keble's *Christian Year* (Sixth Sunday after Epiphany).   [16] Proverbs 12:28. [A]
[17] Proverbs 14:32. [A]   [18] Psalms 16:10, 11. [A]   [19] John 8:51. [A]   [20] John 5:25. [A]
[21] Charles Bradlaugh; see selection by Bradlaugh in this volume.

because they are wholly without his sweet reasonableness, or *epieikeia*. Now this can only be got, first, by knowing that it is in the Bible, and looking for it there; and then, by reading and re-reading the Gospels continually, until we catch something of it.

This, again, is an experimental process. That the *epieikeia* or sweet reasonableness of Jesus may be brought to govern our use of his method and secret, and that it can and will make our use of his method and secret quite a different thing, is proved by our actually finding this to be so when we try. So that the culmination of Christian righteousness in the applying, to guide our use of the method and secret of Jesus, his sweet reasonableness or *epieikeia*, is proved from experience. We end, therefore, as we began,—by experience. And the whole series of experiences, of which the survey is thus completed, rests, primarily, upon one fundamental fact,—itself, eminently, a fact of experience: *the necessity of righteousness*.

Conclusion

BUT now, after all we have been saying of the pre-eminency of righteousness, we remember what we have said formerly in praise of culture and of Hellenism, and against too much Hebraism, too exclusive a pursuit of the 'one thing needful,' as people call it. And we cannot help wondering whether we shall not be reproached with inconsistency, and told that we ought at least to sing, as the Greeks said, a *palinode;* and whether it may not really be so, and we ought. And, certainly, if we had ever said that Hellenism was three-fourths of human life, and conduct or righteousness but one-fourth, a palinode, as well as an unmusical man may, we would sing. But we have never said it. In praising culture, we have never denied that conduct, not culture, is three-fourths of human life.

Only it certainly appears, when the thing is examined, that conduct comes to have relations of a very close kind with culture. And the reason seems to be given by some words of our Bible, which, though they may not be exactly the right rendering of the original in that place, yet in themselves they explain the connection of culture

with conduct very well. 'I have seen the travail,' says the Preacher, 'which God hath given to the sons of men to be exercised in it; he hath made everything beautiful in his time; also, he hath set the world in their heart.'[1] *He hath set the world in their heart!*—that is why art and science, and what we call culture, are necessary. They may be only one-fourth of man's life, but they are *there*, as well as the three-fourths which conduct occupies. 'He hath set *the world* in their heart.' And, really, the reason which we hence gather for the close connection between culture and conduct, is so simple and natural that we are almost ashamed to give it; but we have offered so many simple and natural explanations in place of the abstruse ones which are current, that our hesitation is foolish.

Let us suggest then, that, having this one-fourth of their nature concerned with art and science, men cannot but somehow employ it. If they think that the three-fourths of their nature concerned with conduct are the whole of their nature, and that this is all they have to attend to, still the neglected one-fourth is there, it ferments, it breaks wildly out, it employs itself all at random and amiss. And hence, no doubt, our hymns and our dogmatic theology. Of our hymns we shall say a word presently; but what is our dogmatic theology, except the mis-attribution to the Bible,—the Book of *conduct*,—of a science and an abstruse metaphysic which is not there, because our theologians have in themselves a faculty for science, for it makes one-eighth of them? But they do not employ it on its proper objects; so it invades the Bible and tries to make the Bible what it is not, and to put into it what is not there. And this prevents their attending enough to what *is* in the Bible, and makes them battle for what is *not* in the Bible, but they have put it there;—battle for it in a manner clean contrary, often, to the teaching of the Bible. So has arisen, for instance, all religious persecution. And thus, we say, has conduct itself become impaired.

So that conduct is impaired by the want of science and culture; and our theologians really suffer, not from having too much science, but from having too little. Whereas, if they had turned their faculty for abstruse reasoning towards the proper objects, and had given themselves, in addition, a wide and large acquaintance with the productions of the human spirit and with men's way of thinking and of using words,

[1] Ecclesiastes 3:10, 11. [A]

then, on the one hand, they would not have been tempted to mis-employ on the Bible their faculty for abstruse reasoning, for they would have had plenty of other exercise for it; and, on the other hand, they would have escaped that literary inexperience which now makes them fancy that the Bible-language is scientific, and fit matter for the application of their powers of abstruse reasoning to it, when it is no such thing. Then they would have seen the fallacy of confounding the obscurity attaching to the idea of God,— that vast *not ourselves* which transcends us,— with the obscurity attaching to the idea of their Trinity, a confused metaphysical speculation which puzzles us. The one, they would have perceived, is the obscurity of the immeasurable depth of air, the other is the obscurity of a fog. And fog, they would have known, has no proper place in our conceptions of God; since whatever our minds *can* possess of God they know clearly, for no man, as Goethe says, possesses what he does not understand; but they can possess of Him but a very little. All this our dogmatic theologians would have known, if they had had more science and more literature. And therefore, simple as the Bible and conduct are, still culture seems to be required for them,—required to prevent our mis-handling and sophisticating them.

I I

Culture, then, and literature are required, even in the interest of religion itself, and when, taking nothing but *conduct* into account, we make God, as Israel made him, to be simply and solely 'the Eternal Power, not ourselves, that makes for *righteousness.*' But we are not to forget, that, grand as this conception of God is, and well as it meets the wants of far the largest part of our being, of three-fourths of it, yet there is one-fourth of our being of which it does not strictly meet the wants, the part which is concerned with art and science; or, in other words, with beauty and exact knowledge.

For the total man, therefore, the truer conception of God is as 'the Eternal Power, not ourselves, by which *all things* fulfil the law of their being'; by which, therefore, we fulfil the law of our being so far as our being is æsthetic and intellective, as well as so far as it is moral. And it is evident, as we have before now remarked, that in this wider sense God is

displeased and disserved by many things which cannot be said, except by putting a strain upon words, to displease and disserve him as the God of righteousness. He is displeased and disserved by men uttering such doggerel hymns as: *Sing glory, glory, glory to the great God Triune!* and: *Out of my stony griefs Bethel I'll raise!* and: *My Jesus to know, and feel his blood flow, 'tis life everlasting, 'tis heaven below!* or by theologians uttering such pseudo-science as their *blessed truth that the God of universe is a* PERSON. But it would be harsh to give, at present, this turn to our employment of the phrases, *pleasing God, displeasing God.*

And yet, as man makes progress, we shall surely come to doing this. For, the clearer our conceptions in science and art become, the more will they assimilate themselves to the conceptions of duty in conduct, will become practically stringent like rules of conduct, and will invite the same sort of language in dealing with them. And so far let us venture to poach on M. Emile Burnouf's[2] manor, and to talk about the Aryan genius, as to say, that the love of *science*, the energy and honesty in the pursuit of *science*, in the best of the Aryan races, do seem to correspond in a remarkable way to the love of *conduct*, and the energy and honesty in the pursuit of *conduct*, in the best of the Semitic. To treat science with the same kind of seriousness as conduct, does seem, therefore, to be a not impossible thing for the Aryan genius to come to.

But for all this, however, man is hardly yet ripe. For our race, as we see it now and as ourselves we form a part of it, the true God is and must be pre-eminently the God of the Bible, *the Eternal who makes for righteousness*, from whom Jesus came forth, and whose Spirit governs the course of humanity. Only, we see that even for apprehending this God of the Bible rightly and not wrongly, letters, which so many people now disparage, and what we call, in general, *culture*, seem to be necessary.

And meanwhile, to prevent our at all pluming ourselves on having apprehended what so much baffles our dogmatic friends (although indeed it is not so much we who apprehend it as the 'Zeit-Geist'[3] who discovers it to us), what a chastening and wholesome reflection for us it is, that it is only to our natural inferiority to these ingenious men that we are indebted for our advantage over them! For while *they* were born with talents for metaphysical speculation

---

[2] Émile Louis Burnouf (1821–1907), French philologist, director of a school at Athens.
[3] Literally, "time-spirit," the spirit of the age.

and abstruse reasoning, we are so notoriously deficient in everything of that kind, that our adversaries often taunt us with it, and have held us up to public ridicule as being 'without a system of philosophy based on principles interdependent, subordinate, and coherent.' And so we were thrown on letters; thrown upon reading this and that,—which anybody can do,— and thus gradually getting a notion of the history of the human mind, which enables us (the 'Zeit-Geist' favouring) to correct, in reading the Bible, some of the mistakes into which men of more metaphysical talents than literary experience have fallen. Cripples in like manner have been known, now and then, to be cast by their very infirmity upon some mental pursuit which has turned out happily for them; and a good fortune of this kind has perhaps been ours.

But we do not forget that this good fortune we owe to our weakness, and that the natural superiority remains with our adversaries. And some day, perhaps, the nature of God may be as well known as the nature of a cone or a triangle; and then our two bishops may deduce its properties with success, and make their brilliant logical play about it,—rightly, instead of as now, wrongly; and will resume all their advantage. But this will hardly be in our time. So that the superiority of this pair of distinguished metaphysicians will never perhaps, after all, be of any real advantage to them, but they will be deluded and bemocked by it until they die.

from God and the Bible

The response to Arnold's Literature and Dogma *was such that Arnold felt compelled to answer some of the objections. Accordingly he published a series of seven articles in the* Contemporary Review *between October 1874 and September 1875 under the general title "A Review of Objections to* Literature and Dogma." *These articles were subsequently gathered together and, with a Preface, published in 1875 as* God and the Bible: A Review of Objections to "Literature and Dogma." *In this work Arnold endeavors to justify his arguments in* Literature and Dogma *and to affirm his belief that the Bible is a religious document accessible to all, not only to those previously committed to certain theological propositions. The first chapter and the conclusion are given below.*

CHAPTER I

The God of Miracles

TO PEOPLE disposed to throw the Bible aside *Literature and Dogma* sought to restore the use of it by two considerations: one, that the Bible requires for its basis nothing but what they can verify; the other, that the language of the Bible is not scientific, but *literary.* That is, it is the language of poetry and emotion, approximate language thrown out, as it were, at certain great objects which the human mind augers and feels after, and thrown out by men very liable, many of them, to delusion and error. This has been violently impugned. What we have now to do, therefore, is to ask whoever thought he found profit from what we said, to examine with us whether it has been impugned successfully; whether he and we ought to give it up, or whether we ought to hold by it firmly and hopefully still.

First and foremost has been impugned the definition which, proceeding on the rule to take nothing as a basis for the Bible but what can be verified, we gave of God. And of this we certainly cannot complain. For we have ourselves said, that without a clear understanding in what sense this important but ambiguous term *God* is used, all fruitful discussion in theology is impossible. And yet, in theological discussion, this clear understanding is hardly ever cared for, but people assume that the sense of the term is something perfectly well known. 'A personal First Cause, that thinks and loves, the moral and intelligent governor of the universe,' is the sense which theologians in general assume to be the meaning, properly drawn out and strictly worded, of the term God. We say that by this assumption a great deal which cannot possibly be verified is put into the word God; and we propose, for the God of the Bible and of Christianity, a much less pretentious definition, but which has the advantage of containing nothing that cannot be verified. The God of the Bible and of Christianity is, we say: *The Eternal, not ourselves, that makes for righteousness.*

Almost with one voice our critics have expostulated with us for refusing to admit what they call a personal God. Nothing would be easier for us than, by availing ourselves of the ambiguity natural to the use of the term God, to give such a turn to our expressions as might satisfy some of our critics, or might enable our language to pass muster with the common religious world as permissible. But this would be clean contrary to our design. For we want to recommend the Bible and its religion by showing that they rest on something which can be verified. Now, in the Bible God is everything. Unless therefore we ascertain what it is which we mean by God, and that what we mean we can verify, we cannot recommend the Bible as we desire. So against all ambiguity in the use of this term we wage war. Mr. Llewellyn Davies says that we ourselves admit that the most proper language to use about God is the approximative language of poetry and eloquence, language thrown out at an object which it does not profess to define scientifically, language which cannot, therefore, be adequate and accurate. If Israel, then, might with propriety call God 'the high and holy one that inhabiteth eternity,' why, he asks, may not the Bishop of Gloucester with propriety talk of 'the blessed truth that the God of the universe is a person'? Neither the one expression nor the other is adequate; both are approximate. We answer: Let it be understood, then, that when the Bishop of Gloucester, or others, talk of the blessed truth that the God of the universe is a person, they mean to talk, not science, but rhetoric and poetry. In that case our only criticism on their language will be that it is bad rhetoric and poetry, whereas the rhetoric and poetry of Israel is good. But the truth is they mean it for science; they mean it for a more close and precise account of what Israel called poetically 'the high and holy one that inhabiteth eternity'; and it is false science because it assumes what it cannot verify. However, if it is not meant for science, but for poetry,

let us treat it as poetry; and then it is language not professing to be exact at all, and we are free to use it or not to use it as our sense of poetic propriety may dictate. But at all events let us be clear about one thing: Is it meant for poetry, or is it meant for science?

If we were asked what in our own opinion we had by *Literature and Dogma* effected for the benefit of readers of the Bible, we should answer that we had effected two things above all. First, that we had led the reader to face that primary question, so habitually slurred over, what 'God' means in the Bible, and to see that it means the Eternal not ourselves that makes for righteousness. Secondly, that we had made him ask himself what is meant by 'winning Christ,' 'knowing Christ,' 'the excellency of the knowledge of Christ,' and find that it means laying hold of the method and secret of Jesus. And of these two things achieved by us, as we think, for the Bible-reader's benefit, the first seems to us the more important. Sooner or later he will find the Bible fail him, unless he is provided with a sure meaning for the word 'God.' Until this is done, and to keep steadily before his mind how loosely he and others at present employ the word, we even recommend him to allow to the word no more contents than by its etymology it has, and to render it 'The Shining.' Archbishop Whately[1] blames those who define words by their etymology, and ridicules them as people who should insist upon it that sycophant shall mean 'fig-shewer' and nothing else. But etymological definition, trifling and absurd when a word's imported meaning is sure, becomes valuable when the imported meaning is unfixed. There was at Athens a practice, says Festus, of robbing the fig-orchards; a law was passed to check it; under this law vexatious informations were laid, and those who laid them were called *sycophants*, fig-informers, or, if Archbishop Whately pleases, fig-shewers. Then the name was transferred to vexatious informers or to calumniators generally, and at last to a cheating impostor of any sort. The wider new meaning thus imported into the word was something quite clear, something on which all were agreed; and thenceforward to insist on limiting *sycophant* to its old etymological sense of fig-informer would have been ridiculous.

But the case is different when the fuller meaning imported into a word is something vague and loose, something on which people are by no means agreed. It is then often an excellent

[1] Richard Whately (1787–1863), Archbishop of Dublin.

discipline to revert to the etymology; and to insist on confining ourselves to the sense given by this, until we get for our word a larger sense clear and certain. 'The Shining is our hope and strength.' 'O Shining, thou art my Shining, early will I seek thee!' 'My soul, wait thou only upon The Shining, for my expectation is from him!' 'The fool hath said in his heart: There is no Shining!'[2] This will not give us satisfaction. But it will thereby stimulate us all the more to find a meaning to the word 'God' that does give us satisfaction; and it will keep vivid in our minds the thought how little we outselves or others have such a meaning for the word at present.

Lord Lyttelton[3] lately published in the *Contemporary Review* a disquisition on 'Undogmatic and Unsectarian Teaching,' which signally illustrates the utility of this etymological discipline. Lord Lyttelton is very severe upon those whom he calls 'the shallow sciolists and apostles of modern Unsectarianism'; and very favourable to dogma, or the determined, decreed and received doctrine of so-called orthodox theology. He draws out a formal list of propositions beginning with: 'God is, God made the world, God cares for men, God is the Father of men,' and ending with: 'The Deity of God is in one sense One in another Threefold, God is One in Three Persons.' He defies any one to show where in this list that which is universal ends and that which is dogmatic begins. And his inference apparently is, that therefore the last propositions in the series may be freely taught. But if he examines his thoughts with attention he will find that he cannot tell where the character of his propositions changes because he has been using the word 'God' in the same sense all through the series. Now, the sense given to this word governs the sense of each and all of his propositions, but this sense he omits to furnish us with. Until we have it, we may agree that his latter propositions are dogmatic, but we cannot possibly concede to him that his earlier propositions have universal validity. Yet the whole force of his series of propositions, and of the argument which he founds upon it, depends on this: whether his definition of God, which he does not produce, is unchallengeable or no. Till he produces it, his readers will really best enable themselves to feel the true force of Lord Lyttelton's propositions by substituting for the word God its strict etymol-ogical equivalent Shining,—the only definition to which, until the fuller definition is produced and made good, the word has any right. The propositions will then run: 'The Shining is, The Shining made the world, The Shining cares for men, The Shining is the Father of men'; and so on to the final proposition: 'The Shining is One in Three Persons.' That entire inconclusiveness, of which we are by these means made fully aware, exists just as much in Lord Lyttelton's original propositions, but without being noticed by himself or by most of his readers.

Resolutely clear with himself, then, in using this word 'God,' we urge our reader to be, whatever offence he may give by it. When he is asked in a tone of horrified remonstrance whether he refuses to believe in a personal God, let him steadily examine what it is that people say about a personal God, and what grounds he has for receiving it. People say that there is a personal God, and that a personal God is a God who thinks and loves. That there is an Eternal not ourselves which makes for righteousness and is called God, is admitted; and indeed so much as this human experience proves. For the constitution and history of things show us that happiness, at which we all aim, is dependent on righteousness. Yet certainly we did not make this to be so, and it did not being when we began, nor does it end when we end, but is, so far as we can see, an eternal tendency outside us, prevailing whether we will or no, whether we are here or not. There is no difficulty, therefore, about an Eternal not ourselves that makes for righteousness, and to which men have transferred that ancient high name, *God*, the Brilliant or Shining, by which they once adored a mighty object outside themselves, the sun, which from the first took their notice as powerful for their weal or woe. So that God is, is admitted; but people maintain, besides, that he is personal and thinks and loves. 'The Divine Being cannot,' they say, 'be without the perfection which manifests itself in the human personality as the highest of which we have any knowledge.' Now, 'the deeper elements of personality are,' they add, 'existence, consciousness of this existence and control over it.' These, therefore, they say, God must have. And that the Eternal that makes for righteousness has these, they account (though their language is not always quite consistent on this point) a fact of

---

[2] Psalms 46:1; 63:1; 62:5; 14:1. [A]
[3] George William, 4th Baron Lyttelton (1817–76), under-secretary for the Colonies, sent Anglican settlers to New Zealand.

the same order and of as much certainty as that there is an Eternal that makes for righteousness at all. 'It is this power itself,' says M. Albert Réville,[4] 'this not ourselves which makes for righteousness, that constantly reveals to us the fact that it is a Spirit, that is to say, not merely an influence, but life, consciousness, and love.' Religion, it is affirmed, religion, which is morality touched with emotion, is impossible unless we know of God that he is a person who thinks and loves. 'If the not ourselves which makes for righteousness,' says M. Réville, 'is an unconscious force, I cannot feel for it that sacred emotion which raises morality to the rank of religion. Man no longer worships powers of which he has discovered the action to be impersonal.' All this sort of argumentation, which M. Réville manages with great delicacy and literary skill, is summed up in popular language plainly and well by a writer in the *Edinburgh Review*. 'Is the Power around us not a person? is what you would have us worship a thing? All existing beings must be either persons or things; and no sophistries can deter us from the invincible persuasion which all human creatures possess, that *persons* are superior to *things*.'

Now, before going farther, we have one important remark to make upon all this. M. Réville talks of those who *have discovered* the action of God to be impersonal. In another place he talks of *denying* conscious intelligence to God. The Edinburgh Reviewer talks of those who would have us worship a *thing*. We assure M. Réville that we do not profess to have discovered the nature of God to be impersonal, nor do we deny to God conscious intelligence. We assure the Edinburgh Reviewer that we do not assert God to be a *thing*. All we say is that men do not know enough about the Eternal not ourselves that makes for righteousness, to warrant their pronouncing this either a person or a thing. We say that no one has discovered the nature of God to be personal, or is entitled to assert that God has conscious intelligence. Theologians assert this and make it the basis of religion. It is they who assert and profess to know, not we. We object to their professing to know more than can be known, to their insisting we shall receive it, to their resting religion upon it. We want to rest religion on what can be verified, not on what cannot. And M. Réville himself seems, when he lets us see the bottom of his thoughts, to allow that a personal God who thinks and loves cannot

really be verified, for he says: 'It is in vain to ask how we can verify the fact that God possesses consciousness and intelligence.' But we are for resting religion upon some fact of which it shall not be in vain to ask whether we can verify it. However, the theologians' conception of God is represented as a far more satisfying one in itself than ours, and as having, besides, much to make its truth highly probable, at any rate, if not demonstrable. And the reader of *Literature and Dogma* may think, perhaps, that we have been over-cautious, over-negative; that we are really, as M. Réville says, 'decidedly too much afraid of the idea of the personality of God.' He may think, that though we have given him as his foundation something verifiable and sure, yet that what we have given him is a great deal less than what the theologians offer, and offer with such strong and good reasons for its truth, that it becomes almost certain if not quite, and a man is captious who will not accept it.

Descartes, as is well known, had a famous philosophical method for discovering truths of all kinds; and people heard of his method and used to press him to give them the results which this wonderful organ had enabled him to ascertain. Quite in a contrary fashion, we sometimes flatter ourselves with the hope that we may be of use by the very absence of all scientific pretension, by our very want of 'a philosophy based on principles interdependent, subordinate and coherent'; because we are thus obliged to treat great questions in such a simple way that any one can follow us, while the way, at the same time, may possibly be quite right after all, only overlooked by more ingenious people because it is so very simple.

Now, proceeding in this manner, we venture to ask the plain reader whether it does not strike him as an objection to our making God a person who thinks and loves, that we have really no experience whatever, not the very slightest, of persons who think and love, except in man and the inferior animals. We for our part are by no means disposed to deny that the inferior animals, as they are called, may have consciousness, that they may be said to think and love, in however low a degree. At any rate we can see them before us doing certain things which are like what we do ourselves when we think and love, so that thinking and loving may be attributed to them also without one's failing to understand what is meant, and they may conceivably be called per-

---

[4] Albert Réville (1826–1906), French Protestant theologian.

sons who think and love. But really this is all the experience of any sort that we have of persons who think and love,—the experience afforded by ourselves and the lower animals. True, we easily and naturally attribute all operations that engage our notice to authors who live and think like ourselves. We make persons out of sun, wind, love, envy, war, fortune; in some languages every noun is male or female. But this, we know, is figure and personification. Being ourselves alive and thinking, we naturally invest things with these our attributes, and imagine all action and operation to proceed as our own proceeds. This is a tendency which in common speech and in poetry, where we do not profess to speak exactly, we cannot well help following, and which we follow lawfully. In the language of common speech and of poetry, we speak of the Eternal not ourselves that makes for righteousness, as if he were a person who thinks and loves. Naturally we speak of him so, and there is no objection at all to our so doing.

But it is different when we profess to speak exactly, and yet make God a person who thinks and loves. We then find what difficulty our being actually acquainted with no persons superior to ourselves who think and love brings us into. Some, we know, have made their God in the image of the inferior animals. We have had the God Apis and the God Anubis; but these are extravagances. In general, as God is said to have made man in his own image, the image of God, man has returned the compliment and has made God as being, outwardly or inwardly, in the image of man. What we in general do is to take the best thinking and loving of the best man, to better this best, to call it *perfect*, and to say that this is God. So we construct a magnified and non-natural man, by dropping out all that in man seems a source of weakness and inserting its contrary, and by heightening to the very utmost all that in man seems a source of strength, such as his thought and his love. Take the account of God which begins the Thirty-nine Articles, or the account of God in any Confession of Faith we may choose. The same endeavour shows itself in all of them: to construct a man who thinks and loves, but so immensely bettered that he is a man no longer. Then between this magnified man and ourselves we put, if we please, angels, who are men etherealised. The objection to the magnified man and to the men etherealised is one and the same: that we have absolutely no experience whatever of either the one or the other.

Support, however, is obtained for them from two grounds;—from metaphysical grounds, and from the ground of miracles. Let us take first the ground said to be given by miracles. Interferences and communications of such a kind as to be explainable on no other supposition than that of a magnified and non-natural man, with etherealised men ministering to him, are alleged to have actually happened and to be warranted by sure testimony. And there is something in this. If the alleged interferences and communications have happened, then by this supposition they may fairly be explained. If the progress of the natural day was really stopped to enable the chosen people to win a great victory over its enemies, if a voice out of the sky really said when Jesus was baptized: *This is my beloved Son,*—then the magnified and non-natural man of popular religion, either by himself or with angels, etherealised men, for his ministers, is a supposition made credible, probable, and even almost necessary, by those incidents.

II

Thus we are thrown back on miracles; and the question is, are we to affirm that God is a person who thinks and loves because miracles compel us? Now, the reader of *Literature and Dogma* will recollect that half-a-dozen pages of that book, and not more, were taken up with discussing miracles. The *Guardian* thinks this insufficient. It says that solid replies are demanded to solid treatises, and that we ought to have taken Dr. Mozley's[5] Bampton Lectures on Miracles, and given, if we could, a refutation to them. It tartly adds, however, that to expect this of us 'would be to expect something entirely at variance with Mr. Arnold's antecedents and with his whole nature.' Well, the author of *Supernatural Religion* has occupied half a thick volume in refuting Dr. Mozley's Bampton Lectures. He has written a solid reply to that solid treatise. Sure we are that he has not convinced the *Guardian*, but it ought at least to be pleased with him for having so far done his duty. For our part, although we do justice to Dr. Mozley's ability, yet to write a refutation of his Bampton Lectures is precisely, in our opinion, to do what Strauss has well called 'going out of one's way to assail the paper fortifications which theologians choose to set up.' To engage in an *a priori* argument to prove

---

[5] James Bowling Mozley (1813–78), English theologian. Tractarian, Professor of Divinity at Oxford.

that miracles are impossible, against an adversary who argues *a priori* that they are possible, is the vainest labour in the world. So long as the discussion was of this character, miracles were in no danger. The time for it is now past, because the human mind, whatever may be said for or against miracles *a priori*, is now in fact losing its reliance upon them. And it is losing it for this reason: as its experience widens, it gets acquainted with the natural history of miracles, it sees how they arise, and it slowly but inevitably puts them aside.

Far from excusing ourselves for the brevity and moderation with which the subject of miracles is in *Literature and Dogma* treated, we are disposed to claim praise for it. It is possible to spend a great deal too much time and mental energy over the thesis that miracles cannot be relied on. The thesis, though true, is merely negative, and therefore of secondary importance. The important question is, what becomes of religion,—so precious, as we believe, to the human race,—if miracles cannot be relied on? We ought never so to immerse ourselves in the argument against miracles as to forget that the main question lies beyond, and that we must press forward to it. As soon as we satisfy ourselves that on miracles we cannot build, let us have done with questions about them and begin to build on something surer. Now, it is in a much more simple and unpretending way than controversialists commonly follow that we satisfy ourselves that we cannot build upon miracles.

For it is possible, again, to exaggerate untruly the demonstrative force of the case against miracles. The logical completeness of the case for miracles has been vaunted, and vaunted falsely; some people are now disposed to vaunt falsely the logical completeness of the case against miracles. Poor human nature loves the pretentious forms of exact knowledge, though with the real condition of our thoughts they often ill correspond. The author of *Supernatural Religion* asserts again and again that miracles are contradictory to a complete induction. He quotes Mr. Mill's rule: 'Whatever is contradictory to a complete induction is incredible,' and quotes Mr. Mill's account of a complete induction: 'When observations or experiments have been repeated so often and by so many persons as to exclude all supposition of error in the observer, a law of nature is established'; and he asserts that a law of nature of this kind has been es-

tablished against miracles. He brings forward that famous test by which Paley[6] seeks to establish the Christian miracles, his 'twelve men of known probity and good sense relating a miracle wrought before their eyes, and consenting to be racked and burned sooner than acknowledge that there existed any falsehood or imposture in the case,' and he asserts that no affirmation of any twelve men would be sufficient to overthrow a law of nature, or to save, therefore, the Christian miracles.

Now, these assertions are exaggerated and will not serve. No such law of nature as Mr. Mill describes has been or can be established against the Christian miracles; a complete induction against them, therefore, there is not. Nor does the evidence of their reporters fail because the evidence of no men can make miracles credible. The case against the Christian miracles is that we have an induction, not complete, indeed, but enough more and more to satisfy the mind, and to satisfy it in an ever-increasing number of men, that miracles are untrustworthy. The case against their reporters is, that more and more of us see, and see ever more clearly, that these reporters were not and could not be the sort of picked jury that Paley's argument requires, but that, with all the good faith in the world, they were men likely to fall into error about miracles, to make a miracle where there was none, and that they did fall into error and legend accordingly.

This being so, we have no inclination, even now, either to dwell at excessive length on the subject of miracles, or to make a grand show of victoriously demonstrating their impossibility. But we have to ask ourselves, if necessary, again and again, whenever anything is made to depend upon them, how their case really and truly stands, whether there can be any prospect, either for ourselves or for those in whose interest *Literature and Dogma* was written, of returning to a reliance upon them. And the more we consider it the more we are convinced there is none; and that the cause assigned in *Literature and Dogma* as fatal to miracles;—that the more our experience widens, the more we see and understand the process by which they arose, and their want of solidity,—is fatal to them indeed. The time has come when the minds of men no longer put as a matter of course the Bible-miracles in a class by themselves. Now, from the moment this time commences, from the moment that the comparative history of all miracles is a conception entertained

[6] William Paley (1743–1805), English theologian, author of *Evidences of Christianity* (1794).

and a study admitted, the conclusion is certain, the reign of the Bible-miracles is doomed.

III

Let us see how this is so. Herodotus relates, that, when the Persian invaders came to Delphi, two local heroes buried near the place, Phylacus and Autonous, arose, and were seen, of more than mortal stature, fighting against the Persians.[7] He relates, that before the onset at Salamis the vision of a woman appeared over an Æginetan ship, and cried in a voice which all the Grecian fleet heard: 'Good souls, how long will ye keep backing?'[8] He relates, that at Pedasus, in the neighbourhood of his own city Halicarnassus, the priestess of Athene had a miraculous sprouting of beard whenever any grievous calamity was about to befall the people around; he says in one place that twice this miraculous growth had happened, in another that it had happened thrice.[9] Herodotus writes here of times when he was himself alive, not of a fabulous antiquity. He and his countrymen were not less acute, arguing, critical people than the Jews of Palestine, but much more. Herodotus himself, finally, is a man of a beautiful character and of pure good-faith.

But we do not believe that Phylacus and Autonous arose out of their graves and were seen fighting with the Persians; we know by experience, we all say, how this sort of story grows up. And that after the Crucifixion, then, many dead saints arose and came out of the graves and went into the holy city and appeared unto many, is not this too a story of which we must say, the moment we fairly put it side by side with the other, that it is of the same kind with it, and that we know how the sort of story grows up? That the Phantom-woman called to the Æginetan crew at Salamis, *How long will ye keep backing?* we do not believe any the more because we are told that all the Grecian fleet heard it. We know, we all say, by experience, that this is just the sort of corroboration naturally added to such a story. But we are asked to believe that Jesus after his death actually cried to Paul on his way to Damascus: *It is hard for thee to kick against the pricks*, because the bystanders are said to have heard it, although to be sure in another place, with the looseness natural to such a story, the bystanders are said *not* to have heard this voice. That the Salamis story and the Damascus story

are of one kind, and of what kind, strikes us the moment that we put the two stories together.

The miraculous beard of the priestess of Pedasus is really just like the miraculous dumbness of Zacharias, the father of John the Baptist. The priestess of Pedasus, however, is said by Herodotus in one place to have twice had her marvellous beard, in another to have had it thrice; and the discrepancy proves, we all say, how loose and unhistorical this kind of story is. But yet when Jesus is in the Second Gospel said to have healed as he departed from Jericho one blind man who sate by the wayside, and in the First Gospel to have healed as he departed from Jericho two blind men who sate by the wayside, there is here, we are asked to believe, no discrepancy really at all. Two different healings are meant, which were performed at two different visits to Jericho. Or perhaps they were performed at one and the same visit, but one was performed as Jesus entered the city, and the other as he left it. And the words of St. Mark: 'And he came to Jericho; and as he went out of Jericho blind Bartimæus sate by the wayside,' really mean that Bartimæus sate there as Jesus went *in* to Jericho, and two other blind men sate by the wayside as he went *out*. How arbitrary, unnatural, and vain such an explanation is, what a mere device of our own to make a solid history out of a legend, we never feel so irresistibly as when we put the Jericho story by the side of others like it.

Yet still, in new and popular books, this precious device for reconciling inconsistent accounts of the same thing,—the hypothesis that the incident did really happen more than once,— is furbished up and brought out afresh. So strong, so persistent, so desperate is the endeavour to make that wonderful mixture of truth and fiction, which the Four Gospels give us, into one uniform strain of solid history. The attempt must fail. It will impair the understanding of all who make it, it will mar the reputation of every critic who makes it, and yet will disappoint them after all. The kindest thing one can do to an intelligent reader of the Bible is to convince him of the utter hopelessness of any such attempt, to bring him speedily and once for all to a state of settled clearness on the subject. And this will be done, not so well directly, by arguing how improbable such an hypothesis as that incidents should exactly repeat themselves in itself is, as indirectly, by showing from examples how very prone is the

---

[7] Herodotus viii. 38, 39. [Arnold's note]   [8] Herodotus viii. 84. [Arnold's note]
[9] Herodotus viii. 104. [Arnold's note]

human imagination to reproduce striking incidents a second time, although the incidents have in truth occurred only once.

To save the exactness of the Gospel narratives, the stories of the healing of the blind men at Jericho are made to pass, we have seen, for the stories of two separate miracles. But a more remarkable instance still of the actual production of an incident twice, is alleged in regard to the clearing the Temple of buyers and sellers. The Fourth Gospel, as is well known, puts the clearance at the beginning of Christ's career. The Synoptics put it at the end, shortly before his arrest. Probably the Synoptics are right; for the act was one which, coming from an unknown man, would have merely seemed extravagant and exasperating, whereas, coming from Jesus after his line of teaching and reforming had become familiar, it would have had significance and use. But be this as it may; at any rate, if the act was done at the outset of the career of Jesus, then the Synoptics, one would say, must have made a mistake; if at the close, then the author of the Fourth Gospel. Not at all! The same striking incident with all its circumstances really happened, we are told, twice: first at the outset of Christ's career, and then again at its close. Neither the Synoptics, therefore, nor the author of the Fourth Gospel are in error.

Now, this seems surprising. But some who are lovers of the Bible may be inclined to try and believe it, may seek to cling to such an explanation, may argue for its possiblity *a priori*. Crumble to bits, sooner or later, such explanations will. That which may convince a man, once and for ever, of their hollowness, and save him much loss of time and distress of mind, is the application of such a piece of experience as the following:—

Some years ago a newly-married couple were during their honeymoon travelling in the Alps. They made an excursion on Mont Blanc; the bride met with an accident there, and perished before her husband's eyes. The other day we had, strange to relate, just this touching story over again. Again a newly-married couple were in the Alps during their honeymoon, again Mont Blanc was the scene of an excursion, again the bride met with an accident, again she perished in her husband's sight. Surprising, but there was the fact! People talked of it, the telegraph spread it abroad. But ours is a time of broad daylight and searching inquiry. The matter drew attention, and in a few days the telegraph announced that the second accident had never really happened at all, that it was a mere doubling and

reflection of the first. Men's imagination reiterates in this way things which strike it, and loose relation narrates the doubled fact seriously. As our experience widens, it brings us more and more proof that this is so; and one day a signal example is decisive with us. The Mont Blanc story, or some story of the kind, comes with a sort of magic to make the scales fall from our eyes. It is still possible *a priori* that the Temple may have been cleared twice, and that there is no mistake in the Gospel reports. The induction against it is not a complete induction. But it is henceforth complete enough to serve; it convinces us. In spite of the *a priori* possiblity, we cannot any longer believe in the double clearance of the Temple, and in the exactitude of both the accounts in the Gospels, even though we would.

IV

It is this impossibility of resting religion any more on grounds once supposed to be safe, such as that the Gospel narratives are free from mistake and that the Gospel miracles are trustworthy, which compels us to look for new grounds upon which we may build firmly. Those men do us an ill turn, and we owe them no thanks for it, who compel us to keep going back to examine the old grounds, and declaring their want of solidity. What we need is to have done with all this negative, unfruitful business, and to get to religion again;—to the use of the Bible upon new grounds which shall be secure. The old grounds cannot be used safely any more, and if one opens one's eyes one must see it. Those who inveigh against us could see it, if they chose, as plainly as we do; and they ought to open their eyes and see it, but they will not. And they want us to go on trusting foolishly to the old grounds as they do, until all tumbles in, and there is a great ruin and confusion. Let us not do so. Let those who have read *Literature and Dogma* with satisfaction be sure that what is in that book said against miracles, kept though it be within the narrowest limits possible, is indispensable, and requires so little space just because it is so very certain. Let him accustom himself to treat with steadiness, with rigorous simplicity, all the devices to save those unsaveable things, the Bible miracles.

To reduce the miraculous in them to what are thought reasonable dimensions is now a favourite attempt. But if anything miraculous is left, the whole miracle might as well have been left; if nothing, how has the incident any longer the proving force of a miracle? Let us treat so absurd an attempt as it deserves. Neander supposes that the water at the marriage-feast at Cana was not changed by Jesus into wine, but was only endued by him with wine's brisk taste and exhilarating effects. This has all the difficulties of the miracle, and only gets rid of the poetry. It is as if we were startled by the extravagance of supposing Cinderella's fairy godmother to have actually changed the pumpkin into a coach and six, but suggested that she did really change it it into a one-horse brougham. Many persons, again, feel now an insurmountable suspicion (and no wonder) of Peter's fish with the tribute-money in its mouth, and they suggest that what really happened was that Peter caught a fish, sold it, and paid the tribute with the money he thus got. This is like saying that all Cinderella's godmother really did was to pay a cab for her godchild by selling her vegetables. But then what becomes of the wonder, the miracle? Were there ever such apologists as these? They impair the credit of the Evangelists as much as we do, for they make them transform facts to an extent wholly incompatible with trustworthy reporting. They impair it more; for they make them transform facts with a method incompatible with honest simplicity.

Simple, flexible common-sense is what we most want, in order to be able to follow truly the dealings of that spontaneous, irregular, wonderful power which gives birth to tales of miracle,—the imagination. It is easy to be too systematic. Strauss had the idea, acute and ingenious, of explaining the miracles of the New Testament as a reiteration of the miracles of the Old. Of some miracles this supplies a good explanation. It plausibly explains the story of the Transfiguration, for instance. The story of the illumined face of Jesus,—Jesus, the prophet like unto Moses, whom Moses foretold,—might naturally owe its origin to the illumined face of Moses himself. But of other miracles, such as the walking on the Lake of Gennesaret or the cursing of the barren fig-tree, Strauss' idea affords no admissible explanation whatever. To employ it for these cases can only show the imperturbable resolution of a German professor in making all the facts suit a theory which he has once adopted. But every miracle has its own mode of growth and its own history, and the key to one is not the key to others. Such a rationalising explanation as that above quoted of the money in the mouth of Peter's fish is ridiculous. Yet a clue, a suggestion, however slight, of fact, there probably was to every miracle; and sometimes, not by

any means always, this clue may be traced with likelihood.

The story of the feeding of the thousands may well have had its rise in the suspension, the comparative extinction, of hunger and thirst during hours of rapt interest and intense mental excitement. In such hours a trifling sustenance, which would commonly serve for but a few, will suffice for many. Rumour and imagination make and add details, and swell the thing into a miracle. This sort of incident, again, it is as natural to conceive repeating itself, as it is unnatural to conceive an incident like the clearance of the Temple repeating itself. Or to take the walking on the Sea of Galilee. Here, too, the sort of hint of fact which may have started the miracle will readily occur to every one. Sometimes the hint of fact, lost in our Bibles, is preserved elsewhere. The Gospel of the Hebrews,—an old Gospel outside the Canon of Scripture, but which Jerome quotes and of which we have fragments,— this Gospel, and other records of like character, mention what our Four Gospels do not: a wonderful light at the moment when Jesus was baptized. No one, so far as we know, has yet remarked that in this small and dropped circumstance,— a weird light on Jordan seen while Jesus was baptized,—we not improbably have the little original nucleus of solid fact round which the whole miraculous story of his baptism gathered.

He does well, who, steadily using his own eyes in this manner, and escaping from the barren routine whether of the assailants of the Bible or of its apologists, acquires the serene and imperturbable conviction, indispensable for all fruitful use of the Bible in future, that in travelling through its reports of miracles he moves in a world, not of solid history, but of illusion, rumour, and fairy-tale. Only, when he has acquired this, let him say to himself that he has by so doing achieved nothing, except to get rid of an insecure reliance which inevitably some day or other would have cost him dear, of a staff in religion which must sooner or later have pierced his hand.

One other thing, however, he has done besides this. He has discovered the hollowness of the main ground for making God a person who thinks and loves, a magnified and non-natural man. Only a kind of man magnified could so make man the centre of all things, and interrupt the settled order of nature in his behalf, as miracles imply. But in miracles we are dealing we find, with the unreal world of fairy-tale. Having no reality of their own, they cannot lend it as foundation for the reality of anything else.

Conclusion

THE Canon of the New Testament, then, is not what popular religion supposes; although, on the other hand, its documents are in some quarters the object of far too aggressive and sweeping negations. The most fruitful result to be gained from a sane criticism of the Canon is, that by satisfying oneself how the Gospel records grew up, one is enabled the better to account for much that puzzles us in their representation of Jesus,—of his words more especially. There were facilities for addition and interpolation, for adding touches to what the original accounts made Jesus do, for amplifying, above all, what they made Jesus say. Evidence such as apologists always imagine themselves to be using when they appeal to the Gospels,—the pure, first-hand, well-authenticated evidence of eye-witnesses,—our Gospels are not.

Such evidence is, indeed, remarkably wanting for the whole miraculous side in the doings recorded of Jesus. Sometimes we seem to be near getting such evidence, but it vanishes. Jerome tells us that Quadratus, in the second century, declared that there were yet living in his time persons who had beheld with their eyes Jesus raise the dead to life, and that he himself had seen them and spoken with them. It happens that the declaration of Quadratus is preserved by Eusebius, in whose History Jerome probably read it. Quadratus undoubtedly says that in his time there were yet alive those who had witnessed the raising of the dead by Jesus; but the important addition which alone takes this statement out of the category of hearsay, and makes it personal evidence,—the addition that these alleged witnesses he himself had seen and known,—Quadratus does not make. The addition is merely a rhetorical flourish of Jerome's[1]

No doubt this is so; yet the importance of it all is greatly diminished by one consideration. *If we had the original reports of the eye-witnesses, we should still have reports not essentially differing, probably, from those which we now use.* Certain additions which improved a miraculous story as it grew, certain interpolations which belong to the ideas and circumstances of a later age, would be absent. But we should most likely not have a miracle the less, and we should certainly find a similar misapprehension of Jesus and of what he intended. The people who saw Jesus were as certain to seek for miracles, and to find them, as the people who lived a generation or two later, or as the people who resort to Lourdes or to La Salette now. And this preoccupation with miracles was sure to warp their understanding of Jesus, and their report of his sayings and doings. The recurrence, so much talked of and recommended, to the Apostles, or to the first three centuries, for the pure rule of faith and the genuine doctrine of Jesus, is in truth therefore, however natural an expedient, an utterly futile one. There were indeed, as we have shown in *Literature and Dogma*, certain prominent points in the teaching of Jesus which his immediate followers had not yet lost sight of, and which fell more out of view afterwards. But the pure and genuine doctrine of Jesus neither his immediate followers, nor those whom they instructed, could possess; so immured were they in the ideas of their time and in the belief of the miraculous, so immeasurably was Jesus above them.

II

But our opponents say: 'Everything turns upon the question whether miracles do or did really happen; and you abstain from all attempt to prove their impossibility, you simply assume that they never happen.' And this, which our opponents say, is true, and we have repeatedly admitted it. At the end of this investigation we admit it once more, and lay stress upon it. That miracles *cannot* happen we do not attempt to prove; the demonstration is too ambitious. That they *do not* happen, that what are called miracles are not what the believers in them fancy, but have a natural history of which we can follow the course, the slow action of experience, we say, more and more shows; and shows, too, that there is no exception to be made in favour of the Bible-miracles.

Epiphanius tells us, that at each anniversary of the miracle of Cana, the water of the springs of Cibyra in Caria and Gerasa in Arabia was changed into wine; that he himself had drunk of the transformed water of Cibyra, and his brothers of that of Gerasa.[2] Fifty years ago, a plain Englishman would have had no difficulty in thinking that the Cana miracle was true, and the other two miracles were fables. He is now

---

[1] See Eusebius *Hist. Eccles.* iv. 3; and Routh, *Reliquiae Sacrae*, vol. i. pp. 71, 74. Routh quotes Jerome, and points out his exaggeration. [Arnold's note]

[2] Epiphanius, *Haer.* LI. xxx. [Arnold's note]

irresistibly led to class all these occurrences in one category as unsubstantial tales of marvel. Scales seem to drop from his eyes in regard to miracles; and if he is still to hold fast his Christianity, it must no longer depend upon them.

It was not to discredit miracles that *Literature and Dogma* was written, but because miracles are so widely and deeply discredited already. And it is lost labour, we repeat, to be arguing for or against them. Mankind did not originally accept miracles because it had formal proof of them, but because its imperfect experience inclined it to them. Nor will mankind now drop miracles because it has formal proof against them, but because its more complete experience detaches it from them. The final result was inevitable, as soon as ever miracles began to embarrass people, began to be relegated,—especially the greater miracles,—to a certain limited period long ago over. Irenæus says, that people in his time had arisen from the dead, 'and abode with us a good number of years.'[3] One of his commentators, embarrassed by such stupendous miracles occurring outside of the Bible, makes an attempt to explain away this remarkable allegation; but the most recent editor of Irenæus points out, with truth, that the attempt is vain. Irenæus was as sure to want and to find miracles as the Bible-writers were. And sooner or later mankind was sure to see how universally and easily stories like this of Irenæus arose, and that they arose with the Bible-writers just as they arose with Irenæus, and are not a whit more solid coming from them than from him.

A Catholic imagines that he gets over the difficulty by believing, or professing to believe, the miracles of Irenæus and Epiphanius, as well as those of the Bible-writers. But for him too, even for him, the *Time-Spirit* is gradually becoming too strong. As we may say in general, that, although an educated Protestant may manage to retain for his own lifetime the belief in miracles in which he has been brought up, yet his children will lose it; so to an educated Catholic we may say, putting the change only a little farther off, that (unless some unforeseen deluge should overwhelm European civilisation, leaving everything to be begun anew) his grandchildren will lose it. They will lose it insensibly, as the eighteenth century saw the gradual extinction, among the educated classes, of that

belief in witchcraft which in the century previous a man like Sir Matthew Hale[4] could affirm to have the authority of Scripture and of the wisdom of all nations,—spoke of, in short, just as many religious people speak of miracles now. Witchcraft is but one department of the miraculous; and it was comparatively easy, no doubt, to abandon one department, when men had all the rest of the region to fall back upon. Nevertheless the forces of experience, which have prevailed against witchcraft, will inevitably prevail also against miracles at large, and that by the mere progress of time.

The charge of presumption, and of setting oneself up above all the great men of past days, above 'the wisdom of all nations,' which is often brought against those who pronounce the old view of our religion to be untenable, springs out of a failure to perceive how little the abandonment of certain long-current beliefs depends upon a man's own will, or even upon his sum of powers, natural or acquired. Sir Matthew Hale was not inferior in force of mind to a modern Chief Justice because he believed in witchcraft. Nay, the more enlightened modern, who drops errors of his forefathers by help of that mass of experience which his forefathers aided in accumulating, may often be, according to the well-known saying, 'a dwarf on the giant's shoulders.' His merits may be small compared with those of the giant. Perhaps his only merit is, that he has had the good sense to get up on the giant's shoulders, instead of trotting contentedly along in his shadow. Yet even this, surely, is something.

III

We have to renounce impossible attempts to receive the legendary and miraculous matter of Scripture as grave historical and scientific fact. We have to accustom ourselves to regard henceforth all this part as poetry and legend. In the Old Testament, as an immense poetry growing round and investing an immortal truth, the 'secret of the Eternal':[5] *Righteousness is salvation.* In the New, as an immense poetry growing round and investing an immortal truth, the secret of Jesus: *He that will save his life shall lose it, he that will lose his life shall save it.*

The best friends of mankind are those who can lead it to feel animation and hope in presence

---

[3] See Irenæus, *Adv. Haer.* lib. ii. cap. xxxii. 4; with the note on the passage ,in Stieren's edition. [Arnold's note]
[4] Sir Matthew Hale (1609–76,) English jurist, chief justice of the King's Bench.
[5] Psalms 25:14. [Arnold's note]

of the religious prospect thus profoundly transformed. The way to effect this is by bringing
men to see that our religion, in this altered view
of it, does but at last become again that religion
which Jesus Christ really endeavoured to found,
and of which the truth and grandeur are indestructible. We should do Christians generally
a great injustice, if we thought that the entire
force of their Christianity lay in the fascination
and subjugation of their spirits by the miracles
which they suppose Jesus to have worked, or by
the materialistic promises of heaven which they
suppose him to have offered. Far more does the
vital force of their Christianity lie in the boundless confidence, consolation, and attachment,
which the whole being and discourse of Jesus
inspire. What Jesus then himself thought sufficient, Christians too may bring themselves to
accept with good courage as enough for them.
What Jesus himself dismissed as chimerical,
Christians too may bring themselves to put
aside without dismay.

The central aim of Jesus was to transform
for every religious soul the popular Messias-ideal
of his time, the ideal of happiness and salvation
of the Jewish people; to disengage religion, one
may say, from the materialism of the Book of
Daniel. Fifty years had not gone by after his
death, when the Apocalypse replunged religion
in this materialism; where, indeed, it was from
the first manifest that replunged, by the followers
of Jesus, religion must be. It was replunged
there, but with an addition of inestimable value
and of incalculable working,—the figure and
influence of Jesus. Slowly this influence emerges,
transforms the turbid elements amid which it
was thrown, brings back the imperishable
ideal of its author. To the mind of Jesus, his
own resurrection after a short sojourn in the
grave was the victory of his cause after his death,
and at the price of his death. His disciples
materialised his resurrection; and their version
of the matter falls day by day to ruin. But no
ruin or contradiction befalls the version of Jesus
himself. He *has* risen, his cause has conquered;
the course of events continually attests his
resurrection and victory. The manifest unsoundness of popular Christianity inclines at present
many persons to throw doubts on the truth and
permanence of Christianity in general. Creeds
are discredited, religion is proclaimed to be in

danger, the pious quake, the world laughs.
Nevertheless *the prince of this world is judged;* [6]
the victory of Jesus is won and sure. Conscience
and self-renouncement, the method and the
secret of Jesus, are set up as a leaven in the world,
nevermore to cease working until the world
is leavened. That this is so, that the resurrection
and re-emergent life of Jesus are in this sense
undeniable, and that in this sense Jesus himself
predicted them, may in time, surely, encourage
Christians to lay hold on this sense as Jesus
did.

So, too, with the hope of immortality. Our
common materialistic notions about the resurrection of the body and the world to come are, no
doubt, natural and attractive to ordinary human
nature. But they are in direct conflict with the
new and loftier conceptions of life and death which
Jesus himself strove to establish. His secret, *He
that will save his life shall lose it, he that will lose
his life shall save it,* is of universal application.
It judges, not only the life to which men cling
here, but just as much the life we love to promise
ourselves in the New Jerusalem. The immortality
propounded by Jesus must be looked for elsewhere than in the materialistic aspirations of
our popular religion. *He lived in the eternal order,
and the eternal order never dies;*—this, if we may try
to formulate in one sentence the result of the
sayings of Jesus about life and death, is the sense
in which, according to him, we can rightly
conceive of the righteous man as immortal,
and aspire to be immortal ourselves. And
this conception we shall find to stand us
in good stead when the popular materialistic
version of our future life fails us. So that here
again, too, the version which, unfamiliar and
novel as it may now be to us, has the merit
of standing fast and holding good while other
versions break down, is at the same time the
version of Jesus.

People talk scornfully of a 'sublimated Christianity,' as if the Christianity of Jesus Christ
himself had been a materialistic fairy-tale like
that of Messrs. Moody and Sankey. [7] On the
contrary, insensibly to lift us out of all this sort
of materialism was Jesus Christ's perpetual
endeavour. The parable of the king, who made
a marriage for his son, ends with the episode of
the guest who had not on a wedding garment,
and was cast out. [8] And here, as usual, the

[6] John 16:11. [Arnold's note]
[7] Dwight Moody (1837–99) and Ira David Sankey (1840–1908), American evangelists, noted
preachers.
[8] Matthew 22:1–14. [Arnold's note]

Tübingen critics detect *tendence*. They see in the episode a deliberate invention of the Evangelist; a stroke of Jewish particularism, indemnifying itself for having had to relate that salvation was preached in the highways. We have disagreed often with the Tübingen critics, and we shall venture finally to disagree with them here. We receive the episode as genuine; but what did Jesus mean by it? Shall we not do well in thinking, that he, whose lucidity was so incomparable, and who indicated so much which was to be seized not by the present but by the future, here marked and meant to mark, although but incidentally and in passing, the profound, the utter insufficiency of popular religion? Through the turbid phase of popular religion his religion had to pass. Good and bad it was to bear along with it; the gross and ignorant were to be swept in, by wholesale, from the highways; *the wedding was to be furnished with guests.* On this wise must Christianity needs develop itself, and the necessary law of its development was to be accepted. Vain to be too nice about the unpreparedness of the guests in general, about their inevitable misuse of the favours which they were admitted to enjoy! What could have been the end of such a fastidious scrutiny? To turn them all out into the highways again! But the king's design was, that *the wedding should be furnished with guests.* So the guests shall all stay and fall to;—popular Christianity is founded. But presently, almost as if by accident, a guest even more unprepared and gross than the common, a guest 'not having on a wedding garment,' comes under the king's eye, and is ejected. Only one is noted for decisive ejection; but ah! how many of those guests are as really unapt to seize and follow God's designs for them as he! *Many are called, few chosen.*

The conspicuous delinquent is sentenced to be bound hand and foot, and taken away, and cast into outer darkness. In the severity of this sentence, Jesus marks how utterly those who are gathered to his feast may fail to know him. The misapprehending and materialising of his religion, the long and turbid stage of popular Christianity, was, however, inevitable. But to give light and impulsion to future times, Jesus stamps this Christianity, even from the very moment of its birth, as, though inevitable, not worthy of its name; as ignorant and transient, and requiring all who would be truly children of the kingdom to rise beyond it.

from Discourses in America

Arnold visited America on a lecture tour from October 1883 to March 1884. Despite some difficulties in communicating with American audiences, Arnold on tour was generally a success. He met numerous literary and public figures, such as Oliver Wendell Holmes, Andrew Carnegie, and others. Upon his return to England he gathered the American lectures together as Discourses in America *and published them in 1885. Of the three lectures in the volume, the most distinguished is his "Literature and Science," printed below.*

"Literature and Science," in slightly different form, had been delivered at Cambridge University and published in the Nineteenth Century *in 1882. It was adapted for American audiences and delivered on his American tour. The essay should be compared with T. H. Huxley's "Science and Culture," to which it is an eloquent humanistic reply.*

Literature and Science

Pʀᴀᴄᴛɪᴄᴀʟ people talk with a smile of Plato and of his absolute ideas; and it is impossible to deny that Plato's ideas do often seem unpractical and impracticable, and especially when one views them in connection with the life of a great work-a-day world like the United States. The necessary staple of the life of such a world Plato regards with disdain; handicraft and trade and the working professions he regards with disdain; but what becomes of the life of an industrial modern community if you take handicraft and trade and the working professions out of it? The base mechanic arts and handicrafts, says

Plato, bring about a natural weakness in the principle of excellence in a man, so that he cannot govern the ignoble growths in him, but nurses them, and cannot understand fostering any other. Those who exercise such arts and trades, as they have their bodies, he says, marred by their vulgar businesses, so they have their souls, too, bowed and broken by them. And if one of these uncomely people has a mind to seek self-culture and philosophy, Plato compares him to a bald little tinker, who has scraped together money, and has got his release from service, and has had a bath, and bought a new coat, and is rigged out like a bridegroom about to marry the daughter of his master who has fallen into poor and helpless estate.

Nor do the working professions fare any better than trade at the hands of Plato. He draws for us an inimitable picture of the working lawyer, and of his life of bondage; he shows how this bondage from his youth up has stunted and warped him, and made him small and crooked of soul, encompassing him with difficulties which he is not man enough to rely on justice and truth as means to encounter, but has recourse, for help out of them, to falsehood and wrong. And so, says Plato, this poor creature is bent and broken, and grows up from boy to man without a particle of soundness in him, although exceedingly smart and clever in his own esteem.

One cannot refuse to admire the artist who draws these pictures. But we say to ourselves that his ideas show the influence of a primitive and obsolete order of things, when the warrior caste and the priestly caste were alone in honour, and the humble work of the world was done by slaves. We have now changed all that; the modern majority consists in work, as Emerson declares; and in work, we may add, principally of such plain and dusty kind as the work of cultivators of the ground, handicraftsmen, men of trade and business, men of the working professions. Above all is this true in a great industrious community such as that of the United States.

Now education, many people go on to say, is still mainly governed by the ideas of men like Plato, who lived when the warrior caste and the priestly or philosophical class were alone in honour, and the really useful part of the community were slaves. It is an education fitted for persons of leisure in such a community. This education passed from Greece and Rome to the feudal communities of Europe, where also the warrior caste and the priestly caste were alone held in honour, and where the really useful and working part of the community, though not nominally slaves as in the pagan world, were practically not much better off than slaves, and not more seriously regarded. And how absurd it is, people end by saying, to inflict this education upon an industrious modern community, where very few indeed are persons of leisure, and the mass to be considered has not leisure, but is bound, for its own great good, and for the great good of the world at large, to plain labour and to industrial pursuits, and the education in question tends necessarily to make men dissatisfied with these pursuits and unfitted for them!

That is what is said. So far I must defend Plato, as to plead that his view of education and studies is in the general, as it seems to me, sound enough, and fitted for all sorts and conditions of men, whatever their pursuits may be. 'An intelligent man,' says Plato, 'will prize those studies which result in his soul getting soberness, righteousness, and wisdom, and will less value the others.' I cannot consider *that* a bad description of the aim of education, and of the motives which should govern us in the choice of studies, whether we are preparing ourselves for a hereditary seat in the English House of Lords or for the pork trade in Chicago.

Still I admit that Plato's world was not ours, that his scorn of trade and handicraft is fantastic, that he had no conception of a great industrial community such as that of the United States, and that such a community must and will shape its education to suit its own needs. If the usual education handed down to it from the past does not suit it, it will certainly before long drop this and try another. The usual education in the past has been mainly literary. The question is whether the studies which were long supposed to be the best for all of us are practically the best now; whether others are not better. The tyranny of the past, many think, weighs on us injuriously in the predominance given to letters in education. The question is raised whether, to meet the needs of our modern life, the predominance ought not now to pass from letters to science; and naturally the question is nowhere raised with more energy than here in the United States. The design of abasing what is called 'mere literary instruction and education,' and of exalting what is called 'sound, extensive, and practical scientific knowledge,' is, in this intensely modern world of the United States, even more perhaps than in Europe, a very popular design, and makes great and rapid progress.

I am going to ask whether the present movement for ousting letters from their old pre-dominance in education, and for transferring the predominance in education to the natural sciences, whether this brisk and flourishing movement ought to prevail, and whether it is likely that in the end it really will prevail. An objection may be raised which I will anticipate. My own studies have been almost wholly in letters, and my visits to the field of the natural sciences have been very slight and inadequate, although those sciences have always strongly moved my curiosity. A man of letters, it will perhaps be said, is not competent to discuss the comparative merits of letters and natural science as means of education. To this objection I reply, first of all, that his incompetence, if he attempts the discussion but is really incompetent for it, will be abundantly visible; nobody will be taken in; he will have plenty of sharp observers and critics to save mankind from the danger. But the line I am going to follow is, as you will soon discover, so extremely simple, that perhaps it may be followed without failure even by one who for a more ambitious line of discussion would be quite incompetent.

Some of you may possibly remember a phrase of mine which has been the object of a good deal of comment; an observation to the effect that in our culture, the aim being *to know our-selves and the world*, we have, as the means to this end, *to know the best which has been thought and said in the world*. A man of science, who is also an excellent writer and the very prince of debaters, Professor Huxley, in a discourse at the opening of Sir Josiah Mason's college at Birmingham, laying hold of this phrase, ex-panded it by quoting some more words of mine, which are these: 'The civilised world is to be regarded as now being, for intellectual and spiritual purposes, one great confederation, bound to a joint action and working to a common result; and whose members have for their proper outfit a knowledge of Greek, Roman, and Eastern antiquity, and of one another. Special local and temporary advantages being put out of account, that modern nation will in the intellectual and spiritual sphere make most progress, which most thoroughly carries out this programme.'

Now on my phrase, thus enlarged, Professor Huxley remarks that when I speak of the above-mentioned knowledge as enabling us to know ourselves and the world, I assert *literature* to contain the materials which suffice for thus making us know ourselves and the world. But it is not by any means clear, says he, that after having learnt all which ancient and modern literatures have to tell us, we have laid a suffi-ciently broad and deep foundation for that criticism of life, that knowledge of ourselves and the world, which constitutes culture. On the contrary, Professor Huxley declares that he finds himself 'wholly unable to admit that either nations or individuals will really advance, if their outfit draws nothing from the stores of physical science. An army without weapons of precision, and with no particular base of opera-tions, might more hopefully enter upon a cam-paign on the Rhine, than a man, devoid of a knowledge of what physical science has done in the last century, upon a criticism of life.'

This shows how needful it is for those who are to discuss any matter together, to have a common understanding as to the sense of the terms they employ,—how needful, and how difficult. What Professor Huxley says, implies just the reproach which is so often brought against the study of *belles lettres*, as they are called: that the study is an elegant one, but slight and ineffectual; a smattering of Greek and Latin and other ornamental things, of little use for any one whose object is to get at truth, and to be a practical man. So, too, M. Renan[1] talks of the 'superficial humanism' of a school-course which treats us as if we were all going to be poets, writers, preachers, orators, and he opposes this humanism to positive science, or the critical search after truth. And there is always a tendency in those who are remonstrating against the predominance of letters in education, to understand by letters *belles lettres*, and by *belles lettres* a superficial humanism, the opposite of science or true knowledge.

But when we talk of knowing Greek and Roman antiquity, for instance, which is the knowledge people have called the humanities, I for my part mean a knowledge which is some-thing more than a superficial humanism, mainly decorative. 'I call all teaching *scientific*,' says Wolf,[2] the critic of Homer, 'which is systemati-cally laid out and followed up to its original sources. For example: a knowledge of classical antiquity is scientific when the remains of classical antiquity are correctly studied in the original

---

[1] Ernest Renan (1823–92,) French philosopher and historian.
[2] Friedrich August Wolf (1759–1824), German critic and classical scholar.

languages.' There can be no doubt that Wolf is perfectly right; that all learning is scientific which is systematically laid out and followed up to its original sources, and that a genuine humanism is scientific.

When I speak of knowing Greek and Roman antiquity, therefore, as a help to knowing ourselves and the world, I mean more than a knowledge of so much vocabulary, so much grammar, so many portions of authors in the Greek and Latin languages, I mean knowing the Greeks and Romans, and their life and genius, and what they were and did in the world; what we get from them, and what is its value. That, at least, is the ideal; and when we talk of endeavouring to know Greek and Roman antiquity, as a help to knowing ourselves and the world, we mean endeavouring so to know them as to saitsfy this ideal, however much we may still fall short of it.

The same also as to knowing our own and other modern nations, with the like aim of getting to understand ourselves and the world. To know the best that has been thought and said by the modern nations, is to know, says Professor Huxley, 'only what modern *literatures* have to tell us; it is the criticism of life contained in modern literature.' And yet 'the distinctive character of our times,' he urges, 'lies in the vast and constantly increasing part which is played by natural knowledge.' And how, therefore, can a man, devoid of knowledge of what physical science has done in the last century, enter hopefully upon a criticism of modern life?

Let us, I say, be agreed about the meaning of the terms we are using. I talk of knowing the best which has been thought and uttered in the world; Professor Huxley says this means knowing *literature*. Literature is a large word; it may mean everything written with letters or printed in a book. Euclid's *Elements* and Newton's *Principia* are thus literature. All knowledge that reaches us through books is literature. But by literature Professor Huxley means *belles lettres*. He means to make me say, that knowing the best which has been thought and said by the modern nations is knowing their *belles lettres* and no more. And this is no sufficient equipment, he argues, for a criticism of modern life. But as I do not mean, by knowing ancient Rome, knowing merely more or less of Latin *belles lettres*, and taking no account of Rome's military, and political, and legal, and administrative work in the world; and as, by knowing ancient Greece, I understand knowing her as the giver of Greek art, and the guide to a free and right use of reason and to scientific method, and the founder of our mathematics and physics and astronomy and biology,—I understand knowing her as all this, and not merely knowing certain Greek poems, and histories, and treatises, and speeches,—so as to the knowledge of modern nations also. By knowing modern nations, I mean not merely knowing their *belles lettres*, but knowing also what has been done by such men as Copernicus, Galileo, Newton, Darwin. 'Our ancestors learned,' says Professor Huxley, 'that the earth is the centre of the visible universe, and that man is the cynosure of things terrestrial; and more especially was it inculcated that the course of nature had no fixed order, but that it could be, and constantly was, altered.' But for us now, continues Professor Huxley, 'the notions of the beginning and the end of the world entertained by our forefathers are no longer credible. It is very certain that the earth is not the chief body in the material unigerse, and that the world is not subordinated to man's use. It is even more certain that nature is the expression of a definite order, with which nothing interferes.' 'And yet,' he cries, 'the purely classical education advocated by the representatives of the humanists in our day gives no inkling of all this!'

In due place and time I will just touch upon that vexed question of classical education; but at present the question is as to what is meant by knowing the best which modern nations have thought and said. It is not knowing their *belles lettres* merely which is meant. To know Italian *belles lettres* is not to know Italy, and to know English *belles lettres* is not to know England. Into knowing Italy and England there comes a great deal more, Galileo and Newton amongst it. The reproach of being a superficial humanism, a tincture of *belles lettres*, may attach rightly enough to some other disciplines; but to the particular discipline recommended when I proposed knowing the best that has been thought and said in the world, it does not apply. In that best I certainly include what in modern times has been thought and said by the great observers and knowers of nature.

There is, therefore, really no question between Professor Huxley and me as to whether knowing the great results of the modern scientific study of nature is not required as a part of our culture, as well as knowing the products of literature and art. But to follow the processes by which those results are reached, ought, say the friends of physical science, to be made the staple of education for the bulk of mankind. And here there does arise a question between those whom Professor Huxley calls with playful sarcasm 'the Levites of culture,' and those whom the poor humanist is sometimes apt to regard as its Nebuchadnezzars.[3]

The great result of the scientific investigation of nature we are agreed upon knowing, but how much of our study are we bound to give to the processes by which those results are reached? The results have their visible bearing on human life. But all the processes, too, all the items of fact, by which those results are reached and established, are interesting. All knowledge is interesting to a wise man, and the knowledge of nature is interesting to all men. It is very interesting to know, that, from the albuminous white of the egg, the chick in the egg gets the materials for its flesh, bones, blood, and feathers; while, from the fatty yolk of the egg, it gets the heat and energy which enable it at length to break its shell and begin the world. It is less interesting, perhaps, but still it is interesting, to know that when a taper burns, the wax is converted into carbonic acid and water. Moreover, it is quite true that the habit of dealing with facts, which is given by the study of nature, is, as the friends of physical science praise it for being, an excellent discipline. The appeal, in the study of nature, is constantly to observation and experiment; not only is it said that the thing is so, but we can be made to see that it is so. Not only does a man tell us that when a taper burns the wax is converted into carbonic acid and water, as a man may tell us, if he likes, that Charon is punting his ferry-boat on the river Styx, or that Victor Hugo is a sublime poet, or Mr. Gladstone the most admirable of statesmen; but we are made to see that the conversion into carbonic acid and water does actually happen. This reality of natural knowledge it is, which makes the friends of physical science contrast it, as a knowledge of things, with the humanist's knowledge, which is, say they, a knowledge of words. And hence Professor Huxley is moved to lay it down that, 'for the purpose of attaining real culture, an exclusively scientific education is at least as effectual as an exclusively literary education.' And a certain President of the Section for Mechanical Science in the British Association is, in Scripture phrase, 'very bold,' and declares

that if a man, in his mental training, 'has substituted literature and history for natural science, he has chosen the less useful alternative.' But whether we go these lengths or not, we must all admit that in natural science the habit gained of dealing with facts is a most valuable discipline, and that every one should have some experience of it.

More than this, however, is demanded by the reformers. It is proposed to make the training in natural science the main part of education, for the great majority of mankind at any rate. And here, I confess, I part company with the friends of physical science, with whom up to this point I have been agreeing. In differing from them, however, I wish to proceed with the utmost caution and diffidence. The smallness of my own acquaintance with the disciplines of natural science is ever before my mind, and I am fearful of doing these disciplines an injustice. The ability and pugnacity of the partisans of natural science make them formidable persons to contradict. The tone of tentative inquiry, which befits a being of dim faculties and bounded knowledge, is the tone I would wish to take and not to depart from. At present it seems to me, that those who are for giving to natural knowledge, as they call it, the chief place in the education of the majority of mankind, leave one important thing out of their account: the constitution of human nature. But I put this forward on the strength of some facts not at all recondite, very far from it; facts capable of being stated in the simplest possible fashion, and to which, if I so state them, the man of science will, I am sure, be willing to allow their due weight.

Deny the facts altogether, I think, he hardly can. He can hardly deny, that when we set ourselves to enumerate the powers which go to the building up of human life, and say that they are the power of conduct, the power of intellect and knowledge, the power of beauty, and the power of social life and manners,—he can hardly deny that this scheme, though drawn in rough and plain lines enough, and not pretending to scientific exactness, does yet give a fairly true representation of the matter. Human nature is built up by these powers; we have the need for them all. When we have rightly met and adjusted the claims of them all, we shall then be in a fair way for getting soberness and righteousness, with wisdom. This is evident enough, and the friends of physical science would admit it.

---

[3] The Levites were in charge of ceremonial rites and functions; Nebuchadnezzar, the Babylonian king, captured and destroyed Jerusalem.

But perhaps they may not have sufficiently observed another thing: namely, that the several powers just mentioned are not isolated, but there is, in the generality of mankind, a perpetual tendency to relate them one to another in divers ways. With one such way of relating them I am particularly concerned now. Following our instinct for intellect and knowledge, we acquire pieces of knowledge; and presently, in the generality of men, there arises the desire to relate these pieces of knowledge to our sense for conduct, to our sense for beauty,—and there is weariness and dissatisfaction if the desire is baulked. Now in this desire lies, I think, the strength of that hold which letters have upon us.

All knowledge is, as I said just now, interesting; and even items of knowledge which from the nature of the case cannot well be related, but must stand isolated in our thoughts, have their interest. Even lists of exceptions have their interest. If we are studying Greek accents, it is interesting to know that *pais* and *pas*, and some other monosyllables of the same form of declension, do not take the circumflex upon the last syllable of the genitive plural, but vary, in this respect, from the common rule. If we are studying physiology, it is interesting to know that the pulmonary artery carries dark blood and the pulmonary vein carries bright blood, departing in this respect from the common rule for the division of labour between the veins and the arteries. But every one knows how we seek naturally to combine the pieces of our knowledge together, to bring them under general rules, to relate them to principles; and how unsatisfactory and tiresome it would be to go on for ever learning lists of exceptions, or accumulating items of fact which must stand isolated.

Well, that same need of relating our knowledge, which operates here within the sphere of our knowledge itself, we shall find operating, also, outside that sphere. We experience, as we go on learning and knowing,—the vast majority of us experience,—the need of relating what we have learnt and known to the sense which we have in us for conduct, to the sense which we have in us for beauty.

A certain Greek prophetess of Mantineia in Arcadia, Diotima by name, once explained to the philosopher Socrates that love, and impulse, and bent of all kinds, is, in fact, nothing else but the desire in men that good should for ever be present to them. This desire for good, Diotima assured Socrates, is our fundamental desire, of which fundamental desire every impulse in us is only some one particular form. And therefore this fundamental desire it is, I suppose,— this desire in men that good should be for ever present to them,—which acts in us when we feel the impulse for relating our knowledge to our sense for conduct and to our sense for beauty. At any rate, with men in general the instinct exists. Such is human nature. And the instinct, it will be admitted, is innocent, and human nature is preserved by our following the lead of its innocent instincts. Therefore, in seeking to gratify this instinct in question, we are following the instinct of self-preservation in humanity.

But, no doubt, some kinds of knowledge cannot be made to directly serve the instinct in question, cannot be directly related to the sense for beauty, to the sense for conduct. These are instrument-knowledges; they lead on to other knowledges, which can. A man who passes his life in instrument-knowledges is a specialist. They may be invaluable as instruments to something beyond, for those who have the gift thus to employ them; and they may be disciplines in themselves wherein it is useful for every one to have some schooling. But it is inconceivable that the generality of men should pass all their mental life with Greek accents or with formal logic. My friend Professor Sylvester,[4] who is one of the first mathematicians in the world, holds transcendental doctrines as to the virtue of mathematics, but those doctrines are not for common men. In the very Senate House and heart of our English Cambridge I once ventured, though not without an apology for my profaneness, to hazard the opinion that for the majority of mankind a little of mathematics, even, goes a long way. Of course this is quite consistent with their being of immense importance as an instrument to something else; but it is the few who have the aptitude for thus using them, not the bulk of mankind.

The natural sciences do not, however, stand on the same footing with these instrument-knowledges. Experience shows us that the generality of men will find more interest in learning that, when a taper burns, the wax is converted into carbonic acid and water, or in learning the explanation of the phenomenon of dew, or in learning how the circulation of the

---

[4] James Joseph Sylvester (1814–97), English mathematician, professor at Johns Hopkins and later at Oxford.

blood is carried on, than they find in learning that the genitive plural of *pais* and *pas* does not take the circumflex on the termination. And one piece of natural knowledge is added to another, and others are added to that, and at last we come to propositions so interesting as Mr. Darwin's famous proposition that 'our ancestor was a hairy quadruped furnished with a tail and pointed ears, probably arboreal in his habits.'[5] Or we come to propositions of such reach and magnitude as those which Professor Huxley delivers, when he says that the notions of our forefathers about the beginning and the end of the world were all wrong, and that nature is the expression of a definite order with which nothing interferes.

Interesting, indeed, these results of science are, important they are, and we should all of us be acquainted with them. But what I now wish you to mark is, that we are still, when they are propunded to us and we receive them, we are still in the sphere of intellect and knowledge. And for the generality of men there will be found, I say, to arise, when they have duly taken in the proposition that their ancestor was 'a hairy quadruped furnished with a tail and pointed ears, probably arboreal in his habits,' there will be found to arise an invincible desire to relate this proposition to the sense in us for conduct, and to the sense in us for beauty. But this the men of science will not do for us, and will hardly even profess to do. They will give us other pieces of knowledge, other facts, about other animals and their ancestors, or about plants, or about stones, or about stars; and they may finally bring us to those great 'general conceptions of the universe, which are forced upon us all,' says Professor Huxley, 'by the progress of physical science.' But still it will be *knowledge* only which they give us; knowledge not put for us into relation with our sense for conduct, our sense for beauty, and touched with emotion by being so put; not thus put for us, and therefore, to the majority of mankind, after a certain while, unsatisfying, wearying.

Not to the born naturalist, I admit. But what do we mean by a born naturalist? We mean a man in whom the zeal for observing nature is so uncommonly strong and eminent, that it marks him off from the bulk of mankind. Such a man will pass his life happily in collecting natural knowledge and reasoning upon it, and will ask for nothing, or hardly anything, more. I have heard it said that the sagacious and admirable naturalist whom we lost not very long ago, Mr. Darwin, once owned to a friend that for his part he did not experience the necessity for two things which most men find so necessary to them,—religion and poetry; science and the domestic affections, he thought, were enough. To a born naturalist, I can well understand that this should seem so. So absorbing is his occupation with nature, so strong his love for his occupation, that he goes on acquiring natural knowledge and reasoning upon it, and has little time or inclination for thinking about getting it related to the desire in man for conduct, the desire in man for beauty. He relates it to them for himself as he goes along, so far as he feels the need; and he draws from the domestic affections all the additional solace necessary. But then Darwins are extremely rare. Another great and admirable master of natural knowledge, Faraday, was a Sandemanian.[6] That is to say, he related his knowledge to his instinct for conduct and to his instinct for beauty, by the aid of that respectable Scottish sectary, Robert Sandeman. And so strong, in general, is the demand of religion and poetry to have their share in a man, to associate themselves with his knowing, and to relieve and rejoice it, that, probably, for one man amongst us with the disposition to do as Darwin did in this respect, there are at least fifty with the disposition to do as Faraday.

Education lays hold upon us, in fact, by satisfying this demand. Professor Huxley holds up to scorn mediæval education, with its neglect of the knowledge of nature, its poverty even of literary studies, its formal logic devoted to 'showing how and why that which the Church said was true must be true.' But the great mediæval Universities were not brought into being, we may be sure, by the zeal for giving a jejune and contemptible education. Kings have been their nursing fathers, and queens have been their nursing mothers, but not for this. The mediæval Universities came into being, because the supposed knowledge, delivered by Scripture and the Church, so deeply engaged men's hearts, by so simply, easily, and powerfully relating itself to their desire for conduct, their

---

[5] From Darwin's *Descent of Man* (1871).

[6] Faraday the chemist was a follower of the sect of Sandemanians, named for the Scottish clergyman Robert Sandeman (1718–71).

desire for beauty. All other knowledge was dominated by this supposed knowledge and was subordinated to it, because of the surpassing strength of the hold which it gained upon the affections of men, by allying itself profoundly with their sense for conduct, their sense for beauty.

But now, says Professor Huxley, conceptions of the universe fatal to the notions held by our forefathers have been forced upon as by physical science. Grant to him that they are thus fatal, that the new conceptions must and will soon become current everywhere, and that every one will finally perceive them to be fatal to the beliefs of our forefathers. The need of humane letters, as they are truly called, because they serve the paramount desire in men that good should be for ever present to them,—the need of humane letters, to establish a relation between the new conceptions, and our instinct for beauty, our instinct for conduct, is only the more visible. The Middle Age could do without humane letters, as it could do without the study of nature, because its supposed knowledge was made to engage its emotions so powerfully. Grant that the supposed knowledge disappears, its power of being made to engage the emotions will of course disappear along with it,—but the emotions themselves, and their claim to be engaged and satisfied, will remain. Now if we find by experience that humane letters have an undeniable power of engaging the emotions, the importance of humane letters in a man's training becomes not less, but greater, in proportion to the success of modern science in extirpating what it calls 'mediæval thinking.'

Have humane letters, then, have poetry and eloquence, the power here attributed to them of engaging the emotions, and do they exercise it? And if they have it and exercise it, *how* do they exercise it, so as to exert an influence upon man's sense for conduct, his sense for beauty? Finally, even if they both can and do exert an influence upon the senses in question, how are they to relate to them the results,—the modern results, —of natural science? All these questions may be asked. First, have poetry and elqoence the power of calling out the emotions? The appeal is to experience. Experience shows that for the vast majority of men, for mankind in general, they have the power. Next, do they exercise it? They do. But then, *how* do they exercise it so as to affect man's sense for conduct, his sense for

beauty? And this is perhaps a case for applying the Preacher's words: 'Though a man labour to seek it out, yet he shall not find it; yea, farther, though a wise man think to know it, yet shall he not be able to find it.'[7] Why should it be one thing, in its effect upon the emotions, to say, 'Patience is a virtue,' and quite another thing, in its effect upon the emotions, to say with Homer,

τλητὸν γὰρ Μοῖραι θυμὸν θέσαν ἀνθρώποισιν—[8]

'for an enduring heart have the destinies appointed to the children of men'? Why should it be one thing, in its effect upon the emotions, to say with the philosopher Spinoza, *Felicitas in eo consistit quod homo suum esse conservare potest*— 'Man's happiness consists in his being able to preserve his own essence,' and quite another thing, in its effect upon the emotions, to say with the Gospel, 'What is a man advantaged, if he gain the whole world, and lose himself, forfeit himself?' How does this difference of effect arise? I cannot tell, and I am not much concerned to know; the important thing is that it does arise, and that we can profit by it. But how, finally, are poetry and eloquence to exercise the power of relating the modern results of natural science to man's instinct for conduct, his instinct for beauty? And here again I answer that I do not know *how* they will exercise it, but that they can and will exercise it I am sure. I do not mean that modern philosophical poets and modern philosophical moralists are to come and relate for us, in express terms, the results of modern scientific research to our instinct for conduct, our instinct for beauty. But I mean that we shall find, as a matter of experience, if we know the best that has been thought and uttered in the world, we shall find that the art and poetry and eloquence of men who lived, perhaps, long ago, who had the most limited natural knowledge, who had the most erroneous conceptions about many important matters, we shall find that this art, and poetry, and eloquence, have in fact not only the power of refreshing and delighting us, they have also the power,— such is the strength and worth, in essentials, of their authors' criticism of life,—they have a fortifying, and elevating, and quickening, and suggestive power, capable of wonderfully helping us to relate the results of modern science to our need for conduct, our need for beauty. Homer's conceptions of the physical universe were, I

---

[7] Ecclesiastes, 8:17. [Arnold's note]   [8] *Iliad*, xxiv. 49. [Arnold's note]

imagine, grotesque; but really, under the shock of hearing from modern science that 'the world is not subordinated to man's use, and that man is not the cynosure of things terrestrial,' I could, for my own part, desire no better comfort than Homer's line which I quoted just now,

τλητὸν γὰρ Μοῖραι θυμὸν θέσαν ἀνθρώποισιν—

'for an enduring heart have the destinies appointed to the children of men'!

And the more that men's minds are cleared, the more that the results of science are frankly accepted, the more that poetry and eloquence come to be received and studied as what in truth they really are,—the criticism of life by gifted men, alive and active with extraordinary power at an unusual number of points;—so much the more will the value of humane letters, and of art also, which is an utterance having a like kind of power with theirs, be felt and acknowledged, and their place in education be secured.

Let us therefore, all of us, avoid indeed as much as possible any invidious comparison between the merits of humane letters, as means of education, and the merits of the natural sciences. But when some President of a Section for Mechanical Science insists on making the comparison, and tells us that 'he who in his training has substituted literature and history for natural science has chosen the less useful alternative,' let us make answer to him that the student of humane letters only, will, at least, know also the great general conceptions brought in by modern physical science; for science, as Professor Huxley says, forces them upon us all. But the student of the natural sciences only, will, by our very hypothesis, know nothing of humane letters; not to mention that in setting himself to be perpetually accumulating natural knowledge, he sets himself to do what only specialists have in general the gift for doing genially. And so he will probably be unsatisfied, or at any rate incomplete, and even more incomplete than the student of humane letters only.

I once mentioned in a school-report, how a young man in one of our English training colleges having to paraphrase the passage in *Macbeth* beginning,

Can'st thou not minister to a mind diseased?[9]

turned this line into, 'Can you not wait upon the lunatic?' And I remarked what a curious state of things it would be, if every pupil of our national schools knew, let us say, that the moon is two thousand one hundred and sixty miles in diameter, and thought at the same time that a good paraphrase for

Can'st thou not minister to a mind diseased?

was, 'Can you not wait upon the lunatic?' If one is driven to choose, I think I would rather have a young person ignorant about the moon's diameter, but aware that 'Can you not wait upon the lunatic?' is bad, than a young person whose education had been such as to manage things the other way.

Or to go higher than the pupils of our national schools. I have in my mind's eye a member of our British Parliament who comes to travel here in America, who afterwards relates his travels, and who shows a really masterly knowledge of the geology of this great country and of its mining capabilities, but who ends by gravely suggesting that the United States should borrow a prince from our Royal Family, and should make him their king, and should create a House of Lords of great landed proprietors after the pattern of ours; and then America, he thinks, would have her future happily and perfectly secured. Surely, in this case, the President of the Section for Mechanical Science would himself hardly say that our member of Parliament, by concentrating himself upon geology and mineralogy, and so on, and not attending to literature and history, had 'chosen the more useful alternative.'

If then there is to be separation and option between humane letters on the one hand, and the natural sciences on the other, the great majority of mankind, all who have not exceptional and overpowering aptitudes for the study of nature, would do well, I cannot but think, to choose to be educated in humane letters rather than in the natural sciences. Letters will call out their being at more points, will make them live more.

I said that before I ended I would just touch on the question of classical education, and I will keep my word. Even if literature is to retain a large place in our education, yet Latin and Greek, say the friends of progress, will certainly have to go. Greek is the grand offender in the eyes of these gentlemen. The attackers of the established course of study think that against Greek, at any rate, they have irresistible arguments. Literature may perhaps be needed in education, they say; but why on earth should it be Greek literature?

9 *Macbeth* V, iii, 40.

Why not French or German? Nay, 'has not an Englishman models in his own literature of every kind of excellence?' As before, it is not on any weak pleadings of my own that I rely for convincing the gainsayers; it is on the constitution of human nature itself, and on the instinct of self-preservation in humanity. The instinct for beauty is set in human nature, as surely as the instinct for knowledge is set there, or the instinct for conduct. If the instinct for beauty is served by Greek literature and art as it is served by no other literature and art, we may trust to the instinct of self-preservation in humanity for keeping Greek as part of our culture. We may trust to it for even making the study of Greek more prevalent than it is now. Greek will come, I hope, some day to be studied more rationally than at present; but it will be increasingly studied as men increasingly feel the need in them for beauty, and how powerfully Greek art and Greek literature can serve this need. Women will again study Greek, as Lady Jane Grey did; I believe that in that chain of forts, with which the fair host of the Amazons are now engirdling our English universities, I find that here in America, in colleges like Smith College in Massachusetts, and Vassar College in the State of New York, and in the happy families of the mixed universities out West, they are studying it already.

Defuit una mihi symmetria prisca,—'The antique symmetry was the one thing wanting to me,' said Leonardo da Vinci; and he was an Italian. I will not presume to speak for the Americans, but I am sure that, in the Englishman, the want of this admirable symmetry of the Greeks is a thousand times more great and crying than in any Italian. The results of the want show themselves most glaringly, perhaps, in our architecture, but they show themselves, also, in all our art. *Fit details strictly combined, in view of a large general result nobly conceived;* that is just the beautiful *symmetria prisca* of the Greeks, and it is just where we English fail, where all our art fails. Striking ideas we have, and well-executed details we have; but that high symmetry which, with satisfying and delightful effect, combines them, we seldom or never have. The glorious beauty of the Acropolis at Athens did not come from single fine things stuck about on that hill, a statue here, a gateway there;—no, it arose from all things being perfectly combined for a supreme total effect. What must not an Englishman feel about our deficiencies in this respect, as the sense for beauty, whereof this symmetry is an essential

element, awakens and strengthens within him! what will not one day be his respect and desire for Greece and its *symmetria prisca*, when the scales drop from his eyes as he walks the London streets, and he sees such a lesson in meanness as the Strand, for instance, in its true deformity! But here we are coming to our friend Mr. Ruskin's province, and I will not intrude upon it, for he is its very sufficient guardian.

And so we at last find, it seems, we find flowing in favour of the humanities the natural and necessary stream of things, which seemed against them when we started. The 'hairy quadruped furnished with a tail and pointed ears, probably arboreal in his habits,' this good fellow carried hidden in his nature, apparently, something destined to develop into a necessity for humane letters. Nay, more; we seem finally to be even led to the further conclusion that our hairy ancestor carried in his nature, also, a necessity for Greek.

And therefore, to say the truth, I cannot really think that humane letters are in much actual danger of being thrust out from their leading place in education, in spite of the array of authorities against them at this moment. So long as human nature is what it is, their attractions will remain irresistible. As with Greek, so with letters generally: they will some day come, we may hope, to be studied more rationally, but they will not lose their place. What will happen will rather be that there will be crowded into education other matters besides, far too many; there will be, perhaps, a period of unsettlement and confusion and false tendency; but letters will not in the end lose their leading place. If they lose it for a time, they will get it back again. We shall be brought back to them by our wants and aspirations. And a poor humanist may possess his soul in patience, neither strive nor cry, admit the energy and brilliancy of the partisans of physical science, and their present favour with the public, to be far greater than his own, and still have a happy faith that the nature of things works silently on behalf of the studies which he loves, and that, while we shall all have to acquaint ourselves with the great results reached by modern science and to give ourselves as much training in its disciplines as we can conveniently carry, yet the majority of men will always require humane letters; and so much the more, as they have the more and the greater results of science to relate to the need in man for conduct, and to the need in him for beauty.

from Essays in Criticism, Second Series

The last harvest of Arnold's literary criticism came with the publication in 1888, the year of his death, of Essays in Criticism, Second Series. *Arnold died before writing the proposed preface to the volume. It contains ten essays from the period 1879 to 1888, chiefly on specific literary figures—Milton, Gray, Keats, Wordsworth, Byron, Shelly, Tolstoi, Amiel— and it also contains the magisterial "The Study of Poetry." That essay, given below, had first appeared in 1880 as the introductory essay to a series of volumes of verse edited by T. H. Ward and titled* The English Poets. *It is one of the essays on which Arnold's high standing as a critic has traditionally been based. "Wordsworth," also printed below, had originally been the introduction to a selection by Arnold of Wordsworth's poetry for the Ward series, published in 1879.*

The Study of Poetry

THE future of poetry is immense, because in poetry, where it is worthy of its high destinies, our race, as time goes on, will find an ever surer and surer stay. There is not a creed which is not shaken, not an accredited dogma which is not shown to be questionable, not a received tradition which does not threaten to dissolve. Our religion has materialised itself in the fact, in the supposed fact; it has attached its emotion to the fact, and now the fact is failing it. But for poetry the idea is everything; the rest is a world of illusion, of divine illusion. Poetry attaches its emotion to the idea; the idea *is* the fact. The strongest part of our religion to-day is its unconscious poetry.'

Let me be permitted to quote these words of my own, as uttering the thought which should, in my opinion, go with us and govern us in all our study of poetry. In the present work it is the course of one great contributory stream to the world-river of poetry that we are invited to follow. We are here invited to trace the stream of English poetry. But whether we set ourselves, as here, to follow only one of the several streams that make the mighty river of poetry, or whether we seek to know them all, our governing thought should be the same. We should conceive of poetry worthily, and more highly than it has been the custom to conceive of it. We should conceive of it as capable of higher uses, and called to higher destinies, than those which in general men have assigned to it hitherto. More and more mankind will discover that we have to turn to poetry to interpret life for us, to console us,

to sustain us. Without poetry, our science will appear incomplete; and most of what now passes with us for religion and philosophy will be replaced by poetry. Science, I say, will appear incomplete without it. For finely and truly does Wordsworth call poetry 'the impassioned expression which is in the countenance of all science'; and what is a countenance without its expression? Again, Wordsworth finely and truly calls poetry 'the breath and finer spirit of all knowledge': our religion, parading evidences such as those on which the popular mind relies now; our philosophy, pluming itself on its reasonings about causation and finite and infinite being; what are they but the shadows and dreams and false shows of knowledge? The day will come when we shall wonder at ourselves for having trusted to them, for having taken them seriously; and the more we perceive their hollowness, the more we shall prize 'the breath and finer spirit of knowledge' offered to us by poetry.

But if we conceive thus highly of the destinies of poetry, we must also set our standard for poetry high, since poetry, to be capable of fulfilling such high destinies, must be poetry of a high order of excellence. We must accustom ourselves to a high standard and to a strict judgment. Sainte-Beuve[1] relates that Napoleon one day said, when somebody was spoken of in his presence as a charlatan: 'Charlatan as much as you please; but where is there *not* charlatanism?' —'Yes,' answers Sainte-Beuve, 'in politics, in the art of governing mankind, that is perhaps true. But in the order of thought, in art, the glory, the eternal honour is that charlatanism shall find no entrance; herein lies the inviolable-

---

[1] In Sainte-Beuve's *Cahiers.*

ness of that noble portion of man's being.' It is admirably said, and let us hold fast to it. In poetry, which is thought and art in one, it is the glory, the eternal honour, that charlatanism shall find no entrance; that this noble sphere be kept inviolate and inviolable. Charlatanism is for confusing or obliterating the distinctions between excellent and inferior, sound and unsound or only half-sound, true and untrue or only half-true. It is charlatanism, conscious or unconscious, whenever we confuse or obliterate these. And in poetry, more than anywhere else, it is unpermissible to confuse or obliterate them. For in poetry the distinction between excellent and inferior, sound and unsound or only half-sound, true and untrue or only half-true, is of paramount importance. It is of paramount importance because of the high destinies of poetry. In poetry, as a criticism of life under the conditions fixed for such a criticism by the laws of poetic truth and poetic beauty, the spirit of our race will find, we have said, as time goes on and as other helps fail, its consolation and stay. But the consolation and stay will be of power in proportion to the power of the criticism of life. And the criticism of life will be of power in proportion as the poetry conveying it is excellent rather than inferior, sound rather than unsound or half-sound, true rather than untrue or half-true.

The best poetry is what we want; the best poetry will be found to have a power of forming, sustaining, and delighting us, as nothing else can. A clearer, deeper sense of the best in poetry, and of the strength and joy to be drawn from it, is the most precious benefit which we can gather from a poetical collection such as the present. And yet in the very nature and conduct of such a collection there is inevitably something which tends to obscure in us the consciousness of what our benefit should be, and to distract us from the pursuit of it. We should therefore steadily set it before our minds at the outset, and should compel ourselves to revert constantly to the thought of it as we proceed.

Yes; constantly in reading poetry, a sense for the best, the really excellent, and of the strength and joy to be drawn from it, should be present in our minds and should govern our estimate of what we read. But this real estimate, the only true one, is liable to be superseded, if we are not watchful, by two other kinds of estimate, the historic estimate and the personal estimate, both

of which are fallacious. A poet or a poem may count to us historically, they may count to us on grounds personal to ourselves, and they may count to us really. They may count to us historically. The course of development of a nation's language, thought, and poetry, is profoundly interesting: and by regarding a poet's work as a stage in this course of development we may easily bring ourselves to make it of more importance as poetry than in itself it really is, we may come to use a language of quite exaggerated praise in criticising it; in short, to overrate it. So arises in our poetic judgments the fallacy caused by the estimate which we may call historic. Then, again, a poet or a poem may count to us on grounds personal to ourselves. Our personal affinities, likings, and circumstances, have great power to sway our estimate of this or that poet's work, and to make us attach more importance to it as poetry than in itself it really possesses, because to us it is, or has been, of high importance. Here also we overrate the object of our interest, and apply to it a language of praise which is quite exaggerated. And thus we get the source of a second fallacy in our poetic judgments—the fallacy caused by an estimate which we may call personal.

Both fallacies are natural. It is evident how naturally the study of the history and development of a poetry may incline a man to pause over reputations and works once conspicuous but now obscure, and to quarrel with a careless public for skipping, in obedience to mere tradition and habit, from one famous name or work in its national poetry to another, ignorant of what it misses, and of the reason for keeping what it keeps, and of the whole process of growth in its poetry. The French have become diligent students of their own early poetry, which they long neglected; the study makes many of them dissatisfied with their so-called classical poetry, the court-tragedy of the seventeenth century, a poetry which Pellisson[2] long ago reproached with its want of the true poetic stamp, with its *politesse stérile et rampante,*[3] but which nevertheless has reigned in France as absolutely as if it had been the perfection of classical poetry indeed. The dissatisfaction is natural; yet a lively and accomplished critic, M. Charles d'Héricault, the editor of Clément Marot,[4] goes too far when he says that 'the cloud of glory playing round a classic is a mist as dangerous to

---

[2] Paul Pellisson (1624–93), French critic.   [3] "Sterile and bombastic civility."
[4] Charles d'Héricault edited in 1868–72 the poems of Clément Marot (1496–1544).

the future of a literature as it is intolerable for the purposes of history.' 'It hinders,' he goes on, 'it hinders us from seeing more than one single point, the culminating and exceptional point; the summary, fictitious and arbitrary, of a thought and of a work. It substitutes a halo for a physiognomy, it puts a statue where there was once a man, and hiding from us all trace of the labour, the attempts, the weaknesses, the failures, it claims not study but veneration; it does not show us how the thing is done, it imposes upon us a model. Above all, for the historian this creation of classic personages is inadmissible; for it withdraws the poet from his time, from his proper life, it breaks historical relationships, it blinds criticism by conventional admiration, and renders the investigation of literary origins unacceptable. It gives us a human personage no longer, but a God seated immovable amidst His perfect work, like Jupiter on Olympus; and hardly will it be possible for the young student, to whom such work is exhibited at such a distance from him, to believe that it did not issue ready made from that divine head.'

All this is brilliantly and tellingly said, but we must plead for a distinction. Everything depends on the reality of a poet's classic character. If he is a dubious classic, let us sift him; if he is a false classic, let us explode him. But if he is a real classic, if his work belongs to the class of the very best (for this is the true and right meaning of the word *classic, classical*), then the great thing for us is to feel and enjoy his work as deeply as ever we can, and to appreciate the wide difference between it and all work which has not the same high character. This is what is salutary, this is what is formative; this is the great benefit to be got from the study of poetry. Everything which interferes with it, which hinders it, is injurious. True, we must read our classic with open eyes, and not with eyes blinded with superstition; we must perceive when his work comes short, when it drops out of the class of the very best, and we must rate it, in such cases, at its proper value. But the use of this negative criticism is not in itself, it is entirely in its enabling us to have a clearer sense and a deeper enjoyment of what is truly excellent. To trace the labour, the attempts, the weaknesses, the failures of a genuine classic, to acquaint oneself with his time and his life and his historical relationships, is mere literary dilettantism unless it has that clear sense and deeper enjoyment for its end. It may be said that the more we know about a classic the better we shall enjoy him; and if we lived as long as Methuselah and had all of us heads of perfect clearness and wills of perfect steadfastness, this might be true in fact as it is plausible in theory. But the case here is much the same as the case with the Greek and Latin studies of our schoolboys. The elaborate philological groundwork which we require them to lay is in theory an admirable preparation for appreciating the Greek and Latin authors worthily. The more thoroughly we lay the ground work, the better we shall be able, it may be said, to enjoy the authors. True, if time were not so short, and schoolboy's wits not so soon tired and their power of attention exhausted; only, as it is, the elaborate philological preparation goes on, but the authors are little known and less enjoyed. So with the investigator of 'historic origins' in poetry. He ought to enjoy the true classic all the better for his investigations; he often is distracted from the enjoyment of the best, and with the less good he overbusies himself, and is prone to overrate it in proportion to the trouble which it has cost him.

The idea of tracing historic origins and historical relationships cannot be absent from a compilation like the present. And naturally the poets to be exhibited in it will be assigned to those persons for exhibition who are known to prize them highly, rather than to those who have no special inclination towards them. Moreover the very occupation with an author, and the business of exhibiting him, disposes us to affirm and amplify his importance. In the present work, therefore, we are sure of frequent temptation to adopt the historic estimate, or the personal estimate, and to forget the real estimate; which latter, nevertheless, we must employ if we are to make poetry yield us its full benefit. So high is that benefit, the benefit of clearly feeling and of deeply enjoying the really excellent, the truly classic in poetry, that we do well, I say, to set it fixedly before our minds as our object in studying poets and poetry, and to make the desire of attaining it the one principle to which, as the *Imitation* says, whatever we may read or come to know, we always return. *Cum multa legeris et cognoveris, ad unum semper oportet redire principium.* [5]

---

[5] "When you have read and learned much, you ought always to return to the one principle" (*Imitation of Christ*).

The historic estimate is likely in especial to affect our judgment and our language when we are dealing with ancient poets; the personal estimate when we are are dealing with poets our contemporaries, or at any rate modern. The exaggerations due to the historic estimate are not in themselves, perhaps, of very much gravity. Their report hardly enters the general ear; probably they do not always impose even on the literary men who adopt them. But they lead to a dangerous abuse of language. So we hear Cædmon, amongst our own poets, compared to Milton. I have already noticed the enthusiasm of one accomplished French critic for 'historic origins.' Another eminent French critic, M. Vitet,[6] comments upon that famous document of the early poetry of his nation, the *Chanson de Roland*. It is indeed a most interesting document. The *joculator* or *jongleur* Taillefer, who was with William the Conqueror's army at Hastings, marched before the Norman troops, so said the tradition, singing 'of Charlemagne and of Roland and of Oliver, and of the vassals who died at Roncevaux'; and it is suggested that in the *Chanson de Roland* by one Turoldus or Théroulde, a poem preserved in a manuscript of the twelfth century in the Bodleian Library at Oxford, we have certainly the matter, perhaps even some of the words, of the chant which Taillefer sang. The poem has vigour and freshness; it is not without pathos. But M. Vitet is not satisfied with seeing in it a document of some poetic value, and of very high historic and linguistic value; he sees in it a grand and beautiful work, a monument of epic genius. In its general design he finds the grandiose conception, in its details he finds the constant union of simplicity with greatness, which are the marks, he truly says, of the genuine epic, and distinguish it from the artificial epic of literary ages. One thinks of Homer; this is the sort of praise which is given to Homer, and justly given. Higher praise there cannot well be, and it is the praise due to epic poetry of the highest order only, and to no other. Let us try, then, the *Chanson de Roland* at its best. Roland,

mortally wounded, lays himself down under a pine-tree, with his face turned towards Spain and the enemy—

De plusurs choses à remembrer li prist,
De tantes teres cume li bers cunquist,
De dulce France, des humes de sun lign,
De Carlemagne sun seignor ki l'nurrit.[7]

That is primitive work, I repeat, with an undeniable poetic quality of its own. It deserves such praise, and such praise is sufficient for it. But now turn to Homer—

Ὣς φάτο · τοὺς δ' ἤδη κατέχεν φυσίζοος αἶα
ἐν Λακεδαίμονι αὖθι, φίλῃ ἐν πατρίδι γαίῃ.[8]

We are here in another world, another order of poetry altogether; here is rightly due such supreme praise as that which M. Vitet gives to the *Chanson de Roland*. If our words are to have any meaning, if our judgments are to have any solidity, we must not heap that supreme praise upon poetry of an order immeasurably inferior.

Indeed there can be no more useful help for discovering what poetry belongs to the class of the truly excellent, and can therefore do us most good, than to have always in one's mind lines and expressions of the great masters, and to apply them as a touchstone to other poetry. Of course we are not to require this other poetry to resemble them; it may be very dissimilar. But if we have any tact we shall find them, when we have lodged them well in our minds, an infallible touchstone for detecting the presence or absence of high poetic quality, and also the degree of this quality, in all other poetry which we may place beside them. Short passages, even single lines, will serve our turn quite sufficiently. Take the two lines which I have just quoted from Homer, the poet's comment on Helen's mention of her brothers;—or take his

Ἄ δειλώ, τί σφῶϊ δόμεν Πηλῆϊ ἄνακτι
θνητῷ; ὑμεῖς δ' ἐστὸν ἀγήρω τ' ἀθανάτω τε.
ἦ ἵνα δυστήνοισι μετ' ἀνδράσιν ἄλγε' ἔχητον;[9]

---

[6] Ludovic Vitet (1802–73), French man of letters.

[7] 'Then began he to call many things to remembrance,—all the lands which his valour conquered, and pleasant France, and the men of his lineage, and Charlemagne his liege lord who nourished him.'—*Chanson de Roland*, iii. 939–942. [Arnold's note]

[8] 'So said she; they long since in Earth's soft arms were reposing, There, in their own dear land, their fatherland, Lacedaemon.'

Iliad, iii. 243, 244 (translated by Dr. Hawtrey). [Arnold's note]

[9] 'Ah, unhappy pair, why gave we you to King Peleus, to a mortal? but ye are without old age, and immortal. Was it that with men born to misery ye might have sorrow?'—*Iliad*, xvii. 443–445. [Arnold's note]

the address of Zeus to the horses of Peleus;—or take finally his

Καὶ σέ, γέρον, τὸ πρὶν μὲν ἀκούομεν ὄλβιον εἶναι · [10]

the words of Achilles to Priam, a suppliant before him. Take that incomparable line and a half of Dante, Ugolino's tremendous words—

Io non piangeva; si dentro impietrai.
Piangevan elli . . . [11]

take the lovely words of Beatrice to Virgil—

Io son fatta da Dio, sua mercè, tale,
Che la vostra miseria non mi tange,
Nè fiamma d'esto incendio non m' assale . . . [12]

take the simple, but perfect, single line—

In la sua volontade è nostra pace.[13]

Take of Shakspeare a line or two of Henry the Fourth's expostulation with sleep—

Wilt thou upon the high and giddy mast
Seal up the ship-boy's eyes, and rock his brains
In cradle of the rude imperious surge . . . [14]

and take, as well, Hamlet's dying request to Horatio—

If thou didst ever hold me in thy heart,
Absent thee from felicity awhile,
And in this harsh world draw thy breath in pain
To tell my story . . . [15]

Take of Milton that Miltonic passage—

Darken'd so, yet shone
Above them all the archangel; but his face
Deep scars of thunder had intrench'd, and care
Sat on his faded cheek . . . [16]

add two such lines as—

And courage never to submit or yield
And what is else not to be overcome . . .

and finish with the exquisite close to the loss of Proserpine, the loss

which cost Ceres all that pain
To seek her through the world.

These few lines, if we have tact and can use them, are enough even of themselves to keep clear and sound our judgments about poetry, to save us from fallacious estimates of it, to conduct us to a real estimate.

The specimens I have quoted differ widely from one another, but they have in common this: the possession of the very highest poetical quality. If we are thoroughly penetrated by their power, we shall find that we have acquired a sense enabling us, whatever poetry may be laid before us, to feel the degree in which a high poetical quality is present or wanting there. Critics give themselves great labour to draw out what in the abstract constitutes the characters of a high quality of poetry. It is much better simply to have recourse to concrete examples;—to take specimens of poetry of the high, the very highest quality, and to say: The characters of a high quality of poetry are what is expressed *there*. They are far better recognised by being felt in the verse of the master, than by being perused in the prose of the critic. Nevertheless if we are urgently pressed to give some critical account of them, we may safely, perhaps, venture on laying down, not indeed how and why the characters arise, but where and in what they arise. They are in the matter and substance of the poetry, and they are in its manner and style. Both of these, the substance and matter on the one hand, the style and manner on the other, have a mark, an accent, of high beauty, worth, and power. But if we are asked to define this mark and accent in the abstract, our answer must be: No, for we should thereby be darkening the question, not clearing it. The mark and accent are as given by the substance and matter of that poetry, by the style and manner of that poetry, and of all other poetry which is akin to it in quality.

Only one thing we may add as to the substance and matter of poetry, guiding ourselves by Aristotle's profound observation that the superiority of poetry over history consists in its possessing a higher truth and a higher seriousness (φιλοσοφώτερον καὶ σπουδαιότερον). Let us add, therefore, to what we have said, this: that the substance and matter of the best poetry acquire their special character from possessing, in an eminent degree, truth and seriousness. We may add yet

---

[10] 'Nay, and thou too, old man, in former days wast, as we hear, happy.'—*Iliad*, xxiv. 543. [Arnold's note]

[11] 'I wailed not, so of stone grew I within; *they* wailed.'—*Inferno*, xxxiii. 39, 40. [Arnold's note]

[12] 'Of such sort hath God, thanked be His mercy, made me, that your misery toucheth me not, neither doth the flame of this fire strike me.'—*Inferno*, ii. 91–93. [Arnold's note]

[13] 'In His will is our peace.'—*Paradiso*, iii. 85. [Arnold's note]

[14] *II Henry IV*, III, i, 18–20.   [15] *Hamlet* V, ii, 357–60.

[16] This and the following two passages are from *Paradise Lost*: I, 599–602; I, 108–109; IV, 271–272.

further, what is in itself evident, that to the style and manner of the best poetry their special character, their accent, is given by their diction, and, even yet more, by their movement. And though we distinguish between the two characters, the two accents, of superiority, yet they are nevertheless vitally connected one with the other. The superior character of truth and seriousness, in the matter and substance of the best poetry, is inseparable from the superiority of diction and movement marking its style and manner. The two superiorities are closely related, and are in steadfast proportion one to the other. So far as high poetic truth and seriousness are wanting to a poet's matter and substance, so far also, we may be sure, will a high poetic stamp of diction and movement be wanting to his style and manner. In proportion as this high stamp of diction and movement, again, is absent from a poet's style and manner, we shall find, also, that high poetic truth and seriousness are absent from his substance and matter.

So stated, these are but dry generalities; their whole force lies in their application. And I could wish every student of poetry to make the application of them for himself. Made by himself, the application would impress itself upon his mind far more deeply than made by me. Neither will my limits allow me to make any full application of the generalities above propounded; but in the hope of bringing out, at any rate, some significance in them, and of establishing an important principle more firmly by their means, I will, in the space which remains to me, follow rapidly from the commencement the course of our English poetry with them in my view.

Once more I return to the early poetry of France, with which our own poetry, in its origins, is indissolubly connected. In the twelfth and thirteenth centuries, that seed-time of all modern language and literature, the poetry of France had a clear predominance in Europe. Of the two divisions of that poetry, its productions in the *langue d'oil* and its productions in the *langue d'oc*, the poetry of the *langue d'oc*, of southern France, of the troubadours, is of importance because of its effect on Italian literature;—the first literature of modern Europe to strike the true and grand note, and to bring forth, as in Dante and Petrarch it brought forth, classics. But the predominance of French poetry in Europe, during the twelfth

and thirteenth centuries, is due to its poetry of the *langue d'oil*, the poetry of northern France and of the tongue which is now the French language. In the twelfth century the bloom of this romance-poetry was earlier and stronger in England, at the court of our Anglo-Norman kings, than in France itself. But it was a bloom of French poetry; and as our native poetry formed itself, it formed itself out of this. The romance-poems which took possession of the heart and imagination of Europe in the twelfth and thirteenth centuries are French; 'they are,' as Southey justly says, 'the pride of French literature, nor have we anything which can be placed in competition with them.' Themes were supplied from all quarters; but the romance-setting which was common to them all, and which gained the ear of Europe, was French. This constituted for the French poetry, literature, and language, at the height of the Middle Age, an unchallenged predominance. The Italian Brunetto Latini,[17] the master of Dante, wrote his *Treasure* in French because, he says, 'la parleure en est plus délitable et plus commune à toutes gens.' In the same century, the thirteenth, the French romance-writer, Christian of Troyes,[18] formulates the claims, in chivalry and letters, of France, his native country, as follows:—

> Or vous ert par ce livre apris,
> Que Gresse ot de chevalerie
> Le premier los et de clergie;
> Puis vint chevalerie à Rome,
> Et de la clergie la some,
> Qui ore est en France venue.
> Diex doinst qu'ele i soit retenue,
> Et que li lius li abelisse
> Tant que de France n'isse
> L'onor qui s'i est arestée!

'Now by this book you will learn that first Greece had the renown for chivalry and letters; then chivalry and the primacy in letters passed to Rome, and now it is come to France. God grant it may be kept there; and that the place may please it so well, that the honour which has come to make stay in France may never depart thence!'

Yet it is now all gone, this French romance-poetry, of which the weight of substance and the power of style are not unfairly represented by this extract from Christian of Troyes. Only by means of the historic estimates can we persuade

---

[17] Brunetto Latini (1210?–1294?), Italian scholar, author of *Livres du Trésor,* written in French because "it is a more pleasant language and more common to all people."
[18] Chrétien de Troyes (1140?–1191?), French poet, author of Arthurian romances.

ourselves now to think that any of it is of poetical importance.

But in the fourteenth century there comes an Englishman nourished on this poetry, taught his trade by this poetry, getting words, rhyme, metre from this poetry; for even of that stanza which the Italians used, and which Chaucer derived immediately from the Italians, the basis and suggestion was probably given in France. Chaucer (I have already named him) fascinated his contemporaries, but so too did Christian of Troyes and Wolfram of Eschenbach.[19] Chaucer's power of fascination, however, is enduring; his poetical importance does not need the assistance of the historic estimate; it is real. He is a genuine source of joy and strength, which is flowing still for us and will flow always. He will be read, as time goes on, far more generally than he is read now. His language is a cause of difficulty for us; but so also, and I think in quite as great a degree, is the language of Burns. In Chaucer's case, as in that of Burns, it is a difficulty to be unhesitatingly accepted and overcome.

If we ask ourselves wherein consists the immense superiority of Chaucer's poetry over the romance-poetry—why it is that in passing from this to Chaucer we suddenly feel ourselves to be in another world, we shall find that his superiority is both in the substance of his poetry and in the style of his poetry. His superiority in substance is given by his large, free, simple, clear yet kindly view of human life,—so unlike the total want, in the romance-poets, of all intelligent command of it. Chaucer has not their helplessness; he has gained the power to survey the world from a central, a truly human point of view. We have only to call to mind the Prologue to *The Canterbury Tales.* The right comment upon it is Dryden's: 'It is sufficient to say, according to the proverb, that *here is God's plenty.*' And again: 'He is a perpetual fountain of good sense.' It is by a large, free, sound representation of things, that poetry, this high criticism of life, has truth of substance; and Chaucer's poetry has truth of substance.

Of his style and manner, if we think first of the romance-poetry and then of Chaucer's divine liquidness of diction, his divine fluidity of movement, it is difficult to speak temperately. They are irresistible, and justify all the rapture with which his successors speak of his 'gold dewdrops of speech.' Johnson misses the point entirely

when he finds fault with Dryden for ascribing to Chaucer the first refinement of our numbers, and says that Gower also can show smooth numbers and easy rhymes. The refinement of our numbers means something far more than this. A nation may have versifiers with smooth numbers and easy rhymes, and yet may have no real poetry at all. Chaucer is the father of our splendid English poetry; he is our 'well of English undefiled,' because by the lovely charm of his diction, the lovely charm of his movement, he makes an epoch and founds a tradition. In Spenser, Shakspeare, Milton, Keats, we can follow the tradition of the liquid diction, the fluid movement, of Chaucer; at one time it is his liquid diction of which in these poets we feel the virtue, and at another time it is his fluid movement. And the virtue is irresistible.

Bounded as is my space, I must yet find room for an example of Chaucer's virtue, as I have given examples to show the virtue of the great classics. I feel disposed to say that a single line is enough to show the charm of Chaucer's verse; that merely one line like this—

O martyr souded[20] in virginitee!

has a virtue of manner and movement such as we shall not find in all the verse of romance-poetry; —but this is saying nothing. The virtue is such as we shall not find, perhaps, in all English poetry, outside the poets whom I have named as the special inheritors of Chaucer's tradition. A single line, however, is too little if we have not the strain of Chaucer's verse well in our memory; let us take a stanza. It is from *The Prioress's Tale,* the story of the Christian child murdered in a Jewry—

> My throte is cut unto my nekke-bone
> Saidè this child, and as by way of kindè
> I should have deyd, yea, longè time agone;
> But Jesu Christ, as ye in bookès finde,
> Will that his glory last and be in minde,
> And for the worship of his mother dere
> Yet may I sing O Alma loud and clere.

Wordsworth has modernised this Tale, and to feel how delicate and evanescent is the charm of verse, we have only to read Wordsworth's first three lines of this stanza after Chaucer's—

> My throat is cut unto the bone, I trow,
> Said this young child, and by the law of kind
> I should have died, yea, many hours ago.

---

[19] Wolfram von Eschenbach (c. 1165–c. 1220), German epic poet, author of *Parzival.*
[20] The French *soudé;* soldered, fixed fast. [Arnold's note]

The charm is departed. It is often said that the power of liquidness and fluidity in Chaucer's verse was dependent upon a free, a licentious dealing with language, such as is now impossible; upon a liberty, such as Burns too enjoyed, of making words like *neck, bird,* into a dissyllable by adding to them, and words like *cause, rhyme,* into a dissyllable by sounding the *e* mute. It is true that Chaucer's fluidity is conjoined with this liberty, and is admirably served by it; but we ought not to say that it was dependent upon it. It was dependent upon his talent. Other poets with a like liberty do not attain to the fluidity of Chaucer; Burns himself does not attain to it. Poets, again, who have a talent akin to Chaucer's, such as Shakspeare or Keats, have known how to attain to his fluidity without the like liberty.

And yet Chaucer is not one of the great classics. His poetry transcends and effaces, easily and without effort, all the romance-poetry of Catholic Christendom; it transcends and effaces all the English poetry contemporary with it, it transcends and effaces all the English poetry subsequent to it down to the age of Elizabeth. Of such avail is poetic truth of substance, in its natural and necessary union with poetic truth of style. And yet, I say, Chaucer is not one of the great classics. He has not their accent. What is wanting to him is suggested by the mere mention of the name of the first great classic of Christendom, the immortal poet who died eighty years before Chaucer,—Dante. The accent of such verse as

> In la sua volontade è nostra pace . . .

is altogether beyond Chaucer's reach; we praise him, but we feel that this accent is out of the question for him. It may be said that it was necessarily out of the reach of any poet in the England of that stage of growth. Possibly; but we are to adopt a real, not a historic, estimate of poetry. However we may account for its absence, something is wanting, then, to the poetry of Chaucer, which poetry must have before it can be placed in the glorious class of the best. And there is no doubt what that something is. It is the σπουδαιότης, the high and excellent seriousness, which Aristotle assigns as one of the grand virtues of poetry. The substance of Chaucer's poetry, his view of things and his criticism of life, has largeness, freedom, shrewdness, benignity; but it has not this high seriousness. Homer's criticism of life has it, Dante's has it, Shakspeare's has it. It is this chiefly which gives to our spirits what they can rest upon; and with the increasing demands of our modern ages upon poetry, this virtue of giving us what we can rest upon will be more and more highly esteemed. A voice from the slums of Paris, fifty or sixty years after Chaucer, the voice of poor Villon out of his life of riot and crime, has at its happy moments (as, for instance, in the last stanza of *La Belle Heaulmière*[21]) more of this important poetic virtue of seriousness than all the productions of Chaucer. But its apparition in Villon, and in men like Villon, is fitful; the greatness of the great poets, the power of their criticism of life, is that their virtue is sustained.

To our praise, therefore, of Chaucer as a poet there must be this limitation; he lacks the high seriousness of the great classics, and therewith an important part of their virtue. Still, the main fact for us to bear in mind about Chaucer is his sterling value according to that real estimate which we firmly adopt for all poets. He has poetic truth of substance, though he has not high poetic seriousness, and corresponding to his truth of substance he has an exquisite virtue of style and manner. With him is born our real poetry.

For my present purpose I need not dwell on our Elizabethan poetry, or on the continuation and close of this poetry in Milton. We all of us profess to be agreed in the estimate of this poetry; we all of us recognise it as great poetry, our greatest, and Shakspeare and Milton as our

---

[21] The name *Heaulmière* is said to be derived from a head-dress (helm) worn as a mark by courtesans. In Villon's ballad, a poor old creature of this class laments her days of youth and beauty. The last stanza of the ballad runs thus—

> 'Ainsi le bon temps regretons
> Entre nous, pauvres vieilles sottes,
> Assises bas, à croppetons,
> Tout en ung tas comme pelottes;
> A petit feu de chenevottes
> Tost allumées, tost estainctes.
> Et jadis fusmes si mignottes!
> Ainsi en prend à maintz et maintes.'

'Thus amongst ourselves we regret the good time, poor silly old things, low-seated on our heels, all in a heap like so many balls; by a little fire of hemp-stalks, soon lighted, soon spent. And once we were such darlings! So fares it with many and many a one.' [Arnold's note]

poetical classics. The real estimate, here, has universal currency. With the next age of our poetry divergency and difficulty begin. An historic estimate of that poetry has established itself; and the question is, whether it will be found to coincide with the real estimate.

The age of Dryden, together with our whole eighteenth century which followed it, sincerely believed itself to have produced poetical classics of its own, and even to have made advance, in poetry, beyond all its predecessors. Dryden regards as not seriously disputable the opinion 'that the sweetness of English verse was never understood or practised by our fathers.' Cowley could see nothing at all in Chaucer's poetry. Dryden heartily admired it, and, as we have seen, praised its matter admirably; but of its exquisite manner and movement all he can find to say is that 'there is the rude sweetness of a Scotch tune in it, which is natural and pleasing, though not perfect.' Addison, wishing to praise Chaucer's numbers, compares them with Dryden's own. And all through the eighteenth century, and down even into our own times, the stereotyped phrase of approbation for good verse found in our early poetry has been, that it even approached the verse of Dryden, Addison, Pope, and Johnson.

Are Dryden and Pope poetical classics? Is the historic estimate, which represents them as such, and which has been so long established that it cannot easily give way, the real estimate? Wordsworth and Coleridge, as is well known, denied it; but the authority of Wordsworth and Coleridge does not weigh much with the young generation, and there are many signs to show that the eighteenth century and its judgments are coming into favour again. Are the favourite poets of the eighteenth century classics?

It is impossible within my present limits to discuss the question fully. And what man of letters would not shrink from seeming to dispose dictatorially of the claims of two men who are, at any rate, such masters in letters as Dryden and Pope; two men of such admirable talent, both of them, and one of them, Dryden, a man, on all sides, of such energetic and genial power? And yet, if we are to gain the full benefit from poetry, we must have the real estimate of it. I cast about for some mode of arriving, in the present case, at such an estimate without offence. And perhaps the best way is to begin, as it is easy to begin with cordial praise.

When we find Chapman, the Elizabethan translator of Homer, expressing himself in his preface thus: 'Though truth in her very nakedness sits in so deep a pit, that from Gades to Aurora and Ganges few eyes can sound her, I hope yet those few here will so discover and confirm that, the date being out of her darkness in this morning of our poet, he shall now gird his temples with the sun,'—we pronounce that such a prose is intolerable. When we find Milton writing: 'And long it was not after, when I was confirmed in this opinion, that he, who would not be frustrate of his hope to write well hereafter in laudable things, ought himself to be a true poem,'—we pronounce that such a prose has its own grandeur, but that it is obsolete and inconvenient. But when we find Dryden telling us: 'What Virgil wrote in the vigour of his age, in plenty and at ease, I have undertaken to translate in my declining years; struggling with wants, oppressed with sickness, curbed in my genius, liable to be misconstrued in all I write,'—then we exclaim that here at last we have the true English prose, a prose such as we would all gladly use if we only knew how. Yet Dryden was Milton's contemporary.

But after the Restoration the time had come when our nation felt the imperious need of a fit prose. So, too, the time had likewise come when our nation felt the imperious need of freeing itself from the absorbing preoccupation which religion in the Puritan age had exercised. It was impossible that this freedom should be brought about without some negative excess, without some neglect and impairment of the religious life of the soul; and the spiritual history of the eighteenth century shows us that the freedom was not achieved without them. Still, the freedom was achieved; the preoccupation, an undoubtedly baneful and retarding one if it had continued, was got rid of. And as with religion amongst us at that period, so it was also with letters. A fit prose was a necessity; but it was impossible that a fit prose should establish itself amongst us without some touch of frost to the imaginative life of the soul. The needful qualities for a fit prose are regularity, uniformity, precision, balance. The men of letters, whose destiny it may be to bring their nation to the attainment of a fit prose, must of necessity, whether they work in prose or in verse, give a predominating, an almost exclusive attention to the qualities of regularity, uniformity, precision, balance. But an almost exclusive attention to these qualities involves some repression and silencing of poetry.

We are to regard Dryden as the puissant and

glorious founder, Pope as the splendid high priest, of our age of prose and reason, of our excellent and indispensable eighteenth century. For the purposes of their mission and destiny their poetry, like their prose, is admirable. Do you ask me whether Dryden's verse, take it almost where you will, is not good?

> A milk-white Hind, immortal and unchanged,
> Fed on the lawns and in the forest ranged.[22]

I answer: Admirable for the purposes of the inaugurator of an age of prose and reason. Do you ask me whether Pope's verse, take it almost where you will, is not good?

> To Hounslow Heath I point, and Banstead Down;
> Thence comes your mutton, and these chicks my own.[23]

I answer: Admirable for the purposes of the high priest of an age of prose and reason. But do you ask me whether such verse proceeds from men with an adequate poetic criticism of life, from men whose criticism of life has a high seriousness, or even, without that high seriousness, has poetic largeness, freedom, insight, benignity? Do you ask me whether the application of ideas to life in the verse of these men, often a powerful application, no doubt, is a powerful *poetic* application? Do you ask me whether the poetry of these men has either the matter or the inseparable manner of such an adequate poetic criticism; whether it has the accent of

> Absent thee from felicity awhile . . .

or of

> And what is else not to be overcome . . .

or of

> O martyr souded in virginitee!

I answer: It has not and cannot have them; it is the poetry of the builders of an age of prose and reason. Though they may write in verse, though they may in a certain sense be masters of the art of versification, Dryden and Pope are not classics of our poetry, they are classics of our prose.

Gray is our poetical classic of that literature and age; the position of Gray is singular, and demands a word of notice here. He has not the volume or the power of poets who, coming in times more favourable, have attained to an inde-pendent criticism of life. But he lived with the great poets, he lived, above all, with the Greeks, through perpetually studying and enjoying them; and he caught their poetic point of view for regarding life, caught their poetic manner. The point of view and the manner are not self-sprung in him, he caught them of others; and he had not the free and abundant use of them. But whereas Addison and Pope never had the use of them, Gray had the use of them at times. He is the scantiest and frailest of classics in our poetry, but he is a classic.

And now, after Gray, we are met, as we draw towards the end of the eighteenth century, we are met by the great name of Burns. We enter now on times where the personal estimate of poets begins to be rife, and where the real estimate of them is not reached without difficulty. But in spite of the disturbing pressures of personal partiality, of national partiality, let us try to reach a real estimate of the poetry of Burns.

By his English poetry Burns in general belongs to the eighteenth century, and had little importance for us.

> Mark ruffian Violence, distain'd with crimes,
> Rousing elate in these degenerate times;
> View unsuspecting Innocence a prey,
> As guileful Fraud points out the erring way;
> While subtle Litigation's pliant tongue
> The life-blood equal sucks of Right and Wrong![24]

Evidently this is not the real Burns, or his name and fame would have disappeared long ago. Nor is Clarinda's love-poet, Sylvander, the real Burns either. But he tells us himself: 'These English songs gravel me to death. I have not the command of the language that I have of my native tongue. In fact, I think that my ideas are more barren in English than in Scotch. I have been at *Duncan Gray* to dress it in English, but all I can do is desperately stupid.' We English turn naturally, in Burns, to the poems in our own language, because we can read them easily; but in those poems we have not the real Burns.

The real Burns is of course in his Scotch poems. Let us boldly say that of much of this poetry, a poetry dealing perpetually with Scotch drink, Scotch religion, and Scotch manners, a Scotchman's estimate is apt to be personal. A Scotchman is used to this world of Scotch drink, Scotch religion, and Scotch manners; he has a

---

[22] Dryden's *The Hind and the Panther*.   [23] Pope's *Imitations of Horace*.
[24] Burns's "On the Death of Lord President Dundas."

tenderness for it; he meets its poet half way. In this tender mood he reads pieces like the *Holy Fair* or *Halloween*. But this world of Scotch drink, Scotch religion, and Scotch manners is against a poet, not for him, when it is not a partial countryman who reads him; for in itself it is not a beautiful world, and no one can deny that it is of advantage to a poet to deal with a beautiful world. Burns's world of Scotch drink, Scotch religion, and Scotch manners, is often a harsh, a sordid, a repulsive world; even the world of his *Cotter's Saturday Night* is not a beautiful world. No doubt a poet's criticism of life may have such truth and power that it triumphs over its world and delights us. Burns may triumph over his world, often he does triumph over his world, but let us observe how and where. Burns is the first case we have had where the bias of the personal estimate tends to mislead; let us look at him closely, he can bear it.

Many of his admirers will tell us that we have Burns, convivial, genuine, delightful, here—

> Leeze me on drink! it gies us mair
> 　Than either school or college;
> It kindles wit, it waukens lair,
> 　It pangs us fou o' knowledge.
> Be 't whiskey gill or penny wheep
> 　Or ony stronger potion,
> It never fails, on drinking deep,
> 　To kittle up our notion
> 　　　By might or day.[25]

There is a great deal of that sort of thing in Burns, and it is unsatisfactory, not because it is bacchanalian poetry, but because it has not that accent of sincerity which bacchanalian poetry, to do it justice, very often has. There is something in it of bravado, something which makes us feel that we have not the man speaking to us with his real voice; something, therefore, poetically unsound.

With still more confidence will his admirers tell us that we have the genuine Burns, the great poet, when his strain asserts the independence, equality, dignity, of men, as in the famous song *For a' that and a' that*—

> A prince can mak' a belted knight,
> 　A marquis, duke, and a' that;
> But an honest man's aboon his might,
> 　Guid faith he mauna fa' that!
> For a' that, and a' that,
> 　Their dignities, and a' that,

> The pith o' sense, and pride o' worth,
> 　Are higher rank than a' that.

Here they find his grand, genuine touches; and still more, when this puissant genius, who so often set morality at defiance, falls moralising—

> The sacred lowe o' weel-placed love
> 　Luxuriantly indulge it;
> But never tempt th' illicit rove,
> 　Tho' naething should divulge it.
> I waive the quantum o' the sin,
> 　The hazard o' concealing,
> But och! it hardens a' within,
> 　And petrifies the feeling.[26]

Or in a higher strain—

> Who made the heart, 'tis He alone
> 　Decidedly can try us;
> He knows each chord, its various tone;
> 　Each spring, its various bias.
> Then at the balance let's be mute,
> 　We never can adjust it;
> What's *done* we partly may compute,
> 　But know not what's resisted.[27]

Or in a better strain yet, a strain, his admirers will say, unsurpassable—

> To make a happy fire-side clime
> 　To weans and wife,
> That's the true pathos and sublime
> 　Of human life.[28]

There is criticism of life for you, the admirers of Burns will say to us; there is the application of ideas to life! There is, undoubtedly. The doctrine of the last-quoted lines coincides almost exactly with what was the aim and end, Xenophon tells us, of all the teaching of Socrates. And the application is a powerful one; made by a man of vigorous understanding, and (need I say?) a master of language.

But for supreme poetical success more is required than the powerful application of ideas to life; it must be an application under the conditions fixed by the laws of poetic truth and poetic beauty. Those laws fix as an essential condition, in the poet's treatment of such matters as are here in question, high seriousness;—the high seriousness which comes from absolute sincerity. The accent of high seriousness, born of absolute sincerity, is what gives to such verse as

> In la sua volontade è nostra pace . . .

---

[25] Burns's "The Holy Fair." The next citation is from the same poem.
[26] From "Epistle to a Young Friend."　　[27] From "Address to the Unco Guid."
[28] From "Epistle to Dr. Blacklock."

to such criticism of life as Dante's, its power. Is this accent felt in the passages which I have been quoting from Burns? Surely not; surely, if our sense is quick, we must perceive that we have not in those passages a voice from the very inmost soul of the genuine Burns; he is not speaking to us from these depths, he is more or less preaching. And the compensation for admiring such passages less, from missing the perfect poetic accent in them, will be that we shall admire more the poetry where that accent is found.

No; Burns, like Chaucer, comes short of the high seriousness of the great classics, and the virtue of matter and manner which goes with that high seriousness is wanting to his work. At moments he touches it in a profound and passionate melancholy, as in those four immortal lines taken by Byron as a motto for *The Bride of Abydos*, but which have in them a depth of poetic quality such as resides in no verse of Byron's own—

> Had we never loved sae kindly,
> Had we never loved sae blindly,
> Never met, or never parted,
> We had ne'er been broken-hearted.[29]

But a whole poem of that quality Burns cannot make; the rest, in the *Farewell to Nancy*, is verbiage.

We arrive best at the real estimate of Burns, I think, by conceiving his work as having truth of matter and truth of manner, but not the accent or the poetic virtue of the highest masters. His genuine criticism of life, when the sheer poet in him speaks, is ironic; it is not—

> Thou Power Supreme, whose might scheme
>   These woes of mine fulfil,
> Here firm I rest, they must be best
>   Because they are Thy will![30]

It is far rather: *Whistle owre the lave o't!* Yet we may say of him as of Chaucer, that of life and the world, as they come before him, his view is large, free, shrewd, benignant,—truly poetic, therefore; and his manner of rendering what he sees is to match. But we must note, at the same time, his great difference from Chaucer. The freedom of Chaucer is heightened, in Burns, by a fiery, reckless energy; the benignity of Chaucer deepens, in Burns, into an overwhelming sense of the pathos of things;—of the pathos of human nature, the pathos, also, of non-human nature. Instead of the fluidity of Chaucer's manner, the

manner of Burns has spring, bounding swiftness. Burns is by far the greater force, though he has perhaps less charm. The world of Chaucer is fairer, richer, more significant than that of Burns; but when the largeness and freedom of Burns get full sweep, as in *Tam o' Shanter*, or still more in that puissant and splendid production, *The Jolly Beggars*, his world may be what it will, his poetic genius triumphs over it. In the world of *The Jolly Beggars* there is more than hideousness and squalor, there is bestiality; yet the piece is a superb poetic success. It has a breadth, truth, and power which make the famous scene in Auerbach's Cellar, of Goethe's *Faust*, seem artificial and tame beside it, and which are only matched by Shakspeare and Aristophanes.

Here, where his largeness and freedom serve him so admirably, and also in those poems and songs where to shrewdness he adds infinite arch-, ness and wit, and to benignity infinite pathos, where his manner is flawless, and a perfect poetic whole is the result,—in things like the address to the mouse whose home he had ruined, in things like *Duncan Gray, Tam Glen, Whistle and I'll come to you, my lad, Auld Lang Syne* (this list might be made much longer),—here we have the genuine Burns, of whom the real estimate must be high indeed. Not a classic, nor with the excellent σπουδαιότης of the great classics, nor with a verse rising to a criticism of life and a virtue like theirs; but a poet with thorough truth of substance and an answering truth of style, giving us a poetry sound to the core. We all of us have a leaning towards the pathetic, and may be inclined perhaps to prize Burns most for his touches of piercing, sometimes almost intolerable, pathos; for verse like—

> We twa hae paidl't i' the burn
>   Frae mornin' sun till dine;
> But seas between us braid hae roar'd
>   Sin auld lang syne . . . [31]

where he is as lovely as he is sound. But perhaps it is by the perfection of soundness of his lighter and archer masterpieces that he is poetically most wholesome for us. For the votary misled by a personal estimate of Shelley, as so many of us have been, are, and will be,—of that beautiful spirit building his many-coloured haze of words and images.

> Pinnacled dim in the intense inane—[32]

---

[29] From Burns's "Ae Fond Kiss".   [30] From "Winter: A Dirge."
[31] From "Auld Lang Syne."
[32] This and the following citation are from Shelley's *Prometheus Unbound.*

no contact can be wholesomer than the contact with Burns at his archest and soundest. Side by side with the

> On the brink of the night and the morning
>   My coursers are wont to respire,
> But the Earth has just whispered a warning
>   That their flight must be swifter than fire . . .

of *Prometheus Unbound*, how salutary, how very salutary, to place this from *Tam Glen*—

> My minnie does constantly deave me
>   And bids me beware o' young men;
> They flatter, she says, to deceive me;
>   But wha can think sae o' Tam Glen?

But we enter on burning ground as we approach the poetry of times so near to us—poetry like that of Byron, Shelley, and Wordsworth—of which the estimates are so often not only personal, but personal with passion. For my purpose, it is enough to have taken the single case of Burns, the first poet we come to of whose work the estimate formed is evidently apt to be personal, and to have suggested how we may proceed, using the poetry of the great classics as a sort of touchstone, to correct this estimate, as we had previously corrected by the same means the historic estimate where we met with it. A collection like the present, with its succession of celebrated names and celebrated poems, offers a good opportunity to us for resolutely endeavouring to make our estimates of poetry real. I have sought to point out a method which will help us in making them so, and to exhibit it in use so far as to put any one who likes in a way of applying it for himself.

At any rate the end to which the method and the estimate are designed to lead, and from leading to which, if they do lead to it, they get their whole value,—the benefit of being able clearly to feel and deeply to enjoy the best, the truly classic, in poetry,—is an end, let me say it once more at parting, of supreme importance. We are often told that an era is opening in which we are to see multitudes of a common sort of readers, and masses of a common sort of literature; that such readers do not want and could not relish anything better than such literature, and that to provide it is becoming a vast and profitable industry. Even if good literature entirely lost currency with the world, it would still be abundantly worth while to continue to enjoy it by oneself. But it never will lose currency with the

world, in spite of momentary appearances; it never will lose supremacy. Currency and supremacy are insured to it, not indeed by the world's deliberate and conscious choice, but by something far deeper,—by the instinct of self-preservation in humanity.

Wordsworth

I REMEMBER hearing Lord Macaulay say, after Wordsworth's death, when subscriptions were being collected to found a memorial of him, that ten years earlier more money could have been raised in Cambridge alone, to do honour to Wordsworth, than was now raised all through the country. Lord Macaulay, had, as we know, his own heightened and telling way of putting things, and we must always make allowance for it. But probably it is true that Wordsworth has never, either before or since, been so accepted and popular, so established in possession of the minds of all who profess to care for poetry, as he was between the years 1830 and 1840, and at Cambridge. From the very first, no doubt, he had his believers and witnesses. But I myself heard him declare that, for he knew not how many years, his poetry had never brought him in enough to buy his shoe-strings. The poetry-reading public was very slow to recognise him, and was very easily drawn away from him. Scott effaced him with this public, Byron effaced him.

The death of Byron, seemed, however, to make an opening for Wordsworth. Scott, who had for some time ceased to produce poetry himself, and stood before the public as a great novelist; Scott, too genuine himself not to feel the profound genuineness of Wordsworth, and with an instinctive recognition of his firm hold on nature and of his local truth, always admired him sincerely, and praised him generously. The influence of Coleridge upon young men of ability was then powerful, and was still gathering strength; this influence told entirely in favour of Wordsworth's poetry. Cambridge was a place where Coleridge's influence had great action, and where Wordsworth's poetry, therefore, flourished especially. But even amongst the general public its sale grew large, the eminence of its author was widely recognised, and Rydal Mount[1] became an object

---

[1] Wordsworth's home in the Lake District.

of pilgrimage. I remember Wordsworth relating how one of the pilgrims, a clergyman, asked him if he had ever written anything besides the *Guide to the Lakes.* Yes, he answered modestly, he had written verses. Not every pilgrim was a reader, but the vogue was established, and the stream of pilgrims came.

Mr. Tennyson's decisive appearance dates from 1842. One cannot say that he effaced Wordsworth as Scott and Byron had effaced him. The poetry of Wordsworth had been so long before the public, the suffrage of good judges was so steady and so strong in its favour, that by 1842 the verdict of posterity, one may almost say, had been already pronounced, and Wordsworth's English fame was secure. But the vogue, the ear and applause of the great body of poetry-readers, never quite thoroughly perhaps his, he gradually lost more and more, and Mr. Tennyson gained them. Mr. Tennyson drew to himself, and away from Wordsworth, the poetry-reading public, and the new generations. Even in 1850, when Wordsworth died, this diminution of popularity was visible, and occasioned the remark of Lord Macaulay which I quote at starting.

The diminution has continued. The influence of Coleridge has waned, and Wordsworth's poetry can no longer draw succour from this ally. The poetry has not, however, wanted eulogists; and it may be said to have brought its eulogists luck, for almost every one who has praised Wordsworth's poetry has praised it well. But the public has remained cold, or, at least, undetermined. Even the abundance of Mr. Palgrave's[2] fine and skilfully chosen specimens of Wordsworth, in the *Golden Treasury,* surprised many readers, and gave offence to not a few. To tenth-rate critics and compilers, for whom any violent shock to the public taste would be a temerity not to be risked, it is still quite permissible to speak of Wordsworth's poetry, not only with ignorance, but with impertinence. On the Continent he is almost unknown.

I cannot think, then, that Wordsworth has, up to this time, at all obtained his deserts. "Glory," said M. Renan[3] the other day, "glory after all is the thing which has the best chance of not being altogether vanity." Wordsworth was a homely man, and himself would certainly never have thought of talking of glory as that which, after all, has the best chance of not being altogether vanity. Yet we may well allow that few things are less vain than *real* glory. Let us conceive of the whole group of civilised nations as being, for intellectual and spiritual purposes, one great confederation, bound to a joint action and working towards a common result; a confederation whose members have a due knowledge both of the past, out of which they all proceed, and of one another. This was the ideal of Goethe, and it is an ideal which will impose itself upon the thoughts of our modern societies more and more. Then to be recognised by the verdict of such a confederation as a master, or even as a seriously and eminently worthy workman, in one's own line of intellectual or spiritual activity, is indeed glory; a glory which it would be difficult to rate too highly. For what could be more beneficent, more salutary? The world is forwarded by having its attention fixed on the best things; and here is a tribunal, free from all suspicion of national and provincial partiality, putting a stamp on the best things, and recommending them for general honour and acceptance. A nation, again, is furthered by recognition of its real gifts and successes; it is encouraged to develop them further. And here is an honest verdict, telling us which of our supposed successes are really, in the judgment of the great impartial world, and not in our own private judgment only, successes, and which are not.

It is so easy to feel pride and satisfaction in one's own things, so hard to make sure that one is right in feeling it! We have a great empire. But so had Nebuchadnezzar. We extol the "unrivalled happiness" of our national civilisation. But then comes a candid friend, and remarks that our upper class is materialised, our middle class vulgarised, and our lower class brutalised. We are proud of our painting, our music. But we find that in the judgment of other people our painting is questionable, and our music non-existent. We are proud of our men of science. And here it turns out that the world is with us; we find that in the judgment of other people, too, Newton among the dead, and Mr. Darwin among the living, hold as high a place as they hold in our national opinion.

Finally, we are proud of our poets and poetry. Now poetry is nothing less than the most perfect speech of man, that in which he comes nearest to being able to utter the truth. It is no small thing, therefore, to succeed eminently in poetry. And so much is required for duly estimating success here,

[2] Francis Turner Palgrave (1824–97), compiler of the anthology *The Golden Treasury* (1861).
[3] Ernest Renan (1823–92), French critic frequently cited by Arnold.

that about poetry it is perhaps hardest to arrive at a sure general verdict, and takes longest. Meanwhile, our own conviction of the superiority of our national poets is not decisive, is almost certain to be mingled, as we see constantly in English eulogy of Shakespeare, with much of provincial infatuation. And we know what was the opinion current amongst our neighbours the French—people of taste, acuteness, and quick literary tact—not a hundred years ago, about our great poets. The old *Biographie Universelle* notices the pretension of the English to a place for their poets among the chief poets of the world, and says that this is a pretension which to no one but an Englishman can ever seem admissible. And the scornful, disparaging things said by foreigners about Shakespeare and Milton, and about our national overestimate of them, have been often quoted, and will be in every one's remembrance.

A great change has taken place, and Shakespeare is now generally recognised, even in France, as one of the greatest of poets. Yes, some anti-Gallican cynic will say, the French rank him with Corneille and with Victor Hugo! But let me have the pleasure of quoting a sentence about Shakespeare, which I met with by accident not long ago in the *Correspondant*, a French review which not a dozen English people, I suppose, look at. The writer is praising Shakespeare's prose. With Shakespeare, he says, "prose comes in whenever the subject, being more familiar, is unsuited to the majestic English iambic." And he goes on: "Shakespeare is the king of poetic rhythm and style, as well as the king of the realm of thought; along with his dazzling prose, Shakespeare has succeeded in giving us the most varied, the most harmonious verse which has ever sounded upon the human ear since the verse of the Greeks." M. Henry Cochin,[4] the writer of this sentence, deserves our gratitude for it; it would not be easy to praise Shakespeare, in a single sentence, more justly. And when a foreigner and a Frenchman writes thus of Shakespeare, and when Goethe says of Milton, in whom there was so much to repel Goethe rather than to attract him, that "nothing has been ever done so entirely in the sense of the Greeks as *Samson Agonistes*," and that "Milton is in very truth a poet whom we must treat with all reverence," then we understand what constitutes a European recognition of poets and poetry as contradistinguished from a merely national recognition, and that in favour both of Milton and of Shakes-

peare the judgment of the high court of appeal has finally gone.

I come back to M. Renan's praise of glory, from which I started. Yes, real glory is a most serious thing, glory authenticated by the Amphictyonic Court of final appeal, definitive glory. And even for poets and poetry, long and difficult as may be the process of arriving at the right award, the right award comes at last, the definitive glory rests where it is deserved. Every establishment of such a real glory is good and wholesome for mankind at large, good and wholesome for the nation which produced the poet crowned with it. To the poet himself it can seldom do harm; for he, poor man, is in his grave, probably, long before his glory crowns him.

Wordsworth has been in his grave for some thirty years, and certainly his lovers and admirers cannot flatter themselves that this great and steady light of glory as yet shines over him. He is not fully recognised at home; he is not recognised at all abroad. Yet I firmly believe that the poetical performance of Wordsworth is, after that of Shakespeare and Milton, of which all the world now recognises the worth, undoubtedly the most considerable in our language from the Elizabethan age to the present time. Chaucer is anterior; and on other grounds, too, he cannot well be brought into the comparison. But taking the roll of our chief poetical names, besides Shakespeare and Milton, from the age of Elizabeth downwards, and going through it,—Spenser, Dryden, Pope, Gray, Goldsmith, Cowper, Burns, Coleridge, Scott, Campbell, Moore, Byron, Shelley, Keats (I mention those only who are dead),—I think it certain that Wordsworth's name deserves to stand, and will finally stand, above them all. Several of the poets named have gifts and excellences which Wordsworth has not. But taking the performance of each as a whole, I say that Wordsworth seems to me to have left a body of poetical work superior in power, in interest, in the qualities which give enduring freshness, to that which any one of the others has left.

But this is not enough to say. I think it certain, further, that if we take the chief poetical names of the Continent since the death of Molière, and, omitting Goethe, confront the remaining names with that of Wordsworth, the result is the same. Let us take Klopstock, Lessing, Schiller, Uhland, Rückert, and Heine for Germany; Filicaia, Alfieri, Manzoni, and Leopardi for Italy;

---

[4] In an article on Walt Whitman in *Le Correspondant* in November 1877.

Racine, Boileau, Voltaire, André Chénier, Béranger, Lamartine, Musset, M. Victor Hugo (he has been so long celebrated that although he still lives I may be permitted to name him) for France. Several of these, again, have evidently gifts and excellences to which Wordsworth can make no pretension. But in real poetical achievement it seems to me indubitable that to Wordsworth, here again, belongs the palm. It seems to me that Wordsworth has left behind him a body of poetical work which wears, and will wear, better on the whole than the performance of any one of these personages, so far more brilliant and celebrated, most of them, than the homely poet of Rydal. Wordsworth's performance in poetry is on the whole, in power, in interest, in the qualities which give enduring freshness, superior to theirs.

This is a high claim to make for Wordsworth. But if it is a just claim, if Wordsworth's place among the poets who have appeared in the last two or three centuries is after Shakespeare, Molière, Milton, Goethe, indeed, but before all the rest, then in time Wordsworth will have his due. We shall recognise him in his place, as we recognise Shakespeare and Milton; and not only we ourselves shall recognise him, but he will be recognised by Europe also. Meanwhile, those who recognise him already may do well, perhaps, to ask themselves whether there are not in the case of Wordsworth certain special obstacles which hinder or delay his due recognition by others, and whether these obstacles are not in some measure removable.

The *Excursion* and the *Prelude*, his poems of greatest bulk, are by no means Wordsworth's best work. His best work is in his shorter pieces, and many indeed are there of these which are of first-rate excellence. But in his seven volumes the pieces of high merit are mingled with a mass of pieces very inferior to them; so inferior to them that it seems wonderful how the same poet should have produced both. Shakespeare frequently has lines and passages in a strain quite false, and which are entirely unworthy of him. But one can imagine his smiling if one could meet him in the Elysian Fields and tell him so; smiling and replying that he knew it perfectly well himself, and what did it matter? But with Wordsworth the case is different. Work altogether inferior, work quite uninspired, flat and dull, is produced by him with evident unconsciousness of its defects, and he presents it to us with the same faith and seriousness as his best work. Now a drama or an epic fill the mind, and one does not look beyond them; but in a collection of short pieces the impression made by one piece requires to be continued and sustained by the piece following. In reading Wordsworth the impression made by one of his fine pieces is too often dulled and spoiled by a very inferior piece coming after it.

Wordsworth composed verses during a space of some sixty years; and it is no exaggeration to say that within one single decade of those years, between 1798 and 1808, almost all his really first-rate work was produced. A mass of inferior work remains, work done before and after this golden prime, imbedding the first-rate work and clogging it, obstructing our approach to it, chilling, not unfrequently, the high-wrought mood with which we leave it. To be recognised far and wide as a great poet, to be possible and receivable as a classic, Wordsworth needs to be relieved of a great deal of the poetical baggage which now encumbers him. To administer this relief is indispensable, unless he is to continue to be a poet for the few only,—a poet valued far below his real worth by the world.

There is another thing. Wordsworth classified his poems not according to any commonly received plan of arrangement, but according to a scheme of mental physiology. He has poems of the fancy, poems of the imagination, poems of sentiment and reflection, and so on. His categories are ingenious but far-fetched, and the result of his employment of them is unsatisfactory. Poems are separated one from another which possess a kinship of subject or of treatment far more vital and deep than the supposed unity of mental origin, which was Wordsworth's reason for joining them with others.

The tact of the Greeks in matters of this kind was infallible. We may rely upon it that we shall not improve upon the classification adopted by the Greeks for kinds of poetry; that their categories of epic, dramatic, lyric, and so forth, have a natural propriety, and should be adhered to. It may sometimes seem doubtful to which of two categories a poem belongs; whether this or that poem is to be called, for instance, narrative or lyric, lyric or elegiac. But there is to be found in every good poem a strain, a predominant note, which determines the poem as belonging to one of these kinds rather than the other; and here is the best proof of the value of the classification and of the advantage of adhering to it. Wordsworth's poems will never produce their due effect until they are freed from their present artificial arrangement, and grouped more naturally.

Disengaged from the quantity of inferior work which now obscures them, the best poems of Wordsworth, I hear many people say, would indeed stand out in great beauty, but they would prove to be very few in number, scarcely more than half a dozen. I maintain, on the other hand that what strikes me with admiration, what establishes in my opinion Wordsworth's superiority, is the great and ample body of powerful work which remains to him, even after all his inferior work has been cleared away. He gives us so much to rest upon, so much which communicates his spirit and engages ours!

This is of very great importance. If it were a comparison of single pieces, or of three or four pieces, by each poet, I do not say that Wordsworth would stand decisively above Gray, or Burns, or Coleridge, or Keats, or Manzoni, or Heine. It is in his ampler body of powerful work that I find his superiority. His good work itself, his work which counts, is not all of it, of course, of equal value. Some kinds of poetry are in themselves lower kinds than others. The ballad kind is a lower kind; the didactic kind, still more, is a lower kind. Poetry of this latter sort counts, too, sometimes, by its biographical interest partly, not by its poetical interest pure and simple; but then this can only be when the poet producing it has the power and importance of Wordsworth, a power and importance which he assuredly did not establish by such didactic poetry alone. Altogether, it is, I say, by the great body of powerful and significant work which remains to him, after every reduction and deduction has been made, that Wordsworth's superiority is proved.

To exhibit this body of Wordsworth's best work, to clear away obstructions from around it, and to let it speak for itself, is what every lover of Wordsworth should desire. Until this has been done, Wordsworth, whom we, to whom he is dear, all of us know and feel to be so great a poet, has not had a fair chance before the world. When once it has been done, he will make his way best, not by our advocacy of him, but by his own worth and power. We may safely leave him to make his way thus, we who believe that a superior worth and power in poetry finds in mankind a sense responsive to it and disposed at last to recognise it. Yet at the outset, before he has been duly known and recognised, we may do Wordsworth a service, perhaps by indicating in what

his superior power and worth will be found to consist, and in what it will not.

Long ago, in speaking of Homer, I said that the noble and profound application of ideas to life is the most essential part of poetic greatness. I said that a great poet receives his distinctive character of superiority from his application, under the conditions immutably fixed by the laws of poetic beauty and poetic truth, from his application, I say, to his subject, whatever it may be, of the ideas

"On man, on nature, and on human life,"[5]

which he has acquired for himself. The line quoted is Wordsworth's own; and his superiority arises from his powerful use, in his best pieces, his powerful application to his subject, of ideas "on man, on nature, and on human life."

Voltaire, with his signal acuteness, most truly remarked that "no nation has treated in poetry moral ideas with more energy and depth than the English nation." And he adds: "There, it seems to me, is the great merit of the English poets." Voltaire does not mean, by "treating in poetry moral ideas," the composing moral and didactic poems;—that brings us but a very little way in poetry. He means just the same thing as was meant when I spoke above "of the noble and profound application of ideas to life"; and he means the application of these ideas under the conditions fixed for us by the laws of poetic beauty and poetic truth. If it is said that to call these ideas *moral* ideas is to introduce a strong and injurious limitation, I answer that it is to do nothing of the kind, because moral ideas are really so main a part of human life. The question, *how to live*, is itself a moral idea; and it is the question which most interests every man, and with which, in some way or other, he is perpetually occupied. A large sense is of course to be given to the term *moral*. Whatever bears upon the question, "how to live," comes under it.

"Nor love the life, nor hate; but, what thou liv'st,
  Live well; how long or short, permit to heaven."[6]

In those fine lines Milton utters, as every one at once perceives, a moral idea. Yes, but so too, when Keats consoles the forward-bending lover on the Grecian Urn, the lover arrested and presented in immortal relief by the sculptor's hand before he can kiss, with the line,

"For ever wilt thou love, and she be fair"[7]—

---

[5] Wordsworth's *The Recluse*.   [6] *Paradise Lost*, XI, 553-554.
[7] Keats's "Ode on a Grecian Urn."

he utters a moral idea. When Shakespeare says that

> "We are such stuff
> As dreams are made on, and our little life
> Is rounded with a sleep,"[8]

he utters a moral idea.

Voltaire was right in thinking that the energetic and profound treatment of moral ideas, in this large sense, is what distinguishes the English poetry. He sincerely meant praise, not dispraise or hint of limitation; and they err who suppose that poetic limitation is a necessary consequence of the fact, the fact being granted as Voltaire states it. If what distinguishes the greatest poets is their powerful and profound application of ideas to life, which surely no good critic will deny, then to prefix to the term ideas here the term moral makes hardly any difference, because human life itself is in so preponderating a degree moral.

It is important, therefore, to hold fast to this: that poetry is at bottom a criticism of life; that the greatness of a poet lies in his powerful and beautiful application of ideas to life,—to the question: How to live? Morals are often treated in a narrow and false fashion; they are bound up with systems of thought and belief which have had their day; they are fallen into the hands of pedants and professional dealers; they grow tiresome to some of us. We find attraction, at times, even in a poetry of revolt against them; in a poetry which might take for its motto Omar Kheyam's words: "Let us make up in the tavern for the time which we have wasted in the mosque."[9] Or we find attractions in a poetry indifferent to them; in a poetry where the contents may be what they will, but where the form is studied and exquisite. We delude ourselves in either case; and the best cure for our delusion is to let our minds rest upon that great and inexhaustible word *life*, until we learn to enter into its meaning. A poetry of revolt against moral ideas is a poetry of revolt against *life*; a poetry of indifference towards moral ideas is a poetry of indifference towards *life*.

Epictetus had a happy figure for things like the play of the senses, or literary form and finish, or argumentative ingenuity, in comparison with "the best and master thing," for us, as he called it, the concern, how to live. Some people were afraid of them, he said, or they disliked and under-valued them. Such people were wrong; they were unthankful or cowardly. But the things might also be over-prized, and treated as final when they are not. They bear to life the relation which inns bear to home. "As if a man, journeying home, and finding a nice inn on the road, and liking it, were to stay for ever at the inn! Man, thou hast forgotten thine object; thy journey was not *to* this, but *through* this. 'But this inn is taking.' And how many other inns, too, are taking, and how many fields and meadows! but as places of passage merely. You have an object, which is this: to get home, to do your duty to your family, friends, and fellow-countrymen, to attain inward freedom, serenity, happiness, contentment. Style takes your fancy, arguing takes your fancy, and you forget your home and want to make your abode with them and to stay with them, on the plea that they are taking. Who denies that they are taking? but as places of passage, as inns. And when I say this, you suppose me to be attacking the care for style, the care for argument. I am not; I attack the resting in them, the not looking to the end which is beyond them."

Now, when we come across a poet like Théophile Gautier,[10] we have a poet who has taken up his abode at an inn, and never got farther. There may be inducements to this or that one of us, at this or that moment, to find delight in him, to cleave to him; but after all, we do not change the truth about him,—we only stay ourselves in his inn along with him. And when we come across a poet like Wordsworth, who sings

> "Of truth, of grandeur, beauty, love and hope.
> And melancholy fear subdued by faith,
> Of blessed consolations in distress,
> Of moral strength and intellectual power,
> Of joy in widest commonalty spread"[11]—

then we have a poet intent on "the best and master thing," and who prosecutes his journey home. We say, for brevity's sake, that he deals with *life*, because he deals with that in which life really consists. This is what Voltaire means to praise in the English poets,—this dealing with what is really life. But always it is the mark of the greatest poets that they deal with it; and to say that the English poets are remarkable for dealing with it, is only another way of saying what is true, that in poetry the English genius has especially shown its power.

---

[8] *The Tempest*, IV, i, 156–158.   [9] *The Rubaiyat*, stanza 77.
[10] Théophile Gautier (1881–72), French Romantic poet.   [11] Wordsworth's *Recluse*.

Wordsworth deals with it, and his greatness lies in his dealing with it so powerfully. I have named a number of celebrated poets above all of whom he, in my opinion, deserves to be placed. He is to be placed above poets like Voltaire, Dryden, Pope, Lessing, Schiller, because these famous personages, with a thousand gifts and merits, never, or scarcely ever, attain the distinctive accent and utterance of the high and genuine poets—

"Quique pii vates et Phoebo digna locuti,"[12]

at all. Burns, Keats, Heine, not to speak of others in our list, have this accent;—who can doubt it? And at the same time they have treasures of humour, felicity, passion, for which in Wordsworth we shall look in vain. Where, then, is Wordsworth's superiority? It is here; he deals with more of *life* than they do; he deals with *life*, as a whole, more powerfully.

No Wordsworthian will doubt this. Nay, the fervent Wordsworthian will add, as Mr. Leslie Stephen[13] does, that Wordsworth's poetry is precious because his philosophy is sound; that his "ethical system is as distinctive and capable of exposition as Bishop Butler's"; that his poetry is informed by ideas which "fall spontaneously into a scientific system of thought." But we must be on our guard against the Wordsworthians if we want to secure for Wordsworth his due rank as a poet. The Wordsworthians are apt to praise him for the wrong things, and to lay far too much stress upon what they call his philosophy. His poetry is the reality, his philosophy,—so far, at least, as it may put on the form and habit of "a scientific system of thought," and the more that it puts them on,—is the illusion. Perhaps we shall one day learn to make this proposition general, and to say: Poetry is the reality, philosophy, the illusion. But in Wordsworth's case, at any rate, we cannot do him justice until we dismiss his formal philosophy.

The *Excursion* abounds with philosophy, and therefore the *Excursion* is to the Wordsworthian what it never can be to the disinterested lover of poetry,—a satisfactory work. "Duty exists," says Wordsworth, in the *Excursion*; and then he proceeds thus—

" . . . Immutably survive,
For our support, the measures and the forms,

Which an abstract Intelligence supplies,
Whose kingdom is, where time and space are not."

And the Wordsworthian is delighted, and thinks that here is a sweet union of philosophy and poetry. But the disinterested lover of poetry will feel that the lines carry us really not a step further than the proposition which they would interpret; that they are a tissue of elevated but abstract verbiage, alien to the very nature of poetry.

Or let us come direct to the centre of Wordsworth's philosophy, as "an ethical system, as distinctive and capable of systematical exposition as Bishop Butler's"—

" . . . One adequate support
For the calamities of mortal life
Exists, one only;—an assured belief
That the procession of our fate, howe'er
Sad or disturbed, is ordered by a Being
Of infinite benevolence and power;
Whose everlasting purposes embrace
All accidents, converting them to good."[14]

That is doctrine such as we hear in church too, religious and philosophic doctrine; and the attached Wordsworthian loves passages of such doctrine, and brings them forward in proof of his poet's excellence. But however true the doctrine may be, it has, as here presented, none of the characters of *poetic* truth, the kind of truth which we require from a poet, and in which Wordsworth is really strong.

Even the "intimations" of the famous Ode, those corner-stones of the supposed philosophic system of Wordsworth,—the idea of the high instincts and affections coming out in childhood, testifying of a divine home recently left, and fading away as our life proceeds,—this idea, of undeniable beauty as a play of fancy, has itself not the character of poetic truth of the best kind; it has no real solidity. The instinct of delight in Nature and her beauty had no doubt extraordinary strength in Wordsworth himself as a child. But to say that universally this instinct is mighty in childhood, and tends to die away afterwards, is to say what is extremely doubtful. In many people, perhaps with the majority of educated persons, the love of nature is nearly imperceptible at ten years old, but strong and operative at thirty. In general we may say of these high instincts of early childhood, the base

---

[12] "Those pious prophets who speak things worthy of Phoebus Apollo" *(Aeneid)*.
[13] Leslie Stephen (1832–1904), man of letters, editor of the *Dictionary of National Biography*.
[14] Wordsworth's *Excursion*.

of the alleged systematic philosophy of Wordsworth, what Thucydides says of the early achievements of the Greek race: "It is impossible to speak with certainty of what is so remote; but from all that we can really investigate, I should say that they were no very great things."

Finally, the "scientific system of thought" in Wordsworth gives us at last such poetry as this, which the devout Wordsworthian accepts—

"O for the coming of that glorious time
When, prizing knowledge as her noblest wealth
And best protection, this Imperial Realm,
While she exacts allegiance, shall admit
An obligation, on her part, to *teach*
Them who are born to serve her and obey;
Binding herself by statute to secure,
For all the children whom her soil maintains,
The rudiments of letters, and inform
The mind with moral and religious truth."[15]

Wordsworth calls Voltaire dull, and surely the production of these un-Voltairian lines must have been imposed on him as a judgment! One can hear them being quoted at a Social Science Congress; one can call up the whole scene. A great room in one of our dismal provincial towns; dusty air and jaded afternoon daylight; benches full of men with bald heads and women in spectacles; an orator lifting up his face from a manuscript written within and without to declaim these lines of Wordsworth; and in the soul of any poor child of nature who may have wandered in thither, an unutterable sense of lamentation, and mourning, and woe!

"But turn we," as Wordsworth says, "from these bold, bad men," the haunters of Social Science Congresses. And let us be on our guard, too, against the exhibitors and extollers of a "scientific system of thought" in Wordsworth's poetry. The poetry will never be seen aright while they thus exhibit it. The cause of its greatness is simple, and may be told quite simply. Wordsworth's poetry is great because of the extraordinary power with which Wordsworth feels the joy offered to us in nature, the joy offered to us in the simple primary affections and duties; and because of the extraordinary power with which, in case after case, he shows us this joy, and renders it so as to make us share it.

The source of joy from which he thus draws is the truest and most unfailing source of joy accessible to man. It is also accessible universally. Wordsworth brings us word, therefore, according to his own strong and characteristic line, he brings us word

"Of joy in widest commonalty spread."

Here is an immense advantage for a poet. Wordsworth tells of what all seek, and tells of it at its truest and best source, and yet a source where all may go and draw for it.

Nevertheless, we are not to suppose that everything is precious which Wordsworth, standing even at this perennial and beautiful source, may give us. Wordsworthians are apt to talk as if it must be. They will speak with the same reverence of *The Sailor's Mother*, for example, as of *Lucy Gray*. They do their master harm by such lack of discrimination. *Lucy Gray* is a beautiful success; *The Sailor's Mother* is a failure. To give aright what he wishes to give, to interpret and render successfully, is not always within Wordsworth's own command. It is within no poet's command; here is the part of the Muse, the inspiration, the God, the "not ourselves." In Wordsworth's case, the accident, for so it may almost be called, of inspiration, is of peculiar importance. No poet, perhaps, is so evidently filled with a new and sacred energy when the inspiration is upon him; no poet, when it fails him, is so left "weak as is a breaking wave." I remember hearing him say that "Goethe's poetry was not inevitable enough." The remark is striking and true; no line in Goethe, as Goethe said himself, but its maker knew well how it came there. Wordsworth is right, Goethe's poetry is not inevitable; not inevitable enough. But Wordsworth's poetry, when he is at his best, is inevitable, as inevitable as Nature herself. It might seem that Nature not only gave him the matter for his poem, but wrote his poem for him. He has no style. He was too conversant with Milton not to catch at times his master's manner, and he has fine Miltonic lines; but he has no assured poetic style of his own, like Milton. When he seeks to have a style he falls into ponderosity and pomposity. In the *Excursion* we have his style, as an artistic product of his own creation; and although Jeffrey completely failed to recognise Wordsworth's real greatness, he was yet not wrong in saying of the *Excursion*, as a work of poetic style: "This will never do." And yet magical as is that power, which Wordsworth has not, of assured and possessed poetic style, he has something which is an equivalent for it.

Every one who has any sense for these things feels the subtle turn, the heightening, which is

[15] Wordsworth's *Excursion*.

given to a poet's verse by his genius for style.
We can feel it in the

"After life's fitful fever, he sleeps well"[16]—

of Shakespeare; in the

" . . . though fall'n on evil days,
On evil days though fall'n, and evil tongues"[17]—

of Milton. It is the incomparable charm of
Milton's power of poetic style which gives such
worth to *Paradise Regained,* and makes a great
poem of a work in which Milton's imagination
does not soar high. Wordsworth has in constant
possession, and at command, no style of this kind;
but he had too poetic a nature, and had read the
great poets too well, not to catch, as I have already
remarked, something of it occasionally. We find
it not only in his Miltonic lines; we find it in such
a phrase as this, where the manner is his own,
not Milton's—

" . . . the fierce confederate storm
Of sorrow barricadoed evermore
Within the walls of cities";[18]

although even here, perhaps, the power of style,
which is undeniable, is more properly that of eloquent prose than the subtle heightening and
change wrought by genuine poetic style. It is
style, again, and the elevation given by style,
which chiefly makes the effectiveness of *Laodameia.*
Still the right sort of verse to choose from Wordsworth, if we are to seize his true and most characteristic form of expression, is a line like this from
Michael—

"And never lifted up a single stone."

There is nothing subtle in it, no heightening, no
study of poetic style, strictly so called, at all; yet it
is expression of the highest and most truly expressive kind.

Wordsworth owed much to Burns, and a style
of perfect plainness, relying for effect solely on
the weight and force of that which with entire
fidelity it utters, Burns could show him.

"The poor inhabitant below
Was quick to learn and wise to know,
And keenly felt the friendly glow
And softer flame;
But thoughtless follies laid him low
And stain'd his name."[19]

Every one will be conscious of a likeness here to

Wordsworth; and if Wordsworth did great things
with this nobly plain manner, we must remember,
what indeed he himself would always have been
forward to acknowledge, that Burns used it
before him.

Still Wordsworth's use of it has something
unique and unmatchable. Nature herself seems,
I say, to take the pen out of his hand, and to write
for him with her own bare, sheer, penetrating
power. This arises from two causes; from the
profound sincereness with which Wordsworth
feels his subject, and also from the profoundly
sincere and natural character of his subject itself.
He can and will treat such a subject with nothing
but the most plain, first-hand, almost austere
naturalness. His expression may often be called
bald, as, for instance, in the poem of *Resolution
and Independence*; but it is bald as the bare mountain tops are bald, with a baldness which is full
of grandeur.

Wherever we meet with the successful balance,
in Wordsworth, of profound truth of subject with
profound truth of execution, he is unique. His
best poems are those which most perfectly exhibit this balance. I have a warm admiration for
Laodameia and for the great *Ode*; but if I am to tell
the very truth, I find *Laodameia* not wholly free
from something artificial, and the great *Ode* not
wholly free from something declamatory. If I
had to pick out poems of a kind most perfectly
to show Wordsworth's unique power, I should
rather choose poems such as *Michael, The Fountain,
The Highland Reaper.* And poems with the peculiar
and unique beauty which distinguishes these,
Wordsworth produced in considerable number;
besides very many other poems of which the
worth, although not so rare as the worth of these,
is still exceedingly high.

On the whole, then, as I said at the beginning,
not only is Wordsworth eminent by reason of the
goodness of his best work, but he is eminent also
by reason of the great body of good work which
he has left to us. With the ancients I will not
compare him. In many respects the ancients are
far above us, and yet there is something that we
demand which they can never give. Leaving
the ancients, let us come to the poets and poetry
of Christendom. Dante, Shakespeare, Molière,
Milton, Goethe, are altogether larger and more
splendid luminaries in the poetical heaven than
Wordsworth. But I know not where else, among
the moderns, we are to find his superiors.

[16] *Macbeth* III, ii, 23.   [17] *Paradise Lost,* VII, 25–26.   [18] Wordsworth's *Recluse.*
[19] From Burns's "A Bard's Epitaph."

To disengage the poems which show his power, and to present them to the English-speaking public and to the world, is the object of this volume. I by no means say that it contains all which in Wordsworth's poems is interesting. Expect in the case of *Margaret*, a story composed separately from the rest of the *Excursion*, and which belongs to a different part of England, I have not ventured on detaching portions of poems, or on giving any piece otherwise than as Wordsworth himself gave it. But under the conditions imposed by this reserve, the volume contains, I think, everything, or nearly everything, which may best serve him with the majority of lovers of poetry, nothing which may disserve him.

I have spoken lightly of Wordsworthians; and if we are to get Wordsworth recognised by the public and by the world, we must recommend him not in the spirit of a clique, but in the spirit of disinterested lovers of poetry. But I am a Wordsworthian myself. I can read with pleasure and edification *Peter Bell*, and the whole series of *Ecclesiastical Sonnets*, and the address to Mr. Wilkinson's spade, and even the *Thanksgiving Ode*;—everything of Wordsworth, I think, except *Vaudracour and Julia*. It is not for nothing that one has been brought up in the veneration of a man so truly worthy of homage; that one has seen him and heard him, lived in his neighbourhood, and been familiar with his country. No Wordsworthian has a tenderer affection for this pure and sage master than I, or is less really offended by his defects. But Wordsworth is something more than the pure and sage master of a small band of devoted followers, and we ought not to rest satisfied until he is seen to be what he is. He is one of the very chief glories of English Poetry; and by nothing is England so glorious as by her poetry. Let us lay aside every weight which hinders our getting him recognised as this, and let our one study be to bring to pass, as widely as possible and as truly as possible his own word concerning his poems: "They will co-operate with the benign tendencies in human nature and society, and will, in their degree, be efficacious in making men wiser, better, and happier."

Thomas Henry Huxley

1825-1895

D ARWIN'S BULLDOG was the title Thomas Henry Huxley gave himself in his capacity as the foremost defender and exponent of Darwinian evolution in the period following 1859 when the *Origin of the Species* appeared. Darwin could not have asked for an abler or more tenacious advocate. But Huxley was more than just a spokesman for Darwinism; he was himself a leading scientist and a notable man of letters whose literary gifts place him in the front rank of Victorian essayists.

Huxley was born at Ealing, Middlesex, near London, and educated largely at home and by independent reading. He studied medicine at Charing Cross Hospital and the University of London. Like his mentor-to-be, Darwin, Huxley spent several years at sea on a scientific expedition, this one aboard the H.M.S. *Rattlesnake* charged with surveying the passage between the Great Barrier Reef and the coast of Australia. On the voyage Huxley, serving as a ship's doctor, studied marine life and obtained thereby the material for a series of papers later presented to the Royal Society and the Linnean Society.

By the eighteen-fifties Huxley was established as a leading scientist of the day. He became a fellow of the Royal Society in 1851 and Professor of Natural History at the Royal School of Mines in 1854. But until the publication of the *Origin of the Species* he had been skeptical of the evolutionary hypothesis, and had attacked earlier evolutionary works like Robert Chambers' *Vestiges of Creation* (1844). Darwin's work won him over and thereafter he became Darwin's most eloquent defender.

Huxley, a more gifted writer and controversialist than Darwin, did not hesitate to take on any opponent of evolution. He delighted especially in crossing swords with the clergy, with other scientists, and with public figures. Of his many public debates the most notable is his clash with Bishop Wilberforce at the Oxford debate of 1860; of his written polemic exchanges the most celebrated in its day was that with Prime Minister Gladstone on the accuracy of Genesis and on the subject of the Gadarene swine, while today the most memorable of his written exchanges is held to be his debate with Matthew Arnold on the aims of education.

Because Huxley's talents were so strongly literary, it is not surprising that he went beyond not only his study of science but his role as Darwin's advocate to write generally on intellectual subjects. He was a theorist of education and also deeply interested in philosophy and religion. In this latter area he coined the term "agnostic" to describe his own religious position. The term and the position have since been adopted by others. Huxley's views on the evolutionary hypothesis are best sought in *Man's Place in Nature* (1863); his philosophic views find expression in his *Lay Sermons* (1870), which also contains his well-known Edinburgh lecture from 1863, "The Physical Basis of Life," and his *Ethics and Evolution* (1893); his educational views are contained in his *Science and Education* (1899). His *Essays upon Some Controverted Questions* (1892) contains many of his disputes with other thinkers.

Huxley never ceased studying scientific questions even during a life filled with writing, debate, and public exchange. He served on various royal commissions and exerted an influence on the teaching of sciences in the schools. He served as President of the Royal Society from 1881 to 1885. He was the father of the man of letters Leonard Huxley, who became editor of the *Cornhill Magazine*, and through him the grandfather of the twentieth-century novelist Aldous Huxley and the biologist and social critic Sir Julian Huxley.

T. H. Huxley spent most of his life in London, but after 1885 he lived at Eastbourne for his health. He died there on 29 June 1895.

Apart from his work in purely scientific areas and as the popularizer of Darwinian evolutionary theory, Huxley deserves the attention of the student of literature as a sterling example of the rationalist, scientific mind at work on the major philosophic questions that occupied attention in the second half of the nineteenth century. As a writer Huxley deploys the same brilliant rhetorical armory as that at the disposal of a humanist like Matthew Arnold. Consequently, Huxley can hold his own in literary exchange with the most gifted writers of the imaginative and bellettristic school, even though Huxley affected not to care for rhetorical niceties. Yet many critics see Huxley as first of all a literary man and only secondarily a scientist.

Huxley, the scientist proclaimed his willingness to follow the evidence of science where it led, giving no quarter to previous opinion or dogma. He illustrates this uncompromising commitment best in his refusal to find, as many social Darwinians had, any basis for a social morality in the theory of the evolutionary struggle for survival. At the same time his commitment to certain aspects of evolution and contemporary science is in the nature of a creed or faith that is as impervious to argument as that held by any traditional believer. Still, Huxley stands as the premier spokesman in the latter half of the nineteenth century for scientific rationalism as a basis for philosophy and as a way of life.

CHRONOLOGY

1825	Born 4 May in Ealing, Middlesex.
1842	Studies medicine at University of London and Charing Cross Hospital.
1845	Takes medical degree at University of London.
1846–50	Travels as assistant-surgeon on H.M.S. *Rattlesnake*.
1851	Elected Fellow of Royal Society.
1854	Appointed Professor of Natural History at Royal School of Mines.
1859	Accepts Darwinian theory of evolution.
1860	Oxford Debate with Bishop Wilberforce.
1863	*Man's Place in Nature*.
1868	"The Physical Basis of Life."

1870   *Lay Sermons.*
1881–85   President of the Royal Society.
1886   *Science and Morals.*
1893   *Ethics and Evolution.*
1895   Dies 29 June; buried at Finchley.
1899   *Science and Education.*

EDITIONS

Collected Essays (9 vols., 1893–94).
Lay Sermons, Addresses and Reviews (1870; 3rd ed., 1887).
Critiques and Addressess (1873).
Essays on Some Controverted Questions (1892).
Evolution and Ethics (1893).
Selections from the Essays of T. H. Huxley, ed. A. Castell (1948).
Huxley's Diary of the Voyage of H.M.S. Rattlesnake, ed. J. Huxley (1956).
Religions without Revelation, ed. J. Huxley (1957).
Man's Place in Nature, intro. Ashley Montague (1959).
Science and Education, ed. Charles Winnick (1964).
The Essence of T. H. Huxley, ed. Cyril Bibby (1967).

BIOGRAPHY AND CRITICISM

James McCosh, *The Agnosticism of Hume and Huxley* (1884).
Leonard Huxley, *The Life and Letters of T. H. Huxley* (2 vols., 1900).
P. Chalmers Mitchell, *Huxley* (1901).
Leonard Huxley, *Thomas Henry Huxley* (1920).
Aldous Huxley, *T. H. Huxley as a Man of Letters* (1932).
Clarence Ayres, *Huxley* (1932).
Houston Peterson, *Thomas H. Huxley: Prophet of Science* (1932).
L. T. More, *The Dogma of Evolution* (1933).
William Irvine, *Apes, Angels, and Victorians* (1955).
Cyril Bibby, *Huxley: Scientist, Humanist, and Educator* (1959).
Gertrude Himmelfarb, *Darwin and the Darwinian Revolution* (1959).
A. O. J. Cockshut, *The Unbelievers* (1964).
Ronald Clark, *The Huxleys* (1968).
Albert Ashforth, *Thomas Henry Huxley* (1970).
John W. Bicknell, "The Unbelievers," in *Victorian Prose: A Guide to Research* (1973).

---

from Lay Sermons

The essays collected and published in Lay Sermons *in 1870 were those Huxley had written mainly in the decade of the eighteen-sixties after he had gone forth to defend the doctrine of evolution. Huxley's early inclination to use science as the point of departure for speculations social and philosophic is evident in these essays. The two essays printed below show Huxley in characteristic mode considering the question of education and the question of the physical and material basis of life. "A Liberal Education; And Where to Find It" was an address to the South London Working Man's College on 4 January 1868. It was first published in* Macmillan's Magazine. *"On the Physical Basis of Life," Huxley's best-known single essay, was a lecture delivered at Edinburgh on 8 November 1868 and first published in the* Fortnightly Review *in the following year.*

A Liberal Education; And Where to Find It

THE business which the South London Working Men's College has undertaken is a great work; indeed, I might say, that Education, with which that college proposes to grapple, is the greatest work of all those which lie ready to a man's hand just at present.

And, at length, this fact is becoming generally recognised. You cannot go anywhere without hearing a buzz of more or less confused and contradictory talk on this subject—nor can you fail to notice that, in one point at any rate, there is a very decided advance upon like discussions in former days. Nobody outside the agricultural interest now dares to say that education is a bad thing. If any representative of the once large and powerful party, which, in former days, proclaimed this opinion, still exists in a semi-fossil state, he keeps his thoughts to himself. In fact, there is a chorus of voices, almost distressing in their harmony, raised in favour of the doctrine that education is the great panacea for human troubles, and that, if the country is not shortly to go to the dogs, everybody must be educated.

The politicians tells us, "you must educate the masses because they are going to be masters." The clergy join in the cry for education, for they affirm that the people are drifting away from church and chapel into the broadest infidelity. The manufacturers and the capitalists swell the chorus lustily. They declare that ignorance makes bad workmen; that England will soon be unable to turn out cotton goods, or steam engines, cheaper than other people; and then, Ichabod! Ichabod! the glory will be departed from us. And a few voices are lifted up in favour of the doctrine that the masses should be educated because they are men and women with unlimited capacities of being, doing, and suffering, and that it is as true now, as ever it was, that the people perish for lack of knowledge.

These members of the minority, with whom I confess I have a good deal of sympathy, are doubtful whether any of the other reasons urged in favour of the education of the people are of much value—whether, indeed, some of them are based upon either wise or noble grounds of action. They question if it be wise to tell people that you will do for them, out of fear of their power, what you have left undone, so long as your only motive was compassion for their weakness and their sorrows. And, if ignorance of everything which it is needful a ruler should know is likely to do so much harm in the governing classes of the future, why is it, they ask reasonably enough, that such ignorance in the governing classes of the past has not been viewed with equal horror?

Compare the average artisan and the average country squire, and it may be doubted if you will find a pin to choose between the two in point of ignorance, class feeling, or prejudice. It is true that the ignorance is of a different sort—that the class feeling is in favour of a different class, and that the prejudice has a distinct favour of wrong-headedness in each case—but it is questionable if the one is either a bit better, or a bit worse, than the other. The old protectionist theory is the doctrine of trades unions as applied by the squires, and the modern trades unionism is the doctrine of the squires applied by the artisans. Why should we be worse off under one *régime* than under the other?

Again, this sceptical minority asks the clergy to think whether it is really want of education which keeps the masses away from their ministrations—whether the most completely educated men are not as open to reproach on this score as the workmen; and whether, perchance, this may not indicate that it is not education which lies at the bottom of the matter?

Once more, these people, whom there is no pleasing, venture to doubt whether the glory, which rests upon being able to undersell all the rest of the world, is a very safe kind of glory—whether we may not purchase it too dear; especially if we allow education, which ought to be directed to the making of men, to be diverted into a process of manufacturing human tools, wonderfully adroit in the exercise of some technical industry, but good for nothing else.

And, finally, these people inquire whether it is the masses alone who need a reformed and improved education. They ask whether the richest of our public schools might not well be made to supply knowledge, as well as gentlemanly habits, a strong class feeling, and eminent proficiency in cricket. They seem to think that the noble foundations of our old universities are hardly fulfilling their functions in their present posture of half-clerical seminaries, half racecourses, where men are trained to win a senior wranglership, or a double-first, as horses are trained to win a cup, with as little reference to the needs of after-life in the case of the man as in that of the racer. And, while as zealous for education as the rest, they affirm that, if the education of the richer classes were such as to fit them to be the leaders and the governors of the poorer; and, if the education of the poorer classes were such as to enable them to appreciate really wise guidance and good governance; the politicians need not fear mob-law, nor the clergy lament their want of flocks, nor the capitalists prognosticate the annihilation of the prosperity of the country.

Such is the diversity of opinion upon the why and the wherefore of education. And my hearers will be prepared to expect that the practical recommendations which are put forward are not less discordant. There is a loud cry for compulsory education. We English, in spite of constant experience to the contrary, preserve a touching faith in the efficacy of acts of parliament; and I believe we should have compulsory education in the course of next session, if there were the least probability that half a dozen leading statesmen of different parties would agree what that education should be.

Some hold that education without theology is worse than none. Others maintain, quite as strongly, that education with theology is in the same predicament. But this is certain, that those who hold the first opinion can by no means agree what theology should be taught; and that those who maintain the second are in a small minority.

At any rate "make people learn to read, write, and cipher," say a great many; and the advice is undoubtedly sensible as far as it goes. But, as has happened to me in former days, those who, in despair of getting anything better, advocate this measure, are met with the objection that it is very like making a child practise the use of a knife, fork, and spoon, without giving it a particle of meat. I really don't know what reply is to be made to such an objection.

But it would be unprofitable to spend more time in disentangling, or rather in showing up the knots in, the ravelled skeins of our neighbours. Much more to the purpose is to ask if we possess any clue of our own which may guide us among these entanglements. And by way of a beginning, let us ask ourselves—What is education? Above all things, what is our ideal of a thoroughly liberal education?—of that education which, if we could begin life again, we would give ourselves—of that education which, if we could mould the fates to our own will, we would give our children. Well, I know not what may be your conceptions upon this matter, but I will tell you mine, and I hope I shall find that our views are not very discrepant.

Suppose it were perfectly certain that the life and fortune of every one of us would, one day or other, depend upon his winning or losing a game at chess. Don't you think that we should all consider it to be a primary duty to learn at least the names and the moves of the pieces; to have a notion of a gambit, and a keen eye for all the means of giving and getting out of check? Do you not think that we should look with a disapprobation amounting to scorn, upon the father who allowed his son, or the state which allowed its members, to grow up without knowing a pawn from a knight?

Yet it is a very plain and elementary truth, that the life, the fortune, and the happiness of every one of us, and, more or less, of those who are connected with us, do depend upon our knowing something of the rules of a game infinitely more difficult and complicated than chess. It is a game which has been played for untold ages, every man and woman of us being one of the two players in a game of his or her own. The chessboard is the world, the pieces are the phenomena of the universe, the rules of the game are what we call the laws of Nature. The player on the other side is hidden from us. We know that his play is always fair, just, and patient. But also we know, to our cost, that he never overlooks a mistake, or makes the smallest allowance for ignorance. To the man who plays well, the highest stakes are paid, with that sort of overflowing generosity with which the strong shows delight in strength. And one who plays ill is checkmated—without haste, but without remorse.

My metaphor will remind some of you of the

famous picture in which Retzsch[1] has depicted Satan playing at chess with man for his soul. Substitute for the mocking fiend in that picture, a calm, strong angel who is playing for love, as we say, and would rather lose than win—and I should accept it as an image of human life.

Well, what I mean by Education is learning the rules of this mighty game. In other words, education is the instruction of the intellect in the laws of Nature, under which name I include not merely things and their forces, but men and their ways; and the fashioning of the affections and of the will into an earnest and loving desire to move in harmony with those laws. For me, education means neither more nor less than this. Anything which professes to call itself education must be tried by this standard, and if it fails to stand the test, I will not call it education, whatever may be the force of authority, or of numbers, upon the other side.

It is important to remember that, in strictness, there is no such thing as an uneducated man. Take an extreme case. Suppose that an adult man, in the full vigour of his faculties, could be suddenly placed in the world, as Adam is said to have been, and then left to do as he best might. How long would he be left uneducated? Not five minutes. Nature would begin to teach him, through the eye, the ear, the touch, the properties of objects. Pain and pleasure would be at his elbow telling him to do this and avoid that; and by slow degrees the man would receive an education, which, if narrow, would be thorough, real, and adequate to his circumstances, though there would be no extras and very few accomplishments.

And if to this solitary man entered a second Adam, or, better still, an Eve, a new and greater world, that of social and moral phenomena, would be revealed. Joys and woes, compared with which all others might seem but faint shadows, would spring from the new relations. Happiness and sorrow would take the place of the coarser monitors, pleasure and pain; but conduct would still be shaped by the observation of the natural consequences of actions; or, in other words, by the laws of the nature of man.

To every one of us the world was once as fresh and new as to Adam. And then, long before we were susceptible of any other mode of instruction, Nature took us in hand, and every minute of waking life brought its educational influence, shaping our actions into rough accordance with Nature's laws, so that we might not be ended untimely by too gross disobedience. Nor should I speak of this process of education as past, for any one, be he as old as he may. For every man, the world is as fresh as it was at the first day, and as full of untold novelties for him who has the eyes to see them. And Nature is still continuing her patient education of us in that great university, the universe, of which we are all members—Nature having no Test-Acts.[2]

Those who take honours in Nature's university, who learn the laws which govern men and things and obey them, are the really great and successful men in this world. The great mass of mankind are the "Poll," who pick up just enough to get through without much discredit. Those who won't learn at all are plucked; and then you can't come up again. Nature's pluck means extermination.

Thus the question of compulsory education is settled so far as Nature is concerned. Her bill on that question was framed and passed long ago. But, like all compulsory legislation, that of Nature is harsh and wasteful in its operation. Ignorance is visited as sharply as wilful disobedience—incapacity meets with the same punishment as crime. Nature's discipline is not even a word and a blow, and the blow first; but the blow without the word. It is left to you to find out why your ears are boxed.

The object of what we commonly call education—that education in which man intervenes and which I shall distinguish as artificial education—is to make good these defects in Nature's methods; to prepare the child to receive Nature's education, neither incapably nor ignorantly, nor with wilful disobedience; and to understand the preliminary symptoms of her displeasure, without waiting for the box on the ear. In short, all artificial education ought to be an anticipation of natural education. And a liberal education is an artificial education, which has not only prepared a man to escape the great evils of disobedience to natural laws, but has trained him to appreciate and to seize upon the rewards, which Nature scatters with as free a hand as her penalties.

That man, I think, has had a liberal education,

---

[1] Friedrich August Moritz Retzsch (1779–1857), German painter; his chief work was "The Chess-players."

[2] Laws imposing religious tests for membership in the universities and for public employment.

who has been so trained in youth that his body is the ready servant of his will, and does with ease and pleasure all the work that, as a mechanism, it is capable of; whose intellect is a clear, cold, logic engine, with all its parts of equal strength, and in smooth working order; ready, like a steam engine, to be turned to any kind of work, and spin the gossamers as well as forge the anchors of the mind; whose mind is stored with a knowledge of the great and fundamental truths of Nature and of the laws of her operations; one who, no stunted ascetic, is full of life and fire, but whose passions are trained to come to heel by a vigorous will, the servant of a tender conscience; who has learned to love all beauty, whether of Nature or of art, to hate all vileness, and to respect others as himself.

Such an one and no other, I conceive, has had a liberal education; for he is, as completely as a man can be, in harmony with Nature. He will make the best of her, and she of him. They will get on together rarely; she as his ever beneficent mother; he as her mouth-piece, her conscious self, her minister and interpreter.

Where is such an education as this to be had? Where is there any approximation to it? Has any one tried to found such an education? Looking over the length and breadth of these islands, I am afraid that all these questions must receive a negative answer. Consider our primary schools, and what is taught in them. A child learns:—

1. To read, write, and cipher, more or less well; but in a very large proportion of cases not so well as to take pleasure in reading, or to be able to write the commonest letter properly.

2. A quantity of dogmatic theology, of which the child, nine times out of ten, understands next to nothing.

3. Mixed up with this, so as to seem to stand or fall with it, a few of the broadest and simplest principles of morality. This, to my mind, is much as if a man of science should make the story of the fall of the apple in Newton's garden, an integral part of the doctrine of gravitation, and teach it as of equal authority with the law of the inverse squares.

4. A good deal of Jewish history and Syrian geography, and, perhaps, a little something about English history and the geography of the child's own country. But I doubt if there is a primary school in England in which hangs a map of the hundred in which the village lies, so that the children may be practically taught by it what a map means.

5. A certain amount of regularity, attentive obedience, respect for others: obtained by fear, if the master be incompetent or foolish; by love and reverence, if he be wise.

So far as this school course embraces a training in the theory and practice of obedience to the moral laws of Nature, I gladly admit, not only that it contains a valuable educational element, but that, so far, it deals with the most valuable and important part of all education. Yet, contrast what is done in this direction with what might be done; with the time given to matters of comparatively no importance; with the absence of any attention to things of the highest moment; and one is tempted to think of Falstaff's bill and "the halfpenny worth of bread to all that quantity of sack."

Let us consider what a child thus "educated" knows, and what it does not know. Begin with the most important topic of all—morality, as the guide of conduct. The child knows well enough that some acts meet with approbation and some with disapprobation. But it has never heard that there lies in the nature of things a reason for every moral law, as cogent and as well defined as that which underlies every physical law; that stealing and lying are just as certain to be followed by evil consequences, as putting your hand in the fire, or jumping out of a garret window. Again, though the scholar may have been made acquainted, in dogmatic fashion, with the broad laws of morality, he has had no training in the application of those laws to the difficult problems which result from the complex conditions of modern civilization. Would it not be very hard to expect any one to solve a problem in conic sections who had merely been taught the axioms and definitions of mathematical science?

A workman has to bear hard labour, and perhaps privation, while he sees others rolling in wealth, and feeding their dogs with what would keep his children from starvation. Would it not be well to have helped that man to calm the natural promptings of discontent by showing him, in his youth, the necessary connexion of the moral law which prohibits stealing with the stability of society—by proving to him, once for all, that it is better for his own people, better for himself, better for future generations, that he should starve than steal? If you have no foundation of knowledge, or habit of thought, to work upon, what chance have you of persuading a hungry man that a capitalist is not a thief "with a circumbendibus?" And if he honestly believes that, of what avail is it to quote the commandment against stealing, when he proposes to make the capitalist disgorge?

Again, the child learns absolutely nothing of the history or the political organization of his own country. His general impression is, that everything of much importance happened a very long while ago; and that the Queen and the gentlefolks govern the country much after the fashion of King David and the elders and nobles of Israel—his sole models. Will you give a man with this much information a vote? In easy times he sells it for a pot of beer. Why should he not? It is of about as much use to him as a chignon, and he knows as much what to do with it, for any other purpose. In bad times, on the contrary, he applies his simple theory of government, and believes that his rulers are the cause of his suffer-ings—a belief which sometimes bears remarkable practical fruits.

Least of all, does the child gather from this primary "education" of ours a conception of the laws of the physical world, or of the relations of cause and effect therein. And this is the more to be lamented, as the poor are especially exposed to physical evils, and are more interested in removing them than any other class of the com-munity. If any one is concerned in knowing the ordinary laws of mechanics one would think it is the hand-labourer, whose daily toil lies among levers and pulleys; or among the other imple-ments of artisan work. And if any one is interested in the laws of health, it is the poor workman, whose strength is wasted by ill-prepared food, whose health is sapped by bad ventilation and bad drainage, and half whose children are mas-sacred by disorders which might be prevented. Not only does our present primary education carefully abstain from hinting to the workman that some of his greatest evils are traceable to mere physical agencies, which could be removed by energy, patience, and frugality; but it does worse—it renders him, so far as it can, deaf to those who could help him, and tries to substitute an Oriental submission to what is falsely declared to be the will of God, for his natural tendency to strive after a better condition.

What wonder then, if very recently, an appeal has been made to statistics for the profoundly foolish purpose of showing that education is of no good—that it diminishes neither misery, nor crime, among the masses of mankind? I reply, why should the thing which has been called edu-cation do either the one or the other? If I am a knave or a fool, teaching me to read and write won't make me less of either one or the other—unless somebody shows me how to put my reading and writing to wise and good purposes.

Suppose any one were to argue that medicine is of no use, because it could be proved statistic-ally, that the percentage of deaths was just the same, among people who had been taught how to open a medicine chest, and among those who did not so much as know the key by sight. The argument is absurd; but it is not more preposter-ous than that against which I am contending. The only medicine for suffering, crime, and all the other woes of mankind, is wisdom. Teach a man to read and write, and you have put into his hands the great keys of the wisdom box. But it is quite another matter whether he ever opens the box or not. And he is as likely to poison as to cure himself, if, without guidance, he swallows the first drug that comes to hand. In these times a man may as well be purblind, as unable to read —lame, as unable to write. But I protest that, if I thought the alternative were a necessary one, I would rather that the children of the poor should grow up ignorant of both these mighty arts, than that they should remain ignorant of that knowl-edge to which these arts are means.

It may be said that all these animadversions may apply to primary schools, but that the higher schools, at any rate, must be allowed to give a liberal education. In fact, they professedly sacri-fice everything else to this object.

Let us inquire into this matter. What do the higher schools, those to which the great middle class of the country sends it children, teach, over and above the instruction given in the primary schools? There is a little more reading and writing of English. But, for all that, every one knows that it is a rare thing to find a boy of the middle or upper classes who can read aloud decently, or who can put his thoughts on paper in clear and grammatical (to say nothing of good or elegant) language. The "ciphering" of the lower schools expands into elementary math-ematics in the higher; into arithmetic, with a little algebra, a little Euclid. But I doubt if one boy in five hundred has ever heard the explana-tion of a rule of arithmetic, or knows his Euclid otherwise than by rote.

Of theology, the middle class schoolboy gets rather less than poorer children, less absolutely and less relatively, because there are so many other claims upon his attention. I venture to say that, in the great majority of cases, his ideas on this subject when he leaves school are of the most shadowy and vague description, and associated with painful impressions of the weary hours spent in learning collects and catechism by heart.

Modern geography, modern history, modern literature; the English language as a language; the whole circle of the sciences, physical, moral, and social, are even more completely ignored in the higher than in the lower schools. Up till within a few years back, a boy might have passed through any one of the great public schools with the greatest distinction and credit, and might never so much as have heard of one of the subjects I have just mentioned. He might never have heard that the earth goes round the sun; that England underwent a great revolution in 1688, and France another in 1789; that there once lived certain notable men called Chaucer, Shakspeare, Milton, Voltaire, Goethe, Schiller. The first might be a German and the last an Englishman for anything he could tell you to the contrary. And as for science, the only idea the word would suggest to his mind would be dexterity in boxing.

I have said that this was the state of things a few years back, for the sake of the few righteous who are to be found among the educational cities of the plain. But I would not have you too sanguine about the result, if you sound the minds of the existing generation of public schoolboys, on such topics as those I have mentioned.

Now let us pause to consider this wonderful state of affairs; for the time will come when Englishmen will quote it as the stock example of the stolid stupidity of their ancestors in the nineteenth century. The most thoroughly commercial people, the greatest voluntary wanderers and colonists the world has ever seen, are precisely the middle classes of this country. If there be a people which has been busy making history on the great scale for the last three hundred years—and the most profoundly interesting history—history which, if it happened to be that of Greece or Rome, we should study with avidity—it is the English. If there be a people which, during the same period, has developed a remarkable literature, it is our own. If there be a nation whose prosperity depends absolutely and wholly upon their mastery over the forces of Nature, upon their intelligent apprehension of, and obedience to, the laws of the creation and distribution of wealth, and of the stable equilibrium of the forces of society, it is precisely this nation. And yet this is what these wonderful people tell their sons:—

"At the cost of from one to two thousand pounds of our hard earned money, we devote twelve of the most precious years of your lives to school.

There you shall toil, or be supposed to toil; but there you shall not learn one single thing of all those you will most want to know, directly you leave school and enter upon the practical business of life. You will in all probability go into business, but you shall not know where, or how, any article of commerce is produced, or the difference between an export or an import, or the meaning of the word 'capital.' You will very likely settle in a colony, but you shall not know whether Tasmania is part of New South Wales, or *vice versâ*.

"Very probably you may become a manufacturer, but you shall not be provided with the means of understanding the working of one of your own steam-engines, or the nature of the raw products you employ; and, when you are asked to buy a patent, you shall not have the slightest means of judging whether the inventor is an imposter who is contravening the elementary principles of science, or a man who will make you as rich as Crœsus.

"You will very likely get into the House of Commons. You will have to take your share in making laws which may prove a blessing or a curse to millions of men. But you shall not hear one word respecting the political organization of your country; the meaning of the controversy between freetraders and protectionists shall never have been mentioned to you; you shall not so much as know that there are such things as economical laws.

"The mental power which will be of most importance in your daily life will be the power of seeing things as they are without regard to authority; and of drawing accurate general conclusions from particular facts. But at school and at college you shall know of no source of truth but authority; nor exercise your reasoning faculty upon anything but deduction from that which is laid down by authority.

"You will have to weary your soul with work, and many a time eat your bread in sorrow and in bitterness, and you shall not have learned to take refuge in the great source of pleasure without alloy, the serene resting-place for worn human nature,—the world of art."

Said I not rightly that we are a wonderful people? I am quite prepared to allow, that education entirely devoted to these omitted subjects might not be a completely liberal education. But is an education which ignores them all, a liberal education? Nay, is it too much to say that the education which should embrace these subjects and no others, would be a real education, though an incomplete one; while an education which omits them is really not an education at all, but a more or less useful course of intellectual gymnastics?

For what does the middle-class school put in the place of all these things which are left out? It substitutes what is usually comprised under the compendious title of the "classics"—that is to say, the languages, the literature, and the history of the ancient Greeks and Romans, and the geography of so much of the world as was known to these two great nations of antiquity. Now, do not expect me to depreciate the earnest and enlightened pursuit of classical learning. I have not the least desire to speak ill of such occupations, nor any sympathy with those who run them down. On the contrary, if my opportunities had lain in that direction, there is no investigation into which I could have thrown myself with greater delight than that of antiquity.

What science can present greater attractions than philology? How can a lover of literary excellence fail to rejoice in the ancient masterpieces? And with what consistency could I, whose business lies so much in the attempt to decipher the past, and to build up intelligible forms out of the scattered fragments of long-extinct beings, fail to take a sympathetic, though an unlearned, interest in the labour of a Niebuhr, a Gibbon, or a Grote?[3] Classical history is a great section of the palæontology of man; and I have the same double respect for it as for other kinds of palæontology—that is to say, a respect for the facts which it establishes as for all facts, and a still greater respect for it as a preparation for the discovery of a law of progress.

But if the classics were taught as they might be taught—if boys and girls were instructed in Greek and Latin, not merely as languages, but as illustrations of philological science; if a vivid picture of life on the shores of the Mediterranean, two thousand years ago, were imprinted on the minds of scholars; if ancient history were taught, not as a weary series of feuds and fights, but traced to its causes in such men placed under such conditions; if, lastly, the study of the classical books were followed in such a manner as to impress boys with their beauties, and with the grand simplicity of their statement of the everlasting problems of human life, instead of with their verbal and grammatical peculiarities; I still think it as little proper that they should form the basis

of a liberal education for our contemporaries, as I should think it fitting to make that sort of palæontology with which I am familiar, the back-bone of modern education.

It is wonderful how close a parallel to classical training could be made out of that palæontology to which I refer. In the first place I could get up an osteological primer so arid, so pedantic in its terminology, so altogether distasteful to the youthful mind, as to beat the recent famous production of the head-masters out of the field in all these excellences. Next, I could exercise my boys upon easy fossils, and bring out all their powers of memory and all their ingenuity in the application of my osteo-grammatical rules to the interpretation, or construing, of those fragments. To those who had reached the higher classes, I might supply odd bones to be built up into animals, giving great honour and reward to him who succeeded in fabricating monsters most entirely in accordance with the rules. That would answer to verse-making and essay-writing in the dead languages.

To be sure, if a great comparative anatomist were to look at these fabrications he might shake his head, or laugh. But what then? Would such a catastrophe destroy the parallel? What think you would Cicero, or Horace, say to the production of the best sixth form going? And would not Terence stop his ears and run out if he could be present at an English performance of his own plays? Would Hamlet, in the mouths of a set of French actors, who should insist on pronouncing English after the fashion of their own tongue, be more hideously ridiculous?

But it will be said that I am forgetting the beauty, and the human interest, which appertain to classical studies. To this I reply that it is only a very strong man who can appreciate the charms of a landscape, as he is toiling up a steep hill, along a bad road. What with short-windedness, stones, ruts, and a pervading sense of the wisdom of rest and be thankful, most of us have little enough sense of the beautiful under these circumstances. The ordinary schoolboy is precisely in this case. He finds Parnassus uncommonly steep, and there is no chance of his having much time or inclination to look about him till he gets to the top. And nine times out of ten he does not get to the top.

But if this be a fair picture of the results of classical teaching at its best—and I gather from those who have authority to speak on such mat-

---

[3] Eighteenth- and nineteenth-century historians.

ters that it is so—what is to be said of classical teaching at its worst, or in other words, of the classics of our ordinary middle-class schools?[4] I will tell you. It means getting up endless forms and rules by heart. It means turning Latin and Greek into English, for the mere sake of being able to do it, and without the smallest regard to the worth, or worthlessness, of the author read. It means the learning of innumerable, not always decent, fables in such a shape that the meaning they once had is dried up into utter trash; and the only impression left upon a boy's mind is, that the people who believed such things must have been the greatest idiots the world ever saw. And it means, finally, that after a dozen years spent at this kind of work, the sufferer shall be incompetent to interpret a passage in an author he has not already got up; that he shall loathe the sight of a Greek or Latin book; and that he shall never open, or think of, a classical writer again, until, wonderful to relate, he insists upon submitting his sons to the same process.

These be your gods, O Israel! For the sake of this net result (and respectability) the British father denies his children all the knowledge they might turn to account in life, not merely for the achievement of vulgar success, but for guidance in the great crises of human existence. This is the stone he offers to those whom he is bound by the strongest and tenderest ties to feed with bread.

If primary and secondary education are in this unsatisfactory state, what is to be said to the universities? This is an awful subject, and one I almost fear to touch with my unhallowed hands; but I can tell you what those say who have authority to speak.

The Rector of Lincoln College,[5] in his lately published, valuable "Suggestions for Academical Organization with especial reference to Oxford," tells us (p. 127):—

"The colleges were, in their origin, endowments, not for the elements of a general liberal education, but for the prolonged study of special and professional faculties by men of riper age. The universities embraced both these objects. The colleges, while they incidentally aided in elementary education, were specially devoted to the highest learning. . . . .

"This was the theory of the middle-age university and the design of collegiate foundations in their origin. Time and circumstances have brought about a total change. The colleges no longer promote the researches of science, or direct professional study. Here and there college walls may shelter an occasional student, but not in larger proportions than may be found in private life. Elementary teaching of youths under twenty is now the only function performed by the university, and almost the only object of college endowments. Colleges were homes for the life-study of the highest and most abstruse parts of knowledge. They have become boarding schools in which the elements of the learned languages are taught to youths."

If Mr. Pattison's high position, and his obvious love and respect for his university, be insufficient to convince the outside world that language so severe is yet no more than just, the authority of the Commissioners who reported on the University of Oxford in 1850 is open to no challenge. Yet they write:—

"It is generally acknowledged that both Oxford and the country at large suffer greatly from the absence of a body of learned men devoting their lives to the cultivation of science, and to the direction of academical education.

"The fact that so few books of profound research emanate from the University of Oxford materially impairs its character as a seat of learning, and consequently its hold on the respect of the nation."

Cambridge can claim no exemption from the reproaches addressed to Oxford. And thus there seems no escape from the admission that what we fondly call our great seats of learning are simply "boarding schools" for bigger boys; that learned men are not more numerous in them than out of them; that the advancement of knowledge is not the object of fellows of colleges; that, in the philosophic calm and meditative stillness of their greenswarded courts, philosophy does not thrive and meditation bears few fruits.

It is my great good fortune to reckon amongst my friends resident members of both universities, who are men of learning and research, zealous cultivators of science, keeping before their minds a noble ideal of a university, and doing their best to make that ideal a reality; and, to me, they would necessarily typify the universities, did not the authoritative statements I have quoted compel me to believe that they are exceptional, and

---

[4] For a justification of what is here said about these schools, see that valuable book, "Essays on a Liberal Education," *passim*. [Huxley's note]

[5] Mark Pattison (1813–84).

not representative men. Indeed, upon calm consideration, several circumstances lead me to think that the Rector of Lincoln College and the Commissioners cannot be far wrong.

I believe there can be no doubt that the foreigner who should wish to become acquainted with the scientific, or the literary, activity of modern England, would simply lose his time and his pains if he visited our universities with that object.

And, as for works of profound research on any subject, and, above all, in that classical lore for which the universities profess to sacrifice almost everything else, why, a third-rate, poverty-stricken German university turns out more produce of that kind in one year, than our vast and wealthy foundations elaborate in ten.

Ask the man who is investigating any question, profoundly and thoroughly—be it historical, philosophical, philological, physical, literary, or theological; who is trying to make himself master of any abstract subject (except, perhaps, political economy and geology, both of which are intensely Anglican sciences) whether he is not compelled to read half a dozen times as many German, as English, books? And whether, of these English books, more than one in ten is the work of a fellow of a college, or a professor of an English university?

Is this from any lack of power in the English as compared with the German mind? The countrymen of Grote and of Mill, of Faraday, of Robert Brown, of Lyell, and of Darwin, to go no further back than the contemporaries of men of middle age, can afford to smile at such a suggestion. England can show now, as she has been able to show in every generation since civilization spread over the West, individual men who hold their own against the world, and keep alive the old tradition of her intellectual eminence.

But, in the majority of cases, these men are what they are in virtue of their native intellectual force, and of a strength of character which will not recognize impediments. They are not trained in the courts of the Temple of Science, but storm the walls of that edifice in all sorts of irregular ways, and with much loss of time and power, in order to obtain their legitimate positions.

Our universities not only do not encourage such men; do not offer them positions, in which it should be their highest duty to do, thoroughly, that which they are most capable of doing; but, as far as possible, university training shuts out of

the minds of those among them, who are subjected to it, the prospect that there is anything in the world for which they are specially fitted. Imagine the success of the attempt to still the intellectual hunger of any of the men I have mentioned, by putting before him, as the object of existence, the successful mimicry of the measure of a Greek song, or the roll of Ciceronian prose! Imagine how much success would be likely to attend the attempt to persuade such men, that the education which leads to perfection in such elegancies is alone to be called culture; while the facts of history, the process of thought, the conditions of moral and social existence, and the laws of physical nature, are left to be dealt with as they may, by outside barbarians!

It is not thus that the German universities, from being beneath notice a century ago, have become what they are now—the most intensely cultivated and the most productive intellectual corporations the world has ever seen.

The student who repairs to them sees in the list of classes and of professors a fair picture of the world of knowledge. Whatever he needs to know there is some one ready to teach him, some one competent to discipline him in the way of learning; whatever his special bent, let him but be able and diligent, and in due time he shall find distinction and a career. Among his professors, he sees men whose names are known and revered throughout the civilized world; and their living example infects him with a noble ambition, and a love for the spirit of work.

The Germans dominate the intellectual world by virtue of the same simple secret as that which made Napoleon the master of old Europe. They have declared *la carrière ouverte aux talents*,[6] and every Bursch marches with a professor's gown in his knapsack. Let him become a great scholar, or man of science, and ministers will compete for his services. In Germany, they do not leave the chance of his holding the office he would render illustrious to the tender mercies of a hot canvass, and the final wisdom of a mob of country parsons.

In short, in Germany, the universities are exactly what the Rector of Lincoln and the Commissioners tell us the English universities are not; that is to say, corporations "of learned men devoting their lives to the cultivation of science, and the direction of academical education." They are not "boarding schools for youths," nor clerical seminaries; but institutions for the higher culture of men, in which the theological faculty

[6] The career is open to a man of talents.

is of no more importance, or prominence, than the rest; and which are truly "universities," since they strive to represent and embody the totality of human knowledge, and to find room for all forms of intellectual activity.

May zealous and clear-headed reformers like Mr. Pattison succeed in their noble endeavours to shape our universities towards some such ideal as this, without losing what is valuable and distinctive, in their social tone! But until they have succeeded, a liberal education will be no more obtainable in our Oxford and Cambridge Universities than in our public schools.

If I am justified in my conception of the ideal of a liberal education; and if what I have said about the existing educational institutions of the country is also true, it is clear that the two have no sort of relation to one another; that the best of our schools and the most complete of our university trainings give but a narrow, one-sided, and essentially illiberal education—while the worst give what is really next to no education at all. The South London Working-Men's College could not copy any of these institutions if it would. I am bold enough to express the conviction that it ought not if it could.

For what is wanted is the reality and not the mere name of a liberal education; and this College must steadily set before itself the ambition to be able to give that education sooner or later. At present we are but beginning, sharpening our educational tools, as it were, and, except a modicum of physical science, we are not able to offer much more than is to be found in an ordinary school.

Moral and social science—one of the greatest and most fruitful of our future classes, I hope—at present lacks only one thing in our programme, and that is a teacher. A considerable want, no doubt; but it must be recollected that it is much better to want a teacher than to want the desire to learn.

Further, we need what, for want of a better name, I must call Physical Geography. What I mean is that which the Germans call "*Erdkunde*."[7]

It is a description of the earth, of its place and relation to other bodies; of its general structure, and of its great features—winds, tides, mountains, plains; of the chief forms of the vegetable and animal worlds, of the varieties of man. It is the peg upon which the greatest quantity of useful and entertaining scientific information can be suspended.

Literature is not upon the College programme; but I hope some day to see it there. For literature is the greatest of all sources of refined pleasure, and one of the great uses of a liberal education is to enable us to enjoy that pleasure. There is scope enough for the purposes of liberal education in the study of the rich treasures of our own language alone. All that is needed is direction, and the cultivation of a refined taste by attention to sound criticism. But there is no reason why French and German should not be mastered sufficiently to read what is worth reading in those languages, with pleasure and with profit.

And finally, by-and-by, we must have History; treated not as a succession of battles and dynasties; not as a series of biographies; not as evidence that Providence has always been on the side of either Whigs or Tories; but as the development of man in times past, and in other conditions than our own.

But, as it is one of the principles of our College to be self-supporting, the public must lead, and we must follow, in these matters. If my hearers take to heart what I have said about liberal education, they will desire these things, and I doubt not we shall be able to supply them. But we must wait till the demand is made.

On the Physical Basis of Life[1]

IN ORDER to make the title of this discourse generally intelligible, I have translated the term "Protoplasm," which is the scientific name of the substance of which I am about to speak, by the words "the physical basis of life." I suppose

---

[7] Literally, "knowledge of the earth."

[1] The substance of this paper was contained in a discourse which was delivered in Edinburgh on the evening of Sunday, the 8th of November, 1868—being the first of a series of Sunday evening addresses upon non-theological topics, instituted by the Rev. J. Cranbrook. Some phrases, which could possess only a transitory and local interest, have been omitted; instead of the newspaper report of the Archbishop of York's address, his Grace's subsequently-published pamphlet "On the Limits of Philosophical Inquiry" is quoted; and I have, here and there, endeavoured to express my meaning more fully and clearly than I seem to have done in speaking—if I may judge by sundry criticisms upon what I am supposed to have said, which have appeared. But in substance, and, so far as my recollection serves, in form, what is here written corresponds with what was there said. [Huxley's note]

that, to many, the idea that there is such a thing as a physical basis, or matter, of life may be novel —so widely spread is the conception of life as a something which works through matter, but is independent of it; and even those who are aware that matter and life are inseparably connected, may not be prepared for the conclusion plainly suggested by the phrase, "*the* physical basis or matter of life," that there is some one kind of matter which is common to all living beings, and that their endless diversities are bound together by a physical, as well as an ideal, unity. In fact, when first apprehended, such a doctrine as this appears almost shocking to common sense.

What, truly, can seem to be more obviously different from one another, in faculty, in form, and in substance, than the various kinds of living beings? What community of faculty can there be between the brightly-coloured lichen, which so nearly resembles a mere mineral incrustation of the bare rock on which it grows, and the painter, to whom it is instinct with beauty, or the botanist, whom it feeds with knowledge?

Again, think of the microscopic fungus—a mere infinitesimal ovoid particle, which finds space and duration enough to multiply into countless millions in the body of a living fly; and then of the wealth of foliage, the luxuriance of flower and fruit, which lies between this bald sketch of a plant and the giant pine of California, towering to the dimensions of a cathedral spire, or the Indian fig, which covers acres with its profound shadow, and endures while nations and empires come and go around its vast circumference. Or, turning to the other half of the world of life, picture to yourselves the great Finner whale, hugest of beasts that live, or have lived, disporting his eighty or ninety feet of bone, muscle, and blubber, with easy roll, among waves in which the stoutest ship that ever left dockyard would founder hopelessly; and contrast him with the invisible animalcules—mere gelatinous specks, multitudes of which could, in fact, dance upon the point of a needle with the same ease as the angels of the Schoolmen could, in imagination. With these images before your minds, you may well ask, what community of form, or structure, is there between the animalcule and the whale; or between the fungus and the fig-tree? And, *à fortiori*, between all four?

Finally, if we regard substance, or material composition, what hidden bond can connect the flower which a girl wears in her hair and the blood which courses through her youthful veins; or, what is there in common between the dense and resisting mass of the oak, or the strong fabric of the tortoise, and those broad disks of glassy jelly which may be seen pulsating through the waters of a calm sea, but which drain away to mere films in the hand which raises them out of their element?

Such objections as these must, I think, arise in the mind of every one who ponders, for the first time, upon the conception of a single physical basis of life underlying all the diversities of vital existence; but I propose to demonstrate to you that, notwithstanding these apparent difficulties, a threefold unity—namely, a unity of power or faculty, a unity of form, and a unity of substantial composition—does pervade the whole living world.

No very abstruse argumentation is needed, in the first place, to prove that the powers, or faculties, of all kinds of living matter, diverse as they may be in degree, are substantially similar in kind.

Goethe has condensed a survey of all the powers of mankind into the well-known epigram:—

"Warum treibt sich das Volk so und schreit? Es will sich ernähren
    Kinder zeugen, und die nähren so gut es vermag.
       *   *   *   *   *
    Weiter bringt es kein Mensch, stell' er sich wie er auch will."[2]

In physiological language this means, that all the multifarious and complicated activities of man are comprehensible under three categories. Either they are immediately directed towards the maintenance and development of the body, or they effect transitory changes in the relative positions of parts of the body, or they tend towards the continuance of the species. Even those manifestations of intellect, of feeling, and of will, which we rightly name the higher faculties, are not excluded from this classification, inasmuch as to every one but the subject of them, they are known only as transitory changes in the relative positions of parts of the body. Speech, gesture, and every other form of human action are, in the

---

[2] "Why does humankind so storm and cry? They will feed themselves, produce children, and nourish them as well as they can." "No man can go further than this, let him so place himself however he will."

long run, resolvable into muscular contraction, and muscular contraction is but a transitory change in the relative positions of the parts of a muscle. But the scheme which is large enough to embrace the activities of the highest form of life, covers all those of the lower creatures. The lowest plant, or animalcule, feeds, grows, and reproduces its kind. In addition, all animals manifest those transitory changes of form which we class under irritability and contractility; and, it is more than probable, that when the vegetable world is thoroughly explored, we shall find all plants in possession of the same powers, at one time or other of their existence.

I am not now alluding to such phænomena, at once rare and conspicuous, as those exhibited by the leaflets of the sensitive plant, or the stamens of the barberry, but to much more widely-spread, and, at the same time, more subtle and hidden, manifestations of vegetable contractility. You are doubtless aware that the common nettle owes its stinging property to the innumerable stiff and needle-like, though exquisitely delicate, hairs which cover its surface. Each stinging-needle tapers from a broad base to a slender summit, which, though rounded at the end, is of such microscopic fineness that it readily penetrates, and breaks off in, the skin. The whole hair consists of a very delicate outer case of wood, closely applied to the inner surface of which is a layer of semi-fluid matter, full of innumerable granules of extreme minuteness. This semi-fluid lining is protoplasm, which thus constitutes a kind of bag, full of a limpid liquid, and roughly corresponding in form with the interior of the hair which it fills. When viewed with a sufficiently high magnifying power, the protoplasmic layer of the nettle hair is seen to be in a condition of unceasing activity. Local contractions of the whole thickness of its substance pass slowly and gradually from point to point, and give rise to the appearance of progressive waves, just as the bending of successive stalks of corn by a breeze produces the apparent billows of a corn-field.

But, in addition to these movements, and independently of them, the granules are driven, in relatively rapid streams, through channels in the protoplasm which seem to have a considerable amount of persistence. Most commonly, the currents in adjacent parts of the protoplasm take similar directions; and, thus, there is a general stream up one side of the hair and down the other. But this does not prevent the existence of partial currents which take different routes; and sometimes, trains of granules may be seen coursing swiftly in opposite directions, within a twenty-thousandth of an inch of one another; while, occasionally, opposite streams come into direct collision, and, after a longer or shorter struggle, one predominates. The cause of these currents seems to lie in contractions of the protoplasm which bounds the channels in which they flow, but which are so minute that the best microscopes show only their effects, and not themselves.

The spectacle afforded by the wonderful energies prisoned within the compass of the microscopic hair of a plant, which we commonly regard as a merely passive organism, is not easily forgotten by one who has watched its display, continued hour after hour, without pause or sign of weakening. The possible complexity of many other organic forms, seemingly as simple as the protoplasm of the nettle, dawns upon one; and the comparison of such a protoplasm to a body with an internal circulation, which has been put forward by an eminent physiologist, loses much of its startling character. Currents similar to those of the hairs of the nettle have been observed in a great multitude of very different plants, and weighty authorities have suggested that they probably occur, in more or less perfection, in all young vegetable cells. If such be the case, the wonderful noonday silence of a tropical forest is, after all, due only to the dulness of our hearing; and could our ears catch the murmur of these tiny Maelstroms, as they whirl in the innumerable myriads of living cells which constitute each tree, we should be stunned, as with the roar of a great city.

Among the lower plants, it is the rule rather than the exception, that contractility should be still more openly manifested at some periods of their existence. The protoplasm of *Algæ* and *Fungi* becomes, under many circumstances, partially, or completely, freed from its woody case, and exhibits movements of its whole mass, or is propelled by the contractility of one, or more, hair-like prolongations of its body, which are called vibratile cilia. And, so far as the conditions of the manifestation of the phænomena of contractility have yet been studied, they are the same for the plant as for the animal. Heat and electric shocks influence both, and in the same way, though it may be in different degrees. It is by no means my intention to suggest that there is no difference in faculty between the lowest plant and the highest, or between plants and animals. But the difference between the powers of the lowest plant, or animal, and those of the highest, is one of degree, not of kind, and depends, as Milne-Edwards[3] long ago so well pointed out, upon the extent to which the principle of the division of labour is carried out in the living economy. In the lowest organism all parts are competent to perform all functions, and one and the same portion of protoplasm may successively take on the function of feeding, moving, or reproducing apparatus. In the highest, on the contrary, a great number of parts combine to perform each function, each part doing its alloted share of the work with great accuracy and efficiency, but being useless for any other purpose.

On the other hand, notwithstanding all the fundamental resemblances which exist between the powers of the protoplasm in plants and in animals, they present a striking difference (to which I shall advert more at length presently), in the fact that plants can manufacture fresh protoplasm out of mineral compounds, whereas animals are obliged to procure it ready made, and hence, in the long run, depend upon plants. Upon what condition this difference in the powers of the two great divisions of the world of life depends, nothing is at present known.

With such qualification as arises out of the last-mentioned fact, it may be truly said that the acts of all living things are fundamentally one. Is any such unity predicable of their forms? Let us seek in easily verified facts for a reply to this question. If a drop of blood be drawn by pricking one's finger, and viewed with proper precautions and under a sufficiently high microscopic power, there will be seen, among the innumerable multitude of little, circular, discoidal bodies, or corpuscles, which float in it and give it its colour, a comparatively small number of colourless corpuscles, of somewhat larger size and very irregular shape. If the drop of blood be kept at the temperature of the body, these colourless corpuscles will be seen to exhibit a marvellous activity, changing their forms with great rapidity, drawing in and thrusting out prolongations of their substance, and creeping about as if they were independent organisms.

The substance which is thus active is a mass of protoplasm, and its activity differs in detail, rather than in principle, from that of the protoplasm of the nettle. Under sundry circumstances the corpuscle dies and becomes distended into a round mass, in the midst of which is seen a smaller spherical body, which existed, but was more or less hidden, in the living corpuscle, and is called its *nucleus*. Corpuscles of essentially similar structure are to be found in the skin, in the lining of the mouth, and scattered through the whole framework of the body. Nay, more; in the earliest condition of the human organism, in that state in which it has but just become distinguishable from the egg in which it arises, it is nothing but an aggregation of such corpuscles, and every organ of the body was, once, no more than such an aggregation.

Thus a nucleated mass of protoplasm turns out to be what may be termed the structural unit of the human body. As a matter of fact, the body, in its earliest state, is a mere multiple of such units; and, in its perfect condition, it is a multiple of such units, variously modified.

But does the formula which expresses the essential structural character of the highest animal cover all the rest, as the statement of its powers and faculties covered that of all others? Very nearly. Beast and fowl, reptile and fish, mollusk, worm, and polype, are all composed of structural units of the same character, namely, masses of protoplasm with a nucleus. There are sundry very low animals, each of which, structurally, is a mere colourless blood-corpuscle, leading an independent life. But, at the very bottom of the animal scale, even this simplicity becomes simplified, and all the phænomena of life are manifested by a particle of protoplasm without a nucleus. Nor are such organisms insignificant by reason of their want of complexity. It is a fair question whether the protoplasm of those simplest forms of life, which people an immense extent of the bottom of the sea, would not outweigh that of all the higher living beings which inhabit the land put together. And in ancient times, no less than at the present day, such living beings as these have been the greatest of rock builders.

What has been said of the animal world is no less true of plants. Imbedded in the protoplasm at the broad, or attached, end of the nettle hair, there lies a spheroidal nucleus. Careful examination further proves that the whole substance of the nettle is made up of a repetition of such masses of nucleated protoplasm, each contained in a wooden case, which is modified in form, sometimes into a woody fibre, sometimes into a duct or spiral vessel, sometimes into a pollen grain, or an ovule. Traced back to its earliest state, the nettle arises as the man does, in a particle of nucleated protoplasm. And in the lowest plants, as in the lowest animals, a single mass of such

[3] Henri Milne-Edwards (1800–1885), French naturalist.

protoplasm may constitute the whole plant, or the protoplasm may exist without a nucleus.

Under these circumstances it may well be asked, how is one mass of non-nucleated protoplasm to be distinguished from another? why call one "plant" and the other "animal"?

The only reply is that, so far as form is concerned, plants and animals are not separable, and that, in many cases, it is a mere matter of convention whether we call a given organism an animal or a plant. There is a living body called *Æthalium septicum*, which appears upon decaying vegetable substances, and, in one of its forms, is common upon the surfaces of tan-pits. In this condition it is, to all intents and purposes, a fungus, and formerly was always regarded as such; but the remarkable investigations of De Bary[4] have shown that, in another condition, the *Æthalium* is an actively locomotive creature, and takes in solid matters, upon which, apparently, it feeds, thus exhibiting the most characteristic feature of animality. Is this a plant; or is it an animal? Is it both; or is it neither? Some decide in favour of the last supposition, and establish an intermediate kingdom, a sort of biological No Man's Land for all these questionable forms. But, as it is admittedly impossible to draw any distinct boundary line between this no man's land and the vegetable world on the one hand, or the animal, on the other, it appears to me that this proceeding merely doubles the difficulty which, before, was single.

Protoplasm, simple or nucleated, is the formal basis of all life. It is the clay of the potter: which, bake it and paint it as he will, remains clay, separated by artifice, and not by nature, from the commonest brick or sun-dried clod.

Thus it becomes clear that all living powers are cognate, and that all living forms are fundamentally of one character. The researches of the chemist have revealed a no less striking uniformity of material composition in living matter.

In perfect strictness, it is true that chemical investigation can tell us little or nothing, directly, of the composition of living matter, inasmuch as such matter must needs die in the act of analysis, —and upon this very obvious ground, objections, which I confess seem to me to be somewhat frivolous, have been raised to the drawing of any conclusions whatever respecting the composition of actually living matter, from that of the dead matter of life, which alone is accessible to us. But objectors of this class do not seem to reflect that it is also, in strictness, true that we know nothing about the composition of any body whatever, as it is. The statement that a crystal of calc-spar consists of carbonate of lime, is quite true, if we only mean that, by appropriate processes, it may be resolved into carbonic acid and quicklime. If you pass the same carbonic acid over the very quicklime thus obtained, you will obtain carbonate of lime again; but it will not be calc-spar, nor anything like it. Can it, therefore, be said that chemical analysis teaches nothing about the chemical composition of calc-spar? Such a statement would be absurd; but it is hardly more so than the talk one occasionally hears about the uselessness of applying the results of chemical analysis to the living bodies which have yielded them.

One fact, at any rate, is out of reach of such refinements, and this is, that all the forms of protoplasm which have yet been examined contain the four elements, carbon, hydrogen, oxygen, and nitrogen, in very complex union, and that they behave similarly towards several reagents. To this complex combination, the nature of which has never been determined with exactness, the name of Protein has been applied. And if we use this term with such caution as may properly arise out of our comparative ignorance of the things for which it stands, it may be truly said, that all protoplasm is proteinaceous, or, as the white, or albumen, of an egg is one of the commonest examples of a nearly pure protein matter, we may say that all living matter is more or less albuminoid.

Perhaps it would not yet be safe to say that all forms of protoplasm are affected by the direct action of electric shocks; and yet the number of cases in which the contraction of protoplasm is shown to be effected by this agency increases every day.

Nor can it be affirmed with perfect confidence, that all forms of protoplasm are liable to undergo that peculiar coagulation at a temperature of 40°–50° centigrade, which has been called "heat-stiffening," though Kühne's beautiful researches have proved this occurrence to take place in so many and such diverse living beings, that it is hardly rash to expect that the law holds good for all.

Enough has, perhaps, been said to prove the existence of a general uniformity in the character of the protoplasm, or physical basis, of life, in

---

[4] Heinrich Anton De Bary (1831–88), German botanist.

whatever group of living beings it may be studied. But it will be understood that this general uniformity by no means excludes any amount of special modifications of the fundamental substance. The mineral, carbonate of lime, assumes an immense diversity of characters, though no one doubts that, under all these Protean changes, it is one and the same thing.

And now, what is the ultimate fate, and what the origin, of the matter of life?

Is it, as some of the older naturalists supposed, diffused throughout the universe in molecules, which are indestructible and unchangeable in themselves; but, in endless transmigration, unite in innumerable permutations, into the diversified forms of life we know? Or is the matter of life composed of ordinary matter, differing from it only in the manner in which its atoms are aggregated? Is it built up of ordinary matter, and again resolved into ordinary matter when its work is done?

Modern science does not hesitate a moment between these alternatives. Physiology writes over the portals of life—

"Debemur morti nos nostraque,"[5]

with a profounder meaning than the Roman poet attached to that melancholy line. Under whatever disguise it takes refuge, whether fungus or oak, worm or man, the living protoplasm not only ultimately dies and is resolved into its mineral and lifeless constituents, but is always dying, and, strange as the paradox may sound, could not live unless it died.

In the wonderful story of the "Peau de Chagrin,"[6] the hero becomes possessed of a magical wild ass' skin, which yields him the means of gratifying all his wishes. But its surface represents the duration of the proprietor's life; and for every satisfied desire the skin shrinks in proportion to the intensity of fruition, until at length life and the last handbreadth of the *peau de chagrin* disappear with the gratification of a last wish.

Balzac's studies had led him over a wide range of thought and speculation, and his shadowing forth of physiological truth in this strange story may have been intentional. At any rate, the matter of life is a veritable *peau de chagrin*, and for every vital act it is somewhat the smaller. All work implies waste, and the work of life results, directly or indirectly, in the waste of protoplasm. Every word uttered by a speaker costs him some

physical loss; and, in the strictest sense, he burns that others may have light—so much eloquence, so much of his body resolved into carbonic acid, water, and urea. It is clear that this process of expenditure cannot go on for ever. But, happily, the protoplasmic *peau de chagrin* differs from Balzac's in its capacity of being repaired, and brought back to its full size, after every exertion.

For example, this present lecture, whatever its intellectual worth to you, has a certain physical value to me, which is, conceivably, expressible by the number of grains of protoplasm and other bodily substance wasted in maintaining my vital processes during its delivery. My *peau de chagrin* will be distinctly smaller at the end of the discourse than it was at the beginning. By and by, I shall probably have recourse to the substance commonly called mutton, for the purpose of stretching it back to its original size. Now this mutton was once the living protoplasm, more or less modified, of another animal—a sheep. As I shall eat it, it is the same matter altered, not only by death, but by exposure to sundry artificial operations in the process of cooking.

But these changes, whatever be their extent, have not rendered it incompetent to resume its old functions as matter of life. A singular inward laboratory, which I possess, will dissolve a certain portion of the modified protoplasm; the solution so formed will pass into my veins; and the subtle influences to which it will then be subjected will convert the dead protoplasm into living protoplasm, and transubstantiate sheep into man.

Nor is this all. If digestion were a thing to be trifled with, I might sup upon lobster, and the matter of life of the crustacean would undergo the same wonderful metamorphosis into humanity. And were I to return to my own place by sea, and undergo shipwreck, the crustacea might, and probably would, return the compliment, and demonstrate our common nature by turning my protoplasm into living lobster. Or, if nothing better were to be had, I might supply my wants with mere bread, and I should find the protoplasm of the wheat-plant to be convertible into man, with no more trouble than that of the sheep, and with far less, I fancy, than that of the lobster.

Hence it appears to be a matter of no great moment what animal, or what plant, I lay under contribution for protoplasm, and the fact speaks volumes for the general identity of that substance in all living beings. I share this catholicity of

---

[5] "We owe ourselves and what we have to death."   [6] Literally, "the skin of grief."

assimilation with other animals, all of which, so far as we know, could thrive equally well on the protoplasm of any of their fellows, or of any plant; but here the assimilative powers of the animal world cease. A solution of smelling-salts in water, with an infinitesimal proportion of some other saline matters, contains all the elementary bodies which enter into the composition of protoplasm; but, as I need hardly say, a hogshead of that fluid would not keep a hungry man from starving, nor would it save any animal whatever from a like fate. An animal cannot make protoplasm, but must take it ready-made from some other animal, or some plant—the animal's highest feat of constructive chemistry being to convert dead protoplasm into that living matter of life which is appropriate to itself.

Therefore, in seeking for the origin of protoplasm, we must eventually turn to the vegetable world. The fluid containing carbonic acid, water, and ammonia, which offers such a Barmecide feast to the animal, is a table richly spread to multitudes of plants; and, with a due supply of only such materials, many a plant will not only maintain itself in vigour, but grow and multiply until it has increased a million-fold, or a million million-fold, the quantity of protoplasm which it originally possessed; in this way building up the matter of life, to an indefinite extent, from the common matter of the universe.

Thus, the animal can only raise the complex substance of dead protoplasm, to the higher power, as one may say, of living protoplasm; while the plant can raise the less complex substances—carbonic acid, water, and ammonia—to the same stage of living protoplasm, if not to the same level. But the plant also has its limitations. Some of the fungi, for example, appear to need higher compounds to start with; and no known plant can live upon the uncompounded elements of protoplasm. A plant supplied with pure carbon, hydrogen, oxygen, and nitrogen, phosphorus, sulphur, and the like, would as infallibly die as the animal in his bath of smelling-salts, though it would be surrounded by all the constituents of protoplasm. Nor, indeed, need the process of simplification of vegetable food be carried so far as this, in order to arrive at the limit of the plant's thaumaturgy. Let water, carbonic acid, and all the other needful constituents be supplied with ammonia, and an ordinary plant will still be unable to manufacture protoplasm.

Thus the matter of life, so far as we know it (and we have no right to speculate on any other), breaks up, in consequence of that continual death which is the condition of its manifesting vitality, into carbonic acid, water, and ammonia, which certainly possess no properties but those of ordinary matter. And out of these same forms of ordinary matter, and from none which are simpler, the vegetable world builds up all the protoplasm which keeps the animal world a-going. Plants are the accumulators of the power which animals distribute and disperse.

But it will be observed, that the existence of the matter of life depends on the pre-existence of certain compounds; namely, carbonic acid, water, and ammonia. Withdraw any one of these three from the world, and all vital phænomena come to an end. They are related to the protoplasm of the plant, as the protoplasm of the plant is to that of the animal. Carbon, hydrogen, oxygen, and nitrogen are all lifeless bodies. Of these, carbon and oxygen unite, in certain proportions and under certain conditions, to give rise to carbonic acid; hydrogen and oxygen produce water; nitrogen and hydrogen give rise to ammonia. These new compounds, like the elementary bodies of which they are composed, are lifeless. But when they are brought together, under certain conditions they give rise to the still more complex body, protoplasm, and this protoplasm exhibits the phænomena of life.

I see no break in this series of steps in molecular complication, and I am unable to understand why the language which is applicable to any one term of the series may not be used to any of the others. We think fit to call different kinds of matter carbon, oxygen, hydrogen, and nitrogen, and to speak of the various powers and activities of these substances as the properties of the matter of which they are composed.

When hydrogen and oxygen are mixed in a certain proportion, and an electric spark is passed through them, they disappear, and a quantity of water, equal in weight to the sum of their weights, appears in their place. There is not the slightest parity between the passive and active powers of the waters and those of the oxygen and hydrogen which have given rise to it. At 32° Fahrenheit, and far below that temperature, oxygen and hydrogen are elastic gaseous bodies, whose particles tend to rush away from one another with great force. Water, at the same temperature, is a strong though brittle solid, whose particles tend to cohere into definite geometrical shapes, and sometimes build up frosty imitations of the most complex forms of vegetable foliage.

Nevertheless we call these, and many other

strange phænomena, the properties of the water, and we do not hesitate to believe that, in some way or another, they result from the properties of the component elements of the water. We do not assume that a something called "aquosity" entered into and took possession of the oxide of hydrogen as soon as it was formed, and then guided the aqueous particles to their places in the facets of the crystal, or amongst the leaflets of the hoar-frost. On the contrary, we live in the hope and in the faith that, by the advance of molecular physics, we shall by and by be able to see our way as clearly from the constituents of water to the properties of water, as we are now able to deduce the operations of a watch from the form of its parts and the manner in which they are put together.

Is the case in any way changed when carbonic acid, water, and ammonia disappear, and in their place, under the influence of pre-existing living protoplasm, an equivalent weight of the matter of life makes its appearance?

It is true that there is no sort of parity between the properties of the components and the properties of the resultant, but neither was there in the case of the water. It is also true that what I I have spoken of as the influence of pre-existing living matter is something quite unintelligible; but does anybody quite comprehend the *modus operandi* of an electric spark, which traverses a mixture of oxygen and hydrogen?

What justification is there, then, for the assumption of the existence in the living matter of a something which has no representative, or correlative, in the not living matter which gave rise to it? What better philosophical status has "vitality" than "aquosity"? And why should "vitality" hope for a better fate than the other "itys" which have disappeared since Martinus Scriblerus accounted for the operation of the meat-jack by its inherent "meat-roasting quality", and scorned the "materialism" of those who explained the turning of the spit by a certain mechanism worked by the draught of the chimney?

If scientific language is to possess a definite and constant signification whenever it is employed, it seems to me that we are logically bound to apply to the protoplasm, or physical basis of life, the same conceptions as those which are held to be legitimate elsewhere. If the phænomena exhibited by water are its properties, so are those presented by protoplasm, living or dead, its properties.

If the properties of water may be properly said to result from the nature and disposition of its component molecules, I can find no intelligible

ground for refusing to say that the properties of protoplasm result from the nature and disposition of its molecules.

But I bid you beware that, in accepting these conclusions, you are placing your feet on the first rung of a ladder which, in most people's estimation, is the reverse of Jacob's, and leads to the antipodes of heaven. It may seem a small thing to admit that the dull vital actions of a fungus, or a foraminifer, are the properties of their protoplasm, and are the direct results of the nature of the matter of which they are composed. But if, as I have endeavoured to prove to you, their protoplasm is essentially identical with, and most readily converted into, that of any animal, I can discover no logical halting-place between the admission that such is the case, and the further concession that all vital action may, with equal propriety, be said to be the result of the molecular forces of the protoplasm which displays it. And if so, it must be true, in the same sense and to the same extent, that the thoughts to which I am now giving utterance, and your thoughts regarding them, are the expression of molecular changes in that matter of life which is the source of our other vital phænomena.

Past experience leads me to be tolerably certain that, when the propositions I have just placed before you are accessible to public comment and criticism, they will be condemned by many zealous persons, and perhaps by some few of the wise and thoughtful. I should not wonder if "gross and brutal materialism" were the mildest phrase applied to them in certain quarters. And, most undoubtedly, the terms of the propositions are distinctly materialistic. Nevertheless two things are certain: the one, that I hold the statements to be substantially true; the other, that I, individually, am no materialist, but, on the contrary, believe materialism to involve grave philosophical error.

This union of materialistic terminology with the repudiation of materialistic philosophy I share with some of the most thoughtful men with whom I am acquainted. And, when I first undertook to deliver the present discourse, it appeared to me to be a fitting opportunity to explain how such a union is not only consistent with, but necessitated by, sound logic. I purposed to lead you through the territory of vital phænomena to the materialistic slough in which you find yourselves now plunged, and then to point out to you the sole path by which, in my judgment, extrication is possible.

An occurrence of which I was unaware until my arrival here last night renders this line of argument singularly opportune. I found in your papers the eloquent address "On the Limits of Philosophical Inquiry," which a distinguished prelate of the English Church delivered before the members of the Philosophical Institution on the previous day.[7] My argument, also, turns upon this very point of the limits of philosophical inquiry; and I cannot bring out my own views better than by contrasting them with those so plainly and, in the main, fairly stated by the Archbishop of York.

But I may be permitted to make a preliminary comment upon an occurrence that greatly astonished me. Applying the name of the "New Philosophy" to that estimate of the limits of philosophical inquiry which I, in common with many other men of science, hold to be just, the Archbishop opens his address by identifying this "New Philosophy" with the Positive Philosophy of M. Comte (of whom he speaks as its "founder"); and then proceeds to attack that philosopher and his doctrines vigorously.

Now, so far as I am concerned, the most reverend prelate might dialectically hew M. Comte in pieces, as a modern Agag, and I should not attempt to stay his hand. In so far as my study of what specially characterises the Positive Philosophy has led me, I find therein little or nothing of any scientific value, and a great deal which is as thoroughly antagonistic to the very essence of science as anything in ultramontane Catholicism. In fact, M. Comte's philosophy in practice might be compendiously described as Catholicism *minus* Christianity.

But what has Comtism to do with the "New Philosophy," as the Archbishop defines it in the following passage?

"Let me briefly remind you of the leading principles of this new philosophy.

"All knowledge is experience of facts acquired by the senses. The traditions of older philosophies have obscured our experience by mixing with it much that the senses cannot observe, and until these additions are discarded our knowledge is impure. Thus metaphysics tell us that one fact which we observe is a cause, and another is the effect of that cause; but, upon a rigid analysis, we find that our senses observe nothing of cause or effect: they observe, first, that one fact succeeds another, and, after some opportunity, that this fact has never failed to follow—that for cause and effect we

should substitute invariable succession. An older philosophy teaches us to define an object by distinguishing its essential from its accidental qualities: but experience knows nothing of essential and accidental; she sees only that certain marks attach to an object, and, after many observations, that some of them attach invariably, whilst others may at times be absent. . . . . . As all knowledge is relative, the notion of anything being necessary must be banished with other traditions."[8]

There is much here that expresses the spirit of the "New Philosophy," if by that term be meant the spirit of modern science; but I cannot but marvel that the assembled wisdom and learning of Edinburgh should have uttered no sign of dissent, when Comte was declared to be the founder of these doctrines. No one will accuse Scotchmen of habitually forgetting their great countrymen; but it was enough to make David Hume turn in his grave, that here, almost within earshot of his house, an instructed audience should have listened, without a murmur, while his most characteristic doctrines were attributed to a French writer of fifty years later date, in whose dreary and verbose pages we miss alike the vigour of thought and the exquisite clearness of style of the man whom I make bold to term the most acute thinker of the eighteenth century—even though that century produced Kant.

But I did not come to Scotland to vindicate the honour of one of the greatest men she has ever produced. My business is to point out to you that the only way of escape out of the crass materialism in which we just now landed, is the adoption and strict working-out of the very principles which the Archbishop holds up to reprobation.

Let us suppose that knowledge is absolute, and not relative, and therefore, that our conception of matter represents that which it really is. Let us suppose, further, that we do know more of cause and effect than a certain definite order of succession among facts, and that we have a knowledge of the necessity of that succession—and hence, of necessary laws—and I, for my part, do not see what escape there is from utter materialism and necessarianism. For it is obvious that our knowledge of what we call the material world is, to begin with, at least as certain and definite as that of the spiritual world, and that our acquaintance with law is of as old a date as our knowledge of spontaneity. Further, I take it to be demonstrable that it is utterly impossible to prove that any-

---

[7] See note 1.
[8] "The Limits of Philosophical Inquiry," pp. 4 and 5. [Huxley's note] (The dots are Huxley's.)

thing whatever may not be the effect of a material and necessary cause, and that human logic is equally incompetent to prove that any act is really spontaneous. A really spontaneous act is one which, by the assumption, has no cause; and the attempt to prove such a negative as this is, on the face of the matter, absurd. And while it is thus a philosophical impossibility to demonstrate that any given phænomenon is not the effect of a material cause, any one who is acquainted with the history of science will admit, that its progress has, in all ages, meant, and now, more than ever, means, the extension of the province of what we call matter and causation, and the concomitant gradual banishment from all regions of human thought of what we call spirit and spontaneity.

I have endeavoured, in the first part of this discourse, to give you a conception of the direction towards which modern physiology is tending; and I ask you, what is the difference between the conception of life as the product of a certain disposition of material molecules, and the old notion of an Archæus governing and directing blind matter within each living body, except this—that here, as elsewhere, matter and law have devoured spirit and spontaneity? And as surely as every future grows out of past and present, so will the physiology of the future gradually extend the realm of matter and law until it is co-extensive with knowledge, with feeling, and with action.

The consciousness of this great truth weighs like a nightmare, I believe, upon many of the best minds of these days. They watch what they conceive to be the progress of materialism, in such fear and powerless anger as a savage feels, when, during an eclipse, the great shadow creeps over the face of the sun. The advancing tide of matter threatens to drown their souls; the tightening grasp of law impedes their freedom; they are alarmed lest man's moral nature be debased by the increase of his wisdom.

If the "New Philosophy" be worthy of the reprobation with which it is visited, I confess their fears seem to me to be well founded. While, on the contrary, could David Hume be consulted, I think he would smile at their perplexities, and chide them for doing even as the heathen, and falling down in terror before the hideous idols their own hands have raised.

For, after all, what do we know of this terrible "matter," except as a name for the unknown and hypothetical cause of states of our own consciousness? And what do we know of that "spirit" over whose threatened extinction by matter a great lamentation is arising, like that which was heard

at the death of Pan, except that it is also a name for an unknown and hypothetical cause, or condition, of states of consciousness? In other words, matter and spirit are but names for the imaginary substrata of groups of natural phænomena.

And what is the dire necessity and "iron" law under which men groan? Truly, most gratuitously invented bugbears. I suppose if there be an "iron" law, it is that of gravitation; and if there be a physical necessity, it is that a stone, unsupported, must fall to the ground. But what is all we really know, and can know, about the latter phænomenon? Simply, that, in all human experience, stones have fallen to the ground under these conditions; that we have not the smallest reason for believing that any stone so circumstanced will not fall to the ground; and that we have, on the contrary, every reason to believe that it will so fall. It is very convenient to indicate that all the conditions of belief have been fulfilled in this case, by calling the statement that unsupported stones will fall to the ground, "a law of nature." But when, as commonly happens, we change *will* into *must*, we introduce an idea of necessity which most assuredly does not lie in the observed facts, and has no warranty that I can discover elsewhere. For my part, I utterly repudiate and anathematize the intruder. Fact I know; and Law I know; but what is this Necessity, save an empty shadow of my own mind's throwing?

But, if it is certain that we can have no knowledge of the nature of either matter or spirit, and that the notion of necessity is something illegitimately thrust into the perfectly legitimate conception of law, the materialistic position that there is nothing in the world but matter, force, and necessity, is as utterly devoid of justification as the most baseless of theological dogmas. The fundamental doctrines of materialism, like those of spiritualism, and most other "isms," lie outside "the limits of philosophical inquiry," and David Hume's great service to humanity is his irrefragable demonstration of what these limits are. Hume called himself a sceptic, and therefore others cannot be blamed if they apply the same title to him; but that does not alter the fact that the name, with its existing implications, does him gross injustice.

If a man asks me what the politics of the inhabitants of the moon are, and I reply that I do not know; that neither I, nor any one else, have any means of knowing; and that, under these circumstances, I decline to trouble myself about the subject at all, I do not think he has any right to call me a sceptic. On the contrary, in replying thus, I conceive that I am simply honest and truthful, and show a proper regard for the economy of time. So Hume's strong and subtle intellect takes up a great many problems about which we are naturally curious, and shows us that they are essentially questions of lunar politics, in their essence incapable of being answered, and therefore not worth the attention of men who have work to do in the world. And he thus ends one of his essays:—

"If we take in hand any volume of Divinity, or school metaphysics, for instance, let us ask, *Does it contain any abstract reasoning concerning quantity or number?* No. *Does it contain any experimental reasoning concerning matter of fact and existence?* No. Commit it then to the flames; for it can contain nothing but sophistry and illusion."[9]

Permit me to enforce this most wise advice. Why trouble ourselves about matters of which, however important they may be, we do know nothing, and can know nothing? We live in a world which is full of misery and ignorance, and the plain duty of each and all of us is to try to make the little corner he can influence somewhat less miserable and somewhat less ignorant than it was before he entered it. To do this effectually it is necessary to be fully possessed of only two beliefs: the first, that the order of nature is ascertainable by our faculties to an extent which is practically unlimited; the second, that our volition counts for something as a condition of the course of events.

Each of these beliefs can be verified experimentally, as often as we like to try. Each, therefore, stands upon the strongest foundation upon which any belief can rest, and forms one of our highest truths. If we find that the ascertainment of the order of nature is facilitated by using one terminology, or one set of symbols, rather than another, it is our clear duty to use the former; and no harm can accrue, so long as we bear in mind, that we are dealing merely with terms and symbols.

In itself it is of little moment whether we express the phænomena of matter in terms of spirit; or the phænomena of spirit, in terms of matter: matter may be regarded as a form of thought, thought may be regarded as a property of matter —each statement has a certain relative truth. But with a view to the progress of science, the materialistic terminology is in every way to be preferred. For it connects thought with the other phænomena of the universe, and suggests inquiry into the nature of those physical conditions, or concomitants of thought, which are more or less accessible to us, and a knowledge of which may, in future, help us to exercise the same kind of control over the world of thought, as we already possess in respect of the material world; whereas, the alternative, or spiritualistic, terminology is utterly barren, and leads to nothing but obscurity and confusion of ideas.

Thus there can be little doubt, that the further science advances, the more extensively and consistently will all the phænomena of nature be represented by materialistic formulæ and symbols.

But the man of science, who, forgetting the limits of philosophical inquiry, slides from these formulæ and symbols into what is commonly understood by materialism, seems to me to place himself on a level with the mathematician, who should mistake the x's and y's with which he works his problems, for real entities—and with this further disadvantage, as compared with the mathematician, that the blunders of the latter are of no practical consequence, while the errors of systematic materialism may paralyse the energies and destroy the beauty of a life.

from Science and Education

Science and Education *contains Huxley's essays advocating a larger, indeed a commanding, role for science in the education of the future. The collection was published after Huxley's death. The main essay from the collection, "Science and Culture" (also known as "Science and Education") is Huxley's most highly regarded statement in defense of the new scientific education. It was first delivered as an address on the opening in October of 1880 of Sir Josiah Mason's*

[9] Hume's Essay "Of the Academical or Sceptical Philosophy," in the "Inquiry concerning the Human Understanding." [Huxley's note]

Science College in Birmingham, the institution that later became the University of Birmingham. It is this essay to which Matthew Arnold makes reference in his American discourse, "Literature and Science."

Science and Culture

Six years ago, as some of my present hearers may remember, I had the privilege of addressing a large assemblage of the inhabitants of this city, who had gathered together to do honor to the memory of their famous townsman, Joseph Priestly; and, if any satisfaction attaches to posthumous glory, we may hope that the manes of the burned-out philosopher were then finally appeased.

No man, however, who is endowed with a fair share of common-sense, and not more than a fair share of vanity, will identify either contemporary or posthumous fame with the highest good; and Priestley's life leaves no doubt that he, at any rate, set a much higher value upon the advancement of knowledge, and the promotion of that freedom of thought which is at once the cause and the consequence of intellectual progress.

Hence I am disposed to think that, if Priestley could be among us to-day, the occasion of our meeting would afford him even greater pleasure than the proceedings which celebrated the centenary of his chief discovery. The kindly heart would be moved, the high sense of social duty would be satisfied, by the spectacle of well-earned wealth, neither squandered in tawdry luxury and vainglorious show, nor scattered with the careless charity which blesses neither him that gives nor him that takes, but expended in the execution of a well-considered plan for the aid of present and future generations of those who are willing to help themselves.

We shall all be of one mind thus far. But it is needful to share Priestley's keen interest in physical science; and to have learned, as he had learned, the value of scientific training in fields of inquiry apparently far remote from physical science; in order to appreciate, as he would have appreciated, the value of the noble gift which Sir Josiah Mason has bestowed upon the inhabitants of the Midland district.

For us children of the nineteenth century, however, the establishment of a college under the conditions of Sir Josiah Mason's Trust, has a significance apart from any which it could have possessed a hundred years ago. It appears to be an indication that we are reaching the crisis of the battle, or rather of the long series of battles, which have been fought over education in a campaign which began long before Priestley's time, and will probably not be finished just yet.

In the last century, the combatants were the champions of ancient literature on the one side, and those of modern literature on the other; but, some thirty years[1] ago, the contest became complicated by the appearance of a third army, ranged round the banner of Physical Science.

I am not aware that any one has authority to speak in the name of this new host. For it must be admitted to be somewhat of a guerilla force, composed largely of irregulars, each of whom fights pretty much for his own hand. But the impressions of a full private, who has seen a good deal of service in the ranks, respecting the present position of affairs and the conditions of a permanent peace, may not be devoid of interest; and I do not know that I could make a better use of the present opportunity than by laying them before you.

From the time that the first suggestion to introduce physical science into ordinary education was timidly whispered, until now, the advocates of scientific education have met with opposition of two kinds. On the one hand, they have been pooh-poohed by the men of business who pride themselves on being the representatives of practicality; while, on the other hand, they have been excommunicated by the classical scholars, in their capacity of Levites in charge of the ark of culture and monopolists of liberal education.

The practical men believed that the idol whom they worship—rule of thumb—has been the source of the past prosperity, and will suffice for the future welfare of the arts and manufactures. They were of opinion that science is

[1] The advocacy of the introduction of physical science into general education by George Combe and others commenced a good deal earlier; but the movement had acquired hardly any practical force before the time to which I refer. [Huxley's note]

speculative rubbish; that theory and practice have nothing to do with one another; and that the scientific habit of mind is an impediment, rather than an aid, in the conduct of ordinary affairs.

I have used the past tense in speaking of the practical men—for although they were very formidable thirty years ago, I am not sure that the pure species has not been extirpated. In fact, so far as mere argument goes, they have been subjected to such a *feu d'enfer*[2] that it is a miracle if any have escaped. But I have remarked that your typical practical man has an unexpected resemblance to one of Milton's angels. His spiritual wounds, such as are inflicted by logical weapons, may be as deep as a well and as wide as a church door, but beyond shedding a few drops of ichor, celestial or otherwise, he is no whit the worse. So, if any of these opponents be left, I will not waste time in vain repetition of the demonstrative evidence of the practical value of science; but knowing that a parable will sometimes penetrate where syllogisms fail to effect an entrance, I will offer a story for their consideration.

Once upon a time, a boy,[3] with nothing to depend upon but his own vigorous nature, was thrown into the thick of the struggle for existence in the midst of a great manufacturing population. He seems to have had a hard fight, inasmuch as, by the time he was thirty years of age, his total disposable funds amounted to twenty pounds. Nevertheless, middle life found him giving proof of his comprehension of the practical problems he had been roughly called upon to solve, by a career of remarkable prosperity.

Finally, having reached old age with its well-earned surroundings of "honor, troops of friends," the hero of my story bethought himself of those who were making a like start in life, and how he could stretch out a helping hand to them.

After long and anxious reflection, this successful practical man of business could devise nothing better than to provide them with the means of obtaining "sound, extensive, and practical scientific knowledge." And he devoted a large part of his wealth and five years of incessant work to this end.

I need not point the moral of a tale which, as the solid and spacious fabric of the Scientific College assures us, is no fable, nor can anything which I could say intensify the force of this practical answer to practical objections.

We may take it for granted then that, in the opinion of those best qualified to judge, the diffusion of thorough scientific education is an absolutely essential condition of industrial progress; and that the College which has been opened to-day will confer an inestimable boon upon those whose livelihood is to be gained by the practice of the arts and manufactures of the district.

The only question worth discussion is, whether the conditions, under which the work of the College is to be carried out, are such as to give it the best possible chance of achieving permanent success.

Sir Josiah Mason, without doubt most wisely, has left very large freedom of action to the trustees, to whom he proposes ultimately to commit the administration of the College, so that they may be able to adjust its arrangements in accordance with the changing conditions of the future. But, with respect to three points he has laid most explicit injunctions upon both administrators and teachers.

Party politics are forbidden to enter into the minds of either, so far as the work of the College is concerned; theology is as sternly banished from its precincts; and finally, it is especially declared that the College shall make no provision for "mere literary instruction and education."

It does not concern me at present to dwell upon the first two injunctions any longer than may be needful to express my full conviction of their wisdom. But the third prohibition brings us face to face with those other opponents of scientific education, who are by no means in the moribund condition of the practical man, but alive, alert, and formidable.

It is not impossible that we shall hear this express exclusion of "literary instruction and education" from a College which, nevertheless, professes to give a high and efficient education, sharply criticised. Certainly the time was that the Levites of culture would have sounded their trumpets against its walls as against an educational Jericho.

How often have we not been told that the study of physical science is incompetent to confer culture; that it touches none of the higher problems of life; and, what is worse, that the continual devotion to scientific studies tends to generate a narrow and bigoted belief in the applicability of scientific methods to the search after truth of all kinds? How frequently one has

---

[2] Fire of hell.   [3] Josiah Mason (1795–1881), the subject of the following paragraphs.

reason to observe that no reply to a troublesome argument tells so well as calling its author a "mere scientific specialist." And, as I am afraid it is not permissible to speak of this form of opposition to scientific education in the past tense, may we not expect to be told that this, not only omission, but prohibition, of "mere literary instruction and education" is a patent example of scientific narrow-mindedness?

I am not acquainted with Sir Josiah Mason's reasons for the action which he has taken; but if, as I apprehend is the case, he refers to the ordinary classical course of our schools and universities by the name of "mere literary instruction and education," I venture to offer sundry reasons of my own in support of that action.

For I hold very strongly by two convictions— The first is, that neither the discipline nor the subject-matter of classical education is of such direct value to the student of physical science as to justify the expenditure of valuable time upon either; and the second is, that for the purpose of attaining real culture, an exclusively scientific education is at least as effectual as an exclusively literary education.

I need hardly point out to you that these opinions, especially the latter, are diametrically opposed to those of the great majority of educated Englishmen, influenced as they are by school and university traditions. In their belief, culture is obtainable only by a liberal education; and a liberal education is synonymous, not merely with education and instruction in literature, but in one particular form of literature, namely, that of Greek and Roman antiquity. They hold that the man who has learned Latin and Greek, however little, is educated; while he who is versed in other branches of knowledge, however deeply, is a more or less respectable specialist, not admissible into the cultured caste. The stamp of the educated man, the University degree, is not for him.

I am too well acquainted with the generous catholicity of spirit, the true sympathy with scientific thought, which pervades the writings of our chief apostle of culture[4] to identify him with these opinions; and yet one may cull from one and another of those epistles to the Philistines, which so much delight all who do not answer to that name, sentences which lend them some support.

Mr. Arnold tells us that the meaning of culture is "to know the best that has been thought and said in the world." It is the criticism of life contained in literature. That criticism regards "Europe as being, for intellectual and spiritual purposes, one great confederation, bound to a joint action and working to a common result; and whose members have, for their common outfit, a knowledge of Greek, Roman, and Eastern antiquity, and of one another. Special, local, and temporary advantages being put out of account, that modern nation will in the intellectual and spiritual sphere make most progress which most thoroughly carries out this programme. And what is that but saying that we too, all of us, as individuals, the more thoroughly we carry it out, shall make the more progress?"[5]

We have here to deal with two distinct propositions. The first, that a criticism of life is the essence of culture; the second, that literature contains the materials which suffice for the construction of such a criticism.

I think that we must all assent to the first proposition. For culture certainly means something quite different from learning or technical skill. It implies the possession of an ideal, and the habit of critically estimating the value of things by comparison with a theoretic standard. Perfect culture should supply a complete theory of life, based upon a clear knowledge alike of its possibilities and of its limitations.

But we may agree to all this, and yet strongly dissent from the assumption that literature alone is competent to supply this knowledge. After having learned all that Greek, Roman, and Eastern antiquity have thought and said, and all that modern literatures have to tell us, it is not self-evident that we have laid a sufficiently broad and deep foundation for that criticism of life, which constitutes culture.

Indeed, to any one acquainted with the scope of physical science, it is not at all evident. Considering progress only in the "intellectual and spiritual sphere," I find myself wholly unable to admit that either nations or individuals will really advance, if their common outfit draws nothing from the stores of physical science. I should say that an army, without weapons of precision and with no particular base of operations, might more hopefully enter upon a campaign on the Rhine, than a man, devoid of a knowledge of what physical science has done in the last century, upon a criticism of life.

When a biologist meets with an anomaly, he

---

[4] Matthew Arnold.   [5] "Essays in Criticism," page 37. [Huxley's note]

instinctively turns to the study of development to clear it up. The rationale of contradictory opinions may with equal confidence be sought in history.

It is, happily, no new thing that Englishmen should employ their wealth in building and endowing institutions for educational purposes. But, five or six hundred years ago, deeds of foundation expressed or implied conditions as nearly as possible contrary to those which have been thought expedient by Sir Josiah Mason. That is to say, physical science was practically ignored, while a certain literary training was enjoined as a means to the acquirement of knowledge which was essentially theological.

The reason of this singular contradiction between the actions of men alike animated by a strong and disinterested desire to promote the welfare of their fellows, is easily discovered.

At that time, in fact, if any one desired knowledge beyond such as could be obtained by his own observation, or by common conversation, his first necessity was to learn the Latin language, inasmuch as all the higher knowledge of the western world was contained in works written in that language. Hence, Latin grammar, with logic and rhetoric, studied through Latin, were the fundamentals of education. With respect to the substance of the knowledge imparted through this channel, the Jewish and Christian Scriptures, as interpreted and supplemented by the Romish Church, were held to contain a complete and infallibly true body of information.

Theological dicta were, to the thinkers of those days, that which the axioms and definitions of Euclid are to the geometers of these. The business of the philosophers of the Middle Ages was to deduce, from the data furnished by the theologians, conclusions in accordance with ecclesiastical decrees. They were allowed the high privilege of showing, by logical process, how and why that which the Church said was true, must be true. And if their demonstrations fell short of or exceeded this limit, the Church was maternally ready to check their aberrations; if need were by the help of the secular arm.

Between the two, our ancestors were furnished with a compact and complete criticism of life. They were told how the world began and how it would end; they learned that all material existence was but a base and insignificant blot upon the fair face of the spiritual world, and that nature was, to all intents and purposes, the playground of the devil; they learned that the earth is the centre of the visible universe, and

that man is the cynosure of things terrestrial; and more especially was it inculcated that the course of nature had no fixed order, but that it could be, and constantly was, altered by the agency of innumerable spiritual beings, good and bad, according as they were moved by the deeds and prayers of men. The sum and substance of the whole doctrine was to produce the conviction that the only thing really worth knowing in this world was how to secure that place in a better which, under certain conditions, the Church promised.

Our ancestors had a living belief in this theory of life, and acted upon it in their dealings with education, as in all other matters. Culture meant saintliness—after the fashion of the saints of those days; the education that led to it was, of necessity, theological; and the way to theology lay through Latin.

That the study of nature—further than was requisite for the satisfaction of every-day wants—should have any bearing on human life was far from the thoughts of men thus trained. Indeed, as nature had been cursed for man's sake, it was an obvious conclusion that those who meddled with nature were likely to come into pretty close contact with Satan. And, if any born scientific investigator followed his instincts, he might safely reckon upon earning the reputation, and probably upon suffering the fate, of a sorcerer.

Had the western world been left to itself in Chinese isolation, there is no saying how long this state of things might have endured. But, happily, it was not left to itself. Even earlier than the thirteenth century, the development of Moorish civilization in Spain and the great movement of the Crusades had introduced the leaven which, from that day to this, has never ceased to work. At first, through the intermediation of Arabic translations, afterward by the study of the originals, the western nations of Europe became acquainted with the writings of the ancient philosophers and poets, and, in time, with the whole of the vast literature of antiquity.

Whatever there was of high intellectual aspiration or dominant capacity in Italy, France, Germany and England, spent itself for centuries in taking possession of the rich inheritance left by the dead civilizations of Greece and Rome. Marvellously aided by the invention of printing, classical learning spread and flourished. Those who possessed it prided themselves on having attained the highest culture then within the reach of mankind.

And justly. For, saving Dante on his solitary pinnacle, there was no figure in modern literature at the time of the Renascence to compare with the men of antiquity; there was no art to compete with their sculpture; there was no physical science but that which Greece had created. Above all, there was no other example of perfect intellectual freedom—of the unhesitating acceptance of reason as the sole guide to truth and the supreme arbiter of conduct.

The new learning necessarily soon exerted a profound influence upon education. The language of the monks and schoolmen seemed little better than gibberish to scholars fresh from Virgil and Cicero, and the study of Latin was placed upon a new foundation. Moreover, Latin itself ceased to afford the sole key to knowledge. The student who sought the highest thought of antiquity found only a second-hand reflection of it in Roman literature, and turned his face to the full light of the Greeks. And after a battle, not altogether dissimilar to that which is at present being fought over the teaching of physical science, the study of Greek was recognized as an essential element of all higher education.

Thus the Humanists, as they were called, won the day; and the great reform which they effected was of incalculable service to mankind. But the Nemesis of all reformers is finality; and the reformers of education, like those of religion, fell into the profound, however common, error of mistaking the beginning for the end of the work of reformation.

The representatives of the Humanists, in the nineteenth century, take their stand upon classical education as the sole avenue to culture, as firmly as if we were still in the age of Renascence. Yet, surely, the present intellectual relations of the modern and the ancient worlds are profoundly different from those which obtained three centuries ago. Leaving aside the existence of a great and characteristically modern literature, of modern painting, and, especially, of modern music, there is one feature of the present state of the civilized world which separates it more widely from the Renascence, than the Renascence was separated from the Middle Ages.

This distinctive character of our own times lies in the vast and constantly increasing part which is played by natural knowledge. Not only is our daily life shaped by it, not only does the prosperity of millions of men depend upon it, but our whole theory of life has long been influenced, consciously or unconsciously, by the general conceptions of the universe, which have been forced upon us by physical science.

In fact, the most elementary acquaintance with the results of scientific investigation shows us that they offer a broad and striking contradiction to the opinion so implicitly credited and taught in the Middle Ages.

The notions of the beginning and the end of the world entertained by our forefathers are no longer credible. It is very certain that the earth is not the chief body in the material universe, and that the world is not subordinated to man's use. It is even more certain that nature is the expression of a definite order with which nothing interferes, and that the chief business of mankind is to learn that order and govern themselves accordingly. Moreover, this scientific "criticism of life" presents itself to us with different credentials from any other. It appeals not to authority, nor to what anybody may have thought or said, but to Nature. It admits that all our interpretations of natural fact are more or less imperfect and symbolic, and bids the learner seek for truth not among words but among things. It warns us that the assertion which outstrips evidence is not only a blunder but a crime.

The purely classical education advocated by the representatives of the Humanists in our day, gives no inkling of all this. A man may be a better scholar than Erasmus, and know no more of the chief causes of the present intellectual fermentation than Erasmus did. Scholarly and pious persons, worthy of all respect, favor us with allocutions upon the sadness of the antagonism of science to their medieval way of thinking, which betray an ignorance of the first principles of scientific investigation, an incapacity for understanding what a man of science means by veracity, and an unconsciousness of the weight of established scientific truths, which is almost comical.

There is no great force in the *tu quoque*[6] argument, or else the advocates of scientific education might fairly enough retort upon the modern Humanists that they may be learned specialists, but that they possess no such sound foundation for a criticism of life as deserves the name of culture. And, indeed, if we were disposed to be cruel, we might urge that the Humanists have brought this reproach upon themselves, not because they are too full of the spirit of the ancient Greek, but because they lack it.

[6] And you too.

The period of the Renascence is commonly called that of the "Revival of Letters," as if the influences then brought to bear upon the mind of Western Europe has been wholly exhausted in the field of literature. I think it is very commonly forgotten that the revival of science, effected by the same agency, although less conspicuous, was not less momentous.

In fact, the few and scattered students of nature of that day picked up the clew to her secrets exactly as it fell from the hands of the Greeks a thousand years before. The foundations of mathematics were so well laid by them that our children learn their geometry from a book written for the schools of Alexandria two thousand years ago. Modern astronomy is the natural continuation and development of the work of Hipparchus and of Ptolemy; modern physics of that of Democritus and of Archimedes; it was long before modern biological science outgrew the knowledge bequeathed to us by Aristotle, by Theophrastus, and by Galen.

We cannot know all the best thoughts and sayings of the Greeks unless we know what they thought about natural phenomena. We cannot fully apprehend their criticism of life unless we understand the extent to which that criticism was affected by scientific conceptions. We falsely pretend to be the inheritors of their culture, unless we are penetrated, as the best minds among them were, with an unhesitating faith that the free employment of reason, in accordance with scientific method, is the sole method of reaching truth.

Thus I venture to think that the pretensions of our modern Humanists to the possession of the monopoly of culture and to the exclusive inheritance of the spirit of antiquity must be abated, if not abandoned. But I should be very sorry that anything I have said should be taken to imply a desire on my part to depreciate the value of classical education, as it might be and as it sometimes is. The native capacities of mankind vary no less than their opportunities; and while culture is one, the road by which one man may best reach it is widely different from that which is most advantageous to another. Again, while scientific education is yet inchoate and tentative, classical education is thoroughly well organized upon the practical experience of generations of teachers. So that, given ample time for learning and destination for ordinary life, or for a literary career, I do not think that a young Englishman in search of culture can do better than follow the course usually marked out for him, supplementing its deficiencies by his own efforts.

But for those who mean to make science their serious occupation; or who intend to follow the profession of medicine; or who have to enter early upon the business of life; for all these, in my opinion, classical education is a mistake; and it is for this reason that I am glad to see "mere literary education and instruction" shut out from the curriculum of Sir Josiah Mason's College, seeing that its inclusion would probably lead to the introduction of the ordinary smattering of Latin and Greek.

Nevertheless, I am the last person to question the importance of genuine literary education, or to suppose that intellectual culture can be complete without it. An exclusively scientific training will bring about a mental twist as surely as an exclusively literary training. The value of the cargo does not compensate for a ship's being out of trim; and I should be very sorry to think that the Scientific College would turn out none but lopsided men.

There is no need, however, that such a catastrophe should happen. Instruction in English, French and German is provided, and thus the three greatest literatures of the modern world are made accessible to the student.

French and German, and especially the latter language, are absolutely indispensable to those who desire full knowledge in any department of science. But even supposing that the knowledge of these languages acquired is not more than sufficient for purely scientific purposes, every Englishman has, in his native tongue, an almost perfect instrument of literary expression; and, in his own literature, models of every kind of literary excellence. If an Englishman cannot get literary culture out of his Bible, his Shakespeare, his Milton, neither, in my belief, will the profoundest study of Homer and Sophocles, Virgil and Horace, give it to him.

Thus, since the constitution of the College makes sufficient provision for literary as well as for scientific education, and since artistic instruction is also contemplated, it seems to me that a fairly complete culture is offered to all who are willing to take advantage of it.

But I am not sure that at this point the "practical" man, scotched but not slain, may ask what all this talk about culture has to do with an Institution, the object of which is defined to be "to promote the prosperity of the manufactures and the industry of the country." He may suggest that what is wanted for this end is not culture, nor even a purely scientific discipline, but simply a knowledge of applied science.

I often wish that this phrase, "applied science," had never been invented. For it suggests that there is a sort of scientific knowledge of direct practical use, which can be studied apart from another sort of scientific knowledge, which is of no practical utility, and which is termed "pure science." But there is no more complete fallacy than this. What people call applied science is nothing but the application of pure science to particular classes of problems. It consists of deductions from those general principles, established by reasoning and observation, which constitute pure science. No one can safely make these deductions until he has a firm grasp of the principles; and he can obtain that grasp only by personal experience of the operations of observation and of reasoning on which they are founded.

Almost all the processes employed in the arts and manufactures fall within the range either of physics or of chemistry. In order to improve them, one must thoroughly understand them; and no one has a chance of really understanding them, unless he has obtained that mastery of principles and that habit of dealing with facts which is given by long-continued and well-directed purely scientific training in the physical and the chemical laboratory. So that there really is no question as to the necessity of purely scientific discipline, even if the work of the College were limited by the narrowest interpretation of its stated aims.

And, as to the desirableness of a wider culture than that yielded by science alone, it is to be recollected that the improvement of manufacturing processes is only one of the conditions which contribute to the prosperity of industry. Industry is a means and not an end; and mankind work only to get something which they want. What that something is depends partly on their innate, and partly on their acquired, desires.

If the wealth resulting from prosperous industry is to be spent upon the gratification of unworthy desires, if the increasing perfection of manufacturing processes is to be accompanied by an increasing debasement of those who carry them on, I do not see the good of industry and prosperity.

Now it is perfectly true that men's views of what is desirable depend upon their characters; and that the innate proclivities to which we give

that name are not touched by any amount of instruction. But it does not follow that even mere intellectual education may not, to an indefinite extent, modify the practical manifestation of the characters of men in their actions, by supplying them with motives unknown to the ignorant. A pleasure-loving character will have pleasure of some sort; but, if you give him the choice, he may prefer pleasures which do not degrade him to those which do. And this choice is offered to every man who possesses in literary or artistic culture a never-failing source of pleasures, which are neither withered by age, nor staled by custom, nor imbittered in the recollection by the pangs of self-reproach.

If the Institution opened to-day fulfils the intention of its founder, the picked intelligences among all classes of the population of this district will pass through it. No child born in Birmingham, henceforward, if he have the capacity to profit by the opportunities offered to him, first in the primary and other schools, and afterward in the Scientific College, need fail to obtain, not merely the instruction, but the culture most appropriate to the conditions of his life.

Within these walls, the future employer and the future artisan may sojourn together for a while, and carry, through all their lives, the stamp of the influences then brought to bear upon them. Hence, it is not beside the mark to remind you that the prosperity of industry depends not merely upon the improvement of manufacturing processes, not merely upon the ennobling of the individual character, but upon a third condition, namely, a clear understanding of the conditions of social life, on the part of both the capitalist and the operative, and their agreement upon common principles of social action. They must learn that social phenomena are as much the expression of natural laws as any others; that no social arrangements can be permanent unless they harmonize with the requirements of social statics and dynamics; and that, in the nature of things, there is an arbiter whose decisions execute themselves.

But this knowledge is only to be obtained by the application of the methods of investigation adopted in physical researches to the investigation of the phenomena of society. Hence, I confess, I should like to see one addition made to the excellent scheme of education propounded for the College, in the shape of provision for the teaching of Sociology. For though we are all agreed that party politics are to have no place in the instruction of the College; yet in this country, practically governed as it is now by universal suffrage, every man who does his duty must exercise political functions. And, if the evils which are inseperable from the good of political liberty are to be checked, if the perpetual oscillation of nations between anarchy and despotism is to be replaced by the steady march of self-restraining freedom; it will be because men will gradually bring themselves to deal with political, as they now deal with scientific questions; to be ashamed of undue haste and partisan prejudice in the one case as in the other; and to believe that the machinery of society is at least as delicate as that of a spinning-jenny, and as little likely to be improved by the meddling of those who have not taken the trouble to master the principles of its action.

In conclusion, I am sure that I make myself the mouthpiece of all present in offering to the venerable founder of the Institution, which now commences its beneficent career, our congratulations on the completion of his work; and in expressing the conviction that the remotest posterity will point to it as a crucial instance of the wisdom which natural piety leads all men to ascribe to their ancestors.

Autobiography

Huxley's "Autobiography" is a relatively short essay that was first published in the fourth volume of his Collected Essays *in 1893. It sets forth the central points of his early life, offering thereby a constructive comparison with the equally brief autobiographical reflections of Charles Darwin.*

And when I consider, in one view, the many things . . . . . which I have upon my hands, I feel the burlesque of being employed in this manner at my time of life. But, in another view, and taking in all circumstances, these things, as trifling as they may appear, no less than things of greater importance, seem to be put upon me to do. . . . . .—Bishop Butler to the Duchess of Somerset.

THE "many things" to which the Duchess's correspondent here refers are the repairs and improvements of the episcopal seat at Auckland. I doubt if the great apologist, greater in nothing than in the simple dignity of his character, would have considered the writing an account of himself as a thing which could be put upon him to do whatever circumstances might be taken in. But the good bishop lived in an age when a man might write books and yet be permitted to keep his private existence to himself; in the pre-Boswellian epoch, when the germ of the photographer lay in the womb of the distant future, and the interviewer who pervades our age was an unforeseen, indeed unimaginable, birth of time.

At present, the most convinced believer in the aphorism "Bene qui latuit, bene vixit,"[1] is not always able to act up to it. An importunate person informs him that his portrait is about to be published and will be accompanied by a biography which the importunate person proposes to write. The sufferer knows what that means; either he undertakes to revise the "biography" or he does not. In the former case, he makes himself responsible; in the latter, he allows the publication of a mass of more or less fulsome inaccuracies for which he will be held responsible by those who are familiar with the prevalent art of self-advertisement. On the whole, it may be better to get over the "burlesque of being employed in this manner" and do the thing himself.

It was by reflections of this kind that, some years ago, I was led to write and permit the publication of the subjoined sketch.

I was born about eight o'clock in the morning on the 4th of May, 1825, at Ealing, which was, at that time, as quiet a little country village as could be found within half-a-dozen miles of Hyde Park Corner. Now it is a suburb of London with, I believe, 30,000 inhabitants. My father was one of the masters in a large semi-public school which at one time had a high reputation. I am not aware

[1] "He who hides well his life, lives well" (Ovid).

that any portents preceded my arrival in this world, but, in my childhood, I remember hearing a traditional account of the manner in which I lost the chance of an endowment of great practical value. The windows of my mother's room were open, in consequence of the unusual warmth of the weather. For the same reason, probably, a neighbouring beehive had swarmed, and the new colony, pitching on the window-sill, was making its way into the room when the horrified nurse shut down the sash. If that well-meaning woman had only abstained from her ill-timed interference, the swarm might have settled on my lips, and I should have been endowed with that mellifluous eloquence which, in this country, leads far more surely than worth, capacity, or honest work, to the highest places in Church and State. But the opportunity was lost, and I have been obliged to content myself through life with saying what I mean in the plainest of plain language, than which, I suppose, there is no habit more ruinous to a man's prospects of advancement.

Why I was christened Thomas Henry I do not know; but it is a curious chance than my parents should have fixed for my usual denomination upon the name of that particular Apostle with whom I have always felt most sympathy. Physically and mentally I am the son of my mother so completely—even down to peculiar movements of the hands, which made their appearance in me as I reached the age she had when I noticed them—that I can hardly find any trace of my father in myself, except an inborn faculty for drawing, which unfortunately, in my case, has never been cultivated, a hot temper, and that amount of tenacity of purpose which unfriendly observers sometimes call obstinacy.

My mother was a slender brunette, of an emotional and energetic temperament, and possessed of the most piercing black eyes I ever saw in a woman's head. With no more education than other women of the middle classes in her day, she had an excellent mental capacity. Her most distinguishing characteristic, however, was rapidity of thought. If one ventured to suggest she had not taken much time to arrive at any conclusion, she would say, "I cannot help it, things flash across me." That peculiarity has been passed on to me in full strength; it has often stood me in good stead; it has sometimes played me sad tricks, and it has always been a danger. But, after all, if my time were to come over again, there is nothing I would less willingly part with than my inheritance of mother wit.

I have next to nothing to say about my childhood. In later years my mother, looking at me almost reproachfully, would sometimes say, "Ah! you were such a pretty boy!" whence I had no difficulty in concluding that I had not fulfilled my early promise in the matter of looks. In fact, I have a distinct recollection of certain curls of which I was vain, and of a conviction that I closely resembled that handsome, courtly gentleman, Sir Herbert Oakley, who as vicar of our parish, and who was as a god to us country folk, because he was occasionally visited by the then Prince George of Cambridge. I remember turning my pinafore wrong side forwards in order to represent a surplice, and preaching to my mother's maids in the kitchen as nearly as possible in Sir Herbert's manner one Sunday morning when the rest of the family were at church. That is the earliest indication I can call to mind of the strong clerical affinities which my friend Mr. Herbert Spencer has always ascribed to me, though I fancy they have for the most part remained in a latent state.

My regular school training was of the briefest, perhaps fortunately, for though my way of life has made me acquainted with all sorts and conditions of men, from the highest to the lowest, I deliberately affirm that the society I fell into at school was the worst I have ever known. We boys were average lads, with much the same inherent capacity for good and evil as any others; but the people who were set over us cared about as much for our intellectual and moral welfare as if they were baby-farmers. We were left to the operation of the struggle for existence among ourselves, and bullying was the least of the ill practices current among us. Almost the only cheerful reminiscence in connection with the place which arises in my mind is that of a battle I had with one of my classmates, who had bullied me until I could stand it no longer. I was a very slight lad, but there was a wild-cat element in me which, when roused, made up for lack of weight, and I licked my adversary effectually. However, one of my first experiences of the extremely rough-and-ready nature of justice, as exhibited by the course of things in general, arose out of the fact that I—the victor—had a black eye, while he—the vanquished—had none, so that I got into disgrace and he did not. We made it up, and thereafter I was unmolested. One of the greatest shocks I ever received in my life was to be told a dozen years afterwards by the groom who brought me my horse in a stable-yard in Sydney that he was my quondam antagonist. He had a long story of family misfortune to account for his position, but at that time it was necessary to deal very cautiously with mysterious strangers in New South Wales, and on inquiry I found that the unfortunate young man had not only been "sent out," but had undergone more than one colonial conviction.

As I grew older, my great desire was to be a mechanical engineer, but the fates were against this and, while very young, I commenced the study of medicine under a medical brother-in-law. But, though the Institute of Mechanical Engineers would certainly not own me, I am not sure that I have not all along been a sort of mechanical engineer *in partibus infidelium.*[2] I am now occasionally horrified to think how very little I ever knew or cared about medicine as the art of healing. The only part of my professional course which really and deeply interested me was physiology, which is the mechanical engineering of living machines; and, notwithstanding that natural science has been my proper business, I am afraid there is very little of the genuine naturalist in me. I never collected anything, and species work was always a burden to me; what I cared for was the architectural and engineering part of the business, the working out the wonderful unity of plan in the thousands and thousands of diverse living constructions, and the modifications of similar apparatuses to serve diverse ends. The extraordinary attraction I felt towards the study of the intricacies of living structure nearly proved fatal to me at the outset. I was a mere boy—I think between thirteen and fourteen years of age—when I was taken by some older student friends of mine to the first *post-mortem* examination I ever attended. All my life I have been most unfortunately sensitive to the disagreeables which attend anatomical pursuits, but on this occasion my curiosity overpowered all other feelings, and I spent two or three hours in gratifying it. I did not cut myself, and none of the ordinary symptoms of dissection-poison supervened, but poisoned I was somehow, and I remember sinking into a strange state of apathy. By way of a last chance, I was sent to the care of some good, kind people, friends of my father's, who lived in a farmhouse in the heart of Warwickshire. I remember staggering from my bed to the window on the bright spring morning after my arrival, and throwing open the casement. Life seemed to come back on the wings of the breeze,

and to this day the faint odour of wood-smoke, like that which floated across the farm-yard in the early morning, is as good to me as the "sweet south upon a bed of violets." I soon recovered, but for years I suffered from occasional paroxysms of internal pain, and from that time my constant friend, hypochondriacal dyspepsia, commenced his half century of co-tenancy of my fleshy tabernacle.

Looking back on my "Lehrjahre,"[3] I am sorry to say that I do not think that any account of my doings as a student would tend to edification. In fact, I should distinctly warn ingenuous youth to avoid imitating my example. I worked extremely hard when it pleased me, and when it did not—which was a very frequent case—I was extremely idle (unless making caricatures of one's pastors and masters is to be called a branch of industry), or else wasted my energies in wrong directions. I read everything I could lay hands upon, including novels, and took up all sorts of pursuits to drop them again quite as speedily. No doubt it was very largely my own fault, but the only instruction from which I ever obtained the proper effect of education was that which I received from Mr. Wharton Jones, who was the lecturer on physiology at the Charing Cross School of Medicine. The extent and precision of his knowledge impressed me greatly, and the severe exactness of his method of lecturing was quite to my taste. I do not know that I have ever felt so much respect for anybody as a teacher before or since. I worked hard to obtain his approbation, and he was extremely kind and helpful to the youngster who, I am afraid, took up more of his time than he had any right to do. It was he who suggested the publication of my first scientific paper—a very little one—in the *Medical Gazette* of 1845, and most kindly corrected the literary faults which abounded in it, short as it was; for at that time, and for many years afterwards, I detested the trouble of writing, and would take no pains over it.

It was in the early spring of 1846, that, having finished my obligatory medical studies and passed the first M.B. examination at the London University—though I was still too young to qualify at the College of Surgeons—I was talking to a fellow-student (the present eminent physician, Sir Joseph Fayrer), and wondering what I should do to meet the imperative necessity for earning my own bread, when my friend suggested that I should write to Sir William Burnett, at

---

[2] In the regions of the unfaithful.   [3] Learning years, apprentice years.

that time Director-General for the Medical Service of the Navy, for an appointment. I thought this rather a strong thing to do, as Sir William was personally unknown to me, but my cheery friend would not listen to my scruples, so I went to my lodgings and wrote the best letter I could devise. A few days afterwards I received the usual official circular of acknowledgment, but at the bottom there was written an instruction to call at Somerset House on such a day. I thought that looked like business, so at the appointed time I called and sent in my card, while I waited in Sir William's ante-room. He was a tall, shrewd-looking old gentleman, with a broad Scotch accent—and I think I see him now as he entered with my card in his hand. The first thing he did was to return it, with the frugal reminder that I should probably find it useful on some other occasion. The second was to ask whether I was an Irishman. I suppose the air of modesty about my appeal must have struck him. I satisfied the Director-General that I was English to the backbone, and he made some inquiries as to my student career, finally desiring me to hold myself ready for examination. Having passed this, I was in Her Majesty's Service, and entered on the books of Nelson's old ship, the *Victory*, for duty at Haslar Hospital, about a couple of months after I made my application.

My official chief at Haslar was a very remarkable person, the late Sir John Richardson, an excellent naturalist, and far-famed as an indomitable Arctic traveller. He was a silent, reserved man, outside the circle of his family and intimates; and, having a full share of youthful vanity, I was extremely disgusted to find that "Old John," as we irreverent youngsters called him, took not the slightest notice of my worshipful self either the first time I attended him, as it was my duty to do, or for some weeks afterwards. I am afraid to think of the lengths to which my tongue may have run on the subject of the churlishness of the chief, who was, in truth, one of the kindest-hearted and most considerate of men. But one day, as I was crossing the hospital square, Sir John stopped me, and heaped coals of fire on my head by telling me that he had tried to get me one of the resident appointments, much coveted by the assistant-surgeons, but that the Admiralty had put in another man. "However," said he, "I mean to keep you here till I can get you something you will like," and turned upon his heel without waiting for the thanks I stammered out. That explained how it was I had not been packed off to the West Coast of Africa like some of my juniors, and why, eventually, I remained altogether seven months at Haslar.

After a long interval, during which "Old John" ignored my existence almost as completely as before, he stopped me again as we met in a casual way, and describing the service on which the *Rattlesnake* was likely to be employed, said that Captain Owen Stanley, who was to command the ship, had asked him to recommend an assistant-surgeon who knew something of science; would I like that? Of course I jumped at the offer. "Very well, I give you leave; to go London at once and see Captain Stanley." I went, saw my future commander, who was very civil to me, and promised to ask that I should be appointed to his ship, as in due time I was. It is a singular thing that, during the few months of my stay at Haslar, I had among my messmates two future Directors-General of the Medical Service of the Navy (Sir Alexander Armstrong and Sir John Watt-Reid), with the present President of the College of Physicians and my kindest of doctors, Sir Andrew Clark.

Life on board Her Majesty's ships in those days was a very different affair from what it is now, and ours was exceptionally rough, as we were often many months without receiving letters or seeing any civilised people but ourselves. In exchange, we had the interest of being about the last voyagers, I suppose, to whom it could be possible to meet with people who knew nothing of fire-arms—as we did on the south Coast of New Guinea—and of making acquaintance with a variety of interesting savage and semi-civilised people. But, apart from experience of this kind and the opportunities offered for scientific work, to me, personally, the cruise was extremely valuable. It was good for me to live under sharp discipline; to be down on the realities of existence by living on bare necessaries; to find out how extremely well worth living life seemed to be when one woke up from a night's rest on a soft plank, with the sky for canopy and cocoa and weevilly biscuit the sole prospect for breakfast; and, more especially, to learn to work for the sake of what I got for myself out of it, even if it all went to the bottom and I along with it. My brother officers were as good fellows as sailors ought to be and generally are, but, naturally, they neither knew nor cared anything about my pursuits, nor understood why I should be so zealous in pursuit of the objects which my friends, the middies, christened "Buffons," after the title conspicuous on a volume of the "Suites à Buffon," which stood on my shelf in the chart room.

During the four years of our absence, I sent home communication after communication to the "Linnean Society," with the same result as that obtained by Noah when he sent the raven out of his ark. Tired at last of hearing nothing about them, I determined to do or die, and in 1849 I drew up a more elaborate paper and forwarded it to the Royal Society. This was my dove, if I had only known it. But owing to the movements of the ship, I heard nothing of that either until my return to England in the latter end of the year 1850, when I found that it was printed and published, and that a huge packet of separate copies awaited me. When I hear some of my young friends complain of want of sympathy and encouragement, I am inclined to think that my naval life was not the least valuable part of my education.

Three years after my return were occupied by a battle between my scientific friends on the one hand and the Admiralty on the other, as to whether the latter ought, or ought not, to act up to the spirit of a pledge they had given to encourage officers who had done scientific work by contributing to the expense of publishing mine. At last the Admiralty, getting tired, I suppose, cut short the discussion by ordering me to join a ship, which thing I declined to do, and as Rastignac, in the Père Goriot, says to Paris, I said to London "à nous deux."[4] I desired to obtain a Professorship of either Physiology or Comparative Anatomy, and as vacancies occurred I applied, but in vain. My friend, Professor Tyndall, and I were candidates at the same time, he for the Chair of Physics and I for that of Natural History in the University of Toronto, which, fortunately, as it turned out, would not look at either of us. I say fortunately, not from any lack of respect for Toronto, but because I soon made up my mind that London was the place for me, and hence I have steadily declined the inducements to leave it, which have at various times been offered. At last, in 1854, on the translation of my warm friend Edward Forbes, to Edinburgh, Sir Henry De la Beche, the Director-General of the Geological Survey, offered me the post Forbes vacated of Paleontologist and Lecturer on Natural History. I refused the former point blank, and accepted the latter only provisionally, telling Sir Henry that I did not care for fossils, and that I should give up Natural History as soon as I could get a physiological post. But I held the office for thirty-one years, and a large part of my work has been paleontological.

At that time I disliked public speaking, and had a firm conviction that I should break down every time I opened my mouth. I believe I had every fault a speaker could have (except talking at random or indulging in rhetoric), when I spoke to the first important audience I ever addressed, on a Friday evening at the Royal Institution, in 1852. Yet, I must confess to having been guilty, malgré moi,[5] of as much public speaking as most of my contemporaries, and for the last ten years it ceased to be so much of a bugbear to me. I used to pity myself for having to go through this training, but I am now more disposed to compassionate the unfortunate audiences, especially my ever-friendly hearers at the Royal Institution, who were the subjects of my oratorical experiments.

The last thing that it would be proper for me to do would be to speak of the work of my life, or to say at the end of the day whether I think I have earned my wages or not. Men are said to be partial judges of themselves. Young men may be, I doubt if old men are. Life seems terribly foreshortened as they look back, and the mountain they set themselves to climb in youth turns out to be a mere spur of immeasurably higher ranges when, with failing breath, they reach the top. But if I may speak of the objects I have had more or less definitely in view since I began the ascent of my hillock, they are briefly these: To promote the increase of natural knowledge and to forward the application of scientific methods of investigation to all the problems of life to the best of my ability, in the conviction which has grown with my growth and strengthened with my strength, that there is no alleviation for the sufferings of mankind except veracity of thought and of action, and the resolute facing of the world as it is when the garment of make-believe by which pious hands have hidden its uglier features is stripped off.

It is with this intent that I have subordinated any reasonable, or unreasonable, ambition for scientific fame which I may have permitted myself to entertain to other ends; to the popularisation of science; to the development and organisation of scientific education; to the endless series of battles and skirmishes over evolution; and to untiring opposition to that ecclesiastical spirit, that clericalism, which in England, as everywhere else, and to whatever denomination it may belong, is the deadly enemy of science.

---

[4] "For the two of us, to us together."   [5] In spite of myself.

In striving for the attainment of these objects, I have been but one among many, and I shall be well content to be remembered, or even not remembered, as such. Circumstances, among which I am proud to reckon the devoted kindness of many friends, have led to my occupation of various prominent positions, among which the Presidency of the Royal Society is the highest. It would be mock modesty on my part, with these and other scientific honours which have been bestowed upon me, to pretend that I have not succeeded in the career which I have followed, rather because I was driven into it than of my own free will; but I am afraid I should not count even these things as marks of success if I could not hope that I had somewhat helped that movement of opinion which has been called the New Reformation.

Walter Bagehot

1826-1877

THE HISTORIAN G. M. Young has called Walter Bagehot "the
Greatest Victorian," a judgment modified later in his essay to "most
Victorian of the Victorians." It is a defensible judgment for the
banker, economist, and man of letters who was a distinguished
Victorian liberal with a strong conservative and commonsense undercurrent
in his thinking.

Walter Bagehot was born at Langport in Somerset in 1826. He was educated
at Bristol by an uncle and at University College, London, where he concentrated
on the study of mathematics. He became a lawyer in 1852, but he soon turned
to banking in his father's firm at Langport. His literary inclinations led him to
the joint editorship with Richard Holt Hutton of the *National Review* in 1855.
He married Eliza Wilson in 1858. In 1860 he took over from his father-in-law
the editorship of the *Economist,* an organ of the laissez-faire school of liberal
economics that had earlier given employment to Herbert Spencer. He occupied
this post until his death in 1877.

Much of Bagehot's most important work is in the field of economics and
politics. In the former area his chief contribution, aside from his editorship
of the *Economist,* is his *Economic Studies* (1880). In the latter area his most notable
works are *The English Constitution* (1867), a Burkean justification of the English
system, and his *Physics and Politics* (1876), an effort to apply to political organization the principles derived from Darwinian theories of evolution. In these works
Bagehot shows his kinship with the rational tradition in English thought that
was also open to current thinking in science and philosophy.

As a literary critic Bagehot made his chief contribution with the posthumously published *Literary Studies* (1879), composed of essays originally contributed by him many years before to the *National Review*. These were edited by
his former companion on the *National Review*, R. H. Hutton, who was later
the editor of the *Spectator* and a notable literary critic in his own right.

There is in Bagehot's essays the clarity, the reasonableness, and the effort
to understand that mark the Victorian liberal mind. His literary estimates are
marked by a concern with biography and with a search for the typical and the
representative but not without an awareness of complexity, humor, and irony.
To read Bagehot is thus to gain a glimpse into the literary responses of a
representative, intelligent, prosperous segment of Victorian life.

CHRONOLOGY

1826	Born 3 February at Langport, Somerset.
1846	Takes B.A. at University College, London.
1848	M.A., University of London.
1852	Called to the bar.
1855–60	Coedits *National Review*.
1860	Begins lifelong editorship of the *Economist*.
1867	*The English Constitution*.
1872	*Physics and Politics*.
1877	Dies 24 March; buried at Langport.

EDITIONS

Works, ed. F. Morgan (5 vols., 1889).
Works, ed. E. I. Barrington (10 vols., 1915).
Collected Works, ed. Norman St. John-Stevas (8 vols., 1965—in progress). [Will be the standard edition.]
Literary Studies, ed. R. H. Hutton (2 vols., 1879, 3 vols., 1895), G. Sampson (2 vols., 1906).
Biographical Studies, ed. R. H. Hutton (1881).
Estimations in Criticism, ed. C. Lennox (2 vols., 1908).
The English Constitution, ed. A. J. Balfour (1928), R. H. S. Crossman (1964).
Physics and Politics, ed. Jacques Barzun (1948).

BIOGRAPHY AND CRITICISM

R. H. Hutton, *Criticism of Contemporary Thought and Thinkers* (2 vols., 1894).
E. I. Barrington, *Life of Bagehot* (1914).
William Irvine, *Walter Bagehot* (1939).
The Economist 1843–1943: A Centenary Volume (1943).
Alastair Buchan, *The Spare Chancellor* (1959).
Norman St. John-Stevas, *Walter Bagehot* (1959).
Wendell V. Harris, "The Critics," in *Victorian Prose: A Guide to Research* (1973).

Wordsworth, Tennyson, and Browning; or Pure, Ornate, and Grotesque Art in English Poetry

This essay was collected, after Bagehot's death, in his Literary Studies *in 1879 by his editor Richard Holt Hutton. It had first appeared in November 1864 in the* National Review. *The argument Bagehot advances here should be tested against the three poets he takes as illustrative of the three types of poetic art. In the reprint below, some of Bagehot's lengthy examples from the works of the three poets have been omitted for reasons of space.*

WE COUPLE these two books together,[1] not because of their likeness, for they are as dissimilar as books can be; nor on account of the eminence of their authors, for in general two great authors are too much for one essay: but because they are the best possible illustration of something we have to say upon poetical art,— because they may give to it life and freshness. The accident of contemporaneous publication has here brought together two books very characteristic of modern art, and we want to show how they are characteristic.

Neither English poetry nor English criticism have ever recovered the *eruption* which they both made at the beginning of this century into the fashionable world. The poems of Lord Byron were received with an avidity that resembles our present avidity for sensation novels, and were read by a class which at present reads little but such novels. Old men who remember those days may be heard to say, "We hear nothing of poetry nowadays: it seems quite down." And "down" it certainly is, if for poetry it be a descent to be no longer the favorite excitement of the more frivolous part of the "upper" world. That stimulating poetry is now little read. A stray schoolboy may still be detected in a wild admiration for the "Giaour" or the "Corsair" (and it is suitable to his age, and he should not be reproached for it); but the *real* posterity, the quiet students of a past literature, never read them or think of them. A line or two linger on the memory; a few telling strokes of occasional and felicitous energy are quoted,—but this is all. As wholes, these exaggerated stories were worthless: they taught nothing, and therefore they are forgotten. If nowadays a dismal poet were, like Byron, to lament the fact of his birth, and to hint that he was too good for the world, the *Saturday Reviewers* would say that "they doubted if he *was* too good"; that "a sulky poet was a questionable addition to a tolerable world"; that "he need not have been born, as far as they were concerned." Doubtless, there is much in Byron besides his dismal exaggeration; but it was that exaggeration which made "the sensation" which gave him a wild moment of dangerous fame. As so often happens, the cause of his momentary fashion is the cause also of his lasting oblivion. Moore's[2] former reputation was less excessive, yet it has not been more permanent. The prettiness of a few songs preserves the memory of his name, but as a poet to *read* he is forgotten. There is nothing to read in him: no exquisite thought, no sublime feeling, no consummate description of true character. Almost the sole result of the poetry of that time is the harm which it has done. It degraded for a time the whole character of the art. It said by practice—by a most efficient and successful practice—that it was the aim, the *duty,* of poets to catch the attention of the passing, the fashionable, the busy world. If a poem "fell dead," it was nothing: it was composed to please the "London" of the year, and if that London did not like it, why, it had failed. It fixed upon the minds of a whole generation, it engraved in popular memory and tradition, a vague conviction that poetry is but one of the many *amusements* for the enjoying classes, for the lighter hours of all classes. The mere notion, the bare idea, that poetry is a deep thing, a teaching thing, the most surely and wisely elevating of human things, is even now to the coarse public mind nearly unknown.

As was the fate of poetry, so inevitably was that of criticism. The science that expounds which poetry is good and which is bad is dependent for its popular reputation on the popular estimate of poetry itself. The critics of that day had *a* day, which is more than can be said for some since: they professed to tell the fashionable world in what books it would find new pleasure, and therefore they were read by the fashionable world. Byron counted the critic and poet equal. The *Edinburgh Review* penetrated among the young, and into places of female resort where it does not go now. As people ask, "Have you read 'Henry Dunbar'? and what do you think of it?" so they then asked, "Have you read the 'Giaour'? and what do you think of it?" Lord Jeffrey,[3] a shrewd judge of the world, employed himself in telling it what to think,—not so much what it ought to think, as what at bottom it did think; and so, by dexterous sympathy with current society, he gained contemporary fame and power. Such fame no critic must hope for now. His articles will not penetrate where the poems themselves do not penetrate. When poetry was noisy, criticism was loud; now poetry is a still small voice, and criticism must be smaller and stiller. As the function of such criticism was limited, so was its subject. For the great and (as

---

[1] The two books under review were Tennyson's *Enoch Arden* and Browning's *Dramatis Personae.*
[2] Thomas Moore (1779–1852), Irish poet.
[3] Francis Jeffrey (1773–1850), Scottish critic, editor of the *Edinburgh Review.*

time now proves) the *permanent* part of the poetry of his time,—for Shelley and for Wordsworth,—Lord Jeffrey had but one word. He said, "It won't do." And it will not do, to amuse a drawing-room.

The doctrine that poetry is a light amusement for idle hours, a metrical species of sensational novel, did not indeed become popular without gainsayers. Thirty years ago, Mr. Carlyle most rudely contradicted it. But perhaps this is about all that he has done, He has denied, but he has not disproved. He has contradicted the floating paganism, but he has not founded the deep religion. All about and around us a *faith* in poetry struggles to be extricated, but it is not extricated. Some day, at the touch of the true word, the whole confusion will by magic cease; the broken and shapeless notions will cohere and crystallize into a bright and true theory. But this cannot be yet.

But though no complete theory of the poetic art as yet be possible for us, though perhaps only our children's children will be able to speak on this subject with the assured confidence which belongs to accepted truth, yet something of some certainty may be stated on the easier elements, and something that will throw light on these two new books. But it will be necessary to assign reasons, and the assigning of reasons is a dry task. Years ago, when criticism only tried to show how poetry could be made a good amusement, it was not impossible that criticism itself should be amusing. But now it must at least be serious, for we believe that poetry is a serious and a deep thing.

There should be a word in the language of literary art to express what the word "picturesque" expresses for the fine arts. *Picturesque* means fit to be put into a picture; we want a word *literatesque,* "fit to be put into a book." An artist goes through a hundred different country scenes, rich with beauties, charms, and merits, but he does not paint any of them. He leaves them alone; he idles on till he finds the hundred-and-first,—a scene which many observers would not think much of, but which *he* knows by virtue of his art will look well on canvas,—and this he paints and preserves. Susceptible observers though not artists feel this quality too: they say of a scene, "How picturesque!" meaning by this a quality distinct from that of beauty or sublimity or grandeur,—meaning to speak not only of the scene as it is in itself, but also of its fitness for imitation by art; meaning not only that it is good, but that

its goodness is such as ought to be transferred to paper; meaning not simply that it fascinates, but also that its fascination is such as ought to be copied by man. A fine and insensible instinct has put language to this subtle use: it expresses an idea without which fine-art criticism could not go on; and it is very natural that the language of pictorial art should be better supplied with words than that of literary criticism, for the eye was used before the mind, and language embodies primitive sensuous ideas long ere it expresses or need express abstract and literary ones.

The reason why a landscape is "picturesque" is often said to be, that such landscape represents an "idea." But this explanation, though in the minds of some who use it is near akin to the truth, fails to explain that truth to those who did not know it before; the word "idea" is so often used in these subjects when people do not know anything else to say, it represents so often a kind of intellectual insolvency when philosophers are at their wits' end, that shrewd people will never readily on any occasion give it credit for meaning anything. A wise explainer must therefore look out for other words to convey what he has to say. *Landscapes,* like everything else in nature, divide themselves as we look at them into a sort of rude classification. We go down a river, for example, and we see a hundred landscapes on both sides of it, resembling one another in much, yet differing in something; with trees here, and a farmhouse there, and shadows on one side, and a deep pool far on,—a collection of circumstances most familiar in themselves, but making a perpetual novelty by the magic of their various combinations. We travel so for miles and hours, and then we come to a scene which also has these various circumstances and adjuncts, but which combines them best, which makes the best whole of them, which shows them in their best proportion at a single glance before the eye. Then we say, "This is the place to paint the river: this is the picturesque point!" Or if not artists or critics of art, we feel without analysis or examination that somehow this bend or sweep of the river shall in future *be the river to us:* that it is the image of it which we will retain in our mind's eye, by which we will remember it, which we will call up when we want to describe or think of it. Some fine countries, some beautiful rivers, have not this picturesque quality: they give us elements of beauty, but they do not combine them together; we go on for a time delighted, but *after* a time somehow we get wearied; we feel that we are taking in nothing and learning nothing; we get no collected image before our mind; we see the accidents and circumstances of that sort of scenery, but the summary scene we do not see; we find *disjecta membra,* but no form; various and many and faulty approximations are displayed in succession, but the absolute perfection in that country's or river's scenery—its *type*—is withheld. We go away from such places in part delighted, but in part baffled: we have been puzzled by pretty things; we have beheld a hundred different inconsistent specimens of the same sort of beauty, but the remembered idea, the full development, the characteristic individuality of it, we have not seen.

We find the same sort of quality in all parts of painting. We see a portrait of a person we know, and we say, "It is like—yes, like, of course, but it is not the *man*"; we feel it could not be any one else, but still, somehow it fails to bring home to us the individual as we know him to be. *He* is not there. An accumulation of features like his are painted, but his essence is not painted; an approximation more or less excellent is given, but the characteristic expression, the *typical* form of the man is withheld.

Literature—the painting of words—has the same quality, but wants the analogous word. The word *literatesque* would mean, if we possessed it, that perfect combination in the *subject-matter* of literature which suits the *art* of literature. We often meet people and say of them, sometimes meaning well and sometimes ill, "How well So-and-so would do in a book!" Such people are by no means the best people; but they are the most effective poeple, the most rememberable people. Frequently, when we first know them, we like them because they explain to us so much of our experience. We have known many people "like that," in one way or another, but we did not seem to understand them; they were nothing to us, for their traits were indistinct; we forgot them, for they hitched on to nothing and we could not classify them: but when we see the *type* of the genus, at once we seem to comprehend its character; the inferior specimens are explained by the perfect embodiment; the approximations are definable when we know the ideal to which they draw near. There are an infinite number of classes of human beings; but in each of these classes there is a distinctive type which, if we could expand it in words, would define the class. We cannot expand it in formal terms any more than a landscape, or a species of landscape; but we have an art, an art of words, which can draw it. Travelers and others often bring home, in addition to their long journals,—which, though so living to them, are so dead, so inanimate, so undescriptive to all else,—a pen-and-ink sketch, rudely done very likely, but which, perhaps even the more for the blots and strokes, gives a distinct notion, an emphatic image, to all who see it. We say at once, *Now* we know the sort of thing. The sketch has *hit* the mind. True literature does the same. It describes sorts, varieties, and permutations, by delineating the type of each sort; the ideal of each variety; the central, the marking trait of each permutation.

.   .   .

The great divisions of poetry, and of all other literary art, arise from the different modes in which these *types*—these characteristic men, these characteristic feelings—may be variously described. There are three principal modes which we shall attempt to describe: the *pure,* which is sometimes, but not very wisely, called the "classical"; the *ornate,* which is also unwisely called "romantic"; and the *grotesque,* which might be called the "mediæval." We will describe the nature of these a little. Criticism, we know, must be brief,—not, like poetry, because its charm is too intense to be sustained, but on the contrary, because its interest is too weak to be prolonged; but elementary criticism, if an evil, is a necessary evil: a little while spent among the simple principles of art is the first condition, the absolute prerequisite, for surely apprehending and wisely judging the complete embodiments and miscellaneous forms of actual literature.

The definition of *pure* literature is, that it describes the type in its simplicity; we mean, with the exact amount of accessory circumstance which is necessary to bring it before the mind in finished perfection, and no more than that amount. The *type* needs some accessories from its nature: a picturesque landscape does not consist wholly of picturesque features. There is a setting of surroundings—as the Americans would say, of fixings—without which the reality is not itself. By a traditional mode of speech, as soon as we see a picture in which a complete effect is produced by detail so rare and so harmonized as to escape us, we say, "How classical!" The whole which is to be seen appears at once and through the detail, but the detail itself is not seen: we do not think of that which gives us the idea,—we are absorbed in the idea itself. Just so in literature: the pure art is that which works with the fewest strokes,—the fewest, that is, for its purpose: for its aim is to call up and bring home to men an idea, a form, a character; and if that idea be twisted, that form be involved, that character perplexed, many strokes of literary art will be needful. Pure art does not mutilate its object: it represents it as fully as is possible with the slightest effort which is possible; it shrinks from no needful circumstances, as little as it inserts any which are needless. The precise peculiarity is not merely that no incidental circumstance is inserted which does not tell on the main design,—no art is fit to be called *art* which permits a stroke to be put in without an object,—but that only the minimum of such circumstance is inserted at all. The form is sometimes said to be bare, the accessories are sometimes said to be invisible, because the appendages are so choice that the shape only is perceived.

The English literature undoubtedly contains much impure literature,—impure in its style, if not in its meaning: but it also contains one great, one nearly perfect model of the pure style in the literary expression of typical *sentiment;* and one not perfect, but gigantic and close approximation to perfection in the pure delineation of objective character. Wordsworth, perhaps, comes as near to choice purity of style in sentiment as is possible; Milton, with exceptions and conditions to be explained, approaches perfection by the strenuous purity with which he depicts character.

A wit once said that *"pretty* women had more features than *beautiful* women"; and though the expression may be criticized, the meaning is correct. Pretty women seem to have a great number of attractive points, each of which attracts your attention, and each one of which you remember afterwards; yet these points have not grown together, their features have not linked themselves into a single inseperable whole. But a beautiful woman is a whole as she is: you no more take her to pieces than a Greek statue; she is not an aggregate of divisible charms, she is a charm in herself. Such ever is the dividing test of pure art: if you catch yourself admiring its details, it is defective; you ought to think of it as a single whole which you must remember, which you must admire, which somehow subdues you while you admire it, which is a "possession" to you "forever."

Of course no individual poem embodies this ideal perfectly; of course every human word and phrase has its imperfections: and if we choose an instance to illustrate that ideal, the instance has scarcely a fair chance. By contrasting it with the ideal, we suggest its imperfections; by protruding it as an example, we turn on its defectiveness the microscope of criticism. Yet these two sonnets of Wordsworth may be fitly read in this place, not because they are quite without faults, or because they are the very best examples of their kind of style, but because they are luminous examples: the compactness of the sonnet and the gravity of the sentiment hedging in the thoughts, restraining the fancy, and helping to maintain a singleness of expression.

. . .

. . . Shelley had many merits and many defects. This is not the place for a complete—or indeed for any—estimate of him. But one excellence is most evident. His words are as flexible as any words; the rhythm of some modulating air seems to move them into their place without a struggle by the poet, and almost without his knowledge. This is the perfection of pure art: to embody typical conceptions in the choicest, the fewest accidents; to embody them so that each of these accidents may produce its full effect, and so to embody them without effort.

The extreme opposite to this pure art is what may be called *ornate* art. This species of art aims also at giving a delineation of the typical idea in its perfection and its fullness, but it aims at so doing in a manner most different. It wishes to surround the type with the greatest number of circumstances which it will bear. It works not by choice and selection, but by accumulation and aggregation. The idea is not, as in the pure style, presented with the least clothing which it will endure, but with the richest and most involved clothing that it will admit.

We are fortunate in not having to hunt out of past literature an illustrative specimen of the ornate style. Mr. Tennyson has just given one, admirable in itself and most characteristic of the defects and the merits of this style. The story of "Enoch Arden," as he has enhanced and presented it, is a rich and splendid composit of imagery and illustration. Yet how simple that story is in itself! A sailor who sells fish breaks his leg, gets dismal, gives up selling fish, goes to sea, is wrecked on a desert island, stays there some years, on his return finds his wife married to a miller, speaks to a landlady on the subject, and dies. Told in the pure and simple, the unadorned and classical style, this story would not have taken three pages; but Mr. Tennyson has been able to make it the principal, the largest tale in his new volume. He has done so only by giving to every event and incident in the volume an accompanying commentary. He tells a great deal about the Torrid Zone, which a rough sailor like Enoch Arden certainly would not have perceived; and he gives to the fishing village, to which all the characters belong, a softness and a fascination which such villages scarcely possess in reality.

The description of the tropical island on which the sailor is thrown is an absolute model of adorned art:

"The mountain wooded to the peak, the lawns
And winding glades high up like ways to heaven,
The slender coco's drooping crown of plumes,
The lightning flash of insect and of bird,
The luster of the long convolvuluses
That coiled around the stately stems, and ran
Even to the limit of the land, the glows
And glories of the broad belt of the world,—
All these he saw; but what he fain had seen
He could not see,—the kindly human face,
Nor ever hear a kindly voice, but heard
The myriad shriek of wheeling ocean-fowl,
The league-long roller thundering on the reef,
The moving whisper of huge trees that branched
And blossomed in the zenith, or the sweep
Of some precipitous rivulet to the wave,
As down the shore he ranged, or all day long
Sat often in the seaward-gazing gorge,
A shipwrecked sailor, waiting for a sail:
No sail from day to day, but every day
The sunrise broken into scarlet shafts
Among the palms and ferns and precipices;
The blaze upon the waters to the east;
The blaze upon his island overhead;
The blaze upon the waters to the west;
Then the great stars that globed themselves in heaven,
The hollower-bellowing ocean, and again
The scarlet shafts of sunrise,—but no sail."

No expressive circumstances can be added to this description, no enhancing detail suggested. A much less happy instance is the description of Enoch's life before he sailed:—

"While Enoch was abroad on wrathful seas,
Or often journeying landward; for in truth
Enoch's white horse and Enoch's ocean spoil
In ocean-smelling osier, and his face
Rough-reddened with a thousand winter gales,
Not only to the market-cross were known,
But in the leafy lanes behind the down,
Far as the portal-warding lion-whelp
And peacock yew-tree of the lonely Hall,
Whose Friday fare was Enoch's minist'ring."

So much has not often been made of selling fish. The essence of ornate art is in this manner to accumulate round the typical object everything which can be said about it, every associated thought that can be connected with it, without impairing the essence of the delineation.

The first defect which strikes a student of ornate art—the first which arrests the mere reader of it—is what is called a want of simplicity. Nothing is described as it is; everything has about it an atmosphere of something else. The combined and associated thoughts, though they set off and heighten particular ideas and aspects of the central and typical conception, yet complicate it: a simple thing—"a primrose by the river's brim" is never left by itself; something else is put with it,—something not more connected with it than [the] "lion-whelp" and the "peacock yew-tree" are with the "fresh fish for sale" that Enoch carries past them. Even in the highest cases, ornate art leaves upon a cultured and delicate taste the conviction that it is not the highest art: that it is somehow excessive and over-rich; that it is not chaste in itself or chastening to the mind that sees it; that it is in an [un]explained manner unsatisfactory, "a thing in which we feel there is some hidden want!"

That want is a want of "definition." We must all know landscapes, river landscapes especially, which are in the highest sense beautiful, which when we first see them give us a delicate pleasure, which in some—and these the best—cases give even a gentle sense of surprise that such things should be so beautiful,—and yet when we come to live in them, to spend even a few hours in them, we seem stifled and oppressed. On the other hand, there are people to whom the sea-shore is a companion, an exhilaration; and not so much for the brawl of the shore as for the limited vastness, the finite infinite of the ocean as they see it. Such people often come home braced and nerved, and if they spoke out the truth, would have only to say, "We have seen the horizon line"; if they were let alone, indeed, they would gaze on it hour after hour, so great to them is the fascination, so full the sustaining calm, which they gain from that union of form and greatness. To a very inferior extent,—but still, perhaps, to an extent which most people understand better,—a common arch will have the same effect. A bridge completes a river landscape: if of the old and many-arched sort, it regulates by a long series of defined forms the vague outline of wood and river, which before had nothing to measure it; if of the new scientific sort, it introduces still more strictly a geometrical element,—it stiffens the scenery, which was before too soft, too delicate, too vegetable. Just such is the effect of pure style in literary art: it calms by conciseness. While the ornate style leaves on the mind a mist of beauty, an excess of fascination, a complication of charm, the pure style leaves behind it the simple, defined, measured idea, as it is and by itself. That which is chaste chastens; there is a poised energy—a state half thrill and half tranquillity—which pure art gives, which no other can give; a pleasure justified as well as felt; an ennobled satisfaction at what ought to satisfy us, and must ennoble us.

Ornate art is to pure art what a painted statue is to an unpainted. It is impossible to deny that a touch of color does bring out certain parts, does convey certain expressions, does heighten certain features: but it leaves on the work as a whole a want, as we say, "of something,"—a want of that inseparable chasteness which clings to simple sculpture; an impairing predominance of alluring details, which impairs our satisfaction with our own satisfaction, which makes us doubt whether a higher being than ourselves will be satisfied even though we are so. In the very same manner, though the rouge of ornate literature excites our eye, it also impairs our confidence.

Mr. Arnold has justly observed that this self-justifying, self-proving purity of style is commoner in ancient literature than in modern literature, and also that Shakespeare is not a great or an unmixed example of it. No one can say that he is. His works are full of undergrowth, are full of complexity, are not models of style; except by a miracle, nothing in the Elizabethan age could be a model of style: the restraining taste of that age was feebler and more mistaken than that of any other equally great age. Shakespeare's mind so teemed with creation that he required the most just, most forcible, most constant restraint from without. He most needed to be guided among poets, and he was the least and worst guided. As a whole, no one can call his works finished models of the pure style, or of any style. But he has many passages of the most pure style; passages which could be easily cited if space served. And we must remember that the task which Shakespeare undertook was the most difficult which any poet has ever attempted, and that it is a task in which, after a million efforts, every other poet has failed. The Elizabethan drama—as Shakespeare has immortalized it—undertakes to delineate in five acts, under stage restrictions, and in mere dialogue, a whole list of *dramatis personæ*, a set of characters enough for a modern novel, and with the distinctness of a modern novel. Shakespeare is not content to give two or three great characters in solitude and in dignity, like the classical dramatists: he wishes to give a whole party of characters in the play of life, and according to the nature of each. He would "hold the mirror up to nature," not to catch a monarch in a tragic posture, but a whole group of characters engaged in many actions, intent on many purposes, thinking many thoughts. There is life enough, there is action enough, in single plays of Shakespeare to set up an ancient dramatist for a long career. And Shakespeare succeeded. His characters, taken *en masse* and as a whole, are as well known as any novelist's characters; cultivated men know all about them, as young ladies know all about Mr. Trollope's novels. But no other dramatist has succeeded in such an aim. No one else's characters are staple people in English literature, hereditary people whom every one knows all about in every generation. The contemporary dramatists—Beaumont and Fletcher, Ben Jonson, Marlowe, etc.—had many merits; some of them were great men. But a critic must say of them the worst thing he has to say: "They were men who failed in their characteristic aim;" they attempted to describe numerous sets of complicated characters, and they failed. No one of such characters, or hardly one, lives in common memory; the "Faustus" of Marlowe, a really great idea, is not remembered. They undertook to write what they could not write,—five acts full of real characters; and in consequence, the fine individual things they conceived are forgotten by the mixed multitude, and known only to a few of the few. Of the Spanish theater we cannot speak; but there are no such characters in any French tragedy,—the whole aim of that tragedy forbade it. Goethe has added to literature a few great characters; he may be said almost to have added to literature the idea of "intellectual creation,"—the idea of describing the great characters through the intellect: but he has not added to the common stock what Shakespeare added,—a new multitude of men and women, and these not in simple attitudes, but amid the most complex parts of life, with all their various natures roused, mixed, and strained. The severest art must have allowed many details, much overflowing circumstance, to a poet who undertook to describe what almost defies description. Pure art would have commanded him to use details lavishly; but only by a multiplicity of such could the required effect have been at all produced. Shakespeare could accomplish it, for his mind was a spring, an inexhaustible fountain of human nature; and it is no wonder that, being compelled by the task of his time to let the fullness of his nature overflow, he sometimes let it overflow too much, and covered with erroneous conceits and superfluous images, characters and conceptions which would have been far more justly, far more effectually delineated with conciseness and simplicity. But there is an infinity of pure art in Shakespeare, although there is a great deal else also.

It will be said, If ornate art be, as you say, an inferior species of art, why should it ever be used? If pure art be the best sort of art, why should it not always be used?

The reason is this: Literary art, as we just now explained, is concerned with literatesque characters in literatesque situations; and the *best* art is concerned with the *most* literatesque characters in the *most* literatesque situations. Such are the subjects of pure art; it embodies with the fewest touches, and under the most select and choice circumstances, the highest conceptions: but it does not follow that only the best subjects are to be treated by art, and then only in the very best way. Human nature could not endure such a critical commandment as that, and it would be an erroneous criticism which gave it. *Any* literatesque character may be described in literature under *any* circumstances which exhibit its literatesqueness. . . .

The essence of pure art consists in its describing what is, as it is; and this is very well for what can bear it, but there are many inferior things which will not bear it and which nevertheless ought to be described in books. A certain kind of literature deals with illusions, and this kind of literature has given a coloring to the name "romantic." . . .

There is, however, a third kind of art which differs from these on the point in which they most resemble one another. Ornate art and pure art have this in common, that they paint the types of literature in a form as perfect as they can. Ornate art, indeed, uses undue disguises and unreal enhancements; it does not confine itself to the best types,—on the contrary, it is its office to make the best of imperfect types and lame approximations: but ornate art, as much as pure art, catches its subject in the best light it can, takes the most developed aspect of it which it can find, and throws upon it the most congruous colors it can use. But *grotesque* art does just the contrary. It takes the type, so to say, *in difficulties*. It gives a representation of it in its minimum development, amid the circumstances least favourable to it, just while it is struggling with obstacles, just where it is encumbered with incongruities. It deals, to use the language of science, not with normal types but with abnormal specimens; to use the language of old philosophy, not with what nature is striving to be, but with what some lapse she has happened to become.

This art works by contrast. It enables you to see, it makes you see, the perfect type by painting the opposite deviation. It shows you what ought to be by what ought not to be; when complete, it reminds you of the perfect image by showing you the distorted and imperfect image. Of this art we possess in the present generation one prolific master. Mr. Browning is an artist working by incongruity. Possibly hardly one of his most considerable efforts can be found which is not great because of its odd mixture. He puts together things which no one else would have put together, and produces on our minds a result which no one else would have produced or tried to produce. His admirers may not like all we may have to say of him. But in our way we too are among his admirers. No one ever read him without seeing not only his great ability, but his great *mind*. He not only possesses superficial usable talents, but the strong something, the inner secret something, which uses them and controls them; he is great not in mere accomplishments, but in himself. He has applied a hard strong intellect to real life; he has applied the same intellect to the problems of his age. He has striven to know what *is;* he has endeavoured not to be cheated by counterfeits, not to be infatuated with illusions. His heart is in what he says. He has battered his brain against his creed till he believes it. He has accomplishments too, the more effective because they are mixed. He is at once a student of mysticism and a citizen of the world. He brings to the club sofa distinct visions of old creeds, intense images of strange thoughts; he takes to the bookish student tidings of wild Bohemia and little traces of the *demi-monde*. He puts down what is good for the naughty, and what is naughty for the good. Over women his easier writings exercise that imperious power which belongs to the writings of a great man of the world upon such matters. He knows women, and therefore they wish to know him. If we blame many of Browning's efforts, it is in the interest of art, and not from a wish to hurt or degrade him.

If we wanted to illustrate the nature of grotesque art by an exaggerated instance, we should have selected a poem which the chance of late publication brings us in this new volume. Mr. Browning has undertaken to describe what may be called *mind in difficulties*,—mind set to make out the universe under the worst and hardest circumstances. He takes Caliban,—not perhaps exactly Shakespeare's Caliban, but an analogous and worse creature; a strong thinking power, but a nasty creature,—a gross animal, uncontrolled and unelevated by any feeling of religion or duty. . . .

It is very natural that a poet whose wishes incline or whose genius conducts him to a grotesque art should be attracted towards mediæval subjects. There is no age whose legends are so full of grotesque subjects, and no age whose real life was so fit to suggest them. Then, more than at any other time, good principles have been under great hardships. The vestiges of ancient civilization, the germs of modern civilization, the little remains of what had been, the small beginnings of what is, were buried under a cumbrous mass of barbarism and cruelty. Good elements hidden in horrid accompaniments are the special theme of grotesque art; and these, mediæval life and legends afford more copiously than could have been furnished before Christianity gave its new elements of good, or since modern civilization has removed some few at least of the old elements of destruction. A *buried* life like the spiritual mediæval was Mr. Browning's natural element, and he was right to be attracted by it. His mistake has been, that he has not made it pleasant: that he has forced his art to topics on which no one could charm, or on which he at any rate could not; that on these occasions and in these poems he has failed in fascinating men and women of sane taste.

We say "sane" because there is a most formidable and estimable *insane* taste. The will has great though indirect power over the taste, just as it has over the belief. There are some horrid beliefs from which human nature revolts, from which at first it shrinks, to which at first no effort can force it. But if we fix the mind upon them, they have a power over us just because of their natural offensiveness. They are like the sight of human blood: experienced soldiers tell us that at first, men are sickened by the smell and newness of blood almost to death and fainting; but that as soon as they harden their hearts and stiffen their minds, as soon as they *will* bear it,

then comes an appetite for slaughter, a tendency to gloat on carnage, to love blood (at least for the moment) with a deep, eager love. It is a principle that if we put down a healthy instinctive aversion, nature avenges herself by creating an unhealthy insane attraction. For this reason, the most earnest truth-seeking men fall into the worst delusions. They will not let their mind alone; they force it towards some ugly thing, which a crotchet of argument, a conceit of intellect recommends: and nature punishes their disregard of her warning by subjection to the ugly one, by belief in it. Just so, the most industrious critics get the most admiration. They think it unjust to rest in their instinctive natural horror; they overcome it, and angry nature gives them over to ugly poems and marries them to detestable stanzas.

Mr. Browning possibly, and some of the worst of Mr. Browning's admirers certainly, will say that these grotesque objects exist in real life, and therefore they ought to be, at least may be, described in art. But though pleasure is not the end of poetry, pleasing is a condition of poetry. An exceptional monstrosity of horrid ugliness cannot be made pleasing, except it be made to suggest—to recall—the perfection, the beauty, from which it is a deviation. Perhaps in extreme cases no art is equal to this: but then such self-imposed problems should not be worked by the artist; these out-of-the-way and detestable subjects should be let alone by him. It is rather characteristic of Mr. Browning to neglect this rule. He is the most of a realist, and the least of an idealist, of any poet we know. He evidently sympathizes with some part at least of "Bishop Blougram's Apology." Anyhow this world exists. "There *is* good wine; there *are* pretty women; there *are* comfortable benefices; there *is* money, and it is pleasant to spend it. Accept the creed of your age and you get these, reject that creed and you lose them. And for what do you lose them? For a fancy creed of your own, which no one else will accept, which hardly any one will call a 'creed,' which most people will consider a sort of unbelief." Again, Mr. Browning evidently loves what we may call the "realism," the grotesque realism, of orthodox Christianity. Many parts of it in which great divines have felt keen difficulties are quite pleasant to him. He must *see* his religion, he must have an "object-lesson" in believing. He must have a creed that will *take*, which wins and holds the miscellaneous world, which stout men will heed, which nice women will adore. The spare moments of solitary religion, the "obstinate questionings," the "high instincts," the "first affections," the "shadowy recollections,"

> "Which, be they what they may,
> Are yet the fountain-light of all our day,
> Are yet a master-light of all our seeing."[4]

the great but vague faith, the unutterable tenets, —seem to him worthless, visionary: they are not enough "immersed in matter";[5] they move about "in worlds not realized." We wish he could be tried like the prophet once: he would have found God in the earthquake and the storm; he would have deciphered from them a bracing and a rough religion; he would have known that crude men and ignorant women felt them too, and he would accordingly have trusted them: but he would have distrusted and disregarded the "still small voice"; he would have said it was "fancy,"—a thing you thought you heard to-day, but were not sure you had heard to-morrow; he would call it a nice illusion, an immaterial prettiness; he would ask triumphantly, "How are you to get the mass of men to heed this little thing?" he would have persevered, and insisted, *"My wife* does not hear it."

> On which their neighbors lay such stress,
> To their fathers and mothers having risen
> Out of some subterraneous prison
> Into which they were trepanned
> Long time ago in a mighty band
> Out of Hamelin town in Brunswick land,
> But how or why they don't understand."

Something more we had to say of Mr. Browning, but we must stop. It is singularly characteristic of this age that the poems which rise to the surface should be examples of ornate art and grotesque art, not of pure art. We live in the realm of the *half*-educated. The number of readers grows daily, but the quality of readers does not improve rapidly. The middle class is scattered, headless; it is well-meaning, but aimless: wishing to be wise, but ignorant how to be wise. The aristocracy of England never was a literary aristocracy; never even in the days of its full power, of its unquestioned predominance, did it guide—did it even seriously try to guide— the taste of England. Without guidance, young men and tired men are thrown amongst a mass of books; they have to choose which they like. Many of them would much like to improve their culture, to chasten their taste, if they knew how: but left to themselves, they take not pure art, but showy art; not that which permanently relieves the eye, and makes it happy whenever it looks and as long as it looks, but *glaring* art, which catches and arrests the eye for a moment, but which in the end fatigues it. But before the wholesome remedy of nature—the fatigue— arrives, the hasty reader has passed on to some new excitement, which in its turn stimulates for an instant and then is passed by for ever. These conditions are not favorable to the due appreciation of pure art,—of that art which must be known before it is admired, which must have fastened irrevocably on the brain before you appreciate it, which you must love ere it will seem worthy of your love. Women, too, whose voice in literature counts as well as that of men, and in a light literature counts for more than that of men,—women, such as we know them, such as they are likely to be, ever prefer a delicate unreality to a true or firm art. A dressy literature, an exaggerated literature, seem to be fated to us. These are our curses, as other times had theirs.

---

[4] Wordsworth ,"Intimations of Immortality," ix. [Bagehot's note]
[5] "Locke on the Human Understanding," Book iv., Chap. iii., i. 2. [Bagehot's note]

George Meredith

1828-1909

LIKE SOME others in this volume, Meredith is remembered in the first instance for works of fiction rather than nonfiction: he was an important Victorian novelist and also a poet. But Meredith began as a journalist and his complete works include a number of essays and criticisms notable in the development of nonfiction in the age.

Meredith was the son and grandson of Portsmouth tailors and naval out-fitters, a circumstance that caused him some embarrassment in socially conscious Victorian England. He was born in Portsmouth in 1828, educated privately there and for a few years in Germany at a Moravian school on the Rhine. His mother had died when he was a child, and he was not on good terms with his father. He abandoned a post with a solicitor to turn to journalism in 1849. The following year he married the widowed daughter, nine years his senior, of the satiric novelist Thomas Love Peacock. The marriage was a failure; in 1858 his wife deserted him for a lover with whom she departed for the Continent. A year after her death in 1861 Meredith's cycle of poems called *Modern Love* appeared; it records the course of an unhappy marriage.

Meredith remarried, happily this time, in 1864. His second wife died in 1885. Meantime, from the eighteen-fifties on, Meredith had been publishing both poetry and fiction in considerable quantity. His chief novels include *The Ordeal of Richard Feveral* (1859), *Evan Harrington* (1860), *Sandra Belloni* (1864), *The Adventures of Harry Richmond* (1871), *Beauchamp's Career* (1875), and *The Egoist* (1879). His novels deal acutely with class questions, relations between the sexes, and education. His later novels are often arguments for the equality of women. Meredith also continued to publish various volumes of verse, much of it notable for his concern with evolutionary meliorism through nature. Meredith is perhaps the earliest of the Victorian creative artists to accept the idea of evolution with delight and optimism.

Since Meredith's creative writing brought him little financial reward, he continued to write extensively for the journals, especially the *Fortnightly,* and he served for many years as a publisher's reader for the firm of Chapman and Hall. Of his works of nonfiction, his lecture on comedy has long been regarded as his major achievement. Much of his literary criticism is also of high quality. Meredith lived at Box Hill, Surrey, from 1867. He died there in 1909.

As a writer of nonfiction Meredith is best remembered for *The Idea of Comedy*. Along with a masterful survey of comic writers the work also sets forth as enduring a justification of the uses of comedy as is available in English. It is an excellent illustration of Meredith's wide reading, broad sympathy, and his ability to discourse informatively and concisely.

CHRONOLOGY

1828	Born 12 February in Portsmouth.
1842–44	Studies at Moravian school at Neuwied on the Rhine.
1849	Begins journalistic career; married Mary Ellen Nicolls.
1851	*Poems.*
1858	Wife deserts him.
1859	*The Ordeal of Richard Feverel.*
1861	Wife dies.
1862	*Modern Love.*
1864	Marries Marie Vulliamy.
1875	*Beauchamp's Career.*
1877	*The Idea of Comedy.*
1879	*The Egoist.*
1883	*Poems and Lyrics of the Joy of Earth.*
1885	*Diana of the Crossways.*
1909	Dies 18 May at Box Hill; ashes buried at Dorking.

EDITIONS

Except for *Works,* Meredith's novels are not listed. Many of them exist in various modern editions.
Works. Memorial Edition. (27 vols., 1909–1911).
Works. Edition de luxe. (39 volumes, 1896–1912).
On the Idea of Comedy and the Uses of the Comic Spirit, ed. Lane Cooper (1918).
Letters, ed. W. M. Meredith (1912).

BIOGRAPHY AND CRITICISM

Richard LeGallienne, *George Meredith* (1890).
Joseph Warren Beach, *The Comic Spirit in George Meredith* (1911).
Mary S. H. Gretton, *The Writings and Life of George Meredith* (1926).
J. B. Priestley, *George Meredith* (1926).
Lionel Stevenson, *The Ordeal of George Meredith* (1953).
Walter F. Wright, *Art and Substance in George Meredith* (1953).
Norman Kelvin, *A Troubled Eden* (1961).
C. L. Cline, "George Meredith," in *Victorian Fiction: A Guide to Research* (1964.)

On the Idea of Comedy and the
Uses of the Comic Spirit

Meredith delivered The Idea of Comedy *as a lecture at the London Institute on 1 February 1877. It was then published in the* New Quarterly Magazine *and separately published in book form in 1897 and repeatedly thereafter. It has come to stand as Meredith's most important work in criticism and nonfiction and as one of the classic statements on the idea of comedy. Meredith's central argument, that comedy is restorative and that it prevails over sentimentalism, has been adopted by most theorists of the comic. The entire work is reprinted below.*

GOOD comedies are such rare productions that, notwithstanding the wealth of our literature in the comic element, it would not occupy us long to run over the English list. If they are brought to the test I shall propose, very reputable comedies will be found unworthy of their station, like the ladies of Arthur's Court, when they were reduced to the ordeal of the mantle.

There are plain reasons why the comic poet is not a frequent apparition, and why the great comic poet remains without a fellow. A society of cultivated men and women is required, wherein ideas are current, and the perceptions quick, that he may be supplied with matter and an audience. The semi-barbarism of merely giddy communities, and feverish emotional periods, repel him; and also a state of marked social inequality of the sexes; nor can he whose business is to address the mind be understood where there is not a moderate degree of intellectual activity.

Moreover, to touch and kindle the mind through laughter demands, more than sprightliness, a most subtle delicacy. That must be a natal gift in the comic poet. The substance he deals with will show him a startling exhibition of the dyer's hand, if he is without it. People are ready to surrender themselves to witty thumps on the back, breast, and sides; all except the head—and it is there that he aims. He must be subtle to penetrate. A corresponding acuteness must exist to welcome him. The necessity for the two conditions will explain how it is that we count him during centuries in the singular number.

'*C'est une étrange entreprise que celle de faire rire les honnêtes gens,*'[1] Molière says; and the difficulty of the undertaking cannot be overestimated.

Then again, he is beset with foes to right and left, of a character unknown to the tragic and the lyric poet, or even to philosophers.

We have in this world men whom Rabelais would call 'agelasts'; that is to say, non-laughers—men who are in that respect as dead bodies, which, if you prick them, do not bleed. The old gray boulder-stone, that has finished its peregrination from the rock to the valley, is as easily to be set rolling up again as these men laughing. No collision of circumstances in our mortal career strikes a light for them. It is but one step from being agelastic to misogelastic, and the μισόγελως, the laughter-hating, soon learns to dignify his dislike as an objection in morality.

We have another class of men who are pleased to consider themselves antagonists of the foregoing, and whom we may term 'hypergelasts'; the excessive laughers, ever-laughing, who are as clappers of a bell, that may be rung by a breeze, a grimace; who are so loosely put together that a wink will shake them.

C'est n'estimer rien qu'estimer tout le monde;[2]

and to laugh at everything is to have no appreciation of the comic of comedy.

Neither of these distinct divisions of non-laughers and over-laughers would be entertained by reading *The Rape of the Lock,* or seeing a performance of *Le Tartuffe.* In relation to the stage, they have taken in our land the form and title of Puritan and Bacchanalian; for though the stage is no longer a public offender, and Shakespeare has been revived on it, to give it nobility,

---

[1] "It is a strange enterprise that makes honest people laugh."
[2] "To esteem the whole world is to esteem nothing."

we have not yet entirely raised it above the contention of these two parties. Our speaking on the theme of comedy will appear almost a libertine proceeding to one, while the other will think that the speaking of it seriously brings us into violent contrast with the subject.

Comedy, we have to admit, was never one of the most honored of the Muses. She was in her origin, short of slaughter, the loudest expression of the little civilization of men. The light of Athene over the head of Achilles illuminates the birth of Greek tragedy. But comedy rolled in shouting under the divine protection of the Son of the Wine-jar, as Dionysus is made to proclaim himself by Aristophanes. Our second Charles was the patron, of like benignity, of our Comedy of Manners, which began similarly as a combative performance, under a license to deride and outrage the Puritan, and was here and there Bacchanalian beyond the Aristophanic example— worse, inasmuch as a cynical licentiousness is more abominable than frank filth. An eminent Frenchman judges, from the quality of some of the stuff dredged up for the laughter of men and women who sat through an Athenian comic play, that they could have had small delicacy in other affairs, when they had so little in their choice of entertainment. Perhaps he does not make sufficient allowance for the regulated license of plain-speaking proper to the festival of the god, and claimed by the comic poet as his inalienable right, or for the fact that it was a festival in a season of license, in a city accustomed to give ear to the boldest utterance of both sides of a case. However that may be, there can be no question that the men and women who sat through the acting of Wycherley's *Country Wife* were past blushing. Our tenacity of national impressions has caused the word 'theatre' since then to prod the Puritan nervous system like a satanic instrument; just as one has known anti-papists for whom Smithfield was redolent of a sinister smoke, as though they had a later recollection of the place than the lowing herds. Hereditary Puritanism regarding the stage is met, to this day, in many families quite undistinguished by arrogant piety. It has subsided altogether as a power in the profession of morality; but it is an error to suppose it extinct, and unjust also to forget that it had once good reason to hate, shun, and rebuke our public shows.

We shall find ourselves about where the comic spirit would place us, if we stand at middle distance between the inveterate opponents and the drum-and-fife supporters of comedy. '[*Celui qui s'arrête*] *fait remarquer l'emportement des autres, comme un point fixe*,'[3] as Pascal says. And were there more in this position, comic genius would flourish.

Our English idea of a comedy of manners might be imaged in the person of a blowsy country girl—say Hoyden, the daughter of Sir Tunbelly Clumsey, who, when at home, never disobeyed her father except in the 'eating of green gooseberries'—transforming to a varnished city madam, with a loud laugh and a mincing step; the crazy ancestress of an accountably fallen descendant. She bustles prodigiously, and is punctually smart in her speech, always in a fluster to escape from Dulness, as they say the dogs on the Nile-banks drink at the river running to avoid the crocodile. If the monster catches her, as at times he does, she whips him to a froth, so that those who know Dulness only as a thing of ponderousness shall fail to recognize him in that light and airy shape.

When she had frolicked through her five acts, to surprise you with the information that Mr. Aimwell is converted by a sudden death in the world outside the scenes into Lord Aimwell, and can marry the lady in the light of day, it is to the credit of her vivacious nature that she does not anticipate your calling her Farce. Five is dignity with a trailing robe; whereas one, two, or three acts would be short skirts, and degrading. Advice has been given to householders that they should follow up the shot at a burglar in the dark by hurling the pistol after it, so that if the bullet misses, the weapon may strike, and assure the rascal he has it. The point of her wit is in this fashion supplemented by the rattle of her tongue, and effectively, according to the testimony of her admirers. Her wit is at once, like steam in an engine, the motive force and the warning whistle of her headlong course; and it vanishes like the track of steam when she has reached her terminus, never troubling the brains afterward; a merit that it shares with good wine, to the joy of the Bacchanalians.

As to this wit, it is warlike. In the neatest hands it is like the sword of the cavalier in the Mall, quick to flash out upon slight provocation, and for a similar office—to wound. Commonly its attitude is entirely pugilistic; two blunt fists rallying and countering. When harmless, as when the word 'fool' occurs, or allusions to the state of husband, it has the sound of the smack of

---

[3] "He who stands still can note the demeanor of others as from a fixed point."

harlequin's wand upon clown, and is to the same extent exhilarating. Believe that idle, empty laughter is the most desirable of recreations, and significant comedy will seem pale and shallow in comparison. Our popular idea would be hit by the sculptured group of Laughter holding both his sides, while Comedy pummels, by way of tickling him. As to a meaning, she holds that it does not conduce to making merry; you might as well carry cannon on a racing-yacht. Morality is a duenna to be circumvented. This was the view of English comedy of a sagacious essayist, who said that the end of a comedy would often be the commencement of a tragedy, were the curtain to rise again on the performers. In those old days female modesty was protected by a fan, behind which—and it was of a convenient semicircular breadth—the ladies present in the theatre retired at a signal of decorum, to peep, covertly askant, or with the option of so peeping, through a prettily-fringed eyelet-hole in the eclipsing arch.

> Ego limis specto
> sic per flabellum clanculum.[4]
> —TERENCE.

That fan is the flag and symbol of the society giving us our so-called Comedy of Manners, or comedy of the manners of South-Sea islanders under city veneer; and, as to comic idea, vacuous as the mask without the face behind it.

Elia, whose humor delighted in floating a galleon paradox, and wafting it as far as it would go, bewails the extinction of our artificial comedy, like a poet sighing over the vanished splendor of Cleopatra's Nile-barge; and the sedateness of his plea, for a cause condemned even in his time to the penitentiary, is a novel effect of the ludicrous. When the realism of those 'fictitious, half-believed personages,' as he calls them, had ceased to strike, they were objectionable company, uncaressable as puppets. Their artifices are staringly naked, and have now the effect of a painted face, viewed, after warm hours of dancing, in the morning light. How could the Lurewells and the Plyants ever have been praised for ingenuity in wickedness? Critics apparently sober, and of high reputation, held up their shallow knaveries for the world to admire. These Lurewells, Plyants, Pinchwifes, Fondlewifes, Miss Prue, Peggy, Hoyden, all of them save charming Millamant, are dead as last year's clothes in a fashionable fine lady's wardrobe; and it must be an exceptionably abandoned

Abigail of our period that would look on them with the wish to appear in their likeness. Whether the puppet-show of Punch and Judy inspires our street-urchins to have instant recourse to their fists in a dispute, after the fashion of every one of the actors in that public entertainment who gets possession of the cudgel, is open to question; it has been hinted; and angry moralists have traced the national taste for tales of crime to the smell of blood in our nursery-songs. It will at any rate hardly be questioned that it is unwholesome for men and women to see themselves as they are, if they are no better than they should be; and they will not, when they have improved in manners, care much to see themselves as they once were. That comes of realism in the comic art; and it is not public caprice, but the consequence of a bettering state. The same of an immoral may be said [as] of realistic exhibitions of a vulgar society.

The French make a critical distinction in *ce qui remue* from *ce qui émeut*—that which agitates from that which touches with emotion. In the realistic comedy it is an incessant *remuage;* no calm—merely bustling figures—and no thought. Excepting Congreve's *Way of the World,* which failed on the stage, there was nothing to keep our comedy alive on its merits; neither, with all its realism, true portraiture, nor much quotable fun, nor idea; neither salt nor soul.

The French have a school of stately comedy to which they can fly for renovation whenever they have fallen away from it; and their having such a school is mainly the reason why, as John Stuart Mill pointed out, they know men and women more accurately than we do. Molière followed the Horatian precept, to observe the manners of his age, and give his characters the color befitting them at the time. He did not paint in raw realism. He seized his characters firmly for the central purpose of the play, stamped them in the idea, and, by slightly raising and softening the object of study (as in the case of the ex-Huguenot, Duc de Montausier, for the study of the Misanthrope, and, according to Saint-Simon, the Abbé Roquette for Tartuffe), generalized upon it so as to make it permanently human. Concede that it is natural for human creatures to live in society, and Alceste is an imperishable mark of one, though he is drawn in light outline, without any forcible human coloring.

Our English school has not clearly imagined society; and of the mind hovering above con-

---

[4] "I see the glance thus secretly behind the fan."

gregated men and women it has imagined nothing. The critics who praise it for its down-rightness, and for bringing the situations home to us, as they admiringly say, cannot but dis-approve of Molière's comedy, which appeals to the individual mind to perceive and participate in the social. We have splendid tragedies, we have the most beautiful of poetic plays, and we have literary comedies passingly pleasant to read, and occasionally to see acted. By literary comedies, I mean comedies of classic inspiration, drawn chiefly from Menander and the Greek New Comedy through Terence; or else comedies of the poet's personal conception, that have had no model in life, and are humorous exaggera-tions, happy or otherwise. These are the comedies of Ben Jonson, Massinger, and Fletcher. Mas-singer's Justice Greedy we can all of us refer to a type, 'with good capon lined,' that has been, and will be; and he would be comic, as Panurge is comic, but only a Rabelais could set him moving with real animation. Probably Justice Greedy would be comic to the audience of a country booth, and to some of our friends. If we have lost our youthful relish for the presentation of characters put together to fit a type, we find it hard to put together the mechanism of a civil smile at his enumeration of his dishes. Something of the same is to be said of Bobadill, swearing 'by the foot of Pharaoh'; with a reservation, for he is made to move faster, and to act. The comic of Jonson is a scholar's excogitation of the comic; that of Massinger a moralist's.

Shakespeare is a well-spring of characters which are saturated with the comic spirit; with more of what we will call blood-life than is to be found anywhere out of Shakespeare; and they are of this world, but they are of the world enlarged to our embrace by imagination, and by great poetic imagination. They are, as it were—I put it to suit my present comparison—creatures of the woods and wilds, not in walled towns, not grouped and toned to pursue a comic exhibition of the narrower world of society. Jaques, Falstaff and his regiment, the varied troop of clowns, Malvolio, Sir Hugh Evans and Fluellen (mar-velous Welshmen!) Benedick and Beatrice, Dogberry, and the rest, are subjects of a special study in the poetically comic.

His comedy of incredible imbroglio belongs to the literary section. One may conceive that there was a natural resemblance between him and Menander, both in the scheme and style of his

lighter plays. Has Shakespeare lived in a later and less emotional, less heroical, period of our history, he might have turned to the painting of manners as well as humanity. Euripides would probably, in the time of Menander, when Athens was enslaved but prosperous, have lent his hand to the composition of romantic comedy. He certainly inspired that fine genius.

Politically, it is accounted a misfortune for France that her nobles thronged to the Court of Louis Quatorze. It was a boon to the comic poet. He had that lively quicksilver world of the animalcule passions, the huge pretensions, the placid absurdities, under his eyes in full activity; vociferous quacks and snapping dupes, hypo-crites, posturers, extravagants, pedants, rose-pink ladies and mad grammarians, sonnetteering marquises, high-flying mistresses, plain-minded maids, inter-threading as in a loom, noisy as at a fair. A simply bourgeois circle will not furnish it, for the middle class must have the brilliant, flippant, independent upper for a spur and a pattern; otherwise it is likely to be inwardly dull, as well as outwardly correct. Yet, though the King was benevolent toward Molière, it is not to the French Court that we are indebted for his unrivaled studies of mankind in society. For the amusement of the Court the ballets and farces were written, which are dearer to the rabble upper, as to the rabble lower, class than intellec-tual comedy. The French bourgeoisie of Paris were sufficiently quick-witted and enlightened by education to welcome great works like *Le Tartuffe*, *Les Femmes Savantes*, and *Le Misanthrope*, works that were perilous ventures on the popular intelligence, big vessels to launch on streams running to shallows. The *Tartuffe* hove into view as an enemy's vessel; it offended, not '*Dieu, mais . . . les dévots*,'[5] as the Prince de Condé explained the cabal raised against it to the King.

The *Femmes Savantes* is a capital instance of the uses of comedy in teaching the world to under-stand what ails it. The farce of the *Précieuses* ridiculed, and put a stop to, the monstrous romantic jargon made popular by certain famous novels. The comedy of the *Femmes Savantes* exposed the later and less apparent, but more finely comic, absurdity of an excessive purism in grammar and diction, and the tendency to be idiotic in precision. The French had felt the burden of this new nonsense; but they had to see the comedy several times before they were

---

[5] "Not God, but the pious."

consoled in their suffering by seeing the cause of it exposed.

The *Misanthrope* was yet more frigidly received. Molière thought it dead. 'I can not improve on it, and assuredly never shall,' he said. It is one of the French titles to honor that this quintessential comedy of the opposition of Alceste and Célimène was ultimately understood and applauded. In all countries the middle class presents the public which, fighting the world, and with a good footing in the fight, knows the world best. It may be the most selfish, but that is a question leading us into sophistries. Cultivated men and women who do not skim the cream of life, and are attached to the duties, yet escape the harsher blows, make acute and balanced observers. Molière is their poet.

Of this class in England, a large body, neither Puritan nor Bacchanalian, have a sentimental objection to face the study of the actual world. They take up disdain of it, when its truths appear humiliating; when the facts are not immediately forced on them, they take up the pride of incredulity. They live in a hazy atmosphere that they suppose an ideal one. Humorous writing they will endure, perhaps approve, if it mingles with pathos to shake and elevate the feelings. They approve of satire, because, like the beak of the vulture, it smells of carrion, which they are not. But of comedy they have a shivering dread, for comedy enfolds them with the wretched host of the world, huddles them with us all in an ignoble assimilation, and cannot be used by any exalted variety as a scourge and a broom. Nay, to be an exalted variety is to come under the calm, curious eye of the Comic Spirit, and be probed for what you are. Men are seen among them, and very many cultivated women. You may distinguish them by a favorite phrase: 'Surely we are not so bad!' and the remark: 'If that is human nature, save us from it!'—as if it could be done; but in the peculiar paradise of the wilful people who will not see, the exclamation assumes the saving grace.

Yet, should you ask them whether they dislike sound sense, they vow they do not. And question cultivated women whether it pleases them to be shown moving on an intellectual level with men, they will answer that it does; numbers of them claim the situation. Now comedy is the fountain of sound sense; not the less perfectly sound on account of the sparkle; and comedy lifts women to a station offering them free play for their wit, as they usually show it, when they have it, on the side of sound sense. The higher the comedy,

the more prominent the part they enjoy in it. Dorine in the *Tartuffe* is common sense incarnate, though palpably a waiting-maid. Célimène is undisputed mistress of the same attribute in the *Misanthrope;* wiser as a woman than Alceste as man. In Congreve's *Way of the World,* Millamant overshadows Mirabell, the sprightliest male figure of English comedy.

But those two ravishing women, so copious and so choice of speech, who fence with men and pass their guard, are heartless! Is it not preferable to be the pretty idiot, the passive beauty, the adorable bundle of caprices, very feminine, very sympathetic, of romantic and sentimental fiction? Our women are taught to think so. The Agnès of the *École des Femmes* should be a lesson for men. The heroines of comedy are like women of the world, not necessarily heartless from being clear-sighted; they seem so to the sentimentally reared, only for the reason that they use their wits, and are not wandering vessels crying for a captain or a pilot. Comedy is an exhibition of their battle with men, and that of men with them; and as the two, however divergent, both look on one object, namely, life, the gradual similarity of their impressions must bring them to some resemblance. The comic poet dares to show us men and women coming to this mutual likeness; he is for saying that when they draw together in social life their minds grow liker; just as the philosopher discerns the similarity of boy and girl, until the girl is marched away to the nursery. Philosopher and comic poet are of a cousinship in the eye they cast on life; and they are equally unpopular with our wilful English of the hazy region and the ideal that is not to be disturbed.

Thus, for want of instruction in the comic idea, we lose a large audience among our cultivated middle class that we should expect to support comedy. The sentimentalist is as averse as the Puritan and as the Bacchanalian.

Our traditions are unfortunate. The public taste is with the idle laughers, and still inclines to follow them. It may be shown by an analysis of Wycherley's *Plain Dealer,* a coarse prose adaption of the *Misanthrope,* stuffed with lumps of realism in a vulgarized theme to hit the mark of English appetite, that we have in it the key-note of the comedy of our stage. It is Molière travestied, with the hoof to his foot, and hair on the pointed tip of his ear. And how difficult it is for writers to disentangle themselves from bad traditions is noticeable when we find Goldsmith, who had grave command of the comic in narrative, producing an elegant farce for a comedy; and

Fielding, who was a master of the comic both in narrative and in dialogue, not even approaching to the presentable in farce.

These bad traditions of comedy affect us, not only on the stage, but in our literature, and may be tracked into our social life. They are the ground of the heavy moralizings by which we are outwearied, about life as a comedy, and comedy as a jade, when popular writers, conscious of fatigue in creativeness, desire to be cogent in a modish cynicism; perversions of the idea of life, and of the proper esteem for the society we have wrested from brutishness, and would carry higher. Stock images of this description are accepted by the timid and the sensitive, as well as by the saturnine, quite seriously; for not many look abroad with their own eyes—fewer still have the habit of thinking for themselves. Life, we know too well, is not a comedy, but something strangely mixed; nor is comedy a vile-mask. The corrupted importation from France was noxious, a noble entertainment spoilt to suit the wretched taste of a villainous age; and the later imitations of it, partly drained of its poison and made decorous, became tiresome, notwithstanding their fun, in the perpetual recurring of the same situations, owing to the absence of original study and vigor of conception. Scene 5, Act 2, of the *Misanthrope,* owing, no doubt, to the fact of our not producing matter for original study, is repeated in succession by Wycherley, Congreve, and Sheridan, and, as it is at second hand, we have it done cynically—or such is the tone—in the manner of 'below stairs.' Comedy thus treated may be accepted as a version of the ordinary wordly understanding of our social life; at least, in accord with the current dicta concerning it. The epigrams can be made; but it is uninstructive, rather tending to do disservice. Comedy justly treated, as you find it in Molière, whom we so clownishly mishandled—the comedy of Molière throws no infamous reflection upon life. It is deeply conceived, in the first place, and therefore it cannot be impure. Meditate on that statement. Never did man wield so shrieking a scourge upon vice; but his consummate self-mastery is not shaken while administering it. Tartuffe and Harpagon, in fact, are made each to whip himself and his class—the false pietists, and the insanely covetous. Molière has only set them in motion. He strips Folly to the skin, displays the imposture of the creature, and is content to offer her better clothing, with the lesson Chrysale reads to Philaminte and Bélise. He conceives purely, and he writes purely, in the simplest language, the simplest of French verse. The source of his wit is clear reason; it is a fountain of that soil, and it springs to vindicate reason, common sense, rightness, and justice—for no vain purpose ever. The wit is of such pervading spirit that it inspires a pun with meaning and interest. His moral does not hang like a tail, or preach from one character incessantly cocking an eye at the audience, as in recent realistic French plays, but is in the heart of his work, throbbing with every pulsation of an organic structure. If life is likened to the comedy of Molière, there is no scandal in the comparison.

Congreve's *Way of the World* is an exception to our other comedies, his own among them, by virtue of the remarkable brilliancy of the writing, and the figure of Millamant. The comedy has no idea in it, beyond the stale one that so the world goes; and it concludes with the jaded discovery of a document at a convenient season for the descent of the curtain. A plot was an afterthought with Congreve. By the help of a wooden villain (Maskwell), marked gallows to the flattest eye, he gets a sort of plot in *The Double-Dealer.* His *Way of the World* might be called 'The Conquest of a Town Coquette'; and Millamant is a perfect portrait of a coquette, both in her resistance to Mirabell and the manner of her surrender, and also in her tongue. The wit here is not so salient as in certain passages of *Love for Love,* where Valentine feigns madness, or retorts on his father, or Mrs. Frail rejoices in the harmlessness of wounds to a woman's virtue, if she keeps them 'from air.' In *The Way of the World,* it appears less prepared in the smartness, and is more diffused in the more charactistic style of the speakers. Here, however, as elsewhere, his famous wit is like a bully-fencer, not ashamed to lay traps for its exhibition, transparently petulant for the train between certain ordinary words and the powder-magazine of the improprieties to be fired. Contrast the wit of Congreve with Molière's. That of the first is a Toledo blade, sharp, and wonderfully supple for steel; cast for duelling, restless in the scabbard, being so pretty when out of it. To shine, it must have an adversary. Molière's wit is like a running brook, with innumerable fresh lights on it at every turn of the wood through which its business is to find a way. It does not run in search of obstructions, to be noisy over them; but when dead leaves and viler substances are heaped along the course, its natural song is heightened. Without effort, and with no dazzling flashes of achievement, it is full of healing, the wit of good breeding, the wit of wisdom.

'Genuine humor and true wit,' says Landor, 'require a sound and capacious mind, which is always a grave one. . . . Rabelais and La Fontaine are recorded by their countrymen to have been *rêveurs*. Few men have been graver than Pascal: few have been wittier.' To apply the citation of so great a brain as Pascal's to our countryman would be unfair. Congreve had a certain soundness of mind; of capacity, in the sense intended by Landor, he had little. Judging him by his wit, he performed some happy thrusts; and, taking it for genuine, it is a surface wit, neither rising from a depth nor flowing from a spring:

On voit qu'il se travaille à dire de bons mots.[6]

He drives the poor hack-word, 'fool,' as cruelly to the market for wit as any of his competitors. Here is an example, that has been held up for eulogy:

WITWOUD.   He has brought me a letter from the fool my brother. . . .
MIRABELL.   A fool, and your brother, Witwoud!
WITWOUD.   Ay, ay, my half-brother. My half-brother he is; no nearer, upon honor.
MIRABELL.   Then 'tis possible he may be but half a fool.

—By evident preparation. This is a sort of wit one remembers to have heard at school, of a brilliant outsider; perhaps to have been guilty of oneself a trifle later. It was, no doubt, a blaze of intellectual fireworks to the bumpkin squire who came to London to go to the theatre and learn manners.

Where Congreve excels all his English rivals is in his literary force, and a succinctness of style peculiar to him. He had correct judgment, a correct ear, readiness of illustration within a narrow range—in snap-shots of the obvious at the obvious—and copious language. He hits the mean of a fine style and a natural in dialogue. He is at once precise and voluble. If you have ever thought upon style, you will acknowledge it to be a signal accomplishment. In this he is a classic, and is worthy of treading a measure with Molière. *The Way of the World* may be read out currently at a first glance, so sure are the accents of the emphatic meaning to strike the eye, per-force of the crispness and cunning polish of the sentences. You have not to look over them before you confide yourself to him; he will carry you safe. Sheridan imitated, but was far from sur-

passing, him. The flow of boudoir billingsgate in Lady Wishfort is unmatched for the vigor and pointedness of the tongue. It spins along with a final ring, like the voice of Nature in a fury, and is, indeed, racy eloquence of the elevated fishwife.

Millamant is an admirable, almost a lovable, heroine. It is a piece of genius in a writer to make a woman's manner of speech portray her. You feel sensible of her presence in every line of her speaking. The stipulations with her lover in view of marriage, her fine lady's delicacy, and fine lady's easy evasions of indelicacy, coquettish airs, and playing with irresolution, which in a common maid would be bashfulness, until she submits to 'dwindle into a wife,' as she says, form a picture that lives in the frame, and is in harmony with Mirabell's description of her:

Here she comes, i' faith, full sail, with her fan spread and her streamers out, and a shoal of fools for tenders.

And, after an interview:

Think of you? To think of a whirlwind, though 't were in a whirlwind, were a case of more steady contemplation; a very tranquillity of mind and mansion.

There is a picturesqueness, as of Millamant and no other, in her voice, when she is encouraged to take Mirabell by Mrs. Fainall, who is 'sure' she has 'a mind to him':

MILLAMANT.   Are you? I think I have—and the horrid man looks as if he thought so too.—

One hears the tones, and sees the sketch and color of the whole scene, in reading it.

Célimène is behind Millamant in vividness An air of bewitching whimsicality hovers over the graces of this comic heroine, like the lively conversational play of a beautiful mouth. But in wit she is no rival of Célimène. What she utters adds to her personal witchery, and is not further memorable. She is a flashing portrait, and a type of the superior ladies who do not think, not of those who do. In representing a class, therefore, it is a lower class, in the proportion that one of Gainsborough's full-length aristocratic women is below the permanent impressiveness of a fair Venetian head.

Millamant, side by side with Célimène, is an example of how far the realistic painting of a character can be carried to win our favor, and of where it falls short. Célimène is a woman's mind in movement, armed with an ungovernable wit; with perspicacious, clear eyes for the world,

<hr>

[6] "One sees that he strains to utter witticisms."

and a very distinct knowledge that she belongs to the world, and is most at home in it. She is attracted to Alceste by her esteem for his honesty; she cannot avoid seeing where the good sense of the man is diseased.

Rousseau, in his letter to D'Alembert on the subject of the *Misanthrope,* discusses the character of Alceste as though Molière had put him forth for an absolute example of misanthropy; whereas Alceste is only a misanthrope of the circle he finds himself placed in—he has a touching faith in the virtue residing in the country, and a critical love of sweet simpleness. Nor is he the principal person of the comedy to which he gives a name. He is only passively comic. Célimène is the active spirit. While he is denouncing and railing, the trial is imposed upon her to make the best of him, and control herself, as much as a witty woman, eagerly courted, can do. By appreciating him she practically confesses her faultiness, and she is better disposed to meet him half-way than he is to bend an inch; only she is 'une âme de vingt ans,'[7] the world is pleasant, and, if the gilded flies of the Court are silly, uncompromising fanatics have their ridiculous features as well. Can she abandon the life they make agreeable to her, for a man who will not be guided by the common sense of his class, and who insists on plunging into one extreme—equal to suicide in her eyes—to avoid another? That is the comic question of the *Misanthrope.* Why will he not continue to mix with the world smoothly, appeased by the flattery of her secret and really sincere preference of him, and taking his revenge in satire of it, as she does from her own not very lofty standard, and will by and by do from his more exalted one?

Célimène is worldliness; Alceste is unwordliness. It does not quite imply unselfishness; and that is perceived by her shrewd head. Still, he is a very uncommon figure in her circle, and she esteems him, 'l'homme aux rubans verts,'[8] who 'sometimes diverts,' but more often horribly vexes her—as she can say of him when her satirical tongue is on the run. Unhappily the soul of truth in him, which wins her esteem, refuses to be tamed, or silent, or unsuspicious, and is the perpetual obstacle to their good accord. He is that melancholy person, the critic of everybody save himself; intensely sensitive to the faults of others, wounded by them; in love with his own indubitable honesty, and with his ideal of the simpler form of life befitting it—qualities which constitute the satirist. He is a Jean Jacques of the Court. His proposal to Célimène, when he pardons her, that she should follow him in flying human-kind, and his frenzy of detestation of her at her refusal, are thoroughly in the mood of Jean Jacques. He is an impracticable creature of a priceless virtue; but Célimène may feel that to fly with him to the desert (that is, from the Court to the country),

Où d'etre homme d'honneur on ait la liberté,[9]

she is likely to find herself the companion of a starving satirist, like that poor princess who ran away with the waiting-man, and, when both were hungry in the forest, was ordered to give him flesh. She is a *fieffée*[10] coquette, rejoicing in her wit and her attractions, and distinguished by her inclination for Alceste in the midst of her many other lovers; only she finds it hard to cut them off—what woman with a train does not?—and when the exposure of her naughty wit has laid her under their rebuke, she will do the utmost she can: she will give her hand to honesty, but she cannot quite abandon wordliness. She would be unwise if she did.

The fable is thin. Our pungent contrivers of plots would see no indication of life in the outlines. The life of the comedy is in the idea. As with the singing of the skylark out of sight, you must love the bird to be attentive to the song, so in this highest flight of the comic Muse, you must love pure comedy warmly to understand the *Misanthrope;* you must be receptive of the idea of comedy. And to love comedy you must know the real world, and know men and women well enough not to expect too much of them, though you may still hope for good.

Menander wrote a comedy called *Misogynes,* said to have been the most celebrated of his works. This misogynist is a married man, according to the fragment surviving, and is a hater of women through hatred of his wife. He generalizes upon them from the example of this lamentable adjunct of his fortunes, and seems to have got the worst of it in the contest with her, which is like the issue in reality in the polite world. He seems also to have deserved it, which may be as true to the copy. But we are unable to say whether the wife was a good voice of her sex; or how far Menander in this instance raised the idea of woman from the mire it was plunged into

---

[7] A soul of twenty years.   [8] "The man with green ribbons."
[9] "Where one is free from being a man of honor."   [10] Arrant.

by the comic poets, or rather satiric dramatists, of the middle period of Greek comedy preceding him and the New Comedy, who devoted their wit chiefly to the abuse, and, for a diversity, to the eulogy of extra-mural ladies of conspicuous fame. Menander idealized them, without purposely elevating. He satirized a certain Thais, and his Thais of the *Eunuchus* of Terence is neither professionally attractive nor replusive; his picture of the two Andrians, Chrysis and her sister, is nowhere to be matched for tenderness. But the condition of honest women in his day did not permit of the freedom of action and fencing dialectic of a Célimène, and consequently it is below our mark of pure comedy.

Sainte-Beuve conjures up the ghost of Menander saying: 'For the love of me love Terence.' It is through love of Terence that moderns are able to love Menander; and what is preserved of Terence has not, apparently, given us the best of the friend of Epicurus. Μισούμενος, the lover taken in horror, and Περικειρομένη, the damsel shorn of her locks, have a promising sound for scenes of jealousy and a too masterful display of lordly authority, leading to regrets of the kind known to intemperate men who imagined they were fighting with the weaker, as the fragments indicate.

Of the six comedies of Terence, four are derived from Menander; two, the *Hecyra* and the *Phormio*, from Apollodorus. These two are inferior, in comic action and the peculiar sweetness of Menander, to the *Andria,* the *Adelphi,* the *Heauton Timorumenos,* and the *Eunuchus;* but Phormio is a more dashing and amusing convivial parasite than the Gnatho of the last-named comedy. There were numerous rivals of whom we know next to nothing (except by the quotations of Athenaeus and Plutarch, and the Greek grammarians who cited them to support a dictum) in this, as in the preceding periods of comedy in Athens; for Menander's plays are counted by many scores, and they were crowned by the prize only eight times. The favorite poet with critics, in Greece as in Rome, was Menander; and if some of his rivals here and there surpassed him in comic force, and outstripped him in competition by an appositeness to the occasion that had previously in the same way deprived the genius of Aristophanes of its due reward in *Clouds* and *Birds,* his position as chief of the comic poets of his age was unchallenged. Plutarch

very unnecessarily drags Aristophanes into a comparison with him, to the confusion of the older poet. Their aims, the matter they dealt in, and the times, were quite dissimilar. But it is no wonder that Plutarch, writing when Athenian beauty of style was the delight of his patrons, should rank Menander at the highest. In what degree of faithfulness Terence copied Menander— whether, as he states of the passage in the *Adelphi* taken from Diphilus, '*verbum de verbo*'[11] in the lovelier scenes (the description of the last words of the dying Andrian, and of her funeral, for instance)—remains conjectural. For us, Terence shares with his master the praise of an amenity that is like Elysian speech, equable and ever gracious; like the face of the Andrian's young sister:

Adeo modesto, adeo venusto, ut nil supra.[12]

The celebrated '*flens quam familiariter,*'[13] of which the closest rendering grounds hopelessly on harsh prose, to express the sorrowful confidingness of a young girl who has lost her sister and dearest friend, and has but her lover left to her—'she turned and flung herself on his bosom, weeping as though at home there'—this our instinct tells us must be Greek, though hardly finer in Greek. Certain lines of Terence, compared with the original fragments, show that he embellished them; but his taste was too exquisite for him to do other than devote his genius to the honest translation of such pieces as the above. Menander, then; with him, through the affinity of sympathy, Terence; and Shakespeare and Molière, have this beautiful translucency of language. And the study of the comic poets might be recommended if for that only.

A singular ill fate befell the writings of Menander. What we have of him in Terence was chosen probably to please the cultivated Romans, and is a romantic play with comic intrigue, obtained in two instances, the *Andria* and the *Eunuchus,* by rolling a couple of his originals into one. The titles of certain of the lost plays indicate the comic illumining character; a *Self-Pitier,* a *Self-Chastiser,* an *Ill-tempered Man,* a *Superstitious,* an *Incredulous,* etc., point to suggestive domestic themes. Terence forwarded manuscript translations from Greece that suffered shipwreck; he, who could have restored the treasure, died on the way home. The zealots of Byzantium completed the work of destruction. So we have the four

---

[11] Word for word. [12] "So modest, so charming, like nothing above."
[13] Sorrowful confidingness.

comedies of Terence, numbering six of Menander, with a few sketches of plots (one of them, the *Thesaurus,* introduces a miser, whom we should have liked to contrast with Harpagon), and a multitude of small fragments of a sententious cast, fitted for quotation. Enough remains to make his greatness felt.

Without undervaluing other writers of comedy, I think it may be said that Menander and Molière stand alone specially as comic poets of the feelings and the idea. In each of them there is a conception of the comic that refines even to pain, as in the Menedemus of the *Heauton Timorumenos,* and in the Misanthrope. Menander and Molière have given the principal types to comedy hitherto. The Micio and Demea of the *Adelphi,* with their opposing views of the proper management of youth, are still alive; the Sganarelles and Arnolphes of the *École des Maris* and the *École des Femmes* are not all buried. Tartuffe is the father of the hypocrites; Orgon of the dupes; Thraso of the braggadocios; Alceste of the 'Manlys'; Davus and Syrus of the intriguing valets, the Scapins and Figaros. Ladies that soar in the realms of rose-pink, whose language wears the nodding plumes of intellectual conceit, are traceable to Philaminte and Bélise of the *Femmes Savantes;* and the mordant, witty women have the tongue of Célimène. The reason is that these two poets idealized upon life; the foundation of their types is real and in the quick, but they painted with spiritual strength, which is the solid in art.

The idealistic conception of comedy gives breadth and opportunities of daring to comic genius, and helps to solve the difficulties it creates. How, for example, shall an audience be assured that an evident and monstrous dupe is actually deceived without being an absolute fool? In *Le Tartuffe* the note of high comedy strikes when Orgon on his return home hears of his idol's excellent appetite. *'Le pauvre homme!'*[14] he exclaims. He is told that the wife of his bosom has been unwell. *'Et Tartuffe?'* he asks, impatient to hear him spoken of, his mind suffused with the thought of Tartuffe, crazy with tenderness; and again he croons: *'Le pauvre homme!'* It is the mother's cry of pitying delight at a nurse's recital of the feats in young animal gluttony of her cherished infant. After this master-stroke of the comic, you not only put faith in Orgon's roseate

prepossession, you share it with him by comic sympathy, and can listen with no more than a tremble of the laughing-muscles to the instance he gives of the sublime humanity of Tartuffe:

> Un rien presque suffit pour le scandaliser,
> Jusque-là qu'il se vint, l'autre jour, accuser
> D'avoir pris une puce en faisant sa prière,
> Et de l'avoir tuée avec trop de colère.[15]

'And to have killed it too wrathfully'! Translating Molière is like humming an air one has heard performed by an accomplished violonist of the pure tones without flourish.

Orgon awakening to find another dupe in Madame Pernelle, incredulous of the revelations which have at last opened his own besotted eyes, is a scene of the double comic, vivified by the spell previously cast on the mind. There we feel the power of the poet's creation; and, in the sharp light of that sudden turn, the humanity is livelier than any realistic work can make it.

Italian comedy gives many hints for a Tartuffe; but they may be found in Boccaccio, as well as in Machiavelli's *Mandragola.* The Frate Timoteo of this piece is only a very oily friar, compliantly assisting an intrigue with ecclesiastical sophisms (to use the mildest word) for payment. Frate Timoteo has a fine Italian priestly pose:

DONNA.   Credete voi, che 'l Turco passi questo anno in Italia?

FRATE TIMOTEO.   Se voi non fate orazione, sí.[16]

Priestly arrogance and unctuousness, and trickeries and casuistries, cannot be painted without our discovering a likeness in the long Italian gallery. Goldoni sketched the Venetian manners of the decadence of the Republic with a French pencil, and was an Italian scribe in style.

The Spanish stage is richer in such comedies as that which furnished the idea of the *Menteur* to Corneille. But you must force yourself to believe that this liar is not forcing his vein when he piles lie upon lie. There is no preceding touch to win the mind to credulity. Spanish comedy is generally in sharp outline, as of skeletons; in quick movement, as of marionettes. The comedy might be performed by a troop of the *corps de ballet;* and in the recollection of the reading it resolves to an animated shuffle of feet. It is, in fact, something other than the true idea of comedy. Where the sexes are separated, men and women grow, as the Portuguese call it, *afaimados* of one another,

---

[14] "The poor man!"
[15] "Almost nothing could scandalize him until the other day he was accused of having taken a flea at prayer and of having killed it too wrathfully."
[16] "Do you believe the Turk spent this year in Italy?" "If you don't say your prayers, yes."

famine-stricken; and all the tragic elements are on the stage. Don Juan is a comic character that sends souls flying; nor does the humor of the breaking of a dozen women's hearts conciliate the comic Muse with the drawing of blood.

German attempts at comedy remind one vividly of Heine's image of his country in the dancing of Atta Troll. Lessing tried his hand at it, with a sobering effect upon readers. The intention to produce the reverse effect is just visible, and therein, like the portly graces of the poor old Pyrenean bear poising and twirling on his right hing-leg and his left, consists the fun. Jean Paul Richter gives the best edition of the German comic in the contrast of Siebenkäs with his Lenette. A light of the comic is in Goethe—enough to complete the splendid figure of the man, but no more.

The German literary laugh, like the timed awakenings of their Barbarossa in the hollows of the Untersberg, is infrequent, and rather monstrous—never a laugh of men and women in concert. It comes of unrefined, abstract fancy, grotesque or grim, or gross, like the peculiar humors of their little earthmen. Spiritual laughter they have not yet attained to; sentimentalism waylays them in the flight. Here and there a *volkslied* or *märchen*[17] shows a national aptitude for stout animal laughter; and we see that the literature is built on it, which is hopeful so far; but to enjoy it, to enter into the philosophy of the broad grin that seems to hesitate between the skull and the embryo, and reaches its perfection in breadth from the pulling of two square fingers at the corners of the mouth, one must have aid of 'the good Rhine wine,' and be of German blood unmixed besides. This treble-Dutch lumbersomeness of the Comic Spirit is of itself exclusive of the idea of comedy, and the poor voice allowed to women in German domestic life will account for the absence of comic dialogues reflecting upon life in that land. I shall speak of it again in the second section of this lecture.

Eastward you have total silence of comedy among a people intensely susceptible to laughter, as the *Arabian Nights* will testify. Where the veil is over women's faces, you cannot have society, without which the senses are barbarous and the Comic Spirit is driven to the gutters of grossness to slake its thirst. Arabs in this respect are worse than Italians—much worse than Germans,—just in the degree that their system of treating women is worse.

M. Saint-Marc Girardin, the excellent French essayist and master of critical style, tells of a conversation he had once with an Arab gentleman on the topic of the different management of these difficult creatures in Orient and in Occident; and the Arab spoke in praise of many good results of the greater freedom enjoyed by Western ladies, and the charm of conversing with them. He was questioned why his countrymen took no measures to grant them something of that kind of liberty. He jumped out of his individuality in a twinkling, and entered into the sentiments of his race, replying, from the pinnacle of a splendid conceit, with affected humility of manner: '*You* can look on them without perturbation—but *we*! . . .' And, after this profoundly comic interjection, he added, in deep tones: 'The very face of a woman!' Our representative of temperate notions demurely consented that the Arab's pride of inflammability should insist on the prudery of the veil as the civilizing medium of his race.

There has been fun in Bagdad. But there never will be civilization where comedy is not possible; and that comes of some degree of social equality of the sexes. I am not quoting the Arab to exhort and disturb the somnolent East; rather for cultivated women to recognize that the comic Muse is one of their best friends. They are blind to their interests in swelling the ranks of the sentimentalists. Let them look with their clearest vision abroad and at home. They will see that, where they have no social freedom, comedy is absent; where they are household drudges, the form of comedy is primitive; where they are tolerably independent, but uncultivated, exciting melodrama takes its place, and a sentimental version of them. Yet the comic will out, as they would know if they listened to some of the private conversations of men whose minds are undirected by the comic Muse; as the sentimental man, to his astonishment, would know likewise, if he in similar fashion could receive a lesson. But where women are on the road to an equal footing with men, in attainments and in liberty—in what they have won for themselves, and what has been granted them by a fair civilization—there, and only waiting to be transplanted from life to the stage, or the novel, or the poem, pure comedy flourishes, and is, as it would help them to be, the sweetest of diversions, the wisest of delightful companions.

Now, to look about us in the present time, I

---

[17] Folk song or fairy tale.

think it will be acknowledged that, in neglecting the cultivation of the comic idea, we are losing the aid of a powerful auxiliar. You see Folly perpetually sliding into new shapes in a society possessed of wealth and leisure, with many whims, many strange ailments and strange doctors. Plenty of common sense is in the world to thrust her back when she pretends to empire. But the first-born of common sense, the vigilant Comic, which is the genius of thoughtful laughter, which would readily extinguish her at the outset, is not serving as a public advocate.

You will have noticed the disposition of common sense, under pressure of some pertinacious piece of light-headedness, to grow impatient and angry. That is a sign of the absence, or at least of the dormancy, of the comic idea. For Folly is the natural prey of the Comic, known to it in all her transformations, in every disguise; and it is with the springing delight of hawk over heron, hound after fox, that it gives her chase, never fretting, never tiring, sure of having her, allowing her no rest.

Contempt is a sentiment that cannot be entertained by comic intelligence. What is it but an excuse to be idly-minded, or personally lofty, or comfortably narrow, not perfectly humane? If we do not feign when we say that we despise Folly, we shut the brain. There is a disdainful attitude in the presence of Folly, partaking of the foolishness to comic perception; and anger is not much less foolish than disdain. The struggle we have to conduct is essence against essence. Let no one doubt of the sequel when this emanation of what is firmest in us is launched to strike down the daughter of Unreason and Sentimentalism—such being Folly's parentage, when it is respectable.

Our modern system of combating her is too long defensive, and carried on too ploddingly with concrete engines of war in the attack. She has time to get behind entrenchments. She is ready to stand a siege, before the heavily-armed man of science and the writer of the leading article or elaborate essay have primed their big guns. It should be remembered that she has charms for the multitude; and an English multitude, seeing her make a gallant fight of it, will be half in love with her, certainly willing to lend her a cheer. Benevolent subscriptions assist her to hire her own man of science, her own organ in the press. If ultimately she is cast out and overthrown, she can stretch a finger at gaps in our ranks. She can say that she commanded an army, and seduced men, whom we thought sober men and safe, to act as her lieutenants. We learn rather gloomily, after she has flashed her lantern, that we have in our midst able men, and men with minds, for whom there is no pole-star in intellectual nagivation. Comedy, or the comic element, is the specific for the poison of delusion while Folly is passing from the state of vapor to substantial form.

O for a breath of Aristophanes, Rabelais, Voltaire, Cervantes, Fielding, Molière! These are spirits that, if you know them well, will come when you do call. You will find the very invocation of them act on you like a renovating air—the south-west coming off the sea, or a cry in the Alps.

No one would presume to say that we are deficient in jokers. They abound, and the organization directing their machinery to shoot them in the wake of the leading article and the popular sentiment is good. But the comic differs from them in addressing the wits for laughter; and the sluggish wits want some training to respond to it, whether in public life or private, and particularly when the feelings are excited. The sense of the comic is much blunted by habits of punning and of using humoristic phrase, the trick of employing Johnsonian polysyllables to treat of the infinitely little. And it really may be humorous, of a kind; yet it will miss the point by going too much round about it.

A certain French Duc Pasquier died, some years back, at a very advanced age. He had been the venerable Duc Pasquier, in his later years, up to the period of his death. There was a report of Duc Pasquier that he was a man of profound egoism. Hence an argument arose, and was warmly sustained, upon the excessive selfishness of those who, in a world of troubles, and calls to action, and innumerable duties, husband their strength for the sake of living on. Can it be possible, the argument ran, for a truly generous heart to continue beating up to the age of a hundred? Duc Pasquier was not without his defenders, who likened him to the oak of the forest—a venerable comparison.

The argument was conducted on both sides with spirit and earnestness, lightened here and there by frisky touches of the polysyllabic playful, reminding one of the serious pursuit of their fun by truant boys that are assured they are out of the eye of their master, and now and then indulge in an imitation of him. And well might it be supposed that the comic idea was asleep, not overlooking them! It resolved at last to this, that either Duc Pasquier was a scandal on our humanity in clinging to life so long, or that he honored it by so sturdy a resistance to the enemy. As one who has entangled himself in a labyrinth is glad to get out again at the entrance, the argument ran about, to conclude with its commencement.

Now, imagine a master of the comic treating this theme, and particularly the argument on it. Imagine an Aristophanic comedy of the Centenarian, with choric praises of heroical early death, and the same of a stubborn vitality, and the poet laughing at the Chorus; and the grand question for contention in dialogue, as to the exact age when a man should die, to the identical minute, that he may preserve the respect of his follows, followed by a systematic attempt to make an accurate measurement in parallel lines, with a tough rope-yarn by one party, and a string of yawns by the other, of the veteran's power of enduring life, and our capacity for enduring *him,* with tremendous pulling on both sides. Would not the comic view of the discussion illumine it and the disputants like very lightning? There are questions, as well as persons, that only the comic can fitly touch.

Aristophanes would probably have crowned the ancient tree with the consolatory observation to the haggard line of long-expectant heirs of the Centenarian, that they live to see the blessedness of coming of a strong stock. The shafts of his ridicule would mainly have been aimed at the disputants; for the sole ground of the argument was the old man's character, and sophists are not needed to demonstrate that we can very soon have too much of a bad thing. A centenarian does not necessarily provoke the comic idea, nor does the corpse of a duke. It is not provoked in the order of nature, until we draw its penetrating attentiveness to some circumstance with which we have been mixing our private interests, or our speculative obfuscation. Dulness, insensible to the comic, has the privilege of arousing it; and the laying of a dull finger on matters of human life is the surest method of establishing electrical communications with a battery of laughter—where the comic idea is prevalent.

But if the comic idea prevailed with us, and we had an Aristophanes to barb and wing it, we should be breathing air of Athens. Prosers now pouring forth on us like public fountains would be cut short in the street and left blinking, dumb as pillar-posts with letters thrust into their mouths. We should throw off incubus, our dreadful familiar—by some called boredom—

whom it is our present humiliation to be just alive enough to loathe, never quick enough to foil. There would be a bright and positive, clear Hellenic perception of facts. The vapors of unreason and sentimentalism would be blown away before they were productive. Where would pessimist and optimist be? They would in any case have a diminished audience. Yet possibly the change of despots, from good-natured old obtuseness to keen-edged intelligence, which is by nature merciless, would be more than we could bear. The rupture of the link between dull people, consisting in the fraternal agreement that something is too clever for them, and a shot beyond them, is not to be thought of lightly; for, slender though the link may seem, it is equivalent to a cement forming a concrete of dense cohesion, very desirable in the estimation of the statesman.

A political Aristophanes, taking advantage of his lyrical Bacchic license, was found too much for political Athens. I would not ask to have him revived, but that the sharp light of such a spirit as his might be with us to strike now and then on public affairs, public themes, to make them spin along more briskly.

He hated with the politician's fervor the Sophist who corrupted simplicity of thought, the poet who destroyed purity of style, the demagogue, 'the saw-toothed monster,' who, as he conceived, chicaned the mob; and he held his own against them by strength of laughter, until fines, the curtailing of his comic license in the chorus, and ultimately the ruin of Athens, which could no longer support the expense of the chorus, threw him altogether on dialogue, and brought him under the law. After the catastrophe, the poet, who had ever been gazing back at the men of Marathon and Salamis, must have felt that he had foreseen it; and that he was wise when he pleaded for peace, and derided military coxcombry and the captious old creature Demus, we can admit. He had the comic poet's gift of common sense—which does not always include political intelligence; yet his political tendency raised him above the Old-Comedy turn for uproarious farce. He abused Socrates; but Xenophon, the disciple of Socrates, by his trained rhetoric saved the Ten Thousand. Aristophanes might say that, if his warnings had been followed, there would have been no such thing as a mercenary Greek expedition under Cyrus. Athens, however, was on a landslip, falling; none could arrest it. To gaze back, to uphold the old times, was a most natural conservatism, and fruitless. The aloe had bloomed.

Whether right or wrong in his politics and his criticisms, and bearing in mind the instruments he played on and the audience he had to win, there is an idea in his comedies; it is the idea of good citizenship.

He is not likely to be revived. He stands, like Shakespeare, an unapproachable. Swift says of him, with a loving chuckle:

> But as to comic Aristophanes,
> The rogue too vicious and too profane is.

Aristophanes was 'profane,' under satiric direction; unlike his rivals Cratinus, Phrynichus, Ameipsias, Eupolis, and others, if we are to believe him, who, in their extraordinary Donnybrook Fair of the day of comedy, thumped one another and everybody else with absolute heartiness, as he did, but aimed at small game, and dragged forth particular women, which he did not. He is an aggregate of many men, all of a certain greatness. We may build up a conception of his powers if we mount Rabelais upon *Hudibras,* lift him with the songfulness of Shelley, give him a vein of Heinrich Heine, and cover him with the mantle of the *Anti-Jacobin,* adding (that there may be some Irish in him) a dash of Grattan, before he is in motion.

But such efforts at conceiving one great one by incorporation of minors are vain, and cry for excuse. Supposing Wilkes for leading man in a country constantly plunging into war under some Lamachus, with enemies periodically firing the land up to the gates of London, and a Samuel Foote, of prodigious genius, attacking him with ridicule: I think it gives a notion of the conflict engaged in by Aristophanes. This laughing bald-pate, as he calls himself, was a Titanic pamphleteer, using laughter for his political weapon; a laughter without scruple, the laughter of Hercules. He was primed with wit, as with the garlic he speaks of giving to the game-cocks to make them fight the better. And he was a lyric poet of aerial delicacy, with the homely song of a jolly national poet, and a poet of such feeling that the comic mask is at times no broader than a cloth on a face to show the serious features of our common likeness. He is not to be revived; but, if his method were studied, some of the fire in him would come to us, and *we* might be revived.

Taking them generally, the English public are most in sympathy with this primitive Aristophanic comedy, wherein the comic is capped by the grotesque, irony tips the wit, and satire is a naked sword. They have the basis of the comic in them— an esteem for common sense. They cordially dislike the reverse of it. They have a rich laugh, though it is not the *gros rire* of the Gaul tossing *gros sel,*[18] nor the polished Frenchman's mentally digestive laugh. And if they have now, like a monarch with a troop of dwarfs, too many jesters kicking the dictionary about, to let them *reflect* that they are dull, occasionally (like the pensive monarch surprising himself with an idea of an idea of his own), they *look* so. And they are given to looking in the glass. They must see that something ails them. How much even the better order of them will endure, without a thought of the defensive, when the person afflicting them is protected from satire, we read in memoirs of a preceding age, where the vulgarly tyrannous hostess of a great house of reception shuffled the guests and played them like a pack of cards, with her exact estimate of the strength of each one printed on them; and still this house continued to be the most popular in England, nor did the lady ever appear in print or on the boards as the comic type that she was.

It has been suggested that they have not yet spiritually comprehended the signification of living in society; for who are cheerfuller, brisker of wit, in the fields, and as explorers, colonizers, backwoodsmen? They are happy in rough exercise, and also in complete repose. The intermediate condition, when they are called upon to talk to one another, upon other than affairs of business or their hobbies, reveals them wearing a curious look of vacancy, as it were the socket of an eye wanting. The comic is perpetually springing up in social life, and it oppresses them from not being perceived.

Thus, at a dinner-party, one of the guests, who happens to have enrolled himself in a burial-company, politely entreats the others to inscribe their names as shareholders, expatiating on the advantages accruing to them in the event of their very possible speedy death, the salubrity of the site, the aptitude of the soil for a quick consumption of their remains, etc.; and they drink sadness from the incongruous man, and conceive indigestion not seeing him in a sharply-defined light that would bid them taste the comic of him. Or it is mentioned that a newly-elected member of our Parliament celebrates his arrival at eminence by the publication of a book on cab-fares, dedicated to a beloved female relative deceased, and the comment on it is the word

---

[18] Coarse laugh . . . coarse salt.

'Indeed.' But, merely for a contrast, turn to a not uncommon scene of yesterday in the hunting-field, where a brilliant young rider, having broken his collar-bone, trots away very soon after, against medical interdict, half put together in splinters, to the most distant meet of his neighbourhood, sure of escaping his doctor, who is the first person he encounters. 'I came here purposely to avoid you,' says the patient. 'I came here purposely to take care of you,' says the doctor. Off they go, and come to a swollen brook. The patient clears it handsomely; the doctor tumbles in. All the field are alive with the heartiest relish of every incident and every cross-light on it, and dull would the man have been thought who had not his word to say about it when riding home.

In our prose literature we have had delightful comic writers. Besides Fielding and Goldsmith, there is Miss Austen, whose Emma and Mr. Elton might walk straight into a comedy, were the plot arranged for them. Galt's neglected novels have some characters and strokes of shrewd comedy. In our poetic literature the comic is delicate and graceful above the touch of Italian and French. Generally, however, the English elect excel in satire, and they are noble humorists. The national disposition is for hard-hitting, with a moral purpose to sanction it; or for a rosy, sometimes a larmoyant, geniality, not unmanly in its verging upon tenderness, and with a singular attraction for thickheadedness, to decorate it with asses' ears and the most beautiful sylvan haloes. But the comic is a different spirit.

You may estimate your capacity for comic perception by being able to detect the ridicule of them you love without loving them less; and more by being able to see yourself somewhat ridiculous in dear eyes, and accepting the correction their image of you proposes.

Each one of an affectionate couple may be willing, as we say, to die for the other, yet unwilling to utter the agreeable word at the right moment; but if the wits were sufficiently quick for them to perceive that they are in a comic situation, as affectionate couples must be when they quarrel, they would not wait for the moon or the almanac, or a Dorine, to bring back the flood-tide of tender feelings, that they should join hands and lips.

If you detect the ridicule, and your kindliness is chilled by it, you are slipping into the grasp of Satire.

If, instead of falling foul of the ridiculous person with a satiric rod, to make him writhe and shriek aloud, you prefer to sting him under a semi-caress, by which he shall in his anguish be rendered dubious whether indeed anything has hurt him, you are an engine of Irony.

If you laugh all round him, tumble him, roll him about, deal him a smack, and drop a tear on him, own his likeness to you, and yours to your neighbor, spare him as little as you shun, pity him as much as you expose, it is a spirit of Humor that is moving you.

The comic, which is the perceptive, is the governing spirit, awakening and giving aim to these powers of laughter, but it is not to be confounded with them; it enfolds a thinner form of them, differing from satire in not sharply driving into the quivering sensibilities, and from humor in not comforting them and tucking them up, or indicating a broader than the range of this bustling world to them.

Fielding's Jonathan Wild presents a case of this peculiar distinction, when that man of eminent greatness remarks upon the unfairness of a trial in which the condemnation has been brought about by twelve men of the opposite party; for it is not satiric, it is not humorous; yet it is immensely comic to hear a guilty villain protesting that his own 'party' should have a voice in the law. It opens an avenue into villains' ratiocination. And the comic is not canceled though we should suppose Jonathan to be giving play to his humour. (I may have dreamed this, or had it suggested to me, for, on referring to *Jonathan Wild,* I do not find it.) Apply the case to the man of deep wit, who is ever certain of his condemnation by the opposite party, and then it ceases to be comic, and will be satiric.

The look of Fielding upon Richardson is essentially comic. His method of correcting the sentimental writer is a mixture of the comic and the humorous. Parson Adams is a creation of humor. But both the conception and the presentation of Alceste and of Tartuffe, of Célimène and Philaminte, are purely comic, addressed to the intellect; there is no humour in them, and they refresh the intellect they quicken to detect their comedy, by force of the contrast they offer between themselves and the wiser world about them—that is to say, society, or that assemblage of minds whereof the comic spirit has its origin.

Byron had splendid powers of humour, and the most poetic satire that we have example of, fusing at times to hard irony. He had no strong comic sense, or he would not have taken an anti-social position, which is directly opposed to the comic; and in his philosophy, judged by philosophers, he is a comic figure by reason of this deficiency. '*Sobald er reflectirt ist er ein Kind,*'[19] Goethe says of him. Carlyle sees him in this comic light, treats him in the humorous manner.

The satirist is a moral agent, often a social scavenger, working on a storage of bile.

The ironist is one thing or another, according to his caprice. Irony is the humor of satire; it may be savage, as in Swift, with a moral object, or sedate, as in Gibbon, with a malicious. The foppish irony fretting to be seen, and the irony which leers, that you shall not mistake its intention, are failures in satiric effort pretending to the treasures of ambiguity.

The humorist of mean order is a refreshing laugher, giving tone to the feelings, and sometimes allowing the feelings to be too much for him; but the humorist of high has an embrace of contrasts beyond the scope of the comic poet.

Heart and mind laugh out at Don Quixote, and still you brood on him. The juxtaposition of the knight and squire is a comic conception, the opposition of their natures most humorous. They are as different as the two hemispheres in the time of Columbus, yet they touch, and are bound in one, by laughter. The knight's great aims and constant mishaps, his chivalrous valiancy exercised on absurd objects, his good sense along the high road of the craziest of expeditions, the compassion he plucks out of derision, and the admirable figure he preserves while stalking through the frantically grotesque and burlesque assailing him, are in the loftiest moods of humor, fusing the tragic sentiment with the comic narrative. The stroke of the great humorist is world-wide, with lights of tragedy in his laughter.

Taking a living great, though not creative, humorist to guide our description: the skull of Yorick is in his hands in our seasons of festival; he sees visions of primitive man capering preposterously under the gorgeous robes of ceremonial. Our soles must be on fire when we wear solemnity, if we would not press upon his shrewdest nerve. Finite and infinite flash from one to the other with him, lending him a two-edged thought that peeps out of his peacefullest lines by fits, like the lantern of the fire-watcher at windows, going the rounds at night. The comportment and performances of men in society are to him, by the vivid comparison with their mortality, more grotesque than respectable. But ask yourself: 'Is he always to be relied on for justness?' He will fly straight as the emissary eagle back to Jove at the true Hero. He will also make as determined a swift descent upon the man of his wilful choice, whom we cannot distinguish as a true one. This vast power of his, built up of the feelings and the intellect in union, is often wanting in proportion and in discretion. Humorists touching upon history or society are given to be capricious. They are, as in the case of Sterne, given to be sentimental; for with them the feelings are primary, as with singers. Comedy, on the other hand, is an interpretation of the general mind, and is for that reason of necessity kept in restraint. The French lay marked stress on *mesure et goût,*[20] and they own how much they owe to Molière for leading them in simple justness and taste. We can teach them many things; they can teach us in this.

The comic poet is in the narrow field, or enclosed square, of the society he depicts; and he addresses the still narrower enclosure of men's intellects, with reference to the operation of the social world upon their characters. He is not concerned with beginnings or endings or surroundings, but with what you are now weaving. To understand his work and value it, you must have a sober liking of your kind, and a sober estimate of our civilized qualities. The aim and business of the comic poet are misunderstood, his meaning is not seized nor his point of view taken, when he is accused of dishonoring our nature and being hostile to sentiment, tending to spitefulness and making an unfair use of laughter. Those who detect irony in comedy do so because they choose to see it in life. Poverty, says the satirist, 'has nothing harder in itself than that it makes men ridiculous.' But poverty is never ridiculous to comic perception until it attempts to make its rags conceal its bareness in a forlorn attempt at decency, or foolishly to rival ostentation. Caleb Balderstone, in his endeavour to keep up the honor of a noble household in a state of beggary, is an exquisitely comic character. In the case of 'poor relatives,' on the other hand, it is the rich, whom they perplex, that are really comic; and to laugh at the former, not seeing the comedy of the latter, is to betray dulness of vision. Humorist and satirist frequently hunt together as ironists in pursuit of the grotesque, to the exclusion of the comic. That was an affecting moment in the history of the Prince Regent, when the First Gentleman of Europe burst into tears at a sarcastic remark of Beau Brummell's on the cut of his coat. Humor,

---

[19] "As soon as he reflects, he is a child."   [20] Measure and taste.

satire, irony, pounce on it altogether as their common prey. The Comic Spirit eyes, but does not touch, it. Put into action, it would be farcical. It is too gross for comedy.

Incidents of a kind casting ridicule on our unfortunate nature, instead of our conventional life, provoke derisive laughter, which thwarts the comic idea. But derision is foiled by the play of the intellect. Most of doubtful causes in contest are open to comic interpretation, and any intellectual pleading of a doubtful cause contains germs of an idea of comedy.

The laughter of satire is a blow in the back or the face. The laughter of comedy is impersonal and of unrivaled politeness, nearer a smile—often no more than a smile. It laughs through the mind, for the mind directs it; and it might be called the humor of the mind.

One excellent test of the civilization of a country, as I have said, I take to be the flourishing of the comic idea and comedy; and the test of true comedy is that it shall awaken thoughtful laughter.

If you believe that our civilisation is founded in common sense (and it is the first condition of sanity to believe it), you will, when contemplating men, discern a Spirit overhead; not more heavenly than the light flashed upward from glassy surfaces, but luminous and watchful; never shooting beyond them, nor lagging in the rear; so closely attached to them that it may be taken for a slavish reflex, until its features are studied. It has the sage's brows, and the sunny malice of a faun lurks at the corners of the half-closed lips drawn in an idle wariness of half-tension. That slim feasting smile, shaped like the long-bow, was once a big round satyr's laugh, that flung up the brows like a fortress lifted by gunpowder. The laugh will come again, but it will be of the order of the smile, finely-tempered, showing sunlight of the mind, mental richness rather than noisy enormity. Its common aspect is one of unsolicitous observation, as if surveying a full field and having leisure to dart on its chosen morsels, without any fluttering eagerness. Men's future upon earth docs not attract it; their honesty and shapeliness in the present does; and whenever they wax out of proportion, overblown, affected, pretentious, bombastical, hypocritical, pedantic, fantastically delicate; whenever it sees them self-decieved or hoodwinked, given to run riot in idolatries, drifting into vanities, congregating in absurdities, planning shortsightedly, plotting dementedly; whenever they are at variance with their professions, and violate the unwritten but perceptible laws binding them in consideration one to another; whenever they offend sound reason, fair justice; are false in humility or mined with conceit, individually, or in the bulk; the Spirit overhead will look humanely malign, and cast an oblique light on them, followed by volleys of silvery laughter. That is the Comic Spirit.

Not to distinguish it is to be bull-blind to the spiritual, and to deny the existence of a mind of man where minds of men are in working conjunction.

You must, as I have said, believe that our state of society is founded in common sense, otherwise you will not be struck by the contrasts the Comic Spirit perceives, or have it to look to for your consolation. You will, in fact, be standing in that peculiar oblique beam of light, yourself illuminated to the general eye as the very object of chase and doomed quarry of the thing obscure to you. But to feel its presence, and to see it, is your assurance that many sane and solid minds are with you in what you are experiencing; and this of itself spares you the pain of satirical heat, and the bitter craving to strike heavy blows. You share the sublime of wrath, that would not have hurt the foolish, but merely demonstrate their foolishness. Molière was contented to revenge himself on the critics of the *École des Femmes* by writing the *Critique de l'École des Femmes*, one of the wisest as well as the playfullest of studies in criticism. A perception of the Comic Spirit gives high fellowship. You become a citizen of the selecter world, the highest we know of in connection with our old world, which is not supermundane. Look there for your unchallengeable upper class! You feel that you are one of this our civilised community, that you cannot excape from it, and would not if you could. Good hope sustains you; weariness does not overwhelm you; in isolation you see no charms for vanity; personal pride is greatly moderated. Nor shall your title of citizenship exclude you from worlds of imagination of or devotion. The Comic Spirit is not hostile to the sweetest songfully poetic. Chaucer bubbles with it; Shakespeare overflows; there is a mild moon's ray of it (pale with super-refinement through distance from our flesh and blood planet) in *Comus*. Pope has it, and it is the daylight side of the night half-obscuring Cowper. It is only hostile to the priestly element when that, by baleful swelling, transcends and overlaps the bounds of its office; and then, in extreme cases, it is too true to itself to speak, and veils the lamp—as, for example, the spectacle of Bossuet over the dead body of Molière, at which the dark angels may, but men do not, laugh.

We have had comic pulpits, for a sign that the laughter-moving and the worshipful may be in alliance; I know not how far comic or how much assisted in seeming so by the unexpectedness and the relief of its appearance; at least they are popular—they are said to win the ear. Laughter is open to perversion, like other good things; the scornful and the brutal sorts are not unknown to us; but the laughter directed by the Comic Spirit is a harmless wine, conducing to sobriety in the degree that it enlivens. It enters you like fresh air into a study, as when one of the sudden contrasts of the comic idea floods the brain like reassuring daylight. You are cognizant of the true kind by feeling that you take it in, savor it, and have what flowers live on, natural air for food. That which you give out—the joyful roar—is not the better part; let that go to good-fellowship and the benefit of the lungs. Aristophanes promises his auditors that, if they will retain the ideas of the comic poet carefully, as they keep dried fruits in boxes, their garments shall smell odoriferous of wisdom throughout the year. The boast will not be thought an empty one by those who have choice friends that have stocked themselves according to his directions. Such treasuries of sparkling laughter are wells in our desert. Sensitiveness to the comic laugh is a step in civilization. To shrink from being an object of it is a step in cultivation. We know the degree of refinement in men by the matter they will laugh at, and the ring of the laugh; but we know likewise that the larger natures are distinguished by the great breadth of their power of laughter, and no one really loving Molière is refined by that love to despise or be dense to Aristophanes, though it may be that the lover of Aristophanes will not have risen to the height of Molière. Embrace them both, and you have the whole scale of laughter in your breast. Nothing in the world surpasses in stormy fun the scene in the *Frogs,* when Bacchus and Xanthias receive their thrashings from the hands of business-like Acacus, to discover which is the divinity of the two by his imperviousness to the mortal condition of pain, and each, under the obligation of not crying out, makes believe that his horrible bellow—the god's '*iou! iou!*' being the lustier— means only the stopping of a sneeze, or horsemen sighted, or the prelude to an invocation to some deity, and the salve contrives that the god shall get the bigger lot of blows. Passages of Rabelais,

one or two in *Don Quixote,* and the supper 'in the manner of the ancients' in *Peregrine Pickle,* are of a similar cataract of laughter. But it is not illuminating; it is not the laughter of the mind. Molière's laughter, in his purest comedies, is etheral—as light to our nature, as color to our thoughts. The *Misanthrope* and the *Tartuffe* have no audible laughter, but the characters are steeped in the comic spirit. They quicken the mind through laughter, from coming out of the mind; and the mind accepts them because they are clear interpretations of certain chapters of the Book lying open before us all. Between these two stand Shakespeare and Cervantes, with the richer laugh of heart and mind in one; with much of the Aristophanic robustness, something of Molière's delicacy.

The laughter heard in circles not pervaded by the comic idea will sound harsh and soulless, like versified prose, if you step into them with a sense of the distinction. You will fancy you have changed your habitation to a planet remoter from the sun. You may be among powerful brains, too. You will not find poets—or but a stray one, over-worshipped. You will find learned men undoubtedly, professors, reputed philosophers, and illustrious dilettanti. They have in them, perhaps, every element composing light, except the comic. They read verse, they discourse of art; but their eminent faculties are not under that vigilant sense of a collective supervision, spiritual and present, which we have taken note of. They build a temple of arrogance; they speak much in the voice of oracles; their hilarity, if it does not dip in grossness, is usually a form of pugnacity.

Insufficiency of sight in the eye looking outward has deprived them of the eye that should look inward. They have never weighed themselves in the delicate balance of the comic idea, so as to obtain a suspicion of the rights and dues of the world; and they have, in consequence, an irritable personality. A very learned English professor crushed an argument in a political discussion by asking his adversary angrily: 'Are you aware, Sir, that I am a philologer?'

The practice of polite society will help in training them, and the professor on a sofa, with beautiful ladies on each side of him, may become their pupil and a scholar in manners without knowing it; he is at least a fair and pleasing spectacle to the comic Muse. But the society named polite is volatile in its adorations, and to-morrow will be petting a bronzed soldier, or a black African, or a prince, or a spiritualist; ideas cannot take root in its ever-shifting soil. It is besides addicted in self-defence to gabble exclusively of the affairs of its rapidly revolving world, as children on a whirli-go-round bestow their attention on the wooden horse or cradle ahead of them, to escape from giddiness and preserve a notion of identity. The professor is better out of a circle that often confounds by lionizing, sometimes annoys by abandoning, and always confuses. The school that teaches gently what peril there is lest a cultivated head should still be coxcomb's, and the collisions which may befall high-soaring minds, empty or full, is more to be recommended than the sphere of incessant motion supplying it with material.

Lands where the Comic Spirit is obscure overhead are rank with raw crops of matter. The traveler accustomed to smooth highways and people not covered with burrs and prickles is amazed, amid so much that is fair and cherishable, to come upon such curious barbarism. An Englishman paid a visit of admiration to a professor in the land of culture, and was introduced by him to another distinguished professor, to whom he took so cordially as to walk out with him alone one afternoon. The first professor, an erudite entirely worthy of the sentiment of scholarly esteem prompting the visit, behaved (if we exclude the dagger) with the vindictive jealousy of an injured Spanish beauty. After a short prelude of gloom and obscure explosions, he discharged upon his faithless admirer the bolts of passionate logic familiar to the ears of flighty caballeros: 'Either I am a fit object of your admiration, or I am not. Of these things, one: either you are competent to judge, in which case I stand condemned by you; or you are incompetent, and therefore impertinent, and you may betake yourself to your country again, hypocrite!' The admirer was for persuading the wounded scholar that it is given to us to be able to admire two professors at a time. He was driven forth.

Perhaps this might have occurred in any country, and a comedy of The Pedant, discovering the greedy humanity within the dusty scholar, would not bring it home to one in particular. I am mindful that it was in Germany, when I observe that the Germans have gone through no comic training to warn them of the sly, wise emanation eyeing them from aloft, nor much of satirical. Heinrich Heine has not been enough to cause them to smart and meditate. Nationally, as well as individually, when they are excited they are in danger of the grotesque; as when, for instance, they decline to listen to evidence, and raise a national outcry because one of German blood has been convicted of crime in a foreign country. They are acute critics, yet they still wield clubs in controversy. Compare them in this respect with the people schooled in La Bruyère, La Fontaine, Molière; with the people who have the figures of a Trissotin and a Vadius before them for a comic warning of the personal vanities of the caressed professor. It is more than difference of race. It is the difference of traditions, temper, and style, which comes of schooling.

The French controversialist is a polished swordsman, to be dreaded in his graces and courtesies. The German is Orson, or the mob, or a marching army, in defence of a good case or a bad—a big or a little. His irony is a missile of terrific tonnage; sarcasm he emits like a blast from a dragon's mouth. He must and will be Titan. He stamps his foe underfoot, and is astonished that the creature is not dead, but stinging; for, in truth, the Titan is contending, by comparison, with a god.

When the Germans lie on their arms, looking across the Alsatian frontier at the crowds of Frenchmen rushing to applaud *L'Ami Fritz* at the Théâtre Français, looking and considering the meaning of that applause, which is grimly comic in its political response to the domestic moral of the play—when the Germans watch and are silent, their force of character tells. They are kings in music, we may say princes in poetry, good speculators in philosophy, and our leaders in scholarship. That so gifted a race, possessed, moreover, of the stern good sense which collects the waters of laughter to make the wells, should show at a disadvantage, I hold for a proof, instructive to us, that the discipline of the Comic Spirit is needful to their growth. We see what they can reach to in that great figure of modern manhood, Goethe. They are a growing people; they are conversable as well; and when their men, as in France, and at intervals at Berlin teatables, consent to talk on equal terms with their women, and to listen to them, their growth will be accelerated and be shapelier. Comedy, or, in any form, the Comic Spirit, will then come to them to cut some figures out of the block, show them the mirror, enliven and irradiate the social intelligence.

Modern French comedy is commendable for the directness of the study of actual life, as far as that (which is but the early step in such a scholarship) can be of service in composing and coloring the picture. A consequence of this crude, though well-meant, realism is the collision of the writers in their scenes and incidents, and in their characters. The Muse of most of them is an *Aventurière*. She is clever, and a certain diversion exists in the united scheme for confounding her. The object of this person is to reinstate herself in the decorous world; and either, having accomplished this purpose through deceit, she has a *nostalgie de la boue*[21] that eventually casts her back into it, or she is exposed in her course of deception when she is about to gain her end. A very good, innocent young man is her victim, or a very astute, goodish young man obstructs her path. This latter is enabled to be the champion of the decorous world by knowing the indecorous well. He has assisted in the progress of *aventurières* downward; he will not help them to ascend. The world is with him; and certainly it is not much of an ascension they aspire to; but what sort of a figure is he? The triumph of a candid realism is to show him no hero. You are to admire him (for it must be supposed that realism pretends to waken some admiration) as a credibly living young man; no better, only a little firmer and shrewder, than the rest. If, however, you think at all, after the curtain has fallen, you are likely to think that the *aventurières* have a case to plead against him. True, and the author has not said anything to the contrary; he has but painted from the life; he leaves his audience to the reflections of unphilosophic minds upon life, from the specimen he has presented in the bright and narrow circle of a spy-glass.

I do not know that the fly in amber is of any particular use, but the comic idea enclosed in a comedy makes it more generally perceptible and portable, and that is an advantage. There is a benefit to men in taking the lessons of comedy in congregations, for it enlivens the wits; and to writers it is beneficial, for they must have a clear scheme, and even if they have no idea to present, they must prove that they have made the public sit to them before the sitting, to see the picture. And writing for the stage would be a corrective of a too-incrusted scholarly style, into which some great ones fall at times. It keeps minor writers to a definite plan, and to English. Many of them now swelling a plethoric market in the composition of novels, in pun-manufactories, and in journalism—attached to the machinery forcing perishable matter on a public that swallows voraciously and groans—might, with encouragement, be attending to the study of art in literature. Our critics appear to be fascinated by the quaintness of our public, as the world is when our beast-garden has a new importation of magnitude, and the creature's appetite is reverently consulted. They stipulate for a writer's popularity before they will do much more than take the position of umpires to record his failure or success. Now the pig supplies the most popular of dishes, but it is not accounted the most honored of animals, unless it be by the cottager. Our public might surely be led to try other, perhaps finer, meat. It has good taste in song. It might be taught as justly, on the whole (and the sooner when the cottager's view of the feast shall cease to be the humble one of our literary critics), to extend this capacity for delicate choosing in the direction of the matter arousing laughter.

---

[21] Yearning for the sordid.

Charles Bradlaugh

1833-1891

THE PASSAGE of time has stripped Charles Bradlaugh's name of all but one association—that of crusading atheist. For it was Bradlaugh's destiny to engage in a long struggle with Parliament to be seated as a member despite his refusal to swear an oath on the Bible. In his own day, however, Bradlaugh was known as a general social reformer whose campaign for "atheist liberation," as we might call it, was only one of many crusades.

Bradlaugh was born in 1833 in Hoxton, London, and educated at local schools. His early career was one of economic struggle, and he was variously an office boy, a clerk, and a soldier. He bought his release from the service in 1853 and returned to London. Within a few years he was an active public lecturer and writer. He issued his pamphlets under the name "Iconoclast." In 1862 he helped to found a free-thought periodical, the *National Reformer,* and in its pages and elsewhere he advocated all manner of social reform, ranging from total freedom of the press to birth control. For his advocacy of birth control, which he pursued in conjunction with Annie Besant (later famous as a theosophist), he was fined and imprisoned but subsequently upheld on appeal.

Bradlaugh was elected a Member of Parliament for Northampton in 1880 and this set the stage for his most celebrated confrontation with authority. The House of Commons refused to seat him unless he would take the oath of allegiance on the Bible. As a professed atheist Bradlaugh refused, claiming the right merely to affirm his allegiance. He was not seated. Nor in three succeeding elections that returned him to Parliament could Bradlaugh gain admission. Finally in 1886 he took the oath and was permitted to take his seat in Parliament. He served there for the remainder of his life. He died in 1891 in London.

Bradlaugh is not so much a literary figure as a social and historical one. His interest for the student of letters comes from his vanguard position in the extreme freethinking wing of Victorian thought that gained increasing prominence and ultimately respectability by the end of the century. Bradlaugh's many writings seem now very dated, enmeshed as they are in the particular issues of the day, but his pioneering role in professing unpopular beliefs will strike some as heroic and attractive.

CHRONOLOGY

1833   Born 26 September in London.
1850–53   Serves as soldier.
1853   Leaves army; returns to London.
1862   Founds *National Reformer.*
1876   *The Fruits of Philosophy,* with Annie Besant.
1880   Elected M.P. for Northampton; denied seat in Parliament.
1886   Takes oath and is seated in Parliament.
1891   Dies 30 January; buried in London.

EDITIONS

With the exception of an occasional essay, Bradlaugh's works have rarely been reprinted in this century. Titles below are of a few representative editions.
Autobiography (1873).
Genesis: Its Authorship and Authenticity (1882).
The True Story of My Parliamentary Struggle (1882).
Rules, Customs, and Procedures of the House of Commons (1889).
Speeches (1890).
Humanity's Gain from Unbelief, ed. Hypatia B. Bonner (1929).

BIOGRAPHY AND CRITICISM

Hypatia Bradlaugh Bonner and J. M. Robertson, *Charles Bradlaugh* (2 vols., 1894).
Janet E. Courtney, *Freethinkers of the Nineteenth Century* (1920).
Champion of Liberty: Charles Bradlaugh, A Centenary Volume (1933).
Walter Arnstein, *The Bradlaugh Case* (1965).

A Plea for Atheism

Bradlaugh's extensive writings contain no more representative an essay than his appeal for atheism, a pamphlet first published in 1864 that went through many printings. The work was deliberately simple in form in order to appeal to a wide audience, and it shows the marks of Bradlaugh's long schooling in the writing of polemical pamphlets.

THIS essay is issued in the hope that it may succeed in removing some of the many prejudices prevalent, not only against the actual holders of Atheistic opinions, but also against those wrongfully suspected of Atheism. Men who have been famous for depth of thought, for excellent wit, or great genius, have been recklessly assailed as Atheists by those who lack the high qualifications against which the malice of the calumniators was directed. Thus, not only have Voltaire and Paine been, without ground, accused of Atheism, but Bacon, Locke, and Bishop Berkeley himself, have, amongst others, been denounced by thoughtless or unscrupulous pietists as inclining to Atheism, the ground for the accusation being that they manifested an inclination to push human thought a little in advance of the age in which they lived.

It is too often the fashion with persons of pious reputation to speak in unmeasured language of Atheism as favouring immorality, and of Atheists as men whose conduct is necessarily vicious, and who have adopted Atheistic views as a desperate defiance against a Deity justly offended by the badness of their lives. Such persons urge that amongst the proximate causes of Atheism are vicious training, immoral and profligate companions, licentious living, and the like. Dr. John Pye Smith, in his "Instructions on Christian Theology," goes so far as to declare that "nearly all the Atheists upon record have been men of extremely debauched and vile conduct." Such language from the Christian advocate is not surprising, but there are others who, while professing great desire for the spread of Freethought and having pretensions to rank amongst acute and liberal thinkers, declare Atheism impracticable, and its teachings cold, barren, and negative. Excepting to each of the above allegations, I maintain that thoughtful Atheism affords greater possibility for human happiness than any system yet based on, or possible to be founded on, Theism, and that the lives of true Atheists must be more virtuous—because more human—than those of the believers in Deity, the humanity of the devout believer often finding itself neutralized by a faith with which that humanity is necessarily in constant collision. The devotee piling the faggots at the *auto da fé*[1] of a heretic, and that heretic his son, might notwithstanding be a good father in every other respect (see Deut. xiii. 6–10). Heresy, in the eyes of the believer, is highest criminality, and outweighs all claims of family or affection.

Atheism, properly understood, is no mere disbelief; is in no wise a cold, barren negative; it is, on the contrary, a hearty, fruitful affirmation of all truth, and involves the positive assertion of action of highest humanity.

Let Atheism be fairly examined, and neither condemned—its defence unheard—on the *ex parte* slanders of some of the professional preachers of fashionable orthodoxy, whose courage is bold enough while the pulpit protects the sermon, but whose valour becomes tempered with discretion when a free platform is afforded and discussion claimed; nor misjudged because it has been the custom to regard Atheism as so unpopular as to render its advocacy impolitic. The best policy against all prejudice is to firmly advocate the truth. The Atheist does not say "There is no God," but he says: "I know not what you mean by God; I am without idea of God; the word 'God' is to me a sound conveying no clear or distinct affirmation. I do not deny God, because I cannot deny that of which I have no conception, and the conception of which, by its affirmer, is so imperfect that he is unable to define it to me. If, however, 'God' is defined to mean an existence other than the existence of which I am a mode, then I deny 'God,' and affirm that it is impossible such 'God' can be. That is, I affirm one existence, and deny that there can be more than one." The Pantheist also affirms one existence, and denies that there can be more than one; but the distinction between the Pantheist and the Atheist is, that the Pantheist affirms infinite attributes for existence, while the Atheist maintains that attributes are the characteristics of mode—*i.e.*, the diversities enabling the conditioning in thought.

When the Theist affirms that his God is an existence other than, and separate from, the so-called material universe, and when he invests this separate, hypothetical existence with the several attributes of personality, omniscience, omnipresence, omnipotence, eternity, infinity, immutability, and perfect goodness, then the Atheist in reply says: "I deny the existence of such a being"; and he is entitled to say this because this Theistic definition is self-contradictory, as well as contradictory of every-day experience.

If you speak to the Atheist of God as creator, he answers that the conception of creation is impossible. We are utterly unable to construe it in thought as possible that the complement of existence has been either increased or diminished, much less can we conceive an absolute origination of substance. We cannot conceive either, on the one hand, nothing becoming something, or on the other, something becoming nothing. The words "creation" and "destruction" have no value except as applied to phenomena. You may destroy a gold coin, but you have only destroyed the condition, you have not affected the substance. "Creation" and "destruction" denote change of phenomena; they do not denote origin or cessation of substance. The Theist who speaks of God creating the universe must either suppose that Deity evolved it out of himself, or that he produced it from nothing. But the Theist cannot

---

[1] Literally, act of faith; here, execution.

regard the universe as evolution of Deity, because this would identify Universe and Deity, and be Pantheism rather than Theism. There would be no distinction of substance—no creation. Nor can the Theist regard the universe as created out of nothing, because Deity is, according to him, necessarily eternal and infinite. God's existence being eternal and infinite precludes the possibility of the conception of vacuum to be filled by the universe if created. No one can even think of any point in extent or duration and say: Here is the point of separation between the creator and the created. It is not possible for the Theist to imagine a beginning to the universe. It is not possible to conceive either an absolute commencement, or an absolute termination of existence; that is, it is impossible to conceive beginning, before which you have a period when the universe has yet to be; or to conceive an end, after which the universe, having been, no longer exists. The Atheist affirms that he cognizes to-day effects; that these are, at the same time, causes and effects—causes to the effects they precede, effects to the causes they follow. Cause is simply everything without which the effect would not result, and with which it must result. Cause is the means to an end, consummating itself in that end. Cause is the word we use to include all that determines change. The Theist who argues for creation must assert a point of time—that is, of duration, when the created did not yet exist. At this point of time either something existed or nothing; but something must have existed, for out of nothing nothing can come. Something must have existed, because the point fixed upon is that of the duration of something. This something must have been either finite or infinite; if finite it could not have been God, and if the something were infinite, then creation was impossible: it is impossible to add to infinite existence.

If you leave the question of creation, and deal with the government of the universe, the difficulties of Theism are by no means lessened. The existence of evil is then a terrible stumbling-block to the Theist. Pain, misery, crime, poverty confront the advocate of eternal goodness, and challenge with unanswerable potency his declaration of Deity as all-good, all-wise, and all-powerful. A recent writer in the *Spectator* admits that there is what it regards "as the most painful, as it is often the most incurable, form of Atheism— the Atheism arising from a sort of horror of the idea of an Omnipotent Being permitting such a proportion of misery among the majority of

his creatures." Evil is either caused by God or exists independently; but it cannot be caused by God, as in that case he would not be all-good; nor can it exist hostilely, as in that case he would not be all-powerful. If all-good he would desire to annihilate evil, and continued evil contradicts either God's desire, or God's ability, to prevent it. Evil must either have had a beginning or it must have been eternal; but, according to the Theist, it cannot be eternal, because God alone is eternal. Nor can it have had a beginning, for if it had it must either have originated in God, or outside God; but, according to the Theist, it cannot have originated in God, for he is all-good, and out of all-goodness evil cannot originate; nor can evil have originated outside God, for, according to the Theist, God is infinite, and it is impossible to go outside of or beyond infinity.

To the Atheist this question of evil assumes an entirely different aspect. He declares that each evil is a result, but not a result from God nor Devil. He affirms that conduct founded on knowledge of the laws of existence may ameliorate each present form of evil, and, as our knowledge increases, prevent its future recurrence.

Some declare that the belief in God is necessary as a check to crime. They allege that the Atheist may commit murder, lie, or steal without fear of any consequences. To try the actual value of this argument, it is not unfair to ask: Do Theists ever steal? If yes, then in each such theft the belief in God and his power to punish has been insufficient as a preventive of the crime. Do Theists ever lie or murder? If yes, the same remark has again force—Theism failing against the lesser as against the greater crime. Those who use such an argument overlook that all men seek happiness, though in very diverse fashions. Ignorant and miseducated men often mistake the true path to happiness, and commit crime in the endeavour to obtain it. Atheists hold that by teaching mankind the real road to human happiness it is possible to keep them from the by-ways of criminality and error. Atheists would teach men to be moral now, not because God offers as an inducement reward by and by, but because in the virtuous act itself immediate good is ensured to the doer and the circle surrounding him. Atheism would preserve man from lying, stealing, murdering, not from fear of an eternal agony after death, but because these crimes make this life itself a course of misery.

While Theism, asserting God as the creator and governor of the universe, hinders and checks man's efforts by declaring God's will to be the sole directing and controlling power, Atheism, by declaring all events to be in accordance with natural laws—that is, happening in certain ascertainable sequences—stimulates man to discover the best conditions of life, and offers him the most powerful inducements to morality. While the Theist provides future happiness for a scoundrel repentant on his death-bed, Atheism affirms present and certain happiness for the man who does his best to live here so well as to have little cause for repenting hereafter.

Theism declares that God dispenses health and inflicts disease, and sickness and illness are regarded by the Theists as visitations from an angered Deity, to be borne with meekness and content. Atheism declares that physiological knowledge may preserve us from disease by preventing us from infringing the law of health, and that sickness results not as the ordinance of offended Deity, but from ill-ventilated dwellings and workshops, bad and insufficient food, excessive toil, mental suffering, exposure to inclement weather, and the like—all these finding root in poverty, the chief source of crime and disease; that prayers and piety afford no protection against fever, and that if the human being be kept without food he will starve as quickly whether he be Theist or Atheist, theology being no substitute for bread.

If "Theism is the doctrine that the universe owes its existence to the reason and will of a self-existing Being who is infinitely powerful, wise, and good," then it is a doctrine which involves many difficulties and absurdities. It assumes that the universe has not always existed. The new existence added when the universe was originated was either an improvement or a deterioration on what had always existed; or it was in all respects precisely identical with what had therefore always existed. In the first, if the new universe was an improvement, then the previously self-existent being could not have been infinitely good. If the universe was a deterioration, then the creator could have scarcely been all-wise, or he could not have been all-powerful. If the universe was in all respects precisely identical with the self-existent being, then it must have been infinitely powerful, wise and good, and must have been self-existent. Any of the alternatives is fatal to Theism. Again, if the universe owes its existence to God's reason and will, God must, prior to creation, have thought upon the matter until he ultimately determined to

create; but, if the creation were wise and good, it would never have been delayed while the infinitely wise and good reasoned about it, and, if the creation were not wise and good, the infinitely wise and good would never have commenced it. Either God willed without motive, or he was influenced; if he reasoned, there was—prior to the definite willing—a period of doubt or suspended judgment, all of which is inconsistent with the attributes claimed for deity by Professor Flint. It is hard to understand how whole nations can have been left by their infinitely powerful, wise, and good governor—how many men can have been left by their infinitely powerful, wise, and good father—without any knowledge of himself. Yet this must be so if, as Professor Flint conceives, Thesim is spread over only a comparatively small portion of the earth. The moral effect of Christian and Muhammadan Theism on the nations influenced was well shown in the recent Russo-Turkish War.

Every Theist must admit that, if a God exists, he could have so convinced all men of the fact of his existence that doubt, disagreement, or disbelief would be impossible. If he could not do this, he would not be omnipotent, or he would not be omniscient—that is, he would not be God. Every Theist must also agree that, if a God exists, he would wish all men to have such a clear consciousness of his existence and attributes, that doubt, disagreement, or disbelief on this subject would be impossible. And this, if for no other reason, because that out of doubts and disagreements on religion have too often resulted centuries of persecution, strife, and misery, which a good God would desire to prevent. If God would not desire this, then he is not all good—that is, he is not God. But as many men have doubts, as a large majority of mankind have disagreements, and as some men have disbeliefs as to God's existence and attributes, it must follow that God does not exist, or that he is not all-wise, or that he is not all-powerful, or that he is not all-good.

Many Theists rely on the intuitional argument. It is, perhaps, best to allow the Baird Lecturer[2] to reply to these: "Man, say some, knows God by immediate intuition; he needs no argument for his existence, because he perceives Him directly—face to face—without any medium. It is easy to assert this, but obviously the assertion is the merest dogmatism. Not one man in a thousand who understands what he is affirming will dare

---

[2] Robert Flint (1834–1910), Scottish theologian, author of *Theism* and *Anti-Theistic Theories* (1876–77).

to claim to have an immediate vision of God, and nothing can be more likely than that the man who makes such a claim is self-deluded." And Professor Flint urges that "What seem intuitions are often really inferences, and not unfrequently erroneous inferences; what seem the immediate dictates of pure reason, or the direct and unclouded perceptions of a special spiritual faculty, may be the conceits of fancy, or the products of habits and association, or the reflexions of strong feeling. A man must prove to himself, and he must prove to others, that what he takes to be an intuition is an intuition. Is that proof in this case likely to be easier or more conclusive than the proof of the Divine existence? The so-called immediate perception of God must be shown to be a perception and to be immediate; it must be vindicated and verified; and how this is to be done, especially if there be no other reasons for believing in God than itself, it is difficult to conceive. The history of religion, which is what ought to yield the clearest confirmation of the alleged intuition, appears to be from beginning to end a conspicuous contradiction of it. If all men have the spiritual power of directly beholding their Creator—have an immediate vision of God—how happens it that whole nations believe in the most absurd and monstrous Gods? That millions of men are ignorant whether there be one God or thousands?" And still more strongly he adds: "The opinion that man has an intuition or immediate perception of God is untenable; the opinion that he has an immediate feeling of God is absurd."

Every child is born into the world an Atheist, and, if he grows into a Theist, his Deity differs with the country in which the believer may happen to be born, or the people amongst whom he may happen to be educated. The belief is the result of education or organization. This is practically conceded by Professor Flint, where he speaks of the God-idea as transmitted from the Jews, and says: "We have inherited it from them. If it had not come down to us, if we had not been born into a society pervaded by it, there is no reason to suppose that we should have found it out for ourselves." And, further, he maintains that a child is born "into blank ignorance, and, if left entirely to itself, would, probably, never find out as much religious truth as the most ignorant of parents can teach it." Religious belief is powerful in proportion to the want of scientific knowledge on the part of the believer. The more ignorant the more credulous. In the mind of the Theist "God" is equivalent to the sphere of the unknown; by the use of the word he answers, without thought, problems which might otherwise obtain scientific solution. The more ignorant the Theist, the more numerous his Gods. Belief in God is not a faith founded on reason. Theism is worse than illogical; its teachings are not only without utility, but of itself it has nothing to teach. Separated from Christianity with its almost innumerable sects, from Muhammadanism with its numerous divisions, and separated also from every other preached system, Theism is a Will-o'-the-Wisp, without reality. Apart from orthodoxy, Theism is the veriest dream-form, without substance or coherence.

What does Christian Theism teach? That the first man, made perfect by the all-powerful, all-wise, all-good God, was nevertheless imperfect, and by his imperfection brought misery into the world, where the all-good God must have intended misery should never come; that this God made men to share this misery—men whose fault was their being what he made them; that this God begets a son, who is nevertheless his unbegotten self, and that by belief in the birth of God's eternal son, and in the death of the undying who died as sacrifice to God's vengeance, men may escape the consequences of the first man's error. Christian Theism declares that belief alone can save men, and yet recognizes the fact that man's belief results from teaching, by establishing missionary societies to spread the faith. Christian Theism teaches that God, though no respecter of persons, selected as his favourite one nation in preference to all others; that man can do no good of himself or without God's aid, but yet that each man has a free will; that God is all-powerful, but that few go to heaven, and the majority to hell; that all are to love God, who has predestined from eternity that by far the largest number of human beings are to be burning in hell for ever. Yet the advocates for Theism venture to upbraid those who argue against such a faith.

Either Theism is true or false. If true, discussion must help to spread its influence; if false, the sooner it ceases to influence human conduct the better for human kind. This Plea for Atheism is put forth as a challenge to Theists to do battle for their cause, and in the hope that, the strugglers being sincere, truth may give laurels to the victor and the vanquished; laurels to the victor, in that he has upheld the truth; laurels which should be even more welcome to the vanquished, whose defeat crowns him with a truth he knew not of before.

William Morris

1834-1896

WILLIAM MORRIS must rank as among the most multi-talented men of any age. Artist, architect, decorator, handcraftsman, book designer, poet, novelist, social critic, and reformer—all these and more apply to William Morris. Through his many activities he touched the life of late Victorian England at more points than any single man.

Morris was born near London, the son of a broker. He attended Marlborough School and Exeter College, Oxford. At Oxford he became fast friends with the painter Edward Burne-Jones and was attracted by Anglo-Catholicism, but eventually he turned his energies to art. The first part of his career, to about 1877, was devoted to art and poetry. He studied with the great Gothic revival architect G. E. Street; he was involved with the Rossetti Pre-Raphaelite circle and was one of the founders of the *Oxford and Cambridge Magazine*. He married Jane Burden in 1859 and set up the firm of Morris and Co. in 1861 to produce paintings, furniture, and household decorations. One of their best-known creations was the Morris chair. During his early years Morris published the volume *The Defense of Guenevere* (1858), striking the Arthurian and medieval theme that would occupy much of his attention in subsequent works, such as *The Earthly Paradise*.

In 1871 Morris moved to Kelmscott on the Thames and began his researches into Icelandic sagas. He composed translations of these and also original poems like *Sigurd the Volsung* under the inspiration of the sagas. But by 1877 Morris' interests had shifted to social questions. It was a fulfillment in a later generation of the pattern presented by Ruskin whose works had strongly influenced Morris at Oxford. For the rest of his life Morris was an active campaigner for socialism in Britain. He joined the Social Democratic Federation in 1883 and in the following year established his own Socialist League. Much of his later work in fiction and nonfiction was concerned to advance the cause of socialism. His periodical, *The Commonweal*, founded in 1885, his poetry in *Poems by the Way* (1891), his prose romances, *The Dream of John Ball* (1888) and *News from Nowhere* (1890) were all to some degree undertaken to advance the socialist cause in Morris' own Ruskinian formulation. Although Morris felt himself to be a revolutionary, he came in his later years to agree with the gradualist approach of Fabian socialists like Shaw.

In 1890 Morris established the Kelmscott Press at Hammersmith, London, and began producing there the luxiously illustrated books in the manner of medieval illuminated manuscripts that have their most celebrated example in the Kelmscott *Chaucer* (1896). He died at Hammersmith in 1896.

Leaving aside Morris' extraordinary achievement in various arts and literary endeavors, one must acknowledge that as a prose writer alone Morris occupies a commanding place among the writers of the late Victorian period. Much of his prose, to be sure, is simply propaganda for his program, but much of it is infused with Morris' artistic vision of a society in which the beautiful is accessible to all and in which the sense of community and the sense for art that he found in the Middle Ages is part of the fabric of everyday life.

CHRONOLOGY

1834   Born 24 March in London suburb of Walthamstow.
1848–51   Attends Marlborough School.
1852–56   Attends Exeter College, Oxford.
1858   *The Defense of Guenevere.*
1859   Marries Jane Burden.
1861   Found Morris and Co.
1868–70   *The Earthly Paradise.*
1871   Moves to Kelmscott; first visit to Iceland.
1877   Founds Society for Protection of Ancient Buildings.
1883   Joins Social Democratic Federation.
1884   Organizes Socialist League.
1888   *The Dream of John Ball.*
1890   *News from Nowhere;* founds Kelmscott Press.
1896   Dies 3 October at Kelmscott.

EDITIONS

Except for *Works,* no titles of poetry or fiction are listed below.
Collected Works, ed. May Morris (24 vols., 1910–1915).
William Morris, selec. by H. Newbolt (1923).
Selections from the Prose Works of William Morris, ed. A. H. R. Ball (1931).
Stories in Prose, etc., ed. G. D. H. Cole (1934).
William Morris: Artist, Writer, Socialist, ed. May Morris (2 vols., 1936).
On Art and Socialism, ed. H. Jackson (1947).
Selected Writings and Designs, ed. Asa Briggs (1962).

BIOGRAPHY AND CRITICISM

J. W. Mackail, *The Life of William Morris* (2 vols., 1899).
Elizabeth L. Cary, *William Morris: Poet, Craftsman, Socialist* (1902).
A. Clutton-Brock, *William Morris: His Work and Influence* (1914).
Holbrook Jackson, *William Morris: Craftsman-Socialist* (1926).
P. Bloomfield, *The Life and Work of Morris* (1934).
G. B. Shaw, *Morris As I Knew Him* (1936).
L. W. Eshleman, *A Victorian Rebel* (1940).
Holbrook Jackson, *Dreamers of Dreams* (1948).

Transactions and Other Publications of the William Morris Society (1957—continuing).
R. P. Arnot, *Morris: The Man and the Myth* (1964).
W. E. Fredeman, *Pre-Raphaelitism* (1965).

Whigs, Democrats, and Socialists

The following essay was initially one of the many lectures that Morris delivered in his campaign for socialism in Britain in the last quarter of the nineteenth century. It was first read at a Fabian Society Conference at South Place Institute on 11 June 1886. It was collected in the volume Signs of Change *(1888). In his remarks Morris sets forth what he sees as the future for socialism under the existing constitutional structure of England.*

WHAT is the state of parties in England today? How shall we enumerate them? The Whigs, who stand first on the list in my title, are considered generally to be the survival of an old historical party once looked on as having democratic tendencies, but now the hope of all who would stand soberly on the ancient ways. Besides these, there are Tories also, the descendants of the stout defenders of Church and State and the divine right of kings.

Now, I don't mean to say but that at the back of this ancient name of Tory there lies a great mass of genuine Conservative feeling, held by people who, if they had their own way, would play some rather fantastic tricks, I fancy; nay, even might in the course of time be somewhat rough with such people as are in this hall at present.[1] But this feeling, after all, is only a sentiment now; all practical hope has died out of it, and these worthy people *cannot* have their own way. It is true that they elect members of Parliament, who talk very big to please them, and sometimes even they manage to get a Govern-

ment into power that nominally represents their sentiment, but when that happens the said Government is forced, even when its party has a majority in the House of Commons, to take a much lower standpoint than the high Tory ideal; the utmost that the real Tory party can do, even when backed by the Primrose League and its sham hierarchy, is to delude the electors to return Tories to Parliament to pass measures more akin to Radicalism than the Whigs durst attempt, so that, though there are Tories, there is no Tory party in England.

On the other hand, there is a party, which I can call for the present by no other name than Whig, which is both numerous and very powerful, and which does, in fact govern England, and to my mind will always do so as long as the present constitutional Parliament lasts. Of course, like all parties it includes men of various shades of opinion, from the Tory-tinted Whiggery of Lord Salisbury to the Radical-tinted Whiggery of Mr. Chamberlain's[2] present tail. Neither do I mean to say that they are conscious of being a

---

[1] They *have* been "rather rough," you may say, and have done more than merely hold their sentimental position. Well, I still say (February 1888) that the present open tyranny which sends political opponents to prison, both in England and Ireland, and breaks Radical heads in the street for attempting to attend political meetings, is not Tory, but Whig; not the old Tory "divine right of kings," but the new Tory, *i.e.*, Tory-tinted Whig, "divine right of property," made Bloody Sunday possible. I admit that I did not expect in 1886 that we should in 1887 and 1888 be having such a brilliant example of the tyranny of a parliamentary majority; in fact, I did not reckon on the force of the inpenetrable stupidity of the Prigs in alliance with the Whigs marching under the rather ragged banner of sham Toryism. [Morris' note]

[2] Lord Salisbury (1830–93), Conservative statesman, Prime Minister; Joseph Chamberlain (1836–1914), British statesman, considered leader of the radical wing in Parliament.

united party; on the contrary, the groups will sometimes oppose each other furiously at elections, and perhaps the more simple-minded of them really think that it is a matter of importance to the nation which section of them may be in power; but they may always be reckoned upon to be in their places and vote against any measure which carries with it a real attack on our constitutional system; surely very naturally, since they are there for no other purpose than to do so. They are, and always must be, conscious defenders of the present system, political and economical, as long as they have any cohesion as Tories, Whigs, Liberals, or even Radicals. Not one of them probably would go such a very short journey towards revolution as the abolition of the House of Lords. A one-chamber Parliament would seem to them an impious horror, and the abolition of the monarchy they would consider a serious inconvenience to the London tradesman.

Now this is the real Parliamentary Party, at present divided into jarring sections under the influence of the survival of the party warfare of the last few generations, but which already shows signs of sinking its differences so as to offer a solid front of resistance to the growing instinct which on its side will before long result in a party claiming full economical as well as political freedom for the whole people.

But is there nothing in Parliament, or seeking entrance to it, except this variously tinted Whiggery, this Harlequin of Reaction? Well, inside Parliament, setting aside the Irish party, which is, we may now well hope, merely temporarily there, there is not much. It is not among people of "wealth and local influence," who I see are supposed to be the only available candidates for Parliament of a recognized party, that you will find the elements of revolution. We will grant that there are some few genuine Democrats there, and let them pass. But outside there are undoubtedly many who are genuine Democrats, and who have it in their heads that it is both possible and desirable to capture the constitutional Parliament and turn it into a real popular assembly, which, with the people behind it, might lead us peaceably and constitutionally into the great Revolution which all *thoughtful* men desire to bring about; all thoughtful men, that is, who do not belong to the consciously cynical Tories, *i.e.*, men determined, whether it be just or unjust, good for humanity or bad for it, to keep the people down as long as they can, which they hope, very naturally, will be as long as they live.

To capture Parliament and turn it into a popular but constitutional assembly is, I must conclude, the aspiration of the genuine Democrats wherever they may be found; that is their idea of the first step of the Democratic policy. The questions to be asked of this, as of all other policies, are first, What is the end proposed by it? and secondly, Are they likely to succeed? As to the end proposed, I think there is much difference of opinion. Some Democrats would answer from the merely political point of view, and say · Universal suffrage, payment of members, annual Parliaments, abolition of the House of Lords, abolition of the monarchy, and so forth. I would answer this by saying: After all, these are not ends, but means to an end; and passing by the fact that the last two are not constitutional measures, and so could not be brought about without actual rebellion, I would say if you had gained all these things, and more, all you would have done would have been to establish the ascendancy of the Democratic party; having so established it, you would then have to find out by the usual party means what that Democratic party meant, and you would find that your triumph in mere politics would lead you back again exactly to the place you started from. You would be Whigs under a different name. Monarchy, House of Lords, pensions, standing army, and the rest of it, are only supports to the present social system—the *privilege* based on the wages and capital system of production—and are worth nothing except as supports to it. If you are determined to support that system, therefore, you had better leave these things alone. The real masters of Society, the real tyrants of the people, are the Landlords and the Capitalists, whom your political triumph would not interfere with.

Then, as now, there would be a proletariat and a moneyed class. Then, as now, it would be possible sometimes for a diligent, energetic man, with his mind set wholly on such success, to climb out of the proletariat into the moneyed class, there to sweat as he once was sweated; which, my friends, is, if you will excuse the word, your ridiculous idea of freedom of contract.

The sole and utmost success of your policy would be that it might raise up a strong opposition to the condition of things which it would be your function to uphold; but most probably such opposition would still be outside Parliament, and not in it; you would have made a revolution, probably not without bloodshed, only to show people the necessity for another revolution the very next day.

Will you think the example of America too trite? Anyhow, consider it! A country with universal suffrage, no king, no House of Lords, no privilege as you fondly think; only a little standing army, chiefly used for the murder of red-skins; a democracy after your model; and with all that, a society corrupt to the core, and at this moment engaged in suppressing freedom with just the same reckless brutality and blind ignorance as the Czar of all the Russias uses.[3]

But it will be said, and certainly with much truth, that not all the Democrats are for mere political reform. I say that I believe that this is true, and it is a very important truth too. I will go farther, and will say that all those Democrats who can be distinguished from Whigs do intend social reforms which they hope will somewhat alter the relations of the classes towards each other; and there is, generally speaking, amongst Democrats a leaning towards a kind of limited State Socialism, and it is through that that they hope to bring about a peaceful revolution, which, if it does not introduce a condition of equality, will at least make the workers better off and contented with their lot.

They hope to get a body of representatives elected to Parliament, and by them to get measure after measure passed which will tend towards this goal; nor would some of them, perhaps most of them, be discontented if by this means we could glide into complete State Socialism. I think that the present Democrats are widely tinged with this idea, and to me it is a matter of hope that it is so; whatever of error there is in it, it means advance beyond the complete barrenness of the mere political programme.

Yet I must point out to these semi-Socialist Democrats that in the first place they will be made the cat's-paw of some of the wilier of the Whigs. There are several of these measures which look to some Socialistic, as, for instance, the allotments scheme, and other schemes tending towards peasant proprietorship, co-operation, and the like, but which after all, in spite of their benevolent appearance, are really weapons in the hands of reactionaries, having for their real object the creation of a new middle-class made out of the working-class and at their expense; the raising, in short, of a new army against the attack of the disinherited.

There is no end to this kind of dodge, nor will be apparently till there is an end of the class which tries it on; and a great many of the Demo-crats will be amused and absorbed by it from time to time. They call this sort of nonsense "practical;" it *seems* like doing something, while the steady propaganda of a principle which must prevail in the end is, according to them, doing nothing, and is unpractical. For the rest, it is not likely to become dangerous, further than as it clogs the wheels of the real movement somewhat, because it is sometimes a mere piece of reaction, as when, for instance, it takes the form of peasant proprietorship, flying right in the face of the commercial development of the day, which tends ever more and more towards the aggregation of capital, thereby smoothing the way for the organized possession of the means of production by the workers when the true revolution shall come: while, on the other hand, when this attempt to manufacture a new middle-class takes the form of co-operation and the like, it is not dangerous, because it means nothing more than a slightly altered form of joint-stockery, and everybody almost is beginning to see this. The greed of men stimulated by the spectacle of profit-making all around them, and also by the burden of the interest on the money which they have been obliged to borrow, will not allow them even to approach a true system of co-operation. Those benefited by the transaction presently become eager shareholders in a commercial speculation, and if they are working-men, as they often are, they are also capitalists. The enormous commercial success of the great co-operative societies, and the absolute no-effect of that success on the social conditions of the workers, are sufficient tokens of what this non-political co-operation must come to: "Nothing—it shall not be less."

But again, it may be said, some of the Democrats go farther than this; they take up actual pieces of Socialism, and are more than inclined to support them. Nationalization of the land, or of railways, or cumulative taxation on incomes, or limiting the right of inheritance, or new factory laws, or the restriction by law of the day's labour—one of these, or more than one sometimes, the Democrats will support, and see absolute salvation in these one or two planks of the platform. All this I admit, and once again say it is a hopeful sign, and yet once again I say there is a snare in it—a snake lies lurking in the grass.

Those who think that they can deal with our present system in this piecemeal way very much

---

[3] As true now (Feb. 1888) as then: the murder of the Chicago Anarchists, to wit. [Morris' note]

underrate the strength of the tremendous organization under which we live, and which appoints to each of us his place, and if we do not chance to fit it, grinds us down till we do. Nothing but a tremendous force can deal with this force; it will not suffer itself to be dismembered, nor to lose anything which really is its essence without putting forth all its force in resistance; rather than lose anything which it considers of importance, it will pull the roof of the world down upon its head. For, indeed, I grant these semi-Socialist Democrats that there is one hope for their tampering piecemeal with our Society; if by chance they can excite people into seriously, however blindly, claiming one or other of these things in question, and could be successful in Parliament in driving it through, they would certainly draw on a great civil war, and such a war once let loose would not end but either with the full triumph of Socialism or its extinction for the present; it would be impossible to limit the aim of the struggle; nor can we even guess at the course which it would take, except that it could not be a matter of compromise. But suppose the Democratic party peaceably successful on this new basis of semi-State Socialism, what would it all mean? Attempts to balance the two classes whose interests are opposed to each other, a mere ignoring of this antagonism which has led us through so many centuries to where we are now, and then, after a period of disappointment and disaster, the naked conflict once more; a revolution made, and another immediately necessary on its morrow!

Yet, indeed, it will not come to that; for, whatever may be the aims of the Democrats, they will not succeed in getting themselves into a position from whence they could make the attempt to realize them. I have said there are Tories and yet no real Tory party; so also it seems to me that there are Democrats but no Democratic party; at present they are used by the leaders of the parliamentary factions, and also kept at a distance by them from any real power. If they by hook or crook managed to get a number of members into Parliament, they would find out their differences very speedily under the influence of party rule; in point of fact, the Democrats are not a party; because they have no principles other than the old Whig-Radical ones, extended in some cases so as to take in a little semi-Socialism which the march of events has forced on them— that is, they gravitate on one side to the Whigs and on the other to the Socialists. Whenever, if ever, they begin to be a power in the elections

and get members in the House, the temptation to be members of a real live party which may have the government of the country in its hands, the temptation to what is (facetiously, I suppose) called practical politics, will be too much for many, even of those who gravitate towards Socialism: a quasi-Democratic parliamentary party, therefore, would probably be merely a recruiting ground, a nursery for the left wing of the Whigs; though it would indeed leave behind some small nucleus of opposition, the principles of which, however, would be vague and floating, so that it would be but a powerless group after all.

The future of the constitutional Parliament, therefore, it seems to me, is a perpetual Whig Rump, which will yield to pressure when mere political reforms are attempted to be got out of it, but will be quite immovable towards any real change in social and economical matters; that is to say, so far as it may be conscious of the attack; for I grant that it may be *betrayed* into passing semi-State-Socialistic measures, which will do this amount of good, that they will help to entangle commerce in difficulties, and so add to discontent by creating suffering; suffering of which the people will not understand the causes definitely, but which their instinct will tell them truly is brought about by *government*, and that, too, the only kind of government which they can have so long as the constitutional Parliament lasts.

Now, if you think I have exaggerated the power of the Whigs, that is, of solid, dead, unmoving resistance to progress, I must call your attention to the events of the last few weeks. Here has been a measure of pacification proposed; at the least and worst an attempt to enter upon a pacification of a weary and miserable quarrel many centuries old. The British people, in spite of their hereditary prejudice against the Irish, were not averse to the measure; the Tories were, as usual, powerless against it; yet so strong has been the *vis inertiæ* of Whiggery that it has won a notable victory over common-sense and sentiment combined, and has drawn over to it a section of those hitherto known as Radicals, and probably would have drawn all Radicals over but for the personal ascendancy of Mr. Gladstone. The Whigs, seeing, if but dimly, that this Irish Independence meant an attack on property, have been successful in snatching the promised peace out of the people's hands, and in preparing all kinds of entanglement and confusion for us for a long while in their steady resistance to even the beginnings of revolution.

This, therefore, is what Parliament looks to me: a solid central party, with mere nebulous opposition on the right hand and on the left. The people governed; that is to say, fair play amongst themselves for the money-privileged classes to make the most of their privilege, and to fight sturdily with each other in doing so; but the government concealed as much as possible, and also as long as possible; that is to say, the government resting on an assumed necessary eternity of privilege to monopolize the means of the fructification of labour.

For so long as that assumption is accepted by the ignorance of the people, the Great Whig Rump will remain inexpugnable, but as soon as the people's eyes are opened, even partially— and they begin to understand the meaning of the words, the Emancipation of Labour—we shall begin to have an assured hope of throwing off the basest and most sordid tyranny which the world has yet seen, the tyranny of so-called Constitutionalism.

How, then, are the people's eyes to be opened? By the force evolved from the final triumph and consequent corruption of Commercial Whiggery, which force will include in it a recognition of its constructive activity by intelligent people on the one hand, and on the other half-blind instinctive struggles to use its destructive activity on the part of those who suffer and have not been allowed to think; and, to boot, a great deal that goes between those two extremes.

In this turmoil, all those who can be truly called Socialists will be involved. The modern development of the great class-struggle has forced us to think, our thoughts force us to speak, and our hopes force us to try to get a hearing from the people. Nor can one tell how far our words will carry, so to say. The most moderate exposition of our principles will bear with it the seeds of disruption; nor can we tell what form that disruption will take.

One and all, then, we are responsible for the enunciation of Socialist principles and of the consequences which may flow from their general acceptance, whatever that may be. This responsibility no Socialist can shake off by declarations against physical force and in favour of constitutional methods of agitation; we are attacking the Constitution with the very beginnings, the mere lispings, of Socialism.

Whiggery, therefore, in its various forms, is the representative of Constitutionalism— is the outward expression of monopoly and consequent artificial restraints on labour and life; and there is only one expression of the force which will destroy Whiggery, and that is Socialism; and on the right hand and on the left Toryism and Radicalism will melt into Whiggery—are doing so now—and Socialism has got to absorb all that is not Whig in Radicalism.

Then comes the question, What is the policy of Socialism? If Toryism and Democracy are only nebulous masses of opposition to the solid centre of Whiggery, what can we call Socialism?

Well, at present, in England at least, Socialism is not a party, but a sect. That is sometimes brought against it as a taunt; but I am not dismayed by it; for I can conceive of a sect—nay, I have heard of *one*—becoming a very formidable power, and becoming so by dint of its long remaining a sect. So I think it is quite possible that Socialism will remain a sect till the very eve of the last stroke that completes the revolution, after which it will melt into the new Society. And is it not sects, bodies of definite, uncompromising principles, that lead us into revolutions? Was it not so in the Cromwellian times? Nay, have not the Fenian sect, even in our own days, made Home Rule possible? They may give birth to parties, though not parties themselves. And what should a sect like we are have to do in the parliamentary struggle—we who have an ideal to keep always before ourselves and others, and who cannot accept compromise; who can see nothing that can give us rest for a minute save the emancipation of labour, which will be brought about by the workers gaining possession of all the means of the fructification of labour; and who, even when that is gained, shall have pure Communism ahead to strive for?

What are we to do, then? Stand by and look on? Not exactly. Yet we may look on other people doing their work while we do ours. They are already beginning, as I have said, to stumble about with attempts at State Socialism. Let them make their experiments and blunders, and prepare the way for us by so doing. And our own business? Well, we—sect or party, or group of self-seekers, madmen, and poets, which you will— are at least the only set of people who have been able to see that there is and has been a great class-struggle going on. Further, we can see that this class-struggle cannot come to an end till the classes themselves do: one class must absorb the other. Which, then? Surely the useful one, the one that the world lives by, and on. The business of the people at present is to make it impossible for the useless, non-producing class to live; while the business of Constitutionalism is, on the contrary, to make it possible for them to live. And our business is to help to make the people *conscious* of this great antagonism between the people and Constitutionalism; and meantime to let Constitutionalism go on with its government uphelped by us at least, until it at last becomes *conscious* of its burden of the people's hate, of the people's knowledge that it is disinherited, which we shall have done our best to further by any means that we could.

As to Socialists in Parliament, there are two words about that. If they go there to take a part in carrying on Constitutionalism by palliating the evils of the system, and so helping our rulers to bear their burden of government, I for one, and so far as their action therein goes, cannot call them Socialists at all. But if they go there with the intention of doing what they can towards the disruption of Parliament, that is a matter of tactics for the time being; but even here I cannot help seeing the danger of their being seduced from their true errand, and I fear that they might become, on the terms above mentioned, simply supporters of the very thing they set out to undo.

I say that our work lies quite outside Parliament, and it is to help to educate the people by every and any means that may be effective; and the knowledge we have to help them to is threefold—to know their own, to know how to take their own, and to know how to use their own.

Samuel Butler

1835-1902

THE SATIRICAL novelist and autobiographer Samuel Butler, known chiefly for his novels *Erehwon* ("nowhere" spelled backwards) and *The Way of All Flesh*, was also an essayist, thinker, and intellectual controversialist who involved himself in the late Victorian debate on the exact character and role of evolution.

Butler was the son of a clergyman and the grandson of a bishop. He was born near Bingham, Nottinghamshire, and educated at Shrewsbury School, where his grandfather had been a famous headmaster. He attended St. John's College, Cambridge, destined for the ministry, but he abandoned the scheme to go to New Zealand in 1859 to take up sheep farming. He was successful in this undertaking, and some of his New Zealand background is incorporated into *Erewhon* (1872). He returned to England in 1864 following his father's death and lived in London for the rest of his life. For a time he studied painting, but he gave his chief energy to writing, at first upon subjects having to do with evolution, later more broadly on literature, art, and travel. His highly autobiographical *Way of All Flesh* was written before 1885 but not published until after his death. It is an unsparing account of his turbulent relations with an intensely Victorian father.

Butler's work after 1875 was for a decade mainly concerned with interpretations and modifications of Darwinian theory. The most notable examples. of this concern are *Evolution, Old and New* (1879), *Unconscious Memory* (1880), and *Luck or Cunning?* (1887). Butler had been responsive to Darwin's ideas from the time he read the *Origin of the Species* in New Zealand, but he opposed the explanation of evolution as operating by blind chance or by brute force. He sought to include in evolutionary theory the concept of a vital or creative principle, and his zeal for his ideas led him into frequent disputes with scientists, including Darwin and Huxley. Although most of the scientists of the day tended to ignore or discount Butler's writings on evolution, those writings commended themselves to G. B. Shaw, who also greatly admired Butler as a satirist.

In the eighteen-eighties Butler turned his attention to travel in Italy, to the study of music, which he greatly loved, and to literary criticism and speculation. He advanced the ill-received proposition that the author of the *Odyssey* had been a woman. But his studies in Greek literature led him also to serviceable translations of the *Iliad* and the *Odyssey*. He also wrote on Shakespeare, but his *Shakespeare's Sonnets Reconsidered* (1899) is as irregular from a scholarly point of view as his assertions about the authoress of the *Odyssey*.

Erewhon Revisited (1901) was virtually the last work from Butler's pen, but there was a good deal of posthumously published material. He died in 1902.

Butler's mark as a creative writer is satire, especially in the inversion of expected circumstances that marks the *Erewhon* books. Something of the satirical element is evident too in his nonfiction; and his essays, when not wholly quixotic, are frequently amusing and genial. Butler's gifts as an essayist have been overshadowed by his brilliant *Way of All Flesh* and by some of his crotchets, but they well repay the attention of students of the age of transition from Victorian to modern.

CHRONOLOGY

1835   Born 4 December near Bingham, Nottinghamshire.
1848–54   Attends Shrewsbury School.
1854–58   Attends St. John's College, Cambridge.
1859–64   Engages in sheep farming in New Zealand.
1868–76   Exhibits paintings at Royal Academy.
1872   *Erewhon.*
1875   Visits Canada.
1879   *Evolution, Old and New.*
1897   *The Authoress of the Odyssey.*
1901   *Erewhon Revisited.*
1902   Dies 18 June in London; ashes scattered.
1903   *The Way of All Flesh.*

EDITIONS

Butler's fiction is omitted in the listing below.
Works, ed. H. Festing Jones and A. T. Bartholomew (20 vols., 1923–26).
Essays on Life, Art and Science, ed. R. A. Streatfeild (1904).
Evolution, Old and New, ed. R. A. Streatfeild (1911).
The Note-Books of Samuel Butler, ed. H. Festing Jones (1912).
The Humour of Homer and Other Essays, ed. R. A. Streatfeild (1913).
Luck or Cunning? ed. H. Festing Jones (1920).
The Authoress of the Odyssey, ed. H. Festing Jones (1922).
The Essential Butler, ed. G. D. H. Cole (1961).

BIOGRAPHY AND CRITICISM

R. A. Streatfeild, *Samuel Butler* (1902).
H. Festing Jones, *Samuel Butler: A Memoir* (2 vols., 1919).
Gilbert Cannan, *Samuel Butler* (1915).
C. E. M. Joad, *Samuel Butler* (1924).
Mrs. R. S. Garnett, *Samuel Butler and His Family Relations* (1929).
B. Farrington, *Butler and the Odyssey* (1929).
Malcolm Muggeridge, *The Earnest Atheist* (1936).
P. M. Furbank, *Samuel Butler* (1948).
Philip Henderson, *Samuel Butler: The Incarnate Bachelor* (1953).
Stanley B. Harkness, *The Career of Samuel Butler: A Bibliography* (1955).
Basil Willey, *Darwin and Butler* (1960).
Lee Holt, *Samuel Butler* (1964).

How to Make the Best of Life

This entertaining essay was initially a lecture to the Somerville Club on 27 February 1895.
It was published posthumously in Butler's Essays on Life, Art, and Science.

I HAVE been asked to speak on the question how to make the best of life, but may as well confess at once that I know nothing about it. I cannot think that I have made the best of my own life, nor is it likely that I shall make much better of what may or may not remain to me. I do not even know how to make the best of the twenty minutes that your committee has placed at my disposal, and as for life as a whole, who ever yet made the best of such a colossal opportunity by conscious effort and deliberation? In little things no doubt deliberate and conscious effort will help us, but we are speaking of large issues, and such kingdoms of heaven as the making the best of these come not by observation.

The question, therefore, on which I have undertaken to address you is, as you must all know, fatuous, if it be faced seriously. Life is like playing a violin solo in public and learning the instrument as one goes on. One cannot make the best of such impossibilities, and the question is doubly fatuous until we are told which of our two lives—the conscious or the unconscious—is held by the asker to be the truer life. Which does the question contemplate—the life we know, or the life which others may know, but which we know not?

Death gives a life to some men and women compared with which their so-called existence here is as nothing. Which is the truer life of Shakespeare, Handel, that divine woman who wrote the Odyssey, and of Jane Austen—the life which palpitated with sensible warm motion within their own bodies, or that in virtue of which they are still palpitating in ours? In whose consciousness does their truest life consist—their own, or ours? Can Shakespeare be said to have begun his true life till a hundred years or so after he was dead and buried? His physical life was but as an embryonic stage, a coming up out of darkness, a twilight and dawn before the sunrise of that life of the world to come which he was to enjoy hereafter. We all live for a while after we are gone hence, but we are for the most part stillborn, or at any rate die in infancy, as regards that life which every age and country has recognized as higher and truer than the one of which we are now sentient. As the life of the race is larger, longer, and in all respects more to be considered than that of the individual, so is the life we live in others larger and more important than the one we live in ourselves. This appears nowhere perhaps more plainly than in the case of great teachers, who often in the lives of their pupils produce an effect that reaches far beyond anything produced while their single lives were yet unsupplemented by those other lives into which they infused their own.

Death to such people is the ending of a short life, but it does not touch the life they are already living in those whom they have taught; and happily, as none can know when he shall die, so none can make sure that he too shall not live long beyond the grave; for the life after death is like money before it—no one can be sure that it may not fall to him or her even at the eleventh hour. Money and immortality come in such odd unaccountable ways that no one is cut off from hope. We may not have made either of them for ourselves, but yet another may give them to us in virtue of his or her love, which shall illumine us for ever, and establish us in some heavenly mansion whereof we neither dreamed nor shall ever dream. Look at the Doge Loredano Loredani, the old man's smile upon whose face has been reproduced so faithfully in so many lands that it can never henceforth be forgotten—would he have had one hundredth part of the life he now lives had he not been linked awhile with one of those heaven-sent men who know *che cosa è amor?*[1] Look at Rembrandt's old woman in our National Gallery; had she died before she was eighty-three years old she would not have been living now. Then, when she was eighty-three, immortality perched upon her as a bird on a withered bough.

I seem to hear someone say that this is a mockery, a piece of special pleading, a giving of stones to those that ask for bread. Life is not life unless we can feel it, and a life limited to a knowledge of such fraction of our work as may happen

---

[1] The matter of love.

to survive us is no true life in other people; salve it as we may, death is not life any more than black is white.

The objection is not so true as it sounds. I do not deny that we had rather not die, nor do I pretend that much even in the case of the most favoured few can survive them beyond the grave. It is only because this is so that our own life is possible; others have made room for us, and we should make room for others in our turn without undue repining. What I maintain is that a not inconsiderable number of people do actually attain to a life beyond the grave which we can all feel forcibly enough, whether they can do so or not—that this life tends with increasing civilization to become more and more potent, and that it is better worth considering, in spite of its being unfelt by ourselves, than any which we have felt or can ever feel in our own persons.

Take an extreme case. A group of people are photographed by Edison's new process—say Titiens, Trebelli, and Jenny Lind, with any two of the finest men singers the age has known— let them be photographed incessantly for half an hour while they perform a scene in *Lohengrin*; let all be done stereoscopically. Let them be phonographed at the same time so that their minutest shades of intonation are preserved, let the slides be coloured by a competent artist, and then let the scene be called suddenly into sight and sound, say a hundred years hence. Are those people dead or alive? Dead to themselves they are, but while they live so powerfully and so livingly in us, which is the greater paradox— to say that they are alive or that they are dead? To myself it seems that their life in others would be more truly life than their death to themselves is death. Granted that they do not present all the phenomena of life—who ever does so even when he is held to be alive? We are held to be alive because we present a sufficient number of living phenomena to let the others go without saying; those who see us take the part for the whole here as in everything else, and surely, in the case supposed above, the phenomena of life predominate so powerfully over those of death, that the people themselves must be held to be more alive than dead. Our living personality is, as the word implies, only our mask, and those who still own such a mask as I have supposed have a living personality. Granted again that the case just put is an extreme one; still many a man and many a woman has so stamped him or herself on his work that, though we would gladly have the aid of such accessories as we doubtless

presently shall have to the livingness of our great dead, we can see them very sufficiently through the masterpieces they have left us.

As for their own unconsciousness I do not deny it. The life of the embryo was unconscious before birth, and so is the life—I am speaking only of the life revealed to us by natural religion—after death. But as the embryonic and infant life of which we were unconscious was the most potent factor in our after life of consciousness, so the effect which we may unconsciously produce in others after death, and it may be even before it on those who have never seen us, is in all sober seriousness our truer and more abiding life, and the one which those who would make the best of their sojourn here will take most into their consideration.

Unconsciousness is no bar to livingness. Our conscious actions are a drop in the sea as compared with our unconscious ones. Could we know all the life that is in us by way of circulation, nutrition, breathing, waste, and repair, we should learn what an infinitesimally small part consciousness plays in our present existence; yet our unconscious life is as truly life as our conscious life, and though it is unconscious to itself it emerges into an indirect and vicarious consciousness in our other and conscious self, which exists but in virtue of our unconscious self. So we have also a vicarious consciousness in others. The unconscious life of those that have gone before us has in great part moulded us into such men and women as we are, and our own unconscious lives will in like manner have a vicarious consciousness in others, though we be dead enough to it in ourselves.

If it is again urged that it matters not to us how much we may be alive in others, if we are to know nothing about it, I reply that the common instinct of all who are worth considering gives the lie to such cynicism. I see here present some who have achieved, and others who no doubt will achieve, success in literature. Will one of them hesitate to admit that it is a lively pleasure to her to feel that on the other side of the world someone may be smiling happily over her work, and that she is thus living in that person though she knows nothing about it? Here it seems to me that true faith comes in. Faith does not consist, as the Sunday School pupil said, "in the power of believing that which we know to be untrue." It consists in holding fast that which the healthiest and most kindly instincts of the best and most sensible men and women are intuitively possessed of, without caring to require much evidence further than the fact that such people are so convinced; and for my own part I find the best men and women I know unanimous in feeling that life in others, even though we know nothing about it, is nevertheless a thing to be desired and gratefully accepted if we can get it either before death or after. I observe also that a large number of men and women do actually attain to such life, and in some cases continue so to live, if not for ever, yet to what is practically much the same thing. Our life then in this world is, to natural religion as much as to revealed, a period of probation. The use we make of it is to settle how far we are to enter into another, and whether that other is to be a heaven of just affection or a hell of righteous condemnation.

Who, then, are the most likely so to run that they may obtain this veritable prize of our high calling? Setting aside such lucky numbers, drawn as it were in the lottery of immortality, which I have referred to casually above, and setting aside also the chances and changes from which even immortality is not exempt, who on the whole are most likely to live anew in the affectionate thoughts of those who never so much as saw them in the flesh, and know not even their names? There is a *nisus*,[2] a straining in the dull dumb economy of things, in virtue of which some, whether they will it and know it or no, are more likely to live after death than others, and who are these? Those who aimed at it as by some great thing that they would do to make them famous? Those who have lived most in themselves and for themselves, or those who have been most ensouled consciously, but perhaps better unconsciously, directly but more often indirectly, by the most living souls past and present that have flitted near them? Can we think of a man or woman who grips us firmly, at the thought of whom we kindle when we are alone in our honest daw's plumes, with none to admire or shrug his shoulders, can we think of one such, the secret of whose power does not lie in the charm of his or her personality—that is to say, in the wideness of his or her sympathy with, and therefore life in and communion with other people? In the wreckage that comes ashore from the sea of time there is much tinsel stuff that we must preserve and study if we would know our own times and people; granted that many a dead charlatan lives long and enters largely

and necessarily into our own lives; we use them and throw them away when we have done with them. I do not speak of these, I do not speak of the Virgils and Alexander Popes, and who can say how many more whose names I dare not mention for fear of offending. They are as stuffed birds or beasts in a museum; serviceable no doubt from a scientific standpoint, but with no vivid or vivifying hold upon us. They seem to be alive, but are not. I am speaking of those who do actually live in us, and move us to higher achievements though they be long dead, whose life thrusts out our own and overrides it. I speak of those who draw us ever more towards them from youth to age, and to think of whom is to feel at once that we are in the hands of those we love, and whom we would most wish to resemble. What is the secret of the hold that these people have upon us? Is it not that while, conventionally speaking, alive, they most merged their lives in, and were in fullest communion with those among whom they lived? They found their lives in losing them. We never love the memory of anyone unless we feel that he or she was himself or herself a lover.

I have seen it urged, again, in querulous accents, that the so-called immortality even of the most immortal is not for ever. I see a passage to this effect in a book that is making a stir as I write. I will quote it. The writer says:

"So, it seems to me, is the immortality we so glibly predicate of departed artists. If they survive at all, it is but a shadowy life they live, moving on through the gradations of slow decay to distant but inevitable death. They can no longer, as heretofore, speak directly to the hearts of their fellow-men, evoking their tears or laughter, and all the pleasures, be they sad or merry, of which imagination holds the secret. Driven from the market-place they become first the companions of the student, then the victims of the specialist. He who would still hold familiar intercourse with them must train himself to penetrate the veil which in ever-thickening folds conceals them from the ordinary gaze; he must catch the tone of a vanished society, he must move in a circle of alien associations, he must think in a language not his own."[3]

This is crying for the moon, or rather pretending to cry for it, for the writer is obviously insincere. I see *The Saturday Review* says the passage I have just quoted "reaches almost

---

[2] Ascent.
[3] The Foundations of Belief, by the Right Hon. A. J. Balfour. Longmans, 1895, p. 48. [Butler's note]

to poetry," and indeed I find many blank verses in it, some of them very aggressive. No prose is free from an occasional blank verse, and a good writer will not go hunting over his work to rout them out, but nine or ten in little more than as many lines is indeed reaching too near to poetry for good prose. This, however, is a trifle, and might pass if the tone of the writer was not so obviously that of cheap pessimism. I know not which is cheapest, pessimism or optimism. One forces lights, the other darks; both are equally untrue to good art, and equally sure of their effect with the groundlings. The one extenuates, the other sets down in malice. The first is the more amiable lie, but both are lies, and are known to be so by those who utter them. Talk about catching the tone of a vanished society to understand Rembrandt or Giovanni Bellini! It is nonsense—the folds do not thicken in front of these men; we understand them as well as those among whom they went about in the flesh, and perhaps better. Homer and Shakespeare speak to us probably far more effectually than they did to the men of their own time, and most likely we have them at their best. I cannot think that Shakespeare talked better than we hear him now in *Hamlet* or *Henry the Fourth*; like enough he would have been found a very disappointing person in a drawing-room. People stamp themselves on their work; if they have not done so they are naught, if they have we have them; and for the most part they stamp themselves deeper on their work than on their talk. No doubt Shakespeare and Handel will be one day clean forgotten, as though they had never been born. The world will in the end die; mortality therefore itself is not immortal, and when death dies the life of these men will die with it—but not sooner. It is enough that they should live within us and move us for many ages as they have and will. Such immortality, therefore, as some men and women are born to achieve, or have thrust upon them, is a practical if not a technical immortality, and he who would have more let him have nothing.

I see I have drifted into speaking rather of how to make the best of death than of life, but who can speak of life without his thoughts turning instantly to that which is beyond it? He or she who has made the best of the life after death has made the best of the life before it; who cares one straw for any such chances and changes as will commonly befall him here if he is upheld by the full and certain hope of ever-lasting life in the affections of those that shall come after? If the life after death is happy in the hearts of others, it matters little how unhappy was the life before it.

And now I leave my subject, not without misgiving that I shall have disappointed you. But for the great attention which is being paid to the work from which I have quoted above, I should not have thought it well to insist on points with which you are, I doubt not, as fully impressed as I am: but that book weakens the sanctions of natural religion, and minimizes the comfort which it affords us, while it does more to undermine than to support the foundations of what is commonly called belief. Therefore I was glad to embrace this opportunity of protesting. Otherwise I should not have been so serious on a matter that transcends all seriousness. Lord Beaconsfield cut it shorter with more effect. When asked to give a rule of life for the son of a friend he said, "Do not let him try and find out who wrote the *Letters of Junius*." Pressed for further counsel, he added, "Nor yet who was the Man in the Iron Mask"—and he would say no more. Don't bore people. And yet I am by no means sure that a good many people do not think themselves ill-used unless he who addresses them has thoroughly well bored them—especially if they have paid any money for hearing him. My great namesake said, "Surely the pleasure is as great of being cheated as to cheat," and great as the pleasure both of cheating and boring undoubtedly is, I believe he was right. So I remember a poem which came out some thirty years ago in *Punch*, about a young lady who went forth in quest to "Some burden make or burden bear, but which she did not greatly care, O Miserie." So, again, all the holy men and women who in the Middle Ages professed to have discovered how to make the best of life took care that being bored, if not cheated, should have a large place in their programme. Still there are limits, and I close not without fear that I may have exceeded them.

The "Enfant Terrible" of Literature

This comic piece was first published after Butler's death in The Note-books, *an extensive gathering of Butler's literary jottings. It is one of many illustrations of Butler's simultaneously humorous and frustrated response to his literary position in the late Victorian period.*

MYSELF

I AM THE ENFANT TERRIBLE OF LITERATURE and science. If I cannot, and I know I cannot, get the literary and scientific big-wigs to give me a shilling, I can, and I know I can, heave bricks into the middle of them.

BLAKE, DANTE, VIRGIL, AND TENNYSON

Talking it over, we agreed that Blake was no good because he learnt Italian at sixty in order to study Dante, and we knew Dante was no good because he was so fond of Virgil, and Virgil was no good because Tennyson ran him, and as for Tennyson—well, Tennyson goes without saying.

MY FATHER AND SHAKESPEARE

My father is one of the few men I know who say they do not like Shakespeare. I could forgive my father for not liking Shakespeare if it was only because Shakespeare wrote poetry; but this is not the reason. He dislikes Shakespeare because he finds him so very coarse. He also says he likes Tennyson and this seriously aggravates his offence.

TENNYSON

We were saying what a delightful dispensation of providence it was that prosperous people will write their memoirs. We hoped Tennyson was writing his. [1890.]

P.S. We think his son has done nearly as well. [1898.]

WALTER PATER AND MATTHEW ARNOLD

Mr. Walter Pater's style is, to me, like the face of some old woman who has been to Madame Rachel and had herself enamelled. The bloom is nothing but powder and paint and the odour is cherry-blossom. Mr. Matthew Arnold's odour is as the faint sickliness of hawthorn.

MY RANDOM PASSAGES

At the Century Club a friend very kindly and hesitatingly ventured to suggest to me that I should get some one to go over my MS. before printing; a judicious editor, he said, would have prevented me from printing many a bit which, it seemed to him, was written too recklessly and offhand. The fact is that the more reckless and random a passage appears to be, the more carefully it has been submitted to friends and considered and re-considered; without the support of friends I should never have dared to print one half of what I have printed.

I am not one of those who can repeat the General Confession unreservedly. I should say rather:

"I have left unsaid much that I am sorry I did not say, but I have said little that I am sorry for having said, and I am pretty well on the whole, thank you."

MORAL TRY-YOUR-STRENGTHS

There are people who, if they only had a slot, might turn a pretty penny as moral try-your-strengths, like those we see in railway-stations for telling people their physical strength when they have dropped a penny in the slot. In a way they have a slot, which is their mouths, and people drop pennies in by asking them to dinner, and then they try their strength against them and get snubbed; but this way is roundabout and expensive. We want a good automatic asinometer by which we can tell at a moderate cost how great or how little of a fool we are.

"POPULUS VULT"

If people like being deceived—and this can hardly be doubted—there can rarely have been a time during which they can have had more of the wish than now. The literary, scientific, and religious worlds vie with one another in trying to gratify the public.

MEN AND MONKEYS

In his latest article (Feb. 1892) Prof. Garner says that the chatter of monkeys is not meaningless, but that they are conveying ideas to one another. This seems to me hazardous. The monkeys might with equal justice conclude that in our magazine articles, or literary and artistic criticisms, we are not chattering idly but are conveying ideas to one another.

"ONE TOUCH OF NATURE"

"One touch of nature makes the whole world kin." Should it not be "marks," not "makes"? There is one touch of nature, or natural feature, which marks all mankind as of one family.

P.S. Surely it should be "of ill-nature." "One touch of ill-nature marks—or several touches of ill-nature mark the whole world kin."

GENUINE FEELING

In the *Times* of to-day, 4th June 1887, there is an obituary notice of a Rev. Mr. Knight who wrote about 200 songs, among others "She wore a wreath of roses." The *Times* says that, though these songs have no artistic merit, they are full of genuine feeling, or words to this effect; as though a song which was full of genuine feeling could by any possibility be without artistic merit.

GEORGE MEREDITH

The *Times* in a leading article says (3rd January 1899) "a talker," as Mr. George Meredith has somewhere said, "involves the existence of a talkee," or words to this effect.

I said what comes to the same thing as this in *Life and Habit* in 1877, and I repeated it in the preface to my translation of the Iliad in 1898. I do not believe George Meredith has said anything to the same effect, but I have read so very little of that writer, and have so utterly rejected what I did read, that he may well have done so without my knowing it. He damned *Erewhon*, as Chapman and Hall's reader, in 1871, and, as I am still raw about this after twenty-eight years (I am afraid unless I say something more I shall be taken as writing these words seriously), I prefer to assert that the *Times* writer was quoting from my preface to the Iliad, published a few

weeks earlier, and fathering the remark on George Meredith. By the way, the *Times* did not give so much as a line to my translation in its "Books of the Week," though it was duly sent to them.

FROUDE AND FREEMAN

I think it was last Saturday (Ap. 9) (at any rate it was a day just thereabouts) the *Times* had a leader on Froude's appointment as Reg. Prof. of Mod. Hist. at Oxford. It said Froude was perhaps our greatest living master of style, or words to that effect, only that, like Freeman, he was too long: *i.e.*, only he is an habitual offender against the most fundamental principles of his art. If then Froude is our greatest master of style, what are the rest of us?

There was a much better article yesterday on Marbot, in which my namesake A. J. Butler got a dressing for talking rubbish about style. [1892.]

STYLE

In this day's *Sunday Times* there is an article on Mrs. Browning's letters which begins with some remarks about style. "It is recorded," says the writer, "of Plato, that in a rough draft of one of his Dialogues, found after his death, the first paragraph was written in seventy different forms. Wordsworth spared no pains to sharpen and polish to the utmost the gifts with which nature had endowed him; and Cardinal Newman, one of the greatest masters of English style, has related in an amusing essay the pains he took to acquire his style."

I never knew a writer yet who took the smallest pains with his style and was at the same time readable. Plato's having had seventy shies at one sentence is quite enough to explain to me why I dislike him. A man may, and ought to take a great deal of pains to write clearly, tersely, and euphoniously: he will write many a sentence three or four times over—to do much more than this is worse than not re-writing at all: he will be at great pains to see that he does not repeat himself, to arrange his matter in the way that shall best enable the reader to master it, to cut out superfluous words and, even more, to eschew irrelevant matter: but in each case he will be thinking not of his own style but of his reader's convenience.

Men like Newman and R. L. Stevenson seem to have taken pains to acquire what they called a style as a preliminary measure—as something that they had to form before their writings could be of any value. I should like to put it on record that I never took the smallest pains with my style, have never thought about it, and do not know or want to know whether it is a style at all or whether it is not, as I believe and hope, just common, simple, straightforwardness. I cannot conceive how any man can take thought for his style without loss to himself and his readers.

I have, however, taken all the pains that I had patience to endure in the improvement of my handwriting (which, by the way, has a constant tendency to resume feral characteristics) and also with my MS. generally to keep it clean and legible. I am having a great tidying just now, in the course of which the MS. of *Erewhon* turned up, and I was struck with the great difference between it and the MS. of *The Authoress of the Odyssey*. I have also taken great pains, with what success I know not, to correct impatience, irritability, and other like faults in my own character—and this not because I care two straws about my own character, but because I find the correction of such faults as I have been able to correct makes life easier and saves me from getting into scrapes, and attaches nice people to me more readily. But I suppose this really is attending to style after all. [1897.]

John Morley

1838-1923

J OHN MORLEY, First Viscount Morley of Blackburn, is a classic example of the man of letters in the Victorian age who not only commented upon the contemporary scene but who influenced it by active service in Parliament, thus making for himself two distinguished careers that interacted upon each other.

Morley was born at Blackburn and educated locally, then at Cheltenham College, and finally at Lincoln College, Oxford. His parents hoped for a clerical career for him, but he chose first the law and then literature. He incurred parental disfavor by becoming a freethinker at Oxford, and he was thenceforth obliged to make his own way without financial support from his parents. He did so with difficulty at first but ultimately with great success. He was a contributor to the *Saturday Review* and as a result met most of the liberal intellectuals of the day. He succeeded G. H. Lewes as editor of the *Fortnightly Review* and held the post from 1867 to 1882; he also served as editor of the *Pall Mall Gazette* from 1881 to 1883. He also initiated the English Men of Letters series in 1878 and contributed the volume on Edmund Burke to the series. He had by this time already written a large number of works in the fields of politics and political biography, including *On Compromise* (1874), a work in the John Stuart Mill tradition, *Rousseau* (1876), and *Diderot and the Encyclopaedists* (1878).

In 1883 Morley was elected to Parliament where he served for more than thirty years. Although he continued to write, his main energy went into politics, and some have mourned the resulting loss to literature. He was an ardent supporter of Gladstone and served in Gladstone cabinets as Irish Secretary. Later he was Secretary for India (1905–10), but he never attained the post of Foreign Secretary to which he aspired. In 1903 he published his definitive biography of Gladstone. He was elevated to the peerage in 1908. As a peer he was Lord President of the Council from 1910 to 1914. In that year he resigned from public service. He died in 1923 by which time the Liberal Party of his allegiance had declined to insignificance and new political alignments were in force.

Morley was one of the finest and last flowerings of Victorian liberalism. As heir to the Enlightenment and its nineteenth-century descendant utilitarianism, Morley saw all issues, including literary ones, in the light of logical, practical, and pragmatic considerations. His literary output was prodigious, including several volumes of literary criticism, and no edition of his works contains all his writings. Although he was an agnostic and a radical, his literary judgments are not of a radical kind. They exhibit instead the qualities of sobriety, moral seriousness, and measured eloquence that characterize the earnest Victorian liberal.

CHRONOLOGY

1838	Born 24 December at Blackburn.
1856–60	Attends Lincoln College, Oxford.
1860	Becomes journalist in London.
1867–82	Editor of *Fortnightly Review*.
1871–77	*Critical Miscellanies*, two series.
1874	*On Compromise*.
1878	Initiates EML series.
1881–83	Editor of *Pall Mall Gazette*.
1886	Serves as Irish Secretary.
1892–95	Irish Secretary.
1903	*Life of Gladstone*.
1908	Becomes First Viscount Morley of Blackburn.
1910–14	Lord President of the Council.
1923	Dies 23 September at Wimbledon.

EDITIONS

The Works of John Morley, edition de luxe (15 vols., 1921).
Selected Essays, ed. H. G. Rawlinson (1923).
Nineteenth Century Essays, ed. Peter Stansky (1970).
The Struggle for National Education, ed. Asa Briggs (1970).

BIOGRAPHY AND CRITICISM

Algernon Cecil, *Six Oxford Thinkers* (1909).
G. M. Harper, *Morley and Other Essays* (1920).
J. L. Morrison, *Morley: A Study in Victorianism* (1920).
F. W. Hirst, *The Early Life and Letters of John Morley* (2 vols., 1927).
Edwin M. Everett, *The Party of Humanity* (1939).
Warren Staebler, *The Liberal Mind of John Morley* (1943).
Frances Knickerbocker, *Free Minds: John Morley and His Friends* (1943).
Basil Willey, *More Nineteenth Century Studies* (1956).
M. N. Das, *India under Morley and Minto* (1964).
Peter Stansky, *Ambitions and Strategies* (1964).
Stanley Wolpert, *Morley and India* (1967).
D. A. Hamer, *John Morley: Liberal Intellectual in Politics* (1968).
Stephen E. Koss, *John Morley at the India Office* (1969).
Edward Alexander, *John Morley* (1972).
John Bicknell, "The Unbelievers," in *Victorian Prose: A Guide to Research* (1973).

Memorials of a Man of Letters

*Morley's essay was a review of the then recently published correspondence of Macvey Napier,
editor of the prestigious* Edinburgh Review *from 1829 to 1847. Morley's review first appeared
in 1879 in the* Nineteenth Century. *It provides an opportunity to see a Victorian man of letters at
work on one of his illustrious predecessors in the same field. The essay was variously reprinted
in Morley's* Studies in Literature *and in his* Critical Miscellanies.

WHAT are the qualities of a good contributor? What makes a good Review? Is
the best literature produced by the writer who
does nothing else but write, or by the man who
tempers literature by affairs? What are the
different recommendations of the rival systems
of anonymity and signature? What kind of
change, if any, has passed over periodical literature since those two great periodicals, the
Edinburgh and the *Quarterly*, held sway? These and
a number of other questions in the same matter
must naturally be often present to the mind of
any one who is concerned in the control of a
Review, and a volume has just been printed
[1879] which sets such musings once more astir.
Mr. Macvey Napier was the editor of the
Edinburgh Review from 1829—when Jeffrey,[1] after
a reign of seven-and-twenty years, resigned it
into his hands—until his death in 1847. A portion
of the correspondence addressed to Mr. Napier
during this period is full of personal interest
both to the man of letters and to that more
singular personage, the impresario of men of
letters, the *entrepreneur* of the spiritual power, the
Editor.

To manage an opera-house is usually supposed
to tax human powers more urgently than any
position save that of a general in the very heat
and stress of battle. The orchestra, the chorus, the
subscribers, the first tenor, a pair of rival prima
donnas, the newspapers, the box-agents in Bond
Street, the army of hangers-on in the flies—
all combine to demand such gifts of tact, resolution, patience, foresight, tenacity, flexibility,
as are only expected from the great ruler or the
great soldier. The editor of a periodical of public
consideration—and the *Edinburgh Review* in the
hands of Mr. Napier was the avowed organ of the
ruling Whig powers—is sorely tested in the same
way. The rival house may bribe his stars. His
popular epigrammatist is sometimes as full of

humours as a spoiled soprano. The favourite
pyrotechnist is systematically late and procastin-
atory, or is piqued because his punctuation or his
paragraphs have been meddled with. The contributor whose article would be in excellent time
if it did not appear before the close of the century,
or never appeared at all, pesters you with warnings that a month's delay is a deadly blow to
progress, and stays the procession of the ages.
The contributor who could profitably fill a sheet,
insists on sending a treatise.

Ah, que de choses dans un menuet![2] cried Marcel,
the great dancing-master, and ah, what things
in the type and ἰδέα of an article! cries an editor
with the enthusiasm of his calling; such proportion, measure, comprehension, variety of topics,
pithiness of treatment, all within a space appointed with Procrustean rigour. This is what the
soul of the volunteer contributor is dull to. Of
the minor vexations who can tell? There is one
single tribulation dire enough to poison life—
even if there were no other—and this is disorderly
manuscript. Empson, Mr. Napier's well-known
contributor, was one of the worst offenders;
he would never even take the trouble to mark
his paragraphs. It is my misfortune to have a
manuscript before me at this moment that would
fill thirty of these pages, and yet from beginning
to end there is no indication that it is not to be
read at a single breath. The paragraph ought to
be, and in all good writers it is, as real and as
sensible a division as the sentence. It is an organic
member in prose composition, with a beginning,
a middle, and an end, just as a stanza is an organic
and definite member in the composition of an ode.
'I fear my manuscript is rather disorderly,' says
another, 'but I will correct carefully in print.'
Just so. Because he is too heedless to do his work
in a workmanlike way, he first inflicts fatigue and
vexation on the editor whom he expects to read
his paper; second, he inflicts considerable and

---

[1] Francis Jeffrey (1773–1850), one of the founders and the editor until 1829 of the *Edinburgh Review*.
[2] "Ah, what things there are in a minuet!"

quite needless expense on the publisher; and thirdly, he inflicts a great deal of tedious and thankless labour on the printers, who are for the most part far more meritorious persons than fifth-rate authors. It is true that Burke returned such disordered proofs that the printer usually found it least troublesome to set the whole afresh, and Miss Martineau tells a story of a Scotch compositor who fled from Edinburgh to avoid Carlyle's manuscript, and to his horror was presently confronted after his migration with a piece of the too familiar copy. 'Lord, have mercy!' he cried. 'Have *you* got that man to print for? But most editors will cheerfully forgive such transgressions to all contributors who will guarantee that they write as well as Burke or Carlyle. Alas! it is usually the case that those who have least excuse are the worst offenders. The slovenliest manuscripts come from persons to whom the difference between an hour and a minute is of the very smallest importance. This, however, is a digression, only to be excused by a hope that some persons of sensitive conscience may be led to ponder whether there may not be, after all, some moral obligations even towards editors and printers.

Mr. Napier had one famous contributor, who stands out alone in the history of editors. Lord Brougham's[3] traditional connection with the *Review*,—he had begun to write either in its first or third number, and had written in it ever since—his encyclopaedic ignorance, his power, his fame in the country, and the prestige which his connection reflected on the *Review*, all made him a personage with whom it would have been imprudent or even ruinous to quarrel. Yet the position in which Mr. Napier was placed, after Brougham's breach with the Whigs, was one of the most difficult in which the conductor of a powerful organ could possibly be placed. The *Review* was the representative, the champion, and the mouthpiece of the Whig party, and of the Whigs who were in office. Before William IV. dismissed the Whigs in 1834 as arbitrarily as his father had dismissed the Whigs in 1784, Brougham had covered himself with disrepute among his party by a thousand pranks, and after the dismissal he disgusted them by asking the new Chancellor to make him Chief Baron of the Exchequer. When Lord Melbourne returned to power in the following year, this and other escapades were remembered against him. 'If

left out,' said Lord Melbourne, 'he would indeed be dangerous; but if taken in, he would simply be destructive.' So Brougham was left out, Pepys was made Chancellor, and the Premier compared himself to a man who has broken with a termagant mistress and married the best of cooks. Mr. Napier was not so happy. The termagant was left on his hands. He had to keep terms with a contributor who hated with deadly hatred the very government that the *Review* existed to support. No editor ever had such a contributor as Brougham. He scolds, he storms, he hectors, he lectures; he is for ever threatening desertion and prophesying ruin; he exhausts the vocabulary of opprobrium against his correspondent's best friends; they are silly slaves, base traitors, a vile clique 'whose treatment of me has been the very *ne plus ultra* of ingratitude, baseness, and treachery.' He got the *Review* and its editor into a scrape which shook the world at the time (1834), by betraying Cabinet secrets to spite Lord Durham. His cries against his adversaries are as violent as the threats of Ajax in his tent, and as loud as the bellowings of Philoctetes at the mouth of his cave. Here is one instance out of a hundred:—

That is a trifle, and I only mention it to beg of you to pluck up a little courage, and not be alarmed every time any of the little knot of threateners annoy you. *They want to break off all kind of connection between me and the Edinburgh Review.* I have long seen it. Their fury against the article in the last number knows no bounds, and they will never cease till they worry you out of your connection with me, and get the whole control of the Review into their own hands, by forcing you to resign it yourself. A *party and a personal* engine is all they want to make it. What possible right can any of these silly slaves have to object to my opinion being—what it truly is—against the Holland House theory of Lord Chatham's madness? I *know* that Lord Grenville treated it with contempt. I know others now living who did so too, and I know that so stout a Whig as Sir P. Francis was clearly of that opinion, and he knew Lord Chatham personally. I had every ground to believe that Horace Walpole, a vile, malignant, and unnatural wretch, though a very clever writer of Letters, was nine-tenths of the Holland House authority for the tale. I knew that a baser man in character, or a meaner in capacity than the first Lord Holland existed not, even in those days of job and mediocrity. Why, then, was I bound to take a false view because Lord Holland's family have inherited his hatred of a great rival?

Mr. Napier, who seems to have been one of the

---

[3] Henry Brougham, 1st Baron Brougham and Vaux (1778–1868), statesman, one of the founders of the *Edinburgh Review*.

most considerate and high-minded of men, was moved to energetic remonstrance on this occasion. Lord Brougham explained his strong language away, but he was incapable of really controlling himself and the strain was never lessened until 1843, when the correspondence ceases, and there had been a quarrel between him and his too long-suffering correspondent. Yet, John Allen,— that able scholar and conspicuous figure in the annals of Holland House—wrote of Brougham to Mr. Napier:—'He is not a malignant or bad-hearted man, but he is an unscrupulous one, and where his passions are concerned or his vanity irritated, there is no excess of which he is not capable.' Of Brougham's strong and manly sense, when passion or vanity did not cloud it, and even of a sort of careful justice, these letters give more than one instance. The *Quarterly Review*, for instance, had an article on Romilly's Memoirs, which to Romilly's friends seemed to do him less than justice. Brougham took a more sensible view.

Surely we had no right whatever to expect that they whom Romilly had all his life so stoutly opposed, and who were treated by him with great harshness, should treat him as his friends would do, and at the very moment when a most injudicious act of his family was bringing out all his secret thoughts against them. Only place yourself in the same postion, and suppose that Canning's private journals had been published,—the journals he may have kept while the bitterest enemy of the Whigs, and in every page of which there must have been some passage offensive to the feelings of the living and of the friends of the dead. Would any mercy have been shown to Canning's character and memory by any of the Whig party, either in society or in Reviews? Would the line have been drawn of only attacking Canning's executors, who published the papers, and leaving Canning himself untouched? Clearly and certainly not, and yet I am putting a very much weaker case, for we had joined Canning, and all political enmity was at an end: whereas the Tories and Romilly never had for an hour laid aside their mutual hostility.

If he was capable of equity, Brougham was also capable of hearty admiration, even of an old friend who had on later occasions gone into a line which he intensely disliked. It is a relief in the pages of furious anger and raging censure to come upon what he says of Jeffrey.

I can truly say that there never in all my life crossed my mind one single unkind feeling respecting him, or indeed any feeling but that of the warmest affection and the most unmingled admiration of his character, believing and knowing him to be as excellent and ami-

able as he is great in the ordinary, and, as I think, the far less important sense of the word.

Of the value of Brougham's contributions we cannot now judge. They will not, in spite of their energy and force, bear re-reading to-day, and perhaps the same may be said of three-fourths of Jeffrey's once famous essays. Brougham's self-confidence is heroic. He believed that he could make a speech for Bolingbroke, but by and by he had sense enough to see that, in order to attempt this, he ought to read Bolingbroke for a year, and then practise for another year. In 1838 he thought nothing of undertaking, amid all the demands of active life, such a bagatelle as a History of the French Revolution. 'I have some little knack of narrative,' he says, 'the most difficult by far of all styles, and never yet attained in perfection but by Hume and Livy; and I bring as much oratory and science to the task as most of my predecessors.' But what sort of science? And what has oratory to do with it? And how could he deceive himself into thinking that he could retire to write a history? Nobody that ever lived would have more speedily found out the truth of Voltaire's saying, '*Le repos est une bonne chose, mais l'ennui est son frère.*'[4] The truth is that we learn, after a certain observation of the world, to divide amazement pretty equally between the literary voluptuary or over-fastidious collegian, on the one hand, who is so impressed by the size of his subject that he never does more than collect material and make notes, and the presumptuous politician, on the other hand, who thinks that he can write a history or settle the issues of philosophy and theology in odd half-hours. The one is so enfeebled in will and literary energy after his *viginti annorum lucubrationes*;[5] the other is so accustomed to be content with the hurry, the unfinishedness, the rough-and-ready methods of practical affairs, and they both in different ways measure the worth and seriousness of literature so wrongly in relation to the rest of human interests.

The relations between Lord Brougham and Mr. Napier naturally suggest a good many reflections on the vexed question of the comparative advantages of the old and the new theory of a periodical. The new theory is that a periodical should not be an organ but an open pulpit, and that each writer should sign his name. Without disrespect to ably conducted and eminent contemporaries of long standing, it may be said that

---

[4] "Rest is a good thing, but boredom is its brother."   [5] Lucubrations of twenty years.

the time of opinion and favour is setting in this direction. Yet, on the whole, experience perhaps leads to a doubt whether the gains of the system of signature are so very considerable as some of us once expected. An editor on the new system is no doubt relieved of a certain measure of responsibility. Lord Cockburn's panegyric on the first great editor may show what was expected from a man in such a position as Jeffrey's. 'He had to discover, and to train, authors; to discern what truth and the public mind required; to suggest subjects; to reject, and, more offensive still, to improve, contributions; to keep down absurdities; to infuse spirit; to excite the timid; to repress violence; to soothe jealousies; to quell mutinies; to watch times; and all this in the morning of the reviewing day, before experience had taught editors conciliatory firmness, and contributors reasonable submission. He directed and controlled the elements he presided over with a master's judgment. There was not one of his associates who could have even held these elements together for a single year. . . . Inferior to these excellences, but still important, was his dexterity in revising the writings of others. Without altering the general tone or character of the composition, he had great skill in leaving out defective ideas or words, and in so aiding the original by lively or graceful touches, that reasonable authors were surprised and charmed on seeing how much better they looked than they thought they would' (Cockburn's *Life of Jeffrey*, i. 301).

From such toils and dangers as these the editor of a Review with signed articles is in the main happily free. He has usually suggestions to make, for his experience has probably given him points of view as to the effectiveness of this or that feature of an article for its own purpose, that would not occur to a writer. The writer is absorbed in his subject, and has been less accustomed to think of the public. But this exercise of a claim to a general acquiescence in the judgment and experience of a man who has the best reasons for trying to judge rightly, is a very different thing from the duty of drilling contributors and dressing contributions as they were dressed and drilled by Jeffrey. As Southey said, when groaning under the mutilations inflicted by Gifford on his contributions to the *Quarterly*, 'there must be a power expurgatory in the hands of the editor; and the misfortune is that editors frequently think it incumbent on them to use that power

merely because they have it' (Southey's Life, iv. 18). This is probably true on the anonymous system, where the editor is answerable for every word, and for the literary form no less than for the substantial soundness or interest of an article. In a man of weakish literary vanity—Jeffrey was evidently full of it—there may well be a constant itch to set his betters right in trifles, as Gifford thought that he could mend Southey's adjectives. To a vain editor, or a too masterful editor, the temptation under the anonymous system is no doubt strong. M. Buloz, it is true, the renowned conductor of the *Revue des deux Mondes*, is said to have insisted on, and to have freely practised, the fullest editorial prerogative over articles that were openly signed by the most eminent names in France. But M. Buloz had no competitor, and those who did not choose to submit to his Sultanic despotism were shut out from the only pulpit whence they were sure of addressing the congregation that they wanted. In England contributors are better off; and no editor of a signed periodical would either feel bound or be permitted to take such trouble about mere wording of sentences as Gifford and Jeffrey were in the habit of taking.

There is, however, another side to this, from an editor's point of view. With responsibility—not merely for commas and niceties and literary kick-shaws, but in its old sense—disappears also a portion of the interest of editorial labour. One would suppose it must be more interesting to command a man-of-war than a trading vessel; it would be more interesting to lead a regiment than to keep a tilting-yard. But the times are not ripe for such enterprises. Of literary ability of a good and serviceable kind there is a hundred or five hundred times more in the country than there was when Jeffrey, Smith, Brougham, and Horner devised their *Review* in a ninth story in Edinburgh many years ago.[6] It is the cohesion of a political creed that is gone, and the strength and fervour of a political school. The principles that inspired that group of strong men have been worked out. After their reforms had been achieved, the next great school was economic, and though it produced one fine orator, its work was at no time literary. The Manchester school with all their shortcomings had at least the signal distinction of attaching their views on special political questions to a general and presiding conception of the modern phase of civilisation, as industrial and pacific. The next party of advance, when it is

---

[6] The *Edinburgh Review* was founded in 1802.

formed, might have been expected to borrow from Cobden and Bright their hatred of war and their hatred of imperialism. After the sagacity and enlightenment of this school came the school of persiflage. A knot of vigorous and brilliant men towards 1856 rallied round the late editor of the *Saturday Review*,—and a strange chief he was for such a group,—but their flag was that of the Red Rover. They gave Philistinism many a shrewd blow, but perhaps at the same time helped to some degree—with other far deeper and stronger forces—to produce that sceptical and centrifugal state of mind, which now tends to nullify organised liberalism and paralyse the spirit of improvement. The Benthamites, led first by James Mill, and afterwards in a different key by John Mill, had pushed a number of political improvements in the radical and democratic direction during the time when the *Edinburgh* so powerfully represented more orthodox liberalism. They were the last important group of men who started together from a set of common principles, accepted a common programme of practical applications, and set to work in earnest and with due order and distribution of parts to advocate the common cause.

At present [1879] there is no similar agreement either among the younger men in parliament, or among a sufficiently numerous group of writers outside of parliament. The Edinburgh Reviewers were most of them students of the university of that city. The Westminster Reviewers had all sat at the feet of Bentham. Each group had thus a common doctrine and a positive doctrine. In practical politics it does not much matter by what different roads men have travelled to a given position. But in an organ intended to lead public opinion towards certain changes, or to hold it steadfast against wayward gusts of passion, its strength would be increased a hundredfold if all the writers in it were inspired by that thorough unity of conviction which comes from sincerely accepting a common set of principles to start from, and reaching practical conclusions by the same route. We are probably not very far from a time when such a group might form itself, and its work would for some years lie in the formation of a general body of opinion, rather than in practical realisation of this or that measure. The success of the French Republic, the peaceful order of the United States, perhaps some trouble within our own borders, will lead men with open minds to such a conception of a high and stable type of national life as will unite a sufficient number of them in a common project for pressing

with systematic iteration for a complete set of organic changes. A country with such a land-system, such an electoral system, as ours, has a trying time before it. Those will be doing good service who shall unite to prepare opinion for the inevitable changes. At the present moment the only motto that can be inscribed on the flag of a liberal Review is the general device of Progress, each writer interpreting it in his own sense, and within such limits as he may set for himself. For such a state of things signature is the natural condition, and an editor, even of a signed Review, would hardly decline to accept the account of his function which we find Jeffrey giving to Mr. Napier:—'There are three legitimate considerations by which you should be guided in your conduct as editor generally, and particularly as to the admission or rejection of important articles of a political sort. (1) The effect of your decision on the other contributors upon whom you mainly rely; (2) its effect on the sale and circulation, and on the just authority of the work with the great body of its readers; and (3) your own deliberate opinion as to the safety or danger of the doctrines maintained in the article under consideration, and its tendency either to promote or retard the practical adoption of those liberal principles to which, and *their practical advancement*, you must always consider the journal as devoted.'

As for discovering and training authors, the editor under the new system has inducements that lie entirely the other way; namely, to find as many authors as possible whom the public has already discovered and accepted for itself. Young unknown writers certainly have not gained anything by the new system. Neither perhaps can they be said to have lost, for though of two articles of equal merit an editor would naturally choose the one which should carry the additional recommendation of a name of recognised authority, yet any marked superiority in literary brilliance or effective argument or originality of view would be only too eagerly welcomed in any Review in England. So much public interest is now taken in periodical literature, and the honourable competition in securing variety, weight, and attractiveness is so active, that there is no risk of a literary candle remaining long under a bushel. Miss Martineau has already been quoted as saying:—'I have always been anxious to extend to young or struggling authors the sort of aid which would have been so precious to me in that winter of 1829–1830, and I know that, in above twenty years, I have never succeeded but once.' One of the most distinguished editors in London, who had charge of a periodical for many years, told the present writer what comes to the same thing, namely, that in no single case during all these years did a volunteer contributor of real quality, or with any promise of eminence, present himself or herself. So many hundreds think themselves called, so few are chosen. It used to be argued that the writer under the anonymous system was hidden behind a screen and robbed of his well-earned distinction. In truth, however, it is impossible for a writer of real distinction to remain anonymous. If a writer in a periodical interests the public, they are sure to find out who he is.

Again, there is folly unfathomable in a periodical affecting an eternal consistency, and giving itself the airs of continuous individuality, and being careful not to talk sense on a given question to-day because its founders talked nonsense upon it fifty years ago. This is quite true. There is a monstrous charlatanry about the old editorial We, but perhaps there are some tolerably obvious openings for charlatanry of a different kind under our own system. The man who writes in his own name may sometimes be tempted to say what he knows he is expected from his position or character to say, rather than what he would have said if his personality were not concerned. As far as honesty goes, signature perhaps offers as many inducements to one kind of insincerity, as anonymity offers to another kind. And on the public it might perhaps be contended that there is an effect of a rather similar sort. They are in some cases tempted away from serious discussion of the matter, into frivolous curiosity and gossip about the man. All this criticism of the principle of which the *Fortnightly Review* was the earliest English adherent, will not be taken as the result, in the present writer, of Chamfort's *maladie des désabusés*;[7] that would be both extremely ungrateful and without excuse or reason. It is merely a fragment of disinterested contribution to the study of a remarkable change that is passing over a not unimportant department of literature. One gain alone counter-balances all the drawbacks, and that is gain that could hardly have been foreseen or expected; I mean the freedom with which the great controversies of religion and theology have been discussed in the new Reviews. The removal of the mask has led to an outburst of plain speaking on these subjects, which to Mr. Napier's

generation would have seemed simply incredible. The frank avowal of unpopular beliefs or non-beliefs has raised the whole level of the discussion, and perhaps has been even more advantageous to the orthodox in teaching them more humility, than to the heterodox in teaching them more courage and honesty.

Returning to Mr. Napier's volume, we have said that it is impossible for a great writer to be anonymous. No reader will need to be told who among Mr. Napier's correspondents is the writer of the following:—

I have been thinking sometimes, likewise, of a paper on Napoleon, a man whom, though handled to the extreme of triteness, it will be long years before we understand. Hitherto in the English tongue, there is next to nothing that betokens insight into him, or even sincere belief of such, on the part of the writer. I should like to study the man with what heartiness I could, and form to myself some intelligible picture of him, both as a biographical and as a historical figure, in both of which senses he is our chief contemporary wonder, and in some sort the epitome of his age. This, however, were a task of far more difficulty than Byron, and perhaps not so promising at present.

And if there is any difficulty in recognising the same hand in the next proposal, it arises only from the circumstance that it is Carlyle above all others who has made Benthamism a term of reproach on the lips of men less wise than himself:—

A far finer essay were a faithful, loving, and yet critical, and in part condemnatory, delineation of Jeremy Bentham, and his place and working in this section of the world's history. Bentham will not be put down by logic, and should not be put down, for we need him greatly as a backwoodsman: neither can reconciliation be effected till the one party understands and is just to the other. Bentham is a denyer; he denies with a loud and universally convincing voice; his fault is that he can *affirm* nothing, except that money is pleasant in the purse, and food in the stomach, and that by this simplest of all beliefs he can reorganise society. He can shatter it in pieces—no thanks to him, for its old fastenings are quite rotten—but he cannot reorganise it; this is work for quite others than he. Such an essay on Bentham, however, were a great task for any one; for me a very great one, and perhaps rather out of my road.

Perhaps Carlyle would have agreed that Mill's famous pair of essays on Bentham and Coleridge have served the purpose which he had in his mind, though we may well regret the loss of such a picture of Bentham's philosophic personality

---

[7] Malady of the disillusioned.

as he would surely have given us. It is touching to think of him whom we all know as the most honoured name among living veterans of letters,[8] passing through the vexed ordeal of the young recruit, and battling for his own against the waywardness of critics and the blindness of publishers. In 1831 he writes to Mr. Napier: 'All manner of perplexities have occurred in the publishing of my poor book, which perplexities I could only cut asunder, not unloose; so the MS. like an unhappy ghost still lingers on the wrong side of Styx; the Charon of——Street durst not risk it in his *sutilis cymba*, so it leaped ashore again.' And three months later: 'I have given up the notion of hawking my little Manuscript Book about any further; for a long time it has lain quiet in its drawer, waiting for a better day.' And yet this little book was nothing less than Carlyle's *History of the French Revolution*.

It might be a lesson to small men to see the reasonableness, sense, and patience of these greater men. Macaulay's letters show him to have been a pattern of good sense and considerateness. Carlyle seems indeed to have found Jeffrey's editorial vigour more than could be endured:

My respected friend your predecessor had some difficulty with me in adjusting the respective prerogatives of Author and Editor, for though not, as I hope, insensible to fair reason, I used sometimes to rebel against what I reckoned mere authority, and this partly perhaps as a matter of literary conscience; being wont to write nothing without studying it if possible to the bottom, and writing always with an almost painful feeling of scrupulosity, that light editorial hacking and hewing to right and left was in general nowise to my mind.

But we feel that the fault must have lain with Jeffrey; the qualifications that Lord Cockburn admired so much were not likely to be to the taste of a man of Carlyle's grit. That did not prevent the most original of Mr. Napier's contributors from being one of the most just and reasonable.

I have barely within my time, finished that paper ['Characteristics'], to which you are now heartily welcome, if you have room for it. The doctrines here set forth have mostly long been familiar convictions with me; yet it is perhaps only within the last twelvemonth that the public utterance of some of them could have seemed a duty. I have striven to express myself with what guardedness was possible; and, as there will now be no time for correcting proofs, I must leave it wholly in your editorial hands. Nay, should it on due consideration appear to you in your place (for I see that matter

dimly, and nothing is clear but my own mind and the general condition of the world), unadvisable to print the paper at all, then pray understand, my dear Sir, now and always, that I am no unreasonable man; but if dogmatic enough (as Jeffery used to call it) in my own beliefs, also truly desirous to be just towards those of others. I shall, in all sincerity, beg of you to do, without fear of offence (for in *no* point of view will there be any), what you yourself see good. A mighty work lies before the writers of this time.

It is always interesting, to the man of letters at any rate if not to his neighbours, to find what was first thought by men of admitted competence of the beginnings of writers who are now seen to have made a mark on the world. 'When the reputation of authors is made,' said Sainte-Beuve, 'it is easy to speak of them *convenablement*;[9] we have only to guide ourselves by the common opinion. But at the start, at the moment when they are trying their first flight and are in part ignorant of themselves, then to judge them with tact, with precision, not to exaggerate their scope, to predict their flight, or divine their limits, to put the reasonable objections in the midst of all due respect—this is the quality of the critic who is born to be a critic.' We have been speaking of Carlyle. This is what Jeffrey thought of him in 1832:—

I fear Carlyle will not do, that is, if you do not take the liberties and the pains with him that I did, by striking out freely, and writing in occasionally. The misfortune is, that he is very obstinate, and unluckily in a place like this, he finds people enough to abet and applaud him, to intercept the operation of the otherwise infallible remedy of general avoidance and neglect. It is a great pity, for he is a man of genius and industry, and with the capacity of being an elegant and impressive writer.

The notion of Jeffrey occasionally writing elegantly and impressively into Carlyle's proof-sheets is rather striking. Some of Jeffrey's other criticisms sound very curiously in our ear in these days. It is startling to find Mill's *Logic* described (1843) as a 'great unreadable book, and its elaborate demonstration of axioms and truisms.' A couple of years later Jeffrey admits, in speaking of Mill's paper on Guizot—'Though I have long thought very highly of his powers as a reasoner, I scarcely gave him credit for such large and sound views of *realities* and practical results as are displayed in this article.' Sir James Stephen—the distinguished sire of two distinguished contributors, who may remind more than one editor of our generation of the Horatian saying, that

> Fortes creantur fortibus et bonis,
> . . neque imbellem feroces
> Progenerant aquilae columbam[10]

—this excellent writer took a more just measure of the book which Jeffrey thought unreadable.

My more immediate object in writing is to remind you of John Mill's book [*System of Logic*], of which I have lately been reading a considerable part, and I have done so with the conviction that it is one of the most remarkable productions of this nineteenth century. Exceedingly debatable indeed, but most worthy of debate, are many of his favourite tenets, especially those of the last two or three chapters. No man is fit to encounter him who is not thoroughly conversant with the moral sciences which he handles; and remembering what you told me of your own studies under Dugald Stewart, I cannot but recommend the affair to your own personal attention. You will find very few men fit to be trusted with it. You ought to be aware that, although with great circumspection, not to say timidity, Mill is an opponent of Religion in the abstract, not of any particular form of it. That is, he evidently maintains that superhuman influences on the mind of man are but a dream, whence the inevitable conclusion that all acts of devotion and prayer are but a superstition. That such is his real meaning, however darkly conveyed, is indisputable. You are well aware that it is in direct conflict with my own deepest and most cherished convictions. Yet to condemn him for holding, and for calmly publishing such views, is but to add to the difficulties of fair and full discussion, and to render truth (or supposed truth), less certain and valuable than if it had invited, and encountered, and triumphed over every assault of every honest antagonist. I therefore, wish Mill to be treated respectfully and handsomely.

Few of Mr. Napier's correspondents seem to have been more considerate. At one period (1844) a long time had passed without any contribution from Sir James Stephen's pen appearing in the *Review*. Mr Senior wrote a hint on the subject to the editor, and Mr. Napier seems to have communicated with Sir James Stephen, who replied in a model strain.

Have you any offer of a paper or papers from my friend John Austin? If you have, and if you are not aware what manner of man he is, it may not be amiss that you should be apprised that in these parts he enjoys, and deservedly, a very high and yet a peculiar reputation. I have a great attachment to him. He is, in the best sense of the word, a philosopher, an earnest and humble lover of wisdom. I know not anywhere a larger-minded man, and yet, eloquent as he is in speech,

there is, in his written style, an involution and a lack of vivacity which renders his writings a sealed book to almost every one. Whether he will be able to assume an easier and a lighter manner, I do not know. If not, I rather fear for him when he stands at your bar. All I ask is, that you would convey your judgment in measured and (as far as you can honestly) in courteous terms; for he is, for so considerable a man, strangely sensitive. You must have an odd story to tell of your intercourse with the knights of the Order of the Quill.

And the letter closed with what an editor values more even than decently Christian treatment, namely the suggestion of a fine subject. This became the admirable essay on the Clapham Sect.

The author of one of the two or three most delightful biographies in all literature has published the letter to Mr. Napier in which Macaulay speaks pretty plainly what he thought about Brougham and the extent of his services to the *Review*. Brougham in turn hated Macaulay, whom he calls the third or greatest bore in society that he has ever known. He is furious—and here Brougham was certainly not wrong—over the 'most profligate political morality' of Macaulay's essay on Clive.

In my eyes, his defence of Clive, and the audacious ground of it, merit execration. It is a most serious, and, to me, a painful subject. No—no—all the sentences a man can turn, even if he made them in pure taste, and not in Tom's snip-snap taste of the lower empire,—all won't avail against a rotten morality. The first and most sacred duty of a public man, and, above all an author, is to keep by honest and true doctrine—never to relax—never to countenance vice—ever to hold fast by virtue. What? Are we gravely to be told, at this time of day, that a set-off may be allowed for public, and, therefore, atrocious crimes, though he admits that a common felon pleads it in vain? Gracious God, where is this to end! What horrors will it not excuse! Tiberius's great capacity, his first-rate wit, that which made him the charm of society, will next, I suppose, be set to give a splendour to the inhabitants of Capreae. Why, Clive's address, and his skill, and his courage are not at all more certain, nor are they qualities of a different cast. Every great ruffian, who has filled the world with blood and tears, will be sure of an acquittal, because of his talents and his success. After I had, and chiefly in the *Edinburgh Review*, been trying to restore a better, a purer, a higher standard of morals, and to wean men from the silly love of military glory, for which they are the first to pay, I find the *Edinburgh Review* preaching, not merely the old and common heresies, but ten thousand times worse, adopting a vile

---

[10] "The strong are created by the strong and the good . . . nor will fierce eagles engender gentle doves."

principle never yet avowed in terms, though too often and too much taken for a guide, unknown to those who followed it, in forming their judgments of great and successful criminals.

Of the essay on Warren Hastings he thought better, 'bating some vulgarity and Macaulay's usual want of all power of reasoning.' Lord Cockburn wrote to Mr. Napier (1844) a word or two on Macaulay. 'Delighting as I do,' says Lord Cockburn, 'in his thoughts, views, and knowledge, I feel too often compelled to curse and roar at his words and the structure of his composition. As a corrupter of style, he is more dangerous to the young than Gibbon. His seductive powers greater, his defects worse.' All good critics now accept this as true. Jeffrey, by the way, speaking of the same essay, thinks that Macaulay rates Chatham too high. 'I have always had an impression,' he says, '(though perhaps an ignorant and unjust one), that there was more good luck than wisdom in his foreign policy, and very little to admire (except his personal purity) in any part of his domestic administration.'

It is interesting to find a record, in the energetic speech of contemporary hatred, of the way in which orthodox science regarded a once famous book of heterodox philosophy. Here is Professor Sedgwick on the *Vestiges of Creation*:[11]

I now know the *Vestiges* well, and I detest the book for its shallowness, for the intense vulgarity of its philosophy, for its gross, unblushing materialism, for its silly credulity in catering out of every fool's dish, for its utter ignorance of what is meant by induction, for its gross (and I dare to say, filthy) views of physiology,—most ignorant and most false,—and for its shameful shuffling of the facts of geology so as to make them play a rogue's game. I believe some woman is the author. . . . From the bottom of my soul, I loathe and detest the *Vestiges*. 'Tis a rank pill of asafoetida and arsenic, covered with gold leaf. I do, therefore, trust that your contributor has stamped with an iron heel upon the head of the filthy abortion, and put an end to its crawlings. There is not one subject the author handles bearing on life, of which he does not take a degrading view.

Mr. Napier seems to have asked him to write on the book, and Sedgwick's article, the first he ever wrote for a review, eventually appeared (1845),—without, it is to be hoped, too much of the raging contempt of the above and other letters. 'I do feel contempt, and, I hope, I shall express it. Rats hatched by the incubations of a goose—dogs playing dominos—monkeys breeding men and women—all distinctions between natural and moral done away—the Bible proved all a lie, and mental philosophy one mass of folly, all of it to be pounded down, and done over again in the cooking vessels of Gall and Spurzheim!' This was the beginning of a long campaign, just now drawing near its close. Let us at least be glad that orthodoxy, whether scientific or religious, has mended its temper.

---

[11] Adam Sedgwick (1785–1873), English geologist; Robert Chambers (1802–71) was the author of the pre-Darwinian *Vestiges of Creation* (1844).

Walter Horatio Pater

1839-1894

WALTER PATER, the only major prose writer of the age whose entire life fell within Victoria's reign, was the most retiring and least socially committed of the prose writers of the age. Yet his literary influence was so widespread that he is often thought of as the dominant aesthetic force in the literature of the last quarter of the nineteenth century.

Pater was born in London, the son of a doctor. He showed an early inclination toward the Church, and was encouraged in such interests by his mother and his aunt, who supervised him after the death of his father. He attended King's School in Canterbury with some success, but he did not take gladly to the coarser aspects of public school life. Something of the quality of his childhood is thought to be reflected in his "The Child in the House," but there is no way of separating the fact from the fiction.

In 1858 Pater entered Queen's College, Oxford, from which he graduated in 1862. His religious faith weakened considerably during his Oxford years; yet he sought unsuccessfully as late as 1862 to be ordained by the Bishop of London. In 1864 he was elected a probationary fellow of Brasenose College, and in 1865 the appointment was made permanent. It was as a fellow of Brasenose that Pater spent the rest of his life and from that relatively quiet post that he exerted his profound influence on the thought of the late Victorian period.

Pater's influence was spread in part through his immediate Oxford circle and his teaching. Students influenced by Pater ranged from Gerard Manley Hopkins to Oscar Wilde. But Pater's influence was mainly spread through his writings for periodicals, beginning in 1867 when he published his essay "Winckelmann." This essay and subsequent ones on figures from the Renaissance were gathered together in 1873 to form the volume *Studies in the History of the Renaissance*. The influence of this work on the rising generation of writers and poets can hardly be overestimated. The work seemed the embodiment of the creed of the aesthetes, those inheritors of the Pre-Raphaelite movement who urged art for its own sake as opposed to the dominant Victorian emphasis on art for morality's sake. Such famous Paterian pronouncements from the Conclusion to *The Renaissance* as "To burn always with this hard, gemlike flame, to maintain this ecstasy, is success in life," or, "Not the fruit of experience, but experience itself, is the end," struck many readers as the perfect expression of the aesthetic creed. That such readers had in the author's view misinterpreted him was evident when Pater suppressed the Conclusion in a subsequent printing in order not to give encouragement to such ideas. The suppression may also have been influenced by the satiric attack on his doctrines in W. H. Mallock's *The New Republic* (1877).

Marius the Epicurean (1855) was in part also designed to still criticism of the Mallock type. In this novel of early Christian times Pater portrays a sensitive Roman who responds to the various conflicting spiritual currents of the day, ending finally in something approximating Christian martyrdom. But the chief impact of the work on ardent Paterians was of the response to religions in terms of their qualities of beauty. The exact degree of Pater's commitment to Christianity, in that work or in life, is still debated, but it seems clear that in *Marius* Pater was striving to express a more complex philosophy than art for art's sake.

Pater returned to the area of the essay and nonfiction prose with his *Imaginary Portraits* (1887), *Appreciations* (1889), and *Plato and Platonism* (1893). In his portraits as in some of his fiction proper Pater creates almost a new literary genre between fact and fiction. Many of his portraits are indeed imaginary and thus fictional creations; others are based on historical persons and are thus akin to conventional essays. All of his writing, however, exhibits the play of an extremely cultivated sensibility on subjects relating to art and beauty, a sensibility that detractors found somehow unwholesome but that enthusiasts found exhilarating and inspiring.

Throughout the eighteen-seventies and eighties Pater lived quietly, traveling regularly to the Continent, especially to France, Germany, and Italy, often in the company of his sisters. From 1885 on he lived in London, writing essays for the periodicals, lecturing occasionally, persuing a more active social life but also continuing his historical and literary studies. He moved back to Oxford in 1893 and in 1894 was awarded an honorary doctorate by the University of Glasgow. He died in July of 1894 of heart failure following an earlier attack of rheumatic fever.

Pater was the reluctant spokesman for a movement and a creed that he neither originated nor sought to lead. As a result Pater has been sometimes unfairly and uncritically linked with all aesthetes, decadents, and Wildeans and has been held responsible for their utterances and their aberrations. Pater's own position was certainly that of a highly learned and exquisitely responsive student of literature and philosophy, but it was not necessarily the pure hedonism attributed to him by opponents. The philosophic expression, taken from Pater's own writings, that best describes Pater's stand is neo-Cyrenaicism, the philosophy that refuses to base itself on an unverifiable hypothesis but instead emphasizes the present moment. Such an emphasis, of course, can easily lead in less restrained spirits than Pater's to exactly the hedonism of which Pater was accused, but in Pater himself the philosophy issues in an intense capacity for appreciation through a rigorous disciplining of the sensibility to make it receptive to the highest levels of the beautiful.

Perhaps the reason that Pater became the inadvertent spokesman for aestheticism lay as much in the manner of his writing as in his actual pronouncements, for Pater's style is still recognized as one of the most luminous in all English literature. It was Pater who urged that all art should aspire to the condition of music, and his own art comes close to realizing that aspiration. His attention to melody, cadence, and evocation makes his writing as sensitively wrought as a piece of music, and like music the echoes of an essay by Pater linger in the mind long after the book is closed.

CHRONOLOGY

1839   Born 4 August at Shadwell, East London.
1853–57   Attends King's College, Canterbury.
1858–62   Attends Queen's College, Oxford.
1864   Elected Fellow of Brasenose College, Oxford.
1865   Tours Italy.
1867   Publishes "Winckelmann."
1873   *Studies in the History of the Renaissance.*
1875–80   Engages in Greek studies.
1885   *Marius the Epicurean.* Moves to London.
1889   *Appreciations.*
1893   *Plato and Platonism.* Moves to Oxford.
1894   Honorary LL.D from Glasgow. Dies 30 July; buried St. Giles Cemetery, Oxford.

EDITIONS

Works, New Library Edition (10 vols., 1910).
Imaginary Portraits, ed. Eugene J. Brzenk (1964).
Marius the Epicurean, ed. Anne K. Tuell (1926), Joseph Sagmaster (1935).
Letters, ed. Lawrence G. Evans (1970).
The Renaissance, ed. Kenneth Clark (1961).
Selected Writings, ed. Derek Patmore (1949).
Sketches and Reviews (1919).
Uncollected Essays (1903).
Walter Pater: Selected Works, ed. Richard Aldington (1948).

BIOGRAPHY AND CRITICISM

A. C. Benson, *Walter Pater* (1906).
Edmund Chandler, *Pater on Style* (1958).
Ruth C. Child, *The Aesthetic of Walter Pater* (1940).
Richmond Crinkley, *Walter Pater: Humanist* (1970).
D. J. DeLaura, *Hebrew and Hellene in Victorian England* (1969).
Lawrence G. Evans, "Walter Pater," in *Victorian Prose: A Guide to Research* (1973).
Germain d'Hangest, *Walter Pater: L'Homme et l'oeuvre* (2 vols., 1961).
Graham Hough, *The Last Romantics* (1949).
Wolfgang Iser, *Walter Pater* (1960).
R. V. Johnson, *Walter Pater* (1961).
U. C. Knoepflmacher, *Religious Humanism and the Victorian Novel* (1965).
Gordon McKenzie, *The Literary Character of Walter Pater* (1967).
Gerald C. Monsman, *Pater's Portraits* (1967).
Arthur Symons, *A Study of Walter Pater* (1932).
Anthony Ward, *Walter Pater: The Idea in Nature* (1966).
Thomas Wright, *Life of Walter Pater* (2 vols., 1907).
Helen Hawthorne Young, *The Writings of Walter Pater* (1933).

from The Renaissance

Pater's most influential work, The Renaissance, *was first published in book form in 1873. It was originally titled* Studies in the History of the Renaissance *but appeared in later editions under the title* The Renaissance: Studies in Art and Poetry *and thus it has been known ever since. Ruskin's disapproval of the Renaissance had so commanded assent in Victorian England that Pater seemed to be striking out in a new direction by taking up the subject. The novelty of the material, the elegance of the prose, and the appeal to aesthetic taste of the philosophic doctrine it appeared to advocate combined to make the work and Pater an immediate success.*

The volume contained a total of eight essays, a Preface, and a Conclusion. The Preface and Conclusion and three of the eight essays are given below. Of the three essays printed here, "Leonardo da Vinci" was first published in the Fortnightly Review *in 1871; "Winckelmann" first appeared in the* Westminster Review *in 1867; and "Joachim du Bellay" was a new essay written for the book publication. The Conclusion, suppressed in the second edition, was restored by Pater in the third with an explanatory footnote.*

Preface

MANY attempts have been made by writers on art and poetry to define beauty in the abstract, to express it in the most general terms, to find some universal formula for it. The value of these attempts has most often been in the suggestive and penetrating things said by the way. Such discussions help us very little to enjoy what has been well done in art or poetry, to discriminate between what is more and what is less excellent in them, or to use words like beauty, excellence, art, poetry, with a more precise meaning than they would otherwise have. Beauty, like all other qualities presented to human experience, is relative; and the definition of it becomes unmeaning and useless in proportion to its abstractness. To define beauty, not in the most abstract but in the most concrete terms possible, to find not its universal formula, but the formula which expresses most adequately this or that special manifestation of it, is the aim of the true student of æsthetics.

"To see the object as in itself it really is," has been justly said to be the aim of all true criticism whatever; and in æsthetic criticism the first step towards seeing one's object as it really is, is to know one's own impression as it really is, to discriminate it, to realise it distinctly. The objects with which æsthetic criticism deals— music, poetry, artistic and accomplished forms of human life—are indeed receptacles of so many powers or forces: they possess, like the products of nature, so many virtues or qualities. What is this song or picture, this engaging personality presented in life or in a book, to me? What effect does it really produce on me? Does it give me pleasure? and if so, what sort or degree of pleasure? How is my nature modified by its presence, and under its influence? The answers to these questions are the original facts with which the æsthetic critic has to do; and, as in the study of light, of morals, of number, one must realise such primary data for one's self, or not at all. And he who experiences these impressions strongly, and drives directly at the discrimination and analysis of them, has no need to trouble himself with the abstract question what beauty is in itself, or what its exact relation to truth or experience—metaphysical questions, as unprofitable as metaphysical questions elsewhere. He may pass them all by as being, answerable or not, of no interest to him.

The æsthetic critic, then, regards all the objects with which he has to do, all works of art, and the fairer forms of nature and human life, as powers or forces producing pleasurable sensations, each of a more or less peculiar or unique kind. This influence he feels, and wishes to explain, by analysing and reducing it to its elements. To him, the picture, the landscape, the engaging personality in life or in a book, *La Gioconda,* the hills of Carrara, Pico of Mirandola,[1] are valuable

---

[1] *La Gioconda,* the portrait also known as the Mona Lisa, now in the Louvre, Paris; Carrara, region in Italy where the famous marble is quarried; Pico della Mirandola (1463–94), Italian scholar and philosopher, subject of one of the essays of *The Renaissance.*

for their virtues, as we say, in speaking of a herb, a wine, a gem; for the property each has of affecting one with a special, a unique, impression of pleasure. Our education becomes complete in proportion as our susceptibility to these impressions increases in depth and variety. And the function of the æsthetic critic is to distinguish, to analyse, and separate from its adjuncts, the virtue by which a picture, a landscape, a fair personality in life or in a book, produces this special impression of beauty or pleasure, to indicate what the source of that impression is, and under what conditions it is experienced. His end is reached when he has disengaged that virtue, and noted it, as a chemist notes some natural element, for himself and others; and the rule for those who would reach this end is stated with great exactness in the words of a recent critic of Sainte-Beuve:—*De se borner à connaître de près les belles choses, et à s'en nourrir en exquis amateurs, en humanistes accomplis.*[2]

What is important, then, is not that the critic should possess a correct abstract definition of beauty for the intellect, but a certain kind of temperament, the power of being deeply moved by the presence of beautiful objects. He will remember always that beauty exists in many forms. To him all periods, types, schools of taste, are in themselves equal. In all ages there have been some excellent workmen, and some excellent work done. The question he asks is always: —In whom did the stir, the genius, the sentiment of the period find itself? where was the receptacle of its refinement, its elevation, its taste? "The ages are all equal," says William Blake, "but genius is always above its age."

Often it will require great nicety to disengage this virtue from the commoner elements with which it may be found in combination. Few artists, not Goethe or Byron even, work quite cleanly, casting off all *débris*, and leaving us only what the heat of their imagination has wholly fused and transformed. Take, for instance, the writings of Wordsworth, The heat of his genius, entering into the substance of his work, has crystallised a part, but only a part, of it; and in that great mass of verse there is much which might well be forgotten. But scattered up and down it, sometimes fusing and transforming entire compositions, like the Stanzas on *Resolution and Independence*, or the *Ode on the Recollections of Childhood*, sometimes, as if at random, depositing a fine crystal here or there, in a matter it does not wholly search through and transmute, we trace the action of his unique, incommunicable faculty, that strange, mystical sense of a life in natural things, and of a man's life as a part of nature, drawing strength and colour and character from local influences, from the hills and streams, and from natural sights and sounds. Well! that is the *virtue*, the active principle in Wordsworth's poetry; and then the function of the critic of Wordsworth is to follow up that active principle, to disengage it, to mark the degree in which it penetrates his verse.

The subjects of the following studies are taken from the history of the *Renaissance*, and touch what I think the chief points in that complex, many-sided movement. I have explained in the first of them what I understand by the word, giving it a much wider scope than was intended by those who originally used it to denote that revival of classical antiquity in the fifteenth century which was only one of many results of a general excitement and enlightening of the human mind, but of which the great aim and achievements of what, as Christian art, is often falsely opposed to the Renaissance, were another result. This outbreak of the human spirit may be traced far into the middle age itself, with its motives already clearly pronounced, the care for physical beauty, the worship of the body, the breaking down of those limits which the religious system of the middle age imposed on the heart and the imagination. I have taken as an example of this movement, this earlier Renaissance within the middle age itself, and as an expression of its qualities, two little compositions in early French; not because they constitute the best possible expression of them, but because they help the unity of my series, inasmuch as the Renaissance ends also in France, in French poetry, in a phase of which the writings of Joachim du Bellay[3] are in many ways the most perfect illustration. The Renaissance, in truth, put forth in France an aftermath, a wonderful later growth, the products of which have to the full that subtle and delicate sweetness which belongs to a refined and comely decadence, just as its earliest phases have the freshness which belongs to all periods of growth in art, the charm

[2] "To confine themselves to knowing at first hand beautiful things, and to nourish themselves thereby as do sensitive amateurs and accomplished humanists."
[3] See Pater's essay on du Bellay in this volume.

of *ascêsis*, of the austere and serious girding of the loins in youth.

But it is in Italy, in the fifteenth century, that the interest of the Renaissance mainly lies,—in that solemn fifteenth century which can hardly be studied too much, not merely for its positive results in the things of the intellect and the imagination, its concrete works of art, its special and prominent personalities, with their profound æsthetic charm, but for its general spirit and character, for the ethical qualities of which it is a consummate type.

The various forms of intellectual activity which together make up the culture of an age, move for the most part from different starting-points, and by unconnected roads. As products of the same generation they partake indeed of a common character, and unconsciously illustrate each other; but of the producers themselves, each group is solitary, gaining what advantage or disadvantage there may be in intellectual isolation. Art and poetry, philosophy and the religious life, and that other life of refined pleasure and action in the conspicuous places of the world, are each of them confined to its own circle of ideas, and those who prosecute either of them are generally little curious of the thoughts of others. There come, however, from time to time, eras of more favourable conditions, in which the thoughts of men draw nearer together than is their wont, and the many interests of the intellectual world combine in one complete type of general culture. The fifteenth century in Italy is one of these happier eras, and what is sometimes said of the age of Pericles is true of that of Lorenzo:[4] it is an age productive in personalities, many-sided, centralised, complete. Here, artists and philosophers and those whom the action of the world has elevated and made keen, do not live in isolation, but breathe a common air, and catch light and heat from each other's thoughts. There is a spirit of general elevation and enlightenment in which all alike communicate. The unity of this spirit gives unity to all the various products of the Renaissance; and it is to this intimate alliance with mind, this participation in the best thoughts which that age produced, that the art of Italy in the fifteenth century owes much of its grave dignity and influence.

I have added an essay on Winckelmann, as not incongruous with the studies which precede it, because Winckelmann, coming in the eighteenth century, really belongs in spirit to an earlier age. By his enthusiasm for the things of the intellect and the imagination for their own sake, by his Hellensim, his life-long struggle to attain to the Greek spirit, he is in sympathy with the humanists of a previous century. He is the last fruit of the Renaissance, and explains in a striking way its motive and tendencies.

Leonardo da Vinci

HOMO MINISTER ET INTERPRES NATURÆ [1]

IN VASARI's life of Leonardo da Vinci as we now read it there are some variations from the first edition. There, the painter who has fixed the outward type of Christ for succeeding centuries was a bold speculator, holding lightly by other men's beliefs, setting philosophy above Christianity. Words of his, trenchant enough to justify this impression, are not recorded, and would have been out of keeping with a genius of which one characteristic is the tendency to lose itself in a refined and graceful mystery. The suspicion was but the time-honoured mode in which the world stamps its appreciation of one who has thoughts for himself alone, his high indifference, his intolerance of the common forms of things; and in the second edition the image was changed into something fainter and more conventional. But it is still by a certain mystery in his work, and something enigmatical beyond the usual measure of great men, that he fascinates, or perhaps half repels. His life is one of sudden revolts, with intervals in which he works not at all, or apart from the main scope of his work. By a strange fortune the pictures on which his more popular fame rested disappeared early from the world, like the *Battle of the Standard;* or are mixed obscurely with the product of meaner hands, like the *Last Supper.* His type of beauty is so exotic that it fascinates a larger number than it delights, and seems more than that of any other artist to reflect ideas and views and some scheme of the world within; so that he seemed to his contemporaries to be the possessor of some un-

---

[4] Lorenzo de' Medici (1449–92), also called Lorenzo the Magnificent, Renaissance patron of the arts.
[1] "A Man, the servant and interpreter of Nature."

sanctified and secret wisdom; as to Michelet[2] and others to have anticipated modern ideas. He trifles with his genius, and crowds all his chief work into a few tormented years of later life; yet he is so possessed by his genius that he passes unmoved through the most tragic events, over-whelming his country and friends, like one who comes across them by chance on some secret errand.

His *legend*, as the French say, with the anec-dotes which every one remembers, is one of the most brilliant chapters of Vasari. Later writers merely copied it, until, in 1804, Carlo Amoretti applied to it a criticism which left hardly a date fixed, and not one of those anecdotes untouched. The various questions thus raised have since that time become, one after another, subjects of special study, and mere antiquarianism has in this direc-tion little more to do. For others remain the editing of the thirteen books of his manuscripts, and the separation by technical criticism of what in his reputed works is really his, from what is only half his, or the work of his pupils. But a lover of strange souls may still analyse for himself the impression made on him by those works, and try to reach through it a definition of the chief elements of Leonardo's genius. The *legend*, as corrected and enlarged by its critics, may now and then intervene to support the results of this analysis.

His life has three divisions—thirty years at Florence, nearly twenty years at Milan, then nineteen years of wandering, till he sinks to rest under the protection of Francis the First at the *Château de Clou*. The dishonour of illegitimacy hangs over his birth. Piero Antonio, his father, was of a noble Florentine house, of Vinci in the *Val d'Arno*, and Leonardo, brought up delicately among the true children of that house, was the love-child of his youth, with the keen, puissant nature such children often have. We see him in his boyhood fascinating all men by his beauty, improvising music and songs, buying the caged birds and setting them free, as he walked the streets of Florence, fond of odd bright dresses and spirited horses.

From his earliest years he designed many objects, and constructed models in relief, of which Vasari mentions some of women smiling. His father, pondering over this promise in the child, took him to the workshop of Andrea del Verrocchio, then the most famous artist in Florence. Beautiful objects lay about there—reliquaries, pyxes, silver images for the pope's chapel at Rome, strange fancy-work of the middle age, keeping odd company with fragments of antiquity, then but lately discovered. Another student Leonardo may have seen there—a lad into whose soul the level light and aërial illusions of Italian sunsets had passed, in after days famous as Perugino. Verrocchio was an artist of the earlier Florentine type, carver, painter, and worker in metals, in one; designer, not of pictures only, but of all things for sacred or household use, drinking-vessels, ambries, instru-ments of music, making them all fair to look upon, filling the common ways of life with the reflexion of some far-off brightness; and years of patience had refined his hand till his work was now sought after from distant places.

It happened that Verrocchio was employed by the brethren of Vallombrosa to paint the Baptism of Christ, and Leonardo was allowed to finish an angel in the left-hand corner. It was one of those moments in which the progress of a great thing—here, that of the art of Italy—presses hard on the happiness of an individual, through whose discouragement and decrease, humanity, in more fortunate persons, comes a step nearer to its final success.

For beneath the cheerful exterior of the mere well-paid craftsman, chasing brooches for the copes of *Santa Maria Novella*, or twisting metal screens for the tombs of the Medici, lay the am-bitious desire to expand the destiny of Italian art by a larger knowledge and insight into things, a purpose in art not unlike Leonardo's still unconscious purpose; and often, in the modelling of drapery, or of a lifted arm, or of hair cast back from the face, there came to him something of the freer manner and richer humanity of a later age. But in this *Baptism* the pupil had surpassed the master; and Verrocchio turned away as one stunned, and as if his sweet earlier work must thereafter be distasteful to him, from the bright animated angel of Leonardo's hand.

The angel may still be seen in Florence, a space of sunlight in the cold, laboured old picture; but the legend is true only in sentiment, for painting had always been the art by which Verrocchio set least store. And as in a sense he anticipates Leonardo, so to the last Leonardo recalls the studio of Verrocchio, in the love of beautiful toys, such as the vessel of water for a mirror, and lovely needle-work about the implicated hands in the *Modesty and Vanity*, and

[2] Jules Michelet (1798–1874), French Historian.

of reliefs, like those cameos which in the *Virgin of the Balances* hang all round the girdle of Saint Michael, and of bright variegated stones, such as the agates in the *Saint Anne*, and in a hieratic preciseness and grace, as of a sanctuary swept and garnished. Amid all the cunning and intricacy of his Lombard manner this never left him. Much of it there must have been in that lost picture of *Paradise*, which he prepared as a cartoon for tapestry, to be woven in the looms of Flanders. It was the perfection of the older Florentine style of miniature-painting, with patient putting of each leaf upon the trees and each flower in the grass, where the first man and woman were standing.

And because it was the perfection of that style, it awoke in Leonardo some seed of discontent which lay in the secret places of his nature. For the way to perfection is through a series of disgusts; and this picture—all that he had done so far in his life at Florence—was after all in the old slight manner. His art, if it was to be something in the world, must be weighted with more of the meaning of nature and purpose of humanity. Nature was "the true mistress of higher intelligences." He plunged, then, into the study of nature. And in doing this he followed the manner of the older students; he brooded over the hidden virtues of plants and crystals, the lines traced by the stars as they moved in the sky, over the correspondences which exist between the different orders of living things, through which, to eyes opened, they interpret each other; and for years he seemed to those about him as one listening to a voice, silent for other men.

He learned here the art of going deep, of tracking the sources of expression to their subtlest retreats, the power of an intimate presence in the things he handled. He did not at once or entirely desert his art; only he was no longer the cheerful, objective painter, through whose soul, as through clear glass, the bright figures of Florentine life, only made a little mellower and more pensive by the transit, passed on to the white wall. He wasted many days in curious tricks of design, seeming to lose himself in the spinning of intricate devices of line and colour. He was smitten with a love of the impossible—the perforation of mountains, changing the course of rivers, raising great buildings, such as the church of *San Giovanni*, in the air; all those feats for the performance of which natural magic professed to have the key. Later writers, indeed, see in these efforts an anticipation of modern mechanics;

in him they were rather dreams, thrown off by the overwrought and labouring brain. Two ideas were especially confirmed in him, as reflexes of things that had touched his brain in childhood beyond the depth of other impressions—the smiling of women and the motion of great waters.

And in such studies some interfusion of the extremes of beauty and terror shaped itself, as an image that might be seen and touched, in the mind of this gracious youth, so fixed that for the rest of his life it never left him. As if catching glimpses of it in the strange eyes or hair of chance people, he would follow such about the streets of Florence till the sun went down, of whom many sketches of his remain. Some of these are full of a curious beauty, that remote beauty which may be apprehended only by those who have sought it carefully; who, starting with acknowledged types of beauty, have refined as far upon these, as these refine upon the world of common forms. But mingled inextricably with this there is an element of mockery also; so that, whether in sorrow or scorn, he caricatures Dante even. Legions of grotesques sweep under his hand; for has not nature too her grotesques—the rent rock, the distorting lights of evening on lonely roads, the unveiled structure of man in the embryo, or the skeleton?

All these swarming fancies unite in the *Medusa* of the *Uffizii*. Vasari's story of an earlier Medusa, painted on a wooden shield, is perhaps an invention; and yet, properly told, has more of the air of truth about it than anything else in the whole legend. For its real subject is not the serious work of a man, but the experiment of a child. The lizards and glow-worms and other strange small creatures which haunt an Italian vineyard bring before one the whole picture of a child's life in a Tuscan dwelling—half castle, half farm—and are as true to nature as the pretended astonishment of the father for whom the boy has prepared a surprise. It was not in play that he painted that other Medusa, the one great picture which he left behind him in Florence. The subject has been treated in various ways; Leonardo alone cuts to its centre; he alone realises it as the head of a corpse, exercising its powers through all the circumstances of death. What may be called the fascination of corruption penetrates in every touch its exquisitely finished beauty. About the dainty lines of the cheek the bat flits unheeded. The delicate snakes seem literally strangling each other in terrified struggle to escape from the

Medusa brain. The hue which violent death always brings with it is in the features; features singularly massive and grand, as we catch them inverted, in a dexterous foreshortening, crown foremost, like a great calm stone against which the wave of serpents breaks.

The science of that age was all divination, clairvoyance, unsubjected to our exact modern formulas, seeking in an instant of vision to concentrate a thousand experiences. Later writers, thinking only of the well-ordered treatise on painting which a Frenchman, Raffaelle du Fresne, a hundred years afterwards, compiled from Leonardo's bewildered manuscripts, written strangely, as his manner was, from right to left, have imagined a rigid order in his inquiries. But this rigid order would have been little in accordance with the restlessness of his character; and if we think of him as the mere reasoner who subjects design to anatomy, and composition to mathematical rules, we shall hardly have that impression which those around Leonardo received from him. Poring over his crucibles, making experiments with colour, trying, by a strange variation of the alchemist's dream, to discover the secret, not of an elixir to make man's natural life immortal, but of giving immortality to the subtlest and most delicate effects of painting, he seemed to them rather the sorcerer or the magician, possessed of curious secrets and a hidden knowledge, living in a world of which he alone possessed the key. What his philosophy seems to have been most like is that of Paracelsus or Cardan;[3] and much of the spirit of the older alchemy still hangs about it, with its confidence in short cuts and odd byways to knowledge. To him philosophy was to be something giving strange swiftness and double sight, divining the sources of springs beneath the earth or of expression beneath the human countenance, clairvoyant of occult gifts in common or uncommon things, in the reed at the brook-side, or the star which draws near to us but once in a century. How, in this way, the clear purpose was overclouded, the fine chaser's hand perplexed, we but dimly see; the mystery which at no point quite lifts from Leonardo's life is deepest here. But it is certain that at one period of his life he had almost ceased to be an artist.

The year 1483—the year of the birth of Raphael and the thirty-first of Leonardo's life—is fixed as the date of his visit to Milan by the letter in which he recommends himself to Ludovico Sforza, and offers to tell him, for a price, strange secrets in the art of war. It was that Sforza who murdered his young nephew by slow poison, yet was so susceptible of religious impressions that he blended mere earthly passion with a sort of religious sentimentalism, and who took for his device the mulberry-tree—symbol, in its long delay and sudden yielding of flowers and fruit together, of a wisdom which economises all forces for an opportunity of sudden and sure effect. The fame of Leonardo had gone before him, and he was to model a colossal statue of Francesco, the first Duke of Milan. As for Leonardo himself, he came not as an artist at all, or careful of the fame of one; but as a player on the harp, a strange harp of silver of his own construction, shaped in some curious likeness to a horse's skull. The capricious spirit of Ludovico was susceptible also to the power of music, and Leonardo's nature had a kind of spell in it. Fascination is always the word descriptive of him. No portrait of his youth remains; but all tends to make us believe that up to this time some charm of voice and aspect, strong enough to balance the disadvantage of his birth, and played about him. His physical strength was great; it was said that he could bend a horseshoe like a coil of lead.

The *Duomo*,[4] work of artists from beyond the Alps, so fantastic to the eye of a Florentine used to the mellow, unbroken surfaces of Giotto and Arnolfo, was then in all its freshness; and below, in the streets of Milan, moved a people as fantastic, changeful, and dreamlike. To Leonardo least of all men could there be anything poisonous in the exotic flowers of sentiment which grew there. It was a life of brilliant sins and exquisite amusements: Leonardo became a celebrated designer of pageants; and it suited the quality of his genius, composed, in almost equal parts, of curiosity and the desire of beauty, to take things as they came.

Curiosity and the desire of beauty—these are the two elementary forces in Leonardo's genius; curiosity often in conflict with the desire of beauty, but generating, in union with it, a type of subtle and curious grace.

The movement of the fifteenth century was twofold; partly the Renaissance, partly also the

[3] Paracelsus (1490?–1541), German philosopher; see Browning's poem. Girolamo Cardan (1501–76), Italian scientist.
[4] The Milan Cathedral.

coming of what is called the "modern spirit," with its realism, its appeal to experience. It comprehended a return to antiquity, and a return to nature. Raphael represents the return to antiquity, and Leonardo the return to nature. In this return to nature, he was seeking to satisfy a boundless curiosity by her perpetual surprises, a microscopic sense of finish by her *finesse*, or delicacy of operation, that *subtilitas naturae* which Bacon notices. So we find him often in intimate relations with men of science,—with Fra Luca Paccioli the mathematician, and the anatomist Marc Antonio della Torre. His observations and experiments fill thirteen volumes of manuscript; and those who can judge describe him as anticipating long before, by rapid intuition, the later ideas of science. He explained the obscure light of the unilluminated part of the moon, knew that the sea had once covered the mountains which contain shells, and of the gathering of the equatorial waters above the polar.

He who thus penetrated into the most secret parts of nature preferred always the more to the less remote, what, seeming exceptional, was an instance of law more refined, the construction about things of a peculiar atmosphere and mixed lights. He paints flowers with such curious felicity that different writers have attributed to him a fondness for particular flowers, as Clement the cyclamen, and Rio the jasmin; while, at Venice, there is a stray leaf from his portfolio dotted all over with studies of violets and the wild rose. In him first appears the taste for what is *bizarre* or *recherché* in landscape; hollow places full of the green shadow of bituminous rocks, ridged reefs of trap-rock which cut the water into quaint sheets of light,—their exact antitype is in our own western seas; all the solemn effects of moving water. You may follow it springing from its distant source among the rocks on the heath of the *Madonna of the Balances*, passing, as a little fall, into the treacherous calm of the *Madonna of the Lake*, as a goodly river next, below the cliffs of the *Madonna of the Rocks*, washing the white walls of its distant villages, stealing out in a network of divided streams in *La Gioconda* to the seashore of the *Saint Anne*— that delicate place, where the wind passes like the hand of some fine etcher over the surface, and the untorn shells are lying thick upon the sand, and the tops of the rocks, to which the waves never rise, are green with grass, grown fine as hair. It is the landscape, not of dreams or of fancy, but of places far withdrawn, and hours selected from a thousand with a miracle

of *finesse*. Through Leonardo's strange veil of sight things reach him so; in no ordinary night or day, but as in faint light of eclipse, or in some brief interval of falling rain at daybreak, or through deep water.

And not into nature only; but he plunged also into human personality, and became above all a painter of portraits; faces of a modelling more skilful than has been seen before or since, embodied with a reality which almost amounts to illusion, on the dark air. To take a character as it was, and delicately sound its stops, suited one so curious in observation, curious in invention. He painted thus the portraits of Ludovico's mistresses, Lucretia Crivelli and Cecilia Galerani the poetess, of Ludovico himself, and the Duchess Beatrice. The portrait of Cecilia Galerani is lost, but that of Lucretia Crivelli has been identified with *La Belle Feronière* of the Louvre, and Ludovico's pale, anxious face still remains in the Ambrosian library. Opposite is the portrait of Beatrice d'Este, in whom Leonardo seems to have caught some presentiment of early death, painting her precise and grave, full of the refinement of the dead, in sad earth-coloured raiment, set with pale stones.

Sometimes this curiosity came in conflict with the desire of beauty; it tended to make him go too far below that outside of things in which art really begins and ends. This struggle between the reason and its ideas, and the senses, the desire of beauty, is the key to Leonardo's life at Milan— his restlessness, his endless re-touchings, his odd experiments with colour. How much must he leave unfinished, how much recommence! His problem was the transmutation of ideas into images. What he had attained so far had been the mastery of that earlier Florentine style, with its naïve and limited sensuousness. Now he was to entertain in this narrow medium those divinations of a humanity too wide for it, that larger vision of the opening world, which is only not too much for the great, irregular art of Shakespeare; and everywhere the effort is visible in the work of his hands. This agitation, this perpetual delay, give him an air of weariness and *ennui*. To others he seems to be aiming at an impossible effect, to do something that art, that painting, can never do. Often the expression of physical beauty at this or that point seems strained and marred in the effort, as in those heavy German foreheads—too heavy and German for perfect beauty.

For there was a touch of Germany in that genius which, as Goethe said, had "thought itself weary"—*müde sich gedacht.* What an anticipation of modern Germany, for instance, in that debate on the question whether sculpture or painting is the nobler art![5] But there is this difference between him and the German, that, with all that curious science, the German would have thought nothing more was needed. The name of Goethe himself reminds one how great for the artist may be the danger of overmuch science; how Goethe, who, in the *Elective Affinities* and the first part of *Faust*, does transmute ideas into images, who wrought many such transmutations, did not invariably find the spell-word, and in the second part of *Faust* presents us with a mass of science which has almost no artistic character at all. But Leonardo will never work till the happy moment comes—that moment of *bien-être*, which to imaginative men is a moment of invention. On this he waits with a perfect patience; other moments are but a preparation, or after-taste of it. Few men distinguish between them as jealously as he. Hence so many flaws even in the choicest work. But for Leonardo the distinction is absolute, and, in the moment of *bien-être*, the alchemy complete: the idea is stricken into colour and imagery: a cloudy mysticism is refined to a subdued and graceful mystery, and painting pleases the eye while it satisfies the soul.

This curious beauty is seen above all in his drawings, and in these chiefly in the abstract grace of the bounding lines. Let us take some of these drawings, and pause over them awhile; and, first, one of those at Florence—the heads of a woman and a little child, set side by side, but each in its own separate frame. First of all, there is much pathos in the reappearance, in the fuller curves of the face of the child, of the sharper, more chastened lines of the worn and older face, which leaves no doubt that the heads are those of a little child and its mother. A feeling for maternity is indeed always characteristic of Leonardo; and this feeling is further indicated here by the half-humorous pathos of the diminutive, rounded shoulders of the child. You may note a like pathetic power in drawings of a young man, seated in a stooping posture, his face in his hands, as in sorrow; of a slave sitting in an uneasy inclined attitude, in some brief interval of rest; of a small Madonna and Child, peeping sideways in half-reassured terror, as a

mighty griffin with batlike wings, one of Leonardo's finest *inventions*, descends suddenly from the air to snatch up a great wild beast wandering near them. But note in these, as that which especially belongs to art, the contour of the young man's hair, the poise of the slave's arm above his head, and the curves of the head of the child, following the little skull within, thin and fine as some sea-shell worn by the wind.

Take again another head, still more full of sentiment, but of a different kind, a little drawing in red chalk which every one will remember who has examined at all carefully the drawings by old masters at the Louvre. It is a face of doubtful sex, set in the shadow of its own hair, the cheek-line in high light against it, with something voluptuous and full in the eyelids and the lips. Another drawing might pass for the same face in childhood, with parched and feverish lips, but much sweetness in the loose, short-waisted childish dress, with necklace and *bulla,* and in the daintily bound hair. We might take the thread of suggestion which these two drawings offer, when thus set side by side, and, following it through the drawings at Florence, Venice, and Milan, construct a sort of series, illustrating better than anything else Leonardo's type of womanly beauty. Daughters of Herodias, with their fantastic head-dresses knotted and folded so strangely to leave the dainty oval of the face disengaged, they are not of the Christian family, or of Raphael's. They are the clairvoyants, through whom, as through delicate instruments, one becomes aware of the subtler forces of nature, and the modes of their action, all that is magnetic in it, all those finer conditions wherein material things rise to that subtlety of operation which constitutes them spiritual, where only the final nerve and the keener touch can follow. It is as if in certain significant examples we actually saw those forces at their work on human flesh. Nervous, electric, faint always with some inexplicable faintness, these people seem to be subject to exceptional conditions, to feel powers at work in the common air unfelt by others, to become, as it were, the receptacle of them, and pass them on to us in a chain of secret influences.

But among the more youthful heads there is one at Florence which Love chooses for its own —the head of a young man, which may well be

---

[5] How princely, how characteristic of Leonardo, the answer, *Quanto piu, un' arte porta seco fatica di corpo, tanto piu è vile!* [Pater's note. Leonardo's answer reads: "The more art shows the effect of physical strain in its product, the lower it is!"]

the likeness of Andrea Salaino, beloved of Leonardo for his curled and waving hair—*belli capelli ricci e inanellati*[6]—and afterwards his favourite pupil and servant. Of all the interests in living men and women which may have filled his life at Milan, this attachment alone is recorded. And in return Salaino identified himself so entirely with Leonardo, that the picture of *Saint Anne*, in the Louvre, has been attributed to him. It illustrates Leonardo's usual choice of pupils, men of some natural charm of person or intercourse like Salaino, or men of birth and princely habits of life like Francesco Melzi[7]—men with just enough genius to be capable of initiation into his secret, for the sake of which they were ready to efface their own individuality. Among them, retiring often to the villa of the Melzi at *Canonica al Vaprio*, he worked at his fugitive manuscripts and sketches, working for the present hour, and for a few only, perhaps chiefly for himself. Other artists have been as careless of present or future applause, in self-forgetfulness, or because they set moral or political ends above the ends of art; but in him this solitary culture of beauty seems to have hung upon a kind of self-love, and a carelessness in the work of art of all but art itself. Out of the secret places of a unique temperament he brought strange blossoms and fruits hitherto unknown; and for him, the novel impression conveyed, the exquisite effect woven, counted as an end in itself—a perfect end.

And these pupils of his acquired his manner so thoroughly, that though the number of Leonardo's authentic works is very small indeed, there is a multitude of other men's pictures through which we undoubtedly see him, and come very near to his genius. Sometimes, as in the little picture of the *Madonna of the Balances*, in which, from the bosom of His mother, Christ weighs the pebbles of the brook against the sins of men, we have a hand, rough enough by contrast, working upon some fine hint or sketch of his. Sometimes, as in the subjects of the *Daughter of Herodias* and the *Head of John the Baptist*, the lost originals have been re-echoed and varied upon again and again by Luini and others. At other times the original remains, but has been a mere theme or motive, a type of which the accessories might be modified or changed; and these variations have but brought out the more the purpose, or expression of the original. It is so with the so-called *Saint John the Baptist* of the Louvre—one of the few naked

figures Leonardo painted—whose delicate brown flesh and woman's hair no one would go out into the wilderness to seek, and whose treacherous smile would have us understand something far beyond the outward gesture or circumstance. But the long, reedlike cross in the hand, which suggests Saint John the Baptist, becomes faint in a copy at the Ambrosian Library, and disappears altogether in another version, in the *Palazzo Rosso* at Genoa. Returning from the latter to the original, we are no longer surprised by Saint John's strange likeness to the *Bacchus* which hangs near it, and which set Theophile Gautier thinking of Heine's notion of decayed gods, who, to maintain themselves, after the fall of paganism, took employment in the new religion. We recognise one of those symbolical inventions in which the ostensible subject is used, not as matter for definite pictorial realisation, but as the starting-point of a train of sentiment, subtle and vague as a piece of music. No one ever ruled over the mere *subject* in hand more entirely than Leonardo, or bent it more dexterously to purely artistic ends. And so it comes to pass that though he handles sacred subjects continually, he is the most profane of painters; the given person or subject, Saint John in the Desert, or the Virgin on the knees of Saint Anne, is often merely the pretext for a kind of work which carries one altogether beyond the range of its conventional associations.

About the *Last Supper*, its decay and restorations, a whole literature has risen up, Goethe's pensive sketch of its sad fortunes being perhaps the best. The death in childbirth of the Duchess Beatrice was followed in Ludovico by one of those paroxysms of religious feeling which in him were constitutional. The low, gloomy Dominican church of *Saint Mary of the Graces* had been the favourite oratory of Beatrice. She had spent her last days there, full of sinister presentiments; at last it had been almost necessary to remove her from it by force; and now it was here that mass was said a hundred times a day for her repose. On the damp wall of the refectory, oozing with mineral salts, Leonardo painted the *Last Supper*. Effective anecdotes were told about, it, his retouchings and delays. They show him refusing to work except at the moment of invention, scornful of any one who supposed that art could be a work of mere industry and rule, often coming the whole length of Milan to give a single touch. He painted it, not in fresco, where all must be *impromptu*, but in oils, the new

---

[6] Beautiful hair, curly and abundant.   [7] Francesco Melzi (1492?–1568), pupil of Leonardo.

method which he had been one of the first to welcome, because it allowed of so many after-thoughts, so refined a working out of perfection. It turned out that on a plastered wall no process could have been less durable. Within fifty years it had fallen into decay. And now we have to turn back to Leonardo's own studies, above all to one drawing of the central head at the *Brera*,[8] which, in a union of tenderness and severity in the face-lines, reminds one of the monumental work of Mino da Fiesole, to trace it as it was.

Here was another effort to lift a given subject out of the range of its traditional associations. Strange, after all the mystic developments of the middle age, was the effort to see the Eucharist, not as the pale Host of the altar, but as one taking leave of his friends. Five years afterwards the young Raphael, at Florence, painted it with sweet and solemn effect in the refectory of Saint Onofrio; but still with all the mystical unreality of the school of Perugino. Vasari pretends that the central head was never finished But finished or unfinished, or owing part of its effect to a mellowing decay, the head of Jesus does but consummate the sentiment of the whole company—ghosts through which you see the wall, faint as the shadows of the leaves upon the wall on autumn afternoons. This figure is but the faintest, the most spectral of them all.

The *Last Supper* was finished in 1497; in 1498 the French entered Milan, and whether or not the Gascon bowmen used it as a mark for their arrows, the model of Francesco Sforza certainly did not survive. What, in that age, such work was capable of being—of what nobility, amid what racy truthfulness to fact—we may judge from the bronze statue of Bartolomeo Colleoni on horseback, modelled by Leonardo's master, Verrocchio (he died of grief, it was said, because, the mould accidentally failing, he was unable to complete it), still standing in the *piazza* of Saint John and Saint Paul at Venice. Some traces of the thing may remain in certain of Leonardo's drawings, and perhaps also, by a singular circumstance, in a far-off town of France. For Ludovico became a prisoner, and ended his days at Loches in Touraine. After many years of captivity in the dungeons below, where all seems sick with barbarous feudal memories, he was allowed at last, it is said, to breathe fresher air for awhile in one of the rooms of the great tower still shown, its walls covered with strange painted arabesques, ascribed by tradi-

tion to his hand, amused a little, in this way, through the tedious years. In those vast helmets and human faces and pieces of armour, among which, in great letters, the motto *Infelix Sum*[9] is woven in and out, it is perhaps not too fanciful to see the fruit of a wistful after-dreaming over Leonardo's sundry experiments on the armed figure of the great duke, which had occupied the two so much during the days of their good fortune at Milan.

The remaining years of Leonardo's life are more or less years of wandering. From his brilliant life at court he had saved nothing, and he returned to Florence a poor man. Perhaps necessity kept his spirit excited: the next four years are one prolonged rapture or ecstasy of invention. He painted now the pictures of the Louvre, his most authentic works, which came there straight from the cabinet of Francis the First, at Fontainebleau. One picture of his, the *Saint Anne*—not the *Saint Anne* of the Louvre, but a simple cartoon, now in London—revived for a moment a sort of appreciation more common in an earlier time, when good pictures had still seemed miraculous. For two days a crowd of people of all qualities passed in naïve excitement through the chamber where it hung, and gave Leonardo a taste of the "triumph" of Cimabue. But his work was less with the saints than with the living women of Florence. For he lived still in the polished society that he loved, and in the houses of Florence, left perhaps a little subject to light thoughts by the death of Savonarola—the latest gossip (1869) is of an undraped Monna Lisa, found in some out-of-the-way corner of the late *Orleans* collection—he saw Ginevra di Benci, and Lisa, the young third wife of Francesco del Giocondo. As we have seen him using incidents of sacred story, not for their own sake, or as mere subjects for pictorial realisation, but as a cryptic language for fancies all his own, so now he found a vent for his thought in taking one of these languid women, and raising her, as Leda or Pomona, as Modesty or Vanity, to the seventh heaven of symbolical expression.

La Gioconda is, in the truest sense, Leonardo's masterpiece, the revealing instance of his mode of thought and work. In suggestiveness, only the *Melancholia* of Dürer is comparable to it; and no crude symbolism disturbs the effect of its subdued and graceful mystery. We all know the face and hands of the figure, set in its marble chair, in that circle of fantastic rocks, as in some

---

[8] An art gallery in Milan.   [9] I am unhappy.

faint light under sea. Perhaps of all ancient pictures time has chilled it least.[10] As often happens with works in which invention seems to reach its limit, there is an element in it given to, not invented by, the master. In that inestimable folio of drawings, once in the possession of Vasari, were certain designs by Verrocchio, faces of such impressive beauty that Leonardo in his boyhood copied them many times. It is hard not to connect with these designs of the elder, by-past master, as with its geminal principle, the unfathomable smile, always with a touch of something sinister in it, which plays over all Leonardo's work. Besides, the picture is a portrait. From childhood we see this image defining itself on the fabric of his dreams; and but for express historical testimony, we might fancy that this was but his ideal lady, embodied and beheld at last. What was the relationship of a living Florentine to this creature of his thought? By what strange affinities had the dream and the person grown up thus apart, and yet so closely together? Present from the first incorporeally in Leonardo's brain, dimly traced in the designs of Verrocchio, she is found present at last in *Il Giocondo's* house. That there is much of mere portraiture in the picture is attested by the legend that by artificial means, the presence of mimes and flute-players, that subtle expression was protracted on the face. Again, was it in four years and by renewed labour never really completed, or in four months and as by stroke of magic, that the image was projected?

The presence that rose thus so strangely beside the waters, is expressive of what in the ways of a thousand years men had come to desire. Hers is the head upon which all "the ends of the world are come," and the eyelids are a little weary. It is a beauty wrought out from within upon the flesh, the deposit, little cell by cell, of strange thoughts and fantastic reveries and exquisite passions. Set it for a moment beside one of those white Greek goddesses or beautiful women of antiquity, and how would they be troubled by this beauty, into which the soul with all its maladies has passed! All the thoughts and experience of the world have etched and moulded there, in that which they have of power to refine and make expressive the outward form, the animalism of Greece, the lust of Rome, the mysticism of the middle age with its spiritual ambition and imaginative loves, the return of the Pagan

world, the sins of the Borgias. She is older than the rocks among which she sits; like the vampire, she has been dead many times, and learned the secrets of the grave; and has been a diver in deep seas, and keeps their fallen day about her; and trafficked for strange webs with Eastern merchants and, as Leda, was the mother of Helen of Troy, and, as Saint Anne, the mother of Mary; and all this has been to her but as the sound of lyres and flutes, and lives only in the delicacy with which it has moulded the changing lineaments, and tinged the eyelids and the hands. The fancy of a perpetual life, sweeping together ten thousand experiences, is an old one; and modern philosophy has conceived the idea of humanity as wrought upon by, and summing up in itself, all modes of thought and life. Certainly Lady Lisa might stand as the embodiment of the old fancy, the symbol of the modern idea.

During these years at Florence Leonardo's history is the history of his art; for himself, he is lost in the bright cloud of it. The outward history begins again in 1502, with a wild journey through central Italy, which he makes as the chief engineer of Cæsar Borgia. The biographer, putting together the stray jottings of his manuscripts, may follow him through every day of it, up the strange tower of Siena, elastic like a bent bow, down to the seashore at Piombino, each place appearing as fitfully as in a fever dream.

One other great work was left for him to do, a work all trace of which soon vanished, *The Battle of the Standard*, in which he had Michelangelo for his rival. The citizens of Florence, desiring to decorate the walls of the great councilchamber, had offered the work for competition, and any subject might be chosen from the Florentine wars of the fifteenth century. Michelangelo chose for his cartoon an incident of the war with Pisa, in which the Florentine soldiers, bathing in the Arno, are surprised by the sound of trumpets, and run to arms. His design has reached us only in an old engraving, which helps us less perhaps than our remembrance of the background of his *Holy Family* in the *Uffizii* to imagine in what superhuman form, such as might have beguiled the heart of an earlier world, those figures ascended out of the water. Leonardo chose an incident from the battle of Anghiari, in which two parties of soldiers fight for a standard. Like Michelangelo's, his cartoon is lost,

---

[10] Yet for Vasari there was some further magic of crimson in the lips and cheeks, lost for us. [Pater's note]

and has come to us only in sketches, and in a fragment of Rubens. Through the accounts given we may discern some lust of terrible things in it, so that even the horses tore each other with their teeth. And yet one fragment of it, in a drawing of his at Florence, is far different—a waving field of lovely armour, the chased edgings running like lines of sunlight from side to side. Michelangelo was twenty-seven years old; Leonardo more than fifty; and Raphael, then nineteen years of age, visiting Florence for the first time, came and watched them as they worked.

We catch a glimpse of Leonardo again, at Rome in 1514, surrounded by his mirrors and vials and furnaces, making strange toys that seemed alive of wax and quicksilver. The hesitation which had haunted him all through life, and made him like one under a spell, was upon him now with double force. No one had ever carried political indifferentism farther; it had always been his philosophy to "fly before the storm"; he is for the Sforzas, or against them, as the tide of their fortune turns. Yet now, in the political society of Rome, he came to be suspected of secret French sympathies. It paralysed him to find himself among enemies; and he turned wholly to France, which had long courted him.

France was about to become an Italy more Italian than Italy itself. Francis the First, like Lewis the Twelfth before him, was attracted by the *finesse* of Leonardo's work; *La Gioconda* was already in his cabinet, and he offered Leonardo the little *Château de Clou*, with its vineyards and meadows, in the pleasant valley of the Masse, just outside the walls of the town of Amboise, where, especially in the hunting season, the court then frequently resided. *A Monsieur Lyonard, peinteur du Roy pour Amboyse*[11]—so the letter of Francis the First is headed. It opens a prospect, one of the most interesting in the history of art, where, in a peculiarly blent atmosphere, Italian art dies away as a French exotic.

Two questions remain, after much busy anti-quarianism, concerning Leonardo's death—the question of the exact form of his religion, and the question whether Francis the First was present at the time. They are of about equally little importance in the estimate of Leonardo's genius. The directions in his will concerning the thirty masses and the great candles for the church of Saint Florentin are things of course, their real purpose being immediate and practical; and on no theory of religion could these hurried offices be of much consequence. We forget them in speculating how one who had been always so desirous of beauty, but desired it always in such precise and definite forms, as hands or flowers or hair, looked forward now into the vague land, and experienced the last curiosity.

Joachim du Bellay

IN THE middle of the sixteenth century, when the spirit of the Renaissance was everywhere, and people had begun to look back with distaste on the works of the middle age, the old Gothic manner had still one chance more, in borrowing something from the rival which was about to supplant it. In this way there was produced, chiefly in France, a new and peculiar phase of taste with qualities and a charm of its own, blending the somewhat attentuated grace of Italian ornament with the general outlines of Northern design. It created the *Château de Gaillon*, as you may still see it in the delicate engravings of Israël Silvestre[1]—a Gothic donjon veiled faintly by a surface of dainty Italian traceries—Chenonceaux, Blois, Chambord, and the church of Brou. In painting, there came from Italy workmen like *Maître Roux*[2] and the masters of the school of Fontainebleau, to have their later Italian voluptuousness attempered by the naïve and silvery qualities of the native style; and it was characteristic of these painters that they were most successful in painting on glass, an art so essentially medieval. Taking it up where the middle age had left it, they found their whole work among the last subtleties of colour and line; and keeping within the true limits of their material, they got quite a new order of effects from it, and felt their way to refinements on colour never dreamed of by those older workmen, the glass-painters of Chartres or Le Mans. What is called the *Renaissance in France* is thus not so much the introduction of a wholly new taste ready-made from Italy, but rather the finest and subtlest phase of the middle age itself,

---

[11] "To Mr. Leonardo, painter to the king at Amboise."
[1] Israel Silvestre (1621–91), artist at the court of Louis XIV.
[2] Giovanni Battista Rosso (1495–1540). Florentine artist.

its last fleeting splendour and temperate Saint Martin's summer. In poetry, the Gothic spirit in France had produced a thousand songs; so in the Renaissance, French poetry too did but borrow something to blend with a native growth, and the poems of Ronsard, with their ingenuity, their delicately figured surfaces, their slightness, their fanciful combinations of rhyme, are the correlative of the traceries of the house of Jacques Cœur at Bourges, or the *Maison de Justice* at Rouen.

There was indeed something in the native French taste naturally akin to that Italian *finesse*. The characteristic of French work had always been a certain nicety, a remarkable daintiness of hand, *une netteté remarquable d'exécution*. In the paintings of François Clouet, for example, or rather of the Clouets[3]—for there was a whole family of them—painters remarkable for their resistance to Italian influences, there is a silveriness of colour and a clearness of expression which distinguish them very definitely from their Flemish neighbours, Hemling or the Van Eycks. And this nicety is not less characteristic of old French poetry. A light, aërial delicacy, a simple elegance—*une netteté remarquable d'exécution:* these are essential characteristics alike of Villon's poetry, and of the *Hours of Anne of Brittany*. They are characteristic too of a hundred French Gothic carvings and traceries. Alike in the old Gothic cathedrals, and in their counterpart, the old Gothic *chansons de geste*, the rough and ponderous mass becomes, as if by passing for a moment into happier conditions, or through a more gracious stratum of air, graceful and refined, like the carved ferneries on the granite church at Folgoat, or the lines which describe the fair priestly hands of Archbishop Turpin, in the song of Roland; although below both alike there is a fund of mere Gothic strength, or heaviness.[4]

Now Villon's songs and Clouet's painting are like these. It is the higher touch making itself felt here and there, betraying itself, like nobler blood in a lower stock, by a fine line or gesture or expression, the turn of a wrist, the tapering of a finger. In Ronsard's time that rougher element seemed likely to predominate. No one can turn over the pages of Rabelais without feeling how much need there was of softening, of

castigation. To effect this softening is the object of the revolution in poetry which is connected with Ronsard's name. Casting about for the means of thus refining upon and saving the character of French literature, he accepted that influx of Renaissance taste, which, leaving the buildings, the language, the art, the poetry of France, at bottom, what they were, old French Gothic still, gilds their surfaces with a strange, delightful, foreign aspect passing over all that Northern land, in itself neither deeper nor more permanent than a chance effect of light. He reinforces, he doubles the French diantiness by Italian *finesse*. Thereupon, nearly all the force and all the seriousness of French work disappear; only the elegance, the aërial touch, the perfect manner remain. But this elegance, this manner, this daintiness of execution are consummate, and have an unmistakable æsthetic value.

So the old French *chanson*, which, like the old northern Gothic ornament, though it sometimes refined itself into a sort of weird elegance, was often, in its essence, something rude and formless, became in the hands of Ronsard a Pindaric ode. He gave it structure, a sustained system, *strophe* and *antistrophe*, and taught it a changefulness and variety of metre which keep the curiosity always excited, so that the very aspect of it, as it lies written on the page, carries the eye lightly onwards, and of which this is a good instance:—

> Avril, le grace, et le ris
> De Cypris,
> Le flair et la douce haleine;
> Avril, le parfum des dieux,
> Qui, des cieux,
> Sentent l'odeur de la plaine;
>
> C'est toy, courtois et gentil,
> Qui, d'exil
> Retire ces passageres,
> Ces arondelles qui vont,
> Et qui sont
> Du printemps les messageres.[5]

That is not by Ronsard, but by Remy Belleau, for Ronsard soon came to have a school. Six other poets threw in their lot with him in his literary revolution,—this Remy Belleau, Antoine de Baif, Pontus de Tyard, Étienne Jodelle, Jean Daurat, and lastly Joachim du Bellay; and with

---

[3] François Clouet (1520–72) and his father, Jean Clouet (d. 1540), court painters.
[4] The purely artistic aspects of this subject have been interpreted in a work of great taste and learning, by Mrs. Mark Pattison:—*The Renaissance of Art in France*. [Pater's note]
[5] "April, the grace and the laugh of Venus, the flair and the sweet breath; April, the perfume of the gods, who, from the skies, sense the odor of the field; it is you, gracious and gentle, who brings back from exile these travellers, these swallows who come and who are the messengers of spring."

that strange love of emblems which is characteristic of the time, which covered all the works of Francis the First with the salamander, and all the works of Henry the Second with the double crescent, and all the works of Anne of Brittany with the knotted cord, they called themselves the *Pleiad;* seven in all, although, as happens with the celestial Pleiad, if you scrutinise this constellation of poets more carefully you may find there a great number of minor stars.

The first note of this literary revolution was struck by Joachim du Bellay in a little tract written at the early age of twenty-four, which coming to us through three centuries seems of yesterday, so full is it of those delicate critical distinctions which are sometimes supposed peculiar to modern writers. The piece has for its title *La Deffiense et Illustration de la langue Françoyse;* and its problem is how to illustrate or ennoble the French language, to give it lustre. We are accustomed to speak of the varied critical and creative movement of the fifteenth and sixteenth centuries as the *Renaissance,* and because we have a single name for it we may sometimes fancy that there was more unity in the thing itself than there really was. Even the Reformation, that other great movement of the fifteenth and sixteenth centuries, had far less unity, far less of combined action, than is at first sight supposed; and the Renaissance was infinitely less united, less conscious of combined action, than the Reformation. But if anywhere the Renaissance became conscious, as a German philosopher might say, if ever it was understood as a systematic movement by those who took part in it, it is in this little book of Joachim du Bellay's, which it is impossible to read without feeling the excitement, the animation, of change, of discovery. "It is a remarkable fact," says M. Sainte-Beuve, "and an inversion of what is true of other languages, that, in French, prose has always had the precedence over poetry." Du Bellay's prose is perfectly transparent, flexible, and chaste. In many ways it is a more characteristic example of the culture of the *Pleiad* than any of its verse; and those who love the whole movement of which the *Pleiad* is a part, for a weird foreign grace in it, and may be looking about for a true specimen of it, cannot have a better than Joachim du Bellay and this little treatise of his.

Du Bellay's object is to adjust the existing French culture to the rediscovered classical culture; and in discussing this problem, and developing the theories of the *Pleiad,* he has lighted upon many principles of permanent truth and applicability. There were some who despaired of the French language altogether, who thought it naturally incapable of the fulness and elegance of Greek and Latin—*cette élégance et copie qui est en la langue Greque et Romaine*—that science could be adequately discussed, and poetry nobly written, only in the dead languages. "Those who speak thus," says Du Bellay, "make me think of the relics which one may only see through a little pane of glass, and must not touch with one's hands. That is what these people do with all branches of culture, which they keep shut up in Greek and Latin books, not permitting one to see them otherwise, or transport them out of dead words into those which are alive, and wing their way daily through the mouths of men." "Languages," he says again, "are not born like plants and trees, some naturally feeble and sickly, others healthy and strong and apter to bear the weight of men's conceptions, but all their virtue is generated in the world of choice and men's freewill concerning them. Therefore, I cannot blame too strongly the rashness of some of our countrymen, who being anything rather than Greeks or Latins, depreciate and reject with more than stoical disdain everything written in French; nor can I express my surprise at the odd opinion of some learned men who think that our vulgar tongue is wholly incapable of erudition and good literature."

It was an age of translations. Du Bellay himself translated two books of the *Æneid,* and other poetry, old and new, and there were some who thought that the translation of the classical literature was the true means of *ennobling* the French language:—strangers are ever favourites with us—*nous favorisons toujours les étrangers.* Du Bellay moderates their expectations. "I do not believe that one can learn the right use of them"—he is speaking of figures and ornament in language—"from translations, because it is impossible to reproduce them with the same grace with which the original author used them For each language has I know not what peculiarity of its own; and if you force yourself to express the naturalness (*le naïf*) of this in another language, observing the law of translation,—not to expatiate beyond the limits of the author himself, your words will be constrained, cold and ungraceful." Then he fixes the test of all good translation:—"To prove this, read me Demosthenes and Homer in Latin, Cicero and Virgil in French, and see whether they produce in you the same affections which you experience in reading those authors in the original."

In this effort to ennoble the French language, to give it grace, number, perfection, and as painters do to their pictures, that last, so desirable, touch—*cette dernière main que nous désirons*—what Du Bellay is really pleading for is his mother-tongue, the language, that is, in which one will have the utmost degree of what is moving and passionate. He recognised of what force the music and dignity of languages are, how they enter into the inmost part of things; and in pleading for the cultivation of the French language, he is pleading for no merely scholastic interest, but for freedom, impulse, reality, not in literature only, but in daily communion of speech. After all, it was impossible to have this impulse in Greek and Latin, dead languages shut up in books as in reliquaries—*péris et mises en reliquaires de livres*. By aid of this starveling stock—*pauvre plante et vergette*—of the French language, he must speak delicately, movingly, if he is ever to speak so at all: that, or none, must be for him the medium of what he calls, in one of his great phrases, *le discours fatal des choses mondaines*—that discourse about affairs which decides men's fates. And it is his patriotism not to despair of it; he sees it already perfect in all elegance and beauty of words—*parfait en toute élégance et vénusté de paroles*.

Du Bellay was born in the disastrous year 1525, the year of the battle of Pavia, and the captivity of Francis the First. His parents died early, and to him, as the younger son, his mother's little estate, *ce petit Liré*, the beloved place of his birth, descended. He was brought up by a brother only a little older than himself; and left to themselves, the two boys passed their lives in day-dreams of military glory. Their education was neglected; "The time of my youth," says Du Bellay, "was lost, like the flower which no shower waters, and no hand cultivates." He was just twenty years old when the elder brother died, leaving Joachim to be the guardian of his child. It was with regret, with a shrinking sense of incapacity, that he took upon him the burden of this responsibility. Hitherto he had looked forward to the profession of a soldier, hereditary in his family. But at this time a sickness attacked him which brought him cruel sufferings, and seemed likely to be mortal. It was then for the first time that he read the Greek and Latin poets. These studies came too late to make him what he so much desired to be, a trifler in Greek and Latin verse, like so many others of his time now forgotten; instead, they made him a lover of his own homely native tongue, that poor starveling stock of the French language. It was through this fortunate short-coming in his education that he became national and modern; and he learned afterwards to look back on that wild garden of his youth with only a half regret. A certain Cardinal du Bellay was the successful member of the family, a man often employed in high official business. To him the thoughts of Joachim turned when it became necessary to choose a profession, and in 1552 he accompanied the Cardinal to Rome. He remained there nearly five years, burdened with the weight of affairs, and languishing with home-sickness. Yet it was under these circumstances that his genius yielded its best fruits. From Rome, so full of pleasurable sensation for men of an imaginative temperament such as his, with all the curiosities of the Renaissance still fresh in it, his thoughts went back painfully, longingly, to the country of the Loire, with its wide expanse of waving corn, its homely pointed roofs of grey slate, and its far-off scent of the sea. He reached home at last, but only to die there, quite suddenly, one wintry day, at the early age of thirty-five.

Much of Du Bellay's poetry illustrates rather the age and school to which he belonged than his own temper and genius. As with the writings of Ronsard and the other poets of the *Pleiad*, its interest depends not so much on the impress of individual genius upon it, as on the circumstance that it was once poetry *à la mode*, that it is part of the manner of a time—a time which made much of manner, and carried it to a high degree of perfection. It is one of the decorations of an age which threw a large part of its energy into the work of decoration. We feel a pensive pleasure in gazing on these faded adornments, and observing how a group of actual men and women pleased themselves long ago. Ronsard's poems are a kind of epitome of his age. Of one side of that age, it is true, of the strenuous, the progressive, the serious movement, which was then going on, there is little; but of the catholic side, the losing side, the forlorn hope, hardly a figure is absent. The Queen of Scots, at whose desire Ronsard published his odes, reading him in her northern prison, felt that he was bringing back to her the true flavour of her early days in the court of Catherine at the Louvre, with its exotic Italian gaieties. Those who disliked that poetry, disliked it because they found that age itself distasteful. The poetry of Malherbe[6] came, with

---

[6] François de Malherbe (1555–1628), French poet, leader of a school of clear, correct verse.

its sustained style and weighty sentiment, but with nothing that set people singing; and the lovers of such poetry saw in the poetry of the *Pleiad* only the latest trumpery of the middle age. But the time arrived when the school of Malherbe also had had its day; and the *Romanticists*, who in their eagerness for excitement, for strange music and imagery, went back to the works of the middle age, accepted the *Pleiad* too with the rest; and in that new middle age which their genius has evoked, the poetry of the *Pleiad* has found its place. At first, with Malherbe, you may think it, like the architecture, the whole mode of life, the very dresses of that time, fantastic, faded, *rococo*. But if you look long enough to understand it, to conceive its sentiment, you will find that those wanton lines have a spirit guiding their caprices. For there is *style* there; one temper has shaped the whole; and everything that has style, that has been done as no other man or age could have done it, as it could never, for all our trying, be done again, has its true value and interest. Let us dwell upon it for a moment, and try to gather from it that special flower, *ce fleur particulier*, which Ronsard himself tells us every garden has.

It is poetry not for the people, but for a confined circle, for courtiers, great lords and erudite persons, people who desire to be humoured, to gratify a certain refined voluptuousness they have in them. Ronsard loves, or dreams that he loves, a rare and peculiar type of beauty, *la petite pucelle Angevine*,[7] with golden hair and dark eyes. But he has the ambition not only of being a courtier and a lover, but a great scholar also; he is anxious about orthography, about the letter *è Grecque*, the true spelling of Latin names in French writing, and the restoration of the letter *i* to its primitive liberty—*del' i voyelle en sa première liberté*. His poetry is full of quaint, remote learning. He is just a little pedantic, true always to his own express judgment, that to be natural is not enough for one who in poetry desires to produce work worthy of immortality. And therewithal a certain number of Greek words, which charmed Ronsard and his circle by their gaiety and daintiness, and a certain air of foreign elegance about them, crept into the French language; as there were other strange words which the poets of the *Pleiad* forged for themselves, and which had only an ephemeral existence.

With this was united the desire to taste a more exquisite and various music than that of the older French verse, or of the classical poets. The music of the measured, scanned verse of Latin and Greek poetry is one thing; the music of the rhymed, unscanned verse of Villon and the old French poets, *la poésie chantée*, is another. To combine these two kinds of music in a new school of French poetry, to make verse which should scan and rhyme as well, to search out and harmonise the measure of every syllable, and unite it to the swift, flitting, swallow-like motion of rhyme, to penetrate their poetry with a double music—this was the ambition of the *Pleiad*. They are insatiable of music, they cannot have enough of it; they desire a music of greater compass perhaps than words can possibly yield, to drain out the last drops of sweetness which a certain note or accent contains.

It was Goudimel, the serious and protestant Goudimel, who set Ronsard's songs to music; but except in this eagerness for music the poets of the *Pleiad* seem never quite in earnest. The old Greek and Roman mythology, which the great Italians had found a motive so weighty and severe, becomes with them a mere toy. That "Lord of terrible aspect," *Amor*, has become Love the boy, or the babe. They are full of fine railleries; they delight in diminutives, *ondelette, fontelette, doucelette, Cassandrette*. Their loves are only half real, a vain effort to prolong the imaginative loves of the middle age beyond their natural lifetime. They write love-poems for hire. Like that party of people who tell the tales in Boccaccio's *Decameron*, they form a circle which in an age of great troubles, losses, anxieties, can amuse itself with art, poetry, intrigue. But they amuse themselves with wonderful elegance. And sometimes their gaiety becomes satiric, for, as they play, real passions insinuate themselves, and at least the reality of death. Their dejection at the thought of leaving this fair abode of our common daylight—*le beau sejour du commun jour*—is expressed by them with almost wearisome reiteration. But with this sentiment too they are able to trifle. The imagery of death serves for delicate ornament, and they weave into the airy nothingness of their verses their trite reflections on the vanity of life. Just so the grotesque details of the charnel-house nest themselves, together with birds and flowers and the fancies of the pagan mythology, in the traceries of the architecture of that time, which wantons in its graceful arabesques with the images of old age and death.

---

[7] The little Angevin virgin maid.

Ronsard became deaf at sixteen; and it was this circumstance which finally determined him to be a man of letters instead of a diplomatist, significantly, one might fancy, of a certain premature agedness, and of the tranquil, temperate sweetness appropriate to that, in the school of poetry which he founded. Its charm is that of a thing not vigorous or original, but full of the grace which comes of long study and reiterated refinements, and many steps repeated, and many angles worn down, with an exquisite faintness, *une fadeur exquise*, a certain tenuity and caducity, as for those who can bear nothing vehement or strong; for princes weary of love, like Francis the First, or of pleasure, like Henry the Third, or of action, like Henry the Fourth. Its merits are those of the old,—grace and finish, perfect in minute detail. For these people are a little jaded and have a constant desire for a subdued and delicate excitement, to warm their creeping fancy a little. They love a constant change of rhyme in poetry, and in their houses that strange, fantastic interweaving of thin, reed-like lines, which are a kind of rhetoric in architecture.

But the poetry of the *Pleiad* is true not only to the physiognomy of its age, but also to its country—*ce pays du Vendomois*—the names and scenery of which so often recur in it:—the great Loire, with its long spaces of white sand; the little river Loir; the heathy, upland country, with its scattered pools of water and waste roadsides, and retired manors, with their crazy old feudal defences half fallen into decay; *La Beauce*, where the vast rolling fields seem to anticipate the great western sea itself. It is full of the traits of that country. We see Du Bellay and Ronsard gardening, or hunting with their dogs, or watch the pastimes of a rainy day: and with all this is connected a domesticity, a homeliness and simple goodness, by which the Northern country gains upon the South. They have the love of the aged for warmth, and understand the poetry of winter; for they are not far from the Atlantic, and the west wind which comes up from it, turning the poplars white, spares not this new Italy in France. So the fireside often appears, with the pleasures of the frosty season, about the vast emblazoned chimneys of the time, and with a *bonhomie* as of little children, or old people.

It is in Du Bellay's *Olive*, a collection of sonnets in praise of a half-imaginary lady, *Sonnetz a la louange d'Olive*, that these characteristics are most abundant. Here is a perfectly crystallised example:—

> D'amour, de grace, et de haulte valeur
>   Les feux divins estoient ceinctz et les cieulx
>   S'estoient vestuz d'un manteau precieux
>   A raiz ardens de diverse couleur :
> Tout estoit plein de beauté, de bonheur,
>   La mer tranquille, et le vent gracieulx,
>   Quand celle la nasquit en ces bas lieux
>   Qui a pillé du monde tout l'honneur.
> Ell' prist son teint des beux lyz blanchissans,
>   Son chef de l'or, ses deux levres des rozes,
>   Et du soleil ses yeux replandissans :
> Le ciel usant de liberalité,
>   Mist en l'esprit ses semences encloses,
>   Son nom des Dieux prist l'immortalité.[8]

That he is thus a characteristic specimen of the poetical taste of that age, is indeed Du Bellay's chief interest. But if his work is to have the highest sort of interest, if it is to do something more than satisfy curiosity, if it is to have an æsthetic as distinct from an historical value, it is not enough for a poet to have been the true child of his age, to have conformed to its æsthetic conditions, and by so conforming to have charmed and stimulated that age; it is necessary that there should be perceptible in his work something individual, inventive, unique, the impress there of the writer's own temper and personality. This impress M. Sainte-Beuve thought he found in the *Antiquités de Rome*, and the *Regrets*, which he ranks as what has been called *poésie intime*, that intensely modern sort of poetry in which the writer has for his aim the portraiture of his own most intimate moods, and to take the reader into his confidence. That age had other instances of this intimacy of sentiment: Montaigne's *Essays* are full of it, the carvings of the church of Brou are full of it. M. Sainte-Beuve has perhaps exaggerated the influence of this quality in Du Bellay's *Regrets;* but the very name of the book has a touch of Rousseau about it, and reminds one of a whole generation of self-pitying poets in modern times. It was in the atmosphere of Rome, to him so strange and mournful, that these pale flowers grew up. For that journey to

[8] "Of love, of grace, and of lofty value, the divine fires were cloaked and the skies were vested with a precious garment of gleaming rays of diverse color, all was full of beauty and goodness, the tranquil sea and the gracious wind, when my lady was born in its soft arms, she who brought all honor to the world. She took her color from the beautiful white lilies, her hair from gold, her two lips from roses, and from the sun her dazzling eyes: heaven in its largesse sent to her spirit its riches, her name took immortality from the gods."

Italy, which he deplored as the greatest misfortune of his life, put him in full possession of his talent, and brought out all its originality. And in effect you do find intimacy, *intimité*, here. The trouble of his life is analysed, and the sentiment of it conveyed directly to our minds; not a great sorrow or passion, but only the sense of loss in passing days, the *ennui* of a dreamer who must plunge into the world's affairs, the opposition between actual life and the ideal, a longing for rest, nostalgia, home-sickness—that pre-eminently childish, but so suggestive sorrow, as significant of the final regret of all human creatures for the familiar earth and limited sky.

The feeling for landscape is often described as a modern one; still more so is that for antiquity, the sentiment of ruins. Du Bellay has this sentiment. The duration of the hard, sharp outlines of things is a grief to him and passing his wearisome days among the ruins of ancient Rome, he is consoled by the thought that all must one day end, by the sentiment of the grandeur of nothingness—*la grandeur du rien*. With a strange touch of far-off mysticism, he thinks that the great whole—*le grand tout*—into which all other things pass and lose themselves, ought itself sometimes to perish and pass away. Nothing less can relieve his weariness. From the stately aspects of Rome his thoughts went back continually to France, to the smoking chimneys of his little village, the longer twilight of the North, the soft climate of Anjou—*la douceur Angevine;* yet not so much to the real France, we may be sure, with its dark streets and roofs of rough-hewn slate, as to that other country, with slenderer towers, and more winding rivers, and trees like flowers, and with softer sunshine on more gracefully-proportioned fields and ways, which the fancy of the exile, and the pilgrim, and of the schoolboy far from home, and of those kept at home unwillingly, everywhere builds up before or behind them.

He came home at last, through the *Grisons*, by slow journeys; and there, in the cooler air of his own country, under its skies of milkier blue, the sweetest flower of his genius sprang up. There have been poets whose whole fame has rested on one poem, as Gray's on the *Elegy in a Country Churchyard*, or Ronsard's, as many critics have thought, on the eighteen lines of one famous ode. Du Bellay has almost been the poet of one poem; and this one poem of his is an Italian product transplanted into that green country of Anjou; out of the Latin verses of Andrea Navagero, into French. But it is a composition in which the matter is almost nothing, and the form almost everything; and the form of the poem as it stands, written in old French, is all Du Bellay's own. It is a song which the winnowers are supposed to sing as they winnow the corn, and they invoke the winds to lie lightly on the grain.

D'UN VANNEUR DE BLE AUX VENTS.[9]

A vous trouppe legère
Qui d'aile passagère
Par le monde volez,
Et d'un sifflant murmure
L'ombrageuse verdure
Doulcement esbranlez.

J'offre ces violettes,
Ces lis & ces fleurettes,
Et ces roses icy,
Ces vermeillettes roses
Sont freschement écloses,
Et ces œlliets aussi.

De vostre doulce haleine
Eventez ceste plaine
Eventez ce sejour;
Ce pendant que j'ahanne
A mon blè que je vanne
A la chaleur du jour.

That has, in the highest degree, the qualities, the value, of the whole Pleiad school of poetry, of the whole phase of taste from which that school derives—a certain silvery grace of fancy, nearly all the pleasure of which is in the surprise at the happy and dexterous way in which a thing slight in itself is handled. The sweetness of it is by no means to be got at by crushing, as you crush wild herbs to get at their perfume. One seems to hear the measured motion of the fans, with a child's pleasure on coming across the

[9] A graceful translation of this and some other poems of the Pléiad may be found in *Ballads and Lyrics of Old France*, by Mr. Andrew Lang. [Pater's note. Lang's translation reads: "Hymn to the Winds"—The winds are invoked by the winnowers of corn. "To you, troop so fleet, / That with winged wandering feet, / Through the wide world pass, / And with soft murmuring / Toss the green shades of spring / In woods and grass, / Lily and violet / I give, and blossoms wet, / Roses and dew; / This branch of blushing roses, / Whose fresh bud uncloses, / Wind-flowers too. / Ah, winnow with sweet breath, / Winnow the holt and heath, / Round this retreat; / Where all the golden morn / We fan the gold o' the corn, / In the sun's heat."]

incident for the first time, in one of those great barns of Du Bellay's own country, *La Beauce*, the granary of France. A sudden light transfigures some trivial thing, a weather-vane, a windmill, a winnowing fan, the dust in the barn door. A moment—and the thing has vanished, because it was pure effect; but it leaves a relish behind it, a longing that the accident may happen again.

Winckelmann

ET EGO IN ARCADIA FUI[1]

GOETHE's fragments of art-criticism contain a few pages of strange pregnancy on the character of Winckelmann. He speaks of the teacher who had made his career possible, but whom he had never seen, as of an abstract type of culture, consummate, tranquil, withdrawn already into the region of ideals, yet retaining colour from the incidents of a passionate intellectual life. He classes him with certain works of art, possessing an inexhaustible gift of suggestion, to which criticism may return again and again with renewed freshness. Hegel, in his lectures on the *Philosophy of Art*, estimating the work of his predecessors, has also passed a remarkable judgment on Winckelmann's writings:— "Winckelmann, by contemplation of the ideal works of the ancients, received a sort of inspiration, through which he opened a new sense for the study of art. He is to be regarded as one of those who, in the sphere of art, have known how to initiate a new organ for the human spirit." That it has given a new sense, that it has laid open a new organ, is the highest that can be said of any critical effort. It is interesting then to ask what kind of man it was who thus laid open a new organ. Under what conditions was that effected?

Johann Joachim Winckelmann was born at Stendal, in Brandenburg, in the year 1717. The child of a poor tradesman, he passed through many struggles in early youth, the memory of which ever remained in him as a fitful cause of dejection. In 1763, in the full emancipation of his spirit, looking over the beautiful Roman prospect, he writes—"One gets spoiled here; but God owed me this; in my youth I suffered

too much." Destined to assert and interpret the charm of the Hellenic spirit, he served first a painful apprenticeship in the tarnished intellectual world of Germany in the earlier half of the eighteenth century. Passing out of that into the happy light of the antique, he had a sense of exhilaration almost physical. We find him as a child in the dusky precincts of a German school, hungrily feeding on a few colourless books. The master of this school grows blind; Winckelmann becomes his *famulus*. The old man would have had him study theology. Winckelmann, free of the master's library, chooses rather to become familiar with the Greek classics. Herodotus and Homer win, with their "vowelled" Greek, his warmest enthusiasm; whole nights of fever are devoted to them; disturbing dreams of an Odyssey of his own come to him. "He felt in himself," says Madame de Staël, "an ardent attraction towards the south. In German imaginations even now traces are often to be found of that love of the sun, that weariness of the North (*cette fatigue du nord*), which carried the northern peoples away into the countries of the South. A fine sky brings to birth sentiments not unlike the love of one's Fatherland."

To most of us, after all our steps towards it, the antique world, in spite of its intense outlines, its own perfect self-expression, still remains faint and remote. To him, closely limited except on the side of the ideal, building for his dark poverty "a house not made with hands,"[2] it early came to seem more real than the present. In the fantastic plans of foreign travel continually passing through his mind, to Egypt, for instance, and to France, there seems always to be rather a wistful sense of something lost to be regained, than the desire of discovering anything new. Goethe has told us how, in his eagerness actually to handle the antique, he became interested in the insignificant vestiges of it which the neighbourhood of Strasburg afforded. So we hear of Winckelmann's boyish antiquarian wanderings among the ugly Brandenburg sandhills. Such a conformity between himself and Winckelmann, Goethe would have gladly noted.

At twenty-one he enters the University of Halle, to study theology, as his friends desire; instead he becomes the enthusiastic translator of Herodotus. The condition of Greek learning in German schools and universities had fallen, and there were no professors at Halle who could satisfy his sharp, intellectual craving. Of his

---

[1] "And I was in Arcadia," a famous motto of the pastoral tradition.   [2] II Corinthians 5:1.

professional education he always speaks with scorn, claiming to have been his own teacher from first to last. His appointed teachers did not perceive that a new source of culture was within their hands. *Homo vagus et inconstans!* [3]— one of them pedantically reports of the future pilgrim to Rome, unaware on which side his irony was whetted. When professional education confers nothing but irritation on a Schiller, no one ought to be surprised; for Schiller, and such as he, are primarily spiritual adventurers. But that Winckelmann, the votary of the gravest of intellectual traditions, should get nothing but an attempt at suppression from the professional guardians of learning, is what may well surprise us.

In 1743 he became master of a school at Seehausen. This was the most wearisome period of his life. Notwithstanding a success in dealing with children, which seems to testify to something simple and primeval in his nature, he found the work of teaching very depressing. Engaged in this work, he writes that he still has within him a longing desire to attain to the knowledge of beauty—*sehnlich wünschte zur Kenntniss des Schönen zu gelangen.* He had to shorten his nights, sleeping only four hours, to gain time for reading. And here Winckelmann made a step forward in culture. He multiplied his intellectual force by detaching from it all flaccid interests. He renounced mathematics and law, in which his reading had been considerable,—all but the literature of the arts. Nothing was to enter into his life unpenetrated by its central enthusiasm. At this time he undergoes the charm of Voltaire. Voltaire belongs to that flimsier, more artificial, classical tradition, which Winckelmann was one day to supplant, by the clear ring, the eternal outline, of the genuine antique. But it proves the authority of such a gift as Voltaire's that it allures and wins even those born to supplant it. Voltaire's impression on Winckelmann was never effaced; and it gave him a consideration for French literature which contrasts with his contempt for the literary products of Germany. German literature transformed, siderealised, as we see it in Goethe, reckons Winckelmann among its initiators. But Germany at that time presented nothing in which he could have anticipated *Iphigenie*, and the formation of an effective classical tradition in German literature.

Under this purely literary influence, Winckelmann protests against Christian Wolff [4] and the philosophers. Goethe, in speaking of this protest, alludes to his own obligations to Emmanuel Kant. Kant's influence over the culture of Goethe, which he tells us could not have been resisted by him without loss, consisted in a severe limitation to the concrete. But he adds, that in born antiquaries, like Winckelmann, a constant handling of the antique, with its eternal outline, maintains that limitation as effectually as a critical philosophy. Plato, however, saved so often for his redeeming literary manner, is excepted from Winckelmann's proscription of the philosophers. The modern student most often meets Plato on that side which seems to pass beyond Plato into a world no longer pagan, based upon the conception of a spiritual life. But the element of affinity which he presents to Winckelmann is that which is wholly Greek, and alien from the Christian world, represented by that group of brilliant youths in the *Lysis*, [5] still uninfected by any spiritual sickness, finding the end of all endeavour in the aspects of the human form, the continual stir and motion of a comely human life.

This new-found interest in Plato's dialogues could not fail to increase his desire to visit the countries of the classical tradition. "It is my misfortune," he writes, "that I was not born to great place, wherein I might have had cultivation, and the opportunity of following my instinct and forming myself." A visit to Rome probably was already designed, and he silently preparing for it. Count Bünau, the author of a historical work then of note, had collected at Nöthenitz a valuable library, now part of the library of Dresden. In 1748 Winckelmann wrote to Bünau in halting French:—He is emboldened, he says, by Bünau's indulgence for needy men of letters. He desires only to devote himself to study, having never allowed himself to be dazzled by favourable prospects in the Church. He hints at his doubtful position "in a metaphysical age, by which humane literature is trampled under foot. At present," he goes on, "little value is set on Greek literature, to which I have devoted myself so far as I could penetrate, when good books are so scarce and expensive." Finally, he desires a place in some corner of Bünau's library. "Perhaps, at some future time, I shall become more useful to the public, if, drawn from ob-

---

[3] A man vague and inconstant.
[4] Johann Christian Wolff (1679–1754), German rationalist philosopher.   [5] Platonic dialogue.

scurity in whatever way, I can find means to maintain myself in the capital."

Soon afterwards we find Winckelmann in the library at Nöthenitz. Thence he made many visits to the collection of antiquities at Dresden. He became acquainted with many artists, above all with Oeser, Goethe's future friend and master, who, uniting a high culture with the practical knowledge of art, was fitted to minister to Wickelmann's culture. And now a new channel of communion with the Greek life was opened for him. Hitherto he had handled the words only of Greek poetry, stirred indeed and roused by them, yet divining beyond the words some unexpressed pulsation of sensuous life. Suddenly he is in contact with that life, still fervent in the relics of plastic art. Filled as our culture is with the classical spirit, we can hardly imagine how deeply the human mind was moved, when, at the Renaissance, in the midst of a frozen world, the buried fire of ancient art rose up from under the soil. Winckelmann here reproduces for us the earlier sentiment of the Renaissance. On a sudden the imagination feels itself free. How facile and direct, it seems to say, is this life of the senses and the understanding, when once we have apprehended it! Here, surely, is that more liberal mode of life we have been seeking so long, so near to us all the while. How mistaken and roundabout have been our efforts to reach it by mystic passion, and monastic reverie; how they have deflowered the flesh; how little have they really emancipated us! Hermione[6] melts from her stony posture, and the lost proportions of life right themselves. Here, then, in vivid realisation we see the native tendency of Wincklemann to escape from abstract theory to intuition, to the exercise of sight and touch. Lessing, in the *Laocoon*, has theorised finely on the relation of poetry to sculpture; and philosophy may give us theoretical reasons why not poetry but sculpture should be the most sincere and exact expression of the Greek ideal. By a happy, unperplexed dexterity, Winckelmann solves the question in the concrete. It is what Goethe calls his *Gewahrwerden der griechischen Kunst*, his *finding* of Greek art.

Through the tumultuous richness of Goethe's culture, the influence of Winckelmann is always discernible, as the strong, regulative undercurrent of a clear, antique motive. "One learns nothing from him," he says to Eckermann, "but

one becomes something." If we ask what the secret of this influence was, Goethe himself will tell us—wholeness, unity with one's self, intellectual integrity. And yet these expressions, because they fit Goethe, with his universal culture, so well, seem hardly to describe the narrow, exclusive interest of Winckelmann. Doubtless Winckelmann's perfection is a narrow perfection: his feverish nursing of the one motive of his life is a contrast to Goethe's various energy. But what affected Goethe, what instructed him and ministered to his culture, was the integrity, the truth to its type, of the given force. The development of this force was the single interest of Winckelmann, unembarrassed by anything else in him. Other interests, practical or intellectual, those slighter talents and motives not supreme, which in most men are the waste part of nature, and drain away their vitality, he plucked out and cast from him. The protracted longing of his youth is not a vague, romantic longing: he knows what he longs for, what he wills. Within its severe limits his enthusiasm burns like lava. "You know," says Lavater,[7] speaking of Winckelmann's countenance, "that I consider ardour and indifference by no means incompatible in the same character. If ever there was a striking instance of that union, it is in the countenance before us." "A lowly childhood," says Goethe, "insufficient instruction in youth, broken, distracted studies in early manhood, the burden of school-keeping! He was thirty years old before he enjoyed a single favour of fortune: but so soon as he had attained to an adequate condition of freedom, he appears before us consummate and entire, complete in the ancient sense."

But his hair is turning grey, and he has not yet reached the south. The Saxon court had become Roman Catholic, and the way to favour at Dresden was through Roman ecclesiastics. Probably the thought of a profession of the papal religion was not new to Winckelmann. At one time he had thought of begging his way to Rome, from cloister to cloister, under the pretence of a disposition to change his faith. In 1751, the papal *nuncio*, Archinto, was one of the visitors at Nöthenitz. He suggested Rome as the fitting stage for Winckelmann's accomplishments, and held out the hope of a place in the Pope's library. Cardinal Passionei, charmed with Winckelmann's beautiful Greek writing, was

---

[6] See *The Winter's Tale.*

[7] Johann Kaspar Lavater (1741–1801), Swiss theologian and poet, noted also for studies in physiognomy.

ready to play the part of Mæcenas, if the indispensable change were made. Winckelmann
accepted the bribe, and visited the *nuncio* at
Dresden. Unquiet still at the word "profession,"
not without a struggle, he joined the Roman
Church, July the 11th, 1754.

Goethe boldly pleads that Winckelmann was
a pagan, that the landmarks of Christendom
meant nothing to him. It is clear that he intended to deceive no one by his disguise; fears
of the inquisition are sometimes visible during
his life in Rome; he entered Rome notoriously
with the works of Voltaire in his possession; the
thought of what Count Bünau might be thinking
of him seems to have been his greatest difficulty.
On the other hand, he may have had a sense of
a certain antique and as it were pagan grandeur
in the Roman Catholic religion. Turning from
the crabbed Protestantism, which had been the
ennui of his youth, he might reflect that while
Rome had reconciled itself to the Renaissance,
the Protestant principle in art had cut off
Germany from the supreme tradition of beauty.
And yet to that transparent nature, with its
simplicity as of the earlier world, the loss of
absolute sincerity must have been a real loss.
Goethe understands that Winckelmann had made
this sacrifice. Yet at the bar of the highest
criticism, perhaps, Winckelmann may be absolved. The insincerity of his religious profession
was only one incident of a culture in which the
moral instinct, like the religious or political, was
merged in the artistic. But then the artistic
interest was that, by desperate faithfulness to
which Winckelmann was saved from the mediocrity, which, breaking through no bounds, moves
ever in a bloodless routine, and misses its one
chance in the life of the spirit and the intellect.
There have been instances of culture developed
by every high motive in turn, and yet intense at
every point; and the aim of our culture should
be to attain not only as intense but as complete
a life as possible. But often the higher life is
only possible at all, on condition of the selection
of that in which one's motive is native and strong;
and this selection involves the renunciation of a
crown reserved for others. Which is better?—
to lay open a new sense, to initiate a new organ
for the human spirit, or to cultivate many types
of perfection up to a point which leaves us still
beyond the range of their transforming power?
Savonarola is one type of success; Winckelmann
is another; criticism can reject neither, because

each is true to itself. Winckelmann himself
explains the motive of his life when he says, "It
will be my highest reward, if posterity acknowledges that I have written worthily."

For a time he remained at Dresden. There
his first book appeared, *Thoughts on the Imitation
of Greek Works of Art in Painting and Sculpture.*
Full of obscurities as it was, obscurities which
baffled but did not offend Goethe when he first
turned to art-criticism, its purpose was direct—
an appeal from the artificial classicism of the
day to the study of the antique. The book was
well received, and a pension supplied through
the king's confessor. In September 1755 he
started for Rome, in the company of a young
Jesuit. He was introduced to Raphael Mengs,
a painter then of note, and found a home near
him, in the artists' quarter, in a place where he
could "overlook, far and wide, the eternal city."
At first he was perplexed with the sense of being
a stranger on what was to him, spiritually, native
soil. "Unhappily," he cries in French, often
selected by him as the vehicle of strong feeling,
"I am one of those whom the Greeks call
ὀψιμαθεῖς.[8]—I have come into the world and
into Italy too late." More than thirty years
afterwards, Goethe also, after many aspirations
and severe preparation of mind, visited Italy. In
early manhood, just as he too was *finding* Greek art,
the rumour of that true artist's life of Winckelmann in Italy had strongly moved him. At
Rome, spending a whole year drawing from the
antique, in preparation for *Iphigenie*, he finds the
stimulus of Winckelmann's memory ever active.
Winckelmann's Roman life was simple, primeval,
Greek. His delicate constitution permitted him
the use only of bread and wine. Condemned by
many as a renegade, he had no desire for places
of honour, but only to see his merits acknowledged, and existence assured to him. He was
simple without being niggardly; he desired to
be neither poor nor rich.

Winckelmann's first years in Rome present all
the elements of an intellectual situation of the
highest interest. The beating of the soul against
its bars, the sombre aspect, the alien traditions,
the still barbarous literature of Germany, are
afar off; before him are adequate conditions of
culture, the sacred soil itself, the first tokens of
the advent of the new German literature, with
its broad horizons, its boundless intellectual
promise. Dante, passing from the darkness of
the *Inferno*, is filled with a sharp and joyful sense

[8] Born too late.

of light, which makes him deal with it, in the opening of the *Purgatorio*, in a wonderfully touching and penetrative way. Hellenism, which is the principle pre-eminently of intellectual light (our modern culture may have more colour, the medieval spirit greater heat and profundity, but Hellenism is pre-eminent for light), has always been most effectively conceived by those who have crept into it out of an intellectual world in which the sombre elements predominate. So it had been in the ages of the Renaissance. This repression, removed at last, gave force and glow to Winckelmann's native affinity to the Hellenic spirit. "There had been known before him," says Madame de Staël, "learned men who might be consulted like books; but no one had, if I may say so, made himself a pagan for the purpose of penetrating antiquity." "One is always a poor executant of conceptions not one's own."—*On exécute mal ce qu'on n'a pas conçu soi-même*[9]—are true in their measure of every genuine en-enthusiasm. Enthusiasm,—that, in the broad Platonic sense of the *Phaedrus*, was the secret of his divinatory power over the Hellenic world. This enthusiasm, dependent as it is to a great degree on bodily temperament, has a power of re-enforcing the purer emotions of the intellect with an almost physical excitement. That his affinity with Hellenism was not merely intellectual, that the subtler threads of temperament were inwoven in it, is proved by his romantic, fervent friendships with young men. He has known, he says, many young men more beautiful than Guido's archangel. These friendships, bringing him into contact with the pride of human form, and staining the thoughts with its bloom, perfected his reconciliation to the spirit of Greek sculpture. A letter on taste, addressed from Rome to a young nobleman, Friedrich von Berg, is the record of such a friendship.

"I shall excuse my delay," he begins, "in fulfilling my promise of an essay on the taste for beauty in works of art, in the words of Pindar. He says to Agesidamus, a youth of Locri—ἰδέᾳ τε καλόν, ὥρᾳ τε κεκραμένον[10]—whom he had kept waiting for an intended ode, that a debt paid with usury is the end of reproach. This may win your good-nature on behalf of my present essay, which has turned out far more detailed and circumstantial than I had at first intended.

"It is from yourself that the subject is taken.

Our intercourse has been short, too short both for you and me; but the first time I saw you, the affinity of our spirits was revealed to me: your culture proved that my hope was not groundless; and I found in a beautiful body a soul created for nobleness, gifted with the sense of beauty. My parting from you was therefore one of the most painful in my life; and that this feeling continues our common friend is witness, for your separation from me leaves me no hope of seeing you again. Let this essay be a memorial of our friendship, which, on my side, is free from every selfish motive, and ever remains subject and dedicate to yourself alone."

The following passage is characteristic—

"As it is confessedly the beauty of man which is to be conceived under one general idea, so I have noticed that those who are observant of beauty only in women, and are moved little or not at all by the beauty of men, seldom have an impartial, vital, inborn instinct for beauty in art. To such persons the beauty of Greek art will ever seem wanting, because its supreme beauty is rather male than female. But the beauty of art demands a high sensibility than the beauty of nature, because the beauty of art, like tears shed at a play, gives no pain, is without life, and must be awakened and repaired by culture. Now, as the spirit of culture is much more ardent in youth than in manhood, the instinct of which I am speaking must be exercised and directed to what is beautiful, before that age is reached, at which one would be afraid to confess that one had no taste for it."

Certainly, of that beauty of living form which regulated Winckelmann's friendships, it could not be said that it gave no pain. One notable friendship, the fortune of which we may trace through his letters, begins with an antique, chivalrous letter in French, and ends noisly in a burst of angry fire. Far from reaching the quietism, the bland indifference of art, such attachments are nevertheless more susceptible than any others of equal strength of a purely intellectual culture. Of passion, of physical excitement, they contain only just so much as stimulates the eye to the finest delicacies of colour and form. These friendships, often the caprices of a moment, make Winckelmann's letters, with their troubled colouring, an instructive but bizarre addition to the *History of Art*, that shrine of grave

---

[9] Words of Charlotte Corday before the *Convention*. [Pater's note. "One performs ill that which one has not conceived himself."]

[10] "Beautiful of aspect and gifted with every kind of charm."

and mellow light around the mute Olympian family. The impression which Winckelmann's literary life conveyed to those about him was that of excitement, intuition, inspiration, rather than the contemplative evolution of general principles. The quick, susceptible enthusiast, betraying his temperament even in appearance, by his olive complexion, his deep-seated, piercing eyes, his rapid movements, apprehended the subtlest principles of the Hellenic manner, not through the understanding, but by instinct or touch. A German biographer of Winckelmann has compared him to Columbus. That is not the aptest of comparisons; but it reminds one of a passage in which Edgar Quinet[11] describes the great discoverer's famous voyage. His science was often at fault; but he had a way of estimating at once the slightest indication of land, in a floating weed or passing bird; he seemed actually to come nearer to nature than other men. And that world in which others had moved with so much embarrassment, seems to call out in Winckelmann new senses fitted to deal with it. He is in touch with it; it penetrates him, and becomes part of his temperament. He remodels his writings with constant renewal of insight; he catches the thread of a whole sequence of laws in some hollowing of the hand, or dividing of the hair; he seems to realise that fancy of the reminiscence of a forgotten knowledge hidden for a time in the mind itself; as if the mind of one, lover and philosopher at once in some phase of pre-existence—φιλοσοφήσας πότε μέτ' ἔρωτος—fallen into a new cycle, were beginning its intellectual career over again, yet with a certain power of anticipating its results. So comes the truth of Goethe's judgments on his works; they are a life, a living thing, designed for those who are alive—*ein Lebendiges für die Lebendigen geschrieben, ein Leben selbst.*

In 1758 Cardinal Albani, who had formed in his Roman villa a precious collection of antiquities, became Winckelmann's patron. Pompeii had just opened its treasures; Winckelmann gathered its first-fruits. But his plan of a visit to Greece remained unfulfilled. From his first arrival in Rome he had kept the *History of Ancient Art* ever in view. All his other writings were a preparation for that. It appeared, finally, in 1764; but even after its publication Winckelmann was still employed in perfecting it. It is since his time that many of the most significant examples of Greek art have been submitted to criticism. He had seen little or nothing of what we ascribe to the age of Pheidias; and his conception of Greek art tends, therefore, to put the mere elegance of the imperial society of ancient Rome in place of the severe and chastened grace of the *palaestra*. For the most part he had to penetrate to Greek art through copies, imitations, and later Roman art itself; and it is not surprising that this turbid medium has left in Winckelmann's actual results much that a more privileged criticism can correct.

He had been twelve years in Rome. Admiring Germany had made many calls to him. At last, in 1768, he set out to revisit the country of his birth; and as he left Rome, a strange, inverted home-sickness, a strange reluctance to leave it at all, came over him. He reached Vienna. There he was loaded with honours and presents: other cities were awaiting him. Goethe, then nineteen years old, studying art at Leipsic, was expecting his coming, with that wistful eagerness which marked his youth, when the news of Winckelmann's murder arrived. All his "weariness of the North" had revived with double force. He left Vienna, intending to hasten back to Rome, and at Trieste a delay of a few days occurred. With characteristic openness, Winckelmann had confided his plans to a fellow-traveller, a man named Arcangeli, and had shown him the gold medals received at Vienna. Arcangeli's avarice was aroused. One morning he entered Winckelmann's room, under pretence of taking leave. Winckelmann was then writing "memoranda for the future editor of the *History of Art*," still seeking the perfection of his great work. Arcangeli begged to see the medals once more. As Winckelmann stooped down to take them from the chest, a cord was thrown round his neck. Some time afterwards, a child with whose companionship Winckelmann had beguiled his delay, knocked at the door, and receiving no answer, gave the alarm. Winckelmann was found dangerously wounded, and died a few hours later, after receiving the last sacraments. It seemed as if the gods, in reward for his devotion to them, had given him a death which, for its swiftness and its opportunity, he might well have desired. "He has," says Goethe, "the advantage of figuring in the memory of posterity, as one eternally able and strong; for the image in which one leaves the world is that in which one moves among the shadows." Yet, perhaps, it is not fanciful to regret that his proposed

---

[11] Edgar Quinet (1803–75), French author and politician.

meeting with Goethe never took place. Goethe, then in all the pregnancy of his wonderful youth still unruffled by the "press and storm" of his earlier manhood, was awaiting Winckelmann with a curiosity of the worthiest kind. As it was, Winckelmann became to him something like what Virgil was to Dante. And Winckelmann, with his fiery friendships, had reached that age and that period of culture at which emotions hitherto fitful, sometimes concentrate themselves in a vital, unchangeable relationship. German literary history seems to have lost the chance of one of those famous friendships, the very tradition of which becomes a stimulus to culture, and exercises an imperishable influence.

In one of the frescoes of the Vatican, Raphael has commemorated the tradition of the Catholic religion. Against a space of tranquil sky, broken in upon by the beatific vision, are ranged the great personages of Christian history, with the Sacrament in the midst. Another fresco of Raphael in the same apartment presents a very different company, Dante alone appearing in both. Surrounded by the muses of Greek mythology, under a thicket of laurel, sits Apollo, with the sources of Castalia at his feet. On either side are grouped those on whom the spirit of Apollo descended, the classical and Renaissance poets, to whom the waters of Castalia come down, a river making glad this other "city of God." In this fresco it is the classical tradition, the orthodoxy of taste, that Raphael commemorates. Winckelmann's intellectual history authenticates the claims of this tradition in human culture. In the countries where that tradition arose, where it still lurked about its own artistic relics, and changes of language had not broken its continuity, national pride might sometimes light up anew an enthusiasm for it. Aliens might imitate that enthusiasm, and classicism become from time to time an intellectual fashion. But Winckelmann was not further removed by language, than by local aspects and associations, from those vestiges of the classical spirit; and he lived at a time when, in Germany, classical studies were out of favour. Yet, remote in time and place, he feels after the Hellenic world, divines those channels of ancient art, in which its life still circulates, and, like Scyles, the half-barbarous yet Hellenising king, in the beautiful story of Herodotus, is irresistibly attracted by it. This testimony to the authority of the Hellenic tradition, its fitness to satisfy some vital requirement of the intellect, which Winckel-

mann contributes as a solitary man of genius, is offered also by the general history of the mind. The spiritual forces of the past, which have prompted and informed the culture of a succeeding age, live, indeed, within that culture, but with an absorbed, underground life. The Hellenic element alone has not been so absorbed, or content with this underground life; from time to time it has started to the surface; culture has been drawn back to its sources to be clarified and corrected. Hellenism is not merely an absorbed element in our intellectual life; it is a conscious tradition in it.

Again, individual genius works ever under conditions of time and place: its products are coloured by the varying aspects of nature, and type of human form, and outward manners of life. There is thus an element of change in art; criticism must never for a moment forget that "the artist is the child of his time." But beside these conditions of time and place, and independent of them, there is also an element of permanence, a standard of taste, which genius confesses. This standard is maintained in a purely intellectual tradition. It acts upon the artist, not as one of the influences of his own age, but through those artistic products of the previous generation which first excited, while they directed into a particular channel, his sense of beauty. The supreme artistic products of succeeding generations thus form a series of elevated points, taking each from each the reflection of a strange light, the source of which is not in the atmosphere around and above them, but in a stage of society remote from ours. The standard of taste, then, was fixed in Greece, at a definite historical period. A tradition for all succeeding generations, it originates in a spontaneous growth out of the influences of Greek society. What were the conditions under which this ideal, this standard of artistic orthodoxy, was generated? How was Greece enabled to force its thought upon Europe?

Greek art, when we first catch sight of it, is entangled with Greek religion. We are accustomed to think of Greek religion as the religion of art and beauty, the religion of which the Olympian Zeus and the Athena Polias are the idols, the poems of Homer the sacred books. Thus Cardinal Newman speaks of "the classical polytheism which was gay and graceful, as was natural in a civilised age." Yet such a view is only a partial one. In it the eye is fixed on the sharp, bright edge of high Hellenic culture, but loses sight of the sombre world across which it strikes. Greek religion, where we can observe it most distinctly, is at once a magnificent ritualistic system, and a cycle of poetical conceptions. Religions, as they grow by natural laws out of man's life, are modified by whatever modifies his life. They brighten under a bright sky, they become liberal as the social range widens, they grow intense and shrill in the clefts of human life, where the spirit is narrow and confined, and the stars are visible at noonday; and a fine analysis of these differences is one of the gravest functions of religious criticism. Still, the broad foundation, in mere human nature, of all religions as they exist for the greatest number, is a universal pagan sentiment, a paganism which existed before the Greek religion, and has lingered far onward into the Christian world, ineradicable, like some persistent vegetable growth, because its seed is an element of the very soil out of which it springs.

This pagan sentiment measures the sadness with which the human mind is filled, whenever its thoughts wander far from what is here, and now. It is beset by notions of irresistible natural powers, for the most part ranged against man, but the secret also of his fortune, making the earth golden and the grape fiery for him. He makes gods in his own image, gods smiling and flower-crowned, or bleeding by some sad fatality, to console him by their wounds, never closed from generation to generation. It is with a rush of home-sickness that the thought of death presents itself. He would remain at home for ever on the earth if he could. As it loses its colour and the senses fail, he clings ever closer to it; but since the mouldering of bones and flesh must go on to the end, he is careful for charms and talismans, which may chance to have some friendly power in them, when the inevitable shipwreck comes. Such sentiment is a part of the eternal basis of all religions, modified indeed by changes of time and place, but indestructible, because its root is so deep in the earth of man's nature. The breath of religious initiators passes over them; a few "rise up with wings as eagles,"[12] but the broad level of religious life is not permanently changed. Religious progress, like all purely spritiual progress, is confined to a few. This sentiment attaches itself in the earliest times to certain usages of partriarchal life, the kindling of fire, the washing of the body, the slaughter of the flock, the gathering of harvest, holidays and dances. Here are the beginnings of a ritual, at first as occasional and unfixed as the sentiment

which it expresses, but destined to become the permanent element of religious life. The usages of patriarchal life change; but this germ of ritual remains, promoted now with a consciously religious motive, losing its domestic character, and therefore becoming more and more inexplicable with each generation. Such pagan worship, in spite of local variations, essentially one, is an element in all religions. It is the anodyne which the religious principle, like one administering opiates to the incurable, has added to the law which makes life sombre for the vast majority of mankind.

More definite religious conceptions come from other sources, and fix themselves upon this ritual in various ways, changing it, and giving it new meanings. In Greece they were derived from mythology, itself not due to a religious source at all, but developing in the course of time into a body of religious conceptions, entirely human in form and character. To the unprogressive ritual element it brought these conceptions, itself—ἡ πτεροῦ δύναμις, the power of the wing—an element of refinement, of ascension, with the promise of an endless destiny. While the ritual remains unchanged, the æsthetic element, only accidentally connected with it, expands with the freedom and mobility of the things of the intellect. Always, the fixed element is the religious observance; the fluid, unfixed element is the myth, the religious conception. This religion is itself pagan, and has in any broad view of it the pagan sadness. It does not at once, and for the majority, become the higher Hellenic religion. The country people, of course, cherish the unlovely idols of an earlier time, such as those which Pausanias found still devoutly preserved in Arcadia. Athenæus tells the story of one who, coming to a temple of Latona, had expected to find some worthy presentment of the mother of Apollo, and laughed on seeing only a shapeless wooden figure. The wilder people have wilder gods, which, however, in Athens, or Corinth, or Lacedæmon, changing ever with the worshippers in whom they live and move and have their being, borrow something of the lordliness and distinction of human nature there. Greek religion too has its mendicants, its purifications, its antinomain mysticism, its garments offered to the gods, its statues worn with kissing, its exaggerated superstitions for the vulgar only, its worship of sorrow, its *addolorata*, its mournful mysteries. Scarcely a wild or melancholy note of the medieval church but was

---

[12] Isaiah 40:31.

anticipated by Greek polytheism! What should we have thought of the vertiginous prophetess at the very centre of Greek religion? The supreme Hellenic culture is a sharp edge of light across this gloom. The fiery, stupefying wine becomes in a happier climate clear and exhilarating. The Dorian worship of Apollo, rational, chastened, debonair, with his unbroken daylight, always opposed to the sad Chthonian divinities, is the aspiring element, by force and spring of which Greek religion sublimes itself. Out of Greek religion, under happy conditions, arises Greek art, to minister to human culture. It was the privilege of Greek religion to be able to transform itself into an artistic ideal.

For the thoughts of the Greeks about themselves, and their relation to the world generally, were ever in the happiest readiness to be transformed into objects for the senses. In this lies the main distinction between Greek art and the mystical art of the Christian middle age, which is always struggling to express thoughts beyond itself. Take, for instance, a characteristic work of the middle age, Angelico's *Coronation of the Virgin*, in the cloister of *Saint Mark's* at Florence. In some strange halo of a moon Jesus and the Virgin Mother are seated, clad in mystical white raiment, half shroud, half priestly linen. Jesus, with rosy nimbus and the long pale hair—*tanquam lana alba et tanquam nix*—of the figure in the Apocalypse, with slender finger-tips is setting a crown of pearl on the head of Mary, who, corpse-like in her refinement, is bending forward to receive it, the light lying like snow upon her forehead. Certainly, it cannot be said of Angelico's fresco that it throws into a sensible form our highest thoughts about man and his relation to the world; but it did not do this adequately even for Angelico. For him, all that is outward or sensible in his work—the hair like wool, the rosy nimbus, the crown of pearl—is only the symbol or type of a really inexpressible world, to which he wishes to direct the thoughts; he would have shrunk from the notion that what the eye apprehended was all. Such forms of art, then, are inadequate to the matter they clothe; they remain ever below its level. Something of this kind is true also of oriental art. As in the middle age from an exaggerated inwardness, so in the East from a vagueness, a want of definition, in thought, the matter presented to art is unmanageable, and the forms of sense struggle vainly with it. The many-headed gods of the East, the orientalised, many-breasted Diana of Ephesus, like Angelico's fresco, are at best over-charged symbols, a means of hinting at an idea which art cannot fitly or completely express, which still remains in the world of shadows.

But take a work of Greek art,—the Venus of Melos. That is in no sense a symbol, a suggestion, of anything beyond its own victorious fairness. The mind begins and ends with the finite image, yet loses no part of the spiritual motive. That motive is not lightly and loosely attached to the sensuous form, as its meaning to an allegory, but saturates and is identical with it. The Greek mind had advanced to a particular stage of self-reflexion, but was careful not to pass beyond it. In oriental thought there is a vague conception of life everywhere, but no true appreciation of itself by the mind, no knowledge of the distinction of man's nature: in its consciousness of itself, humanity is still confused with the fantastic, indeterminate life of the animal and vegetable world. In Greek thought, on the other hand, the "lordship of the soul" is recognised; that lordship gives authority and divinity to human eyes and hands and feet; inanimate nature is thrown into the background. But just there Greek thought finds its happy limit; it has not yet become too inward; the mind has not yet learned to boast its independence of the flesh; the spirit has not yet absorbed everything with its emotions, nor reflected its own colour everywhere. It has indeed committed itself to a train of reflexion which must end in defiance of form, of all that is outward, in an exaggerated idealism. But that end is still distant: it has not yet plunged into the depths of religious mysticism.

This ideal art, in which the thought does not outstrip or lie beyond the proper range of its sensible embodiment, could not have arisen out of a phase of life that was uncomely or poor. That delicate pause in Greek reflexion was joined, by some supreme good luck, to the perfect animal nature of the Greeks. Here are the two conditions of an artistic ideal. The influences which perfected the animal nature of the Greeks are part of the process by which "the ideal" was evolved. Those "Mothers" who, in the second part of *Faust*, mould and remould the typical forms that appear in human history, preside, at the beginning of Greek culture, over such a concourse of happy physical conditions as ever generates by natural laws some rare type of intellectual or spiritual life. That delicate air, "nimbly and sweetly recommending itself" to the senses, the finer aspects of nature, the finer lime and clay of the human form, and modelling of the dainty framework of the human countenance:—these are the good luck of the Greek when he enters upon life. Beauty becomes a distinction, like genius, or noble place.

"By no people," says Winckelmann, "has beauty been so highly esteemed as by the Greeks. The priests of a youthful Jupiter at Ægæ, of the Ismenian Apollo, and the priest who at Tangara led the procession of Mercury, bearing a lamb upon his shoulders, were always youths to whom the prize of beauty had been awarded. The citizens of Egesta erected a monument to a certain Philip, who was not their fellow-citizen, but of Croton, for his distinguished beauty; and the people made offerings at it. In an ancient song, ascribed to Simonides or Epicharmus, of four wishes, the first was health, the second beauty. And as beauty was so longed for and prized by the Greeks, every beautiful person sought to become known to the whole people by this distinction, and above all to approve himself to the artists, because they awarded the prize; and this was for the artists an occasion for having supreme beauty ever before their eyes. Beauty even gave a right to fame; and we find in Greek histories the most beautiful people distinguished. Some were famous for the beauty of one single part of their form; as Demetrius Phalereus, for his beautiful eyebrows, was called *Charito belpharos*. It seems even to have been thought that the procreation of beautiful children might be promoted by prizes. This is shown by the existence of contests for beauty, which in ancient times were established by Cypselus, King of Arcadia, by the river Alpheus; and, at the feast of Philæ, a prize was offered to the youths for the deftest kiss. This was decided by an umpire; as also at Megara, by the grave of Diocles. At Sparta, and at Lesbos, in the temple of Juno, and among the Parrhasii, there were contests for beauty among women. The general esteem for beauty went so far, that the Spartan women set up in their bedchambers a Nireus, a Narcissus, or a Hyacinth, that they might bear beautiful children."

So, from a few stray antiquarianisms, a few faces cast up sharply from the waves, Winckelmann, as his manner was, divines the temperament of the antique world, and that in which it had delight. It has passed away with that distant age, and we may venture to dwell upon it. What sharpness and reality it has is the sharpness and reality of suddenly arrested life. The Greek system of gymnastics originated as part of a religious ritual. The worshipper was to recom-

mend himself to the gods by becoming fleet and fair, white and red, like them. The beauty of the *palaestra*, and the beauty of the artist's workshop, reacted on one another. The youth tried to rival his gods; and his increased beauty passed back into them.—"I take the gods to witness, I had rather have a fair body than a king's crown"— Ὄμνυμι πάντας θεοὺς μὴ ἑλέσθαι ἂν τήν βασιλέως ἀρχὴν ἀντὶ τοῦ καλὸς εἶναι.—that is the form in which one age of the world chose the higher life.—A perfect world, if the gods could have seemed for ever only fleet and fair, white and red! Let us not regret that this unperplexed youth of humanity, satisfied with the vision of itself, passed, at the due moment, into a mournful maturity; for already the deep joy was in store for the spirit, of finding the ideal of that youth still red with life in the grave.

It followed that the Greek ideal expressed itself pre-eminently in sculpture. All art has a sensuous element, colour, form, sound—in poetry a dexterous recalling of these, together with the profound, joyful sensuousness of motion, and each of them may be a medium for the ideal: it is partly accident which in any individual case makes the born artist, poet, or painter rather than sculptor. But as the mind itself has had an historical development, one form of art, by the very limitations of its material, may be more adequate than another for the expression of any one phase of that development. Different attitudes of the imagination have a native affinity with different types of sensuous form, so that they combine together, with completeness and ease. The arts may thus be ranged in a series, which corresponds to a series of developments in the human mind itself. Architecture, which begins in a practical need, can only express by vague hint or symbol the spirit or mind of the artist. He closes his sadness over him, or wanders in the perplexed intricacies of things, or projects his purpose from him clean-cut and sincere, or bares himself to the sunlight. But these spiritualities, felt rather than seen, can but lurk about architectural form as volatile effects, to be gathered from it by reflexion. Their expression is, indeed, not really sensuous at all. As human form is not the subject with which it deals, architecture is the mode in which the artistic effort centres, when the thoughts of man concerning himself are still indistinct, when he is still little preoccupied with those harmonies, storms, victories, of the unseen and intellectual world, which, wrought out into the bodily form, give it an interest and significance communicable to it alone. The art of

Egypt, with its supreme architectural effects, is, according to Hegel's beautiful comparison, a Memnon waiting for the day, the day of the Greek spirit, the humanistic spirit, with its power of speech.

Again, painting, music, and poetry, with their endless power of complexity, are the special arts of the romantic and modern ages. Into these, with the utmost attenuation of detail, may be translated every delicacy of thought and feeling, incidental to a consciousness brooding with delight over itself. Through their gradations of shade, their exquisite intervals, they project in an external form that which is most inward in passion or sentiment. Between architecture and those romantic arts of painting, music, and poetry, comes sculpture, which unlike architecture, deals immediately with man, while it contrasts with the romantic arts, because it is not self-analytical. It has to do more exclusively than any other art with the human form, itself one entire medium of spiritual expression, trembling, blushing, melting into dew, with inward excitement. That spirituality which only lurks about architecture as a volatile effect, in sculpture takes up the whole given material, and penetrates it with an imaginative motive; and at first sight sculpture, with its solidity of form, seems a thing more real and full than the faint, abstract world of poetry or painting. Still the fact is the reverse. Discourse and action show man as he is, more directly than the play of the muscles and the moulding of the flesh; and over these poetry has command. Painting, by the flushing of colour in the face of dilatation of light in the eye—music, by its subtle range of tones—can refine most delicately upon a single moment of passion, unravelling its subtlest threads

But why should sculpture thus limit itself to pure form? Because, by this limitation, it becomes a perfect medium of expression for one peculiar motive of the imaginative intellect. It therefore renounces all those attributes of its material which do not forward that motive. It has had, indeed, from the beginning an unfixed claim to colour; but this element of colour in it has always been more or less conventional, with no melting or modulation of tones, never permitting more than a very limited realism. It was maintained chiefly as a religious tradition. In proportion as the art of sculpture ceased to be merely decorative, and subordinate to architecture, it threw itself upon pure form. It renounces the power of expression by lower or heightened tones. In it, no member of the human form is more significant than the rest; the eye is wide, and

without pupil; the lips and brow are hardly less significant than hands, and breasts, and feet. But the limitation of its resources is part of its pride: it has no backgrounds, no sky or atmosphere, to suggest and interpret a train of feeling; a little of suggested motion, and much of pure light on its gleaming surfaces, with pure form—only these. And it gains more than it loses by this limitation to its own distinguishing motives; it unveils man in the repose of his unchanging characteristics. That white light, purged from the angry, bloodlike stains of action and passion, reveals, not what is accidental in man, but the tranquil godship in him, as opposed to the restless accidents of life. The art of sculpture records the first naïve, unperplexed recognition of man by himself; and it is a proof of the high artistic capacity of the Greeks, that they apprehended and remained true to these exquisite limitations, yet, in spite of them, gave to their creations a mobile, a vital, individuality.

Heiterkeit—blitheness or repose, and *Allgemeinheit*—generality or breadth, are, then, the supreme characteristics of the Hellenic ideal. But that generality or breadth has nothing in common with the lax observation, the unlearned thought, the flaccid execution, which have sometimes claimed superiority in art, on the plea of being "broad" or "general." Hellenic breadth and generality come of a culture minute, severe, constantly renewed, rectifying and concentrating its impressions into certain pregnant types.

The basis of all artistic genius lies in the power of conceiving humanity in a new and striking way, of putting a happy world of its own creation in place of the meaner world of our common days, generating around itself an atmosphere with a novel power of refraction, selecting, transforming, recombining the images it transmits, according to the choice of the imaginative intellect. In exercising this power, painting and poetry have a variety of subject almost unlimited. The range of characters or persons open to them is as various as life itself; no character, however trivial, misshapen, or unlovely, can resist their magic. That is because those arts can accomplish their function in the choice and development of some special situation, which lifts or glorifies a character, in itself not poetical. To realise this situation, to define, in a chill and empty atmosphere, the focus where rays, in themselves pale and impotent, unite and begin to burn, the artist may have, indeed, to employ the most cunning detail, to complicate and refine upon thought and passion a thousand-fold. Let us take a brilliant example from the poems of Robert Browning. His poetry is pre-eminently the poetry of situations. The characters themselves are always of secondary importance; often they are characters in themselves of little interest; they seem to come to him by strange accidents from the ends of the world. His gift is shown by the way in which he accepts such a character, throws it into some situation, or apprehends it in some delicate pause of life, in which for a moment it becomes ideal. In the poem entitled *Le Byron de nos Jours*, in his *Dramatis Personae*, we have a single moment of passion thrown into relief after this exquisite fashion. Those two jaded Parisians are not intrinsically interesting: they begin to interest us only when thrown into a choice situation. But to discriminate that moment, to make it appreciable by us, that we may "find" it, what a cobweb of allusions, what double and treble reflexions of the mind upon itself, what an artificial light is constructed and broken over the chosen situation; on how fine a needle's point that little world of passion is balanced! Yet, in spite of this intricacy, the poem has the clear ring of a central motive. We receive from it the impression of one imaginative tone, of a single creative act.

To produce such effects at all requires all the resources of painting, with its power of indirect expression, of subordinate but significant detail, its atmosphere, its foregrounds and backgrounds. To produce them in a pre-eminent degree requires all the resources of poetry, language in its most purged form, its remote associations and suggestions, its double and treble lights. These appliances sculpture cannot command. In it, therefore, not the special situation, but the type, the general character of the subject to be delineated, is all-important. In poetry and painting, the situation predominates over the character; in sculpture, the character over the situation. Excluded by the proper limitation of its material from the development of exquisite situations, it has to choose from a select number of types intrinsically interesting—interesting, that is, independently of any special situation into which they may be thrown. Sculpture finds the secret of its power in presenting these types, in their broad, central, incisive lines. This it effects not by accumulation of detail, but by abstracting from it. All that is accidental, all that distracts the simple effect upon us of the supreme types of humanity, all traces in them of the commonness of the world, it gradually purges away.

Works of art produced under this law, and only these, are really characterised by Hellenic generality or breadth. In every direction it is a law of restraint. It keeps passion always below that degree of intensity at which it must necessarily be transitory, never winding up the features to one note of anger, or desire, or surprise. In some of the feebler allegorical designs of the middle age, we find isolated qualities portrayed as by so many masks; its religious art has familiarised us with faces fixed immovably into blank types of placid reverie. Men and women, again, in the hurry of life, often wear the sharp impress of one absorbing motive, from which it is said death sets their features free. All such instances may be ranged under the *grotesque;* and the Hellenic ideal has nothing in common with the grotesque. It allows passion to play lightly over the surface of the individual form, losing thereby nothing of its central impassivity, its depth and repose. To all but the highest culture, the reserved faces of the gods will ever have something of insipidity.

Again, in the best Greek sculpture, the archaic immobility has been stirred, its forms are in motion; but it is a motion ever kept in reserve, and very seldom committed to any definite action. Endless as are the attitudes of Greek sculpture, exquisite as is the invention of the Greeks in this direction, the actions or situations it permits are simple and few. There is no Greek Madonna; the goddesses are always childless. The actions selected are those which would be without significance, except in a divine person—binding on a sandal or preparing for the bath. When a more complex and significant action is permitted, it is most often represented as just finished, so that eager expectancy is excluded, as in the image of Apollo just after the slaughter of the Python, or of Venus with the apple of Paris already in her hand. The *Laocoon*, with all that patient science through which it has triumphed over an almost unmanageable subject, marks a period in which sculpture has begun to aim at effects legitimate, because delightful, only in painting.

The hair, so rich a source of expression in painting, because, relatively to the eye or the lip, it is mere drapery, is withdrawn from attention; its texture, as well as its colour, is lost, its arrangement but faintly and severely indicated, with no broken or enmeshed light. The eyes are wide and directionless, not fixing anything with their gaze, nor riveting the brain to any special external object, the brows without hair. Again, Greek sculpture deals almost exclusively with youth, where the moulding of the bodily organs is still as if suspended between growth and completion, indicated but not emphasised; where the transition from curve to curve is so delicate and elusive, that Winckelmann compares it to a quiet sea, which, although we understand it to be in motion, we nevertheless regard as an image of repose; where, therefore, the exact degree of development is so hard to apprehend. If a single product only of Hellenic art were to be saved in the wreck of all beside, one might choose perhaps from the "beautiful multitude" of the Panathenaic frieze, that line of youths on horseback, with their level glances, their proud, patient lips, their chastened reins, their whole bodies in exquisite service. This colourless, unclassified purity of life, with its blending and interpenetration of intellectual, spiritual, and physical elements, still folded together, pregnant with the possibilities of a whole world closed within it, is the highest expression of the indifference which lies beyond all that is relative or partial. Everywhere there is the effect of an awaking, of a child's sleep just disturbed. All these effects are united in a single instance—the *adorante* of the museum of Berlin, a youth who has gained the wrestler's prize, with hands lifted and open, in praise for the victory. Fresh, unperplexed, it is the image of a man as he springs first from the sleep of nature, his white light taking no colour from any one-sided experience. He is characterless, so far as *character* involves subjection to the accidental influences of life.

"This sense," says Hegel, "for the consummate modelling of divine and human forms was pre-eminently at home in Greece. In its poets and orators, its historians and philosophers, Greece cannot be conceived from a central point, unless one brings, as a key to the understanding of it, an insight into the ideal forms of sculpture, and regards the images of statesmen and philosophers, as well as epic and dramatic heroes, from the artistic point of view. For those who act, as well as those who create and think, have, in those beautiful days of Greece, this plastic character. They are great and free, and have grown up on the soil of their own individuality, creating themselves out of themselves, and moulding themselves to what they were, and willed to be. The age of Pericles was rich in such characters; Pericles himself, Pheidias, Plato, above all Sophocles, Thucydides also, Xenophon and Socrates, each in his own order, the perfection of one remaining undiminished by that of the others. They are ideal artists of themselves,

cast each in one flawless mould, works of art, which stand before us as an immortal presentment of the gods. Of this modelling also are those bodily works of art, the victors in the Olympic games; yes! and even Phryne, who, as the most beautiful of women, ascended naked out of the water, in the presence of assembled Greece."

This key to the understanding of the Greek spirit, Winckelmann possessed in his own nature, itself like a relic of classical antiquity, laid open by accident to our alien, modern atmosphere. To the criticism of that consummate Greek modelling he brought not only his culture but his temperament. We have seen how definite was the leading motive of that culture; how, like some central root-fibre, it maintained the well-rounded unity of his life through a thousand distractions. Interests not his, nor meant for him, never disturbed him. In morals, as in criticism, he followed the clue of instinct, of an unerring instinct. Penetrating into the antique world by his passion, his temperament, he enunciated no formal principles, always hard and one-sided. Minute and anxious as his culture was, he never became one-sidedly self-analytical. Occupied ever with himself, perfecting himself and developing his genius, he was not content, as so often happens with such natures, that the atmosphere between him and other minds should be thick and clouded; he was ever jealously refining his meaning into a form, express, clear, objective. This temperament he nurtured and invigorated by friendships which kept him always in direct contact with the spirit of youth. The beauty of the Greek statues was a sexless beauty: the statues of the gods had the least traces of sex. Here there is a moral sexlessness, a kind of ineffectual wholeness of nature, yet with a true beauty and significance of its own.

One result of this temperament is a serenity —*Heiterkeit*—which characterises Winckelmann's handling of the sensuous side of Greek art. This serenity is, perhaps, in great measure, a negative quality: it is the absence of any sense of want, or corruption, or shame. With the sensuous element in Greek art he deals in the pagan manner; and what is implied in that? It has been sometimes said that art is a means of escape from "the tyranny of the senses". It may be so for the spectator: he may find that the spectacle of supreme works of art takes from the life of the senses something of its turbid fever. But this is possible for the spectator only because the artist, in producing those works, has gradually sunk his intellectual and spiritual ideas in sensuous form. He may live, as Keats lived, a pure life; but his soul, like that of Plato's false astronomer, becomes more and more immersed in sense, until nothing which lacks the appeal to sense has interest for him. How could such an one ever again endure the greyness of the ideal or spiritual world? The spiritualist is satisfied as he watches the escape of the sensuous elements from his conceptions; his interest grows, as the dyed garment bleaches in the keener air. But the artist steeps his thought again and again into the fire of colour. To the Greek this immersion in the sensuous was, religiously, at least, indifferent. Greek sensuousness, therefore, does not fever the conscience: it is shameless and childlike. Christian asceticism, on the other hand, discrediting the slightest touch of sense, has from time to time provoked into strong emphasis the contrast or antagonism to itself, of the artistic life, with its inevitable sensuousness.—*I did but taste a little honey with the end of the rod that was in mine land, and lo! I must die.*[13]—It has sometimes seemed hard to pursue that life without something of conscious disavowal of a spiritual world; and this imparts to genuine artistic interests a kind of intoxication. From this intoxication Winckelmann is free: he fingers those pagan marbles with unsinged hands, with no sense of shame or loss. That is to deal with the sensuous side of art in the pagan manner.

The longer we contemplate that Hellenic ideal, in which man is at unity with himself, with his physical nature, with the outward world, the more we may be inclined to regret that he should ever have passed beyond it, to contend for a perfection that makes the blood turbid, and frets the flesh, and discredits the actual world about us. But if he was to be saved from the *ennui* which ever attaches itself to realisation, even the realisation of the perfect life, it was necessary that a conflict should come, that some sharper note should grieve the existing harmony, and the spirit chafed by it beat out at last only a larger and profounder music. In Greek tragedy this conflict has begun: man finds himself face to face with rival claims. Greek tragedy shows how such a conflict may be treated with serenity, how the evolution of it may be a spectacle of the dignity, not of the impotence, of the human spirit. But it is not only in tragedy that the Greek spirit showed itself capable of thus bringing joy out of matter in itself full of discouragements. Theocritus too strikes often a note of romantic sadness. But what a blithe and steady poise, above these discouragements, in a clear and sunny stratum of the air!

Into this stage of Greek achievement Winckelmann did not enter. Supreme as he is where his true interest lay, his insight into the typical unity and repose of the highest sort of sculpture seems to have involved limitation in another direction. His conception of art excludes that bolder type of it which deals confidently and serenely with life, conflict, evil. Living in a world of exquisite but abstract and colourless form, he could hardly have conceived of the subtle and penetrative, yet somewhat grotesque art of the modern world. What would he have thought of Gilliatt, in Victor Hugo's *Travailleurs de la Mer*, or of the bleeding mouth of Fantine in the first part of *Les Misérables*, penetrated as those books are with a sense of beauty, as lively and transparent as that of a Greek? Nay, a sort of preparation for the romantic temper is noticeable even within the limits of the Greek ideal itself, which for his part Winckelmann failed to see. For Greek religion has not merely its mournful mysteries of Adonis, of Hyacinthus, of Demeter, but it is conscious also of the fall of earlier divine dynasties. Hyperion gives way to Apollo, Oceanus to Poseidon. Around the feet of that tranquil Olympian family still crowd the weary shadows of an earlier, more formless, divine world. The placid minds even of Olympain gods are troubled with thoughts of a limit to duration, of inevitable decay, of dispossession. Again, the supreme and colourless abstraction of those divine forms, which is the secret of their repose, is also a premonition of the fleshless, consumptive refinements of the pale, medieval artists. That high indifference to the outward, that impassivity, has already a touch of the corpse in it: we see already Angelico and the *Master of the Passion* in the artistic future. The suppression of the sensuous, the shutting of the door upon it, the ascetic interest, may be even now foreseen. Those abstracted gods, "ready to melt out their essence fine into the winds," who can fold up their flesh as a garment and still remain themselves, seem already to feel that bleak air, in which like Helen of Troy, they wander as the spectres of the middle age.

Gradually, as the world came into the church, an artistic interest, native in the human soul, reasserted its claims. But Christian art was still

[13] I Samuel 14:43.

dependent on pagan examples, building the shafts of pagan temples into its churches, perpetuating the form of the *basilica*, in later times working the disused amphitheatres as stone quarries. The sensuous expression of ideas which unreservedly discredit the world of sense, was the delicate problem which Christian art had before it. If we think of medieval painting, as it ranges from the early German schools, still with something of the air of the charnel-house about them, to the clear loveliness of Perugino, we shall see how that problem was solved. In the very "worship of sorrow" the native blitheness of art asserted itself. The religious spirit, as Hegel says, "smiled through its tears." So perfectly did the young Raphael infuse that *Heiterkeit*, that pagan blitheness, into religious works, that his picture of Saint Agatha at Bologna became to Goethe a step in the evolution of *Iphigenie*.[14] But in proportion as the gift of smiling was found once more, there came also an aspiration towards that lost antique art, some relics of which Christian art had buried in itself, ready to work wonders when their day came.

The history of art has suffered as much as any history by trenchant and absolute divisions. Pagan and Christian art are sometimes harshly opposed, and the Renaissance is represented as a fashion which set in at a definite period. That is the superficial view: the deeper view is that which preserves the identity of European culture. The two are really continuous; and there is a sense in which it may be said that the Renaissance was an uninterrupted effort of the middle age, that it was ever taking place. When the actual relics of the antique were restored to the world, in the view of the Christian ascetic it was as if an ancient plague-pit had been opened. All the world took the contagion of the life of nature and of the senses. And now it was seen that the medieval spirit too had done something for the new fortunes of the antique. By hastening the decline of art, by withdrawing interest from it and yet keeping unbroken the thread of its traditions, it had suffered the human mind to repose itself, that when day came it might awake, with eyes refreshed, to those ancient, ideal forms.

The aim of a right criticism is to place Winckelmann in an intellectual perspective, of which Goethe is the foreground. For, after all, he is infinitely less than Goethe; and it is chiefly because at certain points he comes in contact with Goethe, that criticism entertains consideration of him. His relation to modern culture is a peculiar one. He is not of the modern world; nor is he wholly of the eighteenth century, although so much of his outer life is characteristic of it. But that note of revolt against the eighteenth century, which we detect in Goethe, was struck by Winckelmann. Goethe illustrates a union of the Romantic spirit, in its adventure, its variety, its profound subjectivity of soul, with Hellenism, in its transparency, its rationality, its desire of beauty—that marriage of Faust and Helena, of which the art of the nineteenth century is the child, the beautiful lad Euphorion, as Goethe conceives him, on the crags, in the "splendour of battle and in harness as for victory," his brows bound with light.[15] Goethe illustrates, too, the preponderance in this marriage of the Hellenic element; and that element, in its true essence was made known to him by Winckelmann.

Breadth, centrality, with blitheness and repose, are the marks of Hellenic culture. Is such culture a lost art? The local, accidental colouring of its own age has passed from it; and the greatness that is dead looks greater when every link with what is slight and vulgar has been severed. We can only see it at all in the reflected, refined light which a great education creates for us. Can we bring down that ideal into the gaudy, perplexed light of modern life?

Certainly, for us of the modern world, with its conflicting claims, its entangled interests, distracted by so many sorrows, with many preoccupations, so bewildering an experience, the problem of unity with ourselves, in blitheness and repose, is far harder than it was for the Greek within the simple terms of antique life. Yet, not less than ever, the intellect demands completeness, centrality. It is this which Winckelmann imprints on the imagination of Goethe, at the beginning of life, in its original and simplest form, as in a fragment of Greek art itself, stranded on that littered, indeterminate shore of Germany in the eighteenth century. In Winckelmann, this type comes to him, not as in a book or a theory, but more importunately, because in a passionate life, in a personality. For Goethe, possessing all modern interests, ready to be lost in the perplexed currents of modern thought, he defines, in clearest outline, the eternal problem of culture—balance, unity with one's self, consummate Greek modelling.

---

[14] *Italienische Reise*. Bologna, 19 Oct. 1776. [Pater's note]
[15] *Faust*, Th. ii. Act. 3. [Pater's note]

It could no longer be solved, as in Phryne ascending naked out of the water, by perfection of bodily form, or any joyful union with the external world: the shadows had grown too long, the light too solemn, for that. It could hardly be solved, as in Pericles or Pheidias, by the direct exercise of any single talent: amid the manifold claims of our modern intellectual life, that could only have ended in a thin, one-sided growth. Goethe's Hellenism was of another order, the *Allgemeinheit* and *Heiterkeit*, the completeness and serenity, of a watchful, exigent intellectualism. *Im Ganzen, Guten, Wahren, resolut zu leben:*[16]—is Goethe's description of his own higher life; and what is meant by life in the whole—*im Ganzen?* It means the life of one for whom, over and over again, what was once precious has become indifferent. Every one who aims at the life of culture is met by many forms of it, arising out of the intense, laborious, one-sided development of some special talent. They are the brightest enthusiasms the world has to show: and it is not their part to weigh the claims which this or that alien form of genius makes upon them. But the proper instinct of self-culture cares not so much to reap all that those various forms of genius can give, as to find in them its own strength. The demand of the intellect is to feel itself alive. It must see into the laws, the operation, the intellectual reward of every divided form of culture; but only that it may measure the relation between itself and them. It struggles with those forms till its secret is won from each, and then lets each fall back into its place, in the supreme, artistic view of life. With a kind of passionate coldness, such natures rejoice to be away from and past their former selves, and above all, they are jealous of that abandonment to one special gift which really limits their capabilities. It would have been easy for Goethe, with the gift of a sensuous nature, to let it overgrow him. It comes easily and naturally, perhaps, to certain "other-worldly" natures to be even as the *Schöne Seele,*[17] that ideal of gentle pietism, in *Wilhelm Meister:* but to the large vision of Goethe, this seemed to be a phase of life that a man might feel all round, and leave behind him. Again, it is easy to indulge the commonplace metaphysical instinct. But a taste for metaphysics may be one of those things which we must renounce, if we mean to mould our lives to artistic perfection. Philosophy serves culture, not by the fancied gift of absolute or transcendental knowledge, but by

suggesting questions which help one to detect the passion, and strangeness, and dramatic contrasts of life.

But Goethe's culture did not remain "behind the veil": it ever emerged in the practical functions of art, in actual production. For him the problem came to be:—Can the blitheness and universality of the antique ideal be communicated to artistic productions, which shall contain the fulness of the experience of the modern world? We have seen that the development of the various forms of art has corresponded to the development of the thoughts of man concerning humanity, to the growing revelation of the mind to itself. Sculpture corresponds to the unperplexed, emphatic outlines of Hellenic humanism; painting to the mystic depth and intricacy of the middle age; music and poetry have their fortune in the modern world.

Let us understand by poetry all literary production which attains the power of giving pleasure by its form, as distinct from its matter. Only in this varied literary form can art command that width, variety, delicacy of resources, which will enable it to deal with the conditions of modern life. What modern art has to do in the service of culture is so to rearrange the details of modern life, so to reflect it, that it may satisfy the spirit. And what does the spirit need in the face of modern life? The sense of freedom. That naïve, rough sense of freedom, which supposes man's will to be limited, if at all, only by a will stronger than his, he can never have again. The attempt to represent it in art would have so little verisimilitude that it would be flat and uninteresting. The chief factor in the thoughts of the modern mind concerning itself is the intricacy, the universality of natural law, even in the moral order. For us, necessity is not, as of old, a sort of mythological personage without us, with whom we can do warfare. It is rather a magic web woven through and through us, like that magnetic system of which modern science speaks, penetrating us with a network, subtler than our subtlest nerves, yet bearing in it the central forces of the world. Can art represent men and women in these bewildering toils so as to give the spirit at least an equivalent for the sense of freedom? Certainly, in Goethe's romances, and even more in the romances of Victor Hugo, we have high examples of modern art dealing thus with modern life, regarding that life as the modern mind must regard it, yet reflecting upon it blitheness and

---

[16] "In everything to live resolutely in the good and true."   [17] The Beautiful Soul.

repose. Natural laws we shall never modify, embarrass us as they may; but there is still something in the nobler or less noble attitude with which we watch their fatal combinations. In those romances of Goethe and Victor Hugo, in some excellent work done *after* them, this entanglement, this network of law, becomes the tragic situation, in which certain groups of noble men and women work out for themselves a supreme *Dénouement*. Who, if he saw through all, would fret against the chain of circumstance which endows one at the end with those great experiences?

Conclusion[1]

Λέγει που Ἡράκλειτος ὅτι πάντα χωρεῖ καὶ οὐδὲν μένει[2]

To regard all things and principles of things as inconstant modes or fashions has more and more become the tendency of modern thought. Let us begin with that which is without—our physical life. Fix upon it in one of its more exquisite intervals, the moment, for instance, of delicious recoil from the flood of water in summer heat. What is the whole physical life in that moment but a combination of natural elements to which science gives their names? But those elements, phosphorus and lime and delicate fibres, are present not in the human body alone: we detect them in places most remote from it. Our physical life is a perpetual motion of them— the passage of the blood, the waste and repairing of the lenses of the eye, the modification of the tissues of the brain under every ray of light and sound—processes which science reduces to simpler and more elementary forces. Like the elements of which we are composed, the action of these forces extends beyond us: it rusts iron and ripens corn. Far out on every side of us those elements are broadcast, driven in many currents; and birth and gesture and death and the springing of violets from the grave are but a few out of ten thousand resultant combinations. That clear, perpetual outline of face and limb is but an image of ours, under which we group them—

a design in a web, the actual threads of which pass out beyond it. This at least of flamelike our life has, that it is but the concurrence, renewed from moment to moment, of forces parting sooner or later on their ways.

Or if we begin with the inward world of thought and feeling, the whirlpool is still more rapid, the flame more eager and devouring. There it is no longer the gradual darkening of the eye, the gradual fading of colour from the wall —movements of the shore-side, where the water flows down indeed, though in apparent rest—but the race of the mid-stream, a drift of momentary acts of sight and passion and thought. At first sight experience seems to bury us under a flood of external objects, pressing upon us with a sharp and importunate reality, calling us out of ourselves in a thousand forms of action. But when reflexion begins to play upon those objects they are dissipated under its influence; the cohesive force seems suspended like some trick of magic; each object is loosed into a group of impressions —colour, odour, texture—in the mind of the observer. And if we continue to dwell in thought on this world, not of objects in the solidity with which language invests them, but of impressions, unstable, flickering, inconsistent, which burn and are extinguished with our consciousness of them, it contracts still further: the whole scope of observation is dwarfed into the narrow chamber of the individual mind. Experience, already reduced to a group of impressions, is ringed round for each one of us by that thick wall of personality through which no real voice has ever pierced on its way to us, or from us to that which we can only conjecture to be without. Every one of those impressions is the impression of the individual in his isolation, each mind keeping as a solitary prisoner its own dream of a world. Analysis goes a step farther still, and assures us that those impressions of the individual mind to which, for each one of us, experience dwindles down, are in perpetual flight; that each of them is limited by time, and that as time is infinitely divisible, each of them is infinitely divisible also; all that is actual in it being a single moment, gone while we try to apprehend it, of which it may ever be more truly said that it has ceased to be than that it is. To such a tremulous wisp constantly re-forming itself on the

---

[1] This brief "Conclusion" was omitted in the second edition of this book, as I conceived it might possibly mislead some of those young men into whose hands it might fall. On the whole, I have thought it best to reprint it here, with some slight changes which bring it closer to my original meaning. I have dealt more fully in *Marius the Epicurean* with the thoughts suggested by it. [Pater's note]

[2] "Heraclitus says, 'All things give way; nothing remains.' "

stream, to a single sharp impression, with a sense in it, a relic more or less fleeting, of such moments gone by, what is real in our life fines itself down. It is with this movement, with the passage and dissolution of impressions, images, sensations, that analysis leaves off—that continual vanishing away, that strange, perpetual weaving and unweaving of ourselves.

Philosophiren, says Novalis, *ist dephlegmatisiren vivificiren*.[3] The service of philosophy, of speculative culture, towards the human spirit, is to rouse, to startle it to a life of constant and eager observation. Every moment some form grows perfect in hand or face; some tone on the hills or the sea is choicer than the rest; some mood of passion or insight or intellectual excitement is irresistibly real and attractive to us,—for that moment only. Not the fruit of experience, but experience itself, is the end. A counted number of pulses only is given to us of a variegated, dramatic life. How may we see in them all that is to be seen in them by the finest senses? How shall we pass most swiftly from point to point, and be present always at the focus where the greatest number of vital forces unite in their purest energy?

To burn always with this hard, gemlike flame, to maintain this ecstasy, is success in life. In a sense it might even be said that our failure is to form habits: for, after all, habit is relative to a stereotyped world, and meantime it is only the roughness of the eye that makes any two persons, things, situations, seem alike. While all melts under our feet, we may well grasp at any exquisite passion, or any contribution to knowledge that seems by a lifted horizon to set the spirit free for a moment, or any stirring of the senses, strange dyes, strange colours, and curious odours, or work of the artist's hands, or the face of one's friend. Not to discriminate every moment some passionate attitude in those about us, and in the very brilliancy of their gifts some tragic dividing of forces on their ways, is, on this short day of frost and sun, to sleep before evening. With this sense of the splendour of our experience and of its awful brevity, gathering all we are into one desperate effort to see and touch, we shall hardly have time to make theories about the things we see and touch. What we have to do is to be for ever curiously testing new opinions and courting new impressions, never acquiescing in a facile orthodoxy of Comte, or of Hegel, or of our own. Philosophical theories or ideas, as points of view, instruments of criticism, may help us to gather up what might otherwise pass unregarded by us. "Philosophy is the microscope of thought." The theory or idea or system which requires of us the sacrifice of any part of this experience, in consideration of some interest into which we cannot enter, or some abstract theory we have not identified with ourselves, or of what is only conventional, has no real claim upon us.

One of the most beautiful passages of Rousseau is that in the sixth book of the *Confessions*, where he describes the awakening in him of the literary sense. An undefinable taint of death had clung always about him, and now in early manhood he believed himself smitten by mortal disease. He asked himself how he might make as much as possible of the interval that remained; and he was not biassed by anything in his previous life when he decided that it must be by intellectual excitement, which he found just then in the clear, fresh writings of Voltaire. Well! we are all *condamnés*, as Victor Hugo says: we are all under sentence of death but with a sort of indefinite reprieve—*les hommes sont tous condamnés à mort avec des sursis indéfinis*:[4] we have an interval, and then our place knows us no more. Some spend this interval in listlessness, some in high passions, the wisest, at least among "the children of this world,"[5] in art and song. For our one chance lies in expanding that interval, in getting as many pulsations as possible into the given time. Great passions may give us this quickened sense of life, ecstasy and sorrow of love, the various forms of enthusiastic activity, disinterested or otherwise, which come naturally to many of us. Only be sure it is passion—that it does yield you this fruit of a quickened, multiplied consciousness. Of such wisdom, the poetic passion, the desire of beauty, the love of art for its own sake, has most. For art comes to you proposing frankly to give nothing but the highest quality to your moments as they pass, and simply for those moments' sake.

---

[3] "To philosophize is to cast off inertia, to vitalize."
[4] "Men are all condemned to death with indefinite reprieves."
[5] Luke 16:8.

The Child in the House

This autobiographical story was first published in Macmillan's Magazine *in 1878, under the title "Imaginary Portrait: The Child in the House." After Pater's death it was published in his* Miscellaneous Studies *(1895) with the present title. There is little dispute among Pater scholars that Florian Deleal represents Pater himself, but the exact degree of correspondence between details in the story and Pater's own life cannot be established. It is instructive to compare this "imaginary" portrait with other of Pater's portraits to gain a sense of his concept of this original literary mode.*

As Florian Deleal walked, one hot afternoon, he overtook by the wayside a poor aged man, and, as he seemed weary with the road, helped him on with the burden which he carried, a certain distance. And as the man told his story, it chanced that he named the place, a little place in the neighbourhood of a great city, where Florian had passed his earliest years, but which he had never since seen, and, the story told, went forward on his journey comforted. And that night, like a reward for his pity, a dream of that place came to Florian, a dream which did for him the office of the finer sort of memory, bringing its object to mind with a great clearness, yet, as sometimes happens in dreams, raised a little above itself, and above ordinary retrospect. The true aspect of the place, especially of the house there in which he had lived as a child, the fashion of its doors, its hearths, its windows, the very scent upon the air of it, was with him in sleep for a season; only, with tints more musically blent on wall and floor, and some finer light and shadow running in and out along its curves and angles, and with all its little carvings daintier. He awoke with a sigh at the thought of almost thirty years which lay between him and that place, yet with a flutter of pleasure still within him at the fair light, as if it were a smile, upon it. And it happened that this accident of his dream was just the thing needed for the beginning of a certain design he then had in view, the noting, namely, of some things in the story of his spirit—in that process of brain-building by which we are, each one of us, what we are. With the image of the place so clear and favourable upon him, he fell to thinking of himself therein, and how his thoughts had grown up to him. In that half-spiritualised house he could watch the better, over again, the gradual expansion of the soul which had come to be there—of which

indeed, through the law which makes the material objects about them so large an element in children's lives, it had actually become a part; inward and outward being woven through and through each other into one inextricable texture—half, tint and trace and accident of homely colour and form, from the wood and the bricks; half, mere soul-stuff, floated thither from who knows how far. In the house and garden of his dream he saw a child moving, and could divide the main streams at least of the winds that had played on him, and study so the first stage in that mental journey.

The *old house*, as when Florian talked of it afterwards he always called it, (as all children do, who can recollect a change of home, soon enough but not too soon to mark a period in their lives) really was an old house; and an element of French descent in its inmates—descent from Watteau,[1] the old court-painter, one of whose gallant pieces still hung in one of the rooms—might explain, together with some other things, a noticeable trimness and comely whiteness about everything there—the curtains, the couches, the paint on the walls with which the light and shadow played so delicately; might explain also the tolerance of the great poplar in the garden, a tree most often despised by English people, but which French people love, having observed a certain fresh way its leaves have of dealing with the wind, making it sound, in never so slight a stirring of the air, like running water.

The old-fashioned, low wainscoting went round the rooms, and up the staircase with carved balusters and shadowy angles, landing half-way up at a broad window, with a swallow's nest below the sill, and the blossom of an old pear-tree showing across it in late April, against the blue, below which the perfumed juice of the find of fallen fruit in autumn was so fresh. At the next

[1] Jean Antoine Watteau (1684–1721), French painter.

turning came the closet which held on its deep shelves the best china. Little angel faces and reedy flutings stood out round the fire-place of the children's room. And on the top of the house, above the large attic, where the white mice ran in the twilight—an infinite, unexplored wonderland of childish treasures, glass beads, empty scent-bottles still sweet, thrum of coloured silks, among its lumber—a flat space of roof, railed round, gave a view of the neighbouring steeples; for the house, as I said, stood near a great city, which sent up heavenwards, over the twisting weather-vanes, not seldom, its beds of rolling cloud and smoke, touched with storm or sunshine. But the child of whom I am writing did not hate the fog because of the crimson lights which fell from it sometimes upon the chimneys, and the whites which gleamed through its openings, on summer mornings, on turret or pavement. For it is false to suppose that a child's sense of beauty is dependent on any choiceness or special fineness, in the objects which present themselves to it, though this indeed comes to be the rule with most of us in later life; earlier, in some degree, we see inwardly; and the child finds for itself, and with unstinted delight, a difference for the sense, in those whites and reds through the smoke on very homely buildings, and in the gold of the dandelions at the road-side, just beyond the houses, where not a handful of earth is virgin and untouched, in the lack of better ministries to its desire of beauty.

This house then stood not far beyond the gloom and rumours of the town, among high garden-wall, bright all summer-time with Golden-rod, and brown-and-golden Wall-flower—*Flos Parietis,* as the children's Latin-reading father taught them to call it, while he was with them. Tracing back the threads of his complex spiritual habit, as he was used in after years to do, Florian found that he owed to the place many tones of sentiment afterwards customary with him, certain inward lights under which things most naturally presented themselves to him. The coming and going of travellers to the town along the way, the shadow of the streets, the sudden breath of the neighbouring gardens, the singular brightness of bright weather there, its singular darknesses which linked themselves in his mind to certain engraved illustrations in the old big Bible at home, the coolness of the dark, cavernous shops round the great church, with its giddy winding stair up to the pigeons and the bells—a

citadel of peace in the heart of the trouble—all this acted on his childish fancy, so that ever afterwards the like aspects and incidents never failed to throw him into a well-recognised imaginative mood, seeming actually to have become a part of the texture of his mind. Also, Florian could trace home to this point a pervading preference in himself for a kind of comeliness and dignity, an *urbanity* literally, in modes of life, which he connected with the pale people of towns, and which made him susceptible to a kind of exquisite satisfaction in the trimness and well-considered grace of certain things and persons he afterwards met with, here and there, in his way through the world.

So the child of whom I am writing lived on there quietly; things without thus ministering to him, as he sat daily at the window with the birdcage hanging below it, and his mother taught him to read, wondering at the ease with which he learned, and at the quickness of his memory. The perfume of the little flowers of the lime-tree fell through the air upon them like rain; while time seemed to move ever more slowly to the murmur of the bees in it, till it almost stood still on June afternoons. How insignificant, at the moment, seem the influences of the sensible things which are tossed and fall and lie about us, so, or so, in the environment of early childhood. How indelibly, as we afterwards discover, they affect us; with what capricious attractions and associations they figure themselves on the white paper, the smooth wax, of our ingenuous souls, as "with lead in the rock for ever,"[2] giving form and feature, and as it were assigned house-room in our memory, to early experiences of feeling and thought, which abide with us ever afterwards, thus, and not otherwise. The realities and passions, the rumours of the greater world without, steal in upon us, each by its own special little passage-way, through the wall of custom about us; and never afterwards quite detach themselves from this or that accident, or trick, in the mode of their first entrance to us. Our susceptibilities, the discovery of our powers, manifold experiences—our various experiences of the coming and going of bodily pain, for instance—belong to this or the other well-remembered place in the material habitation—that little white room with the window across which the heavy blossoms could beat so peevishly in the wind, with just that particular catch or throb, such a sense of teasing in it, on gusty mornings; and the early

[2] Job 19:23–24.

habitation thus gradually becomes a sort of material shrine or sanctuary of sentiment; a system of visible symbolism interweaves itself through all our thoughts and passions; and irresistibly, little shapes, voices, accidents—the angle at which the sun in the morning fell on the pillow—become parts of the great chain wherewith we are bound.

Thus far, for Florian, what all this had determined was a peculiarly strong sense of home—so forcible a motive with all of us—prompting to us our customary love of the earth, and the larger part of our fear of death, that revulsion we have from it, as from something strange, untried, unfriendly; though life-long imprisonment, they tell you, and final banishment from home is a thing bitterer still; the looking forward to but a short space, a mere childish *goûter*[3] and dessert of it, before the end, being so great a resource of effort to pilgrims and wayfarers, and the soldier in distant quarters, and lending, in lack of that, some power of solace to the thought of sleep in the home churchyard, at least—dead cheek by dead cheek, and with the rain soaking in upon one from above.

So powerful is this instinct, and yet accidents like those I have been speaking of so mechanically determine it; its essence being indeed the early familiar, as constituting our ideal, or typical conception, of rest and security. Out of so many possible conditions, just this for you and that for me, brings ever the unmistakeable realisation of the delightful *chez soi*;[4] this for the Englishman, for me and you, with the closely-drawn white curtain and the shaded lamp; that, quite other, for the wandering Arab, who folds his tent every morning, and makes his sleeping-place among haunted ruins, or in old tombs.

With Florian then the sense of home became singularly intense, his good fortune being that the special character of his home was in itself so essentially home-like. As after many wanderings I have come to fancy that some parts of Surrey and Kent are, for Englishmen, the true landscape, true home-counties, by right, partly, of a certain earthy warmth in the yellow of the sand below their gorse-bushes, and of a certain grey-blue mist after rain, in the hollows of the hills there, welcome to fatigued eyes, and never seen farther south; so I think that the sort of house I have described, with precisely those proportions of red-brick and green, and with a just perceptible monotony in the subdued order of it, for its

distinguishing note, is for Englishmen at least typically home-like. And so for Florian that general human instinct was reinforced by this special home-likeness in the place his wandering soul had happened to light on, as, in the second degree, its body and earthly tabernacle; the sense of harmony between his soul and its physical environment became, for a time at least, like perfectly played music, and the life led there singularly tranquil and filled with a curious sense of self-possession. The love of security, of an habitually undisputed standing-ground or sleeping-place, came to count for much in the generation and correcting of his thoughts, and afterwards as a salutary principle of restraint in all his wanderings of spirit. The wistful yearning towards home, in absence from it, as the shadows of evening deepened, and he followed in thought what was doing there from hour to hour, interpreted to him much of a yearning and regret he experienced afterwards, towards he knew not what, out of strange ways of feeling and thought in which, from time to time, his spirit found itself alone; and in the tears shed in such absences there seemed always to be some soul-subduing foretaste of what his last tears might be.

And the sense of security could hardly have been deeper, the quiet of the child's soul being one with the quite of its home, a place "inclosed" and "sealed." But upon this assured place, upon the child's assured soul which resembled it, there came floating in from the larger world without, as at windows left ajar unknowingly, or over the high garden walls, two streams of impressions, the sentiments of beauty and pain—recognitions of the visible, tangible, audible loveliness of things, as a very real and somewhat tyrannous element in them—and of the sorrow of the world, of grown people and children and animals, as a thing not to be put by in them. From this point he could trace two predominant processes of mental change in him—the growth of an almost diseased sensibility to the spectacle of suffering, and, parallel with this, the rapid growth of a certain capacity of fascination by bright colour and choice form—the sweet curvings, for instance, of the lips of those who seemed to him comely persons, modulated in such delicate unison to the things they said or sang,—marking early the activity in him of a more than customary sensuousness, "the lust of the eye,"[5] as the Preacher says, which might lead him, one day, how far! Could he have foreseen the weariness of the way! In music sometimes the two sorts of impressions came together, and he would weep, to the surprise of older people. Tears of joy too the child knew, also to older people's surprise; real tears, once, of relief from long-strung, childish expectation, when he found returned at evening, with new roses in her cheeks, the little sister who had been to a place where there was a wood, and brought back for him a treasure of fallen acorns, and black crow's feathers, and his peace at finding her again near him mingled all night with some intimate sense of the distant forest, the rumour of its breezes, with the glossy blackbirds aslant and the branches lifted in them, and of the perfect nicety of the little cups that fell. So those two elementary apprehensions of the tenderness and of the colour in things grew apace in him, and were seen by him afterwards to send their roots back into the beginnings of life.

Let me note first some of the occasions of his recognition of the element of pain in things— incidents, now and again, which seemed suddenly to awake in him the whole force of that sentiment which Goethe has called the *Weltschmerz*,[6] and in which the concentrated sorrow of the world seemed suddenly to lie heavy upon him. A book lay in an old book-case, of which he cared to remember one picture—a woman sitting, with hands bound behind her, the dress, the cap, the hair, folded with a simplicity which touched him strangely, as if not by her own hands, but with some ambiguous care at the hands of others— Queen Marie Antoinette, on her way to execution—we all remember David's[7] drawing, meant merely to make her ridiculous. The face that had been so high had learned to be mute and resistless; but out of its very resistlessness, seemed now to call on men to have pity, and forbear; and he took note of that, as he closed the book, as a thing to look at again, if he should at any time find himself tempted to be cruel. Again, he would never quite forget the appeal in the small sister's face, in the garden under the lilacs, terrified at a spider lighted on her sleeve. He could trace back to the look then noted a certain mercy he conceived always for people in fear, even of little things, which seemed to make him, though but for a moment, capable of almost any sacrifice of himself. Impressible, susceptible persons, indeed, who had had their sorrows, lived about him; and this sensibility was due in part to the tacit influence of their presence, enforcing upon him habitually the fact that there are those who pass

their days, as a matter of course, in a sort of "going quietly." Most poignantly of all he could recall, in unfading minutest circumstance, the cry on the stair, sounding bitterly through the house, and struck into his soul for ever, of an aged woman, his father's sister, come now to announce his death in distant India; how it seemed to make the aged woman like a child again; and, he knew not why, but this fancy was full of pity to him. There were the little sorrows of the dumb animals too—of the white angora, with a dark tail like an ermine's, and a face like a flower, who fell into a lingering sickness, and became quite delicately human in its valetudinarianism, and came to have a hundred different expressions of voice—how it grew worse and worse, till it began to feel the light too much for it, and at last, after one wild morning of pain, the little soul flickered away from the body, quite worn to death already, and now but feebly retaining it.

So he wanted another pet; and as there were starlings about the place, which could be taught to speak, one of them was caught, and he meant to treat it kindly; but in the night its young ones could be heard crying after it, and the responsive cry of the mother-bird towards them; and at last, with the first light, though not till after some debate with himself, he went down and opened the cage, and saw a sharp bound of the prisoner up to her nestlings; and therewith came the sense of remorse,—that he too was become an accomplice in moving, to the limit of his small power, the springs and handles of that great machine in things, constructed so ingeniously to play pain-fugues on the delicate nerve-work of living creatures.

I have remarked how, in the process of our brain-building, as the house of thought in which we live gets itself together, like some airy bird's-nest of floating thistle-down and chance straws, compact at last, little accidents have their consequence; and thus it happened that, as he walked one evening, a garden gate, usually closed, stood open; and lo! within, a great red hawthorn in full flower, embossing heavily the bleached and twisted trunk and branches, so aged that there were but few green leaves thereon—a plumage of tender, crimson fire out of the heart of the dry wood. The perfume of the tree had now and again reached him, in the currents of the wind, over the wall, and he had wondered what might be behind it, and was now allowed

---

[6] World-weariness.   [7] Jacques Louis David (1748–1825), French painter.

to fill his arms with the flowers—flowers enough for all the old blue-china pots along the chimney-piece, making *fête* in the children's room. Was it some periodic moment in the expansion of soul within him, or mere trick of heat in the heavily-laden summer air? But the beauty of the thing struck home to him feverishly; and in dreams all night he loitered along a magic roadway of crimson flowers, which seemed to open ruddily in thick, fresh masses about his feet, and fill softly all the little hollows in the banks on either side. Always afterwards, summer by summer, as the flowers came on, the blossom of the red hawthorn still seemed to him absolutely the reddest of all things; and the goodly crimson, still alive in the works of old Venetian masters or old Flemish tapestries, called out always from afar the recollection of the flame in those perishing little petals, as it pulsed gradually out of them, kept long in the drawers of an old cabinet. Also then, for the first time, he seemed to experience a passionateness in his relation to fair outward objects, an inexplicable excitement in their presence, which disturbed him, and from which he half longed to be free. A touch of regret or desire mingled all night with the remembered presence of the red flowers, and their perfume in the darkness about him; and the longing for some undivined, entire possession of them was the beginning of a revelation to him, growing ever clearer, with the coming of the gracious summer guise of fields and trees and persons in each succeeding year, of a certain, at times seemingly exclusive, predominance in his interests, of beautiful physical things, a kind of tyranny of the senses over him.

In later years he came upon philosophies which occupied him much in the estimate of the proportion of the sensuous and the ideal elements in human knowledge, the relative parts they bear in it; and, in his intellectual scheme, was led to assign very little to the abstract thought, and much to its sensible vehicle or occasion. Such metaphysical speculation did but reinforce what was instinctive in his way of receiving the world, and for him, everywhere, that sensible vehicle or occasion became, perhaps only too surely, the necessary concomitant of any perception of things, real enough to be of any weight or reckoning, in his house of thought. There were times when he could think of the necessity he was under of associating all thoughts to touch and sight, as a sympathetic link between himself and actual, feeling, living objects; a protest in favour of real men and women against mere grey, unreal

abstractions; and he remembered gratefully how the Christian religion, hardly less than the religion of the ancient Greeks, translating so much of its spiritual verity into things that may be seen, condescends in part to sanction this infirmity, if so it be, of our human existence, wherein the world of sense is so much with us, and welcomed this thought as a kind of keeper and sentinel over his soul therein. But certainly, he came more and more to be unable to care for, or think of soul but as in an actual body, or of any world but that wherein are water and trees, and where men and women look, so or so, and press actual hands. It was the trick even his pity learned, fastening those who suffered in anywise to his affections by a kind of sensible attachments. He would think of Julian, fallen into incurable sickness, as spoiled in the sweet blossom of his skin like pale amber, and his honey-like hair; of Cecil, early dead, as cut off from the lilies, from golden summer days, from women's voices; and then what comforted him a little was the thought of the turning of the child's flesh to violets in the turf above him. And thinking of the very poor, it was not the things which most men care most for that he yearned to give them; but fairer roses, perhaps, and power to taste quite as they will, at their ease and not task-burdened, a certain desirable, clear light in the new morning, through which sometimes he had noticed them, quite unconscious of it, on their way to their early toil.

So he yielded himself to these things, to be played upon by them like a musical instrument, and began to note with deepening watchfulness, but always with some puzzled, unutterable longing in his enjoyment, the phases of the seasons and of the growing or waning day, down even to the shadowy changes wrought on bare wall or ceiling—the light cast up from the snow, bringing out their darkest angles; the brown light in the cloud, which meant rain; that almost too austere clearness, in the protracted light of the lengthening day, before warm weather began, as if it lingered but to make a severer workday, with the school-books opened earlier and later; that beam of June sunshine, at last, as he lay awake before the time, a way of gold-dust across the darkness; all the humming, the freshness, the perfume of the garden seemed to lie upon it—and coming in one afternoon in September, along the red gravel walk, to look for a basket of yellow crab-apples left in the cool, old parlour, he remembered it the more, and how the colours struck upon him, because a wasp on one bitten apple stung him, and he felt the passion of sudden, severe pain. For this too brought its curious reflexions; and, in relief from it, he would wonder over it—how it had then been with him—puzzled at the depth of the charm or spell over him, which lay, for a little while at least, in the mere absence of pain; once, especially, when an older boy taught him to make flowers of sealing-wax, and he had burnt his hand badly at the lighted taper, and been unable to sleep. He remembered that also afterwards, as a sort of typical thing—a white vision of heat about him, clinging closely, through the languid scent of the ointments put upon the place to make it well.

Also, as he felt this pressure upon him of the sensible world, then, as often afterwards, there would come another sort of curious questioning how the last impressions of eye and ear might happen to him, how they would find him—the scent of the last flower, the soft yellowness of the last morning, the last recognition of some object of affection, hand or voice; it could not be but that the latest look of the eyes, before their final closing, would be strangely vivid; one would go with the hot tears, the cry, the touch of the wistful bystander, impressed how deeply on one! or would it be, perhaps, a mere frail retiring of all things, great or little, away from one, into a level distance?

For with this desire of physical beauty mingled itself early the fear of death—the fear of death intensified by the desire of beauty. Hitherto he had never gazed upon dead faces, as sometimes, afterwards, at the *Morgue* in Paris, or in that fair cemetery at Munich, where all the dead must go and lie in state before burial, behind glass windows, among the flowers and incense and holy candles—the aged clergy with their sacred ornaments, the young men in their dancing-shoes and spotless white linen—after which visits, those waxen, resistless faces would always live with him for many days, making the broadest sunshine sickly. The child had heard indeed of the death of his father, and how, in the Indian station, a fever had taken him, so that though not in action he had yet died as a soldier; and hearing of the "resurrection of the just,"[8] he could think of him as still abroad in the world, somehow, for his protection—a grand, though perhaps rather terrible figure, in beautiful soldier's things, like the figure in the picture of Joshua's Vision in the Bible[9]—and of that, round which the mourners moved so softly, and after-wards with such solemn singing, as but a worn-out garment left at a deserted lodging. So it was, until on a summer day he walked with his mother through a fair churchyard. In a bright dress he rambled among the graves, in the gay weather, and so came, in one corner, upon an open grave for a child—a dark space on the brilliant grass—the black mould lying heaped up round it, weighing down the little jewelled branches of the dwarf rose-bushes in flower. And therewith came, full-grown, never wholly to leave him, with the certainty that even children do sometimes die, the physical horror of death, with its wholly selfish recoil from the association of lower forms of life, and the suffocating weight above. No benign, grave figure in beautiful soldier's things any longer abroad in the world for his protection! only a few poor, piteous bones; and above them, possible, a certain sort of figure he hoped not to see. For sitting one day in the garden below an open window, he heard people talking, and could not but listen, how, in a sleepless hour, a sick woman had seen one of the dead sitting beside her, come to call her hence; and from the broken talk evolved with much clearness the notion that not all those dead people had really departed to the churchyard, nor were quite so motionless as they looked, but led a secret, half-fugitive life in their old homes, quite free by night, though sometimes visible in the day, dodging from room to room, with no great goodwill towards those who shared the place with them. All night the figure sat beside him in the reveries of his broken sleep, and was not quite gone in the morning—an odd, irreconcileable new member of the household, making the sweet familiar chambers unfriendly and suspect by its uncertain presence. He could have hated the dead he had pitied so, for being thus. Afterwards he came to think of those poor, home-returning ghosts, which all men have fancied to themselves —the *revenants*[10]—pathetically, as crying, or beating with vain hands at the doors, as the wind came, their cries distinguishable in it as a wilder inner note. But, always making death more unfamiliar still, that old experience would ever, from time to time, return to him; even in the living he sometimes caught its likeness; at any time or place, in a moment, the faint atmosphere of the chamber of death would be breathed around him, and the image with the bound chin, the quaint smile, the straight, stiff feet, shed itself across the air upon the bright carpet, amid

---

[8] Luke 14:14.   [9] Joshua 5:13–15.   [10] The returning ones, as from the dead.

the gayest company, or happiest communing with himself.

To most children the sombre questionings to which impressions like these attach themselves, if they come at all, are actually suggested by religious books, which therefore they often regard with much secret distaste, and dismiss, as far as possible, from their habitual thoughts as a too depressing element in life. To Florian such impressions, these misgivings as to the ultimate tendency of the years, of the relationship between life and death, had been suggested spontaneously in the natural course of his mental growth by a strong innate sense for the soberer tones in things, further strengthened by actual circumstances; and religious sentiment, that system of biblical ideas in which he had been brought up, presented itself to him as a thing that might soften and light up as with a "lively hope,"[11] a melancholy already deeply settled in him. So he yielded himself easily to religious impressions, and with a kind of mystical appetite for sacred things; the more as they came to him through a saintly person who loved him tenderly, and believed that this early pre-occupation with them already marked the child out for a saint. He began to love, for their own sakes, church lights, holy days, all that belonged to the comely order of the sanctuary, the secrets of its white linen, and holy vessels, and fonts of pure water; and its hieratic purity and simplicity became the type of something he desired always to have about him in actual life. He pored over the pictures in religious books, and knew by heart the exact mode in which the wrestling angel grasped Jacob, how Jacob looked in his mysterious sleep,[12] how the bells and pomegranates were attached to the hem of Aaron's vestment, sounding sweetly as he glided over the turf of the holy place.[13] His way of conceiving religion came then to be in effect what it ever afterwards remained—a sacred history indeed, but still more a sacred ideal, a transcendent version or representation, under intenser and more expressive light and shade, of human life and its familiar or exceptional incidents, birth, death, marriage, youth, age, tears, joy, rest, sleep, waking—a mirror, towards which men might turn away their eyes from vanity and dullness, and see themselves therein as angels, with their daily meat and drink, even, become a kind of sacred transaction—a complementary strain or burden, applied to our every-day existence, whereby the stray snatches of music in it re-set themselves, and fall into the scheme of some higher and more consistent harmony. A place adumbrated itself in his thoughts, wherein those sacred personalities, which are at once the reflex and the pattern of our nobler phases of life, housed themselves; and this region in his intellectual scheme all subsequent experience did but tend still further to realise and define. Some ideal, hieratic persons he would always need to occupy it and keep a warmth there. And he could hardly understand those who felt no such need at all, finding themselves quite happy without such heavenly companionship, and sacred double of their life, beside them.

Thus a constant substitution of the typical for the actual took place in his thoughts. Angels might be met by the way, under English elm or beech-tree; mere messengers seemed like angels, bound on celestial errands; a deep mysticity brooded over real meetings and partings; marriages were made in heaven; and deaths also, with hands of angels thereupon, to bear soul and body quietly asunder, each to its appointed rest. All the acts and accidents of daily life borrowed a sacred colour and significance; the very colours of things became themselves weighty with meanings like the sacred stuffs of Moses' tabernacle, full of penitence or peace.[14] Sentiment, congruous in the first instance only with those divine transactions, the deep, effusive unction of the House of Bethany,[15] was assumed as the due attitude for the reception of our every-day existence; and for a time he walked through the world in a sustained, not unpleasurable awe, generated by the habitual recognition, beside every circumstance and event of life, of its celestial correspondent.

Sensibility—the desire of physical beauty—a strange biblical awe, which made any reference to the unseen act on him like solemn music—these qualities the child took away with him, when, at about the age of twelve years, he left the old house, and was taken to live in another place. He had never left home before, and, anticipating much from this change, had long dreamed over it, jealously counting the days till the time fixed for departure should come; had been a little careless about others even, in his strong desire for it— when Lewis fell sick, for instance, and they must wait still two days longer. At last the morning

---

[11] I Peter 1:3.   [12] Genesis 32:24; 28:11-15.   [13] Exodus 39:24-26.
[14] Exodus 25-27.   [15] Matthew 26:6-13.

came, very fine; and all things—the very pavement with its dust, at the roadside—seemed to have a white, pearl-like lustre in them. They were to travel by a favourite road on which he had often walked a certain distance, and on one of those two prisoner days, when Lewis was sick, had walked farther than ever before, in his great desire to reach the new place. They had started and gone a little way when a pet bird was found to have been left behind, and must even now—so it presented itself to him—have already all the appealing fierceness and wild self-pity at heart of one left by others to perish of hunger in a closed house; and he returned to fetch it, himself in

hardly less stormy distress. But as he passed in search of it from room to room, lying so pale, with a look of meekness in their denudation, and at last through that little, stripped white room, the aspect of the place touched him like the face of one dead; and a clinging back towards it came over him, so intense that he knew it would last long, and spoiling all his pleasure in the realisation of a thing so eagerly anticipated. And so, with the bird found, but himself in an agony of home-sickness, thus capriciously sprung up within him, he was driven quickly away, far into the rural distance, so fondly speculated on, of that favourite country-road.

from Imaginary Portraits

This collection of essays, imaginary and historical, was published in 1887. The essays had originally appeared in various periodicals in the preceding decade. "Sebastian van Storck," given below, was first published in Macmillan's Magazine *in March 1886. It is an instance of a Paterian portrait that is imaginary with the substance of the setting taken from history.*

Sebastian van Storck

IT WAS a winter-scene, by Adrian van de Velde, or by Isaac van Ostade.[1] All the delicate poetry together with all the delicate comfort of the frosty season was in the leafless branches turned to silver, the furred dresses of the skaters, the warmth of the red-brick housefronts under the gauze of white fog, the gleams of pale sunlight on the cuirasses of the mounted soldiers as they receded into the distance. Sebastian van Storck, confessedly the most graceful performer in all that skating multitude, moving in endless maze over the vast surface of the frozen water-meadow, liked best this season of the year for its expression of a perfect impassivity, or at least of a perfect repose. The earth was, or seemed to be, at rest, with a breathlessness or slumber which suited the young man's peculiar temper. The heavy summer, as it dried up the meadows now lying dead below the ice, set free a crowded and competing world of life, which, while it gleamed very pleasantly

russet and yellow for the painter Albert Cuyp,[2] seemed wellnigh to suffocate Sebastian van Storck. Yet with all his appreciation of the national winter, Sebastian was not altogether a Hollander. His mother, of Spanish descent and Catholic, had given a richness of tone and form to the healthy freshness of the Dutch physiognomy, apt to preserve its youthfulness of aspect far beyond the period of life usual with other peoples. This mixed expression charmed the eye of Isaac van Ostade, who had painted his portrait from a sketch taken at one of those skating parties, with his plume of squirrel's tail and fur muff, in all the modest pleasantness of boyhood. When he returned home lately from his studies at a place far inland, at the proposal of his tutor, to recover, as the tutor suggested, a certain loss of robustness, something more than that cheerful indifference of early youth had passed away. The learned man, who held, as was alleged, the doctrines of a surprising new philosophy, reluctant to disturb too early the fine intelligence of the pupil entrusted to him, had found it, perhaps, a matter of honesty to send

[1] Adrian van de Velde (1636–72), Isaac van Ostade (1621–49), Dutch landscape painters.
[2] Albert Cuyp (1620–91), Dutch landscape artist.

back to his parents one likely enough to catch from others any sort of theoretic light; for the letter he wrote dwelt much on the lad's intellectual fearlessness. "At present," he had written, "he is influenced more by curiosity than by a care for truth, according to the character of the young. Certainly, he differs strikingly from his equals in age, by his passion for a vigorous intellectual gymnastic, such as the supine character of their minds renders distasteful to most young men, but in which he shows a fearlessness that at times makes me fancy that his ultimate destination may be the military life; for indeed the rigidly logical tendency of his mind always leads him out upon the practical. Don't misunderstand me! At present, he is strenuous only intellectually; and has given no definite sign of preference, as regards a vocation in life. But he seems to me to be one practical in this sense, that his theorems will shape life for him, directly; that he will always seek, as a matter of course, the effective equivalent to—the line of being which shall be the proper continuation of—his line of thinking. This intellectual rectitude, or candour, which to my mind has a kind of beauty in it, has reacted upon myself, I confess, with a searching quality." That "searching quality," indeed, many others also, people far from being intellectual, had experienced—an agitation of mind in his neighbourhood, oddly at variance with the composure of the young man's manner and surrounding, so jealously preserved.

In the crowd of spectators at the skating, whose eyes followed, so well-satisfied, the movements of Sebastian van Storck, were the mothers of marriageable daughters, who presently became the suitors of this rich and distinguished youth, introduced to them, as now grown to man's estate, by his delighted parents. Dutch aristocracy had put forth all its graces to become the winter morn: and it was characteristic of the period that the artist tribe was there, on a grand footing,—in waiting, for the lights and shadows they liked best. The artists were, in truth, an important body just then, as a natural consequence of the nation's hard-won prosperity; helping it to a full consciousness of the genial yet delicate homeliness it loved, for which it had fought so bravely, and was ready at any moment to fight anew, against man or the sea. Thomas de Keyser,[3] who understood better than any one else the kind of quaint new Atticism which had

found its way into the world over those waste salt marshes, wondering whether quite its finest type as he understood it could ever actually be seen there, saw it at last, in lively motion, in the person of Sebastian van Storck, and desired to paint his portrait. A little to his surprise, the young man declined the offer; not graciously, as was thought.

Holland, just then, was reposing on its laurels after its long contest with Spain, in a short period of complete wellbeing, before troubles of another kind should set in. That a darker time might return again, was clearly enough felt by Sebastian the elder—a time like that of William the Silent, with its insane civil animosities, which would demand similarly energetic personalities, and offer them similar opportunities. And then, it was part of his honest geniality of character to admire those who "get on" in the world. Himself had been, almost from boyhood, in contact with great affairs. A member of the States-General which had taken so hardly the kingly airs of Frederick Henry, he had assisted at the Congress of Munster,[4] and figures conspicuously in Terburgh's picture of that assembly, which had finally established Holland as a first-rate power. The heroism by which the national wellbeing had been achieved was still of recent memory—the air full of its reverberation, and great movement. There was a tradition to be maintained; the sword by no means resting in its sheath. The age was still fitted to evoke a generous ambition; and this son, from whose natural gifts there was so much to hope for, might play his part, at least as a diplomatist, if the present quiet continued. Had not the learned man said that his natural disposition would lead him out always upon practice? And in truth, the memory of that Silent hero had its fascination for the youth. When, about this time, Peter de Keyser, Thomas's brother, unveiled at last his tomb of wrought bronze and marble in the *Nieuwe Kerk* at Delft, the young Sebastian was one of a small company present, and relished much the cold and abstract simplicity of the monument, so conformable to the great, abstract, and unuttered force of the hero who slept beneath.

In complete contrast to all that is abstract or cold in art, the home of Sebastian, the family mansion of the Storcks—a house, the front of which still survives in one of those patient architectural pieces by Jan van der Heyde—was, in its minute and busy wellbeing, like an epitome

---

[3] Thomas de Keyser (1596?–1667), Dutch portrait painter.
[4] When the lowlands concluded a peace with Spain in 1648.

of Holland itself with all the good-fortune of its "thriving genius" reflected, quite spontaneously, in the national taste. The nation had learned to content itself with a religion which told little, or not at all, on the outsides of things. But we may fancy that something of the religious spirit had gone, according to the law of the transmutation of forces, into the scrupulous care for cleanliness, into the grave, old-world, conservative beauty of Dutch houses, which meant that the life people maintained in them was normally affectionate and pure.

The most curious florists of Holland were ambitious to supply the Burgomaster van Storck with the choicest products of their skill for the garden spread below the windows on either side of the portico, and along the central avenue of hoary beeches which led to it. Naturally this house, within a mile of the city of Haarlem, became a resort of the artists, then mixing freely in great society, giving and receiving hints as to the domestic picturesque. Creatures of leisure—of leisure on both sides—they were the appropriate complement of Dutch prosperity, as it was understood just then. Sebastian the elder could almost have wished his son to be one of them: it was the next best thing to being an influential publicist or statesman. The Dutch had just begun to see what a picture their country was—its canals, and *boompjis*,[5] and endless, broadly-lighted meadows, and thousands of miles of quaint water-side: and their painters, the first true masters of landscape for its own sake, were further informing them in the matter. They were bringing proof, for all who cared to see, of the wealth of colour there was all around them in this, supposably, sad land. Above all, they developed the old Low-country taste for interiors. Those innumerable *genre* pieces—conversation, music, play—were in truth the equivalent of novel-reading for that day; its own actual life, in its own proper circumstances, reflected in various degrees of idealisation, with no diminution of the sense of reality (that is to say) but with more and more purged and perfected delightfulness of interest. Themselves illustrating, as every student of their history knows, the good-fellowship of family life, it was the ideal of that life which these artists depicted; the ideal of home in a country

where the preponderant interest of life, after all, could not well be out of doors. Of the earth earthy—genuine red earth of the old Adam—it was an ideal very different from that which the sacred Italian painters had evoked from the life of Italy, yet, in its best types, was not without a kind of natural religiousness. And in the achievement of a type of beauty so national and vernacular, the votaries of purely Dutch art might well feel that the Italianisers, like Berghem, Boll, and Jan Weenix went so far afield in vain.[6]

The fine organisation and acute intelligence of Sebastian would have made him an effective connoisseur of the arts, as he showed by the justice of his remarks in those assemblies of the artists which his father so much loved. But in truth the arts were a matter he could but just tolerate. Why add, by a forced and artificial production, to the monotonous tide of competing, fleeting existence? Only, finding so much fine art actually about him, he was compelled (so to speak) to adjust himself to it; to ascertain and accept that in it which should least collide with, or might even carry forward a little, his own characteristic tendencies. Obviously somewhat jealous of his intellectual interests, he loved inanimate nature, it might have been thought, better than man. He cared nothing, indeed, for the warm sandbanks of Wynants, not for those eerie relics of the ancient Dutch woodland which survive in Hobbema and Ruysdael, still less for the highly-coloured sceneries of the academic band at Rome, in spite of the escape they provide one into clear breadth of atmosphere. For though Sebastian van Storck refused to travel, he loved the distant—enjoyed the sense of things seen from a distance, carrying us, as on wide wings of space itself, far out of one's actual surrounding. His preference in the matter of art was, therefore, for those prospects *à vol d'oiseau*—of the caged bird on the wing at last—of which Rubens had the secret, and still more Philip de Koninck, four of whose choicest works occupied the four walls of his chamber; visionary escapes, north, south, east, and west, into a wide-open though, it must be confessed, a somewhat sullen land. For the fourth of them he had exchanged with his mother a marvellously vivid Metsu, lately bequeathed to him, in which she herself was presented. They

---

[5] Trees.

[6] Seventeenth-century Dutch landscape painters and painters of still lifes. Other seventeenth-century painters cited in following paragraphs are Philip de Koningh (1619–81), Gabriel Metsu (1630–67), Jan Steen (1626–79), Cornelius De Witt (1623–72), Jan De Witt (1625–72), a Dutch statesman, Willem van Aelst (1620–79), Gerhard Douw (1613–75), Pieter de Hoogh (1643–1708), Willem Vandervelde (1610–93), the Hondekoeters, Giles, his son Gysbrecht (1613–53), and grandson Melchior (1636–95).

were the sole ornaments he permitted himself. From the midst of the busy and busy-looking house, crowded with the furniture and the pretty little toys of many generations, a long passage led the rare visitor up a winding staircase, and (again at the end of a long passage) he found himself as if shut off from the whole talkative Dutch world, and in the embrace of that wonderful quiet which is also possible in Holland at its height all around him. It was here that Sebastian could yield himself, with the only sort of love he had ever felt, to the supremacy of his difficult thoughts.—A kind of *empty* place! Here, you felt, all had been mentally put to rights by the working-out of a long equation, which had zero is equal to zero for its result. Here one did, and perhaps felt, nothing; one only thought. Of living creatures only birds came there freely, the sea-birds especially, to attract and detain which there were all sorts of ingenious contrivances about the windows, such as one may see in the cottage sceneries of Jan Steen and others. There was something, doubtless, of his passion for distance in this welcoming of the creatures of the air. An extreme simplicity in their manner of life was, indeed, characteristic of many a distinguished Hollander—William the Silent, Baruch de Spinoza, the brothers de Witt. But the simplicity of Sebastian van Storck was something different from that, and certainly nothing democratic. His mother thought him like one disembarrassing himself carefully, and little by little, of all impediments, habituating himself gradually to make shift with as little as possible, in preparation for a long journey.

The Burgomaster van Storck entertained a party of friends, consisting chiefly of his favourite artists, one summer evening. The guests were seen arriving on foot in the fine weather, some of them accompanied by their wives and daughters, against the light of the low sun, falling red on the old trees of the avenue and the faces of those who advanced along it:—Willem van Aelst, expecting to find hints for a flower-portrait in the exotics which would decorate the banqueting-room; Gerard Dow, to feed his eye, amid all that glittering luxury, on the combat between candle-light and the last rays of the departing sun; Thomas de Keyser, to catch by stealth the likeness of Sebastian the younger. Albert Cuyp was there, who, developing the latent gold in Rembrandt, had brought into his native Dordrecht a heavy wealth of sunshine, as exotic as those flowers or the eastern carpets on the Burgomaster's tables, with Hooch, the indoor Cuyp, and Willem van de

Velde, who painted those shore-pieces with gay ships of war, such as he loved, for his patron's cabinet. Thomas de Keyser came, in company with his brother Peter, his niece, and young Mr. Nicholas Stone from England, pupil of that brother Peter, who afterwards married the niece. For the life of Dutch artists, too, was exemplary in matters of domestic relationship, its history telling many a cheering story of mutual faith in misfortune. Hardly less exemplary was the comradeship which they displayed among themselves, obscuring their own best gifts sometimes, one in the mere accessories of another man's work, so that they came together to-night with no fear of falling out, and spoiling the musical interludes of Madame van Storck in the large back parlour. A little way behind the other guests, three of them together, son, grandson, and the grandfather, moving slowly, came the Hondecoeters—Giles, Gybrecht, and Melchior. They led the party before the house was entered, by fading light, to see the curious poultry of the Burgomaster go to roost; and it was almost night when the supper-room was reached at last. The occasion was an important one to Sebastian, and to others through him. For (was it the music of the duets? he asked himself next morning, with a certain distaste as he remembered it all, or the heady Spanish wines poured out so freely in those narrow but deep Venetian glasses?) on this evening he approached more nearly than he had ever yet done to Mademoiselle van Westrheene, as she sat there beside the *clavecin* looking very ruddy and fresh in her white satin, trimmed with glossy crimson swans-down.

So genially attempered, so warm, was life become, in the land of which Pliny had spoken as scarcely dry land at all. And, in truth, the sea which Sebastian so much loved, and with so great a satisfaction and sense of wellbeing in every hint of its nearness, is never far distant in Holland. Invading all places, stealing under one's feet, insinuating itself everywhere along an endless network of canals (by no means such formal channels as we understand by the name, but picturesque rivers, with sedgy banks and haunted by innumerable birds) its incidents present themselves oddly even in one's park or woodland walks; the ship in full sail appearing suddenly among the great trees or above the garden wall, where we had no suspicion of the presence of water. In the very conditions of life in such a country there was a standing force of pathos. The country itself shared the uncertainty of the individual human life; and there was pathos also in the constantly renewed, heavily-taxed labour, necessary to keep the native soil, fought for so unselfishly, there at all, with a warfare that must still be maintained when that other struggle with the Spaniard was over. But though Sebastian liked to breathe, so nearly, the sea and its influences, those were considerations he scarcely entertained. In his passion for *Schwindsucht*[7]—we haven't the word—he found it pleasant to think of the resistless element which left one hardly a foot-space amidst the yielding sand; of the old beds of lost rivers, surviving now only as deeper channels in the sea; of the remains of a certain ancient town, which within men's memory had lost its few remaining inhabitants, and, with its already empty tombs, dissolved and disappeared in the flood.

It happened, on occasion of an exceptionally low tide, that some remarkable relics were exposed to view on the coast of the island of Vleeland. A countryman's waggon overtaken by the tide, as he returned with merchandise from the shore! you might have supposed, but for a touch of grace in the construction of the thing—lightly wrought timber-work, united and adorned by a multitude of brass fastenings, like the work of children for their simplicity, while the rude, stiff chair, or throne, set upon it, seemed to distinguish it as a chariot of state. To some antiquarians it told the story of the overwhelming of one of the chiefs of the old primeval people of Holland, amid all his gala array, in a great storm. But it was another view which Sebastian preferred; that this object was sepulchral, namely, in its motive—the one surviving relic of a grand burial, in the ancient manner, of a king or hero, whose very tomb was wasted away.—*Sunt metis metæ!*[8] There came with it the odd fancy that he himself would like to have been dead and gone as long ago, with a kind of envy of those whose deceasing was so long since over.

On more peaceful days he would ponder Pliny's account of those primeval forefathers, but without Pliny's contempt for them. A cloyed Roman might despise their humble existence, fixed by necessity from age to age, and with no desire of change, as "the ocean poured in its flood twice a day, making it uncertain whether the country was a part of the continent or of the sea." But for his part Sebastian found something of poetry in all that, as he conceived what thoughts the old Hollander might have had at his fishing,

with nets themselves woven of seaweed, waiting carefully for his drink on the heavy rains, and taking refuge, as the flood rose, on the sand-hills, in a little hut constructed but airily on tall stakes, conformable to the elevation of the highest tides, like a navigator, thought the learned writer, when the sea was risen, like a ship-wrecked mariner when it was retired. For the fancy of Sebastian he lived with great breadths of calm light above and around him, influenced by, and, in a sense, living upon them, and surely might well complain, though to Pliny's so infinite surprise, on being made a Roman citizen.

And certainly Sebastian van Storck did not felicitate his people on the luck which, in the words of another old writer, "hath disposed them to so thriving a genius." Their restless ingenuity in making and maintaining dry land where nature had willed the sea, was even more like the industry of animals than had been that life of their forefathers. Away with that tetchy, feverish, unworthy agitation! with this and that, all too importunate, motive of interest! And then, "My son!" said his father, "be stimulated to action!" he, too, thinking of that heroic industry which had triumphed over nature precisely where the contest had been most difficult.

Yet, in truth, Sebastian was forcibly taken by the simplicity of a great affection, as set forth in an incident of real life of which he heard just then. The eminent Grotius[9] being condemned to perpetual imprisonment, his wife determined to share his fate, alleviated only by the reading of books sent by friends. The books, finished, were returned in a great chest. In this chest the wife enclosed the husband, and was able to reply to the objections of the soldiers who carried it complaining of its weight, with a self-control, which she maintained till the captive was in safety, herself remaining to face the consequences; and there was a kind of absoluteness of affection in that, which attracted Sebastian for a while to ponder on the practical forces which shape men's lives. Had he turned, indeed, to a practical career it would have been less in the direction of the military or political life than of another form of enterprise popular with his countrymen. In the eager, gallant life of that age, if the sword fell for a moment into its sheath, they were for starting off on perilous voyages to the regions of frost and snow in search after that "North-Western passage," for

---

[7] Consumption, or here, spiritual lassitude. [8] There are goals even for goals.
[9] Hugo Grotius (1583–1645), Dutch historian and statesman.

the discovery of which the States-General had offered large rewards. Sebastian, in effect, found a charm in the thought of that still, drowsy, spellbound world of perpetual ice, as in art and life he could always tolerate the sea. Admiral-general of Holland, as painted by Van der Helst, with a marine background by Back-huizen:[10]—at moments his father could fancy him so.

There was still another very different sort of character to which Sebastian would let his thoughts stray, without check, for a time. His mother, whom he much resembled outwardly, a Catholic from Brabant, had had saints in her family, and from time to time the mind of Sebastian had been occupied on the subject of monastic life, its quiet, its negation. The portrait of a certain Carthusian prior, which, like the famous statue of Saint Bruno, the first Carthusian, in the church of Santa Maria degli Angeli at Rome, could it have spoken, would have said, "Silence!" kept strange company with the painted visages of men of affairs. A great theological strife was then raging in Holland. Grave ministers of religion assembled sometimes, as in the painted scene by Rembrandt, in the Burgomaster's house, and once, not however in their company, came a renowned young Jewish divine, Baruch de Spinosa, with whom, most unexpectedly, Sebastian found himself in sympathy, meeting the young Jew's far-reaching thoughts half-way, to the confirmation of his own; and he did not know that his visitor, very ready with the pencil, had taken his likeness as they talked on the fly-leaf of his note-book. Alive to that theological disturbance in the air all around him, he refused to be moved by it, as essentially a strife on small matters, anticipating a vagrant regret which may have visited many other minds since, the regret, namely, that the old, pensive, use-and-wont Catholicism, which had accompanied the nation's earlier struggle for existence, and consoled it therein, had been taken from it. And for himself, indeed, what impressed him in that old Catholicism was a kind of lull in it—a lulling power— like that of the monotonous organ-music, which Holland, Catholic or not, still so greatly loves. But what he could not away with in the Catholic religion was its unfailing drift towards the concrete—the positive imageries of a faith, so richly beset with persons, things, historical incidents.

Rigidly logical in the method of his inferences,

he attained the poetic quality only by the audacity with which he conceived the whole sublime extension of his premises. The contrast was a strange one between the careful, the almost petty fineness of his personal surrounding—all the elegant conventionalities of life, in that rising Dutch family—and the mortal coldness of a temperament, the intellectual tendencies of which seemed to necessitate straightforward flight from all that was positive. He seemed, if one may say so, in love with death; preferring winter to summer; finding only a tranquillising influence in the thought of the earth beneath our feet cooling down for ever from its old cosmic heat; watching pleasurably how their colours fled out of things, and the long sand-bank in the sea, which had been the rampart of a town, was washed down in its turn. One of his acquaintance, a penurious young poet, who, having nothing in his pockets but the imaginative or otherwise barely potential gold of manuscript verses, would have grasped so eagerly, had they lain within his reach, at the elegant outsides of life, thought the fortunate Sebastian, possessed of every possible opportunity of that kind, yet bent only on dispensing with it, certainly a most puzzling and comfortless creature. A few only, half discerning what was in his mind, would fain have shared his intellectual clearness, and found a kind of beauty in this youthful enthusiasm for an abstract theorem. Extremes meeting, his cold and dispassionate detachment from all that is most attractive to ordinary minds came to have the impressiveness of a great passion. And for the most part, people had loved him; feeling instinctively that somewhere there must be the justification of his difference from themselves. It was like being in love: or it was an intellectual malady, such as pleaded for forbearance, like bodily sickness, and gave at times a resigned and touching sweetness to what he did and said. Only once, at a moment of the wild popular excitement which at that period was easy to provoke in Holland, there was a certain group of persons who would have shut him up as no well-wisher to, and perhaps a plotter against, the common-weal. A single traitor might cut the dykes in an hour, in the interest of the English or the French. Or, had he already committed some treasonable act, who was so anxious to expose no writing of his that he left his very letters unsigned, and there were little stratagems to get specimens of his fair manuscript? For

---

[10] Bartholomew Van der Helst (1613–70) and Ludolph Backhuysen (1631–1708), Dutch painters.

with all his breadth of mystic intention, he was persistent, as the hours crept on, to leave all the inevitable details of life at least in order, in equation. And all his singularities appeared to be summed up in his refusal to take his place in the life-sized family group *(très distingué et très soigné,*[11] remarks a modern critic of the work) painted about this time. His mother expostulated with him on the matter:—she must needs feel, a little icily, the emptiness of hope, and something more than the due measure of cold in things for a woman of her age, in the presence of a son who desired but to fade out of the world like a breath—and she suggested filial duty. "Good mother," he answered, "there are duties towards the intellect also, which women can but rarely understand."

The artists and their wives were come to supper again, with the Burgomaster van Storck. Mademoiselle van Westrheene was also come, with her sister and mother. The girl was by this time fallen in love with Sebastian; and she was one of the few who, in spite of his terrible coldness, really loved him for himself. But though of good birth she was poor, while Sebastian could not but perceive that he had many suitors of his wealth. In truth, Madame van Westrheene, her mother, did wish to marry this daughter into the great world, and plied many arts to that end, such as "daughterful" mothers use. Her healthy freshness of mien and mind, her ruddy beauty, some showy presents that had passed, were of a piece with the ruddy colouring of the very house these people lived in; and for a moment the cheerful warmth that may be felt in life seemed to come very close to him,—to come forth, and enfold him. Meantime the girl herself taking note of this, that on a former occasion of their meeting he had seemed likely to respond to her inclination, and that his father would readily consent to such a marriage, surprised him on the sudden with those coquetries and importunities, all those little arts of love, which often succeed with men. Only, to Sebastian they seemed opposed to that absolute nature we suppose in love. And while, in the eyes of all around him to-night, this courtship seemed to promise him, thus early in life, a kind of quiet happiness, he was coming to an estimate of the situation, with strict regard to that ideal of a calm, intellectual indifference, of which he was the sworn chevalier. Set in the cold, hard light of that ideal, this girl, with the pronounced personal views of her mother, and in the

very effectiveness of arts prompted by a real affection, bringing the warm life they prefigured so close to him, seemed vulgar! And still he felt himself bound in honour; or judged from their manner that she and those about them thought him thus bound. He did not reflect on the inconsistency of the feeling of honour (living, as it does essentially, upon the concrete and minute detail of social relationship) for one who, on principle, set so slight a value on anything whatever that is merely relative in its character.

The guests, lively and late, were almost pledging the betrothed in the rich wine. Only Sebastian's mother knew; and at that advanced hour, while the company were thus intently occupied, drew away the Burgomaster to confide to him the misgiving she felt, grown to a great height just then. The young man had slipped from the assembly; but certainly not with Mademoiselle van Westrheene, who was suddenly withdrawn also. And she never appeared again in the world. Already, next day, with the rumour that Sebastian had left his home, it was known that the expected marriage would not take place. The girl, indeed, alleged something in the way of a cause on her part; but seemed to fade away continually afterwards, and in the eyes of all who saw her was like one perishing of wounded pride. But to make a clean breast of her poor girlish wordliness, before she became a *béguine,*[12] she confessed to her mother the receipt of the letter—the cruel letter that had killed her. And in effect, the first copy of this letter, written with a very deliberate fineness, rejecting her—accusing her, so natural, and simply loyal! of a vulgar coarseness of character—was found, oddly tacked on, as their last word, to the studious record of the abstract thoughts which had been the real business of Sebastian's life, in the room whither his mother went to seek him next day, littered with the fragments of the one portrait of him in existence.

The neat and elaborate manuscript volume, of which this letter formed the final page (odd transition! by which a train of thought so abstract drew its conclusion in the sphere of action) afforded at length to the few who were interested in him a much-coveted insight into the curiosity of his existence; and I pause just here to indicate in outline the kind of reasoning through which, making the "Infinite" his beginning and his end, Sebastian had come to think all definite forms of being, the warm pressure of life, the cry of nature

---

[11] "Very distinguished, very carefully done."   [12] Member of a female religious order.

itself, no more than a troublesome irritation of the surface of the one absolute mind, a passing vexatious thought or uneasy dream there, at its height of petulant importunity in the eager, human creature.

The volume was, indeed, a kind of treatise to be:—a hard, systematic, well-concatenated train of thought, still implicated in the circumstances of a journal. Freed from the accidents of that particular literary form with its unavoidable details of place and occasion, the theoretic strain would have been found mathematically continuous. The already so weary Sebastian might perhaps never have taken in hand, or succeeded in, this detachment of his thoughts; every one of which, beginning with himself, as the peculiar and intimate apprehension of this or that particular day and hour, seemed still to protest against such disturbance, as if reluctant to part from those accidental associations of the personal history which had prompted it, and so become a purely intellectual abstraction.

The series began with Sebastian's boyish enthusiasm for a strange, fine saying of Doctor Baruch de Spinosa, concerning the Divine Love: —That whoso loveth God truly must not expect to be loved by him in return.[13] In mere reaction against an actual surrounding of which every circumstance tended to make him a finished egotist, that bold assertion defined for him the ideal of an intellectual disinterestedness, of a domain of unimpassioned mind, with the desire to put one's subjective side out of the way, and let pure reason speak.

And what pure reason affirmed in the first place, as the "beginning of wisdom," was that the world is but a thought, or a series of thoughts: that it exists, therefore, solely in mind. It showed him, as he fixed the mental eye with more and more of self-absorption on the phenomena of his intellectual existence, a picture or vision of the universe as actually the product, so far as he really knew it, of his own lonely thinking power— of himself, there, thinking: as being zero without him: and as possessing a perfectly homogeneous unity in that fact. "Things that have nothing in common with each other," said the axiomatic reason, "cannot be understood or explained by means of each other." But to pure reason things discovered themselves as being, in their essence, thoughts:—all things, even the most opposite things, mere transmutations of a single power, the power of thought. All was but conscious

mind. Therefore, all the more exclusively he must minister to mind, to the intellectual power, submitting himself to the sole direction of that, whithersoever it might lead him. Everything must be referred to, and, as it were, changed into the terms of that, if its essential value was to be ascertained. "Joy," he said, anticipating Spinosa—that, for the attainment of which men are ready to surrender all beside—"is but the name of a passion in which the mind passes to a greater perfection or power of thinking; as grief is the name of the passion in which it passes to a less."

Looking backward for the generative source of that creative power of thought in him, from his own mysterious intellectual being to its first cause, he still reflected, as one can but do, the enlarged pattern of himself into the vague region of hypothesis. In this way, some, at all events, would have explained his mental process. To him that process was nothing less than the apprehension, the revelation, of the greatest and most real of ideas—the true substance of all things. He, too, with his vividly-coloured existence, with this picturesque and sensuous world of Dutch art and Dutch reality all around that would fain have made him the prisoner of its colours, its genial warmth, its struggle for life, its selfish and crafty love, was but a transient perturbation of the one absolute mind; of which, indeed, all finite things whatever, time itself, the most durable achievements of nature and man, and all that seems most like independent energy, are no more than petty accidents or affections. Theorem and corollary! Thus they stood:

"There can be only one substance: (corollary) it is the greatest of errors to think that the non-existent, the world of finite things seen and felt, really is: (theorem): *for, whatever is, is but in that:* (practical corollary): one's wisdom, therefore, consists in hastening, so far as may be, the action of those forces which tend to the restoration of equilibrium, the calm surface of the absolute, untroubled mind, to *tabula rasa,* by the extinction in one's self of all that is but correlative to the finite illusion—by the suppression of ourselves."

In the loneliness which was gathering round him, and, oddly enough, as a somewhat surprising thing, he wondered whether there were, or had been, others possessed of like thoughts, ready to welcome any such as his veritable compatriots. And in fact he became aware just then, in readings difficult indeed, but which from their all-

---

[13] This and the following citations from Spinoza are from his *Ethics.*

absorbing interest seemed almost like an illicit pleasure, a sense of kinship with certain older minds. The study of many an earlier adventurous theorist satisfied his curiosity as the record of daring physical adventure, for instance, might satisfy the curiosity of the healthy. It was a tradition—a constant tradition—that daring thought of his; an echo, or haunting recurrent voice of the human soul itself, and as such sealed with natural truth, which certain minds would not fail to heed; discerning also, if they were really loyal to themselves, its practical conclusion.—The one alone is: and all things beside are but its passing affections, which have no necessary or proper right to be.

As but such "accidents" or "affections," indeed, there might have been found, within the circumference of that one infinite creative thinker, some scope for the joy and love of the creature. There have been dispositions in which that abstract theorem has only induced a renewed value for the finite interests around and within us. Centre of heat and light, truly nothing has seemed to lie beyond the touch of its perpetual summer. It has allied itself to the poetical or artistic sympathy, which feels challenged to acquaint itself with and explore the various forms of finite existence all the more intimately, just because of that sense of one lively spirit circulating through all things—a tiny particle of the one soul, in the sunbeam, or the leaf. Sebastian van Storck, on the contrary, was determined, perhaps by some inherited satiety or fatigue in his nature, to the opposite issue of the practical dilemma. For him, that one abstract being was as the pallid Arctic sun, disclosing itself over the dead level of a glacial, a barren and absolutely lonely sea. The lively purpose of life had been frozen out of it. What he must admire, and love if he could, was "equilibrium," the void, the *tabula rasa*, into which, through all those apparent energies of man and nature, that in truth are but forces of disintegration, the world was really settling. And, himself a mere circumstance in a fatalistic series, to which the clay of the potter was no sufficient parallel, he could not expect to be "loved in return." At first, indeed, he had a kind of delight in his thoughts—in the eager pressure forward, to whatsoever conclusion, of a rigid intellectual gymnastic, which was like the making of Euclid. Only, little by little, under the freezing influence of such propositions, the theoretic energy itself, and with it his old eagerness for truth, the care to track it from proposition to proposition, was chilled out of him. In fact, the

conclusion was there already, and might have been foreseen, in the premises. By a singular perversity, it seemed to him that every one of those passing "affections"—he too, alas! at times—was for ever trying to be, to assert *itself*, to maintain its isolated and petty self, by a kind of practical lie in things; although through every incident of its hypothetic existence it had protested that its proper function was to die. Surely! those transient affections marred the freedom, the truth, the beatific calm, of the absolute selfishness, which could not, if it would, pass beyond the circumference of itself; to which, at times, with a fantastic sense of wellbeing, he was capable of a sort of fanatical devotion. And those, as he conceived, were his moments of genuine theoretic insight, in which, under the abstract "perpetual light," he died to self; while the intellect, after all, had attained a freedom of its own through the vigorous act which assured him that, as nature was but a thought of his, so himself also was but the passing thought of God.

No! rather a puzzle only, an anomaly, upon that one, white, unruffled consciousness! His first principle once recognised, all the rest, the whole array of propositions down to the heartless practical conclusion, must follow of themselves. Detachment: to hasten hence: to fold up one's whole self, as a vesture put aside: to anticipate, by such individual force as he could find in him, the slow disintegration by which nature herself is levelling the eternal hills:—here would be the secret of peace, of such dignity and truth as there could be in a world which after all was essentially an illusion. For Sebastian at least, the world and the individual alike had been divested of all effective purpose. The most vivid of finite objects, the dramatic episodes of Dutch history, the brilliant personalities which had found their parts to play in them, that golden art, surrounding us with an ideal world, beyond which the real world is discernible indeed, but etherealised by the medium through which it comes to one: all this, for most men so powerful a link to existence, only set him on the thought of escape—means of escape—into a formless and nameless infinite world, quite evenly grey. The very emphasis of those objects, their importunity to the eye, the ear, the finite intelligence, was but the measure of their distance from what really is. One's personal presence, the presence, such as it is, of the most incisive things and persons around us, could only lessen by so much, that which really is. To restore *tabula rasa*, then, by a continual effort at self-effacement! Actually proud at times of his curious, well-reasoned nihilism, he could but regard what is called the business of life as no better than a trifling and wearisome delay. Bent on making sacrifice of the rich existence possible for him, as he would readily have sacrificed that of other people, to the bare and formal logic of the answer to a query (never proposed at all to entirely healthy minds) regarding the remote conditions and tendencies of that existence, he did not reflect that if others had inquired as curiously as himself the world could never have come so far at all—that the fact of its having come so far was itself a weighty exception to his hypothesis. His odd devotion, soaring or sinking into fanaticism, into a kind of religious mania, with what was really a vehement assertion of his individual will, he had formulated duty as the principle to hinder as little as possible what he called the restoration of equilibrium, the restora- of the primary consciousness to itself—its relief from that uneasy, tetchy, unworthy dream of a world, made so ill, or dreamt so weakly—to forget, to be forgotten.

And at length this dark fanaticism, losing the support of his pride in the mere novelty of a reasoning so hard and dry, turned round upon him, as our fanaticism will, in black melancholy. The theoretic or imaginative desire to urge Time's creeping footsteps, was felt now as the physical fatigue which leaves the book or the letter unfinished, or finishes eagerly out of hand, for mere finishing's sake, unimportant business. Strange! that the presence to the mind of a metaphysical abstraction should have had this power over one so fortunately endowed for the reception of the sensible world. It could hardly have been so with him but for the concurrence of physical causes with the influences proper to a mere thought. The moralist, indeed, might have noted that a meaner kind of pride, the morbid fear of vulgarity, lent secret strength to the intellectual prejudice, which realised duty as the renunciation of all finite objects, the fastidious refusal to be or do any limited thing. But besides this it was legible in his own admissions from time to time, that the body, following, as it does with powerful temperaments, the lead of mind and the will, the intellectual consumption (so to term it) had been concurrent with, had strengthened and been strengthened by, a vein of physical *phthisis*[14]—by a merely physical accident, after all, of his bodily constitution, such as might have

taken a different turn, had another accident fixed his home among the hills instead of on the shore. Is it only the result of disease? he would ask himself sometimes with a sudden suspicion of his intellectual cogency—this persuasion that myself, and all that surrounds me, are but a diminution of that which really is?—this unkindly melancholy?

The journal, with that "cruel" letter to Mademoiselle van Westrheene coming as the last step in the rigid process of theoretic deduction, circulated among the curious; and people made their judgments upon it. There were some who held that such opinions should be suppressed by law; that they were, or might become, dangerous to society. Perhaps it was the confessor of his mother who thought of the matter most justly. The aged man smiled, observing how, even for minds by no means superficial, the mere dress it wears alters the look of a familiar thought; with a happy sort of smile, as he added (reflecting that such truth as there was in Sebastian's theory was duly covered by the propositions of his own creed, and quoting Sebastian's favourite pagan wisdom from the lips of Saint Paul) "in Him, we live, and move, and have our being."[15]

Next day, as Sebastian escaped to the sea under the long, monotonous line of wind-mills, in comparative calm of mind—reaction of that pleasant morning from the madness of the night before—he was making light, or trying to make light, with some success, of his late distress. He would fain have thought it a small matter, to be adequately set at rest for him by certain well-tested influences of external nature, in a long visit to the place he liked best: a desolate house, amid the sands of the Helder, one of the old lodgings of his family, property now, rather, of the sea-birds, and almost surrounded by the encroaching tide, though there were still relics enough of hardy, sweet things about it. to form what was to Sebastian the most perfect garden in Holland. Here he could make "equation" between himself and what was not himself, and set things in order, in preparation towards such deliberate and final change in his manner of living as circumstances so clearly necessitated.

As he stayed in this place, with one or two silent serving people, a sudden rising of the wind altered, as it might seem, in a few dark, tempestuous hours, the entire world around him. The strong wind changed not again for fourteen days,

---

[14] Tuberculosis.   [15] Acts 17:28.

and its effect was a permanent one; so that people might have fancied that an enemy had indeed cut the dykes somewhere—a pin-hole enough to wreck the ship of Holland, or at least this portion of it, which underwent an inundation of the sea the like of which had not occurred in that province for half a century. Only, when the body of Sebastian was found, apparently not long after death, a child lay asleep, swaddled warmly in his heavy furs, in an upper room of the old tower, to which the tide was almost risen; though the building still stood firmly, and still with the means of life in plenty. And it was in the saving of this child, with a great effort, as certain circumstances seemed to indicate, that Sebastian had lost his life.

His parents were come to seek him, believing him bent on self-destruction, and were almost glad to find him thus. A learned physician, moreover, endeavoured to comfort his mother by remarking that in any case he must certainly have died ere many years were passed, slowly, perhaps painfully, of a disease then coming into the world; disease begotten by the fogs of that country—waters, he observed, not in their place, "above the firmament"[16]—on people grown somewhat over-delicate in their nature by the effects of modern luxury.

from Appreciations

The very title of this volume of Pater's essays says something about his habits as a critic: Pater rarely wrote denunciatory criticism; his strength lay in the appreciation. For Pater an appreciation was an indwelling in the spirit and quality of the original, sometimes to the point of creating a parallel work of art that had been evoked by the work under consideration. The essays from Appreciations *printed below all first appeared in periodicals: "Style" appeared in the* Fortnightly *in December 1888; "D. G. Rossetti" first appeared in T. H. Ward's series* The English Poets *(1883); the "Postscript" was adapted from Pater's "Romanticism," published first in November 1876 in* Macmillan's Magazine.

Style

SINCE all progress of mind consists for the most part in differentiation, in the resolution of an obscure and complex object into its component aspects, it is surely the stupidest of losses to confuse things which right reason has put asunder, to lose the sense of achieved distinctions, the distinction between poetry and prose, for instance, or, to speak more exactly, between the laws and characteristic excellences of verse and prose composition. On the other hand, those who have dwelt most emphatically on the distinction between prose and verse, prose and poetry, may sometimes have been tempted to limit the proper functions of prose too narrowly; and this again is at least false economy, as being, in effect, the renunciation of a certain means or faculty, in a world where after all we must needs make the most of things. Critical efforts to limit art *a priori*, by anticipations regarding the natural incapacity of the material with which this or that artist works, as the sculptor with solid form, or the prose-writer with the ordinary language of men, are always liable to be discredited by the facts of artistic production; and while prose is actually found to be a coloured thing with Bacon, picturesque with Livy and Carlyle, musical with Cicero and Newman, mystical and intimate with Plato and Michelet and Sir Thomas Browne, exalted or florid, it may be, with Milton and Taylor, it will be useless to protest that it can be nothing at all, except something very tamely and narrowly confined to mainly practical ends—a kind of "good round-hand;" as useless as the protest that poetry might not touch prosaic subjects as with Wordsworth, or an abstruse matter as with Browning, or treat contemporary life nobly as with Tennyson. In subordination to

[16] Genesis 1:7.

one essential beauty in all good literary style, in all literature as a fine art, as there are many beauties of poetry so the beauties of prose are many, and it is the business of criticism to estimate them as such; as it is good in the criticism of verse to look for those hard, logical, and quasi-prosaic excellences which that too has, or needs. To find in the poem, amid the flowers, the allusions, the mixed perspectives, of *Lycidas* for instance, the thought, the logical structure:— how wholesome! how delightful! as to identify in prose what we call the poetry, the imaginative power, not treating it as out of place and a kind of vagrant intruder, but by way of an estimate of its rights, that is, of its achieved powers, there.

Dryden, with the characteristic instinct of his age, loved to emphasise the distinction between poetry and prose, the protest against their confusion with each other, coming with somewhat diminished effect from one whose poetry was so prosaic. In truth, his sense of prosaic excellence affected his verse rather than his prose, which is not only fervid, richly figured, poetic, as we say, but vitiated, all unconsciously, by many a scanning line. Setting up correctness, that humble merit of prose, as the central literary excellence, he is really a less correct writer than he may seem, still with an imperfect mastery of the relative pronoun. It might have been foreseen that, in the rotations of mind, the province of poetry in prose would find its assertor; and, a century after Dryden, amid very different intellectual needs, and with the need therefore of great modifications in literary form, the range of the poetic force in literature was effectively enlarged by Wordsworth. The true distinction between prose and poetry he regarded as the almost technical or accidental one of the absence or presence of metrical beauty, or, say! metrical restraint; and for him the opposition came to be between verse and prose of course; but, as the essential dichotomy in this matter, between imaginative and unimaginative writing, parallel to De Quincey's distinction[1] between "the literature of power and the literature of knowledge," in the former of which the composer gives us not fact, but his peculiar sense of fact, whether past or present.

Dismissing then, under sanction of Wordsworth, that harsher opposition of poetry to prose, as savouring in fact of the arbitrary psychology of the last century, and with it the prejudice that there can be but one only beauty of prose style, I propose here to point out certain qualities of all literature as a fine art, which, if they apply to the literature of fact, apply still more to the literature of the imaginative sense of fact, while they apply indifferently to verse and prose, so far as either is really imaginative—certain conditions of true art in both alike, which conditions may also contain in them the secret of the proper discrimination and guardianship of the peculiar excellences of either.

The line between fact and something quite different from external fact is, indeed, hard to draw. In Pascal, for instance, in the persuasive writers generally, how difficult to define the point where, from time to time, argument which, if it is to be worth anything at all, must consist of facts or groups of facts, becomes a pleading— a theorem no longer, but essentially an appeal to the reader to catch the writer's spirit, to think with him, if one can or will—an expression no longer of fact but of his sense of it, his peculiar intuition of a world, prospective, or discerned below the faulty conditions of the present, in either case changed somewhat from the actual world. In science, on the other hand, in history so far as it conforms to scientific rule, we have a literary domain where the imagination may be thought to be always an intruder. And as, in all science, the functions of literature reduce themselves eventually to the transcribing of fact, so all the excellences of literary form in regard to science are reducible to various kinds of painstaking; this good quality being involved in all "skilled work" whatever, in the drafting of an act of parliament, as in sewing. Yet here again, the writer's sense of fact, in history especially, and in all those complex subjects which do but lie on the borders of science, will still take the place of fact, in various degrees. Your historian, for instance, with absolutely truthful intention, amid the multitude of facts presented to him must needs select, and in selecting assert something of his own humour, something that comes not of the world without but of a vision within. So Gibbon moulds his unwieldy material to a preconceived view. Livy, Tacitus, Michelet, moving full of poignant sensibility amid the records of the past, each, after his own sense, modifies—who can tell where and to what degree?—and becomes something else than a transcriber; each, as he thus modifies, passing into the domain of art proper. For just in proportion as the writer's aim, consciously or unconsciously, comes to be the transcribing, not

---

[1] A distinction made in various places by De Quincey. See his "Poetry of Pope."

of the world, not of mere fact, but of his sense of it, he becomes an artist, his work *fine* art; and good art (as I hope ultimately to show) in proportion to the truth of his presentment of that sense; as in those humbler or plainer functions of literature also, truth—truth to bare fact, there—is the essence of such artistic quality as they may have. Truth! there can be no merit, no craft at all, without that. And further, all beauty is in the long run only *fineness* of truth, or what we call expression, the finer accommodation of speech to that vision within.

—The transcript of his sense of fact rather than the fact, as being preferable, pleasanter, more beautiful to the writer himself. In literature, as in every other product of human skill, in the moulding of a bell or a platter for instance, wherever this sense asserts itself, wherever the producer so modifies his work as, over and above its primary use or intention, to make it pleasing (to himself, of course, in the first instance) there, "fine" as opposed to merely serviceable art, exists. Literary art, that is, like all art which is in any way imitative or reproductive of fact— form, or colour, or incident—is the representation of such fact as connected with soul, of a specific personality, in its preferences, its volition and power.

Such is the matter of imaginative or artistic literature—this transcript, not of mere fact, but of fact in its infinite variety, as modified by human preference in all its infinitely varied forms. It will be good literary art not because it is brilliant or sober, or rich, or impulsive, or severe, but just in proportion as its representation of that sense, that soul-fact, is true, verse being only one department of such literature, and imaginative prose, it may be thought, being the special art of the modern world. That imaginative prose should be the special and opportune art of the modern world results from two important facts about the latter: first, the chaotic variety and complexity of its interests, making the intellectual issue, the really master currents of the present time incalculable—a condition of mind little susceptible of the restraint proper to verse form, so that the most characteristic verse of the nineteenth century has been lawless verse; and secondly, an all-pervading naturalism, a

curiosity about everything whatever as it really is, involving a certain humility of attitude, cognate to what must, after all, be the less ambitious form of literature. And prose thus asserting itself as the special and privileged artistic faculty of the present day, will be, however critics may try to narrow its scope, as varied in its excellence as humanity itself reflecting on the facts of its latest experience—an instrument of many stops, meditative, observant, descriptive, eloquent, analytic, plaintive, fervid. Its beauties will be not exclusively "pedestrian": it will exert, in due measure, all the varied charms of poetry, down to the rhythm which, as in Cicero, or Michelet, or Newman, at their best, gives its musical value to every syllable. [2]

The literary artist is of necessity a scholar, and in what he proposes to do will have in mind, first of all, the scholar and the scholarly conscience—the male conscience in this matter, as we must think it, under a system of education which still to so large an extent limits real scholarship to men. In his self-criticism, he supposes always that sort of reader who will go (full of eyes) warily, considerately, though without consideration for him, over the ground which the female conscience traverses so lightly, so amiably. For the material in which he works is no more a creation of his own than the sculptor's marble. Product of a myriad various minds and contending tongues, compact of obscure and minute association, a language has its own abundant and often recondite laws, in the habitual and summary recognition of which scholarship consists. A writer, full of a matter he is before all things anxious to express, may think of those laws, the limitations of vocabulary, structure, and the like, as a restriction, but if a real artist will find in them an opportunity. His punctilious observance of the proprieties of his medium will diffuse through all he writes a general air of sensibility, of refined usage. *Exclusiones debitæ naturæ*—the exclusions, or rejections, which nature demands—we know how large a part these play, according to Bacon, in the science of nature. In a somewhat changed sense, we might say that the art of the scholar is summed up in the observance of those rejections demanded by the nature of his medium,

---

[2] Mr. Saintsbury, in his *Specimens of English Prose, from Malory to Macaulay,* has succeeded in tracing, through successive English prose-writers, the tradition of that severer beauty in them, of which this admirable scholar of our literature is known to be a lover. *English Prose, from Mandeville to Thackeray,* more recently "chosen and edited" by a younger scholar, Mr. Arthur Galton, of New College, Oxford, a lover of our literature at once enthusiastic and discreet, aims at a more various illustration of the eloquent powers of English prose, and is a delightful companion. [Pater's note]

the material he must use. Alive to the value of an atmosphere in which every term finds its utmost degree of expression, and with all the jealousy of a lover of words, he will resist a constant tendency on the part of the majority of those who use them to efface the distinctions of language, the facility of writers often reinforcing in this respect the work of the vulgar. He will feel the obligation not of the laws only, but of those affinities, avoidances, those mere preferences, of his language, which through the associations of literary history have become a part of its nature, prescribing the rejection of many a neology, many a license, many a gipsy phrase which might present itself as actually expressive. His appeal, again, is to the scholar, who has great experience in literature, and will show no favour to short-cuts, or hackneyed illustration, or an affectation of learning designed for the unlearned. Hence a contention, a sense of self-restraint and renunciation, having for the susceptible reader the effect of a challenge for minute consideration; the attention of the writer, in every minutest detail, being a pledge that it is worth the reader's while to be attentive too, that the writer is dealing scrupulously with his instrument, and therefore, indirectly, with the reader himself also, that he has the science of the instrument he plays on, perhaps, after all, with a freedom which in such case will be the freedom of a master.

For meanwhile, braced only by those restraints, he is really vindicating his liberty in the making of a vocabulary, an entire system of composition, for himself, his own true manner; and when we speak of the manner of a true master we mean what is essential in his art. Pedantry being only the scholarship of *le cuistre* [3] (we have no English equivalent) he is no pedant, and does but show his intelligence of the rules of language in his freedoms with it, addition or expansion, which like the spontaneities of manner in a well-bred person will still further illustrate good taste.—The right vocabulary! Translators have not invariably seen how all-important that is in the work of translation, driving for the most part at idiom or construction; whereas, if the original be first-rate, one's first care should be with its elementary particles, Plato, for instance, being often reproducible by an exact following, with no variation in structure, of word after word, as the pencil follows a drawing under tracing-paper, so only

each word or syllable be not of false colour, to change my illustration a little.

Well! that is because any writer worth translating at all has winnowed and searched through his vocabulary, is conscious of the words he would select in systematic reading of a dictionary, and still more of the words he would reject were the dictionary other than Johnson's; and doing this with his peculiar sense of the world ever in view, in search of an instrument for the adequate expression of that, he begets a vocabulary faithful to the colouring of his own spirit, and in the strictest sense original. That living authority which language needs lies, in truth, in its scholars, who recognising always that every language possesses a genius, a very fastidious genius, of its own, expand at once and purify its very elements, which must needs change along with the changing thoughts of living people. Ninety years ago, for instance, great mental force, certainly, was needed by Wordsworth, to break through the consecrated poetic associations of a century, and speak the language that was his, that was to become in a measure the language of the next generation. But he did it with the tact of a scholar also. English, for a quarter of a century past, has been assimilating the phraseology of pictorial art; for half a century, the phraseology of the great German metaphysical movement of eighty years ago; in part also the language of mystical theology: and none but pedants will regret a great consequent increase of its resources. For many years to come its enterprise may well lie in the naturalisation of the vocabulary of science, so only it be under the eye of a sensitive scholarship—in a liberal naturalisation of the ideas of science too, for after all the chief stimulus of good style is to possess a full, rich, complex matter to grapple with. The literary artist, therefore, will be well aware of physical science; science also attaining, in its turn, its true literary ideal. And then, as the scholar is nothing without the historic sense, he will be apt to restore not really obsolete or really worn-out words, but the finer edge of words still in use: *ascertain, communicate, discover,*—words like these it has been part of our "business" to misuse. And still, as language was made for man, he will be no authority for correctnesses which, limiting freedom of utterance, were yet but accidents in their origin; as if one vowed not to say *"its,"* which ought to have been in Shakespeare; *"his"* and

---

[3] The narrow-minded pedant.

"*hers*," for inanimate objects, being but a barbarous and really inexpressive survival. Yet we have known many things like this. Racy Saxon monosyllables, close to us as touch and sight, he will intermix readily with those long, savoursome, Latin words, rich in "second intention." In this late day certainly, no critical process can be conducted reasonably without eclecticism. Of such eclecticism we have a justifying example in one of the first poets of our time. How illustrative of monosyllabic effect, of sonorous Latin, of the phraseology of science, of metaphysic, of colloquialism even, are the writings of Tennyson; yet with what a fine, fastidious scholarship throughout!

A scholar writing for the scholarly, he will of course leave something to the willing intelligence of his reader. "To go preach to the first passer-by," says Montaigne, "to become tutor to the ignorance of the first I meet, is a thing I abhor;" a thing, in fact, naturally distressing to the scholar, who will therefore ever be shy of offering uncomplimentary assistance to the reader's wit. To really strenuous minds there is a pleasurable stimulus in the challenge for a continuous effort on their part, to be rewarded by securer and more intimate grasp of the author's sense. Self-restraint, a skilful economy of means, *ascêsis*, that too has a beauty of its own; and for the reader supposed there will be an æsthetic satisfaction in that frugal closeness of style which makes the most of a word, in the exaction from every sentence of a precise relief, in the just spacing out of word to thought, in the logically filled space connected always with the delightful sense of difficulty overcome.

Different classes of persons, at different times, make, of course, very various demands upon literature. Still, scholars, I suppose, and not only scholars, but all disinterested lovers of books, will always look to it, as to all other fine art, for a refuge, a sort of cloistral refuge, from a certain vulgarity in the actual world. A perfect poem like *Lycidas*, a perfect fiction like *Esmond*, the perfect handling of a theory like Newman's *Idea of a University*, has for them something of the uses of a religious "retreat." Here, then, with a view to the central need of a select few, those "men of a finer thread" who have formed and maintain the literary ideal everything, every component element, will have undergone exact trial, and, above all, there will be no uncharacteristic or tarnished or vulgar decoration, permissible ornament being for the most part

structural, or necessary. As the painter in his picture, so the artist in his book, aims at the production by honourable artifice of a peculiar atmosphere. "The artist," says Schiller, "may be known rather by what he *omits*"; and in literature, too, the true artist may be best recognised by his tact of omission. For to the grave reader words too are grave; and the ornamental word, the figure, the accessory form or colour or reference, is rarely content to die to thought precisely at the right moment, but will inevitably linger awhile, stirring a long "brain-wave" behind it of perhaps quite alien associations.

Just there, it may be, is the detrimental tendency of the sort of scholarly attentiveness of mind I am recommending. But the true artist allows for it. He will remember that, as the very word ornament indicates what is in itself non-essential, so the "one beauty" of all literary style is of its very essence, and independent, in prose and verse alike, of all removable decoration; that it may exist in its fullest lustre, as in Flaubert's *Madame Bovary*, for instance, or in Stendhal's *Le Rouge et Le Noir*, in a composition utterly unadorned, with hardly a single suggestion of visibly beautiful things. Parallel, allusion, the allusive way generally, the flowers in the garden: —he knows the narcotic force of these upon the negligent intelligence to which any *diversion*, literally, is welcome, any vagrant intruder, because one can go wandering away with it from the immediate subject. Jealous, if he have a really quickening motive within, of all that does not hold directly to that, of the facile, the otiose, he will never depart from the strictly pedestrian process, unless he gains a ponderable something thereby. Even assured of its congruity, he will still question its serviceableness. Is it worth while, can we afford, to attend to just that, to just that figure or literary reference, just then?—Surplusage! he will dread that, as the runner on his muscles. For in truth all art does but consist in the removal of surplusage, from the last finish of the gem-engraver blowing away the last particle of invisible dust, back to the earliest divination of the finished work to be, lying somewhere, according to Michelangelo's fancy, in the rough-hewn block of stone.

And what applies to figure or flower must be understood of all other accidental or removable ornaments of writing whatever; and not of specific ornament only, but of all that latent colour and imagery which language as such carries in it. A lover of words for their own sake, to whom nothing about them is unimportant, a minute and constant observer of their physiognomy, he will be on the alert not only for obviously mixed metaphors of course, but for the metaphor that is mixed in all our speech, though a rapid use may involve no cognition of it. Currently recognising the incident, the colour, the physical elements or particles in words like *absorb, consider, extract,* to take the first that occur, he will avail himself of them, as further adding to the resources of expression. The elementary particles of language will be realised as colour and light and shade through his scholarly living in the full sense of them. Still opposing the constant degradation of language by those who use it carelessly, he will not treat coloured glass as if it were clear; and while half the world is using figure unconsciously, will be fully aware not only of all that latent figurative texture in speech, but of the vague, lazy, half-formed personification—a rhetoric, depressing, and worse than nothing, because it has no really rhetorical motive—which plays so large a part there, and, as in the case of more ostentatious ornament, scrupulously exact of it, from syllable to syllable, its precise value.

So far I have been speaking of certain conditions of the literary art arising out of the medium or material in or upon which it works, the essential qualities of language and its aptitudes for contingent ornamentation, matters which define scholarship as science and good taste respectively. They are both subservient to a more intimate quality of good style: more intimate, as coming nearer to the artist himself. The otiose, the facile, surplusage: why are these abhorrent to the true literary artist, except because, in literary as in all other art, structure is all-important, felt, or painfully missed, everywhere?—that architectural conception of work, which forsees the end in the beginning and never loses sight of it, and in every part is conscious of all the rest, till the last sentence does but, with undiminished vigour, unfold and justify the first—a condition of literary art, which, in contradistinction to another quality of the artist himself, to be spoken of later, I shall call the necessity of *mind* in style.

An acute philosophical writer, the late Dean Mansel[4] (a writer whose works illustrate the literary beauty there may be in closeness, and with obvious repression or economy of a fine rhetorical gift) wrote a book, of fascinating precision in a very obscure subject, to show that all the technical laws of logic are but means of securing, in each and all of its apprehensions, the unity, the strict identity with itself, of the apprehending mind. All the laws of good writing aim at a similar unity or identity of the mind in all the processes by which the word is associated to its import. The term is right, and has its essential beauty, when it becomes, in a manner, what it signifies, as with the names of simple sensations. To give the phrase, the sentence, the structural member, the entire composition, song, or essay, a similar unity with its subject and with itself:—style is in the right way when it tends towards that. All depends upon the original unity, the vital wholeness and identity, of the initiatory apprehension or view. So much is true of all art, which therefore requires always its logic, its comprehensive reason—insight, foresight, retrospect, in simultaneous action—true, most of all, of the literary art, as being of all the arts most closely cognate to the abstract intelligence. Such logical coherency may be evidenced not merely in the lines of composition as a whole, but in the choice of a single word, while it by no means interferes with, but may even prescribe, much variety, in the building of the sentence for instance, or in the manner, argumentative, descriptive, discursive, of this or that part or member of the entire design. The blithe, crisp sentence, decisive as a child's expression of its needs, may alternate with the long-contending, victoriously intricate sentence; the sentence, born with the integrity of a single word, relieving the sort of sentence in which, if you look closely, you can see much contrivance, much adjustment, to bring a highly qualified matter into compass at one view. For the literary architecture, if it is to be rich and expressive, involves not only foresight of the end in the beginning, but also development or growth of design, in the process of execution, with many irregularities, surprises, and afterthoughts; the contingent as well as the necessary being subsumed under the unity of the whole. As truly, to the lack of such architectural design, of a single, almost visual, image, vigorously informing an entire, perhaps very intricate, composition, which shall be austere, ornate, argumentative, fanciful, yet true from first to last to that vision within, may be attributed those weaknesses of conscious or unconscious repetition of word, phrase, motive, or member of the whole matter, indicating, as Flaubert was

---

[4] Henry L. Mansel (1820–71), Dean of St. Paul's.

aware, an original structure in thought not organically complete. With such foresight, the actual conclusion will most often get itself written out of hand, before, in the more obvious sense, the work is finished. With some strong and leading sense of the world, the tight hold of which secures true *composition* and not mere loose accretion, the literary artist, I suppose, goes on considerately, setting joint to joint, sustained by yet restraining the productive ardour, retracing the negligences of his first sketch, repeating his steps only that he may give the reader a sense of secure and restful progress, readjusting mere assonances even, that they may soothe the reader, or at least not interrupt him on his way; and then, somewhere before the end comes, is burdened, inspired, with his conclusion, and betimes delivered of it, leaving off, not in weariness and because he finds *himself* at an end, but in all the freshness of volition. His work now structurally complete, with all the accumulating effect of secondary shades of meaning, he finishes the whole up to the just proportion of that ante-penultimate conclusion, and all becomes expressive. The house he has built is rather a body he has informed. And so it happens, to its greater credit, that the better interest even of a narrative to be recounted, a story to be told, will often be in its second reading. And though there are instances of great writers who have been no artists, an unconscious tact sometimes directing work in which we may detect, very pleasurably, many of the effects of conscious art, yet one of the greatest pleasures of really good prose literature is in the critical tracing out of that conscious artistic structure, and the pervading sense of it as we read. Yet of poetic literature too; for, in truth, the kind of constructive intelligence here supposed is one of the forms of the imagination.

That is the special function of mind, in style. Mind and soul:—hard to ascertain philosophically, the distinction is real enough practically, for they often interfere, are sometimes in conflict, with each other. Blake, in the last century, is an instance of preponderating soul, embarrassed, at a loss, in an era of preponderating mind. As a quality of style, at all events, soul is a fact, in certain writers—the way they have of absorbing language, of attracting it into the peculiar spirit they are of, with a subltey which makes the actual result seem like some inexplicable inspiration. By mind, the literary artist reaches us, through static and objective indications of design in his work, legible to all. By soul, he reaches us, somewhat capriciously perhaps, one and not

another, through vagrant sympathy and a kind of immediate contact. Mind we cannot choose but approve where we recognise it; soul may repel us, not because we misunderstand it. The way in which theological interests sometimes avail themselves of language is perhaps the best illustration of the force I mean to indicate generally in literature, by the word *soul*. Ardent religious persuasion may exist, may make its way, without finding any equivalent heat in language: or, again, it may enkindle words to various degrees, and when it really takes hold of them doubles its force. Religious history presents many remarkable instances in which, through no mere phrase-worship, an unconscious literary tact has, for the sensitive, laid open a privileged pathway from one to another. "The altar-fire," people say, "has touched those lips!" The Vulgate, the English Bible, the English Prayer-Book, the writings of Swedenborg, the Tracts for the Times: —there, we have instances of widely different and largely diffused phases of religious feeling in operation as soul in style. But something of the same kind acts with similar power in certain writers of quite other than theological literature, on behalf of some wholly personal and peculiar sense of theirs. Most easily illustrated by theological literature, this quality lends to profane writers a kind of religious influence. At their best, these writers become, as we say sometimes, "prophets"; such character depending on the effect not merely of their matter, but of their matter as allied to, in "electric affinity" with, peculiar form, and working in all cases by an immediate sympathetic contact, on which account it is that it may be called soul, as opposed to mind, in style. And this too is a faculty of choosing and rejecting what is congruous or otherwise, with a drift towards unity—unity of atmosphere here, as there of design—soul securing colour (or perfume, might we say?) as mind secures form, the latter being essentially finite, the former vague or infinite, as the influence of a living person is practically infinite. There are some to whom nothing has any real interest, or real meaning, except as operative in a given person; and it is they who best appreciate the quality of soul in literary art. They seem to know a *person*, in a book, and make way by intuition: yet, although they thus enjoy the completeness of a personal information, it is still a characteristic of soul, in this sense of the word, that it does but suggest what can never be uttered, not as being different from, or more obscure than, what actually gets said, but as containing that plenary substance of which there is only one phase or facet in what is there expressed.

If all high things have their martyrs, Gustave Flaubert might perhaps rank as the martyr of literary style. In his printed correspondence, a curious series of letters, written in his twenty-fifth year, records what seems to have been his one other passion—a series of letters which, with its fine casuistries, its firmly repressed anguish, its tone of harmonious grey, and the sense of disillusion in which the whole matter ends, might have been, a few slight changes supposed, one of his own fictions. Writing to Madame X. certainly he does display, by "taking thought" mainly, by constant and delicate pondering, as in his love for literature, a heart really moved, but still more, and as the pledge of that emotion, a loyalty to his work. Madame X., too, is a literary artist, and the best gifts he can send her are precepts of perfection in art, counsels for the effectual pursuit of that better love. In his love-letters it is the pains and pleasures of art he insists on, its solaces: he communicates secrets, reproves, encourages, with a view to that. Whether the lady was dissatisfied with such divided or indirect service, the reader is not enabled to see; but sees that, in Flaubert's part at least, a living person could be no rival of what was, from first to last, his leading passion, a somewhat solitary and exclusive one.

I must scold you (he writes) for one thing, which shocks, scandalises me, the small concern, namely, you show for art just now. As regards glory be it so: there, I approve. But for art!—the one thing in life that is good and real—can you compare with it an earthly love?—prefer the adoration of a relative beauty to the *cultus* of the true beauty? Well! I tell you the truth. That is the one thing good in me: the one thing I have, to me estimable. For yourself, you blend with the beautiful a heap of alien things, the useful, the agreeable, what not?—

The only way not to be unhappy is to shut yourself up in art, and count everything else as nothing. Pride takes the place of all beside when it is established on a large basis. Work! God wills it. That, it seems to me, is clear.—

I am reading over again the *Æneid*, certain verses of which I repeat to myself to satiety. There are phrases there which stay in one's head, by which I find myself beset, as with those musical airs which are for ever returning, and cause you pain, you love them so much. I observe that I no longer laugh much, and am no longer depressed. I am ripe. You talk of my serenity, and envy me. It may well surprise you. Sick, irritated, the prey a thousand times a day of cruel pain, I continue my labour like a true working-man, who, with

sleeves turned up, in the sweat of his brow, beats away at his anvil, never troubling himself whether it rains or blows, for hail or thunder. I was not like that formerly. The change has taken place naturally, though my will has counted for something in the matter.—

Those who write in good style are sometimes accused of a neglect of ideas, and of the moral end, as if the end of the physician were something else than healing, of the painter than painting—as if the end of art were not, before all else, the beautiful.

What, then, did Flaubert understand by beauty, in the art he pursued with so much fervour, with so much self-command? Let us hear a sympathetic commentator:—

Possessed of an absolute belief that there exists but one way of expressing one thing, one word to call it by, one adjective to qualify, one verb to animate it, he gave himself to superhuman labour for the discovery, in every phase, of that word, that verb, that epithet. In this way, he believed in some mysterious harmony of expression, and when a true word seemed to him to lack euphony still went on seeking another, with invincible patience, certain that he had not yet got hold of the *unique* word. . . . A thousand preoccupations would beset him at the same moment, always with this desperate certitude fixed in his spirit: Among all the expressions in the world, all forms and turns of expression, there is but *one*—one form, one mode—to express what I want to say.

The one word for the one thing, the one thought, amid the multitude of words, terms, that might just do: the problem of style was there!—the unique word, phrase, sentence, paragraph, essay, or song, absolutely proper to the single mental presentation or vision within. In that perfect justice, over and above the many contingent and removable beauties with which beautiful style may charm us, but which it can exist without, independent of them yet dexterously availing itself of them, omnipresent in good work, in function at every point, from single epithets to the rhythm of a whole book, lay the specific, indispensable, very intellectual, beauty of literature, the possibility of which constitutes it a fine art.

One seems to detect the influence of a philosophic idea there, the idea of a natural economy, of some pre-existent adaptation, between a relative, somewhere in the world of thought, and its correlative, somewhere in the world of language—both alike, rather, somewhere in the mind of the artist, desiderative, expectant, inventive—meeting each other with the readiness of "soul and body reunited," in Blake's rapturous design; and, in fact, Flaubert was fond of giving his theory philosophical expression.—

There are no beautiful thoughts (he would say) without beautiful forms, and conversely. As it is impossible to extract from a physical body the qualities which really constitute it—colour, extension, and the like—without reducing it to a hollow abstraction, in a word, without destroying it; just so it is impossible to detach the form from the idea, for the idea only exists by virtue of the form.

All the recognised flowers, the removable ornaments of literature (including harmony and ease in reading aloud, very carefully considered by him) counted, certainly; for these too are part of the actual value of what one says. But still, after all, with Flaubert, the search, the unwearied research, was not for the smooth, or winsome, or forcible word, as such, as with false Ciceronians, but quite simply and honestly, for the word's adjustment to its meaning. The first condition of this must be, of course, to know yourself, to have ascertained your own sense exactly. Then, if we suppose an artist, he says to the reader,—I want you to see precisely what I see. Into the mind sensitive to "form," a flood of random sounds, colours, incidents, is ever penetrating from the world without, to become, by sympathetic selection, a part of its very structure, and, in turn, the visible vesture and expression of that other world it sees so steadily within, nay, already with a partial conformity thereto, to be refined, enlarged, corrected, at a hundred points; and it is just there, just at those doubtful points that the function of style, as tact or taste, intervenes. The unique term will come more quickly to one than another, at one time than another, according also to the kind of matter in question. Quickness and slowness, ease and closeness alike, have nothing to do with the artistic character of the true word found at last. As there is a charm of ease, so there is also a special charm in the signs of discovery, of effort and contention towards a due end, as so often with Flaubert himself—in the style which has been pliant, as only obstinate, durable metal can be, to the inherent perplexities and recusancy of a certain difficult thought.

If Flaubert has not told us, perhaps we should never have guessed how tardy and painful his own procedure really was, and after reading his confession may think that his almost endless hesitation had much to do with diseased nerves. Often, perhaps, the felicity supposed will be the product of a happier, a more exuberant nature

than Flaubert's. Aggravated, certainly, by a morbid physical condition, that anxiety in "seeking the phrase," which gathered all the other small *ennuis* of a really quiet existence into a kind of battle, was connected with his lifelong contention against facile poetry, facile art—art, facile and flimsy; and what constitutes the true artist is not the slowness or quickness of the process, but the absolute success of the result. As with those labourers in the parable, the prize is independent of the mere length of the actual day's work. "You talk," he writes, odd, trying lover, to Madame X.—

"You talk of the exclusiveness of my literary tastes. That might have enabled you to divine what kind of a person I am in the matter of love. I grow so hard to please as a literary artist, that I am driven to despair. I shall end by not writing another line."

"Happy," he cries, in a moment of discouragement at that patient labour, which for him, certainly, was the condition of a great success—

Happy those who have no doubts of themselves! who lengthen out, as the pen runs on, all that flows forth from their brains. As for me, I hesitate, I disappoint myself, turn round upon myself in despite: my taste is augmented in proportion as my natural vigour decreases, and I afflict my soul over some dubious word out of all proportion to the pleasure I get from a whole page of good writing. One would have to live two centuries to attain a true idea of any matter whatever. What Buffon said is a big blasphemy: genius is not long-continued patience. Still, there is some truth in the statement, and more than people think, especially as regards our own day. Art! art! art! bitter deception! phantom that glows with light, only to lead one on to destruction.

Again—

I am growing so peevish about my writing. I am like a man whose ear is true but who plays falsely on the violin: his fingers refuse to reproduce precisely those sounds of which he has the inward sense. Then the tears come rolling down from the poor scraper's eyes and the bow fall from his hand.

Coming slowly or quickly, when it comes, as it came with so much labour of mind, but also with so much lustre, to Gustave Flaubert, this discovery of the word will be, like all artistic success and felicity, incapable of strict analysis: effect of an intuitive condition of mind, it must be recognised by like intuition on the part of the reader, and a sort of immediate sense. In every one of those masterly sentences of Flaubert there was, below all mere contrivance, shaping

and afterthought, by some happy instantaneous
concourse of the various faculties of the mind
with each other, the exact apprehension of what
was *needed* to carry the meaning. And that it
fits with absolute justice will be a judgment of
immediate sense in the appreciative reader. We
all feel this in what may be called inspired
translation. Well! all language involves translation from inward to outward. In literature, as
in all forms of art, there are the absolute and the
merely relative or accessory beauties; and
precisely in that exact proportion of the term to its
purpose is the absolute beauty of style, prose or
verse. All the good qualities, the beauties, of
verse also, are such, only as precise expression.

In the highest as in the lowliest literature, then,
the one indispensable beauty is, after all, truth:—
truth to bare fact in the latter, as to some personal
sense of fact, diverted somewhat from men's
ordinary sense of it, in the former; truth there as
accuracy, truth here as expression, that finest
and most intimate form of truth, the *vraie vérité*.
And what an eclectic principle this really is!
employing for its one sole purpose—that absolute
accordance of expression to idea—all other
literary beauties and excellences whatever: how
many kinds of style it covers, explains, justifies,
and at the same time safeguards! Scott's facility,
Flaubert's deeply pondered evocation of "the
phrase," are equally good art. Say what you have
to say, what you have a will to say, in the simplest,
the most direct and exact manner possible, with
no surplusage:—there, is the justification of the
sentence so fortunately born, "entire, smooth,
and round," that it needs no punctuation, and also
(that is the point!) of the most elaborate period,
if it be right in its elaboration. Here is the
office of ornament: here also the purpose of
restraint in ornament. As the exponent of truth,
that austerity (the beauty, the function, of which
in literature Flaubert understood so well) becomes not the correctness or purism of the
mere scholar, but a security against the otiose, a
jealous exclusion of what does not really tell
towards the pursuit of relief, of life and vigour
in the portraiture of one's sense. License again,
the making free with rule, if it be indeed, as
people fancy, a habit of genius, flinging aside or
transforming all that opposes the liberty of
beautiful production, will be but faith to one's
own meaning. The seeming baldness of *Le Rouge
et Le Noir* is nothing in itself; the wild ornament
of *Les Misérables* is nothing in itself; and the
restraint of Flaubert, amid a real natural opu-

lence, only redoubled beauty—the phrase so
large and so precise at the same time, hard as
bronze, in service to the more perfect adaptation
of words to their matter. Afterthoughts, re-
touchings, finish, will be of profit only so far as
they too really serve to bring out the original,
initiative, generative, sense in them.

In this way, according to the well-known
saying, "The style is the man," complex or
simple, in his individuality, his plenary sense of
what he really has to say, his sense of the world;
all cautions regarding style arising out of so
many natural scruples as to the medium through
which alone he can expose that inward sense of
things, the purity of this medium, its laws or
tricks of refraction: nothing is to be left there
which might give conveyance to any matter save
that. Style in all its varieties, reserved or opulent,
terse, abundant, musical, stimulant, academic, so
long as each is really characteristic or expressive,
finds thus its justification, the sumptuous good
taste of Cicero being as truly the man himself,
and not another, justified, yet insured inalienably
to him, thereby, as would have been his portrait
by Raffaelle, in full consular splendour, on his
ivory chair.

A relegation, you may say perhaps—a relegation of style to the subjectivity, the mere caprice,
of the individual, which must soon transform it
into mannerism. Not so! since there is, under the
conditions supposed, for those elements of the
man, for every lineament of the vision within,
the one word, the one acceptable word, recognisable by the sensitive, by others "who have
intelligence" in the matter, as absolutely as ever
anything can be in the evanescent and delicate
region of human language. The style, the
manner, would be the man, not in his unreasoned
and really uncharacteristic caprices, involuntary
or affected, but in absolutely sincere apprehension of what is most real to him. But let us hear
our French guide again.—

Styles (says Flaubert's commentator), *Styles*, as so
many peculiar moulds, each of which bears the mark of
a particular writer, who is to pour into it the whole content of his ideas, were no part of his theory. What he believed in was *Style*: that is to say, a certain absolute and
unique manner of expressing a thing, in all its intensity
and colour. For him the *form* was the work itself. As in
living creatures, the blood, nourishing the body,
determines its very contour and external aspect, just
so, to his mind, the *matter*, the basis, in a work of art,
imposed, necessarily, the unique, the just expression,
the measure, the rhythm—the *form* in all its
characteristics.

If the style be the man, in all the colour and intensity of a veritable apprehension, it will be in a real sense "impersonal."

I said, thinking of books like Victor Hugo's *Les Misérables,* that prose literature was the characteristic art of the nineteenth century, as others, thinking of its triumphs since the youth of Bach, have assigned that place to music. Music and prose literature are, in one sense, the opposite terms of art; the art of literature presenting to the imagination, through the intelligence, a range of interests, as free and various as those which music presents to it through sense. And certainly the tendency of what has been here said is to bring literature too under those conditions, by conformity to which music takes rank as the typically perfect art. If music be the ideal of all art whatever, precisely because in music it is impossible to distinguish the form from the substance or matter, the subject from the expression, then, literature, by finding its specific excellence in the absolute correspondence of the term to its import, will be but fufilling the condition of all artistic quality in things everywhere, of all good art.

Good art, but not necessarily great art; the distinction between great art and good art depending immediately, as regards literature at all events, not on its form, but on the matter. Thackeray's *Esmond,* surely, is greater art than *Vanity Fair,* by the greater dignity of its interests. It is on the quality of the matter it informs or controls, its compass, its variety, its alliance to great ends, or the depth of the note of revolt, or the largeness of hope in it, that the greatness of literary art depends, as *The Divine Comedy, Paradise Lost, Les Misérables, The English Bible,* are great art. Given the conditions I have tried to explain as constituting good art; then, if it be devoted further to the increase of men's happiness, to the redemption of the oppressed, or the enlargement of our sympathies with each other, or to such presentment of new or old truth about ourselves and our relation to the world as may ennoble and fortify us in our sojourn here, or immediately, as with Dante, to the glory of God, it will be also great art; if, over and above those qualities I summed up as mind and soul—that colour and mystic perfume, and that reasonable structure, it has something of the soul of humanity in it, and finds its logical,

<hr/>

[1] I.e., the Pre-Raphaelites.

its architectural place, in the great structure of human life.

Dante Gabriel Rossetti

IT WAS characteristic of a poet who had ever something about him of mystic isolation, and will still appeal perhaps, though with a name it may seem now established in English literature, to a special and limited audience, that some of his poems had won a kind of exquisite fame before they were in the full sense published. *The Blessed Damozel,* although actually printed twice before the year 1870, was eagerly circulated in manuscript; and the volume which it now opens came at last to satisfy a long-standing curiosity as to the poet, whose pictures also had become an object of the same peculiar kind of interest. For those poems were the work of a painter, understood to belong to, and to be indeed the leader, of a new school then rising into note;[1] and the reader of to-day may observe already, in *The Blessed Damozel,* written at the age of eighteen, a prefiguration of the chief characteristics of that school, as he will recognise in it also, in proportion as he really knows Rossetti, many of the characteristics which are most markedly personal and his own. Common to that school and to him, and in both alike of primary significance, was the quality of sincerity, already felt as one of the charms of that earliest poem—a perfect sincerity, taking effect in the deliberate use of the most direct and unconventional expression, for the conveyance of a poetic sense which recognised no conventional standard of what poetry was called upon to be. At a time when poetic originality in England might seem to have had its utmost play, here was certainly one new poet more, with a structure and music of verse, a vocabulary, an accent, unmistakably novel, yet felt to be no mere tricks of manner adopted with a view to forcing attention—an accent which might rather count as the very seal of reality on one man's own proper speech; as that speech itself was the wholly natural expression of certain wonderful things he really felt and saw. Here was one, who had a matter to present to his readers, to himself at least, in the first instance, so valuable, so real and definite, that his primary aim, as regards form or expression in his verse, would be but its exact equivalence to those *data* within. That he had this gift of transparency in language—the control of a style which did but obediently shift and shape itself to the mental motion, as a well-trained hand can follow on the tracing-paper the outline of an original drawing below it, was proved afterwards by a volume of typically perfect translations from the delightful but difficult "early Italian poets": [2] such transparency being indeed the secret of all genuine style, of all such style as can truly belong to one man and not to another. His own meaning was always personal and even recondite, in a certain sense learned and casuistical, sometimes complex or obscure; but the term was always, one could see, deliberately chosen from many competitors, as the just transcript of that peculiar phase of soul which he alone knew, precisely as he knew it.

One of the peculiarities of *The Blessed Damozel* was a definiteness of sensible imagery, which seemed almost grotesque to some, and was strange, above all, in a theme so profoundly visionary. The gold bar of heaven from which she leaned, her hair yellow like ripe corn, are but examples of a general treatment, as naively detailed as the pictures of those early painters contemporary with Dante, who has shown a similar care for minute and definite imagery in his verse; there, too, in the very midst of profoundly mystic vision. Such definition of outline is indeed one among many points in which Rossetti resembles the great Italian poet, of whom, led to him at first by family circumstances, he was ever a lover—a "servant and singer," faithful as Dante, "of Florence and of Beatrice"—with some close inward conformities of genius also, independent of any mere circumstances of education. It was said by a critic of the last century, not wisely though agreeably to the practice of his time, that poetry rejoices in abstractions. For Rossetti, as for Dante, without question on his part, the first condition of the poetic way of seeing and presenting things is particularisation. "Tell me now," he writes, for Villon's

Dictes-moy ou, n'en quel pays,
Est Flora, la belle Romaine—

Tell me now, in what hidden way is
Lady Flora the lovely Roman:

[2] *The Early Italian Poets* (1861).

—"way," in which one might actually chance to meet her; the unmistakably poetic effect of the couplet in English being dependent on the definiteness of that single word (though actually lighted on in the search after a difficult double rhyme) for which every one else would have written, like Villon himself, a more general one, just equivalent to place or region.

And this delight in concrete definition is allied with another of his conformities to Dante, the really imaginative vividness, namely, of his personifications—his hold upon them, or rather their hold upon him, with the force of a Frankenstein, when once they have taken life from him. Not Death only and Sleep, for instance, and the winged spirit of Love, but certain particular aspects of them, a whole "populace" of special hours and places, "the hour" even "which might have been, yet might not be," are living creatures, with hands and eyes and articulate voices.

> Stands it not by the door—
> Love's Hour—till she and I shall meet;
> With bodiless form and unapparent feet
> That cast no shadow yet before,
> Though round its head the dawn begins to pour
> The breath that makes the day sweet?—
>
> Nay, why
> Name the dead hours? I mind them well:
> Their ghosts in many darkened doorways dwell
> With desolate eyes to know them by.

Poetry as a *mania*—one of Plato's two higher forms of "divine" mania—has, in all its species, a mere insanity incidental to it, the "defect of its quality," into which it may lapse in its moment of weakness; and the insanity which follows a vivid poetic anthropomorphism like that of Rossetti may be noted here and there in his work, in a forced and almost grotesque materialising of abstractions, as Dante also became at times a mere subject of the scholastic realism of the Middle Age.

In *Love's Nocturn* and *The Stream's Secret*, congruously perhaps with a certain feverishness of soul in the moods they present, there is at times a near approach (may it be said?) to such insanity of realism—

> Pity and love shall burn
> In her pressed cheek and cherishing hands;
> And from the living spirit of love that stands
> Between her lips to soothe and yearn,

> Each separate breath shall clasp me round in turn
> And loose my spirit's bands.

But even if we concede this; even if we allow, in the very plan of those two compositions, something of the literary conceit—what exquisite, what novel flowers of poetry, we must admit them to be, as they stand! In the one, what a delight in all the natural beauty of water, all its details for the eye of a painter; in the other, how subtle and fine the imaginative hold upon all the secret ways of sleep and dreams! In both of them, with much the same attitude and tone, Love—sick and doubtful Love—would fain inquire of what lies below the surface of sleep, and below the water; stream or dream being forced to speak by Love's powerful "control"; and the poet would have it foretell the fortune, issue, and event of his wasting passion. Such artifices, indeed, were not unknown in the old Provençal poetry of which Dante had learned something. Only, in Rossetti, at least, they are redeemed by a serious purpose, by that sincerity of his, which allies itself readily to a serious beauty, a sort of grandeur of literary workmanship, to a great style. One seems to hear there a really new kind of poetic utterance, with effects which have nothing else like them; as there is nothing else, for instance, like the narrative of Jacob's Dream in *Genesis,* of Blake's design of the Singing of the Morning Stars, or Addison's Nineteenth Psalm.

With him indeed, as in some revival of the old mythopœic age, common things—dawn, noon, night—are full of human or personal expression, full of sentiment. The lovely little sceneries scattered up and down his poems, glimpses of a landscape, not indeed of broad open-air effects, but rather that of a painter concentrated upon the picturesque effect of one or two selected objects at a time—the "hollow brimmed with mist," or the "ruined weir," as he sees it from one of the windows, or reflected in one of the mirrors of his "house of life" (the vignettes for instance seen by Rose Mary in the magic beryl) attest, by their very freshness and simplicity, to a pictorial or descriptive power in dealing with the inanimate world, which is certainly also one half of the charm, in that other, more remote and mystic, use of it. For with Rossetti this sense of lifeless nature, after all, is translated to a higher service, in which it does but incorporate itself with some phase of strong

emotion. Every one understands how this may happen at critical moments of life; what a weirdly expressive soul may have crept, even in full noonday, into "the white-flower'd elder-thicket," when Godiva saw it "gleam through the Gothic archways in the wall," at the end of her terrible ride. To Rossetti it is so always, because to him life is a crisis at every moment. A sustained impressibility towards the mysterious conditions of man's everyday life, towards the very mystery itself in it, gives a singular gravity to all his work: those matters never became trite to him. But throughout, it is the ideal intensity of love— of love based upon a perfect yet peculiar type of physical or material beauty—which is enthroned in the midst of those mysterious powers; Youth and Death, Destiny and Fortune, Fame, Poetic Fame, Memory, Oblivion, and the like. Rossetti is one of those who, in the words of Mérimée, *se passionnent pour la passion,*[3] one of Love's lovers.

And yet, again as with Dante, to speak of his ideal type of beauty as material, is partly misleading. Spirit and matter, indeed, have been for the most part opposed, with a false contrast or antagonism by schoolmen, whose artificial creation those abstractions really are. In our actual concrete experience, the two trains of phenomena which the words *matter* and *spirit* do but roughly distinguish, play inextricably into each other. Practically, the church of the Middle Age by its æsthetic worship, its sacramentalism, its real faith in the resurrection of the flesh, had set itself against the Manichean opposition of spirit and matter, and its results in men's way of taking life; and in this, Dante is the central representative of its spirit. To him, in the vehement and impassioned heat of his conceptions, the material and the spiritual are fused and blent: if the spiritual attains the definite visibility of a crystal, what is material loses its earthiness and impurity. And here again, by force of instinct, Rossetti is one with him. His chosen type of beauty is one,

> Whose speech Truth knows not from her thought,
> Nor Love her body from her soul.

Like Dante, he knows no region of spirit which shall not be sensuous also, or material. The shadowy world, which he realises so powerfully, has still the ways and houses, the land and water, the light and darkness, the fire and flowers, that had so much to do in the moulding of those

---

[3] "Make themselves get into a passion for the sake of passion."

bodily powers and aspects which counted for so large a part of the soul, here.

For Rossetti, then, the great affections of persons to each other, swayed and determined, in the case of his highly pictorial genius, mainly by that so-called material loveliness, formed the great undeniable reality in things, the solid resisting substance, in a world where all beside might be but shadow. The fortunes of those affections—of the great love so determined; its casuistries, its langour sometimes; above all, its sorrows; its fortunate or unfortunate collisions with those other great matters; how it looks, as the long day of life does round, in the light and shadow of them: all this, conceived with an abundant imagination, and a deep, a philosophic, reflectiveness, is the matter of his verse, and especially of what he designed as his chief poetic work, "a work to be called *The House of Life*," towards which the majority of his sonnets and songs were contributions.

The dwelling-place in which one finds oneself by chance or destiny, yet can partly fashion for oneself; never properly one's own at all, if it be changed too lightly; in which every object has its associations—the dim mirrors, the portraits, the lamps, the books, the hair-tresses of the dead and visionary magic crystals in the secret drawers, the names and words scratched on the windows, windows open upon prospects the saddest or the sweetest; the house one must quit, yet taking perhaps, how much of its quietly active light and colour along with us!—grown now to be a kind of raiment to one's body, as the body, according to Swedenborg, is but the raiment of the soul—under that image, the whole of Rossetti's work might count as a *House of Life*, of which he is but the "Interpreter." And it is a "haunted" house. A sense of power in love, defying distance, and those barriers which are so much more than physical distance, of unutterable desire penetrating into the world of sleep, however "lead-bound," was one of those anticipative notes obscurely struck in *The Blessed Damozel*, and, in his later work, makes him speak sometimes almost like a believer in mesmerism. Dream-land, as we said, with its "phantoms of the body," deftly coming and going on love's service, is to him, in no mere fancy or figure of speech, a real country, a veritable expansion of, or addidion to, our waking life; and he did well perhaps to wait carefully upon sleep, for the lack

of it became mortal disease with him. One may even recognise a sort of morbid and over-hasty making-ready for death itself, which increases on him; thoughts concerning it, its imageries, coming with a frequency and importunity, in excess, one might think, of even the very saddest, quite wholesome wisdom.

And indeed the publication of his second volume of *Ballads and Sonnets* preceded his death by scarcely a twelvemonth. That volume bears witness to the reverse of any failure of power, or falling-off from his early standard of literary perfection, in every one of his then accustomed forms of poetry—the song, the sonnet, and the ballad. The newly printed sonnets, now completing *The House of Life*, certainly advanced beyond those earlier ones, in clearness; his dramatic power in the ballad, was here at its height; while one monumental, gnomic piece, *Soothsay*, testifies, more clearly even than the *Nineveh* of his first volume, to the reflective force, the dry reason, always at work behind his imaginative creations, which at no time dispensed with a genuine intellectual structure. For in matters of pure reflection also, Rossetti maintained the painter's sensuous clearness of conception; and this has something to do with the capacity, largely illustrated by his ballads, of telling some red-hearted story of impassioned action with effect.

Have there, in very deed, been ages, in which the external conditions of poetry such as Rossetti's were of more spontaneous growth than in our own? The archaic side of Rossetti's work, his preferences in regard to earlier poetry, connect him with those who have certainly thought so, who fancied they could have breathed more largely in the age of Chaucer, or of Ronsard, in one of those ages, in the words of Stendhal— *ces siècles de passions où les âmes pouvaient se livrer franchement à la plus haute exaltation, quand les passions qui font la possibilité comme les sujets des beaux arts existaient.*[4] We may think, perhaps, that such old time as that has never really existed except in the fancy of poets; but it was to find it, that Rossetti turned so often from modern life to the chronicle of the past. Old Scotch history, perhaps beyond any other, is strong in the matter of heroic and vehement hatreds and love, the tragic Mary herself being but the perfect blossom of them; and it is from that history that Rossetti has taken the subjects of the

---

[4] "Those ages of passion when souls could release themselves freely to the highest exaltation, when passions existed that were possible subjects for the fine arts."

two longer ballads of his second volume: of the three admirable ballads in it, *The King's Tragedy* (in which Rossetti has dexterously interwoven some relics of James's own exquisite early verse) reaching the highest level of dramatic success, and marking perfection, perhaps, in this kind of poetry; which, in the earlier volume, gave us, among other pieces, *Troy Town, Sister Helen,* and *Eden Bower.*

Like those earlier pieces, the ballads of the second volume bring with them the question of the poetic value of the "refrain"—

> Eden bower's in flower:
> And O the bower and the hour!

—and the like. Two of those ballads—*Troy Town* and *Eden Bower,* are terrible in theme; and the refrain serves, perhaps, to relieve their bold aim at the sentiment of terror. In *Sister Helen* again, the refrain has a real, and sustained purpose (being here duly varied also) and performs the part of a chorus, as the story proceeds. Yet even in these cases, whatever its effect may be in actual recitation, it may fairly be questioned, whether, to the mere reader their actual effect is not that of a positive interruption and drawback, at least in pieces so lengthy; and Rossetti himself, it would seem, came to think so, for in the shortest of his later ballads, *The White Ship*—that old true history of the generosity with which a youth, worthless in life, flung himself upon death—he was contented with a single utterance of the refrain, "given out" like the keynote or tune of a chant.

In *The King's Tragedy,* Rossetti has worked upon motive, broadly human (to adopt the phrase of popular criticism) such as one and all may realise. Rossetti, indeed, with all his self-concentration upon his own peculiar aim, by no means ignored those general interests which are external to poetry as he conceived it; as he has shown here and there, in this poetic, as also in pictorial, work. It was but that, in a life to be shorter even than the average, he found enough to occupy him in the fulfilment of a task, plainly "given him to do." Perhaps, if one had to name a single composition of his to readers desiring to make acquaintance with him for the first time, one would select: *The King's Tragedy*— that poem so moving, so popularly dramatic, and lifelike. Notwithstanding this, his work, it must be conceded, certainly through no

narrowness or egotism, but in the faithfulness of a true workman to a vocation so emphatic, was mainly of the esoteric order. But poetry, at all times, exercises two distinct functions: it may reveal, it may unveil to every eye, the ideal aspects of common things, after Gray's way (though Gray too, it is well to remember, seemed in his own day, seemed even to Johnson, obscure) or it may actually add to the number of motives poetic and uncommon in themselves, by the imaginative creation of things that are ideal from their very birth. Rossetti did something, something excellent, of the former kind; but his characteristic, his really revealing work, lay in the adding to poetry of fresh poetic material, of a new order of phenomena, in the creation of a new ideal.

Postscript

αἰνεῖ δὲ παλαιὸν μὲν οἶνον, ἄνθεα δ' ὕμνων νεωτέρων[1]

THE words, *classical* and *romantic,* although, like many other critical expressions, sometimes abused by those who have understood them too vaguely or too absolutely, yet define two real tendencies in the history of art and literature. Used in an exaggerated sense, to express a greater opposition between those tendencies than really exists, they have at times tended to divide people of taste into opposite camps. But in that *House Beautiful,* which the creative minds of all generations—the artists and those who have treated life in the spirit of art—are always building together, for the refreshment of the human spirit, these oppositions cease; and the *Interpreter* of the *House Beautiful,*[2] the true æsthetic critic, uses these divisions, only so far as they enable him to enter into the peculiarities of the objects with which he has to do. The term *classical,* fixed, as it is, to a well-defined literature, and a well-defined group in art, is clear, indeed; but then it has often been used in a hard, and merely scholastic sense, by the praisers of what is old and accustomed, at the expense of what is new, by critics who would never have discovered for themselves the charm of any work, whether new or old, who value what is old, in art or literature, for

---

[1] "While thou praisest the old wine, thou shalt praise also the flowers of songs that are new" (Pindar).
[2] From Bunyan's *Pilgrim's Progress.*

its accessories, and chiefly for the conventional authority that has gathered about it—people who would never really have been made glad by any Venus fresh-risen from the sea, and who praise the Venus of old Greece and Rome, only because they fancy her grown now into something staid and tame.

And as the term, *classical*, has been used in a too absolute, and therefore in a misleading sense, so the term, *romantic*, has been used much too vaguely, in various accidental senses. The sense in which Scott is called a romantic writer is chiefly this; that, in opposition to the literary tradition of the last century, he loved strange adventure, and sought it in the Middle Age. Much later, in a Yorkshire village, the spirit of romanticism bore a more really characteristic fruit in the work of a young girl, Emily Brontë, the romance of *Wuthering Heights;* the figures of Hareton Earnshaw, of Catherine Linton, and of Heathcliffe—tearing open Catherine's grave, removing one side of her coffin, that he may really lie beside her in death—figures so passionate, yet woven on a background of delicately beautiful, moorland scenery, being typical examples of that spirit. In Germany, again, that spirit is shown less in Tieck, its professional representative, than in Meinhold, the author of *Sidonia the Sorceress* and the *Amber-Witch*.[3] In Germany and France, within the last hundred years, the term has been used to describe a particular school of writers; and, consequently, when Heine criticises the *Romantic School* in Germany—that movement which culminated in Goethe's *Goetz von Berlichingen;* or when Théophile Gautier critises the romantic movement in France, where, indeed, it bore its most characteristic fruits, and its play is hardly yet over where, by a certain audacity, or *bizarrerie* of motive, united with faultless literary execution, it still shows itself in imaginative literature, they use the word, with an exact sense of special artistic qualities, indeed; but use it, nevertheless, with a limited application to the manifestation of those qualities at a particular period. But the romantic spirit is, in reality, an ever-present, an enduring principle, in the artistic temperament; and the qualities of thought and style which that, and other similar uses of the word *romantic* really indicate, are indeed but symptoms of a very continuous and widely working influence.

Though the words *classical* and *romantic,* then, have acquired an almost technical meaning, in application to certain developments of German and French taste, yet this is but one variation of an old opposition, which may be traced from the very beginning of the formation of European art and literature. From the first formation of anything like a standard of taste in these things, the restless curiosity of their more eager lovers necessarily made itself felt, in the craving for new notives, new subjects of interest, new modifications of style. Hence, the opposition between the classicists and the romanticists—between the adherents, in the culture of beauty, of the principles of liberty, and authority, respectively— of strength, and order or what the Greeks called κοσμιότης.[4]

Sainte-Beuve, in the third volume of the *Causeries du Lundi,* has discussed the question, *What is meant by a classic?* It was a question he was well fitted to answer, having himself lived through many phases of taste, and having been in earlier life an enthusiastic member of the romantic school: he was also a great master of that sort of "philosophy of literature," which delights in tracing traditions in it, and the way in which various phases of thought and sentiment maintain themselves, through successive modifications, from epoch to epoch. His aim, then, is to give the word *classic* a wider and, as he says, a more generous sense than it commonly bears, to make it expressly *grandiose et flottant;*[5] and, in doing this, he develops, in a masterly manner, those qualtities of measure, purity, temperance, of which it is the especial function of classical art and literature, whatever meaning, narrower or wider, we attach to the term, to take care.

The charm, therefore, or what is classical, in art or literature, is that of the well-known tale, to which we can, nevertheless, listen over and over again, because it is told so well. To the absolute beauty of its artistic form, is added the accidental, tranquil, charm of familiarity. There are times, indeed, at which these charms fail to work on our spirits at all, because they fail to excite us. "*Romanticism,*" says Stendhal, "is the art of presenting to people the literary works which, in the actual state of their habits and beliefs, are capable of giving them the greatest possible pleasure; *classicism,* on the

---

[3] Ludwig Tieck (1773–1853), German Romantic author; Johann Wilhelm Meinhold (1797–1851), German author of the supernatural.
[4] Decorous behaviour.   [5] Grand and compendious.

contrary, of presenting them with that which gave the greatest possible pleasure to their grandfathers." But then, beneath all changes of habits and beliefs, our love of that mere abstract proportion—of music—which what is classical in literature possesses, still maintains itself in the best of us, and what pleased our grandparents may at least tranquillise us. The "classic" comes to us out of the cool and quiet of other times, as the measure of what a long experience has shown will at least never displease us. And in the classical literature of Greece and Rome, as in the classics of the last century, the essentially classical element is that quality of order in beauty, which they possess, indeed, in a pre-eminent degree, and which impresses some minds to the exclusion of everything else in them.

It is the addition of strangeness to beauty, that constitutes the romantic character in art; and the desire of beauty being a fixed element in every artistic organisation, it is the addition of curiosity to this desire of beauty, that constitutes the romantic temper. Curiosity and the desire of beauty, have each their place in art, as in all true criticism. When one's curiosity is deficient, when one is not eager enough for new impressions, and new pleasures, one is liable to value mere academical proprieties too highly, to be satisfied with worn-out or conventional types, with the insipid ornament of Racine, or the prettiness of that later Greek sculpture, which passed so long for true Hellenic work; to miss those places where the handiwork of nature, or of the artist, has been most cunning; to find the most stimulating products of art a mere irritation. And when one's curiosity is in excess, when it overbalances the desire of beauty, then one is liable to value in works of art what is inartistic in them; to be satisfied with what is exaggerated in art, with productions like some of those of the romantic school in Germany; not to distinguish, jealously enough, between what is admirably done, and what is done not quite so well, in the writings, for instance, of Jean Paul.[6] And if I had to give instances of these defects, then I should say, that Pope, in common with the age of literature to which he belonged, had too little curiosity, so that there is always a certain insipidity in the effect of his work, exquisite as it is; and, coming down to our own time, that Balzac had an excess of curiosity—curiosity not duly tempered with the desire of beauty.

But, however falsely those two tendencies may be opposed by critics, or exaggerated by artists themselves, they are tendencies really at work at all times in art, moulding it, with the balance sometimes a little on one side, sometimes a little on the other, generating, respectively, as the balance inclines on this side or that, two principles, two traditions, in art, and in literature so far as it partakes of the spirit of art. If there is a great overbalance of curiosity, then, we have the grotesque in art: if the union of strangeness and beauty, under very difficult and complex conditions, be a successful one, if the union be entire, then the resultant beauty is very exquisite, very attractive. With a passionate care for beauty, the romantic spirit refuses to have it, unless the condition of strangeness be first fulfilled. Its desire is for a beauty born of unlikely elements, by a profound alchemy, by a difficult initiation, by the charm which wrings it even out of terrible things; and a trace of distortion, of the grotesque, may perhaps linger, as an additional element of expression, about its ultimate grace. Its eager, excited spirit will have strength, the grotesque, first of all—the trees shrieking as you tear off the leaves; for Jean Valjean, the long years of convict life; for Redgauntlet, the quicksands of Solway Moss;[7] then, incorporate with this strangeness, and intensified by restraint, as much sweetness, as much beauty, as is compatible with that. *Énergique, frais, et dispos*—these, according to Sainte-Beuve, are the characteristics of a genuine classic—*les ouvrages anciens ne sont pas classiques parce qu'ils sont vieux, mais parce qu'ils sont énergiques, frais, et dispos.*[8] Energy, freshness, intelligent and masterly disposition:—these are characteristics of Victor Hugo when his alchemy is complete, in certain figures, like Marius and Cosette, in certain scenes, like that in the opening of *Les Travailleurs de la Mer,* where Déruchette writes the name of *Gilliatt* in the snow, on Christmas morning; but always there is a certain note of strangeness discernible there, as well.

The essential elements, then, of the romantic spirit are curiosity and the love of beauty; and it is only as an illustration of these qualities, that it seeks the Middle Age, because, in the overcharged atmosphere of the Middle Age, there

---

[6] Jean Paul Friedrich Richter (1763–1825), German humorist and novelist.

[7] Jean Valjean and Redgauntlet, the heroes respectively of Hugo's *Les Misérables* and Scott's *Redgauntlet.*

[8] "Ancient works are not classics because they are old, but because they are energetic, fresh, and well arranged."

are unworked sources of romantic effect, of a strange beauty, to be won, by strong imagination, out of things unlikely or remote.

Few, probably, now read Madame de Staël's *De l'Allemagne,* though it has its interest, the interest which never quite fades out of work really touched with the enthusiasm of the spiritual adventurer, the pioneer in culture. It was published in 1810, to introduce to French readers a new school of writers—the romantic school, from beyond the Rhine; and it was followed, twenty-three years later, by Heine's *Romantische Schule,* as at once a supplement and a correction. Both these books, then, connect romanticism with Germany, with the names especially of Goethe and Tieck; and, to many English readers, the idea of romanticism is still inseparably connected with Germany—that Germany which, in its quaint old towns, under the spire of Strasburg or the towers of Heidelberg, was always listening in rapt inaction to the melodious, fascinating voices of the Middle Age, and which, now that it has got Strasburg back again, has, I suppose, almost ceased to exist. But neither Germany, with its Goethe and Tieck, nor England, with its Byron and Scott, is nearly so representative of the romantic temper as France, with Murger, and Gautier, and Victor Hugo. It is in French literature that its most characteristic expression is to be found; and that, as most closely derivative, historically, from such peculiar conditions, as ever reinforce it to the utmost.

For, although temperament has much to do with the generation of the romantic spirit, and although this spirit, with its curiosity, its thirst for a curious beauty, may be always traceable in excellent art (traceable even in Sophocles) yet still, in a limited sense, it may be said to be a product of special epochs. Outbreaks of this spirit, that is, come naturally with particular periods—times, when, in men's approaches towards art and poetry, curiosity may be noticed to take the lead, when men come to art and poetry, with a deep thirst for intellectual excitement, after a long *ennui,* or in reaction against the strain of outward, practical things: in the later Middle Age, for instance; so that medieval poetry, centering in Dante, is often opposed to Greek and Roman poetry, as romantic poetry to the classical. What the romanticism of Dante is, may be estimated, if we compare the lines in which Virgil describes the hazelwood, from whose broken twigs flows the blood of Polydorus, not

without the expression of a real shudder at the ghastly incident, with the whole canto of the *Inferno,* into which Dante has expanded them, beautifying and softening it, meanwhile, by a sentiment of profound pity. And it is especially in that period of intellectual disturbance, immediately preceding Dante, amid which the romance languages define themselves at last, that this temper is manifested. Here, in the literature of Provence, the very name of *romanticism* is stamped with its true signification: here we have indeed a romantic world, grotesque even, in the strength of its passions, almost insane in its curious expression of them, drawing all things into its sphere, making the birds, nay! lifeless things, its voices and messengers, yet so penetrated with the desire for beauty and sweetness, that it begets a wholly new species of poetry, in which the *Renaissance* may be said to begin. The last century was pre-eminently a classical age, an age in which, for art and literature, the element of a comely order was in the ascendant; which, passing away, left a hard battle to be fought between the classical and the romantic schools. Yet, it is in the heart of this century, of Goldsmith and Stothard, of Watteau and the *Siècle de Louis XIV.*—in one of its central, if not most characteristic figures, in Rousseau—that the modern or French romanticism really originates. But, what in the eighteenth century is but an exceptional phenomenon, breaking through its fair reserve and discretion only at rare intervals, is the habitual guise of the nineteenth, breaking through it perpetually, with a feverishness, an incomprehensible straining and excitement, which all experience to some degree, but yearning also, in the genuine children of the romantic school to be *énergique, frais, et dispos*—for those qualities of energy, freshness, comely order; and often, in Murger, in Gautier, in Victor Hugo, for instance, with singular felicity attaining them.

It is in the terrible tragedy of Rousseau, in fact, that French romanticism, with much else, begins: reading his *Confessions* we seem actually to assist at the birth of this new, strong spirit in the French mind. The wildness which has shocked so many, and the fascination which has influenced almost every one, in the squalid, yet eloquent figure, we see and hear so clearly in that book, wandering under the apple-blossoms and among the vines of Neuchâtel or Vevey actually give it the quality of a very successful romantic invention. His strangeness or distortion, his profound subjectivity, his passionateness—the *cor laceratum*[9]—Rousseau makes all men in love with these. *Je ne suis fait comme aucun de ceux que j'ai sus. Mais si je ne vaux pas mieux, au moins je suis autre.*—"I am not made like any one else I have ever known: yet, if I am not better, at least I am different." These words, from the first page of the *Confessions,* anticipate all the Werthers, Renés, Obermanns, of the last hundred years. For Rousseau did but anticipate a trouble in the spirit of the whole world; and thirty years afterwards, what in him was a peculiarity, became part of the general consciousness. A storm was coming: Rousseau, with others, felt it in the air, and they helped to bring it down: they introduced a disturbing element into French literature, then so trim and formal, like our own literature of the age of Queen Anne.

In 1815 the storm had come and gone, but had left, in the spirit of "young France," the *ennui* of an immense disillusion. In the last chapter of Edgar Quintet's *Révolution Française,* a work itself full of irony, of disillusion, he distinguishes two books, Senancour's *Obermann* and Chateaubriand's *Génie du Christianisme,* as characteristic of the first decade of the present century. In those two books we detect already the disease and the cure—in *Obermann* the irony, refined into a plaintive philosophy of "indifference"—in Chateaubriand's *Génie du Christianisme,* the refuge from a tarnished actual present, a present of disillusion, into a world of strength and beauty in the Middle Age, as at an earlier period—in *René* and *Atala*—into the free play of them in savage life. It is to minds in this spiritual situation, weary of the present, but yearning for the spectacle of beauty and strength, that the works of French romanticism appeal. They set a positive value on the intense, the exceptional; and a certain distortion is sometimes noticeable in them, as in conceptions like Victor Hugo's *Quasimodo,* or *Gwynplaine,* something of a terrible grotesque, of the *macabre,* as the French themselves call it; though always combined with perfect literary execution, as in Gautier's *La Morte Amoureuse,* or the scene of the "maimed" burial-rites of the player, dead of the frost, in his *Capitaine Fracasse*—true "flowers of the yew." It becomes grim humour in Victor Hugo's combat of Gilliat with the devil-fish, or the incident, with all its ghastly comedy drawn out at length, of the great gun detached from its fastenings on shipboard, in

Quatre-Vingt-Treize (perhaps the most terrible of all the accidents that can happen by sea) and in the entire episode, in that book, of the *Convention.* Not less surely does it reach a genuine pathos; for the habit of noting and distinguishing one's own most intimate passages of sentiment makes one sympathetic, begetting, as it must, the power of entering, by all sorts of finer ways, into the intimate recesses of other minds; so that pity is another quality of romanticism, both Victor Hugo and Gautier being great lovers of animals, and charming writers about them, and Murger being unrivalled in the pathos of his *Scènes de la Vie de Jeunesse.* Penetrating so finely into all situations which appeal to pity, above all, into the special or exceptional phases of such feeling, the romantic humour is not afraid of the quaintness or singularity of its circumstances or expression, pity, indeed, being of the essence of humour; so that Victor Hugo does but turn his romanticism into practice, in his hunger and thirst after practical *Justice!*—a justice which shall no longer wrong children, or animals, for instance, by ignoring in a stupid, mere breadth of view, minute facts about them. Yet the romanticists are antinomian, too, sometimes, because the love of energy and beauty, of distinction in passion, tended naturally to become a little *bizarre,* plunging into the Middle Age, into the secrets of old Italian story. *Are we in the Inferno?*—we are tempted to ask, wondering at something malign in so much beauty. For over all a care for the refreshment of the human spirit by fine art manifests itself, a predominant sense of literary charm, so that, in their search for the secret of exquisite expression, the romantic school went back to the forgotten world of early French poetry, and literature itself became the most delicate of the arts—like "goldsmith's work," says Sainte-Beuve, of Bertrand's *Gaspard de la Nuit*—and that peculiarly French gift, the gift of exquisite speech, *argute loqui,* attained in them a perfection which it had never seen before.

Stendhal, a writer whom I have already quoted, and of whom English readers might well know much more than they do, stands between the earlier and later growths of the romantic spirit. His novels are rich in romantic quality; and his other writings—partly criticism, partly personal reminiscences—are a very curious and interesting illustration of the needs out of

---

[9] Lacerated heart.

which romanticism arose. In his book on *Racine and Shakespeare,* Stendhal argues that all good art was romantic in its day; and this is perhaps true in Stendhal's sense. That little treatise, full of "dry light" and fertile ideas, was published in the year 1823, and its object is to defend an entire independence and liberty in the choice and treatment of subject, both in art and literature, against those who upheld the exclusive authority of precedent. In pleading the cause of romanticism, therefore, it is the novelty, both of form and of motive, in writings like the *Hernani* of Victor Hugo (which soon followed it, raising a storm of criticism) that he is chiefly concerned to justify. To be interesting and really stimulating, to keep us from yawning even, art and literature must follow the subtle movement of that nimbly-shifting *Time-Spirit,* or *Zeit-Geist,* understood by French not less than by German criticism, which is always modifying men's taste, as it modifies their manners and their pleasures. This, he contends, is what all great workmen had always understood. Dante, Shakespeare, Molière, had exercised an absolute independence in their choice of subject and treatment. To turn always with that ever-changing spirit, yet to retain the flavour of what was admirably done in past generations, in the classics, as we say—is the problem of true romanticism. "Dante," he observes, "was pre-eminently the romantic poet. He adored Virgil, yet he wrote the *Divine Comedy,* with the episode of Ugolino, which is as unlike the *Æneid* as can possibly be. And those who thus obey the fundamental principle of romanticism, one by one become classical, and are joined to that ever-increasing common league, formed by men of all countries, to approach nearer and nearer to perfection."

Romanticism, then, although it has its epochs, is in its essential characteristics rather a spirit which shows itself at all times, in various degrees, in individual workmen and their work, and the amount of which criticism has to estimate in them taken one by one, than the peculiarity of a time or a school. Depending on the varying proportion of curiosity and the desire of beauty, natural tendencies of the artistic spirit at all times, it must always be partly a matter of individual temperament. The eighteenth century in England has been regarded as almost exclusively a classical period; yet William Blake, a type of so much which breaks through what are conventionally

thought the influences of that century, is still a noticeable phenomenon in it, and the reaction in favour of naturalism in poetry begins in that century, early. There are, thus, the born romanticists and the born classicists. There are the born classicists who start with *form,* to whose minds the comeliness of the old, immemorial, well-recognised types in art and literature, have revealed themselves impressively; who will entertain no matter which will not go easily and flexibly into them; whose work aspires only to be a variation upon, or study from, the older masters. "'Tis art's decline, my son!"[10] they are always saying, to the progressive element in their own generation; to those who care for that which in fifty years' time every one will be caring for. On the other hand, there are the born romanticists, who start with an original, untried *matter.* still in fusion; who conceive this vividly, and hold by it as the essence of their work; who, by the very vividness and heat of their conception, purge away, sooner or later, all that is not organically appropriate to it, till the whole effect adjusts itself in clear, orderly, proportionate form; which form, after a very little time, becomes classical in its turn.

The romantic or classical character of a picture, a poem, a literary work, depends, then, on the balance of certain qualities in it; and in this sense, a very real distinction may be drawn between good classical and good romantic work. But all critical terms are relative; and there is at least a valuable suggestion in that theory of Stendhal's, that all good art was romantic in its day. In the beauties of Homer and Pheidias, quiet as they now seem, there must have been, for those who confronted them for the first time, excitement and surprise, the sudden, unforeseen satisfaction of the desire of beauty. Yet the *Odyssey,* with its marvellous adventure, is more romantic than the *Iliad,* which nevertheless contains, among many other romantic episodes, that of the immortal horses of Achilles, who weep at the death of Patroclus. Æschylus is more romantic than Sophocles, whose *Philoctetes,* were it written now, might figure, for the strangeness of its motive and the perfectness of its execution, as typically romantic; while, of Euripides, it may be said, that his method in writing his plays is to sacrifice readily almost everything else, so that he may attain the fulness of a single romantic effect. These two

---

[10] Browning, "Fra Lippo Lippi."

tendencies, indeed, might be applied as a measure or standard, all through Greek and Roman art and poetry, with very illuminating results; and for an analyst of the romantic principle in art, no exercise would be more profitable, than to walk through the collection of classical antiquities at the Louvre, or the British Museum, or to examine some representative collection of Greek coins, and note how the element of curiosity, of the love of strangeness, insinuates itself into classical design, and record the effects of the romantic spirit there, the traces of struggle, of the grotesque even, though over-balanced here by sweetness; as in the sculpture of Chartres and Rheims, the real sweetness of mind in the sculptor is often overbalanced by the grotesque, by the rudeness of his strength.

Classicism, then, means for Stendhal, for that younger enthusiastic band of French writers whose unconscious method he formulated into principles, the reign of what is pedantic, conventional, and narrowly academical in art; for him, all good art is romantic. To Sainte-Beuve, who understands the term in a more liberal sense, it is the characteristic of certain epochs, of certain spirits in every epoch, not given to the exercise of original imagination, but rather to the working out of refinements of manner on some authorised matter; and who bring to their perfection, in this way, the elements of sanity, of order and beauty in manner. In general criticism, again, it means the spirit of Greece and Rome, of some phases in literature and art that may seem of equal authority with Greece and Rome, the age of Louis the Fourteenth, the age of Johnson; though this is at best an uncritical use of the term, because in Greek and Roman work there are typical examples of the romantic spirit. But explain the terms as we may, in application to particular epochs, there are these two elements always recognisable; united in perfect art—in Sophocles, in Dante, in the highest work of Goethe, though not always absolutely balanced there; and these two elements may be not in-appropriately termed the classical and romantic tendencies.

Material for the artist, motives of inspiration, are not yet exhausted: our curious, complex, aspiring age still abounds in subjects for æsthetic manipulation by the literary as well as by other forms of art. For the literary art, at all events, the problem just now is, to induce order upon the contorted, proportionless accumulation of our knowledge and experience, our science and history, our hopes and disillusion, and, in effecting this, to do consciously what has been done hitherto for the most part too unconsciously, to write our English language as the Latins wrote theirs, as the French write, as scholars should write. Appealing, as he may, to precedent in this matter, the scholar will still remember that if "the style is the man" it is also the age: that the nineteenth century too will be found to have had its style, justified by necessity—a style very different, alike from the baldness of an impossible "Queen Anne" revival, and an incorrect, incondite exuberance, after the mode of Elizabeth: that we can only return to either at the price of an impoverishment of form or matter, or both, although, an intellecutally rich age such as ours being necessarily an eclectic one, we may well cultivate some of the excellences of literary types so different as those: that in literature as in other matters it is well to unite as many diverse elements as may be: that the individual writer or artist, certainly, is to be estimated by the number of graces he combines, and his power of interpenetrating them in a given work. To discriminate schools, of art, or literature, is, of course, part of the obvious business of literary criticism: but, in the work of literary production, it is easy to be overmuch occupied concerning them. For, in truth, the legitimate contention is, not of one age or school of literary art against another, but of all successive schools alike, against the stupidity which is dead to the substance, and the vulgarity which is dead to form.

Robert Louis Balfour Stevenson

1850-1894

ROBERT LOUIS STEVENSON began his career as an essayist at age sixteen with a pamphlet on Scottish history. Through an active life of extensive travel and of writing novels, adventure stories, and poetry, Stevenson never ceased writing essays and nonfiction. Thereby he made a distinct contribution to the development of the personal essay in the late nineteenth century.

Stevenson, born in 1850, was an only child of an Edinburgh civil engineer. He early suffered from a lung infection, a foreshadowing of the tuberculosis that was to plague him for most of his short life. He attended private school in Edinburgh and Edinburgh University from which he graduated in 1875. He was trained as an engineer but gave it up for law which he in turn gave up for writing. He was called to the bar in 1875 but never practiced.

By 1875 Stevenson was contributing to the *Cornhill Magazine* the essays later collected in *Virginibus Puerisque* (1881) and *Familiar Studies of Men and Books* (1882). In 1879 he traveled to California where he married a British woman in 1880. That year he returned to Britain and lived in Scotland, then later in Switzerland, and then in Bournemouth until 1887, always in search of a place that would improve his health. During this period he wrote some of his best-known works, including *Treasure Island, A Child's Garden of Verses, Dr. Jekyll and Mr. Hyde,* and *Kidnapped.* In 1887 he went to America for his health, staying in Saranac Lake, N.Y.

In 1888 Stevenson left for the South Seas. He established himself in Samoa at an estate called Vailima where he was known affectionately by the natives as "Tusitala," teller of tales. Here he wrote *David Balfour* (1893) and the collection of essays titled *Across the Plains.* He died of a cerebral hemorrhage in 1894.

As a writer of essays Stevenson brings a warmth and intimacy to his subject along with many touches of the masters of the essay like Montaigne that he diligently studied. He believed in the uniqueness of the individual and his capacity for heroism and in living each moment fully. While this latter view does not in Stevenson become pure aestheticism, there is an element of the Paterian appreciation of the moment in his essays which, along with a conscious stylistic elegance, gives them a special intensity. Stevenson's own lifelong awareness, made acute by illness, of the brevity of life combined with his potent spirit of adventure to give his essays and nonfiction a quality that is at once vigorous and reflective.

CHRONOLOGY

1850	Born 13 November in Edinburgh.
1864–67	Attends private school.
1867–75	Attends Edinburgh University.
1879–80	Travels to California; marries Mrs. Osbourne.
1883	*Treasure Island.*
1885	*A Child's Garden of Verses.*
1886	*Kidnapped; Dr. Jekyll and Mr. Hyde.*
1887–88	Travels to Saranac Lake, N.Y., for his health.
1888	Travels to South Seas via Hawaii; settles at Vailima, Samoa.
1889	*The Master of Ballantrae.*
1893	*David Balfour.*
1894	Dies 3 December at Vailima; buried on Mt. Vaea, Samoa.

EDITIONS

There are no fewer than nine separate editions of the Works, of which three are listed below.

Works, Edinburgh Edition, ed. Sidney Colvin (28 vols., 1894–98).

Works, Pentland Edition, ed. Edmund Gosse (20 vols., 1906–7).

Works, Vailima Edition, ed. L. Osbourne and F. Van de G. Stevenson (26 vols., 1922–23).

Letters, ed. Sidney Colvin (2 vols., 1899).

Essays, ed. W. L. Phelps (1906), H. G. Rawlinson (1923), Malcolm Elwin, (1950) George Scott-Moncrieff (1959).

The Stevenson Companion, ed. John Hampden (1950).

The Mind of Robert Louis Stevenson, ed. Roger Ricklefs (1963).

Selected Poetry and Prose, ed. Bradford A. Booth (1968).

BIOGRAPHY AND CRITICISM

Graham Balfour, *The Life of Robert Louis Stevenson* (2 vols., 1912).

John A. Steuart, *Robert Louis Stevenson* (2 vols., 1924).

W. F. Prideaux, *A Bibliography of the Works of Stevenson* (1917).

Lloyd Osbourne, *An Intimate Portrait of R.L.S.* (1924).

D. N. Dalglish, *Presbyterian Pirate: A Portrait of Stevenson* (1937).

Janet A. Smith, *Robert Louis Stevenson* (1937).

Lettice Cooper, *Robert Louis Stevenson* (1947).

David Daiches, *Robert Louis Stevenson* (1947).

Malcolm Elwin, *The Strange Case of Robert Louis Stevenson* (1950).

J. C. Furnas, *Voyage to Windward* (1951).

Richard Aldington, *Portrait of a Rebel* (1957).

E. N. Caldwell, *Last Witness for Stevenson* (1960).

from Virginibus Puerisque

The essays Stevenson wrote for periodicals in the seventies and eighties along with some written in Switzerland where he had gone for his health were collected in 1881 for the volume Virginibus Puerisque. *The title means "for girls and boys" and was designed to be an assertion that the volume contained essays in praise of youth. Of the two essays from the volume printed below, "Crabbed Age and Youth" first appeared in the* Cornhill Magazine *in March 1878, and "Æs Triplex" (triple brass) first appeared in the* Cornhill *in April 1878.*

Crabbed Age and Youth

"You know my mother now and then argues very notably; always very warmly at least. I happen often to differ from her; and we both think so well of our own arguments, that we very seldom are so happy as to convince one another. A pretty common case, I believe, in all *vehement* debatings. She says, I am *too witty;* Anglicè, *too pert;* I, that she is *too wise;* that is to say, being likewise put into English, *not so young as she has been.*"—Miss Howe to Miss Harlowe, *Clarissa,* vol. ii. Letter xiii.

THERE is a strong feeling in favour of cowardly and prudential proverbs. The sentiments of a man while he is full of ardour and hope are to be received, it is supposed, with some qualification. But when the same person has ignominiously failed and begins to eat up his words, he should be listened to like an oracle. Most of our pocket wisdom is conceived for the use of mediocre people, to discourage them from ambitious attempts, and generally console them in their mediocrity. And since mediocre people constitute the bulk of humanity, this is no doubt very properly so. But it does not follow that the one sort of proposition is any less true than the other, or that Icarus is not to be more praised, and perhaps more envied, than Mr. Samuel Budgett the Successful Merchant. The one is dead, to be sure, while the other is still in his counting-house counting out his money; and doubtless this is a consideration. But we have, on the other hand, some bold and magnanimous sayings common to high races and natures, which set forth the advantage of the losing side, and proclaim it better to be a dead lion than a living dog. It is difficult to fancy how the mediocrities reconcile such sayings with their proverbs. According to the latter, every lad who goes to sea is an egregious ass; never to forget your umbrella through a long life would seem a higher and wiser flight of achievement than to go smiling to the stake; and so long as you are a bit of a coward and inflexible in money matters, you fulfil the whole duty of man.

It is a still more difficult consideration for our average men, that while all their teachers, from Solomon down to Benjamin Franklin and the ungodly Binney, have inculcated the same ideal of manners, caution, and respectability, those characters in history who have most notoriously flown in the face of such precepts are spoken of in hyperbolical terms of praise, and honoured with public monuments in the streets of our commercial centres. This is very bewildering to the moral sense. You have Joan of Arc, who left a humble but honest and reputable livelihood under the eyes of her parents, to go a-colonelling, in the company of rowdy soldiers, against the enemies of France; surely a melancholy example for one's daughters! and then you have Columbus, who may have pioneered America, but, when all is said, was a most imprudent navigator. His Life is not the kind of thing one would like to put into the hands of young people; rather, one would do one's utmost to keep it from their knowledge, as a red flag of adventure and disintegrating influence in life. The time would fail me if I were to recite all the big names in history whose exploits are perfectly irrational and even shocking to the business mind. The incongruity is speaking; and I imagine it must engender among the mediocrities a very peculiar attitude towards the nobler and showier sides of national life. They will read of the Charge of Balaclava in much the same spirit as they assist at a performance of the *Lyons Mail.* Persons of substance take in the *Times* and sit composedly in pit or boxes according to the degree of their prosperity in business. As for the generals who go galloping up and down among bomb-shells in absurd cocked hats—as for the actors who raddle their faces and demean themselves for hire upon the stage—they must belong, thank God! to a different order of beings, whom we watch as we watch the clouds careering in the windy, bottomless inane, or read about like characters in ancient and rather fabulous annals. Our offspring would no more think of copying their behaviour, let us hope, than of doffing their clothes and painting themselves blue in consequence of certain admissions in the first chapter of their school history of England.

Discredited as they are in practice, the cowardly proverbs hold their own in theory; and it is another instance of the same spirit, that the opinions of old men about life have been accepted as final. All sorts of allowances are made for the illusions of youth; and none, or almost none, for the disenchantments of age. It is held to be a good taunt, and somehow or other to clinch the question logically, when an old gentleman waggles his head and says: "Ah, so I thought when I was your age." It is not thought an answer at all, if the young man retorts: "My venerable sir, so I shall most probably think when I am yours." and yet the one is as good as the other: pass for pass, tit for tat, a Roland for an Oliver.

"Opinion in good men," says Milton, "is but knowledge in the making." All opinions, properly so called, are stages on the road to truth. It does not follow that a man will travel any further; but if he has really considered the world and drawn a conclusion, he has travelled as far. This does not apply to formulæ got by rote, which are stages on the road to nowhere but second childhood and the grave. To have a catchword in your mouth is not the same thing as to hold an opinion; still less is it the same thing to have made one for yourself. There are too many of these catchwords in the world for people to rap out upon you like an oath and by way of an argument. They have a currency as intellectual counters; and many respectable persons pay their way with nothing else. They seem to stand for vague bodies of theory in the background. The imputed virtue of folios full of knockdown arguments is supposed to reside in them, just as some of the majesty of the British Empire dwells in the constable's truncheon. They are used in pure superstition, as old clodhoppers spoil Latin by way of an exorcism. And yet they are vastly serviceable for checking unprofitable discussion and stopping the mouths of babes and sucklings. And when a young man comes to a certain stage of intellectual growth, the examination of these counters forms a gymnastic at once amusing and fortifying to the mind.

Because I have reached Paris, I am not ashamed of having passed through Newhaven and Dieppe.

They were very good places to pass through, and I am none the less at my destination. All my old opinions were only stages on the way to the one I now hold, as itself is only a stage on the way to something else. I am no more abashed as having been a red-hot Socialist with a panacea of my own than at having been a sucking infant. Doubtless the world is quite right in a million ways; but you have to be kicked about a little to convince you of the fact. And in the meanwhile you must do something, be something, believe something. It is not possible to keep the mind in a state of accurate balance and blank: and even if you could do so, instead of coming ultimately to the right conclusion, you would be very apt to remain in a state of balance and blank to perpetuity. Even in quite intermediate stages, a dash of enthusiasm is not a thing to be ashamed of in the retrospect; if St. Paul had not been a very zealous Pharisee, he would have been a colder Christian. For my part, I look back to the time when I was a Socialist with something like regret. I have convinced myself (for the moment) that we had better leave these great changes to what we call great blind forces; their blindness being so much more perspicacious than the little, peering, partial eyesight of men. I seem to see that my own scheme would not answer; and all the other schemes I ever heard propounded would depress some elements of goodness just as much as they encourgaed others. Now I know that in thus turning Conservative with years, I am going through the normal cycle of change and travelling in the common orbit of men's opinions. I submit to this, as I would submit to gout or grey hair, as a concomitant of growing age or else of failing animal heat; but I do not acknowledge that it is necessarily a change for the better—I dare say it is deplorably for the worse. I have no choice in the business, and can no more resist this tendency of my mind than I could prevent my body from beginning to totter and decay. If I am spared (as the phrase runs) I shall doubtless outlive some troublesome desires; but I am in no hurry about that; nor, when the time comes, shall I plume myself on the immunity. Just in the same way, I do not greatly pride myself on having outlived my belief in the fairy tales of Socialism. Old people have faults of their own; they tend to become cowardly, niggardly, and suspicious. Whether from the growth of experience or the decline of animal heat, I see that age leads to these and certain other faults; and it follows, of course, that while in one sense I hope I am journeying towards the truth, in another I am indubitably posting towards these forms and sources of error.

As we go catching and catching at this or that corner of knowledge, now getting a foresight of generous possibilities, now chilled with a glimpse of prudence, we may compare the headlong course of our years to a swift torrent in which a man is carried away; now he is dashed against a boulder, now he grapples for a moment to a trailing spray; at the end, he is hurled out and overwhelmed in a dark and bottomless ocean. We have no more than glimpses and touches; we are torn away from our theories; we are spun round and round and shown this or the other view of life, until only fools or knaves can hold to their opinions. We take a sight at a condition in life, and say we have studied it; our most elaborate view is no more than an impression. If we had breathing space, we should take the occasion to modify and adjust; but at this breakneck hurry, we are no sooner boys than we are adult, no sooner in love than married or jilted, no sooner one age than we begin to be another, and no sooner in the fulness of our manhood than we begin to decline towards the grave. It is in vain to seek for consistency or expect clear and stable views in a medium so perturbed and fleeting. This is no cabinet science, in which things are tested to a scruple; we theorise with a pistol to our head; we are confronted with a new set of conditions on which we have not only to pass a judgment, but to take action, before the hour is at an end. And we cannot even regard ourselves as a constant; in this flux of things, our identity itself seems in a perpetual variation; and not infrequently we find our own disguise the strangest in the masquerade. In the course of time, we grow to love things we hated and hate things we loved. Milton is not so dull as he once was, nor perhaps Ainsworth so amusing. It is decidedly harder to climb trees, and not nearly so hard to sit still. There is no use pretending; even the thrice royal game of hide-and-seek has somehow lost in zest. All our attributes are modified or changed; and it will be a poor account of us if our views do not modify and change in proportion. To hold the same views at forty as we held at twenty is to have been stupefied for a score of years, and take rank, not as a prophet, but as an unteachable brat, well birched and none the wiser. It is as if a ship captain should sail to India from the Port of London; and having brought a chart of the Thames on deck at his first setting out should obstinately use no other for the whole voyage.

And mark you, it would be no less foolish to begin at Gravesend with a chart of the Red Sea. *Si Jeunesse savait, si Vieillesse pouvait,*[1] is a very pretty sentiment, but not necessarily right. In five cases out of ten, it is not so much that the young people do not know, as that they do not choose. There is something irreverent in the speculation, but perhaps the want of power has more to do with the wise resolutions of age than we are always willing to admit. It would be an instructive experiment to make an old man young again and leave him all his *savoir*. I scarcely think he would put his money in the Savings Bank after all; I doubt if he would be such an admirable son as we are led to expect; and as for his conduct in love, I believe firmly he would out-Herod Herod, and put the whole of his new compeers to the blush. Prudence is a wooden Juggernaut, before whom Benjamin Franklin walks with the portly air of a high-priest, and after whom dances many a successful merchant in the character of Atys. But it is not a deity to cultivate in youth. If a man lives to any considerable age, it cannot be denied that he laments his imprudences, but I notice he often laments his youth a deal more bitterly and with a more genuine intonation.

It is customary to say that age should be considered, because it comes last. It seems just as much to the point, that youth comes first. And the scale fairly kicks the beam, if you go on to add that age, in a majority of cases, never comes at all. Disease and accident make short work of even the most prosperous persons; death costs nothing, and the expense of a headstone is an inconsiderable trifle to the happy heir. To be suddenly snuffed out in the middle of ambitious schemes is tragical enough at best; but when a man has been grudging himself his own life in the meanwhile, and saving up everything for the festival that was never to be, it becomes that hysterically moving sort of tragedy which lies on the confines of farce. The victim is dead—and he has cunningly over-reached himself; a combination of calamities none the less absurd for being grim. To husband a favourite claret until the batch turns sour, is not at all an artful stroke of policy; and how much more with a whole cellar—a whole bodily existence! People may lay down their lives with cheerfulness in the sure expectation of a blessed immortality; but that is a

---

[1] If youth knew, if age could.

different affair from giving up youth with all its admirable pleasures, in the hope of a better quality of gruel in a more than problematical, nay, more than improbable, old age. We should not compliment a hungry man, who should refuse a whole dinner and reserve all his appetite for the dessert, before he knew whether there was to be any dessert or not. If there be such a thing as imprudence in the world, we surely have it here. We sail in leaky bottoms and in great and perilous waters; and to take a cue from the dolorous old naval ballad, we have heard the mermaidens singing, and know that we shall never see dry land any more. Old and young, we are all on our last cruise. If there is a fill of tobacco among the crew, for God's sake pass it round, and let us have a pipe before we go!

Indeed, by the report of our elders, this nervous preparation for old age is only trouble thrown away. We fall on guard, and after all it is a friend who comes to meet us. After the sun is down and the west faded, the heavens begin to fill with shining stars. So, as we grow old, a sort of equable jog-trot of feeling is substituted for the violent ups and downs of passion and disgust; the same influence that restrains our hopes quiets our apprehensions; if the pleasures are less intense, the troubles are milder and more tolerable; and in a word, this period for which we are asked to hoard up everything as for a time of famine, is, in its own right, the richest, easiest, and happiest of life. Nay, by managing its own work and following its own happy inspiration, youth is doing the best it can to endow the leisure of age. A full, busy youth is your only prelude to a self-contained and independent age; and the muff inevitably develops into the bore. There are not many Doctor Johnsons, to set forth upon their first romantic voyage at sixty-four. If we wish to scale Mont Blanc or visit a thieves' kitchen in the East End, to go down in a diving-dress or up in a balloon, we must be about it while we are still young. It will not do to delay until we are clogged with prudence and limping with rheumatism, and people begin to ask us: "What does Gravity out of bed?" Youth is the time to go flashing from one end of the world to the other both in mind and body; to try the manners of different nations; to hear the chimes at midnight; to see sunrise in town and country; to be converted at a revival; to circumnavigate the metaphysics, write halting verses, run a mile to see a fire, and wait all day

long in the theatre to applaud *Hernani*. There is some meaning in the old theory about wild oats; and a man who has not had his green-sickness and got done with it for good, is as little to be depended on as an unvaccinated infant. "It is extraordinary," said Lord Beaconsfield, one of the brightest and best preserved of youths up to the date of his last novel,[2] "it is extraordinary how hourly and how violently change the feelings of an inexperienced young man." And this mobility is a special talent entrusted to his care; a sort of indestructible virginity; a magic armour, with which he can pass unhurt through great dangers and come unbedaubed out of the miriest passages. Let him voyage, speculate, see all that he can, do all that he may; his soul has as many lives as a cat; he will live in all weathers, and never be a halfpenny the worse. Those who go to the devil in youth, with anything like a fair chance, were probably little worth saving from the first; they must have been feeble fellows—creatures made of putty and pack-thread, without steel or fire, anger or true joyfulness, in their composition; we may sympathise with their parents, but there is not much cause to go into mourning for themselves; for to be quite honest, the weak brother is the worst of mankind.

When the old man waggles his head and says, "Ah, so I thought when I was your age," he has proved the youth's case. Doubtless, whether from growth of experience or decline of animal heat, he thinks so no longer; but he thought so while he was young; and all men have thought so while they were young, since there was dew in the morning or hawthorn in May; and here is another young man adding his vote to those of previous generations and rivetting another link to the chain of testimony. It is as natural and as right for a young man to be imprudent and exaggerated, to live in swoops and circles, and beat about his cage like any other wild thing newly captured, as it is for old men to turn grey, or mothers to love their offspring, or heroes to die for something worthier than their lives.

By way of an apologue for the aged, when they feel more than usually tempted to offer their advice, let me recommend the following little tale. A child who had been remarkably fond of toys (and in particular of lead soldiers) found himself growing to the level of acknowledged boyhood without any abatement of this childish taste. He was thirteen; already he had been

2 *Lothair* (1881).

taunted for dallying overlong about the playbox; he had to blush if he was found among his lead soldiers; the shades of the prison-house were closing about him with a vengeance. There is nothing more difficult than to put the thoughts of children into the language of their elders; but this is the effect of his meditations at this juncture: "Plainly," he said, "I must give up my playthings in the meanwhile, since I am not in a position to secure myself against idle jeers. At the same time, I am sure that playthings are the very pick of life; all people give them up out of the same pusillanimous respect for those who are a little older; and if they do not return to them as soon as they can, it is only because they grow stupid and forget. I shall be wiser; I shall conform for a little to the ways of their foolish world; but so soon as I have made enough money, I shall retire and shut myself up among my playthings until the day I die." Nay, as he was passing in the train along the Esterel mountains between Cannes and Fréjus, he remarked a pretty house in an orange garden at the angle of a bay, and decided that this should be his Happy Valley. Astrea Redux; childhood was to come again! The idea has an air of simple nobility to me, not unworthy of Cincinnatus. And yet, as the reader has probably anticipated, it is never likely to be carried into effect. There was a worm i' the bud, a fatal error in the premises. Childhood must pass away, and then youth, as surely as age approaches. The true wisdom is to be always seasonable, and to change with a good grace in changing circumstances. To love playthings well as a child, to lead an adventurous and honourouble youth, and to settle when the time arrives, into a green and smiling age, is to be a good artist in life and deserve well of yourself and your neighbour.

You need repent none of your youthful vagaries. They may have been over the score on one side, just as those of age are probably over the score on the other. But they had a point; they not only befitted your age and expressed its attitude and passions, but they had a relation to what was outside of you, and implied criticisms on the existing state of things, which you need not allow to have been undeserved, because you now see that they were partial. All error, not merely verbal, is a strong way of stating that the current truth is incomplete. The follies of youth have a basis in sound reason, just as much as the embarrassing questions put by babes and sucklings. Their most anti-social acts indicate the defects of our society. When the torrent sweeps the man

against a boulder, you must expect him to scream, and you need not be surprised if the scream is sometimes a theory. Shelley, chafing at the Church of England, discovered the cure of all evils in universal atheism. Generous lads irritated at the injustices of society, see nothing for it but the abolishment of everything and Kingdom Come of anarchy. Shelley was a young fool; so are these cock-sparrow revolutionaries. But it is better to be a fool than to be dead. It is better to emit a scream in the shape of a theory than to be entirely insensible to the jars and incongruities of life and take everything as it comes in a forlorn stupidity. Some people swallow the universe like a pill; they travel on through the world, like smiling images pushed from behind. For God's sake give me the young man who has brains enough to make a fool of himself! As for the others, the irony of facts shall take it out of their hands, and make fools of them in downright earnest, ere the farce be over. There shall be such a mopping and a mowing at the last day, and such blushing and confusion of countenance for all those who have been wise in their own esteem, and have not learnt the rough lessons that youth hands on to age. If we are indeed to perfect and complete our own natures, and grow larger, stronger, and more sympathetic against some nobler career in the future, we had all best bestir ourselves to the utmost while we have the time. To equip a dull, respectable person with wings would be but to make a parody of an angel.

In short, if youth is not quite right in its opinions, there is a strong probability that age is not much more so. Undying hope is co-ruler of the human bosom with infallible credulity. A man finds he has been wrong at every preceding stage of his career, only to deduce the astonishing conclusion that he is at last entirely right. Mankind, after centuries of failure, are still upon the eve of a thoroughly constitutional millennium. Since we have explored the maze so long without result, it follows, for poor human reason, that we cannot have to explore much longer; close by must be the centre, with a champagne luncheon and a piece of ornamental water. How if there were no centre at all, but just one alley after another, and the whole world a labyrinth without end or issue?

I overheard the other day a scrap of conversation, which I take the liberty to reproduce. "What I advance is true," said one. "But not the whole truth," answered the other. "Sir," returned the first (and it seemed to me there was a smack of Dr. Johnson in the speech), "Sir, there is no such thing as the whole truth!" Indeed, there is nothing so evident in life as that there are two sides to a question. History is one long illustration. The forces of nature are engaged, day by day, in cudgelling it into our backward intelligences. We never pause for a moment's consideration, but we admit it as an axiom. An enthusiast sways humanity exactly by disregarding this great truth, and dinning it into our ears that this or that question has only one possible solution; and your enthusiast is a fine florid fellow, dominates things for a while and shakes the world out of a doze; but when once he is gone, an army of quiet and uninfluential people set to work to remind us of the other side and demolish the generous imposture. While Calvin is putting everybody right in his *Institutes,* and hotheaded Knox is thundering in the pulpit, Montaigne is already looking at the other side in his library in Périgord, and predicting that they will find as much to quarrel about in the Bible as they had found already in the Church. Age may have one side, but assuredly Youth has the other. There is nothing more certain than that both are right, except perhaps that both are wrong. Let them agree to differ; for who knows but what agreeing to differ may not be a form of agreement rather than a form of difference?

I suppose it is written that anyone who sets up for a bit of a philosopher, must contradict himself to his very face. For here have I fairly talked myself into thinking that we have the whole thing before us at last; that there is no answer to the mystery, except that there are as many as you please; that there is no centre to the maze because, like the famous sphere, its centre is everywhere; and that agreeing to differ with every ceremony of politeness, is the only "one undisturbed song of pure concent" to which we are ever likely to lend our musical voices.

Æs Triplex

THE changes wrought by death are in themselves so sharp and final, and so terrible and melancholy in their consequences, that the thing stands alone in man's experience, and has no parallel upon earth. It outdoes all other accidents because it is the last of them. Sometimes it leaps suddenly upon its victims, like a Thug; sometimes it lays a regular siege and creeps upon their citadel during a score of years. And when the business is done, there is sore havoc made in other people's lives, and a pin knocked out by which many subsidiary friendships hung together. There are empty chairs, solitary walks, and single beds at night. Again, in taking away our friends, death does not take them away utterly, but leaves behind a mocking, tragical, and soon intolerable residue, which must be hurriedly concealed. Hence a whole chapter of sights and customs striking to the mind, from the pyramids of Egypt to the gibbets and dule trees of mediæval Europe. The poorest persons have a bit of pageant going towards the tomb; memorial stones are set up over the least memorable; and, in order to preserve some show of respect for what remains of our old loves and friendships, we must accompany it with much grimly ludicrous ceremonial, and the hired undertaker parades before the door. All this, and much more of the same sort, accompanied by the eloquence of poets, has gone a great way to put humanity in error; nay, in many philosophies the error has been embodied and laid down with every circumstance of logic; althought in real life the bustle and swiftness, in leaving people little time to think, have not left them time enough to go dangerously wrong in practice.

As a matter of fact, although few things are spoken of with more fearful whisperings than this prospect of death, few have less influence on conduct under healthy circumstances. We have all heard of cities in South America built upon the side of fiery mountains, and how, even in this tremendous neighbourhood, the inhabitants are not a jot more impressed by the solemnity of mortal conditions than if they were delving gardens in the greenest corner of England. There are serenades and suppers and much gallantry among the myrtles overhead; and meanwhile the foundation shudders underfoot, the bowels of the mountain growl, and at any moment living ruin may leap sky-high into the moonlight, and tumble man and his merry-making in the dust. In the eyes of very young people, and very dull old ones, there is something indescribably reckless and desperate in such a picture. It seems not credible that respectable married people, with umbrellas, should find appetite for a bit of supper within quite a long distance of a fiery mountain; ordinary life begins to smell of high-handed debauch when it is carried on so close to a catastrophe; and even cheese and salad, it seems, could hardly be relished in such cir-

cumstances without something like a defiance of
the Creator. It should be a place for nobody but
hermits dwelling in prayer and maceration, or mere
born-devils drowning care in a perpetual carouse.

And yet, when one comes to think upon it
calmly, the situation of these South American
citizens forms only a very pale figure for the
state of ordinary mankind. This world itself,
travelling blindly and swiftly in over-crowded
space, among a million other worlds travelling
blindly and swiftly in contrary directions, may
very well come by a knock that would set it into
explosion like a penny squib. And what, patho-
logically looked at, is the human body with all
its organs, but a mere bagful of petards? The
least of these is as dangerous to the whole economy
as the ship's powder-magazine to the ship; and
with every breath we breathe, and every meal
we eat, we are putting one or more of them in
peril. If we clung as devotedly as some philosophers pretend we do to the abstract idea of life,
or were half as frightened as they make out we are,
for the subversive accident that ends it all, the
trumpets might sound by the hour and no one
would follow them into battle—the blue peter
might fly at the truck, but who would climb into
a sea-going ship? Think (if these philosophers
were right) with what a preparation of spirit
we should affront the daily peril of the dinner-
table: a deadlier spot than any battle-field in
history, where the far greater proportion of our
ancestors have miserably left their bones! What
woman would ever be lured into marriage, so
much more dangerous than the wildest sea?
And what would it be to grow old? For, after a
certain distance, every step we take in life we
find the ice growing thinner below our feet, and
all around us and behind us we see our contemporaries going through. By the time a man
gets well into the seventies, his continued existence
is a mere miracle; and when he lays his old bones
in bed for the night, there is an overwhelming
probability that he will never see the day. Do
the old men mind it, as a matter of fact? Why,
no. They were never merrier; they have their
grog at night, and tell the raciest stories; they
hear of the death of people about their own age,
or even younger, not as if it was a grisly warning,
but with a simple childlike pleasure at having
outlived someone else; and when a draught
might puff them out like a guttering candle, or a
bit of a stumble shatter them like so much glass,
their old hearts keep sound and unaffrighted,
and they go on bubbling with laughter, through
years of man's age compared to which the valley

at Balaclava was as safe and peaceful as a village
cricket-green on Sunday. It may fairly be questioned (if we look to the peril only) whether it
was a much more daring feat for Curtius to
plunge into the gulf, than for any old gentleman
of ninety to doff his clothes and clamber into bed.

Indeed, it is a memorable subject for consideration, with what unconcern and gaiety
mankind pricks on along the Valley of the
Shadow of Death. The whole way is one wilderness
of snares, and the end of it, for those who fear the
last pitch, is irrevocable ruin. And yet we go
spinning through it all, like a party for the Derby.
Perhaps the reader remembers one of the humorous devices of the deified Caligula: how he
encouraged a vast concourse of holiday-makers
on to his bridge over Baiæ bay; and when they
were in the height of their enjoyment, turned
loose the Prætorian guards among the company,
and had them tossed into the sea. This is no bad
miniature of the dealings of nature with the
transitory race of man. Only, what a chequered
picnic we have of it, even while it lasts! and into
what great waters, not to be crossed by any swimmer, God's pale Prætorian throws us over in the end!

We live the time that a match flickers; we
pop the cork of a ginger-beer bottle, and the
earthquake swallows us on the instant. Is it not
odd, is it not incongruous, is it not, in the highest
sense of human speech, incredible, that we
should think so highly of the ginger-beer, and
regard so little the devouring earthquake? The
love of Life and the fear of Death are two famous
phrases that grow harder to understand the more
we think about them. It is a well-known fact that
an immense proportion of boat accidents would
never happen if people held the sheet in their
hands instead of making it fast; and yet, unless
it be some martinet of a professional mariner or
some landsman with shattered nerves, every one
of God's creatures makes it fast. A strange
instance of man's unconcern and brazen boldness
in the face of death!

We confound ourselves with metaphysical
phrases which we import into daily talk with
noble inappropriateness. We have no idea of
what death is, apart from its circumstances and
some of its consequences to others; and although
we have some experience of living, there is not a
man on earth who has flown so high into abstraction as to have any practical guess at the
meaning of the word *life*. All literature, from
Job and Omar Khayyam to Thomas Carlyle or
Walt Whitman, is but an attempt to look upon
the human state with such largeness of view as

shall enable us to rise from the consideration of living to the Definition of life. And our sages give us about the best satisfaction in their power when they say that it is a vapour, or a show, or made out of the same stuff with dreams. Philosophy, in its more rigid sense, has been at the same work for ages; and after a myriad bald heads have wagged over the problem, and piles of words have been heaped one upon another into dry and cloudy volumes without end, philosophy has the honour of laying before us, with modest pride, her contribution towards the subject: that life is a Permanent Possibility of Sensation. Truly a fine result! A man may very well love beef, or hunting, or a woman; but surely, surely, not a Permanent Possibility of Sensation! He may be afraid of a precipice, or a dentist, or a large enemy with a club, or even an undertaker's man; but not certainly of abstract death. We may trick with the word life in its dozen senses until we are weary of tricking; we may argue in terms of all the philosophies on earth, but one fact remains true throughout—that we do not love life, in the sense that we are greatly preoccupied about its conservation; that we do not, properly speaking, love life at all, but living. Into the views of the least careful there will enter some degree of providence; no man's eyes are fixed entirely on the passing hour; but although we have some anticipation of good health, good weather, wine, active employment, love, and self-approval, the sum of these anticipations does not amount to anything like a general view of life's possibilities and issues; nor are those who cherish them most vividly, at all the most scrupulous of their personal safety. To be deeply interested in the accidents of our existence, to enjoy keenly the mixed texture of human experience, rather leads a man to disregard precautions, and risk his neck against a straw. For surely the love of living is stronger in an Alpine climber roping over a peril, or a hunter riding merrily at a stiff fence, than in a creature who lives upon a diet and walks a measured distance in the interest of his constitution.

There is a great deal of very vile nonsense talked upon both sides of the matter: tearing divines reducing life to the dimensions of a mere funeral procession, so short as to be hardly decent; and melancholy unbelievers yearning for the tomb as if it were a world too far away. Both sides must feel a little ashamed of their performances now and again when they draw in their chairs to dinner. Indeed, a good meal and a bottle of wine is an answer to most standard works upon the question. When a man's heart warms to his viands, he forgets a great deal of sophistry, and soars into a rosy zone of contemplation. Death may be knocking at the door, like the Commander's statue; we have something else in hand, thank God, and let him knock. Passing bells are ringing all the world over. All the world over, and every hour, someone is parting company with all his aches and ecstasies. For us also the trap is laid. But we are so fond of life that we have no leisure to entertain the terror of death. It is a honeymoon with us all through, and none of the longest. Small blame to us if we give our whole hearts to this glowing bride of ours, to the appetites, to honour, to the hungry curiosity of the mind, to the pleasure of the eyes in nature, and the pride of our own nimble bodies.

We all of us appreciate the sensations; but as for caring about the Permanence of the Possibility, a man's head is generally very bald, and his senses very dull, before he comes to that. Whether we regard life as a lane leading to a dead wall—a mere bag's end, as the French say—or whether we think of it as a vestibule or gymnasium, where we wait our turn and prepare our faculties for some more noble destiny; whether we thunder in a pulpit, or pule in little atheistic poetry-books, about its vanity and brevity; whether we look justly for years of health and vigour, or are about to mount into a bath-chair, as a step towards the hearse; in each and all of these views and situations there is but one conclusion possible: that a man should stop his ears against paralysing terror, and run the race that is set before him with a single mind. No one surely could have recoiled with more heartache and terror from the thought of death than our respected lexicographer; and yet we know how little it affected his conduct, how wisely and boldly he walked, and in what a fresh and lively vein he spoke of life. Already an old man, he ventured on his Highland tour; and his heart, bound with triple brass, did not recoil before twenty-seven individual cups of tea. As courage and intelligence are the two qualities best worth a good man's cultivation, so it is the first part of intelligence to recognise our precarious estate in life, and the first part of courage to be not at all abashed before the fact. A frank and somewhat headlong carriage, not looking too anxiously before, not dallying in maudlin regret over the past, stamps the man who is well armoured for this world.

And not only well armoured for himself, but a good friend and a good citizen to boot. We do not go to cowards for tender dealing; there is nothing so cruel as panic; the man who has least fear for his own carcase, has most time to consider others. That eminent chemist who took his walks abroad in tin shoes, and subsisted wholly upon tepid milk, had all his work cut out for him in considerable dealings with his own digestion. So soon as prudence has begun to grow up in the brain, like a dismal fungus, it finds its first expression in a paralysis of generous acts. The victim begins to shrink spiritually; he develops a fancy for parlours with a regulated temperature, and takes his morality on the principle of tin shoes and tepid milk. The care of one important body or soul becomes so engrossing, that all the noises of the outer world begin to come thin and faint into the parlour with the regulated temperature; and the shoes go equally forward over blood and rain. To be overwise is to ossify; and the scruple-monger ends by standing stock-still. Now the man who has his heart on his sleeve, and a good whirling weathercock of a brain, who reckons his life as a thing to be dashingly used and cheerfully hazarded, makes a very different acquaintance of the world, keeps all his pulses going true and fast, and gathers impetus as he runs, until, if he be running towards anything better than wild-fire, he may shoot up and become a constellation in the end. Lord look after his health, Lord have a care for his soul, says he; and he has at the key of the position, and swashes through incongruity and peril towards his aim. Death is on all sides of him with pointed batteries, as he is on all sides of all of us; unfortunate surprises gird him round; mim-mouthed friends and relations hold up their hands in quite a little elegiacal synod about his path: and what cares he for all this? Being a true lover of living, a fellow with something pushing and spontaneous in his inside, he must, like any other soldier, in any other stiring, deadly warfare, push on at his best pace until he touch the goal. "A peerage or Westminster Abbey!" cried Nelson in his bright, boyish, heroic manner. These are great incentives; not for any of these, but for the plain satisfaction of living, of being about their business in some sort or other, do the brave, serviceable men of every nation tread down the nettle danger, and pass flyingly over all the stumbling-blocks of prudence. Think of the heroism of Johnson, think of that superb indifference to mortal limitation that set him upon his dictionary, and carried him through triumphantly until the end! Who, if he were wisely considerate of things at large, would ever embark upon any work much more con-

siderable than a half-penny post-card? Who would project a serial novel, after Thackeray and Dickens had each fallen in mid-course? Who would find heart enough to begin to live, if he dallied with the consideration of death?

And, after all, what sorry and pitiful quibbling all this is! To forego all the issues of living in a parlour with a regulated temperature—as if that were not to die a hundred times over, and for ten years at a stretch! As if it were not to die in one's own life-time, and without even the sad immunities of death! As if it were not to die, and yet be the patient spectators of our own pitiable change! The Permanent Possibility is preserved, but the sensations carefully held at arm's length, as if one kept a photographic plate in a dark chamber. It is better to lose health like a spend-thrift than to waste it like a miser. It is better to live and be done with it than to die daily in the sick-room. By all means begin your folio; even if the doctor does not give you a year, even if he hesitates about a month, make one brave push and see what can be accomplished in a week. It is not only in finished undertakings that we ought to honour useful labour. A spirit goes out of the man who means execution, which outlives the most untimely ending. All who have meant good work with their whole hearts, have done good work, although they may die before they have the time to sign it. Every heart that has beat strong and cheerfully has left a hopeful impulse behind it in the world, and bettered the tradition of mankind. And even if death catch people, like an open pitfall, and in mid-career, laying out vast projects, and planning monstrous foundations, flushed with hope, and their mouths full of boastful language, they should be at once tripped up and silenced: is there not something brave and spirited in such a termination? and does not life go down with a better grace, foaming in full body over a precipice, than miserably straggling to an end in sandy deltas? When the Greeks made their fine saying that those whom the gods love die young, I cannot help believing they had this sort of death also in their eye. For surely, at whatever age it overtake the man, this is to die young. Death has not been suffered to take so much as an illusion from his heart. In the hot-fit of life, a-tiptoe on the highest point of being, he passes at a bound on to the other side. The noise of the mallet and chisel is scarcely quenched, the trumpets are hardly done blowing, when, trailing with him clouds of glory, this happy-starred, full-blooded spirit shoots into the spiritual land.

A Note on Realism

Like many of Stevenson's literary essays this one has been published in various collections of his work. It was first published in book form after Stevenson's death in Essays and Criticisms *in 1903, then in* Essays on the Art of Writing *in 1905, and in collected editions of his works in the volume* Essays in Literature. *The essay originally appeared in the* Magazine of Art *in 1883.*

STYLE is the invariable mark of any master; and for the student who does not aspire so high as to be numbered with the giants, it is still the one quality in which he may improve himself at will. Passion, wisdom, creative force, the power of mystery or colour, are allotted in the hour of birth, and can be neither learned nor simulated. But the just and dexterous use of what qualities we have, the proportion of one part to another and to the whole, the elision of the useless, the accentuation of the important, and the preservation of a uniform character from end to end— these, which taken together constitute technical perfection, are to some degree within the reach of industry and intellectual courage. What to put in and what to leave out; whether some particular fact be organically necessary or purely ornamental; whether, if if be purely ornamental, it may not weaken or obscure the general design; and finally, whether, if we decide to use it, we should do so grossly and notably, or in some conventional disguise: are questions of plastic style continually rearising. And the sphinx that patrols the highways of executive art has no more unanswerable riddle to propound.

In literature (from which I must draw my instances) the great change of the past century has been effected by the admission of detail. It was inaugurated by the romantic Scott; and at length, by the semi-romantic Balzac and his more or less wholly unromantic followers, bound like a duty on the novelist. For some time it signified and expressed a more ample contemplation of the conditions of man's life; but it has recently (at least in France) fallen into a merely technical and decorative stage, which it is, perhaps, still too harsh to call survival. With a movement of alarm, the wiser or more timid begin to fall a little back from these extremities; they begin to aspire after a more naked, narrative articulation; after the succinct, the dignified, and the poetic; and as a means to this, after a general lightening of this baggage of detail. After Scott we beheld the starveling story—once, in the hands of Voltaire, as abstract as a parable— begin to be pampered upon facts. The introduction of these details developed a particular ability of hand; and that ability, childishly indulged, has led to the works that now amaze us on a railway journey. A man of the unquestionable force of M. Zola spends himself on technical successes. To afford a popular flavour and attract the mob, he adds a steady current of what I may be allowed to call the rancid. That is exciting to the moralist; but what more particularly interests the artist is this tendency of the extreme of detail, when followed as a principle, to degenerate into mere *feux-de-joie*[1] of literary tricking. The other day even M. Daudet was to be heard babbling of audible colours and visible sounds.

This odd suicide of one branch of the realists may serve to remind us of the fact which underlies a very dusty conflict of the critics. All representative art, which can be said to live, is both realistic and ideal; and the realism about which we quarrel is a matter purely of externals. It is no especial cultus of nature and veracity, but a mere whim of veering fashion, that has made us turn our back upon the larger, more various, and more romantic art of yore. A photographic exactitude in dialogue is now the exclusive fashion; but even in the ablest hands it tells us no more—I think it even tells us less—than Molière, wielding his artificial medium, has told us and to all time of Alceste or Orgon, Dorine or Chrysale. The historical novel is forgotten. Yet truth to the conditions of man's nature and the conditions of man's life, the truth of literary art, is free of the ages. It may be told us in a carpet comedy, in a novel of adventure, or a fairy tale. The scene may be pitched in London, on the sea-coast of Bohemia, or away on the mountains of Beulah. And by an odd and luminous accident,

[1] Bonfires.

if there is any page of literature calculated to awake the envy of M. Zola, it must be that *Troilus and Cressida* which Shakespeare, in a spasm of unmanly anger with the world, grafted on the heroic story of the siege of Troy.

This question of realism, let it then be clearly understood, regards not in the least degree the fundamental truth, but only the technical method, of a work of art. Be as ideal or as abstract as you please, you will be none the less veracious; but if you be weak, you run the risk of being tedious and inexpressive; and if you be very strong and honest, you may chance upon a masterpiece.

A work of art is first cloudily conceived in the mind; during the period of gestation it stands more clearly forward from these swaddling mists, puts on expressive lineaments, and becomes at length that most faultless, but also, alas! that incommunicable product of the human mind, a perfected design. On the approach to execution all is changed. The artist must now step down, don his working clothes, and become the artisan. He now resolutely commits his airy conception, his delicate Ariel, to the touch of matter; he must decide, almost in a breath, the scale, the style, the spirit, and the particularity of execution of his whole design.

The engendering idea of some works is stylistic; a technical preoccupation stands them instead of some robuster principle of life. And with these the execution is but play; for the stylistic problem is resolved beforehand, and all large originality of treatment wilfully foregone. Such are the verses, intricately designed, which we have learnt to admire, with a certain smiling admiration, at the hands of Mr. Lang and Mr. Dobson; such, too, are those canvases where dexterity or even breadth of plastic style takes the place of pictorial nobility of design. So, it may be remarked, it was easier to begin to write *Esmond* than *Vanity Fair,* since, in the first, the style was dictated by the nature of the plan; and Thackeray, a man probably of some indolence of mind, enjoyed and got good profit of this economy of effort. But the case is exceptional. Usually in all works of art that have been conceived from within outwards, and generously nourished from the author's mind, the moment in which he begins to execute is one of extreme perplexity and strain. Artists of in-different energy and an imperfect devotion to their own ideal make this ungrateful effort once for all; and, having formed a style, adhere to it through life. But those of a higher order cannot rest content with a process which, as they

continue to employ it, must infallibly degenerate towards the academic and the cut-and-dried. Every fresh work in which they embark is the signal for a fresh engagement of the whole forces of their mind; and the changing views which accompany the growth of their experience are marked by still more sweeping alterations in the manner of their art. So that criticism loves to dwell upon and distinguish the varying periods of a Raphael, a Shakespeare, or a Beethoven.

It is, then, first of all, at this initial and decisive moment when execution is begun, and thence-forth only in a less degree, that the ideal and the real do indeed, like good and evil angels, content for the direction of the work. Marble, paint, and language, the pen, the needle, and the brush, all have their grossnesses, their ineffable impo-tences, their hours, if I may so express myself, of insubordination. It is the work and it is a great part of the delight of any artist to contend with these unruly tools, and now by brute energy, now by witty expedient, to drive and coax them to effect his will. Given these means, so laugh-ably inadequate, and given the interest, the intensity, and the multiplicity of the actual sensation whose effect he is to render with their aid, the artist has one main and necessary resource which he must, in every case and upon any theory, employ. He must, that is, suppress much and omit more. He must omit what is tedious or irrelevant, and suppress what is tedious and necessary. But such facts as, in regard to the main design, subserve a variety of purposes, he will perforce and eagerly retain. And it is the mark of the very highest order of creative art to be woven exclusively of such. There, any fact that is registered is contrived a double or a treble debt to pay, and is at once an ornament in its place, and a pillar in the main design. Nothing would find room in such a picture that did not serve, at once, to complete the composition, to accentuate the scheme of colour, to distinguish the planes of distance, and to strike the note of the selected sentiment; nothing would be allowed in such a story that did not, at the same time, expedite the progress of the fable, build up the characters, and strike home the moral or the philosophical design. But this is unattainable. As a rule, so far from building the fabric of our works exclusively with these, we are thrown into a rapture if we think we can muster a dozen or a score of them, to be the plums of our confection. And hence, in order that the canvas may be filled or the story proceed from point to point, other details must be admitted. They must be admitted, alas! upon a doubtful title; many without marriage robes. Thus any work of art, as it preceeds towards completion, too often—I had almost written always—loses in force and poignancy of main design. Our little air is swamped and dwarfed among hardly relevant orchestration; our little passionate story drowns in a deep sea of descriptive eloquence or slipshod talk.

But again, we are rather more tempted to admit those particulars which we know we can describe; and hence those most of all which, having been described very often, have grown to be conventionally treated in the practice of our art. These we choose, as the mason chooses the acanthus to adorn his capital, because they come naturally to the accustomed hand. The old stock incidents and accessories, tricks of workmanship and schemes of composition (all being admirably good, or they would long have been forgotten) haunt and tempt our fancy, offer us ready-made but not perfectly appropriate solutions for any problem that arises, and wean us from the study of nature and the uncompromising practice of art. To struggle, to face nature, to find fresh solutions, and give expression to facts which have not yet been adequately or not yet elegantly expressed, is to run a little upon the danger of extreme self-love. Difficulty sets a high price upon achievement; and the artist may easily fall into the error of the French naturalists, and consider any fact as welcome to admission if it be the ground of brilliant handiwork; or, again, into the error of the modern landscape-painter, who is apt to think that difficulty overcome and science well displayed can take the place of what is, after all, the one excuse and breath of art—charm. A little further, and he will regard charm in the light of an unworthy sacrifice to prettiness, and the omission of a tedious passage as an infidelity to art.

We have now the matter of this difference before us. The idealist, his eye singly fixed upon the greater outlines, loves rather to fill up the interval with detail of the conventional order, briefly touched, soberly suppressed in tone, courting neglect. But the realist, with a fine intemperance, will not suffer the presence of anything so dead as a convention; he shall have all fiery, all hot-pressed from nature, all charactered and notable, seizing the eye. The style that befits either of these extremes, once chosen, brings with it its necessary disabilities and dangers. The immediate danger of the realist is to sacrifice the beauty and significance of the whole to local dexterity, or, in the insane pursuit of completion, to immolate his readers under facts; but he comes in the last resort, and as his energy declines, to discard all design, abjure all choice, and, with scientific thoroughness, steadily to communicate matter which is not worth learning. The danger of the idealist is, of course, to become merely null and lose all grip of fact, particularity, or passion.

We talk of bad and good. Everything, indeed, is good which is conceived with honesty and executed with communicative ardour. But though on neither side is dogmatism fitting, and though in every case the artist must decide for himself, and decide afresh and yet afresh for each succeeding work and new creation; yet one thing may be generally said, that we of the last quarter of the nineteenth century, breathing as we do the intellectual atmosphere of our age, are more apt to err upon the side of realism than to sin in quest of the ideal. Upon that theory it may be well to watch and correct our own decisions, always holding back the hand from the least appearance of irrelevant dexterity, and resolutely fixed to begin no work that is not philosophical, passionate, dignified, happily mirthful, or at the last and least, romantic in design.

from Across the Plains

Stevenson's collection of essays in Across the Plains *was first published in 1892 when Stevenson was living in Samoa. It contained essays from his periodical publications of the eighteen-eighties. The essay printed below, "Pulvis et Umbra" (dust and shadow) was first published in* Scribner's Magazine *in 1888. In later editions of Stevenson's works the essay was included in the volume* Memories and Portraits. *"Pulvis et Umbra" is considered to be Stevenson's masterpiece in the vein of the philosophic essay.*

Pulvis et Umbra

WE LOOK for some reward of our endeavours
and are disappointed; not success, not
happiness, not even peace of conscience, crowns
our ineffectual efforts to do well. Our frailties
are invincible, our virtues barren; the battle goes
sore against us to the going down of the sun.
The canting moralist tells us of right and wrong;
and we look abroad, even on the face of our small
earth, and find them change with every climate,
and no country where some action is not honoured
for a virtue and none where it is not branded for
a vice; and we look in our experience, and find
no vital congruity in the wisest rules, but at the
best a municipal fitness. It is not strange if we
are tempted to despair of good. We ask too much.
Our religions and moralities have been trimmed
to flatter us, till they are all emasculate and
sentimentalised, and only please and weaken.
Truth is of a rougher strain. In the harsh face of
life, faith can read a bracing gospel. The human
race is a thing more ancient than the ten commandments; and the bones and revolutions of
the Kosmos, in whose joints we are but moss and
fungus, more ancient still.

I

Of the Kosmos in the last resort, science
reports many doubtful things and all of them
appalling. There seems no substance to this
solid globe on which we stamp: nothing but
symbols and ratios. Symbols and ratios carry us
and bring us forth and beat us down; gravity
that swings the incommensurable suns and worlds
through space, is but a figment varying inversely
as the squares of distances; and the suns and
worlds themselves, imponderable figures of
abstraction, NH_3 and H_2O. Consideration dares
not dwell upon this view; that way madness lies;
science carries us into zones of speculation, where
there is no habitable city for the mind of man.

But take the Kosmos with a grosser faith, as our
senses give it us. We behold space sown with
rotatory islands, suns and worlds and the shards
and wrecks of systems: some, like the sun, still
blazing; some rotting, like the earth; others, like
the moon, stable in desolation. All of these we
take to be made of something we call matter: a
thing which no analysis can help us to conceive;
to whose incredible properties no familiarity can
reconcile our minds. This stuff, when not purified
by the lustration of fire, rots uncleanly into something we call life; seized through all its atoms

with a pediculous malady; swelling in tumours
that become independent, sometimes even (by
an abhorrent prodigy) locomotory; one splitting
into millions, millions cohering into one, as the
malady proceeds through varying stages. This
vital putrescence of the dust, used as we are to it,
yet strikes us with occasional disgust, and the
profusion of worms in a piece of ancient turf, or
the air of a marsh darkened with insects, will
sometimes check our breathing so that we
aspire for cleaner places. But none is clean: the
moving sand is infected with lice; the pure spring,
where it bursts out of the mountain, is a mere
issue of worms; even in the hard rock the crystal
is forming.

In two main shapes this eruption covers the
countenance of the earth: the animal and the
vegetable: one in some degree the inversion of
the other: the second rooted to the spot; the
first coming detached out of its natal mud, and
scurrying abroad with the myriad feet of insects
or towering into the heavens on the wings of
birds: a thing so inconceivable that, if it be well
considered, the heart stops. To what passes with
the anchored vermin, we have little clue:
doubtless they have their joys and sorrows, their
delights and killing agonies: it appears not how.
But of the locomotory, to which we ourselves
belong, we can tell more. These share with us a
thousand miracles: the miracles of sight, of
hearing, of the projection of sound, things that
bridge space; the miracles of memory and reason,
by which the present is conceived, and when it is
gone, its image kept living in the brains of man
and brute; the miracle of reproduction, with its
imperious desires and staggering consequences.
And to put the last touch upon this mountain
mass of the revolting and the inconceivable, all
these prey upon each other, lives tearing other
lives in pieces, cramming them inside themselves,
and by that summary process, growing fat; the
vegetarian, the whale, perhaps the tree, not less
than the lion of the desert; for the vegetarian is
only the eater of the dumb.

Meanwhile our rotatory island, loaded with
predatory life, and more drenched with blood,
both animal and vegetable, than ever mutinied
ship, scuds through space with unimaginable
speed, and turns alternate cheeks to the reverberation of a blazing world, ninety million miles away.

II

What a monstrous spectre is this man, the
disease of the agglutinated dust, lifting alternate
feet or lying drugged with slumber; killing,

feeding, growing, bringing forth small copies of himself; grown upon with hair like grass, fitted with eyes that move and glitter in his face; a thing to set children screaming;—and yet looked at nearlier, known as his fellows know him, how surprising are his attributes! Poor soul, here for so little, cast among so many hardships, filled with desires so incommensurate and so inconsistent, savagely surrounded, savagely descended, irremediably condemned to prey upon his fellow lives: who should have blamed him had he been of a piece with his destiny and a being merely barbarous? and we look and behold him instead filled with imperfect virtues: infinitely childish, often admirably valiant, often touchingly kind; sitting down, amidst his momentary life, to to debate of right and wrong and the attributes of the deity; rising up to do battle for an egg or die for an idea; singling out his friends and his mate with cordial affection; bringing forth in pain, rearing with long-suffering solitude, his young. To touch the heart of his mystery, we find in him one thought, strange to the point of lunacy: the thought of duty; the thought of something owing to himself, to his neighbour, to his God: an ideal of decency, to which he would rise if it were possible; a limit of shame, below which, if it be possible, he will not stoop. The design in most men is one of conformity; here and there, in picked natures, it transcends itself and soars on the other side, arming martyrs with independence; but in all, in their degrees, it is a bosom thought:—Not in man alone, for we trace it in dogs and cats whom we know fairly well, and doubtless some similar point of honour sways the elephant, the oyster, and the louse, of whom we know so little:—But in man, at least, it sways with so complete an empire that merely selfish things come second, even with the selfish: that appetites are starved, fears are conquered, pains supported; that almost the dullest shrinks from the reproof of a glance, although it were a child's; and all but the most cowardly stand amid the risks of war; and the more noble, having strongly conceived an act as due to their ideal, affront and embrace death. Strange enough if, with their singular origin and perverted practice, they think they are to be rewarded in some future life: stranger still, of they are persuaded of the contrary, and think this blow, which they solicit, will strike them senseless for eternity. I shall be reminded what a tragedy of misconception and misconduct man at large presents: of organised injustice, cowardly violence, and treacherous crime; and of the damning imperfections of the best. They cannot be too darkly drawn. Man is indeed marked for failure in his efforts to do right. But where the best consistently miscarry, how tenfold more remarkable that all should continue to strive; and surely we should find it both touching and inspiriting, that in a field from which success is banished, our race should not cease to labour.

If the first view of this creature, stalking in his rotatory isle, be a thing to shake the courage of the stoutest, on this nearer sight, he startles us with an admiring wonder. It matters not where we look, under what climate we observe him, in what stage of society, in what depth of ignorance, burthened with what erroneous morality; by camp-fires in Assiniboia, the snow powdering his shoulders, the wind plucking his blanket, as he sits, passing the ceremonial calumet and uttering his grave opinions like a Roman senator; in ships at sea, a man inured to harship and vile pleasures, his brightest hope a fiddle in a tavern and a bedizened trull who sells herself to rob him, and he for all that simple, innocent, cheerful, kindly like a child, constant to toil, brave to drown, for others; in the slums of cities, moving among indifferent millions to mechanical employments, without hope of change in the future, with scarce a pleasure in the present, and yet true to his virtues, honest up to his lights, kind to his neighbours, tempted perhaps in vain by the bright gin-palace, perhaps long-suffering with the drunken wife that ruins him; in India (a woman this time) kneeling with broken cries and streaming tears, as she drowns her child in the sacred river; in the brothel, the discard of society, living mainly on strong drink fed with affronts, a fool, a thief, the comrade of thieves, and even here keeping the point of honour and the touch of pity, often repaying the world's scorn with service, often standing firm upon a scruple, and at a certain cost, rejecting riches:—everywhere some virtue cherished or affected, everywhere some decency of thought and carriage, everywhere the ensign of man's ineffectual goodness:—ah! if I could show you this! if I could show you these men and women, all the world over, in every stage of history, under every abuse of error, under every circumstance of failure, without hope, without help, without thanks, still obscurely fighting the lost fight of virtue, still clinging, in the brothel or on the scaffold, to some rag of honour, the poor jewel of their souls! They may seek to escape, and yet they cannot; it is not alone their privilege and glory, but their doom; they are condemned to some nobility; all their lives long, the desire of good is at their heels, the implacable hunter.

Of all earth's meteors, here at least is the most strange and consoling: that this ennobled lemur, this hair-crowned bubble of the dust, this inheritor of a few years and sorrows, should yet deny himself his rare delights, and add to his frequent pains, and live for an ideal, however misconceived. Nor can we stop with man. A new doctrine, received with screams a little while ago by canting moralists, and still not properly worked into the body of our thoughts, lights us a step farther into the heart of this rough but noble universe. For nowadays the pride of man denies in vain his kinship with the original dust. He stands no longer like a thing apart. Close at his heels we see the dog, prince of another genus: and in him too, we see dumbly testified the same cultus of an unattainable ideal, the same constancy in failure. Does it stop with the dog? We look at our feet where the ground is blackened with the swarming ant: a creature so small, so far from us in the hierarchy of brutes, that we can scarce trace and scarce comprehend his doings; and here also, in his ordered polities and rigorous justice, we see confessed the law of duty and the fact of individual sin. Does it stop, then, with the ant? Rather this desire of well-doing and this doom of frailty run through all the grades of life: rather is this earth, from the frosty top of Everest to the next margin of the internal fire, one stage of ineffectual virtues and one temple of pious tears and perseverance. The whole creation groaneth and travaileth together. Is is the common and the godlike law of life. The browsers, the biters, the barkers, the hairy coats of field and forest, the squirrel in the oak, the thousand-footed creeper in the dust, as they share with us the gift of life, share with us the love of an ideal: strive like us—like us are tempted to grow weary of the struggle—to do well; like us receive at times unmerited refreshment, visitings of support, returns of courage; and are condemned like us to be crucified between that double law of the members and the will. Are they like us, I wonder, in the timid hope of some reward, some sugar with the drug? do they, too, stand aghast at unrewarded virtues, at the sufferings of those whom, in our partiality, we take to be just, and the prosperity of such as, in our blindness, we call wicked? It may be, and yet God knows what they should look for. Even while they look, even while they repent, the foot of man treads them by thousands in the dust, the yelping hounds burst upon their trail, the bullet speeds, the knives are heating in the den of the vivisectionist; or the dew falls, and the generation of a day is blotted out. For these are creatures, compared with whom our weakness is strength, our ignorance wisdom, our brief span eternity.

And as we dwell, we living things, in our isle of terror and under the imminent hand of death, God forbid it should be man the erected, the reasoner, the wise in his own eyes—God forbid it should be man that wearies in well-doing, that despairs of unrewarded effort, or utters the language of complaint. Let it be enough for faith, that the whole creation groans in mortal frailty, strives with unconquerable constancy: surely not all in vain.

Oscar Fingal O'Flahertie Wills Wilde

1854-1900

T H E flamboyant swath that Oscar Wilde cut across the salons and drawing rooms of the aesthetic period in Victorian England— virtually by himself turning it into the Decadent period—is now at least as well known as any work from his pen, save perhaps *The Importance of Being Earnest*. In his extravagant and often artfully calculated career is found the most extreme expression of the aesthetic-decadent creed in which art not only prevails over morality but becomes the very measure of morality, society, and life itself.

Oscar Wilde was born in Dublin in 1854. He studied at Trinity College, Dublin, and at Magdalen College, Oxford. At Oxford a disciple of Walter Pater's, Wilde established himself as the leader of an aesthetic coterie. Three years after leaving Oxford for London he was notorious enough to be satirized in Gilbert and Sullivan's *Patience* (1881) and a year later prominent enough to make a lecture tour of the United States. Throughout the eighties Wilde commanded attention for his consciously outrageous behavior and for some writing, including essays and a collection of fairy tales, *The Happy Prince* (1888).

But it was the eighteen-nineties that were to prove to be the period of Wilde's triumph and tragedy. In 1891 he published *The Soul of Man under Social-ism,* one of his more serious if derivative works. In the same year appeared his *Picture of Dorian Gray,* the classic work in English of the Decadent period. In the next several years there appeared in rapid succession a series of entertaining comedies, climaxed by his masterpiece *The Importance of Being Earnest* (1895). But in the same year as this triumph came Wilde's downfall. Imprudently suing the Marquis of Queensberry when the latter accused him of homosexuality (an accusation based on Wilde's relationship with Queensberry's son Lord Alfred Douglas), Wilde lost his suit and was himself put on trial and convicted of homosexual practices and sentenced to two years at hard labor. The experi-ence produced Wilde's apologia *DeProfundis* (1897) and his moving poem, *The Ballad of Reading Gaol* (1898). After his release Wilde lived a dismal life on the Continent and died in Paris in 1900.

Wilde's great talents as a writer were primarily in comedy, though his gifts as a writer of short stories and tales should not be under-estimated. His comic writings are marked by brilliant epigrams that not infrequently reverse expectations or play upon well-known platitudes. With all his humour Wilde had a penetrating sense of the follies of society and his pithy remarks oblige the reader to question some of the assumptions on which conventional conduct is based. Like other writers influenced by the aesthetic school Wilde devoted great attention to style and phrasing, so that if the century and the age end without a bang, they nevertheless end on a note of high verbal elegance.

CHRONOLOGY

1854	Born 16 October in Dublin.
1864	Attends private school in Dublin.
1874–76	Attends Trinity College, Dublin.
1776–78	Attends Magdalen College, Oxford.
1881	Satirized in Gilbert and Sullivan's *Patience*.
1882	Tours the United States.
1891	*The Soul of Man under Socialism; The Picture of Dorian Gray*.
1895	*The Importance of Being Earnest*. Loses libel suit; convicted of homosexuality.
1895–97	Prison term.
1900	Dies 30 November in Paris; buried at Père Lachaise Cemetery in Paris.

EDITIONS

Works, (14 vols., 1908).
Works, ed. R. B. Ross (14 vols., 1910).
Complete Works, ed. P. Drake (1966).
The Portable Oscar Wilde, ed. Richard Aldington (1946).
Selected Writings, ed. Richard Ellmann (1961).
Letters, ed. Rupert Hart-Davies (1962).

BIOGRAPHY AND CRITICISM

R. H. Sherard, *Life of Oscar Wilde* (1906, 1928).
W. W. Kenilworth, *A Study of Oscar Wilde* (1912).
Arthur Ransome, *Oscar Wilde* (1912).
O. T. Hopkins, *Oscar Wilde* (1916).
Arthur Symons, *A Study of Oscar Wilde* (1930).
Lord Alfred Douglas, *My Friendship with Oscar Wilde* (1932).
Frances Winwar, *Oscar Wilde and the Yellow Nineties* (1940).
Hesketh Pearson, *Oscar Wilde, His Life and Wit* (1946).
Edward Roditi, *Oscar Wilde* (1947).
Robert Merle, *Oscar Wilde* (1948).
H. Montgomery Hyde, *The Trials of Oscar Wilde* (1949).
St. John Ervine, *Oscar Wilde* (1951).
Vyvyan Holland, *Son of Oscar Wilde* (1954).
Antos Ojala, *Aestheticism and Oscar Wilde* (2 vols., 1954–55).
H. Montgomery Hyde, *Oscar Wilde: The Aftermath* (1963).

from The Picture of Dorian Gray

The Preface to The Picture of Dorian Gray *(1891), printed below, is a characteristic Wildean statement of the aims of art, as seen by the adherents of the philosophy of aestheticism. Typically, Wilde formulates his principles as epigrams, making many memorable and tongue-in-cheek statements to shock the bourgeois and to provoke instant amusement followed perhaps by thoughtful reflection.*

Preface

The artist is the creator of beautiful things.

To reveal art and conceal the artist is art's aim.

The critic is he who can translate into another manner or a new material his impression of beautiful things.

The highest as the lowest form of criticism is a mode of autobiography.

Those who find ugly meanings in beautiful things are corrupt without being charming. This is a fault.

Those who find beautiful meanings in beautiful things are the cultivated. For these there is hope.

They are the elect to whom beautiful things mean only beauty.

There is no such thing as a moral or an immoral book. Books are well written, or badly written. That is all.

The nineteenth-century dislike of realism is the rage of Caliban seeing his own face in a glass.

The nineteenth-century dislike of romanticism is the rage of Caliban not seeing his own face in a glass.

The moral life a man forms part of the subject matter of the artist, but the morality of art consists in the perfect use of an imperfect medium.

No artist desires to prove anything. Even things that are true can be proved.

No artist has ethical sympathies. An ethical sympathy in an artist is an unpardonable mannerism of style.

No artist is ever morbid. The artist can express everything.

Thought and language are to the artist instruments of an art.

Vice and virtue are to the artist materials for an art.

From the point of view of form, the type of all the arts is the art of the musician. From the point of view of feeling, the actor's craft is the type.

All art is at once surface and symbol.

Those who go beneath the surface do so at their peril.

Those who read the symbol do so at their peril.

It is the spectator, and not life, that art really mirrors.

Diversity of opinion about a work of art shows that the work is new, complex, and vital.

When critics disagree the artist is in accord with himself.

We can forgive a man for making a useful thing as long as he does not admire it. The only excuse for making a useless thing is that one admires it intensely.

All art is quite useless.

Index of Authors and Titles